PHILIP'S

WORLD TRAVELLER'S ATLAS

PHILIP'S

WORLD TRAVELLER'S ATLAS

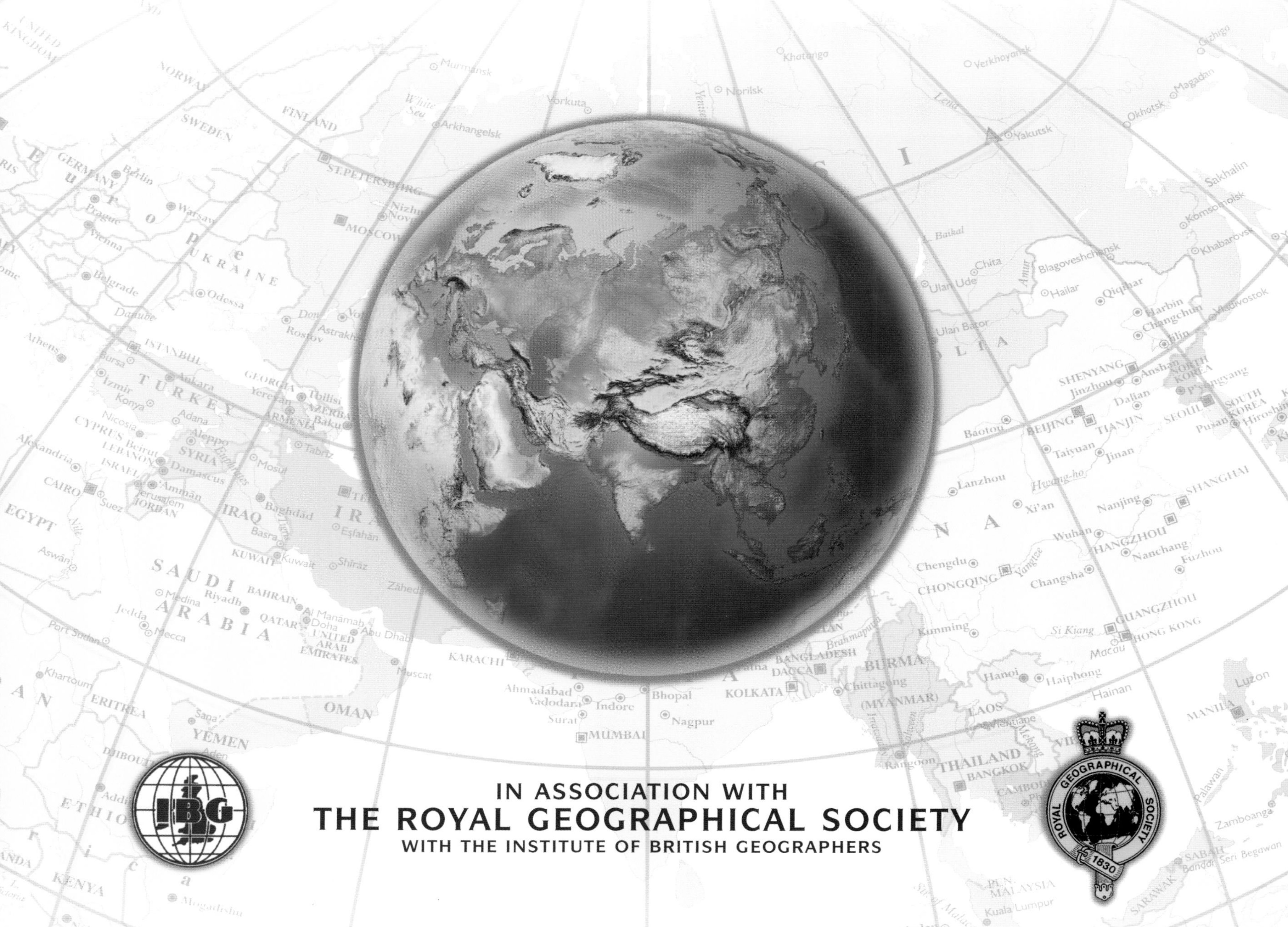

IN ASSOCIATION WITH
THE ROYAL GEOGRAPHICAL SOCIETY
WITH THE INSTITUTE OF BRITISH GEOGRAPHERS

PICTURE ACKNOWLEDGEMENTS

WORLD EXPLORER:
© *CORBIS* 26 bottom, 27 bottom, /Adam Woolfitt 5 centre right, 30 centre left, /AFP 24 top, 25 bottom, /Angelo Hornak 29 centre left, /Australian Picture Library 13 top, /Bob Krist 14 top, /Bob Winsett 20 top, /Brandon D. Cole 11 bottom, /Buddy Mays 26 centre, 22 bottom, /Catherine Karnow 19 bottom, /Charles and Josette Lenars 30 bottom right, /Charles O'Rear 23 left, /Clem Haagner; Gallo Images 10 centre, /Dave G. Houser 30 top, /David Muench 4 left, /Dean Conger 15 bottom, /Derek Hall; Frank Lane Picture Agency 3 centre, /Douglas Peebles 32 bottom, /Duomo 20 right, /Enzo and Paolo Ragazzini 16 bottom, /Galen Rowell 2 left, 9 bottom, 21 top, /George H. H. Huey 4 top, /George Lepp 12 bottom, /Hans Georg Roth 5 top, /Inge Yspeert 10 bottom right, /James Marshall 6 centre right, /John Dakers; Eye Ubiquitous 25 right, /Kevin Schafer 13 bottom, /Marc Muench 20 left, /Michael and Patricia Fogden 8 /Michael Busselle 3 top, /Michael S. Yamashita 22 top, /Milepost 92½ 15 top, /Mimmo Jodice 29 bottom, /Morton Beebe, S. F. 24 centre right, /Nik Wheeler 19 top, /O. Alamany and E. Vicens 5 bottom, /Patrick Ward 7 bottom, 16 centre right, /Peter Johnson 10 top, /Peter Wilson 28 bottom, /Premium Stock 28 top, /Quadrillion 31 bottom, /Raymond Gehman 2 top, 6 top, /Rick Doyle 23 bottom, /Robert Holmes 16 top, /Roger Ressmeyer 3 bottom, /Roger Tidman 9 left, /Stephanie Maze 24 bottom, /Stephen Frink 12 top, 13 centre, /Steve Kaufman 6 bottom, /Tim Thompson 14 centre right, 14 bottom, /Tiziana and Gianni Baldizzone 7 centre right, /Tom Bean 8 bottom, /Tom Brakefield 11 top, /Tom Nebbia 17 right, /Tony Arruza 23 top, /Vanni Archive 29 top, /W. Cody 18 right, 27 top, /Wild Country 26 top, /Wolfgang Kaehler 17 top, 18 top and bottom, 8 top.
© *ALTON TOWERS* 32 left.

CITY GAZETTEER:
© *CORBIS* /Bettmann 41 bottom right, /Carmen Redondo 44 centre left, /Charles E. Rotkin 40 top right, /Chris Lisle 47 centre top, /Hubert Stadler 41 centre top, /John Heseltine 42 top right, /Larry Lee 46 bottom right, /Lindsay Hebberd 42 left, /Patrick Ward 44 bottom right, /Paul A. Souders 47 bottom right, /Richard T. Nowitz 43 bottom centre, /Tim Thompson 41 left, /Todd Gipstein 44 centre top, /Wolfgang Kaehler 45 top right, /Yann Arthus-Bertrand 46 top left.
© *MIKE MOULE* 40 left, 43 top left and centre right, 45 left, 46 centre, 48 centre and right.

CITY MAPS

Cartography by Philip's

PAGE 11, DUBLIN: The town plan of Dublin is based on Ordnance Survey Ireland by permission of the Government Permit Number 7735. © Ordnance Survey Ireland and Government of Ireland.

Ordnance Survey **PAGE 11, EDINBURGH, and PAGE 15, LONDON:**
This product includes mapping data licensed from Ordnance Survey® with the permission of the Controller of Her Majesty's Stationery Office. © Crown copyright 2004. All rights reserved. Licence number 100011710.

VECTOR DATA: Courtesy of Gräfe and Unser Verlag GmbH, München, Germany (city centre maps of Bangkok, Beijing, Cape Town, Jerusalem, Mexico City, Moscow, Singapore, Sydney, Tokyo and Washington D.C.)

NOTE:
For reasons of safety or politics, there may be times when it is not advisable, or desirable, to visit one or more of the places described in the World Explorer and City Gazetteer sections. If in doubt, please check with the Foreign Office.

Published in Great Britain in 2004 by Philip's,
a division of Octopus Publishing Group Limited,
2–4 Heron Quays, London E14 4JP

Cartography by Philip's

ISBN 0-540-08609-6

A CIP catalogue record for this book is available from the British Library.

Printed in Hong Kong

Details of other Philip's titles and services can be found on our website at:
www.philips-maps.co.uk

Philip's World Atlases are published in association with The Royal Geographical Society (with The Institute of British Geographers).

The Society was founded in 1830 and given a Royal Charter in 1859 for 'the advancement of geographical science'. It holds historical collections of national and international importance, many of which relate to the Society's association with and support for scientific exploration and research from the 19th century onwards. It was pivotal in establishing geography as a teaching and research discipline in British universities close to the turn of the century, and has played a key role in geographical and environmental education ever since.

Today the Society is a leading world centre for geographical learning – supporting education, teaching, research and expeditions, and promoting public understanding of the subject.

The Society welcomes those interested in geography as members. For further information, please visit the website at: www.rgs.org

Philip's World Maps

The reference maps which form the main body of this atlas have been prepared in accordance with the highest standards of international cartography to provide an accurate and detailed representation of the Earth. The scales and projections used have been carefully chosen to give balanced coverage of the world, while emphasizing the most densely populated and economically significant regions. A hallmark of Philip's mapping is the use of hill shading and relief colouring to create a graphic impression of landforms: this makes the maps exceptionally easy to read. However, knowledge of the key features employed in the construction and presentation of the maps will enable the reader to derive the fullest benefit from the atlas.

MAP SEQUENCE

The atlas covers the Earth continent by continent: first Europe; then its land neighbour Asia (mapped north before south, in a clockwise sequence), then Africa, Australia and Oceania, North America and South America. This is the classic arrangement adopted by most cartographers since the 16th century. For each continent, there are maps at a variety of scales. First, physical relief and political maps

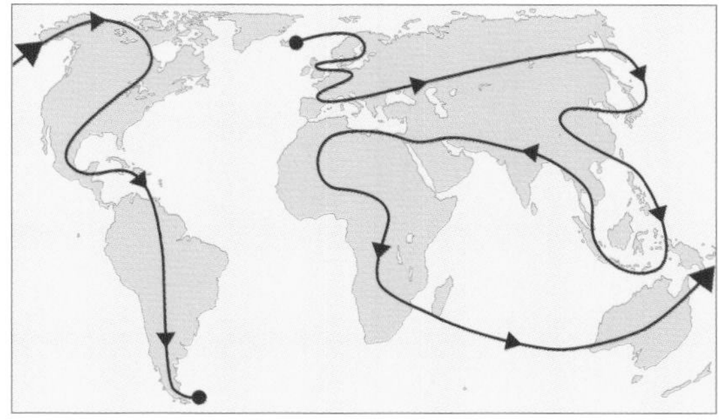

of the whole continent; then a series of larger-scale maps of the regions within the continent, each followed, where required, by still larger-scale maps of the most important or densely populated areas. The governing principle is that by turning the pages of the atlas, the reader moves steadily from north to south through each continent, with each map overlapping its neighbours.

MAP PRESENTATION

With very few exceptions (e.g. for the Arctic and Antarctica), the maps are drawn with north at the top, regardless of whether they are presented upright or sideways on the page. In the borders will be found the map title; a locator diagram showing the area covered; continuation arrows showing the page numbers for maps of adjacent areas; the scale; the projection used; the degrees of latitude and longitude; and the letters and figures used in the index for locating place names and geographical features. Physical relief maps also have a height reference panel identifying the colours used for each layer of contouring.

MAP SYMBOLS

Each map contains a vast amount of detail which can only be conveyed clearly and accurately by the use of symbols. Points and circles of varying sizes locate and identify the relative importance of towns and cities; different styles of type are employed for administrative, geographical and regional place names to aid identification. A variety of pictorial symbols denote landscape features such as glaciers, marshes and coral reefs, and man-made structures including roads, railways, airports, canals and dams. International borders are shown by red lines. Where neighbouring countries are in dispute, for example in parts of the Middle East, the maps show the *de facto* boundary between nations, regardless of the legal or historical situation. The symbols are explained on the first page of the *World Maps* section of the atlas.

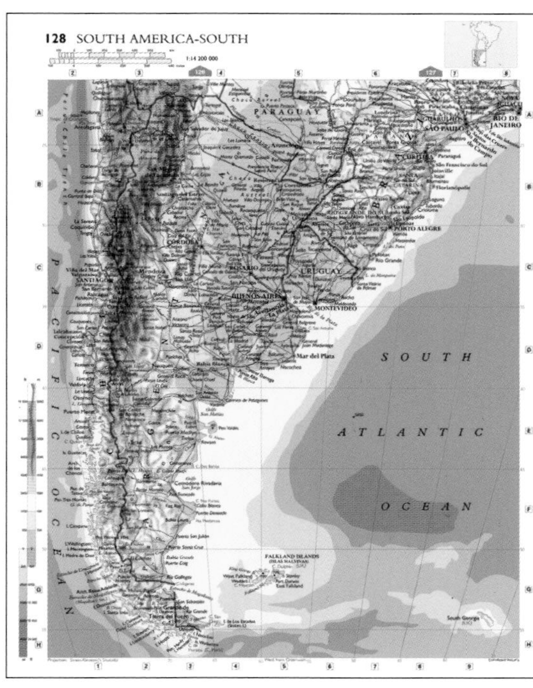

MAP SCALES

1:16 000 000
1 inch = 252 statute miles

The scale of each map is given in the numerical form known as the 'representative fraction'. The first figure is always one, signifying one unit of distance on the map; the second figure, usually in millions, is the number by which the map unit must be multiplied to give the equivalent distance on the Earth's surface. Calculations can easily be made in centimetres and kilometres, by dividing the Earth units figure by 100 000 (i.e. deleting the last five 0s). Thus 1:1 000 000 means 1 cm = 10 km. The calculation for inches and miles is more laborious, but 1 000 000 divided by 63 360 (the number of inches in a mile) shows that 1:1 000 000 means approximately 1 inch = 16 miles. The table below provides distance equivalents for scales down to 1:50 000 000.

LARGE SCALE		
1:1 000 000	1 cm = 10 km	1 inch = 16 miles
1:2 500 000	1 cm = 25 km	1 inch = 39.5 miles
1:5 000 000	1 cm = 50 km	1 inch = 79 miles
1:6 000 000	1 cm = 60 km	1 inch = 95 miles
1:8 000 000	1 cm = 80 km	1 inch = 126 miles
1:10 000 000	1 cm = 100 km	1 inch = 158 miles
1:15 000 000	1 cm = 150 km	1 inch = 237 miles
1:20 000 000	1 cm = 200 km	1 inch = 316 miles
1:50 000 000	1 cm = 500 km	1 inch = 790 miles
SMALL SCALE		

MEASURING DISTANCES

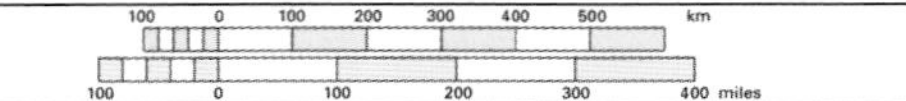

Although each map is accompanied by a scale bar, distances cannot always be measured with confidence because of the distortions involved in portraying the curved surface of the Earth on a flat page. As a general rule, the larger the map scale (i.e. the lower the number of Earth units in the representative fraction), the more accurate and reliable will be the distance measured. On small-scale maps such as those of the world and of entire continents, measurement may only be accurate along the 'standard parallels', or central axes, and should not be attempted without considering the map projection.

MAP PROJECTIONS

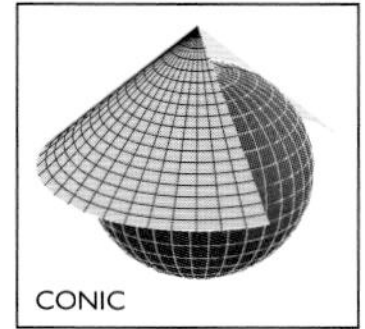

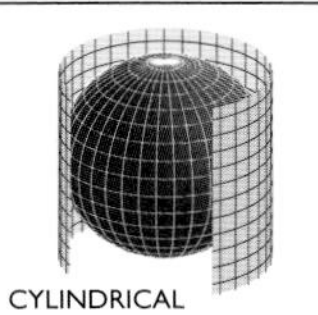

Unlike a globe, no flat map can give a true scale representation of the world in terms of area, shape and position of every region. Each of the numerous systems that have been devised for projecting the curved surface of the Earth on to a flat page involves the sacrifice of accuracy in one or more of these elements. The variations in shape and position of landmasses such as Alaska, Greenland and Australia, for example, can be quite dramatic when different projections are compared.

For this atlas, the guiding principle has been to select projections that involve the least distortion of size and distance. The projection used for each map is noted in the border. Most fall into one of three categories – conic, azimuthal or cylindrical – whose basic concepts are shown above. Each involves plotting the forms of the Earth's surface on a grid of latitude and longitude lines, which may be shown as parallels, curves or radiating spokes.

LATITUDE AND LONGITUDE

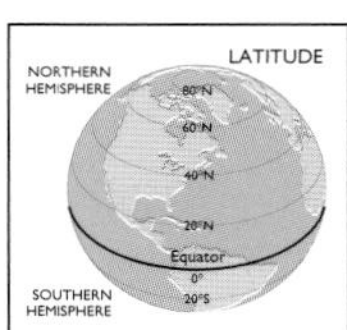

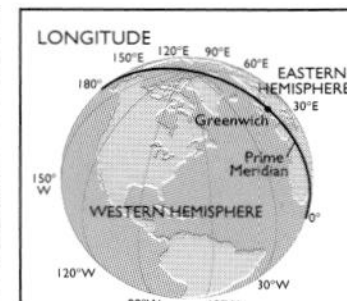

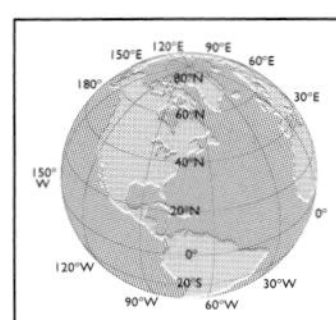

Accurate positioning of individual points on the Earth's surface is made possible by reference to the geometrical system of latitude and longitude. Latitude *parallels* are drawn west–east around the Earth and numbered by degrees north and south of the Equator, which is designated 0° of latitude. Longitude *meridians* are drawn north–south and numbered by degrees east and west of the *prime meridian*, 0° of longitude, which passes through Greenwich in England. By referring to these co-ordinates and their subdivisions of minutes (1/60th of a degree) and seconds (1/60th of a minute), any place on Earth can be located to within a few hundred metres. Latitude and longitude are indicated by blue lines on the maps; they are straight or curved according to the projection employed. Reference to these lines is the easiest way of determining the relative positions of places on different maps, and for plotting compass directions.

NAME FORMS

For ease of reference, both English and local name forms appear in the atlas. Oceans, seas and countries are shown in English throughout the atlas; country names may be abbreviated to their commonly accepted form (e.g. Germany, not The Federal Republic of Germany). Conventional English forms are also used for place names on the smaller-scale maps of the continents. However, local name forms are used on all large-scale and regional maps, with the English form given in brackets only for important cities – the large-scale map of Russia and Central Asia thus shows Moskva (Moscow). For countries which do not use a Roman script, place names have been transcribed according to the systems adopted by the British and US Geographic Names Authorities. For China, the Pin Yin system has been used, with some more widely known forms appearing in brackets, as with Beijing (Peking). Both English and local names appear in the index, the English form being cross-referenced to the local form.

Contents

WORLD STATISTICS

Countries x
Cities xi
Distances xii
Climate xiii
Physical Dimensions xiv–xv
Regions in the News xvi

WORLD EXPLORER

Mountains and volcanoes 2–3
Deserts and canyons 4–5
Lakes and waterfalls 6–7
Wildlife in the Americas and Europe 8–9
Wildlife in Africa, Asia and Australasia 10–11
Marine wildlife 12–13
Great railway journeys 14–15
River and canal journeys 16–17
Sea and ocean cruises 18–19
Winter sports 20–21
Great beaches 22–23
Festivals 24–25
Historic sites in the Americas 26–27
Historic sites in Europe 28–29
Historic sites in Africa, Asia and Australasia 30–31
Theme parks 32

WORLD CITIES

CITY MAPS

Amsterdam 2
Athens 2
Atlanta 3
Baghdad 3
Bangkok 3
Barcelona 4
Beijing 4
Berlin 5
Boston 6
Brussels 6
Budapest 7
Buenos Aires 7
Cairo 7
Calcutta (Kolkata) 8
Canton (Guangzhou) 8
Cape Town 8
Chicago 9
Copenhagen 10
Delhi 10
Dublin 11
Edinburgh 11
Helsinki 12
Hong Kong 12
Istanbul 12
Jakarta 13
Jerusalem 13
Johannesburg 13
Karachi 14
Lagos 14
Lisbon 14
London 15
Lima 16
Los Angeles 16
Madrid 17
Manila 17
Melbourne 17
Mexico City 18
Miami 18
Milan 18
Montréal 19
Moscow 19
Mumbai (Bombay) 20
Munich 20
New York 21
Osaka 22
Oslo 22
Paris 23
Prague 24
Rio de Janeiro 24
Rome 25
San Francisco 25
St Petersburg 26
Santiago 26
São Paulo 26
Seoul 26
Shanghai 27
Singapore 27
Stockholm 28
Sydney 28
Tokyo 29
Tehran 30
Tianjin 30
Toronto 30
Vienna 31
Warsaw 31
Washington 32
Wellington 32

INDEX TO CITY MAPS 33–39

CITY GAZETTEER

Accra, Ghana 40
Agra, India 40
Amsterdam, The Netherlands 40
Antwerp, Belgium 40
Athens, Greece 40
Atlanta, Georgia, USA 40
Auckland, New Zealand 40
Bangkok, Thailand 40
Barcelona, Spain 40
Beijing, China 40
Berlin, Germany 40
Boston, Massachusetts, USA 41
Brisbane, Queensland, Australia 41
Brussels, Belgium 41
Budapest, Hungary 41
Buenos Aires, Argentina 41
Cairo, Egypt 41
Calcutta (Kolkata), India 41
Canton (Guangzhou), China 41
Cape Town, South Africa 41
Cartagena, Colombia 41
Chicago, Illinois, USA 41
Cologne, Germany 42
Copenhagen, Denmark 42
Delhi, India 42
Dublin, Ireland 42
Edinburgh, Scotland 42
Esfahan, Iran 42
Fès, Morocco 42
Florence, Italy 42
Geneva, Switzerland 42
Hamburg, Germany 42
Hanoi, Vietnam 42
Havana, Cuba 42
Helsinki, Finland 43
Hong Kong, China 43
Istanbul, Turkey 43
Jaipur, India 43
Jakarta, Indonesia 43
Jerusalem, Israel 43
Johannesburg, South Africa 43
Kairouan, Tunisia 43
Karachi, Pakistan 43
Katmandu, Nepal 43
Kraków, Poland 43
Kuala Lumpur, Malaysia 44
Kyoto, Japan 44
Lagos, Nigeria 44
Lahore, Pakistan 44
Las Vegas, Nevada, USA 44
Lima, Peru 44
Lisbon, Portugal 44
London, England 44
Los Angeles, California, USA 44
Luxembourg City, Luxembourg 44
Madrid, Spain 44
Manila, Philippines 45
Marrakech, Morocco 45
Melbourne, Victoria, Australia 45
Mexico City, Mexico 45
Miami, Florida, USA 45
Milan, Italy 45
Montréal, Québec, Canada 45
Moscow, Russia 45
Mumbai (Bombay), India 45
Munich, Germany 45
Nairobi, Kenya 45
New Orleans, Louisiana, USA 45
New York, NY, USA 46
Osaka, Japan 46
Oslo, Norway 46
Panama City, Panama 46
Paris, France 46
Perth, Western Australia, Australia 46
Prague, Czech Republic 46
Quito, Ecuador 46
Reykjavik, Iceland 46
Riga, Latvia 46
Rio de Janeiro, Brazil 46
Rome, Italy 46
St Petersburg, Russia 47
San Francisco, California, USA 47
Santiago, Chile 47
São Paulo, Brazil 47
Seattle, Washington, USA 47
Seoul, South Korea 47
Shanghai, China 47
Singapore City, Singapore 47
Stockholm, Sweden 47
Sydney, New South Wales, Australia 47
Tehran, Iran 47
Tianjin, China 48
Tokyo, Japan 48
Toronto, Ontario, Canada 48
Vancouver, British Columbia, Canada 48
Varanasi, India 48
Venice, Italy 48
Vienna, Austria 48
Warsaw, Poland 48
Washington DC, USA 48
Wellington, New Zealand 48
Xi'an, China 48
Yangon (Rangoon), Burma (Myanmar) 48

WORLD MAPS

Map Symbols 1

The World: Political
1:71 100 000 2–3

Arctic Ocean
1:31 100 000 4

Antarctica
1:31 100 000 5

Europe

Europe: Physical
1:17 800 000 6

Europe: Political
1:17 800 000 7

Scandinavia
1:4 400 000
Iceland 1:4 400 000 8–9

Denmark and Southern Sweden
1:2 200 000 10–11

Ireland
1:1 800 000 12

Scotland
1:1 800 000 13

England and Wales
1:1 800 000 14–15

British Isles
1:4 400 000 16

Netherlands, Belgium and Luxembourg
1:2 200 000 17

Northern France
1:2 200 000 18–19

Southern France
1:2 200 000 20–21

Central Europe
1:4 400 000 22–23

Germany
1:2 200 000 24–25

Austria, Czech Republic and Slovak Republic
1:2 200 000 26–27

Hungary, Romania and the Lower Danube
1:2 200 000 28–29

Poland and the Southern Baltic
1:2 200 000 30–31

Baltic States, Belarus and Ukraine
1:4 400 000 32–33

The Volga Basin and the Caucasus
1:4 400 000 34–35

Western Spain and Portugal
1:2 200 000 36–37

Eastern Spain
1:2 200 000 38–39

Northern Italy, Slovenia and Croatia
1:2 200 000 40–41

Southern Italy
1:2 200 000 42–43

Serbia and Montenegro, Bulgaria and Northern Greece
1:2 200 000 44–45

Southern Greece and Western Turkey
1:2 200 000 — 46–47

The Balearics, the Canaries and Madeira
1:900 000 / 1:1 800 000 — 48

Malta, Crete, Corfu, Rhodes and Cyprus
1:900 000 / 1:1 200 000 — 49

Asia

Asia: Physical
1:44 400 000 — 50

Asia: Political
1:44 400 000 — 51

Russia and Central Asia
1:17 800 000 — 52–53

Japan
1:4 400 000 — 54–55

Northern China and Korea
1:5 300 000 — 56–57

Southern China
1:5 300 000 — 58–59

China
1:17 800 000 — 60

The Philippines
1:6 700 000 — 61

Indonesia and the Philippines
1:11 100 000
Java and Madura 1:6 700 000
Bali 1:1 800 000 — 62–63

Mainland South-east Asia
1:5 300 000
Ko Phuket 1:900 000
Ko Samui 1:900 000
Pinang 1:900 000
Singapore 1:900 000 — 64–65

South Asia
1:8 900 000 — 66–67

Northern India and Nepal
1:5 300 000
Jammu and Kashmir 1:5 300 000 — 68–69

The Middle East
1:6 200 000 — 70–71

Turkey and Transcaucasia
1:4 400 000 — 72–73

The Near East
1:2 200 000 — 74

Arabia and the Horn of Africa
1:13 300 000 — 75

Africa

Africa: Physical
1:37 300 000 — 76

Africa: Political
1: 37 300 000 — 77

Northern Africa
1:13 300 000 — 78–79

The Nile Valley
1:7 100 000
The Nile Delta 1:3 600 000 — 80–81

West Africa
1:7 100 000 — 82–83

Central and Southern Africa
1:13 300 000 — 84–85

East Africa
1:7 100 000 — 86–87

Southern Africa
1:7 100 000
Madagascar 1:7 100 000

88–89

Australia and Oceania

Australia and Oceania: Physical and Political
1:44 400 000 90

New Zealand
1:5 300 000
Samoan Islands 1:10 700 000
Fiji and Tonga 1:10 700 000

91

Western Australia
1:7 100 000

92–93

Eastern Australia
1:7 100 000
Whitsunday Islands 1:2 200 000

94–95

Pacific Ocean
1:48 000 000 96–97

North America

North America: Physical
1:31 100 000 98

North America: Political
1:31 100 000 99

Canada
1:13 300 000
Alaska 1:26 700 000

100–101

Western Canada
1:6 200 000

102–103

Eastern Canada
1:6 200 000

104–105

United States
1:10 700 000
Hawaii 1:8 900 000

106–107

Western United States
1:5 300 000

108–109

Central and Southern California and Western Washington
1:2 200 000

110–111

Middle United States
1:5 300 000

112–113

Eastern United States
1:5 300 000

114–115

North-eastern United States
1:2 200 000

116–117

Mexico
1:7 100 000

118–119

Central America and the West Indies
1:7 100 000
Jamaica 1:2 700 000
Guadeloupe 1:1 800 000
Martinique 1:1 800 000
Puerto Rico 1:2 700 000
Virgin Islands 1:1 800 000
St Lucia 1:890 000
Barbados 1:890 000

120–121

South America

South America: Physical
1:31 100 000 122

South America: Political
1:31 100 000 123

South America – North
1:14 200 000
Trinidad and Tobago 1:2 200 000

124–125

Central South America
1:7 100 000

126–127

South America – South
1:14 200 000

128

INDEX TO WORLD MAPS
129–224

World Statistics: Countries

This alphabetical list includes all the countries and territories of the world. If a territory is not completely independent, the country it is associated with is named. The area figures give the total area of land, inland water and ice.

The population figures are 2002 estimates. The annual income is the Gross Domestic Product per capita† in US dollars. The figures are the latest available, usually 2001 estimates.

Country/Territory	Area km^2 Thousands	Area $miles^2$ Thousands	Population Thousands	Capital	Annual Income US $
Afghanistan	652	252	27,756	Kabul	800
Albania	28.8	11.1	3,545	Tirana	3,800
Algeria	2,382	920	32,278	Algiers	5,600
American Samoa (US)	0.2	0.08	69	Pago Pago	8,000
Andorra	0.45	0.17	68	Andorra La Vella	19,000
Angola	1,247	481	10,593	Luanda	1,330
Anguilla (UK)	0.1	0.04	12	The Valley	8,600
Antigua & Barbuda	0.44	0.17	67	St John's	10,000
Argentina	2,767	1,068	37,813	Buenos Aires	12,000
Armenia	29.8	11.5	3,330	Yerevan	3,350
Aruba (Netherlands)	0.19	0.07	70	Oranjestad	28,000
Australia	7,687	2,968	19,547	Canberra	24,000
Austria	83.9	32.4	8,170	Vienna	27,000
Azerbaijan	86.6	33.4	7,798	Baku	3,100
Azores (Portugal)	2.2	0.87	234	Ponta Delgada	12,600
Bahamas	13.9	5.4	301	Nassau	16,800
Bahrain	0.68	0.26	656	Manama	13,000
Bangladesh	144	56	133,377	Dhaka	1,750
Barbados	0.43	0.17	277	Bridgetown	14,500
Belarus	207.6	80.1	10,335	Minsk	8,200
Belgium	30.5	11.8	10,275	Brussels	26,100
Belize	23	8.9	263	Belmopan	3,250
Benin	113	43	6,788	Porto-Novo	1,040
Bermuda (UK)	0.05	0.02	64	Hamilton	34,800
Bhutan	47	18.1	2,094	Thimphu	1,200
Bolivia	1,099	424	8,445	La Paz/Sucre	2,600
Bosnia-Herzegovina	51	20	3,964	Sarajevo	1,800
Botswana	582	225	1,591	Gaborone	7,800
Brazil	8,512	3,286	176,030	Brasília	7,400
Brunei	5.8	2.2	351	Bandar Seri Begawan	18,000
Bulgaria	111	43	7,621	Sofia	6,200
Burkina Faso	274	106	12,603	Ouagadougou	1,040
Burma (= Myanmar)	677	261	42,238	Rangoon	1,500
Burundi	27.8	10.7	6,373	Bujumbura	600
Cambodia	181	70	12,775	Phnom Penh	1,500
Cameroon	475	184	16,185	Yaoundé	1,700
Canada	9,976	3,852	31,902	Ottawa	27,700
Canary Is. (Spain)	7.3	2.8	1,694	Las Palmas/Santa Cruz	18,200
Cape Verde Is.	4	1.6	409	Praia	1,500
Cayman Is. (UK)	0.26	0.1	36	George Town	30,000
Central African Republic	623	241	3,643	Bangui	1,300
Chad	1,284	496	8,997	Ndjaména	1,030
Chile	757	292	15,499	Santiago	10,000
China	9,597	3,705	1,284,304	Beijing	4,300
Colombia	1,139	440	41,008	Bogotá	6,300
Comoros	2.2	0.86	614	Moroni	710
Congo	342	132	2,958	Brazzaville	900
Congo (Dem. Rep. of the)	2,345	905	55,225	Kinshasa	590
Cook Is. (NZ)	0.24	0.09	21	Avarua	5,000
Costa Rica	51.1	19.7	3,835	San José	8,500
Croatia	56.5	21.8	4,391	Zagreb	8,300
Cuba	111	43	11,224	Havana	2,300
Cyprus	9.3	3.6	767	Nicosia	11,500
Czech Republic	78.9	30.4	10,257	Prague	14,400
Denmark	43.1	16.6	5,369	Copenhagen	28,000
Djibouti	23.2	9	473	Djibouti	1,400
Dominica	0.75	0.29	70	Roseau	3,700
Dominican Republic	48.7	18.8	8,722	Santo Domingo	5,800
East Timor	14.9	5.7	953	Dili	500
Ecuador	284	109	13,447	Quito	3,000
Egypt	1,001	387	70,712	Cairo	3,700
El Salvador	21	8.1	6,354	San Salvador	4,600
Equatorial Guinea	28.1	10.8	498	Malabo	2,100
Eritrea	94	36	4,466	Asmara	740
Estonia	44.7	17.3	1,416	Tallinn	10,000
Ethiopia	1,128	436	67,673	Addis Ababa	700
Faroe Is. (Denmark)	1.4	0.54	46	Tórshavn	20,000
Fiji	18.3	7.1	856	Suva	5,200
Finland	338	131	5,184	Helsinki	25,800
France	552	213	59,766	Paris	25,400
French Guiana (France)	90	34.7	182	Cayenne	6,000
French Polynesia (France)	4	1.5	258	Papeete	5,000
Gabon	268	103	1,233	Libreville	5,500
Gambia, The	11.3	4.4	1,456	Banjul	1,770
Gaza Strip (OPT)*	0.36	0.14	1,226	–	630
Georgia	69.7	26.9	4,961	Tbilisi	3,100
Germany	357	138	83,252	Berlin	26,200
Ghana	239	92	20,244	Accra	1,980
Gibraltar (UK)	0.007	0.003	28	Gibraltar Town	17,500
Greece	132	51	10,645	Athens	17,900
Greenland (Denmark)	2,176	840	56	Nuuk (Godthåb)	20,000
Grenada	0.34	0.13	89	St George's	4,750
Guadeloupe (France)	1.7	0.66	436	Basse-Terre	9,000
Guam (US)	0.55	0.21	161	Agana	21,000
Guatemala	109	42	13,314	Guatemala City	3,700
Guinea	246	95	7,775	Conakry	1,970
Guinea-Bissau	36.1	13.9	1,345	Bissau	900
Guyana	215	83	698	Georgetown	3,600
Haiti	27.8	10.7	7,064	Port-au-Prince	1,700
Honduras	112	43	6,561	Tegucigalpa	2,600
Hong Kong (China)	1.1	0.4	7,303	–	25,000
Hungary	93	35.9	10,075	Budapest	12,000
Iceland	103	40	279	Reykjavik	24,800
India	3,288	1,269	1,045,845	New Delhi	2,500
Indonesia	1,890	730	231,328	Jakarta	3,000
Iran	1,648	636	66,623	Tehran	6,400
Iraq	438	169	24,002	Baghdad	2,500
Ireland	70.3	27.1	3,883	Dublin	27,300
Israel	20.6	7.96	6,030	Jerusalem	20,000
Italy	301	116	57,716	Rome	24,300
Ivory Coast (= Côte d'Ivoire)	322	125	16,805	Yamoussoukro	1,550
Jamaica	11	4.2	2,680	Kingston	3,700
Japan	378	146	126,975	Tokyo	27,200
Jordan	89.2	34.4	5,307	Amman	4,200
Kazakhstan	2,717	1,049	16,742	Astana	5,900
Kenya	580	224	31,139	Nairobi	1,000
Kiribati	0.72	0.28	96	Tarawa	840
Korea, North	121	47	22,224	Pyŏngyang	1,000
Korea, South	99	38.2	48,324	Seoul	18,000
Kuwait	17.8	6.9	2,112	Kuwait City	15,100
Kyrgyzstan	198.5	76.6	4,822	Bishkek	2,800
Laos	237	91	5,777	Vientiane	1,630
Latvia	65	25	2,367	Riga	7,800

*OPT = Occupied Palestinian Territory   N/A = Not Available

Country/Territory	Area km^2 Thousands	Area $miles^2$ Thousands	Population Thousands	Capital	Annual Income US $
Lebanon	10.4	4	3,678	Beirut	5,200
Lesotho	30.4	11.7	2,208	Maseru	2,450
Liberia	111	43	3,288	Monrovia	1,100
Libya	1,760	679	5,369	Tripoli	7,600
Liechtenstein	0.16	0.06	33	Vaduz	23,000
Lithuania	65.2	25.2	3,601	Vilnius	7,600
Luxembourg	2.6	1	449	Luxembourg	43,400
Macau (China)	0.02	0.006	462	–	17,600
Macedonia (FYROM)	25.7	9.9	2,055	Skopje	4,400
Madagascar	587	227	16,473	Antananarivo	870
Madeira (Portugal)	0.81	0.31	241	Funchal	16,800
Malawi	118	46	10,702	Lilongwe	660
Malaysia	330	127	22,662	Kuala Lumpur/Putrajaya	9,000
Maldives	0.3	0.12	320	Malé	3,870
Mali	1,240	479	11,340	Bamako	840
Malta	0.32	0.12	397	Valletta	15,000
Marshall Is.	0.18	0.07	74	Majuro	1,600
Martinique (France)	1.1	0.42	422	Fort-de-France	11,000
Mauritania	1,030	398	2,829	Nouakchott	1,800
Mauritius	2	0.72	1,200	Port Louis	10,800
Mayotte (France)	0.37	0.14	171	Mamoundzou	600
Mexico	1,958	756	103,400	Mexico City	9,000
Micronesia, Fed. States of	0.7	0.27	136	Palikir	2,000
Moldova	33.7	13	4,435	Chişinău	2,550
Monaco	0.002	0.001	32	Monaco	27,000
Mongolia	1,567	605	2,694	Ulan Bator	1,770
Montserrat (UK)	0.1	0.04	8	Plymouth	2,400
Morocco	447	172	31,168	Rabat	3,700
Mozambique	802	309	19,608	Maputo	900
Namibia	825	318	1,821	Windhoek	4,500
Nauru	0.02	0.008	12	Yaren District	5,000
Nepal	141	54	25,874	Katmandu	1,400
Netherlands	41.5	16	16,068	Amsterdam/The Hague	25,800
Netherlands Antilles (Neths)	0.99	0.38	214	Willemstad	11,400
New Caledonia (France)	18.6	7.2	208	Nouméa	15,000
New Zealand	269	104	3,908	Wellington	19,500
Nicaragua	130	50	5,024	Managua	2,500
Niger	1,267	489	10,640	Niamey	820
Nigeria	924	357	129,935	Abuja	840
Northern Mariana Is. (US)	0.48	0.18	77	Saipan	12,500
Norway	324	125	4,525	Oslo	30,800
Oman	212	82	2,713	Muscat	8,200
Pakistan	796	307	147,663	Islamabad	2,100
Palau	0.46	0.18	19	Koror	9,000
Panama	77.1	29.8	2,882	Panamá	5,900
Papua New Guinea	463	179	5,172	Port Moresby	2,400
Paraguay	407	157	5,884	Asunción	4,600
Peru	1,285	496	27,950	Lima	4,800
Philippines	300	116	84,526	Manila	4,000
Poland	313	121	38,625	Warsaw	8,800
Portugal	92.4	35.7	9,609	Lisbon	17,300
Puerto Rico (US)	9	3.5	3,958	San Juan	11,200
Qatar	11	4.2	793	Doha	21,200
Réunion (France)	2.5	0.97	744	St-Denis	4,800
Romania	238	92	22,318	Bucharest	6,800
Russia	17,075	6,592	144,979	Moscow	8,300
Rwanda	26.3	10.2	7,398	Kigali	1,000
St Kitts & Nevis	0.36	0.14	39	Basseterre	8,700
St Lucia	0.62	0.24	160	Castries	4,400
St Vincent & Grenadines	0.39	0.15	116	Kingstown	2,900
Samoa	2.8	1.1	179	Apia	3,500
San Marino	0.06	0.02	28	San Marino	34,600
São Tomé & Príncipe	0.96	0.37	170	São Tomé	1,200
Saudi Arabia	2,150	830	23,513	Riyadh	10,600
Senegal	197	76	10,590	Dakar	1,580
Serbia & Montenegro	102.3	39.5	10,657	Belgrade	2,250
Seychelles	0.46	0.18	80	Victoria	7,600
Sierra Leone	71.7	27.7	5,615	Freetown	500
Singapore	0.62	0.24	4,453	Singapore	24,700
Slovak Republic	49	18.9	5,422	Bratislava	11,500
Slovenia	20.3	7.8	1,933	Ljubljana	16,000
Solomon Is.	28.9	11.2	495	Honiara	1,700
Somalia	638	246	7,753	Mogadishu	550
South Africa	1,220	471	43,648	C. Town/Pretoria/Bloem.	9,400
Spain	505	195	38,383	Madrid	18,900
Sri Lanka	65.6	25.3	19,577	Colombo	3,250
Sudan	2,506	967	37,090	Khartoum	1,360
Suriname	163	63	436	Paramaribo	3,500
Swaziland	17.4	6.7	1,124	Mbabane	4,200
Sweden	450	174	8,877	Stockholm	24,700
Switzerland	41.3	15.9	7,302	Bern	31,100
Syria	185	71	17,156	Damascus	3,200
Taiwan	36	13.9	22,548	Taipei	17,200
Tajikistan	143.1	55.2	6,720	Dushanbe	1,140
Tanzania	945	365	37,188	Dodoma	610
Thailand	513	198	62,354	Bangkok	6,600
Togo	56.8	21.9	5,286	Lomé	1,500
Tonga	0.75	0.29	106	Nuku'alofa	2,200
Trinidad & Tobago	5.1	2	1,164	Port of Spain	9,000
Tunisia	164	63	9,816	Tunis	6,600
Turkey	779	301	67,309	Ankara	6,700
Turkmenistan	488.1	188.5	4,689	Ashkhabad	4,700
Turks & Caicos Is. (UK)	0.43	0.17	19	Cockburn Town	7,300
Tuvalu	0.03	0.01	11	Fongafale	1,100
Uganda	236	91	24,699	Kampala	1,200
Ukraine	603.7	233.1	48,396	Kiev	4,200
United Arab Emirates	83.6	32.3	2,446	Abu Dhabi	21,100
United Kingdom	243.3	94	59,778	London	24,700
United States of America	9,373	3,619	280,562	Washington, DC	36,300
Uruguay	177	68	3,387	Montevideo	9,200
Uzbekistan	447.4	172.7	25,563	Tashkent	2,500
Vanuatu	12.2	4.7	196	Port-Vila	1,300
Vatican City	0.0004	0.0002	1	Vatican City	N/A
Venezuela	912	352	24,288	Caracas	6,100
Vietnam	332	127	81,098	Hanoi	2,100
Virgin Is. (UK)	0.15	0.06	21	Road Town	16,000
Virgin Is. (US)	0.34	0.13	123	Charlotte Amalie	15,000
Wallis & Futuna Is. (France)	0.2	0.08	16	Mata-Utu	2,000
West Bank (OPT)*	5.86	2.26	2,164	–	1,000
Western Sahara	266	103	256	El Aaiún	N/A
Yemen	528	204	18,701	Sana	820
Zambia	753	291	9,959	Lusaka	870
Zimbabwe	391	151	11,377	Harare	2,450

† Gross Domestic Product per capita has been measured using the purchasing power parity method. This enables comparisons to be made between countries through their purchasing power (in US dollars), showing real price levels of goods and services rather than using currency exchange rates.

World Statistics: Cities

This list shows the principal cities with more than 500,000 inhabitants (only cities with more than 1 million inhabitants are included for Brazil, China, India, Indonesia, Japan and Russia). The figures are taken from the most recent census or estimate available, and as far as possible are the population of the metropolitan area, e.g. greater New York, Mexico or Paris. All the figures are in thousands. Local name forms have been used for the smaller cities (e.g. Kraków).

AFGHANISTAN	
Kabul	1,565
ALGERIA	
Algiers	1,722
Oran	664
ANGOLA	
Luanda	2,250
ARGENTINA	
Buenos Aires	10,990
Córdoba	1,198
Rosario	1,096
Mendoza	775
La Plata	640
San Miguel de Tucumán	622
Mar del Plata	520
ARMENIA	
Yerevan	1,256
AUSTRALIA	
Sydney	4,041
Melbourne	3,417
Brisbane	1,601
Perth	1,364
Adelaide	1,093
AUSTRIA	
Vienna	1,560
AZERBAIJAN	
Baku	1,713
BANGLADESH	
Dhaka	7,832
Chittagong	2,041
Khulna	877
Rajshahi	517
BELARUS	
Minsk	1,717
Homyel	502
BELGIUM	
Brussels	948
BENIN	
Cotonou	537
BOLIVIA	
La Paz	1,126
Santa Cruz	767
BOSNIA-HERZEGOVINA	
Sarajevo	526
BRAZIL	
São Paulo	10,434
Rio de Janeiro	5,858
Salvador	2,443
Belo Horizonte	2,239
Fortaleza	2,141
Brasília	2,051
Curitiba	1,587
Recife	1,423
Manaus	1,406
Pôrto Alegre	1,361
Belém	1,281
Goiânia	1,093
Guarulhos	1,073
BULGARIA	
Sofia	1,139
BURKINA FASO	
Ouagadougou	690
BURMA (MYANMAR)	
Rangoon	2,513
Mandalay	533
CAMBODIA	
Phnom Penh	570
CAMEROON	
Douala	1,200
Yaoundé	800
CANADA	
Toronto	4,881
Montréal	3,511
Vancouver	2,079
Ottawa–Hull	1,107
Calgary	972
Edmonton	957
Québec	693
Winnipeg	685
Hamilton	681
CENTRAL AFRICAN REPUBLIC	
Bangui	553
CHAD	
Ndjaména	530
CHILE	
Santiago	4,691
CHINA	
Shanghai	15,082
Beijing	12,362
Tianjin	10,687
Hong Kong (SAR)*	6,502
Chongqing	3,870
Shenyang	3,762
Wuhan	3,520
Guangzhou	3,114
Harbin	2,505
Nanjing	2,211
Xi'an	2,115
Chengdu	1,933
Dalian	1,855
Changchun	1,810
Jinan	1,660
Taiyuan	1,642
Qingdao	1,584
Zibo	1,346
Zhengzhou	1,324
Lanzhou	1,296
Anshan	1,252
Fushun	1,246
Kunming	1,242
Changsha	1,198
Hangzhou	1,185
Nanchang	1,169
Shijiazhuang	1,159
Guiyang	1,131
Ürümqi	1,130
Jilin	1,118
Tangshan	1,110
Qiqihar	1,104
Baotou	1,033
COLOMBIA	
Bogotá	6,005
Cali	1,986
Medellín	1,971
Barranquilla	1,158
Cartagena	813
Cúcuta	589
Bucaramanga	508
CONGO	
Brazzaville	938
Pointe-Noire	576
CONGO (DEM. REP.)	
Kinshasa	2,664
Lubumbashi	565
CROATIA	
Zagreb	868
CUBA	
Havana	2,204
CZECH REPUBLIC	
Prague	1,203
DENMARK	
Copenhagen	1,362
DOMINICAN REPUBLIC	
Santo Domingo	2,135
Stgo. de los Caballeros	691
ECUADOR	
Guayaquil	2,070
Quito	1,574
EGYPT	
Cairo	6,800
Alexandria	3,339
El Gîza	2,222
Shubra el Kheima	871
EL SALVADOR	
San Salvador	1,522
ETHIOPIA	
Addis Ababa	2,316
FINLAND	
Helsinki	532
FRANCE	
Paris	11,175
Lyons	1,648
Marseilles	1,516
Lille	1,143
Toulouse	965
Nice	933
Bordeaux	925
Nantes	711
Strasbourg	612
Toulon	565
Douai	553
Rennes	521
Rouen	518
Grenoble	515
GEORGIA	
Tbilisi	1,253
GERMANY	
Berlin	3,426
Hamburg	1,705
Munich	1,206
Cologne	964
Frankfurt	644
Essen	609
Dortmund	595
Stuttgart	585
Düsseldorf	571
Bremen	547
Duisburg	529
Hanover	521
GHANA	
Accra	1,781
GREECE	
Athens	3,097
GUATEMALA	
Guatemala	1,167
GUINEA	
Conakry	1,508
HAITI	
Port-au-Prince	885
HONDURAS	
Tegucigalpa	814
HUNGARY	
Budapest	1,885
INDIA	
Mumbai (Bombay)	16,368
Kolkata (Calcutta)	13,217
Delhi	12,791
Chennai (Madras)	6,425
Bangalore	5,687
Hyderabad	5,534
Ahmadabad	4,519
Pune	3,756
Surat	2,811
Kanpur	2,690
Jaipur	2,324
Lucknow	2,267
Nagpur	2,123
Patna	1,707
Indore	1,639
Vadodara	1,492
Bhopal	1,455
Coimbatore	1,446
Ludhiana	1,395
Cochin	1,355
Vishakhapatnam	1,329
Agra	1,321
Varanasi	1,212
Madurai	1,195
Meerut	1,167
Nasik	1,152
Jabalpur	1,117
Jamshedpur	1,102
Asansol	1,090
Faridabad	1,055
Allahabad	1,050
Amritsar	1,011
Vijayawada	1,011
Rajkot	1,002
INDONESIA	
Jakarta	11,500
Surabaya	2,701
Bandung	2,368
Medan	1,910
Semarang	1,366
Palembang	1,352
Tangerang	1,198
Ujung Pandang	1,092
IRAN	
Tehran	6,759
Mashhad	1,887
Esfahan	1,266
Tabriz	1,191
Shiraz	1,053
Karaj	941
Ahvaz	805
Qom	778
Bakhtaran	693
IRAQ	
Baghdad	3,841
As Sulaymaniyah	952
Arbil	770
Al Mawsil	664
Al Kazimiyah	521
IRELAND	
Dublin	1,024
ISRAEL	
Tel Aviv-Yafo	1,880
Jerusalem	591
ITALY	
Rome	2,654
Milan	1,306
Naples	1,050
Turin	923
Palermo	689
Genoa	659
IVORY COAST	
Abidjan	2,500
JAMAICA	
Kingston	644
JAPAN	
Tokyo	17,950
Yokohama	3,427
Osaka	2,599
Nagoya	2,171
Sapporo	1,822
Kobe	1,494
Kyoto	1,468
Fukuoka	1,341
Kawasaki	1,250
Hiroshima	1,126
Kitakyushu	1,011
Sendai	1,008
JORDAN	
Amman	1,752
KAZAKHSTAN	
Almaty	1,151
Qaraghandy	574
KENYA	
Nairobi	2,000
Mombasa	600
KOREA, NORTH	
Pyŏngyang	2,741
Hamhung	710
Chŏngjin	583
KOREA, SOUTH	
Seoul	10,231
Pusan	3,814
Taegu	2,449
Inch'on	2,308
Taejŏn	1,272
Kwangju	1,258
Ulsan	967
Sŏngnam	869
Puch'on	779
Suwŏn	756
Anyang	590
Chŏnju	563
Chŏngju	531
Ansan	510
P'ohang	509
KYRGYZSTAN	
Bishkek	589
LAOS	
Vientiane	532
LATVIA	
Riga	811
LEBANON	
Beirut	1,500
Tripoli	500
LIBERIA	
Monrovia	962
LIBYA	
Tripoli	960
LITHUANIA	
Vilnius	580
MACEDONIA	
Skopje	541
MADAGASCAR	
Antananarivo	1,053
MALAYSIA	
Kuala Lumpur	1,145
MALI	
Bamako	810
MAURITANIA	
Nouakchott	735
MEXICO	
Mexico City	15,643
Guadalajara	2,847
Monterrey	2,522
Puebla	1,055
León	872
Ciudad Juárez	798
Tijuana	743
Culiacán	602
Mexicali	602
Acapulco	592
Mérida	557
Chihuahua	530
San Luis Potosí	526
Aguascalientés	506
MOLDOVA	
Chişinău	658
MONGOLIA	
Ulan Bator	673
MOROCCO	
Casablanca	2,943
Rabat-Salé	1,220
Marrakesh	602
Fès	564
MOZAMBIQUE	
Maputo	2,000
NEPAL	
Katmandu	535
NETHERLANDS	
Amsterdam	1,115
Rotterdam	1,086
The Hague	700
Utrecht	557
NEW ZEALAND	
Auckland	1,090
NICARAGUA	
Managua	864
NIGERIA	
Lagos	10,287
Ibadan	1,432
Ogbomosho	730
Kano	674
NORWAY	
Oslo	502
PAKISTAN	
Karachi	9,269
Lahore	5,064
Faisalabad	1,977
Rawalpindi	1,406
Multan	1,182
Hyderabad	1,151
Gujranwala	1,125
Peshawar	988
Quetta	560
Islamabad	525
PARAGUAY	
Asunción	945
PERU	
Lima	6,601
Arequipa	620
Trujillo	509
PHILIPPINES	
Manila	8,594
Quezon City	1,989
Caloocan	1,023
Davao	1,009
Cebu	662
Zamboanga	511
POLAND	
Warsaw	1,626
Lódz	815
Kraków	740
Wroclaw	641
Poznań	580
PORTUGAL	
Lisbon	2,561
Oporto	1,174
ROMANIA	
Bucharest	2,028
RUSSIA	
Moscow	8,405
St Petersburg	4,216
Nizhniy Novgorod	1,371
Novosibirsk	1,367
Yekaterinburg	1,275
Samara	1,170
Omsk	1,158
Kazan	1,085
Chelyabinsk	1,084
Ufa	1,082
Perm	1,025
Rostov	1,023
Volgograd	1,005
SAUDI ARABIA	
Riyadh	1,800
Jedda	1,500
Mecca	630
SENEGAL	
Dakar	1,905
SERBIA & MONTENEGRO	
Belgrade	1,598
SIERRA LEONE	
Freetown	505
SINGAPORE	
Singapore	3,866
SOMALIA	
Mogadishu	997
SOUTH AFRICA	
Cape Town	2,350
Johannesburg	1,196
Durban	1,137
Pretoria	1,080
Port Elizabeth	853
Vanderbijlpark–Vereeniging	774
Soweto	597
Sasolburg	540
SPAIN	
Madrid	3,030
Barcelona	1,615
Valencia	763
Sevilla	720
Zaragoza	608
Málaga	532
SRI LANKA	
Colombo	1,863
SUDAN	
Omdurman	1,271
Khartoum	925
Khartoum North	701
SWEDEN	
Stockholm	727
SWITZERLAND	
Zürich	733
SYRIA	
Aleppo	1,813
Damascus	1,394
Homs	659
TAIWAN	
T'aipei	2,596
Kaohsiung	1,435
T'aichung	858
T'ainan	708
Panch'iao	539
TAJIKISTAN	
Dushanbe	524
TANZANIA	
Dar-es-Salaam	1,361
THAILAND	
Bangkok	7,507
TOGO	
Lomé	590
TUNISIA	
Tunis	1,827
TURKEY	
Istanbul	8,506
Ankara	3,294
Izmir	2,554
Bursa	1,485
Adana	1,273
Konya	1,140
Mersin (Içel)	956
Gaziantep	867
Antalya	867
Kayseri	862
Diyarbakir	833
Urfa	785
Manisa	696
Kocaeli	629
Antalya	591
Samsun	590
Kahramanmaras	551
Balikesir	538
Eskisehir	519
Erzurum	512
Malatya	510
TURKMENISTAN	
Ashkhabad	536
UGANDA	
Kampala	954
UKRAINE	
Kiev	2,621
Kharkov	1,521
Dnepropetrovsk	1,122
Donetsk	1,065
Odessa	1,027
Zaporizhzhya	863
Lviv	794
Kryvyy Rih	720
Mykolayiv	518
Mariupol	500
UNITED ARAB EMIRATES	
Abu Dhabi	928
Dubai	674
UNITED KINGDOM	
London	8,089
Birmingham	2,373
Manchester	2,353
Liverpool	852
Glasgow	832
Sheffield	661
Nottingham	649
Newcastle	617
Bristol	552
Leeds	529
UNITED STATES	
New York	21,200
Los Angeles	16,374
Chicago–Gary	9,158
Washington–Baltimore	7,608
San Francisco–San Jose	7,039
Philadelphia–Atlantic City	6,188
Boston–Worcester	5,819
Detroit–Flint	5,456
Dallas–Fort Worth	5,222
Houston–Galveston	4,670
Atlanta	4,112
Miami–Fort Lauderdale	3,876
Seattle–Tacoma	3,554
Phoenix–Mesa	3,252
Minneapolis–St Paul	2,969
Cleveland–Akron	2,946
San Diego	2,814
St Louis	2,604
Denver–Boulder	2,582
San Juan	2,450
Tampa–Saint Petersburg	2,396
Pittsburgh	2,359
Portland–Salem	2,265
Cincinnati–Hamilton	1,979
Sacramento–Yolo	1,797
Kansas City	1,776
Milwaukee–Racine	1,690
Orlando	1,645
Indianapolis	1,607
San Antonio	1,592
Norfolk–Virginia Beach–Newport News	1,570
Las Vegas	1,563
Columbus, OH	1,540
Charlotte–Gastonia	1,499
New Orleans	1,338
Salt Lake City	1,334
Greensboro–Winston Salem–High Point	1,252
Austin–San Marcos	1,250
Nashville	1,231
Providence–Fall River	1,189
Raleigh–Durham	1,188
Hartford	1,183
Buffalo–Niagara Falls	1,170
Memphis	1,136
West Palm Beach	1,131
Jacksonville, FL	1,100
Rochester	1,098
Grand Rapids	1,089
Oklahoma City	1,083
Louisville	1,026
Richmond–Petersburg	997
Greenville	962
Dayton–Springfield	951
Fresno	923
Birmingham	921
Honolulu	876
Albany–Schenectady	876
Tucson	844
Tulsa	803
Syracuse	732
Omaha	717
Albuquerque	713
Knoxville	687
El Paso	680
Bakersfield	662
Allentown	638
Harrisburg	629
Scranton	625
Toledo	618
Baton Rouge	603
Youngstown–Warren	595
Springfield, MA	592
Sarasota	590
Little Rock	584
McAllen	569
Stockton–Lodi	564
Charleston	549
Wichita	545
Mobile	540
Columbia, SC	537
Colorado Springs	517
Fort Wayne	502
URUGUAY	
Montevideo	1,379
UZBEKISTAN	
Tashkent	2,118
VENEZUELA	
Caracas	1,975
Maracaibo	1,706
Valencia	1,263
Barquisimeto	811
Ciudad Guayana	642
VIETNAM	
Ho Chi Minh City	4,322
Hanoi	3,056
Haiphong	783
YEMEN	
Sana'	972
Aden	562
ZAMBIA	
Lusaka	982
ZIMBABWE	
Harare	1,189
Bulawayo	622

* SAR = Special Administrative Region of China

World Statistics: Distances

The table shows air distances in miles and kilometres between 30 major cities. Known as 'Great Circle' distances, these measure the shortest routes between the cities, which aircraft use wherever possible. The maps show the world centred on six cities, and illustrate, for example, why direct flights from Japan to northern America and Europe are across the Arctic regions. The maps have been constructed on an Azimuthal Equidistant projection, on which all distances measured through the centre point are true to scale. The red lines are drawn at 5,000, 10,000 and 15,000 km from the central city.

miles

miles	Bombay (Mumbai)	Buenos Aires	Cairo	Calcutta (Kolkata)	Caracas	Chicago	Hong Kong	Honolulu	Johannesburg	Lagos	London	Los Angeles	Mexico City	Moscow	Nairobi	New York	Paris	Rio de Janeiro	Rome	Singapore	Sydney	Tokyo	Wellington
Beijing	2956	11972	4688	2031	8947	6588	1220	5070	7276	7119	5057	6251	7742	3600	5727	6828	5106	10773	5049	2783	5561	1304	6700
Bombay (Mumbai)		9275	2706	1034	9024	8048	2683	8024	4334	4730	4467	8700	9728	3126	2816	7793	4356	8332	3837	2432	6313	4189	7686
Buenos Aires			7341	10268	3167	5599	11481	7558	5025	4919	6917	6122	4591	8374	6463	5298	6867	1214	6929	9867	7332	11410	6202
Cairo				3541	6340	6127	5064	8838	3894	2432	2180	7580	7687	1803	2197	5605	1994	6149	1325	5137	8959	5947	10268
Calcutta (Kolkata)					9609	7978	1653	7048	5256	5727	4946	8152	9494	3438	3839	7921	4883	9366	4486	1800	5678	3195	7055
Caracas						2502	10166	6009	6847	4810	4664	3612	2228	6175	7173	2131	4738	2825	5196	11407	9534	8801	8154
Chicago							7783	4247	8689	5973	3949	1742	1694	4971	8005	711	4132	5311	4809	9369	9243	6299	8358
Hong Kong								5543	6669	7360	5980	7232	8775	4439	5453	8047	5984	11001	5769	1615	4582	1786	5857
Honolulu									11934	10133	7228	2558	3781	7036	10739	4958	7437	8290	8026	6721	5075	3854	4669
Johannesburg										2799	5637	10362	9063	5692	1818	7979	5426	4420	4811	5381	6860	8418	7308
Lagos											3118	7713	6879	3886	2366	5268	2929	3750	2510	6925	9643	8376	9973
London												5442	5552	1552	4237	3463	212	5778	889	6743	10558	5942	11691
Los Angeles													1549	6070	9659	2446	5645	6310	6331	8776	7502	5475	6719
Mexico City														6664	9207	2090	5717	4780	6365	10321	8058	7024	6897
Moscow															3942	4666	1545	7184	1477	5237	9008	4651	10283
Nairobi																7358	4029	5548	3350	4635	7552	6996	8490
New York																	3626	4832	4280	9531	9935	6741	8951
Paris																		5708	687	6671	10539	6038	11798
Rio de Janeiro																			5725	9763	8389	11551	7367
Rome																				6229	10143	6127	11523
Singapore																					3915	3306	5298
Sydney																						4861	1383
Tokyo																							5762

km

km	Beijing	Bombay (Mumbai)	Buenos Aires	Cairo	Calcutta (Kolkata)	Caracas	Chicago	Hong Kong	Honolulu	Johannesburg	Lagos	London	Los Angeles	Mexico City	Moscow	Nairobi	New York	Paris	Rio de Janeiro	Rome	Singapore	Sydney	Tokyo
Bombay (Mumbai)	4757																						
Buenos Aires	19268	14925																					
Cairo	7544	4355	11814																				
Calcutta (Kolkata)	3269	1664	16524	5699																			
Caracas	14399	14522	5096	10203	15464																		
Chicago	10603	12953	9011	3206	12839	4027																	
Hong Kong	1963	4317	18478	8150	2659	16360	12526																
Honolulu	8160	12914	12164	14223	11343	9670	6836	8921															
Johannesburg	11710	6974	8088	6267	8459	11019	13984	10732	19206														
Lagos	11457	7612	7916	3915	9216	7741	9612	11845	16308	4505													
London	8138	7190	11131	3508	7961	7507	6356	9623	11632	9071	5017												
Los Angeles	10060	14000	9852	12200	13120	5812	2804	11639	4117	16676	12414	8758											
Mexico City	12460	15656	7389	12372	15280	3586	2726	14122	6085	14585	11071	8936	2493										
Moscow	5794	5031	13477	2902	5534	9938	8000	7144	11323	9161	6254	2498	9769	10724									
Nairobi	9216	4532	10402	3536	6179	11544	12883	8776	17282	2927	3807	6819	15544	14818	6344								
New York	10988	12541	8526	9020	12747	3430	1145	12950	7980	12841	8477	5572	3936	3264	7510	11842							
Paris	8217	7010	11051	3210	7858	7625	6650	9630	11968	8732	4714	342	9085	9200	2486	6485	5836						
Rio de Janeiro	17338	13409	1953	9896	15073	4546	8547	17704	13342	7113	6035	9299	10155	7693	11562	8928	7777	9187					
Rome	8126	6175	11151	2133	7219	8363	7739	9284	12916	7743	4039	1431	10188	10243	2376	5391	6888	1105	9214				
Singapore	4478	3914	15879	8267	2897	18359	15078	2599	10816	8660	11145	10852	14123	16610	8428	7460	15339	10737	15712	10025			
Sydney	8949	10160	11800	14418	9138	15343	14875	7374	8168	11040	15519	16992	12073	12969	14497	12153	15989	16962	13501	16324	6300		
Tokyo	2099	6742	18362	9571	5141	14164	10137	2874	6202	13547	13480	9562	8811	11304	7485	11260	10849	9718	18589	9861	5321	7823	
Wellington	10782	12370	9981	16524	11354	13122	13451	9427	7513	11761	16050	18814	10814	11100	16549	13664	14405	18987	11855	18545	8526	2226	9273

Northern Hemisphere

MEXICO CITY
19 26°N 99 4°W

LONDON
51 28°N 0 27°W

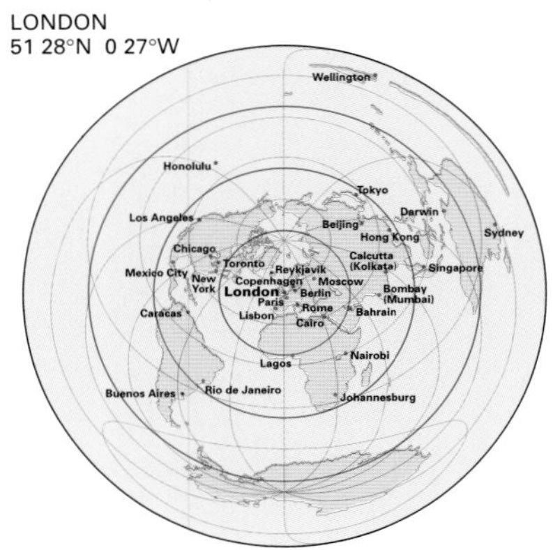

TOKYO
35 33°N 139 46°E

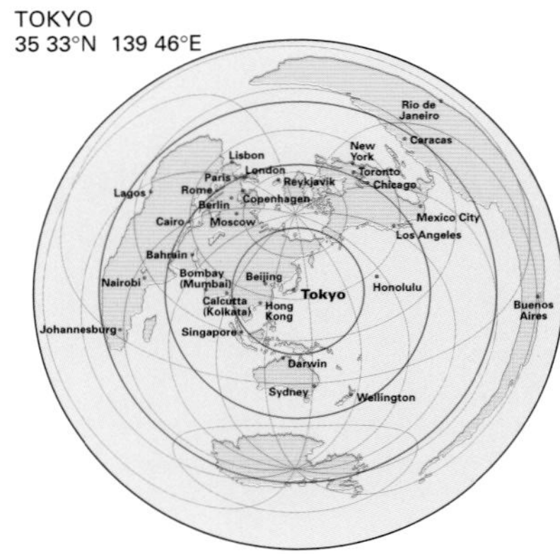

Southern Hemisphere

RIO DE JANEIRO
22 50°S 43 15°W

SINGAPORE
1 21°N 103 54°E

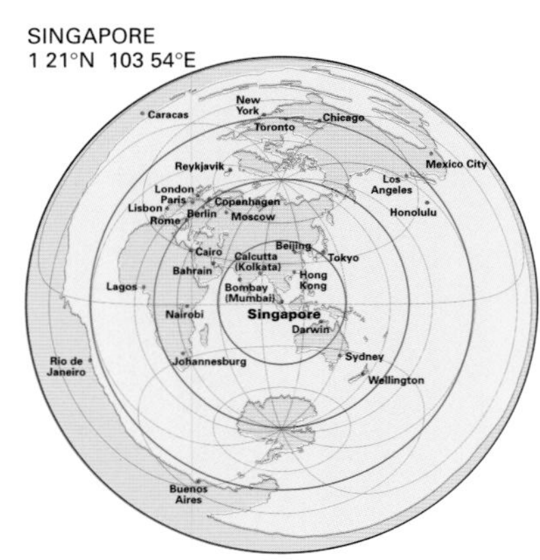

SYDNEY
33 56°S 151 10°E

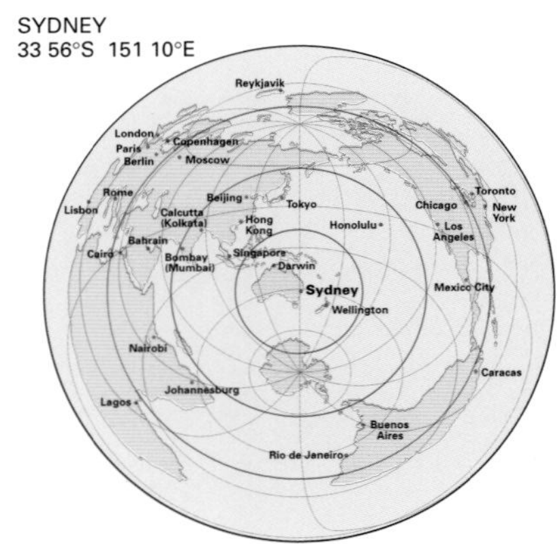

World Statistics: Climate

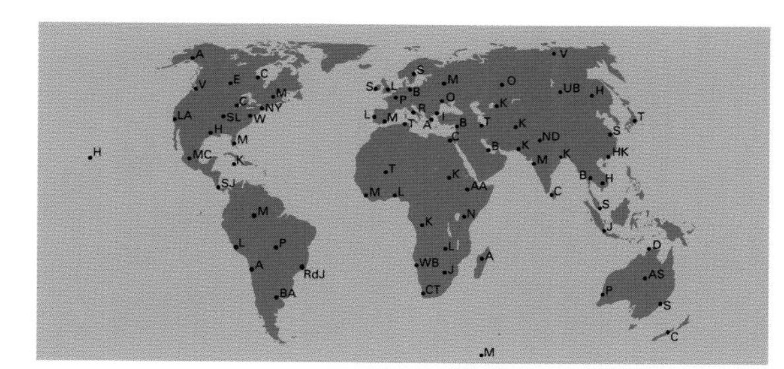

Rainfall and temperature figures are provided for more than 70 cities around the world. As climate is affected by altitude, the height of each city is shown in metres beneath its name. For each location, the top row of figures shows the total rainfall or snow in millimetres, and the bottom row the average temperature in degrees Celsius; the total annual rainfall and average annual temperature are at the end of the rows.

EUROPE	Jan.	Feb.	Mar.	Apr.	May	June	July	Aug.	Sept.	Oct.	Nov.	Dec.	Year
Athens, Greece	62	37	37	23	23	14	6	7	15	51	56	71	402
107 m	10	10	12	16	20	25	28	28	24	20	15	11	18
Berlin, Germany	46	40	33	42	49	65	73	69	48	49	46	43	603
55 m	−1	0	4	9	14	17	19	18	15	9	5	1	9
Istanbul, Turkey	109	92	72	46	38	34	34	30	58	81	103	119	816
14 m	5	6	7	11	16	20	23	23	20	16	12	8	14
Lisbon, Portugal	111	76	109	54	44	16	3	4	33	62	93	103	708
77 m	11	12	14	16	17	20	22	23	21	18	14	12	17
London, UK	54	40	37	37	46	45	57	59	49	57	64	48	593
5 m	4	5	7	9	12	16	18	17	15	11	8	5	11
Málaga, Spain	61	51	62	46	26	5	1	3	29	64	64	62	474
33 m	12	13	16	17	19	29	25	26	23	20	16	13	18
Moscow, Russia	39	38	36	37	53	58	88	71	58	45	47	54	624
156 m	−13	−10	−4	6	13	16	18	17	12	6	−1	−7	4
Odesa, Ukraine	57	62	30	21	34	34	42	37	37	13	35	71	473
64 m	−3	−1	2	9	15	20	22	22	18	12	9	1	10
Paris, France	56	46	35	42	57	54	59	64	55	50	51	50	619
75 m	3	4	8	11	15	18	20	19	17	12	7	4	12
Rome, Italy	71	62	57	51	46	37	15	21	63	99	129	93	744
17 m	8	9	11	14	18	22	25	25	22	17	13	10	16
Shannon, Irish Republic	94	67	56	53	61	57	77	79	86	86	96	117	929
2 m	5	5	7	9	12	14	16	16	14	11	8	6	10
Stockholm, Sweden	43	30	25	31	34	45	61	76	60	48	53	48	554
44 m	−3	−3	−1	5	10	15	18	17	12	7	3	0	7
ASIA													
Bahrain	8	18	13	8	<3	0	0	0	0	0	18	18	81
5 m	17	18	21	25	29	32	33	34	31	28	24	19	26
Bangkok, Thailand	8	20	36	58	198	160	160	175	305	206	66	5	1,397
2 m	26	28	29	30	29	29	28	28	28	28	26	25	28
Beirut, Lebanon	191	158	94	53	18	3	<3	<3	5	51	132	185	892
34 m	14	14	16	18	22	24	27	28	26	24	19	16	21
Colombo, Sri Lanka	89	69	147	231	371	224	135	109	160	348	315	147	2,365
7 m	26	26	27	28	28	27	27	27	27	27	26	26	27
Harbin, China	6	5	10	23	43	94	112	104	46	33	8	5	488
160 m	−18	−15	−5	6	13	19	22	21	14	4	−6	−16	3
Ho Chi Minh, Vietnam	15	3	13	43	221	330	315	269	335	269	114	56	1,984
9 m	26	27	29	30	29	28	28	28	27	27	27	26	28
Hong Kong, China	33	46	74	137	292	394	381	361	257	114	43	31	2,162
33 m	16	15	18	22	26	28	28	28	27	25	21	18	23
Jakarta, Indonesia	300	300	211	147	114	97	64	43	66	112	142	203	1,798
8 m	26	26	27	27	27	27	27	27	27	27	27	26	27
Kabul, Afghanistan	31	36	94	102	20	5	3	3	<3	15	20	10	338
1,815 m	−3	−1	6	13	18	22	25	24	20	14	7	3	12
Karachi, Pakistan	13	10	8	3	3	18	81	41	13	<3	3	5	196
4 m	19	20	24	28	30	31	30	29	28	28	24	20	26
Kazalinsk, Kazakhstan	10	10	13	13	15	5	5	8	8	10	13	15	125
63 m	−12	−11	−3	6	18	23	25	23	16	8	−1	−7	7
Kolkata (Calcutta), India	10	31	36	43	140	297	325	328	252	114	20	5	1,600
6 m	20	22	27	30	30	30	29	29	29	28	23	19	26
Mumbai (Bombay), India	3	3	3	<3	18	485	617	340	264	64	13	3	1,809
11 m	24	24	26	28	30	29	27	27	27	28	27	26	27
New Delhi, India	23	18	13	8	13	74	180	172	117	10	3	10	640
218 m	14	17	23	28	33	34	31	30	29	26	20	15	25
Omsk, Russia	15	8	8	13	31	51	51	51	28	25	18	20	318
85 m	−22	−19	−12	−1	10	16	18	16	10	1	−11	−18	−1
Shanghai, China	48	58	84	94	94	180	147	142	130	71	51	36	1,135
7 m	4	5	9	14	20	24	28	28	23	19	12	7	16
Singapore	252	173	193	188	173	173	170	196	178	208	254	257	2,413
10 m	26	27	28	28	28	28	28	27	27	27	27	27	27
Tehran, Iran	46	38	46	36	13	3	3	3	3	8	20	31	246
1,220 m	2	5	9	16	21	26	30	29	25	18	12	6	17
Tokyo, Japan	48	74	107	135	147	165	142	152	234	208	97	56	1,565
6 m	3	4	7	13	17	21	25	26	23	17	11	6	14
Ulan Bator, Mongolia	<3	<3	3	5	10	28	76	51	23	5	5	3	208
1,325 m	−26	−21	−13	−1	6	14	16	14	8	−1	−13	−22	−3
Verkhoyansk, Russia	5	5	3	5	8	23	28	25	13	8	8	5	134
100 m	−50	−45	−32	−15	0	12	14	9	2	−15	−38	−48	−17
AFRICA													
Addis Ababa, Ethiopia	<3	3	25	135	213	201	206	239	102	28	<3	0	1,151
2,450 m	19	20	20	20	19	18	18	19	21	22	21	20	20
Antananarivo, Madagas.	300	279	178	53	18	8	8	10	18	61	135	287	1,356
1,372 m	21	21	21	19	18	15	14	15	17	19	21	21	19
Cairo, Egypt	5	5	5	3	3	<3	0	0	<3	<3	3	5	28
116 m	13	15	18	21	25	28	28	28	26	24	20	15	22
Cape Town, S. Africa	15	8	18	48	79	84	89	66	43	31	18	10	508
17 m	21	21	20	17	14	13	12	13	14	16	18	19	17
Johannesburg, S. Africa	114	109	89	38	25	8	8	8	23	56	107	125	709
1,665 m	20	20	18	16	13	10	11	13	16	18	19	20	16
Khartoum, Sudan	<3	<3	<3	<3	3	8	53	71	18	5	<3	0	158
390 m	24	25	28	31	33	34	32	31	32	32	28	25	29
Kinshasa, Congo (D.R.)	135	145	196	196	158	8	3	3	31	119	221	142	1,354
325 m	26	26	27	27	26	24	23	24	25	26	26	26	25
Lagos, Nigeria	28	46	102	150	269	460	279	64	140	206	69	25	1,836
3 m	27	28	29	28	28	26	26	25	26	26	28	28	27
Lusaka, Zambia	231	191	142	18	3	<3	<3	0	<3	10	91	150	836
1,277 m	21	22	21	21	19	16	16	18	22	24	23	22	21
Monrovia, Liberia	31	56	97	216	516	973	996	373	744	772	236	130	5,138
23 m	26	26	27	27	26	25	24	25	25	25	26	26	26
Nairobi, Kenya	38	64	125	211	158	46	15	23	31	53	109	86	958
1,820 m	19	19	19	19	18	16	16	16	18	19	18	18	18
Timbuktu, Mali	<3	<3	3	<3	5	23	79	81	38	3	<3	<3	231
301 m	22	24	28	32	34	35	32	30	32	31	28	23	29
Tunis, Tunisia	64	51	41	36	18	8	3	8	33	51	48	61	419
66 m	10	11	13	16	19	23	26	27	25	20	16	11	18
Walvis Bay, Namibia	<3	5	8	3	3	<3	<3	3	<3	<3	<3	<3	23
7 m	19	19	19	18	17	16	15	14	14	15	17	18	18
AUSTRALIA, NEW ZEALAND AND ANTARCTICA													
Alice Springs, Australia	43	33	28	10	15	13	8	8	8	18	31	38	252
579 m	29	28	25	20	15	12	12	14	18	23	26	28	21
Christchurch, N. Zealand	56	43	48	48	66	66	69	48	46	43	48	56	638
10 m	16	16	14	12	9	6	6	7	9	12	14	16	11
Darwin, Australia	386	312	254	97	15	3	<3	3	13	51	119	239	1,491
30 m	29	29	29	29	28	26	25	26	28	29	30	29	28
Mawson, Antarctica	11	30	20	10	44	180	4	40	3	20	0	0	362
14 m	0	−5	−10	−14	−15	−16	−18	−18	−19	−13	−5	−1	−11
Perth, Australia	8	10	20	43	130	180	170	149	86	56	20	13	881
60 m	23	23	22	19	16	14	13	13	15	16	19	22	18
Sydney, Australia	89	102	127	135	127	117	117	76	73	71	73	73	1,181
42 m	22	22	21	18	15	13	12	13	15	18	19	21	17
NORTH AMERICA													
Anchorage, Alaska, USA	20	18	15	10	13	18	41	66	66	56	25	23	371
40 m	−11	−8	−5	2	7	12	14	13	9	2	−5	−11	2
Chicago, Illinois, USA	51	51	66	71	86	89	84	81	79	66	61	51	836
251 m	−4	−3	2	9	14	20	23	22	19	12	5	−1	10
Churchill, Man., Canada	15	13	18	23	32	44	46	58	51	43	39	21	402
13 m	−28	−26	−20	−10	−2	6	12	11	5	−2	−12	−22	−7
Edmonton, Alta., Canada	25	19	19	22	43	77	89	78	39	17	16	25	466
676 m	−15	−10	−5	4	11	15	17	16	11	6	−4	−10	3
Honolulu, Hawaii, USA	104	66	79	48	25	18	23	28	36	48	64	104	643
12 m	23	18	19	20	22	24	25	26	26	24	22	19	22
Houston, Texas, USA	89	76	84	91	119	117	99	99	104	94	89	109	1,171
12 m	12	13	17	21	24	27	28	29	26	22	16	12	21
Kingston, Jamaica	23	15	23	31	102	89	38	91	99	180	74	36	800
34 m	25	25	25	26	26	28	28	28	27	27	26	26	26
Los Angeles, Calif., USA	79	76	71	25	10	3	<3	<3	5	15	31	66	381
95 m	13	14	14	16	17	19	21	22	21	18	16	14	17
Mexico City, Mexico	13	5	10	20	53	119	170	152	130	51	18	8	747
2,309 m	12	13	16	18	19	19	17	18	18	16	14	13	16
Miami, Florida, USA	71	53	64	81	173	178	155	160	203	234	71	51	1,516
8 m	20	20	22	23	25	27	28	28	27	25	22	21	24
Montréal, Que., Canada	72	65	74	74	66	82	90	92	88	76	81	87	946
57 m	−10	−9	−3	−6	13	18	21	20	15	9	2	−7	6
New York City, NY, USA	94	97	91	81	81	84	107	109	86	89	76	91	1,092
96 m	−1	−1	3	10	16	20	23	23	21	15	7	2	11
St Louis, Mo., USA	58	64	89	97	114	114	89	86	81	74	71	64	1,001
173 m	0	1	7	13	19	24	26	26	22	15	8	2	14
San José, Costa Rica	15	5	20	46	229	241	211	241	305	300	145	41	1,798
1,146 m	19	19	21	21	22	21	21	21	21	20	20	19	20
Vancouver, BC, Canada	154	115	101	60	52	45	32	41	67	114	150	182	1,113
14 m	3	5	6	9	12	15	17	17	14	10	6	4	10
Washington, DC, USA	86	76	91	84	94	99	112	109	94	74	66	79	1,064
22 m	1	2	7	12	18	23	25	24	20	14	8	3	13
SOUTH AMERICA													
Antofagasta, Chile	0	0	0	<3	<3	3	5	3	<3	3	<3	0	13
94 m	21	21	20	18	16	15	14	14	15	16	18	19	17
Buenos Aires, Argentina	79	71	109	89	76	61	56	61	79	86	84	99	950
27 m	23	23	21	17	13	9	10	11	13	15	19	22	16
Lima, Peru	3	<3	<3	<3	5	5	8	8	8	3	3	<3	41
120 m	23	24	24	22	19	17	17	16	17	18	19	21	20
Manaus, Brazil	249	231	262	221	170	84	58	38	46	107	142	203	1,811
44 m	28	28	28	27	28	28	28	28	29	29	29	28	28
Paraná, Brazil	287	236	239	102	13	<3	3	5	28	127	231	310	1,582
260 m	23	23	23	23	23	21	21	22	24	24	24	23	23
Rio de Janeiro, Brazil	125	122	130	107	79	53	41	43	66	79	104	137	1,082
61 m	26	26	25	24	22	21	21	21	21	22	23	25	23

World Statistics: Physical Dimensions

Each topic list is divided into continents and within a continent the items are listed in order of size. The bottom part of many of the lists is selective in order to give examples from as many different countries as possible. The order of the continents is as in the atlas, Europe through to South America. The world top ten are shown in square brackets; in the case of mountains this has not been done because the world top 30 are all in Asia. The figures are rounded as appropriate.

WORLD, CONTINENTS, OCEANS

THE WORLD	km²	miles²	%
The World	509,450,000	196,672,000	–
Land	149,450,000	57,688,000	29.3
Water	360,000,000	138,984,000	70.7
Asia	44,500,000	17,177,000	29.8
Africa	30,302,000	11,697,000	20.3
North America	24,241,000	9,357,000	16.2
South America	17,793,000	6,868,000	11.9
Antarctica	14,100,000	5,443,000	9.4
Europe	9,957,000	3,843,000	6.7
Australia & Oceania	8,557,000	3,303,000	5.7
Pacific Ocean	179,679,000	69,356,000	49.9
Atlantic Ocean	92,373,000	35,657,000	25.7
Indian Ocean	73,917,000	28,532,000	20.5
Arctic Ocean	14,090,000	5,439,000	3.9

SEAS

PACIFIC	km²	miles²
South China Sea	2,974,600	1,148,500
Bering Sea	2,268,000	875,000
Sea of Okhotsk	1,528,000	590,000
East China & Yellow	1,249,000	482,000
Sea of Japan	1,008,000	389,000
Gulf of California	162,000	62,500
Bass Strait	75,000	29,000

ATLANTIC	km²	miles²
Caribbean Sea	2,766,000	1,068,000
Mediterranean Sea	2,516,000	971,000
Gulf of Mexico	1,543,000	596,000
Hudson Bay	1,232,000	476,000
North Sea	575,000	223,000
Black Sea	462,000	178,000
Baltic Sea	422,170	163,000
Gulf of St Lawrence	238,000	92,000

INDIAN	km²	miles²
Red Sea	438,000	169,000
The Gulf	239,000	92,000

MOUNTAINS

EUROPE		m	ft
Elbrus	Russia	5,642	18,510
Mont Blanc	France/Italy	4,807	15,771
Monte Rosa	Italy/Switzerland	4,634	15,203
Dom	Switzerland	4,545	14,911
Liskamm	Switzerland	4,527	14,852
Weisshorn	Switzerland	4,505	14,780
Taschorn	Switzerland	4,490	14,730
Matterhorn/Cervino	Italy/Switz.	4,478	14,691
Mont Maudit	France/Italy	4,465	14,649
Dent Blanche	Switzerland	4,356	14,291
Nadelhorn	Switzerland	4,327	14,196
Grandes Jorasses	France/Italy	4,208	13,806
Jungfrau	Switzerland	4,158	13,642
Barre des Ecrins	France	4,103	13,461
Gran Paradiso	Italy	4,061	13,323
Piz Bernina	Italy/Switzerland	4,049	13,284
Eiger	Switzerland	3,970	13,025
Monte Viso	Italy	3,841	12,602
Grossglockner	Austria	3,797	12,457
Wildspitze	Austria	3,772	12,382
Monte Disgrazia	Italy	3,678	12,066
Mulhacén	Spain	3,478	11,411
Pico de Aneto	Spain	3,404	11,168
Marmolada	Italy	3,342	10,964
Etna	Italy	3,340	10,958
Zugspitze	Germany	2,962	9,718
Musala	Bulgaria	2,925	9,596
Olympus	Greece	2,917	9,570
Triglav	Slovenia	2,863	9,393
Monte Cinto	France (Corsica)	2,710	8,891
Galdhöpiggen	Norway	2,468	8,100
Ben Nevis	UK	1,343	4,406

ASIA		m	ft
Everest	China/Nepal	8,850	29,035
K2 (Godwin Austen)	China/Kashmir	8,611	28,251
Kanchenjunga	India/Nepal	8,598	28,208
Lhotse	China/Nepal	8,516	27,939
Makalu	China/Nepal	8,481	27,824
Cho Oyu	China/Nepal	8,201	26,906
Dhaulagiri	Nepal	8,172	26,811
Manaslu	Nepal	8,156	26,758
Nanga Parbat	Kashmir	8,126	26,660
Annapurna	Nepal	8,078	26,502
Gasherbrum	China/Kashmir	8,068	26,469
Broad Peak	China/Kashmir	8,051	26,414
Xixabangma	China	8,012	26,286
Kangbachen	India/Nepal	7,902	25,925
Jannu	India/Nepal	7,902	25,925
Gayachung Kang	Nepal	7,897	25,909
Himalchuli	Nepal	7,893	25,896
Disteghil Sar	Kashmir	7,885	25,869
Nuptse	Nepal	7,879	25,849
Khunyang Chhish	Kashmir	7,852	25,761
Masherbrum	Kashmir	7,821	25,659
Nanda Devi	India	7,817	25,646
Rakaposhi	Kashmir	7,788	25,551
Batura	Kashmir	7,785	25,541
Namche Barwa	China	7,756	25,446
Kamet	India	7,756	25,446
Soltoro Kangri	Kashmir	7,742	25,400
Gurla Mandhata	China	7,728	25,354
Trivor	Pakistan	7,720	25,328
Kongur Shan	China	7,719	25,324
Tirich Mir	Pakistan	7,690	25,229
K'ula Shan	Bhutan/China	7,543	24,747
Pik Kommunizma	Tajikistan	7,495	24,590
Demavend	Iran	5,604	18,386
Ararat	Turkey	5,165	16,945
Gunong Kinabalu	Malaysia (Borneo)	4,101	13,455
Yu Shan	Taiwan	3,997	13,113
Fuji-San	Japan	3,776	12,388

AFRICA		m	ft
Kilimanjaro	Tanzania	5,895	19,340
Mt Kenya	Kenya	5,199	17,057
Ruwenzori (Margherita)	Uganda/Congo (D.R.)	5,109	16,762
Ras Dashan	Ethiopia	4,620	15,157
Meru	Tanzania	4,565	14,977
Karisimbi	Rwanda/Congo (D.R.)	4,507	14,787
Mt Elgon	Kenya/Uganda	4,321	14,176
Batu	Ethiopia	4,307	14,130
Guna	Ethiopia	4,231	13,882
Toubkal	Morocco	4,165	13,665
Irhil Mgoun	Morocco	4,071	13,356
Mt Cameroon	Cameroon	4,070	13,353
Amba Ferit	Ethiopia	3,875	13,042
Pico del Teide	Spain (Tenerife)	3,718	12,198
Thabana Ntlenyana	Lesotho	3,482	11,424
Emi Koussi	Chad	3,415	11,204
Mt aux Sources	Lesotho/S. Africa	3,282	10,768
Mt Piton	Réunion	3,069	10,069

OCEANIA		m	ft
Puncak Jaya	Indonesia	5,029	16,499
Puncak Trikora	Indonesia	4,750	15,584
Puncak Mandala	Indonesia	4,702	15,427
Mt Wilhelm	Papua NG	4,508	14,790
Mauna Kea	USA (Hawaii)	4,205	13,796
Mauna Loa	USA (Hawaii)	4,169	13,681
Mt Cook (Aoraki)	New Zealand	3,753	12,313
Mt Balbi	Solomon Is.	2,439	8,002
Orohena	Tahiti	2,241	7,352
Mt Kosciuszko	Australia	2,230	7,316

NORTH AMERICA		m	ft
Mt McKinley (Denali)	USA (Alaska)	6,194	20,321
Mt Logan	Canada	5,959	19,551
Pico de Orizaba	Mexico	5,610	18,405
Mt St Elias	USA/Canada	5,489	18,008
Popocatepetl	Mexico	5,452	17,887

NORTH AMERICA (continued)		m	ft
Mt Foraker	USA (Alaska)	5,304	17,401
Ixtaccihuatl	Mexico	5,286	17,342
Lucania	Canada	5,227	17,149
Mt Steele	Canada	5,073	16,644
Mt Bona	USA (Alaska)	5,005	16,420
Mt Blackburn	USA (Alaska)	4,996	16,391
Mt Sanford	USA (Alaska)	4,940	16,207
Mt Wood	Canada	4,848	15,905
Nevado de Toluca	Mexico	4,670	15,321
Mt Fairweather	USA (Alaska)	4,663	15,298
Mt Hunter	USA (Alaska)	4,442	14,573
Mt Whitney	USA	4,418	14,495
Mt Elbert	USA	4,399	14,432
Mt Harvard	USA	4,395	14,419
Mt Rainier	USA	4,392	14,409
Blanca Peak	USA	4,372	14,344
Longs Peak	USA	4,345	14,255
Tajumulco	Guatemala	4,220	13,845
Grand Teton	USA	4,197	13,770
Mt Waddington	Canada	3,994	13,104
Mt Robson	Canada	3,954	12,972
Chirripó Grande	Costa Rica	3,837	12,589
Pico Duarte	Dominican Rep.	3,175	10,417

SOUTH AMERICA		m	ft
Aconcagua	Argentina	6,962	22,841
Bonete	Argentina	6,872	22,546
Ojos del Salado	Argentina/Chile	6,863	22,516
Pissis	Argentina	6,779	22,241
Mercedario	Argentina/Chile	6,770	22,211
Huascaran	Peru	6,768	22,204
Llullaillaco	Argentina/Chile	6,723	22,057
Nudo de Cachi	Argentina	6,720	22,047
Yerupaja	Peru	6,632	21,758
N. de Tres Cruces	Argentina/Chile	6,620	21,719
Incahuasi	Argentina/Chile	6,601	21,654
Cerro Galan	Argentina	6,600	21,654
Tupungato	Argentina/Chile	6,570	21,555
Sajama	Bolivia	6,542	21,463
Illimani	Bolivia	6,485	21,276
Coropuna	Peru	6,425	21,079
Ausangate	Peru	6,384	20,945
Cerro del Toro	Argentina	6,380	20,932
Siula Grande	Peru	6,356	20,853
Chimborazo	Ecuador	6,267	20,561
Alpamayo	Peru	5,947	19,511
Cotapaxi	Ecuador	5,896	19,344
Pico Colon	Colombia	5,800	19,029
Pico Bolivar	Venezuela	5,007	16,427

ANTARCTICA		m	ft
Vinson Massif		4,897	16,066
Mt Kirkpatrick		4,528	14,855
Mt Markham		4,349	14,268

OCEAN DEPTHS

ATLANTIC OCEAN	m	ft	
Puerto Rico (Milwaukee) Deep	9,220	30,249	[7]
Cayman Trench	7,680	25,197	[10]
Gulf of Mexico	5,203	17,070	
Mediterranean Sea	5,121	16,801	
Black Sea	2,211	7,254	
North Sea	660	2,165	
Baltic Sea	463	1,519	
Hudson Bay	258	846	

INDIAN OCEAN	m	ft
Java Trench	7,450	24,442
Red Sea	2,635	8,454
Persian Gulf	73	239

PACIFIC OCEAN	m	ft	
Mariana Trench	11,022	36,161	[1]
Tonga Trench	10,882	35,702	[2]
Japan Trench	10,554	34,626	[3]
Kuril Trench	10,542	34,587	[4]
Mindanao Trench	10,497	34,439	[5]
Kermadec Trench	10,047	32,962	[6]

PACIFIC OCEAN (continued)	m	ft	
Peru–Chile Trench	8,050	26,410	[8]
Aleutian Trench	7,822	25,662	[9]

ARCTIC OCEAN	m	ft
Molloy Deep	5,608	18,399

LAND LOWS

		m	ft
Dead Sea	Asia	–411	–1,348
Lake Assal	Africa	–156	–512
Death Valley	N. America	–86	–282
Valdés Peninsula	S. America	–40	–131
Caspian Sea	Europe	–28	–92
Lake Eyre North	Oceania	–16	–52

RIVERS

EUROPE		km	miles
Volga	Caspian Sea	3,700	2,300
Danube	Black Sea	2,850	1,770
Ural	Caspian Sea	2,535	1,575
Dnepr (Dnipro)	Black Sea	2,285	1,420
Kama	Volga	2,030	1,260
Don	Black Sea	1,990	1,240
Petchora	Arctic Ocean	1,790	1,110
Oka	Volga	1,480	920
Belaya	Kama	1,420	880
Dnister (Dniester)	Black Sea	1,400	870
Vyatka	Kama	1,370	850
Rhine	North Sea	1,320	820
N. Dvina	Arctic Ocean	1,290	800
Desna	Dnepr (Dnipro)	1,190	740
Elbe	North Sea	1,145	710
Wisla	Baltic Sea	1,090	675
Loire	Atlantic Ocean	1,020	635

ASIA		km	miles	
Yangtze	Pacific Ocean	6,380	3,960	[3]
Yenisey–Angara	Arctic Ocean	5,550	3,445	[5]
Huang He	Pacific Ocean	5,464	3,395	[6]
Ob–Irtysh	Arctic Ocean	5,410	3,360	[7]
Mekong	Pacific Ocean	4,500	2,795	[9]
Amur	Pacific Ocean	4,400	2,730	[10]
Lena	Arctic Ocean	4,400	2,730	
Irtysh	Ob	4,250	2,640	
Yenisey	Arctic Ocean	4,090	2,540	
Ob	Arctic Ocean	3,680	2,285	
Indus	Indian Ocean	3,100	1,925	
Brahmaputra	Indian Ocean	2,900	1,800	
Syrdarya	Aral Sea	2,860	1,775	
Salween	Indian Ocean	2,800	1,740	
Euphrates	Indian Ocean	2,700	1,675	
Vilyuy	Lena	2,650	1,645	
Kolyma	Arctic Ocean	2,600	1,615	
Amudarya	Aral Sea	2,540	1,575	
Ural	Caspian Sea	2,535	1,575	
Ganges	Indian Ocean	2,510	1,560	
Si Kiang	Pacific Ocean	2,100	1,305	
Irrawaddy	Indian Ocean	2,010	1,250	
Tarim–Yarkand	Lop Nor	2,000	1,240	
Tigris	Indian Ocean	1,900	1,180	

AFRICA		km	miles	
Nile	Mediterranean	6,670	4,140	[1]
Congo	Atlantic Ocean	4,670	2,900	[8]
Niger	Atlantic Ocean	4,180	2,595	
Zambezi	Indian Ocean	3,540	2,200	
Oubangi/Uele	Congo (D.R.)	2,250	1,400	
Kasai	Congo (D.R.)	1,950	1,210	
Shaballe	Indian Ocean	1,930	1,200	
Orange	Atlantic Ocean	1,860	1,155	
Cubango	Okavango Delta	1,800	1,120	
Limpopo	Indian Ocean	1,600	995	
Senegal	Atlantic Ocean	1,600	995	
Volta	Atlantic Ocean	1,500	930	

AUSTRALIA		km	miles
Murray–Darling	Southern Ocean	3,750	2,330
Darling	Murray	3,070	1,905
Murray	Southern Ocean	2,575	1,600
Murrumbidgee	Murray	1,690	1,050

NORTH AMERICA		km	miles	
Mississippi–Missouri	Gulf of Mexico	6,020	3,740	[4]
Mackenzie	Arctic Ocean	4,240	2,630	
Mississippi	Gulf of Mexico	3,780	2,350	
Missouri	Mississippi	3,780	2,350	
Yukon	Pacific Ocean	3,185	1,980	
Rio Grande	Gulf of Mexico	3,030	1,880	

NORTH AMERICA (continued)		km	miles
Arkansas	Mississippi	2,340	1,450
Colorado	Pacific Ocean	2,330	1,445
Red	Mississippi	2,040	1,270
Columbia	Pacific Ocean	1,950	1,210
Saskatchewan	Lake Winnipeg	1,940	1,205
Snake	Columbia	1,670	1,040
Churchill	Hudson Bay	1,600	990
Ohio	Mississippi	1,580	980
Brazos	Gulf of Mexico	1,400	870
St Lawrence	Atlantic Ocean	1,170	730

SOUTH AMERICA		km	miles	
Amazon	Atlantic Ocean	6,450	4,010	[2]
Paraná–Plate	Atlantic Ocean	4,500	2,800	
Purus	Amazon	3,350	2,080	
Madeira	Amazon	3,200	1,990	
São Francisco	Atlantic Ocean	2,900	1,800	
Paraná	Plate	2,800	1,740	
Tocantins	Atlantic Ocean	2,750	1,710	
Paraguay	Paraná	2,550	1,580	
Orinoco	Atlantic Ocean	2,500	1,550	
Pilcomayo	Paraná	2,500	1,550	
Araguaia	Tocantins	2,250	1,400	
Juruá	Amazon	2,000	1,240	
Xingu	Amazon	1,980	1,230	
Ucayali	Amazon	1,900	1,180	
Maranón	Amazon	1,600	990	
Uruguay	Plate	1,600	990	

LAKES

EUROPE		km²	miles²
Lake Ladoga	Russia	17,700	6,800
Lake Onega	Russia	9,700	3,700
Saimaa system	Finland	8,000	3,100
Vänern	Sweden	5,500	2,100
Rybinskoye Res.	Russia	4,700	1,800

ASIA		km²	miles²	
Caspian Sea	Asia	371,800	143,550	[1]
Lake Baykal	Russia	30,500	11,780	[8]
Aral Sea	Kazakhstan/Uzbekistan	28,687	11,086	[10]
Tonlé Sap	Cambodia	20,000	7,700	
Lake Balqash	Kazakhstan	18,500	7,100	
Lake Dongting	China	12,000	4,600	
Lake Ysyk	Kyrgyzstan	6,200	2,400	
Lake Orumiyeh	Iran	5,900	2,300	
Lake Koko	China	5,700	2,200	
Lake Poyang	China	5,000	1,900	
Lake Khanka	China/Russia	4,400	1,700	
Lake Van	Turkey	3,500	1,400	

AFRICA		km²	miles²	
Lake Victoria	E. Africa	68,000	26,000	[3]
Lake Tanganyika	C. Africa	33,000	13,000	[6]
Lake Malawi/Nyasa	E. Africa	29,600	11,430	[9]
Lake Chad	C. Africa	25,000	9,700	
Lake Turkana	Ethiopia/Kenya	8,500	3,300	
Lake Volta	Ghana	8,500	3,300	
Lake Bangweulu	Zambia	8,000	3,100	
Lake Rukwa	Tanzania	7,000	2,700	
Lake Mai-Ndombe	Congo (D.R.)	6,500	2,500	
Lake Kariba	Zambia/Zimbabwe	5,300	2,000	
Lake Albert	Uganda/Congo (D.R.)	5,300	2,000	
Lake Nasser	Egypt/Sudan	5,200	2,000	
Lake Mweru	Zambia/Congo (D.R.)	4,900	1,900	
Lake Cabora Bassa	Mozambique	4,500	1,700	
Lake Kyoga	Uganda	4,400	1,700	
Lake Tana	Ethiopia	3,630	1,400	

AUSTRALIA		km²	miles²
Lake Eyre	Australia	8,900	3,400
Lake Torrens	Australia	5,800	2,200
Lake Gairdner	Australia	4,800	1,900

NORTH AMERICA		km²	miles²	
Lake Superior	Canada/USA	82,350	31,800	[2]
Lake Huron	Canada/USA	59,600	23,010	[4]
Lake Michigan	USA	58,000	22,400	[5]
Great Bear Lake	Canada	31,800	12,280	[7]
Great Slave Lake	Canada	28,500	11,000	
Lake Erie	Canada/USA	25,700	9,900	
Lake Winnipeg	Canada	24,400	9,400	
Lake Ontario	Canada/USA	19,500	7,500	
Lake Nicaragua	Nicaragua	8,200	3,200	
Lake Athabasca	Canada	8,100	3,100	
Smallwood Reservoir	Canada	6,530	2,520	
Reindeer Lake	Canada	6,400	2,500	
Nettilling Lake	Canada	5,500	2,100	
Lake Winnipegosis	Canada	5,400	2,100	

SOUTH AMERICA		km²	miles²
Lake Titicaca	Bolivia/Peru	8,300	3,200
Lake Poopo	Bolivia	2,800	1,100

ISLANDS

EUROPE		km²	miles²	
Great Britain	UK	229,880	88,700	[8]
Iceland	Atlantic Ocean	103,000	39,800	
Ireland	Ireland/UK	84,400	32,600	
Novaya Zemlya (N.)	Russia	48,200	18,600	
W. Spitzbergen	Norway	39,000	15,100	
Novaya Zemlya (S.)	Russia	33,200	12,800	
Sicily	Italy	25,500	9,800	
Sardinia	Italy	24,000	9,300	
N.E. Spitzbergen	Norway	15,000	5,600	
Corsica	France	8,700	3,400	
Crete	Greece	8,350	3,200	
Zealand	Denmark	6,850	2,600	

ASIA		km²	miles²	
Borneo	S. E. Asia	744,360	287,400	[3]
Sumatra	Indonesia	473,600	182,860	[6]
Honshu	Japan	230,500	88,980	[7]
Sulawesi (Celebes)	Indonesia	189,000	73,000	
Java	Indonesia	126,700	48,900	
Luzon	Philippines	104,700	40,400	
Mindanao	Philippines	101,500	39,200	
Hokkaido	Japan	78,400	30,300	
Sakhalin	Russia	74,060	28,600	
Sri Lanka	Indian Ocean	65,600	25,300	
Taiwan	Pacific Ocean	36,000	13,900	
Kyushu	Japan	35,700	13,800	
Hainan	China	34,000	13,100	
Timor	Indonesia	33,600	13,000	
Shikoku	Japan	18,800	7,300	
Halmahera	Indonesia	18,000	6,900	
Ceram	Indonesia	17,150	6,600	
Sumbawa	Indonesia	15,450	6,000	
Flores	Indonesia	15,200	5,900	
Samar	Philippines	13,100	5,100	
Negros	Philippines	12,700	4,900	
Bangka	Indonesia	12,000	4,600	
Palawan	Philippines	12,000	4,600	
Panay	Philippines	11,500	4,400	
Sumba	Indonesia	11,100	4,300	
Mindoro	Philippines	9,750	3,800	

AFRICA		km²	miles²	
Madagascar	Indian Ocean	587,040	226,660	[4]
Socotra	Indian Ocean	3,600	1,400	
Réunion	Indian Ocean	2,500	965	
Tenerife	Atlantic Ocean	2,350	900	
Mauritius	Indian Ocean	1,865	720	

OCEANIA		km²	miles²	
New Guinea	Indon./Papua NG	821,030	317,000	[2]
New Zealand (S.)	Pacific Ocean	150,500	58,100	
New Zealand (N.)	Pacific Ocean	114,700	44,300	
Tasmania	Australia	67,800	26,200	
New Britain	Papua NG	37,800	14,600	
New Caledonia	Pacific Ocean	19,100	7,400	
Viti Levu	Fiji	10,500	4,100	
Hawaii	Pacific Ocean	10,450	4,000	
Bougainville	Papua NG	9,600	3,700	
Guadalcanal	Solomon Is.	6,500	2,500	
Vanua Levu	Fiji	5,550	2,100	
New Ireland	Papua NG	3,200	1,200	

NORTH AMERICA		km²	miles²	
Greenland	Atlantic Ocean	2,175,600	839,800	[1]
Baffin Is.	Canada	508,000	196,100	[5]
Victoria Is.	Canada	212,200	81,900	[9]
Ellesmere Is.	Canada	212,000	81,800	[10]
Cuba	Caribbean Sea	110,860	42,800	
Newfoundland	Canada	110,680	42,700	
Hispaniola	Dom. Rep./Haiti	76,200	29,400	
Banks Is.	Canada	67,000	25,900	
Devon Is.	Canada	54,500	21,000	
Melville Is.	Canada	42,400	16,400	
Vancouver Is.	Canada	32,150	12,400	
Somerset Is.	Canada	24,300	9,400	
Jamaica	Caribbean Sea	11,400	4,400	
Puerto Rico	Atlantic Ocean	8,900	3,400	
Cape Breton Is.	Canada	4,000	1,500	

SOUTH AMERICA		km²	miles²
Tierra del Fuego	Argentina/Chile	47,000	18,100
Falkland Is. (East)	Atlantic Ocean	6,800	2,600
South Georgia	Atlantic Ocean	4,200	1,600
Galapagos (Isabela)	Pacific Ocean	2,250	870

World: Regions in the News

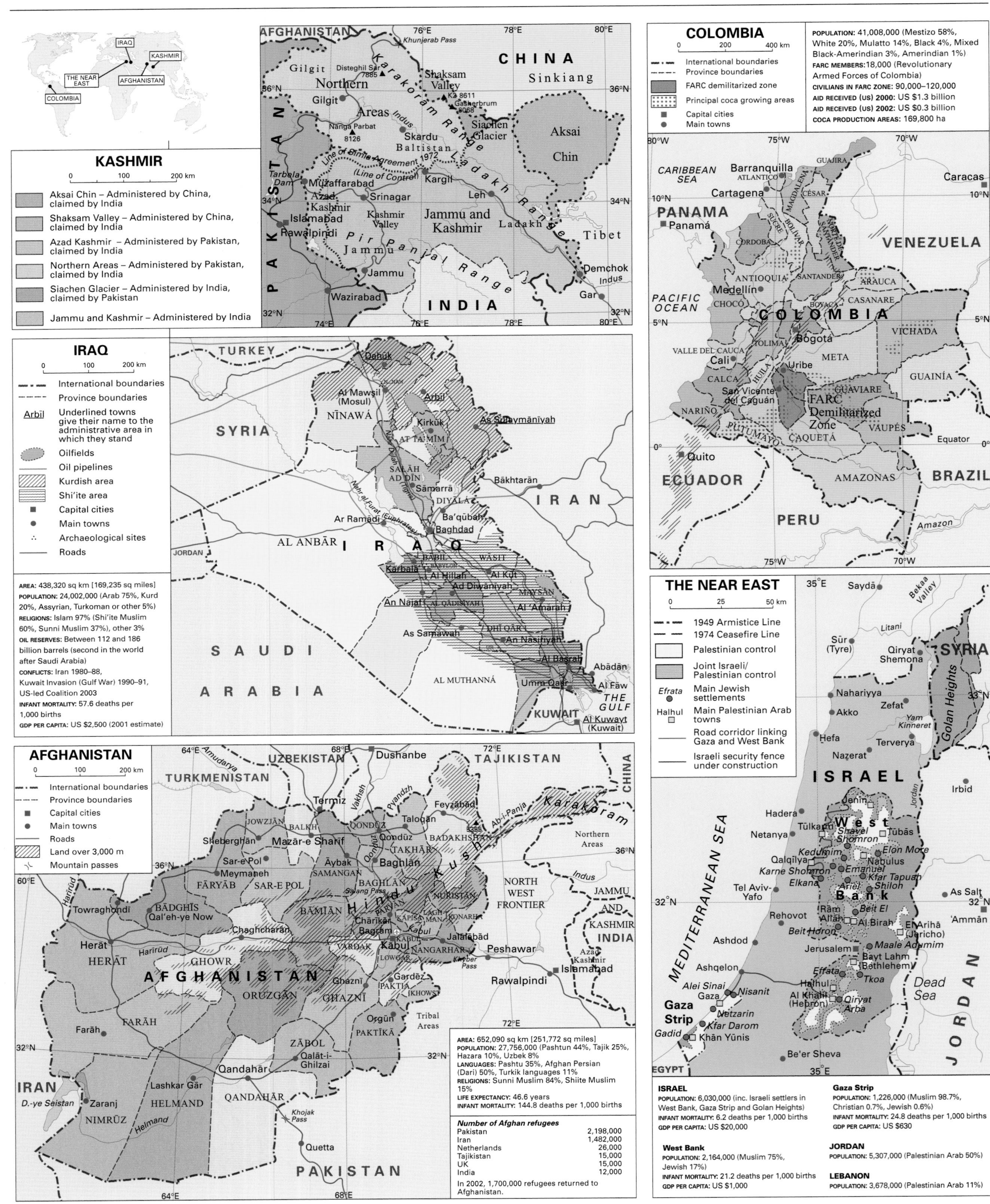

WORLD EXPLORER

CONTENTS

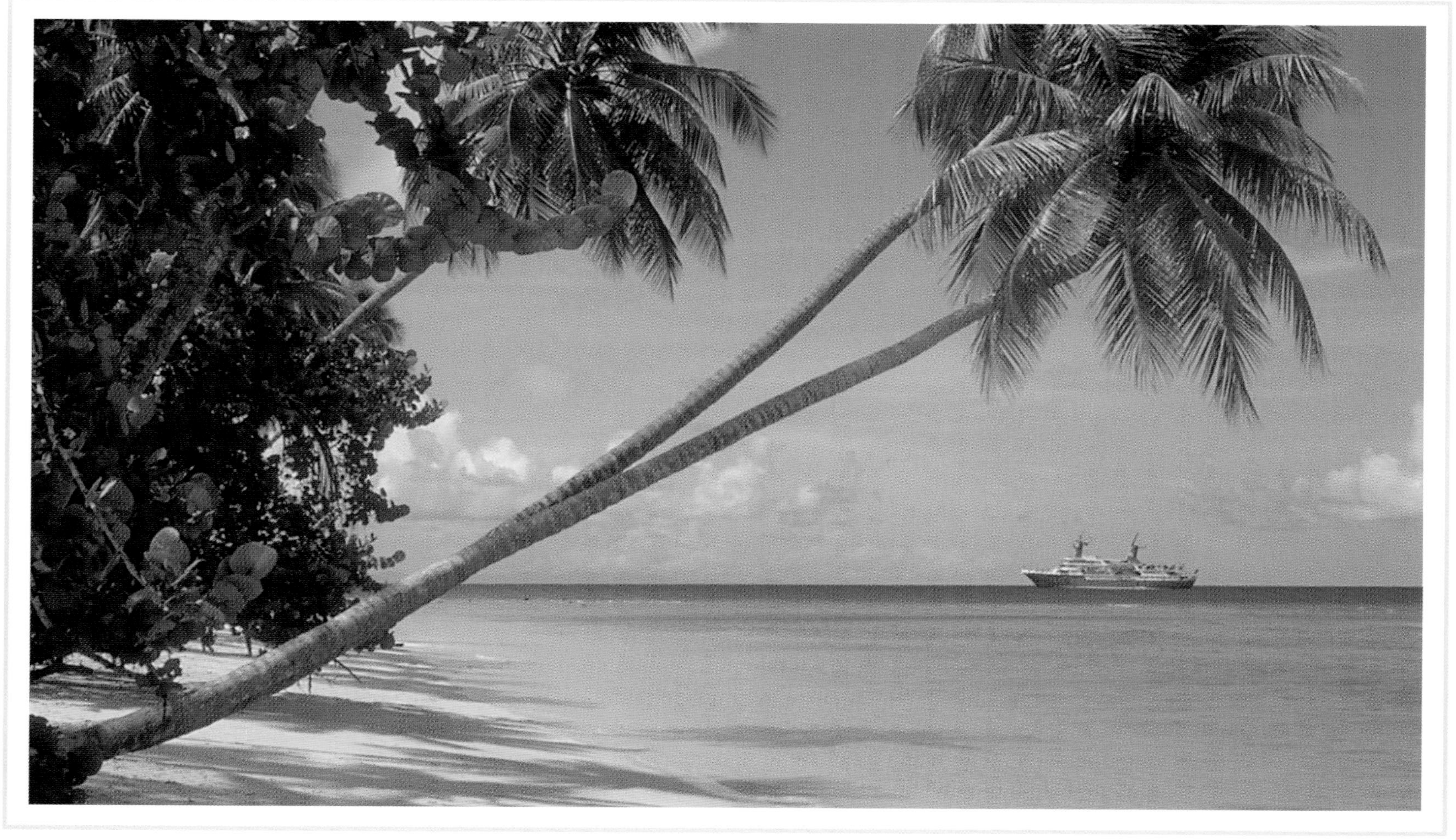

Mountains and volcanoes

The world's mountains provide a huge variety of magnificent scenery, ranging from the tree-covered Blue Mountains of Australia, little more than 1,070 m (3,500 ft) high, to the towering snow-covered Himalayan peaks of Nepal and China, several of which are over 8,000 m (26,000 ft) high. Many are accessible by road, or sometimes by train or cable car, but walking, even if only a short distance, is usually the best way to experience the breathtaking views that they offer.

◄ Rocky Mountains, Banff National Park, Canada
Pointed peaks and sheer cliffs contribute to a magnificent landscape. Over 1,600 km (1,000 miles) of trails pass by glaciers, turquoise lakes and forests of pine, fir and spruce. In the town of Banff a cable car rises to the top of Sulfur Mountain, 2,263 m (7,440 ft) high.
Best time to visit: June–September

THE AMERICAS

Mount McKinley, Denali National Park, Alaska, USA

The USA's highest mountain at 6,194 m (20,321 ft) is in a spectacular wilderness of snow-covered peaks and glaciers with wildlife that includes brown bears, caribou, moose and marmots. Activities include river rafting and sightseeing by plane.
Best time to visit: June–August

Popocatepetl Volcano ('Smoking Mountain'), Sierra Nevada, Mexico

A cloud of smoke often hovers above the massive crater of Popocatepetl, which is 5,452 m (17,887 ft) high. It is possible to climb and descend the mountain in one very long day with the aid of a guide.
Best time to climb: November–March

Cotopaxi and Chimborazo Volcanoes, Ecuador

The two highest active volcanoes in the world are in a country where the main road is known as the 'Avenue of the Volcanoes'. Non-mountaineers can climb Cotopaxi (5,896 m/19,344 ft) and get near to the top of Chimborazo (6,267 m/20,561 ft).
Best time to climb: January–April

Cordillera Blanca, Huascaran National Park, Peru

With 663 glaciers, the peaks of the Cordillera Blanca, more than 50 of which rise to heights of between 5,000 and 6,000 m (16,500 and 19,700 ft), are a great attraction for ice climbers. Huarez is the main climbing centre. An alternative for those who prefer to trek is the richly glaciated Huayhuash range.
Best time to visit: July–September

EUROPE

Landmannalaugar, Iceland

A combination of volcanic and geothermal activity has produced a unique landscape in Landmannalaugar, where mountain peaks (little more than 1,070 m/3,500 ft high) rise above a landscape of convoluted lava fields and blue mountain lakes, and hot springs provide open-air baths.
Best time to visit: July–early September

Mount Vesuvius, Italy

The volcano of Vesuvius dominates the landscape around Naples. Although it lost its plume of smoke after erupting in 1944, it is still active. A bus from Pompeii goes to within 1.5 km (1 mile) of the summit (1,277 m/4,189 ft).
Time to visit: All seasons

AFRICA

Atlas Mountains, Morocco

Canyons with dramatic rock formations are to be found in these rugged mountains that rise to a height of over 3,900 m (13,000 ft). Organized treks pass by numerous isolated Berber villages, far from the road from Marrakech, which winds up to a mountain pass 2,275 m (7,467 ft) high.
Best time to visit: June–October

Mount Kilimanjaro, Tanzania

Africa's highest mountain rises majestically to 5,895 m (19,340 ft) above the plains of Amboseli National Park. It is possible to trek to the top for stunning views over Kenya and Tanzania, along

▲ Sierra Nevada, Yosemite National Park, USA
The Californian Yosemite National Park is famous for its sheer-sided granite domes, such as the Half Dome and the 1,066 m (3,500 ft) high El Capitan, which rise above forests and emerald lakes. Among the many species of flowers and trees to be found in the park are ancient giant sequoias over 60 m (200 ft) high, one of which is estimated to be 2,700 years old. An added attraction are the Yosemite Falls which, with a drop of 739 m (2,425 ft), are the highest in North America. Walkers can escape the summer crowds by using the 1,280 km (800 miles) of trails.
Best time to visit: May–September

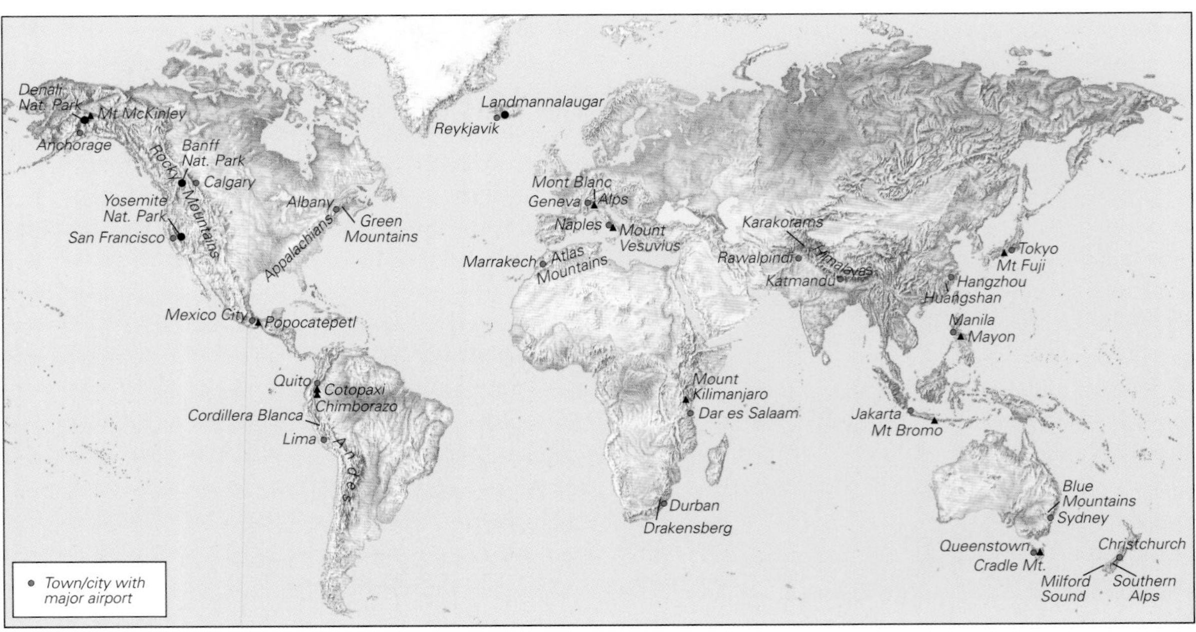

▲ **Mont Blanc, Alps, France** Europe's highest mountain rises to a height of 4,807 m (15,760 ft). A splendid view of it can be had from the peak of the Aiguille de Midi, a granite spear 3,840 m (12,600 ft) high, that is reached by a steep 3 km (2-mile) ascent in a cable car from Chamonix. Below Mont Blanc is the start of a long-distance ski and walking route, which passes ten of the 12 highest peaks in the Alps on its way to the Matterhorn in Switzerland and Italy. *Best time for walking:* May–September

▼ **Mt Bromo, Java** A crater within a vast outer crater, Bromo emits white smoke, as does Mount Semeru, seen here in the distance. Visitors usually stay overnight in a village at the rim of the outer crater, from where it is possible to walk to Bromo at dawn to watch the sun rise up over the outer crater. *Best time to visit:* April–October

routes that pass through farmland and lush forest before reaching alpine-like vegetation and snow-covered rock.
Best time to climb: mid January–late February and late August–September

Drakensberg Mountains, South Africa

Vast pinnacles and blocks of basalt rise to a height of over 3,475 m (11,400 ft) in this range of mountains that also runs through Lesotho. Snowcapped in winter, many of the peaks are an enormous challenge for mountaineers. The Royal Natal National Park has numerous hiking trails.
Best time to visit: April–October

ASIA

Himalayas, Nepal

Within the Himalayas in Nepal are ten of the world's 14 peaks with a height of over 8,000 m (26,000 ft), including Everest (8,850 m/29,035 ft). Far below the snow-capped peaks are terraced hillsides dotted with villages, while above a height of about 2,700 m (9,000 ft) are forests in which rhododendrons bloom between February and April. The most popular base for exploring the mountains is Pokhara. The famous ten-day trek to the mountain town of Jomsom begins here, as does the three- to four-day Annapurna Skyline Trek which provides superb views while being easy enough to be undertaken with children.
Best time to visit: October–April

Karakorams, Pakistan

The jagged peaks of the Karakorams include K2, the world's second highest mountain (8,611 m/28,400 ft). A journey along the Karakoram Highway follows the route of the old Silk Road along the Indus Valley from Rawalpindi to Kashgar in China, sometimes clinging to cliff faces as it winds its way through the mountains up to the Khunjerab Pass at 4,934 m (16,280 ft).
Best time to visit: May–August

Great mountain treks

The following is a selection of great mountain treks that take four or more days. The months given are those in which it is best to undertake each trek.

Long Trail, Vermont, USA (424 km/265 miles; 16–21 days; May–Sept) Easily reached by road, the trail through Vermont's Green Mountains can be walked in sections. It is part of the 3,456 km (2,160-mile) long Appalachian Trail, whose most demanding section is through New Hampshire's White Mountains.

Inca Trail, Peru (4–5 days; April–Sept) By far the best way to approach the spectacular Inca site of Machu Picchu (see *Historic Sites of the Americas*), the Inca Trail begins some distance from Cuzco.

Mont Blanc Circuit, France and Switzerland (10 days; July–Sept) Possibly the finest walk in Europe, it usually starts from Chamonix. With an average altitude of 1,525 m (5,000 ft), it links the seven valleys surrounding Mont Blanc.

Annapurna Circuit, Nepal (17 days; Oct–Nov and March–April) Regarded as Nepal's classic trek, it goes through many types of landscape ***(see picture below)***, and reaches a height of 5,416 m (17,765 ft), as well as providing superb views of Annapurna and Dhaulagiri.

Everest Trek, Nepal (14–16 days; Oct–Nov and March–April) A trek from Jiri to the Everest Base Camp on the Khumbu Glacier provides wonderful views of Everest. It is possible to fly back to Katmandu from Lukla, three days' walk away.

Milford Track, New Zealand (54 km/34 miles; 4 days; Oct–April) A walk that is regarded as a must by most New Zealanders ends at the breathtaking Milford Sound (see *Sea and ocean cruises*). The number of walkers is limited and booking well ahead is necessary.

Mayon Volcano, Philippines

Often described as the world's most perfect volcano cone, Mayon (2,462 m/8,075 ft) is still very active. An eruption in 1993 killed 70 people. It can be climbed in two days but it is essential to do so with a guide.
Best time to climb: December–May

Mt Kinabalu, Borneo, Malaysia

It is possible to walk rather than climb to the top of the highest mountain in South-east Asia (4,010 m/13,455 ft). It does, however, take two days and hiring a guide is compulsory. The view from the top sometimes stretches to the Philippines.
Best time to climb: April–September

Huangshan, China

The Chinese regard the 72-peak Huangshan range as one of the great natural attractions of their country. Some 30 peaks rise to over 1,500 m (4,900 ft). There are two main walking routes up the side of the range, and an eight-minute cable-car ride from Yungusi to the top.
Best time to visit: spring and autumn

Mt Fuji, Japan

The perfectly symmetrical cone of Japan's highest mountain (3,776 m/12,388 ft), which last erupted in 1707, is climbed by people of all ages in the summer. A road goes to the fourth and fifth 'stations', from where it takes four or five hours to climb to the crater. This is best reached at dawn, before the clouds gather.
Best time to climb: July–August

AUSTRALASIA

Blue Mountains, New South Wales, Australia

Reaching a height of just over 1,070 m (3,500 ft), the Blue Mountains – with their densely forested slopes, sandstone chasms, dramatic rock formations and waterfalls – provide a beautiful environment in which to drive and walk. As well as a network of trails there are a number of interesting villages and towns, of which the largest, Katoomba, is served by a railway from Sydney just 80 km (50 miles) away.
Time to visit: All seasons

Cradle Mountain/Lake St Clair National Park, Tasmania, Australia

Australia's best mountain trails and rugged alpine scenery are to be found around Cradle Mountain. Jagged peaks, the highest of which is Mt Ossa (1,617 m/5,300 ft), rise above tarns and lakes in deep valleys.
Best time to visit: November–March

Deserts and canyons

For the adventurous traveller, the stunning landscapes of rock and sand which make up some of the world's most inhospitable environments offer a challenge not to be missed. From the vast sand seas of the Sahara Desert to the deep canyons and distinctive rock formations of the south-western United States, there is an extraordinary range of landforms to explore.

NORTH AMERICA

Bryce Canyon, Utah, USA

On a more human scale than the Grand Canyon, Bryce Canyon is not really a canyon at all but a natural amphitheatre filled with dazzling orange, red and pink rock pinnacles – known as 'hoodoos' – overlooking spectacularly colourful ravines. This surreal landscape can be explored on foot along a network of marked trails, or simply enjoyed from one of the viewpoints along the rim of the amphitheatre.

Monument Valley, Arizona, USA

With its majestic rock pillars towering over a barren, desert landscape, Monument Valley is an awe-inspiring sight. It has been made famous as a backdrop to numerous Hollywood westerns and is now part of the Navajo Reservation. A 27 km (17-mile) road tour of the valley takes two to three hours and offers stunning views of this unforgettable place.

Zion Canyon, Utah, USA

The road through the steep-sided Zion Canyon can become crowded in summer, and it is worth leaving the car to follow one of the short trails to the Emerald Pools or the hanging gardens at Weeping Rock. Longer trails lead from the canyon to the desert plateau above and offer spectacular views of the contrasting landscapes.

▲ Sonoran Desert, USA/Mexico
Almost encircling the Gulf of California and covering 310,000 sq km (120,00 sq miles), the Sonoran Desert is the hottest of North America's deserts. Tucson, Arizona, serves as a base for tours into the desert, including archaeological tours. Nearby are the excellent Arizona-Sonora Desert Museum and the protected desert habitat of Organ Pipe Cactus National Monument where visitors can see the giant saguaro and organ pipe cacti which have come to symbolize the area. There are good trails and scenic drives around the park, and plenty of desert wildlife to watch.

SOUTH AMERICA

Colca Canyon, Peru

High in the Andes the River Colca runs through a gorge which is twice the depth of the Grand Canyon, past ancient Inca granaries cut into the rock and green slopes covered by pre-Inca terracing. This astonishingly beautiful landscape, complete with smoking volcano in the background, is home to the Collagua and Cabana people, whose traditional way of life is punctuated with lively festivals.

Atacama Desert, Chile

Overlooked by a ruined pre-Inca fortress, the picturesque oasis village of San Pedro de Atacama, with its adobe buildings and excellent archeological museum, makes a good base for exploring the canyons, saltpans and stark landscapes of the surrounding desert. One of the most beautiful places to visit is the Valle de la Luna, where the multi-coloured desert formations are a magnet for photographers and filmmakers.

EUROPE

Almerían Desert, Spain

The setting for the film *Lawrence of Arabia* as well as many 'spaghetti westerns', the Almerían Desert is an extraordinary, almost lunar landscape of sand dunes dissected by dried-up river beds and littered with sandstone cones. Film sets are open to the public at Mini-Hollywood.

▲ Grand Canyon, Arizona, USA
Carved by the Colorado River out of the multi-coloured rock of the Arizona Desert, the Grand Canyon is one of North America's most awe-inspiring natural features. Drives and trails around its rim – 443 km (277 miles) in length – provide stunning views. Visitors can walk or ride mules down one of the vertiginous trails to the valley floor, 1.7 km (1 mile) below, or try rafting on the river.

Timanfaya National Park, Lanzarote, Canary Islands

On an island where it rarely rains, a series of volcanic eruptions in the 1730s created an extraordinary apocalyptic landscape. Guided tours go to an area of solidified lava and volcanic cones, aptly called the Mountains of Fire, where a dry bush dropped into a crevice will burst into flames and meals at a solitary restaurant are barbecued on a volcano.

AFRICA

Draa Valley, the Sahara, Morocco

From the town of Ouarzazate, with its dramatic kasbah, the Draa river runs south-east through a rich landscape of dramatic gorges, agricultural land and kasbahs towards the Sahara. After around 160 km (100 miles), the river reaches the former frontier fort of Zagora, which makes a good base for exploring the desert.

Saharan oases, Tunisia
The shifting sand dunes around the town of Douz are an excellent example of the landscape popularly associated with the Sahara Desert. In fact the desert, which covers an area of 8,600,000 sq km (3,320,000 sq miles), has extensive stony plains, rock-strewn plateaux, mountains and large oasis depressions as well as seas of sand. Douz is a good base for camel safaris and for exploring the more isolated southern oases. To the north-west the town of Tozeur, with its beautiful 12th-century mosque, is set beside a vast oasis fed by over 200 springs. It serves as an excellent starting point for four-wheel-drive tours into the desert and to the nearby beautiful mountain oases, such as Tamerza, Mides and Chebika.

Guided expeditions of up to a week can include camel riding and stargazing under the immense Saharan sky.

Ténéré Desert, Niger
For desert purists the seemingly endless sea of sand that is the Ténéré Desert is perhaps the most beautiful part of the Sahara. A two-week round trip from the desert city of Agadez might pass through a massive dinosaur cemetery on the way to the classic oasis town of Bilma and the prehistoric cave paintings of the Djado Plateau. Crossing the Ténéré is notoriously challenging and often dangerous, but the experience is unforgettable.

Sinai Desert, Egypt
Inland from the coastal resorts of the Sinai Peninsula is a hot, desolate wilderness sprinkled with oases and ancient settlements. They include the 6th-century monastery of St Catherine, which stands at the foot of Mount Sinai, where Moses is said to have received the Ten Commandments from God. Camel treks and jeep safaris take visitors into the aptly-named Wilderness of Wanderings, in the centre of the peninsula.

North Kenyan Desert
In sharp contrast to the developed south of Kenya, the North Kenyan Desert is a vast tract of scrubland inhabited by ancient nomadic tribes whose way of life has changed little over the centuries. A rich diversity of desert landscapes here includes scrub desert – which bursts into colour after rainfall – and lunar, volcanic areas. There are lush oases and river-cut canyons too, but the reason most people come here is to see the 'Jade Sea', Lake Turkana, with its profusion of birdlife, hippos and Nile crocodiles.

Namib Desert, Namibia
Stretching for 1,930 km (1,200 miles) down the length of the Namibian coastline to the mouth of the Orange River in South Africa, the Namib is a strip of desert with an average width of 110 km (70 miles). The highest sand dunes in the world – sometimes exceeding 244 m (800 ft) – are to be found at Sossus Vlei, in the Namib-Naukluft National Park. The northern section is known as Skeleton Coast because of the many shipwrecks that lie on the ocean bed nearby.

Blyde River Canyon, South Africa
The view over the canyon from the spot known as God's Window is one of the highlights of any visit to the beautiful Blyde River Nature Reserve, in the Drakensberg. There are two trails down into the canyon – which in some places is over 700 m (2,300 ft) deep – from Bourke's Luck Portholes, where strange natural rock formations can be seen.

ASIA AND AUSTRALASIA

Thar Desert, Rajasthan, India
Within the Rajasthan Desert National Park two areas of interest to tourists can be reached easily from the attractive city of Jaisalmer with its 12th-century fort. One is the Akal Fossil Park where the petrified trunks of 25 trees once covered by the sea lie on a bare hillside. The second is the 3 km (2-mile) long Sam Dunes, just 40 km (25 miles) from Jaisalmer. The dunes are usually crowded with tourists taking camel rides, but it is possible to escape the crowds and go on safaris of several days, by either jeep or camel.

Gobi Desert, Mongolia
For 70 years part of the Soviet Union, the Gobi Desert has only recently become accessible to western travellers. Its greatest attraction is the red sandstone Flaming Cliffs, 80 km (50 miles) north-west of Dalandzadgad, which became famous in the 1920s when the explorer and scientist Roy Chapman Andrews (on whom the character of Indiana Jones was based) discovered fossilized dinosaur remains there. Still rich in dinosaur fossils, the cliffs are just north of the vast Three Beauties National Park with a landscape of mountains, canyons, gravel and sand.

▼ Wadi Rum, Jordan
Soaring vertically from the desert floor of Wadi Rum are the massive rock formations known as jebels for which the area is famous. Vehicles and camels can be hired in the Bedouin settlement of Rum, but it is hard to beat the experience of walking through this extraordinary, silent landscape and sleeping out in the desert under the stars.

◀ Uluru National Park, Northern Territory, Australia
The largest sandstone monolith in the world, Uluru (Ayers Rock) is a magnificent sight, particularly at sunset when it appears to burn from within. Some 40 km (25 miles) to the west are the Olgas – 36 enormous granite domes – which, like Uluru, are an important Aboriginal site. Access is restricted, but visitors can experience their haunting beauty by following the trail through the Valley of the Winds.

Lakes and waterfalls

From the azure tranquillity of Lake Garda in Italy to the thundering roar of Zimbabwe's Victoria Falls, the great lakes and waterfalls of the world are set amidst dramatically beautiful scenery. Many resorts offer watersports as well as long-distance trails for ramblers and horse-riders.

► Lake Maligne, Jasper National Park, Canada
The glacier-fed Lake Maligne – shown here at dawn – is set among the snow-covered peaks of Jasper National Park, the biggest and wildest of Canada's four Rocky Mountain national parks at 10,400 sq km (4,000 sq miles). Boat and hiking tours, fishing, rafting and riding are available, while the independent explorer can hire a boat or walk along the excellent network of trails.

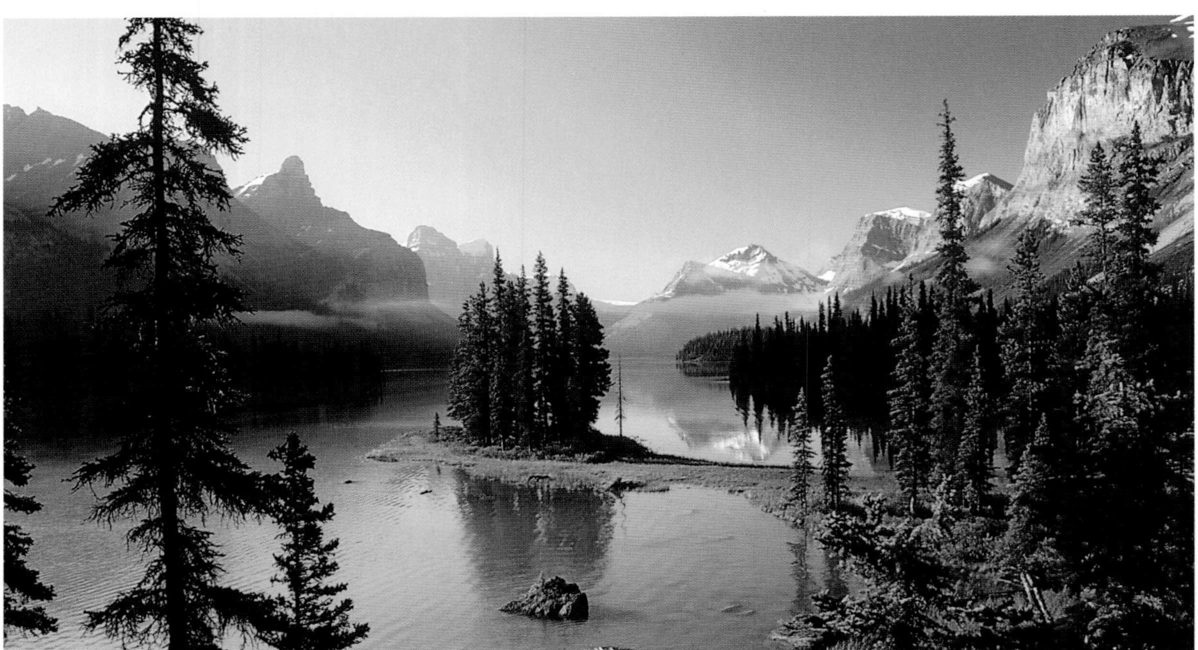

▼ Angel Falls, Venezuela
The world's highest waterfall with an uninterrupted drop of 2,650 ft (807 m), Angel Falls are 16 times the height of Niagara Falls. Although often shrouded in mist, the Falls are at their most spectacular during the rainy season (June–November) when the volume of water is greatest and when visitors can travel by motorized canoe along the river to Devil's Canyon at the foot of the Falls.

▼ Lake Argentino, Argentina
The south-western arm of Lake Argentino is periodically dammed by the Moreno Glacier, from which icebergs regularly break off and crash into the channel below. Visitors can see, hear and photograph the glacier in safety from a series of platforms and viewing points. The massive Upsala Glacier on the northern arm of the lake can be reached by boat from Puerto Bandera.

NORTH AMERICA

Niagara Falls, Canada/USA

The most-visited waterfall in the world, Niagara Falls has been developed as a tourist attraction offering every possible viewing experience, including cable cars, helicopter rides, viewing towers, boats and even tunnels in the rockface. Despite the commercialization, this massive, perpetual curtain of falling water lives up to its reputation as one of the wonders of the natural world.

Waterton-Glacier Park, Montana and Alberta, Canada/USA

Silver lakes are a major feature of the landscape of mountain peaks, waterfalls and hanging valleys, carved by glaciers 10,000 years ago, in the Waterton-Glacier Park. There are spectacular trails for walkers of all levels, and the Going-to-the-Sun Road through the park is considered to be one of the USA's driving highlights.

Lake Tahoe, California, USA

High in the Sierra Nevada mountains on the border between California and Nevada, Lake Tahoe is a popular year-round holiday destination. In winter the area is packed with skiers (see *Winter sports*) while summer brings people seeking the cooler temperatures of the mountains and the crystal waters and sandy beaches of the lake. On the California side, there is swimming, boating, fishing and walking, while the Nevada side offers a glittering nightlife of restaurants and casinos.

SOUTH AMERICA

Iguaçu Falls, Brazil

The torrential waters of the Iguaçu River plunge more than 75 m (250 ft) over a huge, crescent-shaped cliff into the gorge below in a series of some 275 separate waterfalls. Surrounded by lush rainforest, the 4 km (2.5-mile) wide cascades can be viewed from platforms and paths on both sides of the Falls.

Lake Titicaca, Bolivia

High in the Altiplano the clear blue waters of Lake Titicaca bring an oasis of life and colour to the parched landscape. At 8,340 sq km (3,220 sq miles), it is the largest lake in South America, with many lakeside settlements. Boat trips can be made to the floating reed islands inhabited by the Uros, and to ancient Inca ruins on the sacred islands of the Sun and Moon.

Lake Llanquihue, Chile

A reflection of the perfect cone of Volcano Orsono can be seen in this immense lake which lies amid gently rolling pastureland. Towns on the shore include Frutillar Bajo, a popular summer resort with black-sand beaches, and Puerto Varas, a centre for 'adventure' activities such as rafting, riding, hiking and climbing.

EUROPE

Lake Siljan, Sweden

In a land of around 96,000 lakes, Siljan is noted as a centre of Swedish folk tradition and art. Locals and visitors arrive in boats reminiscent of Viking longships during midsummer celebrations at the lakeside church of Rättvik, and traditional mystery plays are performed annually in the open-air theatre at Leksand. Visitors can watch traditional painted wooden horses being made at Nusnäs, and visit the studio of the painter Anders Zorn, who lived in the lakeside town of Mora.

Lake District, England

Famous as the haunt of the Romantic Poets, the Lake District is a beautiful and varied landscape of hills, mountains, lakes and rivers, encompassing a wide range of scenery within a relatively small area. The southern lakes – including Windermere, Coniston and Grasmere – are surrounded by gentle green slopes and attract enormous numbers of visitors in summer.

The wilder north, with its sheer, forbidding crags is more spectacular and much less crowded. Boating is popular on the larger lakes, and a network of paths makes the area a haven for walkers and climbers.

Lake Lucerne, Switzerland

The picturesque medieval town of Lucerne with its famous Kapellbrücke bridge makes an excellent base for exploring this beautiful lake and its mountain surroundings. Visitors can go on a lake cruise and stop off at some of the peaceful villages along the shore, or take the oldest mountain railway in Europe to Mount Rigi for wonderful views of the Alpine scenery.

Lake Garda, Italy

The largest of Italy's lakes, Lake Garda is certainly one of its most beautiful. Sheltered from the north-east by the Dolomites, its climate is particularly gentle, with orange and lemon groves flourishing on its banks. Dotted around the lake are many attractive and historic resort towns – some dating back to Roman times – and romantic hillside villas.

AFRICA

Lake Bosumtwi, Ghana

Sacred to the Asante people, the crater lake of Bosumtwi is the deepest natural lake in Ghana, and its waters are still rising. Its beautiful setting among thickly wooded crater walls makes it a relaxing place to go fishing, boating and swimming. Motorboat trips across the lake are available, and walks around the shore can include visits to lakeside villages.

Murchison Falls, Uganda

The sheer force of the Nile as it shoots through a narrow cleft in the rocks and crashes over a 30 m (100 ft) precipice is what makes Murchison Falls so spectacular. A journey up the river from Paraa Camp to the base of the falls is also an excellent way to see some of the wildlife of the Murchison Falls National Park, including crocodiles, elephants, hippos, giraffes, buffalo, waterbucks and many bird species.

Lake Baringo, Kenya

Encircled by mountains and rich in bird and animal life, Lake Baringo is a fascinating and beautiful place to visit. The shoreline is home to crocodiles and herds of hippos and the area is famous for its hundreds of bird species, attracting birdwatchers from all over the world. A resident ornithologist offers guided walks, and there are also horse rides, camel rides and boat trips to the lake's islands.

ASIA

Lake Toba, Sumatra

Encircled by steep crags – once the rim of an enormous ancient volcano – Lake Toba is the largest crater lake in the world. The area is home to the Toba Batak people, whose brightly painted houses with distinctive crescent-shaped roofs can be seen around the lake. The beautiful island of Samosir is a popular tourist destination

with excellent trekking and rafting as well as interesting megalithic tombs to visit.

Lake Batur, Bali

The largest lake in Bali, Lake Batur is a crater lake and is sacred to the Balinese as the home of the goddess Dewi Danu. The hot springs at Toya Bungkah are said to have healing properties, and the lakeside temple of Pura Jati presides over a holy bathing place. From Toyah Bungkah there are trekking routes up to the summit of Gunung Batur, the soaring 1,717 m (5,630 ft) high volcano which dominates the lake.

Lake Karakul, Tajikistan

At a height of 3,600 m (11,800 ft) in the foothills of the Pamir mountains, Lake Karakul's setting is remote and beautiful. Flanked by the massive Mount Kongur to the north and the magnificent Mount Muztaghata to the south, Karakul is the home of the Kirgiz people and their herds of sheep, goats, horses and camels. It takes a day to walk around the lake, after which walkers can stay overnight in a traditional felt-covered *yurt* at the visitors' camp.

Lake Chuzenji-ko and Kegon Waterfall, Japan

Visitors to Lake Chuzenji-ko and the dramatic Kegon Waterfall are well provided for with cable cars and platforms from which to gaze at the spectacular view, especially popular in autumn when the leaves are changing colour. Beside the lake is a colourful shrine after which both the town and lake are named.

▲ Keli Mutu, Flores, Indonesia
An extinct volcano, Keli Mutu has three extraordinary crater lakes. Not only is each lake a different colour, but the colours change over decades from vivid green through to deep red and intense turquoise as mineral layers dissolve.

AUSTRALASIA

Lake Rotorua, New Zealand

Bubbling hot springs, vertical jets of steam and scalding geysers make Rotorua an exciting place to visit. There are lakeside bath houses where visitors can sample the waters, as well as cruises and facilities for a wide range of watersports on the lake and nearby rivers. Maoris have lived beside the lake for around 700 years, and there are many cultural attractions on offer, some more authentic than others.

◄ Victoria Falls, Zimbabwe
The 1.7 km (1-mile) wide Victoria Falls are made up of five separate waterfalls which plummet more than 100 m (320 ft) into the gorge below. The Falls are a popular base for adrenaline-boosting activities, such as bungee jumping, white-water rafting and riverboarding, and tours of every description can be taken from operators based in Victoria Falls town.

Wildlife in the Americas and Europe

From the bears and moose of the Alaskan wilderness, to the jaguars and toucans of the Central American forests, to the condors and rheas of Patagonia, the Americas have an amazing variety of wildlife. Europe by contrast is famed for its seabirds, and the vast flocks of migrant wildfowl that gather in its wetlands.

► Torres del Paine National Park, Chile
An awe-inspiring landscape of forests, glaciers, shimmering lakes, thundering cascades and soaring granite pillars, Torres del Paine National Park in Patagonia is a haven for wildlife, including guanacos, rheas, flamingos, condors and the shy huemul (Chilean deer). There is an excellent network of short- and long-distance trails through the park.

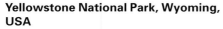

▼ Wrangell-St Elias National Park, Alaska, USA
Of all the Alaskan national parks, Wrangell-St Elias is the best for wildlife watching. This vast landscape of mountains and glaciers is home to moose, wolves, wolverines, bears, beavers and herds of caribou. There are several campsites but few other facilities for visitors in this true wilderness park.

NORTH AMERICA

Wood Buffalo National Park, Alberta/NW Territories, Canada

Canada's largest national park, Wood Buffalo is famous for its free-roaming buffalo herd. Among other inhabitants are lynx, bears and hundreds of bird species, including a river rookery of rare white pelicans and the few remaining whooping cranes in the world. Fort Smith has some accommodation, but canoeing along the rivers and camping are perhaps the best ways to explore this wilderness of forest, marsh and grassland.

Yellowstone National Park, Wyoming, USA

Famous for its many geothermal geysers and hot springs, Yellowstone Park is also home to one of the largest and most diverse populations of mammals in North America. Inhabitants include bison, moose, elks, Bighorn sheep, beavers and marmots as well as lynx, bobcats, wolves and coyotes. Millions of visitors flock to Yellowstone every year, but despite the inevitable tourist development, most of the park is still a true wilderness.

Everglades National Park, Florida, USA

The largest sub-tropical wilderness on the North American mainland, Everglades National Park is a vast area of swamps, mangrove forests and grasslands. It is the only place in the world where alligators and crocodiles live side by side, and there are still a few panthers and black bears. Canoe trails and boat tours are the best way to view the abundant wildlife, which includes a huge variety of bird species.

CENTRAL AMERICA

Braulio Carrillo Park, Costa Rica

Many different habitats exist in Braulio Carrillo, a large area of rainforest covering a range of altitudes from just above sea level to 3,000 m (9,850 ft). Each has its own distinct flora and fauna, although the astonishingly lush vegetation can make spotting animals such as tapirs, sloths, ocelots, jaguars and pumas difficult. The park's abundant birdlife includes toucans, quetzels, umbrella birds, guans and eagles.

Corcovado National Park, Costa Rica

Set on the remote Osa peninsula, Corcovado National Park encompasses coastal mangrove swamps, pristine cloud forests and rocky canyons. Many of Costa Rica's endangered species live here, including tapirs, caymans and jaguars, while crocodiles swim in its waters and turtles lay their eggs on the park's deserted beaches. Ranger stations provide simple accommodation and advice.

Darién National Park, Panama

More than 500 bird species have been seen in the pristine rainforest of Darién National Park, among them many endangered species such as the harpy eagle. Indeed, Cerro Pirre mountain is considered by many birdwatchers to be one of the best sites in the world. Boat trips and forest walks are ideal ways to view the abundant wildlife, although visitors should seek advice on when it is safe to travel because of possible paramilitary activity.

Cockscomb Basin Wildlife Sanctuary, Belize

Beneath the peaks of the Cockscomb mountain range, the dense rainforest of the Cockscomb Basin is home to around 600 jaguars as well as tapirs, anteaters, armadillos and otters. Nearly 300 bird species have been reported in this lush jungle, and a wide variety of reptiles and amphibians are readily visible. Excellent forest trails make this a very rewarding place for wildlife watchers.

SOUTH AMERICA

Podocarpus National Park, Ecuador

Encompassing a wide range of habitats at different altitudes, Podocarpus (near Loja) has many rare plant and animal species, such as the Andean fox, the Andean speckled bear and the mountain tapir. Birdlife is abundant, and it is easy to see many fascinating species. This is, however, a park in peril, with the authorities struggling to protect the environment from poachers, loggers and others. For visitors prepared to rough it, there is much to enjoy in this landscape of lakes, mountains and rainforest.

Manu Biosphere Reserve, Peru

Altitudes range from 200 m (650 ft) to over 4,000 m (13,000 ft) in this area of rainforest near Cuzco. An astonishing 850 bird species are found here, and mammals include jaguars, ocelots, otters and many primate species. The reserve is divided into zones, with restricted visitor access in some areas. A stay in the Reserved Zone, which is set aside for ecotourism and research, must be arranged in advance, but offers the best jungle experience.

▲ Monteverde Cloud Forest Reserve, Costa Rica
Festooned with bromeliads and orchids, the towering rainforest trees of Monteverde Cloud Forest provide shelter for an enormous variety of wildlife including tapirs, monkeys, coatimundis and armadillos, as well as more than 400 bird species. The reserve was established in 1950 by a group of Quakers, who have developed a range of unobtrusive facilities for visitors, including simple accommodation and excellent guided walks.

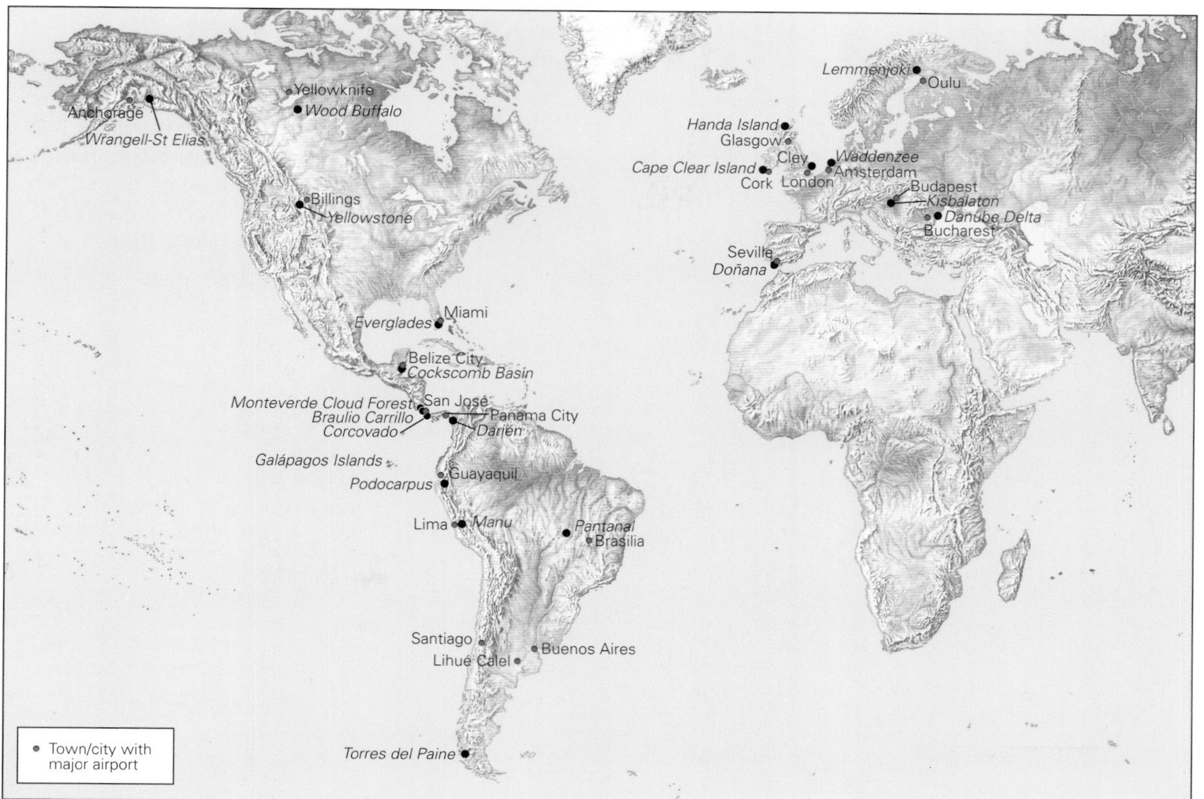

► **Handa Island, Scotland**
The sea cliffs of Handa Island are one of north-west Europe's largest seabird nesting sites, with the high cliff ledges attracting guillemots, razorbills and kittiwakes in enormous numbers. Fulmars, puffins and shags also nest here, while the island's moorland is home to great and Arctic skuas, red-throated divers, shelducks, ringed plovers, wheatears, meadow pipits and skylarks. The island can be visited for the day by boat from the mainland village of Tarbet, near Loch Laxford.

Pantanal, Brazil

A vast swamp covering an area the size of Great Britain, the Pantanal is perhaps the best place to see wildlife in the Americas. Animals wander freely around the wide open spaces, making it relatively easy for visitors to spot such creatures as alligators, jaguars and anacondas, and birds such as the giant red-necked stork. There are organized tours by boat or jeep and on horseback, with overnight accommodation at converted ranch houses.

Lihué Calel National Park, Argentina

An arid landscape of low, pink granite mountains and scrub forest, Lihué Calel (south-west of Santa Rosa) is home to several wild cat species and other mammals such as guanacos, Patagonian foxes, Patagonian hares and chinchillas. Birdlife is plentiful, too, and includes many species of birds of prey. The park has an excellent campsite and visitor centre.

EUROPE

Lemmenjoki National Park, Lappland, Finland

Lemmenjoki (near Inarijärvi) is one of the most extensive areas of uninhabited, forested wilderness in Europe (2,855 sq km/1,102 sq miles). Wide rivers flow through a landscape of peatland and spruce- and birch-forested hills, home to brown bears, golden eagles, foxes, lynx, wolverines and moose. There are also plenty of semi-domesticated reindeer.

Cape Clear Island, Ireland

Ireland's southernmost inhabited island, tiny Cape Clear is famous for its birds. It has breeding populations of chough, black guillemot and rock dove and is visited by many migrant species in August–October, including the rare bee-eater, little bittern, night and purple herons, and great reed warbler, as well as many seabirds. The Bird Observatory has a full-time bird-warden and offers simple accommodation.

Cley Marshes, Norfolk, England

One of Britain's leading birdwatching reserves, Cley Marshes (near Sheringham) has many thatched hides offering excellent views of thousands of water birds. Migrating waders stop in the area on their way to and from their Arctic breeding grounds, and in summer bitterns and avocets breed here. Wildfowl such as teals, widgeons and shovelers are plentiful in winter.

Waddenzee, The Netherlands

Regarded by birdwatchers as the most important intertidal area in Europe, Waddenzee has huge populations of waders and wildfowl. One of the best areas to see the birds is around Schiermonnikoog, particularly at high tide. Among the birds present in summer are avocets, godwits and ruffs, while in winter they include Bewick's swans, barnacle geese, marsh and hen harriers and white-tailed eagles.

Kisbalaton Reserve, Lake Balaton, Hungary

With its reed beds, the Kisbalaton Reserve provides the perfect environment for marsh birds to breed. Night, purple and squacco herons are all to be found here along with little and great white egrets, spoonbills, marsh harriers and several warblers. From October huge flocks of migrating ducks and geese stop in the reserve on their journey south.

Danube Delta, Romania

One of Europe's last unspoiled ecosystems, consisting of forest, lakes, reed beds and marshland, the Danube Delta is home to huge numbers of birds. Due to the lack of tourist facilities, it is probably best-visited in an organized group, ideally from late May–June. Species include bitterns, pygmy cormorants, white pelicans, night, purple and squacco herons, spoonbills, ruddy shelducks, honey buzzards, bee-eaters and white-tailed eagles.

Doñana National Park, Spain

Huge sand dunes and the seasonally flooded plains (*marismas*) behind them provide ideal conditions for a great variety of birdlife in one of Europe's most important wildlife habitats. Peregrines, stone-curlews and short-toed eagles are to be seen in the dunes, while the marismas are feeding grounds for white storks, spoonbills, night and purple herons and colonies of little and cattle egrets.

Galápagos Islands and ecotourism
Lying 960 km (600 miles) off the coast of Ecuador, the fragile wilderness of the Galápagos Islands provides a habitat for a surprising combination of penguins and corals as well as giant tortoises, land and marine iguanas, sperm whales, sea lions, fur seals, orca whales, sharks and a variety of tropical fish. Many of the species living here are found nowhere else in the world, making the Galápagos a vital laboratory for the study of animal and plant life. Access to the islands is strictly controlled and limited to 50 designated visitor sites. The development of ecotourism in the Galápagos Islands aims to ensure the preservation of the habitats and wildlife while enabling tourists to visit and learn about this unique environment.

Wildlife in Africa, Asia and Australasia

An African safari is one of the world's great wildlife-watching experiences. Vast stretches of open savanna are home to the 'big five' – lion, leopard, elephant, rhinoceros and buffalo – as well as herds of zebra and gazelle. The endangered Indian tiger and exotic komodo dragon are just two of the animals that attract visitors to Asia, while Australia has its own unique fauna, including kangaroo, koala and duck-billed platypus.

◀ Masai Mara National Reserve, Kenya
Kenya's greatest concentration of wildlife can be seen in Masai Mara, where cheetahs, hyenas, zebras, hartebeest, hippos and crocodiles share the territory with the 'big five'. During the summer enormous herds of wildebeest, zebras and gazelles arrive from the Serengeti on the first stage of their dramatic annual migration.

AFRICA

Abuko Nature Reserve, Gambia

In this small reserve, mangroves, gallery forest and savanna combine to attract over 270 bird species – including the world's largest and smallest kingfishers – making it one of the best birdwatching sites in West Africa. Abuko is also known for its troops of colobus, patas and vervet monkeys.

Niokolo-Koba National Park, Senegal

Some 80 mammal species, including lions, leopards, elephants, waterbucks, bushbucks, baboons and chimpanzees live in Niokolo-Koba, along with around 350 bird species. The best time to see the animals is when they gather at waterholes during the hot season in April and May.

Tsavo (East and West), Kenya

Tsavo East and Tsavo West combine to make one of the world's biggest national parks, covering an area of 21,000 sq km (8,000 sq miles). As well as the 'big five', the animals include cheetahs, giraffes, zebras, crocodiles, hippos, porcupines and mongooses. Tsavo East is a popular safari destination while at Tsavo West the excellent facilities include underwater hides for hippo watching.

Ngorongoro Crater, Tanzania

Protected within a circle of thickly-forested crater walls, Ngorongoro Crater is an expanse of grassland and forest measuring 14 km (9 miles) across and teeming with wildlife. Elephants, leopards, hyenas, bushbucks, buffalo, wildebeest, elands, warthogs, gazelles and ostriches live alongside the rare black rhinoceros and the handsome black-maned lion, while Lake Makat is home to flocks of flamingos and other water birds.

Jozani Reserve, Zanzibar, Tanzania

The largest remaining area of indigenous forest on Zanzibar, Jozani Reserve is home to a variety of birds and butterflies, as well as a number of rare mammals, including the red colobus monkey, which can only be found here.

Bwindi National Park, Uganda

Half of all the world's endangered mountain gorillas live in Bwindi National Park, an area of hilly rainforest. The park supports a rich variety of animal life including chimpanzees, golden cats, civets, leopards, bushpigs and giant forest hogs. Small groups of visitors who have booked several months in advance can go on guided gorilla-tracking expeditions.

Chobe National Park, Botswana

Encompassing habitats that range from marshland to forest, Chobe is home to a great variety of wildlife, including the rare puku and red lechwe antelope. Other inhabitants include lions, cheetahs, buffalo, giraffes, elephants, zebras, jackals, warthogs, hippos, crocodiles, hyenas, antelopes and wildebeest, as well as an abundance of birdlife. The animals can be viewed from boats on the Chobe River.

Kruger National Park, South Africa

A vast game reserve covering almost 20,000 sq km (7,400 sq miles), Kruger Park is home to around 137 mammal species, including lions, elephants, rhinoceros, leopards, buffalo, zebras, giraffes, impalas, wildebeest, hippos and crocodiles, as well as the rare roan and sable antelopes and oribi. The northern part is especially noted for its birdlife, including the highest density of birds of prey anywhere in the world.

Bird Island, Seychelles

Huge colonies of seabirds nest on the tiny, coral Bird Island. The sooty tern, fairy tern and common noddy are everywhere, while passing migrants add to the interest for birdwatchers. The island is also home to large numbers of giant turtles.

▲ Etosha National Park, Namibia
One of the most important wildlife reserves in Africa, Etosha covers a vast 20,000 sq km (7,720 sq miles) of woodland and grassland surrounding the Etosha Pan – an immense saline desert. Animals living here include springboks, impalas, kudu, wildebeest, hartebeest, roan antelopes, elands, zebras, elephants and the rare white rhinoceros, as well as predators such as lions, leopards, cheetahs, caracals, jackals and hyenas. There are around 340 bird species, including eagles, ostriches and secretary birds. Accommodation to suit all budgets is available.

▼ Serengeti National Park, Tanzania
Covering 14,763 sq km (5,700 sq miles) and including woodland and mountains, as well as huge tracts of open grassland, the Serengeti is home to the 'big five' plus cheetahs, hyenas, zebras, giraffes, gazelles and many others. It also has around 500 bird species. It is most famous for the spectacular summer migration of gazelles, wildebeest and zebras, when around 2 million animals set off on a 800 km (500-mile) trek to fresh feeding grounds.

ASIA

Kaziranga National Park, Assam, India

Famous as the home of the rare one-horned Great Indian Rhinoceros – most of the surviving 1,500 are here – Kaziranga (east of Gauhati) also has tigers, bears, elephants, bison and many bird species. A good way to travel around the tall-grass and swampy terrain is on an elephant. The park is only open from November to April.

Keoladeo Ghana National Park, Rajasthan, India

Formerly known as the Bharatpur Bird Sanctuary, Keoladeo is famous for its breeding populations of native water birds as well as its thousands of migrating birds which arrive every year from China and Siberia, including herons, storks, snake birds and the rare Siberian crane. The best time to visit is from October to February, when the migratory birds are in residence.

Sundarbans Wildlife Sanctuary, India/Bangladesh

Home to one of the largest remaining tiger populations in India, the Sundarbans Wildlife Sanctuary covers 6,695 sq km (2,585 sq miles) of mangrove swamp in the vast Ganges delta. Tigers are not often spotted by visitors, but a boat excursion through the peaceful mangroves will reveal many other animals – monkeys, wild pigs, spotted deer, crocodiles and fishing cats, as well as a profusion of birdlife.

Kanha National Park, Madhya Pradesh, India

Kipling set his *Jungle Book* in this beautiful landscape of forests, rivers and grasslands (near Mandla). Kanha is the only home of the barasingha (swamp deer) and it also plays an important role in the preservation of the tiger, leopard, chital, sambar and gaur (Indian bison). The park is open November–May, with sightings increasing from March onwards as the hot weather brings out the animals in search of water. Excursions are available.

Khao Yai National Park, Thailand

Encompassing a variety of habitats, from mountains clad in evergreen forest to lowland scrub and grassland, Khao Yai (north-east of Bangkok) has an abundance of wildlife, including elephants, gibbons, porcupines, tigers, leopards, Indian munjaks, Malaysian sun bears and several species of deer and monkey. There are over 250 bird species here, too, including the great hornbill and many colourful parrots and parakeets. Visitors can venture deep into the forest on several excellent trails, some of which require guides.

Taman Negara, Malaysia

Covering 4,340 sq km (1,676 sq miles) of ancient tropical rainforest, Taman Negara is a haven for hundreds of species of birds and animals, while its vegetation includes some of the world's rarest orchids. Inhabitants include tapirs, bears, elephants and gibbons. The park, which is the most visited in Pahang, has an elevated canopy walkway, and jungle hides in the trees, where visitors can spend the night.

Komodo National Park, Indonesia

The world's largest lizard, the astonishing 3 m (10 ft) long Komodo dragon, is found only on Komodo and a few neighbouring small islands. Guided treks usually include visits to dragon feeding places, and allow visitors to see some of the other wildlife of the park, such as wild pigs, deer, monkeys, water buffalo and eagles.

Ujung Kulon National Park, Indonesia

The last remaining low-relief forest on Java, in the far west, Ujung Kulon National Park is the only home of the one-horned Javan rhinoceros. Other inhabitants include the Javan gibbon, Javan tiger, muntjac (barking deer), chevrotain (mouse deer), green sea turtle and crocodile.

AUSTRALASIA

Eungella National Park, Queensland, Australia

With its tall, ancient rainforest trees, rocky creeks and spectacular waterfalls, Eungella is an extraordinarily beautiful place to watch wildlife. Among its inhabitants are kangaroos, possums, feathertail gliders, pythons and the native Eungella honey-eater, but the star attraction is the shy duck-billed platypus, which can be seen around the riverbanks at dawn and dusk.

Otago Peninsula, New Zealand

A remarkable variety of wildlife is concentrated on the Otago Peninsula. Seals and other marine life can be seen along the rocky coastline, while the inlets and beaches shelter numerous waders and waterfowl. A protected albatross nesting-site at Taiaroa Head is open to the public once the eggs are laid, and yellow-eyed penguins can be seen at close quarters from an excellent conservation reserve.

Catlins Forest Park, New Zealand

Ancient rainforest runs down to the rocky inlets and estuaries of the coast, offering a variety of habitats for some of New Zealand's rarest plants and animals. There are colonies of Hooker's sea lion and yellow-eyed penguin, and much birdlife. Two- and four-day ecotours are available.

◄ Royal Chitwan National Park, Nepal With its lush sub-tropical jungle and floodplain swamp, Chitwan National Park is a natural habitat for animals such as the tiger, Indian rhinoceros and leopard. Tours on foot, by jeep or on the back of an elephant are best undertaken between October and March.

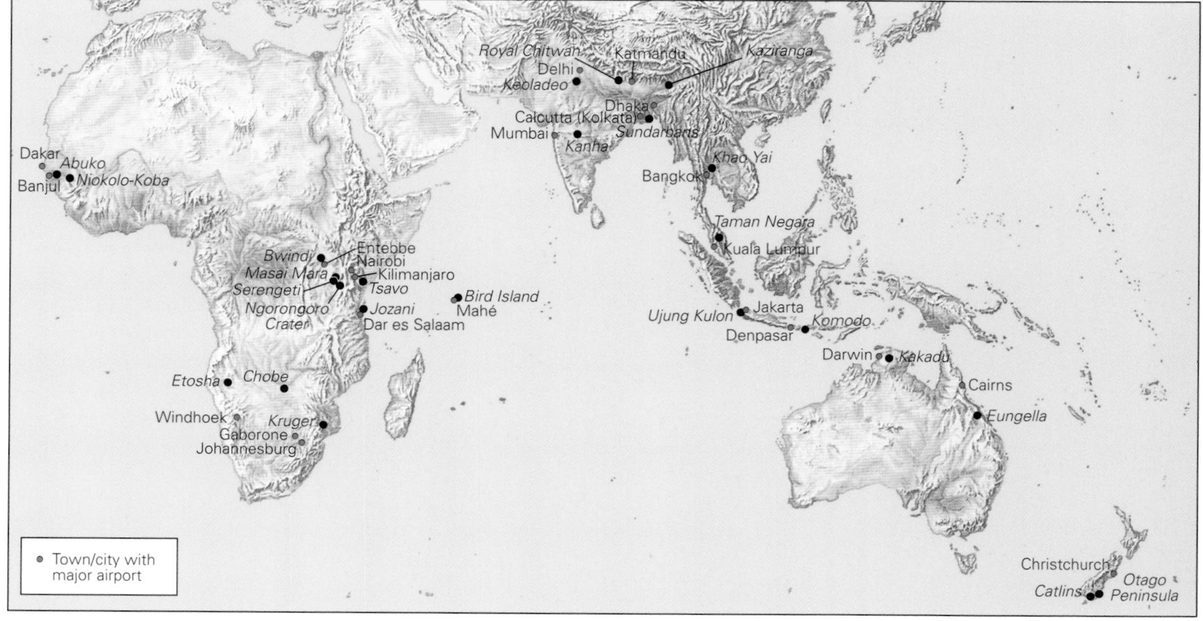

▼ Kakadu National Park, Northern Territory, Australia Australia's largest national park, Kakadu encompasses a spectacular collection of rainforest, ravines and wetlands along the South Alligator River. These varied habitats shelter a vast array of wildlife, including 1,500 species of butterflies and moths, 75 reptile species, including crocodiles, 25 species of frog and one third of all Australia's bird species. Mammals include kangaroos, wallabies, walleroos, dingoes and many species of bat.

Marine wildlife

With whale numbers recovering strongly following the world ban on hunting, many seaports in North America, South Africa and Australasia offer boat trips to watch whales and other large fish and mammals. In the warm waters of the tropics, coral reefs teeming with vividly coloured sealife can be explored by scuba divers and snorkellers or viewed from the comfort of a glass-bottomed boat.

◀ Florida Keys, USA
Among many places in the Caribbean that serve as a base for viewing or swimming with dolphins is Florida Keys. Consisting of 45 islands surrounded by spectacular corals, Florida Keys also provides a perfect environment for scuba diving.

THE AMERICAS

Johnstone Strait, Canada

The sea between Vancouver Island and the mainland is one of the best places in the world to see orcas (killer whales), the largest and most powerful predators on earth, and minke whales.

Hudson Bay, Canada

Beluga whales can be seen in June, July and August in the bay's Arctic waters. Particularly large numbers spend these months in the Churchill River estuary, an area famous for its polar bears.

Cape Breton and Grand Manan Islands, Canada

Whale-watching boat trips take place around both islands. Off Grand Manan, in the Bay of Fundy, up to 20 whale species, including the rare northern right whale and the finback, can be seen.

Massachusetts Bay, USA

Stellwagen Bank in Massachusetts Bay is a feeding ground for humpback, finback and minke whales from April to October. It is a world-renowned whale-watching area, attracting around 1.5 million whale watchers a year. The coastal towns of New England offer a range of boat trips.

Caribbean Sea, Cayman Islands

The islands are famous among scuba divers for their exceptionally clear waters and deep diving with spectacular sponge colonies and a wide range of reef fish. Those interested in larger species can see dolphins, barracudas and sharks – including silky sharks – here.

Caribbean Sea, Belize

The barrier reef of Belize is the largest in the western hemisphere, and second only to Australia's in the world. Between the reef and the mainland lie more than 175 cays and atolls (coral islands and rings) offering some of the best diving opportunities in the world. The extraordinary Blue Hole at the centre of Lighthouse Reef is a circular shaft over 120 m (395 ft) deep which was once a cavern underneath the sea bed. Half Moon Caye offers one of Belize's most spectacular wall dives, with an almost sheer drop overhung with wonderful coral spurs, rich in marine life.

Caribbean Sea, Venezuela

There is good diving to be had around the offshore islands of Venezuela, especially in the archipelago of Los Roques with its white sand beaches and beautiful coral reefs. The Parque Nacional Morrocoy on the north-west coast of Venezuela is very popular for snorkelling.

Paracas National Park, Peru

A boat trip around the offshore islands within this national park provides an opportunity to see dolphins, seals and sea lions, as well as pelicans and the great Andean condors that inhabit the cliffs.

AFRICA AND THE INDIAN OCEAN

Canary Islands

The waters around the islands provide sheltered feeding grounds for pilot whales, not usually seen so close to shore, and there are many boat trips available from Tenerife. Unfortunately, whale watching is not properly regulated here and whales have been injured by the boats.

Red Sea, Egypt

Hurghada is a good base for snorkelling and diving around the coral reefs of the Red Sea. Jolanda Reef, at the tip of the Sinai Peninsula in the Ras Muhammad National Park, is a spectacular column of coral 800 m (2,625 ft) high. The park is best approached from the Sharm el Sheikh resort.

▲ Point Reyes, California, USA
Grey whales can be seen from Point Reyes, north of San Francisco, between October and January as they migrate down the coast of Canada and the USA to the Gulf of California. Between December and March they can be found at Guerrero Negro in Mexico, where they gather to calve.

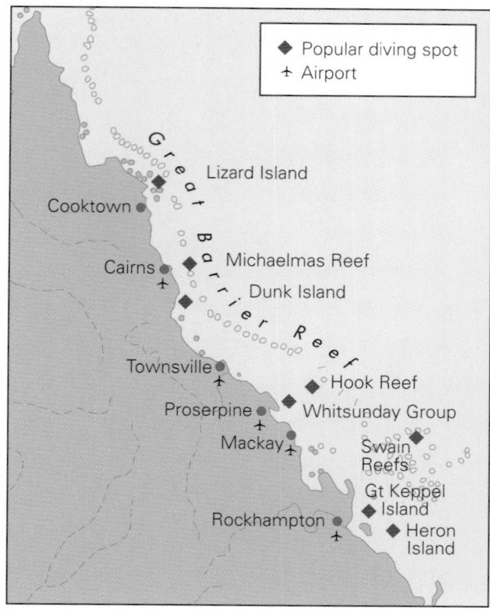

Australia's Great Barrier Reef
The Great Barrier Reef is the largest structure on earth made by living organisms. It is a chain of coral reefs 2,000 km (1,200 miles) long, encompassing more than 600 islands and cays. About 20 of these islands have resort facilities, with Heron Island and Lizard Island both especially popular with divers. There are around 2,000 species of fish living on the reef and the area is home to many marine mammals, including the rare dugong and several species of whale. The best time to visit the reef is between April and December. Cairns is the mainland base for most reef activities and offers all kinds of tours.

Pemba, Zanzibar and Mafia, Tanzania

The three main islands off the Tanzanian coast are surrounded by spectacular coral reefs which are home to a wide variety of marine species including bat fish, lion fish, turtles and rays. They offer some of the best diving opportunities in the world from August to December. Mafia Island is also a favourite breeding ground for giant turtles.

Cape of Good Hope, South Africa

In a country which has the strictest whale protection laws in the world, most whale watching takes place from the shore. The 'Whale Route' is a spectacularly scenic road along the coast from Cape Town, around the Cape of Good Hope, to the Indian Ocean, with many official whale-viewing sites. The town of Hermanus (the self-proclaimed 'whale capital' of South Africa) makes a good base. From June to October southern right whales, once hunted to near-extinction, can be seen swimming in these waters.

Seychelles

The outlying islands in particular offer world-class diving. The reef-ringed shores are a paradise for snorkellers, with over 150 species of tropical reef fish and 30 species of coral. Dophins, porpoises, sharks and barracudas can also be seen. There are four marine national parks and diving schools with good facilities.

Maldives

Without doubt the Maldives are the best place in the Indian Ocean for diving. There are hundreds of diving sites, with something for everyone from beginners to experts. The more adventurous can explore shipwrecks as well as spectacular caves and terraces of coral. There is also plenty of scope for snorkellers.

► **Tortuguero Park, Costa Rica**
In the company of a guide, limited numbers of visitors can watch green turtles at their largest nesting site in the western hemisphere. The turtles lay their eggs on the beach between July and October, the peak time being late August.

ASIA

Ang Thong National Marine Park, Thailand

Boat trips around 42 limestone islands, many eroded into fantastic shapes, provide opportunities for seeing a variety of wildlife – including dolphins, turtles and sea otters – and for snorkelling and diving.

Surin Islands, Thailand

The Surin Islands are noted for diving in moonlight. The wildlife that may be encountered includes wahoo turtles, moray eels, black tip sharks and bat fish.

Sipadan Island, Sabah, Malaysia

An amazing undersea 'wall', teeming with marine life that includes whale sharks, manta rays, turtles and tuna, makes Sipadan one of the world's great diving destinations. The island is the tip of an underwater mountain, making it possible to dive from the beach.

Bunaken Island, Sulawesi, Indonesia

Perhaps the most famous marine destination in Indonesia, Bunaken Island near Manado serves as the main base for exploring the stunning coral reefs known as the 'sea gardens of Sulawesi'.

AUSTRALASIA AND THE PACIFIC

Kaikoura, New Zealand

A world-famous whale-watching centre, Kaikoura caters for 30,000 whale watchers a year. The deepwater canyons near the shore are home to sperm whales.

▲ **Malindi and Wasini Island, Kenya**
One of a number of good diving and snorkelling spots in Kenya, Malindi also offers excursions in glass-bottomed boats to the nearby coral reef. The Kisite Marine National Park on Wasini Island, in the far south, provides spectacular diving safaris.

Hawaii, USA

The extraordinary song of the humpback whale can be heard in the waters around Hawaii from November to May, after which these rare animals return to their summer feeding grounds in the near-polar waters of the north Pacific. Whale watching is strictly regulated, but there are plenty of boat trips on offer. Hawaii also has coral reefs, though with fewer species than on other Indo-Pacific reefs. Diving is popular, with lessons being provided in the crater lake of the extinct Molokini volcano. Excursions in submarines down to a depth of 50 m (160 ft) offer superb views of the underwater world through portholes.

Rangiroa, Tuamotu Islands

Among many excellent diving sites in French Polynesia, this is possibly the best, with outstanding coral, sharks, dolphins, barracudas and rays.

Marquesas Islands

The oxygen-rich water around the islands, which is thick with plankton, supports a variety of marine creatures, including hammerhead and white-tipped sharks, leopard and manta rays, tuna and barracudas. There are around 20 dive sites, including some impressive caves.

Great railway journeys

From the luxury of the Orient-Express to the spartan rigours of the Trans-Siberian Railway, the world's great train journeys exert an irresistible lure for many travellers, passing through spectacular landscapes. Journeys vary in length from a few hours to a fortnight, and the more sought-after trains must be booked well in advance.

► **Palace on Wheels**
India's most luxurious train, originally hauled by the *Desert Queen*, takes passengers on an eight-day tour that begins and ends in Delhi. It includes Jaipur and the other major cities of Rajasthan, and Agra.

NORTH AMERICA

Green Mountain Flyer, Vermont, USA
Distance: 21 km (13 miles)
A vintage train takes passengers through the beautiful Vermont countryside, running alongside the Connecticut River for part of the way. Largely a tourist service, the peak period is during October when the autumn colours are at their best.

Coast Starlight, USA
Distance: 2,235 km (1,389 miles)
A journey from Seattle to Los Angeles, through the magnificent landscapes of the west coast of the USA, includes amongst its highlights the mountains of the Oregon Cascades and the Californian Coast Range. South of Oakland the track runs along the edge of the Pacific Ocean, passing several of California's most popular beaches.

Los Mochis to Chihuahua, Mexico
Distance: 655 km (407 miles)
This 14-hour journey is one of contrasting landscapes, from the tropical Pacific coastlands to the high northern plateau by way of the magnificent Copper Canyon (Barranca del Cobre). Longer and deeper than Arizona's Grand Canyon, this is an area of steeply wooded gorges and spectacular mountain peaks.

SOUTH AMERICA

Guayaquil to Quito, Ecuador
Distance: 463 km (288 miles)
For those who relish danger as well as breathtaking scenery, this line – which has been called 'the world's greatest roller-coaster' – is a must. It climbs high into the Andes, zigzagging perilously to an altitude of 3,609 m (11,840 ft) and passing directly under a waterfall. Trains are erratic and often break down.

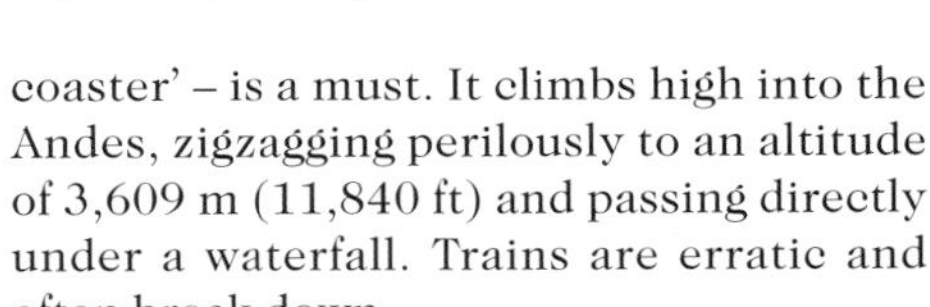

Central Railway, Peru
Distance: 335 km (208 miles)
The highest railway in the world, this takes passengers on an eight- to nine-hour journey across the Andes, from Lima to Huancayo. Dizzy heights, sheer drops, zigzags, loops and tunnels abound.

EUROPE

Flåm Railway, Norway
Distance: 20 km (12 miles)
Dropping 865 m (2,838 ft) in just 20 km (12 miles), this is one of the steepest non-rack railways in the world. Beginning with a view over the Kjosfossen lake and waterfall, the train weaves its way from Myrdal towards Aurlands Fjord and Flåm through a series of tunnels, with spectacular views between tunnels and snow shelters.

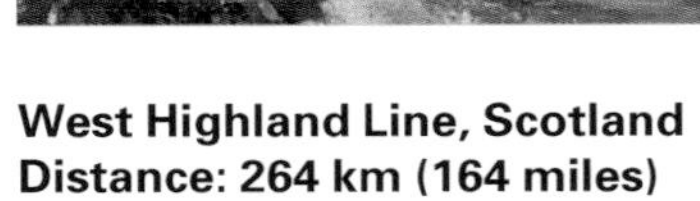

◄ **Glacier Express, Switzerland**
Distance: 290 km (180 miles)
An exhilarating seven-and-a-half hour journey in the Swiss Alps, between the ski resorts of St Moritz and Zermatt, is provided by this train. Extraordinary feats of engineering are displayed as it weaves its way through the mountains, travelling through 91 tunnels, crossing 291 bridges and negotiating hairpin bends and steep ascents.

West Highland Line, Scotland
Distance: 264 km (164 miles)
Running between Glasgow and Mallaig, this line provides one of the most spectacular railway journeys in Britain. The route is particularly dramatic between Fort William and Mallaig, with a series of viaducts and tunnels through the mountains high above the Atlantic coast.

Venice Simplon-Orient-Express, Europe
Distance: 1,714 km (1,065 miles)
Passengers travel in style on a train that re-creates the romance of the golden age of rail as it crosses Europe from London to Venice, via Paris, Zürich, Innsbruck and Verona, in 32 hours. Orient-Express trains also run to Rome and Istanbul on a variety of routes that go through Venice, Florence, Lucerne, Budapest and Bucharest.

Andalusian Express, Spain
Distance: 740 km (460 miles)
The luxurious *Al Andalus* follows a circular route from Seville through the beautiful Andalusian countryside, with its citrus and olive groves, vineyards and hilltop villages. There are opportunties to stop off and see the sites at Córdoba, Granada, Antequera and Ronda.

▲ **Canadian, Canada**
Distance: 2,776 miles (4,4467 km)
On a 69-hour journey that begins in Toronto, this train passes through some of the most beautiful scenery on earth. The prairie lands of Manitoba and Saskatchewan give way to the cattle ranches of Alberta, from where the train climbs into the Rockies. Here it passes lakes, glaciers and the dramatic Fraser Canyon before reaching Vancouver.

Useful web addresses
all preceded by www.

Canadian trains:
cwrr.com
viarail.ca

US trains:
amtrak.com

European trains:
raileurope.com

Orient-Express:
orient-expresstrains.com

Pride of Africa:
rovos.co.za

Palace on Wheels:
palaceonwheels.net

Eastern and Oriental Express:
orient-expresstrains.com/eando/train

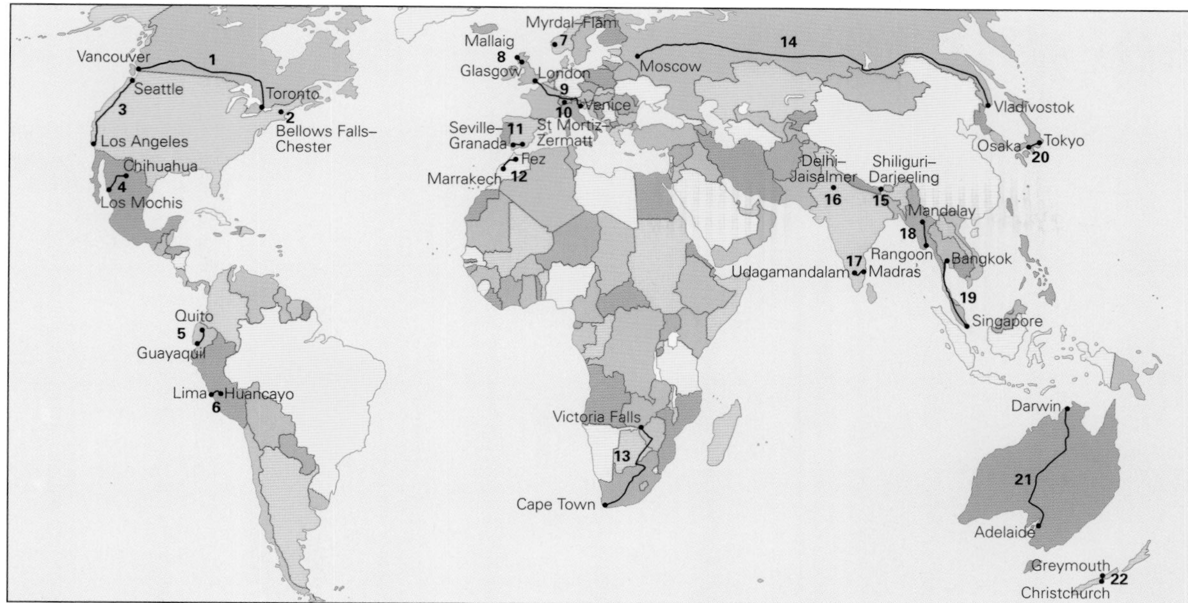

1 Canadian, Canada
2 Green Mountain Flyer, USA
3 Coast Starlight, USA
4 Los Mochis to Chihuahua, Mexico
5 Guayaquil to Quito, Ecuador
6 Central Railway, Peru
7 Flåm Railway, Norway
8 West Highland Line, Scotland
9 Venice Simplon-Orient-Express, Europe
10 Glacier Express, Switzerland
11 Andalusian Express, Spain
12 Marrakech Express, Morocco
13 Pride of Africa, Southern Africa
14 Trans-Siberian Railway, Russia
15 Darjeeling Himalayan Railway, India
16 Palace on Wheels, India
17 Madras to Udagamandalam, India
18 Mandalay Express, Burma (Myanmar)
19 Eastern and Oriental Express, Thailand and Malaysia
20 Tokyo to Osaka, Japan
21 The Ghan, Australia
22 TranzAlpine Express, New Zealand

AFRICA

Marrakech Express, Morocco
Distance: 583 km (362 miles)
Passing through Morocco's four imperial cities, this nine-hour journey begins in Marrakech, near the foot of the High Atlas Mountains, and travels north through the desert to Casablanca. From here the line follows the Atlantic coast to Rabat then gradually heads back inland through orchards and olive groves to Meknès and on to Fès.

Pride of Africa, Southern Africa
Distance: 3,2000 km (2,000 miles)
The journey from Cape Town in this luxurious train is full of romance and drama. In the early stages the train travels through a landscape of vineyards and farmland and across the Karoo Desert to Pretoria. Passengers can enjoy watching wildlife as the journey continues through the African bush across Botswana and Zimbabwe to the spectacular Victoria Falls on the Zambian border.

ASIA

Madras to Udagamandalam, India
Distance: 640 km (400 miles)
This 16-hour journey takes travellers from the plains of Madras through a colourful rural landscape and up into the beautiful Nilgiri hills to the famous hill station of Udagamandalam, formerly known as Ootacamund, or Ooty. The train passes through some of the most dramatic scenery India has to offer, climbing steeply on India's only rack railway to the gentler landscapes of the Deccan Plateau.

Darjeeling Himalayan Railway, India
Distance: 88 km (55 miles)
The tiny engine used on this railway, which is a UNESCO heritage site, takes passengers from Shiliguri on the hot Bengal plains to the mountain climate of Darjeeling in the Himalayas. The journey involves steep ascents and precipitous curves, climbing 2,164 m (7,100 ft). On the way the train passes through Ghoom, which is the second highest station in the world at 2,258 m (7,408 ft) above sea level.

Mandalay Express, Burma (Myanmar)
Distance: 616 km (385 miles)
By no means a tourist train, the Express offers the traveller a truly local experience as it makes its way slowly north from Yangon (formerly Rangoon) through a landscape of rice fields and golden-spired pagodas. The crowded train makes numerous – often unscheduled – stops along the way, making it an unpredictable and colourful journey. Best undertaken between November and February, the journey takes around 16 hours.

Eastern and Oriental Express, Thailand and Malaysia
Distance: 1,943 km (1,207 miles)
Starting in Bangkok, this train takes 52 hours to travel south through the terraced farmlands of Thailand and the rubber plantations and jungles of Malaysia to Singapore. It represents the height of luxury in train travel, while International Express trains that follow the same route provide a more down-to-earth experience.

AUSTRALASIA

The Ghan, Australia
Distance: 2,962 km (1,851 miles)
Named after the Afghan camel-drivers who once transported provisions along its route, the Ghan passenger train made its first journey from Adelaide to Darwin in February 2004. In 47 hours the train passes through vine-covered hills to the craggy mountains of the MacDonnell Ranges, the multi-coloured desert of central Australia and the woodland of the north, much to the delight of train enthusiasts who long campaigned for the line north of Alice Springs to be completed.

◄ Tokyo to Osaka, Japan
Distance: 518 km (322 miles)
The Nozomi Express – the fastest scheduled train service in the world – travels at speeds of up to 300 km/h (186 mph) along this line. Not quite as fast, the Hikari Express completes the journey in just over three hours. However, the scenery, which includes Mount Fuji, can best be appreciated from the slower 'bullet' trains.

TranzAlpine Express, New Zealand
Distance: 233 km (154 miles)
Travelling from Christchurch on the South Island's east coast to Greymouth on the west coast, the Express takes passengers on a four-and-a-half hour journey through a variety of landscapes. After crossing the farmlands of the Canterbury Plains it follows the Waimakariri River gorge into the mountainous Arthur's Pass National Park, where it enters the long Otira tunnel. From here the line descends through lush rainforest, passing lakes Poerua and Brunner, to Greymouth.

Trans-Siberian Railway, Russia
Distance: 9,297 km (5,776 miles)
The southern shore of Lake Baikal is on the route of the Trans-Siberian Railway, the world's longest, and possibly most famous, railway. The eight-day journey takes passengers from Moscow to Vladivostok via the Urals, the forested wilderness of Siberia, and the Transbaikalian Mountains.

In the early days of the railway, built between 1891 and 1916, a ferry was used in summer to carry the train across Lake Baikal, while in winter, when the lake froze, temporary rails were laid over the ice. The Siberian landscape is particularly beautiful in winter when it is covered with snow. In the spring there are carpets of wild flowers while in autumn there are the golden colours of the birch forests.

River and canal journeys

The world's great boat journeys give travellers a unique perspective on the countries through which they pass: rivers and canals were the highways of the past, and there are often opportunities to visit historic sites or natural habitats. Whether you are steaming down the Mississippi in a paddleboat, gliding through the French countryside past castles and vineyards or exploring the tributaries of the Amazon, the pace of the journey gives ample time to enjoy the beauty of the surroundings.

◄ **Lower Mississippi, USA**
A seven-day cruise by paddleboat can be taken from Memphis to New Orleans. The Mississippi twists and turns on its way to the marshlands bordering the coast. There are opportunities to visit some of the historic sites of the Deep South, including the Civil War battlefields of Vicksburg, and the elegant mansion at Oak Alley Plantation, and to sample some of the local Creole and Cajun cuisine.

NORTH AMERICA

St Lawrence, Canada

From Kingston, where Lake Ontario flows into the majestic St Lawrence River, a six-night journey can be made on a replica steamboat to Montréal (see *World Cities*) and Québec (see *Historic sites in the Americas*). Just east of Kingston the river is dotted with literally a Thousand Islands, many of which have summer houses and opulent mansions set amid forests of yellow birch, silver maple and red and white trillium. In the spring the trillium trees are covered by white blossom.

Upper Mississippi, USA

In the summer months, seven-day cruises by paddleboat run between Minneapolis/St Paul and St Louis. There are also three-day cruises between St Louis and Memphis. The upper river, flowing through relatively flat countryside, is wide, slow moving and dotted with islands, but the stretch immediately below St Louis flows between rocky bluffs. Days spent cruising are alternated with sightseeing tours of such places as the boyhood home of Mark Twain, in Hannibal, Memphis, and a historic Native American site in Burlington, Iowa.

► **St Petersburg to Moscow, Russia**
This seven-day cruise passes through a network of rivers, lakes and canals in the richly wooded region of Southern Karelia, and down the upper reaches of the Volga River. Ports of call include the ancient town of Yaroslavl, the attractive Karelian capital of Petrozavodsk, and the Church of the Transfiguration on the island of Kizhi in Lake Onega, with its 22 wooden domes, constructed without a single nail.

CENTRAL AND SOUTH AMERICA

Amazon, Peru and Brazil

Cruises of between three and ten days along the Amazon River, starting from the remote but elegant Peruvian town of Iquitos, or from the brash and bustling Manaus in Brazil, are a relatively comfortable way to see the abundant wildlife of the rainforest. Many companies adopt an educational approach and include lectures on the local flora and fauna. Some include an opportunity to explore smaller tributaries by canoe. For the adventurous independent traveller who is prepared to rough it, a six-day journey by local riverboat from the Atlantic port of Belém to Manaus offers an unforgettable experience of local life and culture.

Orinoco Delta, Venezuela

The vast Orinoco Delta – a maze of channels running between countless forested islands – is one of Venezuela's wildest regions. The area is home to the indigenous Warao people, known for their skilled carving and basketwork, whose houses on stilts can be seen on the riverbanks. Boat tours into the delta can be arranged from the town of Tucupita, and usually last for between two and four days.

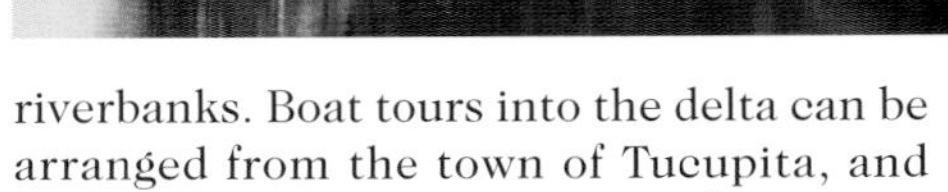

▲ **The Burgundy Canal, France**
Passing through a landscape of wooded valleys and sleepy villages, the six-day journey on a barge from Tonnere to Dijon along the Burgundy Canal provides an opportunity to see the beautiful 16th-century chateaux of Tanlay and Ancy le Franc and the 12th-century Cistercian Abbey of Fontenay. The region is famous for its *grand cru* vineyards and its robust cuisine, and there are plenty of opportunities to enjoy both along the way.

EUROPE

Shropshire Union Canal, UK

From Autherley, a 100 km (60-mile) journey can be taken on a slow-moving barge along the Shropshire Union Canal. Deep wooded cuttings, peaceful rural landscapes, medieval market towns and quiet villages are all passed at little more than walking pace. The ancient city of Chester, with its Roman ruins and medieval city walls, is a highlight of the journey. The canal ends at Ellesmere Port on the River Mersey, where there is an excellent boating museum.

Rhine, Switzerland, Germany and the Netherlands

A ten-day journey down the Rhine from Basel to Arnhem combines stunning scenery with a chance to visit the historic towns and cities along its banks. After flowing through the German Black Forest, the river passes romantic clifftop castles, sloping vineyards and picturesque villages on its way to the cities of the north: Bonn, Cologne and Düsseldorf. A detour up the River Neckar to the historic town of Heidelberg is often included.

◄ Nile, Egypt
A week-long cruise up the Nile from Luxor to Aswan and back combines visits to magnificent historic sites – such as the huge temple of Karnak and the tombs in the Valley of the Kings at Luxor – with periods of relaxation on board an air-conditioned riverboat. There are also opportunities to take camel rides into the desert that lies beyond the narrow fertile strip on either side of the river. From Aswan, where it is possible to sail on the river in a *felucca* (pictured here), a short flight takes passengers to the splendid temple of Abu Simbel, above the shores of Lake Nasser. Abu Simbel can also be reached by taking a luxury three-day cruise on the lake. Created by the building of the Aswan Dam, the lake itself is an impressive sight.

Useful web addresses
all preceded by www.

- cruisein.co.uk
- smallshipcruises.com
- goway.com/cruises
- burgundy-canal.com
- cruise.com

Douro, Portugal

Most cruises on the Douro are round trips of seven to nine days, beginning and ending in Porto. Once the boat leaves the coastal plain, it passes between spectacularly terraced vineyards, in an area unspoilt by major roads. Ports of call include the picturesque towns of Lamego and Vila Real. The region is the centre of Portugal's port wine production, and all cruises include a visit to a vineyard to sample the local produce.

Danube, Hungary, Slovak Republic, Austria and Germany

A Danube cruise of around eight days combines sightseeing tours of some of Central Europe's most historic towns and cities with an opportunity to relax on board, watching rich farmland and terraced slopes slip past. A cruise up-river from Budapest to Regensburg includes frequent stops, enabling passengers to explore Bratislava, Vienna, Linz and Passau, and to visit the sumptuous Baroque palace of Schönbrunn and the Benedictine Abbey in Melk. Since the boat berths overnight, passengers can also enjoy some nightlife ashore, and attend specially organized classical concerts.

AFRICA

River Gambia National Park, Gambia

A day trip on the river from Janjanbureh (Georgetown) or Kuntaur provides an opportunity to view crocodiles and hippos at close range. As the rice fields and coconut trees on the banks give way to dense forest, it may also be possible to glimpse monkeys, baboons and many species of birds.

Niger, Mali

A journey along the River Niger as it curves through the semi-desert of the Sahel is the classic way to see and experience the life of this area. Local passenger boats are scheduled to take seven days, but can take as long as 14 to travel between Gao and Koulikoro. The most popular section is the two days or so between Mopti and Korioumé, the stopping point for visits to the ancient desert city of Timbuktu. Also highly recommended is a detour up the River Bani to the beautiful old town of Djenné, where the mosque is a stunning example of construction using mud bricks and render.

ASIA AND AUSTRALASIA

Backwaters of Kerala, India

The eight-hour journey through the backwaters of Kerala, from Kollam (Quilon) to Alappuzha, is popular with tourists. Passengers are transported along a network of rivers, canals and lagoons, overhung with dense tropical foliage that every so often gives way to open paddy fields. Brightly coloured birds and ancient buildings can be glimpsed on the banks, and the Keralan people can be seen going about their daily lives.

Gorges of the Yangtze, China

Time is running out for those who want to experience the full splendour of a cruise along the Yangtze River as it passes between the rocky pinnacles of the Three Gorges. The controversial Three Gorges Dam project is due to be completed in 2009, and the flooding that will eventually create a 560 km (350-mile) long reservoir has already begun. The dam itself has become a tourist attraction. In the meantime, three- to four-day cruises from Chongqing to Wuhan, through the magnificent Qutang, Wuhang and Xiling gorges, continue to provide stunning views of a dramatic natural landscape. It is also possible to take a longer cruise from Shanghai to Chongqing.

Sepik, Papua New Guinea

The Sepik River twists and turns its way from the central mountains of Papua New Guinea through jungles, swamps and grasslands to the sea. Most cruises start from a remote inland location, to which passengers are transferred from Port Moresby by small plane. There is then a leisurely journey through the rainforest, with stops at riverside villages, some of which are on stilts. The people of the region are renowned for their woodcarving and traditional art, each village having its own distinctive style.

Murray, South Australia

A six-day cruise on a paddelboat, beginning and ending at Mannum, passes through colourful scenery, including verdant wetlands, brick-red plains, sandstone cliffs and deep blue lagoons. The cruise may also include a visit to the old river port of Morgan and an opportunity to hear about Aboriginal customs from elders at the Ngaut Ngaut Conservation Park.

▼ Li, China
The 80 km (50-mile) journey down the Li River from Guilin to the beautiful town of Yangshuo passes through a landscape of precipitous peaks, with names such as Paint Brush Hill and Five Tigers Catch a Goat Hill. Gliding past bamboo-lined riverbanks and picturesque villages, the trip and a bus-ride back to Guilin takes one day.

Sea and ocean cruises

Cruises attract all kinds of travellers and cater for an increasingly wide range of tastes. The steep-sided inlets of Alaska, Chile, Norway and New Zealand allow cruise liners to hug the coast, providing matchless views of these dramatic landscapes. Caribbean cruises allow almost daily shore visits, for shopping and exploring. Transatlantic cruises provide lavish on-board entertainment during the long sea passages. Cruise companies also vary in their appeal: some include lectures on the places they visit; others take a far less serious approach!

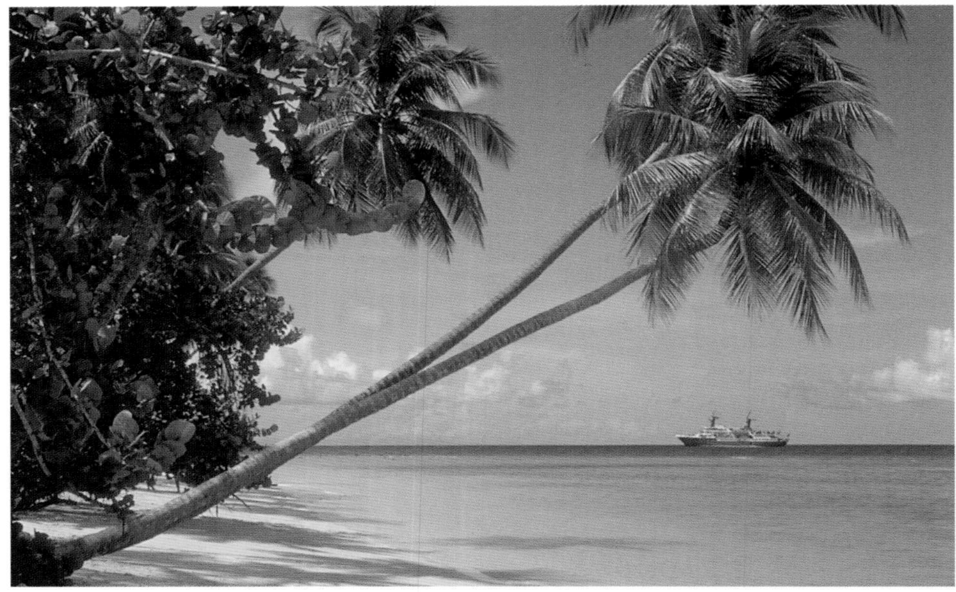

◄ **The Caribbean**
There are numerous variations on the Caribbean cruise, but virtually all have relatively short sea passages and a visit to a different island almost every day. There are organized trips to the rain-forests of Puerto Rico and sites of European colonial history. Some passengers, however, prefer to spend their time simply enjoying the islands' magnificent beaches.

▼ **Antarctic**
Many of the 'expedition cruises' to the Antarctic use converted research ships or ice breakers, which offer less luxurious accom-modation than other cruise ships. Passengers are taken ashore in small inflatable craft, and are thus able to get close to the teeming wildlife. There is always the chance of encountering whales in the surrounding seas, as well as sighting beautifully sculpted icebergs.

NORTH AMERICA AND THE ATLANTIC

Alaska/British Columbia

The main attractions of a cruise in this area are the spectacular mountain scenery and the opportunity to see whales and seals, bears and birds of prey at close hand. Ships hug the coastline, entering steep-sided fjords and sailing close to the mouths of glaciers. Ports of call include Juneau, Alaska's capital, the 'gold rush' town of Skagway, and the Russian settlement of Sitka, with its onion domes.

Mexican Riviera

Mexico's west coast is becoming an increasingly popular area for relatively short cruises to catch the late-summer sunshine. For some tourists, the attractions are miles of unspoilt beaches fringed by jungle, such as those at Manzanillo and Zihuatanejo, and being able to go marlin fishing. For others they are the opportunities to experience Mexican culture and to visit the chic resort of Puerto Vallarta.

Atlantic Isles (Canaries, Madeira)

The Atlantic Isles are a popular cruise destination, particularly in winter and spring, when the lower mountain slopes are brilliant with flowers. Shore visits in Madeira usually include the novelty of a ride in a bullock cart or wicker sled on the mountain roads, while a trip to the summit of Tenerife's Mount Teide (3,718 m/12,000 ft) provides spectacular views of the surrounding islands.

Transatlantic cruises

Cruises link Europe with New York or Boston, with ports further south, such as Miami, and also with various Caribbean islands. The most direct, more northerly, route is for those wishing to enjoy the elaborate onboard entertainment, high standard of cuisine, and formal social life that are typical of the transatlantic liner. On ships plying more southerly waters, passengers can combine a luxury lifestyle with sunbathing, swimming and various other deck activities.

SOUTH AMERICA

Chilean fjords

Cruises along the most southern 1,000 km (625 miles) of Chile's coastline provide magnificent views of mountains and glaciers. The further south, the colder and less predictable the weather becomes, but for many the thrill of travelling the route of Darwin's *Beagle* and visiting Tierra del Fuego outweighs the risk of storms.

EUROPE

Norwegian fjords

Those cruising the fjords of Norway do so primarily to enjoy the majestic mountain scenery. Waterfalls, glaciers and wildlife can all be viewed from the comfort of the ship, while shore visits include a ride on a spectacular mountain railway from Flåm (see *Great railway journeys*). Some cruises extend as far as Europe's most northern point, where passengers can experience the midnight sun.

Western Mediterranean

One of the joys of a cruise in the Western Mediterranean is the opportunity to sample the local cuisine and wines. Most cruises include a day in the vibrant Spanish city of Barcelona. In Italy, there are brief organized trips to view the art treasures of Pisa and Florence, and the Roman remains of Pompeii (see *Historic sites in Europe*). There are also opportunities to enjoy the high-life in some of the fashionable resorts of the French Riviera, such as St Tropez, to visit the casinos of Monte Carlo, and to watch the Spanish flamenco dancers in Cartagena. Some cruises extend as far as the Adriatic, call in at the fortress town of Dubrovnik and include a day's sightseeing in Venice.

Eastern Mediterranean

A region rich in the remains of earlier civilizations, the Eastern Mediterranean provides much of historic interest, and many cruises have on-board experts to give background lectures. Some of the main sites visited include the Roman town of Ephesus in Turkey, the Ancient Greek ruins of Delos, the Crusader castle of Krak des Chevaliers in Syria, and the pyramids in Egypt (see *Historic sites in Africa*). Most cruises also include opportunities for swimming, snorkelling and sunbathing.

▲ **North-east America**
The north-eastern seaboard of America offers areas of great natural beauty such as Acadia National Park in Maine, whose fall colours are the focus of October cruises. There is also an opportunity to see the whales that frequent the waters of Stellwagen Bank off the coast of Massachusetts. Included in a wide variety of shore visits are the Canadian fishing town of Lunenburg, the popular US resort of Martha's Vineyard, and the cities of Boston and New York.

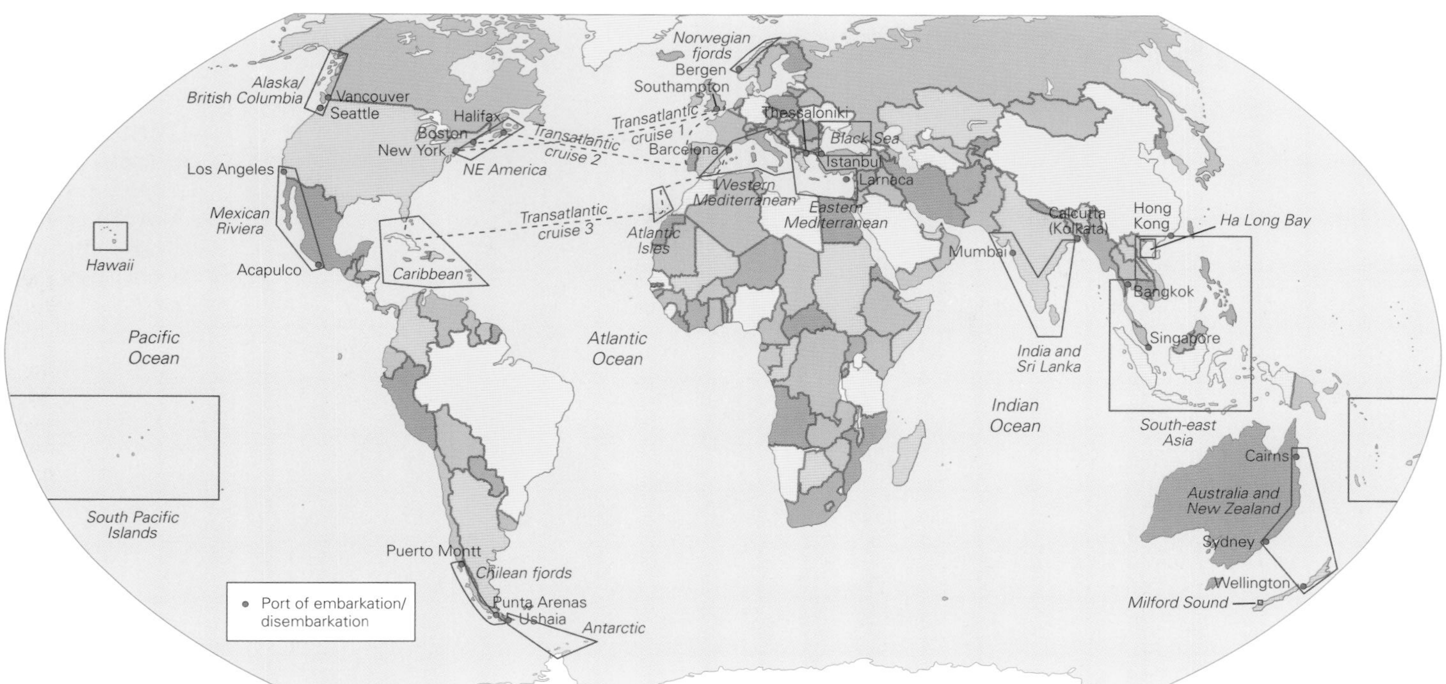

▼ Black Sea
A day in Istanbul (see *World Cities*) is included in most cruises of the Black Sea. The countries bordering the Black Sea provide a rich variety of historic sites, from the medieval churches of Nesebúr in Bulgaria, to the 19th-century opera house in Ukrainian Odessa, the 18th-century palace of Tsar Alexander II on the Crimean peninsula, and the abandoned Byzantine monastery of Sumela, high above the Turkish port of Trabzon.

AFRICA, ASIA AND THE INDIAN OCEAN

India and Sri Lanka

Cruises around the Indian subcontinent provide an opportunity to visit a number of historic sites without the strain of overland travel. A day's sightseeing is followed by a day's relaxation in the relatively cool sea breezes. Many of the sites visited are from India's colonial past – the Dutch fort at Cochin, the former Portuguese colony of Goa, remnants of the British Raj in Madras – but there are also trips to some indigenous sites, such as the Hindu cave temples of Mumbai (Bombay).

South-east Asia

With such a wealth of possible sights and exciting ports of call, there are many varieties of the South-east Asian cruise, which is a popular option for the Christmas break. Most shore visits consist of whistle-stop tours of the port of call, but there are also more adventurous expeditions, such as a visit to an orang-utan sanctuary in Sarawak, or a trek to catch a glimpse of the famous 'Komodo dragon' (see *Wildlife in Asia*). Many of the cruises visit Bali, with its sandy beaches, terraced rice fields and ornate Hindu temples.

Where, when and for how long?

	Main season	Duration of cruise (in days)
Alaska	May–Sept	7–14
NE America	Aug–Oct	7–14
Mexican Riviera	Sept–Oct	7–10
Atlantic Islands	Apr–Dec	9–14
Transatlantic	April and Sep–Nov	14
Caribbean	Oct–Dec	3–23
Chilean fjords	Oct–May	3–7
Antarctica	mid-Oct–early March	9–12
Norwegian fjords	May–July	7–14
Western Mediterranean	Apr–Nov	12–14
Eastern Mediterranean	Aug–Dec	10–14
Black Sea	Aug–Oct	14
India/Sri Lanka	Dec–Feb	14
Southeast Asia	Dec–Feb	8–17
Ha Long, Vietnam	All year	1
Australia/ New Zealand	Nov–Apr	14
Milford Sound	Nov–Apr	half day
Hawaii	Sept–Oct	7–14

AUSTRALASIA AND THE PACIFIC

Australia and New Zealand

Most cruises of Australia's east coast provide more than one opportunity to stop on the 2,000 km (1,250-mile) long Great Barrier Reef (see *Marine wildlife*). By way of contrast, the natural wonders of New Zealand include the spouting geysers and boiling mud of Rotorua (see *Lakes and waterfalls*), and the dolphins, whales and penguins of the verdant Bay of Islands.

Milford Sound, New Zealand

Milford Sound is perfect for a cruise of just a few hours. It is possible to enjoy lunch while gazing out at towering granite peaks and glaciers, and, on the lower slopes, thick beech forests and waterfalls. There is always the chance of sighting the dolphins, seals, penguins and other sea birds that inhabit the sheltered inlet.

Hawaii, USA

The mountainous Hawaiian island chain was formed by a series of volcanoes, many of which are still active. Trips to Volcanoes National Park and the world's most active volcano usually include the memorable experience of getting as close as is safe to the actual lava flow. The lower slopes of the mountains are covered in rainforest, home to 20,000 species of orchid and echoing to the sound of waterfalls. Hawaii is a port of call for most Pacific cruises, but it is also possible to take a cruise exclusively of the islands, and so be able to enjoy some of the dramatic beaches and the local culture.

Useful web addresses
all preceded by www.

- travelshop.de/english/cruises.html
- cruises.about.com
- fieldingtravel.com
- cruisecontrolcruises.co.uk
- cruiseweb.com
- cruiseinformationservice.co.uk

◄ Ha Long Bay, Gulf of Tonkin, Vietnam
'Ha Long' means 'where the dragon plunged into the sea', and the bay contains around 3,000 islands, famous for their sheer, limestone cliffs with honeycombs of caves. A day trip from Haiphong (by motorboat or slower junk) is included in the itineraries of long-distance cruises as well as being available to the independent traveller.

Winter sports

Mountain resorts all over the world are upgrading their facilities: constructing 'ski parks' for snowboarders, installing faster ski-lifts to cut queuing times, and using snow cannons to guarantee good conditions. Now that many of the top resorts can be reached by long-haul flights from either hemisphere, it is possible to enjoy 'winter sports' at any time of year.

◀ **Vail, Colorado, United States**
Vail has runs for all abilities and a special family skiing area. Snowboarders are provided with dedicated pistes, a half-pipe and two fun parks. Numerous winter sports are possible, including dog sledding and snowmobiling.

▼ **Jackson Hole, Wyoming, USA**
One of the most spectacular mountain resorts in the United States, Jackson Hole is most suited to the experienced skier or snowboarder. A 60-person cable car transports skiers from Teton Village to Mount Rendezvous, from where the skilled and intrepid can experience some of the most difficult piste skiing in the world. Other attractions include trips into Yellowstone Park, a swim at 2,460 m (8,000 ft) in the Granite Hot Springs, and sleigh rides to view a huge elk herd.

THE AMERICAS

Whistler, British Columbia, Canada

Considered one of the top ski resorts in the world, the resort provides access to two mountains with vertical drops of around 1,500 m (5,000 ft). As well as a wide variety of runs, Whistler's crowning glory is its five bowls, which provide plenty of scope for expert skiers and boarders, the latter being well catered for. The base village, which is pedestrian-only, has over 100 restaurants.

Banff, Alberta, Canada

The city of Banff is the gateway to three resorts that are linked by a shuttle bus and share a lift pass. **Lake Louise**, a particularly beautiful resort, is a good choice for families of mixed ability, with a beginners' run from the top of every chair lift. **Sunshine Village** includes 'Delirium Dive', one of the most challenging runs in North America. **Mt Norquay/Mystic Ridge** has a number of runs for the very best skiers and also offers night skiing.

Killington, Vermont, USA

The largest ski area in the eastern USA, Killington spreads over seven mountains. It caters for every level of skier, but is especially suitable for beginners, who have their own network of pistes, and for snowboarders who are provided with their own trail map. Snow cannons ensure good coverage throughout an extended season.

Lake Tahoe (Squaw Valley, Heavenly) California/Nevada, USA

Lake Tahoe is surrounded by ski resorts. **Squaw Valley** comprises six inter-linked mountain areas, some of which are still open in June. It has excellent facilities for children, including a family fun snow park. **Heavenly** has a spectacular setting, with something to suit skiers and snowboarders of all abilities. Snowboarders are further catered for by specially constructed mountainside features and by a dedicated fun park. A single ski pass is available for all resorts in the area.

Aspen, Colorado, USA

Long considered the smartest ski resort in the United States, Aspen provides an enormous range of facilities and entertainment, including opera. A linked ticket gives access to four mountains. Aspen Mountain and Aspen Highlands are most suitable for intermediates and experts, Buttermilk for beginners, and Snowmass for all levels. Snowboarding is allowed on all but Aspen Mountain.

Valle Nevado, Chile

A purpose-built resort in the Andes, at an altitude of 2,900 m (9,500 ft), Valle Nevado has wide, open pistes and spectacular views. It is also possible to heli-ski.

Gran Catedral (Bariloche), Argentina

Perched on Catedral Mountain, overlooking Lake Nahuel Huapi, Gran Catedral (formerly Bariloche) is Argentina's best-known and most extensive resort. Many visitors are attracted to the area in August for the National Snow Party.

EUROPE

Geilo, Norway

On the edge of the Hardanger plateau, Geilo provides uncomplicated downhill skiing as well as extensive cross-country trails. It is an excellent family resort, with ski schools giving tuition (in English) in snowboarding and cross-country skiing, as well as alpine skiing.

Soldeu/El Tarter, Andorra

For those on a budget, Andorra is a good option, and Soldeu/El Tarter the best of its resorts. Its reputable ski school and gentle slopes make it ideal for the beginner. A drag lift linking it with the neighbouring resorts of Pas de la Casa/Grau Roig has expanded the quality and quantity of runs available for the more experienced skier.

Three Valleys, France

The vast inter-linked ski area of the Three Valleys can be accessed from several resorts. **Courchevel** provides varied skiing, including wooded slopes, but intrepid skiers can also make their way across the whole Three Valleys system. **Méribel** is conveniently placed in the centre of the system. **Val Thorens**, which at 2,320 m (7,544 ft) is Europe's highest ski resort, has three lifts still open in summer.

Chamonix, France

Chamonix is an attractive town set in a steep-sided valley and dominated by Mont Blanc (see *Mountains and volcanoes*). There is extensive, varied skiing on both sides of the valley, linked by bus services. The most famous run, the Vallée Blanche, involves a cable-car ride up to the Aiguille du Midi, followed by a tough walk to the top of the glacier, and a 20 km (13-mile) run down to the valley. The Mont Blanc Ski Pass includes other resorts, giving access to 1,000 km (625 miles) of piste.

▲ **Val d'Isère/Tignes, France**
Snowboarders and off-piste skiers are among those well catered for by the huge inter-linked system of L'Espace Killy. The system is served by a number of modern resorts. The largest is **Val d'Isère**, which is better suited to more advanced skiers than to beginners, since its easiest skiing is inconveniently located on the upper slopes. **Tignes**, a collection of villages clustered around a mountain lake, offers skiing for much of the year. The lift pass provides access to the whole Espace Killy, as well as a day's skiing at nearby Les Arcs or La Plagne.

Skiing and snowboarding resorts

Level: B = Beginner I = Intermediate A = Advanced Sb = Snowboarding

Resort	Main season	Skiable area or distance	Best-suited level(s)
NORTH AMERICA			
Whistler	Nov–Apr	2,863 ha (7,071 acres)	I/A/Sb
Banff	Dec–Apr	100 km (62 miles)	I
Killington	Oct–Apr	152 km (95 miles)	B/Sb
Squaw Valley	Nov–May	1,600 ha (4,000 acres)	I/A/Sb
Heavenly	Nov–May	1,942 ha (4,800 acres)	I/A
Jackson Hole	Dec–Apr	1,011 ha (2,500 acres)	A
Aspen	late Nov–Apr	1,936 ha (4,785 acres)	all
Vail	early Nov–late May	1,879 ha (4,644 acres)	all
Valle Nevado	mid-June–mid-Oct	64 km (40 miles)	I/A
Gran Catedral	mid-June–end Sept	640 ha (1,600 acres)	I
EUROPE			
Geilo	Nov–May	25 km (16 miles) 250 km (156 miles) cross-country	B/I
Soldeu/El Tarter	Dec–Mar	74 km (46 miles)	B/I
Three Valleys	Dec–Apr	300 km (187 miles)	all/Sb
Val d'Isère/Tignes	Dec–Apr	300 km (187 miles)	I/A/Sb
Chamonix	Dec–Apr	140 km (87 miles)	A/Sb
Zermatt	Dec–Apr	150 km (93 miles)	I/A
Cervinia	Dec–Mar	80 km (50 miles)	B/I
Wengen/Grindelwald	Dec–Mar	195 km (121 miles)	B/I
St Moritz	Dec–Mar	80 km (50 miles)	I
St Anton	Dec–Apr	170 km (106 miles)	I/A
Söll, Ski-Welt	Dec–Mar	250 km (156 miles)	B/I
Cortina	Dec–Mar	140 km (87 miles)	all
ASIA AND AUSTRALASIA			
Hakuba	Dec–Apr	*c.* 500 ha (1,250 acres)	all
Perisher Blue	June–Oct	1,250 ha (3,100 acres)	I
The Remarkables	June–Oct	220 ha (550 acres)	I
Coronet Peak	June–Oct	280 ha (700 acres)	I

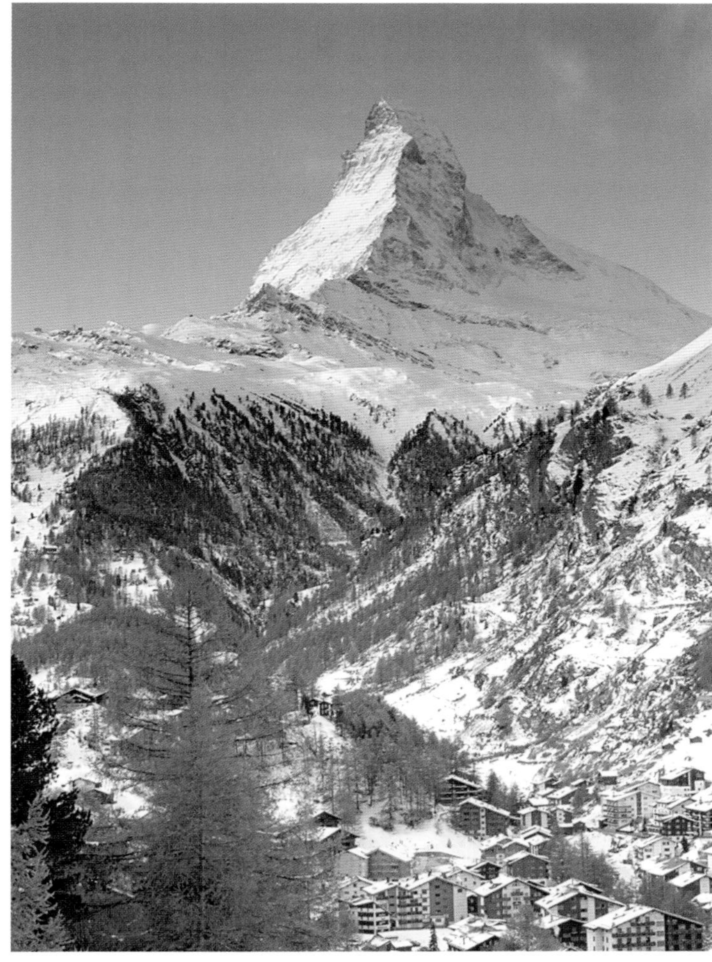

◀ **Matterhorn (Zermatt, Cervinia), Switzerland/Italy** The visitor to the Matterhorn area has the choice of staying in the expensive, car-free, Swiss resort of **Zermatt**, or the cheaper, more lively, Italian resort of **Cervinia**. The lift systems of the two resorts are linked. Zermatt provides a huge variety of skiing, from the wooded slopes immediately above the town to the steep runs below the Kleine Matterhorn. The sunny, south-facing slopes of Cervinia provide plenty of runs of intermediate standard. Summer skiing is possible on the highest slopes.

Jungfrau (Wengen, Grindelwald), Switzerland

The slopes of this famous mountain are served by two of Switzerland's best-known resorts. **Wengen**, which considers itself the 'birthplace of Alpine skiing', is an attractive town whose charm is enhanced by a lack of cars (a mountain railway providing the only access). **Grindelwald** is a larger, livelier town. The two are linked by a lift system that provides access to wonderfully varied skiing.

St Moritz, Switzerland

Famous in particular for its glamorous nightlife, St Moritz serves as a gateway to two major lift systems. Corvatsch/Furtshellas provides an opportunity for glacier skiing in both winter and summer. Corviglia provides varied skiing, interspersed by numerous restaurants in spectacular locations.

St Anton, Austria

St Anton attracts skiers from all over the world to its challenging ski runs, with cannon ensuring a good snow coverage. Dramatic off-piste skiing adds to its attraction for the experienced skier and boarder, but there is little for the beginner.

Söll, Ski-Welt, Austria

Söll provides good family skiing. It is ideal for the beginner and intermediate skier, but is not for the adventurous. Its low altitude results in a short season, although snow cannons have been installed.

Cortina, Italy

Surrounded by the distinctive rocky outcrops of the Dolomites, Cortina provides skiing in five main areas. There are runs for a range of skills, including a difficult descent from the Tofana bowl, and the gentle runs of the Socrepes–Pocol area. Cortina is the smartest of the Italian resorts, with a lively nightlife. Activities off the slopes include ice-skating.

ASIA AND AUSTRALASIA

Hakuba, Japan

The village of Hakuba (near Nagano) is the gateway to seven ski areas, providing runs for different standards of skiers, with beginners and intermediates best served by **Hakuba Goryu-Toomi**, and more advanced skiers by Happo'one (where night skiing is possible) and **Hakuba 47**.

Perisher Blue, Australia

This winter sports area comprises four resorts, spread over seven mountain peaks, accessed by an underground alpine railway and covered by one ski pass. There is a Nordic Ski Centre at Guthega, and 90 km (55 miles) of cross-country skiing. The main resort town is Jindabyne.

Queenstown (Coronet Peak, The Remarkables), New Zealand

Queenstown provides a residential base for two winter sports areas, The Remarkables and Coronet Peak, with shuttles operating between them. As well as good skiing, both areas offer facilities for snowboarders, including pipes and a terrain park. Families are well catered for, with good ski schools. Heli-skiing is also available.

Great beaches

► Negril, Jamaica
Negril beach is 11 km (7 miles) long and fringed by trees that hide low-rise hotels and restaurants. While definitely a tourist resort, it still retains a laid-back Jamaican character. Growing environmentalism has led to planning restrictions and active preservation of the surrounding area, including the creation of the Negril Marine Park. This encompasses the Great Morass swamp behind the beach, and the coral reef, cliffs and grottoes that make Negril so popular with scuba divers and snorkellers.

From California to the Caribbean to Australia, the lure of the beach still has a part in most holiday plans. The range is endless – chic and cosmopolitan in the Mediterranean, wild and rugged along the Atlantic shores or palm-fringed coral in the South Pacific. This small selection highlights some of the great beaches that can be linked into a round-the-world trip – whether for the exhilaration of surfing or sailing, or just to do absolutely nothing.

NORTH AMERICA

Venice Beach, Los Angeles, USA

Venice Beach is famous not so much for its wide stretch of sand as for its curving 'boardwalk'. Here, some of LA's more flamboyant citizens display themselves – on foot, skateboard, rollerblade and cycle. The area was originally developed to imitate its European namesake and, although there is no comparison, it is pleasant to stroll along its canals.

Assateague Island, Maryland/Virginia, USA

Assateague Island National Seashore on the Atlantic coast of the Chesapeake Peninsula consists of 60 km (37 miles) of pristine sandy beach, fringed by pine forest and salt marsh. Only a small area of it is accessible by car and the rest of the beach is deserted, except for the more intrepid campers, many of whom come for the fishing and birdwatching. Herds of wild ponies roam the island.

Sanibel Island, Florida, USA

Sanibel's 19 km (12 miles) of beaches are famous for their seashells. Visitors can be seen scouring the seashore or taking boat trips to more remote locations to find the best shells. Around 40% of the island, which can be toured on rented bicycles, is a wildlife preserve and it is also within striking distance of the Florida Everglades (see *Wildlife in the Americas*).

Puerto Escondido, Mexico

The resort of Puerto Escondido has a beach to suit every taste. 'Playa Zicatela' is considered one of the best surfing beaches in North America, but is suitable only for the strongest swimmers. 'Playa Principal' is a more urban beach, with pleasure craft and waterfront restaurants, while the small coves just out of town provide perfect swimming conditions.

THE CARIBBEAN AND SOUTH AMERICA

Magens Bay, St Thomas, US Virgin Islands

The heart-shaped Magens Bay contains a gently sloping sandy beach, surrounded by overhanging trees that provide welcome shade. Protected from the winds and currents, the bay is safe for bathing. Although nude bathing is not allowed on the main beach, it is permitted on the nearby Little Magens Beach. Interesting rock formations on the fringes of the bay are good for snorkelling. The beach is well served by restaurants and bars, carefully hidden among the trees.

Copacabana Beach, Rio de Janeiro, Brazil

Copacabana's 4 km (2.5 miles) of sand is fringed by a wavy black and white mosaic walkway. The beach is provided with modern amenities, such as public showers, kiosks and restaurants, and the shopping centre is only a short walk away. As well as attracting tourists, the beach is a meeting place for the citizens of Rio, and is the focus of the New Year celebrations. It is framed on one side by a huge granite headland and on the other by an imposing World War I fort, below which is an area from which local fishermen still operate.

Viña del Mar, Chile

Known as 'the Garden City' because of the luscious, tropical foliage that lines its boulevards, Viña del Mar also has a beautiful beach. Visitors who tire of the soft white sand and rolling surf can enjoy a tour of the town by horse-drawn carriage, visit the art museum and the extensive botanical gardens. Evening entertainment comes in the form of gourmet restaurants, casinos, discos and concerts.

▲ Oahu, Hawaiian Islands, USA
Most visitors to the island of Oahu flock to the string of connected beaches in the resort of Waikiki, just to the east of Honolulu, where the curving sand, studded with palm trees, is backed by a towering wall of high-rise hotels. Those looking for a more peaceful holiday, however, head further around the coast and seek out Waimanalo Beach (above), with its gently shelving, near-white sand and mountain backdrop. On the north coast the calm waters of Waimea Bay in summer also provide excellent swimming, but in winter months it is the centre of the surfing scene, as 10 m (30 ft) waves roll in across the Pacific.

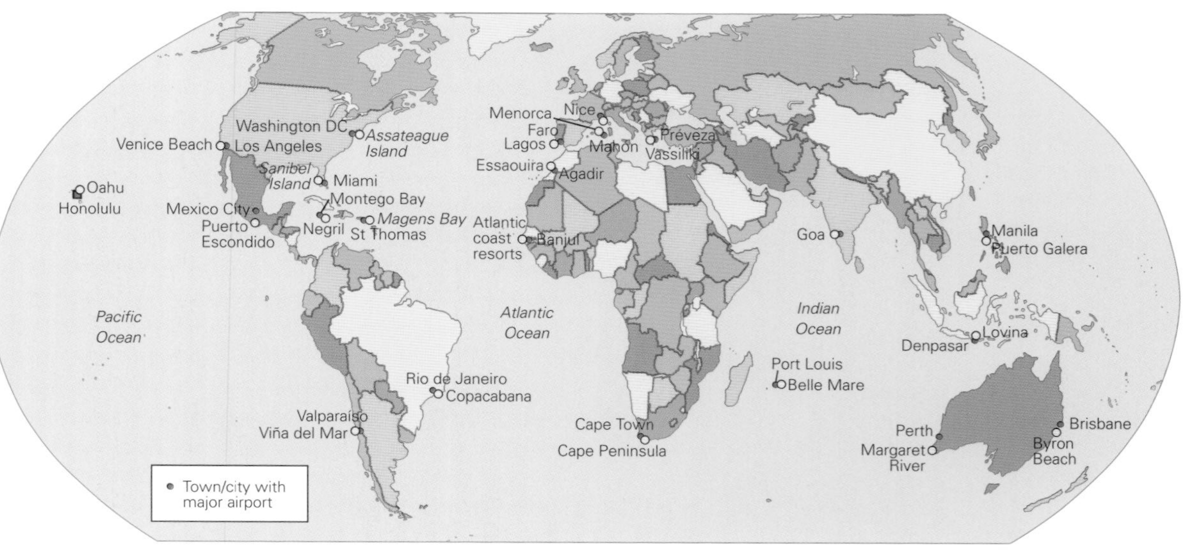

EUROPE

Nice, France

Nice is the largest town on the Côte d'Azur, renowned for the clarity of its light and the colour of its sea. Many famous artists have been inspired by the region, and some are represented in the town's art gallery. The long curved beach is rather pebbly, but its surroundings are attractive, with a wide esplanade on which 'to see and be seen'.

Santa Galdana, Menorca

The Balearic Island least affected by tourism, Menorca is famous for its beaches. The main beach at Santa Galdana can be very crowded in summer, but it is still possible to find relatively unspoilt coves nearby. Just a 1 km (0.5-mile) walk east is the wood-lined sandy beach of Cala Mirjana, where the favourite sport is to jump from rocks into crystal-clear water.

Vassiliki, Levkás, Greece

The small resort of Vassiliki is one of the foremost windsurfing and dinghy sailing centres in the eastern Mediterranean. Set in a bay that provides some shelter for the beginner, it is blessed with reliable winds. The lighter breezes of the morning are followed, after a brief lunchtime lull, by winds strong enough to delight the expert.

AFRICA AND THE INDIAN OCEAN

Essaouira, Morocco

The ancient town of Essaouira provides a fascinating backdrop to 3 km (2 miles) of sandy shoreline. The commercial life of the town tends to spill over on to the beach, with fishermen offering to cook their catch and camel drivers selling rides, although it is possible to find more secluded areas. The town is the centre of the craft of wood inlay, the local Thuya trees providing the raw material.

▲ Cape Peninsula, South Africa
Among the many beaches on the narrow peninsula south of Cape Town is Boulders Beach, so named because of the huge rocks that provide shelter from the wind. Here, visitors share the sands with a colony of jack-ass penguins. Other resorts on the peninsula, where the ocean water to the west is considerably colder than that of False Bay to the east, include some, such as Fish Hoek, which cater specifically for families, and some, such as the fashionable Clifton area, which attract the young and wealthy. Surfers head for the remote Long Beach at Kommetjie.

◄ Lagos, Portugal
Lagos is a busy fishing port and one of the Algarve's oldest settlements, with a long maritime tradition. To the east lie miles of sand dunes and the gently sloping Meia beach. West of the town, the dramatically eroded sandstone cliffs typical of the region form numerous small coves, some of which are only accessible from the sea. Lagos is an excellent base for surfers, who can travel the short distance to Portugal's west-facing beaches if local surf fails. The town provides plenty of interest, from seafood restaurants and bars to the curiosities of the local museum.

Atlantic coast resorts, Gambia

The resorts of Kololi, Kotu, Fajara and Bakau, strung out along a 10 km (6-mile) coastal strip, provide a full range of amenities, including golf courses, equipment for water sports, and swimming pools. Although the sea is relatively safe, there are times when the conditions are unsuitable for all but the strongest swimmer. For those seeking a more authentic African experience, the market town of Serekunda is nearby.

Belle Mare, Mauritius

The coral reef that surrounds much of the island of Mauritius provides a natural breakwater, ensuring calm inshore waters. The beaches are all beautiful, although some have been over-developed or have areas cordoned off by hotels. However, Belle Mare, on the less-developed east coast, still has plenty of public areas. There are also the attractions of a mixed French, Indian and Chinese culture, evident in the island's architecture and cuisine.

ASIA

Goa, India

The dozens of beaches on Goa's 100 km (62-mile) coastline provide plenty of choice. Calangute and Colva, to which young people flocked in the 1970s, are now tourist resorts. However, at both the northern and southern ends of the Goan coast are many relatively unspoilt beaches, including Arambol and Palolem, where beach huts and tree houses provide the main accommodation. At Palolem visitors can take dolphin-watching boat trips.

Puerto Galera, Mindoro, Philippines

A resort area comprising 12 separate coastal districts, Puerto Galera is renowned for its pristine sandy coves, sheltered by a rugged, jungle-covered coastline. Accommodation ranges from bamboo beach huts to air-conditioned bungalows and family-run hotels. The rich marine life of the area attracts scuba-divers, and equipment for underwater and other marine activities is available for hire.

Lovina, Bali

Although second in size only to Kuta, famous for its surf, Lovina manages to retain the relaxed atmosphere its larger rival has long since lost. Situated on Bali's rugged northern coast, the resort comprises six villages, dotted along 8 km (5 miles) of black-sand beach. Those who enjoy some lively nightlife make for the village of Kalibukbuk. Beach-centred activities include snorkelling and dolphin watching. Excursions can be made inland to nearby hot springs and a Buddhist temple, or further afield to the volcanic regions of Bedugul and Batur.

AUSTRALASIA

Byron Beach, New South Wales, Australia

Byron Beach offers a wide range of beaches. Main Beach is ideal for families, with a life-guard patrol and play equipment shaded by trees, while those wishing for more seclusion head for the smaller coves out on Cape Byron. The area also provides some good surfing and the opportunity to watch passing whales and dolphins. The town itself is less commercial, and better suited to those seeking an alternative lifestyle, than the popular resort of Gold Coast, 50 km (30 miles) to the north.

▼ Margaret River, Western Australia
Margaret River is among the best surfing areas in Australia, providing conditions to suit both beginners and experts. It also has much for the non-surfer to enjoy, including swimming beaches, river canoeing trips, and visits to local vineyards to taste some of Australia's best wines.

Festivals

Whether sacred or profane, festivals throughout the world bring thousands of participants and spectators out on to the streets with grand processions often featuring magnificent costumes and dazzling displays of music and dance, drama and sporting prowess.

▼ Chinese New Year, San Francisco, California, USA
For Chinese communities everywhere, the New Year is a week-long festival. Many celebrations are family-based, but they lead up to a very public grand finale. Chinatown in San Francisco is taken over by the Golden Dragon Parade when hundreds of people, including drummers and other musicians, accompany a 23 m (75 ft) dragon through the streets. The Chinese follow a lunar calendar, which means that their New Year occurs in late January or early February.

THE AMERICAS

Corn Dance Festival, Santa Domingo, New Mexico, USA

At Santa Domingo (near Albuquerque) the Pueblo people honour the harvest goddess, Iyatiko, in the Corn Dance Festival. Celebrants, known as the *koshare*, dress in cornhusks and animal skins to enact the history of their people on a day that is filled with drumming, dancing and feasting. The festival which, unlike many Pueblo ceremonies, is a public event, is always held on 4 August.

Heritage and Jazz Festival, New Orleans, Louisiana, USA

Jazz evolved in New Orleans during the late 19th and early 20th centuries, but the first jazz festival was not until 1968. A major event in the musical calendar and organized by the Heritage and Jazz Festival, it runs over two weekends in April or May. Musicians from all over the world perform in large tents at the Fair Grounds and in smaller venues – clubs, theatres and halls – throughout the city.

Fisherman's Festival, Jamaica

29 June is Saint Peter's day. He is the patron saint of fishermen, and in the fishing ports of Jamaica boats are drawn up to the beach where the owners decorate them with shells and flowers. Long processions follow priests to the edge of the sea where they bless the boats, and the beaches become crowded with steel bands, dancers and family picnics.

◄ Palio, Siena, Italy
Celebrated every year on 2 July and 16 August, the Palio is a bare-back horserace that dates from the 16th century. Ten horses, each representing one of Siena's *contrade*, or districts, race three times around the crowded central piazza, sometimes barging into each other and unseating their riders. Before the race there is a procession in which men dressed in medieval clothes whirl and twist the *palio*, or flag, of their *contrada*, to the accompaniment of drummers.

Urkupina, Calvario Hill, Bolivia

Early in the 20th century a girl tending her sheep on Calvario Hill had a vision of the Virgin Mary. Now, on 15 August, thousands of pilgrims carrying candles and flowers, and accompanied by musicians, performers and vendors, climb the hill to pay homage to the Virgin. The festivities that follow last for three days.

National Rodeo Festival, Rancagua, Chile

Rodeos take place all over the country and, in late March, the best competitors go to the National Rodeo in Rancagua. This event celebrates the Chilean *huaso* or cowboy. Thousands come to watch as huasos, wearing traditional costume and the heavy spurs unique to Chile, provide exhibitions of horsemanship. The town is given over to feasts of cowboy food and *la cueca*, the erotic folk dance of Chile.

Mardi Gras Carnaval, Rio de Janeiro, Brazil

All over the Catholic Christian world, there are festivals at Mardi Gras, the last day before the 40 days of Lenten fasting. The Mardi Gras Carnaval in Rio de Janeiro is the most famous. Over the course of two nights the city's 14 main samba schools compete with each other by dancing and parading down the 1 km (0.5-mile) long Sambadrome, watched by thousands of spectators. Each school's parade consists of around 4,000 people in lavish, often extravagant, costumes, accompanied by enormous and elaborate floats, and a band of over 500 drummers. The judging takes place a few days later. Broadcast live on television, it is followed by great celebrations.

EUROPE

Puck Fair, Killorglin, Ireland

A billygoat, King Puck – adorned with ribbons and a crown – opens the three-day Puck Fair every year on 2 August. Musicians from all over Europe perform, and Romanies are among those who entertain the crowds with Irish jigs and stories. The billy is honoured because in the 17th century a herd of goats warned the village of an impending English attack.

Oktober Bierfest, Munich, Germany

The Oktober Bierfest has been an annual event since 1835. It is an important festival for most young visitors to the city and is a huge celebration in honour of beer. It lasts for 16 days from 17 October, and vast beer tents that each house 5,000 drinkers are erected. Food stalls and funfairs add to the festive atmosphere.

Lajkonic, Kraków, Poland

Every year, usually in June, a man dressed as a Tartar rides a mock horse through the streets, accompanied by trumpeters and citizens dressed in medieval costume. He does so in memory of Lajkonic, who in the 13th century killed a Tartar and put on the dead man's clothing before riding into the city to warn that the Tartars were about to attack. The resulting defeat of the Tartars is now celebrated with much pageantry.

San Fermin, Pamplona, Spain

Starting on 6 July and running for eight days, the festival is held in honour of Fermin, patron saint of bullfighters. Each day starts with the playing of drums and pipes, and an effigy of the saint is followed by a procession of matadors and horses, dressed and decorated for the occasion. A rocket signals the release of the bulls from their pen to race through the streets to the bullring. Men run and leap ahead of them, a practice that more than once has resulted in someone being killed. Bull fights and parties fill the evenings.

Aksu Black Sea Festival, Turkey
The origins of this July festival are very old, dating back to pre-Christian fertility rites. Cybele, the fertility goddess, wore a pebble in her crown and women still throw pebbles into the Black Sea in the hope that this will help them conceive. The highlight of the festival is a performance by male dancers dressed in black and silver, and other artists – musicians, potters, painters and weavers – flock to the site where they perform or sell their work.

AFRICA

Odwira, Ghana
The Asante calendar is filled with religious days and ceremonies, of which the Odwira, usually in August or September, is one of the most important. The high chiefs and priests are involved for some days in secret and sacred rituals, and then the roll of drums announces the start of feasting. It all ends with a grand procession, in which the chiefs are carried in splendid palanquins.

Abu El-Haggag, Luxor, Egypt
Among the ancient ruins of Luxor is a small mosque dedicated to a 12th-century Muslim saint, El-Haggag. Each year, in October or November, thousands of people crowd into Luxor for the saint's *mulid*, or festival, during which Sufis and floats parade the streets. Three model boats are carried about by groups of men, though whether this is in memory of the Ancient Egyptian journey into the Underworld, or of the time when the pilgrimage to Mecca involved a sea crossing, is uncertain.

Timket, Ethiopia
Ethiopian Christians celebrate the baptism of Christ for three days starting on 19 January. The priests, after all-night prayers, emerge from churches carrying holy tabots – caskets holding sacred texts – followed by singing children. Multi-coloured umbrellas, signifying high office and authority, are held above the priests. After this religious ceremony, a party mood takes over and there are huge communal meals, music, and excited horse races which sometimes lurch into the spectators.

ASIA AND AUSTRALIA

Urs to Lal Shahbaz Qalandar, Sehwan Sharif, Pakistan
All over Pakistan, Muslims celebrate holy men with *urs*, or saints' days. One of the most popular, attracting many thousands of pilgrims, is held in Sehwan Sharif, around the tomb of the 12th-century Iranian scholar-poet Lal Shahbaz Qalandar. For three days, in October or November, Sufis perform their holy, trance-like dances, while drums and gongs beat hour after hour. The entire crowd dances and chants, and many offer votive offerings to the tomb.

Festival of the Tooth, Kandy, Sri Lanka
In the Esala Perhera temple in Kandy is the Tooth Relic of the Buddha. Usually in July, but occasionally in August, there is a spectacular festival in which there are festive meals and dances to celebrate the relic and Buddha. At the festival's climax a great procession of dancers, drummers, temple chieftains, and over 50 elephants in ceremonial attire, goes to the temple, followed by huge crowds of pilgrims.

Ho Lim, Lim, Vietnam
Singers from all over Vietnam pour into the village of Lim (near Bac Ninh) seven days after Tet, the Chinese New Year, in January or February. They participate in a folk-singing contest, and competition is fierce. The crowds who come to listen are also entertained by a circus, street performers, wrestling competitions, and chess games in which people play the parts of the pieces.

▲ **Sanja Matsuri, Tokyo, Japan**
Matsuri – festivals where shrines, or *mikoshi*, believed to contain a god-spirit, are carried through towns and villages – take place all over Japan. However, the biggest event is in Tokyo in April or May. Here the *mikoshi* weigh about 1 tonne each, and 50 men are needed to hoist one through the streets to the Asakusa Temple. Groups of costumed figures, and musicians playing flutes and beating drums, accompany the *mikoshi* on its journey.

Losar, Tibet
The calendar in Tibet follows the lunar cycle. There are two 'New Year' days, but the significant one is Gyalpo Losar, the King's New Year, which is usually in April. People wear new, decorative clothing; the priests fill the temples with chanting, the beating of gongs and the ringing of bells, and new prayer flags are lifted above the temple roofs. Throughout the city, street theatres and musicians perform while people party and play dice in the parks.

Tano, Kangnung, South Korea
This spring festival, usually in April or May, traditionally involved displays of the Korean form of wrestling, *ssirum*, even in the most remote villages. Now, many Koreans spend the holiday watching *ssirum* on television, except in the village of Kangnung. Here they celebrate for five days, not only with wrestling matches but also with performances of the traditional dance called *nong-ak*. The huge crowds also enjoy a spring drink, *chehotang*.

Gay and Lesbian Mardi Gras, Sydney, Australia
Participants pride themselves on outrageous displays and flamboyant costumes during the annual Mardi Gras parade. The street procession comes at the end of a three- to four-week cultural festival in February–March, and ends in a huge party which is restricted to ticket holders. However, revellers throughout the city regard this as an opportunity to party until dawn and beyond.

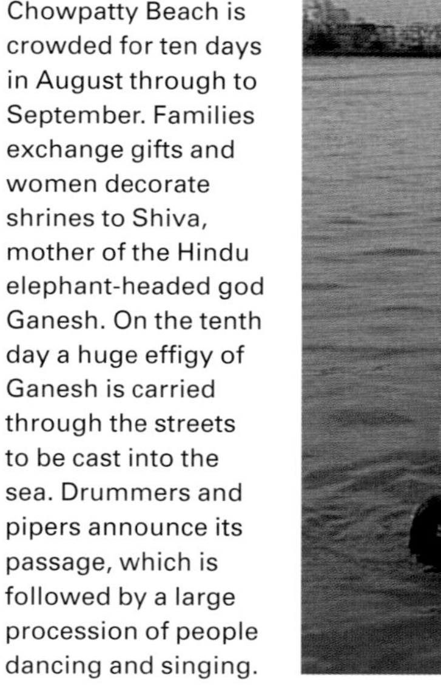

▶ **Ganesh Festival, Mumbai, India**
Chowpatty Beach is crowded for ten days in August through to September. Families exchange gifts and women decorate shrines to Shiva, mother of the Hindu elephant-headed god Ganesh. On the tenth day a huge effigy of Ganesh is carried through the streets to be cast into the sea. Drummers and pipers announce its passage, which is followed by a large procession of people dancing and singing.

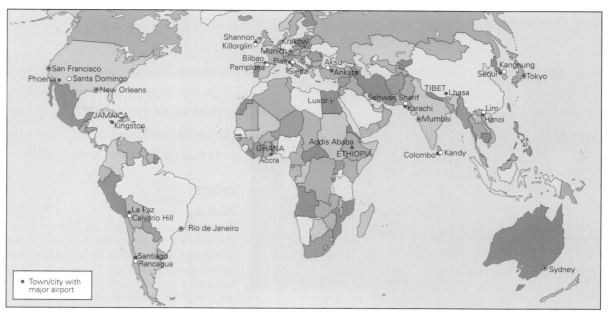

ruins, whose full extent has only recently become apparent, include a pyramid 42 m (140 ft) high.

in the early 17th century. Today it has over 2,000 colonial buildings, including several 18th-century Baroque churches.

only three other missions indicate their former splendour: Sao Miguel in Brazil, and Jesús and Trinidad in Paraguay.

• Sucre
• Washington

beautifully detailed stained glass. A rare 13th-century labyrinth design on the floor, a Renaissance choir screen and the glowing stained glass of the rose window all add to the beauty and impact of the building.

Pompeii and the Romans
Pompeii is an exceptional historic site because, when the eruption of Vesuvius in AD 79 engulfed the city in volcanic debris, the life of the people, their homes and streets, public spaces and palaces were preserved as if frozen in time. Excavations have revealed a wealth of detailed information about the everyday life of citizens of the Roman Empire, including their public notices, graffiti, brothels, latrines, furnishings and food. At its greatest extent, in the 1st–4th centuries AD, the Roman Empire encircled the Mediterranean Sea, reaching north as far as Britain and south into Egypt. Remains of Roman theatres, temples, baths, arenas, villas and other buildings can be found at sites throughout Europe and north Africa.

Dubrovnik, Croatia
The fortifications of the ancient port of Dubrovnik rise straight from the Adriatic, and the double line of city walls encompass two palaces, two monasteries and many churches and other historic buildings, mostly dating from the 15th and 16th centuries. The narrow, winding streets of the old city are free from motor vehicles.

Ephesus, Turkey
The extensive and well-preserved ruins of the ancient city of Ephesus are one of Turkey's most popular historic sites, containing buildings from ancient Greek, Roman and Byzantine times. Among those dating from the Roman period are several temples, a theatre, a library, terraced houses, public baths and latrines, as well as some fine mosaics and wall paintings.

• Istanbul
• Kraków
• Lisbon
• London
• Luxembourg
• Madrid
• Milan
• Moscow
• Munich
• Oslo
• Paris
• Prague
• Reykjavik
• Riga
• Rome
• St Petersburg
• Stockholm
• Vienna
• Warsaw
• Venice

Historic sites in the Americas

Amid the rocky canyons of New Mexico, Arizona and Colorado, the dense jungle

Historic sites in Europe

There is a huge variety of historic sites in Europe, ranging from prehistoric monuments over 5,000 years old to 19th-century castles. Ruins of the architectural achievements of the Classical Greek and Roman civilizations contrast with what are often perfectly preserved cathedrals, churches, monasteries, castles, palaces and civic buildings dating from the 11th century onwards.

Rock of Cashel, Ireland
Poised dramatically above the town of Cashel in County Tipparary stands a limestone outcrop, 109 m (358 ft) high, known as the Rock of Cashel. It is topped by a group of medieval ecclesiastical ruins, which include a bishop's palace, the

◄ Neuschwanstein Castle, Germany
The ultimate fairytale castle, Neuschwanstein (near Fussen) was built in 1869–86 and is the most famous of Ludwig II's castles inspired by Wagner's vision of medieval Germany. It has a wide range of architectural styles, and its tall white marble towers topped by cone-shaped pinnacles, which have been copied by Disney-

Historic sites in Africa, Asia and Australasia

Africa is the home of the imposing ruins of ancient Egypt – one of the world's first civilizations. With the Middle East, it also has historic sites that reflect the competing influences of Christianity and Islam. In Asia, vast temple complexes, often adorned with wonderful sculptures, are among the remains of great empires, while in Australia, Aboriginal rock paintings are evidence of a culture that flourished long before the Europeans arrived.

◄ Angkor, Cambodia
The magnificent ruins at Angkor, capital of the Khmer empire, merit more than one day of sight-seeing. The best-preserved of the buildings is the 12th-century sandstone temple of Angkor Wat, which symbolizes the Hindu universe. Surrounded by pools, it is lavishly decorated with statues and bas-reliefs that are the longest in the world. Around 1.5 km (1 mile) away is the temple complex of Angkor Thom, within which is the Buddhist temple of Bayon with reliefs depicting everyday life.

AFRICA AND THE MIDDLE EAST

Dogon cliffside villages, Mali
Built among the rocks at the foot of the Bandiagara escarpment are the picturesque traditional houses, temples, granaries and meeting places of the Dogon people, whose culture has survived since the 14th century. The area can be reached only on foot and conditions can be gruelling. The best time to visit is December, for the harvest celebrations.

Rock churches of Lalibela, Ethiopia
Carved out of the red volcanic rock of the central highlands are 11 extraordinary medieval churches containing rare and beautiful frescoes, elaborate carvings and bas-reliefs. A complex network of tunnels and passageways connects the churches, some of which are hidden in deep trenches while others have been cut into the cliff face. The best time to visit is the Ethiopian Christmas (7 January) and Easter.

Kilwa Kisiwani, Tanzania
Once an Islamic city-state, the island of Kilwa Kisiwani has extensive ruins, which include a 12th-century mosque, several palaces and grand houses, and a 15th-century Portuguese fort. The impressive 14th-century cliff-top palace of Husuni Kubwa has a 30 m (98 ft) high dome and over 100 rooms.

Zanzibar, Tanzania
The buildings of Zanzibar Town's 'old quarter', Stone Town, reflect its colourful history as an important trading centre, particularly in the 19th century. A maze of narrow streets contain a sultan's palace, an ochre-coloured Arab fort, and the home of the notorious slave trader Tippu Tip, as well as numerous bazaars.

Great Zimbabwe, Zimbabwe
The extensive ruins of a major medieval city dating from the 10th century onwards, Great Zimbabwe is made up of curved stone walls and enclosures which incorporate features of the landscape into their design. The Elliptical Building, with an unusual conical tower and a diameter of almost 100 m (328 ft), is the largest ancient structure in sub-Saharan Africa.

Akko, Israel
The ancient walled port of Akko contains many relics of its long and distinguished history, including the underground 12th-century Crusader vaults and halls, the Ottoman Turkish citadel, and the beautiful 18th-century El Jazzar mosque. A remarkable 18th-century Turkish bath-house has been sensitively restored.

Petra, Jordan
Carved out of red sandstone mountains, the majestic remains of the desert city of Petra include two theatres, the High Place of Sacrifice, a temple and many elaborate tombs. The majority date from the period c. 100 BC –AD 150, when Petra was at the height of its prosperity as an important centre of trade. It had strong links with the Greek Hellenistic world, which are reflected in the Classical facades of its tombs.

The Pyramids and Ancient Egypt
Khafre's Sphinx, 73 m (240 ft) in length and carved from a limestone outcrop, stands near the three pyramids at Giza. The most famous of the Egyptian pyramids, they were built as spectacular royal tombs over 4,500 years ago, during the period of the Old Kingdom. The largest at Giza is nearly 150 m (500 ft) high. The last of the Old Kingdom dynasties collapsed *c.* 2180 BC, but central government was restored by the dynasties of the Middle Kingdom (*c.* 2055–1650 BC) and New Kingdom (*c.* 1550–1070 BC). In the era of the New Kingdom, vast temples and lavishly painted royal tombs were constructed, most notably those either side of the River Nile at Luxor and overlooking Lake Nasser at Abu Simbel (see *River and canal journeys*).

ASIA

Mohenjodaro, Pakistan
The excavated remains of a city, Mohenjodaro is the most impressive of all the sites relating to the civilization that flourished in the Indus Valley c. 2600–1800 BC. The site consists of a raised citadel, with public buildings that include an assembly hall and a Great Bath, and a lower town containing residential and industrial areas.

▼ Ajanta and Ellora Caves, near Aurangabad, India
Cut into a spectacular horseshoe-shaped cliff, the Buddhist temples and monasteries of Ajanta are decorated with wall-paintings which are among the greatest examples of early Indian art. The series of rock-cut temples at Ellora includes the 8th-century Hindu Kailasa temple which is renowned for its exceptional sculptures of gods and mythological figures.

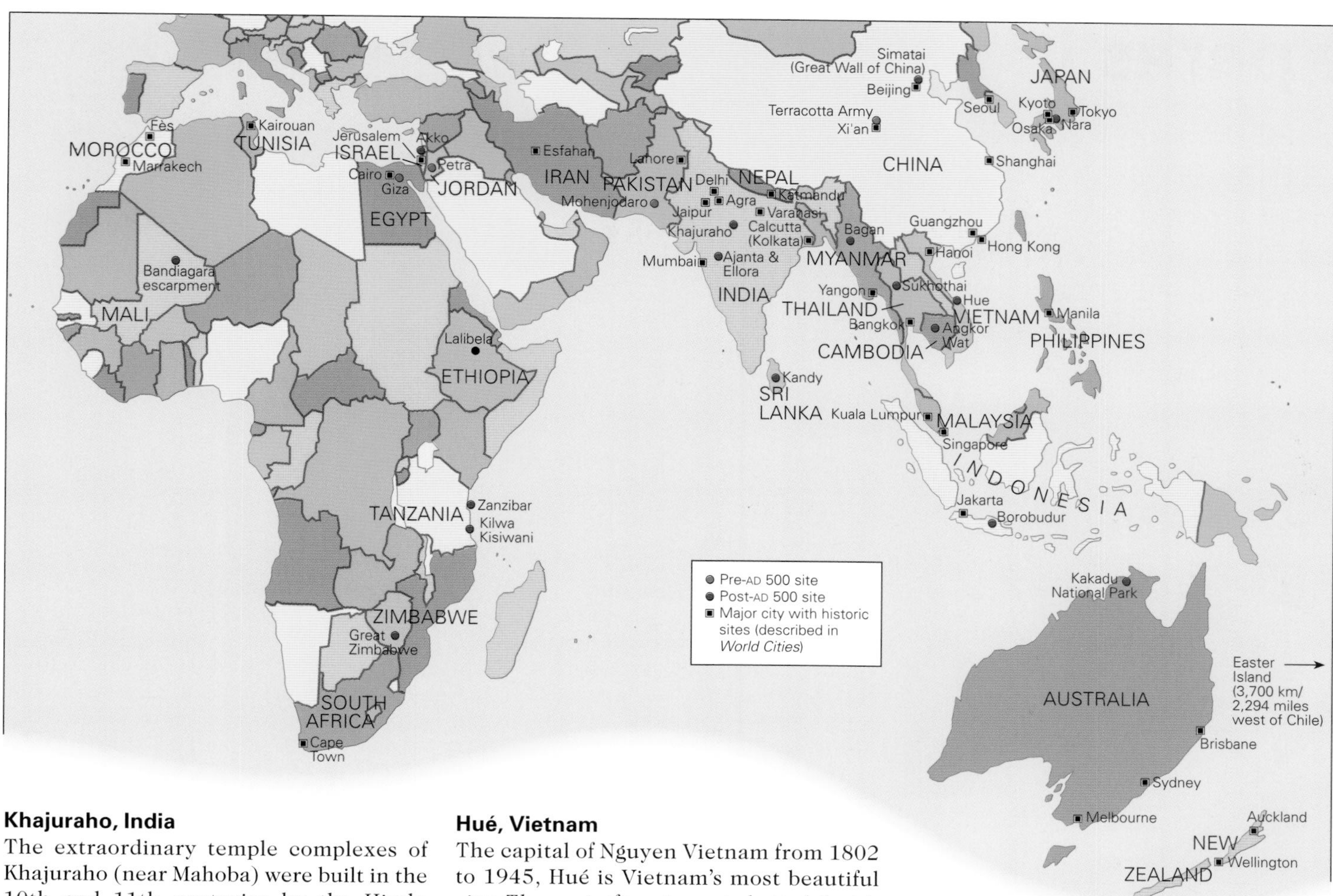

Major cities with historic sites
(see *World Cities*)

AFRICA
- Cairo
- Cape Town
- Fès
- Kairouan
- Marrakech

ASIA
- Agra
- Bangkok
- Beijing
- Calcutta (Kolkata)
- Delhi
- Esfahan
- Guangzhou (Canton)
- Hanoi
- Hong Kong
- Jaipur
- Jakarta
- Jerusalem
- Katmandu
- Kuala Lumpur
- Kyoto
- Lahore
- Manila
- Mumbai
- Osaka
- Seoul
- Singapore
- Tokyo
- Varanasi
- Xi'an
- Yangon

AUSTRALASIA
- Auckland
- Brisbane
- Melbourne
- Sydney
- Wellington

Khajuraho, India
The extraordinary temple complexes of Khajuraho (near Mahoba) were built in the 10th and 11th centuries by the Hindu Chandela dynasty, but were abandoned in the 14th century. Rediscovered in the jungle in 1838, they were carefully restored and are now famous for their sensual and erotic sculptures depicting human, divine, animal and mythological subjects.

Kandy and the Cultural Triangle, Sri Lanka
Famous for its temple and Festival of the Tooth (see *Festivals*), Kandy is one of three former Sinhalese capitals that together form a 'Cultural Triangle'. The other two are Anuradhapura, a huge site with the remains of palaces and temples dating back to the 3rd century BC, and the more compact and better-preserved Polonnaruwa, around 1,000 years old. Within the triangle is the 1st-century BC cave-temple of Dambulla, with 150 Buddha images, and the impressive 6th-century palace-fortress of Sigiriya. Built on top of 'Lion Rock', this is decorated with frescoes and includes a water garden.

Bagan, Burma (Myanmar)
Built between the 11th and the 13th centuries, Bagan (Pagan, near Pakkoku) became known as 'the city of 4 million pagodas', and was the capital of a vast realm. Today it is an important archeological site covering about 40 sq km (15 sq miles) with over 2,000 structures still standing. Among the most impressive are the Temple of Ananda and the Shwezigon Pagoda, with glazed plaques showing scenes from the life of Buddha.

Old Sukhothai, Thailand
The ruins of the 13th-century capital of the Sukhothai empire have been preserved as a 70 sq km (27 sq mile) historical park. They contain numerous temples set in a landscape of lakes, trees and lawns. The most impressive is Wat Mahathat, with fine stucco work and carved Buddhas.

Hué, Vietnam
The capital of Nguyen Vietnam from 1802 to 1945, Hué is Vietnam's most beautiful city. The magnificent moated citadel with its ten fortified gates contains a palace, a mandarin hall and a museum. In the hills to the south of the city there are seven elaborate royal tombs.

Borobudur, Java, Indonesia
Rising like a squat pyramid from the Kedu Plain, Borobudur (near Yogyakarta) is a colossal 9th-century Buddhist stupa (temple) built by the Sailendra dynasty. The largest monument in the southern hemisphere, it covers 200 sq m (2,153 sq ft) and includes over 500 shrines with seated Buddhas. The walls of the stupa, which has five square and four circular terraces, are decorated with bas-reliefs.

Great Wall of China, Simatai, China
Stretching from the Central Asian desert to the Yellow Sea, the Great Wall is over 2,240 km (1,400 miles) long, averages over 6 m (20 ft) in height, and has a central walkway nearly 4 m (13 ft) wide. Much of what exists today dates from the 14th–16th centuries. The Wall can be visited at Badaling, just 70 km (45 miles) from Beijing. However, a less crowded section is at Simatai, 110 km (68 miles) from Beijing, where there are wonderful views to the distant mountains.

Nara, Japan
The ancient city of Nara has many beautiful pagodas, shrines, gardens and temples, the most famous of which is the 8th-century Eastern Great Temple, the Tadai-Ji. Its Great Buddha Hall houses Japan's largest bronze statue of Buddha; the hall itself is the largest wooden building in the world.

AUSTRALASIA AND THE PACIFIC

Kakadu National Park, Australia
Thousands of Aboriginal rock paintings cover the walls of the caves and cliffs of the ancient Aboriginal lands in Kakadu National Park (see also *Wildlife in Australasia*). The paintings, some of which are estimated to be over 20,000 years old, provide a continuous link with the past for the several hundred Aboriginal people who still live there today.

Easter Island statues, Polynesia
The extraordinary stone statues of Easter Island are the legacy of a lost culture which flourished on the island between around AD 400 and 1600. More than 800 colossal stone heads were erected all around the island's coast. The volcanic crater from which the stone was quarried still contains hundreds of unfinished statues, including the 20 m (65 ft) high El Gigante.

◄ Army of Terracotta Warriors, near Xi'an, China
The massive underground mausoleum of China's first emperor, Shi Huang Di, who died in 210 BC, contains an army of around 7,500 life-size terracotta soldiers. Standing in military formation, they are a unique sight.

Theme parks

Inspired by the phenomenon of Disneyland, Los Angeles, the top theme parks around the world are irresistible to children both young and old, as well as adults. The combination of charm and fantasy with white-knuckle rides and superb service guarantees a successful family visit, and since most are located near major cities it is easy to incorporate them into a longer itinerary.

▲ **Alton Towers, England**
The combination of a ruined stately home, wooded parkland and over 100 rides means that Alton Towers (in Staffordshire) provides entertainment for all tastes. For the benefit of its younger visitors it puts on shows featuring characters from storybooks and songs, such as 'Peter Rabbit and Friends on Ice'. Its more challenging rides have a much darker theme, with names such as Nemesis and Oblivion.

Useful web addresses preceded by www.

themeparks.about.com

funguide.com/country

disney.go.com

Disneyland, Los Angeles, USA

Disneyland, founded in 1955, is the original Disney theme park, and Mainstreet, Frontierland and Fantasyland – representations of American life and its dreams – have been duplicated in Disney theme parks around the world. Visitors are attracted not only by rides like the runaway train of Big Thunder Mountain, the parade of Disney characters and the famous nightly firework show, but also out of nostalgia and a desire to experience what is itself now a historic site.

Beto Carrero World, Santa Catarina, Brazil

The most extensive theme park in Brazil, Beto Carrero World (near Itajai) combines thrilling rides, shows and a zoo. Its themed areas cover a range of cultures, including a German House complete with beer cellar, a Viking longboat and a Wild West area. Its shows are similarly wide-ranging and feature the legend of Excalibur. Its white-knuckle rides include the free-falling Tower of Terror, and Star World Mountain, with two 360-degree loops. The animal park includes African wildlife and a large collection of cobras.

Disneyland Paris, France

Although based on the same formula as the Los Angeles theme park, the marketing for Disneyland Paris emphasizes the educational element. There are 'Discovery rides', such as the 'Mississippi Steamboat' which provides information about life in frontier towns, while the Swiss Family Robinson tree-house demonstrates practical survival tips. Most visitors, however, go for the glamour of the shows and parades, and the thrill of the rides. These include being catapaulted 'From the Earth to the Moon' on a Jules Verne style rocket.

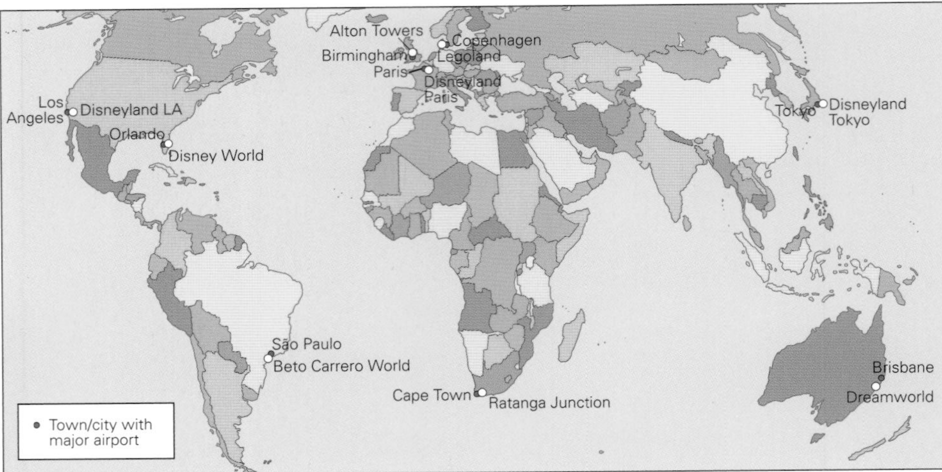

Legoland, Billund, Denmark

Legoland, in which everything is built out of lego, is divided into themed areas, such as Pirateland and Castleland, where children recognize, and are able to interact with, their favourite lego characters. Although the park is aimed primarily at children, providing them with opportunities to play creatively, adults are also charmed by the intricate scale models of real, if somewhat idealized, scenes.

Ratanga Junction, Cape Town, South Africa

Africa's first theme park opened in the late 1990s. It takes as its theme the wildlife of Africa, with rides such as The Cobra, Monkey Falls, and Crocodile Gorge, in which visitors can experience white-water rafting in controlled conditions. A diamond mine is featured, with an underground runaway mine train providing the thrills. There are also less alarming rides for all the family, and 'interactive play areas' for young children.

Disneyland Tokyo, Japan

With many of the same attractions as other Disney theme parks, Disneyland Tokyo is unashamedly American in its culture, although it also offers a journey through Japanese history in Tomorrow Land. The Disney Parade celebrates '100 years of magic', with characters from the earliest cartoons through to the present day, and attempts to predict those of the future.

Dreamworld, Queensland, Australia

Thrilling rides and shows are combined with a wildlife park and conservation zone in Dreamworld (near Gold Coast). The Tower of Terror roller coaster reaches speeds of 160 km (100 miles) per hour as it descends from a height of 115 m (375 ft). The Giant Drop uses the same structure to release passengers vertically so that they experience momentary weightlessness. In an 'interactive tiger exhibition' tigers swim with their trainers, while in the Koala Park visitors can handle koalas and watch other native Australian animals.

Walt Disney World, Orlando, Florida, USA
The massive Walt Disney World in Florida encompasses four separate theme parks. At Magic Kingdom there are rides graded for every taste, from those in Fantasyland aimed specifically at younger children, to the Space Mountain rocket trip, which is not for the faint-hearted. The Epcot Centre aims to re-create the atmosphere and architecture of different countries, including Norway, China and Italy. Visitors can eat food typical of the region, and enjoy themed rides, shows and videos. Disney MGM re-creates urban areas, such as New York Street and Hollywood Boulevard, and uses computer technology to enable visitors to come face to face with characters from recent films. The newest of the parks, Animal Kingdom, combines a safari park with typical Disney features, including thrilling rides, exhibitions and shows.

WORLD CITIES

CITY MAPS

Amsterdam 2
Athens 2
Atlanta 3
Baghdad 3
Bangkok 3
Barcelona 4
Beijing 4
Berlin 5
Boston 6
Brussels 6
Budapest 7
Buenos Aires 7
Cairo 7
Calcutta 8
Canton 8
Cape Town 8
Chicago 9
Copenhagen 10
Delhi 10
Dublin 11
Edinburgh 11
Helsinki 12
Hong Kong 12
Istanbul 12
Jakarta 13
Jerusalem 13
Johannesburg 13
Karachi 14
Lagos 14
Lisbon 14
London 15
Lima 16
Los Angeles 16
Madrid 17
Manila 17
Melbourne 17
Mexico City 18
Miami 18
Milan 18
Montréal 19
Moscow 19
Mumbai 20
Munich 20
New York 21
Osaka 22
Oslo 22
Paris 23
Prague 24
Rio de Janeiro 24
Rome 25
San Francisco 25
St Petersburg 26
Santiago 26
São Paulo 26
Seoul 26
Shanghai 27
Singapore 27
Stockholm 28
Sydney 28
Tokyo 29
Tehran 30
Tianjin 30
Toronto 30
Vienna 31
Warsaw 31
Washington 32
Wellington 32

INDEX 33–39

CITY GAZETTEER 40–48

CITY MAPS

Motorway, freeway, expressway with toll – with road number A10
Motorway, freeway, expressway – with European road number E51
Road junction
Under construction
Tunnel
Primary road – with road number dual carriageway 14 single carriageway 14
Secondary road – with road number dual carriageway 96 single carriageway 96
Other road
Ferry
Railroad
Principal station *Estacion del Norte*
Height above sea level (m) 705
Airport
Airfield
Central area coverage
Urban area
Woodlands and parks

CENTRAL AREA MAPS

Motorway, freeway, expressway
Through route
Secondary road
Dual carriageway
Other road
Tunnel
Limited access/ pedestrian road
Parking (Europe only)
Railroad
Rail/bus station
Underground, metro station
Cable car
Abbey, cathedral
Church of interest
Synagogue
Shrine, temple
Mosque
Public building
Tourist information
Place of interest *Palace*

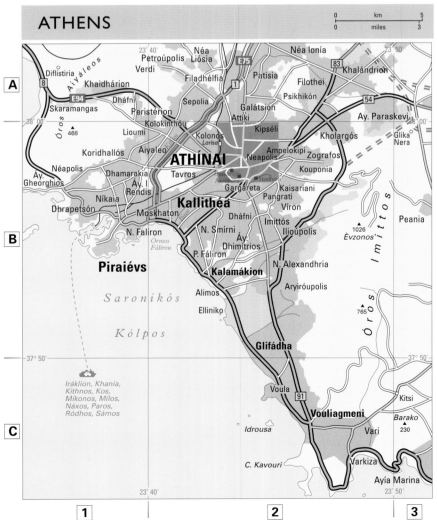

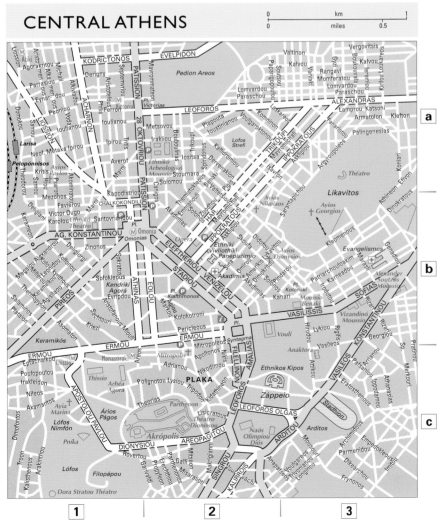

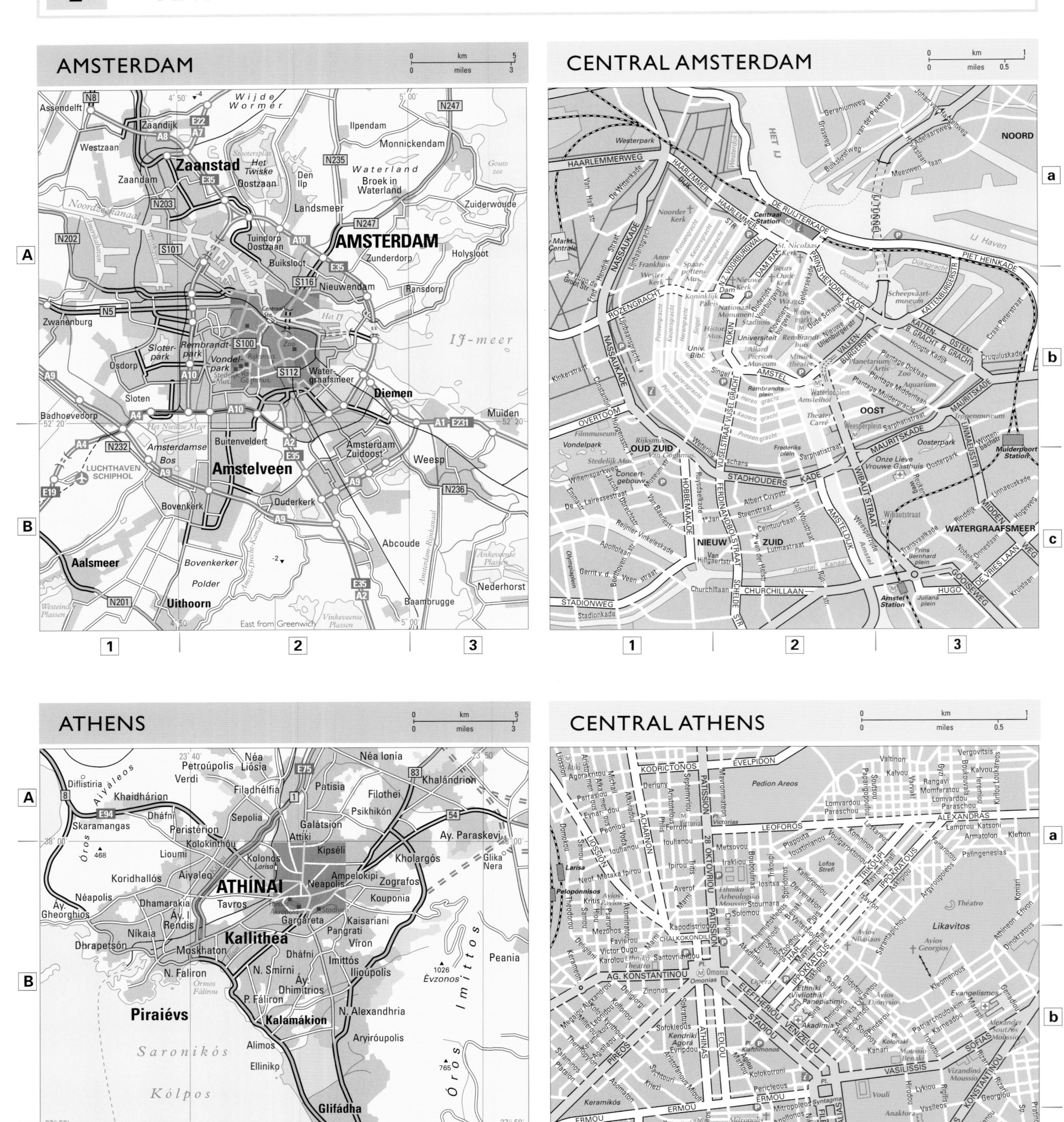
AMSTERDAM
CENTRAL AMSTERDAM
ATHENS
CENTRAL ATHENS
Zaanstad
AMSTERDAM
Amstelveen
Aalsmeer
Uithoorn
Diemen
Weesp
LUCHTHAVEN SCHIPHOL
IJ-meer
East from Greenwich
Centraal Station
Rijksmus.
Universiteit
OUD ZUID
OOST
NOORD
WATERGRAAFSMEER
Muiderpoort Station
Amstel Station
ATHÍNAI
Kallithea
Piraiévs
Glifádha
Vouliagmeni
Saronikós Kólpos
Iráklion, Khania, Kithnos, Kos, Mikonos, Mílos, Náxos, Paros, Ródhos, Sámos
Pedion Areos
Likavitos
PLAKA
Akrópolis
Zappeio
Ethnikos Kipos
Syntagma
Omonia
Stadhion

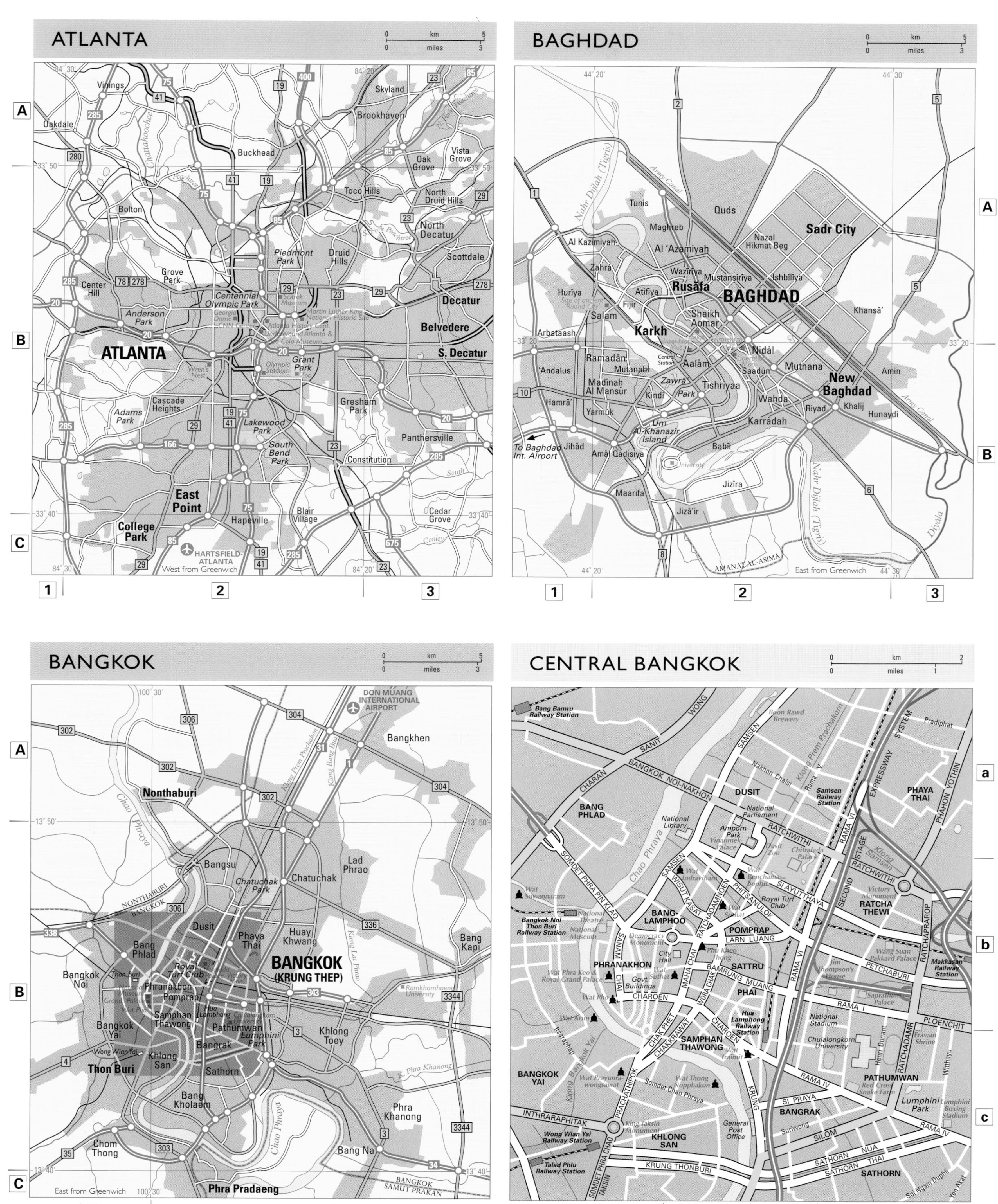
ATLANTA
0 km 5
0 miles 3
Vinings
Skyland
Oakdale
Brookhaven
Buckhead
Vista Grove
Oak Grove
Toco Hills
North Druid Hills
Bolton
North Decatur
Piedmont Park
Druid Hills
Scottdale
Grove Park
Center Hill
Centennial Olympic Park
Decatur
Anderson Park
Belvedere
ATLANTA
S. Decatur
Grant Park
Wren's Nest
Olympic Stadium
Gresham Park
Adams Park
Cascade Heights
Lakewood Park
Panthersville
South Bend Park
Constitution
East Point
College Park
Hapeville
Blair Village
Cedar Grove
HARTSFIELD-ATLANTA
West from Greenwich
BAGHDAD
0 km 5
0 miles 3
Tunis
Quds
Maghreb
Sadr City
Al Kazimiyah
Al 'Azamiyah
Nazal
Hikmat Beg
Zahra
Waziriya
Mustansiriya
Ishbiliya
Huriya
Atifiya
Rusâfa
BAGHDAD
Fijir
Salam
Shaikh Aomar
Khansâ'
Arbataash
Karkh
Nidâl
'Andalus
Ramadân
Aalam
Saadûn
Muthana
Amin
Mutanabi
Madinah Al Mansur
Zawrâ
Tishriyaa
New Baghdad
Hamrâ'
Kindi
Park
Wahda
Yarmûk
Riyad
Khalij
Hunaydi
Um Al-Khanazir Island
Karradah
To Baghdad Int. Airport
Jihâd
Amâl
Qâdisiya
Babil
University
Jizira
Maarifa
Jizâ'ir
AMANAT AL ASIMA
East from Greenwich
BANGKOK
0 km 5
0 miles 3
DON MUANG INTERNATIONAL AIRPORT
Bangkhen
Nonthaburi
Chao Phraya
Bangsu
Lad Phrao
Chatuchak Park
Chatuchak
Dusit
Phaya Thai
Huay Khwang
Bang Kapi
Bang Phlad
BANGKOK (KRUNG THEP)
Bangkok Noi
Phranakhon
Pomprap
Ramkhamhaeng University
Samphan Thawong
Pathumwan
Bangkok Yai
Lumphini Park
Khlong Toey
Bangrak
Khlong San
Thon Buri
Sathorn
Bang Kholaem
Phra Khanong
Chom Thong
Bang Na
BANGKOK SAMUT PRAKAN
Phra Pradaeng
East from Greenwich
CENTRAL BANGKOK
0 km 2
0 miles 1
Bang Bamru Railway Station
Boon Rawd Brewery
Pradiphat
DUSIT
Samsen Railway Station
PHAYA THAI
BANG PHLAD
National Parliament
National Library
Amporn Park
Vinanmek Palace
Dusit Zoo
Chitralada Palace
Wat Suwannaram
Wat Indraviharn
Wat Benchamabophit
Royal Turf Club
Victory Monument
RATCHA THEWI
Bangkok Noi Thon Buri Railway Station
National Theatre
National Museum
BANG-LAMPHOO
POMPRAP
Democracy Monument
City Hall
SATTRU
Wang Suan Pakkard Palace
Makkasan Railway Station
PHRANAKHON
Wat Phra Keo & Royal Grand Palace
Govt. Buildings
Wat Suthat
PHAI
Jim Thompson's House
Saprathum Palace
Wat Arun
National Stadium
Hua Lamphong Railway Station
Chulalongkorn University
Erawan Shrine
SAMPHAN THAWONG
Wat Traimit
BANGKOK YAI
Wat Prayunrawongsawat
Wat Thong Nopphakun
PATHUMWAN
Red Cross Snake Farm
Lumphini Park
Lumphini Boxing Stadium
BANGRAK
King Taksin Monument
Wong Wian Yai Railway Station
KHLONG SAN
General Post Office
Talad Phlu Railway Station
SATHORN

BARCELONA

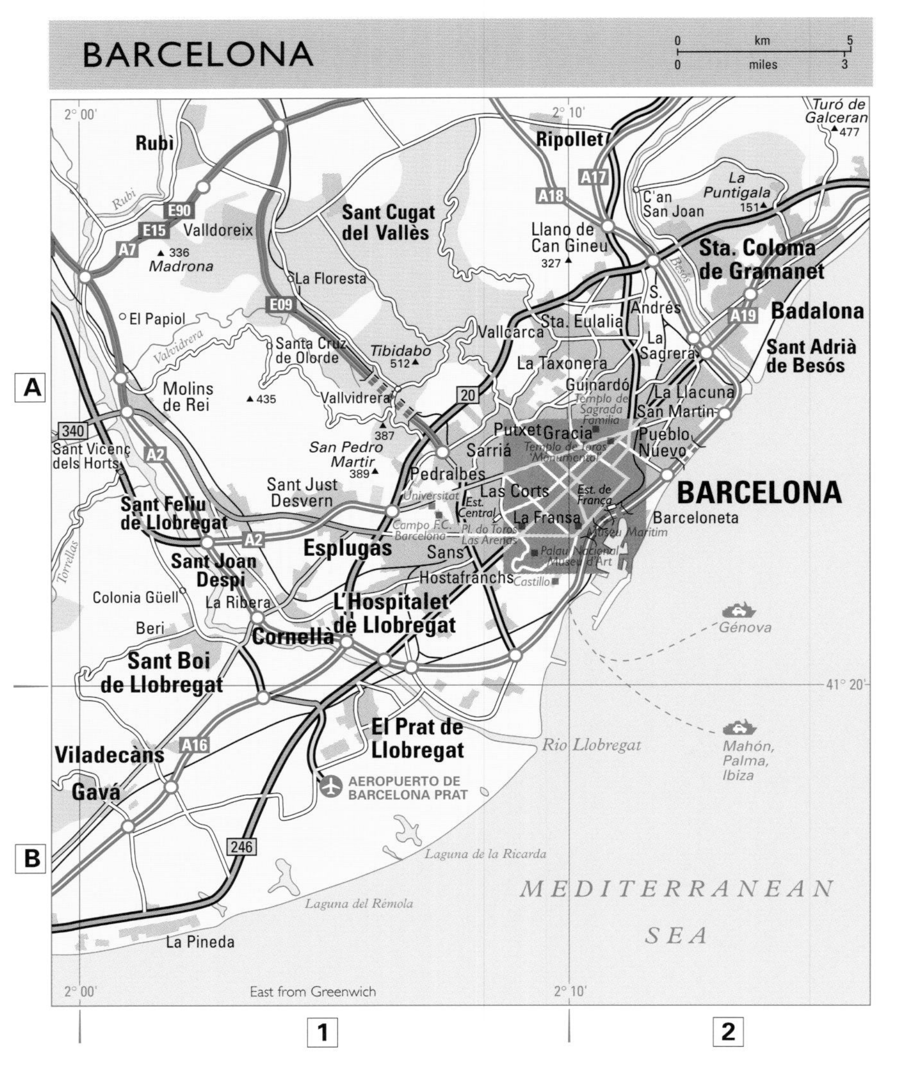

CENTRAL BARCELONA

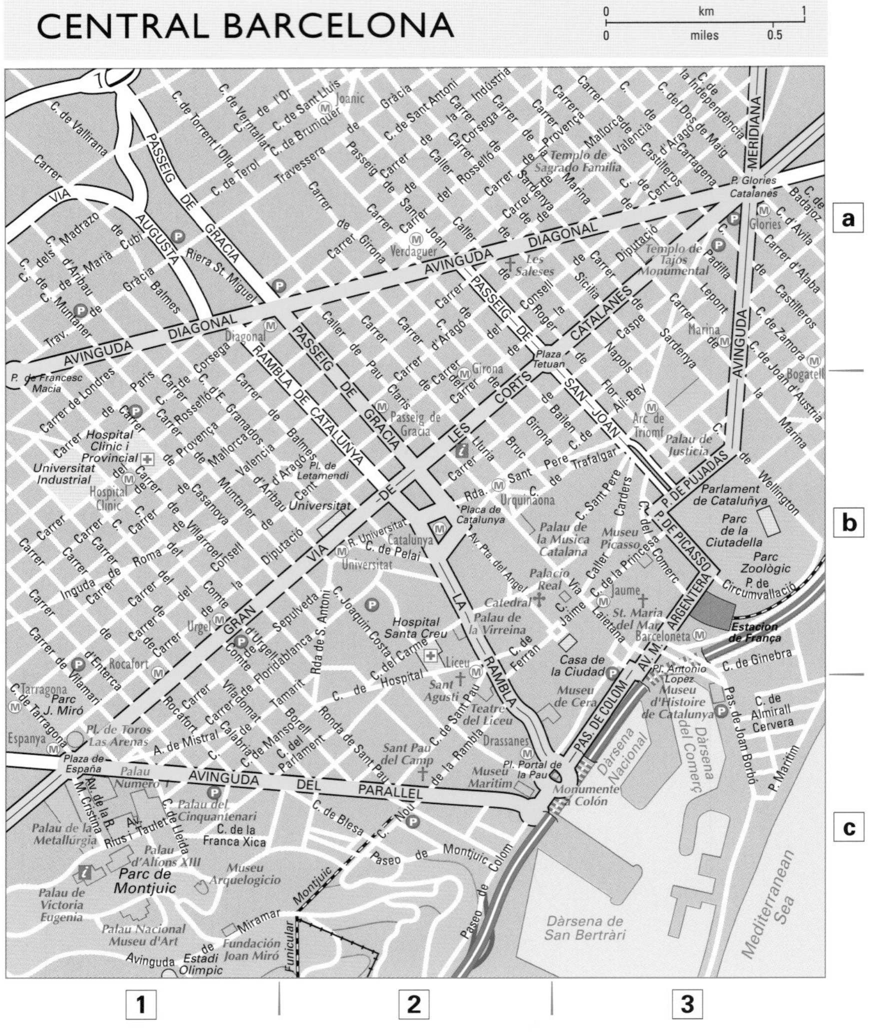

BEIJING

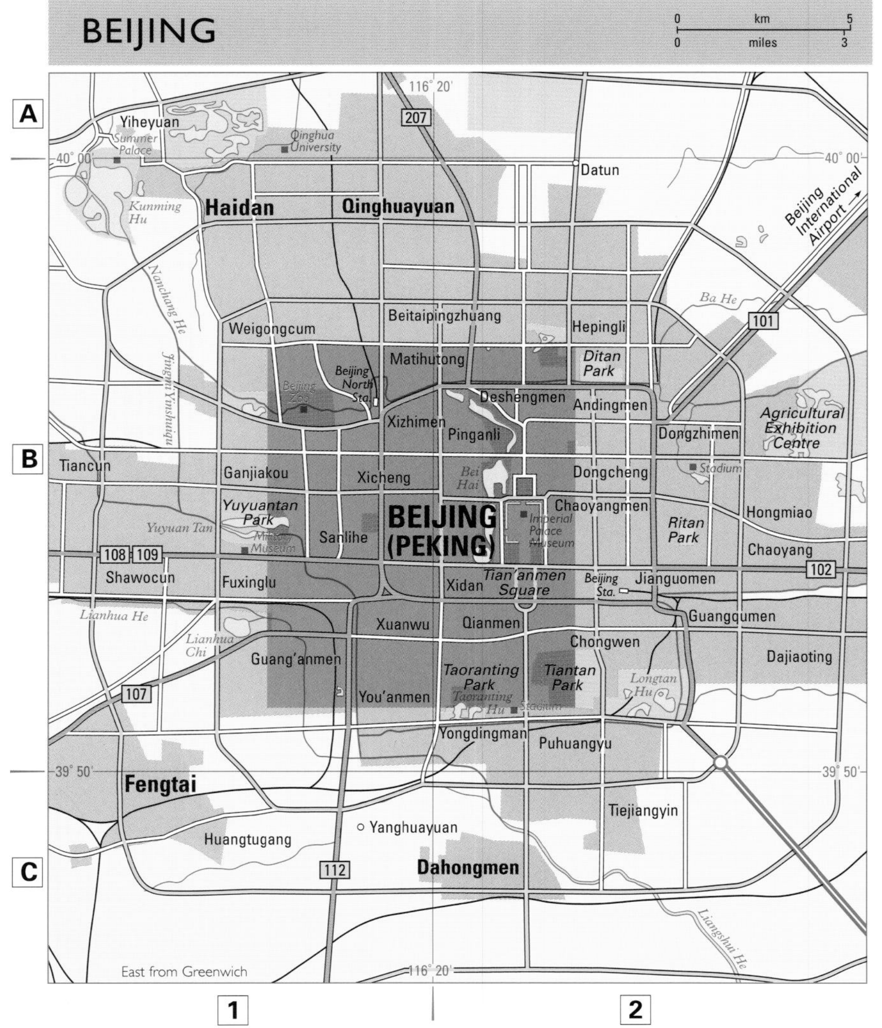

CENTRAL BEIJING

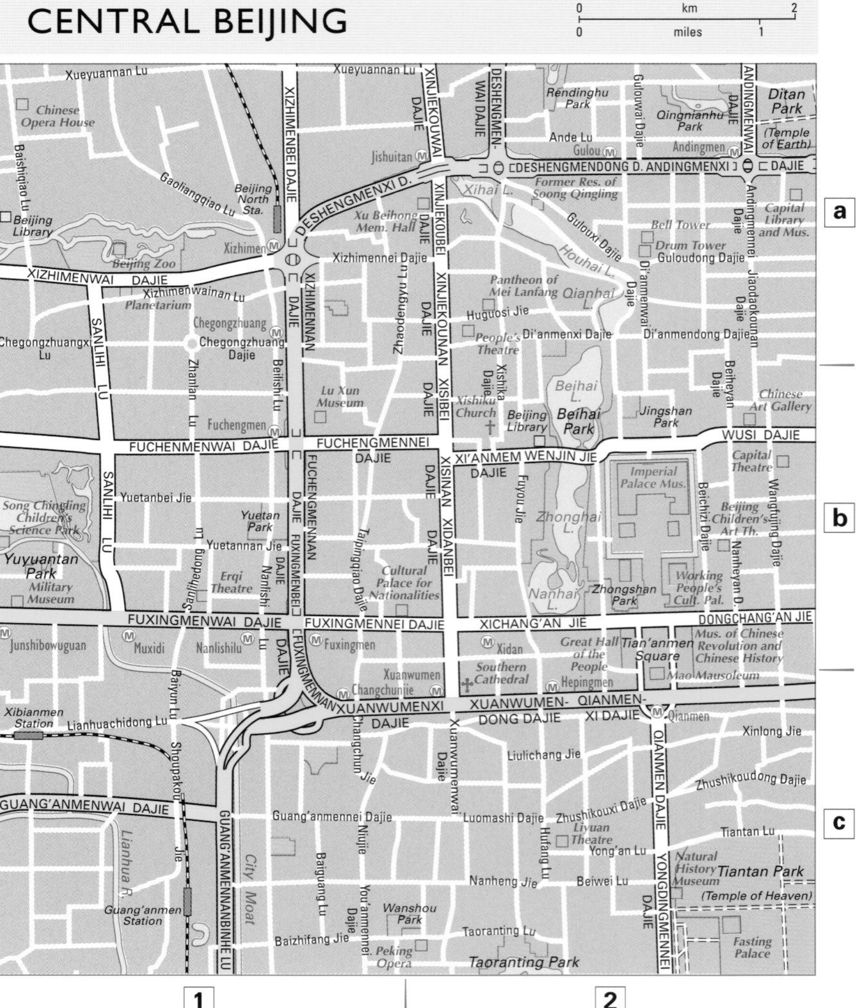

BERLIN

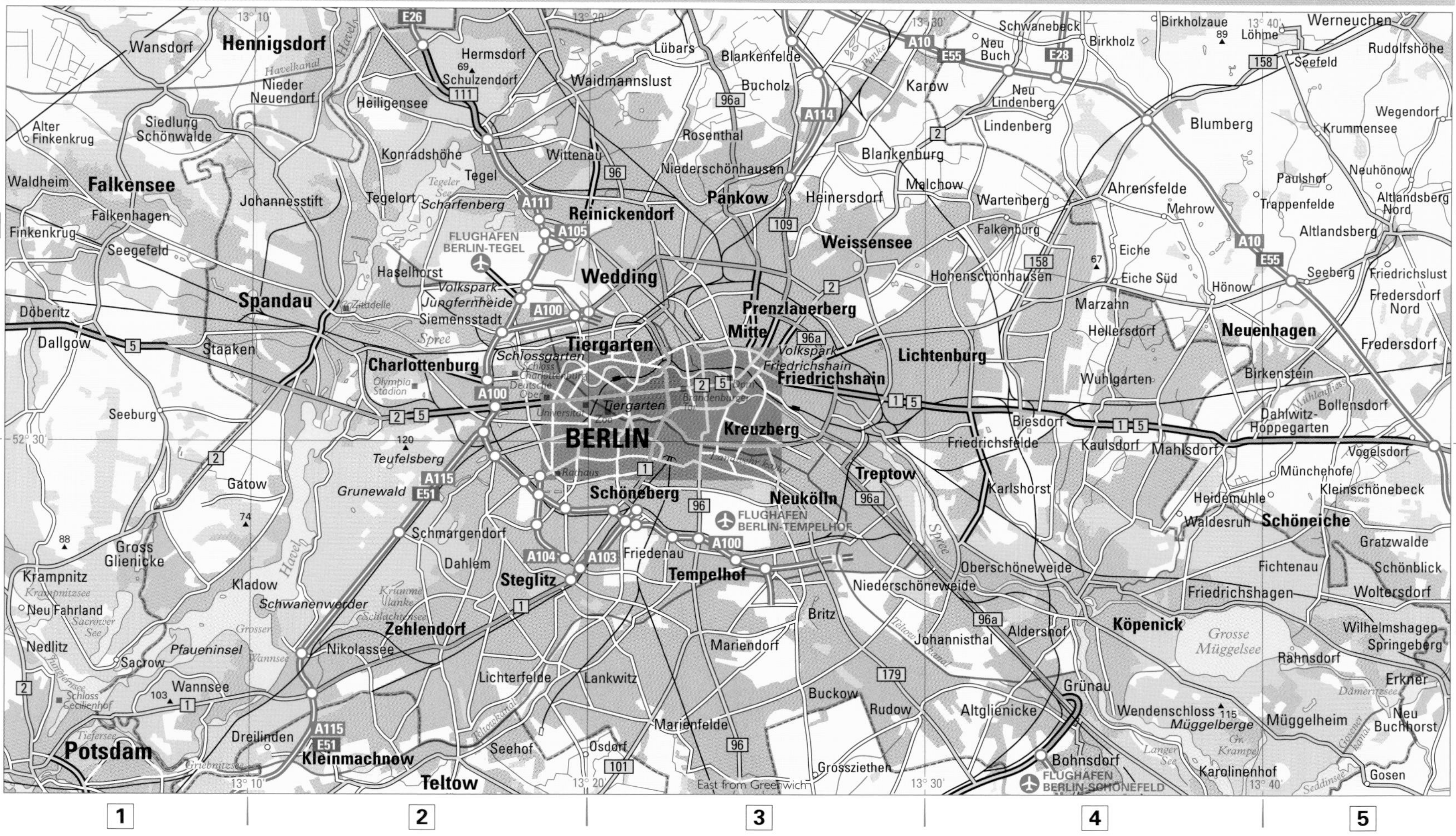

0 km 5
0 miles 3

CENTRAL BERLIN

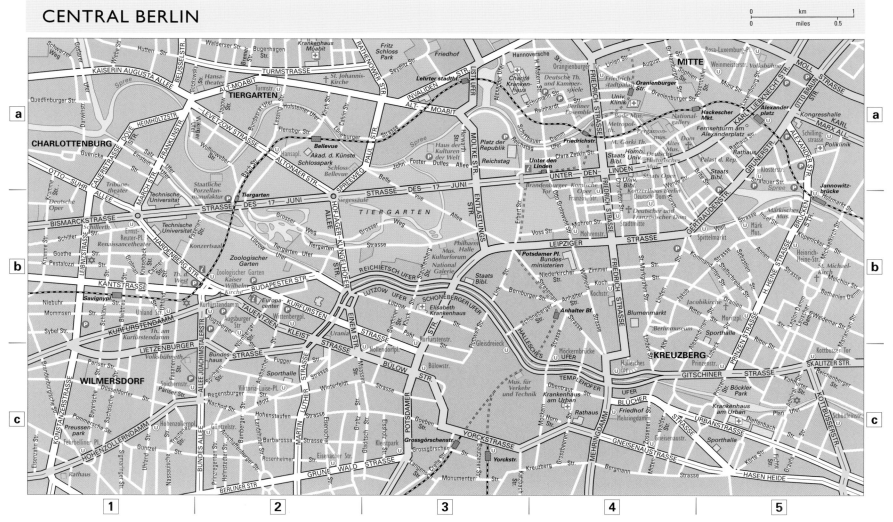

0 km 1
0 miles 0.5

BOSTON
0 km 5
0 miles 3
Burlington
Woburn
Wakefield
Marblehead
Stoneham
Lynn
Swampscott
Saugus
Melrose
Malden
Medford
Winchester
Lexington
Arlington
Revere
Everett
Chelsea
Somerville
Cambridge
Waltham
Watertown
Belmont
Concord
Lincoln
Newton
Brookline
BOSTON
LOGAN INTERNATIONAL AIRPORT
Winthrop
ATLANTIC OCEAN
Nahant Bay
Massachusetts Bay
Boston Harbor
Framingham
Natick
Wellesley
Needham
Dedham
Milton
Quincy
Dorchester
Roxbury
South Boston
Jamaica Plain
Hyde Park
Mattapan
Hingham
Weston
Wayland
Sudbury
BRUSSELS
0 km 5
0 miles 3
Grimbergen
Vilvoorde
Machelen
Zaventem
BRUSSEL NAT. LUCHTHAVEN
Jette
Ganshoren
Evere
Schaerbeek
St-Joose-Ten-Noode
Koekelberg
Molenbeek-St-Jean
Dilbeek
Anderlecht
Woluwe-St-Lambert
Woluwe-St-Pierre
Etterbeek
Ixelles
Auderghem
St-Gilles
Forest
Uccle
Watermael-Boitsfort
BRUSSEL BRUXELLES
Tervuren
Forêt de Soignes
Overijse
Hoeilaart
Beersel
Sint-Genesius-Rode
Halle
Waterloo
Rixensart
La Hulpe
St-Pieters-Leeuw
CENTRAL BRUSSELS
0 km 1
0 miles 0.5
Gare du Nord
Gare du Midi (Eurostar)
Gare Centrale
Grand Place
Jardin Botanique
Parc de Bruxelles
Palais Royal
Palais de Justice
Cath. St-Michel
ST-GILLES
IXELLES
A
B
a
b
c
1
2
3
4

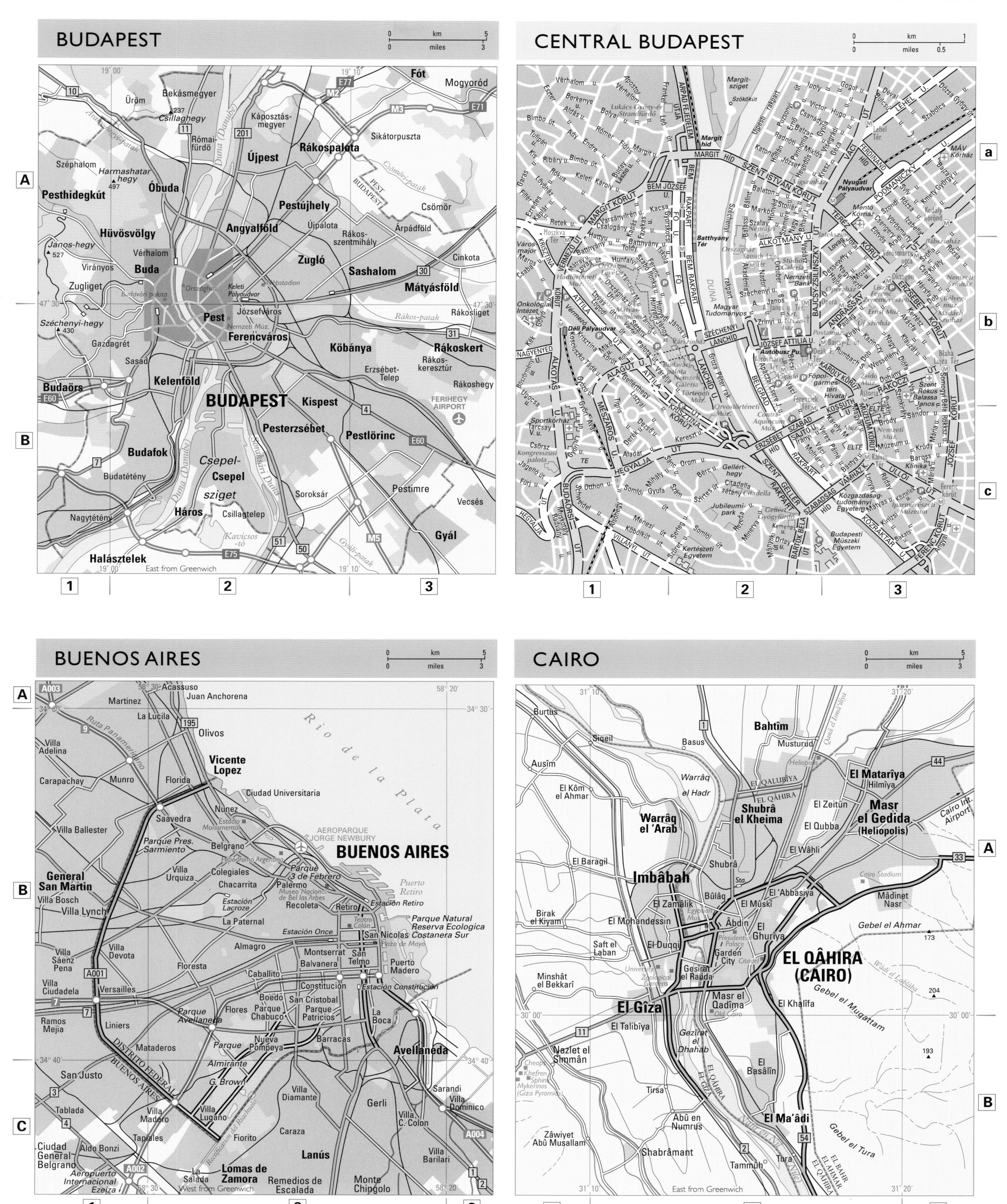
BUDAPEST
0 km 5
0 miles 3
Fót
Mogyoród
Üröm
Békásmegyer
Csillaghegy
Római-fürdő
Káposztás-megyer
Rákospalota
Sikátorpuszta
Újpest
Széphalom
Harmashatar hegy
Óbuda
Pesthidegkút
Pestújhely
Csömör
Hüvösvölgy
Angyalföld
Újpalota
Rákos-szentmihály
Árpádföld
János-hegy
Vérhalom
Zugló
Cinkota
Virányos
Buda
Sashalom
Mátyásföld
Zugliget
Keleti Pályaudvar
Széchenyi-hegy
Józsefváros
Rákosliget
Pest
Ferencváros
Gazdagrét
Kőbánya
Rákoskert
Sasád
Rákos-keresztúr
Erzsébet-Telep
Budaörs
Kelenföld
Rákoshegy
BUDAPEST
Kispest
FERIHEGY AIRPORT
Pesterzsébet
Pestlörinc
Budafok
Csepel
Csepel sziget
Budatétény
Soroksár
Pestimre
Vecsés
Nagytétény
Háros
Csillagtelep
Gyál
Halásztelek
East from Greenwich
A
B
1
2
3
CENTRAL BUDAPEST
0 km 1
0 miles 0.5
Margit-sziget
MARGIT HID
SZENT ISTVÁN KÖRÚT
Nyugati Pályaudvar
Batthyány Tér
DUNA
Magyar Tudományos
SZÉCHENYI LÁNCHID
Déli Pályaudvar
JÓZSEF ATTILA U.
ANDRÁSSY
ERZSÉBET HID
SZABADSÁG HID
Gellért-hegy
Citadella
RÁKÓCZI
KOSSUTH L. U.
Budapesti Műszaki Egyetem
a
b
c
1
2
3
BUENOS AIRES
0 km 5
0 miles 3
Acassuso
Juan Anchorena
Martinez
La Lucila
Olivos
Rio de la Plata
Villa Adelina
Vicente Lopez
Carapachay
Munro
Florida
Ciudad Universitaria
Nunez
Saavedra
AEROPARQUE JORGE NEWBURY
Villa Ballester
Parque Pres. Sarmiento
Belgrano
BUENOS AIRES
General San Martin
Villa Urquiza
Colegiales
Parque 3 de Febrero
Puerto Retiro
Villa Bosch
Chacarrita
Palermo
Villa Lynch
Recoleta
Retiro
Estación Retiro
Parque Natural Reserva Ecologica Costanera Sur
La Paternal
Estación Once
San Nicolas
Villa Sáenz Pena
Villa Devota
Almagro
Montserrat
San Telmo
Floresta
Balvanera
Puerto Madero
Villa Ciudadela
Versailles
Caballito
Constitucion
Estación Constitución
Boedo
San Cristobal
Ramos Mejia
Liniers
Parque Avellaneda
Flores
Parque Chabuco
Parque Patricios
La Boca
Mataderos
Nueva Pompeya
Barracas
Avellaneda
San Justo
DISTRITO FEDERAL BUENOS AIRES
Villa Diamante
Sarandi
Tablada
Villa Madero
Villa Lugano
Gerli
Villa C. Colon
Villa Dominico
Tapiales
Fiorito
Caraza
Ciudad General Belgrano
Aldo Bonzi
Lanús
Villa Barilari
Aeropuerto Internacional Ezeiza
La Salada
Lomas de Zamora
Remedios de Escalada
Monte Chingolo
West from Greenwich
A
B
C
1
2
3
CAIRO
0 km 5
0 miles 3
Burtus
Bahtîm
Siqeil
Basus
Musturud
Ausîm
El Matarîya
Hilmîya
El Kôm el Ahmar
Warrâq el Hadr
Warrâq el 'Arab
Shubrâ el Kheima
El Zeitûn
Masr el Gedida (Heliopolis)
Cairo Int. Airport
El Qubba
El Wâhli
El Baragil
Shubrâ
Imbâbah
El 'Abbasîya
Bûlâq
Mâdinet Nasr
El Zamâlik
El Mûski
Birak el Kiyam
El Mohandessin
Âbdîn
Gebel el Ahmar
El Ghurîya
Saft el Laban
El Duqqi
Garden City
EL QÂHIRA (CAIRO)
Gesîrat el Rauda
Minshât el Bekkarî
Masr el Qadîma
El Khalîfa
El Gîza
Gebel el Mugattam
El Talibîya
Nazlet el Simmân
Gezîrat el Dhahab
El Basâlîn
Tirsa
El Ma'âdi
Gebel el Tura
Zâwiyet Abû Musallam
Abû en Numrus
Shabrâmant
Tammûh
Tura
East from Greenwich
A
B
1
2
3

CALCUTTA (KOLKATA)

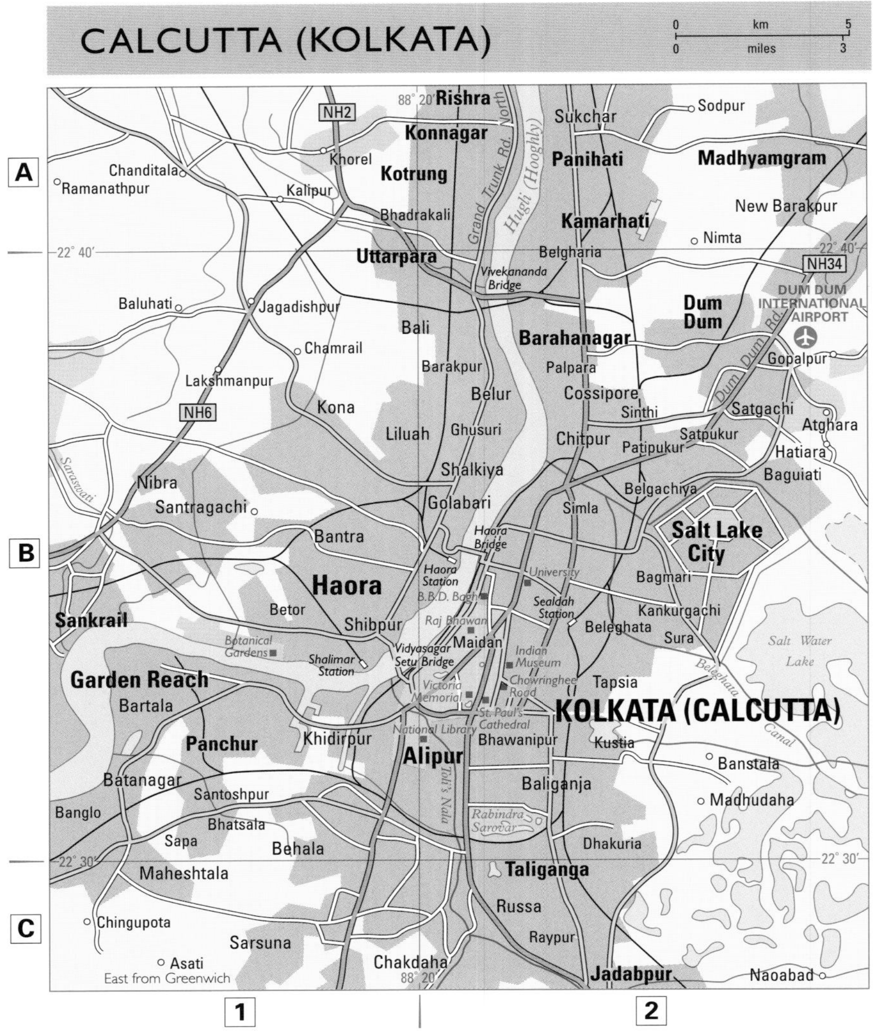

CANTON

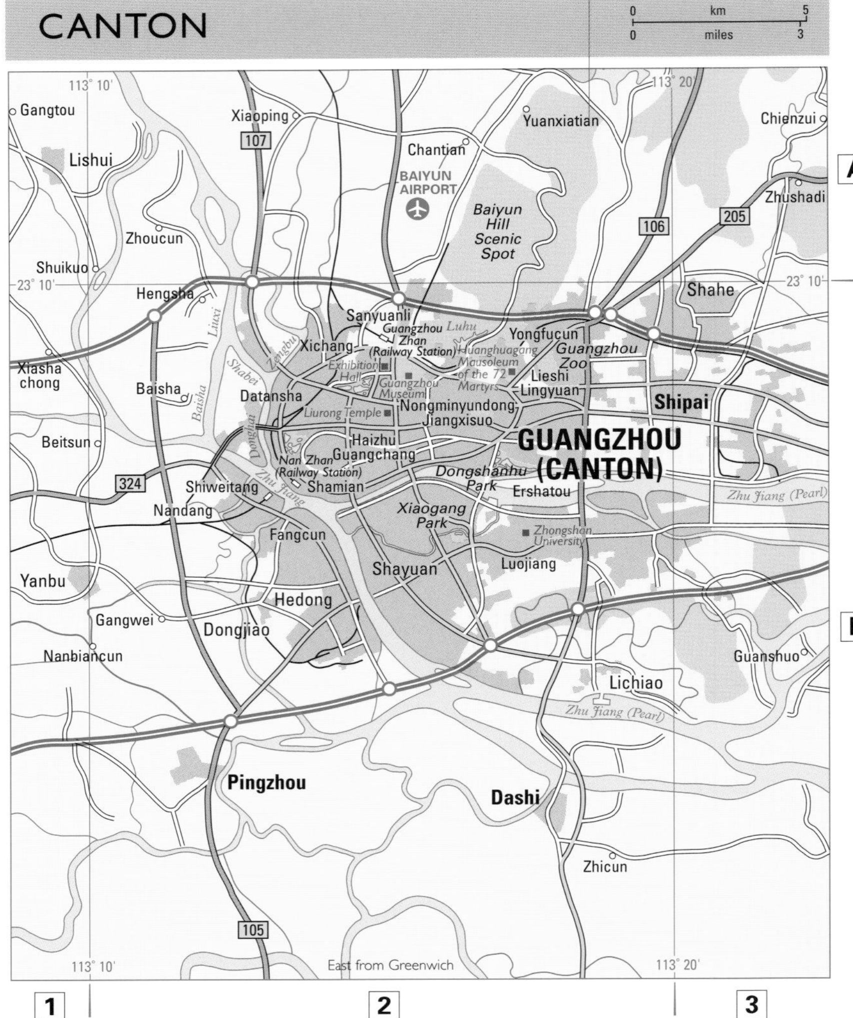

CAPE TOWN

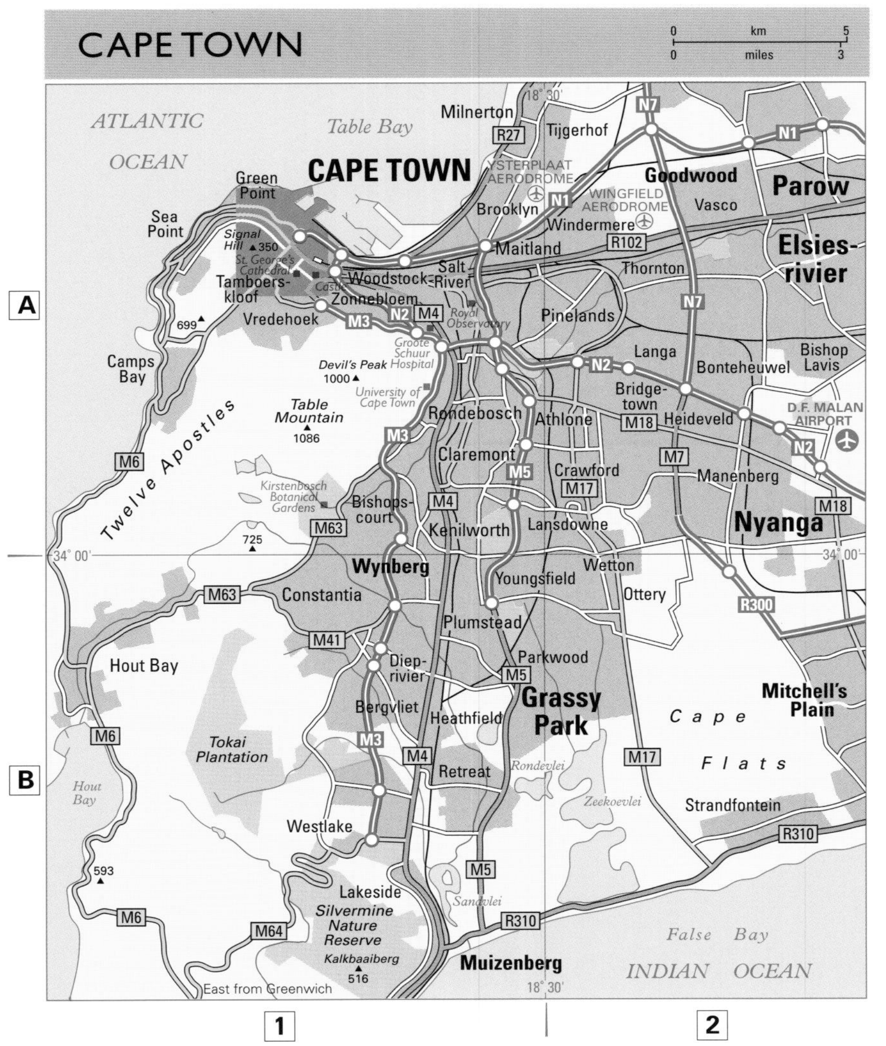

CENTRAL CAPE TOWN

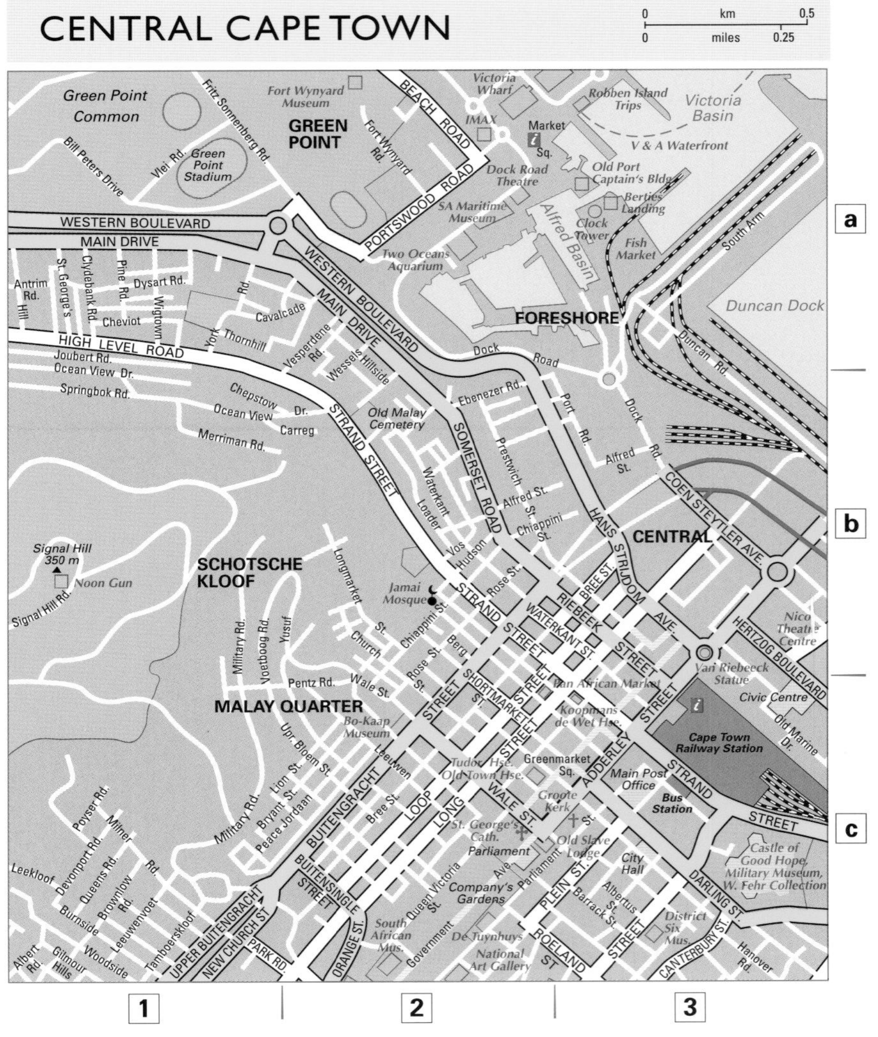

CHICAGO

0 km 5
0 miles 3

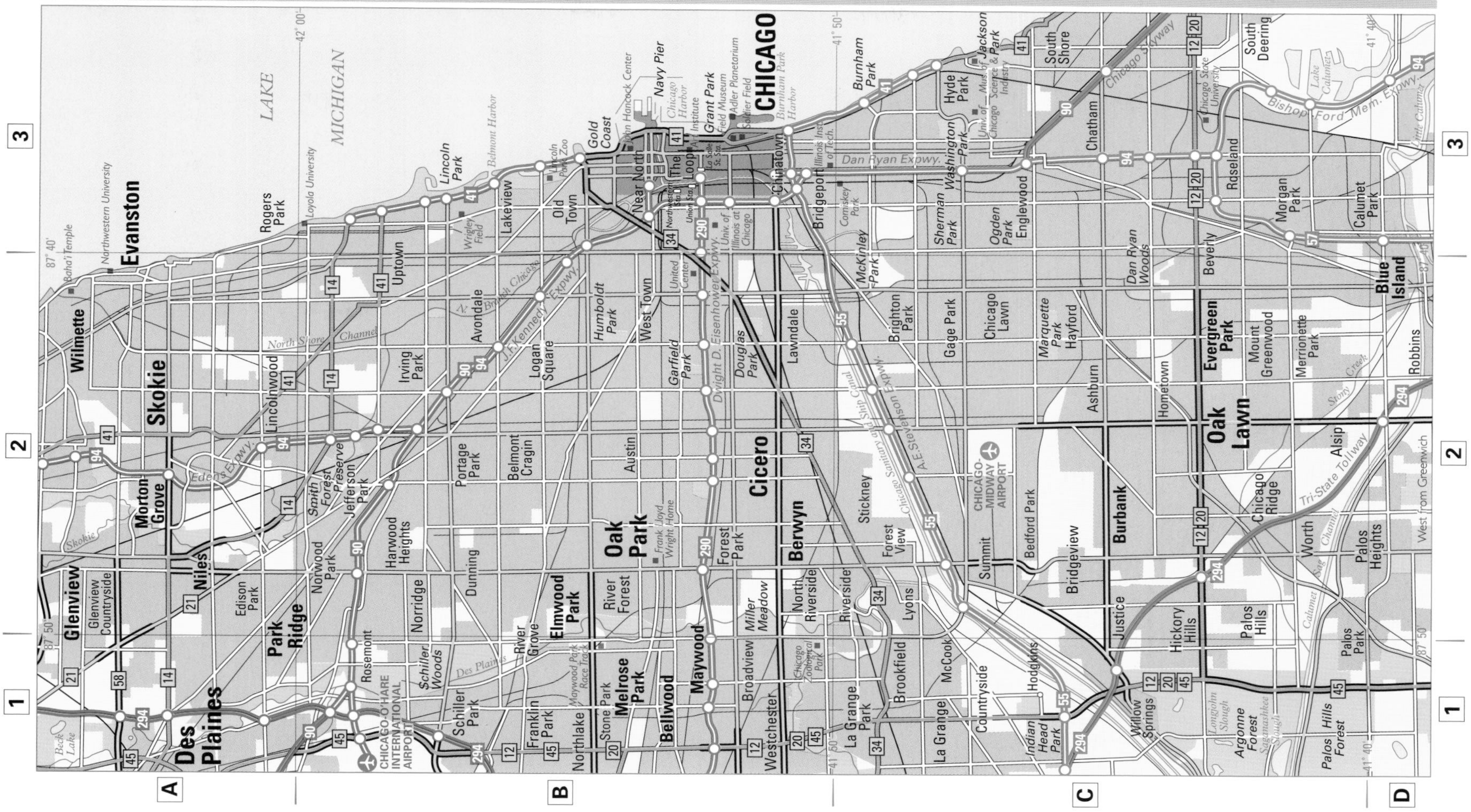

Evanston
Wilmette
Skokie
Morton Grove
Niles
Glenview
Glenview Countryside
Des Plaines
Park Ridge
Edison Park
Rosemont
Norwood Park
Harwood Heights
Norridge
Schiller Woods
Schiller Park
Franklin Park
River Grove
Elmwood Park
Northlake
Stone Park
Melrose Park
Bellwood
Maywood
River Forest
Oak Park
Forest Park
Broadview
Westchester
Berwyn
Cicero
North Riverside
Riverside
La Grange Park
La Grange
Brookfield
Lyons
McCook
Countryside
Hodgkins
Indian Head Park
Willow Springs
Justice
Bridgeview
Summit
Forest View
Stickney
Bedford Park
Burbank
Oak Lawn
Hickory Hills
Palos Hills
Palos Park
Palos Heights
Worth
Chicago Ridge
Alsip
Blue Island
Robbins
Evergreen Park
Beverly
Morgan Park
Calumet Park
Roseland
Chatham
Hyde Park
Washington Park
Englewood
Sherman Park
Ogden Park
Gage Park
Chicago Lawn
Marquette Park
Hayford
Ashburn
Hometown
Mount Greenwood
Merrionette Park
Dan Ryan Woods
Brighton Park
McKinley Park
Bridgeport
Chinatown
Lawndale
Douglas Park
Garfield Park
Humboldt Park
West Town
Austin
Belmont Cragin
Portage Park
Dunning
Jefferson Park
Irving Park
Logan Square
Avondale
Uptown
Rogers Park
Lincolnwood
Lakeview
Lincoln Park
Old Town
Gold Coast
Near North
The Loop
Navy Pier
Grant Park
CHICAGO
Burnham Park
South Shore
South Deering
CHICAGO O'HARE INTERNATIONAL AIRPORT
CHICAGO MIDWAY AIRPORT
LAKE MICHIGAN
Northwestern University
Loyola University
Dan Ryan Expwy.
Dwight D. Eisenhower Expwy.
J.F. Kennedy Expwy.
Edens Expwy.
A.E. Stevenson Expwy.
Chicago Skyway
Bishop Ford Mem. Expwy.
Tri-State Tollway
Chicago Sanitary and Ship Canal
North Shore Channel
Des Plaines
West from Greenwich

CENTRAL CHICAGO

0 km 1
0 miles 0.5

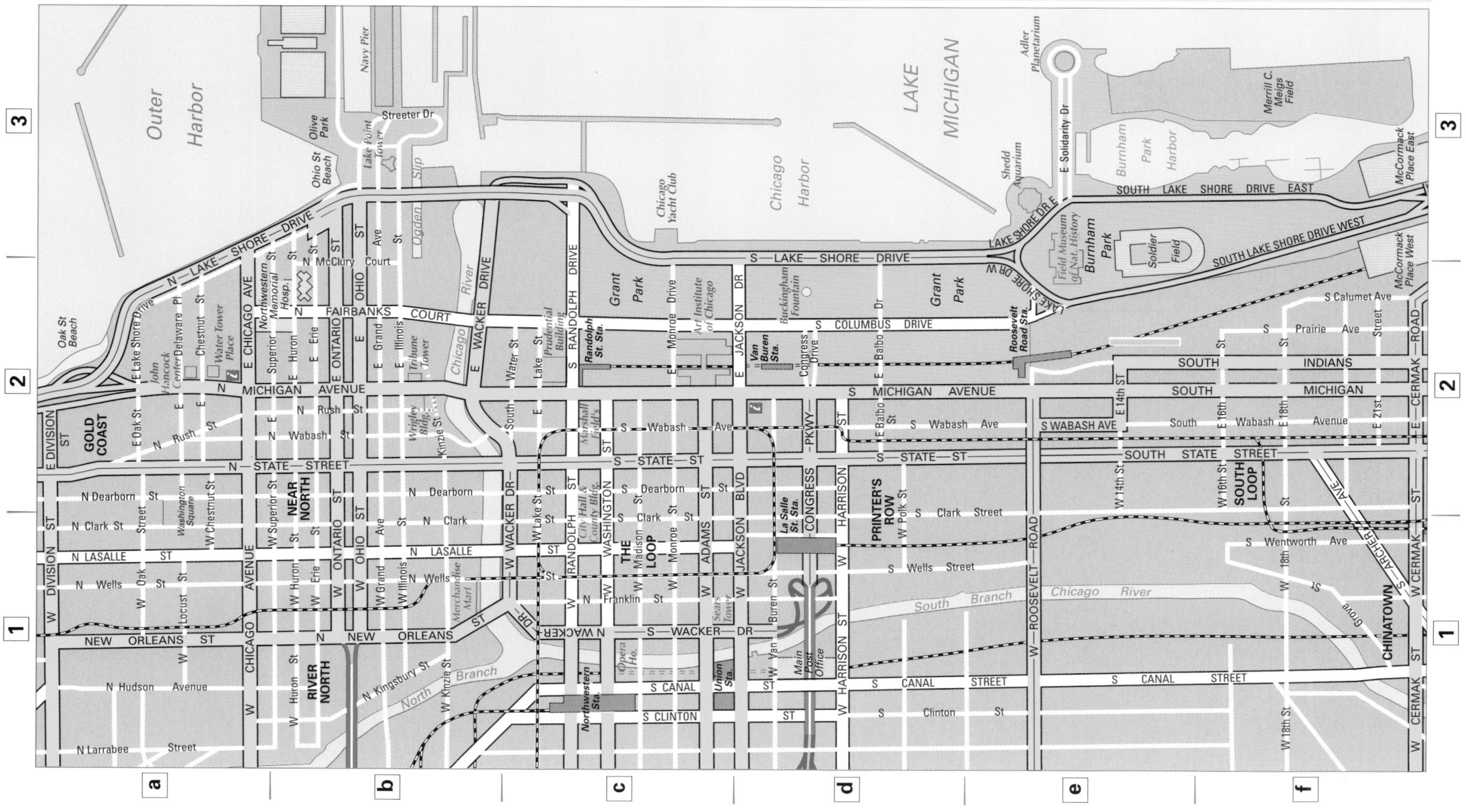

Outer Harbor
Navy Pier
Olive Park
Ohio St Beach
Oak St Beach
Streeter Dr
Lake Point Tower
LAKE MICHIGAN
Adler Planetarium
Shedd Aquarium
Chicago Harbor
Chicago Yacht Club
Burnham Park Harbor
Merrill C. Meigs Field
McCormack Place East
McCormack Place West
Field Museum of Nat. History
Soldier Field
Burnham Park
Grant Park
Buckingham Fountain
Art Institute of Chicago
Prudential Building
Randolph St. Sta.
Van Buren Sta.
Roosevelt Road Sta.
La Salle St. Sta.
Northwestern Sta.
Union Sta.
Sears Tower
Main Post Office
Opera Ho.
City Hall & County Bldg.
Marshall Field's
Merchandise Mart
Wrigley Bldg.
Tribune Tower
Water Tower Place
John Hancock Center
Northwestern Memorial Hosp.
Washington Square
GOLD COAST
NEAR NORTH
RIVER NORTH
THE LOOP
PRINTER'S ROW
SOUTH LOOP
CHINATOWN
N LAKE SHORE DRIVE
S LAKE SHORE DRIVE
SOUTH LAKE SHORE DRIVE EAST
SOUTH LAKE SHORE DRIVE WEST
E FAIRBANKS COURT
S COLUMBUS DRIVE
N MICHIGAN AVENUE
S MICHIGAN AVENUE
N STATE STREET
S STATE ST
E WACKER DRIVE
N WACKER DR
S WACKER DR
S RANDOLPH DRIVE
NEW ORLEANS ST
W ROOSEVELT ROAD
W HARRISON ST
E CERMAK ROAD
W CERMAK ST
S CANAL STREET
S Clinton St
S Wabash Ave
S Clark Street
S Wells Street
S Prairie Ave
S Indiana
S Calumet Ave
S Wentworth Ave
S Archer Ave
Congress Pkwy
Jackson Blvd
Adams
Monroe
Madison
Washington
N Dearborn St
N Clark St
N LaSalle St
N Wells St
N Hudson Avenue
N Larrabee Street
N Kingsbury St
E Oak St
E Rush St
E Chicago Ave
E Ontario St
E Ohio St
W Division St
South Branch Chicago River
North Branch
Chicago River
Ogden Slip

COPENHAGEN

0 km 5
0 miles 3

East from Greenwich

CENTRAL COPENHAGEN

0 km 0.5
0 miles 0.25

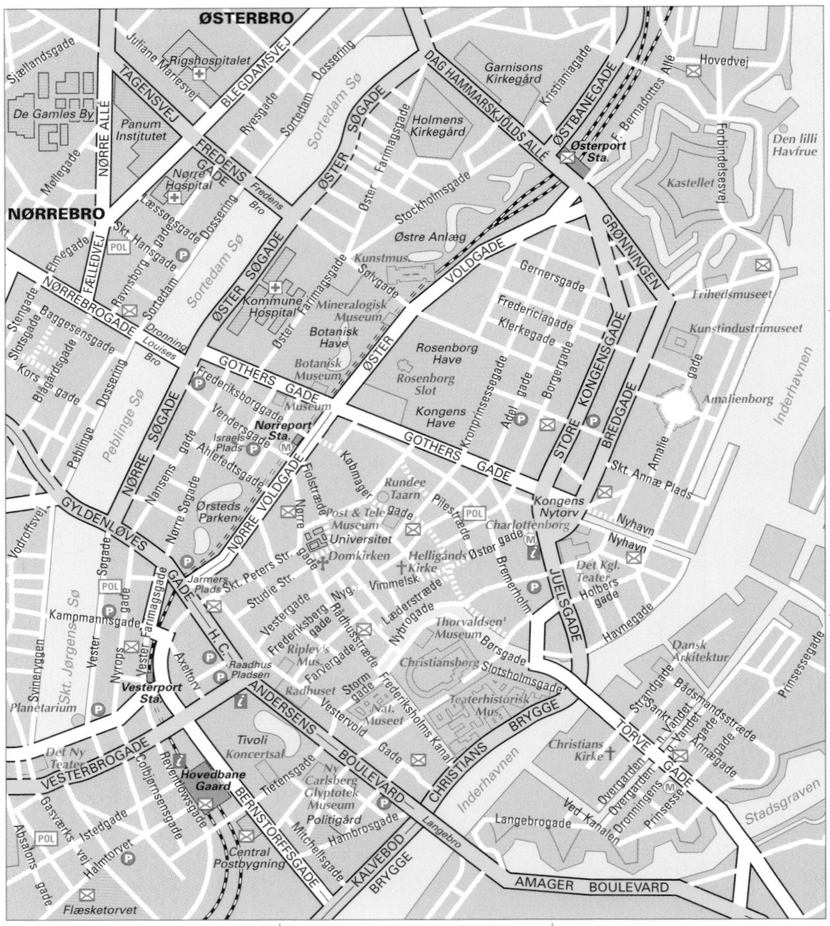

DELHI

0 km 5
0 miles 3

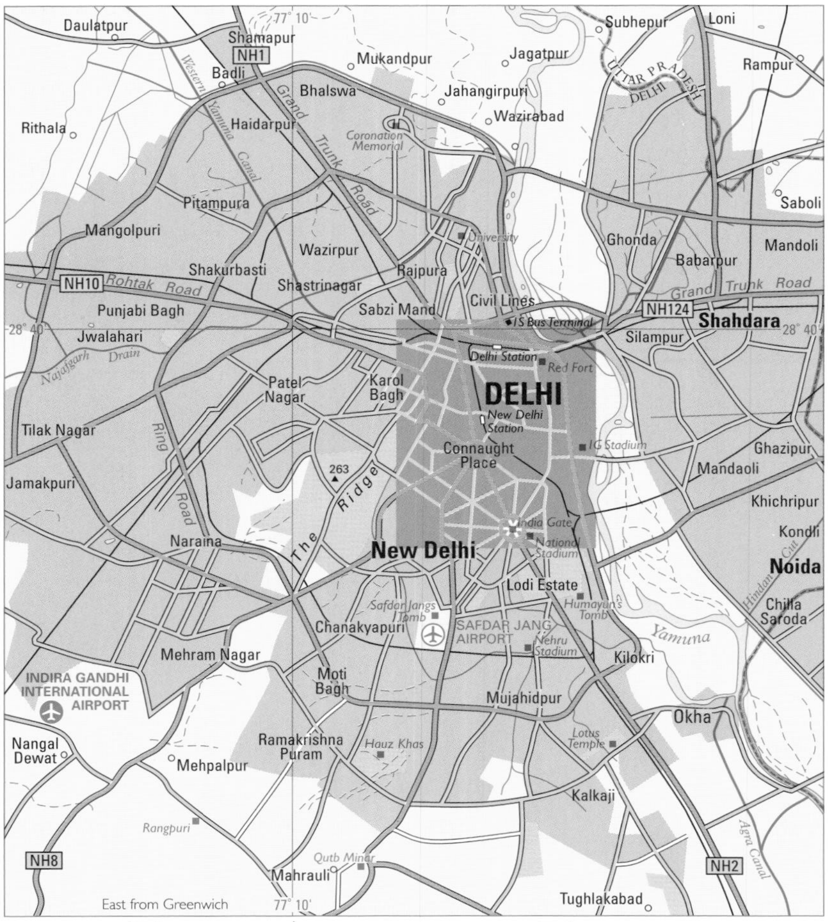

East from Greenwich

CENTRAL DELHI

0 km 2
0 miles 1

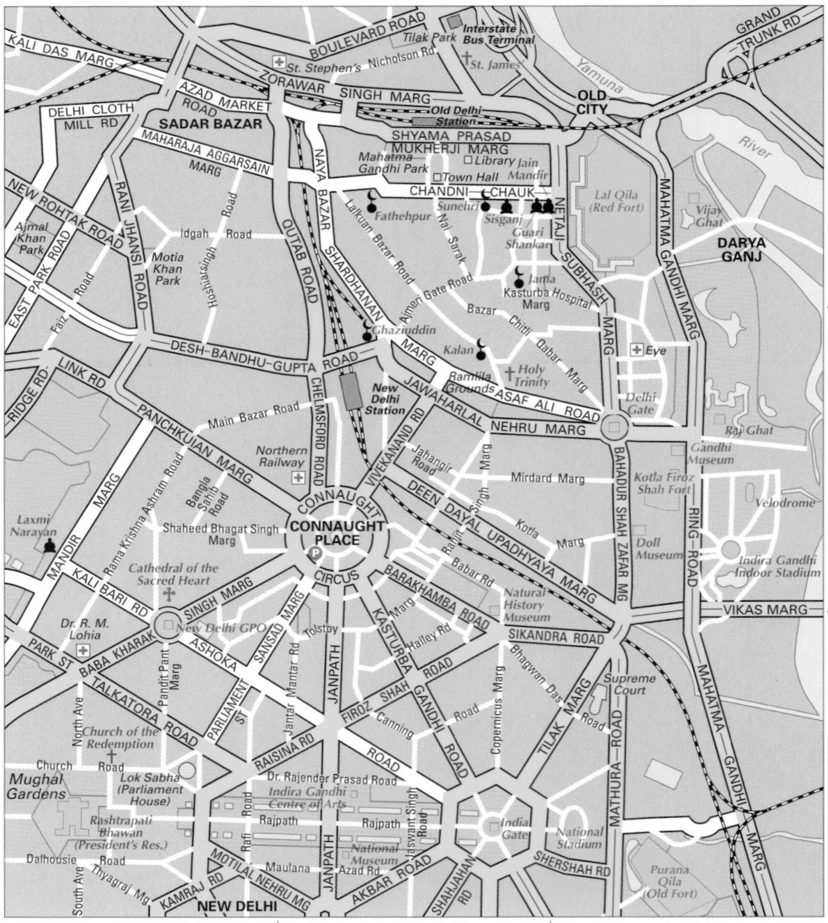

DUBLIN

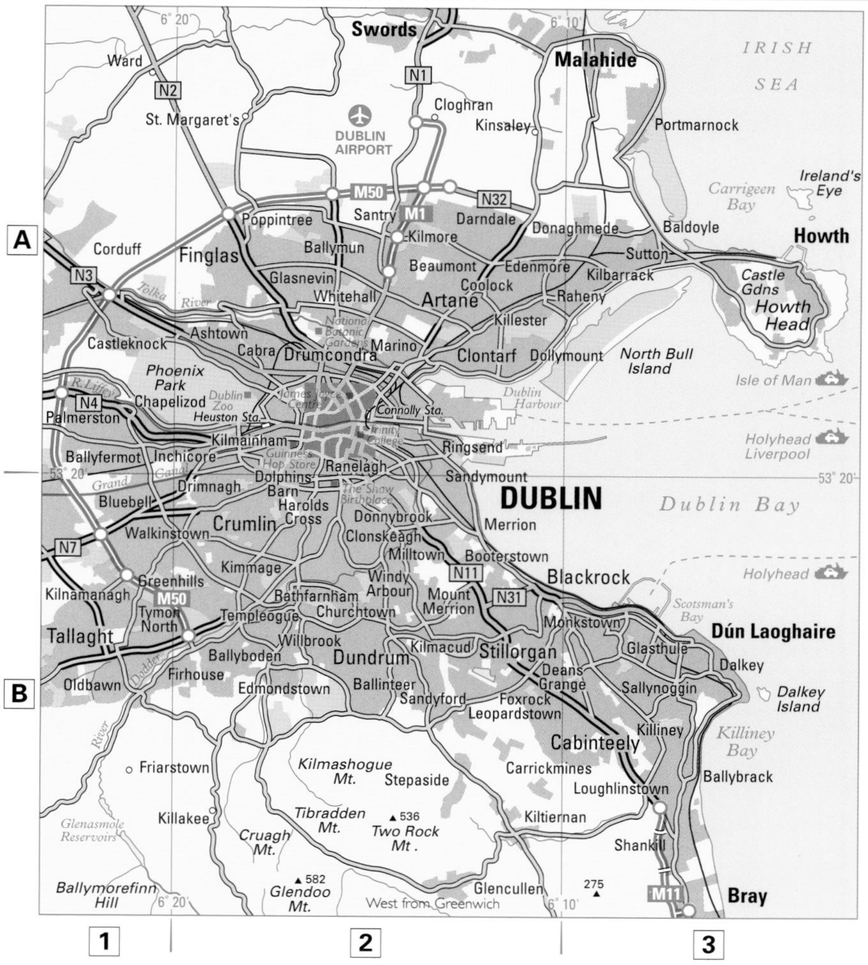

0 km 5
0 miles 3

Swords
Malahide
IRISH SEA
Ward
N2
St. Margaret's
N1
Cloghran
Kinsaley
DUBLIN AIRPORT
Portmarnock
M50
N32
Carrigeen Bay
Ireland's Eye
Poppintree
Santry
M1
Darndale
Donaghmede
Baldoyle
Howth
Corduff
Finglas
Ballymun
Kilmore
Sutton
N3
Glasnevin
Beaumont
Edenmore
Kilbarrack
Castle Gdns
Howth Head
Whitehall
Artane
Coolock
Raheny
Castleknock
Ashtown
Cabra
Drumcondra
Marino
Killester
Clontarf
Dollymount
North Bull Island
Phoenix Park
Chapelizod
Isle of Man
N4
Palmerston
Heuston Sta.
Kilmainham
Connolly Sta.
Holyhead Liverpool
Ballyfermot
Inchicore
Ranelagh
Ringsend
Bluebell
Drimnagh
Dolphins Barn
Sandymount
DUBLIN
Dublin Bay
Walkinstown
Crumlin
Harolds Cross
Donnybrook
Merrion
N7
Clonskeagh
Milltown
Booterstown
Kilnamanagh
Greenhills
Kimmage
Windy Arbour
N11
Blackrock
Holyhead
M50
Tymon North
Templeogue
Rathfarnham
Churchtown
Mount Merrion
N31
Tallaght
Willbrook
Monkstown
Dún Laoghaire
Ballyboden
Dundrum
Kilmacud
Stillorgan
Glasthule
Firhouse
Deans Grange
Dalkey
Oldbawn
Ballinteer
Sallynoggin
Edmondstown
Sandyford
Foxrock
Leopardstown
Dalkey Island
Cabinteely
Killiney
Killiney Bay
Friarstown
Kilmashogue Mt.
Stepaside
Carrickmines
Ballybrack
Loughlinstown
Killakee
Tibradden Mt.
536
Two Rock Mt.
Kiltiernan
Glenasmole Reservoirs
Cruagh Mt.
Shankill
Ballymorefinn Hill
582
Glendoo Mt.
Glencullen
275
M11
Bray
6° 20'
6° 10'
53° 20'
West from Greenwich
1 2 3
A B

CENTRAL DUBLIN

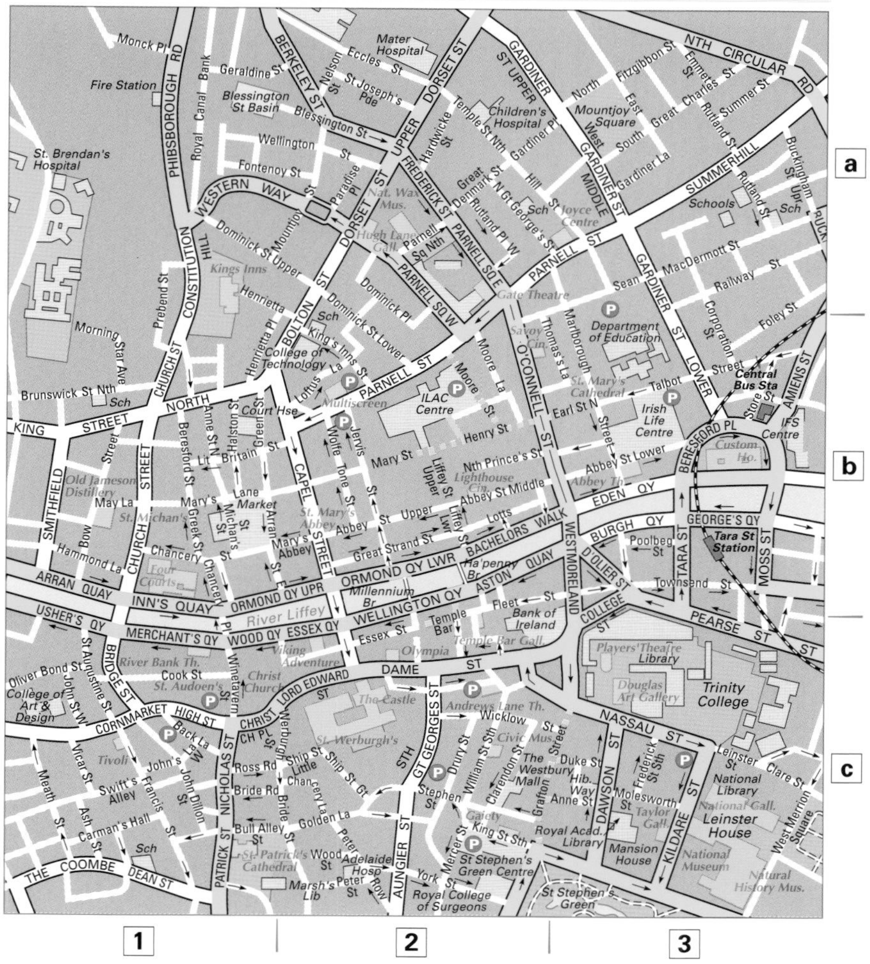

0 km 0,5
0 miles 0,25

Monck Pl
Mater Hospital
NTH CIRCULAR RD
Fire Station
Eccles St
Blessington St Basin
Mountjoy Square
St. Brendan's Hospital
Children's Hospital
WESTERN WAY
Kings Inns
Department of Education
Central Bus Sta
Brunswick St Nth
KING STREET NORTH
Parnell St
ILAC Centre
Irish Life Centre
IFS Centre
SMITHFIELD
Old Jameson Distillery
Custom Ho.
St. Michan's
Abbey St
EDEN QY
GEORGE'S QY
Tara St Station
ARRAN QUAY
INN'S QUAY
ORMOND QY UPR
ORMOND QY LWR
BACHELORS WALK
BURGH QY
USHER'S QY
River Liffey
WELLINGTON QY
ASTON QUAY
PEARSE ST
MERCHANT'S QY
WOOD QY
ESSEX QY
Temple Bar
Bank of Ireland
COLLEGE
Players' Theatre Library
Trinity College
Christ Church
DAME ST
The Castle
Douglas Art Gallery
College of Art & Design
CORNMARKET HIGH ST
NASSAU ST
St. Werburgh's
National Library
Leinster House
National Gall.
National Museum
Mansion House
St. Patrick's Cathedral
St Stephen's Green Centre
Royal College of Surgeons
St. Stephen's Green
Natural History Mus.
THE COOMBE
DEAN ST
PATRICK ST
AUNGIER ST
KILDARE ST
DAWSON ST
1 2 3
a b c

EDINBURGH

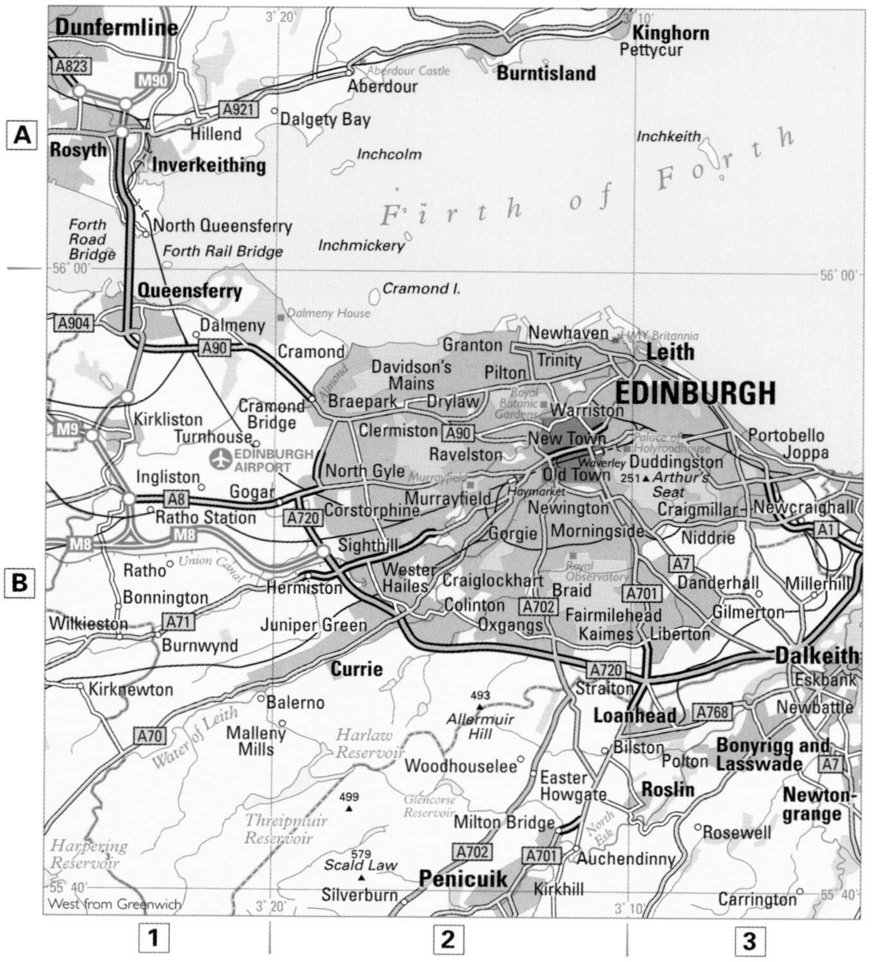

0 km 5
0 miles 3

Dunfermline
Kinghorn
Pettycur
A823
M90
Aberdour Castle
Aberdour
Burntisland
A921
Hillend
Dalgety Bay
Inchkeith
Rosyth
Inverkeithing
Inchcolm
Firth of Forth
Forth Road Bridge
North Queensferry
Forth Rail Bridge
Inchmickery
Queensferry
Cramond I.
A904
Dalmeny
Dalmeny House
A90
Cramond
Granton
Newhaven
Leith
Davidson's Mains
Pilton
Trinity
EDINBURGH
Kirkliston
Cramond Bridge
Braepark
Drylaw
Warriston
Turnhouse
Clermiston
A90
New Town
Portobello
M9
EDINBURGH AIRPORT
Ravelston
Joppa
Ingliston
North Gyle
Old Town
251 Arthur's Seat
Duddingston
Gogar
A8
Corstorphine
Murrayfield
Newington
Craigmillar
Newcraighall
Ratho Station
M8
A720
Sighthill
Gorgie
Morningside
Niddrie
A1
M8
Ratho
Union Canal
Wester Hailes
Craiglockhart
A7
Danderhall
Millerhill
Bonnington
Hermiston
Colinton
Braid
A701
Wilkieston
A71
Juniper Green
Oxgangs
A702
Fairmilehead
Gilmerton
Burnwynd
Kaimes
Liberton
Dalkeith
Currie
A720
Eskbank
Kirknewton
Balerno
493 Allermuir Hill
Straiton
Loanhead
A768
Newbattle
A70
Water of Leith
Malleny Mills
Harlaw Reservoir
Bilston
Polton
Bonnyrigg and Lasswade
Woodhouselee
Easter Howgate
Roslin
A7
Newtongrange
499
Glencorse Reservoir
Threipmuir Reservoir
Milton Bridge
Rosewell
Harperrig Reservoir
579 Scald Law
A702
A701
Auchendinny
Penicuik
Kirkhill
Silverburn
Carrington
3° 20'
3° 10'
56° 00'
55° 40'
West from Greenwich
1 2 3
A B

CENTRAL EDINBURGH

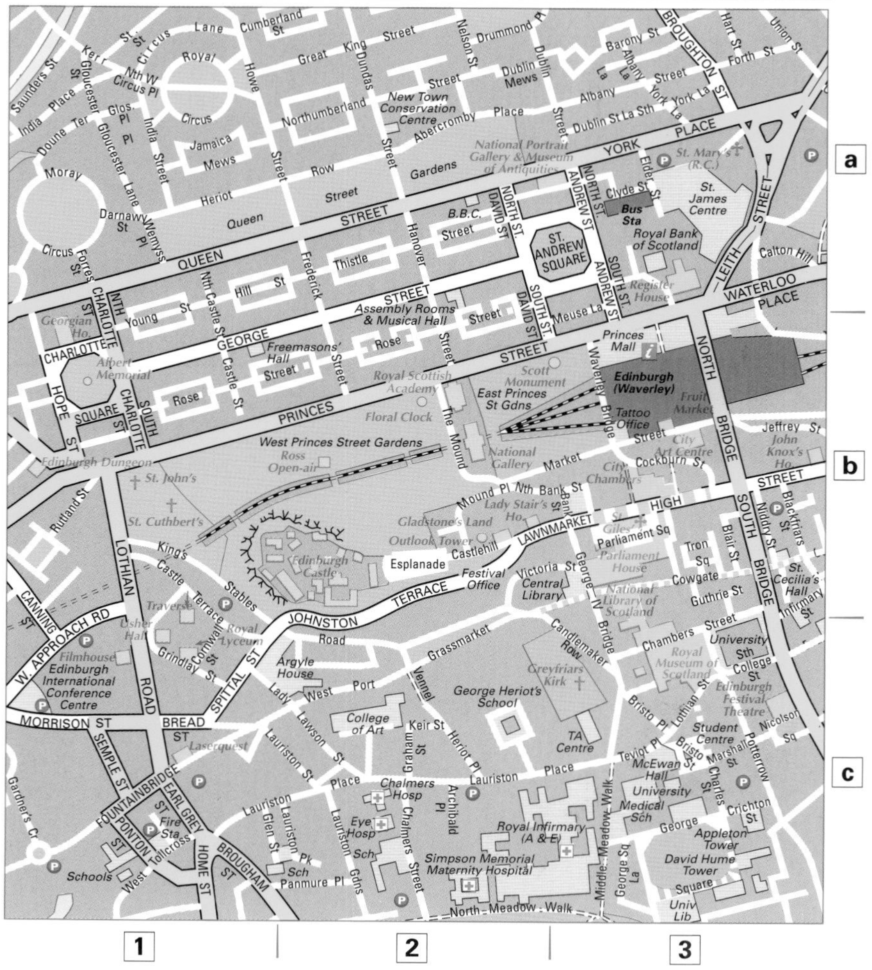

0 km 0,5
0 miles 0,25

Cumberland St
Drummond Pl
BROUGHTON ST
Great King Street
Dublin Mews
New Town Conservation Centre
Royal Circus
Northumberland St
Abercromby Place
YORK PLACE
St. Mary's (R.C.)
Moray Place
Jamaica Mews
National Portrait Gallery & Museum of Antiquities
Heriot Row
Queen Street
Gardens
ST ANDREW SQUARE
Bus Sta
St. James Centre
Royal Bank of Scotland
QUEEN STREET
Thistle Street
Register House
LEITH STREET
Calton Hill
WATERLOO PLACE
Georgian Ho.
CHARLOTTE SQUARE
Young St
Hill St
Assembly Rooms & Musical Hall
Rose Street
GEORGE STREET
Freemasons' Hall
Princes Mall
NORTH BRIDGE
Albert Memorial
PRINCES STREET
Scott Monument
Edinburgh (Waverley)
Royal Scottish Academy
East Princes St Gdns
Fruit Market
Floral Clock
Tattoo Office
West Princes Street Gardens
City Art Centre
Ross Open-air
National Gallery
Market St
City Chambers
Cockburn St
Edinburgh Dungeon
St. John's
St. Cuthbert's
Mound Pl
Lady Stair's Ho.
HIGH ST
John Knox's Ho.
Gladstone's Land
LAWNMARKET
Parliament Sq
Outlook Tower
Castlehill
Esplanade
Parliament House
Tron
Edinburgh Castle
Festival Office
Victoria St
Central Library
National Library of Scotland
Cowgate
St. Cecilia's Hall
Infirmary St
LOTHIAN ROAD
Traverse
Usher Hall
Royal Lyceum
JOHNSTON TERRACE
Grassmarket
Candlemaker Row
Greyfriars Kirk
Chambers Street
Royal Museum of Scotland
University
Old College
Filmhouse
Edinburgh International Conference Centre
Argyle House
West Port
George Heriot's School
SOUTH BRIDGE
Edinburgh Festival Theatre
Nicolson St
MORRISON ST
BREAD ST
College of Art
Lauriston Place
TA Centre
Student Centre
Chalmers Hosp
McEwan Hall
University Medical Sch
Fire Sta
Eye Hosp
Royal Infirmary (A & E)
George Sq
Appleton Tower
David Hume Tower
Simpson Memorial Maternity Hospital
Schools
Panmure Pl
North Meadow Walk
Middle Meadow Walk
Univ Lib
1 2 3
a b c

HELSINKI

0 km 5
0 miles 3

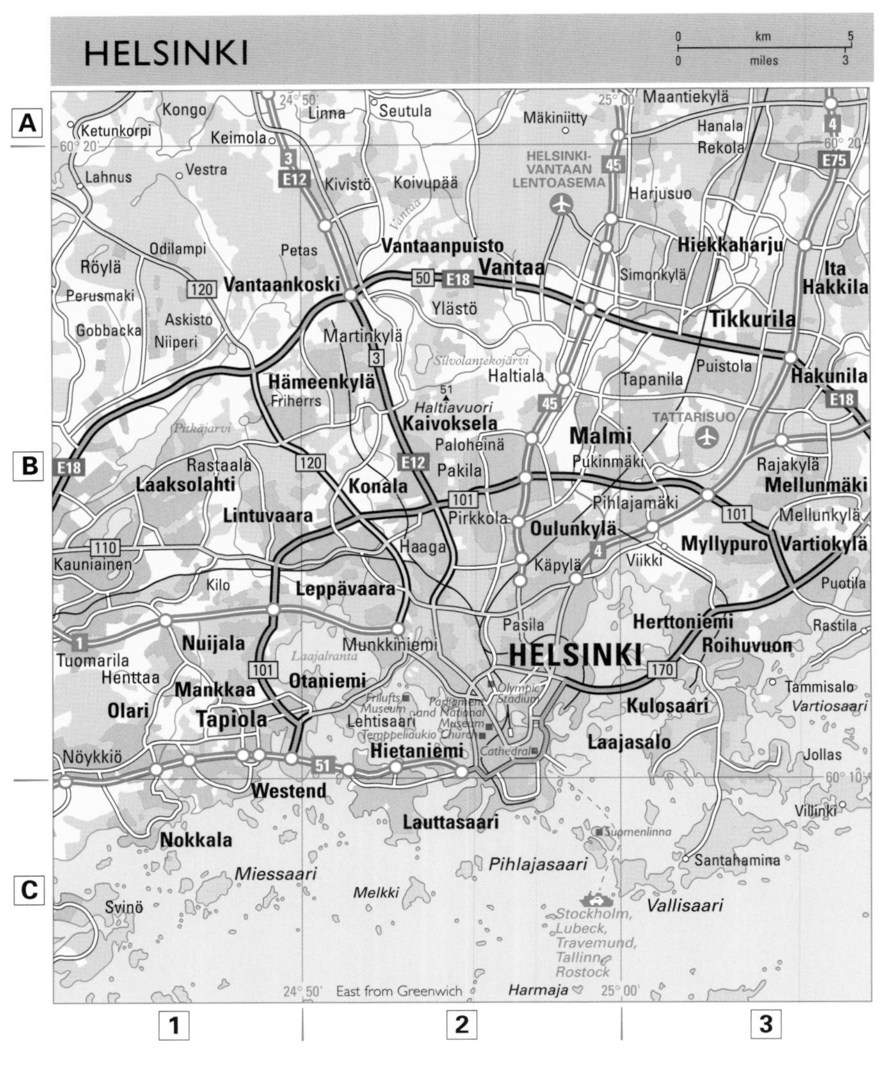

ISTANBUL

0 km 5
0 miles 3

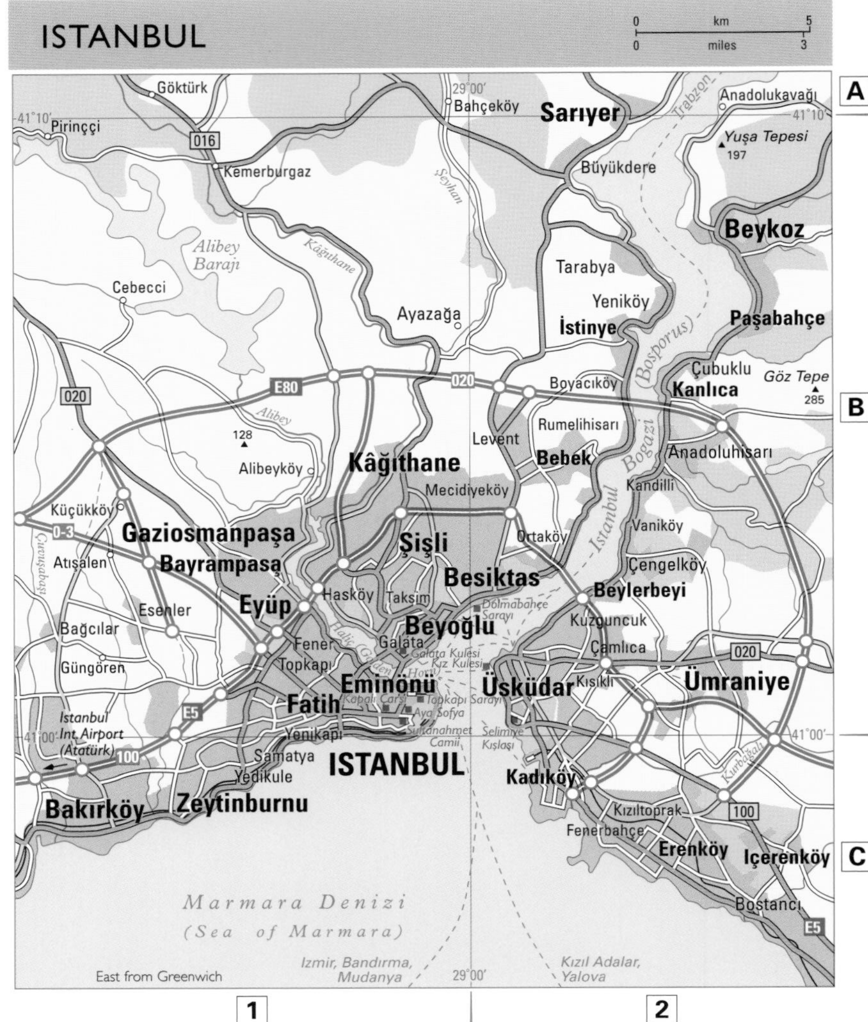

HONG KONG

0 km 5
0 miles 3

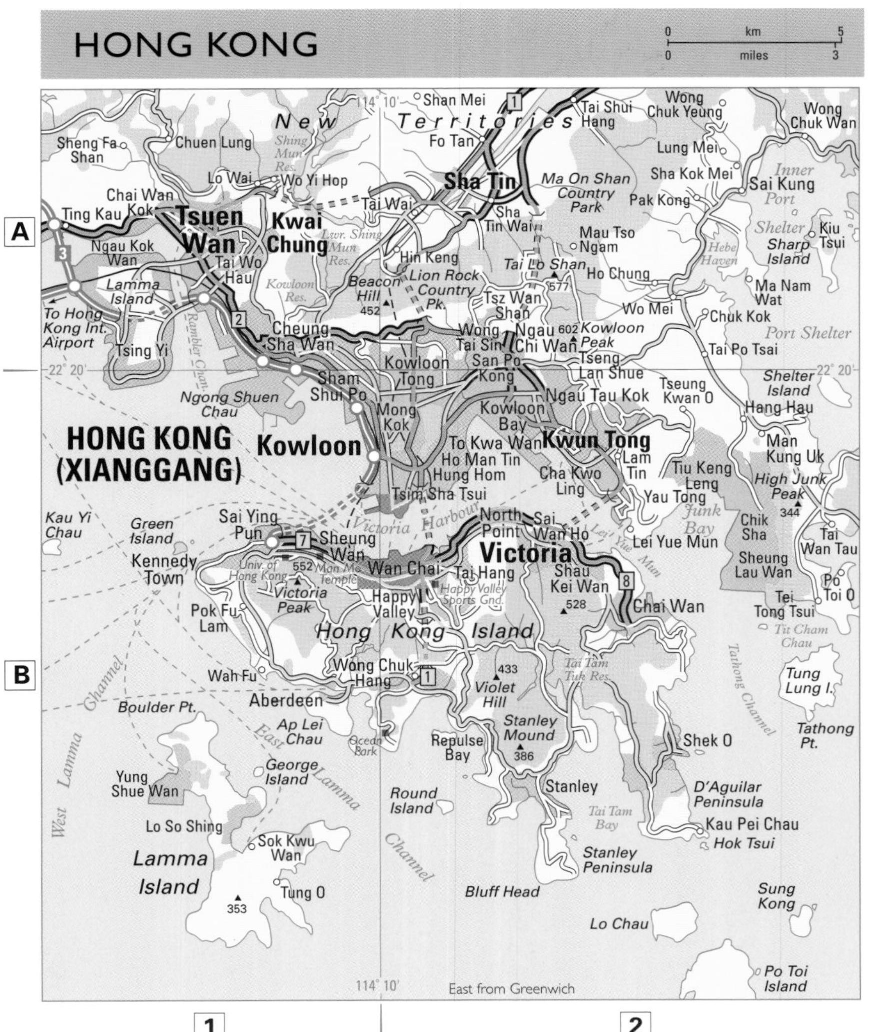

CENTRAL HONG KONG

0 km 0.5
0 miles 0.25

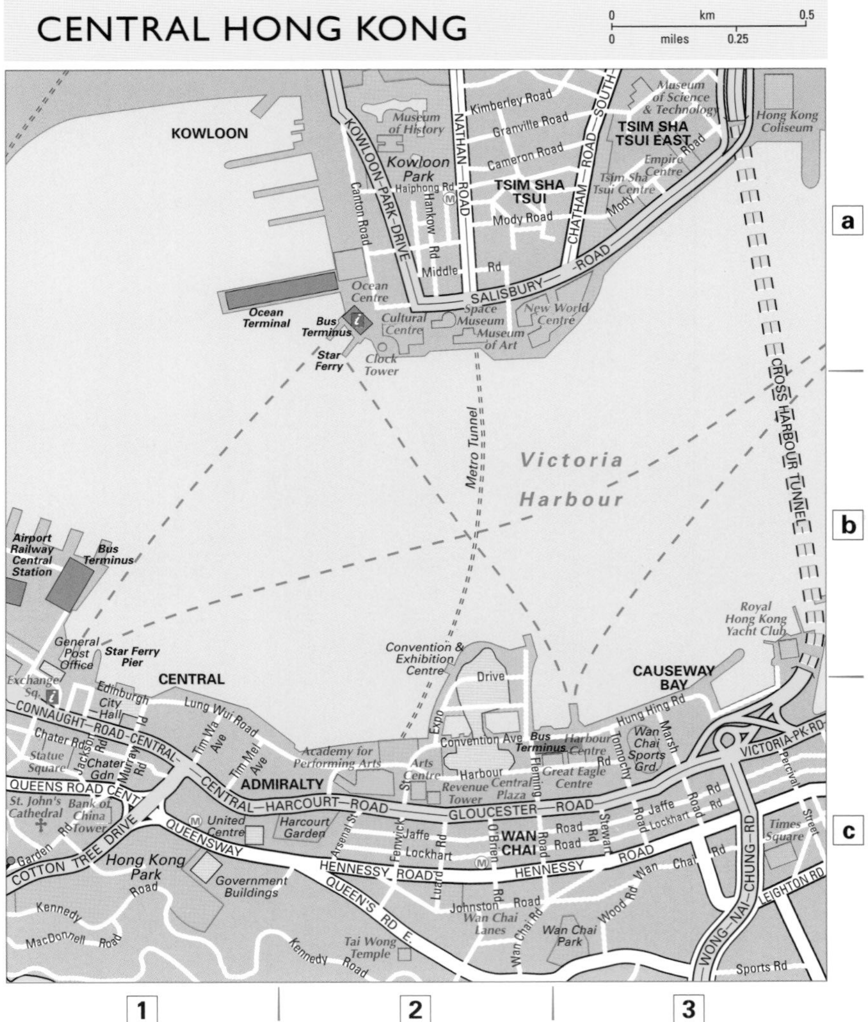

JERUSALEM

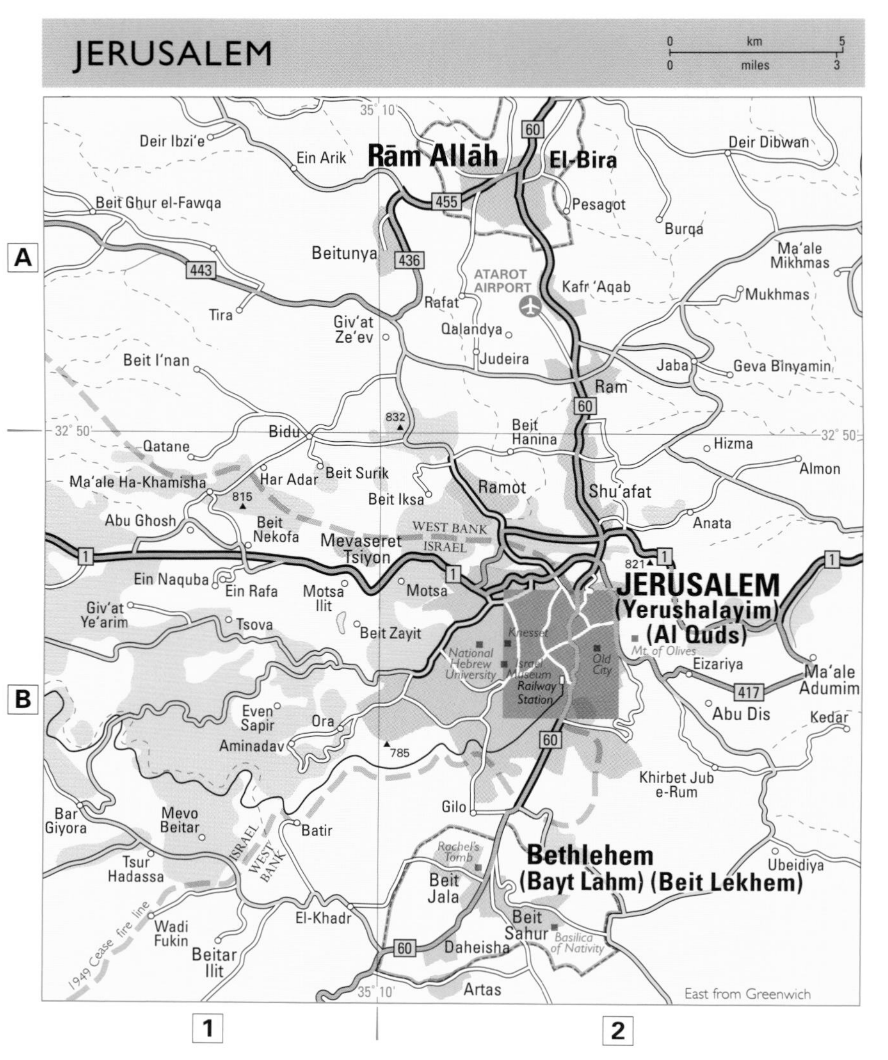

CENTRAL JERUSALEM

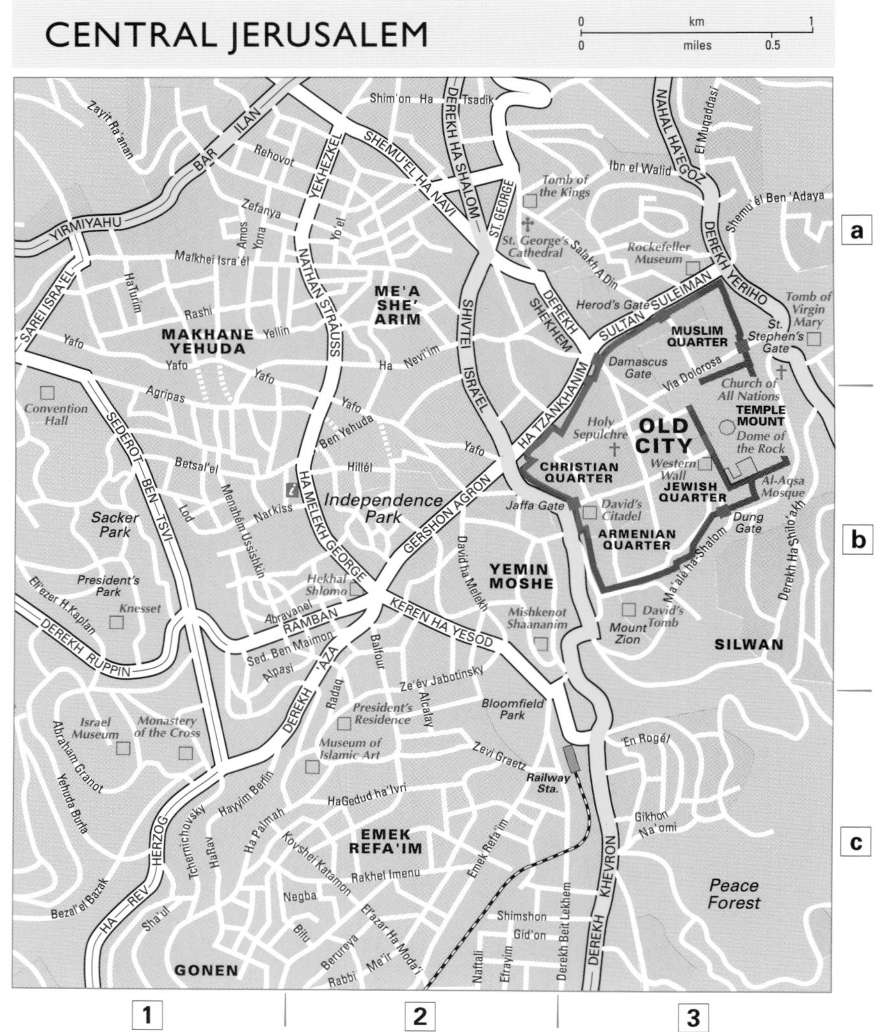

JAKARTA

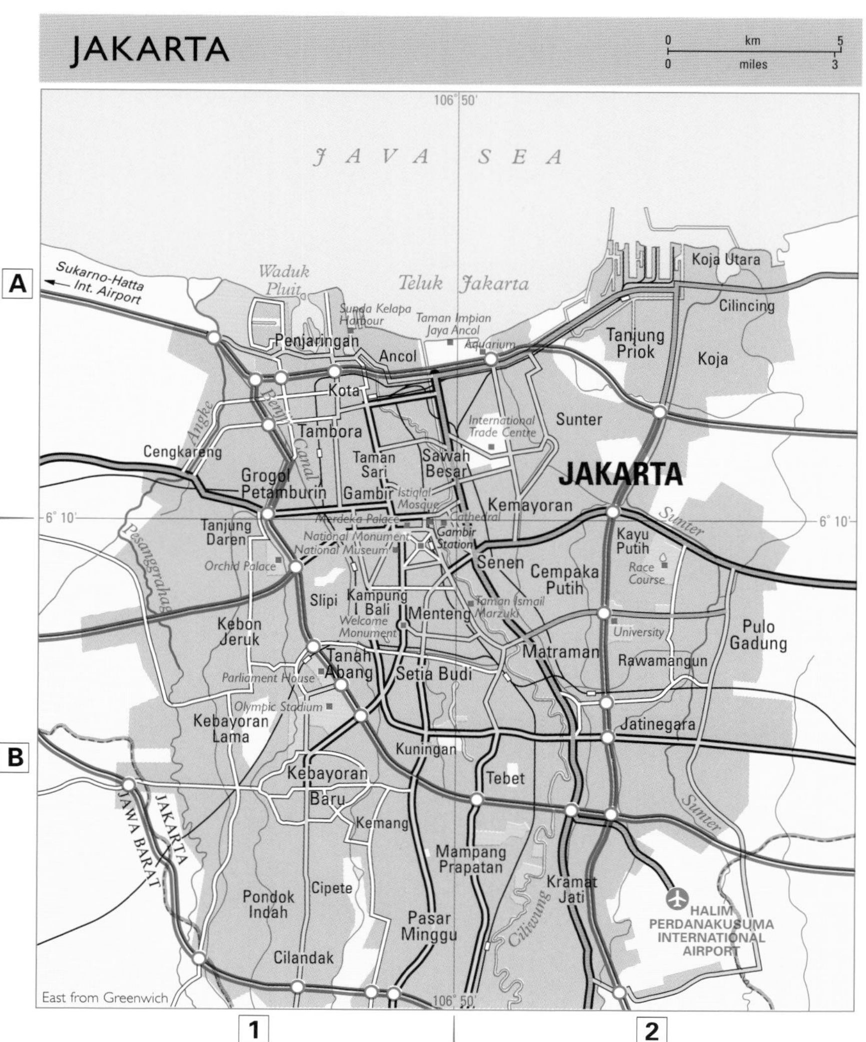

JOHANNESBURG

KARACHI

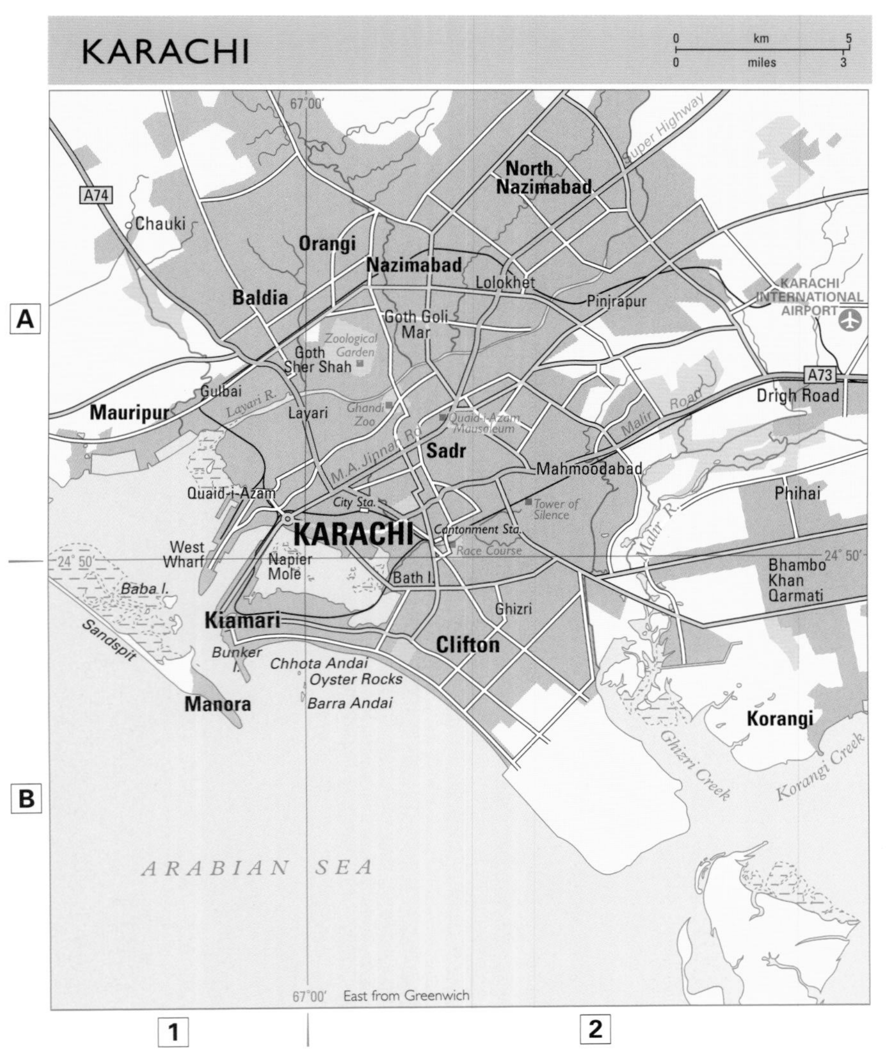

LAGOS

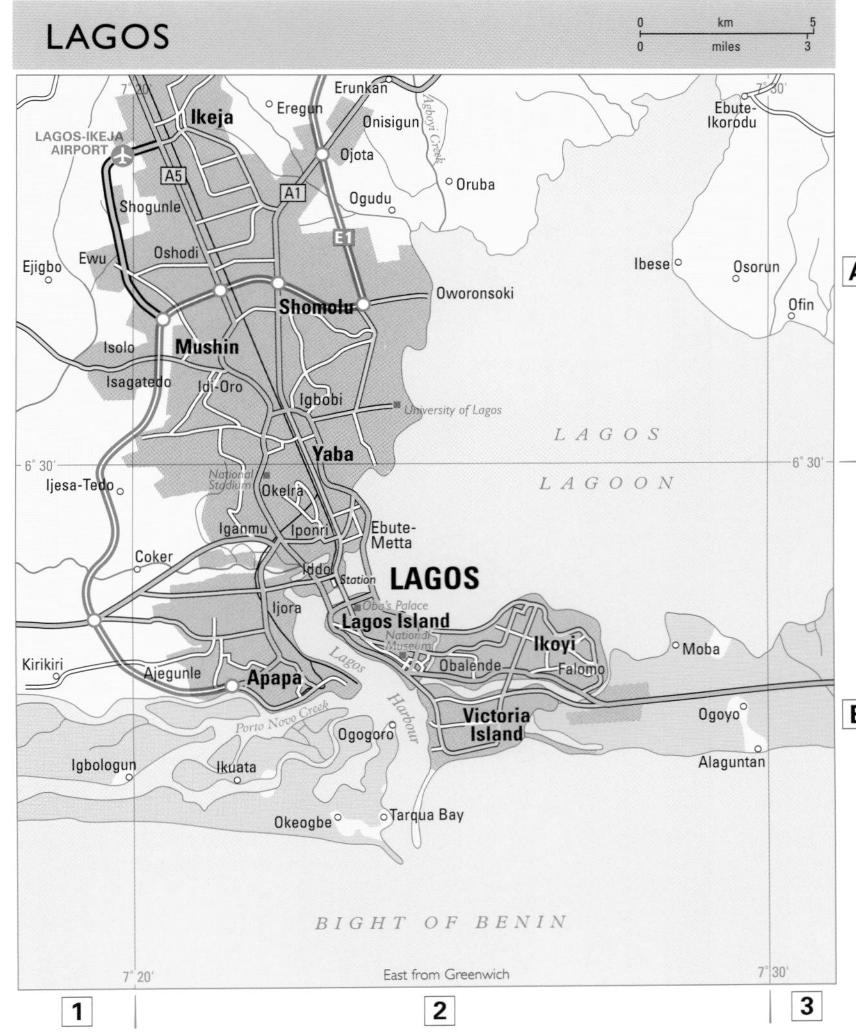

LISBON

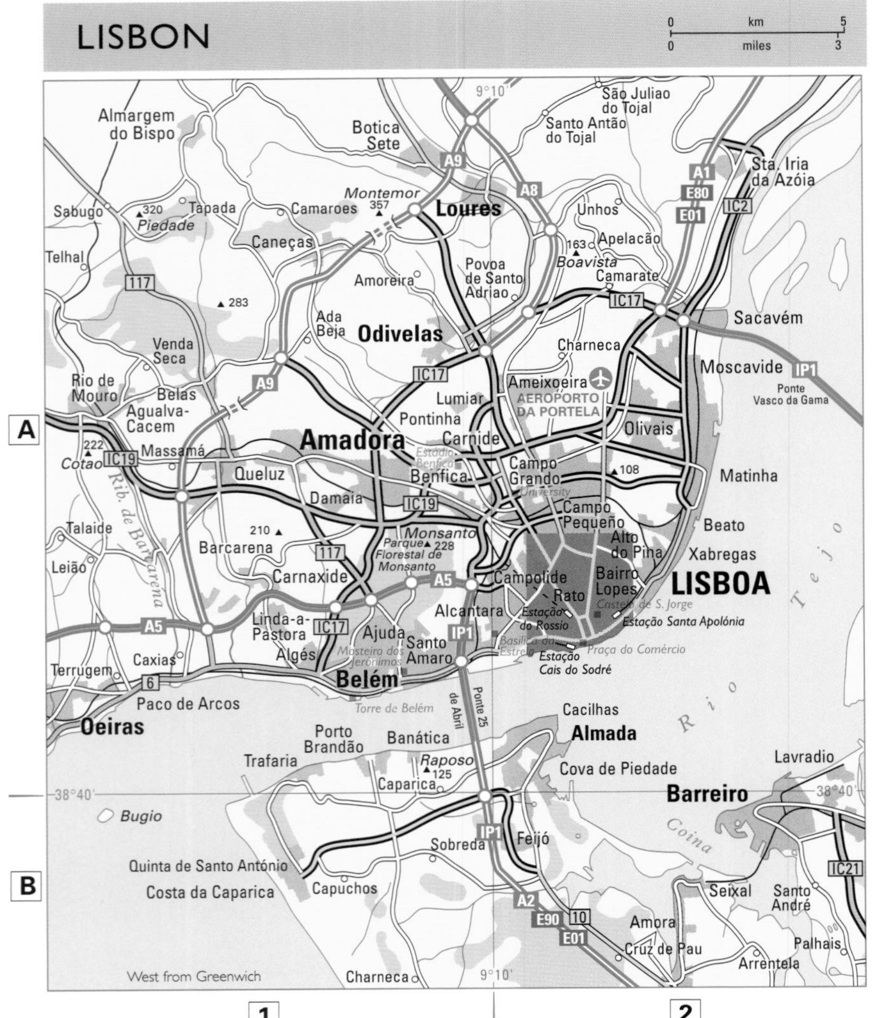

CENTRAL LISBON

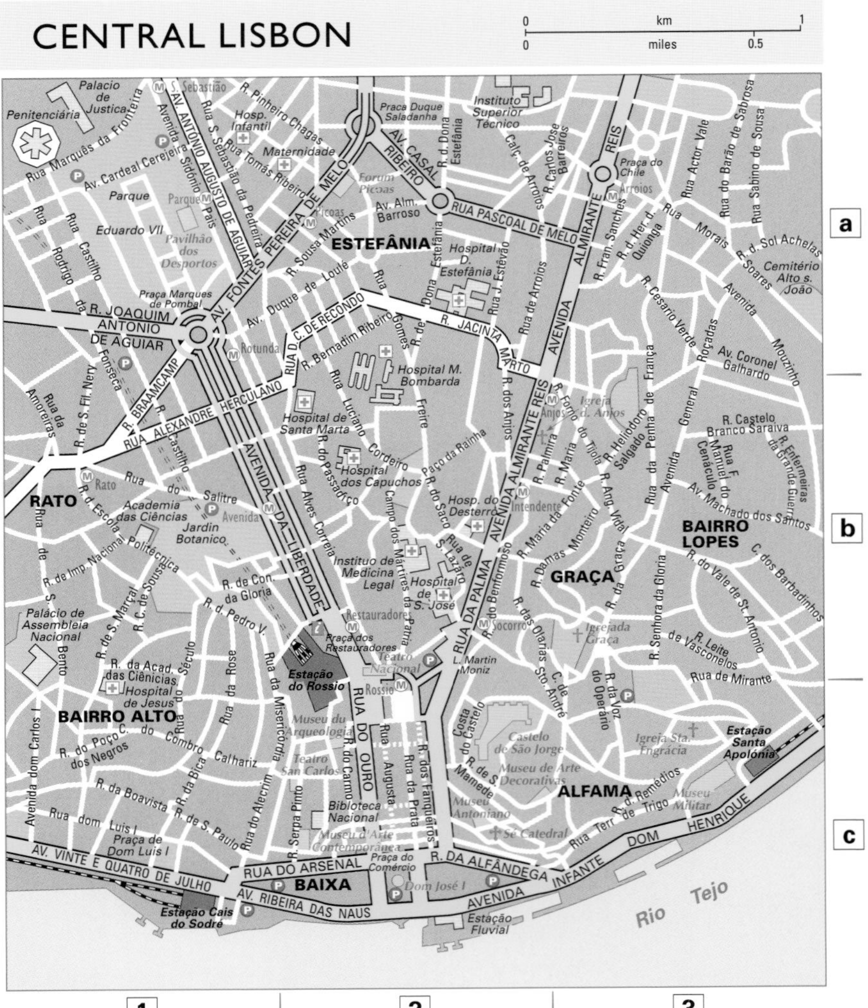

LONDON

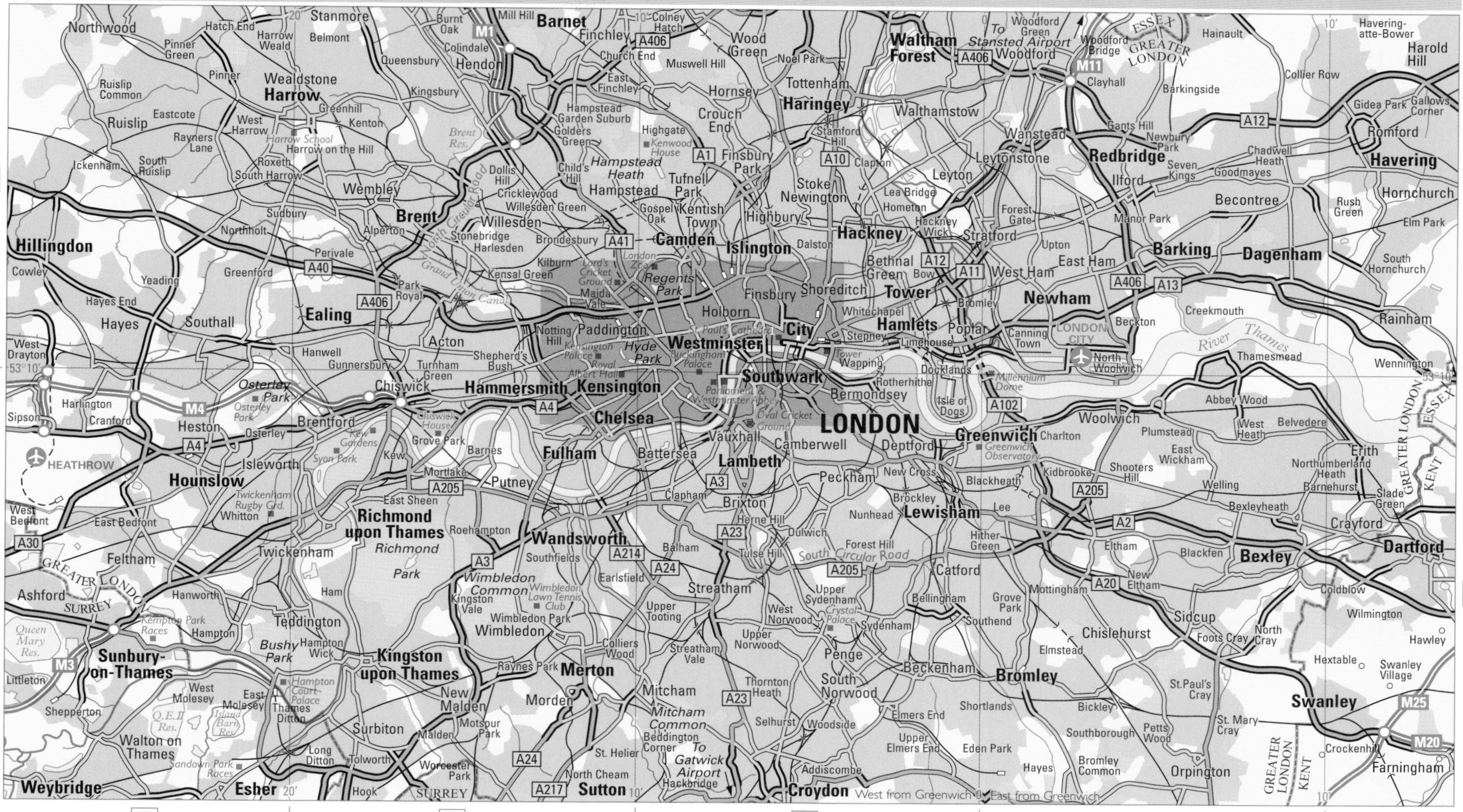

0 km 5
0 miles 3

West from Greenwich | East from Greenwich

CENTRAL LONDON

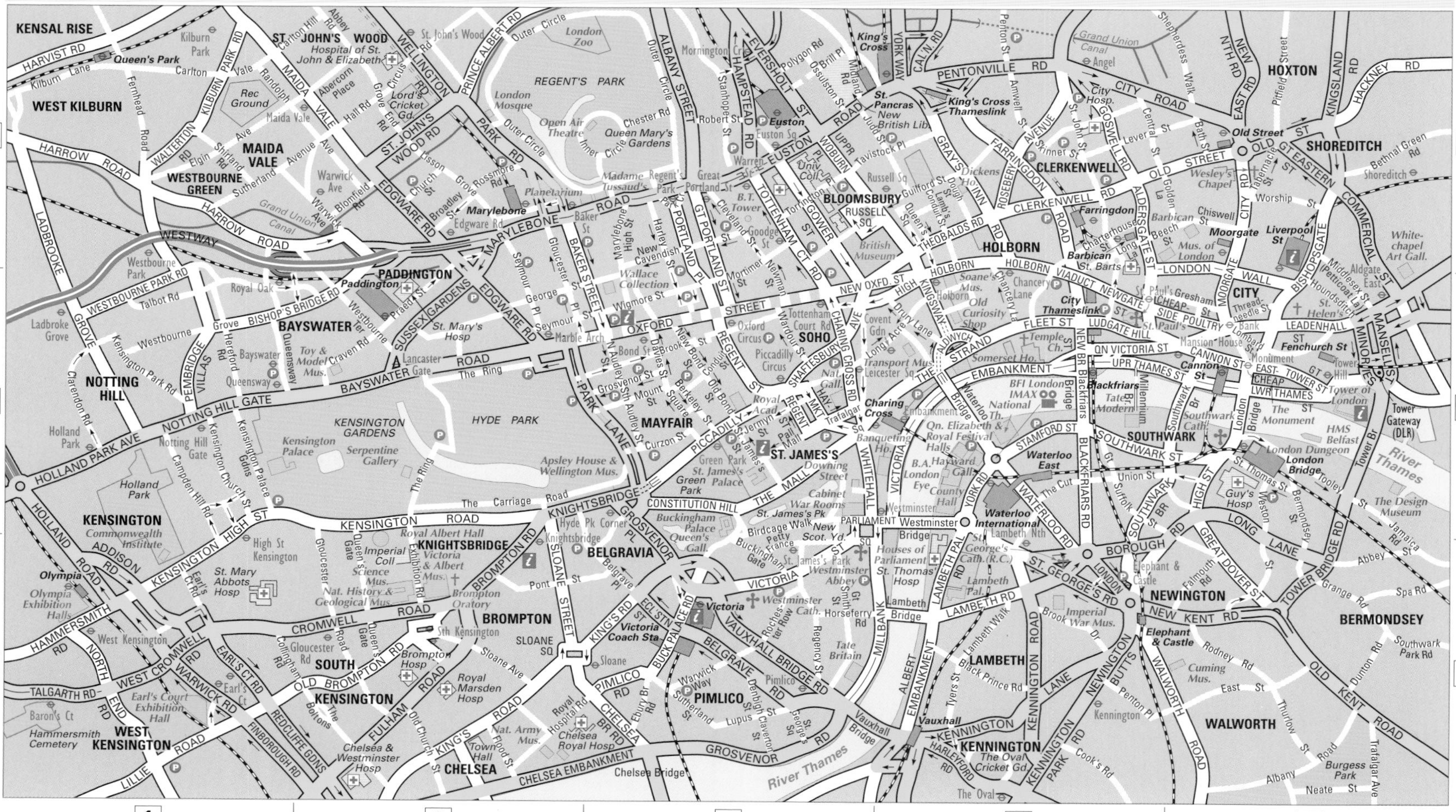

0 km 2
0 miles 1

LOS ANGELES

0 km 5
0 miles 3

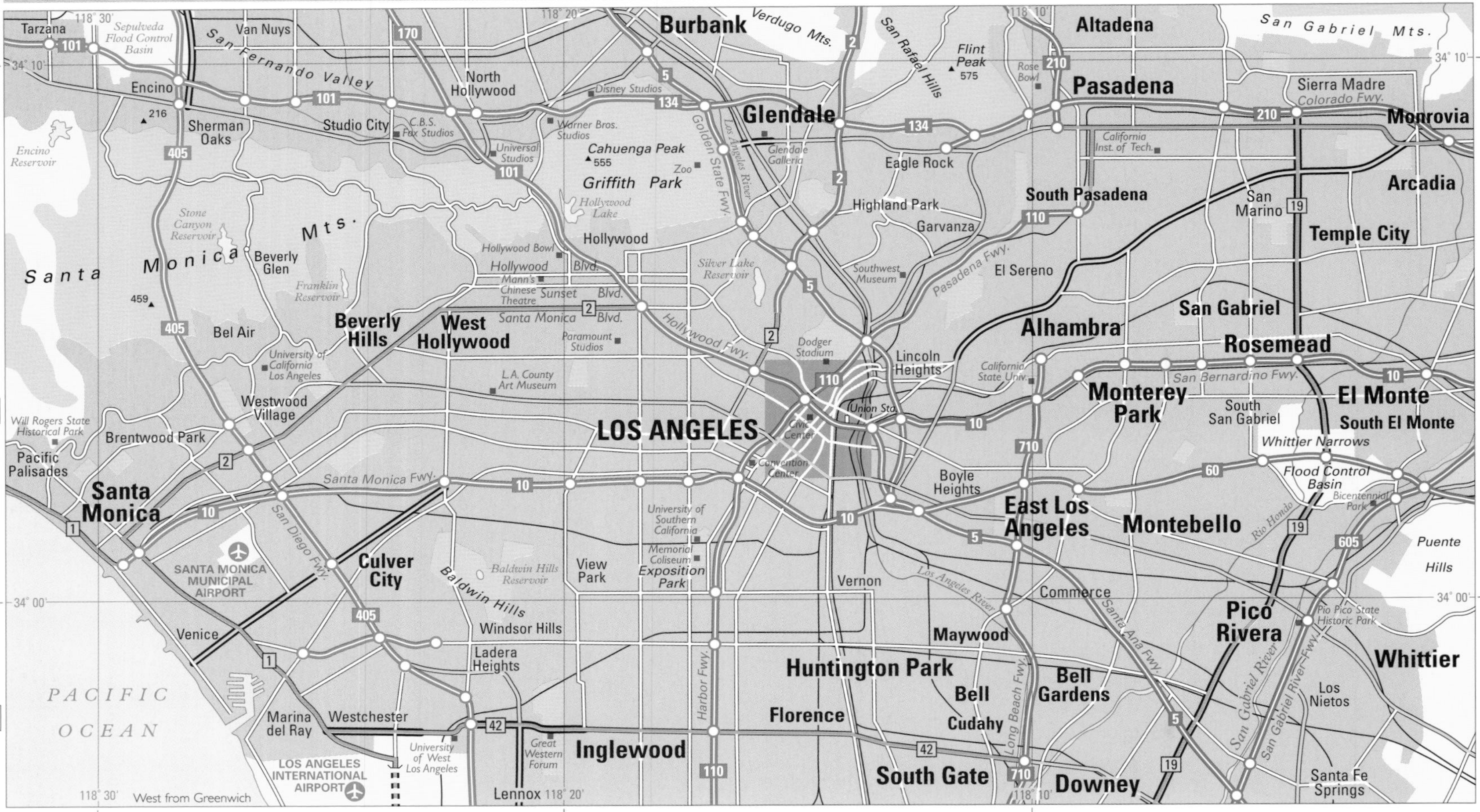

A B C
1 2 3 4

118° 30' 118° 20' 118° 10' 34° 10' 34° 00'

Tarzana
Sepulveda Flood Control Basin
Van Nuys
San Fernando Valley
Encino
216
Encino Reservoir
Sherman Oaks
Studio City
C.B.S. Fox Studios
North Hollywood
Disney Studios
Universal Studios
Warner Bros. Studios
Burbank
Verdugo Mts.
San Rafael Hills
Flint Peak 575
Rose Bowl
Altadena
San Gabriel Mts.
Pasadena
Sierra Madre
Colorado Fwy.
Monrovia
Glendale
Glendale Galleria
Golden State Fwy.
Los Angeles River
Cahuenga Peak 555
Zoo
Griffith Park
Hollywood Lake
Eagle Rock
California Inst. of Tech.
Arcadia
South Pasadena
San Marino
Temple City
Highland Park
Garvanza
Stone Canyon Reservoir
Santa Monica Mts.
Beverly Glen
Franklin Reservoir
459
Hollywood Bowl
Hollywood
Hollywood Blvd.
Mann's Chinese Theatre
Sunset Blvd.
Santa Monica Blvd.
Silver Lake Reservoir
Southwest Museum
Pasadena Fwy.
El Sereno
Bel Air
Beverly Hills
West Hollywood
Paramount Studios
Hollywood Fwy.
Dodger Stadium
Lincoln Heights
Alhambra
San Gabriel
Rosemead
University of California Los Angeles
L.A. County Art Museum
California State Univ.
San Bernardino Fwy.
Westwood Village
Will Rogers State Historical Park
Brentwood Park
Pacific Palisades
LOS ANGELES
Civic Center
Union Sta.
Convention Center
Monterey Park
South San Gabriel
El Monte
South El Monte
Whittier Narrows
Boyle Heights
Flood Control Basin
Bicentennial Park
Santa Monica
Santa Monica Fwy.
San Diego Fwy.
University of Southern California
Memorial Coliseum
Exposition Park
East Los Angeles
Montebello
Rio Hondo
Puente Hills
SANTA MONICA MUNICIPAL AIRPORT
Culver City
Baldwin Hills Reservoir
Baldwin Hills
View Park
Vernon
Los Angeles River
Commerce
Santa Ana Fwy.
Pico Rivera
Pio Pico State Historic Park
Venice
Windsor Hills
Ladera Heights
Maywood
Huntington Park
Bell
Bell Gardens
Whittier
San Gabriel River
San Gabriel River Fwy.
Los Nietos
PACIFIC OCEAN
Marina del Ray
Westchester
Harbor Fwy.
Florence
Cudahy
Long Beach Fwy.
University of West Los Angeles
Great Western Forum
Inglewood
LOS ANGELES INTERNATIONAL AIRPORT
Lennox
South Gate
Downey
Santa Fe Springs
West from Greenwich

LIMA

0 km 5
0 miles 3

A B C
1 2 3

77° 10' 77° 12' 12° 10'

Bocanegra
Los Olivos
Independencia
Huascar
Avenida Panamericana Norte
LIMA
CALLAO
Chavarria
San Juan de Lurigancho
755
Cerro San Jeronimo
Cerro La Milla 242
Cerro Observatorio 465
AEROPUERTO INTERNACIONAL JORGE CHAVEZ
San Martin de Porras
Rimac
Rimac
Carmen de La Legua
Estación Desamparados
Palacio de Gobierno
El Congreso
El Agustino
Cerro El Agustino 482
LIMA
Terminal Maritimo
Callao
Fuerte Real Felipe
La Punta
Bellavista
Breña
La Victoria
Campo de Marte
Museo de Arte
Estadio Nacional
Parque de las Leyendas
Univ. Catolica
Jesús Maria
Parque de la Reserva
La Perla
Museo Nacional
San Luis
Museo de la Nación
San Miguel
Pueblo Libre
Magdalena
Lince
Hipodromo de Monterrico
Paseo de la República
San Isidro
San Borja
Avenida Panamericana Sur
Isla Frontón
Huaca Juliana
Surquillo
Miraflores
Vista Alegre
PACIFIC OCEAN
Santiago de Surco
Barranco
La Campiña
Cerro Morro Solar 273
Chorrillos
Punta La Chira
La Encantada
West from Greenwich

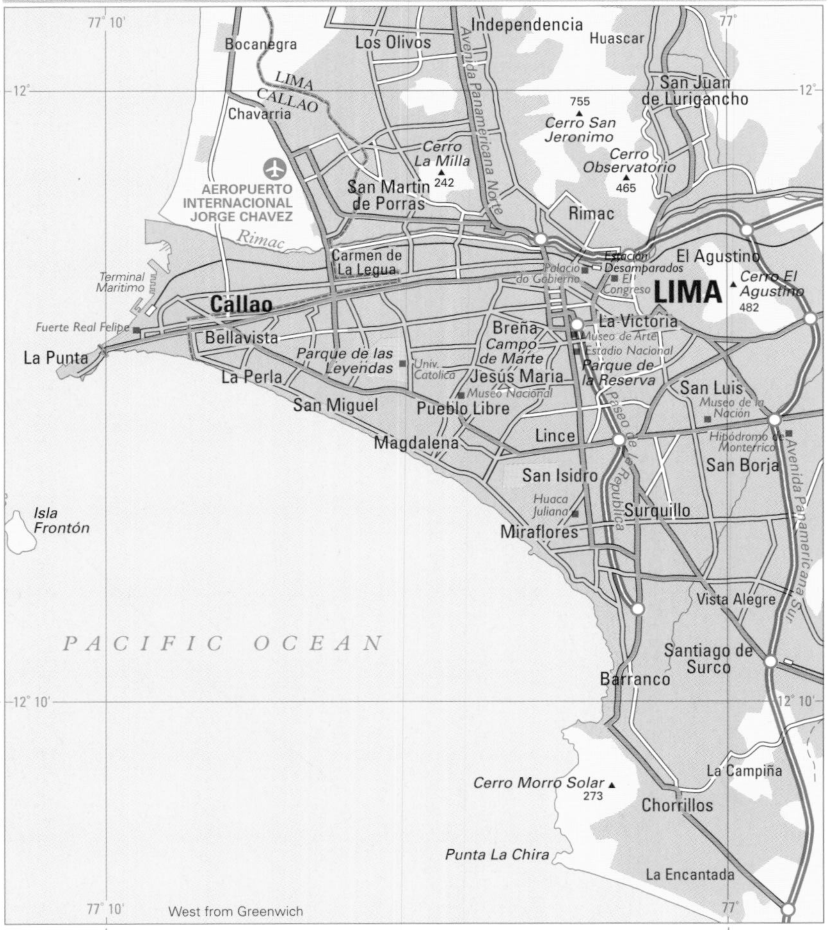

CENTRAL LOS ANGELES

0 km 1
0 miles 0.5

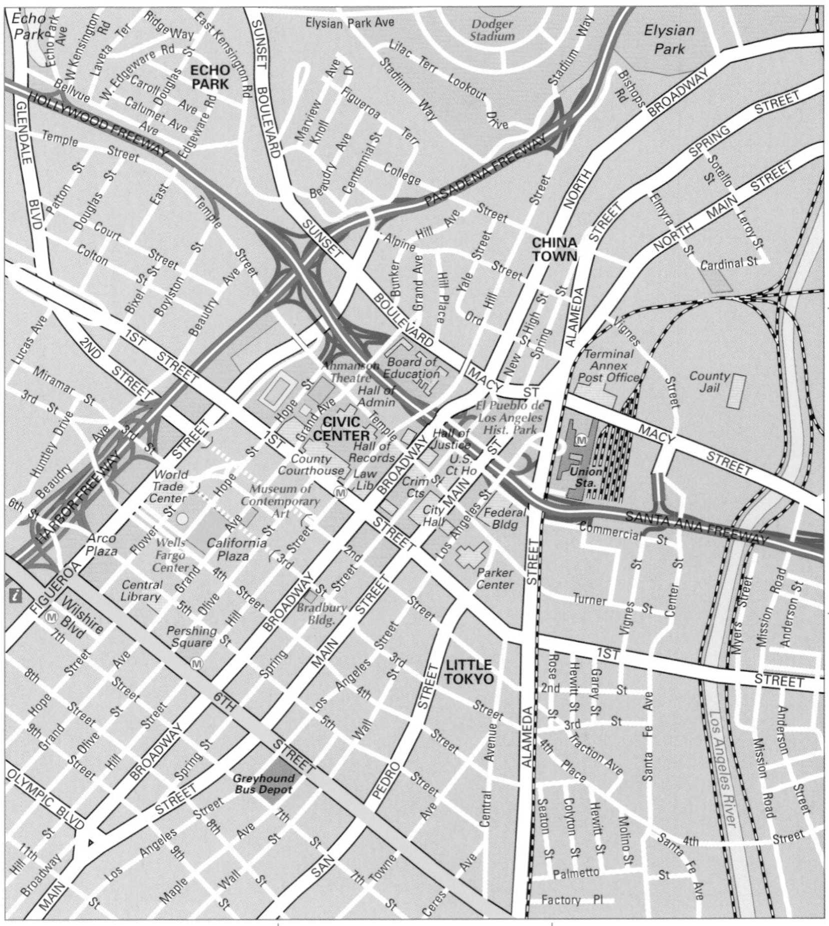

a b c
1 2 3

Echo Park
Elysian Park Ave
Dodger Stadium
Elysian Park
ECHO PARK
SUNSET BOULEVARD
Stadium Way
Lookout Drive
Bishops Rd
BROADWAY
GLENDALE BLVD
HOLLYWOOD FREEWAY
PASADENA FREEWAY
Temple Street
College
CHINA TOWN
NORTH SPRING STREET
NORTH MAIN STREET
ALAMEDA STREET
Cardinal St
SUNSET BOULEVARD
Bunker Hill
Terminal Annex Post Office
County Jail
2ND STREET
1ST STREET
Ahmanson Theatre
Board of Education
Hall of Admin
CIVIC CENTER
El Pueblo de Los Angeles Hist. Park
Hall of Records
Hall of Justice
County Courthouse
Law Lib
Crim Cts
U.S. Ct Ho
MACY STREET
Union Sta.
World Trade Center
Museum of Contemporary Art
City Hall
Federal Bldg
SANTA ANA FREEWAY
HARBOR FREEWAY
Arco Plaza
Wells Fargo Center
California Plaza
Parker Center
Commercial St
Central Library
FIGUEROA
Wilshire Blvd
Pershing Square
Bradbury Bldg.
Turner
1ST STREET
LITTLE TOKYO
ALAMEDA
Los Angeles River
BROADWAY
MAIN STREET
SAN PEDRO STREET
Greyhound Bus Depot
OLYMPIC BLVD
Traction Ave
Santa Fe Ave
Mission Road
Factory Pl
Palmetto

MADRID

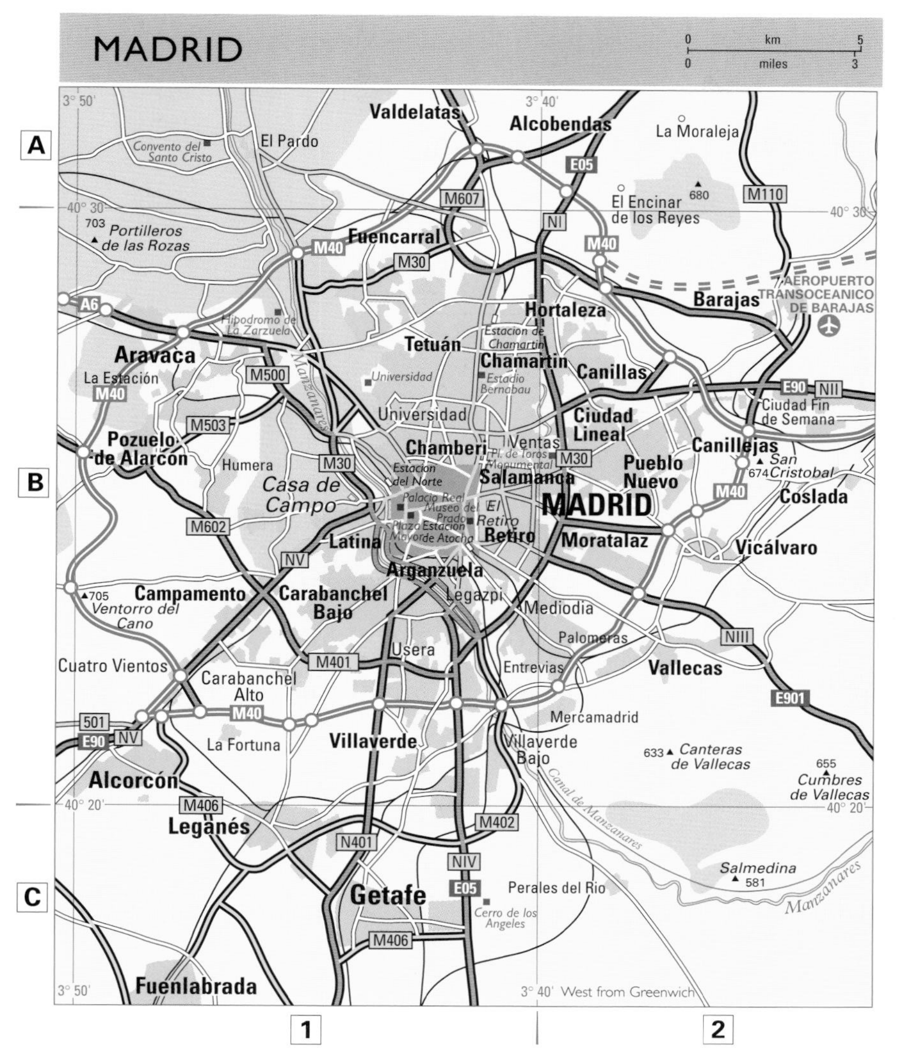

CENTRAL MADRID

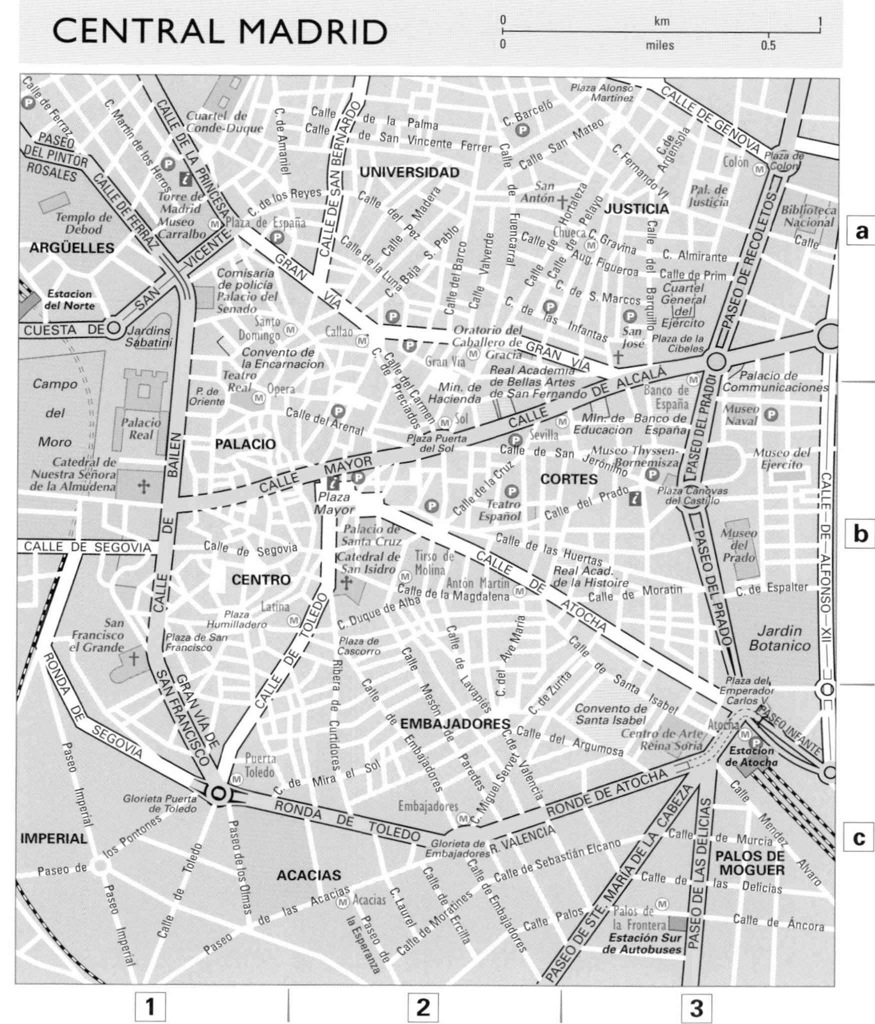

MANILA

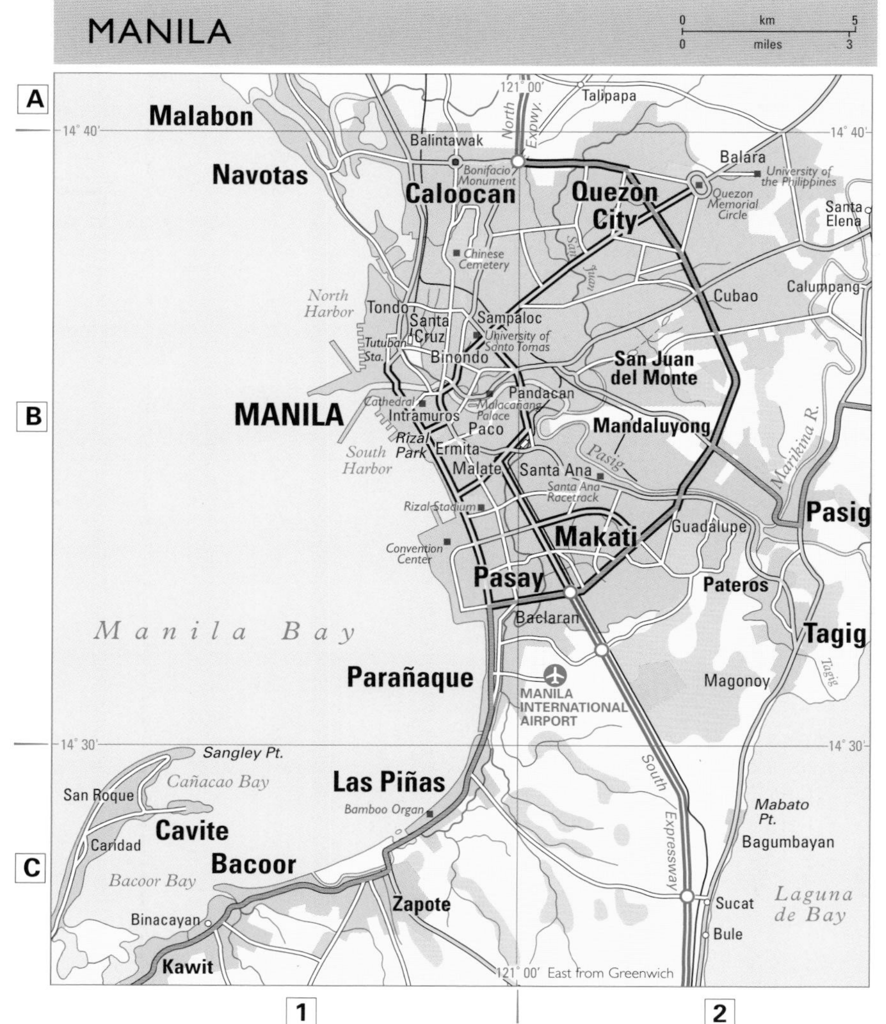

MELBOURNE

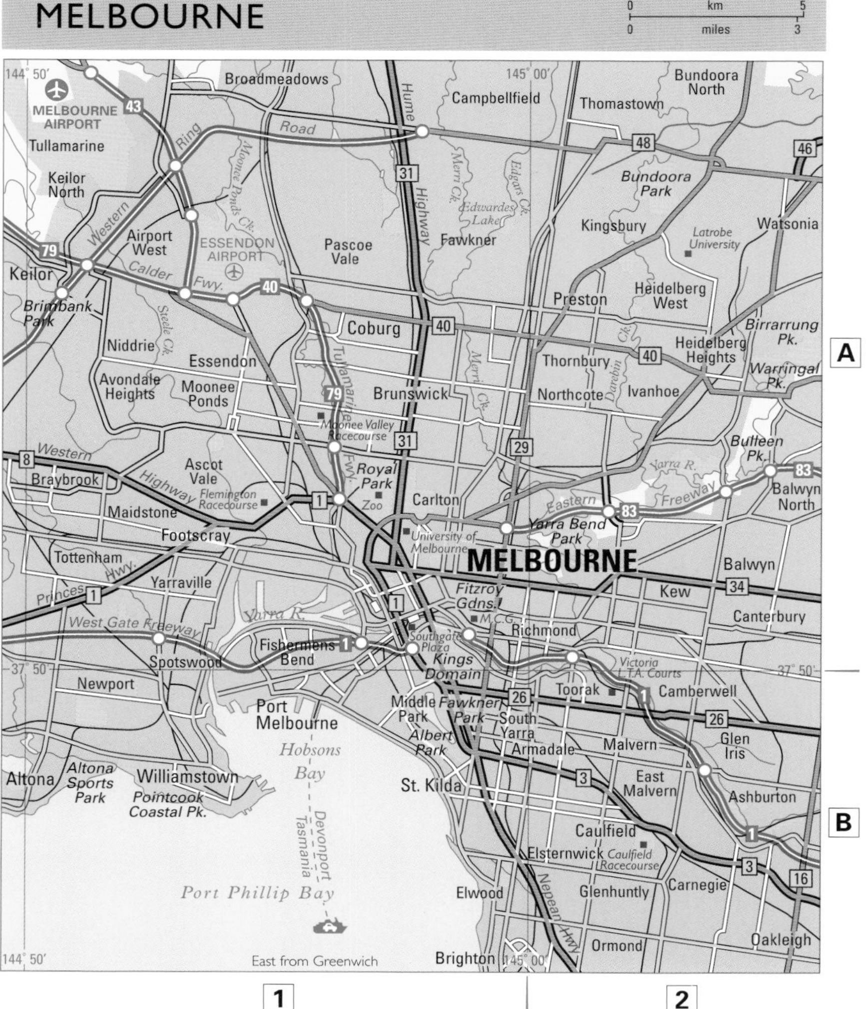

MEXICO CITY

0 km 5
0 miles 3

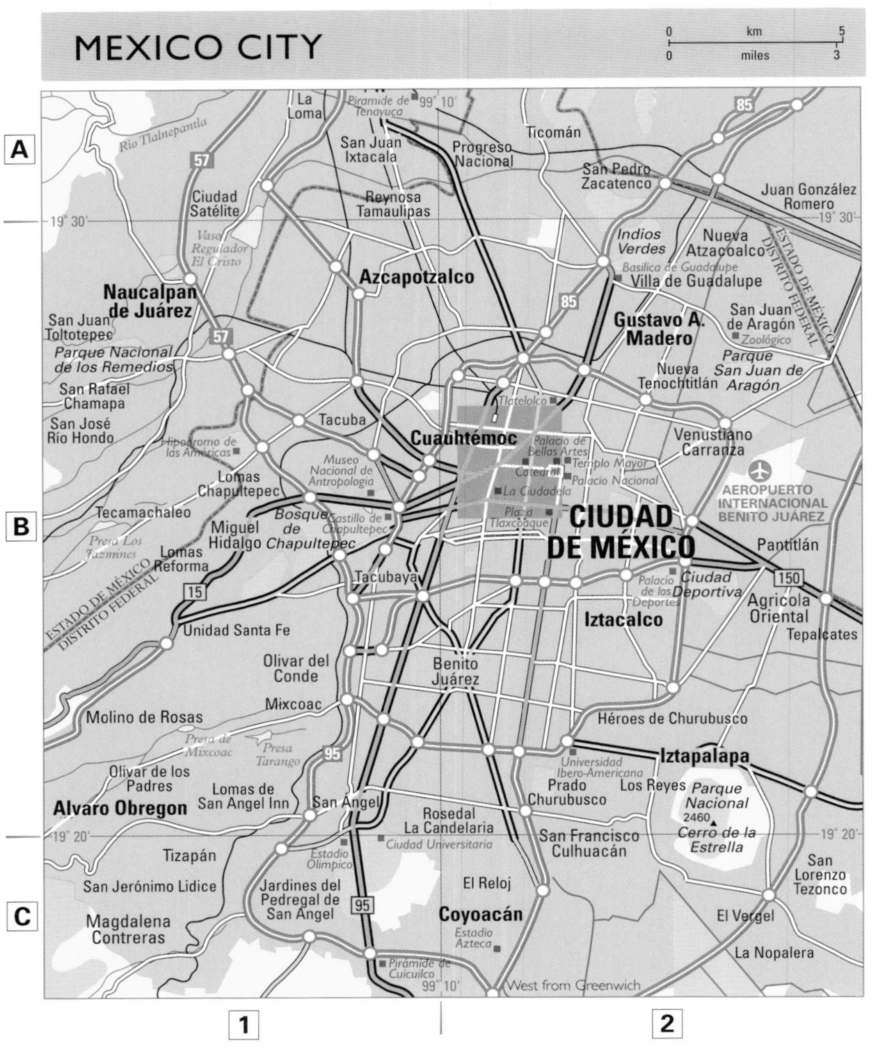

CENTRAL MEXICO CITY

0 km 1
0 miles 0.5

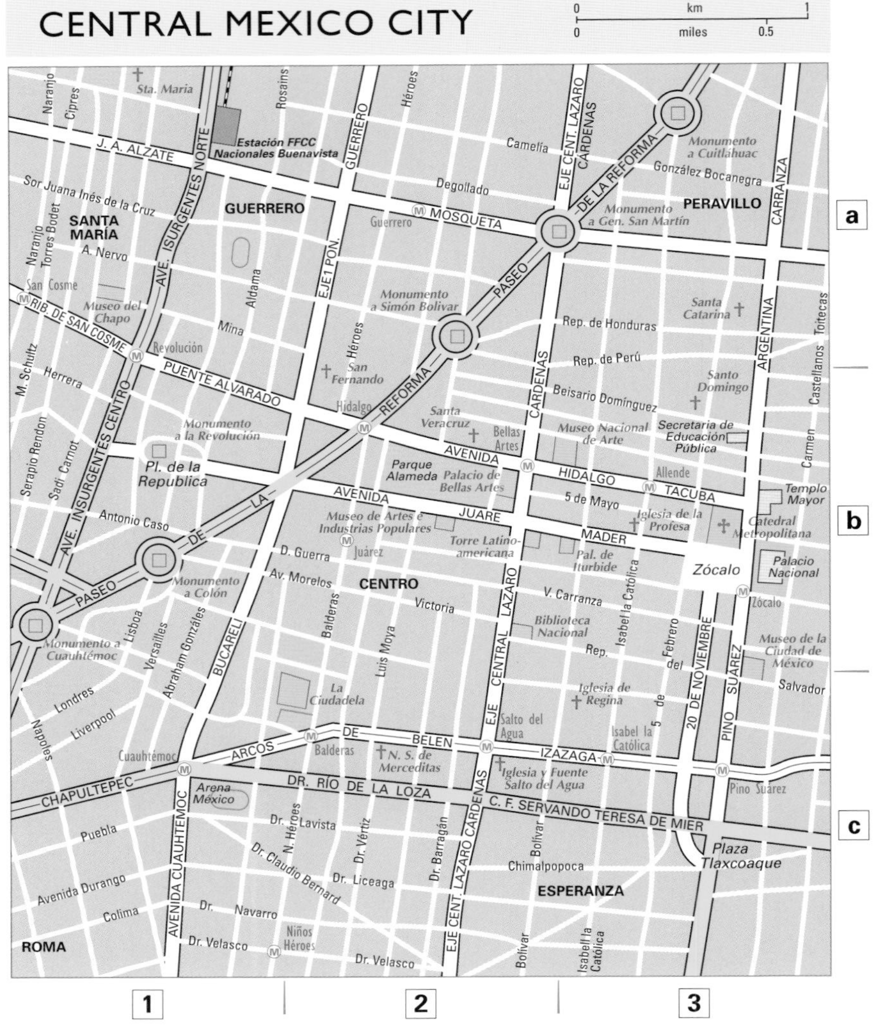

MIAMI

0 km 5
0 miles 3

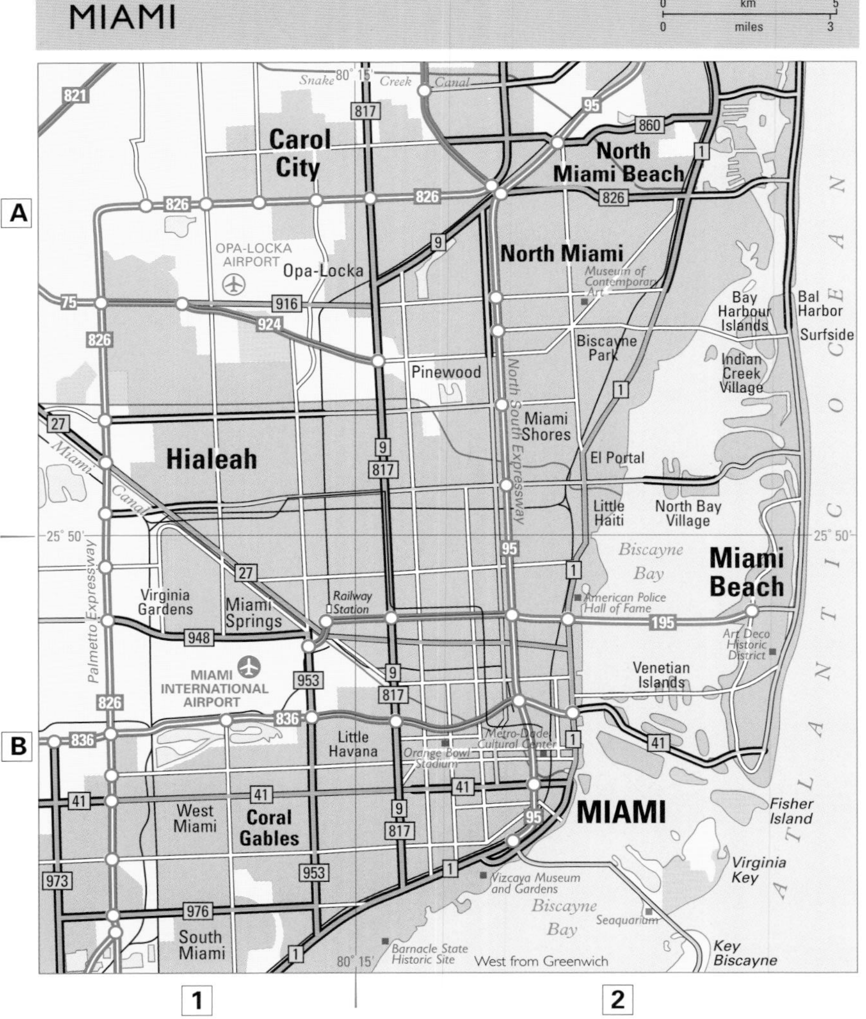

MILAN

0 km 5
0 miles 3

MOSCOW

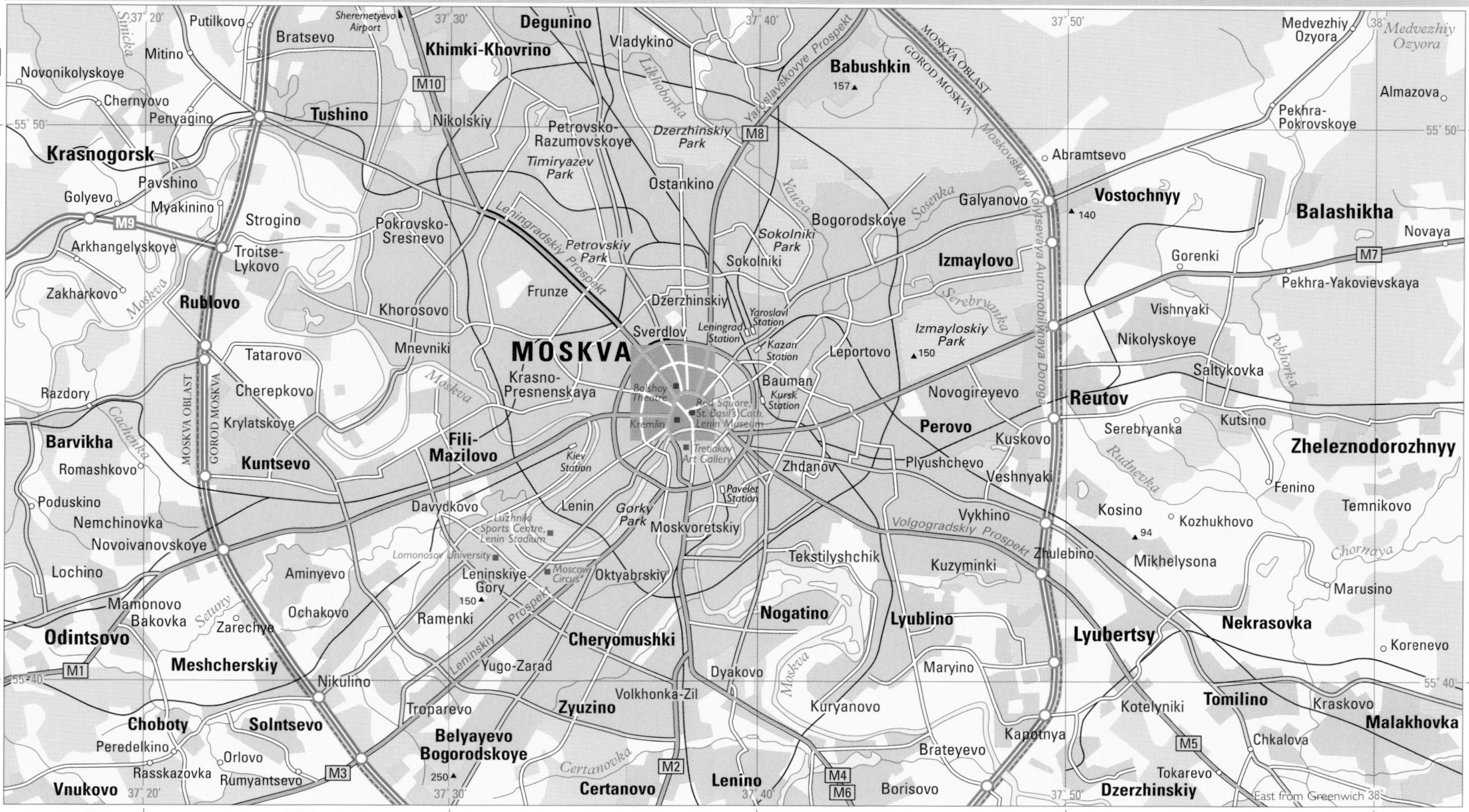

MONTRÉAL

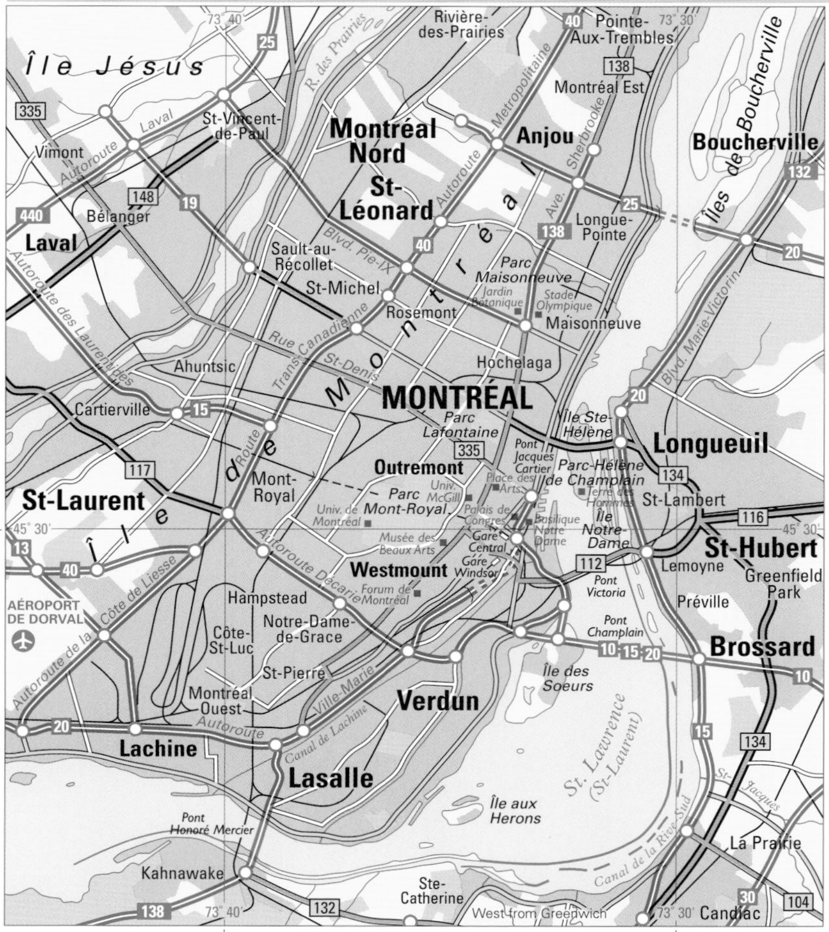

CENTRAL MOSCOW

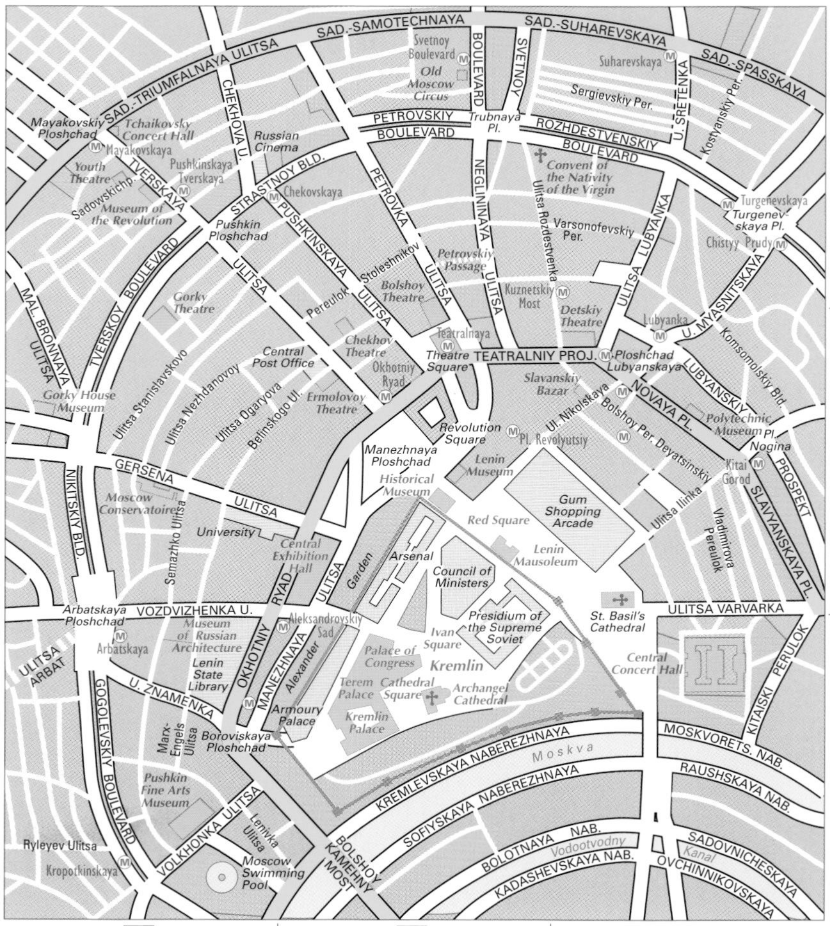

MUMBAI

0 km 5
0 miles 3

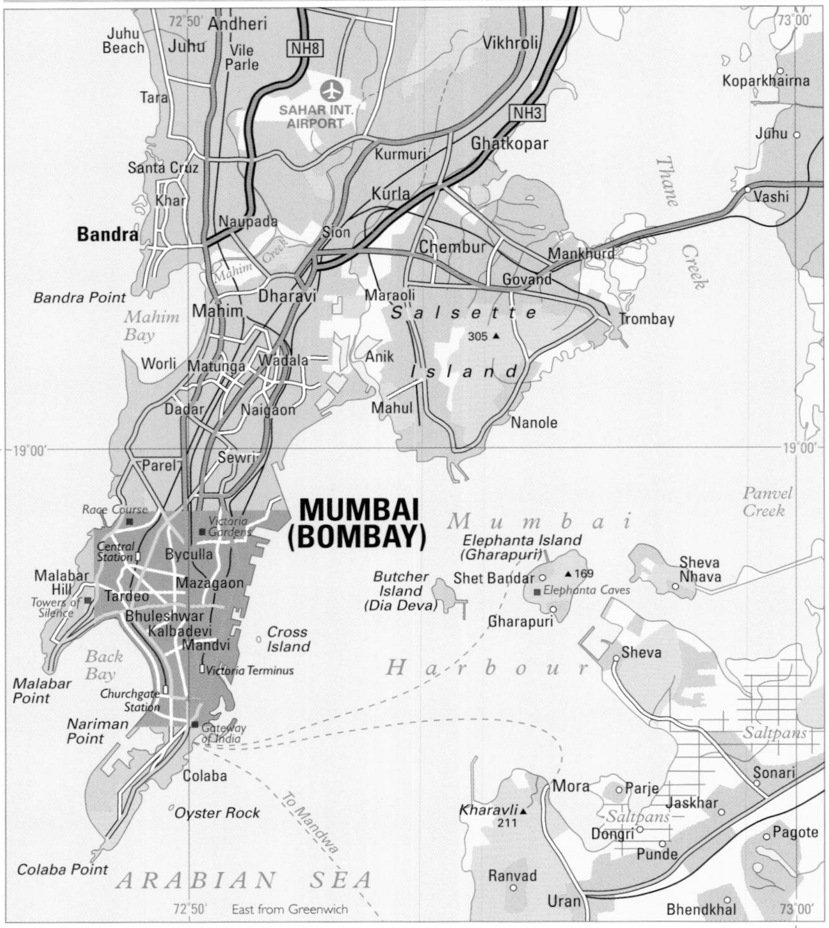

Juhu Beach
Juhu
Andheri
Vile Parle
NH8
Vikhroli
SAHAR INT. AIRPORT
Koparkhairna
Tara
NH3
Ghatkopar
Kurmuri
Juhu
Santa Cruz
Khar
Thane Creek
Kurla
Vashi
Bandra
Naupada
Sion
Chembur
Mankhurd
Mahim Creek
Govand
Bandra Point
Mahim Bay
Mahim
Dharavi
Maraoli
Salsette Island
Trombay
305
Worli
Matunga
Wadala
Anik
Dadar
Naigaon
Mahul
Nanole
19°00'
Parel
Sewri
Race Course
Victoria Gardens
MUMBAI (BOMBAY)
Mumbai Harbour
Panvel Creek
Central Station
Byculla
Elephanta Island (Gharapuri)
Malabar Hill
Mazagaon
Butcher Island (Dia Deva)
Shet Bandar
169
Elephanta Caves
Sheva Nhava
Towers of Silence
Tardeo
Bhuleshwar
Kalbadevi
Gharapuri
Mandvi
Cross Island
Sheva
Back Bay
Victoria Terminus
Malabar Point
Churchgate Station
Saltpans
Nariman Point
Gateway of India
Colaba
Sonari
To Mandwa
Mora
Parje
Oyster Rock
Kharavli 211
Jaskhar
Saltpans
Dongri
Pagote
Punde
Colaba Point
ARABIAN SEA
Ranvad
Uran
Bhendkhal
72°50'
73°00'
East from Greenwich

A B 1 2

CENTRAL MUMBAI

0 km 2
0 miles 1

Haji Ali Tomb
Causeway
Mahalaxmi Race Course
MAHALAXMI
Jijamata Udyan (Victoria Gardens)
BYCULLA
Sant Savta Mg
R. C. Cathedral
Mahalaxmi Temple
Willingdon Sports Club
BREACH CANDY
Boatyard Rd
CUMBALLA HILL
Mumbai Central Sta.
State Road Transport Terminus
MAZAGAON
Dockyard Rd
TARDEO
Wadi Bunder Rd
Clerk Basin
Frere Basin
Kamala Nehru Park (Hanging Gardens)
Mani Bhavan (Gandhi Museum)
Raudat Tahera Mosque
UMERKHADI
Malet Shelf
Babulnath Temple
SARDAR VALLABHBHAI PATEL RD
S. V. PATEL RD
MANDVI
BHULESHWAR
Mumbadevi Temple
Chowpatty Beach
KALBADEVI
Jama Masjid Mosque
GIRGAUM
Taraporewala Aquarium
Crawford Mkt.
PYDHUNI
Cross Island
Carnac Basin
St. George's Hospital
Albless & Cama Hospital
Back Bay
Chatrapathi Shivaji (Victoria) Terminus
Indira Docks
Mumbai Harbour
Wankhede Stadium
G.P.O.
Churchgate Sta.
Brabourne Stadium
FORT
Rajabai Twr.
Town Hall
The Mint
Custom Basin
West Basin
University
Jehangir Art Gallery
Prince of Wales Museum
National Gallery of Modern Art
Nariman Point
National Centre for Performing Arts
COLABA
Gateway of India

a b c 1 2 3

MUNICH

0 km 5
0 miles 3

Dachau-Ost
Flughafen München (Franz Josef Strauss)
Dachau
Obermoos Schwaige
471
Oberschleissheim
E45
Fischerhäuser
Lustheim
Hochbrück
Garching
388
Moos
A92
E53
Rothschwaige
Olympia-Ruder-regatta-strecke
Karlsfeld
Dirnismaning
Ismaning
A9
Würm-kanal
A99
E52
Gröbenried
Ludwigsfeld
Neuherberg
Eschenried
Dachauer
Feldmoching
Am Hasenbergl
Speicher See
E52
Gerberau
304
Allach
500
13
Freimann
Gross-Lappen
Mittl. Isarkanal
Fasanerie-Nord
Untermenzing
A8
304n
11
Unterföhring
Langwald
Moosach
Milbertshofen
Aschheim
Lochhausen
Obermenzing
Gern
Oberföhring
Johanneskirchen
Abfanggraben
48°10'
Aubing
Blutenberg
Nymphenburg
Schloss Nymphenburg
Schwabing
2R
Neu Aubing
Neuhausen
Bogenhausen
Dornach
Feldkirchen
Freiham
Pasing
Würm
Zamdorf
Daglfing
Riem
Lochham
Laim
MÜNCHEN
Frauenkirche
Residenz
Haidhausen
Kirchtrudering
A94
Deutsches Museum
Gräfelfing
A96
E54
Sendling
Gronsdorf
Berg am Laim
Gross-Hadern
Ramersdorf
Planegg
Giesing
Strasstrudering
Neuperlach
Martinsried
Thalkirchen
Haar
Waldtrudering
Perlach
Krailling
Forstenried
Solalinden
Neuried
Fasangarten
Öden-Stockach
Maxhof
Solln
Harlaching
Waldperlach
Perlacher Forst
Unterbiberg
553
Isar
Warnberg
Neubiberg
Gross-hesselohe
A995
Unterhaching
Forstenrieder Park
Geiselgasteig
Westerham
Ottobrunn
A99
Hohenbrunn
Pullach
Am Wald
E533
A95
Taufkirchen
Winning
Höllriegelskreuth
Grünwalder Forst
Furth
Bergham
Wächterhof
Buchenhain
Grünwald
Potzham
E52
Kirchstockbach
Forst
Oberhaching
11°30'
11°40'
East from Greenwich

A B 1 2 3

CENTRAL MUNICH

0 km 1
0 miles 0.5

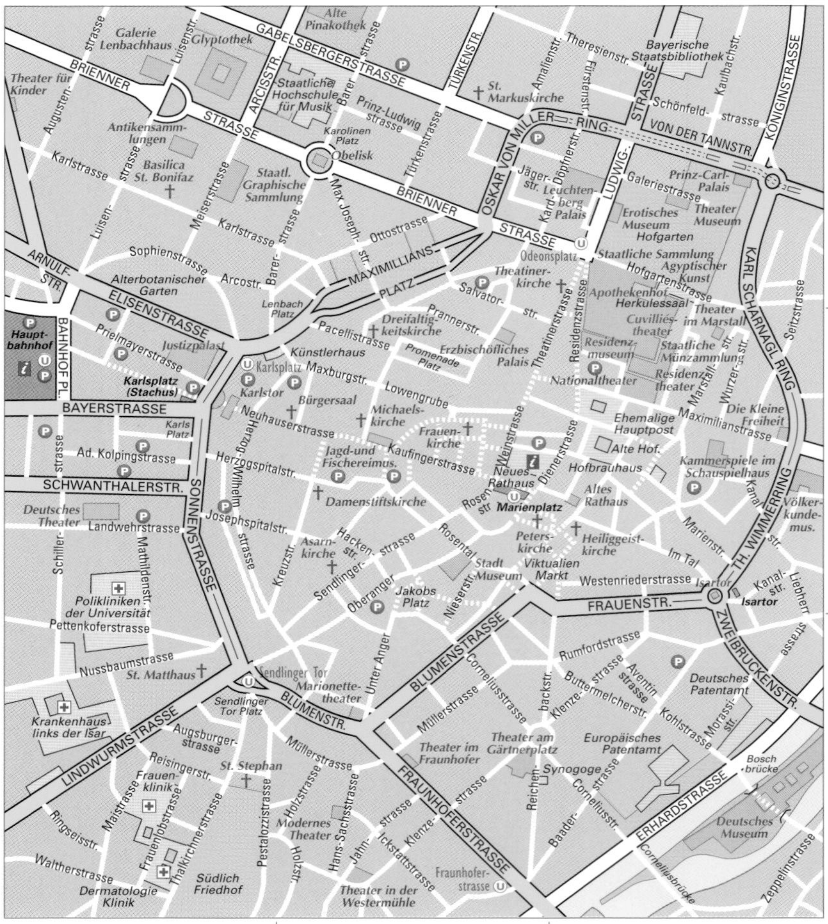

Alte Pinakothek
Galerie Lenbachhaus
Glyptothek
GABELSBERGERSTRASSE
Bayerische Staatsbibliothek
Theater für Kinder
BRIENNER STRASSE
Staatliche Hochschule für Musik
St. Markuskirche
Schönfeldstrasse
Antikensammlungen
Karolinen Platz
Obelisk
Prinz-Ludwig strasse
OSKAR VON MILLER RING
VON DER TANNSTR.
KÖNIGINSTRASSE
Basilica St. Bonifaz
Staatl. Graphische Sammlung
Prinz-Carl-Palais
Leuchtenberg Palais
Erotisches Museum
Theater Museum
Hofgarten
Odeonsplatz
Staatliche Sammlung Ägyptischer Kunst
MAXIMILIANSPLATZ
KARL SCHARNAGL RING
ARNULF STR.
Alterbotanischer Garten
Theatinerkirche
Apothekenhof
Herkulessaal
Theater im Marstall
Hauptbahnhof
ELISENSTRASSE
Lenbach Platz
Dreifaltigkeitskirche
Cuvilliéstheater
Justizpalast
Residenzmuseum
Staatliche Münzsammlung
Künstlerhaus
Erzbischöfliches Palais
Promenade Platz
Residenztheater
Karlsplatz (Stachus)
Nationaltheater
Die Kleine Freiheit
BAYERSTRASSE
Bürgersaal
Michaelskirche
Ehemalige Hauptpost
Maximilianstrasse
Frauenkirche
Alte Hof
Ad. Kolpingstrasse
Jagd-und Fischereimus.
Kaufingerstrasse
Neues Rathaus
Hofbräuhaus
Kammerspiele im Schauspielhaus
SCHWANTHALERSTR.
Damenstiftskirche
Marienplatz
Altes Rathaus
Völkerkundemus.
Deutsches Theater
Landwehrstrasse
Peterskirche
Heiliggeistkirche
Asamkirche
Stadt Museum
Viktualien Markt
Westenriederstrasse
Polikliniken der Universität
Jakobs Platz
FRAUENSTR.
Isartor
TH. WIMMER RING
Pettenkoferstrasse
SONNENSTRASSE
BLUMENSTRASSE
Nussbaumstrasse
St. Matthaus
Sendlinger Tor
Marionettentheater
Deutsches Patentamt
Sendlinger Tor Platz
ZWEIBRÜCKENSTR.
Krankenhaus links der Isar
LINDWURMSTRASSE
Müllerstrasse
Theater im Fraunhofer
Theater am Gärtnerplatz
Europäisches Patentamt
Frauenklinik
St. Stephan
Synogoge
Bosch brücke
ERHARDTSTRASSE
Modernes Theater
FRAUNHOFERSTRASSE
Deutsches Museum
Dermatologie Klinik
Südlich Friedhof
Theater in der Westermühle

a b c 1 2 3

NEW YORK

0 km 5
0 miles 3

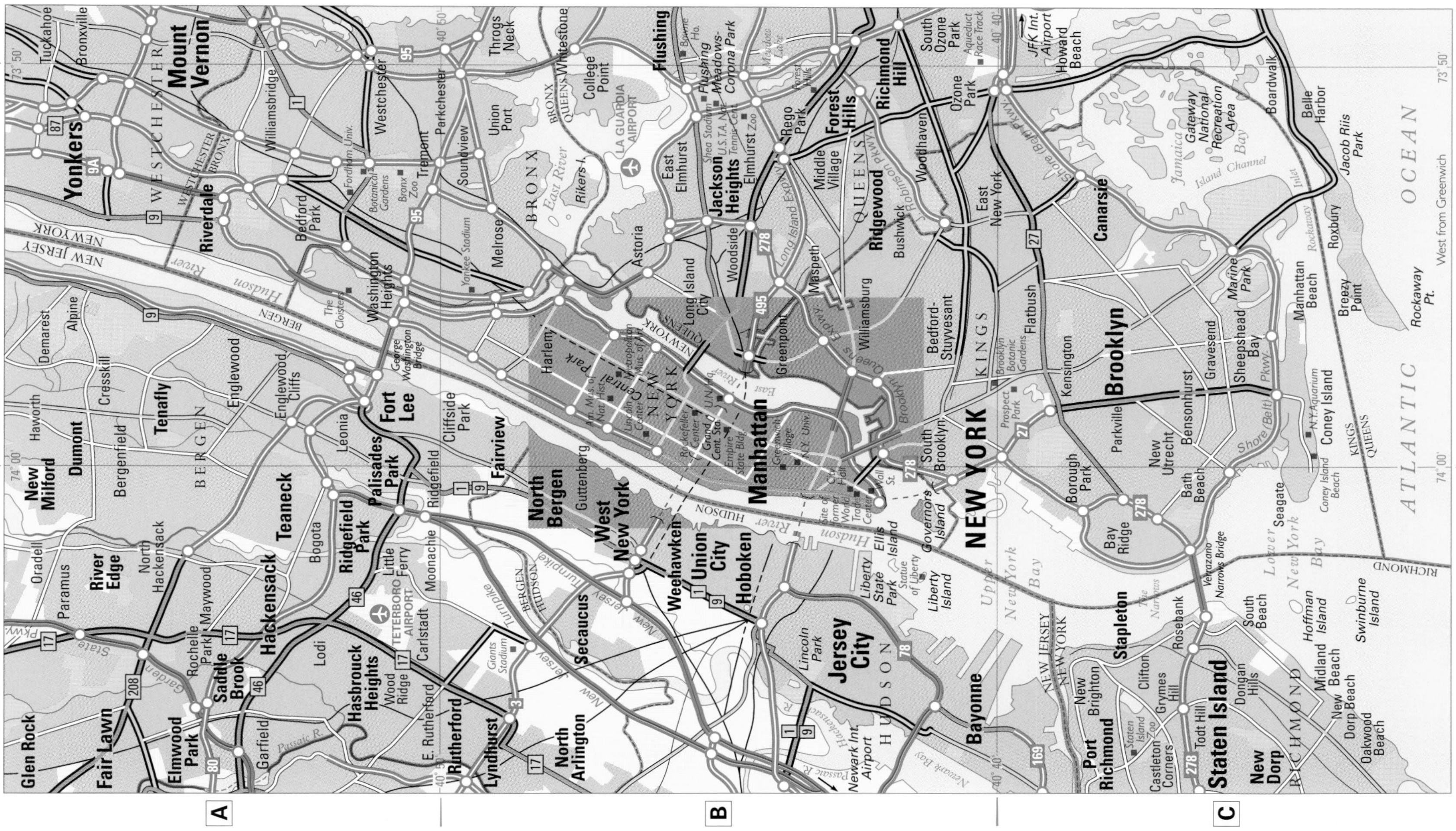

3 2 1

A B C

CENTRAL NEW YORK

0 km 2
0 miles 1

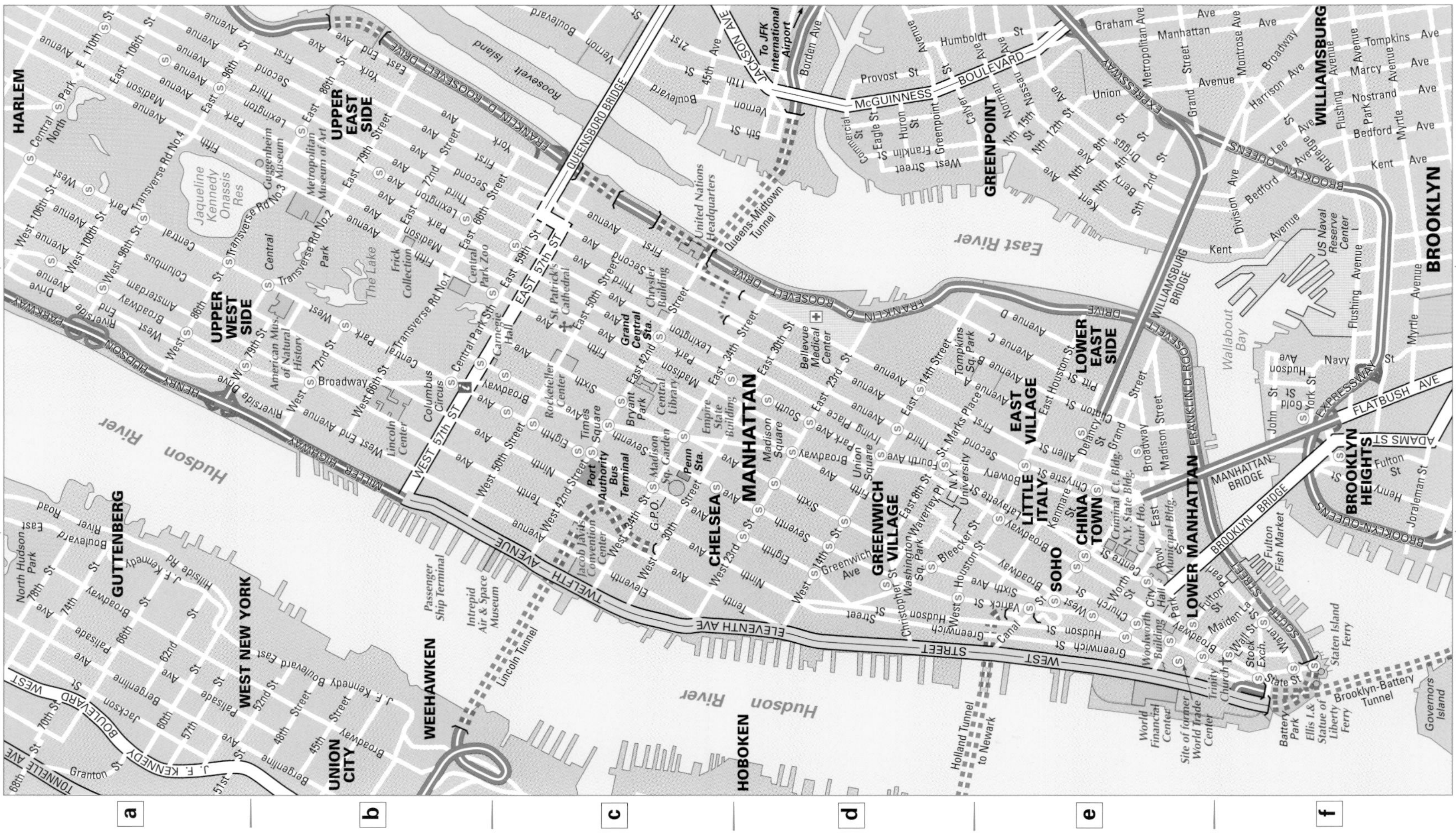

3 2 1

a b c d e f

OSAKA

0 km 5
0 miles 3

East from Greenwich

A B
1 2 3 4

OSLO

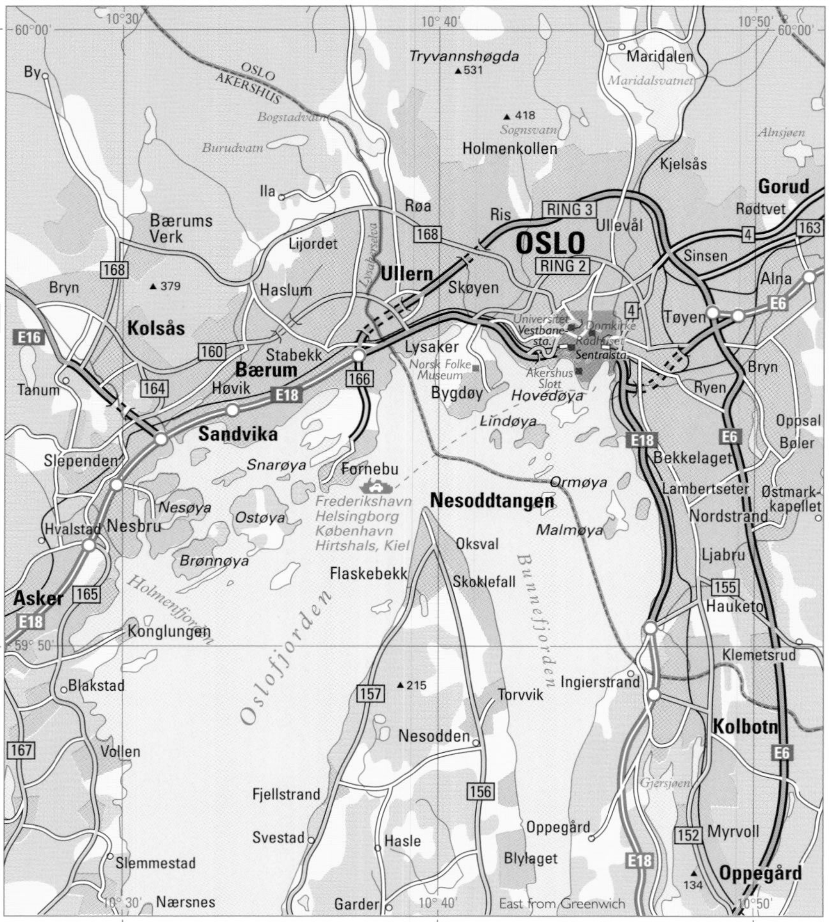

0 km 5
0 miles 3

East from Greenwich

A B
1 2 3 4

CENTRAL OSLO

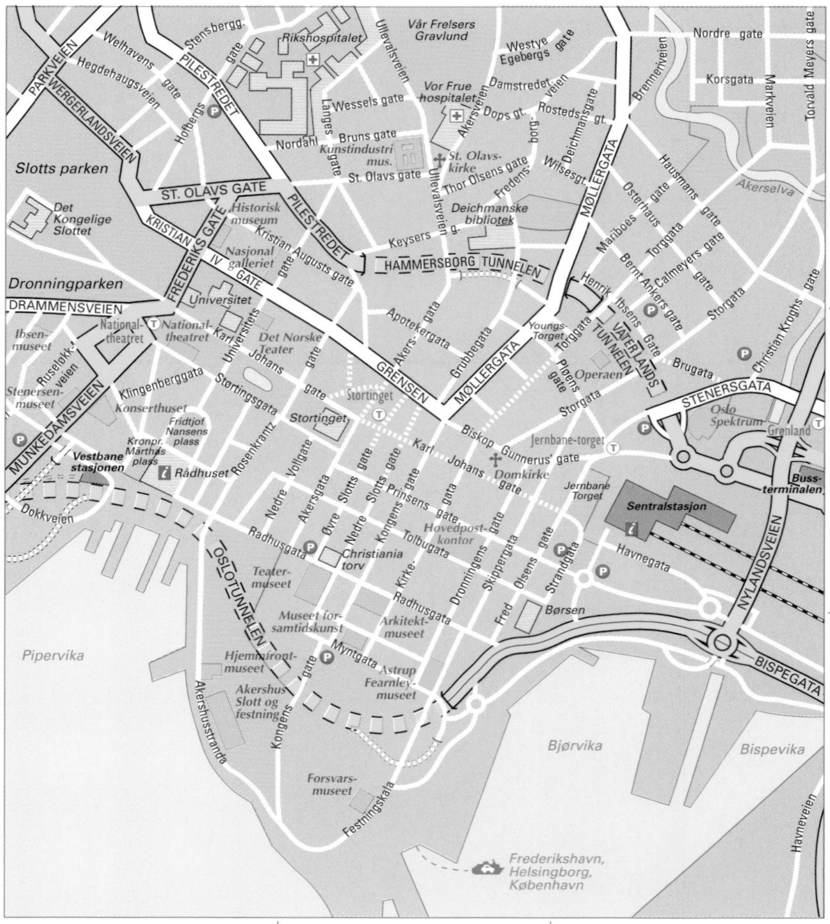

0 km 0.5
0 miles 0.25

a b c
1 2 3

PARIS

1 2 3 4

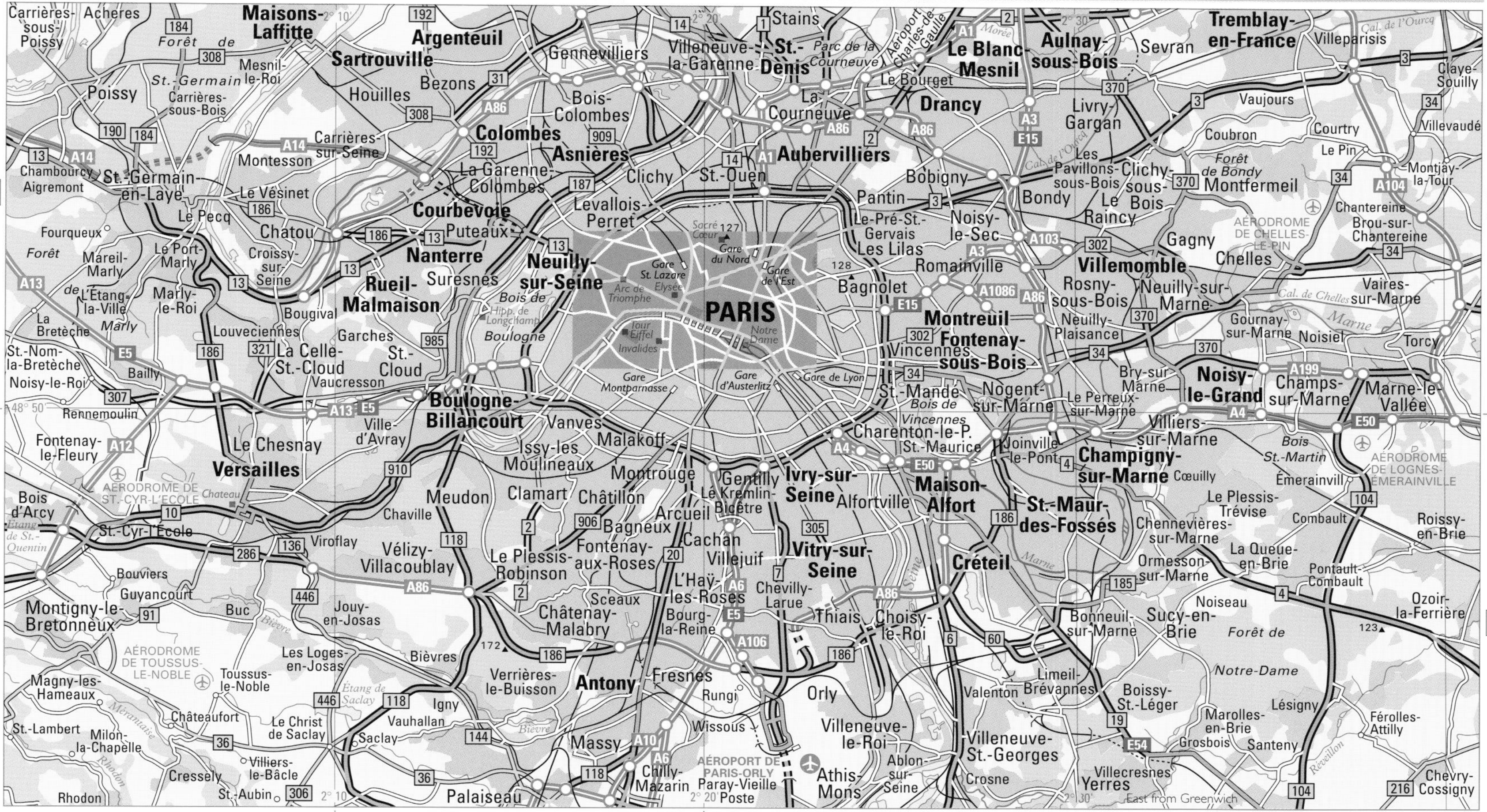

CENTRAL PARIS

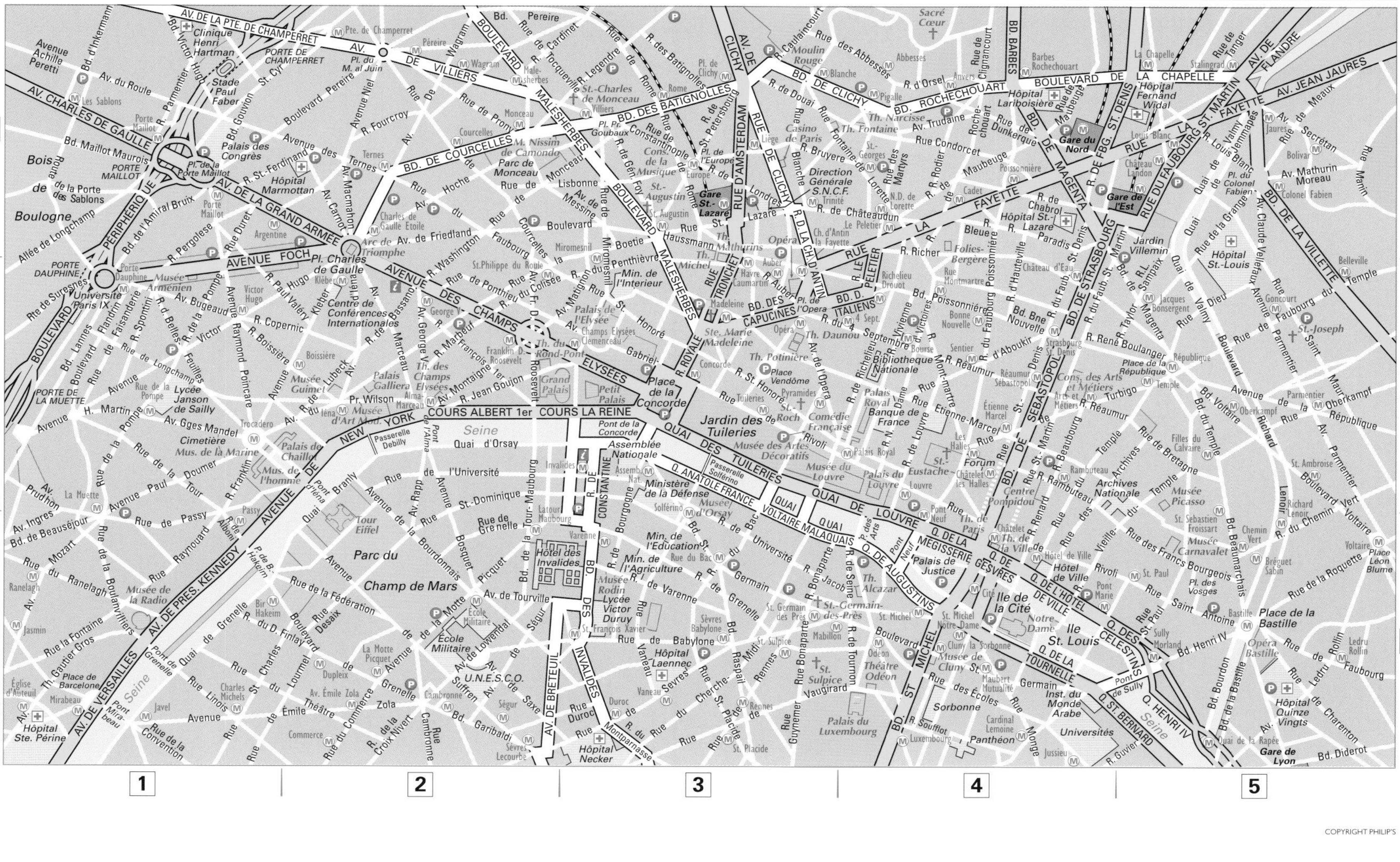

1 2 3 4 5

PRAGUE

0 km 5
0 miles 3

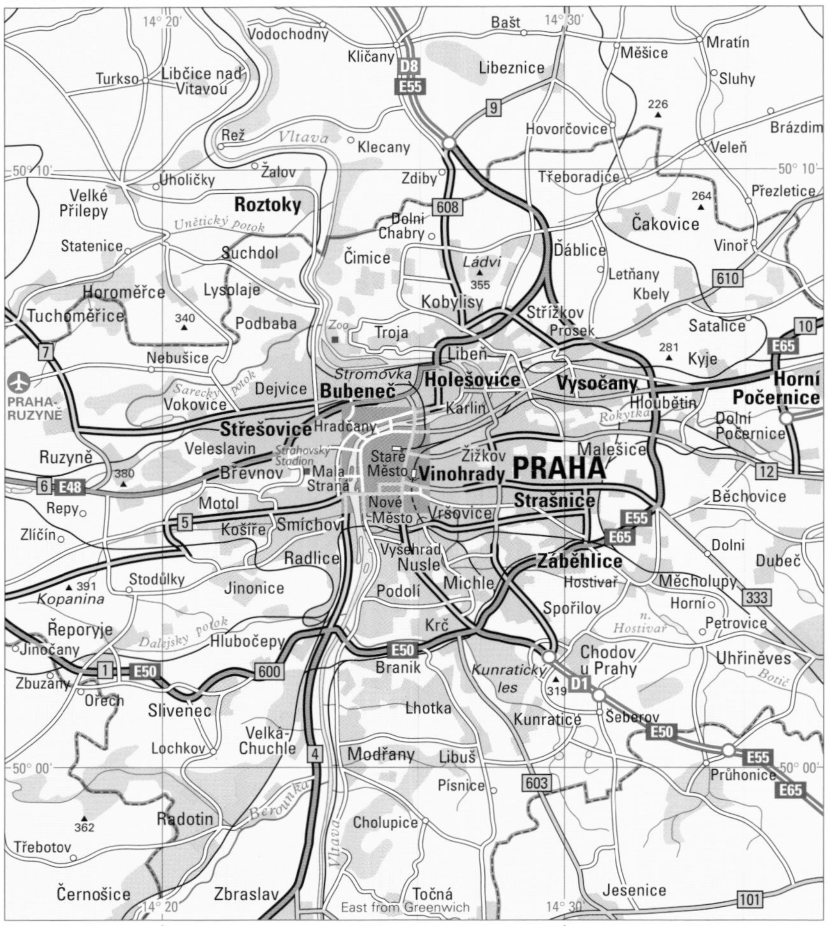

CENTRAL PRAGUE

0 km 1
0 miles 0.5

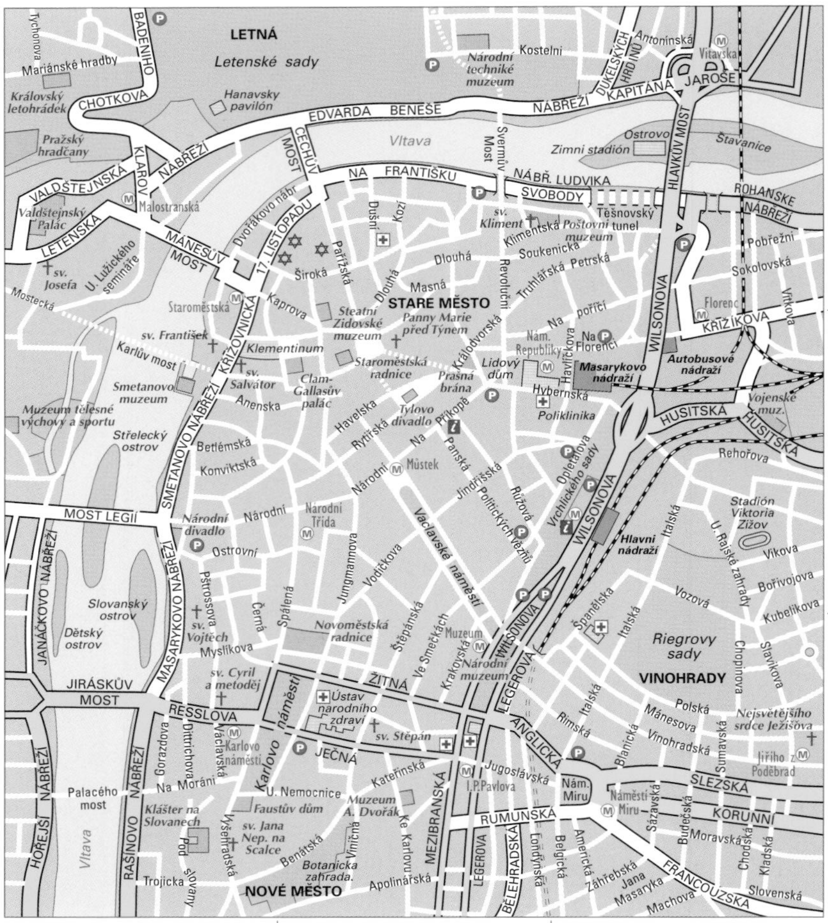

RIO DE JANEIRO

0 km 5
0 miles 3

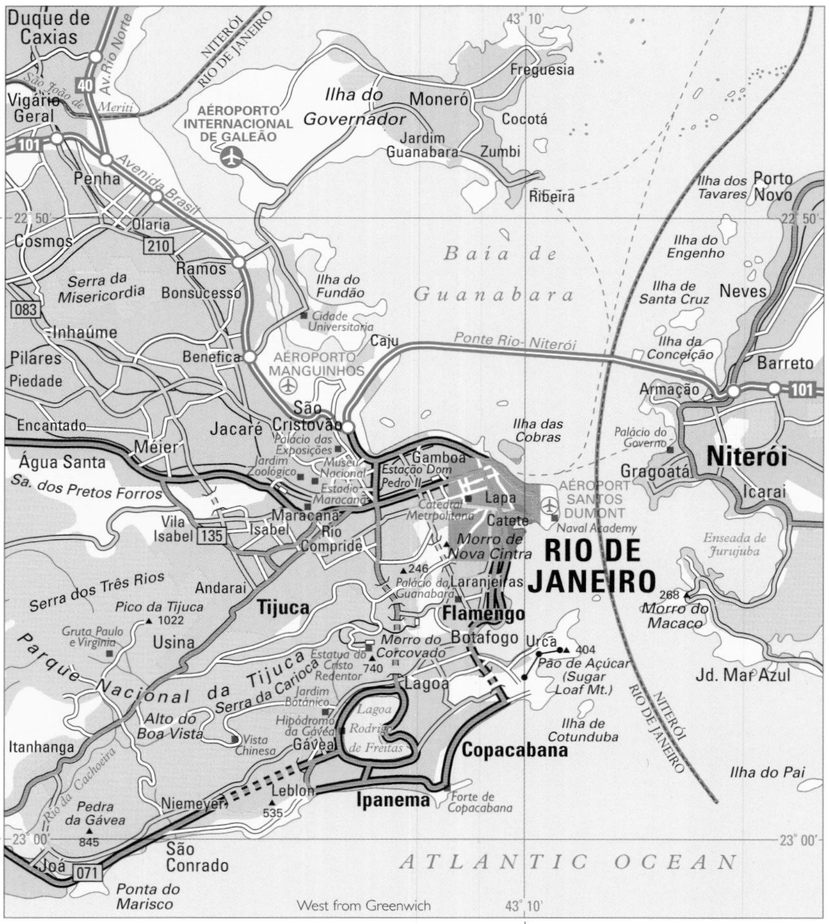

CENTRAL RIO DE JANEIRO

0 km 0.25
0 miles 0.125

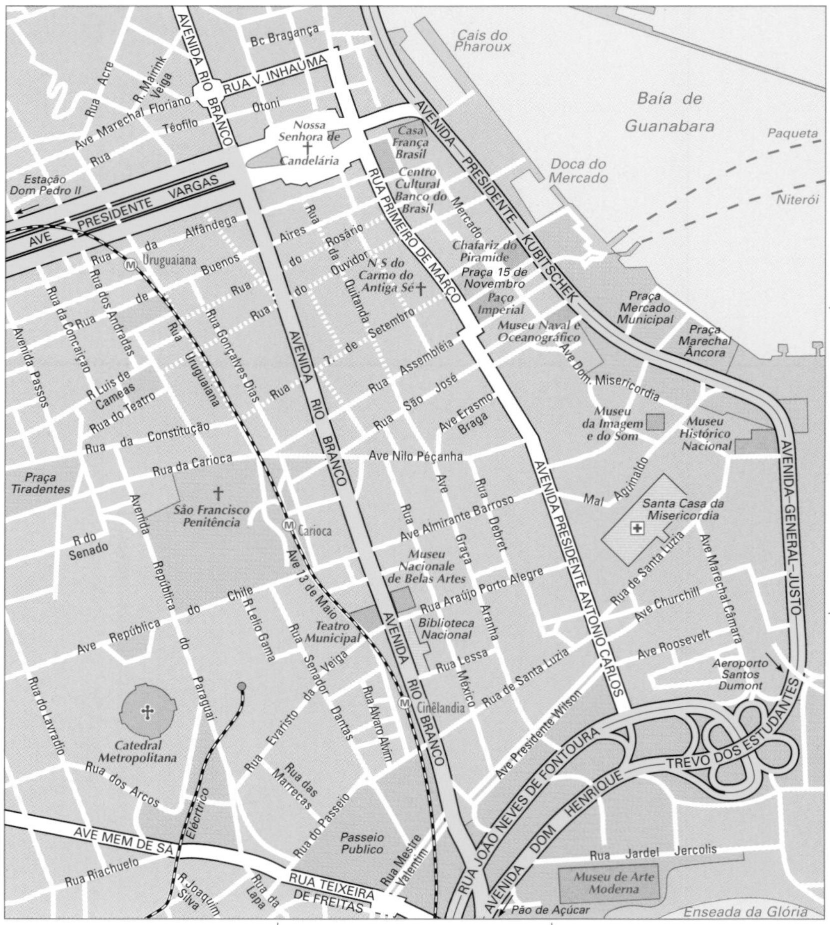

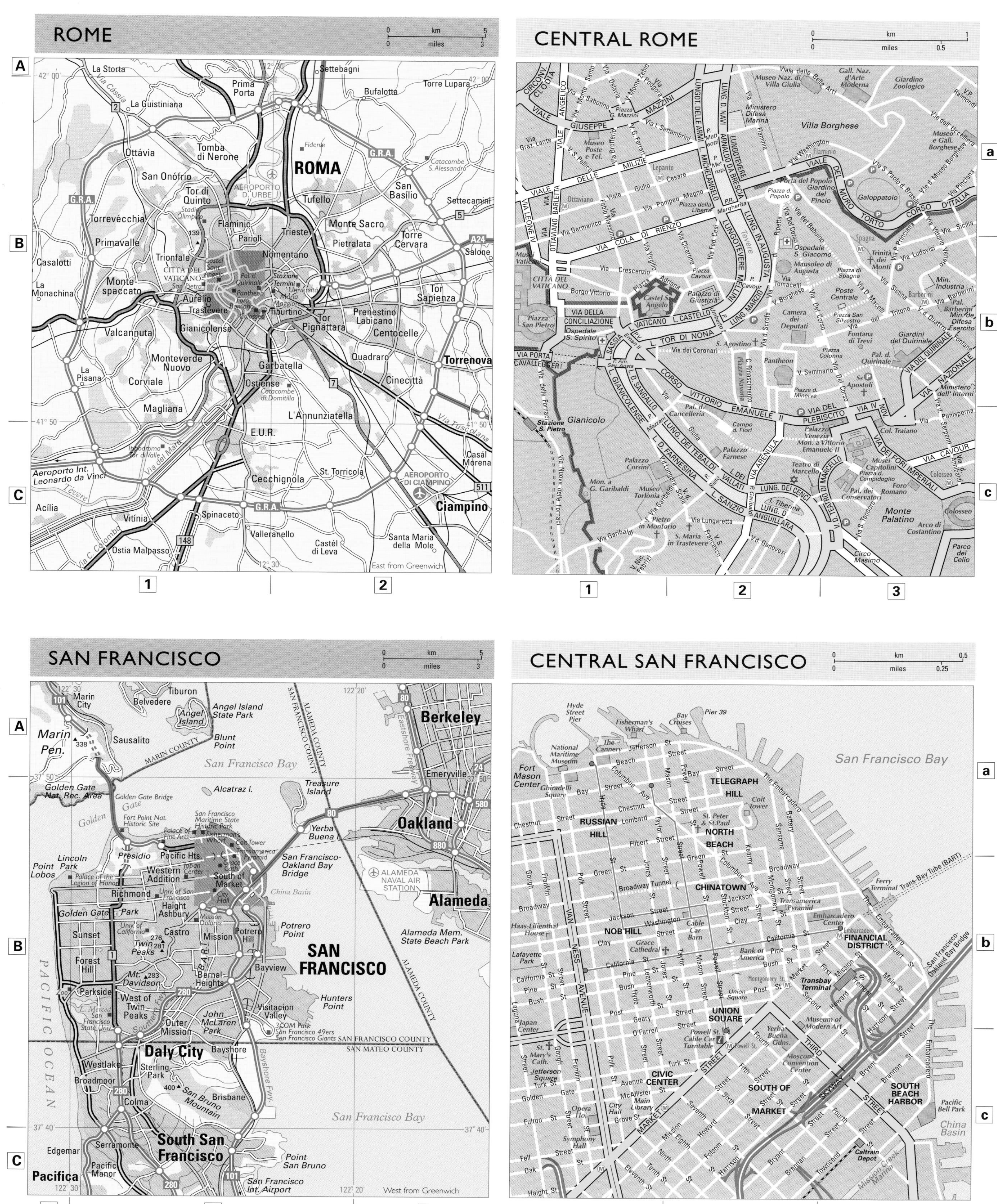
ROME
0 km 5
0 miles 3
La Storta
Prima Porta
Settebagni
Bufalotta
Torre Lupara
La Giustiniana
Ottávia
Tomba di Nerone
ROMA
San Onófrio
Tor di Quinto
Tufello
San Basílio
Settecamini
Torrevécchia
Flaminio
Parioli
Trieste
Monte Sacro
Primavalle
Pietralata
Torre Cervara
Salone
Casalotti
Trionfale
Nomentano
La Monachina
Monte-spaccato
Aurelio
Trastevere
Tiburtino
Tor Sapienza
Prenestino Labicano
Tor Pignattara
Centocelle
Valcannuta
Gianicolense
Quadraro
Torrenova
Monteverde Nuovo
Garbatella
La Pisana
Corviale
Ostiense
Cinecittà
Magliana
L'Annunziatella
E.U.R.
Casál Morena
Aeroporto Int. Leonardo da Vinci
Cecchignola
St. Torricola
AEROPORTO DI CIAMPINO
Ciampino
Acília
Vitinia
Spinaceto
Valleranello
Castél di Leva
Santa Maria della Mole
Ostia Malpasso
East from Greenwich
CENTRAL ROME
0 km 1
0 miles 0.5
Villa Borghese
Galoppatoio
CITTÀ DEL VATICANO
Piazza San Pietro
Castel S. Angelo
VIA DELLA CONCILIAZIONE
Pantheon
Camera dei Deputati
Fontana di Trevi
Palazzo Venezia
Gianicolo
Palazzo Farnese
Teatro di Marcello
Monte Palatino
Colosseo
Circo Massimo
Parco del Celio
SAN FRANCISCO
0 km 5
0 miles 3
Tiburon
Marin City
Belvedere
Angel Island
Angel Island State Park
Sausalito
Blunt Point
Marin Pen.
Berkeley
San Francisco Bay
Emeryville
Golden Gate Nat. Rec. Area
Golden Gate Bridge
Alcatraz I.
Treasure Island
Yerba Buena I.
Oakland
Presidio
Pacific Hts.
San Francisco-Oakland Bay Bridge
Point Lobos
Lincoln Park
Western Addition
South of Market
Richmond
Haight Ashbury
China Basin
ALAMEDA NAVAL AIR STATION
Alameda
Golden Gate Park
Sunset
Castro
Mission
Potrero Hill
Potrero Point
Alameda Mem. State Beach Park
Twin Peaks
SAN FRANCISCO
Forest Hill
Mt. Davidson
Bernal Heights
Bayview
PACIFIC OCEAN
Parkside
West of Twin Peaks
Visitacion Valley
Hunters Point
Outer Mission
John McLaren Park
SAN FRANCISCO COUNTY
SAN MATEO COUNTY
Daly City
Bayshore
Westlake
Sterling Park
Broadmoor
San Bruno Mountain
Brisbane
Colma
San Francisco Bay
Serramonte
South San Francisco
Edgemar
Pacifica
Pacific Manor
Point San Bruno
San Francisco Int. Airport
West from Greenwich
CENTRAL SAN FRANCISCO
0 km 0.5
0 miles 0.25
Hyde Street Pier
Fisherman's Wharf
Pier 39
San Francisco Bay
Fort Mason Center
TELEGRAPH HILL
Coit Tower
RUSSIAN HILL
NORTH BEACH
CHINATOWN
Transamerica Pyramid
Ferry Terminal
Trans-Bay Tube (BART)
Embarcadero Center
NOB HILL
Grace Cathedral
FINANCIAL DISTRICT
Transbay Terminal
UNION SQUARE
Museum of Modern Art
CIVIC CENTER
SOUTH OF MARKET
SOUTH BEACH HARBOR
City Hall
China Basin
Caltrain Depot

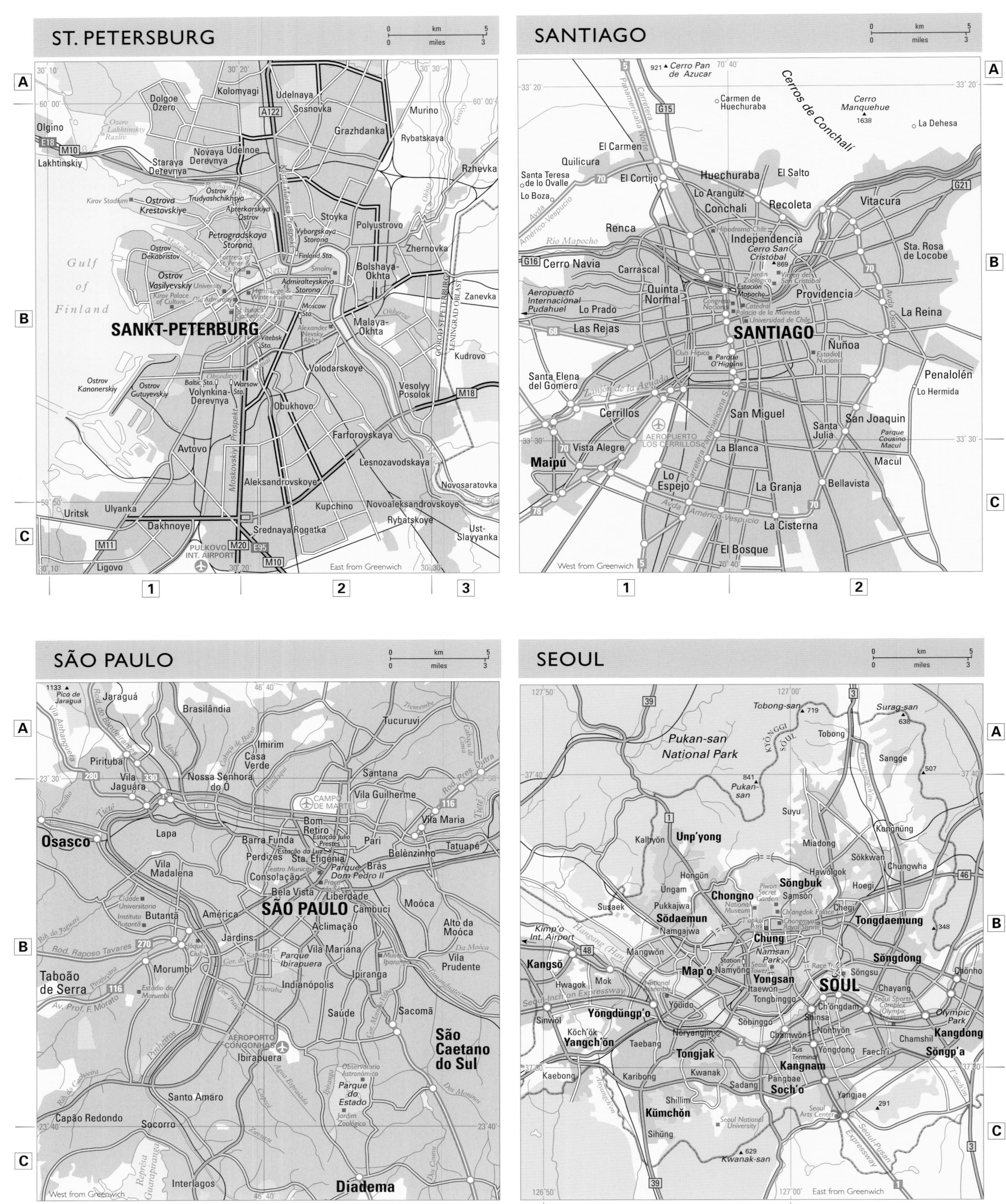
ST. PETERSBURG
0 km 5
0 miles 3
Dolgoe Ozero
Kolomyagi
Udelnaya
Sosnovka
Murino
Olgino
Ozero Lakhtinskiy Razliv
Grazhdanka
Rybatskaya
Lakhtinskiy
Staraya Derevnya
Novaya Derevnya
Udelnoe
Rzhevka
Kirov Stadium
Ostrova Krestovskiye
Ostrov Trudyashchikhsya
Apterkarskiy Ostrov
Stoyka
Polyustrovo
Petrogradskaya Storona
Vyborgskaya Storona
Zhernovka
Ostrov Dekabristov
Finland Sta.
Gulf of Finland
Ostrov Vasilyevskiy
Bolshaya-Okhta
Admiralteyskaya Storona
Zanevka
Kirov Palace of Culture
Old Admiralty
Hermitage & Winter Palace
St. Isaac's Cathedral
Moscow Sta.
Alexander Nevsky Abbey
Malaya-Okhta
SANKT-PETERBURG
Vitebsk Sta.
GOROD ST. PETERBURG
LENINGRAD OBLAST
Kudrovo
Ostrov Kanonerskiy
Ostrov Gutuyevskiy
Baltic Sta.
Warsaw Sta.
Volynkina-Derevnya
Volodarskoye
Vesolyy Posolok
Obukhovo
Farforovskaya
Avtovo
Lesnozavodskaya
Moskovskiy Prospekt
Aleksandrovskoye
Novosaratovka
Uritsk
Ulyanka
Kupchino
Novoaleksandrovskoye
Dakhnoye
Rybatskoye
Srednaya Rogatka
Ust-Slavyanka
PULKOVO INT. AIRPORT
Ligovo
East from Greenwich
SANTIAGO
0 km 5
0 miles 3
921 Cerro Pan de Azucar
Cerros de Conchalí
Carmen de Huechuraba
Cerro Manquehue 1638
La Dehesa
El Carmen
Quilicura
Santa Teresa de lo Ovalle
El Cortijo
Huechuraba
El Salto
Lo Boza
Lo Aranguiz
Conchali
Recoleta
Vitacura
Renca
Hipodromo Chile
Independencia
Cerro San Cristóbal 869
Río Mapocho
Sta. Rosa de Locobe
Cerro Navia
Carrascal
Aeropuerto Internacional Pudahuel
Lo Prado
Quinta Normal
Estación Mapocho
Providencia
La Reina
Las Rejas
SANTIAGO
Ñuñoa
Universidad de Chile
Club Hipico
Parque O'Higgins
Estadio Nacional
Santa Elena del Gomero
Zanjón de la Aguada
Peñalolén
Lo Hermida
Cerrillos
San Miguel
Santa Julia
San Joaquin
AEROPUERTO LOS CERRILLOS
Parque Cousino Macul
Vista Alegre
Maipú
La Blanca
Macul
Lo Espejo
La Granja
Bellavista
La Cisterna
El Bosque
West from Greenwich
SÃO PAULO
0 km 5
0 miles 3
1133 Pico de Jaraguá
Jaraguá
Brasilândia
Tucuruvi
Imirim
Casa Verde
Pirituba
Vila Jaguára
Nossa Senhora do Ó
Santana
CAMPO DE MARTE
Vila Guilherme
Vila Maria
Lapa
Bom Retiro
Osasco
Barra Funda
Pari
Belènzinho
Tatuapé
Perdizes
Sta. Efigênia
Brás
Vila Madalena
Consolação
Parque Dom Pedro II
Bela Vista
Liberdade
Cidade Universitaria
Instituto Butantã
Butantã
América
SÃO PAULO
Cambuci
Moóca
Alto da Moóca
Aclimação
Jardins
Rod. Raposo Tavares
Vila Mariana
Parque Ibirapuera
Vila Prudente
Taboão de Serra
Morumbi
Estadio do Morumbi
Ipiranga
Indianópolis
Av. Prof. F. Morato
Saúde
Sacomã
AEROPORTO CONGONHAS
São Caetano do Sul
Ibirapuera
Observatorio Astronómico
Parque do Estado
Jardim Zoológico
Santo Amaro
Capão Redondo
Socorro
Interlagos
Represa Guarapiranga
Diadema
West from Greenwich
SEOUL
0 km 5
0 miles 3
Tobong-san 719
Surag-san 638
Pukan-san National Park
Tobong
Sangge
841 Pukan-san
507
Suyu
Kongnung
Kalhyŏn
Unp'yong
Miadong
Sŏkkwan
Chungwha
Hawolgok
Hongŭn
Sŏngbuk
Hoegi
Ungam
Chongno
Samsŏn
Piwon Secret Garden
Sŏdaemun
National Museum
Ch'angdok Palace
Chegi
Tongdaemung
Susaek
Pukkajwa
Namgajwa
Chongmyo Royal Shrine
348
Kimp'o Int. Airport
Chung
Hangang (Han)
Mangwŏn
Namsan Park
Sŏngdong
Kangsŏ
Map'o
Seoul Tower
Namyŏng
Race Track
Sŏngsu
Ch'ŏnho
Hwagok
Mok
Yongsan
SŎUL
Chayang
Itaewon
Tongbinggo
National Assembly
Yŏido
Seoul-Inch'on Expressway
Sinwŏl
Yŏngdŭngp'o
Ch'ŏngdam
Seoul Sports Complex (Olympic Stadium)
Olympic Park
Shinsa
Sŏbinggo
Noryangjin
Chamwŏn
Nonhyŏn
Chamshil
Kangdong
Kŏch'ŏk
Yangch'ŏn
Taebang
Tongjak
Bus Terminal
Yŏngdong
Faech'i
Sŏngp'a
Kaebong
Karibong
Kwanak
Kangnam
Pangbae
Sadang
Soch'o
Shillim
Yangjae
291
Kŭmchŏn
Seoul Arts Center
Seoul National University
Sihŭng
629 Kwanak-san
Seoul-Pusan Expressway
East from Greenwich

SHANGHAI

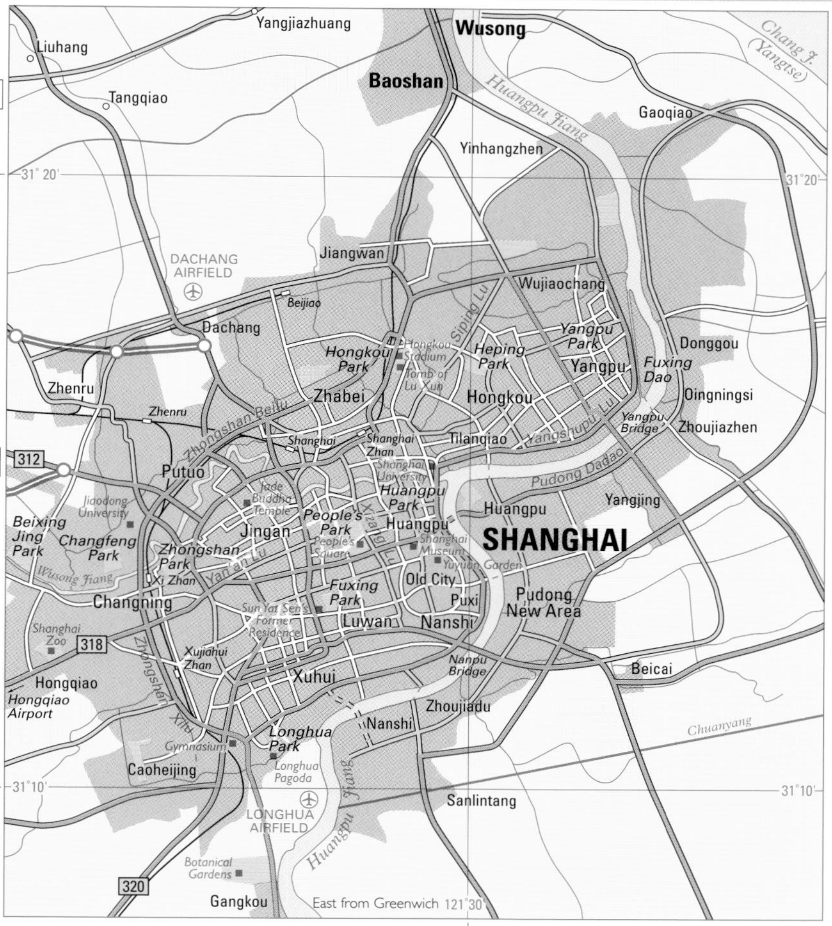

0 km 5
0 miles 3

Yangjiazhuang
Wusong
Chang Jiang (Yangtse)
Liuhang
Baoshan
Tangqiao
Gaoqiao
Huangpu Jiang
Yinhangzhen
31° 20'
31°20'
Jiangwan
DACHANG AIRFIELD
Wujiaochang
Beijiao
Dachang
Siping Lu
Yangpu Park
Donggou
Hongkou Park
Hongkou Stadium
Tomb of Lu Xun
Heping Park
Fuxing Dao
Yangpu
Zhenru
Zhabei
Hongkou
Qiningsi
Zhenru
Yangpu Bridge
Zhoujiazhen
Zhongshan Beilu
Shanghai Zhan
Shanghai University
Tilanqiao
Yangshupu Lu
312
Jade Buddha Temple
Huangpu Park
Pudong Dadao
Putuo
Huangpu
Yangjing
Jiaotong University
Beixing Jing Park
Changfeng Park
Jingan
People's Park
People's Square
Huangpu
Shanghai Museum
Yuyuan Garden
SHANGHAI
Zhongshan Park
Wusong Jiang
Zhan
Yan'an Lu
Old City
Changning
Fuxing Park
Puxi
Pudong New Area
Shanghai Zoo
Sun Yat Sen's Former Residence
Luwan
Nanshi
318
Xujiahui Zhan
Hongqiao
Xuhui
Nanpu Bridge
Beicai
Hongqiao Airport
Zhongshan Xilu
Nanshi
Zhoujiadu
Gymnasium
Longhua Park
Chuanyang
Caoheijing
Longhua Pagoda
31°10'
31°10'
Sanlintang
LONGHUA AIRFIELD
Huangpu Jiang
Botanical Gardens
320
Gangkou
East from Greenwich 121°30'

A B C 1 2

CENTRAL SINGAPORE

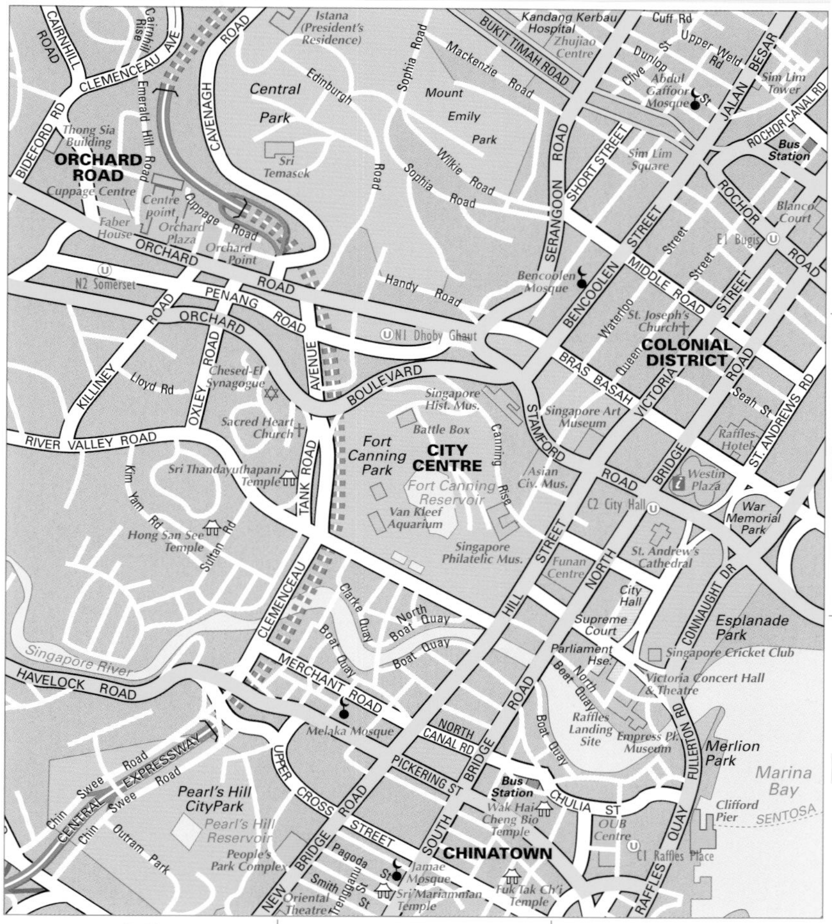

0 km 1
0 miles 0.5

Cairnhill Road
Cairnhill Rise
Istana (President's Residence)
Kandang Kerbau Hospital
Cuff Rd
Clemenceau Ave
Emerald Hill Road
Cavenagh Road
Bukit Timah Road
Zhujiao Centre
Dunlop St
Upper Weld Rd
Jalan Besar
Sim Lim Tower
Central Park
Edinburgh
Sophia Road
Mackenzie Road
Clive St
Abdul Gaffoor Mosque
Mount Emily Park
Rochor Canal Rd
Bideford Rd
Thong Sia Building
ORCHARD ROAD
Sri Temasek
Road
Sophia Road
Wilkie Road
Serangoon Road
Short Street
Sim Lim Square
Bus Station
Cuppage Centre
Centre point
Orchard Plaza
Orchard Point
Cuppage Road
Rochor Street
Blanco Court
Faber House
Orchard Road
Handy Road
Bencoolen Mosque
Middle Road
Street
Bugis
N2 Somerset
Penang Road
Waterloo
Street
Road
Orchard
Killiney Road
N1 Dhoby Ghaut
St Joseph's Church
COLONIAL DISTRICT
Oxley Road
Avenue
Boulevard
Bencoolen
Queen
Lloyd Rd
Chesed-El Synagogue
Singapore Hist. Mus.
Bras Basah
Victoria
Seah St
St. Andrews Rd
Sacred Heart Church
Battle Box
Singapore Art Museum
Raffles Hotel
River Valley Road
Fort Canning Park
CITY CENTRE
Canning Rise
Tank Road
Stamford
Road
Bridge
Westin Plaza
Sri Thandayuthapani Temple
Fort Canning Reservoir
Asian Civ. Mus.
Kim Yam Rd
Van Kleef Aquarium
C2 City Hall
War Memorial Park
Hong San See Temple
Sultan Rd
Singapore Philatelic Mus.
Hill
Street
North
St. Andrew's Cathedral
Clemenceau
Funan Centre
City Hall
Connaught Dr
Clarke Quay
North Boat Quay
Supreme Court
Esplanade Park
Boat Quay
Parliament Hse.
Singapore Cricket Club
Singapore River
Merchant Road
Victoria Concert Hall & Theatre
Havelock Road
Boat Quay
Raffles Landing Site
Road
Melaka Mosque
North Canal Rd
Empress Pl. Museum
Merlion Park
Fullerton Rd
Central Expressway
Chin Swee Road
Pickering St
Bridge
Marina Bay
Bus Station
Chulia St
Upper Cross Road
Wak Hai Cheng Bio Temple
Clifford Pier
Pearl's Hill City Park
Pearl's Hill Reservoir
Street
Quay
SENTOSA
OUB Centre
Chin Swee Road
Outram Park
People's Park Complex
South
CHINATOWN
C1 Raffles Place
New Bridge
Pagoda St
Jamae Mosque
Smith St
Trengganu St
Sri Mariamman Temple
Fuk Tak Ch'i Temple
Raffles Quay
Oriental Theatre

a b c 1 2 3

SINGAPORE

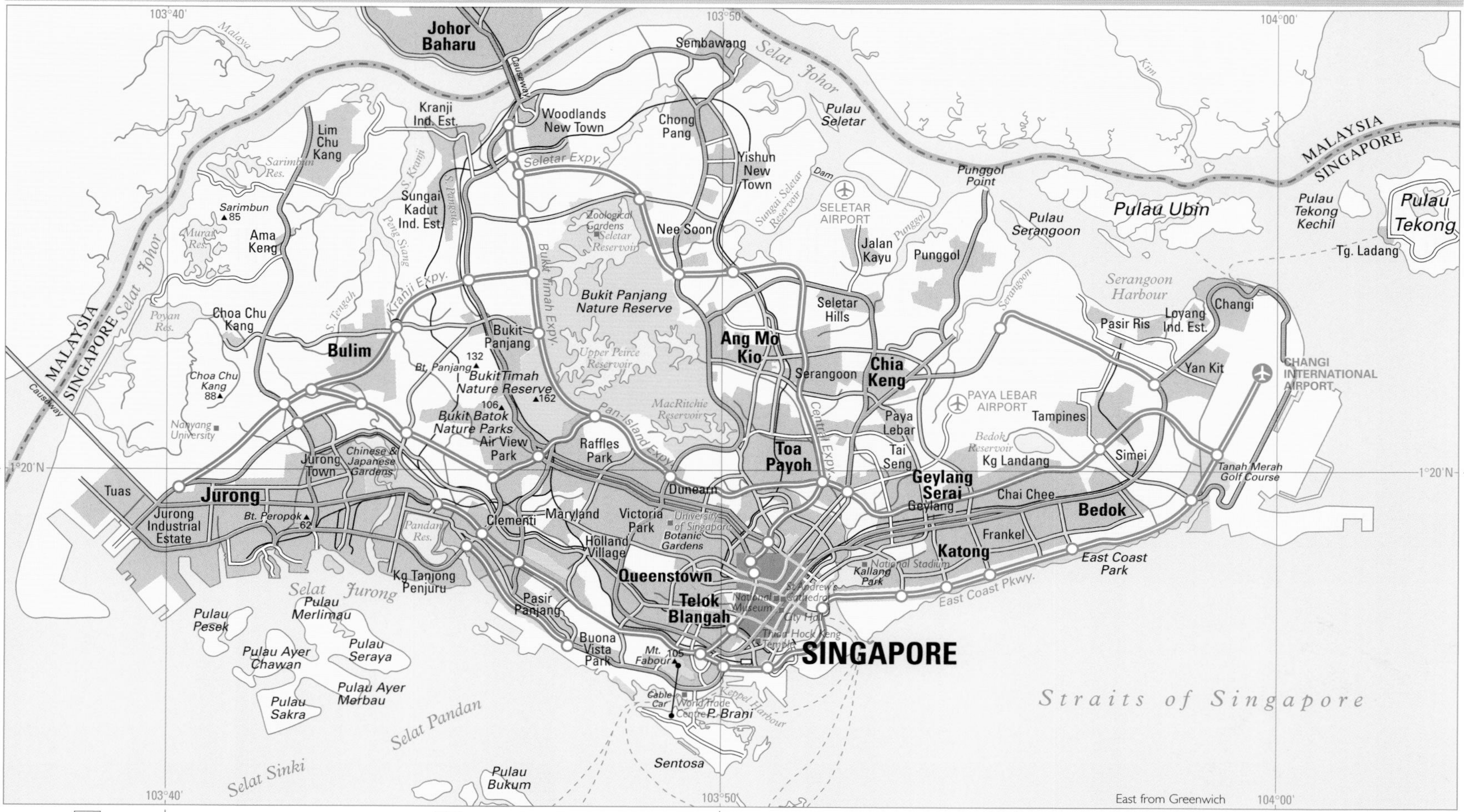

0 km 10
0 miles 6

103°40'
103°50'
104°00'
Johor Baharu
Sembawang
Malaya
Selat Johor
Kim
Kranji Ind. Est.
Causeway
Woodlands New Town
Chong Pang
Pulau Seletar
Lim Chu Kang
Yishun New Town
MALAYSIA SINGAPORE
Sarimbun Res.
Seletar Expy.
Sungai Kadut Ind. Est.
Sungai Seletar Reservoir
Punggol Point
Dam
SELETAR AIRPORT
Sarimbun 85
Zoological Gardens
Seletar Reservoir
Pulau Serangoon
Pulau Ubin
Pulau Tekong Kechil
Pulau Tekong
Ama Keng
Nee Soon
Punggol
Murai Res.
Jalan Kayu
Punggol
Tg. Ladang
Bukit Timah Expy.
Bukit Panjang Nature Reserve
Serangoon Harbour
Seletar Hills
Kranji Expy.
Poyan Res.
Choa Chu Kang
Changi
Bukit Panjang
Loyang Ind. Est.
Ang Mo Kio
Pasir Ris
Bulim
Upper Peirce Reservoir
Bt. Panjang 132
Bukit Timah Nature Reserve
Serangoon
Chia Keng
Yan Kit
CHANGI INTERNATIONAL AIRPORT
MALAYSIA SINGAPORE
Selat Johor
Causeway
Choa Chu Kang 88
MacRitchie Reservoir
PAYA LEBAR AIRPORT
106
Bukit Batok Nature Parks
162
Tampines
Nanyang University
Pan-Island Expy.
Paya Lebar
Air View Park
Raffles Park
Toa Payoh
Central Expy.
Bedok Reservoir
Simei
Jurong Town
Chinese & Japanese Gardens
Tai Seng
1°20'N
1°20'N
Tuas
Dunearn
Geylang Serai
Kg Landang
Tanah Merah Golf Course
Jurong
Geylang
Chai Chee
Jurong Industrial Estate
Bt. Peropok 62
Clementi
Maryland
Victoria Park
University of Singapore
Bedok
Pandan Res.
Botanic Gardens
Frankel
Holland Village
Katong
East Coast Park
Kg Tanjong Penjuru
Queenstown
National Stadium
Kallang Park
Selat Jurong
East Coast Pkwy.
Pulau Pesek
Pulau Merlimau
Pasir Panjang
Telok Blangah
St. Andrew's Cathedral
National Museum
City Hall
Pulau Seraya
Thian Hock Keng Temple
Pulau Ayer Chawan
Buona Vista Park
Mt. Faber 105
SINGAPORE
Pulau Sakra
Pulau Ayer Merbau
Cable Car
World Trade Centre
Keppel Harbour
P. Brani
Straits of Singapore
Selat Pandan
Sentosa
Selat Sinki
Pulau Bukum
103°40'
103°50'
104°00'
East from Greenwich

A B A B 1 2 3 4

STOCKHOLM

0 km 5
0 miles 3

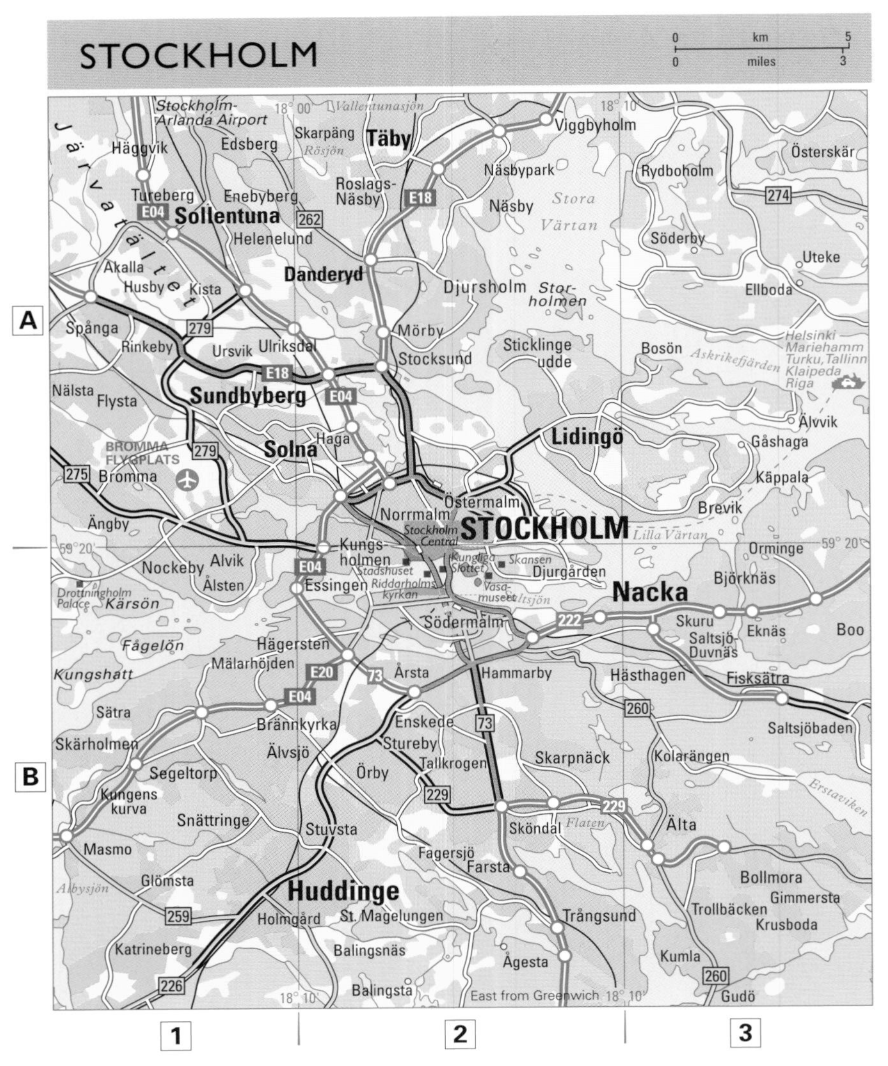

CENTRAL STOCKHOLM

0 km 0.5
0 miles 0.25

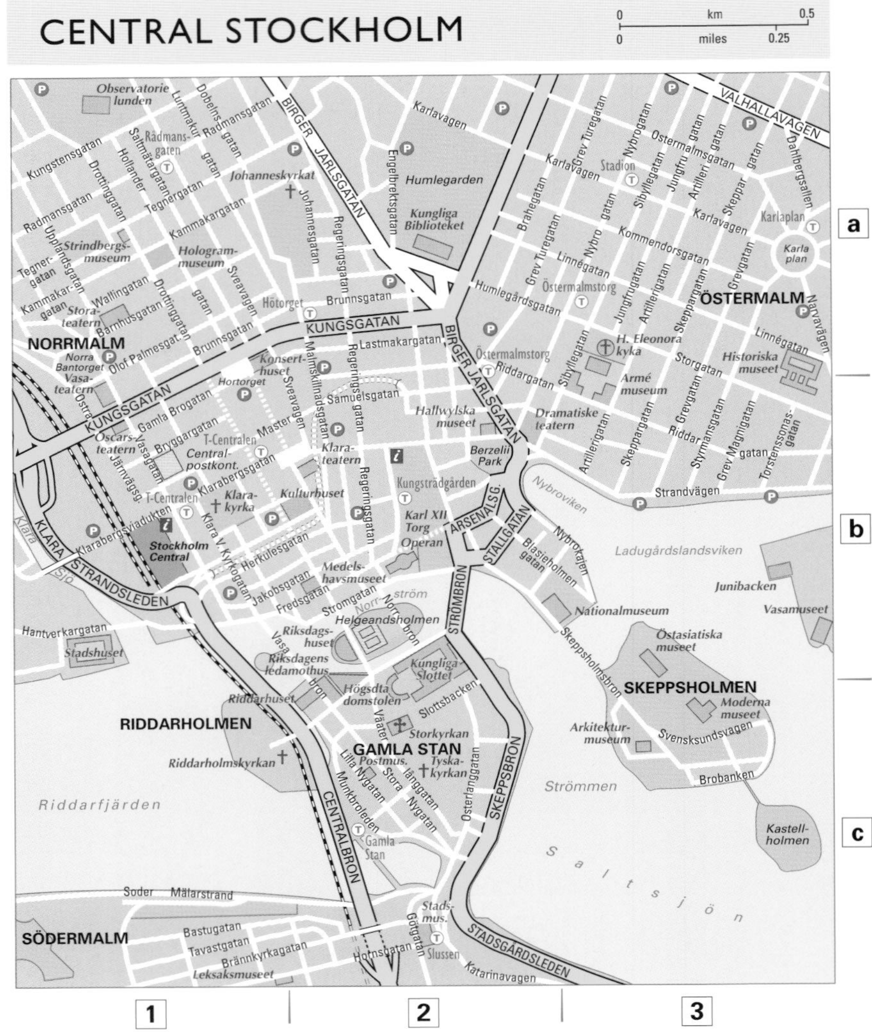

SYDNEY

0 km 5
0 miles 3

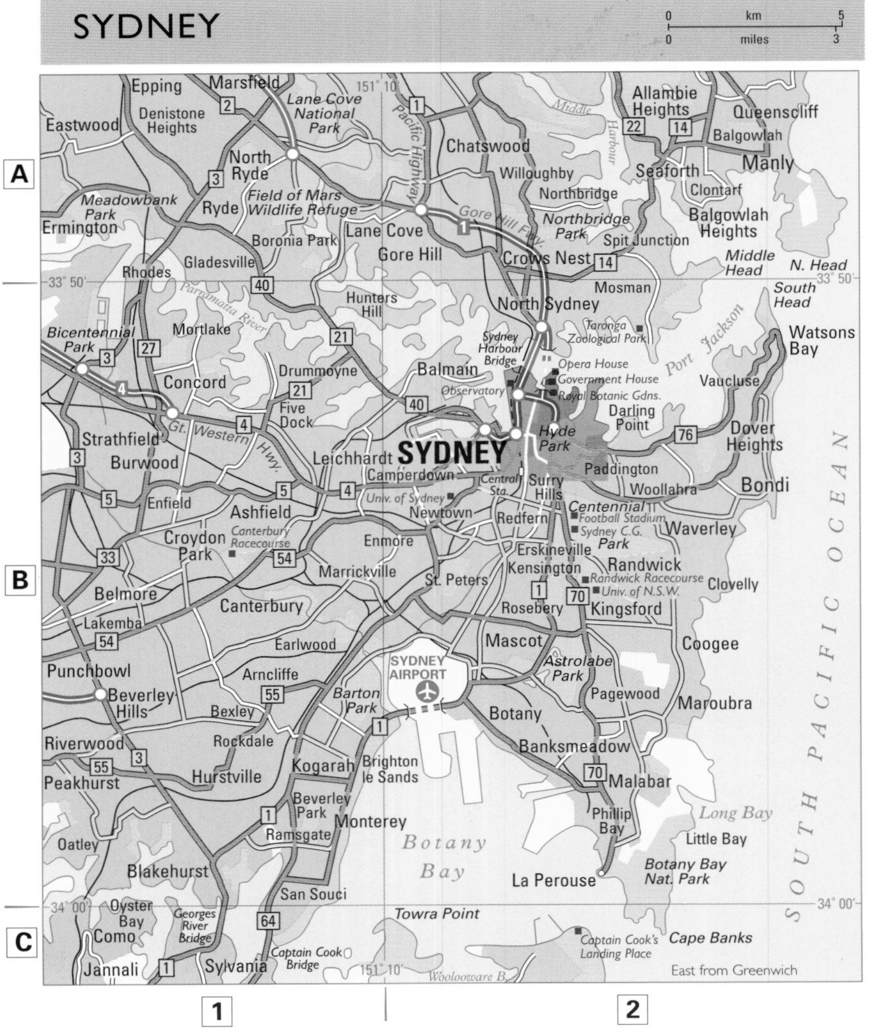

CENTRAL SYDNEY

0 km 2
0 miles 1

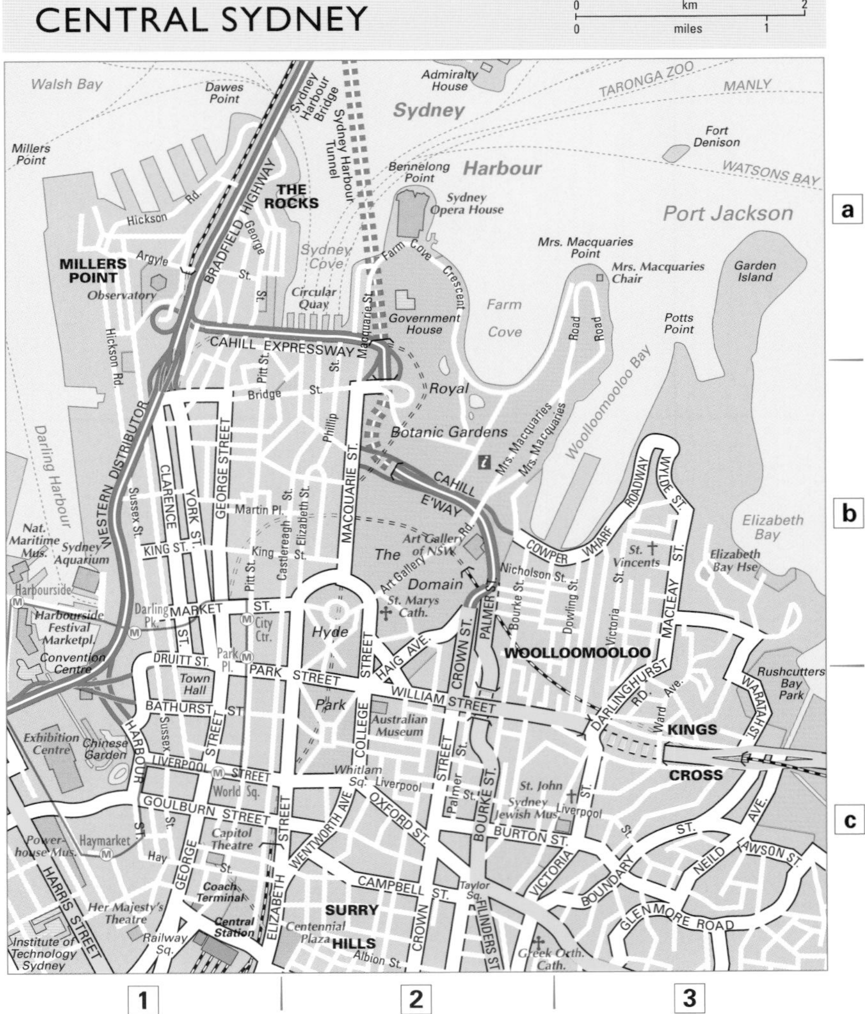

TOKYO

0 km 5
0 miles 3

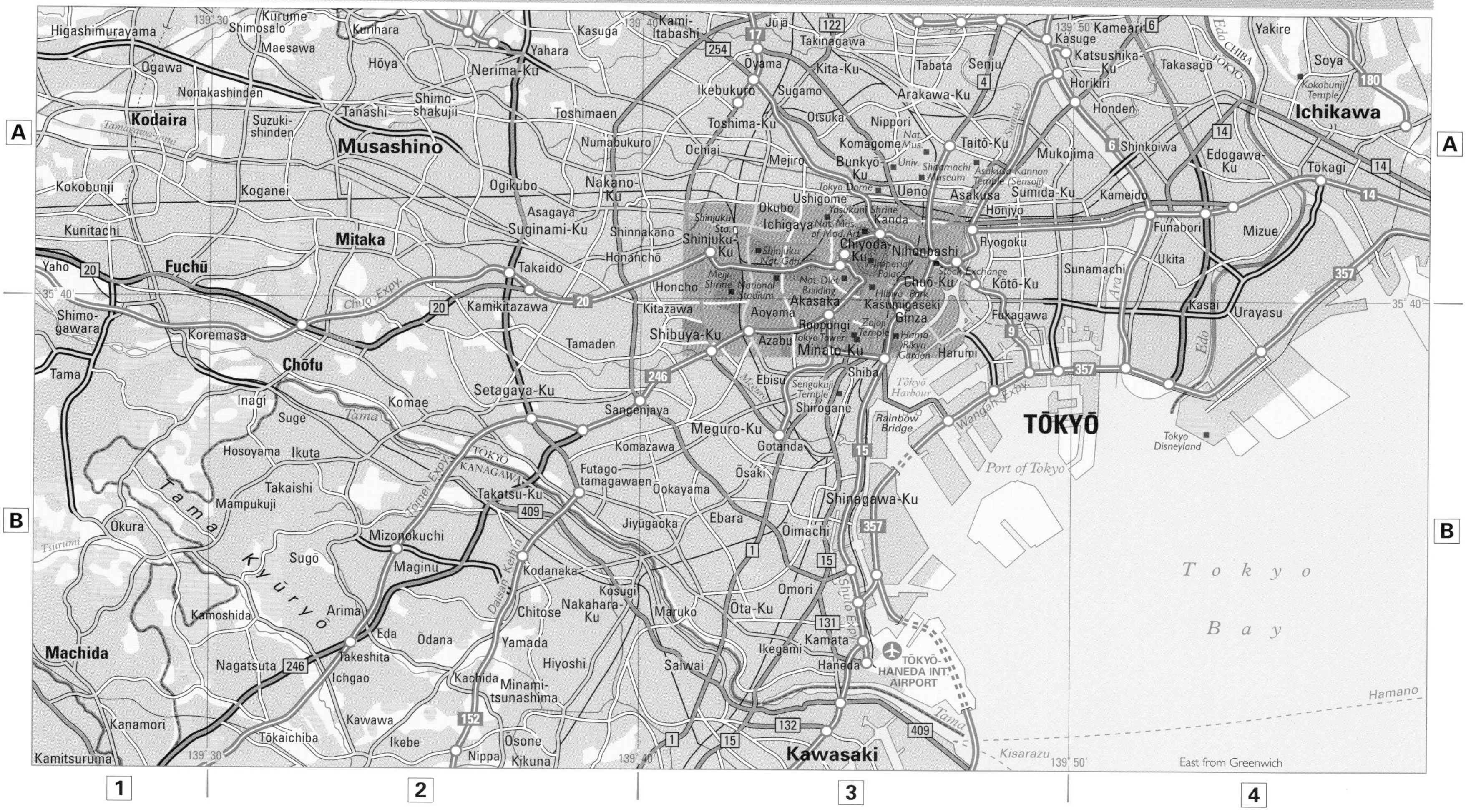

East from Greenwich

CENTRAL TOKYO

0 km 1
0 miles 0.5

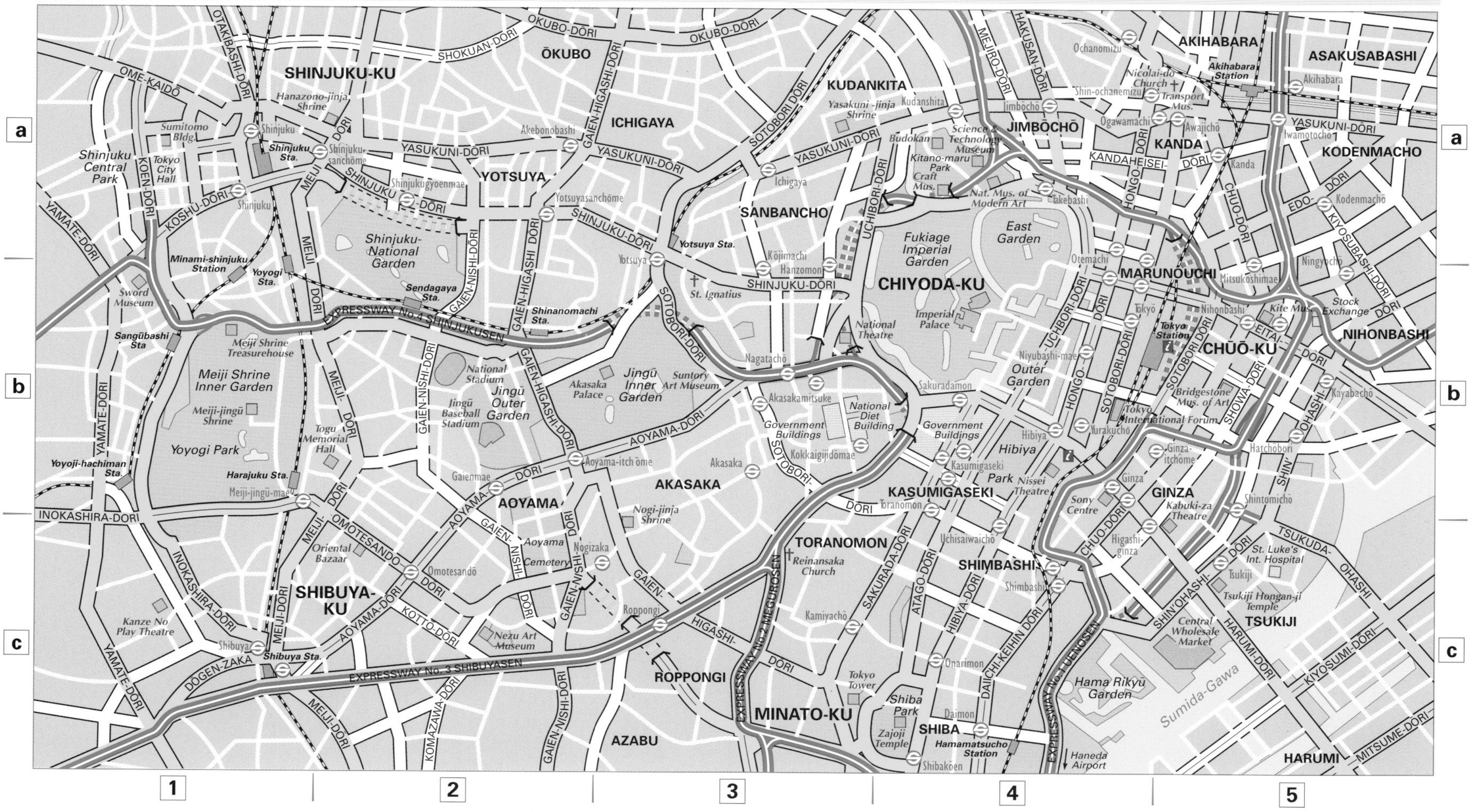

TEHRAN

0 km 5
0 miles 3

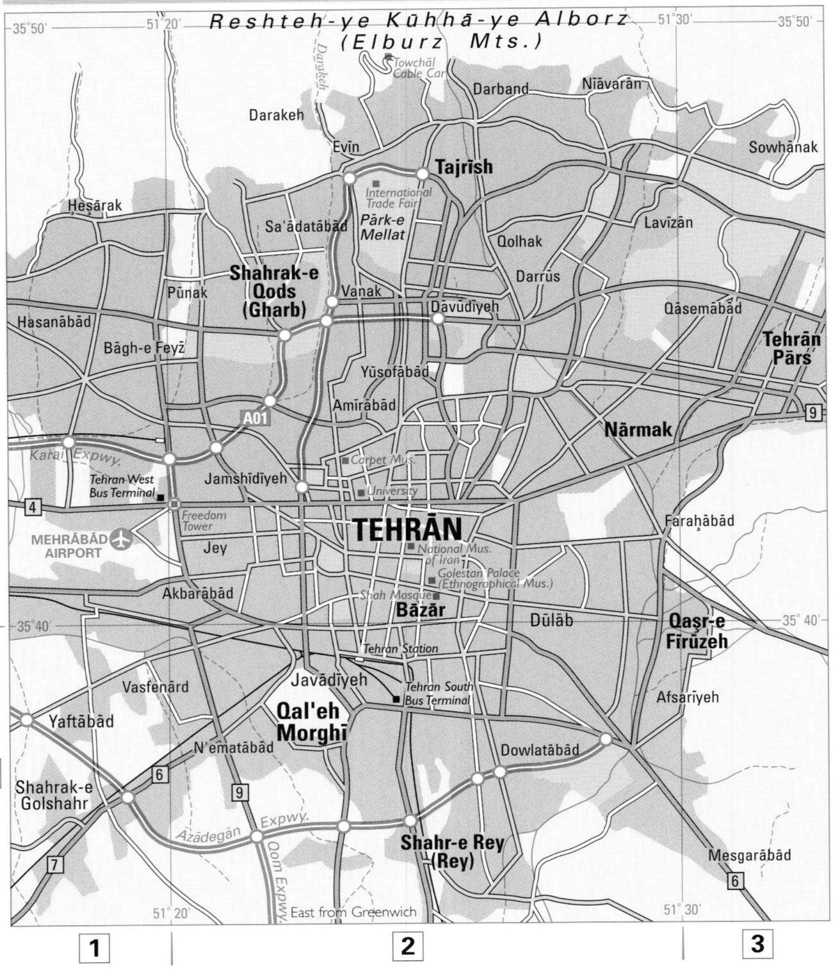

35°50′ 51°20′ 51°30′ 35°50′
Reshteh-ye Kūhhā-ye Alborz
(Elburz Mts.)
Towchāl Cable Car
Darband
Niāvarān
Darakeh
Evīn
Tajrīsh
Sowhānak
Hesārak
International Trade Fair
Pārk-e Mellat
Sa'ādatābād
Lavīzān
Qolhak
Shahrak-e Qods (Gharb)
Pūnak
Vanak
Darrūs
Hasanābād
Dāvūdīyeh
Qāsemābād
Bāgh-e Feyz
Tehrān Pārs
Yūsofābād
Amīrābād
A01
Nārmak
Karaj Expwy.
Carpet Mus.
Tehran West Bus Terminal
Jamshīdīyeh
University
Farahābād
Freedom Tower
MEHRĀBĀD AIRPORT
TEHRĀN
Jey
National Mus. of Iran
Golestan Palace (Ethnographical Mus.)
Akbarābād
Shah Mosque
Bāzār
Dūlāb
Qasr-e Firūzeh
35°40′
Tehran Station
Vasfenārd
Javādīyeh
Tehran South Bus Terminal
Afsarīyeh
Yaftābād
Qal'eh Morghī
N'ematābād
Dowlatābād
Shahrak-e Golshahr
Āzādegān Expwy.
Dom Expwy.
Shahr-e Rey (Rey)
Mesgarābād
East from Greenwich
51°20′ 51°30′
A B 1 2 3

TIANJIN

0 km 5
0 miles 3

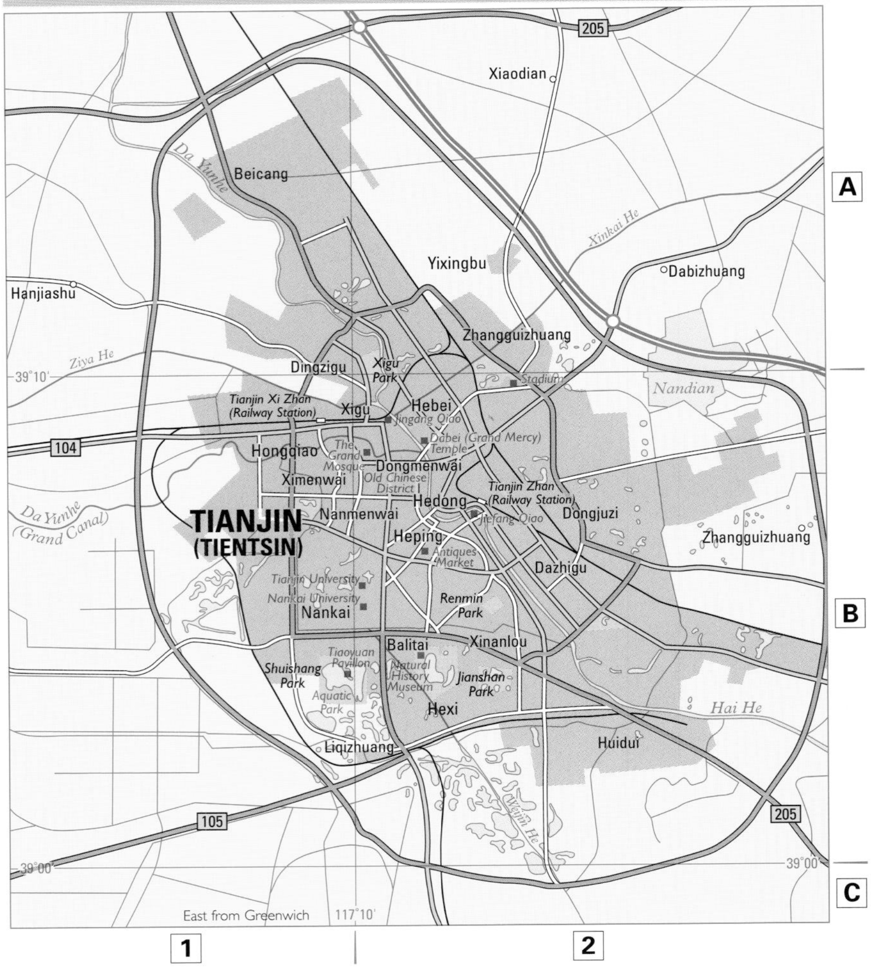

205
Xiaodian
Da Yunhe
Beicang
Xinkai He
Yixingbu
Dabizhuang
Hanjiashu
Zhangguizhuang
Dingzigu
Xigu Park
Stadium
39°10′
Ziya He
Nandian
Tianjin Xi Zhan (Railway Station)
Xigu
Hebei
Jingang Qiao
104
Hongqiao
The Grand Mosque
Dabei (Grand Mercy) Temple
Dongmenwai
Ximenwai
Old Chinese District
Tianjin Zhan (Railway Station)
Hedong
Da Yunhe (Grand Canal)
TIANJIN (TIENTSIN)
Nanmenwai
Jiefang Qiao
Dongjuzi
Heping
Zhangguizhuang
Antiques Market
Dazhigu
Tianjin University
Nankai University
Nankai
Renmin Park
Balitai
Xinanlou
Tiaoyuan Pavilion
Natural History Museum
Shuishang Park
Jianshan Park
Aquatic Park
Hexi
Hai He
Huidui
Liqizhuang
105
205
39°00′
East from Greenwich 117°10′
A B C 1 2

TORONTO

0 km 5
0 miles 3

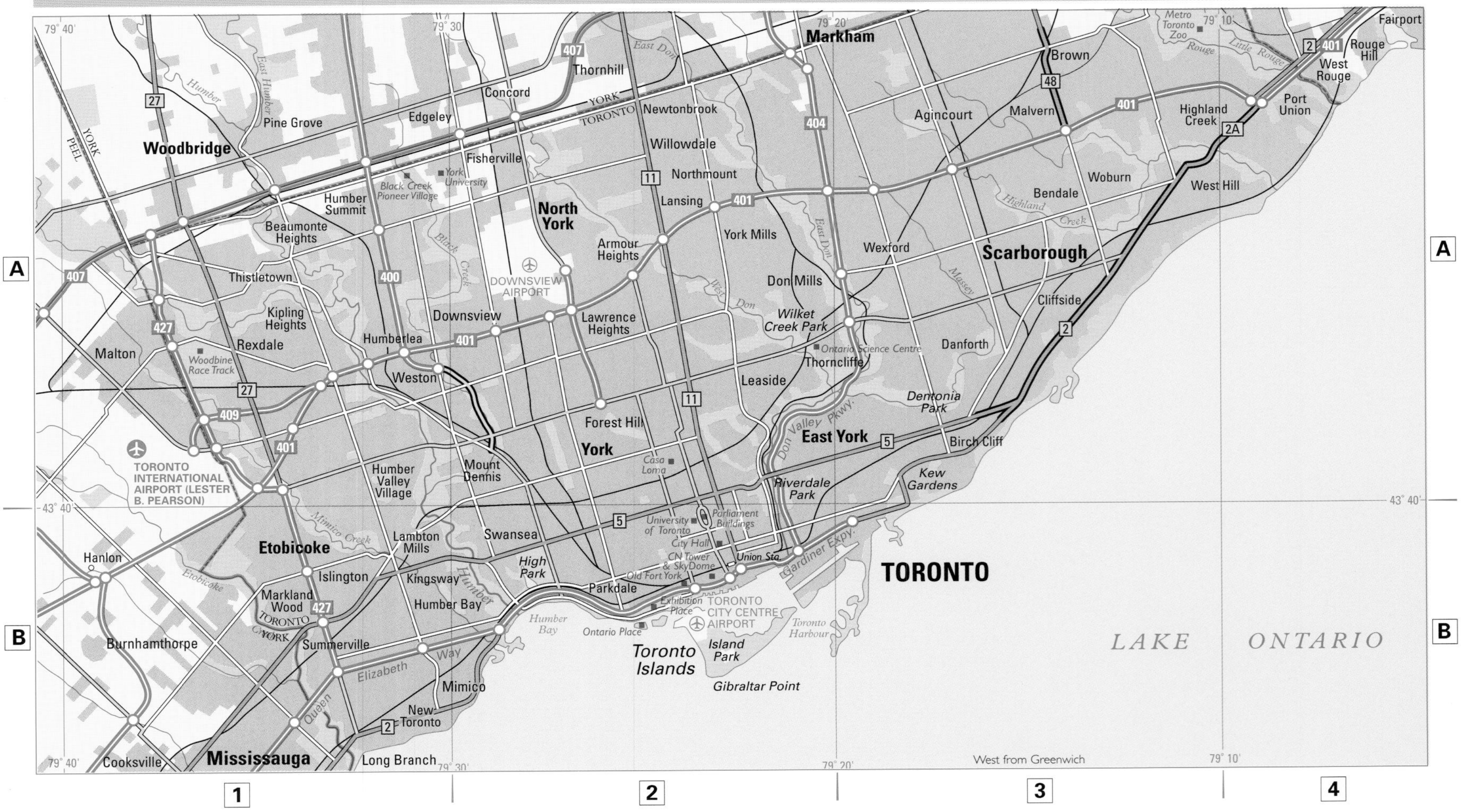

79°40′ 79°30′ 79°20′ 79°10′
Metro Toronto Zoo
Rouge
Little Rouge
Fairport
Markham
407
East Don
Brown
401
Rouge Hill
West Rouge
Thornhill
Humber
East Humber
27
Concord
YORK
TORONTO
Newtonbrook
48
Agincourt
Malvern
401
Highland Creek
2A
Port Union
Pine Grove
Edgeley
Willowdale
404
YORK PEEL
Woodbridge
Fisherville
York University
11
Northmount
Black Creek Pioneer Village
Humber Summit
Lansing
401
Bendale
Woburn
West Hill
Highland Creek
Beaumonte Heights
North York
York Mills
Black Creek
Armour Heights
East Don
Wexford
Scarborough
407
Thistletown
400
DOWNSVIEW AIRPORT
West Don
Don Mills
Massey
Cliffside
Kipling Heights
Downsview
Lawrence Heights
Wilket Creek Park
427
Rexdale
Humberlea
401
Ontario Science Centre
Danforth
Malton
Woodbine Race Track
Thorncliffe
Weston
27
Leaside
11
2
409
Forest Hill
Danforth Park
TORONTO INTERNATIONAL AIRPORT (LESTER B. PEARSON)
401
Don Valley Pkwy.
East York
5
Birch Cliff
Mount Dennis
York
Casa Loma
Humber Valley Village
Riverdale Park
Kew Gardens
43°40′
Mimico Creek
University of Toronto
Parliament Buildings
5
Etobicoke
Lambton Mills
Swansea
City Hall
Hanlon
CN Tower & SkyDome
Union Sta.
Gardiner Expy.
TORONTO
High Park
Etobicoke
Islington
Kingsway
Humber
Old Fort York
Parkdale
Markland Wood
427
Humber Bay
Exhibition Place
TORONTO CITY CENTRE AIRPORT
TORONTO
YORK
Humber Bay
Ontario Place
Toronto Harbour
Burnhamthorpe
Summerville
Toronto Islands
Island Park
LAKE ONTARIO
Elizabeth Way
Queen
Mimico
Gibraltar Point
New Toronto
2
Cooksville
Mississauga
Long Branch
West from Greenwich
A B 1 2 3 4

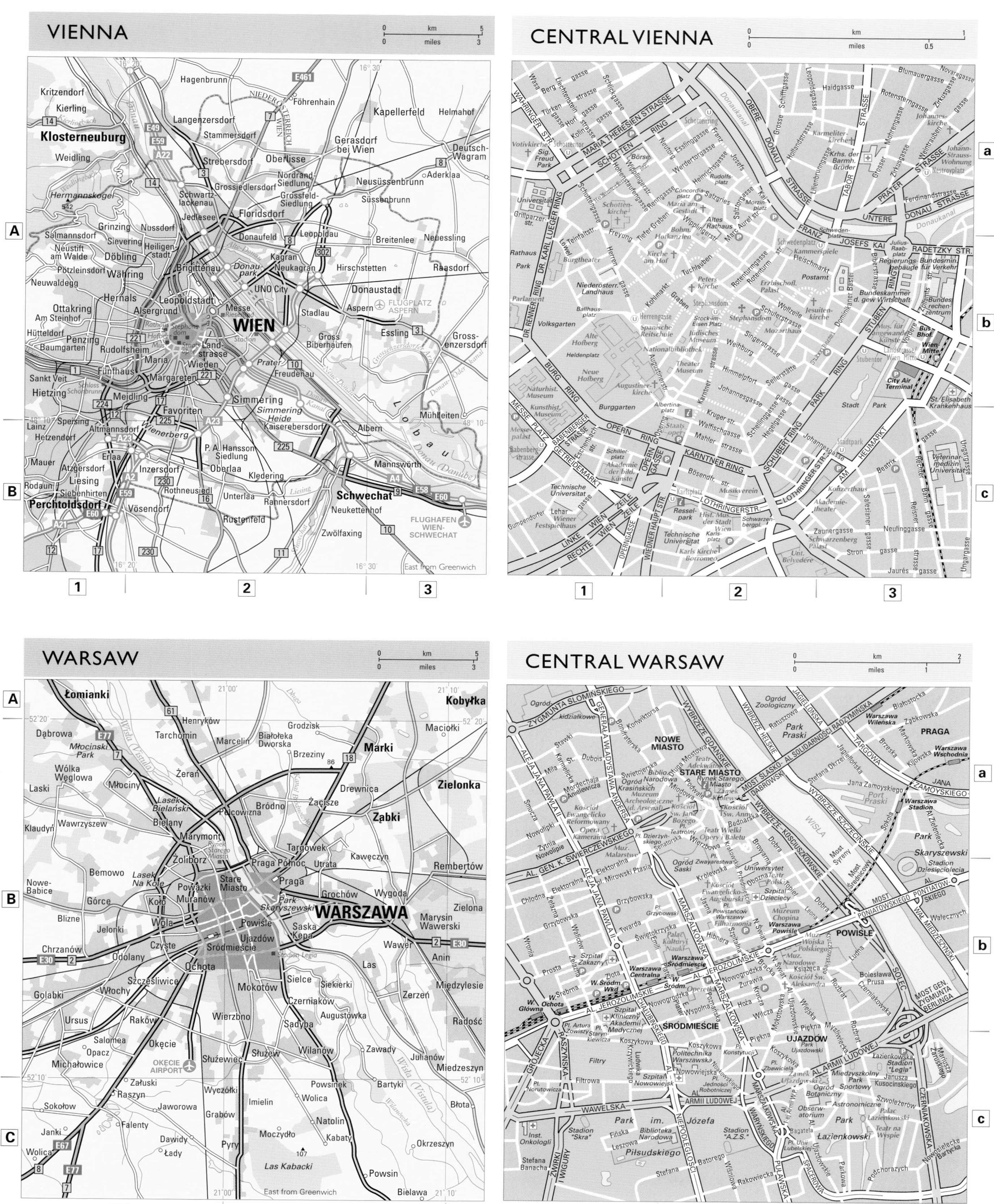
VIENNA
CENTRAL VIENNA
WARSAW
CENTRAL WARSAW
km
miles
East from Greenwich
Klosterneuburg
Kritzendorf
Kierling
Weidling
Hagenbrunn
Föhrenhain
Kapellerfeld
Helmahof
Langenzersdorf
Stammersdorf
Gerasdorf bei Wien
Deutsch-Wagram
Strebersdorf
Oberlisse
Aderklaa
Hermannskogel
Grossjedlersdorf
Neusüssenbrunn
Süssenbrunn
Floridsdorf
Grinzing
Nussdorf
Salmannsdorf
Neustift am Walde
Döbling
Pötzleinsdorf
Währing
Neuwaldegg
Donaufeld
Leopoldau
Breitenlee
Neuessling
Kagran
Neukagran
Hirschstetten
Raasdorf
Brigittenau
UNO City
Donaustadt
Ottakring
Am Steinhof
Hernals
Leopoldstadt
Alsergrund
Messe
WIEN
Stadlau
Aspern
FLUGPLATZ ASPERN
Essling
Gross-enzersdorf
Hütteldorf
Penzing
Baumgarten
Rudolfsheim
Fünfhaus
Landstrasse
Wieden
Gross Biberhaufen
Sankt Veit
Hietzing
Margareten
Freudenau
Meidling
Favoriten
Simmering
Simmering Heide
Mühlleiten
Lainz
Speising
Hetzendorf
Altmannsdorf
Wienerberg
Kaiserebersdorf
Albern
Mauer
P. A. Hansson Siedlung
Oberlaa
Mannswörth
Atzgersdorf
Liesing
Inzersdorf
Kledering
Rodaun
Siebenhirten
Rothneusiedl
Unterlaa
Schwechat
Perchtoldsdorf
Vösendorf
Rannersdorf
Neukettenhof
FLUGHAFEN WIEN-SCHWECHAT
Rustenfeld
Zwölfaxing
Lobau
Donau (Danube)
MARIA THERESIEN STRASSE
SCHOTTEN RING
UNIVERSITÄTS STR.
DR. KARL LUEGER RING
Votivkirche
Sig. Freud Park
Universität
Rathaus Park
Burgtheater
Parlament
Volksgarten
Schottenkirche
Kirche am Hof
Peters Kirche
Graben
Stephansdom
Stephansplatz
Niederösterr. Landhaus
Alte Hofburg
Neue Hofburg
Heldenplatz
Spanische Reitschule
Nationalbibliothek
Jüdisches Museum
Theater Museum
Augustinerkirche
Albertina
Staatsoper
Burggarten
Naturhist. Museum
Kunsthist. Museum
Messepalast
OPERN RING
KÄRNTNER RING
SCHUBERT RING
PARK RING
STUBEN RING
Stadtpark
City Air Terminal
Wien-Mitte
St. Elisabeth Krankenhaus
Schwedenplatz
FRANZ JOSEFS KAI
RADETZKY STR.
OBERE DONAU STRASSE
TABOR STRASSE
PRATER STRASSE
UNTERE DONAU STRASSE
Donaukanal
Karmeliterkirche
Johanneskirche
Postamt
Regierungsgebäude
Bundesministerium für Verkehr
Bundeskammer d. gew Wirtschaft
Mus. für angewandte Künste
Postsparkasse
Akademie der bild. Künste
Technische Universität
Lehar Wiener Festspielhaus
Karlsplatz
Resselpark
Karlskirche
Musikverein
Konzerthaus
Akademietheater
Schwarzenberg Palast
Unt. Belvedere
Veterinär-medizin Universität
LOTHRINGERSTR.
HEUMARKT
LINKE WIEN ZEILE
RECHTE WIEN ZEILE
Łomianki
Kobyłka
Dąbrowa
Henryków
Tarchomin
Marcelin
Białołęka Dworska
Grodzisk
Marki
Maciołki
Młociński Park
Wólka Węglowa
Brzeziny
Żerań
Laski
Młociny
Lasek Bielański
Drewnica
Zielonka
Bielany
Pelcowizna
Bródno
Zacisze
Ząbki
Kłaudyń
Wawrzyszew
Marymont
Targówek
Kawęczyn
Rembertów
Bemowo
Żoliborz
Lasek Na Kole
Praga Północ
Utrata
Nowe-Babice
Powązki
Stare Miasto
Praga
Grochów
Wygoda
Górce
Koło
Muranów
Park Skaryszewski
WARSZAWA
Zielona
Blizne
Wola
Powiśle
Saska Kępa
Marysin Wawerski
Jelonki
Ujazdów
Wawer
Chrzanów
Czyste
Śródmieście
Stadion Legii
Anin
Odolany
Ochota
Las
Szczęśliwice
Sielce
Siekierki
Międzylesie
Gołąbki
Włochy
Mokotów
Zerzeń
Czerniaków
Ursus
Wierzbno
Augustówka
Raków
Sadyba
Radość
Salomea
Okęcie
Opacz
OKĘCIE AIRPORT
Służewiec
Służew
Wilanów
Zawady
Julianów
Michałowice
Miedzeszyn
Załuski
Raszyn
Wyczółki
Powsinek
Bartyki
Jaworowa
Imielin
Wolica
Sokołów
Grabów
Natolin
Błota
Janki
Falenty
Moczydło
Kabaty
Okrzeszyn
Dawidy
Łady
Las Kabacki
Powsin
Bielawa
Wisła (Vistula)
NOWE MIASTO
STARE MIASTO
Rynek Starego Miasta
Park Praski
Ogród Zoologiczny
PRAGA
Warszawa Wileńska
Warszawa Wschodnia
Port Praski
Warszawa Stadion
Park Skaryszewski
Stadion Dziesięciolecia
MOST ŚLĄSKO-DĄBROWSKI
Teatr Wielki Opery i Baletu
Ogród Saski
Ogród Krasińskich
Muzeum Archeologiczne
Plac Kultury i Nauki
Warszawa Centralna
Warszawa Śródmieście
Warszawa Powiśle
POWIŚLE
Muzeum Chopina
Warszawa Filharmonia
MOST PONIATOWSKIEGO
AL. JEROZOLIMSKIE
ŚRÓDMIEŚCIE
UJAZDÓW
Park Ujazdowski
Politechnika Warszawska
Zamek Ujazdowski
Ogród Botaniczny
Obserwatorium Astronomiczne
Park Łazienkowski
Pałac Łazienkowski
Teatr na Wyspie
Stadion "Legia"
Stadion "Skra"
Stadion "A.Z.S."
Park im. Józefa Piłsudskiego
Biblioteka Narodowa
Inst. Onkologii
AL. ARMII LUDOWEJ
WAWELSKA
NIEPODLEGŁOŚCI
MARSZAŁKOWSKA
AL. JANA PAWŁA II
AL. GEN. K. ŚWIERCZEWSKIEGO
WYBRZEŻE KOŚCIUSZKOWSKIE
WYBRZEŻE GDAŃSKIE
WYBRZEŻE SZCZECIŃSKIE
SOLEC
CZERNIAKOWSKA
PUŁAWSKA
GRÓJECKA
RASZYŃSKA

WASHINGTON

0 km 5
0 miles 3

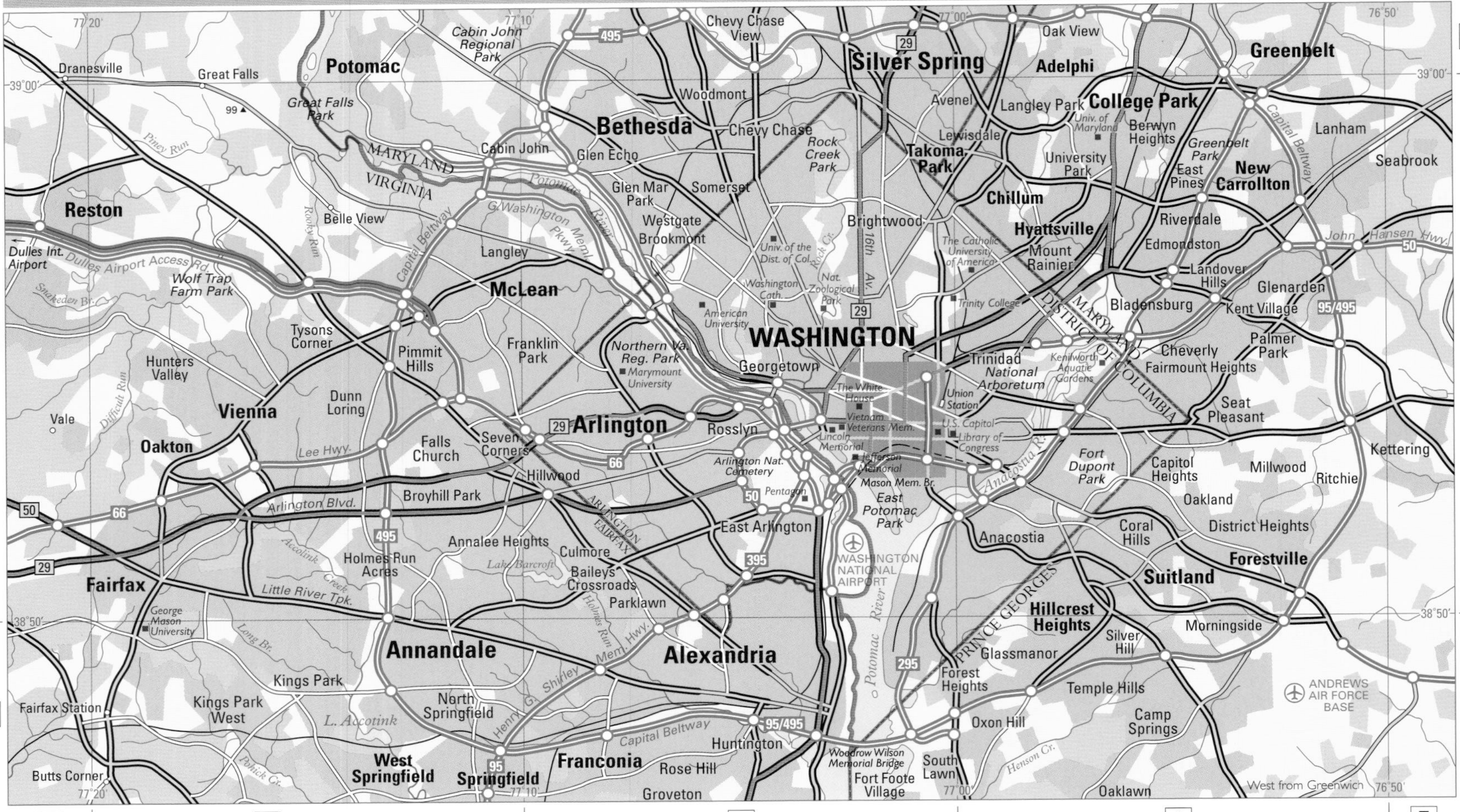

CENTRAL WASHINGTON

0 km 1
0 miles 0.5

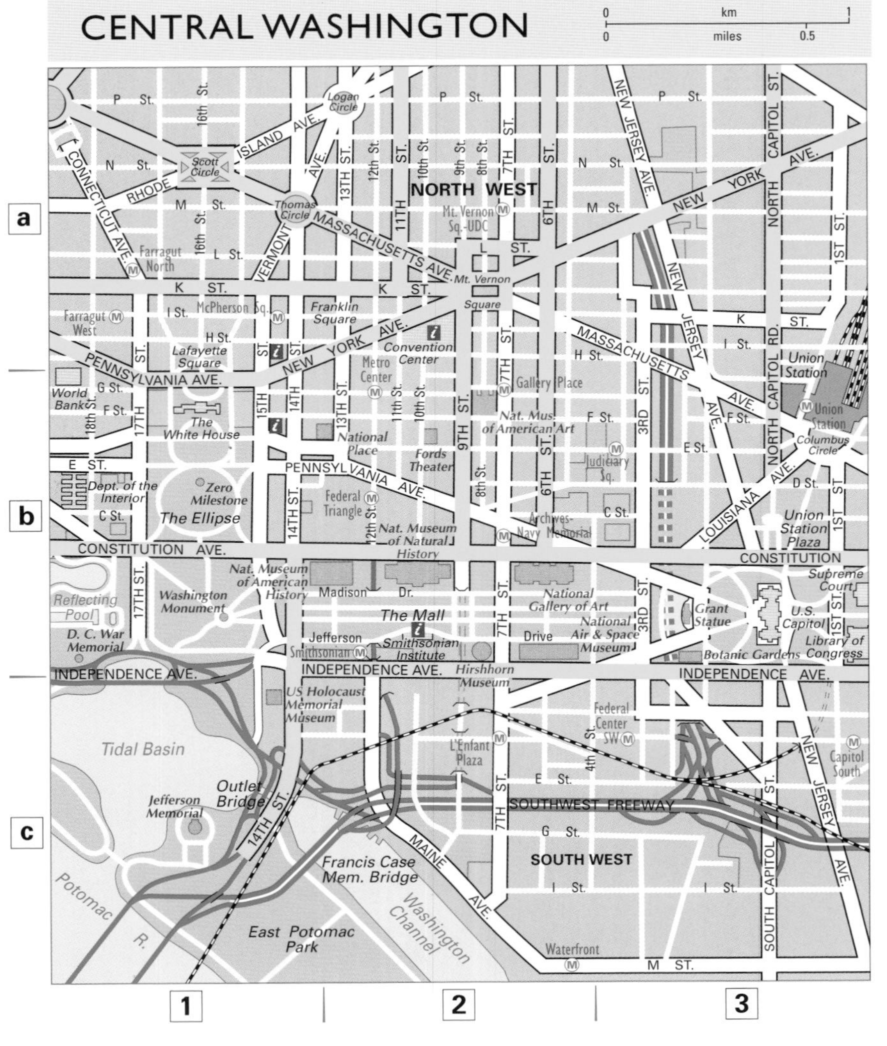

WELLINGTON

0 km 5
0 miles 3

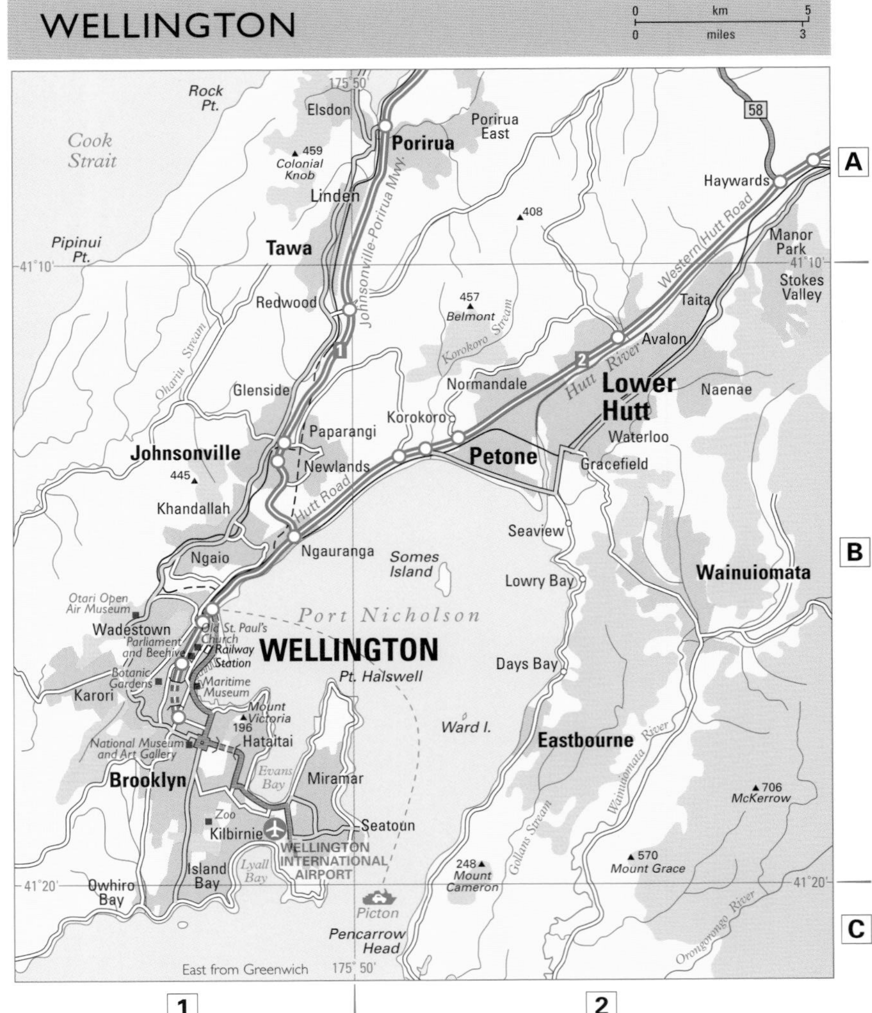

INDEX TO CITY MAPS

The index contains the names of all the principal places and features shown on the City Maps. Each name is followed by an additional entry in italics giving the name of the City Map within which it is located.

The number in bold type which follows each name refers to the number of the City Map page where that feature or place will be found.

The letter and figure which are immediately after the page number give the grid square on the map within which the feature or place is situated. The letter represents the latitude and the figure the longitude. Upper case letters refer to the City Maps, lower case letters to the Central Area Maps. The full geographic reference is provided in the border of the City Maps.

The location given is the centre of the city, suburb or feature and is not necessarily the name. Rivers, canals and roads are indexed to their name. Rivers carry the symbol → after their name.

An explanation of the alphabetical order rules and a list of the abbreviations used are to be found at the beginning of the World Map Index.

A

Aalām, *Baghdad* **3** B2
Aalsmeer, *Amsterdam* **2** B1
Abbey Wood, *London* **15** B4
Abcoude, *Amsterdam* **2** B2
Ābdīn, *Cairo* **7** A2
Abeno, *Osaka* **22** B4
Aberdeen, *Hong Kong* **12** B2
Aberdour, *Edinburgh* **11** A2
Aberdour Castle, *Edinburgh* **11** A2
Abfanggraben →, *Munich* **20** A3
Ablon-sur-Seine, *Paris* **23** B3
Abramtsevo, *Moscow* **19** B4
Abu Dis, *Jerusalem* **13** B2
Abū en Numrus, *Cairo* **7** B2
Abu Ghosh, *Jerusalem* **13** B1
Acacias, *Madrid* **17** c2
Acassuso, *Buenos Aires* **7** A1
Accotink Cr. →, *Washington* **32** B2
Acheres, *Paris* **23** A1
Acilia, *Rome* **25** C1
Aclimação, *São Paulo* **26** B2
Acton, *London* **15** A2
Açúcar, Pão de, *Rio de Janeiro* **24** B2
Ada Beja, *Lisbon* **14** A1
Adams Park, *Atlanta* **3** B2
Adams Shore, *Boston* **6** B4
Addiscombe, *London* **15** B3
Adelphi, *Washington* **32** A4
Aderklaa, *Vienna* **31** A3
Admiralteyskaya Storona, *St. Petersburg* **26** B2
Áffori, *Milan* **18** A2
Aflandshage, *Copenhagen* **10** B3
Afsarīyeh, *Tehran* **30** B2
Agboyi Cr. →, *Lagos* **14** A2
Ågerup, *Copenhagen* **10** A1
Ägesta, *Stockholm* **28** B2
Agincourt, *Toronto* **30** A3
Agora, Arhéa, *Athens* **2** c1
Agra Canal, *Delhi* **10** B2
Agricola Oriental, *Mexico City* **18** B2
Agua Espraiada →, *São Paulo* **26** B2
Agualva-Cacem, *Lisbon* **14** A1
Agustino, Cerro El, *Lima* **16** B2
Ahrensfelde, *Berlin* **5** A4
Ahuntsic, *Montreal* **19** A1
Ai →, *Osaka* **22** A4
Aigremont, *Paris* **23** A1
Air View Park, *Singapore* **27** A2
Airport West, *Melbourne* **17** A1
Aiyaleo, *Athens* **2** B2
Aiyáleos, Óros, *Athens* **2** B1
Ajegunle, *Lagos* **14** B2
Aji, *Osaka* **22** A3
Ajuda, *Lisbon* **14** A1
Akalla, *Stockholm* **28** A1
Akasaka, *Tokyo* **29** b3
Akbarābād, *Tehran* **30** A2
Akershus Slott, *Oslo* **22** A3
Akihabara, *Tokyo* **29** a5
Akrópolis, *Athens* **2** c2
Al 'Azamiyah, *Baghdad* **3** A2
Al Quds = Jerusalem, *Jerusalem* **13** B2
Alaguntan, *Lagos* **14** B2
Alameda, *San Francisco* **25** B3
Alameda, Parque, *Mexico City* **18** b2
Alameda Memorial State Beach Park, *San Francisco* **25** B3
Albern, *Vienna* **31** B2
Albert Park, *Melbourne* **17** B1
Alberton, *Johannesburg* **13** B2
Albertslund, *Copenhagen* **10** B2
Albysjön, *Stockholm* **28** B1
Alcantara, *Lisbon* **14** A1
Alcatraz I., *San Francisco* **25** B2
Alcobendas, *Madrid* **17** A2
Alcorcón, *Madrid* **17** B1
Aldershof, *Berlin* **5** B4
Aldo Bonzi, *Buenos Aires* **7** C1
Aleksandrovskoye, *St. Petersburg* **26** B2
Alexander Nevsky Abbey, *St. Petersburg* **26** B2
Alexander Soutzos Moussío, *Athens* **2** b3
Alexandra, *Johannesburg* **13** A2
Alexandra, *Singapore* **27** B2
Alexandria, *Washington* **32** C3
Alfama, *Lisbon* **14** c3
Alfortville, *Paris* **23** B3
Algés, *Lisbon* **14** A1
Alhambra, *Los Angeles* **16** B4
Alibey →, *Istanbul* **12** B1
Alibey Barajı, *Istanbul* **12** B1
Alibeyköy, *Istanbul* **12** B1
Alimos, *Athens* **2** B2
Alipur, *Calcutta* **8** B1
Allach, *Munich* **20** A1
Allambie Heights, *Sydney* **28** A2
Allard Pierson Museum, *Amsterdam* **2** b2
Allermuir Hill, *Edinburgh* **11** B2
Allerton, Pt., *Boston* **6** B4
Allston, *Boston* **6** A3
Almada, *Lisbon* **14** A2
Almagro, *Buenos Aires* **7** B2
Almargem do Bispo, *Lisbon* **14** A1
Almazovo, *Moscow* **19** A6
Almirante G. Brown, Parque, *Buenos Aires* **7** C2
Almon, *Jerusalem* **13** B2
Almond →, *Edinburgh* **11** B2
Alnabru, *Oslo* **22** A4
Alnsjøen, *Oslo* **22** A4
Alperton, *London* **15** A2
Alpine, *New York* **21** A2
Alrode, *Johannesburg* **13** B2
Alsemerg, *Brussels* **6** B1
Alsergrund, *Vienna* **31** A2
Alsip, *Chicago* **9** C2
Älsten, *Stockholm* **28** B1
Älta, *Stockholm* **28** B3
Altadena, *Los Angeles* **16** A4
Alte-Donau →, *Vienna* **31** A2
Alte Hofburg, *Vienna* **31** b1
Alter Finkenkrug, *Berlin* **5** A1
Altes Rathaus, *Munich* **20** b3
Altglienicke, *Berlin* **5** B4
Altlandsberg, *Berlin* **5** A5
Altlandsberg Nord, *Berlin* **5** A5
Altmannsdorf, *Vienna* **31** B1
Alto da Moóca, *São Paulo* **26** B2
Alto do Pina, *Lisbon* **14** A2
Altona, *Melbourne* **17** B1
Alvaro Obregon, *Mexico City* **18** B1
Alvik, *Stockholm* **28** B1
Älvsjo, *Stockholm* **28** B2
Älvvik, *Stockholm* **28** A3
Am Hasenbergl, *Munich* **20** A2
Am Steinhof, *Vienna* **31** A1
Am Wald, *Munich* **20** B2
Ama Keng, *Singapore* **27** A2
Amadora, *Lisbon* **14** A1
Amagasaki, *Osaka* **22** A3
Amager, *Copenhagen* **10** B3
Amāl Qādisiya, *Baghdad* **3** B2
Amalienborg, *Copenhagen* **10** b3
Amata, *Milan* **18** A1
Ameixoeira, *Lisbon* **14** A2
América, *São Paulo* **26** B1
Amin, *Baghdad* **3** B2
Aminadov, *Jerusalem* **13** B1
Aminyevo, *Moscow* **19** B2
Amīrābād, *Tehran* **30** A2
Amora, *Lisbon* **14** B2
Amoreira, *Lisbon* **14** A1
Ampelokipi, *Athens* **2** B2
Amper →, *Munich* **20** A1
Amstel, *Amsterdam* **2** b2
Amstel →, *Amsterdam* **2** c2
Amstel-Drecht-Kanaal, *Amsterdam* **2** B2
Amstel Station, *Amsterdam* **2** c3
Amstelhof, *Amsterdam* **2** b2
Amstelveen, *Amsterdam* **2** B2
Amsterdam, *Amsterdam* **2** A2
Amsterdam-Rijnkanaal, *Amsterdam* **2** B3
Amsterdam Zoo, *Amsterdam* **2** b3
Amsterdam Zuidoost, *Amsterdam* **2** B2
Amsterdamse Bos, *Amsterdam* **2** B1
Anacostia, *Washington* **32** B4
Anadoluhisarı, *Istanbul* **12** B2
Anadolukavağı, *Istanbul* **12** A2
Anata, *Jerusalem* **13** B2
Ancol, *Jakarta* **13** A1
'Andalus, *Baghdad* **3** B1
Andarai, *Rio de Janeiro* **24** B1
Anderlecht, *Brussels* **6** A1
Anderson Park, *Atlanta* **3** B2
Andingmen, *Beijing* **4** B2
Andrews Air Force Base, *Washington* **32** C4
Ang Mo Kio, *Singapore* **27** A3
Ängby, *Stockholm* **28** A1
Angel I., *San Francisco* **25** A2
Angel Island State Park, *San Francisco* **25** A2
Angke, Kali →, *Jakarta* **13** A1
Angyalföld, *Budapest* **7** A2
Anik, *Mumbai* **20** A2
Anin, *Warsaw* **31** B2
Anjou, *Montreal* **19** A2
Annalee Heights, *Washington* **32** B2
Annandale, *Washington* **32** C2
Anne Frankhuis, *Amsterdam* **2** a1
Antony, *Paris* **23** B2
Anyangch'on, *Seoul* **26** C1
Aoyama, *Tokyo* **29** b2
Ap Lei Chau, *Hong Kong* **12** B1
Apapa, *Lagos* **14** B2
Apelação, *Lisbon* **14** A2
Apterkarskiy Ostrov, *St. Petersburg* **26** B2
Ar Kazimiyah, *Baghdad* **3** B1
Ara →, *Tokyo* **29** A4
Arakawa-Ku, *Tokyo* **29** A3
Arany-hegyi-patak →, *Budapest* **7** A2
Aravaca, *Madrid* **17** B1
Arbataash, *Baghdad* **3** A1
Arc de Triomphe, *Paris* **23** a2
Arcadia, *Los Angeles* **16** B4
Arceuil, *Paris* **23** B2
Arco Plaza, *Los Angeles* **16** b1
Arese, *Milan* **18** A1
Arganzuela, *Madrid* **17** B1
Argenteuil, *Paris* **23** A2
Argonne Forest, *Chicago* **9** C1
Argüelles, *Madrid* **17** a1
Arima, *Osaka* **22** A2
Arima, *Tokyo* **29** B2
Ários Págos, *Athens* **2** c1
Arkhangelskoye, *Moscow* **19** B1
Arlington, *Boston* **6** A2
Arlington, *Washington* **32** B3
Arlington Heights, *Boston* **6** A2
Arlington Nat. Cemetery, *Washington* **32** B3
Armação, *Rio de Janeiro* **24** B2
Armadale, *Melbourne* **17** B2
Armenian Quarter, *Jerusalem* **13** b3
Armour Heights, *Toronto* **30** A2
Arncliffe, *Sydney* **28** B1
Arnold Arboretum, *Boston* **6** B3
Árpádföld, *Budapest* **7** A3
Arrentela, *Lisbon* **14** B2
Årsta, *Stockholm* **28** B2
Art Institute, *Chicago* **9** c2
Artane, *Dublin* **11** A2
Artas, *Jerusalem* **13** B2
Arthur's Seat, *Edinburgh* **11** B3
Aryiróupolis, *Athens* **2** B2
Asagaya, *Tokyo* **29** A2
Asahi, *Osaka* **22** A4
Asakusa, *Tokyo* **29** A3
Asakusabashi, *Tokyo* **29** a5
Asati, *Calcutta* **8** C1
Aschheim, *Munich* **20** A3
Ascot Vale, *Melbourne* **17** A1
Ashburn, *Chicago* **9** C2
Ashburton, *Melbourne* **17** B2
Ashfield, *Sydney* **28** B1
Ashford, *London* **15** B1
Ashiya, *Osaka* **22** A2
Ashiya →, *Osaka* **22** A2
Ashtown, *Dublin* **11** A2
Askisto, *Helsinki* **12** B1
Askrikefjärden, *Stockholm* **28** A3
Asnières, *Paris* **23** A2
Aspern, *Vienna* **31** A2
Aspern, Flugplatz, *Vienna* **31** A3
Assago, *Milan* **18** B1
Assemblée Nationale, *Paris* **23** b3
Assendelft, *Amsterdam* **2** A1
Assiano, *Milan* **18** B1
Astoria, *New York* **21** B2
Astrolabe Park, *Sydney* **28** B2
Atarot Airport, *Jerusalem* **13** A2
Atghara, *Calcutta* **8** B2
Athens = Athínai, *Athens* **2** B2
Athínai, *Athens* **2** B2
Athis-Mons, *Paris* **23** B3
Athlone, *Cape Town* **8** A2
Atholl, *Johannesburg* **13** A2
Atīfīya, *Baghdad* **3** A2
Atişalen, *Istanbul* **12** B1
Atlanta, *Atlanta* **3** B2
Atlanta History Center, *Atlanta* **3** B2
Atomium, *Brussels* **6** A2
Attiki, *Athens* **2** A2
Atzgersdorf, *Vienna* **31** B1
Aubervilliers, *Paris* **23** A3
Aubing, *Munich* **20** B1
Auburndale, *Boston* **6** A2
Aucherdinny, *Edinburgh* **11** B3
Auckland Park, *Johannesburg* **13** B2
Auderghem, *Brussels* **6** B2
Augusta, Mausoleo di, *Rome* **25** b2
Augustówka, *Warsaw* **31** B2
Aulnay-sous-Bois, *Paris* **23** A3
Aurelio, *Rome* **25** B1
Ausīm, *Cairo* **7** A1
Austerlitz, Gare d', *Paris* **23** A3
Austin, *Chicago* **9** B2
Avalon, *Wellington* **32** B2
Avedøre, *Copenhagen* **10** B2
Avellaneda, *Buenos Aires* **7** C2
Avenel, *Washington* **32** B4
Avondale, *Chicago* **9** B2
Avondale Heights, *Melbourne* **17** A1
Avtovo, *St. Petersburg* **26** B1
Ayazağa, *Istanbul* **12** B1
Ayer Chawan, P., *Singapore* **27** B2
Ayer Merbau, P., *Singapore* **27** B2
Ayía Marina, *Athens* **2** C3
Ayía Paraskeví, *Athens* **2** A2
Áyios Dhimitrios, *Athens* **2** B2
Áyios Ioánnis Rendis, *Athens* **2** B1
Azabu, *Tokyo* **29** c3
Azcapotzalco, *Mexico City* **18** B1
Azteca, Estadia, *Mexico City* **18** C2
Azucar, Cerro Pan de, *Santiago* **26** A1

B

Baambrugge, *Amsterdam* **2** B2
Baba I., *Karachi* **14** B1
Babarpur, *Delhi* **10** A2
Babushkin, *Moscow* **19** A4
Back B., *Mumbai* **20** B1
Baclaran, *Manila* **17** B2
Bacoor, *Manila* **17** C1
Bacoor B., *Manila* **17** C1
Badalona, *Barcelona* **4** A2
Badhoevedorp, *Amsterdam* **2** A1
Badli, *Delhi* **10** A1
Bærum, *Oslo* **22** A2
Bağcılar, *Istanbul* **12** B1
Bàggio, *Milan* **18** B1
Bāgh-e-Feyz, *Tehran* **30** A1
Baghdād, *Baghdad* **3** A2
Bagmari, *Calcutta* **8** B2
Bagneux, *Paris* **23** B2
Bagnolet, *Paris* **23** A3
Bagsværd, *Copenhagen* **10** A2
Bagsværd Sø, *Copenhagen* **10** A2
Baguiati, *Calcutta* **8** B2
Bagumbayan, *Manila* **17** C2
Bahçeköy, *Istanbul* **12** A1
Bahtīm, *Cairo* **7** A2
Baileys Crossroads, *Washington* **32** B3
Bailly, *Paris* **23** A1
Bairro Alto, *Lisbon* **14** c1
Bairro Lopes, *Lisbon* **14** b3
Baisha, *Canton* **8** B2
Baisha →, *Canton* **8** B2
Baixa, *Lisbon* **14** c2
Baiyun Airport, *Canton* **8** A2
Baiyun Hill Scenic Spot, *Canton* **8** B2
Bakırköy, *Istanbul* **12** C1
Bakovka, *Moscow* **19** B2
Bal Harbor, *Miami* **18** A2
Balara, *Manila* **17** B2
Balashikha, *Moscow* **19** B5
Baldia, *Karachi* **14** A1
Baldoyle, *Dublin* **11** A3
Baldwin Hills, *Los Angeles* **16** B2
Baldwin Hills Res., *Los Angeles* **16** B2
Balgowlah, *Sydney* **28** A2
Balgowlah Heights, *Sydney* **28** A2
Balham, *London* **15** B3
Bali, *Calcutta* **8** B1
Baliganja, *Calcutta* **8** B2
Balingsnäs, *Stockholm* **28** B2
Balingsta, *Stockholm* **28** B2
Balintawak, *Manila* **17** B1
Balitai, *Tianjin* **30** B2
Ballerup, *Copenhagen* **10** A2
Ballinteer, *Dublin* **11** B2
Ballyboden, *Dublin* **11** B2
Ballybrack, *Dublin* **11** B3
Ballyfermot, *Dublin* **11** A1
Ballymorefinn Hill, *Dublin* **11** B1
Ballymun, *Dublin* **11** A2
Balmain, *Sydney* **28** B2
Baluhati, *Calcutta* **8** B1
Balvanera, *Buenos Aires* **7** B2
Balwyn, *Melbourne* **17** A2
Balwyn North, *Melbourne* **17** A2
Banātica, *Lisbon* **14** A1
Banco do Brasil, Centro Cultural, *Rio de Janeiro* **24** a2
Bandra, *Mumbai* **20** A1
Bandra Pt., *Mumbai* **20** A1
Bang Kapi, *Bangkok* **3** B2
Bang Kholaem, *Bangkok* **3** A2
Bang Na, *Bangkok* **3** B2
Bang Phlad, *Bangkok* **3** a1
Bangkhen, *Bangkok* **3** A2
Bangkok = Krung Thep, *Bangkok* **3** B2
Bangkok Noi, *Bangkok* **3** B1
Bangkok Yai, *Bangkok* **3** B1
Banglamphoo, *Bangkok* **3** b2
Banglo, *Calcutta* **8** B1
Bangrak, *Bangkok* **3** B2
Bangsu, *Bangkok* **3** B2
Bank, *London* **15** b5
Bank of America, *San Francisco* **25** b2
Bank of China Tower, *Hong Kong* **12** c1
Banks, C., *Sydney* **28** C2
Banksmeadow, *Sydney* **28** B2
Banstala, *Calcutta* **8** B2
Bantra, *Calcutta* **8** B1
Baoshan, *Shanghai* **27** A1
Bar Giyora, *Jerusalem* **13** B1
Barahanagar, *Calcutta* **8** B2
Barajas, *Madrid* **17** B2
Barajas, Aeropuerto Transoceanico de, *Madrid* **17** B2
Barakpur, *Calcutta* **8** A2
Barberini, Palazzo, *Rome* **25** b3
Barbican, *London* **15** a4
Barcarena, *Lisbon* **14** A1
Barcarena, Rib. de →, *Lisbon* **14** A1
Barcelona, *Barcelona* **4** A2
Barcelona-Prat, Aeropuerta de, *Barcelona* **4** B1
Barceloneta, *Barcelona* **4** A2
Barking, *London* **15** A4
Barkingside, *London* **15** A4
Barnes, *London* **15** B2
Barnet, *London* **15** A2
Barra Andai, *Karachi* **14** B2
Barra Funda, *São Paulo* **26** B2
Barracas, *Buenos Aires* **7** B2
Barranco, *Lima* **16** B2
Barreiro, *Lisbon* **14** B2
Barreto, *Rio de Janeiro* **24** B2
Bartala, *Calcutta* **8** B1
Barton Park, *Sydney* **28** B1
Bartyki, *Warsaw* **31** C2
Barvikha, *Moscow* **19** B1
Bastille, Place de la, *Paris* **23** c5
Basus, *Cairo* **7** A2
Batanagar, *Calcutta* **8** B1
Bath Beach, *New York* **21** C1
Bath I., *Karachi* **14** B2
Batir, *Jerusalem* **13** B1
Batok, Bukit, *Singapore* **27** A2
Battersea, *London* **15** B3
Battery Park, *New York* **21** f1
Bauman, *Moscow* **19** B4
Baumgarten, *Vienna* **31** A1
Bay Harbour Islands, *Miami* **18** A2
Bay Ridge, *New York* **21** C1
Bayonne, *New York* **21** B1
Bayshore, *San Francisco* **25** B3
Bayswater, *London* **15** b2
Bayt Lahm = Bethlehem, *Jerusalem* **13** B2
Bayview, *San Francisco* **25** B2
Bāzār, *Tehran* **30** A2
Beachmont, *Boston* **6** A4
Beacon Hill, *Hong Kong* **12** A2
Beato, *Lisbon* **14** A2
Beaumont, *Dublin* **11** A2
Beaumonte Heights, *Toronto* **30** A1
Bebek, *Istanbul* **12** B2
Běchovice, *Prague* **24** B3
Beck L., *Chicago* **9** A1
Beckenham, *London* **15** B3
Beckton, *London* **15** A4
Becontree, *London* **15** A4
Beddington Corner, *London* **15** B3
Bedford, *Boston* **6** A2
Bedford Park, *Chicago* **9** C2
Bedford Park, *New York* **21** A2
Bedford Stuyvesant, *New York* **21** B2
Bedford View, *Johannesburg* **13** B2
Bedok, *Singapore* **27** B3
Bedok, Res., *Singapore* **27** A3
Beersel, *Brussels* **6** B1
Behala, *Calcutta* **8** B1
Bei Hai, *Beijing* **4** B2
Beicai, *Shanghai* **27** B2
Beicang, *Tianjin* **30** A1
Beihai Park, *Beijing* **4** b2
Beijing, *Beijing* **4** B1
Beit Ghur el-Fawqa, *Jerusalem* **13** A1
Beit Hanina, *Jerusalem* **13** B2
Beit Iksa, *Jerusalem* **13** B1
Beit I'nan, *Jerusalem* **13** A1
Beit Jala, *Jerusalem* **13** B2
Beit Lekhem = Bethlehem, *Jerusalem* **13** B2
Beit Nekofa, *Jerusalem* **13** B1
Beit Sahur, *Jerusalem* **13** B2
Beit Surik, *Jerusalem* **13** B1
Beit Zayit, *Jerusalem* **13** B1
Beitaipingzhuan, *Beijing* **4** B1
Beitar Illit, *Jerusalem* **13** B1
Beitsun, *Canton* **8** B2
Beitunya, *Jerusalem* **13** A2
Beixing Jing Park, *Shanghai* **27** B1
Békásmegyer, *Budapest* **7** A2
Bekkelaget, *Oslo* **22** A3
Bel Air, *Los Angeles* **16** B2
Bela Vista, *São Paulo* **26** B2
Bélanger, *Montreal* **19** A1
Belas, *Lisbon* **14** A1
Belas Artes, Museu Nacionale de, *Rio de Janeiro* **24** b2
Beleghata, *Calcutta* **8** B2
Belém, *Lisbon* **14** A1
Belém, Torre de, *Lisbon* **14** A1
Belènzinho, *São Paulo* **26** B2
Belgachiya, *Calcutta* **8** B2
Belgharia, *Calcutta* **8** B2
Belgrano, *Buenos Aires* **7** B2
Belgravia, *London* **15** c3
Bell, *Los Angeles* **16** C3
Bell Gardens, *Los Angeles* **16** C4
Bell Tower, *Beijing* **4** a2
Bellavista, *Lima* **16** B2
Bellavista, *Santiago* **26** C2
Belle Harbor, *New York* **21** C2
Belle View, *Washington* **32** B2
Bellevue, Schloss, *Berlin* **5** a2
Bellingham, *London* **15** B3
Bellwood, *Chicago* **9** B1
Belmont, *Boston* **6** A2
Belmont, *London* **15** A2
Belmont, *Wellington* **32** B2
Belmont Harbor, *Chicago* **9** B3
Belmore, *Sydney* **28** B1
Belur, *Calcutta* **8** B2
Belvedere, *Atlanta* **3** B3
Belvedere, *London* **15** B4
Belvedere, *San Francisco* **25** A2
Belyayevo Bogorodskoye, *Moscow* **19** C3
Bemowo, *Warsaw* **31** B1
Benaki, Mousío, *Athens* **2** b3
Bendale, *Toronto* **30** A3
Bendkhal, *Mumbai* **20** B2
Benefica, *Rio de Janeiro* **24** B1
Benfica, *Lisbon* **14** A1
Benito Juárez, *Mexico City* **18** B2
Benito Juárez, Aeropuerto Int., *Mexico City* **18** B2
Bensonhurst, *New York* **21** C2
Berchem-Sainte-Agathe, *Brussels* **6** A1
Berg am Laim, *Munich* **20** B2
Bergenfield, *New York* **21** A2
Bergham, *Munich* **20** B2
Bergvliet, *Cape Town* **8** B1
Beri, *Barcelona* **4** A1
Berkeley, *San Francisco* **25** A3
Berlin, *Berlin* **5** A3
Bermondsey, *London* **15** B3
Bernabeu, Estadio, *Madrid* **17** B1
Bernal Heights, *San Francisco* **25** B2
Berwyn, *Chicago* **9** B2
Berwyn Heights, *Washington* **32** B4
Besiktas, *Istanbul* **12** B2
Besós →, *Barcelona* **4** A2
Bethesda, *Washington* **32** B3
Bethlehem, *Jerusalem* **13** B2
Bethnal Green, *London* **15** A3
Betor, *Calcutta* **8** B1
Beurs, *Amsterdam* **2** b2
Beverley Hills, *Sydney* **28** B1
Beverley Park, *Sydney* **28** B1
Beverly, *Chicago* **9** C3
Beverly Glen, *Los Angeles* **16** B2
Beverly Hills, *Los Angeles* **16** B2
Bexley, *London* **15** B4
Bexley, *Sydney* **28** B1
Bexleyheath, *London* **15** B4
Beykoz, *Istanbul* **12** B2
Beylerbeyi, *Istanbul* **12** B2
Beyoğlu, *Istanbul* **12** B1
Bezons, *Paris* **23** A2
Bezuidenhout Park, *Johannesburg* **13** B2
Bhadrakali, *Calcutta* **8** A2
Bhalswa, *Delhi* **10** A2
Bhambo Khan Qarmati, *Karachi* **14** B2
Bhatsala, *Calcutta* **8** B1
Bhawanipur, *Calcutta* **8** B2
Bhuleshwar, *Mumbai* **20** b2
Białołeka Dworska, *Warsaw* **31** B2
Biblioteca Nacional, *Rio de Janeiro* **24** c2
Bicentennial Park, *Sydney* **28** B1
Bickley, *London* **15** B4
Bidu, *Jerusalem* **13** B1
Bielany, *Warsaw* **31** B1
Bielawa, *Warsaw* **31** C2
Biesdorf, *Berlin* **5** A4
Bièvre →, *Paris* **23** B1
Bièvres, *Paris* **23** B2
Bilston, *Edinburgh* **11** B2
Binacayan, *Manila* **17** C1
Binondo, *Manila* **17** B1
Birak el Kiyam, *Cairo* **7** A1
Birch Cliff, *Toronto* **30** A3
Birkenstein, *Berlin* **5** A5
Birkholz, *Berlin* **5** A4
Birkholzaue, *Berlin* **5** A4
Birrarung Park, *Melbourne* **17** A2
Biscayne Bay, *Miami* **18** B2
Biscayne Park, *Miami* **18** A2
Bishop Lavis, *Cape Town* **8** A2
Bishopscourt, *Cape Town* **8** A1
Bispebjerg, *Copenhagen* **10** A3
Biwon Secret Garden, *Seoul* **26** B1
Björknas, *Stockholm* **28** B3
Black Cr. →, *Toronto* **30** A2
Blackfen, *London* **15** B4
Blackheath, *London* **15** B4
Blackrock, *Dublin* **11** B2
Bladensburg, *Washington* **32** B4
Blair Village, *Atlanta* **3** C2
Blairgowrie, *Johannesburg* **13** A2
Blakehurst, *Sydney* **28** B1
Blakstad, *Oslo* **22** B1
Blankenburg, *Berlin* **5** A3
Blankenfelde, *Berlin* **5** A3
Blizne, *Warsaw* **31** B1
Bloomsbury, *London* **15** a3
Błota, *Warsaw* **31** C3
Blue Island, *Chicago* **9** C2
Bluebell, *Dublin* **11** B1
Bluff Hd., *Hong Kong* **12** B2
Blumberg, *Berlin* **5** A4
Blunt Pt., *San Francisco* **25** A2
Blutenberg, *Munich* **20** B1
Blylaget, *Oslo* **22** B3
Bo-Kaap Museum, *Cape Town* **8** c2
Boa Vista, Alto do, *Rio de Janeiro* **24** B1
Boardwalk, *New York* **21** C3
Boavista, *Lisbon* **14** A2
Bobigny, *Paris* **23** A3
Bocanegra, *Lima* **16** A2
Boedo, *Buenos Aires* **7** B2
Bogenhausen, *Munich* **20** B2
Bogorodskoye, *Moscow* **19** B4
Bogota, *New York* **21** A1
Bogstadvatnet, *Oslo* **22** A2
Bohnsdorf, *Berlin* **5** B4
Bois-Colombes, *Paris* **23** A2
Bois-d'Arcy, *Paris* **23** B1
Boissy-St-Léger, *Paris* **23** B4
Boldinasco, *Milan* **18** B1
Bøler, *Oslo* **22** A4
Bollate, *Milan* **18** A1
Bollebeek, *Brussels* **6** A1
Bollensdorf, *Berlin* **5** A5
Bollmora, *Stockholm* **28** B3
Bolshaya-Okhta, *St. Petersburg* **26** B2
Bolton, *Atlanta* **3** B2
Bom Retiro, *São Paulo* **26** B2
Bombay = Mumbai, *Mumbai* **20** B2
Bondi, *Sydney* **28** B2
Bondy, *Paris* **23** A3
Bondy, Forêt de, *Paris* **23** A4
Bonifacio Monument, *Manila* **17** B1
Bonneuil-sur-Marne, *Paris* **23** B4
Bonnington, *Edinburgh* **11** B1
Bonnyrig and Lasswade, *Edinburgh* **11** B3
Bonsucesso, *Rio de Janeiro* **24** B1
Bontebeuwel, *Cape Town* **8** A2
Boo, *Stockholm* **28** A3
Booterstown, *Dublin* **11** B2
Borisovo, *Moscow* **19** C4
Borle, *Mumbai* **20** A2
Boronia Park, *Sydney* **28** A1
Borough Park, *New York* **21** C2
Bosmont, *Johannesburg* **13** B1
Bosön, *Stockholm* **28** A3
Bosporus = Istanbul Boğazi, *Istanbul* **12** B2
Bostancı, *Istanbul* **12** C2
Boston Harbor, *Boston* **6** A4
Botafogo, *Rio de Janeiro* **24** B1
Botanisk Have, *Copenhagen* **10** b2
Botany, *Sydney* **28** B2
Botany B., *Sydney* **28** B2
Botany Bay Nat. Park, *Sydney* **28** B2
Botič →, *Prague* **24** B3
Botica Sete, *Lisbon* **14** A1
Boucherville, *Montreal* **19** A3
Boucherville, Îs. de, *Montreal* **19** A3
Bougival, *Paris* **23** A1
Boulder Pt., *Hong Kong* **12** B1
Boulogne, Bois de, *Paris* **23** A2
Boulogne-Billancourt, *Paris* **23** A2
Bourg-la-Reine, *Paris* **23** B2
Bouviers, *Paris* **23** B1
Bovenkerk, *Amsterdam* **2** B2
Bovenkerker Polder, *Amsterdam* **2** B2
Bovisa, *Milan* **18** A2
Bow, *London* **15** A3
Bowery, *New York* **21** e2
Boyacıköy, *Istanbul* **12** B2
Boyle Heights, *Los Angeles* **16** B3
Bradbury Building, *Los Angeles* **16** b2
Braepark, *Edinburgh* **11** B2
Braid, *Edinburgh* **11** B2
Bramley, *Johannesburg* **13** A2
Brandenburger Tor, *Berlin* **5** A3
Brani, P., *Singapore* **27** B3
Branik, *Prague* **24** B2
Brännkyrka, *Stockholm* **28** B2
Brás, *São Paulo* **26** B2
Brasilândia, *São Paulo* **26** A1
Brateyevo, *Moscow* **19** C4
Bratsevo, *Moscow* **19** A2
Bray, *Dublin* **11** B3
Braybrook, *Melbourne* **17** A1
Brázdim, *Prague* **24** A3
Breach Candy, *Mumbai* **20** a1
Breakheart Reservation, *Boston* **6** A3
Brede, *Copenhagen* **10** A3
Breeds Pond, *Boston* **6** A4
Breezy Point, *New York* **21** C2
Breitenlee, *Vienna* **31** A3
Breña, *Lima* **16** B2
Brent, *London* **15** A2
Brent Res., *London* **15** A2
Brentford, *London* **15** B2
Brentwood Park, *Los Angeles* **16** B2
Brera, *Milan* **18** B2
Bresso, *Milan* **18** A2
Brevik, *Stockholm* **28** A3
Břevnov, *Prague* **24** B2
Bridgeport, *Chicago* **9** B3
Bridgetown, *Cape Town* **8** A2
Bridgeview, *Chicago* **9** C2
Brighton, *Boston* **6** A3
Brighton, *Melbourne* **17** B1
Brighton le Sands, *Sydney* **28** B1
Brighton Park, *Chicago* **9** C2
Brightwood, *Washington* **32** B3
Brigittenau, *Vienna* **31** A2
Brimbank Park, *Melbourne* **17** A1
Brisbane, *San Francisco* **25** B2
British Museum, *London* **15** a3
Britz, *Berlin* **5** B3
Brixton, *London* **15** B3
Broad Sd., *Boston* **6** A4
Broadmeadows, *Melbourne* **17** A1
Broadmoor, *San Francisco* **25** B2
Broadview, *Chicago* **9** B1
Broadway, *New York* **21** e1
Brockley, *London* **15** B3
Bródno, *Warsaw* **31** B2
Bródnowski, Kanal, *Warsaw* **31** B2
Broek in Waterland, *Amsterdam* **2** A2
Bromley, *London* **15** B4
Bromley Common, *London* **15** B4
Bromma, *Stockholm* **28** A1
Bromma flygplats, *Stockholm* **28** A1
Brompton, *London* **15** c2
Brøndby Strand, *Copenhagen* **10** B2
Brøndbyøster, *Copenhagen* **10** B2
Brøndbyvester, *Copenhagen* **10** B2
Brondesbury, *London* **15** A2
Brønnøya, *Oslo* **22** A2
Brønshøj, *Copenhagen* **10** A2
Bronxville, *New York* **21** A3
Brookfield, *Chicago* **9** C1

Brookhaven, *Atlanta* 3 A2
Brookline, *Boston* 6 B3
Brooklyn, *Cape Town* 8 A1
Brooklyn, *New York* 21 C2
Brooklyn, *Wellington* 32 B1
Brooklyn Bridge, *New York* 21 f2
Brookmont, *Washington* 32 B3
Brossard, *Montreal* 19 B3
Brou-sur-Chantereine, *Paris* 23 A4
Brown, *Toronto* 30 A3
Broyhill Park, *Washington* 32 B2
Brughério, *Milan* 18 A2
Brunswick, *Melbourne* 17 A1
Brush Hill, *Boston* 6 B1
Brussegem, *Brussels* 6 A1
Brussel Nat. Luchthaven, *Brussels* 6 A2
Brussels = Bruxelles, *Brussels* 6 A2
Bruxelles, *Brussels* 6 A2
Bruzzano, *Milan* 18 A2
Bry-sur-Marne, *Paris* 23 A4
Bryanston, *Johannesburg* 13 A1
Bryn, *Oslo* 22 A1
Brzeziny, *Warsaw* 31 B2
Bubeneč, *Prague* 24 B2
Buc, *Paris* 23 B1
Buchenhain, *Munich* 20 B1
Buchholz, *Berlin* 5 A3
Buckhead, *Atlanta* 3 A2
Buckingham Palace, *London* 15 b3
Buckow, *Berlin* 5 B3
Buda, *Budapest* 7 A2
Budafok, *Budapest* 7 B2
Budaörs, *Budapest* 7 B1
Budapest, *Budapest* 7 B2
Budatétény, *Budapest* 7 B2
Budavaripalota, *Budapest* 7 b2
Buddinge, *Copenhagen* 10 A3
Budokan, *Tokyo* 29 a4
Buena Vista, *San Francisco* 25 B2
Buenos Aires, *Buenos Aires* 7 B2
Bufalotta, *Rome* 25 B2
Bugio, *Lisbon* 14 B1
Buiksloot, *Amsterdam* 2 A2
Buitenveldert, *Amsterdam* 2 B2
Buizingen, *Brussels* 6 B1
Bukit Panjang Nature Reserve, *Singapore* 27 A2
Bukit Timah Nature Reserve, *Singapore* 27 A2
Bukum, P., *Singapore* 27 B2
Bûlâq, *Cairo* 7 A2
Bule, *Manila* 17 C2
Bulim, *Singapore* 27 A2
Bullen Park, *Melbourne* 17 A2
Bundoora North, *Melbourne* 17 A2
Bundoora Park, *Melbourne* 17 A2
Bunker I., *Karachi* 14 B1
Bunkyo-Ku, *Tokyo* 29 A3
Bunnefjorden, *Oslo* 22 A3
Buona Vista Park, *Singapore* 27 B2
Burbank, *Chicago* 9 C2
Burbank, *Los Angeles* 16 A3
Burlington, *Boston* 6 A2
Burnham Park, *Chicago* 9 c2
Burnham Park Harbor, *Chicago* 9 B3
Burnhamthorpe, *Toronto* 30 B1
Burnt Oak, *London* 15 A2
Burntisland, *Edinburgh* 11 A2
Burnwynd, *Edinburgh* 11 B1
Burqa, *Jerusalem* 13 A2
Burtus, *Cairo* 7 A1
Burudvatn, *Oslo* 22 A2
Burwood, *Sydney* 28 B1
Bushwick, *New York* 21 B2
Bushy Park, *London* 15 B1
Butantã, *São Paulo* 26 B1
Butcher I., *Mumbai* 20 B2
Butts Corner, *Washington* 32 C2
Büyükdere, *Istanbul* 12 B2
Byculla, *Mumbai* 20 B2
Bygdøy, *Oslo* 22 A3

C

C.N. Tower, *Toronto* 30 B2
Cabaçu de Cima →, *São Paulo* 26 A2
Caballito, *Buenos Aires* 7 B2
Cabin John, *Washington* 32 B2
Cabin John Regional Park, *Washington* 32 A2
Cabinteely, *Dublin* 11 B3
Cabra, *Dublin* 11 A2
Cabuçú de Baixo →, *São Paulo* 26 A1
Cachan, *Paris* 23 B2
Cachenka →, *Moscow* 19 B1
Cachoeira, Rib. da →, *São Paulo* 26 B1
Cacilhas, *Lisbon* 14 A2
Cahuenga Pk., *Los Angeles* 16 B3
Cairo = El Qâhira, *Cairo* 7 A2
Caju, *Rio de Janeiro* 24 B1
Čakovice, *Prague* 24 B3
Calcutta = Kolkata, *Calcutta* 8 B2
California Inst. of Tech., *Los Angeles* 16 B4
California Plaza, *Los Angeles* 16 b1
California State Univ., *Los Angeles* 16 B3
Callao, *Lima* 16 B2
Caloocan, *Manila* 17 B1
Calumet Park, *Chicago* 9 C3
Calumet Sag Channel →, *Chicago* 9 C2
Calumpang, *Manila* 17 B2
Calvairate, *Milan* 18 B2
Camarate, *Lisbon* 14 A2
Camaroes, *Lisbon* 14 A1
Camberwell, *London* 15 B3
Camberwell, *Melbourne* 17 B2
Cambridge, *Boston* 6 A3
Cambridge Res., *Boston* 6 A2
Cambuci, *São Paulo* 26 B2
Camden, *London* 15 A3
Cameron, Mt., *Wellington* 32 B2
Çamlica, *Istanbul* 12 B2
Camp Springs, *Washington* 32 C4
Campamento, *Madrid* 17 B1
Campbellfield, *Melbourne* 17 A1
Camperdown, *Sydney* 28 B2
Campidoglio, *Rome* 25 c3
Campo, Casa de, *Madrid* 17 B1
Campo F.C. Barcelona, *Barcelona* 4 A1
Campo Grando, *Lisbon* 14 A2
Campo Pequeño, *Lisbon* 14 A2
Campolide, *Lisbon* 14 A2
Camps Bay, *Cape Town* 8 A1
C'an San Joan, *Barcelona* 4 A2
Cañacao B., *Manila* 17 C1
Canarsie, *New York* 21 C2
Cancelleria, Palazzo dei, *Rome* 25 c2
Candiac, *Montreal* 19 B3
Caneças, *Lisbon* 14 A1
Canillas, *Madrid* 17 B2
Canillejas, *Madrid* 17 B2
Canning Town, *London* 15 A4
Canteras de Vallecas, *Madrid* 17 B2
Canterbury, *Melbourne* 17 A2
Canterbury, *Sydney* 28 B1
Canton = Guangzhou, *Canton* 8 B2
Caoheijing, *Shanghai* 27 B1
Capão Redondo, *São Paulo* 26 B1
Caparica, *Lisbon* 14 A2
Caparica, Costa da, *Lisbon* 14 B1
Cape Flats, *Cape Town* 8 B2
Cape Town, *Cape Town* 8 A1
Capitol Heights, *Washington* 32 B4
Capitol Hill, *Washington* 32 B4
Capitolini, Musei, *Rome* 25 c3
Captain Cook Bridge, *Sydney* 28 C1
Captain Cook Landing Place Park, *Sydney* 28 C2
Capuchos, *Lisbon* 14 B1
Carabanchel Alto, *Madrid* 17 B1
Carabanchel Bajo, *Madrid* 17 B1
Carapachay, *Buenos Aires* 7 B1
Caraza, *Buenos Aires* 7 C2
Caridad, *Manila* 17 C1
Carioca, Sa. da, *Rio de Janeiro* 24 B1
Carlstadt, *New York* 21 A1
Carlton, *Melbourne* 17 A1
Carmen de Huechuraba, *Santiago* 26 B1
Carmen de la Legua, *Lima* 16 B2
Carnaxide, *Lisbon* 14 A1
Carnegie, *Melbourne* 17 B2
Carnegie Hall, *New York* 21 c2
Carnide, *Lisbon* 14 A1
Carol City, *Miami* 18 A1
Carrascal, *Santiago* 26 B1
Carrickmines, *Dublin* 11 B3
Carrières-sous-Bois, *Paris* 23 A1
Carrières-sous-Poissy, *Paris* 23 A1
Carrières-sur-Seine, *Paris* 23 A2
Carrigeen Bay, *Dublin* 11 A3
Cartierville, *Montreal* 19 A1
Casa Verde, *São Paulo* 26 A1
Casal Morena, *Rome* 25 C2
Casalotti, *Rome* 25 B1
Cascade Heights, *Atlanta* 3 B2
Castel Sant'Angelo, *Rome* 25 B1
Castle, *Dublin* 11 c2
Castle, *Edinburgh* 11 b2
Castle of Good Hope, *Cape Town* 8 c3
Castleknock, *Dublin* 11 A1
Castleton Corners, *New York* 21 C1
Catedral Metropolitana, *Mexico City* 18 b3
Catedral Metropolitana, *Rio de Janeiro* 24 c1
Catete, *Rio de Janeiro* 24 B1
Catford, *London* 15 B3
Caulfield, *Melbourne* 17 B2
Causeway Bay, *Hong Kong* 12 c3
Cavite, *Manila* 17 C1
Caxias, *Lisbon* 14 A1
Cebecci, *Istanbul* 12 B1
Cecchignola, *Rome* 25 C2
Cecilienhof, Schloss, *Berlin* 5 B1
Cedar Grove, *Atlanta* 3 C3
Cempaka Putih, *Jakarta* 13 B2
Çengelköy, *Istanbul* 12 B2
Cengkareng, *Jakarta* 13 A1
Centennial Park, *Sydney* 28 B2
Center Hill, *Atlanta* 3 B2
Centocelle, *Rome* 25 B2
Centraal Station, *Amsterdam* 2 a2
Central Park, *New York* 21 B2
Cerillos, *Santiago* 26 B1
Cerro de la Estrella, *Mexico City* 18 B2
Cerro de los Angeles, *Madrid* 17 C1
Cerro Navia, *Santiago* 26 B1
Certanovka →, *Moscow* 19 C3
Certanovo, *Moscow* 19 C3
Cesano Boscone, *Milan* 18 B1
Cesate, *Milan* 18 A1
Cha Kwo Ling, *Hong Kong* 12 B2
Chacarrita, *Buenos Aires* 7 B2
Chadwell Heath, *London* 15 A4
Chai Chee, *Singapore* 27 B3
Chai Wan, *Hong Kong* 12 B2
Chai Wan Kok, *Hong Kong* 12 A1
Chaillot, Palais de, *Paris* 23 b2
Chakdaha, *Calcutta* 8 C1
Chamartin, *Madrid* 17 B1
Chamberi, *Madrid* 17 B1
Chambourcy, *Paris* 23 A1
Champ de Mars, Parc du, *Paris* 23 c2
Champigny-sur-Marne, *Paris* 23 B4
Champlain, Pont, *Montreal* 19 B2
Champs Elysées, Avenue des, *Paris* 23 b2
Champs-sur-Marne, *Paris* 23 A4
Chamrail, *Calcutta* 8 B1
Chamshil, *Seoul* 26 B2
Chamwŏn, *Seoul* 26 B2
Chanakyapuri, *Delhi* 10 B2
Chanditala, *Calcutta* 8 A1
Changfeng Park, *Shanghai* 27 B1
Changi, *Singapore* 27 A3
Changi Int. Airport, *Singapore* 27 A3
Changning, *Shanghai* 27 B1
Chantereine, *Paris* 23 A4
Chantian, *Canton* 8 A2
Chao Phraya →, *Bangkok* 3 B2
Chaoyang, *Beijing* 4 B2
Chaoyangmen, *Beijing* 4 B2
Chapelizod, *Dublin* 11 A1
Chapultepec, Bosque de, *Mexico City* 18 B1
Chapultepec, Castillo de, *Mexico City* 18 B1
Charenton-le-Pont, *Paris* 23 B3
Charing Cross, *London* 15 b4
Charleroi, Kanal de →, *Brussels* 6 B1
Charles Bridge, *Prague* 24 b1
Charles Square, *Prague* 24 c1
Charlestown, *Boston* 6 A3
Charlottenburg, *Berlin* 5 A2
Charlottenburg, Schloss, *Berlin* 5 A2
Charlottenlund, *Copenhagen* 10 A3
Charlton, *London* 15 B4
Charneca, *Lisbon* 14 A2
Charneca, *Lisbon* 14 B1
Châteaufort, *Paris* 23 B1
Châtenay-Malabry, *Paris* 23 B2
Chatham, *Chicago* 9 C3
Châtillon, *Paris* 23 B2
Chatou, *Paris* 23 A1
Chatpur, *Calcutta* 8 B2
Chatswood, *Sydney* 28 A2
Chatuchak, *Bangkok* 3 B2
Chatuchak Park, *Bangkok* 3 B2
Chauki, *Karachi* 14 A1
Chavarria, *Lima* 16 B2
Chaville, *Paris* 23 B2
Chayang, *Seoul* 26 B2
Chegi, *Seoul* 26 B2
Chelles, *Paris* 23 A4
Chelles, Canal de, *Paris* 23 A4
Chells-le-Pin, Aérodrome, *Paris* 23 A4
Chelsea, *Boston* 6 A3
Chelsea, *London* 15 B2
Chelsea, *New York* 21 c1
Chembur, *Mumbai* 20 A2
Chennevières-sur-Marne, *Paris* 23 B4
Cheops, *Cairo* 7 B1
Cherepkovo, *Moscow* 19 B2
Chernyovo, *Moscow* 19 A1
Cheryomushki, *Moscow* 19 B3
Chestnut Hill, *Boston* 6 B2
Cheung Sha Wan, *Hong Kong* 12 A1
Cheverly, *Washington* 32 B4
Chevilly-Larue, *Paris* 23 B3
Chevry-Cossigny, *Paris* 23 B4
Chevy Chase, *Washington* 32 B3
Chevy Chase View, *Washington* 32 A3
Chia Keng, *Singapore* 27 A3
Chiaravalle Milanese, *Milan* 18 B2
Chicago, *Chicago* 9 B3
Chicago Harbor, *Chicago* 9 B3
Chicago Lawn, *Chicago* 9 C2
Chicago-Midway Airport, *Chicago* 9 C2
Chicago-O'Hare Int. Airport, *Chicago* 9 B1
Chicago Ridge, *Chicago* 9 C2
Chicago Sanitary and Ship Canal, *Chicago* 9 C2
Chienzui, *Canton* 8 A3
Chik Sha, *Hong Kong* 12 B2
Child's Hill, *London* 15 A2
Chilla Saroda, *Delhi* 10 B2
Chillum, *Washington* 32 B4
Chilly-Mazarin, *Paris* 23 B2
Chinatown, *Los Angeles* 16 a3
Chinatown, *New York* 21 e2
Chinatown, *San Francisco* 25 b2
Chinatown, *Singapore* 27 c2
Chingupota, *Calcutta* 8 C1
Chislehurst, *London* 15 B4
Chiswick, *London* 15 B2
Chiswick House, *London* 15 B2
Chitose, *Tokyo* 29 B2
Chitralada Palace, *Bangkok* 3 B2
Chiyoda-Ku, *Tokyo* 29 b4
Chkalova, *Moscow* 19 C5
Choa Chu Kang, *Singapore* 27 A2
Choboty, *Moscow* 19 C2
Chodov u Prahy, *Prague* 24 B3
Chōfu, *Tokyo* 29 B2
Choisy-le-Roi, *Paris* 23 B3
Cholupice, *Prague* 24 C2
Chom Thong, *Bangkok* 3 B1
Chong Pang, *Singapore* 27 A2
Ch'ŏngdam, *Seoul* 26 B2
Chongmyo Royal Shrine, *Seoul* 26 B1
Chongno, *Seoul* 26 B1
Chongwen, *Beijing* 4 B2
Chŏnho, *Seoul* 26 B2
Chopin, Muzeum, *Warsaw* 31 b2
Chornaya →, *Moscow* 19 B6
Chorrillos, *Lima* 16 C2
Chowpatty Beach, *Mumbai* 20 b1
Christian Quarter, *Jerusalem* 13 b3
Christiansborg, *Copenhagen* 10 c2
Christianshavn, *Copenhagen* 10 A3
Chrysler Building, *New York* 21 c2
Chrzanów, *Warsaw* 31 B1
Chuen Lung, *Hong Kong* 12 A1
Chuk Kok, *Hong Kong* 12 A2
Chulalongkorn Univ., *Bangkok* 3 B2
Chung, *Seoul* 26 B1
Chunghwa, *Seoul* 26 B2
Chungnangch'on →, *Seoul* 26 B1
Chūō-Ku, *Tokyo* 29 b5
Church End, *London* 15 A2
Churchtown, *Dublin* 11 B2
Ciampino, *Rome* 25 C2
Ciampino, Aeroporto di, *Rome* 25 C2
Cicero, *Chicago* 9 B2
Cilandak, *Jakarta* 13 B1
Cilincing, *Jakarta* 13 A2
Ciliwung →, *Jakarta* 13 B2
Cimice, *Prague* 24 B2
Cinecittà, *Rome* 25 B2
Cinisello Bálsamo, *Milan* 18 A2
Cinkota, *Budapest* 7 A3
Cipete, *Jakarta* 13 B1
Citadella, *Budapest* 7 c2
Citta degli Studi, *Milan* 18 B2
Città del Vaticano, *Rome* 25 B1
City, *London* 15 A3
City Hall, *New York* 21 e1
Ciudad Deportiva, *Mexico City* 18 B2
Ciudad Fin de Semana, *Madrid* 17 B2
Ciudad General Belgrano, *Buenos Aires* 7 C1
Ciudad Lineál, *Madrid* 17 B2
Ciudad Satélite, *Mexico City* 18 A1
Ciudad Universitaria, *Buenos Aires* 7 B2
Ciudad Universitaria, *Mexico City* 18 C1
Ciutadella, Parc de la, *Barcelona* 4 b3
Civic Center, *Los Angeles* 16 b2
Clamart, *Paris* 23 B2
Clapham, *London* 15 B3
Clapton, *London* 15 A3
Claremont, *Cape Town* 8 A1
Clayhall, *London* 15 A4
Clerkenwell, *London* 15 a4
Clermiston, *Edinburgh* 11 B2
Clichy, *Paris* 23 A2
Clichy-sous-Bois, *Paris* 23 A4
Cliffside, *Toronto* 30 A3
Cliffside Park, *New York* 21 B2
Clifton, *Boston* 6 A4
Clifton, *Karachi* 14 B2
Clifton, *New York* 21 C1
Cliftondale, *Boston* 6 A3
Cloghran, *Dublin* 11 A2
Clonskeagh, *Dublin* 11 B2
Clontarf, *Dublin* 11 A2
Clontarf, *Sydney* 28 A2
Clovelly, *Sydney* 28 B2
Cobras, I. das, *Rio de Janeiro* 24 B2
Coburg, *Melbourne* 17 A1
Cochituate, *Boston* 6 A1
Cochituate, L., *Boston* 6 B1
Cocotá, *Rio de Janeiro* 24 A1
Cœuilly, *Paris* 23 B4
Coina, *Lisbon* 14 B2
Coit Tower, *San Francisco* 25 a2
Coker, *Lagos* 14 B2
Colaba, *Mumbai* 20 B1
Colaba Pt., *Mumbai* 20 B1
Colegiales, *Buenos Aires* 7 B2
Colindale, *London* 15 A2
Colinton, *Edinburgh* 11 B2
College Park, *Atlanta* 3 C2
College Park, *Washington* 32 B4
College Point, *New York* 21 B2
Collégien, *Paris* 23 A4
Collier Row, *London* 15 A4
Colliers Wood, *London* 15 B2
Colma, *San Francisco* 25 B2
Colney Hatch, *London* 15 A3
Cologno Monzese, *Milan* 18 A2
Colombes, *Paris* 23 A2
Colón, Monumente, *Barcelona* 4 c3
Colon, Plaza de, *Madrid* 17 a3
Colonia Güell, *Barcelona* 4 A1
Colonial Knob, *Wellington* 32 A1
Colosseo, *Rome* 25 c3
Columbus Circus, *New York* 21 b2
Combault, *Paris* 23 B4
Comércio, Praça do, *Lisbon* 14 A2
Commerce, *Los Angeles* 16 B4
Como, *Sydney* 28 C1
Company's Gardens, *Cape Town* 8 c2
Conceição, I. da, *Rio de Janeiro* 24 B2
Concertgebouw, *Amsterdam* 2 c1
Conchali, *Santiago* 26 B2
Concord, *Boston* 6 A1
Concord, *Sydney* 28 B1
Concord, *Toronto* 30 A2
Concorde, Place de la, *Paris* 23 b3
Concorezzo, *Milan* 18 A2
Coney Island, *New York* 21 C2
Congonhas, Aéroporto, *São Paulo* 26 B2
Connaught Place, *Delhi* 10 B2
Conservatori, Palazzo dei, *Rome* 25 c3
Consolação, *São Paulo* 26 B2
Constantia, *Cape Town* 8 B1
Constitución, *Buenos Aires* 7 B2
Constitution, *Atlanta* 3 B2
Convention and Exhibition Centre, *Hong Kong* 12 b2
Coogee, *Sydney* 28 B2
Cook Str., *Wellington* 32 A1
Cooksville, *Toronto* 30 B1
Coolock, *Dublin* 11 A2
Copacabana, *Rio de Janeiro* 24 B1
Copenhagen = København, *Copenhagen* 10 A2
Coral Gables, *Miami* 18 B2
Coral Hills, *Washington* 32 B4
Corcovado, Morro do, *Rio de Janeiro* 24 B1
Corduff, *Dublin* 11 A1
Cormano, *Milan* 18 A2
Cornaredo, *Milan* 18 A1
Córsico, *Milan* 18 B1
Corsini, Palazzo, *Rome* 25 c1
Corviale, *Rome* 25 B1
Coslada, *Madrid* 17 B2
Cossigny, *Paris* 23 B4
Cossipore, *Calcutta* 8 B2
Costantino, Arco di, *Rome* 25 c3
Costorphine, *Edinburgh* 11 B2
Cotao, *Lisbon* 14 A1
Côte St.-Luc, *Montreal* 19 B2
Cotunduba, I. de, *Rio de Janeiro* 24 B2
Coubron, *Paris* 23 A4
Countryside, *Chicago* 9 C1
Courbevoie, *Paris* 23 A2
Courtry, *Paris* 23 A4
Covent Garden, *London* 15 b4
Cowgate, *Edinburgh* 11 b3
Cowley, *London* 15 A1
Coyoacán, *Mexico City* 18 B2
Cragin, *Chicago* 9 B2
Craighall Park, *Johannesburg* 13 A2
Craiglockhart, *Edinburgh* 11 B2
Craigmillar, *Edinburgh* 11 B3
Cramond, *Edinburgh* 11 B2
Cramond Bridge, *Edinburgh* 11 B1
Cramond I., *Edinburgh* 11 B2
Cranford, *London* 15 B1
Crawford, *Cape Town* 8 A2
Crayford, *London* 15 B5
Creekmouth, *London* 15 A4
Crescenzago, *Milan* 18 A2
Cressely, *Paris* 23 B1
Cresskill, *New York* 21 A2
Creteil, *Paris* 23 B3
Cricklewood, *London* 15 A2
Cristo Redentor, Estatua do, *Rio de Janeiro* 24 B1
Crockenhill, *London* 15 B4
Croissy-Beaubourg, *Paris* 23 B4
Croissy-sur-Seine, *Paris* 23 A1
Crosby, *Johannesburg* 13 B1
Crosne, *Paris* 23 B3
Cross I., *Mumbai* 20 B2
Crouch End, *London* 15 A3
Crown Mine, *Johannesburg* 13 B1
Crows Nest, *Sydney* 28 A2
Croydon, *London* 15 B3
Croydon Park, *Sydney* 28 B1
Cruagh Mt., *Dublin* 11 B2
Crumlin, *Dublin* 11 B2
Cruz de Pau, *Lisbon* 14 B2
Crystal Palace, *London* 15 B3
Csepel, *Budapest* 7 B2
Csepelsziget, *Budapest* 7 B2
Csillaghegy, *Budapest* 7 A2
Csillagtelep, *Budapest* 7 B2
Csömör, *Budapest* 7 A3
Csömöri-patak →, *Budapest* 7 A3
Cuauhtémoc, *Mexico City* 18 B2
Cubao, *Manila* 17 B2
Çubuklu, *Istanbul* 12 B2
Cudahy, *Los Angeles* 16 C3
Cuicuilco, Pirámido de, *Mexico City* 18 C1
Culver City, *Los Angeles* 16 B2
Cumballa Hill, *Mumbai* 20 a1
Cumbres de Vallecas, *Madrid* 17 B2
Cupecé, *São Paulo* 26 B1
Currie, *Edinburgh* 11 B2
Cusago, *Milan* 18 B1
Cusano Milanino, *Milan* 18 A2
Custom House, *Dublin* 11 b3
Çuvuşabaşi →, *Istanbul* 12 B1
Czernriaków, *Warsaw* 31 B2
Czyste, *Warsaw* 31 B1

D

D.F. Malan Airport, *Cape Town* 8 A2
Da Moóca →, *São Paulo* 26 B2
Da Yunhe →, *Tianjin* 30 A1
Dabizhuang, *Tianjin* 30 A2
Ďáblice, *Prague* 24 B2
Dąbrowa, *Warsaw* 31 B1
Dachang, *Shanghai* 27 B1
Dachang Airfield, *Shanghai* 27 B1
Dachau-Ost, *Munich* 20 A1
Dachauer Moos, *Munich* 20 A1
Dadar, *Mumbai* 20 A1
Dagenham, *London* 15 A4
Daglfing, *Munich* 20 B2
Daheisha, *Jerusalem* 13 B2
Dahlem, *Berlin* 5 B2
Dahlwitz-Hoppegarten, *Berlin* 5 A5
Dahongmen, *Beijing* 4 C2
Daitō, *Osaka* 22 A4
Dajiaoting, *Beijing* 4 B2
Dakhnoye, *St. Petersburg* 26 C1
Dalejsky potok →, *Prague* 24 B2
Dalgety Bay, *Edinburgh* 11 A1
Dalkeith, *Edinburgh* 11 B3
Dalkey, *Dublin* 11 B3
Dalkey Island, *Dublin* 11 B3
Dallgow, *Berlin* 5 A1
Dalmeny, *Edinburgh* 11 B1
Dalston, *London* 15 A3
Daly City, *San Francisco* 25 B2
Dam, *Amsterdam* 2 b2
Dam Rak, *Amsterdam* 2 a2
Damaia, *Lisbon* 14 A1
Dämeritzsee, *Berlin* 5 B5
Dan Ryan Woods, *Chicago* 9 C2
Danderhall, *Edinburgh* 11 B3
Danderyd, *Stockholm* 28 A2
Danforth, *Toronto* 30 A3
Darakeh, *Tehran* 30 A2
Darband, *Tehran* 30 A2
Darling Harbour, *Sydney* 28 b1
Darling Point, *Sydney* 28 B2
Darndale, *Dublin* 11 A2
Darrūs, *Tehran* 30 A2
Dartford, *London* 15 B5
Darya Ganj, *Delhi* 1 a3
Dashi, *Canton* 8 B2
Datansha, *Canton* 8 B2
Datun, *Beijing* 4 B2
Daulatpur, *Delhi* 10 A1
David's Citadel, *Jerusalem* 13 b3
David's Tomb, *Jerusalem* 13 b3
Davidson, Mt., *San Francisco* 25 B2
Davidson's Mains, *Edinburgh* 11 B2
Dāvūdiyeh, *Tehran* 30 A2
Davydkovo, *Moscow* 19 B2
Dawidy, *Warsaw* 31 C1
Days Bay, *Wellington* 32 B2
Dazhigu, *Tianjin* 30 B2
De Waag, *Amsterdam* 2 b2
Decatur, *Atlanta* 3 B2
Dedham, *Boston* 6 B2
Deer I., *Boston* 6 A4
Degunino, *Moscow* 19 A3
Deir Dibwan, *Jerusalem* 13 A2
Deir Ibzi'e, *Jerusalem* 13 A1
Dejvice, *Prague* 24 B2
Dekabristov, Ostrov, *St. Petersburg* 26 B1
Delhi, *Delhi* 10 B2
Delhi Gate, *Delhi* 1 b3
Demarest, *New York* 21 A2
Den Ilp, *Amsterdam* 2 A2
Denistone Heights, *Sydney* 28 A1
Denmark Park, *Toronto* 30 A3
Deptford, *London* 15 B3
Deputati, Camera dei, *Rome* 25 b2
Des Plaines, *Chicago* 9 A1
Des Plaines →, *Chicago* 9 B1
Deshengmen, *Beijing* 4 B2
Deutsch-Wagram, *Vienna* 31 A3
Deutsche Oper, *Berlin* 5 A2
Deutscher Museum, *Munich* 20 B2
Devil's Peak, *Cape Town* 8 A1
Dháfni, *Athens* 2 B2
Dhakuria, *Calcutta* 8 B2
Dhamarakia, *Athens* 2 B1
Dharavi, *Mumbai* 20 A2
Dhrapersón, *Athens* 2 B1
Diadema, *São Paulo* 26 C2
Diegen, *Brussels* 6 A2
Diemen, *Amsterdam* 2 A2
Diepkloof, *Johannesburg* 13 B1
Dieprivier, *Cape Town* 8 B1
Difficult Run →, *Washington* 32 B2
Dilbeek, *Brussels* 6 A1
Dinzigu, *Tianjin* 30 A1
Dirnismaning, *Munich* 20 A2
District Heights, *Washington* 32 B4
Ditan Park, *Beijing* 4 a2
Diyāla →, *Baghdad* 3 B3
Djursholm, *Stockholm* 28 A2
Döberitz, *Berlin* 5 A1
Döbling, *Vienna* 31 A2
Docklands, *London* 15 A3
Dodder, R. →, *Dublin* 11 B1
Dodger Stadium, *Los Angeles* 16 B3
Dolgoe Ozero, *St. Petersburg* 26 A1
Doll Museum, *Delhi* 1 b3
Dollis Hill, *London* 15 A2
Dollymount, *Dublin* 11 A3
Dolni, *Prague* 24 B3
Dolni Chabry, *Prague* 24 B2
Dolní Počernice, *Prague* 24 B3
Dolphins Barn, *Dublin* 11 B2
Dom Pedro II, Parque, *São Paulo* 26 B2
Domain, The, *Sydney* 28 b2
Dome of the Rock, *Jerusalem* 13 b3
Don Mills, *Toronto* 30 A2
Don Muang Int. Airport, *Bangkok* 3 A2
Donaghmede, *Dublin* 11 A3
Donau-Oder Kanal, *Vienna* 31 A3
Donaufeld, *Vienna* 31 A2
Donaupark, *Vienna* 31 A2
Donaustadt, *Vienna* 31 A2
Dongan Hills, *New York* 21 C1
Dongcheng, *Beijing* 4 B2
Donggou, *Shanghai* 27 B2
Dongjiao, *Canton* 8 B2
Dongjuzi, *Tianjin* 30 B2
Dongmenwai, *Tianjin* 30 B2
Dongri, *Mumbai* 20 B2
Dongshanhu Park, *Canton* 8 B2
Dongzhimen, *Beijing* 4 B2
Donnybrook, *Dublin* 11 B2
Doornfontein, *Johannesburg* 13 B2
Dorchester, *Boston* 6 B3
Dorchester B., *Boston* 6 B3
Dornach, *Munich* 20 B3
Dorval, Aéroport de, *Montreal* 19 B1
Dos Couros →, *São Paulo* 26 C2
Dos Moninos →, *São Paulo* 26 C2
Douglas Park, *Chicago* 9 B2
Dover Heights, *Sydney* 28 B2
Dowlatābād, *Tehran* 30 B2
Downey, *Los Angeles* 16 C4
Downsview, *Toronto* 30 A1
Dragør, *Copenhagen* 10 B3
Drancy, *Paris* 23 A3
Dranesville, *Washington* 32 A1
Dreilinden, *Berlin* 5 B2
Drewnica, *Warsaw* 31 B2
Drigh Road, *Karachi* 14 A2
Drimnagh, *Dublin* 11 B2
Drogenbos, *Brussels* 6 B1
Druid Hills, *Atlanta* 3 B2
Drum Towwer, *Beijing* 4 a2
Drumcondra, *Dublin* 11 A2
Drummoyne, *Sydney* 28 B1
Drylaw, *Edinburgh* 11 B2
Dubeč, *Prague* 24 B3
Dublin, *Dublin* 11 A2
Dublin Airport, *Dublin* 11 A2
Dublin Bay, *Dublin* 11 B3
Dublin Harbour, *Dublin* 11 A2
Duddingston, *Edinburgh* 11 B3
Dugnano, *Milan* 18 A2
Dūlāb, *Tehran* 30 B2
Dulwich, *London* 15 B3
Dum Dum, *Calcutta* 8 B2
Dum Dum Int. Airport, *Calcutta* 8 B2
Dumont, *New York* 21 A2
Dún Laoghaire, *Dublin* 11 B3
Duna →, *Budapest* 7 A2
Duncan Dock, *Cape Town* 8 a3
Dundrum, *Dublin* 11 B2
Dunearn, *Singapore* 27 B2
Dunfermline, *Edinburgh* 11 A1
Dunn Loring, *Washington* 32 B2
Dunning, *Chicago* 9 B2
Dunvegan, *Johannesburg* 13 A2
Duomo, *Milan* 18 B2
Duque de Caxias, *Rio de Janeiro* 24 A1
Dusit, *Bangkok* 3 B2
Dusit Zoo, *Bangkok* 3 a2
Dworp, *Brussels* 6 B1
Dyakovo, *Moscow* 19 B3
Dzerzhinskiy, *Moscow* 19 C5
Dzerzhinskiy, *Moscow* 19 B3
Dzerzhinskiy Park, *Moscow* 19 B3

E

Eagle Rock, *Los Angeles* 16 B3
Ealing, *London* 15 A2
Earl's Court, *London* 15 c1
Earlsfield, *London* 15 B2
Earlwood, *Sydney* 28 B1
East Acton, *Boston* 6 A1
East Arlington, *Boston* 6 A3
East Arlington, *Washington* 32 B3
East Bedfont, *London* 15 B1
East Boston, *Boston* 6 A3
East Don →, *Toronto* 30 A2
East Elmhurst, *New York* 21 B2
East Finchley, *London* 15 A2
East Ham, *London* 15 A4
East Humber →, *Toronto* 30 A1
East Lamma Channel, *Hong Kong* 12 B1
East Lexington, *Boston* 6 A2
East Los Angeles, *Los Angeles* 16 B3
East Molesey, *London* 15 B1
East New York, *New York* 21 B2
East Pines, *Washington* 32 B4
East Point, *Atlanta* 3 B2
East Potomac Park, *Washington* 32 B3
East Pt., *Boston* 6 A4
East River →, *New York* 21 B2
East Rutherford, *New York* 21 A1
East Sheen, *London* 15 B2
East Village, *New York* 21 e2
East Wickham, *London* 15 B4
East York, *Toronto* 30 A2
Eastbourne, *Wellington* 32 B2
Eastcote, *London* 15 A1
Easter Howgate, *Edinburgh* 11 B2
Eastwood, *Sydney* 28 A1
Ebara, *Tokyo* 29 B3
Ebisu, *Tokyo* 29 B3
Ebute-Ikorodu, *Lagos* 14 A2
Ebute-Metta, *Lagos* 14 B2
Echo Park, *Los Angeles* 16 a1
Eda, *Tokyo* 29 B2
Edenvale, *Johannesburg* 13 A2
Edenmore, *Dublin* 11 A2
Edgars Cr. →, *Melbourne* 17 A1
Edgeley, *Toronto* 30 A1
Edgemar, *San Francisco* 25 C2
Edinburgh, *Edinburgh* 11 B2
Edison Park, *Chicago* 9 A2
Edmondston, *Washington* 32 B4
Edmonstown, *Dublin* 11 B2
Edo →, *Tokyo* 29 B4
Edogawa-Ku, *Tokyo* 29 A4
Edsberg, *Stockholm* 28 A1
Edwards L., *Melbourne* 17 A1
Eiche, *Berlin* 5 A4
Eiche Sud, *Berlin* 5 A4
Eiffel, Tour, *Paris* 23 A2
Ein Arik, *Jerusalem* 13 B1
Ein Naquba, *Jerusalem* 13 B1
Ein Rafa, *Jerusalem* 13 B1
Eizariya, *Jerusalem* 13 B2
Ejby, *Copenhagen* 10 A2
Ejigbo, *Lagos* 14 A1
Ekeberg, *Oslo* 22 A3
Eknäs, *Stockholm* 28 B3
El 'Abbasiya, *Cairo* 7 A2
El Agustino, *Lima* 16 B2
El Baragil, *Cairo* 7 A2
El Basâtîn, *Cairo* 7 B2
El-Bira, *Jerusalem* 13 A2
El Bosque, *Santiago* 26 C2
El Carmen, *Santiago* 26 B1
El Cortijo, *Santiago* 26 B1
El Duqqi, *Cairo* 7 A2
El Encinar de los Reyes, *Madrid* 17 A2
El Ghurîya, *Cairo* 7 A2
El Gîza, *Cairo* 7 A2
El-Khadr, *Jerusalem* 13 B1
El Khalîfa, *Cairo* 7 A2
El Kôm el Ahmar, *Cairo* 7 A2
El Ma'âdi, *Cairo* 7 B2
El Matarîya, *Cairo* 7 A2
El Mohandessin, *Cairo* 7 A2
El Monte, *Los Angeles* 16 B4
El Mûskî, *Cairo* 7 A2
El Pardo, *Madrid* 17 A1
El Portal, *Miami* 18 A2
El Prat de Llobregat, *Barcelona* 4 B1
El Pueblo de L.A. Historic Park, *Los Angeles* 16 b2
El Qâhira, *Cairo* 7 A2
El Qubba, *Cairo* 7 A2
El Reloj, *Mexico City* 18 C2
El Retiro, *Madrid* 17 B1
El Salto, *Santiago* 26 B2
El Sereno, *Los Angeles* 16 B3
El Talibîya, *Cairo* 7 B2
El Vergel, *Mexico City* 18 C2
El Wâhli, *Cairo* 7 A2
El Zamâlik, *Cairo* 7 A2
El Zeitûn, *Cairo* 7 A2
Elephanta Caves, *Mumbai* 20 B2
Elephanta I., *Mumbai* 20 B2
Ellboda, *Stockholm* 28 A3
Ellinikón, *Athens* 2 B2
Ellis I., *New York* 21 B1
Elm Park, *London* 15 A5
Elmers End, *London* 15 B3
Elmhurst, *New York* 21 B2
Elmstead, *London* 15 B4
Elmwood Park, *Chicago* 9 B2
Elmwood Park, *New York* 21 A1
Elsdon, *Wellington* 32 A1
Elsiesrivier, *Cape Town* 8 A2
Elsternwick, *Melbourne* 17 B2
Eltham, *London* 15 B4
Elwood, *Melbourne* 17 B1
Élysée, *Paris* 23 A2
Elysian Park, *Los Angeles* 16 a3
Embajadores, *Madrid* 17 c2
Embarcadero Center, *San Francisco* 25 b3
Emek Refa'im, *Jerusalem* 13 c2
Émerainville, *Paris* 23 B4
Emeryville, *San Francisco* 25 A3
Eminönü, *Istanbul* 12 B1
Emmarentia, *Johannesburg* 13 A2
Empire State Building, *New York* 21 c2
Encantado, *Rio de Janeiro* 24 B1
Encino, *Los Angeles* 16 B2
Encino Res., *Los Angeles* 16 B1
Enebyberg, *Stockholm* 28 A1
Enfield, *Sydney* 28 B1
Engenho, I. do, *Rio de Janeiro* 24 B2
Englewood, *Chicago* 9 C3
Englewood, *New York* 21 A2
Englewood Cliffs, *New York* 21 A2
Enmore, *Sydney* 28 B2
Enskede, *Stockholm* 28 B2
Entrevias, *Madrid* 17 B1
Epping, *Sydney* 28 A1
Erawan Shrine, *Bangkok* 3 c3
Eregun, *Lagos* 14 A2
Erenköy, *Istanbul* 12 C2
Erith, *London* 15 B5
Erlaa, *Vienna* 31 B1
Ermington, *Sydney* 28 A1
Ermita, *Manila* 17 B1
Erskineville, *Sydney* 28 B2
Erunkan, *Lagos* 14 A2
Erzsébet-Telep, *Budapest* 7 B3
Eschenried, *Munich* 20 A1
Esenler, *Istanbul* 12 B1
Esher, *London* 15 B1
Eskbank, *Edinburgh* 11 B3
Esperanza, *Mexico City* 18 c3
Esplanade Park, *Singapore* 27 c3
Esplugas, *Barcelona* 4 A1
Esposizione Univ. di Roma (E.U.R.), *Rome* 25 C1
Essendon, *Melbourne* 17 A1
Essendon Airport, *Melbourne* 17 A1
Essingen, *Stockholm* 28 B1
Essling, *Vienna* 31 A3
Est, Gare de l', *Paris* 23 a5
Estadio Maracanã, *Rio de Janeiro* 24 B1
Estado, Parque do, *São Paulo* 26 B2
Estefânia, *Lisbon* 14 a2
Estrela, Basilica da, *Lisbon* 14 A2
Ethnikó Arheologiko Mousio, *Athens* 2 a2
Etobicoke, *Toronto* 30 B1
Etobicoke Cr. →, *Toronto* 30 B1
Etterbeek, *Brussels* 6 B2
Euston, *London* 15 a3
Evanston, *Chicago* 9 A2
Even Sapir, *Jerusalem* 13 B1
Evere, *Brussels* 6 A2
Everett, *Boston* 6 A3
Evergreen Park, *Chicago* 9 C2
Evin, *Tehran* 30 A2
Évzonos, *Athens* 2 B2
Ewu, *Lagos* 14 A1
Exchange Square, *Hong Kong* 12 c1
Exposições, Palácio das, *Rio de Janeiro* 24 B1
Eyüp, *Istanbul* 12 B1

F

Fabour, Mt., *Singapore* 27 B2
Faechi, *Seoul* 26 B2
Fælledparken, *Copenhagen* 10 A3
Fågelön, *Stockholm* 28 B1
Fagersjö, *Stockholm* 28 B2
Fair Lawn, *New York* 21 A1
Fairfax, *Washington* 32 B2
Fairfax Station, *Washington* 32 C2
Fairhaven Bay, *Boston* 6 A1
Fairhaven Hill, *Boston* 6 A1
Fairland, *Johannesburg* 13 A1
Fairmilehead, *Edinburgh* 11 B2
Fairmount Heights, *Washington* 32 B4
Fairport, *Toronto* 30 A4
Fairview, *New York* 21 B2
Falenty, *Warsaw* 31 C1
Fáliro, Órmos, *Athens* 2 B2
Falkenberg, *Berlin* 5 A4
Falkenhagen, *Berlin* 5 A1
Falkensee, *Berlin* 5 A1
Falls Church, *Washington* 32 B2
Falomo, *Lagos* 14 B2
False Bay, *Cape Town* 8 B2
Fangcun, *Canton* 8 B2
Farahābād, *Tehran* 30 A2
Farforovskaya, *St. Petersburg* 26 B2
Farningham, *London* 15 B5
Farrar Pond, *Boston* 6 A1
Farsta, *Stockholm* 28 B2
Fasanerie-Nord, *Munich* 20 A2
Fasangarten, *Munich* 20 B2
Fasting Palace, *Beijing* 4 c2
Fatih, *Istanbul* 12 B1
Favoriten, *Vienna* 31 B2
Fawkner, *Melbourne* 17 A1

Montebello, *Los Angeles* 16 B4
Montemor, *Lisbon* 14 A1
Monterey Park, *Los Angeles* 16 B4
Montespaccato, *Rome* 25 B1
Montesson, *Paris* 23 A1
Monteverde Nuovo, *Rome* 25 B1
Montfermeil, *Paris* 23 A4
Montigny-le-Bretonneux, *Paris* 23 B1
Montjay-la-Tour, *Paris* 23 A4
Montjuic, Parc de, *Barcelona* 4 c1
Montparnasse, Gare, *Paris* 23 A2
Montréal, *Montreal* 19 A2
Montréal, Î. de, *Montreal* 19 A2
Montréal, Univ. de, *Montreal* 19 B2
Montréal Est, *Montreal* 19 A2
Montréal Nord, *Montreal* 19 A2
Montréal Ouest, *Montreal* 19 B1
Montreuil, *Paris* 23 A3
Montrouge, *Paris* 23 B2
Montserrat, *Buenos Aires* 7 B2
Monza, *Milan* 18 A2
Monzoro, *Milan* 18 B1
Moóca, *São Paulo* 26 B2
Moonachie, *New York* 21 B1
Moonee Ponds, *Melbourne* 17 A1
Moonee Valley Racecourse, *Melbourne* 17 A1
Moosach, *Munich* 20 A2
Mora, *Mumbai* 20 B2
Moratalaz, *Madrid* 17 B2
Mörby, *Stockholm* 28 A2
Morden, *London* 15 B2
Morée →, *Paris* 23 A3
Morgan Park, *Chicago* 9 C3
Moriguchi, *Osaka* 22 A4
Morivione, *Milan* 18 B2
Morningside, *Edinburgh* 11 B2
Morningside, *Johannesburg* 13 A2
Morningside, *Washington* 32 C4
Morro Solar, Cerro, *Lima* 16 C2
Mortlake, *London* 15 B2
Mortlake, *Sydney* 28 B1
Morton Grove, *Chicago* 9 A2
Morumbi, *São Paulo* 26 B1
Moscavide, *Lisbon* 14 A2
Moscow = Moskva, *Moscow* 19 B3
Moskhaton, *Athens* 2 B2
Moskva, *Moscow* 19 B3
Moskva →, *Moscow* 19 B2
Moskvoretskiy, *Moscow* 19 B3
Mosman, *Sydney* 28 A2
Móstoles, *Madrid* 17 C1
Moti Bagh, *Delhi* 10 B2
Motol, *Prague* 24 B1
Motsa, *Jerusalem* 13 B2
Motsa Ilit, *Jerusalem* 13 B1
Motspur Park, *London* 15 B2
Mottingham, *London* 15 B4
Moulin Rouge, *Paris* 23 a3
Mount Dennis, *Toronto* 30 A2
Mount Greenwood, *Chicago* 9 C2
Mount Hood Memorial Park, *Boston* 6 A3
Mount Merrion, *Dublin* 11 B2
Mount Rainier, *Washington* 32 B4
Mount Vernon, *New York* 21 A3
Mount Vernon Square, *Washington* 32 a2
Mount Zion, *Jerusalem* 13 b3
Mozarthaus, *Vienna* 31 b2
Müggelberge, *Berlin* 5 B4
Müggelheim, *Berlin* 5 B5
Muggiò, *Milan* 18 A2
Mughal Gardens, *Delhi* 1 c1
Mühleiten, *Vienna* 31 A3
Mühlenfliess →, *Berlin* 5 A5
Muiden, *Amsterdam* 2 A3
Muiderpoort Station, *Amsterdam* 2 b3
Muizenberg, *Cape Town* 8 B1
Mujahidpur, *Delhi* 10 B2
Mukandpur, *Delhi* 10 A2
Mukhmas, *Jerusalem* 13 A2
Muko →, *Osaka* 22 A3
Mukojima, *Tokyo* 29 A3
Mulbarton, *Johannesburg* 13 B2
Mumbai, *Mumbai* 20 B2
Mumbai Harbour, *Mumbai* 20 B2
Münchehofe, *Berlin* 5 B5
München, *Munich* 20 B2
Munich = München, *Munich* 20 B2
Munkkiniemi, *Helsinki* 12 B2
Munro, *Buenos Aires* 7 B1
Murai Res., *Singapore* 27 A2
Muranów, *Warsaw* 31 B1
Murino, *St. Petersburg* 26 B2
Murrayfield, *Edinburgh* 11 B2
Musashino, *Tokyo* 29 A2
Museu Nacional, *Rio de Janeiro* 24 B1
Mushin, *Lagos* 14 A2
Musiektheater, *Amsterdam* 2 b2
Muslim Quarter, *Jerusalem* 13 a3
Musocco, *Milan* 18 B1
Mustansiriya, *Baghdad* 3 A2
Musturud, *Cairo* 7 A2
Muswell Hill, *London* 15 A3
Mutanabi, *Baghdad* 3 B2
Muthana, *Baghdad* 3 B2
Myakinino, *Moscow* 19 B2
Mykerinos, *Cairo* 7 B1
Myllypuro, *Helsinki* 12 B3

N

Nacka, *Stockholm* 28 B3
Nada, *Osaka* 22 A2
Naenae, *Wellington* 32 B2
Nærsnes, *Oslo* 22 B1
Nagata, *Osaka* 22 B1
Nagatsuta, *Tokyo* 29 B2
Nagytétény, *Budapest* 7 B1
Nahant, *Boston* 6 A4
Nahant B., *Boston* 6 A4
Nahant Harbor, *Boston* 6 A4
Nahr Dijlah →, *Baghdad* 3 B2
Najafgarh Drain →, *Delhi* 10 B1
Nakahara-Ku, *Tokyo* 29 B2
Nakano-Ku, *Tokyo* 29 A2
Namgajwa, *Seoul* 26 B1
Namsan Park, *Seoul* 26 B1
Namyŏng, *Seoul* 26 B1
Nanbiancun, *Canton* 8 B1
Nanchang He →, *Beijing* 4 B1
Nandang, *Canton* 8 B2
Nandian, *Tianjin* 30 A2
Nangal Dewat, *Delhi* 10 B1
Naniwa, *Osaka* 22 B3
Nankai, *Tianjin* 30 B1
Nanmenwai, *Tianjin* 30 B1
Nanole, *Mumbai* 20 A2
Nanpu Bridge, *Shanghai* 27 B2
Nanshi, *Shanghai* 27 B1
Nantasket Beach, *Boston* 6 B4
Nanterre, *Paris* 23 A2
Naoabad, *Calcutta* 8 C2
Napier Mole, *Karachi* 14 B1
Naraina, *Delhi* 10 B1
Nariman Point, *Mumbai* 20 c1
Nariman Pt., *Mumbai* 20 B1
Nārmak, *Tehran* 30 A2
Naruo, *Osaka* 22 A3
Näsby, *Stockholm* 28 A2
Näsbypark, *Stockholm* 28 A2
Nathan Road, *Hong Kong* 12 a2
Natick, *Boston* 6 B2
National Maritime Museum, *San Francisco* 25 a1
National Museum, *Bangkok* 3 b1
Nationalmuseum, *Stockholm* 28 b2
Natolin, *Warsaw* 31 C2
Naturhistorischesmuseum, *Vienna* 31 b1
Naucalpan de Juárez, *Mexico City* 18 B1
Naupada, *Mumbai* 20 A2
Navíglio di Pavia, *Milan* 18 B1
Navíglio Grande, *Milan* 18 B1
Navona, Piazza, *Rome* 25 b2
Navotas, *Manila* 17 B1
Navy Pier, *Chicago* 9 b3
Nazal Hikmat Beg, *Baghdad* 3 A2
Nazimabad, *Karachi* 14 A2
Nazlet el Simmân, *Cairo* 7 B1
Néa Alexandhria, *Athens* 2 B2
Néa Faliron, *Athens* 2 B1
Néa Ionía, *Athens* 2 A2
Néa Liósia, *Athens* 2 A2
Néa Smírni, *Athens* 2 B2
Neapolis, *Athens* 2 B2
Near North, *Chicago* 9 b2
Nebušice, *Prague* 24 B1
Nederhorst, *Amsterdam* 2 B3
Nedlitz, *Berlin* 5 B1
Nee Soon, *Singapore* 27 A2
Needham Heights, *Boston* 6 B2
Nekrasovka, *Moscow* 19 B5
N'ematābād, *Tehran* 30 B2
Nemchinovka, *Moscow* 19 B1
Nemzeti Muz, *Budapest* 7 c3
Neponsit, *New York* 21 C2
Nerima-Ku, *Tokyo* 29 A3
Nesodden, *Oslo* 22 B3
Nesoddtangen, *Oslo* 22 A3
Nesøya, *Oslo* 22 A2
Neu Aubing, *Munich* 20 B1
Neu Buch, *Berlin* 5 A4
Neu Buchhorst, *Berlin* 5 B5
Neu Fahrland, *Berlin* 5 B1
Neu Lindenberg, *Berlin* 5 A4
Neubiberg, *Munich* 20 B3
Neue Hofburg, *Vienna* 31 b1
Neuenhagen, *Berlin* 5 A4
Neuessling, *Vienna* 31 A3
Neuhausen, *Munich* 20 B2
Neuherberg, *Munich* 20 A2
Neuhönow, *Berlin* 5 A5
Neuilly-Plaisance, *Paris* 23 A4
Neuilly-sur-Marne, *Paris* 23 A4
Neuilly-sur-Seine, *Paris* 23 A2
Neukagran, *Vienna* 31 A2
Neukettenhof, *Vienna* 31 B2
Neukölln, *Berlin* 5 B3
Neuperlach, *Munich* 20 B2
Neuried, *Munich* 20 B1
Neustift am Walde, *Vienna* 31 A1
Neusüssenbrunn, *Vienna* 31 A2
Neuwaldegg, *Vienna* 31 A1
Neva →, *St. Petersburg* 26 B2
Neves, *Rio de Janeiro* 24 B2
New Baghdād, *Baghdad* 3 B2
New Barakpur, *Calcutta* 8 A2
New Brighton, *New York* 21 C1
New Canada, *Johannesburg* 13 B1
New Canada Dam, *Johannesburg* 13 B1
New Carrollton, *Washington* 32 B4
New Cross, *London* 15 B3
New Delhi, *Delhi* 10 B2
New Dorp, *New York* 21 C1
New Dorp Beach, *New York* 21 C1
New Malden, *London* 15 B2
New Milford, *New York* 21 A1
New Territories, *Hong Kong* 12 A1
New Toronto, *Toronto* 30 B1
New Town, *Edinburgh* 11 B2
New Utrecht, *New York* 21 C2
Newark B., *New York* 21 B1
Newbattle, *Edinburgh* 11 B3
Newbury Park, *London* 15 A4
Newcraighall, *Edinburgh* 11 B3
Newham, *London* 15 A4
Newhaven, *Edinburgh* 11 B2
Newington, *Edinburgh* 11 B2
Newington, *London* 15 c5
Newlands, *Johannesburg* 13 B1
Newlands, *Wellington* 32 B1
Newport, *Melbourne* 17 B1
Newton, *Boston* 6 B2
Newtonbrook, *Toronto* 30 A2
Newtongrange, *Edinburgh* 11 B3
Newtonville, *Boston* 6 A2
Newtown, *Sydney* 28 B2
Neyagawa, *Osaka* 22 A4
Ngaio, *Wellington* 32 B1
Ngau Chi Wan, *Hong Kong* 12 A2
Ngau Tau Kok, *Hong Kong* 12 B2
Ngauranga, *Wellington* 32 B1
Ngong Shuen Chau, *Hong Kong* 12 B1
Ngua Kok Wan, *Hong Kong* 12 A1
Nīāvarān, *Tehran* 30 A2
Nibra, *Calcutta* 8 B1
Nidāl, *Baghdad* 3 B2
Niddrie, *Edinburgh* 11 B3
Niddrie, *Melbourne* 17 A1
Nieder Neuendorf, *Berlin* 5 A2
Niederschöneweide, *Berlin* 5 B3
Niederschönhausen, *Berlin* 5 A3
Niemeyer, *Rio de Janeiro* 24 B1
Nieuw Zuid, *Amsterdam* 2 c2
Nieuwe Kerk, *Amsterdam* 2 b2
Nieuwendam, *Amsterdam* 2 A2
Nihonbashi, *Tokyo* 29 b5
Niipperi, *Helsinki* 12 B1
Nīkaia, *Athens* 2 B1
Nikolassee, *Berlin* 5 B2
Nikolskiy, *Moscow* 19 B2
Nikolskoye, *Moscow* 19 B5
Nikulino, *Moscow* 19 B2
Nil, Nahr en →, *Cairo* 7 B2
Nile = Nil, Nahr en →, *Cairo* 7 B2
Niles, *Chicago* 9 A2
Nimta, *Calcutta* 8 A2
Ningyuan, *Tianjin* 30 B2
Nippa, *Tokyo* 29 B2
Nippori, *Tokyo* 29 A3
Nishi, *Osaka* 22 A3
Nishinari, *Osaka* 22 B3
Nishiyodogawa, *Osaka* 22 A3
Niterói, *Rio de Janeiro* 24 B2
Nob Hill, *San Francisco* 25 b1
Nockeby, *Stockholm* 28 B1
Noel Park, *London* 15 A3
Nogatino, *Moscow* 19 B4
Nogent-sur-Marne, *Paris* 23 A3
Noida, *Delhi* 10 B2
Noiseau, *Paris* 23 B4
Noisiel, *Paris* 23 A4
Noisy-le-Grand, *Paris* 23 A4
Noisy-le-Roi, *Paris* 23 A1
Noisy-le-Sec, *Paris* 23 A3
Nokkala, *Helsinki* 12 C1
Nomentano, *Rome* 25 B2
Nonakashinden, *Tokyo* 29 A2
Nongminyundong Jiangxisuo, *Canton* 8 B2
Nonhyŏn, *Seoul* 26 B2
Nonthaburi, *Bangkok* 3 A1
Noon Gun, *Cape Town* 8 b1
Noorder Kerk, *Amsterdam* 2 a1
Noordgesig, *Johannesburg* 13 B1
Noordzeekanaal, *Amsterdam* 2 A1
Nord, Gare du, *Paris* 23 a4
Nordrand-Siedlung, *Vienna* 31 A2
Nordstrand, *Oslo* 22 A3
Normandale, *Wellington* 32 B2
Nørrebro, *Copenhagen* 10 a1
Norridge, *Chicago* 9 B2
Norrmalm, *Stockholm* 28 a1
North Arlington, *New York* 21 B1
North Bay Village, *Miami* 18 A2
North Bergen, *New York* 21 B1
North Branch Chicago River →, *Chicago* 9 B2
North Bull Island, *Dublin* 11 A3
North Cambridge, *Boston* 6 A3
North Cheam, *London* 15 B2
North Cohasset, *Boston* 6 B4
North Cray, *London* 15 B4
North Decatur, *Atlanta* 3 B3
North Druid Hills, *Atlanta* 3 B3
North Esk →, *Edinburgh* 11 B2
North Gyle, *Edinburgh* 11 B2
North Hackensack, *New York* 21 A1
North Harbor, *Manila* 17 B1
North Hd., *Sydney* 28 A2
North Hollywood, *Los Angeles* 16 B2
North Lexington, *Boston* 6 A2
North Miami, *Miami* 18 A2
North Miami Beach, *Miami* 18 A2
North Nazimabad, *Karachi* 14 A2
North Pt., *Hong Kong* 12 B2
North Queensferry, *Edinburgh* 11 A1
North Quincy, *Boston* 6 B3
North Res., *Boston* 6 A3
North Riverside, *Chicago* 9 B2
North Saugus, *Boston* 6 A3
North Shore Channel →, *Chicago* 9 B2
North Springfield, *Washington* 32 C2
North Sudbury, *Boston* 6 A1
North Sydney, *Sydney* 28 B2
North Woolwich, *London* 15 A4
North York, *Toronto* 30 A2
Northbridge, *Sydney* 28 A2
Northbridge Park, *Sydney* 28 A2
Northcliff, *Johannesburg* 13 A1
Northcote, *Melbourne* 17 A2
Northlake, *Chicago* 9 B1
Northmount, *Toronto* 30 A2
Northolt, *London* 15 A1
Northumberland Heath, *London* 15 B5
Northwood, *London* 15 A1
Norumbega Res., *Boston* 6 B2
Norwood, *Johannesburg* 13 A2
Norwood Park, *Chicago* 9 B2
Noryangjin, *Seoul* 26 B1
Nossa Senhora de Candelária, *Rio de Janeiro* 24 a2
Nossa Senhora do Ó, *São Paulo* 26 B1
Nossegem, *Brussels* 6 A3
Notre-Dame, *Paris* 23 c4
Notre-Dame, Bois, *Paris* 23 B4
Notre-Dame-de-Grace, *Montreal* 19 B2
Notting Hill, *London* 15 A2
Nova Milanese, *Milan* 18 A2
Novate Milanese, *Milan* 18 A1
Novaya Derevnya, *St. Petersburg* 26 A1
Nové Město, *Prague* 24 B2
Novoaleksandrovskoye, *St. Petersburg* 26 B2
Novogireyevo, *Moscow* 19 B4
Novoivanovskoye, *Moscow* 19 B1
Novonikolyskoye, *Moscow* 19 A1
Novosaratovka, *St. Petersburg* 26 B3
Nowe-Babice, *Warsaw* 31 B1
Nöykkiö, *Helsinki* 12 B1
Nueva Atzacoalco, *Mexico City* 18 B2
Nueva Pompeya, *Buenos Aires* 7 C2
Nueva Tenochtitlán, *Mexico City* 18 B2
Nuijala, *Helsinki* 12 B1
Numabukuro, *Tokyo* 29 A2
Nunez, *Buenos Aires* 7 B2
Nunhead, *London* 15 B3
Ñuñoa, *Santiago* 26 B2
Nusle, *Prague* 24 B2
Nussdorf, *Vienna* 31 A2
Nyanga, *Cape Town* 8 A2
Nymphenburg, *Munich* 20 B2
Nymphenburg, Schloss, *Munich* 20 B2

O

Oak Grove, *Atlanta* 3 A3
Oak Island, *Boston* 6 A4
Oak Lawn, *Chicago* 9 C2
Oak Park, *Chicago* 9 B2
Oak View, *Washington* 32 A4
Oakdale, *Atlanta* 3 A2
Oakland, *San Francisco* 25 B3
Oakland, *Washington* 32 B4
Oaklawn, *Washington* 32 C4
Oakleigh, *Melbourne* 17 B2
Oakton, *Washington* 32 B2
Oakwood Beach, *New York* 21 C1
Oatley, *Sydney* 28 B1
Obalende, *Lagos* 14 B2
Oba's Palace, *Lagos* 14 B2
Oberföhring, *Munich* 20 B2
Oberhaching, *Munich* 20 B2
Oberlaa, *Vienna* 31 B2
Oberlisse, *Vienna* 31 A2
Obermenzing, *Munich* 20 A1
Obermoos Schwaige, *Munich* 20 A1
Oberschleissheim, *Munich* 20 A2
Oberschöneweide, *Berlin* 5 B4
Observatory, *Johannesburg* 13 B2
Observatory, *Sydney* 28 a1
Obu, *Osaka* 22 A1
Obu-tôge, *Osaka* 22 A1
Óbuda, *Budapest* 7 A2
Obukhovo, *St. Petersburg* 26 B2
Obvodnyy Kanal, *St. Petersburg* 26 B1
Ocean Park, *Hong Kong* 12 B2
Ochakovo, *Moscow* 19 B2
Ochota, *Warsaw* 31 B1
O'Connell Street, *Dublin* 11 b2
Ōdana, *Tokyo* 29 B2
Oden-Stockach, *Munich* 20 B3
Odilampi, *Helsinki* 12 B1
Odintsovo, *Moscow* 19 B1
Odivelas, *Lisbon* 14 A1
Odolany, *Warsaw* 31 B1
Oeiras, *Lisbon* 14 A1
Ofin, *Lagos* 14 A3
Ogawa, *Tokyo* 29 A1
Ogden Park, *Chicago* 9 C2
Ogikubo, *Tokyo* 29 A2
Ogogoro, *Lagos* 14 B2
Ogoyo, *Lagos* 14 B2
Ogudu, *Lagos* 14 A2
Ohariu Stream →, *Wellington* 32 B1
O'Higgins, Parque, *Santiago* 26 B2
Oimachi, *Tokyo* 29 B3
Ojota, *Lagos* 14 A2
Okamoto, *Osaka* 22 A2
Okęcie, *Warsaw* 31 B1
Okęcie Airport, *Warsaw* 31 B1
Okelra, *Lagos* 14 B2
Okeogbe, *Lagos* 14 B2
Okha, *Delhi* 10 B2
Okhta →, *St. Petersburg* 26 B2
Okkervil →, *St. Petersburg* 26 B2
Okrzeszyn, *Warsaw* 31 C2
Oksval, *Oslo* 22 A3
Oktyabrskiy, *Moscow* 19 B3
Ōkubo, *Tokyo* 29 a2
Ōkura, *Tokyo* 29 B1
Olari, *Helsinki* 12 B1
Olaria, *Rio de Janeiro* 24 B1
Old Admiralty, *St. Petersburg* 26 B1
Old City, *Delhi* 1 a3
Old City, *Jerusalem* 13 b3
Old City, *Shanghai* 27 B1
Old Fort = Purana Qila, *Delhi* 1 c3
Old Harbor, *Boston* 6 B3
Old Town, *Chicago* 9 B3
Old Town, *Edinburgh* 11 B2
Oldbawn, *Dublin* 11 B1
Olgino, *St. Petersburg* 26 A1
Olimpico, Estadio, *Mexico City* 18 C1
Olivais, *Lisbon* 14 A2
Olivar de los Padres, *Mexico City* 18 B1
Olivar del Conde, *Mexico City* 18 B1
Olivos, *Buenos Aires* 7 B2
Olona →, *Milan* 18 B1
Olympia, *London* 15 c1
Olympic Stadium, *Helsinki* 12 B2
Olympique, Stade, *Montreal* 19 A2
Omonias, Pl., *Athens* 2 b1
Ōmori, *Tokyo* 29 B3
Onchi, *Osaka* 22 B4
Onchi →, *Osaka* 22 B4
Onisigun, *Lagos* 14 A2
Ōokayama, *Tokyo* 29 B3
Oosterpark, *Amsterdam* 2 b3
Oostzaan, *Amsterdam* 2 A2
Opa-Locka, *Miami* 18 A1
Opa-Locka Airport, *Miami* 18 A1
Opacz, *Warsaw* 31 B1
Opera House, *Sydney* 28 a2
Ophirton, *Johannesburg* 13 B2
Oppegård, *Oslo* 22 B3
Oppem, *Brussels* 6 A1
Oppsal, *Oslo* 22 A4
Ora, *Jerusalem* 13 B1
Oradell, *New York* 21 A1
Orange Bowl Stadium, *Miami* 18 B2
Orangi, *Karachi* 14 A2
Orchard Road, *Singapore* 27 a1
Ordrup, *Copenhagen* 10 A3
Orech, *Prague* 24 B1
Øresund, *Copenhagen* 10 A3
Orient Heights, *Boston* 6 A3
Orlando Dam, *Johannesburg* 13 B1
Orlando East, *Johannesburg* 13 B1
Orlovo, *Moscow* 19 C2
Orly, *Paris* 23 B3
Ormesson-sur-Marne, *Paris* 23 B4
Ormond, *Melbourne* 17 B2
Ormøya, *Oslo* 22 A3
Orpington, *London* 15 B4
Orsay, Musée d', *Paris* 23 b3
Országház, *Budapest* 7 b2
Országos Levétár, *Budapest* 7 b1
Ortaköy, *Istanbul* 12 B2
Ortica, *Milan* 18 B2
Oruba, *Lagos* 14 B2
Orvostörteneti Múz., *Budapest* 7 c2
Ōsaka, *Osaka* 22 B4
Osaka B., *Osaka* 22 B2
Osaka Castle, *Osaka* 22 A4
Osaka Harbour, *Osaka* 22 B3
Osaka International Airport, *Osaka* 22 A3
Ōsaki, *Tokyo* 29 B3
Osasco, *São Paulo* 26 B1
Osdorf, *Berlin* 5 B3
Osdorp, *Amsterdam* 2 A1
Oshodi, *Lagos* 14 A2
Oslo, *Oslo* 22 A3
Oslofjorden, *Oslo* 22 B3
Ōsone, *Tokyo* 29 B2
Osorun, *Lagos* 14 A2
Ospiate, *Milan* 18 A1
Ostankino, *Moscow* 19 B3
Östasiatiskamuséet, *Stockholm* 28 b3
Österalm, *Stockholm* 28 a3
Østerbro, *Copenhagen* 10 a1
Osterley, *London* 15 B1
Osterley Park, *London* 15 B1
Östermalm, *Stockholm* 28 A2
Österskär, *Stockholm* 28 A3
Ostiense, *Rome* 25 B1
Østmarkkapellet, *Oslo* 22 A4
Østøya, *Oslo* 22 B2
Østre Aker, *Oslo* 22 A3
Ōta-Ku, *Tokyo* 29 B3
Otaniemi, *Helsinki* 12 B1
Otari Open Air Museum, *Wellington* 32 B1
Otsuka, *Tokyo* 29 A3
Ottakring, *Vienna* 31 A1
Ottávia, *Rome* 25 B1
Ottery, *Cape Town* 8 B2
Ottobrunn, *Munich* 20 B3
Oud Zuid, *Amsterdam* 2 b1
Oude Kerk, *Amsterdam* 2 b2
Ouderkerk, *Amsterdam* 2 B2
Oulunkylä, *Helsinki* 12 B2
Ourcq, Canal de l', *Paris* 23 A3
Outer Mission, *San Francisco* 25 B2
Outremont, *Montreal* 19 A2
Overijse, *Brussels* 6 B3
Owhiro Bay, *Wellington* 32 C1
Oworonsoki, *Lagos* 14 A2
Oxford Street, *London* 15 b3
Oxgangs, *Edinburgh* 11 B2
Oxon Hill, *Washington* 32 C4
Oyodo, *Osaka* 22 A3
Oyster B., *Sydney* 28 C1
Oyster Rock, *Mumbai* 20 B1
Oyster Rocks, *Karachi* 14 B2
Ozoir-la-Ferrière, *Paris* 23 B4
Ozone Park, *New York* 21 B2

P

Pacific Heights, *San Francisco* 25 B2
Pacific Manor, *San Francisco* 25 C2
Pacific Palisades, *Los Angeles* 16 B1
Pacifica, *San Francisco* 25 C2
Paco, *Manila* 17 B1
Paco de Arcos, *Lisbon* 14 A1
Paco Imperial, *Rio de Janeiro* 24 a2
Paddington, *London* 15 b2
Paddington, *Sydney* 28 B2
Paderno, *Milan* 18 A1
Pagewood, *Sydney* 28 B2
Pagote, *Mumbai* 20 B2
Pai, I. do, *Rio de Janeiro* 24 B2
Pak Kong, *Hong Kong* 12 A2
Pakila, *Helsinki* 12 B2
Palacio de Bellas Artes, *Mexico City* 18 b2
Palacio de Communicaciones, *Madrid* 17 a3
Palacio Nacional, *Mexico City* 18 B2
Palacio Real, *Barcelona* 4 b3
Palacio Real, *Madrid* 17 b1
Palaión Fáliron, *Athens* 2 B2
Palais de Justice, *Brussels* 6 c2
Palais Royal, *Paris* 23 b4
Palais Royale, *Brussels* 6 b3
Palaiseau, *Paris* 23 B2
Palau Nacional Museu d'Art, *Barcelona* 4 c1
Palazzolo, *Milan* 18 A1
Palermo, *Buenos Aires* 7 B2
Palhais, *Lisbon* 14 B2
Palisades Park, *New York* 21 A1
Palmer Park, *Washington* 32 B4
Palmerston, *Dublin* 11 A1
Paloheinä, *Helsinki* 12 B2
Palomeras, *Madrid* 17 B2
Palos Heights, *Chicago* 9 D2
Palos Hills, *Chicago* 9 C2
Palos Hills Forest, *Chicago* 9 C1
Palos Park, *Chicago* 9 C1
Palpara, *Calcutta* 8 B2
Panchur, *Calcutta* 8 B1
Pandacan, *Manila* 17 B2
Pandan, Selat, *Singapore* 27 B2
Pandan Res., *Singapore* 27 B2
Panepistimio, *Athens* 2 b2
Pangbae, *Seoul* 26 C1
Pangrati, *Athens* 2 B2
Pangsua, Sungei →, *Singapore* 27 A2
Panihati, *Calcutta* 8 A2
Panjang, Bukit, *Singapore* 27 A2
Panje, *Mumbai* 20 B2
Panke →, *Berlin* 5 A3
Pankow, *Berlin* 5 A3
Panthéon, *Paris* 23 c4
Pantheon, *Rome* 25 b2
Pantin, *Paris* 23 A3
Pantitlán, *Mexico City* 18 B2
Panvel Cr. →, *Mumbai* 20 B2
Paparangi, *Wellington* 32 B1
Papiol, *Barcelona* 4 A1
Paramus, *New York* 21 A1
Paranaque, *Manila* 17 B1
Paray-Vieille-Poste, *Paris* 23 B3
Parco Regionale, *Milan* 18 A1
Parel, *Mumbai* 20 B1
Pari, *São Paulo* 26 B2
Parioli, *Rome* 25 B2
Paris, *Paris* 23 A3
Paris-Orly, Aéroport de, *Paris* 23 B3
Pārk-e Mellat, *Tehran* 30 A2
Park Ridge, *Chicago* 9 A1
Park Royal, *London* 15 A2
Parkchester, *New York* 21 B2
Parkdale, *Toronto* 30 B2
Parkhurst, *Johannesburg* 13 A2
Parklawn, *Washington* 32 B3
Parkmore, *Johannesburg* 13 A2
Parkside, *San Francisco* 25 B2
Parktown, *Johannesburg* 13 B2
Parktown North, *Johannesburg* 13 A2
Parkview, *Johannesburg* 13 A2
Parkville, *New York* 21 C2
Parkwood, *Cape Town* 8 B1
Parkwood, *Johannesburg* 13 A2
Parow, *Cape Town* 8 A2
Parque Chabuco, *Buenos Aires* 7 B2
Parque Patricios, *Buenos Aires* 7 B2
Parramatta →, *Sydney* 28 A1
Parthenon, *Athens* 2 c2
Paşabahçe, *Istanbul* 12 B2
Pasadena, *Los Angeles* 16 B4
Pasar Minggu, *Jakarta* 13 B1
Pasay, *Manila* 17 B1
Pascoe Vale, *Melbourne* 17 A1
Paseo de la Reforma, *Mexico City* 18 b2
Pasig, *Manila* 17 B2
Pasig →, *Manila* 17 B2
Pasila, *Helsinki* 12 B2
Pasing, *Munich* 20 B1
Pasir Panjang, *Singapore* 27 B2
Pasir Ris, *Singapore* 27 A3
Passaic →, *New York* 21 B1
Passirana, *Milan* 18 A1
Patel Nagar, *Delhi* 10 B2
Pateros, *Manila* 17 B2
Pathersville, *Atlanta* 3 B3
Pathumwan, *Bangkok* 3 B2
Patipukur, *Calcutta* 8 B2
Patisia, *Athens* 2 A2
Paulo E. Virginia, Gruta, *Rio de Janeiro* 24 B1
Paulshof, *Berlin* 5 A5
Pavshino, *Moscow* 19 B1
Paya Lebar, *Singapore* 27 A3
Peachtree →, *Atlanta* 3 B2
Peakhurst, *Sydney* 28 B1
Peania, *Athens* 2 B3
Peckham, *London* 15 B3
Peddocks I., *Boston* 6 B4
Pederstrup, *Copenhagen* 10 A2
Pedralbes, *Barcelona* 4 A1
Pedregal de San Angel, Jardines del, *Mexico City* 18 C1
Pekhorka →, *Moscow* 19 C6
Pekhra-Pokrovskoye, *Moscow* 19 A5
Pekhra-Yakovievskaya, *Moscow* 19 B5
Peking = Beijing, *Beijing* 4 B1
Pelcowizna, *Warsaw* 31 B2
Pelopónnisos Sta., *Athens* 2 a1
Penalolén, *Santiago* 26 B2
Pencarrow Hd., *Wellington* 32 C2
Peng Siang →, *Singapore* 27 A2
Penge, *London* 15 B3
Penha, *Rio de Janeiro* 24 A1
Penicuik, *Edinburgh* 11 B2
Penjaringan, *Jakarta* 13 A1
Penn Station, *New York* 21 c2
Pennsylvania Avenue, *Washington* 32 b1
Pentland Hills, *Edinburgh* 11 B1
Penyagino, *Moscow* 19 A2
Penzing, *Vienna* 31 A1
People's Park, *Shanghai* 27 B1
People's Square, *Shanghai* 27 B1
Perales del Rio, *Madrid* 17 C2
Peravillo, *Mexico City* 18 a3
Perchtoldsdorf, *Vienna* 31 B1
Perdizes, *São Paulo* 26 B2
Peredelkino, *Moscow* 19 C2
Pergamon Museum, *Berlin* 5 a4
Peristérion, *Athens* 2 A2
Perivale, *London* 15 A2
Perk, *Brussels* 6 A2
Perlach, *Munich* 20 B2
Perlacher Forst, *Munich* 20 B2
Pero, *Milan* 18 A1
Peropok, Bukit, *Singapore* 27 B2
Perovo, *Moscow* 19 B4
Pershing Square, *Los Angeles* 16 c1
Pertusella, *Milan* 18 A1
Pesagot, *Jerusalem* 13 A2
Pesanggrahag, Kali →, *Jakarta* 13 B1
Peschiera Borromeo, *Milan* 18 B2
Pesek, P., *Singapore* 27 B2
Pest, *Budapest* 7 B2
Pesterzsébet, *Budapest* 7 B2
Pesthidegkút, *Budapest* 7 A1
Pestimre, *Budapest* 7 B3
Pestlörinc, *Budapest* 7 B3
Pestújhely, *Budapest* 7 A3
Petas, *Helsinki* 12 B2
Petone, *Wellington* 32 B2
Petrogradskaya Storona, *St. Petersburg* 26 B2
Petroúpolis, *Athens* 2 A2
Petrovice, *Prague* 24 B3
Petrovskiy Park, *Moscow* 19 B3
Petrovsko-Razumovskoye, *Moscow* 19 B3
Pettycur, *Edinburgh* 11 A2
Peutie, *Brussels* 6 A2
Pfaueninsel, *Berlin* 5 B1
Phaya Thai, *Bangkok* 3 B2
Phihai, *Karachi* 14 A2
Phillip B., *Sydney* 28 B2
Phoenix Park, *Dublin* 11 A2
Phra Khanong, *Bangkok* 3 B2
Phra Pradaeng, *Bangkok* 3 C2
Phranakhon, *Bangkok* 3 B1
Picasso, Museu, *Barcelona* 4 c2
Piccadilly, *London* 15 b3
Pico Rivera, *Los Angeles* 16 C4
Piedade, *Lisbon* 14 A1
Piedade, *Rio de Janeiro* 24 B1
Piedade, Cova da, *Lisbon* 14 A2
Piedmont Park, *Atlanta* 3 B2
Pietralata, *Rome* 25 B2
Pihlajamäki, *Helsinki* 12 B2
Pihlajasaari, *Helsinki* 12 C2
Pilares, *Rio de Janeiro* 24 B1
Pilton, *Edinburgh* 11 B2
Pimlico, *London* 15 c3
Pimmit Hills, *Washington* 32 B2
Pine Grove, *Toronto* 30 A1
Pinewood, *Miami* 18 A2
Piney Run →, *Washington* 32 B1
Pinganli, *Beijing* 4 B2
Pingzhou, *Canton* 8 B2
Pinheiros →, *São Paulo* 26 B1
Pinjrapur, *Karachi* 14 A2
Pinner, *London* 15 A1
Pinner Green, *London* 15 A1
Pioltello, *Milan* 18 A2
Pipinui Pt., *Wellington* 32 A1
Piraévs, *Athens* 2 B1
Pirajuçara →, *São Paulo* 26 B1
Pirinçci, *Istanbul* 12 B1
Pirituba, *São Paulo* 26 A1
Pirkkola, *Helsinki* 12 B2
Písnice, *Prague* 24 C2
Pitampura, *Delhi* 10 A1
Pitkäjärvi, *Helsinki* 12 B1
Planegg, *Munich* 20 B1
Plumstead, *Cape Town* 8 B1
Plumstead, *London* 15 B4
Plyushchevo, *Moscow* 19 B4
Pníka, *Athens* 2 c1
Po Toi I., *Hong Kong* 12 B2
Po Toi O, *Hong Kong* 12 B2
Poasco, *Milan* 18 B2
Podbaba, *Prague* 24 B2
Podolí, *Prague* 24 B2
Poduskino, *Moscow* 19 B1
Pointe-Aux-Trembles, *Montreal* 19 A2
Poissy, *Paris* 23 A1
Pok Fu Lam, *Hong Kong* 12 B1
Pokrovsko-Sresnevo, *Moscow* 19 B2
Polton, *Edinburgh* 11 B3
Polyustrovo, *St. Petersburg* 26 B2
Pompidou, Centre, *Paris* 23 b4
Pomprap, *Bangkok* 3 b2
Pondok Indah, *Jakarta* 13 B1
Ponta do Marisco, *Rio de Janeiro* 24 C1
Pontault-Combault, *Paris* 23 B4
Pontinha, *Lisbon* 14 A1
Poplar, *London* 15 A3
Popolo, Porta del, *Rome* 25 a2
Poppintree, *Dublin* 11 A2
Porirua, *Wellington* 32 A2
Porirua East, *Wellington* 32 A2
Port I., *Osaka* 22 A2
Port Melbourne, *Melbourne* 17 B1
Port Nicholson, *Wellington* 32 B2
Port Philip Bay, *Melbourne* 17 B1
Port Richmond, *New York* 21 C1
Port Shelter, *Hong Kong* 12 B2
Port Union, *Toronto* 30 A4
Portage Park, *Chicago* 9 B2
Portal de la Pau, Pl., *Barcelona* 4 c2
Portela, Aeroporto da, *Lisbon* 14 A2
Portmarnock, *Dublin* 11 A3
Porto Brandão, *Lisbon* 14 A1
Porto Novo, *Rio de Janeiro* 24 A2
Porto Novo Cr. →, *Lagos* 14 B2
Portobello, *Edinburgh* 11 B3
Portrero, *San Francisco* 25 B3
Potomac, *Washington* 32 A2
Potomac →, *Washington* 32 B3
Potrero Pt., *San Francisco* 25 B2
Potsdam, *Berlin* 5 B1
Potsdamer Platz, *Berlin* 5 b3
Potzham, *Munich* 20 B2
Pötzleinsdorf, *Vienna* 31 A1
Povoa de Santo Adriao, *Lisbon* 14 A2
Powązki, *Warsaw* 31 B1
Powiśle, *Warsaw* 31 B2
Powsin, *Warsaw* 31 C2
Powsinek, *Warsaw* 31 C2
Poyan Res., *Singapore* 27 A2
Pozuelo de Alarcon, *Madrid* 17 B1
Prado, Museo del, *Madrid* 17 b3
Prado Churubusco, *Mexico City* 18 B2
Praga, *Warsaw* 31 B2
Praha = Prague, *Prague* 24 B2
Praha, *Prague* 24 B2
Praha-Ruzyně Airport, *Prague* 24 B1
Prairies, R. des →, *Montreal* 19 A2
Prater, *Vienna* 31 A2
Precotto, *Milan* 18 A2
Prenestino Labicano, *Rome* 25 B2
Prenzlauerberg, *Berlin* 5 A3
Preston, *Melbourne* 17 A1
Pretos Forros, Sa. dos, *Rio de Janeiro* 24 B1
Préville, *Montreal* 19 B3
Přezletice, *Prague* 24 B3
Prima Porta, *Rome* 25 B1
Primavalle, *Rome* 25 B1
Primrose, *Johannesburg* 13 B2
Princes Street, *Edinburgh* 11 b2
Printer's Row, *Chicago* 9 d2
Progreso Nacional, *Mexico City* 18 A2
Prosek, *Prague* 24 B3
Prospect Hill Park, *Boston* 6 A2
Providencia, *Santiago* 26 B2
Prudential Building, *Chicago* 9 c2
Průhonice, *Prague* 24 C3
Psikhikón, *Athens* 2 A2
Pudong New Area, *Shanghai* 27 B2
Pueblo Libre, *Lima* 16 B2
Pueblo Nuevo, *Barcelona* 4 A2
Pueblo Nuevo, *Madrid* 17 B2
Puerta del Sol, Plaza, *Madrid* 17 b2
Puerto Madero, *Buenos Aires* 7 B2
Puerto Retiro, *Buenos Aires* 7 B2
Puhuangyu, *Beijing* 4 B2
Puistola, *Helsinki* 12 B3
Pukan-san, *Seoul* 26 B1
Pukinmäki, *Helsinki* 12 B2
Pukkajwa, *Seoul* 26 B1
Pulkovo Int. Airport, *St. Petersburg* 26 C1
Pullach, *Munich* 20 B1
Pulo Gadung, *Jakarta* 13 B2
Pūnak, *Tehran* 30 A2
Punchbowl, *Sydney* 28 B1
Punde, *Mumbai* 20 B2
Punggol, *Singapore* 27 A3
Punggol, Sungei →, *Singapore* 27 A3
Punggol Pt., *Singapore* 27 A3
Punjabi Bagh, *Delhi* 10 A1
Puotila, *Helsinki* 12 B3
Purana Qila, *Delhi* 1 c3
Puteaux, *Paris* 23 A2
Putilkovo, *Moscow* 19 A2
Putney, *London* 15 B2
Putuo, *Shanghai* 27 B1
Putxet, *Barcelona* 4 A1
Puxi, *Shanghai* 27 B1
Pydhuni, *Mumbai* 20 b2
Pyramids, *Cairo* 7 B1
Pyry, *Warsaw* 31 C1

Q

Qalandya, *Jerusalem* 13 A2
Qal'eh Morghī, *Tehran* 30 B2
Qanâ el Ismâ'îlîya, *Cairo* 7 A2
Qāsemābād, *Tehran* 30 A3
Qasr-e Firūzeh, *Tehran* 30 B3
Qatane, *Jerusalem* 13 B1
Qianmen, *Beijing* 4 B2
Qinghuayuan, *Beijing* 4 B1
Qingningsi, *Shanghai* 27 B2
Qolhak, *Tehran* 30 A2
Quadraro, *Rome* 25 B2
Quaid-i-Azam, *Karachi* 14 A1
Quartiere Zingone, *Milan* 18 B1
Quds, *Baghdad* 3 A2
Queen Mary Res., *London* 15 B1
Queen Street, *Edinburgh* 11 a1
Queensbury, *London* 15 A2
Queenscliffe, *Sydney* 28 A2
Queensferry, *Edinburgh* 11 B1
Queenstown, *Singapore* 27 B2
Quellerina, *Johannesburg* 13 A1
Queluz, *Lisbon* 14 A1
Quezon City, *Manila* 17 B2
Quezon Memorial Circle, *Manila* 17 B2
Quilicura, *Santiago* 26 B1
Quincy, *Boston* 6 B3
Quincy B., *Boston* 6 B4
Quinta Normal, *Santiago* 26 B1
Quinto de Stampi, *Milan* 18 B2
Quinto Romano, *Milan* 18 B1
Quirinale, *Rome* 25 b1
Quirinale, Palazzo dei, *Rome* 25 b3

R

Raasdorf, *Vienna* 31 A3
Rådhuset, *Oslo* 22 a3
Radlice, *Prague* 24 B2
Radość, *Warsaw* 31 B3
Radotin, *Prague* 24 C2
Rafat, *Jerusalem* 13 A2
Raffles Hotel, *Singapore* 27 b3
Raffles Park, *Singapore* 27 B2
Raheny, *Dublin* 11 A3
Rahnsdorf, *Berlin* 5 B5
Rainham, *London* 15 A5

Raj Ghat, *Delhi* 1 b3
Rajakylä, *Helsinki* 12 B3
Rajpath, *Delhi* 1 c2
Rajpura, *Delhi* 10 A2
Rákos-patak →, *Budapest* 7 B3
Rákoshegy, *Budapest* 7 B3
Rákoskeresztúr, *Budapest* 7 B3
Rákoskert, *Budapest* 7 B3
Rákosliget, *Budapest* 7 B3
Rákospalota, *Budapest* 7 A2
Rákosszentmihály, *Budapest* 7 A2
Raków, *Warsaw* 31 B1
Ram, *Jerusalem* 13 A2
Râm Allâh, *Jerusalem* 13 A2
Ramadân, *Baghdad* 3 B2
Ramakrishna Puram, *Delhi* 10 B1
Ramanathpur, *Calcutta* 8 A1
Rambla, La, *Barcelona* 4 b2
Rambler Channel, *Hong Kong* 12 A1
Ramenki, *Moscow* 19 B2
Ramersdorf, *Munich* 20 B2
Ramos, *Rio de Janeiro* 24 B1
Ramos Mejia, *Buenos Aires* 7 B1
Ramot, *Jerusalem* 13 B2
Rampur, *Delhi* 10 A2
Ramsgate, *Sydney* 28 B1
Rand Afrikaans Univ., *Johannesburg* 13 B2
Rand Airport, *Johannesburg* 13 B2
Randburg, *Johannesburg* 13 A1
Randhart, *Johannesburg* 13 B2
Randpark Ridge, *Johannesburg* 13 A1
Randwick, *Sydney* 28 B2
Ranelagh, *Dublin* 11 A2
Rannersdorf, *Vienna* 31 B2
Ransbèche, *Brussels* 6 B2
Ransdorp, *Amsterdam* 2 A2
Ranvad, *Mumbai* 20 B2
Raposo, *Lisbon* 14 A1
Rashtrapati Bhawan, *Delhi* 1 c1
Rasskazovka, *Moscow* 19 C2
Rastaala, *Helsinki* 12 B1
Rastila, *Helsinki* 12 B3
Raszyn, *Warsaw* 31 C1
Ratcha Thewi, *Bangkok* 3 b3
Rathfarnham, *Dublin* 11 B2
Ratho, *Edinburgh* 11 B1
Ratho Station, *Edinburgh* 11 B1
Rato, *Lisbon* 14 A2
Ravelston, *Edinburgh* 11 B2
Rawamangun, *Jakarta* 13 B2
Rayners Lane, *London* 15 A1
Raynes Park, *London* 15 B2
Raypur, *Calcutta* 8 C2
Razdory, *Moscow* 19 B1
Real Felipe, Fuerte, *Lima* 16 B2
Recoleta, *Buenos Aires* 7 B2
Recoleta, *Santiago* 26 B2
Red Fort = Lal Qila, *Delhi* 1 a3
Redbridge, *London* 15 A4
Redfern, *Sydney* 28 B2
Redwood, *Wellington* 32 B1
Reeves Hill, *Boston* 6 A1
Refshaleøen, *Copenhagen* 10 A3
Regents Park, *Johannesburg* 13 B2
Regent's Park, *London* 15 a2
Rego Park, *New York* 21 B2
Reichstag, *Berlin* 5 a3
Reina Sofía, Centro de Arte, *Madrid* 17 c3
Reinickendorf, *Berlin* 5 A3
Rekola, *Helsinki* 12 B3
Rembertów, *Warsaw* 31 B2
Rembrandthuis, *Amsterdam* 2 b2
Rembrandtpark, *Amsterdam* 2 A2
Rembrandtsplein, *Amsterdam* 2 b2
Remedios, Parque Nacional de los, *Mexico City* 18 B1
Remedios de Escalada, *Buenos Aires* 7 C2
Rémola, Laguna del, *Barcelona* 4 B1
Renca, *Santiago* 26 B1
Renmin Park, *Tianjin* 30 B2
Rennemoulin, *Paris* 23 A1
Reporyje, *Prague* 24 B1
Republica, Plaza de la, *Mexico City* 18 b1
République, Place de la, *Paris* 23 b5
Repulse Bay, *Hong Kong* 12 B2
Repy, *Prague* 24 B1
Residenz, *Munich* 20 B2
Residenzmuseum, *Munich* 20 b3
Reston, *Washington* 32 B2
Retiro, *Buenos Aires* 7 B2
Retiro, *Madrid* 17 B1
Retreat, *Cape Town* 8 B1
Reutov, *Moscow* 19 B5
Réveillon →, *Paris* 23 B4
Revere, *Boston* 6 A3
Rexdale, *Toronto* 30 A1
Reynosa Tamaulipas, *Mexico City* 18 A1
Rho, *Milan* 18 A1
Rhodes, *Sydney* 28 A1
Rhodon, *Paris* 23 B1
Rhodon →, *Paris* 23 B1
Ribeira, *Rio de Janeiro* 24 A1
Ricarda, Laguna de la, *Barcelona* 4 B1
Richmond, *Melbourne* 17 A2
Richmond, *San Francisco* 25 B2
Richmond Hill, *New York* 21 B2
Richmond Park, *London* 15 B2
Richmond upon Thames, *London* 15 B2
Riddarholmen, *Stockholm* 28 c1
Riddarhuset, *Stockholm* 28 c2
Ridgefield, *New York* 21 B1
Ridgefield Park, *New York* 21 A1
Ridgewood, *New York* 21 B2
Riem, *Munich* 20 B3
Rijksmuseum, *Amsterdam* 2 b1
Rikers I., *New York* 21 B2
Riksdagenshusdamothus, *Stockholm* 28 b2
Riksdagshuset, *Stockholm* 28 b2
Rimac, *Lima* 16 B2
Ringsend, *Dublin* 11 A2
Rinkeby, *Stockholm* 28 A1
Rio Comprido, *Rio de Janeiro* 24 B1
Rio de Janeiro, *Rio de Janeiro* 24 B1
Rio de la Plata, *Buenos Aires* 7 B2
Rio de Mouro, *Lisbon* 14 A1
Ripollet, *Barcelona* 4 A1
Ris, *Oslo* 22 A3
Risby, *Copenhagen* 10 A1
Rishra, *Calcutta* 8 A2
Ritchie, *Washington* 32 B4
Rithala, *Delhi* 10 A1
Rive Sud, Canal de la, *Montreal* 19 B2
River Edge, *New York* 21 A1
River Forest, *Chicago* 9 B2
River Grove, *Chicago* 9 B1
Riverdale, *New York* 21 A2
Riverdale, *Washington* 32 B4
Riverdale Park, *Toronto* 30 A2
Riverlea, *Johannesburg* 13 B1
Riverside, *Chicago* 9 C2
Riverwood, *Sydney* 28 B1
Rivière-des-Praires, *Montreal* 19 A2
Rixensart, *Brussels* 6 B3
Riyad, *Baghdad* 3 B2
Rizal Park, *Manila* 17 B1
Rizal Stadium, *Manila* 17 B1
Røa, *Oslo* 22 A2
Robbins, *Chicago* 9 D2
Robertsham, *Johannesburg* 13 B2
Rochelle Park, *New York* 21 A1
Rock Cr. →, *Washington* 32 B3
Rock Creek Park, *Washington* 32 B3
Rock Pt., *Wellington* 32 A1
Rockaway Pt., *New York* 21 C2
Rockdale, *Sydney* 28 B1
Rockefeller Center, *New York* 21 c2
Rodaon, *Vienna* 31 B1
Rødovre, *Copenhagen* 10 A2
Rodrigo de Freitas, L., *Rio de Janeiro* 24 B1
Roehampton, *London* 15 B2
Rogers Park, *Chicago* 9 A2
Roihuvuori, *Helsinki* 12 B3
Roissy-en-Brie, *Paris* 23 B4
Rokin, *Amsterdam* 2 b2
Rokkō I., *Osaka* 22 A2
Rokkō Sanchi, *Osaka* 22 A2
Rokkō-Zan, *Osaka* 22 A2
Rokytka →, *Prague* 24 B3
Roma, *Rome* 25 B1
Római-Fürdő, *Budapest* 7 A2
Romainville, *Paris* 23 A3
Romano Banco, *Milan* 18 B1
Romashkovo, *Moscow* 19 B1
Rome = Roma, *Rome* 25 B1
Romford, *London* 15 A5
Rondebosch, *Cape Town* 8 A1
Roppongi, *Tokyo* 29 c3
Rose Hill, *Washington* 32 C3
Rosebank, *New York* 21 C1
Rosebery, *Sydney* 28 B2
Rosedal La Candelaria, *Mexico City* 18 B2
Roseland, *Chicago* 9 C3
Rosemead, *Los Angeles* 16 B4
Rosemont, *Montreal* 19 A2
Rosenborg Have, *Copenhagen* 10 A3
Rosenthal, *Berlin* 5 A3
Rosettenville, *Johannesburg* 13 B2
Rosewell, *Edinburgh* 11 B3
Rosherville Dam, *Johannesburg* 13 B2
Rösjön, *Stockholm* 28 A2
Roslags-Näsby, *Stockholm* 28 A2
Roslin, *Edinburgh* 11 B3
Roslindale, *Boston* 6 B3
Rosny-sous-Bois, *Paris* 23 A4
Rosslyn, *Washington* 32 B3
Rosyth, *Edinburgh* 11 A1
Rotherhithe, *London* 15 B3
Rothneusiedl, *Vienna* 31 B2
Rothschmaige, *Munich* 20 A1
Rouge Hill, *Toronto* 30 A4
Round I., *Hong Kong* 12 B2
Roxbury, *Boston* 6 B3
Roxeth, *London* 15 A1
Royal Botanic Garden, *Edinburgh* 11 B2
Royal Botanic Gardens, *Sydney* 28 b2
Royal Grand Palace, *Bangkok* 3 b1
Royal Observatory, *Edinburgh* 11 B2
Royal Park, *Melbourne* 17 A1
Royal Turf Club, *Bangkok* 3 b2
Röylä, *Helsinki* 12 B1
Rozas, Portilleros de las, *Madrid* 17 B1
Roztoky, *Prague* 24 B2
Rozzano, *Milan* 18 B1
Rubí →, *Barcelona* 4 A1
Rublovo, *Moscow* 19 B2
Rudnevka →, *Moscow* 19 B5
Rudolfsheim, *Vienna* 31 A2
Rudolfshöhe, *Berlin* 5 A5
Rudow, *Berlin* 5 B3
Rueil-Malmaison, *Paris* 23 A2
Ruisbroek, *Brussels* 6 B1
Ruislip, *London* 15 A1
Rumelihisarı, *Istanbul* 12 B2
Rumyantsevo, *Moscow* 19 C2
Rungis, *Paris* 23 B3
Rusāfa, *Baghdad* 3 A2
Rush Green, *London* 15 A5
Russa, *Calcutta* 8 C2
Russian Hill, *San Francisco* 25 a1
Rustenfeld, *Vienna* 31 B2
Rutherford, *New York* 21 B1
Ruzyně, *Prague* 24 B1
Rybatskaya, *St. Petersburg* 26 B2
Rydboholm, *Stockholm* 28 A3
Ryde, *Sydney* 28 A1
Rynek, *Warsaw* 31 a2
Ryogoku, *Tokyo* 29 A3
Rzhevka, *St. Petersburg* 26 B3

S

Sa'ādatābād, *Tehran* 30 A2
Saadūn, *Baghdad* 3 B2
Saavedra, *Buenos Aires* 7 B2
Saboli, *Delhi* 10 A2
Sabugo, *Lisbon* 14 A1
Sabzi Mand, *Delhi* 10 A2
Sacavém, *Lisbon* 14 A2
Saclay, *Paris* 23 B2
Saclay, Étang de, *Paris* 23 B1
Sacomã, *São Paulo* 26 B2
Sacré Cœur, *Paris* 23 a3
Sacrow, *Berlin* 5 B1
Sacrower See, *Berlin* 5 B1
Sadang, *Seoul* 26 C1
Sadar Bazar, *Delhi* 1 a1
Saddle Brook, *New York* 21 A1
Sadr, *Karachi* 14 A2
Sadr City, *Baghdad* 3 A2
Sadyba, *Warsaw* 31 B2
Saft el Laban, *Cairo* 7 A2
Saganashkee Slough, *Chicago* 9 C1
Sagene, *Oslo* 22 A3
Sagrada Família, Templo de, *Barcelona* 4 A2
Sagrado Familia, Templo de, *Barcelona* 4 a2
Sahar Int. Airport, *Mumbai* 20 A2
Sai Kung, *Hong Kong* 12 A2
Sai Wan Ho, *Hong Kong* 12 B2
Sai Ying Pun, *Hong Kong* 12 B1
St.-Aubin, *Paris* 23 B1
St.-Cloud, *Paris* 23 A2
St.-Cyr-l'École, *Paris* 23 B1
St.-Cyr-l'École, Aérodrome de, *Paris* 23 B1
St.-Denis, *Paris* 23 A3
St.-Germain, Forêt de, *Paris* 23 A1
St.-Germain-en-Laye, *Paris* 23 A1
St. Giles Cathedral, *Edinburgh* 11 b2
St-Gilles, *Brussels* 6 B2
St. Helier, *London* 15 B2
St.-Hubert, *Montreal* 19 B3
St. Hubert, Galerie, *Brussels* 6 b2
St. Isaac's Cathedral, *St. Petersburg* 26 B1
St. Jacques →, *Montreal* 19 B3
St. James's, *London* 15 b3
St. John's Cathedral, *Hong Kong* 12 c1
St-Joose-Ten-Noode, *Brussels* 6 A2
St. Kilda, *Melbourne* 17 B1
St. Lambert, *Montreal* 19 A3
St.-Lambert, *Paris* 23 B1
St.-Laurent, *Montreal* 19 A1
St. Lawrence →, *Montreal* 19 B2
St.-Lazare, Gare, *Paris* 23 A2
St.-Léonard, *Montreal* 19 A2
St. Magelungen, *Stockholm* 28 B2
St.-Mandé, *Paris* 23 A3
St. Margaret's, *Dublin* 11 A2
St.-Martin, Bois, *Paris* 23 B4
St. Mary Cray, *London* 15 B4
St.-Maur-des-Fossés, *Paris* 23 B3
St.-Maurice, *Paris* 23 B3
St.-Michel, *Montreal* 19 A2
St. Nikolaus-Kirken, *Prague* 24 B2
St.-Ouen, *Paris* 23 A3
St. Patrick's Cathedral, *Dublin* 11 c1
St. Patrick's Cathedral, *New York* 21 c2
St. Paul's Cathedral, *London* 15 b4
St. Paul's Cray, *London* 15 B4
St. Peters, *Sydney* 28 B2
St. Petersburg = Sankt Peterburg, *St. Petersburg* 26 B1
St.-Pierre, *Montreal* 19 B2
St.-Pieters-Leeuw, *Brussels* 6 B1
St.-Quentin, Étang de, *Paris* 23 B1
St. Stephen's Green, *Dublin* 11 c3
St-Stevens-Woluwe, *Brussels* 6 A2
St.-Vincent-de-Paul, *Montreal* 19 A2
Ste.-Catherine, *Montreal* 19 B2
Ste.-Hélène, Î., *Montreal* 19 A2
Saiwai, *Tokyo* 29 B3
Sakai, *Osaka* 22 B3
Sakai Harbour, *Osaka* 22 B3
Sakra, P., *Singapore* 27 B2
Salam, *Baghdad* 3 A2
Salamanca, *Madrid* 17 B1
Sällynoggin, *Dublin* 11 B3
Salmannsdorf, *Vienna* 31 A1
Salmedina, *Madrid* 17 C2
Salomea, *Warsaw* 31 B1
Salsette I., *Mumbai* 20 A2
Salt Lake City, *Calcutta* 8 B2
Salt River, *Cape Town* 8 A1
Salt Water L., *Calcutta* 8 B2
Saltsjö-Duvnäs, *Stockholm* 28 B3
Saltykovka, *Moscow* 19 B5
Samatya, *Istanbul* 12 C1
Sampaloc, *Manila* 17 B1
Samphan Thawong, *Bangkok* 3 B2
Samsŏn, *Seoul* 26 B2
San Andrés, *Barcelona* 4 A2
San Angel, *Mexico City* 18 B1
San Angelo, Castel, *Rome* 25 b1
San Basilio, *Rome* 25 B2
San Borja, *Lima* 16 B3
San Bóvio, *Milan* 18 B2
San Bruno, Pt., *San Francisco* 25 C2
San Bruno Mt., *San Francisco* 25 B2
San Cristobal, *Buenos Aires* 7 B2
San Cristobal, *Madrid* 17 B2
San Cristóbal, Cerro, *Santiago* 26 B2
San Cristoforo, *Milan* 18 B1
San Donato Milanese, *Milan* 18 B2
San Francisco, *San Francisco* 25 B2
San Francisco B., *San Francisco* 25 B3
San Francisco Culhuacán, *Mexico City* 18 C2
San Fruttuoso, *Milan* 18 A2
San Gabriel, *Los Angeles* 16 B4
San Giuliano Milanese, *Milan* 18 B2
San Isidro, *Lima* 16 B2
San Jerónimo Lidice, *Mexico City* 18 C1
San Joaquin, *Santiago* 26 B2
San José Rio Hondo, *Mexico City* 18 B1
San Juan →, *Manila* 17 B2
San Juan de Aragón, *Mexico City* 18 B2
San Juan de Aragón, Parque, *Mexico City* 18 B2
San Juan de Lurigancho, *Lima* 16 A2
San Juan del Monte, *Manila* 17 B2
San Juan Ixtacala, *Mexico City* 18 A1
San Juan Toltotepec, *Mexico City* 18 B1
San Just Desvern, *Barcelona* 4 A1
San Justo, *Buenos Aires* 7 C1
San Lorenzo Tezonco, *Mexico City* 18 C2
San Luis, *Lima* 16 B2
San Marino, *Los Angeles* 16 B4
San Martin, *Barcelona* 4 A2
San Martin de Porras, *Lima* 16 B2
San Miguel, *Lima* 16 B2
San Miguel, *Santiago* 26 B2
San Nicolas, *Buenos Aires* 7 B2
San Onófrio, *Rome* 25 B1
San Pedro Martir, *Barcelona* 4 A1
San Pedro Zacatenco, *Mexico City* 18 A2
San Pietro, Piazza, *Rome* 25 b1
San Po Kong, *Hong Kong* 12 A2
San Rafael Chamapa, *Mexico City* 18 B1
San Rafael Hills, *Los Angeles* 16 A3
San Roque, *Manila* 17 B2
San Siro, *Milan* 18 B1
San Souci, *Sydney* 28 B1
San Telmo, *Buenos Aires* 7 B2
San Vicenc dels Horts, *Barcelona* 4 A1
Sanbancho, *Tokyo* 29 a3
Sandown, *Johannesburg* 13 A2
Sandown Park Races, *London* 15 B1
Sandton, *Johannesburg* 13 A2
Sandvika, *Oslo* 22 A2
Sandy Pond, *Boston* 6 A2
Sandyford, *Dublin* 11 B2
Sandymount, *Dublin* 11 B2
Sangenjaya, *Tokyo* 29 B2
Sangge, *Seoul* 26 B2
Sangley Pt., *Manila* 17 C1
Sankrail, *Calcutta* 8 B1
Sankt Peterburg, *St. Petersburg* 26 B1
Sankt Veit, *Vienna* 31 A1
Sanlihe, *Beijing* 4 B1
Sanlintang, *Shanghai* 27 C1
Sans, *Barcelona* 4 A1
Sant Agusti, *Barcelona* 4 c2
Sant Ambrogio, Basilica di, *Milan* 18 B2
Sant Boi de Llobregat, *Barcelona* 4 A1
Sant Cugat, *Barcelona* 4 A1
Sant Feliu de Llobregat, *Barcelona* 4 A1
Sant Joan Despi, *Barcelona* 4 A1
Sant Maria del Mar, *Barcelona* 4 b3
Sant Pau del Camp, *Barcelona* 4 c2
Santa Ana, *Manila* 17 B2
Santa Coloma de Gramanet, *Barcelona* 4 A2
Santa Cruz, *Manila* 17 B1
Santa Cruz, *Mumbai* 20 A1
Santa Cruz, I. de, *Rio de Janeiro* 24 B2
Santa Cruz de Olorde, *Barcelona* 4 A1
Santa Efigénia, *São Paulo* 26 B2
Santa Elena, *Manila* 17 B2
Santa Elena del Gomero, *Santiago* 26 B1
Santa Eulalia, *Barcelona* 4 A2
Santa Fe Springs, *Los Angeles* 16 C4
Santa Iria da Azóia, *Lisbon* 14 A2
Santa Julia, *Santiago* 26 C2
Santa Maria, *Mexico City* 18 a1
Santa Monica, *Los Angeles* 16 B2
Santa Monica Mts., *Los Angeles* 16 B2
Santa Rosa De Locobe, *Santiago* 26 B2
Santa Teresa de la Ovalle, *Santiago* 26 B1
Santahamina, *Helsinki* 12 C3
Santana, *São Paulo* 26 A2
Santeny, *Paris* 23 B4
Santiago, *Santiago* 26 B2
Santiago de Surco, *Lima* 16 B2
Santo Amaro, *Lisbon* 14 A1
Santo Amaro, *São Paulo* 26 B1
Santo Andre, *Lisbon* 14 B2
Santo Antão do Tojal, *Lisbon* 14 A2
Santo António, Qta. de, *Lisbon* 14 B1
Santo Tomas, Univ. of, *Manila* 17 B1
Santos Dumont, Aéroport, *Rio de Janeiro* 24 B2
Santoshpur, *Calcutta* 8 B1
Santragachi, *Calcutta* 8 B1
Santry, *Dublin* 11 A2
Sanyuanli, *Canton* 8 B2
São Caetano do Sul, *São Paulo* 26 B2
São Conrado, *Rio de Janeiro* 24 C1
São Cristovão, *Rio de Janeiro* 24 B1
São Francisco Penitência, *Rio de Janeiro* 24 b1
São Jorge, Castelo de, *Lisbon* 14 A2
São Juliao do Tojal, *Lisbon* 14 A2
São Paulo, *São Paulo* 26 B2
Sapa, *Calcutta* 8 B1
Sapateiro, Cor. do →, *São Paulo* 26 B1
Sarandi, *Buenos Aires* 7 C2
Saraswati →, *Calcutta* 8 A1
Sarecky potok →, *Prague* 24 B2
Sarimbun, *Singapore* 27 A2
Sarimbun Res., *Singapore* 27 A2
Sarıyer, *Istanbul* 12 A2
Saronikós Kólpos, *Athens* 2 B1
Sarriá, *Barcelona* 4 A1
Sarsuna, *Calcutta* 8 C1
Sartrouville, *Paris* 23 A2
Sasad, *Budapest* 7 B2
Sashalom, *Budapest* 7 A3
Saska, *Warsaw* 31 B2
Satalice, *Prague* 24 B3
Satgachi, *Calcutta* 8 B2
Sathorn, *Bangkok* 3 B2
Satpukur, *Calcutta* 8 B2
Sätra, *Stockholm* 28 B1
Sattru Pha, *Bangkok* 3 b2
Saúde, *São Paulo* 26 B2
Saugus, *Boston* 6 A3
Saugus →, *Boston* 6 A3
Sault-au-Récollet, *Montreal* 19 A2
Sausalito, *San Francisco* 25 A2
Sawah Besar, *Jakarta* 13 A1
Saxonville, *Boston* 6 B1
Scald Law, *Edinburgh* 11 B2
Scarborough, *Toronto* 30 A3
Sceaux, *Paris* 23 B2
Schaerbeek, *Brussels* 6 A2
Scharfenberg, *Berlin* 5 A2
Scheepvartmuseum, *Amsterdam* 2 b3
Schiller Park, *Chicago* 9 B1
Schiller Woods, *Chicago* 9 B1
Schiphol, Luchthaven, *Amsterdam* 2 B1
Schlachtensee, *Berlin* 5 B2
Schlossgarten, *Berlin* 5 A2
Schmargendorf, *Berlin* 5 B2
Schönblick, *Berlin* 5 B5
Schönbrunn, Schloss, *Vienna* 31 A1
Schöneberg, *Berlin* 5 B3
Schöneiche, *Berlin* 5 B5
Schönwalde, *Berlin* 5 A1
Schotschekloof, *Cape Town* 8 b1
Schulzendorf, *Berlin* 5 A2
Schwabing, *Munich* 20 B2
Schwanebeck, *Berlin* 5 A4
Schwanenwerder, *Berlin* 5 B2
Schwarzlackenau, *Vienna* 31 A2
Schwechat, *Vienna* 31 B2
Scitrek Museum, *Atlanta* 3 B2
Scott Monument, *Edinburgh* 11 b2
Scottdale, *Atlanta* 3 B3
Sea Point, *Cape Town* 8 A1
Seabrook, *Washington* 32 B5
Seacliff, *San Francisco* 25 B2
Seaforth, *Sydney* 28 A2
Seagate, *New York* 21 C1
Sears Tower, *Chicago* 9 c1
Seat Pleasant, *Washington* 32 B4
Seaview, *Wellington* 32 B2
Šeberov, *Prague* 24 B3
Secaucus, *New York* 21 B1
Seddinsee, *Berlin* 5 B5
Seeberg, *Berlin* 5 A5
Seeburg, *Berlin* 5 A1
Seefeld, *Berlin* 5 A5
Seegefeld, *Berlin* 5 A1
Seehof, *Berlin* 5 B2
Segeltorp, *Stockholm* 28 B1
Segrate, *Milan* 18 B2
Seguro, *Milan* 18 B1
Seine →, *Paris* 23 B3
Seixal, *Lisbon* 14 B2
Selby, *Johannesburg* 13 B2
Seletar, P., *Singapore* 27 A3
Seletar Hills, *Singapore* 27 A3
Seletar Res., *Singapore* 27 A2
Selhurst, *London* 15 B3
Sembawang, *Singapore* 27 A2
Senago, *Milan* 18 A1
Sendinger Tor Platz, *Munich* 20 c1
Sendling, *Munich* 20 B2
Senju, *Tokyo* 29 A3
Senriyama, *Osaka* 22 A4
Sentosa, P., *Singapore* 27 B2
Seoul = Sŏul, *Seoul* 26 B2
Seoul National Univ., *Seoul* 26 C1
Seoul Tower, *Seoul* 26 B1
Sepolia, *Athens* 2 A2
Sepulveda Flood Control Basin, *Los Angeles* 16 A2
Serangoon, *Singapore* 27 A3
Serangoon, P., *Singapore* 27 A3
Serangoon, Sungei →, *Singapore* 27 A3
Serangoon Harbour, *Singapore* 27 A3
Seraya, P., *Singapore* 27 B2
Serebryanka, *Moscow* 19 B5
Serebryanka →, *Moscow* 19 B4
Serramonte, *San Francisco* 25 C2
Sesto San Giovanni, *Milan* 18 A2
Sesto Ulteriano, *Milan* 18 B2
Setagaya-Ku, *Tokyo* 29 B2
Seter, *Oslo* 22 A3
Setia Budi, *Jakarta* 13 B1
Settebagni, *Rome* 25 A2
Settecamini, *Rome* 25 B2
Séttimo Milanese, *Milan* 18 B1
Settsu, *Osaka* 22 A4
Setuny →, *Moscow* 19 B2
Seutula, *Helsinki* 12 A2
Seven Corners, *Washington* 32 B3
Seven Kings, *London* 15 A4
Sévesco →, *Milan* 18 A1
Sevran, *Paris* 23 A4
Sewri, *Mumbai* 20 B2
Sforzesso, Castello, *Milan* 18 B2
Sha Kok Mei, *Hong Kong* 12 A2
Sha Tin, *Hong Kong* 12 A2
Sha Tin Wai, *Hong Kong* 12 A2
Shabrâmant, *Cairo* 7 B2
Shahdara, *Delhi* 10 A2
Shahe, *Canton* 8 B2
Shahr-e Rey, *Tehran* 30 B2
Shahrak-e Golshahr, *Tehran* 30 B1
Shahrak-e Qods, *Tehran* 30 A2
Shaikh Aomar, *Baghdad* 3 A2
Shakurbasti, *Delhi* 10 A1
Shalkiya, *Calcutta* 8 B2
Sham Shui Po, *Hong Kong* 12 B1
Shamapur, *Delhi* 10 A1
Shamian, *Canton* 8 B2
Shan Mei, *Hong Kong* 12 A2
Shanghai, *Shanghai* 27 B2
Shankill, *Dublin* 11 B3
Sharp I., *Hong Kong* 12 A2
Shastrinagar, *Delhi* 10 A2
Shau Kei Wan, *Hong Kong* 12 B2
Shawocun, *Beijing* 4 B1
Shayuan, *Canton* 8 B2
Sheepshead Bay, *New York* 21 C2
Shek O, *Hong Kong* 12 B2
Shelter I., *Hong Kong* 12 B2
Sheng Fa Shan, *Hong Kong* 12 A1
Shepherds Bush, *London* 15 A2
Shepperton, *London* 15 B1
Sherman Oaks, *Los Angeles* 16 B2
Sherman Park, *Chicago* 9 C2
Shet Bandar, *Mumbai* 20 B2
Sheung Lau Wan, *Hong Kong* 12 B2
Sheung Wan, *Hong Kong* 12 B1
Sheva, *Mumbai* 20 B2
Sheva Nhava, *Mumbai* 20 B2
Shiba, *Tokyo* 29 c4
Shibpur, *Calcutta* 8 B1
Shibuya-Ku, *Tokyo* 29 c1
Shijōnawate, *Osaka* 22 A4
Shillim, *Seoul* 26 C1
Shimogawara, *Tokyo* 29 B1
Shimosalo, *Tokyo* 29 A2
Shimoshakujii, *Tokyo* 29 A2
Shinagawa-Ku, *Tokyo* 29 B3
Shing Mun Res., *Hong Kong* 12 A1
Shinjuku-Ku, *Tokyo* 29 a1
Shinjuku National Garden, *Tokyo* 29 a2
Shinkoiwa, *Tokyo* 29 A4
Shinnakano, *Tokyo* 29 A3
Shinsa, *Seoul* 26 B2
Shipai, *Canton* 8 B3
Shirinashi →, *Osaka* 22 B3
Shirogane, *Tokyo* 29 B3
Shiweitang, *Canton* 8 B2
Shogunle, *Lagos* 14 A2
Shomolu, *Lagos* 14 A2
Shooters Hill, *London* 15 B4
Shoreditch, *London* 15 a5
Shortlands, *London* 15 B4
Shu' afat, *Jerusalem* 13 B2
Shubrâ, *Cairo* 7 A2
Shubrâ el Kheima, *Cairo* 7 A2
Shuikuo, *Canton* 8 A2
Shuishang Park, *Tianjin* 30 B1
Sidcup, *London* 15 B4
Siebenhirten, *Vienna* 31 B1
Siedlung, *Berlin* 5 A1
Siekierki, *Warsaw* 31 B2
Sielce, *Warsaw* 31 B2
Siemensstadt, *Berlin* 5 A2
Sierra Madre, *Los Angeles* 16 B4
Sievering, *Vienna* 31 A2
Sighthill, *Edinburgh* 11 B2
Signal Hill, *Cape Town* 8 A1
Sihŭng, *Seoul* 26 C1
Sikátorpuszta, *Budapest* 7 A3
Silampur, *Delhi* 10 B2
Silver Hill, *Boston* 6 A2
Silver Hill, *Washington* 32 C4
Silver Spring, *Washington* 32 A3
Silvermine Nature Reserve, *Cape Town* 8 B1
Silvolantekojärvi, *Helsinki* 12 B2
Simei, *Singapore* 27 A3
Simla, *Calcutta* 8 B2
Simmering, *Vienna* 31 A2
Simmering Heide, *Vienna* 31 A2
Simonkylä, *Helsinki* 12 B3
Singapore, *Singapore* 27 B3
Singapore, Univ. of, *Singapore* 27 B2
Sinicka →, *Moscow* 19 A1
Sinki, Selat, *Singapore* 27 B2
Sint-Genesius-Rode, *Brussels* 6 B2
Sinwŏl, *Seoul* 26 B1
Sion, *Mumbai* 20 A2
Sipson, *London* 15 B1
Siqeil, *Cairo* 7 A1
Şişli, *Istanbul* 12 B1
Skansen, *Stockholm* 28 B2
Skärholmen, *Stockholm* 28 B1
Skarpäng, *Stockholm* 28 A2
Skarpnäck, *Stockholm* 28 B2
Skaryszewski Park, *Warsaw* 31 B2
Skeppsholmen, *Stockholm* 28 c3
Skokie, *Chicago* 9 A2
Skokie →, *Chicago* 9 A2
Skoklefall, *Oslo* 22 A3
Sköndal, *Stockholm* 28 B2
Skovlunde, *Copenhagen* 10 A2
Skovshoved, *Copenhagen* 10 A3
Skuru, *Stockholm* 28 B3
Skyland, *Atlanta* 3 A3
Slade Green, *London* 15 B5
Slemmestad, *Oslo* 22 B1
Slependen, *Oslo* 22 A2
Slipi, *Jakarta* 13 B1
Slivenec, *Prague* 24 B2
Sloten, *Amsterdam* 2 A1
Sloterpark, *Amsterdam* 2 A1
Sluhy, *Prague* 24 A3
Służew, *Warsaw* 31 B2
Służewiec, *Warsaw* 31 B2
Smíchov, *Prague* 24 B2
Smith Forest Preserve, *Chicago* 9 B2
Smithsonian Institute, *Washington* 32 b2
Smolny, *St. Petersburg* 26 B2
Snake Creek Canal →, *Miami* 18 A2
Snarøya, *Oslo* 22 A2
Snättringe, *Stockholm* 28 B1
Söbinggo, *Seoul* 26 B1
Søborg, *Copenhagen* 10 A2
Sobreda, *Lisbon* 14 B1
Soch'o, *Seoul* 26 C1
Sōdaemun, *Seoul* 26 B1
Söderby, *Stockholm* 28 A3
Södermalm, *Stockholm* 28 B2
Sodpur, *Calcutta* 8 A2
Soeurs, Î. des, *Montreal* 19 B2
Sognsvatn, *Oslo* 22 A3
Soho, *London* 15 b3
Soho, *New York* 21 e1
Soignes, Forêt de, *Brussels* 6 B2
Sok Kwu Wan, *Hong Kong* 12 B1
Sökkwan, *Seoul* 26 B2
Sokolniki, *Moscow* 19 B4
Sokolniki Park, *Moscow* 19 B4
Sokołów, *Warsaw* 31 C1
Solalinden, *Munich* 20 B3
Soldier Field, *Chicago* 9 e3
Sollentuna, *Stockholm* 28 A1
Solln, *Munich* 20 B2
Solna, *Stockholm* 28 A1
Solntsevo, *Moscow* 19 C2
Somerset, *Washington* 32 B3
Somerville, *Boston* 6 A3
Somes Is., *Wellington* 32 B2
Sonari, *Mumbai* 20 B2
Søndersø, *Copenhagen* 10 A2
Sŏngbuk, *Seoul* 26 B2
Sŏngdong, *Seoul* 26 B2
Sŏngp'a, *Seoul* 26 B2
Sŏngsu, *Seoul* 26 B2
Soong Qingling, Former Res. of, *Beijing* 4 a2
Soroksár, *Budapest* 7 B2
Soroksari Duna →, *Budapest* 7 B2
Sosenka →, *Moscow* 19 B4
Sosnovka, *St. Petersburg* 26 B2
Sŏul, *Seoul* 26 B2
Soundview, *New York* 21 B2
South Beach, *New York* 21 C1
South Beach Harbor, *San Francisco* 25 c3
South Bend Park, *Atlanta* 3 B2
South Boston, *Boston* 6 A3
South Brooklyn, *New York* 21 B2
South Decatur, *Atlanta* 3 B3
South Deering, *Chicago* 9 C3
South El Monte, *Los Angeles* 16 B4
South Gate, *Los Angeles* 16 C3
South Harbor, *Manila* 17 B1
South Harrow, *London* 15 A1
South Hd., *Sydney* 28 B2
South Hills, *Johannesburg* 13 B2
South Hornchurch, *London* 15 A5
South Kensington, *London* 15 c2
South Lawn, *Washington* 32 C3
South Lincoln, *Boston* 6 A2
South Miami, *Miami* 18 B1
South Norwood, *London* 15 B3
South of Market, *San Francisco* 25 B2
South Ozone Park, *New York* 21 B3
South Pasadena, *Los Angeles* 16 B4
South Res., *Boston* 6 A3
South Ruislip, *London* 15 A1
South San Francisco, *San Francisco* 25 C2
South San Gabriel, *Los Angeles* 16 B4
South Shore, *Chicago* 9 C3
South Sudbury, *Boston* 6 A1
Southall, *London* 15 A1
Southborough, *London* 15 B4
Southend, *London* 15 B3
Southfields, *London* 15 B2
Southwark, *London* 15 B3
Søvang, *Copenhagen* 10 B3
Soweto, *Johannesburg* 13 B1
Sowhānak, *Tehran* 30 A3
Soya, *Tokyo* 29 A4
Spandau, *Berlin* 5 A1
Spånga, *Stockholm* 28 A1
Spanische Reitschule, *Vienna* 31 b1
Spectacle I., *Boston* 6 A4
Speicher-See, *Munich* 20 A3
Speising, *Vienna* 31 B1
Sphinx, *Cairo* 7 B1
Spinaceto, *Rome* 25 C1
Spit Junction, *Sydney* 28 A2
Spořilov, *Prague* 24 B3
Spot Pond, *Boston* 6 A3
Spotswood, *Melbourne* 17 B1
Spree →, *Berlin* 5 A2
Spring Pond, *Boston* 6 A4
Springeberg, *Berlin* 5 B5
Springfield, *Washington* 32 C2
Squantum, *Boston* 6 B3
Srednaya Rogatka, *St. Petersburg* 26 C2
Śródmieście, *Warsaw* 31 B2
Staaken, *Berlin* 5 A1
Stabekk, *Oslo* 22 A2
Stadhion, *Athens* 2 c3
Stadhuis, *Amsterdam* 2 b2
Stadlau, *Vienna* 31 A2
Stadshuset, *Stockholm* 28 b1
Stains, *Paris* 23 A3
Stamford Hill, *London* 15 A3
Stammersdorf, *Vienna* 31 A2
Stanley, *Hong Kong* 12 B2
Stanley Mound, *Hong Kong* 12 B2
Stanley Pen., *Hong Kong* 12 B2
Stanmore, *London* 15 A2
Stapleton, *New York* 21 C1
Star Ferry, *Hong Kong* 12 a2
Staraya Derevnya, *St. Petersburg* 26 B1
Stare, *Warsaw* 31 B2
Staré Město, *Prague* 24 B2
Starego Miasto, *Warsaw* 31 a2
Staten Island Zoo, *New York* 21 C1
Statenice, *Prague* 24 B1
Statue Square, *Hong Kong* 12 c1
Stedelijk Museum, *Amsterdam* 2 c1
Steele Creek, *Melbourne* 17 A1
Steenokkerzeel, *Brussels* 6 A2
Steglitz, *Berlin* 5 B2
Stepaside, *Dublin* 11 B2
Stephansdom, *Vienna* 31 b2
Stepney, *London* 15 A3
Sterling Park, *San Francisco* 25 B2
Sticklinge udde, *Stockholm* 28 A2
Stickney, *Chicago* 9 C2
Stillorgan, *Dublin* 11 B2
Stockholm, *Stockholm* 28 B2
Stocksund, *Stockholm* 28 A2
Stodůlky, *Prague* 24 B1
Stoke Newington, *London* 15 A3
Stokes Valley, *Wellington* 32 B2
Stone Canyon Res., *Los Angeles* 16 B2
Stone Park, *Chicago* 9 B1
Stonebridge, *London* 15 A2
Stoneham, *Boston* 6 A3
Stony Brook Res., *Boston* 6 B3
Stora Värtan, *Stockholm* 28 A2
Store Hareskov, *Copenhagen* 10 A2
Store Magleby, *Copenhagen* 10 B3
Storholmen, *Stockholm* 28 A2
Stoyka, *St. Petersburg* 26 B2
Straiton, *Edinburgh* 11 B3
Strand, *London* 15 b4
Strandfontein, *Cape Town* 8 B2
Strašnice, *Prague* 24 B2
Strasstrudering, *Munich* 20 B3
Stratford, *London* 15 A4
Strathfield, *Sydney* 28 B1
Streatham, *London* 15 B3
Streatham Vale, *London* 15 B3
Strebersdorf, *Vienna* 31 A2
Střešovice, *Prague* 24 B2
Stříkov, *Prague* 24 B2
Strogino, *Moscow* 19 B2
Strombeek-Bever, *Brussels* 6 A2
Stromovka, *Prague* 24 B2
Studio City, *Los Angeles* 16 B2
Stureby, *Stockholm* 28 B2
Stuvsta, *Stockholm* 28 B2
Subhepur, *Delhi* 10 A2
Sucat, *Manila* 17 C2
Suchdol, *Prague* 24 B2
Sucy-en-Brie, *Paris* 23 B4
Sudbury, *Boston* 6 A1
Sugamo, *Tokyo* 29 A3
Sugar Loaf Mt. = Açúcar, Pão de, *Rio de Janeiro* 24 B2
Suge, *Tokyo* 29 B2
Suginami-Ku, *Tokyo* 29 A2
Sugō, *Tokyo* 29 B2
Suita, *Osaka* 22 A4
Suitland, *Washington* 32 B4
Sukchar, *Calcutta* 8 A2
Suma, *Osaka* 22 B1
Sumida →, *Tokyo* 29 A3
Sumida-Ku, *Tokyo* 29 A3
Sumiyoshi, *Osaka* 22 B4
Summerville, *Toronto* 30 B1
Summit, *Chicago* 9 C2
Sunamachi, *Tokyo* 29 A4
Sunbury-on-Thames, *London* 15 B1
Sundbyberg, *Stockholm* 28 A1
Sundbyerne, *Copenhagen* 10 B3
Sung Kong, *Hong Kong* 12 B2
Sungei Kadut Industrial Estate, *Singapore* 27 A2
Sungei Selatar Res., *Singapore* 27 A3
Sunter, *Jakarta* 13 A2
Sunter, Kali →, *Jakarta* 13 B2
Suomenlinna, *Helsinki* 12 C2
Supreme Court, *Washington* 32 b3
Sura, *Calcutta* 8 B2
Surag-san, *Seoul* 26 A2
Surbiton, *London* 15 B2
Suresnes, *Paris* 23 A2
Surfside, *Miami* 18 A2
Surquillo, *Lima* 16 B2
Surrey Hills, *Sydney* 28 B2
Susaek, *Seoul* 26 B1
Süssenbrunn, *Vienna* 31 A2
Sutton, *Dublin* 11 A3
Sutton, *London* 15 B2
Suyu, *Seoul* 26 B2
Suzukishinden, *Tokyo* 29 A2
Svanemøllen, *Copenhagen* 10 A3
Sverdlov, *Moscow* 19 B3
Svestad, *Oslo* 22 B2
Svinö, *Helsinki* 12 C1
Swampscott, *Boston* 6 A4
Swanley, *London* 15 B4
Swansea, *Toronto* 30 B2
Swinburne I., *New York* 21 C1
Swords, *Dublin* 11 A2
Sydenham, *Johannesburg* 13 A2
Sydney, *Sydney* 28 B2
Sydney, Univ. of, *Sydney* 28 B2
Sydney Airport, *Sydney* 28 B2
Sydney Harbour Bridge, *Sydney* 28 B2
Sydstranden, *Copenhagen* 10 B3
Sylvania, *Sydney* 28 C1
Syntagma, Pl., *Athens* 2 b3
Syon Park, *London* 15 B2
Szczęśliwice, *Warsaw* 31 B1
Széchnenyi-hegy, *Budapest* 7 B1
Szent Istvánbaz, *Budapest* 7 b2
Széphalom, *Budapest* 7 A1

T

Tabata, *Tokyo* 29 A3
Tablada, *Buenos Aires* 7 C1
Table Bay, *Cape Town* 8 A1
Table Mountain, *Cape Town* 8 A1
Taboão da Serra, *São Paulo* 26 B1
Täby, *Stockholm* 28 A2
Tacuba, *Mexico City* 18 B1
Tacubaya, *Mexico City* 18 B1
Taebang, *Seoul* 26 B1

Tagig, *Manila* 17 B2
Tagig →, *Manila* 17 B2
Tai Hang, *Hong Kong* 12 B2
Tai Lo Shan, *Hong Kong* 12 A2
Tai Po Tsai, *Hong Kong* 12 A2
Tai Seng, *Singapore* 27 A3
Tai Shui Hang, *Hong Kong* 12 A2
Tai Tam B., *Hong Kong* 12 B2
Tai Tam Tuk Res., *Hong Kong* 12 B2
Tai Wai, *Hong Kong* 12 A1
Tai Wan Tau, *Hong Kong* 12 B2
Tai Wo Hau, *Hong Kong* 12 A1
Tainaka, *Osaka* 22 B4
Taishō, *Osaka* 22 B3
Taita, *Wellington* 32 B2
Tajrīsh, *Tehran* 30 A2
Takaido, *Tokyo* 29 A2
Takaishi, *Tokyo* 29 B2
Takarazuka, *Osaka* 22 A2
Takasago, *Tokyo* 29 A4
Takatsu-Ku, *Tokyo* 29 B2
Takeshita, *Tokyo* 29 B2
Takinegawa, *Tokyo* 29 A3
Takoma Park, *Washington* 32 B3
Taksim, *Istanbul* 12 B1
Talaide, *Lisbon* 14 A1
Taliganga, *Calcutta* 8 B2
Talipapa, *Manila* 17 A2
Tallaght, *Dublin* 11 B1
Tallkrogen, *Stockholm* 28 B2
Tama, *Tokyo* 29 B1
Tama →, *Tokyo* 29 B2
Tama Kyūryō, *Tokyo* 29 B2
Tamaden, *Tokyo* 29 B2
Tamagawa-josui →, *Tokyo* 29 A1
Taman Sari, *Jakarta* 13 A1
Tamanduateí →, *São Paulo* 26 B2
Tamboerskloof, *Cape Town* 8 A1
Tambora, *Jakarta* 13 A1
Tammisalo, *Helsinki* 12 B3
Tammūh, *Cairo* 7 B2
Tampines, *Singapore* 27 A3
Tanah Abang, *Jakarta* 13 B1
Tanigami, *Osaka* 22 A2
Tanjung Duren, *Jakarta* 13 B1
Tanjung Priok, *Jakarta* 13 A2
Tanum, *Oslo* 22 A1
Taoranting Park, *Beijing* 4 c2
Tapada, *Lisbon* 14 A1
Tapanila, *Helsinki* 12 B3
Tapiales, *Buenos Aires* 7 C1
Tapiola, *Helsinki* 12 B1
Tapsia, *Calcutta* 8 B2
Tara, *Mumbai* 20 A1
Tarabya, *Istanbul* 12 B2
Tarango, Presa, *Mexico City* 18 B1
Tårbæk, *Copenhagen* 10 A3
Tarchomin, *Warsaw* 31 B1
Tardeo, *Mumbai* 20 B1
Targówek, *Warsaw* 31 B2
Tårnby, *Copenhagen* 10 B3
Tarqua Bay, *Lagos* 14 B2
Tåstrup, *Copenhagen* 10 B1
Tatarovo, *Moscow* 19 B2
Tathong Channel, *Hong Kong* 12 B2
Tathong Pt., *Hong Kong* 12 B2
Tatuapé, *São Paulo* 26 B2
Taufkirchen, *Munich* 20 B2
Tavares, I. dos, *Rio de Janeiro* 24 A2
Távros, *Athens* 2 B2
Tawa, *Wellington* 32 A1
Teaneck, *New York* 21 A1
Teatro Municipal, *Rio de Janeiro* 24 c2
Tebet, *Jakarta* 13 B2
Tecamachaleo, *Mexico City* 18 B1
Teddington, *London* 15 B1
Tegel, *Berlin* 5 A2
Tegel, Flughafen, *Berlin* 5 A2
Tegeler See, *Berlin* 5 A2
Tegelort, *Berlin* 5 A2
Tehrān, *Tehran* 30 A2
Tehrān Pārs, *Tehran* 30 A3
Tei Tong Tsui, *Hong Kong* 12 B2
Tejo, Rio →, *Lisbon* 14 A2
Tekstilyshchik, *Moscow* 19 B4
Telegraph hill, *San Francisco* 25 a2
Telhal, *Lisbon* 14 A1
Telok Blangah, *Singapore* 27 B2
Teltow, *Berlin* 5 B2
Teltow kanal, *Berlin* 5 B3
Temnikovo, *Moscow* 19 B6
Tempelhof, *Berlin* 5 B3
Tempelhof, Flughafen, *Berlin* 5 B3
Temple City, *Los Angeles* 16 B4
Temple Hills Park, *Washington* 32 C4
Temple Mount, *Jerusalem* 13 b3
Templeogue, *Dublin* 11 B2
Templo Mayor, *Mexico City* 18 b3
Tenafly, *New York* 21 A2
Tenayuca, Piramide de, *Mexico City* 18 A1
Tengah →, *Singapore* 27 A2
Tennoji, *Osaka* 22 B4
Tepalcates, *Mexico City* 18 B2
Terrazzano, *Milan* 18 A1
Terrugem, *Lisbon* 14 A1
Tervuren, *Brussels* 6 B3
Tervuren, Park van, *Brussels* 6 B3
Tetuán, *Madrid* 17 B1
Teufelsberg, *Berlin* 5 B2
Tévere →, *Rome* 25 B1
Thalkirchen, *Munich* 20 B2
Thames →, *London* 15 A4
Thames Ditton, *London* 15 B1
Thamesmead, *London* 15 A4
Thana Cr. →, *Mumbai* 20 A2
The Loop, *Chicago* 9 B3
The Ridge, *Delhi* 10 B2
The Wilds, *Johannesburg* 13 B2
Theater Carré, *Amsterdam* 2 b2
Théatro Dionissou, *Athens* 2 c2
Thiais, *Paris* 23 B3
Thissío, *Athens* 2 c1
Thistletown, *Toronto* 30 A1
Thomastown, *Melbourne* 17 A2
Thompson I., *Boston* 6 B4
Thon Buri, *Bangkok* 3 B1
Thornbury, *Melbourne* 17 A2
Thorncliffe, *Toronto* 30 A2
Thornhill, *Toronto* 30 A2
Thornton, *Cape Town* 8 A2
Thornton Heath, *London* 15 B3
Threipmuir Res., *Edinburgh* 11 B2
Throgs Neck, *New York* 21 B3
Thyssen Bornemisza, Museo, *Madrid* 17 b3
Tian'anmen Square, *Beijing* 4 B2
Tiancun, *Beijing* 4 B1
Tianjin, *Tianjin* 30 B1
Tiantan Park, *Beijing* 4 c2
Tibidabo, *Barcelona* 4 A1
Tibradden Mt., *Dublin* 11 B2
Tiburon, *San Francisco* 25 A2
Tiburtino, *Rome* 25 B2
Ticomán, *Mexico City* 18 A2
Tiefersee, *Berlin* 5 B1
Tiejiangyin, *Beijing* 4 C2
Tientsin = Tianjin, *Tianjin* 30 B1
Tiergarten, *Berlin* 5 A3
Tietê →, *São Paulo* 26 B2
Tigerhof, *Cape Town* 8 A2
Tigris = Nahr Dijlah →, *Baghdad* 3 B2
Tijuca, *Rio de Janeiro* 24 B1
Tijuca, Parque Nacional da, *Rio de Janeiro* 24 B1
Tijuca, Pico da, *Rio de Janeiro* 24 B1
Tikkurila, *Helsinki* 12 B3
Tilak Nagar, *Delhi* 10 B1
Tilanqiao, *Shanghai* 27 B1
Timah, Bukit, *Singapore* 27 A2
Times Square, *New York* 21 c2
Timiryazev Park, *Moscow* 19 B3
Ting Kau, *Hong Kong* 12 A1
Tira, *Jerusalem* 13 A1
Tirsa, *Cairo* 7 B2
Tishrīyaa, *Baghdad* 3 B2
Tiu Keng Leng, *Hong Kong* 12 B2
Tivoli, *Copenhagen* 10 a3
Tizapán, *Mexico City* 18 C1
Tlalnepantla →, *Mexico City* 18 A1
To Kwai Wan, *Hong Kong* 12 B2
Toa Payoh, *Singapore* 27 A3
Tobong, *Seoul* 26 B2
Tobong-san, *Seoul* 26 A2
Točná, *Prague* 24 C2
Toco Hills, *Atlanta* 3 B2
Todt Hill, *New York* 21 C1
Tōkagi, *Tokyo* 29 A4
Tokai Plantation, *Cape Town* 8 B1
Tōkaichiba, *Tokyo* 29 B2
Tokarevo, *Moscow* 19 C5
Tōkyō, *Tokyo* 29 B3
Tokyo B., *Tokyo* 29 B4
Tokyo-Haneda Int. Airport, *Tokyo* 29 B3
Tokyo Harbour, *Tokyo* 29 B3
Tolka R. →, *Dublin* 11 A1
Tolworth, *London* 15 B2
Tomb of Lu Xun, *Shanghai* 27 B1
Tomb of the Kings, *Jerusalem* 13 a2
Tomba di Nerone, *Rome* 25 B1
Tomilino, *Moscow* 19 C5
Tondo, *Manila* 17 B1
Tongbinggo, *Seoul* 26 B1
Tongjak, *Seoul* 26 B1
Tongmaemung, *Seoul* 26 B2
Tongqiao, *Shanghai* 27 A1
Toorak, *Melbourne* 17 B2
Topkapı, *Istanbul* 12 B1
Tor di Quinto, *Rome* 25 B1
Tor Pignattara, *Rome* 25 B2
Tor Sapienza, *Rome* 25 B2
Toranomon, *Tokyo* 29 c3
Torcy, *Paris* 23 A4
Toronto, *Toronto* 30 B3
Toronto, Univ. of, *Toronto* 30 B2
Toronto Harbour, *Toronto* 30 B2
Toronto I., *Toronto* 30 B2
Toronto Int. Airport, *Toronto* 30 A1
Toros Las Arenas, Pl. de, *Barcelona* 4 c1
Toros Monumental, Templo de, *Barcelona* 4 a3
Torre Latino-americana, *Mexico City* 18 b2
Torre Lupara, *Rome* 25 B2
Torre Nova, *Rome* 25 B2
Torrellas →, *Barcelona* 4 A1
Torrevécchia, *Rome* 25 B1
Toshima-Ku, *Tokyo* 29 A3
Toshimaen, *Tokyo* 29 A2
Tottenham, *London* 15 A3
Tottenham, *Melbourne* 17 A1
Tour Eiffel, *Paris* 23 c2
Toussus-le-Noble, *Paris* 23 B1
Toussus-le-Noble, Aérodrome de, *Paris* 23 B1
Tower Bridge, *London* 15 b5
Tower Hamlets, *London* 15 A3
Tower of London, *London* 15 A3
Towra Pt., *Sydney* 28 C2
Tøyen, *Oslo* 22 A3
Toyonaka, *Osaka* 22 A3
Trafalgar Square, *London* 15 b3
Trafaria, *Lisbon* 14 A1
Traição, Cor. →, *São Paulo* 26 B2
Tranegilde, *Copenhagen* 10 B2
Trångsund, *Stockholm* 28 B2
Transamerica Pyramid, *San Francisco* 25 b2
Transbay Terminal, *San Francisco* 25 b3
Trappenfelde, *Berlin* 5 A4
Trastévere, *Rome* 25 B1
Treasure I., *San Francisco* 25 B2
Třeboradice, *Prague* 24 B3
Třebotov, *Prague* 24 C1
Tremblay-en-France, *Paris* 23 A4
Tremembe →, *São Paulo* 26 A2
Tremont, *New York* 21 A2
Trenno, *Milan* 18 B1
Treptow, *Berlin* 5 B3
Trés Rios, Sa. dos, *Rio de Janeiro* 24 B1
Trevi, Fontana di, *Rome* 25 b3
Trezzano sul Naviglio, *Milan* 18 B1
Tribune Tower, *Chicago* 9 b2
Trieste, *Rome* 25 B2
Trinidad, *Washington* 32 B4
Trinity, *Edinburgh* 11 B2
Trinity College, *Dublin* 11 c3
Trionfale, *Rome* 25 B1
Triulzo, *Milan* 18 B2
Trocadero, *Paris* 23 b1
Troitse-Lykovo, *Moscow* 19 B2
Troja, *Prague* 24 B2
Trollbäcken, *Stockholm* 28 B3
Trombay, *Mumbai* 20 A2
Troparevo, *Moscow* 19 C2
Tropenmuseum, *Amsterdam* 2 b3
Trudyashchikhsya, Ostrov, *St. Petersburg* 26 B1
Tryvasshøgda, *Oslo* 22 A3
Tseng Lan Shue, *Hong Kong* 12 A2
Tsim Sha Tsui, *Hong Kong* 12 a2
Tsing Yi, *Hong Kong* 12 A1
Tsova, *Jerusalem* 13 B1
Tsuen Wan, *Hong Kong* 12 A1
Tsukiji, *Tokyo* 29 c5
Tsur Hadassa, *Jerusalem* 13 B1
Tsurumi →, *Tokyo* 29 B3
Tsz Wan Shan, *Hong Kong* 12 A2
Tuas, *Singapore* 27 B1
Tuchoměřice, *Prague* 24 B1
Tuckahoe, *New York* 21 A3
Tucuruvi, *São Paulo* 26 A2
Tufello, *Rome* 25 B2
Tufnell Park, *London* 15 A3
Tughlakabad, *Delhi* 10 B2
Tuileries, Jardin des, *Paris* 23 b3
Tuindorp Oostzaan, *Amsterdam* 2 A2
Tullamarine, *Melbourne* 17 A1
Tulse Hill, *London* 15 B3
Tung Lung I., *Hong Kong* 12 B2
Tung O, *Hong Kong* 12 B1
Tunis, *Baghdad* 3 A2
Tuomarila, *Helsinki* 12 B1
Tureberg, *Stockholm* 28 A1
Turffontein, *Johannesburg* 13 B2
Turkso, *Prague* 24 A1
Turnham Green, *London* 15 B2
Turnhouse, *Edinburgh* 11 B1
Tuscolana, Via, *Rome* 25 B2
Tushino, *Moscow* 19 A2
Twelve Apostles, *Cape Town* 8 A1
Twickenham, *London* 15 B1
Twickenham Rugby Ground, *London* 15 B1
Twin Peaks, *San Francisco* 25 B2
Two Rock Mt., *Dublin* 11 B2
Tymon North, *Dublin* 11 B1
Tysons Corner, *Washington* 32 B2

U

U.S. Capitol, *Washington* 32 b3
Ubeidiya, *Jerusalem* 13 B2
Uberaba →, *São Paulo* 26 B2
Ubin, P., *Singapore* 27 A3
Uccle, *Brussels* 6 B2
Udelnaya, *St. Petersburg* 26 A2
Udelnoe, *St. Petersburg* 26 B1
Udlding, *Munich* 20 A1
Ueno, *Tokyo* 29 A3
Úholičky, *Prague* 24 B1
Uhříněves, *Prague* 24 B3
Uithoorn, *Amsterdam* 2 B1
Újpalota, *Budapest* 7 A2
Újpest, *Budapest* 7 A2
Ukita, *Tokyo* 29 A4
Ullerup, *Copenhagen* 10 B3
Ullevål, *Oslo* 22 A3
Ulriksdal, *Stockholm* 28 A1
Ulyanka, *St. Petersburg* 26 B1
Um Al-Khanazir Island, *Baghdad* 3 B2
Umeda, *Osaka* 22 A3
Umerkhadi, *Mumbai* 20 b2
Ümraniye, *Istanbul* 12 B2
Underground Atlanta, *Atlanta* 3 B2
Unětický potok →, *Prague* 24 B2
Ŭngam, *Seoul* 26 B1
Unhos, *Lisbon* 14 A2
Unidad Santa Fe, *Mexico City* 18 B1
Union City, *New York* 21 B1
Union Port, *New York* 21 B2
Union Square, *New York* 21 d2
Union Square, *San Francisco* 25 b2
Union Station, *Washington* 32 b3
United Nations H.Q., *New York* 21 c3
Universidad, *Madrid* 17 B1
Universidad de Chile, *Santiago* 26 B2
University Park, *Washington* 32 B4
Unp'yong, *Seoul* 26 B1
Unter den Linden, *Berlin* 5 a4
Unterbiberg, *Munich* 20 B2
Unterföhring, *Munich* 20 A3
Unterhaching, *Munich* 20 B2
Unterlaa, *Vienna* 31 B2
Untermenzing, *Munich* 20 A1
Upper East Side, *New York* 21 b3
Upper Elmers End, *London* 15 B3
Upper New York B., *New York* 21 C1
Upper Norwood, *London* 15 B3
Upper Peirce Res., *Singapore* 27 A2
Upper Sydenham, *London* 15 B3
Upper Tooting, *London* 15 B3
Upper West Side, *New York* 21 a2
Upton, *London* 15 A4
Uptown, *Chicago* 9 B2
Uran, *Mumbai* 20 B2
Urayasu, *Tokyo* 29 B4
Urbe, Aeroporto d', *Rome* 25 B2
Urca, *Rio de Janeiro* 24 B2
Uritsk, *St. Petersburg* 26 C1
Üröm, *Budapest* 7 A2
Ursus, *Warsaw* 31 B1
Ursvik, *Stockholm* 28 A1
Usera, *Madrid* 17 B1
Ushigome, *Tokyo* 29 A3
Usina, *Rio de Janeiro* 24 B1
Üsküdar, *Istanbul* 12 B2
Ust-Slavyanka, *St. Petersburg* 26 C3
Uteke, *Stockholm* 28 A3
Utrata, *Warsaw* 31 B2
Uttarpara, *Calcutta* 8 B1
Utterslev Mose, *Copenhagen* 10 A2

V

Vadaul, *Mumbai* 20 A2
Vaires-sur-Marne, *Paris* 23 A4
Valby, *Copenhagen* 10 B2
Valcannuta, *Rome* 25 B1
Valdelatas, *Madrid* 17 A1
Vale, *Washington* 32 B2
Valenton, *Paris* 23 B3
Valera, *Milan* 18 A1
Vallcarca, *Barcelona* 4 A1
Valldoreix, *Barcelona* 4 A1
Vallecas, *Madrid* 17 B2
Vallensbæk, *Copenhagen* 10 B2
Vallensbæk Strand, *Copenhagen* 10 B2
Vallentunasjön, *Stockholm* 28 A2
Valleranello, *Rome* 25 C1
Vallisaari, *Helsinki* 12 C3
Vallvidrera, *Barcelona* 4 A1
Valvidrera →, *Barcelona* 4 A1
Van Goghmuseum, *Amsterdam* 2 c1
Vanak, *Tehran* 30 A2
Vangede, *Copenhagen* 10 A3
Vaniköy, *Istanbul* 12 B2
Vanløse, *Copenhagen* 10 A2
Vantaa, *Helsinki* 12 B2
Vantaa →, *Helsinki* 12 B2
Vantaankoski, *Helsinki* 12 B2
Vantaanpuisto, *Helsinki* 12 B2
Vanves, *Paris* 23 B2
Varedo, *Milan* 18 A1
Varkiza, *Athens* 2 C2
Varszínház, *Budapest* 7 b2
Vartiokylä, *Helsinki* 12 B3
Vartiosaari, *Helsinki* 12 B3
Vasamuseet, *Stockholm* 28 b3
Vasco, *Cape Town* 8 A2
Vasfanārd, *Tehran* 30 B2
Vashi, *Mumbai* 20 A2
Vasilyevskiy, Ostrov, *St. Petersburg* 26 B1
Vaso Regulador El Cristo, *Mexico City* 18 B1
Vaucluse, *Sydney* 28 B2
Vaucresson, *Paris* 23 A1
Vauhallan, *Paris* 23 B2
Vaujours, *Paris* 23 A4
Vauxhall, *London* 15 c4
Vecsés, *Budapest* 7 B3
Veleň, *Prague* 24 A3
Veleslavín, *Prague* 24 B2
Vélizy-Villacoublay, *Paris* 23 B2
Velká-Chuchle, *Prague* 24 B2
Velké Přílepy, *Prague* 24 B1
Venda Seca, *Lisbon* 14 A1
Venetian Islands, *Miami* 18 B2
Venezia, Palazzo, *Rome* 25 c2
Venice, *Los Angeles* 16 C2
Ventas, *Madrid* 17 B1
Ventorro del Cano, *Madrid* 17 B1
Venustiano Carranza, *Mexico City* 18 B2
Verde →, *São Paulo* 26 A1
Verdi, *Athens* 2 A2
Verdun, *Montreal* 19 B2
Vérhalom, *Budapest* 7 A2
Vermelho →, *São Paulo* 26 B1
Vernon, *Los Angeles* 16 B3
Verrières-le-Buisson, *Paris* 23 B2
Versailles, *Buenos Aires* 7 B1
Versailles, *Paris* 23 B1
Veshnyaki, *Moscow* 19 B4
Vesolyy Posolok, *St. Petersburg* 26 B2
Vestra, *Helsinki* 12 B1
Vestskoven, *Copenhagen* 10 A2
Vicálvaro, *Madrid* 17 B2
Vicente Lopez, *Buenos Aires* 7 B2
Victoria, *Hong Kong* 12 B2
Victoria, *London* 15 c3
Victoria, Mt., *Wellington* 32 B1
Victoria, Pont, *Montreal* 19 B2
Victoria and Albert Waterfront, *Cape Town* 8 a1
Victoria Gardens, *Mumbai* 20 B2
Victoria Harbour, *Hong Kong* 12 B1
Victoria Island, *Lagos* 14 B2
Victoria L., *Johannesburg* 13 B2
Victoria Lawn Tennis Courts, *Melbourne* 17 B2
Victoria Park, *Singapore* 27 B2
Victoria Peak, *Hong Kong* 12 B1
Victoria Wharf, *Cape Town* 8 a2
Vienna = Wien, *Vienna* 31 A2
Vienna, *Washington* 32 B2
View Park, *Los Angeles* 16 B3
Vigário Geral, *Rio de Janeiro* 24 A1
Vigentino, *Milan* 18 B2
Viggbyholm, *Stockholm* 28 A2
Vighignolo, *Milan* 18 B1
Viikki, *Helsinki* 12 B3
Vikhroli, *Mumbai* 20 A2
Vila Guilherme, *São Paulo* 26 B2
Vila Isabel, *Rio de Janeiro* 24 B1
Vila Jaguára, *São Paulo* 26 B1
Vila Madalena, *São Paulo* 26 B1
Vila Maria, *São Paulo* 26 B2
Vila Mariana, *São Paulo* 26 B2
Vila Prudente, *São Paulo* 26 B2
Viladecans, *Barcelona* 4 B1
Vile Parle, *Mumbai* 20 A2
Villa Adelina, *Buenos Aires* 7 B1
Villa Ballester, *Buenos Aires* 7 B1
Villa Barilari, *Buenos Aires* 7 C2
Villa Borghese, *Rome* 25 a3
Villa Bosch, *Buenos Aires* 7 B1
Villa C. Colon, *Buenos Aires* 7 C2
Villa Ciudadela, *Buenos Aires* 7 B1
Villa de Guadalupe, *Mexico City* 18 B2
Villa Devoto, *Buenos Aires* 7 B1
Villa Diamante, *Buenos Aires* 7 C2
Villa Dominico, *Buenos Aires* 7 C3
Villa Lugano, *Buenos Aires* 7 C2
Villa Lynch, *Buenos Aires* 7 B1
Villa Madero, *Buenos Aires* 7 C1
Villa Sáenz Pena, *Buenos Aires* 7 B1
Villa Urquiza, *Buenos Aires* 7 B1
Villaverde, *Madrid* 17 B1
Villaverde Bajo, *Madrid* 17 B1
Ville-d'Avray, *Paris* 23 B2
Villecresnes, *Paris* 23 B4
Villejuif, *Paris* 23 B3
Villemomble, *Paris* 23 A4
Villeneuve-la-Garenne, *Paris* 23 A3
Villeneuve-le-Roi, *Paris* 23 B3
Villeneuve-St.-Georges, *Paris* 23 B3
Villeparisis, *Paris* 23 A4
Villevaudé, *Paris* 23 A4
Villiers-le-Bâcle, *Paris* 23 B1
Villiers-sur-Marne, *Paris* 23 B4
Villinki, *Helsinki* 12 C3
Villoresi, Canale, *Milan* 18 A1
Vilvoorde, *Brussels* 6 A2
Vimodrone, *Milan* 18 A2
Vimont, *Montreal* 19 A1
Vinanmek Palace, *Bangkok* 3 a2
Vincennes, *Paris* 23 A3
Vincennes, Bois de, *Paris* 23 B3
Vinings, *Atlanta* 3 A2
Vinohrady, *Prague* 24 c3
Vinoř, *Prague* 24 B3
Violet Hill, *Hong Kong* 12 B2
Virányos, *Budapest* 7 A2
Virgen del San Cristóbal, *Santiago* 26 B2
Virginia Gardens, *Miami* 18 B1
Virginia Key, *Miami* 18 B2
Viroflay, *Paris* 23 B2
Víron, *Athens* 2 B2
Virum, *Copenhagen* 10 A2
Vishnyaki, *Moscow* 19 B5
Visitacion Valley, *San Francisco* 25 B2
Vista Alegre, *Lima* 16 B3
Vista Alegre, *Santiago* 26 C1
Vista Grove, *Atlanta* 3 A3
Vitacura, *Santiago* 26 B2
Vitinia, *Rome* 25 C1
Vitry-sur-Seine, *Paris* 23 B3
Vizandinó, Moussío, *Athens* 2 b3
Vladykino, *Moscow* 19 A3
Vlezenbeek, *Brussels* 6 B1
Vltava →, *Prague* 24 A2
Vnukovo, *Moscow* 19 C1
Vokovice, *Prague* 24 B2
Volgelsdorf, *Berlin* 5 B5
Volkhonka-Zil, *Moscow* 19 C3
Vollen, *Oslo* 22 B1
Volodarskoye, *St. Petersburg* 26 B2
Volynkina-Derevnya, *St. Petersburg* 26 B1
Vondelpark, *Amsterdam* 2 A2
Vösendorf, *Vienna* 31 B2
Vostochnyy, *Moscow* 19 B5
Voula, *Athens* 2 C2
Vouliagmeni, *Athens* 2 C2
Vredehoek, *Cape Town* 8 A1
Vršovice, *Prague* 24 B2
Vyborgskaya Storona, *St. Petersburg* 26 B2
Vykhino, *Moscow* 19 B4
Vyšehrad, *Prague* 24 B2

W

Wachterhof, *Munich* 20 B3
Wadala, *Mumbai* 20 A2
Wadestown, *Wellington* 32 B1
Wadi Fukin, *Jerusalem* 13 B1
Wah Fu, *Hong Kong* 12 B1
Wahda, *Baghdad* 3 B2
Währing, *Vienna* 31 A2
Waidmannslust, *Berlin* 5 A3
Wainuiomata, *Wellington* 32 B2
Wainuiomata R. →, *Wellington* 32 B2
Wakefield, *Boston* 6 A3
Waldesruh, *Berlin* 5 B4
Waldperlach, *Munich* 20 B3
Waldtrudering, *Munich* 20 B3
Walkinstown, *Dublin* 11 B1
Wall Street, *New York* 21 f1
Waltham, *Boston* 6 A2
Waltham Forest, *London* 15 A3
Walthamstow, *London* 15 A3
Walton on Thames, *London* 15 B1
Wambeek, *Brussels* 6 A3
Wan Chai, *Hong Kong* 12 B2
Wan Chai Lanes, *Hong Kong* 12 c2
Wandsworth, *London* 15 B2
Wankhede Stadium, *Mumbai* 20 c2
Wannsee, *Berlin* 5 B1
Wansdorf, *Berlin* 5 A1
Wanstead, *London* 15 A4
Wapping, *London* 15 A3
Ward, *Dublin* 11 A1
Ward I., *Wellington* 32 B2
Warnberg, *Munich* 20 B2
Warrāq el 'Arab, *Cairo* 7 A2
Warrâq el Hadr, *Cairo* 7 A2
Warringen Park, *Melbourne* 17 A2
Warriston, *Edinburgh* 11 B2
Warsaw = Warszawa, *Warsaw* 31 B2
Warszawa, *Warsaw* 31 B2
Wartenberg, *Berlin* 5 A4
Washington, *Washington* 32 B3
Washington Heights, *New York* 21 A2
Washington Monument, *Washington* 32 b1
Washington Nat. Airport, *Washington* 32 B3
Washington Park, *Chicago* 9 C3
Wat Arun, *Bangkok* 3 b1
Wat Pho, *Bangkok* 3 b1
Wat Phra Keo, *Bangkok* 3 b1
Water of Leith, *Edinburgh* 11 B1
Water Tower Place, *Chicago* 9 a2
Watergraafsmeer, *Amsterdam* 2 A2
Waterland, *Amsterdam* 2 A2
Waterloo, *Brussels* 6 B2
Waterloo, *Wellington* 32 B2
Waterloo International, *London* 15 b4
Watermael-Boitsfort, *Brussels* 6 B2
Watertown, *Boston* 6 A2
Watsonia, *Melbourne* 17 A2
Waverley, *Boston* 6 A2
Waverley, *Johannesburg* 13 A2
Waverley, *Sydney* 28 B2
Waverley Station, *Edinburgh* 11 b3
Wawer, *Warsaw* 31 B2
Wawrzyszew, *Warsaw* 31 B1
Wayland, *Boston* 6 A1
Wazirabad, *Delhi* 10 A2
Wazīrīya, *Baghdad* 3 A2
Wazirpur, *Delhi* 10 A2
Wealdstone, *London* 15 A1
Wedding, *Berlin* 5 A3
Weehawken, *New York* 21 B1
Weesp, *Amsterdam* 2 B3
Weidling, *Vienna* 31 A1
Weidlingbach, *Vienna* 31 A1
Weigongcun, *Beijing* 4 B1
Weijin He →, *Tianjin* 30 B2
Weissensee, *Berlin* 5 A3
Wellesley, *Boston* 6 B2
Wellesley Falls, *Boston* 6 B2
Wellesley Hills, *Boston* 6 B2
Welling, *London* 15 B4
Wellington, *Boston* 6 A3
Wellington, *Wellington* 32 B1
Wells Fargo Center, *Los Angeles* 16 b1
Weltevreden Park, *Johannesburg* 13 A1
Wembley, *London* 15 A2
Wemmel, *Brussels* 6 A1
Wemmer Pan, *Johannesburg* 13 B2
Wenceslas Square, *Prague* 24 b2
Wendenschloss, *Berlin* 5 B4
Wenhuagong, *Tianjin* 30 B2
Wennington, *London* 15 A5
Werneuchen, *Berlin* 5 A5
West Bedford, *Boston* 6 A2
West Concord, *Boston* 6 A1
West Don →, *Toronto* 30 A2
West Drayton, *London* 15 A1
West Ham, *London* 15 A4
West Harrow, *London* 15 A1
West Heath, *London* 15 B4
West Hill, *Toronto* 30 A3
West Hollywood, *Los Angeles* 16 B2
West Kensington, *London* 15 c1
West Kilburn, *London* 15 a1
West Lamma Channel, *Hong Kong* 12 B1
West Lynn, *Boston* 6 A4
West Medford, *Boston* 6 A3
West Miami, *Miami* 18 B1
West Molesey, *London* 15 B1
West New York, *New York* 21 B1
West of Twin Peaks, *San Francisco* 25 B2
West Park, *Johannesburg* 13 A1
West Rouge, *Toronto* 30 A4
West Roxbury, *Boston* 6 B3
West Springfield, *Washington* 32 C2
West Town, *Chicago* 9 B2
West Wharf, *Karachi* 14 B1
Westbourne Green, *London* 15 a1
Westchester, *Chicago* 9 B1
Westchester, *Los Angeles* 16 C2
Westchester, *New York* 21 A2
Westcliff, *Johannesburg* 13 B2
Westdene, *Johannesburg* 13 B1
Westend, *Helsinki* 12 C1
Wester Hailes, *Edinburgh* 11 B2
Westerham, *Munich* 20 B2
Western Addition, *San Francisco* 25 B2
Western Wall, *Jerusalem* 13 b3
Westgate, *Washington* 32 B3
Westlake, *Cape Town* 8 B1
Westlake, *San Francisco* 25 B2
Westminster, *London* 15 A3
Westmount, *Montreal* 19 B2
Weston, *Boston* 6 A2
Weston, *Toronto* 30 A1
Weston Res., *Boston* 6 A2
Westwood Village, *Los Angeles* 16 B2
Westzaan, *Amsterdam* 2 A1
Wetton, *Cape Town* 8 B2
Wexford, *Toronto* 30 A3
Weybridge, *London* 15 B1
Wezembeek-Oppem, *Brussels* 6 A2
White House, The, *Washington* 32 b1
Whitechapel, *London* 15 A3
Whitehall, *Dublin* 11 A2
Whitehall, *London* 15 b3
Whittier, *Los Angeles* 16 C4
Whitton, *London* 15 B1
Wieden, *Vienna* 31 A2
Wien, *Vienna* 31 A2
Wien-Schwechat, Flughafen, *Vienna* 31 B3
Wienerberg, *Vienna* 31 B2
Wierzbno, *Warsaw* 31 B2
Wijde Wormer, *Amsterdam* 2 A2
Wilanów, *Warsaw* 31 B2
Wilanówka →, *Warsaw* 31 C2
Wilhelmshagen, *Berlin* 5 B5
Wilket Creek Park, *Toronto* 30 A2
Wilkieston, *Edinburgh* 11 B1
Willbrook, *Dublin* 11 B2
Willesden, *London* 15 A2
Willesden Green, *London* 15 A2
Williamsbridge, *New York* 21 A2
Williamsburg, *New York* 21 B2
Williamstown, *Melbourne* 17 B1
Willoughby, *Sydney* 28 A2
Willow Springs, *Chicago* 9 C1
Willowdale, *Toronto* 30 A2
Wilmersdorf, *Berlin* 5 c1
Wilmette, *Chicago* 9 A2
Wilmington, *London* 15 B5
Wilshire Boulevard, *Los Angeles* 16 c1
Wimbledon, *London* 15 B2
Wimbledon Common, *London* 15 B2
Wimbledon Park, *London* 15 B2
Wimbledon Tennis Ground, *London* 15 B2
Winchester, *Boston* 6 A3
Windermere, *Cape Town* 8 A2
Windsor, *Johannesburg* 13 A1
Windsor Hills, *Los Angeles* 16 C2
Windy Arbour, *Dublin* 11 B2
Winning, *Munich* 20 B2
Winthrop, *Boston* 6 A4
Wissous, *Paris* 23 B2
Wittenau, *Berlin* 5 A2
Witwatersrand, Univ. of, *Johannesburg* 13 B2
Włochy, *Warsaw* 31 B1
Wo Mei, *Hong Kong* 12 B2
Wo Yi Hop, *Hong Kong* 12 A1
Woburn, *Boston* 6 A3
Woburn, *Toronto* 30 A3
Woduk Pluit, *Jakarta* 13 A1
Wola, *Warsaw* 31 B1
Wolf Trap Farm Park, *Washington* 32 B2
Wolica, *Warsaw* 31 C2
Wolica, *Warsaw* 31 C1
Wólka Węglowa, *Warsaw* 31 B1
Wollaston, *Boston* 6 B3
Woltersdorf, *Berlin* 5 B5
Woluwe-Saint-Lambert, *Brussels* 6 A2
Woluwe-Saint-Pierre, *Brussels* 6 A2
Wong Chuk Hang, *Hong Kong* 12 B2
Wong Chuk Wan, *Hong Kong* 12 A2
Wong Chuk Yeung, *Hong Kong* 12 A2
Wong Tai Sin, *Hong Kong* 12 A2
Wood Green, *London* 15 A3
Wood Ridge, *New York* 21 A1
Woodbridge, *Toronto* 30 A1
Woodford, *London* 15 A4
Woodford Bridge, *London* 15 A4
Woodford Green, *London* 15 A4
Woodhaven, *New York* 21 B2
Woodhouselee, *Edinburgh* 11 B2
Woodlands New Town, *Singapore* 27 A2
Woodmont, *Washington* 32 B3
Woodside, *London* 15 B3
Woodside, *New York* 21 B2
Woodstock, *Cape Town* 8 A1
Woollahra, *Sydney* 28 B2
Woolloomooloo, *Sydney* 28 b2
Woolooware B., *Sydney* 28 C1
Woolwich, *London* 15 B4
Woolworth Building, *New York* 21 e1
World Trade Center, site of former, *New York* 21 B1
Worli, *Mumbai* 20 A1
Worth, *Chicago* 9 C2
Wren's Nest, *Atlanta* 3 B2
Wrigley Building, *Chicago* 9 b2
Wuhlgarten, *Berlin* 5 A4
Wujiaochang, *Shanghai* 27 B2
Würm →, *Munich* 20 B1
Würm-kanal, *Munich* 20 A1
Wusong, *Shanghai* 27 A1
Wyczółki, *Warsaw* 31 C1
Wygoda, *Warsaw* 31 B2
Wynberg, *Cape Town* 8 B1

X

Xabregas, *Lisbon* 14 A2
Xianggang = Hong Kong, *Hong Kong* 12 B1
Xiaodian, *Tianjin* 30 A2
Xiaogang Park, *Canton* 8 B2
Xiaoping, *Canton* 8 A2
Xiasha chong, *Canton* 8 B1
Xichang, *Canton* 8 B2
Xicheng, *Beijing* 4 B1
Xidan, *Beijing* 4 B2
Xigu Park, *Tianjin* 30 A2
Xigucun, *Tianjin* 30 A1
Ximenwai, *Tianjin* 30 B1
Xinanlou, *Tianjin* 30 B2
Xinkai He →, *Tianjin* 30 A2
Xizhimen, *Beijing* 4 B1
Xu Beihong Mem. Hall, *Beijing* 4 a1
Xuanwu, *Beijing* 4 B1
Xuhui, *Shanghai* 27 B1

Y

Yaba, *Lagos* 14 A2
Yaftābād, *Tehran* 30 B1
Yahara, *Tokyo* 29 A2
Yaho, *Tokyo* 29 A1
Yakire, *Tokyo* 29 A4
Yamada, *Osaka* 22 A4
Yamada, *Tokyo* 29 B2
Yamamoto, *Osaka* 22 B4
Yamato →, *Osaka* 22 B3
Yamuna →, *Delhi* 10 B2
Yan Kit, *Singapore* 27 A3
Yanbu, *Canton* 8 B1
Yangch'ŏn, *Seoul* 26 B1
Yanghuayuan, *Beijing* 4 C1
Yangjae, *Seoul* 26 C2
Yangjiazhuang, *Shanghai* 27 A1
Yangpu, *Shanghai* 27 B2
Yangpu Park, *Shanghai* 27 B2
Yao, *Osaka* 22 B4
Yao Airport, *Osaka* 22 B4
Yarmūk, *Baghdad* 3 B1
Yarra →, *Melbourne* 17 A1
Yarra Bend Park, *Melbourne* 17 A2
Yarraville, *Melbourne* 17 A1
Yau Tong, *Hong Kong* 12 B2
Yauza →, *Moscow* 19 A4
Yeading, *London* 15 A1
Yedikule, *Istanbul* 12 C1
Yemin Moshe, *Jerusalem* 13 b2
Yenikapı, *Istanbul* 12 B1
Yeniköy, *Istanbul* 12 B2
Yerba Buena Gardens, *San Francisco* 25 c2
Yerba Buena I., *San Francisco* 25 B2
Yerres, *Paris* 23 B4
Yerushalayim = Jerusalem, *Jerusalem* 13 B2
Yiheyuan, *Beijing* 4 A1
Yinhangzhen, *Shanghai* 27 A2
Yishun New Town, *Singapore* 27 A3
Yixingbu, *Tianjin* 30 B2
Ylästö, *Helsinki* 12 B2
Yodo →, *Osaka* 22 A4
Yongdingman, *Beijing* 4 B2
Yŏngdong, *Seoul* 26 B2
Yŏngdŭngp'o, *Seoul* 26 B1
Yongfucun, *Canton* 8 B2
Yongjing, *Shanghai* 27 B2
Yongsan, *Seoul* 26 B1
Yonkers, *New York* 21 A2
York, *Toronto* 30 A2
York Mills, *Toronto* 30 A2
Yotsuya, *Tokyo* 29 a2
You'anmen, *Beijing* 4 B1
Yŏŭido, *Seoul* 26 B1
Youndsfield, *Cape Town* 8 B1
Yuanxiatian, *Canton* 8 A2
Yugo-Zarad, *Moscow* 19 B3
Yung Shue Wan, *Hong Kong* 12 B1
Yūsofābād, *Tehran* 30 A2
Yuyuantan Park, *Beijing* 4 b2

Z

Zaandam, *Amsterdam* 2 A1
Zaandijk, *Amsterdam* 2 A1
Zaanstad, *Amsterdam* 2 A1
Záběhlice, *Prague* 24 B2
Ząbki, *Warsaw* 31 B2
Żacisze, *Warsaw* 31 B2
Zahrā, *Baghdad* 3 A1
Zakharkovo, *Moscow* 19 B1
Žalov, *Prague* 24 A2
Załuski, *Warsaw* 31 C1
Zamdorf, *Munich* 20 B2
Zamek Królewski, *Warsaw* 31 a2
Zamek Ujazdowski, *Warsaw* 31 c3
Zanevka, *St. Petersburg* 26 B3
Zapote, *Manila* 17 C1
Zappeio, *Athens* 2 c2
Zarechye, *Moscow* 19 B2
Zaventem, *Brussels* 6 A2
Zawady, *Warsaw* 31 B2
Zâwiyet Abû Musallam, *Cairo* 7 B1
Zawrā' Park, *Baghdad* 3 B2
Zbraslav, *Prague* 24 C2
Zbuzany, *Prague* 24 B1
Zdiby, *Prague* 24 B2
Zeekoevlei, *Cape Town* 8 B2
Zehlendorf, *Berlin* 5 B2
Zenne →, *Brussels* 6 B1
Żerań, *Warsaw* 31 B2
Zerzeń, *Warsaw* 31 B2
Zeytinburnu, *Istanbul* 12 C1
Zhabei, *Shanghai* 27 B1
Zhangguizhuang, *Tianjin* 30 B2
Zhdanov, *Moscow* 19 B4
Zheleznodorozhnyy, *Moscow* 19 B6
Zhenru, *Shanghai* 27 B1
Zhernovka, *St. Petersburg* 26 B2
Zhicun, *Canton* 8 B2
Zhongshan Park, *Beijing* 4 b2
Zhongshan Park, *Shanghai* 27 B1
Zhoucun, *Canton* 8 A2
Zhoujiadu, *Shanghai* 27 B1
Zhoujiazhen, *Shanghai* 27 B2
Zhu Jiang →, *Canton* 8 B3
Zhulebino, *Moscow* 19 B5
Zhushadi, *Canton* 8 B3
Zielona, *Warsaw* 31 B3
Zielonka, *Warsaw* 31 B2
Ziya He →, *Tianjin* 30 A1
Žižkov, *Prague* 24 B2
Zličín, *Prague* 24 B1
Zócalo, *Mexico City* 18 b3
Zografos, *Athens* 2 B2
Żoliborz, *Warsaw* 31 B1
Zonnenbloem, *Cape Town* 8 A1
Zoo, *Beijing* 4 a1
Zugliget, *Budapest* 7 B1
Zugló, *Budapest* 7 A2
Zuiderwoude, *Amsterdam* 2 A3
Zumbi, *Rio de Janeiro* 24 A1
Zunderdorp, *Amsterdam* 2 A2
Zuvuvu →, *São Paulo* 26 C1
Zwanenburg, *Amsterdam* 2 A1
Zwölfaxing, *Vienna* 31 B2
Zyuzino, *Moscow* 19 C3

CITY GAZETTEER

The entries below provide information on places of interest in cities throughout the world that have particularly large numbers of visitors, whether in a business or tourist capacity. The map page reference at the start of an entry indicates that one or more relevant maps are included in the City Maps section.

Accra, Ghana

Accra is not the most beautiful city in West Africa, but its people are considered to be among the friendliest and best educated. It has several lively markets and a National Museum with displays of West African art and artefacts. Near the city are some beautiful sandy beaches, although visitors should be alert to the powerful undertow. Further along the coast are forts and castles that once served as slave-trading centres, including St George's Castle at Elmina, the oldest European structure in sub-Saharan Africa.

Agra, India

Agra is visited primarily for its architectural wonders, especially the 17th-century Taj Mahal. This magical building, a symbol of Mughal emperor Shah Jahan's love for his favourite wife, Mumtaz Mahal, captures the imagination even when crowded with tourists in the heat of the day. Agra's 16th-century Red Fort contains elaborately decorated royal apartments and gardens that give a vivid impression of life at the Mughal court. Just 40 km (25 miles) away is the Mughal 'ghost city' of Fatehpur Sikri which was abandoned almost immediately after it had been built in the 1570s.

Taj Mahal, Agra

Amsterdam, The Netherlands

Map page 2

In the centre of Amsterdam is a network of canals, crossed by around a thousand bridges and edged with tree-lined streets of 17th- and 18th-century gabled houses. Canal cruises are an excellent way to get to know the city, and visitors can also hire bicycles – a major form of transport in Amsterdam. Among the museums are the Rijksmuseum, with its famous art collection, the Van Gogh Museum, and the Stedelijk Museum, housing modern art. The heart of the city is Dam Square, with the royal palace and Anne Frank's house (now a museum) close by. Rembrandt's house can also be visited in an area full of bars, nightclubs and restaurants.

Antwerp, Belgium

A vibrant city with much to see, Antwerp – on the River Scheldt and Europe's second largest port – deserves to be a highly rated tourist destination. At the heart of its beautiful old town is the Great Market, with a 16th-century town hall. Nearby, among cobbled streets lined with bars, restaurants and shops, is the impressive Gothic cathedral with paintings by Rubens, the city's most famous artist. There is also much to attract those who want a really enjoyable night on the town.

Athens, Greece

Map page 2

Athens is a curious mixture of ancient and modern, where ugly concrete tower blocks rub shoulders with Classical monuments. Dominating the centre of the city are the ruins on the Acropolis, dating from the 5th century BC and crowned by the magnificent Parthenon. Other interesting ruins include the Temple of Olympian Zeus, the largest temple in Greece. The National Archaeological Museum houses gold artefacts from Mycenae and spectacular Minoan frescoes. Nestling beneath the Acropolis is the engaging Pláka quarter, with its small Byzantine churches and bustling tavernas. For most visitors the centre of Athens is Sindagma Square, with its large hotels, banks and open-air cafés. Ferries to the islands depart from the port of Piraeus, 10 km (6 miles) from the square.

Atlanta, Georgia, USA

Map page 3

Beneath the glittering high-rise buildings of Atlanta's modern financial centre lies 'Underground Atlanta' – the revitalized old centre, complete with cobbled, gas-lit streets and packed with shops and restaurants. The piazza above it is filled with street entertainers and flanked by the Coca-Cola Museum. Atlanta is most famously associated with Martin Luther King, and an area of the city is devoted to his memory and to the history of the civil rights movement. The Centennial Olympic Park, with its Fountain of Rings, is an entertaining outdoor venue, and the adjacent CNN Center provides an interesting studio tour.

Auckland, New Zealand

The heart of Auckland is the magnificent Waitemata Harbour, where sailing is a popular pastime. The city is not renowned for its nightlife, but it is pleasant to walk its streets, perhaps following the 13 km (8-mile) Coast-to-Coast Walkway from the Ferry Building to Manukau Harbour. On the route, in an area of parkland known as The Domain, is the Auckland Museum, with a unique collection of Maori and Pacific Island artefacts. Beyond is the inner suburb of Parnell, with its colonial buildings, east of which is Underwater World, a particularly impressive aquarium. There are several city beaches, and surfing beaches beyond the Waitakere Ranges.

Bangkok, Thailand

Map page 3

With its choking traffic, Bangkok can be both a daunting and an exhilarating city for short-stay visitors. Something of the old Siam can be uncovered by using the river-bus service to visit the Royal Grand Palace and the ornate Temple of the Emerald Buddha (Wat Phra Keo). Other Buddhist temples include the Temple of the Dawn (Wat Arun), whose 82 m (266 ft) high gilded stupa is best seen from the Chao Phraya River. At Jim Thompson's House there is an extraordinary private museum of Thai domestic architecture. The network of canals, with their floating markets, is well worth exploring, as are the shops for silk and other textiles, clothes, jewellery and handicrafts. Night-time entertainment includes traditional dancing and Thai boxing.

Floating market, Bangkok

Barcelona, Spain

Map page 4

The capital of Catalonia and Spain's second city, Barcelona is a major port with a fashionable, cosmopolitan cultural life. Particularly enjoyable is strolling along the Ramblas, a broad avenue which bisects central Barcelona, and has a vibrant street life. At the southern end is the renovated harbour area, with shops, restaurants and tapas bars. The district of greatest historic interest is the Barri Gòtic, where medieval houses cluster around the great Gothic cathedral, La Seu. Barcelona has over 50 museums and galleries, including world-class museums dedicated to the works of Picasso and Miró, but it is the buildings of Antonio Gaudí that are most often associated with the city. His incomplete Sagrada Família Cathedral has become a symbol for Barcelona, and is perhaps the most fantastic of all his eccentric creations.

Beijing, China

Map page 4

Despite Beijing's daunting scale, extreme climate and heavy traffic, its sights are well worth visiting. They include the massive Tiananmen Square, the Mao Mausoleum, the Great Hall of the People, the Imperial Palace (Forbidden City), the buildings of the Summer Palace along the shore of Kunming Lake, and the 15th-century Temple of Heaven. Beijing has many interesting parks, including Beihai Park with its historic buildings and exquisite Jade Island. However, perhaps the most famous attraction of all is the Great Wall, which can be visited at Badaling, just 70 km (40 miles) north-west of the city, on a trip that also takes in the Ming tombs in the Shisan Ling Valley.

Berlin, Germany

Map page 5

After decades of being divided into West and East Berlin, the city is once again the capital of a united Germany. From the modern dome on the renovated Reichstag building there are fine views of the new buildings rising in the former no-man's-land between the two sectors, whose distinct character can still be felt. The city's youthful 'alternative' scene also continues to thrive, as does its famous nightlife in and around, for example, Savignyplatz in the west and the Scheunenviertel in the east. To the east of the Brandenburg Gate is an area of grand old squares and streets containing Berlin's main museums, including the Pergamon, with its collection of Ancient, Oriental and Islamic art. To the west is the landscaped Tiergarten, the famous zoo, with its exotic pastiche architecture, and the wealthy, modern heart of former West Berlin.

Boston, Massachusetts, USA

Map page 6

The oldest areas of Boston have a European feel, their street plan based on meandering farm tracks. The Beacon Hill district contains splendid 19th-century brick houses and narrow alleyways, and the Massachusetts State House. A 'Freedom Trail', marked by a line of red bricks, takes the visitor past 17th- and 18th-century buildings, some of which are associated with the American Revolution. There are also guided tours of the USA's oldest surviving battleship – the USS *Constitution*, built in 1797 – moored in Boston Harbour. Across the Charles River lies Cambridge, with Harvard University and Square. Boston is a relatively unthreatening city for visitors, with a lively intellectual and artistic life, and a 'necklace' of city parks and tree-lined streets within a compact central area.

Brisbane, Queensland, Australia

The relaxed atmosphere and compactness of its centre make Brisbane a pleasant place to stroll around. Its historic precinct, next to the Botanic Gardens, contains some fine 19th-century buildings, among them the Treasury. South of the River Brisbane is the State Art Gallery and the Cultural Centre, which includes two theatres and a superb concert hall. Day trips are possible to the beaches of the Gold and Sunshine Coasts.

Brussels, Belgium

Map page 6

The centre of government for the European Union, Brussels is renowned for its excellent restaurants and shops, with everything from flea markets to the designer boutiques in the Galéries St Hubert. The imposing Hôtel de Ville, the gilded 17th-century houses and the Maison du Roi make the Grand-Place one of the world's most beautiful central squares. To the east lies the Gothic cathedral, the Palais Royale and the Royal Art Museums, containing both ancient and modern art. The city is full of fine examples of Art Nouveau architecture, including the museum dedicated to the founder of the movement, Victor Horta. A popular tourist site is the irreverent 17th-century statue, Manneken Pis.

Budapest, Hungary

Map page 7

The Danube and Parliament building, Budapest

Formerly two cities, Buda and Pest, on opposite sides of the Danube, the capital of Hungary is a fascinating destination. The Castle Hill district of Buda includes the cobbled streets and medieval houses of the Old Town, and the Royal Palace (Budavári palota), containing the national art gallery and museum. The Fishermen's Bastion gives sweeping views over the city. A network of grand 19th-century boulevards forms the centre of the larger, more cosmopolitan Pest, with its imposing Parliament building (Országház). There are many elegant spa baths (gyógyfürdo) dotted around the city, and extensive Roman remains, including an amphitheatre, at Óbuda and Rómaifürdo. Famous for its cafés, Budapest has excellent restaurants and offers a huge range of entertainment, including opera, jazz and discos.

Buenos Aires, Argentina

Map page 7

The centre of Buenos Aires is laid out on a grand scale, with wide boulevards, imposing 19th-century buildings, modern tower blocks, and spacious plazas. Around this area, however, are the more intimate districts (*barrios*), each with its distinctive character. San Telmo is the artists' quarter, while La Boca, with its brightly painted houses, is the city's port district. The most fashionable district, Recoleta, houses the National Museum of Art, but is best known for the ornate tombs of its cemetery.

La Boca, Buenos Aires

Cairo, Egypt

Map page 7

The largest city in Africa, Cairo is full of hooting taxis and bustling crowds. Modern buildings have risen next to the minarets of the old mosques, while a maze of markets provide potential bargains. The Pyramids of Giza are visible from the upper storeys of buildings all over the city. Famous worldwide for its unrivalled collection of antiquities, the Egyptian Museum houses the treasures of the Pharaoh Tutankhamun, and more than 100,000 other relics and antiquities from all periods of ancient Egyptian history. Experiences not to be missed include the *Son et Lumière* that takes place daily by the Sphinx at Giza, and drifting on the Nile in a *felucca* while watching the sun sink below the Cairo skyline.

Calcutta (Kolkata), India

Map page 8

The capital of West Bengal, Calcutta (Kolkata) is regarded by many as the cultural and intellectual centre of India. It also has a reputation for extreme poverty and squalor. One of the great colonial cities of Asia, its main historic sites date from the days of the British Raj and include the white marble Victoria Memorial, the neo-Gothic St Paul's Cathedral, and the Indian Museum, with sculptures from all over India. These buildings are all in the vicinity of the Maidan, one of the largest city parks in the world, where hundreds of different interests – among them yoga, cricket and riding – are regularly pursued, and live entertainment is provided.

Canton (Guangzhou), China

Map page 8

An economic success but a planning disaster, Guangzhou holds more attraction for the business traveller than for those seeking historic sites. There are, however, numerous decaying French and British colonial buildings on Shamian Island, which provides a haven of peace from the bustle of Guangzhou's streets. A climb to the top of the 11th-century Temple of Six Banyan Trees provides a fine view. Another way of seeing the city is to take a cruise on the Pearl River.

Cape Town, South Africa

Map page 8

South Africa's oldest city, Cape Town has several buildings of historic interest, including the Castle of Good Hope, the Old Town House, the Tuynhuis and the Parliament building. Artefacts from all over Africa are sold at the Saturday market in Greenmarket Square. The city lies below the spectacular Table Mountain, accessible by cable car. There are numerous good beaches, such as those at Clifton and Camps Bay on the cold Atlantic Ocean, and at Muizenberg and Fishoek on the warmer Indian Ocean. The old docks have been developed as the Victoria and Albert Waterfront, which boasts a range of restaurants. Boat trips run from here to the infamous Robben Island, where Nelson Mandela was imprisoned.

Cartagena, Colombia

Several impressive 16th-century forts overlook the channel leading to the bay of Cartagena, evidence of the city's origins as an imperial Spanish stronghold. Huge 17th- and 18th-century walls surround narrow streets, palaces, churches, monasteries and plazas. The Palace of the Inquisition is a fine example of colonial architecture, with its magnificent Baroque gateway.

Chicago, Illinois, USA

Map page 9

Built on the shore of Lake Michigan, Chicago played a key role in the economic development of the USA, serving as a railhead for the cattle trade of the Midwest. Its skyline includes skyscrapers dating from the 1890s, buildings in the International Style of the 1950s, and particularly fine examples of more recent architecture. The Sears Tower provides fantastic views of four states from its Space Deck. A closer view can be had on a boat trip up the Chicago River or from 'The Loop', an elevated railway that lends its name to the area it encircles. There are several important museums, including the vast Museum of Science and Industry and the Art Institute of Chicago. For outdoor pursuits, there is the extensive Grant Park, bordering the lake. The city is renowned for its rich musical life and, as well as a world-class symphony orchestra, there is a multitude of clubs offering blues, jazz, rock and folk music.

Skyline with Sears Tower, Chicago

Cologne, Germany

Despite the almost total destruction of central Cologne during World War II, many historic buildings have been restored to their former glory, including the massive and beautiful twin-towered Gothic cathedral (Dom). Among the museums and art galleries are the Roman-Germanic Museum and the Imhoff-Stollwek Museum of Chocolate. The city's unique beer, *kslsch*, can be sampled in the numerous beer halls. Short boat trips on the Rhine provide views of the impressive riverfront, while longer boat excursions go to, for example, Königswinter and Linz.

Copenhagen, Denmark

Map page 10

Scandinavia's largest and liveliest city, Copenhagen has excellent art collections, royal palaces, churches and other historic buildings as well as entertainment late into the night. Punctuated by parks, lakes, fountains and squares, the city is easily explored on foot or bicycle. The old harbour of Nyhavn, with its tall, brightly painted buildings, is packed with pavement cafés and bars, while the Latin Quarter is good for restaurants. From the top of the Round Tower (Rundee Taarn), Europe's oldest functioning observatory, there are magnificent views over the city. The famous Tivoli Gardens is a delightfully varied amusement park dating from 1843. A bridge now links Copenhagen to the attractive Swedish city of Malmö.

Delhi, India

Map page 10

Red Fort, Delhi

The capital of India, Delhi is a city with two centres: New Delhi, which was established by the British in 1911, and Old Delhi, whose present layout dates from the 17th century. The streets of the old town, and in particular Chandni Chauk, are famously frenetic. The massive walls of the Red Fort and the Lahore Gate enclose a host of palace buildings, although many have been stripped of their fine decoration. India's largest mosque, the Jama Masjid, is also in the old town. The new city, with its broad avenues and imposing marble buildings, contains some older sites, including the 16th-century tomb of Humayun and the 12th-century Qutb Minar tower.

Dublin, Ireland

Map page 11

Built on the River Liffey, Ireland's capital contains elegant 18th-century buildings, two Norman cathedrals, a castle, and some fine museums, three of them in Leinster House. One of the oldest books in the world, the 9th-century illuminated Book of Kells, is housed in Trinity College library, while the Writers' Museum pays homage to local literary figures such as W. B. Yeats, James Joyce and Oscar Wilde. Dublin has a relaxed, friendly atmosphere, and plenty of pubs and restaurants. In summer, outdoor events are often held in Phoenix Park. The famous Easter Uprising of 1916 is commemorated at Kilmainham Jail, where many heroes of Irish independence were once incarcerated.

Edinburgh, Scotland

Map page 11

Set on a dramatic rock that soars 76 m (250 ft) from the valley floor, the Old Town of Edinburgh is a collection of historic buildings, towering tenements and narrow passages huddling beneath a romantic castle. The Royal Mile, lined with 16th- and 17th-century buildings, leads from the castle to the royal residence of Holyrood. The Royal Museum lies to its south, as does the lively Grassmarket district with its bars and restaurants. The small but elegant National Gallery sits in Princes Street Gardens to the north. Beyond lie graceful Georgian squares, terraces and crescents of the New Town. Scotland's capital has a rich cultural life, including the world-famous International and Fringe festivals.

Esfahan, Iran

On the four sides of the vast central square of Esfahan, with its formal lawns and pool, are the delicately tiled façades of public buildings. These include the opulent Royal Mosque and the magnificent entrance to the bazaar, whose crowded streets twist and turn towards the steps of the Great Mosque, a complex of buildings spanning a 700-year period. Among other historic sites are the shrine of Imamzadeh Ahmad and several royal palaces. Esfahan's high altitude keeps it relatively cool, making it pleasant to stroll through the streets and parks, and sample the many teahouses.

Fès, Morocco

The old part of Fès – Fès el-Bali – is one of the largest living medieval cities in the world. A fascinating labyrinth of some 94,000 streets and lanes, its covered bazaars are crammed with every conceivable sort of craft workshop, restaurants and market stalls, as well as extensive dye pits and tanneries. On the edge of the old town, the Museum of Moroccan Arts houses a splendid collection of artefacts, including colourful tribal carpets and the city's famous blue pottery.

Florence, Italy

The pedestrianized streets in the beautiful centre of Florence enable visitors to wander about freely, visiting such well-known Renaissance sites as the cathedral, with its red-roofed dome, and the spacious Piazza della Signoria, dominated by the crenellated Palazzo Vecchio. Between the piazza and the River Arno is the Uffizi Gallery, containing famous works by Botticelli and Titian among many others. The 14th-century Ponte Vecchio bridge, lined on both sides with jewellery and gift shops, provides a route to the imposing Pitti Palace. The city's churches range in style from the exquisite San Miniato, through the austere Santo Croce to the classically inspired San Lorenzo. Of the many religious frescoes, those by Fra Angelico in the monastery of San Marco, and by Masaccio in the church of Santa Maria del Carmine, stand out. The Bargello has a fine collection of sculpture, while the Accademia houses Michelangelo's *David*.

Cathedral with Brunelleshci's dome, Florence

Geneva, Switzerland

Geneva enjoys one of the world's most dramatic locations, straddling the Rhône where it leaves Lake Geneva, and overlooked by the Alps on one side and the Jura mountains on the other. A cosmopolitan, French-speaking city, it is a world centre for banking and commerce as well as for international organizations, such as the Red Cross. South of the river, the oldest part has excellent museums, galleries and historic buildings, including St Peter's Cathedral, where John Calvin preached. Geneva lives up to its reputation for efficiency, cleanliness and safety, but all this comes at a price: restaurants, clubs and other entertainments are smart and expensive.

Hamburg, Germany

Germany's largest port (there are daily harbour tours from March to November), Hamburg combines its busy commercial life with a graceful, old-world charm. Situated on the River Elbe and criss-crossed by a network of canals, at its heart is the Alster lake, where boating is a popular pastime in the summer. The city has many extensive parks, stylish shopping arcades, elegant boulevards, museums and art galleries, among them the Kunsthalle with a fine collection of art spanning several centuries. There are numerous inviting café-bars and all-night entertainment, most notably in the St Pauli Quarter, where The Beatles famously performed in the 1960s.

Hanoi, Vietnam

Built on the Red River, around several large lakes, Hanoi has both peaceful tree-lined avenues and parks, and a bustling old city where almost anything can be purchased, including silk, lacquerware, puppets and jewellery. Bikes are the main form of transport. The city's many religious buildings include the One-Pillar Pagoda and the 11th-century Temple of Literature. Ho Chi Minh's mausoleum provides a memorable experience, with visitors being escorted to view the embalmed body. A day trip can be made to the Perfume Pagoda – actually a complex of pagodas and Buddhist shrines carved out of limestone cliffs. A cruise from Haiphong around the limestone islands of Halong Bay is also recommended.

Havana, Cuba

Ironically for a country that is proud of its independence from imperialism, one of the main attractions of Cuba's capital is its colonial past. The vast open space of Plaza de la Revolución and the post-colonial buildings of the Vedado district are worth seeing, but it is the boulevards and squares of Old Havana that are most fascinating.

The palaces surrounding the Plaza de Armas, the Baroque cathedral and the elegant thoroughfare 'The Paseo' are all fine examples of colonial architecture. There are few cars on the streets, but many bicycles. There are also many nightclubs, where salsa is the predominant dance style.

Capitol building and Grand Theatre, Havana

Helsinki, Finland

Map page 12

Helsinki is almost surrounded by water and is full of the sounds and scents of the sea. Among its architectural gems are the 19th-century Neo-classical buildings of Senate Square – which also contains the blue-domed Lutheran Cathedral – and the rock-hewn church of Temppeliauko (1969) where many concerts are held. Although its combination of attractive buildings, good restaurants and excellent art galleries and museums make it a year-round tourist destination, Helsinki really comes to life in summer, with open-air cafés, concerts, and boat trips to the ruined fortress on nearby Suomenlinna Island.

Hong Kong, China

Map page 12

Most visitors to Hong Kong take the short ferry ride from Kowloon across the harbour, with its spectacular view of the high-rise buildings on the waterfront of Hong Kong Island. A visit to the Man Mo temple, with its ornate interior, provides a complete contrast. A funicular goes to the top of Victoria Peak where there are shady paths through lush vegetation. The Tsim Sha Tsui area of Kowloon contains a group of modern exhibition buildings, including the Space Museum and the Hong Kong Museum of History, as well as air-conditioned shopping malls. A ferry goes to the islands of Lamma, where there are relatively uncrowded beaches, country walks and seafood restaurants. A hydrofoil goes to Macau.

Istanbul, Turkey

Map page 12

Formerly known as Constantinople, Istanbul has an imperial history dating back to the time of the Roman Empire. Its strategic position straddling the Bosporus Strait makes it both a European and an Asian city. Among the churches built in the 6th century by Emperor Constantine is the domed Hagia Sophia (Aya Sofya), which was converted into a mosque in 1453 and is now a museum. The 17th-century Blue Mosque (Sultanahmet Camii) is a masterpiece of Ottoman architecture, while the Topkapi Palace, with its imperial treasury stuffed with gold and jewels, is on every itinerary. In old Istanbul is the labyrinthine Kapali Carsi (the world's largest covered bazaar) where more than 4,000 shops and stalls sell carpets, jewellery, ceramics, brass and leatherware. A fascinating mixture of both the ancient and modern, Istanbul also has a renowned cuisine.

Jaipur, India

Known as the 'Pink City' because of the salmon-coloured wash applied to many of its buildings, Jaipur is the capital of the colourful state of Rajasthan. It is divided into areas dedicated to specialist activities, such as elephant-handling or the sale of textiles, silver or gems. Within the walled town are the Palace of Winds (Hawa Mahal), with its delicately screened windows, the City Palace – now a museum – and Jai Singh's extraordinary Observatory, with its huge angular stone instruments. Nearby is the hill town and Rajput palace complex of Amber.

Jakarta, Indonesia

Map page 13

Jakarta's glinting high-rise office blocks contrast sharply with the cobbled square at the heart of what was 18th-century Batavia (now known as Kota). Much can be discovered of this colonial period at the dock of Sunda Kelapa, where many magnificent schooners are moored and a maritime museum has been created in an old warehouse. The National Museum has excellent displays on Indonesia's ethnic groups. There is a theme park at Taman Impian Jaya Ancol, and Balinese dancing and traditional music at Taman Ismail Marzuki. Jakarta also offers a fine range of restaurants.

Jerusalem, Israel

Map page 13

The focus of most visits to Jerusalem is the Old City with its different quarters. The heart of the Christian quarter is the Church of the Holy Sepulchre, the site of Christ's crucifixion. This is reached along the Via Dolorosa, much of which passes through the Muslim quarter, with its impressive Mamluk architecture. The Western (Wailing) Wall is in the Jewish quarter, which also contains the multi-layered Temple Mount Excavations. The Armenian quarter, the centre of the Armenian Church, contains the impressive Citadel. Towering over all these is the golden Dome of the Rock, a sacred Muslim site in the Temple Mount compound.

Dome of the Rock, Jerusalem

Johannesburg, South Africa

Map page 13

The richest city in Africa, Johannesburg is also a lively centre of South African culture. Museum-Africa has collections relating to the history and art of all sections of the community, while the nearby Market Theatre Complex, which contains four theatres, is an attractive place in which to eat and drink, and listen to music. Visitors, however, should be aware of the high crime rate in the downtown area, and enjoy instead the restaurants and gardens of northern suburbs such as Rosebank and Melville. Outside the city is Soweto, the vast black township which has a lively music and theatre scene but is best visited on a guided tour.

Kairouan, Tunisia

An important centre for the Muslim faith, Tunisia's holy city has over 130 mosques, including the 9th-century Great Mosque, which once doubled as a fortress. A special permit is required to visit the holy sites. Kairouan's maze of buildings and narrow, winding streets is enclosed by ancient city walls, and it is a fascinating place in which to stroll. Artisans carry out the traditional trades of weaving and carpentry, and carpet sellers try to attract visitors to their stalls in the souk (bazaar).

Karachi, Pakistan

Map page 14

Developed as a city by the British from the 1840s, Karachi is a business rather than a tourist centre. It does, however, have many colourful bazaars in Saddar, the central district, which specialize in such products as jewellery, cloth, dried fruit and bottles. It also has a fascinating coastline which can be viewed on a traditional lateen-sailed boat trip from the harbour. Clifton Beach, with its camel rides and fairground, is well equipped for families, while other, rather less commercialized beaches are a short drive away.

Katmandu, Nepal

Street scene, Katmandu

Katmandu is a popular holiday destination – an intriguing mixture of modern buildings and narrow, traffic-clogged streets with intricately carved temples and shrines. Many of these ancient buildings are grouped around Durbar Square, including the Jaganath Temple, with its erotic carvings. The Old Royal Palace houses an interesting museum. Jochne, better known as 'Freak Street', is a focal point for many visitors, with its fascinating shops, cheap hotels and restaurants. Outside the city are three huge temples: the Hindu Pashupatinath complex, with its riverside ghats, and the Buddhist stupas of Boudhanath and Swayambunath.

Kraków, Poland

Having come through World War II virtually unscathed, and with not a high-rise building in sight, Kraków's densely packed old centre is full of historic churches and picturesque streets and squares. The central market square, which is reputed to be the largest medieval town square in Europe, contains a number of interesting buildings, among them the largely 16th-century Cloth Hall. The square is also the focus of the city's vigorous cultural life. There are several jazz and cabaret clubs in the Old Town, as well as numerous attractive cafés, bars and restaurants. To the south are the castle and cathedral of Wawel, behind which lies Kazimierz, the gradually reviving Jewish district.

Kuala Lumpur, Malaysia

A city that has sprung up since the 1860s, Kuala Lumpur is short on historic sites but has plenty to offer the visitor. Its colonial, 19th-century heart is Merdeka Square. Nearby is the most spectacular of the city's mosques, Masjid Jamek. Chinatown and Little India provide much of interest, and Malaysian craftwork and antiques can be bought at the Art Deco Central Market. The 'Golden Triangle' business area includes the Petronas Twin Towers, one of the world's tallest buildings. The Lake Gardens contain a Bird Park, Orchid Garden and Butterfly Park. A half-hour drive outside the city are the Batu Caves, used as Hindu temples. Day trips can be made to the historic city of Malacca and the Genting Highlands Casino Complex.

Kyoto, Japan

Japan's capital for over 1,000 years, Kyoto has numerous Buddhist temples, Shinto shrines, palaces and gardens. Despite extensive modern development, there are still traditional wooden houses and craft shops in the back streets. A city that is particularly spectacular when clad in either cherry blossom or autumnal colours, its main sights include the 1,001 gilded statues of Buddha lined up in the Hall of the Thirty-Three Bays, the view from the temple of Kiyomizu-dera, and the intriguing gardens of Ginkaku-ji. Other famous gardens include the lake-garden of Kinkaku-ji, and the 500-year-old garden of Ryoan-ji. The city of Nara, 35 km (22 miles) south, contains the huge bronze Buddha of Todai-ji, and other fine examples of early Japanese art and architecture.

Temple of Kiyomizu-dera, Kyoto

Lagos, Nigeria

Map page 14

Although no longer the capital of Nigeria, Lagos is by far the largest city in West Africa. At its heart lies Lagos Island, a business centre whose skyline is spiked by skyscrapers. The National Museum provides a fascinating insight into the country's cultural heritage and includes works of art dating back 2,800 years, including beautiful Benin bronzes. The city's main attraction, however, is modern African music, and many of the country's best-known singers have nightclubs here.

Lahore, Pakistan

Lahore is renowned for its Mughal architecture. The most attractive of its many mosques is that of Wazir Kahn, covered in intricate glazed mosaic tiles, but the largest is the Badshahi Mosque. The massive walls of Lahore Fort surround a compound of elegant buildings. Away from the centre is Jahangir's tomb and the Shalimar Garden, with its geometrically arranged terraces, ponds, fountains and, in February and March, its spectacular flowers.

Las Vegas, Nevada, USA

A city whose population grew from 30 to half a million in just 90 years, Las Vegas is continually reinventing itself, with the casinos on The Strip providing ever bigger and better spectacles. The most famous is Caesar's Palace, with staff dressed as centurions and Cleopatra lookalikes. New York, New York entices with its replica skyscrapers and a Statue of Liberty. Treasure Island has a mock sea battle, Mirage an erupting volcano and Circus Circus live fire-eaters. Food and lodging are cheap, particularly midweek, with the real profits being made on the gambling tables and slot machines. Las Vegas is popular for outrageous weddings, with services being conducted in the most unlikely places – in a 'drive-through' chapel, the nearby Grand Canyon, or even in mid-air.

The Strip, Las Vegas

Lima, Peru

Map page 16

A once-beautiful city, Lima has suffered badly at the hands of modern developers. It is worth visiting primarily for its fine museums, which provide background information about Peru's Inca sites. It is also a useful base from which to explore the surrounding countryside, including the beautiful beaches to the south, over which towers the temple complex of Pachacamac.

Lisbon, Portugal

Map page 14

There are many hills to climb and much to see in Portugal's capital. Stretching north from the Rio Tejo, the Baixa district – rebuilt after the devastating earthquake of 1755 – contains many of the city's museums and theatres. The old Moorish area, the Alfama, survived the earthquake and its warren of narrow streets, stairways and squares leads up to the hilltop Castle of St George, with magnificent views. On the edge of the city the Belém area contains fine examples of 16th-century architecture, including the marvellous Jerônimos Monastery and the famous white Belém Tower. At night the haunting traditional *fado* music is played in bars in, for example, the Bairro Alto district. Day trips can be made to the hill town of Sintra or to the beaches on the Estoril coast.

London, England

Map page 15

Europe's largest city, London is a lively, cosmopolitan metropolis, offering a huge range of attractions to the visitor. From the grand squares of Knightsbridge and Belgravia to the business district of the City, central London is made up of a mosaic of areas, each with its own distinctive atmosphere and architectural style. Historic buildings include the Tower of London (containing the Crown Jewels), St Paul's Cathedral, Westminster Abbey, the Houses of Parliament and Buckingham Palace. Among the many art galleries are the Tate Modern, housed in a converted power station on the South Bank of the River Thames, and The National Gallery, overlooking Trafalgar Square. The British Museum contains a monumental collection of Egyptian, Greek and Roman artefacts. Soho, Piccadilly and Covent Garden form the heart of the theatre district, with numerous restaurants, clubs and bars. Day excursions can be made to Hampton Court Palace, Windsor Castle, Canterbury Cathedral, the Royal Pavilion in Brighton, and the historic university towns of Oxford and Cambridge.

Los Angeles, California, USA

Map page 16

Among the skyscrapers in Los Angeles' downtown area are some notable public buildings, including the Museum of Contemporary Art. To the southwest is Exposition Park, home to three museums, including the interactive California Space Center. Most visitors, however, flock to Hollywood in search of film stars, although the big names have long since left for more salubrious neighbourhoods, such as Beverly Hills and elegant Bel Air. Other attractions include the Warner Bros. Studio Tour, and the thrilling rides at Universal Studios. On the coast, the long sandy beach linking Santa Monica and Venice is a magnet for Los Angeles' more colourful characters.

Luxembourg City, Luxembourg

The picturesque old walled city of Luxembourg perches above the Pétrusse and Alzette valleys, overlooked by the ruins of its ancient fortress with a labyrinth of defensive tunnels and underground chambers (the casemates), which is a UNESCO World Heritage Site. Running between the Citadelle du St Esprit, which provides spectacular views, and the Grand Ducal Palace is the elegant Chemin de la Corniche, one of Europe's most beautiful pedestrian promenades.

Madrid, Spain

Map page 17

Spain's capital is a huge metropolis with a remarkable collection of museums and art galleries, beautiful parks and a famously vibrant nightlife centred on Plaza de Santa Ana. The city is made up of a number of districts (*barrios*), each with its own distinct character. The area of most interest to visitors is around the 17th-century Plaza Mayor, with the elaborately decorated Royal Palace, the Opera House (Teatro Real) and the famous Prado Museum all within easy reach. The city has a vivacious character and a buzzing street life. Tapas bars are everywhere, and shoppers can explore the busy Gran Via or the atmospheric Rastro flea market centred on Plaza de Cascorro. Excursions can be made to the austere monastery of El Escorial and to the historic towns of Toledo, Segovia, Avila and Aranjuez.

Plaza Mayor, Madrid

Manila, Philippines

Map page 17

Many people visit Manila purely for its bars and nightlife, and the city provides plenty to choose from in the business district of Makati and the streets behind Roxes Boulevard. The walled area known as Intramuros contains the most significant historic sites, including Fort Santiago and the imposing Romanesque cathedral. Rizal Park, projecting out into Manila Bay, contains a lagoon, a spectacular fountain, a replica of Beijing's Summer Palace, a Japanese Garden and planetarium. Manila's Chinatown (on the border of Santa Cruz and Binondo) is the place to go for silk, porcelain and Chinese dumplings.

Marrakech, Morocco

Famous for its lively street life, Marrakech is also known for the pink colour that dominates the city from the earth walls around the old town centre to the flat-roofed houses. Every evening in Djemaa El Fna, the old town's central square, acrobats, snake charmers and storytellers perform. Nearby is the labyrinthine souk (bazaar), with its hundreds of small shops selling jewellery, carpets, metalware and leather. There are several beautiful gardens, and the Museum of Arts contains a magnificent display of carpets. Just an hour's drive away are the spectacular High Atlas mountains.

The souk, Marrakech

Melbourne, Victoria, Australia

Map page 17

Central Melbourne, on the north bank of the River Yarra, is a striking blend of past and present. Ornate 19th-century buildings sit alongside towering skyscrapers, as in Collins Street where the 1980s Rialto Towers provide splendid views from an Observation Deck. Elsewhere, the Old Melbourne Gaol is a major historic attraction and there are many fine parks and gardens, including the outstanding Botanic Gardens. The city's multi-ethnic nature is apparent in the popular Queen Victoria Market and in the huge variety of restaurants. Outside the centre several inner suburbs, each with a distinct character, can be explored by tram. Places of interest nearby include the Yarra Valley with its wineries and wildlife sanctuaries, and Phillip Island with its penguins.

Mexico City, Mexico

Map page 18

It is worth braving the traffic and pollution of Mexico City to see the impressive architecture of the buildings surrounding the main square (Zócalo), including the National Palace, with its murals by Diego Rivera. Nearby are the fascinating excavations of an Aztec temple (Templo Mayor). Bosque de Chapultepec, with its boating lakes, gardens and zoo, provides some relief from the hectic street life. It is also home to the outstanding Museo de Antropologia, whose indoor and outdoor exhibition spaces house the world's greatest collection of Mexican art and artefacts. Just 48 km (30 miles) away from the centre are the splendid ruins of the ancient city of Teotihuacán.

Miami, Florida, USA

Map page 18

Miami is spread out along the fragmented coastline of Biscayne Bay. The Spanish language predominates and the downtown area, with its modern tower blocks, is greatly enlivened by the Latin American street life. Little Havana and Little Haiti are two areas worth visiting for their strong culture. The city's most elegant neighbourhood is Coral Gables, built as a 'model suburb' in the 1920s. Miami Beach, on an island linked to the mainland by causeways, has many fine examples of Art Deco buildings and miles of sandy beaches, hotels and bars.

Milan, Italy

Map page 18

Famous as a world centre for design and fashion, and for its grand opera house, La Scala, Milan has many historic buildings alongside its modern skyscrapers. The enormous Gothic cathedral dominates the main square, Piazza del Duomo, and the nearby convent of Santa Maria delle Grazie houses Leonardo da Vinci's fresco *The Last Supper*. Italy's most beautiful shopping arcade, the Galleria Vittorio Emanuele II, runs between the cathedral and La Scala. The Castello Sforzesco, a striking red-brick castle which was once the seat of the Dukes of Milan, houses the excellent municipal art collections. Excursions can be made to the old university town of Pavia and to the lake resorts such as Varenna and Bellagio on Lake Como, and Stresa on Lake Maggiore.

Montréal, Québec, Canada

Map page 19

Situated on the St Lawrence River, Montréal is Canada's second-largest city. The multi-ethnic nature of its population, of whom around 60% are French-speaking, is evident in the diversity of its cuisine and cultural festivals. The Parisian-style old city has numerous 17th-, 18th- and 19th-century buildings, among them the Neo-gothic Basilique Notre-Dame. By the river a public space has been created out of the old shipyards, complete with exhibitions and amusements. Boat trips can be taken up and down the St Lawrence, including one through the Lachine Rapids. The collection in the Art Museum is wide-ranging and includes a display of Inuit art. There are also particularly interesting Botanic Gardens.

Moscow, Russia

Map page 19

Moscow radiates outwards from the Kremlin in a series of rings, of which the innermost is of greatest interest to visitors and is small enough to be explored on foot. Among the buildings enclosed by the thick red-brick walls of the Kremlin are three imposing palaces and the Archangel Cathedral. Outside is Red Square, with the exotic, multi-coloured domes of St Basil's Cathedral, the Lenin Mausoleum, the Historical Museum and the magnificent 19th-century state department store, GUM, facing each other across the famous cobbled parade ground. There are also numerous literary museums and art galleries. The palatial metro system with its glittering chandeliers and fabulous marble architecture should not be missed.

St Basil's Cathedral, Moscow

Mumbai (Bombay), India

Map page 20

Home to India's thriving film industry, Mumbai also has the largest slum area of any city in Asia. The influence of the British colonial heritage is apparent in the Victorian Gothic buildings of the Fort district, the triumphal Gateway of India arch, and the red double-decker buses. The frenetic streets and bazaars are, however, pure India. Malabar Hill, with its Hanging Gardens, provides some relief from the crowds, as do the Mahatma Gandhi Museum and an impressive new National Gallery of Modern Art. Most visitors take a boat trip across the large harbour to Elephanta Island, to see the Hindu temples hewn out of the rock.

Munich, Germany

Map page 20

Munich is a cosmopolitan city, close to the Bavarian Alps, with many beautiful buildings and a wide variety of theatres, museums, galleries and restaurants. In the centre of the old town is the Marienplatz with its famous old town hall (Rathaus), and several historic churches. Many visitors shop in the glamorous Maximilianstrasse and spend an evening at the opera or drink in one of the city's many historic beer cellars, such as the famous Hofbräuhaus. Another attraction is the beer festival in October. Just outside the city is the Baroque palace of Nymphenburg.

Nairobi, Kenya

East Africa's most modern city has broad streets lined with jacaranda trees. The compact city centre can be walked in 20 minutes, but visitors should be aware that street robberies are a growing problem. The National Museum details the history of Kenyan tribal groups. Close to the city is the Bomas of Kenya, where traditional dances and songs are performed, and the Nairobi National Park where zebras, giraffes, lions, leopards and rhinos are among the animals that can be seen, particularly from July to September.

New Orleans, Louisiana, USA

Its fantastic mix of cultures – French, Spanish, Native American, African and Caribbean – makes New Orleans one of America's most stimulating cities. It is famous as the 'cradle of jazz', and trad jazz is still played in Preservation Hall. The best way to see the elegant architecture of the French Quarter is on foot, starting in Jackson Square – a park that is surrounded by some of the city's most important public buildings, including the Louisiana State Museum. Many visitors go to New Orleans simply to enjoy its restaurants, including the Creole and Cajun cuisines, both variations on the French. Popular times to visit are during the Mardi Gras carnival in February or March, and the annual Jazz Festival in April or May.

New York, NY, USA

Map page 21

Manhattan and the Statue of Liberty, New York

New York is the ultimate destination for those who love cities, with most of its main attractions on Manhattan Island. However, its famous skyline was changed forever following the destruction of the twin towers of the World Trade Center on 11 September 2001; the 1930s Empire State Building is now the city's tallest building. The dozens of art galleries include the Metropolitan Museum of Art and the Guggenheim Museum of predominantly 20th-century art. The ferry to Staten Island provides panoramic views of Manhattan, while the Circle Line runs ferries across the harbour to the Statue of Liberty and Ellis Island. Districts to be toured on foot include Greenwich Village, with its cafés, SoHo, renowned for its art galleries and boutiques, and Little Italy. Some visitors are drawn to the city by stores such as Bloomingdales, others by its nightlife. Providing a haven from the big-city traffic is Central Park, where there is often live entertainment.

Osaka, Japan

Map page 22

The Japanese city most welcoming to foreign visitors, Osaka is enjoyed mainly for its lively nightlife and varied cuisine. It has some fine historic sites, such as the castle and the red-painted Sumiyoshi Shinto shrine to the gods of the sea. Its museums include the Liberty Osaka Museum of Human Rights and the Suntory Museum of 20th-century graphic art. The spectacular Osaka Aquarium is another attraction.

Oslo, Norway

Map page 22

The oldest of Scandinavia's capitals, Oslo is an attractive city situated at the head of Oslofjord. The impressive medieval Akershus castle contains grand staterooms, dungeons and the Norwegian Resistance Museum. The Munch Museum has over 5,000 drawings and paintings by Edvard Munch, while in the beautiful Vigeland Park, sculptures by Gustav Vigeland are on permanent display. Across the harbour is the BygdØy peninsula with good beaches, an open-air folk museum and maritime museums containing Viking ships as well as Thor Heyerdahl's raft, *Kon-Tiki*.

Panama City, Panama

Bristling with skyscrapers and fronted by palm-fringed beaches, Panama is a thriving modern city. In the Casco Viejo district, grand Spanish colonial buildings overlook the Bay of Panama from the tip of a fortified peninsula. The old sea wall provides excellent views across the bay and there are restaurants in its restored colonial dungeons. Other attractions include the 17th-century Presidential Palace, the cathedral and the Panama Canal. The 16th-century ruins of Old Panama (Panamá Viejo) lie 6.5 km (4 miles) to the east.

Paris, France

Map page 23

Famously beautiful in springtime, Paris is fascinating at any time of year. Packed with historic buildings, world-famous art collections, fine restaurants and street cafés, it is one of the world's most elegant cities. Compact enough to explore on foot, the centre is made up of a number of distinct areas or *quartiers*, each with its own character. On a hill crowned by the basilica of Sacré-Coeur is Montmartre, with its village-like atmosphere, street artists, nearby flea markets and a splendid view over the city. The Notre Dame Cathedral and Sainte Chapelle are on the peaceful Île de la Cité, an island in the River Seine. The Picasso Museum is set among the beautiful old houses and courtyards of the Marais. The colourful Pompidou Centre looms above the galleries and cafés of the Beaubourg. The Louvre occupies a vast stretch of the Right Bank of the Seine, and there is a magnificent unbroken view through the Tuileries gardens and along the Champs Elysées to the Arc de Triomphe. Attractions on the Left Bank include the Musée d'Orsay – containing a huge collection of Impressionist art – and the Eiffel Tower. Excursions can be made to the royal palaces of Versailles and Fontainebleu, Monet's house at Giverney, and the beautiful cathedral at Chartres.

The Seine and Notre Dame, Paris

Perth, Western Australia, Australia

Situated on a sweep of the Swan River, Perth has lots of sunshine and an easy-going atmosphere. Its centre is relatively compact and dominated by skyscrapers, among which are scattered some Victorian buildings, such as the ornate Government House and the Old Flour Mill. A few miles to the west lie excellent sandy beaches and opportunities for surfing, while cruise companies offer dolphin- and whale-watching trips. The port of Fremantle, just 20 km (12 miles) away, is worth visiting, as is Rottnest Island.

Prague, Czech Republic

Map page 24

With a centre full of beautiful buildings covering 900 years of architecture it is easy to see why Prague, on the River Vitava, is one of Europe's top tourist attractions. Prague Castle (Prazsky Hrad), encompassing the 10th-century Church of St George and the Gothic St Vitus' Cathedral, is the focus of most visits to the city. Other architectural treasures include Baroque and Rococo palaces and the Neoclassical National Theatre (Náordní divadlo). The Old Jewish Quarter (Josefov) contains the Jewish Cemetery and several synagogues, including the Old-New Synagogue (Staranová). Prague's rich cultural life centres especially on its music – it is home to two fine orchestras. It is also arguably the beer-drinking capital of the world, and has several famous beer halls as well as numerous pubs and bars.

Quito, Ecuador

At a height of 2,850 m (9,350 ft), Quito escapes the oppressive temperature and pollution of many Latin American cities. The historic centre, with its whitewashed buildings and red roofs, is a UNESCO heritage site and includes a 16th-century monastery and cathedral, as well as a number of museums. There is also a fascinating vivarium, with displays of many of Ecuador's reptiles, both living and dead.

Reykjavik, Iceland

The world's northernmost capital, Reykjavik is a small modern city with colourful buildings, fashionable shops and a lively nightlife. The Arni Magnússon Institute houses a famous collection of Icelandic saga manuscripts, while the National Museum in the Old Town displays relics from the earliest days of settlement. The modern church of Hallgrímskirkja is built in the shape of a lava mountain and offers excellent views over the city from its 75 m (246 ft) high tower.

Riga, Latvia

A bustling industrial city, Riga also has a waterfront castle, a medieval centre and a lively cultural life. Places to visit include the cavernous Dome Cathedral, the Riga Motor Museum, an open-air ethnographical museum and St Peter's Church – with a view over Old Riga from the spire, which is reached by a lift. To the west, a string of resort towns known collectively as Jurmala stretches for 20 km (12 miles) along the coast, with peaceful beaches and good restaurants.

Rio de Janeiro, Brazil

Map page 24

With a spectacular location at the entrance to a bay, Rio has two famous landmarks that provide breathtaking views: Corcovado Mountain, topped by a huge statue of Christ, and Sugar Loaf Mountain. There are many museums, including the National Historical and the wide-ranging National. The city is best known, however, for its lively beaches, including Copacabana, and the more upmarket Ipanema. At night, the bars, clubs and discos of Rio resound to jazz and rock. There are samba shows primarily for tourists as well as more authentic dancehalls. A particularly popular time to visit is during the spectacular Mardi Gras Carnaval, in February or March.

View from Sugar Loaf Mountain, Rio de Janeiro

Rome, Italy

Map page 25

The historic capital of the Roman Empire, of Latin Christendom and now of Italy, Rome is exceptionally rich in treasures from many eras. Ancient buildings include the Colosseum, the Arch of Constantine, Trajan's Column, the Roman Forum and the Pantheon. Among the early Christian sites are the famous catacombs and the basilicas of Santa Maria Maggiore and San Giovanni in Laterano (near the Colosseum). Michelangelo's Piazza del Campidoglio – bordered by three palaces – is a fine example of Renaissance town planning, but Rome is known more for its Baroque buildings and squares, and landmarks such as the Trevi Fountain and the Spanish Steps. In the centre of Rome, the Vatican City is the world's smallest independent state, containing St Peter's Square, St Peter's Basilica, the Sistine Chapel and ten museums. Increased pedestrianization of the centre has made it easier to enjoy the exuberant street life for which the city is famous.

St Petersburg, Russia

Map page 26

Situated in the Neva River delta, St Petersburg is a city of canals, bridges and elegant architecture. Founded in 1703 by Peter the Great, its oldest landmark is the massive Peter-Paul Fortress, with the slender spire of the Cathedral of St Peter and St Paul rising above it. At the heart of the city is Palace Square, dominated by the pastel-coloured façade of the Winter Palace. The palace is part of the Hermitage Museum, which contains one of the world's greatest collections of European art. Along the Nevsky Prospekt are the former homes of many famous Russians as well as several palaces, department stores, theatres, restaurants, churches and the richly decorated Kazan Cathedral. Day trips can be taken to several summer palaces, among them Pushkin and Petrodvorets.

San Francisco, California, USA

Map page 25

One of the USA's most spectacular cities, San Francisco's trademarks are its elegant suspension bridges (Golden Gate and Oakland Bay Bridge) and the street cars that service the steep streets. It is also famous as America's gay capital, the main focus of the gay community being the Castro district. The city has a thriving Chinatown, and its North Beach area (between Russian and Telegraph hills) has long been associated with alternative culture. The northern waterfront includes the famous and crowded Fisherman's Wharf development, with its numerous restaurants. The Golden Gate Park is home to several specialist gardens, art galleries and museums. A boat takes visitors to Alcatraz, the notorious island prison.

Santiago, Chile

Map page 26

Santiago is a sprawling city set on a wide plain at the foot of the Andes. However, its central area is relatively compact, and its tree-lined streets and landscaped parks are pleasant to explore on foot, with diversions to the Museum of Pre-Colombian Art in the Real Casa de Aduana and the Santiago Museum, close to the cathedral. A funicular goes to the peak of San Cristóbal and the Pablo Neruda Museum. Day trips can be made to the beaches of Valparaiso and the ski resort of Valle Nevado.

São Paulo, Brazil

Map page 26

Although much of São Paulo is modern, the area around the central square (Praça da Sé) contains several interesting old buildings, such as the whitewashed Palácio do Colégio, (a 19th-century replica of Baroque buildings), the Igreja de Santo Antônio and the Solar da Marquesa de Santos. The city has plenty of nightlife and a varied cuisine, some of its best bars and restaurants being in the suburb known as the Jardins. The nearby Parque do Ibirapuera is a centre for sporting activities and home to several of the city's museums, as well as providing a haven of peace in its 'reading woods'.

Seattle, Washington, USA

The sparkling skyscrapers of downtown Seattle, including the trademark 'flying saucer' of the Space Needle, rise from the shores of Elliott Bay against the spectacular backdrop of the snowy peak of Mount Rainier. A recent surge in the city's prosperity (Seattle is home to the Microsoft Corporation) has led to much new building and the restoration of the historic centre. The city is a centre for contemporary arts and music, the embodiment of which is the high-tech Experience Music Project building. It also contains the headquarters of the Boeing Corporation, whose out-of-town Museum of Flight is a popular attraction.

Seoul, South Korea

Map page 26

Secret Garden of palace of Ch'angdok , Seoul

Selected as the site of the ruling dynasty's capital in 1394, Seoul today consists of a series of linked districts, each with its own centre. The National Assembly and financial institutions are on the small island of Youido. Spread around the old centre is a series of royal palaces, the best preserved of which is Ch'angdok, with its Secret Garden of wooded hills and ponds. T'apkol Park is a good place to meet the locals, while Namsan Park is home to the Botanic Gardens, and also to Seoul Tower, which provides a fine view of the city.

Shanghai, China

Map page 27

Rapidly regaining its status as a major trading and commercial centre, Shanghai's colonial past is clearly visible in the massive 1920s Neoclassical buildings of its waterfront trading area, famous as 'The Bund'. The maze of narrow streets in the Old City and the crowded bazaar of Yuyuan Park provide a complete contrast. Chinese culture is celebrated in the impressive collection of paintings, ceramics, calligraphy, and sculpture in the new Shanghai Museum. Just 80 km (50 miles) away are the famous city gardens of Suzhou, some of which are over 1,000 years old.

Singapore City, Singapore

Map page 27

Singapore is a popular 'stopover' city because it is relatively compact, has an efficient infrastructure and its shopping malls are a source of bargains. Amid the high-rise developments are colonial, Chinese, Malay and Indian enclaves that have retained their character, and some fine historic buildings, such as Coleman's Parliament building, the Buddhist Temple of Heavenly Happiness (Thian Hock Keng Temple) and the colourful Sri Mariamman Hindu Temple. On the riverside are the restored old shops of Boat and Clarke Quays, both of which are relatively lively nightspots. To the south a cable car and causeway go to the island of Sentosa, which has beaches and attractions such as the impressive Underwater World, while to the north is the well-designed zoo, which features a night safari park. To the west attractions include the Jurong Bird Park and Tang Dynasty City.

Stockholm, Sweden

Map page 28

Built on 14 islands, between Lake Mälaren and the Baltic Sea, Stockholm is a beautiful city with numerous parks. It has an essentially modern feel, with many fine 20th-century buildings, although there is still a medieval Old Town (Gamla Stan), with narrow streets and a 15th-century cathedral (Storkyrkan). A ferry goes to Drottningholm – the royal family's island castle, complete with lakeside gardens and an 18th-century theatre. The island of Djurgarden is home to an open-air museum of Swedish vernacular architecture (Skansen) and the cathedral-like building that covers the *Vasa* – a beautifully restored 17th-century warship.

Sydney, NSW, Australia

Map page 28

Australia's oldest and largest city is built around a beautiful harbour that is both a major port and recreational area. Best known for its sail-shaped opera house and striking steel-arched harbour bridge, Sydney also has excellent beaches such as Manly, which can be reached by ferry, and the famous Bondi. In the centre, ferries and harbour cruises set out from Circular Quay, near which is The Rocks, with a restored historic quarter. Another area of waterside redevelopment is Darling Harbour, not far from which is the bustling Sydney Fish Market. Away from the harbour, inner suburbs worth visiting include Glebe, Newtown and Paddington, each with a distinct character and attractive 19th-century terraced houses. With an exciting mix of Asian and European cultures, the city offers a cosmopolitan choice of restaurants, theatres and music. The many museums and art galleries include the Australian Museum, which has a gallery devoted to Aboriginal history. A day trip can be made by train to the spectacular Blue Mountains only 80 km (50 miles) away.

Opera House, Sydney

Tehran, Iran

Map page 30

Most visitors to Tehran concentrate on its excellent museums. The National Museum and the Golestan Palace Museum house many ancient objects, including those taken from famous sites such as Persepolis. The Museum of Glass and Ceramics is well designed and organized, and the Reza Abbasis Museum displays Islamic art. For those willing to brave the heat and noise, Iran has an extensive bazaar.

Tianjin, China

Map page 30

The centre of Tianjin, for decades an important trading port, is a mixture of international architectural styles – British, French, German and Japanese – from the late 19th century. The Ancient Culture Street, a major draw for visitors, is an attempt to re-create the feel of ancient China. For a more authentic experience of Chinese culture, it is worth going to the Antiques Market and taking a walk through the Hai River Park.

Tokyo, Japan

Map page 29

Visitors to Tokyo, faced with a vast urban sprawl, normally work outwards from the Imperial Palace and the surrounding gardens, which contain the remains of Edo Castle. Immediately to the east is the downtown area, with a wide choice of restaurants and shops and some fine examples of modern architecture, including the Tokyo International Forum, with a 60 m (200 ft) high glass atrium. To the west is the Meiji Shrine, set in attractive gardens. The city centre has many art galleries, exhibiting both Japanese and European art. However, many of the largest museums, including the Tokyo National Museum, are further north, in Ueno. The adjacent Asakusa district reveals a more tranquil world of wooden houses, temples and shrines, including the magnificent temple of Senso-ji.

Toronto, Ontario, Canada

Map page 30

Standing on the shore of Lake Ontario, Toronto is Canada's leading commercial city. In its centre is the tallest free-standing structure in the world: the CN Tower. Glass-fronted lifts transport visitors to the Space Deck, 442 m (1,400 ft high), from where it is possible to see as far as Niagara Falls. The city's museums include the Royal Ontario Museum and the Gallery of Inuit Art. Along the waterfront an area of old warehouses has been developed as the Harbourfront Park, with hotels, theatres, shops and restaurants. Toronto's large immigrant population has helped create a vibrant city culture, with a thriving music scene.

Vancouver, British Columbia, Canada

Built around a natural harbour, Vancouver is a major port and city of inlets and green spaces, set against a mountain backdrop. The downtown area contains a cluster of sparkling, glass-fronted skyscrapers. Vancouver has a thriving Chinatown and a dynamic artistic and musical scene that encompasses classical, jazz and rock music. Of the many museums, the Museum of Anthropology is the finest. Stanley Park – a peninsula containing a large area of semi-wilderness – has three of Vancouver's many city beaches and the Vancouver Aquarium. Nearby is Vancouver Island, with its rainforest and glacial mountain peaks.

Varanasi, India

Built on the banks of the sacred River Ganges, Varanasi is famous for the flights of stone steps (ghats), lining 5 km (3 miles) of the river banks, where Hindu pilgrims bathe in the waters and cremate their dead. The old town consists of a maze of narrow alleyways at the heart of which is the Golden Temple, dedicated to the god Shiva. The city is also sacred for Buddhists, and at nearby Sarnath there is a collection of restored temples.

Venice, Italy

Distant view of Church of Santa Maria delle Salute, Venice

Built on a collection of islands and criss-crossed by 177 canals, Venice is a city like no other, where boats are the only means of transport. A journey by gondola or vaporetto along the Grand Canal passes many grand palaces, including the Gothic Ca' d'Oro and Ca' Foscari, the Renaissance Palazzo Grimani and the Baroque Rezzonico. The familiar landmark of the Rialto Bridge presides over the busiest shopping area in Venice. Around St Mark's Square is the stunning 11th-century Byzantine Basilica, the Pala d'Oro, and the Doge's Palace. A lift to the top of the towering Campanile provides exceptional views over the city and the lagoon, across which lies the Lido, with beaches and hotels. The Accademia contains the world's most comprehensive collection of Venetian art, including paintings by Titian, while the Peggy Guggenheim collection is one of the most important of 20th-century art outside the USA.

Vienna, Austria

Map page 31

Formerly the capital of the Habsburg and Austro-Hungarian empires, today's Vienna preserves an atmosphere of historic grandeur. A city of cafés, beer cellars, parks and elegant boulevards, it has a centre, the Innere Stadt, that is sufficiently compact to be explored on foot. It contains numerous Baroque churches and palaces, the magnificent Gothic St Stephen's Cathedral, and the Hofburg – the Habsburgs' imperial palace, which is now home to the famous Spanish Riding School. Among the city's many museums are the Kunsthistorisches (Art History Museum), with an unrivalled collection of paintings by Peter Breugel the Elder, and the fine 18th-century Belvedere palace complex which features paintings by Klimt and Schiele among others. Outside the centre is Schönbrunn, the Habsburgs' impressive summer palace, and the Prater (in Leopoldstadt), a vast park featuring Vienna's giant ferris wheel. To the north the hills of Kahlenberg and Leopoldsberg provide magnificent views over the city.

Warsaw, Poland

Map page 31

The old centre of Warsaw, on the left bank of the River Vistula, was reduced to rubble during World War II, but it has been meticulously rebuilt and is now a UNESCO World Heritage site. All the buildings appear to date from the 18th century or earlier. They include St John's Cathedral and the Renaissance and Baroque merchants' houses surrounding the Old Market Square (Rynek Starego Miasta). There is also the excellent Historical Museum of Warsaw, many lively cafés and some fine restaurants. Outside the Old Town is the beautiful Lazienki park and palace complex and, 6 km (4 miles) further south, the restored Baroque Wilanów park and palace.

Washington DC, USA

Map page 32

The main public buildings of Washington DC are grouped on and around the National Mall – a broad swathe of parkland containing the Washington Monument, the Lincoln and Jefferson memorials, and the V-shaped polished black stone wall incised with thousands of names, which commemorates the Americans who fell in Vietnam. On the north side of the Mall is the White House, and overlooking all from the eastern end is the Capitol building, with its 55 m (180 ft) high rotunda. Home to the House of Representatives and the Senate, it is open to visitors. The National Gallery of Art and the National Air and Space Museum are two of the many museums. Central Washington DC can be dangerous at night. Georgetown is more relaxed, with its restaurants, bars and handsome streets. Within easy reach of the city are Chesapeake Bay and several Civil War battle sites.

Wellington, New Zealand

Map page 32

Overlooked by Mount Victoria, Wellington is the political and commercial capital of New Zealand. Wooden Victorian houses climb the steep hills surrounding the magnificent harbour of Port Nicholson, and a cable car provides a spectacular view of the city. Among the historic buildings in the centre are the Old Government Buildings, while the city's museums include the recently opened Museum of New Zealand (Te Papa). A lively, cosmopolitan city, Wellington has an exciting cultural scene, as evidenced in February and March by the annual Fringe Festival and the biennial International Festival of the Arts.

View over the harbour, Wellington

Xi'an, China

As well as being a base from which to visit the famous Army of Terracotta Warriors, Xi'an possesses its own historic sites. These include the impressive city walls that all but surround the old town, and the 64 m (200 ft) high Big Goose Pagoda. Xi'an also has a strong Islamic culture and its Great Mosque is the largest in China. The Shaanxi Provincial Museum presents a fascinating history of the Silk Road.

Yangon (Rangoon), Burma (Myanmar)

The main focus of any visit to Yangon will be the magnificent Shwedagon stupa. The stupa is 90 m (290 ft) high and shaped like a bell. Completely covered in gold, it is surrounded by a host of smaller gilded stupas, statues, temples and pavilions. Of the many other Buddhist sites around the city, the huge reclining Buddha at Chaukhtatgyi Paya is the most impressive. Two large lakes provide areas of recreation, and the many tree-lined streets and areas of near-jungle give some parts an almost rural feel.

WORLD MAPS

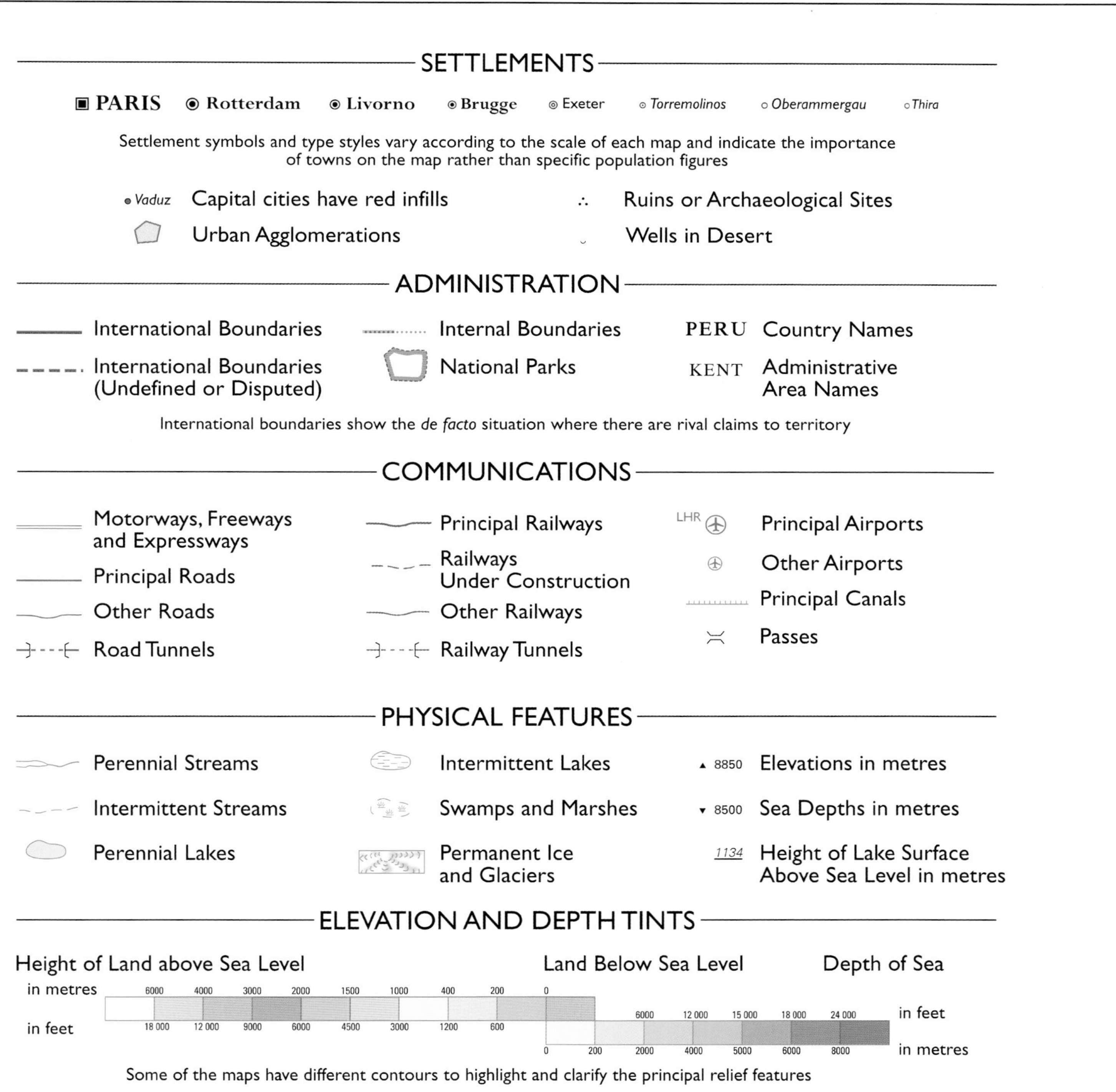
SETTLEMENTS
PARIS
Rotterdam
Livorno
Brugge
Exeter
Torremolinos
Oberammergau
Thira
Settlement symbols and type styles vary according to the scale of each map and indicate the importance of towns on the map rather than specific population figures
Vaduz
Capital cities have red infills
Urban Agglomerations
Ruins or Archaeological Sites
Wells in Desert
ADMINISTRATION
International Boundaries
International Boundaries (Undefined or Disputed)
Internal Boundaries
National Parks
PERU
Country Names
KENT
Administrative Area Names
International boundaries show the de facto situation where there are rival claims to territory
COMMUNICATIONS
Motorways, Freeways and Expressways
Principal Roads
Other Roads
Road Tunnels
Principal Railways
Railways Under Construction
Other Railways
Railway Tunnels
LHR
Principal Airports
Other Airports
Principal Canals
Passes
PHYSICAL FEATURES
Perennial Streams
Intermittent Streams
Perennial Lakes
Intermittent Lakes
Swamps and Marshes
Permanent Ice and Glaciers
8850
Elevations in metres
8500
Sea Depths in metres
1134
Height of Lake Surface Above Sea Level in metres
ELEVATION AND DEPTH TINTS
Height of Land above Sea Level
in metres
6000
4000
3000
2000
1500
1000
400
200
0
in feet
18 000
12 000
9000
6000
4500
3000
1200
600
Land Below Sea Level
Depth of Sea
6000
12 000
15 000
18 000
24 000
in feet
0
200
2000
4000
5000
6000
8000
in metres
Some of the maps have different contours to highlight and clarify the principal relief features

THE WORLD : Political

Equatorial Scale 1:84 000 000

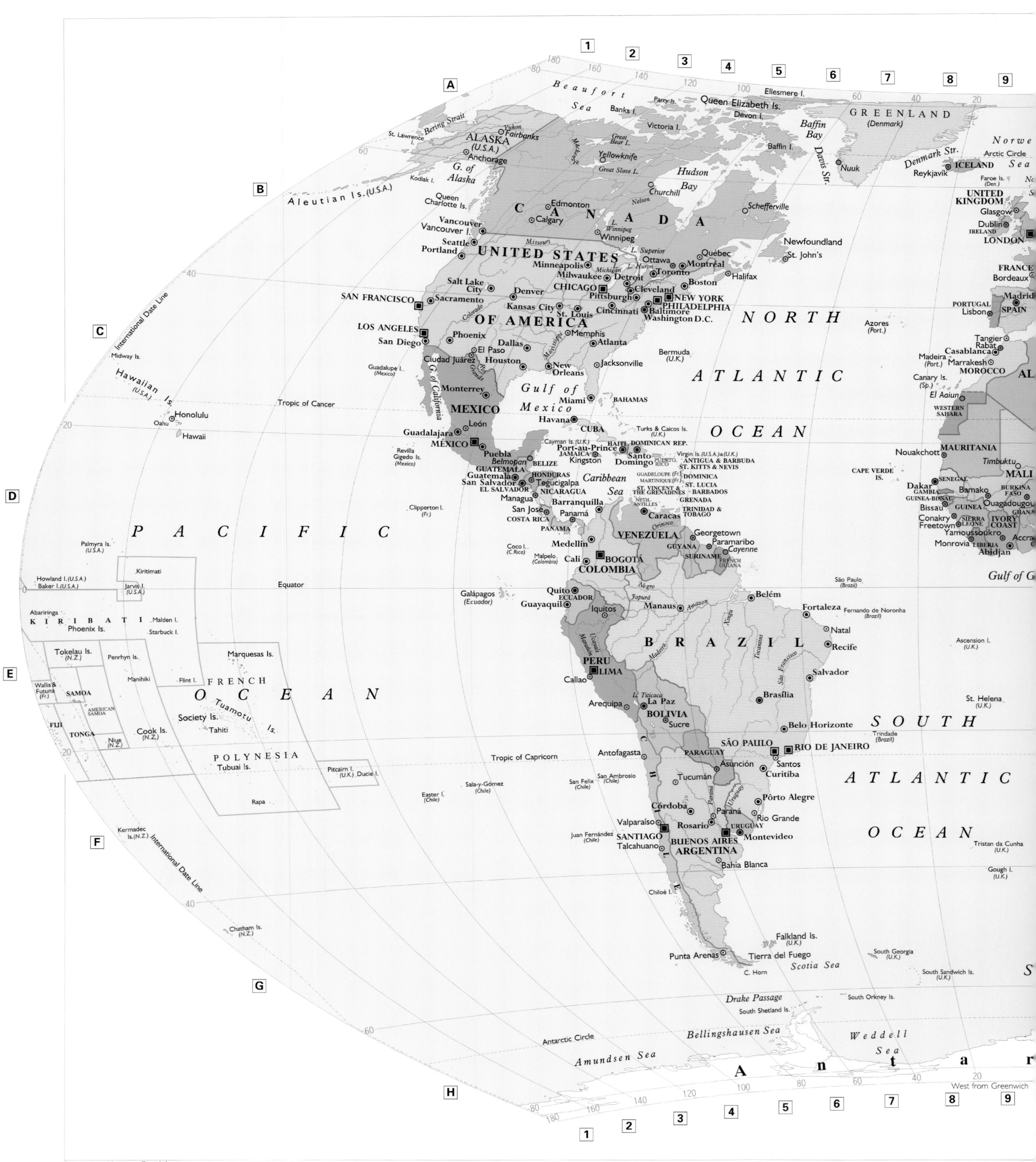

Projection: Hammer Equal Area

Hanoi ◉ Capital Cities

4 ARCTIC OCEAN

100 0 200 400 600 800 1000 1200 1400 km

1:31 100 000

100 0 200 400 600 800 1000 miles

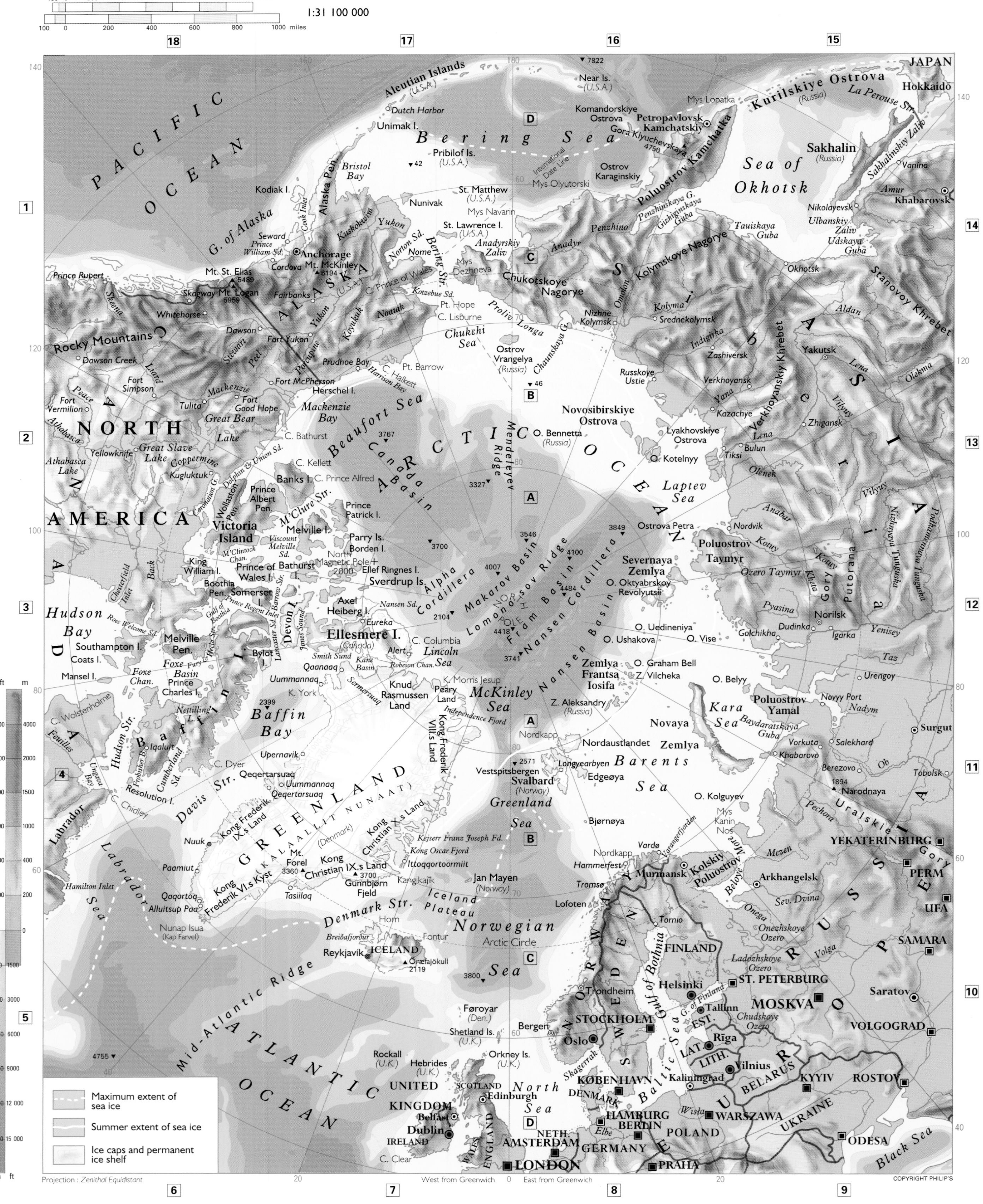

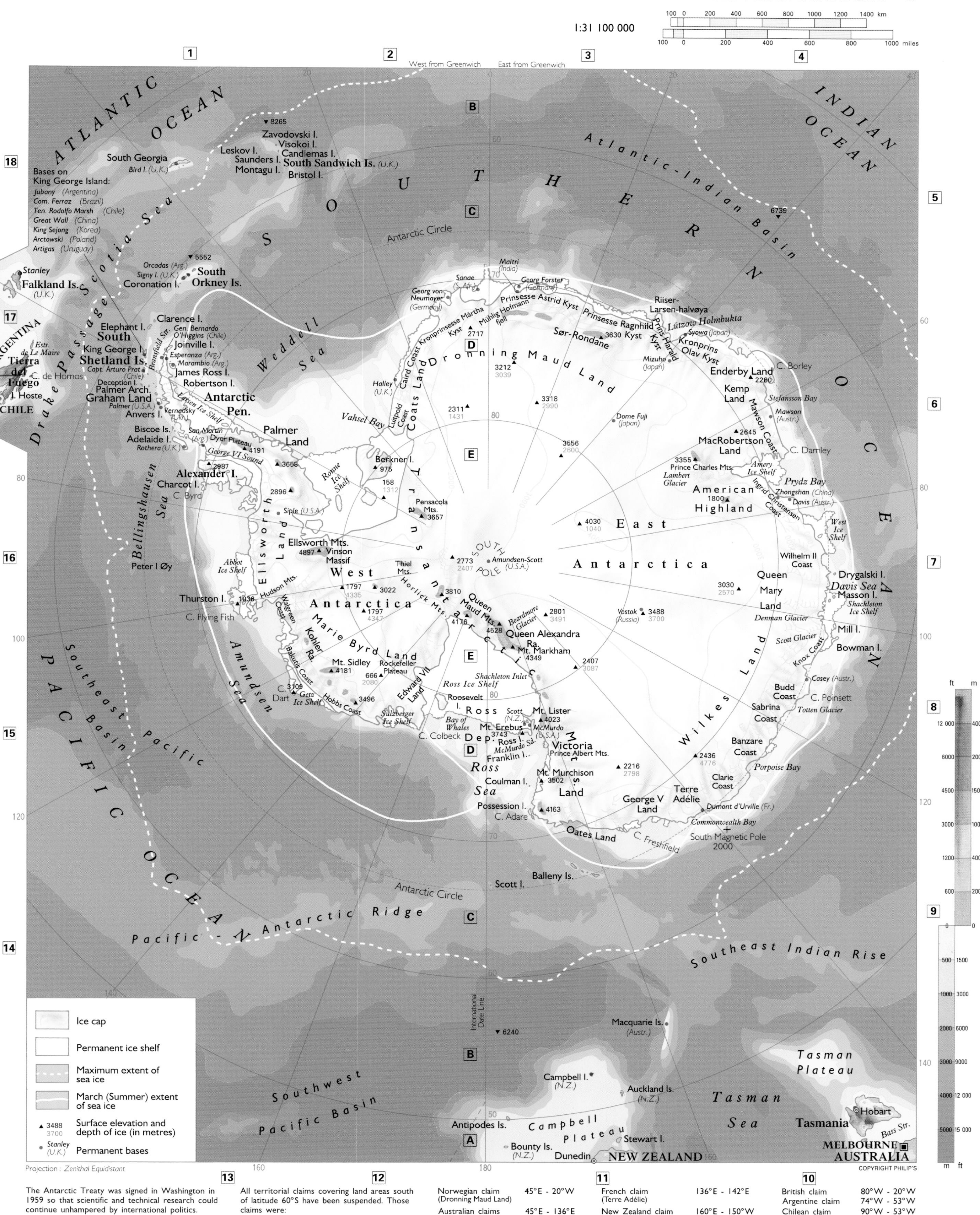

The Antarctic Treaty was signed in Washington in 1959 so that scientific and technical research could continue unhampered by international politics.

All territorial claims covering land areas south of latitude 60°S have been suspended. Those claims were:

Norwegian claim (Dronning Maud Land)	45°E - 20°W
Australian claims	45°E - 136°E 142°E - 160°E
French claim (Terre Adélie)	136°E - 142°E
New Zealand claim (Ross Dependency)	160°E - 150°W
British claim	80°W - 20°W
Argentine claim	74°W - 53°W
Chilean claim	90°W - 53°W

1:17 800 000

Norwegian Sea
North Sea
ATLANTIC OCEAN
Bay of Biscay
Mediterranean Sea
Black Sea
Caspian Sea
Baltic Sea
Adriatic Sea
Ionian Sea
Tyrrhenian Sea
Aegean Sea
Ligurian Sea
Celtic Sea
English Channel
Irish Sea
White Sea
Sea of Azov
Ural Mountains
Caspian Depression
Volga Hts.
Central Russian Uplands
North European Plain
Scandinavia
Lapland
Finland
Ukraine
Carpathians
Alps
Apennines
Pyrenees
Iberian Peninsula
Massif Central
Caucasus
Balkans
Dinaric Alps
Pindus
Anatolia (Asia Minor)
Taurus Mts.
Pontine Mts.
Armenia
Kurdistan
Mesopotamia
Iceland
British Isles
Great Britain
Ireland
Corsica
Sardinia
Sicily
Crete
Cyprus
Africa
Plateau of the Shotts
COPYRIGHT PHILIP'S
Projection: Bonne
Sea areas named in weather forecasts

1:31 100 000

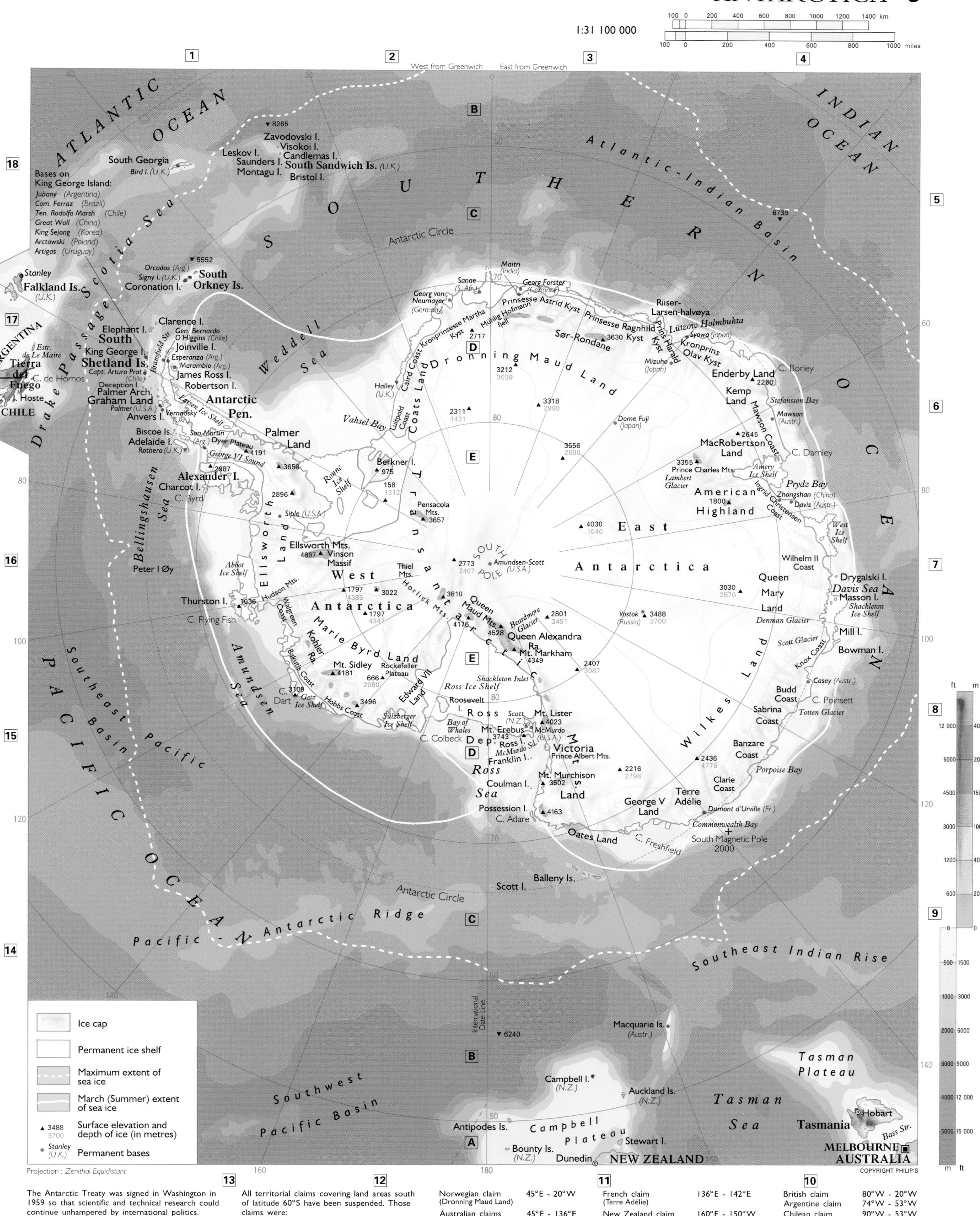

Projection: Zenithal Equidistant

The Antarctic Treaty was signed in Washington in 1959 so that scientific and technical research could continue unhampered by international politics.

All territorial claims covering land areas south of latitude 60°S have been suspended. Those claims were:

Norwegian claim (Dronning Maud Land)	45°E - 20°W	French claim (Terre Adélie)	136°E - 142°E
Australian claims	45°E - 136°E 142°E - 160°E	New Zealand claim (Ross Dependency)	160°E - 150°W
British claim	80°W - 20°W		
Argentine claim	74°W - 53°W		
Chilean claim	90°W - 53°W		

EUROPE : Physical

100 0 100 200 300 400 500 600 700 800 km

1:17 800 000

100 0 100 200 300 400 500 miles

Projection: Bonne

West from Greenwich 0 East from Greenwich

Sea areas named in weather forecasts

m 5000 4000 2000 1000 400 200 0 -200 -1000 -2000 -4000

ft 15 000 12 000 6000 3000 1200 600 0 -600 -3000 -6000 -12 000

1:17 800 000

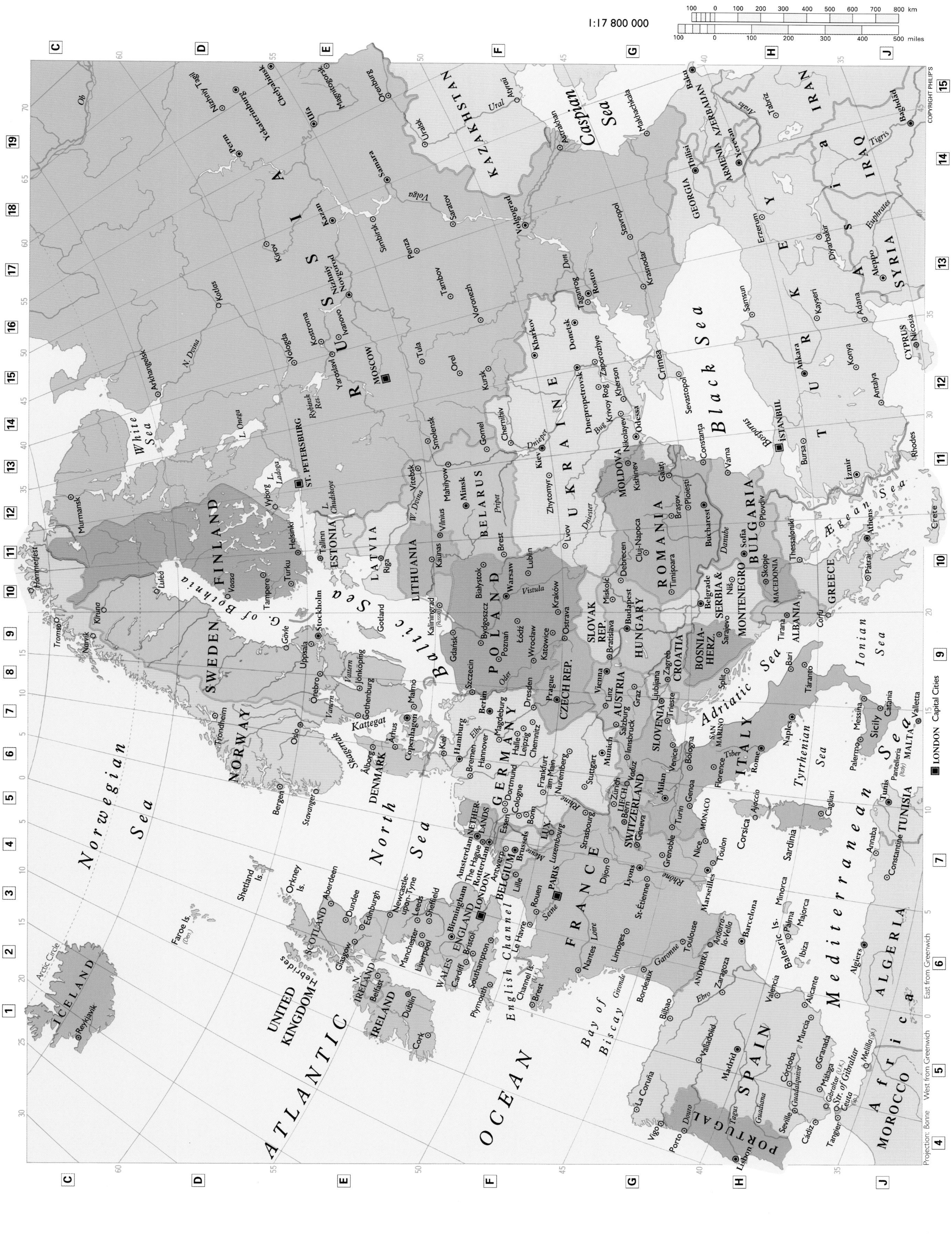

100 0 100 200 300 400 500 600 700 800 km
100 0 100 200 300 400 500 miles
ICELAND
Reykjavik
Norwegian Sea
NORWAY
SWEDEN
FINLAND
DENMARK
UNITED KINGDOM
IRELAND
ATLANTIC OCEAN
North Sea
Baltic Sea
G. of Bothnia
White Sea
ESTONIA
LATVIA
LITHUANIA
BELARUS
POLAND
GERMANY
NETHERLANDS
BELGIUM
LUX.
FRANCE
SWITZERLAND
AUSTRIA
CZECH REP.
SLOVAK REP.
HUNGARY
SLOVENIA
CROATIA
BOSNIA-HERZ.
SERBIA & MONTENEGRO
MACEDONIA
ALBANIA
GREECE
BULGARIA
ROMANIA
MOLDOVA
UKRAINE
RUSSIA
KAZAKHSTAN
GEORGIA
ARMENIA
AZERBAIJAN
TURKEY
IRAN
IRAQ
SYRIA
CYPRUS
ITALY
SPAIN
PORTUGAL
ANDORRA
MONACO
SAN MARINO
MALTA
MOROCCO
ALGERIA
TUNISIA
Africa
Bay of Biscay
English Channel
Mediterranean Sea
Tyrrhenian Sea
Ionian Sea
Adriatic Sea
Ægean Sea
Black Sea
Caspian Sea
MOSCOW
ST. PETERSBURG
LONDON
PARIS
■ LONDON Capital Cities
Projection: Bonne
West from Greenwich
East from Greenwich
COPYRIGHT PHILIP'S

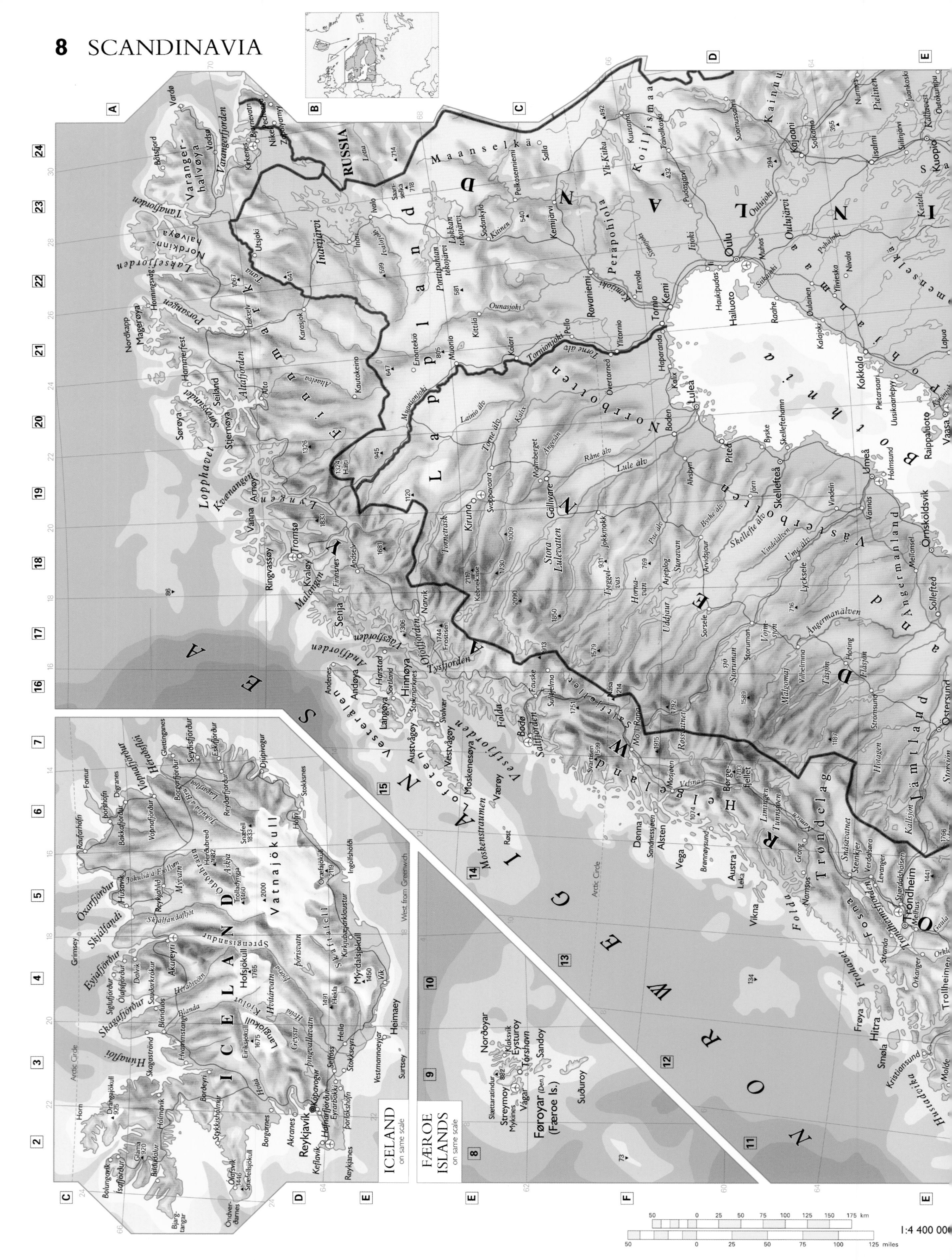
RUSSIA
FINLAND
NORWAY
NORWEGIAN SEA
Lappland
Norrbotten
Västerbotten
ICELAND
Vatnajökull
ICELAND
on same scale
FÆROE ISLANDS
on same scale
Føroyar (Den.)
(Færoe Is.)
Tórshavn
Reykjavík
Akureyri
Tromsø
Narvik
Bodø
Trondheim
Kiruna
Gällivare
Luleå
Umeå
Oulu
Kemi
Kajaani
Kuopio
Kokkola
Vaasa
Östersund
Hammerfest
Nordkapp
Kirkenes
Vardø
Lofoten
Vesterålen
Senja
Hinnøya
Lyngen
Lofothavet
Vestfjorden
Moskenstraumen
Trøndelag
Jämtland
Ångermanland
Finnmarksvidda
Maanselkä
Kainuu
Koillismaa
Pohjanmaa
Arctic Circle
West from Greenwich
1:4 400 000
50 0 25 50 75 100 125 150 175 km
50 0 25 50 75 100 125 miles

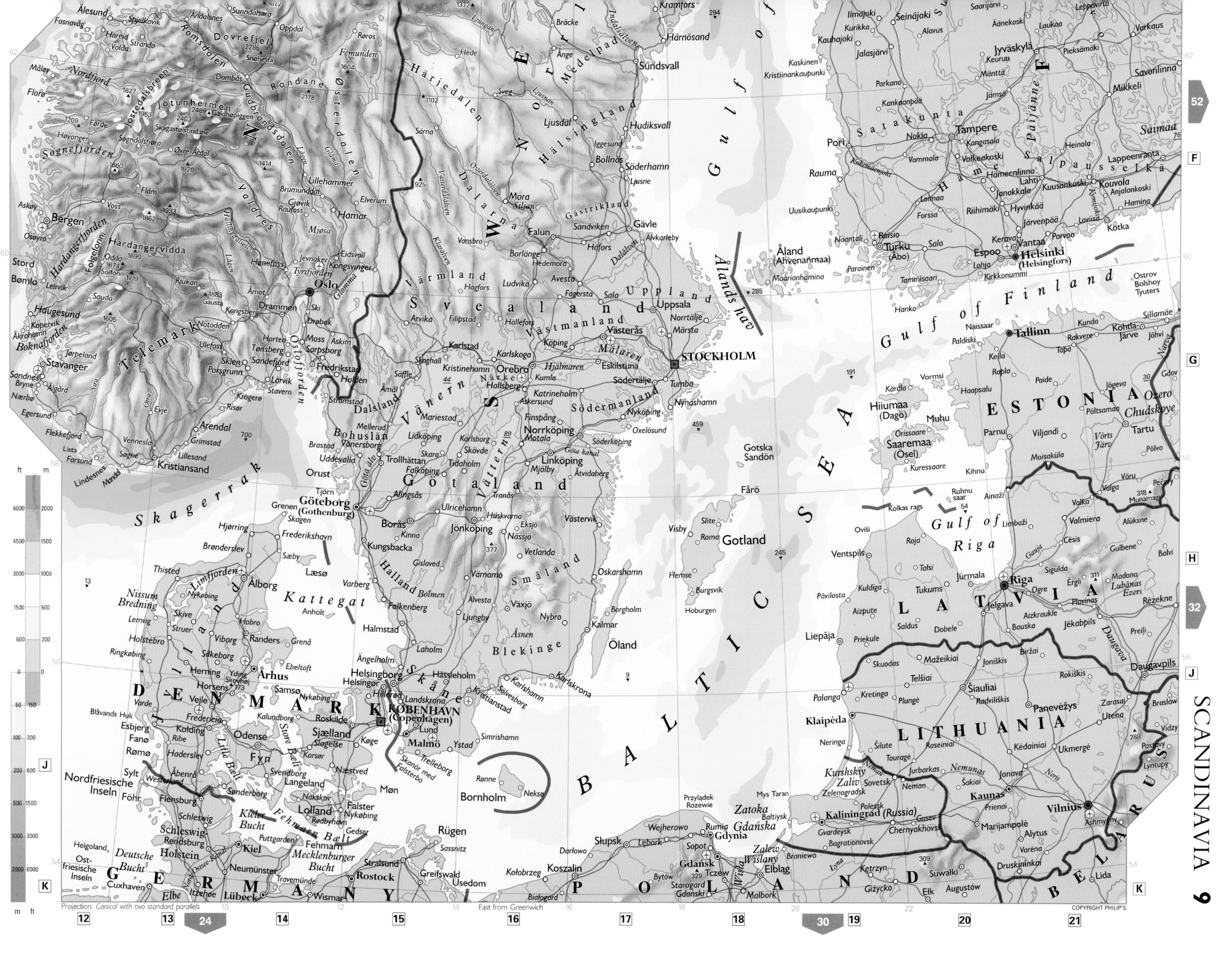

Gulf of Bothnia
Gulf of Finland
Gulf of Riga
BALTIC SEA
Ålands hav
Skagerrak
Kattegat
FINLAND
ESTONIA
LATVIA
LITHUANIA
DENMARK
NORWAY
SWEDEN
POLAND
GERMANY
RUSSIA
BELARUS
Helsinki (Helsingfors)
Tallinn
Riga
Vilnius
STOCKHOLM
Oslo
KØBENHAVN (Copenhagen)
Göteborg (Gothenburg)
Bergen
Stavanger
Kristiansand
Tampere
Turku (Åbo)
Tartu
Kaunas
Kaliningrad (Russia)
Klaipėda
Liepāja
Gdańsk
Gdynia
Malmö
Århus
Odense
Uppsala
Västerås
Örebro
Norrköping
Linköping
Jönköping
Kalmar
Karlskrona
Gotland
Öland
Bornholm
Fyn
Sjælland
Lolland
Falster
Rügen
Hiiumaa (Dagö)
Saaremaa (Ösel)
Åland (Ahvenanmaa)
Vänern
Vättern
Mälaren
Saimaa
Päijänne
Hardangervidda
Jotunheimen
Telemark
Dalarna
Värmland
Småland
Skåne
Svealand
Götaland
Lübeck
Kiel
Rostock
Flensburg
Deutsche Bucht
Nordfriesische Inseln
Projection: Conical with two standard parallels
East from Greenwich
COPYRIGHT PHILIP'S
ft m
6000 2000
4500 1500
3000 1000
1500 500
600 200
0 0
50 150
100 300
200 600
500 1500
1000 3000
2000 6000

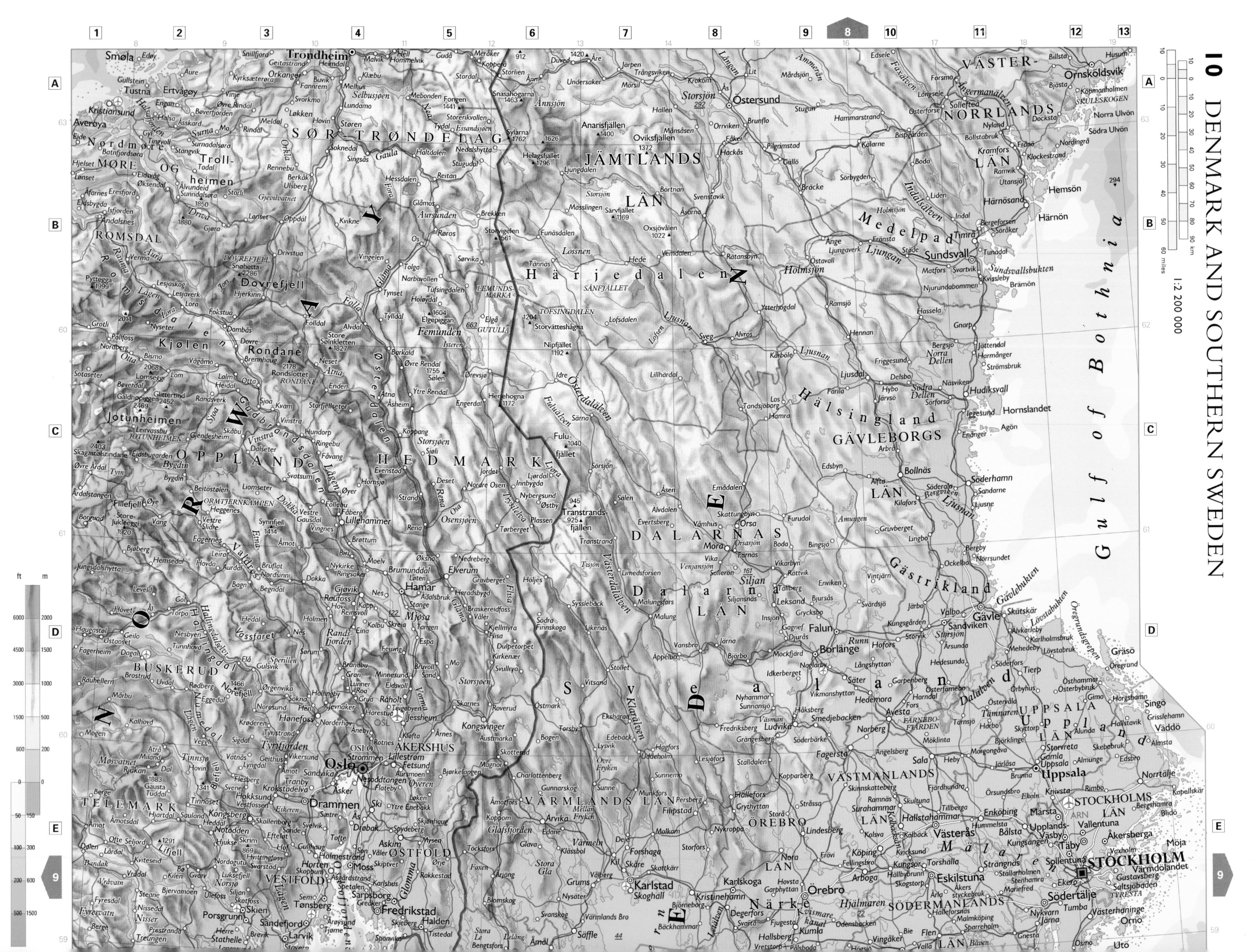
1:2 200 000
km
miles
Gulf of Bothnia
NORWAY
SWEDEN
STOCKHOLM
Oslo
Uppsala
Gävle
Sundsvall
Östersund
Trondheim
Karlstad
Örebro
Västerås
Drammen
Lillehammer
Hamar
JÄMTLANDS LÄN
GÄVLEBORGS LÄN
DALARNAS LÄN
VÄRMLANDS LÄN
ÖREBRO LÄN
UPPSALA LÄN
STOCKHOLMS LÄN
HEDMARK
OPPLAND
BUSKERUD
TELEMARK
AKERSHUS
ØSTFOLD
VESTFOLD
SØR-TRØNDELAG
Jotunheimen
Dovrefjell
Rondane
Siljan
Klarälven
Glomma
Mjøsa
ft
m

Skagerrak
Kattegat
BALTIC SEA
DENMARK
GERMANY
POLAND
Jylland
Sjælland
Fyn
Lolland
Falster
Møn
Bornholm (Denmark)
Götaland
Småland
Skåne
Öland (Sweden)
Gotland (Sweden)
Læsø (Denmark)
Anholt (Denmark)
Samsø
Fehmarn
Sylt
Föhr
Amrum
KØBENHAVN
Göteborg
Malmö
Helsingborg
Jönköping
Norrköping
Linköping
Nyköping
Västervik
Kalmar
Karlskrona
Växjö
Halmstad
Borås
Trollhättan
Uddevalla
Ålborg
Århus
Odense
Esbjerg
Kolding
Vejle
Randers
Silkeborg
Herning
Viborg
Fredericia
Flensburg
Kiel
Visby
Rønne
Kristianstad
Lund
Trelleborg
Ystad
Vänern
Vättern
Bohuslän
Dalsland
ÖSTERGÖTLANDS LÄN
VÄSTRA GÖTALANDS LÄN
JÖNKÖPINGS LÄN
KRONOBERGS LÄN
KALMAR LÄN
BLEKINGE LÄN
SKÅNE LÄN
HALLANDS LÄN
GOTLANDS LÄN
NORDJYLLANDS AMT.
VIBORG AMT.
ÅRHUS AMT.
RINGKØBING AMT.
VEJLE AMT.
RIBE AMT.
SØNDERJYLLANDS AMT.
FYNS AMT.
VESTSJÆLLANDS AMT.
STORSTRØMS AMT.
FREDERIKSBORG AMT.
ROSKILDE AMT.
KØBENHAVNS AMT.
BORNHOLMS AMT.
AUST-AGDER
Arendal
Kalmarsund
Hanöbukten
Øresund
Store Bælt
Lille Bælt
Fehmarn Belt
Bornholmsgattet
Ålborg Bugt
Projection: Lambert's Conformal Conic
East from Greenwich
COPYRIGHT PHILIP'S
National Parks
24
30
11

1:1 800 000

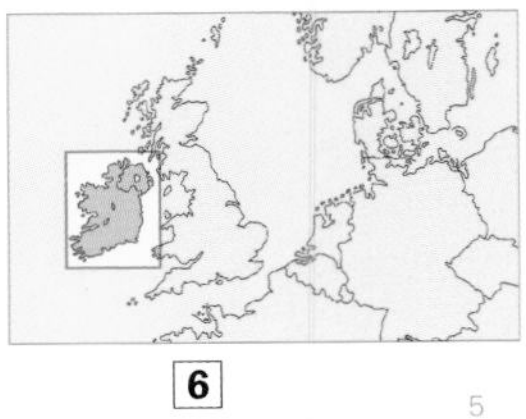

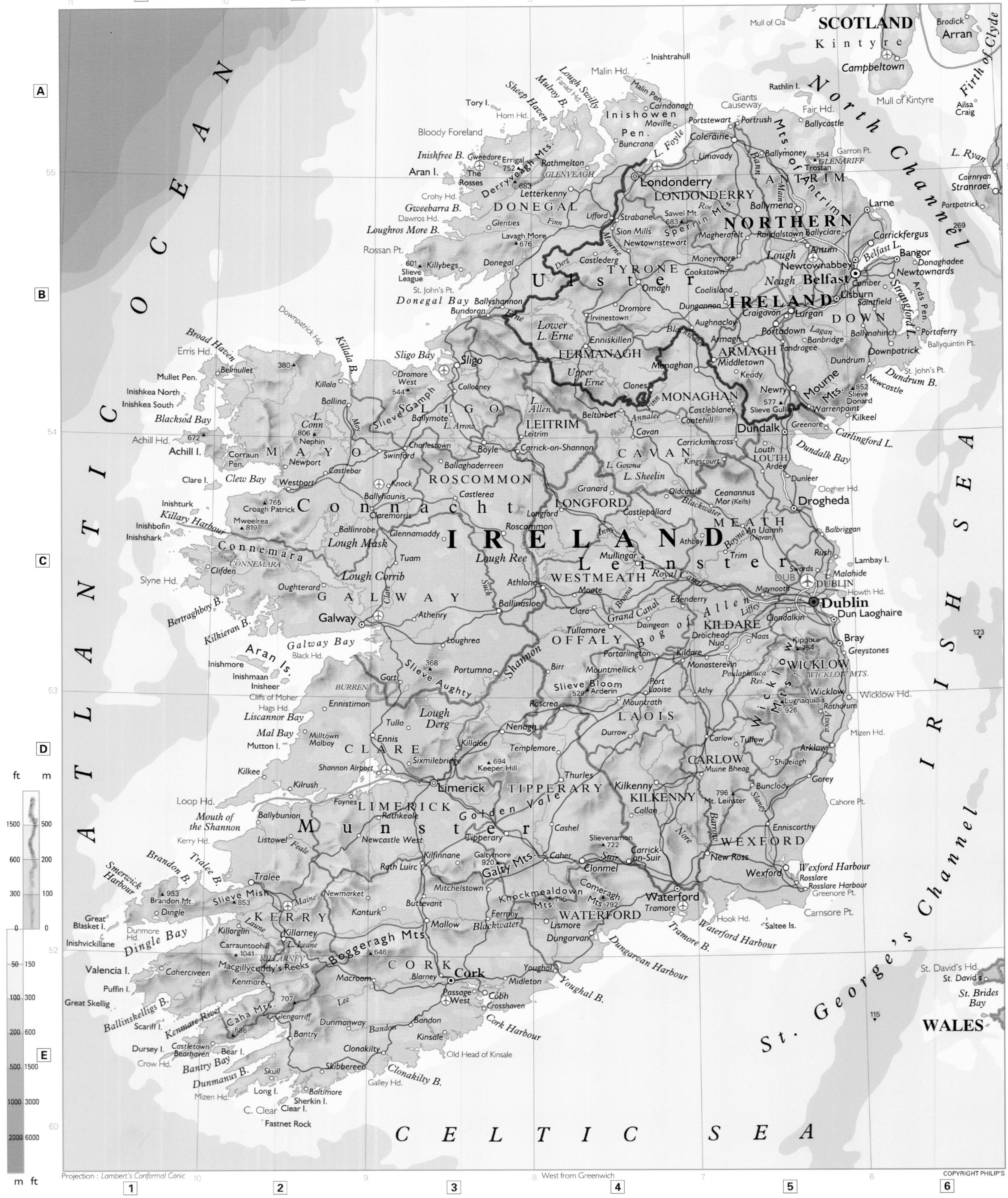

Projection : Lambert's Conformal Conic

West from Greenwich

National Parks

12
14

Forest Parks in Scotland

ENGLAND AND WALES

1:1 800 000

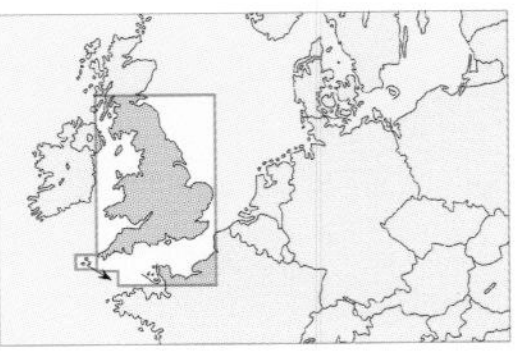

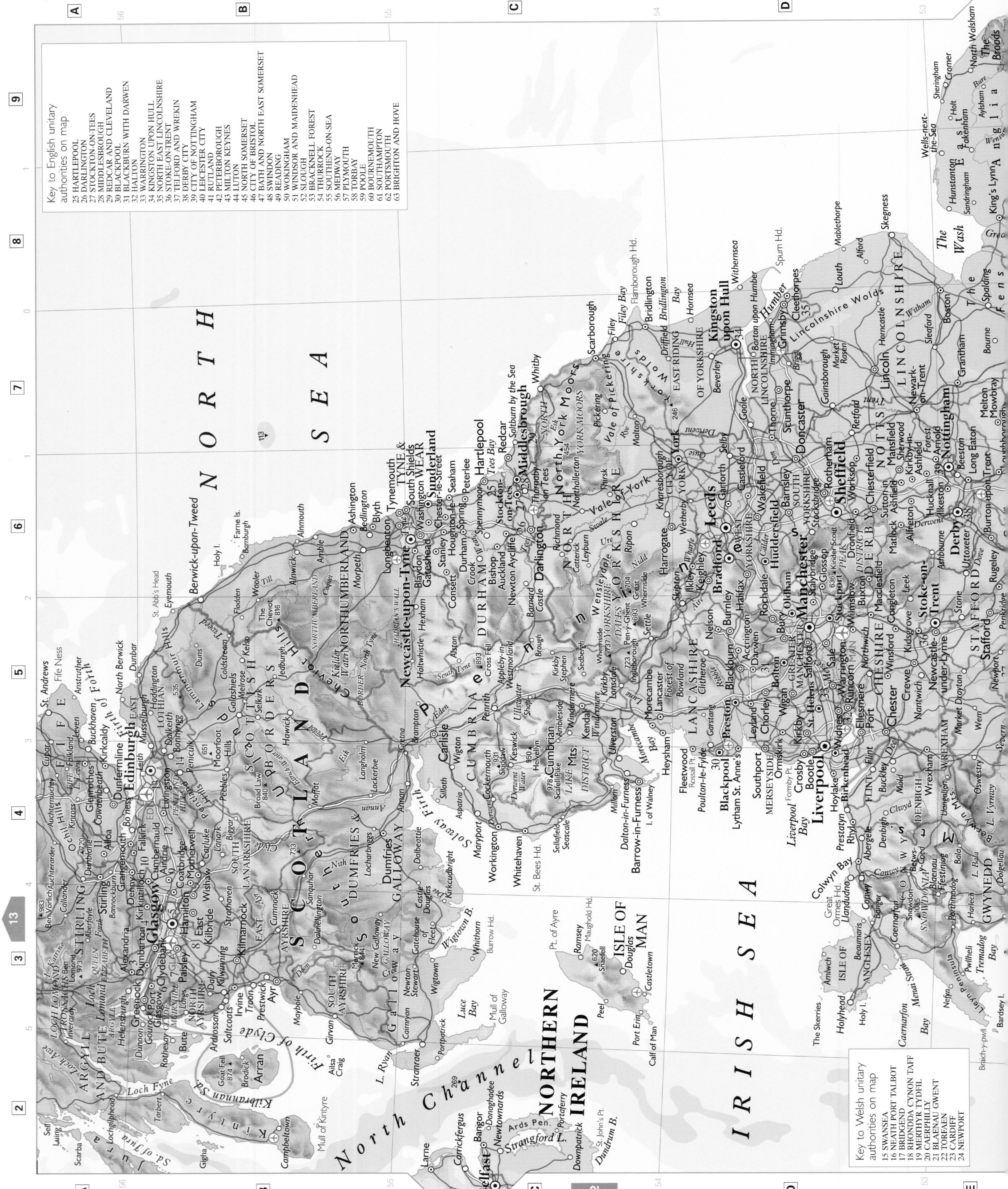
Key to English unitary authorities on map
25 HARTLEPOOL
26 DARLINGTON
27 STOCKTON-ON-TEES
28 MIDDLESBROUGH
29 REDCAR AND CLEVELAND
30 BLACKPOOL
31 BLACKBURN WITH DARWEN
32 HALTON
33 WARRINGTON
34 KINGSTON UPON HULL
35 NORTH EAST LINCOLNSHIRE
36 STOKE-ON-TRENT
37 TELFORD AND WREKIN
38 DERBY CITY
39 CITY OF NOTTINGHAM
40 LEICESTER CITY
41 RUTLAND
42 PETERBOROUGH
43 MILTON KEYNES
44 LUTON
45 NORTH SOMERSET
46 CITY OF BRISTOL
47 BATH AND NORTH EAST SOMERSET
48 SWINDON
49 READING
50 WOKINGHAM
51 WINDSOR AND MAIDENHEAD
52 SLOUGH
53 BRACKNELL FOREST
54 THURROCK
55 SOUTHEND-ON-SEA
56 MEDWAY
57 PLYMOUTH
58 TORBAY
59 POOLE
60 BOURNEMOUTH
61 SOUTHAMPTON
62 PORTSMOUTH
63 BRIGHTON AND HOVE
Key to Welsh unitary authorities on map
15 SWANSEA
16 NEATH PORT TALBOT
17 BRIDGEND
18 RHONDDA CYNON TAFF
19 MERTHYR TYDFIL
20 CAERPHILLY
21 BLAENAU GWENT
22 TORFAEN
23 CARDIFF
24 NEWPORT
NORTH SEA
IRISH SEA
North Channel
NORTHERN IRELAND
ISLE OF MAN
13
12

ENGLAND

WALES

ENGLISH CHANNEL

FRANCE

CHANNEL ISLANDS (U.K.)

ISLES OF SCILLY
on same scale

National Parks in England and Wales

Forest Parks in Scotland

m	ft
1000	3000
500	1500
200	600
100	300
0	0
50	150
100	300
200	600

Projection: Lambert's Conformal Conic

West from Greenwich

East from Greenwich

1:4 400 000
km
miles
Projection: Conical with two standard parallels
East from Greenwich
West from Greenwich
COPYRIGHT PHILIP'S
ATLANTIC OCEAN
NORTH SEA
CELTIC SEA
IRISH SEA
English Channel
St. George's Channel
Bristol Channel
North Channel
North Minch
Pentland Firth
Moray Firth
Firth of Clyde
Cardigan Bay
Str. of Dover
The Wash
UNITED KINGDOM
IRELAND
NORTHERN IRELAND
SCOTLAND
ENGLAND
WALES
FRANCE
NETHERLANDS
BELGIUM
NORWAY
Shetland Is.
Yell
Unst
Fetlar
Mainland
Lerwick
Foula
Fair Isle
Orkney Is.
Westray
Sanday
Stronsay
Kirkwall
Hoy
South Ronaldsay
C. Wrath
Thurso
Wick
Helmsdale
Outer Hebrides
Inner Hebrides
Lewis
Stornoway
Harris
St. Kilda
North Uist
Benbecula
South Uist
Barra
Skye
Portree
Rhum
Eigg
Coll
Tiree
Mull
Colonsay
Jura
Islay
Arran
North West Highlands
Grampian Mts.
Southern Uplands
Cheviot Hills
Pennines
Cambrian Mts.
Cotswold Hills
Wicklow Mts.
Ullapool
Lairg
Golspie
Tain
Invergordon
Dingwall
Inverness
Nairn
Elgin
Buckie
Banff
Fraserburgh
Peterhead
Huntly
Inverurie
Aberdeen
Stonehaven
Ballater
Aviemore
L. Ness
Mallaig
Fort William
Ben Nevis
Tobermory
Oban
Montrose
Arbroath
Forfar
Dundee
Perth
St. Andrews
Glenrothes
Kirkcaldy
L. Lomond
Stirling
Dunfermline
Edinburgh
Dunbar
Greenock
Glasgow
Paisley
East Kilbride
Hamilton
Irvine
Kilmarnock
Ayr
Campbeltown
Galashiels
Jedburgh
Hawick
Berwick-upon-Tweed
Alnwick
Girvan
Dumfries
Stranraer
Kirkcudbright
Annan
Carlisle
Newcastle-upon-Tyne
South Shields
Sunderland
Gateshead
Hexham
Durham
Hartlepool
Redcar
Middlesbrough
Darlington
Stockton-on-Tees
Scarborough
Workington
Whitehaven
Cumbrian Mts.
Barrow-in-Furness
Lancaster
Douglas
I. of Man
Harrogate
York
Bridlington
Beverley
Kingston upon Hull
Leeds
Bradford
Keighley
Burnley
Blackpool
Preston
Blackburn
Bolton
Halifax
Huddersfield
Barnsley
Scunthorpe
Grimsby
Humber
Doncaster
Rotherham
Sheffield
Manchester
Oldham
Stockport
Liverpool
Warrington
Lincoln
Louth
Skegness
Chesterfield
Mansfield
Nottingham
Derby
Crewe
Chester
Stoke on Trent
Stafford
Boston
Grantham
Cromer
King's Lynn
Norwich
Great Yarmouth
Lowestoft
Shrewsbury
Telford
Welshpool
Wolverhampton
BIRMINGHAM
Leicester
Nuneaton
Coventry
Corby
Peterborough
Thetford
Redditch
Rugby
Northampton
Bury St. Edmunds
Ely
Cambridge
Bedford
Ipswich
Felixstowe
Harwich
Colchester
Chelmsford
Worcester
Hereford
Royal Leamington Spa
Milton Keynes
Luton
Stevenage
Hemel Hempstead
Harlow
Cheltenham
Gloucester
Oxford
High Wycombe
Watford
Basildon
Southend-on-Sea
Brecon
Merthyr Tydfil
Neath
Cwmbran
Newport
Rhondda
Cardiff
Bristol
Bath
Swindon
Newbury
Slough
LONDON
Thames
Reading
Chatham
Canterbury
Margate
Maidstone
Dover
Folkestone
Ashford
Guildford
Reigate
Crawley
Basingstoke
Salisbury
Winchester
Southampton
Fareham
Havant
Portsmouth
Brighton
Worthing
Hastings
Eastbourne
Isle of Wight
Newport
Bournemouth
Poole
Weymouth
Yeovil
Taunton
Weston-super-Mare
Exmoor
Barnstaple
Bude
Exeter
Exmouth
Dartmoor
Torbay
Plymouth
Newquay
Truro
St. Austell
Falmouth
Penzance
Land's End
Isles of Scilly
Anglesey
Holyhead
Bangor
Colwyn Bay
Snowdon
Wrexham
Pwllheli
Aberystwyth
Fishguard
Carmarthen
Haverfordwest
Milford Haven
Pembroke
Llanelli
Swansea
Port Talbot
Barry
Malin Hd.
Buncrana
Aran I.
Letterkenny
Coleraine
Londonderry
Ballymena
Larne
Lifford
Antrim
Bangor
Donegal
Lough Neagh
Belfast
Bundoran
Lower L. Erne
Omagh
Lisburn
Portadown
Lurgan
Enniskillen
Armagh
Newry
Sligo
Clones
Ballina
Achill I.
L. Conn
Castlebar
Leitrim
Cavan
Castleblaney
Dundalk
Westport
Connacht
Roscommon
Ceanannus Mor
Drogheda
Lough Mask
Connemara
Longford
Lough Ree
Mullingar
Boyne
Lough Corrib
Athlone
Galway
Galway B.
Aran Is.
Ballinasloe
Tullamore
Liffey
Dublin
Dun Laoghaire
Bray
Birr
Port Laoise
Athy
Ennis
Lough Derg
Nenagh
Carlow
Kilkenny
Leinster
Kilrush
Limerick
Thurles
Arklow
Shannon
Listowel
Tipperary
Tralee
Munster
Clonmel
Carrick-on-Suir
Wexford
Rosslare
Dingle
Carrauntoohill
Macgillycuddy's Reeks
Killarney
Mallow
Blackwater
Waterford
Dungarvan
Valencia I.
Cork
Youghal
Cobh
Bandon
Bantry
Kinsale
C. Clear
Bergen
Askøy
Osøyro
Stord
Bømlo
Leirvik
Haugesund
Kopervik
Åkrahamn
Boknafjorden
Stavanger
Sandnes
Bryne
Nærbø
's-Gravenhage (Den Haag)
Hoek van Holland
ROTTERDAM
Dordrecht
Haarlem
Alkmaar
Den Helder
Vlissingen
Zeebrugge
Antwerpen
Oostende
Brugge
Gent
Mechelen
BRUSSEL (Bruxelles)
Dunkerque
Calais
Gris-Nez
Boulogne-sur-Mer
St-Omer
Lille
Tourcoing
Tournai
Béthune
Villeneuve-d'Ascq
Bruay-la-Buissière
Lens
Valenciennes
Le Touquet-Paris-Plage
Abbeville
Cambrai
St-Quentin
Picardie
Somme
Le Tréport
Dieppe
Amiens
Fécamp
Pays de Caux
Rouen
Le Havre
Bolbec
Seine
Elbeuf
Trouville-sur-Mer
Caen
Lisieux
Bayeux
Valognes
Cherbourg
Cotentin
Pte. de Barfleur
C. de la Hague
Alderney
Guernsey
St. Peter Port
Sark
Channel Is. (U.K.)
Jersey
St. Helier
18
19
9
17

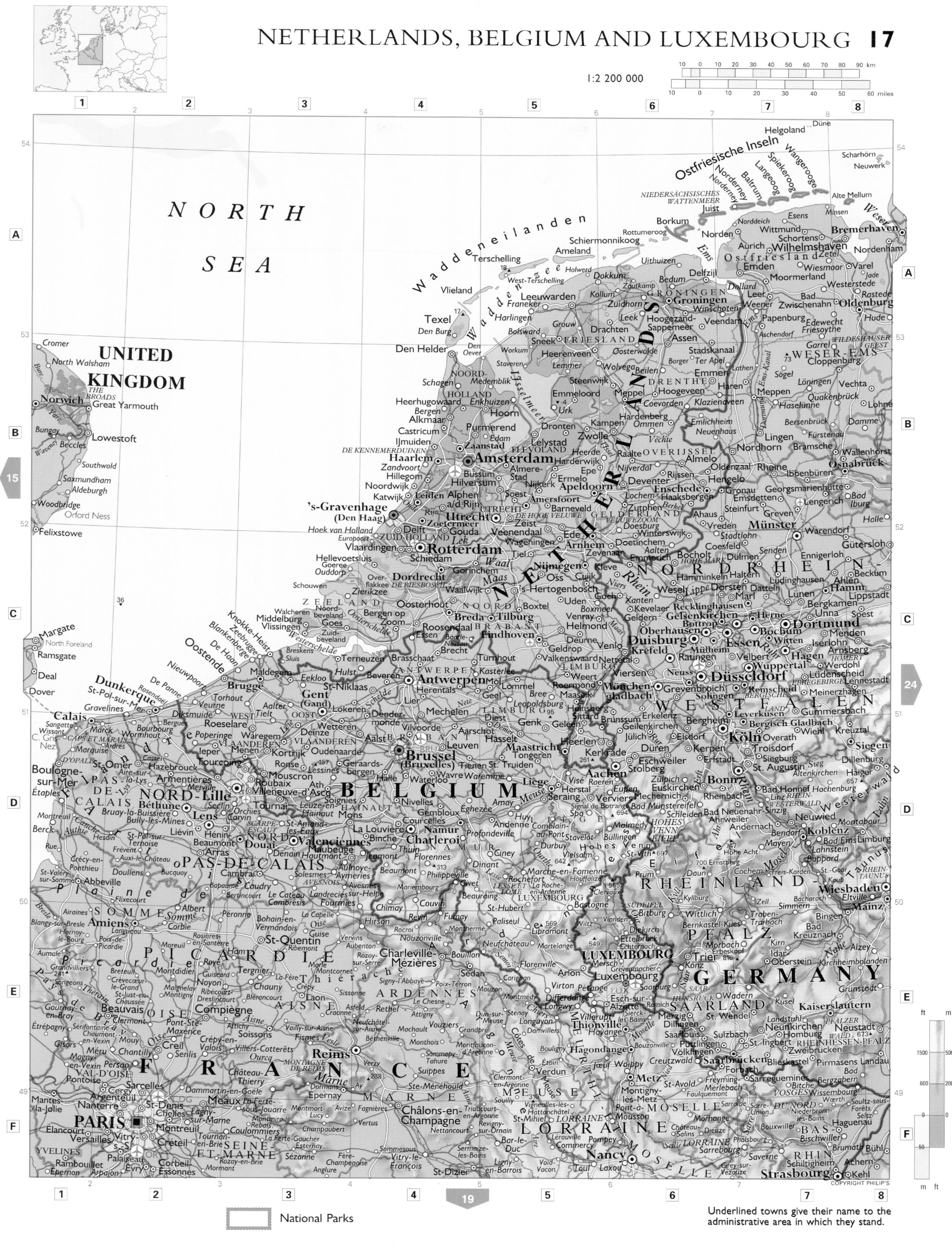
1:2 200 000
km
miles
NORTH SEA
UNITED KINGDOM
NETHERLANDS
BELGIUM
LUXEMBOURG
GERMANY
FRANCE
Waddeneilanden
Waddenzee
Ostfriesische Inseln
IJsselmeer
Amsterdam
's-Gravenhage (Den Haag)
Rotterdam
Utrecht
Groningen
Leeuwarden
Arnhem
Nijmegen
Eindhoven
Antwerpen
Brussel (Bruxelles)
Gent (Gand)
Brugge
Oostende
Liège
Namur
Charleroi
Luxembourg
Lille
Dunkerque
Calais
Amiens
Reims
PARIS
Metz
Nancy
Strasbourg
Saarbrücken
Köln
Düsseldorf
Dortmund
Essen
Duisburg
Münster
Bremerhaven
Oldenburg
Koblenz
Wiesbaden
NORDRHEIN-WESTFALEN
RHEINLAND-PFALZ
SAARLAND
WESER-EMS
PICARDIE
NORD-PAS-DE-CALAIS
LORRAINE
ARDENNES
Norwich
Great Yarmouth
Lowestoft
Margate
Ramsgate
Dover
15
19
24
COPYRIGHT PHILIP'S
National Parks
Underlined towns give their name to the administrative area in which they stand.

DÉPARTEMENTS IN THE PARIS AREA
1 Ville de Paris
2 Seine-St-Denis
3 Val-de-Marne
4 Hauts-de-Seine

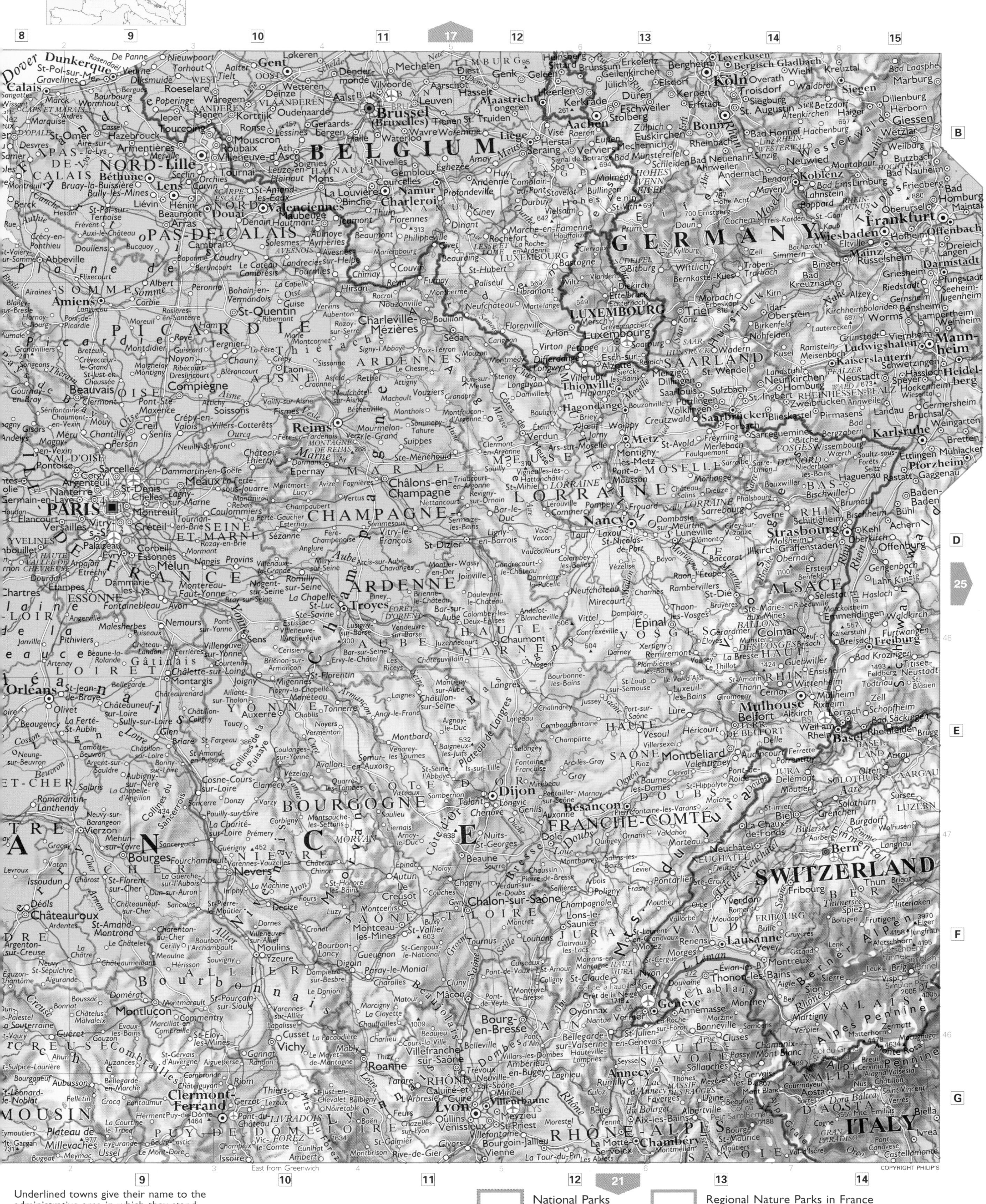

17 21 25

Underlined towns give their name to the administrative area in which they stand.

National Parks

Regional Nature Parks in France

1:2 200 000

ATLANTIC OCEAN
Golfe de Gascogne
Golfe du Lion
FRANCE
SPAIN
ANDORRA
AQUITAINE
POITOU-CHARENTES
LIMOUSIN
AUVERGNE
MIDI-PYRÉNÉES
LANGUEDOC-ROUSSILLON
PYRÉNÉES-ATLANTIQUES
HAUTES-PYRÉNÉES
PYRÉNÉES-ORIENTALES
HAUTE-GARONNE
NAVARRA
HUESCA
LLEIDA
GIRONA
BARCELONA
CATALUÑA
ZARAGOZA
Massif Central
Bordeaux
Toulouse
Limoges
Poitiers
La Rochelle
Angoulême
Périgueux
Clermont-Ferrand
Montpellier
Perpignan
Carcassonne
Pau
Bayonne
Tarbes
Agen
Montauban
Albi
Rodez
Béziers
Narbonne
Nevers
Bourges
Châteauroux
Montluçon
Niort
Cholet
Pamplona
Zaragoza
Huesca
Lleida
Girona
BARCELONA
Donostia-San Sebastián
Andorra la Vella
Île d'Yeu
Île de Ré
Île d'Oléron
Costa Brava
Projection : Lambert's Conformal Conic
West from Greenwich
East from Greenwich

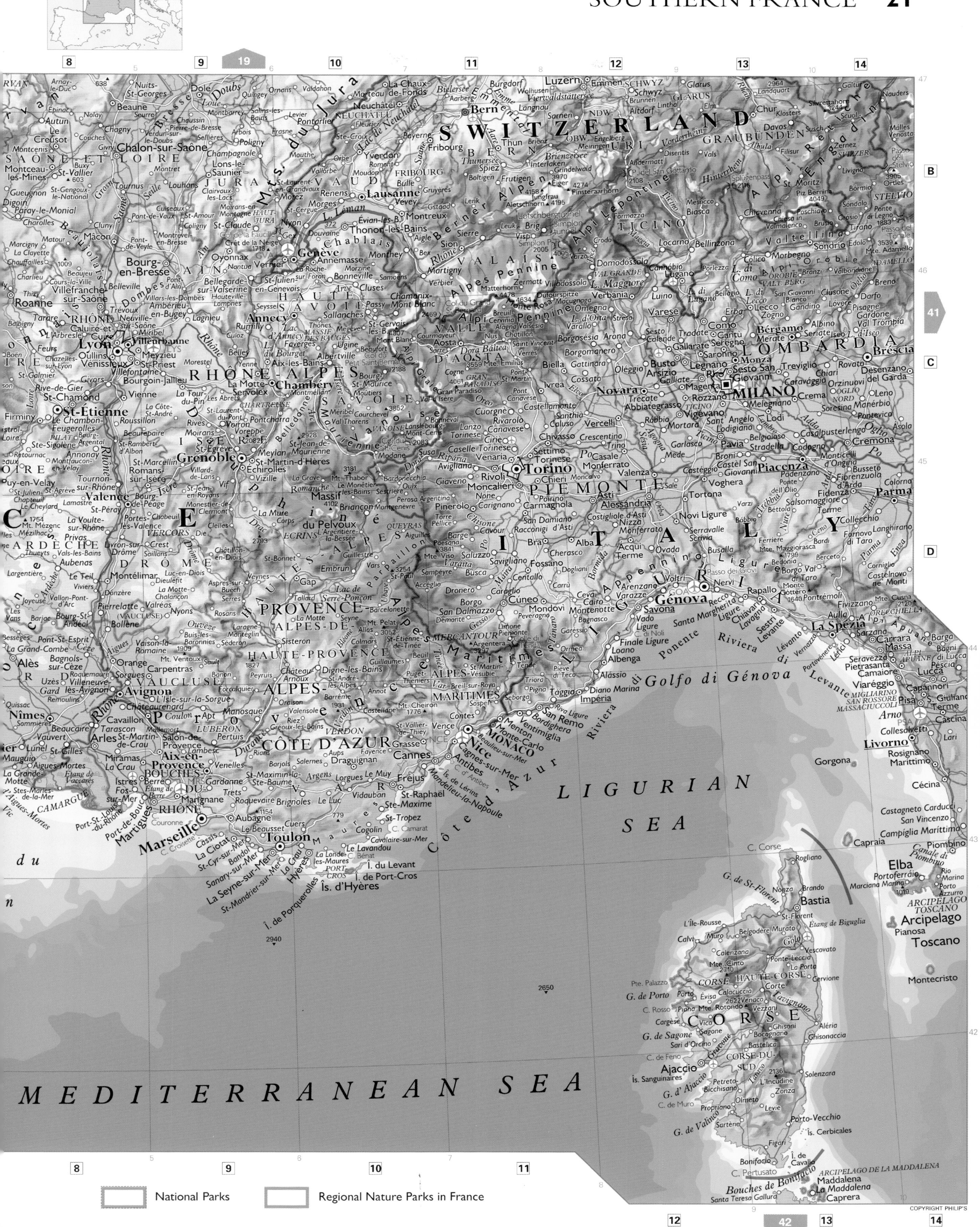

8
9
19
10
11
12
13
14
SWITZERLAND
Bern
Luzern
Neuchâtel
Lausanne
Genève
Montreux
Sion
VALAIS
Fribourg
Chur
Davos
GRAUBÜNDEN
TICINO
Lugano
Locarno
Bellinzona
Como
Lecco
Bérgamo
Brescia
LOMBÁRDIA
MILANO
Varese
Monza
Novara
Vercelli
Biella
Aosta
VALLE D'AOSTA
Torino
PIEMONTE
Asti
Alessándria
Cuneo
Génova
LIGURIA
Savona
La Spézia
Massa
Carrara
Lucca
Pisa
Livorno
Piacenza
Parma
Cremona
Pavia
ITALY
FRANCE
RHÔNE-ALPES
Lyon
Villeurbanne
St-Étienne
Grenoble
Chambéry
Annecy
Valence
Avignon
Nîmes
Arles
Marseille
Toulon
Aix-en-Provence
Nice
Cannes
Antibes
Menton
MONACO
Monte-Carlo
San Remo
Imperia
PROVENCE-ALPES-CÔTE D'AZUR
CÔTE D'AZUR
Hyères
Îs. d'Hyères
Chalon-sur-Saône
Mâcon
Bourg-en-Bresse
Roanne
Montélimar
Gap
Digne-les-Bains
DRÔME
ARDÈCHE
VAUCLUSE
SAVOIE
HAUTE-SAVOIE
ISÈRE
HAUTES-ALPES
ALPES-MARITIMES
CAMARGUE
Golfo di Génova
Riviera di Ponente
Riviera di Levante
LIGURIAN SEA
MEDITERRANEAN SEA
Côte d'Azur
CORSE
HAUTE-CORSE
CORSE-DU-SUD
Bastia
Ajaccio
Calvi
Corte
Porto-Vecchio
Bonifacio
Bouches de Bonifacio
Elba
Arcipelago Toscano
Capraia
Gorgona
Montecristo
Pianosa
Maddalena
Caprera
ARCIPELAGO DE LA MADDALENA
Mont Blanc
Matterhorn
Monte Rosa
Gran Paradiso
Alpi Pennine
Alpes Maritimes
Mts. du Jura
Rhône
8
9
10
11
12
42
13
14
41
B
C
D
National Parks
Regional Nature Parks in France

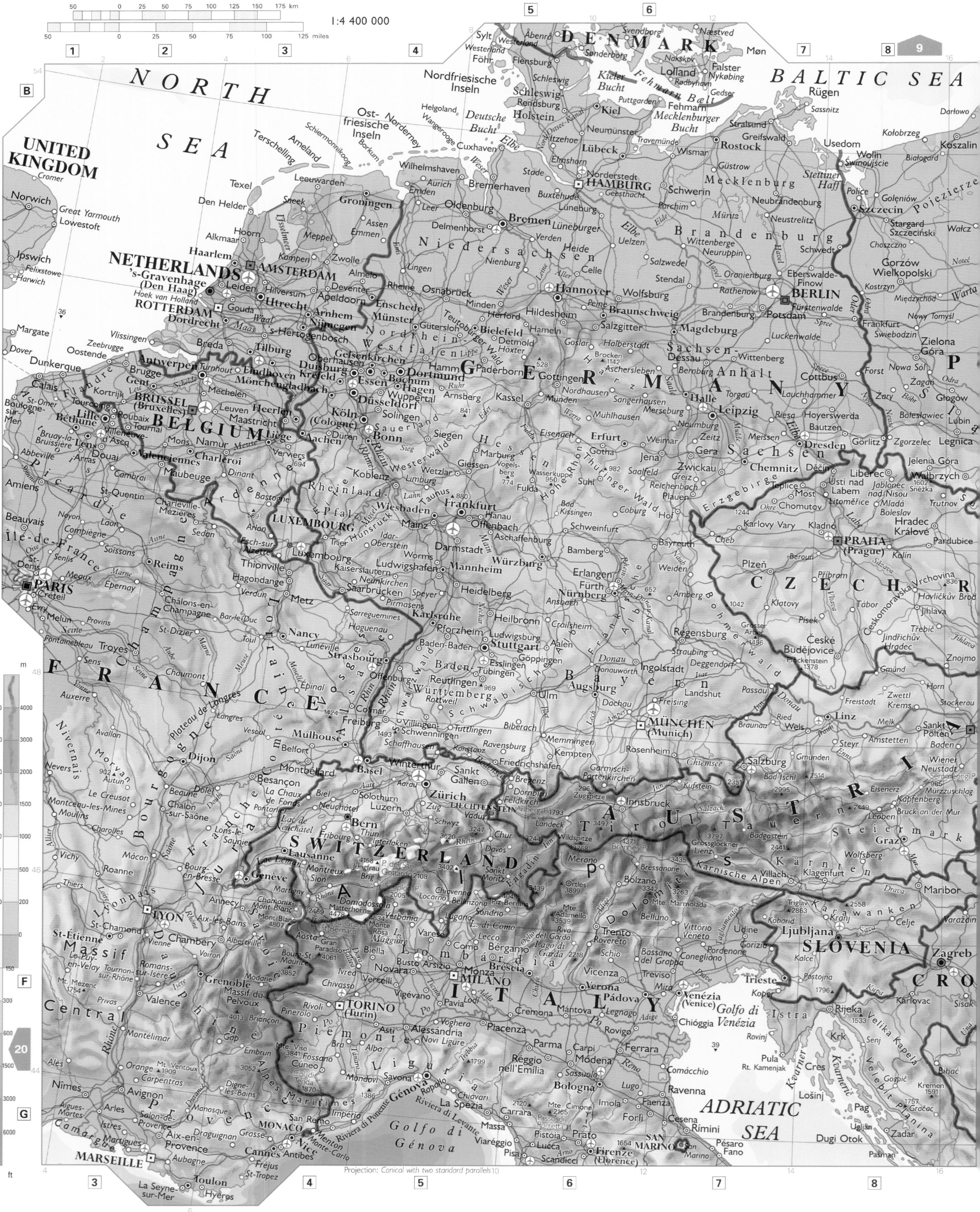

50 0 25 50 75 100 125 150 175 km

50 0 25 50 75 100 125 miles

1:4 400 000

NORTH SEA

BALTIC SEA

UNITED KINGDOM

NETHERLANDS

BELGIUM

LUXEMBOURG

DENMARK

GERMANY

FRANCE

SWITZERLAND

LIECHTENSTEIN

AUSTRIA

CZECH R.

SLOVENIA

ITALY

MONACO

SAN MARINO

ADRIATIC SEA

Golfo di Génova

Golfo di Venézia

Projection: Conical with two standard parallels

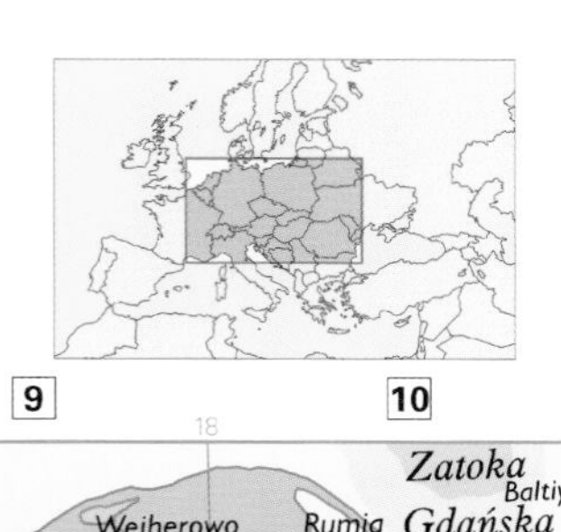

32

34

East from Greenwich

44

45

10 0 10 20 30 40 50 60 70 80 90 km

10 0 10 20 30 40 50 60 miles

1:2 200 000

FRANCE
SWITZERLAND
LUXEMBOURG
SLOVENIA
BAYERN
BADEN-WÜRTTEMBERG
PRAHA
MÜNCHEN
Stuttgart
Frankfurt
Nürnberg
Zürich
Bern
Innsbruck
Salzburg
Underlined towns give their name to the administrative area in which they stand.
National Parks
Nature Parks in Germany
East from Greenwich
Projection: Lambert's Conformal Conic
COPYRIGHT PHILIP'S

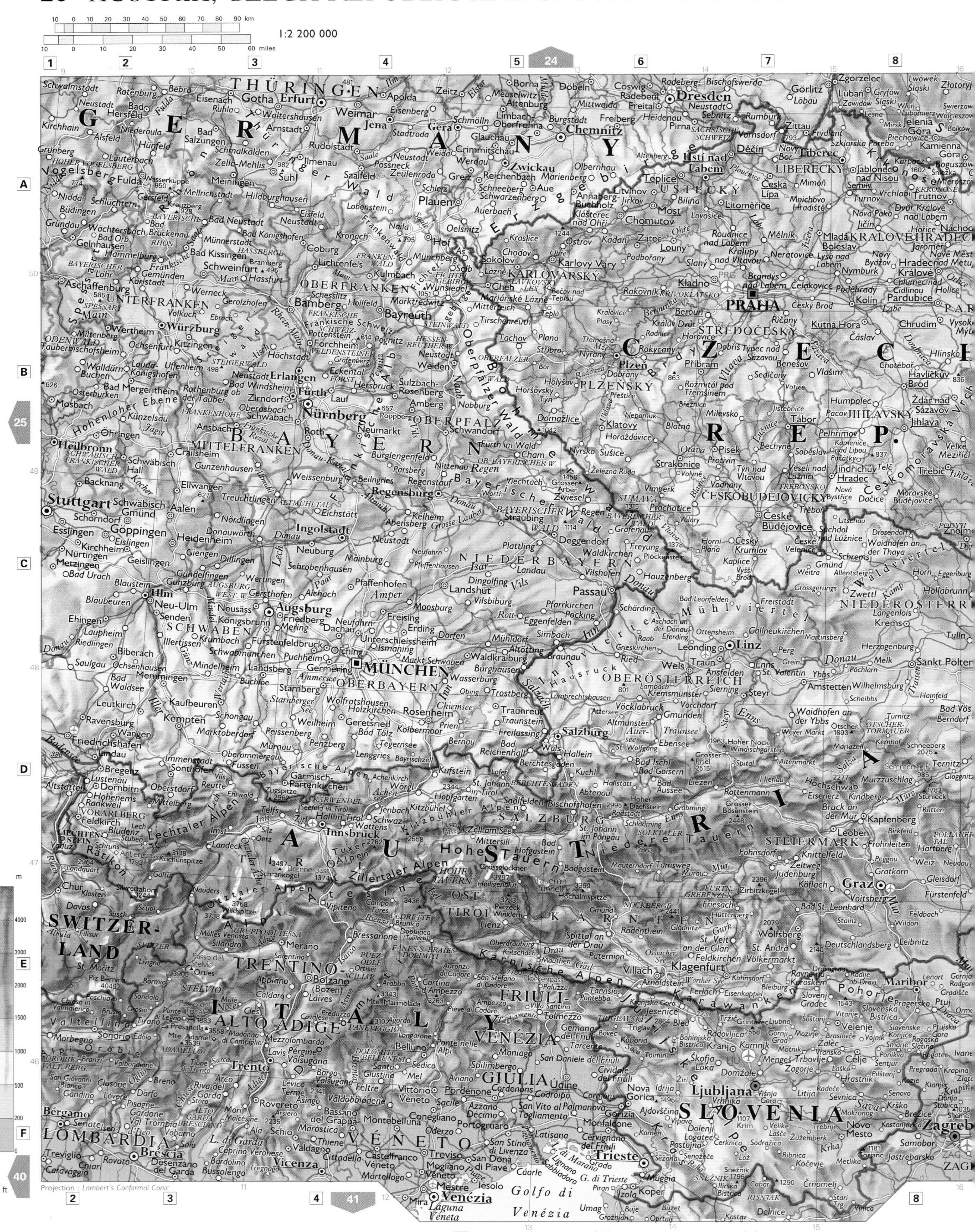
1:2 200 000
km
miles
24
25
40
41
GERMANY
THÜRINGEN
BAYERN
OBERFRANKEN
UNTERFRANKEN
MITTELFRANKEN
OBERPFALZ
NIEDERBAYERN
SCHWABEN
OBERBAYERN
CZECH REP.
KARLOVARSKÝ
PLZEŇSKÝ
STŘEDOČESKÝ
ÚSTECKÝ
LIBERECKÝ
JIHOČESKÝ
ČESKOBUDĚJOVICKÝ
JIHLAVSKÝ
AUSTRIA
NIEDERÖSTERREICH
OBERÖSTERREICH
SALZBURG
STEIERMARK
KÄRNTEN
TIROL
VORARLBERG
SWITZERLAND
LIECHTENSTEIN
ITALY
TRENTINO-ALTO ADIGE
FRIULI-VENEZIA GIULIA
VENETO
LOMBARDIA
SLOVENIA
PRAHA
MÜNCHEN
Dresden
Chemnitz
Erfurt
Nürnberg
Regensburg
Augsburg
Stuttgart
Würzburg
Plzeň
České Budějovice
Linz
Salzburg
Innsbruck
Graz
Klagenfurt
Ljubljana
Trieste
Venézia
Bolzano (Bozen)
Trento
Zagreb
Donau
Golfo di Venézia
Projection: Lambert's Conformal Conic

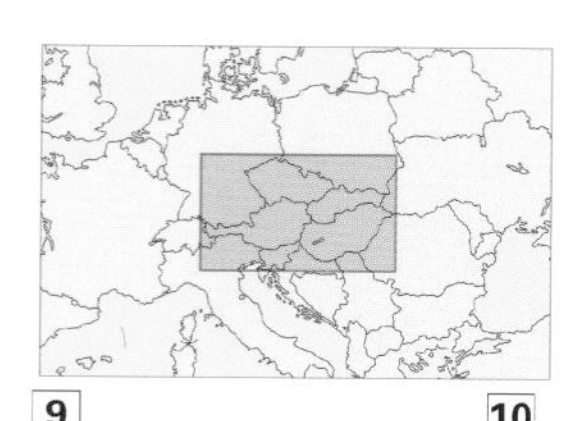

31

33

29

28

East from Greenwich

National Parks

Underlined towns give their name to the administrative area in which they stand.

Administrative divisions in Croatia:
1 Brodsko-Posavska
2 Koprivničko-Križevačka
4 Medimurska
5 Osječko-Baranjska
6 Požeško-Slavonska
8 Virovitičko-Podravska
9 Vukovarsko-Srijemska

Inter-entity boundaries as agreed at the 1995 Dayton Peace Agreement

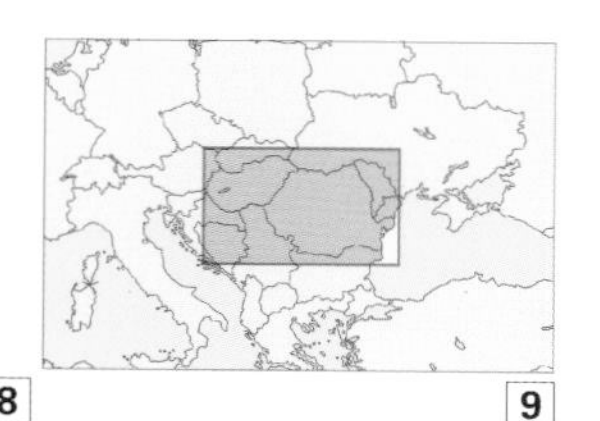

National Parks

Underlined towns give their name to the administrative area in which they stand.

10 0 10 20 30 40 50 60 70 80 90 km

1:2 200 000

10 0 10 20 30 40 50 60 miles

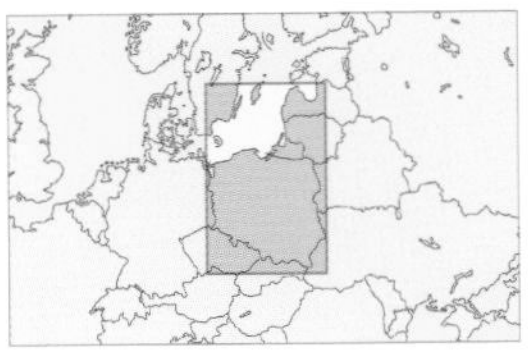

BALTIC SEA
LATVIA
LITHUANIA
KALININGRAD (Russia)
SWEDEN
Gulf of Riga
Irbes šaurums (Kura kurk)
Gotland (Sweden)
Öland (Sweden)
Bornholm (Denmark)
Riga
Kaunas
Klaipėda
Liepāja
Ventspils
Kaliningrad
Gdańsk
Gdynia
Elbląg
Olsztyn
Koszalin
Słupsk
Szczecin
Karlskrona
Kalmar
Visby
Växjö
Jönköping
POMORSKIE
WARMIŃSKO-MAZURSKIE
ZACHODNIO-POMORSKIE
Zatoka Gdańska
Hanöbukten

POLAND
GERMANY
BELARUS
UKRAINE
CZECH REP.
SLOVAK REP.
AUSTRIA
POMORSKIE
PODLASKIE
MAZOWIECKIE
LUBUSKIE
WIELKOPOLSKIE
ŁÓDZKIE
LUBELSKIE
DOLNOŚLĄSKIE
OPOLSKIE
ŚLĄSKIE
ŚWIĘTOKRZYSKIE
MAŁOPOLSKIE
PODKARPACKIE
WARSZAWA
Kraków
Wrocław
Poznań
Łódź
Lublin
Białystok
Brest
Brno
Ostrava
Projection: Lambert's Conformal Conic
East from Greenwich
COPYRIGHT PHILIP'S
National Parks
Underlined towns give their name to the administrative area in which they stand.

1:4 400 000

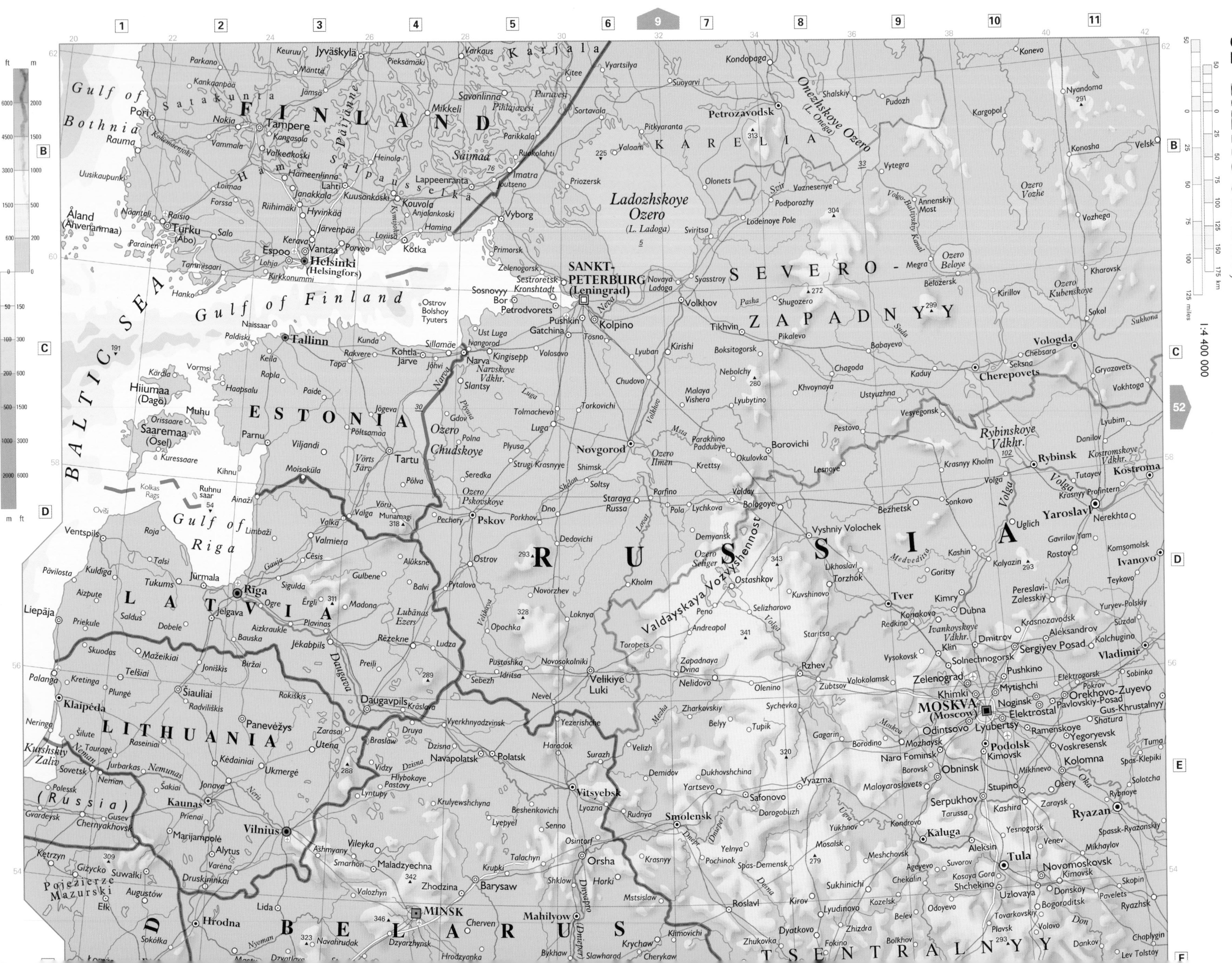

50 0 25 50 75 100 125 150 175 km
50 0 25 50 75 100 125 miles
BALTIC SEA
Gulf of Finland
Gulf of Riga
Gulf of Bothnia
FINLAND
ESTONIA
LATVIA
LITHUANIA
BELARUS
RUSSIA
SEVERO-ZAPADNYY
TSENTRALNYY
KARELIA
Ladozhskoye Ozero (L. Ladoga)
Onezhskoye Ozero (L. Onega)
SANKT-PETERBURG (Leningrad)
MOSKVA (Moscow)
MINSK
Helsinki (Helsingfors)
Tallinn
Riga
Vilnius
Daugava
Volga
Dnyapro (Dnieper)

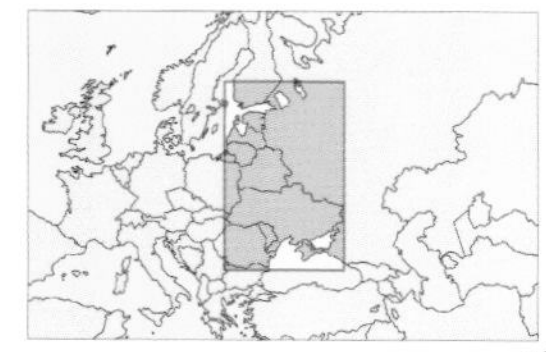

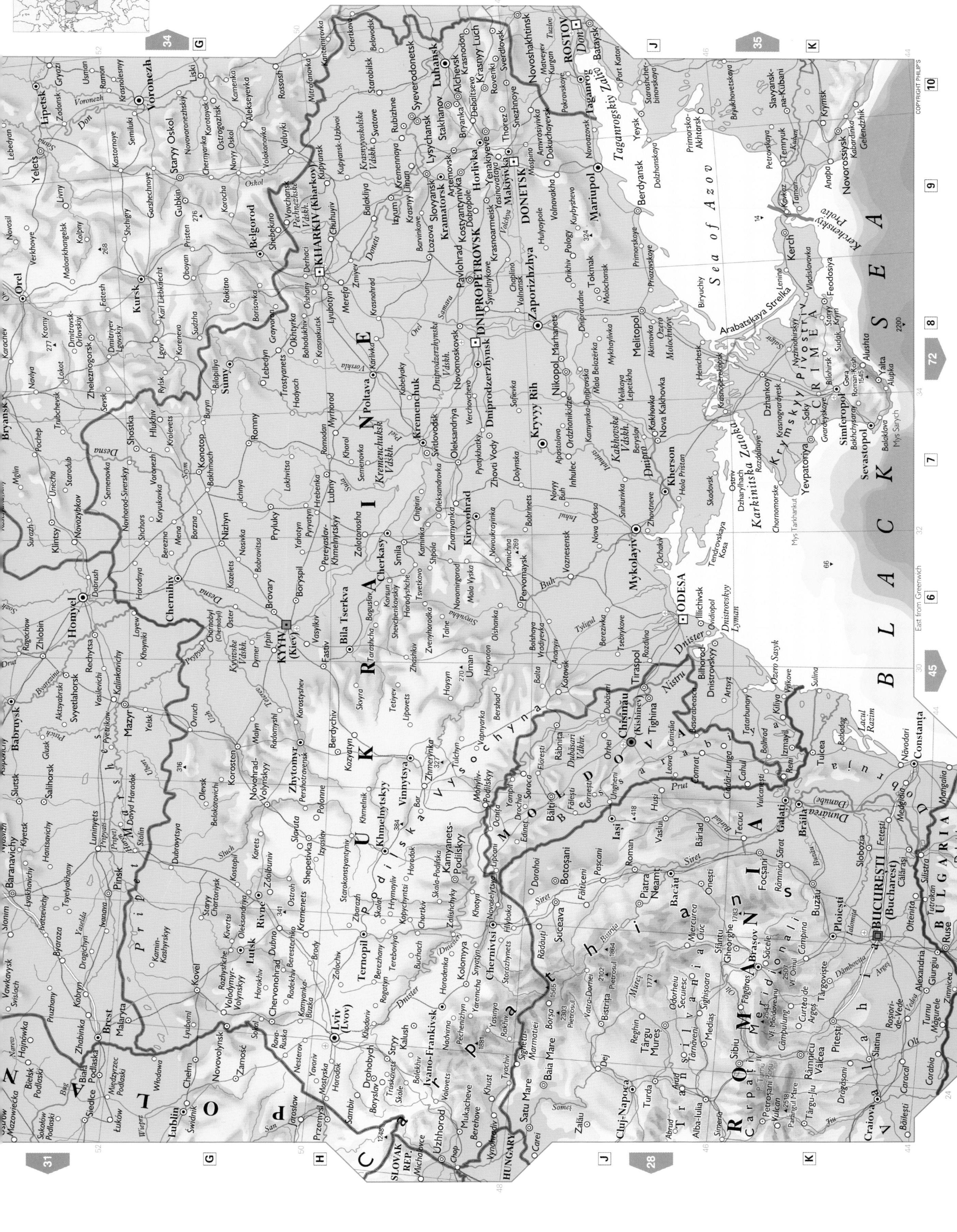
U K R A I N E
B L A C K S E A
Sea of Azov
R O M A N I A
M O L D O V A
B U L G A R I A
HUNGARY
SLOVAK REP.
CRIMEA
KYIV (Kiev)
KHARKIV (Kharkov)
DNIPROPETROVSK
DONETSK
ODESA
CHIȘINĂU (Kishinev)
BUCUREȘTI (Bucharest)
ROSTOV
Lviv (Lvov)
Zaporizhzhya
Kryvyy Rih
Mykolayiv
Kherson
Sevastopol
Simferopol
Mariupol
Luhansk
Homyel
Voronezh
Kursk
Belgorod
Poltava
Cherkasy
Vinnytsya
Zhytomyr
Rivne
Lutsk
Ternopil
Chernivtsi
Khmelnytskyy
Chernihiv
Sumy
Kirovohrad
Constanța
Galați
Brăila
Iași
Projection: Conical with two standard parallels
COPYRIGHT PHILIP'S
East from Greenwich

1:4 400 000

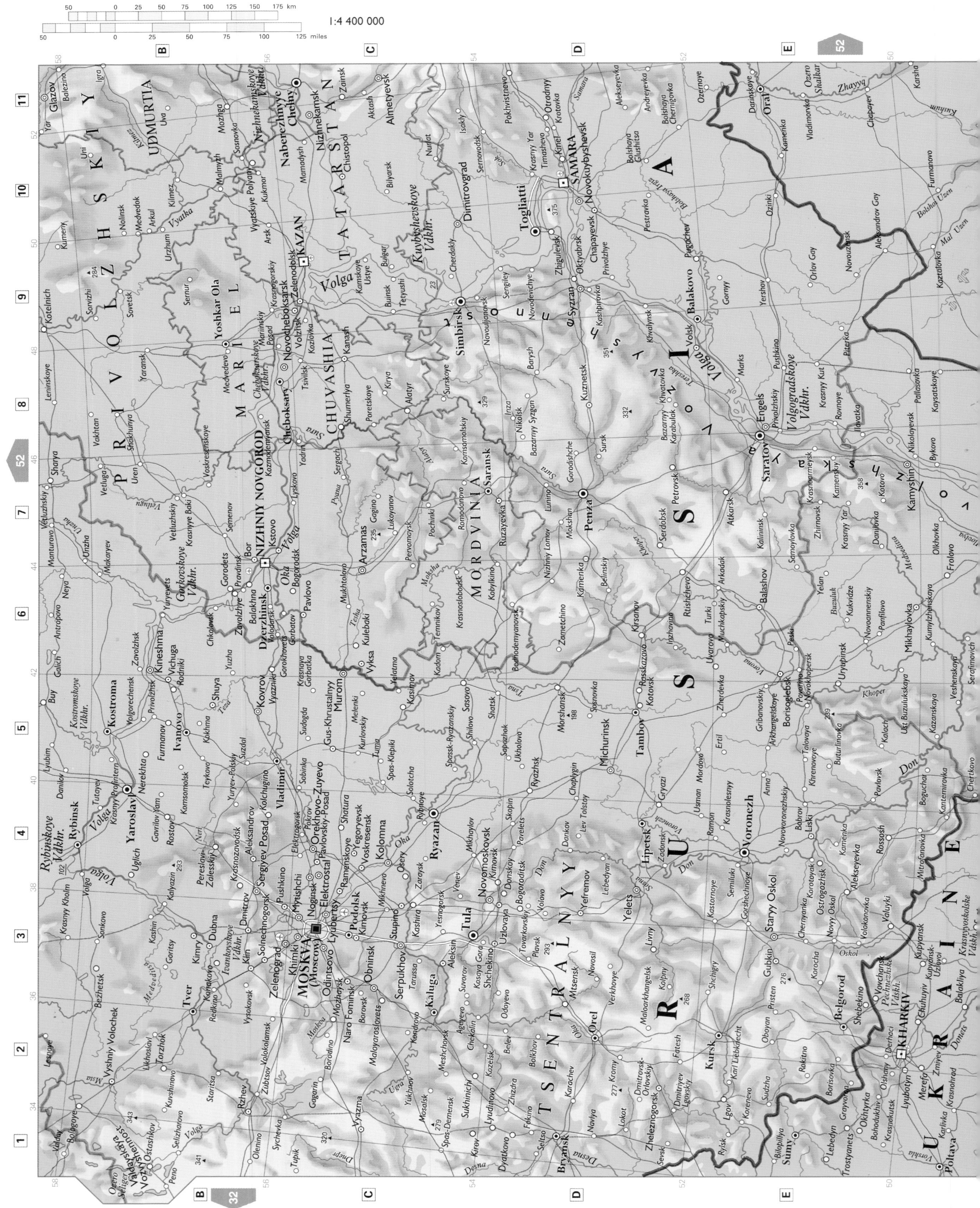

50 0 25 50 75 100 125 150 175 km
50 0 25 50 75 100 125 miles
52
32
PRIVOLZHSKIY
UDMURTIA
MARI EL
TATARSTAN
CHUVASHIA
MORDVINIA
TSENTRAL'NYY
RUSSIA
UKRAINE
MOSKVA (Moscow)
NIZHNIY NOVGOROD
KAZAN
SAMARA
KHARKIV
Yaroslavl
Kostroma
Ivanovo
Vladimir
Ryazan
Tula
Kaluga
Tver
Orel
Bryansk
Kursk
Belgorod
Voronezh
Lipetsk
Tambov
Penza
Saransk
Saratov
Engels
Simbirsk
Togliatti
Syzran
Cheboksary
Yoshkar Ola
Dzerzhinsk
Arzamas
Naberezhnyye Chelny
Nizhnekamsk
Kamyshin
Balakovo
Oral
Sumy
Poltava
Volga
Oka
Don
Kuybyshevskoye Vdkhr.
Volgogradskoye Vdkhr.
Rybinskoye Vdkhr.
Gorkovskoye Vdkhr.

CASPIAN SEA
BLACK SEA
Sea of Azov
Taganrogskiy Zaliv
KAZAKHSTAN
Caspian Depression
Ryn Peski
KALMYKIA
Chernyye Zemli
YUZHNYY
Prikubanskaya Nizmennost
Ergeni Vozvyshennost
Tsimlyanskoye Vdkhr.
Caucasus Mountains
DAGESTAN
CHECHENIA
INGUSHETIA
NORTH OSSETIA
KABARDINO-BALKARIA
KARACHAY-CHERKESSIA
ADYGEA
ABKHAZIA
AJARIA
GEORGIA
ARMENIA
AZERBAIJAN
TURKEY
Kuzey Anadolu Dağları
VOLGOGRAD
Astrakhan
ROSTOV
DONETSK
DNIPROPETROVSK
Luhansk
Zaporizhzhya
Mariupol
Krasnodar
Stavropol
Grozny
Vladikavkaz
Nalchik
Makhachkala
Derbent
TBILISI
YEREVAN
BAKI (Baku)
Sochi
Sokhumi
Kutaisi
Batumi
Trabzon
Samsun
Projection: Conical with two standard parallels
East from Greenwich

1:2 200 000

Bay of Biscay
Costa Verde
Donostia-San Sebastián
Bilbao
Santander
Gijón
Oviedo
León
Burgos
Valladolid
Palencia
Salamanca
Zamora
Segovia
Ávila
MADRID
Toledo
A Coruña (La Coruña)
Santiago de Compostela
Lugo
Ourense (Orense)
Pontevedra
Vigo
Porto
Braga
Coimbra
Logroño
Vitoria-Gasteiz
GALICIA
ASTURIAS
CANTABRIA
PAÍS VASCO
LA RIOJA
CASTILLA Y LEÓN
MADRID
SPAIN

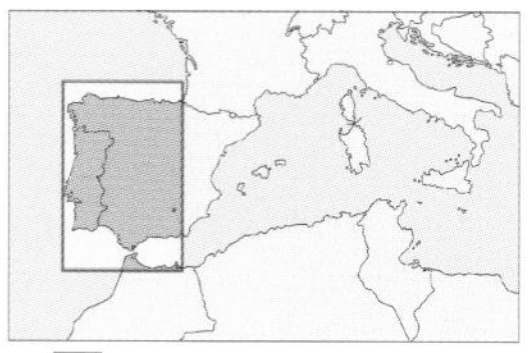

National Parks

Nature Parks in Spain and Portugal

Projection: Lambert's Conformal Conic

West from Greenwich

1:2 200 000

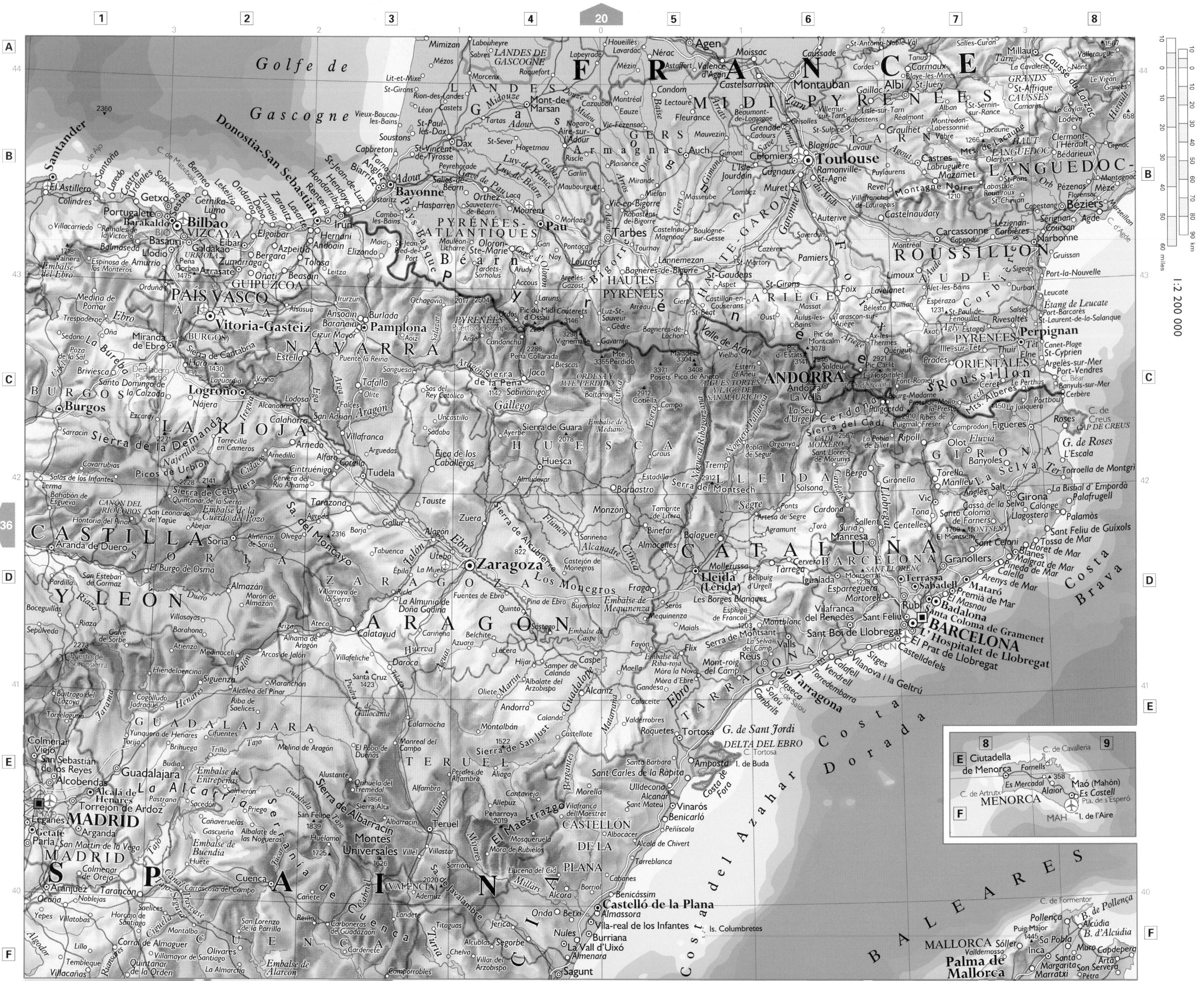
FRANCE
SPAIN
ARAGÓN
CATALUÑA
NAVARRA
PAÍS VASCO
LA RIOJA
CASTILLA Y LEÓN
MADRID
ROUSSILLON
LANGUEDOC-
MIDI-PYRÉNÉES
ANDORRA
BALEARES
Golfe de Gascogne
Costa Brava
Costa Dorada
Costa del Azahar
MALLORCA
MENORCA
Toulouse
Perpignan
Narbonne
Béziers
Carcassonne
Bayonne
Biarritz
Pau
Tarbes
Donostia-San Sebastián
Santander
Bilbao
Vitoria-Gasteiz
Pamplona
Logroño
Burgos
Zaragoza
Huesca
Lleida (Lérida)
Girona
BARCELONA
L'Hospitalet de Llobregat
Tarragona
Castelló de la Plana
Teruel
Guadalajara
MADRID
Cuenca
Soria
Palma de Mallorca
Andorra la Vella
Ciutadella de Menorca
Maó (Mahón)
Ebro
DELTA DEL EBRO
G. de Sant Jordi
Sierra de Guara
Sa. del Moncayo
Montes Universales
Sierra de Albarracín

M E D I T E R R A N E A N S E A
Golfo de Valencia
ISLAS
Costa Blanca
Costa del Sol
CASTILLA-LA MANCHA
VALENCIA
MURCIA
ALICANTE
ALBACETE
ALMERÍA
GRANADA
JAÉN
CIUDAD REAL
Valencia
Alicante
Murcia
Cartagena
Albacete
Almería
Granada
Elche
Torrevieja
Benidorm
Denia
Gandia
Lorca
Linares
Úbeda
EIVISSA (IBIZA)
Eivissa (Ibiza)
Formentera
Cabrera
Palma
Mar Menor
G. de Mazarrón
G. de Almería
Golfe d'Arzew
Alborán (Sp.)
Melilla (Sp.)
Islas Chafarinas (Sp.)
Nador
Oran (Ouahran)
Mostaganem
Ech Cheliff
Blida
ALGER (Algiers)
Médéa
Tiaret
Sidi-bel-Abbès
Mascara
Relizane
Tissemsilt
A L G E R I A
National Parks
Nature Parks in Spain
Projection: Lambert's Conformal Conic
East from Greenwich
West from Greenwich
COPYRIGHT PHILIP'S
37
78

1:2 200 000
10 0 10 20 30 40 50 60 70 80 90 km
10 0 10 20 30 40 50 60 miles
25
21
42
SWITZERLAND
FRANCE
LIGURIAN SEA
Golfo di Génova
Riviera di Ponente
Riviera di Levante
Côte d'Azur
RHÔNE-ALPES
PROVENCE-ALPES-CÔTE D'AZUR
LOMBARDIA
PIEMONTE
LIGURIA
VALLE D'AOSTA
EMILIA-ROMAGNA
TOSCANA
CORSE
HAUTE-CORSE
CORSE-DU-SUD
ALPES-MARITIMES
HAUTE-SAVOIE
SAVOIE
ISÈRE
DRÔME
HAUTES-ALPES
ALPES-DE-HAUTE-PROVENCE
VAUCLUSE
BOUCHES-DU-RHÔNE
VAR
AIN
JURA
MONACO
Arcipelago Toscano
Alpes Pennine
Alpi Lepontine
Berner Alpen
Mts. du Jura
L. Léman
L. Maggiore
L. di Como
L. di Garda
Milano
Torino
Genova
Lyon
Grenoble
Genève
Lausanne
Bern
Marseille
Toulon
Nice
Cannes
Avignon
Chambéry
Annecy
Bastia
Ajaccio
Elba
Livorno
La Spezia
Parma
Piacenza
Novara
Bergamo
Brescia
Cuneo
Savona
Pisa
Lucca
Projection : Lambert's Conformal Conic
East from Greenwich
m 4000 3000 2000 1500 1000 500 200 0
ft 12 000 9000 6000 4500 3000 1500 600
150 300 600 1500 3000 6000 ft
0 50 100 200 500 1000 2000 m
National Parks
Underlined towns give their name to the administrative area in which they stand.

Administrative divisions in Croatia:

1 Brodsko-Posavska
2 Koprivničko-Križevačka
3 Krapinsko-Zagorska
4 Medimurska
6 Požeško-Slavonska
7 Varaždinska
8 Virovitičko-Podravska
10 Zagreba čka

Nature Parks in Italy

Inter-entity boundaries as agreed at the 1995 Dayton Peace Agreement

26 28 44 43

1:2 200 000

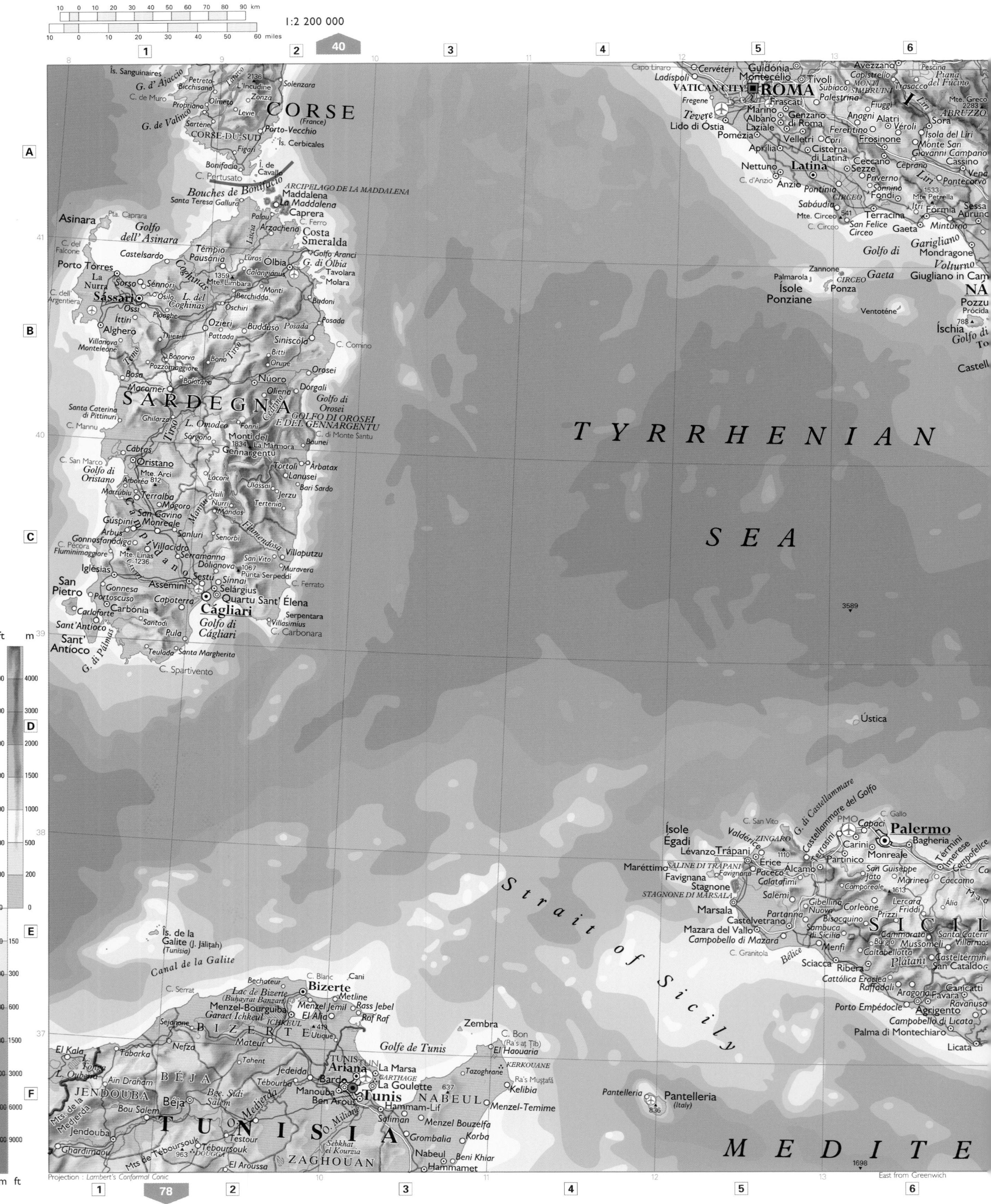

40
78

Nature Parks in Italy

National Parks

Underlined towns give their name to the administrative area in which they stand.

1:2 200 000
km
miles
28
41
43
46
SERBIA
& MONTENEGRO
MONTENEGRO
BOSNIA-HERZEGOVINA
CROATIA
VOJVODINA
KOSOVO
MACEDONIA
ALBANIA
ITALY
ADRIATIC SEA
Strait of Otranto
BEOGRAD (Belgrade)
Novi Sad
Sarajevo
Podgorica
Priština
Skopje
Tiranë
Durrës
Sofiya
Thessaloníki (Salonica)
Craiova
Niš
Kragujevac
Bitola
Ohrid
Vlorë
Kérkira (Corfu)
Lecce
Brindisi
KENTRIKÍ MAKEDHONÍA
DYTIKÍ MAKEDHONÍA
Thermaïkós Kólpos
Projection : Lambert's Conformal Conic
East from Greenwich
Inter-entity boundaries as agreed at the 1995 Dayton Peace Agreement

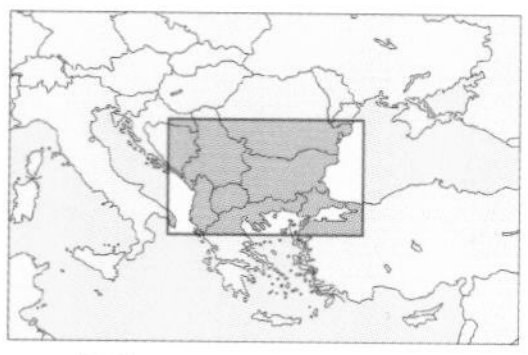

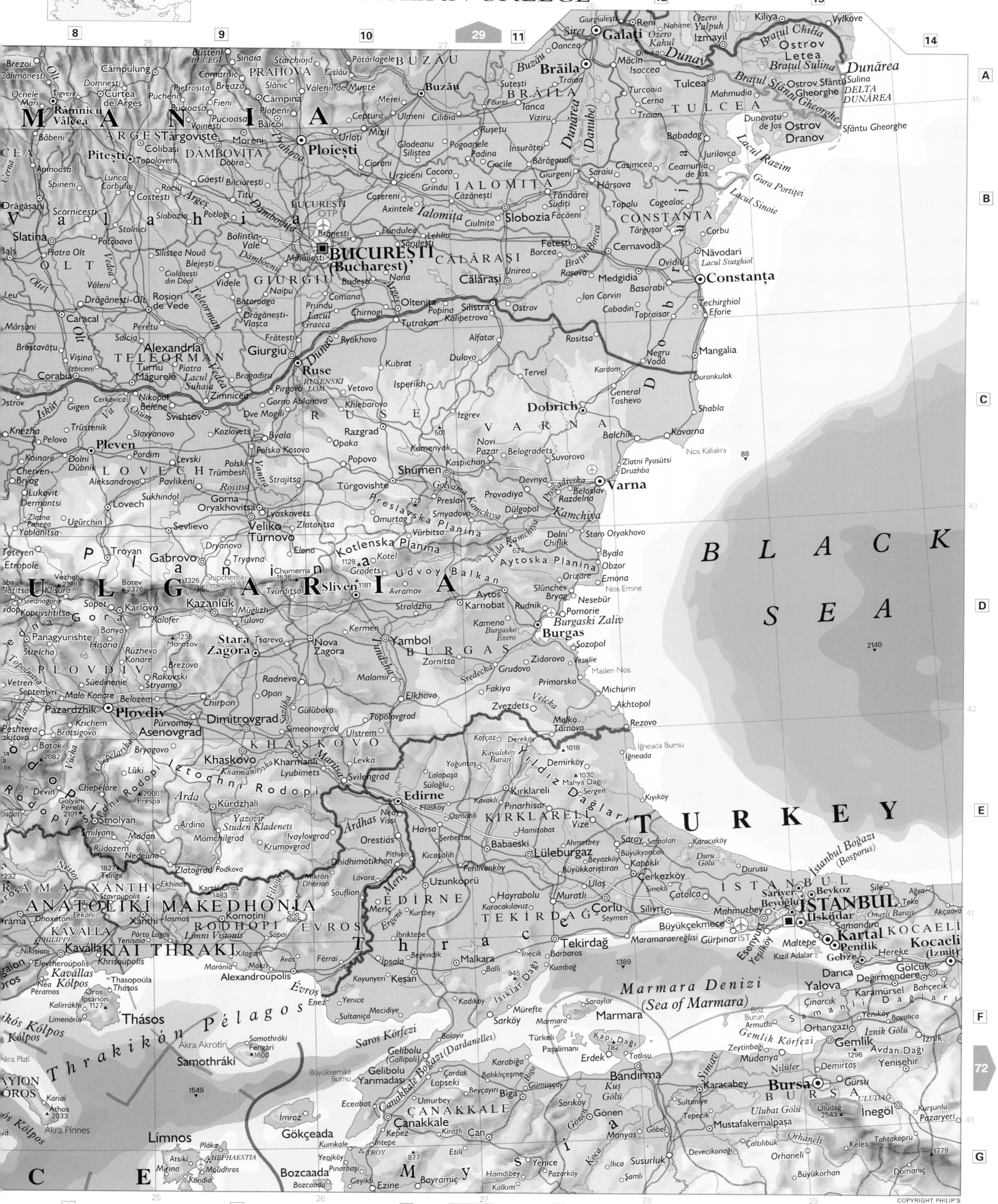

National Parks

Underlined towns give their name to the administrative area in which they stand.

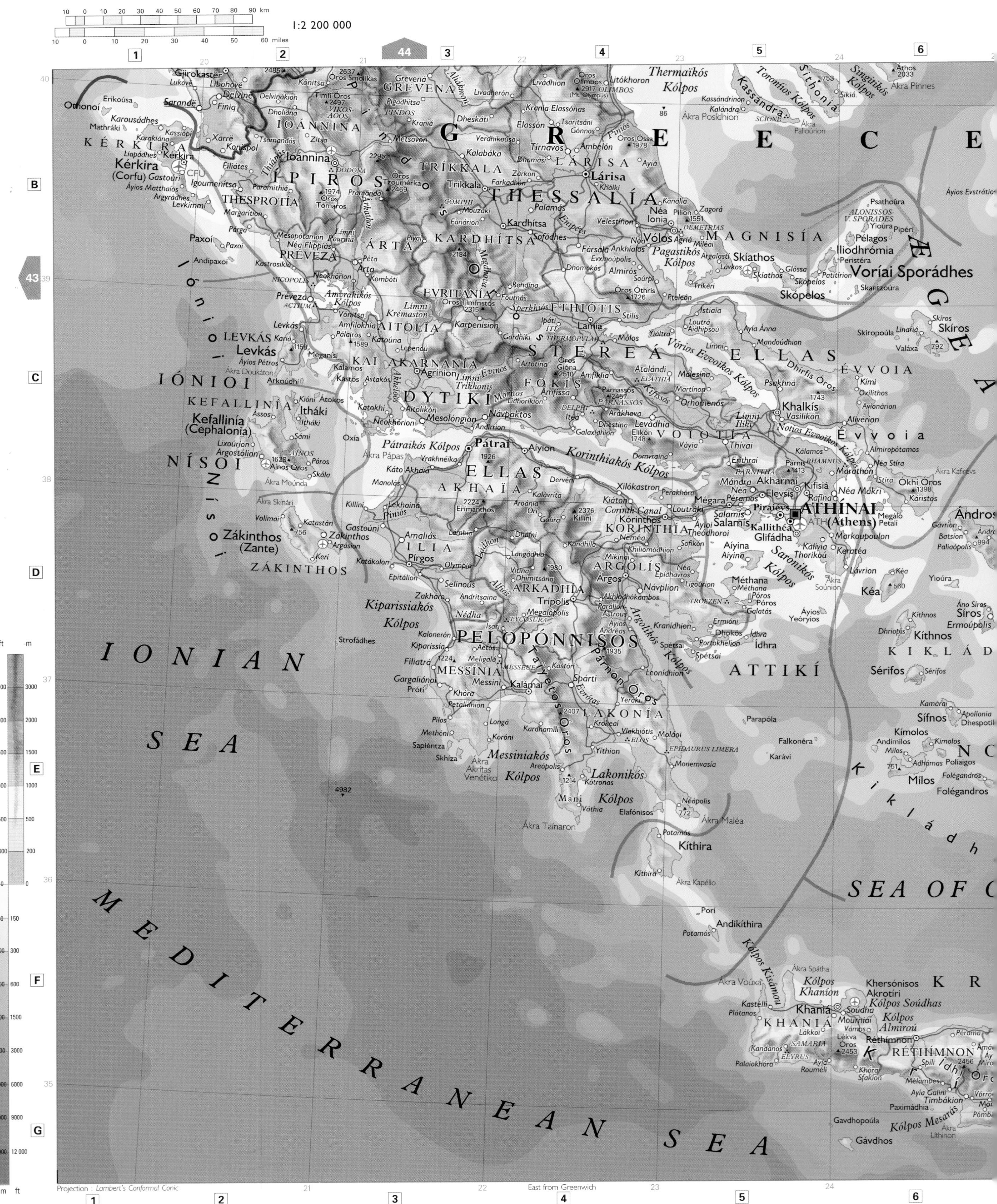
1:2 200 000
IONIAN SEA
MEDITERRANEAN SEA
SEA OF CRETE
GREECE
PELOPÓNNISOS
ATTIKÍ
THESSALÍA
STEREÁ ELLÁS
ÍPIROS
ÍONIOI NÍSOI
Voríai Sporádhes
Kikládhes
ATHÍNAI (Athens)
Kérkira (Corfu)
Kefallinía (Cephalonia)
Zákinthos (Zante)
Pátrai
Lárisa
Vólos
Kórinthos
Trípolis
Kalámai
Spárti
Khaniá
Kíthira
Évvoia
Projection : Lambert's Conformal Conic
East from Greenwich

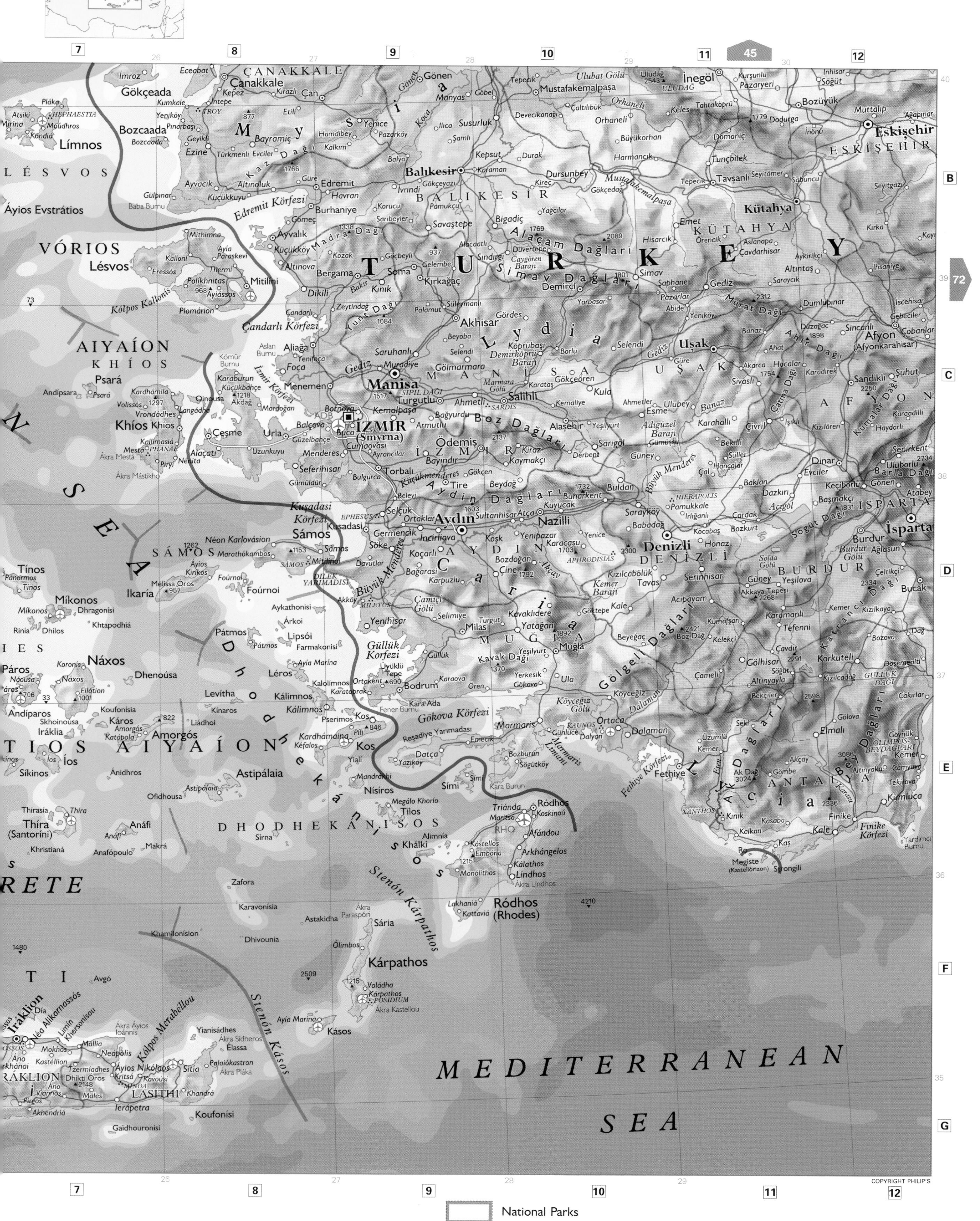

National Parks

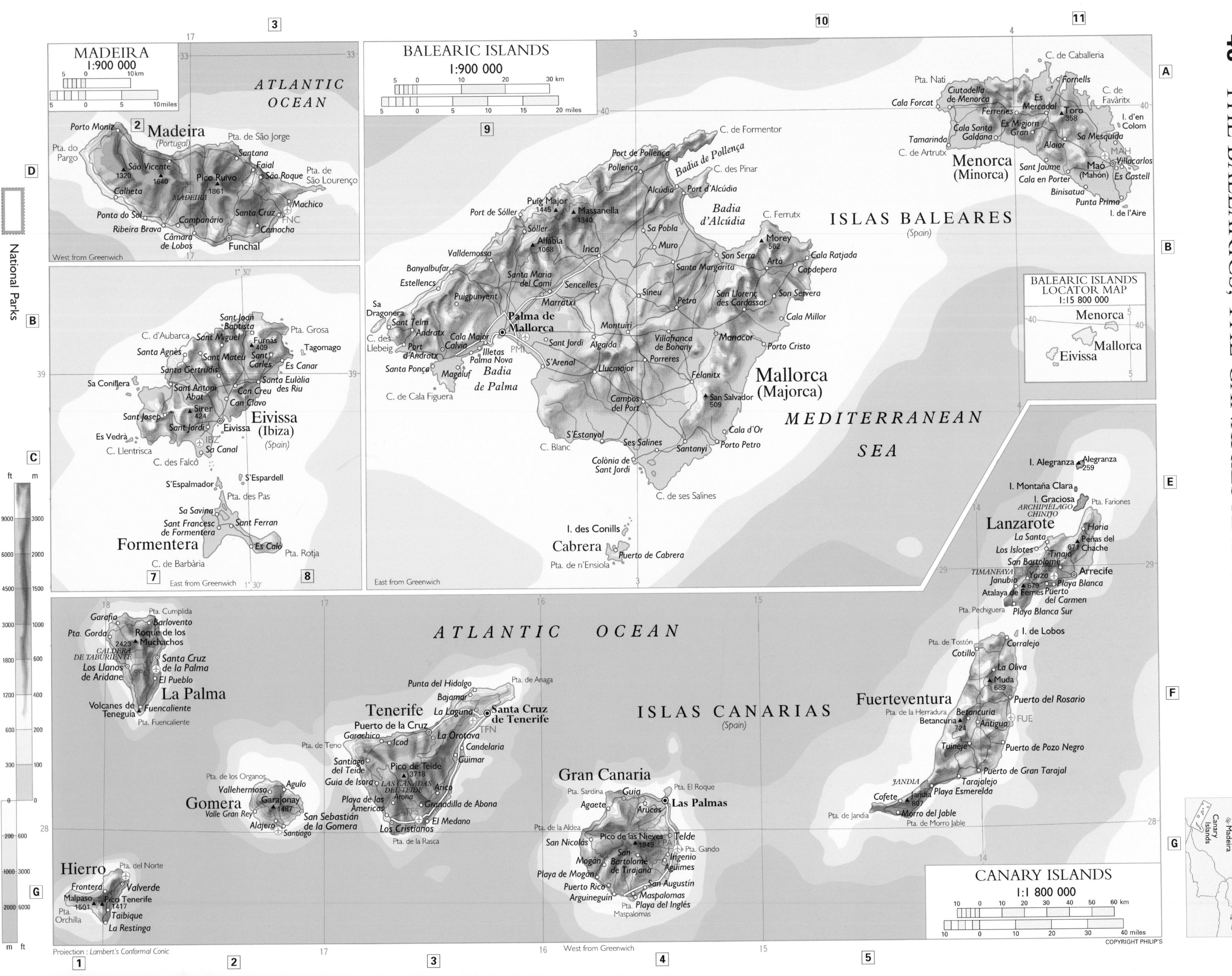

MADEIRA
1:900 000
ATLANTIC OCEAN
Madeira
(Portugal)
Funchal
BALEARIC ISLANDS
1:900 000
ISLAS BALEARES
(Spain)
Menorca
(Minorca)
Mallorca
(Majorca)
Palma de Mallorca
Eivissa
(Ibiza)
Formentera
Cabrera
MEDITERRANEAN SEA
BALEARIC ISLANDS LOCATOR MAP
1:15 800 000
ATLANTIC OCEAN
ISLAS CANARIAS
(Spain)
La Palma
Hierro
Gomera
Tenerife
Santa Cruz de Tenerife
Gran Canaria
Las Palmas
Fuerteventura
Lanzarote
Arrecife
CANARY ISLANDS
1:1 800 000
National Parks
Projection : Lambert's Conformal Conic
West from Greenwich
East from Greenwich
COPYRIGHT PHILIP'S

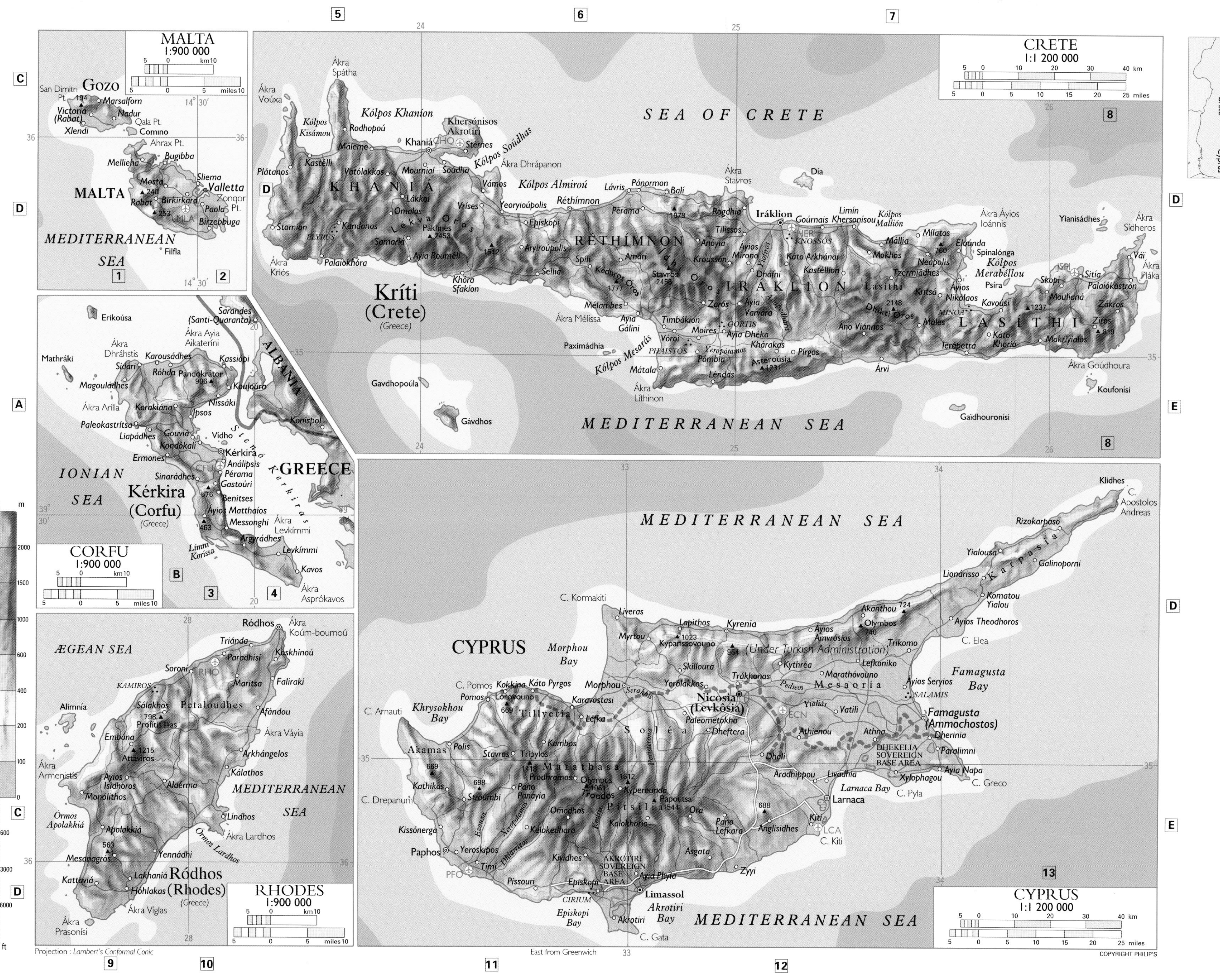
CRETE
1:1 200 000
SEA OF CRETE
MEDITERRANEAN SEA
Kríti
(Crete)
(Greece)
CYPRUS
1:1 200 000
CYPRUS
MEDITERRANEAN SEA
Famagusta Bay
Morphou Bay
Nicosia (Levkosía)
Limassol
Larnaca
Paphos
Famagusta (Ammochostos)
MALTA
1:900 000
Gozo
MALTA
Valletta
MEDITERRANEAN SEA
CORFU
1:900 000
Kérkira
(Corfu)
(Greece)
IONIAN SEA
ALBANIA
GREECE
RHODES
1:900 000
Ródhos
(Rhodes)
(Greece)
ÆGEAN SEA
MEDITERRANEAN SEA
Projection : Lambert's Conformal Conic
East from Greenwich
COPYRIGHT PHILIP'S

500 0 250 500 750 1000 1250 1500 1750 km

500 0 250 500 750 1000 1250 miles

1:44 400 000

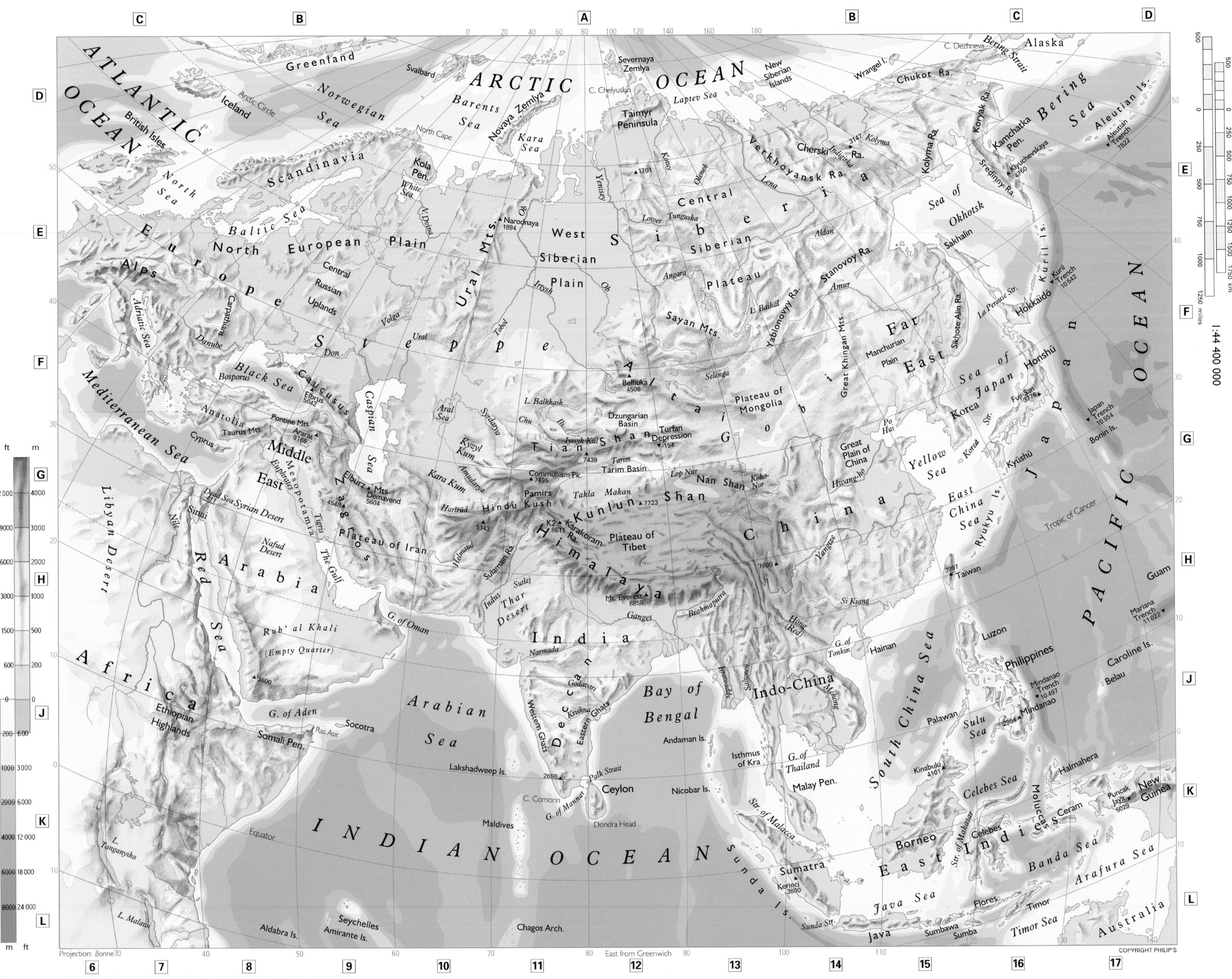

ft m 12 000 4000 9000 3000 6000 2000 3000 1000 1500 500 600 200 0 0

200 600 1000 3000 2000 6000 4000 12 000 6000 18 000 8000 24 000 m ft

1:44 400 000

500 0 250 500 750 1000 1250 1500 1750 km

500 0 250 500 750 1000 1250 miles

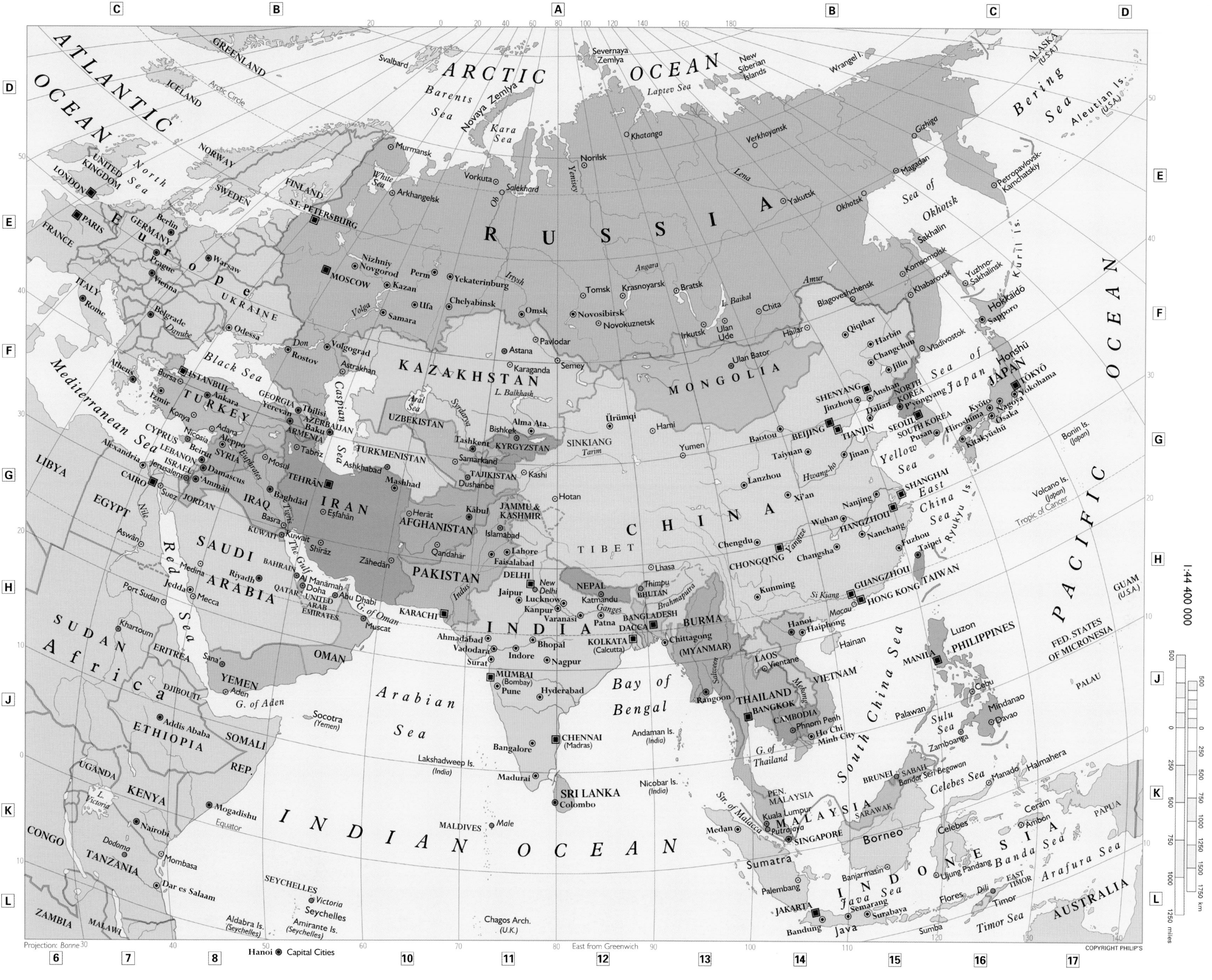

1:17 800 000
100 0 100 200 300 400 500 600 700 800 km
100 0 100 200 300 400 500 miles
RUSSIA
1 Adygea
2 Karachey-Cherkessia
3 Kabardino-Balkaria
4 North Ossetia
5 Ingushetia
6 Chechenia
7 Dagestan
8 Mordvinia
9 Chuvashia
10 Mari El
11 Tatarstan
12 Udmurtia
13 Khakassia
AZERBAIJAN
14 Naxçıvan
GEORGIA
15 Ajaria
16 Abkhazia
UKRAINE
17 Crimea
Projection: Conical Orthomorphic with two standard parallels
East from Greenwich
ft m
12 000 4000
9000 3000
6000 2000
3000 1000
1200 400
600 200
0 0
200 600
2000 6000
4000 12 000
m ft
RUSSIA
KAZAKHSTAN
UZBEKISTAN
TURKMENISTAN
KYRGYZSTAN
TAJIKISTAN
AFGHANISTAN
IRAN
IRAQ
TURKEY
GEORGIA
ARMENIA
AZERBAIJAN
UKRAINE
BELARUS
POLAND
LITHUANIA
LATVIA
ESTONIA
FINLAND
SWEDEN
NORWAY
DENMARK
GERMANY
MOLDOVA
ROMANIA
Barents Sea
Kara Sea
Baltic Sea
Black Sea
Caspian Sea
Aral Sea
Sea of Azov
North Sea
Gulf of Bothnia
Beloye More
Zemlya Frantsa Iosifa
Novaya Zemlya
SEVERO-ZAPADNYY
TSENTRALNYY
PRIVOLZHSKIY
YUZHNYY
URALSKIY
MOSKVA
SANKT-PETERBURG
ASTANA
ALMATY
TOSHKENT
BAKI
TEHRĀN
ÜRÜMQI

D C B
E F G
6 7 8 9

East Siberian Sea
Laptev Sea
OCEAN
Chukchi Sea
Bering Sea
Sea of Okhotsk
Sea of Japan (East Sea)
Ostrov Vrangelya
Severnaya Zemlya
Ostrov Komsomolets
Ostrov Oktyabrskoy Revolyutsii
Ostrov Bolshevik
Ostrov Shmidta
Ostrov Pioner
Mys Arkticheskiy
Mys Chelyuskin
Proliv Vilkitskogo
Novosibirskiye Ostrova
Ostrov Kotelnyy
Ostrov Belkovskiy
Ostrov Stolbovoy
Lyakhovskiye Ostrova
Proliv Dmitriya Lapteva
Ostrov Novaya Sibir
Ostrov Faddeyevskiy
Ostrova Delonga
Ostrov Zhokhova
Ostrov Bennetta
Poluostrov Taymyr
Gory Byrranga
Oz. Taymyr
Ostrov Bolshoy Begichev
Nordvik
Khatanga
Volochanka
Dudinka
Norilsk
Gory Putorana
Turukhansk
Noginsk
Nizhnyaya Tunguska
Tura
Yukta
Podkamennaya Tunguska
Yartsevo
Vanavara
Kezhma
Yeniseysk
Boguchany
Krasnoyarsk
Achinsk
Kansk
Tayshet
Bratsk
Ust-Ilimsk
Ust-Kut
Kirensk
Nizhneudinsk
Tulun
Zima
Irkutsk
Angarsk
Usolye Sibirskoye
Cheremkhovo
Ulan Ude
Chita
Vostochnyy Sayan
Zapadnyy Sayan
Abakan
Minusinsk
Kyzyl
TUVA
Tannu Ola
Uvs Nuur
Hovsgol Nuur
Kyakhta
Darhan
Ulaanbaatar
Hentiyn Nuruu
Hangayn Nuruu
Hovd
Uliastay
Tsetserleg
Altay
Choybalsan
Tamsagbulag
Ondorhaan
Saynshand
Erenhot
Dalandzadgad
Hami
Gaxun Nur
MONGOLIA
Gobi
Baotou
Hohhot
Zhangjiakou
BEIJING
Chengde
Chifeng
Linxi
Xilinhot
CHINA
Hailar
Manzhouli
Hulun Nur
Da Hinggan Ling
QIQIHAR
HARBIN
Dongbei
CHANGCHUN
JILIN
SHENYANG
ANSHAN
FUSHUN
DALIAN
Yingkou
Dandong
NORTH KOREA
PYONGYANG
Nampo
Wonsan
Chongjin
SOUL (Seoul)
INCH'ON
TAEJON
TAEGU
PUSAN
SOUTH KOREA
JAPAN
Hokkaido
SAPPORO
Hakodate
Aomori
Akita
Honshu
Niigata
Kanazawa
OSAKA
Vladivostok
Nakhodka
Ussuriysk
Khabarovsk
Komsomolsk
Sikhote Alin
Blagoveshchensk
Svobodnyy
Tynda
Skovorodino
Stanovoy Khrebet
Yablonovyy Khrebet
Ozero Baykal
Sakhalin
Yuzhno-Sakhalinsk
Kurilskiye Ostrova
Okha
Nikolayevsk-na-Amure
Ayan
Okhotsk
Magadan
Khrebet Dzhugdzhur
Aldan
Neryungri
Olekminsk
Lensk
Vilyuysk
Yakutsk
Mirnyy
Verkhoyanskiy Khrebet
Verkhoyansk
Khrebet Cherskogo
Kolymskoye Nagorye
DALNEVOSTOCHNYY
SAKHA
RUSSIA
Zhigansk
Tiksi
Arctic Circle
Srednekolymsk
Nizhne Kolymsk
Cherskiy
Pevek
Chukotskoye Nagorye
Anadyr
Koryakskoye Nagorye
Sredinnyy Khrebet
Poluostrov Kamchatka
Petropavlovsk-Kamchatskiy
Ust-Kamchatsk
Komandorskiye Ostrova
Mys Dezhneva (East C.)
Uelen
Provideniya
Anadyrskiy Zaliv
St. Lawrence I. (U.S.A.)
Zaliv Shelikhova
COPYRIGHT PHILIP'S

1:4 400 000
50 0 25 50 75 100 125 150 175 km
50 0 25 50 75 100 125 miles
SEA OF OKHOTSK
SEA OF JAPAN
(EAST SEA)
La Perouse Strait
(Sōya-Kaikyō)
Sakhalin
(Russia)
Ostrov Kunashir
Nemuro-Kaikyō
HOKKAIDŌ
Hokkaidō
SAPPORO
Otaru
Asahikawa
Kitami
Abashiri
Abashiri-Wan
Wakkanai
Rishiri-Tō
Rebun-Tō
Kushiro
Nemuro
Obihiro
Tomakomai
Muroran
Uchiura-Wan
Ishikari-Wan
(Otaru-Wan)
Hakodate
Tsugaru-Kaikyō
Okushiri-Tō
Hidaka-Sammyaku
Kitami-Sammyaku
Erimo-Misaki
Sōya-Misaki
Honshū
TŌHOKU
CHŪBU
Aomori
Hachinohe
Mutsu-Wan
Morioka
Akita
Sendai
Sendai-Wan
Yamagata
Fukushima
Niigata
Sado
Sakata
Hirosaki
Miyako
Ishinomaki
RUSSIA
Khrebet Sikhote Alin
Vladivostok
Nakhodka
Ussuriysk
Lake Khanka
Zaliv Petra Velikogo
Dalnerechensk
Dalnegorsk
Olga
Svetlaya
CHINA
HEILONGJIANG
JILIN
Jixi
Shuangyashan
Jiamusi
Hunchun
NORTH KOREA
Chŏngjin
Najin
53
57

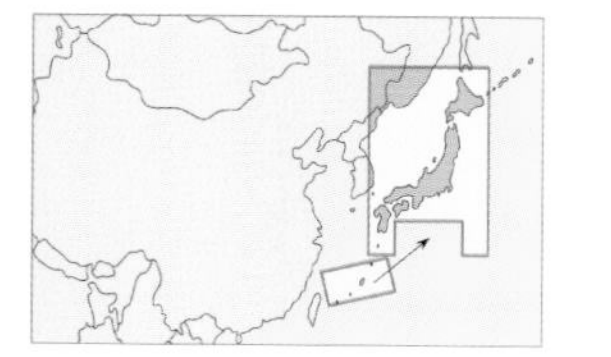

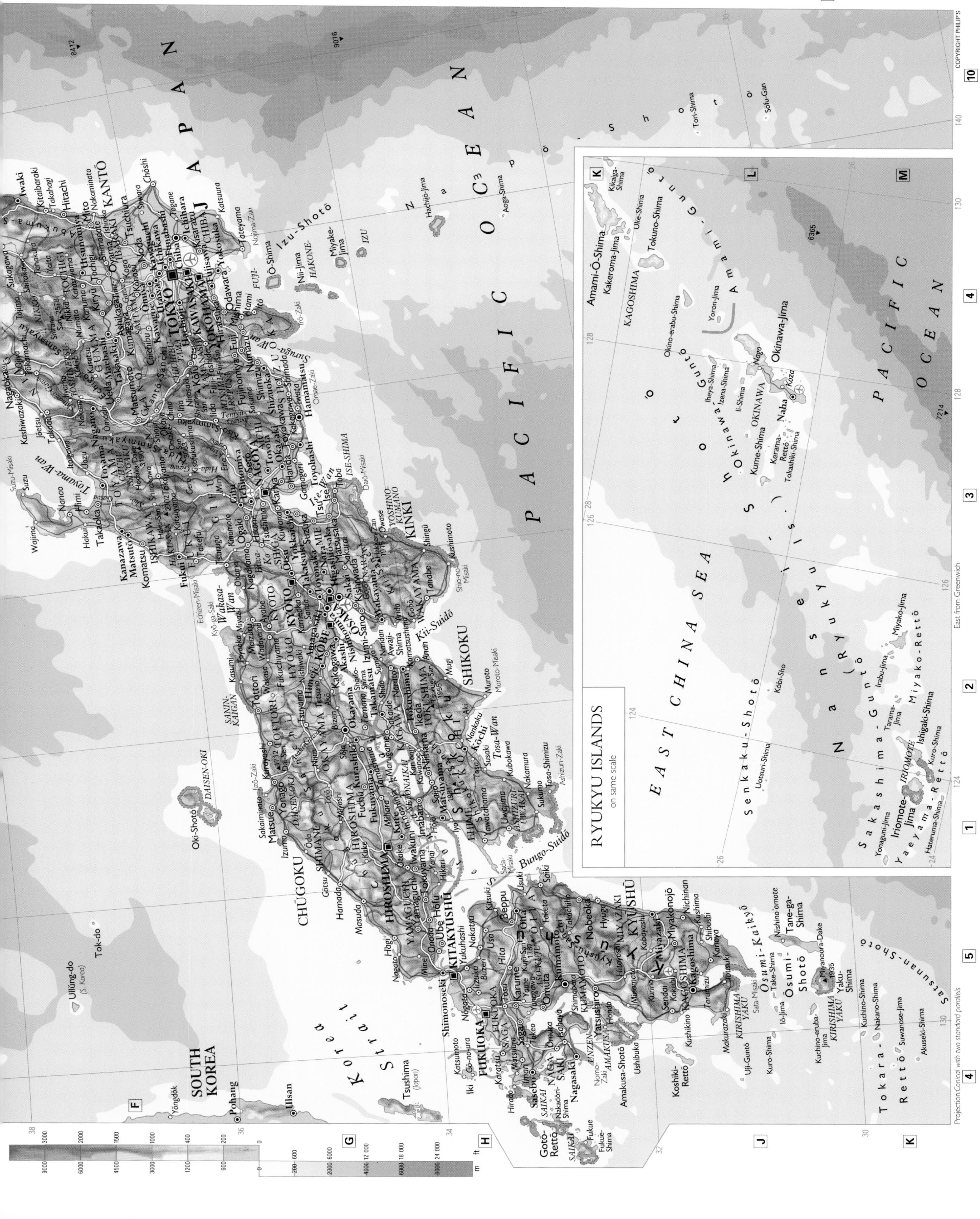

RYUKYU ISLANDS
on same scale

Projection: Conical with two standard parallels

East from Greenwich

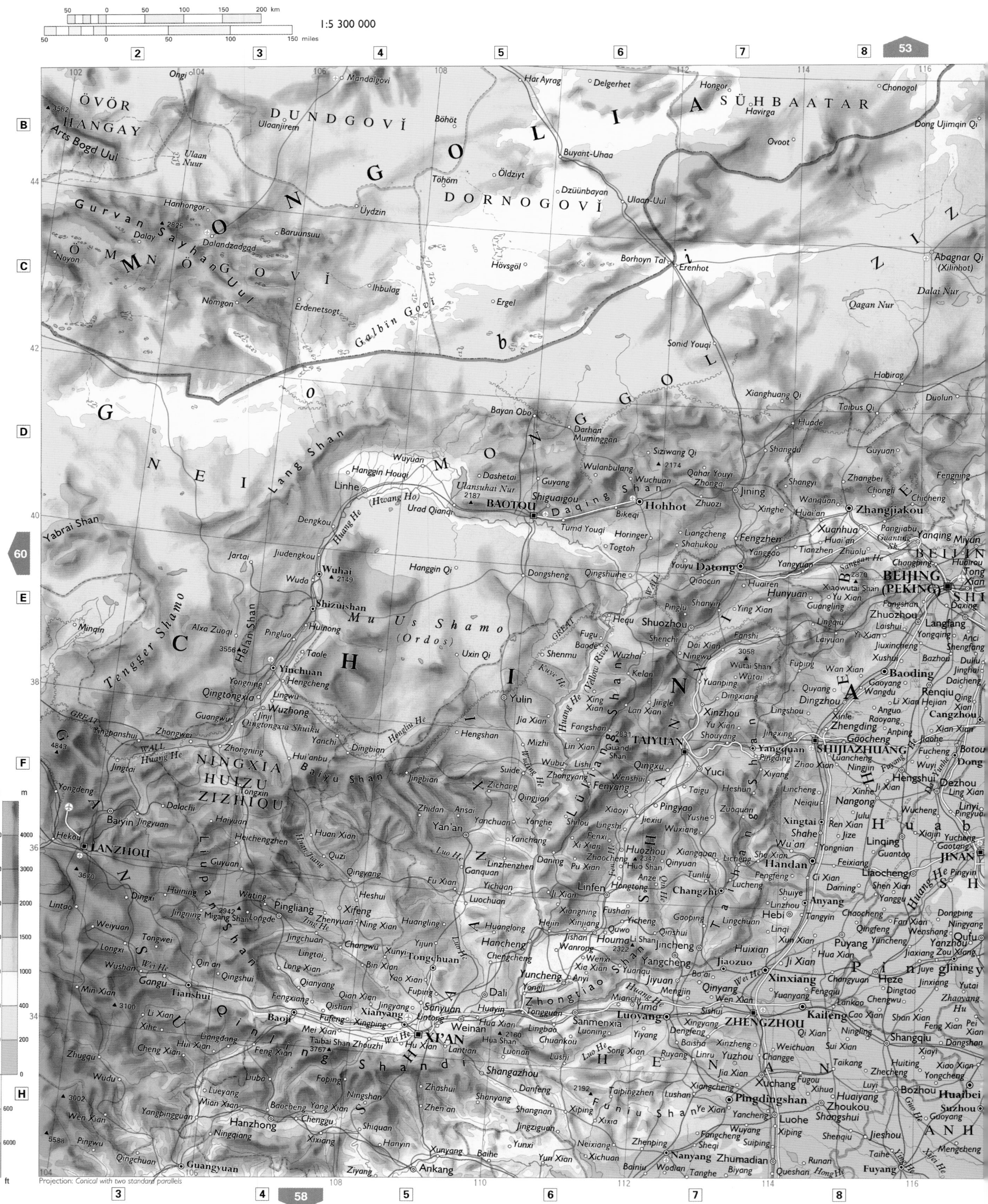
1:5 300 000
km
miles
Projection: Conical with two standard parallels
ÖVÖR HANGAY
DUNDGOVĬ
DORNOGOVĬ
SÜHBAATAR
ÖMNÖGOVĬ
MONGOLIA
Gobi
Galbin Govĭ
Gurvan Sayhan Uul
Arts Bogd Uul
NEI MONGOL
Mu Us Shamo (Ordos)
Tengger Shamo
Lang Shan
Daqing Shan
Helan Shan
NINGXIA HUIZU ZIZHIQU
GANSU
SHAANXI
SHANXI
HENAN
HEBEI
SHANDONG
ANHUI
Liupan Shan
Qinling Shandi
Lüliang Shan
Taihang Shan
Zhongtiao Shan
Funiu Shan
GREAT WALL
Huang He (Hwang Ho)
Huang He (Yellow River)
Wei He
Luo He
BEIJING (PEKING)
TAIYUAN
SHIJIAZHUANG
ZHENGZHOU
XI'AN
LANZHOU
JINAN
BAOTOU
Hohhot
Yinchuan
Datong
Zhangjiakou
Baoding
Handan
Luoyang
Kaifeng
Xinxiang
Anyang
Changzhi
Yan'an
Yulin
Wuhai
Baoji
Tianshui
Hanzhong
Guangyuan
Ankang
Pingdingshan
Nanyang
Erenhot
Abagnar Qi (Xilinhot)
Ulaan-Uul
Buyant-Uhaa
Dalandzadgad
Mandalgovi
Qagan Nur
Dalai Nur
Ulansuhai Nur
Ulaan Nuur
Yabrai Shan
12 000 / 4000
9000 / 3000
6000 / 2000
4500 / 1500
3000 / 1000
1200 / 400
600 / 200
0 / 0
200 / 600
2000 / 6000
m / ft

53
60
58

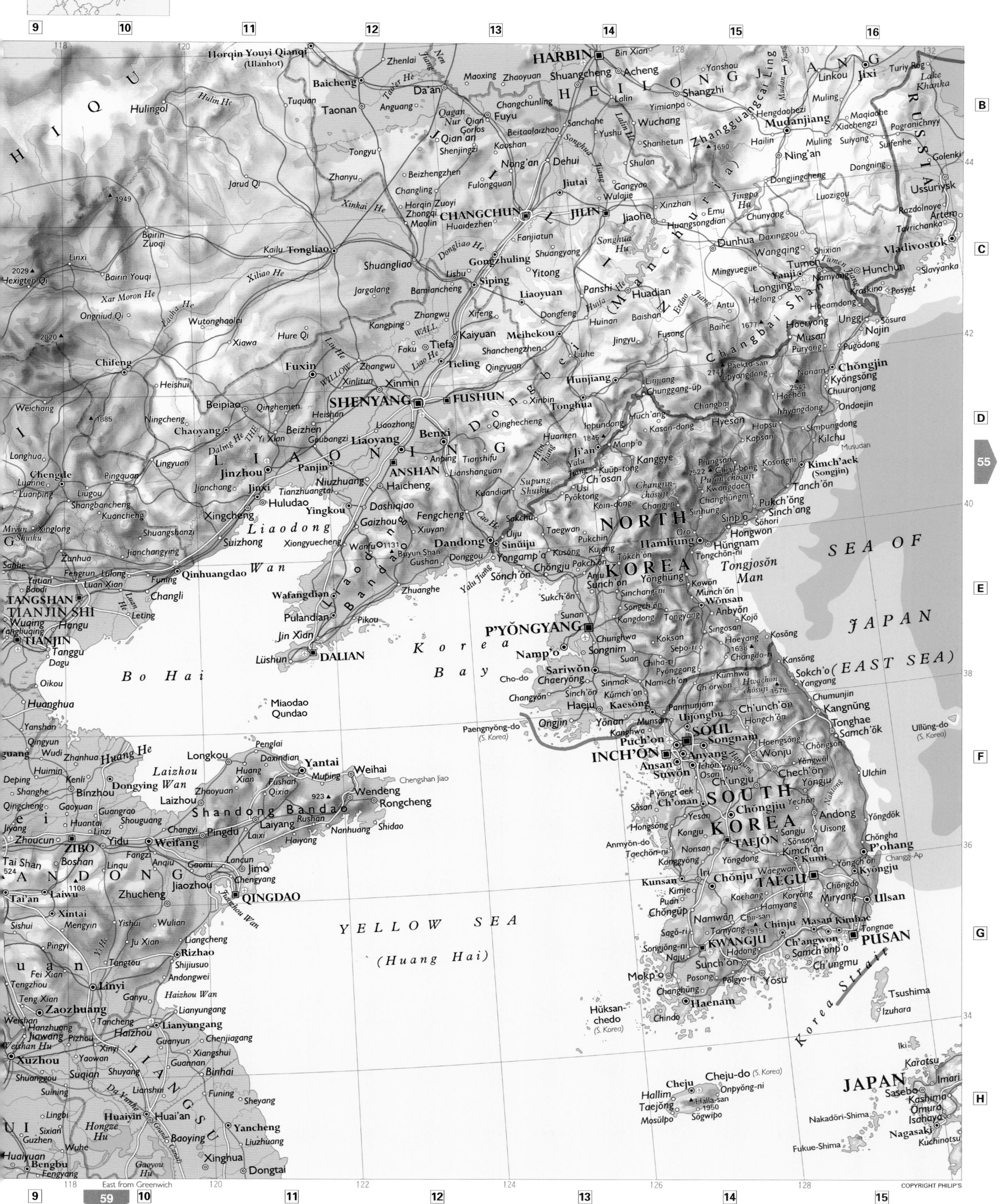

1:5 300 000

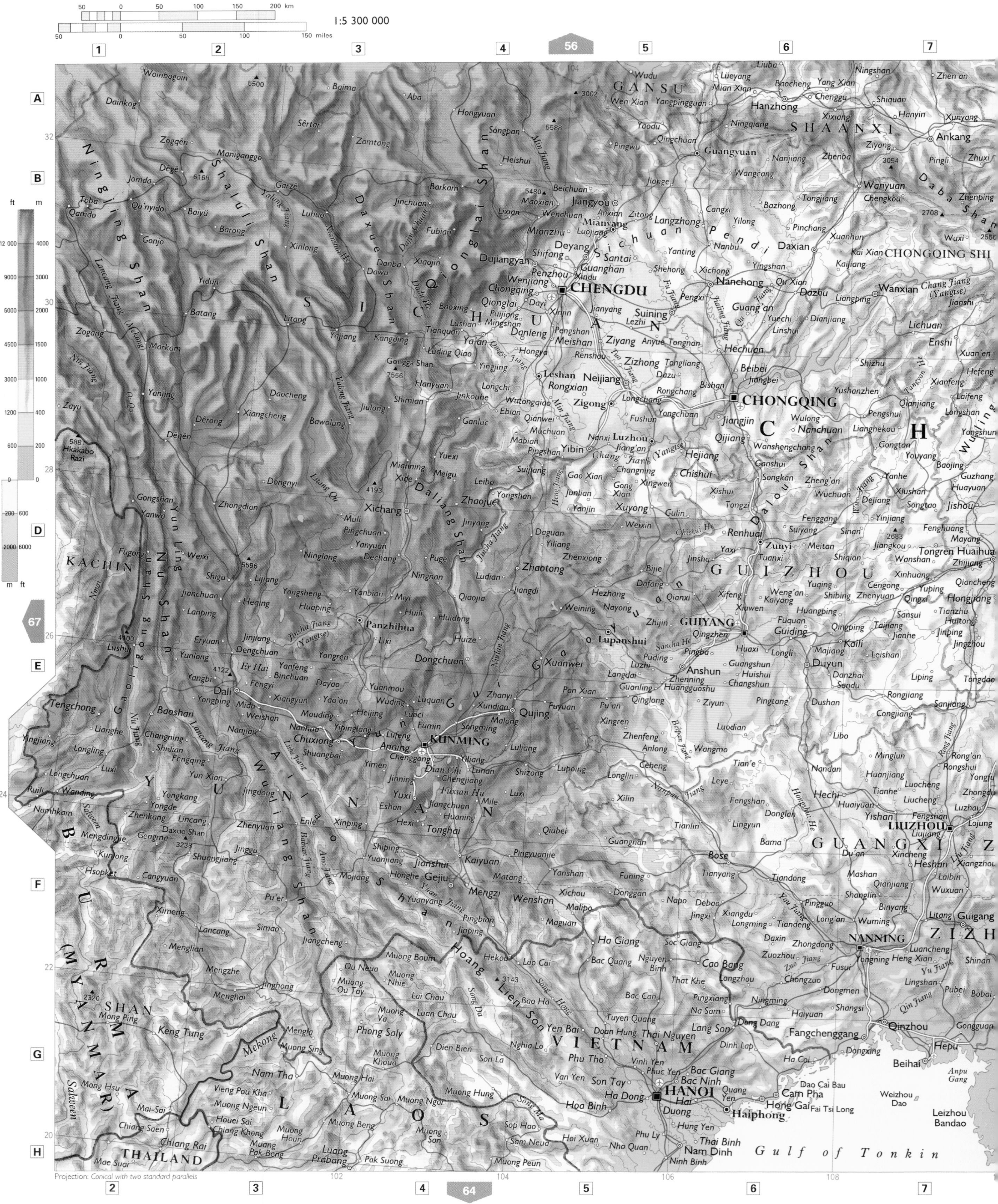

50 0 50 100 150 200 km
50 0 50 100 150 miles
1 2 3 4 5 6 7
56
A B D E F G H
67
64
Projection: Conical with two standard parallels
GANSU
SHAANXI
SICHUAN
Sichuan Pendi
CHONGQING SHI
GUIZHOU
YUNNAN
GUANGXI
VIETNAM
LAOS
THAILAND
BURMA (MYANMAR)
KACHIN
SHAN
CHENGDU
CHONGQING
GUIYANG
KUNMING
HANOI
NANNING
LIUZHOU
Gulf of Tonkin
Hanzhong
Ankang
Guangyuan
Mianyang
Deyang
Nanchong
Suining
Neijiang
Zigong
Leshan
Yibin
Luzhou
Zunyi
Anshun
Liupanshui
Qujing
Dali
Panzhihua
Xichang
Lijiang
Baoshan
Tengchong
Jinghong
Gejiu
Kaiyuan
Mengzi
Wenshan
Bose
Hechi
Qinzhou
Beihai
Hepu
Fangchenggang
Haiphong
Nam Dinh
Thai Binh
Hoa Binh
Yen Bai
Lao Cai
Cao Bang
Lang Son
Ha Giang
Dien Bien
Luang Prabang
Keng Tung
Chiang Rai
Chiang Saen
Ningjing Shan
Shaluli Shan
Daxue Shan
Qionglai Shan
Daba Shan
Daliang Shan
Dalou Shan
Wuliang Shan
Ailao Shan
Yun Ling
Nu Shan
Gaoligong Shan
Hoang Lien Son
Wuling Shan
Gongga Shan
7556
Hkakabo Razi
5881
Lancang Jiang (Mekong)
Nu Jiang
Jinsha Jiang (Yangtse)
Chang Jiang (Yangtse)
Min Jiang
Jialing Jiang
Wu Jiang
Nanpan Jiang
Hongshui He
Yalong Jiang
Dadu He
Song Hong
Song Da
Mekong
Salween
Er Hai
Dian Chi
Fuxian Hu

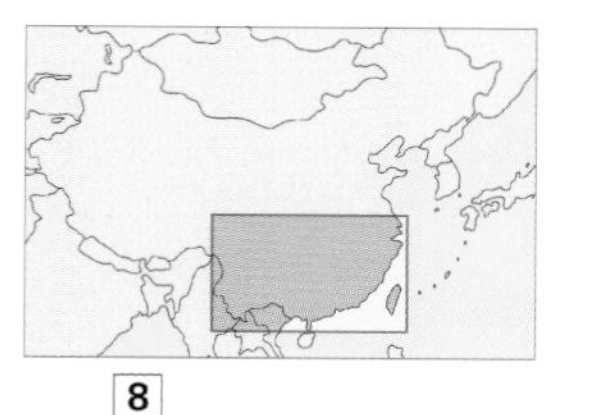

57

8 9 10 11 12 13 14

A B C D E F G H

Shangnan Xiping Xixia Fangcheng Wuyang Suiping Xiping Shenqiu Jieshou Mengcheng Guzhen Hongze Hu Xinghua Dongtai
Jingziguan Yun Xian Neixiang Zhenping Nanyang Sheqi Zhumadian Runan Hong He Taihe Fuyang Madian Guo He Huaiyuan Wuhe Fengyang Bengbu Mingguang Gaoyou Hu Gaoyou J I A N G S U Hai'an Rugao Rudong
Baihe Xichuan Danjiangkou Shuiku Wadian Tanghe Biyang Queshan Xincai Yingshang Fengtai Huainan Shou Xian Tianchang Yangzhou Taizhou Jiangyan Yangzhong Jiangdu Luhe Yizheng Dingyuan Changfeng
Shiyan Bainiu Dengzhou Xinye H E N A N Zhengyang Huai He Xi Xian Huaibin Zhengyangguan Taixing Nantong Haimen Qidong
Danjiangkou Laohekou Minggang Tongbai Luoshan Huangchuan Huoqiu Chengxi Hu Chengdong Hu Wabu Hu Chuzhou NANJING Zhenjiang Danyang Jingjiang Jiangyin Chang Jiang (Yangtse) Chongming Dao
Zhushan Gucheng Zaoyang Xinyang Gushi Hefei Jurong Changzhou Chongming Changshu
Fang Xian Bookang Xiangfan Nanzhang Suizhou Lu'an Feixi Chao Hu Zhegao Jiangning Ma'anshan Jintan Wuxi Kunshan Jiading Baoshan
Shennongjia Jing Shan Yicheng Dahong Shan Maping 1636 Guangshui Dawu Shangcheng Jinzhai Huoshan Shucheng Chaohu He Xian Lishui Dangtu Shijiu Hu Liyang Suzhou Qingpu SHANGHAI Nanhui
Xuejiaping Xiemahe Fengle Hong'an Dabie Shan A N H U I Wuwei Wuhu Gaochun Yixing Tai Hu Wujiang Songjiang Jinshan SHANGHAI SHI
Yangping Zhongxiang Anlu Macheng 1834 Tongcheng Lujiang Fangchang Nanyi Hu Langxi Changxing Huzhou Jiaxing Pinghu
Xingshan Yuan'an Jingmen Yunmeng Xiaogan Yuexi Tongling Datong Nanling Xuanzhou Guangde Anji Tongxiang Haining Hangzhou Wan Daqu Shan
Three Gorges Dam H U B E I Jingshan Yingcheng Hanchuan Huangpi Xinzhou Luotian Gaohebu Zongyang Guichi Qingyang Jing Xian Xiaofeng Ningguo Chongde Haiyan Dai Shan Daishan
Yichang Dangyang Tianmen Hankou WUHAN Tuanfeng Yingshan Qianshan Anqing Taiping HANGZHOU Shangyu Cixi Zhoushan Zhoushan Dao
Changyang Zhijiang Jiangling Shayang Caidian Huanggang Jinkou Xishui Taihu Wangjiang Huaining Dongliu Shitai 1610 Qianyang Jingde Lin'an Xiaoshan Yuyao Zhenhai Putuo Taohua Dao
Zhicheng Shashi Qianjiang Xiantao Paizhou Ezhou Huangshi Qichun Susong Changhua Fuyang Shaoxing Ningbo
Wufeng Songzi Gong'an Haoxue Hong Hu Jiayu Daye Meichuan Wuxue Huangmei Dongzhi Yi Xian Jixi She Xian Zhuji Shengzhou Fenghua Liuheng Dao
2393 Jianli Honghu Yangxin Pengze Qimen Huangshan Tonglu Xinchang Xiangshan
Nanping Shishou Xianning Ruichang Jiujiang Hukou Shimenjie Xiuning Chun'an Meicheng Pujiang Ninghai
Shimen Jinshi Li Xian Huarong Linxiang Puqi Mufu Shan Lu Shan 1474 De'an Fuliang Jingdezhen Wuyuan Jiande Shouchang Z H E J I A N G Yiwu Dongyang Tiantai Niutou Shan
Sangzhi Cili Linli Anxiang Nan Xian Yueyang Tongcheng Wuning Duchang Kaihua Lanxi Jinhua Anwen Sanmen
Li Shui Changde Dongting Hu Xiu Shui Yongxiu Poyang Hu Leping Changshan Longyou Quzhou Tangxi Wuyi Yongkang Xianju Linhai
Dayong Hanshou 1596 Xiushui Jiuling Shan Jing'an Anyi Boyang Dexing Yushan Jiangshan Jinyun Huangyan Jiaojiang Wenling Taizhou Liedao
Yuan Jiang Taoyuan Yuanjiang Pingjiang 1794 Fengxin Xinjian NANCHANG Nanchang Wannian Hengfeng Shangrao Suichang Lishui Yongjia
Zi Shui Yiyang Miluo Xiangyin Tonggu Gao'an Jinxian Yiyang Guangfeng 1725 Xiping Qingtian Yueqing Yuhuan Yuhuan Dao
Luxi Yuanling Anhua Wangcheng Yifeng Fengcheng Dongxiang Yingtan Yanshan Guixi Xin Jiang Yunhe Wenzhou Dongtou
Meichengzhen Ningxiang CHANGSHA Liuyang Shanggao Zhangshu Linchuan Yujiang Longquan Hexi Rui'an
Chenxi Xupu Shaoshan Xiangtan Zhuzhou Wanzai Yichun Fenyi Xinyu Chongren Jinxi 2120 Pucheng Wencheng Pingyang
Xinhua Loudi Xiangxiang Liling Xingan Zixi Guangze Wuyishan Qingyuan Taishun Cangnan Nanji Shan
Lengshuijiang Lianyuan Pingxiang J I A N G X I Gaokeng Xiajiang Yihuang Nancheng Jianyang Songxi Shouning Fuding
H U N A N Shuangfeng Anfu Gujiang Yongfeng Le'an Shaowu Shuiji Zhenghe Zherong
1963 Xinshao Longhui Shaodong Hengshan Wugong Shan Lianhua Ji'an Jishui Xinfeng Nanfeng Lichuan Jian'ou Zhouning Pingnan Fu'an Sansha
Qianyang Dongkou Shaoyang You Xian Hengyang Yongxin Taining 1629 Ningde Xiapu
Xuefeng Shan Shaoyang Qidong Hengyang Chaling Xincheng Taihe Guangchang Jianning Jiangle Nanping Gutian Fuying Dao
Wugong Huangyangsi Qiyang Anren Lei Shui Ninggang Jinggangshan Wan'an Ningdu Min Jiang Luoyuan Lianjiang Matsu Tao (Taiwan)
Suining Xinning Lengshuitan Xiang Jiang Changning Ling Xian Luoxiao Shan Xingguo Shicheng Mingxi Sha Xian Sanming Minqing Fuzhou
Chengbu Dong'an Yongzhou Leiyang Yongxing 2164 Suichuan Longkou Ninghua Qingliu Youxi Minhou Changle
Ziyuan Guidong Shadi Yudu Ruijin F U J I A N Yongtai Fuqing
Quanzhou Xintian Zixing Ganzhou Changting Yong'an Datian Hanjiang Haitan Dao
Longsheng Xing'an Ningyuan Guiyang Jiahe 1510 Chenzhou Shangyou Chongyi Huichang Liancheng Maiyuan Dehua Xianyou Putian Xinghua Wan Pingtan Tanshui Chilung
Lingchuan Guanyang Dao Xian Yizhang Rucheng Dayu Nankang Xinfeng Anyuan Ting Jiang Zhangping Yongchun Anxi Hui'an Nanri Dao T'AIPEI T'aoyuan Panch'iao
Wutong Guilin Jiangyong Lanshan Linwu Nanxiong Wuping Longyan Nanan Quanzhou Chunghi Hsinchu Tach'i Ilan
Lingui Jianghua Nan Ling Lechang Renhua Xunwu Shanghang Hua'an Jinjiang T'uch'eng Lotung
Gongcheng Fuchuan Lianzhou Shixing Longnan Dingnan Jiaoling Yongding Changtai Zhangzhou Tong'an Shishi Yüanli Miaoli
Yangshuo Pingle Zhongshan Lianshan Ruyuan Shaoguan Quannan Pingyuan Xiamen Chinmen (Quemoy) Chinmen Tao (Taiwan) Tachia 3931 Tungshih Toiluko
Lipu He Xian Yangshan Wengcheng Heping Lianping Meizhou Nanjing Pinghe Longhai Taiwan Strait Fengyüan T'aichung Chungyang Shanmo Hualien
Xiaren Mengshan Zhaoping Yingde Wengyuan Longchuan Xingning Dabu Zhangpu Changhua Lukang Yüanlin Erhlin Nantou Fenglin
G U A N G X I Z H U A N G Z U Huaiji Xinfeng Fengshun Han Jiang Yunxiao TAIWAN Tounan Yunlin Alishan
Gui Jiang Nanfeng Qingyuan Bei Jiang Fogang Xinfengjiang Shuiku Longmen Dong Jiang Heyuan Huacheng Chaozhou Raoping Dongshan Makung P'enghu Ch'üntou (Pescadores) (Taiwan) Pekang Chiai Yu Shan 3997 Paiho Yüli
Pingnan Wuzhou Guangning G U A N G D O N G Conghua Zijin Jieyang Chenghai Zhao'an Nan'ao Tropic of Cancer P'otzu Hsinying Kuanshan
Xun Jiang Teng Xian Fengkai Sihui Huadu Zengcheng Puning Chaoyang Shantou Chiali Ch'ishan
Guiping Cangwu Xi Jiang Zhaoqing Hekou Sanshui GUANGZHOU Boluo Huizhou Haifeng Lufeng Haimen T'ainan T'aitung
Deqing Gaoyao Foshan Shilong Dongguan Huidong Shanwei Huilai Fengshan Lü-Tao
Q U Yunan Yunfu Jiujiang Panyu Shunde Shenzhen Honghai Wan KAOHSIUNG P'ingtung
Beiliu Rong Xian Cenxi Yunkai Dashan Luoding Xinxing Jiangmen Xiaolan Zhongshan Tsuen Wan Kowloon Fangliao Tawu
Yulin Kaiping Xinhui Enping Zhuhai Zhu Jiang HONG KONG (XIANGGANG) Fengkang Hengchun Hung'ou Hsü
Luchuan 1703 Xinyi Taishan Doumen Macau Chixi Dangan Liedao Maopi T'ou Oluanpi
Yangchun Gaolan Dao
Gaozhou Yangjiang Luzon Strait
Huazhou Maoming Shangchuan Dao
Lianjiang Dianbai Diancheng Hailing Dao Xiachuan Dao
Suixi Wuchuan
Zhanjiang
Leizhou Donghai Dao Naozhou Dao
Leizhou Wan
Dongsha Dao (Pratas I.) (China)
S O U T H C H I N A S E A
Xuwen Hai'an

112 114 116 118 120 122

32 30 28 26 24 22 20

East from Greenwich

61

CHINA

1:17 800 000

100 0 100 200 300 400 500 600 700 800 km

100 0 100 200 300 400 500 miles

m: 6000, 4000, 3000, 2000, 1500, 1000, 400, 200, 0, 200, 2000, 4000, 6000

ft: 18 000, 12 000, 9000, 6000, 4500, 3000, 1200, 600, 0, 600, 6000, 12 000, 18 000

Projection: Bonne

East from Greenwich

53

52

62

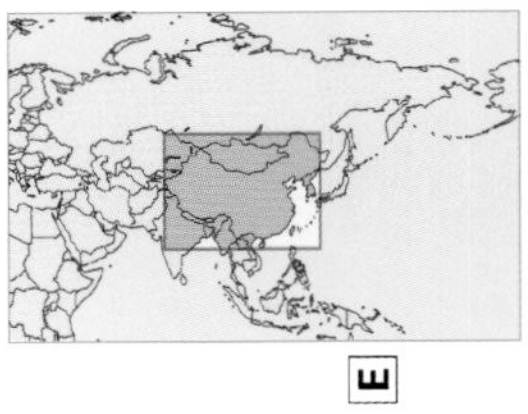

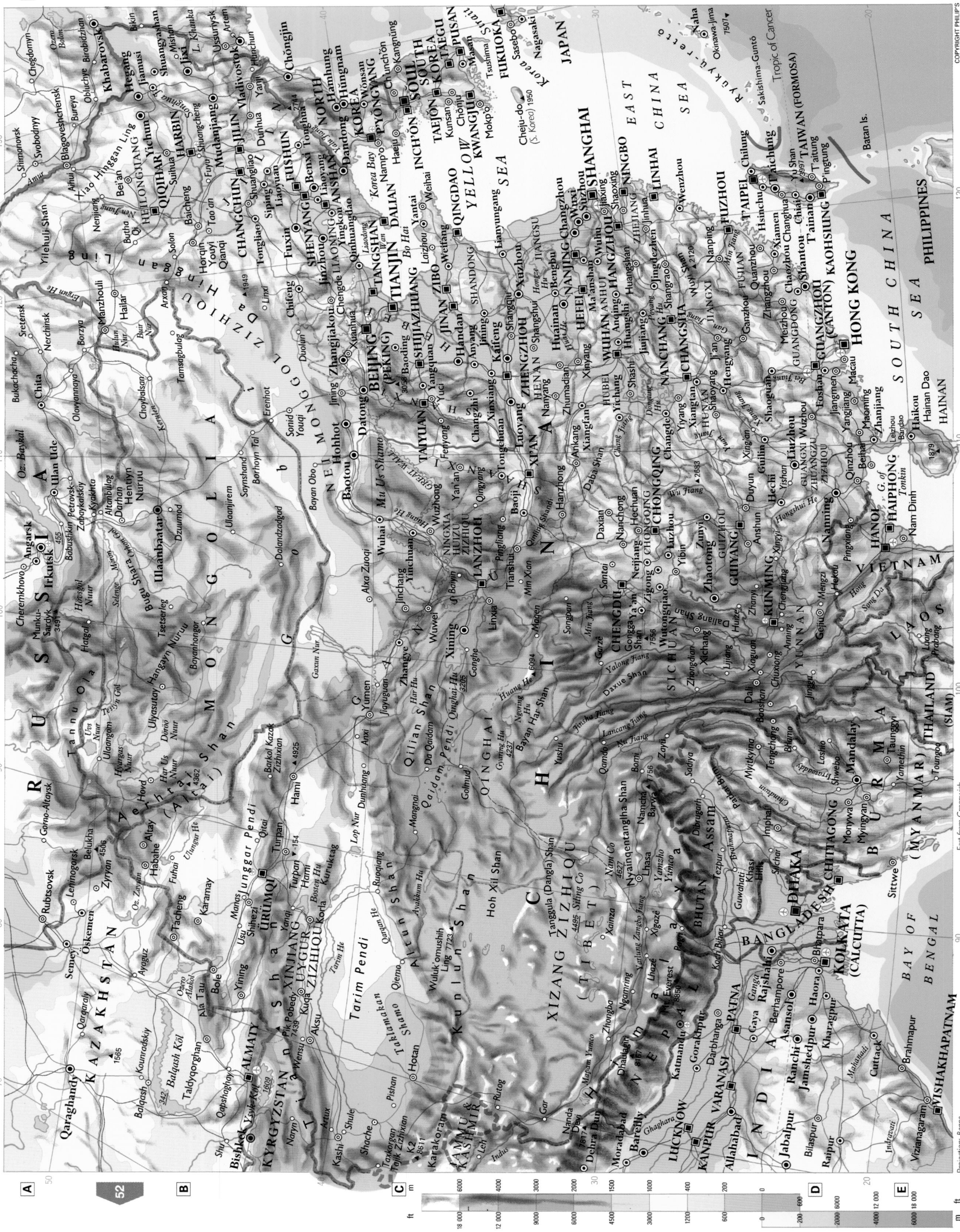

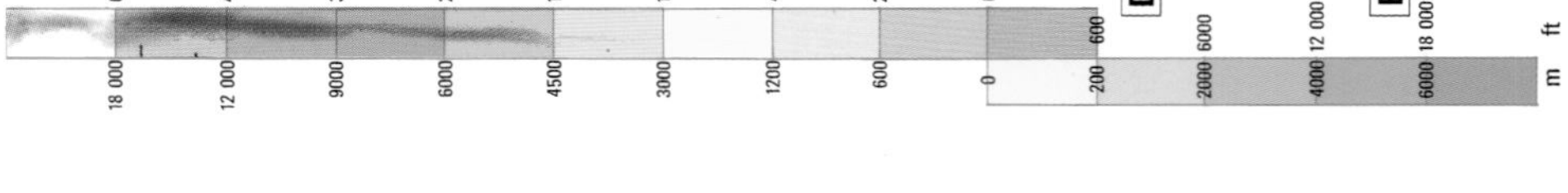

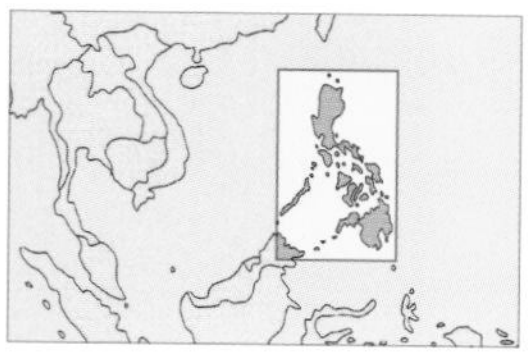

1:6 700 000

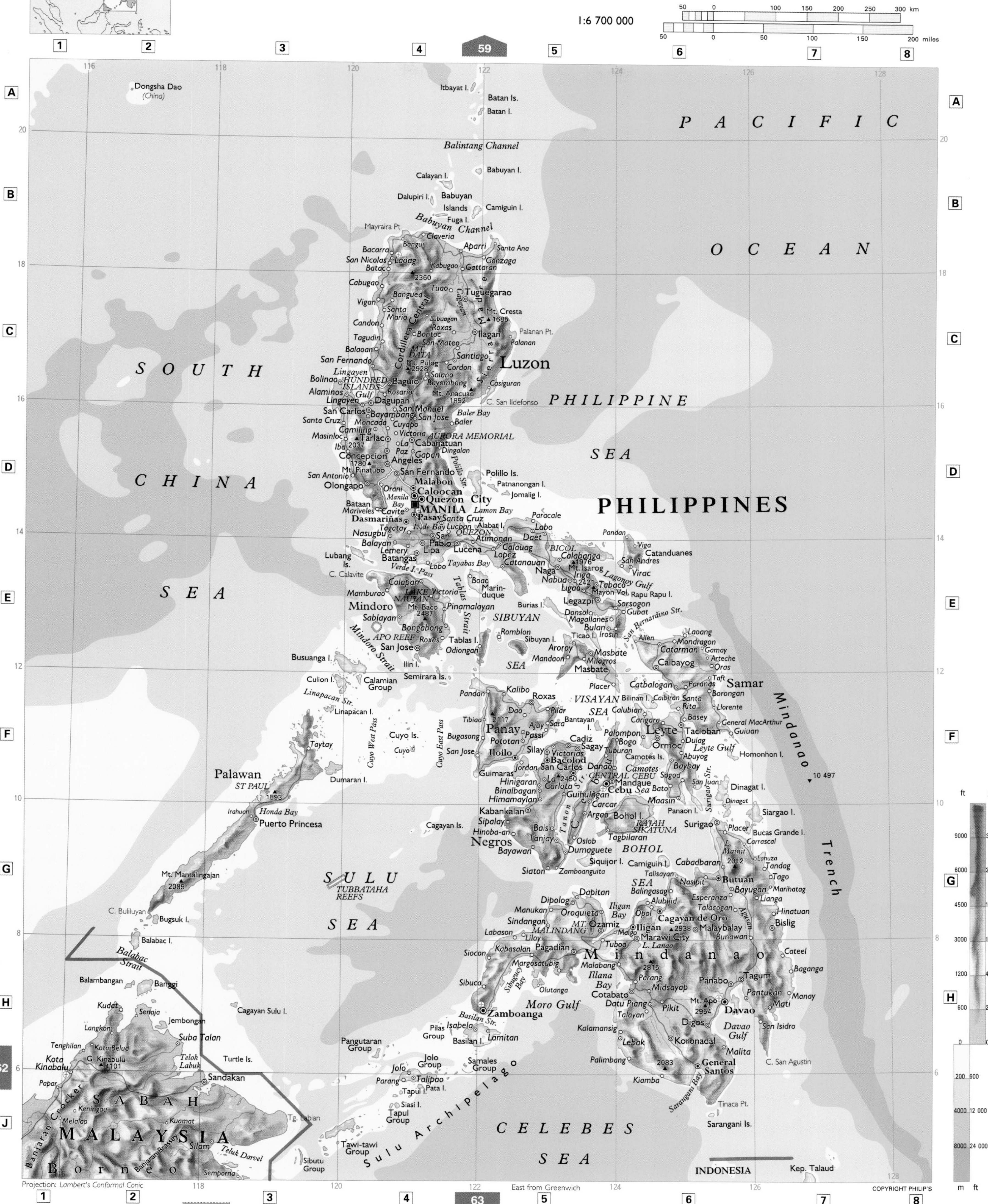

THE PHILIPPINES

Projection: Lambert's Conformal Conic

East from Greenwich

National Parks

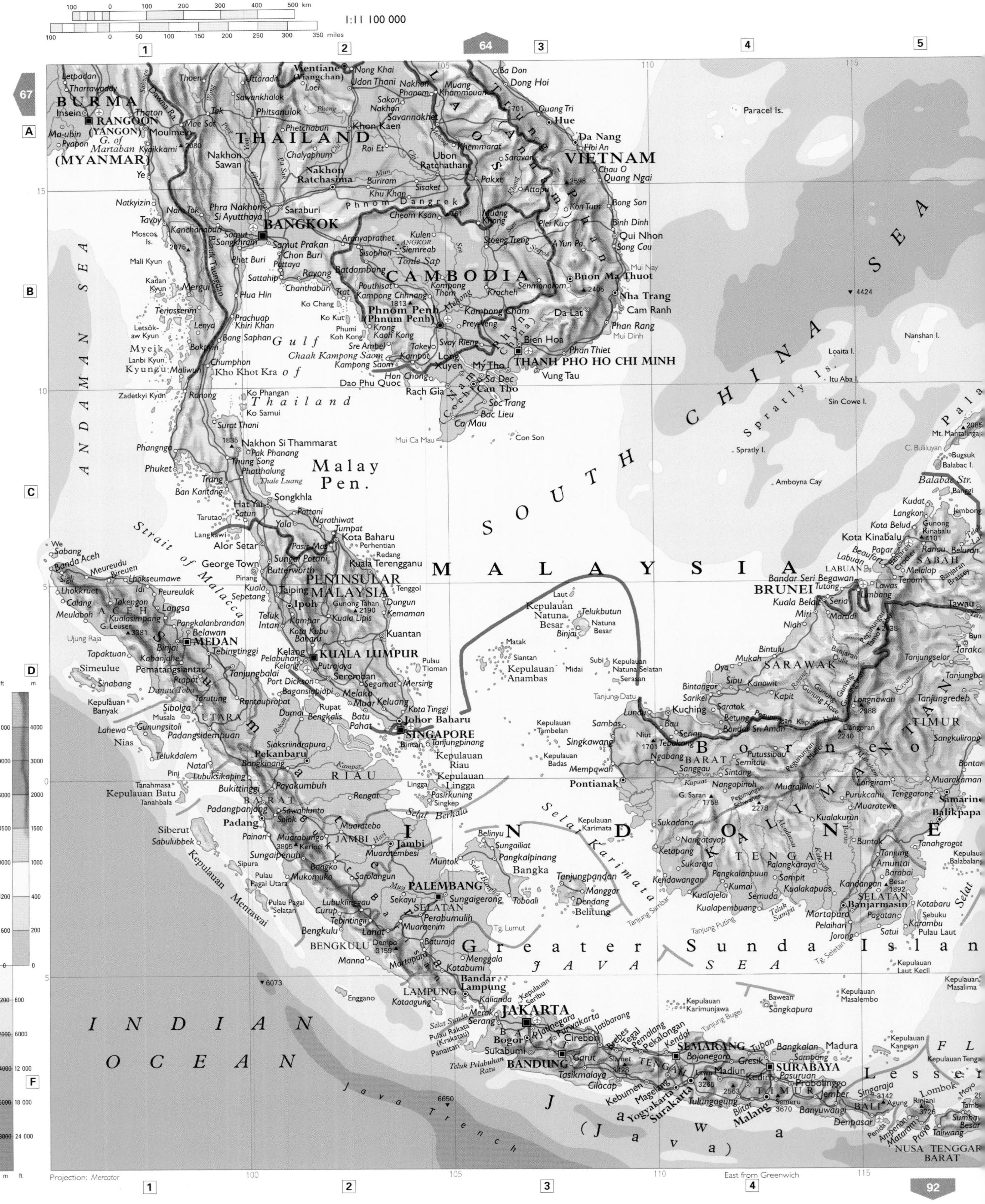
1:11 100 000
Projection: Mercator
East from Greenwich
BURMA
(MYANMAR)
RANGOON
(YANGON)
G. of
Martaban
THAILAND
BANGKOK
LAOS
Vientiane
(Viangchan)
VIETNAM
Hue
Da Nang
CAMBODIA
Phnom Penh
(Phnum Penh)
THANH PHO HO CHI MINH
Gulf of Thailand
ANDAMAN SEA
SOUTH CHINA SEA
Paracel Is.
Spratly Is.
Malay Pen.
MALAYSIA
PENINSULAR MALAYSIA
KUALA LUMPUR
SINGAPORE
Strait of Malacca
BRUNEI
Bandar Seri Begawan
SABAH
SARAWAK
Kota Kinabalu
Kuching
Pontianak
Borneo
KALIMANTAN
MEDAN
Padang
Pekanbaru
Jambi
PALEMBANG
Bangka
Sumatra
INDONESIA
JAKARTA
BANDUNG
SEMARANG
SURABAYA
Yogyakarta
Malang
Denpasar
BALI
Banjarmasin
Balikpapan
Samarinda
Greater Sunda Islands
JAVA SEA
Java
Java Trench
INDIAN OCEAN
Sela Karimata
Kepulauan Natuna
Kepulauan Anambas
Kepulauan Riau
Kepulauan Mentawai
Siberut
Nias
Simeulue
Enggano
NUSA TENGGARA BARAT
Lombok

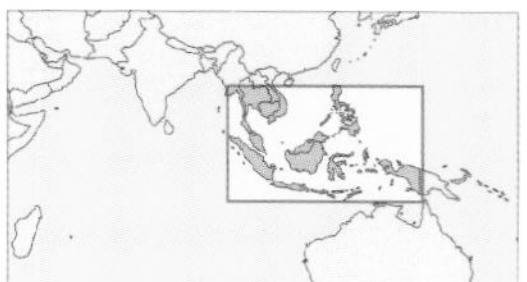

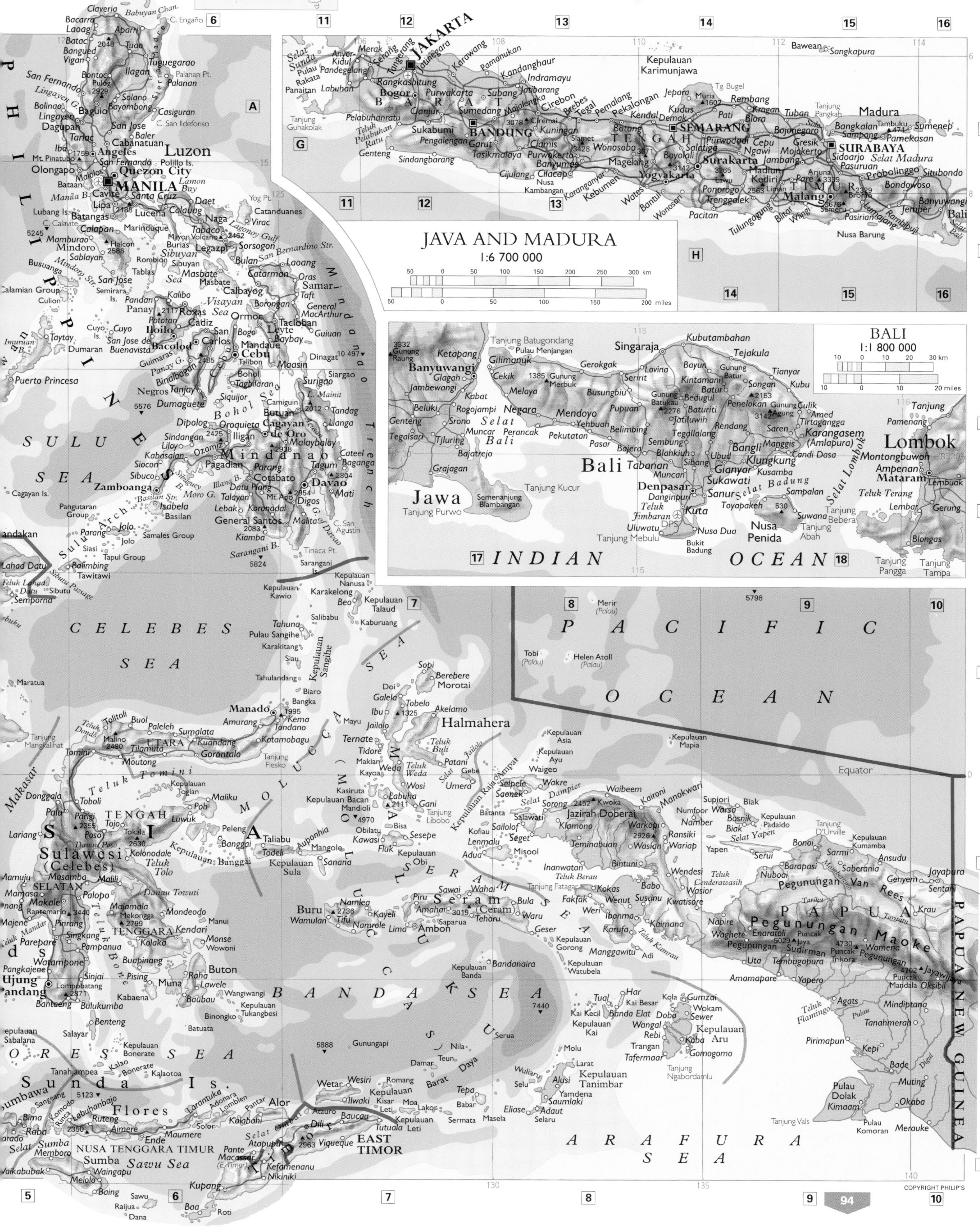

JAVA AND MADURA

1:6 700 000

BALI

1:1 800 000

94

50 0 50 100 150 200 km

1:5 300 000

50 0 50 100 150 miles

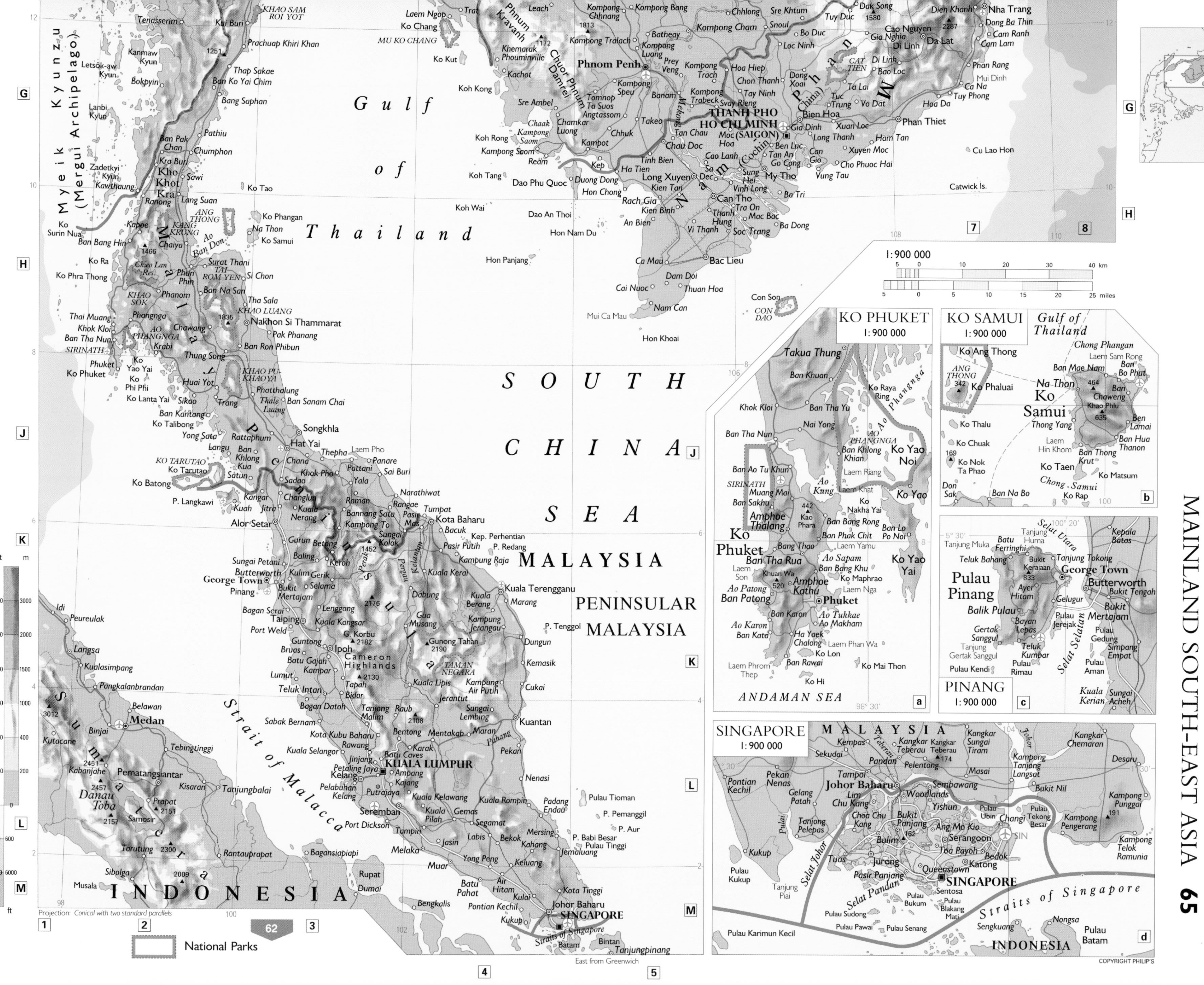
Gulf of Thailand
SOUTH CHINA SEA
MALAYSIA
PENINSULAR MALAYSIA
INDONESIA
Strait of Malacca
Phnom Penh
THANH PHO HO CHI MINH (SAIGON)
KUALA LUMPUR
SINGAPORE
Myeik Kyunzu (Mergui Archipelago)
KO PHUKET
1:900 000
KO SAMUI
1:900 000
PINANG
1:900 000
SINGAPORE
1:900 000
1:900 000
ANDAMAN SEA
Straits of Singapore
National Parks
Projection: Conical with two standard parallels
East from Greenwich
COPYRIGHT PHILIP'S

1:8 900 000
km
miles
Projection: Conical with two standard parallels
Continuation Southwards on same scale
ft
m
ARABIAN SEA
AFGHANISTAN
PAKISTAN
IRAN
INDIA
SRI LANKA
TURKMENISTAN
KARACHI
Hyderabad
Quetta
Kābul
Islamabad
Rawalpindi
Peshawar
Lahore
Faisalabad
Multan
Amritsar
Ludhiana
Chandigarh
DELHI
New Delhi
Jaipur
Agra
Kanpur
Jodhpur
Udaipur
AHMADABAD
Vadodara
Surat
MUMBAI (BOMBAY)
PUNE (Poona)
Nagpur
Indore
Bhopal
HYDERABAD
CHENNAI (Madras)
BANGALORE
Madurai
Colombo
Kandy
Jaffna
Trincomalee
Herat
Qandahār
RAJASTHAN
GUJARAT
PUNJAB
HARYANA
MAHARASHTRA
MADHYA PRADESH
ANDHRA PRADESH
KARNATAKA
TAMIL NADU
KERALA
JAMMU & KASHMIR
HIMACHAL PRADESH
UTTARANCHAL
BALUCHISTAN
SIND
Thar Desert
Great Indian Desert
Hindu Kush
Karakoram
Western Ghats
Eastern Ghats
Gulf of Kachchh
Gulf of Khambhat
Rann of Kachchh
Coromandel Coast
Malabar Coast
Gulf of Mannar
Palk Strait
Makran Coast Range
Central Makran Range
Sulaiman Range
Kirthar Range
Mouths of the Indus
C. Comorin
Dondra Head

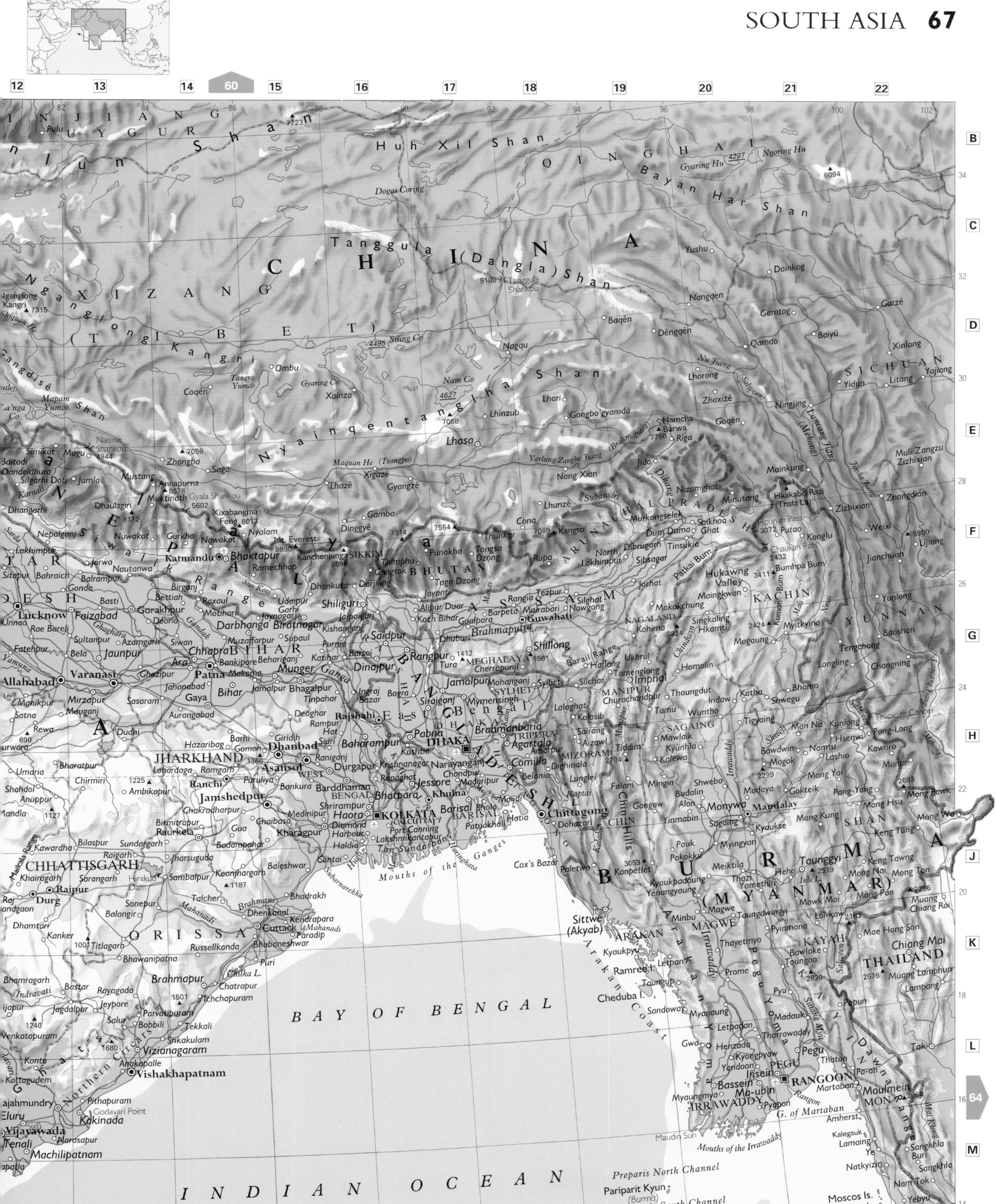
CHINA
XIZANG (TIBET)
QINGHAI
SICHUAN
YUNNAN
NEPAL
BHUTAN
SIKKIM
BANGLADESH
BURMA (MYANMAR)
THAILAND
BIHAR
JHARKHAND
CHHATTISGARH
ORISSA
ASSAM
ARUNACHAL PRADESH
NAGALAND
MANIPUR
MIZORAM
TRIPURA
MEGHALAYA
WEST BENGAL
KACHIN
SAGAING
CHIN
MAGWE
ARAKAN
SHAN
KAYAH
IRRAWADDY
PEGU
MON
Tanggula (Dangla) Shan
Huh Xil Shan
Bayan Har Shan
Nyainqentanglha Shan
Siwalik Range
Chin Hills
Arakan Yoma
Pegu Yoma
Dawna Range
BAY OF BENGAL
INDIAN OCEAN
Mouths of the Ganges
Mouths of the Irrawaddy
G. of Martaban
Preparis North Channel
Preparis South Channel
Arakan Coast
Lhasa
Katmandu
DHAKA
KOLKATA (CALCUTTA)
RANGOON
Patna
Lucknow
Varanasi
Allahabad
Chittagong
Mandalay
Guwahati
Shillong
Vishakhapatnam
Cuttack
Bhubaneshwar
Mt. Everest 8850
Kanchenjunga 8598
Namcha Barwa 7756
East from Greenwich
COPYRIGHT PHILIP'S

1:5 300 000

50 0 50 100 150 200 km

50 0 50 100 150 miles

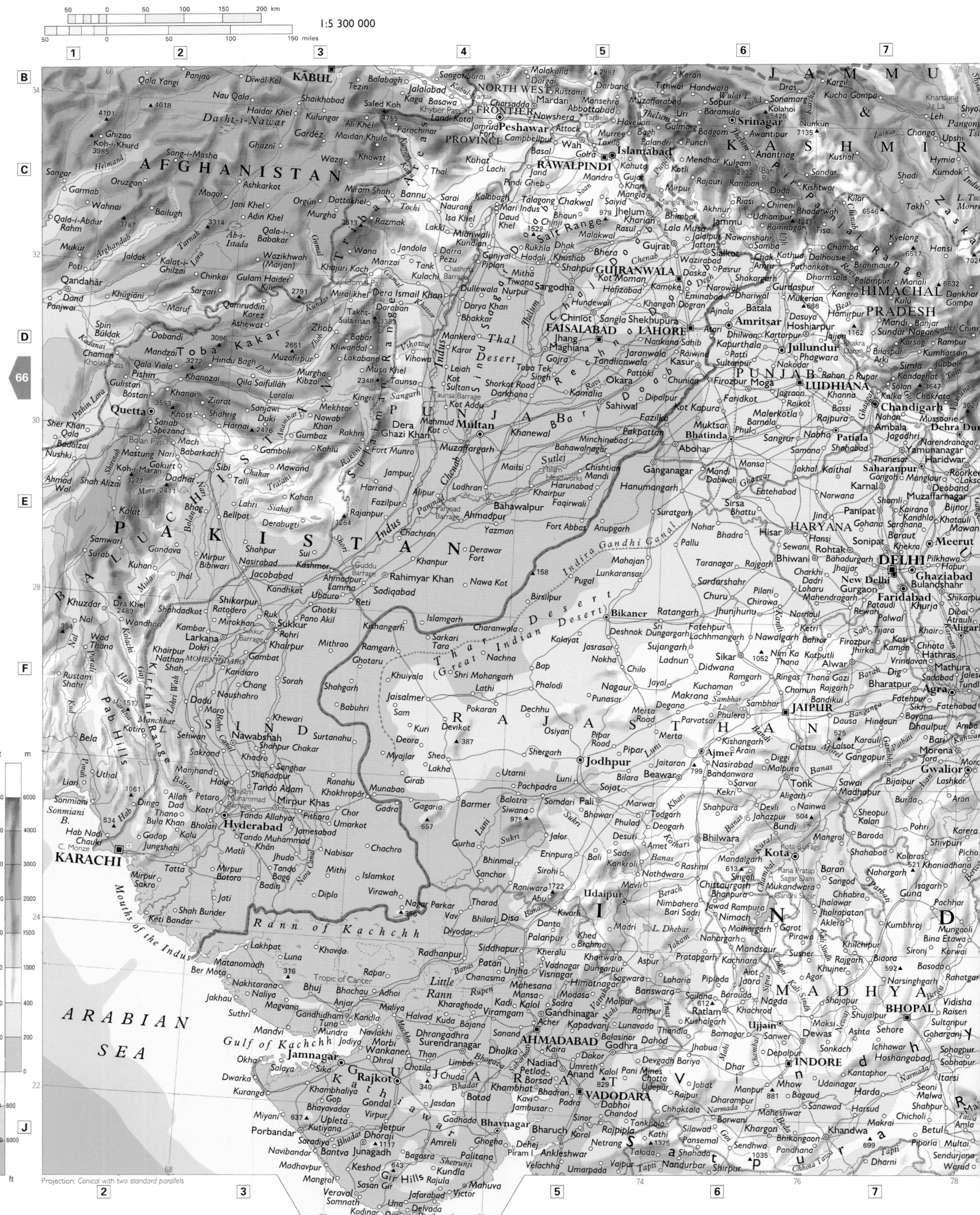

66

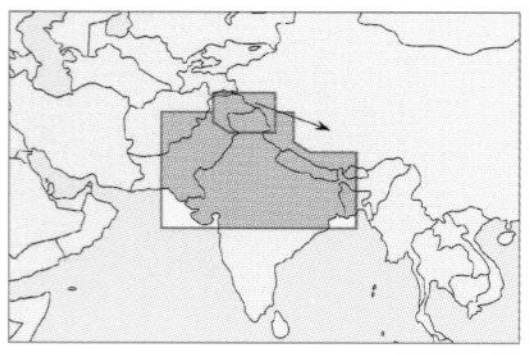

JAMMU AND KASHMIR
on same scale
AFGHANISTAN
CHINA
NORTH WEST FRONTIER
Northern Areas
Karakoram Range
JAMMU & KASHMIR
Zaskar Mountains
Ladakh Range
Kunlun Shan
Aksai Chin
Soda Plains
Islamabad
RAWALPINDI
PUNJAB
Srinagar
Kashmir
Azad
K2
Gasherbrum
Nanga Parbat
HIMACHAL PRADESH
Nganglong Kangri
Gangdisê Shan
XIZANG ZIZHIQU (TIBET)
Yarlung Zangbo Jiang (Brahmaputra)
Mt. Everest (Chomolungma or Sagarmatha)
NEPAL
Katmandu
Himalaya
Mahabharat Lekh
Siwalik Range
UTTARANCHAL
UTTAR PRADESH
LUCKNOW
KANPUR
Allahabad
VARANASI
PATNA
BIHAR
JHARKHAND
Ranchi
Jamshedpur
Dhanbad
WEST BENGAL
KOLKATA
Haora
BANGLADESH
DHAKA
Rajshahi
Khulna
KHULNA
RAJSHAHI
SIKKIM
BHUTAN
Thimphu
ASSAM
Garo Hills
CHHATTISGARH
MADHYA PRADESH
Jabalpur
Kaimur Hills
Maikala Ra.
Sundarbans
Mouths of the Ganges
The Sandheads
East from Greenwich
COPYRIGHT PHILIP'S

1:6 200 000

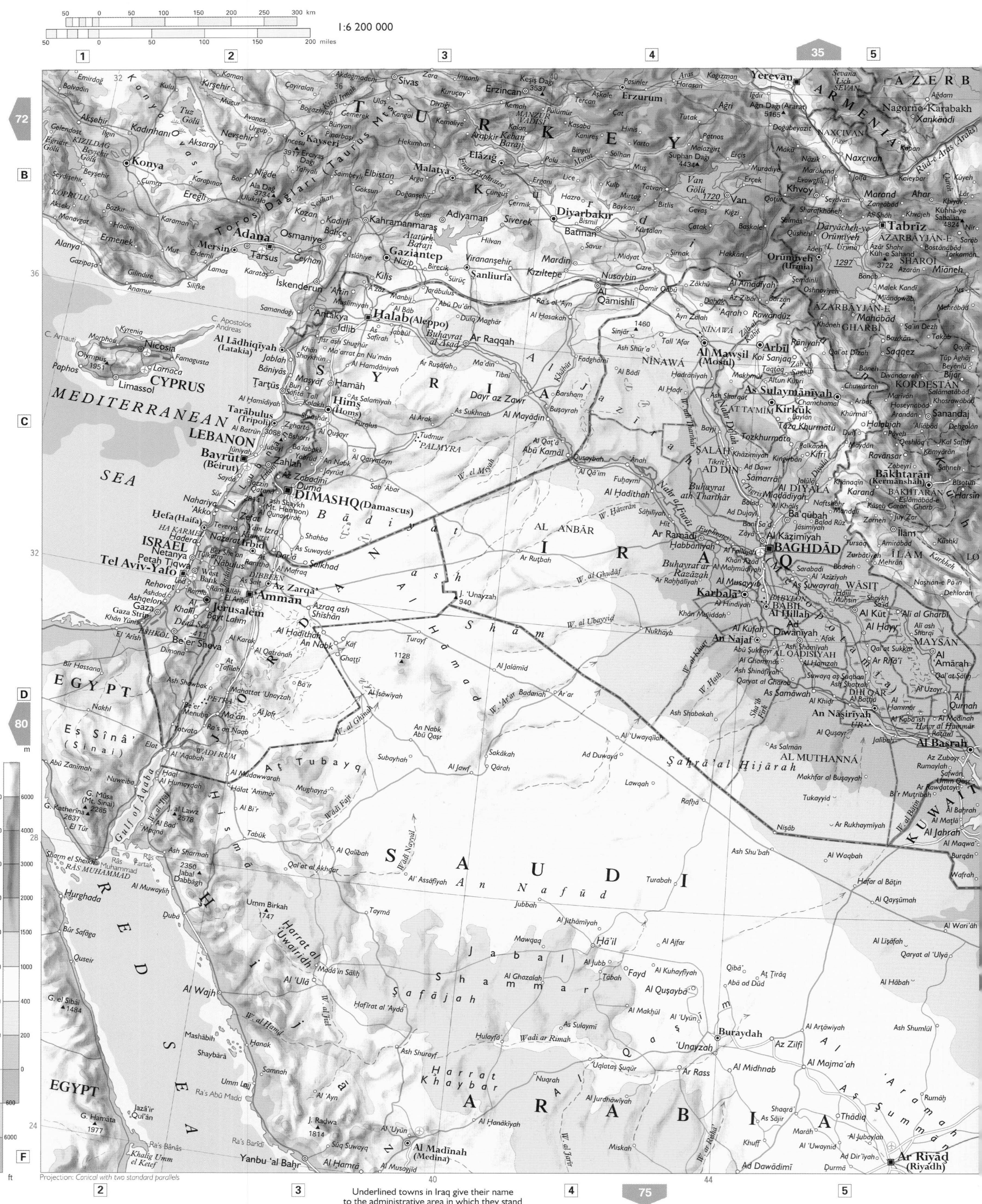

Projection: Conical with two standard parallels

Underlined towns in Iraq give their name to the administrative area in which they stand

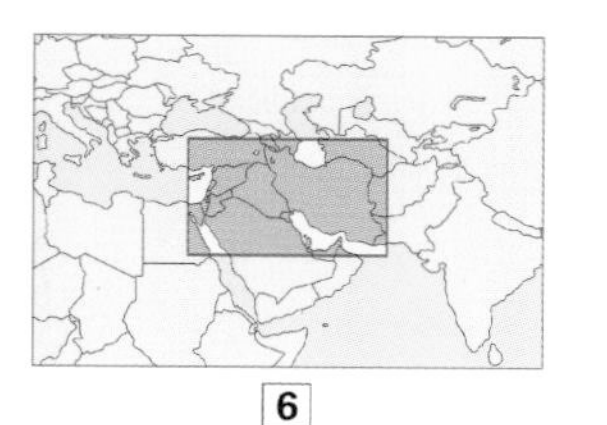

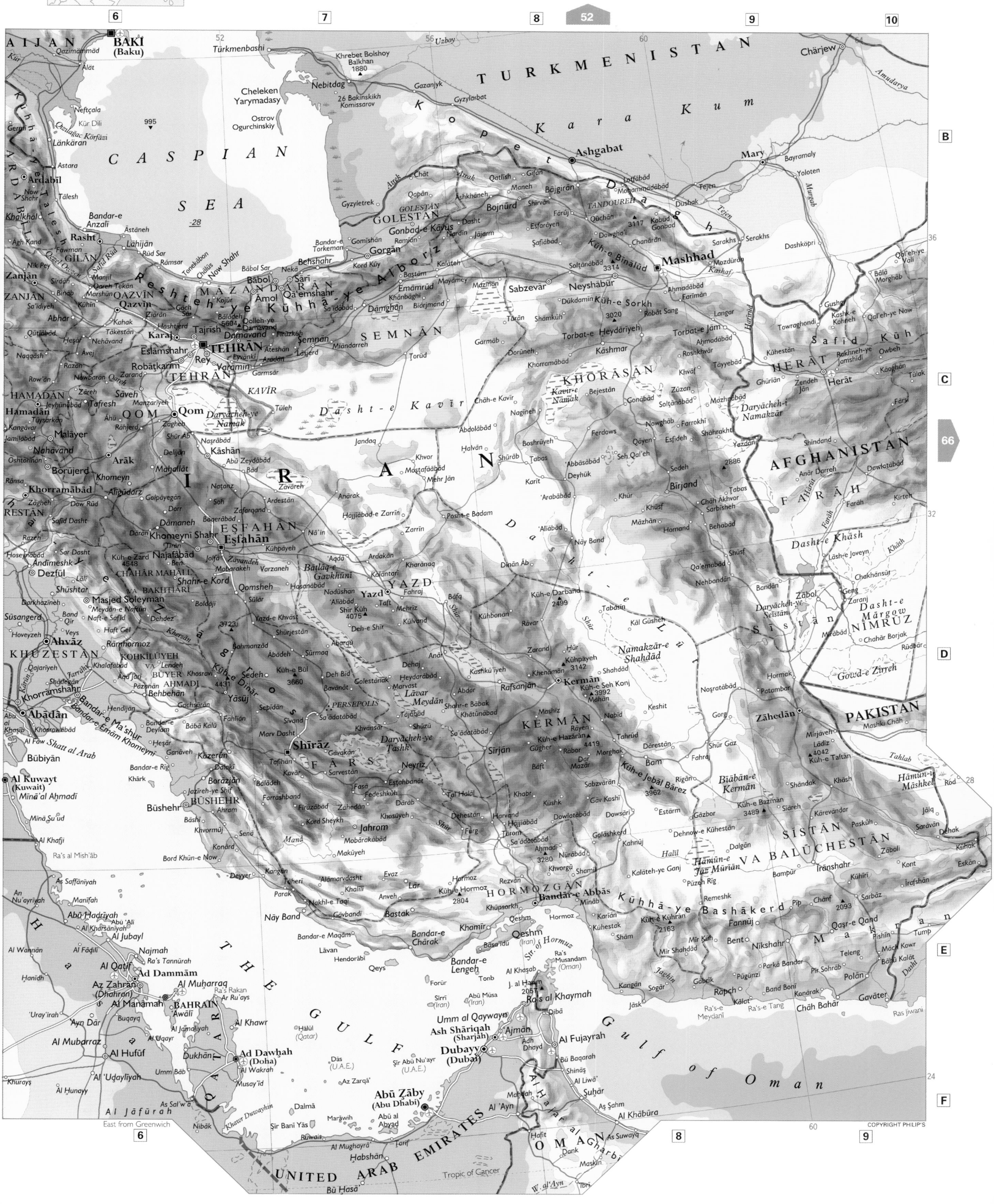

6 7 8 52 9 10

B C 66 D E F

TURKMENISTAN

CASPIAN SEA

IRAN

AFGHANISTAN

PAKISTAN

THE GULF

Gulf of Oman

QATAR

BAHRAIN

UNITED ARAB EMIRATES

OMAN

East from Greenwich 6 8 9

1: 4 400 000

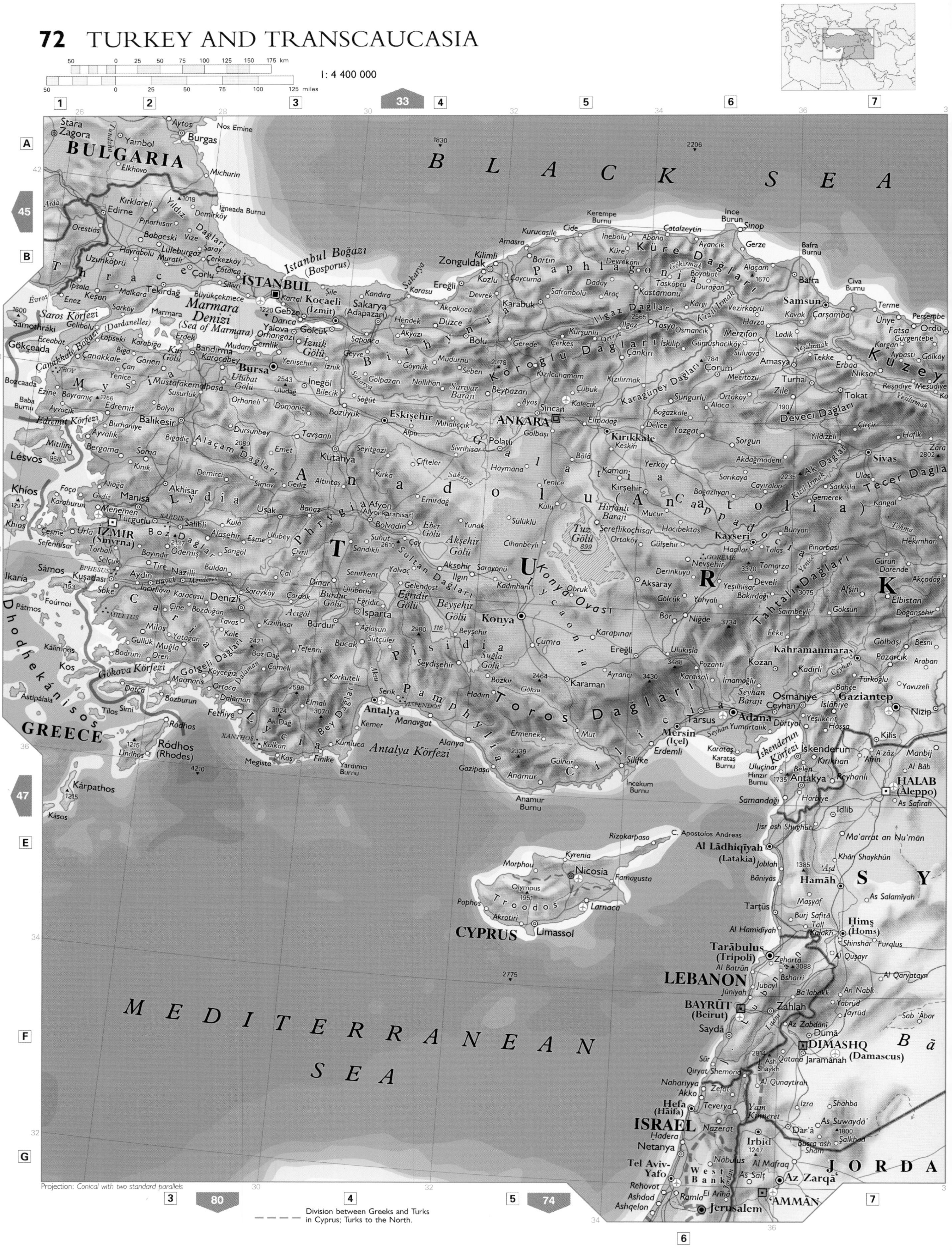

50 0 25 50 75 100 125 150 175 km

50 0 25 50 75 100 125 miles

Projection: Conical with two standard parallels

Division between Greeks and Turks in Cyprus; Turks to the North.

9 35 10 11 12

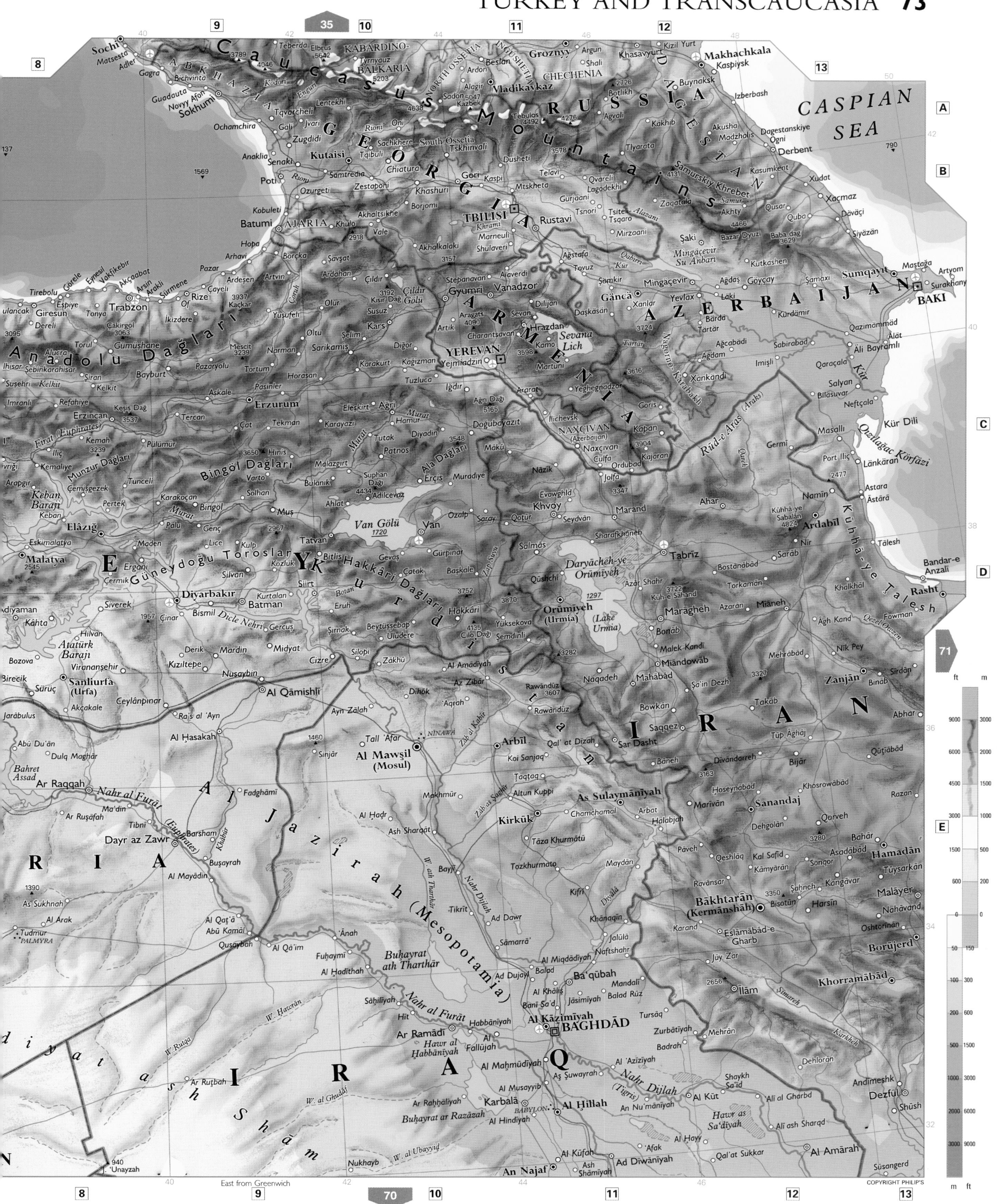

8 13 A B C D E 71 70 10 11 12 13 8 9

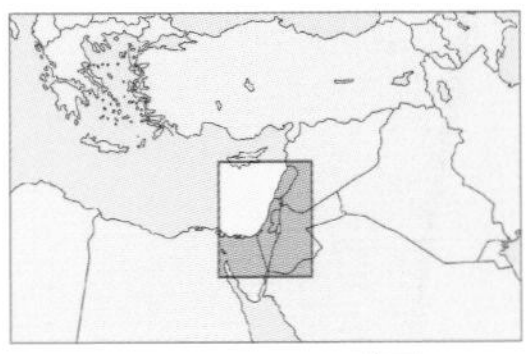

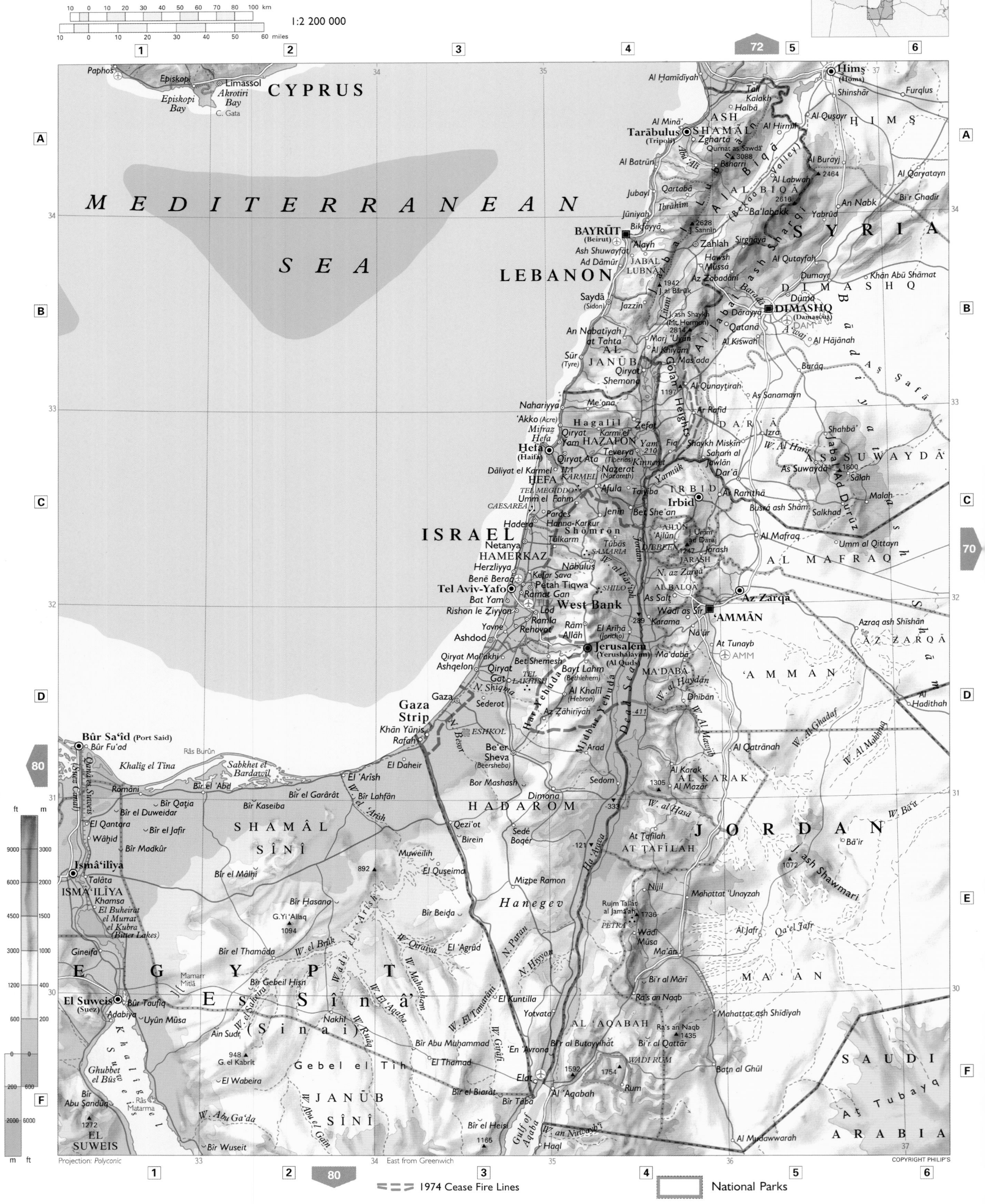
10 0 10 20 30 40 50 60 70 80 100 km
1:2 200 000
10 0 10 20 30 40 50 60 miles
1
2
3
4
72
5
6
A
B
C
D
E
F
70
80
Paphos
Episkopi
Limassol
Episkopi Bay
Akrotiri Bay
C. Gata
CYPRUS
MEDITERRANEAN
SEA
LEBANON
ISRAEL
SYRIA
JORDAN
EGYPT
SAUDI ARABIA
Ḥimṣ (Homs)
Al Ḥamīdīyah
Tall Kalakh
Halbā
Shinshār
Furqlus
Al Minā'
Ṭarābulus (Tripoli)
ASH SHAMĀL
Zghartā
Qurnat as Sawdā' 3088
Al Hirmil
Al Quṣayr
ḤIMṢ
Al Batrūn
Bsharri
Al Burayj
2464
Al Qaryatayn
Jubayl
Qarṭabā
AL BIQĀ'
Al Labwah
2616
An Nabk
Bi'r Ghadīr
Ibrāhīm
Ba'labakk
Yabrūd
Jūniyah
Bikfayyā
2628 J. Sannīn
BAYRŪT (Beirut)
'Alayh
Zaḥlah
Sirghayā
Ash Shuwayfāt
Ad Dāmūr
JABAL LUBNĀN
Ḥawsh Mūssā
Al Quṭayfah
Az Zabadānī
Ḍumayr
Khān Abū Shāmat
1942 J. al Bārūk
DIMASHQ
Ṣaydā (Sidon)
Jazzīn
Dūmā
DIMASHQ (Damascus)
J. ash Shaykh (Mt. Hermon) 2814
Dārayyā
Qaṭanā
An Nabaṭīyah at Taḥtā
Marj 'Uyūn
Al Khiyām
Al Kiswah
Al Hājānah
Ṣūr (Tyre)
AL JANŪB
Mas'ada
Qiryat Shemona
Golan Heights
Barāq
1197
Al Qunayṭirah
Aṣ Ṣanamayn
Nahariyya
Me'ona
Ar Rafid
'Akko (Acre)
Hagalil
Mifraz Hefa
Qiryat Yam
Karmi'el
Zefat
HAZAFON
DAR'Ā
Izra'
Shahbā'
Hefa (Haifa)
Yam -210
Fiq
Shaykh Miskīn
Teverya (Tiberias)
Kinneret
Saḥam al Jawlān
AS SUWAYDĀ'
Qiryat Ata
Nazerat (Nazareth)
As Suwaydā'
1800
Dāliyat el Karmel
HA KARMEL
HEFA
Dar'ā
Ṣalkhad
TEL MEGIDDO
Afula
Taiyiba
IRBID
Irbid
Ar Ramthā
Umm el Fahm
CAESAREA
Pardes
Jenin
Bet She'an
Buṣrá ash Shām
Ṣalkhad
Malaḥ
Hadera
Hanna-Karkur
Shomron
'Ajlūn
J. Umm ad Daraj 1247
Al Mafraq
Netanya
Tulkarm
Ṭūbās
SAMARIA
DIBBEEN
Jarash
Umm al Qiṭṭayn
HAMERKAZ
Herzliyya
Nābulus
JARASH
AL MAFRAQ
Kefar Sava
N. az Zarqā
Benē Beraq
Petah Tiqwa
SHILO
AL BALQĀ'
Tel Aviv-Yafo
Ramat Gan
As Salt
Az Zarqā
Bat Yam
West Bank
Wādī as Sīr
'AMMĀN
Rishon le Ẕiyyon
Lod
Ramla
Rām Allāh
Karama
Yavne
Rehovot
Arīḥā (Jericho)
Na'ūr
Azraq ash Shīshān
Ashdod
Jerusalem (Yerushalayim) (Al Quds)
At Tunayb
AZ ZARQĀ'
Qiryat Mal'akhi
Mādabā
AMM
Ashqelon
Qiryat Gat
Bet Shemesh
Bayt Laḥm (Bethlehem)
MA'DABĀ
'AMMĀN
TEL LAKHISH
Al Khalīl (Hebron)
Dhībān
Gaza
N. Shiqma
Sederot
Aẓ Ẓāhirīyah
Al Ḥadīthah
Gaza Strip
Dead Sea
-411
Khān Yūnis
Rafah
ESHKOL
Al Qaṭrānah
Be'er Sheva (Beersheba)
Arad
Bûr Sa'îd (Port Said)
Bûr Fu'ad
Râs Burûn
Khalîg el Tîna
Sabkhet el Bardawîl
El Daheir
Al Karak
AL KARAK
Bîr el 'Abd
El 'Arîsh
Bor Mashash
Sedom
1305
Al Mazār
Români
Bîr Lahfân
Dimona
Bîr Qaṭia
Bîr el Garârât
Bîr Kaseiba
HADAROM
-333
Bîr el Duweidar
W. al Ḥasā
El Qantara
Bîr el Jafir
Qezi'ot
W. Ba'ir
Wâḥid
SHAMÂL SÎNÎ
Birein
Sedé Boqér
Aṭ Ṭafīlah
AṬ ṬAFĪLAH
Bā'ir
Bîr Madkûr
-121
Ismâ'ilîya
Muweilih
892
El Quṣeima
1072
Bîr el Mâlḥi
J. ash Shawmarī
Talâta
ISMÂ'ILÎYA
Mizpe Ramon
Khamsa
Nijil
Mahattat 'Unayzah
El Buheirat el Murrat el Kubra (Bitter Lakes)
Bîr Ḥasana
Hanegev
Rujm Tal'at al Jamā'ah 1736
G.Yi 'Allaq 1094
Bîr Beida
PETRA
Wādī Mūsā
Al Jafr
Qa'el Jafr
Geneifa
Bîr el Thamâda
W. el Brûk
W. Qurayya
El 'Agrûd
N. Paran
Ma'ān
MA'ĀN
N. Ḥiyyon
Mamarr Mitlâ
Bîr Gebeil Ḥiṣn
W. Mahashsham
Bi'r al Mārī
El Suweis (Suez)
Bûr Taufîq
SÎNÂ' (Sinai)
El Kuntilla
Ra's an Naqb
Adabiya
'Uyûn Mûsa
Yotvata
Mahattat ash Shīdīyah
Nakhl
AL 'AQABAH
Ras an Naqb 1435
Ain Sudr
W. Rudg
Bîr Abu Muhammad
Bi'r al Qattar
948 G. el Kabrît
'En 'Avrona
Bîr al Butayyihāt
WADI RUM
Gebel el Tîh
El Thamad
1592
1754
Baṭn al Ghūl
Ghubbet el Bûs
El Wabeira
Elat
Rum
Al 'Aqabah
Bîr el Biarât
Bîr Tâba
At Tubayq
Bîr Abu Ṣandûq
Râs Matarma
JANÛB SÎNÎ
1272
EL SUWEIS
W. Abu Ga'da
Bîr el Heisi
Gulf of Aqaba
W. an Nuwaybi'
Al Mudawwarah
1165
Ḥaql
Bîr Wuseit
Khalîg el Suweis
ft m
9000 3000
6000 2000
4500 1500
3000 1000
1200 400
600 200
0 0
200 600
2000 6000
m ft
Projection: Polyconic
East from Greenwich
33
34
35
36
37
31
32
COPYRIGHT PHILIP'S
1974 Cease Fire Lines
National Parks

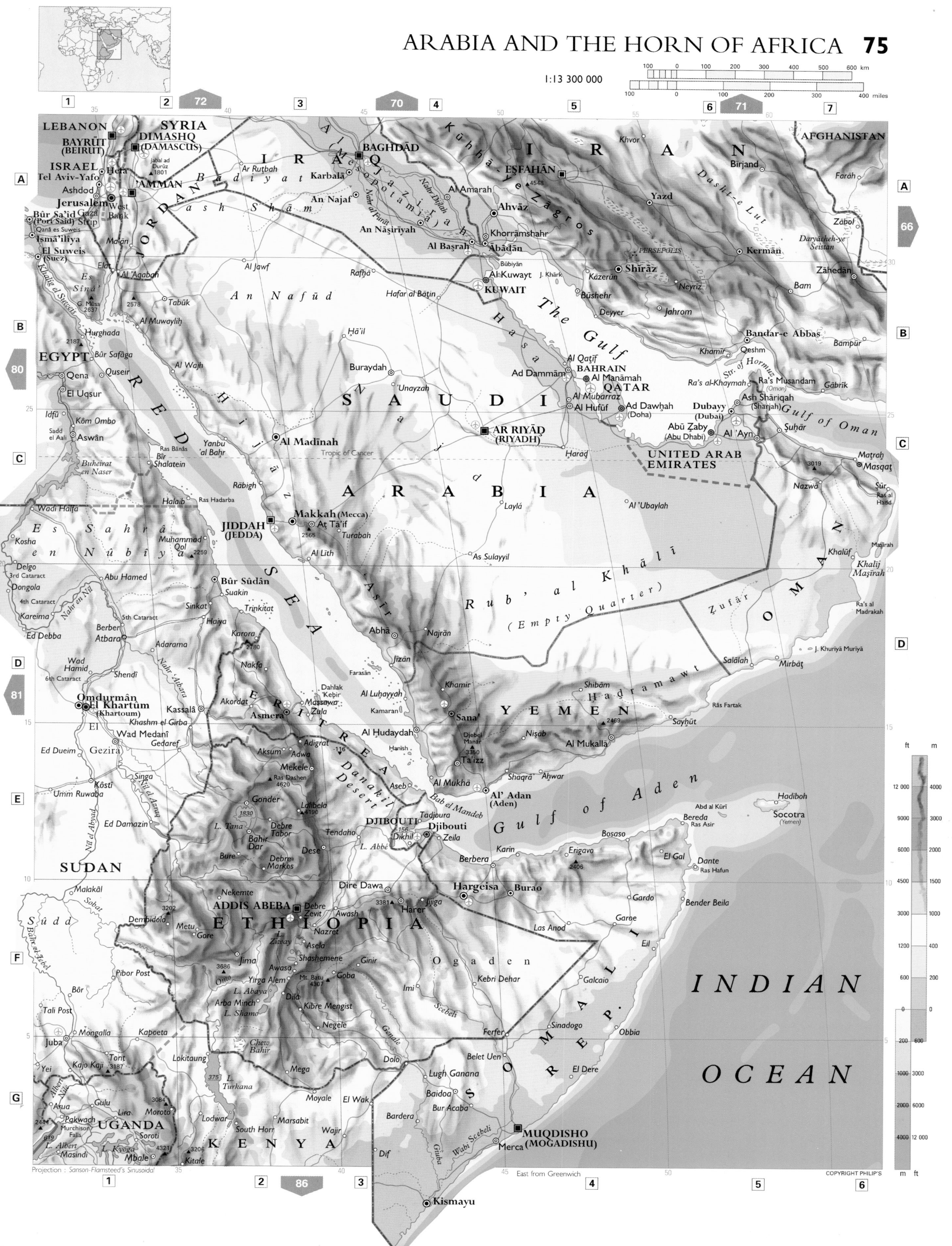
1:13 300 000
LEBANON
SYRIA
IRAQ
IRAN
AFGHANISTAN
ISRAEL
JORDAN
EGYPT
SAUDI ARABIA
KUWAIT
BAHRAIN
QATAR
UNITED ARAB EMIRATES
OMAN
YEMEN
ERITREA
DJIBOUTI
ETHIOPIA
SUDAN
SOMALI REP.
KENYA
UGANDA
BAGHDĀD
AR RIYĀD (RIYADH)
ADDIS ABEBA
MUQDISHO (MOGADISHU)
RED SEA
The Gulf
Gulf of Oman
Gulf of Aden
INDIAN OCEAN
Rub' al Khālī (Empty Quarter)
An Nafūd
Projection : Sanson-Flamsteed's Sinusoidal
East from Greenwich
COPYRIGHT PHILIP'S

1:37 300 000

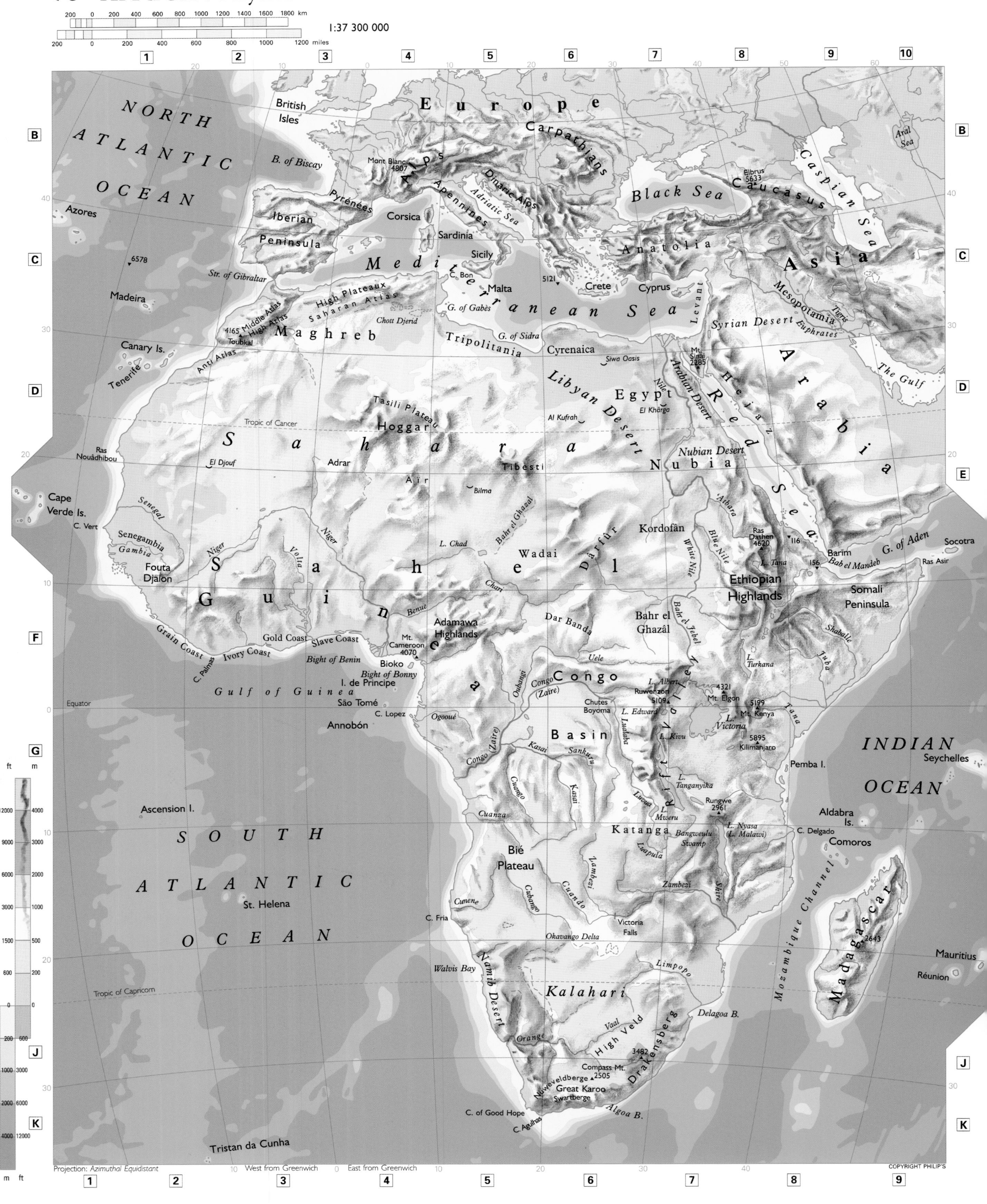
NORTH ATLANTIC OCEAN
British Isles
Europe
Carpathians
B. of Biscay
Mont Blanc 4807
Alps
Dinaric Alps
Apennines
Adriatic Sea
Black Sea
Caucasus
Elbrus 5633
Caspian Sea
Aral Sea
Azores
Pyrénées
Iberian Peninsula
Corsica
Sardinia
Sicily
Anatolia
Asia
6578
Str. of Gibraltar
Mediterranean Sea
C. Bon
Malta
5121
Crete
Cyprus
Levant
Mesopotamia
Tigris
Madeira
High Plateaux
Saharan Atlas
Middle Atlas
High Atlas
4165 Toubkal
G. of Gabès
Chott Djerid
Syrian Desert
Euphrates
Maghreb
G. of Sidra
Tripolitania
Cyrenaica
Canary Is.
Anti Atlas
Tenerife
Siwa Oasis
Mt. Sinai 2285
Arabia
The Gulf
Libyan Desert
Egypt
Nile
El Khârga
Arabian Desert
Hejaz
Red Sea
Tasili Plateau
Hoggar
Tropic of Cancer
Al Kufrah
Sahara
Ras Nouâdhibou
El Djouf
Adrar
Tibesti
Nubian Desert
Nubia
Aïr
Bilma
Cape Verde Is.
C. Vert
Senegal
Niger
'Atbara
Kordofân
Ras Dashen 4620
116
Senegambia
Gambia
Volta
L. Chad
Bahr el Ghazal
Dârfûr
Wadai
White Nile
Blue Nile
L. Tana
156
Barim
Bab el Mandeb
G. of Aden
Socotra
Ras Asir
Fouta Djalon
Sahel
Chari
Ethiopian Highlands
Somali Peninsula
Guinea
Benue
Dar Banda
Bahr el Ghazâl
Bahr el Jebel
Shabelle
Grain Coast
Gold Coast
Slave Coast
Adamawa Highlands
Mt. Cameroon 4070
Ivory Coast
Bight of Benin
Bight of Bonny
Bioko
C. Palmas
Uele
Rift Valley
L. Turkana
Juba
Congo
Oubangui
Congo (Zaïre)
L. Albert
Ruwenzori 5109
4321 Mt. Elgon
Gulf of Guinea
I. de Principe
São Tomé
Equator
C. Lopez
Annobón
Ogooué
Chutes Boyoma
L. Edward
5199 Mt. Kenya
Tana
L. Victoria
Lualaba
Basin
L. Kivu
5895 Kilimanjaro
Congo (Zaïre)
Kasai
Sankuru
INDIAN OCEAN
Seychelles
Pemba I.
Cuango
Kasai
L. Tanganyika
Ascension I.
Lukuga
L. Mweru
Rungwe 2961
Cuanza
Aldabra Is.
SOUTH ATLANTIC OCEAN
Katanga
Bangweulu Swamp
L. Nyasa L. Malawi
C. Delgado
Comoros
Luapula
Bié Plateau
Zambezi
Zambezi
Shire
Mozambique Channel
Cunene
Cubango
Cuando
C. Fria
St. Helena
Victoria Falls
Okavango Delta
Madagascar
2643
Mauritius
Walvis Bay
Namib Desert
Limpopo
Réunion
Tropic of Capricorn
Kalahari
Delagoa B.
Vaal
High Veld
Drakensberg
Orange
3482
Compass Mt. 2505
Nuweveldberge
Great Karoo
Swartberge
C. of Good Hope
C. Agulhas
Algoa B.
Tristan da Cunha
Projection: Azimuthal Equidistant
West from Greenwich
East from Greenwich

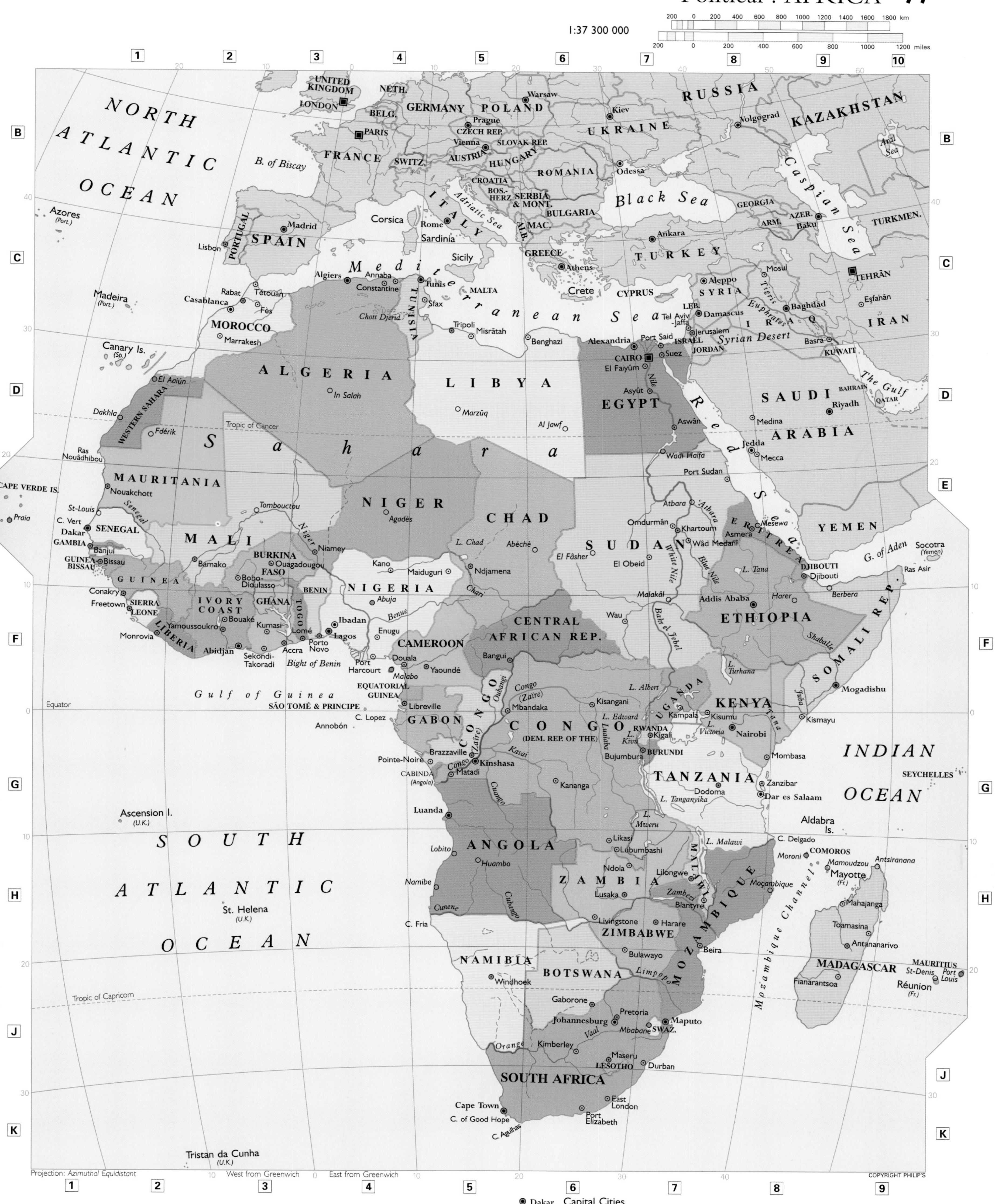
1:37 300 000
NORTH ATLANTIC OCEAN
SOUTH ATLANTIC OCEAN
INDIAN OCEAN
Mediterranean Sea
Black Sea
Caspian Sea
Red Sea
Sahara
UNITED KINGDOM
LONDON
NETH.
BELG.
GERMANY
POLAND
Warsaw
RUSSIA
KAZAKHSTAN
UKRAINE
Kiev
Volgograd
PARIS
FRANCE
SWITZ.
CZECH REP.
Prague
Vienna
AUSTRIA
SLOVAK REP.
HUNGARY
ROMANIA
Odessa
CROATIA
BOS.-HERZ
SERBIA & MONT.
BULGARIA
ALB.
MAC.
GREECE
Athens
ITALY
Rome
Corsica
Sardinia
Sicily
MALTA
Crete
CYPRUS
TURKEY
Ankara
GEORGIA
ARM.
AZER.
Baku
TURKMEN.
TEHRĀN
Esfahān
IRAN
Mosul
SYRIA
Aleppo
Damascus
LEB.
Tel Aviv-Jaffa
Jerusalem
ISRAEL
JORDAN
IRAQ
Baghdād
Basra
KUWAIT
Syrian Desert
Tigris
Euphrates
The Gulf
BAHRAIN
QATAR
Riyadh
SAUDI ARABIA
Medina
Jedda
Mecca
YEMEN
Socotra (Yemen)
G. of Aden
Ras Asir
Aral Sea
B. of Biscay
Azores (Port.)
Madeira (Port.)
Canary Is. (Sp.)
CAPE VERDE IS.
Praia
PORTUGAL
Lisbon
SPAIN
Madrid
Rabat
Tétouan
Casablanca
Fès
MOROCCO
Marrakesh
Algiers
Annaba
Constantine
Tunis
Sfax
TUNISIA
Chott Djerid
ALGERIA
In Salah
Tripoli
Misrātah
Benghazi
LIBYA
Marzūq
Al Jawf
Alexandria
Port Said
Suez
CAIRO
El Faiyûm
Asyût
Nile
EGYPT
Aswân
Wadi Halfa
Port Sudan
El Aaiún
WESTERN SAHARA
Dakhla
Fdérik
Tropic of Cancer
Ras Nouâdhibou
MAURITANIA
Nouakchott
St-Louis
C. Vert
Dakar
SENEGAL
Senegal
GAMBIA
Banjul
GUINEA-BISSAU
Bissau
GUINEA
Conakry
Freetown
SIERRA LEONE
LIBERIA
Monrovia
Tombouctou
MALI
Bamako
Niger
NIGER
Agadès
Niamey
BURKINA FASO
Ouagadougou
Bobo-Dioulasso
IVORY COAST
Bouaké
Yamoussoukro
Abidjan
GHANA
Kumasi
Sekondi-Takoradi
Accra
TOGO
Lomé
BENIN
Porto Novo
NIGERIA
Kano
Maiduguri
Abuja
Ibadan
Lagos
Enugu
Benue
Port Harcourt
Bight of Benin
Gulf of Guinea
CHAD
L. Chad
Abéché
Ndjamena
Chari
SUDAN
El Fâsher
El Obeid
Omdurmân
Khartoum
Wâd Medanî
Atbara
'Atbara
White Nile
Blue Nile
Malakâl
Wau
Bahr el Jebel
ERITREA
Asmera
Mesewa
DJIBOUTI
Djibouti
L. Tana
ETHIOPIA
Addis Ababa
Harer
Berbera
SOMALI REP.
Shaballe
Mogadishu
Juba
Kismayu
CAMEROON
Douala
Yaoundé
Malabo
EQUATORIAL GUINEA
SÃO TOMÉ & PRINCIPE
Annobón
Libreville
C. Lopez
GABON
CENTRAL AFRICAN REP.
Bangui
Oubangi
CONGO
Congo (Zaire)
Mbandaka
CONGO (DEM. REP. OF THE)
Brazzaville
Kinshasa
Pointe-Noire
CABINDA (Angola)
Matadi
Kasai
Kwango
Lualaba
Kisangani
Kananga
L. Albert
UGANDA
Kampala
L. Edward
RWANDA
Kigali
L. Kivu
BURUNDI
Bujumbura
KENYA
Kisumu
L. Victoria
Nairobi
Tana
L. Turkana
Mombasa
TANZANIA
Dodoma
Zanzibar
Dar es Salaam
L. Tanganyika
L. Mweru
SEYCHELLES
Aldabra Is.
C. Delgado
COMOROS
Moroni
Mamoudzou
Mayotte (Fr.)
Antsiranana
Mahajanga
Toamasina
Antananarivo
MADAGASCAR
Fianarantsoa
MAURITIUS
St-Denis
Port Louis
Réunion (Fr.)
Mozambique Channel
Equator
Ascension I. (U.K.)
St. Helena (U.K.)
Tristan da Cunha (U.K.)
Luanda
ANGOLA
Lobito
Huambo
Namibe
Cunene
Cubango
C. Fria
Likasi
Lubumbashi
Ndola
ZAMBIA
Lusaka
Lilongwe
L. Malawi
MALAWI
Zambezi
Blantyre
Moçambique
MOZAMBIQUE
Beira
Livingstone
Harare
ZIMBABWE
Bulawayo
Limpopo
NAMIBIA
Windhoek
BOTSWANA
Gaborone
Tropic of Capricorn
Pretoria
Johannesburg
Mbabane
SWAZ.
Maputo
Vaal
Orange
Kimberley
Maseru
LESOTHO
Durban
SOUTH AFRICA
East London
Port Elizabeth
Cape Town
C. of Good Hope
C. Agulhas
Projection: Azimuthal Equidistant
West from Greenwich
East from Greenwich
COPYRIGHT PHILIP'S
Dakar Capital Cities

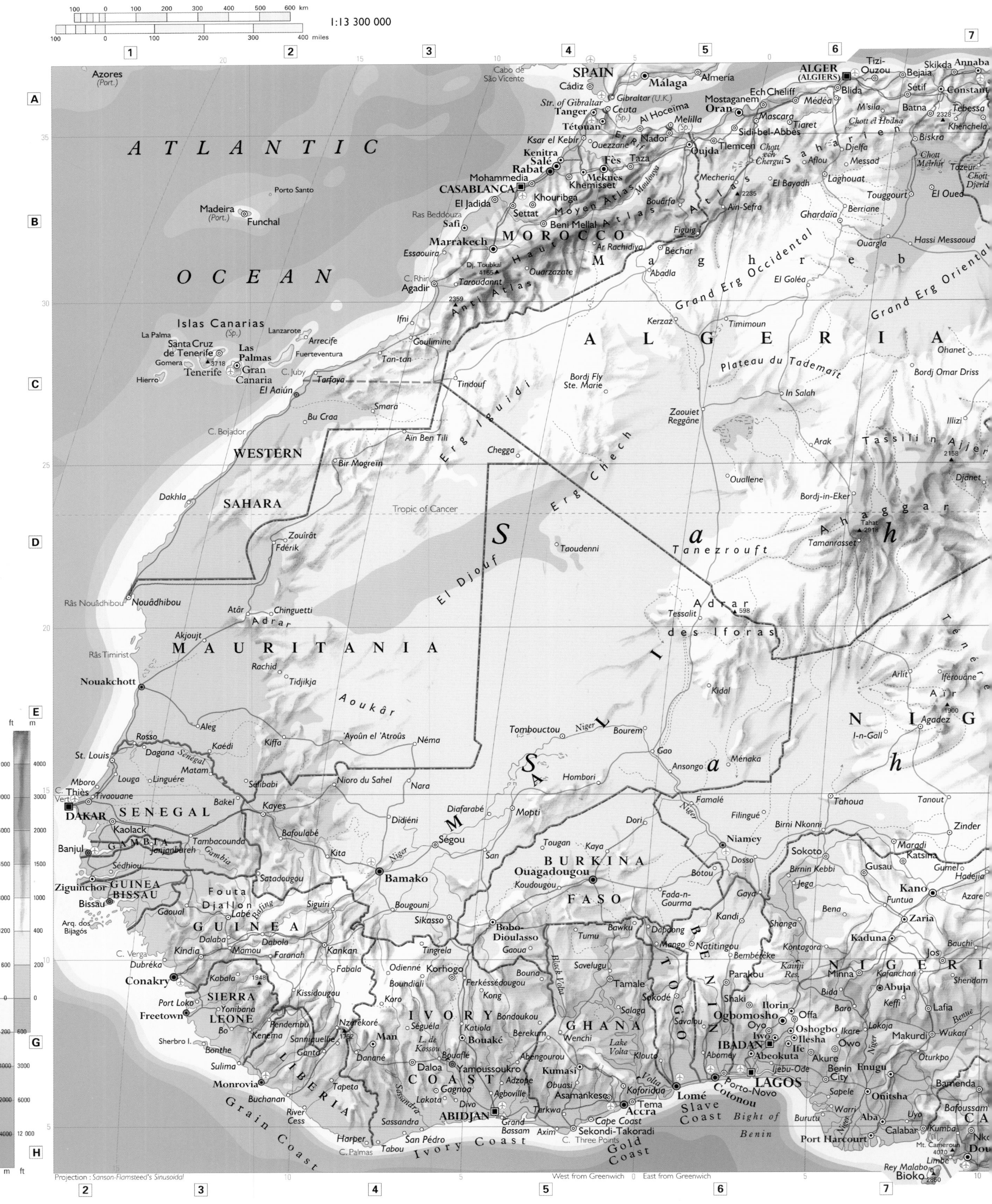

1:13 300 000
km
miles
ATLANTIC OCEAN
Azores (Port.)
Madeira (Port.)
Funchal
Porto Santo
Islas Canarias (Sp.)
La Palma
Santa Cruz de Tenerife
Tenerife
Gomera
Hierro
Las Palmas
Gran Canaria
Lanzarote
Arrecife
Fuerteventura
SPAIN
Cádiz
Málaga
Almería
Str. of Gibraltar
Gibraltar (U.K.)
Tanger
Ceuta (Sp.)
Tétouan
Al Hoceima
Melilla (Sp.)
MOROCCO
Rabat
Salé
Kenitra
Fès
Meknès
Taza
Oujda
CASABLANCA
Mohammedia
El Jadida
Settat
Khouribga
Safi
Marrakech
Essaouira
Agadir
Taroudannt
Ouarzazate
Er Rachidiya
Beni Mellal
Moyen Atlas
Haut Atlas
Anti Atlas
Ifni
Goulimine
Tan-tan
Tarfaya
El Aaiún
Smara
WESTERN SAHARA
Bu Craa
C. Bojador
Dakhla
Bir Mogreïn
Tropic of Cancer
Nouâdhibou
Râs Nouâdhibou
MAURITANIA
Zouîrât
Fdérik
Atâr
Chinguetti
Adrar
Akjoujt
Nouakchott
Râs Timirist
Rachid
Tidjikja
Aoukâr
Aleg
Rosso
Kaédi
Kiffa
'Ayoûn el 'Atroûs
Néma
St. Louis
SENEGAL
DAKAR
Thiès
Kaolack
Tambacounda
GAMBIA
Banjul
Ziguinchor
GUINEA-BISSAU
Bissau
Arq. dos Bijagós
Fouta Djallon
GUINEA
Labé
Kankan
Conakry
SIERRA LEONE
Freetown
LIBERIA
Monrovia
Grain Coast
IVORY COAST
Man
Bouaké
Yamoussoukro
ABIDJAN
San Pédro
Ivory Coast
MALI
Bamako
Ségou
Mopti
Tombouctou
Gao
Kidal
Niger
Taoudenni
El Djouf
Sahara
Tanezrouft
Adrar des Iforas
Tessalit
BURKINA FASO
Ouagadougou
Bobo-Dioulasso
GHANA
Kumasi
Accra
Tema
Gold Coast
Lake Volta
TOGO
Lomé
BENIN
Porto-Novo
Cotonou
Slave Coast
Bight of Benin
NIGERIA
LAGOS
IBADAN
Ogbomosho
Kano
Kaduna
Zaria
Sokoto
Abuja
Enugu
Port Harcourt
Niamey
NIGER
Agadez
Aïr
ALGERIA
ALGER (ALGIERS)
Oran
Tlemcen
Sidi-bel-Abbès
Mostaganem
Blida
Médéa
Constantine
Sétif
Batna
Biskra
Ghardaia
Ouargla
Hassi Messaoud
Touggourt
Béchar
Timimoun
In Salah
Tindouf
Erg Iguidi
Erg Chech
Grand Erg Occidental
Grand Erg Oriental
Plateau du Tademaït
Tassili n Ajjer
Ahaggar
Tamanrasset
Tahat 2918
Maghreb
Bioko
Mt. Cameroun 4070
Projection : Sanson-Flamsteed's Sinusoidal
West from Greenwich
East from Greenwich

Bizerte
CARTHAGE
Ariana
TUNIS
Béja
Sicilia
Nabeul
Sousse
Kairouan
MALTA
Valletta
Mahdia
Sfax
Gafsa
Golfe de Gabès
Île de Djerba
Gabès
Zarzis
Médenine
Zuwārah
Tarābulus (Tripoli)
Tatahouine
Az Zāwiyah
Al Khums
Misrātah
Dehibat
Gharyān
968
Mizdah
Tripolitania
Surt
Khalīj Surt
Daraj
Ghudāmis
Hūn
GREECE
Kríti
Iráklion
Ródhos
Antalya
TURKEY
ADANA
Antakya
HALAB
Nahr al Furāt
CYPRUS
Nicosia
Al Lādhiqīyah
SYRIA
Tarābulus
Hims
LEBANON
BAYRŪT (BEIRUT)
DIMASHQ (DAMASCUS)
IRAQ
Jabal ad Durūz
1801
Ar Rutbah
Bādiyat ash Shām
ISRAEL
Tel Aviv-Yafo
Ashdod
Hefa
Jerusalem
West Bank
'AMMĀN
JORDAN
MEDITERRANEAN SEA
Zāwiyat al Baydā
Darnah
Banghāzī
Al Marj
Tubruq
Bardīyah
Salûm
Suluq
Ajdābiyā
Cyrenaica
Al Jaghbūb
Awjilah
Zillah
Marsā Matrūh
El Alamein
EL ISKANDARIYA (ALEXANDRIA)
Damanhûr
El Mahalla el Kubra
Dumyât
Bûr Sa'îd
El Mansûra
Qanâ es Suweis
Ismâ'iliya
Tanta
Zagazig
EL GÎZA
EL QÂHIRA (CAIRO)
El Suweis
Helwân
El Faiyûm
Beni Suef
-133
Munkhafed el Qattâra
Sîwa
Maghâgha
El Minyâ
Mallawi
Manfalût
Asyût
Nahr en Nil
Es Sahrâ Esh Sharqîya
Khalîg el Suweis
Es Sînâ'
G. Mûsa 2637
Elat
Al 'Aqabah
Al Jawf
75
SAUDI ARABIA
Tabūk
2578
Al Muwaylih
Hurghada
2187
Bûr Safâga
Quseir
Al Wajh
Hijaz
RED SEA
Qasr Farâfra
Tahta
Sohâg
Girga
Qena
THEBES
KARNAK
El Uqsur
El Khârga
El Wâhât el-Khârga
Mût
El Wâhât el-Dakhla
Idfû
Kom Ombo
Sadd el Aali
Aswân
Yanbu 'al Bahr
Ras Bânâs
Bîr Shalatein
Buheirat en Naser
ABU SIMBEL
Halaib
Ras Hadarba
Râbigh
LIBYA
Sahrâ' Lîbîya
EGYPT
Idehan Awbārī
Brach
Sabhah
Awbārī
1200
Marzūq
Fezzan
Wāw al Kabīr
Ghat
Al Qatrūn
Sahrâ' Rebiana
Al Kufrah
Al Jawf
Sahara
1082
J. Uweinat 1893
Tummo
Madama
Aozou Strip
Aozou
Bardai
Pic Toussidé 3265
3150 Tarso Emissi
Tibesti
Zouar
Emi Koussi 3415
Ma'tan as Sarra
Chirfa
Wadi Halfa
El Wâhât el Selîma
Es Sahrâ en Nûbîya
Kosha
Delgo
Muhammad Qol
2259
Bûr Sûdân
Suakin
3rd Cataract
Dongola
Abu Hamed
Ounianga Sérir
Dépression du Mourdi
Borkou
Faya-Largeau
Bilma
Grand Erg du Bilma
Fachi
Bir 'Atrun
Kareima
4th Cataract
5th Cataract
Sinkat
Trinkitat
Haiya
Ed Debba
Berber
Atbara
Karora
2780
Nakfa
Adarama
Nahr Atbara
Fada
1310
Ennedi
Erg du Djourab
Zagaoua
Wad Hamid
6th Cataract
Shendî
ERITREA
Oum Chalouba
SUDAN
Omdurmân
El Khartûm (Khartoum)
Kassalâ
Akordat
NIGER
CHAD
Zigey
Biltine
Malha
1954
El Wuz
Khashm el Girba
Boultoum
Nguigmi
Mao
Bahr el Ghazal
Lac Tchad
Moussoro
Al Junaynah
Kutum
Umm Keddada
Sodiri
Wâd Medanî
El Gezira
Gedaref
Bosso
Abéché
Ed Dueim
Gashua
Nguru
Geidam
Ati
Massakory
Oum Hadjer
Zalingei
Djebel Mara 3088
Dârfûr
El Fâsher
El Obeid
Singa
Kôstî
Umm Ruwaba
Gonder
Maiduguri
Ndjamena
Kousseri
Bokoro
Mongo
Goz Beïda
Nyâlâ
En Nahud
Er Rahad
Kordofân
Abû Zabad
Nîl el Azraq
1830
Potiskum
Bama
Massenya
Abou-Deïa
El Odaiya
Ed Damazin
L. Tana
Bahir Dar
Nîl el Abyad
1325
Kâdugli
Bure
Bajoga
Chari
Maroua
Am-Timan
Biu
Bongor
Mubi
Kumo
Guider
Logone
Birao
Bahr el Arab
Songo
Debre Markos
Numan
Garoua
Pala
Laï
Sarh
1276
Malakâl
Sobat
Nekemte
Yola
Moundou
Koumra
Doba
Ndélé
Sa'id Bundas
Bahr el Ghazâl
Raga
Jur
Bahr el Ghazâl
Sudd
Bahr el Jebel
Dembidolo
3202
ETHIOPIA
Metu
Gore
Gashaka
Baïbokoum
Gogriâl
Wâw
Tonj
Ngaoundéré
Banyo
Paoua
Kaga Bandoro
Rumbêk
Pibor Post
Jima
3686
Omo
Adamawa Highlands
Bossangoa
CENTRAL AFRICAN REPUBLIC
Yalinga
Toinya
Bôr
L. Abaya
Arba Minch
L. Shamo
Bétaré Oya
Bouar
Bozoum
Sibut
Ippy
Bakouma
Tali Post
Amâdi
Yoko
Foumban
Sahr el Istiwa'iya
Carnot
Bossembélé
Bambari
Bangassou
Obo
Mongalla
Kapoeta
Chew Bahir
CAMEROON
Bertoua
Batouri
Oubangi
Mobaye
Bomu
Yambio
Juba
Torit
Kinyeti 3187
Lokitaung
L. Turkana
Sanaga
Nanga-Eboko
Abong-Mbang
Berbérati
Bangui
Zongo
Bosobolo
Mobayi
Bondo
Ango
Faradje
Yei
Kajo Kaji
Yaoundé
Mbaïki
Libenge
Uele
Dungu
375
COPYRIGHT PHILIPS

84
86

1:7 100 000

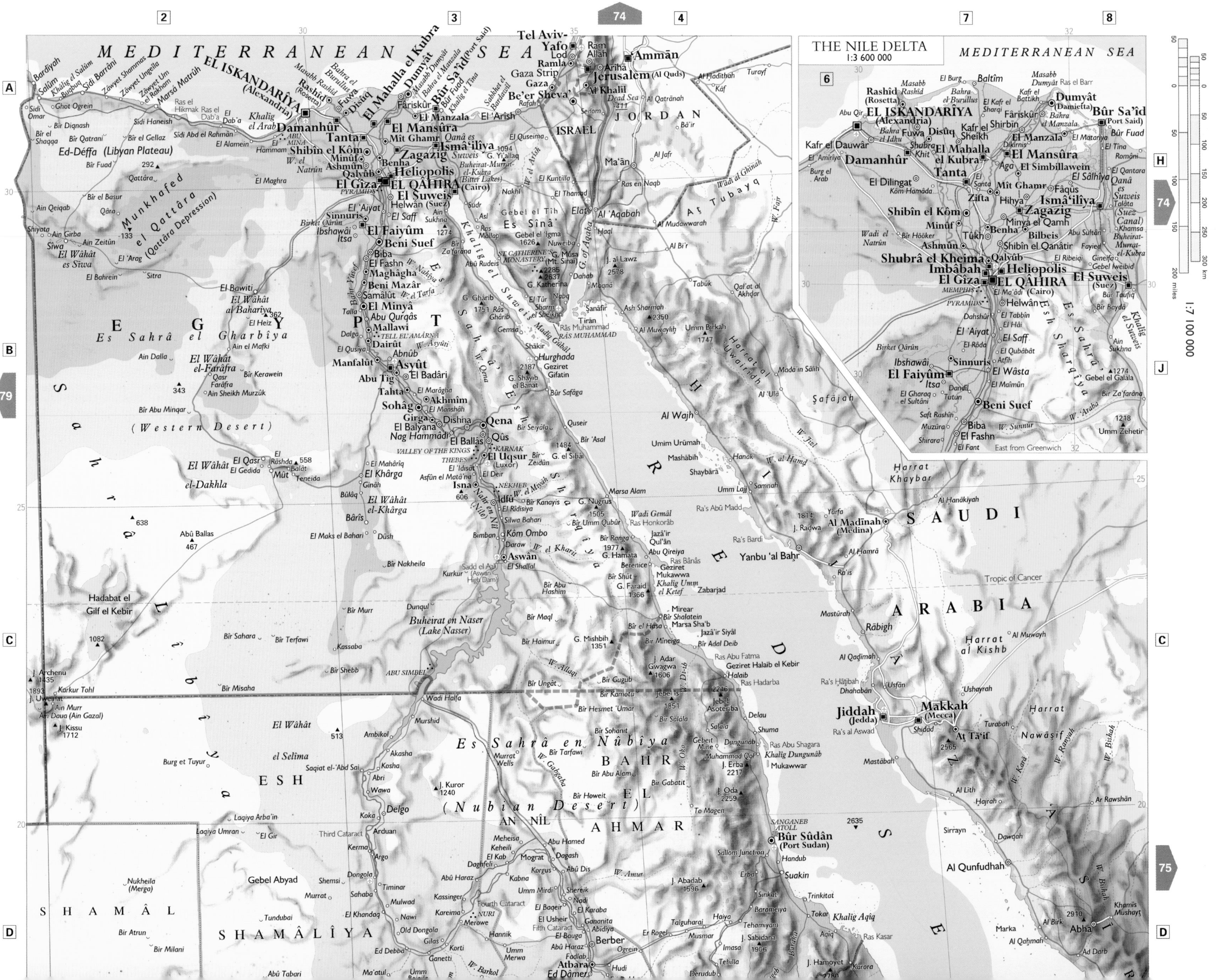

50 0 50 100 150 200 250 300 km
50 0 50 100 150 200 miles
THE NILE DELTA
1:3 600 000
East from Greenwich
MEDITERRANEAN SEA
EL ISKANDARÎYA (Alexandria)
Rashîd (Rosetta)
Damanhûr
Tanta
El Mahalla el Kubra
El Mansûra
Dumyât (Damietta)
Bûr Sa'îd (Port Said)
Ismâ'ilîya
Zagazig
Benha
Heliopolis
EL QÂHIRA (Cairo)
El Gîza
El Suweis (Suez)
Helwân
El Faiyûm
Beni Suef
El Minyâ
Asyût
Sohâg
Qena
El Uqsur (Luxor)
Aswân
Buheirat en Naser (Lake Nasser)
Wadi Halfa
Tel Aviv-Yafo
Jerusalem (Al Quds)
Ammân
Be'er Sheva'
Gaza Strip
ISRAEL
JORDAN
Ma'ân
Al 'Aqabah
Es Sînâ'
Khalig el Suweis
G. of Aqaba
SAUDI ARABIA
Al Madînah (Medina)
Yanbu 'al Bahr
Jiddah (Jedda)
Makkah (Mecca)
Aţ Ţâ'if
Al Qunfudhah
Abhâ
Tropic of Cancer
Bûr Sûdân (Port Sudan)
Suakin
Berber
Atbara
Ed Dâmer
Dongola
Merowe
EGYPT
Es Sahrâ el Gharbîya (Western Desert)
Es Sahrâ esh Sharqîya
Munkhafed el Qattâra (Qattâra Depression)
El Wâhât el-Khârga
El Wâhât el-Dakhla
El Wâhât el-Farâfra
El Wâhât el Bahariya
El Wâhât es Sîwa
Sîwa
Marsâ Matrûh
Ed-Déffa (Libyan Plateau)
Sahrâ Lîbîya
Es Sahrâ en Nûbîya (Nubian Desert)
Hadabat el Gilf el Kebir
BAHR EL AHMAR
ESH SHAMÂLÎYA

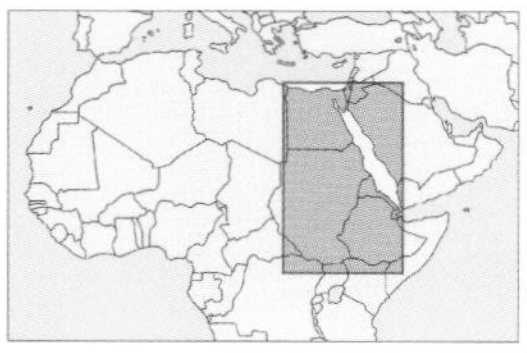

National Parks

Nature Reserves and Game Reserves

∴ UNESCO World Heritage Sites

m	ft
4000	12 000
3000	9000
2000	6000
1500	4500
1000	3000
400	1200
200	600
0	0

Projection: Lambert's Equivalent Azimuthal

East from Greenwich

75
84
86

1:7 100 000

MAURITANIA
SAHARA
Nouakchott
Tagânt
Aoukâr
El Mreyyé
Trarza
SENEGAL
DAKAR
Thiès
Kaolack
St. Louis
GAMBIA
Banjul
GUINEA-BISSAU
Bissau
Arquipélago dos Bijagós
GUINEA
Conakry
Fouta Djalon
Kankan
Labé
SIERRA LEONE
Freetown
LIBERIA
Monrovia
IVORY COAST
Yamoussoukro
ABIDJAN
Bouaké
Korhogo
BAMAKO
Ségou
Kayes
Mopti
Tombouctou (Timbuktu)
Bobo-Dioulasso
ATLANTIC OCEAN
Grain Coast
Ivory Coast
GULF
Projection : Lambert's Equivalent Azimuthal
West from Greenwich

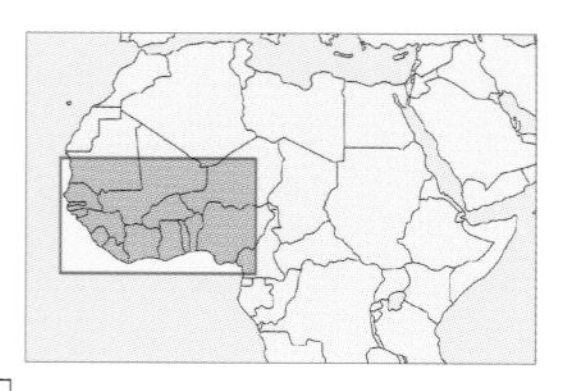

N. E. NIGERIA
on same scale

National Parks

Nature Reserves and Game Reserves

∴ UNESCO World Heritage Sites

East from Greenwich

79

84

1:13 300 000

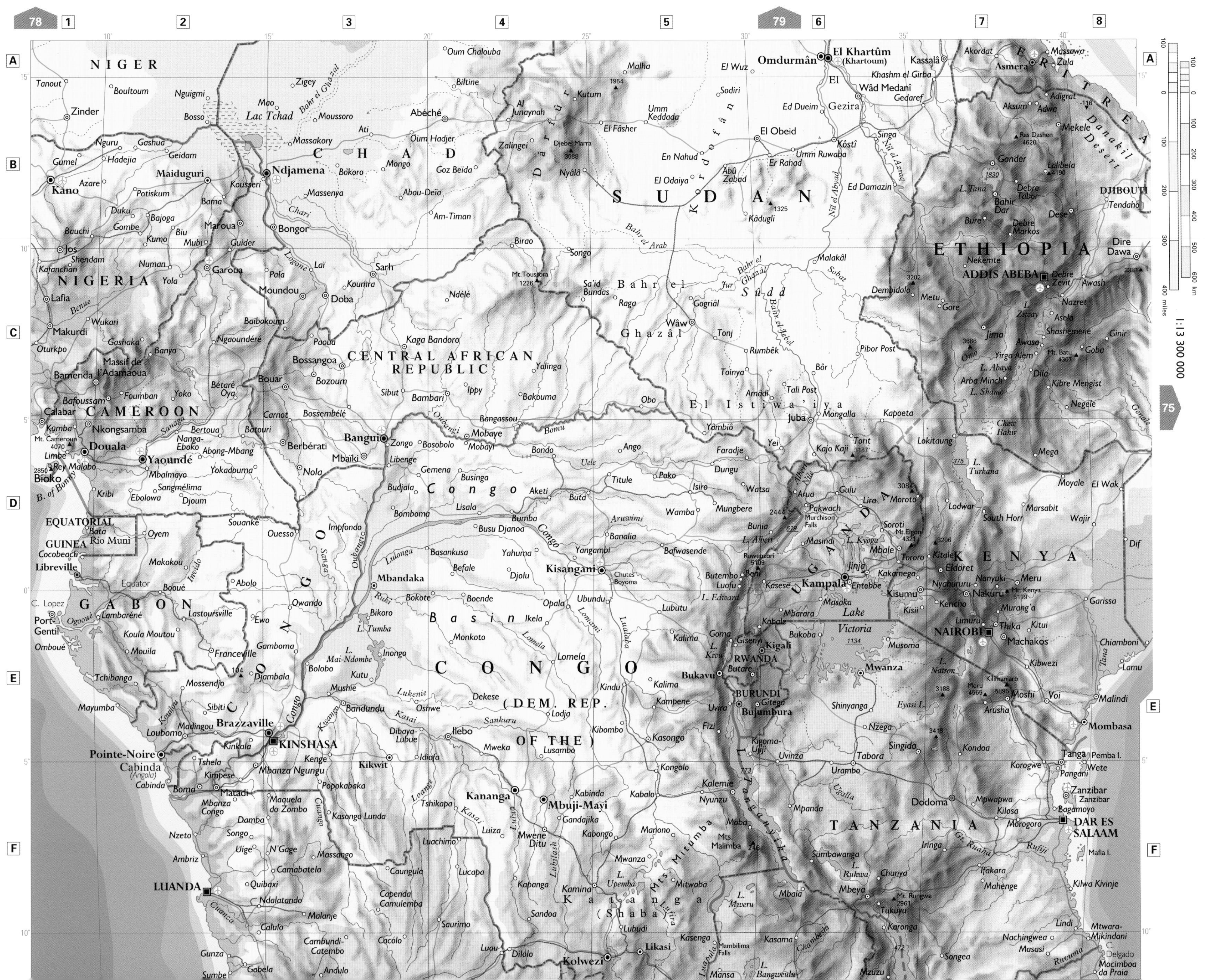
100 0 100 200 300 400 500 600 km
100 0 100 200 300 400 miles
78
79
75
A B C D E F
1 2 3 4 5 6 7 8
NIGER
CHAD
Lac Tchad
Ndjamena
SUDAN
Omdurmân
El Khartûm (Khartoum)
Bahr el Ghazâl
El Istiwa'iya
Juba
ERITREA
Asmera
Danakil Desert
DJIBOUTI
ETHIOPIA
ADDIS ABEBA
NIGERIA
Kano
CAMEROON
Yaoundé
Douala
CENTRAL AFRICAN REPUBLIC
Bangui
EQUATORIAL GUINEA
Rio Muni
Bioko
Libreville
GABON
Equator
CONGO
Brazzaville
Pointe-Noire
Congo Basin
CONGO (DEM. REP. OF THE)
KINSHASA
Kisangani
Mbandaka
Kananga
Mbuji-Mayi
Katanga (Shaba)
Kolwezi
Likasi
Cabinda (Angola)
LUANDA
UGANDA
Kampala
Lake Victoria
RWANDA
Kigali
BURUNDI
Bujumbura
L. Tanganyika
KENYA
NAIROBI
Mombasa
L. Turkana
TANZANIA
Dodoma
Zanzibar
DAR ES SALAAM

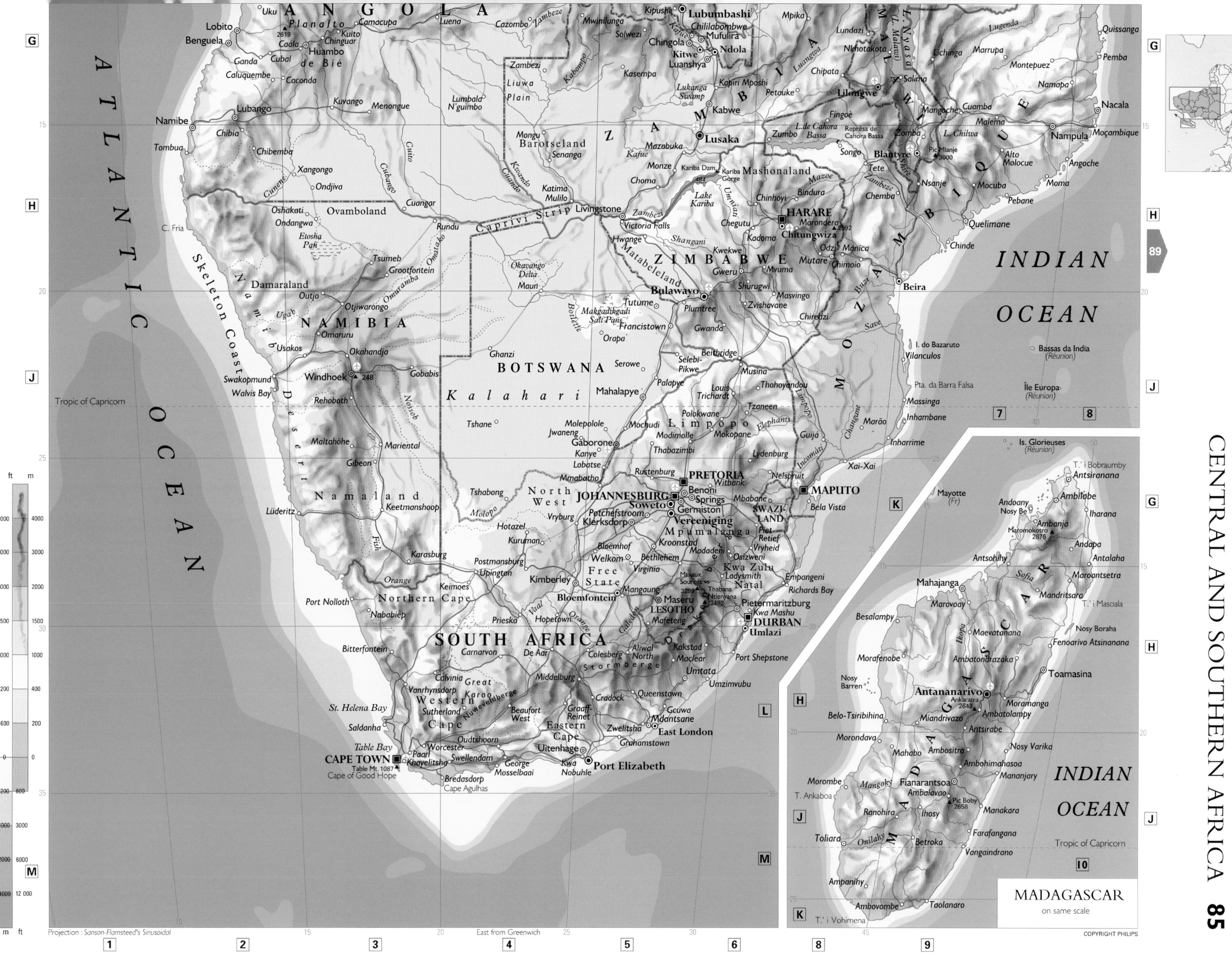
ATLANTIC OCEAN
INDIAN OCEAN
ANGOLA
ZAMBIA
MALAWI
MOZAMBIQUE
ZIMBABWE
NAMIBIA
BOTSWANA
SOUTH AFRICA
LESOTHO
SWAZILAND
MADAGASCAR
Kalahari
Namib Desert
Skeleton Coast
Caprivi Strip
HARARE
Lusaka
Lilongwe
MAPUTO
PRETORIA
JOHANNESBURG
Windhoek
Gaborone
Bulawayo
Beira
Blantyre
DURBAN
CAPE TOWN
Port Elizabeth
East London
Bloemfontein
Kimberley
Maseru
Antananarivo
Toamasina
Tropic of Capricorn
MADAGASCAR
on same scale
Projection : Sanson-Flamsteed's Sinusoidal
East from Greenwich
COPYRIGHT PHILIPS

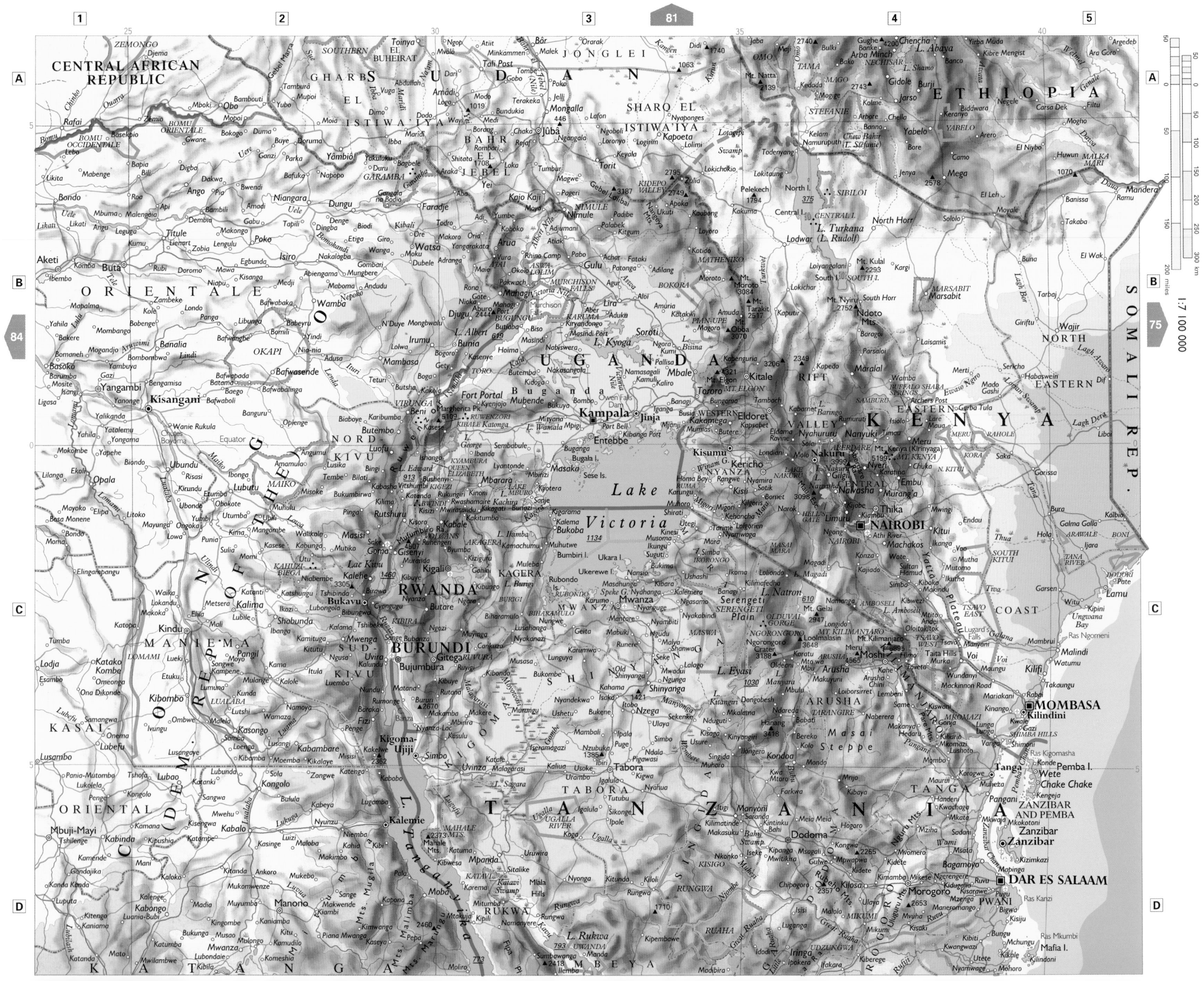
1:7 100 000
SOMALI REP.
ETHIOPIA
KENYA
UGANDA
SUDAN
TANZANIA
RWANDA
BURUNDI
CENTRAL AFRICAN REPUBLIC
ORIENTALE
NAIROBI
MOMBASA
DAR ES SALAAM
Kampala
Lake Victoria
L. Tanganyika
L. Turkana (L. Rudolf)
L. Albert
L. Kyoga
L. Rukwa
ZANZIBAR AND PEMBA
Zanzibar
Pemba I.
Mafia I.
Kisangani
Dodoma
Tabora
Kigali
Bujumbura
Juba
Mwanza
Arusha
Moshi
Nakuru
Kisumu
Eldoret
Entebbe
Jinja
Tanga
Morogoro
Kigoma-Ujiji
Kalemie
Bukavu
Goma
Kindu
Mbuji-Mayi
Marsabit
Malindi
Lamu

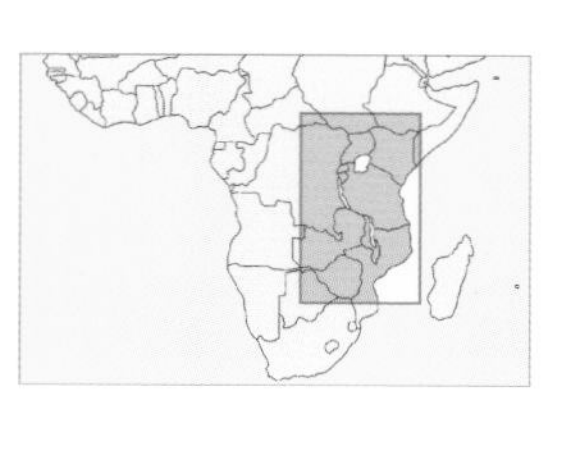

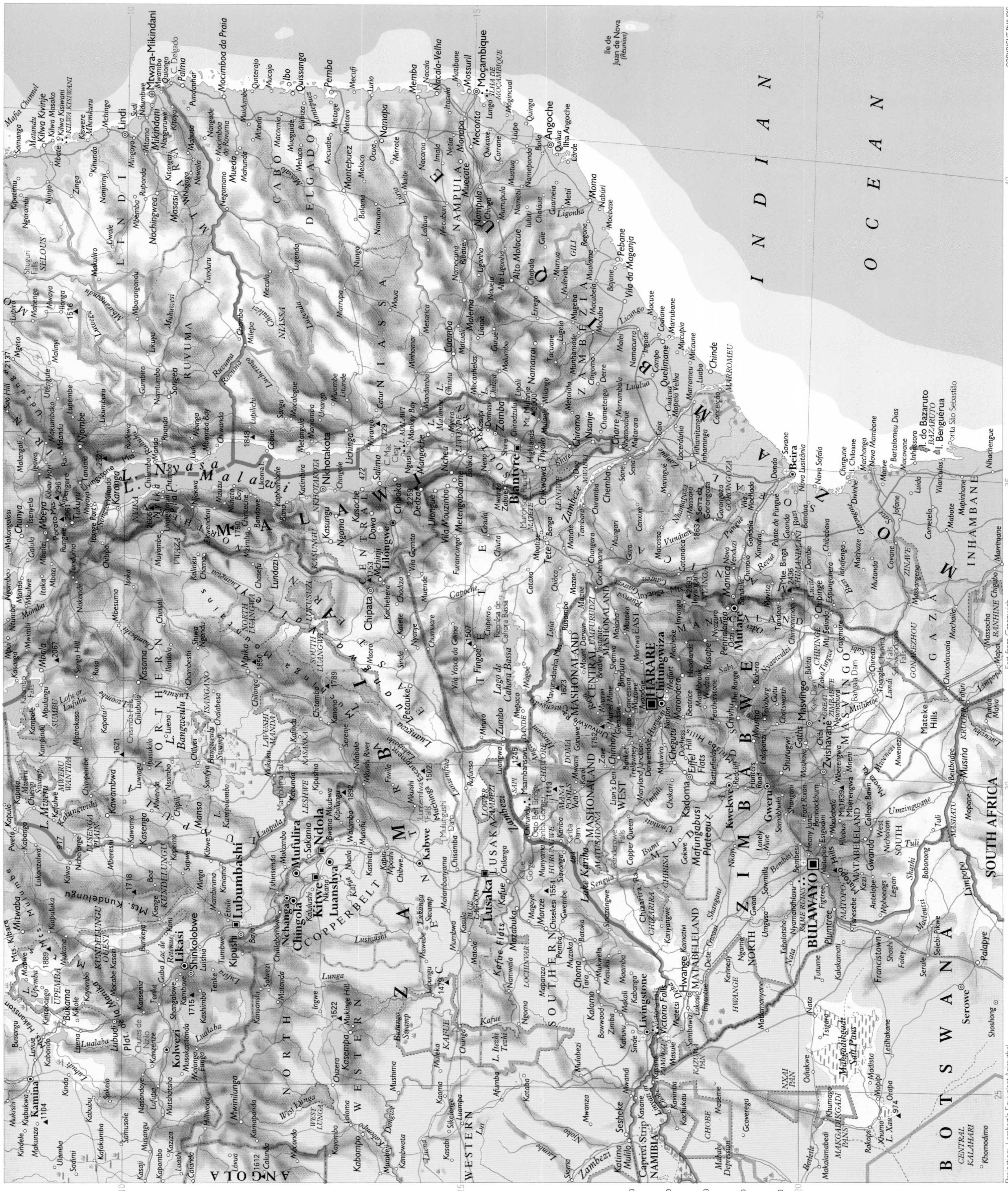

National Parks

Nature Reserves and Game Reserves

∴ UNESCO World Heritage Sites

Projection: Lambert's Equivalent Azimuthal

East from Greenwich

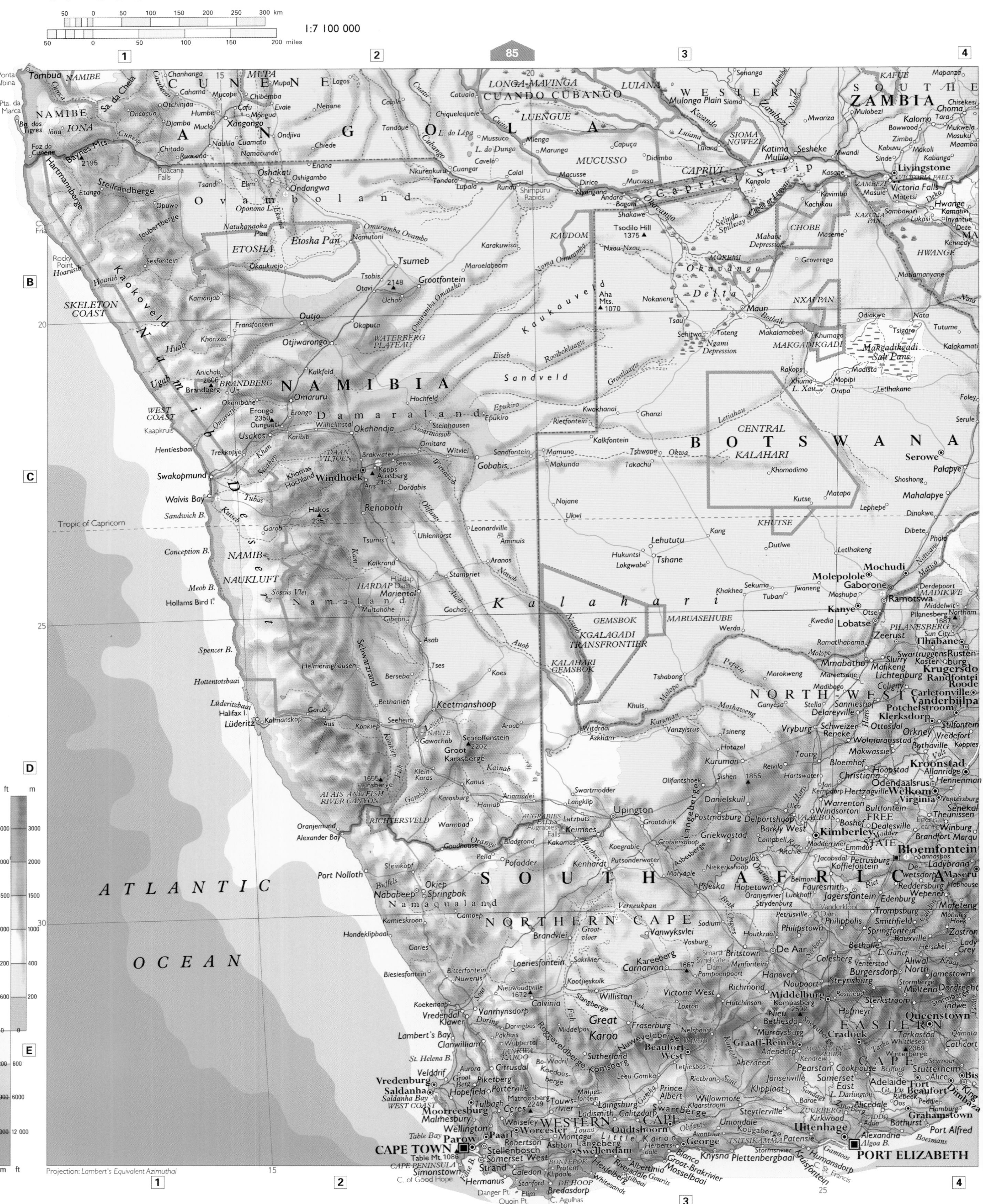
1:7 100 000
85
A N G O L A
ZAMBIA
NAMIBIA
BOTSWANA
SOUTH AFRICA
ATLANTIC OCEAN
NORTHERN CAPE
NORTH-WEST
EASTERN CAPE
WESTERN CAPE
FREE STATE
CAPRIVI Strip
Okavango Delta
Kalahari
Damaraland
Namaqualand
Ovamboland
Kaokoveld
Namib Desert
Great Karoo
Little Karoo
Sandveld
Etosha Pan
Makgadikgadi Salt Pans
SKELETON COAST
Tropic of Capricorn
Windhoek
Walvis Bay
Swakopmund
Lüderitz
Keetmanshoop
Rehoboth
Otjiwarongo
Tsumeb
Grootfontein
Okahandja
Gobabis
Mariental
Oranjemund
Port Nolloth
Springbok
Upington
Kimberley
Bloemfontein
Welkom
Vryburg
Mafikeng
Mmabatho
Gaborone
Molepolole
Mochudi
Kanye
Lobatse
Serowe
Palapye
Mahalapye
Maun
Ghanzi
Livingstone
Victoria Falls
Hwange
Kasane
De Aar
Beaufort West
Middelburg
Graaff-Reinet
Cradock
Queenstown
Grahamstown
Port Alfred
PORT ELIZABETH
Uitenhage
Oudtshoorn
George
Knysna
Plettenbergbaai
Mossel Baai
Swellendam
Worcester
Paarl
Stellenbosch
CAPE TOWN
Table Mt. 1088
Hermanus
C. of Good Hope
C. Agulhas
Saldanha
Vredenburg
Kuruman
Postmasburg
Colesberg
Orange
Projection: Lambert's Equivalent Azimuthal

National Parks

Nature Reserves and Game Reserves

∴ UNESCO World Heritage Sites

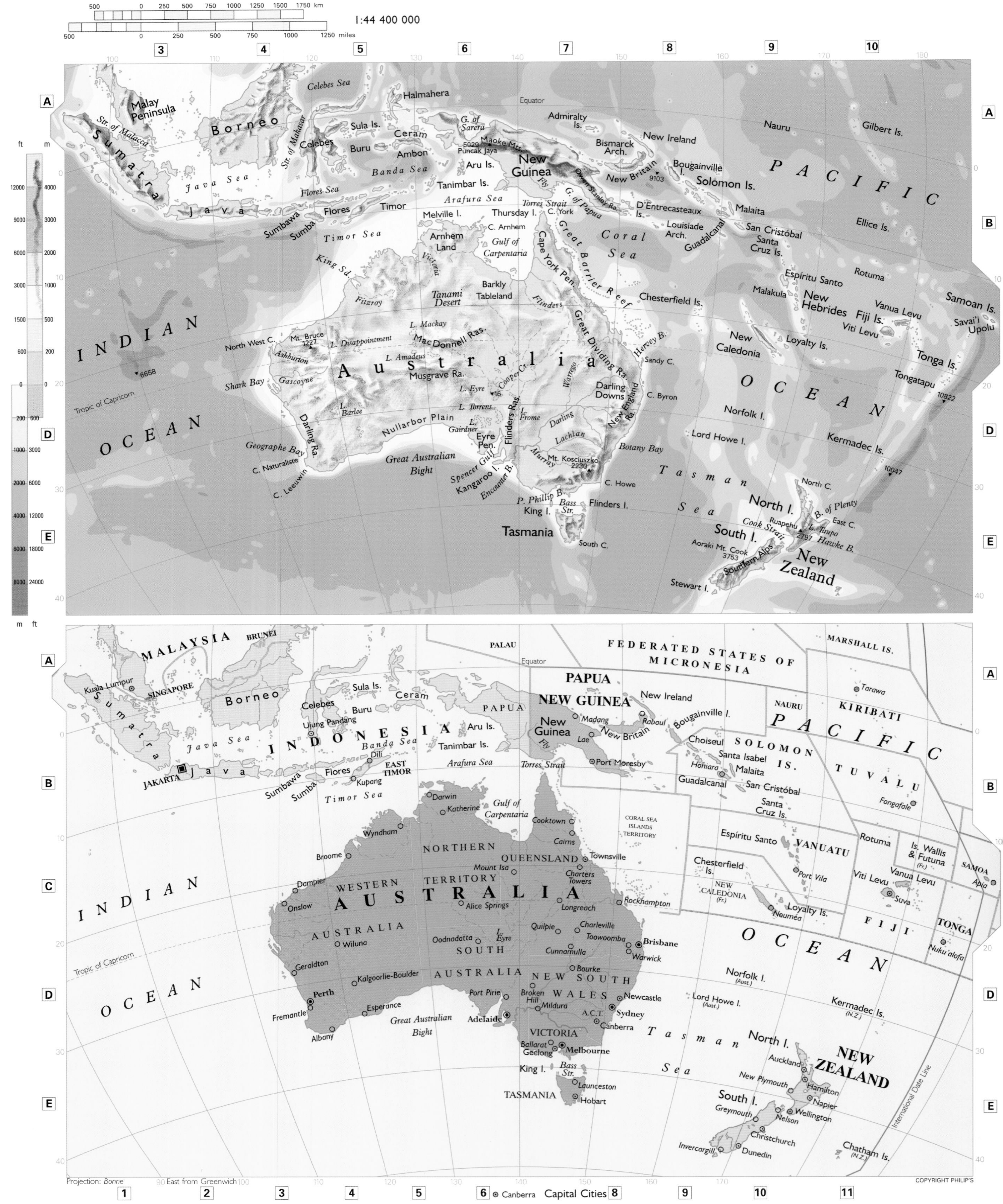
1:44 400 000
INDIAN OCEAN
PACIFIC OCEAN
Australia
New Guinea
Borneo
Sumatra
Java
Celebes
Tasmania
New Zealand
North I.
South I.
Tasman Sea
Coral Sea
Arafura Sea
Timor Sea
Banda Sea
Java Sea
Celebes Sea
Great Australian Bight
Great Barrier Reef
Great Dividing Ra.
Nullarbor Plain
MacDonnell Ras.
Tanami Desert
Barkly Tableland
Mt. Kosciuszko 2230
Aoraki Mt. Cook 3753
Puncak Jaya 5029
Tropic of Capricorn
Equator
MALAYSIA
BRUNEI
SINGAPORE
INDONESIA
EAST TIMOR
PAPUA NEW GUINEA
FEDERATED STATES OF MICRONESIA
PALAU
MARSHALL IS.
NAURU
KIRIBATI
SOLOMON IS.
TUVALU
VANUATU
FIJI
TONGA
SAMOA
NEW CALEDONIA (Fr.)
CORAL SEA ISLANDS TERRITORY
WESTERN AUSTRALIA
NORTHERN TERRITORY
SOUTH AUSTRALIA
QUEENSLAND
NEW SOUTH WALES
VICTORIA
A.C.T.
TASMANIA
NEW ZEALAND
JAKARTA
Canberra
Sydney
Melbourne
Brisbane
Adelaide
Perth
Hobart
Darwin
Auckland
Wellington
Christchurch
Port Moresby
Honiara
Port Vila
Nouméa
Suva
Nuku'alofa
Apia
International Date Line
Projection: Bonne
East from Greenwich
Capital Cities
COPYRIGHT PHILIP'S

1:5 300 000

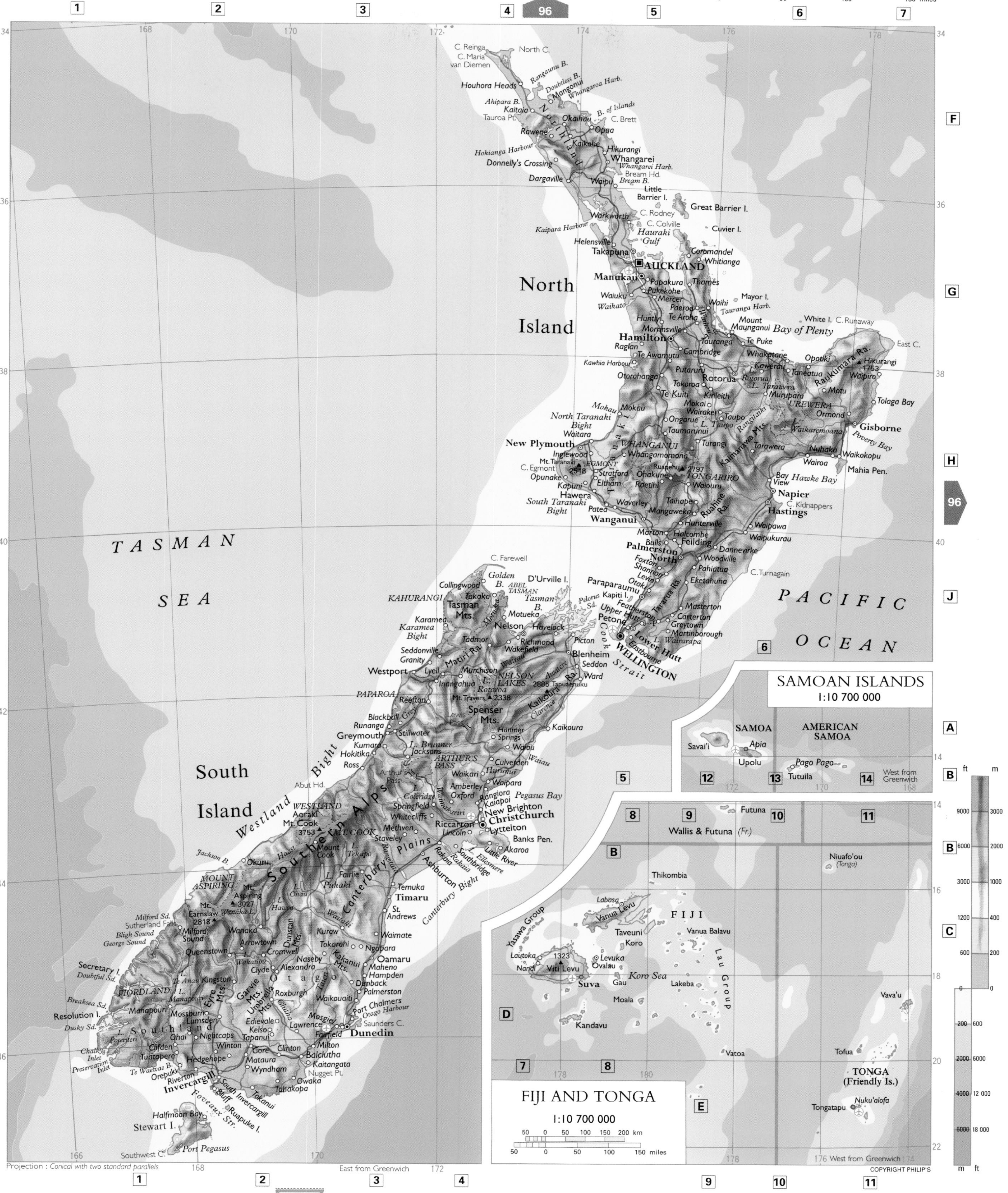

50 0 50 100 150 200 km

50 0 50 100 150 miles

96

North Island

C. Reinga
North C.
C. Maria van Diemen
Rangaunu B.
Doubtless B.
Mangonui
Whangaroa Harb.
Houhora Heads
Ahipara B.
Kaitaia
Tauroa Pt.
Northland
B. of Islands
Okaihau
C. Brett
Opua
Rawene
Kaikohe
Hokianga Harbour
Hikurangi
Whangarei
Whangarei Harb.
Donnelly's Crossing
Bream Hd.
Dargaville
Waipu
Bream B.
Little Barrier I.
Great Barrier I.
Warkworth
C. Rodney
C. Colville
Kaipara Harbour
Hauraki Gulf
Cuvier I.
Helensville
Takapuna
Coromandel
Whitianga
AUCKLAND
Manukau
Papakura
Thames
Pukekohe
Mercer
Waiuku
Waikato
Paeroa
Waihi
Mayor I.
Tauranga Harb.
Huntly
Te Aroha
Morrinsville
Mount Maunganui
Bay of Plenty
White I.
C. Runaway
Hamilton
Tauranga
Te Puke
Raglan
Cambridge
East C.
Te Awamutu
Whakatane
Opotiki
Hikurangi 1753
Kawhia Harbour
Putaruru
Kawerau
Taneatua
Raukumara Ra.
Otorohanga
Rotorua
L. Rotorua
L. Tarawera
Murupara
Waipiro
Tokoroa
Motu
Te Kuiti
Kinleith
UREWERA
Tolaga Bay
Mokau
Mokai
Wairakei
Ormond
North Taranaki Bight
Ongarue
Taupo
L. Taupo
Gisborne
Waitara
Taumarunui
L. Waikaremoana
Poverty Bay
New Plymouth
WHANGANUI
Turangi
Tarawera
Nuhaka
Waikokopu
Inglewood
Whangamomona
Kaimanawa Mts.
Mt. Taranaki 2518
EGMONT
Ruapehu 2797
Wairoa
Mahia Pen.
C. Egmont
Stratford
TONGARIRO
Opunake
Ohakune
Eltham
Raetihi
Waiouru
Bay View
Hawke Bay
Kaponga
Hawera
Napier
South Taranaki Bight
Taihape
Ruahine Ra.
Patea
Waverley
Mangaweka
Hastings
C. Kidnappers
Wanganui
Hunterville
Waipawa
Marton
Halcombe
Waipukurau
Bulls
Feilding
Palmerston North
Dannevirke
Foxton
Woodville
Shannon
Pahiatua
Levin
Eketahuna
C. Turnagain
Paraparaumu
Otaki
Kapiti I.
Tararua Ra.
Featherston
Masterton
Upper Hutt
Carterton
Greytown
Martinborough
Petone
Lower Hutt
L. Wairarapa
WELLINGTON
Eastbourne
Cook Strait

TASMAN SEA

PACIFIC OCEAN

South Island

C. Farewell
Golden B.
ABEL TASMAN
D'Urville I.
Collingwood
Takaka
Tasman B.
KAHURANGI
Tasman Mts.
Motueka
Pelorus Sd.
Karamea
Karamea Bight
Nelson
Havelock
Richmond
Tadmor
Wakefield
Picton
Seddonville
Granity
Matiri Ra.
Blenheim
Seddon
Westport
Lyell
Murchison
NELSON LAKES
Ward
Inangahua
L. Rotoroa
2885 Tapuaenuku
PAPAROA
Reefton
Mt. Travers 2338
Spenser Mts.
Kaikoura Ra.
Blackball
Runanga
Kaikoura
Greymouth
Stillwater
Hanmer Springs
Kumara
L. Brunner
Hokitika
Jacksons
Waiau
ARTHUR'S PASS
Ross
Culverden
Hurunui
Waikari
Waipara
Abut Hd.
Amberley
Oxford
Pegasus Bay
Rangiora
Kaiapoi
WESTLAND
Springfield
New Brighton
Aoraki Mt. Cook 3753
Whitecliffs
Christchurch
Riccarton
Lyttelton
Westland Bight
Methven
Lincoln
Banks Pen.
MT. COOK
Staveley
Akaroa
Southern Alps
Plains
L. Ellesmere
Little River
Jackson B.
Mount Cook
L. Tekapo
Rakaia
Southbridge
Okuru
Ashburton
MOUNT ASPIRING
L. Pukaki
Fairlie
Canterbury
Canterbury Bight
Mt. Aspiring 3027
Temuka
Timaru
Mt. Earnslaw 2818
L. Wanaka
L. Ohau
L. Hawea
Milford Sd.
St. Andrews
Sutherland Falls
Bligh Sound
Milford Sound
Wanaka
Dunstan Mts.
Waimate
George Sound
Kurow
Queenstown
Arrowtown
Cromwell
Tokarahi
Ngapara
Oamaru
Secretary I.
Naseby
Kakanui Mts.
Doubtful Sd.
Clyde
Alexandra
Maheno
Hampden
L. Te Anau
Kingston
Dunback
Eyre Mts.
Otago
Palmerston
FIORDLAND
Garvie Mts.
Roxburgh
Breaksea Sd.
L. Manapouri
Umbrella Mts.
Waikouaiti
Port Chalmers
Otago Harbour
Resolution I.
Manapouri
Mossburn
Lumsden
Saunders C.
Dusky Sd.
Edievale
Mosgiel
Southland
Lawrence
Kelso
Fairfield
Dunedin
Ohai
Nightcaps
Tapanui
L. Poteriteri
Milton
Chalky Inlet
Winton
Gore
Clinton
Balclutha
Preservation Inlet
Tuatapere
Hedgehope
Mataura
Kaitangata
Clifden
Wyndham
Nugget Pt.
Te Waewae B.
Orepuki
Riverton
Owaka
Invercargill
Tahakopa
Bluff
South Invercargill
Tokanui
Foveaux Str.
Ruapuke I.
Halfmoon Bay
Stewart I.
Port Pegasus
Southwest C.

SAMOAN ISLANDS

1:10 700 000

SAMOA
AMERICAN SAMOA
Savai'i
Apia
Upolu
Pago Pago
Tutuila
West from Greenwich

Futuna
Wallis & Futuna (Fr.)
Niuafo'ou (Tonga)
Thikombia
Labasa
Vanua Levu
FIJI
Yasawa Group
Taveuni
Vanua Balavu
Koro
Lautoka
1323
Levuka
Ovalau
Nandi
Viti Levu
Lau Group
Suva
Koro Sea
Gau
Lakeba
Vava'u
Moala
Kandavu
Vatoa
Tofua
TONGA (Friendly Is.)
Tongatapu
Nuku'alofa

FIJI AND TONGA

1:10 700 000

50 0 50 100 150 200 km

50 0 50 100 150 miles

176 West from Greenwich

ft m
9000 3000
6000 2000
3000 1000
1200 400
600 200
0 0
200 600
2000 6000
4000 12 000
6000 18 000
m ft

Projection : Conical with two standard parallels

East from Greenwich

National Parks

1:7 100 000

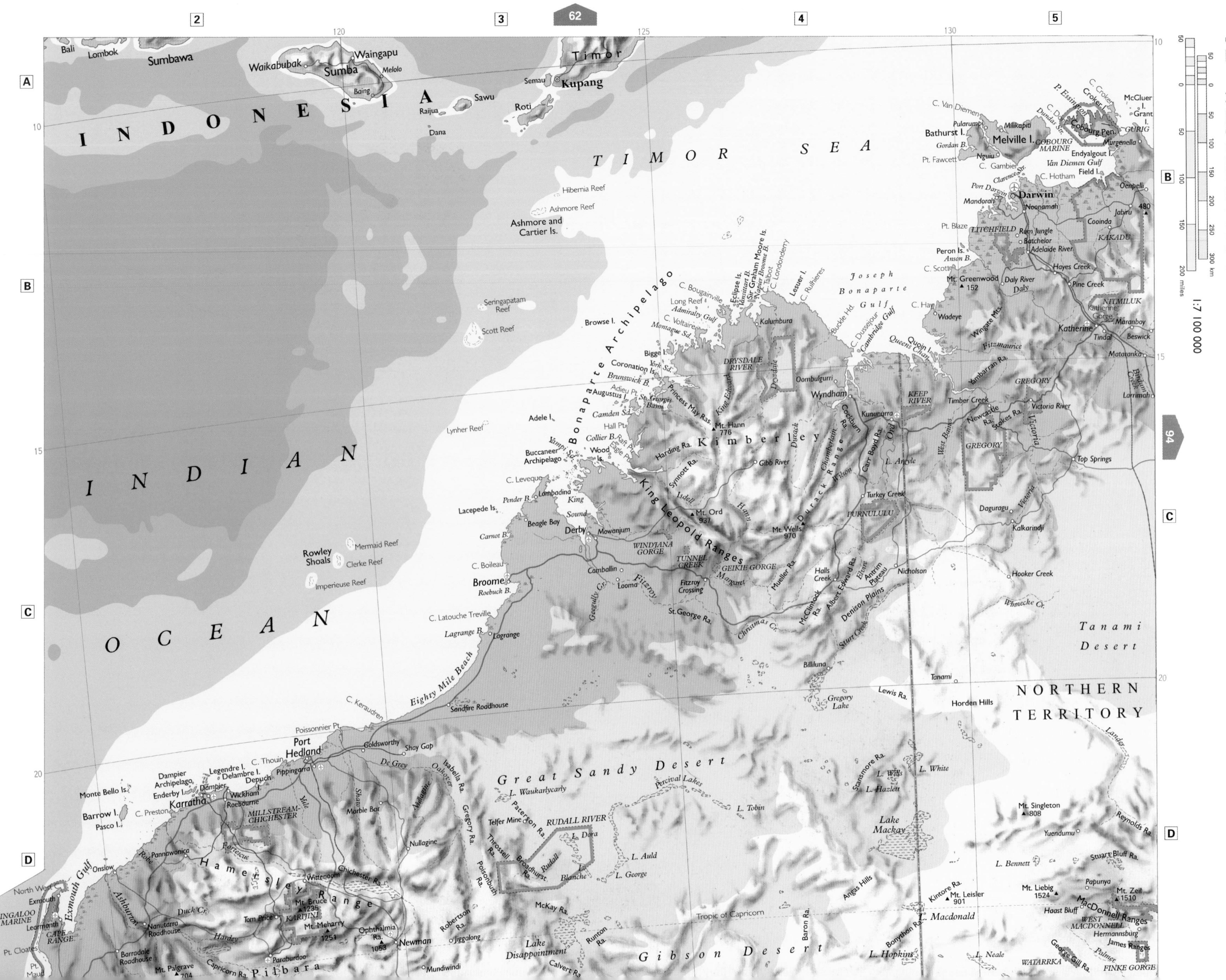
50 0 50 100 150 200 250 300 km
50 0 50 100 150 200 miles
62
94
TIMOR SEA
INDIAN OCEAN
INDONESIA
NORTHERN TERRITORY
Tanami Desert
Great Sandy Desert
Gibson Desert
Kimberley
King Leopold Ranges
Bonaparte Archipelago
Joseph Bonaparte Gulf
Hamersley Range
Pilbara
Eighty Mile Beach
Timor
Kupang
Sumba
Waingapu
Waikabubak
Sumbawa
Lombok
Bali
Roti
Sawu
Darwin
Melville I.
Bathurst I.
Katherine
Wyndham
Kununurra
Derby
Broome
Port Hedland
Karratha
Dampier
Onslow
Newman
Fitzroy Crossing
Halls Creek
Exmouth Gulf
Ashmore and Cartier Is.
Rowley Shoals
Lake Mackay
Lake Disappointment
Tropic of Capricorn
A
B
C
D
2
3
4
5

95
WESTERN AUSTRALIA
SOUTH AUSTRALIA
Great Victoria Desert
Nullarbor Plain
Hampton Tableland
Great Australian Bight
INDIAN OCEAN
SOUTHERN OCEAN
PERTH
Fremantle
Kwinana
Rockingham
Mandurah
Bunbury
Busselton
Albany
Esperance
Geraldton
Carnarvon
Kalgoorlie-Boulder
Norseman
Northam
Merredin
Leonora
Laverton
Meekatharra
Wiluna
Cue
Denham
Kalbarri
Eucla
Nullarbor
Ayers Rock
Mt. Woodroffe 1440
Musgrave Ranges
Petermann Ranges
Everard Ranges
Archipelago of the Recherche
Houtman Abrolhos
Dirk Hartog I.
Shark Bay
National Parks
Projection: Bonne
East from Greenwich
COPYRIGHT PHILIP'S

1:7 100 000

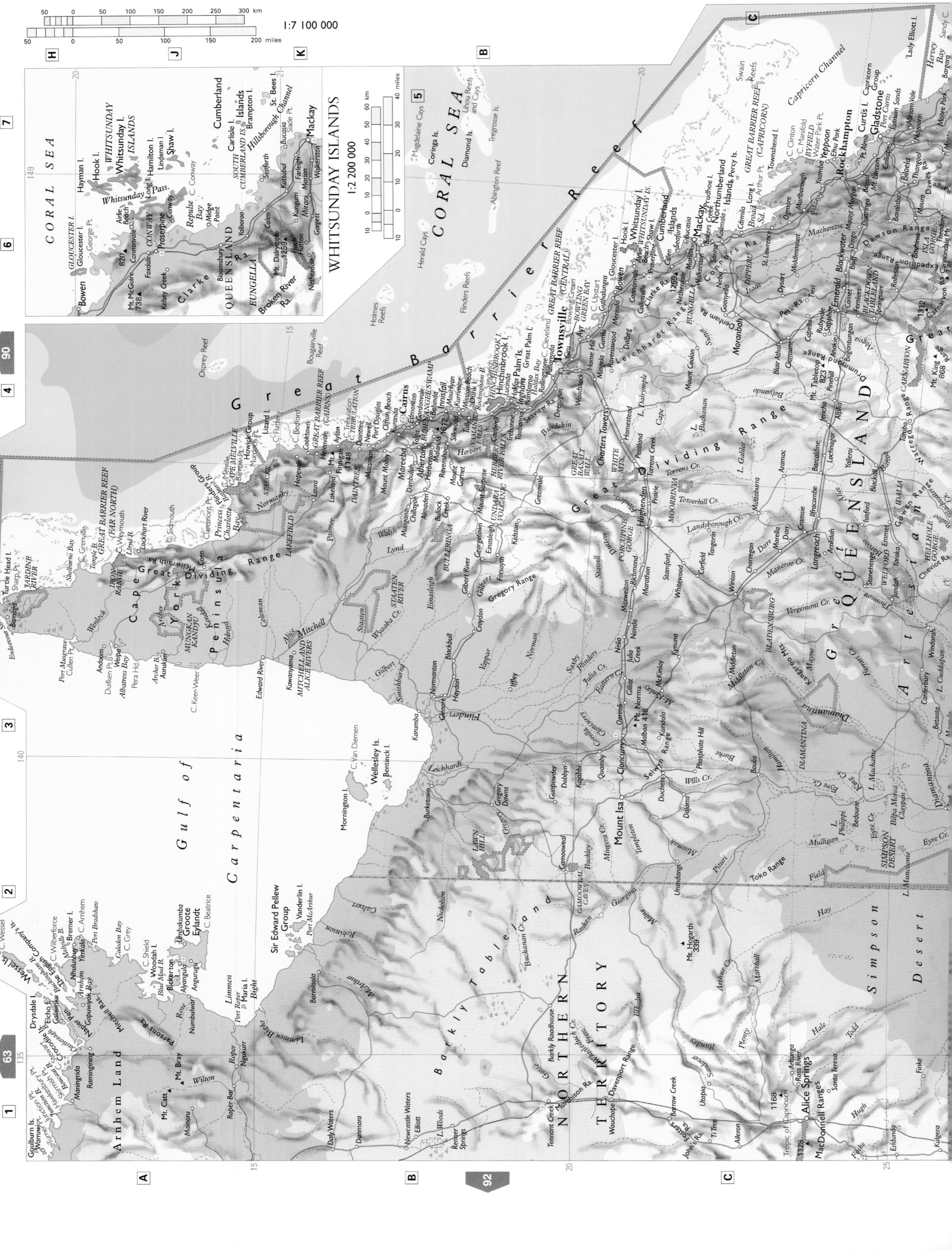

50 0 50 100 150 200 250 300 km
50 0 50 100 150 200 miles
WHITSUNDAY ISLANDS
1:2 200 000
CORAL SEA
Whitsunday I.
Hook I.
Hayman I.
Lindeman I.
Shaw I.
Cumberland Islands
Brampton I.
Carlisle I.
St. Bees I.
Hillsborough Channel
Mackay
Proserpine
Bowen
Clarke Ra.
EUNGELLA
Broken River Ra.
Mt. Dalrymple 1259
Mt. McGuire 738
Great Barrier Reef
GREAT BARRIER REEF (CAIRNS)
GREAT BARRIER REEF (CENTRAL)
GREAT BARRIER REEF (CAPRICORN)
GREAT BARRIER REEF (FAR NORTH)
Gulf of Carpentaria
Cape York Peninsula
Great Dividing Range
QUEENSLAND
NORTHERN TERRITORY
Barkly Tableland
Simpson Desert
Arnhem Land
Great Artesian Basin
Capricorn Channel
Tropic of Capricorn
Thursday I.
Prince of Wales I.
Horn I.
Turtle Head I.
Weipa
Cooktown
Cairns
Innisfail
Hinchinbrook I.
Townsville
Charters Towers
Bowen
Mackay
Rockhampton
Gladstone
Yeppoon
Emerald
Blackwater
Longreach
Winton
Hughenden
Richmond
Cloncurry
Mount Isa
Normanton
Karumba
Burketown
Mornington I.
Wellesley Is.
Groote Eylandt
Sir Edward Pellew Group
Borroloola
Roper Bar
Tennant Creek
Alice Springs
MacDonnell Ranges
Barkly Roadhouse
Newcastle Waters
Daly Waters
Camooweal
Boulia
Birdsville
Mt. Bartle Frere 1612
Mt. Hogarth 339
Mitchell
Gilbert
Flinders
Leichhardt
Diamantina
Georgina
Selwyn Range
Gregory Range
Coral Sea
Swain Reefs
Flinders Reefs
Holmes Reefs
Osprey Reef
Dawson Range
Expedition Range
Carnarvon Range
Drummond Range
Leichhardt Range
Denham Ra.
Peak Ra.
Connors Ra.

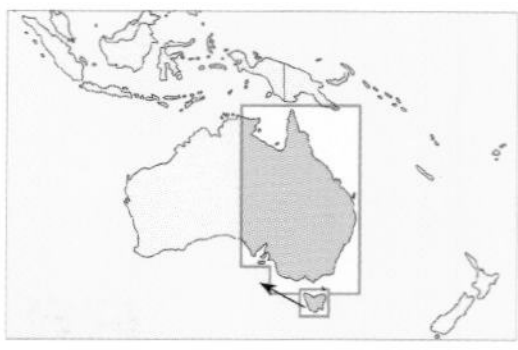

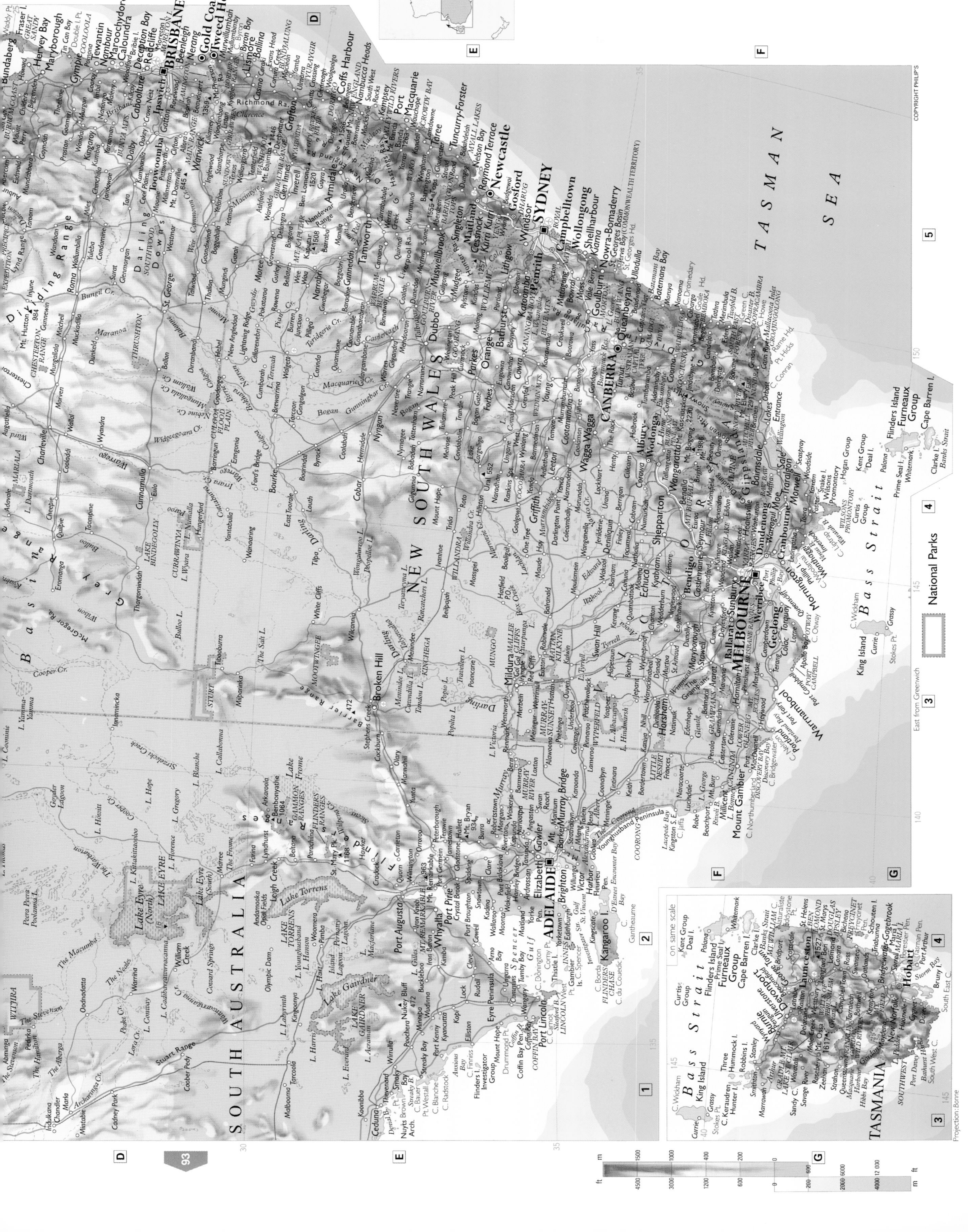

National Parks

on same scale

East from Greenwich

Projection: Bonne

93

m	ft
1500	4500
1000	3000
400	1200
200	600
0	0
200	600
2000	6000
4000	12 000

Equatorial Scale 1:48 000 000

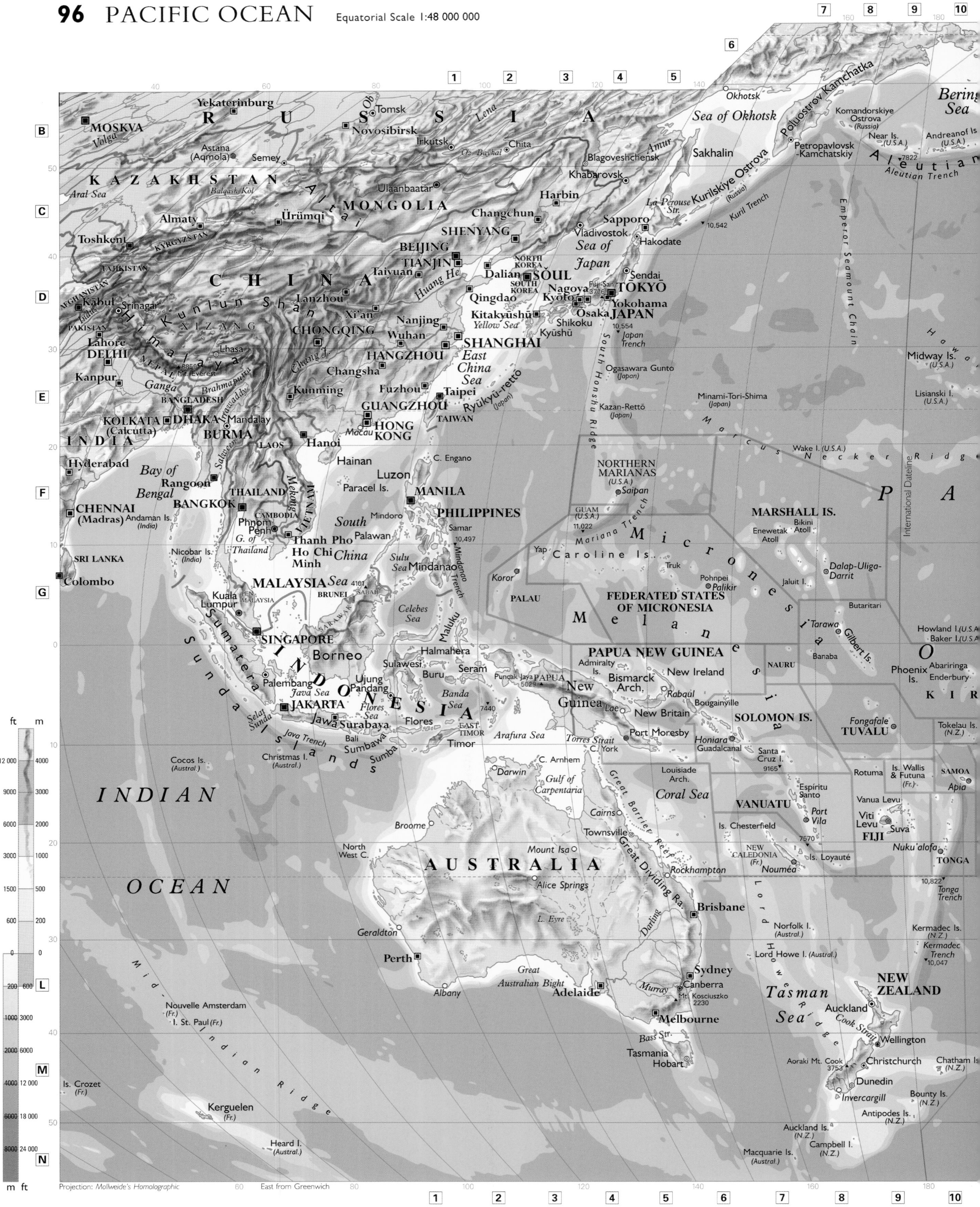

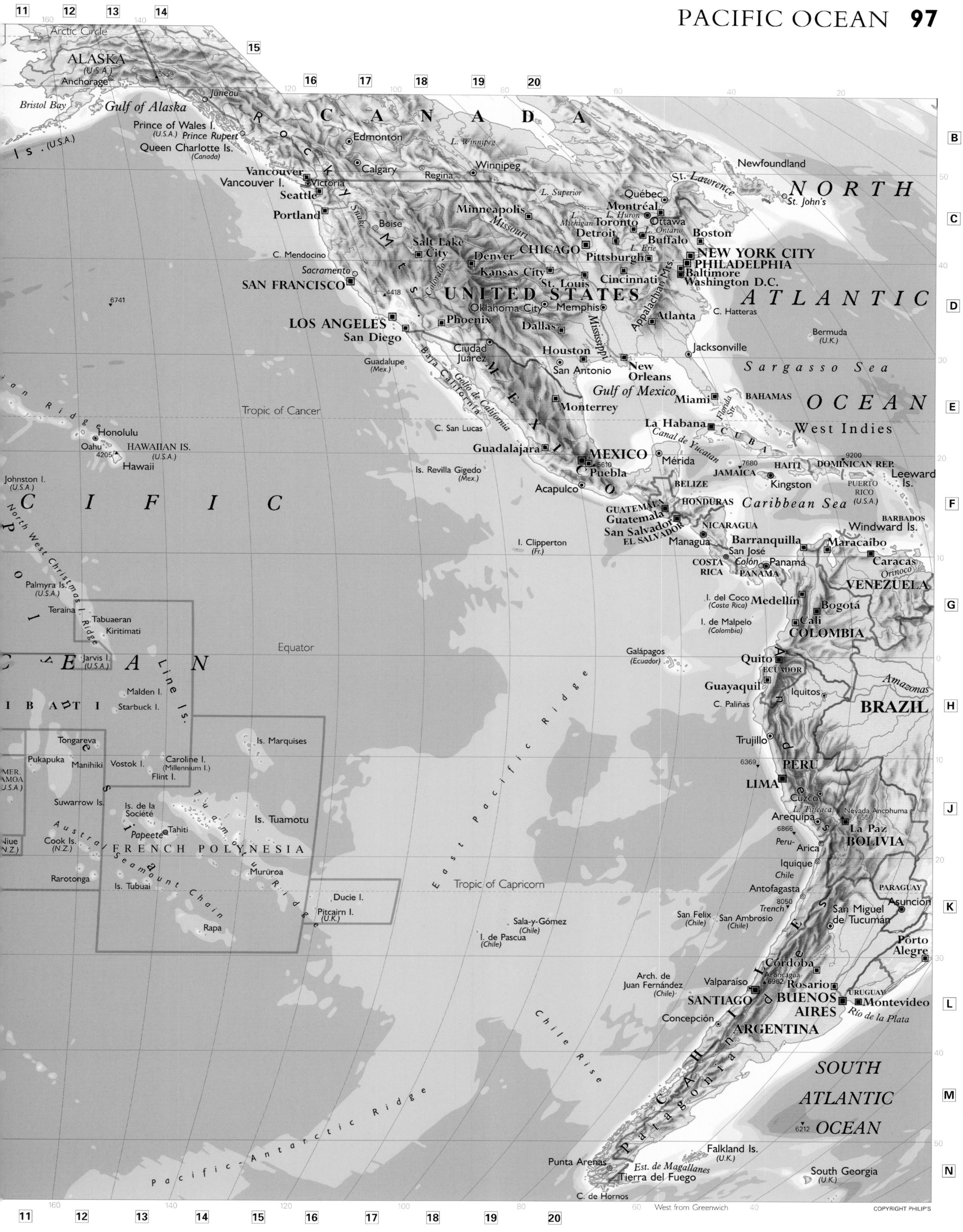
11
12
13
14
15
16
17
18
19
20
B
C
D
E
F
G
H
J
K
L
M
N
Arctic Circle
ALASKA
(U.S.A.)
Anchorage
5959
Juneau
Bristol Bay
Gulf of Alaska
Is. (U.S.A.)
Prince of Wales I.
(U.S.A.) Prince Rupert
Queen Charlotte Is.
(Canada)
ROCKY MTS.
CANADA
Edmonton
Calgary
L. Winnipeg
Winnipeg
Regina
Newfoundland
Vancouver
Vancouver I.
Victoria
Seattle
Portland
Boise
Snake
Missouri
Minneapolis
L. Superior
St. Lawrence
Québec
Montréal
Ottawa
L. Huron
L. Michigan
Toronto
L. Ontario
Detroit
Buffalo
Boston
L. Erie
St. John's
NORTH
Salt Lake City
CHICAGO
Pittsburgh
NEW YORK CITY
PHILADELPHIA
Baltimore
Washington D.C.
C. Mendocino
Sacramento
SAN FRANCISCO
Denver
Kansas City
St. Louis
Cincinnati
Colorado
Appalachian Mts.
4418
UNITED STATES
Oklahoma City
Memphis
ATLANTIC
6741
LOS ANGELES
San Diego
Phoenix
Dallas
Atlanta
C. Hatteras
Mississippi
Bermuda
(U.K.)
Ciudad Juárez
Houston
Jacksonville
Guadalupe
(Mex.)
San Antonio
New Orleans
Sargasso Sea
Baja California
Golfo de California
Gulf of Mexico
Miami
BAHAMAS
Florida Str.
OCEAN
Tropic of Cancer
Monterrey
MEXICO
La Habana
CUBA
West Indies
Honolulu
Oahu
HAWAIIAN IS.
(U.S.A.)
4205
Hawaii
C. San Lucas
Canal de Yucatán
Guadalajara
MEXICO
6610
Puebla
Mérida
9200
7680
HAITI
DOMINICAN REP.
Leeward Is.
Johnston I.
(U.S.A.)
Is. Revilla Gigedo
(Mex.)
JAMAICA
Kingston
PUERTO RICO
(U.S.A.)
BELIZE
Acapulco
PACIFIC
HONDURAS
Caribbean Sea
GUATEMALA
Guatemala
BARBADOS
Windward Is.
San Salvador
EL SALVADOR
NICARAGUA
Managua
North West Christmas I. Ridge
I. Clipperton
(Fr.)
Barranquilla
Maracaibo
San José
Caracas
COSTA RICA
Colón
Panamá
PANAMA
Orinoco
Palmyra Is.
(U.S.A.)
VENEZUELA
I. del Coco
(Costa Rica)
Medellín
Bogotá
Teraina
Tabuaeran
Kiritimati
I. de Malpelo
(Colombia)
Cali
COLOMBIA
Equator
Galápagos
(Ecuador)
Quito
Jarvis I.
(U.S.A.)
ECUADOR
OCEAN
Amazonas
Guayaquil
Iquitos
Malden I.
KIRIBATI
Starbuck I.
Line Is.
C. Paliñas
BRAZIL
East Pacific Ridge
Tongareva
Is. Marquises
Trujillo
Pukapuka
Manihiki
Vostok I.
Caroline I.
(Millennium I.)
Flint I.
6369
PERU
AMER. SAMOA
(U.S.A.)
LIMA
Suwarrow Is.
Is. de la Société
Tuamotu Ridge
Is. Tuamotu
Cuzco
L. Titicaca
Nevada Ancohuma
6550
Arequipa
La Paz
Tahiti
Papeete
6866
BOLIVIA
Niue
(N.Z.)
Cook Is.
(N.Z.)
Austral Seamount Chain
FRENCH POLYNESIA
Peru-Chile Trench
Arica
Iquique
Mururoa
Tropic of Capricorn
Antofagasta
PARAGUAY
Rarotonga
Is. Tubuai
Ducie I.
Pitcairn I.
(U.K.)
8050
Asunción
San Felix
(Chile)
San Ambrosio
(Chile)
San Miguel de Tucumán
Rapa
Sala-y-Gómez
(Chile)
I. de Pascua
(Chile)
Porto Alegre
Córdoba
Arch. de Juan Fernández
(Chile)
Aconcagua
6962
Valparaíso
Rosario
URUGUAY
SANTIAGO
BUENOS AIRES
Montevideo
Río de la Plata
Concepción
ARGENTINA
Chile Rise
ANDES
CHILE
SOUTH ATLANTIC OCEAN
Patagonia
6212
Pacific-Antarctic Ridge
Falkland Is.
(U.K.)
Punta Arenas
Est. de Magallanes
Tierra del Fuego
South Georgia
(U.K.)
C. de Hornos
160
140
120
100
80
60
40
20
West from Greenwich

NORTH AMERICA : Physical

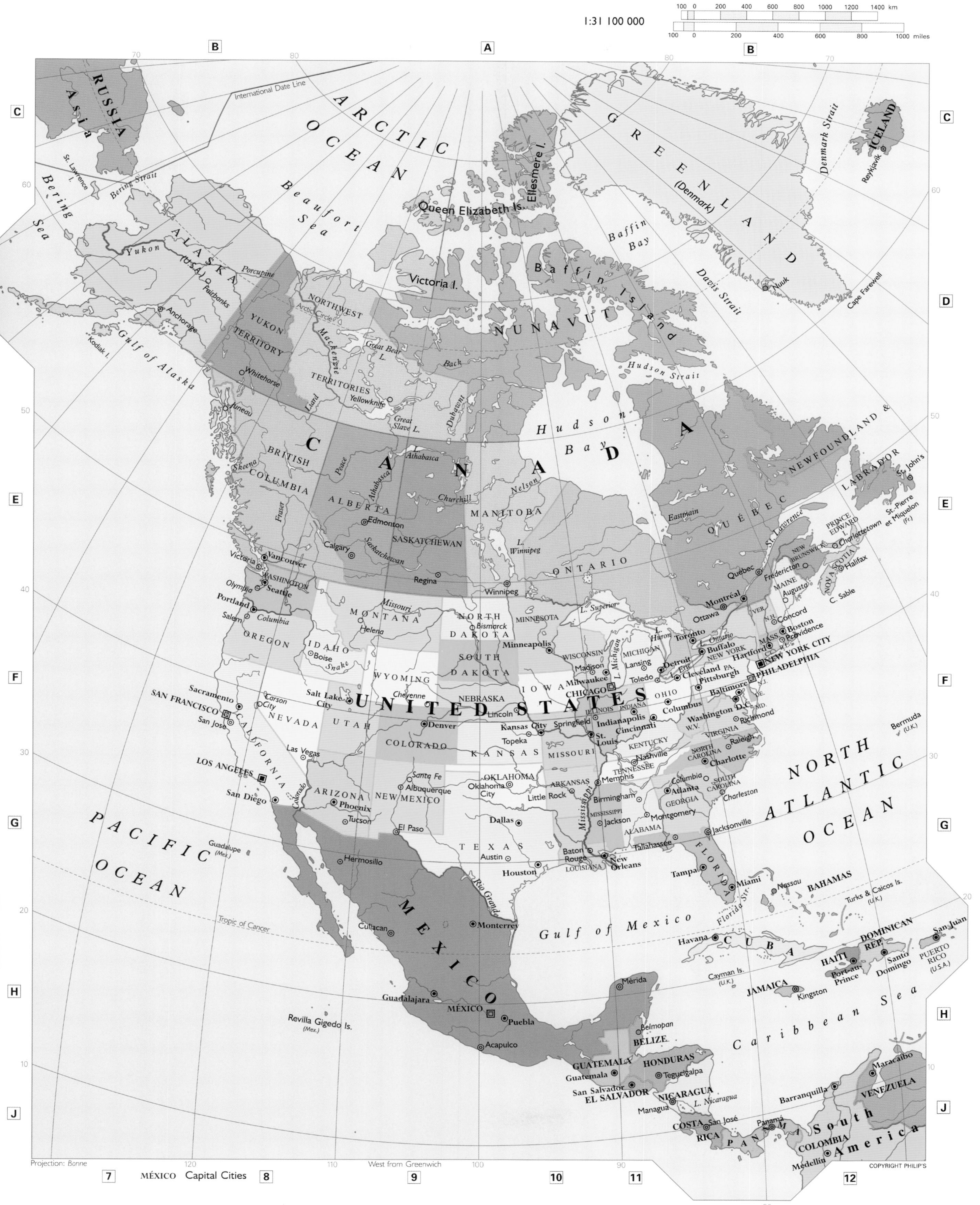
1:31 100 000
100 0 200 400 600 800 1000 1200 1400 km
100 0 200 400 600 800 1000 miles
ARCTIC OCEAN
Beaufort Sea
Bering Sea
Bering Strait
International Date Line
RUSSIA
Asia
St. Lawrence I.
Queen Elizabeth Is.
Ellesmere I.
GREENLAND (Denmark)
Denmark Strait
ICELAND
Reykjavík
Baffin Bay
Baffin Island
Davis Strait
Nuuk
Cape Farewell
Victoria I.
NUNAVUT
Hudson Strait
Hudson Bay
ALASKA (U.S.A.)
Yukon
Porcupine
Fairbanks
Anchorage
Kodiak I.
Gulf of Alaska
YUKON TERRITORY
Whitehorse
Juneau
NORTHWEST TERRITORIES
Arctic Circle
Mackenzie
Great Bear L.
Back
Yellowknife
Great Slave L.
Liard
Dubawnt
CANADA
BRITISH COLUMBIA
Skeena
Fraser
Peace
Athabasca
ALBERTA
Edmonton
Calgary
SASKATCHEWAN
Saskatchewan
Regina
Churchill
Nelson
MANITOBA
L. Winnipeg
Winnipeg
ONTARIO
Eastmain
QUÉBEC
St. Lawrence
Québec
Montréal
Ottawa
Toronto
NEWFOUNDLAND & LABRADOR
St John's
St.-Pierre et Miquelon (Fr.)
PRINCE EDWARD I.
Charlottetown
NEW BRUNSWICK
Fredericton
NOVA SCOTIA
Halifax
C. Sable
Vancouver
Victoria
WASHINGTON
Olympia
Seattle
Portland
Salem
Columbia
OREGON
IDAHO
Boise
Snake
MONTANA
Missouri
Helena
NORTH DAKOTA
Bismarck
MINNESOTA
Minneapolis
L. Superior
SOUTH DAKOTA
WYOMING
Cheyenne
NEBRASKA
Lincoln
IOWA
WISCONSIN
Madison
L. Michigan
Milwaukee
CHICAGO
MICHIGAN
Lansing
L. Huron
Detroit
L. Erie
L. Ontario
Toledo
Cleveland
Buffalo
NEW YORK
PA.
Pittsburgh
Hartford
NEW YORK CITY
PHILADELPHIA
MAINE
Augusta
N.H.
VER.
Concord
MASS.
Boston
Providence
N.J.
DE.
MD.
Baltimore
Washington D.C.
Richmond
W.V.
VIRGINIA
Raleigh
NORTH CAROLINA
Charlotte
SOUTH CAROLINA
Columbia
Charleston
GEORGIA
Atlanta
Jacksonville
Tallahassee
FLORIDA
Tampa
Miami
Florida Str.
ALABAMA
Montgomery
Birmingham
MISSISSIPPI
Jackson
Mississippi
LOUISIANA
Baton Rouge
New Orleans
TENNESSEE
Nashville
Memphis
KENTUCKY
OHIO
Columbus
INDIANA
Indianapolis
Cincinnati
ILLINOIS
Springfield
St. Louis
MISSOURI
Kansas City
Topeka
KANSAS
ARKANSAS
Little Rock
OKLAHOMA
Oklahoma City
TEXAS
Dallas
Austin
Houston
Rio Grande
El Paso
NEW MEXICO
Santa Fe
Albuquerque
COLORADO
Denver
UTAH
Salt Lake City
UNITED STATES
NEVADA
Carson City
Las Vegas
CALIFORNIA
Sacramento
SAN FRANCISCO
San Jose
LOS ANGELES
San Diego
Colorado
ARIZONA
Phoenix
Tucson
PACIFIC OCEAN
Guadalupe (Mex.)
Hermosillo
MEXICO
Culiacan
Monterrey
Guadalajara
MÉXICO
Puebla
Acapulco
Mérida
Revilla Gigedo Is. (Mex.)
Tropic of Cancer
Gulf of Mexico
NORTH ATLANTIC OCEAN
Bermuda (U.K.)
BAHAMAS
Nassau
Turks & Caicos Is. (U.K.)
CUBA
Havana
Cayman Is. (U.K.)
JAMAICA
Kingston
HAITI
Port-au-Prince
DOMINICAN REP.
Santo Domingo
PUERTO RICO (U.S.A.)
San Juan
Caribbean Sea
BELIZE
Belmopan
GUATEMALA
Guatemala
HONDURAS
Tegucigalpa
San Salvador
EL SALVADOR
NICARAGUA
Managua
L. Nicaragua
COSTA RICA
San José
PANAMA
Panamá
Barranquilla
Maracaibo
VENEZUELA
COLOMBIA
Medellín
South America
Projection: Bonne
West from Greenwich
MÉXICO Capital Cities
COPYRIGHT PHILIP'S

1:13 300 000
km
miles
Projection : Bonne
PACIFIC OCEAN
ALASKA
YUKON TERRITORY
NORTHWEST TERRITORIES
BRITISH COLUMBIA
ALBERTA
SASKATCHEWAN
MANITOBA
MONTANA
NORTH DAKOTA
SOUTH DAKOTA
NEBRASKA
MINNESOTA
IOWA
WASHINGTON
UNITED STATES
Banks Island
Victoria Island
Prince of Wales I.
Somerset Island
Viscount Melville Sound
M'Clintock Channel
Amundsen Gulf
Coronation Gulf
Queen Maud Gulf
King William I.
Boothia Peninsula
Great Bear L.
Great Slave L.
Lake Athabasca
Reindeer Lake
Lake Winnipeg
L. Winnipegosis
L. Manitoba
L. of the Woods
Alexander Archipelago
Queen Charlotte Is.
Queen Charlotte Sound
Vancouver I.
Juan de Fuca Str.
Hecate Str.
Mackenzie Mountains
Selwyn Mts.
Cassiar Mountains
Rocky Mountains
Coast Mountains
Wrangell Mts.
St. Elias Mts.
Caribou Mts.
Mt. Logan 5959
Mt. Robson 3954
Anchorage
Fairbanks
Whitehorse
Dawson
Inuvik
Yellowknife
Edmonton
Calgary
VANCOUVER
Victoria
SEATTLE
Saskatoon
Regina
Winnipeg
Churchill
Prince George
Prince Rupert
Kamloops
Fort Nelson
Fort McMurray
Lethbridge
Medicine Hat
Bismarck
Fargo
Minneapolis
St. Paul
Omaha
Sioux Falls
Des Moines
ALASKA
1:26 700 000
CHUKCHI SEA
BERING SEA
GULF OF ALASKA
PACIFIC OCEAN
RUSSIA
CANADA
Aleutian Is.
Brooks Range
Alaska Range
Alaska Peninsula
Kodiak I.
Mt. McKinley 6194
Barrow
Prudhoe Bay
Nome
Bethel
Juneau
Sitka
West from Greenwich
ft
m

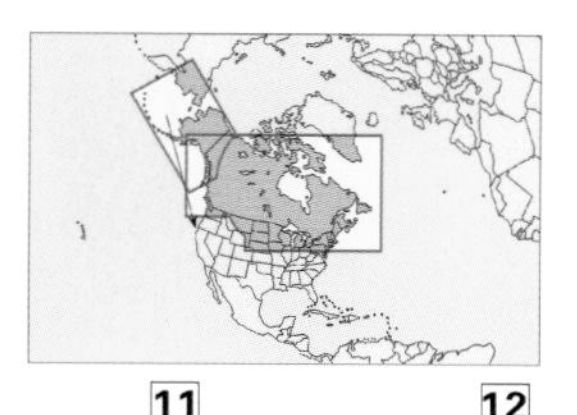

107

1:6 200 000

100

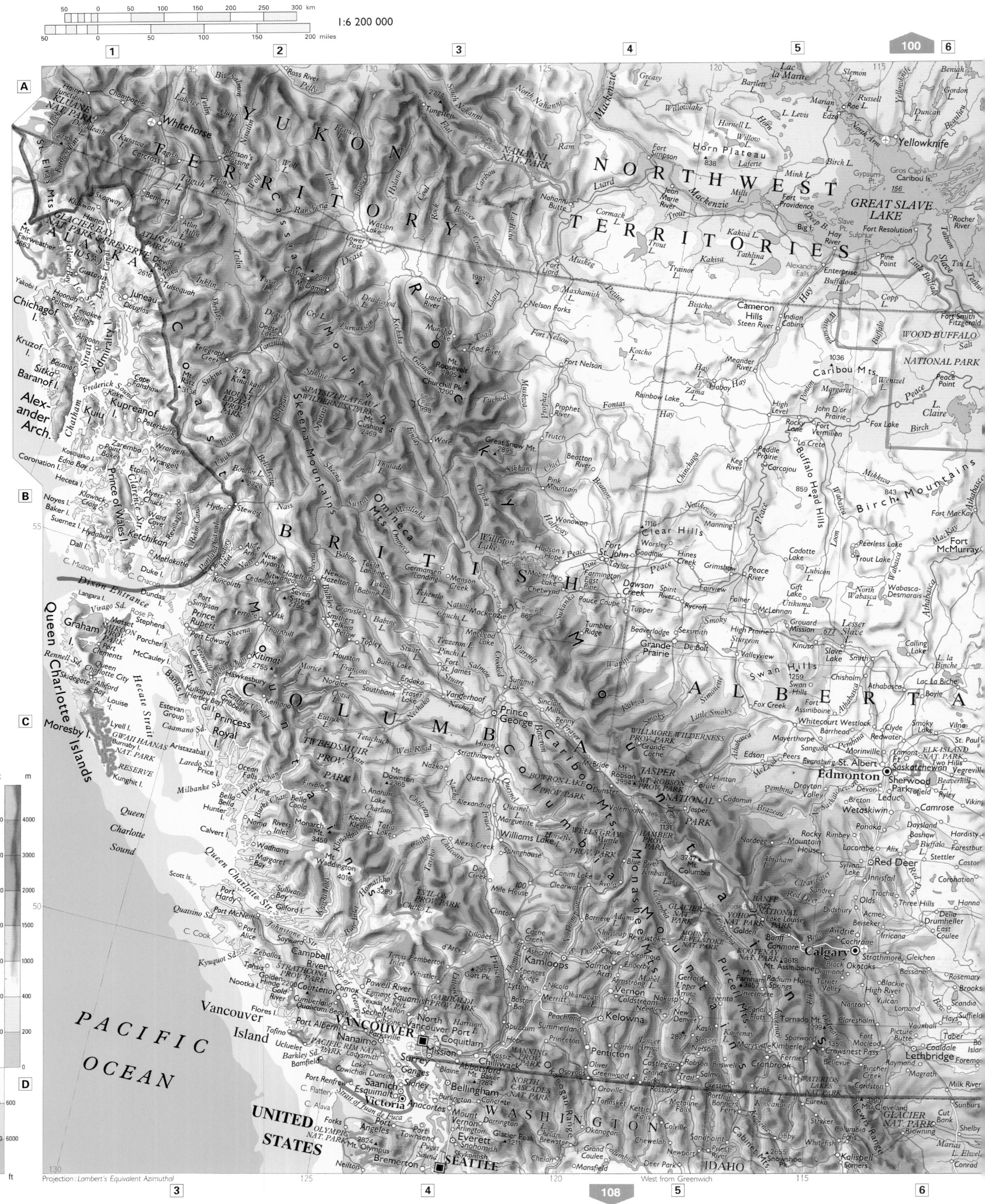

108

National Parks

1:6 200 000

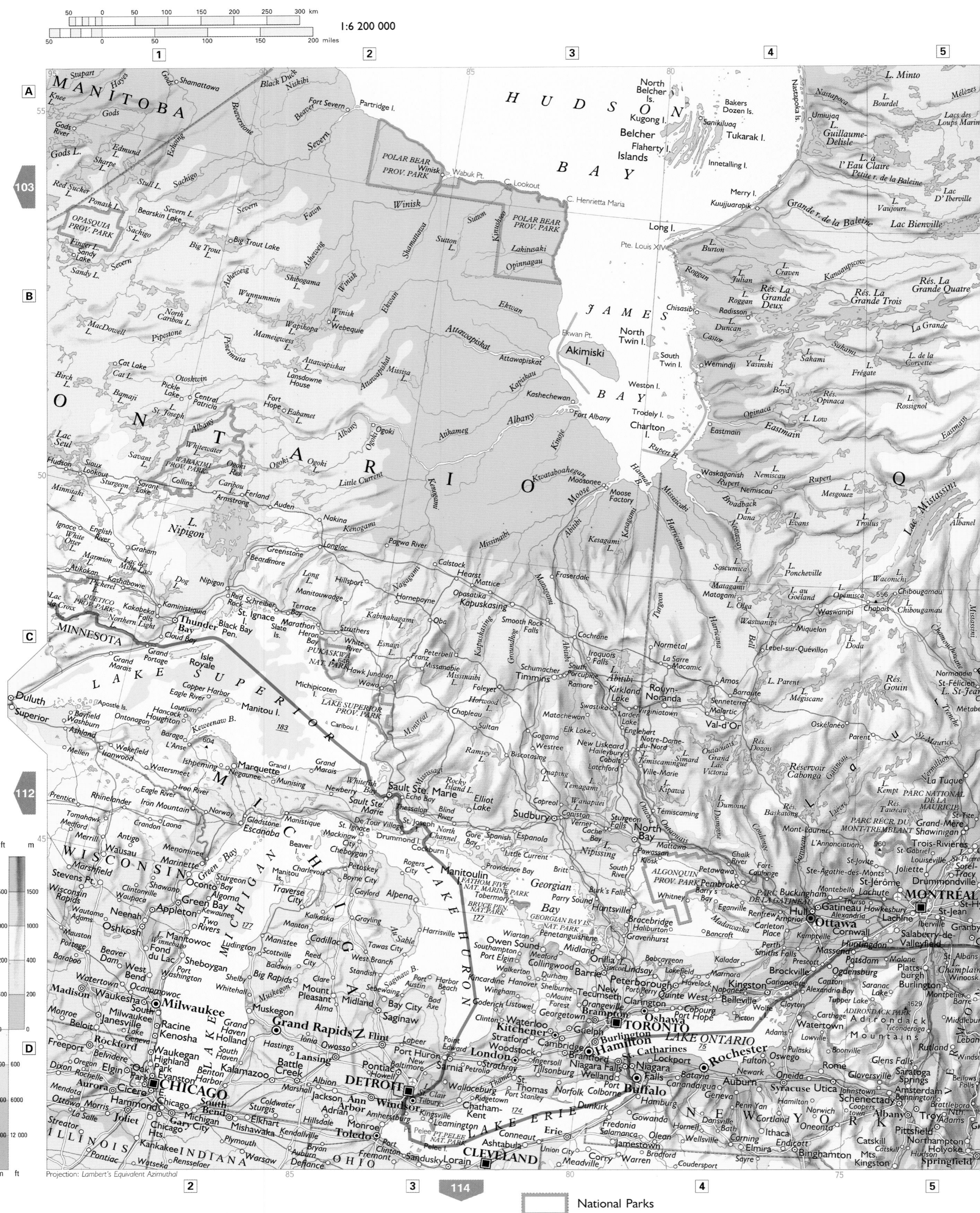

103
112
114

National Parks

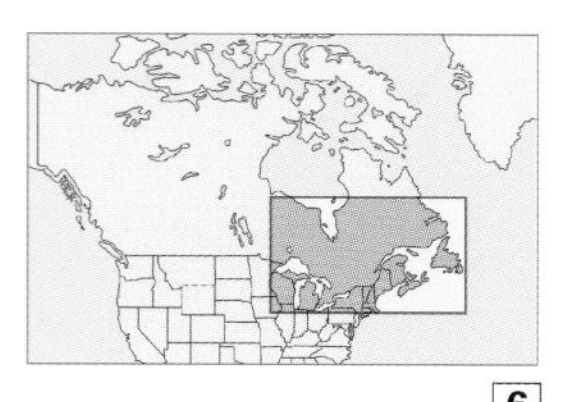

101

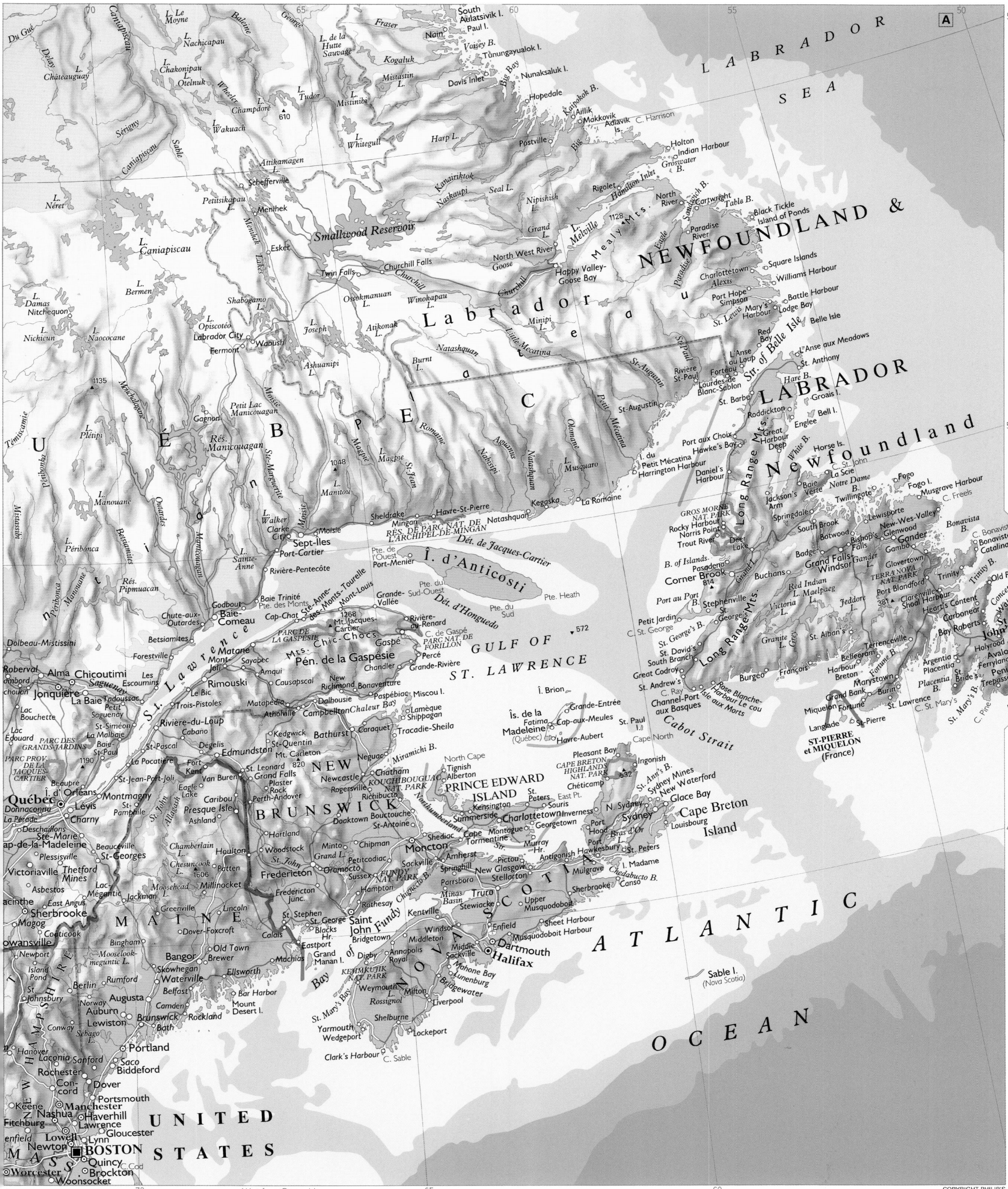

6 7 8 9

A B C D

LABRADOR SEA

NEWFOUNDLAND & LABRADOR

Labrador

Newfoundland

QUÉBEC

GULF OF ST. LAWRENCE

NEW BRUNSWICK

PRINCE EDWARD ISLAND

NOVA SCOTIA

Cape Breton Island

Î. d'Anticosti

Cabot Strait

ST-PIERRE et MIQUELON (France)

MAINE

UNITED STATES

ATLANTIC OCEAN

West from Greenwich

70 65 60

6 7 8

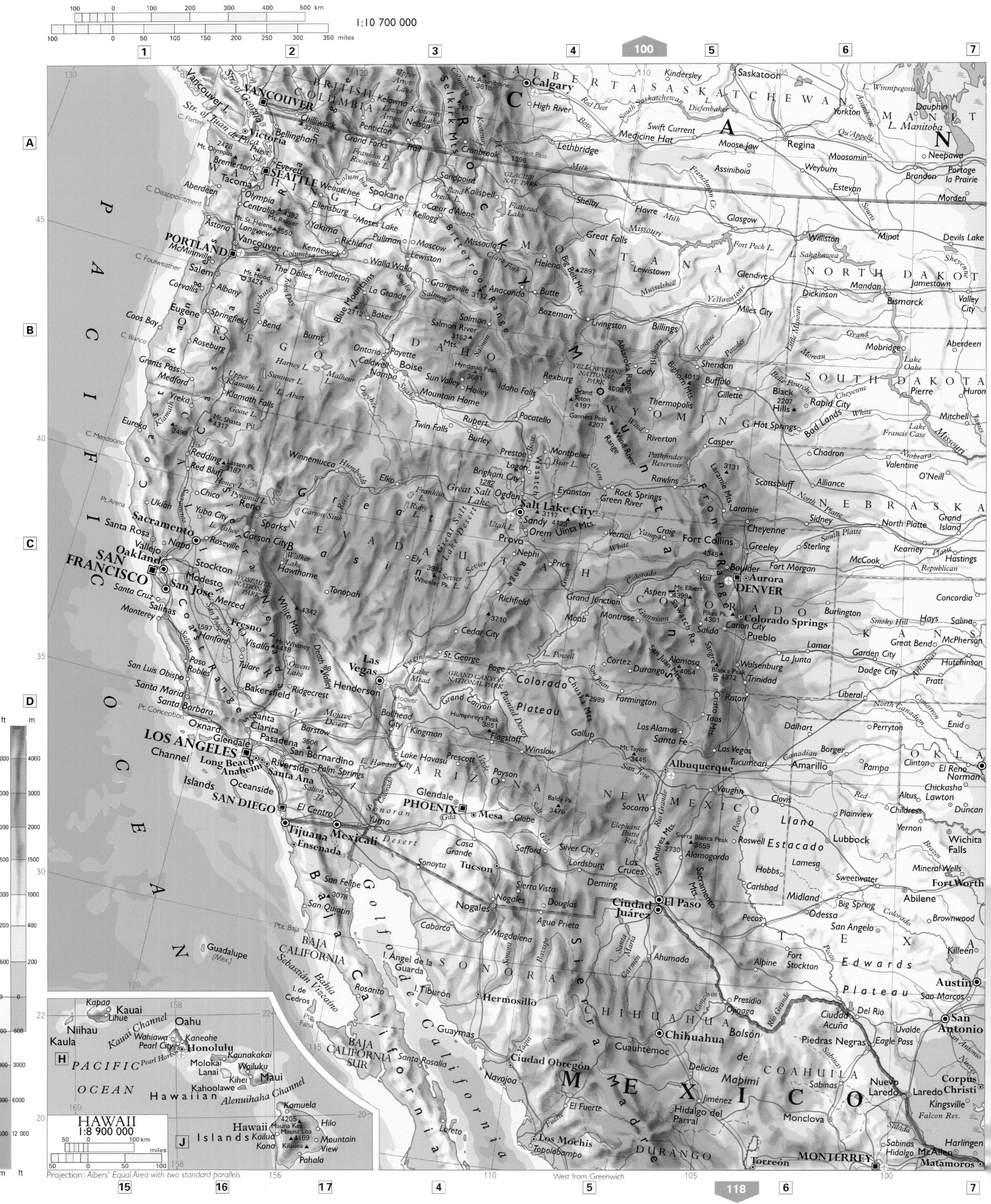

1:10 700 000
100 0 100 200 300 400 500 km
100 0 50 100 150 200 250 300 350 miles
100
118
West from Greenwich
Projection: Albers' Equal Area with two standard parallels
PACIFIC OCEAN
C A N A D A
BRITISH COLUMBIA
ALBERTA
SASKATCHEWAN
MANITOBA
WASHINGTON
OREGON
IDAHO
MONTANA
WYOMING
NORTH DAKOTA
SOUTH DAKOTA
NEBRASKA
KANSAS
OKLA
CALIFORNIA
NEVADA
UTAH
COLORADO
ARIZONA
NEW MEXICO
TEXAS
M E X I C O
BAJA CALIFORNIA
BAJA CALIFORNIA SUR
SONORA
CHIHUAHUA
COAHUILA
DURANGO
ROCKY MOUNTAINS
Great Basin
Sierra Nevada
Coast Ranges
Cascade Range
Colorado Plateau
Llano Estacado
Edwards Plateau
Sierra Madre
Bolsón de Mapimí
Sonoran Desert
Mojave Desert
Golfo de California
Gulf of California
Channel Islands
VANCOUVER
Victoria
SEATTLE
Tacoma
Olympia
Spokane
PORTLAND
Salem
Eugene
Boise
Helena
Great Falls
Billings
Calgary
Regina
Saskatoon
Bismarck
Pierre
Cheyenne
DENVER
Aurora
Colorado Springs
Salt Lake City
Reno
Sacramento
SAN FRANCISCO
Oakland
San Jose
Fresno
LOS ANGELES
SAN DIEGO
Las Vegas
PHOENIX
Tucson
Albuquerque
Santa Fe
El Paso
Ciudad Juárez
Chihuahua
Hermosillo
Tijuana
Mexicali
MONTERREY
San Antonio
Austin
Fort Worth
Amarillo
Lubbock
Mt. Rainier 4392
Mt. Hood 3424
Mt. Shasta 4317
Lassen Pk. 3187
Mt. Whitney 4418
Mt. Elbert 4399
Pikes Pk. 4301
Grand Teton 4197
Gannett Peak 4207
Humphreys Peak 3851
Wheeler Pk. 3982
Kings Pk. 4123
Great Salt Lake
Salton Sea -72
L. Tahoe
YELLOWSTONE NATIONAL PARK
YOSEMITE NATIONAL PARK
GRAND CANYON NATIONAL PARK
GLACIER NAT. PARK
Columbia
Snake
Missouri
Yellowstone
Colorado
Rio Grande
Pecos
Platte
Arkansas
Red
HAWAII
1:8 900 000
50 0 100 km
50 0 50 100 miles
Kauai
Oahu
Honolulu
Molokai
Lanai
Maui
Kahoolawe
Hawaii
Hilo
Niihau
Kaula
Mauna Kea 4205
Mauna Loa 4169
Kilauea
Hawaiian Islands
PACIFIC OCEAN
Kauai Channel
Alenuihaha Channel
ft m
12 000 4000
9000 3000
6000 2000
4500 1500
3000 1000
1200 400
600 200
0 0
200 600
1000 3000
2000 6000
4000 12 000
m ft

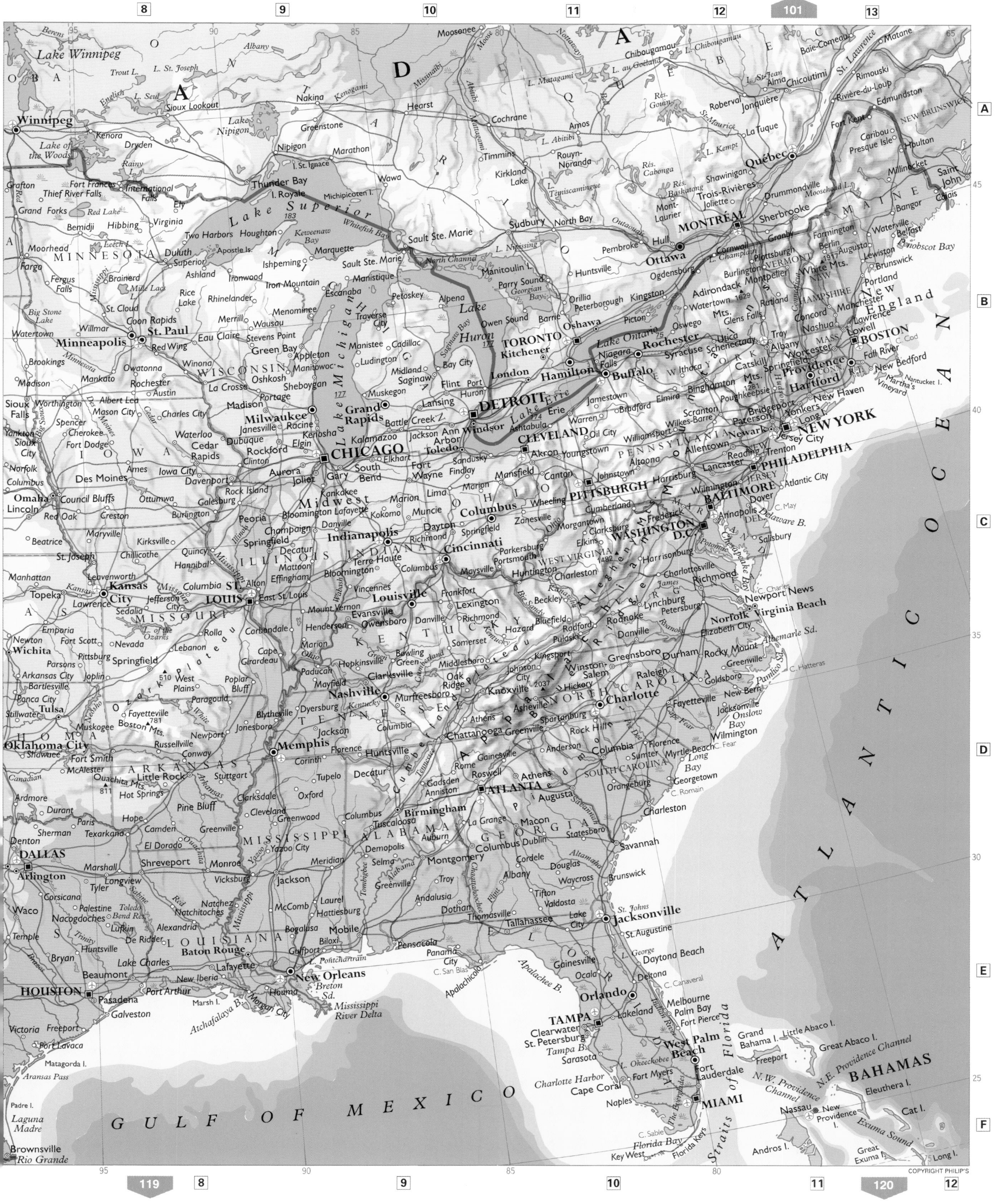

8 9 10 11 12 101 13

A B C D E F

Lake Winnipeg
Winnipeg
Lake of the Woods
Kenora
Dryden
Sioux Lookout
Nakina
Lake Nipigon
Greenstone
Nipigon
Thunder Bay
Marathon
Hearst
Moosonee
Cochrane
Timmins
Kirkland Lake
Amos
Rouyn-Noranda
Chibougamau
Chicoutimi
Jonquière
Roberval
La Tuque
Québec
Baie-Comeau
Matane
Rimouski
Rivière-du-Loup
Edmundston
Fort Kent
Caribou
Presque Isle
Houlton
Millinocket
Saint John
Calais
Fort Frances
International Falls
Thief River Falls
Grand Forks
Red Lake
Bemidji
Hibbing
Virginia
Ely
Lake Superior
Two Harbors
Houghton
Keweenaw Bay
Marquette
Sault Ste. Marie
Wawa
Sudbury
North Bay
Pembroke
Ottawa
Hull
MONTREAL
Sherbrooke
Trois-Rivières
Joliette
Drummondville
Shawinigan
Mont-Laurier
Bangor
Waterville
Belfast
Penobscot Bay
Augusta
Lewiston
Brunswick
Portland
Berlin
Farmington
White Mts.
Moorhead
Fargo
Duluth
Superior
Ashland
Ironwood
Ishpeming
Iron Mountain
Escanaba
Manistique
Petoskey
Alpena
Manitoulin I.
Parry Sound
Georgian Bay
Orillia
Peterborough
Kingston
Ogdensburg
Cornwall
Burlington
Montpelier
Plattsburgh
Adirondack Mts.
Watertown
Glens Falls
Rutland
Concord
Manchester
New England
Lawrence
Lowell
BOSTON
C. Cod
Fergus Falls
Brainerd
Mille Lacs L.
St. Cloud
Rice Lake
Rhinelander
Menominee
Traverse City
Lake Huron
Lake Michigan
Owen Sound
Barrie
Oshawa
TORONTO
Kitchener
Lake Ontario
Niagara Falls
Rochester
Oswego
Syracuse
Utica
Schenectady
Albany
Troy
Worcester
Providence
Fall River
New Bedford
Nantucket I.
Martha's Vineyard
Big Stone Lake
Willmar
Coon Rapids
Minneapolis
St. Paul
Red Wing
Eau Claire
Merrill
Wausau
Stevens Point
Green Bay
Appleton
Manitowoc
Oshkosh
Sheboygan
Manistee
Cadillac
Ludington
Midland
Saginaw
Bay City
Flint
Port Huron
London
Hamilton
Buffalo
Ithaca
Binghamton
Catskill Mts.
Springfield
Hartford
New Haven
Poughkeepsie
Brookings
Mankato
Owatonna
Rochester
Austin
Winona
La Crosse
Madison
Portage
Milwaukee
Racine
Kenosha
Muskegon
Grand Rapids
Lansing
DETROIT
Windsor
Lake Erie
Erie
Jamestown
Bradford
Elmira
Scranton
Wilkes-Barre
Bridgeport
Yonkers
Long I.
NEW YORK
Jersey City
Newark
Paterson
Sioux Falls
Worthington
Albert Lea
Mason City
Charles City
Janesville
Spencer
Cherokee
Fort Dodge
Waterloo
Cedar Rapids
Dubuque
Rockford
Elgin
CHICAGO
Kalamazoo
Battle Creek
Jackson
Ann Arbor
Toledo
Ashtabula
CLEVELAND
Warren
Oil City
Williamsport
Allentown
Reading
Trenton
PHILADELPHIA
Yankton
Sioux City
Clinton
Iowa City
Ames
Des Moines
Davenport
Rock Island
Aurora
Joliet
Gary
South Bend
Elkhart
Fort Wayne
Sandusky
Findlay
Mansfield
Akron
Youngstown
Canton
Johnstown
Altoona
Harrisburg
Lancaster
Wilmington
Atlantic City
Norfolk
Columbus
Omaha
Council Bluffs
Lincoln
Red Oak
Creston
Ottumwa
Burlington
Galesburg
Peoria
Kankakee
Midwest
Bloomington
Lafayette
Kokomo
Marion
Muncie
Lima
Columbus
Wheeling
PITTSBURGH
Cumberland
Frederick
BALTIMORE
Annapolis
Dover
Delaware B.
C. May
Beatrice
Maryville
Kirksville
Quincy
Springfield
Champaign
Danville
Decatur
Indianapolis
Dayton
Richmond
Springfield
Zanesville
Morgantown
Clarksburg
Elkins
WASHINGTON D.C.
Salisbury
St. Joseph
Chillicothe
Hannibal
Mattoon
Effingham
Terre Haute
Cincinnati
Parkersburg
Portsmouth
Huntington
Charleston
Harrisonburg
Charlottesville
Richmond
Chesapeake Bay
Manhattan
Topeka
Leavenworth
Kansas City
Lawrence
Columbia
Jefferson City
Sedalia
ST. LOUIS
Alton
East St. Louis
Vincennes
Louisville
Frankfort
Lexington
Maysville
Beckley
Lynchburg
Petersburg
Newport News
Virginia Beach
C. Charles
Emporia
Newton
Wichita
Fort Scott
Nevada
Rolla
Carbondale
Mount Vernon
Evansville
Owensboro
Henderson
Danville
Richmond
Hazard
Bluefield
Roanoke
Danville
Norfolk
Elizabeth City
Albemarle Sd.
Pittsburg
Springfield
Lebanon
Cape Girardeau
Paducah
Marion
Hopkinsville
Bowling Green
Somerset
Middlesboro
Kingsport
Radford
Pulaski
Greensboro
Durham
Rocky Mount
Greenville
Pamlico Sd.
C. Hatteras
Parsons
Joplin
Arkansas City
Bartlesville
Ponca City
Tulsa
Stillwater
Ozark Plateau
West Plains
Poplar Bluff
Paragould
Mayfield
Clarksville
Nashville
Oak Ridge
Johnson City
Knoxville
Winston-Salem
Hickory
Raleigh
Goldsboro
New Bern
Muskogee
Fayetteville
Boston Mts.
Blytheville
Dyersburg
Jonesboro
Murfreesboro
Asheville
Charlotte
NORTH CAROLINA
Fayetteville
Jacksonville
Onslow Bay
Wilmington
C. Fear
Oklahoma City
Shawnee
Fort Smith
McAlester
Russellville
Newport
Conway
Memphis
Jackson
Columbia
Athens
Chattanooga
Greenville
Spartanburg
Rock Hill
Florence
Myrtle Beach
Long Bay
Sumter
Columbia
Anderson
Ouachita Mts.
Little Rock
Hot Springs
Stuttgart
Clarksdale
Oxford
Corinth
Tupelo
Florence
Huntsville
Decatur
Gadsden
Anniston
Rome
Gainesville
Roswell
ATLANTA
Athens
Augusta
Orangeburg
Georgetown
C. Romain
Charleston
Ardmore
Durant
Paris
Hope
Pine Bluff
Cleveland
Greenwood
Columbus
Tuscaloosa
Birmingham
La Grange
Macon
Statesboro
Sherman
Texarkana
Camden
El Dorado
Greenville
Yazoo City
Demopolis
Auburn
Columbus
Dublin
Savannah
Denton
DALLAS
Arlington
Marshall
Shreveport
Monroe
Vicksburg
Meridian
Selma
Montgomery
Cordele
Douglas
Waycross
Brunswick
Longview
Tyler
Jackson
Troy
Albany
Tifton
Valdosta
Corsicana
Waco
Palestine
Nacogdoches
Natchez
Natchitoches
McComb
Laurel
Hattiesburg
Greenville
Andalusia
Dothan
Thomasville
Tallahassee
Lake City
Jacksonville
St. Johns
St. Augustine
Temple
Lufkin
Alexandria
De Ridder
Bogalusa
Mobile
Biloxi
Gulfport
Pensacola
Panama City
Bryan
Huntsville
Baton Rouge
Lafayette
Lake Charles
Beaumont
L. Pontchartrain
New Orleans
Houma
Breton Sd.
Mississippi River Delta
C. San Blas
Apalachicola
Apalachee B.
Gainesville
Ocala
Daytona Beach
Deltona
C. Canaveral
Orlando
Melbourne
Palm Bay
Fort Pierce
HOUSTON
Pasadena
Port Arthur
New Iberia
Marsh I.
Atchafalaya B.
Morgan City
Galveston
Victoria
Freeport
Port Lavaca
Matagorda I.
Aransas Pass
TAMPA
Clearwater
St. Petersburg
Tampa B.
Sarasota
Lakeland
L. Okeechobee
West Palm Beach
Fort Myers
Charlotte Harbor
Cape Coral
Naples
Fort Lauderdale
MIAMI
Grand Bahama I.
Little Abaco I.
Great Abaco I.
Freeport
N.E. Providence Channel
N.W. Providence Channel
BAHAMAS
Eleuthera I.
Nassau
New Providence I.
Exuma Sound
Cat I.
Andros I.
Great Exuma I.
Long I.
Padre I.
Laguna Madre
Brownsville
Rio Grande
GULF OF MEXICO
C. Sable
Florida Bay
Key West
Florida Keys
Straits of Florida
ATLANTIC OCEAN
CANADA
ONTARIO
QUEBEC
NEW BRUNSWICK
MAINE
VERMONT
NEW HAMPSHIRE
MASS.
CONN.
NEW YORK
NEW JERSEY
PENNSYLVANIA
MARYLAND
DEL.
OHIO
WEST VIRGINIA
VIRGINIA
KENTUCKY
TENNESSEE
INDIANA
ILLINOIS
MICHIGAN
WISCONSIN
MINNESOTA
IOWA
MISSOURI
KANSAS
OKLAHOMA
ARKANSAS
MISSISSIPPI
ALABAMA
GEORGIA
SOUTH CAROLINA
FLORIDA
LOUISIANA
TEXAS
Appalachian Mts.
Cumberland Plateau
Blue Ridge
Allegheny Mts.
Mississippi
Missouri
Ohio

95 90 85 80

50 0 50 100 150 200 km
1:5 300 000
50 0 50 100 150 miles
A B C D E F
112
102
BRITISH COLUMBIA
ALBERTA
SASKATCHEWAN
CANADA
WASHINGTON
OREGON
IDAHO
MONTANA
WYOMING
UTAH
NEVADA
CALIFORNIA
SEATTLE
PORTLAND
VANCOUVER
Spokane
Boise
Salt Lake City
Sacramento
Reno
Helena
Great Falls
Billings
Casper
Laramie
Ogden
Provo
Pocatello
Idaho Falls
Missoula
Butte
Bozeman
Eugene
Salem
Medford
Redding
Eureka
Tacoma
Olympia
Yakima
Kennewick
Walla Walla
Lewiston
Elko
Winnemucca
Carson City
Great Salt Lake
Great Salt Lake Desert
Columbia Basin
Columbia Plateau
Snake River Plain
Rocky Mountains
Bitterroot Range
Salmon River Mountains
Sawtooth Range
Blue Mountains
Wallowa Mts.
Cascade Range
Coast Ranges
Klamath Mts.
Sierra Nevada
Great Basin
Bighorn Mountains
Absaroka Range
Wind River Range
Uinta Mountains
Medicine Bow Mts.
Park Ra.
Roan Plateau
Clearwater Mountains
Lemhi Range
Little Belt Mts.
Big Belt Mts.
Lewis Range
Swan Range
Cabinet Mountains
Olympic Mts.
Steens Mountain
Harney Basin
Warner Mts.
Independence Mts.
Ruby Mts.
Toiyabe Ra.
Shoshone Mountains
Stillwater Ra.
Santa Rosa Range
Strait of Juan de Fuca
Puget Sound

PACIFIC
OCEAN
Golfo de California
BAJA CALIFORNIA
ARIZONA
NEW MEXICO
COLORADO
TEXAS
SONORA
CHIHUAHUA
MEXICO
Colorado Plateau
Mojave Desert
Sonoran Desert
Death Valley
LOS ANGELES
SAN DIEGO
SAN FRANCISCO
PHOENIX
Tucson
Las Vegas
Albuquerque
Santa Fe
El Paso
Ciudad Juárez
Chihuahua
Hermosillo
Tijuana
Mexicali
Ensenada
San Jose
Fresno
Bakersfield
Isla Guadalupe (Mexico)
National Parks
West from Greenwich
Projection: Albers' Equal Area with two standard parallels
COPYRIGHT PHILIP'S
113
118

1:2 200 000

WESTERN WASHINGTON REGION
on same scale
PACIFIC OCEAN
SACRAMENTO
SAN FRANCISCO
SEATTLE
PORTLAND
VANCOUVER
WASHINGTON
OREGON
BRITISH COLUMBIA
CANADA

NEVADA
ARIZONA
MEXICO
BAJA CALIFORNIA
PACIFIC OCEAN
Mojave Desert
Sonoran Desert
Death Valley
Amargosa Range
Chocolate Mts.
San Bernardino Mts.
San Gabriel Mts.
San Rafael Mts.
Temblor Range
Channel Islands
Santa Barbara Channel
San Pedro Channel
Gulf of Santa Catalina
Salton Sea
Imperial Valley
Lake Mead
Lake Mohave
LAS VEGAS
Henderson
North Las Vegas
Kingman
Bullhead City
Needles
Lake Havasu City
Barstow
Victorville
Hesperia
Apple Valley
Lancaster
Palmdale
Bakersfield
Ridgecrest
Santa Clarita
LOS ANGELES
Long Beach
Anaheim
Santa Ana
Riverside
San Bernardino
Palm Springs
Indio
Oxnard
Ventura
Santa Barbara
Santa Maria
San Luis Obispo
Lompoc
Oceanside
Escondido
SAN DIEGO
Chula Vista
Tijuana
Mexicali
El Centro
Yuma
Santa Cruz I.
Santa Rosa I.
San Miguel I.
Santa Catalina I.
San Clemente I.
San Nicolas I.
Santa Barbara I.
National Parks
118
Projection: Bonne
West from Greenwich
COPYRIGHT PHILIP'S

50 0 50 100 150 200 km

50 0 50 100 150 miles

1:5 300 000

114

103

108

109

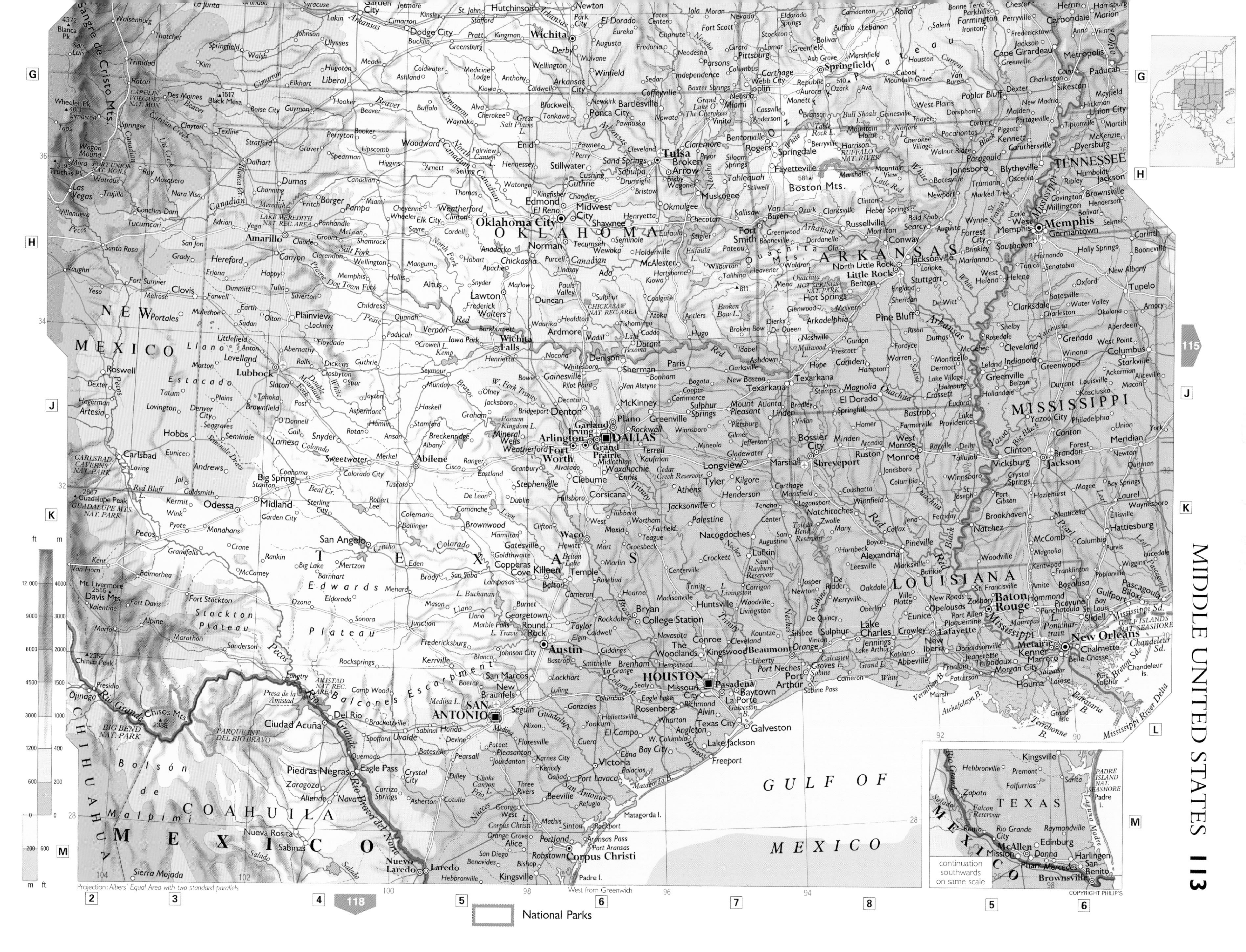
OKLAHOMA
TEXAS
NEW MEXICO
ARKANSAS
LOUISIANA
MISSISSIPPI
TENNESSEE
MEXICO
COAHUILA
CHIHUAHUA
GULF OF MEXICO
Oklahoma City
Tulsa
Dallas
Fort Worth
Houston
San Antonio
Austin
Little Rock
Memphis
New Orleans
Jackson
Shreveport
Baton Rouge
Corpus Christi
Amarillo
Lubbock
Wichita
Springfield
Edwards Plateau
Llano Estacado
Stockton Plateau
Bolsón de Mapimí
Sangre de Cristo Mts.
Boston Mts.
Ouachita Mts.
Balcones Escarpment
Rio Grande
Red
Arkansas
Canadian
Pecos
Brazos
Colorado
Mississippi
National Parks
continuation southwards on same scale
Projection: Albers' Equal Area with two standard parallels
West from Greenwich
COPYRIGHT PHILIP'S
m
ft
4000
3000
2000
1500
1000
400
200
0
200
12 000
9000
6000
4500
3000
1200
600
0
600
115
118

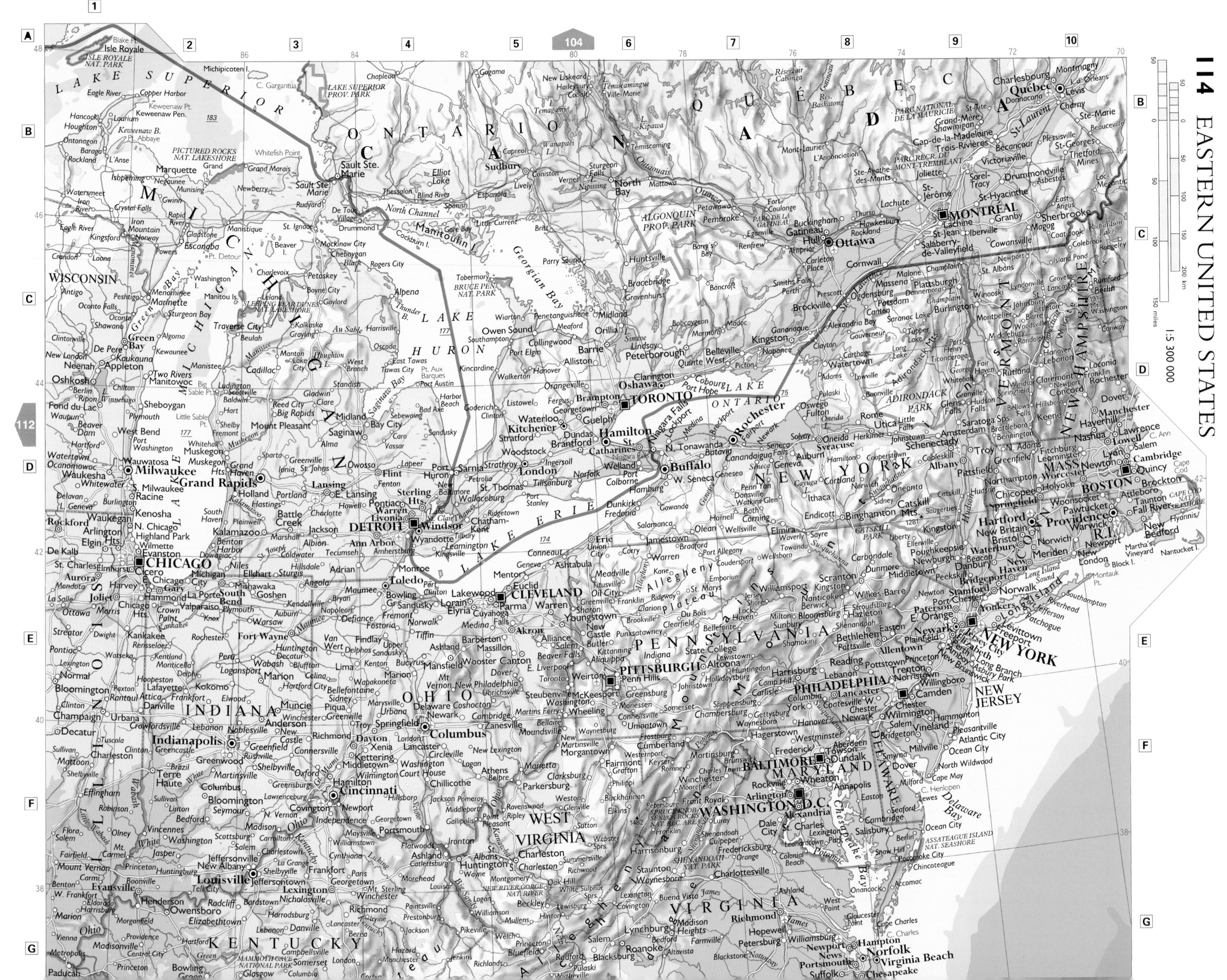

1:5 300 000
50 0 50 100 150 200 km
50 0 50 100 150 miles
LAKE SUPERIOR
LAKE HURON
Georgian Bay
LAKE ERIE
LAKE ONTARIO
LAKE MICHIGAN
ONTARIO
QUÉBEC
CANADA
MICHIGAN
WISCONSIN
ILLINOIS
INDIANA
OHIO
KENTUCKY
WEST VIRGINIA
VIRGINIA
PENNSYLVANIA
NEW YORK
NEW JERSEY
DELAWARE
MARYLAND
VERMONT
NEW HAMPSHIRE
MASS.
CONN.
R.I.
CHICAGO
DETROIT
CLEVELAND
PITTSBURGH
TORONTO
MONTRÉAL
Ottawa
BOSTON
NEW YORK
PHILADELPHIA
BALTIMORE
WASHINGTON D.C.
Chesapeake Bay
Delaware Bay

104
112

ATLANTIC OCEAN
GULF OF MEXICO
BAHAMAS
TENNESSEE
NORTH CAROLINA
SOUTH CAROLINA
GEORGIA
ALABAMA
FLORIDA
MAINE
CANADA
continuation eastwards on same scale
National Parks
Projection: Albers' Equal Area with two standard parallels
West from Greenwich
COPYRIGHT PHILIP'S

1:2 200 000

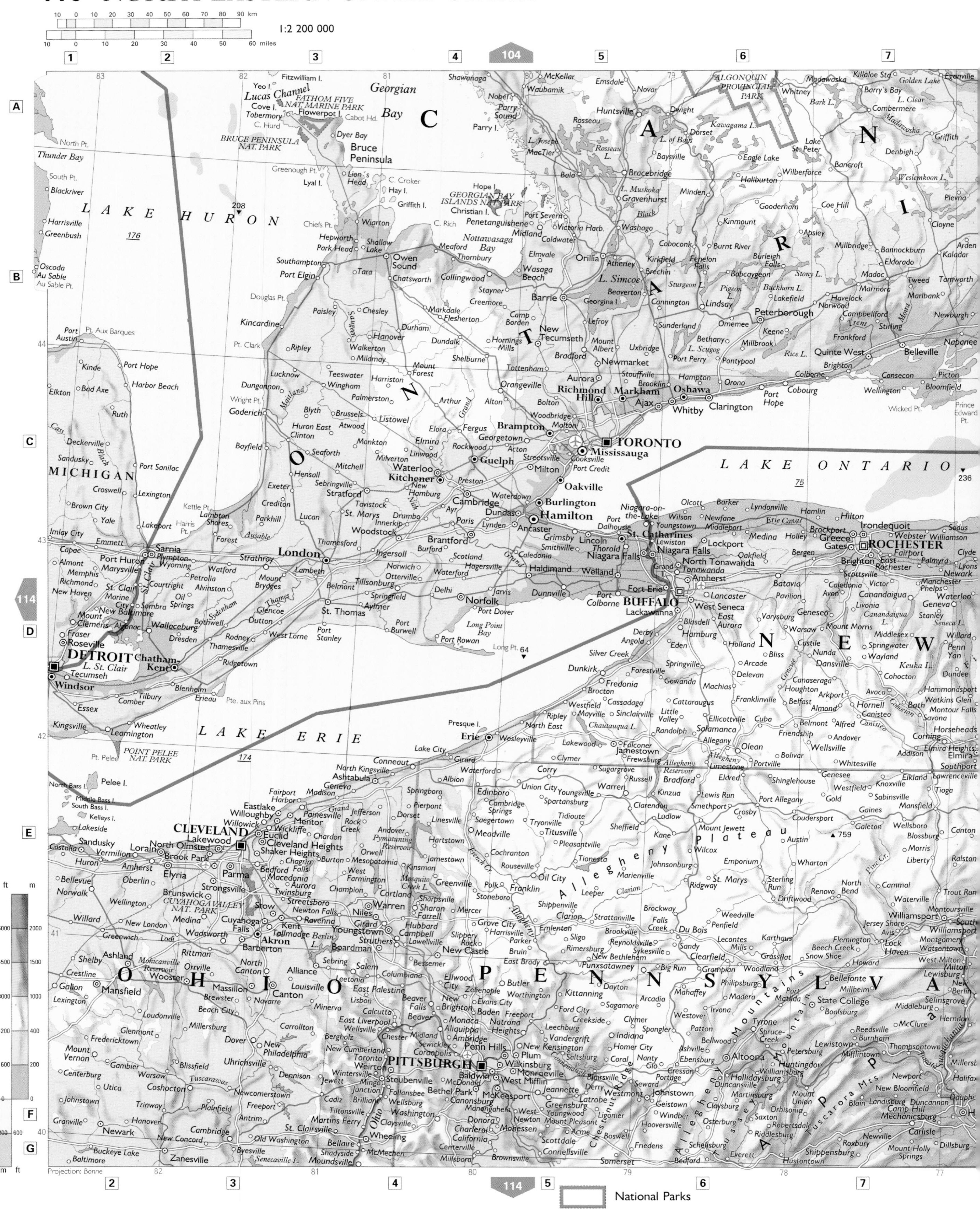

10 0 10 20 30 40 50 60 70 80 90 km
10 0 10 20 30 40 50 60 miles
1 2 3 4 5 6 7
104
A B C D E F G
114
Georgian Bay
Lucas Channel
FATHOM FIVE NAT. MARINE PARK
BRUCE PENINSULA NAT. PARK
Bruce Peninsula
GEORGIAN BAY ISLANDS NAT. PARK
ALGONQUIN PROVINCIAL PARK
LAKE HURON
ONTARIO
CANADA
Thunder Bay
Nottawasaga Bay
L. Simcoe
Barrie
Orillia
Owen Sound
Peterborough
Belleville
Newmarket
Richmond Hill
Markham
Oshawa
Whitby
Clarington
TORONTO
Mississauga
Brampton
Oakville
Burlington
Hamilton
Guelph
Waterloo
Kitchener
Cambridge
Brantford
Stratford
London
Sarnia
Port Huron
DETROIT
Windsor
Chatham-Kent
L. St. Clair
MICHIGAN
LAKE ONTARIO
LAKE ERIE
St. Catharines
Niagara Falls
BUFFALO
ROCHESTER
Erie
Jamestown
Olean
POINT PELEE NAT. PARK
Pelee I.
CLEVELAND
Lakewood
Parma
Akron
Canton
Youngstown
Warren
Mansfield
OHIO
CUYAHOGA VALLEY NAT. PARK
PENNSYLVANIA
PITTSBURGH
Allegheny Plateau
Allegheny Mountains
Tussey Mts.
Tuscarora Mts.
Appalachian
State College
Altoona
Williamsport
NEW YORK
Projection: Bonne
ft m
6000 2000
4500 1500
3000 1000
1200 400
600 200
0 0
200 600
m ft
National Parks

104

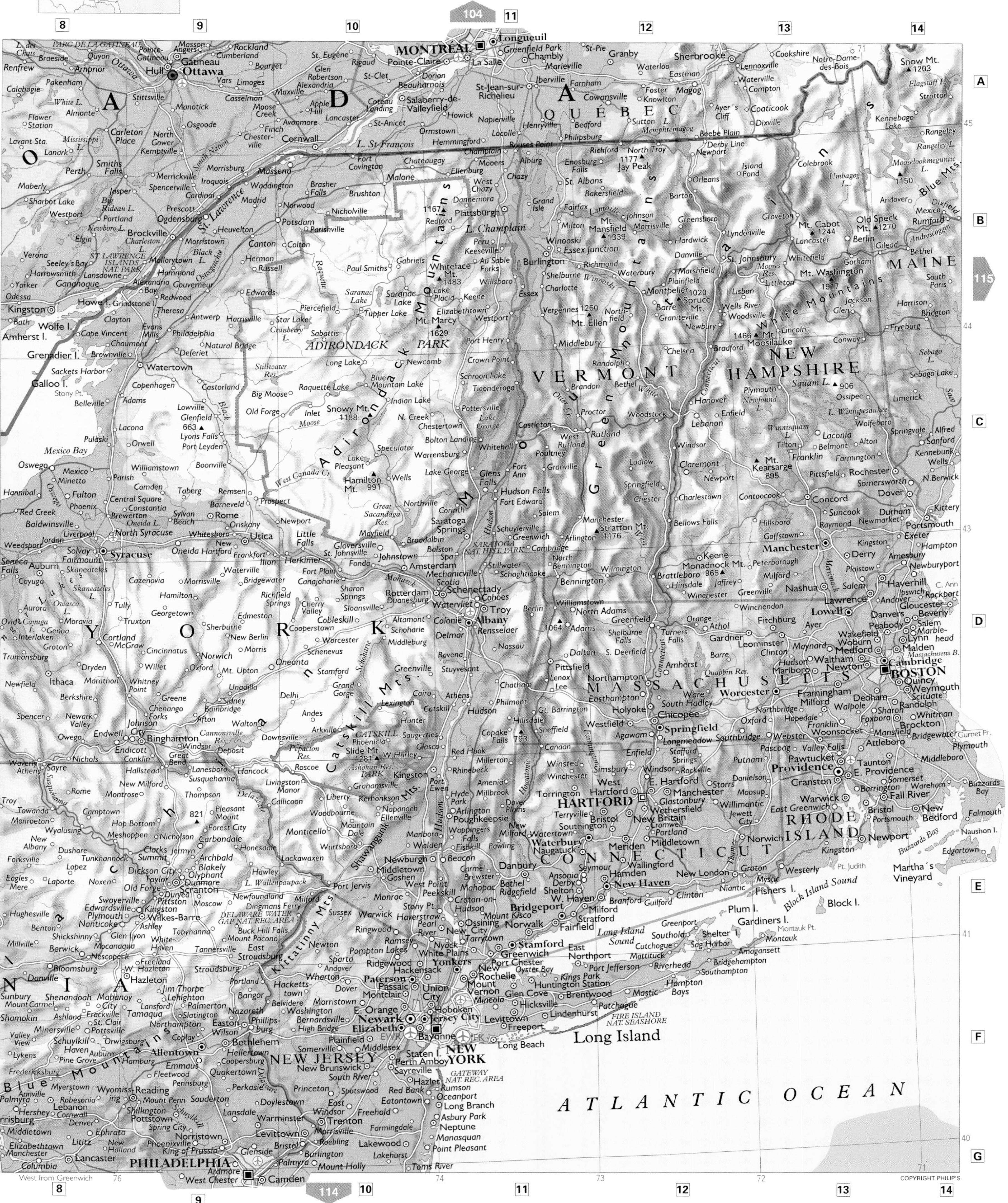
8
9
10
11
12
13
14
A
B
C
D
E
F
G
MONTREAL
Longueuil
Ottawa
Hull
Gatineau
Sherbrooke
Q U É B E C
O
A
D
A
Kingston
Wolfe I.
Amherst I.
Galloo I.
Watertown
Ogdensburg
St. Lawrence
L. St-François
L. Champlain
Plattsburgh
Burlington
Montpelier
Barre
Rutland
Mt. Marcy
1629
ADIRONDACK PARK
Adirondack Mountains
VERMONT
Green Mountains
NEW HAMPSHIRE
White Mountains
Mt. Washington
1917
MAINE
Portland
Concord
Manchester
Nashua
Portsmouth
Syracuse
Utica
Rome
Albany
Schenectady
Troy
Binghamton
Catskill Mts.
Y
O
R
K
MASSACHUSETTS
BOSTON
Worcester
Springfield
Cambridge
Lowell
Pittsfield
Providence
RHODE ISLAND
HARTFORD
New Haven
Bridgeport
Stamford
CONNECTICUT
Waterbury
New London
Block Island Sound
Block I.
Long Island Sound
Long Island
Martha's Vineyard
Nantucket Sound
Yonkers
Newark
Jersey City
NEW YORK
Staten I.
NEW JERSEY
Paterson
Elizabeth
Trenton
PHILADELPHIA
Camden
Allentown
Bethlehem
Reading
Scranton
Wilkes-Barre
Blue Mountains
ATLANTIC OCEAN
45
44
43
42
41
40
76
75
74
73
72
71
West from Greenwich

115

114

1:7 100 000

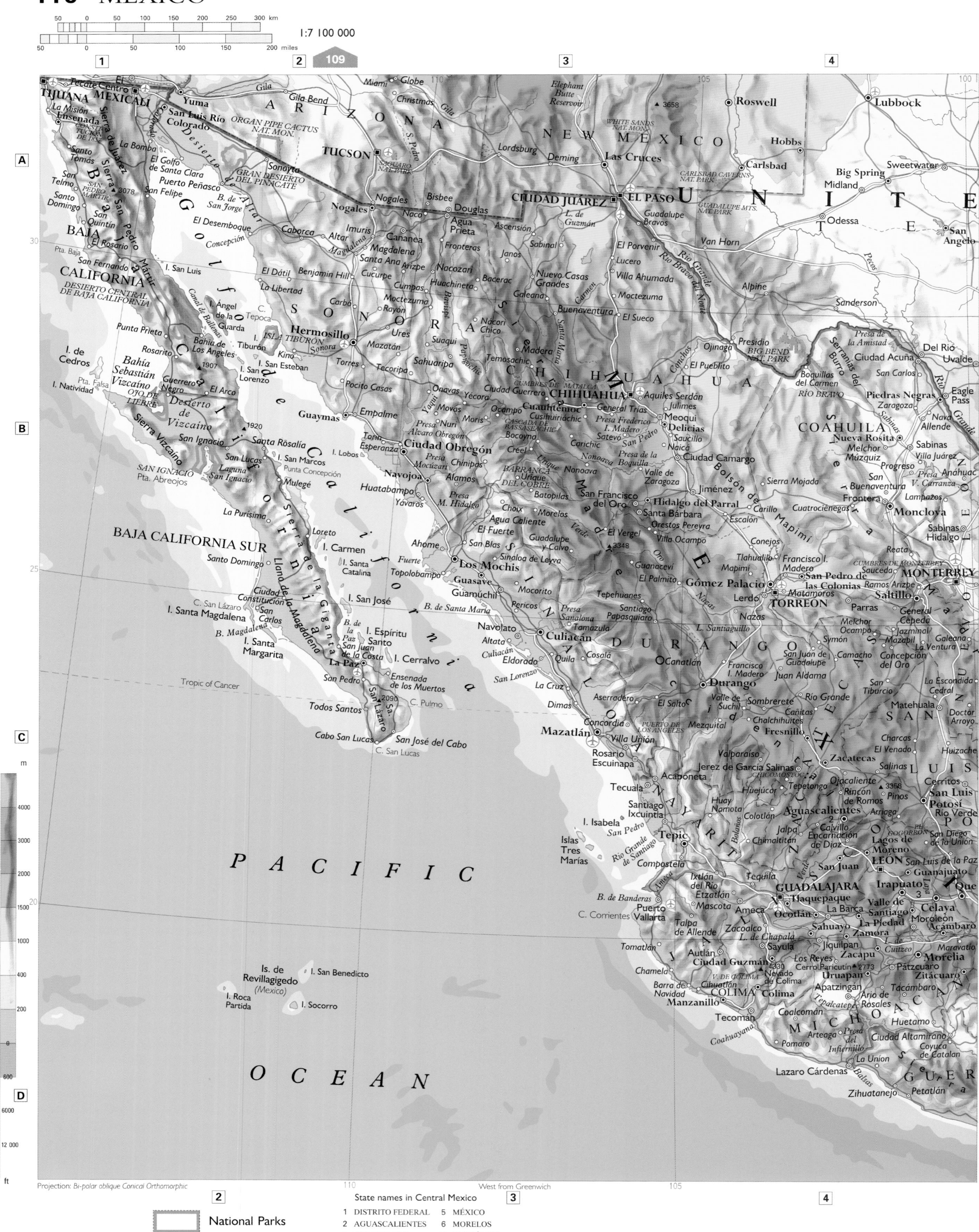

Projection: Bi-polar oblique Conical Orthomorphic

West from Greenwich

National Parks

State names in Central Mexico

1 DISTRITO FEDERAL
2 AGUASCALIENTES
3 GUANAJUATO
4 HIDALGO
5 MÉXICO
6 MORELOS
7 QUERÉTARO
8 TLAXCALA

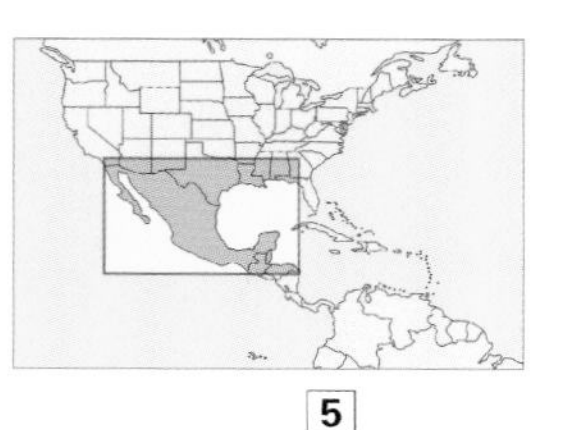

113

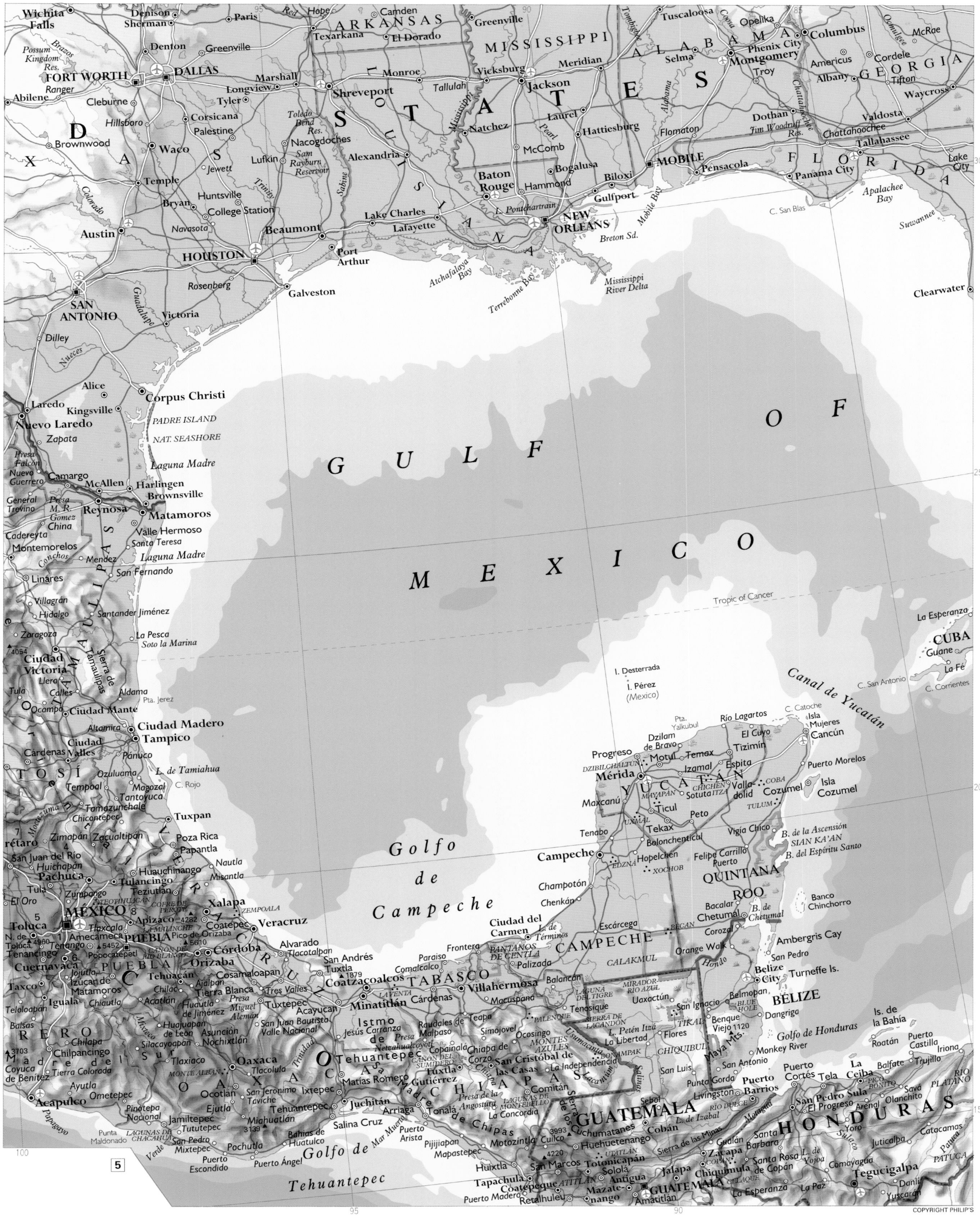

5 6 7 8

A B C D E

GULF OF MEXICO

Golfo de Campeche

UNITED STATES

TEXAS

LOUISIANA

MISSISSIPPI

ALABAMA

GEORGIA

FLORIDA

CUBA

Canal de Yucatán

YUCATÁN

CAMPECHE

QUINTANA ROO

TABASCO

CHIAPAS

OAXACA

GUATEMALA

BELIZE

HONDURAS

Golfo de Honduras

Golfo de Tehuantepec

Tropic of Cancer

120

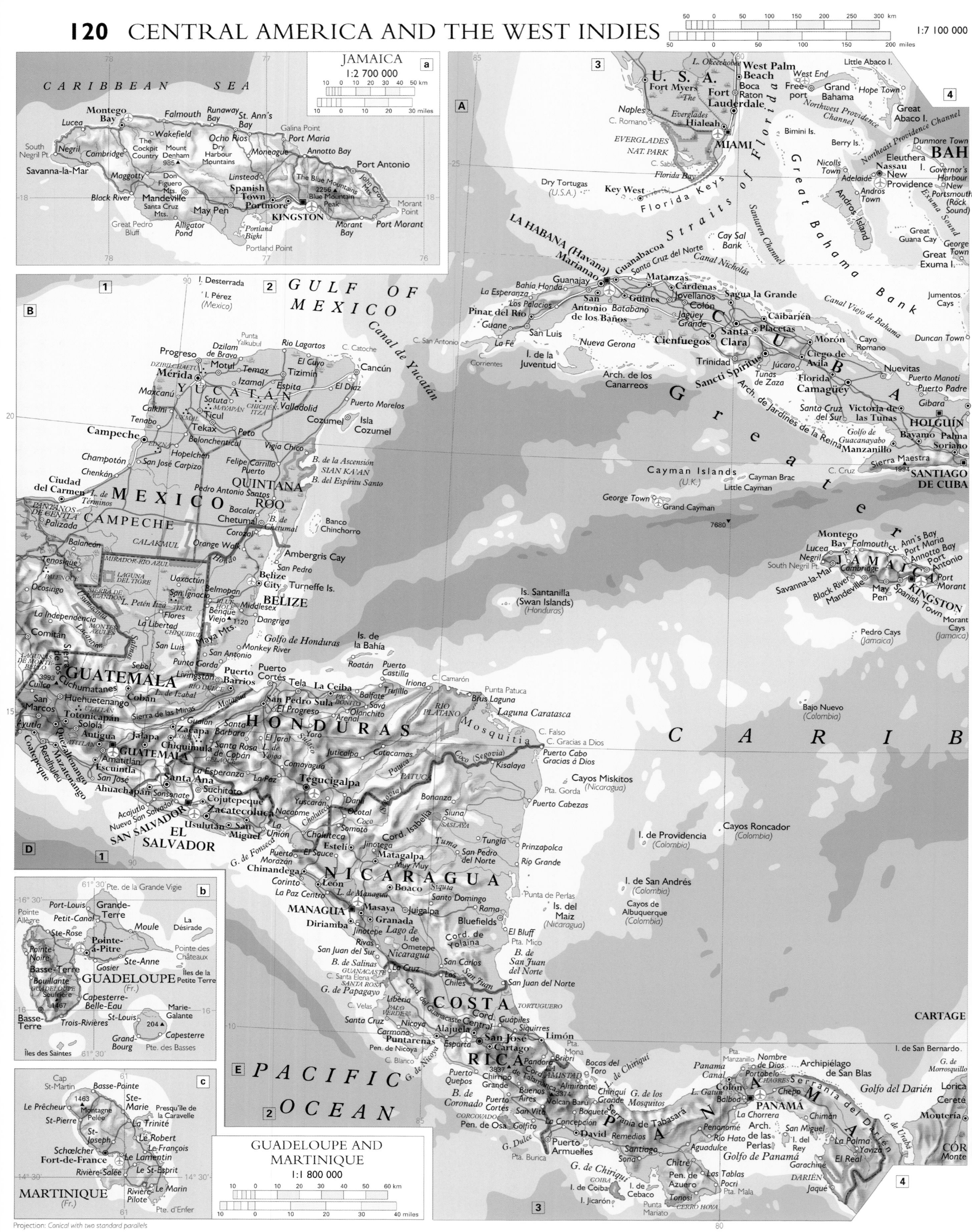
1:7 100 000
JAMAICA
1:2 700 000
CARIBBEAN SEA
Montego Bay
Falmouth
Runaway Bay
St. Ann's Bay
Lucea
Negril
Savanna-la-Mar
Black River
Mandeville
May Pen
Spanish Town
Portmore
KINGSTON
Port Antonio
Port Morant
Blue Mountain Peak
GULF OF MEXICO
U. S. A.
MIAMI
West Palm Beach
Fort Lauderdale
Key West
Straits of Florida
Great Bahama Bank
Nassau
New Providence
Andros Island
LA HABANA (Havana)
Matanzas
Cienfuegos
Santa Clara
CUBA
Camagüey
HOLGUÍN
SANTIAGO DE CUBA
Cayman Islands (U.K.)
George Town
Grand Cayman
Canal de Yucatán
YUCATÁN
Mérida
Cancún
Cozumel
Campeche
MEXICO
QUINTANA ROO
CAMPECHE
BELIZE
Belize City
Belmopan
GUATEMALA
Golfo de Honduras
HONDURAS
Tegucigalpa
San Pedro Sula
La Ceiba
EL SALVADOR
SAN SALVADOR
NICARAGUA
MANAGUA
Lago de Nicaragua
COSTA RICA
San José
Limón
PANAMÁ
Golfo de Panamá
Serranía del Darién
Golfo del Darién
PACIFIC OCEAN
C A R I B
Cayos Miskitos (Nicaragua)
I. de Providencia (Colombia)
I. de San Andrés (Colombia)
Is. Santanilla (Swan Islands) (Honduras)
CARTAGE
GUADELOUPE (Fr.)
Pointe-à-Pitre
Basse-Terre
Grande-Terre
Marie-Galante
MARTINIQUE (Fr.)
Fort-de-France
GUADELOUPE AND MARTINIQUE
1:1 800 000
Projection: Conical with two standard parallels

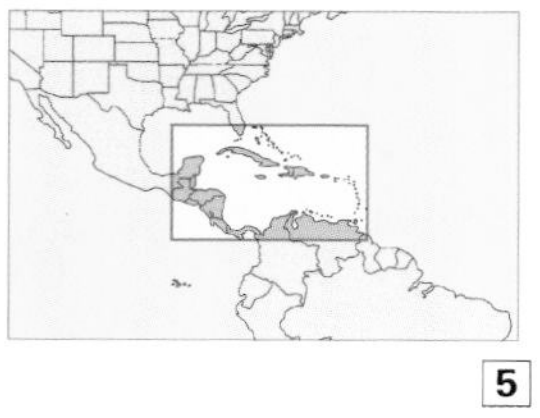
5

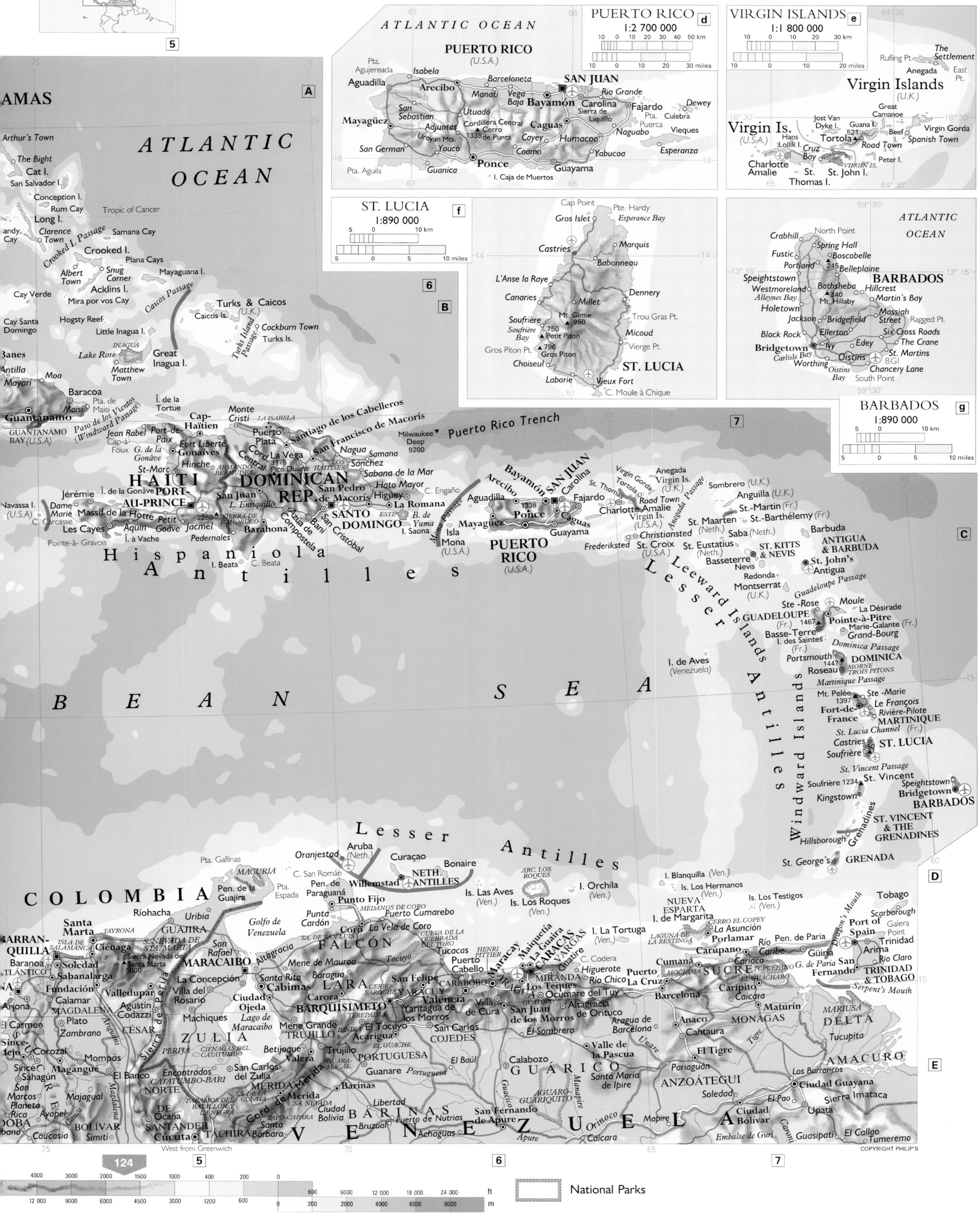
PUERTO RICO
d
1:2 700 000
ATLANTIC OCEAN
PUERTO RICO
(U.S.A.)
Pta. Agujereada
Isabela
Aguadilla
Arecibo
Barceloneta
SAN JUAN
Manatí
Vega Baja
Bayamón
Carolina
Rio Grande
Fajardo
Dewey
Culebra
Vieques
Esperanza
San Sebastian
Utuado
Mayagüez
Adjuntas
Cordillera Central
Cerro de Punta
Caguas
Cayey
Humacao
Naguabo
Uroyan Mts.
Yauco
Coamo
Yabucoa
San German
Ponce
Guanica
Guayama
Pta. Aguila
I. Caja de Muertos
VIRGIN ISLANDS
e
1:1 800 000
Rufling Pt.
The Settlement
Anegada
East Pt.
Virgin Islands
(U.K.)
Great Camanoe
Jost Van Dyke I.
Guana I.
Virgin Is.
(U.S.A.)
Hans Lollik I.
Tortola
Beef I.
Virgin Gorda
Spanish Town
Road Town
Cruz Bay
Peter I.
Charlotte Amalie
St. Thomas I.
St. John I.
ST. LUCIA
f
1:890 000
Cap Point
Pte. Hardy
Esperance Bay
Gros Islet
Castries
Marquis
Babonneau
L'Anse la Raye
Dennery
Canaries
Millet
Mt. Gimie
Trou Gras Pt.
Soufrière
Soufrière Bay
Petit Piton
Micoud
Gros Piton Pt.
Gros Piton
Vierge Pt.
Choiseul
ST. LUCIA
Laborie
Vieux Fort
C. Moule à Chique
ATLANTIC OCEAN
Crabhill
North Point
Spring Hall
Fustic
Boscobelle
Portland
Belleplaine
Speightstown
BARBADOS
Westmoreland
Bathsheba
Hillcrest
Alleynes Bay
Mt. Hillaby
Martin's Bay
Holetown
Massiah Street
Jackson
Bridgefield
Ragged Pt.
Black Rock
Ellerton
Six Cross Roads
Edey
The Crane
Bridgetown
Ivy
Carlisle Bay
Oistins
St. Martins
Worthing
Oistins Bay
Chancery Lane
South Point
BARBADOS
g
1:890 000
AMAS
ATLANTIC OCEAN
Arthur's Town
The Bight
Cat I.
San Salvador I.
Conception I.
Rum Cay
Tropic of Cancer
Long I.
Clarence Town
Samana Cay
Crooked I. Passage
Crooked I.
Plana Cays
Albert Town
Snug Corner
Mayaguana I.
Acklins I.
Cay Verde
Mira por vos Cay
Caicos Passage
Turks & Caicos
(U.K.)
Caicos Is.
Cockburn Town
Turks Is.
Cay Santa Domingo
Hogsty Reef
Little Inagua I.
Turks Island Passage
Lake Rose
Great Inagua I.
Matthew Town
Moa
Baracoa
Pta. de Maisi
Guantánamo
GUANTANAMO BAY (U.S.A.)
Paso de los Vientos (Windward Passage)
Î. de la Tortue
Monte Cristi
Cap-Haïtien
Port-de-Paix
Jean Rabel
Fort Liberté
Puerto Plata
Santiago de los Caballeros
San Francisco de Macorís
Milwaukee Deep 9200
Puerto Rico Trench
Gonaïves
La Vega
Nagua
Samana
Hinche
Pico Duarte
Sánchez
Sabana de la Mar
St-Marc
HAITI
DOMINICAN REP.
Hato Mayor
C. Engaño
Jérémie
Î. de la Gonâve
PORT-AU-PRINCE
San Juan
San Pedro de Macorís
Higüey
La Romana
Navassa I. (U.S.A)
Dame Marie
Massif de la Hotte
L. Enriquillo
SANTO DOMINGO
B. de Yuma
Les Cayes
Aquin
Petit Goâve
Jacmel
Barahona
Azua de Compostela
Baní
San Cristóbal
I. Saona
Mona Passage
Isla Mona (U.S.A.)
Î. à Vache
Pedernales
Pointe-à-Gravois
Hispaniola
I. Beata
C. Beata
Antilles
Arecibo
Bayamón
SAN JUAN
Carolina
Aguadilla
Fajardo
Mayagüez
Ponce
Caguas
Guayama
PUERTO RICO
(U.S.A.)
Virgin Gorda
Tortola
St. Thomas
Anegada
Virgin Is. (U.K.)
Road Town
Charlotte Amalie
Virgin Is. (U.S.A.)
Anegada Passage
Sombrero (U.K.)
Anguilla (U.K.)
St.-Martin (Fr.)
St. Maarten (Neth.)
St.-Barthélemy (Fr.)
Saba (Neth.)
Barbuda
Christiansted
Frederiksted
St. Croix (U.S.A.)
St. Eustatius (Neth.)
ST. KITTS & NEVIS
ANTIGUA & BARBUDA
Basseterre
Nevis
St. John's
Antigua
Redonda
Montserrat (U.K.)
Leeward Islands
Lesser Antilles
Guadeloupe Passage
Ste-Rose
Moule
La Désirade
GUADELOUPE (Fr.)
Pointe-à-Pitre
Marie-Galante (Fr.)
Basse-Terre
Grand-Bourg
I. des Saintes (Fr.)
Dominica Passage
Portsmouth
DOMINICA
Roseau
MORNE TROIS PITONS
Martinique Passage
I. de Aves (Venezuela)
Mt. Pelée
Ste-Marie
Le François
Fort-de-France
Rivière-Pilote
MARTINIQUE (Fr.)
St. Lucia Channel
Castries
ST. LUCIA
Soufrière
St. Vincent Passage
Soufrière
St. Vincent
Speightstown
Bridgetown
BARBADOS
Kingstown
Windward Islands
Grenadines
ST. VINCENT & THE GRENADINES
Hillsborough
St. George's
GRENADA
BEAN SEA
Lesser Antilles
Aruba (Neth.)
Oranjestad
Curaçao
Bonaire
Willemstad
NETH. ANTILLES
Pta. Gallinas
MACURIA
C. San Román
Pen. de Paraguaná
Pta. Espada
Pen. de la Guajira
Punto Fijo
MÉDANOS DE CORO
Puerto Cumarebo
Punta Cardón
Coro
La Vela de Coro
ARC. LOS ROQUES
Is. Las Aves (Ven.)
Is. Los Roques (Ven.)
I. Orchila (Ven.)
I. Blanquilla (Ven.)
Is. Los Hermanos (Ven.)
Is. Los Testigos (Ven.)
NUEVA ESPARTA
I. de Margarita
La Asunción
Porlamar
Tobago
Scarborough
Port of Spain
Galera Point
Trinidad
Dragon's Mouth
COLOMBIA
Ríohacha
Uribia
Golfo de Venezuela
Santa Marta
GUAJIRA
TAYRONA
BARRANQUILLA
Ciénaga
Sierra Nevada de Santa Marta
San Rafael
MARACAIBO
Altagracia
FALCÓN
Tucacas
HENRI PITTIER
Puerto Cabello
Maracay
Maiquetía
La Guaira
CARACAS
VARGAS
C. Codera
I. La Tortuga (Ven.)
LAGUNA DE LA RESTINGA
CERRO EL COPEY
Carúpano
Río Caribe
Pen. de Paria
Güiria
Arima
Rio Claro
San Fernando
TRINIDAD & TOBAGO
Serpent's Mouth
G. de Paria
Baranoa
Soledad
Sabanalarga
Fundación
Valledupar
Villa del Rosario
La Concepción
Santa Rita
Cabimas
Mene de Mauroa
Baragua
LARA
San Felipe
YARACUY
Valencia
CARABOBO
ARAGUA
Higuerote
MIRANDA
Los Teques
Río Chico
Puerto La Cruz
Cumaná
SUCRE
Caripito
Caicara
Barcelona
Maturín
MONAGAS
Calamar
MAGDALENA
Agustín Codazzi
Ciudad Ojeda
Carora
BARQUISIMETO
Yaritagua
Villa de Cura
San Juan de los Morros
Ocumare del Tuy
Altagracia de Orituco
Aragua de Barcelona
Anaco
Cantaura
El Carmen
Plato
CÉSAR
Machiques
Lago de Maracaibo
Mene Grande
TRUJILLO
El Tocuyo
Acarigua
San Carlos
COJEDES
El Sombrero
Zambrano
ZULIA
Sierra de Perijá
PERIJÁ
CIÉNAGAS DEL CATATUMBO
Betijoque
Valera
Trujillo
PORTUGUESA
El Baúl
Calabozo
GUÁRICO
Valle de la Pascua
El Tigre
Pariaguán
ANZOÁTEGUI
Soledad
Ciudad Guayana
Sierra Imataca
MARIUSA
DELTA AMACURO
Tucupita
Los Barrancos
Corozal
Mompós
Magangué
Sincé
Sahagún
El Banco
Encontrados
San Carlos del Zulia
CATATUMBO-BARI
NORTE DE SANTANDER
MERIDA
Cord. de Mérida
Mérida
SIERRA NEVADA
Guanare
Barinas
Ciudad Bolivia
BARINAS
Libertad
Santa María de Ipire
AGUARO-GUARIQUITO
San Fernando de Apure
Ocaña
BOLÍVAR
Cúcuta
TÁCHIRA
Santa Bárbara
Puerto de Nutrias
Bruzual
Achaguas
Apure
VENEZUELA
Orinoco
Mapire
Caicara
Ciudad Bolívar
El Pao
Upata
Embalse de Guri
Guasipati
El Callao
Tumeremo
Caucasia
Simití
Magdalena
Cauca
West from Greenwich
COPYRIGHT PHILIP'S
124
National Parks
ft
m
A
B
C
D
E
5
6
7

1:31 100 000

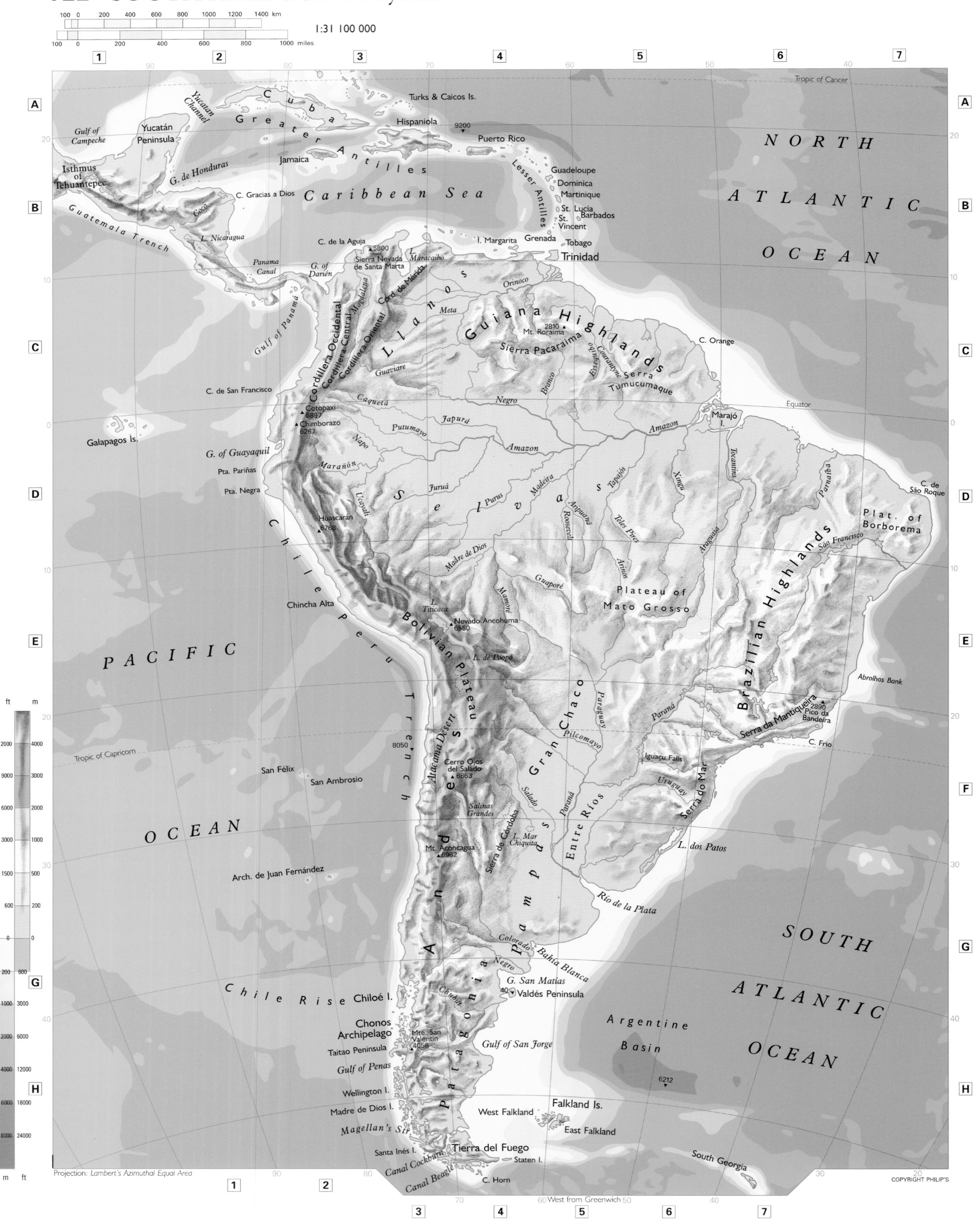

NORTH ATLANTIC OCEAN
Caribbean Sea
Cuba
Greater Antilles
Lesser Antilles
Hispaniola
Turks & Caicos Is.
Puerto Rico
Jamaica
Yucatan Channel
Yucatán Peninsula
Gulf of Campeche
Isthmus of Tehuantepec
G. de Honduras
C. Gracias a Dios
Guatemala Trench
Coco
L. Nicaragua
Panama Canal
G. of Darién
Gulf of Panamá
Guadeloupe
Dominica
Martinique
St. Lucia
St. Vincent
Barbados
Grenada
Tobago
Trinidad
I. Margarita
C. de la Aguja
Sierra Nevada de Santa Marta
L. Maracaibo
Cord. de Mérida
Cordillera Occidental
Cordillera Central
Cordillera Oriental
Magdalena
Llanos
Orinoco
Meta
Guaviare
Guiana Highlands
Mt. Roraima
Sierra Pacaraima
Serra Tumucumaque
Essequibo
Courantyne
Branco
C. Orange
C. de San Francisco
Cotopaxi 5897
Chimborazo 6267
Galapagos Is.
G. of Guayaquil
Pta. Pariñas
Pta. Negra
Caquetá
Negro
Equator
Marajó I.
Amazon
Putumayo
Japurá
Napo
Marañón
Ucayali
Juruá
Purus
Madeira
Tapajós
Xingu
Tocantins
Parnaíba
C. de São Roque
Selvas
Aripuanã
Roosevelt
Teles Pires
Huascarán 6768
Madre de Dios
Guaporé
Mamoré
Arinos
Araguaia
Plat. of Borborema
São Francisco
Brazilian Highlands
Plateau of Mato Grosso
Chile Peru Trench
Chincha Alta
L. Titicaca
Nevado Ancohuma 6550
Bolivian Plateau
L. de Poopó
PACIFIC OCEAN
Tropic of Cancer
Tropic of Capricorn
Abrolhos Bank
Serra da Mantiqueira
Pico da Bandeira 2890
C. Frio
Gran Chaco
Paraguay
Pilcomayo
Paraná
Iguaçu Falls
Uruguay
Serra do Mar
Atacama Desert
San Félix
San Ambrosio
Cerro Ojos del Salado 6863
Salinas Grandes
Salado
Sierra de Córdoba
L. Mar Chiquita
Entre Ríos
L. dos Patos
Mt. Aconcagua 6962
Arch. de Juan Fernández
Andes
Pampas
Río de la Plata
Colorado
Bahía Blanca
Negro
G. San Matías
Valdés Peninsula
Chubut
Patagonia
Chile Rise
Chiloé I.
Chonos Archipelago
Mte. San Valentín 4058
Taitao Peninsula
Gulf of Penas
Gulf of San Jorge
Argentine Basin
6212
SOUTH ATLANTIC OCEAN
Wellington I.
Madre de Dios I.
Magellan's Str.
West Falkland
Falkland Is.
East Falkland
Santa Inés I.
Tierra del Fuego
Staten I.
Canal Cockburn
Canal Beagle
C. Horn
South Georgia
9200
8050
West from Greenwich
Projection: Lambert's Azimuthal Equal Area
COPYRIGHT PHILIP'S

1:31 100 000
100 0 200 400 600 800 1000 1200 1400 km
100 0 200 400 600 800 1000 miles
Tropic of Cancer
Havana
C U B A
BAHAMAS
Turks & Caicos Is. (U.K.)
MEXICO
BELIZE
JAMAICA
Kingston
HAITI
Port-au-Prince
DOMINICAN REP.
San Juan
Virgin Is. (U.K.)
PUERTO RICO (U.S.A.)
ST. KITTS & NEVIS
Basse-Terre
ANTIGUA & BARBUDA
GUADELOUPE (Fr.)
DOMINICA
Fort-de-France
MARTINIQUE (Fr.)
Castries
ST. LUCIA
ST. VINCENT
Kingstown
BARBADOS
Bridgetown
GRENADA
St. George's
NORTH ATLANTIC OCEAN
GUATEMALA
Guatemala
HONDURAS
Tegucigalpa
San Salvador
EL SALVADOR
NICARAGUA
Managua
C a r i b b e a n S e a
Aruba
Curaçao
C. de la Aguja
Barranquilla
Maracaibo
Caracas
Port of Spain
TRINIDAD & TOBAGO
COSTA RICA
San José
Panamá
P A N A M A
G. of Darién
Cartagena
Barquisimeto
Valencia
Cúcuta
San Cristóbal
Orinoco
Ciudad Guayana
Georgetown
Medellín
Bucaramanga
VENEZUELA
GUYANA
Paramaribo
Cayenne
C. Orange
SURINAME
FRENCH GUIANA
Gulf of Panamá
Bogotá
Magdalena
Cali
COLOMBIA
RORAIMA
Branco
Essequibo
AMAPÁ
Galapagos Is. (Ecuador)
Quito
Equator
ECUADOR
Putumayo
Japurá
Napo
Marajó I.
Belém
Amazon
Manaus
Santarém
Guayaquil
G. of Guayaquil
Iquitos
Amazon
São Luís
Marañón
AMAZONAS
P A R Á
Tocantins
Fortaleza
Juruá
Madeira
Tapajós
Xingu
MARANHÃO
Teresina
C. de São Roque
Chiclayo
Ucayali
Purus
CEARÁ
RIO G. DO NORTE
Natal
Parnaíba
PARAÍBA
Trujillo
A C R E
Pôrto Velho
Araguaia
P I A U Í
Campina Grande
Chimbote
PERNAMBUCO
Recife
P E R U
Madre de Dios
RONDÔNIA
TOCANTINS
ALAGOAS
Maceió
Callao
LIMA
B R A Z I L
SERGIPE
Aracaju
Cuzco
Mamoré
MATO GROSSO
B A H Í A
Salvador
L. Titicaca
Arequipa
La Paz
BOLIVIA
G O I Á S
DIS. FED.
Brasília
Cuiabá
São Francisco
Cochabamba
Santa Cruz
Goiânia
PACIFIC OCEAN
Sucre
Paraguay
MATO GROSSO DO SUL
MINAS GERAIS
Iquique
Belo Horizonte
ESPÍRITO SANTO
Vitória
Ribeirão Prêto
Paraná
Juiz de Fora
PARAGUAY
SÃO PAULO
Campinas
R. DE J.
Campos
Antofagasta
Salta
Pilcomayo
PARANÁ
SÃO PAULO
Niterói
RIO DE JANEIRO
Tropic of Capricorn
Asunción
Curitiba
San Félix (Chile)
San Ambrosio (Chile)
San Miguel de Tucumán
Resistencia
SANTA CATARINA
Salado
Corrientes
Uruguay
RIO GRANDE DO SUL
Pôrto Alegre
Córdoba
Santa Fe
San Juan
Paraná
Pelotas
Viña del Mar
Valparaíso
SANTIAGO
Mendoza
Rosario
URUGUAY
Arch. de Juan Fernández (Chile)
BUENOS AIRES
Montevideo
La Plata
Río de la Plata
Talca
Concepción
Bahía Blanca
Mar del Plata
SOUTH ATLANTIC OCEAN
Colorado
Valdivia
Negro
Viedma
Puerto Montt
Chubut
C H I L E
A R G E N T I N A
Comodoro Rivadavia
Gulf of San Jorge
Gulf of Penas
West Falkland
FALKLAND IS. (U.K.)
Stanley
East Falkland
Magellan's Str.
Punta Arenas
Tierra del Fuego
South Georgia (U.K.)
C. Horn
Projection: Lambert's Azimuthal Equal Area
West from Greenwich
COPYRIGHT PHILIP'S
LIMA Capital Cities

km 100 0 100 200 300 400 500

1:14 200 000

100 0 100 200 300 400 miles

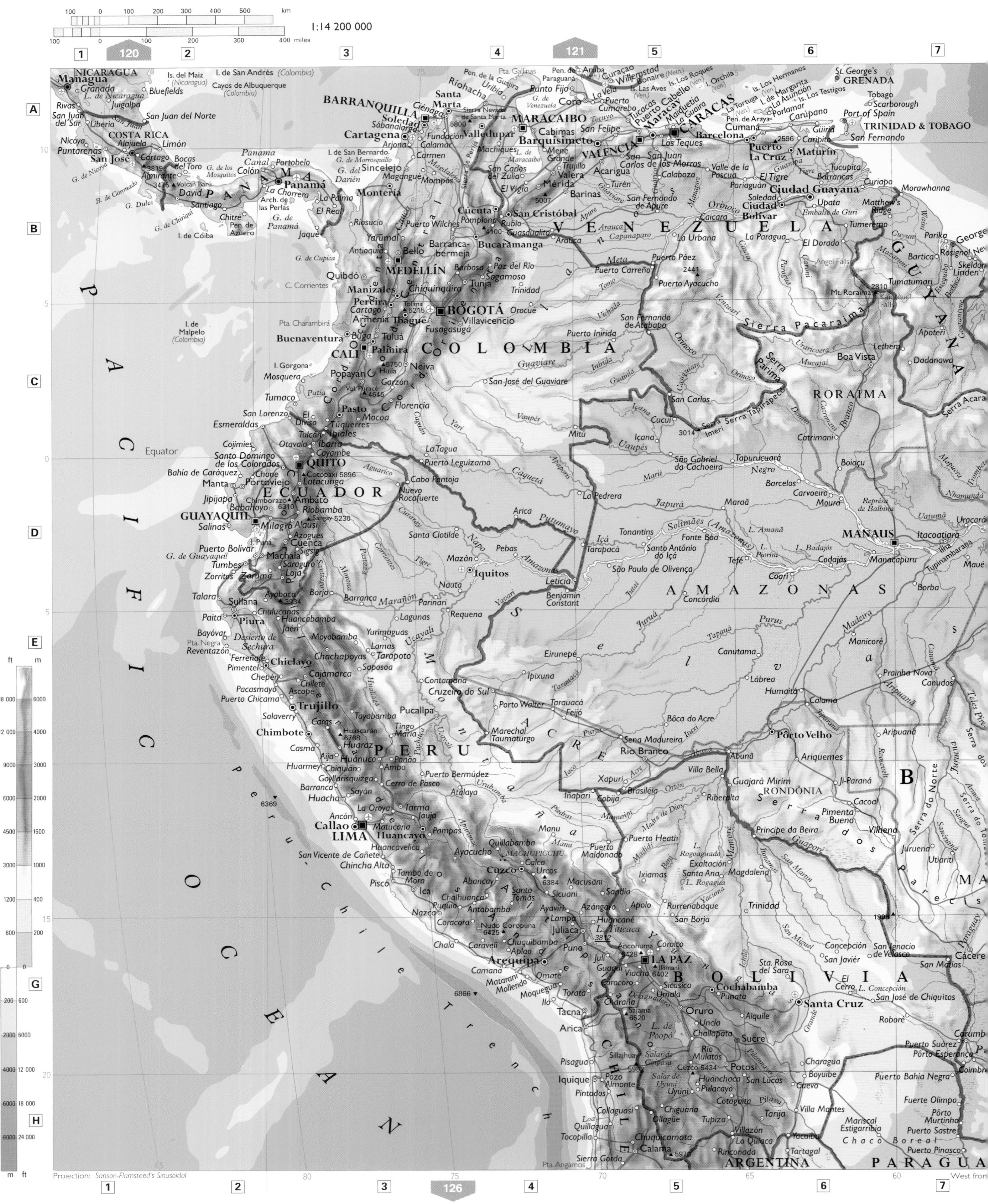

120 121 126

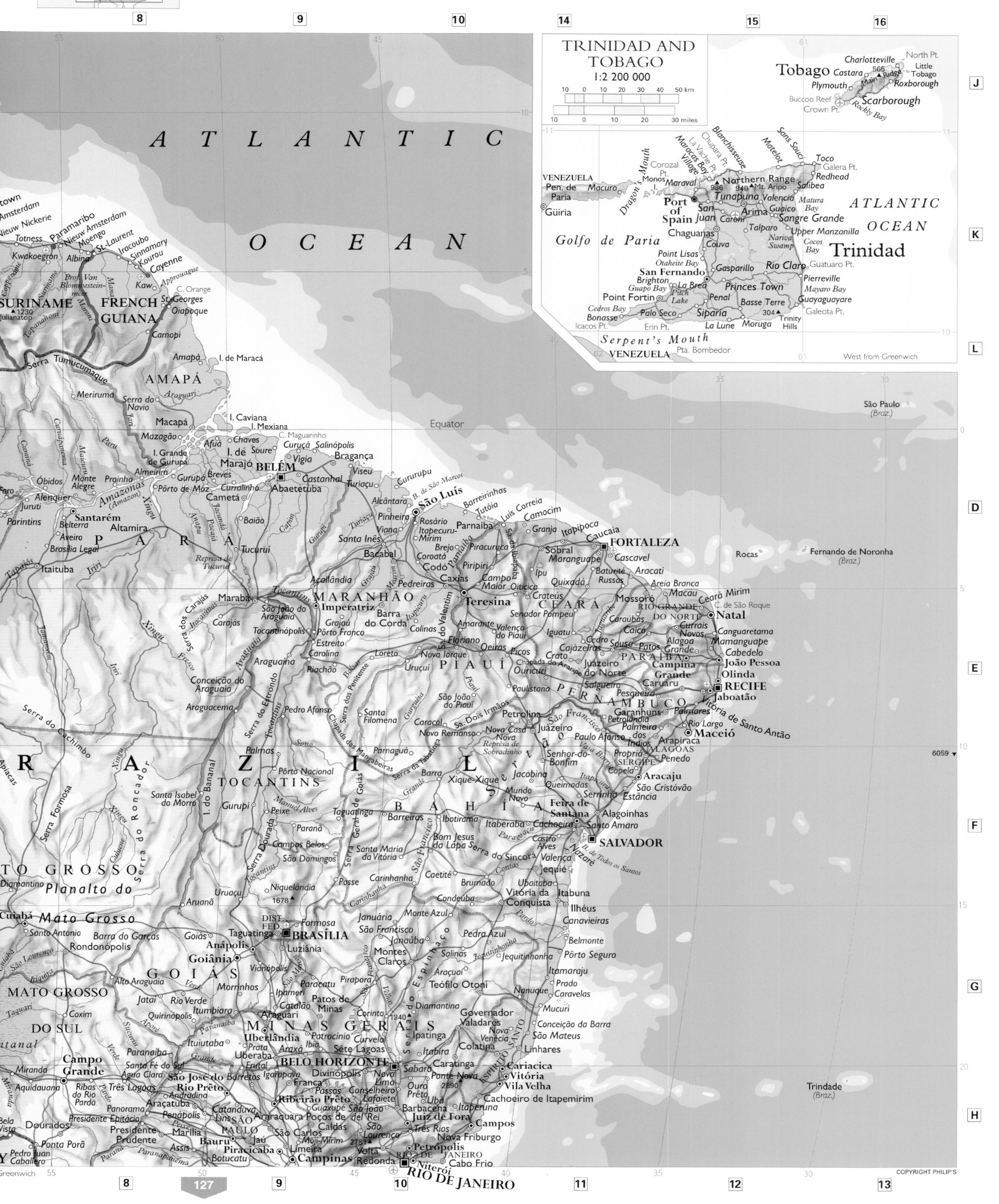
ATLANTIC OCEAN
TRINIDAD AND TOBAGO
1:2 200 000
Tobago
Trinidad
Port of Spain
Golfo de Paria
Serpent's Mouth
SURINAME
FRENCH GUIANA
AMAPÁ
PARÁ
MARANHÃO
PIAUÍ
CEARÁ
RIO GRANDE DO NORTE
PARAÍBA
PERNAMBUCO
ALAGOAS
SERGIPE
BAHIA
TOCANTINS
GOIÁS
MINAS GERAIS
MATO GROSSO
MATO GROSSO DO SUL
BRASÍLIA
BELÉM
São Luís
FORTALEZA
Natal
João Pessoa
RECIFE
Maceió
SALVADOR
BELO HORIZONTE
RIO DE JANEIRO
Equator
Fernando de Noronha (Braz.)
São Paulo (Braz.)
Trindade (Braz.)
West from Greenwich
COPYRIGHT PHILIP'S

127

50 0 50 100 150 200 250 300 km

1:7 100 000

50 0 50 100 150 200 miles

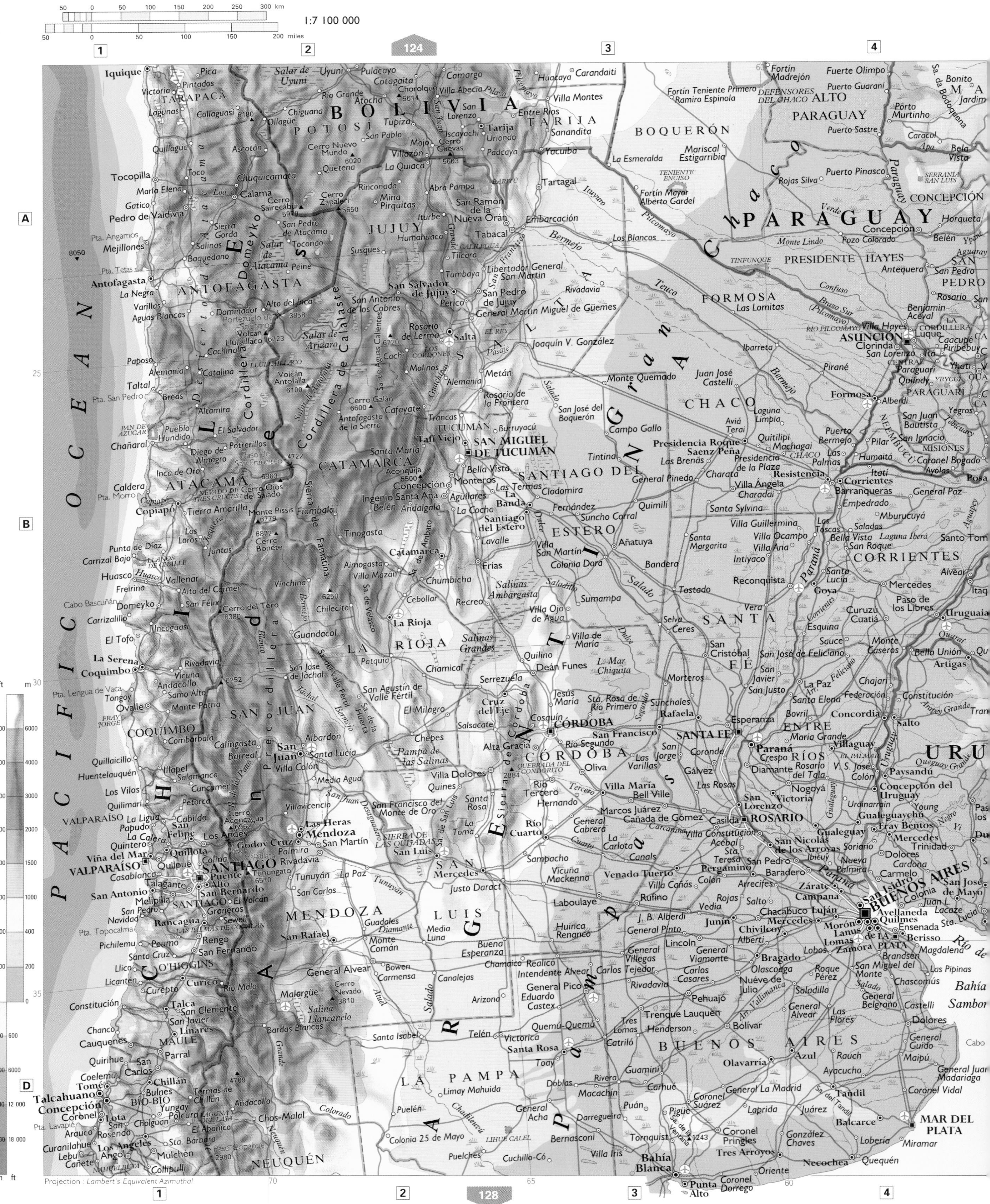

National Parks

1:14 200 000

100 0 100 200 300 400 500 km

100 0 100 200 300 400 miles

126 127

PACIFIC OCEAN

SOUTH ATLANTIC OCEAN

Peru-Chile Trench

Tropic of Capricorn

PARAGUAY

URUGUAY

ARGENTINA

CHILE

BRAZIL

PATAGONIA

Chaco Boreal

Chaco Central

Chaco Austral

SÃO PAULO

PARANÁ

SANTA CATARINA

RIO GRANDE DO SUL

Puna de Atacama

Desierto de Atacama

Salar de Atacama

Sierras de Córdoba

BUENOS AIRES

MONTEVIDEO

SANTIAGO

Asunción

CÓRDOBA

ROSARIO

SÃO PAULO

RIO DE JANEIRO

CURITIBA

PÔRTO ALEGRE

GUARULHOS

NOVA IGUAÇU

Mendoza

San Miguel de Tucumán

Santiago del Estero

Corrientes

Resistencia

Santa Fe

Paraná

Mar del Plata

Bahía Blanca

Neuquén

Comodoro Rivadavia

Río Gallegos

Punta Arenas

Ushuaia

Antofagasta

Valparaíso

Viña del Mar

Concepción

Talcahuano

Temuco

Valdivia

Osorno

Puerto Montt

Salta

San Salvador de Jujuy

Florianópolis

Joinville

Londrina

Campinas

Santos

Pelotas

Rio Grande

Río de la Plata

Golfo San Matías

Golfo San Jorge

Pen. Valdés

Estrecho de Magallanes (Magellan's Str.)

Tierra del Fuego

Isla Grande de Tierra del Fuego

I. de Los Estados (Staten I.)

Cabo de Hornos (C. Horn)

I. de Chiloé

Arch. de los Chonos

I. Wellington

Arch. Reina Adelaida

FALKLAND ISLANDS (ISLAS MALVINAS) (U.K.)

West Falkland

East Falkland

Stanley

Falkland Sd.

South Georgia (U.K.)

Cerro Aconcagua 6962

Ojos del Salado 6863

Volcán Llullaillaco 6723

Mte. San Valentín 4058

Mt. Fitzroy 3375

Mte. Tronador 3554

5830

ft m

18 000 6000

12 000 4000

9000 3000

6000 2000

4500 1500

3000 1000

1200 400

600 200

0 0

200 600

2000 6000

4000 12 000

6000 18 000

8000 24 000

m ft

A B C D E F G H

2 3 4 5 6 7 8

1 2 3 4 5 6 7 8 9

Projection: Sanson-Flamsteed's Sinusoidal

West from Greenwich

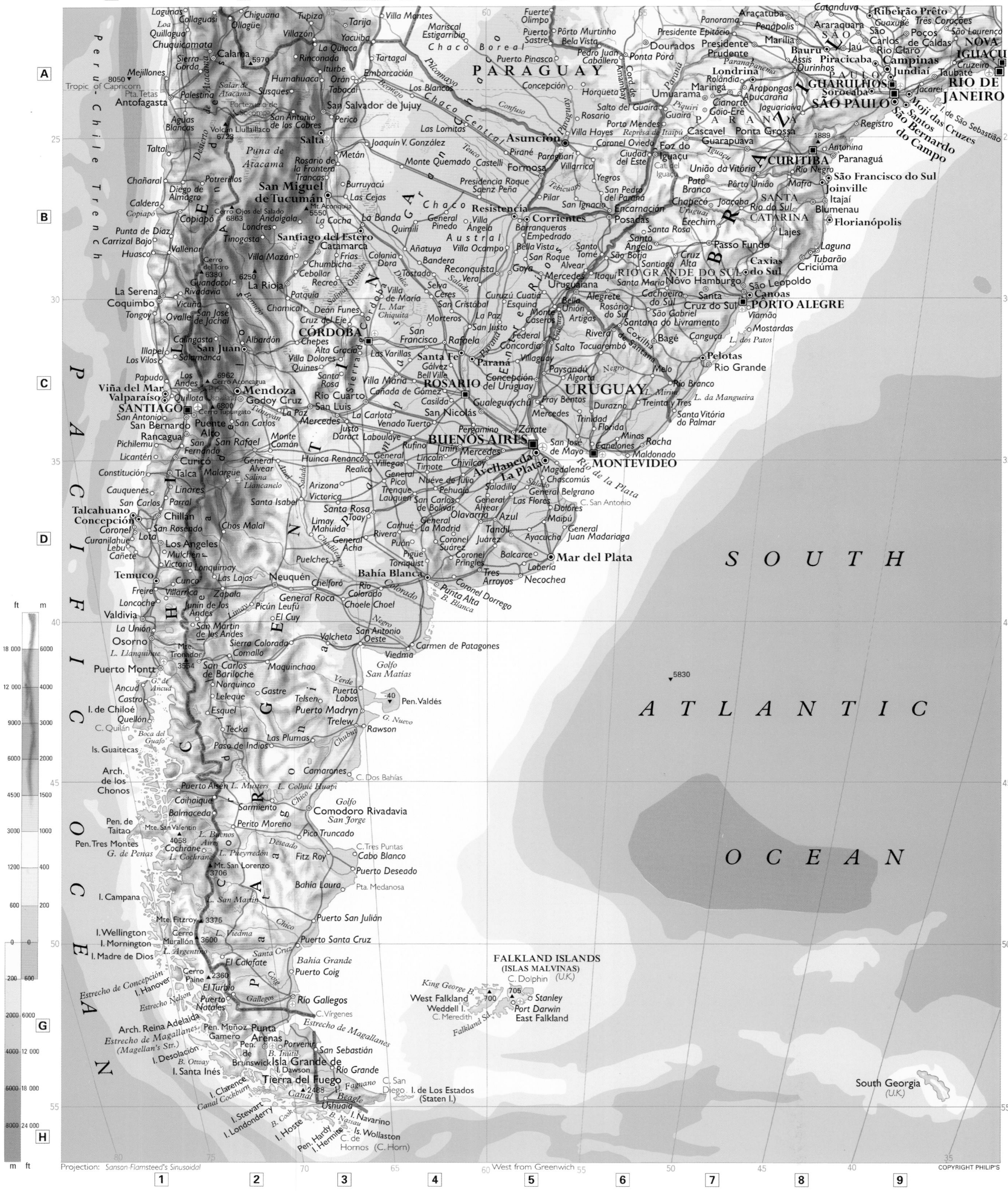

INDEX TO WORLD MAPS

How to use the index

The index contains the names of all the principal places and features shown on the World Maps. Each name is followed by an additional entry in italics giving the country or region within which it is located. The alphabetical order of names composed of two or more words is governed primarily by the first word and then by the second. This is an example of the rule:

Mīr Kūh, *Iran* **71 E8**
Mīr Shahdād, *Iran* **71 E8**
Mira, *Italy* **41 C9**
Mira por vos Cay, *Bahamas* .. **121 B5**
Miraj, *India* **66 F2**

Physical features composed of a proper name (Erie) and a description (Lake) are positioned alphabetically by the proper name. The description is positioned after the proper name and is usually abbreviated:

Erie, L., *N. Amer.* **116 D4**

Where a description forms part of a settlement or administrative name however, it is always written in full and put in its true alphabetic position:

Mount Morris, *U.S.A.* **116 D7**

Names beginning with M' and Mc are indexed as if they were spelled Mac. Names beginning St. are alphabetised under Saint, but Sankt, Sint, Sant', Santa and San are all spelt in full and are alphabetised accordingly. If the same place name occurs two or more times in the index and all are in the same country, each is followed by the name of the administrative subdivision in which it is located. For example:

Jackson, Ky., *U.S.A.* **114 G4**
Jackson, Mich., *U.S.A.* **114 D3**
Jackson, Minn., *U.S.A.* **112 D7**

The number in bold type which follows each name in the index refers to the number of the map page where that feature or place will be found. This is usually the largest scale at which the place or feature appears.

The letter and figure which are in bold type immediately after the page number give the grid square on the map page, within which the feature is situated. The letter represents the latitude and the figure the longitude. A lower case letter immediately after the page number refers to an inset map on that page.

In some cases the feature itself may fall within the specified square, while the name is outside. This is usually the case only with features which are larger than a grid square.

Rivers are indexed to their mouths or confluences, and carry the symbol → after their names. The following symbols are also used in the index: ■ country, ☒ overseas territory or dependency, □ first order administrative area, △ national park, ⌓ other park (provincial park, nature reserve or game reserve), ✈ (LHR) principal airport (and location identifier).

How to pronounce place names

English-speaking people usually have no difficulty in reading and pronouncing correctly English place names. However, foreign place name pronunciations may present many problems. Such problems can be minimised by following some simple rules. However, these rules cannot be applied to all situations, and there will be many exceptions.

1. In general, stress each syllable equally, unless your experience suggests otherwise.
2. Pronounce the letter 'a' as a broad 'a' as in 'arm'.
3. Pronounce the letter 'e' as a short 'e' as in 'elm'.
4. Pronounce the letter 'i' as a cross between a short 'i' and long 'e', as the two 'i's in 'California'.
5. Pronounce the letter 'o' as an intermediate 'o' as in 'soft'.
6. Pronounce the letter 'u' as an intermediate 'u' as in 'sure'.
7. Pronounce consonants hard, except in the Romance-language areas where 'g's are likely to be pronounced softly like 'j' in 'jam'; 'j' itself may be pronounced as 'y'; and 'x's may be pronounced as 'h'.
8. For names in mainland China, pronounce 'q' like the 'ch' in 'chin', 'x' like the 'sh' in 'she', 'zh' like the 'j' in 'jam', and 'z' as if it were spelled 'dz'. In general pronounce 'a' as in 'father', 'e' as in 'but', 'i' as in 'keep', 'o' as in 'or', and 'u' as in 'rule'.

Moreover, English has no diacritical marks (accent and pronunciation signs), although some languages do. The following is a brief and general guide to the pronunciation of those most frequently used in the principal Western European languages.

		Pronunciation as in
French	é	day and shows that the e is to be pronounced; e.g. Orléans.
	è	mare
	î	used over any vowel and does not affect pronunciation; shows contraction of the name, usually omission of 's' following a vowel.
	ç	's' before 'a', 'o' and 'u'.
	ë, ï, ü	over 'e', 'i' and 'u' when they are used with another vowel and shows that each is to be pronounced.
German	ä	fate
	ö	fur
	ü	no English equivalent; like French 'tu'
Italian	à, é	over vowels and indicates stress.
Portuguese	ã, õ	vowels pronounced nasally.
	ç	boss
	á	shows stress
	ô	shows that a vowel has an 'i' or 'u' sound combined with it.
Spanish	ñ	canyon
	ü	pronounced as w and separately from adjoining vowels.
	á	usually indicates that this is a stressed vowel.

Abbreviations

A.C.T. – Australian Capital Territory
A.R. – Autonomous Region
Afghan. – Afghanistan
Afr. – Africa
Ala. – Alabama
Alta. – Alberta
Amer. – America(n)
Arch. – Archipelago
Ariz. – Arizona
Ark. – Arkansas
Atl. Oc. – Atlantic Ocean
B. – Baie, Bahía, Bay, Bucht, Bugt
B.C. – British Columbia
Bangla. – Bangladesh
Barr. – Barrage
Bos.-H. – Bosnia-Herzegovina
C. – Cabo, Cap, Cape, Coast
C.A.R. – Central African Republic
C. Prov. – Cape Province
Calif. – California
Cat. – Catarata
Cent. – Central
Chan. – Channel
Colo. – Colorado
Conn. – Connecticut
Cord. – Cordillera
Cr. – Creek
Czech. – Czech Republic
D.C. – District of Columbia
Del. – Delaware
Dem. – Democratic
Dep. – Dependency
Des. – Desert
Dét. – Détroit
Dist. – District
Dj. – Djebel
Domin. – Dominica
Dom. Rep. – Dominican Republic
E. – East
E. Salv. – El Salvador
Eq. Guin. – Equatorial Guinea
Est. – Estrecho
Falk. Is. – Falkland Is.
Fd. – Fjord
Fla. – Florida
Fr. – French
G. – Golfe, Golfo, Gulf, Guba, Gebel
Ga. – Georgia
Gt. – Great, Greater
Guinea-Biss. – Guinea-Bissau
H.K. – Hong Kong
H.P. – Himachal Pradesh
Hants. – Hampshire
Harb. – Harbor, Harbour
Hd. – Head
Hts. – Heights
I.(s). – Île, Ilha, Insel, Isla, Island, Isle
Ill. – Illinois
Ind. – Indiana
Ind. Oc. – Indian Ocean
Ivory C. – Ivory Coast
J. – Jabal, Jebel
Jaz. – Jazīrah
Junc. – Junction
K. – Kap, Kapp
Kans. – Kansas
Kep. – Kepulauan
Ky. – Kentucky
L. – Lac, Lacul, Lago, Lagoa, Lake, Limni, Loch, Lough
La. – Louisiana
Ld. – Land
Liech. – Liechtenstein
Lux. – Luxembourg
Mad. P. – Madhya Pradesh
Madag. – Madagascar
Man. – Manitoba
Mass. – Massachusetts
Md. – Maryland
Me. – Maine
Medit. S. – Mediterranean Sea
Mich. – Michigan
Minn. – Minnesota
Miss. – Mississippi
Mo. – Missouri
Mont. – Montana
Mozam. – Mozambique
Mt.(s) – Mont, Montaña, Mountain
Mte. – Monte
Mti. – Monti
N. – Nord, Norte, North, Northern, Nouveau
N.B. – New Brunswick
N.C. – North Carolina
N. Cal. – New Caledonia
N. Dak. – North Dakota
N.H. – New Hampshire
N.I. – North Island
N.J. – New Jersey
N. Mex. – New Mexico
N.S. – Nova Scotia
N.S.W. – New South Wales
N.W.T. – North West Territory
N.Y. – New York
N.Z. – New Zealand
Nac. – Nacional
Nat. – National
Nebr. – Nebraska
Neths. – Netherlands
Nev. – Nevada
Nfld. – Newfoundland
Nic. – Nicaragua
O. – Oued, Ouadi
Occ. – Occidentale
Okla. – Oklahoma
Ont. – Ontario
Or. – Orientale
Oreg. – Oregon
Os. – Ostrov
Oz. – Ozero
P. – Pass, Passo, Pasul, Pulau
P.E.I. – Prince Edward Island
Pa. – Pennsylvania
Pac. Oc. – Pacific Ocean
Papua N.G. – Papua New Guinea
Pass. – Passage
Peg. – Pegunungan
Pen. – Peninsula, Péninsule
Phil. – Philippines
Pk. – Peak
Plat. – Plateau
Prov. – Province, Provincial
Pt. – Point
Pta. – Ponta, Punta
Pte. – Pointe
Qué. – Québec
Queens. – Queensland
R. – Rio, River
R.I. – Rhode Island
Ra. – Range
Raj. – Rajasthan
Recr. – Recreational, Récréatif
Reg. – Region
Rep. – Republic
Res. – Reserve, Reservoir
Rhld-Pfz. – Rheinland-Pfalz
S. – South, Southern, Sur
Si. Arabia – Saudi Arabia
S.C. – South Carolina
S. Dak. – South Dakota
S.I. – South Island
S. Leone – Sierra Leone
Sa. – Serra, Sierra
Sask. – Saskatchewan
Scot. – Scotland
Sd. – Sound
Serbia & M.. – Serbia & Montenegro
Sev. – Severnaya
Sib. – Siberia
Sprs. – Springs
St. – Saint
Sta. – Santa
Ste. – Sainte
Sto. – Santo
Str. – Strait, Stretto
Switz. – Switzerland
Tas. – Tasmania
Tenn. – Tennessee
Terr. – Territory, Territoire
Tex. – Texas
Tg. – Tanjung
Trin. & Tob. – Trinidad & Tobago
U.A.E. – United Arab Emirates
U.K. – United Kingdom
U.S.A. – United States of America
Ut. P. – Uttar Pradesh
Va. – Virginia
Vdkhr. – Vodokhranilishche
Vdskh. – Vodoskhovyshche
Vf. – Vírful
Vic. – Victoria
Vol. – Volcano
Vt. – Vermont
W. – Wadi, West
W. Va. – West Virginia
Wall. & F. Is. – Wallis and Futuna Is.
Wash. – Washington
Wis. – Wisconsin
Wlkp. – Wielkopolski
Wyo. – Wyoming
Yorks. – Yorkshire

A

A 'Âli an Nîl □, *Sudan* 81 F3
A Baña, *Spain* 36 C2
A Cañiza, *Spain* 36 C2
A Coruña, *Spain* 36 B2
A Estrada, *Spain* 36 C2
A Fonsagrada, *Spain* 36 B3
A Guarda, *Spain* 36 D2
A Gudiña, *Spain* 36 C3
A Rúa, *Spain* 36 C3
Aachen, *Germany* 24 E2
Aalborg = Ålborg, *Denmark* 11 G3
Aalen, *Germany* 25 G6
Aalst, *Belgium* 17 D4
Aalten, *Neths.* 17 C6
Aalter, *Belgium* 17 C3
Äänekoski, *Finland* 9 E21
Aarau, *Switz.* 25 H4
Aarberg, *Switz.* 25 H3
Aare →, *Switz.* 25 H4
Aargau □, *Switz.* 25 H4
Aarhus = Århus, *Denmark* 11 H4
Aarschot, *Belgium* 17 D4
Aba, *China* 58 A3
Aba, *Dem. Rep. of the Congo* 86 B3
Aba, *Nigeria* 83 D6
Âbâ, Jazîrat, *Sudan* 81 E3
Abadab, J., *Sudan* 80 D4
Ābādān, *Iran* 71 D6
Abade, *Ethiopia* 81 F4
Ābādeh, *Iran* 71 D7
Abadin, *Spain* 36 B3
Abadla, *Algeria* 78 B5
Abaetetuba, *Brazil* 125 D9
Abagnar Qi, *China* 56 C9
Abah, Tanjung, *Indonesia* 63 K18
Abai, *Paraguay* 127 B4
Abak, *Nigeria* 83 E6
Abakaliki, *Nigeria* 83 D6
Abakan, *Russia* 53 D10
Abala, *Niger* 83 C5
Abalak, *Niger* 83 B6
Abalemma, *Niger* 83 B6
Abana, *Turkey* 72 B6
Abancay, *Peru* 124 F4
Abano Terme, *Italy* 41 C8
Abarán, *Spain* 39 G3
Abariringa, *Kiribati* 96 H10
Abarqū, *Iran* 71 D7
Abashiri, *Japan* 54 B12
Abashiri-Wan, *Japan* 54 C12
Abaújszántó, *Hungary* 28 B6
Abava →, *Latvia* 30 A8
Ābay = Nîl el Azraq →, *Sudan* 81 D3
Abay, *Kazakhstan* 52 E8
Abaya, L., *Ethiopia* 81 F4
Abayita-Shala Lakes △, *Ethiopia* 81 F4
Abaza, *Russia* 52 D9
Abbadia di Fiastra ⌂, *Italy* 41 E10
Abbadia San Salvatore, *Italy* 41 F8
'Abbāsābād, *Iran* 71 C8
Abbay = Nîl el Azraq →, *Sudan* 81 D3
Abbaye, Pt., *U.S.A.* 114 B1
Abbé, L., *Ethiopia* 81 E5
Abbeville, *France* 19 B8
Abbeville, *Ala., U.S.A.* 115 K3
Abbeville, *La., U.S.A.* 113 L8
Abbeville, *S.C., U.S.A.* 115 H4
Abbiategrasso, *Italy* 40 C5
Abbot Ice Shelf, *Antarctica* 5 D16
Abbottabad, *Pakistan* 68 B5
Abd al Kūrī, *Yemen* 75 E5
Ābdar, *Iran* 71 D7
'Abdolābād, *Iran* 71 C8
Abdulpur, *Bangla.* 69 G13
Abéché, *Chad* 79 F10
Abejar, *Spain* 38 D2
Abekr, *Sudan* 81 E2
Abel Tasman △, *N.Z.* 91 J4
Abengourou, *Ivory C.* 82 D4
Abenójar, *Spain* 37 G6
Åbenrå, *Denmark* 11 J3
Abensberg, *Germany* 25 G7
Abeokuta, *Nigeria* 83 D5
Aber, *Uganda* 86 B3
Aberaeron, *U.K.* 15 E3
Aberayron = Aberaeron, *U.K.* 15 E3
Aberchirder, *U.K.* 13 D6
Abercorn = Mbala, *Zambia* 87 D3
Abercorn, *Australia* 95 D5
Aberdare, *U.K.* 15 F4
Aberdare △, *Kenya* 86 C4
Aberdare Ra., *Kenya* 86 C4
Aberdeen, *Australia* 95 E5
Aberdeen, *Canada* 103 C7
Aberdeen, *S. Africa* 88 E3
Aberdeen, *U.K.* 13 D6
Aberdeen, *Ala., U.S.A.* 115 J1
Aberdeen, *Idaho, U.S.A.* 108 E7
Aberdeen, *Md., U.S.A.* 114 F7
Aberdeen, *S. Dak., U.S.A.* 112 C5
Aberdeen, *Wash., U.S.A.* 110 D3
Aberdeen, City of □, *U.K.* 13 D6
Aberdeenshire □, *U.K.* 13 D6
Aberdovey = Aberdyfi, *U.K.* 15 E3
Aberdyfi, *U.K.* 15 E3
Aberfeldy, *U.K.* 13 E5
Aberfoyle, *U.K.* 13 E4
Abergavenny, *U.K.* 15 F4
Abergele, *U.K.* 14 D4
Abernathy, *U.S.A.* 113 J4
Abert, L., *U.S.A.* 108 E3
Aberystwyth, *U.K.* 15 E3
Abhā, *Si. Arabia* 75 D3
Abhar, *Iran* 71 B6
Abhayapuri, *India* 69 F14
Abia □, *Nigeria* 83 D6
Abide, *Turkey* 47 C11
Abidiya, *Sudan* 80 D3
Abidjan, *Ivory C.* 82 D4
Abilene, *Kans., U.S.A.* 112 F6
Abilene, *Tex., U.S.A.* 113 J5
Abingdon, *U.K.* 15 F6
Abingdon, *U.S.A.* 115 G5
Abington Reef, *Australia* 94 B4
Abitau →, *Canada* 103 B7
Abitibi →, *Canada* 104 B3
Abitibi, L., *Canada* 104 C4
Abiy Adi, *Ethiopia* 81 E4
Abkhaz Republic = Abkhazia □, *Georgia* 35 J5
Abkhazia □, *Georgia* 35 J5
Abminga, *Australia* 95 D1
Abnûb, *Egypt* 80 B3
Åbo = Turku, *Finland* 9 F20
Abocho, *Nigeria* 83 D6
Abohar, *India* 68 D6
Aboisso, *Ivory C.* 82 D4
Abomey, *Benin* 83 D5
Abong-Mbang, *Cameroon* 84 D2
Abonnema, *Nigeria* 83 E6
Abony, *Hungary* 28 C5
Aboso, *Ghana* 82 D4
Abou-Deïa, *Chad* 79 F9
Aboyne, *U.K.* 13 D6
Abra Pampa, *Argentina* 126 A2
Abraham L., *Canada* 102 C5
Abrantes, *Portugal* 37 F2
Abreojos, Pta., *Mexico* 118 B2
Abri, *Esh Shamâliya, Sudan* 80 C3
Abri, *Janub Kordofân, Sudan* 81 E3
Abrolhos, Banka, *Brazil* 122 E7
Abrud, *Romania* 28 D8
Abruzzo □, *Italy* 41 F10
Absaroka Range, *U.S.A.* 108 D9
Abtenau, *Austria* 26 D6
Abu, *India* 68 G5
Abū al Abyad, *U.A.E.* 71 E7
Abū al Khaşīb, *Iraq* 71 D6
Abū 'Alī, *Si. Arabia* 71 E6
Abū 'Alī →, *Lebanon* 74 A4
Abu Ballas, *Egypt* 80 C2
Abu Deleiq, *Sudan* 81 D3
Abu Dhabi = Abū Ẓāby, *U.A.E.* 71 E7
Abu Dis, *Sudan* 80 D3
Abu Dom, *Sudan* 81 D3
Abū Du'ān, *Syria* 70 B3
Abu el Gairi, W. →, *Egypt* 74 F2
Abu Fatma, Ras, *Sudan* 80 C4
Abu Gabra, *Sudan* 81 E2
Abu Ga'da, W. →, *Egypt* 74 F1
Abu Gelba, *Sudan* 81 E3
Abu Gubeiha, *Sudan* 81 E3
Abu Habl, Khawr →, *Sudan* 81 E3
Abū Ḩadrīyah, *Si. Arabia* 71 E6
Abu Hamed, *Sudan* 80 D3
Abu Haraz, *An Nîl el Azraq, Sudan* 80 D3
Abu Haraz, *El Gezira, Sudan* 81 E3
Abu Haraz, *Esh Shamâliya, Sudan* 80 D3
Abu Higar, *Sudan* 81 E3
Abū Kamāl, *Syria* 70 C4
Abu Kuleiwat, *Sudan* 81 E2
Abū Madd, Ra's, *Si. Arabia* 70 E3
Abu Matariq, *Sudan* 81 E2
Abu Mendi, *Ethiopia* 81 E4
Abū Mūsā, *U.A.E.* 71 E7
Abū Qaşr, *Si. Arabia* 70 D3
Abu Qir, *Egypt* 80 H7
Abu Qireiya, *Egypt* 80 C4
Abu Qurqâs, *Egypt* 80 B3
Abu Shagara, Ras, *Sudan* 80 C4
Abu Shanab, *Sudan* 81 E2
Abu Simbel, *Egypt* 80 C3
Abū Şukhayr, *Iraq* 70 D5
Abū Sultān, *Egypt* 80 H8
Abu Tabari, *Sudan* 80 D2
Abu Tig, *Egypt* 80 B3
Abu Tiga, *Sudan* 81 E3
Abu Tineitin, *Sudan* 81 E3
Abu Uruq, *Sudan* 81 D3
Abu Zabad, *Sudan* 81 E2
Abū Ẓāby, *U.A.E.* 71 E7
Abū Zeydābād, *Iran* 71 C6
Abuja, *Nigeria* 83 D6
Abukuma-Gawa →, *Japan* 54 E10
Abukuma-Sammyaku, *Japan* 54 F10
Abunã, *Brazil* 124 E5
Abunã →, *Brazil* 124 E5
Abune Yosef, *Ethiopia* 81 E4
Aburo, *Dem. Rep. of the Congo* 86 B3
Abut Hd., *N.Z.* 91 K3
Abuye Meda, *Ethiopia* 81 E4
Abwong, *Sudan* 81 F3
Åby, *Sweden* 11 F10
Aby, Lagune, *Ivory C.* 82 D4
Abyad, *Sudan* 81 E2
Åbybro, *Denmark* 11 G3
Acadia △, *U.S.A.* 115 C11
Açailândia, *Brazil* 125 D9
Acajutla, *El Salv.* 120 D2
Acámbaro, *Mexico* 118 D4
Acanthus, *Greece* 44 F7
Acaponeta, *Mexico* 118 C3
Acapulco, *Mexico* 119 D5
Acarai, Serra, *Brazil* 124 C7
Acarigua, *Venezuela* 124 B5
Acatlán, *Mexico* 119 D5
Acayucan, *Mexico* 119 D6
Accéglio, *Italy* 40 D4
Accomac, *U.S.A.* 114 G8
Accous, *France* 20 E3
Accra, *Ghana* 83 D4
Accrington, *U.K.* 14 D5
Acebal, *Argentina* 126 C3
Aceh □, *Indonesia* 62 D1
Acerra, *Italy* 43 B7
Aceuchal, *Spain* 37 G4
Achalpur, *India* 66 J10
Acheng, *China* 57 B14
Achenkirch, *Austria* 26 D4
Achensee, *Austria* 26 D4
Acher, *India* 68 H5
Achern, *Germany* 25 G4
Achill Hd., *Ireland* 12 C1
Achill I., *Ireland* 12 C1
Achim, *Germany* 24 B5
Achinsk, *Russia* 53 D10
Acıgöl, *Turkey* 47 D11
Acıpayam, *Turkey* 47 D11
Acireale, *Italy* 43 E8
Ackerman, *U.S.A.* 113 J10
Acklins I., *Bahamas* 121 B5
Acme, *Canada* 102 C6
Acme, *U.S.A.* 116 F5
Aconcagua, Cerro, *Argentina* 126 C2
Aconquija, Mt., *Argentina* 126 B2
Açores, Is. dos, *Atl. Oc.* 78 A1
Acornhoek, *S. Africa* 89 C5
Acquapendente, *Italy* 41 F8
Acquasanta Terme, *Italy* 41 F10
Acquasparta, *Italy* 41 F9
Acquaviva delle Fonti, *Italy* 43 B9
Ácqui Terme, *Italy* 40 D5
Acraman, L., *Australia* 95 E2
Acre = 'Akko, *Israel* 74 C4
Acre □, *Brazil* 124 E4
Acre →, *Brazil* 124 E5
Acri, *Italy* 43 C9
Acs, *Hungary* 28 C3
Actium, *Greece* 46 C2
Acton, *Canada* 116 C4
Acuña, *Mexico* 118 B4
Ad Dammām, *Si. Arabia* 71 E6
Ad Dāmūr, *Lebanon* 74 B4
Ad Dawādimī, *Si. Arabia* 70 E5
Ad Dawḩah, *Qatar* 71 E6
Ad Dawr, *Iraq* 70 C4
Ad Dir'īyah, *Si. Arabia* 70 E5
Ad Dīwānīyah, *Iraq* 70 D5
Ad Dujayl, *Iraq* 70 C5
Ad Duwayd, *Si. Arabia* 70 D4
Ada, *Ghana* 83 D5
Ada, *Serbia & M.* 28 E5
Ada, *Minn., U.S.A.* 112 B6
Ada, *Okla., U.S.A.* 113 H6
Adabiya, *Egypt* 74 F1
Adair, C., *Canada* 101 A12
Adaja →, *Spain* 36 D6
Adak I., *U.S.A.* 100 C2
Adamaoua, Massif de l', *Cameroon* 83 D7
Adamawa □, *Nigeria* 83 D7
Adamawa Highlands = Adamaoua, Massif de l', *Cameroon* 83 D7
Adamello ⌂, *Italy* 40 B7
Adamello, Mte., *Italy* 40 B7
Adami Tulu, *Ethiopia* 81 F4
Adaminaby, *Australia* 95 F4
Adams, *Mass., U.S.A.* 117 D11
Adams, *N.Y., U.S.A.* 117 C8
Adams, *Wis., U.S.A.* 112 D10
Adams, Mt., *U.S.A.* 110 D5
Adam's Bridge, *Sri Lanka* 66 Q11
Adams L., *Canada* 102 C5
Adam's Peak, *Sri Lanka* 66 R12
Adamuz, *Spain* 37 G6
Adana, *Turkey* 70 B2
Adanero, *Spain* 36 E6
Adapazarı = Sakarya, *Turkey* 72 B4
Adar Gwagwa, J., *Sudan* 80 C4
Adarama, *Sudan* 81 D3
Adare, C., *Antarctica* 5 D11
Adarte, *Eritrea* 81 E5
Adaut, *Indonesia* 63 F8
Adavale, *Australia* 95 D3
Adda →, *Italy* 40 C6
Addis Ababa = Addis Abeba, *Ethiopia* 81 F4
Addis Abeba, *Ethiopia* 81 F4
Addis Alem, *Ethiopia* 81 F4
Addis Zemen, *Ethiopia* 81 E4
Addison, *U.S.A.* 116 D7
Addo, *S. Africa* 88 E4
Addo △, *S. Africa* 88 E4
Adebour, *Niger* 83 C7
Ādeh, *Iran* 70 B5
Adel, *U.S.A.* 115 K4
Adelaide, *Australia* 95 E2
Adelaide, *Bahamas* 120 A4
Adelaide, *S. Africa* 88 E4
Adelaide I., *Antarctica* 5 C17
Adelaide Pen., *Canada* 100 B10
Adelaide River, *Australia* 92 B5
Adelanto, *U.S.A.* 111 L9
Adele I., *Australia* 92 C3
Adélie, Terre, *Antarctica* 5 C10
Adélie Land = Adélie, Terre, *Antarctica* 5 C10
Ademuz, *Spain* 38 E3
Aden = Al 'Adan, *Yemen* 75 E4
Aden, G. of, *Asia* 75 E4
Adendorp, *S. Africa* 88 E3
Aderbissinat, *Niger* 83 B6
Adh Dhayd, *U.A.E.* 71 E7
Adhoi, *India* 68 H4
Adi, *Indonesia* 63 E8
Adi Arkai, *Ethiopia* 81 E4
Adi Daro, *Ethiopia* 81 E4
Adi Keyih, *Eritrea* 81 E4
Adi Kwala, *Eritrea* 81 E4
Adi Ugri, *Eritrea* 81 E4
Adieu, C., *Australia* 93 F5
Adieu Pt., *Australia* 92 C3
Adigala, *Ethiopia* 81 E5
Adige →, *Italy* 41 C9
Adigrat, *Ethiopia* 81 E4
Adıgüzel Barajı, *Turkey* 47 C11
Adilabad, *India* 66 K11
Adilcevaz, *Turkey* 73 C10
Adirondack ⌂, *U.S.A.* 117 C10
Adirondack Mts., *U.S.A.* 117 C10
Adıyaman, *Turkey* 73 D8
Adjohon, *Benin* 83 D5
Adjud, *Romania* 29 D12
Adjumani, *Uganda* 86 B3
Adjuntas, *Puerto Rico* 121 d
Adlavik Is., *Canada* 105 B8
Adler, *Russia* 35 J4
Admer, *Algeria* 83 A6
Admiralty G., *Australia* 92 B4
Admiralty I., *U.S.A.* 102 B2
Admiralty Is., *Papua N. G.* 96 H6
Adnan Menderes, İzmir ✕ (ADB), *Turkey* 47 C9
Ado, *Nigeria* 83 D5
Ado-Ekiti, *Nigeria* 83 D6
Adok, *Sudan* 81 F3
Adola, *Ethiopia* 81 E5
Adonara, *Indonesia* 63 F6
Adoni, *India* 66 M10
Adony, *Hungary* 28 C3
Adour →, *France* 20 E2
Adra, *India* 69 H12
Adra, *Spain* 37 J7
Adrano, *Italy* 43 E7
Adrar, *Mauritania* 78 D3
Adrar des Iforas, *Algeria* 78 C5
Ádria, *Italy* 41 C9
Adrian, *Mich., U.S.A.* 114 E3
Adrian, *Tex., U.S.A.* 113 H3
Adriatic Sea, *Medit. S.* 6 G9
Adua, *Indonesia* 63 E7
Adwa, *Ethiopia* 81 E4
Adygea □, *Russia* 35 H5
Adzhar Republic = Ajaria □, *Georgia* 35 K6
Adzopé, *Ivory C.* 82 D4
Ægean Sea, *Medit. S.* 47 C7
Aerhtai Shan, *Mongolia* 60 B4
Ærø, *Denmark* 11 K4
Ærøskøbing, *Denmark* 11 K4
Aëtós, *Greece* 46 D3
'Afak, *Iraq* 70 C5
Afándou, *Greece* 49 C10
Afghanistan ■, *Asia* 66 C4
Afikpo, *Nigeria* 83 D6
Aflou, *Algeria* 78 B6
Afragóla, *Italy* 43 B7
Afram →, *Ghana* 83 D4
Afrera, *Ethiopia* 81 E5
Africa 76 E6
'Afrīn, *Syria* 70 B3
Afşin, *Turkey* 72 C7
Afton, *N.Y., U.S.A.* 117 D9
Afton, *Wyo., U.S.A.* 108 E8
Afuá, *Brazil* 125 D8
'Afula, *Israel* 74 C4
Afyon, *Turkey* 47 C12
Afyon □, *Turkey* 47 C12
Afyonkarahisar = Afyon, *Turkey* 47 C12
Aga, *Egypt* 80 H7
Agadès = Agadez, *Niger* 83 B6
Agadez, *Niger* 83 B6
Agadir, *Morocco* 78 B4
Agaete, *Canary Is.* 48 F4
Agaie, *Nigeria* 83 D6
Again, *Sudan* 81 F2
Ağapınar, *Turkey* 47 B12
Agar, *India* 68 H7
Agaro, *Ethiopia* 81 F4
Agartala, *India* 67 H17
Agăş, *Romania* 29 D11
Agassiz, *Canada* 102 D4
Agats, *Indonesia* 63 F9
Agawam, *U.S.A.* 117 D12
Agbélouvé, *Togo* 83 D5
Agboville, *Ivory C.* 82 D4
Ağcabädi, *Azerbaijan* 35 K8
Ağdam, *Azerbaijan* 35 L8
Ağdaş, *Azerbaijan* 35 K8
Agde, *France* 20 E7
Agde, C. d', *France* 20 E7
Agdzhabedi = Ağcabädi, *Azerbaijan* 35 K8
Agen, *France* 20 D4
Agerbæk, *Denmark* 11 J2
Agersø, *Denmark* 11 J5
Ageyevo, *Russia* 32 E9
Aggteleki △, *Hungary* 28 B5
Āgh Kand, *Iran* 71 B6
Aghireşu, *Romania* 29 D8
Aginskoye, *Russia* 53 D12
Ağlasun, *Turkey* 47 D12
Agly →, *France* 20 F7
Agnew, *Australia* 93 E3
Agnibilékrou, *Ivory C.* 82 D4
Agnita, *Romania* 29 E9
Agnone, *Italy* 41 G11
Agofie, *Ghana* 83 D5
Agogna →, *Italy* 40 C5
Agogo, *Sudan* 81 F2
Agön, *Sweden* 10 C11
Agon Coutainville, *France* 18 C5
Ágordo, *Italy* 41 B9
Agori, *India* 69 G10
Agouna, *Benin* 83 D5
Agout →, *France* 20 E5
Agra, *India* 68 F7
Agrakhanskiy Poluostrov, *Russia* 35 J8
Agramunt, *Spain* 38 D6
Agreda, *Spain* 38 D3
Ağri, *Turkey* 73 C10
Agri →, *Italy* 43 B9
Ağrı Dağı, *Turkey* 70 B5
Ağri Karakose = Ağri, *Turkey* 73 C10
Agriá, *Greece* 46 B5
Agrigento, *Italy* 42 E6
Agrínion, *Greece* 46 C3
Agrópoli, *Italy* 43 B7
Ağstafa, *Azerbaijan* 35 K7
Agua Caliente, *Baja Calif., Mexico* 111 N10
Agua Caliente, *Sinaloa, Mexico* 118 B3
Agua Caliente Springs, *U.S.A.* 111 N10
Água Clara, *Brazil* 125 H8
Agua Fria ⌂, *U.S.A.* 109 J8
Agua Hechicero, *Mexico* 111 N10
Agua Prieta, *Mexico* 118 A3
Aguadilla, *Puerto Rico* 121 d
Aguadulce, *Panama* 120 E3
Aguanga, *U.S.A.* 111 M10
Aguanish, *Canada* 105 B7
Aguanus →, *Canada* 105 B7
Aguapey →, *Argentina* 126 B4
Aguaray Guazú →, *Paraguay* 126 A4
Aguarico →, *Ecuador* 124 D3
Aguaro-Guariquito △, *Venezuela* 121 E6
Aguas →, *Spain* 38 D4
Aguas Blancas, *Chile* 126 A2
Aguas Calientes, Sierra de, *Argentina* 126 B2
Aguascalientes, *Mexico* 118 C4
Aguascalientes □, *Mexico* 118 C4
Agudo, *Spain* 37 G6
Águeda, *Portugal* 36 E2
Agueda →, *Spain* 36 D4
Aguelhok, *Mali* 83 B5
Aguié, *Niger* 83 C6
Aguila, Punta, *Puerto Rico* 121 d
Aguilafuente, *Spain* 36 D6
Aguilar, *Spain* 37 H6
Aguilar de Campóo, *Spain* 36 C6
Aguilares, *Argentina* 126 B2
Aguilas, *Spain* 39 H3
Agüimes, *Canary Is.* 48 G4
Aguja, C. de la, *Colombia* 122 B3
Agujereada, Pta., *Puerto Rico* 121 d
Agulaa, *Ethiopia* 81 E4
Agulhas, C., *S. Africa* 88 E3
Agulo, *Canary Is.* 48 F2
Agung, Gunung, *Indonesia* 63 J18
Agur, *Uganda* 86 B3
Agusan →, *Phil.* 61 G6
Ağva, *Turkey* 45 E13
Agvali, *Russia* 35 J8
Aha Mts., *Botswana* 88 B3
Ahaggar, *Algeria* 78 D7
Ahamansu, *Ghana* 83 D5
Ahar, *Iran* 70 B5
Ahat, *Turkey* 47 C11
Ahaus, *Germany* 24 C2
Ahipara B., *N.Z.* 91 F4
Ahir Dağı, *Turkey* 47 C12
Ahiri, *India* 66 K12
Ahlat, *Turkey* 73 C10
Ahlen, *Germany* 24 D3
Ahmad Wal, *Pakistan* 68 E1
Ahmadabad, *India* 68 H5
Aḩmadābād, *Khorāsān, Iran* 71 C9
Aḩmadābād, *Khorāsān, Iran* 71 C8
Aḩmadī, *Iran* 71 E8
Ahmadnagar, *India* 66 K9
Ahmadpur, *Pakistan* 68 E4
Ahmadpur Lamma, *Pakistan* 68 E4
Ahmar, *Ethiopia* 81 F5
Ahmedabad = Ahmadabad, *India* 68 H5
Ahmednagar = Ahmadnagar, *India* 66 K9
Ahmetbey, *Turkey* 45 E11
Ahmetler, *Turkey* 47 C11
Ahmetli, *Turkey* 47 C9
Ahoada, *Nigeria* 83 D6
Ahome, *Mexico* 118 B3
Ahoskie, *U.S.A.* 115 G7
Ahr →, *Germany* 24 E3
Ahram, *Iran* 71 D6
Ahrax Pt., *Malta* 49 D1
Ahrensbök, *Germany* 24 A6
Ahrensburg, *Germany* 24 B6
Āhū, *Iran* 71 C6
Ahuachapán, *El Salv.* 120 D2
Ahun, *France* 19 F9
Åhus, *Sweden* 11 J8
Ahvāz, *Iran* 71 D6
Ahvenanmaa = Åland, *Finland* 9 F19
Aḩwar, *Yemen* 75 E4
Ahzar →, *Mali* 83 B5
Ai →, *India* 69 F14
Ai-Ais, *Namibia* 88 D2
Ai-Ais and Fish River Canyon △, *Namibia* 88 C2
Aichach, *Germany* 25 G7
Aichi □, *Japan* 55 G8
Aigle, *Switz.* 25 J2
Aignay-le-Duc, *France* 19 E11
Aigoual, Mt., *France* 20 D7
Aigre, *France* 20 C4
Aigua, *Uruguay* 127 C5
Aigueperse, *France* 19 F10
Aigues →, *France* 21 D8
Aigues-Mortes, *France* 21 E8
Aigues-Mortes, G. d', *France* 21 E8
Aigües Tortes y Lago San Mauricio △, *Spain* 38 C4
Aiguilles, *France* 21 D10
Aiguillon, *France* 20 D4
Aigurande, *France* 19 F8
Aihui, *China* 60 A7
Aija, *Peru* 124 E3
Aikawa, *Japan* 54 E9
Aiken, *U.S.A.* 115 J5
Ailao Shan, *China* 58 F3
Aileron, *Australia* 94 C1
Aillant-sur-Tholon, *France* 19 E10
Aillik, *Canada* 105 A8
Ailsa Craig, *U.K.* 13 F3
Aim, *Russia* 53 D14
Aimere, *Indonesia* 63 F6

Aimogasta, *Argentina* 126 B2
Ain □, *France* 19 F12
Ain →, *France* 21 C9
Aïn Ben Tili, *Mauritania* 78 C4
Aïn Dalla, *Egypt* 80 B2
Ain el Mafki, *Egypt* 80 B2
Ain Girba, *Egypt* 80 B2
Ain Murr, *Sudan* 80 C2
Ain Qeiqab, *Egypt* 80 B1
Aïn Sefra, *Algeria* 78 B5
Ain Sheikh Murzûk, *Egypt* 80 B2
Ain Sudr, *Egypt* 74 F2
Ain Sukhna, *Egypt* 80 J8
Ain Zeitûn, *Egypt* 80 B2
Ainaži, *Latvia* 9 H21
Aínos Óros, *Greece* 46 C2
Ainsworth, *U.S.A.* 112 D5
Aiquile, *Bolivia* 124 G5
Aïr, *Niger* 83 B6
Air Force I., *Canada* 101 B12
Air Hitam, *Malaysia* 65 M4
Airaines, *France* 19 C8
Airdrie, *Canada* 102 C6
Airdrie, *U.K.* 13 F5
Aire →, *France* 19 C11
Aire →, *U.K.* 14 D7
Aire, I. de l', *Spain* 48 B11
Aire-sur-la-Lys, *France* 19 B9
Aire-sur-l'Adour, *France* 20 E3
Airlie Beach, *Australia* 94 J6
Airvault, *France* 18 F6
Aisch →, *Germany* 25 F6
Aisne □, *France* 19 C10
Aisne →, *France* 19 C9
Ait, *India* 69 G8
Aitana, Sierra de, *Spain* 39 G4
Aitkin, *U.S.A.* 112 B8
Aitolía Kai Akarnanía □, *Greece* 46 C3
Aitolikón, *Greece* 46 C3
Aiud, *Romania* 29 D8
Aix-en-Provence, *France* 21 E9
Aix-la-Chapelle = Aachen, *Germany* 24 E2
Aix-les-Bains, *France* 21 C9
Aixe-sur-Vienne, *France* 20 C5
Áíyina, *Greece* 46 D5
Aiyínion, *Greece* 44 F6
Aíyion, *Greece* 46 C4
Aizawl, *India* 67 H18
Aizenay, *France* 18 F5
Aizkraukle, *Latvia* 9 H21
Aizpute, *Latvia* 9 H19
Aizuwakamatsu, *Japan* 54 F9
Ajaccio, *France* 21 G12
Ajaccio, G. d', *France* 21 G12
Ajai ⌂, *Uganda* 86 B3
Ajaigarh, *India* 69 G9
Ajalpan, *Mexico* 119 D5
Ajanta Ra., *India* 66 J9
Ajari Rep. = Ajaria □, *Georgia* 35 K6
Ajaria □, *Georgia* 35 K6
Ajax, *Canada* 116 C5
Ajdâbiyâ, *Libya* 79 B10
Ajdovščina, *Slovenia* 41 C10
Ajibar, *Ethiopia* 81 E4
Ajka, *Hungary* 28 C2
'Ajlūn, *Jordan* 74 C4
'Ajlūn □, *Jordan* 74 C4
'Ajmān, *U.A.E.* 71 E7
Ajmer, *India* 68 F6
Ajnala, *India* 68 D6
Ajo, *U.S.A.* 109 K7
Ajo, C. de, *Spain* 36 B7
Ajok, *Sudan* 81 F2
Ajuy, *Phil.* 61 F5
Ak Dağ, *Turkey* 47 E11
Ak Dağları, *Muğla, Turkey* 47 E11
Ak Dağları, *Sivas, Turkey* 72 C7
Akaba, *Togo* 83 D5
Akabira, *Japan* 54 C11
Akagera △, *Rwanda* 86 C3
Akaki Beseka, *Ethiopia* 81 F4
Akala, *Sudan* 81 D4
Akamas, *Cyprus* 49 D11
Akan △, *Japan* 54 C12
Akanthou, *Cyprus* 49 D12
Akarca, *Turkey* 47 C11
Akaroa, *N.Z.* 91 K4
Akasha, *Sudan* 80 C3
Akashi, *Japan* 55 G7
Akbarpur, *Bihar, India* 69 G10
Akbarpur, *Ut. P., India* 69 F10
Akçaabat, *Turkey* 73 B8
Akçadağ, *Turkey* 72 C7
Akçakale, *Turkey* 73 D8
Akçakoca, *Turkey* 72 B4
Akçaova, *Turkey* 45 E13
Akçay, *Turkey* 47 E11
Akçay →, *Turkey* 47 D10
Akdağ, *Turkey* 47 C8
Akdağmadeni, *Turkey* 72 C6
Akelamo, *Indonesia* 63 D7
Åkers styckebruk, *Sweden* 10 E11
Åkersberga, *Sweden* 10 E12
Aketi, *Dem. Rep. of the Congo* 84 D4
Akhaïa □, *Greece* 46 C3
Akhalkalaki, *Georgia* 35 K6
Akhaltsikhe, *Georgia* 35 K6
Akharnaí, *Greece* 46 C5
Akhelóös →, *Greece* 46 C3
Akhendriá, *Greece* 47 G7
Akhisar, *Turkey* 47 C9
Akhladhókambos, *Greece* 46 D4
Akhmîm, *Egypt* 80 B3
Akhnur, *India* 69 C6
Akhtopol, *Bulgaria* 45 D11
Akhtuba →, *Russia* 35 G8
Akhtubinsk, *Russia* 35 F8
Akhty, *Russia* 35 K8
Akhtyrka = Okhtyrka, *Ukraine* 33 G8
Aki, *Japan* 55 H6
Akimiski I., *Canada* 104 B3
Akimovka, *Ukraine* 33 J8
Åkirkeby, *Denmark* 11 J8
Akita, *Japan* 54 E10
Akita □, *Japan* 54 E10
Akjoujt, *Mauritania* 82 B2
Akka, *Mali* 82 B4
Akkaya Tepesi, *Turkey* 47 D11
Akkeshi, *Japan* 54 C12
'Akko, *Israel* 74 C4
Akköy, *Turkey* 47 D9
Aklampa, *Benin* 83 D5
Aklavik, *Canada* 100 B6
Aklera, *India* 68 G7
Akmenė, *Lithuania* 30 B9
Akmenrags, *Latvia* 30 B8
Akmolinsk = Astana, *Kazakhstan* 52 D8
Akmonte = Almonte, *Spain* 37 H4
Akō, *Japan* 55 G7
Ako, *Nigeria* 83 C7
Akôbô, *Sudan* 81 F3
Akobo →, *Ethiopia* 81 F3
Akola, *India* 66 J10
Akonolinga, *Cameroon* 83 E7
Akor, *Mali* 82 C3
Akordat, *Eritrea* 81 D4
Akosombo Dam, *Ghana* 83 D5
Akot, *Sudan* 81 F3
Akoupé, *Ivory C.* 82 D4
Akpatok I., *Canada* 101 B13
Åkrahamn, *Norway* 9 G11
Akranes, *Iceland* 8 D2
Akreïjit, *Mauritania* 82 B3
Akrítas Venétiko, Ákra, *Greece* 46 E3
Akron, *Colo., U.S.A.* 112 E3
Akron, *Ohio, U.S.A.* 116 E3
Akrotiri, *Cyprus* 49 E11
Akrotíri, Ákra, *Greece* 45 F9
Akrotiri Bay, *Cyprus* 49 E12
Aksai Chin, *China* 69 B8
Aksaray, *Turkey* 70 B2
Aksay, *Kazakhstan* 52 D6
Akşehir, *Turkey* 70 B1
Akşehir Gölü, *Turkey* 72 C4
Akstafa = Ağstafa, *Azerbaijan* 35 K7
Aksu, *China* 60 B3
Aksu →, *Turkey* 72 D4
Aksum, *Ethiopia* 81 E4
Aktash, *Russia* 34 C11
Aktogay, *Kazakhstan* 52 E8
Aktsyabrski, *Belarus* 33 F5
Aktyubinsk = Aqtöbe, *Kazakhstan* 52 D6
Aku, *Nigeria* 83 D6
Akure, *Nigeria* 83 D6
Akureyri, *Iceland* 8 D4
Akuseki-Shima, *Japan* 55 K4
Akusha, *Russia* 35 J8
Akwa-Ibom □, *Nigeria* 83 E6
Akyab = Sittwe, *Burma* 67 J18
Akyazı, *Turkey* 72 B4
Al 'Adan, *Yemen* 75 E4
Al Aḥsā = Hasa □, *Si. Arabia* 71 E6
Al Ajfar, *Si. Arabia* 70 E4
Al Amādīyah, *Iraq* 70 B4
Al 'Amārah, *Iraq* 70 D5
Al 'Aqabah, *Jordan* 74 F4
Al 'Aqabah □, *Jordan* 74 F4
Al Arak, *Syria* 70 C3
Al 'Aramah, *Si. Arabia* 70 E5
Al 'Arṭāwīyah, *Si. Arabia* 70 E5
Al 'Āṣimah = 'Ammān □, *Jordan* 74 D5
Al 'Assāfīyah, *Si. Arabia* 70 D3
Al 'Ayn, *Si. Arabia* 70 E3
Al 'Ayn, *U.A.E.* 71 E7
Al 'Azīzīyah, *Iraq* 70 C5
Al Bāb, *Syria* 70 B3
Al Bad', *Si. Arabia* 70 D2
Al Bādī, *Iraq* 70 C4
Al Baḥrah, *Kuwait* 70 D5
Al Baḥral Mayyit = Dead Sea, *Asia* 74 D4
Al Balqā' □, *Jordan* 74 C4
Al Bārūk, J., *Lebanon* 74 B4
Al Baṣrah, *Iraq* 70 D5
Al Baṭḥā, *Iraq* 70 D5
Al Batrūn, *Lebanon* 74 A4
Al Bayḍā, *Libya* 79 B10
Al Biqā, *Lebanon* 74 A5
Al Bi'r, *Si. Arabia* 70 D3
Al Burayj, *Syria* 74 A5
Al Faḍilī, *Si. Arabia* 71 E6
Al Fallūjah, *Iraq* 70 C4
Al Fāw, *Iraq* 71 D6
Al Fujayrah, *U.A.E.* 71 E8
Al Ghadaf, W. →, *Jordan* 74 D5
Al Ghammās, *Iraq* 70 D5
Al Ghazālah, *Si. Arabia* 70 E4
Al Ḥadīthah, *Iraq* 70 C4
Al Ḥadīthah, *Si. Arabia* 74 D6
Al Ḥaḍr, *Iraq* 70 C4
Al Ḥājānah, *Syria* 74 B5
Al Ḥajar al Gharbī, *Oman* 71 E8
Al Ḥāmad, *Si. Arabia* 70 D3
Al Hamdānīyah, *Syria* 70 C3
Al Ḥamīdīyah, *Syria* 74 A4
Al Ḥammār, *Iraq* 70 D5
Al Ḥamrā', *Si. Arabia* 70 E3
Al Ḥamzah, *Iraq* 70 D5
Al Ḥanākīyah, *Si. Arabia* 70 E4
Al Harīr, W. →, *Syria* 74 C4
Al Ḥasā, W. →, *Jordan* 74 D4
Al Ḥasakah, *Syria* 70 B4
Al Haydān, W. →, *Jordan* 74 D4
Al Ḥayy, *Iraq* 70 C5
Al Ḥijarah, *Asia* 70 D4
Al Ḥillah, *Iraq* 70 C5
Al Ḥillah, *Si. Arabia* 75 B4
Al Hindīyah, *Iraq* 70 C5
Al Hirmil, *Lebanon* 74 A5
Al Hoceïma, *Morocco* 78 A5
Al Ḥudaydah, *Yemen* 75 E3
Al Hufūf, *Si. Arabia* 71 E6
Al Ḥumayḍah, *Si. Arabia* 70 D2
Al Ḥunayy, *Si. Arabia* 71 E6
Al Īsāwīyah, *Si. Arabia* 70 D3
Al Jafr, *Jordan* 74 E5
Al Jāfūrah, *Si. Arabia* 71 E7
Al Jaghbūb, *Libya* 79 C10
Al Jahrah, *Kuwait* 70 D5
Al Jalāmīd, *Si. Arabia* 70 D3
Al Jamalīyah, *Qatar* 71 E6
Al Janūb □, *Lebanon* 74 B4
Al Jawf, *Libya* 79 D10
Al Jawf, *Si. Arabia* 70 D3
Al Jazirah, *Iraq* 70 C5
Al Jithāmīyah, *Si. Arabia* 70 E4
Al Jubayl, *Si. Arabia* 71 E6
Al Jubaylah, *Si. Arabia* 70 E5
Al Jubb, *Si. Arabia* 70 E4
Al Junaynah, *Sudan* 79 F10
Al Kabā'ish, *Iraq* 70 D5
Al Karak, *Jordan* 74 D4
Al Karak □, *Jordan* 74 E5
Al Kāẓimīyah, *Iraq* 70 C5
Al Khābūra, *Oman* 71 F8
Al Khafji, *Si. Arabia* 71 E6
Al Khalīl, *West Bank* 74 D4
Al Khāliṣ, *Iraq* 70 C5
Al Kharsānīyah, *Si. Arabia* 71 E6
Al Khaṣab, *Oman* 71 E8
Al Khawr, *Qatar* 71 E6
Al Khiḍr, *Iraq* 70 D5
Al Khiyām, *Lebanon* 74 B4
Al Khums, *Libya* 79 B8
Al Kiswah, *Syria* 74 B5
Al Kūfah, *Iraq* 70 C5
Al Kufrah, *Libya* 79 D10
Al Kuhayfīyah, *Si. Arabia* 70 E4
Al Kūt, *Iraq* 70 C5
Al Kuwayt, *Kuwait* 70 D5
Al Labwah, *Lebanon* 74 A5
Al Lādhiqīyah, *Syria* 70 C2
Al Līth, *Si. Arabia* 75 C3
Al Liwā', *Oman* 71 E8
Al Luḥayyah, *Yemen* 75 D3
Al Madīnah, *Iraq* 70 D5
Al Madīnah, *Si. Arabia* 70 E3
Al Mafraq, *Jordan* 74 C5
Al Mafraq □, *Jordan* 74 C5
Al Maḥmūdīyah, *Iraq* 70 C5
Al Majma'ah, *Si. Arabia* 70 E5
Al Makhruq, W. →, *Jordan* 74 D6
Al Makḥūl, *Si. Arabia* 70 E4
Al Manāmah, *Bahrain* 71 E6
Al Maqwa', *Kuwait* 70 D5
Al Marj, *Libya* 79 B10
Al Maṭlā, *Kuwait* 70 D5
Al Mawjib, W. →, *Jordan* 74 D4
Al Mawṣil, *Iraq* 70 B4
Al Mayādin, *Syria* 70 C4
Al Mazār, *Jordan* 74 D4
Al Midhnab, *Si. Arabia* 70 E5
Al Minā', *Lebanon* 74 A4
Al Miqdādīyah, *Iraq* 70 C5
Al Mubarraz, *Si. Arabia* 71 E6
Al Mudawwarah, *Jordan* 74 F5
Al Mughayrā', *U.A.E.* 71 E7
Al Muḥarraq, *Bahrain* 71 E6
Al Mukallā, *Yemen* 75 E4
Al Mukhā, *Yemen* 75 E3
Al Musayjīd, *Si. Arabia* 70 E3
Al Musayyib, *Iraq* 70 C5
Al Muthanná □, *Iraq* 70 D5
Al Muwayh, *Si. Arabia* 80 C5
Al Muwayliḥ, *Si. Arabia* 70 E2
Al Owuho = Otukpa, *Nigeria* 83 D6
Al Qādisīyah □, *Iraq* 70 D5
Al Qā'im, *Iraq* 70 C4
Al Qalībah, *Si. Arabia* 70 D3
Al Qāmishlī, *Syria* 70 B4
Al Qaryatayn, *Syria* 74 A6
Al Qaṣīm, *Si. Arabia* 70 E4
Al Qaṭ'ā, *Syria* 70 C4
Al Qaṭīf, *Si. Arabia* 71 E6
Al Qaṭrānah, *Jordan* 74 D5
Al Qaṭrūn, *Libya* 79 D9
Al Qayṣūmah, *Si. Arabia* 70 D5
Al Quds = Jerusalem, *Israel* 74 D4
Al Qunayṭirah, *Syria* 74 C4
Al Qunfudhah, *Si. Arabia* 80 D5
Al Qurnah, *Iraq* 70 D5
Al Quṣayr, *Iraq* 70 D5
Al Quṣayr, *Syria* 74 A5
Al Qutayfah, *Syria* 74 B5
Al 'Ubaylah, *Si. Arabia* 75 C5
Al 'Uḍaylīyah, *Si. Arabia* 71 E6
Al 'Ulā, *Si. Arabia* 70 E3
Al 'Uqayr, *Si. Arabia* 71 E6
Al 'Uwaynid, *Si. Arabia* 70 E5
Al 'Uwayqīlah, *Si. Arabia* 70 D4
Al 'Uyūn, *Ḥijāz, Si. Arabia* 70 E3
Al 'Uyūn, *Najd, Si. Arabia* 70 E4
Al 'Uzayr, *Iraq* 70 D5
Al Wajh, *Si. Arabia* 70 E3
Al Wakrah, *Qatar* 71 E6
Al Waqbah, *Si. Arabia* 70 D5
Al Wari'āh, *Si. Arabia* 70 E5
Ala, *Italy* 40 C8
Ala Dağ, *Turkey* 70 B2
Ala Dağları, *Turkey* 73 C10
Alabama □, *U.S.A.* 115 J2
Alabama →, *U.S.A.* 115 K2
Alabaster, *U.S.A.* 115 J2
Alaca, *Turkey* 72 B6
Alacaatlı, *Turkey* 47 B10
Alaçam, *Turkey* 72 B6
Alaçam Dağları, *Turkey* 47 B10
Alaçatı, *Turkey* 47 C8
Alachua, *U.S.A.* 115 L4
Alaejos, *Spain* 36 D5
Alaérma, *Greece* 49 C9
Alagir, *Russia* 35 J7
Alagna Valsésia, *Italy* 40 C4
Alagoa Grande, *Brazil* 125 E11
Alagoas □, *Brazil* 125 E11
Alagoinhas, *Brazil* 125 F11
Alagón, *Spain* 38 D3
Alagón →, *Spain* 36 F4
Alaior, *Spain* 48 B11
Alajero, *Canary Is.* 48 F2
Alajuela, *Costa Rica* 120 D3
Alakamisy, *Madag.* 89 C8
Alaknanda →, *India* 69 D8
Alakol, Ozero, *Kazakhstan* 60 B3
Alamarvdasht, *Iran* 71 E7
Alamata, *Ethiopia* 81 E4
Alameda, *Calif., U.S.A.* 110 H4
Alameda, *N. Mex., U.S.A.* 109 J10
Alaminos, *Phil.* 61 C3
Alamo, *U.S.A.* 111 J11
Alamo Crossing, *U.S.A.* 111 L13
Alamogordo, *U.S.A.* 109 K11
Alamos, *Mexico* 118 B3
Alamosa, *U.S.A.* 109 H11
Åland, *Finland* 9 F19
Alandroal, *Portugal* 37 G3
Ålands hav, *Sweden* 9 F18
Alange, Presa de, *Spain* 37 G4
Alania = North Ossetia □, *Russia* 35 J7
Alanís, *Spain* 37 G5
Alanya, *Turkey* 70 B1
Alaotra, Farihin', *Madag.* 89 B8
Alapayevsk, *Russia* 52 D7
Alappuzha = Alleppey, *India* 66 Q10
Alar del Rey, *Spain* 36 C6
Alaraz, *Spain* 36 E5
Alarcón, Embalse de, *Spain* 38 F2
Alarobia-Vohiposa, *Madag.* 89 C8
Alaşehir, *Turkey* 47 C10
Alaska □, *U.S.A.* 100 B5
Alaska, G. of, *Pac. Oc.* 100 C5
Alaska Peninsula, *U.S.A.* 100 C4
Alaska Range, *U.S.A.* 100 B4
Alássio, *Italy* 40 E5
Älät, *Azerbaijan* 35 L9
Alatri, *Italy* 41 G10
Alatyr, *Russia* 34 C8
Alatyr →, *Russia* 34 C8
Alausi, *Ecuador* 124 D3
Álava □, *Spain* 38 C2
Alava, C., *U.S.A.* 108 B1
Alaverdi, *Armenia* 35 K7
Alavus, *Finland* 9 E20
Alawoona, *Australia* 95 E3
'Alayh, *Lebanon* 74 B4
Alazani →, *Azerbaijan* 35 K8
Alba, *Italy* 40 D5
Alba □, *Romania* 29 D8
Alba Adriática, *Italy* 41 F10
Alba de Tormes, *Spain* 36 E5
Alba-Iulia, *Romania* 29 D8
Albac, *Romania* 28 D7
Albacete, *Spain* 39 F3
Albacete □, *Spain* 39 G3
Albacutya, L., *Australia* 95 F3
Ålbæk, *Denmark* 11 G4
Ålbæk Bugt, *Denmark* 11 G4
Albaida, *Spain* 39 G4
Albalate de las Nogueras, *Spain* 38 E2
Albalate del Arzobispo, *Spain* 38 D4
Alban, *France* 20 E6
Albanel, L., *Canada* 104 B5
Albania ■, *Europe* 44 E4
Albano Laziale, *Italy* 41 G9
Albany, *Australia* 93 G2
Albany, *Ga., U.S.A.* 115 K3
Albany, *N.Y., U.S.A.* 117 D11
Albany, *Oreg., U.S.A.* 108 D2
Albany, *Tex., U.S.A.* 113 J5
Albany →, *Canada* 104 B3
Albardón, *Argentina* 126 C2
Albarracín, *Spain* 38 E3
Albarracín, Sierra de, *Spain* 38 E3
Albatera, *Spain* 39 G4
Albatross B., *Australia* 94 A3
Albegna →, *Italy* 41 F8
Albemarle, *U.S.A.* 115 H5
Albemarle Sd., *U.S.A.* 115 H7
Albenga, *Italy* 40 D5
Alberche →, *Spain* 36 F6
Alberdi, *Paraguay* 126 B4
Alberes, Mts., *France* 20 F6
Ålberga, *Sweden* 11 F10
Albersdorf, *Germany* 24 A5
Albert, *France* 19 C9
Albert, L., *Africa* 86 B3
Albert, L., *Australia* 95 F2
Albert Edward Ra., *Australia* 92 C4
Albert Lea, *U.S.A.* 112 D8
Albert Nile →, *Uganda* 86 B3
Albert Town, *Bahamas* 121 B5
Alberta □, *Canada* 102 C6
Alberti, *Argentina* 126 D3
Albertinia, *S. Africa* 88 E3
Albertirsa, *Hungary* 28 C4
Alberton, *Canada* 105 C7
Albertville = Kalemie, *Dem. Rep. of the Congo* 86 D2
Albertville, *France* 21 C10
Albertville, *U.S.A.* 115 H2
Albi, *France* 20 E6
Albia, *U.S.A.* 112 E8
Albina, *Suriname* 125 B8
Albina, Ponta, *Angola* 88 B1
Albino, *Italy* 40 C6
Albion, *Mich., U.S.A.* 114 D3
Albion, *Nebr., U.S.A.* 112 E6
Albion, *Pa., U.S.A.* 116 E4
Albocácer, *Spain* 38 E5
Albolote, *Spain* 37 H7
Alborán, *Medit. S.* 37 K7
Alborea, *Spain* 39 F3
Ålborg, *Denmark* 11 G3
Ålborg Bugt, *Denmark* 11 H4
Alborz, Reshteh-ye Kūhhā-ye, *Iran* 71 C7
Albox, *Spain* 39 H2
Albufeira, *Portugal* 37 H2
Albula →, *Switz.* 25 J5
Albuñol, *Spain* 37 J7
Albuquerque, *U.S.A.* 109 J10
Albuquerque, Cayos de, *Caribbean* 120 D3
Alburg, *U.S.A.* 117 B11
Alburno, Mte., *Italy* 43 B8
Alburquerque, *Spain* 37 F4
Albury = Albury-Wodonga, *Australia* 95 F4
Albury-Wodonga, *Australia* 95 F4
Alcácer do Sal, *Portugal* 37 G2
Alcáçovas, *Portugal* 37 G2
Alcalá de Chivert, *Spain* 38 E5
Alcalá de Guadaira, *Spain* 37 H5
Alcalá de Henares, *Spain* 36 E7
Alcalá de los Gazules, *Spain* 37 J5
Alcalá del Júcar, *Spain* 39 F3
Alcalá del Río, *Spain* 37 H5
Alcalá del Valle, *Spain* 37 J5
Alcalá la Real, *Spain* 37 H7
Álcamo, *Italy* 42 E5
Alcanadre, *Spain* 38 C2
Alcanadre →, *Spain* 38 D4
Alcanar, *Spain* 38 E5
Alcanede, *Portugal* 37 F2
Alcanena, *Portugal* 37 F2
Alcañices, *Spain* 36 D4
Alcañiz, *Spain* 38 D4
Alcântara, *Brazil* 125 D10
Alcántara, *Spain* 36 F4
Alcántara, Embalse de, *Spain* 36 F4
Alcantarilla, *Spain* 39 H3
Alcaracejos, *Spain* 37 G6
Alcaraz, *Spain* 39 G2
Alcaraz, Sierra de, *Spain* 39 G2
Alcaudete, *Spain* 37 H6
Alcázar de San Juan, *Spain* 37 F7
Alchevsk, *Ukraine* 33 H10
Alcira = Alzira, *Spain* 39 F4
Alcobaça, *Portugal* 37 F2
Alcobendas, *Spain* 36 E7
Alcolea del Pinar, *Spain* 38 D2
Alcora, *Spain* 38 E4
Alcorcón, *Spain* 36 E7
Alcoutim, *Portugal* 37 H3
Alcova, *U.S.A.* 108 E10
Alcoy, *Spain* 39 G4
Alcubierre, Sierra de, *Spain* 38 D4
Alcublas, *Spain* 38 F4
Alcúdia, *Spain* 48 B10
Alcúdia, B. d', *Spain* 48 B10
Alcudia, Sierra de la, *Spain* 37 G6
Aldabra Is., *Seychelles* 77 G8
Aldama, *Mexico* 119 C5
Aldan, *Russia* 53 D13
Aldan →, *Russia* 53 C13
Aldea, Pta. de la, *Canary Is.* 48 G4
Aldeburgh, *U.K.* 15 E9
Alder Pk., *U.S.A.* 110 K5
Alderney, *U.K.* 15 H5
Aldershot, *U.K.* 15 F7
Åled, *Sweden* 11 H6
Aledo, *U.S.A.* 112 E9
Alefa, *Ethiopia* 81 E4
Aleg, *Mauritania* 82 B2
Alegranza, *Canary Is.* 48 E6
Alegranza, I., *Canary Is.* 48 E6
Alegre, *Brazil* 127 A7
Alegrete, *Brazil* 127 B4
Aleisk, *Russia* 52 D9
Aleksandriya = Oleksandriya, *Kirovohrad, Ukraine* 33 H7
Aleksandriya = Oleksandriya, *Rivne, Ukraine* 33 G4
Aleksandriyskaya, *Russia* 35 J8
Aleksandrov, *Russia* 32 D10
Aleksandrov Gay, *Russia* 34 E9
Aleksandrovac, *Serbia & M.* 44 C5
Aleksandrovac, *Serbia & M.* 44 B5
Aleksandrovka = Oleksandrovka, *Ukraine* 33 H7
Aleksandrovo, *Bulgaria* 45 C8
Aleksandrovsk-Sakhalinskiy, *Russia* 53 D15
Aleksandrów Kujawski, *Poland* 31 F5
Aleksandrów Łódźki, *Poland* 31 G6
Aleksandry, Z., *Russia* 4 A10
Alekseyevka, *Samara, Russia* 34 D10
Alekseyevka, *Voronezh, Russia* 33 G10
Aleksin, *Russia* 32 E9
Aleksinac, *Serbia & M.* 44 C5
Além Paraíba, *Brazil* 127 A7
Alemania, *Argentina* 126 B2
Alemania, *Chile* 126 B2
Alençon, *France* 18 D7
Alenquer, *Brazil* 125 D8
Alenuihaha Channel, *U.S.A.* 106 H17
Alépé, *Ivory C.* 82 D4
Aleppo = Ḥalab, *Syria* 70 B3
Aléria, *France* 21 F13
Alert, *Canada* 4 A4
Alès, *France* 21 D8
Aleşd, *Romania* 28 C7
Alessándria, *Italy* 40 D5
Ålestrup, *Denmark* 11 H3
Ålesund, *Norway* 9 E12
Alet-les-Bains, *France* 20 F6
Aletschhorn, *Switz.* 25 J4
Aleutian Is., *Pac. Oc.* 100 C2
Aleutian Trench, *Pac. Oc.* 96 C10
Alexander, *U.S.A.* 112 B3
Alexander, Mt., *Australia* 93 E3
Alexander Arch., *U.S.A.* 100 C6
Alexander Bay, *S. Africa* 88 D2

Alexander City, U.S.A. 115 J3
Alexander I., Antarctica 5 C17
Alexandra, Australia 95 F4
Alexandra, N.Z. 91 L2
Alexandra Falls, Canada 102 A5
Alexandria = El Iskandarîya, Egypt 80 H7
Alexandria, B.C., Canada 102 C4
Alexandria, Ont., Canada 117 A10
Alexandria, Romania 29 G10
Alexandria, S. Africa 88 E4
Alexandria, U.K. 13 F4
Alexandria, La., U.S.A. 113 K8
Alexandria, Minn., U.S.A. 112 C7
Alexandria, S. Dak., U.S.A. 112 D6
Alexandria, Va., U.S.A. 114 F7
Alexandria Bay, U.S.A. 117 B9
Alexandrina, L., Australia 95 F2
Alexandroúpolis, Greece 45 F9
Alexis →, Canada 105 B8
Alexis Creek, Canada 102 C4
Alfabia, Spain 48 B9
Alfambra, Spain 38 E3
Alfândega da Fé, Portugal 36 D4
Alfaro, Spain 38 C3
Alfatar, Bulgaria 45 C11
Alfaz del Pi, Spain 39 G4
Alfeld, Germany 24 D5
Alfenas, Brazil 127 A6
Alfiós →, Greece 46 D3
Alföld, Hungary 28 D5
Alfonsine, Italy 41 D9
Alford, Aberds., U.K. 13 D6
Alford, Lincs., U.K. 14 D8
Alfred, Maine, U.S.A. 117 C14
Alfred, N.Y., U.S.A. 116 D7
Alfreton, U.K. 14 D6
Alfta, Sweden 10 C10
Alga, Kazakhstan 52 E6
Algaida, Spain 48 B9
Algar, Spain 37 J5
Ålgård, Norway 9 G11
Algarinejo, Spain 37 H6
Algarve, Portugal 37 J2
Algeciras, Spain 37 J5
Algemesí, Spain 39 F4
Alger, Algeria 78 A6
Algeria ■, Africa 78 C6
Alghero, Italy 42 B1
Älghult, Sweden 11 G9
Algiers = Alger, Algeria 78 A6
Algiers ✕ (ALG), Algeria 39 J8
Algoa B., S. Africa 88 E4
Algodonales, Spain 37 J5
Algodor →, Spain 36 F7
Algoma, U.S.A. 114 C2
Algona, U.S.A. 112 D7
Algonac, U.S.A. 116 D2
Algonquin ⌂, Canada 104 C4
Algorta, Uruguay 128 C5
Alhama de Almería, Spain 37 J8
Alhama de Aragón, Spain 38 D3
Alhama de Granada, Spain 37 H7
Alhama de Murcia, Spain 39 H3
Alhambra, U.S.A. 111 L8
Alhaurín el Grande, Spain 37 J6
Alhucemas = Al Hoceïma, Morocco 78 A5
'Alī al Gharbī, Iraq 70 C5
'Alī ash Sharqī, Iraq 70 C5
Äli Bayramlı, Azerbaijan 35 L9
'Alī Khēl, Afghan. 68 C3
Ali Sahîh, Djibouti 81 E5
Alī Shāh, Iran 70 B5
Ália, Italy 42 E6
'Alīābād, Khorāsān, Iran 71 C8
'Alīābād, Kordestān, Iran 70 C5
'Alīābād, Yazd, Iran 71 D7
Aliaga, Spain 38 E4
Aliağa, Turkey 47 C8
Aliákmon →, Greece 44 F6
Alibo, Ethiopia 81 F4
Alibori →, Benin 83 C5
Alibunar, Serbia & M. 28 E5
Alicante, Spain 39 G4
Alicante □, Spain 39 G4
Alicante ✕ (ALC), Spain 39 G4
Alice, S. Africa 88 E4
Alice, U.S.A. 113 M5
Alice →, Queens., Australia 94 C3
Alice →, Queens., Australia 94 B3
Alice, Punta, Italy 43 C10
Alice Arm, Canada 102 B3
Alice Springs, Australia 94 C1
Alicedale, S. Africa 88 E4
Aliceville, U.S.A. 115 J1
Alicudi, Italy 43 D7
Aliganj, India 69 F8
Aligarh, Raj., India 68 G7
Aligarh, Ut. P., India 68 F8
Alīgūdarz, Iran 71 C6
Alijó, Portugal 36 D3
Alimnía, Greece 49 C9
Alingsås, Sweden 11 G6
Alipur, Pakistan 68 E4
Alipur Duar, India 67 F16
Aliquippa, U.S.A. 116 F4
Alishan, Taiwan 59 F13
Aliste →, Spain 36 D5
Alitus = Alytus, Lithuania 9 J21
Alivérion, Greece 46 C6
Aliwal North, S. Africa 88 E4
Alix, Canada 102 C6
Aljezur, Portugal 37 H2
Aljustrel, Portugal 37 H2
Alkamari, Niger 83 C7
Alkmaar, Neths. 17 B4
All American Canal, U.S.A. 109 K6
Allada, Benin 83 D5
Allagash →, U.S.A. 115 B11
Allah Dad, Pakistan 68 G2
Allahabad, India 69 G9
Allan, Canada 103 C7
Allanche, France 20 C6
Allanridge, S. Africa 88 D4
Allaqi, Wadi →, Egypt 80 C3
Allariz, Spain 36 C3
Allassac, France 20 C5
Ålleberg, Sweden 11 F7
Allegany, U.S.A. 116 D6
Allegheny →, U.S.A. 116 F5
Allegheny Mts., U.S.A. 114 G6
Allegheny Reservoir, U.S.A. 116 E6
Allègre, France 20 C7
Allègre, Pte., Guadeloupe 120 b
Allen, Bog of, Ireland 12 C5
Allen, L., Ireland 12 B3
Allendale, U.S.A. 115 J5
Allende, Mexico 118 B4
Allentown, U.S.A. 117 F9
Allentsteig, Austria 26 C8
Alleppey, India 66 Q10
Allepuz, Spain 38 E4
Aller →, Germany 24 C5
Alleynes B., Barbados 121 g
Alliance, Nebr., U.S.A. 112 D3
Alliance, Ohio, U.S.A. 116 F3
Allier □, France 19 F9
Allier →, France 19 F10
Alliford Bay, Canada 102 C2
Alligator Pond, Jamaica 120 a
Allinge, Denmark 11 J8
Alliston = New Tecumseth, Canada 116 B5
Alloa, U.K. 13 E5
Allones, France 18 D8
Allora, Australia 95 D5
Allos, France 21 D10
Alluitsup Paa, Greenland 101 B15
Alma, Canada 105 C5
Alma, Ga., U.S.A. 115 K4
Alma, Kans., U.S.A. 112 F6
Alma, Mich., U.S.A. 114 D3
Alma, Nebr., U.S.A. 112 E5
Alma Ata = Almaty, Kazakhstan 52 E8
Almacelles, Spain 38 D5
Almada, Portugal 37 G1
Almaden, Australia 94 B3
Almadén, Spain 37 G6
Almanor, L., U.S.A. 108 F3
Almansa, Spain 39 G3
Almanza, Spain 36 C5
Almanzor, Pico, Spain 36 E5
Almanzora →, Spain 39 H3
Almaş, Munţii, Romania 28 F7
Almassora, Spain 38 F4
Almaty, Kazakhstan 52 E8
Almazán, Spain 38 D2
Almeirim, Brazil 125 D8
Almeirim, Portugal 37 F2
Almelo, Neths. 17 B6
Almenar de Soria, Spain 38 D2
Almenara, Spain 38 F4
Almenara, Sierra de la, Spain 39 H3
Almendra, Embalse de, Spain 36 D4
Almendralejo, Spain 37 G4
Almere-Stad, Neths. 17 B5
Almería, Spain 37 J8
Almería □, Spain 39 H2
Almería, G. de, Spain 39 J2
Almetyevsk, Russia 34 C11
Älmhult, Sweden 11 H8
Almirante, Panama 120 E3
Almiropótamos, Greece 46 C6
Almirós, Greece 46 B4
Almiroú, Kólpos, Greece 49 D6
Almodôvar, Portugal 37 H2
Almodóvar del Campo, Spain 37 G6
Almodóvar del Río, Spain 37 H5
Almond, U.S.A. 116 D7
Almont, U.S.A. 116 D1
Almonte, Canada 117 A8
Almonte, Spain 37 H4
Almora, India 69 E8
Almoradí, Spain 39 G4
Almorox, Spain 36 E6
Almoustarat, Mali 83 B5
Älmsta, Sweden 10 E12
Almudévar, Spain 38 C4
Almuñécar, Spain 37 J7
Almunge, Sweden 10 E12
Almuradiel, Spain 37 G7
Alness, U.K. 13 D4
Alnmouth, U.K. 14 B6
Alnwick, U.K. 14 B6
Aloi, Uganda 86 B3
Alon, Burma 67 H19
Alonissos-Voríai Sporades △, Greece 46 B6
Alor, Indonesia 63 F6
Alor Setar, Malaysia 65 J3
Álora, Spain 37 J6
Alosno, Spain 37 H3
Alot, India 68 H6
Aloysius, Mt., Australia 93 E4
Alpaugh, U.S.A. 110 K7
Alpe Apuane ⌂, Italy 40 D7
Alpedrinha, Portugal 36 E3
Alpena, U.S.A. 114 C4
Alpes-de-Haute-Provence □, France 21 D10
Alpes-Maritimes □, France 21 E11
Alpha, Australia 94 C4
Alpha Cordillera, Arctic 4 A2
Alphen aan den Rijn, Neths. 17 B4
Alpiarça, Portugal 37 F2
Alpine, Ariz., U.S.A. 109 K9
Alpine, Calif., U.S.A. 111 N10
Alpine, Tex., U.S.A. 113 K3
Alps, Europe 6 F7
Alpu, Turkey 72 C4
Alqueta, Barragem do, Portugal 37 G3
Alrø, Denmark 11 J4
Als, Denmark 11 K3
Alsace, France 19 D14
Alsask, Canada 103 C7
Alsasua, Spain 38 C2
Alsek →, U.S.A. 102 B1
Alsfeld, Germany 24 E5
Alsten, Norway 8 D15
Alstermo, Sweden 11 H9
Alston, U.K. 14 C5
Alta, Norway 8 B20
Alta, Sierra, Spain 38 E3
Alta Gracia, Argentina 126 C3
Alta Sierra, U.S.A. 111 K8
Altaelva →, Norway 8 B20
Altafjorden, Norway 8 A20
Altai = Aerhtai Shan, Mongolia 60 B4
Altamaha →, U.S.A. 115 K5
Altamira, Brazil 125 D8
Altamira, Chile 126 B2
Altamira, Mexico 119 C5
Altamira, Cuevas de, Spain 36 B6
Altamont, U.S.A. 117 D10
Altamura, Italy 43 B9
Altanbulag, Mongolia 60 A5
Altar, Mexico 118 A2
Altar, Desierto de, Mexico 118 B2
Altata, Mexico 118 C3
Altavista, U.S.A. 114 G6
Altay, China 60 B3
Altdorf, Switz. 25 J4
Alte Mellum, Germany 24 B4
Altea, Spain 39 G4
Altenberg, Germany 24 E9
Altenbruch, Germany 24 B4
Altenburg, Germany 24 E8
Altenkirchen, Mecklenburg-Vorpommern, Germany 24 A9
Altenkirchen, Rhld-Pfz., Germany 24 E3
Altenmarkt, Austria 26 D7
Alter do Chão, Portugal 37 F3
Altınoluk, Turkey 47 B8
Altınova, Turkey 47 B8
Altıntaş, Turkey 47 B12
Altınyaka, Turkey 47 E12
Altınyayla, Turkey 47 D11
Altiplano, Bolivia 122 E4
Altkirch, France 19 E14
Altmark, Germany 24 C7
Altmühl →, Germany 25 G7
Altmühltal ⌂, Germany 25 G7
Altmunster, Austria 26 D6
Alto Adige = Trentino-Alto Adige □, Italy 41 B8
Alto Araguaia, Brazil 125 G8
Alto Cuchumatanes = Cuchumatanes, Sierra de los, Guatemala 120 C1
Alto del Carmen, Chile 126 B1
Alto del Inca, Chile 126 A2
Alto Garda Bresciano ⌂, Italy 40 C7
Alto Ligonha, Mozam. 87 F4
Alto Molocue, Mozam. 87 F4
Alto Paraguay □, Paraguay 126 A4
Alto Paraná □, Paraguay 127 B5
Alton, Canada 116 C4
Alton, U.K. 15 F7
Alton, Ill., U.S.A. 112 F9
Alton, N.H., U.S.A. 117 C13
Altona, Canada 103 D9
Altoona, U.S.A. 116 F6
Altötting, Germany 25 G8
Altstätten, Switz. 25 H5
Altun Kupri, Iraq 70 C5
Altun Shan, China 60 C3
Alturas, U.S.A. 108 F3
Altus, U.S.A. 113 H5
Alubijid, Phil. 61 G6
Alucra, Turkey 73 B8
Aluk, Sudan 81 F2
Alūksne, Latvia 9 H22
Alunda, Sweden 10 D12
Alunite, U.S.A. 111 K12
Aluoro →, Ethiopia 81 F3
Alupka, Ukraine 33 K8
Alushta, Ukraine 33 K8
Alusi, Indonesia 63 F8
Alustante, Spain 38 E3
Alva, U.S.A. 113 G5
Alvaiázere, Portugal 36 F2
Älvängen, Sweden 11 G6
Alvão ⌂, Portugal 36 D3
Alvarado, Mexico 119 D5
Alvarado, U.S.A. 113 J6
Alvaro Obregón, Presa, Mexico 118 B3
Älvdalen, Sweden 10 C8
Alvear, Argentina 126 B4
Alverca, Portugal 37 G1
Alvesta, Sweden 11 H8
Alvin, U.S.A. 113 L7
Alvinston, Canada 116 D3
Alvito, Portugal 37 G3
Älvkarleby, Sweden 10 D11
Alvord Desert, U.S.A. 108 E4
Älvros, Sweden 10 B8
Älvsbyn, Sweden 8 D19
Alwar, India 68 F7
Alxa Zuoqi, China 56 E3
Alyangula, Australia 94 A2
Alyata = Älät, Azerbaijan 35 L9
Alyth, U.K. 13 E5
Alytus, Lithuania 9 J21
Alzada, U.S.A. 112 C2
Alzey, Germany 25 F4
Alzira, Spain 39 F4
Am Timan, Chad 79 F10
Amadeus, L., Australia 93 D5
Amadi, Dem. Rep. of the Congo 86 B2
Amâdi, Sudan 81 F3
Amadjuak L., Canada 101 B12
Amadora, Portugal 37 G1
Amagansett, U.S.A. 117 F12
Amagasaki, Japan 55 G7
Amager, Denmark 11 J6
Amagunze, Nigeria 83 D6
Amahai, Indonesia 63 E7
Amakusa-Shotō, Japan 55 H5
Åmål, Sweden 10 E6
Amalfi, Italy 43 B7
Amaliás, Greece 46 D3
Amalner, India 66 J9
Amamapare, Indonesia 63 E9
Amambaí, Brazil 127 A4
Amambaí →, Brazil 127 A5
Amambay □, Paraguay 127 A4
Amambay, Cordillera de, S. Amer. 127 A4
Amami-Guntō, Japan 55 L4
Amami-Ō-Shima, Japan 55 L4
Aman, Pulau, Malaysia 65 c
Amaná, L., Brazil 124 D6
Amanat →, India 69 G11
Amanda Park, U.S.A. 110 C3
Amangeldy, Kazakhstan 52 D7
Amantea, Italy 43 C9
Amapá, Brazil 125 C8
Amapá □, Brazil 125 C8
Amara, Sudan 81 E3
Amarante, Brazil 125 E10
Amarante, Portugal 36 D2
Amaranth, Canada 103 C9
Amareleja, Portugal 37 G3
Amargosa →, U.S.A. 111 J10
Amargosa Range, U.S.A. 111 J10
Amári, Greece 49 D6
Amarillo, U.S.A. 113 H4
Amarkantak, India 69 H9
Amârna, Tell el', Sudan 80 B3
Amaro, Mte., Italy 41 F11
Amarpur, India 69 G12
Amarti, Eritrea 81 E5
Amarwara, India 69 H8
Amasra, Turkey 72 B5
Amassama, Nigeria 83 D6
Amasya, Turkey 72 B6
Amata, Australia 93 E5
Amatikulu, S. Africa 89 D5
Amatitlán, Guatemala 120 D1
Amatrice, Italy 41 F10
Amay, Belgium 17 D5
Amazon = Amazonas →, S. Amer. 125 D9
Amazonas □, Brazil 124 E6
Amazonas →, S. Amer. 125 D9
Amba Ferit, Ethiopia 81 E4
Ambah, India 68 F8
Ambahakily, Madag. 89 C7
Ambahita, Madag. 89 C8
Ambala, India 68 D7
Ambalavao, Madag. 89 C8
Ambanja, Madag. 89 A8
Ambararata, Madag. 89 B8
Ambarchik, Russia 53 C17
Ambarijeby, Madag. 89 A8
Ambaro, Helodranon', Madag. 89 A8
Ambato, Ecuador 124 D3
Ambato, Madag. 89 A8
Ambato, Sierra de, Argentina 126 B2
Ambato Boeny, Madag. 89 B8
Ambatofinandrahana, Madag. 89 C8
Ambatolampy, Madag. 89 B8
Ambatomainty, Madag. 89 B8
Ambatomanoina, Madag. 89 B8
Ambatondrazaka, Madag. 89 B8
Ambatosoratra, Madag. 89 B8
Ambelón, Greece 46 B4
Ambenja, Madag. 89 B8
Amberg, Germany 25 F7
Ambergris Cay, Belize 119 D7
Ambérieu-en-Bugey, France 21 C9
Amberley, N.Z. 91 K4
Ambert, France 20 C7
Ambidédi, Mali 82 C2
Ambikapur, India 69 H10
Ambikol, Sudan 80 C3
Ambilobé, Madag. 89 A8
Ambinanindrano, Madag. 89 C8
Ambinanitelo, Madag. 89 B8
Ambinda, Madag. 89 B8
Amble, U.K. 14 B6
Ambleside, U.K. 14 C5
Ambo, Peru 124 F3
Amboahangy, Madag. 89 C8
Ambodifototra, Madag. 89 B8
Ambodilazana, Madag. 89 B8
Ambodiriana, Madag. 89 B8
Ambohidratrimo, Madag. 89 B8
Ambohidray, Madag. 89 B8
Ambohimahamasina, Madag. 89 C8
Ambohimahasoa, Madag. 89 C8
Ambohimanga, Madag. 89 C8
Ambohimitombo, Madag. 89 C8
Ambohitra, Madag. 89 A8
Amboise, France 18 E8
Ambon, Indonesia 63 E7
Ambondro, Madag. 89 D8
Amboseli △, Kenya 86 C4
Amboseli, L., Kenya 86 C4
Ambositra, Madag. 89 C8
Ambovombe, Madag. 89 D8
Amboy, U.S.A. 111 L11
Amboyna Cay, S. China Sea 62 C4
Ambridge, U.S.A. 116 F4
Ambriz, Angola 84 F2
Amchitka I., U.S.A. 100 C1
Amderma, Russia 52 C7
Amdhi, India 69 H9
Ameca, Mexico 118 C4
Ameca →, Mexico 118 C3
Amecameca, Mexico 119 D5
Ameland, Neths. 17 A5
Amélia, Italy 41 F9
Amendolara, Italy 43 C9
Amenia, U.S.A. 117 E11
American Falls, U.S.A. 108 E7
American Falls Reservoir, U.S.A. 108 E7
American Fork, U.S.A. 108 F8
American Highland, Antarctica 5 D6
American Samoa ☑, Pac. Oc. 91 B13
Americana, Brazil 127 A6
Americus, U.S.A. 115 K3
Amerigo Vespucci, Florence ✕ (FLR), Italy 40 E8
Amersfoort, Neths. 17 B5
Amersfoort, S. Africa 89 D4
Amery Ice Shelf, Antarctica 5 C6
Ames, Spain 36 C2
Ames, U.S.A. 112 E8
Amesbury, U.S.A. 117 D14
Amet, India 68 G5
Amfíklia, Greece 46 C4
Amfilokhía, Greece 46 C3
Amfípolis, Greece 44 F7
Ámfissa, Greece 46 C4
Amga, Russia 53 C14
Amga →, Russia 53 C14
Amgu, Russia 53 E14
Amgun →, Russia 53 D14
Amherst, Canada 105 C7
Amherst, Mass., U.S.A. 117 D12
Amherst, N.Y., U.S.A. 116 D6
Amherst, Ohio, U.S.A. 116 E2
Amherst I., Canada 117 B8
Amherstburg, Canada 104 D3
Amiata, Mte., Italy 41 F8
Amidon, U.S.A. 112 B3
Amiens, France 19 C9
Amindaion, Greece 44 F5
Åminne, Sweden 11 G7
Amino, Ethiopia 81 G5
Aminuis, Namibia 88 C2
Amīrābād, Iran 70 C5
Amirante Is., Seychelles 50 K9
Amisk ⌂, Canada 103 B9
Amisk L., Canada 103 C8
Amistad ⌂, U.S.A. 113 L4
Amistad, Presa de la, Mexico 118 B4
Amite, U.S.A. 113 K9
Amla, India 68 J8
Amlapura = Karangasem, Indonesia 63 J18
Amlia I., U.S.A. 100 C2
Amlwch, U.K. 14 D3
Amm Adam, Sudan 81 D4
'Ammān, Jordan 74 D4
'Ammān □, Jordan 74 D5
'Ammān ✕ (AMM), Jordan 74 D5
Ammanford, U.K. 15 F4
Ammassalik = Tasiilaq, Greenland 4 C6
Ammerån →, Sweden 10 A10
Ammersee, Germany 25 G7
Ammochostos = Famagusta, Cyprus 49 D12
Ammon, U.S.A. 108 E8
Amnat Charoen, Thailand 64 E5
Amnura, Bangla. 69 G13
Amo Jiang →, China 58 F3
Āmol, Iran 71 B7
Amorgós, Greece 47 E7
Amory, U.S.A. 115 J1
Amos, Canada 104 C4
Åmot, Norway 9 G13
Åmotfors, Sweden 10 E6
Amoy = Xiamen, China 59 E12
Ampanavoana, Madag. 89 B9
Ampang, Malaysia 65 L3
Ampangalana, Lakandranon', Madag. 89 C8
Ampanihy, Madag. 89 C7
Amparafaravola, Madag. 89 B8
Ampasinambo, Madag. 89 C8
Ampasindava, Helodranon', Madag. 89 A8
Ampasindava, Saikanosy, Madag. 89 A8
Ampenan, Indonesia 63 K18
Amper, Nigeria 83 D6
Amper →, Germany 25 G7
Ampezzo, Italy 41 B9
Amphoe Kathu, Thailand 65 a
Amphoe Thalang, Thailand 65 a
Ampitsikinana, Réunion 89 A8
Ampombiantambo, Madag. 89 A8
Amposta, Spain 38 E5
Ampotaka, Madag. 89 D7
Ampoza, Madag. 89 C7
Amqui, Canada 105 C6
Amravati, India 66 J10
Amreli, India 68 J4
Amritsar, India 68 D6
Amroha, India 69 E8
Amrum, Germany 24 A4
Amsterdam, Neths. 17 B4
Amsterdam, U.S.A. 117 D10
Amsterdam ✕ (AMS), Neths. 17 B4
Amsterdam, I. = Nouvelle-Amsterdam, I., Ind. Oc. 3 F13
Amstetten, Austria 26 C7
Amudarya →, Uzbekistan 52 E6
Amundsen Gulf, Canada 100 A7
Amundsen-Scott, Antarctica 5 E
Amundsen Sea, Antarctica 5 D15
Amungen, Sweden 10 C9
Amuntai, Indonesia 62 E5
Amur →, Russia 53 D15
Amur, W. →, Sudan 80 D3
Amurang, Indonesia 63 D6
Amurrio, Spain 38 B1
Amursk, Russia 53 D14
Amusco, Spain 36 C6
Amvrakikós Kólpos, Greece 46 C2

Amvrosiyivka, *Ukraine* 33 J10
Amyderya = Amudarya →, *Uzbekistan* 52 E6
An Anbār □, *Iraq* 70 C4
An Bien, *Vietnam* 65 H5
An Hoa, *Vietnam* 64 E7
An Nabatīyah at Tahta, *Lebanon* 74 B4
An Nabk, *Si. Arabia* 70 D3
An Nabk, *Syria* 74 A5
An Nafūd, *Si. Arabia* 70 D4
An Najaf, *Iraq* 70 C5
An Nāşirīyah, *Iraq* 70 D5
An Nhon, *Vietnam* 64 F7
An Nîl □, *Sudan* 80 D3
An Nîl el Abyad □, *Sudan* 81 E3
An Nîl el Azraq □, *Sudan* 81 E3
An Nu'ayrīyah, *Si. Arabia* 71 E6
An Nu'mānīyah, *Iraq* 73 F11
An Nuwaybi', W. →, *Si. Arabia* 74 F3
An Thoi, Dao, *Vietnam* 65 H4
An Uaimh, *Ireland* 12 C5
Anabar →, *Russia* 53 B12
'Anabtā, *West Bank* 74 C4
Anaconda, *U.S.A.* 108 C7
Anacortes, *U.S.A.* 110 B4
Anacuao, Mt., *Phil.* 61 C4
Anadarko, *U.S.A.* 113 H5
Anadia, *Portugal* 36 E2
Anadolu, *Turkey* 72 C5
Anadyr, *Russia* 53 C18
Anadyr →, *Russia* 53 C18
Anadyrskiy Zaliv, *Russia* 53 C19
Anáfi, *Greece* 47 E7
Anafópoulo, *Greece* 47 E7
Anaga, Pta. de, *Canary Is.* 48 F3
Anagni, *Italy* 41 G10
'Ānah, *Iraq* 70 C4
Anaheim, *U.S.A.* 111 M9
Anahim Lake, *Canada* 102 C3
Anáhuac, *Mexico* 118 B4
Anakapalle, *India* 67 L13
Anakie, *Australia* 94 C4
Anaklia, *Georgia* 35 J5
Analalava, *Madag.* 89 A8
Analavoka, *Madag.* 89 C8
Análipsis, *Greece* 49 A3
Anambar →, *Pakistan* 68 D3
Anambas, Kepulauan, *Indonesia* 62 D3
Anambas Is. = Anambas, Kepulauan, *Indonesia* 62 D3
Anambra □, *Nigeria* 83 D6
Anamosa, *U.S.A.* 112 D9
Anamur, *Turkey* 70 B2
Anamur Burnu, *Turkey* 72 D5
Anan, *Japan* 55 H7
Anand, *India* 68 H5
Anánes, *Greece* 46 E6
Anantapur, *India* 66 M10
Anantnag, *India* 69 C6
Ananyiv, *Ukraine* 33 J5
Anapa, *Russia* 33 K9
Anapodháris →, *Greece* 49 E7
Anápolis, *Brazil* 125 G9
Anapu →, *Brazil* 125 D8
Anār, *Iran* 71 D7
Anārak, *Iran* 71 C7
Anarisfjällen, *Sweden* 10 A7
Anas →, *India* 68 H5
Anatolia = Anadolu, *Turkey* 72 C5
Anatsogno, *Madag.* 89 C7
Añatuya, *Argentina* 126 B3
Anaunethad L., *Canada* 103 A8
Anbyŏn, *N. Korea* 57 E14
Ancares ⌓, *Spain* 36 C4
Ancares, Sierra de, *Spain* 36 C4
Ancaster, *Canada* 116 C5
Ancenis, *France* 18 E5
Anchor Bay, *U.S.A.* 110 G3
Anchorage, *U.S.A.* 100 B5
Anci, *China* 56 E9
Ancohuma, Nevado, *Bolivia* 124 G5
Ancón, *Peru* 124 F3
Ancona, *Italy* 41 E10
Ancud, *Chile* 128 E2
Ancud, G. de, *Chile* 128 E2
Ancy-le-Franc, *France* 19 E11
Andacollo, *Argentina* 126 D1
Andacollo, *Chile* 126 C1
Andaingo, *Madag.* 89 B8
Andalgalá, *Argentina* 126 B2
Åndalsnes, *Norway* 9 E12
Andalucía □, *Spain* 37 H6
Andalusia = Andalucía □, *Spain* 37 H6
Andalusia, *U.S.A.* 115 K2
Andaman Is., *Ind. Oc.* 50 H13
Andaman Sea, *Ind. Oc.* 62 B1
Andamooka Opal Fields, *Australia* 95 E2
Andapa, *Madag.* 89 A8
Andara, *Namibia* 88 B3
Andelot-Blancheville, *France* 19 D12
Andenes, *Norway* 8 B17
Andenne, *Belgium* 17 D5
Andéranboukane, *Mali* 83 B5
Andermatt, *Switz.* 25 J4
Andernach, *Germany* 24 E3
Andernos-les-Bains, *France* 20 D2
Anderslöv, *Sweden* 11 J7
Anderson, *Alaska, U.S.A.* 100 B5
Anderson, *Calif., U.S.A.* 108 F2
Anderson, *Ind., U.S.A.* 114 E3
Anderson, *Mo., U.S.A.* 113 G7
Anderson, *S.C., U.S.A.* 115 H4
Anderson →, *Canada* 100 B7
Anderstorp, *Sweden* 11 G7
Andes, *U.S.A.* 117 D10
Andes, Cord. de los, *S. Amer.* 124 H5
Andfjorden, *Norway* 8 B17
Andhra Pradesh □, *India* 66 L11
Andijon, *Uzbekistan* 52 E8
Andikíthira, *Greece* 46 F5
Andilamena, *Madag.* 89 B8
Andīmeshk, *Iran* 71 C6
Andímilos, *Greece* 46 E6
Andíparos, *Greece* 47 D7
Andípaxoi, *Greece* 46 B2
Andípsara, *Greece* 47 C7
Andírrion, *Greece* 46 C3
Andizhan = Andijon, *Uzbekistan* 52 E8
Andoain, *Spain* 38 B2
Andoany, *Madag.* 89 A8
Andohahela ⌓, *Madag.* 89 C8
Andong, *S. Korea* 57 F15
Andongwei, *China* 57 G10
Andoom, *Australia* 94 A3
Andorra, *Spain* 38 E4
Andorra ■, *Europe* 20 F5
Andorra La Vella, *Andorra* 20 F5
Andover, *U.K.* 15 F6
Andover, *Maine, U.S.A.* 117 B14
Andover, *Mass., U.S.A.* 117 D13
Andover, *N.J., U.S.A.* 117 F10
Andover, *N.Y., U.S.A.* 116 D7
Andover, *Ohio, U.S.A.* 116 E4
Andøya, *Norway* 8 B16
Andradina, *Brazil* 125 H8
Andrahary, Mt., *Madag.* 89 A8
Andramasina, *Madag.* 89 B8
Andranopasy, *Madag.* 89 C7
Andranovory, *Madag.* 89 C7
Andratx, *Spain* 48 B9
Andreanof Is., *U.S.A.* 100 C2
Andreapol, *Russia* 32 D7
Andrews, *S.C., U.S.A.* 115 J6
Andrews, *Tex., U.S.A.* 113 J3
Andreyevka, *Russia* 34 D10
Ándria, *Italy* 43 A9
Andriamena, *Madag.* 89 B8
Andriandampy, *Madag.* 89 C8
Andriba, *Madag.* 89 B8
Andrijevica, *Serbia & M.* 44 D3
Andringitra ⌓, *Madag.* 89 C8
Andrítsaina, *Greece* 46 D3
Androka, *Madag.* 89 C7
Andropov = Rybinsk, *Russia* 32 C10
Ándros, *Greece* 46 D6
Andros I., *Bahamas* 120 B4
Andros Town, *Bahamas* 120 B4
Androscoggin →, *U.S.A.* 117 C14
Andrychów, *Poland* 31 J6
Andselv, *Norway* 8 B18
Andújar, *Spain* 37 G6
Andulo, *Angola* 84 G3
Aneby, *Sweden* 11 G8
Anegada I., *Br. Virgin Is.* 121 e
Anegada Passage, *W. Indies* 121 C7
Anécho, *Togo* 83 D5
Anenni-Noi, *Moldova* 29 D14
Aneto, Pico de, *Spain* 38 C5
Anfu, *China* 59 D10
Ang Mo Kio, *Singapore* 65 d
Ang Thong, *Thailand* 64 E3
Ang Thong △, *Thailand* 65 H2
Ang Thong, Ko, *Thailand* 65 b
Angamos, Punta, *Chile* 126 A1
Angara →, *Russia* 53 D10
Angara-Débou, *Benin* 83 C5
Angarab, *Ethiopia* 81 E4
Angarbaka, *Sudan* 81 F1
Angarsk, *Russia* 53 D11
Angas Hills, *Australia* 92 D4
Angaston, *Australia* 95 E2
Ånge, *Sweden* 10 B9
Ángel, Salto = Angel Falls, *Venezuela* 124 B6
Ángel de la Guarda, I., *Mexico* 118 B2
Angel Falls, *Venezuela* 124 B6
Angeles, *Phil.* 61 D4
Ängelholm, *Sweden* 11 H6
Angels Camp, *U.S.A.* 110 G6
Ängelsberg, *Sweden* 10 E10
Anger →, *Ethiopia* 81 F4
Angereb →, *Ethiopia* 81 E4
Ångermanälven →, *Sweden* 10 B11
Ångermanland, *Sweden* 8 E18
Angermünde, *Germany* 24 B9
Angers, *Canada* 117 A9
Angers, *France* 18 E6
Angerville, *France* 19 D9
Ångesån →, *Sweden* 8 C20
Angikuni L., *Canada* 103 A9
Angkor, *Cambodia* 64 F4
Anglès, *Spain* 38 D7
Anglesey, Isle of □, *U.K.* 14 D3
Anglet, *France* 20 E2
Angleton, *U.S.A.* 113 L7
Anglin →, *France* 20 B4
Anglisidhes, *Cyprus* 49 E12
Anglure, *France* 19 D10
Angmagssalik = Tasiilaq, *Greenland* 4 C6
Ango, *Dem. Rep. of the Congo* 86 B2
Angoche, *Mozam.* 87 F4
Angoche, I., *Mozam.* 87 F4
Angol, *Chile* 126 D1
Angola, *Ind., U.S.A.* 114 E3
Angola, *N.Y., U.S.A.* 116 D5
Angola ■, *Africa* 85 G3
Angoulême, *France* 20 C4
Angoumois, *France* 20 C4
Angra dos Reis, *Brazil* 127 A7
Angren, *Uzbekistan* 52 E8
Angtassom, *Cambodia* 65 G5
Angu, *Dem. Rep. of the Congo* 86 B1
Anguang, *China* 57 B12
Anguilla ☑, *W. Indies* 121 C7
Anguo, *China* 56 E8
Angurugu, *Australia* 94 A2
Angus □, *U.K.* 13 E6
Angwa →, *Zimbabwe* 89 B5
Anhanduí →, *Brazil* 127 A5
Anholt, *Denmark* 11 H5
Anhua, *China* 59 C8
Anhui □, *China* 59 B11
Anhwei = Anhui □, *China* 59 B11
Anichab, *Namibia* 88 C1
Ánidhros, *Greece* 47 E7
Anié, *Togo* 83 D5
Animas →, *U.S.A.* 109 H9
Anina, *Romania* 28 E6
Aninoasa, *Romania* 29 F9
Anivorano, *Madag.* 89 B8
Anjalankoski, *Finland* 9 F22
Anjar, *India* 68 H4
Anji, *China* 59 B12
Anjou, *France* 18 E6
Anjozorobe, *Madag.* 89 B8
Anju, *N. Korea* 57 E13
Anka, *Nigeria* 83 C6
Ankaboa, Tanjona, *Madag.* 89 C7
Ankang, *China* 56 H5
Ankara, *Turkey* 72 C5
Ankarafantsika ⌓, *Madag.* 89 B8
Ankaramena, *Madag.* 89 C8
Ankaratra, *Madag.* 85 H9
Ankarsrum, *Sweden* 11 G10
Ankasakasa, *Madag.* 89 B7
Ankavandra, *Madag.* 89 B8
Ankazoabo, *Madag.* 89 C7
Ankazobe, *Madag.* 89 B8
Ankeny, *U.S.A.* 112 E8
Ankilimalinika, *Madag.* 89 C7
Ankilizato, *Madag.* 89 C8
Ankisabe, *Madag.* 89 B8
Anklam, *Germany* 24 B9
Ankober, *Ethiopia* 81 F4
Ankoro, *Dem. Rep. of the Congo* 86 D2
Ankororoka, *Madag.* 89 D8
Anlong, *China* 58 E5
Anlu, *China* 59 B9
Anmyŏn-do, *S. Korea* 57 F14
Ånn, *Sweden* 10 A6
Ann, C., *U.S.A.* 117 D14
Ann Arbor, *U.S.A.* 114 D4
Anna, *Russia* 34 E5
Anna, *U.S.A.* 113 G10
Annaba, *Algeria* 78 A7
Annaberg-Buchholz, *Germany* 24 E9
Annalee →, *Ireland* 12 B4
Annam, *Vietnam* 64 E7
Annamitique, Chaîne, *Asia* 64 D6
Annan, *U.K.* 13 G5
Annan →, *U.K.* 13 G5
Annapolis, *U.S.A.* 114 F7
Annapolis Royal, *Canada* 105 D6
Annapurna, *Nepal* 69 E10
Annean, L., *Australia* 93 E2
Anneberg, *Sweden* 11 G8
Annecy, *France* 21 C10
Annecy, Lac d', *France* 21 C10
Annemasse, *France* 19 F13
Annenskiy Most, *Russia* 32 B9
Anning, *China* 58 E4
Anniston, *U.S.A.* 115 J3
Annobón, *Atl. Oc.* 77 G4
Annonay, *France* 21 C8
Annot, *France* 21 E10
Annotto Bay, *Jamaica* 120 a
Ånnsjön, *Sweden* 10 A6
Annville, *U.S.A.* 117 F8
Annweiler, *Germany* 25 F3
Áno Arkhánai, *Greece* 47 F7
Áno Porróia, *Greece* 44 E7
Áno Síros, *Greece* 46 D6
Áno Viánnos, *Greece* 49 D7
Anorotsangana, *Madag.* 89 A8
Anosibe, *Madag.* 89 B8
Anou Mellene, *Mali* 83 B5
Anoumaba, *Ivory C.* 82 D4
Anóyia, *Greece* 49 D6
Anping, *Hebei, China* 56 E8
Anping, *Liaoning, China* 57 D12
Anpu Gang, *China* 58 G7
Anqing, *China* 59 B11
Anqiu, *China* 57 F10
Anren, *China* 59 D9
Ansager, *Denmark* 11 J2
Ansai, *China* 56 F5
Ansbach, *Germany* 25 F6
Anseba →, *Eritrea* 81 D4
Ansfelden, *Austria* 26 C7
Anshan, *China* 57 D12
Anshun, *China* 58 D5
Ansião, *Portugal* 36 F2
Ansley, *U.S.A.* 112 E5
Ansó, *Spain* 38 C4
Ansoain, *Spain* 38 C3
Anson, *U.S.A.* 113 J5
Anson B., *Australia* 92 B5
Ansongo, *Mali* 83 B5
Ansongo-Ménaka ⌓, *Mali* 83 B5
Ansonia, *U.S.A.* 117 E11
Anstruther, *U.K.* 13 E6
Ansudu, *Indonesia* 63 E9
Antabamba, *Peru* 124 F4
Antakya, *Turkey* 70 B3
Antalaha, *Madag.* 89 A9
Antalya, *Turkey* 72 D4
Antalya □, *Turkey* 47 E12
Antalya Körfezi, *Turkey* 72 D4
Antambohobe, *Madag.* 89 C8
Antanambao-Manampotsy, *Madag.* 89 B8
Antanambe, *Madag.* 89 B8
Antananarivo, *Madag.* 89 B8
Antananarivo □, *Madag.* 89 B8
Antanifotsy, *Madag.* 89 B8
Antanimbaribe, *Madag.* 89 C7
Antanimora, *Madag.* 89 C8
Antarctic Pen., *Antarctica* 5 C18
Antarctica 5 E3
Antelope, *Zimbabwe* 87 G2
Antequera, *Paraguay* 126 A4
Antequera, *Spain* 37 H6
Antero, Mt., *U.S.A.* 109 G10
Antevamena, *Madag.* 89 C7
Anthemoús, *Greece* 44 F7
Anthony, *Kans., U.S.A.* 113 G5
Anthony, *N. Mex., U.S.A.* 109 K10
Anti Atlas, *Morocco* 78 C4
Anti-Lebanon = Ash Sharqi, Al Jabal, *Lebanon* 74 B5
Antibes, *France* 21 E11
Antibes, C. d', *France* 21 E11
Anticosti, Î. d', *Canada* 105 C7
Antifer, C. d', *France* 18 C7
Antigo, *U.S.A.* 112 C10
Antigonish, *Canada* 105 C7
Antigua, *Canary Is.* 48 F5
Antigua, *Guatemala* 120 D1
Antigua, *W. Indies* 121 C7
Antigua & Barbuda ■, *W. Indies* 121 C7
Antilla, *Cuba* 120 B4
Antilles = West Indies, *Cent. Amer.* 121 D7
Antioch, *U.S.A.* 110 G5
Antioche, Pertuis d', *France* 20 B2
Antioquia, *Colombia* 124 B3
Antipodes Is., *Pac. Oc.* 96 M9
Antlers, *U.S.A.* 113 H7
Antoetra, *Madag.* 89 C8
Antofagasta, *Chile* 126 A1
Antofagasta □, *Chile* 126 A2
Antofagasta de la Sierra, *Argentina* 126 B2
Antofalla, *Argentina* 126 B2
Antofalla, Salar de, *Argentina* 126 B2
Anton, *U.S.A.* 113 J3
Antongila, Helodrano, *Madag.* 89 B8
Antonibé, *Madag.* 89 B8
Antonibé, Presqu'île d', *Madag.* 89 A8
Antonina, *Brazil* 127 B6
Antrain, *France* 18 D5
Antrim, *U.K.* 12 B5
Antrim, *U.S.A.* 116 F3
Antrim □, *U.K.* 12 B5
Antrim, Mts. of, *U.K.* 12 A5
Antrim Plateau, *Australia* 92 C4
Antrodoco, *Italy* 41 F10
Antropovo, *Russia* 34 A6
Antsakabary, *Madag.* 89 B8
Antsalova, *Madag.* 89 B7
Antsenavolo, *Madag.* 89 C8
Antsiafabositra, *Madag.* 89 B8
Antsirabe, *Antananarivo, Madag.* 89 B8
Antsirabe, *Antsiranana, Madag.* 89 A8
Antsirabe, *Mahajanga, Madag.* 89 B8
Antsiranana, *Madag.* 89 A8
Antsiranana □, *Madag.* 89 A8
Antsohihy, *Madag.* 89 A8
Antsohimbondrona Seranana, *Madag.* 89 A8
Antu, *China* 57 C15
Antwerp = Antwerpen, *Belgium* 17 C4
Antwerp, *U.S.A.* 117 B9
Antwerpen, *Belgium* 17 C4
Antwerpen □, *Belgium* 17 C4
Anupgarh, *India* 68 E5
Anuppur, *India* 69 H9
Anuradhapura, *Sri Lanka* 66 Q12
Anveh, *Iran* 71 E7
Anvers = Antwerpen, *Belgium* 17 C4
Anvers I., *Antarctica* 5 C17
Anwen, *China* 59 C13
Anxi, *Fujian, China* 59 E12
Anxi, *Gansu, China* 60 B4
Anxian, *China* 58 B5
Anxiang, *China* 59 C9
Anxious B., *Australia* 95 E1
Anyama, *Ivory C.* 82 D4
Anyang, *China* 56 F8
Anyer-Kidul, *Indonesia* 63 G11
Anyi, *Jiangxi, China* 59 C10
Anyi, *Shanxi, China* 56 G6
Anyuan, *China* 59 E10
Anyue, *China* 58 B5
Anza, *U.S.A.* 111 M10
Anze, *China* 56 F7
Anzhero-Sudzhensk, *Russia* 52 D9
Ánzio, *Italy* 42 A5
Ao Makham, *Thailand* 65 a
Ao Phangnga △, *Thailand* 65 a
Aoga-Shima, *Japan* 55 H9
Aoiz, *Spain* 38 C3
Aomen = Macau, *China* 59 F9
Aomori, *Japan* 54 D10
Aomori □, *Japan* 54 D10
Aonla, *India* 69 E8
Aoraki Mount Cook, *N.Z.* 91 K3
Aosta, *Italy* 40 C4
Aotearoa = New Zealand ■, *Oceania* 91 J6
Aoudéras, *Niger* 83 B6
Aoukâr, *Mauritania* 82 B3
Aozou Strip, *Chad* 79 D9
Apa →, *S. Amer.* 126 A4
Apache, *U.S.A.* 113 H5
Apache Junction, *U.S.A.* 109 K8
Apalachee B., *U.S.A.* 115 L4
Apalachicola, *U.S.A.* 115 L3
Apalachicola →, *U.S.A.* 115 L3
Apam, *Ghana* 83 D4
Apapa, *Nigeria* 83 D5
Apaporis →, *Colombia* 124 D5
Aparados da Serra △, *Brazil* 127 B5
Aparri, *Phil.* 61 B4
Apateu, *Romania* 28 D6
Apatin, *Serbia & M.* 28 E4
Apatity, *Russia* 52 C4
Apatzingán, *Mexico* 118 D4
Apeldoorn, *Neths.* 17 B5
Apen, *Germany* 24 B3
Apennines = Appennini, *Italy* 40 E7
Aphrodisias, *Turkey* 47 D10
Apia, *Samoa* 91 A13
Apiacás, Serra dos, *Brazil* 124 E7
Apies →, *S. Africa* 89 D4
Apizaco, *Mexico* 119 D5
Aplao, *Peru* 124 G4
Apo, Mt., *Phil.* 63 C7
Apolakkiá, *Greece* 49 C9
Apolakkiá, Órmos, *Greece* 49 C9
Apolda, *Germany* 24 D7
Apollonia, *Greece* 46 E6
Apolo, *Bolivia* 124 F5
Aporé →, *Brazil* 125 G8
Apostle Is., *U.S.A.* 112 B9
Apostle Islands Nat. Lakeshore, *U.S.A.* 112 B9
Apóstoles, *Argentina* 127 B4
Apostolos Andreas, C., *Cyprus* 49 D13
Apostolovo, *Ukraine* 33 J7
Apoteri, *Guyana* 124 C7
Appalachian Mts., *U.S.A.* 114 G6
Äppelbo, *Sweden* 10 D8
Appennini, *Italy* 40 E7
Appennino Ligure, *Italy* 40 D6
Appenzell-Ausser Rhoden □, *Switz.* 25 H5
Appenzell-Inner Rhoden □, *Switz.* 25 H5
Appiano, *Italy* 41 B8
Apple Hill, *Canada* 117 A10
Apple Valley, *U.S.A.* 111 L9
Appleby-in-Westmorland, *U.K.* 14 C5
Appledore, *U.K.* 15 F3
Appleton, *U.S.A.* 114 C1
Approuague →, *Fr. Guiana* 125 C8
Apricena, *Italy* 41 G12
Aprília, *Italy* 42 A5
Apsheronsk, *Russia* 35 H4
Apsley, *Canada* 116 B6
Apt, *France* 21 E9
Apuane, Alpi, *Italy* 40 D7
Apucarana, *Brazil* 127 A5
Apulia = Púglia □, *Italy* 43 A9
Apure →, *Venezuela* 124 B5
Apurimac →, *Peru* 124 F4
Apuseni, Munţii, *Romania* 28 D7
Āqā Jarī, *Iran* 71 D6
Aqaba = Al 'Aqabah, *Jordan* 74 F4
Aqaba, G. of, *Red Sea* 70 D2
'Aqabah, Khalīj al = Aqaba, G. of, *Red Sea* 70 D2
'Aqdā, *Iran* 71 C7
Aqîq, *Sudan* 80 D4
Aqîq, Khalîg, *Sudan* 80 D4
Aqmola = Astana, *Kazakhstan* 52 D8
'Aqrah, *Iraq* 70 B4
Aqtaū, *Kazakhstan* 52 E6
Aqtöbe, *Kazakhstan* 52 D6
Aquidauana, *Brazil* 125 H7
Aquiles Serdán, *Mexico* 118 B3
Aquin, *Haiti* 121 C5
Aquitaine □, *France* 20 D3
Ar Rachidiya = Er Rachidia, *Morocco* 78 B5
Ar Rafīd, *Syria* 74 C4
Ar Raḩḩālīyah, *Iraq* 70 C4
Ar Ramādī, *Iraq* 70 C4
Ar Ramthā, *Jordan* 74 C5
Ar Raqqah, *Syria* 70 C3
Ar Rass, *Si. Arabia* 70 E4
Ar Rawshān, *Si. Arabia* 80 C5
Ar Rifā'ī, *Iraq* 70 D5
Ar Riyāḑ, *Si. Arabia* 70 E5
Ar Ru'ays, *Qatar* 71 E6
Ar Rukhaymīyah, *Iraq* 70 D5
Ar Ruşāfah, *Syria* 70 C3
Ar Ruţbah, *Iraq* 70 C4
Ara, *India* 69 G11
Ara Goro, *Ethiopia* 81 F5
Ara Tera, *Ethiopia* 81 F5
Arab, *U.S.A.* 115 H2
'Arab, Bahr el →, *Sudan* 81 F2
Arab, Khalîg el, *Egypt* 80 A2
Arab, Shatt al →, *Asia* 71 D6
'Araba, W. →, *Egypt* 80 J8
'Arabābād, *Iran* 71 C8
Araban, *Turkey* 72 D7
Arabatskaya Strelka, *Ukraine* 33 K8
Arabba, *Italy* 41 B8
Arabia, *Asia* 50 G8
Arabian Desert = Es Sahrâ' Esh Sharqîya, *Egypt* 80 B3
Arabian Gulf = Gulf, The, *Asia* 71 E6
Arabian Sea, *Ind. Oc.* 50 H10
Araç, *Turkey* 72 B5
Aracaju, *Brazil* 125 F11
Aracati, *Brazil* 125 D11
Araçatuba, *Brazil* 127 A5
Aracena, *Spain* 37 H4
Aracena, Sierra de, *Spain* 37 H4
Aračinovo, *Macedonia* 44 D5
Araçuaí, *Brazil* 125 G10
'Arad, *Israel* 74 D4
Arad, *Romania* 28 D6
Arad □, *Romania* 28 D6
Arādān, *Iran* 71 C7
Aradhippou, *Cyprus* 49 E12
Arafura Sea, *E. Indies* 96 H5
Aragats, *Armenia* 35 K7
Aragón □, *Spain* 38 D4
Aragón →, *Spain* 38 C3
Aragona, *Italy* 42 E6
Araguacema, *Brazil* 125 E9
Araguaia →, *Brazil* 125 E9
Araguaína, *Brazil* 125 E9
Araguari, *Brazil* 125 G9
Araguari →, *Brazil* 125 C9
Arain, *India* 68 F6
Arak, *Algeria* 78 C6
Arāk, *Iran* 71 C6
Araka, *Sudan* 81 G3
Arakan Coast, *Burma* 67 K19

Arakan Yoma, *Burma* 67 K19
Arákhova, *Greece* 46 C4
Arakli, *Turkey* 73 B8
Araks = Aras, Rūd-e →, *Asia* 35 K9
Aral, *Kazakhstan* 52 E7
Aral Sea, *Asia* 52 E7
Aral Tengizi = Aral Sea, *Asia* 52 E7
Aralsk = Aral, *Kazakhstan* 52 E7
Aralskoye More = Aral Sea, *Asia* 52 E7
Aralsor, Ozero, *Kazakhstan* 35 F9
Aramac, *Australia* 94 C4
Aran I., *Ireland* 12 A3
Aran Is., *Ireland* 12 C2
Aranda de Duero, *Spain* 36 D7
Arandān, *Iran* 70 C5
Aranđelovac, *Serbia & M.* 44 B4
Aranjuez, *Spain* 36 E7
Aranos, *Namibia* 88 C2
Aransas Pass, *U.S.A.* 113 M6
Aranyaprathet, *Thailand* 64 F4
Araouane, *Mali* 82 B4
Arapahoe, *U.S.A.* 112 E5
Arapey Grande →, *Uruguay* 126 C4
Arapgir, *Turkey* 70 B3
Arapiraca, *Brazil* 125 E11
Arapongas, *Brazil* 127 A5
Ar'ar, *Si. Arabia* 70 D4
Araranguá, *Brazil* 127 B6
Araraquara, *Brazil* 125 H9
Ararás, Serra das, *Brazil* 127 B5
Ararat, *Armenia* 73 C11
Ararat, *Australia* 95 F3
Ararat, Mt. = Ağrı Dağı, *Turkey* 70 B5
Araria, *India* 69 F12
Araripe, Chapada do, *Brazil* 125 E11
Araruama, L. de, *Brazil* 127 A7
Aras, Rūd-e →, *Asia* 35 K9
Aratāne, *Mauritania* 82 B3
Arauca, *Colombia* 124 B4
Arauca →, *Venezuela* 124 B5
Arauco, *Chile* 126 D1
Arawa, *Ethiopia* 81 F5
Arawale ⌂, *Kenya* 86 C5
Araxá, *Brazil* 125 G9
Araya, Pen. de, *Venezuela* 124 A6
Arba Gugu, *Ethiopia* 81 F5
Arba Minch, *Ethiopia* 81 F4
Arbat, *Iraq* 70 C5
Árbatax, *Italy* 42 C2
Arbi, *Ethiopia* 81 F4
Arbīl, *Iraq* 70 B5
Arboga, *Sweden* 10 E9
Arbois, *France* 19 F12
Arbore, *Ethiopia* 81 F4
Arboréa, *Italy* 42 C1
Arborfield, *Canada* 103 C8
Arborg, *Canada* 103 C9
Arbre du Ténéré, *Niger* 83 B7
Arbroath, *U.K.* 13 E6
Arbuckle, *U.S.A.* 110 F4
Arbus, *Italy* 42 C1
Arc →, *France* 21 C10
Arc-lès-Gray, *France* 19 E12
Arcachon, *France* 20 D2
Arcachon, Bassin d', *France* 20 D2
Arcade, *Calif., U.S.A.* 111 L8
Arcade, *N.Y., U.S.A.* 116 D6
Arcadia, *Fla., U.S.A.* 115 M5
Arcadia, *La., U.S.A.* 113 J8
Arcadia, *Pa., U.S.A.* 116 F6
Arcata, *U.S.A.* 108 F1
Arcévia, *Italy* 41 E9
Archangel = Arkhangelsk, *Russia* 52 C5
Archar, *Bulgaria* 44 C6
Archbald, *U.S.A.* 117 E9
Archena, *Spain* 39 G3
Archer →, *Australia* 94 A3
Archer B., *Australia* 94 A3
Archer Bend = Mungkan Kandju △, *Australia* 94 A3
Archers Post, *Kenya* 86 B4
Arches △, *U.S.A.* 109 G9
Archidona, *Spain* 37 H6
Archipel-de-Mingan △, *Canada* 105 B7
Archipiélago Chinijo △, *Canary Is.* 48 E6
Archipiélago Los Roques △, *Venezuela* 121 D6
Arci, Mte., *Italy* 42 C1
Arcidosso, *Italy* 41 F8
Arcipelago de la Maddalena △, *Italy* 42 A2
Arcipelago Toscano △, *Italy* 40 F7
Arcis-sur-Aube, *France* 19 D11
Arckaringa Cr. →, *Australia* 95 D2
Arco, *Italy* 40 C7
Arco, *U.S.A.* 108 E7
Arcos = Arcos de Jalón, *Spain* 38 D2
Arcos de Jalón, *Spain* 38 D2
Arcos de la Frontera, *Spain* 37 J5
Arcos de Valdevez, *Portugal* 36 D2
Arcot, *India* 66 N11
Arcozelo, *Portugal* 36 E3
Arctic Bay, *Canada* 101 A11
Arctic Ocean, *Arctic* 4 B18
Arctic Red River = Tsiigehtchic, *Canada* 100 B6
Arctowski, *Antarctica* 5 C18
Arda →, *Bulgaria* 45 E10
Arda →, *Italy* 40 C7
Ardabīl, *Iran* 71 B6
Ardabīl □, *Iran* 71 B6
Ardahan, *Turkey* 73 B10
Ardakān = Sepīdān, *Iran* 71 D7
Ardakān, *Iran* 71 C7
Ardala, *Sweden* 11 F7
Ardales, *Spain* 37 J6
Ardèche □, *France* 21 D8
Ardèche →, *France* 21 D8
Ardee, *Ireland* 12 C5
Arden, *Canada* 116 B8
Arden, *Denmark* 11 H3
Arden, *Calif., U.S.A.* 110 G5
Arden, *Nev., U.S.A.* 111 J11
Ardenne, *Belgium* 17 E5
Ardennes = Ardenne, *Belgium* 17 E5
Ardennes □, *France* 19 C11
Ardentes, *France* 19 F8
Arderin, *Ireland* 12 C4
Ardeşen, *Turkey* 73 B9
Ardestān, *Iran* 71 C7
Árdhas →, *Greece* 45 E10
Ardhéa, *Greece* 44 F6
Ardila →, *Portugal* 37 G3
Ardino, *Bulgaria* 45 E9
Ardivachar Pt., *U.K.* 13 D1
Ardlethan, *Australia* 95 E4
Ardmore, *Okla., U.S.A.* 113 H6
Ardmore, *Pa., U.S.A.* 117 G9
Ardnamurchan, Pt. of, *U.K.* 13 E2
Ardnave Pt., *U.K.* 13 F2
Ardon, *Russia* 35 J7
Ardore, *Italy* 43 D9
Ardres, *France* 19 B8
Ardrossan, *Australia* 95 E2
Ardrossan, *U.K.* 13 F4
Ards Pen., *U.K.* 12 B6
Arduan, *Sudan* 80 D3
Ardud, *Romania* 28 C7
Åre, *Sweden* 10 A7
Arecibo, *Puerto Rico* 121 d
Areia Branca, *Brazil* 125 E11
Arena, Pt., *U.S.A.* 110 G3
Arenal, *Honduras* 120 C2
Arenas = Las Arenas, *Spain* 36 B6
Arenas de San Pedro, *Spain* 36 E5
Arendal, *Norway* 9 G13
Arendsee, *Germany* 24 C7
Arenys de Mar, *Spain* 38 D7
Arenzano, *Italy* 40 D5
Areópolis, *Greece* 46 E4
Arequipa, *Peru* 124 G4
Arero, *Ethiopia* 81 G4
Arès, *France* 20 D2
Arévalo, *Spain* 36 D6
Arezzo, *Italy* 41 E8
Arga, *Turkey* 70 B3
Arga →, *Spain* 38 C3
Argalasti, *Greece* 46 B5
Argamasilla de Alba, *Spain* 37 F7
Argamasilla de Calatrava, *Spain* 37 G6
Arganda, *Spain* 36 E7
Arganil, *Portugal* 36 E2
Argedeb, *Ethiopia* 81 F5
Argelès-Gazost, *France* 20 E3
Argelès-sur-Mer, *France* 20 F7
Argens →, *France* 21 E10
Argent-sur-Sauldre, *France* 19 E9
Argenta, *Canada* 102 C5
Argenta, *Italy* 41 D8
Argentan, *France* 18 D6
Argentário, Mte., *Italy* 41 F8
Argentat, *France* 20 C5
Argentera, *Italy* 40 D4
Argenteuil, *France* 19 D9
Argentia, *Canada* 105 C9
Argentiera, C. dell', *Italy* 42 B1
Argentina ■, *S. Amer.* 128 D3
Argentino, L., *Argentina* 128 G2
Argenton-Château, *France* 18 F6
Argenton-sur-Creuse, *France* 19 F8
Argeş □, *Romania* 29 F9
Argeş →, *Romania* 29 F11
Arghandab →, *Afghan.* 68 D1
Argheile, *Ethiopia* 81 F5
Argo, *Sudan* 80 D3
Argolikós Kólpos, *Greece* 46 D4
Argolís □, *Greece* 46 D4
Argonne, *France* 19 C12
Árgos, *Greece* 46 D4
Árgos Orestikón, *Greece* 44 F5
Argostólion, *Greece* 46 C2
Arguedas, *Spain* 38 C3
Arguello, Pt., *U.S.A.* 111 L6
Arguineguín, *Canary Is.* 48 G4
Argun, *Russia* 35 J7
Argun →, *Russia* 53 D13
Argungu, *Nigeria* 83 C5
Argus Pk., *U.S.A.* 111 K9
Argyle, L., *Australia* 92 C4
Argyll ⌂, *U.K.* 13 E4
Argyll & Bute □, *U.K.* 13 E3
Arhavi, *Turkey* 73 B9
Århus, *Denmark* 11 H4
Århus Amtskommune □, *Denmark* 11 H4
Ariadnoye, *Russia* 54 B7
Ariamsvlei, *Namibia* 88 D2
Ariano Irpino, *Italy* 43 A8
Aribinda, *Burkina Faso* 83 C4
Arica, *Chile* 124 G4
Arica, *Colombia* 124 D4
Arico, *Canary Is.* 48 F3
Arid, C., *Australia* 93 F3
Arida, *Japan* 55 G7
Ariège □, *France* 20 F5
Ariège →, *France* 20 E5
Arieş →, *Romania* 29 D8
Arihā, *Israel* 80 A4
Arilje, *Serbia & M.* 44 C4
Arílla, Ákra, *Greece* 49 A3
Arima, *Trin. & Tob.* 121 D7
Arinos →, *Brazil* 124 F7
Ario de Rosales, *Mexico* 118 D4
Ariogala, *Lithuania* 30 C10
Aripo, Mt., *Trin. & Tob.* 125 K15
Aripuanã, *Brazil* 124 E6
Aripuanã →, *Brazil* 124 E6
Ariquemes, *Brazil* 124 E6
Arisaig, *U.K.* 13 E3
Arîsh, W. el →, *Egypt* 80 A3
Arissa, *Ethiopia* 81 E5
Aristazabal I., *Canada* 102 C3
Arivonimamo, *Madag.* 89 B8
Ariza, *Spain* 38 D2
Arizaro, Salar de, *Argentina* 126 A2
Arizona, *Argentina* 126 D2
Arizona □, *U.S.A.* 109 J8
Arizpe, *Mexico* 118 A2
Årjäng, *Sweden* 10 E6
Arjeplog, *Sweden* 8 D18
Arjona, *Colombia* 124 A3
Arjona, *Spain* 37 H6
Arjuna, *Indonesia* 63 G15
Arka, *Russia* 53 C15
Arkadak, *Russia* 34 E6
Arkadelphia, *U.S.A.* 113 H8
Arkadhía □, *Greece* 46 D4
Arkaig, L., *U.K.* 13 E3
Arkalyk = Arqalyk, *Kazakhstan* 52 D7
Arkansas □, *U.S.A.* 113 H8
Arkansas →, *U.S.A.* 113 J9
Arkansas City, *U.S.A.* 113 G6
Arkaroola, *Australia* 95 E2
Árkathos →, *Greece* 46 B3
Arkhángelos, *Greece* 49 C10
Arkhangelsk, *Russia* 52 C5
Arkhangelskoye, *Russia* 34 E5
Arki, *India* 68 D7
Arkiko, *Eritrea* 81 D4
Arklow, *Ireland* 12 D5
Árkoi, *Greece* 47 D8
Arkona, Kap, *Germany* 24 A9
Arkösund, *Sweden* 11 F10
Arkoúdhi Nisís, *Greece* 46 C2
Arkport, *U.S.A.* 116 D7
Arkticheskiy, Mys, *Russia* 53 A10
Arkul, *Russia* 34 B10
Arkville, *U.S.A.* 117 D10
Ärla, *Sweden* 10 E10
Arlanda, Stockholm ✈ (ARN), *Sweden* 10 E11
Arlanza →, *Spain* 36 C6
Arlanzón →, *Spain* 36 C6
Arlbergpass, *Austria* 26 D3
Arles, *France* 21 E8
Arli, *Burkina Faso* 83 C5
Arli △, *Burkina Faso* 83 C5
Arlington, *S. Africa* 89 D4
Arlington, *N.Y., U.S.A.* 117 E11
Arlington, *Oreg., U.S.A.* 108 D3
Arlington, *S. Dak., U.S.A.* 112 C6
Arlington, *Tex., U.S.A.* 113 J6
Arlington, *Va., U.S.A.* 114 F7
Arlington, *Vt., U.S.A.* 117 C11
Arlington, *Wash., U.S.A.* 110 B4
Arlington Heights, *U.S.A.* 114 D2
Arlit, *Niger* 78 E7
Arlon, *Belgium* 17 E5
Arltunga, *Australia* 94 C1
Armagh, *U.K.* 12 B5
Armagh □, *U.K.* 12 B5
Armagnac, *France* 20 E4
Armançon →, *France* 19 E10
Armando Bermudez △, *Dom. Rep.* 121 C5
Armavir, *Russia* 35 H5
Armenia, *Colombia* 124 C3
Armenia ■, *Asia* 35 K7
Armeniş, *Romania* 28 E7
Armenistís, Ákra, *Greece* 49 C9
Armentières, *France* 19 B9
Armidale, *Australia* 95 E5
Armilla, *Spain* 37 H7
Armorique ⌂, *France* 18 D3
Armour, *U.S.A.* 112 D5
Armstrong, *B.C., Canada* 102 C5
Armstrong, *Ont., Canada* 104 B2
Armutlu, *Bursa, Turkey* 45 F12
Armutlu, *İzmir, Turkey* 47 C9
Arnaía, *Greece* 44 F7
Arnarfjörður, *Iceland* 8 D2
Arnaud →, *Canada* 101 B12
Arnauti, C., *Cyprus* 49 D11
Arnay-le-Duc, *France* 19 E11
Arnedillo, *Spain* 38 C2
Arnedo, *Spain* 38 C2
Arnett, *U.S.A.* 113 G5
Arnhem, *Neths.* 17 C5
Arnhem, C., *Australia* 94 A2
Arnhem B., *Australia* 94 A2
Arnhem Land, *Australia* 94 A1
Árnissa, *Greece* 44 F5
Arno →, *Italy* 40 E7
Arno Bay, *Australia* 95 E2
Arnold, *U.K.* 14 D6
Arnold, *U.S.A.* 110 G6
Arnoldstein, *Austria* 26 E6
Arnon →, *France* 19 E9
Arnot, *Canada* 103 B9
Arnøy, *Norway* 8 A19
Arnprior, *Canada* 117 A8
Arnsberg, *Germany* 24 D4
Arnsberger Wald ⌂, *Germany* 24 D4
Arnstadt, *Germany* 24 E6
Aroab, *Namibia* 88 D2
Aroánia Óri, *Greece* 46 D4
Aroche, *Spain* 37 H4
Arochuku, *Nigeria* 83 D6
Arolsen, *Germany* 24 D5
Aron, *India* 68 G6
Aron →, *France* 19 F10
Arona, *Canary Is.* 48 F3
Arona, *Italy* 40 C5
Aroroy, *Phil.* 61 E5
Arosa, Ría de, *Spain* 36 C2
Arpajon, *France* 19 D9
Arpajon-sur-Cère, *France* 20 D6
Arpaşu de Jos, *Romania* 29 E9
Arqalyk, *Kazakhstan* 52 D7
Arrah = Ara, *India* 69 G11
Arrah, *Ivory C.* 82 D4
Arraiolos, *Portugal* 37 G3
Arran, *U.K.* 13 F3
Arras, *France* 19 B9
Arrasate, *Spain* 38 B2
Arrats →, *France* 20 D4
Arreau, *France* 20 F4
Arrecife, *Canary Is.* 48 F6
Arrecifes, *Argentina* 126 C3
Arrée, Mts. d', *France* 18 D3
Arresø, *Denmark* 11 J6
Arriaga, *Chiapas, Mexico* 119 D6
Arriaga, *San Luis Potosí, Mexico* 118 C4
Arribes del Duero ⌂, *Spain* 36 D4
Arrilalah, *Australia* 94 C3
Arrino, *Australia* 93 E2
Arriondas, *Spain* 36 B5
Arromanches-les-Bains, *France* 18 C6
Arronches, *Portugal* 37 F3
Arros →, *France* 20 E3
Arrow, L., *Ireland* 12 B3
Arrowhead, L., *U.S.A.* 111 L9
Arrowtown, *N.Z.* 91 L2
Arroyo de la Luz, *Spain* 37 F4
Arroyo Grande, *U.S.A.* 111 K6
Års, *Denmark* 11 H3
Ars, *Iran* 70 B5
Ars-sur-Moselle, *France* 19 C13
Arsenault L., *Canada* 103 B7
Arsenev, *Russia* 54 B6
Arsi □, *Ethiopia* 81 F4
Arsiero, *Italy* 41 C8
Arsin, *Turkey* 73 B8
Arsk, *Russia* 34 B9
Årsunda, *Sweden* 10 D10
Árta, *Greece* 46 B3
Artà, *Spain* 48 B10
Árta □, *Greece* 46 B3
Arteaga, *Mexico* 118 D4
Arteche, *Phil.* 61 E6
Arteijo = Arteixo, *Spain* 36 B2
Arteixo, *Spain* 36 B2
Artem = Artyom, *Azerbaijan* 35 K10
Artem, *Russia* 54 C6
Artemovsk, *Russia* 53 D10
Artemovsk, *Ukraine* 33 H9
Artemovskiy, *Russia* 35 G5
Artenay, *France* 19 D8
Artern, *Germany* 24 D7
Artesa de Segre, *Spain* 38 D6
Artesia = Mosomane, *Botswana* 88 C4
Artesia, *U.S.A.* 113 J2
Arthington, *Liberia* 82 D2
Arthur, *Canada* 116 C4
Arthur →, *Australia* 95 G3
Arthur Cr. →, *Australia* 94 C2
Arthur Pt., *Australia* 94 C5
Arthur River, *Australia* 93 F2
Arthur's Pass, *N.Z.* 91 K3
Arthur's Pass △, *N.Z.* 91 K3
Arthur's Town, *Bahamas* 121 B4
Artigas, *Antarctica* 5 C18
Artigas, *Uruguay* 126 C4
Artik, *Armenia* 35 K6
Artillery L., *Canada* 103 A7
Artois, *France* 19 B9
Artotína, *Greece* 46 C4
Artrutx, C. de, *Spain* 48 B10
Artsyz, *Ukraine* 33 J5
Artvin, *Turkey* 73 B9
Artyom, *Azerbaijan* 35 K10
Aru, Kepulauan, *Indonesia* 63 F8
Aru Is. = Aru, Kepulauan, *Indonesia* 63 F8
Arua, *Uganda* 86 B3
Aruanã, *Brazil* 125 F8
Aruba ☒, *W. Indies* 121 D6
Arucas, *Canary Is.* 48 F4
Arudy, *France* 20 E3
Arun →, *Nepal* 69 F12
Arun →, *U.K.* 15 G7
Arunachal Pradesh □, *India* 67 F19
Arusha, *Tanzania* 86 C4
Arusha □, *Tanzania* 86 C4
Arusha △, *Tanzania* 86 C4
Arusha Chini, *Tanzania* 86 C4
Aruwimi →, *Dem. Rep. of the Congo* 86 B1
Arvada, *Colo., U.S.A.* 112 F2
Arvada, *Wyo., U.S.A.* 108 D10
Arve →, *France* 19 F13
Árvi, *Greece* 49 E7
Arviat, *Canada* 100 B10
Arviat, *Canada* 103 A10
Arvidsjaur, *Sweden* 8 D18
Arvika, *Sweden* 10 E6
Arvin, *U.S.A.* 111 K8
Arwal, *India* 69 G11
Arxan, *China* 60 B6
Åryd, *Sweden* 11 H8
Aryirádhes, *Greece* 49 B3
Aryiroúpolis, *Greece* 49 D6
Arys, *Kazakhstan* 52 E7
Arzachena, *Italy* 42 A2
Arzamas, *Russia* 34 C6
Arzgir, *Russia* 35 H7
Arzignano, *Italy* 41 C8
Arzúa, *Spain* 36 C2
Aš, *Czech Rep.* 26 A5
Ås, *Sweden* 10 A8
As Pontes de García Rodríguez, *Spain* 36 B3
Aş Şafā, *Syria* 74 B6
As Saffānīyah, *Si. Arabia* 71 E6
As Safīrah, *Syria* 70 B3
Aş Şahm, *Oman* 71 E8
As Sājir, *Si. Arabia* 70 E5
As Salamīyah, *Syria* 70 C3
As Salmān, *Iraq* 70 D5
As Salṭ, *Jordan* 74 C4
As Sal'w'a, *Qatar* 71 E6
As Samāwah, *Iraq* 70 D5
As Sanamayn, *Syria* 74 B5
As Sohar = Şuḥār, *Oman* 71 E8
As Sukhnah, *Syria* 70 C3
As Sulaymānīyah, *Iraq* 70 C5
As Sulaymī, *Si. Arabia* 70 E4
As Sulayyil, *Si. Arabia* 75 C4
As Summān, *Si. Arabia* 70 E5
As Suwaydā', *Syria* 74 C5
As Suwaydā' □, *Syria* 74 C5
As Suwayq, *Oman* 71 F8
Aş Şuwayrah, *Iraq* 70 C5
Åsa, *Sweden* 11 G6
Asab, *Namibia* 88 D2
Asaba, *Nigeria* 83 D6
Asad, Buḩayrat al, *Syria* 70 C3
Asadābād, *Iran* 73 E13
Asafo, *Ghana* 82 D4
Asahi-Gawa →, *Japan* 55 G6
Asahigawa, *Japan* 54 C11
Asale, L., *Ethiopia* 81 E5
Asamankese, *Ghana* 83 D4
Asan →, *India* 69 F8
Asansol, *India* 69 H12
Åsarna, *Sweden* 10 B8
Asayita, *Ethiopia* 81 E5
Asbe Teferi, *Ethiopia* 81 F5
Asbesberge, *S. Africa* 88 D3
Asbestos, *Canada* 105 C5
Asbury Park, *U.S.A.* 117 F10
Ascea, *Italy* 43 B8
Ascensión, *Mexico* 118 A3
Ascensión, B. de la, *Mexico* 119 D7
Ascension I., *Atl. Oc.* 77 G2
Aschach an der Donau, *Austria* 26 C7
Aschaffenburg, *Germany* 25 F5
Aschendorf, *Germany* 24 B3
Aschersleben, *Germany* 24 D7
Asciano, *Italy* 41 E8
Áscoli Piceno, *Italy* 41 F10
Áscoli Satriano, *Italy* 43 A8
Ascope, *Peru* 124 E3
Ascotán, *Chile* 126 A2
Aseb, *Eritrea* 81 E5
Åseda, *Sweden* 11 G9
Asela, *Ethiopia* 81 F4
Åsen, *Sweden* 10 C7
Asenovgrad, *Bulgaria* 45 D8
Aserradero, *Mexico* 118 C3
Asfeld, *France* 19 C11
Asfûn el Matâ'na, *Egypt* 80 B3
Asgata, *Cyprus* 49 E12
Ash Fork, *U.S.A.* 109 J7
Ash Grove, *U.S.A.* 113 G8
Ash Shabakah, *Iraq* 70 D4
Ash Shamāl □, *Lebanon* 74 A5
Ash Shāmīyah, *Iraq* 70 D5
Ash Shāriqah, *U.A.E.* 71 E7
Ash Sharmah, *Si. Arabia* 70 D2
Ash Sharqāt, *Iraq* 70 C4
Ash Sharqi, Al Jabal, *Lebanon* 74 B5
Ash Shaṭrah, *Iraq* 70 D5
Ash Shawbak, *Jordan* 70 D2
Ash Shawmari, J., *Jordan* 74 E5
Ash Shināfīyah, *Iraq* 70 D5
Ash Shu'bah, *Si. Arabia* 70 D5
Ash Shumlūl, *Si. Arabia* 70 E5
Ash Shūr'a, *Iraq* 70 C4
Ash Shurayf, *Si. Arabia* 70 E3
Ash Shuwayfāt, *Lebanon* 74 B4
Ashanti □, *Ghana* 83 D4
Ashau, *Vietnam* 64 D6
Ashbourne, *U.K.* 14 D6
Ashburn, *U.S.A.* 115 K4
Ashburton, *N.Z.* 91 K3
Ashburton →, *Australia* 92 D1
Ashcroft, *Canada* 102 C4
Ashdod, *Israel* 74 D3
Ashdown, *U.S.A.* 113 J7
Asheboro, *U.S.A.* 115 H6
Ashern, *Canada* 103 C9
Asherton, *U.S.A.* 113 L5
Asheville, *U.S.A.* 115 H4
Ashewat, *Pakistan* 68 D3
Asheweig →, *Canada* 104 B2
Ashford, *Australia* 95 D5
Ashford, *U.K.* 15 F8
Ashgabat, *Turkmenistan* 52 F6
Ashibetsu, *Japan* 54 C11
Ashikaga, *Japan* 55 F9
Ashington, *U.K.* 14 B6
Ashizuri-Uwakai △, *Japan* 55 H6
Ashizuri-Zaki, *Japan* 55 H6
Ashkarkot, *Afghan.* 68 C2
Ashkhabad = Ashgabat, *Turkmenistan* 52 F6
Āshkhāneh, *Iran* 71 B8
Ashland, *Kans., U.S.A.* 113 G5
Ashland, *Ky., U.S.A.* 114 F4
Ashland, *Mont., U.S.A.* 108 D10
Ashland, *Ohio, U.S.A.* 116 F2
Ashland, *Oreg., U.S.A.* 108 E2
Ashland, *Pa., U.S.A.* 117 F8
Ashland, *Va., U.S.A.* 114 G7
Ashland, *Wis., U.S.A.* 112 B9
Ashley, *N. Dak., U.S.A.* 112 B5
Ashley, *Pa., U.S.A.* 117 E9
Ashmore and Cartier Is., *Ind. Oc.* 92 B3
Ashmore Reef, *Australia* 92 B3
Ashmûn, *Egypt* 80 H7
Ashmyany, *Belarus* 9 J21
Ashokan Reservoir, *U.S.A.* 117 E10
Ashqelon, *Israel* 74 D3
Ashta, *India* 68 H7
Ashtabula, *U.S.A.* 116 E4
Ashton, *S. Africa* 88 E3
Ashton, *U.S.A.* 108 D8
Ashuanipi, L., *Canada* 105 B6
Ashuapmushuan →, *Canada* 104 C5
Ashville, *U.S.A.* 116 F6
'Āṣī →, *Asia* 72 D6
Asia 50 E11
Asia, Kepulauan, *Indonesia* 63 D8

Asiago, *Italy* 41 C8
Asifabad, *India* 66 K11
Asinara, *Italy* 42 A1
Asinara, G. dell', *Italy* 42 A1
Asino, *Russia* 52 D9
Asipovichy, *Belarus* 32 F5
'Asīr □, *Si. Arabia* 75 D3
Asir, Ras, *Somali Rep.* 75 E5
Aşkale, *Turkey* 73 C9
Askersund, *Sweden* 11 F8
Askham, *S. Africa* 88 D3
Askim, *Norway* 9 G14
Askja, *Iceland* 8 D5
Askøy, *Norway* 9 F11
Asl, *Egypt* 80 B3
Aslan Burnu, *Turkey* 47 C8
Aslanapa, *Turkey* 47 B11
Asmara = Asmera, *Eritrea* 81 D4
Asmera, *Eritrea* 81 D4
Asnæs, *Denmark* 11 J4
Åsnen, *Sweden* 11 H8
Aso Kuju △, *Japan* 55 H5
Ásola, *Italy* 40 C7
Asosa, *Ethiopia* 81 E3
Asoteriba, Jebel, *Sudan* 80 C4
Aspatria, *U.K.* 14 C4
Aspe, *Spain* 39 G4
Aspen, *U.S.A.* 109 G10
Aspendos, *Turkey* 72 D4
Aspermont, *U.S.A.* 113 J4
Aspet, *France* 20 E4
Aspiring, Mt., *N.Z.* 91 L2
Aspres-sur-Buëch, *France* 21 D9
Asprókavos, Ákra, *Greece* 49 B4
Aspromonte △, *Italy* 43 D8
Aspur, *India* 68 H6
Asquith, *Canada* 103 C7
Assab = Aseb, *Eritrea* 81 E5
Assâba, Massif de l', *Mauritania* 82 B2
Assagny △, *Ivory C.* 82 D4
Assaikio, *Nigeria* 83 D6
Assal, L., *Djibouti* 81 E5
Assam □, *India* 67 G18
Assamakka, *Niger* 83 B6
Assateague Island ⌓, *U.S.A.* 114 F8
Asse, *Belgium* 17 D4
Assémini, *Italy* 42 C1
Assen, *Neths.* 17 A6
Assens, *Denmark* 11 J3
Assini, *Ivory C.* 82 D4
Assiniboia, *Canada* 103 D7
Assiniboine →, *Canada* 103 D9
Assiniboine, Mt., *Canada* 102 C5
Assis, *Brazil* 127 A5
Assisi, *Italy* 41 E9
Ássos, *Greece* 46 C2
Assynt, L., *U.K.* 13 C3
Astaffort, *France* 20 D4
Astakidha, *Greece* 47 F8
Astakós, *Greece* 46 C3
Astana, *Kazakhstan* 52 D8
Āstāneh, *Iran* 71 B6
Astara, *Azerbaijan* 71 B6
Āstārā, *Iran* 73 C13
Asteroúsia, *Greece* 49 E7
Asti, *Italy* 40 D5
Astipálaia, *Greece* 47 E8
Astorga, *Spain* 36 C4
Astoria, *U.S.A.* 110 D3
Åstorp, *Sweden* 11 H6
Astrakhan, *Russia* 35 G9
Astudillo, *Spain* 36 C6
Asturias □, *Spain* 36 B5
Asturias ✕ (OVD), *Spain* 36 B4
Asunción, *Paraguay* 126 B4
Asunción Nochixtlán, *Mexico* 119 D5
Åsunden, *Sweden* 11 F9
Asutri, *Sudan* 81 D4
Aswa →, *Uganda* 86 B3
Aswa-Lolim ⌓, *Uganda* 86 B3
Aswad, Ra's al, *Si. Arabia* 80 C4
Aswân, *Egypt* 80 C3
Aswan Dam = Sadd el Aali, *Egypt* 80 C3
Asyût, *Egypt* 80 B3
Asyûti, Wadi →, *Egypt* 80 B3
Aszód, *Hungary* 28 C4
At Ţafīlah, *Jordan* 74 E4
At Ţafīlah □, *Jordan* 74 E4
Aţ Tā'if, *Si. Arabia* 75 C3
At Ta'mīm □, *Iraq* 70 C5
Aţ Ţirāq, *Si. Arabia* 70 E5
Aţ Ţubayq, *Si. Arabia* 70 D3
Atabey, *Turkey* 47 D12
Atacama □, *Chile* 126 B2
Atacama, Desierto de, *Chile* 126 A2
Atacama, Salar de, *Chile* 126 A2
Atakpamé, *Togo* 83 D5
Atalándi, *Greece* 46 C4
Atalaya, *Peru* 124 F4
Atalaya de Femes, *Canary Is.* 48 F6
Atami, *Japan* 55 G9
Atapupu, *E. Timor* 63 F6
Atâr, *Mauritania* 78 D3
Atarfe, *Spain* 37 H7
Atari, *Pakistan* 68 D6
Atascadero, *U.S.A.* 110 K6
Atasu, *Kazakhstan* 52 E8
Ataturk, Istanbul ✕ (IST), *Turkey* 45 F12
Atatürk Baraji, *Turkey* 73 D8
Atauro, *E. Timor* 63 F7
'Atbara, *Sudan* 80 D3
'Atbara, Nahr →, *Sudan* 80 D3
Atbasar, *Kazakhstan* 52 D7
Atça, *Turkey* 47 D10
Atchafalaya B., *U.S.A.* 113 L9
Atchison, *U.S.A.* 112 F7
Atebubu, *Ghana* 83 D4
Ateca, *Spain* 38 D3
Aterno →, *Italy* 41 F10
Āteshān, *Iran* 71 C7
Atesine, Alpi, *Italy* 41 B8
Atessa, *Italy* 41 F11
Atfîh, *Egypt* 80 J7
Ath, *Belgium* 17 D3
Athabasca, *Canada* 102 C6
Athabasca →, *Canada* 103 B6
Athabasca, L., *Canada* 103 B7
Athabasca Sand Dunes ⌓, *Canada* 103 B7
Athboy, *Ireland* 12 C5
Athenry, *Ireland* 12 C3
Athens = Athínai, *Greece* 46 D5
Athens, *Ala., U.S.A.* 115 H2
Athens, *Ga., U.S.A.* 115 J4
Athens, *N.Y., U.S.A.* 117 D11
Athens, *Ohio, U.S.A.* 114 F4
Athens, *Pa., U.S.A.* 117 E8
Athens, *Tenn., U.S.A.* 115 H3
Athens, *Tex., U.S.A.* 113 J7
Athens International ✕ (ATH), *Greece* 46 D5
Atherley, *Canada* 116 B5
Atherton, *Australia* 94 B4
Athiéme, *Benin* 83 D5
Athienou, *Cyprus* 49 D12
Athínai, *Greece* 46 D5
Athlone, *Ireland* 12 C4
Athna, *Cyprus* 49 D12
Athol, *U.S.A.* 117 D12
Atholl, Forest of, *U.K.* 13 E5
Atholville, *Canada* 105 C6
Áthos, *Greece* 45 F8
Athy, *Ireland* 12 C5
Ati, *Chad* 79 F9
Ati, *Sudan* 81 E2
Atiak, *Uganda* 86 B3
Atienza, *Spain* 38 D2
Atiit, *Sudan* 81 F3
Atik L., *Canada* 103 B9
Atikaki ⌓, *Canada* 103 C9
Atikameg →, *Canada* 104 B3
Atikokan, *Canada* 104 C1
Atikonak L., *Canada* 105 B7
Atimonan, *Phil.* 61 E4
Atitlán △, *Cent. Amer.* 119 E6
Atka, *Russia* 53 C16
Atka I., *U.S.A.* 100 C2
Atkarsk, *Russia* 34 E7
Atkinson, *U.S.A.* 112 D5
Atlanta, *Ga., U.S.A.* 115 J3
Atlanta, *Tex., U.S.A.* 113 J7
Atlantic, *U.S.A.* 112 E7
Atlantic City, *U.S.A.* 114 F8
Atlantic-Indian Basin, *Antarctica* 5 B4
Atlantic Ocean 2 E9
Atlas Mts. = Haut Atlas, *Morocco* 78 B4
Atlin, *Canada* 102 B2
Atlin ⌓, *Canada* 102 B2
Atlin, L., *Canada* 102 B2
Atmore, *U.S.A.* 115 K2
Atoka, *U.S.A.* 113 H6
Átokos Nisís, *Greece* 46 C2
Atolia, *U.S.A.* 111 K9
Atrai →, *Bangla.* 69 G13
Atrak = Atrek →, *Turkmenistan* 71 B8
Ätran, *Sweden* 11 G6
Ätran →, *Sweden* 11 H6
Atrauli, *India* 68 E8
Atrek →, *Turkmenistan* 71 B8
Atri, *Italy* 41 F10
Atsiki, *Greece* 47 B7
Atsoum, Mts., *Cameroon* 83 D7
Atsuta, *Japan* 54 C10
Attalla, *U.S.A.* 115 H2
Attapu, *Laos* 64 E6
Attáviros, *Greece* 49 C9
Attawapiskat, *Canada* 104 B3
Attawapiskat →, *Canada* 104 B3
Attawapiskat L., *Canada* 104 B2
Attersee, *Austria* 26 D6
Attica, *Ind., U.S.A.* 114 E2
Attica, *Ohio, U.S.A.* 116 E2
Attichy, *France* 19 C10
Attigny, *France* 19 C11
Attika = Attikí □, *Greece* 46 D5
Attikamagen L., *Canada* 105 B6
Attikí □, *Greece* 46 D5
Attleboro, *U.S.A.* 117 E13
Attock, *Pakistan* 68 C5
Attopeu = Attapu, *Laos* 64 E6
Attu I., *U.S.A.* 100 C1
Attur, *India* 66 P11
Atuel →, *Argentina* 126 D2
Åtvidaberg, *Sweden* 11 F10
Atwater, *U.S.A.* 110 H6
Atwood, *Canada* 116 C3
Atwood, *U.S.A.* 112 F4
Atyraū, *Kazakhstan* 52 E6
Au Sable, *U.S.A.* 116 B1
Au Sable →, *U.S.A.* 114 C4
Au Sable Forks, *U.S.A.* 117 B11
Au Sable Pt., *U.S.A.* 116 B1
Aubagne, *France* 21 E9
Aubarca, C. d', *Spain* 48 B7
Aube □, *France* 19 D11
Aube →, *France* 19 D10
Aubenas, *France* 21 D8
Aubenton, *France* 19 C11
Auberry, *U.S.A.* 110 H7
Aubigny-sur-Nère, *France* 19 E9
Aubin, *France* 20 D6
Aubrac, Mts. d', *France* 20 D7
Auburn, *Ala., U.S.A.* 115 J3
Auburn, *Calif., U.S.A.* 110 G5
Auburn, *Ind., U.S.A.* 114 E3
Auburn, *Maine, U.S.A.* 115 C10
Auburn, *N.Y., U.S.A.* 117 D8
Auburn, *Nebr., U.S.A.* 112 E7
Auburn, *Pa., U.S.A.* 117 F8
Auburn, *Wash., U.S.A.* 110 C4
Auburn Ra., *Australia* 95 D5
Auburndale, *U.S.A.* 115 L5
Aubusson, *France* 20 C6
Auce, *Latvia* 30 B9
Auch, *France* 20 E4
Auchi, *Nigeria* 83 D6
Auchterarder, *U.K.* 13 E5
Auchtermuchty, *U.K.* 13 E5
Auckland, *N.Z.* 91 G5
Auckland Is., *Pac. Oc.* 96 N8
Aude □, *France* 20 E6
Aude →, *France* 20 E7
Auden, *Canada* 104 B2
Auderville, *France* 18 C5
Audierne, *France* 18 D2
Audincourt, *France* 19 E13
Audo Mts., *Ethiopia* 81 F5
Audubon, *U.S.A.* 112 E7
Aue, *Germany* 24 E8
Auerbach, *Germany* 24 E8
Augathella, *Australia* 95 D4
Aughnacloy, *U.K.* 12 B5
Augrabies Falls, *S. Africa* 88 D3
Augrabies Falls △, *S. Africa* 88 D3
Augsburg, *Germany* 25 G6
Augsburg-Westliche Wälder ⌓, *Germany* 25 G6
Augusta, *Australia* 93 F2
Augusta, *Italy* 43 E8
Augusta, *Ark., U.S.A.* 113 H9
Augusta, *Ga., U.S.A.* 115 J5
Augusta, *Kans., U.S.A.* 113 G6
Augusta, *Maine, U.S.A.* 101 D13
Augusta, *Mont., U.S.A.* 108 C7
Augustenborg, *Denmark* 11 K3
Augustów, *Poland* 30 E9
Augustus, Mt., *Australia* 93 D2
Augustus I., *Australia* 92 C3
Aukan, *Eritrea* 81 D5
Aukrug ⌓, *Germany* 24 A5
Aukum, *U.S.A.* 110 G6
Auld, L., *Australia* 92 D3
Aulla, *Italy* 40 D6
Aulnay, *France* 20 B3
Aulne →, *France* 18 D2
Aulnoye-Aymeries, *France* 19 B10
Ault, *France* 18 B8
Ault, *U.S.A.* 112 E2
Aulus-les-Bains, *France* 20 F5
Aumale, *France* 19 C8
Aumont-Aubrac, *France* 20 D7
Auna, *Nigeria* 83 C5
Auning, *Denmark* 11 H4
Aunis, *France* 20 B3
Auponhia, *Indonesia* 63 E7
Aups, *France* 21 E10
Aur, Pulau, *Malaysia* 65 L5
Auraiya, *India* 69 F8
Aurangabad, *Bihar, India* 69 G11
Aurangabad, *Maharashtra, India* 66 K9
Auray, *France* 18 E4
Aurich, *Germany* 24 B3
Aurillac, *France* 20 D6
Auronzo di Cadore, *Italy* 41 B9
Aurora, *Canada* 116 C5
Aurora, *S. Africa* 88 E2
Aurora, *Colo., U.S.A.* 112 F2
Aurora, *Ill., U.S.A.* 114 E1
Aurora, *Mo., U.S.A.* 113 G8
Aurora, *N.Y., U.S.A.* 117 D8
Aurora, *Nebr., U.S.A.* 112 E6
Aurora, *Ohio, U.S.A.* 116 E3
Aurukun, *Australia* 94 A3
Aus, *Namibia* 88 D2
Ausable →, *Canada* 116 C3
Auschwitz = Oświęcim, *Poland* 31 H6
Austerlitz = Slavkov u Brna, *Czech Rep.* 27 B9
Austin, *Minn., U.S.A.* 112 D8
Austin, *Nev., U.S.A.* 108 G5
Austin, *Pa., U.S.A.* 116 E6
Austin, *Tex., U.S.A.* 113 K6
Austin, L., *Australia* 93 E2
Austin I., *Canada* 103 A10
Austra, *Norway* 8 D14
Austral Is. = Tubuai Is., *Pac. Oc.* 97 K13
Austral Seamount Chain, *Pac. Oc.* 97 K13
Australia ■, *Oceania* 96 K5
Australian Capital Territory □, *Australia* 95 F4
Australind, *Australia* 93 F2
Austria ■, *Europe* 26 E7
Austvågøy, *Norway* 8 B16
Autazes, *Brazil* 124 D7
Auterive, *France* 20 E5
Authie →, *France* 19 B8
Authon-du-Perche, *France* 18 D7
Autlán, *Mexico* 118 D4
Autun, *France* 19 F11
Auvergne, *France* 20 C7
Auvergne, Mts. d', *France* 20 C6
Auvézère →, *France* 20 C4
Auxerre, *France* 19 E10
Auxi-le-Château, *France* 19 B9
Auxonne, *France* 19 E12
Auzances, *France* 19 F9
Ava, *U.S.A.* 113 G8
Avallon, *France* 19 E10
Avalon, *U.S.A.* 111 M8
Avalon Pen., *Canada* 105 C9
Avanos, *Turkey* 70 B2
Avaré, *Brazil* 127 A6
Ávas, *Greece* 45 F9
Avawatz Mts., *U.S.A.* 111 K10
Avdan Daği, *Turkey* 45 F13
Aveiro, *Brazil* 125 D7
Aveiro, *Portugal* 36 E2
Aveiro □, *Portugal* 36 E2
Āvej, *Iran* 71 C6
Avellaneda, *Argentina* 126 C4
Avellino, *Italy* 43 B7
Avenal, *U.S.A.* 110 K6
Aversa, *Italy* 43 B7
Avery, *U.S.A.* 108 C6
Aves, Is. las, *Venezuela* 121 D6
Avesnes-sur-Helpe, *France* 19 B10
Avesnois ⌓, *France* 19 B10
Avesta, *Sweden* 10 D10
Aveyron □, *France* 20 D6
Aveyron →, *France* 20 D5
Avezzano, *Italy* 41 F10
Avgó, *Greece* 47 F7
Aviá Terai, *Argentina* 126 B3
Aviano, *Italy* 41 B9
Aviemore, *U.K.* 13 D5
Avigliana, *Italy* 40 C4
Avigliano, *Italy* 43 B8
Avignon, *France* 21 E8
Ávila, *Spain* 36 E6
Ávila □, *Spain* 36 E6
Ávila, Sierra de, *Spain* 36 E5
Avila Beach, *U.S.A.* 111 K6
Avilés, *Spain* 36 B5
Avintes, *Portugal* 36 D2
Avionárion, *Greece* 46 C6
Avis, *Portugal* 37 F3
Avis, *U.S.A.* 116 E7
Avísio →, *Italy* 40 B8
Aviz = Avis, *Portugal* 37 F3
Avize, *France* 19 D11
Avlum, *Denmark* 11 H2
Avoca, *U.S.A.* 116 D7
Avoca →, *Australia* 95 F3
Avoca →, *Ireland* 12 D5
Avola, *Canada* 102 C5
Avola, *Italy* 43 F8
Avon, *U.S.A.* 116 D7
Avon →, *Australia* 93 F2
Avon →, *Bristol, U.K.* 15 F5
Avon →, *Dorset, U.K.* 15 G6
Avon →, *Warks., U.K.* 15 E5
Avon Park, *U.S.A.* 115 M5
Avondale, *Zimbabwe* 87 F3
Avonlea, *Canada* 103 D8
Avonmore, *Canada* 117 A10
Avonmouth, *U.K.* 15 F5
Avramov, *Bulgaria* 45 D10
Avranches, *France* 18 D5
Avre →, *France* 18 D8
Avrig, *Romania* 29 E9
Avrillé, *France* 18 E6
Avtovac, *Bos.-H.* 44 C2
Awag el Baqar, *Sudan* 81 E3
A'waj →, *Syria* 74 B5
Awaji-Shima, *Japan* 55 G7
'Awālī, *Bahrain* 71 E6
Awantipur, *India* 69 C6
Awasa, *Ethiopia* 81 F4
Awasa, L., *Ethiopia* 81 F4
Awash, *Ethiopia* 81 F5
Awash △, *Ethiopia* 81 F5
Awash →, *Ethiopia* 81 E5
Awaso, *Ghana* 82 D4
Awatere →, *N.Z.* 91 J5
Awbārī, *Libya* 79 C8
Awbārī, Idehan, *Libya* 79 C8
Awe, L., *U.K.* 13 E3
Aweil, *Sudan* 81 F2
Awgu, *Nigeria* 83 D6
Awjilah, *Libya* 79 C10
Awka, *Nigeria* 83 D6
Ax-les-Thermes, *France* 20 F5
Axat, *France* 20 F6
Axe →, *U.K.* 15 F5
Axel Heiberg I., *Canada* 98 A10
Axim, *Ghana* 82 E4
Axintele, *Romania* 29 F11
Axiós →, *Greece* 44 F6
Axminster, *U.K.* 15 G4
Axvall, *Sweden* 11 F7
Ay, *France* 19 C11
Ayabaca, *Peru* 124 D3
Ayabe, *Japan* 55 G7
Ayacucho, *Argentina* 126 D4
Ayacucho, *Peru* 124 F4
Ayaguz, *Kazakhstan* 52 E9
Ayamé, *Ivory C.* 82 D4
Ayamonte, *Spain* 37 H3
Ayan, *Russia* 53 D14
Ayancık, *Turkey* 72 B6
Ayas, *Turkey* 72 B5
Ayaviri, *Peru* 124 F4
Aybastı, *Turkey* 72 B7
Aydın, *Turkey* 72 D2
Aydin □, *Turkey* 47 D9
Aydin Dağları, *Turkey* 47 D10
Ayelu, *Ethiopia* 81 E5
Ayenngré, *Togo* 83 D5
Ayer, *U.S.A.* 117 D13
Ayer Hitam, *Malaysia* 65 c
Ayerbe, *Spain* 38 C4
Ayer's Cliff, *Canada* 117 A12
Ayers Rock, *Australia* 93 E5
Ayiá, *Greece* 46 B4
Ayia Aikateríni, Ákra, *Greece* 49 A3
Ayía Ánna, *Greece* 46 C5
Ayia Dhéka, *Greece* 49 D6
Ayia Gálini, *Greece* 49 D6
Ayía Marína, *Kásos, Greece* 47 F8
Ayia Marína, *Léros, Greece* 47 D8
Áyia Napa, *Cyprus* 49 E13
Ayía Paraskeví, *Greece* 47 B8
Áyia Phyla, *Cyprus* 49 E12
Ayia Rouméli, *Greece* 46 F5
Ayia Varvára, *Greece* 49 D7
Ayiássos, *Greece* 47 B8
Ayioi Theódhoroi, *Greece* 46 D5
Áyion Óros □, *Greece* 45 F8
Áyios Amvrósios, *Cyprus* 49 D12
Áyios Andréas, *Greece* 46 D4
Áyios Evstrátios, *Greece* 46 B6
Áyios Ioánnis, Ákra, *Greece* 49 D7
Áyios Isídhoros, *Greece* 49 C9
Áyios Kiríkos, *Greece* 47 D8
Áyios Matthaíos, *Greece* 49 B3
Áyios Mírono, *Greece* 47 F7
Áyios Nikólaos, *Greece* 49 D7
Áyios Pétros, *Greece* 46 C2
Áyios Seryios, *Cyprus* 49 D12
Áyios Theodhoros, *Cyprus* 49 D13
Áyios Yeóryios, *Greece* 46 D5
Aykathonisi, *Greece* 47 D8
Aykirikçi, *Turkey* 47 B12
Aylesbury, *U.K.* 15 F7
Aylmer, *Canada* 116 D4
Aylmer, L., *Canada* 100 B8
'Ayn, Wādī al, *Oman* 71 F7
Ayn Dār, *Si. Arabia* 71 E7
Ayn Zālah, *Iraq* 70 B4
Ayna, *Spain* 39 G2
Ayod, *Sudan* 81 F3
Ayolas, *Paraguay* 126 B4
Ayom, *Sudan* 81 F2
Ayon, Ostrov, *Russia* 53 C17
Ayora, *Spain* 39 F3
Ayorou, *Niger* 83 C5
'Ayoûn el 'Atroûs, *Mauritania* 82 B3
Ayr, *Australia* 94 B4
Ayr, *Canada* 116 C4
Ayr, *U.K.* 13 F4
Ayr →, *U.K.* 13 F4
Ayrancı, *Turkey* 72 D5
Ayrancılar, *Turkey* 47 C9
Ayre, Pt. of, *U.K.* 14 C3
Aysha, *Ethiopia* 81 E5
Ayton, *Australia* 94 B4
Aytos, *Bulgaria* 45 D11
Aytoska Planina, *Bulgaria* 45 D11
Ayu, Kepulauan, *Indonesia* 63 D8
Ayutla, *Guatemala* 120 D1
Ayutla, *Mexico* 119 D5
Ayvacık, *Turkey* 72 C2
Ayvalık, *Turkey* 47 B8
Az Zabadānī, *Syria* 74 B5
Az Ẓāhirīyah, *West Bank* 74 D3
Az Ẓahrān, *Si. Arabia* 71 E6
Az Zarqā, *Jordan* 74 C5
Az Zarqā', *U.A.E.* 71 E7
Az Zarqā □, *Jordan* 74 C5
Az Zāwiyah, *Libya* 79 B8
Az Zībār, *Iraq* 70 B5
Az Zilfī, *Si. Arabia* 70 E5
Az Zubayr, *Iraq* 70 D5
Az Zuqur, *Yemen* 81 E5
Azad Kashmir □, *Pakistan* 69 C5
Azambuja, *Portugal* 37 F2
Azamgarh, *India* 69 F10
Azangaro, *Peru* 124 F4
Azaoua, *Niger* 83 B5
Azaouad, *Mali* 82 B4
Azaouak, Vallée de l', *Mali* 83 B5
Āzār Shahr, *Iran* 70 B5
Azara, *Nigeria* 83 D6
Azarān, *Iran* 70 B5
Azärbayjan = Azerbaijan ■, *Asia* 35 K9
Āzarbāyjān-e Gharbī □, *Iran* 70 B5
Āzarbāyjān-e Sharqī □, *Iran* 70 B5
Azare, *Nigeria* 83 C7
Azay-le-Rideau, *France* 18 E7
A'zāz, *Syria* 70 B3
Azbine = Aïr, *Niger* 83 B6
Azerbaijan ■, *Asia* 35 K9
Azerbaijchan = Azerbaijan ■, *Asia* 35 K9
Azezo, *Ethiopia* 81 E4
Azimganj, *India* 69 G13
Aznalcóllar, *Spain* 37 H4
Azogues, *Ecuador* 124 D3
Azores = Açores, Is. dos, *Atl. Oc.* 78 A1
Azov, *Russia* 35 G4
Azov, Sea of, *Europe* 33 J9
Azovskoye More = Azov, Sea of, *Europe* 33 J9
Azpeitia, *Spain* 38 B2
Azraq ash Shīshān, *Jordan* 74 D5
Aztec, *U.S.A.* 109 H10
Azúa de Compostela, *Dom. Rep.* 121 C5
Azuaga, *Spain* 37 G5
Azuara, *Spain* 38 D4
Azuer →, *Spain* 37 F7
Azuero, Pen. de, *Panama* 120 E3
Azuga, *Romania* 29 E10
Azul, *Argentina* 126 D4
Azusa, *U.S.A.* 111 L9
Azzano Décimo, *Italy* 41 C9

B

Ba Be △, *Vietnam* 64 A5
Ba Don, *Vietnam* 64 D6
Ba Dong, *Vietnam* 65 H6
Ba Ngoi = Cam Lam, *Vietnam* 65 G7
Ba Tri, *Vietnam* 65 G6
Ba Vi △, *Vietnam* 64 B5
Ba Xian = Bazhou, *China* 56 E9
Baa, *Indonesia* 63 F6
Baamonde, *Spain* 36 B3
Baardeere = Bardera, *Somali Rep.* 75 G3
Baarle-Nassau, *Belgium* 17 C4
Bab el Mandeb, *Red Sea* 75 E3
Baba, *Bulgaria* 44 D7
Bābā, Koh-i-, *Afghan.* 66 B5
Baba Burnu, *Turkey* 47 B8
Baba dag, *Azerbaijan* 35 K9
Bābā Kalū, *Iran* 71 D6
Babadag, *Romania* 29 F13
Babadağ, *Turkey* 47 D10
Babadayhan, *Turkmenistan* 52 F7
Babaeski, *Turkey* 45 E11
Babahoyo, *Ecuador* 124 D3
Babai = Sarju →, *India* 69 F9
Babana, *Nigeria* 83 C5
Babanusa, *Sudan* 81 E2

Babar, *Indonesia* 63 F7
Babar, *Pakistan* 68 D3
Babarkach, *Pakistan* 68 E3
Babayevo, *Russia* 32 C8
Babb, *U.S.A.* 108 B7
Babenhausen, *Germany* 25 F4
Băbeni, *Romania* 29 F9
Baberu, *India* 69 G9
Babi Besar, Pulau, *Malaysia* 65 L4
Babia Gora, *Europe* 31 J6
Babian Jiang →, *China* 58 F3
Babīl □, *Iraq* 70 C5
Babile, *Ethiopia* 81 F5
Babimost, *Poland* 31 F2
Babinda, *Australia* 94 B4
Babine, *Canada* 102 B3
Babine →, *Canada* 102 B3
Babine L., *Canada* 102 C3
Babiogórski △, *Poland* 31 J6
Babo, *Indonesia* 63 E8
Babócsa, *Hungary* 28 D2
Bābol, *Iran* 71 B7
Bābol Sar, *Iran* 71 B7
Baborów, *Poland* 31 H5
Babruysk, *Belarus* 33 F5
Babuhri, *India* 68 F3
Babuna, *Macedonia* 44 E5
Babura, *Nigeria* 83 C6
Babusar Pass, *Pakistan* 69 B5
Babushkin, *Russia* 60 A5
Babušnica, *Serbia & M.* 44 C6
Babuyan Chan., *Phil.* 61 B4
Babylon, *Iraq* 70 C5
Bač, *Serbia & M.* 28 E4
Bâc →, *Moldova* 29 D14
Bac Can, *Vietnam* 58 F5
Bac Giang, *Vietnam* 58 G6
Bac Lieu, *Vietnam* 65 H5
Bac Ninh, *Vietnam* 58 G6
Bac Phan, *Vietnam* 64 B5
Bac Quang, *Vietnam* 58 F5
Bacabal, *Brazil* 125 D10
Bacalar, *Mexico* 119 D7
Bacan, Kepulauan, *Indonesia* 63 E7
Bacarra, *Phil.* 61 B4
Bacău, *Romania* 29 D11
Bacău □, *Romania* 29 D11
Baccarat, *France* 19 D13
Bacerac, *Mexico* 118 A3
Băceşti, *Romania* 29 D12
Bach Long Vi, Dao, *Vietnam* 64 B6
Bach Ma △, *Vietnam* 64 D6
Bacharach, *Germany* 25 E3
Bachelina, *Russia* 52 D7
Bachhwara, *India* 69 G11
Bachuma, *Ethiopia* 81 F4
Bačina, *Serbia & M.* 44 C5
Back →, *Canada* 100 B9
Bačka Palanka, *Serbia & M.* 28 E4
Bačka Topola, *Serbia & M.* 28 E4
Bäckebo, *Sweden* 11 H10
Bäckefors, *Sweden* 11 F6
Bäckhammar, *Sweden* 10 E8
Bački Petrovac, *Serbia & M.* 28 E4
Backnang, *Germany* 25 G5
Baco, Mt., *Phil.* 61 E4
Bacolod, *Phil.* 61 F5
Bacqueville-en-Caux, *France* 18 C8
Bács-Kiskun □, *Hungary* 28 D4
Bácsalmás, *Hungary* 28 D4
Bacuag = Placer, *Phil.* 61 G6
Bacuk, *Malaysia* 65 J4
Bād, *Iran* 71 C7
Bad →, *U.S.A.* 112 C4
Bad Aussee, *Austria* 26 D6
Bad Axe, *U.S.A.* 116 C2
Bad Bergzabern, *Germany* 25 F3
Bad Berleburg, *Germany* 24 D4
Bad Bevensen, *Germany* 24 B6
Bad Bramstedt, *Germany* 24 B5
Bad Brückenau, *Germany* 25 E5
Bad Doberan, *Germany* 24 A7
Bad Driburg, *Germany* 24 D5
Bad Ems, *Germany* 25 E3
Bad Frankenhausen, *Germany* 24 D7
Bad Freienwalde, *Germany* 24 C10
Bad Goisern, *Austria* 26 D6
Bad Harzburg, *Germany* 24 D6
Bad Hersfeld, *Germany* 24 E5
Bad Hofgastein, *Austria* 26 D6
Bad Homburg, *Germany* 25 E4
Bad Honnef, *Germany* 24 E3
Bad Iburg, *Germany* 24 C4
Bad Ischl, *Austria* 26 D6
Bad Kissingen, *Germany* 25 E6
Bad Königshofen, *Germany* 25 E6
Bad Kreuznach, *Germany* 25 F3
Bad Krozingen, *Germany* 25 H3
Bad Laasphe, *Germany* 24 E4
Bad Lands, *U.S.A.* 112 D3
Bad Langensalza, *Germany* 24 D6
Bad Lauterberg, *Germany* 24 D6
Bad Leonfelden, *Austria* 26 C7
Bad Liebenwerda, *Germany* 24 D9
Bad Mergentheim, *Germany* 25 F5
Bad Münstereifel, *Germany* 24 E2
Bad Nauheim, *Germany* 25 E4
Bad Neuenahr-Ahrweiler, *Germany* 24 E3
Bad Neustadt, *Germany* 25 E6
Bad Oeynhausen, *Germany* 24 C4
Bad Oldesloe, *Germany* 24 B6
Bad Orb, *Germany* 25 E5
Bad Pyrmont, *Germany* 24 D5
Bad Reichenhall, *Germany* 25 H8
Bad Säckingen, *Germany* 25 H3
Bad Salzuflen, *Germany* 24 C4
Bad Salzungen, *Germany* 24 E6
Bad Schwartau, *Germany* 24 B6
Bad Segeberg, *Germany* 24 B6
Bad St. Leonhard, *Austria* 26 E7
Bad Tölz, *Germany* 25 H7
Bad Urach, *Germany* 25 G5
Bad Vöslau, *Austria* 27 D9
Bad Waldsee, *Germany* 25 H5
Bad Wildungen, *Germany* 24 D5
Bad Wimpfen, *Germany* 25 F5
Bad Windsheim, *Germany* 25 F6
Bad Zwischenahn, *Germany* 24 B4
Bada Barabil, *India* 69 H11
Badagara, *India* 66 P9
Badagri, *Nigeria* 83 D5
Badajós, L., *Brazil* 124 D6
Badajoz, *Spain* 37 G4
Badajoz □, *Spain* 37 G4
Badakhshān □, *Afghan.* 66 A7
Badalona, *Spain* 38 D7
Badalzai, *Afghan.* 68 E1
Badampahar, *India* 67 H15
Badanah, *Si. Arabia* 70 D4
Badarinath, *India* 69 D8
Badas, Kepulauan, *Indonesia* 62 D3
Baddo →, *Pakistan* 66 F4
Bade, *Indonesia* 63 F9
Badeggi, *Nigeria* 83 D6
Badéguichéri, *Niger* 83 C6
Baden, *Austria* 27 C9
Baden, *Switz.* 25 H4
Baden, *U.S.A.* 116 F4
Baden-Baden, *Germany* 25 G4
Baden-Württemberg □, *Germany* 25 G4
Badgastein, *Austria* 26 D6
Badger, *Canada* 105 C8
Badger, *U.S.A.* 110 J7
Bādghīs □, *Afghan.* 66 B3
Badgingarra △, *Australia* 93 F2
Badgom, *India* 69 B6
Badia Polésine, *Italy* 41 C8
Badiar △, *Guinea* 82 C2
Badin, *Pakistan* 68 G3
Badinka ⌓, *Mali* 82 C3
Badlands △, *U.S.A.* 112 D3
Badogo, *Mali* 82 C3
Badoumbé, *Mali* 82 C2
Badrah, *Iraq* 70 C5
Badrinath, *India* 69 D8
Badulla, *Sri Lanka* 66 R12
Badung, Selat, *Indonesia* 63 K18
Baena, *Spain* 37 H6
Baeza, *Spain* 37 H7
Bafang, *Cameroon* 83 D7
Bafatá, *Guinea-Biss.* 82 C2
Baffin B., *Canada* 101 A13
Baffin I., *Canada* 101 B12
Bafia, *Cameroon* 83 E7
Bafilo, *Togo* 83 D5
Bafing △, *Mali* 82 C2
Bafing →, *Mali* 82 C2
Bafliyūn, *Syria* 70 B3
Bafoulabé, *Mali* 82 C2
Bafoussam, *Cameroon* 83 D7
Bāfq, *Iran* 71 D7
Bafra, *Turkey* 72 B6
Bafra Burnu, *Turkey* 72 B7
Bāft, *Iran* 71 D8
Bafut, *Cameroon* 83 D7
Bafwasende, *Dem. Rep. of the Congo* 86 B2
Bagam, *Niger* 83 B6
Bagamoyo, *Tanzania* 86 D4
Bagan Datoh, *Malaysia* 65 L3
Bagan Serai, *Malaysia* 65 K3
Baganga, *Phil.* 61 H7
Bagani, *Namibia* 88 B3
Bagansiapiapi, *Indonesia* 62 D2
Bagasra, *India* 68 J4
Bagaud, *India* 68 H6
Bagawi, *Sudan* 81 E3
Bagbag, *Sudan* 81 D3
Bagdad, *U.S.A.* 111 L11
Bagdarin, *Russia* 53 D12
Bagé, *Brazil* 127 C5
Bagenalstown = Muine Bheag, *Ireland* 12 D5
Baggs, *U.S.A.* 108 F10
Bagh, *Pakistan* 69 C5
Baghain →, *India* 69 G9
Baghdād, *Iraq* 70 C5
Bagheria, *Italy* 42 D6
Baghlān, *Afghan.* 66 A6
Baghlān □, *Afghan.* 66 B6
Bagley, *U.S.A.* 112 B7
Bagnara Cálabra, *Italy* 43 D8
Bagnasco, *Italy* 40 D5
Bagnères-de-Bigorre, *France* 20 E4
Bagnères-de-Luchon, *France* 20 F4
Bagni di Lucca, *Italy* 40 D7
Bagno di Romagna, *Italy* 41 E8
Bagnoles-de-l'Orne, *France* 18 D6
Bagnols-sur-Cèze, *France* 21 D8
Bagnorégio, *Italy* 41 F9
Bago = Pegu, *Burma* 67 L20
Bagodar, *India* 69 G11
Bagrationovsk, *Russia* 9 J19
Bagrdan, *Serbia & M.* 44 B5
Baguio, *Phil.* 61 C4
Bağyurdu, *Turkey* 47 C9
Bagzane, Monts, *Niger* 83 B6
Bah, *India* 69 F8
Bahabón de Esgueva, *Spain* 36 D7
Bahadurganj, *India* 69 F12
Bahadurgarh, *India* 68 E7
Bahama, Canal Viejo de, *W. Indies* 120 B4
Bahamas ■, *N. Amer.* 121 B5
Bahār, *Iran* 73 E13
Baharampur, *India* 69 G13
Baharîya, El Wâhât al, *Egypt* 80 B2
Baharu Pandan = Pandan, *Malaysia* 65 d
Bahawalnagar, *Pakistan* 68 E5
Bahawalpur, *Pakistan* 68 E4
Bahçe, *Turkey* 72 D7
Bahçecik, *Turkey* 45 F13
Baheri, *India* 69 E8
Bahgul →, *India* 69 F8
Bahi, *Tanzania* 86 D4
Bahi Swamp, *Tanzania* 86 D4
Bahía = Salvador, *Brazil* 125 F11
Bahía □, *Brazil* 125 F10
Bahía, Is. de la, *Honduras* 120 C2
Bahía Blanca, *Argentina* 126 D3
Bahía de Caráquez, *Ecuador* 124 D2
Bahía Honda, *Cuba* 120 B3
Bahía Laura, *Argentina* 128 F3
Bahía Negra, *Paraguay* 124 H7
Bahir Dar, *Ethiopia* 81 E4
Bahmanzād, *Iran* 71 D6
Bahr el Ahmar □, *Sudan* 80 D4
Bahr el Ghazâl □, *Sudan* 81 F2
Bahr el Jabal □, *Sudan* 81 G3
Bahraich, *India* 69 F9
Bahrain ■, *Asia* 71 E6
Bahror, *India* 68 F7
Bāhū Kalāt, *Iran* 71 E9
Bai, *Mali* 82 C4
Bai Bung, Mui = Ca Mau, Mui, *Vietnam* 65 H5
Bai Duc, *Vietnam* 64 C5
Bai Thuong, *Vietnam* 64 C5
Baia de Aramă, *Romania* 28 E7
Baia Mare, *Romania* 29 C8
Baia-Sprie, *Romania* 29 C8
Baião, *Brazil* 125 D9
Baïbokoum, *Chad* 79 G9
Baicheng, *China* 57 B12
Băicoi, *Romania* 29 E10
Baidoa, *Somali Rep.* 75 G3
Baie-Comeau, *Canada* 105 C6
Baie-St-Paul, *Canada* 105 C5
Baie-Trinité, *Canada* 105 C6
Baie Verte, *Canada* 105 C8
Baignes-Ste-Radegonde, *France* 20 C3
Baigneux-les-Juifs, *France* 19 E11
Baihar, *India* 69 H9
Baihe, *China* 56 H6
Baijnath, *India* 69 E8
Baikal, L. = Baykal, Oz., *Russia* 53 D11
Baikunthpur, *India* 69 H10
Baile Atha Cliath = Dublin, *Ireland* 12 C5
Băile Govora, *Romania* 29 E9
Băile Herculane, *Romania* 28 F7
Băile Olăneşti, *Romania* 29 E9
Băile Tuşnad, *Romania* 29 D10
Bailén, *Spain* 37 G7
Băileşti, *Romania* 29 F8
Baima, *China* 58 A3
Bain-de-Bretagne, *France* 18 E5
Bainbridge, *Ga., U.S.A.* 115 K3
Bainbridge, *N.Y., U.S.A.* 117 D9
Baing, *Indonesia* 63 F6
Bainiu, *China* 56 H7
Baiona, *Spain* 36 C2
Bā'ir, *Jordan* 74 E5
Bairin Youqi, *China* 57 C10
Bairin Zuoqi, *China* 57 C10
Bairnsdale, *Australia* 95 F4
Bais, *Phil.* 61 G5
Baisha, *China* 56 G7
Baissa, *Nigeria* 83 D7
Baitadi, *Nepal* 69 E9
Baixa Limia-Sierra do Xurés ⌓, *Spain* 36 D2
Baiyin, *China* 56 F3
Baiyü, *China* 58 B2
Baiyu Shan, *China* 56 F4
Baiyuda, *Sudan* 80 D3
Baj Baj, *India* 69 H13
Baja, *Hungary* 28 D3
Baja, Pta., *Mexico* 118 B1
Baja California, *Mexico* 118 A1
Baja California □, *Mexico* 118 B2
Baja California Sur □, *Mexico* 118 B2
Bajag, *India* 69 H9
Bajamar, *Canary Is.* 48 F3
Bajana, *India* 68 H4
Bajatrejo, *Indonesia* 63 J17
Bajera, *Indonesia* 63 J18
Bājgīrān, *Iran* 71 B8
Bajimba, Mt., *Australia* 95 D5
Bajina Bašta, *Serbia & M.* 44 C3
Bajmok, *Serbia & M.* 28 E4
Bajo Nuevo, *Caribbean* 120 C4
Bajoga, *Nigeria* 83 C7
Bajool, *Australia* 94 C5
Bak, *Hungary* 28 D1
Bakar, *Croatia* 41 C11
Bakasi Pen., *Cameroon* 83 E6
Bakel, *Senegal* 82 C2
Baker, *Calif., U.S.A.* 111 K10
Baker, *Mont., U.S.A.* 112 B2
Baker, L., *Canada* 100 B10
Baker, Mt., *U.S.A.* 108 B3
Baker City, *U.S.A.* 108 D5
Baker I., *Pac. Oc.* 96 G10
Baker I., *U.S.A.* 102 B2
Baker L., *Australia* 93 E4
Baker Lake, *Canada* 100 B10
Bakers Creek, *Australia* 94 C4
Bakers Dozen Is., *Canada* 104 A4
Bakersfield, *Calif., U.S.A.* 111 K8
Bakersfield, *Vt., U.S.A.* 117 B12
Bakhchysaray, *Ukraine* 33 K7
Bakhmach, *Ukraine* 33 G7
Bākhtarān, *Iran* 70 C5
Bākhtarān □, *Iran* 70 C5
Bakı, *Azerbaijan* 35 K9
Bakır →, *Turkey* 47 C9
Bakırdağı, *Turkey* 72 C6
Bakkafjörður, *Iceland* 8 C6
Baklan, *Turkey* 47 C11
Bako, *Ethiopia* 81 F4
Bako, *Ivory C.* 82 D3
Bakony, *Hungary* 28 C2
Bakony Forest = Bakony, *Hungary* 28 C2
Bakori, *Nigeria* 83 C6
Bakouma, *C.A.R.* 84 C4
Baksan, *Russia* 35 J6
Bakswaho, *India* 69 G8
Baku = Bakı, *Azerbaijan* 35 K9
Bakundi, *Nigeria* 83 D7
Bakutis Coast, *Antarctica* 5 D15
Baky = Bakı, *Azerbaijan* 35 K9
Bala, *Canada* 116 A5
Bala, *Senegal* 82 C2
Bâlâ, *Turkey* 72 C5
Bala, *U.K.* 14 E4
Bala, L., *U.K.* 14 E4
Balabac I., *Phil.* 62 C5
Balabac Str., *E. Indies* 62 C5
Balabagh, *Afghan.* 68 B4
Ba'labakk, *Lebanon* 74 B5
Balabalangan, Kepulauan, *Indonesia* 62 E5
Bălăciţa, *Romania* 29 F8
Balad, *Iraq* 70 C5
Balad Rūz, *Iraq* 70 C5
Bālādeh, *Fārs, Iran* 71 D6
Bālādeh, *Māzandaran, Iran* 71 B6
Balaghat, *India* 66 J12
Balaghat Ra., *India* 66 K10
Balaguer, *Spain* 38 D5
Balakhna, *Russia* 34 B6
Balaklava, *Ukraine* 33 K7
Balakliya, *Ukraine* 33 H9
Balakovo, *Russia* 34 D8
Balamau, *India* 69 F9
Bălan, *Romania* 29 D10
Balancán, *Mexico* 119 D6
Balashov, *Russia* 34 E6
Balasinor, *India* 68 H5
Balasore = Baleshwar, *India* 67 J15
Balassagyarmat, *Hungary* 28 B4
Balât, *Egypt* 80 B2
Balaton, *Hungary* 28 D2
Balaton-felvidéki △, *Hungary* 28 D2
Balatonboglár, *Hungary* 28 D2
Balatonfüred, *Hungary* 28 D2
Balatonszentgyörgy, *Hungary* 28 D2
Balayan, *Phil.* 61 E4
Balazote, *Spain* 39 G2
Balbieriškis, *Lithuania* 30 D10
Balbigny, *France* 21 C8
Balbina, Reprêsa de, *Brazil* 124 D7
Balboa, *Panama* 120 E4
Balbriggan, *Ireland* 12 C5
Balcarce, *Argentina* 126 D4
Balcarres, *Canada* 103 C8
Bălceşti, *Romania* 29 F8
Balchik, *Bulgaria* 45 C12
Balclutha, *N.Z.* 91 M2
Balcones Escarpment, *U.S.A.* 113 L5
Balçova, *Turkey* 47 C9
Bald Hd., *Australia* 93 G2
Bald I., *Australia* 93 F2
Bald Knob, *U.S.A.* 113 H9
Baldock L., *Canada* 103 B9
Baldwin, *Mich., U.S.A.* 114 D3
Baldwin, *Pa., U.S.A.* 116 F5
Baldwinsville, *U.S.A.* 117 C8
Baldy Mt., *U.S.A.* 108 B9
Baldy Peak, *U.S.A.* 109 K9
Bale, *Croatia* 41 C10
Bale, *Ethiopia* 81 F5
Bale □, *Ethiopia* 81 F5
Bale Mts. △, *Ethiopia* 81 F4
Baleares, Is., *Spain* 48 B10
Balearic Is. = Baleares, Is., *Spain* 48 B10
Baleine = Whale →, *Canada* 105 A6
Baleine, Petite R. de la →, *Canada* 104 A4
Băleni, *Romania* 29 E12
Baler, *Phil.* 61 D4
Baler Bay, *Phil.* 61 D4
Baleshare, *U.K.* 13 D1
Baleshwar, *India* 67 J15
Balezino, *Russia* 34 B11
Balfate, *Honduras* 120 C2
Bali, *Cameroon* 83 D7
Balí, *Greece* 49 D6
Bali, *India* 68 G5
Bali, *Indonesia* 63 J18
Bali □, *Indonesia* 63 J18
Bali, Selat, *Indonesia* 63 J17
Bali Sea, *Indonesia* 63 J17
Balia, *S. Leone* 82 D2
Baliapal, *India* 69 J12
Baligród, *Poland* 31 J9
Balik Pulau, *Malaysia* 65 c
Balıkeşir, *Turkey* 47 B9
Balıkeşir □, *Turkey* 47 B9
Balıklıçeşme, *Turkey* 45 F11
Balikpapan, *Indonesia* 62 E5
Balimbing, *Phil.* 63 C5
Baling, *Malaysia* 65 K3
Balingen, *Germany* 25 G4
Balinţ, *Romania* 28 E6
Balintang Channel, *Phil.* 61 B4
Balipara, *India* 67 F18
Balkan Mts. = Stara Planina, *Bulgaria* 44 C7
Balkhash = Balqash, *Kazakhstan* 52 E8
Balkhash, Ozero = Balqash Köl, *Kazakhstan* 52 E8
Balla, *Bangla.* 67 G17
Ballachulish, *U.K.* 13 E3
Balladonia, *Australia* 93 F3
Ballaghaderreen, *Ireland* 12 C3
Ballarat, *Australia* 95 F3
Ballard, L., *Australia* 93 E3
Ballater, *U.K.* 13 D5
Ballé, *Mali* 82 B3
Ballena Gris = Ojo de Liebre ⌓, *Mexico* 118 B2
Ballenas, Canal de, *Mexico* 118 B2
Balleny Is., *Antarctica* 5 C11
Balleroy, *France* 18 C6
Ballerup, *Denmark* 11 J6
Ballı, *Turkey* 45 F11
Ballia, *India* 69 G11
Ballina, *Australia* 95 D5
Ballina, *Ireland* 12 B2
Ballinasloe, *Ireland* 12 C3
Ballinger, *U.S.A.* 113 K5
Ballinrobe, *Ireland* 12 C2
Ballinskelligs B., *Ireland* 12 E1
Ballon, *France* 18 D7
Ballons des Vosges ⌓, *France* 19 E14
Ballsh, *Albania* 44 F3
Ballston Spa, *U.S.A.* 117 D11
Ballybunion, *Ireland* 12 D2
Ballycastle, *U.K.* 12 A5
Ballyclare, *U.K.* 12 B5
Ballyhaunis, *Ireland* 12 C3
Ballymena, *U.K.* 12 B5
Ballymoney, *U.K.* 12 A5
Ballymote, *Ireland* 12 B3
Ballynahinch, *U.K.* 12 B6
Ballyquintin Pt., *U.K.* 12 B6
Ballyshannon, *Ireland* 12 B3
Balmaceda, *Chile* 128 F2
Balmaseda, *Spain* 38 B1
Balmazújváros, *Hungary* 28 C6
Balmertown, *Canada* 103 C10
Balmoral, *Australia* 95 F3
Balmorhea, *U.S.A.* 113 K3
Balochistan = Baluchistan □, *Pakistan* 66 F4
Balonne →, *Australia* 95 D4
Balotra, *India* 68 G5
Balqash, *Kazakhstan* 52 E8
Balqash Köl, *Kazakhstan* 52 E8
Balrampur, *India* 69 F10
Balranald, *Australia* 95 E3
Balş, *Romania* 29 F9
Balsas, *Mexico* 119 D5
Balsas →, *Brazil* 125 E9
Balsas →, *Mexico* 118 D4
Bålsta, *Sweden* 10 E11
Balston Spa, *U.S.A.* 117 D11
Balta, *Romania* 28 F7
Balta, *Ukraine* 33 J5
Baltanás, *Spain* 36 D6
Bălţi, *Moldova* 29 C12
Baltic Sea, *Europe* 9 H18
Baltîm, *Egypt* 80 H7
Baltimore, *Ireland* 12 E2
Baltimore, *Md., U.S.A.* 114 F7
Baltimore, *Ohio, U.S.A.* 116 G2
Baltit, *Pakistan* 69 A6
Baltiysk, *Russia* 9 J18
Baltrum, *Germany* 24 B3
Baluchistan □, *Pakistan* 66 F4
Balurghat, *India* 69 G13
Balvi, *Latvia* 9 H22
Balya, *Turkey* 47 B9
Bam, *Iran* 71 D8
Bama, *China* 58 E6
Bama, *Nigeria* 83 C7
Bamaga, *Australia* 94 A3
Bamaji L., *Canada* 104 B1
Bamako, *Mali* 82 C3
Bamba, *Mali* 83 B4
Bambara Maoundé, *Mali* 82 B4
Bambari, *C.A.R.* 84 C4
Bambaroo, *Australia* 94 B4
Bambaya, *Guinea* 82 D2
Bamberg, *Germany* 25 F6
Bamberg, *U.S.A.* 115 J5
Bambesi, *Ethiopia* 81 F3
Bambey, *Senegal* 82 C1
Bambili, *Dem. Rep. of the Congo* 86 B2
Bamboi, *Ghana* 82 D4
Bamburgh, *U.K.* 14 B6
Bamenda, *Cameroon* 83 D7
Bamfield, *Canada* 102 D3
Bāmīān □, *Afghan.* 66 B5
Bamiancheng, *China* 57 C13
Bamkin, *Cameroon* 83 D7
Bampūr, *Iran* 71 E9
Ban, *Burkina Faso* 82 C4
Ban Ao Tu Khun, *Thailand* 65 a
Ban Ban, *Laos* 64 C4
Ban Bang Hin, *Thailand* 65 H2
Ban Bang Khu, *Thailand* 65 a
Ban Bang Rong, *Thailand* 65 a
Ban Bo Phut, *Thailand* 65 b
Ban Chaweng, *Thailand* 65 b
Ban Chiang Klang, *Thailand* 64 C3
Ban Chik, *Laos* 64 D4
Ban Choho, *Thailand* 64 E4
Ban Dan Lan Hoi, *Thailand* 64 D2
Ban Don = Surat Thani, *Thailand* 65 H2
Ban Don, *Vietnam* 64 F6
Ban Don, Ao →, *Thailand* 65 H2
Ban Dong, *Thailand* 64 C3
Ban Hong, *Thailand* 64 C2
Ban Hua Thanon, *Thailand* 65 b
Ban Kaeng, *Thailand* 64 D3
Ban Kantang, *Thailand* 65 J2
Ban Karon, *Thailand* 65 a
Ban Kata, *Thailand* 65 a
Ban Keun, *Laos* 64 C4
Ban Khai, *Thailand* 64 F3
Ban Kheun, *Laos* 64 B3
Ban Khlong Khian, *Thailand* 65 a
Ban Khlong Kua, *Thailand* 65 J3
Ban Khuan, *Thailand* 65 a
Ban Khuan Mao, *Thailand* 65 J2
Ban Ko Yai Chim, *Thailand* 65 G2
Ban Kok, *Thailand* 64 D4
Ban Laem, *Thailand* 64 F2
Ban Lamai, *Thailand* 65 b

Ban Lao Ngam, *Laos* 64 E6
Ban Le Kathe, *Thailand* 64 E2
Ban Lo Po Noi, *Thailand* 65 a
Ban Mae Chedi, *Thailand* 64 C2
Ban Mae Laeng, *Thailand* 64 B2
Ban Mae Nam, *Thailand* 65 b
Ban Mae Sariang, *Thailand* 64 C1
Ban Mê Thuôt = Buon Ma Thuot, *Vietnam* 64 F7
Ban Mi, *Thailand* 64 E3
Ban Muong Mo, *Laos* 64 C4
Ban Na Bo, *Thailand* 65 b
Ban Na Mo, *Laos* 64 D5
Ban Na San, *Thailand* 65 H2
Ban Na Tong, *Laos* 64 B3
Ban Nam Bac, *Laos* 64 B4
Ban Nam Ma, *Laos* 64 A3
Ban Ngang, *Laos* 64 E6
Ban Nong Bok, *Laos* 64 D5
Ban Nong Boua, *Laos* 64 E6
Ban Nong Pling, *Thailand* 64 E3
Ban Pak Chan, *Thailand* 65 G2
Ban Patong, *Thailand* 65 a
Ban Phai, *Thailand* 64 D4
Ban Phak Chit, *Thailand* 65 a
Ban Pong, *Thailand* 64 F2
Ban Rawai, *Thailand* 65 a
Ban Ron Phibun, *Thailand* 65 H2
Ban Sakhu, *Thailand* 65 a
Ban Sanam Chai, *Thailand* 65 J3
Ban Sangkha, *Thailand* 64 E4
Ban Tak, *Thailand* 64 D2
Ban Tako, *Thailand* 64 E4
Ban Tha Dua, *Thailand* 64 D2
Ban Tha Li, *Thailand* 64 D3
Ban Tha Nun, *Thailand* 65 a
Ban Tha Rua, *Thailand* 65 a
Ban Tha Yu, *Thailand* 65 a
Ban Thahine, *Laos* 64 E5
Ban Thong Krut, *Thailand* 65 b
Ban Xien Kok, *Laos* 64 B3
Ban Yen Nhan, *Vietnam* 64 B6
Banaba, *Kiribati* 96 H8
Banalia, *Dem. Rep. of the Congo* 86 B2
Banam, *Cambodia* 65 G5
Banamba, *Mali* 82 C3
Banana Is., *S. Leone* 82 D2
Bananal, I. do, *Brazil* 125 F8
Banaras = Varanasi, *India* 69 G10
Banas →, *Gujarat, India* 68 H4
Banas →, *Mad. P., India* 69 G9
Bânâs, Ras, *Egypt* 80 C4
Banaz, *Turkey* 47 C11
Banaz →, *Turkey* 47 C11
Banbridge, *U.K.* 12 B5
Banbury, *U.K.* 15 E6
Banchory, *U.K.* 13 D6
Banco, *Ethiopia* 81 F4
Bancroft, *Canada* 116 A7
Band, *Romania* 29 D9
Band Bonī, *Iran* 71 E8
Band Qīr, *Iran* 71 D6
Banda, *Mad. P., India* 69 G8
Banda, *Ut. P., India* 69 G9
Banda, Kepulauan, *Indonesia* 63 E7
Banda Aceh, *Indonesia* 62 C1
Banda Banda, Mt., *Australia* 95 E5
Banda Elat, *Indonesia* 63 F8
Banda Is. = Banda, Kepulauan, *Indonesia* 63 E7
Banda Sea, *Indonesia* 63 F7
Bandai-Asahi △, *Japan* 54 F10
Bandai-San, *Japan* 54 F10
Bandama →, *Ivory C.* 82 D3
Bandama Blanc →, *Ivory C.* 82 D3
Bandama Rouge →, *Ivory C.* 82 D4
Bandān, *Iran* 71 D9
Bandanaira, *Indonesia* 63 E7
Bandanwara, *India* 68 F6
Bandar = Machilipatnam, *India* 67 L12
Bandar-e Abbās, *Iran* 71 E8
Bandar-e Anzalī, *Iran* 71 B6
Bandar-e Bushehr = Būshehr, *Iran* 71 D6
Bandar-e Chārak, *Iran* 71 E7
Bandar-e Deylam, *Iran* 71 D6
Bandar-e Emām Khomeynı, *Iran* 71 D6
Bandar-e Lengeh, *Iran* 71 E7
Bandar-e Maqām, *Iran* 71 E7
Bandar-e Ma'shur, *Iran* 71 D6
Bandar-e Rīg, *Iran* 71 D6
Bandar-e Torkeman, *Iran* 71 B7
Bandar Lampung = Tanjungkarang Telukbetung, *Indonesia* 62 F3
Bandar Maharani = Muar, *Malaysia* 65 L4
Bandar Penggaram = Batu Pahat, *Malaysia* 65 M4
Bandar Seri Begawan, *Brunei* 62 C4
Bandar Sri Aman, *Malaysia* 62 D4
Bandawe, *Malawi* 87 E3
Bande, *Spain* 36 C3
Bandeira, Pico da, *Brazil* 127 A7
Bandera, *Argentina* 126 B3
Banderas, B. de, *Mexico* 118 C3
Bandhogarh, *India* 69 H9
Bandi →, *India* 68 F6
Bandiagara, *Mali* 82 C4
Bandikui, *India* 68 F7
Bandırma, *Turkey* 45 F11
Bandjarmasin = Banjarmasin, *Indonesia* 62 E4
Bandol, *France* 21 E9
Bandon, *Ireland* 12 E3
Bandon →, *Ireland* 12 E3
Bandula, *Mozam.* 87 F3
Bandundu, *Dem. Rep. of the Congo* 84 E3
Bandung, *Indonesia* 63 G12
Bané, *Burkina Faso* 83 C4
Băneasa, *Romania* 29 E12
Bāneh, *Iran* 70 C5
Bañeres, *Spain* 39 G4
Banes, *Cuba* 121 B4
Banff, *Canada* 102 C5
Banff, *U.K.* 13 D6
Banff △, *Canada* 102 C5
Banfora, *Burkina Faso* 82 C4
Bang Fai →, *Laos* 64 D5
Bang Hieng →, *Laos* 64 D5
Bang Krathum, *Thailand* 64 D3
Bang Lamung, *Thailand* 64 F3
Bang Mun Nak, *Thailand* 64 D3
Bang Pa In, *Thailand* 64 E3
Bang Rakam, *Thailand* 64 D3
Bang Saphan, *Thailand* 65 G2
Bang Thao, *Thailand* 65 a
Bangaduni I., *India* 69 J13
Bangala Dam, *Zimbabwe* 87 G3
Bangalore, *India* 66 N10
Banganga →, *India* 68 F6
Bangangté, *Cameroon* 83 D7
Bangaon, *India* 69 H13
Bangassou, *C.A.R.* 84 D4
Banggai, *Indonesia* 63 E6
Banggai, Kepulauan, *Indonesia* 63 E6
Banggai Arch. = Banggai, Kepulauan, *Indonesia* 63 E6
Banggi, *Malaysia* 62 C5
Banghāzī, *Libya* 79 B10
Bangjang, *Sudan* 81 E3
Bangka, *Sulawesi, Indonesia* 63 D7
Bangka, *Sumatera, Indonesia* 62 E3
Bangka, Selat, *Indonesia* 62 E3
Bangkalan, *Indonesia* 63 G15
Bangkinang, *Indonesia* 62 D2
Bangko, *Indonesia* 62 E2
Bangkok, *Thailand* 64 F3
Bangladesh ■, *Asia* 67 H17
Bangli, *Indonesia* 63 J18
Bangolo, *Ivory C.* 82 D3
Bangong Co, *India* 69 B8
Bangor, *Down, U.K.* 12 B6
Bangor, *Gwynedd, U.K.* 14 D3
Bangor, *Maine, U.S.A.* 101 D13
Bangor, *Pa., U.S.A.* 117 F9
Bangued, *Phil.* 61 C4
Bangui, *C.A.R.* 84 D3
Bangui, *Phil.* 61 B4
Banguru, *Dem. Rep. of the Congo* 86 B2
Bangweulu, L., *Zambia* 87 E3
Bangweulu Swamp, *Zambia* 87 E3
Banhine △, *Mozam.* 89 C5
Bani, *Dom. Rep.* 121 C5
Bani →, *Mali* 82 C4
Bani Bangou, *Niger* 83 B5
Banī Sa'd, *Iraq* 70 C5
Bania, *Ivory C.* 82 D4
Banihal Pass, *India* 69 C6
Banikoara, *Benin* 83 C5
Bāniyās, *Syria* 70 C3
Banja Luka, *Bos.-H.* 28 F2
Banjar, *India* 68 D7
Banjar →, *India* 69 H9
Banjarmasin, *Indonesia* 62 E4
Banjul, *Gambia* 82 C1
Banka, *India* 69 G12
Bankas, *Mali* 82 C4
Bankeryd, *Sweden* 11 G8
Banket, *Zimbabwe* 87 F3
Bankilaré, *Niger* 83 C5
Bankipore, *India* 67 G14
Banks I., *B.C., Canada* 102 C3
Banks I., *N.W.T., Canada* 100 A7
Banks Pen., *N.Z.* 91 K4
Banks Str., *Australia* 95 G4
Bankura, *India* 69 H12
Bankya, *Bulgaria* 44 D7
Banmankhi, *India* 69 G12
Bann →, *Arm., U.K.* 12 B5
Bann →, *L'derry., U.K.* 12 A5
Bannalec, *France* 18 E3
Bannang Sata, *Thailand* 65 J3
Banning, *U.S.A.* 111 M10
Banningville = Bandundu, *Dem. Rep. of the Congo* 84 E3
Banno, *Ethiopia* 81 G4
Bannockburn, *Canada* 116 B7
Bannockburn, *U.K.* 13 E5
Bannockburn, *Zimbabwe* 87 G2
Bannu, *Pakistan* 66 C7
Bano, *India* 69 H11
Bañolas = Banyoles, *Spain* 38 C7
Banon, *France* 21 D9
Baños de la Encina, *Spain* 37 G7
Baños de Molgas, *Spain* 36 C3
Bánovce nad Bebravou, *Slovak Rep.* 27 C11
Banovići, *Bos.-H.* 28 F3
Bansgaon, *India* 69 F10
Banská Bystrica, *Slovak Rep.* 27 C12
Banská Štiavnica, *Slovak Rep.* 27 C11
Bansko, *Bulgaria* 44 E7
Banskobystrický □, *Slovak Rep.* 27 C12
Banswara, *India* 68 H6
Bantaeng, *Indonesia* 63 F5
Bantaji, *Nigeria* 83 D7
Bantayan, *Phil.* 61 F5
Bantry, *Ireland* 12 E2
Bantry B., *Ireland* 12 E2
Bantul, *Indonesia* 63 G14
Bantva, *India* 68 J4
Banya, *Bulgaria* 45 D8
Banyak, Kepulauan, *Indonesia* 62 D1
Banyalbufar, *Spain* 48 B9
Banyo, *Cameroon* 83 D7
Banyoles, *Spain* 38 C7
Banyuls-sur-Mer, *France* 20 F7
Banyumas, *Indonesia* 63 G13
Banyuwangi, *Indonesia* 63 J17
Banzare Coast, *Antarctica* 5 C9
Bao Ha, *Vietnam* 58 F5
Bao Lac, *Vietnam* 64 A5
Bao Loc, *Vietnam* 65 G6
Bao'an = Shenzhen, *China* 59 F10
Baocheng, *China* 56 H4
Baode, *China* 56 E6
Baodi, *China* 57 E9
Baoding, *China* 56 E8
Baoji, *China* 56 G4
Baojing, *China* 58 C7
Baokang, *China* 59 B8
Baoshan, *Shanghai, China* 59 B13
Baoshan, *Yunnan, China* 58 E2
Baotou, *China* 56 D6
Baoxing, *China* 58 B4
Baoying, *China* 57 H10
Bap, *India* 68 F5
Bapatla, *India* 67 M12
Bapaume, *France* 19 B9
Bāqerābād, *Iran* 71 C6
Ba'qūbah, *Iraq* 70 C5
Baquedano, *Chile* 126 A2
Bar, *Serbia & M.* 44 D3
Bar, *Ukraine* 33 H4
Bar Bigha, *India* 69 G11
Bar Harbor, *U.S.A.* 115 C11
Bar-le-Duc, *France* 19 D12
Bar-sur-Aube, *France* 19 D11
Bar-sur-Seine, *France* 19 D11
Bara, *India* 69 G9
Bâra, *Romania* 29 C12
Bara Banki, *India* 69 F9
Barabai, *Indonesia* 62 E5
Baraboo, *U.S.A.* 112 D10
Baracoa, *Cuba* 121 B5
Baradā →, *Syria* 74 B5
Baradero, *Argentina* 126 C4
Baraga, *U.S.A.* 112 B10
Bărăganul, *Romania* 29 F12
Barah →, *India* 68 F6
Barahona, *Dom. Rep.* 121 C5
Barahona, *Spain* 38 D2
Barail Range, *India* 67 G18
Barajas, Madrid ✕ (MAD), *Spain* 36 E7
Baraka, *Sudan* 81 E2
Baraka →, *Sudan* 80 D4
Barakaldo, *Spain* 38 B2
Barakar →, *India* 69 G12
Barakhola, *India* 67 G18
Barakot, *India* 69 J11
Barakpur, *India* 69 H13
Baralaba, *Australia* 94 C4
Baralla, *Spain* 36 C3
Baralzon L., *Canada* 103 B9
Barameiya, *Sudan* 80 D4
Baramula, *India* 69 B6
Baran, *India* 68 G7
Baran →, *Pakistan* 68 G3
Barañain, *Spain* 38 C3
Baranavichy, *Belarus* 33 F4
Barani, *Burkina Faso* 82 C4
Baranof, *U.S.A.* 102 B2
Baranof I., *U.S.A.* 100 C6
Baranów Sandomierski, *Poland* 31 H8
Baranya □, *Hungary* 28 E3
Baraolt, *Romania* 29 D10
Barapasi, *Indonesia* 63 E9
Barasat, *India* 69 H13
Barat Daya, Kepulauan, *Indonesia* 63 F7
Barataria B., *U.S.A.* 113 L10
Barauda, *India* 68 H6
Baraut, *India* 68 E7
Barbacena, *Brazil* 127 A7
Barbados ■, *W. Indies* 121 g
Barban, *Croatia* 41 C11
Barbària, C. de, *Spain* 48 C7
Barbaros, *Turkey* 45 F11
Barbastro, *Spain* 38 C5
Barbate = Barbate de Franco, *Spain* 37 J5
Barbate de Franco, *Spain* 37 J5
Barberino di Mugello, *Italy* 41 E8
Barberton, *S. Africa* 89 D5
Barberton, *U.S.A.* 116 E3
Barbezieux-St-Hilaire, *France* 20 C3
Barbonneau, *St. Lucia* 121 f
Barbosa, *Colombia* 124 B4
Barbourville, *U.S.A.* 115 G4
Barbuda, *W. Indies* 121 C7
Bârca, *Romania* 29 G8
Barcaldine, *Australia* 94 C4
Barcarrota, *Spain* 37 G4
Barcellona Pozzo di Gotto, *Italy* 43 D8
Barcelona, *Spain* 38 D7
Barcelona, *Venezuela* 124 A6
Barcelona □, *Spain* 38 D7
Barcelona ✕ (BCN), *Spain* 38 D7
Barceloneta, *Puerto Rico* 121 d
Barcelonette, *France* 21 D10
Barcelos, *Brazil* 124 D6
Barcin, *Poland* 31 F4
Barclayville, *Liberia* 82 E3
Barcoo →, *Australia* 94 D3
Barcs, *Hungary* 28 E2
Barczewo, *Poland* 30 E7
Bärdä, *Azerbaijan* 35 K8
Bardaï, *Chad* 79 D9
Bardas Blancas, *Argentina* 126 D2
Bardawîl, Sabkhet el, *Egypt* 74 D2
Barddhaman, *India* 69 H12
Bardejov, *Slovak Rep.* 27 B14
Bardera, *Somali Rep.* 75 G3
Bardi, *Italy* 40 D6
Bardīyah, *Libya* 79 B10
Bardolino, *Italy* 40 C7
Bardonécchia, *Italy* 40 C3
Bardsey I., *U.K.* 14 E3
Bardstown, *U.S.A.* 114 G3
Bareilly, *India* 69 E8
Barela, *India* 69 H9
Barentin, *France* 18 C7
Barenton, *France* 18 D6
Barents Sea, *Arctic* 50 B7
Barentu, *Eritrea* 81 D4
Barfleur, *France* 18 C5
Barfleur, Pte. de, *France* 18 C5
Barga, *Italy* 40 D7
Bargara, *Australia* 94 C5
Bargas, *Spain* 36 F6
Bârgăului Bistrița, *Romania* 29 C9
Barge, *Italy* 40 D4
Bargnop, *Sudan* 81 F2
Bargteheide, *Germany* 24 B6
Barguzin, *Russia* 53 D11
Barh, *India* 69 G11
Barhaj, *India* 69 F10
Barharwa, *India* 69 G12
Barhi, *India* 69 G11
Bari, *India* 68 F7
Bari, *Italy* 43 A9
Bari Doab, *Pakistan* 68 D5
Bari Sadri, *India* 68 G6
Bari Sardo, *Italy* 42 C2
Barīdī, Ra's, *Si. Arabia* 70 E3
Barīm, *Yemen* 76 E8
Barinas, *Venezuela* 124 B4
Baring, C., *Canada* 100 B8
Baringo, L., *Kenya* 86 B4
Bârîs, *Egypt* 80 C3
Barisal, *Bangla.* 67 H17
Barisal □, *Bangla.* 67 H17
Barisan, Bukit, *Indonesia* 62 E2
Barito →, *Indonesia* 62 E4
Baritú △, *Argentina* 126 A3
Barjac, *France* 21 D8
Barjols, *France* 21 E10
Bark L., *Canada* 116 A7
Barka = Baraka →, *Sudan* 80 D4
Barkakana, *India* 69 H11
Barkam, *China* 58 B4
Barker, *U.S.A.* 116 C6
Barkley, L., *U.S.A.* 115 G2
Barkley Sound, *Canada* 102 D3
Barkly East, *S. Africa* 88 E4
Barkly Roadhouse, *Australia* 94 B2
Barkly Tableland, *Australia* 94 B2
Barkly West, *S. Africa* 88 D3
Barkol, Wadi →, *Sudan* 80 D3
Barla Dağı, *Turkey* 47 C12
Bârlad, *Romania* 29 D12
Bârlad →, *Romania* 29 E12
Barlee, L., *Australia* 93 E2
Barlee, Mt., *Australia* 93 D4
Barletta, *Italy* 43 A9
Barlinek, *Poland* 31 F2
Barlovento, *Canary Is.* 48 F2
Barlow L., *Canada* 103 A8
Barmedman, *Australia* 95 E4
Barmer, *India* 68 G4
Barmera, *Australia* 95 E3
Barmouth, *U.K.* 14 E3
Barmstedt, *Germany* 24 B5
Barna →, *India* 69 G10
Barnagar, *India* 68 H6
Barnala, *India* 68 D6
Barnard Castle, *U.K.* 14 C6
Barnaul, *Russia* 52 D9
Barnesville, *U.S.A.* 115 J3
Barnet □, *U.K.* 15 F7
Barneveld, *Neths.* 17 B5
Barneveld, *U.S.A.* 117 C9
Barneville-Cartevert, *France* 18 C5
Barnhart, *U.S.A.* 113 K4
Barnsley, *U.K.* 14 D6
Barnstaple, *U.K.* 15 F3
Barnstaple Bay = Bideford Bay, *U.K.* 15 F3
Barnsville, *U.S.A.* 112 B6
Barnwell, *U.S.A.* 115 J5
Baro, *Nigeria* 83 D6
Baro →, *Ethiopia* 81 F3
Baroda = Vadodara, *India* 68 H5
Baroda, *India* 68 G7
Baroe, *S. Africa* 88 E3
Baron Ra., *Australia* 92 D4
Barong, *China* 58 B2
Barotseland, *Zambia* 85 H4
Barouéli, *Mali* 82 C3
Barpeta, *India* 67 F17
Barques, Pt. Aux, *U.S.A.* 116 B2
Barquísimeto, *Venezuela* 124 A5
Barr, Ras el, *Egypt* 80 H7
Barr Smith Range, *Australia* 93 E3
Barra, *Brazil* 125 F10
Barra, *U.K.* 13 E1
Barra, Sd. of, *U.K.* 13 D1
Barra de Navidad, *Mexico* 118 D4
Barra do Corda, *Brazil* 125 E9
Barra do Piraí, *Brazil* 127 A7
Barra Falsa, Pta. da, *Mozam.* 89 C6
Barra Hd., *U.K.* 13 E1
Barra Mansa, *Brazil* 127 A7
Barraba, *Australia* 95 E5
Barrackpur = Barakpur, *India* 69 H13
Barradale Roadhouse, *Australia* 92 D1
Barrafranca, *Italy* 43 E7
Barraigh = Barra, *U.K.* 13 E1
Barranca, *Lima, Peru* 124 F3
Barranca, *Loreto, Peru* 124 D3
Barranca del Cobre △, *Mexico* 118 B3
Barrancabermeja, *Colombia* 124 B4
Barrancas, *Venezuela* 124 B6
Barrancos, *Portugal* 37 G4
Barranqueras, *Argentina* 126 B4
Barranquilla, *Colombia* 124 A4
Barraute, *Canada* 104 C4
Barre, *Mass., U.S.A.* 117 D12
Barre, *Vt., U.S.A.* 117 B12
Barreal, *Argentina* 126 C2
Barreiras, *Brazil* 125 F10
Barreirinhas, *Brazil* 125 D10
Barreiro, *Portugal* 37 G1
Barrême, *France* 21 E10
Barren, Nosy, *Madag.* 89 B7
Barretos, *Brazil* 125 H9
Barrhead, *Canada* 102 C6
Barrie, *Canada* 116 B5
Barrier Ra., *Australia* 95 E3
Barrière, *Canada* 102 C4
Barrington, *U.S.A.* 117 E13
Barrington L., *Canada* 103 B8
Barrington Tops, *Australia* 95 E5
Barringun, *Australia* 95 D4
Barro do Garças, *Brazil* 125 G8
Barron, *U.S.A.* 112 C9
Barrow, *U.S.A.* 100 A4
Barrow →, *Ireland* 12 D5
Barrow Creek, *Australia* 94 C1
Barrow I., *Australia* 92 D2
Barrow-in-Furness, *U.K.* 14 C4
Barrow Pt., *Australia* 94 A3
Barrow Pt., *U.S.A.* 98 B4
Barrow Ra., *Australia* 93 E4
Barrow Str., *Canada* 4 B3
Barruecopardo, *Spain* 36 D4
Barruelo de Santullán, *Spain* 36 C6
Barry, *U.K.* 15 F4
Barry's Bay, *Canada* 116 A7
Barsalogho, *Burkina Faso* 83 C4
Barsat, *Pakistan* 69 A5
Barsham, *Syria* 70 C4
Barsi, *India* 66 K9
Barsinghausen, *Germany* 24 C5
Barsoi, *India* 67 G15
Barstow, *U.S.A.* 111 L9
Barth, *Germany* 24 A8
Barthélemy, Col, *Vietnam* 64 C5
Bartica, *Guyana* 124 B7
Bartin, *Turkey* 72 B5
Bartlesville, *U.S.A.* 113 G7
Bartlett, *U.S.A.* 110 J8
Bartlett, L., *Canada* 102 A5
Bartolomeu Dias, *Mozam.* 87 G4
Barton, *U.S.A.* 117 B12
Barton upon Humber, *U.K.* 14 D7
Bartoszyce, *Poland* 30 D7
Bartow, *U.S.A.* 115 M5
Barú, Volcan, *Panama* 120 E3
Barumba, *Dem. Rep. of the Congo* 86 B1
Baruth, *Germany* 24 C9
Baruunsuu, *Mongolia* 56 C3
Barvinkove, *Ukraine* 33 H9
Barwani, *India* 68 H6
Barwice, *Poland* 30 E3
Barycz →, *Poland* 31 G3
Barysaw, *Belarus* 32 E5
Barysh, *Russia* 34 D8
Barzān, *Iraq* 70 B5
Bârzava, *Romania* 28 D6
Bas-Rhin □, *France* 19 D14
Bašaid, *Serbia & M.* 28 E5
Bāsa'idū, *Iran* 71 E7
Basal, *Pakistan* 68 C5
Basankusa, *Dem. Rep. of the Congo* 84 D3
Basarabeasca, *Moldova* 29 D13
Basarabi, *Romania* 29 F13
Basarabia = Bessarabiya, *Moldova* 33 J5
Basauri, *Spain* 38 B2
Basawa, *Afghan.* 68 B4
Bascuñán, C., *Chile* 126 B1
Basel, *Switz.* 25 H3
Basel, Euroairport ✕ (BSL), *Europe* 19 E14
Basel-Landschaft □, *Switz.* 25 H3
Basento →, *Italy* 43 B9
Bashākerd, Kūhhā-ye, *Iran* 71 E8
Bashaw, *Canada* 102 C6
Bāshī, *Iran* 71 D6
Bashkir Republic = Bashkortostan □, *Russia* 52 D6
Bashkortostan □, *Russia* 52 D6
Basibasy, *Madag.* 89 C7
Basilan I., *Phil.* 61 H5
Basilan Str., *Phil.* 61 H5
Basildon, *U.K.* 15 F8
Basile, *Eq. Guin.* 83 E6
Basilicata □, *Italy* 43 B9
Basim = Washim, *India* 66 J10
Basin, *U.S.A.* 108 D9
Basingstoke, *U.K.* 15 F6
Baška, *Croatia* 41 D11
Başkale, *Turkey* 73 C10
Baskatong, Rés., *Canada* 104 C4
Basle = Basel, *Switz.* 25 H3
Başmakçı, *Turkey* 47 D12
Basoda, *India* 68 H7
Basoko, *Dem. Rep. of the Congo* 86 B1
Basque, Pays, *France* 20 E2
Basque Provinces = País Vasco □, *Spain* 38 C2
Basra = Al Başrah, *Iraq* 70 D5
Bass Str., *Australia* 95 F4
Bassano, *Canada* 102 C6
Bassano del Grappa, *Italy* 41 C8
Bassar, *Togo* 83 D5
Bassas da India, *Ind. Oc.* 85 J7
Basse-Normandie □, *France* 18 D6
Basse-Pointe, *Martinique* 120 c
Basse Santa-Su, *Gambia* 82 C2
Basse-Terre, *Guadeloupe* 120 b
Basse Terre, *Trin. & Tob.* 125 K15
Bassein, *Burma* 67 L19
Basses, Pte. des, *Guadeloupe* 120 b
Basseterre, *St. Kitts & Nevis* 121 C7
Bassett, *U.S.A.* 112 D5
Bassi, *India* 68 D7
Bassigny, *France* 19 E12
Bassikounou, *Mauritania* 82 B3
Bassila, *Benin* 83 D5
Bassum, *Germany* 24 C4

Båstad, Sweden 11 H6
Bastak, Iran 71 E7
Baştām, Iran 71 B7
Bastar, India 67 K12
Bastelica, France 21 F13
Basti, India 69 F10
Bastia, France 21 F13
Bastogne, Belgium 17 D5
Bastrop, La., U.S.A. 113 J9
Bastrop, Tex., U.S.A. 113 K6
Bat Yam, Israel 74 C3
Bata, Eq. Guin. 84 D1
Bata, Romania 28 D7
Bataan □, Phil. 61 D4
Batabanó, Cuba 120 B3
Batabanó, G. de, Cuba 120 B3
Batac, Phil. 61 B4
Batagai, Russia 53 C14
Batajnica, Serbia & M. 44 B4
Batak, Bulgaria 45 E8
Batala, India 68 D6
Batalha, Portugal 36 F2
Batama, Dem. Rep. of the Congo 86 B2
Batamay, Russia 53 C13
Batang, China 58 B2
Batang, Indonesia 63 G13
Batangas, Phil. 61 E4
Batanta, Indonesia 63 E8
Batatais, Brazil 127 A6
Batavia, U.S.A. 116 D6
Bataysk, Russia 33 J10
Batchelor, Australia 92 B5
Batdambang, Cambodia 64 F4
Batemans B., Australia 95 F5
Batemans Bay, Australia 95 F5
Bates Ra., Australia 93 E3
Batesburg-Leesville, U.S.A. 115 J5
Batesville, Ark., U.S.A. 113 H9
Batesville, Miss., U.S.A. 113 H10
Batesville, Tex., U.S.A. 113 L5
Bath, Canada 117 B8
Bath, U.K. 15 F5
Bath, Maine, U.S.A. 115 D11
Bath, N.Y., U.S.A. 116 D7
Bath & North East Somerset □, U.K. 15 F5
Batheay, Cambodia 65 G5
Bathsheba, Barbados 121 g
Bathurst = Banjul, Gambia 82 C1
Bathurst, Australia 95 E4
Bathurst, Canada 105 C6
Bathurst, S. Africa 88 E4
Bathurst, C., Canada 100 A7
Bathurst B., Australia 94 A3
Bathurst Harb., Australia 95 G4
Bathurst I., Australia 92 B5
Bathurst I., Canada 98 B9
Bathurst Inlet, Canada 100 B9
Bati, Ethiopia 81 E5
Batie, Burkina Faso 82 D4
Batlow, Australia 95 F4
Batman, Turkey 70 B4
Baṭn al Ghūl, Jordan 74 F4
Batna, Algeria 78 A7
Batobato = San Isidro, Phil. 61 H7
Batočina, Serbia & M. 44 B5
Batoka, Zambia 87 F2
Baton Rouge, U.S.A. 113 K9
Batong, Ko, Thailand 65 J2
Bátonyterenye, Hungary 28 C4
Batopilas, Mexico 118 B3
Batouri, Cameroon 84 D2
Båtsfjord, Norway 8 A23
Battambang = Batdambang, Cambodia 64 F4
Batticaloa, Sri Lanka 66 R12
Battipáglia, Italy 43 B7
Battle, U.K. 15 G8
Battle →, Canada 103 C7
Battle Creek, U.S.A. 114 D3
Battle Ground, U.S.A. 110 E4
Battle Harbour, Canada 105 B8
Battle Lake, U.S.A. 112 B7
Battle Mountain, U.S.A. 108 F5
Battlefields, Zimbabwe 87 F2
Battleford, Canada 103 C7
Battonya, Hungary 28 D6
Batu, Ethiopia 81 F4
Batu, Kepulauan, Indonesia 62 E1
Batu Caves, Malaysia 65 L3
Batu Ferringhi, Malaysia 65 c
Batu Gajah, Malaysia 65 K3
Batu Is. = Batu, Kepulauan, Indonesia 62 E1
Batu Pahat, Malaysia 65 M4
Batuata, Indonesia 63 F6
Batugondang, Tanjung, Indonesia 63 J17
Batukau, Gunung, Indonesia 63 J18
Batumi, Georgia 35 K5
Batur, Indonesia 63 J18
Batur, Gunung, Indonesia 63 J18
Baturaja, Indonesia 62 E2
Baturité, Brazil 125 D11
Baturiti, Indonesia 63 J18
Bau, Malaysia 62 D4
Baubau, Indonesia 63 F6
Baucau, E. Timor 63 F7
Bauchi, Nigeria 83 C6
Bauchi □, Nigeria 83 C7
Baud, France 18 E3
Baudette, U.S.A. 112 A7
Bauer, C., Australia 95 E1
Bauhinia, Australia 94 C4
Baukau = Baucau, E. Timor 63 F7
Bauld, C., Canada 101 C14
Baume-les-Dames, France 19 E13
Baunatal, Germany 24 D5
Baunei, Italy 42 B2
Baure, Nigeria 83 C6
Bauru, Brazil 127 A6
Bausi, India 69 G12
Bauska, Latvia 9 H21
Bautino, Kazakhstan 35 H10
Bautzen, Germany 24 D10
Bauya, S. Leone 82 D2
Bavānāt, Iran 71 D7
Bavanište, Serbia & M. 28 F5
Bavaria = Bayern □, Germany 25 G7
Båven, Sweden 10 E10
Bavispe →, Mexico 118 B3
Bawdwin, Burma 67 H20
Bawean, Indonesia 62 F4
Bawku, Ghana 83 C4
Bawlake, Burma 67 K20
Bawolung, China 58 C3
Baxley, U.S.A. 115 K4
Baxoi, China 58 B1
Baxter, U.S.A. 112 B7
Baxter Springs, U.S.A. 113 G7
Baxter State △, U.S.A. 115 B11
Bay, L. de, Phil. 61 D4
Bay City, Mich., U.S.A. 114 D4
Bay City, Tex., U.S.A. 113 L7
Bay Minette, U.S.A. 115 K2
Bay Roberts, Canada 105 C9
Bay St. Louis, U.S.A. 113 K10
Bay Springs, U.S.A. 113 K10
Bay View, N.Z. 91 H6
Baya, Dem. Rep. of the Congo 87 E2
Bayamo, Cuba 120 B4
Bayamón, Puerto Rico 121 d
Bayan Har Shan, China 60 C4
Bayan Hot = Alxa Zuoqi, China 56 E3
Bayan Lepas, Malaysia 65 c
Bayan Obo, China 56 D5
Bayan-Ovoo = Erdenetsogt, Mongolia 56 C4
Bayana, India 68 F7
Bayanaūyl, Kazakhstan 52 D8
Bayandalay, Mongolia 56 C2
Bayanhongor, Mongolia 60 B5
Bayard, N. Mex., U.S.A. 109 K9
Bayard, Nebr., U.S.A. 112 E3
Bayawan, Phil. 61 G5
Baybay, Phil. 61 F6
Bayburt, Turkey 73 B9
Baydhabo = Baidoa, Somali Rep. 75 G3
Bayelsa □, Nigeria 83 E6
Bayerische Alpen, Germany 25 H7
Bayerische Rhön △, Germany 25 E6
Bayerischer Spessart △, Germany 25 F6
Bayerischer Wald, Germany 25 G8
Bayern □, Germany 25 G7
Bayeux, France 18 C6
Bayfield, Canada 116 C3
Bayfield, U.S.A. 112 B9
Bayındır, Turkey 47 C9
Bayjī, Iraq 70 C4
Baykal, Oz., Russia 53 D11
Baykan, Turkey 70 B4
Baykonur = Bayqongyr, Kazakhstan 52 E7
Baynes Mts., Namibia 88 B1
Bayombong, Phil. 61 C4
Bayon, France 19 D13
Bayona = Baiona, Spain 36 C2
Bayonne, France 20 E2
Bayonne, U.S.A. 117 F10
Bayovar, Peru 124 E2
Bayqongyr, Kazakhstan 52 E7
Bayram-Ali = Bayramaly, Turkmenistan 52 F7
Bayramaly, Turkmenistan 52 F7
Bayramiç, Turkey 47 B8
Bayreuth, Germany 25 F7
Bayrischzell, Germany 25 H8
Bayrūt, Lebanon 74 B4
Bays, L. of, Canada 116 A5
Baysville, Canada 116 A5
Bayt Lahm, West Bank 74 D4
Baytown, U.S.A. 113 L7
Bayun, Indonesia 63 J18
Bayzo, Niger 83 C5
Baza, Spain 37 H8
Bazar Dyuzi, Russia 35 K8
Bazardüzü = Bazar Dyuzi, Russia 35 K8
Bazarny Karabulak, Russia 34 D8
Bazarnyy Syzgan, Russia 34 D8
Bazaruto △, Mozam. 89 C6
Bazaruto, I. do, Mozam. 89 C6
Bazas, France 20 D3
Bazhong, China 58 B6
Bazhou, China 56 E9
Bazmān, Kūh-e, Iran 71 D9
Beach, U.S.A. 112 B3
Beach City, U.S.A. 116 F3
Beachport, Australia 95 F3
Beachy Hd., U.K. 15 G8
Beacon, Australia 93 F2
Beacon, U.S.A. 117 E11
Beaconsfield, Australia 95 G4
Beagle, Canal, S. Amer. 128 H3
Beagle Bay, Australia 92 C3
Bealanana, Madag. 89 A8
Beals Cr. →, U.S.A. 113 J4
Beamsville, Canada 116 C5
Bear →, Calif., U.S.A. 110 G5
Bear →, Utah, U.S.A. 106 B4
Béar, C., France 20 F7
Bear I., Ireland 12 E2
Bear L., Canada 103 B9
Bear L., U.S.A. 108 F8
Beardmore, Canada 104 C2
Beardmore Glacier, Antarctica 5 E11
Beardstown, U.S.A. 112 F9
Bearma →, India 69 G8
Béarn, France 20 E3
Bearpaw Mts., U.S.A. 108 B9
Bearskin Lake, Canada 104 B1
Beas →, India 68 D6
Beas de Segura, Spain 37 G8
Beasain, Spain 38 B2
Beata, C., Dom. Rep. 121 C5
Beata, I., Dom. Rep. 121 C5
Beatrice, U.S.A. 112 E6
Beatrice, Zimbabwe 87 F3
Beatrice, C., Australia 94 A2
Beatton →, Canada 102 B4
Beatton River, Canada 102 B4
Beatty, U.S.A. 110 J10
Beaucaire, France 21 E8
Beauce, Plaine de la, France 19 D8
Beauceville, Canada 105 C5
Beaudesert, Australia 95 D5
Beaufort, France 21 C10
Beaufort, Malaysia 62 C5
Beaufort, N.C., U.S.A. 115 H7
Beaufort, S.C., U.S.A. 115 J5
Beaufort Sea, Arctic 98 B5
Beaufort West, S. Africa 88 E3
Beaugency, France 19 E8
Beauharnois, Canada 117 A11
Beaujeu, France 19 F11
Beaujolais, France 19 F11
Beaulieu →, Canada 102 A6
Beaulieu-sur-Dordogne, France 20 D5
Beaulieu-sur-Mer, France 21 E11
Beauly, U.K. 13 D4
Beauly →, U.K. 13 D4
Beaumaris, U.K. 14 D3
Beaumont, Belgium 17 D4
Beaumont, France 20 D4
Beaumont, U.S.A. 113 K7
Beaumont-de-Lomagne, France 20 E5
Beaumont-le-Roger, France 18 C7
Beaumont-sur-Sarthe, France 18 D7
Beaune, France 19 E11
Beaune-la-Rolande, France 19 D9
Beaupré, Canada 105 C5
Beaupréau, France 18 E6
Beauraing, Belgium 17 D4
Beaurepaire, France 21 C9
Beausejour, Canada 103 C9
Beauvais, France 19 C9
Beauval, Canada 103 B7
Beauvoir-sur-Mer, France 18 F4
Beauvoir-sur-Niort, France 20 B3
Beaver, Okla., U.S.A. 113 G4
Beaver, Pa., U.S.A. 116 F4
Beaver, Utah, U.S.A. 109 G7
Beaver →, B.C., Canada 102 B4
Beaver →, Ont., Canada 104 A2
Beaver →, Sask., Canada 103 B7
Beaver →, U.S.A. 113 G5
Beaver City, U.S.A. 112 E5
Beaver Creek, Canada 100 B5
Beaver Dam, U.S.A. 112 D10
Beaver Falls, U.S.A. 116 F4
Beaver Hill L., Canada 103 C10
Beaver I., U.S.A. 114 C3
Beaverhill L., Canada 102 C6
Beaverlodge, Canada 102 B5
Beaverstone →, Canada 104 B2
Beaverton, Canada 116 B5
Beaverton, U.S.A. 110 E4
Beawar, India 68 F6
Bebedouro, Brazil 127 A6
Bebera, Tanjung, Indonesia 63 K18
Beboa, Madag. 89 B7
Bebra, Germany 24 E5
Becan, Mexico 119 D7
Beccles, U.K. 15 E9
Bečej, Serbia & M. 28 E5
Beceni, Romania 29 E11
Becerreá, Spain 36 C3
Béchar, Algeria 78 B5
Bechyně, Czech Rep. 26 B7
Beckley, U.S.A. 114 G5
Beckum, Germany 24 D4
Beclean, Romania 29 C9
Bečov nad Teplou, Czech Rep. 26 A5
Bečva →, Czech Rep. 27 B10
Bédar, Spain 39 H3
Bédarieux, France 20 E7
Beddouza, Ras, Morocco 78 B4
Bedele, Ethiopia 81 F4
Bederkesa, Germany 24 B4
Bedeso, Ethiopia 81 F5
Bedford, Canada 117 A12
Bedford, S. Africa 88 E4
Bedford, U.K. 15 E7
Bedford, Ind., U.S.A. 114 F2
Bedford, Iowa, U.S.A. 112 E7
Bedford, Ohio, U.S.A. 116 E3
Bedford, Pa., U.S.A. 116 F6
Bedford, Va., U.S.A. 114 G6
Bedford, C., Australia 94 B4
Bedfordshire □, U.K. 15 E7
Będków, Poland 31 G6
Bednja →, Croatia 41 B13
Bednodemyanovsk, Russia 34 D6
Bedok, Singapore 65 d
Bedónia, Italy 40 D6
Bedourie, Australia 94 C2
Bedum, Neths. 17 A6
Będzin, Poland 31 H6
Beebe Plain, Canada 117 A12
Beech Creek, U.S.A. 116 E7
Beef I., Br. Virgin Is. 121 e
Beelitz, Germany 24 C8
Beenleigh, Australia 95 D5
Be'er Menuha, Israel 70 D2
Be'er Sheva, Israel 74 D3
Beersheba = Be'er Sheva, Israel 74 D3
Beeskow, Germany 24 C10
Beestekraal, S. Africa 89 D4
Beeston, U.K. 14 E6
Beetzendorf, Germany 24 C7
Beeville, U.S.A. 113 L6
Befale, Dem. Rep. of the Congo 84 D4
Befandriana, Mahajanga, Madag. 89 B8
Befandriana, Toliara, Madag. 89 C7
Befasy, Madag. 89 C7
Befotaka, Antsiranana, Madag. 89 A8
Befotaka, Fianarantsoa, Madag. 89 C8
Bega, Australia 95 F4
Bega, Canalul, Romania 28 E5
Bégard, France 18 D3
Beğendik, Turkey 45 F10
Begoro, Ghana 83 D4
Begusarai, India 69 G12
Behābād, Iran 71 C8
Behala, India 69 H13
Behara, Madag. 89 C8
Behbehān, Iran 71 D6
Behm Canal, U.S.A. 102 B2
Behshahr, Iran 71 B7
Bei Jiang →, China 59 F9
Bei'an, China 60 B7
Beibei, China 58 C6
Beichuan, China 58 B5
Beihai, China 58 G7
Beijing, China 56 E9
Beijing □, China 56 E9
Beilen, Neths. 17 B6
Beiliu, China 59 F8
Beilngries, Germany 25 F7
Beilpajah, Australia 95 E3
Beilul, Eritrea 81 E5
Beinn na Faoghla = Benbecula, U.K. 13 D1
Beipan Jiang, China 58 E5
Beipiao, China 57 D11
Beira, Mozam. 87 F3
Beirut = Bayrūt, Lebanon 74 B4
Beiseker, Canada 102 C6
Beitaolaizhao, China 57 B13
Beitbridge, Zimbabwe 87 G3
Beiuş, Romania 28 D7
Beizhen = Binzhou, China 57 F10
Beizhen, China 57 D11
Beizhengzhen, China 57 B12
Beja, Portugal 37 G3
Béja, Tunisia 79 A7
Beja □, Portugal 37 H3
Bejaïa, Algeria 78 A7
Béjar, Spain 36 E5
Bejestān, Iran 71 C8
Bekaa Valley = Al Biqā, Lebanon 74 A5
Bekçiler, Turkey 47 E11
Békés, Hungary 28 D6
Békés □, Hungary 28 D6
Békéscsaba, Hungary 28 D6
Bekilli, Turkey 47 C11
Bekily, Madag. 89 C8
Bekisopa, Madag. 89 C8
Bekitro, Madag. 89 C8
Bekodoka, Madag. 89 B8
Bekoji, Ethiopia 81 F4
Bekok, Malaysia 65 L4
Bekopaka, Madag. 89 B7
Bekuli, Indonesia 63 J17
Bekwai, Ghana 83 D4
Bela, India 69 G10
Bela, Pakistan 68 F2
Bela Bela, S. Africa 89 C4
Bela Crkva, Serbia & M. 28 F6
Bela Palanka, Serbia & M. 44 C6
Bela Vista, Brazil 126 A4
Bela Vista, Mozam. 89 D5
Bélâbre, France 20 B5
Belalcázar, Spain 37 G5
Belan →, India 69 G9
Belanovica, Serbia & M. 44 B4
Belarus ■, Europe 32 F4
Belau = Palau ■, Pac. Oc. 96 G5
Belavenona, Madag. 89 C8
Belawan, Indonesia 62 D1
Belaya, Ethiopia 81 E4
Belaya Glina, Russia 35 G5
Belaya Kalitva, Russia 35 F5
Belaya Tserkov = Bila Tserkva, Ukraine 33 H6
Belceşti, Romania 29 C12
Bełchatów, Poland 31 G6
Belcher Is., Canada 104 A3
Belchite, Spain 38 D4
Belden, U.S.A. 110 E5
Beled Weyne = Belet Uen, Somali Rep. 75 G4
Belém, Brazil 125 D9
Belén, Argentina 126 B2
Belén, Paraguay 126 A4
Belen, U.S.A. 109 J10
Belene, Bulgaria 45 C9
Beleni, Turkey 72 D7
Bélesta, France 20 F5
Belet Uen, Somali Rep. 75 G4
Belev, Russia 32 F9
Belevi, Turkey 47 C9
Belfair, U.S.A. 110 C4
Belfast, S. Africa 89 D5
Belfast, U.K. 12 B6
Belfast, Maine, U.S.A. 115 C11
Belfast, N.Y., U.S.A. 116 D6
Belfast L., U.K. 12 B6
Belfield, U.S.A. 112 B3
Belfort, France 19 E13
Belfort, Territoire de □, France 19 E13
Belfry, U.S.A. 108 D9
Belgaum, India 66 M9
Belgioioso, Italy 40 C6
Belgium ■, Europe 17 D4
Belgodère, France 21 F13
Belgorod, Russia 33 G9
Belgorod-Dnestrovskiy = Bilhorod-Dnistrovskyy, Ukraine 33 J6
Belgrade = Beograd, Serbia & M. 44 B4
Belgrade, U.S.A. 108 D8
Belgrade ✕ (BEG), Serbia & M. 44 C4
Belhaven, U.S.A. 115 H7
Beli Drim →, Europe 44 D4
Beli Manastir, Croatia 28 E3
Beli Timok →, Serbia & M. 44 C6
Bélice →, Italy 42 E5
Belimbing, Indonesia 63 J18
Belinskiy, Russia 34 D6
Belinyu, Indonesia 62 E3
Beliton Is. = Belitung, Indonesia 62 E3
Belitung, Indonesia 62 E3
Beliu, Romania 28 D6
Belize ■, Cent. Amer. 119 D7
Belize City, Belize 119 D7
Beljakovci, Macedonia 44 D5
Beljanica, Serbia & M. 44 B5
Belkovskiy, Ostrov, Russia 53 B14
Bell →, Canada 104 C4
Bell I., Canada 105 B8
Bell-Irving →, Canada 102 B3
Bell Peninsula, Canada 101 B11
Bell Ville, Argentina 126 C3
Bella, Italy 43 B8
Bella Bella, Canada 102 C3
Bella Coola, Canada 102 C3
Bella Unión, Uruguay 126 C4
Bella Vista, Corrientes, Argentina 126 B4
Bella Vista, Tucuman, Argentina 126 B2
Bellac, France 20 B5
Bellágio, Italy 40 C6
Bellaire, U.S.A. 116 F4
Bellária, Italy 41 D9
Bellary, India 66 M10
Bellata, Australia 95 D4
Belle-Chasse, U.S.A. 113 L10
Belle Fourche, U.S.A. 112 C3
Belle Fourche →, U.S.A. 112 C3
Belle Glade, U.S.A. 115 M5
Belle-Île, France 18 E3
Belle Isle, Canada 105 B8
Belle Isle, Str. of, Canada 105 B8
Belle Plaine, U.S.A. 112 E8
Belle Yella, Liberia 82 D3
Belledonne, France 21 C10
Bellefontaine, U.S.A. 114 E4
Bellefonte, U.S.A. 116 F7
Bellegarde, France 19 E9
Bellegarde-en-Marche, France 20 C6
Bellegarde-sur-Valserine, France 19 F12
Bellême, France 18 D7
Belleoram, Canada 105 C8
Belleplaine, Barbados 121 g
Belleville, Canada 116 B7
Belleville, France 19 F11
Belleville, Ill., U.S.A. 112 F10
Belleville, Kans., U.S.A. 112 F6
Belleville, N.Y., U.S.A. 117 C8
Belleville-sur-Vie, France 18 F5
Bellevue, Canada 102 D6
Bellevue, Idaho, U.S.A. 108 E6
Bellevue, Nebr., U.S.A. 112 E7
Bellevue, Ohio, U.S.A. 116 E2
Bellevue, Wash., U.S.A. 110 C4
Belley, France 21 C9
Bellin = Kangirsuk, Canada 101 B13
Bellinge, Denmark 11 J4
Bellingen, Australia 95 E5
Bellingham, U.S.A. 100 D7
Bellingshausen Sea, Antarctica 5 C17
Bellinzona, Switz. 25 J5
Bello, Colombia 124 B3
Bellows Falls, U.S.A. 117 C12
Bellpat, Pakistan 68 E3
Bellpuig d'Urgell, Spain 38 D6
Belluno, Italy 41 B9
Bellwood, U.S.A. 116 F6
Bélmez, Spain 37 G5
Belmont, Canada 116 D3
Belmont, S. Africa 88 D3
Belmont, U.S.A. 116 D6
Belmonte, Brazil 125 G11
Belmonte, Portugal 36 E3
Belmonte, Spain 39 F2
Belmopan, Belize 119 D7
Belmullet, Ireland 12 B2
Belo Horizonte, Brazil 125 G10
Belo-sur-Mer, Madag. 89 C7
Belo-Tsiribihina, Madag. 89 B7
Belogorsk = Bilohirsk, Ukraine 33 K8
Belogorsk, Russia 53 D13
Belogradchik, Bulgaria 44 C6
Belogradets, Bulgaria 45 C11
Beloha, Madag. 89 D8
Beloit, Kans., U.S.A. 112 F5
Beloit, Wis., U.S.A. 112 D10
Belokorovichi, Ukraine 33 G5
Belomorsk, Russia 52 C4
Belonia, India 67 H17
Belopolye = Bilopillya, Ukraine 33 G8
Belorechensk, Russia 35 H4
Belorussia = Belarus ■, Europe 32 F4
Beloslav, Bulgaria 45 C11
Belovo, Bulgaria 45 D8
Belovo, Russia 52 D9
Belovodsk, Ukraine 33 H10
Beloye, Ozero, Russia 32 B9
Beloye More, Russia 52 C4
Belozem, Bulgaria 45 D9
Belozersk, Russia 32 B9
Belpasso, Italy 43 E7
Belpre, U.S.A. 114 F5
Belrain, India 69 E9
Belt, U.S.A. 108 C8
Beltana, Australia 95 E2
Belterra, Brazil 125 D8
Beltinci, Slovenia 41 B13
Belton, U.S.A. 113 K6
Belton L., U.S.A. 113 K6
Beltsy = Bălţi, Moldova 29 C12
Belturbet, Ireland 12 B4
Belukha, Russia 52 E9
Beluran, Malaysia 62 C5
Beluša, Slovak Rep. 27 B11
Belušić, Serbia & M. 44 C5
Belvedere Maríttimo, Italy 43 C8

Belvès, *France* 20 D5
Belvidere, *Ill., U.S.A.* 112 D10
Belvidere, *N.J., U.S.A.* 117 F9
Belvis de la Jara, *Spain* 36 F6
Belyando →, *Australia* 94 C4
Belyy, *Russia* 32 E7
Belyy, Ostrov, *Russia* 52 B8
Belyy Yar, *Russia* 52 D9
Bełżec, *Poland* 31 H10
Belzig, *Germany* 24 C8
Belzoni, *U.S.A.* 113 J9
Bełżyce, *Poland* 31 G9
Bemaraha, Lembalemban' i, *Madag.* 89 B7
Bemarivo, *Madag.* 89 C7
Bemarivo →, *Antsiranana, Madag.* 89 A9
Bemarivo →, *Mahajanga, Madag.* 89 B8
Bemavo, *Madag.* 89 C8
Bembéréke, *Benin* 83 C5
Bembesi, *Zimbabwe* 87 G2
Bembesi →, *Zimbabwe* 87 F2
Bembézar →, *Spain* 37 H5
Bembibre, *Spain* 36 C4
Bemetara, *India* 69 J9
Bemidji, *U.S.A.* 112 B7
Bemolanga, *Madag.* 89 B8
Ben, *Iran* 71 C6
Ben Cruachan, *U.K.* 13 E3
Ben Dearg, *U.K.* 13 D4
Ben En △, *Vietnam* 64 C5
Ben Hope, *U.K.* 13 C4
Ben Lawers, *U.K.* 13 E4
Ben Lomond, *N.S.W., Australia* 95 E5
Ben Lomond, *Tas., Australia* 95 G4
Ben Lomond, *U.K.* 13 E4
Ben Lomond △, *Australia* 95 G4
Ben Luc, *Vietnam* 65 G6
Ben Macdhui, *U.K.* 13 D5
Ben Mhor, *U.K.* 13 D1
Ben More, *Arg. & Bute, U.K.* 13 E2
Ben More, *Stirl., U.K.* 13 E4
Ben More Assynt, *U.K.* 13 C4
Ben Nevis, *U.K.* 13 E3
Ben Quang, *Vietnam* 64 D6
Ben Vorlich, *U.K.* 13 E4
Ben Wyvis, *U.K.* 13 D4
Bena, *Nigeria* 83 C6
Benalla, *Australia* 95 F4
Benalmádena, *Spain* 37 J6
Benares = Varanasi, *India* 69 G10
Bénat, C., *France* 21 E10
Benavente, *Portugal* 37 G2
Benavente, *Spain* 36 C5
Benavides, *U.S.A.* 113 M5
Benavides de Órbigo, *Spain* 36 C5
Benbecula, *U.K.* 13 D1
Benbonyathe, *Australia* 95 E2
Bend, *U.S.A.* 108 D3
Bender Beila, *Somali Rep.* 75 F5
Bendery = Tighina, *Moldova* 29 D14
Bendigo, *Australia* 95 F3
Bendorf, *Germany* 24 E3
Benē Beraq, *Israel* 74 C3
Bénéna, *Mali* 82 C4
Benenitra, *Madag.* 89 C8
Benešov, *Czech Rep.* 26 B7
Benevento, *Italy* 43 A7
Benfeld, *France* 19 D14
Benga, *Mozam.* 87 F3
Bengal, Bay of, *Ind. Oc.* 67 M17
Bengalûru = Bangalore, *India* 66 N10
Bengbis, *Cameroon* 83 E7
Bengbu, *China* 57 H9
Benghazi = Banghāzī, *Libya* 79 B10
Bengkalis, *Indonesia* 62 D2
Bengkulu, *Indonesia* 62 E2
Bengkulu □, *Indonesia* 62 E2
Bengough, *Canada* 103 D7
Bengtsfors, *Sweden* 10 E6
Benguela, *Angola* 85 G2
Benguérua, I., *Mozam.* 89 C6
Benha, *Egypt* 80 H7
Beni, *Dem. Rep. of the Congo* 86 B2
Beni →, *Bolivia* 124 F5
Beni Mazâr, *Egypt* 80 B3
Beni Mellal, *Morocco* 78 B4
Beni Suef, *Egypt* 80 J7
Beniah L., *Canada* 102 A6
Benicarló, *Spain* 38 E5
Benicássim, *Spain* 38 E5
Benicia, *U.S.A.* 110 G4
Benidorm, *Spain* 39 G4
Benin ■, *Africa* 83 D5
Benin →, *Nigeria* 83 D6
Benin, Bight of, *W. Afr.* 83 E5
Benin City, *Nigeria* 83 D6
Benisa, *Spain* 39 G5
Benitses, *Greece* 49 A3
Benjamin Aceval, *Paraguay* 126 A4
Benjamin Constant, *Brazil* 124 D4
Benjamin Hill, *Mexico* 118 A2
Benkelman, *U.S.A.* 112 E4
Benkovac, *Croatia* 41 D12
Bennett, *Canada* 102 B2
Bennett, L., *Australia* 92 D5
Bennetta, Ostrov, *Russia* 53 B15
Bennettsville, *U.S.A.* 115 H6
Bennichchāb, *Mauritania* 82 B1
Bennington, *N.H., U.S.A.* 117 D11
Bennington, *Vt., U.S.A.* 117 D11
Bénodet, *France* 18 E2
Benoni, *S. Africa* 89 D4
Benque Viejo, *Belize* 119 D7
Bensheim, *Germany* 25 F4
Benson, *Ariz., U.S.A.* 109 L8
Benson, *Minn., U.S.A.* 112 C7
Bent, *Iran* 71 E8
Benteng, *Indonesia* 63 F6
Bentinck I., *Australia* 94 B2
Bentiu, *Sudan* 81 F2
Bento Gonçalves, *Brazil* 127 B5
Benton, *Ark., U.S.A.* 113 H8
Benton, *Calif., U.S.A.* 110 H8
Benton, *Ill., U.S.A.* 112 G10
Benton, *Pa., U.S.A.* 117 E8
Benton Harbor, *U.S.A.* 114 D2
Bentong, *Malaysia* 65 L3
Bentonville, *U.S.A.* 113 G7
Bentu Liben, *Ethiopia* 81 F4
Benue □, *Nigeria* 83 D6
Benue →, *Nigeria* 83 D6
Benxi, *China* 57 D12
Beo, *Indonesia* 63 D7
Beograd, *Serbia & M.* 44 B4
Beoumi, *Ivory C.* 82 D3
Bepan Jiang →, *China* 58 E6
Beppu, *Japan* 55 H5
Beqaa Valley = Al Biqā, *Lebanon* 74 A5
Ber Mota, *India* 68 H3
Berach →, *India* 68 G6
Beraketa, *Madag.* 89 C7
Berane, *Serbia & M.* 44 D3
Berat, *Albania* 44 F3
Berau, Teluk, *Indonesia* 63 E8
Beravina, *Madag.* 89 B8
Berber, *Sudan* 80 D3
Berbera, *Somali Rep.* 75 E4
Berbérati, *C.A.R.* 84 D3
Berbice →, *Guyana* 124 B7
Berceto, *Italy* 40 D6
Berchidda, *Italy* 42 B2
Berchtesgaden, *Germany* 25 H8
Berchtesgaden △, *Germany* 25 H8
Berck, *France* 19 B8
Berdichev = Berdychiv, *Ukraine* 33 H5
Berdsk, *Russia* 52 D9
Berdyansk, *Ukraine* 33 J9
Berdychiv, *Ukraine* 33 H5
Berea, *U.S.A.* 114 G3
Berebere, *Indonesia* 63 D7
Bereda, *Somali Rep.* 75 E5
Berehove, *Ukraine* 33 H2
Berekum, *Ghana* 82 D4
Berenice, *Egypt* 80 C4
Berens →, *Canada* 103 C9
Berens I., *Canada* 103 C9
Berens River, *Canada* 103 C9
Beresford, *U.S.A.* 112 D6
Berestechko, *Ukraine* 33 G3
Bereşti, *Romania* 29 D12
Beretău →, *Romania* 28 C6
Berettyó →, *Hungary* 28 D6
Berettyóújfalu, *Hungary* 28 C6
Berevo, *Mahajanga, Madag.* 89 B7
Berevo, *Toliara, Madag.* 89 B7
Bereza = Byaroza, *Belarus* 33 F3
Berezhany, *Ukraine* 33 H3
Berezina = Byarezina →, *Belarus* 33 F6
Berezivka, *Ukraine* 33 J6
Berezna, *Ukraine* 33 G6
Bereznik, *Russia* 52 C5
Berezniki, *Russia* 52 D6
Berezovo, *Russia* 52 C7
Berga, *Spain* 38 C6
Berga, *Sweden* 11 G10
Bergama, *Turkey* 47 B9
Bérgamo, *Italy* 40 C6
Bergara, *Spain* 38 B2
Bergby, *Sweden* 10 D11
Bergedorf, *Germany* 24 B6
Bergeforsen, *Sweden* 10 B11
Bergen, *Mecklenburg-Vorpommern, Germany* 24 A9
Bergen, *Niedersachsen, Germany* 24 C5
Bergen, *Neths.* 17 B4
Bergen, *Norway* 9 F11
Bergen, *U.S.A.* 116 C7
Bergen op Zoom, *Neths.* 17 C4
Bergerac, *France* 20 D4
Bergheim, *Germany* 24 E2
Bergholz, *U.S.A.* 116 F4
Bergisch Gladbach, *Germany* 17 D7
Bergisches Land ⌓, *Germany* 24 E3
Bergkamen, *Germany* 24 D3
Bergkvara, *Sweden* 11 H10
Bergshamra, *Sweden* 10 E12
Bergsjö, *Sweden* 10 C11
Bergstrasse-Odenwald ⌓, *Germany* 25 F1
Bergues, *France* 19 B9
Bergviken, *Sweden* 10 C10
Bergville, *S. Africa* 89 D4
Berhala, Selat, *Indonesia* 62 E2
Berhampore = Baharampur, *India* 69 G13
Berhampur = Brahmapur, *India* 67 K14
Berheci →, *Romania* 29 E12
Bering Sea, *Pac. Oc.* 100 C1
Bering Strait, *Pac. Oc.* 100 B3
Beringovskiy, *Russia* 53 C18
Berisso, *Argentina* 126 C4
Berja, *Spain* 37 J8
Berkeley, *U.S.A.* 110 H4
Berkner I., *Antarctica* 5 D18
Berkovitsa, *Bulgaria* 44 C7
Berkshire, *U.S.A.* 117 D8
Berkshire Downs, *U.K.* 15 F6
Berlanga, *Spain* 37 G5
Berlenga, I., *Portugal* 37 F1
Berlin, *Germany* 24 C9
Berlin, *Md., U.S.A.* 114 F8
Berlin, *N.H., U.S.A.* 117 B13
Berlin, *N.Y., U.S.A.* 117 D11
Berlin, *Wis., U.S.A.* 114 D1
Berlin □, *Germany* 24 C9
Berlin L., *U.S.A.* 116 E4
Berlin Tegel ✕ (TXL), *Germany* 24 C9
Bermeja, Sierra, *Spain* 37 J5
Bermejo →, *Formosa, Argentina* 126 B4
Bermejo →, *San Juan, Argentina* 126 C2
Bermen, L., *Canada* 105 B6
Bermeo, *Spain* 38 B2
Bermillo de Sayago, *Spain* 36 D4
Bermuda ⧄, *Atl. Oc.* 98 F13
Bern, *Switz.* 25 J3
Bern □, *Switz.* 25 J3
Bernalda, *Italy* 43 B9
Bernalillo, *U.S.A.* 109 J10
Bernardo de Irigoyen, *Argentina* 127 B5
Bernardo O'Higgins □, *Chile* 126 C1
Bernardsville, *U.S.A.* 117 F10
Bernasconi, *Argentina* 126 D3
Bernau, *Bayern, Germany* 25 H8
Bernau, *Brandenburg, Germany* 24 C9
Bernay, *France* 18 C7
Bernburg, *Germany* 24 D7
Berndorf, *Austria* 26 D9
Berne = Bern, *Switz.* 25 J3
Berne = Bern □, *Switz.* 25 J3
Berner Alpen, *Switz.* 25 J3
Berneray, *U.K.* 13 D1
Bernier I., *Australia* 93 D1
Bernina, Piz, *Switz.* 25 J5
Bernkastel-Kues, *Germany* 25 F3
Beroroha, *Madag.* 89 C8
Béroubouay, *Benin* 83 C5
Beroun, *Czech Rep.* 26 B7
Berounka →, *Czech Rep.* 26 B7
Berovo, *Macedonia* 44 E6
Berre, Étang de, *France* 21 E9
Berre-l'Étang, *France* 21 E9
Berri, *Australia* 95 E3
Berriane, *Algeria* 78 B6
Berry, *Australia* 95 E5
Berry, *France* 19 F8
Berry Is., *Bahamas* 120 A4
Berryessa L., *U.S.A.* 110 G4
Berryville, *U.S.A.* 113 G8
Berseba, *Namibia* 88 D2
Bersenbrück, *Germany* 24 C3
Bershad, *Ukraine* 33 H5
Berthold, *U.S.A.* 112 A4
Berthoud, *U.S.A.* 112 E2
Bertincourt, *France* 19 B9
Bertoua, *Cameroon* 84 D2
Bertraghboy B., *Ireland* 12 C2
Berwick, *U.S.A.* 117 E8
Berwick-upon-Tweed, *U.K.* 14 B6
Berwyn Mts., *U.K.* 14 E4
Beryslav, *Ukraine* 33 J7
Berzasca, *Romania* 28 F6
Berzence, *Hungary* 28 D2
Besal, *Pakistan* 69 B5
Besalampy, *Madag.* 89 B7
Besançon, *France* 19 E13
Besar, *Indonesia* 62 E5
Beshenkovichi, *Belarus* 32 E5
Beška, *Serbia & M.* 28 E5
Beslan, *Russia* 35 J7
Besna Kobila, *Serbia & M.* 44 D6
Besnard L., *Canada* 103 B7
Besni, *Turkey* 70 B3
Besor, N. →, *Egypt* 74 D3
Bessarabiya, *Moldova* 33 J5
Bessarabka = Basarabeasca, *Moldova* 29 D13
Bessèges, *France* 21 D8
Bessemer, *Ala., U.S.A.* 115 J2
Bessemer, *Mich., U.S.A.* 112 B9
Bessemer, *Pa., U.S.A.* 116 F4
Bessin, *France* 18 C6
Bessines-sur-Gartempe, *France* 20 B5
Beswick, *Australia* 92 B5
Bet She'an, *Israel* 74 C4
Bet Shemesh, *Israel* 74 D4
Betafo, *Madag.* 89 B8
Betancuria, *Canary Is.* 48 F5
Betanzos, *Spain* 36 B2
Bétaré Oya, *Cameroon* 84 C2
Betatao, *Madag.* 89 B8
Bétera, *Spain* 39 F4
Bétérou, *Benin* 83 D5
Bethal, *S. Africa* 89 D4
Bethanien, *Namibia* 88 D2
Bethany, *Canada* 116 B6
Bethany, *U.S.A.* 112 E7
Bethel, *Alaska, U.S.A.* 100 B3
Bethel, *Conn., U.S.A.* 117 E11
Bethel, *Maine, U.S.A.* 117 B14
Bethel, *Vt., U.S.A.* 117 C12
Bethel Park, *U.S.A.* 116 F4
Béthenville, *France* 19 C11
Bethlehem = Bayt Lahm, *West Bank* 74 D4
Bethlehem, *S. Africa* 89 D4
Bethlehem, *U.S.A.* 117 F9
Bethulie, *S. Africa* 88 E4
Béthune, *France* 19 B9
Béthune →, *France* 18 C8
Betioky, *Madag.* 89 C7
Betong, *Thailand* 65 K3
Betoota, *Australia* 94 D3
Betor, *Ethiopia* 81 E4
Betroka, *Madag.* 89 C8
Betsiamites, *Canada* 105 C6
Betsiamites →, *Canada* 105 C6
Betsiboka →, *Madag.* 89 B8
Bettendorf, *U.S.A.* 112 E9
Bettiah, *India* 69 F11
Bettna, *Sweden* 11 F10
Béttola, *Italy* 40 D6
Betul, *India* 66 J10
Betung, *Malaysia* 62 D4
Betws-y-Coed, *U.K.* 14 D4
Betxi, *Spain* 38 F4
Betzdorf, *Germany* 24 E3
Beuil, *France* 21 D10
Beulah, *Mich., U.S.A.* 114 C2
Beulah, *N. Dak., U.S.A.* 112 B4
Beuvron →, *France* 18 E8
Beveren, *Belgium* 17 C4
Beverley, *Australia* 93 F2
Beverley, *U.K.* 14 D7
Beverley Hills, *U.S.A.* 115 L4
Beverly, *U.S.A.* 117 D14
Beverly Hills, *U.S.A.* 111 L8
Beverungen, *Germany* 24 D5
Bevoalavo, *Madag.* 89 D7
Bewas →, *India* 69 H8
Bex, *Switz.* 25 J3
Bexhill, *U.K.* 15 G8
Bey Dağları, *Turkey* 47 E12
Beyānlū, *Iran* 70 C5
Beyazköy, *Turkey* 45 E11
Beyçayırı, *Turkey* 45 F10
Beydağ, *Turkey* 47 C10
Beyeğaç, *Turkey* 47 D10
Beyin, *Ghana* 82 D4
Beykoz, *Turkey* 45 E13
Beyla, *Guinea* 82 D3
Beynat, *France* 20 C5
Beyneu, *Kazakhstan* 52 E6
Beyoba, *Turkey* 47 C9
Beyoğlu, *Turkey* 45 E12
Beypazarı, *Turkey* 72 B4
Beyşehir, *Turkey* 72 D4
Beyşehir Gölü, *Turkey* 70 B1
Beytüşşebap, *Turkey* 73 D10
Bezdan, *Serbia & M.* 28 E3
Bezhetsk, *Russia* 32 D9
Béziers, *France* 20 E7
Bezwada = Vijayawada, *India* 67 L12
Bhabua, *India* 69 G10
Bhachau, *India* 66 H7
Bhadar →, *Gujarat, India* 68 H5
Bhadar →, *Gujarat, India* 68 J3
Bhadarwah, *India* 69 C6
Bhadgaon = Bhaktapur, *Nepal* 69 F11
Bhadohi, *India* 69 G10
Bhadra, *India* 68 E6
Bhadrakh, *India* 67 J15
Bhadran, *India* 68 H5
Bhadravati, *India* 66 N9
Bhag, *Pakistan* 68 E2
Bhagalpur, *India* 69 G12
Bhagirathi →, *Uttaranchal, India* 69 D8
Bhagirathi →, *W. Bengal, India* 69 H13
Bhakkar, *Pakistan* 68 D4
Bhakra Dam, *India* 68 D7
Bhaktapur, *Nepal* 69 F11
Bhamo, *Burma* 67 G20
Bhandara, *India* 66 J11
Bhanpura, *India* 68 G6
Bhanrer Ra., *India* 69 H8
Bhaptiahi, *India* 69 F12
Bharat = India ■, *Asia* 66 K11
Bharatpur, *Chhattisgarh, India* 69 H9
Bharatpur, *Raj., India* 68 F7
Bharno, *India* 69 H11
Bharuch, *India* 66 J8
Bhatinda, *India* 68 D6
Bhatpara, *India* 69 H13
Bhattu, *India* 68 E6
Bhaun, *Pakistan* 68 C5
Bhaunagar = Bhavnagar, *India* 66 J8
Bhavnagar, *India* 66 J8
Bhawari, *India* 68 G5
Bhayavadar, *India* 68 J4
Bhera, *Pakistan* 68 C5
Bhikangaon, *India* 68 J6
Bhilsa = Vidisha, *India* 68 H7
Bhilwara, *India* 68 G6
Bhima →, *India* 66 L10
Bhimbar, *Pakistan* 69 C6
Bhind, *India* 69 F8
Bhinga, *India* 69 F9
Bhinmal, *India* 68 G5
Bhiwandi, *India* 66 K8
Bhiwani, *India* 68 E7
Bhogava →, *India* 68 H5
Bhola, *Bangla.* 67 H17
Bholari, *Pakistan* 68 G3
Bhopal, *India* 68 H7
Bhubaneshwar, *India* 67 J14
Bhuj, *India* 68 H3
Bhusawal, *India* 66 J9
Bhutan ■, *Asia* 67 F17
Biafra, B. of = Bonny, Bight of, *Africa* 83 E6
Biak, *Indonesia* 63 E9
Biała, *Poland* 31 H4
Biała →, *Poland* 31 H7
Biała Piska, *Poland* 30 E9
Biała Podlaska, *Poland* 31 F10
Biała Rawska, *Poland* 31 G7
Białobrzegi, *Poland* 31 G7
Białogard, *Poland* 30 D2
Białowieski △, *Poland* 31 F10
Białowieża, *Poland* 31 F10
Biały Bór, *Poland* 30 E3
Białystok, *Poland* 31 E10
Biancavilla, *Italy* 43 E7
Bianco, *Italy* 43 D9
Biankouma, *Ivory C.* 82 D3
Biaora, *India* 68 H7
Bīārjmand, *Iran* 71 B7
Biaro, *Indonesia* 63 D7
Biarritz, *France* 20 E2
Bias, *Indonesia* 63 J18
Biasca, *Switz.* 25 J4
Biba, *Egypt* 80 J7
Bibai, *Japan* 54 C10
Bibbiena, *Italy* 41 E8
Bibby I., *Canada* 103 A10
Bibel →, *Spain* 36 C3
Biberach, *Germany* 25 G5
Bibiani, *Ghana* 82 D4
Bibungwa, *Dem. Rep. of the Congo* 86 C2
Bicaj, *Albania* 44 E4
Bicaz, *Romania* 29 D11
Bicazu Ardelean, *Romania* 29 D10
Bíccari, *Italy* 43 A8
Bicester, *U.K.* 15 F6
Bichena, *Ethiopia* 81 E4
Bicheno, *Australia* 95 G4
Bichia, *India* 69 H9
Bichvinta, *Georgia* 35 J5
Bickerton I., *Australia* 94 A2
Bicske, *Hungary* 28 C3
Bida, *Nigeria* 83 D6
Bidar, *India* 66 L10
Biddeford, *U.S.A.* 115 D10
Biddwara, *Ethiopia* 81 F4
Bideford, *U.K.* 15 F3
Bideford Bay, *U.K.* 15 F3
Bidhuna, *India* 69 F8
Bidor, *Malaysia* 65 K3
Bie, *Sweden* 10 E10
Bié, Planalto de, *Angola* 85 G3
Bieber, *U.S.A.* 108 F3
Biebrza →, *Poland* 31 E9
Biebrzański △, *Poland* 30 E9
Biecz, *Poland* 31 J8
Biel, *Switz.* 25 H3
Bielawa, *Poland* 31 H3
Bielefeld, *Germany* 24 C4
Bielersee, *Switz.* 25 H3
Biella, *Italy* 40 C5
Bielsk Podlaski, *Poland* 31 F10
Bielsko-Biała, *Poland* 31 J6
Bien Hoa, *Vietnam* 65 G6
Bienne = Biel, *Switz.* 25 H3
Bienvenida, *Spain* 37 G4
Bienville, L., *Canada* 104 A5
Bierné, *France* 18 E6
Bierun, *Poland* 31 H6
Bierutów, *Poland* 31 G4
Biescas, *Spain* 38 C4
Biese →, *Germany* 24 C7
Biesiesfontein, *S. Africa* 88 E2
Bieszczadzki △, *Poland* 31 J9
Bietigheim-Bissingen, *Germany* 25 G5
Bieżuń, *Poland* 31 F6
Biferno →, *Italy* 41 G12
Big →, *Canada* 105 B8
Big B., *Canada* 105 A7
Big Bear City, *U.S.A.* 111 L10
Big Bear Lake, *U.S.A.* 111 L10
Big Belt Mts., *U.S.A.* 108 C8
Big Bend, *Swaziland* 89 D5
Big Bend △, *U.S.A.* 113 L3
Big Black →, *U.S.A.* 113 K9
Big Blue →, *U.S.A.* 112 F6
Big Creek, *U.S.A.* 110 H7
Big Cypress ⌓, *U.S.A.* 115 M5
Big Cypress Swamp, *U.S.A.* 115 M5
Big Falls, *U.S.A.* 112 A8
Big Fork →, *U.S.A.* 112 A8
Big Horn Mts. = Bighorn Mts., *U.S.A.* 108 D10
Big I., *Canada* 102 A5
Big Lake, *U.S.A.* 113 K4
Big Moose, *U.S.A.* 117 C10
Big Muddy Cr. →, *U.S.A.* 112 A2
Big Pine, *U.S.A.* 110 H8
Big Piney, *U.S.A.* 108 E8
Big Rapids, *U.S.A.* 114 D3
Big Rideau L., *Canada* 117 B8
Big River, *Canada* 103 C7
Big Run, *U.S.A.* 116 F6
Big Sable Pt., *U.S.A.* 114 C2
Big Salmon →, *Canada* 102 A2
Big Sand L., *Canada* 103 B9
Big Sandy, *U.S.A.* 108 B8
Big Sandy →, *U.S.A.* 114 F4
Big Sandy Cr. →, *U.S.A.* 112 F3
Big Sioux →, *U.S.A.* 112 D6
Big South Fork △, *U.S.A.* 115 G3
Big Spring, *U.S.A.* 113 J4
Big Stone City, *U.S.A.* 112 C6
Big Stone Gap, *U.S.A.* 115 G4
Big Stone L., *U.S.A.* 112 C6
Big Sur, *U.S.A.* 110 J5
Big Timber, *U.S.A.* 108 D9
Big Trout L., *Canada* 104 B2
Big Trout Lake, *Canada* 104 B2
Biğa, *Turkey* 45 F11
Biga →, *Turkey* 45 F11
Bigadiç, *Turkey* 47 B10
Biganos, *France* 20 D3
Biggar, *Canada* 103 C7
Biggar, *U.K.* 13 F5
Bigge I., *Australia* 92 B4
Biggenden, *Australia* 95 D5
Biggleswade, *U.K.* 15 E7
Biggs, *U.S.A.* 110 F5
Bighorn, *U.S.A.* 108 C10
Bighorn →, *U.S.A.* 108 C10
Bighorn Canyon ⌓, *U.S.A.* 108 D9
Bighorn L., *U.S.A.* 108 D9
Bighorn Mts., *U.S.A.* 108 D10
Bignona, *Senegal* 82 C1
Bigorre, *France* 20 E4
Bigstone L., *Canada* 103 C9
Biguglia, Étang de, *France* 21 F13
Bigwa, *Tanzania* 86 D4
Bihać, *Bos.-H.* 41 D12
Bihar, *India* 69 G11
Bihar □, *India* 69 G12
Biharamulo, *Tanzania* 86 C3
Biharamulo ⌓, *Tanzania* 86 C3
Bihariganj, *India* 69 G12
Biharkeresztes, *Hungary* 28 C6
Bihor □, *Romania* 28 D7
Bihor, Munţii, *Romania* 28 D7
Bijagós, Arquipélago dos, *Guinea-Biss.* 82 C1
Bijaipur, *India* 68 F7
Bijapur, *Chhattisgarh, India* 67 K12
Bijapur, *Karnataka, India* 66 L9
Bījār, *Iran* 70 C5
Bijawar, *India* 69 G8
Bijeljina, *Bos.-H.* 28 F4

Bijelo Polje, Serbia & M. 44 C3
Bijie, China 58 D5
Bijnor, India 68 E8
Bikaner, India 68 E5
Bikapur, India 69 F10
Bikeqi, China 56 D6
Bikfayyā, Lebanon 74 B4
Bikin, Russia 53 E14
Bikin →, Russia 54 A7
Bikini Atoll, Marshall Is. 96 F8
Bikita, Zimbabwe 89 C5
Bikoué, Cameroon 83 E7
Bila Tserkva, Ukraine 33 H6
Bilanga, Burkina Faso 83 C4
Bilara, India 68 F5
Bilaspur, Chhattisgarh, India 69 H10
Bilaspur, Punjab, India 68 D7
Biläsuvar, Azerbaijan 73 C13
Bilauk Taungdan, Thailand 64 F2
Bilbao, Spain 38 B2
Bilbao ✕ (BIO), Spain 36 B8
Bilbeis, Egypt 80 H7
Bilbo = Bilbao, Spain 38 B2
Bilbor, Romania 29 C10
Bilciureşti, Romania 29 F10
Bíldudalur, Iceland 8 D2
Bílé Karpaty, Europe 27 B11
Bileća, Bos.-H. 44 D2
Bilecik, Turkey 72 B4
Biłgoraj, Poland 31 H9
Bilgram, India 69 F9
Bilhaur, India 69 F9
Bilhorod-Dnistrovskyy, Ukraine 33 J6
Bilibino, Russia 53 C17
Bilibiza, Mozam. 87 E5
Bilisht, Albania 44 F5
Billabalong Roadhouse, Australia 93 E2
Billdal, Sweden 11 G5
Billiluna, Australia 92 C4
Billings, U.S.A. 108 D9
Billiton Is. = Belitung, Indonesia 62 E3
Billsta, Sweden 10 A12
Billund, Denmark 11 J3
Bilma, Niger 79 E8
Bilo Gora, Croatia 28 E2
Biloela, Australia 94 C5
Bilohirsk, Ukraine 33 K8
Bilopillya, Ukraine 33 G8
Biloxi, U.S.A. 113 K10
Bilpa Morea Claypan, Australia 94 D3
Biltine, Chad 79 F10
Bilyarsk, Russia 34 C10
Bima, Indonesia 63 F5
Bimban, Egypt 80 C3
Bimbila, Ghana 83 D5
Bimini Is., Bahamas 120 A4
Bin Xian, Heilongjiang, China 57 B14
Bin Xian, Shaanxi, China 56 G5
Bin Yauri, Nigeria 83 C5
Bina-Etawah, India 68 G8
Bināb, Iran 71 B6
Binalbagan, Phil. 61 F5
Binalong, Australia 95 E4
Bīnālūd, Kūh-e, Iran 71 B8
Binatang = Bintangor, Malaysia 62 D4
Binche, Belgium 17 D4
Binchuan, China 58 E3
Binder, Chad 83 D7
Bindki, India 69 F9
Bindslev, Denmark 11 G4
Bindura, Zimbabwe 87 F3
Binefar, Spain 38 D5
Bingara, Australia 95 D5
Bingen, Germany 25 F3
Bingerville, Ivory C. 82 D4
Bingham, U.S.A. 115 C11
Binghamton, U.S.A. 117 D9
Bingöl, Turkey 70 B4
Bingöl Dağları, Turkey 73 C9
Bingsjö, Sweden 10 C9
Binh Dinh = An Nhon, Vietnam 64 F7
Binh Khe, Vietnam 64 F7
Binh Son, Vietnam 64 E7
Binhai, China 57 G10
Binic, France 18 D4
Binisatua, Spain 48 B11
Binjai, Indonesia 62 D3
Binji, Nigeria 83 C5
Binnaway, Australia 95 E4
Binongko, Indonesia 63 F6
Binscarth, Canada 103 C8
Bint Goda, Sudan 81 E3
Bintan, Indonesia 62 D2
Bintangor, Malaysia 62 D4
Bintulu, Malaysia 62 D4
Bintuni, Indonesia 63 E8
Binyang, China 58 F7
Binz, Germany 24 A9
Binzert = Bizerte, Tunisia 79 A7
Binzhou, China 57 F10
Bío Bío □, Chile 126 D1
Biograd na Moru, Croatia 41 E12
Biogradska Gora △, Serbia & M. 44 D3
Bioko, Eq. Guin. 83 E6
Biokovo, Croatia 41 E14
Bipindi, Cameroon 83 E7
Bir, India 66 K9
Bir, Ras, Djibouti 81 E5
Bîr Abu Hashim, Egypt 80 C3
Bîr Abu Minqar, Egypt 80 B2
Bîr Abu Muḥammad, Egypt 74 F3
Bi'r ad Dabbāghāt, Jordan 74 E4
Bîr Adal Deib, Sudan 80 C4
Bi'r al Butayyihāt, Jordan 74 F4
Bi'r al Mārī, Jordan 74 E4
Bi'r al Qattār, Jordan 74 F4
Bir 'Asal, Egypt 80 B3
Bîr Atrun, Sudan 80 D2
Bîr Beiḍa, Egypt 74 E3
Bîr Diqnash, Egypt 80 A2
Bîr el 'Abd, Egypt 74 D2
Bîr el Basur, Egypt 80 B2
Bîr el Biarât, Egypt 74 F3
Bîr el Duweidar, Egypt 74 E1
Bîr el Garârât, Egypt 74 D2
Bîr el Gellaz, Egypt 80 A2
Bîr el Heisi, Egypt 74 F3
Bîr el Jafir, Egypt 74 E1
Bîr el Mâlḥi, Egypt 74 E2
Bîr el Shaqqa, Egypt 80 A2
Bîr el Thamâda, Egypt 74 E2
Bîr Fuad, Egypt 80 A2
Bîr Gebeil Ḥiṣn, Egypt 74 E2
Bi'r Ghadīr, Syria 74 A6
Bîr Haimur, Egypt 80 C3
Bîr Ḥasana, Egypt 74 E2
Bîr Hôôker, Egypt 80 H7
Bîr Kanayis, Egypt 80 C3
Bîr Kaseiba, Egypt 74 E2
Bîr Kerawein, Egypt 80 B2
Bîr Lahfân, Egypt 74 E2
Bîr Madkûr, Egypt 74 E1
Bîr Maql, Egypt 80 C3
Bîr Mîneiga, Sudan 80 C4
Bîr Misaha, Egypt 80 C2
Bîr Mogreïn, Mauritania 78 C3
Bîr Murr, Egypt 80 C3
Bi'r Muṭribah, Kuwait 70 D5
Bîr Nakheila, Egypt 80 C3
Bîr Qaṭia, Egypt 74 E1
Bîr Qatrani, Egypt 80 A2
Bîr Ranga, Egypt 80 C4
Bîr Sahara, Egypt 80 C2
Bîr Seiyâla, Egypt 80 B3
Bîr Shalatein, Egypt 80 C4
Bîr Shebb, Egypt 80 C2
Bîr Shût, Egypt 80 C4
Bîr Terfawi, Egypt 80 C2
Bîr Umm Qubûr, Egypt 80 C3
Bîr Ungât, Egypt 80 C3
Bîr Za'farâna, Egypt 80 J8
Bîr Zeidûn, Egypt 80 B3
Biramféro, Guinea 82 C3
Biratnagar, Nepal 69 F12
Birawa, Dem. Rep. of the Congo 86 C2
Birch →, Canada 102 B6
Birch Hills, Canada 103 C7
Birch I., Canada 103 C9
Birch L., N.W.T., Canada 102 A5
Birch L., Ont., Canada 104 B1
Birch Mts., Canada 102 B6
Birch River, Canada 103 C8
Birchip, Australia 95 F3
Birchiş, Romania 28 E7
Bird, Canada 103 B10
Bird I. = Las Aves, Is., W. Indies 121 C7
Bird I., Antarctica 5 B1
Birdsville, Australia 94 D2
Birdum Cr. →, Australia 92 C5
Birecik, Turkey 70 B3
Birein, Israel 74 E3
Bireuen, Indonesia 62 C1
Biri →, Sudan 81 F2
Birifo, Gambia 82 C2
Birigui, Brazil 127 A5
Birjand, Iran 71 C8
Birkenfeld, Germany 25 F3
Birkenhead, U.K. 14 D4
Birkerød, Denmark 11 J6
Birket Qârûn, Egypt 80 J7
Birkfeld, Austria 26 D8
Bîrlad = Bârlad, Romania 29 D12
Birmingham, U.K. 15 E6
Birmingham, U.S.A. 115 J2
Birmingham International ✕ (BHX), U.K. 15 E6
Birmitrapur, India 67 H14
Birni Ngaouré, Niger 83 C5
Birni Nkonni, Niger 83 C6
Birnin Gwari, Nigeria 83 C6
Birnin Kebbi, Nigeria 83 C5
Birnin Kudu, Nigeria 83 C6
Birobidzhan, Russia 53 E14
Birr, Ireland 12 C4
Birrie →, Australia 95 D4
Birsilpur, India 68 E5
Birsk, Russia 52 D6
Birštonas, Lithuania 30 D11
Birtle, Canada 103 C8
Birur, India 66 N9
Biryuchiy, Ukraine 33 J8
Biržai, Lithuania 9 H21
Birzebbugga, Malta 49 D2
Bisa, Indonesia 63 E7
Bisáccia, Italy 43 A8
Bisacquino, Italy 42 E6
Bisalpur, India 69 E8
Bisbee, U.S.A. 109 L9
Biscarrosse, France 20 D2
Biscarrosse et de Parentis, Étang de, France 20 D2
Biscay, B. of, Atl. Oc. 6 F5
Biscayne B., U.S.A. 115 N5
Biscéglie, Italy 43 A9
Bischheim, France 19 D14
Bischofshofen, Austria 26 D6
Bischofswerda, Germany 24 D10
Bischwiller, France 19 D14
Biscoe Is., Antarctica 5 C17
Biscotasing, Canada 104 C3
Biševo, Croatia 41 F13
Bisha, Eritrea 81 D4
Bishah, W. →, Si. Arabia 80 C5
Bishan, China 58 C6
Bishkek, Kyrgyzstan 52 E8
Bishnupur, India 69 H12
Bisho, S. Africa 89 E4
Bishop, Calif., U.S.A. 110 H8
Bishop, Tex., U.S.A. 113 M6
Bishop Auckland, U.K. 14 C6
Bishop's Falls, Canada 105 C8
Bishop's Stortford, U.K. 15 F8
Bisignano, Italy 43 C9
Bisina, L., Uganda 86 B3
Biskra, Algeria 78 B7
Biskupiec, Poland 30 E7
Bismarck, U.S.A. 112 B4
Bismarck Arch., Papua N. G. 96 H7
Bismark, Germany 24 C7
Bismil, Turkey 73 D9
Biso, Uganda 86 B3
Bison, U.S.A. 112 C3
Bīsotūn, Iran 70 C5
Bispgården, Sweden 10 A10
Bissagos = Bijagós, Arquipélago dos, Guinea-Biss. 82 C1
Bissau, Guinea-Biss. 82 C1
Bissaula, Nigeria 83 D7
Bissikrima, Guinea 82 C2
Bissorã, Guinea-Biss. 82 C1
Bistcho L., Canada 102 B5
Bistreţ, Romania 29 G8
Bistrica = Ilirska-Bistrica, Slovenia 41 C11
Bistriţa, Romania 29 C9
Bistriţa →, Romania 29 D11
Bistriţa Năsăud □, Romania 29 C9
Bistriţei, Munţii, Romania 29 C10
Biswan, India 69 F9
Bisztynek, Poland 30 D7
Bitburg, Germany 25 F2
Bitche, France 19 C14
Bithynia, Turkey 72 B4
Bitlis, Turkey 70 B4
Bitola, Macedonia 44 E5
Bitolj = Bitola, Macedonia 44 E5
Bitonto, Italy 43 A9
Bitter Creek, U.S.A. 108 F9
Bitter L. = Buheirat-Murrat-el-Kubra, Egypt 80 H8
Bitterfeld, Germany 24 D8
Bitterfontein, S. Africa 88 E2
Bitterroot →, U.S.A. 108 C6
Bitterroot Range, U.S.A. 108 D6
Bitterwater, U.S.A. 110 J6
Bitti, Italy 42 B2
Bittou, Burkina Faso 83 C4
Biu, Nigeria 83 C7
Bivolari, Romania 29 C12
Bivolu, Vf., Romania 29 C10
Biwa-Ko, Japan 55 G8
Biwabik, U.S.A. 112 B8
Bixad, Romania 29 C8
Bixby, U.S.A. 113 H7
Biyang, China 56 H7
Biysk, Russia 52 D9
Bizana, S. Africa 89 E4
Bizen, Japan 55 G7
Bizerte, Tunisia 79 A7
Bjargtangar, Iceland 8 D1
Bjärnum, Sweden 11 H7
Bjästa, Sweden 10 A12
Bjelasica, Serbia & M. 44 D3
Bjelašnica, Bos.-H. 28 G3
Bjelovar, Croatia 41 C13
Bjerringbro, Denmark 11 H3
Björbo, Sweden 10 D8
Björklinge, Sweden 10 D11
Björneborg, Sweden 10 E8
Bjørnevatn, Norway 8 B23
Bjørnøya, Arctic 4 B8
Bjursås, Sweden 10 D9
Bjuv, Sweden 11 H6
Bla, Mali 82 C3
Blace, Serbia & M. 44 C5
Blachownia, Poland 31 H5
Black = Da →, Vietnam 58 G5
Black →, Canada 116 B5
Black →, Ariz., U.S.A. 109 K8
Black →, Ark., U.S.A. 113 H9
Black →, Mich., U.S.A. 116 D2
Black →, N.Y., U.S.A. 117 C8
Black →, Wis., U.S.A. 112 D9
Black Bay Pen., Canada 104 C2
Black Birch L., Canada 103 B7
Black Canyon of the Gunnison ⌓, U.S.A. 109 G10
Black Diamond, Canada 102 C6
Black Duck →, Canada 104 A2
Black Forest = Schwarzwald, Germany 25 G4
Black Forest, U.S.A. 112 F2
Black Hd., Ireland 12 C2
Black Hills, U.S.A. 112 D3
Black I., Canada 103 C9
Black L., Canada 103 B7
Black L., Mich., U.S.A. 114 C3
Black L., N.Y., U.S.A. 117 B9
Black Lake, Canada 103 B7
Black Mesa, U.S.A. 113 G3
Black Mt. = Mynydd Du, U.K. 15 F4
Black Mts., U.K. 15 F4
Black Range, U.S.A. 109 K10
Black River, Jamaica 120 a
Black River Falls, U.S.A. 112 C9
Black Rock, Barbados 121 g
Black Sea, Eurasia 6 G12
Black Tickle, Canada 105 B8
Black Volta →, Africa 82 D4
Black Warrior →, U.S.A. 115 J2
Blackall, Australia 94 C4
Blackball, N.Z. 91 K3
Blackbull, Australia 94 B3
Blackburn, U.K. 14 D5
Blackburn with Darwen □, U.K. 14 D5
Blackdown Tableland △, Australia 94 C4
Blackfoot, U.S.A. 108 E7
Blackfoot →, U.S.A. 108 C7
Blackfoot River Reservoir, U.S.A. 108 E8
Blackpool, U.K. 14 D4
Blackpool □, U.K. 14 D4
Blackriver, U.S.A. 116 B1
Blacks Harbour, Canada 105 C6
Blacksburg, U.S.A. 114 G5
Blacksod B., Ireland 12 B1
Blackstone, U.S.A. 114 G7
Blackstone Ra., Australia 93 E4
Blackwater = West Road →, Canada 102 C4
Blackwater, Australia 94 C4
Blackwater →, Meath, Ireland 12 C4
Blackwater →, Waterford, Ireland 12 D4
Blackwater →, U.K. 12 B5
Blackwell, U.S.A. 113 G6
Blackwells Corner, U.S.A. 111 K7
Bladensburg △, Australia 94 C3
Blaenau Ffestiniog, U.K. 14 E4
Blaenau Gwent □, U.K. 15 F4
Blagaj, Bos.-H. 44 C1
Blagnac, France 20 E5
Blagnac, Toulouse ✕ (TLS), France 20 E5
Blagodarnoye = Blagodarnyy, Russia 35 H6
Blagodarnyy, Russia 35 H6
Blagoevgrad, Bulgaria 44 D7
Blagoveshchensk, Russia 53 D13
Blahkiuh, Indonesia 63 J18
Blain, France 18 E5
Blain, U.S.A. 116 F7
Blaine, Minn., U.S.A. 112 C8
Blaine, Wash., U.S.A. 110 B4
Blaine Lake, Canada 103 C7
Blair, U.S.A. 112 E6
Blair Athol, Australia 94 C4
Blair Atholl, U.K. 13 E5
Blairgowrie, U.K. 13 E5
Blairsden, U.S.A. 110 F6
Blairsville, U.S.A. 116 F5
Blaj, Romania 29 D8
Blakang Mati, Pulau, Singapore 65 d
Blake Pt., U.S.A. 112 A10
Blakely, Ga., U.S.A. 115 K3
Blakely, Pa., U.S.A. 117 E9
Blâmont, France 19 D13
Blanc, C., Spain 48 B9
Blanc, Mont, Alps 21 C10
Blanc-Sablon, Canada 105 B8
Blanca, B., Argentina 128 D4
Blanca Peak, U.S.A. 109 H11
Blanche, C., Australia 95 E1
Blanche, L., S. Austral., Australia 95 D2
Blanche, L., W. Austral., Australia 92 D3
Blanchisseuse, Trin. & Tob. 125 K15
Blanco, S. Africa 88 E3
Blanco, U.S.A. 113 K5
Blanco →, Argentina 126 C2
Blanco, C., Costa Rica 120 E2
Blanco, C., U.S.A. 108 E1
Blanda →, Iceland 8 D3
Blandford Forum, U.K. 15 G5
Blanding, U.S.A. 109 H9
Blanes, Spain 38 D7
Blangy-sur-Bresle, France 19 C8
Blanice →, Czech Rep. 26 B7
Blankaholm, Sweden 11 G10
Blankenberge, Belgium 17 C3
Blankenburg, Germany 24 D6
Blanquefort, France 20 D3
Blanquilla, I., Venezuela 121 D7
Blanquillo, Uruguay 127 C4
Blansko, Czech Rep. 27 B9
Blantyre, Malawi 87 F4
Blarney, Ireland 12 E3
Blasdell, U.S.A. 116 D6
Błaszki, Poland 31 G5
Blatná, Czech Rep. 26 B6
Blato, Croatia 41 F13
Blaubeuren, Germany 25 G5
Blaustein, Germany 25 G5
Blåvands Huk, Denmark 11 J2
Blaydon, U.K. 14 C6
Blaye, France 20 C3
Blaye-les-Mines, France 20 D6
Blayney, Australia 95 E4
Blaze, Pt., Australia 92 B5
Błażowa, Poland 31 J9
Bleckede, Germany 24 B6
Bled, Slovenia 41 B11
Bleiburg, Austria 26 E7
Blejeşti, Romania 29 F10
Blekinge, Sweden 9 H16
Blekinge län □, Sweden 11 H9
Blenheim, Canada 116 D3
Blenheim, N.Z. 91 J4
Bléone →, France 21 D10
Blérancourt, France 19 C10
Bletchley, U.K. 15 F7
Blida, Algeria 78 A6
Blidö, Sweden 10 E12
Blidsberg, Sweden 11 G7
Blieskastel, Germany 25 F3
Bligh Sound, N.Z. 91 L1
Blind River, Canada 104 C3
Blinisht, Albania 44 E3
Bliss, Idaho, U.S.A. 108 E6
Bliss, N.Y., U.S.A. 116 D6
Blissfield, U.S.A. 116 F3
Blitar, Indonesia 63 H15
Blitta, Togo 83 D5
Block I., U.S.A. 117 E13
Block Island Sd., U.S.A. 117 E13
Bloemfontein, S. Africa 88 D4
Bloemhof, S. Africa 88 D4
Blois, France 18 E8
Blomskog, Sweden 10 E6
Blomstermåla, Sweden 11 H10
Blönduós, Iceland 8 D3
Blongas, Indonesia 63 K19
Blonie, Poland 31 F7
Bloodvein →, Canada 103 C9
Bloody Foreland, Ireland 12 A3
Bloomer, U.S.A. 112 C9
Bloomfield, Canada 116 C7
Bloomfield, Iowa, U.S.A. 112 E8
Bloomfield, N. Mex., U.S.A. 109 H10
Bloomfield, Nebr., U.S.A. 112 D6
Bloomington, Ill., U.S.A. 112 E10
Bloomington, Ind., U.S.A. 114 F2
Bloomington, Minn., U.S.A. 112 C8
Bloomsburg, U.S.A. 117 F8
Bloomsbury, Australia 94 J6
Blora, Indonesia 63 G14
Blossburg, U.S.A. 116 E7
Blouberg, S. Africa 89 C4
Blountstown, U.S.A. 115 K3
Bludenz, Austria 26 D2
Blue Earth, U.S.A. 112 D8
Blue Hole △, Belize 120 C2
Blue Lagoon △, Zambia 87 F2
Blue Mesa Reservoir, U.S.A. 109 G10
Blue Mountain Lake, U.S.A. 117 C10
Blue Mountain Pk., Jamaica 120 a
Blue Mts., Jamaica 120 a
Blue Mts., Maine, U.S.A. 117 B14
Blue Mts., Oreg., U.S.A. 108 D4
Blue Mts., Pa., U.S.A. 117 F8
Blue Mud B., Australia 94 A2
Blue Nile = Nîl el Azraq →, Sudan 81 D3
Blue Rapids, U.S.A. 112 F6
Blue Ridge Mts., U.S.A. 115 G5
Blue River, Canada 102 C5
Bluefield, U.S.A. 114 G5
Bluefields, Nic. 120 D3
Bluff, Australia 94 C4
Bluff, N.Z. 91 M2
Bluff, U.S.A. 109 H9
Bluff Knoll, Australia 93 F2
Bluff Pt., Australia 93 E1
Bluffton, U.S.A. 114 E3
Blumenau, Brazil 127 B6
Blunt, U.S.A. 112 C5
Bly, U.S.A. 108 E3
Blyde River Canyon ⌓, S. Africa 89 C5
Blyth, Canada 116 C3
Blyth, U.K. 14 B6
Blythe, U.S.A. 111 M12
Blytheville, U.S.A. 113 H10
Bo, S. Leone 82 D2
Bo Duc, Vietnam 65 G6
Bo Hai, China 57 E10
Bo Xian = Bozhou, China 56 H8
Boa Vista, Brazil 124 C6
Boac, Phil. 61 E4
Boaco, Nic. 120 D2
Bo'ai, China 56 G7
Boal, Spain 36 B4
Boalsburg, U.S.A. 116 F7
Boane, Mozam. 89 D5
Boardman, U.S.A. 116 E4
Bobadah, Australia 95 E4
Bobai, China 58 F7
Bobbili, India 67 K13
Bóbbio, Italy 40 D6
Bobcaygeon, Canada 116 B6
Böblingen, Germany 25 G5
Bobo-Dioulasso, Burkina Faso 82 C4
Bobolice, Poland 30 E3
Boboshevo, Bulgaria 44 D7
Bobov Dol, Bulgaria 44 D6
Bóbr →, Poland 31 F2
Bobraomby, Tanjon' i, Madag. 89 A8
Bobrinets, Ukraine 33 H7
Bobrov, Russia 34 E5
Bobrovitsa, Ukraine 33 G6
Bobruysk = Babruysk, Belarus 33 F5
Boby, Pic, Madag. 85 J9
Boca de Drago, Venezuela 125 K15
Bôca do Acre, Brazil 124 E5
Boca Raton, U.S.A. 115 M5
Bocanda, Ivory C. 82 D4
Bocas del Toro, Panama 120 E3
Boceguillas, Spain 36 D7
Bochnia, Poland 31 J7
Bocholt, Germany 24 D2
Bochum, Germany 24 D3
Bockenem, Germany 24 C6
Boćki, Poland 31 F10
Bocognano, France 21 F13
Bocoyna, Mexico 118 B3
Bocşa, Romania 28 E6
Boda, Dalarnas, Sweden 10 C9
Böda, Kalmar, Sweden 11 G11
Boda, Västernorrland, Sweden 10 B10
Bodafors, Sweden 11 G8
Bodaybo, Russia 53 D12
Boddam, U.K. 13 B7
Boddington, Australia 93 F2
Bode Sadu, Nigeria 83 D5
Bodega Bay, U.S.A. 110 G3
Boden, Sweden 8 D19
Bodensee, Europe 25 H5
Bodenteich, Germany 24 C6
Bodhan, India 66 K10
Bodinga, Nigeria 83 C6
Bodmin, U.K. 15 G3
Bodmin Moor, U.K. 15 G3
Bodø, Norway 8 C16
Bodrog →, Hungary 28 B6
Bodrum, Turkey 47 D9
Bódva →, Hungary 28 B5
Boën, France 21 C8
Boende, Dem. Rep. of the Congo 84 E4
Boerne, U.S.A. 113 L5
Boesmans →, S. Africa 88 E4
Boffa, Guinea 82 C2
Bogalusa, U.S.A. 113 K10
Bogan →, Australia 95 D4
Bogan Gate, Australia 95 E4
Bogandé, Burkina Faso 83 C4
Bogantungan, Australia 94 C4
Bogata, U.S.A. 113 J7
Bogatić, Serbia & M. 44 B3

Boğazkale, *Turkey* 72 B6
Boğazlıyan, *Turkey* 72 C6
Bogen, *Sweden* 10 D6
Bogense, *Denmark* 11 J4
Bogetići, *Serbia & M.* 44 D2
Boggabilla, *Australia* 95 D5
Boggabri, *Australia* 95 E5
Boggeragh Mts., *Ireland* 12 D3
Boglan = Solhan, *Turkey* 70 B4
Bognor Regis, *U.K.* 15 G7
Bogo, *Phil.* 61 F6
Bogodukhov = Bohodukhiv, *Ukraine* 33 G8
Bogol Manya, *Ethiopia* 81 G5
Bogong, Mt., *Australia* 95 F4
Bogor, *Indonesia* 63 G12
Bogoroditsk, *Russia* 32 F10
Bogorodsk, *Russia* 34 B6
Bogoso, *Ghana* 82 D4
Bogotá, *Colombia* 124 C4
Bogotol, *Russia* 52 D9
Bogou, *Togo* 83 C5
Bogra, *Bangla.* 67 G16
Boguchany, *Russia* 53 D10
Boguchar, *Russia* 34 F5
Bogué, *Mauritania* 82 B2
Boguslav, *Ukraine* 33 H6
Boguszów-Gorce, *Poland* 31 H3
Bohain-en-Vermandois, *France* 19 C10
Bohemian Forest = Böhmerwald, *Germany* 25 F9
Bohinjska Bistrica, *Slovenia* 41 B11
Böhmerwald, *Germany* 25 F9
Bohmte, *Germany* 24 C4
Bohodukhiv, *Ukraine* 33 G8
Bohol □, *Phil.* 61 G6
Bohol Sea, *Phil.* 63 C6
Bohongou, *Burkina Faso* 83 C5
Böhönye, *Hungary* 28 D2
Bohuslän, *Sweden* 11 F5
Boi, *Nigeria* 83 D6
Boi, Pta. de, *Brazil* 127 A6
Boiaçu, *Brazil* 124 D6
Boileau, C., *Australia* 92 C3
Boing'o, *Sudan* 81 F3
Boiro, *Spain* 36 C2
Boise, *U.S.A.* 108 E5
Boise City, *U.S.A.* 113 G3
Boissevain, *Canada* 103 D8
Bóite →, *Italy* 41 B9
Boitzenburg, *Germany* 24 B9
Boizenburg, *Germany* 24 B6
Bojador, C., *W. Sahara* 78 C3
Bojana →, *Albania* 44 E3
Bojano, *Italy* 43 A7
Bojanowo, *Poland* 31 G3
Bøjden, *Denmark* 11 J4
Bojnūrd, *Iran* 71 B8
Bojonegoro, *Indonesia* 63 G14
Boju, *Nigeria* 83 D6
Boka, *Serbia & M.* 28 E5
Boka Kotorska, *Serbia & M.* 44 D2
Bokala, *Ivory C.* 82 D4
Bokani, *Nigeria* 83 D6
Bokaro, *India* 69 H11
Boké, *Guinea* 82 C2
Bokhara →, *Australia* 95 D4
Bokkos, *Nigeria* 83 D6
Boknafjorden, *Norway* 9 G11
Bokora ⌓, *Uganda* 86 B3
Bokoro, *Chad* 79 F9
Bokpyin, *Burma* 65 G2
Boksitogorsk, *Russia* 32 C7
Bol, *Croatia* 41 E13
Bolama, *Guinea-Biss.* 82 C1
Bolan →, *Pakistan* 68 E2
Bolan Pass, *Pakistan* 66 E5
Bolaños →, *Mexico* 118 C4
Bolaños de Calatrava, *Spain* 37 G7
Bolayır, *Turkey* 45 F10
Bolbec, *France* 18 C7
Boldājī, *Iran* 71 D6
Boldeşti-Scăeni, *Romania* 29 E11
Bole, *China* 60 B3
Bole, *Ethiopia* 81 F4
Bole, *Ghana* 82 D4
Bolekhiv, *Ukraine* 33 H2
Bolesławiec, *Poland* 31 G2
Bolgatanga, *Ghana* 83 C4
Bolgrad = Bolhrad, *Ukraine* 33 K5
Bolhrad, *Ukraine* 33 K5
Bolinao, *Phil.* 61 C3
Bolintin-Vale, *Romania* 29 F10
Bolívar, *Argentina* 126 D3
Bolivar, *Mo., U.S.A.* 113 G8
Bolivar, *N.Y., U.S.A.* 116 D6
Bolivar, *Tenn., U.S.A.* 113 H10
Bolivia ■, *S. Amer.* 124 G6
Bolivian Plateau = Altiplano, *Bolivia* 122 E4
Boljevac, *Serbia & M.* 44 C5
Bolkhov, *Russia* 32 F9
Bolków, *Poland* 31 H3
Bollebygd, *Sweden* 11 G6
Bollène, *France* 21 D8
Bollnäs, *Sweden* 10 C10
Bollon, *Australia* 95 D4
Bollstabruk, *Sweden* 10 B11
Bolmen, *Sweden* 11 H7
Bolobo, *Dem. Rep. of the Congo* 84 E3
Bologna, *Italy* 41 D8
Bologna ✕ (BLQ), *Italy* 41 D8
Bologoye, *Russia* 32 D8
Bolon, Ozero, *Russia* 60 B8
Bolonchenticul, *Mexico* 119 D7
Bolótana, *Italy* 42 B1
Boloven, Cao Nguyen, *Laos* 64 E6
Bolpur, *India* 69 H12
Bolsena, *Italy* 41 F8
Bolsena, L. di, *Italy* 41 F8
Bolshaya Chernigovka, *Russia* 34 D10
Bolshaya Glushitsa, *Russia* 34 D10
Bolshaya Martynovka, *Russia* 35 G5
Bolshaya Vradiyevka, *Ukraine* 33 J6
Bolshevik, Ostrov, *Russia* 53 B11
Bolshoy Anyuy →, *Russia* 53 C17
Bolshoy Begichev, Ostrov, *Russia* 53 B12
Bolshoy Kavkas = Caucasus Mountains, *Eurasia* 35 J7
Bolshoy Lyakhovskiy, Ostrov, *Russia* 53 B15
Bolshoy Tokmak = Tokmak, *Ukraine* 33 J8
Bolshoy Tyuters, Ostrov, *Russia* 9 G22
Bolsward, *Neths.* 17 A5
Bolt Head, *U.K.* 15 G4
Boltaña, *Spain* 38 C5
Boltigen, *Switz.* 25 J3
Bolton, *Canada* 116 C5
Bolton, *U.K.* 14 D5
Bolton Landing, *U.S.A.* 117 C11
Bolu, *Turkey* 72 B4
Bolungavík, *Iceland* 8 C2
Boluo, *China* 59 F10
Bolvadin, *Turkey* 70 B1
Bolzano, *Italy* 41 B8
Bom Jesus da Lapa, *Brazil* 125 F10
Boma, *Dem. Rep. of the Congo* 84 F2
Bombala, *Australia* 95 F4
Bombarral, *Portugal* 37 F1
Bombay = Mumbai, *India* 66 K8
Bombedor, Pta., *Venezuela* 125 L15
Bomboma, *Dem. Rep. of the Congo* 84 D3
Bombombwa, *Dem. Rep. of the Congo* 86 B2
Bomi Hills, *Liberia* 82 D2
Bomili, *Dem. Rep. of the Congo* 86 B2
Bømlo, *Norway* 9 G11
Bomokandi →, *Dem. Rep. of the Congo* 86 B2
Bomu →, *C.A.R.* 84 D4
Bon, C., *Tunisia* 76 C5
Bon Sar Pa, *Vietnam* 64 F6
Bonāb, *Iran* 73 D12
Bonaigarh, *India* 69 J11
Bonaire, *Neth. Ant.* 121 D6
Bonampak, *Mexico* 119 D6
Bonang, *Australia* 95 F4
Bonanza, *Nic.* 120 D3
Bonaparte Arch., *Australia* 92 B3
Boñar, *Spain* 36 C5
Bonar Bridge, *U.K.* 13 D4
Bonasse, *Trin. & Tob.* 125 K15
Bonaventure, *Canada* 105 C6
Bonavista, *Canada* 105 C9
Bonavista, C., *Canada* 105 C9
Bonavista B., *Canada* 105 C9
Bondeno, *Italy* 41 D8
Bondo, *Dem. Rep. of the Congo* 86 B1
Bondoukou, *Ivory C.* 82 D4
Bondowoso, *Indonesia* 63 G15
Bone, Teluk, *Indonesia* 63 E6
Bonerate, *Indonesia* 63 F6
Bonerate, Kepulauan, *Indonesia* 63 F6
Bo'ness, *U.K.* 13 E5
Bonete, Cerro, *Argentina* 126 B2
Bong Son = Hoai Nhon, *Vietnam* 64 E7
Bonga, *Ethiopia* 81 F4
Bongabong, *Phil.* 61 E4
Bongor, *Chad* 79 F9
Bongouanou, *Ivory C.* 82 D4
Bonham, *U.S.A.* 113 J6
Boni, *Mali* 82 B4
Boni ⌓, *Kenya* 86 C5
Bonifacio, *France* 21 G13
Bonifacio, Bouches de, *Medit. S.* 42 A2
Bonin Is. = Ogasawara Gunto, *Pac. Oc.* 96 E6
Bonke, *Ethiopia* 81 F4
Bonkoukou, *Niger* 83 C5
Bonn, *Germany* 24 E3
Bonnat, *France* 19 F8
Bonne Terre, *U.S.A.* 113 G9
Bonners Ferry, *U.S.A.* 108 B5
Bonnétable, *France* 18 D7
Bonneval, *Eure-et-Loir, France* 18 D8
Bonneval, *Savoie, France* 21 C11
Bonneville, *France* 19 F13
Bonney, L., *Australia* 95 F3
Bonnie Rock, *Australia* 93 F2
Bonny, *Nigeria* 83 E6
Bonny →, *Nigeria* 83 E6
Bonny, Bight of, *Africa* 83 E6
Bonny-sur-Loire, *France* 19 E9
Bonnyrigg, *U.K.* 13 F5
Bonnyville, *Canada* 103 C6
Bono, *Italy* 42 B2
Bonoi, *Indonesia* 63 E9
Bonorva, *Italy* 42 B1
Bonsall, *U.S.A.* 111 M9
Bontang, *Indonesia* 62 D5
Bontebok △, *S. Africa* 88 E3
Bonthe, *S. Leone* 82 D2
Bontoc, *Phil.* 61 C4
Bonyeri, *Ghana* 82 D4
Bonyhád, *Hungary* 28 D3
Bonython Ra., *Australia* 92 D4
Bookabie, *Australia* 93 F5
Booker, *U.S.A.* 113 G4
Boola, *Guinea* 82 D3
Booligal, *Australia* 95 E3
Boonah, *Australia* 95 D5
Boone, *Iowa, U.S.A.* 112 D8
Boone, *N.C., U.S.A.* 115 G5
Booneville, *Ark., U.S.A.* 113 H8
Booneville, *Miss., U.S.A.* 115 H1
Boonville, *Calif., U.S.A.* 110 F3
Boonville, *Ind., U.S.A.* 114 F2
Boonville, *Mo., U.S.A.* 112 F8
Boonville, *N.Y., U.S.A.* 117 C9
Boorabbin △, *Australia* 93 F4
Boorindal, *Australia* 95 E4
Boorowa, *Australia* 95 E4
Boosaaso = Bosaso, *Somali Rep.* 75 E4
Boothia, Gulf of, *Canada* 101 A11
Boothia Pen., *Canada* 100 A10
Bootle, *U.K.* 14 D4
Booué, *Gabon* 84 E2
Boppard, *Germany* 25 E3
Boquete, *Panama* 120 E3
Boquilla, Presa de la, *Mexico* 118 B3
Boquillas del Carmen, *Mexico* 118 B4
Bor, *Czech Rep.* 26 B5
Bor, *Russia* 34 B7
Bor, *Serbia & M.* 44 B6
Bôr, *Sudan* 81 F3
Bor, *Sweden* 11 G8
Bor, *Turkey* 72 D6
Bor Mashash, *Israel* 74 D3
Borah Peak, *U.S.A.* 108 D7
Borang, *Sudan* 81 G3
Borås, *Sweden* 11 G6
Borāzjān, *Iran* 71 D6
Borba, *Brazil* 124 D7
Borba, *Portugal* 37 G3
Borborema, Planalto da, *Brazil* 122 D7
Borcea, *Romania* 29 F12
Borçka, *Turkey* 73 B9
Bord Khūn-e Now, *Iran* 71 D6
Borda, C., *Australia* 95 F2
Bordeaux, *France* 20 D3
Bordeaux ✕ (BOD), *France* 20 D3
Borden, *Australia* 93 F2
Borden-Carleton, *Canada* 105 C7
Borden I., *Canada* 4 B2
Borden Pen., *Canada* 101 A11
Border Ranges △, *Australia* 95 D5
Borders = Scottish Borders □, *U.K.* 13 F6
Bordertown, *Australia* 95 F3
Borðeyri, *Iceland* 8 D3
Bordighera, *Italy* 40 E4
Bordj Fly Ste. Marie, *Algeria* 78 C5
Bordj-in-Eker, *Algeria* 78 D7
Bordj Omar Driss, *Algeria* 78 C7
Bore, *Ethiopia* 81 G4
Borehamwood, *U.K.* 15 F7
Borek Wielkopolski, *Poland* 31 G4
Borensberg, *Sweden* 11 F9
Borgå = Porvoo, *Finland* 9 F21
Borgarfjörður, *Iceland* 8 D7
Borgarnes, *Iceland* 8 D3
Børgefjellet, *Norway* 8 D15
Borger, *Neths.* 17 B6
Borger, *U.S.A.* 113 H4
Borgholm, *Sweden* 11 H10
Bórgia, *Italy* 43 D9
Borgo San Dalmazzo, *Italy* 40 D4
Borgo San Lorenzo, *Italy* 41 E8
Borgo Val di Taro, *Italy* 40 D6
Borgo Valsugana, *Italy* 41 B8
Borgomanero, *Italy* 40 C5
Borgorose, *Italy* 41 F10
Borgosésia, *Italy* 40 C5
Borhoyn Tal, *Mongolia* 56 C6
Bori, *Nigeria* 83 E6
Borikhane, *Laos* 64 C4
Borisoglebsk, *Russia* 34 E6
Borisov = Barysaw, *Belarus* 32 E5
Borisovka, *Russia* 33 G9
Borja, *Peru* 124 D3
Borja, *Spain* 38 D3
Borjas Blancas = Les Borges Blanques, *Spain* 38 D5
Borjomi, *Georgia* 35 K6
Børkop, *Denmark* 11 J3
Borkou, *Chad* 79 E9
Borkum, *Germany* 24 B2
Borlänge, *Sweden* 10 D9
Borley, C., *Antarctica* 5 C5
Borlu, *Turkey* 47 C10
Bormida →, *Italy* 40 D5
Bórmio, *Italy* 40 B7
Borna, *Germany* 24 D8
Borne Sulinowo, *Poland* 30 E3
Borneo, *E. Indies* 62 D5
Bornholm, *Denmark* 11 J8
Bornholms Amtskommune □, *Denmark* 11 J8
Bornholmsgattet, *Europe* 11 J8
Borno □, *Nigeria* 83 C7
Bornos, *Spain* 37 J5
Bornova, *Turkey* 47 C9
Bornu Yassa, *Nigeria* 83 C7
Boro →, *Sudan* 81 F2
Borodino, *Russia* 32 E8
Borogontsy, *Russia* 53 C14
Boromo, *Burkina Faso* 82 C4
Boron, *U.S.A.* 111 L9
Borongan, *Phil.* 61 F6
Borotangba Mts., *C.A.R.* 81 F2
Borotou, *Ivory C.* 82 D3
Borovan, *Bulgaria* 44 C7
Borovichi, *Russia* 32 C7
Borovsk, *Russia* 32 E9
Borrby, *Sweden* 11 J8
Borrego Springs, *U.S.A.* 111 M10
Borriol, *Spain* 38 E4
Borroloola, *Australia* 94 B2
Borşa, *Cluj, Romania* 29 D8
Borşa, *Maramureş, Romania* 29 C9
Borsad, *India* 68 H5
Borsec, *Romania* 29 D10
Borsod-Abaúj-Zemplén □, *Hungary* 28 B6
Bort-les-Orgues, *France* 20 C6
Borth, *U.K.* 15 E3
Börtnan, *Sweden* 10 B7
Borūjerd, *Iran* 71 C6
Boryslav, *Ukraine* 33 H2
Boryspil, *Ukraine* 33 G6
Borzhomi = Borjomi, *Georgia* 35 K6
Borzna, *Ukraine* 33 G7
Borzya, *Russia* 53 D12
Bosa, *Italy* 42 B1
Bosanska Dubica, *Bos.-H.* 41 C13
Bosanska Gradiška, *Bos.-H.* 28 E2
Bosanska Kostajnica, *Bos.-H.* 41 C13
Bosanska Krupa, *Bos.-H.* 41 D13
Bosanski Brod, *Bos.-H.* 28 E2
Bosanski Novi, *Bos.-H.* 41 C13
Bosanski Petrovac, *Bos.-H.* 41 D13
Bosanski Šamac, *Bos.-H.* 28 E3
Bosansko Grahovo, *Bos.-H.* 41 D13
Bosaso, *Somali Rep.* 75 E4
Boscastle, *U.K.* 15 G3
Boscobelle, *Barbados* 121 g
Bose, *China* 58 F6
Boshan, *China* 57 F9
Boshof, *S. Africa* 88 D4
Boshrūyeh, *Iran* 71 C8
Bosilegrad, *Serbia & M.* 44 D6
Boskovice, *Czech Rep.* 27 B9
Bosna →, *Bos.-H.* 28 E3
Bosna i Hercegovina = Bosnia-Herzegovina ■, *Europe* 28 G2
Bosnia-Herzegovina ■, *Europe* 28 G2
Bosnik, *Indonesia* 63 E9
Bosobolo, *Dem. Rep. of the Congo* 84 D3
Bosporus = Istanbul Boğazı, *Turkey* 45 E13
Bosque Farms, *U.S.A.* 109 J10
Bossangoa, *C.A.R.* 84 C3
Bossé Bangou, *Niger* 83 C5
Bossier City, *U.S.A.* 113 J8
Bosso, *Niger* 83 C7
Bosso, Dallol →, *Niger* 83 C5
Bostan, *Pakistan* 68 D2
Bostānābād, *Iran* 70 B5
Bosten Hu, *China* 60 B3
Boston, *U.K.* 14 E7
Boston, *U.S.A.* 117 D13
Boston Bar, *Canada* 102 D4
Boston Mts., *U.S.A.* 113 H8
Bosumtwi, L., *Ghana* 83 D4
Bosut →, *Croatia* 28 E3
Boswell, *Canada* 102 D5
Boswell, *U.S.A.* 116 F5
Botad, *India* 68 H4
Botan →, *Turkey* 73 D10
Botene, *Laos* 64 D3
Botev, *Bulgaria* 45 D8
Botevgrad, *Bulgaria* 44 D7
Bothaville, *S. Africa* 88 D4
Bothnia, G. of, *Europe* 8 E19
Bothwell, *Australia* 95 G4
Bothwell, *Canada* 116 D3
Boticas, *Portugal* 36 D3
Botletle →, *Botswana* 88 C3
Botlikh, *Russia* 35 J8
Botna →, *Moldova* 29 D14
Botoroaga, *Romania* 29 F10
Botoşani, *Romania* 29 C11
Botoşani □, *Romania* 29 C11
Botou, *Burkina Faso* 83 C5
Botricello, *Italy* 43 D9
Botro, *Ivory C.* 82 D3
Botswana ■, *Africa* 88 C3
Bottineau, *U.S.A.* 112 A4
Bottnaryd, *Sweden* 11 G7
Bottrop, *Germany* 17 C6
Botucatu, *Brazil* 127 A6
Botwood, *Canada* 105 C8
Bou Djébéha, *Mali* 82 B4
Boû Rjeïmât, *Mauritania* 82 B1
Bouaflé, *Ivory C.* 82 D3
Bouaké, *Ivory C.* 82 D3
Bouar, *C.A.R.* 84 C3
Bouârfa, *Morocco* 78 B5
Boucaut B., *Australia* 94 A1
Bouches-du-Rhône □, *France* 21 E9
Boucle de Baoule △, *Mali* 82 C3
Boucles de la Seine Normande ⌓, *France* 18 C7
Bouctouche, *Canada* 105 C7
Bougainville, C., *Australia* 92 B4
Bougainville I., *Papua N. G.* 96 H7
Bougainville Reef, *Australia* 94 B4
Bougie = Bejaïa, *Algeria* 78 A7
Bougouni, *Mali* 82 C3
Bouillon, *Belgium* 17 E5
Boukombé, *Benin* 83 C5
Boulal, *Mali* 82 B3
Boulazac, *France* 20 C4
Boulder, *Colo., U.S.A.* 112 E2
Boulder, *Mont., U.S.A.* 108 C7
Boulder City, *U.S.A.* 111 K12
Boulder Creek, *U.S.A.* 110 H4
Boulder Dam = Hoover Dam, *U.S.A.* 111 K12
Bouli, *Mauritania* 82 B2
Boulia, *Australia* 94 C2
Bouligny, *France* 19 C12
Boulogne →, *France* 18 E5
Boulogne-sur-Gesse, *France* 20 E4
Boulogne-sur-Mer, *France* 19 B8
Bouloire, *France* 18 E7
Boulouli, *Mali* 82 B3
Boulsa, *Burkina Faso* 83 C4
Boultoum, *Niger* 83 C7
Boûmdeïd, *Mauritania* 82 B2
Boun Neua, *Laos* 64 B3
Boun Tai, *Laos* 64 B3
Bouna, *Ivory C.* 82 D4
Boundary Peak, *U.S.A.* 110 H8
Boundiali, *Ivory C.* 82 D3
Bountiful, *U.S.A.* 108 F8
Bounty Is., *Pac. Oc.* 96 M9
Boura, *Mali* 82 C4
Bourbon-Lancy, *France* 19 F10
Bourbon-l'Archambault, *France* 19 F10
Bourbonnais, *France* 19 F10
Bourbonne-les-Bains, *France* 19 E12
Bourbourg, *France* 19 B9
Bourdel L., *Canada* 104 A5
Bourem, *Mali* 83 B4
Bourg, *France* 20 C3
Bourg-Argental, *France* 21 C8
Bourg-de-Péage, *France* 21 C9
Bourg-en-Bresse, *France* 19 F12
Bourg-Lastic, *France* 20 C6
Bourg-Madame, *France* 20 F5
Bourg-St-Andéol, *France* 21 D8
Bourg-St-Maurice, *France* 21 C10
Bourganeuf, *France* 20 C5
Bourges, *France* 19 E9
Bourget, *Canada* 117 A9
Bourget, Lac du, *France* 21 C9
Bourgneuf, B. de, *France* 18 E4
Bourgneuf-en-Retz, *France* 18 E5
Bourgogne, *France* 19 F11
Bourgoin-Jallieu, *France* 21 C9
Bourgueil, *France* 18 E7
Bourke, *Australia* 95 E4
Bourne, *U.K.* 14 E7
Bournemouth, *U.K.* 15 G6
Bournemouth □, *U.K.* 15 G6
Bouroum, *Burkina Faso* 83 C4
Bouse, *U.S.A.* 111 M13
Boussac, *France* 19 F9
Boussé, *Burkina Faso* 83 C4
Boussouma, *Burkina Faso* 83 C4
Boutilimit, *Mauritania* 82 B2
Boutonne →, *France* 20 C3
Bouvet I. = Bouvetøya, *Antarctica* 3 G10
Bouvetøya, *Antarctica* 3 G10
Bouxwiller, *France* 19 D14
Bouza, *Niger* 83 C6
Bouzonville, *France* 19 C13
Bova Marina, *Italy* 43 E8
Bovalino Marina, *Italy* 43 D9
Bovec, *Slovenia* 41 B10
Bovill, *U.S.A.* 108 C5
Bovino, *Italy* 43 A8
Bovril, *Argentina* 126 C4
Bow →, *Canada* 102 C6
Bow Island, *Canada* 102 D6
Bowbells, *U.S.A.* 112 A3
Bowdle, *U.S.A.* 112 C5
Bowelling, *Australia* 93 F2
Bowen, *Argentina* 126 D2
Bowen, *Australia* 94 J6
Bowen Mts., *Australia* 95 F4
Bowie, *Ariz., U.S.A.* 109 K9
Bowie, *Tex., U.S.A.* 113 J6
Bowkān, *Iran* 70 B5
Bowland, Forest of, *U.K.* 14 D5
Bowling Green, *Ky., U.S.A.* 114 G2
Bowling Green, *Ohio, U.S.A.* 114 E4
Bowling Green, C., *Australia* 94 B4
Bowling Green Bay △, *Australia* 94 B4
Bowman, *U.S.A.* 112 B3
Bowman I., *Antarctica* 5 C8
Bowmanville = Clarington, *Canada* 116 C6
Bowmore, *U.K.* 13 F2
Bowral, *Australia* 95 E5
Bowraville, *Australia* 95 E5
Bowron →, *Canada* 102 C4
Bowron Lake ⌓, *Canada* 102 C4
Bowser L., *Canada* 102 B3
Bowsman, *Canada* 103 C8
Bowwood, *Zambia* 87 F2
Box Cr. →, *Australia* 95 E3
Boxholm, *Sweden* 11 F9
Boxmeer, *Neths.* 17 C5
Boxtel, *Neths.* 17 C5
Boyabat, *Turkey* 72 B6
Boyalıca, *Turkey* 45 F13
Boyang, *China* 59 C11
Boyce, *U.S.A.* 113 K8
Boyd L., *Canada* 104 B4
Boyle, *Canada* 102 C6
Boyle, *Ireland* 12 C3
Boyne →, *Ireland* 12 C5
Boyne City, *U.S.A.* 114 C3
Boynitsa, *Bulgaria* 44 C6
Boynton Beach, *U.S.A.* 115 M5
Boyolali, *Indonesia* 63 G14
Boyoma, Chutes, *Dem. Rep. of the Congo* 86 B2
Boysen Reservoir, *U.S.A.* 108 E9
Boyuibe, *Bolivia* 124 G6
Boyup Brook, *Australia* 93 F2
Boz Burun, *Turkey* 45 F12
Boz Dağ, *Turkey* 47 D11
Boz Dağları, *Turkey* 47 C10
Bozburun, *Turkey* 47 E10
Bozcaada, *Turkey* 72 C2
Bozdoğan, *Turkey* 47 D10
Bozeman, *U.S.A.* 108 D8
Bozen = Bolzano, *Italy* 41 B8
Boževac, *Serbia & M.* 44 B5
Bozhou, *China* 56 H8
Bozkır, *Turkey* 72 D5
Bozkurt, *Turkey* 47 D11
Bozouls, *France* 20 D6
Bozoum, *C.A.R.* 84 C3
Bozova, *Antalya, Turkey* 47 D12
Bozova, *Sanliurfa, Turkey* 73 D8
Bozovici, *Romania* 28 F7
Bozüyük, *Turkey* 47 B12
Bra, *Italy* 40 D4
Braås, *Sweden* 11 G9
Brabant □, *Belgium* 17 D4
Brabant L., *Canada* 103 B8
Brabrand, *Denmark* 11 H4
Brač, *Croatia* 41 E13
Bracadale, L., *U.K.* 13 D2
Bracciano, *Italy* 41 F9
Bracciano, L. di, *Italy* 41 F9
Bracebridge, *Canada* 116 A5
Brach, *Libya* 79 C8

Bracieux, *France* 18 E8
Bräcke, *Sweden* 10 B9
Brackettville, *U.S.A.* 113 L4
Bracki Kanal, *Croatia* 41 E13
Bracknell, *U.K.* 15 F7
Bracknell Forest □, *U.K.* 15 F7
Brad, *Romania* 28 D7
Brádano →, *Italy* 43 B9
Bradenton, *U.S.A.* 115 M4
Bradford, *Canada* 116 B5
Bradford, *U.K.* 14 D6
Bradford, *Pa., U.S.A.* 116 E6
Bradford, *Vt., U.S.A.* 117 C12
Bradley, *Ark., U.S.A.* 113 J8
Bradley, *Calif., U.S.A.* 110 K6
Bradley Institute, *Zimbabwe* 87 F3
Brady, *U.S.A.* 113 K5
Brædstrup, *Denmark* 11 J3
Braeside, *Canada* 117 A8
Braga, *Portugal* 36 D2
Braga □, *Portugal* 36 D2
Bragadiru, *Romania* 29 G10
Bragado, *Argentina* 126 D3
Bragança, *Brazil* 125 D9
Bragança, *Portugal* 36 D4
Bragança □, *Portugal* 36 D4
Bragança Paulista, *Brazil* 127 A6
Brahmanbaria, *Bangla.* 67 H17
Brahmani →, *India* 67 J15
Brahmapur, *India* 67 K14
Brahmaputra →, *Asia* 69 H13
Braich-y-pwll, *U.K.* 14 E3
Braidwood, *Australia* 95 F4
Brăila, *Romania* 29 E12
Brăila □, *Romania* 29 E12
Brainerd, *U.S.A.* 112 B7
Braintree, *U.K.* 15 F8
Braintree, *U.S.A.* 117 D14
Brak →, *S. Africa* 88 D3
Brake, *Germany* 24 B4
Brakel, *Germany* 24 D5
Bräkne-Hoby, *Sweden* 11 H9
Brakwater, *Namibia* 88 C2
Brålanda, *Sweden* 11 F6
Bramberg, *Germany* 25 E6
Bramdrupdam, *Denmark* 11 J3
Bramming, *Denmark* 11 J2
Brämön, *Sweden* 10 B11
Brampton, *Canada* 116 C5
Brampton, *U.K.* 14 C5
Bramsche, *Germany* 24 C3
Bramton I., *Australia* 94 J7
Branco →, *Brazil* 124 D6
Brandberg, *Namibia* 88 C1
Brandberg ⌂, *Namibia* 88 C1
Brande, *Denmark* 11 J3
Brandenburg = Neubrandenburg, *Germany* 24 B9
Brandenburg, *Germany* 24 C8
Brandenburg □, *Germany* 24 C9
Brandfort, *S. Africa* 88 D4
Brando, *France* 21 F13
Brandon, *Canada* 103 D9
Brandon, *U.S.A.* 117 C11
Brandon B., *Ireland* 12 D1
Brandon Mt., *Ireland* 12 D1
Brandsen, *Argentina* 126 D4
Brandvlei, *S. Africa* 88 E3
Brandýs nad Labem, *Czech Rep.* 26 A7
Brănești, *Romania* 29 F11
Branford, *U.S.A.* 117 E12
Braniewo, *Poland* 30 D6
Bransfield Str., *Antarctica* 5 C18
Brańsk, *Poland* 31 F9
Branson, *U.S.A.* 113 G8
Brantford, *Canada* 116 C4
Brantôme, *France* 20 C4
Branzi, *Italy* 40 B6
Bras d'Or L., *Canada* 105 C7
Brasher Falls, *U.S.A.* 117 B10
Brasil, Planalto, *Brazil* 122 E6
Brasiléia, *Brazil* 124 F5
Brasília, *Brazil* 125 G9
Brasília Legal, *Brazil* 125 D7
Braslaw, *Belarus* 9 J22
Braslovče, *Slovenia* 41 B12
Brașov, *Romania* 29 E10
Brașov □, *Romania* 29 E10
Brass, *Nigeria* 83 E6
Brass →, *Nigeria* 83 E6
Brassac-les-Mines, *France* 20 C7
Brasschaat, *Belgium* 17 C4
Brassey, Banjaran, *Malaysia* 62 D5
Brassey Ra., *Australia* 93 E3
Brasstown Bald, *U.S.A.* 115 H4
Brastad, *Sweden* 11 F5
Brastavățu, *Romania* 29 G9
Bratan = Morozov, *Bulgaria* 45 D9
Brateș, *Romania* 29 E11
Bratislava, *Slovak Rep.* 27 C10
Bratislava M.R. Stefanik ✕ (BTS), *Slovak Rep.* 27 C10
Bratislavský □, *Slovak Rep.* 27 C10
Bratsigovo, *Bulgaria* 45 D8
Bratsk, *Russia* 53 D11
Brattleboro, *U.S.A.* 117 D12
Bratunac, *Bos.-H.* 28 F4
Braunau, *Austria* 26 C6
Braunschweig, *Germany* 24 C6
Braunton, *U.K.* 15 F3
Bravicea, *Moldova* 29 C13
Bråviken, *Sweden* 11 F10
Bravo del Norte, Rio = Grande, Rio →, *U.S.A.* 113 N6
Brawley, *U.S.A.* 111 N11
Bray, *Ireland* 12 C5
Bray, Mt., *Australia* 94 A1
Bray-sur-Seine, *France* 19 D10
Brazeau →, *Canada* 102 C5
Brazil, *U.S.A.* 114 F2
Brazil ■, *S. Amer.* 125 F9
Brazilian Highlands = Brasil, Planalto, *Brazil* 122 E6
Brazo Sur →, *S. Amer.* 126 B4
Brazos →, *U.S.A.* 113 L7
Brazzaville, *Congo* 84 E3
Brčko, *Bos.-H.* 28 F3
Brda →, *Poland* 31 E5
Brdy, *Czech Rep.* 26 B6
Breaden, L., *Australia* 93 E4
Breaksea Sd., *N.Z.* 91 L1
Bream B., *N.Z.* 91 F5
Bream Hd., *N.Z.* 91 F5
Breas, *Chile* 126 B1
Breaza, *Romania* 29 E10
Brebes, *Indonesia* 63 G13
Brechin, *Canada* 116 B5
Brechin, *U.K.* 13 E6
Brecht, *Belgium* 17 C4
Breckenridge, *Colo., U.S.A.* 108 G10
Breckenridge, *Minn., U.S.A.* 112 B6
Breckenridge, *Tex., U.S.A.* 113 J5
Breckland, *U.K.* 15 E8
Břeclav, *Czech Rep.* 27 C9
Brecon, *U.K.* 15 F4
Brecon Beacons, *U.K.* 15 F4
Brecon Beacons △, *U.K.* 15 F4
Breda, *Neths.* 17 C4
Bredaryd, *Sweden* 11 G7
Bredasdorp, *S. Africa* 88 E3
Bredebro, *Denmark* 11 J2
Bredstedt, *Germany* 24 A4
Bree, *Belgium* 17 C5
Bregalnica →, *Macedonia* 44 E6
Bregenz, *Austria* 26 D2
Bregovo, *Bulgaria* 44 B6
Bréhal, *France* 18 D5
Bréhat, Î. de, *France* 18 D4
Breiðafjörður, *Iceland* 8 D2
Breil-sur-Roya, *France* 21 E11
Breisach, *Germany* 25 G3
Brejo, *Brazil* 125 D10
Bremen, *Germany* 24 B4
Bremen □, *Germany* 24 B4
Bremer Bay, *Australia* 93 F2
Bremer I., *Australia* 94 A2
Bremerhaven, *Germany* 24 B4
Bremerton, *U.S.A.* 110 C4
Bremervörde, *Germany* 24 B5
Brenes, *Spain* 37 H5
Brenham, *U.S.A.* 113 K6
Brenne, *France* 20 B5
Brenne ⌂, *France* 20 B5
Brennerpass, *Austria* 26 D4
Breno, *Italy* 40 C7
Brent, *U.S.A.* 115 J2
Brenta →, *Italy* 41 C9
Brentwood, *U.K.* 15 F8
Brentwood, *Calif., U.S.A.* 110 H5
Brentwood, *N.Y., U.S.A.* 117 F11
Bréscia, *Italy* 40 C7
Breskens, *Neths.* 17 C3
Breslau = Wrocław, *Poland* 31 G4
Bresle →, *France* 18 B8
Bressanone, *Italy* 41 B8
Bressay, *U.K.* 13 A7
Bresse, *France* 19 F12
Bressuire, *France* 18 F6
Brest, *Belarus* 33 F2
Brest, *France* 18 D2
Brest-Litovsk = Brest, *Belarus* 33 F2
Bretagne, *France* 18 D3
Bretçu, *Romania* 29 D11
Bretenoux, *France* 20 D5
Breteuil, *Eure, France* 18 D7
Breteuil, *Oise, France* 19 C9
Breton, *Canada* 102 C6
Breton, Pertuis, *France* 20 B2
Breton Sd., *U.S.A.* 113 L10
Brett, C., *N.Z.* 91 F5
Bretten, *Germany* 25 F4
Breuil-Cervínia, *Italy* 40 C4
Brevard, *U.S.A.* 115 H4
Breves, *Brazil* 125 D8
Brewarrina, *Australia* 95 E4
Brewer, *U.S.A.* 115 C11
Brewer, Mt., *U.S.A.* 110 J8
Brewerville, *Liberia* 82 D2
Brewster, *N.Y., U.S.A.* 117 E11
Brewster, *Ohio, U.S.A.* 116 F3
Brewster, *Wash., U.S.A.* 108 B4
Brewster, Kap = Kangikajik, *Greenland* 4 B6
Brewton, *U.S.A.* 115 K2
Breyten, *S. Africa* 89 D5
Breza, *Bos.-H.* 28 F3
Brezhnev = Naberezhnyye Chelny, *Russia* 34 C11
Brežice, *Slovenia* 41 C12
Březnice, *Czech Rep.* 26 B6
Breznik, *Bulgaria* 44 D6
Brezno, *Slovak Rep.* 27 C12
Brezoi, *Romania* 29 E9
Brezovica, *Serbia & M.* 44 D5
Brezovo, *Bulgaria* 45 D9
Briançon, *France* 21 D10
Briare, *France* 19 E9
Briático, *Italy* 43 D9
Bribie I., *Australia* 95 D5
Bribri, *Costa Rica* 120 E3
Briceni, *Moldova* 29 B12
Bricquebec, *France* 18 C5
Bridgefield, *Barbados* 121 g
Bridgehampton, *U.S.A.* 117 F12
Bridgend, *U.K.* 15 F4
Bridgend □, *U.K.* 15 F4
Bridgeport, *Calif., U.S.A.* 110 G7
Bridgeport, *Conn., U.S.A.* 117 E11
Bridgeport, *Nebr., U.S.A.* 112 E3
Bridgeport, *Tex., U.S.A.* 113 J6
Bridger, *U.S.A.* 108 D9
Bridgeton, *U.S.A.* 114 F8
Bridgetown, *Australia* 93 F2
Bridgetown, *Barbados* 121 g
Bridgetown, *Canada* 105 D6
Bridgewater, *Canada* 105 D7
Bridgewater, *Mass., U.S.A.* 117 E14
Bridgewater, *N.Y., U.S.A.* 117 D9
Bridgewater, C., *Australia* 95 F3
Bridgewater-Gagebrook, *Australia* 95 G4
Bridgnorth, *U.K.* 15 E5
Bridgton, *U.S.A.* 117 B14
Bridgwater, *U.K.* 15 F5
Bridgwater B., *U.K.* 15 F4
Bridlington, *U.K.* 14 C7
Bridlington B., *U.K.* 14 C7
Bridport, *Australia* 95 G4
Bridport, *U.K.* 15 G5
Briec, *France* 18 D2
Brienne-le-Château, *France* 19 D11
Brienon-sur-Armançon, *France* 19 E10
Brienz, *Switz.* 25 J4
Brienzersee, *Switz.* 25 J3
Brière ⌂, *France* 18 E4
Brig, *Switz.* 25 J3
Brigg, *U.K.* 14 D7
Brigham City, *U.S.A.* 108 F7
Bright, *Australia* 95 F4
Brighton, *Australia* 95 F2
Brighton, *Canada* 116 B7
Brighton, *Trin. & Tob.* 125 K15
Brighton, *U.K.* 15 G7
Brighton, *Colo., U.S.A.* 112 F2
Brighton, *N.Y., U.S.A.* 116 C7
Brignogan-Plage, *France* 18 D2
Brignoles, *France* 21 E10
Brihuega, *Spain* 38 E2
Brikama, *Gambia* 82 C1
Brilliant, *U.S.A.* 116 F4
Brilon, *Germany* 24 D4
Bríndisi, *Italy* 43 B10
Brinje, *Croatia* 41 D12
Brinkley, *U.S.A.* 113 H9
Brinnon, *U.S.A.* 110 C4
Brion, Î., *Canada* 105 C7
Brionne, *France* 18 C7
Brionski, *Croatia* 41 D10
Brioude, *France* 20 C7
Briouze, *France* 18 D6
Brisbane, *Australia* 95 D5
Brisbane →, *Australia* 95 D5
Brisighella, *Italy* 41 D8
Bristol, *U.K.* 15 F5
Bristol, *Conn., U.S.A.* 117 E12
Bristol, *Pa., U.S.A.* 117 F10
Bristol, *R.I., U.S.A.* 117 E13
Bristol, *Tenn., U.S.A.* 115 G4
Bristol, City of □, *U.K.* 15 F5
Bristol B., *U.S.A.* 100 C4
Bristol Channel, *U.K.* 15 F3
Bristol I., *Antarctica* 5 B1
Bristol L., *U.S.A.* 109 J5
Bristow, *U.S.A.* 113 H6
Britain = Great Britain, *Europe* 6 E5
British Columbia □, *Canada* 102 C3
British Indian Ocean Terr. = Chagos Arch. ⊠, *Ind. Oc.* 50 K11
British Isles, *Europe* 6 E5
British Virgin Is. ⊠, *W. Indies* 121 e
Brits, *S. Africa* 89 D4
Britstown, *S. Africa* 88 E3
Britt, *Canada* 104 C3
Brittany = Bretagne, *France* 18 D3
Britton, *U.S.A.* 112 C6
Brive-la-Gaillarde, *France* 20 C5
Briviesca, *Spain* 36 C7
Brixen = Bressanone, *Italy* 41 B8
Brixham, *U.K.* 15 G4
Brnaze, *Croatia* 41 E13
Brněnský □, *Czech Rep.* 27 B9
Brno, *Czech Rep.* 27 B9
Broach = Bharuch, *India* 66 J8
Broad →, *U.S.A.* 115 J5
Broad Arrow, *Australia* 93 F3
Broad B., *U.K.* 13 C2
Broad Haven, *Ireland* 12 B2
Broad Law, *U.K.* 13 F5
Broad Sd., *Australia* 94 C4
Broadalbin, *U.S.A.* 117 C10
Broadback →, *Canada* 104 B4
Broadhurst Ra., *Australia* 92 D3
Broads △, *U.K.* 15 E9
Broads, The, *U.K.* 14 E9
Broadus, *U.S.A.* 112 C2
Broager, *Denmark* 11 K3
Broby, *Sweden* 11 H8
Brocēni, *Latvia* 30 B9
Brochet, *Canada* 103 B8
Brochet, L., *Canada* 103 B8
Brocken, *Germany* 24 D6
Brockport, *U.S.A.* 116 C7
Brockton, *U.S.A.* 117 D13
Brockville, *Canada* 117 B9
Brockway, *Mont., U.S.A.* 112 B2
Brockway, *Pa., U.S.A.* 116 E6
Brocton, *U.S.A.* 116 D5
Brod, *Macedonia* 44 E5
Brodarevo, *Serbia & M.* 44 C3
Brodeur Pen., *Canada* 101 A11
Brodhead, Mt., *U.S.A.* 116 E7
Brodick, *U.K.* 13 F3
Brodnica, *Poland* 31 E6
Brody, *Ukraine* 33 G3
Brogan, *U.S.A.* 108 D5
Broglie, *France* 18 C7
Brok, *Poland* 31 F8
Broken Arrow, *U.S.A.* 113 G7
Broken Bow, *Nebr., U.S.A.* 112 E5
Broken Bow, *Okla., U.S.A.* 113 H7
Broken Bow Lake, *U.S.A.* 113 H7
Broken Hill = Kabwe, *Zambia* 87 E2
Broken Hill, *Australia* 95 E3
Broken River Ra., *Australia* 94 K6
Brokind, *Sweden* 11 F9
Bromley □, *U.K.* 15 F8
Bromo, *Indonesia* 63 G15
Bromölla, *Sweden* 11 H8
Bromsgrove, *U.K.* 15 E5
Brønderslev, *Denmark* 11 G3
Brong-Ahafo □, *Ghana* 82 D4
Broni, *Italy* 40 C6
Bronkhorstspruit, *S. Africa* 89 D4
Brønnøysund, *Norway* 8 D15
Bronte, *Italy* 43 E7
Brook Park, *U.S.A.* 116 E4
Brookhaven, *U.S.A.* 113 K9
Brookings, *Oreg., U.S.A.* 108 E1
Brookings, *S. Dak., U.S.A.* 112 C6
Brooklin, *Canada* 116 C6
Brooklyn Park, *U.S.A.* 112 C8
Brooks, *Canada* 102 C6
Brooks Range, *U.S.A.* 100 B5
Brooksville, *U.S.A.* 115 L4
Brookton, *Australia* 93 F2
Brookville, *U.S.A.* 116 E5
Broom, L., *U.K.* 13 D3
Broome, *Australia* 92 C3
Broons, *France* 18 D4
Brora, *U.K.* 13 C5
Brora →, *U.K.* 13 C5
Brørup, *Denmark* 11 J2
Brösarp, *Sweden* 11 J8
Brosna →, *Ireland* 12 C4
Broșteni, *Mehedinți, Romania* 28 F7
Broșteni, *Suceava, Romania* 29 C10
Brothers, *U.S.A.* 108 E3
Brou, *France* 18 D8
Brouage, *France* 20 C2
Brough, *U.K.* 14 C5
Brough Hd., *U.K.* 13 B5
Broughton Island = Qikiqtarjuaq, *Canada* 101 B13
Broumov, *Czech Rep.* 27 A9
Brovary, *Ukraine* 33 G6
Brovst, *Denmark* 11 G3
Brown, L., *Australia* 93 F2
Brown, Pt., *Australia* 95 E1
Brown City, *U.S.A.* 116 C2
Brown Willy, *U.K.* 15 G3
Brownfield, *U.S.A.* 113 J3
Browning, *U.S.A.* 108 B7
Brownsville, *Oreg., U.S.A.* 108 D2
Brownsville, *Pa., U.S.A.* 116 F5
Brownsville, *Tenn., U.S.A.* 113 H10
Brownsville, *Tex., U.S.A.* 113 N6
Brownville, *U.S.A.* 117 C9
Brownwood, *U.S.A.* 113 K5
Browse I., *Australia* 92 B3
Bruas, *Malaysia* 65 K3
Bruay-la-Buissière, *France* 19 B9
Bruce, Mt., *Australia* 92 D2
Bruce Pen., *Canada* 116 B3
Bruce Peninsula △, *Canada* 116 A3
Bruce Rock, *Australia* 93 F2
Bruche →, *France* 19 D14
Bruchsal, *Germany* 25 F4
Bruck an der Leitha, *Austria* 27 C9
Bruck an der Mur, *Austria* 26 D8
Brue →, *U.K.* 15 F5
Bruges = Brugge, *Belgium* 17 C3
Brugg, *Switz.* 25 H4
Brugge, *Belgium* 17 C3
Bruin, *U.S.A.* 116 E5
Brûlé, *Canada* 102 C5
Brûlon, *France* 18 E6
Brumado, *Brazil* 125 F10
Brumath, *France* 19 D14
Brumunddal, *Norway* 9 F14
Bruneau, *U.S.A.* 108 E6
Bruneau →, *U.S.A.* 108 E6
Bruneck = Brunico, *Italy* 41 B8
Brunei = Bandar Seri Begawan, *Brunei* 62 C4
Brunei ■, *Asia* 62 D4
Brunflo, *Sweden* 10 A8
Brunico, *Italy* 41 B8
Brunna, *Sweden* 10 E11
Brunnen, *Switz.* 25 J4
Brunner, L., *N.Z.* 91 K3
Brunsbüttel, *Germany* 24 B5
Brunssum, *Neths.* 17 D5
Brunswick = Braunschweig, *Germany* 24 C6
Brunswick, *Ga., U.S.A.* 115 K5
Brunswick, *Maine, U.S.A.* 115 D11
Brunswick, *Md., U.S.A.* 114 F7
Brunswick, *Mo., U.S.A.* 112 F8
Brunswick, *Ohio, U.S.A.* 116 E3
Brunswick, Pen. de, *Chile* 128 G2
Brunswick B., *Australia* 92 C3
Brunswick Junction, *Australia* 93 F2
Bruntál, *Czech Rep.* 27 B10
Bruny I., *Australia* 95 G4
Brus Laguna, *Honduras* 120 C3
Brusartsi, *Bulgaria* 44 C7
Brush, *U.S.A.* 112 E3
Brushton, *U.S.A.* 117 B10
Brusio, *Switz.* 25 J6
Brusque, *Brazil* 127 B6
Brussel, *Belgium* 17 D4
Brussels = Brussel, *Belgium* 17 D4
Brussels, *Canada* 116 C3
Brussels Nat. ✕ (BRU), *Belgium* 17 D5
Brusy, *Poland* 30 E4
Bruthen, *Australia* 95 F4
Bruxelles = Brussel, *Belgium* 17 D4
Bruyères, *France* 19 D13
Bruz, *France* 18 D5
Brwinów, *Poland* 31 F7
Bryagovo, *Bulgaria* 45 E9
Bryan, *Ohio, U.S.A.* 114 E3
Bryan, *Tex., U.S.A.* 113 K6
Bryan, Mt., *Australia* 95 E2
Bryanka, *Ukraine* 33 H10
Bryansk, *Bryansk, Russia* 33 F8
Bryansk, *Dagestan, Russia* 35 H8
Bryanskoye = Bryansk, *Russia* 35 H8
Bryce Canyon △, *U.S.A.* 109 H7
Bryne, *Norway* 9 G11
Bryson City, *U.S.A.* 115 H4
Bryukhovetskaya, *Russia* 33 K10
Brza Palanka, *Serbia & M.* 44 B6
Brzeg, *Poland* 31 H4
Brzeg Dolny, *Poland* 31 G3
Brześć Kujawski, *Poland* 31 F5
Brzesko, *Poland* 31 J7
Brzeziny, *Poland* 31 G6
Brzozów, *Poland* 31 J9
Bsharri, *Lebanon* 74 A5
Bū Baqarah, *U.A.E.* 71 E8
Bu Craa, *W. Sahara* 78 C3
Bū Ḥasā, *U.A.E.* 71 F7
Bua, *Sweden* 11 G6
Bua Yai, *Thailand* 64 E4
Buapinang, *Indonesia* 63 E6
Buba, *Guinea-Biss.* 82 C2
Bubanza, *Burundi* 86 C2
Bubaque, *Guinea-Biss.* 82 C1
Bube, *Ethiopia* 81 F4
Būbiyān, *Kuwait* 71 D6
Buca, *Turkey* 47 C9
Bucak, *Turkey* 47 D12
Bucaramanga, *Colombia* 124 B4
Bucas Grande I., *Phil.* 61 G6
Bucasia, *Australia* 94 K7
Buccaneer Arch., *Australia* 92 C3
Buccino, *Italy* 43 B8
Buccoo Reef, *Trin. & Tob.* 125 J16
Bucecea, *Romania* 29 C11
Bucegi △, *Romania* 29 E10
Buchach, *Ukraine* 33 H3
Buchan, *U.K.* 13 D6
Buchan Ness, *U.K.* 13 D7
Buchanan, *Canada* 103 C8
Buchanan, *Liberia* 82 D2
Buchanan, L., *Queens., Australia* 94 C4
Buchanan, L., *W. Austral., Australia* 93 E3
Buchanan, L., *U.S.A.* 113 K5
Buchanan Cr. →, *Australia* 94 B2
Buchans, *Canada* 105 C8
Bucharest = București, *Romania* 29 F11
Bucharest Otopeni ✕ (OTP), *Romania* 45 B10
Buchen, *Germany* 25 F5
Buchholz, *Germany* 24 B5
Buchloe, *Germany* 25 G6
Buchon, Pt., *U.S.A.* 110 K6
Buciumi, *Romania* 28 C8
Buck Hill Falls, *U.S.A.* 117 E9
Bückeburg, *Germany* 24 C5
Buckeye, *U.S.A.* 109 K7
Buckeye Lake, *U.S.A.* 116 G2
Buckhannon, *U.S.A.* 114 F5
Buckhaven, *U.K.* 13 E5
Buckhorn L., *Canada* 116 B6
Buckie, *U.K.* 13 D6
Buckingham, *Canada* 104 C4
Buckingham, *U.K.* 15 F7
Buckingham B., *Australia* 94 A2
Buckinghamshire □, *U.K.* 15 F7
Buckle Hd., *Australia* 92 B4
Buckleboo, *Australia* 95 E2
Buckley, *U.K.* 14 D4
Buckley →, *Australia* 94 C2
Bucklin, *U.S.A.* 113 G5
Bucks L., *U.S.A.* 110 F5
Bucquoy, *France* 19 B9
București, *Romania* 29 F11
Bucyrus, *U.S.A.* 114 E4
Budacu, Vf., *Romania* 29 C10
Budalin, *Burma* 67 H19
Budaörs, *Hungary* 28 C3
Budapest, *Hungary* 28 C4
Budapest □, *Hungary* 28 C4
Budapest ✕ (BUD), *Hungary* 28 C4
Budaun, *India* 69 E8
Budd Coast, *Antarctica* 5 C8
Buddusò, *Italy* 42 B2
Bude, *U.K.* 15 G3
Budennovsk, *Russia* 35 H7
Budești, *Romania* 29 F11
Budge Budge = Baj Baj, *India* 69 H13
Budgewoi, *Australia* 95 E5
Budia, *Spain* 38 E2
Büdingen, *Germany* 25 E5
Budjala, *Dem. Rep. of the Congo* 84 D3
Budoni, *Italy* 42 B2
Búdrio, *Italy* 41 D8
Budva, *Serbia & M.* 44 D2
Budzyń, *Poland* 31 F3
Buea, *Cameroon* 83 E6
Buellton, *U.S.A.* 111 L6
Buena Esperanza, *Argentina* 126 C2
Buena Park, *U.S.A.* 111 M9
Buena Vista, *Colo., U.S.A.* 109 G10
Buena Vista, *Va., U.S.A.* 114 G6
Buena Vista Lake Bed, *U.S.A.* 111 K7
Buenaventura, *Colombia* 124 C3
Buenaventura, *Mexico* 118 B3
Buendía, Embalse de, *Spain* 38 E2
Buenos Aires, *Argentina* 126 C4
Buenos Aires, *Costa Rica* 120 E3
Buenos Aires □, *Argentina* 126 D4
Buenos Aires, L., *Chile* 128 F2
Buffalo, *Mo., U.S.A.* 113 G8
Buffalo, *N.Y., U.S.A.* 116 D6
Buffalo, *Okla., U.S.A.* 113 G5
Buffalo, *S. Dak., U.S.A.* 112 C3
Buffalo, *Wyo., U.S.A.* 108 D10
Buffalo △, *U.S.A.* 113 G8
Buffalo →, *Canada* 102 A5
Buffalo →, *S. Africa* 89 D5
Buffalo Head Hills, *Canada* 102 B5

Buffalo L., *Alta., Canada* 102 C6
Buffalo L., *N.W.T., Canada* 102 A5
Buffalo Narrows, *Canada* 103 B7
Buffalo Springs ⌓, *Kenya* 86 B4
Buffels →, *S. Africa* 88 D2
Buford, *U.S.A.* 115 H4
Bug = Buh →, *Ukraine* 33 J6
Bug →, *Poland* 31 F8
Buga, *Colombia* 124 C3
Bugala I., *Uganda* 86 C3
Buganda, *Uganda* 86 C3
Buganga, *Uganda* 86 C3
Bugasong, *Phil.* 61 F5
Bugeat, *France* 20 C5
Bugel, Tanjung, *Indonesia* 63 G14
Bugibba, *Malta* 49 D1
Bugojno, *Bos.-H.* 28 F2
Bugsuk, *Phil.* 62 C5
Buguma, *Nigeria* 83 E6
Bugun Shara, *Mongolia* 60 B5
Bugungu ⌓, *Uganda* 86 B3
Buguruslan, *Russia* 52 D6
Buh →, *Ukraine* 33 J6
Buharkent, *Turkey* 47 D10
Buheirat-Murrat-el-Kubra, *Egypt* 80 H8
Buhera, *Zimbabwe* 89 B5
Bühl, *Germany* 25 G4
Buhl, *U.S.A.* 108 E6
Buhuşi, *Romania* 29 D11
Bui △, *Ghana* 82 D4
Builth Wells, *U.K.* 15 E4
Buinsk, *Russia* 34 C9
Buir Nur, *Mongolia* 60 B6
Buis-les-Baronnies, *France* 21 D9
Buitrago = Buitrago del Lozoya, *Spain* 36 E7
Buitrago del Lozoya, *Spain* 36 E7
Bujalance, *Spain* 37 H6
Bujanovac, *Serbia & M.* 44 D5
Bujaraloz, *Spain* 38 D4
Buje, *Croatia* 41 C10
Bujumbura, *Burundi* 86 C2
Bük, *Hungary* 28 C1
Buk, *Poland* 31 F3
Bukachacha, *Russia* 53 D12
Bukama, *Dem. Rep. of the Congo* 87 D2
Bukavu, *Dem. Rep. of the Congo* 86 C2
Bukene, *Tanzania* 86 C3
Bukhara = Bukhoro, *Uzbekistan* 52 F7
Bukhoro, *Uzbekistan* 52 F7
Bukima, *Tanzania* 86 C3
Bukit Badung, *Indonesia* 63 K18
Bukit Kerajaan, *Malaysia* 65 c
Bukit Mertajam, *Malaysia* 65 c
Bukit Ni, *Malaysia* 65 d
Bukit Panjang, *Singapore* 65 d
Bukit Tengah, *Malaysia* 65 c
Bukittinggi, *Indonesia* 62 E2
Bükk, *Hungary* 28 B5
Bükki △, *Hungary* 28 B5
Bukoba, *Tanzania* 86 C3
Bukum, Pulau, *Singapore* 65 d
Bukuru, *Nigeria* 83 D6
Bukuya, *Uganda* 86 B3
Būl, Kuh-e, *Iran* 71 D7
Bula, *Guinea-Biss.* 82 C1
Bula, *Indonesia* 63 E8
Bülach, *Switz.* 25 H4
Bulahdelah, *Australia* 95 E5
Bulan, *Phil.* 61 E5
Bulancak, *Turkey* 73 B8
Bulandshahr, *India* 68 E7
Bulanık, *Turkey* 73 C10
Bûlâq, *Egypt* 80 B3
Bulawayo, *Zimbabwe* 87 G2
Buldan, *Turkey* 47 C10
Bulgar, *Russia* 34 C9
Bulgaria ■, *Europe* 45 D9
Bulgheria, Monte, *Italy* 43 B8
Bulgurca, *Turkey* 47 C9
Buli, Teluk, *Indonesia* 63 D7
Buliluyan, C., *Phil.* 61 G2
Bulim, *Singapore* 65 d
Bulki, *Ethiopia* 81 F4
Bulkley →, *Canada* 102 B3
Bull Shoals L., *U.S.A.* 113 G8
Bullaque →, *Spain* 37 G6
Bullas, *Spain* 39 G3
Bulle, *Switz.* 25 J3
Bulleringa △, *Australia* 94 B3
Bullhead City, *U.S.A.* 111 K12
Büllingen, *Belgium* 17 D6
Bullock Creek, *Australia* 94 B3
Bulloo →, *Australia* 95 D3
Bulloo L., *Australia* 95 D3
Bulls, *N.Z.* 91 J5
Bully-les-Mines, *France* 19 B9
Bulnes, *Chile* 126 D1
Bulqizë, *Albania* 44 E4
Bulsar = Valsad, *India* 66 J8
Bultfontein, *S. Africa* 88 D4
Bulukumba, *Indonesia* 63 F6
Bulun, *Russia* 53 B13
Bumba, *Dem. Rep. of the Congo* 84 D4
Bumbeşti-Jiu, *Romania* 29 E8
Bumbiri I., *Tanzania* 86 C3
Bumbuna, *S. Leone* 82 D2
Bumhpa Bum, *Burma* 67 F20
Bumi →, *Zimbabwe* 87 F2
Buna, *Kenya* 86 B4
Bunawan, *Phil.* 61 G6
Bunazi, *Tanzania* 86 C3
Bunbury, *Australia* 93 F2
Bunclody, *Ireland* 12 D5
Buncrana, *Ireland* 12 A4
Bundaberg, *Australia* 95 C5
Bünde, *Germany* 24 C4
Bundey →, *Australia* 94 C2
Bundi, *India* 68 G6
Bundjalung △, *Australia* 95 D5
Bundoran, *Ireland* 12 B3
Bundukia, *Sudan* 81 F3
Bung Kan, *Thailand* 64 C4
Bunga →, *Nigeria* 83 C6
Bungay, *U.K.* 15 E9
Bungil Cr. →, *Australia* 95 D4
Bungo-Suidō, *Japan* 55 H6
Bungoma, *Kenya* 86 B3
Bungotakada, *Japan* 55 H5
Bungu, *Tanzania* 86 D4
Bunia, *Dem. Rep. of the Congo* 86 B3
Bunji, *Pakistan* 69 B6
Bunkie, *U.S.A.* 113 K8
Bunnell, *U.S.A.* 115 L5
Buñol, *Spain* 39 F4
Bunsuru, *Nigeria* 83 C5
Buntok, *Indonesia* 62 E4
Bununu Dass, *Nigeria* 83 C6
Bununu Kasa, *Nigeria* 83 D6
Bunya Mts. △, *Australia* 95 D5
Bünyan, *Turkey* 72 C6
Bunyu, *Indonesia* 62 D5
Bunza, *Nigeria* 83 C5
Buol, *Indonesia* 63 D6
Buon Brieng, *Vietnam* 64 F7
Buon Ma Thuot, *Vietnam* 64 F7
Buong Long, *Cambodia* 64 F6
Buorkhaya, Mys, *Russia* 53 B14
Buqayq, *Si. Arabia* 71 E6
Buqbuq, *Egypt* 80 A2
Bur Acaba, *Somali Rep.* 75 G3
Bûr Fuad, *Egypt* 80 H8
Bûr Safâga, *Egypt* 70 E2
Bûr Sa'îd, *Egypt* 80 H8
Bûr Sûdân, *Sudan* 80 D4
Bûr Taufiq, *Egypt* 80 J8
Bura, *Kenya* 86 C4
Burakin, *Australia* 93 F2
Buram, *Sudan* 81 E2
Burao, *Somali Rep.* 75 F4
Burāq, *Syria* 74 B5
Buraydah, *Si. Arabia* 70 E4
Burbank, *U.S.A.* 111 L8
Burda, *India* 68 G6
Burdekin →, *Australia* 94 B4
Burdur, *Turkey* 47 D12
Burdur □, *Turkey* 47 D12
Burdur Gölü, *Turkey* 47 D12
Burdwan = Barddhaman, *India* 69 H12
Bure, *Gojam, Ethiopia* 81 E4
Bure, *Ilubabor, Ethiopia* 81 F4
Bure →, *U.K.* 14 E9
Büren, *Germany* 24 D4
Bureya →, *Russia* 53 E13
Burford, *Canada* 116 C4
Burg, *Germany* 24 C7
Burg auf Fehmarn, *Germany* 24 A7
Burg el Arab, *Egypt* 80 H6
Burg et Tuyur, *Sudan* 80 C2
Burg Stargard, *Germany* 24 B9
Burgas, *Bulgaria* 45 D11
Burgas □, *Bulgaria* 45 D10
Burgaski Zaliv, *Bulgaria* 45 D11
Burgdorf, *Germany* 24 C6
Burgdorf, *Switz.* 25 H3
Burgenland □, *Austria* 27 D9
Burgeo, *Canada* 105 C8
Burgersdorp, *S. Africa* 88 E4
Burges, Mt., *Australia* 93 F3
Burghausen, *Germany* 25 G8
Burghead, *U.K.* 13 D5
Búrgio, *Italy* 42 E6
Burglengenfeld, *Germany* 25 F8
Burgohondo, *Spain* 36 E6
Burgos, *Spain* 36 C7
Burgos □, *Spain* 36 C7
Burgstädt, *Germany* 24 E8
Burgsvik, *Sweden* 11 G12
Burguillos del Cerro, *Spain* 37 G4
Burgundy = Bourgogne, *France* 19 F11
Burhaniye, *Turkey* 47 B8
Burhanpur, *India* 66 J10
Burhi Gandak →, *India* 69 G12
Burhner →, *India* 69 H9
Buri Pen., *Eritrea* 81 D4
Burias I., *Phil.* 61 E5
Burica, Pta., *Costa Rica* 120 E3
Burien, *U.S.A.* 110 C4
Burigi ⌓, *Tanzania* 86 C3
Burigi, L., *Tanzania* 86 C3
Burin, *Canada* 105 C8
Buriram, *Thailand* 64 E4
Burj Sāfitā, *Syria* 70 C3
Burji, *Ethiopia* 81 F4
Burkburnett, *U.S.A.* 113 H5
Burke →, *Australia* 94 C2
Burke Chan., *Canada* 102 C3
Burketown, *Australia* 94 B2
Burkina Faso ■, *Africa* 82 C4
Burk's Falls, *Canada* 104 C4
Burlada, *Spain* 38 C3
Burleigh Falls, *Canada* 116 B6
Burley, *U.S.A.* 108 E7
Burlingame, *U.S.A.* 110 H4
Burlington, *Canada* 116 C5
Burlington, *Colo., U.S.A.* 112 F3
Burlington, *Iowa, U.S.A.* 112 E9
Burlington, *Kans., U.S.A.* 112 F7
Burlington, *N.C., U.S.A.* 115 G6
Burlington, *N.J., U.S.A.* 117 F10
Burlington, *Vt., U.S.A.* 117 B11
Burlington, *Wash., U.S.A.* 110 B4
Burlington, *Wis., U.S.A.* 114 D1
Burlyu-Tyube, *Kazakhstan* 52 E8
Burma ■, *Asia* 67 J20
Burnaby I., *Canada* 102 C2
Burnet, *U.S.A.* 113 K5
Burney, *U.S.A.* 108 F3
Burnham, *U.S.A.* 116 F7
Burnham-on-Sea, *U.K.* 15 F5
Burnie, *Australia* 95 G4
Burnley, *U.K.* 14 D5
Burns, *U.S.A.* 108 E4
Burns Lake, *Canada* 102 C3
Burnside →, *Canada* 100 B9
Burnside, L., *Australia* 93 E3
Burnsville, *U.S.A.* 112 C8
Burnt, L., *Canada* 105 B7
Burnt River, *Canada* 116 B6
Burntwood →, *Canada* 103 B9
Burntwood L., *Canada* 103 B8
Burqān, *Kuwait* 70 D5
Burra, *Australia* 95 E2
Burra, *Nigeria* 83 C6
Burray, *U.K.* 13 C6
Burrel, *Albania* 44 E4
Burren △, *Ireland* 12 C3
Burren Junction, *Australia* 95 E4
Burriana, *Spain* 38 F4
Burrinjuck Res., *Australia* 95 F4
Burro, Serranías del, *Mexico* 118 B4
Burrow Hd., *U.K.* 13 G4
Burrum Coast △, *Australia* 95 D5
Burruyacú, *Argentina* 126 B3
Burry Port, *U.K.* 15 F3
Bursa, *Turkey* 45 F13
Burseryd, *Sweden* 11 G7
Burstall, *Canada* 103 C7
Burton, *Ohio, U.S.A.* 116 E3
Burton, *S.C., U.S.A.* 115 J5
Burton, L., *Canada* 104 B4
Burton upon Trent, *U.K.* 14 E6
Buru, *Indonesia* 63 E7
Burullus, Bahra el, *Egypt* 80 H7
Burûn, Râs, *Egypt* 74 D2
Burundi ■, *Africa* 86 C3
Bururi, *Burundi* 86 C2
Burutu, *Nigeria* 83 D6
Burwell, *U.S.A.* 112 E5
Burwick, *U.K.* 13 C5
Bury, *U.K.* 14 D5
Bury St. Edmunds, *U.K.* 15 E8
Buryatia □, *Russia* 53 D11
Buryn, *Ukraine* 33 G7
Burzenin, *Poland* 31 G5
Busalla, *Italy* 40 D5
Busan = Pusan, *S. Korea* 57 G15
Busango Swamp, *Zambia* 87 E2
Buşayrah, *Syria* 70 C4
Busca, *Italy* 40 D4
Bushat, *Albania* 44 E3
Būshehr, *Iran* 71 D6
Būshehr □, *Iran* 71 D6
Bushell, *Canada* 103 B7
Bushenyi, *Uganda* 86 C3
Bushire = Būshehr, *Iran* 71 D6
Busie, *Ghana* 82 C4
Businga, *Dem. Rep. of the Congo* 84 D4
Busko-Zdrój, *Poland* 31 H7
Busovača, *Bos.-H.* 28 F2
Buşra ash Shām, *Syria* 74 C5
Busselton, *Australia* 93 F2
Busseri →, *Sudan* 81 F2
Busseto, *Italy* 40 D7
Bussière-Badil, *France* 20 C4
Bussolengo, *Italy* 40 C7
Bussum, *Neths.* 17 B5
Buşteni, *Romania* 29 E10
Busto, C., *Spain* 36 B4
Busto Arsízio, *Italy* 40 C5
Busu Djanoa, *Dem. Rep. of the Congo* 84 D4
Busuanga I., *Phil.* 61 E3
Büsum, *Germany* 24 A4
Busungbiu, *Indonesia* 63 J17
Buta, *Dem. Rep. of the Congo* 86 B1
Butare, *Rwanda* 86 C2
Butaritari, *Kiribati* 96 G9
Bute, *U.K.* 13 F3
Bute Inlet, *Canada* 102 C4
Butemba, *Uganda* 86 B3
Butembo, *Dem. Rep. of the Congo* 86 B2
Buteni, *Romania* 28 D7
Butera, *Italy* 43 E7
Butha Qi, *China* 60 B7
Butiaba, *Uganda* 86 B3
Butler, *Mo., U.S.A.* 112 F7
Butler, *Pa., U.S.A.* 116 F5
Buton, *Indonesia* 63 E6
Butte, *Mont., U.S.A.* 108 C7
Butte, *Nebr., U.S.A.* 112 D5
Butte Creek →, *U.S.A.* 110 F5
Butterworth = Gcuwa, *S. Africa* 89 E4
Butterworth, *Malaysia* 65 c
Buttevant, *Ireland* 12 D3
Buttfield, Mt., *Australia* 93 D4
Button B., *Canada* 103 B10
Buttonwillow, *U.S.A.* 111 K7
Butty Hd., *Australia* 93 F3
Butuan, *Phil.* 61 G6
Butuku-Luba, *Eq. Guin.* 83 E6
Butung = Buton, *Indonesia* 63 E6
Buturlinovka, *Russia* 34 E5
Butzbach, *Germany* 25 E4
Bützow, *Germany* 24 B7
Buur Hakaba = Bur Acaba, *Somali Rep.* 75 G3
Buxa Duar, *India* 69 F13
Buxar, *India* 69 G10
Buxtehude, *Germany* 24 B5
Buxton, *U.K.* 14 D6
Buxy, *France* 19 F11
Buy, *Russia* 34 A5
Buynaksk, *Russia* 35 J8
Buyo, *Ivory C.* 82 D3
Buyo, L. de, *Ivory C.* 82 D3
Büyük Menderes →, *Turkey* 47 D9
Büyükçekmece, *Turkey* 45 E12
Büyükkarıştiran, *Turkey* 45 E11
Büyükkemikli Burnu, *Turkey* 45 F10
Büyükorhan, *Turkey* 47 B10
Büyükyoncalı, *Turkey* 45 E11
Buzançais, *France* 18 F8
Buzău, *Romania* 29 E11
Buzău □, *Romania* 29 E11
Buzău →, *Romania* 29 E12
Buzău, Pasul, *Romania* 29 E11
Buzen, *Japan* 55 H5
Buzet, *Croatia* 41 C10
Buzi →, *Mozam.* 87 F3
Buziaş, *Romania* 28 E6
Buzuluk, *Russia* 52 D6
Buzuluk →, *Russia* 34 E6
Buzzards B., *U.S.A.* 117 E14
Buzzards Bay, *U.S.A.* 117 E14
Bwana Mkubwe, *Dem. Rep. of the Congo* 87 E2
Bwindi △, *Uganda* 86 C2
Byala, *Ruse, Bulgaria* 45 C9
Byala, *Varna, Bulgaria* 45 D11
Byala Slatina, *Bulgaria* 44 C7
Byarezina →, *Belarus* 33 F6
Byaroza, *Belarus* 33 F3
Bychawa, *Poland* 31 G9
Byczyna, *Poland* 31 G5
Bydgoszcz, *Poland* 31 E5
Byelarus = Belarus ■, *Europe* 32 F4
Byelorussia = Belarus ■, *Europe* 32 F4
Byers, *U.S.A.* 112 F2
Byesville, *U.S.A.* 116 G3
Byfield △, *Australia* 94 C5
Byford, *Australia* 93 F2
Bykhaw, *Belarus* 32 F6
Bykhov = Bykhaw, *Belarus* 32 F6
Bykovo, *Russia* 34 F7
Bylas, *U.S.A.* 109 K8
Bylot, *Canada* 103 B10
Bylot I., *Canada* 101 A12
Byrd, C., *Antarctica* 5 C17
Byrock, *Australia* 95 E4
Byron, C., *Australia* 95 D5
Byron Bay, *Australia* 95 D5
Byrranga, Gory, *Russia* 53 B11
Byrranga Mts. = Byrranga, Gory, *Russia* 53 B11
Byrum, *Denmark* 11 G5
Byske, *Sweden* 8 D19
Byske älv →, *Sweden* 8 D19
Bystrzyca →, *Dolnośląskie, Poland* 31 G3
Bystrzyca →, *Lubelskie, Poland* 31 G9
Bystrzyca Kłodzka, *Poland* 31 H3
Bytča, *Slovak Rep.* 27 B11
Bytom, *Poland* 31 H5
Bytom Odrzański, *Poland* 31 G2
Bytów, *Poland* 30 D4
Byumba, *Rwanda* 86 C3
Bzenec, *Czech Rep.* 27 C10
Bzura →, *Poland* 31 F7

C

Ca →, *Vietnam* 64 C5
Ca Mau, *Vietnam* 65 H5
Ca Mau, Mui, *Vietnam* 65 H5
Ca Na, *Vietnam* 65 G7
Caacupé, *Paraguay* 126 B4
Caaguazú △, *Paraguay* 127 B4
Caála, *Angola* 85 G3
Caamaño Sd., *Canada* 102 C3
Caazapá, *Paraguay* 126 B4
Caazapá □, *Paraguay* 127 B4
Cabadbaran, *Phil.* 61 G6
Cabalian = San Juan, *Phil.* 61 F6
Caballeria, C. de, *Spain* 48 A11
Cabana, *Spain* 36 B2
Cabañaquinta, *Spain* 36 B5
Cabanatuan, *Phil.* 61 D4
Cabañeros ⌓, *Spain* 37 F6
Cabanes, *Spain* 38 E5
Cabano, *Canada* 105 C6
Čabar, *Croatia* 41 C11
Cabazon, *U.S.A.* 111 M10
Cabedelo, *Brazil* 125 E12
Cabeza del Buey, *Spain* 37 G5
Cabezón de la Sal, *Spain* 36 B6
Cabildo, *Chile* 126 C1
Cabimas, *Venezuela* 124 A4
Cabinda, *Angola* 84 F2
Cabinda □, *Angola* 84 F2
Cabinet Mts., *U.S.A.* 108 C6
Cabo Blanco, *Argentina* 128 F3
Cabo de Gata-Níjar ⌓, *Spain* 39 J2
Cabo Frio, *Brazil* 127 A7
Cabo Pantoja, *Peru* 124 D3
Cabonga, Réservoir, *Canada* 104 C4
Cabool, *U.S.A.* 113 G8
Caboolture, *Australia* 95 D5
Cabora Bassa Dam = Cahora Bassa, Reprêsa de, *Mozam.* 87 F3
Caborca, *Mexico* 118 A2
Cabot, Mt., *U.S.A.* 117 B13
Cabot Hd., *Canada* 116 A3
Cabot Str., *Canada* 105 C8
Cabra, *Spain* 37 H6
Cabra del Santo Cristo, *Spain* 37 H7
Cābras, *Italy* 42 C1
Cabrera, *Spain* 48 B9
Cabrera △, *Spain* 39 F7
Cabrera, Sierra, *Spain* 36 C4
Cabri, *Canada* 103 C7
Cabriel →, *Spain* 39 F3
Cabugao, *Phil.* 61 C4
Cacabelos, *Spain* 36 C4
Caçador, *Brazil* 127 B5
Čačak, *Serbia & M.* 44 C4
Caçapava do Sul, *Brazil* 127 C5
Cáccamo, *Italy* 42 E6
Cacém, *Portugal* 37 G1
Cáceres, *Brazil* 124 G7
Cáceres, *Spain* 37 F4
Cáceres □, *Spain* 36 F5
Cache Bay, *Canada* 104 C4
Cache Cr. →, *U.S.A.* 110 G5
Cache Creek, *Canada* 102 C4
Cacheu, *Guinea-Biss.* 82 C1
Cachi, *Argentina* 126 B2
Cachimbo, Serra do, *Brazil* 125 E7
Cachinal de la Sierra, *Chile* 126 A2
Cachoeira, *Brazil* 125 F11
Cachoeira do Sul, *Brazil* 127 C5
Cachoeiro de Itapemirim, *Brazil* 127 A7
Cachopo, *Portugal* 37 H3
Cacine, *Guinea-Biss.* 82 C1
Cacoal, *Brazil* 124 F6
Cacólo, *Angola* 84 G3
Caconda, *Angola* 85 G3
Čadca, *Slovak Rep.* 27 B11
Caddo, *U.S.A.* 113 H6
Cader Idris, *U.K.* 15 E4
Cadereyta, *Mexico* 118 B5
Cadí, Sierra del, *Spain* 38 C6
Cadí-Moixeró ⌓, *Spain* 38 C3
Cadibarrawirracanna, L., *Australia* 95 D2
Cadillac, *France* 20 D3
Cadillac, *U.S.A.* 114 C3
Cadiz, *Phil.* 61 F5
Cádiz, *Spain* 37 J4
Cadiz, *Calif., U.S.A.* 111 L11
Cadiz, *Ohio, U.S.A.* 116 F4
Cádiz □, *Spain* 37 J5
Cádiz, G. de, *Spain* 37 J3
Cadiz L., *U.S.A.* 109 J6
Cadney Park, *Australia* 95 D1
Cadomin, *Canada* 102 C5
Cadotte Lake, *Canada* 102 B5
Cadours, *France* 20 E5
Cadoux, *Australia* 93 F2
Caen, *France* 18 C6
Caernarfon, *U.K.* 14 D3
Caernarfon B., *U.K.* 14 D3
Caernarvon = Caernarfon, *U.K.* 14 D3
Caerphilly, *U.K.* 15 F4
Caerphilly □, *U.K.* 15 F4
Caesarea, *Israel* 74 C3
Caetité, *Brazil* 125 F10
Cafayate, *Argentina* 126 B2
Cafu, *Angola* 88 B2
Cagayan →, *Phil.* 61 B4
Cagayan de Oro, *Phil.* 61 G6
Cagayan Is., *Phil.* 61 G4
Cagayan Sulu I., *Phil.* 61 H3
Cagli, *Italy* 41 E9
Cágliari, *Italy* 42 C2
Cágliari, G. di, *Italy* 42 C2
Cagnano Varano, *Italy* 41 G12
Cagnes-sur-Mer, *France* 21 E11
Caguán →, *Colombia* 124 D4
Caguas, *Puerto Rico* 121 d
Caha Mts., *Ireland* 12 E2
Cahama, *Angola* 88 B1
Caher, *Ireland* 12 D4
Caherciveen, *Ireland* 12 E1
Cahora Bassa, L. de, *Mozam.* 87 F3
Cahora Bassa, Reprêsa de, *Mozam.* 87 F3
Cahore Pt., *Ireland* 12 D5
Cahors, *France* 20 D5
Cahul, *Moldova* 29 E13
Cai Bau, Dao, *Vietnam* 58 G6
Cai Nuoc, *Vietnam* 65 H5
Caia, *Mozam.* 87 F4
Caianda, *Angola* 87 E1
Caibarién, *Cuba* 120 B4
Caibiran, *Phil.* 61 F6
Caicara, *Venezuela* 124 B5
Caicó, *Brazil* 125 E11
Caicos Is., *Turks & Caicos* 121 B5
Caicos Passage, *W. Indies* 121 B5
Caidian, *China* 59 B10
Căinari, *Moldova* 29 D14
Caird Coast, *Antarctica* 5 D1
Cairn Gorm, *U.K.* 13 D5
Cairngorm Mts., *U.K.* 13 D5
Cairngorms △, *U.K.* 13 D5
Cairnryan, *U.K.* 13 G3
Cairns, *Australia* 94 B4
Cairns L., *Canada* 103 C10
Cairo = El Qâhira, *Egypt* 80 H7
Cairo, *Ga., U.S.A.* 115 K3
Cairo, *Ill., U.S.A.* 113 G10
Cairo, *N.Y., U.S.A.* 117 D11
Cairo Montenotte, *Italy* 40 D5
Caithness, *U.K.* 13 C5
Caithness, Ord of, *U.K.* 13 C5
Caja de Muertos, I., *Puerto Rico* 121 d
Cajamarca, *Peru* 124 E3
Cajarc, *France* 20 D5
Cajàzeiras, *Brazil* 125 E11
Čajetina, *Serbia & M.* 44 C3
Çakirgol, *Turkey* 73 B8
Çakırlar, *Turkey* 47 E12
Čakovec, *Croatia* 41 B13
Çal, *Turkey* 47 C11
Cala, *Spain* 37 H4
Cala →, *Spain* 37 H4
Cala Cadolar, Punta de = Rotja, Pta., *Spain* 39 G6
Cala d'Or, *Spain* 48 B10
Cala en Porter, *Spain* 48 B11
Cala Figuera, C. de, *Spain* 48 B9
Cala Forcat, *Spain* 48 B10
Cala Major, *Spain* 48 B9
Cala Mezquida = Sa Mesquida, *Spain* 48 B11
Cala Millor, *Spain* 48 B10
Cala Ratjada, *Spain* 48 B10
Cala Santa Galdana, *Spain* 48 B10
Calabanga, *Phil.* 61 E5
Calabar, *Nigeria* 83 E6
Calabogie, *Canada* 117 A8

Calabozo, *Venezuela* 124 B5
Calábria □, *Italy* 43 C9
Calábria △, *Italy* 43 C9
Calaburras, Pta. de, *Spain* 37 J6
Calaceite, *Spain* 38 D5
Calacuccia, *France* 21 F13
Calafat, *Romania* 28 G7
Calafate, *Argentina* 128 G2
Calafell, *Spain* 38 D6
Calahorra, *Spain* 38 C3
Calais, *France* 19 B8
Calais, *U.S.A.* 115 C12
Calakmul ⌓, *Mexico* 119 D7
Calalaste, Cord. de, *Argentina* 126 B2
Calama, *Brazil* 124 E6
Calama, *Chile* 126 A2
Calamar, *Colombia* 124 A4
Calamian Group, *Phil.* 61 F3
Calamocha, *Spain* 38 E3
Calamonte, *Spain* 37 G4
Călan, *Romania* 28 E7
Calañas, *Spain* 37 H4
Calanda, *Spain* 38 E4
Calang, *Indonesia* 62 D1
Calangiánus, *Italy* 42 B2
Calapan, *Phil.* 61 E4
Călărasi, *Moldova* 29 C13
Călăraşi, *Romania* 29 F12
Călăraşi □, *Romania* 29 F12
Calasparra, *Spain* 39 G3
Calatafimi, *Italy* 42 E5
Calatayud, *Spain* 38 D3
Călăţele, *Romania* 28 D8
Calato = Kálathos, *Greece* 47 E10
Calauag, *Phil.* 61 E5
Calavà, C., *Italy* 43 D7
Calavite, C., *Phil.* 61 E4
Calayan, *Phil.* 61 B4
Calbayog, *Phil.* 61 E6
Calca, *Peru* 124 F4
Calcasieu L., *U.S.A.* 113 L8
Calcutta = Kolkata, *India* 69 H13
Calcutta, *U.S.A.* 116 F4
Caldaro, *Italy* 41 B8
Caldas da Rainha, *Portugal* 37 F1
Caldas de Reis, *Spain* 36 C2
Calder →, *U.K.* 14 D6
Caldera, *Chile* 126 B1
Caldera de Taburiente △, *Canary Is.* 48 F2
Caldwell, *Idaho, U.S.A.* 108 E5
Caldwell, *Kans., U.S.A.* 113 G6
Caldwell, *Tex., U.S.A.* 113 K6
Caledon, *S. Africa* 88 E2
Caledon →, *S. Africa* 88 E4
Caledon B., *Australia* 94 A2
Caledonia, *Canada* 116 C5
Caledonia, *U.S.A.* 116 D7
Calella, *Spain* 38 D7
Calemba, *Angola* 88 B2
Calen, *Australia* 94 J6
Calenzana, *France* 21 F12
Caletones, *Chile* 126 C1
Calexico, *U.S.A.* 111 N11
Calf of Man, *U.K.* 14 C3
Calgary, *Canada* 102 C6
Calheta, *Madeira* 48 D2
Calhoun, *U.S.A.* 115 H3
Cali, *Colombia* 124 C3
Calicut, *India* 66 P9
Caliente, *U.S.A.* 109 H6
California, *Mo., U.S.A.* 112 F8
California, *Pa., U.S.A.* 116 F5
California □, *U.S.A.* 110 H7
California, Baja, *Mexico* 118 A1
California, Baja, T.N. = Baja California □, *Mexico* 118 B2
California, Baja, T.S. = Baja California Sur □, *Mexico* 118 B2
California, G. de, *Mexico* 118 B2
California City, *U.S.A.* 111 K9
California Hot Springs, *U.S.A.* 111 K8
Calilegua △, *Argentina* 126 B3
Călimăneşti, *Romania* 29 E9
Călimani, Munţii, *Romania* 29 C10
Calingasta, *Argentina* 126 C2
Calipatria, *U.S.A.* 111 M11
Calistoga, *U.S.A.* 110 G4
Calitri, *Italy* 43 B8
Calitzdorp, *S. Africa* 88 E3
Callabonna, L., *Australia* 95 D3
Callac, *France* 18 D3
Callan, *Ireland* 12 D4
Callander, *U.K.* 13 E4
Callao, *Peru* 124 F3
Calles, *Mexico* 119 C5
Callicoon, *U.S.A.* 117 E9
Calling Lake, *Canada* 102 B6
Calliope, *Australia* 94 C5
Callosa de Ensarriá, *Spain* 39 G4
Callosa de Segura, *Spain* 39 G4
Calne, *U.K.* 15 F6
Calola, *Angola* 88 B2
Calolbon = San Andres, *Phil.* 61 E6
Calonge, *Spain* 38 D8
Caloocan, *Phil.* 61 D4
Calore →, *Italy* 43 A7
Caloundra, *Australia* 95 D5
Calpe, *Spain* 39 G5
Calpella, *U.S.A.* 110 F3
Calpine, *U.S.A.* 110 F6
Calstock, *Canada* 104 C3
Caltabellotta, *Italy* 42 E6
Caltagirone, *Italy* 43 E7
Caltanissetta, *Italy* 43 E7
Çaltılıbük, *Turkey* 45 G12
Caluire-et-Cuire, *France* 19 G11
Calulo, *Angola* 84 G2
Caluso, *Italy* 40 C4
Calvados □, *France* 18 C6
Calvert →, *Australia* 94 B2
Calvert I., *Canada* 102 C3
Calvert Ra., *Australia* 92 D3
Calvi, *France* 21 F12
Calviá, *Spain* 39 F7
Calvillo, *Mexico* 118 C4
Calvinia, *S. Africa* 88 E2
Calvo = Calvo, Mte., *Italy* 41 G12
Calvo, Mte., *Italy* 41 G12
Calwa, *U.S.A.* 110 J7
Calzada Almuradiel = Almuradiel, *Spain* 37 G7
Calzada de Calatrava, *Spain* 37 G7
Cam →, *U.K.* 15 E8
Cam Lam, *Vietnam* 65 G7
Cam Pha, *Vietnam* 58 G6
Cam Ranh, *Vietnam* 65 G7
Cam Xuyen, *Vietnam* 64 C6
Camabatela, *Angola* 84 F3
Camacha, *Madeira* 48 D3
Camacho, *Mexico* 118 C4
Camacupa, *Angola* 85 G3
Camagüey, *Cuba* 120 B4
Camaiore, *Italy* 40 E7
Camaná, *Peru* 124 G4
Camanche Reservoir, *U.S.A.* 110 G6
Camaquã, *Brazil* 127 C5
Camaquã →, *Brazil* 127 C5
Câmara de Lobos, *Madeira* 48 D3
Camarat, C., *France* 21 E10
Camarès, *France* 20 E6
Camaret-sur-Mer, *France* 18 D2
Camargo, *Mexico* 119 B5
Camargue, *France* 21 E8
Camargue ⌓, *France* 21 E8
Camarillo, *U.S.A.* 111 L7
Camariñas, *Spain* 36 B1
Camarón, C., *Honduras* 120 C2
Camarones, *Argentina* 128 E3
Camas, *Spain* 37 H4
Camas, *U.S.A.* 110 E4
Camas Valley, *U.S.A.* 108 E2
Camballin, *Australia* 92 C3
Cambará, *Brazil* 127 A5
Cambay = Khambhat, *India* 68 H5
Cambay, G. of = Khambhat, G. of, *India* 66 J8
Cambil, *Spain* 37 H7
Cambo-les-Bains, *France* 20 E2
Cambodia ■, *Asia* 64 F5
Camborne, *U.K.* 15 G2
Cambrai, *France* 19 B10
Cambre, *Spain* 36 B2
Cambria, *U.S.A.* 110 K5
Cambrian Mts., *U.K.* 15 E4
Cambridge, *Canada* 116 C4
Cambridge, *Jamaica* 120 a
Cambridge, *N.Z.* 91 G5
Cambridge, *U.K.* 15 E8
Cambridge, *Mass., U.S.A.* 117 D13
Cambridge, *Minn., U.S.A.* 112 C8
Cambridge, *N.Y., U.S.A.* 117 C11
Cambridge, *Nebr., U.S.A.* 112 E4
Cambridge, *Ohio, U.S.A.* 116 F3
Cambridge Bay = Ikaluktutiak, *Canada* 100 B9
Cambridge G., *Australia* 92 B4
Cambridge Springs, *U.S.A.* 116 E4
Cambridgeshire □, *U.K.* 15 E7
Cambrils, *Spain* 38 D6
Cambuci, *Brazil* 127 A7
Cambundi-Catembo, *Angola* 84 G3
Camden, *Ala., U.S.A.* 115 K2
Camden, *Ark., U.S.A.* 113 J8
Camden, *Maine, U.S.A.* 115 C11
Camden, *N.J., U.S.A.* 117 G9
Camden, *N.Y., U.S.A.* 117 C9
Camden, *S.C., U.S.A.* 115 H5
Camden Sd., *Australia* 92 C3
Camdenton, *U.S.A.* 113 F8
Camelford, *U.K.* 15 G3
Çameli, *Turkey* 47 D11
Camenca, *Moldova* 29 B13
Camerino, *Italy* 41 E10
Cameron, *Ariz., U.S.A.* 109 J8
Cameron, *La., U.S.A.* 113 L8
Cameron, *Mo., U.S.A.* 112 F7
Cameron, *Tex., U.S.A.* 113 K6
Cameron Highlands, *Malaysia* 65 K3
Cameron Hills, *Canada* 102 B5
Cameroon ■, *Africa* 79 G7
Camerota, *Italy* 43 B8
Cameroun →, *Cameroon* 83 E6
Cameroun, Mt., *Cameroon* 83 E6
Cametá, *Brazil* 125 D9
Çamiçi Gölü, *Turkey* 47 D9
Camiguin □, *Phil.* 61 G6
Camiguin I., *Phil.* 61 B4
Camiling, *Phil.* 61 D4
Camilla, *U.S.A.* 115 K3
Caminha, *Portugal* 36 D2
Camino, *U.S.A.* 110 G6
Camira Creek, *Australia* 95 D5
Cammal, *U.S.A.* 116 E7
Cammarata, *Italy* 42 E6
Camocim, *Brazil* 125 D10
Camooweal, *Australia* 94 B2
Camooweal Caves △, *Australia* 94 C2
Camopi, *Fr. Guiana* 125 C8
Camotes Is., *Phil.* 61 F6
Camotes Sea, *Phil.* 61 F6
Camp Borden, *Canada* 116 B5
Camp Hill, *U.S.A.* 116 F8
Camp Nelson, *U.S.A.* 111 J8
Camp Pendleton, *U.S.A.* 111 M9
Camp Verde, *U.S.A.* 109 J8
Camp Wood, *U.S.A.* 113 L5
Campagna, *Italy* 43 B8
Campana, *Argentina* 126 C4
Campana, I., *Chile* 128 F1
Campanário, *Madeira* 48 D2
Campanario, *Spain* 37 G5
Campánia □, *Italy* 43 B7
Campbell, *S. Africa* 88 D3
Campbell, *Calif., U.S.A.* 110 H5
Campbell, *Ohio, U.S.A.* 116 E4
Campbell I., *Pac. Oc.* 96 N8
Campbell L., *Canada* 103 A7
Campbell River, *Canada* 102 C3
Campbell Town, *Australia* 95 G4
Campbellford, *Canada* 116 B7
Campbellpur, *Pakistan* 68 C5
Campbellsville, *U.S.A.* 114 G3
Campbellton, *Canada* 105 C6
Campbelltown, *Australia* 95 E5
Campbeltown, *U.K.* 13 F3
Campeche, *Mexico* 119 D6
Campeche □, *Mexico* 119 D6
Campeche, Golfo de, *Mexico* 119 D6
Campello, *Spain* 39 G4
Câmpeni, *Romania* 28 D8
Camperdown, *Australia* 95 F3
Camperville, *Canada* 103 C8
Campi Salentina, *Italy* 43 B11
Câmpia Turzii, *Romania* 29 D8
Campidano, *Italy* 42 C1
Campíglia Maríttima, *Italy* 40 E7
Campillo de Altobuey, *Spain* 39 F3
Campillos, *Spain* 37 H6
Câmpina, *Romania* 29 E10
Campina Grande, *Brazil* 125 E11
Campinas, *Brazil* 127 A6
Campli, *Italy* 41 F10
Campo, *Spain* 38 C5
Campo de Criptana, *Spain* 37 F7
Campo de Gibraltar, *Spain* 37 J5
Campo Grande, *Brazil* 125 H8
Campo Maior, *Brazil* 125 D10
Campo Maior, *Portugal* 37 F3
Campo Mourão, *Brazil* 127 A5
Campo Túres, *Italy* 41 B8
Campobasso, *Italy* 43 A7
Campobello di Licata, *Italy* 42 E6
Campobello di Mazara, *Italy* 42 E5
Campofelice di Roccella, *Italy* 42 E6
Campomarino, *Italy* 41 G12
Camporeale, *Italy* 42 E6
Camporrobles, *Spain* 38 F3
Campos, *Brazil* 127 A7
Campos Belos, *Brazil* 125 F9
Campos del Port, *Spain* 48 B10
Campos Novos, *Brazil* 127 B5
Camprodón, *Spain* 38 C7
Camptonville, *U.S.A.* 110 F5
Camptown, *U.S.A.* 117 E8
Câmpulung, *Argeş, Romania* 29 E10
Câmpulung, *Suceava, Romania* 29 C10
Câmpuri, *Romania* 29 D11
Camrose, *Canada* 102 C6
Camsell Portage, *Canada* 103 B7
Çamyuva, *Turkey* 47 E12
Çan, *Turkey* 45 F11
Can Clavo, *Spain* 48 C7
Can Creu, *Spain* 48 C7
Can Gio, *Vietnam* 65 G6
Can Tho, *Vietnam* 65 G5
Canaan, *U.S.A.* 117 D11
Canada ■, *N. Amer.* 100 C10
Canada Basin, *Arctic* 4 B18
Cañada de Gómez, *Argentina* 126 C3
Canadian, *U.S.A.* 113 H4
Canadian →, *U.S.A.* 113 H7
Canajoharie, *U.S.A.* 117 D10
Çanakkale, *Turkey* 45 F10
Çanakkale □, *Turkey* 45 F10
Çanakkale Boğazı, *Turkey* 45 F10
Canal Flats, *Canada* 102 C5
Canalejas, *Argentina* 126 D2
Canals, *Argentina* 126 C3
Canals, *Spain* 39 G4
Canandaigua, *U.S.A.* 116 D7
Canandaigua L., *U.S.A.* 116 D7
Cananea, *Mexico* 118 A2
Canarias, Is., *Atl. Oc.* 48 F4
Canaries, *St. Lucia* 121 f
Canarreos, Arch. de los, *Cuba* 120 B3
Canary Is. = Canarias, Is., *Atl. Oc.* 48 F4
Canaseraga, *U.S.A.* 116 D7
Canatlán, *Mexico* 118 C4
Canaveral ⌓, *U.S.A.* 115 L5
Canaveral, C., *U.S.A.* 115 L5
Cañaveruelas, *Spain* 38 E2
Canavieiras, *Brazil* 125 G11
Canberra, *Australia* 95 F4
Canby, *Calif., U.S.A.* 108 F3
Canby, *Minn., U.S.A.* 112 C6
Canby, *Oreg., U.S.A.* 110 E4
Cancale, *France* 18 D5
Canche →, *France* 19 B8
Cancún, *Mexico* 119 C7
Candanchu, *Spain* 38 C4
Çandarlı, *Turkey* 47 C8
Çandarlı Körfezi, *Turkey* 47 C8
Candas, *Spain* 36 B5
Candé, *France* 18 E5
Candela, *Italy* 43 A8
Candelaria, *Argentina* 127 B4
Candelaria, *Canary Is.* 48 F3
Candelario ⌓, *Spain* 36 E5
Candeleda, *Spain* 36 E5
Candelo, *Australia* 95 F4
Candi Dasa, *Indonesia* 63 J18
Candia = Iráklion, *Greece* 49 D7
Candia, Sea of = Crete, Sea of, *Greece* 47 E7
Candle L., *Canada* 103 C7
Candlemas I., *Antarctica* 5 B1
Cando, *U.S.A.* 112 A5
Candon, *Phil.* 61 C4
Canea = Khaniá, *Greece* 49 D6
Canelli, *Italy* 40 D5
Canelones, *Uruguay* 127 C4
Canet-Plage, *France* 20 F7
Cañete, *Chile* 126 D1
Cañete, *Peru* 124 F3
Cañete, *Spain* 38 E3
Cañete de las Torres, *Spain* 37 H6
Cangas, *Spain* 36 C2
Cangas de Narcea, *Spain* 36 B4
Cangas de Onís, *Spain* 36 B5
Cangnan, *China* 59 D13
Canguaretama, *Brazil* 125 E11
Canguçu, *Brazil* 127 C5
Canguçu, Serra do, *Brazil* 127 C5
Cangwu, *China* 59 F8
Cangxi, *China* 58 B5
Cangyuan, *China* 58 F2
Cangzhou, *China* 56 E9
Caniapiscau →, *Canada* 105 A6
Caniapiscau, L. de, *Canada* 105 B6
Canicattì, *Italy* 42 E6
Canicattini Bagni, *Italy* 43 E8
Caniles, *Spain* 37 H8
Canim Lake, *Canada* 102 C4
Canindeyu □, *Paraguay* 127 A5
Canino, *Italy* 41 F8
Canisteo, *U.S.A.* 116 D7
Canisteo →, *U.S.A.* 116 D7
Cañitas, *Mexico* 118 C4
Cañizal, *Spain* 36 D5
Canjáyar, *Spain* 37 H8
Çankırı, *Turkey* 72 B5
Cankuzo, *Burundi* 86 C3
Canmore, *Canada* 102 C5
Cann River, *Australia* 95 F4
Canna, *U.K.* 13 D2
Cannanore, *India* 66 P9
Cannes, *France* 21 E11
Canning Town = Port Canning, *India* 69 H13
Cannington, *Canada* 116 B5
Cannóbio, *Italy* 40 B5
Cannock, *U.K.* 15 E5
Cannon Ball →, *U.S.A.* 112 B4
Cannondale Mt., *Australia* 94 D4
Cannonsville Reservoir, *U.S.A.* 117 D9
Cannonvale, *Australia* 94 J6
Canoas, *Brazil* 127 B5
Canoe L., *Canada* 103 B7
Canon City, *U.S.A.* 112 F2
Cañón de Río Blanco △, *Mexico* 119 D5
Cañón del Río Lobos ⌓, *Spain* 36 D7
Cañón del Sumidero △, *Mexico* 119 D5
Canora, *Canada* 103 C8
Canosa di Púglia, *Italy* 43 A9
Canowindra, *Australia* 95 E4
Canso, *Canada* 105 C7
Cantabria □, *Spain* 36 B7
Cantabria, Sierra de, *Spain* 38 C2
Cantabrian Mts. = Cantábrica, Cordillera, *Spain* 36 C5
Cantábrica, Cordillera, *Spain* 36 C5
Cantal □, *France* 20 C6
Cantal, Plomb du, *France* 20 C6
Cantanhede, *Portugal* 36 E2
Cantavieja, *Spain* 38 E4
Čantavir, *Serbia & M.* 28 E4
Cantemir, *Moldova* 29 D13
Canterbury, *Australia* 94 D3
Canterbury, *U.K.* 15 F9
Canterbury Bight, *N.Z.* 91 L3
Canterbury Plains, *N.Z.* 91 K3
Cantil, *U.S.A.* 111 K9
Cantillana, *Spain* 37 H5
Canton = Guangzhou, *China* 59 F9
Canton, *Ga., U.S.A.* 115 H3
Canton, *Ill., U.S.A.* 112 E9
Canton, *Miss., U.S.A.* 113 J9
Canton, *Mo., U.S.A.* 112 E9
Canton, *N.Y., U.S.A.* 117 B9
Canton, *Ohio, U.S.A.* 116 F3
Canton, *Pa., U.S.A.* 116 E8
Canton, *S. Dak., U.S.A.* 112 D6
Canton L., *U.S.A.* 113 G5
Cantù, *Italy* 40 C6
Canudos, *Brazil* 124 E7
Canumã →, *Brazil* 124 D7
Canutama, *Brazil* 124 E6
Canutillo, *U.S.A.* 109 L10
Canvey, *U.K.* 15 F8
Canyon, *U.S.A.* 113 H4
Canyon De Chelly ⌓, *U.S.A.* 109 H9
Canyon of the Ancients ⌓, *U.S.A.* 109 H9
Canyonlands △, *U.S.A.* 109 G9
Canyonville, *U.S.A.* 108 E2
Cao Bang, *Vietnam* 58 F6
Cao He →, *China* 57 D13
Cao Lanh, *Vietnam* 65 G5
Cao Xian, *China* 56 G8
Cáorle, *Italy* 41 C9
Cap-aux-Meules, *Canada* 105 C7
Cap-Chat, *Canada* 105 C6
Cap-de-la-Madeleine, *Canada* 104 C5
Cap-Haïtien, *Haiti* 121 C5
Cap Pt., *St. Lucia* 121 f
Capac, *U.S.A.* 116 C2
Capáccio, *Italy* 43 B8
Capaci, *Italy* 42 D6
Capanaparo →, *Venezuela* 124 B5
Capánnori, *Italy* 40 E7
Capbreton, *France* 20 E2
Capdenac, *France* 20 D6
Capdepera, *Spain* 38 F8
Cape →, *Australia* 94 C4
Cape Arid △, *Australia* 93 F3
Cape Barren I., *Australia* 95 G4
Cape Breton Highlands △, *Canada* 105 C7
Cape Breton I., *Canada* 105 C7
Cape Charles, *U.S.A.* 114 G8
Cape Coast, *Ghana* 83 D4
Cape Cod ⌓, *U.S.A.* 114 E10
Cape Coral, *U.S.A.* 115 M5
Cape Dorset, *Canada* 101 B12
Cape Fear →, *U.S.A.* 115 H6
Cape Girardeau, *U.S.A.* 113 G10
Cape Hatteras ⌓, *U.S.A.* 115 H8
Cape Lee △, *Australia* 93 F3
Cape Lookout ⌓, *U.S.A.* 115 H7
Cape May, *U.S.A.* 114 F8
Cape May Point, *U.S.A.* 114 F8
Cape Melville △, *Australia* 94 A3
Cape Mount △, *Liberia* 82 D2
Cape Peninsula △, *S. Africa* 88 E2
Cape Range △, *Australia* 92 D1
Cape Tormentine, *Canada* 105 C7
Cape Town, *S. Africa* 88 E2
Cape Tribulation △, *Australia* 94 B4
Cape Verde Is. ■, *Atl. Oc.* 77 E1
Cape Vincent, *U.S.A.* 117 B8
Cape York Peninsula, *Australia* 94 A3
Capela, *Brazil* 125 F11
Capella, *Australia* 94 C4
Capendu, *France* 20 E6
Capestang, *France* 20 E7
Capesterre, *Guadeloupe* 120 b
Capesterre-Belle-Eau, *Guadeloupe* 120 b
Capim →, *Brazil* 125 D9
Capistrello, *Italy* 41 G10
Capitan, *U.S.A.* 109 K11
Capitán Arturo Prat, *Antarctica* 5 C17
Capitol Reef △, *U.S.A.* 109 G8
Capitola, *U.S.A.* 110 J5
Capizzi, *Italy* 43 E7
Capoche →, *Mozam.* 87 F3
Capodichino, Naples ✈ (NAP), *Italy* 43 B7
Capoterra, *Italy* 42 C1
Cappadocia, *Turkey* 72 C6
Capraia, *Italy* 40 E6
Caprara, Pta., *Italy* 42 A1
Caprarola, *Italy* 41 F9
Capreol, *Canada* 104 C3
Caprera, *Italy* 42 A2
Capri, *Italy* 43 B7
Capricorn Group, *Australia* 94 C5
Capricorn Ra., *Australia* 92 D2
Caprino Veronese, *Italy* 40 C7
Caprivi Game ⌓, *Namibia* 88 B3
Caprivi Strip, *Namibia* 88 B3
Caps et Marais d'Opale ⌓, *France* 19 B9
Captain's Flat, *Australia* 95 F4
Captieux, *France* 20 D3
Capulin Volcano ⌓, *U.S.A.* 113 G3
Caquetá →, *Colombia* 124 D5
Caracal, *Romania* 29 F9
Caracas, *Venezuela* 124 A5
Caracol, *Mato Grosso do Sul, Brazil* 126 A4
Caracol, *Piauí, Brazil* 125 E10
Caráglio, *Italy* 40 D4
Carajas, *Brazil* 125 E8
Carajás, Serra dos, *Brazil* 125 E8
Carangola, *Brazil* 127 A7
Caransebeş, *Romania* 28 E7
Carantec, *France* 18 D3
Caraquet, *Canada* 105 C6
Caras, *Peru* 124 E3
Caraş Severin □, *Romania* 28 E7
Caraşova, *Romania* 28 E6
Caratasca, L., *Honduras* 120 C3
Caratinga, *Brazil* 125 G10
Caraúbas, *Brazil* 125 E11
Caravaca = Caravaca de la Cruz, *Spain* 39 G3
Caravaca de la Cruz, *Spain* 39 G3
Caravággio, *Italy* 40 C6
Caravela, *Guinea-Biss.* 82 C1
Caravelas, *Brazil* 125 G11
Caraveli, *Peru* 124 G4
Caravelle, Presqu'île de la, *Martinique* 120 c
Caràzinho, *Brazil* 127 B5
Carballino = O Carballiño, *Spain* 36 C2
Carballo, *Spain* 36 B2
Carberry, *Canada* 103 D9
Carbó, *Mexico* 118 B2
Carbonara, C., *Italy* 42 C2
Carbondale, *Colo., U.S.A.* 108 G10
Carbondale, *Ill., U.S.A.* 113 G10
Carbondale, *Pa., U.S.A.* 117 E9
Carbonear, *Canada* 105 C9
Carboneras, *Spain* 39 J3
Carboneras de Guadazón, *Spain* 38 F3
Carbónia, *Italy* 42 C1
Carcabuey, *Spain* 37 H6
Carcagente = Carcaixent, *Spain* 39 F4
Carcaixent, *Spain* 39 F4
Carcajou, *Canada* 102 B5
Carcar, *Phil.* 61 F5
Carcarana →, *Argentina* 126 C3
Carcasse, C., *Haiti* 121 C5
Carcassonne, *France* 20 E6
Carcross, *Canada* 102 A2
Çardak, *Çanakkale, Turkey* 45 F10
Çardak, *Denizli, Turkey* 47 D11
Cardamon Hills, *India* 66 Q10
Cardeña, *Spain* 37 G6
Cárdenas, *Cuba* 120 B3
Cárdenas, *San Luis Potosí, Mexico* 119 C5
Cárdenas, *Tabasco, Mexico* 119 D6
Cardenete, *Spain* 38 F3
Cardiff, *U.K.* 15 F4
Cardiff □, *U.K.* 15 F4
Cardiff-by-the-Sea, *U.S.A.* 111 M9
Cardigan, *U.K.* 15 E3
Cardigan B., *U.K.* 15 E3
Cardinal, *Canada* 117 B9
Cardona, *Spain* 38 D6
Cardona, *Uruguay* 126 C4
Cardoner →, *Spain* 38 D6
Cardoso, Ilha do, *Brazil* 127 B5
Cardston, *Canada* 102 D6

Cardwell, *Australia* 94 B4
Careen L., *Canada* 103 B7
Carei, *Romania* 28 C7
Careme = Ciremay, *Indonesia* 63 G13
Carentan, *France* 18 C5
Carey, *U.S.A.* 108 E7
Carey, L., *Australia* 93 E3
Carey L., *Canada* 103 A8
Careysburg, *Liberia* 82 D2
Cargèse, *France* 21 F12
Carhaix-Plouguer, *France* 18 D3
Carhué, *Argentina* 126 D3
Caria, *Turkey* 47 D10
Cariacica, *Brazil* 125 H10
Cariati, *Italy* 43 C9
Caribbean Sea, *W. Indies* 121 D5
Cariboo Mts., *Canada* 102 C4
Caribou, *U.S.A.* 115 B12
Caribou →, *Man., Canada* 103 B10
Caribou →, *N.W.T., Canada* 102 A3
Caribou I., *Canada* 104 C2
Caribou Is., *Canada* 102 A6
Caribou L., *Man., Canada* 103 B9
Caribou L., *Ont., Canada* 104 B2
Caribou Mts., *Canada* 102 B5
Caribou River ⌓, *Canada* 103 B9
Caribrod = Dimitrovgrad, *Serbia & M.* 44 C6
Carichic, *Mexico* 118 B3
Carigara, *Phil.* 61 F6
Carignan, *France* 19 C12
Carignano, *Italy* 40 D4
Carillo, *Mexico* 118 B4
Carinda, *Australia* 95 E4
Cariñena, *Spain* 38 D3
Carinhanha, *Brazil* 125 F10
Carinhanha →, *Brazil* 125 F10
Carini, *Italy* 42 D6
Cariño, *Spain* 36 B3
Carínola, *Italy* 42 A6
Carinthia = Kärnten □, *Austria* 26 E6
Caripito, *Venezuela* 124 A6
Carlet, *Spain* 39 F4
Carleton, Mt., *Canada* 105 C6
Carleton Place, *Canada* 117 A8
Carletonville, *S. Africa* 88 D4
Cârlibaba, *Romania* 29 C10
Carlin, *U.S.A.* 108 F5
Carlingford L., *U.K.* 12 B5
Carlinville, *U.S.A.* 112 F10
Carlisle, *U.K.* 14 C5
Carlisle, *U.S.A.* 116 F7
Carlisle B., *Barbados* 121 g
Carlisle I., *Australia* 94 J7
Carlit, Pic, *France* 20 F5
Carloforte, *Italy* 42 C1
Carlos Casares, *Argentina* 126 D3
Carlos Tejedor, *Argentina* 126 D3
Carlow, *Ireland* 12 D5
Carlow □, *Ireland* 12 D5
Carlsbad, *Calif., U.S.A.* 111 M9
Carlsbad, *N. Mex., U.S.A.* 113 J2
Carlsbad Caverns △, *U.S.A.* 113 J2
Carluke, *U.K.* 13 F5
Carlyle, *Canada* 103 D8
Carmacks, *Canada* 100 B6
Carmagnola, *Italy* 40 D4
Carman, *Canada* 103 D9
Carmarthen, *U.K.* 15 F3
Carmarthen B., *U.K.* 15 F3
Carmarthenshire □, *U.K.* 15 F3
Carmaux, *France* 20 D6
Carmel, *U.S.A.* 117 E11
Carmel-by-the-Sea, *U.S.A.* 110 J5
Carmel Valley, *U.S.A.* 110 J5
Carmelo, *Uruguay* 126 C4
Carmen, *Colombia* 124 B3
Carmen, *Paraguay* 127 B4
Carmen →, *Mexico* 118 A3
Carmen, I., *Mexico* 118 B2
Carmen de Patagones, *Argentina* 128 E4
Cármenes, *Spain* 36 C5
Carmensa, *Argentina* 126 D2
Carmi, *Canada* 102 D5
Carmi, *U.S.A.* 114 F1
Carmichael, *U.S.A.* 110 G5
Carmila, *Australia* 94 C4
Carmona, *Costa Rica* 120 E2
Carmona, *Spain* 37 H5
Carn Ban, *U.K.* 13 D4
Carn Eige, *U.K.* 13 D3
Carnamah, *Australia* 93 E2
Carnarvon, *Australia* 93 D1
Carnarvon, *S. Africa* 88 E3
Carnarvon △, *Australia* 94 C4
Carnarvon Ra., *Queens., Australia* 94 D4
Carnarvon Ra., *W. Austral., Australia* 93 E3
Carnation, *U.S.A.* 110 C5
Carndonagh, *Ireland* 12 A4
Carnduff, *Canada* 103 D8
Carnegie, *U.S.A.* 116 F4
Carnegie, L., *Australia* 93 E3
Carnic Alps = Karnische Alpen, *Europe* 26 E6
Carniche Alpi = Karnische Alpen, *Europe* 26 E6
Carnot, *C.A.R.* 84 D3
Carnot, C., *Australia* 95 E2
Carnot B., *Australia* 92 C3
Carnoustie, *U.K.* 13 E6
Carnsore Pt., *Ireland* 12 D5
Caro, *U.S.A.* 114 D4
Carol City, *U.S.A.* 115 N5
Carolina, *Brazil* 125 E9
Carolina, *Puerto Rico* 121 d
Carolina, *S. Africa* 89 D5
Caroline I., *Kiribati* 97 H12
Caroline Is., *Micronesia* 96 G7
Caroni, *Trin. & Tob.* 125 K15
Caroni →, *Venezuela* 124 B6
Caroníe = Nébrodi, Monti, *Italy* 43 E7
Caroona, *Australia* 95 E5
Carpathians, *Europe* 6 F10
Carpaţii Meridionali, *Romania* 29 E9
Carpentaria, G. of, *Australia* 94 A2
Carpentras, *France* 21 D9
Carpi, *Italy* 40 D7
Cărpineni, *Moldova* 29 D13
Carpinteria, *U.S.A.* 111 L7
Carpio, *Spain* 36 D5
Carr Boyd Ra., *Australia* 92 C4
Carrabelle, *U.S.A.* 115 L3
Carral, *Spain* 36 B2
Carranza, Presa V., *Mexico* 118 B4
Carrara, *Italy* 40 D7
Carrascal, *Phil.* 61 G6
Carrascosa del Campo, *Spain* 38 E2
Carrauntoohill, *Ireland* 12 D2
Carrick-on-Shannon, *Ireland* 12 C3
Carrick-on-Suir, *Ireland* 12 D4
Carrickfergus, *U.K.* 12 B6
Carrickmacross, *Ireland* 12 C5
Carrieton, *Australia* 95 E2
Carrington, *U.S.A.* 112 B5
Carrión →, *Spain* 36 D6
Carrión de los Condes, *Spain* 36 C6
Carrizal Bajo, *Chile* 126 B1
Carrizalillo, *Chile* 126 B1
Carrizo Cr. →, *U.S.A.* 113 G3
Carrizo Plain ⌓, *U.S.A.* 110 K7
Carrizo Springs, *U.S.A.* 113 L5
Carrizozo, *U.S.A.* 109 K11
Carroll, *U.S.A.* 112 D7
Carrollton, *Ga., U.S.A.* 115 J3
Carrollton, *Ill., U.S.A.* 112 F9
Carrollton, *Ky., U.S.A.* 114 F3
Carrollton, *Mo., U.S.A.* 112 F8
Carrollton, *Ohio, U.S.A.* 116 F3
Carron →, *U.K.* 13 D4
Carron, L., *U.K.* 13 D3
Carrot →, *Canada* 103 C8
Carrot River, *Canada* 103 C8
Carrouges, *France* 18 D6
Carrù, *Italy* 40 D4
Carruthers, *Canada* 103 C7
Carsa Dek, *Ethiopia* 81 F4
Çarşamba, *Turkey* 72 B7
Carsòli, *Italy* 41 F10
Carson, *Calif., U.S.A.* 111 M8
Carson, *N. Dak., U.S.A.* 112 B4
Carson →, *U.S.A.* 110 F8
Carson City, *U.S.A.* 110 F7
Carson Sink, *U.S.A.* 108 G4
Cartagena, *Colombia* 124 A3
Cartagena, *Spain* 39 H4
Cartago, *Colombia* 124 C3
Cartago, *Costa Rica* 120 E3
Cártama, *Spain* 37 J6
Cartaxo, *Portugal* 37 F2
Cartaya, *Spain* 37 H3
Cartersville, *U.S.A.* 115 H3
Carterton, *N.Z.* 91 J5
Carthage, *Tunisia* 42 F3
Carthage, *Ill., U.S.A.* 112 E9
Carthage, *Mo., U.S.A.* 113 G7
Carthage, *N.Y., U.S.A.* 114 D8
Carthage, *Tex., U.S.A.* 113 J7
Cartier I., *Australia* 92 B3
Cartwright, *Canada* 105 B8
Caruaru, *Brazil* 125 E11
Carúpano, *Venezuela* 124 A6
Caruthersville, *U.S.A.* 113 G10
Carvin, *France* 19 B9
Carvoeiro, *Brazil* 124 D6
Carvoeiro, C., *Portugal* 37 F1
Cary, *U.S.A.* 115 H6
Casa, Pas de la = Envalira, Port d', *Europe* 38 C6
Casa Branca, *Portugal* 37 G2
Casa Grande, *U.S.A.* 109 K8
Casablanca, *Chile* 126 C1
Casablanca, *Morocco* 78 B4
Casacalenda, *Italy* 41 G11
Casalbordino, *Italy* 41 F11
Casale Monferrato, *Italy* 40 C5
Casalmaggiore, *Italy* 40 D7
Casalpusterlengo, *Italy* 40 C6
Casamance →, *Senegal* 82 C1
Casarano, *Italy* 43 B11
Casares, *Spain* 37 J5
Casas Ibáñez, *Spain* 39 F3
Casasimarro, *Spain* 39 F2
Casatejada, *Spain* 36 F5
Casavieja, *Spain* 36 E6
Cascada de Basaseachic △, *Mexico* 118 B3
Cascade, *Idaho, U.S.A.* 108 D5
Cascade, *Mont., U.S.A.* 108 C8
Cascade Locks, *U.S.A.* 110 E5
Cascade Ra., *U.S.A.* 110 D5
Cascade Reservoir, *U.S.A.* 108 D5
Cascais, *Portugal* 37 G1
Cascavel, *Brazil* 127 A5
Cáscina, *Italy* 40 E7
Casco B., *U.S.A.* 115 D10
Caselle Torinese, *Italy* 40 C4
Caserta, *Italy* 43 A7
Casey, *Antarctica* 5 C8
Caseyr, Raas = Asir, Ras, *Somali Rep.* 75 E5
Cashel, *Ireland* 12 D4
Casiguran, *Phil.* 61 C5
Casilda, *Argentina* 126 C3
Casimcea, *Romania* 29 F13
Casino, *Australia* 95 D5
Casiquiare →, *Venezuela* 124 C5
Čáslav, *Czech Rep.* 26 B8
Casma, *Peru* 124 E3
Casmalia, *U.S.A.* 111 L6
Cásola Valsénio, *Italy* 41 D8
Cásoli, *Italy* 41 F11
Caspe, *Spain* 38 D4
Casper, *U.S.A.* 108 E10
Caspian Depression, *Eurasia* 35 G9
Caspian Sea, *Eurasia* 52 E6
Cass Lake, *U.S.A.* 112 B7
Cassà de la Selva, *Spain* 38 D7
Cassadaga, *U.S.A.* 116 D5
Cassano allo Iónio, *Italy* 43 C9
Casse, Grande, *France* 21 C10
Cassel, *France* 19 B9
Casselman, *Canada* 117 A9
Casselton, *U.S.A.* 112 B6
Cassiar, *Canada* 102 B3
Cassiar Mts., *Canada* 102 B2
Cassino, *Italy* 42 A6
Cassis, *France* 21 E9
Cassville, *U.S.A.* 113 G8
Castagneto Carducci, *Italy* 40 E7
Castaic, *U.S.A.* 111 L8
Castalia, *U.S.A.* 116 E2
Castanhal, *Brazil* 125 D9
Castara, *Trin. & Tob.* 125 J16
Castéggio, *Italy* 40 C6
Castejón de Monegros, *Spain* 38 D4
Castèl di Sangro, *Italy* 41 G11
Castèl San Giovanni, *Italy* 40 C6
Castèl San Pietro Terme, *Italy* 41 D8
Castelbuono, *Italy* 43 E7
Castelfidardo, *Italy* 41 E10
Castelfiorentino, *Italy* 40 E7
Castelfranco Emília, *Italy* 40 D8
Castelfranco Véneto, *Italy* 41 C8
Casteljaloux, *France* 20 D4
Castellabate, *Italy* 43 B7
Castellammare, G. di, *Italy* 42 D5
Castellammare del Golfo, *Italy* 42 D5
Castellammare di Stábia, *Italy* 43 B7
Castellamonte, *Italy* 40 C4
Castellane, *France* 21 E10
Castellaneta, *Italy* 43 B9
Castelli, *Argentina* 126 D4
Castelló de la Plana, *Spain* 38 F4
Castellón de la Plana □, *Spain* 38 E4
Castellote, *Spain* 38 E4
Castelmáuro, *Italy* 41 G11
Castelnau-de-Médoc, *France* 20 C3
Castelnau-Magnoac, *France* 20 E4
Castelnaudary, *France* 20 E5
Castelnovo ne' Monti, *Italy* 40 D7
Castelnuovo di Val di Cécina, *Italy* 40 E7
Castelo, *Brazil* 127 A7
Castelo Branco, *Portugal* 36 F3
Castelo Branco □, *Portugal* 36 F3
Castelo de Paiva, *Portugal* 36 D2
Castelo de Vide, *Portugal* 37 F3
Castelsardo, *Italy* 42 B1
Castelsarrasin, *France* 20 D5
Casteltérmini, *Italy* 42 E6
Castelvetrano, *Italy* 42 E5
Casterton, *Australia* 95 F3
Castets, *France* 20 E2
Castiglion Fiorentino, *Italy* 41 E8
Castiglione del Lago, *Italy* 41 E9
Castiglione della Pescáia, *Italy* 40 F7
Castiglione delle Stiviere, *Italy* 40 C7
Castilblanco, *Spain* 37 F5
Castile, *U.S.A.* 116 D6
Castilla, Playa de, *Spain* 37 J4
Castilla-La Mancha □, *Spain* 6 H5
Castilla y Leon □, *Spain* 36 D6
Castillo de Locubín, *Spain* 37 H7
Castillon-en-Couserans, *France* 20 F5
Castillonès, *France* 20 D4
Castillos, *Uruguay* 127 C5
Castle Dale, *U.S.A.* 108 G8
Castle Douglas, *U.K.* 13 G5
Castle Rock, *Colo., U.S.A.* 112 F2
Castle Rock, *Wash., U.S.A.* 110 D4
Castlebar, *Ireland* 12 C2
Castlebay, *U.K.* 13 E1
Castleblaney, *Ireland* 12 B5
Castlederg, *U.K.* 12 B4
Castleford, *U.K.* 14 D6
Castlegar, *Canada* 102 D5
Castlemaine, *Australia* 95 F3
Castlepollard, *Ireland* 12 C4
Castlerea, *Ireland* 12 C3
Castlereagh →, *Australia* 95 E4
Castlereagh B., *Australia* 94 A2
Castleton, *U.S.A.* 117 C11
Castletown, *U.K.* 14 C3
Castletown Bearhaven, *Ireland* 12 E2
Castor, *Canada* 102 C6
Castor →, *Canada* 104 B4
Castorland, *U.S.A.* 117 C9
Castres, *France* 20 E6
Castricum, *Neths.* 17 B4
Castries, *St. Lucia* 121 f
Castril, *Spain* 37 H8
Castro, *Brazil* 127 A6
Castro, *Chile* 128 E2
Castro Alves, *Brazil* 125 F11
Castro del Río, *Spain* 37 H6
Castro-Urdiales, *Spain* 36 B7
Castro Verde, *Portugal* 37 H2
Castrojeriz, *Spain* 36 C6
Castropol, *Spain* 36 B4
Castroreale, *Italy* 43 D8
Castrovíllari, *Italy* 43 C9
Castroville, *U.S.A.* 110 J5
Castuera, *Spain* 37 G5
Çat, *Turkey* 73 C9
Cat Ba △, *Vietnam* 64 B6
Cat Ba, Dao, *Vietnam* 64 B6
Cat I., *Bahamas* 121 B4
Cat L., *Canada* 104 B1
Cat Lake, *Canada* 104 B1
Cat Tien △, *Vietnam* 65 G6
Čata, *Slovak Rep.* 27 D11
Catacamas, *Honduras* 120 D2
Cataguases, *Brazil* 127 A7
Çatak, *Turkey* 73 C10
Catalão, *Brazil* 125 G9
Çatalca, *Turkey* 45 E12
Catalina, *Canada* 105 C9
Catalina, *Chile* 126 B2
Catalina, *U.S.A.* 109 K8
Catalonia = Cataluña □, *Spain* 38 D6
Cataluña □, *Spain* 38 D6
Çatalzeytin, *Turkey* 72 B6
Catamarca, *Argentina* 126 B2
Catamarca □, *Argentina* 126 B2
Catanauan, *Phil.* 61 E5
Catanduanes □, *Phil.* 61 E6
Catanduva, *Brazil* 127 A6
Catánia, *Italy* 43 E8
Catánia, G. di, *Italy* 43 E8
Catanzaro, *Italy* 43 D9
Catarman, *Phil.* 61 E6
Catatumbo-Bari △, *Colombia* 121 E5
Catatumbo-Bari △, *Colombia* 121 E5
Catbalogan, *Phil.* 61 F6
Cateel, *Phil.* 61 H7
Catembe, *Mozam.* 89 D5
Caterham, *U.K.* 15 F7
Cathcart, *S. Africa* 88 E4
Cathlamet, *U.S.A.* 110 D3
Catio, *Guinea-Biss.* 82 C1
Catlettsburg, *U.S.A.* 114 F4
Çatma Dağı, *Turkey* 47 C11
Catoche, C., *Mexico* 119 C7
Cátria, Mte., *Italy* 41 E9
Catriló, *Argentina* 126 D3
Catrimani, *Brazil* 124 C6
Catrimani →, *Brazil* 124 C6
Catskill, *U.S.A.* 117 D11
Catskill ⌓, *U.S.A.* 117 D10
Catskill Mts., *U.S.A.* 117 D10
Catt, Mt., *Australia* 94 A1
Cattaraugus, *U.S.A.* 116 D6
Catterick, *U.K.* 14 C6
Cattólica, *Italy* 41 E9
Cattólica Eraclea, *Italy* 42 E6
Catuala, *Angola* 88 B2
Catuane, *Mozam.* 89 D5
Catur, *Mozam.* 87 E4
Catwick Is., *Vietnam* 65 G7
Cauca →, *Colombia* 124 B4
Caucaia, *Brazil* 125 D11
Caucasus Mountains, *Eurasia* 35 J7
Caudete, *Spain* 39 G3
Caudry, *France* 19 B10
Caulnes, *France* 18 D4
Caulónia, *Italy* 43 D9
Caungula, *Angola* 84 F3
Cauquenes, *Chile* 126 D1
Caura →, *Venezuela* 124 B6
Cauresi →, *Mozam.* 87 F3
Căuşani, *Moldova* 29 D14
Causapscal, *Canada* 105 C6
Caussade, *France* 20 D5
Causse-Méjean, *France* 20 D7
Causses du Quercy ⌓, *France* 20 D5
Cauterets, *France* 20 F3
Cauvery →, *India* 66 P11
Caux, Pays de, *France* 18 C7
Cava de' Tirreni, *Italy* 43 B7
Cávado →, *Portugal* 36 D2
Cavagrande del Cassibile ⌓, *Italy* 43 F8
Cavaillon, *France* 21 E9
Cavalaire-sur-Mer, *France* 21 E10
Cavalese, *Italy* 41 B8
Cavalier, *U.S.A.* 112 A6
Cavalla = Cavally →, *Africa* 82 E3
Cavallo, I. de, *France* 21 G13
Cavally →, *Africa* 82 E3
Cavan, *Ireland* 12 B4
Cavan □, *Ireland* 12 C4
Cavárzere, *Italy* 41 C9
Çavdarhisar, *Turkey* 47 B11
Çavdır, *Turkey* 47 D11
Cave Creek, *U.S.A.* 109 K7
Cavenagh Ra., *Australia* 93 E4
Cavendish, *Australia* 95 F3
Caviana, I., *Brazil* 125 C8
Cavite, *Phil.* 61 D4
Cavnic, *Romania* 29 C8
Cavour, *Italy* 40 D4
Cavtat, *Croatia* 44 D2
Cawndilla L., *Australia* 95 E3
Cawnpore = Kanpur, *India* 69 F9
Caxias, *Brazil* 125 D10
Caxias do Sul, *Brazil* 127 B5
Çay, *Turkey* 72 C4
Cay Sal Bank, *Bahamas* 120 B4
Cayambe, *Ecuador* 124 C3
Çaycuma, *Turkey* 72 B5
Çayeli, *Turkey* 73 B9
Cayenne, *Fr. Guiana* 125 B8
Cayey, *Puerto Rico* 121 d
Caygören Barajı, *Turkey* 47 B10
Cayiralan, *Turkey* 72 C6
Caylus, *France* 20 D5
Cayman Brac, *Cayman Is.* 120 C4
Cayman Is. ⊠, *W. Indies* 120 C3
Cayo Romano, *Cuba* 120 B4
Cayres, *France* 20 D7
Cayuga, *U.S.A.* 117 D8
Cayuga L., *U.S.A.* 117 D8
Cazalla de la Sierra, *Spain* 37 H5
Căzăneşti, *Romania* 29 F12
Cazaubon, *France* 20 E3
Cazaux et de Sanguinet, Étang de, *France* 20 D2
Cazenovia, *U.S.A.* 117 D9
Cazères, *France* 20 E5
Cazin, *Bos.-H.* 41 D12
Čazma, *Croatia* 41 C13
Cazombo, *Angola* 85 G4
Cazorla, *Spain* 37 H7
Cazorla, Sierra de, *Spain* 37 G8
Cea →, *Spain* 36 C5
Ceamurlia de Jos, *Romania* 29 F13
Ceanannus Mor, *Ireland* 12 C5
Ceará = Fortaleza, *Brazil* 125 D11
Ceará □, *Brazil* 125 E11
Ceará Mirim, *Brazil* 125 E11
Ceauru, L., *Romania* 29 F8
Cebaco, I. de, *Panama* 120 E3
Cebollar, *Argentina* 126 B2
Cebollera, Sierra de, *Spain* 38 D2
Cebreros, *Spain* 36 E6
Cebu, *Phil.* 61 F5
Čečava, *Bos.-H.* 28 F2
Ceccano, *Italy* 42 A6
Cece, *Hungary* 28 D3
Cechi, *Ivory C.* 82 D4
Cecil Plains, *Australia* 95 D5
Cécina, *Italy* 40 E7
Cécina →, *Italy* 40 E7
Ceclavín, *Spain* 36 F4
Cedar →, *U.S.A.* 112 E9
Cedar City, *U.S.A.* 109 H7
Cedar Creek Reservoir, *U.S.A.* 113 J6
Cedar Falls, *Iowa, U.S.A.* 112 D8
Cedar Falls, *Wash., U.S.A.* 110 C5
Cedar Key, *U.S.A.* 115 L4
Cedar L., *Canada* 103 C9
Cedar Rapids, *U.S.A.* 112 E9
Cedartown, *U.S.A.* 115 H3
Cedarvale, *Canada* 102 B3
Cedarville, *S. Africa* 89 E4
Cedeira, *Spain* 36 B2
Cedral, *Mexico* 118 C4
Cedrino →, *Italy* 42 B2
Cedro, *Brazil* 125 E11
Cedros, I. de, *Mexico* 118 B1
Cedros B., *Trin. & Tob.* 125 K15
Ceduna, *Australia* 95 E1
Cedynia, *Poland* 31 F1
Cée, *Spain* 36 C1
Ceerigaabo = Erigavo, *Somali Rep.* 75 E4
Cefalù, *Italy* 43 D7
Cega →, *Spain* 36 D6
Cegléd, *Hungary* 28 C4
Céglie Messápico, *Italy* 43 B10
Cehegín, *Spain* 39 G3
Ceheng, *China* 58 E5
Cehu-Silvaniei, *Romania* 29 C8
Ceica, *Romania* 28 D7
Ceira →, *Portugal* 36 E2
Cekik, *Indonesia* 63 J17
Čelákovice, *Czech Rep.* 26 A7
Celano, *Italy* 41 F10
Celanova, *Spain* 36 C3
Celaque △, *Honduras* 120 D2
Celaya, *Mexico* 118 C4
Celebes = Sulawesi, *Indonesia* 63 E6
Celebes Sea, *Indonesia* 63 D6
Čelić, *Bos.-H.* 28 F3
Celina, *U.S.A.* 114 E3
Celinac, *Bos.-H.* 28 F2
Celje, *Slovenia* 41 B12
Celldömölk, *Hungary* 28 C2
Celle, *Germany* 24 C6
Celorico da Beira, *Portugal* 36 E3
Celtic Sea, *Atl. Oc.* 6 E4
Çeltikçi, *Turkey* 47 D12
Çemişgezek, *Turkey* 73 C8
Cenderwasih, Teluk, *Indonesia* 63 E9
Cengong, *China* 58 D7
Ceno →, *Italy* 40 D7
Centallo, *Italy* 40 D4
Centelles, *Spain* 38 D7
Center, *N. Dak., U.S.A.* 112 B4
Center, *Tex., U.S.A.* 113 K7
Centerburg, *U.S.A.* 116 F2
Centerville, *Calif., U.S.A.* 110 J7
Centerville, *Iowa, U.S.A.* 112 E8
Centerville, *Pa., U.S.A.* 116 F5
Centerville, *Tenn., U.S.A.* 115 H2
Centerville, *Tex., U.S.A.* 113 K7
Cento, *Italy* 41 D8
Central = Tsentralnyy □, *Russia* 34 D4
Central □, *Ghana* 83 D4
Central □, *Kenya* 86 C4
Central □, *Malawi* 87 E3
Central □, *Zambia* 87 E2
Central, Cordillera, *Colombia* 124 C4
Central, Cordillera, *Costa Rica* 120 D3
Central, Cordillera, *Dom. Rep.* 121 C5
Central, Cordillera, *Phil.* 61 C4
Central, Cordillera, *Puerto Rico* 121 d
Central African Rep. ■, *Africa* 79 G9
Central America, *America* 98 H11
Central Butte, *Canada* 103 C7
Central City, *Colo., U.S.A.* 108 G11
Central City, *Ky., U.S.A.* 114 G2
Central City, *Nebr., U.S.A.* 112 E6
Central I., *Kenya* 86 B4
Central Island △, *Kenya* 86 B4
Central Kalahari ⌓, *Botswana* 88 C3
Central Makran Range, *Pakistan* 66 F4
Central Patricia, *Canada* 104 B1
Central Point, *U.S.A.* 108 E2
Central Russian Uplands, *Europe* 6 E13
Central Siberian Plateau, *Russia* 50 C14
Central Square, *U.S.A.* 117 C8
Centralia, *Ill., U.S.A.* 112 F10
Centralia, *Mo., U.S.A.* 112 F8
Centralia, *Wash., U.S.A.* 110 D4
Cenxi, *China* 59 F8
Ceotina →, *Bos.-H.* 44 C2
Cephalonia = Kefallinía, *Greece* 46 C2
Čepin, *Croatia* 28 E3
Ceprano, *Italy* 42 A6
Ceptura, *Romania* 29 E11
Cepu, *Indonesia* 63 G14
Ceram = Seram, *Indonesia* 63 E7
Ceram Sea = Seram Sea, *Indonesia* 63 E7

Cerbère, *France* 20 F7
Cerbicales, Is., *France* 21 G13
Cercal, *Portugal* 37 H2
Cerdaña, *Spain* 38 C6
Cère →, *France* 20 D5
Cerea, *Italy* 41 C8
Ceredigion □, *U.K.* 15 E3
Ceres, *Argentina* 126 B3
Ceres, *S. Africa* 88 E2
Ceres, *U.S.A.* 110 H6
Céret, *France* 20 F6
Cergy, *France* 19 C9
Cerignola, *Italy* 43 A8
Cerigo = Kíthira, *Greece* 46 E5
Cérilly, *France* 19 F9
Cerisiers, *France* 19 D10
Cerizay, *France* 18 F6
Çerkeş, *Turkey* 72 B5
Çerkezköy, *Turkey* 45 E12
Cerknica, *Slovenia* 41 C11
Cerkovica, *Bulgaria* 45 C8
Cermerno, *Serbia & M.* 44 C4
Çermik, *Turkey* 73 C8
Cerna, *Romania* 29 E13
Cerna →, *Romania* 29 F8
Cernavodă, *Romania* 29 F13
Cernay, *France* 19 E14
Cernik, *Croatia* 28 E2
Cerralvo, I., *Mexico* 118 C3
Cërrik, *Albania* 44 E3
Cerritos, *Mexico* 118 C4
Cerro Chato, *Uruguay* 127 C4
Cerro Corá △, *Paraguay* 127 A4
Cerro el Copey △, *Venezuela* 121 D7
Cerro El Copey △, *Venezuela* 121 D7
Cerro Hoya △, *Panama* 120 E3
Cerro Saoche △, *Venezuela* 121 D6
Cerro Saroche △, *Venezuela* 121 D6
Certaldo, *Italy* 40 E8
Cervaro →, *Italy* 43 A8
Cervati, Monte, *Italy* 43 B8
Cervantes, *Australia* 93 F2
Cervera, *Spain* 38 D6
Cervera de Pisuerga, *Spain* 36 C6
Cervera del Río Alhama, *Spain* 38 C3
Cervéteri, *Italy* 41 F9
Cérvia, *Italy* 41 D9
Cervignano del Friuli, *Italy* 41 C10
Cervinara, *Italy* 43 A7
Cervione, *France* 21 F13
Cervo, *Spain* 36 B3
Cesarò, *Italy* 43 E7
Cesena, *Italy* 41 D9
Cesenático, *Italy* 41 D9
Cēsis, *Latvia* 9 H21
Česká Lípa, *Czech Rep.* 26 A7
Česká Třebová, *Czech Rep.* 27 B9
České Budějovice, *Czech Rep.* 26 C7
České Velenice, *Czech Rep.* 26 C7
Českobudějovický □, *Czech Rep.* 26 B7
Českomoravská Vrchovina, *Czech Rep.* 26 B8
Český Brod, *Czech Rep.* 26 A7
Český Krumlov, *Czech Rep.* 26 C7
Český Těšín, *Czech Rep.* 27 B11
Česma →, *Croatia* 41 C13
Çeşme, *Turkey* 47 C8
Cessnock, *Australia* 95 E5
Cesson-Sévigné, *France* 18 D5
Cestas, *France* 20 D3
Cestos →, *Liberia* 82 D3
Cestos Sehnkwehn △, *Liberia* 82 D3
Cetate, *Romania* 28 F8
Cetin Grad, *Croatia* 41 C12
Cetina →, *Croatia* 41 E13
Cetinje, *Serbia & M.* 44 D2
Cetraro, *Italy* 43 C8
Ceuta, *N. Afr.* 78 A4
Ceva, *Italy* 40 D5
Cévennes, *France* 20 D7
Cévennes △, *France* 20 D7
Ceyhan, *Turkey* 70 B2
Ceyhan →, *Turkey* 72 D6
Ceylânpınar, *Turkey* 73 D9
Ceylon = Sri Lanka ■, *Asia* 66 R12
Cèze →, *France* 21 D8
Cha-am, *Thailand* 64 F2
Cha Pa, *Vietnam* 64 A4
Chabanais, *France* 20 C4
Chabeuil, *France* 21 D9
Chablais, *France* 19 F13
Chablis, *France* 19 E10
Chacabuco, *Argentina* 126 C3
Chachapoyas, *Peru* 124 E3
Chachoengsao, *Thailand* 64 F3
Chachran, *Pakistan* 66 E7
Chachro, *Pakistan* 68 G4
Chaco △, *Argentina* 126 B4
Chaco □, *Argentina* 126 B3
Chaco □, *Paraguay* 126 B4
Chaco →, *U.S.A.* 109 H9
Chaco Austral, *S. Amer.* 128 B4
Chaco Boreal, *S. Amer.* 124 H6
Chaco Central, *S. Amer.* 128 A4
Chaco Culture △, *U.S.A.* 109 H10
Chacon, C., *U.S.A.* 102 C2
Chad ■, *Africa* 79 F8
Chad, L. = Tchad, L., *Chad* 79 F8
Chadan, *Russia* 53 D10
Chadileuvú →, *Argentina* 126 D2
Chadiza, *Zambia* 87 E3
Chadron, *U.S.A.* 112 D3
Chadyr-Lunga = Ciadâr-Lunga, *Moldova* 29 D13
Chae Hom, *Thailand* 64 C2
Chae Son △, *Thailand* 64 C2
Chaem →, *Thailand* 64 C2
Chaeryŏng, *N. Korea* 57 E13
Chagai Hills = Chāh Gay Hills, *Afghan.* 66 E3
Chagda, *Russia* 53 D14
Chaghcharān, *Afghan.* 66 B4
Chagny, *France* 19 F11
Chagoda, *Russia* 32 C8
Chagos Arch. ☒, *Ind. Oc.* 50 K11
Chagres △, *Panama* 120 E4
Chagrin Falls, *U.S.A.* 116 E3
Chaguanas, *Trin. & Tob.* 125 K15
Chāh Ākhvor, *Iran* 71 C8
Chāh Bahar, *Iran* 71 E9
Chāh-e Kavīr, *Iran* 71 C8
Chāh Gay Hills, *Afghan.* 66 E3
Chahar Burjak, *Afghan.* 66 D3
Chahār Mahāll va Bakhtīarī □, *Iran* 71 C6
Chaibasa, *India* 67 H14
Chaillé-les-Marais, *France* 20 B2
Chainat, *Thailand* 64 E3
Chaiya, *Thailand* 65 H2
Chaiyaphum, *Thailand* 64 E4
Chaj Doab, *Pakistan* 68 C5
Chajari, *Argentina* 126 C4
Chak Amru, *Pakistan* 68 C6
Chaka, *Sudan* 81 G3
Chakar →, *Pakistan* 68 E3
Chakari, *Zimbabwe* 89 B4
Chake Chake, *Tanzania* 86 D4
Chakhānsūr, *Afghan.* 66 D3
Chakonipau, L., *Canada* 105 A6
Chakradharpur, *India* 69 H11
Chakrata, *India* 68 D7
Chakwal, *Pakistan* 68 C5
Chala, *Peru* 124 G4
Chalais, *France* 20 C4
Chalchihuites, *Mexico* 118 C4
Chalcis = Khalkís, *Greece* 46 C5
Châlette-sur-Loing, *France* 19 D9
Chaleur B., *Canada* 105 C6
Chalfant, *U.S.A.* 110 H8
Chalhuanca, *Peru* 124 F4
Chalindrey, *France* 19 E12
Chaling, *China* 59 D9
Chalisgaon, *India* 66 J9
Chalk River, *Canada* 104 C4
Chalky Inlet, *N.Z.* 91 M1
Challans, *France* 18 F5
Challapata, *Bolivia* 124 G5
Challis, *U.S.A.* 108 D6
Chalmette, *U.S.A.* 113 L10
Chalon-sur-Saône, *France* 19 F11
Chalonnes-sur-Loire, *France* 18 E6
Châlons-en-Champagne, *France* 19 D11
Châlus, *France* 20 C4
Chālūs, *Iran* 71 B6
Cham, *Germany* 25 F8
Cham, Cu Lao, *Vietnam* 64 E7
Chama, *U.S.A.* 109 H10
Chamaicó, *Argentina* 126 D3
Chaman, *Pakistan* 66 D5
Chamba, *India* 68 C7
Chamba, *Tanzania* 87 E4
Chambal →, *India* 69 F8
Chamberlain, *U.S.A.* 112 D5
Chamberlain →, *Australia* 92 C4
Chamberlain L., *U.S.A.* 115 B11
Chambers, *U.S.A.* 109 J9
Chambersburg, *U.S.A.* 114 F7
Chambéry, *France* 21 C9
Chambeshi →, *Zambia* 84 G6
Chambly, *Canada* 117 A11
Chambord, *Canada* 105 C5
Chamboulive, *France* 20 C5
Chamchamal, *Iraq* 70 C5
Chamela, *Mexico* 118 D3
Chamical, *Argentina* 126 C2
Chamkar Luong, *Cambodia* 65 G4
Chamoli, *India* 69 D8
Chamonix-Mont Blanc, *France* 21 C10
Champa, *India* 69 H10
Champagne, *Canada* 102 A1
Champagne, *France* 19 D11
Champagnole, *France* 19 F12
Champaign, *U.S.A.* 114 E1
Champassak, *Laos* 64 E5
Champaubert, *France* 19 D10
Champawat, *India* 69 E9
Champdeniers-St-Denis, *France* 20 B3
Champdoré, L., *Canada* 105 A6
Champeix, *France* 20 C7
Champion, *U.S.A.* 116 E4
Champlain, *U.S.A.* 117 B11
Champlain, L., *U.S.A.* 117 B11
Champlitte, *France* 19 E12
Champotón, *Mexico* 119 D6
Champua, *India* 69 H11
Chamusca, *Portugal* 37 F2
Chana, *Thailand* 65 J3
Chañaral, *Chile* 126 B1
Chanārān, *Iran* 71 B8
Chanasma, *India* 68 H5
Chancery Lane, *Barbados* 121 g
Chanco, *Chile* 126 D1
Chand, *India* 69 J8
Chandan, *India* 69 G12
Chandan Chauki, *India* 69 E9
Chandannagar, *India* 69 H13
Chandausi, *India* 69 E8
Chandeleur Is., *U.S.A.* 113 L10
Chandeleur Sd., *U.S.A.* 113 L10
Chandigarh, *India* 68 D7
Chandil, *India* 69 H12
Chandler, *Australia* 95 D1
Chandler, *Canada* 105 C7
Chandler, *Ariz., U.S.A.* 109 K8
Chandler, *Okla., U.S.A.* 113 H6
Chandod, *India* 68 J5
Chandpur, *Bangla.* 67 H17
Chandrapur, *India* 66 K11
Chānf, *Iran* 71 E9
Chang, *Pakistan* 68 F3
Chang, Ko, *Thailand* 65 F4
Ch'ang Chiang = Chang Jiang →, *China* 59 B13
Chang Jiang →, *China* 59 B13
Changa, *India* 69 C7
Changanacheri, *India* 66 Q10
Changane →, *Mozam.* 89 C5
Changbai, *China* 57 D15
Changbai Shan, *China* 57 C15
Changchiak'ou = Zhangjiakou, *China* 56 D8
Ch'angchou = Changzhou, *China* 59 B12
Changchun, *China* 57 C13
Changchunling, *China* 57 B13
Changde, *China* 59 C8
Changdo-ri, *N. Korea* 57 E14
Changfeng, *China* 59 A11
Changhai = Shanghai, *China* 59 B13
Changhua, *China* 59 B12
Changhua, *Taiwan* 59 E13
Changhŭng, *S. Korea* 57 G14
Changhŭngni, *N. Korea* 57 D15
Changi, *Singapore* 65 d
Changi, Singapore ✕ (SIN), *Singapore* 65 M4
Changjiang, *China* 64 C7
Changjin, *N. Korea* 57 D14
Changjin-chŏsuji, *N. Korea* 57 D14
Changle, *China* 59 E12
Changli, *China* 57 E10
Changling, *China* 57 B12
Changlun, *Malaysia* 65 J3
Changning, *Hunan, China* 59 D9
Changning, *Sichuan, China* 58 C5
Changning, *Yunnan, China* 58 E2
Changping, *China* 56 D9
Changsha, *China* 59 C9
Changshan, *China* 59 C12
Changshu, *China* 59 B13
Changshun, *China* 58 D6
Changtai, *China* 59 E11
Changting, *China* 59 E11
Changwu, *China* 56 G4
Changxing, *China* 59 B12
Changyang, *China* 59 B8
Changyi, *China* 57 F10
Changyŏn, *N. Korea* 57 E13
Changyuan, *China* 56 G8
Changzhi, *China* 56 F7
Changzhou, *China* 59 B12
Chanhanga, *Angola* 88 B1
Chania = Khaniá, *Greece* 49 D6
Chanlar = Xanlar, *Azerbaijan* 35 K8
Channapatna, *India* 66 N10
Channel Is., *U.K.* 15 H5
Channel Is., *U.S.A.* 111 M7
Channel Islands △, *U.S.A.* 111 L7
Channel-Port aux Basques, *Canada* 105 C8
Channel Tunnel, *Europe* 15 F9
Channing, *U.S.A.* 113 H3
Chantada, *Spain* 36 C3
Chanthaburi, *Thailand* 64 F4
Chantilly, *France* 19 C9
Chantonnay, *France* 18 F5
Chantrey Inlet, *Canada* 100 B10
Chanute, *U.S.A.* 113 G7
Chanza →, *Spain* 37 H3
Chao Hu, *China* 59 B11
Chao Phraya →, *Thailand* 64 F3
Chao Phraya Lowlands, *Thailand* 64 E3
Chaocheng, *China* 56 F8
Chaohu, *China* 59 B11
Chaoyang, *Guangdong, China* 59 F11
Chaoyang, *Liaoning, China* 57 D11
Chaozhou, *China* 59 F11
Chapais, *Canada* 104 C5
Chapala, *Mozam.* 87 F4
Chapala, L. de, *Mexico* 118 C4
Chapayev, *Kazakhstan* 34 E10
Chapayevsk, *Russia* 34 D9
Chapecó, *Brazil* 127 B5
Chapel Hill, *U.S.A.* 115 H6
Chapleau, *Canada* 104 C3
Chaplin, *Canada* 103 C7
Chaplin L., *Canada* 103 C7
Chaplino, *Ukraine* 33 H9
Chaplygin, *Russia* 32 F11
Chappell, *U.S.A.* 112 E3
Chapra = Chhapra, *India* 69 G11
Chara, *Russia* 53 D12
Charadai, *Argentina* 126 B4
Charagua, *Bolivia* 124 G6
Charambirá, Punta, *Colombia* 124 C3
Charaña, *Bolivia* 124 G5
Charantsavan, *Armenia* 35 K7
Charanwala, *India* 68 F5
Charata, *Argentina* 126 B3
Charcas, *Mexico* 118 C4
Charcot I., *Antarctica* 5 C17
Chard, *U.K.* 15 G5
Chardon, *U.S.A.* 116 E3
Chardzhou = Chärjew, *Turkmenistan* 52 F7
Charente □, *France* 20 C4
Charente →, *France* 20 C2
Charente-Maritime □, *France* 20 C3
Charenton-du-Cher, *France* 19 F9
Chari →, *Chad* 79 F8
Chārīkār, *Afghan.* 66 B6
Chariton →, *U.S.A.* 112 F8
Chärjew, *Turkmenistan* 52 F7
Charkhari, *India* 69 G8
Charkhi Dadri, *India* 68 E7
Charleroi, *Belgium* 17 D4
Charleroi, *U.S.A.* 116 F5
Charles, C., *U.S.A.* 114 G8
Charles City, *U.S.A.* 112 D8
Charles de Gaulle, Paris ✕ (CDG), *France* 19 D9
Charles L., *Canada* 103 B6
Charles Town, *U.S.A.* 114 F7
Charleston, *Ill., U.S.A.* 114 F1
Charleston, *Miss., U.S.A.* 113 H9
Charleston, *Mo., U.S.A.* 113 G10
Charleston, *S.C., U.S.A.* 115 J6
Charleston, *W. Va., U.S.A.* 114 F5
Charleston L., *Canada* 117 B9
Charleston Peak, *U.S.A.* 111 J11
Charlestown, *Ireland* 12 C3
Charlestown, *S. Africa* 89 D4
Charlestown, *Ind., U.S.A.* 114 F3
Charlestown, *N.H., U.S.A.* 117 C12
Charlestown of Aberlour, *U.K.* 13 D5
Charleville = Rath Luirc, *Ireland* 12 D3
Charleville, *Australia* 95 D4
Charleville-Mézières, *France* 19 C11
Charlevoix, *U.S.A.* 114 C3
Charlieu, *France* 19 F11
Charlotte, *Mich., U.S.A.* 114 D3
Charlotte, *N.C., U.S.A.* 115 H5
Charlotte, *Vt., U.S.A.* 117 B11
Charlotte Amalie, *U.S. Virgin Is.* 121 e
Charlotte Harbor, *U.S.A.* 115 M4
Charlotte L., *Canada* 102 C3
Charlottenberg, *Sweden* 10 E6
Charlottesville, *U.S.A.* 114 F6
Charlottetown, *Nfld., Canada* 105 B8
Charlottetown, *P.E.I., Canada* 105 C7
Charlotteville, *Trin. & Tob.* 125 J16
Charlton, *Australia* 95 F3
Charlton, *U.S.A.* 112 E8
Charlton I., *Canada* 104 B4
Charmes, *France* 19 D13
Charny, *Canada* 105 C5
Charolles, *France* 19 F11
Chârost, *France* 19 F9
Charre, *Mozam.* 87 F4
Charroux, *France* 20 B4
Charsadda, *Pakistan* 68 B4
Charters Towers, *Australia* 94 C4
Chartres, *France* 18 D8
Chartreuse ⌂, *France* 21 C9
Chascomús, *Argentina* 126 D4
Chasefu, *Zambia* 87 E3
Chashma Barrage, *Pakistan* 68 C4
Chasseneuil-sur-Bonnieure, *France* 20 C4
Chāt, *Iran* 71 B7
Chatal Balkan = Udvoy Balkan, *Bulgaria* 45 D10
Château-Arnoux, *France* 21 D10
Château-Chinon, *France* 19 E10
Château-d'Olonne, *France* 20 B2
Château-du-Loir, *France* 18 E7
Château-Gontier, *France* 18 E6
Château-la-Vallière, *France* 18 E7
Château-Landon, *France* 19 D9
Château-Renault, *France* 18 E7
Château-Salins, *France* 19 D13
Château-Thierry, *France* 19 C10
Châteaubourg, *France* 18 D5
Châteaubriant, *France* 18 E5
Châteaudun, *France* 18 D8
Châteaugay, *U.S.A.* 117 B10
Châteaugiron, *France* 18 D5
Châteauguay, L., *Canada* 105 A5
Châteaulin, *France* 18 D2
Châteaumeillant, *France* 19 F9
Châteauneuf-du-Faou, *France* 18 D3
Châteauneuf-sur-Charente, *France* 20 C3
Châteauneuf-sur-Cher, *France* 19 F9
Châteauneuf-sur-Loire, *France* 19 E9
Châteaurenard, *Bouches-du-Rhône, France* 21 E8
Châteaurenard, *Loiret, France* 19 E9
Châteauroux, *France* 19 F8
Châteauvillain, *France* 19 D11
Châteaux, Pte. des, *Guadeloupe* 120 b
Châtelaillon-Plage, *France* 20 B2
Châtelguyon, *France* 20 C7
Châtellerault, *France* 18 F7
Châtelus-Malvaleix, *France* 19 F9
Chatham = Chatham-Kent, *Canada* 116 D2
Chatham = Miramichi, *Canada* 105 C6
Chatham, *U.K.* 15 F8
Chatham, *U.S.A.* 117 D11
Chatham Is., *Pac. Oc.* 96 M10
Chatham-Kent, *Canada* 116 D2
Châtillon, *Italy* 40 C4
Châtillon-Coligny, *France* 19 E9
Châtillon-en-Diois, *France* 21 D9
Châtillon-sur-Indre, *France* 18 F8
Châtillon-sur-Loire, *France* 19 E9
Châtillon-sur-Seine, *France* 19 E11
Chatmohar, *Bangla.* 69 G13
Chatra, *India* 69 G11
Chatrapur, *India* 67 K14
Chats, L. des, *Canada* 117 A8
Chatsu, *India* 68 F6
Chatsworth, *Canada* 116 B4
Chatsworth, *Zimbabwe* 87 F3
Chāttagām = Chittagong, *Bangla.* 67 H17
Chattahoochee, *U.S.A.* 115 K3
Chattahoochee →, *U.S.A.* 115 K3
Chattanooga, *U.S.A.* 115 H3
Chatteris, *U.K.* 15 E8
Chaturat, *Thailand* 64 E3
Chau Doc, *Vietnam* 65 G5
Chaudes-Aigues, *France* 20 D7
Chauffailles, *France* 19 F11
Chaukan Pass, *Burma* 67 F20
Chaumont, *France* 19 D12
Chaumont, *U.S.A.* 117 B8
Chaumont-en-Vexin, *France* 19 C8
Chaumont-sur-Loire, *France* 18 E8
Chaunay, *France* 20 B4
Chaunskaya G., *Russia* 4 C16
Chauny, *France* 19 C10
Chausey, Îs., *France* 18 D5
Chaussin, *France* 19 F12
Chautauqua L., *U.S.A.* 116 D5
Chauvigny, *France* 18 F7
Chauvin, *Canada* 103 C6
Chavanges, *France* 19 D11
Chaves, *Brazil* 125 D9
Chaves, *Portugal* 36 D3
Chawang, *Thailand* 65 H2
Chazelles-sur-Lyon, *France* 21 C8
Chazy, *U.S.A.* 117 B11
Cheb, *Czech Rep.* 26 A5
Cheboksarskoye Vdkhr., *Russia* 34 B8
Cheboksary, *Russia* 34 B8
Cheboygan, *U.S.A.* 114 C3
Chebsara, *Russia* 32 C10
Chech, Erg, *Africa* 78 D5
Chechen, Ostrov, *Russia* 35 H8
Chechenia □, *Russia* 35 J7
Checheno-Ingush Republic = Chechenia □, *Russia* 35 J7
Chechnya = Chechenia □, *Russia* 35 J7
Chech'ŏn, *S. Korea* 57 F15
Chęciny, *Poland* 31 H7
Checotah, *U.S.A.* 113 H7
Chedabucto B., *Canada* 105 C7
Cheduba I., *Burma* 67 K18
Cheepie, *Australia* 95 D4
Chef-Boutonne, *France* 20 B3
Chegdomyn, *Russia* 53 D14
Chegga, *Mauritania* 78 C4
Chegutu, *Zimbabwe* 87 F3
Chehalis, *U.S.A.* 110 D4
Chehalis →, *U.S.A.* 110 D3
Cheile Nerei-Beusnita △, *Romania* 28 F6
Cheiron, Mt., *France* 21 E10
Cheju do, *S. Korea* 57 H14
Chekalin, *Russia* 32 E9
Chekiang = Zhejiang □, *China* 59 C13
Chel = Kuru, Bahr el →, *Sudan* 81 F2
Chela, Sa. da, *Angola* 88 B1
Chelan, *U.S.A.* 108 C4
Chelan, L., *U.S.A.* 108 B3
Cheleken, *Turkmenistan* 52 F6
Cheleken Yarymadasy, *Turkmenistan* 71 B7
Chelforó, *Argentina* 128 D3
Chelkar = Shalqar, *Kazakhstan* 52 E6
Chelkar Tengiz, Solonchak, *Kazakhstan* 52 E7
Chella, *Ethiopia* 81 F4
Chelles, *France* 19 D9
Chełm, *Poland* 31 G10
Chełmno, *Poland* 31 E5
Chelmsford, *U.K.* 15 F8
Chełmża, *Poland* 31 E5
Chelsea, *U.S.A.* 117 C12
Cheltenham, *U.K.* 15 F5
Chelva, *Spain* 38 F4
Chelyabinsk, *Russia* 52 D7
Chelyuskin, C. = Chelyuskin, Mys, *Russia* 53 B11
Chelyuskin, Mys, *Russia* 53 B11
Chemainus, *Canada* 110 B3
Chemba, *Mozam.* 85 H6
Chembar = Belinskiy, *Russia* 34 D6
Chemillé, *France* 18 E6
Chemnitz, *Germany* 24 E8
Chemult, *U.S.A.* 108 E3
Chen, Gora, *Russia* 53 C15
Chenab →, *Pakistan* 68 D4
Chenango Forks, *U.S.A.* 117 D9
Chencha, *Ethiopia* 81 F4
Chenchiang = Zhenjiang, *China* 59 A12
Cheney, *U.S.A.* 108 C5
Cheng Xian, *China* 56 H3
Chengbu, *China* 59 D8
Chengcheng, *China* 56 G5
Chengchou = Zhengzhou, *China* 56 G7
Chengde, *China* 57 D9
Chengdong Hu, *China* 59 A11
Chengdu, *China* 58 B5
Chenggong, *China* 58 E4
Chenggu, *China* 56 H4
Chenghai, *China* 59 F11
Chengjiang, *China* 58 E4
Chengkou, *China* 58 B7
Ch'engmai, *China* 64 C7
Ch'engtu = Chengdu, *China* 58 B5
Chengwu, *China* 56 G8
Chengxi Hu, *China* 59 A11
Chengyang, *China* 57 F11
Chenjiagang, *China* 57 G10
Chenkán, *Mexico* 119 D6
Chennai, *India* 66 N12
Chenôve, *France* 19 E12
Chenxi, *China* 59 C8
Chenzhou, *China* 59 E9
Cheo Reo, *Vietnam* 62 B3
Cheom Ksan, *Cambodia* 64 E5
Chepelare, *Bulgaria* 45 E8
Chepén, *Peru* 124 E3
Chepes, *Argentina* 126 C2
Chepo, *Panama* 120 E4
Chepstow, *U.K.* 15 F5
Chequamegon B., *U.S.A.* 112 B9
Cher □, *France* 19 E9
Cher →, *France* 18 E7
Chéradi, *Italy* 43 B10
Cherasco, *Italy* 40 D4
Cheraw, *U.S.A.* 115 H6
Cherbourg, *France* 18 C5
Cherdakly, *Russia* 34 C9
Cherdyn, *Russia* 52 C6
Cheremkhovo, *Russia* 53 D11
Cherepanovo, *Russia* 52 D9
Cherepovets, *Russia* 32 C9
Chergui, Chott ech, *Algeria* 78 B6
Cherikov = Cherykaw, *Belarus* 32 F6
Cherkasy, *Ukraine* 33 H7
Cherkessk, *Russia* 35 H6
Cherlak, *Russia* 52 D8
Chernaya, *Russia* 53 B9
Cherni, *Bulgaria* 44 D7

Chernigov = Chernihiv, *Ukraine* 33 G6
Chernihiv, *Ukraine* 33 G6
Chernivtsi, *Ukraine* 33 H3
Chernobyl = Chornobyl, *Ukraine* 33 G6
Chernogorsk, *Russia* 53 D10
Chernomorskoye = Chornomorske, *Ukraine* 33 K7
Chernovtsy = Chernivtsi, *Ukraine* 33 H3
Chernyakhovsk, *Russia* 9 J19
Chernyanka, *Russia* 33 G9
Chernysheyskiy, *Russia* 53 C12
Chernyye Zemli, *Russia* 35 H8
Cherokee, *Iowa, U.S.A.* 112 D7
Cherokee, *Okla., U.S.A.* 113 G5
Cherokee Village, *U.S.A.* 113 G9
Cherokees, Grand Lake O' The, *U.S.A.* 113 G7
Cherrapunji, *India* 67 G17
Cherry Valley, *Calif., U.S.A.* 111 M10
Cherry Valley, *N.Y., U.S.A.* 117 D10
Cherskiy, *Russia* 53 C17
Cherskogo Khrebet, *Russia* 53 C15
Chertkovo, *Russia* 33 H11
Cherven, *Belarus* 32 F5
Cherven-Bryag, *Bulgaria* 45 C8
Chervonohrad, *Ukraine* 33 G3
Cherwell →, *U.K.* 15 F6
Cherykaw, *Belarus* 32 F6
Chesapeake, *U.S.A.* 114 G7
Chesapeake B., *U.S.A.* 114 G7
Cheshire □, *U.K.* 14 D5
Cheshskaya Guba, *Russia* 52 C5
Cheshunt, *U.K.* 15 F7
Chesil Beach, *U.K.* 15 G5
Chesley, *Canada* 116 B3
Cheste, *Spain* 39 F4
Chester, *U.K.* 14 D5
Chester, *Calif., U.S.A.* 108 F3
Chester, *Ill., U.S.A.* 113 G10
Chester, *Mont., U.S.A.* 108 B8
Chester, *Pa., U.S.A.* 114 F8
Chester, *S.C., U.S.A.* 115 H5
Chester, *Vt., U.S.A.* 117 C12
Chester, *W. Va., U.S.A.* 116 F4
Chester-le-Street, *U.K.* 14 C6
Chesterfield, *U.K.* 14 D6
Chesterfield, Is., *N. Cal.* 96 J7
Chesterfield Inlet, *Canada* 100 B10
Chesterton Ra., *Australia* 95 D4
Chesterton Range △, *Australia* 95 D4
Chestertown, *U.S.A.* 117 C11
Chesterville, *Canada* 117 A9
Chestnut Ridge, *U.S.A.* 116 F5
Chesuncook L., *U.S.A.* 115 C11
Chéticamp, *Canada* 105 C7
Chetrosu, *Moldova* 29 B12
Chetumal, *Mexico* 119 D7
Chetumal, B. de, *Mexico* 119 D7
Chetwynd, *Canada* 102 B4
Chevanceaux, *France* 20 C3
Cheviot, The, *U.K.* 14 B5
Cheviot Hills, *U.K.* 14 B5
Cheviot Ra., *Australia* 94 D3
Chew Bahir, *Ethiopia* 81 G4
Chewelah, *U.S.A.* 108 B5
Chewore ⌓, *Zimbabwe* 87 F2
Cheyenne, *Okla., U.S.A.* 113 H5
Cheyenne, *Wyo., U.S.A.* 112 E2
Cheyenne →, *U.S.A.* 112 C4
Cheyenne Wells, *U.S.A.* 112 F3
Cheyne B., *Australia* 93 F2
Chhabra, *India* 68 G7
Chhaktala, *India* 68 H6
Chhapra, *India* 69 G11
Chhata, *India* 68 F7
Chhatarpur, *Jharkhand, India* 69 G11
Chhatarpur, *Mad. P., India* 69 G8
Chhattisgarh □, *India* 69 J10
Chhep, *Cambodia* 64 F5
Chhindwara, *Mad. P., India* 69 H8
Chhindwara, *Mad. P., India* 69 H8
Chhlong, *Cambodia* 65 F5
Chhota Tawa →, *India* 68 H7
Chhoti Kali Sindh →, *India* 68 G6
Chhuikhadan, *India* 69 J9
Chhuk, *Cambodia* 65 G5
Chi →, *Thailand* 64 E5
Chiai, *Taiwan* 59 F13
Chiali, *Taiwan* 59 F13
Chiamboni, *Somali Rep.* 84 E8
Chiamussu = Jiamusi, *China* 60 B8
Chianciano Terme, *Italy* 41 E8
Chiang Dao, *Thailand* 64 C2
Chiang Kham, *Thailand* 64 C3
Chiang Khan, *Thailand* 64 D3
Chiang Khong, *Thailand* 58 G3
Chiang Mai, *Thailand* 64 C2
Chiang Rai, *Thailand* 58 H2
Chiang Saen, *Thailand* 58 G3
Chianti, *Italy* 41 E8
Chiapa →, *Mexico* 119 D6
Chiapa de Corzo, *Mexico* 119 D6
Chiapas □, *Mexico* 119 D6
Chiaramonte Gulfi, *Italy* 43 E7
Chiaravalle, *Italy* 41 E10
Chiaravalle Centrale, *Italy* 43 D9
Chiari, *Italy* 40 C6
Chiatura, *Georgia* 35 J6
Chiautla, *Mexico* 119 D5
Chiávari, *Italy* 40 D6
Chiavenna, *Italy* 40 B6
Chiba, *Japan* 55 G10
Chiba □, *Japan* 55 G10
Chibabava, *Mozam.* 89 C5
Chibemba, *Cunene, Angola* 85 H2
Chibemba, *Huila, Angola* 88 B2
Chibi, *Zimbabwe* 89 C5
Chibia, *Angola* 85 H2
Chibougamau, *Canada* 104 C5
Chibougamau, L., *Canada* 104 C5
Chibuk, *Nigeria* 83 C7
Chibuto, *Mozam.* 89 C5
Chic-Chocs, Mts., *Canada* 105 C6
Chicacole = Srikakulam, *India* 67 K13
Chicago, *U.S.A.* 114 E2
Chicago Heights, *U.S.A.* 114 E2
Chichagof I., *U.S.A.* 100 C6
Chichén-Itzá, *Mexico* 119 C7
Chichén-Itzá, Ruinas, *Mexico* 119 C7
Chicheng, *China* 56 D8
Chichester, *U.K.* 15 G7
Chichester Ra., *Australia* 92 D2
Chichibu, *Japan* 55 F9
Chichibu-Tama △, *Japan* 55 G9
Ch'ich'ihaerh = Qiqihar, *China* 53 E13
Chicholi, *India* 68 H8
Chickasaw ⌓, *U.S.A.* 113 H6
Chickasha, *U.S.A.* 113 H6
Chiclana de la Frontera, *Spain* 37 J4
Chiclayo, *Peru* 124 E3
Chico, *U.S.A.* 110 F5
Chico →, *Chubut, Argentina* 128 E3
Chico →, *Santa Cruz, Argentina* 128 G3
Chicomo, *Mozam.* 89 C5
Chicomostoc, *Mexico* 118 C4
Chicontepec, *Mexico* 119 C5
Chicopee, *U.S.A.* 117 D12
Chicoutimi, *Canada* 105 C5
Chicualacuala, *Mozam.* 89 C5
Chidambaram, *India* 66 P11
Chidenguele, *Mozam.* 89 C5
Chidley, C., *Canada* 101 B13
Chiducuane, *Mozam.* 89 C5
Chiede, *Angola* 88 B2
Chiefs Pt., *Canada* 116 B3
Chiem Hoa, *Vietnam* 64 A5
Chiemsee, *Germany* 25 H8
Chiengi, *Zambia* 87 D2
Chiengmai = Chiang Mai, *Thailand* 64 C2
Chienti →, *Italy* 41 E10
Chieri, *Italy* 40 C4
Chiers →, *France* 19 C11
Chiesa in Valmalenco, *Italy* 40 B6
Chiese →, *Italy* 40 C7
Chieti, *Italy* 41 F11
Chifeng, *China* 57 C10
Chigirin, *Ukraine* 33 H7
Chignecto B., *Canada* 105 C7
Chiguana, *Bolivia* 126 A2
Chigwell, *U.K.* 15 F8
Chiha-ri, *N. Korea* 57 E14
Chihli, G. of = Bo Hai, *China* 57 E10
Chihuahua, *Mexico* 118 B3
Chihuahua □, *Mexico* 118 B3
Chiili = Shīeli, *Kazakhstan* 52 E7
Chik Bollapur, *India* 66 N10
Chikmagalur, *India* 66 N9
Chikwawa, *Malawi* 87 F3
Chilac, *Mexico* 119 D5
Chilam Chavki, *Pakistan* 69 B6
Chilanga, *Zambia* 87 F2
Chilapa, *Mexico* 119 D5
Chilas, *Pakistan* 69 B6
Chilaw, *Sri Lanka* 66 R11
Chilcotin →, *Canada* 102 C4
Childers, *Australia* 95 D5
Childress, *U.S.A.* 113 H4
Chile ■, *S. Amer.* 128 D2
Chile Rise, *Pac. Oc.* 97 L18
Chilecito, *Argentina* 126 B2
Chilete, *Peru* 124 E3
Chilia, Braţul →, *Romania* 29 E14
Chililabombwe, *Zambia* 87 E2
Chilin = Jilin, *China* 57 C14
Chilka L., *India* 67 K14
Chilko →, *Canada* 102 C4
Chilko L., *Canada* 102 C4
Chillagoe, *Australia* 94 B3
Chillán, *Chile* 126 D1
Chillicothe, *Ill., U.S.A.* 112 E10
Chillicothe, *Mo., U.S.A.* 112 F8
Chillicothe, *Ohio, U.S.A.* 114 F4
Chilliwack, *Canada* 102 D4
Chilo, *India* 68 F5
Chiloane, I., *Mozam.* 89 C5
Chiloé, I. de, *Chile* 128 E2
Chilpancingo, *Mexico* 119 D5
Chiltern Hills, *U.K.* 15 F7
Chilton, *U.S.A.* 114 C1
Chilubi, *Zambia* 87 E2
Chilubula, *Zambia* 87 E3
Chilumba, *Malawi* 87 E3
Chilung, *Taiwan* 59 E13
Chilwa, L., *Malawi* 87 F4
Chimaltitán, *Mexico* 118 C4
Chimán, *Panama* 120 E4
Chimanimani, *Zimbabwe* 89 B5
Chimanimani △, *Zimbabwe* 87 F3
Chimay, *Belgium* 17 D4
Chimayo, *U.S.A.* 109 H11
Chimbay, *Uzbekistan* 52 E6
Chimborazo, *Ecuador* 124 D3
Chimbote, *Peru* 124 E3
Chimkent = Shymkent, *Kazakhstan* 52 E7
Chimoio, *Mozam.* 87 F3
Chimpembe, *Zambia* 87 D2
Chin □, *Burma* 67 J18
Chin Ling Shan = Qinling Shandi, *China* 56 H5
China, *Mexico* 119 B5
China ■, *Asia* 60 D6
China Lake, *U.S.A.* 111 K9
Chinan = Jinan, *China* 56 F9
Chinandega, *Nic.* 120 D2
Chinati Peak, *U.S.A.* 113 L2
Chincha Alta, *Peru* 124 F3
Chinchaga →, *Canada* 102 B5
Chinchilla, *Australia* 95 D5
Chinchilla de Monte Aragón, *Spain* 39 G3
Chinchorro, Banco, *Mexico* 119 D7
Chinchou = Jinzhou, *China* 57 D11
Chincoteague, *U.S.A.* 114 G8
Chinde, *Mozam.* 87 F4
Chindo, *S. Korea* 57 G14
Chindwin →, *Burma* 67 J19
Chineni, *India* 69 C6
Chinga, *Mozam.* 87 F4
Chingola, *Zambia* 87 E2
Chingole, *Malawi* 87 E3
Ch'ingtao = Qingdao, *China* 57 F11
Chinguetti, *Mauritania* 78 D3
Chingune, *Mozam.* 89 C5
Chinhae, *S. Korea* 57 G15
Chinhanguanine, *Mozam.* 89 D5
Chinhoyi, *Zimbabwe* 87 F3
Chini, *India* 68 D8
Chiniot, *Pakistan* 68 D5
Chínipas, *Mexico* 118 B3
Chinji, *Pakistan* 68 C5
Chinju, *S. Korea* 57 G15
Chinle, *U.S.A.* 109 H9
Chinmen, *Taiwan* 59 E13
Chinmen Tao, *Taiwan* 59 E12
Chinnampo = Namp'o, *N. Korea* 57 E13
Chino, *Japan* 55 G9
Chino, *U.S.A.* 111 L9
Chino Valley, *U.S.A.* 109 J7
Chinon, *France* 18 E7
Chinook, *U.S.A.* 108 B9
Chinsali, *Zambia* 87 E3
Chióggia, *Italy* 41 C9
Chíos = Khíos, *Greece* 47 C8
Chipata, *Zambia* 87 E3
Chiperceni, *Moldova* 29 C13
Chipinge, *Zimbabwe* 87 G3
Chipinge ⌓, *Zimbabwe* 87 G3
Chipiona, *Spain* 37 J4
Chipley, *U.S.A.* 115 K3
Chipman, *Canada* 105 C6
Chipoka, *Malawi* 87 E3
Chippenham, *U.K.* 15 F5
Chippewa →, *U.S.A.* 112 C8
Chippewa Falls, *U.S.A.* 112 C9
Chipping Norton, *U.K.* 15 F6
Chiprovtsi, *Bulgaria* 44 C6
Chiputneticook Lakes, *U.S.A.* 115 C11
Chiquián, *Peru* 124 F3
Chiquibul △, *Belize* 120 C2
Chiquimula, *Guatemala* 120 D2
Chiquinquira, *Colombia* 124 B4
Chir →, *Russia* 35 F6
Chirala, *India* 66 M12
Chiramba, *Mozam.* 87 F3
Chirawa, *India* 68 E6
Chirchiq, *Uzbekistan* 52 E7
Chiredzi, *Zimbabwe* 89 C5
Chiricahua ⌓, *U.S.A.* 109 K9
Chiricahua Peak, *U.S.A.* 109 L9
Chiriquí, G. de, *Panama* 120 E3
Chiriquí, L. de, *Panama* 120 E3
Chirisa ⌓, *Zimbabwe* 87 F2
Chirivira Falls, *Zimbabwe* 87 G3
Chirmiri, *India* 67 H13
Chirnogi, *Romania* 29 F11
Chirpan, *Bulgaria* 45 D9
Chirripó Grande, Cerro, *Costa Rica* 120 E3
Chirundu, *Zimbabwe* 89 B4
Chisamba, *Zambia* 87 E2
Chisapani Garhi, *Nepal* 67 F14
Chisasibi, *Canada* 104 B4
Ch'ishan, *Taiwan* 59 F13
Chisholm, *Canada* 102 C6
Chisholm, *U.S.A.* 112 B8
Chishtian Mandi, *Pakistan* 68 E5
Chishui, *China* 58 C5
Chishui He →, *China* 58 C5
Chisimaio, *Somali Rep.* 77 G8
Chisimba Falls, *Zambia* 87 E3
Chişinău, *Moldova* 29 C13
Chişinău ✕ (KIV), *Moldova* 29 C13
Chişineu Criş, *Romania* 28 D6
Chisone →, *Italy* 40 D4
Chisos Mts., *U.S.A.* 113 L3
Chistopol, *Russia* 34 C10
Chita, *Russia* 53 D12
Chitipa, *Malawi* 87 D3
Chitose, *Japan* 54 C10
Chitral, *Pakistan* 66 B7
Chitré, *Panama* 120 E3
Chittagong, *Bangla.* 67 H17
Chittagong □, *Bangla.* 67 G17
Chittaurgarh, *India* 68 G6
Chittoor, *India* 66 N11
Chitungwiza, *Zimbabwe* 87 F3
Chiusi, *Italy* 41 E8
Chiva, *Spain* 39 F4
Chivasso, *Italy* 40 C4
Chivhu, *Zimbabwe* 87 F3
Chivilcoy, *Argentina* 126 C4
Chiwanda, *Tanzania* 87 E3
Chixi, *China* 59 G9
Chizarira, *Zimbabwe* 87 F2
Chizarira △, *Zimbabwe* 87 F2
Chizera, *Zambia* 87 E2
Chkalov = Orenburg, *Russia* 52 D6
Chkolovsk, *Russia* 34 B6
Chloride, *U.S.A.* 111 K12
Chlumec nad Cidlinou, *Czech Rep.* 26 A8
Chmielnik, *Poland* 31 H7
Cho Bo, *Vietnam* 58 G5
Cho-do, *N. Korea* 57 E13
Cho Phuoc Hai, *Vietnam* 65 G6
Choa Chu Kang, *Singapore* 65 d
Choba, *Kenya* 86 B4
Chobe △, *Botswana* 88 B4
Choch'iwŏn, *S. Korea* 57 F14
Chocianów, *Poland* 31 G2
Chociwel, *Poland* 30 E2
Chocolate Mts., *U.S.A.* 111 M11
Choctawhatchee →, *U.S.A.* 115 K3
Chodecz, *Poland* 31 F6
Chodov, *Czech Rep.* 26 A5
Chodziez, *Poland* 31 F3
Choele Choel, *Argentina* 128 D3
Choiseul, *St. Lucia* 121 f
Choix, *Mexico* 118 B3
Chojna, *Poland* 31 F1
Chojnice, *Poland* 30 E4
Chojnów, *Poland* 31 G2
Chōkai-San, *Japan* 54 E10
Choke Canyon L., *U.S.A.* 113 L5
Choke Mts., *Ethiopia* 81 E4
Chokurdakh, *Russia* 53 B15
Cholame, *U.S.A.* 110 K6
Cholet, *France* 18 E6
Cholguan, *Chile* 126 D1
Choluteca, *Honduras* 120 D2
Choluteca →, *Honduras* 120 D2
Chom Bung, *Thailand* 64 F2
Chom Thong, *Thailand* 64 C2
Choma, *Zambia* 87 F2
Chomolungma = Everest, Mt., *Nepal* 69 E12
Chomun, *India* 68 F6
Chomutov, *Czech Rep.* 26 A6
Chon Buri, *Thailand* 64 F3
Chon Thanh, *Vietnam* 65 G6
Ch'onan, *S. Korea* 57 F14
Chone, *Ecuador* 124 D3
Chong Kai, *Cambodia* 64 F4
Chong Mek, *Thailand* 64 E5
Chong Phangan, *Thailand* 65 b
Chong Samui, *Thailand* 65 b
Chongde, *China* 59 B13
Chŏngdo, *S. Korea* 57 G15
Chŏngha, *S. Korea* 57 F15
Chŏngjin, *N. Korea* 57 D15
Chŏngjiu, *S. Korea* 57 F14
Chŏngju, *N. Korea* 57 E13
Chongli, *China* 56 D8
Chongming, *China* 59 B13
Chongming Dao, *China* 59 B13
Chongqing, *Chongqing, China* 58 C6
Chongqing, *Sichuan, China* 58 B4
Chongqing Shi □, *China* 58 C6
Chongren, *China* 59 D11
Chonguene, *Mozam.* 89 C5
Chŏngŭp, *S. Korea* 57 G14
Chongyi, *China* 59 E10
Chongzuo, *China* 58 F6
Chŏnju, *S. Korea* 57 G14
Chonos, Arch. de los, *Chile* 128 F2
Chop, *Ukraine* 33 H2
Chopim →, *Brazil* 127 B5
Chor, *Pakistan* 68 G3
Chorbat La, *India* 69 B7
Chorley, *U.K.* 14 D5
Chornobyl, *Ukraine* 33 G6
Chornomorske, *Ukraine* 33 K7
Chorolque, Cerro, *Bolivia* 126 A2
Choroszcz, *Poland* 31 E9
Chorregon, *Australia* 94 C3
Chorro el Indio △, *Venezuela* 121 E5
Chortkiv, *Ukraine* 33 H3
Ch'ŏrwon, *S. Korea* 57 E14
Chorzele, *Poland* 31 E7
Chorzów, *Poland* 31 H5
Chos-Malal, *Argentina* 126 D1
Ch'osan, *N. Korea* 57 D13
Choszczno, *Poland* 31 E2
Choteau, *U.S.A.* 108 C7
Chotěboř, *Czech Rep.* 26 B8
Chotila, *India* 68 H4
Chotta Udepur, *India* 68 H6
Chowchilla, *U.S.A.* 110 H6
Choybalsan, *Mongolia* 60 B6
Christchurch, *N.Z.* 91 K4
Christchurch, *U.K.* 15 G6
Christian I., *Canada* 116 B4
Christiana, *S. Africa* 88 D4
Christiansfeld, *Denmark* 11 J3
Christiansted, *U.S. Virgin Is.* 121 C7
Christie B., *Canada* 103 A6
Christina →, *Canada* 103 B6
Christmas Cr. →, *Australia* 92 C4
Christmas I. = Kiritimati, *Kiribati* 97 G12
Christmas I., *Ind. Oc.* 96 J2
Christopher L., *Australia* 93 D4
Chrudim, *Czech Rep.* 26 B8
Chrzanów, *Poland* 31 H6
Chtimba, *Malawi* 87 E3
Chu = Shū, *Kazakhstan* 52 E8
Chu →, *Vietnam* 64 C5
Chu Lai, *Vietnam* 64 E7
Chuak, Ko, *Thailand* 65 b
Ch'uanchou = Quanzhou, *China* 59 E12
Chuankou, *China* 56 G6
Chubbuck, *U.S.A.* 108 E7
Chūbu □, *Japan* 55 F8
Chubu-Sangaku △, *Japan* 55 F8
Chubut →, *Argentina* 128 E3
Chuchi L., *Canada* 102 B4
Chuda, *India* 68 H4
Chudovo, *Russia* 32 C6
Chudskoye, Ozero, *Russia* 9 G22
Chūgoku □, *Japan* 55 G6
Chūgoku-Sanchi, *Japan* 55 G6
Chuguyev = Chuhuyiv, *Ukraine* 33 H9
Chugwater, *U.S.A.* 112 E2
Chuhuyiv, *Ukraine* 33 H9
Chukchi Sea, *Russia* 53 C19
Chukotskoye Nagorye, *Russia* 53 C18
Chula Vista, *U.S.A.* 111 N9
Chulucanas, *Peru* 124 E2
Chulym →, *Russia* 52 D9
Chum Phae, *Thailand* 64 D4
Chum Saeng, *Thailand* 64 E3
Chumar, *India* 69 C8
Chumbicha, *Argentina* 126 B2
Chumerna, *Bulgaria* 45 D9
Chumikan, *Russia* 53 D14
Chumphon, *Thailand* 65 G2
Chumuare, *Mozam.* 87 E3
Chumunjin, *S. Korea* 57 F15
Chuna →, *Russia* 53 D10
Chun'an, *China* 59 C12
Ch'unch'ŏn, *S. Korea* 57 F14
Chunchura, *India* 69 H13
Chunga, *Zambia* 87 F2
Chunggang-ŭp, *N. Korea* 57 D14
Chunghwa, *N. Korea* 57 E13
Ch'ungju, *S. Korea* 57 F14
Chungking = Chongqing, *China* 58 C6
Chungli, *Taiwan* 59 E13
Ch'ungmu, *S. Korea* 57 G15
Chungt'iaoshan = Zhongtiao Shan, *China* 56 G6
Chungyang Shanmo, *Taiwan* 59 F13
Chunian, *Pakistan* 68 D6
Chunya, *Tanzania* 87 D3
Chunyang, *China* 57 C15
Chupara Pt., *Trin. & Tob.* 125 K15
Chuquibamba, *Peru* 124 G4
Chuquicamata, *Chile* 126 A2
Chur, *Switz.* 25 J5
Churachandpur, *India* 67 G18
Church Stretton, *U.K.* 15 E5
Churchill, *Canada* 103 B10
Churchill →, *Man., Canada* 103 B10
Churchill →, *Nfld., Canada* 105 B7
Churchill, C., *Canada* 103 B10
Churchill Falls, *Canada* 105 B7
Churchill L., *Canada* 103 B7
Churchill Pk., *Canada* 102 B3
Churki, *India* 69 H10
Churu, *India* 68 E6
Churún Merú = Angel Falls, *Venezuela* 124 B6
Chushal, *India* 69 C8
Chuska Mts., *U.S.A.* 109 H9
Chusovoy, *Russia* 52 D6
Chute-aux-Outardes, *Canada* 105 C6
Chuuronjang, *N. Korea* 57 D15
Chuvash Republic = Chuvashia □, *Russia* 34 C8
Chuvashia □, *Russia* 34 C8
Chuwārtah, *Iraq* 70 C5
Chuxiong, *China* 58 E3
Chūy = Shū →, *Kazakhstan* 50 E10
Chuy, *Uruguay* 127 C5
Chuzhou, *China* 59 A12
Ci Xian, *China* 56 F8
Ciacova, *Romania* 28 E6
Ciadâr-Lunga, *Moldova* 29 D13
Ciamis, *Indonesia* 63 G13
Cianjur, *Indonesia* 63 G12
Cianorte, *Brazil* 127 A5
Cibola, *U.S.A.* 111 M12
Cicero, *U.S.A.* 114 E2
Cidacos →, *Spain* 38 C3
Cide, *Turkey* 72 B5
Ciéagas del Cataumbo △, *Venezuela* 121 E5
Ciechanów, *Poland* 31 F7
Ciechanowiec, *Poland* 31 F9
Ciechocinek, *Poland* 31 F5
Ciego de Avila, *Cuba* 120 B4
Ciénaga, *Colombia* 124 A4
Cienfuegos, *Cuba* 120 B3
Cierp, *France* 20 F4
Cíes, Is., *Spain* 36 C2
Cieszanów, *Poland* 31 H10
Cieszyn, *Poland* 31 J5
Cieza, *Spain* 39 G3
Çifteler, *Turkey* 72 C4
Cifuentes, *Spain* 38 E2
Cihanbeyli, *Turkey* 72 C5
Cihuatlán, *Mexico* 118 D4
Cijara ⌓, *Spain* 37 F6
Cijara, Embalse de, *Spain* 37 F6
Cijulang, *Indonesia* 63 G13
Cilacap, *Indonesia* 63 G13
Çıldır, *Turkey* 73 B10
Çıldır Gölü, *Turkey* 73 B10
Cilento e Vallo di Diano △, *Italy* 43 B8
Cili, *China* 59 C8
Cilibia, *Romania* 29 E12
Cilicia, *Turkey* 72 D5
Cill Chainnigh = Kilkenny, *Ireland* 12 D4
Cilo Dağı, *Turkey* 73 D10
Cima, *U.S.A.* 111 K11
Cimarron, *Kans., U.S.A.* 113 G4
Cimarron, *N. Mex., U.S.A.* 113 G2
Cimarron →, *U.S.A.* 113 G6
Cimişlia, *Moldova* 29 D13
Cimone, Mte., *Italy* 40 D7
Çinar, *Turkey* 73 D9
Çınarcık, *Turkey* 45 F13
Cinca →, *Spain* 38 D5
Cincar, *Bos.-H.* 28 G2
Cincinnati, *U.S.A.* 114 F3
Cincinnatus, *U.S.A.* 117 D9
Çine, *Turkey* 47 D10
Ciney, *Belgium* 17 D5
Cíngoli, *Italy* 41 E10
Cinigiano, *Italy* 41 F8
Cinto, Mte., *France* 21 F12
Cintruénigo, *Spain* 38 C3
Ciocile, *Romania* 29 F12
Ciolăneşti din Deal, *Romania* 29 F10
Ciorani, *Romania* 29 F11
Čiovo, *Croatia* 41 E13
Circeo, Mte., *Italy* 42 A6
Çirçir, *Turkey* 72 C7
Circle, *Alaska, U.S.A.* 100 B5
Circle, *Mont., U.S.A.* 112 B2
Circleville, *U.S.A.* 114 F4
Cirebon, *Indonesia* 63 G13
Ciremay, *Indonesia* 63 G13

Cirencester, *U.K.* 15 F6
Cireşu, *Romania* 28 F7
Cirey-sur-Vezouze, *France* 19 D13
Ciriè, *Italy* 40 C4
Cirium, *Cyprus* 49 E11
Cirò, *Italy* 43 C10
Cirò Marina, *Italy* 43 C10
Ciron →, *France* 20 D3
Cisco, *U.S.A.* 113 J5
Cislău, *Romania* 29 E11
Cisna, *Poland* 31 J9
Cisnădie, *Romania* 29 E9
Cisterna di Latina, *Italy* 42 A5
Cisternino, *Italy* 43 B10
Cistierna, *Spain* 36 C5
Citeli-Ckaro = Tsiteli-Tsqaro, *Georgia* 35 K8
Citlaltépetl = Orizaba, Pico de, *Mexico* 119 D5
Citrus Heights, *U.S.A.* 110 G5
Citrusdal, *S. Africa* 88 E2
Città della Pieve, *Italy* 41 F9
Città di Castello, *Italy* 41 E9
Città Sant' Angelo, *Italy* 41 F11
Cittadella, *Italy* 41 C8
Cittaducale, *Italy* 41 F9
Cittanova, *Italy* 43 D9
Ciuc, Munţii, *Romania* 29 D11
Ciucaş, Vf., *Romania* 29 E10
Ciucea, *Romania* 28 D7
Ciuciulea, *Moldova* 29 C12
Ciuciuleni, *Moldova* 29 C13
Ciudad Altamirano, *Mexico* 118 D4
Ciudad Bolívar, *Venezuela* 124 B6
Ciudad Camargo, *Mexico* 118 B3
Ciudad de Valles, *Mexico* 119 C5
Ciudad del Carmen, *Mexico* 119 D6
Ciudad del Este, *Paraguay* 127 B5
Ciudad Delicias = Delicias, *Mexico* 118 B3
Ciudad Guayana, *Venezuela* 124 B6
Ciudad Guerrero, *Mexico* 118 B3
Ciudad Guzmán, *Mexico* 118 D4
Ciudad Juárez, *Mexico* 118 A3
Ciudad Madero, *Mexico* 119 C5
Ciudad Mante, *Mexico* 119 C5
Ciudad Obregón, *Mexico* 118 B3
Ciudad Real, *Spain* 37 G7
Ciudad Real □, *Spain* 37 G7
Ciudad Rodrigo, *Spain* 36 E4
Ciudad Trujillo = Santo Domingo, *Dom. Rep.* 121 C6
Ciudad Victoria, *Mexico* 119 C5
Ciudadela, *Spain* 48 B10
Ciulniţa, *Romania* 29 F12
Ciumeghiu, *Romania* 28 D6
Ciuperceni, *Romania* 28 F8
Civa Burnu, *Turkey* 72 B7
Cividale del Friuli, *Italy* 41 B10
Civita Castellana, *Italy* 41 F9
Civitanova Marche, *Italy* 41 E10
Civitavécchia, *Italy* 41 F8
Civray, *France* 20 B4
Çivril, *Turkey* 47 C11
Cixerri →, *Italy* 42 C1
Cixi, *China* 59 B13
Cizre, *Turkey* 70 B4
Cizur Mayor, *Spain* 38 C3
Clackmannanshire □, *U.K.* 13 E5
Clacton-on-Sea, *U.K.* 15 F9
Clain →, *France* 18 F7
Claire, L., *Canada* 102 B6
Clairton, *U.S.A.* 116 F5
Clairvaux-les-Lacs, *France* 19 F12
Claise →, *France* 20 B5
Clallam Bay, *U.S.A.* 110 B2
Clamecy, *France* 19 E10
Clanton, *U.S.A.* 115 J2
Clanwilliam, *S. Africa* 88 E2
Clara, *Ireland* 12 C4
Claraville, *U.S.A.* 111 K8
Clare, *Australia* 95 E2
Clare, *U.S.A.* 114 D3
Clare □, *Ireland* 12 D3
Clare →, *Ireland* 12 C2
Clare I., *Ireland* 12 C1
Claremont, *Calif., U.S.A.* 111 L9
Claremont, *N.H., U.S.A.* 117 C12
Claremont Pt., *Australia* 94 A3
Claremore, *U.S.A.* 113 G7
Claremorris, *Ireland* 12 C3
Clarence →, *Australia* 95 D5
Clarence →, *N.Z.* 91 K4
Clarence, I., *Chile* 128 G2
Clarence I., *Antarctica* 5 C18
Clarence Str., *Australia* 92 B5
Clarence Town, *Bahamas* 121 B5
Clarendon, *Pa., U.S.A.* 116 E5
Clarendon, *Tex., U.S.A.* 113 H4
Clarenville-Shoal Harbour, *Canada* 105 C9
Claresholm, *Canada* 102 D6
Clarie Coast, *Antarctica* 5 C9
Clarinda, *U.S.A.* 112 E7
Clarington, *Canada* 116 C6
Clarion, *Iowa, U.S.A.* 112 D8
Clarion, *Pa., U.S.A.* 116 E5
Clarion →, *U.S.A.* 116 E5
Clark, *U.S.A.* 112 C6
Clark, Pt., *Canada* 116 B3
Clark Fork, *U.S.A.* 108 B5
Clark Fork →, *U.S.A.* 108 B5
Clarkdale, *U.S.A.* 109 J7
Clarke City, *Canada* 105 B6
Clarke I., *Australia* 95 G4
Clarke Ra., *Australia* 94 J6
Clark's Fork →, *U.S.A.* 108 D9
Clark's Harbour, *Canada* 105 D6
Clarks Hill L., *U.S.A.* 115 J4
Clarks Summit, *U.S.A.* 117 E9
Clarksburg, *U.S.A.* 114 F5
Clarksdale, *U.S.A.* 113 H9
Clarksville, *Ark., U.S.A.* 113 H8
Clarksville, *Tenn., U.S.A.* 115 G2
Clarksville, *Tex., U.S.A.* 113 J7
Clatskanie, *U.S.A.* 110 D3
Claude, *U.S.A.* 113 H4
Claveria, *Phil.* 61 B4
Clay, *U.S.A.* 110 G5
Clay Center, *U.S.A.* 112 F6
Claypool, *U.S.A.* 109 K8
Claysburg, *U.S.A.* 116 F6
Claysville, *U.S.A.* 116 F4
Clayton, *N. Mex., U.S.A.* 113 G3
Clayton, *N.Y., U.S.A.* 117 B8
Clear, C., *Ireland* 12 E2
Clear, L., *Canada* 116 A7
Clear Hills, *Canada* 102 B5
Clear I., *Ireland* 12 E2
Clear L., *U.S.A.* 110 F4
Clear Lake, *Iowa, U.S.A.* 112 D8
Clear Lake, *S. Dak., U.S.A.* 112 C6
Clear Lake Reservoir, *U.S.A.* 108 F3
Clearfield, *Pa., U.S.A.* 116 E6
Clearfield, *Utah, U.S.A.* 108 F8
Clearlake, *U.S.A.* 108 G2
Clearlake Highlands, *U.S.A.* 110 G4
Clearwater, *Canada* 102 C4
Clearwater, *U.S.A.* 115 M4
Clearwater →, *Alta., Canada* 102 C6
Clearwater →, *Alta., Canada* 103 B6
Clearwater L., *Canada* 103 C9
Clearwater Lake ⌂, *Canada* 103 C8
Clearwater Mts., *U.S.A.* 108 C6
Clearwater River ⌂, *Canada* 103 B7
Cleburne, *U.S.A.* 113 J6
Clee Hills, *U.K.* 15 E5
Cleethorpes, *U.K.* 14 D7
Cleeve Cloud, *U.K.* 15 F6
Clelles, *France* 21 D9
Clemson, *U.S.A.* 115 H4
Clerke Reef, *Australia* 92 C2
Clermont, *Australia* 94 C4
Clermont, *France* 19 C9
Clermont, *U.S.A.* 115 L5
Clermont-en-Argonne, *France* 19 C12
Clermont-Ferrand, *France* 20 C7
Clermont-l'Hérault, *France* 20 E7
Clerval, *France* 19 E13
Clervaux, *Lux.* 17 D6
Cles, *Italy* 40 B8
Clevedon, *U.K.* 15 F5
Cleveland, *Miss., U.S.A.* 113 J9
Cleveland, *Ohio, U.S.A.* 116 E3
Cleveland, *Okla., U.S.A.* 113 G6
Cleveland, *Tenn., U.S.A.* 115 H3
Cleveland, *Tex., U.S.A.* 113 K7
Cleveland, C., *Australia* 94 B4
Cleveland, Mt., *U.S.A.* 108 B7
Cleveland Heights, *U.S.A.* 116 E3
Clevelândia, *Brazil* 127 B5
Clew B., *Ireland* 12 C2
Clewiston, *U.S.A.* 115 M5
Clifden, *Ireland* 12 C1
Clifden, *N.Z.* 91 M1
Cliffdell, *U.S.A.* 110 D5
Cliffy Hd., *Australia* 93 G2
Clifton, *Australia* 95 D5
Clifton, *Ariz., U.S.A.* 109 K9
Clifton, *Colo., U.S.A.* 109 G9
Clifton, *Tex., U.S.A.* 113 K6
Clifton Beach, *Australia* 94 B4
Climax, *Canada* 103 D7
Clinch →, *U.S.A.* 115 H3
Clingmans Dome, *U.S.A.* 115 H4
Clint, *U.S.A.* 109 L10
Clinton, *B.C., Canada* 102 C4
Clinton, *Ont., Canada* 116 C3
Clinton, *N.Z.* 91 M2
Clinton, *Ark., U.S.A.* 113 H8
Clinton, *Conn., U.S.A.* 117 E12
Clinton, *Ill., U.S.A.* 112 E10
Clinton, *Ind., U.S.A.* 114 F2
Clinton, *Iowa, U.S.A.* 112 E9
Clinton, *Mass., U.S.A.* 117 D13
Clinton, *Miss., U.S.A.* 113 J9
Clinton, *Mo., U.S.A.* 112 F8
Clinton, *N.C., U.S.A.* 115 H6
Clinton, *Okla., U.S.A.* 113 H5
Clinton, *S.C., U.S.A.* 115 H5
Clinton, *Tenn., U.S.A.* 115 G3
Clinton, *Wash., U.S.A.* 110 C4
Clinton C., *Australia* 94 C5
Clinton Colden L., *Canada* 100 B9
Clintonville, *U.S.A.* 112 C10
Clipperton, I., *Pac. Oc.* 97 F17
Clisham, *U.K.* 13 D2
Clisson, *France* 18 E5
Clitheroe, *U.K.* 14 D5
Clo-oose, *Canada* 110 B2
Cloates, Pt., *Australia* 92 D1
Clocolan, *S. Africa* 89 D4
Clodomira, *Argentina* 126 B3
Clogher Hd., *Ireland* 12 C5
Clonakilty, *Ireland* 12 E3
Clonakilty B., *Ireland* 12 E3
Cloncurry, *Australia* 94 C3
Cloncurry →, *Australia* 94 B3
Clondalkin, *Ireland* 12 C5
Clones, *Ireland* 12 B4
Clonmel, *Ireland* 12 D4
Cloppenburg, *Germany* 24 C4
Cloquet, *U.S.A.* 112 B8
Clorinda, *Argentina* 126 B4
Cloud Bay, *Canada* 104 C2
Cloud Peak, *U.S.A.* 108 D10
Cloudcroft, *U.S.A.* 109 K11
Cloverdale, *U.S.A.* 110 G4
Clovis, *Calif., U.S.A.* 110 J7
Clovis, *N. Mex., U.S.A.* 113 H3
Cloyes-sur-le-Loir, *France* 18 E8
Cloyne, *Canada* 116 B7
Cluj □, *Romania* 29 D8
Cluj-Napoca, *Romania* 29 D8
Clunes, *Australia* 95 F3
Cluny, *France* 19 F11
Cluses, *France* 19 F13
Clusone, *Italy* 40 C6
Clutha →, *N.Z.* 91 M2
Clwyd →, *U.K.* 14 D4
Clyde, *Canada* 102 C6
Clyde, *N.Z.* 91 L2
Clyde, *U.S.A.* 116 C8
Clyde →, *U.K.* 13 F4
Clyde, Firth of, *U.K.* 13 F3
Clyde Muirshiel ⌂, *U.K.* 13 F4
Clyde River, *Canada* 101 A13
Clydebank, *U.K.* 13 F4
Clymer, *N.Y., U.S.A.* 116 D5
Clymer, *Pa., U.S.A.* 116 D5
Ćmielów, *Poland* 31 H8
Côa →, *Portugal* 36 D3
Coachella, *U.S.A.* 111 M10
Coachella Canal, *U.S.A.* 111 N12
Coahoma, *U.S.A.* 113 J4
Coahuayana →, *Mexico* 118 D4
Coahuila □, *Mexico* 118 B4
Coal →, *Canada* 102 B3
Coalane, *Mozam.* 87 F4
Coalcomán, *Mexico* 118 D4
Coaldale, *Canada* 102 D6
Coalgate, *U.S.A.* 113 H6
Coalinga, *U.S.A.* 110 J6
Coalisland, *U.K.* 12 B5
Coalville, *U.K.* 14 E6
Coalville, *U.S.A.* 108 F8
Coamo, *Puerto Rico* 121 d
Coari, *Brazil* 124 D6
Coast □, *Kenya* 86 C4
Coast Mts., *Canada* 102 C3
Coast Ranges, *U.S.A.* 110 G4
Coatbridge, *U.K.* 13 F4
Coatepec, *Mexico* 119 D5
Coatepeque, *Guatemala* 120 D1
Coatesville, *U.S.A.* 114 F8
Coaticook, *Canada* 117 A13
Coats I., *Canada* 101 B11
Coats Land, *Antarctica* 5 D1
Coatzacoalcos, *Mexico* 119 D6
Coba, *Mexico* 119 C7
Cobadin, *Romania* 29 F13
Cobalt, *Canada* 104 C4
Cobán, *Guatemala* 120 C1
Çobanlar, *Turkey* 47 C12
Cobar, *Australia* 95 E4
Cóbh, *Ireland* 12 E3
Cobija, *Bolivia* 124 F5
Cobleskill, *U.S.A.* 117 D10
Coboconk, *Canada* 116 B6
Cobourg, *Canada* 116 C6
Cobourg ⌂, *Australia* 92 B5
Cobourg Pen., *Australia* 92 B5
Cobram, *Australia* 95 F4
Cóbué, *Mozam.* 87 E3
Coburg, *Germany* 25 E6
Coca, *Spain* 36 D6
Cocanada = Kakinada, *India* 67 L13
Cocentaina, *Spain* 39 G4
Cochabamba, *Bolivia* 124 G5
Cochem, *Germany* 25 E3
Cochemane, *Mozam.* 87 F3
Cochin, *India* 66 Q10
Cochin China = Nam-Phan, *Vietnam* 65 G6
Cochran, *U.S.A.* 115 J4
Cochrane, *Alta., Canada* 102 C6
Cochrane, *Ont., Canada* 104 C3
Cochrane, *Chile* 128 F2
Cochrane →, *Canada* 103 B8
Cochrane, L., *Chile* 128 F2
Cochranton, *U.S.A.* 116 E4
Cockburn, *Australia* 95 E3
Cockburn, Canal, *Chile* 128 G2
Cockburn I., *Canada* 104 C3
Cockburn Ra., *Australia* 92 C4
Cockermouth, *U.K.* 14 C4
Cocklebiddy, *Australia* 93 F4
Cockpit Country, The, *Jamaica* 120 a
Coco →, *Cent. Amer.* 120 D3
Coco, I. del, *Pac. Oc.* 97 G19
Cocoa, *U.S.A.* 115 L5
Cocobeach, *Gabon* 84 D1
Cocora, *Romania* 29 F12
Cocos B., *Trin. & Tob.* 125 K15
Cocos Is., *Ind. Oc.* 96 J1
Cod, C., *U.S.A.* 114 D10
Codajás, *Brazil* 124 D6
Codigoro, *Italy* 41 D9
Codlea, *Romania* 29 E10
Codó, *Brazil* 125 D10
Codogno, *Italy* 40 C6
Codróipo, *Italy* 41 C10
Codru, Munţii, *Romania* 28 D7
Cody, *U.S.A.* 108 D9
Coe Hill, *Canada* 116 B7
Coelemu, *Chile* 126 D1
Coen, *Australia* 94 A3
Coesfeld, *Germany* 24 D3
Cœur d'Alene, *U.S.A.* 108 C5
Cœur d'Alene L., *U.S.A.* 108 C5
Coevorden, *Neths.* 17 B6
Cofete, *Canary Is.* 48 F5
Coffeyville, *U.S.A.* 113 G7
Coffin B., *Australia* 95 E2
Coffin Bay, *Australia* 95 E2
Coffin Bay △, *Australia* 95 E2
Coffin Bay Peninsula, *Australia* 95 E2
Coffs Harbour, *Australia* 95 E5
Cofre de Perote △, *Mexico* 119 D5
Cofrentes, *Spain* 39 F3
Cogalnic →, *Moldova* 29 E14
Cogealac, *Romania* 29 F13
Coghinas →, *Italy* 42 B1
Coghinas, L. del, *Italy* 42 B2
Cognac, *France* 20 C3
Cogne, *Italy* 40 C4
Cogolin, *France* 21 E10
Cogolludo, *Spain* 38 E1
Cohocton, *U.S.A.* 116 D7
Cohocton →, *U.S.A.* 116 D7
Cohoes, *U.S.A.* 117 D11
Cohuna, *Australia* 95 F3
Coiba, I., *Panama* 120 E3
Coig →, *Argentina* 128 G3
Coigeach, Rubha, *U.K.* 13 C3
Coihaique, *Chile* 128 F2
Coimbatore, *India* 66 P10
Coimbra, *Brazil* 124 G7
Coimbra, *Portugal* 36 E2
Coimbra □, *Portugal* 36 E2
Coín, *Spain* 37 J6
Coipasa, Salar de, *Bolivia* 124 G5
Cojimies, *Ecuador* 124 C3
Cojocna, *Romania* 29 D8
Cojutepequé, *El Salv.* 120 D2
Čoka, *Serbia & M.* 28 E5
Cokeville, *U.S.A.* 108 E8
Colac, *Australia* 95 F3
Colatina, *Brazil* 125 G10
Colbeck, C., *Antarctica* 5 D13
Colborne, *Canada* 116 C7
Colby, *U.S.A.* 112 F4
Colchester, *U.K.* 15 F8
Cold L., *Canada* 103 C7
Coldstream, *Canada* 102 C5
Coldstream, *U.K.* 13 F6
Coldwater, *Canada* 116 B5
Coldwater, *Kans., U.S.A.* 113 G5
Coldwater, *Mich., U.S.A.* 114 E3
Colebrook, *U.S.A.* 117 B13
Coleman, *U.S.A.* 113 K5
Coleman →, *Australia* 94 B3
Colenso, *S. Africa* 89 D4
Coleraine, *Australia* 95 F3
Coleraine, *U.K.* 12 A5
Coleridge, L., *N.Z.* 91 K3
Colesberg, *S. Africa* 88 E4
Coleville, *U.S.A.* 110 G7
Colfax, *Calif., U.S.A.* 110 F6
Colfax, *La., U.S.A.* 113 K8
Colfax, *Wash., U.S.A.* 108 C5
Colhué Huapi, L., *Argentina* 128 F3
Colibaşi, *Moldova* 29 E13
Colibaşi, *Romania* 29 F9
Cólico, *Italy* 40 B6
Coligny, *France* 19 F12
Coligny, *S. Africa* 89 D4
Colima, *Mexico* 118 D4
Colima □, *Mexico* 118 D4
Colima, Nevado de, *Mexico* 118 D4
Colina, *Chile* 126 C1
Colina do Norte, *Guinea-Biss.* 82 C2
Colinas, *Brazil* 125 E10
Colindres, *Spain* 36 B7
Coll, *U.K.* 13 E2
Collaguasi, *Chile* 126 A2
Collarada, Peña, *Spain* 38 C4
Collarenebri, *Australia* 95 D4
Colle di Val d'Elsa, *Italy* 40 E8
Collécchio, *Italy* 40 D7
Colleen Bawn, *Zimbabwe* 87 G2
College Park, *U.S.A.* 115 J3
College Station, *U.S.A.* 113 K6
Collesalvetti, *Italy* 40 E7
Colli Euganei ⌂, *Italy* 41 C8
Collie, *Australia* 93 F2
Collier B., *Australia* 92 C3
Collier Ra., *Australia* 93 D2
Collier Range △, *Australia* 93 D2
Collina, Passo di, *Italy* 40 D7
Collingwood, *Canada* 116 B4
Collingwood, *N.Z.* 91 J4
Collins, *Canada* 104 B2
Collinsville, *Australia* 94 C4
Collipulli, *Chile* 126 D1
Collooney, *Ireland* 12 B3
Colmar, *France* 19 D14
Colmars, *France* 21 D10
Colmenar, *Spain* 37 J6
Colmenar de Oreja, *Spain* 36 E7
Colmenar Viejo, *Spain* 36 E7
Colo →, *Australia* 95 E5
Cologne = Köln, *Germany* 24 E2
Colom, I. d'en, *Spain* 48 B11
Coloma, *U.S.A.* 110 G6
Colomb-Béchar = Béchar, *Algeria* 78 B5
Colombey-les-Belles, *France* 19 D12
Colombey-les-Deux-Églises, *France* 19 D11
Colombia ■, *S. Amer.* 124 C4
Colombian Basin, *S. Amer.* 98 H12
Colombo, *Sri Lanka* 66 R11
Colomiers, *France* 20 E5
Colón, *Buenos Aires, Argentina* 126 C3
Colón, *Entre Ríos, Argentina* 126 C4
Colón, *Cuba* 120 B3
Colón, *Panama* 120 E4
Colón, Arch. de, *Ecuador* 97 H18
Colònia de Sant Jordi, *Spain* 48 B9
Colonia del Sacramento, *Uruguay* 126 C4
Colonia Dora, *Argentina* 126 B3
Colonial Beach, *U.S.A.* 114 F7
Colonie, *U.S.A.* 117 D11
Colonna, C., *Italy* 43 C10
Colonsay, *Canada* 103 C7
Colonsay, *U.K.* 13 E2
Colorado □, *U.S.A.* 109 G10
Colorado →, *Argentina* 128 D4
Colorado →, *N. Amer.* 109 L6
Colorado →, *U.S.A.* 113 L7
Colorado City, *U.S.A.* 113 J4
Colorado Plateau, *U.S.A.* 109 H8
Colorado River Aqueduct, *U.S.A.* 111 L12
Colorado Springs, *U.S.A.* 112 F2
Colorno, *Italy* 40 D7
Colotlán, *Mexico* 118 C4
Colstrip, *U.S.A.* 108 D10
Colton, *U.S.A.* 117 B10
Columbia, *Ky., U.S.A.* 114 G3
Columbia, *La., U.S.A.* 113 J8
Columbia, *Miss., U.S.A.* 113 K10
Columbia, *Mo., U.S.A.* 112 F8
Columbia, *Pa., U.S.A.* 117 F8
Columbia, *S.C., U.S.A.* 115 J5
Columbia, *Tenn., U.S.A.* 115 H2
Columbia →, *N. Amer.* 110 D2
Columbia, C., *Canada* 4 A4
Columbia, District of □, *U.S.A.* 114 F7
Columbia, Mt., *Canada* 102 C5
Columbia Basin, *U.S.A.* 108 C4
Columbia Falls, *U.S.A.* 108 B6
Columbia Mts., *Canada* 102 C5
Columbia Plateau, *U.S.A.* 108 D5
Columbiana, *U.S.A.* 116 F4
Columbretes, Is., *Spain* 38 F5
Columbus, *Ga., U.S.A.* 115 J3
Columbus, *Ind., U.S.A.* 114 F3
Columbus, *Kans., U.S.A.* 113 G7
Columbus, *Miss., U.S.A.* 115 J1
Columbus, *Mont., U.S.A.* 108 D9
Columbus, *N. Mex., U.S.A.* 109 L10
Columbus, *Nebr., U.S.A.* 112 E6
Columbus, *Ohio, U.S.A.* 114 F4
Columbus, *Tex., U.S.A.* 113 L6
Colunga, *Spain* 36 B5
Colusa, *U.S.A.* 110 F4
Colville, *U.S.A.* 108 B5
Colville →, *U.S.A.* 100 A4
Colville, C., *N.Z.* 91 G5
Colwood, *Canada* 110 B3
Colwyn Bay, *U.K.* 14 D4
Coma, *Ethiopia* 81 F4
Comácchio, *Italy* 41 D9
Comalcalco, *Mexico* 119 D6
Comallo, *Argentina* 128 E2
Comana, *Romania* 29 F11
Comanche, *U.S.A.* 113 K5
Comandante Ferraz, *Antarctica* 5 C18
Comăneşti, *Romania* 29 D11
Comarnic, *Romania* 29 E10
Comayagua, *Honduras* 120 D2
Combahee →, *U.S.A.* 115 J5
Combarbalá, *Chile* 126 C1
Combe Martin, *U.K.* 15 F3
Combeaufontaine, *France* 19 E12
Comber, *Canada* 116 D2
Comber, *U.K.* 12 B6
Combermere, *Canada* 116 A7
Comblain-au-Pont, *Belgium* 17 D5
Combourg, *France* 18 D5
Combrailles, *France* 19 F9
Combronde, *France* 20 C7
Comeragh Mts., *Ireland* 12 D4
Comet, *Australia* 94 C4
Comilla, *Bangla.* 67 H17
Comino, *Malta* 49 C1
Comino, C., *Italy* 42 B2
Cómiso, *Italy* 43 F7
Comitán, *Mexico* 119 D6
Commentry, *France* 19 F9
Commerce, *Ga., U.S.A.* 115 H4
Commerce, *Tex., U.S.A.* 113 J7
Commercy, *France* 19 D12
Committee B., *Canada* 101 B11
Commonwealth B., *Antarctica* 5 C10
Commoron Cr. →, *Australia* 95 D5
Communism Pk. = Kommunizma, Pik, *Tajikistan* 52 F8
Como, *Italy* 40 C6
Como, Lago di, *Italy* 40 B6
Comodoro Rivadavia, *Argentina* 128 F3
Comoé △, *Ivory C.* 82 D4
Comorâşte, *Romania* 28 E6
Comorin, C., *India* 66 Q10
Comoro Is. = Comoros ■, *Ind. Oc.* 77 H8
Comoros ■, *Ind. Oc.* 77 H8
Comox, *Canada* 102 D4
Compiègne, *France* 19 C9
Comporta, *Portugal* 37 G2
Compostela, *Mexico* 118 C4
Comprida, I., *Brazil* 127 A6
Compton, *Canada* 117 A13
Compton, *U.S.A.* 111 M8
Comrat, *Moldova* 29 D13
Con Cuong, *Vietnam* 64 C5
Con Dao △, *Vietnam* 65 H6
Con Son, *Vietnam* 65 H6
Conakry, *Guinea* 82 D2
Conara, *Australia* 95 G4
Concarneau, *France* 18 E3
Conceição, *Mozam.* 87 F4
Conceição da Barra, *Brazil* 125 G11
Conceição do Araguaia, *Brazil* 125 E9
Concepción, *Argentina* 126 B2
Concepción, *Bolivia* 124 G6
Concepción, *Chile* 126 D1
Concepción, *Mexico* 119 D6
Concepción, *Paraguay* 126 A4
Concepción □, *Chile* 126 D1
Concepción →, *Mexico* 118 A2
Concepción, Est. de, *Chile* 128 G2
Concepción, L., *Bolivia* 124 G6
Concepción, Punta, *Mexico* 118 B2
Concepción del Oro, *Mexico* 118 C4
Concepción del Uruguay, *Argentina* 126 C4
Conception, Pt., *U.S.A.* 111 L6
Conception B., *Canada* 105 C9
Conception B., *Namibia* 88 C1
Conception I., *Bahamas* 121 B4
Concession, *Zimbabwe* 87 F3
Conchas Dam, *U.S.A.* 113 H2
Conches-en-Ouche, *France* 18 D7
Concho, *U.S.A.* 109 J9

Concho →, *U.S.A.* 113 K5
Conchos →, *Chihuahua, Mexico* 118 B4
Conchos →, *Tamaulipas, Mexico* 119 B5
Concord, *Calif., U.S.A.* 110 H4
Concord, *N.C., U.S.A.* 115 H5
Concord, *N.H., U.S.A.* 117 C13
Concordia, *Argentina* 126 C4
Concórdia, *Brazil* 124 D5
Concordia, *Mexico* 118 C3
Concordia, *U.S.A.* 112 F6
Concrete, *U.S.A.* 108 B3
Condamine, *Australia* 95 D5
Condat, *France* 20 C6
Conde, *U.S.A.* 112 C5
Condé-sur-Noireau, *France* 18 D6
Condeúba, *Brazil* 125 F10
Condobolin, *Australia* 95 E4
Condom, *France* 20 E4
Condon, *U.S.A.* 108 D3
Conegliano, *Italy* 41 C9
Conejera, I. = Conills, I. des, *Spain* 48 B9
Conejos, *Mexico* 118 B4
Conero ⌂, *Italy* 41 E10
Confolens, *France* 20 B4
Confuso →, *Paraguay* 126 B4
Congaz, *Moldova* 29 D13
Conghua, *China* 59 F9
Congjiang, *China* 58 E7
Congleton, *U.K.* 14 D5
Congo (Brazzaville) = Congo ■, *Africa* 84 E3
Congo (Kinshasa) = Congo, Dem. Rep. of the ■, *Africa* 84 E4
Congo ■, *Africa* 84 E3
Congo →, *Africa* 84 F2
Congo, Dem. Rep. of the ■, *Africa* 84 E4
Congo Basin, *Africa* 84 E4
Congonhas, *Brazil* 127 A7
Congress, *U.S.A.* 109 J7
Conil = Conil de la Frontera, *Spain* 37 J4
Conil de la Frontera, *Spain* 37 J4
Conills, I. des, *Spain* 48 B9
Coniston, *Canada* 104 C3
Conjeeveram = Kanchipuram, *India* 66 N11
Conklin, *Canada* 103 B6
Conklin, *U.S.A.* 117 D9
Conn, L., *Ireland* 12 B2
Connacht □, *Ireland* 12 C2
Conneaut, *U.S.A.* 116 E4
Connecticut □, *U.S.A.* 117 E12
Connecticut →, *U.S.A.* 117 E12
Connell, *U.S.A.* 108 C4
Connellsville, *U.S.A.* 116 F5
Connemara, *Ireland* 12 C2
Connemara △, *Ireland* 12 C2
Connemaugh →, *U.S.A.* 116 F5
Connerré, *France* 18 D7
Connersville, *U.S.A.* 114 F3
Connors Ra., *Australia* 94 C4
Conques, *France* 20 D6
Conquest, *Canada* 103 C7
Conrad, *U.S.A.* 108 B8
Conran, C., *Australia* 95 F4
Conroe, *U.S.A.* 113 K7
Consecon, *Canada* 116 C7
Conselheiro Lafaiete, *Brazil* 127 A7
Conselve, *Italy* 41 C8
Consett, *U.K.* 14 C6
Consort, *Canada* 103 C6
Constance = Konstanz, *Germany* 25 H5
Constance, L. = Bodensee, *Europe* 25 H5
Constanţa, *Romania* 29 F13
Constanţa □, *Romania* 29 F13
Constantia, *U.S.A.* 117 C8
Constantina, *Spain* 37 H5
Constantine, *Algeria* 78 A7
Constitución, *Chile* 126 D1
Constitución, *Uruguay* 126 C4
Constitucion de 1857 △, *Mexico* 118 A1
Consuegra, *Spain* 37 F7
Consul, *Canada* 103 D7
Contact, *U.S.A.* 108 F6
Contai, *India* 69 J12
Contamana, *Peru* 124 E4
Contarina, *Italy* 41 C9
Contas →, *Brazil* 125 F11
Contes, *France* 21 E11
Contoocook, *U.S.A.* 117 C13
Contra Costa, *Mozam.* 89 D5
Contres, *France* 18 E8
Contrexéville, *France* 19 D12
Contwoyto L., *Canada* 100 B8
Conversano, *Italy* 43 B10
Conway = Conwy, *U.K.* 14 D4
Conway = Conwy →, *U.K.* 14 D4
Conway, *Australia* 94 J6
Conway, *Ark., U.S.A.* 113 H8
Conway, *N.H., U.S.A.* 117 C13
Conway, *S.C., U.S.A.* 115 J6
Conway, C., *Australia* 94 J6
Conway, L., *Australia* 95 D2
Conwy, *U.K.* 14 D4
Conwy □, *U.K.* 14 D4
Conwy →, *U.K.* 14 D4
Coober Pedy, *Australia* 95 D1
Cooch Behar = Koch Bihar, *India* 67 F16
Cooinda, *Australia* 92 B5
Cook, *Australia* 93 F5
Cook, *U.S.A.* 112 B8
Cook, B., *Chile* 128 H3
Cook, C., *Canada* 102 C3
Cook, Mt. = Aoraki Mount Cook, *N.Z.* 91 K3
Cook Inlet, *U.S.A.* 100 C4
Cook Is., *Pac. Oc.* 97 J12
Cook Strait, *N.Z.* 91 J5
Cookeville, *U.S.A.* 115 G3
Cookhouse, *S. Africa* 88 E4
Cookshire, *Canada* 117 A13
Cookstown, *U.K.* 12 B5
Cooksville, *Canada* 116 C5
Cooktown, *Australia* 94 B4
Coolabah, *Australia* 95 E4
Cooladdi, *Australia* 95 D4
Coolah, *Australia* 95 E4
Coolamon, *Australia* 95 E4
Coolgardie, *Australia* 93 F3
Coolidge, *U.S.A.* 109 K8
Coolidge Dam, *U.S.A.* 109 K8
Cooloola △, *Australia* 95 D5
Cooma, *Australia* 95 F4
Coon Rapids, *U.S.A.* 112 C8
Coonabarabran, *Australia* 95 E4
Coonamble, *Australia* 95 E4
Coonana, *Australia* 93 F3
Coondapoor, *India* 66 N9
Cooninie, L., *Australia* 95 D2
Cooper, *U.S.A.* 113 J7
Cooper Cr. →, *Australia* 95 D2
Cooperstown, *N. Dak., U.S.A.* 112 B5
Cooperstown, *N.Y., U.S.A.* 117 D10
Coorabie, *Australia* 93 F5
Coorong, The, *Australia* 95 F2
Coorow, *Australia* 93 E2
Cooroy, *Australia* 95 D5
Coos Bay, *U.S.A.* 108 E1
Coosa →, *U.S.A.* 115 J2
Cootamundra, *Australia* 95 E4
Cootehill, *Ireland* 12 B4
Copahue Paso, *Argentina* 126 D1
Copainalá, *Mexico* 119 D6
Copake Falls, *U.S.A.* 117 D11
Copalnic Mănăştur, *Romania* 29 C8
Copán, *Honduras* 120 D2
Cope, *U.S.A.* 112 F3
Cope, C., *Spain* 39 H3
Copenhagen = København, *Denmark* 11 J6
Copenhagen, *U.S.A.* 117 C9
Copenhagen ✕ (CPH), *Denmark* 11 J6
Copertino, *Italy* 43 B11
Copiapó, *Chile* 126 B1
Copiapó →, *Chile* 126 B1
Coplay, *U.S.A.* 117 F9
Copp L., *Canada* 102 A6
Copparo, *Italy* 41 D8
Coppename →, *Suriname* 125 B7
Copper Harbor, *U.S.A.* 114 B2
Copper Queen, *Zimbabwe* 87 F2
Copperas Cove, *U.S.A.* 113 K6
Copperbelt □, *Zambia* 87 E2
Coppermine = Kugluktuk, *Canada* 100 B8
Coppermine →, *Canada* 100 B8
Copperopolis, *U.S.A.* 110 H6
Copşa Mică, *Romania* 29 D9
Coquet →, *U.K.* 14 B6
Coquille, *U.S.A.* 108 E1
Coquimbo, *Chile* 126 C1
Coquimbo □, *Chile* 126 C1
Corabia, *Romania* 29 G9
Coracora, *Peru* 124 G4
Coraki, *Australia* 95 D5
Coral, *U.S.A.* 116 F5
Coral Gables, *U.S.A.* 115 N5
Coral Harbour, *Canada* 101 B11
Coral Sea, *Pac. Oc.* 96 J7
Coral Springs, *U.S.A.* 115 M5
Coraopolis, *U.S.A.* 116 F4
Corato, *Italy* 43 A9
Corbeil-Essonnes, *France* 19 D9
Corbie, *France* 19 C9
Corbières, *France* 20 F6
Corbigny, *France* 19 E10
Corbin, *U.S.A.* 114 G3
Corbones →, *Spain* 37 H5
Corbu, *Romania* 29 F13
Corby, *U.K.* 15 E7
Corcaigh = Cork, *Ireland* 12 E3
Corcoran, *U.S.A.* 110 J7
Corcovado △, *Costa Rica* 120 E3
Cordele, *U.S.A.* 115 K4
Cordell, *U.S.A.* 113 H5
Cordenòns, *Italy* 41 C9
Cordes, *France* 20 D5
Córdoba, *Argentina* 126 C3
Córdoba, *Mexico* 119 D5
Córdoba, *Spain* 37 H6
Córdoba □, *Argentina* 126 C3
Córdoba □, *Spain* 37 G6
Córdoba, Sierra de, *Argentina* 126 C3
Cordon, *Phil.* 61 C4
Cordova, *U.S.A.* 100 B5
Corella, *Spain* 38 C3
Corella →, *Australia* 94 B3
Corfield, *Australia* 94 C3
Corfu = Kérkira, *Greece* 49 A3
Corfu ✕ (CFU), *Greece* 46 B1
Corfu, Str. of, *Greece* 49 A4
Corgo = O Corgo, *Spain* 36 C3
Cori, *Italy* 42 A5
Coria, *Spain* 36 F4
Coria del Río, *Spain* 37 H4
Corigliano Cálabro, *Italy* 43 C9
Coringa Is., *Australia* 94 B4
Corinth = Kórinthos, *Greece* 46 D4
Corinth, *Miss., U.S.A.* 115 H1
Corinth, *N.Y., U.S.A.* 117 C11
Corinth, G. of = Korinthiakós Kólpos, *Greece* 46 C4
Corinth Canal, *Greece* 46 D4
Corinto, *Brazil* 125 G10
Corinto, *Nic.* 120 D2
Cork, *Ireland* 12 E3
Cork □, *Ireland* 12 E3
Cork Harbour, *Ireland* 12 E3
Corlay, *France* 18 D3
Corleone, *Italy* 42 E6
Corleto Perticara, *Italy* 43 B9
Çorlu, *Turkey* 45 E11
Cormack L., *Canada* 102 A4
Cormòns, *Italy* 41 C10
Cormorant, *Canada* 103 C8
Cormorant L., *Canada* 103 C8
Corn Is. = Maiz, Is. del, *Nic.* 120 D3
Cornalvo ⌂, *Spain* 37 F4
Cornélio Procópio, *Brazil* 127 A5
Corner Brook, *Canada* 105 C8
Corneşti, *Moldova* 29 C13
Corníglio, *Italy* 40 D7
Corning, *Ark., U.S.A.* 113 G9
Corning, *Calif., U.S.A.* 108 G2
Corning, *Iowa, U.S.A.* 112 E7
Corning, *N.Y., U.S.A.* 116 D7
Corno Grande, *Italy* 41 F10
Cornwall, *Canada* 117 A10
Cornwall, *U.S.A.* 117 F8
Cornwall □, *U.K.* 15 G3
Corny Pt., *Australia* 95 E2
Coro, *Venezuela* 124 A5
Coroatá, *Brazil* 125 D10
Corocoro, *Bolivia* 124 G5
Coroico, *Bolivia* 124 G5
Coromandel, *N.Z.* 91 G5
Coromandel Coast, *India* 66 N12
Corona, *Calif., U.S.A.* 111 M9
Corona, *N. Mex., U.S.A.* 109 J11
Coronach, *Canada* 103 D7
Coronado, *U.S.A.* 111 N9
Coronado, B. de, *Costa Rica* 120 E3
Coronados, Is. los, *U.S.A.* 111 N9
Coronation, *Canada* 102 C6
Coronation Gulf, *Canada* 100 B8
Coronation I., *Antarctica* 5 C18
Coronation Is., *Australia* 92 B3
Coronda, *Argentina* 126 C3
Coronel, *Chile* 126 D1
Coronel Bogado, *Paraguay* 126 B4
Coronel Dorrego, *Argentina* 126 D3
Coronel Oviedo, *Paraguay* 126 B4
Coronel Pringles, *Argentina* 126 D3
Coronel Suárez, *Argentina* 126 D3
Coronel Vidal, *Argentina* 126 D4
Coropuna, Nevado, *Peru* 124 G4
Çorovodë, *Albania* 44 F4
Corowa, *Australia* 95 F4
Corozal, *Belize* 119 D7
Corozal Pt., *Trin. & Tob.* 125 K15
Corps, *France* 21 D9
Corpus, *Argentina* 127 B4
Corpus Christi, *U.S.A.* 113 M6
Corpus Christi, L., *U.S.A.* 113 L6
Corral de Almaguer, *Spain* 36 F7
Corralejo, *Canary Is.* 48 F6
Corraun Pen., *Ireland* 12 C2
Corréggio, *Italy* 40 D7
Correntes, C. das, *Mozam.* 89 C6
Corrèze □, *France* 20 C5
Corrèze →, *France* 20 C5
Corrib, L., *Ireland* 12 C2
Corridónia, *Italy* 41 E10
Corrientes, *Argentina* 126 B4
Corrientes □, *Argentina* 126 B4
Corrientes →, *Argentina* 126 C4
Corrientes →, *Peru* 124 D4
Corrientes, C., *Colombia* 124 B3
Corrientes, C., *Cuba* 120 B3
Corrientes, C., *Mexico* 118 C3
Corrigan, *U.S.A.* 113 K7
Corrigin, *Australia* 93 F2
Corry, *U.S.A.* 116 E5
Corse, *France* 21 G13
Corse ⌂, *France* 21 F13
Corse, C., *France* 21 E13
Corse-du-Sud □, *France* 21 G13
Corsica = Corse, *France* 21 G13
Corsicana, *U.S.A.* 113 J6
Corte, *France* 21 F13
Corte Pinto, *Portugal* 37 H3
Cortegana, *Spain* 37 H4
Cortez, *U.S.A.* 109 H9
Cortina d'Ampezzo, *Italy* 41 B9
Cortland, *N.Y., U.S.A.* 117 D8
Cortland, *Ohio, U.S.A.* 116 E4
Cortona, *Italy* 41 E8
Corubal →, *Guinea-Biss.* 82 C2
Coruche, *Portugal* 37 G2
Çoruh →, *Turkey* 35 K5
Çorum, *Turkey* 72 B6
Corumbá, *Brazil* 124 G7
Corund, *Romania* 29 D10
Corunna = A Coruña, *Spain* 36 B2
Corvallis, *U.S.A.* 108 D2
Corvette, L. de la, *Canada* 104 B5
Corydon, *U.S.A.* 112 E8
Cosalá, *Mexico* 118 C3
Cosamaloapan, *Mexico* 119 D5
Cosenza, *Italy* 43 C9
Coşereni, *Romania* 29 F11
Coshocton, *U.S.A.* 116 F3
Cosmo Newberry, *Australia* 93 E3
Cosne-Cours-sur-Loire, *France* 19 E9
Coso Junction, *U.S.A.* 111 J9
Coso Pk., *U.S.A.* 111 J9
Cospeito, *Spain* 36 B3
Cosquín, *Argentina* 126 C3
Cossato, *Italy* 40 C5
Cossé-le-Vivien, *France* 18 E6
Cosson →, *France* 18 E8
Costa Blanca, *Spain* 39 G4
Costa Brava, *Spain* 38 D8
Costa del Sol, *Spain* 37 J6
Costa Dorada, *Spain* 38 D6
Costa Mesa, *U.S.A.* 111 M9
Costa Rica ■, *Cent. Amer.* 120 E3
Costa Smeralda, *Italy* 42 A2
Costeşti, *Romania* 29 F9
Costigliole d'Asti, *Italy* 40 D5
Cosumnes →, *U.S.A.* 110 G5
Coswig, *Sachsen, Germany* 24 D9
Coswig, *Sachsen-Anhalt, Germany* 24 D8
Cotabato, *Phil.* 61 H6
Cotagaita, *Bolivia* 126 A2
Côte d'Azur, *France* 21 E11
Côte-d'Ivoire = Ivory Coast ■, *Africa* 82 D4
Côte d'Or, *France* 19 E11
Côte-d'Or □, *France* 19 E11
Coteau des Prairies, *U.S.A.* 112 C6
Coteau du Missouri, *U.S.A.* 112 B4
Cotentin, *France* 18 C5
Côtes-d'Armor □, *France* 18 D4
Côtes de Meuse, *France* 19 C12
Côtes-du-Nord = Côtes-d'Armor □, *France* 18 D4
Cotiella, *Spain* 38 C5
Cotillo, *Canary Is.* 48 F5
Cotiujeni, *Moldova* 29 C13
Cotonou, *Benin* 83 D5
Cotopaxi, *Ecuador* 124 D3
Cotronei, *Italy* 43 C9
Cotswold Hills, *U.K.* 15 F5
Cottage Grove, *U.S.A.* 108 E2
Cottbus, *Germany* 24 D10
Cottonwood, *U.S.A.* 109 J7
Cotulla, *U.S.A.* 113 L5
Coubre, Pte. de la, *France* 20 C2
Couches, *France* 19 F11
Couço, *Portugal* 37 G2
Coudersport, *U.S.A.* 116 E6
Couedic, C. du, *Australia* 95 F2
Couëron, *France* 18 E5
Couesnon →, *France* 18 D5
Couhé, *France* 20 B4
Coulanges-sur-Yonne, *France* 19 E10
Coulee City, *U.S.A.* 108 C4
Coulman I., *Antarctica* 5 D11
Coulommiers, *France* 19 D10
Coulon →, *France* 21 E9
Coulonge →, *Canada* 104 C4
Coulonges-sur-l'Autize, *France* 20 B3
Coulounieix-Chamiers, *France* 20 C4
Coulterville, *U.S.A.* 110 H6
Council, *U.S.A.* 108 D5
Council Bluffs, *U.S.A.* 112 E7
Council Grove, *U.S.A.* 112 F6
Coupeville, *U.S.A.* 110 B4
Courantyne →, *S. Amer.* 124 B7
Courcelles, *Belgium* 17 D4
Courchevel, *France* 21 C10
Courçon, *France* 20 B3
Courmayeur, *Italy* 40 C3
Couronne, C., *France* 21 E9
Cours-la-Ville, *France* 19 F11
Coursan, *France* 20 E7
Courseulles-sur-Mer, *France* 18 C6
Courtenay, *Canada* 102 D4
Courtenay, *France* 19 D10
Courtland, *U.S.A.* 110 G5
Courtrai = Kortrijk, *Belgium* 17 D3
Courtright, *Canada* 116 D2
Coushatta, *U.S.A.* 113 J8
Coutances, *France* 18 C5
Coutras, *France* 20 C3
Coutts Crossing, *Australia* 95 D5
Couva, *Trin. & Tob.* 125 K15
Couvin, *Belgium* 17 D4
Covarrubias, *Spain* 36 C7
Covasna, *Romania* 29 E11
Covasna □, *Romania* 29 E10
Cove I., *Canada* 116 A3
Coventry, *U.K.* 15 E6
Covilhã, *Portugal* 36 E3
Covington, *Ga., U.S.A.* 115 J4
Covington, *Ky., U.S.A.* 114 F3
Covington, *Okla., U.S.A.* 113 G6
Covington, *Tenn., U.S.A.* 113 H10
Covington, *Va., U.S.A.* 114 G5
Cowal, L., *Australia* 95 E4
Cowan, L., *Australia* 93 F3
Cowan L., *Canada* 103 C7
Cowangie, *Australia* 95 F3
Cowansville, *Canada* 117 A12
Coward Springs, *Australia* 95 D2
Cowcowing Lakes, *Australia* 93 F2
Cowdenbeath, *U.K.* 13 E5
Cowell, *Australia* 95 E2
Cowes, *U.K.* 15 G6
Cowichan L., *Canada* 110 B2
Cowlitz →, *U.S.A.* 110 D4
Cowra, *Australia* 95 E4
Cox, *Spain* 39 G4
Coxilha Grande, *Brazil* 127 B5
Coxim, *Brazil* 125 G8
Cox's Bazar, *Bangla.* 67 J17
Coyote Wells, *U.S.A.* 111 N11
Coyuca de Benítez, *Mexico* 119 D4
Coyuca de Catalan, *Mexico* 118 D4
Cozad, *U.S.A.* 112 E5
Cozes, *France* 20 C3
Cozumel, *Mexico* 119 C7
Cozumel, Isla, *Mexico* 119 C7
Crabhill, *Barbados* 121 g
Cracow = Kraków, *Poland* 31 H6
Cracow, *Australia* 95 D5
Cradle Mt.-Lake St. Clair △, *Australia* 95 G4
Cradock, *Australia* 95 E2
Cradock, *S. Africa* 88 E4
Craig, *U.S.A.* 108 F10
Craigavon, *U.K.* 12 B5
Craigmore, *Zimbabwe* 87 G3
Craik, *Canada* 103 C7
Crailsheim, *Germany* 25 F6
Craiova, *Romania* 29 F8
Cramsie, *Australia* 94 C3
Cranberry L., *U.S.A.* 117 B10
Cranberry Portage, *Canada* 103 C8
Cranbrook, *Australia* 93 F2
Cranbrook, *Canada* 102 D5
Crandon, *U.S.A.* 112 C10
Crane, *Oreg., U.S.A.* 108 E4
Crane, *Tex., U.S.A.* 113 K3
Cranston, *U.S.A.* 117 E13
Craon, *France* 18 E6
Craonne, *France* 19 C10
Craponne-sur-Arzon, *France* 20 C7
Crasna, *Romania* 29 D12
Crasna →, *Romania* 28 C7
Crasnei, Munţii, *Romania* 29 C8
Crater L., *U.S.A.* 108 E2
Crater Lake △, *U.S.A.* 108 E2
Craters of the Moon △, *U.S.A.* 108 E7
Crateús, *Brazil* 125 E10
Crati →, *Italy* 43 C9
Crato, *Brazil* 125 E11
Crato, *Portugal* 37 F3
Craven, L., *Canada* 104 B4
Crawford, *U.S.A.* 112 D3
Crawfordsville, *U.S.A.* 114 E2
Crawley, *U.K.* 15 F7
Crazy Mts., *U.S.A.* 108 C8
Crean L., *Canada* 103 C7
Crécy-en-Ponthieu, *France* 19 B8
Crediton, *Canada* 116 C3
Crediton, *U.K.* 15 G4
Cree →, *Canada* 103 B7
Cree →, *U.K.* 13 G4
Cree L., *Canada* 103 B7
Creede, *U.S.A.* 109 H10
Creekside, *U.S.A.* 116 F5
Creel, *Mexico* 118 B3
Creemore, *Canada* 116 B4
Creighton, *Canada* 103 C8
Creighton, *U.S.A.* 112 D6
Creil, *France* 19 C9
Crema, *Italy* 40 C6
Cremona, *Italy* 40 C7
Crepaja, *Serbia & M.* 28 E5
Crépy, *France* 19 C10
Crépy-en-Valois, *France* 19 C9
Cres, *Croatia* 41 D11
Crescent City, *U.S.A.* 108 F1
Crescentino, *Italy* 40 C5
Crespo, *Argentina* 126 C3
Cresson, *U.S.A.* 116 F6
Crest, *France* 21 D9
Cresta, Mt., *Phil.* 61 C5
Crestline, *Calif., U.S.A.* 111 L9
Crestline, *Ohio, U.S.A.* 116 F2
Creston, *Canada* 102 D5
Creston, *Calif., U.S.A.* 110 K6
Creston, *Iowa, U.S.A.* 112 E7
Crestview, *Calif., U.S.A.* 110 H8
Crestview, *Fla., U.S.A.* 115 K2
Crêt de la Neige, *France* 19 F12
Crete = Kríti, *Greece* 49 D7
Crete, *U.S.A.* 112 E6
Crete, Sea of, *Greece* 47 E7
Créteil, *France* 19 D9
Creus, C. de, *Spain* 38 C8
Creuse □, *France* 19 F9
Creuse →, *France* 20 B4
Creutzwald, *France* 19 C13
Creuzburg, *Germany* 24 D6
Crèvecœur-le-Grand, *France* 19 C9
Crevillente, *Spain* 39 G4
Crewe, *U.K.* 14 D5
Crewkerne, *U.K.* 15 G5
Crianlarich, *U.K.* 13 E4
Criciúma, *Brazil* 127 B6
Cricova, *Moldova* 29 C13
Crieff, *U.K.* 13 E5
Crikvenica, *Croatia* 41 C11
Crimea □, *Ukraine* 33 K8
Crimean Pen. = Krymskyy Pivostriv, *Ukraine* 33 K8
Crimmitschau, *Germany* 24 E8
Cristuru Secuiesc, *Romania* 29 D10
Crişul Alb →, *Romania* 28 D6
Crişul Negru →, *Romania* 28 D6
Crişul Repede →, *Romania* 28 D5
Criuleni, *Moldova* 29 C14
Crivitz, *Germany* 24 B7
Crna →, *Macedonia* 44 E5
Crna Gora = Montenegro □, *Serbia & M.* 44 D3
Crna Gora, *Macedonia* 44 D5
Crna Reka = Crna →, *Macedonia* 44 E5
Crna Trava, *Serbia & M.* 44 D6
Crni Drim →, *Macedonia* 44 E4
Crni Timok →, *Serbia & M.* 44 C6
Crnoljeva Planina, *Serbia & M.* 44 D5
Črnomelj, *Slovenia* 41 C12
Croagh Patrick, *Ireland* 12 C2
Croatia ■, *Europe* 41 C13
Crocker, Banjaran, *Malaysia* 62 C5
Crockett, *U.S.A.* 113 K7
Crocodile = Krokodil →, *Mozam.* 89 D5
Crocodile Is., *Australia* 94 A1
Crocq, *France* 20 C6
Crodo, *Italy* 40 B5
Crohy Hd., *Ireland* 12 B3
Croisette, C., *France* 21 E9
Croisic, Pte. du, *France* 18 E4
Croix, L. La, *Canada* 104 C1
Croker, C., *Australia* 92 B5
Croker, C., *Canada* 116 B4
Croker I., *Australia* 92 B5
Cromarty, *U.K.* 13 D4
Cromer, *U.K.* 14 E9
Cromwell, *N.Z.* 91 L2
Cromwell, *U.S.A.* 117 E12
Cronat, *France* 19 F10
Crook, *U.K.* 14 C6
Crooked →, *Canada* 102 C4
Crooked →, *U.S.A.* 108 D3
Crooked I., *Bahamas* 121 B5
Crooked Island Passage, *Bahamas* 121 B5
Crookston, *Minn., U.S.A.* 112 B6

Crookston, *Nebr., U.S.A.* 112 D4
Crookwell, *Australia* 95 E4
Cropane-Micone ⌓, *Italy* 43 D9
Crosby, *U.K.* 14 D4
Crosby, *N. Dak., U.S.A.* 112 A3
Crosby, *Pa., U.S.A.* 116 E6
Crosbyton, *U.S.A.* 113 J4
Crosía, *Italy* 43 C9
Cross →, *Nigeria* 83 E6
Cross City, *U.S.A.* 115 L4
Cross Fell, *U.K.* 14 C5
Cross L., *Canada* 103 C9
Cross Lake, *Canada* 103 C9
Cross River □, *Nigeria* 83 D6
Cross River △, *Nigeria* 83 D6
Cross Sound, *U.S.A.* 100 C6
Crossett, *U.S.A.* 113 J9
Crosshaven, *Ireland* 12 E3
Crossville, *U.S.A.* 115 G3
Croswell, *U.S.A.* 116 C2
Croton-on-Hudson, *U.S.A.* 117 E11
Crotone, *Italy* 43 C10
Crow →, *Canada* 102 B4
Crow Agency, *U.S.A.* 108 D10
Crow Hd., *Ireland* 12 E1
Crowell, *U.S.A.* 113 J5
Crowley, *U.S.A.* 113 K8
Crowley, L., *U.S.A.* 110 H8
Crown Point, *Ind., U.S.A.* 114 E2
Crown Point, *N.Y., U.S.A.* 117 C11
Crown Pt., *Trin. & Tob.* 125 J16
Crownpoint, *U.S.A.* 109 J9
Crows Landing, *U.S.A.* 110 H5
Crows Nest, *Australia* 95 D5
Crowsnest Pass, *Canada* 102 D6
Croydon, *Australia* 94 B3
Croydon □, *U.K.* 15 F7
Crozet, Is., *Ind. Oc.* 3 G12
Crozon, *France* 18 D2
Cruz, C., *Cuba* 120 C4
Cruz Alta, *Brazil* 127 B5
Cruz Bay, *U.S. Virgin Is.* 121 e
Cruz de Incio, *Spain* 36 C3
Cruz del Eje, *Argentina* 126 C3
Cruzeiro, *Brazil* 127 A7
Cruzeiro do Oeste, *Brazil* 127 A5
Cruzeiro do Sul, *Brazil* 124 E4
Cry L., *Canada* 102 B3
Crystal Bay, *U.S.A.* 110 F7
Crystal Brook, *Australia* 95 E2
Crystal City, *U.S.A.* 113 L5
Crystal Falls, *U.S.A.* 114 B1
Crystal River, *U.S.A.* 115 L4
Crystal Springs, *U.S.A.* 113 K9
Csenger, *Hungary* 28 C7
Csongrád, *Hungary* 28 D5
Csongrád □, *Hungary* 28 D5
Csorna, *Hungary* 28 C2
Csurgo, *Hungary* 28 D2
Cu Lao Hon, *Vietnam* 65 G7
Cua Rao, *Vietnam* 64 C5
Cuácua →, *Mozam.* 87 F4
Cuamato, *Angola* 88 B2
Cuamba, *Mozam.* 87 E4
Cuando →, *Angola* 85 H4
Cuando Cubango □, *Angola* 88 B3
Cuangar, *Angola* 88 B2
Cuango = Kwango →, *Dem. Rep. of the Congo* 84 E3
Cuanza →, *Angola* 84 F2
Cuarto →, *Argentina* 126 C3
Cuatrociénegas, *Mexico* 118 B4
Cuauhtémoc, *Mexico* 118 B3
Cuba, *Portugal* 37 G3
Cuba, *N. Mex., U.S.A.* 109 J10
Cuba, *N.Y., U.S.A.* 116 D6
Cuba ■, *W. Indies* 120 B4
Cubango →, *Africa* 88 B3
Çubuk, *Turkey* 72 B5
Cuc Phuong △, *Vietnam* 64 B5
Cuchumatanes, Sierra de los, *Guatemala* 120 C1
Cuckfield, *U.K.* 15 F7
Cucuí, *Brazil* 124 C5
Cucurpe, *Mexico* 118 A2
Cúcuta, *Colombia* 124 B4
Cudalbi, *Romania* 29 E12
Cuddalore, *India* 66 P11
Cuddapah, *India* 66 M11
Cuddapan, L., *Australia* 94 D3
Cudillero, *Spain* 36 B4
Cue, *Australia* 93 E2
Cuéllar, *Spain* 36 D6
Cuenca, *Ecuador* 124 D3
Cuenca, *Spain* 38 E2
Cuenca □, *Spain* 38 F3
Cuenca, Serranía de, *Spain* 38 F3
Cuenca Alta del Manzanares ⌓, *Spain* 36 E7
Cuerdo del Pozo, Embalse de la, *Spain* 38 D2
Cuernavaca, *Mexico* 119 D5
Cuero, *U.S.A.* 113 L6
Cuers, *France* 21 E10
Cueva de la Quebrado del Toro △, *Venezuela* 121 D6
Cuevas del Almanzora, *Spain* 39 H3
Cuevo, *Bolivia* 124 H6
Cugir, *Romania* 29 E8
Cugnaux, *France* 20 E5
Cuhai-Bakony →, *Hungary* 28 C2
Cuiabá, *Brazil* 125 G7
Cuiabá →, *Brazil* 125 G7
Cuijk, *Neths.* 17 C5
Cuilco, *Guatemala* 120 C1
Cuillin Hills, *U.K.* 13 D2
Cuillin Sd., *U.K.* 13 D2
Cuiseaux, *France* 19 F12
Cuito →, *Angola* 88 B3
Cuitzeo, L. de, *Mexico* 118 D4
Cujmir, *Romania* 28 F7
Cukai, *Malaysia* 65 K4
Culbertson, *U.S.A.* 112 A2
Culcairn, *Australia* 95 F4
Culebra, Isla de, *Puerto Rico* 121 d
Culebra, Sierra de la, *Spain* 36 D4
Culfa, *Azerbaijan* 73 C11
Culgoa →, *Australia* 95 D4
Culgoa Flood Plain △, *Australia* 95 D4
Culiacán, *Mexico* 118 C3
Culiacán →, *Mexico* 118 C3
Culik, *Indonesia* 63 J18
Culion, *Phil.* 61 F4
Cúllar, *Spain* 37 H8
Cullarin Ra., *Australia* 95 E4
Cullen, *U.K.* 13 D6
Cullen Pt., *Australia* 94 A3
Cullera, *Spain* 39 F4
Cullman, *U.S.A.* 115 H2
Cullompton, *U.K.* 15 G4
Culoz, *France* 21 C9
Culpeper, *U.S.A.* 114 F7
Culuene →, *Brazil* 125 F8
Culver, Pt., *Australia* 93 F3
Culverden, *N.Z.* 91 K4
Cumaná, *Venezuela* 124 A6
Cumaovası, *Turkey* 47 C9
Cumberland, *B.C., Canada* 102 D4
Cumberland, *Ont., Canada* 117 A9
Cumberland, *U.S.A.* 114 F6
Cumberland →, *U.S.A.* 115 G2
Cumberland, L., *U.S.A.* 115 G3
Cumberland Gap △, *U.S.A.* 115 G4
Cumberland I., *U.S.A.* 115 K5
Cumberland Is., *Australia* 94 J7
Cumberland Island ⌓, *U.S.A.* 115 K5
Cumberland L., *Canada* 103 C8
Cumberland Pen., *Canada* 101 B13
Cumberland Plateau, *U.S.A.* 115 H3
Cumberland Sd., *Canada* 101 B13
Cumbernauld, *U.K.* 13 F5
Cumborah, *Australia* 95 D4
Cumbres de Majalca △, *Mexico* 118 B3
Cumbres de Monterrey △, *Mexico* 118 B4
Cumbres Mayores, *Spain* 37 G4
Cumbria □, *U.K.* 14 C5
Cumbrian Mts., *U.K.* 14 C5
Cumbum, *India* 66 M11
Cuminá →, *Brazil* 125 D7
Cummings Mt., *U.S.A.* 111 K8
Cummins, *Australia* 95 E2
Cumnock, *Australia* 95 E4
Cumnock, *U.K.* 13 F4
Cumpas, *Mexico* 118 B3
Cumplida, Pta., *Canary Is.* 48 F2
Çumra, *Turkey* 72 D5
Cunco, *Chile* 128 D2
Cuncumén, *Chile* 126 C1
Cunderdin, *Australia* 93 F2
Cunene →, *Angola* 88 B1
Cúneo, *Italy* 40 D4
Çüngüş, *Turkey* 70 B3
Cunillera, I. = Sa Conillera, *Spain* 48 C7
Cunlhat, *France* 20 C7
Cunnamulla, *Australia* 95 D4
Cuorgnè, *Italy* 40 C4
Cupar, *Canada* 103 C8
Cupar, *U.K.* 13 E5
Cupcini, *Moldova* 29 B12
Cupica, G. de, *Colombia* 124 B3
Ćuprija, *Serbia & M.* 44 C5
Curaçao, *Neth. Ant.* 121 D6
Curanilahue, *Chile* 126 D1
Curaray →, *Peru* 124 D4
Cure →, *France* 19 E10
Curepto, *Chile* 126 D1
Curiapo, *Venezuela* 124 B6
Curicó, *Chile* 126 C1
Curinga, *Italy* 43 D9
Curitiba, *Brazil* 127 B6
Curitibanos, *Brazil* 127 B5
Currabubula, *Australia* 95 E5
Currais Novos, *Brazil* 125 E11
Curralinho, *Brazil* 125 D9
Currant, *U.S.A.* 108 G6
Currawinya △, *Australia* 95 D3
Current →, *U.S.A.* 113 G9
Currie, *Australia* 95 F3
Currie, *U.S.A.* 108 F6
Curtea de Argeş, *Romania* 29 E9
Curtici, *Romania* 28 D6
Curtis, *U.S.A.* 112 E4
Curtis Group, *Australia* 95 F4
Curtis I., *Australia* 94 C5
Curuápanema →, *Brazil* 125 D7
Curuçá, *Brazil* 125 D9
Curuguaty, *Paraguay* 127 A4
Curup, *Indonesia* 62 E2
Cururupu, *Brazil* 125 D10
Curuzú Cuatiá, *Argentina* 126 B4
Curvelo, *Brazil* 125 G10
Cushing, *U.S.A.* 113 H6
Cushing, Mt., *Canada* 102 B3
Cusihuiriáchic, *Mexico* 118 B3
Cusna, Mte., *Italy* 40 D7
Cusset, *France* 19 F10
Custer, *U.S.A.* 112 D3
Cut Bank, *U.S.A.* 108 B7
Cutchogue, *U.S.A.* 117 E12
Cuthbert, *U.S.A.* 115 K3
Cutler, *U.S.A.* 110 J7
Cutro, *Italy* 43 C9
Cuttaburra →, *Australia* 95 D3
Cuttack, *India* 67 J14
Cuvier, C., *Australia* 93 D1
Cuvier I., *N.Z.* 91 G5
Cuxhaven, *Germany* 24 B4
Cuyahoga Falls, *U.S.A.* 116 E3
Cuyahoga Valley △, *U.S.A.* 116 E3
Cuyapo, *Phil.* 61 D4
Cuyo, *Phil.* 61 F4
Cuyo East Pass, *Phil.* 61 F4
Cuyo West Pass, *Phil.* 61 F4
Cuyuni →, *Guyana* 124 B7
Cuzco, *Bolivia* 124 H5
Cuzco, *Peru* 124 F4
Čvrsnica, *Bos.-H.* 28 G2
Cwmbran, *U.K.* 15 F4
Cyangugu, *Rwanda* 86 C2
Cybinka, *Poland* 31 F1
Cyclades = Kikládhes, *Greece* 46 E6
Cygnet, *Australia* 95 G4
Cynthiana, *U.S.A.* 114 F3
Cypress Hills, *Canada* 103 D7
Cypress Hills ⌓, *Canada* 103 D7
Cyprus ■, *Asia* 49 E12
Cyrenaica, *Libya* 79 C10
Czaplinek, *Poland* 30 E3
Czar, *Canada* 103 C6
Czarna →, *Łódzkie, Poland* 31 G6
Czarna →, *Świętokrzyskie, Poland* 31 H8
Czarna Białostocka, *Poland* 31 E10
Czarna Woda, *Poland* 30 E5
Czarne, *Poland* 30 E3
Czarnków, *Poland* 31 F3
Czech Rep. ■, *Europe* 26 B8
Czechowice-Dziedzice, *Poland* 31 J5
Czempiń, *Poland* 31 F3
Czeremcha, *Poland* 31 F10
Czerniejewo, *Poland* 31 F4
Czersk, *Poland* 30 E4
Czerwieńsk, *Poland* 31 F2
Czerwionka-Leszczyny, *Poland* 31 H5
Częstochowa, *Poland* 31 H6
Człopa, *Poland* 31 E3
Człuchów, *Poland* 30 E4
Czyżew-Osada, *Poland* 31 F9

D

Da →, *Vietnam* 58 G5
Da Hinggan Ling, *China* 60 B7
Da Lat, *Vietnam* 65 G7
Da Nang, *Vietnam* 64 D7
Da Qaidam, *China* 60 C4
Da Yunhe →, *China* 57 G11
Da'an, *China* 57 B13
Daan Viljoen ⌓, *Namibia* 88 C2
Dab'a, Ras el, *Egypt* 80 H6
Daba Shan, *China* 58 B7
Dabai, *Nigeria* 83 C6
Dabakala, *Ivory C.* 82 D4
Dabas, *Hungary* 28 C4
Dabat, *Ethiopia* 81 E4
Dabbagh, Jabal, *Si. Arabia* 70 E2
Dabhoi, *India* 68 H5
Dąbie, *Poland* 31 F5
Dabie Shan, *China* 59 B10
Dabilda, *Cameroon* 83 C7
Dabnou, *Niger* 83 C6
Dabo = Pasirkuning, *Indonesia* 62 E2
Dabola, *Guinea* 82 C2
Dabou, *Ivory C.* 82 D4
Daboya, *Ghana* 83 D4
Dąbrowa Białostocka, *Poland* 30 E10
Dąbrowa Górnicza, *Poland* 31 H6
Dąbrowa Tarnowska, *Poland* 31 H7
Dabu, *China* 59 E11
Dabung, *Malaysia* 65 K4
Dabus →, *Ethiopia* 81 E4
Dacato →, *Ethiopia* 81 F5
Dacca = Dhaka, *Bangla.* 69 H14
Dacca = Dhaka □, *Bangla.* 69 G14
Dachau, *Germany* 25 G7
Dachstein, Hoher, *Austria* 26 D6
Dačice, *Czech Rep.* 26 B8
Dadanawa, *Guyana* 124 C7
Daday, *Turkey* 72 B5
Dade City, *U.S.A.* 115 L4
Dadhar, *Pakistan* 68 E2
Dadiya, *Nigeria* 83 D7
Dadra & Nagar Haveli □, *India* 66 J8
Dadri = Charkhi Dadri, *India* 68 E7
Dadu, *Pakistan* 68 F2
Dadu He →, *China* 58 C4
Daet, *Phil.* 61 D5
Dafang, *China* 58 D5
Dağ, *Turkey* 47 D12
Dagana, *Senegal* 82 B1
Dagash, *Sudan* 80 D3
Dagestan □, *Russia* 35 J8
Dagestanskiye Ogni, *Russia* 35 J9
Daggett, *U.S.A.* 111 L10
Daghestan Republic = Dagestan □, *Russia* 35 J8
Daghfeli, *Sudan* 80 D3
Dağlıq Qarabağ = Nagorno-Karabakh □, *Azerbaijan* 70 B5
Dagö = Hiiumaa, *Estonia* 9 G20
Dagu, *China* 57 E9
Daguan, *China* 58 D4
Dagupan, *Phil.* 61 C4
Daguragu, *Australia* 92 C5
Dahab, *Egypt* 80 B3
Dahlak △, *Eritrea* 81 D5
Dahlak Kebir, *Eritrea* 81 D5
Dahlenburg, *Germany* 24 B6
Dahlonega, *U.S.A.* 115 H4
Dahme, *Germany* 24 D9
Dahod, *India* 68 H6
Dahomey = Benin ■, *Africa* 83 D5
Dahong Shan, *China* 59 B9
Dahra, *Senegal* 82 B1
Dahshûr, *Egypt* 80 J7
Dahūk, *Iraq* 70 B3
Dai Hao, *Vietnam* 64 C6
Dai-Sen, *Japan* 55 G6
Dai Shan, *China* 59 B14
Dai Xian, *China* 56 E7
Daicheng, *China* 56 E9
Daimiel, *Spain* 37 F7
Daingean, *Ireland* 12 C4
Dainkog, *China* 58 A1
Daintree, *Australia* 94 B4
Daintree △, *Australia* 94 B4
Daiō-Misaki, *Japan* 55 G8
Dair, J. ed, *Sudan* 81 E3
Dairût, *Egypt* 80 B3
Daisen-Oki △, *Japan* 55 G6
Daisetsu-Zan, *Japan* 54 C11
Daisetsu-Zan △, *Japan* 54 C11
Dajarra, *Australia* 94 C2
Dajin Chuan →, *China* 58 B3
Dak Dam, *Cambodia* 64 F6
Dak Nhe, *Vietnam* 64 E6
Dak Pek, *Vietnam* 64 E6
Dak Song, *Vietnam* 65 F6
Dak Sui, *Vietnam* 64 E6
Dakar, *Senegal* 82 C1
Dakhla, *W. Sahara* 78 D2
Dakhla, El Wâhât el-, *Egypt* 80 B2
Dakingari, *Nigeria* 83 C5
Dakor, *India* 68 H5
Dakoro, *Niger* 83 C6
Dakota City, *U.S.A.* 112 D6
Đakovica, *Serbia & M.* 44 D4
Đakovo, *Croatia* 28 E3
Dalaba, *Guinea* 82 C2
Dalachi, *China* 56 F3
Dalai Nur, *China* 56 C9
Dālakī, *Iran* 71 D6
Dalälven →, *Sweden* 10 D10
Dalaman, *Turkey* 47 E10
Dalaman →, *Turkey* 47 E10
Dalandzadgad, *Mongolia* 56 C3
Dalap-Uliga-Darrit, *Marshall Is.* 96 G9
Dalarna, *Sweden* 10 D8
Dalarnas län □, *Sweden* 10 C8
Dālbandīn, *Pakistan* 66 E4
Dalbeattie, *U.K.* 13 G5
Dalbeg, *Australia* 94 C4
Dalbosjön, *Sweden* 11 F6
Dalby, *Australia* 95 D5
Dalby, *Sweden* 11 J7
Dalby Söderskog △, *Sweden* 11 J7
Dale City, *U.S.A.* 114 F7
Dale Hollow L., *U.S.A.* 115 G3
Dalga, *Egypt* 80 B3
Dalgān, *Iran* 71 E8
Dalhart, *U.S.A.* 113 G3
Dalhousie, *Canada* 105 C6
Dalhousie, *India* 68 C6
Dali, *Shaanxi, China* 56 G5
Dali, *Yunnan, China* 58 E3
Dalian, *China* 57 E11
Daliang Shan, *China* 58 D4
Daling He →, *China* 57 D11
Dāliyat el Karmel, *Israel* 74 C4
Dalj, *Croatia* 28 E3
Dalkeith, *U.K.* 13 F5
Dallas, *Oreg., U.S.A.* 108 D2
Dallas, *Tex., U.S.A.* 113 J6
Dallol, *Ethiopia* 81 E5
Dalmā, *U.A.E.* 71 E7
Dalmacija, *Croatia* 41 E13
Dalmas, L., *Canada* 105 B5
Dalmatia = Dalmacija, *Croatia* 41 E13
Dalmau, *India* 69 F9
Dalmellington, *U.K.* 13 F4
Dalnegorsk, *Russia* 53 E14
Dalnerechensk, *Russia* 53 E14
Dalnevostochnyy □, *Russia* 53 C14
Daloa, *Ivory C.* 82 D3
Dalou Shan, *China* 58 C6
Dalry, *U.K.* 13 F4
Dalrymple, L., *Australia* 94 C4
Dalrymple, Mt., *Australia* 94 K6
Dals Långed, *Sweden* 11 F6
Dalsjöfors, *Sweden* 11 G7
Dalsland, *Sweden* 11 F6
Daltenganj, *India* 69 H11
Dalton, *Ga., U.S.A.* 115 H3
Dalton, *Mass., U.S.A.* 117 D11
Dalton, *Nebr., U.S.A.* 112 E3
Dalton-in-Furness, *U.K.* 14 C4
Dalupiri I., *Phil.* 61 B4
Dalvík, *Iceland* 8 D4
Dalwallinu, *Australia* 93 F2
Daly →, *Australia* 92 B5
Daly City, *U.S.A.* 110 H4
Daly L., *Canada* 103 B7
Daly River, *Australia* 92 B5
Daly Waters, *Australia* 94 B1
Dalyan, *Turkey* 47 E10
Dam Doi, *Vietnam* 65 H5
Dam Ha, *Vietnam* 64 B6
Daman, *India* 66 J8
Dāmaneh, *Iran* 71 C6
Damanhûr, *Egypt* 80 H7
Damant L., *Canada* 103 A7
Damanzhuang, *China* 56 E9
Damar, *Indonesia* 63 F7
Damaraland, *Namibia* 88 C2
Damascus = Dimashq, *Syria* 74 B5
Damaturu, *Nigeria* 83 C7
Damāvand, *Iran* 71 C7
Damāvand, Qolleh-ye, *Iran* 71 C7
Damba, *Angola* 84 F3
Dâmboviţa □, *Romania* 29 F10
Dâmboviţa →, *Romania* 29 F11
Dâmbovnic →, *Romania* 29 F10
Dame Marie, *Haiti* 121 C5
Dāmghān, *Iran* 71 B7
Dămienesti, *Romania* 29 D11
Damietta = Dumyât, *Egypt* 80 H7
Daming, *China* 56 F8
Damīr Qābū, *Syria* 70 B4
Dammam = Ad Dammām, *Si. Arabia* 71 E6
Dammarie-les-Lys, *France* 19 D9
Dammartin-en-Goële, *France* 19 C9
Damme, *Germany* 24 C4
Damodar →, *India* 69 H12
Damoh, *India* 69 H8
Dampier, *Australia* 92 D2
Dampier, Selat, *Indonesia* 63 E8
Dampier Arch., *Australia* 92 D2
Damrei, Chuor Phnum, *Cambodia* 65 G4
Damvillers, *France* 19 C12
Dan-Gulbi, *Nigeria* 83 C6
Dan Xian, *China* 64 C7
Dana, *Indonesia* 63 F6
Dana, L., *Canada* 104 B4
Dana, Mt., *U.S.A.* 110 H7
Danakil Desert, *Ethiopia* 81 E5
Danané, *Ivory C.* 82 D3
Danao, *Phil.* 61 F6
Danau Poso, *Indonesia* 63 E6
Danba, *China* 58 B3
Danbury, *U.S.A.* 117 E11
Danby L., *U.S.A.* 109 J6
Dand, *Afghan.* 68 D1
Dande ⌓, *Zimbabwe* 87 F3
Dandeldhura, *Nepal* 69 E9
Dandeli, *India* 66 M9
Dandenong, *Australia* 95 F4
Dandîl, *Egypt* 80 J7
Dandong, *China* 57 D13
Danfeng, *China* 56 H6
Dangan Liedao, *China* 59 F10
Dangé-St-Romain, *France* 20 B4
Dângeni, *Romania* 29 C11
Danger Is. = Pukapuka, *Cook Is.* 97 J11
Danger Pt., *S. Africa* 88 E2
Danginpuri, *Indonesia* 63 K18
Dangla, *Ethiopia* 81 E4
Dangla Shan = Tanggula Shan, *China* 60 C4
Dangora, *Nigeria* 83 C6
Dangouadougou, *Burkina Faso* 82 D4
Dangrek, Phnom, *Thailand* 64 E5
Dangriga, *Belize* 119 D7
Dangshan, *China* 56 G9
Dangtu, *China* 59 B12
Dangyang, *China* 59 B8
Dani, *Burkina Faso* 83 C4
Daniel, *U.S.A.* 108 E8
Daniel's Harbour, *Canada* 105 B8
Danielskuil, *S. Africa* 88 D3
Danielson, *U.S.A.* 117 E13
Danilov, *Russia* 32 C11
Danilovgrad, *Serbia & M.* 44 D3
Danilovka, *Russia* 34 E7
Daning, *China* 56 F6
Danja, *Nigeria* 83 C6
Danjiangkou, *China* 59 A8
Danjiangkou Shuiku, *China* 59 A8
Ḑank, *Oman* 71 F8
Dankalwa, *Nigeria* 83 C7
Dankama, *Nigeria* 83 C6
Dankhar Gompa, *India* 66 C11
Dankov, *Russia* 32 F10
Danleng, *China* 58 B4
Danlí, *Honduras* 120 D2
Dannemora, *U.S.A.* 117 B11
Dannenberg, *Germany* 24 B7
Dannevirke, *N.Z.* 91 J6
Dannhauser, *S. Africa* 89 D5
Dansville, *U.S.A.* 116 D7
Danta, *India* 68 G5
Dantan, *India* 69 J12
Danube = Dunărea →, *Europe* 29 E14
Danvers, *U.S.A.* 117 D14
Danville, *Ill., U.S.A.* 114 E2
Danville, *Ky., U.S.A.* 114 G3
Danville, *Pa., U.S.A.* 117 F8
Danville, *Va., U.S.A.* 115 G6
Danville, *Vt., U.S.A.* 117 B12
Danyang, *China* 59 B12
Danzhai, *China* 58 D6
Danzig = Gdańsk, *Poland* 30 D5
Dão →, *Portugal* 36 E2
Dao Xian, *China* 59 E8
Daocheng, *China* 58 C3
Daoukro, *Ivory C.* 82 D4
Dapaong, *Togo* 83 C5
Dapchi, *Nigeria* 83 C7
Dapitan, *Phil.* 61 G5
Daqing Shan, *China* 56 D6
Daqu Shan, *China* 59 B14
Dar Banda, *Africa* 76 F6
Dar el Beida = Casablanca, *Morocco* 78 B4
Dar es Salaam, *Tanzania* 86 D4
Dar Mazār, *Iran* 71 D8
Dar'ā, *Syria* 74 C5
Dar'ā □, *Syria* 74 C5
Dārāb, *Iran* 71 D7
Daraban, *Pakistan* 68 D4
Darabani, *Romania* 29 B11
Daraina, *Madag.* 89 A8
Daraj, *Libya* 79 B8
Dārān, *Iran* 71 C6
Daravica, *Serbia & M.* 44 D4
Daraw, *Egypt* 80 C3
Dārayyā, *Syria* 74 B5
Darazo, *Nigeria* 83 C7
Darband, *Pakistan* 68 B5
Darband, Kūh-e, *Iran* 71 D8
Darbhanga, *India* 69 F11
D'Arcy, *Canada* 102 C4
Darda, *Croatia* 28 E3
Dardanelle, *Ark., U.S.A.* 113 H8
Dardanelle, *Calif., U.S.A.* 110 G7
Dardanelles = Çanakkale Boğazı, *Turkey* 45 F10
Dare →, *Ethiopia* 81 F5
Darende, *Turkey* 72 C7
Dārestān, *Iran* 71 D8
Darfo, *Italy* 40 C7

Dârfûr, Sudan 79 F10
Dargai, Pakistan 68 B4
Dargan Ata, Turkmenistan 52 E7
Dargaville, N.Z. 91 F4
Dargol, Niger 83 C5
Darhan, Mongolia 60 B5
Darhan Muminggan Lianheqi, China 56 D6
Dari, Sudan 81 F3
Darıca, Turkey 72 B3
Darién △, Panama 120 E4
Darién, G. del, Colombia 124 B3
Dariganga = Ovoot, Mongolia 56 B7
Darinskoye, Kazakhstan 34 E10
Darjeeling = Darjiling, India 69 F13
Darjiling, India 69 F13
Darkan, Australia 93 F2
Darkhana, Pakistan 68 D5
Darkhazīneh, Iran 71 D6
Darkot Pass, Pakistan 69 A5
Darling →, Australia 95 E3
Darling Downs, Australia 95 D5
Darling Ra., Australia 93 F2
Darlington, U.K. 14 C6
Darlington, U.S.A. 115 H6
Darlington □, U.K. 14 C6
Darlington, L., S. Africa 88 E4
Darlot, L., Australia 93 E3
Darłowo, Poland 30 D3
Dărmăneşti, Bacău, Romania 29 D11
Dărmăneşti, Suceava, Romania 29 C11
Darmstadt, Germany 25 F4
Darnah, Libya 79 B10
Darnall, S. Africa 89 D5
Darney, France 19 D13
Darnley, C., Antarctica 5 C6
Darnley B., Canada 100 B7
Daroca, Spain 38 D3
Darou-Mousti, Senegal 82 B1
Darr →, Australia 94 C3
Darra Pezu, Pakistan 68 C4
Darrequeira, Argentina 126 D3
Darrington, U.S.A. 108 B3
Darsser Ort, Germany 24 A8
Dart →, U.K. 15 G4
Dart, C., Antarctica 5 D14
Dartford, U.K. 15 F8
Dartmoor, U.K. 15 G4
Dartmoor △, U.K. 15 G4
Dartmouth, Canada 105 D7
Dartmouth, U.K. 15 G4
Dartmouth Res., Australia 95 D4
Dartuch, C. = Artrutx, C. de, Spain 48 B10
Daruvar, Croatia 28 E2
Darvaza, Turkmenistan 52 E6
Darvel, Teluk = Lahad Datu, Teluk, Malaysia 63 D5
Darwen, U.K. 14 D5
Darwendale, Zimbabwe 89 B5
Darwha, India 66 J10
Darwin, Australia 92 B5
Darwin, U.S.A. 111 J9
Darya Khan, Pakistan 68 D4
Daryoi Amu = Amudarya →, Uzbekistan 52 E6
Dās, U.A.E. 71 E7
Dashen, Ras, Ethiopia 81 E4
Dashetai, China 56 D5
Dashhowuz, Turkmenistan 52 E6
Dashkesan = Daşkäsän, Azerbaijan 35 K7
Dashköpri, Turkmenistan 71 B9
Dasht, Iran 71 B8
Dasht →, Pakistan 66 G2
Daska, Pakistan 68 C6
Daşkäsän, Azerbaijan 35 K7
Dassa, Benin 83 D5
Dasuya, India 68 D6
Datça, Turkey 47 E9
Datia, India 69 G8
Datian, China 59 E11
Datong, Anhui, China 59 B11
Datong, Shanxi, China 56 D7
Dattakhel, Pakistan 68 C3
Datteln, Germany 24 D3
Datu, Tanjung, Indonesia 62 D3
Datu Piang, Phil. 61 H6
Datuk, Tanjong = Datu, Tanjung, Indonesia 62 D3
Daua = Dawa →, Africa 81 G5
Daud Khel, Pakistan 68 C4
Daudnagar, India 69 G11
Daugava →, Latvia 9 H21
Daugavpils, Latvia 9 J22
Daulpur, India 68 F7
Daun, Germany 25 E2
Dauphin, Canada 103 C8
Dauphin, U.S.A. 116 F8
Dauphin L., Canada 103 C9
Dauphiné, France 21 C9
Daura, Borno, Nigeria 83 C7
Daura, Katsina, Nigeria 83 C6
Dausa, India 68 F7
Däväçi, Azerbaijan 35 K9
Davangere, India 66 M9
Davao, Phil. 61 H6
Davao G., Phil. 61 H6
Dāvar Panāh = Sarāvān, Iran 71 E9
Davenport, Calif., U.S.A. 110 H4
Davenport, Iowa, U.S.A. 112 E9
Davenport, Wash., U.S.A. 108 C4
Davenport Ra., Australia 94 C1
Daventry, U.K. 15 E6
David, Panama 120 E3
David City, U.S.A. 112 E6
David Gorodok = Davyd Haradok, Belarus 33 F4
Davidson, Canada 103 C7
Davis, Antarctica 5 C6
Davis, U.S.A. 110 G5
Davis Dam, U.S.A. 111 K12
Davis Inlet, Canada 105 A7
Davis Mts., U.S.A. 113 K2
Davis Sea, Antarctica 5 C7
Davis Str., N. Amer. 101 B14
Davo →, Ivory C. 82 D3
Davos, Switz. 25 J5
Davutlar, Turkey 47 D9
Davy L., Canada 103 B7
Davyd Haradok, Belarus 33 F4
Dawa →, Africa 81 G5
Dawaki, Bauchi, Nigeria 83 D6
Dawaki, Kano, Nigeria 83 C6
Dawei = Tavoy, Burma 64 E2
Dawes Ra., Australia 94 C5
Dawlish, U.K. 15 G4
Dawna Ra., Burma 64 D2
Dawros Hd., Ireland 12 B3
Dawson, Canada 100 B6
Dawson, U.S.A. 115 K3
Dawson, I., Chile 128 G2
Dawson B., Canada 103 C8
Dawson Creek, Canada 102 B4
Dawson Inlet, Canada 103 A10
Dawson Ra., Australia 94 C4
Dawu, Hubei, China 59 B9
Dawu, Sichuan, China 58 B3
Dax, France 20 E2
Daxian, China 58 B6
Daxin, China 58 F6
Daxindian, China 57 F11
Daxinggou, China 57 C15
Daxue Shan, Sichuan, China 58 B3
Daxue Shan, Yunnan, China 58 F2
Dayao, China 58 E3
Daye, China 59 B10
Dayet en Naharat, Mali 82 B4
Dayi, China 58 B4
Daylesford, Australia 95 F3
Dayong, China 59 C8
Dayr az Zawr, Syria 70 C4
Daysland, Canada 102 C6
Dayton, Nev., U.S.A. 110 F7
Dayton, Ohio, U.S.A. 114 F3
Dayton, Pa., U.S.A. 116 F5
Dayton, Tenn., U.S.A. 115 H3
Dayton, Wash., U.S.A. 108 C4
Dayton, Wyo., U.S.A. 108 D10
Daytona Beach, U.S.A. 115 L5
Dayu, China 59 E10
Dayville, U.S.A. 108 D4
Dazhu, China 58 B6
Dazkırı, Turkey 47 D11
Dazu, China 58 C5
De Aar, S. Africa 88 E3
De Biesbosch △, Neths. 17 C4
De Funiak Springs, U.S.A. 115 K2
De Grey →, Australia 92 D2
De Haan, Belgium 17 C3
De Hoge Veluwe △, Neths. 17 B5
De Hoop ⌂, S. Africa 88 E3
De Kalb, U.S.A. 112 E10
De Kennemerduinen △, Neths. 17 B4
De Land, U.S.A. 115 L5
De Leon, U.S.A. 113 J5
De Panne, Belgium 17 C2
De Pere, U.S.A. 114 C1
De Queen, U.S.A. 113 H7
De Quincy, U.S.A. 113 K8
De Ridder, U.S.A. 113 K8
De Smet, U.S.A. 112 C6
De Soto, U.S.A. 112 F9
De Tour Village, U.S.A. 114 C4
De Witt, U.S.A. 113 H9
Dead Sea, Asia 74 D4
Deadwood, U.S.A. 112 C3
Deadwood L., Canada 102 B3
Deal, U.K. 15 F9
Deal I., Australia 95 F4
Dealesville, S. Africa 88 D4
De'an, China 59 C10
Dean →, Canada 102 C3
Dean, Forest of, U.K. 15 F5
Dean Chan., Canada 102 C3
Deán Funes, Argentina 126 C3
Dease →, Canada 102 B3
Dease L., Canada 102 B2
Dease Lake, Canada 102 B2
Death Valley, U.S.A. 111 J10
Death Valley △, U.S.A. 111 J10
Death Valley Junction, U.S.A. 111 J10
Deauville, France 18 C7
Deba, Spain 38 B2
Deba Habe, Nigeria 83 C7
Debaltsevo, Ukraine 33 H10
Debao, China 58 F6
Debar, Macedonia 44 E4
Debark, Ethiopia 81 E4
Debden, Canada 103 C7
Dębica, Poland 31 H8
Dęblin, Poland 31 G8
Dębno, Poland 31 F1
Débo, L., Mali 82 B4
DeBolt, Canada 102 B5
Deborah East, L., Australia 93 F2
Deborah West, L., Australia 93 F2
Debrc, Serbia & M. 44 B3
Debre Birhan, Ethiopia 81 F4
Debre Markos, Ethiopia 81 E4
Debre May, Ethiopia 81 E4
Debre Sina, Ethiopia 81 F4
Debre Tabor, Ethiopia 81 E4
Debre Zevit, Ethiopia 81 F4
Debre Zeyit, Ethiopia 81 E4
Debrecen, Hungary 28 C6
Debrzno, Poland 30 E4
Dečani, Serbia & M. 44 D4
Decatur, Ala., U.S.A. 115 H2
Decatur, Ga., U.S.A. 115 J3
Decatur, Ill., U.S.A. 112 F10
Decatur, Ind., U.S.A. 114 E3
Decatur, Tex., U.S.A. 113 J6
Decazeville, France 20 D6
Deccan, India 66 L11
Deception Bay, Australia 95 D5
Deception I., Antarctica 5 C17
Deception L., Canada 103 B8
Dechang, China 58 D4
Dechhu, India 68 F5
Děčín, Czech Rep. 26 A7
Decize, France 19 F10
Deckerville, U.S.A. 116 C2
Decollatura, Italy 43 C9
Decorah, U.S.A. 112 D9
Deda, Romania 29 D9
Dedéagach = Alexandroúpolis, Greece 45 F9
Deder, Ethiopia 81 F5
Dedham, U.S.A. 117 D13
Dédougou, Burkina Faso 82 C4
Dedovichi, Russia 32 D5
Dedza, Malawi 87 E3
Dee →, Aberds., U.K. 13 D6
Dee →, Dumf. & Gall., U.K. 13 G4
Dee →, Wales, U.K. 14 D4
Deep B., Canada 102 A5
Deepwater, Australia 95 D5
Deer →, Canada 103 B10
Deer L., Canada 103 C10
Deer Lake, Nfld., Canada 105 C8
Deer Lake, Ont., Canada 103 C10
Deer Lodge, U.S.A. 108 C7
Deer Park, U.S.A. 108 C5
Deer River, U.S.A. 112 B8
Deeragun, Australia 94 B4
Deerdepoort, S. Africa 88 C4
Deferiet, U.S.A. 117 B9
Defiance, U.S.A. 114 E3
Degana, India 68 F6
Dêgê, China 58 B2
Degebe →, Portugal 37 G3
Degeberga, Sweden 11 J8
Dégelis, Canada 105 C6
Degema, Nigeria 83 E6
Degerfors, Sweden 10 E8
Degerhamn, Sweden 11 H10
Deggendorf, Germany 25 G8
Degh →, Pakistan 68 D5
Değirmendere, Turkey 45 F13
Deh Bīd, Iran 71 D7
Deh-e Shīr, Iran 71 D7
Dehaj, Iran 71 D7
Dehak, Iran 71 E9
Dehdez, Iran 71 D6
Dehej, India 68 J5
Dehestān, Iran 71 D7
Dehgolān, Iran 70 C5
Dehibat, Tunisia 79 B8
Dehlorān, Iran 70 C5
Dehnow-e Kūhestān, Iran 71 E8
Dehra Dun, India 68 D8
Dehri, India 69 G11
Dehua, China 59 E12
Dehui, China 57 B13
Deim Zubeir, Sudan 81 F2
Deinze, Belgium 17 D3
Dej, Romania 29 C8
Deje, Sweden 10 E7
Dejiang, China 58 C7
Deka →, Zimbabwe 88 B4
Dekemhare, Eritrea 81 D4
Dekese, Dem. Rep. of the Congo 84 E4
Del Mar, U.S.A. 111 N9
Del Norte, U.S.A. 109 H10
Del Rio, U.S.A. 113 L4
Delai, Sudan 80 D4
Delambre I., Australia 92 D2
Delami, Sudan 81 E3
Delano, U.S.A. 111 K7
Delano Peak, U.S.A. 109 G7
Delareyville, S. Africa 88 D4
Delaronde L., Canada 103 C7
Delavan, U.S.A. 112 D10
Delaware, U.S.A. 114 E4
Delaware □, U.S.A. 114 F8
Delaware →, U.S.A. 117 G9
Delaware B., U.S.A. 114 F8
Delaware Water Gap ⌂, U.S.A. 117 E10
Delay →, Canada 105 A5
Delbrück, Germany 24 D4
Delčevo, Macedonia 44 E6
Delegate, Australia 95 F4
Delémont, Switz. 25 H3
Delevan, U.S.A. 116 D6
Delft, Neths. 17 B4
Delfzijl, Neths. 17 A6
Delgado, C., Mozam. 87 E5
Delgerhet, Mongolia 56 B6
Delgo, Sudan 80 C3
Delhi, Canada 116 D4
Delhi, India 68 E7
Delhi, La., U.S.A. 113 J9
Delhi, N.Y., U.S.A. 117 D10
Deli Jovan, Serbia & M. 44 B6
Delia, Canada 102 C6
Delice, Turkey 72 C6
Delicias, Mexico 118 B3
Delījān, Iran 71 C6
Déline, Canada 100 B7
Delisle, Canada 103 C7
Delitzsch, Germany 24 D8
Dell City, U.S.A. 109 L11
Dell Rapids, U.S.A. 112 D6
Delle, France 19 E14
Delmar, U.S.A. 117 D11
Delmenhorst, Germany 24 B4
Delnice, Croatia 41 C11
Delonga, Ostrova, Russia 53 B15
Deloraine, Australia 95 G4
Deloraine, Canada 103 D8
Delphi, Greece 46 C4
Delphi, U.S.A. 114 E2
Delphos, U.S.A. 114 E3
Delportshoop, S. Africa 88 D3
Delray Beach, U.S.A. 115 M5
Delsbo, Sweden 10 C10
Delta, Colo., U.S.A. 109 G9
Delta, Utah, U.S.A. 108 G7
Delta □, Nigeria 83 D6
Delta del Ebro ⌂, Spain 38 E5
Delta del Po ⌂, Italy 41 D9
Delta du Saloum △, Senegal 82 C1
Delta Dunărea ⌂, Romania 29 E14
Delta Junction, U.S.A. 100 B5
Deltona, U.S.A. 115 L5
Delungra, Australia 95 D5
Delvada, India 68 J4
Delvinákion, Greece 46 B2
Delvinë, Albania 44 G4
Demak, Indonesia 63 G14
Demanda, Sierra de la, Spain 38 C2
Demavend = Damāvand, Qolleh-ye, Iran 71 C7
Dembecha, Ethiopia 81 E4
Dembi, Ethiopia 81 F4
Dembia, Dem. Rep. of the Congo 86 B2
Dembidolo, Ethiopia 81 F3
Demchok, India 69 C8
Demer →, Belgium 17 D4
Demetrias, Greece 46 B5
Demidov, Russia 32 E6
Deming, N. Mex., U.S.A. 109 K10
Deming, Wash., U.S.A. 110 B4
Demini →, Brazil 124 D6
Demirci, Turkey 47 B10
Demirköprü Barajı, Turkey 47 C10
Demirköy, Turkey 45 E11
Demmin, Germany 24 B9
Demonte, Italy 40 D4
Demopolis, U.S.A. 115 J2
Dempo, Indonesia 62 E2
Demyansk, Russia 32 D7
Den Burg, Neths. 17 A4
Den Chai, Thailand 64 D3
Den Haag = 's-Gravenhage, Neths. 17 B4
Den Helder, Neths. 17 B4
Den Oever, Neths. 17 B5
Denain, France 19 B10
Denair, U.S.A. 110 H6
Denau, Uzbekistan 52 F7
Denbigh, Canada 116 A7
Denbigh, U.K. 14 D4
Denbighshire □, U.K. 14 D4
Dendang, Indonesia 62 E3
Dendermonde, Belgium 17 C4
Deneba, Ethiopia 81 F4
Dengchuan, China 58 E3
Denge, Nigeria 83 C6
Dengfeng, China 56 G7
Dengi, Nigeria 83 D6
Dengkou, China 56 D4
Dengzhou, China 59 A9
Denham, Australia 93 E1
Denham, Mt., Jamaica 120 a
Denham Ra., Australia 94 C4
Denham Sd., Australia 93 E1
Denholm, Canada 103 C7
Denia, Spain 39 G5
Denial B., Australia 95 E1
Deniliquin, Australia 95 F3
Denison, Iowa, U.S.A. 112 E7
Denison, Tex., U.S.A. 113 J6
Denison Plains, Australia 92 C4
Denizli, Turkey 47 D11
Denizli □, Turkey 47 D11
Denman Glacier, Antarctica 5 C7
Denmark, Australia 93 F2
Denmark ■, Europe 11 J3
Denmark Str., Atl. Oc. 98 C17
Dennery, St. Lucia 121 f
Dennison, U.S.A. 116 F3
Denny, U.K. 13 E5
Denpasar, Indonesia 63 K18
Denpasar ✕ (DPS), Indonesia 63 K18
Denton, Mont., U.S.A. 108 C9
Denton, Tex., U.S.A. 113 J6
D'Entrecasteaux △, Australia 93 F2
D'Entrecasteaux, Pt., Australia 93 F2
Denu, Ghana 83 D5
Denver, Colo., U.S.A. 112 F2
Denver, Pa., U.S.A. 117 F8
Denver City, U.S.A. 113 J3
Deoband, India 68 E7
Deogarh, India 68 G5
Deoghar, India 69 G12
Deolali, India 66 K8
Deoli = Devli, India 68 G6
Déols, France 19 F8
Deora, India 68 F4
Deori, India 69 H8
Deoria, India 69 F10
Deosai Mts., Pakistan 69 B6
Deosri, India 69 F14
Depalpur, India 68 H6
Deping, China 57 F9
Deposit, U.S.A. 117 D9
Depuch I., Australia 92 D2
Deputatskiy, Russia 53 C14
Dêqên, China 58 C2
Deqing, China 59 F8
Dera Ghazi Khan, Pakistan 68 D4
Dera Ismail Khan, Pakistan 68 D4
Derabugti, Pakistan 68 E3
Derawar Fort, Pakistan 68 E4
Derbent, Russia 35 J9
Derbent, Turkey 47 C10
Derby, Australia 92 C3
Derby, U.K. 14 E6
Derby, Conn., U.S.A. 117 E11
Derby, Kans., U.S.A. 113 G6
Derby, N.Y., U.S.A. 116 D6
Derby City □, U.K. 14 E6
Derby Line, U.S.A. 117 B12
Derbyshire □, U.K. 14 D6
Đerdap △, Serbia & M. 44 B6
Derdepoort, S. Africa 88 C4
Derecske, Hungary 28 C6
Dereham, U.K. 15 E8
Dereköy, Turkey 45 E11
Dereli, Turkey 73 B8
Derg →, U.K. 12 B4
Derg, L., Ireland 12 D3
Dergachi = Derhaci, Ukraine 33 G9
Dergaon, India 67 F19
Derhaci, Ukraine 33 G9
Derik, Turkey 73 D9
Derinkuyu, Turkey 72 C6
Dermantsi, Bulgaria 45 C8
Dermott, U.S.A. 113 J9
Dêrong, China 58 C2
Derry = Londonderry, U.K. 12 B4
Derry = Londonderry □, U.K. 12 B4
Derry, N.H., U.S.A. 117 D13
Derry, Pa., U.S.A. 116 F5
Derryveagh Mts., Ireland 12 B3
Derudub, Sudan 80 D4
Derval, France 18 E5
Dervéni, Greece 46 C4
Derventa, Bos.-H. 28 F2
Derwent →, Cumb., U.K. 14 C4
Derwent →, Derby, U.K. 14 E6
Derwent →, N. Yorks., U.K. 14 D7
Derwent Water, U.K. 14 C4
Des Moines, Iowa, U.S.A. 112 E8
Des Moines, N. Mex., U.S.A. 113 G3
Des Moines →, U.S.A. 112 E9
Desa, Romania 28 G8
Desaguadero →, Argentina 126 C2
Desaguadero →, Bolivia 124 G5
Desar, Malaysia 65 d
Descanso, Pta., Mexico 111 N9
Descartes, France 20 B4
Deschaillons-sur-St-Laurent, Canada 105 C5
Deschambault L., Canada 103 C8
Deschutes →, U.S.A. 108 D3
Dese, Ethiopia 81 E4
Deseado →, Argentina 128 F3
Desenzano del Garda, Italy 40 C7
Desert Center, U.S.A. 111 M11
Desert Hot Springs, U.S.A. 111 M10
Deshnok, India 68 F5
Desierto Central de Baja California ⌂, Mexico 118 B2
Desna →, Ukraine 33 G6
Desnătui →, Romania 29 G8
Desolación, I., Chile 128 G2
Despeñaperros ⌂, Spain 37 G7
Despeñaperros, Paso, Spain 37 G7
Despotovac, Serbia & M. 44 B5
Dessau, Germany 24 D8
Dessye = Dese, Ethiopia 81 E4
D'Estrees B., Australia 95 F2
Desuri, India 68 G5
Desvres, France 19 B8
Det Udom, Thailand 64 E5
Deta, Romania 28 E6
Dete, Zimbabwe 88 B4
Đetinja →, Serbia & M. 44 C4
Detmold, Germany 24 D4
Detour, Pt., U.S.A. 114 C2
Detroit, U.S.A. 116 D1
Detroit Lakes, U.S.A. 112 B7
Detva, Slovak Rep. 27 C12
Deurne, Neths. 17 C5
Deutsch-Luxemburgischer ⌂, Germany 25 F2
Deutsche Bucht, Germany 24 A4
Deutschlandsberg, Austria 26 E8
Deux-Sèvres □, France 18 F6
Deva, Romania 28 E7
Devakottai, India 66 Q11
Devaprayag, India 69 D8
Dévaványa, Hungary 28 C5
Deveci Dağları, Turkey 72 B7
Devecikonağı, Turkey 45 G12
Devecser, Hungary 28 C2
Develi, Turkey 72 C6
Deventer, Neths. 17 B6
Deveron →, U.K. 13 D6
Devesel, Romania 28 F7
Devgadh Bariya, India 68 H5
Devikot, India 68 F4
Devils Den, U.S.A. 110 K7
Devils Lake, U.S.A. 112 A5
Devils Paw, Canada 102 B2
Devils Postpile ⌂, U.S.A. 110 H7
Devils Tower Junction, U.S.A. 112 C2
Devils Tower Nat. Monument, U.S.A. 112 C2
Devin, Bulgaria 45 E8
Devine, U.S.A. 113 L5
Devizes, U.K. 15 F6
Devli, India 68 G6
Devnya, Bulgaria 45 C11
Devoll →, Albania 44 F4
Devon, Canada 102 C6
Devon □, U.K. 15 G4
Devon I., Canada 98 B11
Devonport, Australia 95 G4
Devonport, N.Z. 91 G5
Devrek, Turkey 72 B4
Devrekâni, Turkey 72 B5
Devrez →, Turkey 72 B6
Dewas, India 68 H7
Dewetsdorp, S. Africa 88 D4
Dewey, Puerto Rico 121 d
Dexing, China 59 C11
Dexter, Maine, U.S.A. 115 C11
Dexter, Mo., U.S.A. 113 G10
Dexter, N. Mex., U.S.A. 113 J2
Dey-Dey, L., Australia 93 E5
Deyang, China 58 B5

Deyhūk, *Iran* 71 C8
Deyyer, *Iran* 71 E6
Dezadeash L., *Canada* 102 A1
Dezfūl, *Iran* 71 C6
Dezhneva, Mys, *Russia* 53 C19
Dezhou, *China* 56 F9
Dhadhar →, *India* 69 G11
Dháfni, *Kríti, Greece* 49 D7
Dháfni, *Pelóponnisos, Greece* 46 D4
Dhahabān, *Si. Arabia* 80 C4
Dhahiriya = Aẓ Ẓāhirīyah, *West Bank* 74 D3
Dhahran = Aẓ Ẓahrān, *Si. Arabia* 71 E6
Dhak, *Pakistan* 68 C5
Dhaka, *Bangla.* 69 H14
Dhaka □, *Bangla.* 69 G14
Dhali, *Cyprus* 49 D12
Dhamási, *Greece* 46 B4
Dhampur, *India* 69 E8
Dhamtari, *India* 67 J12
Dhanbad, *India* 69 H12
Dhangarhi, *Nepal* 67 E12
Dhankuta, *Nepal* 69 F12
Dhar, *India* 68 H6
Dharampur, *India* 68 H6
Dharamsala = Dharmsala, *India* 68 C7
Dhariwal, *India* 68 D6
Dharla →, *Bangla.* 69 G13
Dharmapuri, *India* 66 N11
Dharmjaygarh, *India* 69 H10
Dharmsala, *India* 68 C7
Dharni, *India* 68 J7
Dharwad, *India* 66 M9
Dhasan →, *India* 69 G8
Dhaulagiri, *Nepal* 69 E10
Dhebar, L., *India* 68 G6
Dheftera, *Cyprus* 49 D12
Dhenkanal, *India* 67 J14
Dhenoúsa, *Greece* 47 D7
Dherinia, *Cyprus* 49 D12
Dheskáti, *Greece* 44 G5
Dhespotikó, *Greece* 46 E6
Dhestina, *Greece* 46 C4
Dhī Qār □, *Iraq* 70 D5
Dhiarrizos →, *Cyprus* 49 E11
Dhībān, *Jordan* 74 D4
Dhidhimótikhon, *Greece* 45 E10
Dhíkti Óros, *Greece* 49 D7
Dhilianáta, *Greece* 46 C2
Dhílos, *Greece* 47 D7
Dhilwan, *India* 68 D6
Dhimarkhera, *India* 69 H9
Dhimitsána, *Greece* 46 D4
Dhírfis Óros, *Greece* 46 C5
Dhodhekánisos, *Greece* 47 E8
Dhodhekánisos □, *Greece* 47 E8
Dhokós, *Greece* 46 D5
Dholiana, *Greece* 46 B2
Dholka, *India* 68 H5
Dhomokós, *Greece* 46 B4
Dhoraji, *India* 68 J4
Dhoxáton, *Greece* 45 E8
Dhragonísi, *Greece* 47 D7
Dhráhstis, Ákra, *Greece* 49 A3
Dhrangadhra, *India* 68 H4
Dhrápanon, Ákra, *Greece* 49 D6
Dhriopís, *Greece* 46 D6
Dhrol, *India* 68 H4
Dhuburi, *India* 67 F16
Dhule, *India* 66 J9
Di-ib, W. →, *Sudan* 80 C4
Di Linh, *Vietnam* 65 G7
Di Linh, Cao Nguyen, *Vietnam* 65 G7
Día, *Greece* 49 D7
Diabakania, *Guinea* 82 C2
Diablo, Mt., *U.S.A.* 110 H5
Diablo Range, *U.S.A.* 110 J5
Diafarabé, *Mali* 82 C4
Diala, *Mali* 82 C3
Dialakoro, *Mali* 82 C3
Dialakoto, *Senegal* 82 C2
Diallassagou, *Mali* 82 C4
Diamante, *Argentina* 126 C3
Diamante, *Italy* 43 C8
Diamante →, *Argentina* 126 C2
Diamantina, *Brazil* 125 G10
Diamantina △, *Australia* 94 C3
Diamantina →, *Australia* 95 D2
Diamantino, *Brazil* 125 F7
Diamond Bar, *U.S.A.* 111 L9
Diamond Harbour, *India* 69 H13
Diamond Is., *Australia* 94 B5
Diamond Mts., *U.S.A.* 108 G6
Diamond Springs, *U.S.A.* 110 G6
Dian Chi, *China* 58 E4
Dianalund, *Denmark* 11 J5
Dianbai, *China* 59 G8
Diancheng, *China* 59 G8
Dianjiang, *China* 58 B6
Diano Marina, *Italy* 40 E5
Dianra, *Ivory C.* 82 D3
Diapaga, *Burkina Faso* 83 C5
Diapangou, *Burkina Faso* 83 C5
Diariguila, *Guinea* 82 C2
Dibā, *U.A.E.* 71 E8
Dibai, *India* 68 E8
Dibaya-Lubue, *Dem. Rep. of the Congo* 84 E3
Dibbeen △, *Jordan* 74 C4
Dibete, *Botswana* 88 C4
Dibrugarh, *India* 67 F19
Dickens, *U.S.A.* 113 J4
Dickinson, *U.S.A.* 112 B3
Dickson = Dikson, *Russia* 52 B9
Dickson, *U.S.A.* 115 G2
Dickson City, *U.S.A.* 117 E9
Dicle Nehri →, *Turkey* 73 D9
Dicomano, *Italy* 41 E8
Didesa, W. →, *Ethiopia* 81 E4
Didi, *Sudan* 81 F3
Didiéni, *Mali* 82 C3
Didsbury, *Canada* 102 C6
Didwana, *India* 68 F6
Die, *France* 21 D9
Diébougou, *Burkina Faso* 82 C4
Diecke, *Guinea* 82 D3
Diefenbaker, L., *Canada* 103 C7
Diego de Almagro, *Chile* 126 B1
Diego Garcia, *Ind. Oc.* 3 E13
Diekirch, *Lux.* 17 E6
Diéma, *Mali* 82 C3
Diembéring, *Senegal* 82 C1
Diemelsee ⌂, *Germany* 24 D4
Dien Ban, *Vietnam* 64 E7
Dien Bien, *Vietnam* 58 G4
Dien Khanh, *Vietnam* 65 F7
Diepholz, *Germany* 24 C4
Dieppe, *France* 18 C8
Dierks, *U.S.A.* 113 H8
Diest, *Belgium* 17 D5
Dietikon, *Switz.* 25 H4
Dieulefit, *France* 21 D9
Dieuze, *France* 19 D13
Dif, *Somali Rep.* 75 G3
Differdange, *Lux.* 17 E5
Dig, *India* 68 F7
Digba, *Dem. Rep. of the Congo* 86 B2
Digby, *Canada* 105 D6
Diggi, *India* 68 F6
Dighinala, *Bangla.* 67 H18
Dighton, *U.S.A.* 112 F4
Digna, *Mali* 82 C3
Digne-les-Bains, *France* 21 D10
Digoin, *France* 19 F11
Digor, *Turkey* 73 B10
Digos, *Phil.* 61 H6
Digranes, *Iceland* 8 C6
Digul →, *Indonesia* 63 F9
Digya △, *Ghana* 83 D5
Dihang = Brahmaputra →, *Asia* 69 H13
Dijlah, Nahr →, *Asia* 70 D5
Dijon, *France* 19 E12
Dikhil, *Djibouti* 81 E5
Dikili, *Turkey* 47 B8
Dikirnis, *Egypt* 80 H7
Dikkil = Dikhil, *Djibouti* 81 E5
Dikodougou, *Ivory C.* 82 D3
Diksmuide, *Belgium* 17 C2
Dikson, *Russia* 52 B9
Dikwa, *Nigeria* 83 C7
Dila, *Ethiopia* 81 F4
Dilek Yarimadisi △, *Turkey* 47 D9
Dili, *E. Timor* 63 F7
Dilijan, *Armenia* 35 K7
Dilizhan = Dilijan, *Armenia* 35 K7
Dilj, *Croatia* 28 E3
Dillenburg, *Germany* 24 E4
Dilley, *U.S.A.* 113 L5
Dilli = Delhi, *India* 68 E7
Dilling, *Sudan* 81 E2
Dillingen, *Bayern, Germany* 25 G6
Dillingen, *Saarland, Germany* 25 F2
Dillingham, *U.S.A.* 100 C4
Dillon, *Canada* 103 B7
Dillon, *Mont., U.S.A.* 108 D7
Dillon, *S.C., U.S.A.* 115 H6
Dillon →, *Canada* 103 B7
Dillsburg, *U.S.A.* 116 F7
Dilly, *Mali* 82 C3
Dilolo, *Dem. Rep. of the Congo* 84 G4
Dimas, *Mexico* 118 C3
Dimashq, *Syria* 74 B5
Dimashq □, *Syria* 74 B5
Dimbaza, *S. Africa* 89 E4
Dimbokro, *Ivory C.* 82 D4
Dimboola, *Australia* 95 F3
Dîmboviţa = Dâmboviţa →, *Romania* 29 F11
Dimbulah, *Australia* 94 B4
Dimitrovgrad, *Bulgaria* 45 D9
Dimitrovgrad, *Russia* 34 C9
Dimitrovgrad, *Serbia & M.* 44 C6
Dimitrovo = Pernik, *Bulgaria* 44 D7
Dimmitt, *U.S.A.* 113 H3
Dimo, *Sudan* 81 F2
Dimona, *Israel* 74 D4
Dimovo, *Bulgaria* 44 C6
Dinagat, *Phil.* 61 F6
Dinajpur, *Bangla.* 67 G16
Dinan, *France* 18 D4
Dīnān Āb, *Iran* 71 C8
Dinant, *Belgium* 17 D4
Dinapur, *India* 69 G11
Dinar, *Turkey* 47 C12
Dīnār, Kūh-e, *Iran* 71 D6
Dinara Planina, *Croatia* 41 D13
Dinard, *France* 18 D4
Dinaric Alps = Dinara Planina, *Croatia* 41 D13
Dindanko, *Mali* 82 C3
Dinder △, *Sudan* 81 E4
Dinder, Nahr ed →, *Sudan* 81 E3
Dindigul, *India* 66 P11
Dindori, *India* 69 H9
Ding Xian = Dingzhou, *China* 56 E8
Dinga, *Pakistan* 68 G2
Dingalan, *Phil.* 61 D4
Dingbian, *China* 56 F4
Dingelstädt, *Germany* 24 D6
Dingle, *Ireland* 12 D1
Dingle, *Sweden* 11 F5
Dingle B., *Ireland* 12 D1
Dingmans Ferry, *U.S.A.* 117 E10
Dingnan, *China* 59 E10
Dingo, *Australia* 94 C4
Dingolfing, *Germany* 25 G8
Dingtao, *China* 56 G8
Dinguira, *Mali* 82 C2
Dinguiraye, *Guinea* 82 C2
Dingwall, *U.K.* 13 D4
Dingxi, *China* 56 G3
Dingxiang, *China* 56 E7
Dingyuan, *China* 59 A11
Dingzhou, *China* 56 E8
Dinh, Mui, *Vietnam* 65 G7
Dinh Lap, *Vietnam* 58 G6
Dinira △, *Venezuela* 121 E6
Dinira △, *Venezuela* 121 E5
Dinokwe, *Botswana* 88 C4
Dinorwic, *Canada* 103 D10
Dinosaur ⌂, *Canada* 102 C6
Dinosaur ⌂, *U.S.A.* 108 F9
Dinuba, *U.S.A.* 110 J7
Diö, *Sweden* 11 H8
Dioïla, *Mali* 82 C3
Dioka, *Mali* 82 C2
Diongoï, *Mali* 82 C3
Diósgyör, *Hungary* 28 B5
Diosig, *Romania* 28 C7
Diougani, *Mali* 82 C4
Diouloulou, *Senegal* 82 C1
Dioura, *Mali* 82 C3
Diourbel, *Senegal* 82 C1
Dipalpur, *Pakistan* 68 D5
Diplo, *Pakistan* 68 G3
Dipolog, *Phil.* 61 G5
Dipperu △, *Australia* 94 C4
Dir, *Pakistan* 66 B7
Diré, *Mali* 82 B4
Dire Dawa, *Ethiopia* 81 F5
Diriamba, *Nic.* 120 D2
Dirk Hartog I., *Australia* 93 E1
Dirranbandi, *Australia* 95 D4
Disa, *India* 68 G5
Disa, *Sudan* 81 E3
Disappointment, C., *U.S.A.* 108 C2
Disappointment, L., *Australia* 92 D3
Disaster B., *Australia* 95 F4
Discovery B., *Australia* 95 F3
Disentis Muster, *Switz.* 25 J4
Dishna, *Egypt* 80 B3
Disina, *Nigeria* 83 C6
Disko = Qeqertarsuaq, *Greenland* 101 B5
Disna = Dzisna →, *Belarus* 32 E5
Diss, *U.K.* 15 E9
Disteghil Sar, *Pakistan* 69 A6
Distrito Federal □, *Brazil* 125 G9
Distrito Federal □, *Mexico* 119 D5
Disûq, *Egypt* 80 H7
Diu, *India* 68 J4
Dīvāndarreh, *Iran* 70 C5
Dives →, *France* 18 C6
Dives-sur-Mer, *France* 18 C6
Divichi = Däväçi, *Azerbaijan* 35 K9
Divide, *U.S.A.* 108 D7
Dividing Ra., *Australia* 93 E2
Divinópolis, *Brazil* 125 H10
Divjake, *Albania* 44 F3
Divnoye, *Russia* 35 H6
Divo, *Ivory C.* 82 D3
Divriği, *Turkey* 73 C8
Dīwāl Kol, *Afghan.* 68 B2
Dixie Mt., *U.S.A.* 110 F6
Dixon, *Calif., U.S.A.* 110 G5
Dixon, *Ill., U.S.A.* 112 E10
Dixon Entrance, *U.S.A.* 100 C6
Dixville, *Canada* 117 A13
Diyadin, *Turkey* 73 C10
Diyālā □, *Iraq* 70 C5
Diyālā →, *Iraq* 70 C5
Diyarbakır, *Turkey* 70 B4
Diyodar, *India* 68 G4
Djakarta = Jakarta, *Indonesia* 63 G12
Djamba, *Angola* 88 B1
Djambala, *Congo* 84 E2
Djanet, *Algeria* 78 D7
Djawa = Jawa, *Indonesia* 62 F3
Djelfa, *Algeria* 78 B6
Djema, *C.A.R.* 86 A2
Djenné, *Mali* 82 C4
Djerba, I. de, *Tunisia* 79 B8
Djerid, Chott, *Tunisia* 78 B7
Djibo, *Burkina Faso* 83 C4
Djibouti, *Djibouti* 81 E5
Djibouti ■, *Africa* 81 E5
Djolu, *Dem. Rep. of the Congo* 84 D4
Djougou, *Benin* 83 D5
Djoum, *Cameroon* 84 D2
Djourab, Erg du, *Chad* 79 E9
Djugu, *Dem. Rep. of the Congo* 86 B3
Djúpivogur, *Iceland* 8 D6
Djurås, *Sweden* 10 D9
Djurö △, *Sweden* 11 F7
Djursland, *Denmark* 11 H4
Dmitriya Lapteva, Proliv, *Russia* 53 B15
Dmitriyev Lgovskiy, *Russia* 33 F8
Dmitrov, *Russia* 32 D9
Dmitrovsk-Orlovskiy, *Russia* 33 F8
Dnepr = Dnipro →, *Ukraine* 33 J7
Dneprodzerzhinsk = Dniprodzerzhynsk, *Ukraine* 33 H8
Dneprodzerzhinskoye Vdkhr. = Dniprodzerzhynske Vdskh., *Ukraine* 33 H8
Dnepropetrovsk = Dnipropetrovsk, *Ukraine* 33 H8
Dneprorudnoye = Dniprorudne, *Ukraine* 33 J8
Dnestr = Dnister →, *Europe* 33 J6
Dnestrovski = Belgorod, *Russia* 33 G9
Dnieper = Dnipro →, *Ukraine* 33 J7
Dniester = Dnister →, *Europe* 33 J6
Dnipro →, *Ukraine* 33 J7
Dniprodzerzhynsk, *Ukraine* 33 H8
Dniprodzerzhynske Vdskh., *Ukraine* 33 H8
Dnipropetrovsk, *Ukraine* 33 H8
Dniprorudne, *Ukraine* 33 J8
Dnister →, *Europe* 33 J6
Dnistrovskyy Lyman, *Ukraine* 33 J6
Dno, *Russia* 32 D5
Dnyapro = Dnipro →, *Ukraine* 33 J7
Doaktown, *Canada* 105 C6
Doan Hung, *Vietnam* 58 G5
Doany, *Madag.* 89 A8
Doba, *Chad* 79 G9
Dobandi, *Pakistan* 68 D2
Dobbiaco, *Italy* 41 B9
Dobbyn, *Australia* 94 B3
Dobczyce, *Poland* 31 J7
Dobele, *Latvia* 9 H20
Dobele □, *Latvia* 30 B10
Döbeln, *Germany* 24 D9
Doberai, Jazirah, *Indonesia* 63 E8
Dobiegniew, *Poland* 31 F2
Doblas, *Argentina* 126 D3
Dobo, *Indonesia* 63 F8
Doboj, *Bos.-H.* 28 F3
Dobra, *Wielkopolskie, Poland* 31 G5
Dobra, *Zachodnio-Pomorskie, Poland* 30 E2
Dobra, *Dâmbovita, Romania* 29 F10
Dobra, *Hunedoara, Romania* 28 E7
Dobre Miasto, *Poland* 30 E7
Dobreşti, *Romania* 28 D7
Dobrich, *Bulgaria* 45 C11
Dobrinishta, *Bulgaria* 44 E7
Dobříš, *Czech Rep.* 26 B7
Dobrodzień, *Poland* 31 H5
Dobropole, *Ukraine* 33 H9
Dobruja, *Europe* 29 F13
Dobrush, *Belarus* 33 F6
Dobrzany, *Poland* 30 E2
Dobrzyń nad Wisłą, *Poland* 31 F6
Doc, Mui, *Vietnam* 64 D6
Docker River, *Australia* 93 D4
Docksta, *Sweden* 10 A12
Doctor Arroyo, *Mexico* 118 C4
Doda, *India* 69 C6
Doda, L., *Canada* 104 C4
Dodecanese = Dhodhekánisos, *Greece* 47 E8
Dodge City, *U.S.A.* 113 G5
Dodge L., *Canada* 103 B7
Dodgeville, *U.S.A.* 112 D9
Dodo, *Cameroon* 83 D7
Dodo, *Sudan* 81 F2
Dodola, *Ethiopia* 81 F4
Dodoma, *Tanzania* 86 D4
Dodoma □, *Tanzania* 86 D4
Dodona, *Greece* 46 B2
Dodori ⌂, *Kenya* 86 C5
Dodsland, *Canada* 103 C7
Dodson, *U.S.A.* 108 B9
Dodurga, *Turkey* 47 B11
Doesburg, *Neths.* 17 B6
Doetinchem, *Neths.* 17 C6
Dog Creek, *Canada* 102 C4
Dog L., *Man., Canada* 103 C9
Dog L., *Ont., Canada* 104 C2
Doğanşehir, *Turkey* 72 C7
Dogliani, *Italy* 40 D4
Dogondoutchi, *Niger* 83 C5
Dogran, *Pakistan* 68 D5
Doğubayazıt, *Turkey* 70 B5
Doguéraoua, *Niger* 83 C6
Doha = Ad Dawḥah, *Qatar* 71 E6
Dohazari, *Bangla.* 67 H18
Dohrighat, *India* 69 F10
Doi, *Indonesia* 63 D7
Doi Inthanon △, *Thailand* 64 C2
Doi Khuntan △, *Thailand* 64 C2
Doi Luang, *Thailand* 64 C3
Doi Luang △, *Thailand* 64 C2
Doi Saket, *Thailand* 64 C2
Doi Suthep △, *Thailand* 64 C2
Dois Irmãos, Sa., *Brazil* 125 E10
Dojransko Jezero, *Macedonia* 44 E6
Dokkum, *Neths.* 17 A5
Dokri, *Pakistan* 68 F3
Dokuchayevsk, *Ukraine* 33 J9
Dol-de-Bretagne, *France* 18 D5
Dolac, *Serbia & M.* 44 D4
Dolak, Pulau, *Indonesia* 63 F9
Dolbeau-Mistassini, *Canada* 105 C5
Dole, *France* 19 E12
Doleib, Wadi →, *Sudan* 81 E3
Dolenji Logatec, *Slovenia* 41 C11
Dolgellau, *U.K.* 14 E4
Dolgelley = Dolgellau, *U.K.* 14 E4
Dolhasca, *Romania* 29 C11
Dolianova, *Italy* 42 C2
Dolinskaya = Dolynska, *Ukraine* 33 H7
Dolj □, *Romania* 29 F8
Dollard, *Neths.* 17 A7
Dolna Banya, *Bulgaria* 44 D7
Dolni Chiflik, *Bulgaria* 45 D11
Dolni Dŭbnik, *Bulgaria* 45 C8
Dolnośląskie □, *Poland* 31 G3
Dolný Kubín, *Slovak Rep.* 27 B12
Dolo, *Ethiopia* 81 G5
Dolo, *Italy* 41 C9
Dolomites = Dolomiti, *Italy* 41 B8
Dolomiti, *Italy* 41 B8
Dolomiti Bellunesi △, *Italy* 41 B9
Dolores, *Argentina* 126 D4
Dolores, *Uruguay* 126 C4
Dolores, *U.S.A.* 109 H9
Dolores →, *U.S.A.* 109 G9
Dolovo, *Serbia & M.* 28 F5
Dolphin, C., *Falk. Is.* 128 G5
Dolphin and Union Str., *Canada* 100 B8
Dolsk, *Poland* 31 G4
Dolynska, *Ukraine* 33 H7
Dolzhanskaya, *Russia* 33 J9
Dom Pedrito, *Brazil* 127 C5
Doma, *Nigeria* 83 D6
Doma ⌂, *Zimbabwe* 87 F3
Domaniç, *Turkey* 47 B11
Domariaganj →, *India* 69 F10
Domasi, *Malawi* 87 F4
Domažlice, *Czech Rep.* 26 B5
Dombarovskiy, *Russia* 52 D6
Dombås, *Norway* 9 E13
Dombasle-sur-Meurthe, *France* 19 D13
Dombes, *France* 21 C9
Dombóvár, *Hungary* 28 D3
Dombrád, *Hungary* 28 B6
Dome Fuji, *Antarctica* 5 D5
Domel I. = Letsôk-aw Kyun, *Burma* 65 G2
Domérat, *France* 19 F9
Domeyko, *Chile* 126 B1
Domeyko, Cordillera, *Chile* 126 A2
Domfront, *France* 18 D6
Dominador, *Chile* 126 A2
Dominica ■, *W. Indies* 121 C7
Dominica Passage, *W. Indies* 121 C7
Dominican Rep. ■, *W. Indies* 121 C5
Dömitz, *Germany* 24 B7
Domme, *France* 20 D5
Domneşti, *Romania* 29 E9
Domodóssola, *Italy* 40 B5
Domogled-Valea Cernei △, *Romania* 28 F7
Dompaire, *France* 19 D13
Dompierre-sur-Besbre, *France* 19 F10
Dompim, *Ghana* 82 D4
Domrémy-la-Pucelle, *France* 19 D12
Domville, Mt., *Australia* 95 D5
Domvraína, *Greece* 46 C4
Domžale, *Slovenia* 41 B11
Don →, *Russia* 33 J10
Don →, *Aberds., U.K.* 13 D6
Don →, *S. Yorks., U.K.* 14 D7
Don, C., *Australia* 92 B5
Don Benito, *Spain* 37 G5
Don Figuero Mts., *Jamaica* 120 a
Don Sak, *Thailand* 65 b
Dona Ana = Nhamabué, *Mozam.* 87 F4
Doña Mencía, *Spain* 37 H6
Donaghadee, *U.K.* 12 B6
Donald, *Australia* 95 F3
Donaldsonville, *U.S.A.* 113 K9
Donalsonville, *U.S.A.* 115 K3
Doñana △, *Spain* 37 J4
Donau = Dunărea →, *Europe* 29 E14
Donau →, *Austria* 27 C10
Donau Auen △, *Austria* 27 C9
Donaueschingen, *Germany* 25 H4
Donauwörth, *Germany* 25 G6
Doncaster, *U.K.* 14 D6
Dondo, *Mozam.* 87 F3
Dondo, Teluk, *Indonesia* 63 D6
Dondra Head, *Sri Lanka* 66 S12
Donduşeni, *Moldova* 29 B12
Donegal, *Ireland* 12 B3
Donegal □, *Ireland* 12 B4
Donegal B., *Ireland* 12 B3
Donets →, *Russia* 35 G5
Donets Basin, *Ukraine* 6 F13
Donetsk, *Ukraine* 33 J9
Dong Ba Thin, *Vietnam* 65 F7
Dong Dang, *Vietnam* 58 G6
Dong Giam, *Vietnam* 64 C5
Dong Ha, *Vietnam* 64 D6
Dong Hene, *Laos* 64 D5
Dong Hoi, *Vietnam* 64 D6
Dong Jiang →, *China* 59 F10
Dong Khe, *Vietnam* 64 A6
Dong Ujimqin Qi, *China* 56 B9
Dong Van, *Vietnam* 64 A5
Dong Xoai, *Vietnam* 65 G6
Donga, *Nigeria* 83 D7
Donga →, *Nigeria* 83 D7
Dong'an, *China* 59 D8
Dongara, *Australia* 93 E1
Dongbei, *China* 53 E13
Dongchuan, *China* 58 D4
Donges, *France* 18 E4
Dongfang, *China* 64 C7
Dongfeng, *China* 57 C13
Donggala, *Indonesia* 63 E5
Donggan, *China* 58 F5
Donggou, *China* 57 E13
Dongguan, *China* 59 F9
Dongguang, *China* 56 F9
Donghai Dao, *China* 59 G8
Dongjingcheng, *China* 57 B15
Dongkou, *China* 59 D8
Donglan, *China* 58 E6
Dongliu, *China* 59 B11
Dongmen, *China* 58 F6
Dongning, *China* 57 B16
Dongnyi, *China* 58 C3
Dongola, *Sudan* 80 D3
Dongping, *China* 56 G9
Dongsha Dao, *China* 59 G11
Dongshan, *China* 59 F11
Dongsheng, *China* 56 E6
Dongtai, *China* 57 H11
Dongting Hu, *China* 59 C9
Dongtou, *China* 59 D13
Dongxiang, *China* 59 C11
Dongxing, *China* 58 G7
Dongyang, *China* 59 C13
Dongzhi, *China* 59 B11
Donington, C., *Australia* 95 E2
Doniphan, *U.S.A.* 113 G9
Donja Stubica, *Croatia* 41 C12
Donji Dušnik, *Serbia & M.* 44 C6
Donji Miholjac, *Croatia* 28 E3
Donji Milanovac, *Serbia & M.* 44 B6
Donji Vakuf, *Bos.-H.* 28 F2
Dønna, *Norway* 8 C15
Donna, *U.S.A.* 113 M5
Donnacona, *Canada* 105 C5
Donnelly's Crossing, *N.Z.* 91 F4
Donnybrook, *Australia* 93 F2
Donnybrook, *S. Africa* 89 D4
Donora, *U.S.A.* 116 F5
Donostia = Donostia-San Sebastián, *Spain* 38 B3
Donostia-San Sebastián, *Spain* 38 B3

Donskoy, *Russia* 32 F10
Donsol, *Phil.* 61 E5
Donzère, *France* 21 D8
Donzy, *France* 19 E10
Doon →, *U.K.* 13 F4
Dora, L., *Australia* 92 D3
Dora Báltea →, *Italy* 40 C5
Dora Ripária →, *Italy* 40 C4
Doran L., *Canada* 103 A7
Dorchester, *U.K.* 15 G5
Dorchester, C., *Canada* 101 B12
Dordabis, *Namibia* 88 C2
Dordogne □, *France* 20 C4
Dordogne →, *France* 20 C3
Dordrecht, *Neths.* 17 C4
Dordrecht, *S. Africa* 88 E4
Dore →, *France* 20 C7
Dore, Mts., *France* 20 C6
Doré L., *Canada* 103 C7
Doré Lake, *Canada* 103 C7
Dorfen, *Germany* 25 G8
Dorgali, *Italy* 42 B2
Dori, *Burkina Faso* 83 C4
Doring →, *S. Africa* 88 E2
Doringbos, *S. Africa* 88 E2
Dorking, *U.K.* 15 F7
Dormaa-Ahenkro, *Ghana* 82 D4
Dormans, *France* 19 C10
Dormo, Ras, *Eritrea* 81 E5
Dornbirn, *Austria* 26 D2
Dornes, *France* 19 F10
Dorneşti, *Romania* 29 C11
Dornie, *U.K.* 13 D3
Dornoch, *U.K.* 13 D4
Dornoch Firth, *U.K.* 13 D4
Dornogovĭ □, *Mongolia* 56 C6
Doro, *Mali* 83 B4
Dorog, *Hungary* 28 C3
Dorogobuzh, *Russia* 32 E7
Dorohoi, *Romania* 29 C11
Döröö Nuur, *Mongolia* 60 B4
Dorr, *Iran* 71 C6
Dorre I., *Australia* 93 E1
Dorrigo, *Australia* 95 E5
Dorris, *U.S.A.* 108 F3
Dorset, *Canada* 116 A6
Dorset, *U.S.A.* 116 E4
Dorset □, *U.K.* 15 G5
Dorsten, *Germany* 24 D2
Dortmund, *Germany* 24 D3
Dortmund-Ems-Kanal →, *Germany* 24 D3
Dörtyol, *Turkey* 72 D7
Dorum, *Germany* 24 B4
Doruma, *Dem. Rep. of the Congo* 86 B2
Dorūneh, *Iran* 71 C8
Dos Bahías, C., *Argentina* 128 E3
Dos Hermanas, *Spain* 37 H5
Dos Palos, *U.S.A.* 110 J6
Döşemealtı, *Turkey* 47 D12
Dosso, *Niger* 83 C5
Dosso ⌂, *Niger* 83 C5
Dothan, *U.S.A.* 115 K3
Doty, *U.S.A.* 110 D3
Douai, *France* 19 B10
Douako, *Guinea* 82 D2
Douala, *Cameroon* 83 E6
Douarnenez, *France* 18 D2
Doubabougou, *Mali* 82 C3
Double Island Pt., *Australia* 95 D5
Double Mountain Fork →, *U.S.A.* 113 J4
Doubrava →, *Czech Rep.* 26 A8
Doubs □, *France* 19 E13
Doubs →, *France* 19 F12
Doubtful Sd., *N.Z.* 91 L1
Doubtless B., *N.Z.* 91 F4
Doudeville, *France* 18 C7
Doué-la-Fontaine, *France* 18 E6
Douentza, *Mali* 82 C4
Douentza ⌂, *Mali* 82 B4
Douglas, *S. Africa* 88 D3
Douglas, *U.K.* 14 C3
Douglas, *Ariz., U.S.A.* 109 L9
Douglas, *Ga., U.S.A.* 115 K4
Douglas, *Wyo., U.S.A.* 112 D2
Douglas Apsley △, *Australia* 95 G4
Douglas Chan., *Canada* 102 C3
Douglas Pt., *Canada* 116 B3
Douglasville, *U.S.A.* 115 J3
Doukáton, Ákra, *Greece* 46 C2
Doulevant-le-Château, *France* 19 D11
Doullens, *France* 19 B9
Doumen, *China* 59 F9
Douna, *Mali* 82 C3
Dounreay, *U.K.* 13 C5
Dourada, Serra, *Brazil* 125 F9
Dourados, *Brazil* 127 A5
Dourados →, *Brazil* 127 A5
Dourados, Serra dos, *Brazil* 127 A5
Dourdan, *France* 19 D9
Douro →, *Europe* 36 D2
Douvaine, *France* 19 F13
Douvres-la-Délivrande, *France* 18 C6
Douze →, *France* 20 E3
Dove →, *U.K.* 14 E6
Dove Creek, *U.S.A.* 109 H9
Dover, *Australia* 95 G4
Dover, *U.K.* 15 F9
Dover, *Del., U.S.A.* 114 F8
Dover, *N.H., U.S.A.* 117 C14
Dover, *N.J., U.S.A.* 117 F10
Dover, *Ohio, U.S.A.* 116 F3
Dover, Pt., *Australia* 93 F4
Dover, Str. of, *Europe* 15 G9
Dover-Foxcroft, *U.S.A.* 115 C11
Dover Plains, *U.S.A.* 117 E11
Dovey = Dyfi →, *U.K.* 15 E3
Dovrefjell, *Norway* 9 E13
Dow Rūd, *Iran* 71 C6
Dowa, *Malawi* 87 E3
Dowagiac, *U.S.A.* 114 E2
Dowerin, *Australia* 93 F2
Dowgha'i, *Iran* 71 B8
Dowlatābād, *Iran* 71 D8
Down □, *U.K.* 12 B5
Downey, *Calif., U.S.A.* 111 M8
Downey, *Idaho, U.S.A.* 108 E7
Downham Market, *U.K.* 15 E8
Downieville, *U.S.A.* 110 F6
Downpatrick, *U.K.* 12 B6
Downpatrick Hd., *Ireland* 12 B2
Downsville, *U.S.A.* 117 D10
Downton, Mt., *Canada* 102 C4
Dowsārī, *Iran* 71 D8
Doyle, *U.S.A.* 110 E6
Doylestown, *U.S.A.* 117 F9
Dozois, Rés., *Canada* 104 C4
Dra Khel, *Pakistan* 68 F2
Drac →, *France* 21 C9
Dračevo, *Macedonia* 44 E5
Drachten, *Neths.* 17 A6
Drăgănești, *Moldova* 29 C13
Drăgănești-Olt, *Romania* 29 F9
Drăgănești-Vlașca, *Romania* 29 F10
Dragaš, *Serbia & M.* 44 D4
Drăgășani, *Romania* 29 F9
Dragichyn, *Belarus* 33 F3
Dragocvet, *Serbia & M.* 44 C5
Dragon's Mouth = Boca de Drago, *Venezuela* 125 K15
Dragovishtitsa, *Bulgaria* 44 D6
Draguignan, *France* 21 E10
Drain, *U.S.A.* 108 E2
Drake, *U.S.A.* 112 B4
Drake Passage, *S. Ocean* 5 B17
Drakensberg, *S. Africa* 89 D4
Dráma, *Greece* 45 E8
Dráma □, *Greece* 45 E8
Drammen, *Norway* 9 G14
Drangajökull, *Iceland* 8 C2
Dranov, Ostrov, *Romania* 29 F14
Dras, *India* 69 B6
Drau = Drava →, *Croatia* 28 E3
Drava →, *Croatia* 28 E3
Dravograd, *Slovenia* 41 B12
Drawa →, *Poland* 31 F2
Drawieński △, *Poland* 31 E2
Drawno, *Poland* 31 E2
Drawsko Pomorskie, *Poland* 30 E2
Drayton Valley, *Canada* 102 C6
Dreieich, *Germany* 25 E4
Dren, *Serbia & M.* 44 C4
Drenthe □, *Neths.* 17 B6
Drepanum, C., *Cyprus* 49 E11
Dresden, *Canada* 116 D2
Dresden, *Germany* 24 D9
Dreux, *France* 18 D8
Drezdenko, *Poland* 31 F2
Driffield, *U.K.* 14 C7
Driftwood, *U.S.A.* 116 E6
Driggs, *U.S.A.* 108 E8
Drin →, *Albania* 44 D3
Drin i Zi →, *Albania* 44 E4
Drina →, *Bos.-H.* 44 B3
Drincea →, *Romania* 28 F7
Drinjača →, *Bos.-H.* 28 F4
Drissa = Vyerkhnyadzvinsk, *Belarus* 32 E4
Drniš, *Croatia* 41 E13
Drøbak, *Norway* 9 G14
Drobeta-Turnu Severin, *Romania* 28 F7
Drobin, *Poland* 31 F6
Drochia, *Moldova* 29 B12
Drogheda, *Ireland* 12 C5
Drogichin = Dragichyn, *Belarus* 33 F3
Drogobych = Drohobych, *Ukraine* 33 H2
Drohiczyn, *Poland* 31 F9
Drohobych, *Ukraine* 33 H2
Droichead Atha = Drogheda, *Ireland* 12 C5
Droichead Nua, *Ireland* 12 C5
Droitwich, *U.K.* 15 E5
Drôme □, *France* 21 D9
Drôme →, *France* 21 D8
Dromedary, C., *Australia* 95 F5
Drómling ⌂, *Germany* 24 C7
Dromore, *U.K.* 12 B4
Dromore West, *Ireland* 12 B3
Dronero, *Italy* 40 D4
Dronfield, *U.K.* 14 D6
Dronne →, *France* 20 C3
Dronning Maud Land, *Antarctica* 5 D3
Dronninglund, *Denmark* 11 G4
Dronten, *Neths.* 17 B5
Dropt →, *France* 20 D3
Drosendorf, *Austria* 26 C8
Droué, *France* 18 D8
Drumbo, *Canada* 116 C4
Drumheller, *Canada* 102 C6
Drummond, *U.S.A.* 108 C7
Drummond I., *U.S.A.* 114 C4
Drummond Pt., *Australia* 95 E2
Drummond Ra., *Australia* 94 C4
Drummondville, *Canada* 104 C5
Drumright, *U.S.A.* 113 H6
Druskininkai, *Lithuania* 9 J20
Drut →, *Belarus* 33 F6
Druya, *Belarus* 32 E4
Druzhba, *Bulgaria* 45 C12
Druzhina, *Russia* 53 C15
Drvar, *Bos.-H.* 41 D13
Drvenik, *Croatia* 41 E13
Drwęca →, *Poland* 31 E5
Dry Harbour Mts., *Jamaica* 120 a
Dry Tortugas, *U.S.A.* 120 B3
Dryanovo, *Bulgaria* 45 D9
Dryden, *Canada* 103 D10
Dryden, *U.S.A.* 117 D8
Drygalski I., *Antarctica* 5 C7
Drysdale →, *Australia* 92 B4
Drysdale I., *Australia* 94 A2
Drysdale River △, *Australia* 92 B4
Drzewica, *Poland* 31 G7
Drzewiczka →, *Poland* 31 G7
Dschang, *Cameroon* 83 D7
Du Bois, *U.S.A.* 116 E6
Du Gué →, *Canada* 104 A5
Du He, *China* 59 A8
Du Quoin, *U.S.A.* 112 G10
Du'an, *China* 58 F7
Duanesburg, *U.S.A.* 117 D10
Duaringa, *Australia* 94 C4
Duarte, Pico, *Dom. Rep.* 121 D5
Ḑubā, *Si. Arabia* 70 E2
Dubai = Dubayy, *U.A.E.* 71 E7
Dubăsari, *Moldova* 29 C14
Dubăsari Vdkhr., *Moldova* 29 C13
Dubawnt →, *Canada* 103 A8
Dubawnt L., *Canada* 103 A8
Dubayy, *U.A.E.* 71 E7
Dubbo, *Australia* 95 E4
Dubele, *Dem. Rep. of the Congo* 86 B2
Dübendorf, *Switz.* 25 H4
Dubica, *Croatia* 41 C13
Dublin, *Ireland* 12 C5
Dublin, *Ga., U.S.A.* 115 J4
Dublin, *Tex., U.S.A.* 113 J5
Dublin □, *Ireland* 12 C5
Dublin ✕ (DUB), *Ireland* 12 C5
Dubna, *Russia* 32 D9
Dubnica nad Váhom, *Slovak Rep.* 27 C11
Dubno, *Ukraine* 33 G3
Dubois, *U.S.A.* 108 D7
Dubossary = Dubăsari, *Moldova* 29 C14
Dubossary Vdkhr. = Dubăsari Vdkhr., *Moldova* 29 C13
Dubovka, *Russia* 35 F7
Dubovskoye, *Russia* 35 G6
Dubrajpur, *India* 69 H12
Dubréka, *Guinea* 82 D2
Dubrovitsa = Dubrovytsya, *Ukraine* 33 G4
Dubrovnik, *Croatia* 44 D2
Dubrovytsya, *Ukraine* 33 G4
Dubuque, *U.S.A.* 112 D9
Dubysa →, *Lithuania* 30 C10
Duchang, *China* 59 C11
Duchesne, *U.S.A.* 108 F8
Duchess, *Australia* 94 C2
Ducie I., *Pac. Oc.* 97 K15
Duck →, *U.S.A.* 115 G2
Duck Cr. →, *Australia* 92 D2
Duck Lake, *Canada* 103 C7
Duck Mountain ⌂, *Canada* 103 C8
Duckwall, Mt., *U.S.A.* 110 H6
Duderstadt, *Germany* 24 D6
Dudhi, *India* 67 G13
Dudinka, *Russia* 53 C9
Dudley, *U.K.* 15 E5
Dudwa, *India* 69 E9
Duékoué, *Ivory C.* 82 D3
Dueñas, *Spain* 36 D6
Duero = Douro →, *Europe* 36 D2
Dufftown, *U.K.* 13 D5
Dufourspitz, *Switz.* 25 K3
Dūghī Kalā, *Afghan.* 66 C3
Dugi Otok, *Croatia* 41 D11
Dugo Selo, *Croatia* 41 C13
Duifken Pt., *Australia* 94 A3
Duisburg, *Germany* 24 D2
Duiwelskloof, *S. Africa* 89 C5
Dujiangyan, *China* 58 B4
Duk Fadiat, *Sudan* 81 F3
Duk Faiwil, *Sudan* 81 F3
Dukat, *Albania* 44 F3
Dūkdamīn, *Iran* 71 C8
Dukelský Průsmyk, *Slovak Rep.* 27 B14
Dukhān, *Qatar* 71 E6
Dukhovshchina, *Russia* 32 E7
Duki, *Pakistan* 66 D6
Dukla, *Poland* 31 J8
Duku, *Bauchi, Nigeria* 83 C7
Duku, *Sokoto, Nigeria* 83 C5
Dulag, *Phil.* 61 F6
Dulce, *U.S.A.* 109 H10
Dulce →, *Argentina* 126 C3
Dulce, G., *Costa Rica* 120 E3
Dulf, *Iraq* 70 C5
Dŭlgopol, *Bulgaria* 45 C11
Dulit, Banjaran, *Malaysia* 62 D4
Duliu, *China* 56 E9
Dullewala, *Pakistan* 68 D4
Dullstroom, *S. Africa* 89 D5
Dülmen, *Germany* 24 D3
Dulovo, *Bulgaria* 45 C11
Dulq Maghār, *Syria* 70 B3
Duluth, *U.S.A.* 112 B8
Dum Dum, *India* 69 H13
Dum Duma, *India* 67 F19
Dūmā, *Syria* 74 B5
Dumaguete, *Phil.* 61 G5
Dumai, *Indonesia* 62 D2
Dumaran, *Phil.* 61 F3
Dumas, *Ark., U.S.A.* 113 J9
Dumas, *Tex., U.S.A.* 113 H4
Ḑumayr, *Syria* 74 B5
Dumbarton, *U.K.* 13 F4
Ďumbier, *Slovak Rep.* 27 C12
Dumbleyung, *Australia* 93 F2
Dumboa, *Nigeria* 83 C7
Dumbrăveni, *Romania* 29 D9
Dumfries, *U.K.* 13 F5
Dumfries & Galloway □, *U.K.* 13 F5
Dumitrești, *Romania* 29 E11
Dumka, *India* 69 G12
Dumlupınar, *Turkey* 47 C12
Dümmer, *Germany* 24 C4
Dümmer ⌂, *Germany* 24 C4
Dumoine →, *Canada* 104 C4
Dumoine, L., *Canada* 104 C4
Dumont d'Urville, *Antarctica* 5 C10
Dumraon, *India* 69 G11
Dumyât, *Egypt* 80 H7
Dumyât, Masabb, *Egypt* 80 H7
Dún Dealgan = Dundalk, *Ireland* 12 B5
Dún Laoghaire, *Ireland* 12 C5
Dun-le-Palestel, *France* 19 F8
Dun-sur-Auron, *France* 19 F9
Dun-sur-Meuse, *France* 19 C12
Duna = Dunărea →, *Europe* 29 E14
Duna →, *Hungary* 28 E3
Duna-Drava △, *Hungary* 28 D3
Duna-völgyi-főcsatorna, *Hungary* 28 D4
Dunaföldvár, *Hungary* 28 D3
Dunagiri, *India* 69 D8
Dunaj = Dunărea →, *Europe* 29 E14
Dunaj →, *Slovak Rep.* 27 D11
Dunajec →, *Poland* 31 H7
Dunajská Streda, *Slovak Rep.* 27 C10
Dunakeszi, *Hungary* 28 C4
Dunapataj, *Hungary* 28 D4
Dunărea →, *Europe* 29 E14
Dunaszekcső, *Hungary* 28 D3
Dunaújváros, *Hungary* 28 D3
Dunav = Dunărea →, *Europe* 29 E14
Dunavațu de Jos, *Romania* 29 F14
Dunavtsi, *Bulgaria* 44 C6
Dunay, *Russia* 54 C6
Dunback, *N.Z.* 91 L3
Dunbar, *U.K.* 13 E6
Dunblane, *U.K.* 13 E5
Duncan, *Canada* 102 D4
Duncan, *Ariz., U.S.A.* 109 K9
Duncan, *Okla., U.S.A.* 113 H6
Duncan, L., *Canada* 104 B4
Duncan L., *Canada* 102 A6
Duncan Town, *Bahamas* 120 B4
Duncannon, *U.S.A.* 116 F7
Duncansby Head, *U.K.* 13 C5
Duncansville, *U.S.A.* 116 F6
Dundaga, *Latvia* 30 A9
Dundalk, *Canada* 116 B4
Dundalk, *Ireland* 12 B5
Dundalk, *U.S.A.* 114 F7
Dundalk Bay, *Ireland* 12 C5
Dundas = Uummannaq, *Greenland* 4 B4
Dundas = Uummannaq, *Greenland* 4 B5
Dundas, *Canada* 116 C5
Dundas, L., *Australia* 93 F3
Dundas I., *Canada* 102 C2
Dundas Str., *Australia* 92 B5
Dundee, *S. Africa* 89 D5
Dundee, *U.K.* 13 E6
Dundee, *U.S.A.* 116 D8
Dundee City □, *U.K.* 13 E6
Dundgovĭ □, *Mongolia* 56 B4
Dundrum, *U.K.* 12 B6
Dundrum B., *U.K.* 12 B6
Dunedin, *N.Z.* 91 L3
Dunedin, *U.S.A.* 115 L4
Dunfermline, *U.K.* 13 E5
Dungannon, *Canada* 116 C3
Dungannon, *U.K.* 12 B5
Dungarpur, *India* 68 H5
Dungarvan, *Ireland* 12 D4
Dungarvan Harbour, *Ireland* 12 D4
Dungeness, *U.K.* 15 G8
Dungo, L. do, *Angola* 88 B2
Dungog, *Australia* 95 E5
Dungu, *Dem. Rep. of the Congo* 86 B2
Dungun, *Malaysia* 65 K4
Dungunâb, *Sudan* 80 C4
Dungunâb, Khalîg, *Sudan* 80 C4
Dunhua, *China* 57 C15
Dunhuang, *China* 60 B4
Dunk I., *Australia* 94 B4
Dunkassa, *Benin* 83 C5
Dunkeld, *Australia* 95 E4
Dunkeld, *U.K.* 13 E5
Dunkerque, *France* 19 A9
Dunkery Beacon, *U.K.* 15 F4
Dunkirk = Dunkerque, *France* 19 A9
Dunkirk, *U.S.A.* 116 D5
Dunkuj, *Sudan* 81 E3
Dunkwa, *Central, Ghana* 82 D4
Dunkwa, *Central, Ghana* 83 D4
Dúnleary = Dún Laoghaire, *Ireland* 12 C5
Dunleer, *Ireland* 12 C5
Dunmanus B., *Ireland* 12 E2
Dunmanway, *Ireland* 12 E2
Dunmara, *Australia* 94 B1
Dunmore, *U.S.A.* 117 E9
Dunmore Hd., *Ireland* 12 D1
Dunmore Town, *Bahamas* 120 A4
Dunn, *U.S.A.* 115 H6
Dunnellon, *U.S.A.* 115 L4
Dunnet Hd., *U.K.* 13 C5
Dunning, *U.S.A.* 112 E4
Dunnville, *Canada* 116 D5
Dunolly, *Australia* 95 F3
Dunoon, *U.K.* 13 F4
Dunphy, *U.S.A.* 108 F5
Dunqul, *Egypt* 80 C3
Duns, *U.K.* 13 F6
Dunseith, *U.S.A.* 112 A4
Dunsmuir, *U.S.A.* 108 F2
Dunstable, *U.K.* 15 F7
Dunstan Mts., *N.Z.* 91 L2
Dunster, *Canada* 102 C5
Dunvegan, *U.K.* 13 D2
Dunvegan L., *Canada* 103 A7
Duolun, *China* 56 C9
Duong Dong, *Vietnam* 65 G4
Dupree, *U.S.A.* 112 C4
Dupuyer, *U.S.A.* 108 B7
Duque de Caxias, *Brazil* 127 A7
Durack →, *Australia* 92 C4
Durack Ra., *Australia* 92 C4
Durağan, *Turkey* 72 B6
Durak, *Turkey* 47 B10
Đurakovac, *Serbia & M.* 44 D4
Durance →, *France* 21 E8
Durand, *U.S.A.* 112 C9
Durango, *Mexico* 118 C4
Durango, *U.S.A.* 109 H10
Durango □, *Mexico* 118 C4
Durankulak, *Bulgaria* 45 C12
Durant, *Miss., U.S.A.* 113 J10
Durant, *Okla., U.S.A.* 113 J6
Duratón →, *Spain* 36 D6
Durazno, *Uruguay* 126 C4
Durazzo = Durrës, *Albania* 44 E3
Durban, *France* 20 F6
Durban, *S. Africa* 89 D5
Durbuy, *Belgium* 17 D5
Dúrcal, *Spain* 37 J7
Đurđevac, *Croatia* 28 D2
Düren, *Germany* 24 E2
Durg, *India* 67 J12
Durgapur, *India* 69 H12
Durham, *Canada* 116 B4
Durham, *U.K.* 14 C6
Durham, *Calif., U.S.A.* 110 F5
Durham, *N.C., U.S.A.* 115 H6
Durham, *N.H., U.S.A.* 117 C14
Durham □, *U.K.* 14 C6
Durlești, *Moldova* 29 C13
Ḑurmā, *Si. Arabia* 70 E5
Durmitor, *Serbia & M.* 44 C2
Durmitor △, *Serbia & M.* 44 C3
Durness, *U.K.* 13 C4
Durrës, *Albania* 44 E3
Durrow, *Ireland* 12 D4
Dursey I., *Ireland* 12 E1
Dursley, *U.K.* 15 F5
Dursunbey, *Turkey* 47 B10
Durtal, *France* 18 E6
Duru, *Dem. Rep. of the Congo* 86 B2
Duru Gölü, *Turkey* 45 E12
Durusu, *Turkey* 45 E12
Durūz, Jabal ad, *Jordan* 74 C5
D'Urville, Tanjung, *Indonesia* 63 E9
D'Urville I., *N.Z.* 91 J4
Duryea, *U.S.A.* 117 E9
Dûsh, *Egypt* 80 C3
Dushak, *Turkmenistan* 52 F7
Dushan, *China* 58 E6
Dushanbe, *Tajikistan* 52 F7
Dusheti, *Georgia* 35 J7
Dushore, *U.S.A.* 117 E8
Dusky Sd., *N.Z.* 91 L1
Dussejour, C., *Australia* 92 B4
Düsseldorf, *Germany* 24 D2
Düsseldorf Rhein-Ruhr ✕ (DUS), *Germany* 24 D2
Duszniki-Zdrój, *Poland* 31 H3
Dutch Harbor, *U.S.A.* 100 C3
Dutlwe, *Botswana* 88 C3
Dutsan Wai, *Nigeria* 83 C6
Dutton, *Canada* 116 D3
Dutton →, *Australia* 94 C3
Duved, *Sweden* 10 A6
Düvertepe, *Turkey* 47 B10
Duwayhin, Khawr, *U.A.E.* 71 E6
Duyun, *China* 58 D6
Düzağac, *Turkey* 47 C12
Düzce, *Turkey* 72 B4
Duzdab = Zāhedān, *Iran* 71 D9
Dve Mogili, *Bulgaria* 45 C9
Dvina, Severnaya →, *Russia* 52 C5
Dvinsk = Daugavpils, *Latvia* 9 J22
Dvor, *Croatia* 41 C13
Dvůr Králové nad Labem, *Czech Rep.* 26 A8
Dwarka, *India* 68 H3
Dwellingup, *Australia* 93 F2
Dwight, *Canada* 116 A5
Dwight, *U.S.A.* 114 E1
Dyatkovo, *Russia* 32 F8
Dyatlovo = Dzyatlava, *Belarus* 32 F3
Dyce, *U.K.* 13 D6
Dyer, C., *Canada* 101 B13
Dyer Bay, *Canada* 116 A3
Dyer Plateau, *Antarctica* 5 D17
Dyersburg, *U.S.A.* 113 G10
Dyfi →, *U.K.* 15 E3
Dyje →, *Czech Rep.* 27 C9
Dymer, *Ukraine* 33 G6
Dynów, *Poland* 31 J9
Dysart, *Australia* 94 C4
Dzamin Üüd = Borhoyn Tal, *Mongolia* 56 C6
Dzerzhinsk, *Russia* 34 B6
Dzhalinda, *Russia* 53 D13
Dzhambul = Taraz, *Kazakhstan* 52 E8
Dzhankoy, *Ukraine* 33 K8
Dzhanybek, *Kazakhstan* 34 F8
Dzharylhach, Ostriv, *Ukraine* 33 J7
Dzhezkazgan = Zhezqazghan, *Kazakhstan* 52 E7
Dzhizak = Jizzakh, *Uzbekistan* 52 E7
Dzhugdzur, Khrebet, *Russia* 53 D14
Dzhvari = Jvari, *Georgia* 35 J6
Działdowo, *Poland* 31 E7
Działoszyce, *Poland* 31 H7
Działoszyn, *Poland* 31 G5
Dzibilchaltún, *Mexico* 119 C7
Dzibilchaltun, *Yucatán, Mexico* 119 C7
Dzierzgoń, *Poland* 30 E6
Dzierżoniów, *Poland* 31 H3
Dzilam de Bravo, *Mexico* 119 C7
Dzisna, *Belarus* 32 E5
Dzisna →, *Belarus* 32 E5
Dziwnów, *Poland* 30 D1
Dzungaria = Junggar Pendi, *China* 60 B3
Dzuumod, *Mongolia* 60 B5
Dzyarzhynsk, *Belarus* 32 F4
Dzyatlava, *Belarus* 32 F3

E

E.C. Manning ⌂, *Canada* **102 D4**
Eabamet L., *Canada* **104 B2**
Eads, *U.S.A.* **112 F3**
Eagar, *U.S.A.* **109 J9**
Eagle, *Alaska, U.S.A.* **100 B5**
Eagle, *Colo., U.S.A.* **108 G10**
Eagle →, *Canada* **105 B8**
Eagle Butte, *U.S.A.* **112 C4**
Eagle Grove, *U.S.A.* **112 D8**
Eagle L., *Canada* **103 D10**
Eagle L., *Calif., U.S.A.* **108 F3**
Eagle L., *Maine, U.S.A.* **115 B11**
Eagle Lake, *Canada* **116 A6**
Eagle Lake, *Maine, U.S.A.* **115 B11**
Eagle Lake, *Tex., U.S.A.* **113 L6**
Eagle Mountain, *U.S.A.* **111 M11**
Eagle Nest, *U.S.A.* **109 H11**
Eagle Pass, *U.S.A.* **113 L4**
Eagle Pk., *U.S.A.* **110 G7**
Eagle Pt., *Australia* **92 C3**
Eagle River, *Mich., U.S.A.* **114 B1**
Eagle River, *Wis., U.S.A.* **112 C10**
Eaglehawk, *Australia* **95 F3**
Eagles Mere, *U.S.A.* **117 E8**
Ealing □, *U.K.* **15 F7**
Ear Falls, *Canada* **103 C10**
Earle, *U.S.A.* **113 H9**
Earlimart, *U.S.A.* **111 K7**
Earn →, *U.K.* **13 E5**
Earn, L., *U.K.* **13 E4**
Earnslaw, Mt., *N.Z.* **91 L2**
Earth, *U.S.A.* **113 H3**
Easley, *U.S.A.* **115 H4**
East Anglia, *U.K.* **14 E9**
East Angus, *Canada* **105 C5**
East Antarctica, *Antarctica* **5 D7**
East Aurora, *U.S.A.* **116 D6**
East Ayrshire □, *U.K.* **13 F4**
East Bengal, *Bangla.* **67 H17**
East Beskids = Vychodné Beskydy, *Europe* **27 B15**
East Brady, *U.S.A.* **116 F5**
East C., *N.Z.* **91 G7**
East Chicago, *U.S.A.* **114 E2**
East China Sea, *Asia* **60 C7**
East Coulee, *Canada* **102 C6**
East Dereham = Dereham, *U.K.* **15 E8**
East Dunbartonshire □, *U.K.* **13 F4**
East Falkland, *Falk. Is.* **128 G5**
East Grand Forks, *U.S.A.* **112 B6**
East Greenwich, *U.S.A.* **117 E13**
East Grinstead, *U.K.* **15 F8**
East Hartford, *U.S.A.* **117 E12**
East Helena, *U.S.A.* **108 C8**
East Indies, *Asia* **50 K15**
East Kilbride, *U.K.* **13 F4**
East Lansing, *U.S.A.* **114 D3**
East Liverpool, *U.S.A.* **116 F4**
East London, *S. Africa* **89 E4**
East Lothian □, *U.K.* **13 F6**
East Main = Eastmain, *Canada* **104 B4**
East Northport, *U.S.A.* **117 F11**
East Orange, *U.S.A.* **117 F10**
East Pacific Ridge, *Pac. Oc.* **97 J17**
East Palestine, *U.S.A.* **116 F4**
East Pine, *Canada* **102 B4**
East Point, *U.S.A.* **115 J3**
East Providence, *U.S.A.* **117 E13**
East Pt., *Br. Virgin Is.* **121 e**
East Pt., *Canada* **105 C7**
East Renfrewshire □, *U.K.* **13 F4**
East Retford = Retford, *U.K.* **14 D7**
East Riding of Yorkshire □, *U.K.* **14 D7**
East Rochester, *U.S.A.* **116 C7**
East St. Louis, *U.S.A.* **112 F9**
East Schelde = Oosterschelde →, *Neths.* **17 C4**
East Sea = Japan, Sea of, *Asia* **54 E7**
East Siberian Sea, *Russia* **53 B17**
East Stroudsburg, *U.S.A.* **117 E9**
East Sussex □, *U.K.* **15 G8**
East Tawas, *U.S.A.* **114 C4**
East Timor ■, *Asia* **63 F7**
East Toorale, *Australia* **95 E4**
East Walker →, *U.S.A.* **110 G7**
East Windsor, *U.S.A.* **117 F10**
Eastbourne, *N.Z.* **91 J5**
Eastbourne, *U.K.* **15 G8**
Eastend, *Canada* **103 D7**
Easter I. = Pascua, I. de, *Chile* **97 K17**
Eastern □, *Ghana* **83 D4**
Eastern □, *Kenya* **86 C4**
Eastern Cape □, *S. Africa* **88 E4**
Eastern Cr. →, *Australia* **94 C3**
Eastern Ghats, *India* **66 N11**
Eastern Group = Lau Group, *Fiji* **91 C9**
Eastern Group, *Australia* **93 F3**
Eastern Province □, *S. Leone* **82 D2**
Eastern Transvaal = Mpumalanga □, *S. Africa* **89 D5**
Easterville, *Canada* **103 C9**
Easthampton, *U.S.A.* **117 D12**
Eastlake, *U.S.A.* **116 E3**
Eastland, *U.S.A.* **113 J5**
Eastleigh, *U.K.* **15 G6**
Eastmain, *Canada* **104 B4**
Eastmain →, *Canada* **104 B4**
Eastman, *Canada* **117 A12**
Eastman, *U.S.A.* **115 J4**
Easton, *Md., U.S.A.* **114 F7**
Easton, *Pa., U.S.A.* **117 F9**
Easton, *Wash., U.S.A.* **110 C5**
Eastpointe, *U.S.A.* **116 D2**
Eastport, *U.S.A.* **115 C12**
Eastsound, *U.S.A.* **110 B4**
Eaton, *U.S.A.* **112 E2**
Eatonia, *Canada* **103 C7**
Eatonton, *U.S.A.* **115 J4**
Eatontown, *U.S.A.* **117 F10**
Eatonville, *U.S.A.* **110 D4**
Eau Claire, *U.S.A.* **112 C9**
Eau Claire, L. à l', *Canada* **104 A5**
Eauze, *France* **20 E4**
Eban, *Nigeria* **83 D5**
Ebbegebirge ⌂, *Germany* **24 D3**
Ebbw Vale, *U.K.* **15 F4**
Ebeltoft, *Denmark* **11 H4**
Ebeltoft Vig, *Denmark* **11 H4**
Ebensburg, *U.S.A.* **116 F6**
Ebensee, *Austria* **26 D6**
Eber Gölü, *Turkey* **72 C4**
Eberbach, *Germany* **25 F4**
Eberswalde-Finow, *Germany* **24 C9**
Ebetsu, *Japan* **54 C10**
Ebey's Landing ⌂, *U.S.A.* **110 B4**
Ebian, *China* **58 C4**
Ebingen, *Germany* **25 G5**
Éboli, *Italy* **43 B8**
Ebolowa, *Cameroon* **83 E7**
Ebonyi □, *Nigeria* **83 D6**
Ebrach, *Germany* **25 F6**
Ébrié, Lagune, *Ivory C.* **82 D4**
Ebro →, *Spain* **38 E5**
Ebro, Embalse del, *Spain* **36 C7**
Ebstorf, *Germany* **24 B6**
Eceabat, *Turkey* **45 F10**
Ech Chéliff, *Algeria* **78 A6**
Echigo-Sammyaku, *Japan* **55 F9**
Échirolles, *France* **21 C9**
Echizen-Misaki, *Japan* **55 G7**
Echmiadzin = Yejmiadzin, *Armenia* **35 K7**
Echo Bay, *N.W.T., Canada* **100 B8**
Echo Bay, *Ont., Canada* **104 C3**
Echoing →, *Canada* **104 B1**
Echterdingen, Stuttgart ✕ (STR), *Germany* **25 G5**
Echternach, *Lux.* **17 E6**
Echuca, *Australia* **95 F3**
Ecija, *Spain* **37 H5**
Eckental, *Germany* **25 F7**
Eckernförde, *Germany* **24 A5**
Eclipse I., *Australia* **93 G2**
Eclipse Is., *Australia* **92 B4**
Eclipse Sd., *Canada* **101 A11**
Écommoy, *France* **18 E7**
Écouché, *France* **18 D6**
Ecrins △, *France* **21 D10**
Ecuador ■, *S. Amer.* **124 D3**
Écueillé, *France* **18 E8**
Ed, *Sweden* **11 F5**
Ed Dabbura, *Sudan* **80 D3**
Ed Da'ein, *Sudan* **81 E2**
Ed Damazin, *Sudan* **79 F12**
Ed Dâmer, *Sudan* **80 D3**
Ed Dar el Beida = Casablanca, *Morocco* **78 B4**
Ed Debba, *Sudan* **80 D3**
Ed-Déffa, *Egypt* **80 A2**
Ed Deim, *Sudan* **81 E2**
Ed Dueim, *Sudan* **81 E3**
Edam, *Canada* **103 C7**
Edam, *Neths.* **17 B5**
Edane, *Sweden* **10 E6**
Eday, *U.K.* **13 B6**
Edd, *Eritrea* **81 E5**
Eddrachillis B., *U.K.* **13 C3**
Eddystone, *U.K.* **15 G3**
Eddystone Pt., *Australia* **95 G4**
Ede, *Neths.* **17 B5**
Ede, *Nigeria* **83 D5**
Edéa, *Cameroon* **83 E7**
Edebäck, *Sweden* **10 D7**
Edehon L., *Canada* **103 A9**
Edelény, *Hungary* **28 B5**
Eden, *Australia* **95 F4**
Eden, *N.C., U.S.A.* **115 G6**
Eden, *N.Y., U.S.A.* **116 D6**
Eden, *Tex., U.S.A.* **113 K5**
Eden →, *U.K.* **14 C4**
Edenburg, *S. Africa* **88 D4**
Edendale, *S. Africa* **89 D5**
Edenderry, *Ireland* **12 C4**
Edenton, *U.S.A.* **115 G7**
Edenville, *S. Africa* **89 D4**
Eder →, *Germany* **24 D5**
Eder-Stausee, *Germany* **24 D4**
Edewecht, *Germany* **24 B3**
Edgar, *U.S.A.* **112 E6**
Edgartown, *U.S.A.* **117 E14**
Edge Hill, *U.K.* **15 E6**
Edgefield, *U.S.A.* **115 J5**
Edgeley, *U.S.A.* **112 B5**
Edgemont, *U.S.A.* **112 D3**
Edgeøya, *Svalbard* **4 B9**
Édhessa, *Greece* **44 F6**
Edievale, *N.Z.* **91 L2**
Edina, *Liberia* **82 D2**
Edina, *U.S.A.* **112 E8**
Edinboro, *U.S.A.* **116 E4**
Edinburg, *U.S.A.* **113 M5**
Edinburgh, *U.K.* **13 F5**
Edinburgh ✕ (EDI), *U.K.* **13 F5**
Edinburgh, City of □, *U.K.* **13 F5**
Edineț, *Moldova* **29 B12**
Edirne, *Turkey* **45 E10**
Edirne □, *Turkey* **45 E10**
Edison, *U.S.A.* **110 B4**
Edithburgh, *Australia* **95 F2**
Edmeston, *U.S.A.* **117 D9**
Edmond, *U.S.A.* **113 H6**
Edmonds, *U.S.A.* **110 C4**
Edmonton, *Australia* **94 B4**
Edmonton, *Canada* **102 C6**
Edmund L., *Canada* **104 B1**
Edmundston, *Canada* **105 C6**
Edna, *U.S.A.* **113 L6**
Edo □, *Nigeria* **83 D6**
Edolo, *Italy* **40 B7**
Edremit, *Turkey* **47 B9**
Edremit Körfezi, *Turkey* **47 B8**
Edsbro, *Sweden* **10 E12**
Edsbyn, *Sweden* **10 C9**
Edson, *Canada* **102 C5**
Eduardo Castex, *Argentina* **126 D3**
Edward →, *Australia* **95 F3**
Edward, L., *Africa* **86 C2**
Edward River, *Australia* **94 A3**
Edward VII Land, *Antarctica* **5 E13**
Edwards, *Calif., U.S.A.* **111 L9**
Edwards, *N.Y., U.S.A.* **117 B9**
Edwards Air Force Base, *U.S.A.* **111 L9**
Edwards Plateau, *U.S.A.* **113 K4**
Edwardsville, *U.S.A.* **117 E9**
Edzná, *Mexico* **119 D6**
Edzo, *Canada* **102 A5**
Eeklo, *Belgium* **17 C3**
Eferding, *Austria* **26 C7**
Effigy Mounds ⌂, *U.S.A.* **112 D9**
Effingham, *U.S.A.* **114 F1**
Eforie, *Romania* **29 F13**
Ega →, *Spain* **38 C3**
Égadi, Ísole, *Italy* **42 E5**
Egan Range, *U.S.A.* **108 G6**
Eganville, *Canada* **116 A7**
Eger = Cheb, *Czech Rep.* **26 A5**
Eger, *Hungary* **28 C5**
Eger →, *Hungary* **28 C5**
Egersund, *Norway* **9 G12**
Egg L., *Canada* **103 B7**
Eggegebirge Südlicher Teutoburger Wald ⌂, *Germany* **24 D4**
Eggenburg, *Austria* **26 C8**
Eggenfelden, *Germany* **25 G8**
Éghezée, *Belgium* **17 D4**
Égletons, *France* **20 C6**
Egmont, *Canada* **102 D4**
Egmont △, *N.Z.* **91 H5**
Egmont, C., *N.Z.* **91 H4**
Egmont, Mt. = Taranaki, Mt., *N.Z.* **91 H5**
Egra, *India* **69 J12**
Eğridir, *Turkey* **72 D4**
Eğridir Gölü, *Turkey* **70 B1**
Egtved, *Denmark* **11 J3**
Egume, *Nigeria* **83 D6**
Éguzon-Chantôme, *France* **19 F8**
Egvekinot, *Russia* **53 C19**
Egyek, *Hungary* **28 C5**
Egypt ■, *Africa* **80 B3**
Eha Amufu, *Nigeria* **83 D6**
Ehime □, *Japan* **55 H6**
Ehingen, *Germany* **25 G5**
Ehrenberg, *U.S.A.* **111 M12**
Ehrwald, *Austria* **26 D3**
Eibar, *Spain* **38 B2**
Eichstätt, *Germany* **25 G7**
Eider →, *Germany* **24 A4**
Eidsvold, *Australia* **95 D5**
Eidsvoll, *Norway* **9 F14**
Eifel, *Germany* **25 E2**
Eiffel Flats, *Zimbabwe* **87 F3**
Eiger, *Switz.* **40 B5**
Eigg, *U.K.* **13 E2**
Eighty Mile Beach, *Australia* **92 C3**
Eil, *Somali Rep.* **75 F4**
Eil, L., *U.K.* **13 E3**
Eildon, L., *Australia* **95 F4**
Eilenburg, *Germany* **24 D8**
Ein el Luweiqa, *Sudan* **81 E3**
Einasleigh, *Australia* **94 B3**
Einasleigh →, *Australia* **94 B3**
Einbeck, *Germany* **24 D5**
Eindhoven, *Neths.* **17 C5**
Einsiedeln, *Switz.* **25 H4**
Eire ■, *Europe* **12 C4**
Eiríksjökull, *Iceland* **8 D3**
Eirunepé, *Brazil* **124 E5**
Eiseb →, *Namibia* **88 C2**
Eisenach, *Germany* **24 E6**
Eisenberg, *Germany* **24 E7**
Eisenerz, *Austria* **26 D7**
Eisenhüttenstadt, *Germany* **24 C10**
Eisenkappel, *Austria* **26 E7**
Eisenstadt, *Austria* **27 D9**
Eisfeld, *Germany* **25 E6**
Eisleben, *Germany* **24 D7**
Eislingen, *Germany* **25 G5**
Eivissa, *Spain* **48 C7**
Eixe, Serra do, *Spain* **36 C4**
Ejea de los Caballeros, *Spain* **38 C3**
Ejeda, *Madag.* **89 C7**
Ejura, *Ghana* **83 D4**
Ejutla, *Mexico* **119 D5**
Ekalaka, *U.S.A.* **112 C2**
Ekenässjön, *Sweden* **11 G9**
Ekerö, *Sweden* **10 E11**
Eket, *Nigeria* **83 E6**
Eketahuna, *N.Z.* **91 J5**
Ekhínos, *Greece* **45 E9**
Ekibastuz, *Kazakhstan* **52 D8**
Ekiti □, *Nigeria* **83 D6**
Ekoli, *Dem. Rep. of the Congo* **86 C1**
Ekoln, *Sweden* **10 E11**
Ekshärad, *Sweden* **10 D7**
Eksjö, *Sweden* **11 G8**
Ekuma →, *Namibia* **88 B2**
Ekwan →, *Canada* **104 B3**
Ekwan Pt., *Canada* **104 B3**
El Aaiún, *W. Sahara* **78 C3**
El Abanico, *Chile* **126 D1**
El Abbasiya, *Sudan* **81 E3**
El 'Agrûd, *Egypt* **74 E3**
El Ait, *Sudan* **81 E2**
El 'Aiyat, *Egypt* **80 J7**
El 'Alamein, *Egypt* **80 A2**
El 'Aqaba, W. →, *Egypt* **74 E2**
El 'Arag, *Egypt* **80 B2**
El Arahal, *Spain* **37 H5**
El Arīḥā, *West Bank* **74 D4**
El 'Arîsh, *Egypt* **74 D2**
El 'Arîsh, W. →, *Egypt* **74 D2**
El Asnam = Ech Chéliff, *Algeria* **78 A6**
El Astillero, *Spain* **36 B7**
El Badâri, *Egypt* **80 B3**
El Bahrein, *Egypt* **80 B2**
El Ballâs, *Egypt* **80 B3**
El Balyana, *Egypt* **80 B3**
El Baqeir, *Sudan* **80 D3**
El Barco de Ávila, *Spain* **36 E5**
El Barco de Valdeorras = O Barco, *Spain* **36 C4**
El Bauga, *Sudan* **80 D3**
El Bawiti, *Egypt* **80 B2**
El Bayadh, *Algeria* **78 B6**
El Bierzo, *Spain* **36 C4**
El Bluff, *Nic.* **120 D3**
El Bonillo, *Spain* **39 G2**
El Brûk, W. →, *Egypt* **74 E2**
El Buheirat □, *Sudan* **81 F3**
El Burgo de Osma, *Spain* **38 D1**
El Cajon, *U.S.A.* **111 N10**
El Campo, *U.S.A.* **113 L6**
El Centro, *U.S.A.* **111 N11**
El Cerro, *Bolivia* **124 G6**
El Cerro de Andévalo, *Spain* **37 H4**
El Compadre, *Mexico* **111 N10**
El Coronil, *Spain* **37 H5**
El Cuy, *Argentina* **128 D3**
El Cuyo, *Mexico* **119 C7**
El Dab'a, *Egypt* **80 H6**
El Daheir, *Egypt* **74 D3**
El Dátil, *Mexico* **118 B2**
El Deir, *Egypt* **80 B3**
El Dere, *Somali Rep.* **75 G4**
El Descanso, *Mexico* **111 N10**
El Desemboque, *Mexico* **118 A2**
El Dilingat, *Egypt* **80 H7**
El Diviso, *Colombia* **124 C3**
El Djouf, *Mauritania* **78 D4**
El Dorado, *Ark., U.S.A.* **113 J8**
El Dorado, *Kans., U.S.A.* **113 G6**
El Dorado, *Venezuela* **124 B6**
El 'Ein, *Sudan* **81 D2**
El Ejido, *Spain* **37 J8**
El Escorial, *Spain* **36 E6**
El Espinar, *Spain* **36 D6**
El Faiyûm, *Egypt* **80 J7**
El Fâsher, *Sudan* **81 E2**
El Fashn, *Egypt* **80 J7**
El Ferrol = Ferrol, *Spain* **36 B2**
El Fifi, *Sudan* **81 E2**
El Fuerte, *Mexico* **118 B3**
El Ga'a, *Sudan* **81 E2**
El Gal, *Somali Rep.* **75 E5**
El Garef, *Sudan* **81 E3**
El Gebir, *Sudan* **81 E2**
El Gedida, *Egypt* **80 B2**
El Geneina = Al Junaynah, *Sudan* **79 F10**
El Geteina, *Sudan* **81 E3**
El Gezira □, *Sudan* **81 E3**
El Gir, *Sudan* **80 D2**
El Gîza, *Egypt* **80 J7**
El Gogorron △, *Mexico* **118 C4**
El Goléa, *Algeria* **78 B6**
El Grau, *Spain* **39 G4**
El Guácharo △, *Venezuela* **121 D7**
El Guache △, *Venezuela* **121 E6**
El Guache △, *Venezuela* **121 E6**
El Hagiz, *Sudan* **81 D4**
El Hâi, *Egypt* **80 J7**
El Hammam, *Egypt* **80 A2**
El Hawata, *Sudan* **81 E3**
El Heiz, *Egypt* **80 B2**
El Hideib, *Sudan* **81 E3**
El Hilla, *Sudan* **81 E2**
El 'Idisât, *Egypt* **80 B3**
El Iskandarîya, *Egypt* **80 H7**
El Istiwa'iya, *Sudan* **79 G11**
El Jadida, *Morocco* **78 B4**
El Jardal, *Honduras* **120 D2**
El Jebelein, *Sudan* **81 E3**
El Kab, *Sudan* **80 D3**
El Kabrît, G., *Egypt* **74 F2**
El Kafr el Sharqi, *Egypt* **80 H7**
El Kamlin, *Sudan* **81 D3**
El Karaba, *Sudan* **80 D3**
El Kere, *Ethiopia* **81 F5**
El Khandaq, *Sudan* **80 D3**
El Khârga, *Egypt* **80 B3**
El Khartûm, *Sudan* **81 D3**
El Khartûm □, *Sudan* **81 D3**
El Khartûm Bahrî, *Sudan* **81 D3**
El Kuntilla, *Egypt* **74 E3**
El Laqâwa, *Sudan* **81 E2**
El Leh, *Ethiopia* **81 G4**
El Leiya, *Sudan* **81 D4**
El Maestrazgo, *Spain* **38 E4**
El Mafâza, *Sudan* **81 E3**
El Maghra, *Egypt* **80 A2**
El Mahalla el Kubra, *Egypt* **80 H7**
El Mahârîq, *Egypt* **80 B3**
El Maîmûn, *Egypt* **80 J7**
El Maks el Bahari, *Egypt* **80 C3**
El Malpais ⌂, *U.S.A.* **109 J10**
El Manshâh, *Egypt* **80 B3**
El Mansûra, *Egypt* **80 H7**
El Manzala, *Egypt* **80 H7**
El Marâgha, *Egypt* **80 B3**
El Masid, *Sudan* **81 D3**
El Masnou, *Spain* **38 D7**
El Matariya, *Egypt* **80 H8**
El Meda, *Ethiopia* **81 F5**
El Medano, *Canary Is.* **48 F3**
El Metemma, *Sudan* **81 D3**
El Milagro, *Argentina* **126 C2**
El Minyâ, *Egypt* **80 B3**
El Monte, *U.S.A.* **111 L8**
El Montseny, *Spain* **38 D7**
El Mreyye, *Mauritania* **82 B3**
El Niybo, *Ethiopia* **81 G4**
El Obeid, *Sudan* **81 E3**
El Odaiya, *Sudan* **81 E2**
El Oro, *Mexico* **119 D4**
El Oued, *Algeria* **78 B7**
El Palmar △, *Argentina* **126 C4**
El Palmito, Presa, *Mexico* **118 B3**
El Paso, *U.S.A.* **109 L10**
El Paso Robles, *U.S.A.* **110 K6**
El Pedernoso, *Spain* **39 F2**
El Pedroso, *Spain* **37 H5**
El Pinacate y Gran Desierto del Altar = Gran Desierto del Pinacate ⌂, *Mexico* **118 A2**
El Pobo de Dueñas, *Spain* **38 E3**
El Portal, *U.S.A.* **110 H7**
El Porvenir, *Mexico* **118 A3**
El Prat de Llobregat, *Spain* **38 D7**
El Progreso, *Honduras* **120 C2**
El Pueblito, *Mexico* **118 B3**
El Pueblo, *Canary Is.* **48 F2**
El Puente del Arzobispo, *Spain* **36 F5**
El Puerto de Santa María, *Spain* **37 J4**
El Qâhira, *Egypt* **80 H7**
El Qantara, *Egypt* **74 E1**
El Qasr, *Egypt* **80 B2**
El Qubâbât, *Egypt* **80 J7**
El Quseima, *Egypt* **74 E3**
El Qusîya, *Egypt* **80 B3**
El Râshda, *Egypt* **80 B2**
El Real, *Panama* **124 B3**
El Reno, *U.S.A.* **113 H6**
El Rey △, *Argentina* **126 A3**
El Rîdisiya, *Egypt* **80 C3**
El Rio, *U.S.A.* **111 L7**
El Ronquillo, *Spain* **37 H4**
El Roque, Pta., *Canary Is.* **48 F4**
El Rosarito, *Mexico* **118 B2**
El Rubio, *Spain* **37 H5**
El Saff, *Egypt* **80 J7**
El Saheira, W. →, *Egypt* **74 E2**
El Salto, *Mexico* **118 C3**
El Salvador ■, *Cent. Amer.* **120 D2**
El Sauce, *Nic.* **120 D2**
El Saucejo, *Spain* **37 H5**
El Shallal, *Egypt* **80 C3**
El Simbillawein, *Egypt* **80 H7**
El Sueco, *Mexico* **118 B3**
El Suweis, *Egypt* **80 J8**
El Tabbîn, *Egypt* **80 J7**
El Tamarâni, W. →, *Egypt* **74 E3**
El Thamad, *Egypt* **74 F3**
El Tigre, *Venezuela* **124 B6**
El Tîh, Gebal, *Egypt* **74 F2**
El Tîna, *Egypt* **80 H8**
El Tîna, Khalîg, *Egypt* **74 D1**
El Tofo, *Chile* **126 B1**
El Tránsito, *Chile* **126 B1**
El Tûr, *Egypt* **70 D2**
El Turbio, *Argentina* **128 G2**
El Uqsur, *Egypt* **80 B3**
El Valle ⌂, *Spain* **39 H3**
El Venado, *Mexico* **118 C4**
El Vendrell, *Spain* **38 D6**
El Vergel, *Mexico* **118 B3**
El Vigía, *Venezuela* **124 B4**
El Viso del Alcor, *Spain* **37 H5**
El Wabeira, *Egypt* **74 F2**
El Wak, *Kenya* **86 B5**
El Waqf, *Egypt* **80 B3**
El Weguet, *Ethiopia* **81 F5**
El Wuz, *Sudan* **81 D3**
Elafónisos, *Greece* **46 E4**
Élancourt, *France* **19 D8**
Élassa, *Greece* **47 F8**
Elassón, *Greece* **46 B4**
Elat, *Israel* **74 F3**
Eláthia, *Greece* **46 C4**
Elâzığ, *Turkey* **70 B3**
Elba, *Italy* **40 F7**
Elba, *U.S.A.* **115 K2**
Elbasan, *Albania* **44 E4**
Elbe, *U.S.A.* **110 D4**
Elbe →, *Europe* **24 B4**
Elbe-Seitenkanal, *Germany* **24 C6**
Elbert, Mt., *U.S.A.* **109 G10**
Elberton, *U.S.A.* **115 H4**
Elbeuf, *France* **18 C8**
Elbidtan, *Turkey* **70 B3**
Elbing = Elbląg, *Poland* **30 D6**
Elbistan, *Turkey* **72 C7**
Elbląg, *Poland* **30 D6**
Elbow, *Canada* **103 C7**
Elbrus, *Asia* **35 J6**
Elbufer-Drawehn ⌂, *Germany* **24 B6**
Elburz Mts. = Alborz, Reshteh-ye Kūhhā-ye, *Iran* **71 C7**
Elche, *Spain* **39 G4**
Elche de la Sierra, *Spain* **39 G2**
Elcho I., *Australia* **94 A2**
Elda, *Spain* **39 G4**
Elde →, *Germany* **24 B7**
Eldon, *Mo., U.S.A.* **112 F8**
Eldon, *Wash., U.S.A.* **110 C3**
Eldora, *U.S.A.* **112 D8**
Eldorado, *Argentina* **127 B5**
Eldorado, *Canada* **116 B7**
Eldorado, *Mexico* **118 C3**
Eldorado, *Ill., U.S.A.* **114 G1**
Eldorado, *Tex., U.S.A.* **113 K4**
Eldorado Springs, *U.S.A.* **113 G8**
Eldoret, *Kenya* **86 B4**
Eldred, *U.S.A.* **116 E6**
Elea, C., *Cyprus* **49 D13**
Eleanora, Pk., *Australia* **93 F3**
Elefantes →, *Africa* **89 C5**
Elektrogorsk, *Russia* **32 E10**
Elektrostal, *Russia* **32 E10**
Elele, *Nigeria* **83 D6**
Elena, *Bulgaria* **45 D9**
Elephant Butte Reservoir, *U.S.A.* **109 K10**

Elephant I., *Antarctica* **5 C18**
Eleshnitsa, *Bulgaria* **44 E7**
Eleşkirt, *Turkey* **73 C10**
Eleuthera, *Bahamas* **120 B4**
Elevsís, *Greece* **46 C5**
Elevtheroúpolis, *Greece* **45 F8**
Elgin, *Canada* **117 B8**
Elgin, *U.K.* **13 D5**
Elgin, *Ill., U.S.A.* **114 D1**
Elgin, *N. Dak., U.S.A.* **112 B4**
Elgin, *Oreg., U.S.A.* **108 D5**
Elgin, *Tex., U.S.A.* **113 K6**
Elgoibar, *Spain* **38 B2**
Elgon, Mt., *Africa* **86 B3**
Eliase, *Indonesia* **63 F8**
Elikón, *Greece* **46 C4**
Elim, *Namibia* **88 B2**
Elim, *S. Africa* **88 E2**
Elin Pelin, *Bulgaria* **44 D7**
Elista, *Russia* **35 G7**
Elizabeth, *Australia* **95 E2**
Elizabeth, *U.S.A.* **117 F10**
Elizabeth City, *U.S.A.* **115 G7**
Elizabethton, *U.S.A.* **115 G4**
Elizabethtown, *Ky., U.S.A.* **114 G3**
Elizabethtown, *N.Y., U.S.A.* **117 B11**
Elizabethtown, *Pa., U.S.A.* **117 F8**
Elizondo, *Spain* **38 B3**
Ełk, *Poland* **30 E9**
Elk →, *Canada* **102 C5**
Ełk →, *Poland* **30 E9**
Elk →, *U.S.A.* **115 H2**
Elk City, *U.S.A.* **113 H5**
Elk Creek, *U.S.A.* **110 F4**
Elk Grove, *U.S.A.* **110 G5**
Elk Island △, *Canada* **102 C6**
Elk Lake, *Canada* **104 C3**
Elk Point, *Canada* **103 C6**
Elk River, *Idaho, U.S.A.* **108 C5**
Elk River, *Minn., U.S.A.* **112 C8**
Elkedra →, *Australia* **94 C2**
Elkhart, *Ind., U.S.A.* **114 E3**
Elkhart, *Kans., U.S.A.* **113 G4**
Elkhorn, *Canada* **103 D8**
Elkhorn →, *U.S.A.* **112 E6**
Elkhovo, *Bulgaria* **45 D10**
Elkin, *U.S.A.* **115 G5**
Elkins, *U.S.A.* **114 F6**
Elkland, *U.S.A.* **116 E7**
Elko, *Canada* **102 D5**
Elko, *U.S.A.* **108 F6**
Elkton, *U.S.A.* **116 C1**
Ell, L., *Australia* **93 E4**
Ellef Ringnes I., *Canada* **4 B2**
Ellen, Mt., *U.S.A.* **117 B12**
Ellenburg, *U.S.A.* **117 B11**
Ellendale, *U.S.A.* **112 B5**
Ellensburg, *U.S.A.* **108 C3**
Ellenville, *U.S.A.* **117 E10**
Ellerton, *Barbados* **121 g**
Ellery, Mt., *Australia* **95 F4**
Ellesmere, L., *N.Z.* **91 M4**
Ellesmere I., *Canada* **98 B11**
Ellesmere Port, *U.K.* **14 D5**
Ellice Is. = Tuvalu ■, *Pac. Oc.* **96 H9**
Ellicottville, *U.S.A.* **116 D6**
Ellinikón, Athens, ✈ (ATH), *Greece* **46 D5**
Elliot, *Australia* **94 B1**
Elliot, *S. Africa* **89 E4**
Elliot Lake, *Canada* **104 C3**
Elliotdale = Xhora, *S. Africa* **89 E4**
Ellis, *U.S.A.* **112 F5**
Elliston, *Australia* **95 E1**
Ellisville, *U.S.A.* **113 K10**
Ellon, *U.K.* **13 D6**
Ellore = Eluru, *India* **67 L12**
Ellsworth, *Kans., U.S.A.* **112 F5**
Ellsworth, *Maine, U.S.A.* **115 C11**
Ellsworth Land, *Antarctica* **5 D16**
Ellsworth Mts., *Antarctica* **5 D16**
Ellwangen, *Germany* **25 G6**
Ellwood City, *U.S.A.* **116 F4**
Elm, *Switz.* **25 J5**
Elm-Lappwald ⌂, *Germany* **24 C6**
Elma, *Canada* **103 D9**
Elma, *U.S.A.* **110 D3**
Elmadağ, *Turkey* **72 C5**
Elmalı, *Turkey* **47 E11**
Elmhurst, *U.S.A.* **114 E2**
Elmina, *Ghana* **83 D4**
Elmira, *Canada* **116 C4**
Elmira, *U.S.A.* **116 D8**
Elmira Heights, *U.S.A.* **116 D8**
Elmore, *Australia* **95 F3**
Elmore, *U.S.A.* **111 M11**
Elmshorn, *Germany* **24 B5**
Elmvale, *Canada* **116 B5**
Elne, *France* **20 F6**
Elora, *Canada* **116 C4**
Elos, *Greece* **46 E4**
Eloúnda, *Greece* **49 D7**
Eloy, *U.S.A.* **109 K8**
Éloyes, *France* **19 D13**
Elrose, *Canada* **103 C7**
Elsdorf, *Germany* **24 E2**
Elsie, *U.S.A.* **110 E3**
Elsinore = Helsingør, *Denmark* **11 H6**
Elster →, *Germany* **24 D7**
Elsterwerda, *Germany* **24 D9**
Eltham, *N.Z.* **91 H5**
Elton, *Russia* **35 F8**
Elton, Ozero, *Russia* **35 F8**
Eltville, *Germany* **25 E4**
Eluru, *India* **67 L12**
Elvas, *Portugal* **37 G3**
Elven, *France* **18 E4**
Elverum, *Norway* **9 F14**
Elvire →, *Australia* **92 C4**
Elvire, Mt., *Australia* **93 E2**
Elvo →, *Italy* **40 C5**
Elwell, L., *U.S.A.* **108 B8**
Elwood, *Ind., U.S.A.* **114 E3**
Elwood, *Nebr., U.S.A.* **112 E5**
Elx = Elche, *Spain* **39 G4**
Ely, *U.K.* **15 E8**
Ely, *Minn., U.S.A.* **112 B9**
Ely, *Nev., U.S.A.* **108 G6**
Elyria, *U.S.A.* **116 E2**
Elyrus, *Greece* **46 F5**
Elz →, *Germany* **25 G3**
Emådalen, *Sweden* **10 C8**
Emāmrūd, *Iran* **71 B7**
Emån →, *Sweden* **11 G10**
Emba, *Kazakhstan* **52 E6**
Emba →, *Kazakhstan* **52 E6**
Embarcación, *Argentina* **126 A3**
Embarras Portage, *Canada* **103 B6**
Embetsu, *Japan* **54 B10**
Embi = Emba, *Kazakhstan* **52 E6**
Embi = Emba →, *Kazakhstan* **52 E6**
Embóna, *Greece* **49 C9**
Embrun, *France* **21 D10**
Embu, *Kenya* **86 C4**
Emden, *Germany* **24 B3**
Emecik, *Turkey* **47 E9**
Emerald, *Australia* **94 C4**
Emerson, *Canada* **103 D9**
Emet, *Turkey* **47 B11**
Emi Koussi, *Chad* **79 E9**
Emília-Romagna □, *Italy* **40 D8**
Emilius, Mte., *Italy* **40 C4**
Eminabad, *Pakistan* **68 C6**
Emine, Nos, *Bulgaria* **45 D11**
Emirdağ, *Turkey* **72 C4**
Emissi, Tarso, *Chad* **79 D9**
Emlenton, *U.S.A.* **116 E5**
Emlichheim, *Germany* **24 C2**
Emmaboda, *Sweden* **11 H9**
Emmaus, *S. Africa* **88 D4**
Emmaus, *U.S.A.* **117 F9**
Emme →, *Switz.* **25 H3**
Emmeloord, *Neths.* **17 B5**
Emmen, *Neths.* **17 B6**
Emmen, *Switz.* **25 H4**
Emmendingen, *Germany* **25 G3**
Emmental, *Switz.* **25 J3**
Emmerich, *Germany* **24 D2**
Emmet, *Australia* **94 C3**
Emmetsburg, *U.S.A.* **112 D7**
Emmett, *Idaho, U.S.A.* **108 E5**
Emmett, *Mich., U.S.A.* **116 D2**
Emmonak, *U.S.A.* **100 B3**
Emo, *Canada* **103 D10**
Emőd, *Hungary* **28 C5**
Emona, *Bulgaria* **45 D11**
Empalme, *Mexico* **118 B2**
Empangeni, *S. Africa* **89 D5**
Empedrado, *Argentina* **126 B4**
Emperor Seamount Chain, *Pac. Oc.* **96 D9**
Empoli, *Italy* **40 E7**
Emporia, *Kans., U.S.A.* **112 F6**
Emporia, *Va., U.S.A.* **115 G7**
Emporium, *U.S.A.* **116 E6**
Empress, *Canada* **103 C7**
Empty Quarter = Rub' al Khālī, *Si. Arabia* **75 D4**
Ems →, *Germany* **24 B3**
Emsdale, *Canada* **116 A5**
Emsdetten, *Germany* **24 C3**
Emu, *China* **57 C15**
Emu Park, *Australia* **94 C5**
'En 'Avrona, *Israel* **74 F4**
En Nahud, *Sudan* **81 E2**
En Nofalab, *Sudan* **81 D3**
Ena, *Japan* **55 G8**
Enana, *Namibia* **88 B2**
Enånger, *Sweden* **10 C11**
Enard B., *U.K.* **13 C3**
Enare = Inarijärvi, *Finland* **8 B22**
Enarotali, *Indonesia* **63 E9**
Encampment, *U.S.A.* **108 F10**
Encantadas, Serra, *Brazil* **127 C5**
Encarnación, *Paraguay* **127 B4**
Encarnación de Diaz, *Mexico* **118 C4**
Enchi, *Ghana* **82 D4**
Encinitas, *U.S.A.* **111 M9**
Encino, *U.S.A.* **109 J11**
Encounter B., *Australia* **95 F2**
Encs, *Hungary* **28 B6**
Endako, *Canada* **102 C3**
Ende, *Indonesia* **63 F6**
Endeavour Str., *Australia* **94 A3**
Endelave, *Denmark* **11 J4**
Enderbury I., *Kiribati* **96 H10**
Enderby, *Canada* **102 C5**
Enderby I., *Australia* **92 D2**
Enderby Land, *Antarctica* **5 C5**
Enderlin, *U.S.A.* **112 B6**
Endicott, *U.S.A.* **117 D8**
Endwell, *U.S.A.* **117 D8**
Endyalgout I., *Australia* **92 B5**
Eneabba, *Australia* **93 E2**
Enewetak Atoll, *Marshall Is.* **96 F8**
Enez, *Turkey* **45 F10**
Enfer, Pte. d', *Martinique* **120 c**
Enfield, *Canada* **105 D7**
Enfield, *Conn., U.S.A.* **117 E12**
Enfield, *N.H., U.S.A.* **117 C12**
Engadin, *Switz.* **25 J6**
Engaño, C., *Dom. Rep.* **121 C6**
Engaño, C., *Phil.* **63 A6**
Engaru, *Japan* **54 B11**
Engcobo, *S. Africa* **89 E4**
Engelberg, *Switz.* **25 J4**
Engels, *Russia* **34 E8**
Engemann L., *Canada* **103 B7**
Engershatu, *Eritrea* **81 D4**
Enggano, *Indonesia* **62 F2**
England, *U.S.A.* **113 H9**
England □, *U.K.* **14 D7**
Englee, *Canada* **105 B8**
Englehart, *Canada* **104 C4**
Englewood, *U.S.A.* **112 F2**
English →, *Canada* **103 C10**
English Bazar = Ingraj Bazar, *India* **69 G13**
English Channel, *Europe* **15 G6**
English River, *Canada* **104 C1**
Engures ezers, *Latvia* **30 A10**
Enguri →, *Georgia* **35 J5**
Enid, *U.S.A.* **113 G6**
Enipévs →, *Greece* **46 B4**
Enkhuizen, *Neths.* **17 B5**
Enköping, *Sweden* **10 E11**
Enle, *China* **58 F3**
Enna, *Italy* **43 E7**
Ennadai, *Canada* **103 A8**
Ennadai L., *Canada* **103 A8**
Ennedi, *Chad* **79 E10**
Enngonia, *Australia* **95 D4**
Ennigerloh, *Germany* **24 D4**
Ennis, *Ireland* **12 D3**
Ennis, *Mont., U.S.A.* **108 D8**
Ennis, *Tex., U.S.A.* **113 J6**
Enniscorthy, *Ireland* **12 D5**
Enniskillen, *U.K.* **12 B4**
Ennistimon, *Ireland* **12 D2**
Enns, *Austria* **26 C7**
Enns →, *Austria* **26 C7**
Enontekiö, *Finland* **8 B20**
Enosburg Falls, *U.S.A.* **117 B12**
Enping, *China* **59 F9**
Enriquillo, L., *Dom. Rep.* **121 C5**
Enschede, *Neths.* **17 B6**
Ensenada, *Argentina* **126 C4**
Ensenada, *Mexico* **118 A1**
Ensenada de los Muertos, *Mexico* **118 C2**
Enshi, *China* **58 B7**
Ensiola, Pta. de n', *Spain* **48 B9**
Ensisheim, *France* **19 E14**
Entebbe, *Uganda* **86 B3**
Enterprise, *Canada* **102 A5**
Enterprise, *Ala., U.S.A.* **115 K3**
Enterprise, *Oreg., U.S.A.* **108 D5**
Entorno de Doñana ⌂, *Spain* **37 J4**
Entraygues-sur-Truyère, *France* **20 D6**
Entre Ríos, *Bolivia* **126 A3**
Entre Ríos □, *Argentina* **126 C4**
Entrepeñas, Embalse de, *Spain* **38 E2**
Entroncamento, *Portugal* **37 F2**
Enugu, *Nigeria* **83 D6**
Enugu □, *Nigeria* **83 D6**
Enugu Ezike, *Nigeria* **83 D6**
Enumclaw, *U.S.A.* **110 C5**
Envalira, Port d', *Europe* **38 C6**
Envermeu, *France* **18 C8**
Enviken, *Sweden* **10 D9**
Enying, *Hungary* **28 D3**
Enza →, *Italy* **40 D7**
Éolie, Ís., *Italy* **43 D7**
Epanomí, *Greece* **44 F6**
Epe, *Neths.* **17 B5**
Epe, *Nigeria* **83 D5**
Épernay, *France* **19 C10**
Épernon, *France* **19 D8**
Ephesus, *Turkey* **47 D9**
Ephraim, *U.S.A.* **108 G8**
Ephrata, *Pa., U.S.A.* **117 F8**
Ephrata, *Wash., U.S.A.* **108 C4**
Epidaurus Limera, *Greece* **46 E5**
Épila, *Spain* **38 D3**
Épinac, *France* **19 F11**
Épinal, *France* **19 D13**
Episkopi, *Cyprus* **49 E11**
Episkopí, *Greece* **49 D6**
Episkopi Bay, *Cyprus* **49 E11**
Epitálion, *Greece* **46 D3**
Eppan = Appiano, *Italy* **41 B8**
Eppingen, *Germany* **25 F4**
Epsom, *U.K.* **15 F7**
Epukiro, *Namibia* **88 C2**
Equatorial Guinea ■, *Africa* **84 D1**
Er Hai, *China* **58 E3**
Er Rachidia, *Morocco* **78 B5**
Er Rahad, *Sudan* **81 E3**
Er Rif, *Morocco* **78 A5**
Er Rogel, *Sudan* **80 D4**
Er Roseires, *Sudan* **81 E3**
Er Rua'at, *Sudan* **81 E3**
Eraclea, *Italy* **41 C9**
Erāwadī Myit = Irrawaddy →, *Burma* **67 M19**
Erāwadī Myitwanya = Irrawaddy, Mouths of the, *Burma* **67 M19**
Erba, *Italy* **40 C6**
Erba, *Sudan* **80 D4**
Erba, J., *Sudan* **80 C4**
Erbaa, *Turkey* **72 B7**
Erbeskopf, *Germany* **25 F3**
Erbil = Arbīl, *Iraq* **70 B5**
Erbu, *Ethiopia* **81 E3**
Erçek, *Turkey* **70 B4**
Erçiş, *Turkey* **73 C10**
Erciyaş Dağı, *Turkey* **70 B2**
Érd, *Hungary* **28 C3**
Erdao Jiang →, *China* **57 C14**
Erdek, *Turkey* **45 F11**
Erdemli, *Turkey* **72 D6**
Erdene = Ulaan-Uul, *Mongolia* **56 B6**
Erdenetsogt, *Mongolia* **56 C4**
Erding, *Germany* **25 G7**
Erdre →, *France* **18 E5**
Erebus, Mt., *Antarctica* **5 D11**
Erechim, *Brazil* **127 B5**
Ereğli, *Konya, Turkey* **70 B2**
Ereğli, *Zonguldak, Turkey* **72 B4**
Erei, Monti, *Italy* **43 E7**
Erenhot, *China* **56 C7**
Eresma →, *Spain* **36 D6**
Eressós, *Greece* **47 B7**
Erfenisdam, *S. Africa* **88 D4**
Erfstadt, *Germany* **24 E2**
Erft →, *Germany* **24 D2**
Erfurt, *Germany* **24 E7**
Ergani, *Turkey* **70 B3**
Ergel, *Mongolia* **56 C5**
Ergene →, *Turkey* **45 E10**
Ergeni Vozvyshennost, *Russia* **35 G7**
Ērgli, *Latvia* **9 H21**
Erhlin, *Taiwan* **59 F13**
Eria →, *Spain* **36 C5**
Eriba, *Sudan* **81 D4**
Eriboll, L., *U.K.* **13 C4**
Érice, *Italy* **42 D5**
Erie, *U.S.A.* **116 D4**
Erie, L., *N. Amer.* **116 D4**
Erie Canal, *U.S.A.* **116 C7**
Erieau, *Canada* **116 D3**
Erigavo, *Somali Rep.* **75 E4**
Erikoúsa, *Greece* **49 A3**
Eriksdale, *Canada* **103 C9**
Erímanthos, *Greece* **46 D3**
Erimo-misaki, *Japan* **54 D11**
Erin Pt., *Trin. & Tob.* **125 K15**
Erinpura, *India* **68 G5**
Eriskay, *U.K.* **13 D1**
Erithraí, *Greece* **46 C5**
Eritrea ■, *Africa* **81 E4**
Erjas →, *Portugal* **36 F3**
Erkelenz, *Germany* **24 D2**
Erkner, *Germany* **24 C9**
Erlangen, *Germany* **25 F6**
Erldunda, *Australia* **94 D1**
Ermelo, *Neths.* **17 B5**
Ermelo, *S. Africa* **89 D4**
Ermenek, *Turkey* **70 B2**
Ermil, *Sudan* **81 E2**
Ermióni, *Greece* **46 D5**
Ermones, *Greece* **49 A3**
Ermoúpolis = Síros, *Greece* **46 D6**
Ernakulam, *India* **66 Q10**
Erne →, *Ireland* **12 B3**
Erne, Lower L., *U.K.* **12 B4**
Erne, Upper L., *U.K.* **12 B4**
Ernée, *France* **18 D6**
Ernest Giles Ra., *Australia* **93 E3**
Ernstberg, *Germany* **25 E2**
Erode, *India* **66 P10**
Eromanga, *Australia* **95 D3**
Erongo, *Namibia* **88 C2**
Erquy, *France* **18 D4**
Erramala Hills, *India* **66 M11**
Errer →, *Ethiopia* **81 F5**
Errigal, *Ireland* **12 A3**
Erris Hd., *Ireland* **12 B1**
Ersekë, *Albania* **44 F4**
Erskine, *U.S.A.* **112 B7**
Erstein, *France* **19 D14**
Ertholmene, *Denmark* **11 J9**
Ertil, *Russia* **34 E5**
Ertis = Irtysh →, *Russia* **52 C7**
Eruh, *Turkey* **73 D10**
Eruwa, *Nigeria* **83 D5**
Ervy-le-Châtel, *France* **19 D10**
Erwin, *U.S.A.* **115 G4**
Eryuan, *China* **58 D2**
Erzgebirge, *Germany* **24 E8**
Erzin, *Russia* **53 D10**
Erzincan, *Turkey* **70 B3**
Erzurum, *Turkey* **70 B4**
Es Caló, *Spain* **48 C8**
Es Canar, *Spain* **48 B8**
Es Mercadal, *Spain* **48 B11**
Es Migjorn Gran, *Spain* **48 B11**
Es Safiya, *Sudan* **81 D3**
Es Sahrâ' Esh Sharqîya, *Egypt* **80 B3**
Es Sînâ', *Egypt* **74 F3**
Es Sûkî, *Sudan* **81 E3**
Es Vedrà, *Spain* **48 C7**
Esambo, *Dem. Rep. of the Congo* **86 C1**
Esan-Misaki, *Japan* **54 D10**
Esashi, *Hokkaidō, Japan* **54 B11**
Esashi, *Hokkaidō, Japan* **54 D10**
Esbjerg, *Denmark* **11 J2**
Escalante, *U.S.A.* **109 H8**
Escalante →, *U.S.A.* **109 H8**
Escalón, *Mexico* **118 B4**
Escambia →, *U.S.A.* **115 K2**
Escanaba, *U.S.A.* **114 C2**
Esch-sur-Alzette, *Lux.* **17 E6**
Eschede, *Germany* **24 C6**
Eschwege, *Germany* **24 D6**
Eschweiler, *Germany* **24 E2**
Escondido, *U.S.A.* **111 M9**
Escravos →, *Nigeria* **83 D6**
Escuinapa, *Mexico* **118 C3**
Escuintla, *Guatemala* **120 D1**
Eséka, *Cameroon* **83 E7**
Eşen →, *Turkey* **47 E11**
Esenguly, *Turkmenistan* **52 F6**
Esens, *Germany* **24 B3**
Esenyurt, *Turkey* **45 E12**
Esera →, *Spain* **38 C5**
Eşfahān, *Iran* **71 C6**
Eşfahān □, *Iran* **71 C6**
Esfarāyen, *Iran* **71 B8**
Esfīdeh, *Iran* **71 C8**
Esgueva →, *Spain* **36 D6**
Esh Sham = Dimashq, *Syria* **74 B5**
Esh Shamâlîya □, *Sudan* **80 D2**
Esha Ness, *U.K.* **13 A7**
Eshan, *China* **58 E4**
Esher, *U.K.* **15 F7**
Eshkol △, *Israel* **74 D3**
Eshowe, *S. Africa* **89 D5**
Esiama, *Ghana* **82 E4**
Esigodini, *Zimbabwe* **89 C4**
Esil = Ishim →, *Russia* **52 D8**
Esino →, *Italy* **41 E10**
Esira, *Madag.* **89 C8**
Esk →, *Cumb., U.K.* **13 G5**
Esk →, *N. Yorks., U.K.* **14 C7**
Eskān, *Iran* **71 E9**
Esker, *Canada* **105 B6**
Eskifjörður, *Iceland* **8 D7**
Eskilsäter, *Sweden* **11 F7**
Eskilstuna, *Sweden* **10 E10**
Eskimalatya, *Turkey* **73 C8**
Eskimo Point = Arviat, *Canada* **100 B10**
Eskişehir, *Turkey* **47 B12**
Eskişehir □, *Turkey* **47 B12**
Esla →, *Spain* **36 D4**
Eslāmābād-e Gharb, *Iran* **70 C5**
Eslāmshahr, *Iran* **71 C6**
Eslöv, *Sweden* **11 J7**
Eşme, *Turkey* **47 C10**
Esmeraldas, *Ecuador* **124 C3**
Esnagi L., *Canada* **104 C3**
Espalion, *France* **20 D6**
Espanola, *Canada* **104 C3**
Espanola, *U.S.A.* **109 H10**
Esparreguera, *Spain* **38 D6**
Esparta, *Costa Rica* **120 E3**
Espelkamp, *Germany* **24 C4**
Esperance, *Australia* **93 F3**
Esperance B., *Australia* **93 F3**
Esperance B., *St. Lucia* **121 f**
Esperanza, *Antarctica* **5 C18**
Esperanza, *Argentina* **126 C3**
Esperanza, *Phil.* **61 G6**
Esperanza, *Puerto Rico* **121 d**
Espéraza, *France* **20 F6**
Espichel, C., *Portugal* **37 G1**
Espiel, *Spain* **37 G5**
Espigão, Serra do, *Brazil* **127 B5**
Espinazo, Sierra del = Espinhaço, Serra do, *Brazil* **125 G10**
Espinhaço, Serra do, *Brazil* **125 G10**
Espinho, *Portugal* **36 D2**
Espinilho, Serra do, *Brazil* **127 B5**
Espinosa de los Monteros, *Spain* **36 B7**
Espírito Santo □, *Brazil* **125 H10**
Espíritu Santo, *Vanuatu* **96 J8**
Espíritu Santo, B. del, *Mexico* **119 D7**
Espíritu Santo, I., *Mexico* **118 C2**
Espita, *Mexico* **119 C7**
Espiye, *Turkey* **73 B8**
Espluga de Francolí, *Spain* **38 D6**
Espoo, *Finland* **9 F21**
Espuña, Sierra de, *Spain* **39 H3**
Espungabera, *Mozam.* **89 C5**
Esquel, *Argentina* **128 E2**
Esquimalt, *Canada* **102 D4**
Esquina, *Argentina* **126 C4**
Essaouira, *Morocco* **78 B4**
Essebie, *Dem. Rep. of the Congo* **86 B3**
Essen, *Belgium* **17 C4**
Essen, *Germany* **24 D3**
Essendon, Mt., *Australia* **93 E3**
Essequibo →, *Guyana* **124 B7**
Essex, *Canada* **116 D2**
Essex, *Calif., U.S.A.* **111 L11**
Essex, *N.Y., U.S.A.* **117 B11**
Essex □, *U.K.* **15 F8**
Essex Junction, *U.S.A.* **117 B11**
Esslingen, *Germany* **25 G5**
Essonne □, *France* **19 D9**
Estaca de Bares, C. de, *Spain* **36 B3**
Estadilla, *Spain* **38 C5**
Estados, I. de Los, *Argentina* **128 G4**
Estagel, *France* **20 F6**
Eşţahbānāt, *Iran* **71 D7**
Estância, *Brazil* **125 F11**
Estancia, *U.S.A.* **109 J10**
Estārm, *Iran* **71 D8**
Estarreja, *Portugal* **36 E2**
Estats, Pic d', *Spain* **38 C6**
Estcourt, *S. Africa* **89 D4**
Este, *Italy* **41 C8**
Este △, *Dom. Rep.* **121 C6**
Estelí, *Nic.* **120 D2**
Estella, *Spain* **38 C2**
Estellencs, *Spain* **48 B9**
Estena →, *Spain* **37 F6**
Estepa, *Spain* **37 H6**
Estepona, *Spain* **37 J5**
Esterhazy, *Canada* **103 C8**
Esternay, *France* **19 D10**
Esterri d'Aneu, *Spain* **38 C6**
Estevan, *Canada* **103 D8**
Estevan Group, *Canada* **102 C3**
Estherville, *U.S.A.* **112 D7**
Estissac, *France* **19 D10**
Eston, *Canada* **103 C7**
Estonia ■, *Europe* **9 G21**
Estoril, *Portugal* **37 G1**
Estouk, *Mali* **83 B5**
Estreito, *Brazil* **125 E9**
Estrela, Serra da, *Portugal* **36 E3**
Estrella, *Spain* **37 G7**
Estremoz, *Portugal* **37 G3**
Estrondo, Serra do, *Brazil* **125 E9**
Esztergom, *Hungary* **28 C3**
Et Tîdra, *Mauritania* **82 B1**
Etah, *India* **69 F8**
Étain, *France* **19 C12**
Étampes, *France* **19 D9**
Etanga, *Namibia* **88 B1**
Étaples, *France* **19 B8**
Etawah, *India* **69 F8**
Etawney L., *Canada* **103 B9**
Ete, *Nigeria* **83 D6**
Ethel, *U.S.A.* **110 D4**
Ethelbert, *Canada* **103 C8**
Ethiopia ■, *Africa* **75 F3**
Ethiopian Highlands, *Ethiopia* **50 J7**
Etili, *Turkey* **45 G10**
Etive, L., *U.K.* **13 E3**
Etna, *Italy* **43 E7**
Etoile, *Dem. Rep. of the Congo* **87 E2**
Etosha △, *Namibia* **88 B2**
Etosha Pan, *Namibia* **88 B2**
Etowah, *U.S.A.* **115 H3**

Étréchy, *France* 19 D9
Étrépagny, *France* 19 C8
Étretat, *France* 18 C7
Etropole, *Bulgaria* 45 D8
Ettelbruck, *Lux.* 17 E6
Ettlingen, *Germany* 25 G4
Ettrick Water →, *U.K.* 13 F6
Etuku, *Dem. Rep. of the Congo* 86 C2
Etulia, *Moldova* 29 E13
Etzatlán, *Mexico* 118 C4
Etzná, *Mexico* 119 D6
Etzná-Tixmucuy = Edxná, *Mexico* 119 D6
Eu, *France* 18 B8
Eubenangee Swamp △, *Australia* 94 B4
Euboea = Évvoia, *Greece* 46 C6
Eucla, *Australia* 93 F4
Euclid, *U.S.A.* 116 E3
Eucumbene, L., *Australia* 95 F4
Eudora, *U.S.A.* 113 J9
Eufaula, *Ala., U.S.A.* 115 K3
Eufaula, *Okla., U.S.A.* 113 H7
Eufaula L., *U.S.A.* 113 H7
Eugene, *U.S.A.* 108 E2
Eugowra, *Australia* 95 E4
Eulo, *Australia* 95 D4
Eungella △, *Australia* 94 C4
Eunice, *La., U.S.A.* 113 K8
Eunice, *N. Mex., U.S.A.* 113 J3
Eupen, *Belgium* 17 D6
Euphrates = Furāt, Nahr al →, *Asia* 70 D5
Eure □, *France* 18 C8
Eure →, *France* 18 C8
Eure-et-Loir □, *France* 18 D8
Eureka, *Canada* 4 B3
Eureka, *Calif., U.S.A.* 108 F1
Eureka, *Kans., U.S.A.* 113 G6
Eureka, *Mont., U.S.A.* 108 B6
Eureka, *Nev., U.S.A.* 108 G5
Eureka, *S. Dak., U.S.A.* 112 C5
Eureka, Mt., *Australia* 93 E3
Euroa, *Australia* 95 F4
Europa, Île, *Ind. Oc.* 85 J8
Europa, Picos de, *Spain* 36 B6
Europa, Pta. de, *Gib.* 37 J5
Europe 6 E10
Europoort, *Neths.* 17 C4
Euskirchen, *Germany* 24 E2
Eustis, *U.S.A.* 115 L5
Eutin, *Germany* 24 A6
Eutsuk L., *Canada* 102 C3
Evale, *Angola* 88 B2
Evans, *U.S.A.* 112 E2
Evans, L., *Canada* 104 B4
Evans City, *U.S.A.* 116 F4
Evans Head, *Australia* 95 D5
Evans Mills, *U.S.A.* 117 B9
Evansburg, *Canada* 102 C5
Evanston, *Ill., U.S.A.* 114 E2
Evanston, *Wyo., U.S.A.* 108 F8
Evansville, *U.S.A.* 114 G2
Évaux-les-Bains, *France* 19 F9
Evaz, *Iran* 71 E7
Evciler, *Afyon, Turkey* 47 C11
Evciler, *Çanakkale, Turkey* 47 B8
Eveleth, *U.S.A.* 112 B8
Evensk, *Russia* 53 C16
Everard, L., *Australia* 95 E2
Everard Ranges, *Australia* 93 E5
Everest, Mt., *Nepal* 69 E12
Everett, *Pa., U.S.A.* 116 F6
Everett, *Wash., U.S.A.* 110 C4
Everglades △, *U.S.A.* 115 N5
Everglades, The, *U.S.A.* 115 N5
Everglades City, *U.S.A.* 115 N5
Evergreen, *Ala., U.S.A.* 115 K2
Evergreen, *Mont., U.S.A.* 108 B6
Everöd, *Sweden* 11 J8
Evertsberg, *Sweden* 10 C7
Evesham, *U.K.* 15 E6
Évian-les-Bains, *France* 19 F13
Évinos →, *Greece* 46 C3
Évisa, *France* 21 F12
Evje, *Norway* 9 G12
Évora, *Portugal* 37 G3
Évora □, *Portugal* 37 G3
Evowghlī, *Iran* 70 B5
Évreux, *France* 18 C8
Evritanía □, *Greece* 46 B3
Évron, *France* 18 D6
Évros □, *Greece* 45 E10
Évros →, *Greece* 72 B2
Evrótas →, *Greece* 46 E4
Évry, *France* 19 D9
Évvoia, *Greece* 46 C6
Évvoia □, *Greece* 46 C5
Evxinoúpolis, *Greece* 46 B4
Ewe, L., *U.K.* 13 D3
Ewing, *U.S.A.* 112 D5
Ewo, *Congo* 84 E2
Exaltación, *Bolivia* 124 F5
Excelsior Springs, *U.S.A.* 112 F7
Excideuil, *France* 20 C5
Exe →, *U.K.* 15 G4
Exeter, *Canada* 116 C3
Exeter, *U.K.* 15 G4
Exeter, *Calif., U.S.A.* 110 J7
Exeter, *N.H., U.S.A.* 117 D14
Exmoor, *U.K.* 15 F4
Exmoor △, *U.K.* 15 F4
Exmouth, *Australia* 92 D1
Exmouth, *U.K.* 15 G4
Exmouth G., *Australia* 92 D1
Expedition △, *Australia* 95 D4
Expedition Ra., *Australia* 94 C4
Extremadura □, *Spain* 37 F4
Exuma Sound, *Bahamas* 120 B4
Eyasi, L., *Tanzania* 86 C4
Eye Pen., *U.K.* 13 C2
Eyemouth, *U.K.* 13 F6
Eygurande, *France* 19 G9
Eyjafjörður, *Iceland* 8 C4
Eymet, *France* 20 D4
Eymoutiers, *France* 20 C5
Eynesil, *Turkey* 73 B8
Eyre (North), L., *Australia* 95 D2
Eyre (South), L., *Australia* 95 D2
Eyre Mts., *N.Z.* 91 L2
Eyre Pen., *Australia* 95 E2
Eysturoy, *Færoe Is.* 8 E9
Eyvānkī, *Iran* 71 C6
Ez Zeidab, *Sudan* 80 D3
Ezcaray, *Spain* 38 C1
Ežerėlis, *Lithuania* 30 D10
Ezhou, *China* 59 B10
Ezine, *Turkey* 47 B8
Ezouza →, *Cyprus* 49 E11

F

F.Y.R.O.M. = Macedonia ■, *Europe* 44 E5
Fabala, *Guinea* 82 D3
Fabens, *U.S.A.* 109 L10
Fabero, *Spain* 36 C4
Fåborg, *Denmark* 11 J4
Fabriano, *Italy* 41 E9
Făcăeni, *Romania* 29 F12
Fachi, *Niger* 79 E8
Fada, *Chad* 79 E10
Fada-n-Gourma, *Burkina Faso* 83 C5
Fadd, *Hungary* 28 D3
Faddeyevskiy, Ostrov, *Russia* 53 B15
Faddor, *Sudan* 81 F3
Fadghāmī, *Syria* 70 C4
Fadlab, *Sudan* 80 D3
Faenza, *Italy* 41 D8
Færoe Is. = Føroyar, *Atl. Oc.* 8 F9
Fafa, *Mali* 83 B5
Fafe, *Portugal* 36 D2
Fagam, *Nigeria* 83 C7
Făgăras, *Romania* 29 E9
Făgăras, Munții, *Romania* 29 E9
Fågelmara, *Sweden* 11 H9
Fagerhult, *Sweden* 11 G9
Fagersta, *Sweden* 10 D9
Făget, *Romania* 28 E7
Făget, Munții, *Romania* 29 C8
Fagnano, L., *Argentina* 128 G3
Fagnières, *France* 19 D11
Faguibine, L., *Mali* 82 B4
Fahlīān, *Iran* 71 D6
Fahraj, *Kermān, Iran* 71 D8
Fahraj, *Yazd, Iran* 71 D7
Fai Tsi Long, *Vietnam* 58 G6
Faial, *Madeira* 48 D3
Fair Haven, *U.S.A.* 114 D9
Fair Hd., *U.K.* 12 A5
Fair Oaks, *U.S.A.* 110 G5
Fairbanks, *U.S.A.* 100 B5
Fairbury, *U.S.A.* 112 E6
Fairfax, *U.S.A.* 117 B11
Fairfield, *Ala., U.S.A.* 115 J2
Fairfield, *Calif., U.S.A.* 110 G4
Fairfield, *Conn., U.S.A.* 117 E11
Fairfield, *Idaho, U.S.A.* 108 E6
Fairfield, *Ill., U.S.A.* 114 F1
Fairfield, *Iowa, U.S.A.* 112 E9
Fairfield, *Tex., U.S.A.* 113 K7
Fairford, *Canada* 103 C9
Fairhope, *U.S.A.* 115 K2
Fairlie, *N.Z.* 91 L3
Fairmead, *U.S.A.* 110 H6
Fairmont, *Minn., U.S.A.* 112 D7
Fairmont, *W. Va., U.S.A.* 114 F5
Fairmount, *Calif., U.S.A.* 111 L8
Fairmount, *N.Y., U.S.A.* 117 C8
Fairplay, *U.S.A.* 109 G11
Fairport, *U.S.A.* 116 C7
Fairport Harbor, *U.S.A.* 116 E3
Fairview, *Canada* 102 B5
Fairview, *Mont., U.S.A.* 112 B2
Fairview, *Okla., U.S.A.* 113 G5
Fairweather, Mt., *U.S.A.* 102 B1
Faisalabad, *Pakistan* 68 D5
Faith, *U.S.A.* 112 C3
Faizabad, *India* 69 F10
Fajardo, *Puerto Rico* 121 d
Fajr, W. →, *Si. Arabia* 70 D3
Fakenham, *U.K.* 14 E8
Fåker, *Sweden* 10 A8
Fakfak, *Indonesia* 63 E8
Fakiya, *Bulgaria* 45 D11
Fakobli, *Ivory C.* 82 D3
Fakse, *Denmark* 11 J6
Fakse Bugt, *Denmark* 11 J6
Fakse Ladeplads, *Denmark* 11 J6
Faku, *China* 57 C12
Falaba, *S. Leone* 82 D2
Falaise, *France* 18 D6
Falaise, Mui, *Vietnam* 64 C5
Falakrón Óros, *Greece* 44 E7
Falam, *Burma* 67 H18
Falces, *Spain* 38 C3
Fălciu, *Romania* 29 D13
Falcó, C. des, *Spain* 48 C7
Falcón, Presa, *Mexico* 119 B5
Falcon Lake, *Canada* 103 D9
Falcon Reservoir, *U.S.A.* 113 M5
Falconara Marittima, *Italy* 41 E10
Falcone, C. del, *Italy* 42 B1
Falconer, *U.S.A.* 116 D5
Faléa, *Mali* 82 C2
Falémé →, *Senegal* 82 C2
Falerum, *Sweden* 11 F10
Faleshty = Fălești, *Moldova* 29 C12
Fălești, *Moldova* 29 C12
Falfurrias, *U.S.A.* 113 M5
Falher, *Canada* 102 B5
Falirakí, *Greece* 49 C10
Falkenberg, *Germany* 24 D9
Falkenberg, *Sweden* 11 H6
Falkensee, *Germany* 24 C9
Falkirk, *U.K.* 13 F5
Falkirk □, *U.K.* 13 F5
Falkland, *U.K.* 13 E5
Falkland Is. ☒, *Atl. Oc.* 128 G5
Falkland Sd., *Falk. Is.* 128 G5
Falkonéra, *Greece* 46 E5
Falköping, *Sweden* 11 F7
Fall River, *U.S.A.* 117 E13
Fallbrook, *U.S.A.* 111 M9
Fallon, *U.S.A.* 108 G4
Falls City, *U.S.A.* 112 E7
Falls Creek, *U.S.A.* 116 E6
Falmouth, *Jamaica* 120 a
Falmouth, *U.K.* 15 G2
Falmouth, *U.S.A.* 117 E14
Falsa, Pta., *Mexico* 118 B1
False B., *S. Africa* 88 E2
Falso, C., *Honduras* 120 C3
Falster, *Denmark* 11 K5
Falsterbo, *Sweden* 9 J15
Fălticeni, *Romania* 29 C11
Falun, *Sweden* 10 D9
Famagusta, *Cyprus* 49 D12
Famagusta Bay, *Cyprus* 49 D13
Famalé, *Niger* 78 F6
Famatina, Sierra de, *Argentina* 126 B2
Family L., *Canada* 103 C9
Famoso, *U.S.A.* 111 K7
Fan Xian, *China* 56 G8
Fana, *Mali* 82 C3
Fanad Hd., *Ireland* 12 A4
Fanárion, *Greece* 46 B3
Fandriana, *Madag.* 89 C8
Fánes-Sénnes e Braies ⌓, *Italy* 41 B9
Fang, *Thailand* 58 H2
Fang Xian, *China* 59 A8
Fangaga, *Sudan* 80 D4
Fangak, *Sudan* 81 F3
Fangchang, *China* 59 B12
Fangcheng, *China* 56 H7
Fangchenggang, *China* 58 G7
Fangliao, *Taiwan* 59 F13
Fangshan, *China* 56 E6
Fangzi, *China* 57 F10
Fani i Madh →, *Albania* 44 E4
Fanjakana, *Madag.* 89 C8
Fanjiatun, *China* 57 C13
Fannich, L., *U.K.* 13 D4
Fannūj, *Iran* 71 E8
Fanø, *Denmark* 11 J2
Fano, *Italy* 41 E10
Fanshi, *China* 56 E7
Fao = Al Fāw, *Iraq* 71 D6
Faqirwali, *Pakistan* 68 E5
Fâqûs, *Egypt* 80 H7
Far East = Dalnevostochnyy □, *Russia* 53 C14
Far East, *Asia* 50 E16
Fara in Sabina, *Italy* 41 F9
Faradje, *Dem. Rep. of the Congo* 86 B2
Farafangana, *Madag.* 89 C8
Farâfra, El Wâhât el-, *Egypt* 80 B2
Farāh, *Afghan.* 66 C3
Farāh □, *Afghan.* 66 C3
Farahalana, *Madag.* 89 A9
Faraid, Gebel, *Egypt* 80 C4
Farako, *Ivory C.* 82 D4
Faramana, *Burkina Faso* 82 C4
Faranah, *Guinea* 82 C2
Farasān, Jazā'ir, *Si. Arabia* 75 D3
Farasan Is. = Farasān, Jazā'ir, *Si. Arabia* 75 D3
Faratsiho, *Madag.* 89 B8
Fardes →, *Spain* 37 H7
Fareham, *U.K.* 15 G6
Farewell, C., *N.Z.* 91 J4
Farewell C. = Nunap Isua, *Greenland* 101 C15
Färgelanda, *Sweden* 11 F5
Farghona, *Uzbekistan* 52 E8
Fargo, *U.S.A.* 112 B6
Fār'iah, W. al →, *West Bank* 74 C4
Faribault, *U.S.A.* 112 C8
Faridabad, *India* 68 E6
Faridkot, *India* 68 D6
Faridpur, *Bangla.* 69 H13
Faridpur, *India* 69 E8
Färila, *Sweden* 10 C9
Farim, *Guinea-Biss.* 82 C1
Farīmān, *Iran* 71 C8
Farina, *Australia* 95 E2
Fariones, Pta., *Canary Is.* 48 E6
Fâriskûr, *Egypt* 80 H7
Färjestaden, *Sweden* 11 H10
Farkadhón, *Greece* 46 B4
Farleigh, *Australia* 94 K7
Farmakonisi, *Greece* 47 D9
Farmerville, *U.S.A.* 113 J8
Farmingdale, *U.S.A.* 117 F10
Farmington, *Canada* 102 B4
Farmington, *Calif., U.S.A.* 110 H6
Farmington, *Maine, U.S.A.* 115 C10
Farmington, *Mo., U.S.A.* 113 G9
Farmington, *N.H., U.S.A.* 117 C13
Farmington, *N. Mex., U.S.A.* 109 H9
Farmington, *Utah, U.S.A.* 108 F8
Farmington →, *U.S.A.* 117 E12
Farmville, *U.S.A.* 114 G6
Färnäs, *Sweden* 10 D8
Farne Is., *U.K.* 14 B6
Färnebofjärden △, *Sweden* 10 D10
Farnham, *Canada* 117 A12
Farnham, Mt., *Canada* 102 C5
Faro, *Brazil* 125 D7
Faro, *Canada* 100 B6
Faro, *Portugal* 37 H3
Fårö, *Sweden* 9 H18
Faro □, *Portugal* 37 H2
Faro ✕ (FAO), *Portugal* 37 H3
Fårösund, *Sweden* 11 G13
Farquhar, C., *Australia* 93 D1
Farrars Cr. →, *Australia* 94 D3
Farrāshband, *Iran* 71 D7
Farrell, *U.S.A.* 116 E4
Farrokhī, *Iran* 71 C8
Farruch, C. = Ferrutx, C., *Spain* 48 B10
Fārs □, *Iran* 71 D7
Fársala, *Greece* 46 B4
Farsø, *Denmark* 11 H3
Farson, *U.S.A.* 108 E9
Farsund, *Norway* 9 G12
Fartak, Râs, *Si. Arabia* 70 D2
Fartak, Ra's, *Yemen* 75 D5
Fârțănești, *Romania* 29 E12
Fartura, Serra da, *Brazil* 127 B5
Faru, *Nigeria* 83 C6
Fārūj, *Iran* 71 B8
Fårup, *Denmark* 11 H3
Farvel, Kap = Nunap Isua, *Greenland* 101 C15
Farwell, *U.S.A.* 113 H3
Fāryāb □, *Afghan.* 66 B4
Fasā, *Iran* 71 D7
Fasano, *Italy* 43 B10
Fashoda, *Sudan* 81 F3
Fassa, *Mali* 82 C3
Fastiv, *Ukraine* 33 G5
Fastnet Rock, *Ireland* 12 E2
Fastov = Fastiv, *Ukraine* 33 G5
Fatagar, Tanjung, *Indonesia* 63 E8
Fatehabad, *Haryana, India* 68 E6
Fatehabad, *Ut. P., India* 68 F8
Fatehgarh, *India* 69 F8
Fatehpur, *Bihar, India* 69 G11
Fatehpur, *Raj., India* 68 F6
Fatehpur, *Ut. P., India* 69 G9
Fatehpur, *Ut. P., India* 69 F9
Fatehpur Sikri, *India* 68 F6
Fatesh, *Russia* 33 F8
Fathai, *Sudan* 81 F3
Fathom Five ⌓, *Canada* 116 A3
Fatick, *Senegal* 82 C1
Fatima, *Canada* 105 C7
Fátima, *Portugal* 37 F2
Fatoya, *Guinea* 82 C3
Fatsa, *Turkey* 72 B7
Faucille, Col de la, *France* 19 F13
Faulkton, *U.S.A.* 112 C5
Faulquemont, *France* 19 C13
Faure I., *Australia* 93 E1
Făurei, *Romania* 29 E12
Fauresmith, *S. Africa* 88 D4
Fauske, *Norway* 8 C16
Favara, *Italy* 42 E6
Faváritx, C. de, *Spain* 48 B11
Faverges, *France* 21 C10
Favignana, *Italy* 42 E5
Favignana, I., *Italy* 42 E5
Fawcett, Pt., *Australia* 92 B5
Fawn →, *Canada* 104 A2
Fawnskin, *U.S.A.* 111 L10
Faxaflói, *Iceland* 8 D2
Faxälven →, *Sweden* 10 A10
Faya-Largeau, *Chad* 79 E9
Fayd, *Si. Arabia* 70 E4
Fayence, *France* 21 E10
Fayette, *Ala., U.S.A.* 115 J2
Fayette, *Mo., U.S.A.* 112 F8
Fayetteville, *Ark., U.S.A.* 113 G7
Fayetteville, *N.C., U.S.A.* 115 H6
Fayetteville, *Tenn., U.S.A.* 115 H2
Fayied, *Egypt* 80 H8
Fayón, *Spain* 38 D5
Fazao-Malfakassa △, *Togo* 83 D5
Fazilka, *India* 68 D6
Fazilpur, *Pakistan* 68 E4
Fdérik, *Mauritania* 78 D3
Feale →, *Ireland* 12 D2
Fear, C., *U.S.A.* 115 J7
Feather →, *U.S.A.* 108 G3
Feather Falls, *U.S.A.* 110 F5
Featherston, *N.Z.* 91 J5
Featherstone, *Zimbabwe* 87 F3
Fécamp, *France* 18 C7
Fedala = Mohammedia, *Morocco* 78 B4
Federación, *Argentina* 126 C4
Féderal, *Argentina* 128 C5
Federal Capital Terr. □, *Nigeria* 83 D6
Federal Way, *U.S.A.* 110 C4
Fedeshkūh, *Iran* 71 D7
Fehérgyarmat, *Hungary* 28 C7
Fehmarn, *Germany* 24 A7
Fehmarn Bælt, *Europe* 11 K5
Fehmarn Belt = Fehmarn Bælt, *Europe* 11 K5
Fei Xian, *China* 57 G9
Feijó, *Brazil* 124 E4
Feilding, *N.Z.* 91 J5
Feira de Santana, *Brazil* 125 F11
Feixi, *China* 59 B11
Feixiang, *China* 56 F8
Fejér □, *Hungary* 28 C3
Fejø, *Denmark* 11 K5
Feke, *Turkey* 72 D6
Fekete →, *Hungary* 28 E3
Felanitx, *Spain* 48 B10
Feldbach, *Austria* 26 E8
Feldberg, *Baden-W., Germany* 25 H3
Feldberg, *Mecklenburg-Vorpommern, Germany* 24 B9
Feldkirch, *Austria* 26 D2
Feldkirchen, *Austria* 26 E7
Felipe Carrillo Puerto, *Mexico* 119 D7
Felixburg, *Zimbabwe* 89 B5
Felixstowe, *U.K.* 15 F9
Felletin, *France* 20 C6
Fellingsbro, *Sweden* 10 E9
Felton, *U.S.A.* 110 H4
Feltre, *Italy* 41 B8
Femer Bælt = Fehmarn Bælt, *Europe* 11 K5
Femø, *Denmark* 11 K5
Femunden, *Norway* 9 E14
Fen He →, *China* 56 G6
Fene, *Spain* 36 B2
Fenelon Falls, *Canada* 116 B6
Fener Burnu, *Turkey* 47 E9
Feneroa, *Ethiopia* 81 E4
Feng Xian, *Jiangsu, China* 56 G9
Feng Xian, *Shaanxi, China* 56 H4
Fengári, *Greece* 45 F9
Fengcheng, *Jiangxi, China* 59 C10
Fengcheng, *Liaoning, China* 57 D13
Fengfeng, *China* 56 F8
Fenggang, *China* 58 D6
Fenghua, *China* 59 C13
Fenghuang, *China* 58 D7
Fengkai, *China* 59 F8
Fengkang, *Taiwan* 59 F13
Fengle, *China* 59 B9
Fenglin, *Taiwan* 59 F13
Fengning, *China* 56 D9
Fengqing, *China* 58 E2
Fengqiu, *China* 56 G8
Fengrun, *China* 57 E10
Fengshan, *Guangxi Zhuangzu, China* 58 E7
Fengshan, *Guangxi Zhuangzu, China* 58 E6
Fengshan, *Taiwan* 59 F13
Fengshun, *China* 59 F11
Fengtai, *Anhui, China* 59 A11
Fengtai, *Beijing, China* 56 E9
Fengxian, *China* 59 B13
Fengxiang, *China* 56 G4
Fengxin, *China* 59 C10
Fengyang, *China* 57 H9
Fengyi, *China* 58 E3
Fengyüan, *Taiwan* 59 E13
Fengzhen, *China* 56 D7
Feno, C. de, *France* 21 G12
Fenoarivo, *Fianarantsoa, Madag.* 89 C8
Fenoarivo, *Fianarantsoa, Madag.* 89 C8
Fenoarivo Afovoany, *Madag.* 89 B8
Fenoarivo Atsinanana, *Madag.* 89 B8
Fens, The, *U.K.* 14 E7
Fensmark, *Denmark* 11 J5
Fenton, *U.S.A.* 114 D4
Fenxi, *China* 56 F6
Fenyang, *China* 56 F6
Fenyi, *China* 59 D10
Feodosiya, *Ukraine* 33 K8
Ferdows, *Iran* 71 C8
Fère-Champenoise, *France* 19 D10
Fère-en-Tardenois, *France* 19 C10
Ferentino, *Italy* 41 G10
Ferfer, *Somali Rep.* 75 F4
Fergana = Farghona, *Uzbekistan* 52 E8
Fergus, *Canada* 116 C4
Fergus Falls, *U.S.A.* 112 B6
Feričanci, *Croatia* 28 E2
Ferihegy, Budapest ✕ (BUD), *Hungary* 28 C4
Ferkéssédougou, *Ivory C.* 82 D3
Ferlach, *Austria* 26 E7
Ferland, *Canada* 104 B2
Ferlo, Vallée du, *Senegal* 82 B2
Ferlo-Nord ⌓, *Senegal* 82 B2
Ferlo-Sud ⌓, *Senegal* 82 B2
Fermanagh □, *U.K.* 12 B4
Fermo, *Italy* 41 E10
Fermont, *Canada* 105 B6
Fermoselle, *Spain* 36 D4
Fermoy, *Ireland* 12 D3
Fernán Nuñéz, *Spain* 37 H6
Fernández, *Argentina* 126 B3
Fernandina Beach, *U.S.A.* 115 K5
Fernando de Noronha, *Brazil* 125 D12
Fernando Póo = Bioko, *Eq. Guin.* 83 E6
Ferndale, *U.S.A.* 110 B4
Fernie, *Canada* 102 D5
Fernlees, *Australia* 94 C4
Fernley, *U.S.A.* 108 G4
Ferozepore = Firozpur, *India* 68 D6
Férrai, *Greece* 45 F10
Ferrandina, *Italy* 43 B9
Ferrara, *Italy* 41 D8
Ferrato, C., *Italy* 42 C2
Ferreira do Alentejo, *Portugal* 37 G2
Ferreñafe, *Peru* 124 E3
Ferrerías, *Spain* 48 B11
Ferret, C., *France* 20 D2
Ferrette, *France* 19 E14
Ferriday, *U.S.A.* 113 K9
Ferriere, *Italy* 40 D6
Ferrières, *France* 19 D9
Ferro, Capo, *Italy* 42 A2
Ferrol, *Spain* 36 B2
Ferron, *U.S.A.* 109 G8
Ferrutx, C., *Spain* 48 B10
Ferryland, *Canada* 105 C9
Fertile, *U.S.A.* 112 B6
Fertőszentmiklós, *Hungary* 28 C1
Fertotavi △, *Hungary* 28 C1
Fès, *Morocco* 78 B5
Fessenden, *U.S.A.* 112 B5
Festus, *U.S.A.* 112 F9
Feté Bowé, *Senegal* 82 C2
Fetești, *Romania* 29 F12
Fethiye, *Turkey* 47 E11
Fethiye Körfezi, *Turkey* 47 E10
Fetlar, *U.K.* 13 A8
Feuilles →, *Canada* 101 C12
Feurs, *France* 21 C8
Fez = Fès, *Morocco* 78 B5
Fezzan, *Libya* 79 C8
Fiambalá, *Argentina* 126 B2
Fianarantsoa, *Madag.* 89 C8

Fianarantsoa □, *Madag.* 89 B8
Fiche, *Ethiopia* 81 F4
Fichtelgebirge, *Germany* 25 E7
Fichtelgebirge ⌓, *Germany* 25 E8
Ficksburg, *S. Africa* 89 D4
Fidenza, *Italy* 40 D7
Fiditi, *Nigeria* 83 D5
Field →, *Australia* 94 C2
Field I., *Australia* 92 B5
Fieni, *Romania* 29 E10
Fier, *Albania* 44 F3
Fierzë, *Albania* 44 D4
Fife ⌓, *U.K.* 13 E5
Fife □, *U.K.* 13 E5
Fife Ness, *U.K.* 13 E6
Fifth Cataract, *Sudan* 80 D3
Figari, *France* 21 G13
Figeac, *France* 20 D6
Figeholm, *Sweden* 11 G10
Figline Valdarno, *Italy* 41 E8
Figtree, *Zimbabwe* 87 G2
Figueira Castelo Rodrigo, *Portugal* 36 E4
Figueira da Foz, *Portugal* 36 E2
Figueiró dos Vinhos, *Portugal* 36 F2
Figueres, *Spain* 38 C7
Figuig, *Morocco* 78 B5
Fihaonana, *Madag.* 89 B8
Fiherenana, *Madag.* 89 B8
Fiherenana →, *Madag.* 89 C7
Fiji ■, *Pac. Oc.* 91 C8
Fik, *Ethiopia* 81 F5
Fika, *Nigeria* 83 C7
Filabres, Sierra de los, *Spain* 37 H8
Filabusi, *Zimbabwe* 89 C4
Filadélfia, *Italy* 43 D9
Fil'akovo, *Slovak Rep.* 27 C12
Filey, *U.K.* 14 C7
Filey B., *U.K.* 14 C7
Filfla, *Malta* 49 D1
Filiaşi, *Romania* 29 F8
Filiátes, *Greece* 46 B2
Filiatrá, *Greece* 46 D3
Filicudi, *Italy* 43 D7
Filingué, *Niger* 83 C5
Filiourí →, *Greece* 45 E9
Filipstad, *Sweden* 10 E8
Filisur, *Switz.* 25 J5
Fillmore, *Calif., U.S.A.* 111 L8
Fillmore, *Utah, U.S.A.* 109 G7
Filótion, *Greece* 47 D7
Filottrano, *Italy* 41 E10
Filtu, *Ethiopia* 81 F5
Fina ⌓, *Mali* 82 C3
Finale Emília, *Italy* 41 D8
Finale Lígure, *Italy* 40 D5
Fiñana, *Spain* 37 H8
Finch, *Canada* 117 A9
Finch Hatton, *Australia* 94 K6
Findhorn →, *U.K.* 13 D5
Findlay, *U.S.A.* 114 E4
Finger L., *Canada* 104 B1
Finger Lakes, *U.S.A.* 117 D8
Fíngoè, *Mozam.* 87 E3
Finike, *Turkey* 47 E12
Finike Körfezi, *Turkey* 47 E12
Finiq, *Albania* 44 G4
Finistère □, *France* 18 D3
Finisterre = Fisterra, *Spain* 36 C1
Finisterre, C. = Fisterra, C., *Spain* 36 C1
Finke, *Australia* 94 D1
Finke Gorge △, *Australia* 92 D5
Finland ■, *Europe* 8 E22
Finland, G. of, *Europe* 9 G21
Finlay →, *Canada* 102 B3
Finley, *Australia* 95 F4
Finley, *U.S.A.* 112 B6
Finn →, *Ireland* 12 B4
Finnerödja, *Sweden* 11 F8
Finnigan, Mt., *Australia* 94 B4
Finniss, C., *Australia* 95 E1
Finnmark, *Norway* 8 B20
Finnsnes, *Norway* 8 B18
Finspång, *Sweden* 11 F9
Finsteraarhorn, *Switz.* 25 J4
Finsterwalde, *Germany* 24 D9
Fiora →, *Italy* 41 F8
Fiordland △, *N.Z.* 91 L1
Fiorenzuola d'Arda, *Italy* 40 D6
Fīq, *Syria* 74 C4
Firat = Furāt, Nahr al →, *Asia* 70 D5
Fire Island ⌓, *U.S.A.* 117 F11
Firebag →, *Canada* 103 B6
Firebaugh, *U.S.A.* 110 J6
Firedrake L., *Canada* 103 A8
Firenze, *Italy* 41 E8
Firenzuola, *Italy* 41 D8
Firk, Sha'ib →, *Iraq* 70 D5
Firmi, *France* 20 D6
Firminy, *France* 21 C8
Firozabad, *India* 69 F8
Firozpur, *India* 68 D6
Firozpur-Jhirka, *India* 68 F7
Fīrūzābād, *Iran* 71 D7
Fīrūzkūh, *Iran* 71 C7
Firvale, *Canada* 102 C3
Fish →, *Namibia* 88 D2
Fish →, *S. Africa* 88 E3
Fish River Canyon, *Namibia* 88 D2
Fisher, *Australia* 93 F5
Fisher B., *Canada* 103 C9
Fishers I., *U.S.A.* 117 E13
Fishguard, *U.K.* 15 E3
Fishing L., *Canada* 103 C9
Fishkill, *U.S.A.* 117 E11
Fismes, *France* 19 C10
Fisterra, *Spain* 36 C1
Fisterra, C., *Spain* 36 C1
Fitchburg, *U.S.A.* 117 D13
Fitz Roy, *Argentina* 128 F3
Fitzgerald, *Canada* 102 B6
Fitzgerald, *U.S.A.* 115 K4
Fitzgerald River △, *Australia* 93 F3
Fitzmaurice →, *Australia* 92 B5
Fitzroy →, *Queens., Australia* 94 C5
Fitzroy →, *W. Austral., Australia* 92 C3
Fitzroy, Mte., *Argentina* 128 F2
Fitzroy Crossing, *Australia* 92 C4
Fitzwilliam I., *Canada* 116 A3
Fiuggi, *Italy* 41 G10
Fiume = Rijeka, *Croatia* 41 C11
Fiumicino, Rome ✕ (FCO), *Italy* 41 G9
Five Points, *U.S.A.* 110 J6
Fivizzano, *Italy* 40 D7
Fizi, *Dem. Rep. of the Congo* 86 C2
Fjällbacka, *Sweden* 11 F5
Fjärdhundra, *Sweden* 10 E10
Fjellerup, *Denmark* 11 H4
Fjerritslev, *Denmark* 11 G3
Fjugesta, *Sweden* 10 E8
Flagstaff, *U.S.A.* 109 J8
Flagstaff L., *U.S.A.* 115 C10
Flaherty I., *Canada* 104 A4
Flåm, *Norway* 9 F12
Flambeau →, *U.S.A.* 112 C9
Flamborough Hd., *U.K.* 14 C7
Fläming, *Germany* 24 C8
Flaming Gorge ⌓, *U.S.A.* 108 F9
Flaming Gorge Reservoir, *U.S.A.* 108 F9
Flamingo, Teluk, *Indonesia* 63 F9
Flanders = Flandre, *Europe* 19 B9
Flandre, *Europe* 19 B9
Flandre Occidentale = West-Vlaanderen □, *Belgium* 17 D2
Flandre Orientale = Oost-Vlaanderen □, *Belgium* 17 C3
Flandreau, *U.S.A.* 112 C6
Flanigan, *U.S.A.* 110 E7
Flannan Is., *U.K.* 13 C1
Flåsjön, *Sweden* 8 D16
Flat →, *Canada* 102 A3
Flathead L., *U.S.A.* 108 C7
Flattery, C., *Australia* 94 A4
Flattery, C., *U.S.A.* 110 B2
Flatwoods, *U.S.A.* 114 F4
Fleetwood, *U.K.* 14 D4
Fleetwood, *U.S.A.* 117 F9
Flekkefjord, *Norway* 9 G12
Flemington, *U.S.A.* 116 E7
Flen, *Sweden* 10 E10
Flensburg, *Germany* 24 A5
Flers, *France* 18 D6
Flesherton, *Canada* 116 B4
Flesko, Tanjung, *Indonesia* 63 D6
Fleurance, *France* 20 E4
Fleurier, *Switz.* 25 J2
Fleurieu Pen., *Australia* 95 F2
Flevoland □, *Neths.* 17 B5
Flin Flon, *Canada* 103 C8
Flinders →, *Australia* 94 B3
Flinders B., *Australia* 93 F2
Flinders Group, *Australia* 94 A3
Flinders I., *S. Austral., Australia* 95 E1
Flinders I., *Tas., Australia* 95 G4
Flinders Ranges, *Australia* 95 E2
Flinders Reefs, *Australia* 94 B4
Flint, *U.K.* 14 D4
Flint, *U.S.A.* 114 D4
Flint →, *U.S.A.* 115 K3
Flint I., *Kiribati* 97 J12
Flintshire □, *U.K.* 14 D4
Fliseryd, *Sweden* 11 G10
Flix, *Spain* 38 D5
Flixecourt, *France* 19 B9
Floby, *Sweden* 11 F7
Floda, *Sweden* 11 G6
Flodden, *U.K.* 14 B5
Flogny-la-Chapelle, *France* 19 E10
Floodwood, *U.S.A.* 112 B8
Flora, *U.S.A.* 114 F1
Florac, *France* 20 D7
Florala, *U.S.A.* 115 K2
Florence = Firenze, *Italy* 41 E8
Florence, *Ala., U.S.A.* 115 H2
Florence, *Ariz., U.S.A.* 109 K8
Florence, *Colo., U.S.A.* 112 F2
Florence, *Oreg., U.S.A.* 108 E1
Florence, *S.C., U.S.A.* 115 H6
Florence, L., *Australia* 95 D2
Florence Amerigo Vespucci ✕ (FLR), *Italy* 40 E8
Florence Pisa ✕ (PSA), *Italy* 40 E7
Florencia, *Colombia* 124 C3
Florennes, *Belgium* 17 D4
Florensac, *France* 20 E7
Florenville, *Belgium* 17 E5
Flores, *Guatemala* 120 C2
Flores, *Indonesia* 63 F6
Flores I., *Canada* 102 D3
Flores Sea, *Indonesia* 63 F6
Floreşti, *Moldova* 29 C13
Floresville, *U.S.A.* 113 L5
Floriano, *Brazil* 125 E10
Florianópolis, *Brazil* 127 B6
Florida, *Cuba* 120 B4
Florida, *Uruguay* 127 C4
Florida □, *U.S.A.* 115 L5
Florida, Straits of, *U.S.A.* 120 B4
Florida B., *U.S.A.* 120 B3
Florida Keys, *U.S.A.* 115 N5
Florídia, *Italy* 43 E8
Flórina, *Greece* 44 F5
Flórina □, *Greece* 44 F5
Florø, *Norway* 9 F11
Flower Station, *Canada* 117 A8
Flowerpot I., *Canada* 116 A3
Floydada, *U.S.A.* 113 J4
Fluk, *Indonesia* 63 E7
Flúmen →, *Spain* 38 D4
Flumendosa →, *Italy* 42 C2
Fluminimaggiore, *Italy* 42 C1
Flushing = Vlissingen, *Neths.* 17 C3
Fluviá →, *Spain* 38 C8
Flying Fish, C., *Antarctica* 5 D15
Foam Lake, *Canada* 103 C8
Foča, *Bos.-H.* 44 C2
Foça, *Turkey* 47 C8
Fochabers, *U.K.* 13 D5
Focşani, *Romania* 29 E12
Fodécontéa, *Guinea* 82 C2
Fogang, *China* 59 F9
Fóggia, *Italy* 43 A8
Foggo, *Nigeria* 83 C6
Foglia →, *Italy* 41 E9
Fogo, *Canada* 105 C9
Fogo I., *Canada* 105 C9
Fohnsdorf, *Austria* 26 D7
Föhr, *Germany* 24 A4
Foia, *Portugal* 37 H2
Foix, *France* 20 E5
Fojnica, *Bos.-H.* 28 G2
Fokino, *Russia* 32 F8
Fokís □, *Greece* 46 C4
Fokku, *Nigeria* 83 C5
Folda, *Nord-Trøndelag, Norway* 8 D14
Folda, *Nordland, Norway* 8 C16
Földeák, *Hungary* 28 D5
Folégandros, *Greece* 46 E6
Foley, *Botswana* 88 C4
Foley, *U.S.A.* 115 K2
Foleyet, *Canada* 104 C3
Folgefonni, *Norway* 9 F12
Foligno, *Italy* 41 F9
Folkestone, *U.K.* 15 F9
Folkston, *U.S.A.* 115 K5
Follansbee, *U.S.A.* 116 F4
Follónica, *Italy* 40 F7
Follónica, G. di, *Italy* 40 F7
Folsom L., *U.S.A.* 110 G5
Folteşti, *Romania* 29 E13
Fond-du-Lac, *Canada* 103 B7
Fond du Lac, *U.S.A.* 112 D10
Fond-du-Lac →, *Canada* 103 B7
Fonda, *U.S.A.* 117 D10
Fondi, *Italy* 42 A6
Fonfría, *Spain* 36 D4
Fongafale, *Tuvalu* 96 H9
Fonni, *Italy* 42 B2
Fonsagrada = A Fonsagrada, *Spain* 36 B3
Fonseca, G. de, *Cent. Amer.* 120 D2
Font-Romeu, *France* 20 F5
Fontaine-Française, *France* 19 E12
Fontainebleau, *France* 19 D9
Fontana, *U.S.A.* 111 L9
Fontas →, *Canada* 102 B4
Fonte Boa, *Brazil* 124 D5
Fontem, *Cameroon* 83 D6
Fontenay-le-Comte, *France* 20 B3
Fontenelle Reservoir, *U.S.A.* 108 E8
Fontur, *Iceland* 8 C6
Fonyód, *Hungary* 28 D2
Foochow = Fuzhou, *China* 59 D12
Foping, *China* 56 H5
Forbach, *France* 19 C13
Forbes, *Australia* 95 E4
Forbesganj, *India* 69 F12
Forcados, *Nigeria* 83 D6
Forcados →, *Nigeria* 83 D6
Forcalquier, *France* 21 E9
Forchheim, *Germany* 25 F7
Ford City, *Calif., U.S.A.* 111 K7
Ford City, *Pa., U.S.A.* 116 F5
Førde, *Norway* 9 F11
Ford's Bridge, *Australia* 95 D4
Fordyce, *U.S.A.* 113 J8
Forécariah, *Guinea* 82 D2
Forel, Mt., *Greenland* 98 C16
Foremost, *Canada* 102 D6
Forest, *Canada* 116 C3
Forest, *U.S.A.* 113 J10
Forest City, *Iowa, U.S.A.* 112 D8
Forest City, *N.C., U.S.A.* 115 H5
Forest City, *Pa., U.S.A.* 117 E9
Forest Grove, *U.S.A.* 110 E3
Forestburg, *Canada* 102 C6
Foreste Casentinesi-Monte Falterona-Campigna △, *Italy* 41 E8
Foresthill, *U.S.A.* 110 F6
Forestier Pen., *Australia* 95 G4
Forestville, *Canada* 105 C6
Forestville, *Calif., U.S.A.* 110 G4
Forestville, *N.Y., U.S.A.* 116 D5
Forêt d'Orient ⌓, *France* 19 D11
Forez, Mts. du, *France* 20 C7
Forfar, *U.K.* 13 E6
Forillon △, *Canada* 105 C7
Forks, *U.S.A.* 110 C2
Forksville, *U.S.A.* 117 E8
Forlì, *Italy* 41 D9
Forman, *U.S.A.* 112 B6
Formazza, *Italy* 40 B5
Formby Pt., *U.K.* 14 D4
Formentera, *Spain* 48 C7
Formentor, C. de, *Spain* 48 B10
Former Yugoslav Republic of Macedonia = Macedonia ■, *Europe* 44 E5
Fórmia, *Italy* 42 A6
Formígine, *Italy* 40 D7
Formosa = Taiwan ■, *Asia* 59 F13
Formosa, *Argentina* 126 B4
Formosa, *Brazil* 125 G9
Formosa □, *Argentina* 126 B3
Formosa, Serra, *Brazil* 125 F8
Formosa B. = Ungwana B., *Kenya* 86 C5
Formosa Strait = Taiwan Strait, *Asia* 59 E12
Fornells, *Spain* 48 A11
Fornos de Algodres, *Portugal* 36 E3
Fornovo di Taro, *Italy* 40 D7
Føroyar, *Atl. Oc.* 8 F9
Forres, *U.K.* 13 D5
Forrest, *Australia* 93 F4
Forrest, Mt., *Australia* 93 D4
Forrest City, *U.S.A.* 113 H9
Fors, *Sweden* 10 D10
Forsayth, *Australia* 94 B3
Forshaga, *Sweden* 10 E7
Förslöv, *Sweden* 11 H6
Forsmo, *Sweden* 10 A11
Forssa, *Finland* 9 F20
Forst, *Germany* 24 D10
Forsvik, *Sweden* 11 F8
Forsyth, *U.S.A.* 108 C10
Fort Abbas, *Pakistan* 68 E5
Fort Albany, *Canada* 104 B3
Fort Ann, *U.S.A.* 117 C11
Fort Assiniboine, *Canada* 102 C6
Fort Augustus, *U.K.* 13 D4
Fort Beaufort, *S. Africa* 88 E4
Fort Benton, *U.S.A.* 108 C8
Fort Bragg, *U.S.A.* 108 G2
Fort Bridger, *U.S.A.* 108 F8
Fort Chipewyan, *Canada* 103 B6
Fort Clatsop ⌓, *U.S.A.* 110 D3
Fort Collins, *U.S.A.* 112 E2
Fort-Coulonge, *Canada* 104 C4
Fort Covington, *U.S.A.* 117 B10
Fort Davis, *U.S.A.* 113 K3
Fort-de-France, *Martinique* 120 c
Fort Defiance, *U.S.A.* 109 J9
Fort Dodge, *U.S.A.* 112 D7
Fort Edward, *U.S.A.* 117 C11
Fort Erie, *Canada* 116 D6
Fort Fairfield, *U.S.A.* 115 B12
Fort Frances, *Canada* 103 D10
Fort Franklin = Déline, *Canada* 100 B7
Fort Garland, *U.S.A.* 109 H11
Fort George = Chisasibi, *Canada* 104 B4
Fort Good Hope, *Canada* 100 B7
Fort Hancock, *U.S.A.* 109 L11
Fort Hertz = Putao, *Burma* 67 F20
Fort Hope, *Canada* 104 B2
Fort Irwin, *U.S.A.* 111 K10
Fort Kent, *U.S.A.* 115 B11
Fort Klamath, *U.S.A.* 108 E3
Fort Laramie, *U.S.A.* 112 D2
Fort Lauderdale, *U.S.A.* 115 M5
Fort Liard, *Canada* 102 A4
Fort Liberté, *Haiti* 121 C5
Fort Lupton, *U.S.A.* 112 E2
Fort MacKay, *Canada* 102 B6
Fort Macleod, *Canada* 102 D6
Fort McMurray, *Canada* 102 B6
Fort McPherson, *Canada* 100 B6
Fort Madison, *U.S.A.* 112 E9
Fort Meade, *U.S.A.* 115 M5
Fort Morgan, *U.S.A.* 112 E3
Fort Myers, *U.S.A.* 115 M5
Fort Nelson, *Canada* 102 B4
Fort Nelson →, *Canada* 102 B4
Fort Norman = Tulita, *Canada* 100 B7
Fort Payne, *U.S.A.* 115 H3
Fort Peck, *U.S.A.* 108 B10
Fort Peck Dam, *U.S.A.* 108 C10
Fort Peck L., *U.S.A.* 108 C10
Fort Pierce, *U.S.A.* 115 M5
Fort Pierre, *U.S.A.* 112 C4
Fort Pierre Bordes = Ti-n-Zaouatene, *Algeria* 83 B5
Fort Plain, *U.S.A.* 117 D10
Fort Portal, *Uganda* 86 B3
Fort Providence, *Canada* 102 A5
Fort Qu'Appelle, *Canada* 103 C8
Fort Resolution, *Canada* 102 A6
Fort Rixon, *Zimbabwe* 87 G2
Fort Ross, *U.S.A.* 110 G3
Fort Rupert = Waskaganish, *Canada* 104 B4
Fort St. James, *Canada* 102 C4
Fort St. John, *Canada* 102 B4
Fort Saskatchewan, *Canada* 102 C6
Fort Scott, *U.S.A.* 113 G7
Fort Severn, *Canada* 104 A2
Fort Shevchenko, *Kazakhstan* 35 H10
Fort Simpson, *Canada* 102 A4
Fort Smith, *Canada* 102 B6
Fort Smith, *U.S.A.* 113 H7
Fort Stockton, *U.S.A.* 113 K3
Fort Sumner, *U.S.A.* 113 H2
Fort Thompson, *U.S.A.* 112 C5
Fort Union ⌓, *U.S.A.* 113 H2
Fort Valley, *U.S.A.* 115 J4
Fort Vermilion, *Canada* 102 B5
Fort Walton Beach, *U.S.A.* 115 K2
Fort Wayne, *U.S.A.* 114 E3
Fort William, *U.K.* 13 E3
Fort Worth, *U.S.A.* 113 J6
Fort Yates, *U.S.A.* 112 B4
Fort Yukon, *U.S.A.* 100 B5
Fortaleza, *Brazil* 125 D11
Forteau, *Canada* 105 B8
Fortescue →, *Australia* 92 D2
Forth →, *U.K.* 13 E5
Forth, Firth of, *U.K.* 13 E6
Fortore →, *Italy* 41 G12
Fortrose, *U.K.* 13 D4
Fortuna, *Spain* 39 G3
Fortuna, *Calif., U.S.A.* 108 F1
Fortuna, *N. Dak., U.S.A.* 112 A3
Fortune, *Canada* 105 C8
Fortune B., *Canada* 105 C8
Forūr, *Iran* 71 E7
Fos-sur-Mer, *France* 21 E8
Foshan, *China* 59 F9
Fosna, *Norway* 8 E14
Fosnavåg, *Norway* 9 E11
Foso, *Ghana* 83 D4
Fossano, *Italy* 40 D4
Fossil, *U.S.A.* 108 D3
Fossil Butte ⌓, *U.S.A.* 108 F8
Fossombrone, *Italy* 41 E9
Foster, *Canada* 117 A12
Foster →, *Canada* 103 B7
Fosters Ra., *Australia* 94 C1
Fostoria, *U.S.A.* 114 E4
Fotadrevo, *Madag.* 89 C8
Fouesnant, *France* 18 E2
Fougères, *France* 18 D5
Foul Pt., *Sri Lanka* 66 Q12
Foula, *U.K.* 13 A6
Foulalaba, *Mali* 82 C3
Foulness I., *U.K.* 15 F8
Foulpointe, *Madag.* 89 B8
Foulweather, C., *U.S.A.* 106 B2
Foumban, *Cameroon* 83 D7
Foumbot, *Cameroon* 83 D7
Foundiougne, *Senegal* 82 C1
Fountain, *U.S.A.* 112 F2
Fountain Springs, *U.S.A.* 111 K8
Fourchambault, *France* 19 E10
Fouriesburg, *S. Africa* 88 D4
Fourmies, *France* 19 B11
Fournás, *Greece* 46 B3
Foúrnoi, *Greece* 47 D8
Fours, *France* 19 F10
Fourth Cataract, *Sudan* 80 D3
Fouta Djallon, *Guinea* 82 C2
Foux, Cap-à-, *Haiti* 121 C5
Foveaux Str., *N.Z.* 91 M2
Fowey, *U.K.* 15 G3
Fowler, *Calif., U.S.A.* 110 J7
Fowler, *Colo., U.S.A.* 112 F3
Fowlers B., *Australia* 93 F5
Fowman, *Iran* 71 B6
Fox →, *Canada* 103 B10
Fox Creek, *Canada* 102 C5
Fox Lake, *Canada* 102 B6
Fox Valley, *Canada* 103 C7
Foxboro, *U.S.A.* 117 D13
Foxdale, *Australia* 94 J6
Foxe Basin, *Canada* 101 B12
Foxe Chan., *Canada* 101 B11
Foxe Pen., *Canada* 101 B12
Foxen, *Sweden* 10 E5
Foxton, *N.Z.* 91 J5
Foyle, Lough, *U.K.* 12 A4
Foynes, *Ireland* 12 D2
Foz, *Spain* 36 B3
Foz do Cunene, *Angola* 88 B1
Foz do Iguaçu, *Brazil* 127 B5
Frackville, *U.S.A.* 117 F8
Fraga, *Spain* 38 D5
Fraile Muerto, *Uruguay* 127 C5
Fram Basin, *Arctic* 4 A
Framingham, *U.S.A.* 117 D13
Frampol, *Poland* 31 H9
Franca, *Brazil* 125 H9
Francavilla al Mare, *Italy* 41 F11
Francavilla Fontana, *Italy* 43 B10
France ■, *Europe* 7 F6
Frances, *Australia* 95 F3
Frances →, *Canada* 102 A3
Frances L., *Canada* 102 A3
Franceville, *Gabon* 84 E2
Franche-Comté, *France* 19 F12
Francis Case, L., *U.S.A.* 112 D5
Francisco Beltrão, *Brazil* 127 B5
Francisco I. Madero, *Coahuila, Mexico* 118 B4
Francisco I. Madero, *Durango, Mexico* 118 C4
Francistown, *Botswana* 89 C4
Francofonte, *Italy* 43 E7
François, *Canada* 105 C8
François L., *Canada* 102 C3
Francois Peron △, *Australia* 93 E1
Franeker, *Neths.* 17 A5
Frank Hann △, *Australia* 93 F3
Frankado, *Djibouti* 81 E5
Frankenberg, *Germany* 24 D4
Frankenhöhe ⌓, *Germany* 25 F6
Frankenwald, *Germany* 25 E7
Frankenwald ⌓, *Germany* 25 E7
Frankford, *Canada* 116 B7
Frankfort, *S. Africa* 89 D4
Frankfort, *Ind., U.S.A.* 114 E2
Frankfort, *Kans., U.S.A.* 112 F6
Frankfort, *Ky., U.S.A.* 114 F3
Frankfort, *N.Y., U.S.A.* 117 C9
Frankfurt, *Brandenburg, Germany* 24 C10
Frankfurt, *Hessen, Germany* 25 E4
Frankfurt International ✕ (FRA), *Germany* 25 E4
Fränkische Alb, *Germany* 25 F7
Fränkische Rezat →, *Germany* 25 F7
Fränkische Saale →, *Germany* 25 E5
Fränkische Schweiz, *Germany* 25 F7
Fränkische Schweiz-Veldensteiner Forst ⌓, *Germany* 25 F7
Frankland →, *Australia* 93 G2
Franklin, *Ky., U.S.A.* 115 G2
Franklin, *La., U.S.A.* 113 L9
Franklin, *Mass., U.S.A.* 117 D13
Franklin, *N.H., U.S.A.* 117 C13
Franklin, *Nebr., U.S.A.* 112 E5
Franklin, *Pa., U.S.A.* 116 E5
Franklin, *Va., U.S.A.* 115 G7
Franklin, *W. Va., U.S.A.* 114 F6
Franklin B., *Canada* 100 B7
Franklin D. Roosevelt L., *U.S.A.* 108 B4
Franklin-Gordon Wild Rivers △, *Australia* 95 G4
Franklin I., *Antarctica* 5 D11
Franklin L., *U.S.A.* 108 F6
Franklin Mts., *Canada* 100 B7
Franklin Str., *Canada* 100 A10
Franklinton, *U.S.A.* 113 K9
Franklinville, *U.S.A.* 116 D6
Franks Pk., *U.S.A.* 108 E9
Frankston, *Australia* 95 F4
Frånö, *Sweden* 10 B11

Fransfontein, *Namibia* 88 C2
Fränsta, *Sweden* 10 B10
Frantsa Iosifa, Zemlya, *Russia* 52 A6
Franz, *Canada* 104 C3
Franz Josef Land = Frantsa Iosifa, Zemlya, *Russia* 52 A6
Franz Josef Strauss, Munich ✕ (MUC), *Germany* 25 G7
Franzburg, *Germany* 24 A8
Frascati, *Italy* 41 G9
Fraser, *U.S.A.* 116 D2
Fraser ➛, *B.C., Canada* 102 D4
Fraser ➛, *Nfld., Canada* 105 A7
Fraser, Mt., *Australia* 93 E2
Fraser I., *Australia* 95 D5
Fraser Lake, *Canada* 102 C4
Fraserburg, *S. Africa* 88 E3
Fraserburgh, *U.K.* 13 D6
Fraserdale, *Canada* 104 C3
Frashër, *Albania* 44 F4
Frasne, *France* 19 F13
Frăteşti, *Romania* 29 G10
Frauenfeld, *Switz.* 25 H4
Fray Bentos, *Uruguay* 126 C4
Fray Jorge △, *Chile* 126 C1
Frechilla, *Spain* 36 C6
Fredericia, *Denmark* 11 J3
Frederick, *Md., U.S.A.* 114 F7
Frederick, *Okla., U.S.A.* 113 H5
Frederick, *S. Dak., U.S.A.* 112 C5
Fredericksburg, *Pa., U.S.A.* 117 F8
Fredericksburg, *Tex., U.S.A.* 113 K5
Fredericksburg, *Va., U.S.A.* 114 F7
Fredericktown, *Mo., U.S.A.* 113 G9
Fredericktown, *Ohio, U.S.A.* 116 F2
Frederico I. Madero, Presa, *Mexico* 118 B3
Frederico Westphalen, *Brazil* 127 B5
Fredericton, *Canada* 105 C6
Fredericton Junction, *Canada* 105 C6
Frederiksborg Amtskommune □, *Denmark* 11 J6
Frederikshåb = Paamiut, *Greenland* 101 B15
Frederikshavn, *Denmark* 11 G4
Frederikssund, *Denmark* 11 J6
Frederiksted, *U.S. Virgin Is.* 121 C7
Frederiksværk, *Denmark* 11 J6
Fredonia, *Ariz., U.S.A.* 109 H7
Fredonia, *Kans., U.S.A.* 113 G7
Fredonia, *N.Y., U.S.A.* 116 D5
Fredriksberg, *Sweden* 10 D8
Fredrikstad, *Norway* 9 G14
Free State □, *S. Africa* 88 D4
Freehold, *U.S.A.* 117 F10
Freel Peak, *U.S.A.* 110 G7
Freeland, *U.S.A.* 117 E9
Freels, C., *Canada* 105 C9
Freeman, *Calif., U.S.A.* 111 K9
Freeman, *S. Dak., U.S.A.* 112 D6
Freeport, *Bahamas* 120 A4
Freeport, *Ill., U.S.A.* 112 D10
Freeport, *N.Y., U.S.A.* 117 F11
Freeport, *Ohio, U.S.A.* 116 F3
Freeport, *Pa., U.S.A.* 116 F5
Freeport, *Tex., U.S.A.* 113 L7
Freetown, *S. Leone* 82 D2
Frégate, L. de la, *Canada* 104 B5
Fregenal de la Sierra, *Spain* 37 G4
Fregene, *Italy* 41 G9
Fréhel, C., *France* 18 D4
Freiberg, *Germany* 24 E9
Freibourg = Fribourg, *Switz.* 25 J3
Freiburg, *Baden-W., Germany* 25 H3
Freiburg, *Niedersachsen, Germany* 24 B5
Freilassing, *Germany* 25 H8
Freire, *Chile* 128 D2
Freirina, *Chile* 126 B1
Freising, *Germany* 25 G7
Freistadt, *Austria* 26 C7
Freital, *Germany* 24 D9
Fréjus, *France* 21 E10
Fremantle, *Australia* 93 F2
Fremont, *Calif., U.S.A.* 110 H4
Fremont, *Mich., U.S.A.* 114 D3
Fremont, *Nebr., U.S.A.* 112 E6
Fremont, *Ohio, U.S.A.* 114 E4
Fremont ➛, *U.S.A.* 109 G8
French Camp, *U.S.A.* 110 H5
French Creek ➛, *U.S.A.* 116 E5
French Guiana ⊠, *S. Amer.* 125 C8
French Polynesia ⊠, *Pac. Oc.* 97 K13
Frenchman Cr. ➛, *N. Amer.* 108 B10
Frenchman Cr. ➛, *U.S.A.* 112 E4
Frenštát pod Radhoštěm, *Czech Rep.* 27 B11
Fresco, *Ivory C.* 82 D3
Fresco ➛, *Brazil* 125 E8
Freshfield, C., *Antarctica* 5 C10
Fresnay-sur-Sarthe, *France* 18 D7
Fresnillo, *Mexico* 118 C4
Fresno, *U.S.A.* 110 J7
Fresno Alhandiga, *Spain* 36 E5
Fresno Reservoir, *U.S.A.* 108 B9
Freudenstadt, *Germany* 25 G4
Frévent, *France* 19 B9
Frew ➛, *Australia* 94 C2
Frewsburg, *U.S.A.* 116 D5
Freycinet △, *Australia* 95 G4
Freycinet Pen., *Australia* 95 G4
Freyming-Merlebach, *France* 19 C13
Freyung, *Germany* 25 G9
Fria, *Guinea* 82 C2
Fria, C., *Namibia* 88 B1
Friant, *U.S.A.* 110 J7
Frías, *Argentina* 126 B2
Fribourg, *Switz.* 25 J3
Fribourg □, *Switz.* 25 J3
Fridafors, *Sweden* 11 H8
Friday Harbor, *U.S.A.* 110 B3
Friedberg, *Bayern, Germany* 25 G6
Friedberg, *Hessen, Germany* 25 E4
Friedens, *U.S.A.* 116 F6
Friedland, *Germany* 24 B9
Friedrichshafen, *Germany* 25 H5
Friedrichskoog, *Germany* 24 A4
Friedrichstadt, *Germany* 24 A5
Friendly Is. = Tonga ■, *Pac. Oc.* 91 D11
Friendship, *U.S.A.* 116 D6
Friesach, *Austria* 26 E7
Friesack, *Germany* 24 C8
Friesland □, *Neths.* 17 A5
Friesoythe, *Germany* 24 B3
Friggesund, *Sweden* 10 C10
Frillesås, *Sweden* 11 G6
Frinnaryd, *Sweden* 11 G8
Frio ➛, *U.S.A.* 113 L5
Frio, C., *Brazil* 122 F6
Friol, *Spain* 36 B3
Friona, *U.S.A.* 113 H3
Fristad, *Sweden* 11 G6
Fritch, *U.S.A.* 113 H4
Fritsla, *Sweden* 11 G6
Fritzlar, *Germany* 24 D5
Friuli-Venézia Giulia □, *Italy* 41 B9
Frobisher B., *Canada* 101 B13
Frobisher Bay = Iqaluit, *Canada* 101 B13
Frobisher L., *Canada* 103 B7
Frohavet, *Norway* 8 E13
Frohnleiten, *Austria* 26 D8
Frolovo, *Russia* 34 F6
Frombork, *Poland* 30 D6
Frome, *U.K.* 15 F5
Frome ➛, *U.K.* 15 G5
Frome, L., *Australia* 95 E2
Frómista, *Spain* 36 C6
Front Range, *U.S.A.* 106 C5
Front Royal, *U.S.A.* 114 F6
Fronteira, *Portugal* 37 F3
Frontera, *Canary Is.* 48 G2
Frontera, *Mexico* 119 D6
Fronteras, *Mexico* 118 A3
Frontignan, *France* 20 E7
Frosinone, *Italy* 42 A6
Frostburg, *U.S.A.* 114 F6
Frostisen, *Norway* 8 B17
Frouard, *France* 19 D13
Frövi, *Sweden* 10 E9
Frøya, *Norway* 8 E13
Frumoasa, *Romania* 29 D10
Frunze = Bishkek, *Kyrgyzstan* 52 E8
Fruška Gora, *Serbia & M.* 28 E4
Fruška Gora △, *Serbia & M.* 44 A3
Frutal, *Brazil* 125 H9
Frutigen, *Switz.* 25 J3
Frýdek-Místek, *Czech Rep.* 27 B11
Frýdlant, *Czech Rep.* 26 A8
Fryeburg, *U.S.A.* 117 B14
Fryvaldov = Jeseník, *Czech Rep.* 27 A10
Fthiótis □, *Greece* 46 C4
Fu Jiang ➛, *China* 58 C6
Fu Xian = Wafangdian, *China* 57 E11
Fu Xian, *China* 56 G5
Fu'an, *China* 59 D12
Fubian, *China* 58 B4
Fucécchio, *Italy* 40 E7
Fucheng, *China* 56 F9
Fuchou = Fuzhou, *China* 59 D12
Fuchū, *Japan* 55 G6
Fuchuan, *China* 59 E8
Fuchun Jiang ➛, *China* 59 B13
Fúcino, Piana del, *Italy* 41 F10
Fuding, *China* 59 D13
Fuencaliente, *Canary Is.* 48 F2
Fuencaliente, *Spain* 37 G6
Fuencaliente, Pta., *Canary Is.* 48 F2
Fuengirola, *Spain* 37 J6
Fuenlabrada, *Spain* 36 E7
Fuensalida, *Spain* 36 E6
Fuente-Álamo, *Spain* 39 G3
Fuente-Álamo de Murcia, *Spain* 39 H3
Fuente de Cantos, *Spain* 37 G4
Fuente del Maestre, *Spain* 37 G4
Fuente el Fresno, *Spain* 37 F7
Fuente Obejuna, *Spain* 37 G5
Fuente Palmera, *Spain* 37 H5
Fuentes de Andalucía, *Spain* 37 H5
Fuentes de Ebro, *Spain* 38 D4
Fuentes de León, *Spain* 37 G4
Fuentes de Oñoro, *Spain* 36 E4
Fuentesaúco, *Spain* 36 D5
Fuerte ➛, *Mexico* 118 B3
Fuerte Olimpo, *Paraguay* 126 A4
Fuerteventura, *Canary Is.* 48 F6
Fuerteventura ✕ (FUE), *Canary Is.* 48 F6
Fufeng, *China* 56 G5
Fuga I., *Phil.* 61 B4
Fugong, *China* 58 D2
Fugou, *China* 56 G8
Fugu, *China* 56 E6
Fuhai, *China* 60 B3
Fuḩaymī, *Iraq* 70 C4
Fuhlsbüttel, Hamburg ✕ (HAM), *Germany* 24 B5
Fuji, *Japan* 55 G9
Fuji-Hakone-Izu △, *Japan* 55 G9
Fuji-San, *Japan* 55 G9
Fuji-Yoshida, *Japan* 55 G9
Fujian □, *China* 59 E12
Fujinomiya, *Japan* 55 G9
Fujisawa, *Japan* 55 G9
Fujiyama, Mt. = Fuji-San, *Japan* 55 G9
Fukagawa, *Japan* 54 C11
Fukien = Fujian □, *China* 59 E12
Fukuchiyama, *Japan* 55 G7
Fukue-Shima, *Japan* 55 H4
Fukui, *Japan* 55 F8
Fukui □, *Japan* 55 G8
Fukuoka, *Japan* 55 H5
Fukuoka □, *Japan* 55 H5
Fukushima, *Japan* 54 F10
Fukushima □, *Japan* 54 F10
Fukuyama, *Japan* 55 G6
Fulacunda, *Guinea-Biss.* 82 C1
Fulda, *Germany* 24 E5
Fulda ➛, *Germany* 24 D5
Fulford Harbour, *Canada* 110 B3
Fuliang, *China* 59 C11
Fullerton, *Calif., U.S.A.* 111 M9
Fullerton, *Nebr., U.S.A.* 112 E6
Fulongquan, *China* 57 B13
Fülöpszállás, *Hungary* 28 D4
Fulton, *Mo., U.S.A.* 112 F9
Fulton, *N.Y., U.S.A.* 117 C8
Fuluälven ➛, *Sweden* 10 C7
Fulufjället, *Sweden* 10 C6
Fumay, *France* 19 C11
Fumel, *France* 20 D4
Fumin, *China* 58 E4
Funabashi, *Japan* 55 G10
Funafuti = Fongafale, *Tuvalu* 96 H9
Funäsdalen, *Sweden* 10 B6
Funchal, *Madeira* 48 D3
Funchal ✕ (FNC), *Madeira* 48 D3
Fundación, *Colombia* 124 A4
Fundão, *Portugal* 36 E3
Fundu Moldovei, *Romania* 29 C10
Fundulea, *Romania* 29 F11
Fundy △, *Canada* 105 C6
Fundy, B. of, *Canada* 105 D6
Funhalouro, *Mozam.* 89 C5
Funing, *Hebei, China* 57 E10
Funing, *Jiangsu, China* 57 H10
Funing, *Yunnan, China* 58 F5
Funiu Shan, *China* 56 H7
Funsi, *Ghana* 82 C4
Funtua, *Nigeria* 83 C6
Fuping, *Hebei, China* 56 E8
Fuping, *Shaanxi, China* 56 G5
Fuqing, *China* 59 E12
Fuquan, *China* 58 D6
Furano, *Japan* 54 C11
Furāt, Nahr al ➛, *Asia* 70 D5
Fūrg, *Iran* 71 D7
Furmanov, *Russia* 34 B5
Furmanovo, *Kazakhstan* 34 F9
Furnás, *Spain* 48 B8
Furnas, Represa de, *Brazil* 127 A6
Furneaux Group, *Australia* 95 G4
Furqlus, *Syria* 74 A6
Fürstenau, *Germany* 24 C3
Fürstenberg, *Germany* 24 B9
Fürstenfeld, *Austria* 26 D9
Fürstenfeldbruck, *Germany* 25 G7
Fürstenwalde, *Germany* 24 C10
Fürth, *Germany* 25 F6
Furth im Wald, *Germany* 25 F8
Furtwangen, *Germany* 25 G4
Furudal, *Sweden* 10 C9
Furukawa, *Japan* 54 E10
Furulund, *Sweden* 11 J7
Fury and Hecla Str., *Canada* 101 B11
Fusagasuga, *Colombia* 124 C4
Fuscaldo, *Italy* 43 C9
Fushan, *Shandong, China* 57 F11
Fushan, *Shanxi, China* 56 G6
Fushë Arrëz, *Albania* 44 D4
Fushë Krujë, *Albania* 44 E3
Fushun, *Liaoning, China* 57 D12
Fushun, *Sichuan, China* 58 C5
Fusong, *China* 57 C14
Füssen, *Germany* 25 H6
Fustic, *Barbados* 121 g
Fusui, *China* 58 F6
Futog, *Serbia & M.* 28 E4
Futuna, *Wall. & F. Is.* 91 B8
Fuwa, *Egypt* 80 H7
Fuxian Hu, *China* 58 E4
Fuxin, *China* 57 C11
Fuyang, *Anhui, China* 56 H8
Fuyang, *Zhejiang, China* 59 B12
Fuyang He ➛, *China* 56 E9
Fuying Dao, *China* 59 D13
Fuyu, *China* 57 B13
Fuyuan, *China* 58 E5
Füzesgyarmat, *Hungary* 28 C6
Fuzhou, *China* 59 D12
Fylde, *U.K.* 14 D5
Fyn, *Denmark* 11 J4
Fyne, L., *U.K.* 13 F3
Fyns Amtskommune □, *Denmark* 11 J4
Fynshav, *Denmark* 11 K3

G

Ga, *Ghana* 82 D4
Gaanda, *Nigeria* 83 C7
Gabarin, *Nigeria* 83 C7
Gabas ➛, *France* 20 E3
Gabela, *Angola* 84 G2
Gabès, *Tunisia* 79 B8
Gabès, G. de, *Tunisia* 79 B8
Gabgaba, W. ➛, *Egypt* 80 C3
Gąbin, *Poland* 31 F6
Gabon ■, *Africa* 84 E2
Gaborone, *Botswana* 88 C4
Gabriels, *U.S.A.* 117 B10
Gābrīk, *Iran* 71 E8
Gabrovo, *Bulgaria* 45 D9
Gacé, *France* 18 D7
Gāch Sār, *Iran* 71 B6
Gachsārān, *Iran* 71 D6
Gacko, *Bos.-H.* 44 C2
Gadag, *India* 66 M9
Gadamai, *Sudan* 81 D4
Gadap, *Pakistan* 68 G2
Gadarwara, *India* 69 H8
Gadebusch, *Germany* 24 B7
Gadein, *Sudan* 81 F2
Gadhada, *India* 68 J4
Gádor, Sierra de, *Spain* 37 J8
Gadra, *Pakistan* 68 G4
Gadsden, *U.S.A.* 115 H3
Gadwal, *India* 66 L10
Gadyach = Hadyach, *Ukraine* 33 G8
Găeşti, *Romania* 29 F10
Gaeta, *Italy* 42 A6
Gaeta, G. di, *Italy* 42 A6
Gaffney, *U.S.A.* 115 H5
Gafsa, *Tunisia* 78 B7
Gagarawa, *Nigeria* 83 C6
Gagaria, *India* 68 G4
Gagarin, *Russia* 32 E8
Găgăuzia □, *Moldova* 29 D13
Gaggenau, *Germany* 25 G4
Gaghamni, *Sudan* 81 E2
Gagino, *Russia* 34 C7
Gagliano del Capo, *Italy* 43 C11
Gagnef, *Sweden* 10 D9
Gagnoa, *Ivory C.* 82 D3
Gagnon, *Canada* 105 B6
Gagnon, L., *Canada* 103 A6
Gagra, *Georgia* 35 J5
Gahini, *Rwanda* 86 C3
Gahmar, *India* 69 G10
Gai Xian = Gaizhou, *China* 57 D12
Gaïdhouronísi, *Greece* 49 E7
Gail, *U.S.A.* 113 J4
Gail ➛, *Austria* 26 E6
Gaillac, *France* 20 E5
Gaillimh = Galway, *Ireland* 12 C2
Gaillon, *France* 18 C8
Gaines, *U.S.A.* 116 E7
Gainesville, *Fla., U.S.A.* 115 L4
Gainesville, *Ga., U.S.A.* 115 H4
Gainesville, *Mo., U.S.A.* 113 G8
Gainesville, *Tex., U.S.A.* 113 J6
Gainsborough, *U.K.* 14 D7
Gairdner, L., *Australia* 95 E2
Gairloch, *U.K.* 13 D3
Gairloch, L., *U.K.* 13 D3
Gaizhou, *China* 57 D12
Gaj, *Croatia* 28 E2
Gaj ➛, *Pakistan* 68 F2
Gakuch, *Pakistan* 69 A5
Galala, Gebel el, *Egypt* 80 J8
Galán, Cerro, *Argentina* 126 B2
Galana ➛, *Kenya* 86 C5
Galanta, *Slovak Rep.* 27 C10
Galapagar, *Spain* 36 E7
Galápagos = Colón, Arch. de, *Ecuador* 97 H18
Galashiels, *U.K.* 13 F6
Galatás, *Greece* 46 D5
Galaţi, *Romania* 29 E13
Galaţi □, *Romania* 29 E12
Galatia, *Turkey* 72 C5
Galatina, *Italy* 43 B11
Galátone, *Italy* 43 B11
Galax, *U.S.A.* 115 G5
Galaxídhion, *Greece* 46 C4
Galcaio, *Somali Rep.* 75 F4
Galdhøpiggen, *Norway* 9 F12
Galeana, *Chihuahua, Mexico* 118 A3
Galeana, *Nuevo León, Mexico* 118 A3
Galegu, *Sudan* 81 E4
Galela, *Indonesia* 63 D7
Galena, *U.S.A.* 100 B4
Galeota Pt., *Trin. & Tob.* 125 K16
Galera, *Spain* 39 H2
Galera Pt., *Trin. & Tob.* 121 D7
Galesburg, *U.S.A.* 112 E9
Galeton, *U.S.A.* 116 E7
Galga, *Ethiopia* 81 F4
Gali, *Georgia* 35 J5
Galicea Mare, *Romania* 29 F8
Galich, *Russia* 34 A6
Galiche, *Bulgaria* 44 C7
Galicia □, *Spain* 36 C3
Galičica △, *Macedonia* 44 E4
Galilee = Hagalil, *Israel* 74 C4
Galilee, L., *Australia* 94 C4
Galilee, Sea of = Yam Kinneret, *Israel* 74 C4
Galim, *Cameroon* 83 D7
Galina Pt., *Jamaica* 120 a
Galinoporni, *Cyprus* 49 D13
Galion, *U.S.A.* 116 F2
Galiuro Mts., *U.S.A.* 109 K8
Galiwinku, *Australia* 94 A2
Gallabat, *Sudan* 81 E4
Gallan Hd., *U.K.* 13 C1
Gallarate, *Italy* 40 C5
Gallatin, *U.S.A.* 115 G2
Galle, *Sri Lanka* 66 R12
Gállego ➛, *Spain* 38 D4
Gallegos ➛, *Argentina* 128 G3
Galletti ➛, *Ethiopia* 81 F5
Galley Hd., *Ireland* 12 E3
Galliate, *Italy* 40 C5
Gallinas, Pta., *Colombia* 124 A4
Gallipoli = Gelibolu, *Turkey* 45 F10
Gallípoli, *Italy* 43 B10
Gallipolis, *U.S.A.* 114 F4
Gällivare, *Sweden* 8 C19
Gallneukirchen, *Austria* 26 C7
Gällö, *Sweden* 10 B9
Gallo, C., *Italy* 42 D6
Gallocanta, L. de, *Spain* 38 E3
Galloo I., *U.S.A.* 117 C8
Galloway, *U.K.* 13 F4
Galloway ⌓, *U.K.* 13 F4
Galloway, Mull of, *U.K.* 13 G4
Gallup, *U.S.A.* 109 J9
Gallur, *Spain* 38 D3
Galoya, *Sri Lanka* 66 Q12
Galt, *U.S.A.* 110 G5
Galten, *Denmark* 11 H3
Galtür, *Austria* 26 E3
Galty Mts., *Ireland* 12 D3
Galtymore, *Ireland* 12 D3
Galva, *U.S.A.* 112 E9
Galve de Sorbe, *Spain* 38 D1
Galveston, *U.S.A.* 113 L7
Galveston B., *U.S.A.* 113 L7
Gálvez, *Argentina* 126 C3
Galway, *Ireland* 12 C2
Galway □, *Ireland* 12 C2
Galway B., *Ireland* 12 C2
Gam ➛, *Vietnam* 64 B5
Gamagōri, *Japan* 55 G8
Gamari, L., *Ethiopia* 81 E5
Gamawa, *Nigeria* 83 C7
Gamay, *Phil.* 61 E6
Gambaga, *Ghana* 83 C4
Gambat, *Pakistan* 68 F3
Gambela, *Ethiopia* 81 F3
Gambela △, *Ethiopia* 81 F3
Gambhir ➛, *India* 68 F6
Gambia ■, *W. Afr.* 82 C1
Gambia ➛, *W. Afr.* 82 C1
Gambier, *U.S.A.* 116 F2
Gambier, C., *Australia* 92 B5
Gambier Is., *Australia* 95 F2
Gambo, *Canada* 105 C9
Gamboli, *Pakistan* 68 E3
Gamboma, *Congo* 84 E3
Gamka ➛, *S. Africa* 88 E3
Gamkab ➛, *Namibia* 88 D2
Gamla Uppsala, *Sweden* 10 E11
Gamlakarleby = Kokkola, *Finland* 8 E20
Gamleby, *Sweden* 11 G10
Gammon ➛, *Canada* 103 C9
Gammon Ranges △, *Australia* 95 E2
Gamo-Gofa □, *Ethiopia* 81 F4
Gamou, *Niger* 83 C6
Gamtoos ➛, *S. Africa* 88 E4
Gan, *France* 20 E3
Gan Goriama, Mts., *Cameroon* 83 D7
Gan Jiang ➛, *China* 59 C11
Ganado, *U.S.A.* 109 J9
Gananita, *Sudan* 80 D3
Gananoque, *Canada* 117 B8
Ganāveh, *Iran* 71 D6
Gäncä, *Azerbaijan* 35 K8
Gancheng, *China* 64 C7
Gand = Gent, *Belgium* 17 C3
Ganda, *Angola* 85 G2
Gandajika, *Dem. Rep. of the Congo* 84 F4
Gandak ➛, *India* 69 G11
Gandava, *Pakistan* 68 E2
Gander, *Canada* 105 C9
Gander L., *Canada* 105 C9
Ganderkesee, *Germany* 24 B4
Ganderowe Falls, *Zimbabwe* 87 F2
Gandesa, *Spain* 38 D5
Gandhi Sagar, *India* 68 G6
Gandhinagar, *India* 68 H5
Gandi, *Nigeria* 83 C6
Gandía, *Spain* 39 G4
Gandino, *Italy* 40 C6
Gando, Pta., *Canary Is.* 48 G4
Gandole, *Nigeria* 83 D7
Gâneb, *Mauritania* 82 B2
Ganedidalem = Gani, *Indonesia* 63 E7
Ganetti, *Sudan* 80 D3
Ganga ➛, *India* 69 H14
Ganga Sagar, *India* 69 J13
Gangafani, *Mali* 82 C4
Gangan ➛, *India* 69 E8
Ganganagar, *India* 68 E5
Gangapur, *India* 68 F7
Gangara, *Niger* 83 C6
Gangaw, *Burma* 67 H19
Gangdisê Shan, *China* 67 D12
Ganges = Ganga ➛, *India* 69 H14
Ganges, *Canada* 102 D4
Ganges, *France* 20 E7
Ganges, Mouths of the, *India* 69 J14
Gånghester, *Sweden* 11 G7
Gangi, *Italy* 43 E7
Gângiova, *Romania* 29 G8
Gangoh, *India* 68 E7
Gangotri, *India* 69 D8
Gangtok, *India* 67 F16
Gangu, *China* 56 G3
Gangyao, *China* 57 B14
Gani, *Indonesia* 63 E7
Ganj, *India* 69 F8
Ganluc, *China* 58 C4
Gannat, *France* 19 F10
Gannett Peak, *U.S.A.* 108 E9
Ganquan, *China* 56 F5
Gänserdorf, *Austria* 27 C9
Ganshui, *China* 58 C6
Gansu □, *China* 56 G3
Ganta, *Liberia* 82 D3
Gantheaume, C., *Australia* 95 F2
Gantheaume B., *Australia* 93 E1
Gantsevichi = Hantsavichy, *Belarus* 33 F4
Ganye, *Nigeria* 83 D7
Ganyem = Genyem, *Indonesia* 63 E10
Ganyu, *China* 57 G10
Ganyushkino, *Kazakhstan* 35 G9
Ganzhou, *China* 59 E10
Gao, *Mali* 83 B4
Gao Xian, *China* 58 C5
Gao'an, *China* 59 C10
Gaochun, *China* 59 B12
Gaohe, *China* 59 F9
Gaohebu, *China* 59 B11
Gaokeng, *China* 59 D9
Gaolan Dao, *China* 59 G9
Gaoligong Shan, *China* 58 E2
Gaomi, *China* 57 F10
Gaoming, *China* 59 F9
Gaoping, *China* 56 G7
Gaotang, *China* 56 F9

Gaoua, *Burkina Faso* 82 C4
Gaoual, *Guinea* 82 C2
Gaoxiong = Kaohsiung, *Taiwan* 59 F13
Gaoyang, *China* 56 E8
Gaoyao, *China* 59 F9
Gaoyou, *China* 59 A12
Gaoyou Hu, *China* 57 H10
Gaoyuan, *China* 57 F9
Gaozhou, *China* 59 G8
Gap, *France* 21 D10
Gapan, *Phil.* 61 D4
Gapat →, *India* 69 G10
Gapuwiyak, *Australia* 94 A2
Gar, *China* 60 C2
Garabogazköl Aylagy, *Turkmenistan* 52 E6
Garachico, *Canary Is.* 48 F3
Garachiné, *Panama* 120 E4
Garafía, *Canary Is.* 48 F2
Garah, *Australia* 95 D4
Garajonay, *Canary Is.* 48 F2
Garamba △, *Dem. Rep. of the Congo* 86 B2
Garango, *Burkina Faso* 83 C4
Garanhuns, *Brazil* 125 E11
Garautha, *India* 69 G8
Garawe, *Liberia* 82 E3
Garba Tula, *Kenya* 86 B4
Garberville, *U.S.A.* 108 F2
Garbiyang, *India* 69 D9
Garbsen, *Germany* 24 C5
Gard □, *France* 21 D8
Gard →, *France* 21 E8
Garda, L. di, *Italy* 40 C7
Gardanne, *France* 21 E9
Gårdby, *Sweden* 11 H10
Garde L., *Canada* 103 A7
Gardelegen, *Germany* 24 C7
Garden City, *Ga., U.S.A.* 115 J5
Garden City, *Kans., U.S.A.* 113 G4
Garden City, *Tex., U.S.A.* 113 K4
Garden Grove, *U.S.A.* 111 M9
Gardēz, *Afghan.* 68 C3
Gardhíki, *Greece* 46 C3
Gardiner, *Maine, U.S.A.* 115 C11
Gardiner, *Mont., U.S.A.* 108 D8
Gardiners I., *U.S.A.* 117 E12
Gardner, *U.S.A.* 117 D13
Gardner Canal, *Canada* 102 C3
Gardnerville, *U.S.A.* 110 G7
Gardno, Jezioro, *Poland* 30 D4
Gardo, *Somali Rep.* 75 F4
Gardone Val Trómpia, *Italy* 40 C7
Gárdony, *Hungary* 28 C3
Garešnica, *Croatia* 41 C13
Garéssio, *Italy* 40 D5
Garey, *U.S.A.* 111 L6
Garfield, *U.S.A.* 108 C5
Garforth, *U.K.* 14 D6
Gargaliánoi, *Greece* 46 D3
Gargan, Mt., *France* 20 C5
Gargano △, *Italy* 41 G12
Gargett, *Australia* 94 K6
Gargouna, *Mali* 83 B5
Gargždai, *Lithuania* 30 C8
Garibaldi ⌂, *Canada* 102 D4
Gariep, L., *S. Africa* 88 E4
Garies, *S. Africa* 88 E2
Garigliano →, *Italy* 42 A6
Garissa, *Kenya* 86 C4
Garkida, *Nigeria* 83 C7
Garko, *Nigeria* 83 C6
Garland, *Tex., U.S.A.* 113 J6
Garland, *Utah, U.S.A.* 108 F7
Garlasco, *Italy* 40 C5
Garliava, *Lithuania* 30 D10
Garlin, *France* 20 E3
Garm, *Tajikistan* 52 F8
Garmāb, *Iran* 71 C8
Garmisch-Partenkirchen, *Germany* 25 H7
Garmo, Qullai = Kommunizma, Pik, *Tajikistan* 52 F8
Garmsār, *Iran* 71 C7
Garner, *U.S.A.* 112 D8
Garnett, *U.S.A.* 112 F7
Garo Hills, *India* 69 G14
Garoe, *Somali Rep.* 75 F4
Garonne →, *France* 20 C3
Garonne, Canal Latéral à la, *France* 20 D4
Garoowe = Garoe, *Somali Rep.* 75 F4
Garot, *India* 68 G6
Garoua, *Cameroon* 83 D7
Garpenberg, *Sweden* 10 D10
Garphyttan, *Sweden* 10 E8
Garrauli, *India* 69 G8
Garrel, *Germany* 24 C4
Garrigue = Garrigues, *France* 20 E7
Garrigues, *France* 20 E7
Garrison, *Mont., U.S.A.* 108 C7
Garrison, *N. Dak., U.S.A.* 112 B4
Garrison Res. = Sakakawea, L., *U.S.A.* 112 B4
Garron Pt., *U.K.* 12 A6
Garrovillas, *Spain* 37 F4
Garrucha, *Spain* 39 H3
Garry →, *U.K.* 13 E5
Garry, L., *Canada* 100 B9
Garsen, *Kenya* 86 C5
Gärsnäs, *Sweden* 11 J8
Garson L., *Canada* 103 B6
Garstang, *U.K.* 14 D5
Gartempe →, *France* 20 B4
Gartz, *Germany* 24 B10
Garu, *Ghana* 83 C4
Garu, *India* 69 H11
Garub, *Namibia* 88 D2
Garut, *Indonesia* 63 G12
Garvão, *Portugal* 37 H2
Garvie Mts., *N.Z.* 91 L2
Garwa = Garoua, *Cameroon* 83 D7
Garwa, *India* 69 G10
Garwolin, *Poland* 31 G8
Gary, *U.S.A.* 114 E2
Garz, *Germany* 24 A9
Garzê, *China* 58 B3
Garzón, *Colombia* 124 C3
Gas-San, *Japan* 54 E10
Gasan Kuli = Esenguly, *Turkmenistan* 52 F6
Gascogne, *France* 20 E4
Gascogne, G. de, *Europe* 20 E2
Gascony = Gascogne, *France* 20 E4
Gascoyne →, *Australia* 93 D1
Gascoyne Junction, *Australia* 93 E2
Gascueña, *Spain* 38 E2
Gash, Wadi →, *Ethiopia* 81 D4
Gash-Setit ⌂, *Eritrea* 81 D4
Gashagar, *Nigeria* 83 C7
Gashaka, *Nigeria* 83 D7
Gashaka-Gumti △, *Nigeria* 83 D7
Gasherbrum, *Pakistan* 69 B7
Gashua, *Nigeria* 83 C7
Gasparillo, *Trin. & Tob.* 125 K15
Gaspé, *Canada* 105 C7
Gaspé, C., *Canada* 105 C7
Gaspé Pen. = Gaspésie, Pén. de la, *Canada* 105 C6
Gaspésie ⌂, *Canada* 105 C6
Gaspésie, Pén. de la, *Canada* 105 C6
Gassan, *Burkina Faso* 82 C4
Gassol, *Nigeria* 83 D7
Gasteiz = Vitoria-Gasteiz, *Spain* 38 C2
Gastonia, *U.S.A.* 115 H5
Gastoúni, *Greece* 46 D3
Gastoúri, *Greece* 46 B1
Gastre, *Argentina* 128 E3
Gästrikland, *Sweden* 10 D10
Gata, C., *Cyprus* 49 E12
Gata, C. de, *Spain* 39 J2
Gata, Sierra de, *Spain* 36 E4
Gataga →, *Canada* 102 B3
Gătaia, *Romania* 28 E6
Gatchina, *Russia* 32 C6
Gatehouse of Fleet, *U.K.* 13 G4
Gates, *U.S.A.* 116 C7
Gateshead, *U.K.* 14 C6
Gatesville, *U.S.A.* 113 K6
Gateway ⌂, *U.S.A.* 117 F11
Gaths, *Zimbabwe* 87 G3
Gatico, *Chile* 126 A1
Gâtinais, *France* 19 D9
Gâtine, Hauteurs de, *France* 20 B3
Gatineau, *Canada* 117 A9
Gatineau △, *Canada* 104 C4
Gatineau →, *Canada* 104 C4
Gattaran, *Phil.* 61 B4
Gattinara, *Italy* 40 C5
Gatton, *Australia* 95 D5
Gatun, L., *Panama* 120 E4
Gatwick, London ✕ (LGW), *U.K.* 15 F7
Gatyana, *S. Africa* 89 E4
Gau, *Fiji* 91 D8
Gaucín, *Spain* 37 J5
Gauer L., *Canada* 103 B9
Gauhati = Guwahati, *India* 67 F17
Gauja →, *Latvia* 9 H21
Gaula →, *Norway* 8 E14
Gauri Phanta, *India* 69 E9
Gausta, *Norway* 9 G13
Gauteng □, *S. Africa* 89 D4
Gāv Koshī, *Iran* 71 D8
Gāvakān, *Iran* 71 D7
Gavallai △, *Liberia* 82 D3
Gavarnie, *France* 20 F3
Gavāter, *Iran* 71 E9
Gāvbandī, *Iran* 71 E7
Gavdhopoúla, *Greece* 49 E6
Gávdhos, *Greece* 49 E6
Gavi, *Italy* 40 D5
Gavião, *Portugal* 37 F3
Gaviota, *U.S.A.* 111 L6
Gāvkhūnī, Bāţlāq-e, *Iran* 71 C7
Gävle, *Sweden* 10 D11
Gävleborgs län □, *Sweden* 10 C10
Gävlebukten, *Sweden* 10 D11
Gavorrano, *Italy* 40 F7
Gavray, *France* 18 D5
Gavrilov Yam, *Russia* 32 D10
Gávrion, *Greece* 46 D6
Gawachab, *Namibia* 88 D2
Gawilgarh Hills, *India* 66 J10
Gawler, *Australia* 95 E2
Gawu, *Nigeria* 83 D6
Gaxun Nur, *China* 60 B5
Gaya, *India* 69 G11
Gaya, *Niger* 83 C5
Gaya, *Nigeria* 83 C6
Gayéri, *Burkina Faso* 83 C5
Gaylord, *U.S.A.* 114 C3
Gayndah, *Australia* 95 D5
Gaysin = Haysyn, *Ukraine* 33 H5
Gayvoron = Hayvoron, *Ukraine* 33 H5
Gaza, *Gaza Strip* 74 D3
Gaza □, *Mozam.* 89 C5
Gaza Strip ☒, *Asia* 74 D3
Gazanjyk, *Turkmenistan* 71 B7
Gazaoua, *Niger* 83 C6
Gāzbor, *Iran* 71 D8
Gazi, *Dem. Rep. of the Congo* 86 B1
Gaziantep, *Turkey* 70 B3
Gazimağosa = Famagusta, *Cyprus* 49 D12
Gazipaşa, *Turkey* 72 D5
Gbarnga, *Liberia* 82 D3
Gbekebo, *Nigeria* 83 D5
Gboko, *Nigeria* 83 D6
Gbongan, *Nigeria* 83 D5
Gcoverega, *Botswana* 88 B3
Gcuwa, *S. Africa* 89 E4
Gdańsk, *Poland* 30 D5
Gdansk ✕ (GDN), *Poland* 30 D5
Gdańska, Zatoka, *Poland* 30 D6
Gdov, *Russia* 9 G22
Gdynia, *Poland* 30 D5
Geba →, *Guinea-Biss.* 82 C1
Gebe, *Indonesia* 63 D7
Gebeciler, *Turkey* 47 C12
Gebeit Mine, *Sudan* 80 C4
Gebel Abyad, *Sudan* 80 D2
Gebel Iweibid, *Egypt* 80 H8
Gebze, *Turkey* 45 F13
Gecha, *Ethiopia* 81 F4
Gedaref, *Sudan* 81 E4
Gedaref □, *Sudan* 81 E4
Gediz, *Turkey* 47 B11
Gediz →, *Turkey* 47 C8
Gedo, *Ethiopia* 81 F4
Gèdre, *France* 20 F4
Gedser, *Denmark* 11 K5
Gedung, Pulau, *Malaysia* 65 c
Geegully Cr. →, *Australia* 92 C3
Geel, *Belgium* 17 C4
Geelong, *Australia* 95 F3
Geelvink B. = Cenderwasih, Teluk, *Indonesia* 63 E9
Geelvink Chan., *Australia* 93 E1
Geesthacht, *Germany* 24 B6
Geidam, *Nigeria* 83 C7
Geikie →, *Canada* 103 B8
Geikie Gorge △, *Australia* 92 C4
Geilenkirchen, *Germany* 24 E2
Geili, *Sudan* 81 D3
Geisingen, *Germany* 25 H4
Geislingen, *Germany* 25 G5
Geistown, *U.S.A.* 116 F6
Geita, *Tanzania* 86 C3
Gejiu, *China* 58 F4
Gel →, *Sudan* 81 F2
Gel, Meydān-e, *Iran* 71 D7
Gel River, *Sudan* 81 F2
Gela, *Italy* 43 E7
Gela, G. di, *Italy* 43 F7
Gelahun, *Liberia* 82 D2
Gelang Patah, *Malaysia* 65 d
Gelderland □, *Neths.* 17 B6
Geldern, *Germany* 24 D2
Geldrop, *Neths.* 17 C5
Geleen, *Neths.* 17 D5
Gelehun, *S. Leone* 82 D2
Gelembe, *Turkey* 47 B9
Gelemso, *Ethiopia* 81 F5
Gelendost, *Turkey* 72 C4
Gelendzhik, *Russia* 33 K10
Gelibolu, *Turkey* 45 F10
Gelibolu Yarımadası, *Turkey* 45 F10
Gelidonya Burnu, *Turkey* 72 D4
Gelnhausen, *Germany* 25 E5
Gelnica, *Slovak Rep.* 27 C13
Gelsenkirchen, *Germany* 24 D3
Gelting, *Germany* 24 A5
Gelugur, *Malaysia* 65 c
Gemas, *Malaysia* 65 L4
Gembloux, *Belgium* 17 D4
Gembu, *Nigeria* 83 D7
Gemena, *Dem. Rep. of the Congo* 84 D3
Gemerek, *Turkey* 70 B3
Gemla, *Sweden* 11 H8
Gemlik, *Turkey* 45 F13
Gemlik Körfezi, *Turkey* 45 F12
Gemona del Friuli, *Italy* 41 B10
Gemsa, *Egypt* 80 B3
Gemsbok △, *Botswana* 88 D3
Gemünden, *Germany* 25 E5
Genale →, *Ethiopia* 81 F4
Genç, *Turkey* 73 C9
Gençay, *France* 20 B4
Geneina, Gebel, *Egypt* 80 B3
General Acha, *Argentina* 126 D3
General Alvear, *Buenos Aires, Argentina* 126 D4
General Alvear, *Mendoza, Argentina* 126 D2
General Artigas, *Paraguay* 126 B4
General Belgrano, *Argentina* 126 D4
General Bernardo O'Higgins, *Antarctica* 5 C18
General Cabrera, *Argentina* 126 C3
General Cepeda, *Mexico* 118 B4
General Guido, *Argentina* 126 D4
General Juan Madariaga, *Argentina* 126 D4
General La Madrid, *Argentina* 126 D3
General MacArthur, *Phil.* 61 F6
General Martin Miguel de Güemes, *Argentina* 126 A3
General Paz, *Argentina* 126 B4
General Pico, *Argentina* 126 D3
General Pinedo, *Argentina* 126 B3
General Pinto, *Argentina* 126 C3
General Roca, *Argentina* 128 D3
General Santos, *Phil.* 61 H6
General Toshevo, *Bulgaria* 45 C12
General Trevino, *Mexico* 119 B5
General Trías, *Mexico* 118 B3
General Viamonte, *Argentina* 126 D3
General Villegas, *Argentina* 126 D3
Genesee, *Idaho, U.S.A.* 108 C5
Genesee, *Pa., U.S.A.* 116 E7
Genesee →, *U.S.A.* 116 C7
Geneseo, *Ill., U.S.A.* 112 E9
Geneseo, *N.Y., U.S.A.* 116 D7
Geneva = Genève, *Switz.* 25 J2
Geneva, *Ala., U.S.A.* 115 K3
Geneva, *N.Y., U.S.A.* 116 D8
Geneva, *Nebr., U.S.A.* 112 E6
Geneva, *Ohio, U.S.A.* 116 E4
Geneva, L. = Léman, L., *Europe* 19 F13
Geneva, L., *U.S.A.* 114 D1
Genève, *Switz.* 25 J2
Gengenbach, *Germany* 25 G4
Gengma, *China* 58 F2
Genichesk = Henichesk, *Ukraine* 33 J8
Genil →, *Spain* 37 H5
Genk, *Belgium* 17 D5
Genlis, *France* 19 E12
Gennargentu, Mti. del, *Italy* 42 B2
Gennes, *France* 18 E6
Genoa = Génova, *Italy* 40 D5
Genoa, *Australia* 95 F4
Genoa, *N.Y., U.S.A.* 117 D8
Genoa, *Nebr., U.S.A.* 112 E6
Genoa, *Nev., U.S.A.* 110 F7
Genoa ✕ (GOA), *Italy* 40 D5
Génova, *Italy* 40 D5
Génova, G. di, *Italy* 40 E6
Genriyetty, Ostrov, *Russia* 53 B16
Gent, *Belgium* 17 C3
Genteng, *Bali, Indonesia* 63 J17
Genteng, *Jawa, Indonesia* 63 G12
Genthin, *Germany* 24 C8
Genyem, *Indonesia* 63 E10
Genzano di Lucánia, *Italy* 43 B9
Genzano di Roma, *Italy* 41 G9
Geoagiu, *Romania* 29 E8
Geographe B., *Australia* 93 F2
Geographe Chan., *Australia* 93 D1
Geokchay = Göyçay, *Azerbaijan* 35 K8
Georg Forster, *Antarctica* 5 D3
Georg von Neumayer, *Antarctica* 5 D17
Georga, Zemlya, *Russia* 52 A5
George, *S. Africa* 88 E3
George →, *Canada* 105 A6
George, L., *N.S.W., Australia* 95 F4
George, L., *S. Austral., Australia* 95 F3
George, L., *W. Austral., Australia* 92 D3
George, L., *Uganda* 86 B3
George, L., *Fla., U.S.A.* 115 L5
George, L., *N.Y., U.S.A.* 117 C11
George Gill Ra., *Australia* 92 D5
George Pt., *Australia* 94 J6
George River = Kangiqsualujjuaq, *Canada* 101 C13
George Sound, *N.Z.* 91 L1
George Town, *Australia* 95 G4
George Town, *Bahamas* 120 B4
George Town, *Cayman Is.* 120 C3
George Town, *Malaysia* 65 c
George V Land, *Antarctica* 5 C10
George VI Sound, *Antarctica* 5 D17
George West, *U.S.A.* 113 L5
Georgetown = Janjanbureh, *Gambia* 82 C2
Georgetown, *Australia* 94 B3
Georgetown, *Ont., Canada* 116 C5
Georgetown, *P.E.I., Canada* 105 C7
Georgetown, *Guyana* 124 B7
Georgetown, *Calif., U.S.A.* 110 G6
Georgetown, *Colo., U.S.A.* 108 G11
Georgetown, *Ky., U.S.A.* 114 F3
Georgetown, *N.Y., U.S.A.* 117 D9
Georgetown, *Ohio, U.S.A.* 114 F4
Georgetown, *S.C., U.S.A.* 115 J6
Georgetown, *Tex., U.S.A.* 113 K6
Georgia □, *U.S.A.* 115 K5
Georgia ■, *Asia* 35 J6
Georgia, Str. of, *Canada* 102 D4
Georgian B., *Canada* 116 A4
Georgian Bay Islands △, *Canada* 116 B5
Georgina →, *Australia* 94 C2
Georgina I., *Canada* 116 B5
Georgiu-Dezh = Liski, *Russia* 33 G10
Georgiyevsk, *Russia* 35 H6
Georgsmarienhütte, *Germany* 24 C4
Gera, *Germany* 24 E8
Geraardsbergen, *Belgium* 17 D3
Geral, Serra, *Brazil* 127 B6
Geral de Goiás, Serra, *Brazil* 125 F9
Geraldine, *U.S.A.* 108 C8
Geraldton, *Australia* 93 E1
Geraldton, *Canada* 104 C2
Gérardmer, *France* 19 D13
Gercüş, *Turkey* 73 D9
Gerede, *Turkey* 72 B5
Gerês, Sierra do, *Portugal* 36 D3
Gereshk, *Afghan.* 66 D4
Geretsried, *Germany* 25 H7
Gérgal, *Spain* 39 H2
Gerik, *Malaysia* 65 K3
Gering, *U.S.A.* 112 E3
Gerlach, *U.S.A.* 108 F4
Gerlachovský štít, *Slovak Rep.* 27 B13
German Planina, *Macedonia* 44 D6
Germansen Landing, *Canada* 102 B4
Germantown, *U.S.A.* 113 M10
Germany ■, *Europe* 24 E6
Germencik, *Turkey* 47 D9
Germering, *Germany* 25 G7
Germersheim, *Germany* 25 F4
Germī, *Iran* 71 B6
Germiston, *S. Africa* 89 D4
Gernika-Lumo, *Spain* 38 B2
Gernsheim, *Germany* 25 F4
Gero, *Japan* 55 G8
Gerokgak, *Indonesia* 63 J17
Gerolzhofen, *Germany* 25 F6
Gerona = Girona, *Spain* 38 D7
Gerrard, *Canada* 102 C5
Gers □, *France* 20 E4
Gers →, *France* 20 D4
Gersfeld, *Germany* 24 E5
Gersthofen, *Germany* 25 G6
Gertak Sanggul, *Malaysia* 65 c
Gertak Sanggul, Tanjung, *Malaysia* 65 c
Gerung, *Indonesia* 63 K19
Gerzat, *France* 20 C7
Gerze, *Turkey* 72 B6
Geseke, *Germany* 24 D4
Geser, *Indonesia* 63 E8
Gesso →, *Italy* 40 D4
Gestro, Wabi →, *Ethiopia* 81 G5
Getafe, *Spain* 36 E7
Getinge, *Sweden* 11 H6
Gettysburg, *Pa., U.S.A.* 114 F7
Gettysburg, *S. Dak., U.S.A.* 112 C5
Getxo, *Spain* 38 B2
Getz Ice Shelf, *Antarctica* 5 D14
Gevaş, *Turkey* 73 C10
Gévaudan, *France* 20 D7
Gevgelija, *Macedonia* 44 E6
Gévora →, *Spain* 37 G4
Gewani, *Ethiopia* 81 E5
Gex, *France* 19 F13
Geyikli, *Turkey* 47 B8
Geyser, *U.S.A.* 108 C8
Geyserville, *U.S.A.* 110 G4
Geyve, *Turkey* 72 B4
Ghâbat el Arab = Wang Kai, *Sudan* 81 F2
Ghabeish, *Sudan* 81 E2
Ghaggar →, *India* 68 E6
Ghaghara →, *India* 69 G11
Ghaghat →, *Bangla.* 69 G13
Ghagra, *India* 69 H11
Ghagra →, *India* 69 F9
Ghalla, Wadi el →, *Sudan* 81 E2
Ghana ■, *W. Afr.* 83 D4
Ghansor, *India* 69 H9
Ghanzi, *Botswana* 88 C3
Gharb el Istiwa'iya □, *Sudan* 81 G3
Gharb Kordofân, *Sudan* 81 E2
Gharbîya, Es Sahrâ el, *Egypt* 80 B2
Ghardaïa, *Algeria* 78 B6
Ghârib, G., *Egypt* 80 B3
Gharig, *Sudan* 81 E2
Gharyān, *Libya* 79 B8
Ghat, *Libya* 79 D8
Ghatal, *India* 69 H12
Ghatampur, *India* 69 F9
Ghats, Eastern, *India* 66 N11
Ghats, Western, *India* 66 N9
Ghatsila, *India* 69 H12
Ghaţţī, *Si. Arabia* 70 D3
Ghawdex = Gozo, *Malta* 49 C1
Ghazal, Bahr el →, *Chad* 79 F9
Ghazâl, Bahr el →, *Sudan* 81 F3
Ghaziabad, *India* 68 E7
Ghazipur, *India* 69 G10
Ghaznī, *Afghan.* 68 C3
Ghaznī □, *Afghan.* 66 C6
Ghedi, *Italy* 40 C7
Ghelari, *Romania* 28 E7
Ghent = Gent, *Belgium* 17 C3
Gheorghe Gheorghiu-Dej = Oneşti, *Romania* 29 D11
Gheorgheni, *Romania* 29 D10
Gherla, *Romania* 29 C8
Ghidigeni, *Romania* 29 D12
Ghilarza, *Italy* 42 B1
Ghimeş-Făget, *Romania* 29 D11
Ghīnah, Wādī al →, *Si. Arabia* 70 D3
Ghisonaccia, *France* 21 F13
Ghisoni, *France* 21 F13
Ghizao, *Afghan.* 68 C1
Ghizar →, *Pakistan* 69 A5
Ghot Ogrein, *Egypt* 80 A2
Ghotaru, *India* 68 F4
Ghotki, *Pakistan* 68 E3
Ghowr □, *Afghan.* 66 C4
Ghudāf, W. al →, *Iraq* 70 C4
Ghudāmis, *Libya* 77 C4
Ghudāmis □, *Libya* 79 B8
Ghughri, *India* 69 H9
Ghugus, *India* 66 K11
Ghulam Mohammad Barrage, *Pakistan* 68 G3
Ghūrīān, *Afghan.* 66 B2
Gia Dinh, *Vietnam* 65 G6
Gia Lai = Plei Ku, *Vietnam* 64 F7
Gia Nghia, *Vietnam* 65 G6
Gia Ngoc, *Vietnam* 64 E7
Gia Vuc, *Vietnam* 64 E7
Giannutri, *Italy* 40 F8
Giant Forest, *U.S.A.* 110 J8
Giant Mts. = Krkonoše, *Czech Rep.* 26 A8
Giant Sequoia ⌂, *U.S.A.* 110 K8
Giants Causeway, *U.K.* 12 A5
Gianyar, *Indonesia* 63 K18
Giarabub = Al Jaghbūb, *Libya* 79 C10
Giarre, *Italy* 43 E8
Giaveno, *Italy* 40 C4
Gibara, *Cuba* 120 B4
Gibb River, *Australia* 92 C4
Gibbon, *U.S.A.* 112 E5
Gibe →, *Ethiopia* 81 F4
Gibellina Nuova, *Italy* 42 E5
Gibeon, *Namibia* 88 D2
Gibraleón, *Spain* 37 H4
Gibraltar ☒, *Europe* 37 J5
Gibraltar, Str. of, *Medit. S.* 37 K5
Gibraltar Range △, *Australia* 95 D5
Gibson Desert, *Australia* 92 D4
Gibsons, *Canada* 102 D4
Gibsonville, *U.S.A.* 110 F6
Giddings, *U.S.A.* 113 K6
Gidole, *Ethiopia* 81 F4
Giebnegáisi = Kebnekaise, *Sweden* 8 C18
Gien, *France* 19 E9
Giengen, *Germany* 25 G6
Giessen, *Germany* 24 E4
Gīfān, *Iran* 71 B8
Gifatin, Geziret, *Egypt* 80 B3
Gifhorn, *Germany* 24 C6
Gift Lake, *Canada* 102 B5
Gifu, *Japan* 55 G8
Gifu □, *Japan* 55 G8
Gigant, *Russia* 35 G5
Giganta, Sa. de la, *Mexico* 118 B2
Gigen, *Bulgaria* 45 C8
Gigha, *U.K.* 13 F3
Gíglio, *Italy* 40 F7
Gignac, *France* 20 E7

Gigüela →, *Spain* 37 F7
Gijón, *Spain* 36 B5
Gil I., *Canada* 102 C3
Gila →, *U.S.A.* 109 K6
Gila Bend, *U.S.A.* 109 K7
Gila Bend Mts., *U.S.A.* 109 K7
Gila Cliff Dwellings ⌂, *U.S.A.* 109 K9
Gīlān □, *Iran* 71 B6
Gilău, *Romania* 29 D8
Gilbert →, *Australia* 94 B3
Gilbert Is., *Kiribati* 96 G9
Gilbert River, *Australia* 94 B3
Gilead, *U.S.A.* 117 B14
Gilf el Kebîr, Hadabat el, *Egypt* 80 C2
Gilford I., *Canada* 102 C3
Gilgandra, *Australia* 95 E4
Gilgil, *Kenya* 86 C4
Gilgit, *India* 69 B6
Gilgit →, *Pakistan* 69 B6
Gili ⌂, *Mozam.* 87 F4
Gilimanuk, *Indonesia* 63 J17
Giljeva Planina, *Serbia & M.* 44 C3
Gillam, *Canada* 103 B10
Gilleleje, *Denmark* 11 H6
Gillen, L., *Australia* 93 E3
Gilles, L., *Australia* 95 E2
Gillette, *U.S.A.* 112 C2
Gilliat, *Australia* 94 C3
Gillingham, *U.K.* 15 F8
Gilmer, *U.S.A.* 113 J7
Gilmore, L., *Australia* 93 F3
Gilo →, *Ethiopia* 81 F3
Gilort →, *Romania* 29 F8
Gilroy, *U.S.A.* 110 H5
Gimbi, *Ethiopia* 81 F4
Gimie, Mt, *St. Lucia* 121 f
Gimli, *Canada* 103 C9
Gimo, *Sweden* 10 D12
Gimone →, *France* 20 E5
Gimont, *France* 20 E4
Gin Gin, *Australia* 95 D5
Ginâh, *Egypt* 80 B3
Gineifa, *Egypt* 80 H8
Gingin, *Australia* 93 F2
Gingindlovu, *S. Africa* 89 D5
Ginir, *Ethiopia* 81 F5
Ginosa, *Italy* 43 B9
Ginzo de Limia = Xinzo de Limia, *Spain* 36 C3
Gióia, G. di, *Italy* 43 D8
Gióia del Colle, *Italy* 43 B9
Gióia Tauro, *Italy* 43 D8
Gioiosa Iónica, *Italy* 43 D9
Gioiosa Marea, *Italy* 43 D7
Gióna, Óros, *Greece* 46 C4
Giovi, Passo dei, *Italy* 40 D5
Giovinazzo, *Italy* 43 A9
Gir Hills, *India* 68 J4
Girab, *India* 68 F4
Girâfi, W. →, *Egypt* 74 F3
Giraltovce, *Slovak Rep.* 27 B14
Girard, *Kans., U.S.A.* 113 G7
Girard, *Ohio, U.S.A.* 116 E4
Girard, *Pa., U.S.A.* 116 E4
Girdle Ness, *U.K.* 13 D6
Giresun, *Turkey* 73 B8
Girga, *Egypt* 80 B3
Giri →, *India* 68 D7
Giridih, *India* 69 G12
Girifalco, *Italy* 43 D9
Girne = Kyrenia, *Cyprus* 49 D12
Giro, *Nigeria* 83 C5
Giromagny, *France* 19 E13
Girona, *Spain* 38 D7
Girona □, *Spain* 38 C7
Gironde □, *France* 20 D3
Gironde →, *France* 20 C2
Gironella, *Spain* 38 C6
Girraween △, *Australia* 95 D5
Giru, *Australia* 94 B4
Girvan, *U.K.* 13 F4
Gisborne, *N.Z.* 91 H7
Gisenyi, *Rwanda* 86 C2
Gislaved, *Sweden* 11 G7
Gisors, *France* 19 C8
Gitega, *Burundi* 86 C2
Giuba →, *Somali Rep.* 75 G3
Giugliano in Campania, *Italy* 43 B7
Giulianova, *Italy* 41 F10
Giurgeni, *Romania* 29 F12
Giurgiu, *Romania* 29 G10
Giurgiu □, *Romania* 29 F10
Giurgiuleşti, *Moldova* 29 E13
Give, *Denmark* 11 J3
Givet, *France* 19 B11
Givors, *France* 21 C8
Givry, *France* 19 F11
Giyon, *Ethiopia* 81 F4
Giza = El Gîza, *Egypt* 80 J7
Gizhiga, *Russia* 53 C17
Gizhiginskaya Guba, *Russia* 53 C16
Giżycko, *Poland* 30 D8
Gizzeria, *Italy* 43 D9
Gjalicë e Lumës, Mal., *Albania* 44 D4
Gjegjan, *Albania* 44 E4
Gjirokastër, *Albania* 44 F4
Gjoa Haven, *Canada* 100 B10
Gjøvik, *Norway* 9 F14
Gjuhës, Kep i, *Albania* 44 F3
Glace Bay, *Canada* 105 C8
Glacier △, *Canada* 102 C5
Glacier △, *U.S.A.* 108 B7
Glacier Bay △, *U.S.A.* 102 B1
Glacier Peak, *U.S.A.* 108 B3
Gladewater, *U.S.A.* 113 J7
Gladstone, *Queens., Australia* 94 C5
Gladstone, *S. Austral., Australia* 95 E2
Gladstone, *Canada* 103 C9
Gladstone, *U.S.A.* 114 C2
Gladwin, *U.S.A.* 114 D3
Glafsfjorden, *Sweden* 10 E6
Glagah, *Indonesia* 63 J17
Głagów Małapolski, *Poland* 31 H8
Glåma = Glomma →, *Norway* 9 G14
Gláma, *Iceland* 8 D2
Glamis, *U.S.A.* 111 N11
Glamoč, *Bos.-H.* 41 D13
Glamorgan, Vale of □, *U.K.* 15 F4
Glamsbjerg, *Denmark* 11 J4
Glarus, *Switz.* 25 H5
Glarus □, *Switz.* 25 J5
Glasco, *Kans., U.S.A.* 112 F6
Glasco, *N.Y., U.S.A.* 117 D11
Glasgow, *U.K.* 13 F4
Glasgow, *Ky., U.S.A.* 114 G3
Glasgow, *Mont., U.S.A.* 108 B10
Glasgow, City of □, *U.K.* 13 F4
Glasgow International ✕ (GLA), *U.K.* 13 F4
Glaslyn, *Canada* 103 C7
Glastonbury, *U.K.* 15 F5
Glastonbury, *U.S.A.* 117 E12
Glauchau, *Germany* 24 E8
Glava, *Sweden* 10 E6
Glavice, *Croatia* 41 E13
Glazov, *Russia* 34 A11
Gleichen, *Canada* 102 C6
Gleisdorf, *Austria* 26 D8
Gleiwitz = Gliwice, *Poland* 31 H5
Glen, *U.S.A.* 117 B13
Glen Affric, *U.K.* 13 D3
Glen Canyon, *U.S.A.* 109 H8
Glen Canyon ⌂, *U.S.A.* 109 H8
Glen Canyon Dam, *U.S.A.* 109 H8
Glen Coe, *U.K.* 13 E3
Glen Cove, *U.S.A.* 117 F11
Glen Garry, *U.K.* 13 D3
Glen Innes, *Australia* 95 D5
Glen Lyon, *U.S.A.* 117 E8
Glen Mor, *U.K.* 13 D4
Glen More ⌂, *U.K.* 13 D5
Glen Moriston, *U.K.* 13 D4
Glen Robertson, *Canada* 117 A10
Glen Spean, *U.K.* 13 E4
Glen Ullin, *U.S.A.* 112 B4
Glénan, Îs. de, *France* 18 E3
Glenariff △, *Ireland* 12 A5
Glencoe, *Canada* 116 D3
Glencoe, *S. Africa* 89 D5
Glencoe, *U.S.A.* 112 C7
Glendale, *Ariz., U.S.A.* 109 K7
Glendale, *Calif., U.S.A.* 111 L8
Glendale, *Zimbabwe* 87 F3
Glendive, *U.S.A.* 112 B2
Glendo, *U.S.A.* 112 D2
Glenelg →, *Australia* 95 F3
Glenfield, *U.S.A.* 117 C9
Glengarriff, *Ireland* 12 E2
Glenmont, *U.S.A.* 116 F2
Glenmorgan, *Australia* 95 D4
Glenn, *U.S.A.* 110 F4
Glennallen, *U.S.A.* 100 B5
Glennamaddy, *Ireland* 12 C3
Glenns Ferry, *U.S.A.* 108 E6
Glenore, *Australia* 94 B3
Glenreagh, *Australia* 95 E5
Glenrock, *U.S.A.* 108 E11
Glenrothes, *U.K.* 13 E5
Glens Falls, *U.S.A.* 117 C11
Glenside, *U.S.A.* 117 F9
Glenties, *Ireland* 12 B3
Glenveagh △, *Ireland* 12 A3
Glenville, *U.S.A.* 114 F5
Glenwood, *Canada* 105 C9
Glenwood, *Ark., U.S.A.* 113 H8
Glenwood, *Iowa, U.S.A.* 112 E7
Glenwood, *Minn., U.S.A.* 112 C7
Glenwood, *Wash., U.S.A.* 110 D5
Glenwood Springs, *U.S.A.* 108 G10
Glettinganes, *Iceland* 8 D7
Glifádha, *Greece* 46 D5
Glimåkra, *Sweden* 11 H8
Glina, *Croatia* 41 C13
Glinojeck, *Poland* 31 F7
Gliwice, *Poland* 31 H5
Globe, *U.S.A.* 109 K8
Glodeanu Siliştea, *Romania* 29 F11
Glodeni, *Moldova* 29 C12
Glödnitz, *Austria* 26 E7
Gloggnitz, *Austria* 26 D8
Głogów, *Poland* 31 G3
Głogówek, *Poland* 31 H4
Glomma →, *Norway* 9 G14
Glorieuses, Is., *Ind. Oc.* 89 A8
Glóssa, *Greece* 46 B5
Glossop, *U.K.* 14 D6
Gloucester, *Australia* 95 E5
Gloucester, *U.K.* 15 F5
Gloucester, *U.S.A.* 117 D14
Gloucester I., *Australia* 94 J6
Gloucester Island △, *Australia* 94 J6
Gloucester Point, *U.S.A.* 114 G7
Gloucestershire □, *U.K.* 15 F5
Gloversville, *U.S.A.* 117 C10
Glovertown, *Canada* 105 C9
Główno, *Poland* 31 G6
Głubczyce, *Poland* 31 H4
Glubokiy, *Russia* 35 F5
Glubokoye = Hlybokaye, *Belarus* 32 E4
Głuchołazy, *Poland* 31 H4
Glücksburg, *Germany* 24 A5
Glückstadt, *Germany* 24 B5
Glukhov = Hlukhiv, *Ukraine* 33 G7
Glusk, *Belarus* 33 F5
Głuszyca, *Poland* 31 H3
Glyngøre, *Denmark* 11 H2
Gmünd, *Kärnten, Austria* 26 E6
Gmünd, *Niederösterreich, Austria* 26 C8
Gmunden, *Austria* 26 D6
Gnarp, *Sweden* 10 B11
Gnesta, *Sweden* 10 E11
Gniew, *Poland* 30 E5
Gniewkowo, *Poland* 31 F5
Gniezno, *Poland* 31 F4
Gnjilane, *Serbia & M.* 44 D5
Gnoien, *Germany* 24 B8
Gnosjö, *Sweden* 11 G7
Gnowangerup, *Australia* 93 F2
Go Cong, *Vietnam* 65 G6
Gō-no-ura, *Japan* 55 H4
Goa, *India* 66 M8
Goa □, *India* 66 M8
Goalen Hd., *Australia* 95 F5
Goalpara, *India* 67 F17
Goaltor, *India* 69 H12
Goalundo Ghat, *Bangla.* 69 H13
Goaso, *Ghana* 82 D4
Goat Fell, *U.K.* 13 F3
Goba, *Ethiopia* 81 F4
Goba, *Mozam.* 89 D5
Gobabis, *Namibia* 88 C2
Göbel, *Turkey* 45 F12
Gobi, *Asia* 56 C6
Gobō, *Japan* 55 H7
Gobo, *Sudan* 81 F3
Göçbeyli, *Turkey* 47 B9
Goch, *Germany* 24 D2
Gochas, *Namibia* 88 C2
Godalming, *U.K.* 15 F7
Godavari →, *India* 67 L13
Godavari Pt., *India* 67 L13
Godbout, *Canada* 105 C6
Godda, *India* 69 G12
Godech, *Bulgaria* 44 C7
Goderich, *Canada* 116 C3
Goderville, *France* 18 C7
Godfrey Ra., *Australia* 93 D2
Godhavn = Qeqertarsuaq, *Greenland* 101 B14
Godhra, *India* 68 H5
Gödöllő, *Hungary* 28 C4
Godoy Cruz, *Argentina* 126 C2
Gods →, *Canada* 104 A1
Gods L., *Canada* 104 B1
Gods River, *Canada* 103 C10
Godthåb = Nuuk, *Greenland* 101 B14
Godwin Austen = K2, *Pakistan* 69 B7
Goeie Hoop, Kaap die = Good Hope, C. of, *S. Africa* 88 E2
Goéland, L. au, *Canada* 104 C4
Goélands, L. aux, *Canada* 105 A7
Goeree, *Neths.* 17 C3
Goes, *Neths.* 17 C3
Goffstown, *U.S.A.* 117 C13
Gogama, *Canada* 104 C3
Gogebic, L., *U.S.A.* 112 B10
Goggetti, *Ethiopia* 81 F4
Gogolin, *Poland* 31 H5
Gogonou, *Benin* 83 C5
Gogra = Ghaghara →, *India* 69 G11
Gogriâl, *Sudan* 81 F2
Gogti, *Ethiopia* 81 E5
Gohana, *India* 68 E7
Goharganj, *India* 68 H7
Goi →, *India* 68 H6
Goiânia, *Brazil* 125 G9
Goiás, *Brazil* 125 G8
Goiás □, *Brazil* 125 F9
Goio-Erê, *Brazil* 127 A5
Góis, *Portugal* 36 E2
Gojam □, *Ethiopia* 81 E4
Gojeb, Wabi →, *Ethiopia* 81 F4
Gojō, *Japan* 55 G7
Gojra, *Pakistan* 68 D5
Gökçeada, *Turkey* 45 F9
Gökçedağ, *Turkey* 47 B10
Gökçen, *Turkey* 47 C9
Gökçeören, *Turkey* 47 C10
Gökçeyazı, *Turkey* 47 B9
Gökırmak →, *Turkey* 72 B6
Gökova, *Turkey* 47 D10
Gökova Körfezi, *Turkey* 47 E9
Göksu →, *Turkey* 72 D6
Göksun, *Turkey* 72 C7
Gokteik, *Burma* 67 H20
Göktepe, *Turkey* 47 D10
Gokurt, *Pakistan* 68 E2
Gokwe, *Zimbabwe* 89 B4
Gola, *India* 69 E9
Golakganj, *India* 69 F13
Golan Heights = Hagolan, *Syria* 74 C4
Gołańcz, *Poland* 31 F4
Golāshkerd, *Iran* 71 E8
Golaya Pristen = Hola Pristan, *Ukraine* 33 J7
Gölbaşı, *Adiyaman, Turkey* 72 D7
Gölbaşı, *Ankara, Turkey* 72 C5
Golchikha, *Russia* 4 B12
Golconda, *U.S.A.* 108 F5
Gölcük, *Kocaeli, Turkey* 45 F13
Gölcük, *Niğde, Turkey* 72 C6
Gold, *U.S.A.* 116 E7
Gold Beach, *U.S.A.* 108 E1
Gold Coast, *W. Afr.* 83 E4
Gold Hill, *U.S.A.* 108 E2
Gold River, *Canada* 102 D3
Gołdap, *Poland* 30 D9
Goldberg, *Germany* 24 B8
Golden, *Canada* 102 C5
Golden B., *N.Z.* 91 J4
Golden Gate, *U.S.A.* 108 H2
Golden Gate Highlands △, *S. Africa* 89 D4
Golden Hinde, *Canada* 102 D3
Golden Lake, *Canada* 116 A7
Golden Spike ⌂, *U.S.A.* 108 F7
Golden Vale, *Ireland* 12 D3
Goldendale, *U.S.A.* 108 D3
Goldfield, *U.S.A.* 109 H5
Goldsand L., *Canada* 103 B8
Goldsboro, *U.S.A.* 115 H7
Goldsmith, *U.S.A.* 113 K3
Goldsworthy, *Australia* 92 D2
Goldthwaite, *U.S.A.* 113 K5
Golegã, *Portugal* 37 F2
Goleniów, *Poland* 30 E1
Golestān □, *Iran* 71 B7
Golestānak, *Iran* 71 D7
Goleta, *U.S.A.* 111 L7
Golfito, *Costa Rica* 120 E3
Golfo Aranci, *Italy* 42 B2
Golfo di Orosei e del Gennargentu △, *Italy* 42 B2
Gölgeli Dağları, *Turkey* 47 D10
Gölhisar, *Turkey* 47 D11
Goliad, *U.S.A.* 113 L6
Golija, *Serbia & M.* 44 C2
Golija, *Serbia & M.* 44 C4
Golina, *Poland* 31 F5
Gölköy, *Turkey* 72 B7
Göllersdorf, *Austria* 26 C9
Gölmarmara, *Turkey* 47 C9
Golo →, *France* 21 F13
Gölova, *Turkey* 47 E12
Golpāyegān, *Iran* 71 C6
Gölpazarı, *Turkey* 72 B4
Golra, *Pakistan* 68 C5
Golspie, *U.K.* 13 D5
Golub-Dobrzyń, *Poland* 31 E6
Golubac, *Serbia & M.* 44 B5
Golyam Perelik, *Bulgaria* 45 E8
Golyama Kamchiya →, *Bulgaria* 45 C11
Goma, *Dem. Rep. of the Congo* 86 C2
Gomal Pass, *Pakistan* 68 D3
Gomati →, *India* 69 G10
Gombari, *Dem. Rep. of the Congo* 86 B2
Gombe, *Nigeria* 83 C7
Gömbe, *Turkey* 47 E11
Gombe □, *Nigeria* 83 C7
Gombe →, *Tanzania* 86 C3
Gombi, *Nigeria* 83 C7
Gomel = Homyel, *Belarus* 33 F6
Gomera, *Canary Is.* 48 F2
Gómez Palacio, *Mexico* 118 B4
Gomīshān, *Iran* 71 B7
Gommern, *Germany* 24 C7
Gomogomo, *Indonesia* 63 F8
Gomoh, *India* 67 H15
Gomotartsi, *Bulgaria* 44 B6
Gompa = Ganta, *Liberia* 82 D3
Gomphi, *Greece* 46 B3
Gonābād, *Iran* 71 C8
Gonaïves, *Haiti* 121 C5
Gonarezhou △, *Zimbabwe* 87 G3
Gonâve, G. de la, *Haiti* 121 C5
Gonâve, I. de la, *Haiti* 121 C5
Gonbad-e Kāvūs, *Iran* 71 B7
Gönc, *Hungary* 28 B6
Gonda, *India* 69 F9
Gondal, *India* 68 J4
Gonder, *Ethiopia* 81 E4
Gonder □, *Ethiopia* 81 E4
Gondia, *India* 66 J12
Gondola, *Mozam.* 87 F3
Gondomar, *Portugal* 36 D2
Gondrecourt-le-Château, *France* 19 D12
Gönen, *Balıkesir, Turkey* 45 F11
Gönen, *Isparta, Turkey* 47 D12
Gönen →, *Turkey* 45 F11
Gong Xian, *China* 58 C5
Gong'an, *China* 59 B9
Gongcheng, *China* 59 E8
Gongga Shan, *China* 58 C3
Gongguan, *China* 58 G7
Gonghe, *China* 60 C5
Gongola →, *Nigeria* 83 D7
Gongolgon, *Australia* 95 E4
Gongshan, *China* 58 D2
Gongtan, *China* 58 C7
Gongzhuling, *China* 57 C13
Goniadz, *Poland* 30 E9
Goniri, *Nigeria* 83 C7
Gonjo, *China* 58 B2
Gonnesa, *Italy* 42 C1
Gónnos, *Greece* 46 B4
Gonnosfanádiga, *Italy* 42 C1
Gonzaga, *Phil.* 61 B5
Gonzales, *Calif., U.S.A.* 110 J5
Gonzales, *Tex., U.S.A.* 113 L6
González Chaves, *Argentina* 126 D3
Good Hope, C. of, *S. Africa* 88 E2
Gooderham, *Canada* 116 B6
Goodhouse, *S. Africa* 88 D2
Gooding, *U.S.A.* 108 E6
Goodland, *U.S.A.* 112 F4
Goodlow, *Canada* 102 B4
Goodooga, *Australia* 95 D4
Goodsprings, *U.S.A.* 111 K11
Goole, *U.K.* 14 D7
Goolgowi, *Australia* 95 E4
Goomalling, *Australia* 93 F2
Goomeri, *Australia* 95 D5
Goonda, *Mozam.* 87 F3
Goondiwindi, *Australia* 95 D5
Goongarrie △, *Australia* 93 F3
Goongarrie, L., *Australia* 93 F3
Goonyella, *Australia* 94 C4
Goose →, *Canada* 105 B7
Goose Creek, *U.S.A.* 115 J5
Goose L., *U.S.A.* 108 F3
Gop, *India* 66 H6
Gopalganj, *India* 69 F11
Göppingen, *Germany* 25 G5
Gor, *Spain* 37 H8
Góra, *Dolnośląskie, Poland* 31 G3
Góra, *Mazowieckie, Poland* 31 F7
Góra Kalwaria, *Poland* 31 G8
Gorakhpur, *India* 69 F10
Goražde, *Bos.-H.* 28 G3
Gorbatov, *Russia* 34 B6
Gorbea, Peña, *Spain* 38 B2
Gorczański △, *Poland* 31 J7
Gorda, *U.S.A.* 110 K5
Gorda, Pta., *Canary Is.* 48 F2
Gorda, Pta., *Nic.* 120 D3
Gordan B., *Australia* 92 B5
Gördes, *Turkey* 47 C10
Gordon, *U.S.A.* 112 D3
Gordon →, *Australia* 95 G4
Gordon L., *Alta., Canada* 103 B6
Gordon L., *N.W.T., Canada* 102 A6
Gordonvale, *Australia* 94 B4
Gore, *Ethiopia* 81 F4
Gore, *N.Z.* 91 M2
Gore Bay, *Canada* 104 C3
Görele, *Turkey* 73 B8
Goreme, *Turkey* 72 C6
Gorey, *Ireland* 12 D5
Gorg, *Iran* 71 D8
Gorgān, *Iran* 71 B7
Gorgona, *Italy* 40 E6
Gorgona, I., *Colombia* 124 C3
Gorgora, *Ethiopia* 81 E4
Gorgoram, *Nigeria* 83 C7
Gorham, *U.S.A.* 117 B13
Gori, *Georgia* 35 J7
Goriganga →, *India* 69 E9
Gorinchem, *Neths.* 17 C4
Goris, *Armenia* 73 C12
Goritsy, *Russia* 32 D9
Gorízia, *Italy* 41 C10
Gorj □, *Romania* 29 E8
Gorki = Horki, *Belarus* 32 E6
Gorkiy = Nizhniy Novgorod, *Russia* 34 B7
Gorkovskoye Vdkhr., *Russia* 34 B6
Gorleston, *U.K.* 15 E9
Gorlice, *Poland* 31 J8
Görlitz, *Germany* 24 D10
Gorlovka = Horlivka, *Ukraine* 33 H10
Gorman, *U.S.A.* 111 L8
Gorna Dzhumayo = Blagoevgrad, *Bulgaria* 44 D7
Gorna Oryakhovitsa, *Bulgaria* 45 C9
Gornja Radgona, *Slovenia* 41 B13
Gornja Tuzla, *Bos.-H.* 28 F3
Gornji Grad, *Slovenia* 41 B11
Gornji Milanovac, *Serbia & M.* 44 B4
Gornji Vakuf, *Bos.-H.* 28 G2
Gorno Ablanovo, *Bulgaria* 45 C9
Gorno-Altay □, *Russia* 52 D9
Gorno-Altaysk, *Russia* 52 D9
Gornyatskiy, *Russia* 35 F5
Gornyy, *Saratov, Russia* 34 E9
Gornyy, *Sib., Russia* 54 B6
Gorodenka = Horodenka, *Ukraine* 33 H3
Gorodets, *Russia* 34 B6
Gorodishche = Horodyshche, *Ukraine* 33 H6
Gorodishche, *Russia* 34 D7
Gorodnya = Horodnya, *Ukraine* 33 G6
Gorodok = Haradok, *Belarus* 32 E6
Gorodok = Horodok, *Ukraine* 33 H2
Gorodovikovsk, *Russia* 35 G5
Gorokhov = Horokhiv, *Ukraine* 33 G3
Gorokhovets, *Russia* 34 B6
Gorom Gorom, *Burkina Faso* 83 C4
Goromonzi, *Zimbabwe* 87 F3
Gorong, Kepulauan, *Indonesia* 63 E8
Gorongosa △, *Mozam.* 89 B5
Gorongose →, *Mozam.* 89 C5
Gorongoza, *Mozam.* 87 F3
Gorongoza, Sa. da, *Mozam.* 87 F3
Gorontalo, *Indonesia* 63 D6
Goronyo, *Nigeria* 83 C6
Górowo Iławeckie, *Poland* 30 D7
Gorron, *France* 18 D6
Gorshechnoye, *Russia* 33 G10
Gort, *Ireland* 12 C3
Gortis, *Greece* 49 D6
Góry Bystrzyckie, *Poland* 31 H3
Goryachiy Klyuch, *Russia* 35 H4
Gorzkowice, *Poland* 31 G6
Górzno, *Poland* 31 E6
Gorzów Śląski, *Poland* 31 G5
Gorzów Wielkopolski, *Poland* 31 F2
Gosford, *Australia* 95 E5
Goshen, *Calif., U.S.A.* 110 J7
Goshen, *Ind., U.S.A.* 114 E3
Goshen, *N.Y., U.S.A.* 117 E10
Goshogawara, *Japan* 54 D10
Gosier, *Guadeloupe* 120 b
Goslar, *Germany* 24 D6
Gospič, *Croatia* 41 D12
Gosport, *U.K.* 15 G6
Gossas, *Senegal* 82 C1
Gosse →, *Australia* 94 B1
Gossi, *Mali* 83 B4
Gossinga, *Sudan* 81 F2
Gostivar, *Macedonia* 44 E4
Gostyń, *Poland* 31 G4
Gostynin, *Poland* 31 F6
Göta älv →, *Sweden* 11 G5
Göta kanal, *Sweden* 11 F9
Götaland, *Sweden* 11 G8
Göteborg, *Sweden* 11 G5
Götene, *Sweden* 11 F7
Goteşti, *Moldova* 29 D13
Gotha, *Germany* 24 E6
Gothenburg = Göteborg, *Sweden* 11 G5
Gothenburg, *U.S.A.* 112 E4
Gothèye, *Niger* 83 C5
Gotland, *Sweden* 11 G12
Gotlands län □, *Sweden* 11 G12
Gotō-Rettō, *Japan* 55 H4
Gotse Delchev, *Bulgaria* 44 E7
Gotska Sandön, *Sweden* 9 G18
Gōtsu, *Japan* 55 G6
Gott Pk., *Canada* 102 C4
Góttero, Monte, *Italy* 40 D6
Göttingen, *Germany* 24 D5
Gottwald = Zmiyev, *Ukraine* 33 H9
Gottwaldov = Zlín, *Czech Rep.* 27 B10
Goubangzi, *China* 57 D11

Gouda, *Neths.* 17 **B4**
Goúdhoura, Ákra, *Greece* 49 **E8**
Goudiry, *Senegal* 82 **C2**
Goudoumaria, *Niger* 83 **C7**
Gouéké, *Guinea* 82 **D3**
Gough I., *Atl. Oc.* 2 **G9**
Gouin, Rés., *Canada* 104 **C5**
Gouitafla, *Ivory C.* 82 **D3**
Goulburn, *Australia* 95 **E4**
Goulburn Is., *Australia* 94 **A1**
Goulia, *Ivory C.* 82 **C3**
Goulimine, *Morocco* 78 **C3**
Goumbou, *Mali* 82 **B3**
Gouménissa, *Greece* 44 **F6**
Goundam, *Mali* 82 **B4**
Goúra, *Greece* 46 **D4**
Gourbassi, *Mali* 82 **C2**
Gourdon, *France* 20 **D5**
Gouré, *Niger* 83 **C7**
Gourin, *France* 18 **D3**
Gourits →, *S. Africa* 88 **E3**
Gourma-Rharous, *Mali* 83 **B4**
Goúrnais, *Greece* 49 **D7**
Gournay-en-Bray, *France* 19 **C8**
Gourock, *U.K.* 13 **F4**
Goursi, *Burkina Faso* 82 **C4**
Gouverneur, *U.S.A.* 117 **B9**
Gouviá, *Greece* 49 **A3**
Gouzon, *France* 19 **F9**
Governador Valadares, *Brazil* 125 **G10**
Governor's Harbour, *Bahamas* 120 **A4**
Govindgarh, *India* 69 **G9**
Gowan Ra., *Australia* 94 **D4**
Gowanda, *U.S.A.* 116 **D6**
Gower, *U.K.* 15 **F3**
Gowna, L., *Ireland* 12 **C4**
Goya, *Argentina* 126 **B4**
Göyçay, *Azerbaijan* 35 **K8**
Goyder Lagoon, *Australia* 95 **D2**
Goyllarisquisga, *Peru* 124 **F3**
Göynük, *Antalya, Turkey* 47 **E12**
Göynük, *Bolu, Turkey* 72 **B4**
Goz Beïda, *Chad* 79 **F10**
Goz Regeb, *Sudan* 81 **D4**
Gozdnica, *Poland* 31 **G2**
Gozo, *Malta* 49 **C1**
Graaff-Reinet, *S. Africa* 88 **E3**
Grabo, *Ivory C.* 82 **D3**
Grabow, *Germany* 24 **B7**
Grabów nad Prosną, *Poland* 31 **G5**
Gračac, *Croatia* 41 **D12**
Gračanica, *Bos.-H.* 28 **F3**
Graçay, *France* 19 **E8**
Gracias a Dios, C., *Honduras* 120 **D3**
Graciosa, I., *Canary Is.* 48 **E6**
Grad Sofiya □, *Bulgaria* 44 **D7**
Gradac, *Serbia & M.* 44 **C3**
Gradačac, *Bos.-H.* 28 **F3**
Gradeška Planina, *Macedonia* 44 **E6**
Gradets, *Bulgaria* 45 **D10**
Gradišče, *Slovenia* 41 **B12**
Grădiştea de Munte, *Romania* 29 **E8**
Grado, *Italy* 41 **C10**
Grado, *Spain* 36 **B4**
Grady, *U.S.A.* 113 **H3**
Graeca, Lacul, *Romania* 29 **F11**
Grafenau, *Germany* 25 **G9**
Gräfenberg, *Germany* 25 **F7**
Grafham Water, *U.K.* 15 **E7**
Grafton, *Australia* 95 **D5**
Grafton, *N. Dak., U.S.A.* 112 **A6**
Grafton, *W. Va., U.S.A.* 114 **F5**
Graham, *Canada* 104 **C1**
Graham, *U.S.A.* 113 **J5**
Graham, Mt., *U.S.A.* 109 **K9**
Graham Bell, Ostrov = Greem-Bell, Ostrov, *Russia* 52 **A7**
Graham I., *Canada* 102 **C2**
Graham Land, *Antarctica* 5 **C17**
Grahamstown, *S. Africa* 88 **E4**
Grahamsville, *U.S.A.* 117 **E10**
Grahovo, *Serbia & M.* 44 **D2**
Graie, Alpi, *Europe* 21 **C11**
Grain Coast, *W. Afr.* 82 **E3**
Grajagan, *Indonesia* 63 **K17**
Grajagan, Teluk, *Indonesia* 63 **K17**
Grajaú, *Brazil* 125 **E9**
Grajaú →, *Brazil* 125 **D10**
Grajewo, *Poland* 30 **E9**
Gramada, *Bulgaria* 44 **C6**
Gramat, *France* 20 **D5**
Grammichele, *Italy* 43 **E7**
Grámmos, Óros, *Greece* 44 **F4**
Grampian, *U.S.A.* 116 **F6**
Grampian Highlands = Grampian Mts., *U.K.* 13 **E5**
Grampian Mts., *U.K.* 13 **E5**
Grampians, The, *Australia* 95 **F3**
Gramsh, *Albania* 44 **F4**
Gran Canaria, *Canary Is.* 48 **G4**
Gran Chaco, *S. Amer.* 126 **B3**
Gran Desierto del Pinacate ⌂, *Mexico* 118 **A2**
Gran Paradiso, *Italy* 40 **C4**
Gran Sasso d'Itália, *Italy* 41 **F10**
Gran Sasso e Monti Della Laga △, *Italy* 41 **F10**
Granada, *Nic.* 120 **D2**
Granada, *Spain* 37 **H7**
Granada, *U.S.A.* 113 **F3**
Granada □, *Spain* 37 **H7**
Granadilla de Abona, *Canary Is.* 48 **F3**
Granard, *Ireland* 12 **C4**
Granbury, *U.S.A.* 113 **J6**
Granby, *Canada* 117 **A12**
Granby, *U.S.A.* 108 **F11**
Grand →, *Canada* 116 **D5**
Grand →, *Mo., U.S.A.* 112 **F8**
Grand →, *S. Dak., U.S.A.* 112 **C4**
Grand Bahama, *Bahamas* 120 **A4**
Grand Bank, *Canada* 105 **C8**
Grand Bassam, *Ivory C.* 82 **D4**
Grand Béréby, *Ivory C.* 82 **E3**
Grand-Bourg, *Guadeloupe* 120 **b**
Grand Canal = Yun Ho →, *China* 57 **E9**
Grand Canyon, *U.S.A.* 109 **H7**
Grand Canyon △, *U.S.A.* 109 **H7**
Grand Canyon-Parashant ⌂, *U.S.A.* 109 **H7**
Grand Cayman, *Cayman Is.* 120 **C3**
Grand Centre, *Canada* 103 **C6**
Grand Cess, *Liberia* 82 **E3**
Grand Coulee, *U.S.A.* 108 **C4**
Grand Coulee Dam, *U.S.A.* 108 **C4**
Grand Falls, *Canada* 105 **C6**
Grand Falls-Windsor, *Canada* 105 **C8**
Grand Forks, *Canada* 102 **D5**
Grand Forks, *U.S.A.* 112 **B6**
Grand Gorge, *U.S.A.* 117 **D10**
Grand Haven, *U.S.A.* 114 **D2**
Grand I., *Mich., U.S.A.* 114 **B2**
Grand I., *N.Y., U.S.A.* 116 **D6**
Grand Island, *U.S.A.* 112 **E5**
Grand Isle, *La., U.S.A.* 113 **L9**
Grand Isle, *Vt., U.S.A.* 117 **B11**
Grand Junction, *U.S.A.* 109 **G9**
Grand L., *N.B., Canada* 105 **C6**
Grand L., *Nfld., Canada* 105 **C8**
Grand L., *Nfld., Canada* 105 **B7**
Grand L., *U.S.A.* 113 **L8**
Grand Lahou, *Ivory C.* 82 **D3**
Grand Lake, *U.S.A.* 108 **F11**
Grand-Lieu, L. de, *France* 18 **E5**
Grand Manan I., *Canada* 105 **D6**
Grand Marais, *Canada* 112 **B9**
Grand Marais, *U.S.A.* 114 **B3**
Grand-Mère, *Canada* 104 **C5**
Grand Popo, *Benin* 83 **D5**
Grand Portage, *U.S.A.* 112 **B10**
Grand Prairie, *U.S.A.* 113 **J6**
Grand Rapids, *Canada* 103 **C9**
Grand Rapids, *Mich., U.S.A.* 114 **D2**
Grand Rapids, *Minn., U.S.A.* 112 **B8**
Grand St-Bernard, Col du, *Europe* 25 **K3**
Grand Staircase-Escalante ⌂, *U.S.A.* 109 **H8**
Grand Teton, *U.S.A.* 108 **E8**
Grand Teton △, *U.S.A.* 108 **D8**
Grand Union Canal, *U.K.* 15 **E7**
Grand-Vigie, Pte. de la, *Guadeloupe* 120 **b**
Grandas de Salime, *Spain* 36 **B4**
Grande →, *Jujuy, Argentina* 126 **A2**
Grande →, *Mendoza, Argentina* 126 **D2**
Grande →, *Bolivia* 124 **G6**
Grande →, *Bahia, Brazil* 125 **F10**
Grande →, *Minas Gerais, Brazil* 125 **H8**
Grande, B., *Argentina* 128 **G3**
Grande, Rio →, *U.S.A.* 113 **N6**
Grande Baleine, R. de la →, *Canada* 104 **A4**
Grande Cache, *Canada* 102 **C5**
Grande-Entrée, *Canada* 105 **C7**
Grande Prairie, *Canada* 102 **B5**
Grande-Rivière, *Canada* 105 **C7**
Grande-Terre, I., *Guadeloupe* 120 **b**
Grande-Vallée, *Canada* 105 **C6**
Grandfalls, *U.S.A.* 113 **K3**
Grândola, *Portugal* 37 **G2**
Grandpré, *France* 19 **C11**
Grands Causses ⌂, *France* 20 **D6**
Grands-Jardins ⌂, *Canada* 105 **C5**
Grandview, *Canada* 103 **C8**
Grandview, *U.S.A.* 108 **C4**
Grandvilliers, *France* 19 **C8**
Graneros, *Chile* 126 **C1**
Grangemouth, *U.K.* 13 **E5**
Granger, *U.S.A.* 108 **F9**
Grängesberg, *Sweden* 10 **D9**
Grangeville, *U.S.A.* 108 **D5**
Granisle, *Canada* 102 **C3**
Granite City, *U.S.A.* 112 **F9**
Granite Falls, *U.S.A.* 112 **C7**
Granite L., *Canada* 105 **C8**
Granite Mt., *U.S.A.* 111 **M10**
Granite Pk., *U.S.A.* 108 **D9**
Graniteville, *U.S.A.* 117 **B12**
Granitola, C., *Italy* 42 **E5**
Granity, *N.Z.* 91 **J3**
Granja, *Brazil* 125 **D10**
Granja de Moreruela, *Spain* 36 **D5**
Granja de Torrehermosa, *Spain* 37 **G5**
Gränna, *Sweden* 11 **F8**
Granollers, *Spain* 38 **D7**
Gransee, *Germany* 24 **B9**
Grant, *U.S.A.* 112 **E4**
Grant, Mt., *U.S.A.* 108 **G4**
Grant City, *U.S.A.* 112 **E7**
Grant I., *Australia* 92 **B5**
Grant Range, *U.S.A.* 109 **G6**
Grantham, *U.K.* 14 **E7**
Grantown-on-Spey, *U.K.* 13 **D5**
Grants, *U.S.A.* 109 **J10**
Grants Pass, *U.S.A.* 108 **E2**
Grantsville, *U.S.A.* 108 **F7**
Granville, *France* 18 **D5**
Granville, *N. Dak., U.S.A.* 112 **A4**
Granville, *N.Y., U.S.A.* 117 **C11**
Granville, *Ohio, U.S.A.* 116 **F2**
Granville L., *Canada* 103 **B8**
Graskop, *S. Africa* 89 **C5**
Gräsö, *Sweden* 10 **D12**
Grass →, *Canada* 103 **B9**
Grass Range, *U.S.A.* 108 **C9**
Grass River ⌂, *Canada* 103 **C8**
Grass Valley, *Calif., U.S.A.* 110 **F6**
Grass Valley, *Oreg., U.S.A.* 108 **D3**
Grassano, *Italy* 43 **B9**
Grasse, *France* 21 **E10**
Grassflat, *U.S.A.* 116 **F6**
Grasslands △, *Canada* 103 **D7**
Grassy, *Australia* 95 **G3**
Gråsten, *Denmark* 11 **K3**
Grästorp, *Sweden* 11 **F6**
Gratkorn, *Austria* 26 **D8**
Graubünden □, *Switz.* 25 **J5**
Graulhet, *France* 20 **E5**
Graus, *Spain* 38 **C5**
Grave, Pte. de, *France* 20 **C2**
Gravelbourg, *Canada* 103 **D7**
Gravelines, *France* 19 **A9**
's-Gravenhage, *Neths.* 17 **B4**
Gravenhurst, *Canada* 116 **B5**
Gravesend, *Australia* 95 **D5**
Gravesend, *U.K.* 15 **F8**
Gravina in Púglia, *Italy* 43 **B9**
Gravois, Pointe-à-, *Haiti* 121 **C5**
Gravone →, *France* 21 **G12**
Gray, *France* 19 **E12**
Grayling, *U.S.A.* 114 **C3**
Grays, *U.K.* 15 **F8**
Grays Harbor, *U.S.A.* 108 **C1**
Grays L., *U.S.A.* 108 **E8**
Grays River, *U.S.A.* 110 **D3**
Grayvoron, *Russia* 33 **G8**
Graz, *Austria* 26 **D8**
Grdelica, *Serbia & M.* 44 **D6**
Greasy L., *Canada* 102 **A4**
Great Abaco I., *Bahamas* 120 **A4**
Great Artesian Basin, *Australia* 94 **C3**
Great Australian Bight, *Australia* 93 **F5**
Great Bahama Bank, *Bahamas* 120 **B4**
Great Barrier I., *N.Z.* 91 **G5**
Great Barrier Reef, *Australia* 94 **B4**
Great Barrier Reef ⌂, *Australia* 94 **B4**
Great Barrington, *U.S.A.* 117 **D11**
Great Basalt Wall △, *Australia* 94 **B4**
Great Basin, *U.S.A.* 108 **G5**
Great Basin △, *U.S.A.* 108 **G6**
Great Bear →, *Canada* 100 **B7**
Great Bear L., *Canada* 100 **B7**
Great Belt = Store Bælt, *Denmark* 11 **J4**
Great Bend, *Kans., U.S.A.* 112 **F5**
Great Bend, *Pa., U.S.A.* 117 **E9**
Great Blasket I., *Ireland* 12 **D1**
Great Britain, *Europe* 6 **E5**
Great Camanoe, *Br. Virgin Is.* 121 **e**
Great Codroy, *Canada* 105 **C8**
Great Dividing Ra., *Australia* 94 **C4**
Great Driffield = Driffield, *U.K.* 14 **C7**
Great Exuma I., *Bahamas* 120 **B4**
Great Falls, *U.S.A.* 108 **C8**
Great Fish = Groot Vis →, *S. Africa* 88 **E4**
Great Guana Cay, *Bahamas* 120 **B4**
Great Inagua I., *Bahamas* 121 **B5**
Great Indian Desert = Thar Desert, *India* 68 **F5**
Great Karoo, *S. Africa* 88 **E3**
Great Lake, *Australia* 95 **G4**
Great Lakes, *N. Amer.* 98 **E11**
Great Malvern, *U.K.* 15 **E5**
Great Miami →, *U.S.A.* 114 **F3**
Great Ormes Head, *U.K.* 14 **D4**
Great Ouse →, *U.K.* 14 **E8**
Great Palm I., *Australia* 94 **B4**
Great Pedro Bluff, *Jamaica* 120 **a**
Great Plains, *N. Amer.* 98 **E9**
Great Ruaha →, *Tanzania* 86 **D4**
Great Sacandaga Res., *U.S.A.* 117 **C10**
Great Saint Bernard Pass = Grand St-Bernard, Col du, *Europe* 25 **K3**
Great Salt L., *U.S.A.* 108 **F7**
Great Salt Lake Desert, *U.S.A.* 108 **F7**
Great Salt Plains L., *U.S.A.* 113 **G5**
Great Sand Dunes ⌂, *U.S.A.* 109 **H11**
Great Sandy △, *Australia* 95 **D5**
Great Sandy Desert, *Australia* 92 **D3**
Great Sangi = Sangihe, Pulau, *Indonesia* 63 **D7**
Great Scarcies →, *S. Leone* 82 **D2**
Great Skellig, *Ireland* 12 **E1**
Great Slave L., *Canada* 102 **A5**
Great Smoky Mts. △, *U.S.A.* 115 **H4**
Great Snow Mt., *Canada* 102 **B4**
Great Stour = Stour →, *U.K.* 15 **F9**
Great Victoria Desert, *Australia* 93 **E4**
Great Wall, *Antarctica* 5 **C18**
Great Wall, *China* 56 **E5**
Great Whernside, *U.K.* 14 **C6**
Great Yarmouth, *U.K.* 15 **E9**
Great Zab = Zāb al Kabīr →, *Iraq* 70 **C4**
Great Zimbabwe, *Zimbabwe* 87 **G3**
Greater Antilles, *W. Indies* 121 **C5**
Greater London □, *U.K.* 15 **F7**
Greater Manchester □, *U.K.* 14 **D5**
Greater St. Lucia Wetlands ⌂, *S. Africa* 89 **D5**
Greater Sudbury = Sudbury, *Canada* 104 **C3**
Greater Sunda Is., *Indonesia* 62 **F4**
Grebbestad, *Sweden* 11 **F5**
Grebenka = Hrebenka, *Ukraine* 33 **G7**
Greco, C., *Cyprus* 49 **E13**
Greco, Mte., *Italy* 41 **G10**
Gredos, Sierra de, *Spain* 36 **E6**
Greece, *U.S.A.* 116 **C7**
Greece ■, *Europe* 46 **B3**
Greeley, *Colo., U.S.A.* 112 **E2**
Greeley, *Nebr., U.S.A.* 112 **E5**
Greem-Bell, Ostrov, *Russia* 52 **A7**
Green, *U.S.A.* 108 **E2**
Green →, *Ky., U.S.A.* 114 **G2**
Green →, *Utah, U.S.A.* 109 **G9**
Green B., *U.S.A.* 114 **C2**
Green Bay, *U.S.A.* 114 **C2**
Green C., *Australia* 95 **F5**
Green Cove Springs, *U.S.A.* 115 **L5**
Green Lake, *Canada* 103 **C7**
Green Mts., *U.S.A.* 117 **C12**
Green River, *Utah, U.S.A.* 109 **G8**
Green River, *Wyo., U.S.A.* 108 **F9**
Green Valley, *U.S.A.* 109 **L8**
Greenbank, *U.S.A.* 110 **B4**
Greenbush, *Mich., U.S.A.* 116 **B1**
Greenbush, *Minn., U.S.A.* 112 **A6**
Greencastle, *U.S.A.* 114 **F2**
Greene, *U.S.A.* 117 **D9**
Greenfield, *Calif., U.S.A.* 110 **J5**
Greenfield, *Calif., U.S.A.* 111 **K8**
Greenfield, *Ind., U.S.A.* 114 **F3**
Greenfield, *Iowa, U.S.A.* 112 **E7**
Greenfield, *Mass., U.S.A.* 117 **D12**
Greenfield, *Mo., U.S.A.* 113 **G8**
Greenfield Park, *Canada* 117 **A11**
Greenland ☑, *N. Amer.* 98 **C15**
Greenland Sea, *Arctic* 4 **B7**
Greenock, *U.K.* 13 **F4**
Greenore, *Ireland* 12 **B5**
Greenore Pt., *Ireland* 12 **D5**
Greenough, *Australia* 93 **E1**
Greenough →, *Australia* 93 **E1**
Greenough Pt., *Canada* 116 **B3**
Greenport, *U.S.A.* 117 **E12**
Greensboro, *Ga., U.S.A.* 115 **J4**
Greensboro, *N.C., U.S.A.* 115 **G6**
Greensboro, *Vt., U.S.A.* 117 **B12**
Greensburg, *Ind., U.S.A.* 114 **F3**
Greensburg, *Kans., U.S.A.* 113 **G5**
Greensburg, *Pa., U.S.A.* 116 **F5**
Greenstone Pt., *U.K.* 13 **D3**
Greenvale, *Australia* 94 **B4**
Greenville, *Liberia* 82 **D3**
Greenville, *Ala., U.S.A.* 115 **K2**
Greenville, *Calif., U.S.A.* 110 **E6**
Greenville, *Maine, U.S.A.* 115 **C11**
Greenville, *Mich., U.S.A.* 114 **D3**
Greenville, *Miss., U.S.A.* 113 **J9**
Greenville, *Mo., U.S.A.* 113 **G9**
Greenville, *N.C., U.S.A.* 115 **H7**
Greenville, *N.H., U.S.A.* 117 **D13**
Greenville, *N.Y., U.S.A.* 117 **D10**
Greenville, *Ohio, U.S.A.* 114 **E3**
Greenville, *Pa., U.S.A.* 116 **E4**
Greenville, *S.C., U.S.A.* 115 **H4**
Greenville, *Tenn., U.S.A.* 115 **G4**
Greenville, *Tex., U.S.A.* 113 **J6**
Greenwater Lake ⌂, *Canada* 103 **C8**
Greenwich, *Conn., U.S.A.* 117 **E11**
Greenwich, *N.Y., U.S.A.* 117 **C11**
Greenwich, *Ohio, U.S.A.* 116 **E2**
Greenwich □, *U.K.* 15 **F8**
Greenwood, *Canada* 102 **D5**
Greenwood, *Ark., U.S.A.* 113 **H7**
Greenwood, *Ind., U.S.A.* 114 **F2**
Greenwood, *Miss., U.S.A.* 113 **J9**
Greenwood, *S.C., U.S.A.* 115 **H4**
Greenwood, Mt., *Australia* 92 **B5**
Gregbe, *Ivory C.* 82 **D3**
Gregory, *U.S.A.* 112 **D5**
Gregory △, *Australia* 92 **C5**
Gregory →, *Australia* 94 **B2**
Gregory, L., *S. Austral., Australia* 95 **D2**
Gregory, L., *W. Austral., Australia* 93 **E2**
Gregory Downs, *Australia* 94 **B2**
Gregory L., *Australia* 92 **D4**
Gregory Ra., *Queens., Australia* 94 **B3**
Gregory Ra., *W. Austral., Australia* 92 **D3**
Greiffenberg, *Germany* 24 **B9**
Greifswald, *Germany* 24 **A9**
Greifswalder Bodden, *Germany* 24 **A9**
Grein, *Austria* 26 **C7**
Greiz, *Germany* 24 **E8**
Gremikha, *Russia* 52 **C4**
Grenå, *Denmark* 11 **H4**
Grenada, *U.S.A.* 113 **J10**
Grenada ■, *W. Indies* 121 **D7**
Grenade, *France* 20 **E5**
Grenadier I., *U.S.A.* 117 **B8**
Grenadines, *St. Vincent* 121 **D7**
Grenchen, *Switz.* 25 **H3**
Grenen, *Denmark* 11 **G4**
Grenfell, *Australia* 95 **E4**
Grenfell, *Canada* 103 **C8**
Grenoble, *France* 21 **C9**
Grenville, C., *Australia* 94 **A3**
Grenville Chan., *Canada* 102 **C3**
Gréoux-les-Bains, *France* 21 **E9**
Gresham, *U.S.A.* 110 **E4**
Gresik, *Indonesia* 63 **G15**
Gretna, *U.K.* 13 **F5**
Greven, *Germany* 24 **C3**
Grevená, *Greece* 44 **F5**
Grevená □, *Greece* 44 **F5**
Grevenbroich, *Germany* 24 **D2**
Grevenmacher, *Lux.* 17 **E6**
Grevesmühlen, *Germany* 24 **B7**
Grevestrand, *Denmark* 11 **J6**
Grey →, *Canada* 105 **C8**
Grey →, *N.Z.* 91 **K3**
Grey, C., *Australia* 94 **A2**
Grey Ra., *Australia* 95 **D3**
Greybull, *U.S.A.* 108 **D9**
Greymouth, *N.Z.* 91 **K3**
Greystones, *Ireland* 12 **C5**
Greytown, *N.Z.* 91 **J5**
Greytown, *S. Africa* 89 **D5**
Gribanovskiy, *Russia* 34 **E5**
Gribbell I., *Canada* 102 **C3**
Gribës, Mal i, *Albania* 44 **F3**
Gridley, *U.S.A.* 110 **F5**
Griekwastad, *S. Africa* 88 **D3**
Griesheim, *Germany* 25 **F4**
Grieskirchen, *Austria* 26 **C6**
Griffin, *U.S.A.* 115 **J3**
Griffith, *Australia* 95 **E4**
Griffith, *Canada* 116 **A7**
Griffith I., *Canada* 116 **B4**
Grignols, *France* 20 **D3**
Grigoriopol, *Moldova* 29 **C14**
Grimaylov = Hrymayliv, *Ukraine* 33 **H4**
Grimes, *U.S.A.* 110 **F5**
Grimma, *Germany* 24 **D8**
Grimmen, *Germany* 24 **A9**
Grimsay, *U.K.* 13 **D1**
Grimsby, *Canada* 116 **C5**
Grimsby, *U.K.* 14 **D7**
Grímsey, *Iceland* 8 **C5**
Grimshaw, *Canada* 102 **B5**
Grimslöv, *Sweden* 11 **H8**
Grimstad, *Norway* 9 **G13**
Grindelwald, *Switz.* 25 **J4**
Grindsted, *Denmark* 11 **J2**
Grindstone I., *Canada* 117 **B8**
Grindu, *Romania* 29 **F11**
Grinnell, *U.S.A.* 112 **E8**
Grintavec, *Slovenia* 41 **B11**
Gris-Nez, C., *France* 19 **B8**
Grisolles, *France* 20 **E5**
Grisons = Graubünden □, *Switz.* 25 **J5**
Grisslehamn, *Sweden* 10 **D12**
Grmeč Planina, *Bos.-H.* 41 **D13**
Groais I., *Canada* 105 **B8**
Grobiņa, *Latvia* 30 **B8**
Groblersdal, *S. Africa* 89 **D4**
Grobming, *Austria* 26 **D6**
Grocka, *Serbia & M.* 44 **B4**
Gródek, *Poland* 31 **E10**
Grodków, *Poland* 31 **H4**
Grodno = Hrodna, *Belarus* 32 **F2**
Grodzisk Mazowiecki, *Poland* 31 **F7**
Grodzisk Wielkopolski, *Poland* 31 **F3**
Grodzyanka = Hrodzyanka, *Belarus* 32 **F5**
Groesbeck, *U.S.A.* 113 **K6**
Groix, *France* 18 **E3**
Groix, Î. de, *France* 18 **E3**
Grójec, *Poland* 31 **G7**
Gronau, *Niedersachsen, Germany* 24 **C5**
Gronau, *Nordrhein-Westfalen, Germany* 24 **C3**
Grong, *Norway* 8 **D15**
Grönhögen, *Sweden* 11 **H10**
Groningen, *Neths.* 17 **A6**
Groningen □, *Neths.* 17 **A6**
Groom, *U.S.A.* 113 **H4**
Groot →, *S. Africa* 88 **E3**
Groot Berg →, *S. Africa* 88 **E2**
Groot-Brakrivier, *S. Africa* 88 **E3**
Groot Karasberge, *Namibia* 88 **D2**
Groot-Kei →, *S. Africa* 89 **E4**
Groot Vis →, *S. Africa* 88 **E4**
Grootdrink, *S. Africa* 88 **D3**
Groote Eylandt, *Australia* 94 **A2**
Grootfontein, *Namibia* 88 **B2**
Grootlaagte →, *Africa* 88 **C3**
Grootvloer →, *S. Africa* 88 **E3**
Gros C., *Canada* 102 **A6**
Gros Islet, *St. Lucia* 121 **f**
Gros Morne △, *Canada* 105 **C8**
Gros Piton, *St. Lucia* 121 **f**
Gros Piton Pt., *St. Lucia* 121 **f**
Grósio, *Italy* 40 **B7**
Grosne →, *France* 19 **F11**
Grossa, Pta., *Spain* 48 **B8**
Grossenbrode, *Germany* 24 **A7**
Grossenhain, *Germany* 24 **D9**
Grosser Arber, *Germany* 25 **F9**
Grosser Plöner See, *Germany* 24 **A6**
Grosseto, *Italy* 41 **F8**
Grossgerungs, *Austria* 26 **C7**
Grossglockner, *Austria* 26 **D5**
Groswater B., *Canada* 105 **B8**
Groton, *Conn., U.S.A.* 117 **E12**
Groton, *N.Y., U.S.A.* 117 **D8**
Groton, *S. Dak., U.S.A.* 112 **C5**
Grottáglie, *Italy* 43 **B10**
Grottaminarda, *Italy* 43 **A8**
Grottammare, *Italy* 41 **F10**
Grouard Mission, *Canada* 102 **B5**
Grouin, Pte. du, *France* 18 **D5**
Groundhog →, *Canada* 104 **C3**
Grouw, *Neths.* 17 **A5**
Grove City, *U.S.A.* 116 **E4**
Grove Hill, *U.S.A.* 115 **K2**
Groveland, *U.S.A.* 110 **H6**
Grover City, *U.S.A.* 111 **K6**
Groves, *U.S.A.* 113 **L8**
Groveton, *U.S.A.* 117 **B13**
Grožnjan, *Croatia* 41 **C10**
Groznyy, *Russia* 35 **J7**
Grubišno Polje, *Croatia* 28 **E2**
Grudovo, *Bulgaria* 45 **D11**
Grudusk, *Poland* 31 **E7**
Grudziądz, *Poland* 30 **E5**
Gruinard B., *U.K.* 13 **D3**
Gruissan, *France* 20 **E7**
Grumo Áppula, *Italy* 43 **A9**
Grums, *Sweden* 10 **E7**
Grünberg, *Germany* 24 **E4**
Gründau, *Germany* 25 **E5**
Grundy Center, *U.S.A.* 112 **D8**
Grünstadt, *Germany* 25 **F4**
Gruppo di Tessa ⌂, *Italy* 40 **B8**
Gruvberget, *Sweden* 10 **C10**
Gruver, *U.S.A.* 113 **G4**
Gruyères, *Switz.* 25 **J3**
Gruža, *Serbia & M.* 44 **C4**
Gryazi, *Russia* 33 **F10**
Gryazovets, *Russia* 32 **C11**
Grybów, *Poland* 31 **J7**
Grycksbo, *Sweden* 10 **D9**
Gryfice, *Poland* 30 **E2**
Gryfino, *Poland* 31 **E1**
Gryfów Śląski, *Poland* 31 **G2**
Grythyttan, *Sweden* 10 **E8**
Gstaad, *Switz.* 25 **J3**
Gua, *India* 67 **H14**
Gua Musang, *Malaysia* 65 **K3**
Guacanayabo, G. de, *Cuba* 120 **B4**
Guachípas →, *Argentina* 126 **B2**
Guadajoz →, *Spain* 37 **H6**

Guadalajara, *Mexico* 118 C4
Guadalajara, *Spain* 38 E1
Guadalajara □, *Spain* 38 E2
Guadalcanal, *Solomon Is.* 96 H8
Guadalcanal, *Spain* 37 G5
Guadalén →, *Spain* 37 G7
Guadales, *Argentina* 126 C2
Guadalete →, *Spain* 37 J4
Guadalimar →, *Spain* 37 G7
Guadalmena →, *Spain* 37 G8
Guadalmez →, *Spain* 37 G5
Guadalope →, *Spain* 38 D4
Guadalquivir →, *Spain* 37 J4
Guadalupe = Guadeloupe ⊠, *W. Indies* 120 b
Guadalupe, *Mexico* 111 N10
Guadalupe, *Spain* 37 F5
Guadalupe, *U.S.A.* 111 L6
Guadalupe →, *Mexico* 111 N10
Guadalupe →, *U.S.A.* 113 L6
Guadalupe, Sierra de, *Spain* 37 F5
Guadalupe Bravos, *Mexico* 118 A3
Guadalupe I., *Pac. Oc.* 98 G8
Guadalupe Mts. △, *U.S.A.* 113 K2
Guadalupe Peak, *U.S.A.* 113 K2
Guadalupe y Calvo, *Mexico* 118 B3
Guadarrama, Sierra de, *Spain* 36 E7
Guadauta, *Georgia* 35 J5
Guadeloupe △, *Guadeloupe* 120 b
Guadeloupe ⊠, *W. Indies* 120 b
Guadeloupe Passage, *W. Indies* 121 C7
Guadiamar →, *Spain* 37 J4
Guadiana →, *Portugal* 37 H3
Guadiana Menor →, *Spain* 37 H7
Guadiaro →, *Spain* 37 J5
Guadiato →, *Spain* 37 H5
Guadiela →, *Spain* 38 E2
Guadix, *Spain* 37 H7
Guafo, Boca del, *Chile* 128 E2
Guaico, *Trin. & Tob.* 125 K15
Guainía →, *Colombia* 124 C5
Guaíra, *Brazil* 127 A5
Guaíra □, *Paraguay* 126 B4
Guaitecas, Is., *Chile* 128 E2
Guajará-Mirim, *Brazil* 124 F5
Guajira, Pen. de la, *Colombia* 124 A4
Gualán, *Guatemala* 120 C2
Gualdo Tadino, *Italy* 41 E9
Gualeguay, *Argentina* 126 C4
Gualeguaychú, *Argentina* 126 C4
Gualequay →, *Argentina* 126 C4
Guam ⊠, *Pac. Oc.* 96 F6
Guaminí, *Argentina* 126 D3
Guamúchil, *Mexico* 118 B3
Guana I., *Br. Virgin Is.* 121 e
Guanabacoa, *Cuba* 120 B3
Guanacaste △, *Costa Rica* 120 D2
Guanacaste, Cordillera del, *Costa Rica* 120 D2
Guanaceví, *Mexico* 118 B3
Guanahani = San Salvador I., *Bahamas* 121 B5
Guanajay, *Cuba* 120 B3
Guanajuato, *Mexico* 118 C4
Guanajuato □, *Mexico* 118 C4
Guandacol, *Argentina* 126 B2
Guane, *Cuba* 120 B3
Guang'an, *China* 58 B6
Guangchang, *China* 59 D11
Guangde, *China* 59 B12
Guangdong □, *China* 59 F9
Guangfeng, *China* 59 C12
Guanghan, *China* 58 B5
Guangling, *China* 56 E8
Guangnan, *China* 58 E5
Guangning, *China* 59 F9
Guangrao, *China* 57 F10
Guangshui, *China* 59 B9
Guangshun, *China* 58 D6
Guangwu, *China* 56 F3
Guangxi Zhuangzu Zizhiqu □, *China* 58 F7
Guangyuan, *China* 58 A5
Guangze, *China* 59 D11
Guangzhou, *China* 59 F9
Guanica, *Puerto Rico* 121 d
Guanipa →, *Venezuela* 124 B6
Guanling, *China* 58 E5
Guannan, *China* 57 G10
Guantánamo, *Cuba* 121 B4
Guantánamo B., *Cuba* 121 C4
Guantao, *China* 56 F8
Guanyang, *China* 59 E8
Guanyun, *China* 57 G10
Guápiles, *Costa Rica* 120 D3
Guapo B., *Trin. & Tob.* 125 K15
Guaporé, *Brazil* 127 B5
Guaporé →, *Brazil* 124 F5
Guaqui, *Bolivia* 124 G5
Guara, Sierra de, *Spain* 38 C4
Guaramacal △, *Venezuela* 121 E5
Guaramacal △, *Venezuela* 121 E5
Guarapari, *Brazil* 127 A7
Guarapuava, *Brazil* 127 B5
Guaratinguetá, *Brazil* 127 A6
Guaratuba, *Brazil* 127 B6
Guarda, *Portugal* 36 E3
Guarda □, *Portugal* 36 E3
Guardafui, C. = Asir, Ras, *Somali Rep.* 75 E5
Guardamar del Segura, *Spain* 39 G4
Guardavalle, *Italy* 43 D9
Guárdia Sanframondi, *Italy* 43 A7
Guardiagrele, *Italy* 41 F11
Guardo, *Spain* 36 C6
Guareña, *Spain* 37 G4
Guareña →, *Spain* 36 D5
Guárico □, *Venezuela* 124 B5
Guarujá, *Brazil* 127 A6
Guarulhos, *Brazil* 127 A6
Guarus, *Brazil* 127 A7
Guasave, *Mexico* 118 B3
Guasdualito, *Venezuela* 124 B4
Guastalla, *Italy* 40 D7
Guatemala, *Guatemala* 120 D1
Guatemala ■, *Cent. Amer.* 120 C1
Guatopo △, *Venezuela* 121 D6
Guatuaro Pt., *Trin. & Tob.* 125 K16
Guaviare →, *Colombia* 124 C5
Guaxupé, *Brazil* 127 A6
Guayaguayare, *Trin. & Tob.* 125 K15
Guayama, *Puerto Rico* 121 d
Guayaquil, *Ecuador* 124 D3
Guayaquil, G. de, *Ecuador* 124 D2
Guaymas, *Mexico* 118 B2
Guba, *Dem. Rep. of the Congo* 87 E2
Guba, *Ethiopia* 81 E4
Gûbâl, Madîq, *Egypt* 80 B3
Gubat, *Phil.* 61 E6
Gúbbio, *Italy* 41 E9
Guben, *Germany* 24 D10
Gubin, *Poland* 31 G1
Gubio, *Nigeria* 83 C7
Gubkin, *Russia* 33 G9
Guča, *Serbia & M.* 44 C4
Gucheng, *China* 59 A8
Gudata = Guadauta, *Georgia* 35 J5
Gudbrandsdalen, *Norway* 9 F14
Guddu Barrage, *Pakistan* 66 E6
Gudenå →, *Denmark* 11 H4
Gudermes, *Russia* 35 J8
Gudhjem, *Denmark* 11 J8
Gudur, *India* 66 M11
Guebwiller, *France* 19 E14
Guecho = Getxo, *Spain* 38 B2
Guékédou, *Guinea* 82 D2
Guéle Mendouka, *Cameroon* 83 E7
Guelmine = Goulimine, *Morocco* 78 C3
Guelph, *Canada* 116 C4
Guéméné-Penfao, *France* 18 E5
Guéméné-sur-Scorff, *France* 18 D3
Guéné, *Benin* 83 C5
Guer, *France* 18 E4
Guérande, *France* 18 E4
Guéret, *France* 19 F8
Guérigny, *France* 19 E10
Guerneville, *U.S.A.* 110 G4
Guernica = Gernika-Lumo, *Spain* 38 B2
Guernsey, *U.K.* 15 H5
Guernsey, *U.S.A.* 112 D2
Guerrero □, *Mexico* 119 D5
Guessou-Sud, *Benin* 83 C5
Gueugnon, *France* 19 F11
Guéyo, *Ivory C.* 82 D3
Gughe, *Ethiopia* 81 F4
Gügher, *Iran* 71 D8
Guglionesi, *Italy* 41 G11
Guhakolak, Tanjung, *Indonesia* 63 G11
Gui Jiang →, *China* 59 F8
Guia, *Canary Is.* 48 F4
Guia de Isora, *Canary Is.* 48 F3
Guia Lopes da Laguna, *Brazil* 127 A4
Guiana Highlands, *S. Amer.* 122 C4
Guibéroua, *Ivory C.* 82 D3
Guichi, *China* 59 B11
Guider, *Cameroon* 83 D7
Guidiguir, *Niger* 83 C6
Guidimouni, *Niger* 83 C6
Guiding, *China* 58 D6
Guidong, *China* 59 D9
Guidónia-Montecélio, *Italy* 41 F9
Guiers, L. de, *Senegal* 82 B1
Guigang, *China* 58 F7
Guiglo, *Ivory C.* 82 D3
Guihulñgan, *Phil.* 61 F5
Guijá, *Mozam.* 89 C5
Guijuelo, *Spain* 36 E5
Guildford, *U.K.* 15 F7
Guilford, *U.S.A.* 117 E12
Guilin, *China* 59 E8
Guillaume-Delisle, L., *Canada* 104 A4
Guillaumes, *France* 21 D10
Guillestre, *France* 21 D10
Guilvinec, *France* 18 E2
Güimar, *Canary Is.* 48 F3
Guimarães, *Portugal* 36 D2
Guimaras □, *Phil.* 61 F5
Guinda, *U.S.A.* 110 G4
Guinea, *Africa* 76 F4
Guinea ■, *W. Afr.* 82 C2
Guinea, Gulf of, *Atl. Oc.* 83 E5
Guinea-Bissau ■, *Africa* 82 C2
Güines, *Cuba* 120 B3
Guingamp, *France* 18 D3
Guinguinéo, *Senegal* 82 C1
Guipavas, *France* 18 D2
Guiping, *China* 59 F8
Guipúzcoa □, *Spain* 38 B2
Guir, *Mali* 82 B4
Guirel, *Mauritania* 82 B3
Güiria, *Venezuela* 124 A6
Guiscard, *France* 19 C10
Guise, *France* 19 C10
Guitiriz, *Spain* 36 B3
Guitri, *Ivory C.* 82 D3
Guiuan, *Phil.* 61 F6
Guixi, *China* 59 C11
Guiyang, *Guizhou, China* 58 D6
Guiyang, *Hunan, China* 59 E9
Guizhou □, *China* 58 D6
Gujan-Mestras, *France* 20 D2
Gujar Khan, *Pakistan* 68 C5
Gujarat □, *India* 68 H4
Gujiang, *China* 59 D10
Gujranwala, *Pakistan* 68 C6
Gujrat, *Pakistan* 68 C6
Gukovo, *Russia* 35 F5
Gulbarga, *India* 66 L10
Gulbene, *Latvia* 9 H22
Gulf, The, *Asia* 71 E6
Gulf Islands ⌂, *U.S.A.* 115 E2
Gulfport, *U.S.A.* 113 K10
Gulgong, *Australia* 95 E4
Gulin, *China* 58 C5
Gulistan, *Pakistan* 68 D2
Gull Lake, *Canada* 103 C7
Gullbrandstorp, *Sweden* 11 H6
Gullspång, *Sweden* 11 F8
Güllük, *Turkey* 47 D9
Gulluk Daği △, *Turkey* 47 E12
Güllük Korfezi, *Turkey* 47 D9
Gulma, *Nigeria* 83 C5
Gulmarg, *India* 69 B6
Gülnar, *Turkey* 72 D5
Gülpınar, *Turkey* 47 B8
Gülşehir, *Turkey* 72 C6
Gulshad, *Kazakhstan* 52 E8
Gulu, *Uganda* 86 B3
Gŭlŭbovo, *Bulgaria* 45 D9
Gulud, J., *Sudan* 81 E2
Gulwe, *Tanzania* 86 D4
Gulyaypole = Hulyaypole, *Ukraine* 33 J9
Gumal →, *Pakistan* 68 D4
Gumbaz, *Pakistan* 68 D3
Gumel, *Nigeria* 83 C6
Gumiel de Hizán, *Spain* 36 D7
Gumla, *India* 69 H11
Gumlu, *Australia* 94 B4
Gumma □, *Japan* 55 F9
Gummersbach, *Germany* 24 D3
Gummi, *Nigeria* 83 C6
Gümüldür, *Turkey* 47 C9
Gümüşçay, *Turkey* 45 F11
Gümüşhaciköy, *Turkey* 72 B6
Gümüşhane, *Turkey* 73 B8
Gümüşsu, *Turkey* 47 C11
Gumzai, *Indonesia* 63 F8
Guna, *Ethiopia* 81 F4
Guna, *India* 68 G7
Gundelfingen, *Germany* 25 G6
Güney, *Burdur, Turkey* 47 D11
Güney, *Denizli, Turkey* 47 C11
Güneydoğu Toroslar, *Turkey* 73 C9
Gunisao →, *Canada* 103 C9
Gunisao L., *Canada* 103 C9
Gunjyal, *Pakistan* 68 C4
Günlüce, *Turkey* 47 E10
Gunnarskog, *Sweden* 10 E6
Gunnbjørn Fjeld, *Greenland* 4 C6
Gunnebo, *Sweden* 11 G10
Gunnedah, *Australia* 95 E5
Gunnewin, *Australia* 95 D4
Gunningbar Cr. →, *Australia* 95 E4
Gunnison, *Colo., U.S.A.* 109 G10
Gunnison, *Utah, U.S.A.* 108 G8
Gunnison →, *U.S.A.* 109 G9
Gunpowder, *Australia* 94 B2
Guntakal, *India* 66 M10
Guntersville, *U.S.A.* 115 H2
Guntong, *Malaysia* 65 K3
Guntur, *India* 67 L12
Gunungapi, *Indonesia* 63 F7
Gunungsitoli, *Indonesia* 62 D1
Günz →, *Germany* 25 G6
Gunza, *Angola* 84 G2
Günzburg, *Germany* 25 G6
Gunzenhausen, *Germany* 25 F6
Guo He →, *China* 57 H9
Guoyang, *China* 56 H9
Gupis, *Pakistan* 69 A5
Gura Humorului, *Romania* 29 C10
Gura-Teghii, *Romania* 29 E11
Gurag, *Ethiopia* 81 F4
Gurahonţ, *Romania* 28 D7
Gurdaspur, *India* 68 C6
Gurdon, *U.S.A.* 113 J8
Güre, *Balıkesir, Turkey* 47 B8
Güre, *Uşak, Turkey* 47 C11
Gurgaon, *India* 68 E7
Gürgentepe, *Turkey* 72 B7
Gurghiu, Munţii, *Romania* 29 D10
Gurgueia →, *Brazil* 125 E10
Gurha, *India* 68 G4
Guri, Embalse de, *Venezuela* 124 B6
Gurig △, *Australia* 92 B5
Gurin, *Nigeria* 83 D7
Gurjaani, *Georgia* 35 K7
Gurk →, *Austria* 26 E7
Gurkha, *Nepal* 69 E11
Gurley, *Australia* 95 D4
Gurnet Point, *U.S.A.* 117 D14
Guro, *Mozam.* 87 F3
Gürpınar, *İst., Turkey* 45 F12
Gürpınar, *Van, Turkey* 73 C10
Gürsu, *Turkey* 45 F13
Gurué, *Mozam.* 87 F4
Gurun, *Malaysia* 65 K3
Gürün, *Turkey* 72 C7
Gurupá, *Brazil* 125 D8
Gurupá, I. Grande de, *Brazil* 125 D8
Gurupi, *Brazil* 125 F9
Gurupi →, *Brazil* 125 D9
Guruwe, *Zimbabwe* 89 B5
Guryev = Atyraū, *Kazakhstan* 52 E6
Gus-Khrustalnyy, *Russia* 34 C5
Gusau, *Nigeria* 83 C6
Gusev, *Russia* 9 J20
Gushan, *China* 57 E12
Gushgy, *Turkmenistan* 52 F7
Gushi, *China* 59 A10
Gushiago, *Ghana* 83 D4
Gusinje, *Serbia & M.* 44 D3
Gusinoozersk, *Russia* 53 D11
Gúspini, *Italy* 42 C1
Güssing, *Austria* 27 D9
Gustavsberg, *Sweden* 10 E12
Gustavus, *U.S.A.* 102 B1
Gustine, *U.S.A.* 110 H6
Güstrow, *Germany* 24 B8
Gusum, *Sweden* 11 F10
Guta = Kolárovo, *Slovak Rep.* 27 D10
Gütersloh, *Germany* 24 D4
Gutha, *Australia* 93 E2
Guthalungra, *Australia* 94 B4
Guthrie, *Okla., U.S.A.* 113 H6
Guthrie, *Tex., U.S.A.* 113 J4
Gutian, *China* 59 D12
Guttenberg, *U.S.A.* 112 D9
Gutu, *Zimbabwe* 89 B5
Guwahati, *India* 67 F17
Guy Fawkes River △, *Australia* 95 D5
Guyana ■, *S. Amer.* 124 C7
Guyane française = French Guiana ⊠, *S. Amer.* 125 C8
Guyang, *China* 56 D6
Guyenne, *France* 20 D4
Guymon, *U.S.A.* 113 G4
Guyra, *Australia* 95 E5
Guyuan, *Hebei, China* 56 D8
Guyuan, *Ningxia Huizu, China* 56 G4
Güzelbahçe, *Turkey* 47 C8
Güzelyurt = Morphou, *Cyprus* 49 D11
Guzhang, *China* 58 C7
Guzhen, *China* 57 H9
Guzmán, L. de, *Mexico* 118 A3
Gvardeysk, *Russia* 9 J19
Gvardeyskoye, *Ukraine* 33 K8
Gwa, *Burma* 67 L19
Gwaai, *Zimbabwe* 87 F2
Gwaai →, *Zimbabwe* 87 F2
Gwabegar, *Australia* 95 E4
Gwadabawa, *Nigeria* 83 C6
Gwādar, *Pakistan* 66 G3
Gwagwada, *Nigeria* 83 C6
Gwaii Haanas △, *Canada* 102 C2
Gwalior, *India* 68 F8
Gwanara, *Nigeria* 83 D5
Gwanda, *Zimbabwe* 87 G2
Gwandu, *Nigeria* 83 C5
Gwane, *Dem. Rep. of the Congo* 86 B2
Gwaram, *Nigeria* 83 C7
Gwarzo, *Nigeria* 83 C6
Gwasero, *Nigeria* 83 D5
Gwda →, *Poland* 31 E3
Gweebarra B., *Ireland* 12 B3
Gweedore, *Ireland* 12 A3
Gweru, *Zimbabwe* 87 F2
Gwi, *Nigeria* 83 D6
Gwinn, *U.S.A.* 114 B2
Gwio Kura, *Nigeria* 83 C7
Gwoza, *Nigeria* 83 C7
Gwydir →, *Australia* 95 D4
Gwynedd □, *U.K.* 14 E3
Gyandzha = Gäncä, *Azerbaijan* 35 K8
Gyaring Hu, *China* 60 C4
Gydanskiy Poluostrov, *Russia* 52 C8
Gympie, *Australia* 95 D5
Gyomaendrőd, *Hungary* 28 D5
Gyöngyös, *Hungary* 28 C4
Győr, *Hungary* 28 C2
Győr-Moson-Sopron □, *Hungary* 28 C2
Gypsum Pt., *Canada* 102 A6
Gypsumville, *Canada* 103 C9
Gyueshevo, *Bulgaria* 44 D6
Gyula, *Hungary* 28 D6
Gyumri, *Armenia* 35 K6
Gyzylarbat, *Turkmenistan* 52 F6
Gyzyletrek, *Turkmenistan* 71 B7
Gzhatsk = Gagarin, *Russia* 32 E8

H

Ha 'Arava →, *Israel* 74 E4
Ha Coi, *Vietnam* 58 G6
Ha Dong, *Vietnam* 58 G5
Ha Giang, *Vietnam* 58 F5
Ha Karmel △, *Israel* 74 C4
Ha Tien, *Vietnam* 65 G5
Ha Tinh, *Vietnam* 64 C5
Ha Trung, *Vietnam* 64 C5
Ha Yaek Chalong, *Thailand* 65 a
Haaksbergen, *Neths.* 17 B6
Haapsalu, *Estonia* 9 G20
Haarlem, *Neths.* 17 B4
Haast →, *N.Z.* 91 K2
Haast Bluff, *Australia* 92 D5
Hab →, *Pakistan* 68 G3
Hab Nadi Chauki, *Pakistan* 68 G2
Habahe, *China* 60 B3
Habaswein, *Kenya* 86 B4
Habay, *Canada* 102 B5
Ḩabbānīyah, *Iraq* 70 C4
Ḩabbānīyah, Hawr al, *Iraq* 73 F10
Habichtswald ⌂, *Germany* 24 D5
Habo, *Sweden* 11 G8
Haboro, *Japan* 54 B10
Ḩabshān, *U.A.E.* 71 F7
Hachenburg, *Germany* 24 E3
Hachijō-Jima, *Japan* 55 H9
Hachinohe, *Japan* 54 D10
Hachiōji, *Japan* 55 G9
Hachŏn, *N. Korea* 57 D15
Hacıbektaş, *Turkey* 72 C6
Hacılar, *Turkey* 72 C6
Hackås, *Sweden* 10 B8
Hackensack, *U.S.A.* 117 F10
Hackettstown, *U.S.A.* 117 F10
Hadali, *Pakistan* 68 C5
Hadarba, Ras, *Sudan* 80 C4
Hadarom □, *Israel* 74 E4
Ḩadd, Ra's al, *Oman* 75 C6
Haddington, *U.K.* 13 F6
Hadejia, *Nigeria* 83 C7
Hadejia →, *Nigeria* 83 C7
Ḩadera, *Israel* 74 C3
Ḩadera, N. →, *Israel* 74 C3
Haderslev, *Denmark* 11 J3
Hadhramaut = Ḩaḑramawt, *Yemen* 75 D4
Hadiboh, *Yemen* 75 E5
Hadım, *Turkey* 72 D5
Hadong, *S. Korea* 57 G14
Ḩaḑramawt, *Yemen* 75 D4
Ḩadrānīyah, *Iraq* 70 C4
Hadrian's Wall, *U.K.* 14 B5
Hadsten, *Denmark* 11 H4
Hadsund, *Denmark* 11 H4
Hadyach, *Ukraine* 33 G8
Haeju, *N. Korea* 57 E13
Haenam, *S. Korea* 57 G14
Haenertsburg, *S. Africa* 89 C4
Haerhpin = Harbin, *China* 57 B14
Hafar al Bāţin, *Si. Arabia* 70 D5
Hafik, *Turkey* 72 C7
Ḩafīrat al 'Aydā, *Si. Arabia* 70 E3
Ḩafit, *Oman* 71 F7
Hafizabad, *Pakistan* 68 C5
Haflong, *India* 67 G18
Hafnarfjörður, *Iceland* 8 D3
Haft Gel, *Iran* 71 D6
Hafun, Ras, *Somali Rep.* 75 E5
Hagalil, *Israel* 74 C4
Hagby, *Sweden* 11 H10
Hagen, *Germany* 24 D3
Hagenow, *Germany* 24 B7
Hagerman, *U.S.A.* 113 J2
Hagerman Fossil Beds ⌂, *U.S.A.* 108 E6
Hagerstown, *U.S.A.* 114 F7
Hagersville, *Canada* 116 D4
Hagetmau, *France* 20 E3
Hagfors, *Sweden* 10 D7
Hagi, *Japan* 55 G5
Hagolan, *Syria* 74 C4
Hagondange, *France* 19 C13
Hags Hd., *Ireland* 12 D2
Hague, C. de la, *France* 18 C5
Hague, The = 's-Gravenhage, *Neths.* 17 B4
Haguenau, *France* 19 D14
Hai Duong, *Vietnam* 58 G6
Hai'an, *Guangdong, China* 59 G8
Hai'an, *Jiangsu, China* 59 A13
Haicheng, *Fujian, China* 59 E11
Haicheng, *Liaoning, China* 57 D12
Haidar Khel, *Afghan.* 68 C3
Haidarâbâd = Hyderabad, *India* 66 L11
Haidargarh, *India* 69 F9
Haifa = Ḩefa, *Israel* 74 C4
Haifeng, *China* 59 F10
Haiger, *Germany* 24 E4
Haikou, *China* 60 D6
Ḩā'il, *Si. Arabia* 70 E4
Hailar, *China* 60 B6
Hailey, *U.S.A.* 108 E6
Haileybury, *Canada* 104 C4
Hailin, *China* 57 B15
Hailing Dao, *China* 59 G8
Hailong, *China* 57 C13
Hailuoto, *Finland* 8 D21
Haimen, *Guangdong, China* 59 F11
Haimen, *Jiangsu, China* 59 B13
Hainan □, *China* 60 E5
Hainaut □, *Belgium* 17 D4
Hainburg, *Austria* 27 C9
Haines, *Alaska, U.S.A.* 102 B1
Haines, *Oreg., U.S.A.* 108 D5
Haines City, *U.S.A.* 115 L5
Haines Junction, *Canada* 102 A1
Hainfeld, *Austria* 26 C8
Haining, *China* 59 B13
Haiphong, *Vietnam* 58 G6
Haitan Dao, *China* 59 E12
Haiti ■, *W. Indies* 121 C5
Haiya, *Sudan* 80 D4
Haiyan, *China* 59 B13
Haiyang, *China* 57 F11
Haiyuan, *Guangxi Zhuangzu, China* 58 F6
Haiyuan, *Ningxia Huizu, China* 56 F3
Haizhou, *China* 57 G10
Haizhou Wan, *China* 57 G10
Hajdú-Bihar □, *Hungary* 28 C6
Hajdúböszörmény, *Hungary* 28 C6
Hajdúdorog, *Hungary* 28 C6
Hajdúhadház, *Hungary* 28 C6
Hajdúnánás, *Hungary* 28 C6
Hajdúsámson, *Hungary* 28 C6
Hajdúszoboszló, *Hungary* 28 C6
Hajipur, *India* 69 G11
Ḩājjī Muḩsin, *Iraq* 70 C5
Ḩājjīābād, *Iran* 71 D7
Ḩājjīābād-e Zarrīn, *Iran* 71 C7
Hajnówka, *Poland* 31 F10
Hakansson, Mts., *Dem. Rep. of the Congo* 87 D2
Hakkâri, *Turkey* 70 B4
Hakkâri Dağları, *Turkey* 73 C10
Hakken-Zan, *Japan* 55 G7
Hakodate, *Japan* 54 D10
Hakos, *Namibia* 88 C2
Håksberg, *Sweden* 10 D9
Haku-San, *Japan* 55 F8
Haku-San △, *Japan* 55 F8
Hakui, *Japan* 55 F8
Hala, *Pakistan* 66 G6
Ḩalab, *Syria* 70 B3
Ḩalabjah, *Iraq* 70 C5
Halaib, *Sudan* 80 C4
Halasa, *Sudan* 81 E3
Hālat 'Ammār, *Si. Arabia* 70 D3
Halbā, *Lebanon* 74 A5
Halberstadt, *Germany* 24 D7
Halcombe, *N.Z.* 91 J5
Halcon, *Phil.* 63 B6
Halden, *Norway* 9 G14
Haldensleben, *Germany* 24 C7
Haldia, *India* 67 H16
Haldimand, *Canada* 116 D5
Haldwani, *India* 69 E8
Hale →, *Australia* 94 C2
Halesowen, *U.K.* 15 E5

Halesworth, *U.K.* 15 E9
Haleyville, *U.S.A.* 115 H2
Half Assini, *Ghana* 82 D4
Halfmoon Bay, *N.Z.* 91 M2
Halfway →, *Canada* 102 B4
Halia, *India* 69 G10
Haliburton, *Canada* 116 A6
Halifax, *Australia* 94 B4
Halifax, *Canada* 105 D7
Halifax, *U.K.* 14 D6
Halifax, *U.S.A.* 116 F8
Halifax B., *Australia* 94 B4
Halifax I., *Namibia* 88 D2
Halīl →, *Iran* 71 E8
Halkirk, *U.K.* 13 C5
Hall Beach = Sanirajak, *Canada* 101 B11
Hall in Tirol, *Austria* 26 D4
Hall Pen., *Canada* 101 B13
Hall Pt., *Australia* 92 C3
Hallabro, *Sweden* 11 H9
Halland, *Sweden* 9 H15
Hallands län □, *Sweden* 11 H6
Hallands Väderö, *Sweden* 11 H6
Hallandsås, *Sweden* 11 H7
Hällbybrunn, *Sweden* 10 E10
Halle, *Belgium* 17 D4
Halle, *Nordrhein-Westfalen, Germany* 24 C4
Halle, *Sachsen-Anhalt, Germany* 24 D7
Hällefors, *Sweden* 10 E8
Hälleforsnäs, *Sweden* 10 E10
Hallein, *Austria* 26 D6
Hällekis, *Sweden* 11 F7
Hallen, *Sweden* 10 A8
Hallett, *Australia* 95 E2
Hallettsville, *U.S.A.* 113 L6
Hallim, *S. Korea* 57 H14
Hallingdalselvi →, *Norway* 9 F13
Hallock, *U.S.A.* 112 A6
Halls Creek, *Australia* 92 C4
Hallsberg, *Sweden* 10 E9
Hallstahammar, *Sweden* 10 E10
Hallstatt, *Austria* 26 D6
Hallstavik, *Sweden* 10 D12
Hallstead, *U.S.A.* 117 E9
Halmahera, *Indonesia* 63 D7
Halmeu, *Romania* 28 C8
Halmstad, *Sweden* 11 H6
Hals, *Denmark* 11 H4
Hälsingborg = Helsingborg, *Sweden* 11 H6
Hälsingland, *Sweden* 10 C10
Halstead, *U.K.* 15 F8
Haltern, *Germany* 24 D3
Halti, *Finland* 8 B19
Halton □, *U.K.* 14 D5
Haltwhistle, *U.K.* 14 C5
Ḩālūl, *Qatar* 71 E7
Halvad, *India* 68 H4
Ḩalvān, *Iran* 71 C8
Ham, *France* 19 C10
Ham Tan, *Vietnam* 65 G6
Ham Yen, *Vietnam* 64 A5
Hamab, *Namibia* 88 D2
Hamad, *Sudan* 81 D3
Hamada, *Japan* 55 G6
Hamadān, *Iran* 71 C6
Hamadān □, *Iran* 71 C6
Hamāh, *Syria* 70 C3
Hamamatsu, *Japan* 55 G8
Hamar, *Norway* 9 F14
Hamâta, Gebel, *Egypt* 70 E2
Hambantota, *Sri Lanka* 66 R12
Hamber ⌓, *Canada* 102 C5
Hamburg, *Germany* 24 B5
Hamburg, *Ark., U.S.A.* 113 J9
Hamburg, *N.Y., U.S.A.* 116 D6
Hamburg, *Pa., U.S.A.* 117 F9
Hamburg □, *Germany* 24 B5
Hamburg Fuhlsbüttel ✕ (HAM), *Germany* 24 B5
Ḩamḑ, W. al →, *Si. Arabia* 70 E3
Hamden, *U.S.A.* 117 E12
Hamdibey, *Turkey* 47 B9
Häme, *Finland* 9 F20
Hämeenlinna, *Finland* 9 F21
Hamélé, *Ghana* 82 C4
Hamelin Pool, *Australia* 93 E1
Hameln, *Germany* 24 C5
Hamerkaz □, *Israel* 74 C3
Hamersley Ra., *Australia* 92 D2
Hamhung, *N. Korea* 57 E14
Hami, *China* 60 B4
Hamilton, *Australia* 95 F3
Hamilton, *Canada* 116 C5
Hamilton, *N.Z.* 91 G5
Hamilton, *U.K.* 13 F4
Hamilton, *Ala., U.S.A.* 115 H1
Hamilton, *Mont., U.S.A.* 108 C6
Hamilton, *N.Y., U.S.A.* 117 D9
Hamilton, *Ohio, U.S.A.* 114 F3
Hamilton, *Tex., U.S.A.* 113 K5
Hamilton →, *Australia* 94 C2
Hamilton City, *U.S.A.* 110 F4
Hamilton I., *Australia* 94 J6
Hamilton Inlet, *Canada* 105 B8
Hamilton Mt., *U.S.A.* 117 C10
Hamina, *Finland* 9 F22
Hamirpur, *H.P., India* 68 D7
Hamirpur, *Ut. P., India* 69 G9
Hamitabat, *Turkey* 45 E11
Hamlet, *U.S.A.* 115 H6
Hamley Bridge, *Australia* 95 E2
Hamlin = Hameln, *Germany* 24 C5
Hamlin, *N.Y., U.S.A.* 116 C7
Hamlin, *Tex., U.S.A.* 113 J4
Hamm, *Germany* 24 D3
Ḩammār, Hawr al, *Iraq* 70 D5
Hammarstrand, *Sweden* 10 A10
Hammelburg, *Germany* 25 E5
Hammeren, *Denmark* 11 J8
Hammerfest, *Norway* 8 A20
Hammerum, *Denmark* 11 H3
Hamminkeln, *Germany* 24 D2
Hammond, *Ind., U.S.A.* 114 E2
Hammond, *La., U.S.A.* 113 K9
Hammond, *N.Y., U.S.A.* 117 B9
Hammondsport, *U.S.A.* 116 D7
Hammonton, *U.S.A.* 114 F8
Hamneda, *Sweden* 11 H7
Hamoyet, Jebel, *Sudan* 80 D4
Hampden, *N.Z.* 91 L3
Hampshire □, *U.K.* 15 F6
Hampshire Downs, *U.K.* 15 F6
Hampton, *N.B., Canada* 105 C6
Hampton, *Ont., Canada* 116 C6
Hampton, *Ark., U.S.A.* 113 J8
Hampton, *Iowa, U.S.A.* 112 D8
Hampton, *N.H., U.S.A.* 117 D14
Hampton, *S.C., U.S.A.* 115 J5
Hampton, *Va., U.S.A.* 114 G7
Hampton Bays, *U.S.A.* 117 F12
Hampton Tableland, *Australia* 93 F4
Hamra, *Sweden* 10 C8
Hamrat esh Sheykh, *Sudan* 81 E2
Hamur, *Turkey* 73 C10
Hamyang, *S. Korea* 57 G14
Han Jiang →, *China* 59 F11
Han Shui, *China* 58 A7
Han Shui →, *China* 59 B10
Hanak, *Si. Arabia* 70 E3
Hanamaki, *Japan* 54 E10
Hanang, *Tanzania* 86 C4
Hanau, *Germany* 25 E4
Hanbogd = Ihbulag, *Mongolia* 56 C4
Hançalar, *Turkey* 47 C11
Hâncești, *Moldova* 29 D13
Hancheng, *China* 56 G6
Hanchuan, *China* 59 B9
Hancock, *Mich., U.S.A.* 112 B10
Hancock, *N.Y., U.S.A.* 117 E9
Handa, *Japan* 55 G8
Handan, *China* 56 F8
Handeni, *Tanzania* 86 D4
Handlová, *Slovak Rep.* 27 C11
Handub, *Sudan* 80 D4
Handwara, *India* 69 B6
Hanegev, *Israel* 74 E4
Hanford, *U.S.A.* 110 J7
Hanford Reach ⌓, *U.S.A.* 108 C4
Hang Chat, *Thailand* 64 C2
Hang Dong, *Thailand* 64 C2
Hangang →, *S. Korea* 57 F14
Hangayn Nuruu, *Mongolia* 60 B4
Hangchou = Hangzhou, *China* 59 B13
Hanggin Houqi, *China* 56 D4
Hanggin Qi, *China* 56 E5
Hangu, *China* 57 E9
Hangzhou, *China* 59 B13
Hangzhou Wan, *China* 59 B13
Hanhongor, *Mongolia* 56 C3
Ḩanīdh, *Si. Arabia* 71 E6
Ḩanīsh, *Yemen* 75 E3
Haniska, *Slovak Rep.* 27 C14
Hanjiang, *China* 59 E12
Hankinson, *U.S.A.* 112 B6
Hanko, *Finland* 9 G20
Hankou, *China* 59 B10
Hanksville, *U.S.A.* 109 G8
Hanle, *India* 69 C8
Hanmer Springs, *N.Z.* 91 K4
Hann →, *Australia* 92 C4
Hann, Mt., *Australia* 92 C4
Hanna, *Canada* 102 C6
Hanna, *U.S.A.* 108 F10
Hannah B., *Canada* 104 B4
Hannibal, *Mo., U.S.A.* 112 F9
Hannibal, *N.Y., U.S.A.* 117 C8
Hannik, *Sudan* 80 D3
Hannover, *Germany* 24 C5
Hanö, *Sweden* 11 H8
Hanöbukten, *Sweden* 11 J8
Hanoi, *Vietnam* 58 G5
Hanover = Hannover, *Germany* 24 C5
Hanover, *Canada* 116 B3
Hanover, *S. Africa* 88 E3
Hanover, *N.H., U.S.A.* 117 C12
Hanover, *Ohio, U.S.A.* 116 F2
Hanover, *Pa., U.S.A.* 114 F7
Hanover, I., *Chile* 128 G2
Hans Lollik I., *U.S. Virgin Is.* 121 e
Hansdiha, *India* 69 G12
Hanshou, *China* 59 C8
Hansi, *India* 68 E6
Hanson, L., *Australia* 95 E2
Hanstholm, *Denmark* 11 G2
Hantsavichy, *Belarus* 33 F4
Hanumangarh, *India* 68 E6
Hanyin, *China* 58 A7
Hanyuan, *China* 58 C4
Hanzhong, *China* 56 H4
Hanzhuang, *China* 57 G9
Haora, *India* 69 H13
Haoxue, *China* 59 B9
Haparanda, *Sweden* 8 D21
Happy, *U.S.A.* 113 H4
Happy Camp, *U.S.A.* 108 F2
Happy Valley-Goose Bay, *Canada* 105 B7
Hapsu, *N. Korea* 57 D15
Hapur, *India* 68 E7
Ḩaql, *Si. Arabia* 74 F3
Har, *Indonesia* 63 F8
Har-Ayrag, *Mongolia* 56 B5
Har Hu, *China* 60 C4
Har Us Nuur, *Mongolia* 60 B4
Har Yehuda, *Israel* 74 D3
Ḩaraḑ, *Si. Arabia* 75 C4
Haradok, *Belarus* 32 E6
Häradsbäck, *Sweden* 11 H8
Haranomachi, *Japan* 54 F10
Harare, *Zimbabwe* 87 F3
Harat, *Eritrea* 81 D4
Harbin, *China* 57 B14
Harbiye, *Turkey* 72 D7
Harbo, *Sweden* 10 D11
Harboør, *Denmark* 11 H2
Harbor Beach, *U.S.A.* 116 C2
Harbour Breton, *Canada* 105 C8
Harbour Deep, *Canada* 105 B8
Harburg, *Germany* 24 B5
Harburger Berge ⌓, *Germany* 24 B5
Hårby, *Denmark* 11 J4
Harda, *India* 68 H7
Hardangerfjorden, *Norway* 9 F12
Hardangervidda, *Norway* 9 F12
Hardap ⌓, *Namibia* 88 C2
Hardap Dam, *Namibia* 88 C2
Hardenberg, *Neths.* 17 B6
Harderwijk, *Neths.* 17 B5
Hardey →, *Australia* 92 D2
Hardin, *U.S.A.* 108 D10
Harding, *S. Africa* 89 E4
Harding Ra., *Australia* 92 C3
Hardisty, *Canada* 102 C6
Hardoi, *India* 69 F9
Hardwar = Haridwar, *India* 68 E8
Hardwick, *U.S.A.* 117 B12
Hardy, Pen., *Chile* 128 H3
Hardy, Pte., *St. Lucia* 121 f
Hare B., *Canada* 105 B8
Hareid, *Norway* 9 E12
Haren, *Germany* 24 C3
Harer, *Ethiopia* 81 F5
Harerge □, *Ethiopia* 81 F5
Hareto, *Ethiopia* 81 F4
Harfleur, *France* 18 C7
Hargeisa, *Somali Rep.* 75 F3
Harghita □, *Romania* 29 D10
Harghita, Munții, *Romania* 29 D10
Hargshamn, *Sweden* 10 D12
Hari →, *Indonesia* 62 E2
Haria, *Canary Is.* 48 E6
Haridwar, *India* 68 E8
Harim, Jabal al, *Oman* 71 E8
Haringhata →, *Bangla.* 67 J16
Harīrūd →, *Asia* 66 A2
Härjedalen, *Sweden* 10 B7
Harlan, *Iowa, U.S.A.* 112 E7
Harlan, *Ky., U.S.A.* 115 G4
Hârlău, *Romania* 29 C11
Harlech, *U.K.* 14 E3
Harlem, *U.S.A.* 108 B9
Hårlev, *Denmark* 11 J6
Harlingen, *Neths.* 17 A5
Harlingen, *U.S.A.* 113 M6
Harlow, *U.K.* 15 F8
Harlowton, *U.S.A.* 108 C9
Harmancık, *Turkey* 47 B11
Harmånger, *Sweden* 10 C11
Harmil, *Eritrea* 81 D5
Harnai, *Pakistan* 68 D2
Harney Basin, *U.S.A.* 108 E4
Harney L., *U.S.A.* 108 E4
Harney Peak, *U.S.A.* 112 D3
Härnön, *Sweden* 10 B12
Härnösand, *Sweden* 10 B11
Haro, *Spain* 38 C2
Haroldswick, *U.K.* 13 A8
Harp L., *Canada* 105 A7
Harper, *Liberia* 82 E3
Harplinge, *Sweden* 11 H6
Harr, *Mauritania* 82 B2
Harrai, *India* 69 H8
Harrand, *Pakistan* 68 E4
Ḩarrat Khaybar, *Si. Arabia* 80 B5
Ḩarrat Nawāṣīf, *Si. Arabia* 80 C5
Harricana →, *Canada* 104 B4
Harriman, *U.S.A.* 115 H3
Harrington Harbour, *Canada* 105 B8
Harris, *U.K.* 13 D2
Harris, L., *Australia* 95 E2
Harris, Sd. of, *U.K.* 13 D1
Harris Pt., *Canada* 116 C2
Harrisburg, *Ill., U.S.A.* 113 G10
Harrisburg, *Nebr., U.S.A.* 112 E3
Harrisburg, *Pa., U.S.A.* 116 F8
Harrismith, *S. Africa* 89 D4
Harrison, *Ark., U.S.A.* 113 G8
Harrison, *Maine, U.S.A.* 117 B14
Harrison, *Nebr., U.S.A.* 112 D3
Harrison, C., *Canada* 105 B8
Harrison L., *Canada* 102 D4
Harrisonburg, *U.S.A.* 114 F6
Harrisonville, *U.S.A.* 112 F7
Harriston, *Canada* 116 C4
Harrisville, *Mich., U.S.A.* 116 B1
Harrisville, *N.Y., U.S.A.* 117 B9
Harrisville, *Pa., U.S.A.* 116 E5
Harrodsburg, *U.S.A.* 114 G3
Harrogate, *U.K.* 14 C6
Harrow □, *U.K.* 15 F7
Harrowsmith, *Canada* 117 B8
Harry S. Truman Reservoir, *U.S.A.* 112 F7
Harsefeld, *Germany* 24 B5
Harsewinkel, *Germany* 24 D4
Harsīn, *Iran* 70 C5
Hârșova, *Romania* 29 F12
Harstad, *Norway* 8 B17
Harsud, *India* 68 H7
Hart, *U.S.A.* 114 D2
Hart, L., *Australia* 95 E2
Hartbees →, *S. Africa* 88 D3
Hartberg, *Austria* 26 D8
Hartford, *Conn., U.S.A.* 117 E12
Hartford, *Ky., U.S.A.* 114 G2
Hartford, *S. Dak., U.S.A.* 112 D6
Hartford, *Wis., U.S.A.* 112 D10
Hartford City, *U.S.A.* 114 E3
Hartland, *Canada* 105 C6
Hartland Pt., *U.K.* 15 F3
Hartlepool, *U.K.* 14 C6
Hartlepool □, *U.K.* 14 C6
Hartley Bay, *Canada* 102 C3
Hartmannberge, *Namibia* 88 B1
Hartney, *Canada* 103 D8
Hârtop, *Moldova* 29 D13
Harts →, *S. Africa* 88 D3
Hartselle, *U.S.A.* 115 H2
Hartshorne, *U.S.A.* 113 H7
Hartstown, *U.S.A.* 116 E4
Hartsville, *U.S.A.* 115 H5
Hartswater, *S. Africa* 88 D3
Hartwell, *U.S.A.* 115 H4
Harunabad, *Pakistan* 68 E5
Harvand, *Iran* 71 D7
Harvey, *Australia* 93 F2
Harvey, *Ill., U.S.A.* 114 E2
Harvey, *N. Dak., U.S.A.* 112 B5
Harwich, *U.K.* 15 F9
Haryana □, *India* 68 E7
Haryn →, *Belarus* 33 F4
Harz, *Germany* 24 D6
Harz △, *Germany* 24 D6
Harzgerode, *Germany* 24 D7
Hasa □, *Si. Arabia* 71 E6
Hasaheisa, *Sudan* 81 E3
Ḩasanābād, *Iran* 71 C7
Ḩasb, W. →, *Iraq* 70 D5
Hasdo →, *India* 69 J10
Haselünne, *Germany* 24 C3
Hashimoto, *Japan* 55 G7
Hashtjerd, *Iran* 71 C6
Haskell, *U.S.A.* 113 J5
Hasköy, *Turkey* 45 E10
Haslach, *Germany* 25 G4
Hasle, *Denmark* 11 J8
Haslemere, *U.K.* 15 F7
Haslev, *Denmark* 11 J5
Hasparren, *France* 20 E2
Hassa, *Turkey* 72 D7
Hassberge ⌓, *Germany* 25 E6
Hassela, *Sweden* 10 B10
Hasselt, *Belgium* 17 D5
Hassfurt, *Germany* 25 E6
Hassi Messaoud, *Algeria* 78 B7
Hässleholm, *Sweden* 11 H7
Hassloch, *Germany* 25 F4
Hästholmen, *Sweden* 11 F8
Hastings, *N.Z.* 91 H6
Hastings, *U.K.* 15 G8
Hastings, *Mich., U.S.A.* 114 D3
Hastings, *Minn., U.S.A.* 112 C8
Hastings, *Nebr., U.S.A.* 112 E5
Hastings Ra., *Australia* 95 E5
Hästveda, *Sweden* 11 H7
Hat Yai, *Thailand* 65 J3
Hatanbulag = Ergel, *Mongolia* 56 C5
Hatay = Antalya, *Turkey* 72 D4
Hatch, *U.S.A.* 109 K10
Hatchet L., *Canada* 103 B8
Hațeg, *Romania* 28 E7
Hateruma-Shima, *Japan* 55 M1
Hatfield P.O., *Australia* 95 E3
Hatgal, *Mongolia* 60 A5
Hathras, *India* 68 F8
Hatia, *Bangla.* 67 H17
Ḩāṭibah, Ra's, *Si. Arabia* 80 C4
Hato Mayor, *Dom. Rep.* 121 C6
Hatta, *India* 69 G8
Hattah, *Australia* 95 E3
Hatteras, C., *U.S.A.* 115 H8
Hattiesburg, *U.S.A.* 113 K10
Hatvan, *Hungary* 28 C4
Hau Bon = Cheo Reo, *Vietnam* 62 B3
Hau Duc, *Vietnam* 64 E7
Haugesund, *Norway* 9 G11
Haukipudas, *Finland* 8 D21
Haultain →, *Canada* 103 B7
Hauraki G., *N.Z.* 91 G5
Hausruck, *Austria* 26 C6
Haut Atlas, *Morocco* 78 B4
Haut-Jura ⌓, *France* 19 F9
Haut-Languedoc ⌓, *France* 20 E6
Haut Niger △, *Guinea* 82 C2
Haut-Rhin □, *France* 19 E14
Haut-Zaïre = Orientale □, *Dem. Rep. of the Congo* 86 B2
Haute-Corse □, *France* 21 F13
Haute-Garonne □, *France* 20 E5
Haute-Loire □, *France* 20 C7
Haute-Marne □, *France* 19 D12
Haute-Normandie □, *France* 18 C7
Haute-Saône □, *France* 19 E13
Haute-Savoie □, *France* 21 C10
Haute-Vienne □, *France* 20 C5
Hautes-Alpes □, *France* 21 D10
Hautes Fagnes = Hohe Venn, *Belgium* 17 D6
Hautes Fagnes = Hohes Venn-Eifel ⌓, *Europe* 24 E2
Hautes-Pyrénées □, *France* 20 F4
Hauteville-Lompnès, *France* 21 C9
Hautmont, *France* 19 B10
Hauts-de-Seine □, *France* 19 D9
Hauts Plateaux, *Algeria* 76 C4
Hauzenberg, *Germany* 25 G9
Havana = La Habana, *Cuba* 120 B3
Havana, *U.S.A.* 112 E9
Havant, *U.K.* 15 G7
Havârna, *Romania* 29 B11
Havasor = Kığzı, *Turkey* 70 B4
Havasu, L., *U.S.A.* 111 L12
Havdhem, *Sweden* 11 G12
Havel →, *Germany* 24 C8
Havelian, *Pakistan* 68 B5
Havelock, *Canada* 116 B7
Havelock, *N.Z.* 91 J4
Havelock, *U.S.A.* 115 H7
Haverfordwest, *U.K.* 15 F3
Haverhill, *U.K.* 15 E8
Haverhill, *U.S.A.* 117 D13
Haverstraw, *U.S.A.* 117 E11
Håverud, *Sweden* 11 F6
Havirga, *Mongolia* 56 B7
Havířov, *Czech Rep.* 27 B11
Havlíčkův Brod, *Czech Rep.* 26 B8
Havneby, *Denmark* 11 J2
Havran, *Turkey* 47 B9
Havre, *U.S.A.* 108 B9
Havre-Aubert, *Canada* 105 C7
Havre-St.-Pierre, *Canada* 105 B7
Havsa, *Turkey* 45 E10
Havza, *Turkey* 72 B6
Haw →, *U.S.A.* 115 H6
Hawaii □, *U.S.A.* 106 H16
Hawaii I., *Pac. Oc.* 106 J17
Hawaiian Is., *Pac. Oc.* 106 H17
Hawaiian Ridge, *Pac. Oc.* 97 E11
Hawarden, *U.S.A.* 112 D6
Hawea, L., *N.Z.* 91 L2
Hawera, *N.Z.* 91 H5
Hawick, *U.K.* 13 F6
Hawk Junction, *Canada* 104 C3
Hawke B., *N.Z.* 91 H6
Hawker, *Australia* 95 E2
Hawkesbury, *Canada* 104 C5
Hawkesbury I., *Canada* 102 C3
Hawkesbury Pt., *Australia* 94 A1
Hawkinsville, *U.S.A.* 115 J4
Hawley, *Minn., U.S.A.* 112 B6
Hawley, *Pa., U.S.A.* 117 E9
Ḩawrān, W. →, *Iraq* 70 C4
Hawsh Mūssá, *Lebanon* 74 B4
Hawthorne, *U.S.A.* 108 G4
Hay, *Australia* 95 E3
Hay →, *Australia* 94 C2
Hay →, *Canada* 102 A5
Hay, C., *Australia* 92 B4
Hay I., *Canada* 116 B4
Hay L., *Canada* 102 B5
Hay-on-Wye, *U.K.* 15 E4
Hay River, *Canada* 102 A5
Hay Springs, *U.S.A.* 112 D3
Haya = Tehoru, *Indonesia* 63 E7
Hayachine-San, *Japan* 54 E10
Hayange, *France* 19 C13
Haydarlı, *Turkey* 47 C12
Hayden, *U.S.A.* 108 F10
Haydon, *Australia* 94 B3
Hayes, *U.S.A.* 112 C4
Hayes →, *Canada* 104 A1
Hayes Creek, *Australia* 92 B5
Hayle, *U.K.* 15 G2
Hayling I., *U.K.* 15 G7
Haymana, *Turkey* 72 C5
Haymen I., *Australia* 94 J6
Hayrabolu, *Turkey* 45 E11
Hays, *Canada* 102 C6
Hays, *U.S.A.* 112 F5
Haysyn, *Ukraine* 33 H5
Hayvoron, *Ukraine* 33 H5
Hayward, *Calif., U.S.A.* 110 H4
Hayward, *Wis., U.S.A.* 112 B9
Haywards Heath, *U.K.* 15 G7
Hazafon □, *Israel* 74 C4
Hazārān, Kūh-e, *Iran* 71 D8
Hazard, *U.S.A.* 114 G4
Hazaribag, *India* 69 H11
Hazaribag Road, *India* 69 G11
Hazebrouck, *France* 19 B9
Hazelton, *Canada* 102 B3
Hazelton, *U.S.A.* 112 B4
Hazen, *U.S.A.* 112 B4
Hazlehurst, *Ga., U.S.A.* 115 K4
Hazlehurst, *Miss., U.S.A.* 113 K9
Hazlet, *U.S.A.* 117 F10
Hazleton, *U.S.A.* 117 F9
Hazlett, L., *Australia* 92 D4
Hazro, *Turkey* 70 B4
He Xian, *Anhui, China* 59 B12
He Xian, *Guangxi Zhuangzu, China* 59 E8
Head of Bight, *Australia* 93 F5
Headlands, *Zimbabwe* 87 F3
Healdsburg, *U.S.A.* 110 G4
Healdton, *U.S.A.* 113 H6
Healesville, *Australia* 95 F4
Heany Junction, *Zimbabwe* 89 C4
Heard I., *Ind. Oc.* 3 G13
Hearne, *U.S.A.* 113 K6
Hearst, *Canada* 104 C3
Heart →, *U.S.A.* 112 B4
Heart's Content, *Canada* 105 C9
Heath, Pte., *Canada* 105 C7
Heathrow, London ✕ (LHR), *U.K.* 15 F7
Heavener, *U.S.A.* 113 H7
Hebbronville, *U.S.A.* 113 M5
Hebei □, *China* 56 E9
Hebel, *Australia* 95 D4
Heber, *U.S.A.* 111 N11
Heber City, *U.S.A.* 108 F8
Heber Springs, *U.S.A.* 113 H9
Hebert, *Canada* 103 C7
Hebgen L., *U.S.A.* 108 D8
Hebi, *China* 56 G8
Hebrides, *U.K.* 6 D4
Hebrides, Sea of the, *U.K.* 13 D2
Hebron = Al Khalīl, *West Bank* 74 D4
Hebron, *Canada* 101 C13
Hebron, *N. Dak., U.S.A.* 112 B3
Hebron, *Nebr., U.S.A.* 112 E6
Heby, *Sweden* 10 E10
Hecate Str., *Canada* 102 C2
Heceta I., *U.S.A.* 102 B2
Hechi, *China* 58 E7
Hechingen, *Germany* 25 G4
Hechuan, *China* 58 B6
Hecla, *U.S.A.* 112 C5
Hecla I., *Canada* 103 C9
Hédé, *France* 18 D5
Hede, *Sweden* 10 B7
Hedemora, *Sweden* 10 D9

Hedensted, *Denmark* 11 J3
Hedesunda, *Sweden* 10 D10
Heerde, *Neths.* 17 B6
Heerenveen, *Neths.* 17 B5
Heerhugowaard, *Neths.* 17 B4
Heerlen, *Neths.* 17 D5
Ḥefa, *Israel* 74 C4
Ḥefa □, *Israel* 74 C4
Hefei, *China* 59 B11
Hefeng, *China* 59 C8
Hegalig, *Sudan* 81 E3
Hegang, *China* 60 B8
Heiban, *Sudan* 81 E3
Heichengzhen, *China* 56 F4
Heide, *Germany* 24 A5
Heidelberg, *Germany* 25 F4
Heidelberg, *S. Africa* 88 E3
Heidenau, *Germany* 24 E9
Heidenheim, *Germany* 25 G6
Heijing, *China* 58 E3
Heilbad Heiligenstadt, *Germany* 24 D6
Heilbron, *S. Africa* 89 D4
Heilbronn, *Germany* 25 F5
Heiligenblut, *Austria* 26 D5
Heiligenhafen, *Germany* 24 A6
Heilongjiang □, *China* 60 B7
Heilunkiang = Heilongjiang □, *China* 60 B7
Heimaey, *Iceland* 8 E3
Heinola, *Finland* 9 F22
Heinsberg, *Germany* 24 D2
Heinze Kyun, *Burma* 64 E1
Heishan, *China* 57 D12
Heishui, *Liaoning, China* 57 C10
Heishui, *Sichuan, China* 58 A4
Hejaz = Ḥijāz □, *Si. Arabia* 70 E3
Hejian, *China* 56 E9
Hejiang, *China* 58 C5
Hejin, *China* 56 G6
Hekımhan, *Turkey* 70 B3
Hekla, *Iceland* 8 E4
Hekou, *Guangdong, China* 59 F9
Hekou, *Yunnan, China* 58 F4
Hel, *Poland* 30 D5
Helagsfjället, *Sweden* 10 B6
Helan Shan, *China* 56 E3
Helechosa, *Spain* 37 F6
Helen Atoll, *Pac. Oc.* 63 D8
Helena, *Ark., U.S.A.* 113 H9
Helena, *Mont., U.S.A.* 108 C7
Helendale, *U.S.A.* 111 L9
Helensburgh, *U.K.* 13 E4
Helensville, *N.Z.* 91 G5
Helenvale, *Australia* 94 B4
Helgasjön, *Sweden* 11 H8
Helgeland, *Norway* 8 C15
Helgoland, *Germany* 24 A3
Heligoland = Helgoland, *Germany* 24 A3
Heligoland B. = Deutsche Bucht, *Germany* 24 A4
Heliopolis, *Egypt* 80 H7
Hella, *Iceland* 8 E3
Hellertown, *U.S.A.* 117 F9
Hellespont = Çanakkale Boğazı, *Turkey* 45 F10
Hellevoetsluis, *Neths.* 17 C4
Hellhole Gorge △, *Australia* 94 D3
Hellín, *Spain* 39 G3
Hells Canyon ⌓, *U.S.A.* 108 D5
Hell's Gate △, *Kenya* 86 C4
Helmand □, *Afghan.* 66 D4
Helmand →, *Afghan.* 66 D2
Helme →, *Germany* 24 D7
Helmeringhausen, *Namibia* 88 D2
Helmond, *Neths.* 17 C5
Helmsdale, *U.K.* 13 C5
Helmsdale →, *U.K.* 13 C5
Helmstedt, *Germany* 24 C7
Helong, *China* 57 C15
Helper, *U.S.A.* 108 G8
Helsingborg, *Sweden* 11 H6
Helsinge, *Denmark* 11 H6
Helsingfors = Helsinki, *Finland* 9 F21
Helsingør, *Denmark* 11 H6
Helsinki, *Finland* 9 F21
Helska, Mierzeja, *Poland* 30 D5
Helston, *U.K.* 15 G2
Helvellyn, *U.K.* 14 C4
Helwân, *Egypt* 80 J7
Hemel Hempstead, *U.K.* 15 F7
Hemet, *U.S.A.* 111 M10
Hemingford, *U.S.A.* 112 D3
Hemmingford, *Canada* 117 A11
Hempstead, *U.S.A.* 113 K6
Hemse, *Sweden* 11 G12
Hemsön, *Sweden* 10 B12
Henån, *Sweden* 11 F5
Henan □, *China* 56 H8
Henares →, *Spain* 36 E7
Henashi-Misaki, *Japan* 54 D9
Hendaye, *France* 20 E2
Hendek, *Turkey* 72 B4
Henderson, *Argentina* 126 D3
Henderson, *Ky., U.S.A.* 114 G2
Henderson, *N.C., U.S.A.* 115 G6
Henderson, *Nev., U.S.A.* 111 J12
Henderson, *Tenn., U.S.A.* 115 H1
Henderson, *Tex., U.S.A.* 113 J7
Hendersonville, *N.C., U.S.A.* 115 H4
Hendersonville, *Tenn., U.S.A.* 115 G2
Hendījān, *Iran* 71 D6
Hendorābī, *Iran* 71 E7
Heng Jiang, *China* 58 C5
Heng Xian, *China* 58 F7
Hengcheng, *China* 56 E4
Hëngchun, *Taiwan* 59 F13
Hengdaohezi, *China* 57 B15
Hengelo, *Neths.* 17 B6
Hengfeng, *China* 59 C10
Hengshan, *Hunan, China* 59 D9
Hengshan, *Shaanxi, China* 56 F5
Hengshui, *China* 56 F8
Hengyang, *China* 59 D9
Henichesk, *Ukraine* 33 J8
Hénin-Beaumont, *France* 19 B9
Henley-on-Thames, *U.K.* 15 F7
Henlopen, C., *U.S.A.* 114 F8
Hennan, *Sweden* 10 B9
Hennebont, *France* 18 E3
Hennenman, *S. Africa* 88 D4
Hennessey, *U.S.A.* 113 G6
Hennigsdorf, *Germany* 24 C9
Henri Pittier △, *Venezuela* 121 D6
Henri Pittler △, *Venezuela* 121 D6
Henrietta, *U.S.A.* 113 J5
Henrietta, Ostrov = Genriyetty, Ostrov, *Russia* 53 B16
Henrietta Maria, C., *Canada* 104 A3
Henry, *U.S.A.* 112 E10
Henryetta, *U.S.A.* 113 H7
Henryville, *Canada* 117 A11
Hensall, *Canada* 116 C3
Henstedt-Ulzburg, *Germany* 24 B6
Hentiesbaai, *Namibia* 88 C1
Hentiyn Nuruu, *Mongolia* 60 B5
Henty, *Australia* 95 F4
Henzada, *Burma* 67 L19
Hephaestia, *Greece* 47 B7
Heping, *China* 59 E10
Heppner, *U.S.A.* 108 D4
Hepu, *China* 58 G7
Hepworth, *Canada* 116 B3
Heqing, *China* 58 D3
Hequ, *China* 56 E6
Héraðsflói, *Iceland* 8 D6
Héraðsvötn →, *Iceland* 8 D4
Heraklion = Iráklion, *Greece* 49 D7
Herald Cays, *Australia* 94 B4
Herāt, *Afghan.* 66 B3
Herāt □, *Afghan.* 66 B3
Hérault □, *France* 20 E7
Hérault →, *France* 20 E7
Herbault, *France* 18 E8
Herbert →, *Australia* 94 B4
Herbert River Falls △, *Australia* 94 B4
Herberton, *Australia* 94 B4
Herbertsdale, *S. Africa* 88 E3
Herbignac, *France* 18 E4
Herborn, *Germany* 24 E4
Herby, *Poland* 31 H5
Herceg-Novi, *Serbia & M.* 44 D2
Herchmer, *Canada* 103 B10
Herðubreið, *Iceland* 8 D5
Hereford, *U.K.* 15 E5
Hereford, *U.S.A.* 113 H3
Herefordshire □, *U.K.* 15 E5
Hereke, *Turkey* 45 F13
Herencia, *Spain* 37 F7
Herentals, *Belgium* 17 C4
Herford, *Germany* 24 C4
Héricourt, *France* 19 E13
Herington, *U.S.A.* 112 F6
Herisau, *Switz.* 25 H5
Hérisson, *France* 19 F9
Herkimer, *U.S.A.* 117 D10
Herlong, *U.S.A.* 110 E6
Herm, *U.K.* 15 H5
Hermann, *U.S.A.* 112 F9
Hermannsburg, *Australia* 92 D5
Hermannsburg, *Germany* 24 C6
Hermanus, *S. Africa* 88 E2
Herment, *France* 20 C6
Hermidale, *Australia* 95 E4
Hermiston, *U.S.A.* 108 D4
Hermite, I., *Chile* 128 H3
Hermon, *U.S.A.* 117 B9
Hermon, Mt. = Shaykh, J. ash, *Lebanon* 74 B4
Hermosillo, *Mexico* 118 B2
Hernád →, *Hungary* 28 C6
Hernandarias, *Paraguay* 127 B5
Hernandez, *U.S.A.* 110 J6
Hernando, *Argentina* 126 C3
Hernando, *U.S.A.* 113 H10
Hernani, *Spain* 38 B3
Herndon, *U.S.A.* 116 F8
Herne, *Germany* 17 C7
Herne Bay, *U.K.* 15 F9
Herning, *Denmark* 11 H2
Heroica = Caborca, *Mexico* 118 A2
Heroica Nogales = Nogales, *Mexico* 118 A2
Heron Bay, *Canada* 104 C2
Herradura, Pta. de la, *Canary Is.* 48 F5
Herreid, *U.S.A.* 112 C4
Herrenberg, *Germany* 25 G4
Herrera, *Spain* 37 H6
Herrera de Alcántara, *Spain* 37 F3
Herrera de Pisuerga, *Spain* 36 C6
Herrera del Duque, *Spain* 37 F5
Herrestad, *Sweden* 11 F5
Herrin, *U.S.A.* 113 G10
Herriot, *Canada* 103 B8
Herrljunga, *Sweden* 11 F7
Hersbruck, *Germany* 25 F7
Herschel I., *Canada* 4 C1
Hershey, *U.S.A.* 117 F8
Hersonissos, *Greece* 49 D7
Herstal, *Belgium* 17 D5
Hertford, *U.K.* 15 F7
Hertfordshire □, *U.K.* 15 F7
's-Hertogenbosch, *Neths.* 17 C5
Hertzogville, *S. Africa* 88 D4
Hervás, *Spain* 36 E5
Hervey B., *Australia* 94 C5
Herzberg, *Brandenburg, Germany* 24 D9
Herzberg, *Niedersachsen, Germany* 24 D6
Herzliyya, *Israel* 74 C3
Herzogenburg, *Austria* 26 C8
Ḥeşār, *Fārs, Iran* 71 D6
Ḥeşār, *Markazī, Iran* 71 C6
Hesdin, *France* 19 B9
Heshan, *China* 58 F7
Heshui, *China* 56 G5
Heshun, *China* 56 F7
Hesperia, *U.S.A.* 111 L9
Hesse = Hessen □, *Germany* 24 E4
Hessen □, *Germany* 24 E4
Hessenreuther und Manteler Wald ⌓, *Germany* 25 F8
Hestra, *Sweden* 11 G7
Hetch Hetchy Aqueduct, *U.S.A.* 110 H5
Hettinger, *U.S.A.* 112 C3
Hettstedt, *Germany* 24 D7
Heuvelton, *U.S.A.* 117 B9
Heves, *Hungary* 28 C5
Heves □, *Hungary* 28 C5
Hewitt, *U.S.A.* 113 K6
Hexham, *U.K.* 14 C5
Hexi, *Yunnan, China* 58 E4
Hexi, *Zhejiang, China* 59 D12
Hexigten Qi, *China* 57 C9
Ḥeydarābād, *Iran* 71 D7
Heysham, *U.K.* 14 C5
Heyuan, *China* 59 F10
Heywood, *Australia* 95 F3
Heze, *China* 56 G8
Hezhang, *China* 58 D5
Hi, Ko, *Thailand* 65 a
Hi Vista, *U.S.A.* 111 L9
Hialeah, *U.S.A.* 115 N5
Hiawatha, *U.S.A.* 112 F7
Hibbing, *U.S.A.* 112 B8
Hibbs B., *Australia* 95 G4
Hibernia Reef, *Australia* 92 B3
Hickman, *U.S.A.* 113 G10
Hickory, *U.S.A.* 115 H5
Hicks, Pt., *Australia* 95 F4
Hicks L., *Canada* 103 A9
Hicksville, *U.S.A.* 117 F11
Hida, *Romania* 29 C8
Hida-Gawa →, *Japan* 55 G8
Hida-Sammyaku, *Japan* 55 F8
Hidaka-Sammyaku, *Japan* 54 C11
Hidalgo, *Mexico* 119 C5
Hidalgo □, *Mexico* 119 C5
Hidalgo, Presa M., *Mexico* 118 B3
Hidalgo del Parral, *Mexico* 118 B3
Hiddensee, *Germany* 24 A9
Hieflau, *Austria* 26 D7
Hiendelaencina, *Spain* 38 D2
Hierro, *Canary Is.* 48 G1
Higashiajima-San, *Japan* 54 F10
Higashiōsaka, *Japan* 55 G7
Higgins, *U.S.A.* 113 G4
Higgins Corner, *U.S.A.* 110 F5
High Bridge, *U.S.A.* 117 F10
High Level, *Canada* 102 B5
High Point, *U.S.A.* 115 H6
High Prairie, *Canada* 102 B5
High River, *Canada* 102 C6
High Tatra = Tatry, *Slovak Rep.* 27 B13
High Veld, *Africa* 76 J6
High Wycombe, *U.K.* 15 F7
Highland □, *U.K.* 13 D4
Highland Park, *U.S.A.* 114 D2
Highmore, *U.S.A.* 112 C5
Highrock L., *Man., Canada* 103 B8
Highrock L., *Sask., Canada* 103 B7
Higüey, *Dom. Rep.* 121 C6
Hihya, *Egypt* 80 H7
Hiiumaa, *Estonia* 9 G20
Híjar, *Spain* 38 D4
Ḥijāz □, *Si. Arabia* 70 E3
Hijo = Tagum, *Phil.* 61 H6
Hikari, *Japan* 55 H5
Hikmak, Ras el, *Egypt* 80 A2
Hiko, *U.S.A.* 110 H11
Hikone, *Japan* 55 G8
Hikurangi, *Gisborne, N.Z.* 91 H6
Hikurangi, *Northland, N.Z.* 91 F5
Hildburghausen, *Germany* 24 E6
Hildesheim, *Germany* 24 C5
Hill →, *Australia* 93 F2
Hill City, *Idaho, U.S.A.* 108 E6
Hill City, *Kans., U.S.A.* 112 F5
Hill City, *S. Dak., U.S.A.* 112 D3
Hill Island L., *Canada* 103 A7
Hillaby, Mt., *Barbados* 121 g
Hillared, *Sweden* 11 G7
Hillcrest, *Barbados* 121 g
Hillcrest Center, *U.S.A.* 111 K8
Hillegom, *Neths.* 17 B4
Hillerød, *Denmark* 11 J6
Hillerstorp, *Sweden* 11 G7
Hillsboro, *Kans., U.S.A.* 112 F6
Hillsboro, *N. Dak., U.S.A.* 112 B6
Hillsboro, *N.H., U.S.A.* 117 C13
Hillsboro, *Ohio, U.S.A.* 114 F4
Hillsboro, *Oreg., U.S.A.* 110 E4
Hillsboro, *Tex., U.S.A.* 113 J6
Hillsborough, *Grenada* 121 D7
Hillsborough Channel, *Australia* 94 J7
Hillsdale, *Mich., U.S.A.* 114 E3
Hillsdale, *N.Y., U.S.A.* 117 D11
Hillsport, *Canada* 104 C2
Hillston, *Australia* 95 E4
Hilo, *U.S.A.* 106 J17
Hilton, *U.S.A.* 116 C7
Hilton Head Island, *U.S.A.* 115 J5
Hilvan, *Turkey* 73 D8
Hilversum, *Neths.* 17 B5
Himachal Pradesh □, *India* 68 D7
Himalaya, *Asia* 69 E11
Himamaylan, *Phil.* 61 F5
Himarë, *Albania* 44 F3
Himatnagar, *India* 66 H8
Himeji, *Japan* 55 G7
Himi, *Japan* 55 F8
Himmerland, *Denmark* 11 H3
Ḥimş, *Syria* 74 A5
Ḥimş □, *Syria* 74 A6
Hinche, *Haiti* 121 C5
Hinchinbrook I., *Australia* 94 B4
Hinchinbrook Island △, *Australia* 94 B4
Hinckley, *U.K.* 15 E6
Hinckley, *U.S.A.* 112 B8
Hindaun, *India* 68 F7
Hindmarsh, L., *Australia* 95 F3
Hindsholm, *Denmark* 11 J4
Hindu Bagh, *Pakistan* 68 D2
Hindu Kush, *Asia* 66 B7
Hindupur, *India* 66 N10
Hines Creek, *Canada* 102 B5
Hinesville, *U.S.A.* 115 K5
Hinganghat, *India* 66 J11
Hingham, *U.S.A.* 108 B8
Hingir, *India* 69 J10
Hingoli, *India* 66 K10
Hinigaran, *Phil.* 61 F5
Hinis, *Turkey* 73 C9
Hinna = Imi, *Ethiopia* 81 F5
Hinna, *Nigeria* 83 C7
Hinnerup, *Denmark* 11 H4
Hinnøya, *Norway* 8 B16
Hinojosa del Duque, *Spain* 37 G5
Hinsdale, *U.S.A.* 117 D12
Hinterrhein →, *Switz.* 25 J5
Hinton, *Canada* 102 C5
Hinton, *U.S.A.* 114 G5
Hınzır Burnu, *Turkey* 72 D6
Hirado, *Japan* 55 H4
Hirakud Dam, *India* 67 J13
Hiran →, *India* 69 H8
Hirapur, *India* 69 G8
Hiratsuka, *Japan* 55 G9
Hirfanlı Barajı, *Turkey* 72 C5
Hiroo, *Japan* 54 C11
Hirosaki, *Japan* 54 D10
Hiroshima, *Japan* 55 G6
Hiroshima □, *Japan* 55 G6
Hirson, *France* 19 C11
Hirtshals, *Denmark* 11 G3
Hisar, *India* 68 E6
Hisarcık, *Turkey* 47 B11
Hisarya, *Bulgaria* 45 D8
Hisb, Sha'ib = Ḥasb, W. →, *Iraq* 70 D5
Ḥismá, *Si. Arabia* 70 D3
Hispaniola, *W. Indies* 121 C5
Hīt, *Iraq* 70 C4
Hita, *Japan* 55 H5
Hitachi, *Japan* 55 F10
Hitchin, *U.K.* 15 F7
Hitoyoshi, *Japan* 55 H5
Hitra, *Norway* 8 E13
Hitzacker, *Germany* 24 B7
Hixon, *Canada* 102 C4
Ḥiyyon, N. →, *Israel* 74 E4
Hjalmar L., *Canada* 103 A7
Hjälmaren, *Sweden* 10 E9
Hjältevad, *Sweden* 11 G9
Hjo, *Sweden* 11 F8
Hjørring, *Denmark* 11 G3
Hjortkvarn, *Sweden* 11 F9
Hkakabo Razi, *Burma* 67 E20
Hlinsko, *Czech Rep.* 26 B8
Hlobane, *S. Africa* 89 D5
Hlohovec, *Slovak Rep.* 27 C10
Hlučín, *Czech Rep.* 27 B11
Hluhluwe, *S. Africa* 89 D5
Hluhluwe ⌓, *S. Africa* 89 C5
Hlukhiv, *Ukraine* 33 G7
Hlyboka, *Ukraine* 33 H3
Hlybokaye, *Belarus* 32 E4
Hnúšť'a, *Slovak Rep.* 27 C12
Ho, *Ghana* 83 D5
Ho Chi Minh City = Thanh Pho Ho Chi Minh, *Vietnam* 65 G6
Ho Thuong, *Vietnam* 64 C5
Hoa Binh, *Vietnam* 58 G5
Hoa Da, *Vietnam* 65 G7
Hoa Hiep, *Vietnam* 65 G5
Hoai Nhon, *Vietnam* 64 E7
Hoang Lien Son, *Vietnam* 58 F4
Hoanib →, *Namibia* 88 B2
Hoare B., *Canada* 101 B13
Hoarusib →, *Namibia* 88 B2
Hobart, *Australia* 95 G4
Hobart, *U.S.A.* 113 H5
Hobbs, *U.S.A.* 113 J3
Hobbs Coast, *Antarctica* 5 D14
Hobe Sound, *U.S.A.* 115 M5
Hoboken, *U.S.A.* 117 F10
Hobro, *Denmark* 11 H3
Hoburgen, *Sweden* 11 H12
Hocalar, *Turkey* 47 C11
Hochfeld, *Namibia* 88 C2
Hochharz △, *Germany* 24 D6
Hochschwab, *Austria* 26 D8
Höchstadt, *Germany* 25 F6
Hochtaunus ⌓, *Germany* 25 E4
Hockenheim, *Germany* 25 F4
Hodaka-Dake, *Japan* 55 F8
Hodeida = Al Ḥudaydah, *Yemen* 75 E3
Hodgeville, *Canada* 103 C7
Hodgson, *Canada* 103 C9
Hódmezővásárhely, *Hungary* 28 D5
Hodna, Chott el, *Algeria* 78 A6
Hodonín, *Czech Rep.* 27 C10
Hoeamdong, *N. Korea* 57 C16
Hœdic, Î. de, *France* 18 E4
Hoek van Holland, *Neths.* 17 C4
Hoengsŏng, *S. Korea* 57 F14
Hoeryong, *N. Korea* 57 C15
Hoeyang, *N. Korea* 57 E14
Hof, *Germany* 25 E7
Hofgeismar, *Germany* 24 D5
Hofheim, *Germany* 25 E4
Hofmeyr, *S. Africa* 88 E4
Höfn, *Iceland* 8 D6
Hofors, *Sweden* 10 D10
Hofsjökull, *Iceland* 8 D4
Hōfu, *Japan* 55 G5
Hogan Group, *Australia* 95 F4
Höganäs, *Sweden* 11 H6
Hogarth, Mt., *Australia* 94 C2
Hoggar = Ahaggar, *Algeria* 78 D7
Högsäter, *Sweden* 11 F6
Högsby, *Sweden* 11 G10
Högsjö, *Sweden* 10 E9
Hogsty Reef, *Bahamas* 121 B5
Hoh →, *U.S.A.* 110 C2
Hohe Acht, *Germany* 25 E3
Hohe Tauern, *Austria* 26 D5
Hohe Tauern △, *Austria* 26 D5
Hohe Venn, *Belgium* 17 D6
Hohenau, *Austria* 27 C9
Hohenems, *Austria* 26 D2
Hohenloher Ebene, *Germany* 25 F5
Hohenwald, *U.S.A.* 115 H2
Hohenwestedt, *Germany* 24 A5
Hoher Rhön = Rhön, *Germany* 24 E5
Hoher Vogelsberg ⌓, *Germany* 24 D5
Hohes Venn-Eifel ⌓, *Europe* 24 E2
Hohhot, *China* 56 D6
Hóhlakas, *Greece* 49 D9
Hohoe, *Ghana* 83 D5
Hoi An, *Vietnam* 64 E7
Hoi Xuan, *Vietnam* 58 G5
Hoisington, *U.S.A.* 112 F5
Højer, *Denmark* 11 K2
Hōjō, *Japan* 55 H6
Hok, *Sweden* 11 G8
Hökensås, *Sweden* 11 G8
Hökerum, *Sweden* 11 G7
Hokianga Harbour, *N.Z.* 91 F4
Hokitika, *N.Z.* 91 K3
Hokkaidō □, *Japan* 54 C11
Hol-Hol, *Djibouti* 81 E5
Hola Pristan, *Ukraine* 33 J7
Holbæk, *Denmark* 11 J5
Holbrook, *Australia* 95 F4
Holbrook, *U.S.A.* 109 J8
Holden, *U.S.A.* 108 G7
Holdenville, *U.S.A.* 113 H6
Holdrege, *U.S.A.* 112 E5
Holešov, *Czech Rep.* 27 B10
Holetown, *Barbados* 121 g
Holguín, *Cuba* 120 B4
Holíč, *Slovak Rep.* 27 C10
Holice, *Czech Rep.* 26 A8
Höljes, *Sweden* 10 D6
Hollabrunn, *Austria* 26 C9
Hollams Bird I., *Namibia* 88 C1
Holland, *Mich., U.S.A.* 114 D2
Holland, *N.Y., U.S.A.* 116 D6
Hollandale, *U.S.A.* 113 J9
Hollandia = Jayapura, *Indonesia* 63 E10
Holley, *U.S.A.* 116 C6
Hollfeld, *Germany* 25 F7
Hollidaysburg, *U.S.A.* 116 F6
Hollis, *U.S.A.* 113 H5
Hollister, *Calif., U.S.A.* 110 J5
Hollister, *Idaho, U.S.A.* 108 E6
Höllviken = Höllviksnäs, *Sweden* 11 J6
Höllviksnäs, *Sweden* 11 J6
Holly Hill, *U.S.A.* 115 L5
Holly Springs, *U.S.A.* 113 H10
Hollywood, *U.S.A.* 115 N5
Holman, *Canada* 100 A8
Hólmavík, *Iceland* 8 D3
Holmen, *U.S.A.* 112 D9
Holmes Reefs, *Australia* 94 B4
Holmsjö, *Sweden* 11 H9
Holmsjön, *Västernorrland, Sweden* 10 B10
Holmsjön, *Västernorrland, Sweden* 10 B9
Holmsland Klit, *Denmark* 11 J2
Holmsund, *Sweden* 8 E19
Holod, *Romania* 28 D7
Holroyd →, *Australia* 94 A3
Holstebro, *Denmark* 11 H2
Holsteinische Schweiz ⌓, *Germany* 24 A6
Holsworthy, *U.K.* 15 G3
Holton, *Canada* 105 B8
Holton, *U.S.A.* 112 F7
Holtville, *U.S.A.* 111 N11
Holwerd, *Neths.* 17 A5
Holy I., *Angl., U.K.* 14 D3
Holy I., *Northumb., U.K.* 14 B6
Holyhead, *U.K.* 14 D3
Holyoke, *Colo., U.S.A.* 112 E3
Holyoke, *Mass., U.S.A.* 117 D12
Holyrood, *Canada* 105 C9
Holzkirchen, *Germany* 25 H7
Holzminden, *Germany* 24 D5
Homa Bay, *Kenya* 86 C3
Homalin, *Burma* 67 G19
Homand, *Iran* 71 C8
Homathko →, *Canada* 102 C4
Homberg, *Germany* 24 D5
Hombori, *Mali* 83 B4
Homburg, *Germany* 25 F3
Home B., *Canada* 101 B13
Home Hill, *Australia* 94 B4
Homedale, *U.S.A.* 108 E5
Homer, *Alaska, U.S.A.* 100 C4
Homer, *La., U.S.A.* 113 J8
Homer City, *U.S.A.* 116 F5
Homert ⌓, *Germany* 24 D4
Homestead, *Australia* 94 C4
Homestead, *U.S.A.* 115 N5
Homestead ⌓, *U.S.A.* 112 E6
Homewood, *U.S.A.* 110 F6
Homoine, *Mozam.* 89 C6
Homoljske Planina, *Serbia & M.* 44 B5
Homorod, *Romania* 29 D10
Homs = Ḥimş, *Syria* 74 A5
Homyel, *Belarus* 33 F6
Hon Chong, *Vietnam* 65 G5
Hon Me, *Vietnam* 64 C5

Honan = Henan □, *China* 56 H8
Honaz, *Turkey* 47 D11
Honbetsu, *Japan* 54 C11
Honcut, *U.S.A.* 110 F5
Honda Bay, *Phil.* 61 G3
Hondarribia, *Spain* 38 B3
Hondeklipbaai, *S. Africa* 88 E2
Hondo, *Japan* 55 H5
Hondo, *U.S.A.* 113 L5
Hondo →, *Belize* 119 D7
Honduras ■, *Cent. Amer.* 120 D2
Honduras, G. de, *Caribbean* 120 C2
Hønefoss, *Norway* 9 F14
Honesdale, *U.S.A.* 117 E9
Honey L., *U.S.A.* 110 E6
Honfleur, *France* 18 C7
Høng, *Denmark* 11 J5
Hong →, *Vietnam* 58 F5
Hong Gai, *Vietnam* 58 G6
Hong He →, *China* 56 H8
Hong Hu, *China* 59 C9
Hong Kong □, *China* 59 F10
Hong'an, *China* 59 B10
Hongch'ŏn, *S. Korea* 57 F14
Honghai Wan, *China* 59 F10
Honghe, *China* 58 F4
Honghu, *China* 59 C9
Hongjiang, *China* 58 D7
Hongliu He →, *China* 56 F5
Hongor, *Mongolia* 56 B7
Hongsa, *Laos* 64 C3
Hongshui He →, *China* 58 F7
Hongsŏng, *S. Korea* 57 F14
Hongtong, *China* 56 F6
Honguedo, Détroit d', *Canada* 105 C7
Hongwon, *N. Korea* 57 E14
Hongya, *China* 58 C4
Hongyuan, *China* 58 A4
Hongze Hu, *China* 57 H10
Honiara, *Solomon Is.* 96 H7
Honiton, *U.K.* 15 G4
Honjō, *Japan* 54 E10
Honkorâb, Ras, *Egypt* 80 C4
Honningsvåg, *Norway* 8 A21
Hönö, *Sweden* 11 G5
Honolulu, *U.S.A.* 106 H16
Honshū, *Japan* 54 F9
Hontoria del Pinar, *Spain* 38 D1
Hood, Mt., *U.S.A.* 108 D3
Hood, Pt., *Australia* 93 F2
Hood River, *U.S.A.* 108 D3
Hoodsport, *U.S.A.* 110 C3
Hooge, *Germany* 24 A4
Hoogeveen, *Neths.* 17 B6
Hoogezand-Sappemeer, *Neths.* 17 A6
Hooghly = Hugli →, *India* 69 J13
Hooghly-Chinsura = Chunchura, *India* 69 H13
Hook Hd., *Ireland* 12 D5
Hook I., *Australia* 94 J6
Hook of Holland = Hoek van Holland, *Neths.* 17 C4
Hooker, *U.S.A.* 113 G4
Hooker Creek, *Australia* 92 C5
Hoonah, *U.S.A.* 102 B1
Hooper Bay, *U.S.A.* 100 B3
Hoopeston, *U.S.A.* 114 E2
Hoopstad, *S. Africa* 88 D4
Höör, *Sweden* 11 J7
Hoorn, *Neths.* 17 B5
Hoover, *U.S.A.* 115 J2
Hoover Dam, *U.S.A.* 111 K12
Hooversville, *U.S.A.* 116 F6
Hop Bottom, *U.S.A.* 117 E9
Hopa, *Turkey* 73 B9
Hope, *Canada* 102 D4
Hope, *Ariz., U.S.A.* 111 M13
Hope, *Ark., U.S.A.* 113 J8
Hope, L., *S. Austral., Australia* 95 D2
Hope, L., *W. Austral., Australia* 93 F3
Hope, Pt., *U.S.A.* 4 C17
Hope I., *Canada* 116 B4
Hope Town, *Bahamas* 120 A4
Hopedale, *Canada* 105 A7
Hopedale, *U.S.A.* 117 D13
Hopefield, *S. Africa* 88 E2
Hopei = Hebei □, *China* 56 E9
Hopelchén, *Mexico* 119 D7
Hopetoun, *Vic., Australia* 95 F3
Hopetoun, *W. Austral., Australia* 93 F3
Hopetown, *S. Africa* 88 D3
Hopevale, *Australia* 94 B4
Hopewell, *U.S.A.* 114 G7
Hopfgarten, *Austria* 26 D5
Hopkins, L., *Australia* 92 D4
Hopkinsville, *U.S.A.* 115 G2
Hopland, *U.S.A.* 110 G3
Hoquiam, *U.S.A.* 110 D3
Horasan, *Turkey* 73 B10
Horažďovice, *Czech Rep.* 26 B6
Horb, *Germany* 25 G4
Hörby, *Sweden* 11 J7
Horcajo de Santiago, *Spain* 38 F1
Horden Hills, *Australia* 92 D5
Horezu, *Romania* 29 E8
Horgen, *Switz.* 25 H4
Horgoš, *Serbia & M.* 28 D4
Hořice, *Czech Rep.* 26 A8
Horinger, *China* 56 D6
Horki, *Belarus* 32 E6
Horlick Mts., *Antarctica* 5 E15
Horlivka, *Ukraine* 33 H10
Hormak, *Iran* 71 D9
Hormoz, *Iran* 71 E7
Hormoz, Jaz.-ye, *Iran* 71 E8
Hormozgān □, *Iran* 71 E8
Hormuz, Kūh-e, *Iran* 71 E7
Hormuz, Str. of, *The Gulf* 71 E8
Horn, *Austria* 26 C8
Horn, *Iceland* 8 C2
Horn, *Sweden* 11 G9
Horn →, *Canada* 102 A5
Horn, Cape = Hornos, C. de, *Chile* 128 H3
Horn Head, *Ireland* 12 A3
Horn I., *Australia* 94 A3
Horn Plateau, *Canada* 102 A5
Hornachuelos, *Spain* 37 H5
Hornavan, *Sweden* 8 C17
Hornbeck, *U.S.A.* 113 K8
Hornbrook, *U.S.A.* 108 F2
Hornburg, *Germany* 24 C6
Horncastle, *U.K.* 14 D7
Horndal, *Sweden* 10 D10
Hornell, *U.S.A.* 116 D7
Hornell L., *Canada* 102 A5
Hornepayne, *Canada* 104 C3
Horní Planá, *Czech Rep.* 26 C7
Hornings Mills, *Canada* 116 B4
Hornitos, *U.S.A.* 110 H6
Hornos, C. de, *Chile* 128 H3
Hornoy-le-Bourg, *France* 19 C8
Hornsea, *U.K.* 14 D7
Hornslandet, *Sweden* 10 C11
Hörnum, *Germany* 24 A4
Horobetsu = Noboribetsu, *Japan* 54 C10
Horodenka, *Ukraine* 33 H3
Horodnya, *Ukraine* 33 G6
Horodok, *Khmelnytskyy, Ukraine* 33 H4
Horodok, *Lviv, Ukraine* 33 H2
Horodyshche, *Ukraine* 33 H6
Horokhiv, *Ukraine* 33 G3
Horovice, *Czech Rep.* 26 B6
Horqin Youyi Qianqi, *China* 57 A12
Horqueta, *Paraguay* 126 A4
Horred, *Sweden* 11 G6
Horse Creek, *U.S.A.* 112 E3
Horse I., *Canada* 103 C9
Horse Is., *Canada* 105 B8
Horsefly L., *Canada* 102 C4
Horseheads, *U.S.A.* 116 D8
Horsens, *Denmark* 11 J3
Horsham, *Australia* 95 F3
Horsham, *U.K.* 15 F7
Horšovský Týn, *Czech Rep.* 26 B5
Horten, *Norway* 9 G14
Hortobágy →, *Hungary* 28 C6
Hortobágyi △, *Hungary* 28 C6
Horton, *U.S.A.* 112 F7
Horton →, *Canada* 100 B7
Horwood L., *Canada* 104 C3
Hosaina, *Ethiopia* 81 F4
Hose, Gunung-Gunung, *Malaysia* 62 D4
Ḩoseynābād, *Khuzestān, Iran* 71 C6
Ḩoseynābād, *Kordestān, Iran* 70 C5
Hoshangabad, *India* 68 H7
Hoshiarpur, *India* 68 D6
Hospet, *India* 66 M10
Hoste, I., *Chile* 128 H3
Hostens, *France* 20 D3
Hot, *Thailand* 64 C2
Hot Creek Range, *U.S.A.* 108 G6
Hot Springs, *Ark., U.S.A.* 113 H8
Hot Springs, *S. Dak., U.S.A.* 112 D3
Hot Springs △, *U.S.A.* 113 H8
Hotagen, *Sweden* 8 E16
Hotan, *China* 60 C2
Hotazel, *S. Africa* 88 D3
Hotchkiss, *U.S.A.* 109 G10
Hotham, C., *Australia* 92 B5
Hoting, *Sweden* 8 D17
Hotolisht, *Albania* 44 E4
Hotte, Massif de la, *Haiti* 121 C5
Hottentotsbaai, *Namibia* 88 D1
Houat, Î. de, *France* 18 E4
Houdan, *France* 19 D8
Houei Sai, *Laos* 58 G3
Houeillès, *France* 20 D4
Houffalize, *Belgium* 17 D5
Houghton, *Mich., U.S.A.* 112 B10
Houghton, *N.Y., U.S.A.* 116 D6
Houghton L., *U.S.A.* 114 C3
Houghton-le-Spring, *U.K.* 14 C6
Houhora Heads, *N.Z.* 91 F4
Houlton, *U.S.A.* 115 B12
Houma, *U.S.A.* 113 L9
Houndé, *Burkina Faso* 82 C4
Hourtin, *France* 20 C2
Hourtin-Carcans, Étang d', *France* 20 C2
Housatonic →, *U.S.A.* 117 E11
Houston, *Canada* 102 C3
Houston, *Mo., U.S.A.* 113 G9
Houston, *Tex., U.S.A.* 113 L7
Hout →, *S. Africa* 89 C4
Houtkraal, *S. Africa* 88 E3
Houtman Abrolhos, *Australia* 93 E1
Hovd, *Mongolia* 60 B4
Hove, *U.K.* 15 G7
Hovenweep ⌓, *U.S.A.* 109 H9
Hoveyzeh, *Iran* 71 D6
Hovmantorp, *Sweden* 11 H9
Hövsgöl, *Mongolia* 56 C5
Hövsgöl Nuur, *Mongolia* 60 A5
Hovsta, *Sweden* 10 E9
Howakil, *Eritrea* 81 D5
Howar, Wadi →, *Sudan* 81 D2
Howard, *Australia* 95 D5
Howard, *Pa., U.S.A.* 116 F7
Howard, *S. Dak., U.S.A.* 112 C6
Howe, *U.S.A.* 108 E7
Howe, C., *Australia* 95 F5
Howe I., *Canada* 117 B8
Howell, *U.S.A.* 114 D4
Howick, *Canada* 117 A11
Howick, *S. Africa* 89 D5
Howick Group, *Australia* 94 A4
Howitt, L., *Australia* 95 D2
Howland I., *Pac. Oc.* 96 G10
Howrah = Haora, *India* 69 H13
Howth Hd., *Ireland* 12 C5
Höxter, *Germany* 24 D5
Hoy, *U.K.* 13 C5
Hoya, *Germany* 24 C5
Høyanger, *Norway* 9 F12
Hoyerswerda, *Germany* 24 D10
Hoylake, *U.K.* 14 D4
Hoyos, *Spain* 36 E4
Hpa-an = Pa-an, *Burma* 67 L20
Hpungan Pass, *Burma* 67 F20
Hradec Králové, *Czech Rep.* 26 A8
Hrádek, *Czech Rep.* 27 C9
Hranice, *Czech Rep.* 27 B10
Hrazdan, *Armenia* 35 K7
Hrebenka, *Ukraine* 33 G7
Hrodna, *Belarus* 32 F2
Hrodzyanka, *Belarus* 32 F5
Hron →, *Slovak Rep.* 27 D11
Hrubieszów, *Poland* 31 H10
Hrubý Jeseník, *Czech Rep.* 27 A10
Hrvatska = Croatia ■, *Europe* 41 C13
Hrymayliv, *Ukraine* 33 H4
Hsenwi, *Burma* 67 H20
Hsiamen = Xiamen, *China* 59 E12
Hsian = Xi'an, *China* 56 G5
Hsinchu, *Taiwan* 59 E13
Hsinhailien = Lianyungang, *China* 57 G10
Hsinying, *Taiwan* 59 F13
Hsopket, *Burma* 58 F2
Hsüchou = Xuzhou, *China* 57 G9
Hu Xian, *China* 56 G5
Hua Hin, *Thailand* 64 F2
Hua Xian, *Henan, China* 56 G8
Hua Xian, *Shaanxi, China* 56 G5
Hua'an, *China* 59 E11
Huab →, *Namibia* 88 B2
Huacheng, *China* 59 E10
Huachinera, *Mexico* 118 A3
Huacho, *Peru* 124 F3
Huade, *China* 56 D7
Huadian, *China* 57 C14
Huadu, *China* 59 F9
Huai Had △, *Thailand* 64 D5
Huai He →, *China* 59 A12
Huai Nam Dang △, *Thailand* 64 C2
Huai Yot, *Thailand* 65 J2
Huai'an, *Hebei, China* 56 D8
Huai'an, *Jiangsu, China* 57 H10
Huaibei, *China* 56 G9
Huaibin, *China* 59 A10
Huaide = Gongzhuling, *China* 57 C13
Huaidezhen, *China* 57 C13
Huaihua, *China* 58 D7
Huaiji, *China* 59 F9
Huainan, *China* 59 A11
Huaining, *China* 59 B11
Huairen, *China* 56 E7
Huairou, *China* 56 D9
Huaiyang, *China* 56 H8
Huaiyin, *China* 57 H10
Huaiyuan, *Anhui, China* 57 H9
Huaiyuan, *Guangxi Zhuangzu, China* 58 E7
Huajianzi, *China* 57 D13
Huajuapan de Leon, *Mexico* 119 D5
Hualapai Peak, *U.S.A.* 109 J7
Hualien, *Taiwan* 59 E13
Huallaga →, *Peru* 124 E3
Huambo, *Angola* 85 G3
Huan Jiang →, *China* 56 G5
Huan Xian, *China* 56 F4
Huancabamba, *Peru* 124 E3
Huancane, *Peru* 124 G5
Huancavelica, *Peru* 124 F3
Huancayo, *Peru* 124 F3
Huanchaca, *Bolivia* 124 H5
Huang Hai = Yellow Sea, *China* 57 G12
Huang He →, *China* 57 F10
Huang Xian, *China* 57 F11
Huangchuan, *China* 59 A10
Huanggang, *China* 59 B10
Huangguoshu, *China* 58 E5
Huangling, *China* 56 G5
Huanglong, *China* 56 G5
Huanglongtan, *China* 59 A8
Huangmei, *China* 59 B10
Huangpi, *China* 59 B10
Huangping, *China* 58 D6
Huangshan, *China* 59 C12
Huangshi, *China* 59 B10
Huangsongdian, *China* 57 C14
Huangyan, *China* 59 C13
Huangyangsi, *China* 59 D8
Huaning, *China* 58 E4
Huanjiang, *China* 58 E7
Huantai, *China* 57 F9
Huánuco, *Peru* 124 E3
Huaping, *China* 58 D3
Huaraz, *Peru* 124 E3
Huarmey, *Peru* 124 F3
Huarong, *China* 59 C9
Huascarán, *Peru* 124 E3
Huasco, *Chile* 126 B1
Huasco →, *Chile* 126 B1
Huasna, *U.S.A.* 111 K6
Huatabampo, *Mexico* 118 B3
Huauchinango, *Mexico* 119 C5
Huautla de Jiménez, *Mexico* 119 D5
Huaxi, *China* 58 D6
Huay Namota, *Mexico* 118 C4
Huayin, *China* 56 G6
Huayuan, *China* 58 C7
Huayun, *China* 58 B6
Huazhou, *China* 59 G8
Hubbard, *Ohio, U.S.A.* 116 E4
Hubbard, *Tex., U.S.A.* 113 K6
Hubbart Pt., *Canada* 103 B10
Hubei □, *China* 59 B9
Hubli, *India* 66 M9
Huch'ang, *N. Korea* 57 D14
Hucknall, *U.K.* 14 D6
Huddersfield, *U.K.* 14 D6
Hude, *Germany* 24 B4
Hudi, *Sudan* 80 D3
Hudiksvall, *Sweden* 10 C11
Hudson, *Canada* 104 B1
Hudson, *Mass., U.S.A.* 117 D13
Hudson, *N.Y., U.S.A.* 117 D11
Hudson, *Wis., U.S.A.* 112 C8
Hudson, *Wyo., U.S.A.* 108 E9
Hudson →, *U.S.A.* 117 F10
Hudson Bay, *Nunavut, Canada* 101 C11
Hudson Bay, *Sask., Canada* 103 C8
Hudson Falls, *U.S.A.* 117 C11
Hudson Mts., *Antarctica* 5 D16
Hudson Str., *Canada* 101 B13
Hudson's Hope, *Canada* 102 B4
Hue, *Vietnam* 64 D6
Huebra →, *Spain* 36 D4
Huedin, *Romania* 28 D8
Huehuetenango, *Guatemala* 120 C1
Huejúcar, *Mexico* 118 C4
Huélamo, *Spain* 38 E3
Huelgoat, *France* 18 D3
Huelma, *Spain* 37 H7
Huelva, *Spain* 37 H4
Huelva □, *Spain* 37 H4
Huelva →, *Spain* 37 H5
Huentelauquén, *Chile* 126 C1
Huércal-Overa, *Spain* 39 H3
Huerta, Sa. de la, *Argentina* 126 C2
Huertas, C. de las, *Spain* 39 G4
Huerva →, *Spain* 38 D4
Huesca, *Spain* 38 C4
Huesca □, *Spain* 38 C5
Huéscar, *Spain* 39 H2
Huetamo, *Mexico* 118 D4
Huete, *Spain* 38 E2
Hugh →, *Australia* 94 D1
Hughenden, *Australia* 94 C3
Hughes, *Australia* 93 F4
Hughesville, *U.S.A.* 117 E8
Hugli →, *India* 69 J13
Hugo, *Colo., U.S.A.* 112 F3
Hugo, *Okla., U.S.A.* 113 H7
Hugoton, *U.S.A.* 113 G4
Hui Xian = Huixian, *China* 56 G7
Hui Xian, *China* 56 H4
Hui'an, *China* 59 E12
Hui'anbu, *China* 56 F4
Huichang, *China* 59 E10
Huichapán, *Mexico* 119 C5
Huidong, *Guangdong, China* 59 F10
Huidong, *Sichuan, China* 58 D4
Huifa He →, *China* 57 C14
Huila, Nevado del, *Colombia* 124 C3
Huilai, *China* 59 F11
Huili, *China* 58 D4
Huimin, *China* 57 F9
Huinan, *China* 57 C14
Huinca Renancó, *Argentina* 126 C3
Huining, *China* 56 G3
Huinong, *China* 56 E4
Huisache, *Mexico* 118 C4
Huishui, *China* 58 D6
Huisne →, *France* 18 E7
Huiting, *China* 56 G9
Huitong, *China* 58 D7
Huixian, *China* 56 G7
Huixtla, *Mexico* 119 D6
Huize, *China* 58 D4
Huizhou, *China* 59 F10
Hukawng Valley, *Burma* 67 F20
Hukou, *China* 59 C11
Hŭksan-chedo, *S. Korea* 57 G13
Hukuntsi, *Botswana* 88 C3
Ḩulayfā', *Si. Arabia* 70 E4
Huld = Ulaanjirem, *Mongolia* 56 B3
Hulin He →, *China* 57 B12
Hull = Kingston upon Hull, *U.K.* 14 D7
Hull, *Canada* 117 A9
Hull →, *U.K.* 14 D7
Hulst, *Neths.* 17 C4
Hultsfred, *Sweden* 11 G9
Hulun Nur, *China* 60 B6
Hulyaypole, *Ukraine* 33 J9
Huma, Tanjung, *Malaysia* 65 c
Humacao, *Puerto Rico* 121 d
Humahuaca, *Argentina* 126 A2
Humaitá, *Brazil* 124 E6
Humaitá, *Paraguay* 126 B4
Humansdorp, *S. Africa* 88 E3
Humara, J., *Sudan* 81 D3
Humbe, *Angola* 88 B1
Humber →, *U.K.* 14 D7
Humboldt, *Canada* 103 C7
Humboldt, *Iowa, U.S.A.* 112 D7
Humboldt, *Tenn., U.S.A.* 113 H10
Humboldt →, *U.S.A.* 108 F4
Humboldt Gletscher = Sermersuaq, *Greenland* 4 B4
Hume, *U.S.A.* 110 J8
Hume, L., *Australia* 95 F4
Humenné, *Slovak Rep.* 27 C14
Hummelsta, *Sweden* 10 E10
Humphreys, Mt., *U.S.A.* 110 H8
Humphreys Peak, *U.S.A.* 109 J8
Humpolec, *Czech Rep.* 26 B8
Humptulips, *U.S.A.* 110 C3
Hūn, *Libya* 79 C9
Hun Jiang →, *China* 57 D13
Húnaflói, *Iceland* 8 D3
Hunan □, *China* 59 D9
Hunchun, *China* 57 C16
Hundested, *Denmark* 11 J5
Hundewali, *Pakistan* 68 D5
Hundred Mile House, *Canada* 102 C4
Hunedoara, *Romania* 28 E7
Hunedoara □, *Romania* 28 E7
Hünfeld, *Germany* 24 E5
Hung Yen, *Vietnam* 58 G6
Hungary ■, *Europe* 27 D12
Hungary, Plain of, *Europe* 6 F10
Hungerford, *Australia* 95 D3
Hŭngnam, *N. Korea* 57 E14
Hungt'ou Hsü, *Taiwan* 59 G13
Huni Valley, *Ghana* 82 D4
Hunneberg, *Sweden* 11 F6
Hunnebostrand, *Sweden* 11 F5
Hunsberge, *Namibia* 88 D2
Hunsrück, *Germany* 25 F3
Hunstanton, *U.K.* 14 E8
Hunte →, *Germany* 24 B4
Hunter, *U.S.A.* 117 D10
Hunter I., *Australia* 95 G3
Hunter I., *Canada* 102 C3
Hunter Ra., *Australia* 95 E5
Hunters Road, *Zimbabwe* 87 F2
Hunterville, *N.Z.* 91 H5
Huntingburg, *U.S.A.* 114 F2
Huntingdon, *Canada* 104 C5
Huntingdon, *U.K.* 15 E7
Huntingdon, *U.S.A.* 116 F6
Huntington, *Ind., U.S.A.* 114 E3
Huntington, *Oreg., U.S.A.* 108 D5
Huntington, *Utah, U.S.A.* 108 G8
Huntington, *W. Va., U.S.A.* 114 F4
Huntington Beach, *U.S.A.* 111 M9
Huntington Station, *U.S.A.* 117 F11
Huntly, *N.Z.* 91 G5
Huntly, *U.K.* 13 D6
Huntsville, *Canada* 116 A5
Huntsville, *Ala., U.S.A.* 115 H2
Huntsville, *Tex., U.S.A.* 113 K7
Hunyani →, *Zimbabwe* 87 F3
Hunyuan, *China* 56 E7
Hunza →, *India* 69 B6
Huo Xian = Huozhou, *China* 56 F6
Huong Khe, *Vietnam* 64 C5
Huonville, *Australia* 95 G4
Huoqiu, *China* 59 A11
Huoshan, *Anhui, China* 59 A12
Huoshan, *Anhui, China* 59 B11
Huoshao Dao = Lü-Tao, *Taiwan* 59 F13
Huozhou, *China* 56 F6
Hupeh = Hubei □, *China* 59 B9
Ḩūr, *Iran* 71 D8
Hurbanovo, *Slovak Rep.* 27 D11
Hurd, C., *Canada* 116 A3
Hure Qi, *China* 57 C11
Hurezani, *Romania* 29 F8
Hurghada, *Egypt* 80 B3
Hurley, *N. Mex., U.S.A.* 109 K9
Hurley, *Wis., U.S.A.* 112 B9
Huron, *Calif., U.S.A.* 110 J6
Huron, *Ohio, U.S.A.* 116 E2
Huron, *S. Dak., U.S.A.* 112 C5
Huron, L., *U.S.A.* 116 B2
Huron East, *Canada* 116 C3
Hurricane, *U.S.A.* 109 H7
Hurso, *Ethiopia* 81 F5
Hurungwe ⌓, *Zimbabwe* 87 F2
Hurunui →, *N.Z.* 91 K4
Hurup, *Denmark* 11 H2
Húsavík, *Iceland* 8 C5
Huşi, *Romania* 29 D13
Huskvarna, *Sweden* 11 G8
Hustadvika, *Norway* 8 E12
Hustontown, *U.S.A.* 116 F6
Hustopeče, *Czech Rep.* 27 C9
Husum, *Germany* 24 A5
Husum, *Sweden* 10 A13
Hutchinson, *Kans., U.S.A.* 113 F6
Hutchinson, *Minn., U.S.A.* 112 C7
Hutte Sauvage, L. de la, *Canada* 105 A7
Hüttenberg, *Austria* 26 E7
Hüttener Berge ⌓, *Germany* 24 A5
Hutton, Mt., *Australia* 95 D4
Huwun, *Ethiopia* 81 G5
Huy, *Belgium* 17 D5
Huzhou, *China* 59 B13
Hvalpsund, *Denmark* 11 H3
Hvammstangi, *Iceland* 8 D3
Hvar, *Croatia* 41 E13
Hvarski Kanal, *Croatia* 41 E13
Hvítá →, *Iceland* 8 D3
Hwachŏn-chŏsuji, *S. Korea* 57 E14
Hwang Ho = Huang He →, *China* 57 F10
Hwange, *Zimbabwe* 87 F2
Hwange △, *Zimbabwe* 88 B4
Hyannis, *Mass., U.S.A.* 114 E10
Hyannis, *Nebr., U.S.A.* 112 E4
Hyargas Nuur, *Mongolia* 60 B4
Hybo, *Sweden* 10 C10
Hydaburg, *U.S.A.* 102 B2
Hyde Park, *U.S.A.* 117 E11
Hyden, *Australia* 93 F2
Hyder, *U.S.A.* 102 B2
Hyderabad, *India* 66 L11
Hyderabad, *Pakistan* 68 G3
Hyères, *France* 21 E10
Hyères, Îs. d', *France* 21 F10
Hyesan, *N. Korea* 57 D15
Hyland →, *Canada* 102 B3
Hyltebruk, *Sweden* 11 H7
Hymia, *India* 69 C8
Hyndman Peak, *U.S.A.* 108 E6
Hyōgo □, *Japan* 55 G7
Hyrum, *U.S.A.* 108 F8
Hysham, *U.S.A.* 108 C10
Hythe, *U.K.* 15 F9
Hyūga, *Japan* 55 H5
Hyvinge = Hyvinkää, *Finland* 9 F21
Hyvinkää, *Finland* 9 F21

I

I-n-Gall, *Niger* 83 B6
I-n-Oudad, *Algeria* 83 A5
I-n-Ouzzal, *Algeria* 83 A5
I-n-Tadreft, *Niger* 83 B6
Iablaniţa, *Romania* 28 F7
Iaco →, *Brazil* 124 E5

Iacobeni, *Romania* 29 C10
Iakora, *Madag.* 89 C8
Ialomiţa □, *Romania* 29 F12
Ialomiţa →, *Romania* 29 F12
Ialoveni, *Moldova* 29 D13
Ialpug →, *Moldova* 29 E13
Ianca, *Romania* 29 E12
Iara, *Romania* 29 D8
Iarda, *Ethiopia* 81 E4
Iargara, *Moldova* 29 D13
Iaşi, *Romania* 29 C12
Iaşi □, *Romania* 29 C12
Íasmos, *Greece* 45 E9
Ib →, *India* 69 J10
Iba, *Phil.* 61 D3
Ibadan, *Nigeria* 83 D5
Ibagué, *Colombia* 124 C3
Iballë, *Albania* 44 D4
Ibăneşti, *Botoşani, Romania* 29 B11
Ibăneşti, *Mureş, Romania* 29 D9
Ibar →, *Serbia & M.* 44 C4
Ibaraki □, *Japan* 55 F10
Ibarra, *Ecuador* 124 C3
Ibba, *Sudan* 81 G2
Ibba, Bahr el →, *Sudan* 81 F2
Ibbenbüren, *Germany* 24 C3
Ibembo, *Dem. Rep. of the Congo* 86 B1
Ibera, L., *Argentina* 126 B4
Iberian Peninsula, *Europe* 6 H5
Iberville, *Canada* 117 A11
Iberville, Lac d', *Canada* 104 A5
Ibi, *Nigeria* 83 D6
Ibi, *Spain* 39 G4
Ibiá, *Brazil* 125 G9
Ibiapaba, Sa. da, *Brazil* 125 D10
Ibicuí →, *Brazil* 127 B4
Ibicuy, *Argentina* 126 C4
Ibiza = Eivissa, *Spain* 48 C7
Ibiza ✕ (IBZ), *Spain* 39 G6
Íblei, Monti, *Italy* 43 E7
Ibo, *Mozam.* 87 E5
Ibonma, *Indonesia* 63 E8
Ibotirama, *Brazil* 125 F10
Ibrāhīm →, *Lebanon* 74 A4
'Ibrī, *Oman* 71 F8
İbriktepe, *Turkey* 45 E10
Ibshawâi, *Egypt* 80 J7
Ibu, *Indonesia* 63 D7
Ibusuki, *Japan* 55 J5
Ica, *Peru* 124 F3
Iça →, *Brazil* 124 D5
Icacos Pt., *Trin. & Tob.* 125 K15
Içana, *Brazil* 124 C5
Içana →, *Brazil* 124 C5
İçel = Mersin, *Turkey* 70 B2
Iceland ■, *Europe* 8 D4
Iceland Plateau, *Arctic* 4 C7
Ich'ang = Yichang, *China* 59 B8
Ichchapuram, *India* 67 K14
Ichhawar, *India* 68 H7
Ichihara, *Japan* 55 G10
Ichikawa, *Japan* 55 G9
Ichilo →, *Bolivia* 124 G6
Ichinohe, *Japan* 54 D10
Ichinomiya, *Japan* 55 G8
Ichinoseki, *Japan* 54 E10
Ichnya, *Ukraine* 33 G7
Icod, *Canary Is.* 48 F3
Ida Grove, *U.S.A.* 112 D7
Idabel, *U.S.A.* 113 J7
Idaga Hamus, *Ethiopia* 81 E4
Idah, *Nigeria* 83 D6
Idaho □, *U.S.A.* 108 D7
Idaho City, *U.S.A.* 108 E6
Idaho Falls, *U.S.A.* 108 E7
Idalia △, *Australia* 94 C3
Idanha-a-Nova, *Portugal* 36 F3
Idar-Oberstein, *Germany* 25 F3
Idfû, *Egypt* 80 C3
Ídhi Óros, *Greece* 49 D6
Ídhra, *Greece* 46 D5
Idi, *Indonesia* 62 C1
Idiofa, *Dem. Rep. of the Congo* 84 E3
Idkerberget, *Sweden* 10 D9
Idku, Bahra el, *Egypt* 80 H7
Idlib, *Syria* 70 C3
Idre, *Sweden* 10 C6
Idria, *U.S.A.* 110 J6
Idrija, *Slovenia* 41 C11
Idritsa, *Russia* 32 D5
Idutywa, *S. Africa* 89 E4
Ieper, *Belgium* 17 D2
Ierápetra, *Greece* 49 E7
Ierissós, *Greece* 44 F7
Ierissóu Kólpos, *Greece* 44 F7
Iernut, *Romania* 29 D9
Iesi, *Italy* 41 E10
Iésolo, *Italy* 41 C9
Ifach, Peñón de, *Spain* 39 G5
Ifakara, *Tanzania* 84 F7
'Ifâl, W. al →, *Si. Arabia* 70 D2
Ifanadiana, *Madag.* 89 C8
Ife, *Nigeria* 83 D5
Iférouâne, *Niger* 83 B6
Iffley, *Australia* 94 B3
Ifon, *Nigeria* 83 D6
Iforas, Adrar des, *Africa* 83 B5
Ifould, L., *Australia* 93 F5
Iganga, *Uganda* 86 B3
Igarapava, *Brazil* 125 H9
Igarka, *Russia* 52 C9
Igatimi, *Paraguay* 127 A4
Igbetti, *Nigeria* 83 D5
Igbo-Ora, *Nigeria* 83 D5
Igboho, *Nigeria* 83 D5
Igbor, *Nigeria* 83 D6
Iğdır, *Turkey* 73 C11
Igelfors, *Sweden* 11 F9
Iggesund, *Sweden* 10 C11
Iglésias, *Italy* 42 C1
Igloolik, *Canada* 101 B11
Igluligaarjuk = Chesterfield Inlet, *Canada* 100 B10
Iglulik = Igloolik, *Canada* 101 B11
'Igma, Gebel el, *Egypt* 80 B3
Ignace, *Canada* 104 C1
İğneada, *Turkey* 45 E11
İğneada Burnu, *Turkey* 45 E12
Igoumenítsa, *Greece* 46 B2
Igra, *Russia* 34 B11
Iguaçu △, *Brazil* 127 B5
Iguaçu →, *Brazil* 127 B5
Iguaçu, Cat. del, *Brazil* 127 B5
Iguaçu Falls = Iguaçu, Cat. del, *Brazil* 127 B5
Iguala, *Mexico* 119 D5
Igualada, *Spain* 38 D6
Iguassu = Iguaçu →, *Brazil* 127 B5
Iguatu, *Brazil* 125 E11
Iguazú △, *Argentina* 127 B5
Iguidi, Erg, *Africa* 78 C4
Iharana, *Madag.* 89 A9
Ihbulag, *Mongolia* 56 C4
Iheya-Shima, *Japan* 55 L3
Ihiala, *Nigeria* 83 D6
Ihosy, *Madag.* 89 C8
Ihotry, Farihy, *Madag.* 89 C7
Ihugh, *Nigeria* 83 D6
Ii, *Finland* 8 D21
Ii-Shima, *Japan* 55 L3
Iida, *Japan* 55 G8
Iijoki →, *Finland* 8 D21
Iisalmi, *Finland* 8 E22
Iiyama, *Japan* 55 F9
Iizuka, *Japan* 55 H5
Ijebu-Igbo, *Nigeria* 83 D5
Ijebu-Ode, *Nigeria* 83 D5
IJmuiden, *Neths.* 17 B4
IJssel →, *Neths.* 17 B5
IJsselmeer, *Neths.* 17 B5
Ijuí, *Brazil* 127 B5
Ijuí →, *Brazil* 127 B4
Ikalamavony, *Madag.* 89 C8
Ikale, *Nigeria* 83 D6
Ikaluktutiak, *Canada* 100 B9
Ikang, *Nigeria* 83 E6
Ikara, *Nigeria* 83 C6
Ikare, *Nigeria* 83 D6
Ikaría, *Greece* 47 D8
Ikast, *Denmark* 11 H3
Ikeda, *Japan* 55 G6
Ikeja, *Nigeria* 83 D5
Ikela, *Dem. Rep. of the Congo* 84 E4
Ikerre-Ekiti, *Nigeria* 83 D6
Ikhtiman, *Bulgaria* 44 D7
Iki, *Japan* 55 H4
Ikimba L., *Tanzania* 86 C3
Ikire, *Nigeria* 83 D5
İkizdere, *Turkey* 73 B9
Ikom, *Nigeria* 83 D6
Ikongo, *Madag.* 89 C8
Ikopa →, *Madag.* 89 B8
Ikorongo ⌂, *Tanzania* 86 C3
Ikot Ekpene, *Nigeria* 83 D6
Ikparjuk = Arctic Bay, *Canada* 101 A11
Ikungu, *Tanzania* 86 C3
Ikurun, *Nigeria* 83 D5
Ila, *Nigeria* 83 D5
Ilagan, *Phil.* 61 C4
Ilaka, *Madag.* 89 B8
Īlām, *Iran* 70 C5
Ilam, *Nepal* 69 F12
Īlām □, *Iran* 70 C5
Ilan, *Taiwan* 59 E13
Ilanskiy, *Russia* 53 D10
Ilaro, *Nigeria* 83 D5
Ilatane, *Niger* 83 B5
Iława, *Poland* 30 E6
Ile →, *Kazakhstan* 52 E8
Île-à-la-Crosse, *Canada* 103 B7
Île-à-la-Crosse, Lac, *Canada* 103 B7
Île-de-France □, *France* 19 D9
Ileanda, *Romania* 29 C8
Ilebo, *Dem. Rep. of the Congo* 84 E4
Ilek, *Russia* 52 D6
Ilero, *Nigeria* 83 D5
Ilesha, *Kwara, Nigeria* 83 D5
Ilesha, *Oyo, Nigeria* 83 D5
Ilford, *Canada* 103 B9
Ilfracombe, *Australia* 94 C3
Ilfracombe, *U.K.* 15 F3
Ilgaz, *Turkey* 72 B5
Ilgaz Dağları, *Turkey* 72 B5
Ilgın, *Turkey* 72 C4
Ilha de Moçambique, *Mozam.* 87 F5
Ílhavo, *Portugal* 36 E2
Ilhéus, *Brazil* 125 F11
Ili = Ile →, *Kazakhstan* 52 E8
Ilia, *Romania* 28 E7
Ilia □, *Greece* 46 D3
Iliamna L., *U.S.A.* 100 C4
Iliç, *Turkey* 73 C8
Ilıca, *Turkey* 47 B9
Ilichevsk, *Azerbaijan* 73 C11
Iligan, *Phil.* 61 G6
Iligan Bay, *Phil.* 61 G6
Ilíki, L., *Greece* 46 C5
Ilin I., *Phil.* 61 E4
Iliodhrómia, *Greece* 46 B5
Ilion, *U.S.A.* 117 D9
Ilirska-Bistrica, *Slovenia* 41 C11
Ilkeston, *U.K.* 14 E6
Ilkley, *U.K.* 14 D6
Illampu = Ancohuma, Nevado, *Bolivia* 124 G5
Illana B., *Phil.* 61 H5
Illapel, *Chile* 126 C1
Ille-et-Vilaine □, *France* 18 D5
Ille-sur-Têt, *France* 20 F6
Illéla, *Niger* 83 C6
Iller →, *Germany* 25 G5
Illertissen, *Germany* 25 G6
Illescas, *Spain* 36 E7
Illetas, *Spain* 48 B9
Illichivsk, *Ukraine* 33 J6
Illiers-Combray, *France* 18 D8
Illimani, Nevado, *Bolivia* 124 G5
Illinois □, *U.S.A.* 112 E10
Illinois →, *U.S.A.* 112 F9
Illium = Troy, *Turkey* 47 B8
Illizi, *Algeria* 78 C7
Illkirch-Graffenstaden, *France* 19 D14
Íllora, *Spain* 37 H7
Ilm →, *Germany* 24 D7
Ilmajoki, *Finland* 9 E20
Ilmen, Ozero, *Russia* 32 C6
Ilmenau, *Germany* 24 E6
Ilo, *Peru* 124 G4
Ilobu, *Nigeria* 83 D5
Iloilo, *Phil.* 61 F5
Ilora, *Nigeria* 83 D5
Ilorin, *Nigeria* 83 D5
Ilovatka, *Russia* 34 E7
Ilovlya, *Russia* 35 F7
Ilovlya →, *Russia* 35 F7
Iłowa, *Poland* 31 G2
Ilubabor □, *Ethiopia* 81 F4
Ilva Mică, *Romania* 29 C9
Ilwaco, *U.S.A.* 110 D2
Ilwaki, *Indonesia* 63 F7
Ilyichevsk = Illichivsk, *Ukraine* 33 J6
Iłża, *Poland* 31 G8
Iłżanka →, *Poland* 31 G8
Imabari, *Japan* 55 G6
Imaloto →, *Madag.* 89 C8
İmamoğlu, *Turkey* 72 D6
Imandra, Ozero, *Russia* 52 C4
Imanombo, *Madag.* 89 C8
Imari, *Japan* 55 H4
Imasa, *Sudan* 80 D4
Imathía □, *Greece* 44 F6
Imatra, *Finland* 32 B5
Imbil, *Australia* 95 D5
Iménas, *Mali* 83 B5
imeni 26 Bakinskikh Komissarov = Neftçala, *Azerbaijan* 71 B6
imeni 26 Bakinskikh Komissarov, *Turkmenistan* 71 B7
Imeri, Serra, *Brazil* 124 C5
Imerimandroso, *Madag.* 89 B8
Imi, *Ethiopia* 81 F5
Imishly = Imişli, *Azerbaijan* 35 L9
Imişli, *Azerbaijan* 35 L9
Imlay, *U.S.A.* 108 F4
Imlay City, *U.S.A.* 116 D1
Immaseri, *Sudan* 81 D2
Immenstadt, *Germany* 25 H6
Immingham, *U.K.* 14 D7
Immokalee, *U.S.A.* 115 M5
Imo □, *Nigeria* 83 D6
Imo →, *Nigeria* 83 E6
Ímola, *Italy* 41 D8
Imotski, *Croatia* 41 E14
Imperatriz, *Brazil* 125 E9
Impéria, *Italy* 40 E5
Imperial, *Canada* 103 C7
Imperial, *Calif., U.S.A.* 111 N11
Imperial, *Nebr., U.S.A.* 112 E4
Imperial Beach, *U.S.A.* 111 N9
Imperial Dam, *U.S.A.* 111 N12
Imperial Reservoir, *U.S.A.* 111 N12
Imperial Valley, *U.S.A.* 111 N11
Imperieuse Reef, *Australia* 92 C2
Impfondo, *Congo* 84 D3
Imphal, *India* 67 G18
Imphy, *France* 19 F10
Imranlı, *Turkey* 73 C8
İmroz = Gökçeada, *Turkey* 45 F9
İmroz, *Turkey* 45 F9
Imst, *Austria* 26 D3
Imuris, *Mexico* 118 A2
Imuruan B., *Phil.* 63 B5
In Akhmed, *Mali* 83 B4
In Aleï, *Mali* 82 B4
In Delimane, *Mali* 83 B5
In Guezzam, *Algeria* 83 B6
In Koufi, *Mali* 83 B5
In Salah, *Algeria* 78 C6
In Tallak, *Mali* 83 B5
In Tebezas, *Mali* 83 B5
Ina, *Japan* 55 G8
Inagua △, *Bahamas* 121 B5
Inangahua, *N.Z.* 91 J3
Inanwatan, *Indonesia* 63 E8
Iñapari, *Peru* 124 F5
Inari, *Finland* 8 B22
Inarijärvi, *Finland* 8 B22
Inawashiro-Ko, *Japan* 54 F10
Inca, *Spain* 48 B9
Inca de Oro, *Chile* 126 B2
Incaguasi, *Chile* 126 B1
İnce Burun, *Turkey* 72 A6
İncekum Burnu, *Turkey* 72 D5
İncesu, *Turkey* 70 B2
Inch'ŏn, *S. Korea* 57 F14
Incio = Cruz de Incio, *Spain* 36 C3
İncirliova, *Turkey* 47 D9
Incline Village, *U.S.A.* 108 G4
Incomáti →, *Mozam.* 89 D5
Inda Silase, *Ethiopia* 81 E4
Indal, *Sweden* 10 B11
Indalsälven →, *Sweden* 10 B11
Indaw, *Burma* 67 G20
Indbir, *Ethiopia* 81 F4
Independence, *Calif., U.S.A.* 110 J8
Independence, *Iowa, U.S.A.* 112 D9
Independence, *Kans., U.S.A.* 113 G7
Independence, *Ky., U.S.A.* 114 F3
Independence, *Mo., U.S.A.* 112 F7
Independence Fjord, *Greenland* 4 A6
Independence Mts., *U.S.A.* 108 F5
Independenţa, *Romania* 29 E12
Index, *U.S.A.* 110 C5
India ■, *Asia* 66 K11
Indian →, *U.S.A.* 115 M5
Indian Cabins, *Canada* 102 B5
Indian Harbour, *Canada* 105 B8
Indian Head, *Canada* 103 C8
Indian Lake, *U.S.A.* 117 C10
Indian Ocean 50 K11
Indian Springs, *U.S.A.* 111 J11
Indiana, *U.S.A.* 116 F5
Indiana □, *U.S.A.* 114 F3
Indianapolis, *U.S.A.* 114 F2
Indianola, *Iowa, U.S.A.* 112 E8
Indianola, *Miss., U.S.A.* 113 J9
Indigirka →, *Russia* 53 B15
Inđija, *Serbia & M.* 28 E5
Indio, *U.S.A.* 111 M10
Indira Gandhi Canal, *India* 68 F5
Indo-China, *Asia* 50 H14
Indonesia ■, *Asia* 62 F5
Indore, *India* 68 H6
Indramayu, *Indonesia* 63 G13
Indravati →, *India* 67 K12
Indre □, *France* 19 F8
Indre →, *France* 18 E7
Indre-et-Loire □, *France* 18 E7
Indulkana, *Australia* 95 D1
Indus →, *Pakistan* 68 G2
Indus, Mouths of the, *Pakistan* 68 H3
İnebolu, *Turkey* 72 B5
İnecik, *Turkey* 45 F11
İnegöl, *Turkey* 45 F13
Ineu, *Romania* 28 D6
Infantes = Villanueva de los Infantes, *Spain* 37 G7
Infiernillo, Presa del, *Mexico* 118 D4
Infiesto, *Spain* 36 B5
Ingelstad, *Sweden* 11 H8
Ingenio, *Canary Is.* 48 G4
Ingenio Santa Ana, *Argentina* 126 B2
Ingersoll, *Canada* 116 C4
Ingham, *Australia* 94 B4
Ingleborough, *U.K.* 14 C5
Inglewood, *Queens., Australia* 95 D5
Inglewood, *Vic., Australia* 95 F3
Inglewood, *N.Z.* 91 H5
Inglewood, *U.S.A.* 111 M8
Ingólfshöfði, *Iceland* 8 E5
Ingolstadt, *Germany* 25 G7
Ingomar, *U.S.A.* 108 C10
Ingonish, *Canada* 105 C7
Ingore, *Guinea-Biss.* 82 C1
Ingraj Bazar, *India* 69 G13
Ingrid Christensen Coast, *Antarctica* 5 C6
Ingul = Inhul →, *Ukraine* 33 J7
Ingulec = Inhulec, *Ukraine* 33 J7
Ingulets = Inhulets →, *Ukraine* 33 J7
Inguri = Enguri →, *Georgia* 35 J5
Ingushetia □, *Russia* 35 J7
Ingwavuma, *S. Africa* 89 D5
Inhaca, *Mozam.* 89 D5
Inhafenga, *Mozam.* 89 C5
Inhambane, *Mozam.* 89 C6
Inhambane □, *Mozam.* 89 C5
Inhaminga, *Mozam.* 87 F4
Inharrime, *Mozam.* 89 C6
Inharrime →, *Mozam.* 89 C6
Inhisar, *Turkey* 47 A12
Inhul →, *Ukraine* 33 J7
Inhulec, *Ukraine* 33 J7
Inhulets →, *Ukraine* 33 J7
Iniesta, *Spain* 39 F3
Ining = Yining, *China* 52 E9
Inírida →, *Colombia* 124 C5
Inishbofin, *Ireland* 12 C1
Inisheer, *Ireland* 12 C2
Inishfree B., *Ireland* 12 A3
Inishkea North, *Ireland* 12 B1
Inishkea South, *Ireland* 12 B1
Inishmaan, *Ireland* 12 C2
Inishmore, *Ireland* 12 C2
Inishowen Pen., *Ireland* 12 A4
Inishshark, *Ireland* 12 C1
Inishturk, *Ireland* 12 C1
Inishvickillane, *Ireland* 12 D1
Injibara, *Ethiopia* 81 E4
Injune, *Australia* 95 D4
Inklin →, *Canada* 102 B2
Inland Kaikoura Ra., *N.Z.* 91 J4
Inland Sea = Setonaikai, *Japan* 55 G6
Inle L., *Burma* 67 J20
Inlet, *U.S.A.* 117 C10
Inn →, *Austria* 26 C6
Innamincka, *Australia* 95 D3
Inner Hebrides, *U.K.* 13 E2
Inner Mongolia = Nei Monggol Zizhiqu □, *China* 56 D7
Inner Sound, *U.K.* 13 D3
Innerkip, *Canada* 116 C4
Innetalling I., *Canada* 104 A4
Innisfail, *Australia* 94 B4
Innisfail, *Canada* 102 C6
In'noshima, *Japan* 55 G6
Innsbruck, *Austria* 26 D4
Innviertel, *Austria* 26 C6
Inny →, *Ireland* 12 C4
Inongo, *Dem. Rep. of the Congo* 84 E3
İnönü, *Turkey* 47 B12
Inoucdjouac = Inukjuak, *Canada* 101 C12
Inowrocław, *Poland* 31 F5
Inpundong, *N. Korea* 57 D14
Inscription, C., *Australia* 93 E1
Insein, *Burma* 67 L20
Insjön, *Sweden* 10 D9
Ińsko, *Poland* 30 E2
Însurăţei, *Romania* 29 F12
Inta, *Russia* 52 C6
Intendente Alvear, *Argentina* 126 D3
İntepe, *Turkey* 47 A8
Interlaken, *Switz.* 25 J3
Interlaken, *U.S.A.* 117 D8
International Falls, *U.S.A.* 112 A8
Intiyaco, *Argentina* 126 B3
Întorsura Buzăului, *Romania* 29 E11
Inukjuak, *Canada* 101 C12
Inútil, B., *Chile* 128 G2
Inuvik, *Canada* 100 B6
Inveraray, *U.K.* 13 E3
Inverbervie, *U.K.* 13 E6
Invercargill, *N.Z.* 91 M2
Inverclyde □, *U.K.* 13 F4
Inverell, *Australia* 95 D5
Invergordon, *U.K.* 13 D4
Inverloch, *Australia* 95 F4
Invermere, *Canada* 102 C5
Inverness, *Canada* 105 C7
Inverness, *U.K.* 13 D4
Inverness, *U.S.A.* 115 L4
Inverurie, *U.K.* 13 D6
Investigator Group, *Australia* 95 E1
Investigator Str., *Australia* 95 F2
Inya, *Russia* 52 D9
Inyanga, *Zimbabwe* 87 F3
Inyangani, *Zimbabwe* 87 F3
Inyantue, *Zimbabwe* 88 B4
Inyo Mts., *U.S.A.* 110 J9
Inyokern, *U.S.A.* 111 K9
Inza, *Russia* 34 D8
Inzhavino, *Russia* 34 D6
Iō-Jima, *Japan* 55 J5
Ioánnina, *Greece* 46 B2
Ioánnina □, *Greece* 46 B2
Iola, *U.S.A.* 113 G7
Ion Corvin, *Romania* 29 F12
Iona, *U.K.* 13 E2
Ione, *U.S.A.* 110 G6
Ionia, *U.S.A.* 114 D3
Ionian Is. = Iónioi Nísoi, *Greece* 46 C2
Ionian Sea, *Medit. S.* 6 H9
Iónioi Nísoi, *Greece* 46 C2
Iónioi Nísoi □, *Greece* 46 C2
Íos, *Greece* 47 E7
Iowa □, *U.S.A.* 112 D8
Iowa →, *U.S.A.* 112 E9
Iowa City, *U.S.A.* 112 E9
Iowa Falls, *U.S.A.* 112 D8
Iowa Park, *U.S.A.* 113 J5
Ipala, *Tanzania* 86 C3
Ipameri, *Brazil* 125 G9
Ipáti, *Greece* 46 C4
Ipatinga, *Brazil* 125 G10
Ipatovo, *Russia* 35 H6
Ipel' →, *Europe* 27 D11
Ipiales, *Colombia* 124 C3
Ipin = Yibin, *China* 58 C5
Ípiros □, *Greece* 46 B2
Ipixuna, *Brazil* 124 E4
Ipoh, *Malaysia* 65 K3
Ippy, *C.A.R.* 84 C4
Ipsala, *Turkey* 45 F10
Ipsárion, Óros, *Greece* 45 F8
Ipswich, *Australia* 95 D5
Ipswich, *U.K.* 15 E9
Ipswich, *Mass., U.S.A.* 117 D14
Ipswich, *S. Dak., U.S.A.* 112 C5
Ipu, *Brazil* 125 D10
Iqaluit, *Canada* 101 B13
Iquique, *Chile* 124 H4
Iquitos, *Peru* 124 D4
Irabu-Jima, *Japan* 55 M2
Iracoubo, *Fr. Guiana* 125 B8
Īrafshān, *Iran* 71 E9
Irahuan, *Phil.* 61 G3
Iráklia, *Kikládhes, Greece* 47 E7
Iráklia, *Sérrai, Greece* 44 E7
Iráklion, *Greece* 49 D7
Iráklion □, *Greece* 49 D7
Irala, *Paraguay* 127 B5
Iran ■, *Asia* 71 C7
Iran, Gunung-Gunung, *Malaysia* 62 D4
Iran, Plateau of, *Asia* 50 F9
Iran Ra. = Iran, Gunung-Gunung, *Malaysia* 62 D4
Īrānshahr, *Iran* 71 E9
Irapuato, *Mexico* 118 C4
Iraq ■, *Asia* 70 C5
Irati, *Brazil* 127 B5
Irbes saurums, *Latvia* 30 A9
Irbid, *Jordan* 74 C4
Irbid □, *Jordan* 74 C5
Iregua →, *Spain* 38 C7
Ireland ■, *Europe* 12 C4
Irele, *Nigeria* 83 D6
Irgiz, Bolshaya →, *Russia* 34 D9
Irhyangdong, *N. Korea* 57 D15
Iri, *S. Korea* 57 G14
Irian Jaya = Papua □, *Indonesia* 63 E9
Irié, *Guinea* 82 D3
Iriga, *Phil.* 61 E5
Iringa, *Tanzania* 86 D4
Iringa □, *Tanzania* 86 D4
Iriomote △, *Japan* 55 M1
Iriomote-Jima, *Japan* 55 M1
Iriona, *Honduras* 120 C2
Iriri →, *Brazil* 125 D8
Irish Republic ■, *Europe* 12 C4
Irish Sea, *U.K.* 14 D3
Irkutsk, *Russia* 53 D11
Irlığanlı, *Turkey* 47 D11
Irma, *Canada* 103 C6
Irō-Zaki, *Japan* 55 G9
Iroise, Mer d', *France* 18 D2
Iron Baron, *Australia* 95 E2
Iron Gate = Portile de Fier, *Europe* 28 F7
Iron Knob, *Australia* 95 E2
Iron Mountain, *U.S.A.* 114 C1
Iron Range △, *Australia* 94 A3
Iron River, *U.S.A.* 112 B10
Irondequoit, *U.S.A.* 116 C7
Ironton, *Mo., U.S.A.* 113 G9

Ironton, *Ohio, U.S.A.* 114 F4
Ironwood, *U.S.A.* 112 B9
Ironwood Forest ⌓, *U.S.A.* 109 K8
Iroquois, *Canada* 117 B9
Iroquois Falls, *Canada* 104 C3
Irosin, *Phil.* 61 E6
Irpin, *Ukraine* 33 G6
Irrara Cr. →, *Australia* 95 D4
Irrawaddy □, *Burma* 67 L19
Irrawaddy →, *Burma* 67 M19
Irrawaddy, Mouths of the, *Burma* 67 M19
Irricana, *Canada* 102 C6
Irsina, *Italy* 43 B9
Irtysh →, *Russia* 52 C7
Irumu, *Dem. Rep. of the Congo* 86 B2
Irún, *Spain* 38 B3
Irunea = Pamplona, *Spain* 38 C3
Irurzun, *Spain* 38 C3
Irvine, *U.K.* 13 F4
Irvine, *Calif., U.S.A.* 111 M9
Irvine, *Ky., U.S.A.* 114 G4
Irvinestown, *U.K.* 12 B4
Irving, *U.S.A.* 113 J6
Irvona, *U.S.A.* 116 F6
Irwin →, *Australia* 93 E1
Irymple, *Australia* 95 E3
Is, Jebel, *Sudan* 80 C4
Is-sur-Tille, *France* 19 E12
Isa, *Nigeria* 83 C6
Isa Khel, *Pakistan* 68 C4
Isaac →, *Australia* 94 C4
Isabel, *U.S.A.* 112 C4
Isabela, *Phil.* 61 H5
Isabela, *Puerto Rico* 121 d
Isabela, I., *Mexico* 118 C3
Isabelia, Cord., *Nic.* 120 D2
Isabella Ra., *Australia* 92 D3
Isaccea, *Romania* 29 E13
Ísafjarðardjúp, *Iceland* 8 C2
Ísafjörður, *Iceland* 8 C2
Isagarh, *India* 68 G7
Isahaya, *Japan* 55 H5
Isaka, *Tanzania* 86 C3
Isakly, *Russia* 34 C10
Işalniţa, *Romania* 29 F8
Isalo △, *Madag.* 89 C8
Isan →, *India* 69 F9
Isana = Içana →, *Brazil* 124 C5
Isangano △, *Zambia* 87 E3
Isanlu Makutu, *Nigeria* 83 D6
Isar →, *Germany* 25 G8
Isarco →, *Italy* 41 B8
Ísari, *Greece* 46 D3
Íscar, *Spain* 36 D6
İscehisar, *Turkey* 47 C12
Íschia, *Italy* 42 B6
Isdell →, *Australia* 92 C3
Ise, *Japan* 55 G8
Ise-Shima △, *Japan* 55 G8
Ise-Wan, *Japan* 55 G8
Isefjord, *Denmark* 11 J5
Isel →, *Austria* 26 E5
Iseo, *Italy* 40 C7
Iseo, L. d', *Italy* 40 C7
Iseramagazi, *Tanzania* 86 C3
Isère □, *France* 21 C9
Isère →, *France* 21 D8
Iserlohn, *Germany* 24 D3
Isérnia, *Italy* 43 A7
Iseyin, *Nigeria* 83 D5
Isfahan = Eşfahān, *Iran* 71 C6
Ishëm, *Albania* 44 E3
Ishigaki-Shima, *Japan* 55 M2
Ishikari-Gawa →, *Japan* 54 C10
Ishikari-Sammyaku, *Japan* 54 C11
Ishikari-Wan, *Japan* 54 C10
Ishikawa □, *Japan* 55 F8
Ishim, *Russia* 52 D7
Ishim →, *Russia* 52 D8
Ishinomaki, *Japan* 54 E10
Ishioka, *Japan* 55 F10
Ishkuman, *Pakistan* 69 A5
Ishpeming, *U.S.A.* 114 B2
Isigny-sur-Mer, *France* 18 C5
Isıklar Dağı, *Turkey* 45 F11
Işıklı, *Turkey* 47 C11
Isil Kul, *Russia* 52 D8
Ísili, *Italy* 42 C2
Isiolo, *Kenya* 86 B4
Isiro, *Dem. Rep. of the Congo* 86 B2
Isisford, *Australia* 94 C3
İskenderun, *Turkey* 70 B3
İskenderun Körfezi, *Turkey* 72 D6
İskilip, *Turkey* 72 B6
Iskŭr →, *Bulgaria* 45 C8
Iskŭr, Yazovir, *Bulgaria* 44 D7
Iskut →, *Canada* 102 B2
Isla →, *U.K.* 13 E5
Isla Coiba △, *Panama* 120 E3
Isla Cristina, *Spain* 37 H3
Isla de Salamanca △, *Colombia* 121 D5
Isla de Salamanca △, *Colombia* 121 D5
Isla Gorge △, *Australia* 94 D4
Isla Tiburón y San Esteban ⌓, *Mexico* 118 B2
Isla Vista, *U.S.A.* 111 L7
Islâhiye, *Turkey* 72 D7
Islam Headworks, *Pakistan* 68 E5
Islamabad, *Pakistan* 68 C5
Islamgarh, *Pakistan* 68 F4
Islamkot, *Pakistan* 68 G4
Islampur, *India* 69 G11
Island L., *Canada* 103 C10
Island Lagoon, *Australia* 95 E2
Island Pond, *U.S.A.* 117 B13
Islands, B. of, *Canada* 105 C8
Islands, B. of, *N.Z.* 91 F5
Islay, *U.K.* 13 F2
Isle →, *France* 20 D3
Isle aux Morts, *Canada* 105 C8
Isle of Wight □, *U.K.* 15 G6
Isle Royale △, *U.S.A.* 114 B1
Isleton, *U.S.A.* 110 G5
Ismail = Izmayil, *Ukraine* 33 K5
Ismâ'ilîya, *Egypt* 80 H8
Ismaning, *Germany* 25 G7
Isna, *Egypt* 80 B3
Isoanala, *Madag.* 89 C8
Isogstalo, *India* 69 B8
Ísola del Liri, *Italy* 41 G10
Ísola della Scala, *Italy* 40 C7
Ísola di Capo Rizzuto, *Italy* 43 D10
Isparta, *Turkey* 47 D12
Isperikh, *Bulgaria* 45 C10
Íspica, *Italy* 43 F7
Israel ■, *Asia* 74 D3
Isratu, *Eritrea* 81 D4
Issia, *Ivory C.* 82 D3
Issoire, *France* 20 C7
Issoudun, *France* 19 F8
Issyk-Kul, Ozero = Ysyk-Köl, *Kyrgyzstan* 52 E8
Ist, *Croatia* 41 D11
Istállós-kő, *Hungary* 28 B5
İstanbul, *Turkey* 45 E12
İstanbul □, *Turkey* 45 E12
İstanbul ✕ (IST), *Turkey* 45 F12
İstanbul Boğazı, *Turkey* 45 E13
Istiaía, *Greece* 46 C5
Istok, *Serbia & M.* 44 D4
Istokpoga, L., *U.S.A.* 115 M5
Istra, *Croatia* 41 C10
Istres, *France* 21 E8
Istria = Istra, *Croatia* 41 C10
Itá, *Paraguay* 126 B4
Itaberaba, *Brazil* 125 F10
Itabira, *Brazil* 125 G10
Itabirito, *Brazil* 127 A7
Itabuna, *Brazil* 125 F11
Itacaunas →, *Brazil* 125 E9
Itacoatiara, *Brazil* 124 D7
Itaipú, Represa de, *Brazil* 127 B5
Itaituba, *Brazil* 125 D7
Itajaí, *Brazil* 127 B6
Itajubá, *Brazil* 127 A6
Itaka, *Tanzania* 87 D3
Itala ⌓, *S. Africa* 89 D5
Italy ■, *Europe* 7 G8
Itamaraju, *Brazil* 125 G11
Itampolo, *Madag.* 89 C7
Itandrano, *Madag.* 89 C8
Itapecuru-Mirim, *Brazil* 125 D10
Itaperuna, *Brazil* 127 A7
Itapetininga, *Brazil* 127 A6
Itapeva, *Brazil* 127 A6
Itapicuru →, *Bahia, Brazil* 125 F11
Itapicuru →, *Maranhão, Brazil* 125 D10
Itapipoca, *Brazil* 125 D11
Itapuá □, *Paraguay* 127 B4
Itaquari, *Brazil* 127 A7
Itaquí, *Brazil* 126 B4
Itararé, *Brazil* 127 A6
Itarsi, *India* 68 H7
Itatí, *Argentina* 126 B4
Itatiaia △, *Brazil* 127 A7
Itbayat, *Phil.* 61 A4
Itchen →, *U.K.* 15 G6
Itéa, *Greece* 46 C4
Itezhi Tezhi, L., *Zambia* 87 F2
Ithaca = Itháki, *Greece* 46 C2
Ithaca, *U.S.A.* 117 D8
Itháki, *Greece* 46 C2
Íti △, *Greece* 46 C4
Itiquira →, *Brazil* 125 G7
Itō, *Japan* 55 G9
Itoigawa, *Japan* 55 F8
Iton →, *France* 18 C8
Itonamas →, *Bolivia* 124 F6
Itri, *Italy* 42 A6
Itsa, *Egypt* 80 J7
Íttiri, *Italy* 42 B1
Ittoqqortoormiit, *Greenland* 4 B6
Itu, *Brazil* 127 A6
Itu, *Nigeria* 83 D6
Itu Aba I., *S. China Sea* 62 B4
Ituiutaba, *Brazil* 125 G9
Itumbiara, *Brazil* 125 G9
Ituna, *Canada* 103 C8
Itunge Port, *Tanzania* 87 D3
Iturbe, *Argentina* 126 A2
Ituri →, *Dem. Rep. of the Congo* 86 B2
Iturup, Ostrov, *Russia* 53 E15
Ituxi →, *Brazil* 124 E6
Ituyuro →, *Argentina* 126 A3
Itzehoe, *Germany* 24 B5
Ivahona, *Madag.* 89 C8
Ivaí →, *Brazil* 127 A5
Ivalo, *Finland* 8 B22
Ivalojoki →, *Finland* 8 B22
Ivanava, *Belarus* 33 F3
Ivančice, *Czech Rep.* 27 B9
Ivăneşti, *Romania* 29 D12
Ivangorod, *Russia* 32 C5
Ivanhoe, *Australia* 95 E3
Ivanhoe, *Calif., U.S.A.* 110 J7
Ivanhoe, *Minn., U.S.A.* 112 C6
Ivanić Grad, *Croatia* 41 C13
Ivanjica, *Serbia & M.* 44 C4
Ivanjska, *Bos.-H.* 28 F2
Ivankoyskoye Vdkhr., *Russia* 32 D9
Ivano-Frankivsk, *Ukraine* 33 H3
Ivano-Frankovsk = Ivano-Frankivsk, *Ukraine* 33 H3
Ivanovo = Ivanava, *Belarus* 33 F3
Ivanovo, *Russia* 34 B5
Ivanšćica, *Croatia* 41 B13
Ivato, *Madag.* 89 C8
Ivatsevichy, *Belarus* 33 F3
Ivaylovgrad, *Bulgaria* 45 E10
Ivinheima →, *Brazil* 127 A5
Ivinhema, *Brazil* 127 A5
Ivohibe, *Madag.* 89 C8
Ivory Coast, *W. Afr.* 82 E4
Ivory Coast ■, *Africa* 82 D4
Ivösjön, *Sweden* 11 H8
Ivrea, *Italy* 40 C4
Ivrindi, *Turkey* 47 B9
Ivujivik, *Canada* 101 B12
Ivybridge, *U.K.* 15 G4
Iwaizumi, *Japan* 54 E10
Iwaki, *Japan* 55 F10
Iwakuni, *Japan* 55 G6
Iwamizawa, *Japan* 54 C10
Iwanai, *Japan* 54 C10
Iwata, *Japan* 55 G8
Iwate □, *Japan* 54 E10
Iwate-San, *Japan* 54 E10
Iwo, *Nigeria* 83 D5
Iwonicz-Zdrój, *Poland* 31 J8
Ixiamas, *Bolivia* 124 F5
Ixopo, *S. Africa* 89 E5
Ixtepec, *Mexico* 119 D5
Ixtlán del Río, *Mexico* 118 C4
Iyal Bakhit, *Sudan* 81 E2
Iyo, *Japan* 55 H6
Izabal, L. de, *Guatemala* 120 C2
Izamal, *Mexico* 119 C7
Izberbash, *Russia* 35 J8
Izbica, *Poland* 31 H10
Izbica Kujawska, *Poland* 31 F5
Izbiceni, *Romania* 29 G9
Izena-Shima, *Japan* 55 L3
Izgrev, *Bulgaria* 45 C10
Izhevsk, *Russia* 52 D6
Izmayil, *Ukraine* 33 K5
İzmir, *Turkey* 47 C9
İzmir □, *Turkey* 47 C9
İzmir Adnan Menderes ✕ (ADB), *Turkey* 47 C9
İzmir Körfezi, *Turkey* 47 C8
İzmit = Kocaeli, *Turkey* 45 F13
Iznájar, *Spain* 37 H6
Iznalloz, *Spain* 37 H7
Iznik, *Turkey* 72 B3
Iznik Gölü, *Turkey* 45 F13
Izobil'nyy, *Russia* 35 H5
Izola, *Slovenia* 41 C10
Izra, *Syria* 74 C5
Iztochni Rodopi, *Bulgaria* 45 E9
Izu-Shotō, *Japan* 55 G10
Izúcar de Matamoros, *Mexico* 119 D5
Izumi-Sano, *Japan* 55 G7
Izumo, *Japan* 55 G6
Izyaslav, *Ukraine* 33 G4
Izyum, *Ukraine* 33 H9

J

Jaba, *Ethiopia* 81 F4
Jabal at Tā'ir, *Red Sea* 81 D5
Jabalón →, *Spain* 37 G6
Jabalpur, *India* 69 H8
Jabbūl, *Syria* 70 B3
Jabiru, *Australia* 92 B5
Jablah, *Syria* 70 C3
Jablanac, *Croatia* 41 D11
Jablanica, *Bos.-H.* 28 G2
Jablonec nad Nisou, *Czech Rep.* 26 A8
Jablonica, *Slovak Rep.* 27 C10
Jabłonowo Pomorskie, *Poland* 30 E6
Jablunkov, *Czech Rep.* 27 B11
Jaboatão, *Brazil* 125 E11
Jaboticabal, *Brazil* 127 A6
Jabukovac, *Serbia & M.* 44 B6
Jaca, *Spain* 38 C4
Jacareí, *Brazil* 127 A6
Jacarèzinho, *Brazil* 127 A6
Jackman, *U.S.A.* 115 C10
Jacksboro, *U.S.A.* 113 J5
Jackson, *Barbados* 121 g
Jackson, *Ala., U.S.A.* 115 K2
Jackson, *Calif., U.S.A.* 110 G6
Jackson, *Ky., U.S.A.* 114 G4
Jackson, *Mich., U.S.A.* 114 D3
Jackson, *Minn., U.S.A.* 112 D7
Jackson, *Miss., U.S.A.* 113 J9
Jackson, *Mo., U.S.A.* 113 G10
Jackson, *N.H., U.S.A.* 117 B13
Jackson, *Ohio, U.S.A.* 114 F4
Jackson, *Tenn., U.S.A.* 115 H1
Jackson, *Wyo., U.S.A.* 108 E8
Jackson B., *N.Z.* 91 K2
Jackson L., *U.S.A.* 108 E8
Jacksons, *N.Z.* 91 K3
Jackson's Arm, *Canada* 105 C8
Jacksonville, *Ala., U.S.A.* 115 J3
Jacksonville, *Ark., U.S.A.* 113 H8
Jacksonville, *Calif., U.S.A.* 110 H6
Jacksonville, *Fla., U.S.A.* 115 K5
Jacksonville, *Ill., U.S.A.* 112 F9
Jacksonville, *N.C., U.S.A.* 115 H7
Jacksonville, *Tex., U.S.A.* 113 K7
Jacksonville Beach, *U.S.A.* 115 K5
Jacmel, *Haiti* 121 C5
Jacob Lake, *U.S.A.* 109 H7
Jacobabad, *Pakistan* 68 E3
Jacobina, *Brazil* 125 F10
Jacques-Cartier ⌓, *Canada* 105 C5
Jacques-Cartier, Dét. de, *Canada* 105 C7
Jacques-Cartier, Mt., *Canada* 105 C6
Jacqueville, *Ivory C.* 82 D4
Jacuí →, *Brazil* 127 C5
Jacumba, *U.S.A.* 111 N10
Jacundá →, *Brazil* 125 D8
Jade, *Germany* 24 B4
Jadebusen, *Germany* 24 B4
Jadotville = Likasi, *Dem. Rep. of the Congo* 87 E2
Jadovnik, *Serbia & M.* 44 C3
Jadraque, *Spain* 38 E2
Jaén, *Peru* 124 E3
Jaén, *Spain* 37 H7
Jaén □, *Spain* 37 H7
Jafarabad, *India* 68 J4
Jaffa = Tel Aviv-Yafo, *Israel* 74 C3
Jaffa, C., *Australia* 95 F2
Jaffna, *Sri Lanka* 66 Q12
Jaffray, *Canada* 103 D10
Jaffrey, *U.S.A.* 117 D12
Jagadhri, *India* 68 D7
Jagadishpur, *India* 69 G11
Jagdalpur, *India* 67 K13
Jagersfontein, *S. Africa* 88 D4
Jaghīn →, *Iran* 71 E8
Jagodina, *Serbia & M.* 44 B5
Jagraon, *India* 66 D9
Jagst →, *Germany* 25 F5
Jagtial, *India* 66 K11
Jaguariaíva, *Brazil* 127 A6
Jaguaribe →, *Brazil* 125 D11
Jagüey Grande, *Cuba* 120 B3
Jahanabad, *India* 69 G11
Jahazpur, *India* 68 G6
Jahrom, *Iran* 71 D7
Jaijon, *India* 68 D7
Jailolo, *Indonesia* 63 D7
Jailolo, Selat, *Indonesia* 63 D7
Jaipur, *India* 68 F6
Jais, *India* 69 F9
Jaisalmer, *India* 68 F4
Jaisinghnagar, *India* 69 H8
Jaitaran, *India* 68 F5
Jaithari, *India* 69 H8
Jājarm, *Iran* 71 B8
Jajce, *Bos.-H.* 28 F2
Jakam →, *India* 68 H6
Jakarta, *Indonesia* 63 G12
Jakhal, *India* 68 E6
Jakhau, *India* 68 H3
Jakobstad = Pietarsaari, *Finland* 8 E20
Jakupica, *Macedonia* 44 E5
Jal, *U.S.A.* 113 J3
Jalālābād, *Afghan.* 68 B4
Jalalabad, *India* 69 F8
Jalalpur Jattan, *Pakistan* 68 C6
Jalama, *U.S.A.* 111 L6
Jalapa, *Guatemala* 120 D2
Jalapa Enríquez = Xalapa, *Mexico* 119 D5
Jalasjärvi, *Finland* 9 E20
Jalaun, *India* 69 F8
Jaldhaka →, *Bangla.* 69 F13
Jalesar, *India* 68 F8
Jaleswar, *Nepal* 69 F11
Jalgaon, *India* 66 J9
Jalībah, *Iraq* 70 D5
Jalingo, *Nigeria* 83 D7
Jalisco □, *Mexico* 118 D4
Jalkot, *Pakistan* 69 B5
Jallas →, *Spain* 36 C1
Jalna, *India* 66 K9
Jalón →, *Spain* 38 D3
Jalor, *India* 68 G5
Jalpa, *Mexico* 118 C4
Jalpaiguri, *India* 67 F16
Jaluit I., *Marshall Is.* 96 G8
Jalūlā, *Iraq* 70 C5
Jamaari, *Nigeria* 83 C6
Jamaica ■, *W. Indies* 120 a
Jamalpur, *Bangla.* 67 G16
Jamalpur, *India* 69 G12
Jamalpurganj, *India* 69 H13
Jamanxim →, *Brazil* 125 D7
Jambewangi, *Indonesia* 63 J17
Jambi, *Indonesia* 62 E2
Jambi □, *Indonesia* 62 E2
Jambusar, *India* 68 H5
James →, *S. Dak., U.S.A.* 112 D6
James →, *Va., U.S.A.* 114 G7
James B., *Canada* 104 B3
James Ranges, *Australia* 92 D5
James Ross I., *Antarctica* 5 C18
Jamesabad, *Pakistan* 68 G3
Jamestown, *Australia* 95 E2
Jamestown, *S. Africa* 88 E4
Jamestown, *N. Dak., U.S.A.* 112 B5
Jamestown, *N.Y., U.S.A.* 116 D5
Jamestown, *Pa., U.S.A.* 116 E4
Jamīlābād, *Iran* 71 C6
Jamiltepec, *Mexico* 119 D5
Jamira →, *India* 69 J13
Jämjö, *Sweden* 11 H9
Jamkhandi, *India* 66 L9
Jammerbugt, *Denmark* 11 G3
Jammu, *India* 68 C6
Jammu & Kashmir □, *India* 69 B7
Jamnagar, *India* 68 H4
Jamni →, *India* 69 G8
Jampur, *Pakistan* 68 E4
Jamrud, *Pakistan* 68 C4
Jämsä, *Finland* 9 F21
Jamshedpur, *India* 69 H12
Jamtara, *India* 69 H12
Jämtland, *Sweden* 8 E15
Jämtlands län □, *Sweden* 10 B7
Jan L., *Canada* 103 C8
Jan Mayen, *Arctic* 4 B7
Janakkala, *Finland* 9 F21
Janaúba, *Brazil* 125 G10
Jand, *Pakistan* 68 C5
Jandaq, *Iran* 71 C7
Jandía, *Canary Is.* 48 F5
Jandía △, *Canary Is.* 48 F5
Jandía, Pta. de, *Canary Is.* 48 F5
Jandola, *Pakistan* 68 C4
Jandowae, *Australia* 95 D5
Jándula →, *Spain* 37 G6
Janesville, *U.S.A.* 112 D10
Janga, *Ghana* 83 C4
Jangamo, *Mozam.* 89 C6
Janghai, *India* 69 G10
Janikowo, *Poland* 31 F5
Janinà = Ioánnina □, *Greece* 46 B2
Janja, *Bos.-H.* 28 F4
Janjanbureh, *Gambia* 82 C2
Janjevo, *Serbia & M.* 44 D5
Janjgir, *India* 69 J10
Janjina, *Croatia* 41 F14
Janjina, *Madag.* 89 C8
Janos, *Mexico* 118 A3
Jánoshalma, *Hungary* 28 D4
Jánosháza, *Hungary* 28 C2
Jánossomorja, *Hungary* 28 C2
Janów, *Poland* 31 H6
Janów Lubelski, *Poland* 31 H9
Janów Podlaski, *Poland* 31 F10
Janowiec Wielkopolski, *Poland* 31 F4
Januária, *Brazil* 125 G10
Janub Dârfûr □, *Sudan* 81 E2
Janub Kordofân □, *Sudan* 81 E3
Janûb Sînî □, *Egypt* 74 F2
Janubio, *Canary Is.* 48 F6
Janville, *France* 19 D8
Janzé, *France* 18 E5
Jaora, *India* 68 H6
Japan ■, *Asia* 55 G8
Japan, Sea of, *Asia* 54 E7
Japan Trench, *Pac. Oc.* 96 D6
Japen = Yapen, *Indonesia* 63 E9
Japla, *India* 69 G11
Japurá →, *Brazil* 124 D5
Jaquarão, *Brazil* 127 C5
Jaqué, *Panama* 120 E4
Jarābulus, *Syria* 70 B3
Jaraicejo, *Spain* 37 F5
Jaraíz de la Vera, *Spain* 36 E5
Jarama →, *Spain* 36 E7
Jaramānah, *Syria* 72 F7
Jarandilla, *Spain* 36 E5
Jaranwala, *Pakistan* 68 D5
Jarash, *Jordan* 74 C4
Jarash □, *Jordan* 74 C4
Järbo, *Sweden* 10 D10
Jardim, *Brazil* 126 A4
Jardín →, *Spain* 39 G2
Jardine River △, *Australia* 94 A3
Jardines de la Reina, Arch. de los, *Cuba* 120 B4
Jargalang, *China* 57 C12
Jargalant = Hovd, *Mongolia* 60 B4
Jari →, *Brazil* 125 D8
Jarīr, W. al →, *Si. Arabia* 70 E4
Järlåsa, *Sweden* 10 E11
Jarmen, *Germany* 24 B9
Järna, *Dalarnas, Sweden* 10 D8
Järna, *Stockholm, Sweden* 10 E11
Jarnac, *France* 20 C3
Jarny, *France* 19 C12
Jarocin, *Poland* 31 G4
Jaroměř, *Czech Rep.* 26 A8
Jarosław, *Poland* 31 H9
Järpås, *Sweden* 11 F6
Järpen, *Sweden* 10 A7
Jarrahdale, *Australia* 93 F2
Jarrahi →, *Iran* 71 D6
Jarres, Plaine des, *Laos* 64 C4
Jarso, *Ethiopia* 81 F4
Jartai, *China* 56 E3
Jarud Qi, *China* 57 B11
Järvenpää, *Finland* 9 F21
Jarvis, *Canada* 116 D4
Jarvis I., *Pac. Oc.* 97 H12
Jarvorník, *Czech Rep.* 27 A10
Järvsö, *Sweden* 10 C10
Jarwa, *India* 69 F10
Jaša Tomić, *Serbia & M.* 28 E5
Jasdan, *India* 68 H4
Jashpurnagar, *India* 69 H11
Jasidih, *India* 69 G12
Jasień, *Poland* 31 G2
Jāsimīyah, *Iraq* 70 C5
Jasin, *Malaysia* 65 L4
Jāsk, *Iran* 71 E8
Jasło, *Poland* 31 J8
Jasmund, *Germany* 24 A9
Jasmund △, *Germany* 24 A9
Jaso, *India* 69 G9
Jasper, *Alta., Canada* 102 C5
Jasper, *Ont., Canada* 117 B9
Jasper, *Ala., U.S.A.* 115 J2
Jasper, *Fla., U.S.A.* 115 K4
Jasper, *Ind., U.S.A.* 114 F2
Jasper, *Tex., U.S.A.* 113 K8
Jasper △, *Canada* 102 C5
Jasrasar, *India* 68 F5
Jastarnia, *Poland* 30 D5
Jastrebarsko, *Croatia* 41 C12
Jastrowie, *Poland* 30 E3
Jastrzębie Zdrój, *Poland* 31 J5
Jász-Nagykun-Szolnok □, *Hungary* 28 C5
Jászapáti, *Hungary* 28 C5
Jászárokszállás, *Hungary* 28 C4
Jászberény, *Hungary* 28 C4
Jászkisér, *Hungary* 28 C5
Jászladány, *Hungary* 28 C5
Jataí, *Brazil* 125 G8
Jati, *Pakistan* 68 G3
Jatibarang, *Indonesia* 63 G13
Jatiluwih, *Indonesia* 63 J18
Jatinegara, *Indonesia* 63 G12
Játiva = Xátiva, *Spain* 39 G4
Jättendal, *Sweden* 10 C11
Jaú, *Brazil* 127 A6
Jauja, *Peru* 124 F3
Jaunpur, *India* 69 G10
Java = Jawa, *Indonesia* 62 F3
Java Barat □, *Indonesia* 63 G12
Java Sea, *Indonesia* 62 E3
Java Tengah □, *Indonesia* 63 G14
Java Timur □, *Indonesia* 63 G15
Java Trench, *Ind. Oc.* 62 F3
Javalambre, Sa. de, *Spain* 38 E4

Jávea, Spain 39 G5
Jawa, Indonesia 62 F3
Jawad, India 68 G6
Jawor, Poland 31 G3
Jaworzno, Poland 31 H6
Jaworzyna Śląska, Poland 31 H3
Jay Peak, U.S.A. 117 B12
Jaya, Puncak, Indonesia 63 E9
Jayanti, India 67 F16
Jayapura, Indonesia 63 E10
Jayawijaya, Pegunungan, Indonesia 63 E9
Jaynagar, India 67 F15
Jayrūd, Syria 70 C3
Jayton, U.S.A. 113 J4
Jāz Mūrīān, Hāmūn-e, Iran 71 E8
Jazīreh-ye Shīf, Iran 71 D6
Jazminal, Mexico 118 C4
Jazzīn, Lebanon 74 B4
Jean, U.S.A. 111 K11
Jean Marie River, Canada 102 A4
Jean Rabel, Haiti 121 C5
Jeanerette, U.S.A. 113 L9
Jeanette, Ostrov = Zhannetty, Ostrov, Russia 53 B16
Jeannette, U.S.A. 116 F5
Jebāl Bārez, Kūh-e, Iran 71 D8
Jebba, Nigeria 83 D5
Jebel, Bahr el →, Sudan 81 F3
Jebel Dud, Sudan 81 E3
Jebel Qerri, Sudan 81 D3
Jedburgh, U.K. 13 F6
Jedda = Jiddah, Si. Arabia 75 C2
Jeddore L., Canada 105 C8
Jedlicze, Poland 31 J8
Jędrzejów, Poland 31 H7
Jedwabne, Poland 31 E9
Jeetzel →, Germany 24 B7
Jefferson, Iowa, U.S.A. 112 D7
Jefferson, Ohio, U.S.A. 116 E4
Jefferson, Tex., U.S.A. 113 J7
Jefferson, Mt., Nev., U.S.A. 108 G5
Jefferson, Mt., Oreg., U.S.A. 108 D3
Jefferson City, Mo., U.S.A. 112 F8
Jefferson City, Tenn., U.S.A. 115 G4
Jeffersontown, U.S.A. 114 F3
Jeffersonville, U.S.A. 114 F3
Jeffrey City, U.S.A. 108 E10
Jega, Nigeria 83 C5
Jeju = Cheju do, S. Korea 57 H14
Jēkabpils, Latvia 9 H21
Jekyll I., U.S.A. 115 K5
Jelcz-Laskowice, Poland 31 G4
Jelenia Góra, Poland 31 H2
Jelgava, Latvia 9 H20
Jelgava □, Latvia 30 B10
Jelica, Serbia & M. 44 C4
Jelli, Sudan 81 F3
Jelšava, Slovak Rep. 27 C13
Jemaja, Indonesia 65 L5
Jemaluang, Malaysia 65 L4
Jember, Indonesia 63 H15
Jembongan, Malaysia 62 C5
Jena, Germany 24 E7
Jena, U.S.A. 113 K8
Jenbach, Austria 26 D4
Jenīn, West Bank 74 C4
Jenkins, U.S.A. 114 G4
Jenner, U.S.A. 110 G3
Jennings, U.S.A. 113 K8
Jepara, Indonesia 63 G14
Jeparit, Australia 95 F3
Jequié, Brazil 125 F10
Jequitinhonha, Brazil 125 G10
Jequitinhonha →, Brazil 125 G11
Jerantut, Malaysia 65 L4
Jerejak, Pulau, Malaysia 65 c
Jérémie, Haiti 121 C5
Jerez, Punta, Mexico 119 C5
Jerez de García Salinas, Mexico 118 C4
Jerez de la Frontera, Spain 37 J4
Jerez de los Caballeros, Spain 37 G4
Jericho = El Arīḩā, West Bank 74 D4
Jericho, Australia 94 C4
Jerichow, Germany 24 C8
Jerid, Chott el = Djerid, Chott, Tunisia 78 B7
Jerilderie, Australia 95 F4
Jermyn, U.S.A. 117 E9
Jerome, U.S.A. 108 E6
Jerramungup, Australia 93 F2
Jersey, U.K. 15 H5
Jersey City, U.S.A. 117 F10
Jersey Shore, U.S.A. 116 E7
Jerseyville, U.S.A. 112 F9
Jerusalem, Israel 74 D4
Jervis B., Australia 95 F5
Jervis Inlet, Canada 102 C4
Jerzu, Italy 42 C2
Jesenice, Slovenia 41 B11
Jeseník, Czech Rep. 27 A10
Jesenké, Slovak Rep. 27 C13
Jesi = Iesi, Italy 41 E10
Jesselton = Kota Kinabalu, Malaysia 62 C5
Jessnitz, Germany 24 D8
Jessore, Bangla. 67 H16
Jesup, U.S.A. 115 K5
Jesús Carranza, Mexico 119 D5
Jesús María, Argentina 126 C3
Jetmore, U.S.A. 113 F5
Jetpur, India 68 J4
Jeumont, France 19 B11
Jevnaker, Norway 9 F14
Jewett, U.S.A. 116 F3
Jewett City, U.S.A. 117 E13
Jeyḩūnābād, Iran 71 C6
Jeypore, India 67 K13
Jeziorak, Jezioro, Poland 30 E6
Jeziorany, Poland 30 E7
Jeziorka →, Poland 31 F8
Jha Jha, India 69 G12
Jhaarkand = Jharkhand □, India 69 H11
Jhabua, India 68 H6
Jhajjar, India 68 E7
Jhal, Pakistan 68 E2
Jhal Jhao, Pakistan 66 F4
Jhalawar, India 68 G7
Jhalida, India 69 H11
Jhalrapatan, India 68 G7
Jhang Maghiana, Pakistan 68 D5
Jhansi, India 69 G8
Jhargram, India 69 H12
Jharia, India 69 H12
Jharkhand □, India 69 H11
Jharsuguda, India 67 J14
Jhelum, Pakistan 68 C5
Jhelum →, Pakistan 68 D5
Jhilmilli, India 69 H10
Jhudo, Pakistan 68 G3
Jhunjhunu, India 68 E6
Ji-Paraná, Brazil 124 F6
Ji Xian, Hebei, China 56 F8
Ji Xian, Henan, China 56 G8
Ji Xian, Shanxi, China 56 F6
Jia Xian, Henan, China 56 H7
Jia Xian, Shaanxi, China 56 E6
Jiading, China 59 B13
Jiahe, China 59 E9
Jialing Jiang →, China 58 C6
Jiamusi, China 60 B8
Ji'an, Jiangxi, China 59 D10
Ji'an, Jilin, China 57 D14
Jianchang, China 57 D11
Jianchangying, China 57 D10
Jianchuan, China 58 D2
Jiande, China 59 C12
Jiang'an, China 58 C5
Jiangbei, China 58 C6
Jiangcheng, China 58 F3
Jiangchuan, China 58 E4
Jiangdi, China 58 D4
Jiangdu, China 59 A12
Jiange, China 58 A5
Jianghua, China 59 E8
Jiangjin, China 58 C6
Jiangkou, China 58 D7
Jiangle, China 59 D11
Jiangling, China 59 B9
Jiangmen, China 59 F9
Jiangning, China 59 B12
Jiangshan, China 59 C12
Jiangsu □, China 57 H11
Jiangxi □, China 59 D11
Jiangyan, China 59 A13
Jiangyin, China 59 B13
Jiangyong, China 59 E8
Jiangyou, China 58 B5
Jianhe, China 58 D7
Jianli, China 59 C9
Jianning, China 59 D11
Jian'ou, China 59 D12
Jianshi, China 58 B7
Jianshui, China 58 F4
Jianyang, Fujian, China 59 D12
Jianyang, Sichuan, China 58 B5
Jiao Xian = Jiaozhou, China 57 F11
Jiaohe, Hebei, China 56 E9
Jiaohe, Jilin, China 57 C14
Jiaojiang, China 59 C13
Jiaoling, China 59 E11
Jiaozhou, China 57 F11
Jiaozhou Wan, China 57 F11
Jiaozuo, China 56 G7
Jiashan, China 59 B13
Jiawang, China 57 G9
Jiaxiang, China 56 G9
Jiaxing, China 59 B13
Jiayi = Chiai, Taiwan 59 F13
Jiayu, China 59 C9
Jibiya, Nigeria 83 C6
Jibou, Romania 29 C8
Jibuti = Djibouti ■, Africa 81 E5
Jicarón, I., Panama 120 E3
Jičín, Czech Rep. 26 A8
Jiddah, Si. Arabia 75 C2
Jido, India 67 E19
Jieshou, China 56 H8
Jiexiu, China 56 F6
Jieyang, China 59 F11
Jigawa □, Nigeria 83 C6
Jiggalong, Australia 92 D3
Jigni, India 69 G8
Jihlava, Czech Rep. 26 B8
Jihlava →, Czech Rep. 27 C9
Jihlavský □, Czech Rep. 26 B8
Jihočeský □, Czech Rep. 26 B7
Jihomoravský □, Czech Rep. 27 B9
Jijiga, Ethiopia 75 F3
Jikamshi, Nigeria 83 C6
Jikau, Sudan 81 F3
Jilin, China 57 C14
Jilin □, China 57 C14
Jiloca →, Spain 38 D3
Jilong = Chilung, Taiwan 59 E13
Jim Thorpe, U.S.A. 117 F9
Jima, Ethiopia 81 F4
Jimbaran, Teluk, Indonesia 63 K18
Jimbolia, Romania 28 E5
Jimena de la Frontera, Spain 37 J5
Jiménez, Mexico 118 B4
Jimo, China 57 F11
Jin Jiang →, China 59 C10
Jin Xian = Jinzhou, China 56 E8
Jin Xian, China 57 E11
Jinan, China 56 F9
Jinchang, China 60 C5
Jincheng, China 56 G7
Jinchuan, China 58 B4
Jind, India 68 E7
Jindabyne, Australia 95 F4
Jindřichův Hradec, Czech Rep. 26 B8
Jing He →, China 56 G5
Jing Shan, China 59 B8
Jing Xian, China 59 B12
Jing'an, China 59 C10
Jingbian, China 56 F5
Jingchuan, China 56 G4
Jingde, China 59 B12
Jingdezhen, China 59 C11
Jingdong, China 58 E3
Jinggangshan, China 59 D10
Jinggu, China 58 F3
Jinghai, China 56 E9
Jinghong, China 58 G3
Jingjiang, China 59 A13
Jingle, China 56 E6
Jingmen, China 59 B9
Jingning, China 56 G3
Jingpo Hu, China 57 C15
Jingshan, China 59 B9
Jingtai, China 56 F3
Jingxi, China 58 F6
Jingxing, China 56 E8
Jingyang, China 56 G5
Jingyu, China 57 C14
Jingyuan, China 56 F3
Jingzhou, China 58 D7
Jingziguan, China 56 H6
Jinhua, China 59 C12
Jining, Nei Monggol Zizhiqu, China 56 D7
Jining, Shandong, China 56 G9
Jinja, Uganda 86 B3
Jinjang, Malaysia 65 L3
Jinji, China 56 F4
Jinjiang, Fujian, China 59 E12
Jinjiang, Yunnan, China 58 D3
Jinjini, Ghana 82 D4
Jinkou, China 59 B10
Jinkouhe, China 58 C4
Jinmen Dao, China 59 E12
Jinnah Barrage, Pakistan 66 C7
Jinning, China 58 E4
Jinotega, Nic. 120 D2
Jinotepe, Nic. 120 D2
Jinping, Guizhou, China 58 D7
Jinping, Yunnan, China 58 F4
Jinsha, China 58 D6
Jinsha Jiang →, China 58 C5
Jinshan, China 59 B13
Jinshi, China 59 C8
Jintan, China 59 B12
Jinxi, Jiangxi, China 59 D11
Jinxi, Liaoning, China 57 D11
Jinxian, China 59 C11
Jinxiang, China 56 G9
Jinyang, China 58 D4
Jinyun, China 59 C13
Jinzhai, China 59 B10
Jinzhou, Hebei, China 56 E8
Jinzhou, Liaoning, China 57 D11
Jiparaná →, Brazil 124 E6
Jipijapa, Ecuador 124 D2
Jiquilpan, Mexico 118 D4
Jishan, China 56 G6
Jishou, China 58 C7
Jishui, China 59 D10
Jisr ash Shughūr, Syria 70 C3
Jitarning, Australia 93 F2
Jitra, Malaysia 65 J3
Jiu →, Romania 29 G8
Jiudengkou, China 56 E4
Jiujiang, Guangdong, China 59 F9
Jiujiang, Jiangxi, China 59 C10
Jiuling Shan, China 59 C10
Jiulong = Kowloon, China 59 F10
Jiulong, China 58 C3
Jiutai, China 57 B13
Jiuxincheng, China 56 E8
Jiuyuhang, China 59 B12
Jixi, Anhui, China 59 B12
Jixi, Heilongjiang, China 57 B16
Jiyang, China 57 F9
Jiyuan, China 56 G7
Jīzān, Si. Arabia 75 D3
Jize, China 56 F8
Jizera →, Czech Rep. 26 A7
Jizl, Wādī al →, Si. Arabia 70 E3
Jizō-Zaki, Japan 55 G6
Jizzakh, Uzbekistan 52 E7
Joaçaba, Brazil 127 B5
Joal Fadiout, Senegal 82 C1
João Pessoa, Brazil 125 E12
Joaquín V. González, Argentina 126 B3
Jobat, India 68 H6
Jobourg, Nez de, France 18 C5
Jódar, Spain 37 H7
Jodhpur, India 68 F5
Jodiya, India 68 H4
Jōetsu, Japan 55 F9
Jœuf, France 19 C12
Jofane, Mozam. 89 C5
Jogbani, India 69 F12
Jõgeva, Estonia 9 G22
Jogjakarta = Yogyakarta, Indonesia 63 G14
Johannesburg, S. Africa 89 D4
Johannesburg, U.S.A. 111 K9
Johansfors, Sweden 11 H9
Johilla →, India 69 H9
John Crow Mts., Jamaica 120 a
John Day, U.S.A. 108 D4
John Day →, U.S.A. 108 D3
John Day Fossil Beds ⌓, U.S.A. 108 D4
John D'Or Prairie, Canada 102 B5
John F. Kennedy International, New York ✕ (JFK), U.S.A. 117 F11
John H. Kerr Reservoir, U.S.A. 115 G6
John o' Groats, U.K. 13 C5
Johnnie, U.S.A. 111 J10
John's Ra., Australia 94 C1
Johnson, Kans., U.S.A. 113 G4
Johnson, Vt., U.S.A. 117 B12
Johnson City, N.Y., U.S.A. 117 D9
Johnson City, Tenn., U.S.A. 115 G4
Johnson City, Tex., U.S.A. 113 K5
Johnsonburg, U.S.A. 116 E6
Johnsondale, U.S.A. 111 K8
Johnsons Crossing, Canada 102 A2
Johnston, L., Australia 93 F3
Johnston Falls = Mambilima Falls, Zambia 87 E2
Johnston I., Pac. Oc. 97 F11
Johnstone Str., Canada 102 C3
Johnstown, N.Y., U.S.A. 117 C10
Johnstown, Ohio, U.S.A. 116 F2
Johnstown, Pa., U.S.A. 116 F6
Johor, Selat, Asia 65 d
Johor Baharu, Malaysia 65 d
Jõhvi, Estonia 9 G22
Joigny, France 19 E10
Joinville, Brazil 127 B6
Joinville, France 19 D12
Joinville I., Antarctica 5 C18
Jojutla, Mexico 119 D5
Jokkmokk, Sweden 8 C18
Jökulsá á Bru →, Iceland 8 D6
Jökulsá á Fjöllum →, Iceland 8 C5
Jolfā, Āzarbājān-e Sharqī, Iran 70 B5
Jolfā, Eşfahan, Iran 71 C6
Joliet, U.S.A. 114 E1
Joliette, Canada 104 C5
Jolo, Phil. 61 J4
Jolon, U.S.A. 110 K5
Jomalig I., Phil. 61 D5
Jombang, Indonesia 63 G15
Jomda, China 58 B2
Jonava, Lithuania 9 J21
Jones Sound, Canada 4 B3
Jonesboro, Ark., U.S.A. 113 H9
Jonesboro, La., U.S.A. 113 J8
Jong →, S. Leone 82 D2
Jonglei, Sudan 81 F3
Jonglei □, Sudan 81 F3
Joniškis, Lithuania 9 H20
Jönköping, Sweden 11 G8
Jönköpings län □, Sweden 11 G8
Jonquière, Canada 105 C5
Jonsered, Sweden 11 G6
Jonzac, France 20 C3
Joplin, U.S.A. 113 G7
Jora, India 68 F6
Jordan, Mont., U.S.A. 108 C10
Jordan, N.Y., U.S.A. 117 C8
Jordan ■, Asia 74 E5
Jordan →, Asia 74 D4
Jordan Valley, U.S.A. 108 E5
Jordanów, Poland 31 J6
Jorhat, India 67 F19
Jörn, Sweden 8 D19
Jorong, Indonesia 62 E4
Jørpeland, Norway 9 G11
Jorquera →, Chile 126 B2
Jos, Nigeria 83 D6
Jos Plateau, Nigeria 83 D6
Jošanička Banja, Serbia & M. 44 C4
José Batlle y Ordóñez, Uruguay 127 C4
Joseni, Romania 29 D10
Joseph, L., Nfld., Canada 105 B6
Joseph, L., Ont., Canada 116 A5
Joseph Bonaparte G., Australia 92 B4
Joshinath, India 69 D8
Joshinetsu-Kōgen △, Japan 55 F9
Joshua Tree, U.S.A. 111 L10
Joshua Tree △, U.S.A. 111 M10
Josselin, France 18 E4
Jost Van Dyke, Br. Virgin Is. 121 e
Jostedalsbreen, Norway 9 F12
Jotunheimen, Norway 9 F13
Joubertberge, Namibia 88 B1
Joué-lès-Tours, France 18 E7
Jourdanton, U.S.A. 113 L5
Joutseno, Finland 32 B5
Jovellanos, Cuba 120 B3
Joyeuse, France 21 D8
Józefów, Lubelskie, Poland 31 H10
Józefów, Mazowieckie, Poland 31 F8
Ju Xian, China 57 F10
Juan Aldama, Mexico 118 C4
Juan Bautista Alberdi, Argentina 126 C3
Juan de Fuca Str., Canada 110 B3
Juan de Nova, Ind. Oc. 89 B7
Juan Fernández, Arch. de, Pac. Oc. 97 L20
Juan José Castelli, Argentina 126 B3
Juan L. Lacaze, Uruguay 126 C4
Juankoski, Finland 8 E23
Juárez, Argentina 126 D4
Juárez, Mexico 111 N11
Juárez, Sierra de, Mexico 118 A1
Juàzeiro, Brazil 125 E10
Juàzeiro do Norte, Brazil 125 E11
Juba = Giuba →, Somali Rep. 75 G3
Juba, Sudan 81 G3
Jubany, Antarctica 5 C18
Jubayl, Lebanon 74 A4
Jubbah, Si. Arabia 70 D4
Jubbal, India 68 D7
Jubbulpore = Jabalpur, India 69 H8
Jübek, Germany 24 A5
Jubga, Russia 35 H4
Jubilee L., Australia 93 E4
Juby, C., Morocco 78 C3
Júcar = Xúquer →, Spain 39 F4
Júcaro, Cuba 120 B4
Juchitán, Mexico 119 D5
Judaea = Har Yehuda, Israel 74 D3
Judenburg, Austria 26 D7
Judith →, U.S.A. 108 C9
Judith, Pt., U.S.A. 117 E13
Judith Gap, U.S.A. 108 C9
Juelsminde, Denmark 11 J4
Jugoslavia = Serbia & Montenegro ■, Europe 44 C4
Juigalpa, Nic. 120 D2
Juillac, France 20 C5
Juist, Germany 24 B2
Juiz de Fora, Brazil 127 A7
Jujuy □, Argentina 126 A2
Julesburg, U.S.A. 112 E3
Juli, Peru 124 G5
Julia Cr. →, Australia 94 C3
Julia Creek, Australia 94 C3
Juliaca, Peru 124 G4
Julian, U.S.A. 111 M10
Julian, L., Canada 104 B4
Julian Alps = Julijske Alpe, Slovenia 41 B11
Julianatop, Suriname 125 C7
Julianehåb = Qaqortoq, Greenland 101 B6
Jülich, Germany 24 E2
Julijske Alpe, Slovenia 41 B11
Julimes, Mexico 118 B3
Jullundur, India 68 D6
Julu, China 56 F8
Jumbo, Zimbabwe 87 F3
Jumbo Pk., U.S.A. 111 J12
Jumentos Cays, Bahamas 120 B4
Jumilla, Spain 39 G3
Jumla, Nepal 69 E10
Jumna = Yamuna →, India 69 G9
Junagadh, India 68 J4
Junction, Tex., U.S.A. 113 K5
Junction, Utah, U.S.A. 109 G7
Junction B., Australia 94 A1
Junction City, Kans., U.S.A. 112 F6
Junction City, Oreg., U.S.A. 108 D2
Junction Pt., Australia 94 A1
Jundah, Australia 94 C3
Jundiaí, Brazil 127 A6
Juneau, U.S.A. 102 B2
Junee, Australia 95 E4
Jungfrau, Switz. 25 J3
Junggar Pendi, China 60 B3
Jungshahi, Pakistan 68 G2
Juniata →, U.S.A. 116 F7
Junín, Argentina 126 C3
Junín de los Andes, Argentina 128 D2
Jūniyah, Lebanon 74 B4
Junlian, China 58 C5
Juntas, Chile 126 B2
Juntura, U.S.A. 108 E4
Jur, Nahr el →, Sudan 81 F2
Jura = Jura, Mts. du, Europe 19 F13
Jura = Schwäbische Alb, Germany 25 G5
Jura, U.K. 13 F3
Jura □, France 19 F12
Jura □, Switz. 25 H3
Jūra →, Lithuania 30 C9
Jura, Mts. du, Europe 19 F13
Jura, Sd. of, U.K. 13 F3
Jurbarkas, Lithuania 9 J20
Jurien, Australia 93 F2
Jurilovca, Romania 29 F13
Jūrmala, Latvia 9 H20
Jurong, China 59 B12
Jurong, Singapore 65 d
Juruá →, Brazil 124 D5
Juruena, Brazil 124 F7
Juruena →, Brazil 124 E7
Juruti, Brazil 125 D7
Jussey, France 19 E12
Justo Daract, Argentina 126 C2
Jutaí →, Brazil 124 D5
Jüterbog, Germany 24 D9
Juticalpa, Honduras 120 D2
Jutland = Jylland, Denmark 11 H3
Juventud, I. de la, Cuba 120 B3
Juvigny-sous-Andaine, France 18 D6
Jūy Zar, Iran 70 C5
Juye, China 56 G9
Juzennecourt, France 19 D11
Jvari, Georgia 35 J6
Jwaneng, Botswana 85 J4
Jyderup, Denmark 11 J5
Jylland, Denmark 11 H3
Jyväskylä, Finland 9 E21

K

K2, Pakistan 69 B7
Ka →, Nigeria 83 C5
Kaap Plateau, S. Africa 88 D3
Kaapkruis, Namibia 88 C1
Kaapstad = Cape Town, S. Africa 88 E2
Kaba, Guinea 82 C2
Kabaena, Indonesia 63 F6
Kabala, S. Leone 82 D2
Kabale, Uganda 86 C3
Kabalo, Dem. Rep. of the Congo 86 D2
Kabambare, Dem. Rep. of the Congo 86 C2
Kabango, Dem. Rep. of the Congo 87 D2
Kabanjahe, Indonesia 62 D1
Kabankalan, Phil. 61 G5
Kabara, Mali 82 B4
Kabardinka, Russia 33 K10
Kabardino-Balkar Republic = Kabardino-Balkaria □, Russia 35 J6
Kabardino-Balkaria □, Russia 35 J6
Kabarega Falls = Murchison Falls, Uganda 86 B3
Kabasalan, Phil. 61 H5
Kabat, Indonesia 63 J17
Kabba, Nigeria 83 D6
Kabetogama, U.S.A. 112 A8
Kabi, Niger 83 C7
Kabin Buri, Thailand 64 F3
Kabinakagami L., Canada 104 C3
Kabinda, Dem. Rep. of the Congo 84 F4
Kabna, Sudan 80 D3

Kabompo, Zambia 87 E1
Kabompo →, Zambia 85 G4
Kabondo, Dem. Rep. of the Congo 87 D2
Kabongo, Dem. Rep. of the Congo 86 D2
Kabot, Guinea 82 C2
Kabou, Togo 83 D5
Kabr, Sudan 81 E2
Kabrousse, Senegal 82 C1
Kabūd Gonbad, Iran 71 B8
Kabugao, Phil. 61 B4
Kābul, Afghan. 68 B3
Kābul □, Afghan. 66 B6
Kābul →, Pakistan 68 C5
Kabunga, Dem. Rep. of the Congo 86 C2
Kaburuang, Indonesia 63 D7
Kabushiya, Sudan 81 D3
Kabwe, Zambia 87 E2
Kačanik, Serbia & M. 44 D5
Kačerginė, Lithuania 30 D10
Kachchh, Gulf of, India 68 H3
Kachchh, Rann of, India 68 H4
Kachchhidhana, India 69 J8
Kachebera, Zambia 87 E3
Kachia, Nigeria 83 D6
Kachikau, Botswana 88 B3
Kachin □, Burma 58 D1
Kachira, L., Uganda 86 C3
Kachiry, Kazakhstan 52 D8
Kachisi, Ethiopia 81 F4
Kachnara, India 68 H6
Kachot, Cambodia 65 G4
Kaçkar, Turkey 73 B9
Kadan, Czech Rep. 26 A6
Kadan Kyun, Burma 64 F2
Kadanai →, Afghan. 68 D1
Kadarkút, Hungary 28 D2
Kadavu, Fiji 91 D8
Kade, Ghana 83 D4
Kadhimain = Al Kāẓimīyah, Iraq 70 C5
Kadi, India 68 H5
Kadina, Australia 95 E2
Kadınhanı, Turkey 72 C5
Kadiolo, Mali 82 C3
Kadipur, India 69 F10
Kadirli, Turkey 70 B3
Kadiyevka = Stakhanov, Ukraine 33 H10
Kadodo, Sudan 81 E2
Kadoka, U.S.A. 112 D4
Kadom, Russia 34 C6
Kadoma, Zimbabwe 87 F2
Kâdugli, Sudan 81 E2
Kaduna, Nigeria 83 C6
Kaduna □, Nigeria 83 C6
Kaduy, Russia 32 C9
Kaédi, Mauritania 82 B2
Kaélé, Cameroon 83 C7
Kaeng Khoï, Thailand 64 E3
Kaeng Kra Chan △, Thailand 64 F2
Kaeng Tana △, Thailand 64 E5
Kaesŏng, N. Korea 57 F14
Kāf, Si. Arabia 70 D3
Kafan = Kapan, Armenia 70 B5
Kafanchan, Nigeria 83 D6
Kafareti, Nigeria 83 C7
Kaffrine, Senegal 82 C1
Kafin, Nigeria 83 D6
Kafin Madaki, Nigeria 83 C6
Kafinda, Zambia 87 E3
Kafirévs, Ákra, Greece 46 C6
Kafr el Battikh, Egypt 80 H7
Kafr el Dauwâr, Egypt 80 H7
Kafr el Sheikh, Egypt 80 H7
Kafue, Zambia 87 F2
Kafue △, Zambia 87 F2
Kafue →, Zambia 85 H5
Kafue Flats, Zambia 87 F2
Kafulwe, Zambia 87 D2
Kaga, Afghan. 68 B4
Kaga Bandoro, C.A.R. 84 C3
Kagan, Uzbekistan 52 F7
Kagarko, Nigeria 83 D6
Kagawa □, Japan 55 G7
Kagera □, Tanzania 86 C3
Kagera →, Uganda 86 C3
Kağızman, Turkey 70 B4
Kagmar, Sudan 81 E3
Kagoshima, Japan 55 J5
Kagoshima □, Japan 55 J5
Kagul = Cahul, Moldova 29 E13
Kahak, Iran 71 B6
Kahama, Tanzania 86 C3
Kahan, Pakistan 68 E3
Kahang, Malaysia 65 L4
Kahayan →, Indonesia 62 E4
Kahe, Tanzania 86 C4
Kahnūj, Iran 71 E8
Kahoka, U.S.A. 112 E9
Kahoolawe, U.S.A. 106 H16
Kahramanmaraş, Turkey 70 B3
Kâhta, Turkey 73 D8
Kahurangi △, N.Z. 91 J4
Kahuta, Pakistan 68 C5
Kahuzi-Biega △, Dem. Rep. of the Congo 86 C2
Kai, Kepulauan, Indonesia 63 F8
Kai Besar, Indonesia 63 F8
Kai Is. = Kai, Kepulauan, Indonesia 63 F8
Kai Kecil, Indonesia 63 F8
Kai Xian, China 58 B7
Kaiama, Nigeria 83 D5
Kaiapoi, N.Z. 91 K4
Kaieteur Falls, Guyana 124 B7
Kaifeng, China 56 G8
Kaihua, China 59 C12
Kaijiang, China 58 B6
Kaikohe, N.Z. 91 F4
Kaikoura, N.Z. 91 K4
Kailahun, S. Leone 82 D2
Kailash = Kangrinboqe Feng, China 69 D9
Kaili, China 58 D6
Kailu, China 57 C11
Kailua Kona, U.S.A. 106 J17
Kaimana, Indonesia 63 E8
Kaimanawa Mts., N.Z. 91 H5
Kaimganj, India 69 F8
Kaimur Hills, India 69 G10
Kainab →, Namibia 88 D2
Kainji Dam, Nigeria 83 D5
Kainji Lake △, Nigeria 83 C5
Kainji Res., Nigeria 83 C5
Kainuu, Finland 8 D23
Kaipara Harbour, N.Z. 91 G5
Kaiping, China 59 F9
Kaipokok B., Canada 105 B8
Kaira, India 68 H5
Kairana, India 68 E7
Kaironi, Indonesia 63 E8
Kairouan, Tunisia 79 A8
Kaiserslautern, Germany 25 F3
Kaiserstuhl, Germany 25 G3
Kaitaia, N.Z. 91 F4
Kaitangata, N.Z. 91 M2
Kaithal, India 68 E7
Kaitu →, Pakistan 68 C4
Kaiyang, China 58 D6
Kaiyuan, Liaoning, China 57 C13
Kaiyuan, Yunnan, China 58 F4
Kajaani, Finland 8 D22
Kajabbi, Australia 94 C3
Kajana = Kajaani, Finland 8 D22
Kajang, Malaysia 65 L3
Kajaran, Armenia 73 C12
Kajiado, Kenya 86 C4
Kajo Kaji, Sudan 81 G3
Kajuru, Nigeria 83 C6
Kaka, Sudan 81 E3
Kakabeka Falls, Canada 104 C2
Kakadu △, Australia 92 B5
Kakamas, S. Africa 88 D3
Kakamega, Kenya 86 B3
Kakanj, Bos.-H. 28 F3
Kakanui Mts., N.Z. 91 L3
Kakata, Liberia 82 D2
Kakdwip, India 69 J13
Kake, Japan 55 G6
Kake, U.S.A. 102 B2
Kakegawa, Japan 55 G9
Kakeroma-Jima, Japan 55 K4
Kakhib, Russia 35 J8
Kakhovka, Ukraine 33 J7
Kakhovske Vdskh., Ukraine 33 J7
Kakinada, India 67 L13
Kakisa →, Canada 102 A5
Kakisa L., Canada 102 A5
Kakogawa, Japan 55 G7
Kakum △, Ghana 83 D4
Kakwa →, Canada 102 C5
Kāl Gūsheh, Iran 71 D8
Kal Safīd, Iran 70 C5
Kala, Nigeria 83 C7
Kalaallit Nunaat = Greenland ∅, N. Amer. 98 C15
Kalabagh, Pakistan 68 C4
Kalabahi, Indonesia 63 F6
Kalabáka, Greece 46 B3
Kalabana, Mali 82 C3
Kalach, Russia 34 E5
Kalach na Donu, Russia 35 F6
Kaladan →, Burma 67 J18
Kaladar, Canada 116 B7
Kalahari, Africa 88 C3
Kalahari Gemsbok △, S. Africa 88 D3
Kalajoki, Finland 8 D20
Kalakamati, Botswana 89 C4
Kalakan, Russia 53 D12
K'alak'unlun Shank'ou = Karakoram Pass, Asia 69 B7
Kalam, Pakistan 69 B5
Kalama, Dem. Rep. of the Congo 86 C2
Kalama, U.S.A. 110 E4
Kalámai, Greece 46 D4
Kalamariá, Greece 44 F6
Kalamata = Kalámai, Greece 46 D4
Kalamazoo, U.S.A. 114 D3
Kalamazoo →, U.S.A. 114 D2
Kalambo Falls, Tanzania 87 D3
Kálamos, Greece 46 C5
Kálamos Nisís, Greece 46 C2
Kalan, Turkey 70 B3
Kalankalan, Guinea 82 C3
Kalannie, Australia 93 F2
Kalāntarī, Iran 71 C7
Kalao, Indonesia 63 F6
Kalaotoa, Indonesia 63 F6
Kälarne, Sweden 10 B10
Kalasin, Thailand 64 D4
Kālat, Iran 71 E8
Kalat, Pakistan 66 E5
Kalāteh, Iran 71 B7
Kalāteh-ye Ganj, Iran 71 E8
Kálathos, Greece 47 E10
Kalaus →, Russia 35 H7
Kalávrita, Greece 46 C4
Kalbarri, Australia 93 E1
Kalbarri △, Australia 93 E1
Kale, Antalya, Turkey 47 E12
Kale, Denizli, Turkey 47 D10
Kalecik, Turkey 72 B5
Kalegauk Kyun, Burma 67 M20
Kalehe, Dem. Rep. of the Congo 86 C2
Kalema, Tanzania 86 C3
Kalemie, Dem. Rep. of the Congo 86 D2
Kalety, Poland 31 H5
Kalewa, Burma 67 H19
Kaleybar, Iran 70 B5
Kalgan = Zhangjiakou, China 56 D8
Kalgoorlie-Boulder, Australia 93 F3
Kali →, India 69 F8
Kali Sindh →, India 68 G6
Kaliakra, Nos, Bulgaria 45 C12
Kalianda, Indonesia 62 F3
Kalibo, Phil. 61 F5
Kalima, Dem. Rep. of the Congo 86 C2
Kalimantan, Indonesia 62 E4
Kalimantan Barat □, Indonesia 62 E4
Kalimantan Selatan □, Indonesia 62 E5
Kalimantan Tengah □, Indonesia 62 E4
Kalimantan Timur □, Indonesia 62 D5
Kálimnos, Greece 47 D8
Kalimpong, India 69 F13
Kalinin = Tver, Russia 32 D8
Kaliningrad, Russia 9 J19
Kaliningrad ✕ (KGD), Russia 30 D7
Kalininsk, Russia 34 E7
Kalinkavichy, Belarus 33 F5
Kalinkovichi = Kalinkavichy, Belarus 33 F5
Kalinovik, Bos.-H. 44 C2
Kalipetrovo, Bulgaria 45 B11
Kaliro, Uganda 86 B3
Kalirrákhi, Greece 45 F8
Kalispell, U.S.A. 108 B6
Kalisz, Poland 31 G5
Kalisz Pomorski, Poland 31 E2
Kaliua, Tanzania 86 D3
Kaiívia Thorikoú, Greece 46 D5
Kalix, Sweden 8 D20
Kalix →, Sweden 8 D20
Kalka, India 68 D7
Kalkan, Turkey 47 E11
Kalkarindji, Australia 92 C5
Kalkaska, U.S.A. 114 C3
Kalkfeld, Namibia 88 C2
Kalkfontein, Botswana 88 C3
Kalkım, Turkey 47 B9
Kalkrand, Namibia 88 C2
Kållandsö, Sweden 11 F7
Kallavesi, Finland 8 E22
Källby, Sweden 11 F7
Kållered, Sweden 11 G6
Kallimasiá, Greece 47 C8
Kallinge, Sweden 11 H9
Kallithéa, Greece 46 D5
Kallmet, Albania 44 E3
Kalloní, Greece 47 B8
Kallonís, Kólpos, Greece 47 B8
Kallsjön, Sweden 8 E15
Kalmalo, Nigeria 83 C6
Kalmar, Sweden 11 H10
Kalmar län □, Sweden 11 G10
Kalmar sund, Sweden 11 H10
Kalmyk Republic = Kalmykia □, Russia 35 G8
Kalmykia □, Russia 35 G8
Kalmykovo, Kazakhstan 52 E6
Kalna, India 69 H13
Kalnai, India 69 H10
Kalocsa, Hungary 28 D4
Kalofer, Bulgaria 45 D8
Kalokhorio, Cyprus 49 E12
Kaloko, Dem. Rep. of the Congo 86 D2
Kalol, Gujarat, India 68 H5
Kalol, Gujarat, India 68 H5
Kalolímnos, Greece 47 D9
Kalomo, Zambia 87 F2
Kalonerón, Greece 46 D3
Kalpi, India 69 F8
Kaltern = Caldaro, Italy 41 B8
Kaltungo, Nigeria 83 D7
Kalu, Pakistan 68 G2
Kaluga, Russia 32 E9
Kalulushi, Zambia 87 E2
Kalundborg, Denmark 11 J5
Kalush, Ukraine 33 H3
Kałuszyn, Poland 31 F8
Kalutara, Sri Lanka 66 R12
Kalvarija, Lithuania 30 D10
Kalyan, India 66 K8
Kalyazin, Russia 32 D9
Kam, Albania 44 D4
Kam →, Nigeria 83 D7
Kama, Dem. Rep. of the Congo 86 C2
Kama →, Russia 52 D6
Kamachumu, Tanzania 86 C3
Kamaishi, Japan 54 E10
Kamalia, Pakistan 68 D5
Kaman, India 68 F6
Kaman, Turkey 72 C5
Kamanjab, Namibia 88 B2
Kamapanda, Zambia 87 E1
Kamarān, Yemen 75 D3
Kamativi, Zimbabwe 88 B4
Kamba, Nigeria 83 C5
Kambalda, Australia 93 F3
Kambar, Pakistan 68 F3
Kambia, S. Leone 82 D2
Kambolé, Togo 83 D5
Kambolé, Zambia 87 D3
Kambos, Cyprus 49 D11
Kambove, Dem. Rep. of the Congo 87 E2
Kamchatka, Poluostrov, Russia 53 D16
Kamchatka Pen. = Kamchatka, Poluostrov, Russia 53 D16
Kamchiya →, Bulgaria 45 C11
Kame Ruins, Zimbabwe 87 G2
Kamen, Russia 52 D9
Kamen-Rybolov, Russia 54 B6
Kamenica, Serbia & M. 44 C6
Kamenica, Serbia & M. 44 B3
Kamenice nad Lipou, Czech Rep. 26 B8
Kamenjak, Rt, Croatia 41 D10
Kamenka = Kaminka, Ukraine 33 H7
Kamenka, Kazakhstan 34 E10
Kamenka, Penza, Russia 34 D6
Kamenka, Voronezh, Russia 33 G10
Kamenka Bugskaya = Kamyanka-Buzka, Ukraine 33 G3
Kamenka Dneprovskaya = Kamyanka-Dniprovska, Ukraine 33 J8
Kamennomostskiy, Russia 35 H5
Kameno, Bulgaria 45 D11
Kamenolomini, Russia 35 G5
Kamensk-Shakhtinskiy, Russia 35 F5
Kamensk Uralskiy, Russia 52 D7
Kamenskiy, Russia 34 E7
Kamenskoye, Russia 53 C17
Kamenyak, Bulgaria 45 C10
Kamenz, Germany 24 D10
Kameoka, Japan 55 G7
Kamiah, U.S.A. 108 C5
Kamień Krajeński, Poland 30 E4
Kamień Pomorski, Poland 30 E1
Kamienna →, Poland 31 G8
Kamienna Góra, Poland 31 H3
Kamieńsk, Poland 31 G6
Kamieskroon, S. Africa 88 E2
Kamilukuak L., Canada 103 A8
Kamin-Kashyrskyy, Ukraine 33 G3
Kamina, Dem. Rep. of the Congo 87 D2
Kaminak L., Canada 103 A10
Kaministiquia, Canada 104 C1
Kaminka, Ukraine 33 H7
Kaminoyama, Japan 54 E10
Kamiros, Greece 49 C9
Kamituga, Dem. Rep. of the Congo 86 C2
Kamla →, India 69 G12
Kamloops, Canada 102 C4
Kamnik, Slovenia 41 B11
Kamo, Armenia 35 K7
Kamo, Japan 54 F9
Kamoke, Pakistan 68 C6
Kamp →, Austria 26 C8
Kampala, Uganda 86 B3
Kampar, Malaysia 65 K3
Kampar →, Indonesia 62 D2
Kampen, Neths. 17 B5
Kampene, Dem. Rep. of the Congo 84 E5
Kamphaeng Phet, Thailand 64 D2
Kampinoski △, Poland 31 F7
Kampolombo, L., Zambia 87 E2
Kampong Chhnang, Cambodia 65 F5
Kampong Pengerang, Malaysia 65 d
Kampong Punggai, Malaysia 65 d
Kampong Saom, Cambodia 65 G4
Kampong Saom, Chaak, Cambodia 65 G4
Kampong Tanjong Langsat, Malaysia 65 d
Kampong Telok Ramunia, Malaysia 65 d
Kampong To, Thailand 65 J3
Kampot, Cambodia 65 G5
Kampti, Burkina Faso 82 C4
Kampuchea = Cambodia ■, Asia 64 F5
Kampung Air Putih, Malaysia 65 K4
Kampung Jerangau, Malaysia 65 K4
Kampung Raja, Malaysia 65 K4
Kampungbaru = Tolitoli, Indonesia 63 D6
Kamrau, Teluk, Indonesia 63 E8
Kamsack, Canada 103 C8
Kamsai, Guinea 82 C2
Kamskoye Ustye, Russia 34 C9
Kamuchawie L., Canada 103 B8
Kamui-Misaki, Japan 54 C10
Kamyanets-Podilskyy, Ukraine 33 H4
Kamyanka-Buzka, Ukraine 33 G3
Kamyanka-Dniprovska, Ukraine 33 J8
Kāmyārān, Iran 70 C5
Kamyshin, Russia 34 E7
Kamyzyak, Russia 35 G9
Kan, Sudan 81 F3
Kanaaupscow, Canada 101 C12
Kanaaupscow →, Canada 104 B4
Kanab, U.S.A. 109 H7
Kanab →, U.S.A. 109 H7
Kanagi, Japan 54 D10
Kanairiktok →, Canada 105 A7
Kanália, Greece 46 B4
Kananga, Dem. Rep. of the Congo 84 F4
Kanash, Russia 34 C8
Kanaskat, U.S.A. 110 C5
Kanastraíon, Ákra = Palioúrion, Ákra, Greece 44 G7
Kanawha →, U.S.A. 114 F4
Kanazawa, Japan 55 F8
Kanchanaburi, Thailand 64 E2
Kanchenjunga, Nepal 69 F13
Kanchipuram, India 66 N11
Kańczuga, Poland 31 J9
Kandaghat, India 68 D7
Kandahar = Qandahār, Afghan. 66 D4
Kandalaksha, Russia 52 C4
Kandangan, Indonesia 62 E5
Kandanghaur, Indonesia 63 G13
Kandanos, Greece 49 D5
Kandava, Latvia 30 A9
Kandavu = Kadavu, Fiji 91 D8
Kandhíla, Greece 46 D4
Kandhkot, Pakistan 68 E3
Kandhla, India 68 E7
Kandi, Benin 83 C5
Kandi, India 69 H13
Kandiaro, Pakistan 68 F3
Kandıra, Turkey 72 B4
Kandla, India 68 H4
Kandos, Australia 95 E4
Kandreho, Madag. 89 B8
Kandy, Sri Lanka 66 R12
Kane, U.S.A. 116 E6
Kane Basin, Greenland 98 B12
Kanel, Senegal 82 B2
Kaneohe, U.S.A. 106 H16
Kanevskaya, Russia 35 G4
Kanfanar, Croatia 41 C10
Kang, Botswana 88 C3
Kang Krung △, Thailand 65 H2
Kangaba, Mali 82 C3
Kangal, Turkey 72 C7
Kangān, Fārs, Iran 71 E7
Kangān, Hormozgān, Iran 71 E8
Kangar, Malaysia 65 J3
Kangaré, Mali 82 C3
Kangaroo I., Australia 95 F2
Kangaroo Mts., Australia 94 C3
Kangasala, Finland 9 F21
Kangāvar, Iran 71 C6
Kangding, China 58 B3
Kangdong, N. Korea 57 E14
Kangean, Kepulauan, Indonesia 62 F5
Kangean Is. = Kangean, Kepulauan, Indonesia 62 F5
Kangen →, Sudan 81 F3
Kanggye, N. Korea 57 D14
Kanggyŏng, S. Korea 57 F14
Kanghwa, S. Korea 57 F14
Kangikajik, Greenland 4 B6
Kangiqliniq = Rankin Inlet, Canada 100 B10
Kangiqsualujjuaq, Canada 101 C13
Kangiqsujuaq, Canada 101 B12
Kangiqtugaapik = Clyde River, Canada 101 A13
Kangirsuk, Canada 101 B13
Kangkar Chemaran, Malaysia 65 d
Kangkar Sungai Tiram, Malaysia 65 d
Kangkar Teberau, Malaysia 65 d
Kangnŭng, S. Korea 57 F15
Kangping, China 57 C12
Kangra, India 68 C7
Kangrinboqe Feng, China 69 D9
Kangto, India 67 F18
Kanhar →, India 69 G10
Kani, Ivory C. 82 D3
Kaniama, Dem. Rep. of the Congo 86 D1
Kaniapiskau = Caniapiscau →, Canada 105 A6
Kaniapiskau, L. = Caniapiscau, L. de, Canada 105 B6
Kanin, Poluostrov, Russia 52 C5
Kanin Nos, Mys, Russia 52 C5
Kanin Pen. = Kanin, Poluostrov, Russia 52 C5
Kaninë, Albania 44 F3
Kaniva, Australia 95 F3
Kanjiža, Serbia & M. 28 D5
Kanjut Sar, Pakistan 69 A6
Kankaanpää, Finland 9 F20
Kankakee, U.S.A. 114 E2
Kankakee →, U.S.A. 114 E1
Kankan, Guinea 82 C3
Kankendy = Xankändi, Azerbaijan 70 B5
Kanker, India 67 J12
Kankossa, Mauritania 82 B2
Kankroli, India 68 G5
Kannapolis, U.S.A. 115 H5
Kannauj, India 69 F8
Kannod, India 66 H10
Kano, Nigeria 83 C6
Kano □, Nigeria 83 C6
Kan'onji, Japan 55 G6
Kanoroba, Ivory C. 82 D3
Kanowit, Malaysia 62 D4
Kanoya, Japan 55 J5
Kanpetlet, Burma 67 J18
Kanpur, India 69 F9
Kansas □, U.S.A. 112 F6
Kansas →, U.S.A. 112 F7
Kansas City, Kans., U.S.A. 112 F7
Kansas City, Mo., U.S.A. 112 F7
Kansenia, Dem. Rep. of the Congo 87 E2
Kansk, Russia 53 D10
Kansŏng, S. Korea 57 E15
Kansu = Gansu □, China 56 G3
Kantaphor, India 68 H7
Kantchari, Burkina Faso 83 C5
Kantché, Niger 83 C6
Kanté, Togo 83 D5
Kantemirovka, Russia 33 H10
Kantharalak, Thailand 64 E5
Kantli →, India 68 E6
Kantō □, Japan 55 F9
Kantō-Sanchi, Japan 55 G9
Kanturk, Ireland 12 D3
Kanuma, Japan 55 F9
Kanus, Namibia 88 D2
Kanye, Botswana 88 C4
Kanzenze, Dem. Rep. of the Congo 87 E2
Kanzi, Ras, Tanzania 86 D4
Kao Phara, Thailand 65 a
Kaohsiung, Taiwan 59 F13
Kaokoveld, Namibia 88 B1
Kaolack, Senegal 82 C1
Kaoshan, China 57 B13
Kapaa, U.S.A. 106 G15
Kapadvanj, India 68 H5
Kapaklı, Turkey 45 E11
Kapan, Armenia 70 B5
Kapanga, Dem. Rep. of the Congo 84 F4
Kapchagai = Qapshaghay, Kazakhstan 52 E8
Kapela = Velika Kapela, Croatia 41 C12
Kapéllo, Ákra, Greece 46 E5
Kapema, Dem. Rep. of the Congo 87 E2
Kapfenberg, Austria 26 D8
Kapı Dağı, Turkey 45 F11
Kapiri Mposhi, Zambia 87 E2
Kāpīsā □, Afghan. 66 B6
Kapiskau →, Canada 104 B3
Kapit, Malaysia 62 D4
Kapiti I., N.Z. 91 J5
Kaplan, U.S.A. 113 K8
Kaplice, Czech Rep. 26 C7
Kapoe, Thailand 65 H2
Kapoeta, Sudan 81 G3
Kápolnásnyék, Hungary 28 C3
Kapos →, Hungary 28 D3

Kaposvár, *Hungary* 28 D2
Kapowsin, *U.S.A.* 110 D4
Kappeln, *Germany* 24 A5
Kappelshamn, *Sweden* 11 G12
Kapps, *Namibia* 88 C2
Kaprije, *Croatia* 41 E12
Kapsan, *N. Korea* 57 D15
Kapsukas = Marijampolė, *Lithuania* 9 J20
Kaptai L., *Bangla.* 67 H18
Kapuas ➝, *Indonesia* 62 E3
Kapuas Hulu, Pegunungan, *Malaysia* 62 D4
Kapuas Hulu Ra. = Kapuas Hulu, Pegunungan, *Malaysia* 62 D4
Kapulo, *Dem. Rep. of the Congo* 87 D2
Kapunda, *Australia* 95 E2
Kapuni, *N.Z.* 91 H5
Kapurthala, *India* 68 D6
Kapuskasing, *Canada* 104 C3
Kapuskasing ➝, *Canada* 104 C3
Kapustin Yar, *Russia* 35 F7
Kaputar, *Australia* 95 E5
Kaputir, *Kenya* 86 B4
Kapuvár, *Hungary* 28 C2
Kara, *Russia* 52 C7
Karā, W. ➝, *Si. Arabia* 80 C5
Kara Ada, *Turkey* 47 E9
Kara Bogaz Gol, Zaliv = Garabogazköl Aylagy, *Turkmenistan* 52 E6
Kara Burun, *Turkey* 47 E9
Kara Kalpak Republic = Qoraqalpoghistan □, *Uzbekistan* 52 E6
Kara Kum, *Turkmenistan* 52 F6
Kara Sea, *Russia* 52 B7
Karaadilli, *Turkey* 47 C12
Karabiğa, *Turkey* 45 F11
Karabük, *Turkey* 72 B5
Karaburun, *Albania* 44 F3
Karaburun, *Turkey* 47 C8
Karabutak = Qarabutaq, *Kazakhstan* 52 E7
Karacabey, *Turkey* 45 F12
Karacakılavuz, *Turkey* 45 E11
Karacaköy, *Turkey* 45 E12
Karacasu, *Turkey* 47 D10
Karachala = Qaraçala, *Azerbaijan* 35 L9
Karachayevsk, *Russia* 35 J5
Karachev, *Russia* 33 F8
Karachey-Cherkessia □, *Russia* 35 J5
Karachi, *Pakistan* 68 G2
Karad, *India* 66 L9
Karadirek, *Turkey* 47 C12
Karaga, *Ghana* 83 D4
Karaganda = Qaraghandy, *Kazakhstan* 52 E8
Karagayly, *Kazakhstan* 52 E8
Karaginskiy, Ostrov, *Russia* 53 D17
Karagola Road, *India* 69 G12
Karagüney Dağları, *Turkey* 72 B6
Karahallı, *Turkey* 47 C11
Karaikal, *India* 66 P11
Karaikkudi, *India* 66 P11
Karaisali, *Turkey* 72 D6
Karaj, *Iran* 71 C6
Karak, *Malaysia* 65 L4
Karakalpakstan = Qoraqalpoghistan □, *Uzbekistan* 52 E6
Karakelong, *Indonesia* 63 D7
Karakitang, *Indonesia* 63 D7
Karaklis = Vanadzor, *Armenia* 35 K7
Karakoçan, *Turkey* 73 C9
Karakol, *Kyrgyzstan* 52 E8
Karakoram Pass, *Asia* 69 B7
Karakoram Ra., *Pakistan* 69 B7
Karakurt, *Turkey* 73 B10
Karakuwisa, *Namibia* 88 B2
Karalon, *Russia* 53 D12
Karama, *Jordan* 74 D4
Karaman, *Balıkesir, Turkey* 47 B9
Karaman, *Konya, Turkey* 70 B2
Karamanlı, *Turkey* 47 D11
Karamay, *China* 60 B3
Karambu, *Indonesia* 62 E5
Karamea Bight, *N.Z.* 91 J3
Karamnasa ➝, *India* 69 G10
Karamürsel, *Turkey* 45 F13
Karand, *Iran* 70 C5
Karangana, *Mali* 82 C3
Karanganyar, *Indonesia* 63 G13
Karangasem, *Indonesia* 63 J18
Karanjia, *India* 69 J11
Karankasso, *Burkina Faso* 82 C4
Karaova, *Turkey* 47 D9
Karapınar, *Turkey* 72 D5
Karasburg, *Namibia* 88 D2
Karasino, *Russia* 52 C9
Karasjok, *Norway* 8 B21
Karasu, *Turkey* 72 B4
Karasu ➝, *Turkey* 47 E12
Karasuk, *Russia* 52 D8
Karasuyama, *Japan* 55 F10
Karataş, *Adana, Turkey* 72 D6
Karataş, *Manisa, Turkey* 47 C10
Karataş Burnu, *Turkey* 72 D6
Karatau, Khrebet = Qarataū, *Kazakhstan* 52 E7
Karatoprak, *Turkey* 47 D9
Karatsu, *Japan* 55 H5
Karaul, *Russia* 52 B9
Karauli, *India* 68 F7
Karavastasë, L. e, *Albania* 44 F3
Karávi, *Greece* 46 E5
Karavostasi, *Cyprus* 49 D11
Karawang, *Indonesia* 63 G12
Karawanken, *Europe* 26 E7
Karayazı, *Turkey* 73 C10
Karazhal, *Kazakhstan* 52 E8
Karbalā', *Iraq* 70 C5
Kårböle, *Sweden* 10 C9
Karcag, *Hungary* 28 C5
Karcha ➝, *Pakistan* 69 B7
Karchana, *India* 69 G9
Karczew, *Poland* 31 F8
Kardam, *Bulgaria* 45 C12
Kardeljovo = Ploče, *Croatia* 41 E14
Kardhámila, *Greece* 47 C8
Kardhamíli, *Greece* 46 E4
Kardhítsa, *Greece* 46 B3
Kardhítsa □, *Greece* 46 B3
Kärdla, *Estonia* 9 G20
Kareeberge, *S. Africa* 88 E3
Kareha ➝, *India* 69 G12
Kareima, *Sudan* 80 D3
Karelia □, *Russia* 52 C4
Karelian Republic = Karelia □, *Russia* 52 C4
Karera, *India* 68 G8
Kārevāndar, *Iran* 71 E9
Kargasok, *Russia* 52 D9
Kargat, *Russia* 52 D9
Kargı, *Turkey* 72 B6
Kargil, *India* 69 B7
Kargopol, *Russia* 32 B10
Kargowa, *Poland* 31 F2
Karguéri, *Niger* 83 C7
Karhal, *India* 69 F8
Kariá, *Greece* 46 C2
Kariaí, *Greece* 45 F8
Karīān, *Iran* 71 E8
Karianga, *Madag.* 89 C8
Kariba, *Zimbabwe* 87 F2
Kariba, L., *Zimbabwe* 87 F2
Kariba Dam, *Zimbabwe* 87 F2
Kariba Gorge, *Zambia* 87 F2
Karibib, *Namibia* 88 C2
Karijini △, *Australia* 92 D2
Karimata, Kepulauan, *Indonesia* 62 E3
Karimata, Selat, *Indonesia* 62 E3
Karimata Is. = Karimata, Kepulauan, *Indonesia* 62 E3
Karimnagar, *India* 66 K11
Karimun Kecil, Pulau, *Indonesia* 65 d
Karimunjawa, Kepulauan, *Indonesia* 62 F4
Karin, *Somali Rep.* 75 E4
Káristos, *Greece* 46 C6
Karīt, *Iran* 71 C8
Kariya, *Japan* 55 G8
Kariyangwe, *Zimbabwe* 89 B4
Karjala, *Finland* 32 A5
Karkaralinsk = Qarqaraly, *Kazakhstan* 52 E8
Karkheh ➝, *Iran* 70 D5
Karkinitska Zatoka, *Ukraine* 33 K7
Karkinitskiy Zaliv = Karkinitska Zatoka, *Ukraine* 33 K7
Karkur Tohl, *Egypt* 80 C2
Karl Liebknecht, *Russia* 33 G8
Karl-Marx-Stadt = Chemnitz, *Germany* 24 E8
Karlholmsbruk, *Sweden* 10 D11
Karlino, *Poland* 30 D2
Karlivka, *Ukraine* 33 H8
Karlobag, *Croatia* 41 D12
Karlovac, *Croatia* 41 C12
Karlovarský □, *Czech Rep.* 26 A5
Karlovka = Karlivka, *Ukraine* 33 H8
Karlovo, *Bulgaria* 45 D8
Karlovy Vary, *Czech Rep.* 26 A5
Karlsbad = Karlovy Vary, *Czech Rep.* 26 A5
Karlsborg, *Sweden* 11 F8
Karlshamn, *Sweden* 11 H8
Karlskoga, *Sweden* 10 E8
Karlskrona, *Sweden* 11 H9
Karlsruhe, *Germany* 25 F4
Karlstad, *Sweden* 10 E7
Karlstad, *U.S.A.* 112 A6
Karlstadt, *Germany* 25 F5
Karma, *Niger* 83 C5
Karmėlava, *Lithuania* 30 D11
Karmi'el, *Israel* 74 C4
Karnak, *Egypt* 80 B3
Karnal, *India* 68 E7
Karnali ➝, *Nepal* 69 E9
Karnaphuli Res. = Kaptai L., *Bangla.* 67 H18
Karnaprayag, *India* 69 D8
Karnataka □, *India* 66 N10
Karnes City, *U.S.A.* 113 L6
Karnische Alpen, *Europe* 26 E6
Karnobat, *Bulgaria* 45 D10
Kärnten □, *Austria* 26 E6
Karo, *Mali* 82 C4
Karoi, *Zimbabwe* 87 F2
Karon, Ao, *Thailand* 65 a
Karonga, *Malawi* 87 D3
Karoo △, *S. Africa* 88 E3
Karoonda, *Australia* 95 F2
Karor, *Pakistan* 68 D4
Karora, *Sudan* 80 D4
Káros, *Greece* 47 E7
Karounga, *Mali* 82 B3
Karousádhes, *Greece* 46 B1
Karpacz, *Poland* 31 H2
Karpasia, *Cyprus* 49 D13
Kárpathos, *Greece* 47 F9
Kárpathos, Stenón, *Greece* 47 F9
Karpatsky △, *Ukraine* 29 B9
Karpenísion, *Greece* 46 C3
Karpuz Burnu = Apostolos Andreas, C., *Cyprus* 49 D13
Karpuzlu, *Turkey* 47 D9
Karratha, *Australia* 92 D2
Kars, *Turkey* 73 B10
Karsakpay, *Kazakhstan* 52 E7
Karsha, *Kazakhstan* 34 F10
Karshi = Qarshi, *Uzbekistan* 52 F7
Karsiyang, *India* 69 F13
Karsog, *India* 68 D7
Karst = Kras, *Croatia* 41 C10
Kartal, *Turkey* 45 F13
Kartál Óros, *Greece* 45 E9
Kartaly, *Russia* 52 D7
Kartapur, *India* 68 D6
Karthaus, *U.S.A.* 116 E6
Kartuzy, *Poland* 30 D5
Karufa, *Indonesia* 63 E8
Karuma ⌂, *Uganda* 86 B3
Karumba, *Australia* 94 B3
Karumo, *Tanzania* 86 C3
Karumwa, *Tanzania* 86 C3
Kārūn ➝, *Iran* 71 D6
Karungu, *Kenya* 86 C3
Karup, *Denmark* 11 H3
Karviná, *Czech Rep.* 27 B11
Karwan ➝, *India* 68 F8
Karwar, *India* 66 M9
Karwendel ⌂, *Austria* 26 D4
Karwi, *India* 69 G9
Kaş, *Turkey* 47 E11
Kasaba, *Turkey* 47 E11
Kasache, *Malawi* 87 E3
Kasai ➝, *Dem. Rep. of the Congo* 84 E3
Kasai-Oriental □, *Dem. Rep. of the Congo* 86 D1
Kasaji, *Dem. Rep. of the Congo* 87 E1
Kasama, *Zambia* 87 E3
Kasan-dong, *N. Korea* 57 D14
Kasane, *Namibia* 88 B3
Kasanga, *Tanzania* 87 D3
Kasanka △, *Zambia* 87 E3
Kasar, Ras, *Sudan* 80 D4
Kasaragod, *India* 66 N9
Kasba L., *Canada* 103 A8
Kāseh Garān, *Iran* 70 C5
Kasempa, *Zambia* 87 E2
Kasenga, *Dem. Rep. of the Congo* 87 E2
Kasese, *Uganda* 86 B3
Kasewa, *Zambia* 87 E2
Kasganj, *India* 69 F8
Kashabowie, *Canada* 104 C1
Kashaf, *Iran* 71 C9
Kāshān, *Iran* 71 C6
Kashechewan, *Canada* 104 B3
Kashgar = Kashi, *China* 60 C2
Kashi, *China* 60 C2
Kashimbo, *Dem. Rep. of the Congo* 87 E2
Kashin, *Russia* 32 D9
Kashipur, *India* 69 E8
Kashira, *Russia* 32 E10
Kashiwazaki, *Japan* 55 F9
Kashk-e Kohneh, *Afghan.* 66 B3
Kashkū'īyeh, *Iran* 71 D7
Kāshmar, *Iran* 71 C8
Kashmir, *Asia* 69 C7
Kashmor, *Pakistan* 68 E3
Kashpirovka, *Russia* 34 D9
Kashun Noerh = Gaxun Nur, *China* 60 B5
Kasiari, *India* 69 H12
Kasimov, *Russia* 34 C5
Kasinge, *Dem. Rep. of the Congo* 86 D2
Kasiruta, *Indonesia* 63 E7
Kaskaskia ➝, *U.S.A.* 112 G10
Kaskattama ➝, *Canada* 103 B10
Kaskinen, *Finland* 9 E19
Kaslo, *Canada* 102 D5
Kasmere L., *Canada* 103 B8
Kasongo, *Dem. Rep. of the Congo* 86 C2
Kasongo Lunda, *Dem. Rep. of the Congo* 84 F3
Kásos, *Greece* 47 F8
Kásos, Stenón, *Greece* 47 F8
Kaspi, *Georgia* 35 K7
Kaspichan, *Bulgaria* 45 C11
Kaspiysk, *Russia* 35 J8
Kaspiyskiy = Lagan, *Russia* 35 H8
Kassab ed Doleib, *Sudan* 81 E3
Kassaba, *Egypt* 80 C2
Kassalâ, *Sudan* 81 D4
Kassalâ □, *Sudan* 81 D4
Kassándra, *Greece* 44 F7
Kassándrinon, *Greece* 44 F7
Kassel, *Germany* 24 D5
Kassinger, *Sudan* 80 D3
Kassiópi, *Greece* 49 A3
Kasson, *U.S.A.* 112 C8
Kastamonu, *Turkey* 72 B5
Kastav, *Croatia* 41 C11
Kastélli, *Greece* 49 D5
Kastéllion, *Greece* 49 D7
Kastellórizon = Megiste, *Greece* 47 E11
Kástellos, *Greece* 47 E9
Kastellou, Ákra, *Greece* 47 F9
Kasterlee, *Belgium* 17 C4
Kastlösa, *Sweden* 11 H10
Kastóri, *Greece* 46 D4
Kastoría, *Greece* 44 F5
Kastoría □, *Greece* 44 F5
Kastorías, Límni, *Greece* 44 F5
Kastornoye, *Russia* 33 G10
Kastós Nisís, *Greece* 46 C2
Kastrosikiá, *Greece* 46 B2
Kastrup, København ✕ (CPH), *Denmark* 11 J6
Kastsyukovichy, *Belarus* 32 F7
Kasulu, *Tanzania* 86 C3
Kasumi, *Japan* 55 G7
Kasumkent, *Russia* 35 K9
Kasungu, *Malawi* 87 E3
Kasungu △, *Malawi* 87 E3
Kasur, *Pakistan* 68 D6
Kataba, *Zambia* 87 F2
Katagum, *Nigeria* 83 C7
Katahdin, Mt., *U.S.A.* 115 C11
Katako Kombe, *Dem. Rep. of the Congo* 86 C1
Katákolon, *Greece* 46 D3
Katale, *Tanzania* 86 C3
Katanda, *Katanga, Dem. Rep. of the Congo* 86 D1
Katanda, *Nord-Kivu, Dem. Rep. of the Congo* 86 C2
Katanga □, *Dem. Rep. of the Congo* 86 D2
Katangi, *India* 66 J11
Katanning, *Australia* 93 F2
Katastári, *Greece* 46 D2
Katavi △, *Tanzania* 86 D3
Katavi Swamp, *Tanzania* 86 D3
Kateríni, *Greece* 44 F6
Katghora, *India* 69 H10
Katha, *Burma* 67 G20
Katherîna, Gebel, *Egypt* 70 D2
Katherine, *Australia* 92 B5
Katherine Gorge, *Australia* 92 B5
Kathi, *India* 68 J6
Kathiawar, *India* 68 H4
Kathikas, *Cyprus* 49 E11
Kathmandu = Katmandu, *Nepal* 69 F11
Kathua, *India* 68 C6
Kati, *Mali* 82 C3
Katihar, *India* 69 G12
Katima Mulilo, *Zambia* 88 B3
Katimbira, *Malawi* 87 E3
Katingan = Mendawai ➝, *Indonesia* 62 E4
Katiola, *Ivory C.* 82 D3
Katlanovo, *Macedonia* 44 E5
Katmandu, *Nepal* 69 F11
Katni, *India* 69 H9
Káto Akhaïa, *Greece* 46 C3
Káto Arkhánai, *Greece* 49 D7
Káto Khorió, *Greece* 49 D7
Káto Pyrgos, *Cyprus* 49 D11
Káto Stavros, *Greece* 44 F7
Katokhí, *Greece* 46 C3
Katompe, *Dem. Rep. of the Congo* 86 D2
Katong, *Singapore* 65 d
Katonga ➝, *Uganda* 86 B3
Katoomba, *Australia* 95 E5
Katoúna, *Greece* 46 C3
Katowice, *Poland* 31 H6
Katrancı Dağı, *Turkey* 47 D12
Katrine, L., *U.K.* 13 E4
Katrineholm, *Sweden* 11 E10
Katsepe, *Madag.* 89 B8
Katsina, *Nigeria* 83 C6
Katsina □, *Nigeria* 83 C6
Katsina Ala, *Nigeria* 83 D6
Katsina Ala ➝, *Nigeria* 83 D6
Katsumoto, *Japan* 55 H4
Katsuura, *Japan* 55 G10
Katsuyama, *Japan* 55 F8
Kattaviá, *Greece* 49 D9
Kattegat, *Denmark* 11 H5
Katthammarsvik, *Sweden* 11 G12
Katul, J., *Sudan* 81 E2
Katumba, *Dem. Rep. of the Congo* 86 D2
Katwa, *India* 69 H13
Katwijk, *Neths.* 17 B4
Katy Wrocławskie, *Poland* 31 G3
Kauai, *U.S.A.* 106 H15
Kauai Channel, *U.S.A.* 106 H15
Kaub, *Germany* 25 E3
Kaudom ⌂, *Namibia* 88 B3
Kaufbeuren, *Germany* 25 H6
Kaufman, *U.S.A.* 113 J6
Kauhajoki, *Finland* 9 E20
Kaukauna, *U.S.A.* 114 C1
Kaukauveld, *Namibia* 88 C3
Kaunakakai, *U.S.A.* 106 H16
Kaunas, *Lithuania* 9 J20
Kaunas ✕ (KUN), *Lithuania* 30 D11
Kaunia, *Bangla.* 69 G13
Kaunos, *Turkey* 47 E10
Kaura Namoda, *Nigeria* 83 C6
Kauru, *Nigeria* 83 C6
Kautokeino, *Norway* 8 B20
Kauwapur, *India* 69 F10
Kavacha, *Russia* 53 C17
Kavadarci, *Macedonia* 44 E6
Kavajë, *Albania* 44 E3
Kavak, *Turkey* 72 B7
Kavak Dağı, *Turkey* 47 D10
Kavaklı, *Turkey* 45 E11
Kavaklıdere, *Turkey* 47 D10
Kavalerovo, *Russia* 54 B7
Kavali, *India* 66 M12
Kavála, *Greece* 45 F8
Kavála □, *Greece* 45 E8
Kavála Kólpos, *Greece* 45 F8
Kavār, *Iran* 71 D7
Kavarna, *Bulgaria* 45 C12
Kavi, *India* 68 H5
Kavimba, *Botswana* 88 B3
Kavīr, Dasht-e, *Iran* 71 C7
Kavkaz, *Russia* 33 K9
Kävlinge, *Sweden* 11 J7
Kavos, *Greece* 49 B4
Kavoúsi, *Greece* 47 F7
Kaw, *Fr. Guiana* 125 C8
Kawa, *Sudan* 81 E3
Kawagama L., *Canada* 116 A6
Kawagoe, *Japan* 55 G9
Kawaguchi, *Japan* 55 G9
Kawambwa, *Zambia* 87 D2
Kawanoe, *Japan* 55 G6
Kawardha, *India* 69 J9
Kawasaki, *Japan* 55 G9
Kawasi, *Indonesia* 63 E7
Kawerau, *N.Z.* 91 H6
Kawhia Harbour, *N.Z.* 91 H5
Kawio, Kepulauan, *Indonesia* 63 D7
Kawnro, *Burma* 67 H21
Kawthaung, *Burma* 65 H2
Kawthoolei = Kayin □, *Burma* 67 L20
Kawthule = Kayin □, *Burma* 67 L20
Kaxholmen, *Sweden* 11 G8
Kaya, *Burkina Faso* 83 C4
Kayah □, *Burma* 67 K20
Kayalıköy Barajı, *Turkey* 45 E11
Kayan ➝, *Indonesia* 62 D5
Kaycee, *U.S.A.* 108 E10
Kayeli, *Indonesia* 63 E7
Kayenta, *U.S.A.* 109 H8
Kayes, *Mali* 82 C2
Kayı, *Turkey* 47 B12
Kayima, *S. Leone* 82 D2
Kayin □, *Burma* 67 L20
Kaymakçı, *Turkey* 47 C10
Kayoa, *Indonesia* 63 D7
Kayomba, *Zambia* 87 E1
Kaysatskoye, *Russia* 34 F8
Kayseri, *Turkey* 70 B2
Kaysville, *U.S.A.* 108 F8
Kaz Dağı, *Turkey* 47 B8
Kazachye, *Russia* 53 B14
Kazakhstan ■, *Asia* 52 E7
Kazan, *Russia* 34 C9
Kazan ➝, *Canada* 103 A9
Kazan-Rettō, *Pac. Oc.* 96 E6
Kazanlŭk, *Bulgaria* 45 D9
Kazanskaya, *Russia* 34 F5
Kazatin = Kozyatyn, *Ukraine* 33 H5
Kazaure, *Nigeria* 83 C6
Kazbek, *Russia* 35 J7
Kāzerūn, *Iran* 71 D6
Kazi Magomed = Qazimämmäd, *Azerbaijan* 35 K9
Kazimierz Dolny, *Poland* 31 G8
Kazimierza Wielka, *Poland* 31 H7
Kazincbarcika, *Hungary* 28 B5
Kazlų Rūda, *Lithuania* 30 D10
Kaztalovka, *Kazakhstan* 34 F9
Kazuma Pan △, *Zimbabwe* 87 F2
Kazuno, *Japan* 54 D10
Kazym ➝, *Russia* 52 C7
Kcynia, *Poland* 31 F4
Ké-Macina, *Mali* 82 C3
Kéa, *Greece* 46 D6
Keady, *U.K.* 12 B5
Kearney, *U.S.A.* 112 E5
Kearny, *U.S.A.* 109 K8
Kearsarge, Mt., *U.S.A.* 117 C13
Keban, *Turkey* 73 C8
Keban Barajı, *Turkey* 70 B3
Kebbi □, *Nigeria* 83 C5
Kébi, *Ivory C.* 82 D3
Kebnekaise, *Sweden* 8 C18
Kebri Dehar, *Ethiopia* 75 F3
Kebumen, *Indonesia* 63 G13
Kecel, *Hungary* 28 D4
Kechika ➝, *Canada* 102 B3
Keçiborlu, *Turkey* 47 D12
Kecskemét, *Hungary* 28 D4
Kedada, *Ethiopia* 81 F4
Kėdainiai, *Lithuania* 9 J21
Kedarnath, *India* 69 D8
Kedgwick, *Canada* 105 C6
Kédhros Óros, *Greece* 49 D6
Kediri, *Indonesia* 63 G15
Kedjebi, *Ghana* 83 D5
Kédougou, *Senegal* 82 C2
Kędzierzyn-Koźle, *Poland* 31 H5
Keeler, *U.S.A.* 110 J9
Keeley L., *Canada* 103 C7
Keeling Is. = Cocos Is., *Ind. Oc.* 96 J1
Keelung = Chilung, *Taiwan* 59 E13
Keene, *Canada* 116 B6
Keene, *Calif., U.S.A.* 111 K8
Keene, *N.H., U.S.A.* 117 D12
Keene, *N.Y., U.S.A.* 117 B11
Keep River △, *Australia* 92 C4
Keeper Hill, *Ireland* 12 D3
Keer-Weer, C., *Australia* 94 A3
Keeseville, *U.S.A.* 117 B11
Keetmanshoop, *Namibia* 88 D2
Keewatin, *Canada* 103 D10
Keewatin ➝, *Canada* 103 B8
Kefa □, *Ethiopia* 81 F4
Kefallinía, *Greece* 46 C2
Kefallinía □, *Greece* 46 C2
Kéfalos, *Greece* 47 E8
Kefamenanu, *Indonesia* 63 F6
Kefar Sava, *Israel* 74 C3
Keffi, *Nigeria* 83 D6
Keffin Hausa, *Nigeria* 83 C6
Keflavík, *Iceland* 8 D2
Keftya, *Ethiopia* 81 E4
Keg River, *Canada* 102 B5
Kegaska, *Canada* 105 B7
Keheili, *Sudan* 80 D3
Kehl, *Germany* 25 G3
Keighley, *U.K.* 14 D6
Keila, *Estonia* 9 G21
Keimoes, *S. Africa* 88 D3
Keita, *Niger* 83 C6
Keitele, *Finland* 8 E22
Keith, *Australia* 95 F3
Keith, *U.K.* 13 D6
Keizer, *U.S.A.* 108 D2
Kejimkujik △, *Canada* 105 D6
Kejserr Franz Joseph Fd., *Greenland* 4 B6
Kekri, *India* 68 G6
Kelam, *Ethiopia* 81 G4
Kelamet, *Eritrea* 81 D4
Kelan, *China* 56 E6
Kelang, *Malaysia* 65 L3
Kelantan ➝, *Malaysia* 65 J4
Këlcyrë, *Albania* 44 F4
Kelekçi, *Turkey* 47 D11
Keles, *Turkey* 45 G13
Keleti-főcsatorna, *Hungary* 28 C6
Kelheim, *Germany* 25 G7
Kelkit, *Turkey* 73 B8
Kelkit ➝, *Turkey* 72 B7
Kellerberrin, *Australia* 93 F2

Kellett, C., *Canada* 4 B1
Kelleys I., *U.S.A.* 116 E2
Kellogg, *U.S.A.* 108 C5
Kells = Ceanannus Mor, *Ireland* 12 C5
Kelmė, *Lithuania* 30 C9
Kelokedhara, *Cyprus* 49 E11
Kelowna, *Canada* 102 D5
Kelsey Creek, *Australia* 94 J6
Kelseyville, *U.S.A.* 110 G4
Kelso, *N.Z.* 91 L2
Kelso, *U.K.* 13 F6
Kelso, *U.S.A.* 110 D4
Keluang, *Malaysia* 65 L4
Kelvington, *Canada* 103 C8
Kem, *Russia* 52 C4
Kema, *Indonesia* 63 D7
Kemah, *Turkey* 70 B3
Kemaliye, *Erzincan, Turkey* 73 C8
Kemaliye, *Manisa, Turkey* 47 C10
Kemalpaşa, *Turkey* 47 C9
Kemaman, *Malaysia* 62 D2
Kemano, *Canada* 102 C3
Kemasik, *Malaysia* 65 K4
Kembolcha, *Ethiopia* 81 E4
Kemer, *Antalya, Turkey* 47 E12
Kemer, *Burdur, Turkey* 47 D12
Kemer, *Muğla, Turkey* 47 E11
Kemer Barajı, *Turkey* 47 D10
Kemerovo, *Russia* 52 D9
Ķemeru △, *Latvia* 30 B10
Kemi, *Finland* 8 D21
Kemi älv = Kemijoki →, *Finland* 8 D21
Kemijärvi, *Finland* 8 C22
Kemijoki →, *Finland* 8 D21
Kemmerer, *U.S.A.* 108 F8
Kemmuna = Comino, *Malta* 49 C1
Kemp, L., *U.S.A.* 113 J5
Kemp Land, *Antarctica* 5 C5
Kempas, *Malaysia* 65 d
Kempsey, *Australia* 95 E5
Kempt, L., *Canada* 104 C5
Kempten, *Germany* 25 H6
Kempton, *Australia* 95 G4
Kemptville, *Canada* 117 B9
Ken →, *India* 69 G9
Kenai, *U.S.A.* 100 B4
Kendai, *India* 69 H10
Kendal, *Indonesia* 63 G14
Kendal, *U.K.* 14 C5
Kendall, *Australia* 95 E5
Kendall, *U.S.A.* 115 N5
Kendall →, *Australia* 94 A3
Kendallville, *U.S.A.* 114 E3
Kendari, *Indonesia* 63 E6
Kendawangan, *Indonesia* 62 E4
Kende, *Nigeria* 83 C5
Kendi, Pulau, *Malaysia* 65 c
Kendrapara, *India* 67 J15
Këndrevicës, Maja e, *Albania* 44 F3
Kendrew, *S. Africa* 88 E3
Kene Thao, *Laos* 64 D3
Kenedy, *U.S.A.* 113 L6
Kenema, *S. Leone* 82 D2
Keng Kok, *Laos* 64 D5
Keng Tawng, *Burma* 67 J21
Keng Tung, *Burma* 58 G2
Kengeja, *Tanzania* 86 D4
Kenhardt, *S. Africa* 88 D3
Kéniéba, *Mali* 82 C2
Kenitra, *Morocco* 78 B4
Kenli, *China* 57 F10
Kenmare, *Ireland* 12 E2
Kenmare, *U.S.A.* 112 A3
Kenmare River, *Ireland* 12 E2
Kennebago Lake, *U.S.A.* 117 A14
Kennebec, *U.S.A.* 112 D5
Kennebec →, *U.S.A.* 115 D11
Kennebunk, *U.S.A.* 117 C14
Kennedy, *Zimbabwe* 88 B4
Kennedy Ra., *Australia* 93 D2
Kennedy Range △, *Australia* 93 D2
Kenner, *U.S.A.* 113 L9
Kennet →, *U.K.* 15 F7
Kenneth Ra., *Australia* 93 D2
Kennett, *U.S.A.* 113 G9
Kennewick, *U.S.A.* 108 C4
Kenogami →, *Canada* 104 B3
Kenora, *Canada* 103 D10
Kenosha, *U.S.A.* 114 D2
Kensington, *Canada* 105 C7
Kent, *Ohio, U.S.A.* 116 E3
Kent, *Tex., U.S.A.* 113 K2
Kent, *Wash., U.S.A.* 110 C4
Kent □, *U.K.* 15 F8
Kent Group, *Australia* 95 F4
Kent Pen., *Canada* 100 B9
Kentaū, *Kazakhstan* 52 E7
Kentland, *U.S.A.* 114 E2
Kenton, *U.S.A.* 114 E4
Kentucky □, *U.S.A.* 114 G3
Kentucky →, *U.S.A.* 114 F3
Kentucky L., *U.S.A.* 115 G2
Kentville, *Canada* 105 C7
Kentwood, *U.S.A.* 113 K9
Kenya ■, *Africa* 86 B4
Kenya, Mt., *Kenya* 86 C4
Keo Neua, Deo, *Vietnam* 64 C5
Keokuk, *U.S.A.* 112 E9
Keonjhargarh, *India* 69 J11
Kep, *Cambodia* 65 G5
Kep, *Vietnam* 64 B6
Kepala Batas, *Malaysia* 65 c
Kepez, *Turkey* 45 F10
Kepi, *Indonesia* 63 F9
Kępice, *Poland* 30 D3
Kępno, *Poland* 31 G4
Kepsut, *Turkey* 47 B10
Kerala □, *India* 66 P10
Kerama-Rettō, *Japan* 55 L3
Keran, *Pakistan* 69 B5
Keran △, *Togo* 83 C5
Kerang, *Australia* 95 F3
Keranyo, *Ethiopia* 81 F4
Kerao →, *Sudan* 81 E3
Keratéa, *Greece* 46 D5
Keraudren, C., *Australia* 92 C2
Kerava, *Finland* 9 F21
Kerch, *Ukraine* 33 K9
Kerchenskiy Proliv, *Black Sea* 33 K9
Kerchoual, *Mali* 83 B5
Kerempe Burnu, *Turkey* 72 A5
Keren, *Eritrea* 81 D4
Kerewan, *Gambia* 82 C1
Kerguelen, *Ind. Oc.* 3 G13
Keri, *Greece* 46 D2
Keri Kera, *Sudan* 81 E3
Kericho, *Kenya* 86 C4
Kerinci, *Indonesia* 62 E2
Kerki, *Turkmenistan* 52 F7
Kerkinítis, Límni, *Greece* 44 E7
Kérkira, *Greece* 49 A3
Kérkira □, *Greece* 46 B1
Kérkira ✕ (CFU), *Greece* 46 B1
Kerkouane, *Tunisia* 42 F4
Kerkrade, *Neths.* 17 D6
Kerma, *Sudan* 80 D3
Kermadec Is., *Pac. Oc.* 96 L10
Kermadec Trench, *Pac. Oc.* 96 L10
Kermān, *Iran* 71 D8
Kerman, *U.S.A.* 110 J6
Kermān □, *Iran* 71 D8
Kermān, Bīābān-e, *Iran* 71 D8
Kermānshāh = Bākhtarān, *Iran* 70 C5
Kermen, *Bulgaria* 45 D10
Kermit, *U.S.A.* 113 K3
Kern →, *U.S.A.* 111 K7
Kernhof, *Austria* 26 D8
Kernow = Cornwall □, *U.K.* 15 G3
Kernville, *U.S.A.* 111 K8
Keroh, *Malaysia* 65 K3
Kérou, *Benin* 83 C5
Kérouane, *Guinea* 82 D3
Kerpen, *Germany* 24 E2
Kerrera, *U.K.* 13 E3
Kerrobert, *Canada* 103 C7
Kerrville, *U.S.A.* 113 K5
Kerry □, *Ireland* 12 D2
Kerry Hd., *Ireland* 12 D2
Kersa, *Ethiopia* 81 F5
Kerulen →, *Asia* 60 B6
Kerzaz, *Algeria* 78 C5
Kesagami →, *Canada* 104 B4
Kesagami L., *Canada* 104 B3
Keşan, *Turkey* 45 F10
Kesennuma, *Japan* 54 E10
Keshit, *Iran* 71 D8
Keşiş Dağ, *Turkey* 73 C8
Keskin, *Turkey* 72 C5
Kestell, *S. Africa* 89 D4
Kestenga, *Russia* 52 C4
Keswick, *U.K.* 14 C4
Keszthely, *Hungary* 28 D2
Ket →, *Russia* 52 D9
Keta, *Ghana* 83 D5
Keta Lagoon, *Ghana* 83 D5
Ketapang, *Bali, Indonesia* 63 J17
Ketapang, *Kalimantan, Indonesia* 62 E4
Ketchenery, *Russia* 35 G7
Ketchikan, *U.S.A.* 102 B2
Ketchum, *U.S.A.* 108 E6
Kete Krachi, *Ghana* 83 D4
Ketef, Khalîg Umm el, *Egypt* 70 F2
Keti Bandar, *Pakistan* 68 G2
Kétou, *Benin* 83 D5
Ketri, *India* 68 E6
Kętrzyn, *Poland* 30 D8
Kettering, *U.K.* 15 E7
Kettering, *U.S.A.* 114 F3
Kettle →, *Canada* 103 B11
Kettle Falls, *U.S.A.* 108 B4
Kettle Pt., *Canada* 116 C2
Kettleman City, *U.S.A.* 110 J7
Kęty, *Poland* 31 J6
Keuka L., *U.S.A.* 116 D7
Keuruu, *Finland* 9 E21
Kevelaer, *Germany* 24 D2
Kewanee, *U.S.A.* 112 E10
Kewaunee, *U.S.A.* 114 C2
Keweenaw B., *U.S.A.* 114 B1
Keweenaw Pen., *U.S.A.* 114 B2
Keweenaw Pt., *U.S.A.* 114 B2
Key Largo, *U.S.A.* 115 N5
Key West, *U.S.A.* 107 F10
Keyala, *Sudan* 81 G3
Keynsham, *U.K.* 15 F5
Keyser, *U.S.A.* 114 F6
Kezhma, *Russia* 53 D11
Kezi, *Zimbabwe* 89 C4
Kežmarok, *Slovak Rep.* 27 B13
Kgalagadi Transfrontier ⌓, *Africa* 88 D3
Khabarovsk, *Russia* 53 E14
Khabr, *Iran* 71 D8
Khābūr →, *Syria* 70 C4
Khachmas = Xaçmaz, *Azerbaijan* 35 K9
Khachrod, *India* 68 H6
Khadari, W. el →, *Sudan* 81 E2
Khadro, *Pakistan* 68 F3
Khadyzhensk, *Russia* 35 H4
Khadzhilyangar, *China* 69 B8
Khaga, *India* 69 G9
Khagaria, *India* 69 G12
Khaipur, *Pakistan* 68 E5
Khair, *India* 68 F7
Khairabad, *India* 69 F9
Khairagarh, *India* 69 J9
Khairpur, *Pakistan* 68 F3
Khairpur Nathan Shah, *Pakistan* 68 F2
Khairwara, *India* 68 H5
Khaisor →, *Pakistan* 68 D3
Khajuri Kach, *Pakistan* 68 C3
Khakassia □, *Russia* 52 D9
Khakhea, *Botswana* 88 C3
Khalafābād, *Iran* 71 D6
Khalilabad, *India* 69 F10
Khalīlī, *Iran* 71 E7
Khalkhāl, *Iran* 71 B6
Khálki, *Dhodhekánisos, Greece* 47 E9
Khálki, *Thessalía, Greece* 46 B4
Khalkidhikí □, *Greece* 44 F7
Khalkís, *Greece* 46 C5
Khalmer-Sede = Tazovskiy, *Russia* 52 C8
Khalmer Yu, *Russia* 52 C7
Khalūf, *Oman* 75 C6
Kham Keut, *Laos* 64 C5
Khamaria, *India* 69 H9
Khambhaliya, *India* 68 H3
Khambhat, *India* 68 H5
Khambhat, G. of, *India* 66 J8
Khamilonísion, *Greece* 47 F8
Khamīr, *Iran* 71 E7
Khamir, *Yemen* 75 D3
Khamsa, *Egypt* 74 E1
Khan →, *Namibia* 88 C2
Khān Abū Shāmat, *Syria* 74 B5
Khān Azād, *Iraq* 70 C5
Khān Mujiddah, *Iraq* 70 C4
Khān Shaykhūn, *Syria* 70 C3
Khān Yūnis, *Gaza Strip* 74 D3
Khanai, *Pakistan* 68 D2
Khānaqīn, *Iraq* 70 C5
Khānbāghī, *Iran* 71 B7
Khandrá, *Greece* 47 F8
Khandwa, *India* 66 J10
Khandyga, *Russia* 53 C14
Khāneh, *Iran* 70 B5
Khanewal, *Pakistan* 68 D4
Khangah Dogran, *Pakistan* 68 D5
Khanh Duong, *Vietnam* 64 F7
Khaniá, *Greece* 49 D6
Khaniá □, *Greece* 49 D6
Khaniadhana, *India* 68 G8
Khaníon, Kólpos, *Greece* 49 D5
Khanka, L., *Asia* 53 E14
Khankendy = Xankändi, *Azerbaijan* 70 B5
Khanna, *India* 68 D7
Khanozai, *Pakistan* 68 D2
Khanpur, *Pakistan* 68 E4
Khanty-Mansiysk, *Russia* 52 C7
Khao Laem △, *Thailand* 64 E2
Khao Luang △, *Thailand* 65 H2
Khao Phlu, *Thailand* 65 b
Khao Pu-Khao Ya △, *Thailand* 65 J2
Khao Sam Roi Yot △, *Thailand* 65 F2
Khao Sok △, *Thailand* 65 H2
Khao Yai △, *Thailand* 64 E3
Khaoen Si Nakarin △, *Thailand* 64 E2
Khapalu, *Pakistan* 69 B7
Khapcheranga, *Russia* 53 E12
Kharabali, *Russia* 35 G8
Kharaghoda, *India* 68 H4
Kharagpur, *India* 69 H12
Khárakas, *Greece* 49 D7
Kharan Kalat, *Pakistan* 66 E4
Kharānaq, *Iran* 71 C7
Kharda, *India* 66 K9
Khardung La, *India* 69 B7
Kharg = Khārk, Jazīreh-ye, *Iran* 71 D6
Khârga, El Wâhât-el, *Egypt* 80 B3
Khargon, *India* 66 J9
Khari →, *India* 68 G6
Kharian, *Pakistan* 68 C5
Kharit, Wadi el →, *Egypt* 80 C3
Khārk, Jazīreh-ye, *Iran* 71 D6
Kharkiv, *Ukraine* 33 H9
Kharkov = Kharkiv, *Ukraine* 33 H9
Kharmanli, *Bulgaria* 45 E9
Kharovsk, *Russia* 32 C11
Kharsawangarh, *India* 69 H11
Kharta, *Turkey* 72 B3
Khartoum = El Khartûm, *Sudan* 81 D3
Khasan, *Russia* 54 C5
Khasavyurt, *Russia* 35 J8
Khāsh, *Iran* 66 E2
Khashm el Girba, *Sudan* 81 E4
Khashum, *Sudan* 81 E2
Khashuri, *Georgia* 35 J6
Khaskovo, *Bulgaria* 45 E9
Khaskovo □, *Bulgaria* 45 E9
Khatanga, *Russia* 53 B11
Khatanga →, *Russia* 53 B11
Khatauli, *India* 68 E7
Khatra, *India* 69 H12
Khātūnābād, *Iran* 71 D7
Khatyrka, *Russia* 53 C18
Khavda, *India* 68 H3
Khaybar, Ḩarrat, *Si. Arabia* 70 E4
Khayelitsha, *S. Africa* 85 L3
Khāzimiyah, *Iraq* 70 C4
Khazzān Jabal al Awliyā, *Sudan* 81 D3
Khe Bo, *Vietnam* 64 C5
Khe Long, *Vietnam* 64 B5
Khe Sanh, *Vietnam* 64 D6
Khed Brahma, *India* 66 G8
Khekra, *India* 68 E7
Khemarak Phouminville, *Cambodia* 65 G4
Khemisset, *Morocco* 78 B4
Khemmarat, *Thailand* 64 D5
Khenāmān, *Iran* 71 D8
Khenchela, *Algeria* 78 A7
Khersān →, *Iran* 71 D6
Khérson, *Greece* 44 E6
Kherson, *Ukraine* 33 J7
Khersónisos Akrotíri, *Greece* 49 D6
Kheta →, *Russia* 53 B11
Khewari, *Pakistan* 68 F3
Khilchipur, *India* 68 G7
Khilioméodhion, *Greece* 46 D4
Khilok, *Russia* 53 D12
Khimki, *Russia* 32 E9
Khíos, *Greece* 47 C8
Khíos □, *Greece* 47 C8
Khirsadoh, *India* 69 H8
Khiuma = Hiiumaa, *Estonia* 9 G20
Khiva, *Uzbekistan* 52 E7
Khīyāv, *Iran* 70 B5
Khlebarovo, *Bulgaria* 45 C10
Khlong Khlung, *Thailand* 64 D2
Khmelnik, *Ukraine* 33 H4
Khmelnitskiy = Khmelnytskyy, *Ukraine* 33 H4
Khmelnytskyy, *Ukraine* 33 H4
Khmer Rep. = Cambodia ■, *Asia* 64 F5
Khoai, Hon, *Vietnam* 65 H5
Khodoriv, *Ukraine* 33 H3
Khodzent = Khŭjand, *Tajikistan* 52 E7
Khojak Pass, *Afghan.* 68 D2
Khok Kloi, *Thailand* 65 a
Khok Pho, *Thailand* 65 J3
Kholm, *Russia* 32 D6
Kholmsk, *Russia* 53 E15
Khomas Hochland, *Namibia* 88 C2
Khombole, *Senegal* 82 C1
Khomeyn, *Iran* 71 C6
Khomeynī Shahr, *Iran* 71 C6
Khomodino, *Botswana* 88 C3
Khon Kaen, *Thailand* 64 D4
Khong →, *Cambodia* 64 F5
Khong Sedone, *Laos* 64 E5
Khonuu, *Russia* 53 C15
Khoper →, *Russia* 34 F6
Khor el 'Atash, *Sudan* 81 E3
Khóra, *Greece* 46 D3
Khóra Sfakíon, *Greece* 49 D6
Khorāsān □, *Iran* 71 C8
Khorat = Nakhon Ratchasima, *Thailand* 64 E4
Khorat, Cao Nguyen, *Thailand* 64 E4
Khorixas, *Namibia* 88 C1
Khorol, *Ukraine* 33 H7
Khorramābād, *Khorāsān, Iran* 71 C8
Khorramābād, *Lorestān, Iran* 71 C6
Khorrāmshahr, *Iran* 71 D6
Khorugh, *Tajikistan* 52 F8
Khosravī, *Iran* 71 D6
Khosrowābād, *Khuzestān, Iran* 71 D6
Khosrowābād, *Kordestān, Iran* 70 C5
Khost, *Pakistan* 68 D2
Khosūyeh, *Iran* 71 D7
Khotyn, *Ukraine* 33 H4
Khouribga, *Morocco* 78 B4
Khowst, *Afghan.* 68 C3
Khowst □, *Afghan.* 66 C6
Khoyniki, *Belarus* 33 G5
Khrami →, *Georgia* 35 K7
Khrenovoye, *Russia* 34 E5
Khrisoúpolis, *Greece* 45 F8
Khristianá, *Greece* 47 E7
Khrysokhou B., *Cyprus* 49 D11
Khtapodhiá, *Greece* 47 D7
Khu Khan, *Thailand* 64 E5
Khuan Wa, *Thailand* 65 a
Khudzhand = Khŭjand, *Tajikistan* 52 E7
Khuff, *Si. Arabia* 70 E5
Khūgīānī, *Afghan.* 68 D2
Khuis, *Botswana* 88 D3
Khuiyala, *India* 68 F4
Khŭjand, *Tajikistan* 52 E7
Khujner, *India* 68 H7
Khulna, *Bangla.* 67 H16
Khulna □, *Bangla.* 67 H16
Khulo, *Georgia* 35 K6
Khumago, *Botswana* 88 C3
Khūnsorkh, *Iran* 71 E8
Khunti, *India* 69 H11
Khūr, *Iran* 71 C8
Khurai, *India* 68 G8
Khurayş, *Si. Arabia* 71 E6
Khureit, *Sudan* 81 E2
Khurīyā Murīyā, Jazā'ir, *Oman* 75 D6
Khurja, *India* 68 E7
Khūrmāl, *Iraq* 70 C5
Khurr, Wādī al, *Iraq* 70 C4
Khūsf, *Iran* 71 C8
Khush, *Afghan.* 66 C3
Khushab, *Pakistan* 68 C5
Khust, *Ukraine* 33 H2
Khutse ⌓, *Botswana* 88 C3
Khuzdar, *Pakistan* 68 F2
Khūzestān □, *Iran* 71 D6
Khvāf, *Iran* 71 C9
Khvājeh, *Iran* 70 B5
Khvalynsk, *Russia* 34 D9
Khvānsār, *Iran* 71 D7
Khvatovka, *Russia* 34 D8
Khvor, *Iran* 71 C7
Khvorgū, *Iran* 71 E8
Khvormūj, *Iran* 71 D6
Khvoy, *Iran* 70 B5
Khvoynaya, *Russia* 32 C8
Khyber Pass, *Afghan.* 68 B4
Kiabukwa, *Dem. Rep. of the Congo* 87 D1
Kiama, *Australia* 95 E5
Kiamba, *Phil.* 61 H6
Kiambi, *Dem. Rep. of the Congo* 86 D2
Kiambu, *Kenya* 86 C4
Kiang West △, *Gambia* 82 C1
Kiangara, *Madag.* 89 B8
Kiangsi = Jiangxi □, *China* 59 D11
Kiangsu = Jiangsu □, *China* 57 H11
Kiáton, *Greece* 46 C4
Kibæk, *Denmark* 11 H2
Kibale △, *Uganda* 86 B3
Kibanga Port, *Uganda* 86 B3
Kibara, *Tanzania* 86 C3
Kibare, Mts., *Dem. Rep. of the Congo* 86 D2
Kibira △, *Burundi* 86 C3
Kibombo, *Dem. Rep. of the Congo* 86 C2
Kibondo, *Tanzania* 86 C3
Kibre Mengist, *Ethiopia* 81 F4
Kibumbu, *Burundi* 86 C2
Kibungo, *Rwanda* 86 C3
Kibuye, *Burundi* 86 C2
Kibuye, *Rwanda* 86 C2
Kibwesa, *Tanzania* 86 D2
Kibwezi, *Kenya* 86 C4
Kicasalih, *Turkey* 45 E10
Kičevo, *Macedonia* 44 E4
Kichha, *India* 69 E8
Kichha →, *India* 69 E8
Kicking Horse Pass, *Canada* 102 C5
Kidal, *Mali* 83 B5
Kidderminster, *U.K.* 15 E5
Kidepo Valley △, *Uganda* 86 B3
Kidete, *Tanzania* 86 D4
Kidira, *Senegal* 82 C2
Kidnappers, C., *N.Z.* 91 H6
Kidsgrove, *U.K.* 14 D5
Kidston, *Australia* 94 B3
Kidugallo, *Tanzania* 86 D4
Kiel, *Germany* 24 A6
Kiel Canal = Nord-Ostsee-Kanal, *Germany* 24 A5
Kielce, *Poland* 31 H7
Kielder Water, *U.K.* 14 B5
Kieler Bucht, *Germany* 24 A6
Kiembara, *Burkina Faso* 82 C4
Kien Binh, *Vietnam* 65 H5
Kien Tan, *Vietnam* 65 G5
Kienge, *Dem. Rep. of the Congo* 87 E2
Kiessé, *Niger* 83 C5
Kiev = Kyyiv, *Ukraine* 33 G6
Kifaya, *Guinea* 82 C2
Kiffa, *Mauritania* 82 B2
Kifisiá, *Greece* 46 C5
Kifissós →, *Greece* 46 C5
Kifrī, *Iraq* 70 C5
Kigali, *Rwanda* 86 C3
Kigarama, *Tanzania* 86 C3
Kigelle, *Sudan* 81 F3
Kigezi ⌓, *Uganda* 86 C2
Kigoma □, *Tanzania* 86 D3
Kigoma-Ujiji, *Tanzania* 86 C2
Kigomasha, Ras, *Tanzania* 86 C4
Kığzı, *Turkey* 70 B4
Kihei, *U.S.A.* 106 H16
Kihnu, *Estonia* 9 G21
Kii-Sanchi, *Japan* 55 G8
Kii-Suidō, *Japan* 55 H7
Kikaiga-Shima, *Japan* 55 K4
Kikinda, *Serbia & M.* 28 E5
Kikládhes, *Greece* 46 E6
Kikládhes □, *Greece* 46 D6
Kikwit, *Dem. Rep. of the Congo* 84 E3
Kil, *Sweden* 10 E7
Kilafors, *Sweden* 10 C10
Kilar, *India* 68 C7
Kilauea Crater, *U.S.A.* 106 J17
Kilbrannan Sd., *U.K.* 13 F3
Kilchu, *N. Korea* 57 D15
Kilcoy, *Australia* 95 D5
Kildare, *Ireland* 12 C5
Kildare □, *Ireland* 12 C5
Kileikli, *Sudan* 81 E2
Kilfinnane, *Ireland* 12 D3
Kilgore, *U.S.A.* 113 J7
Kilibo, *Benin* 83 D5
Kilifi, *Kenya* 86 C4
Kilimanjaro, *Tanzania* 86 C4
Kilimanjaro □, *Tanzania* 86 C4
Kilimli, *Turkey* 72 B4
Kilindini, *Kenya* 86 C4
Kilis, *Turkey* 70 B3
Kiliya, *Ukraine* 33 K5
Kilkee, *Ireland* 12 D2
Kilkeel, *U.K.* 12 B5
Kilkenny, *Ireland* 12 D4
Kilkenny □, *Ireland* 12 D4
Kilkieran B., *Ireland* 12 C2
Kilkís, *Greece* 44 F6
Kilkís □, *Greece* 44 E6
Killala, *Ireland* 12 B2
Killala B., *Ireland* 12 B2
Killaloe, *Canada* 116 A7
Killaloe, *Ireland* 12 D3
Killarney, *Australia* 95 D5
Killarney, *Canada* 103 D9
Killarney, *Ireland* 12 D2
Killarney △, *Ireland* 12 D2
Killary Harbour, *Ireland* 12 C2
Killdeer, *U.S.A.* 112 B3
Killeberg, *Sweden* 11 H8
Killeen, *U.S.A.* 113 K6
Killin, *U.K.* 13 E4
Killíni, *Ilía, Greece* 46 D3
Killíni, *Korinthía, Greece* 46 D4
Killorglin, *Ireland* 12 D2
Killybegs, *Ireland* 12 B3
Kilmarnock, *U.K.* 13 F4
Kilmez, *Russia* 34 B10
Kilmez →, *Russia* 34 B10
Kilmore, *Australia* 95 F3
Kilondo, *Tanzania* 87 D3
Kilosa, *Tanzania* 86 D4
Kilrush, *Ireland* 12 D2
Kilwa Kisiwani, *Tanzania* 87 D4
Kilwa Kivinje, *Tanzania* 87 D4
Kilwa Masoko, *Tanzania* 87 D4
Kilwinning, *U.K.* 13 F4
Kim, *U.S.A.* 113 G3
Kim →, *Cameroon* 83 D7
Kimaam, *Indonesia* 63 F9
Kimamba, *Tanzania* 86 D4
Kimba, *Australia* 95 E2
Kimball, *Nebr., U.S.A.* 112 E3
Kimball, *S. Dak., U.S.A.* 112 D5
Kimberley, *Australia* 92 C4
Kimberley, *Canada* 102 D5
Kimberley, *S. Africa* 88 D3
Kimberly, *U.S.A.* 108 E6

Kimch'aek, *N. Korea* 57 **D15**
Kimch'ŏn, *S. Korea* 57 **F15**
Kími, *Greece* 46 **C6**
Kimje, *S. Korea* 57 **G14**
Kimmirut, *Canada* 101 **B13**
Kímolos, *Greece* 46 **E6**
Kimovsk, *Moskva, Russia* 32 **E9**
Kimovsk, *Tula, Russia* 32 **E10**
Kimparana, *Mali* 82 **C4**
Kimpese, *Dem. Rep. of the Congo* 84 **F2**
Kimry, *Russia* 32 **D9**
Kimstad, *Sweden* 11 **F9**
Kinabalu, Gunong, *Malaysia* 62 **C5**
Kínaros, *Greece* 47 **E8**
Kinaskan L., *Canada* 102 **B2**
Kinbasket L., *Canada* 102 **C5**
Kincardine, *Canada* 116 **B3**
Kincolith, *Canada* 102 **C3**
Kinda, *Dem. Rep. of the Congo* 87 **D2**
Kindberg, *Austria* 26 **D8**
Kinde, *U.S.A.* 116 **C2**
Kinder Scout, *U.K.* 14 **D6**
Kindersley, *Canada* 103 **C7**
Kindia, *Guinea* 82 **D2**
Kindu, *Dem. Rep. of the Congo* 86 **C2**
Kinel, *Russia* 34 **D10**
Kineshma, *Russia* 34 **B6**
Kinesi, *Tanzania* 86 **C3**
King, L., *Australia* 93 **F2**
King, Mt., *Australia* 94 **D4**
King City, *U.S.A.* 110 **J5**
King Cr. →, *Australia* 94 **C2**
King Edward →, *Australia* 92 **B4**
King Frederick VI Land = Kong Frederik VI Kyst, *Greenland* 101 **B15**
King George B., *Falk. Is.* 128 **G4**
King George I., *Antarctica* 5 **C18**
King George Is., *Canada* 101 **C11**
King I. = Kadan Kyun, *Burma* 64 **F2**
King I., *Australia* 95 **F3**
King I., *Canada* 102 **C3**
King Leopold Ranges, *Australia* 92 **C4**
King of Prussia, *U.S.A.* 117 **F9**
King Sd., *Australia* 92 **C3**
King Sejong, *Antarctica* 5 **C18**
King William I., *Canada* 100 **B10**
King William's Town, *S. Africa* 88 **E4**
Kingait = Cape Dorset, *Canada* 101 **B12**
Kingaok = Bathurst Inlet, *Canada* 100 **B9**
Kingaroy, *Australia* 95 **D5**
Kingfisher, *U.S.A.* 113 **H6**
Kingirbān, *Iraq* 70 **C5**
Kingisepp = Kuressaare, *Estonia* 9 **G20**
Kingisepp, *Russia* 32 **C5**
Kingman, *Ariz., U.S.A.* 111 **K12**
Kingman, *Kans., U.S.A.* 113 **G5**
Kingoonya, *Australia* 95 **E2**
Kingri, *Pakistan* 68 **D3**
Kings →, *U.S.A.* 110 **J7**
Kings Canyon △, *U.S.A.* 110 **J8**
King's Lynn, *U.K.* 14 **E8**
Kings Mountain, *U.S.A.* 115 **H5**
Kings Park, *U.S.A.* 117 **F11**
King's Peak, *U.S.A.* 108 **F8**
Kingsbridge, *U.K.* 15 **G4**
Kingsburg, *U.S.A.* 110 **J7**
Kingscote, *Australia* 95 **F2**
Kingscourt, *Ireland* 12 **C5**
Kingsford, *U.S.A.* 114 **C1**
Kingsland, *U.S.A.* 115 **K5**
Kingsley, *U.S.A.* 112 **D7**
Kingsport, *U.S.A.* 115 **G4**
Kingston, *Canada* 117 **B8**
Kingston, *Jamaica* 120 **a**
Kingston, *N.Z.* 91 **L2**
Kingston, *N.H., U.S.A.* 117 **D13**
Kingston, *N.Y., U.S.A.* 117 **E11**
Kingston, *Pa., U.S.A.* 117 **E9**
Kingston, *R.I., U.S.A.* 117 **E13**
Kingston Pk., *U.S.A.* 111 **K11**
Kingston South East, *Australia* 95 **F2**
Kingston upon Hull, *U.K.* 14 **D7**
Kingston upon Hull □, *U.K.* 14 **D7**
Kingston-upon-Thames □, *U.K.* 15 **F7**
Kingstown, *St. Vincent* 121 **D7**
Kingstree, *U.S.A.* 115 **J6**
Kingsville, *Canada* 116 **D2**
Kingsville, *U.S.A.* 113 **M6**
Kingussie, *U.K.* 13 **D4**
Kingwood, *U.S.A.* 113 **K7**
Kınık, *Antalya, Turkey* 47 **E11**
Kınık, *İzmir, Turkey* 47 **B9**
Kinistino, *Canada* 103 **C7**
Kinkala, *Congo* 84 **E2**
Kinki □, *Japan* 55 **H8**
Kinleith, *N.Z.* 91 **H5**
Kinlochleven, *U.K.* 13 **E4**
Kinmount, *Canada* 116 **B6**
Kinna, *Sweden* 11 **G6**
Kinnairds Hd., *U.K.* 13 **D6**
Kinnared, *Sweden* 11 **G7**
Kinnarodden, *Norway* 6 **A11**
Kinnarp, *Sweden* 11 **F7**
Kinneviken, *Sweden* 11 **F7**
Kino, *Mexico* 118 **B2**
Kinoje →, *Canada* 104 **B3**
Kinomoto, *Japan* 55 **G8**
Kinoni, *Uganda* 86 **C3**
Kinoosao, *Canada* 103 **B8**
Kinross, *U.K.* 13 **E5**
Kinsale, *Ireland* 12 **E3**
Kinsale, Old Hd. of, *Ireland* 12 **E3**
Kinsha = Chang Jiang →, *China* 59 **B13**
Kinshasa, *Dem. Rep. of the Congo* 84 **E3**
Kinsley, *U.S.A.* 113 **G5**
Kinsman, *U.S.A.* 116 **E4**
Kinston, *U.S.A.* 115 **H7**
Kintamani, *Indonesia* 63 **J18**
Kintampo, *Ghana* 83 **D4**
Kintore, *U.K.* 13 **D6**
Kintore Ra., *Australia* 92 **D4**
Kintyre, *U.K.* 13 **F3**
Kintyre, Mull of, *U.K.* 13 **F3**
Kinushseo →, *Canada* 104 **A3**
Kinuso, *Canada* 102 **B5**
Kinyangiri, *Tanzania* 86 **C3**
Kinyeti, *Sudan* 81 **G3**
Kinzig →, *Germany* 25 **G3**
Kinzua, *U.S.A.* 116 **E6**
Kinzua Dam, *U.S.A.* 116 **E6**
Kióni, *Greece* 46 **C2**
Kiosk, *Canada* 104 **C4**
Kiowa, *Kans., U.S.A.* 113 **G5**
Kiowa, *Okla., U.S.A.* 113 **H7**
Kipahigan L., *Canada* 103 **B8**
Kipanga, *Tanzania* 86 **D4**
Kiparissía, *Greece* 46 **D3**
Kiparissiakós Kólpos, *Greece* 46 **D3**
Kipawa, L., *Canada* 104 **C4**
Kipembawe, *Tanzania* 86 **D3**
Kipengere Ra., *Tanzania* 87 **D3**
Kipili, *Tanzania* 86 **D3**
Kipini, *Kenya* 86 **C5**
Kipling, *Canada* 103 **C8**
Kippure, *Ireland* 12 **C5**
Kipushi, *Dem. Rep. of the Congo* 87 **E2**
Kirane, *Mali* 82 **B2**
Kiranomena, *Madag.* 89 **B8**
Kiraz, *Turkey* 47 **C10**
Kirazlı, *Turkey* 45 **F10**
Kirchhain, *Germany* 24 **E4**
Kirchheim, *Germany* 25 **G5**
Kirchheimbolanden, *Germany* 25 **F3**
Kirchschlag, *Austria* 27 **D9**
Kireç, *Turkey* 47 **B10**
Kirensk, *Russia* 53 **D11**
Kirghizia = Kyrgyzstan ■, *Asia* 52 **E8**
Kirghizstan = Kyrgyzstan ■, *Asia* 52 **E8**
Kiribati ■, *Pac. Oc.* 96 **H10**
Kırıkhan, *Turkey* 72 **D7**
Kırıkkale, *Turkey* 72 **C5**
Kirillov, *Russia* 32 **C10**
Kirin = Jilin, *China* 57 **C14**
Kirinyaga = Kenya, Mt., *Kenya* 86 **C4**
Kirishi, *Russia* 32 **C7**
Kirishima Yaku △, *Japan* 55 **J5**
Kiritimati, *Kiribati* 97 **G12**
Kırka, *Turkey* 47 **B12**
Kırkağaç, *Turkey* 47 **B9**
Kirkby, *U.K.* 14 **D5**
Kirkby-in-Ashfield, *U.K.* 14 **D6**
Kirkby Lonsdale, *U.K.* 14 **C5**
Kirkby Stephen, *U.K.* 14 **C5**
Kirkcaldy, *U.K.* 13 **E5**
Kirkcudbright, *U.K.* 13 **G4**
Kirkee, *India* 66 **K8**
Kirkenes, *Norway* 8 **B23**
Kirkfield, *Canada* 116 **B6**
Kirkintilloch, *U.K.* 13 **F4**
Kirkjubæjarklaustur, *Iceland* 8 **E4**
Kirkkonummi, *Finland* 9 **F21**
Kirkland Lake, *Canada* 104 **C3**
Kırklareli, *Turkey* 45 **E11**
Kırklareli □, *Turkey* 45 **E11**
Kirksville, *U.S.A.* 112 **E8**
Kirkūk, *Iraq* 70 **C5**
Kirkwall, *U.K.* 13 **C6**
Kirkwood, *S. Africa* 88 **E4**
Kirn, *Germany* 25 **F3**
Kirov, *Kaluga, Russia* 32 **E8**
Kirov, *Kirov, Russia* 52 **D5**
Kirovabad = Gäncä, *Azerbaijan* 35 **K8**
Kirovakan = Vanadzor, *Armenia* 35 **K7**
Kirovograd = Kirovohrad, *Ukraine* 33 **H7**
Kirovohrad, *Ukraine* 33 **H7**
Kirovsk = Babadayhan, *Turkmenistan* 52 **F7**
Kirovskiy, *Astrakhan, Russia* 35 **H9**
Kirovskiy, *Kamchatka, Russia* 53 **D16**
Kirovskiy, *Primorsk, Russia* 54 **B6**
Kirriemuir, *U.K.* 13 **E5**
Kirsanov, *Russia* 34 **D6**
Kırşehir, *Turkey* 70 **B2**
Kirtachi, *Niger* 83 **C5**
Kirthar Range, *Pakistan* 68 **F2**
Kirtland, *U.S.A.* 109 **H9**
Kiruna, *Sweden* 8 **C19**
Kirundu, *Dem. Rep. of the Congo* 86 **C2**
Kirya, *Russia* 34 **C8**
Kiryū, *Japan* 55 **F9**
Kisa, *Sweden* 11 **G9**
Kisaga, *Tanzania* 86 **C3**
Kisalaya, *Nic.* 120 **D3**
Kisalföld, *Hungary* 28 **C2**
Kisámou, Kólpos, *Greece* 49 **D5**
Kisanga, *Dem. Rep. of the Congo* 86 **B2**
Kisangani, *Dem. Rep. of the Congo* 86 **B2**
Kisar, *Indonesia* 63 **F7**
Kisarawe, *Tanzania* 86 **D4**
Kisarazu, *Japan* 55 **G9**
Kisbér, *Hungary* 28 **C3**
Kishanganga →, *Pakistan* 69 **B5**
Kishanganj, *India* 69 **F13**
Kishangarh, *Raj., India* 68 **F6**
Kishangarh, *Raj., India* 68 **F4**
Kishi, *Nigeria* 83 **D5**
Kishinev = Chişinău, *Moldova* 29 **C13**
Kishiwada, *Japan* 55 **G7**
Kishtwar, *India* 69 **C6**
Kisielice, *Poland* 30 **E6**
Kisigo ⌓, *Tanzania* 86 **D3**
Kisii, *Kenya* 86 **C3**
Kisiju, *Tanzania* 86 **D4**
Kisir, *Turkey* 73 **B10**
Kisizi, *Uganda* 86 **C2**
Kiskomárom = Zalakomár, *Hungary* 28 **D2**
Kiskőrei-víztároló, *Hungary* 28 **C5**
Kiskőrös, *Hungary* 28 **D4**
Kiskundorozsma, *Hungary* 28 **D5**
Kiskunfélegyháza, *Hungary* 28 **D4**
Kiskunhalas, *Hungary* 28 **D4**
Kiskunmajsa, *Hungary* 28 **D4**
Kiskunsági △, *Hungary* 28 **D4**
Kislovodsk, *Russia* 35 **J6**
Kismayu = Chisimaio, *Somali Rep.* 77 **G8**
Kiso-Gawa →, *Japan* 55 **G8**
Kiso-Sammyaku, *Japan* 55 **G8**
Kisofukushima, *Japan* 55 **G8**
Kisoro, *Uganda* 86 **C2**
Kissidougou, *Guinea* 82 **D2**
Kissimmee, *U.S.A.* 115 **L5**
Kissimmee →, *U.S.A.* 115 **M5**
Kississing L., *Canada* 103 **B8**
Kissónerga, *Cyprus* 49 **E11**
Kissu, J., *Sudan* 80 **C2**
Kistanje, *Croatia* 41 **E12**
Kisújszállás, *Hungary* 28 **C5**
Kisumu, *Kenya* 86 **C3**
Kisvárda, *Hungary* 28 **B7**
Kiswani, *Tanzania* 86 **C4**
Kiswere, *Tanzania* 87 **D4**
Kit Carson, *U.S.A.* 112 **F3**
Kita, *Mali* 82 **C3**
Kitaibaraki, *Japan* 55 **F10**
Kitakami, *Japan* 54 **E10**
Kitakami-Gawa →, *Japan* 54 **E10**
Kitakami-Sammyaku, *Japan* 54 **E10**
Kitakata, *Japan* 54 **F9**
Kitakyūshū, *Japan* 55 **H5**
Kitale, *Kenya* 86 **B4**
Kitami, *Japan* 54 **C11**
Kitami-Sammyaku, *Japan* 54 **B11**
Kitangiri, L., *Tanzania* 86 **C3**
Kitaya, *Tanzania* 87 **E5**
Kitchener, *Canada* 116 **C4**
Kitee, *Finland* 32 **A6**
Kitega = Gitega, *Burundi* 86 **C2**
Kitengo, *Dem. Rep. of the Congo* 86 **D1**
Kitgum, *Uganda* 86 **B3**
Kíthira, *Greece* 46 **E5**
Kíthnos, *Greece* 46 **D6**
Kiti, *Cyprus* 49 **E12**
Kiti, C., *Cyprus* 49 **E12**
Kitimat, *Canada* 102 **C3**
Kitinen →, *Finland* 8 **C22**
Kitiyab, *Sudan* 81 **D3**
Kítros, *Greece* 44 **F6**
Kitsuki, *Japan* 55 **H5**
Kittakittaooloo, L., *Australia* 95 **D2**
Kittanning, *U.S.A.* 116 **F5**
Kittatinny Mts., *U.S.A.* 117 **F10**
Kittery, *U.S.A.* 115 **D10**
Kittilä, *Finland* 8 **C21**
Kitui, *Kenya* 86 **C4**
Kitwanga, *Canada* 102 **B3**
Kitwe, *Zambia* 87 **E2**
Kitzbühel, *Austria* 26 **D5**
Kitzbühler Alpen, *Austria* 26 **D5**
Kitzingen, *Germany* 25 **F6**
Kivarli, *India* 68 **G5**
Kivertsi, *Ukraine* 33 **G3**
Kividhes, *Cyprus* 49 **E11**
Kivik, *Sweden* 11 **J8**
Kivotós, *Greece* 44 **F5**
Kivu, L., *Dem. Rep. of the Congo* 86 **C2**
Kiyev = Kyyiv, *Ukraine* 33 **G6**
Kiyevskoye Vdkhr. = Kyyivske Vdskh., *Ukraine* 33 **G6**
Kıyıköy, *Turkey* 45 **E12**
Kiziguru, *Rwanda* 86 **C3**
Kızıl Adalar, *Turkey* 45 **F13**
Kızıl Irmak →, *Turkey* 72 **B6**
Kizil Jilga, *China* 69 **B8**
Kizil Yurt, *Russia* 35 **J8**
Kızılcabölük, *Turkey* 47 **D11**
Kızılcadağ, *Turkey* 47 **D11**
Kızılcahamam, *Turkey* 72 **B5**
Kızılhisar, *Turkey* 72 **D3**
Kızılırmak, *Turkey* 72 **B5**
Kızılkaya, *Turkey* 47 **D12**
Kızılören, *Turkey* 47 **C12**
Kızıltepe, *Turkey* 70 **B4**
Kizimkazi, *Tanzania* 86 **D4**
Kizlyar, *Russia* 35 **J8**
Kizyl-Arvat = Gyzylarbat, *Turkmenistan* 52 **F6**
Kjellerup, *Denmark* 11 **H3**
Kjölur, *Iceland* 8 **D4**
Kladanj, *Bos.-H.* 28 **F3**
Kladnica, *Serbia & M.* 44 **C4**
Kladno, *Czech Rep.* 26 **A7**
Kladovo, *Serbia & M.* 44 **B6**
Klaeng, *Thailand* 64 **F3**
Klagenfurt, *Austria* 26 **E7**
Klaipėda, *Lithuania* 9 **J19**
Klaipėda □, *Lithuania* 30 **C8**
Klaksvík, *Færoe Is.* 8 **E9**
Klamath →, *U.S.A.* 108 **F1**
Klamath Falls, *U.S.A.* 108 **E3**
Klamath Mts., *U.S.A.* 108 **F2**
Klamono, *Indonesia* 63 **E8**
Klanjec, *Croatia* 41 **B12**
Klappan →, *Canada* 102 **B3**
Klarälven →, *Sweden* 10 **E7**
Klässbol, *Sweden* 10 **E6**
Klatovy, *Czech Rep.* 26 **B6**
Klawer, *S. Africa* 88 **E2**
Klazienaveen, *Neths.* 17 **B6**
Klé, *Mali* 82 **C3**
Klecko, *Poland* 31 **F4**
Kleczew, *Poland* 31 **F5**
Kleena Kleene, *Canada* 102 **C4**
Klein-Karas, *Namibia* 88 **D2**
Klekovača, *Bos.-H.* 41 **D13**
Klenoec, *Macedonia* 44 **E4**
Klenovec, *Slovak Rep.* 27 **C12**
Klerksdorp, *S. Africa* 88 **D4**
Kleszczele, *Poland* 31 **F10**
Kletnya, *Russia* 32 **F7**
Kletsk = Klyetsk, *Belarus* 33 **F4**
Kletskiy, *Russia* 35 **F6**
Kleve, *Germany* 24 **D2**
Klickitat, *U.S.A.* 108 **D3**
Klickitat →, *U.S.A.* 110 **E5**
Klidhes, *Cyprus* 49 **D13**
Klimovichi, *Belarus* 32 **F6**
Klin, *Russia* 32 **D9**
Klina, *Serbia & M.* 44 **D4**
Klinaklini →, *Canada* 102 **C3**
Klintehamn, *Sweden* 11 **G12**
Klintsy, *Russia* 33 **F7**
Klip →, *S. Africa* 89 **D4**
Klipdale, *S. Africa* 88 **E2**
Klippan, *Sweden* 11 **H7**
Klipplaat, *S. Africa* 88 **E3**
Klisura, *Bulgaria* 45 **D8**
Kljajićevo, *Serbia & M.* 28 **E4**
Ključ, *Bos.-H.* 41 **D13**
Kłobuck, *Poland* 31 **H5**
Klockestrand, *Sweden* 10 **B11**
Kłodawa, *Poland* 31 **F5**
Kłodzko, *Poland* 31 **H3**
Klong Wang Chao △, *Thailand* 64 **D2**
Klos, *Albania* 44 **E4**
Klosterneuburg, *Austria* 27 **C9**
Klosters, *Switz.* 25 **J5**
Klötze, *Germany* 24 **C7**
Klouto, *Togo* 83 **D5**
Kluane △, *Canada* 102 **A1**
Kluane L., *Canada* 100 **B6**
Kluczbork, *Poland* 31 **H5**
Klukwan, *U.S.A.* 102 **B1**
Klungkung, *Indonesia* 63 **K18**
Klyetsk, *Belarus* 33 **F4**
Klyuchevskaya, Gora, *Russia* 53 **D17**
Knäred, *Sweden* 11 **H7**
Knaresborough, *U.K.* 14 **C6**
Knee L., *Man., Canada* 104 **A1**
Knee L., *Sask., Canada* 103 **B7**
Knezha, *Bulgaria* 45 **C8**
Knight Inlet, *Canada* 102 **C3**
Knighton, *U.K.* 15 **E4**
Knights Ferry, *U.S.A.* 110 **H6**
Knights Landing, *U.S.A.* 110 **G5**
Knin, *Croatia* 41 **D13**
Knislinge, *Sweden* 11 **H8**
Knittelfeld, *Austria* 26 **D7**
Knivsta, *Sweden* 10 **E11**
Knjaževac, *Serbia & M.* 44 **C6**
Knob, C., *Australia* 93 **F2**
Knock, *Ireland* 12 **C3**
Knockmealdown Mts., *Ireland* 12 **D4**
Knokke-Heist, *Belgium* 17 **C3**
Knossós, *Greece* 49 **D7**
Knowlton, *Canada* 117 **A12**
Knox, *U.S.A.* 114 **E2**
Knox Coast, *Antarctica* 5 **C8**
Knoxville, *Iowa, U.S.A.* 112 **E8**
Knoxville, *Pa., U.S.A.* 116 **E7**
Knoxville, *Tenn., U.S.A.* 115 **H4**
Knud Rasmussen Land, *Greenland* 4 **A5**
Knysna, *S. Africa* 88 **E3**
Knyszyn, *Poland* 30 **E9**
Ko Kha, *Thailand* 64 **C2**
Ko Tarutao △, *Thailand* 65 **J2**
Ko Yao, *Thailand* 65 **a**
Koartac = Quaqtaq, *Canada* 101 **B13**
Koba, *Indonesia* 63 **F8**
Kobarid, *Slovenia* 41 **B10**
Kobayashi, *Japan* 55 **J5**
Kobdo = Hovd, *Mongolia* 60 **B4**
Kōbe, *Japan* 55 **G7**
Kobelyaky, *Ukraine* 33 **H8**
København, *Denmark* 11 **J6**
Københavns Amtskommune □, *Denmark* 11 **J6**
Kobenni, *Mauritania* 82 **B3**
Kōbi-Sho, *Japan* 55 **M1**
Koblenz, *Germany* 25 **E3**
Kobo, *Ethiopia* 81 **E4**
Kobryn, *Belarus* 33 **F3**
Kobuleti, *Georgia* 35 **K5**
Kobylin, *Poland* 31 **G4**
Kobyłka, *Poland* 31 **F8**
Kobylkino, *Russia* 34 **C6**
Koca →, *Turkey* 45 **F11**
Kocabaş, *Turkey* 47 **D11**
Kocaeli, *Turkey* 45 **F13**
Kocaeli □, *Turkey* 45 **F13**
Kočane, *Serbia & M.* 44 **C5**
Kočani, *Macedonia* 44 **E6**
Koçarlı, *Turkey* 47 **D9**
Koceljevo, *Serbia & M.* 44 **B3**
Kočevje, *Slovenia* 41 **C11**
Koch Bihar, *India* 67 **F16**
Kochang, *S. Korea* 57 **G14**
Kochas, *India* 69 **G10**
Kocher →, *Germany* 25 **F5**
Kochi = Cochin, *India* 66 **Q10**
Kōchi, *Japan* 55 **H6**
Kōchi □, *Japan* 55 **H6**
Kochiu = Gejiu, *China* 58 **F4**
Kock, *Poland* 31 **G9**
Kodarma, *India* 69 **G11**
Kode, *Sweden* 11 **G5**
Kodiak, *U.S.A.* 100 **C4**
Kodiak I., *U.S.A.* 100 **C4**
Kodinar, *India* 68 **J4**
Kodok, *Sudan* 81 **F3**
Kodori →, *Georgia* 35 **J5**
Koedoesberge, *S. Africa* 88 **E3**
Koes, *Namibia* 88 **D2**
Kofçaz, *Turkey* 45 **E11**
Koffiefontein, *S. Africa* 88 **D4**
Kofiau, *Indonesia* 63 **E7**
Köflach, *Austria* 26 **D8**
Koforidua, *Ghana* 83 **D4**
Kōfu, *Japan* 55 **G9**
Koga, *Japan* 55 **F9**
Kogaluc →, *Canada* 105 **A7**
Køge, *Denmark* 11 **J6**
Køge Bugt, *Denmark* 11 **J6**
Kogi □, *Nigeria* 83 **D6**
Kogin Baba, *Nigeria* 83 **D7**
Koh-i-Khurd, *Afghan.* 68 **C1**
Koh-i-Maran, *Pakistan* 68 **E2**
Kohat, *Pakistan* 68 **C4**
Kohima, *India* 67 **G19**
Kohkīlūyeh va Būyer Aḩmadi □, *Iran* 71 **D6**
Kohler Ra., *Antarctica* 5 **D15**
Kohlu, *Pakistan* 68 **E3**
Kohtla-Järve, *Estonia* 9 **G22**
Koi Sanjaq, *Iraq* 70 **B5**
Koillismaa, *Finland* 8 **D23**
Koin-dong, *N. Korea* 57 **D14**
Koinare, *Bulgaria* 45 **C8**
Koindu, *S. Leone* 82 **D2**
Kojetín, *Czech Rep.* 27 **B10**
Kojŏ, *N. Korea* 57 **E14**
Kojonup, *Australia* 93 **F2**
Kojūr, *Iran* 71 **B6**
Koka, *Sudan* 80 **C3**
Kokand = Qŭqon, *Uzbekistan* 52 **E8**
Kokas, *Indonesia* 63 **E8**
Kokava, *Slovak Rep.* 27 **C12**
Kokchetav = Kökshetaū, *Kazakhstan* 52 **D7**
Kokemäenjoki →, *Finland* 9 **F19**
Kokhma, *Russia* 34 **B5**
Koki, *Senegal* 82 **B1**
Kokkola, *Finland* 8 **E20**
Koko, *Nigeria* 83 **C5**
Koko Kyunzu, *Burma* 67 **M18**
Kokolopozo, *Ivory C.* 82 **D3**
Kokomo, *U.S.A.* 114 **E2**
Kokoro, *Niger* 83 **C5**
Koksan, *N. Korea* 57 **E14**
Kökshetaū, *Kazakhstan* 52 **D7**
Koksoak →, *Canada* 101 **C13**
Kokstad, *S. Africa* 89 **E4**
Kokubu, *Japan* 55 **J5**
Kola, *Indonesia* 63 **F8**
Kola Pen. = Kolskiy Poluostrov, *Russia* 52 **C4**
Kolachi →, *Pakistan* 68 **F2**
Kolahoi, *India* 69 **B6**
Kolahun, *Liberia* 82 **D2**
Kolaka, *Indonesia* 63 **E6**
Kolar, *India* 66 **N11**
Kolar Gold Fields, *India* 66 **N11**
Kolaras, *India* 68 **G6**
Kolari, *Finland* 8 **C20**
Kolárovo, *Slovak Rep.* 27 **D10**
Kolašin, *Serbia & M.* 44 **D3**
Kolayat, *India* 66 **F8**
Kolbäck, *Sweden* 10 **E10**
Kolbäcksån →, *Sweden* 10 **E10**
Kolbermoor, *Germany* 25 **H8**
Kolbuszowa, *Poland* 31 **H8**
Kolchugino = Leninsk-Kuznetskiy, *Russia* 52 **D9**
Kolchugino, *Russia* 32 **D10**
Kolda, *Senegal* 82 **C2**
Koldegi, *Sudan* 81 **E3**
Kolding, *Denmark* 11 **J3**
Kolepom = Dolak, Pulau, *Indonesia* 63 **F9**
Kolguyev, Ostrov, *Russia* 52 **C5**
Kolhapur, *India* 66 **L9**
Kolia, *Ivory C.* 82 **D3**
Kolín, *Czech Rep.* 26 **A8**
Kolind, *Denmark* 11 **H4**
Kolkas rags, *Latvia* 9 **H20**
Kolkata, *India* 69 **H13**
Kollam = Quilon, *India* 66 **Q10**
Kölleda, *Germany* 24 **D7**
Kollum, *Neths.* 17 **A6**
Kolmanskop, *Namibia* 88 **D2**
Köln, *Germany* 24 **E2**
Kolno, *Poland* 30 **E8**
Koło, *Poland* 31 **F5**
Kołobrzeg, *Poland* 30 **D2**
Kolokani, *Mali* 82 **C3**
Koloko, *Burkina Faso* 82 **C3**
Kololo, *Ethiopia* 81 **F5**
Kolomna, *Russia* 32 **E10**
Kolomyya, *Ukraine* 33 **H3**
Kolondiéba, *Mali* 82 **C3**
Kolonodale, *Indonesia* 63 **E6**
Kolonowskie, *Poland* 31 **H5**
Kolosib, *India* 67 **G18**
Kolpashevo, *Russia* 52 **D9**
Kolpino, *Russia* 32 **C6**
Kolpny, *Russia* 33 **F9**
Kolskiy Poluostrov, *Russia* 52 **C4**
Kolsva, *Sweden* 10 **E9**
Kolubara →, *Serbia & M.* 44 **B4**
Koluszki, *Poland* 31 **G6**
Kolwezi, *Dem. Rep. of the Congo* 87 **E2**
Kolyma →, *Russia* 53 **C17**
Kolymskoye Nagorye, *Russia* 53 **C16**
Kôm Hamâda, *Egypt* 80 **H7**
Kôm Ombo, *Egypt* 80 **C3**
Komadugu Gana →, *Nigeria* 83 **C7**
Komandorskiye Is. = Komandorskiye Ostrova, *Russia* 53 **D17**
Komandorskiye Ostrova, *Russia* 53 **D17**
Komárno, *Slovak Rep.* 27 **D11**
Komárom, *Hungary* 28 **C3**
Komárom-Esztergom □, *Hungary* 28 **C3**
Komatipoort, *S. Africa* 89 **D5**
Komatou Yialou, *Cyprus* 49 **D13**
Komatsu, *Japan* 55 **F8**
Komatsushima, *Japan* 55 **H7**
Kombissiri, *Burkina Faso* 83 **C4**
Kombori, *Burkina Faso* 82 **C4**
Kombóti, *Greece* 46 **B3**
Komen, *Slovenia* 41 **C10**

Komenda, *Ghana* 83 D4
Komi □, *Russia* 52 C6
Komiža, *Croatia* 41 E13
Komló, *Hungary* 28 D3
Kommunarsk = Alchevsk, *Ukraine* 33 H10
Kommunizma, Pik, *Tajikistan* 52 F8
Komodo, *Indonesia* 63 F5
Komoé →, *Ivory C.* 82 D4
Komoran, Pulau, *Indonesia* 63 F9
Komoro, *Japan* 55 F9
Komotini, *Greece* 45 E9
Komovi, *Serbia & M.* 44 D3
Kompasberg, *S. Africa* 88 E3
Kompong Bang, *Cambodia* 65 F5
Kompong Cham, *Cambodia* 65 F5
Kompong Chhnang = Kampong Chhnang, *Cambodia* 65 F5
Kompong Chikreng, *Cambodia* 64 F5
Kompong Kleang, *Cambodia* 64 F5
Kompong Luong, *Cambodia* 65 G5
Kompong Pranak, *Cambodia* 64 F5
Kompong Som = Kampong Saom, *Cambodia* 65 G4
Kompong Som, Chhung = Kampong Saom, Chaak, *Cambodia* 65 G4
Kompong Speu, *Cambodia* 65 G5
Kompong Sralau, *Cambodia* 64 E5
Kompong Thom, *Cambodia* 64 F5
Kompong Trabeck, *Cambodia* 64 F5
Kompong Trabeck, *Cambodia* 65 G5
Kompong Trach, *Cambodia* 65 G5
Kompong Tralach, *Cambodia* 65 G5
Komrat = Comrat, *Moldova* 29 D13
Komsberg, *S. Africa* 88 E3
Komsomolets, Ostrov, *Russia* 53 A10
Komsomolsk, *Amur, Russia* 53 D14
Komsomolsk, *Ivanovo, Russia* 32 D11
Komsomolskiy, *Russia* 34 C7
Kömür Burnu, *Turkey* 47 C8
Kon Tum, *Vietnam* 64 E7
Kon Tum, Plateau du, *Vietnam* 64 E7
Kona, *Mali* 82 C4
Konakovo, *Russia* 32 D9
Konarhā □, *Afghan.* 66 B7
Konārī, *Iran* 71 D6
Konch, *India* 69 G8
Konde, *Tanzania* 86 C4
Kondiá, *Greece* 47 B7
Kondinin, *Australia* 93 F2
Kondoa, *Tanzania* 86 C4
Kondókali, *Greece* 49 A3
Kondopaga, *Russia* 32 A8
Kondratyevo, *Russia* 53 D10
Kondrovo, *Russia* 32 E8
Konduga, *Nigeria* 83 C7
Köneürgench, *Turkmenistan* 52 E6
Konevo, *Russia* 32 A10
Kong = Khong →, *Cambodia* 64 F5
Kong, *Ivory C.* 82 D4
Kong, Koh, *Cambodia* 65 G4
Kong Christian IX Land, *Greenland* 4 C6
Kong Christian X Land, *Greenland* 4 B6
Kong Frederik IX Land, *Greenland* 4 C5
Kong Frederik VI Kyst, *Greenland* 101 B15
Kong Frederik VIII Land, *Greenland* 4 B6
Kong Oscar Fjord, *Greenland* 4 B6
Kongeå →, *Denmark* 11 J2
Kongerslev, *Denmark* 11 H4
Kongju, *S. Korea* 57 F14
Konglu, *Burma* 67 F20
Kongola, *Namibia* 88 B3
Kongolo, *Kasai-Or., Dem. Rep. of the Congo* 86 D1
Kongolo, *Katanga, Dem. Rep. of the Congo* 86 D2
Kongor, *Sudan* 81 F3
Kongoussi, *Burkina Faso* 83 C4
Kongsberg, *Norway* 9 G13
Kongsvinger, *Norway* 9 F15
Kongwa, *Tanzania* 86 D4
Koni, *Dem. Rep. of the Congo* 87 E2
Koni, Mts., *Dem. Rep. of the Congo* 87 E2
Koniakari, *Mali* 82 C2
Koniecpol, *Poland* 31 H6
Königs Wusterhausen, *Germany* 24 C9
Königsberg = Kaliningrad, *Russia* 9 J19
Königsbrunn, *Germany* 25 G6
Königslutter, *Germany* 24 C6
Konin, *Poland* 31 F5
Konispol, *Albania* 44 G4
Kónitsa, *Greece* 46 A2
Konjic, *Bos.-H.* 28 G2
Konkiep, *Namibia* 88 D2
Konkouré →, *Guinea* 82 D2
Könnern, *Germany* 24 D7
Kono, *S. Leone* 82 D2
Konongo, *Ghana* 83 D4
Konosha, *Russia* 32 B11
Kōnosu, *Japan* 55 F9
Konotop, *Ukraine* 33 G7
Konsankoro, *Guinea* 82 D3
Końskie, *Poland* 31 G7
Konstancin-Jeziorna, *Poland* 31 F8
Konstantinovka = Kostyantynivka, *Ukraine* 33 H9
Konstantinovsk, *Russia* 35 G5
Konstantynów Łódźki, *Poland* 31 G6
Konstanz, *Germany* 25 H5
Kont, *Iran* 71 E9
Kontagora, *Nigeria* 83 C6
Kontcha, *Cameroon* 83 D7
Konya, *Turkey* 70 B2
Konya Ovası, *Turkey* 72 C5
Konz, *Germany* 25 F2
Konza, *Kenya* 86 C4
Koocanusa, L., *Canada* 108 B6
Kookynie, *Australia* 93 E3
Koolyanobbing, *Australia* 93 F2
Koonibba, *Australia* 95 E1
Koorawatha, *Australia* 95 E4
Koorda, *Australia* 93 F2
Kooskia, *U.S.A.* 108 C6
Kootenay △, *Canada* 102 C5
Kootenay →, *U.S.A.* 102 D5
Kootenay L., *Canada* 102 D5
Kootjieskolk, *S. Africa* 88 E3
Kopanovka, *Russia* 35 G8
Kopaonik, *Serbia & M.* 44 C4
Kopaonik △, *Serbia & M.* 44 C4
Kópavogur, *Iceland* 8 D3
Koper, *Slovenia* 41 C10
Kopervik, *Norway* 9 G11
Kopet Dagh, *Asia* 71 B8
Kopi, *Australia* 95 E2
Köping, *Sweden* 10 E10
Köpingsvik, *Sweden* 11 H10
Kopište, *Croatia* 41 F13
Koplik, *Albania* 44 D3
Köpmanholmen, *Sweden* 10 A12
Kopparberg, *Sweden* 10 E9
Koppeh Dāgh = Kopet Dagh, *Asia* 71 B8
Koppies, *S. Africa* 89 D4
Koppom, *Sweden* 10 E6
Koprivlen, *Bulgaria* 44 E7
Koprivnica, *Croatia* 41 B13
Kopřivnice, *Czech Rep.* 27 B11
Koprivshtitsa, *Bulgaria* 45 D8
Köprübaşı, *Turkey* 47 C10
Kopychyntsi, *Ukraine* 33 H3
Kora △, *Kenya* 86 C4
Korab, *Macedonia* 44 E4
Korakiána, *Greece* 49 A3
Koral, *India* 68 J5
Korarou, L., *Mali* 82 B4
Korba, *India* 69 H10
Korbach, *Germany* 24 D4
Korbu, G., *Malaysia* 65 K3
Korçë, *Albania* 44 F4
Korčula, *Croatia* 41 F13
Korčulanski Kanal, *Croatia* 41 E13
Kord Kūy, *Iran* 71 B7
Kord Sheykh, *Iran* 71 D7
Kordestan = Kurdistan, *Asia* 73 D10
Kordestān □, *Iran* 70 C5
Kordofân, *Sudan* 79 F11
Koré Mayroua, *Niger* 83 C5
Korea, North ■, *Asia* 57 E14
Korea, South ■, *Asia* 57 G15
Korea Bay, *Korea* 57 E13
Korea Strait, *Asia* 57 H15
Korem, *Ethiopia* 81 E4
Korenevo, *Russia* 33 G8
Korenovsk, *Russia* 35 H4
Korets, *Ukraine* 33 G4
Korfantów, *Poland* 31 H4
Korgan, *Turkey* 72 B7
Korgus, *Sudan* 80 D3
Korhogo, *Ivory C.* 82 D3
Koribundu, *S. Leone* 82 D2
Korienzé, *Mali* 82 B4
Korinthía □, *Greece* 46 D4
Korinthiakós Kólpos, *Greece* 46 C4
Kórinthos, *Greece* 46 D4
Korioumé, *Mali* 82 B4
Koríssa, Límni, *Greece* 49 B3
Kōriyama, *Japan* 54 F10
Korkuteli, *Turkey* 47 D12
Kormakiti, C., *Cyprus* 49 D11
Körmend, *Hungary* 28 C1
Kornat, *Croatia* 41 E12
Kornat △, *Croatia* 41 E12
Korneshty = Corneşti, *Moldova* 29 C13
Korneuburg, *Austria* 27 C9
Kórnik, *Poland* 31 F4
Koro, *Fiji* 91 C8
Koro, *Ivory C.* 82 D3
Koro, *Mali* 82 C4
Koro Sea, *Fiji* 91 C9
Korocha, *Russia* 33 G9
Köroğlu Dağları, *Turkey* 72 B5
Korogwe, *Tanzania* 86 D4
Koronadal, *Phil.* 61 H6
Koróni, *Greece* 46 E3
Korónia, Limni, *Greece* 44 F7
Koronís, *Greece* 47 D7
Koronowo, *Poland* 31 E4
Koror, *Palau* 96 G5
Körös →, *Hungary* 28 D5
Körös Maros △, *Hungary* 28 C5
Köröstarcsa, *Hungary* 28 D6
Korosten, *Ukraine* 33 G5
Korostyshev, *Ukraine* 33 G5
Korotoyak, *Russia* 33 G10
Korraraika, Helodranon' i, *Madag.* 89 B7
Korsakov, *Russia* 53 E15
Korsberga, *Sweden* 11 G9
Korshunovo, *Russia* 53 D12
Korsør, *Denmark* 11 J5
Korsun Shevchenkovskiy, *Ukraine* 33 H6
Korsze, *Poland* 30 D8
Korti, *Sudan* 80 D3
Kortrijk, *Belgium* 17 D3
Korucu, *Turkey* 47 B9
Korwai, *India* 68 G8
Koryakskoye Nagorye, *Russia* 53 C18
Koryŏng, *S. Korea* 57 G15
Koryukovka, *Ukraine* 33 G7
Kos, *Greece* 47 E9
Kosa, *Ethiopia* 81 F4
Kosaya Gora, *Russia* 32 E9
Kościan, *Poland* 31 F3
Kościerzyna, *Poland* 30 D4
Kosciusko, *U.S.A.* 113 J10
Kosciuszko, Mt., *Australia* 95 F4
Köséły →, *Hungary* 28 C6
Kosha, *Sudan* 80 C3
Koshava, *Bulgaria* 44 B7
K'oshih = Kashi, *China* 60 C2
Koshiki-Rettō, *Japan* 55 J4
Kosi, *India* 68 F7
Kosi →, *India* 69 E8
Košice, *Slovak Rep.* 27 C14
Košický □, *Slovak Rep.* 27 C14
Kosjerić, *Serbia & M.* 44 B3
Köşk, *Turkey* 47 D10
Koskinoú, *Greece* 49 C10
Koslan, *Russia* 52 C5
Kosŏng, *N. Korea* 57 E15
Kosovo □, *Serbia & M.* 44 D4
Kosovo Polje, *Serbia & M.* 44 D5
Kosovska Kamenica, *Serbia & M.* 44 D5
Kosovska Mitrovica, *Serbia & M.* 44 D4
Kossou, L. de, *Ivory C.* 82 D3
Kosta, *Sweden* 11 H9
Kostajnica, *Croatia* 41 C13
Kostanjevica, *Slovenia* 41 C12
Kostenets, *Bulgaria* 44 D7
Koster, *S. Africa* 88 D4
Kôstî, *Sudan* 81 E3
Kostinbrod, *Bulgaria* 44 D7
Kostolac, *Serbia & M.* 44 B5
Kostopil, *Ukraine* 33 G4
Kostroma, *Russia* 32 D11
Kostromskoye Vdkhr., *Russia* 32 D11
Kostrzyn, *Lubuskie, Poland* 31 F1
Kostrzyn, *Wielkopolskie, Poland* 31 F4
Kostyantynivka, *Ukraine* 33 H9
Kostyukovichi = Kastsyukovichy, *Belarus* 32 F7
Koszalin, *Poland* 30 D3
Kőszeg, *Hungary* 28 C1
Kot Addu, *Pakistan* 68 D4
Kot Kapura, *India* 68 D6
Kot Moman, *Pakistan* 68 C5
Kot Sultan, *Pakistan* 68 D4
Kota, *India* 68 G6
Kota Baharu, *Malaysia* 65 J4
Kota Barrage, *India* 68 G6
Kota Belud, *Malaysia* 62 C5
Kota Kinabalu, *Malaysia* 62 C5
Kota Kubu Baharu, *Malaysia* 65 L3
Kota Tinggi, *Malaysia* 65 M4
Kotaagung, *Indonesia* 62 F2
Kotabaru, *Indonesia* 62 E5
Kotabumi, *Indonesia* 62 E2
Kotamobagu, *Indonesia* 63 D6
Kotcho L., *Canada* 102 B4
Kotdwara, *India* 69 E8
Kotel, *Bulgaria* 45 D10
Kotelnich, *Russia* 34 A9
Kotelnikovo, *Russia* 35 G6
Kotelnyy, Ostrov, *Russia* 53 B14
Kothari →, *India* 68 G6
Köthen, *Germany* 24 D7
Kothi, *Chhattisgarh, India* 69 H10
Kothi, *Mad. P., India* 69 G9
Kotiro, *Pakistan* 68 F2
Kotka, *Finland* 9 F22
Kotlas, *Russia* 52 C5
Kotlenska Planina, *Bulgaria* 45 D10
Kotli, *Pakistan* 68 C5
Kotma, *India* 69 H9
Kotmul, *Pakistan* 69 B6
Koton-Karifi, *Nigeria* 83 D6
Kotonkoro, *Nigeria* 83 C6
Kotor, *Serbia & M.* 44 D2
Kotor Varoš, *Bos.-H.* 28 F2
Kotoriba, *Croatia* 41 B13
Kotovo, *Russia* 34 E7
Kotovsk, *Russia* 34 D5
Kotovsk, *Ukraine* 33 J5
Kotputli, *India* 68 F7
Kotri, *Pakistan* 68 G3
Kótronas, *Greece* 46 E4
Kötschach-Mauthen, *Austria* 26 E6
Kotturu, *India* 66 M10
Kotuy →, *Russia* 53 B11
Kotzebue, *U.S.A.* 100 B3
Kouchibouguac △, *Canada* 105 C6
Koudougou, *Burkina Faso* 82 C4
Koufonísi, *Greece* 49 E8
Koufonísia, *Greece* 47 E7
Kougaberge, *S. Africa* 88 E3
Kouibli, *Ivory C.* 82 D3
Kouilou →, *Congo* 84 E2
Koula Moutou, *Gabon* 84 E2
Koulen = Kulen, *Cambodia* 64 F5
Koulikoro, *Mali* 82 C3
Kouloúra, *Greece* 49 A3
Koúm-bournoú, Ákra, *Greece* 49 C10
Koumala, *Australia* 94 C4
Koumankou, *Mali* 82 C3
Koumbia, *Burkina Faso* 82 C4
Koumbia, *Guinea* 82 C2
Koumboum, *Guinea* 82 C2
Koumpenntoum, *Senegal* 82 C2
Koumra, *Chad* 79 G9
Koun-Fao, *Ivory C.* 82 D4
Koundara, *Guinea* 82 C2
Koundian, *Guinea* 82 C3
Koungheul, *Senegal* 82 C2
Kounradskiy, *Kazakhstan* 52 E8
Kountze, *U.S.A.* 113 K7
Koupéla, *Burkina Faso* 83 C4
Kourémalé, *Mali* 82 C3
Kouris →, *Cyprus* 49 E11
Kourou, *Fr. Guiana* 125 B8
Kourouba, *Mali* 82 C2
Kouroukoto, *Mali* 82 C2
Kourouma, *Burkina Faso* 82 C4
Kourouninkoto, *Mali* 82 C3
Kouroussa, *Guinea* 82 C3
Koussanar, *Senegal* 82 C2
Koussané, *Mali* 82 C2
Koussane, *Senegal* 82 C2
Kousseri, *Cameroon* 79 F8
Koutiala, *Mali* 82 C3
Kouto, *Ivory C.* 82 D3
Kouvé, *Togo* 83 D5
Kouvola, *Finland* 9 F22
Kovačica, *Serbia & M.* 28 E5
Kovel, *Ukraine* 33 G3
Kovin, *Serbia & M.* 28 F5
Kovrov, *Russia* 34 B5
Kowal, *Poland* 31 F6
Kowalewo Pomorskie, *Poland* 31 E5
Kowanyama, *Australia* 94 B3
Kowloon, *China* 59 F10
Kowŏn, *N. Korea* 57 E14
Koyampattur = Coimbatore, *India* 66 P10
Köyceğiz, *Turkey* 47 E10
Köyceğız Gölü, *Turkey* 47 E10
Koyulhisar, *Turkey* 72 B7
Koyunyeri, *Turkey* 45 F10
Koza, *Japan* 55 L3
Kozak, *Turkey* 47 B9
Kozan, *Turkey* 70 B2
Kozáni, *Greece* 44 F5
Kozáni □, *Greece* 44 F5
Kozara, *Bos.-H.* 41 D14
Kozara △, *Bos.-H.* 28 F2
Kozarac, *Bos.-H.* 41 D13
Kozelets, *Ukraine* 33 G6
Kozelsk, *Russia* 32 E8
Kozhikode = Calicut, *India* 66 P9
Koziegłowy, *Poland* 31 H6
Kozienice, *Poland* 31 G8
Kozje, *Slovenia* 41 B12
Kozloduy, *Bulgaria* 44 C7
Kozlovets, *Bulgaria* 45 C9
Kozlovka, *Russia* 34 C9
Kozlu, *Turkey* 72 B4
Kozluk, *Turkey* 73 C9
Koźmin, *Poland* 31 G4
Kozmodemyansk, *Russia* 34 B8
Kożuchów, *Poland* 31 G2
Kozyatyn, *Ukraine* 33 H5
Kpabia, *Ghana* 83 D4
Kpalimé, *Togo* 83 D5
Kpandae, *Ghana* 83 D4
Kpessi, *Togo* 83 D5
Kra, Isthmus of = Kra, Kho Khot, *Thailand* 65 G2
Kra, Kho Khot, *Thailand* 65 G2
Kra Buri, *Thailand* 65 G2
Kraai →, *S. Africa* 88 E4
Krabi, *Thailand* 65 H2
Kracheh, *Cambodia* 64 F6
Kragan, *Indonesia* 63 G14
Kragerø, *Norway* 9 G13
Kragujevac, *Serbia & M.* 44 B4
Krajenka, *Poland* 31 E3
Krakatau = Rakata, Pulau, *Indonesia* 62 F3
Krakatoa = Rakata, Pulau, *Indonesia* 62 F3
Krakor, *Cambodia* 64 F5
Kraków, *Poland* 31 H6
Kraków ✕ (KRK), *Poland* 31 H6
Kralanh, *Cambodia* 64 F4
Králíky, *Czech Rep.* 27 A9
Kraljevo, *Serbia & M.* 44 C4
Kralovéhradecký □, *Czech Rep.* 26 A8
Královský Chlmec, *Slovak Rep.* 27 C14
Kralupy nad Vltavou, *Czech Rep.* 26 A7
Kramatorsk, *Ukraine* 33 H9
Kramfors, *Sweden* 10 B11
Kraniá, *Greece* 44 G5
Kranía Elassónas, *Greece* 46 B4
Kranídhion, *Greece* 46 D5
Kranj, *Slovenia* 41 B11
Kranjska Gora, *Slovenia* 41 B10
Krankskop, *S. Africa* 89 D5
Krapina, *Croatia* 41 B12
Krapina →, *Croatia* 41 C12
Krapkowice, *Poland* 31 H4
Kras, *Croatia* 41 C10
Kraskino, *Russia* 53 E14
Krāslava, *Latvia* 32 E4
Kraslice, *Czech Rep.* 26 A5
Krasnaya Gorbatka, *Russia* 34 C5
Krasnaya Polyana, *Russia* 35 J5
Kraśnik, *Poland* 31 H9
Krasnoarmeisk, *Ukraine* 33 H9
Krasnoarmeysk, *Russia* 34 E7
Krasnoarmeyskiy, *Russia* 35 G6
Krasnobrod, *Poland* 31 H10
Krasnodar, *Russia* 35 H4
Krasnodon, *Ukraine* 33 H10
Krasnogorskiy, *Russia* 34 B9
Krasnograd = Krasnohrad, *Ukraine* 33 H8
Krasnogvardeyskoye, *Russia* 35 H5
Krasnogvardyesk, *Ukraine* 33 K8
Krasnohrad, *Ukraine* 33 H8
Krasnokutsk, *Ukraine* 33 G8
Krasnolesnyy, *Russia* 33 G10
Krasnoperekopsk, *Ukraine* 33 J7
Krasnorechenskiy, *Russia* 54 B7
Krasnoselkup, *Russia* 52 C9
Krasnoslobodsk, *Mordvinia, Russia* 34 C6
Krasnoslobodsk, *Volgograd, Russia* 35 F7
Krasnoturinsk, *Russia* 52 D7
Krasnovodsk = Türkmenbashi, *Turkmenistan* 52 E6
Krasnoyarsk, *Russia* 53 D10
Krasnoye = Krasnyy, *Russia* 32 E6
Krasnozavodsk, *Russia* 32 D10
Krasny Sulin, *Russia* 33 J11
Krasnystaw, *Poland* 31 H10
Krasnyy, *Russia* 32 E6
Krasnyy Kholm, *Russia* 32 C9
Krasnyy Kut, *Russia* 34 E8
Krasnyy Liman, *Ukraine* 33 H9
Krasnyy Luch, *Ukraine* 33 H10
Krasnyy Profintern, *Russia* 32 D11
Krasnyy Yar, *Astrakhan, Russia* 35 G9
Krasnyy Yar, *Samara, Russia* 34 D10
Krasnyy Yar, *Volgograd, Russia* 34 E7
Krasnyye Baki, *Russia* 34 B7
Krasnyyoskolske Vdskh., *Ukraine* 33 H9
Kraszna →, *Hungary* 28 B7
Kratie = Kracheh, *Cambodia* 64 F6
Kratovo, *Macedonia* 44 D6
Krau, *Indonesia* 63 E10
Kravanh, Chuor Phnum, *Cambodia* 65 G4
Krefeld, *Germany* 24 D2
Krémaston, Límni, *Greece* 46 C3
Kremen, *Croatia* 41 D12
Kremenchuk, *Ukraine* 33 H7
Kremenchuksk Vdskh., *Ukraine* 33 H7
Kremenets, *Ukraine* 33 G3
Kremennaya, *Ukraine* 33 H10
Kremges = Svitlovodsk, *Ukraine* 33 H7
Kremmen, *Germany* 24 C9
Kremmling, *U.S.A.* 108 F10
Kremnica, *Slovak Rep.* 27 C11
Krems, *Austria* 26 C8
Kremsmünster, *Austria* 26 C7
Kretinga, *Lithuania* 9 J19
Krettsy, *Russia* 32 C7
Kreuzberg, *Germany* 25 E5
Kreuztal, *Germany* 24 E4
Kría Vrísi, *Greece* 44 F6
Kribi, *Cameroon* 83 E6
Krichem, *Bulgaria* 45 D8
Krichev = Krychaw, *Belarus* 32 F6
Krim, *Slovenia* 41 C11
Kriós, Ákra, *Greece* 49 D5
Krishna →, *India* 67 M12
Krishnanagar, *India* 69 H13
Kristdala, *Sweden* 11 G10
Kristiansand, *Norway* 9 G13
Kristianstad, *Sweden* 11 H8
Kristiansund, *Norway* 8 E12
Kristiinankaupunki, *Finland* 9 E19
Kristinehamn, *Sweden* 10 E8
Kristinestad = Kristiinankaupunki, *Finland* 9 E19
Kríti, *Greece* 49 D7
Kritsá, *Greece* 49 D7
Kriva →, *Macedonia* 44 D5
Kriva Palanka, *Macedonia* 44 D6
Krivaja →, *Bos.-H.* 28 F3
Krivelj, *Serbia & M.* 44 B6
Křivoklátsko ⌂, *Czech Rep.* 26 A6
Krivoy Rog = Kryvyy Rih, *Ukraine* 33 J7
Križevci, *Croatia* 41 B13
Krk, *Croatia* 41 C11
Krka △, *Croatia* 41 E12
Krka →, *Slovenia* 41 C12
Krkonoše, *Czech Rep.* 26 A8
Krkonoše △, *Czech Rep.* 26 A8
Krnov, *Czech Rep.* 27 A10
Krobia, *Poland* 31 G3
Krokeaí, *Greece* 46 E4
Krokek, *Sweden* 11 F10
Krokodil →, *Mozam.* 89 D5
Krokom, *Sweden* 10 A8
Krokowa, *Poland* 30 D5
Krolevets, *Ukraine* 33 G7
Kroměříž, *Czech Rep.* 27 B10
Krompachy, *Slovak Rep.* 27 C13
Kromy, *Russia* 33 F8
Kronach, *Germany* 25 E7
Krong Kaoh Kong, *Cambodia* 62 B2
Kronobergs län □, *Sweden* 11 H8
Kronprins Olav Kyst, *Antarctica* 5 C5
Kronprinsesse Märtha Kyst, *Antarctica* 5 D2
Kronshtadt, *Russia* 32 C5
Kroonstad, *S. Africa* 88 D4
Kröpelin, *Germany* 24 A7
Kropotkin, *Russia* 35 H5
Kropp, *Germany* 24 A5
Krosna, *Lithuania* 30 D10
Krośniewice, *Poland* 31 F6
Krosno, *Poland* 31 J8
Krosno Odrzańskie, *Poland* 31 F2
Krotoszyn, *Poland* 31 G4
Krotovka, *Russia* 34 D10
Kroussón, *Greece* 49 D6
Krrabë, *Albania* 44 E3
Krško, *Slovenia* 41 C12
Krstača, *Serbia & M.* 44 D4
Kruger △, *S. Africa* 89 C5
Krugersdorp, *S. Africa* 89 D4
Kruisfontein, *S. Africa* 88 E3
Krujë, *Albania* 44 E3
Krulevshchina = Krulyewshchyna, *Belarus* 32 E4
Krulyewshchyna, *Belarus* 32 E4
Krumbach, *Germany* 25 G6
Krumë, *Albania* 44 D4
Krumovgrad, *Bulgaria* 45 E9
Krung Thep = Bangkok, *Thailand* 64 F3
Krupanj, *Serbia & M.* 44 B3
Krupina, *Slovak Rep.* 27 C12
Krupinica →, *Slovak Rep.* 27 C11
Krupki, *Belarus* 32 E5
Kruševac, *Serbia & M.* 44 C5
Kruševo, *Macedonia* 44 E5
Kruszwica, *Poland* 31 F5
Krychaw, *Belarus* 32 F6
Krymsk, *Russia* 33 K10
Krymskiy Poluostrov = Krymskyy Pivostriv, *Ukraine* 33 K8
Krymskyy Pivostriv, *Ukraine* 33 K8
Krynica, *Poland* 31 J7
Krynica Morska, *Poland* 30 D6

Krynki, *Poland* 31 E10
Kryvyy Rih, *Ukraine* 33 J7
Krzepice, *Poland* 31 H5
Krzeszów, *Poland* 31 H9
Krzna →, *Poland* 31 F10
Krzywiń, *Poland* 31 G3
Krzyż Wielkopolski, *Poland* 31 F2
Ksar el Kebir, *Morocco* 78 B4
Ksar es Souk = Er Rachidia, *Morocco* 78 B5
Ksiąz Wielkopolski, *Poland* 31 F4
Kstovo, *Russia* 34 B7
Ku, W. el →, *Sudan* 81 E2
Kuah, *Malaysia* 65 J2
Kuala Belait, *Malaysia* 62 D4
Kuala Berang, *Malaysia* 65 K4
Kuala Dungun = Dungun, *Malaysia* 65 K4
Kuala Kangsar, *Malaysia* 65 K3
Kuala Kelawang, *Malaysia* 65 L4
Kuala Kerai, *Malaysia* 65 K4
Kuala Kerian, *Malaysia* 65 c
Kuala Lipis, *Malaysia* 65 K4
Kuala Lumpur, *Malaysia* 65 L3
Kuala Nerang, *Malaysia* 65 J3
Kuala Pilah, *Malaysia* 65 L4
Kuala Rompin, *Malaysia* 65 L4
Kuala Selangor, *Malaysia* 65 L3
Kuala Sepetang, *Malaysia* 65 K3
Kuala Terengganu, *Malaysia* 65 K4
Kualajelai, *Indonesia* 62 E4
Kualakapuas, *Indonesia* 62 E4
Kualakurun, *Indonesia* 62 E4
Kualapembuang, *Indonesia* 62 E4
Kualasimpang, *Indonesia* 62 D1
Kuancheng, *China* 57 D10
Kuandang, *Indonesia* 63 D6
Kuandian, *China* 57 D13
Kuangchou = Guangzhou, *China* 59 F9
Kuanshan, *Taiwan* 59 F13
Kuantan, *Malaysia* 65 L4
Kuba = Quba, *Azerbaijan* 35 K9
Kuban →, *Russia* 33 K9
Kuban Depression = Prikubanskaya Nizmennost, *Russia* 35 H4
Kubenskoye, Ozero, *Russia* 32 C10
Kubokawa, *Japan* 55 H6
Kubrat, *Bulgaria* 45 C10
Kubu, *Indonesia* 63 J18
Kubutambahan, *Indonesia* 63 J18
Kucar, Tanjung, *Indonesia* 63 K18
Kučevo, *Serbia & M.* 44 B5
Kucha Gompa, *India* 69 B7
Kuchaman, *India* 68 F6
Kuchenspitze, *Austria* 26 D3
Kuchinda, *India* 69 J11
Kuching, *Malaysia* 62 D4
Kuchino-eruba-Jima, *Japan* 55 J5
Kuchino-Shima, *Japan* 55 K4
Kuchinotsu, *Japan* 55 H5
Kuchl, *Austria* 26 D6
Kucing = Kuching, *Malaysia* 62 D4
Kuçovë, *Albania* 44 F3
Küçükbahçe, *Turkey* 47 C8
Küçükköy, *Turkey* 47 B8
Küçükkuyu, *Turkey* 47 B8
Küçükmenderes →, *Turkey* 47 D9
Kud →, *Pakistan* 68 F2
Kuda, *India* 66 H7
Kudat, *Malaysia* 62 C5
Kudirkos Naumiestis, *Lithuania* 30 D9
Kudowa-Zdrój, *Poland* 31 H3
Kudus, *Indonesia* 63 G14
Kudymkar, *Russia* 52 D6
Kueiyang = Guiyang, *China* 58 D6
Kufra Oasis = Al Kufrah, *Libya* 79 D10
Kufstein, *Austria* 26 D5
Kugaaruk = Pelly Bay, *Canada* 101 B11
Kugluktuk, *Canada* 100 B8
Kugong I., *Canada* 104 A4
Kūhak, *Iran* 66 F3
Kuhan, *Pakistan* 68 E2
Kūhbonān, *Iran* 71 D8
Kūhestak, *Iran* 71 E8
Kuhin, *Iran* 71 B6
Kūhīrī, *Iran* 71 E9
Kuhnsdorf, *Austria* 26 E7
Kūhpāyeh, *Eşfahan, Iran* 71 C7
Kūhpāyeh, *Kermān, Iran* 71 D8
Kūhrān, Kūh-e, *Iran* 71 E8
Kui Buri, *Thailand* 65 F2
Kuiseb →, *Namibia* 88 C1
Kuito, *Angola* 85 G3
Kuiu I., *U.S.A.* 102 B2
Kujang, *N. Korea* 57 E14
Kujawsko-Pomorskie □, *Poland* 30 E5
Kuji, *Japan* 54 D10
Kujū-San, *Japan* 55 H5
Kukavica, *Serbia & M.* 44 D5
Kukawa, *Nigeria* 83 C7
Kukës, *Albania* 44 D4
Kukmor, *Russia* 34 B10
Kukup, *Malaysia* 65 d
Kukup, Pulau, *Malaysia* 65 d
Kukvidze, *Russia* 34 E6
Kula, *Bulgaria* 44 C6
Kula, *Serbia & M.* 28 E4
Kula, *Turkey* 47 C10
Kulachi, *Pakistan* 68 D4
Kulai, *Malaysia* 65 M4
Kulaly, Ostrov, *Kazakhstan* 35 H10
Kulasekarappattinam, *India* 66 Q11
Kulautuva, *Lithuania* 30 D10
Kuldīga, *Latvia* 9 H19
Kuldīga □, *Latvia* 30 B8
Kuldja = Yining, *China* 52 E9
Kuldu, *Sudan* 81 E2
Kulebaki, *Russia* 34 C6
Kulen, *Cambodia* 64 F5
Kulen Vakuf, *Bos.-H.* 41 D13
Kulgam, *India* 69 C6
Kulgera, *Australia* 94 D1
Kulim, *Malaysia* 65 K3
Kulin, *Australia* 93 F2
Kulkayu = Hartley Bay, *Canada* 102 C3
Kullen, *Sweden* 11 H6
Kulmbach, *Germany* 25 E7
Kŭlob, *Tajikistan* 52 F7
Kulp, *Turkey* 73 C9
Kulpawn →, *Ghana* 83 D4
Kulsary, *Kazakhstan* 52 E6
Kulti, *India* 69 H12
Kulu, *India* 68 D7
Kulu, *Turkey* 72 C5
Kulumbura, *Australia* 92 B4
Kulunda, *Russia* 52 D8
Kulungar, *Afghan.* 68 C3
Külvand, *Iran* 71 D7
Kulwin, *Australia* 95 F3
Kulyab = Kŭlob, *Tajikistan* 52 F7
Kuma →, *Russia* 35 H8
Kumafşarı, *Turkey* 47 D11
Kumaganum, *Nigeria* 83 C7
Kumagaya, *Japan* 55 F9
Kumai, *Indonesia* 62 E4
Kumalar Dağı, *Turkey* 47 C12
Kumamba, Kepulauan, *Indonesia* 63 E9
Kumamoto, *Japan* 55 H5
Kumamoto □, *Japan* 55 H5
Kumanovo, *Macedonia* 44 D5
Kumara, *N.Z.* 91 K3
Kumarina, *Australia* 93 D2
Kumasi, *Ghana* 82 D4
Kumayri = Gyumri, *Armenia* 35 K6
Kumba, *Cameroon* 83 E6
Kumbağ, *Turkey* 45 F11
Kumbakonam, *India* 66 P11
Kumbarilla, *Australia* 95 D5
Kumbhraj, *India* 68 G7
Kumbia, *Australia* 95 D5
Kumbo, *Cameroon* 83 D7
Kŭmch'ŏn, *N. Korea* 57 E14
Kumdok, *India* 69 C8
Kume-Shima, *Japan* 55 L3
Kumeny, *Russia* 34 A9
Kumharsain, *India* 68 D7
Kŭmhwa, *S. Korea* 57 E14
Kumi, *Uganda* 86 B3
Kumkale, *Turkey* 45 G10
Kumla, *Sweden* 10 E9
Kumluca, *Turkey* 47 E12
Kummerower See, *Germany* 24 B8
Kumo, *Nigeria* 83 C7
Kumon Bum, *Burma* 67 F20
Kumylzhenskaya, *Russia* 34 F6
Kunágota, *Hungary* 28 D6
Kunashir, Ostrov, *Russia* 53 E15
Kunda, *Estonia* 9 G22
Kunda, *India* 69 G9
Kundar →, *Pakistan* 68 D3
Kundelungu △, *Dem. Rep. of the Congo* 87 E2
Kundelungu Ouest △, *Dem. Rep. of the Congo* 87 D2
Kundian, *Pakistan* 68 C4
Kundla, *India* 68 J4
Kung, Ao, *Thailand* 65 a
Kunga →, *Bangla.* 69 J13
Kungälv, *Sweden* 11 G5
Kunghit I., *Canada* 102 C2
Kungrad = Qŭnghirot, *Uzbekistan* 52 E6
Kungsängen, *Sweden* 10 E11
Kungsbacka, *Sweden* 11 G6
Kungsgården, *Sweden* 10 D10
Kungshamn, *Sweden* 11 F5
Kungsör, *Sweden* 10 E10
Kungur, *Russia* 52 D6
Kungurri, *Australia* 94 K6
Kunhar →, *Pakistan* 69 B5
Kunhegyes, *Hungary* 28 C5
Kuningan, *Indonesia* 63 G13
Kunlong, *Burma* 58 F2
Kunlun Shan, *Asia* 60 C3
Kunmadaras, *Hungary* 28 C5
Kunming, *China* 58 E4
Kunów, *Poland* 31 H8
Kunsan, *S. Korea* 57 G14
Kunshan, *China* 59 B13
Kunszentmárton, *Hungary* 28 D5
Kunszentmiklós, *Hungary* 28 C4
Kuntaur, *Senegal* 82 C2
Kununurra, *Australia* 92 C4
Kunwari →, *India* 69 F8
Kunya-Urgench = Köneürgench, *Turkmenistan* 52 E6
Künzelsau, *Germany* 25 F5
Kuopio, *Finland* 8 E22
Kupa →, *Croatia* 41 C13
Kupang, *Indonesia* 63 F6
Kupreanof I., *U.S.A.* 102 B2
Kupres, *Bos.-H.* 28 G2
Kupyansk, *Ukraine* 33 H9
Kupyansk-Uzlovoi, *Ukraine* 33 H9
Kuqa, *China* 60 B3
Kür →, *Azerbaijan* 73 C13
Kür Dili, *Azerbaijan* 71 B6
Kura = Kür →, *Azerbaijan* 73 C13
Kuranda, *Australia* 94 B4
Kuranga, *India* 68 H3
Kurashiki, *Japan* 55 G6
Kurayoshi, *Japan* 55 G6
Kürdämir, *Azerbaijan* 35 K9
Kurdistan, *Asia* 73 D10
Kŭrdzhali, *Bulgaria* 45 E9
Kure, *Japan* 55 G6
Küre, *Turkey* 72 B5
Küre Dağları, *Turkey* 72 B6
Kuressaare, *Estonia* 9 G20
Kurgan, *Russia* 52 D7
Kurganinsk, *Russia* 35 H5
Kurgannaya = Kurganinsk, *Russia* 35 H5
Kuri, *India* 68 F4
Kuria Maria Is. = Khurīyā Murīyā, Jazā'ir, *Oman* 75 D6
Kuridala, *Australia* 94 C3
Kurigram, *Bangla.* 67 G16
Kurikka, *Finland* 9 E20
Kuril Is. = Kurilskiye Ostrova, *Russia* 53 E15
Kuril Trench, *Pac. Oc.* 96 C7
Kurilsk, *Russia* 53 E15
Kurilskiye Ostrova, *Russia* 53 E15
Kurino, *Japan* 55 J5
Kurinskaya Kosa = Kür Dili, *Azerbaijan* 71 B6
Kurkur, *Egypt* 80 C3
Kurlovskiy, *Russia* 34 C5
Kurmuk, *Sudan* 81 E3
Kurnool, *India* 66 M11
Kuro-Shima, *Kagoshima, Japan* 55 J4
Kuro-Shima, *Okinawa, Japan* 55 M2
Kuror, J., *Sudan* 80 C3
Kurow, *N.Z.* 91 L3
Kurów, *Poland* 31 G9
Kurram →, *Pakistan* 68 C4
Kurri Kurri, *Australia* 95 E5
Kurrimine, *Australia* 94 B4
Kursavka, *Russia* 35 H6
Kurshskaya Kosa ⌓, *Russia* 30 C7
Kurshskiy Zaliv, *Russia* 9 J19
Kuršių Nerijos △, *Lithuania* 30 C8
Kursk, *Russia* 33 G9
Kuršumlija, *Serbia & M.* 44 C5
Kuršumlijska Banja, *Serbia & M.* 44 C5
Kurşunlu, *Bursa, Turkey* 45 F13
Kurşunlu, *Çankırı, Turkey* 72 B5
Kurtalan, *Turkey* 73 D9
Kurtbey, *Turkey* 45 E10
Kuru, *Sudan* 81 F2
Kuru, Bahr el →, *Sudan* 81 F2
Kurucaşile, *Turkey* 72 B5
Kuruçay, *Turkey* 70 B3
Kuruktag, *China* 60 B3
Kuruman, *S. Africa* 88 D3
Kuruman →, *S. Africa* 88 D3
Kurume, *Japan* 55 H5
Kurun →, *Sudan* 81 F3
Kurunegala, *Sri Lanka* 66 R12
Kurya, *Russia* 52 C6
Kus Gölü, *Turkey* 45 F11
Kuşadası, *Turkey* 72 D2
Kuşadası Körfezi, *Turkey* 47 D8
Kusamba, *Indonesia* 63 K18
Kusatsu, *Japan* 55 F9
Kusawa L., *Canada* 102 A1
Kusel, *Germany* 25 F3
Kushaka, *Nigeria* 83 C6
Kushalgarh, *India* 68 H6
Kushchevskaya, *Russia* 35 G4
Kusheriki, *Nigeria* 83 C6
Kushikino, *Japan* 55 J5
Kushima, *Japan* 55 J5
Kushimoto, *Japan* 55 H7
Kushiro, *Japan* 54 C12
Kushiro-Gawa →, *Japan* 54 C12
Kushiro Shitsugen △, *Japan* 54 C12
Küshk, *Iran* 71 D8
Kushka = Gushgy, *Turkmenistan* 52 F7
Kūshkī, *Iran* 70 C5
Kushol, *India* 69 C7
Kushtia, *Bangla.* 67 H16
Kushum →, *Kazakhstan* 34 F10
Kuskokwim B., *U.S.A.* 100 C3
Kusmi, *India* 69 H10
Kussharo-Ko, *Japan* 54 C12
Kustanay = Qostanay, *Kazakhstan* 52 D7
Kut, Ko, *Thailand* 65 G4
Kuta, *Indonesia* 63 K18
Kütahya, *Turkey* 47 B12
Kütahya □, *Turkey* 47 B11
Kutaisi, *Georgia* 35 J6
Kutaraja = Banda Aceh, *Indonesia* 62 C1
Kutch, Gulf of = Kachchh, Gulf of, *India* 68 H3
Kutch, Rann of = Kachchh, Rann of, *India* 68 H4
Kutina, *Croatia* 41 C13
Kutiyana, *India* 68 J4
Kutjevo, *Croatia* 28 E2
Kutkashen, *Azerbaijan* 35 K8
Kutná Hora, *Czech Rep.* 26 B8
Kutno, *Poland* 31 F6
Kutse, *Botswana* 88 C3
Kuttabul, *Australia* 94 K6
Kutu, *Dem. Rep. of the Congo* 84 E3
Kutum, *Sudan* 81 E1
Kúty, *Slovak Rep.* 27 C10
Kuujjuaq, *Canada* 101 C13
Kuujjuarapik, *Canada* 104 A4
Kuŭp-tong, *N. Korea* 57 D14
Kuusamo, *Finland* 8 D23
Kuusankoski, *Finland* 9 F22
Kuvshinovo, *Russia* 32 D8
Kuwait = Al Kuwayt, *Kuwait* 70 D5
Kuwait ■, *Asia* 70 D5
Kuwana, *Japan* 55 G8
Kuwana →, *India* 69 F10
Kuybyshev = Samara, *Russia* 34 D10
Kuybyshev, *Russia* 52 D8
Kuybyshevo, *Ukraine* 33 J9
Kuybyshevskoye Vdkhr., *Russia* 34 C9
Kuye He →, *China* 56 E6
Küyeh, *Iran* 70 B5
Kuyucak, *Turkey* 47 D10
Kuyumba, *Russia* 53 C10
Kuzey Anadolu Dağları, *Turkey* 72 B7
Kuzmin, *Serbia & M.* 28 E4
Kuznetsk, *Russia* 34 D8
Kuzomen, *Russia* 52 C4
Kvænangen, *Norway* 8 A19
Kværndrup, *Denmark* 11 J4
Kvaløy, *Norway* 8 B18
Kvänum, *Sweden* 11 F7
Kvareli = Qvareli, *Georgia* 35 K7
Kvarner, *Croatia* 41 D11
Kvarnerič, *Croatia* 41 D11
Kvicksund, *Sweden* 10 E10
Kvillsfors, *Sweden* 11 G9
Kvismare kanal, *Sweden* 10 E9
Kvissleby, *Sweden* 10 B11
Kwa-Nobuhle, *S. Africa* 85 L5
Kwabhaca, *S. Africa* 89 E4
Kwakhanai, *Botswana* 88 C3
Kwakoegron, *Suriname* 125 B7
Kwale, *Kenya* 86 C4
Kwale, *Nigeria* 83 D6
KwaMashu, *S. Africa* 89 D5
Kwando →, *Africa* 88 B3
Kwangchow = Guangzhou, *China* 59 F9
Kwangdaeri, *N. Korea* 57 D14
Kwangju, *S. Korea* 57 G14
Kwango →, *Dem. Rep. of the Congo* 84 E3
Kwangsi-Chuang = Guangxi Zhuangzu Zizhiqu □, *China* 58 F7
Kwangtung = Guangdong □, *China* 59 F9
Kwara □, *Nigeria* 83 D6
Kwataboahegan →, *Canada* 104 B3
Kwatisore, *Indonesia* 63 E8
KwaZulu Natal □, *S. Africa* 89 D5
Kweichow = Guizhou □, *China* 58 D6
Kwekwe, *Zimbabwe* 87 F2
Kwidzyn, *Poland* 30 E5
Kwiha, *Ethiopia* 81 E4
Kwinana New Town, *Australia* 93 F2
Kwisa →, *Poland* 31 G2
Kwoka, *Indonesia* 63 E8
Kwolla, *Nigeria* 83 D6
Kyabra Cr. →, *Australia* 95 D3
Kyabram, *Australia* 95 F4
Kyaikto, *Burma* 64 D1
Kyakhta, *Russia* 53 D11
Kyambura ⌓, *Uganda* 86 C3
Kyancutta, *Australia* 95 E2
Kyaukpadaung, *Burma* 67 J19
Kyaukpyu, *Burma* 67 K18
Kyaukse, *Burma* 67 J20
Kybartai, *Lithuania* 30 D9
Kyburz, *U.S.A.* 110 G6
Kyelang, *India* 68 C7
Kyenjojo, *Uganda* 86 B3
Kyjov, *Czech Rep.* 27 B10
Kyle, *Canada* 103 C7
Kyle Dam, *Zimbabwe* 87 G3
Kyle of Lochalsh, *U.K.* 13 D3
Kyll →, *Germany* 25 F2
Kyllburg, *Germany* 25 E2
Kymijoki →, *Finland* 9 F22
Kyneton, *Australia* 95 F3
Kynuna, *Australia* 94 C3
Kyō-ga-Saki, *Japan* 55 G7
Kyoga, L., *Uganda* 86 B3
Kyogle, *Australia* 95 D5
Kyom →, *Sudan* 81 F2
Kyongju, *S. Korea* 57 G15
Kyongpyaw, *Burma* 67 L19
Kyŏngsŏng, *N. Korea* 57 D15
Kyōto, *Japan* 55 G7
Kyōto □, *Japan* 55 G7
Kyparissovouno, *Cyprus* 49 D12
Kyperounda, *Cyprus* 49 E11
Kyrenia, *Cyprus* 49 D12
Kyrgyzstan ■, *Asia* 52 E8
Kyritz, *Germany* 24 C8
Kyrkhult, *Sweden* 11 H8
Kyrönjoki →, *Finland* 8 E19
Kystatyam, *Russia* 53 C13
Kysucké Nové Mesto, *Slovak Rep.* 27 B11
Kythréa, *Cyprus* 49 D12
Kyunhla, *Burma* 67 H19
Kyuquot Sound, *Canada* 102 D3
Kyurdamir = Kürdämir, *Azerbaijan* 35 K9
Kyūshū, *Japan* 55 H5
Kyūshū □, *Japan* 55 H5
Kyūshū-Sanchi, *Japan* 55 H5
Kyustendil, *Bulgaria* 44 D6
Kyusyur, *Russia* 53 B13
Kyyiv, *Ukraine* 33 G6
Kyyivske Vdskh., *Ukraine* 33 G6
Kyzyl, *Russia* 53 D10
Kyzyl Kum, *Uzbekistan* 52 E7
Kyzyl-Kyya, *Kyrgyzstan* 52 E8
Kyzyl-Orda = Qyzylorda, *Kazakhstan* 52 E7

L

La Albuera, *Spain* 37 G4
La Alcarria, *Spain* 38 E2
La Almarcha, *Spain* 38 F2
La Almunia de Doña Godina, *Spain* 38 D3
La Amistad △, *Cent. Amer.* 120 E3
La Asunción, *Venezuela* 124 A6
La Baie, *Canada* 105 C5
La Banda, *Argentina* 126 B3
La Bañeza, *Spain* 36 C5
La Barca, *Mexico* 118 C4
La Barge, *U.S.A.* 108 E8
La Bastide-Puylaurent, *France* 20 D7
La Baule-Escoubiac, *France* 18 E4
La Belle, *U.S.A.* 115 M5
La Biche →, *Canada* 102 B4
La Biche, L., *Canada* 102 C6
La Bisbal d'Empordà, *Spain* 38 D8
La Bomba, *Mexico* 118 A1
La Brea, *Trin. & Tob.* 125 K15
La Brède, *France* 20 D3
La Bresse, *France* 19 D13
La Bureba, *Spain* 36 C7
La Calera, *Chile* 126 C1
La Campana △, *Chile* 126 C1
La Campiña, *Spain* 37 H6
La Canal = Sa Canal, *Spain* 48 C7
La Cañiza = A Cañiza, *Spain* 36 C2
La Canourgue, *France* 20 D7
La Capelle, *France* 19 C10
La Carlota, *Argentina* 126 C3
La Carlota, *Phil.* 61 F5
La Carlota, *Spain* 37 H6
La Carolina, *Spain* 37 G7
La Cavalerie, *France* 20 D7
La Ceiba, *Honduras* 120 C2
La Chaise-Dieu, *France* 20 C7
La Chapelle d'Angillon, *France* 19 E9
La Chapelle-St-Luc, *France* 19 D11
La Chapelle-sur-Erdre, *France* 18 E5
La Charité-sur-Loire, *France* 19 E10
La Chartre-sur-le-Loir, *France* 18 E7
La Châtaigneraie, *France* 20 B3
La Châtre, *France* 19 F9
La Chaux-de-Fonds, *Switz.* 25 H2
La Chorrera, *Panama* 120 E4
La Ciotat, *France* 21 E9
La Clayette, *France* 19 F11
La Cocha, *Argentina* 126 B2
La Concepción = Ri-Aba, *Eq. Guin.* 83 E6
La Concepción, *Panama* 120 E3
La Concordia, *Mexico* 119 D6
La Coruña = A Coruña, *Spain* 36 B2
La Coruña □, *Spain* 36 B2
La Côte-St-André, *France* 21 C9
La Courtine-le-Trucq, *France* 20 C6
La Crau, *Bouches-du-Rhône, France* 21 E8
La Crau, *Var, France* 21 E10
La Crescent, *U.S.A.* 112 D9
La Crete, *Canada* 102 B5
La Crosse, *Kans., U.S.A.* 112 F5
La Crosse, *Wis., U.S.A.* 112 D9
La Cruz, *Costa Rica* 120 D2
La Cruz, *Mexico* 118 C3
La Désirade, *Guadeloupe* 120 b
La Escondida, *Mexico* 118 C5
La Esmeralda, *Paraguay* 126 A3
La Esperanza, *Cuba* 120 B3
La Esperanza, *Honduras* 120 D2
La Estrada = A Estrada, *Spain* 36 C2
La Faouët, *France* 18 D3
La Fayette, *U.S.A.* 115 H3
La Fé, *Cuba* 120 B3
La Fère, *France* 19 C10
La Ferté-Bernard, *France* 18 D7
La Ferté-Gaucher, *France* 19 D10
La Ferté-Macé, *France* 18 D6
La Ferté-St-Aubin, *France* 19 E8
La Ferté-sous-Jouarre, *France* 19 D10
La Ferté-Vidame, *France* 18 D7
La Flèche, *France* 18 E6
La Follette, *U.S.A.* 115 G3
La Fregeneda, *Spain* 36 E4
La Fuente de San Esteban, *Spain* 36 E4
La Gacilly, *France* 18 E4
La Gineta, *Spain* 39 F2
La Grand-Combe, *France* 21 D8
La Grande, *U.S.A.* 108 D4
La Grande →, *Canada* 104 B5
La Grande Deux, Rés., *Canada* 104 B4
La Grande-Motte, *France* 21 E8
La Grande Quatre, Rés., *Canada* 104 B5
La Grande Trois, Rés., *Canada* 104 B4
La Grange, *Calif., U.S.A.* 110 H6
La Grange, *Ga., U.S.A.* 115 J3
La Grange, *Ky., U.S.A.* 114 F3
La Grange, *Tex., U.S.A.* 113 L6
La Grave, *France* 21 C10
La Guaira, *Venezuela* 124 A5
La Guardia = A Guarda, *Spain* 36 D2
La Gudiña = A Gudiña, *Spain* 36 C3
La Guerche-de-Bretagne, *France* 18 E5
La Guerche-sur-l'Aubois, *France* 19 F9
La Habana, *Cuba* 120 B3
La Haute Vallée de Chevreuse ⌓, *France* 19 D8
La Haye-du-Puits, *France* 18 C5
La Horra, *Spain* 36 D7
La Independencia, *Mexico* 119 D6
La Isabela, *Dom. Rep.* 121 C5
La Jonquera, *Spain* 38 C7
La Junta, *U.S.A.* 113 F3
La Laguna, *Canary Is.* 48 F3
La Libertad, *Guatemala* 120 C1
La Libertad, *Mexico* 118 B2
La Ligua, *Chile* 126 C1
La Línea de la Concepción, *Spain* 37 J5
La Loche, *Canada* 103 B7
La Londe-les-Maures, *France* 21 E10
La Lora, *Spain* 36 C7
La Loupe, *France* 18 D8
La Louvière, *Belgium* 17 D4
La Lune, *Trin. & Tob.* 125 K15
La Machine, *France* 19 F10
La Maddalena, *Italy* 42 A2
La Malbaie, *Canada* 105 C5
La Malinche △, *Mexico* 119 D5
La Mancha, *Spain* 39 F2
La Mariña, *Spain* 36 B3
La Martre, L., *Canada* 102 A5
La Mesa, *U.S.A.* 111 N9
La Misión, *Mexico* 118 A1
La Mothe-Achard, *France* 18 F5
La Motte, *France* 21 D10
La Motte-Chalançon, *France* 21 D9
La Motte-Servolex, *France* 21 C9
La Moure, *U.S.A.* 112 B5
La Muela, *Spain* 38 D3

La Mure, *France* 21 D9
La Negra, *Chile* 126 A1
La Oliva, *Canary Is.* 48 F6
La Orotava, *Canary Is.* 48 F3
La Oroya, *Peru* 124 F3
La Pacaudière, *France* 19 F10
La Palma, *Canary Is.* 48 F2
La Palma, *Panama* 120 E4
La Palma del Condado, *Spain* 37 H4
La Paloma, *Chile* 126 C1
La Pampa □, *Argentina* 126 D2
La Paragua, *Venezuela* 124 B6
La Paz, *Entre Ríos, Argentina* 126 C4
La Paz, *San Luis, Argentina* 126 C2
La Paz, *Bolivia* 124 G5
La Paz, *Honduras* 120 D2
La Paz, *Mexico* 118 C2
La Paz, *Phil.* 61 D4
La Paz Centro, *Nic.* 120 D2
La Pedrera, *Colombia* 124 D5
La Pérade, *Canada* 105 C5
La Perouse Str., *Asia* 54 B11
La Pesca, *Mexico* 119 C5
La Piedad, *Mexico* 118 C4
La Pine, *U.S.A.* 108 E3
La Plata, *Argentina* 126 D4
La Pobla de Lillet, *Spain* 38 C6
La Pocatière, *Canada* 105 C5
La Pola de Gordón, *Spain* 36 C5
La Porta, *France* 21 F13
La Porte, *Ind., U.S.A.* 114 E2
La Porte, *Tex., U.S.A.* 113 L7
La Presanella, *Italy* 40 B7
La Puebla = Sa Pobla, *Spain* 38 F8
La Puebla de Cazalla, *Spain* 37 H5
La Puebla de los Infantes, *Spain* 37 H5
La Puebla de Montalbán, *Spain* 36 F6
La Puebla del Río, *Spain* 37 H4
La Puerta de Segura, *Spain* 37 G8
La Purísima, *Mexico* 118 B2
La Push, *U.S.A.* 110 C2
La Quiaca, *Argentina* 126 A2
La Réole, *France* 20 D3
La Restinga, *Canary Is.* 48 G2
La Rioja, *Argentina* 126 B2
La Rioja □, *Argentina* 126 B2
La Rioja □, *Spain* 38 C2
La Robla, *Spain* 36 C5
La Roche-Bernard, *France* 18 E4
La Roche-Canillac, *France* 20 C5
La Roche-en-Ardenne, *Belgium* 17 D5
La Roche-sur-Foron, *France* 19 F13
La Roche-sur-Yon, *France* 18 F5
La Rochefoucauld, *France* 20 C4
La Rochelle, *France* 20 B2
La Roda, *Spain* 39 F2
La Roda de Andalucía, *Spain* 37 H6
La Romana, *Dom. Rep.* 121 C6
La Ronge, *Canada* 103 B7
La Rumorosa, *Mexico* 111 N10
La Sabina = Sa Savina, *Spain* 48 C7
La Sagra, *Spain* 39 H2
La Salle, *U.S.A.* 112 E10
La Sanabria, *Spain* 36 C4
La Santa, *Canary Is.* 48 E6
La Sarre, *Canada* 104 C4
La Scie, *Canada* 105 C8
La Selva, *Spain* 38 C7
La Selva Beach, *U.S.A.* 110 J5
La Selva del Camp, *Spain* 38 D6
La Serena, *Chile* 126 B1
La Serena, *Spain* 37 G5
La Seu d'Urgell, *Spain* 38 C6
La Seyne-sur-Mer, *France* 21 E9
La Sila, *Italy* 43 C9
La Solana, *Spain* 37 G7
La Soufrière, *St. Vincent* 121 D7
La Souterraine, *France* 19 F8
La Spézia, *Italy* 40 D6
La Suze-sur-Sarthe, *France* 18 E7
La Tagua, *Colombia* 124 C4
La Teste, *France* 20 D2
La Tortuga, *Venezuela* 121 D6
La Tour-du-Pin, *France* 21 C9
La Tranche-sur-Mer, *France* 18 F5
La Tremblade, *France* 20 C2
La Trinité, *Martinique* 120 c
La Tuque, *Canada* 104 C5
La Unión, *Chile* 128 E2
La Unión, *El Salv.* 120 D2
La Unión, *Mexico* 118 D4
La Unión, *Spain* 39 H4
La Urbana, *Venezuela* 124 B5
La Vache Pt., *Trin. & Tob.* 125 K15
La Vall d'Uixó, *Spain* 38 F4
La Vecilla de Curveño, *Spain* 36 C5
La Vega, *Dom. Rep.* 121 C5
La Vela de Coro, *Venezuela* 124 A5
La Veleta, *Spain* 37 H7
La Venta, *Mexico* 119 D6
La Ventura, *Mexico* 118 C4
La Voulte-sur-Rhône, *France* 21 D8
Laa an der Thaya, *Austria* 27 C9
Laaber, Grosse →, *Germany* 25 G8
Laage, *Germany* 24 B8
Laas Caanood = Las Anod, *Somali Rep.* 75 F4
Laatzen, *Germany* 24 C5
Laba →, *Russia* 35 H4
Labasa, *Fiji* 91 C8
Labason, *Phil.* 61 G5
Labastide-Murat, *France* 20 D5
Labastide-Rouairoux, *France* 20 E6
Labbézenga, *Mali* 83 B5
Labe = Elbe →, *Europe* 24 B4
Labé, *Guinea* 82 C2
Laberge, L., *Canada* 102 A1
Labin, *Croatia* 41 C11
Labinsk, *Russia* 35 H5
Labis, *Malaysia* 65 L4
Łabiszyn, *Poland* 31 F4
Labo, *Phil.* 61 D5
Laboe, *Germany* 24 A6
Laborec →, *Slovak Rep.* 27 C14
Laborie, *St. Lucia* 121 f
Labouheyre, *France* 20 D3
Laboulaye, *Argentina* 126 C3
Labrador, *Canada* 105 B7
Labrador City, *Canada* 105 B6
Labrador Sea, *Atl. Oc.* 101 C14
Lábrea, *Brazil* 124 E6
Labruguière, *France* 20 E6
Labuan, *Malaysia* 62 C5
Labuan, Pulau, *Malaysia* 62 C5
Labuha, *Indonesia* 63 E7
Labuhan, *Indonesia* 63 G11
Labuhanbajo, *Indonesia* 63 F6
Labuk, Telok, *Malaysia* 62 C5
Labyrinth, L., *Australia* 95 E2
Labytnangi, *Russia* 52 C7
Laç, *Albania* 44 E3
Lac-Bouchette, *Canada* 105 C5
Lac Édouard, *Canada* 104 C5
Lac La Biche, *Canada* 102 C6
Lac la Martre = Wha Ti, *Canada* 100 B8
Lac La Ronge ⌓, *Canada* 103 B7
Lac-Mégantic, *Canada* 105 C5
Lac Thien, *Vietnam* 64 F7
Lacanau, *France* 20 D2
Lacanau, Étang de, *France* 20 D2
Lacantúm →, *Mexico* 119 D6
Lacara →, *Spain* 37 G4
Lacaune, *France* 20 E6
Lacaune, Mts. de, *France* 20 E6
Laccadive Is. = Lakshadweep Is., *India* 50 H11
Lacepede B., *Australia* 95 F2
Lacepede Is., *Australia* 92 C3
Lacerdónia, *Mozam.* 87 F4
Lacey, *U.S.A.* 110 C4
Lachhmangarh, *India* 68 F6
Lachi, *Pakistan* 68 C4
Lachine, *Canada* 104 C5
Lachlan →, *Australia* 95 E3
Lachute, *Canada* 104 C5
Lackawanna, *U.S.A.* 116 D6
Lackawaxen, *U.S.A.* 117 E10
Lacolle, *Canada* 117 A11
Lacombe, *Canada* 102 C6
Lacona, *U.S.A.* 117 C8
Láconi, *Italy* 42 C2
Laconia, *U.S.A.* 117 C13
Lacq, *France* 20 E3
Ladakh Ra., *India* 69 C8
Lądek-Zdrój, *Poland* 31 H3
Ládhon →, *Greece* 46 D3
Ladik, *Turkey* 72 B6
Ladismith, *S. Africa* 88 E3
Ladíspoli, *Italy* 41 G9
Lādīz, *Iran* 71 D9
Ladnun, *India* 68 F6
Ladoga, L. = Ladozhskoye Ozero, *Russia* 32 B6
Ladozhskoye Ozero, *Russia* 32 B6
Lady Elliott I., *Australia* 94 C5
Lady Grey, *S. Africa* 88 E4
Ladybrand, *S. Africa* 88 D4
Ladysmith, *Canada* 102 D4
Ladysmith, *S. Africa* 89 D4
Ladysmith, *U.S.A.* 112 C9
Lae, *Papua N. G.* 96 H6
Laem Hin Khom, *Thailand* 65 b
Laem Khat, *Thailand* 65 a
Laem Nga, *Thailand* 65 a
Laem Ngop, *Thailand* 65 F4
Laem Phan Wa, *Thailand* 65 a
Laem Pho, *Thailand* 65 J3
Laem Phrom Thep, *Thailand* 65 a
Laem Riang, *Thailand* 65 a
Laem Sam Rong, *Thailand* 65 b
Laem Son, *Thailand* 65 a
Laem Yamu, *Thailand* 65 a
Læsø, *Denmark* 11 G5
Læsø Rende, *Denmark* 11 G4
Lafayette, *Colo., U.S.A.* 112 F2
Lafayette, *Ind., U.S.A.* 114 E2
Lafayette, *La., U.S.A.* 113 K9
Lafayette, *Tenn., U.S.A.* 115 G2
Laferte →, *Canada* 102 A5
Lafia, *Nigeria* 83 D6
Lafiagi, *Nigeria* 83 D6
Lafleche, *Canada* 103 D7
Lafon, *Sudan* 81 F3
Lagan, *Russia* 35 H8
Lagan, *Sweden* 11 H7
Lagan →, *Sweden* 11 H6
Lagan →, *U.K.* 12 B6
Lagarfljót →, *Iceland* 8 D6
Lage, *Germany* 24 D4
Lågen →, *Oppland, Norway* 9 F14
Lågen →, *Vestfold, Norway* 9 G14
Lägerdorf, *Germany* 24 B5
Laghouat, *Algeria* 78 B6
Lagnieu, *France* 21 C9
Lagny-sur-Marne, *France* 19 D9
Lago, *Italy* 43 C9
Lago de Sanabria y Entorno ⌓, *Spain* 36 C4
Lagôa, *Portugal* 37 H2
Lagoa do Peixe △, *Brazil* 127 C5
Lagoa Vermelha, *Brazil* 127 B5
Lagoaça, *Portugal* 36 D4
Lagodekhi, *Georgia* 35 K8
Lagónegro, *Italy* 43 B8
Lagonoy G., *Phil.* 61 E5
Lagos, *Nigeria* 83 D5
Lagos, *Portugal* 37 H2
Lagos □, *Nigeria* 83 D5
Lagos de Moreno, *Mexico* 118 C4
Lagrange, *Australia* 92 C3
Lagrange B., *Australia* 92 C3
Laguardia, *Spain* 38 C2
Laguépie, *France* 20 D5
Laguna, *Brazil* 127 B6
Laguna, *U.S.A.* 109 J10
Laguna Beach, *U.S.A.* 111 M9
Laguna de Duera, *Spain* 36 D6
Laguna de La Restinga △, *Venezuela* 121 D7
Laguna de la Restinga △, *Venezuela* 121 D6
Laguna del Laja △, *Chile* 126 D1
Laguna del Tigre △, *Guatemala* 120 C1
Laguna Limpia, *Argentina* 126 B4
Lagunas, *Chile* 126 A2
Lagunas, *Peru* 124 E3
Lagunas de Chacahua △, *Mexico* 119 D5
Lagunas de Montebello △, *Mexico* 119 D6
Lagunas de Ruidera ⌓, *Spain* 39 G2
Lahad Datu, *Malaysia* 63 C5
Lahad Datu, Teluk, *Malaysia* 63 D5
Lahan Sai, *Thailand* 64 E4
Lahanam, *Laos* 64 D5
Lahar, *India* 69 F8
Laharpur, *India* 69 F9
Lahat, *Indonesia* 62 E2
Lahewa, *Indonesia* 62 D1
Lāhījān, *Iran* 71 B6
Lahn →, *Germany* 25 E3
Lahnstein, *Germany* 25 E3
Laholm, *Sweden* 11 H7
Laholmsbukten, *Sweden* 11 H6
Lahore, *Pakistan* 68 D6
Lahr, *Germany* 25 G3
Lahri, *Pakistan* 68 E3
Lahti, *Finland* 9 F21
Lahtis = Lahti, *Finland* 9 F21
Laï, *Chad* 79 G9
Lai Chau, *Vietnam* 58 F4
Lai'an, *China* 59 A12
Laibin, *China* 58 F7
Laifeng, *China* 58 C7
L'Aigle, *France* 18 D7
Laignes, *France* 19 E11
L'Aiguillon-sur-Mer, *France* 20 B2
Laila = Layla, *Si. Arabia* 75 C4
Laingsburg, *S. Africa* 88 E3
Lainio älv →, *Sweden* 8 C20
Lairg, *U.K.* 13 C4
Laishui, *China* 56 E8
Laissac, *France* 20 D6
Láives, *Italy* 41 B8
Laiwu, *China* 57 F9
Laixi, *China* 57 F11
Laiyang, *China* 57 F11
Laiyuan, *China* 56 E8
Laizhou, *China* 57 F10
Laizhou Wan, *China* 57 F10
Laja →, *Mexico* 118 C4
Lajere, *Nigeria* 83 C7
Lajes, *Brazil* 127 B5
Lajkovac, *Serbia & M.* 44 B4
Lajosmizse, *Hungary* 28 C4
Lak Sao, *Laos* 64 C5
Lakaband, *Pakistan* 68 D3
Lakamané, *Mali* 82 C3
Lake Alpine, *U.S.A.* 110 G7
Lake Andes, *U.S.A.* 112 D5
Lake Arthur, *U.S.A.* 113 K8
Lake Bindegolly △, *Australia* 95 D3
Lake Cargelligo, *Australia* 95 E4
Lake Charles, *U.S.A.* 113 K8
Lake City, *Colo., U.S.A.* 109 G10
Lake City, *Fla., U.S.A.* 115 K4
Lake City, *Mich., U.S.A.* 114 C3
Lake City, *Minn., U.S.A.* 112 C8
Lake City, *Pa., U.S.A.* 116 D4
Lake City, *S.C., U.S.A.* 115 J6
Lake Cowichan, *Canada* 102 D4
Lake District △, *U.K.* 14 C4
Lake Elsinore, *U.S.A.* 111 M9
Lake Eyre △, *Australia* 95 D2
Lake Gairdner △, *Australia* 95 E2
Lake George, *U.S.A.* 117 C11
Lake Grace, *Australia* 93 F2
Lake Harbour = Kimmirut, *Canada* 101 B13
Lake Havasu City, *U.S.A.* 111 L12
Lake Hughes, *U.S.A.* 111 L8
Lake Isabella, *U.S.A.* 111 K8
Lake Jackson, *U.S.A.* 113 L7
Lake Junction, *U.S.A.* 108 D8
Lake King, *Australia* 93 F2
Lake Lenore, *Canada* 103 C8
Lake Louise, *Canada* 102 C5
Lake Malawi △, *Malawi* 87 E3
Lake Mburo △, *Uganda* 86 C3
Lake Mead ⌓, *U.S.A.* 111 K12
Lake Meredith ⌓, *U.S.A.* 113 H4
Lake Mills, *U.S.A.* 112 D8
Lake Nakura △, *Kenya* 86 C4
Lake Placid, *U.S.A.* 117 B11
Lake Pleasant, *U.S.A.* 117 C10
Lake Providence, *U.S.A.* 113 J9
Lake Roosevelt ⌓, *U.S.A.* 108 C4
Lake St. Peter, *Canada* 116 A6
Lake Superior ⌓, *Canada* 104 C3
Lake Torrens △, *Australia* 95 E2
Lake Village, *U.S.A.* 113 J9
Lake Wales, *U.S.A.* 115 M5
Lake Worth, *U.S.A.* 115 M5
Lakeba, *Fiji* 91 D9
Lakefield, *Canada* 116 B6
Lakefield △, *Australia* 94 B3
Lakehurst, *U.S.A.* 117 F10
Lakeland, *Australia* 94 B3
Lakeland, *U.S.A.* 115 M5
Lakemba = Lakeba, *Fiji* 91 D9
Lakeport, *Calif., U.S.A.* 110 F4
Lakeport, *Mich., U.S.A.* 116 C2
Lakes Entrance, *Australia* 95 F4
Lakeside, *Ariz., U.S.A.* 109 J9
Lakeside, *Calif., U.S.A.* 111 N10
Lakeside, *Nebr., U.S.A.* 112 D3
Lakeside, *Ohio, U.S.A.* 116 E2
Lakeview, *U.S.A.* 108 E3
Lakeville, *U.S.A.* 112 C8
Lakewood, *Colo., U.S.A.* 112 F2
Lakewood, *N.J., U.S.A.* 117 F10
Lakewood, *N.Y., U.S.A.* 116 D5
Lakewood, *Ohio, U.S.A.* 116 E3
Lakewood, *Wash., U.S.A.* 110 C4
Lakha, *India* 68 F4
Lakhaniá, *Greece* 49 D9
Lakhimpur, *India* 69 F9
Lakhnadon, *India* 69 H8
Lakhnau = Lucknow, *India* 69 F9
Lakhonpheng, *Laos* 64 E5
Lakhpat, *India* 68 H3
Läki, *Azerbaijan* 35 K8
Lakin, *U.S.A.* 113 G4
Lakitusaki →, *Canada* 104 B3
Lakki, *Pakistan* 68 C4
Lákkoi, *Greece* 49 D5
Lakonía □, *Greece* 46 E4
Lakonikós Kólpos, *Greece* 46 E4
Lakor, *Indonesia* 63 F7
Lakota, *Ivory C.* 82 D3
Lakota, *U.S.A.* 112 A5
Laksar, *India* 68 E8
Laksefjorden, *Norway* 8 A22
Lakselv, *Norway* 8 A21
Lakshadweep Is., *India* 50 H11
Lakshmanpur, *India* 69 H10
Lakshmikantapur, *India* 69 H13
Lala Musa, *Pakistan* 68 C5
Lalaghat, *India* 67 G18
Lalago, *Tanzania* 86 C3
Lalapanzi, *Zimbabwe* 87 F3
Lalapaşa, *Turkey* 45 E10
Lalbenque, *France* 20 D5
L'Albufera, *Spain* 39 F4
Lalganj, *India* 69 G11
Lalgola, *India* 69 G13
Lālī, *Iran* 71 C6
Lalibela, *Ethiopia* 81 E4
Lalin, *China* 57 B14
Lalín, *Spain* 36 C2
Lalin He →, *China* 57 B13
Lalinde, *France* 20 D4
Lalitapur, *Nepal* 69 F11
Lalitpur, *India* 69 G8
Lalkua, *India* 69 E8
Lalsot, *India* 68 F7
Lam, *Vietnam* 64 B6
Lam Pao Res., *Thailand* 64 D4
Lama Kara, *Togo* 83 D5
Lamaing, *Burma* 67 M20
Lamar, *Colo., U.S.A.* 112 F3
Lamar, *Mo., U.S.A.* 113 G7
Lamas, *Peru* 124 E3
Lamastre, *France* 21 D8
Lambach, *Austria* 26 C6
Lamballe, *France* 18 D4
Lambaréné, *Gabon* 84 E2
Lambasa = Labasa, *Fiji* 91 C8
Lambay I., *Ireland* 12 C5
Lambert Glacier, *Antarctica* 5 D6
Lambert's Bay, *S. Africa* 88 E2
Lambesc, *France* 21 E9
Lambeth, *Canada* 116 D3
Lámbia, *Greece* 46 D3
Lambomakondro, *Madag.* 89 C7
Lambro →, *Italy* 40 C6
Lambton Shores, *Canada* 116 C3
Lame, *Nigeria* 83 C6
Lame Deer, *U.S.A.* 108 D10
Lamego, *Portugal* 36 D3
Lamèque, *Canada* 105 C7
Lameroo, *Australia* 95 F3
Lamesa, *U.S.A.* 113 J4
Lamía, *Greece* 46 C4
Lamington △, *Australia* 95 D5
Lamitan, *Phil.* 61 H5
Lammermuir Hills, *U.K.* 13 F6
Lammhult, *Sweden* 11 G8
Lamoille →, *U.S.A.* 117 B11
Lamon B., *Phil.* 61 D5
Lamont, *Canada* 102 C6
Lamont, *Calif., U.S.A.* 111 K8
Lamont, *Wyo., U.S.A.* 108 E10
Lamotte-Beuvron, *France* 19 E9
Lampa, *Peru* 124 G4
Lampang, *Thailand* 64 C2
Lampasas, *U.S.A.* 113 K5
Lampazos de Naranjo, *Mexico* 118 B4
Lampertheim, *Germany* 25 F4
Lampeter, *U.K.* 15 E3
Lampman, *Canada* 103 D8
Lamprechtshausen, *Austria* 26 D5
Lampung □, *Indonesia* 62 F2
Lamta, *India* 69 H9
Lamu, *Kenya* 86 C5
Lamy, *U.S.A.* 109 J11
Lan Xian, *China* 56 E6
Lan Yu = Hungt'ou Hsü, *Taiwan* 59 G13
Lanak La, *China* 69 B8
Lanak'o Shank'ou = Lanak La, *China* 69 B8
Lanao, L., *Phil.* 61 H6
Lanark, *Canada* 117 A8
Lanark, *U.K.* 13 F5
Lanbi Kyun, *Burma* 65 G2
Lancang, *China* 58 F2
Lancang Jiang →, *China* 58 G3
Lancashire □, *U.K.* 14 D5
Lancaster, *Canada* 117 A10
Lancaster, *U.K.* 14 C5
Lancaster, *Calif., U.S.A.* 111 L8
Lancaster, *Ky., U.S.A.* 114 G3
Lancaster, *N.H., U.S.A.* 117 B13
Lancaster, *N.Y., U.S.A.* 116 D6
Lancaster, *Ohio, U.S.A.* 114 F4
Lancaster, *Pa., U.S.A.* 117 F8
Lancaster, *S.C., U.S.A.* 115 H5
Lancaster, *Wis., U.S.A.* 112 D9
Lancaster Sd., *Canada* 101 A11
Lancelin, *Australia* 93 F2
Lanchow = Lanzhou, *China* 56 F2
Lanciano, *Italy* 41 F11
Lancun, *China* 57 F11
Łańcut, *Poland* 31 H9
Land Between the Lakes ⌓, *U.S.A.* 115 G1
Landau, *Bayern, Germany* 25 G8
Landau, *Rhld-Pfz., Germany* 25 F4
Landeck, *Austria* 26 D3
Lander, *U.S.A.* 108 E9
Lander →, *Australia* 92 D5
Landerneau, *France* 18 D2
Landeryd, *Sweden* 11 G7
Landes, *France* 20 D2
Landes □, *France* 20 E3
Landes de Gascogne ⌓, *France* 20 D3
Landete, *Spain* 38 F3
Landi Kotal, *Pakistan* 68 B4
Landisburg, *U.S.A.* 116 F7
Landivisiau, *France* 18 D2
Landquart, *Switz.* 25 J5
Landrecies, *France* 19 B10
Land's End, *U.K.* 15 G2
Landsberg, *Germany* 25 G6
Landsborough Cr. →, *Australia* 94 C3
Landsbro, *Sweden* 11 G8
Landshut, *Germany* 25 G8
Landskrona, *Sweden* 11 J6
Landstuhl, *Germany* 25 F3
Landvetter, *Sweden* 11 G6
Lanesboro, *U.S.A.* 117 E9
Lanester, *France* 18 E3
Lanett, *U.S.A.* 115 J3
Lang Qua, *Vietnam* 64 A5
Lang Shan, *China* 56 D4
Lang Son, *Vietnam* 58 G6
Lang Suan, *Thailand* 65 H2
Langå, *Denmark* 11 H3
La'nga Co, *China* 67 D12
Lángadhás, *Greece* 44 F7
Langádhia, *Greece* 46 D4
Långan →, *Sweden* 10 A8
Langano, L., *Ethiopia* 81 F4
Langar, *Iran* 71 C9
Langara I., *Canada* 102 C2
Långås, *Sweden* 11 H6
Langdai, *China* 58 D5
Langdon, *U.S.A.* 112 A5
Långe Jan = Ölands södra udde, *Sweden* 11 H10
Langeac, *France* 20 C7
Langeais, *France* 18 E7
Langeb Baraka →, *Sudan* 80 D4
Langeberg, *S. Africa* 88 E3
Langeberge, *S. Africa* 88 D3
Langeland, *Denmark* 11 K4
Langelands Bælt, *Denmark* 11 K4
Langen, *Hessen, Germany* 25 F4
Langen, *Niedersachsen, Germany* 24 B4
Langenburg, *Canada* 103 C8
Langeneß, *Germany* 24 A4
Langenlois, *Austria* 26 C8
Langeoog, *Germany* 24 B3
Langeskov, *Denmark* 11 J4
Länghem, *Sweden* 11 G7
Langhirano, *Italy* 40 D7
Langholm, *U.K.* 13 F5
Langjökull, *Iceland* 8 D3
Langkawi, Pulau, *Malaysia* 65 J2
Langklip, *S. Africa* 88 D3
Langkon, *Malaysia* 62 C5
Langlade, *St- P. & M.* 105 C8
Langley, *Canada* 110 A4
Langnau, *Switz.* 25 J3
Langogne, *France* 20 D7
Langon, *France* 20 D3
Langøya, *Norway* 8 B16
Langreo, *Spain* 36 B5
Langres, *France* 19 E12
Langres, Plateau de, *France* 19 E12
Langsa, *Indonesia* 62 D1
Långsele, *Sweden* 10 A11
Långshyttan, *Sweden* 10 D10
Langtry, *U.S.A.* 113 L4
Langu, *Thailand* 65 J2
Langue de Barbarie △, *Senegal* 82 C1
Languedoc, *France* 20 E7
Languedoc-Roussillon □, *France* 20 E6
Langxi, *China* 59 B12
Langxiangzhen, *China* 56 E9
Langzhong, *China* 58 B5
Lanigan, *Canada* 103 C7
Lankao, *China* 56 G8
Länkäran, *Azerbaijan* 71 B6
Lanmeur, *France* 18 D3
Lannemezan, *France* 20 E4
Lannilis, *France* 18 D2
Lannion, *France* 18 D3
L'Annonciation, *Canada* 104 C5
Lanouaille, *France* 20 C5
Lanping, *China* 58 D2
Lansdale, *U.S.A.* 117 F9
Lansdowne, *Australia* 95 E5
Lansdowne, *Canada* 117 B8
Lansdowne, *India* 69 E8
Lansdowne House, *Canada* 104 B2
L'Anse, *U.S.A.* 114 B1
L'Anse au Loup, *Canada* 105 B8
L'Anse aux Meadows, *Canada* 105 B8
L'Anse la Raye, *St. Lucia* 121 f
Lansford, *U.S.A.* 117 F9
Lanshan, *China* 59 E9
Lansing, *U.S.A.* 114 D3
Lanslebourg-Mont-Cenis, *France* 21 C10
Lanta Yai, Ko, *Thailand* 65 J2
Lantewa, *Nigeria* 83 C7

Lantian, *China* 56 G5
Lanus, *Argentina* 126 C4
Lanusei, *Italy* 42 C2
Lanuza, *Phil.* 61 G7
Lanxi, *China* 59 C12
Lanzarote, *Canary Is.* 48 F6
Lanzarote ✕ (ACE), *Canary Is.* 48 F6
Lanzhou, *China* 56 F2
Lanzo Torinese, *Italy* 40 C4
Lao →, *Italy* 43 C8
Lao Bao, *Laos* 64 D6
Lao Cai, *Vietnam* 58 F4
Laoag, *Phil.* 61 B4
Laoang, *Phil.* 61 E6
Laoha He →, *China* 57 C11
Laohekou, *China* 59 A8
Laois □, *Ireland* 12 D4
Laon, *France* 19 C10
Laona, *U.S.A.* 114 C1
Laos ■, *Asia* 64 D5
Lapa, *Brazil* 127 B6
Lapai, *Nigeria* 83 D6
Lapalisse, *France* 19 F10
Lapeer, *U.S.A.* 114 D4
Lapeyrade, *France* 20 D3
Lapithos, *Cyprus* 49 D12
Lapland = Lappland, *Europe* 8 B21
Laporte, *U.S.A.* 117 E8
Lapovo, *Serbia & M.* 44 B5
Lappeenranta, *Finland* 9 F23
Lappland, *Europe* 8 B21
Laprida, *Argentina* 126 D3
Lapseki, *Turkey* 45 F10
Laptev Sea, *Russia* 53 B13
Lapua, *Finland* 8 E20
Lăpuş →, *Romania* 29 C8
Lapuş, Munţii, *Romania* 29 C8
Lăpuşna, *Moldova* 29 D13
Łapy, *Poland* 31 F9
Laqiya Arba'in, *Sudan* 80 C2
Laqiya Umran, *Sudan* 80 D2
L'Áquila, *Italy* 41 F10
Lār, *Āzarbājān-e Sharqī, Iran* 70 B5
Lār, *Fārs, Iran* 71 E7
Larabanga, *Ghana* 82 D4
Laragne-Montéglin, *France* 21 D9
Laramie, *U.S.A.* 112 E2
Laramie →, *U.S.A.* 108 F11
Laramie Mts., *U.S.A.* 112 E2
Laranjeiras do Sul, *Brazil* 127 B5
Larantuka, *Indonesia* 63 F6
Larat, *Indonesia* 63 F8
L'Arbresle, *France* 21 C8
Lärbro, *Sweden* 11 G12
Larde, *Mozam.* 87 F4
Larder Lake, *Canada* 104 C4
Lardhos, Ákra = Líndhos, Ákra, *Greece* 49 C10
Lardhos, Órmos, *Greece* 49 C10
Laredo, *Spain* 36 B7
Laredo, *U.S.A.* 113 M5
Laredo Sd., *Canada* 102 C3
Largentière, *France* 21 D8
L'Argentière-la-Bessée, *France* 21 D10
Largo, *U.S.A.* 115 M4
Largs, *U.K.* 13 F4
Lari, *Italy* 40 E7
Lariang, *Indonesia* 63 E5
Larimore, *U.S.A.* 112 B6
Larino, *Italy* 41 G11
Lárisa, *Greece* 46 B4
Lárisa □, *Greece* 46 B4
Larkana, *Pakistan* 68 F3
Larnaca, *Cyprus* 49 E12
Larnaca Bay, *Cyprus* 49 E12
Larne, *U.K.* 12 B6
Larned, *U.S.A.* 112 F5
Laroquebrou, *France* 20 D6
Larose, *U.S.A.* 113 L9
Larrimah, *Australia* 92 C5
Larsen Ice Shelf, *Antarctica* 5 C17
Laruns, *France* 20 F3
Larvik, *Norway* 9 G14
Larzac, Causse du, *France* 20 E7
Las Alpujarras, *Spain* 39 J1
Las Animas, *U.S.A.* 112 F3
Las Anod, *Somali Rep.* 75 F4
Las Arenas, *Spain* 36 B6
Las Aves, Is., *W. Indies* 121 C7
Las Batuecas ⌓, *Spain* 36 E4
Las Brenãs, *Argentina* 126 B3
Las Cabezas de San Juan, *Spain* 37 J5
Las Cañadas del Teide △, *Canary Is.* 48 F3
Las Cejas, *Argentina* 128 B4
Las Chimeneas, *Mexico* 111 N10
Las Cruces, *U.S.A.* 109 K10
Las Flores, *Argentina* 126 D4
Las Heras, *Argentina* 126 C2
Las Lajas, *Argentina* 128 D2
Las Lomitas, *Argentina* 126 A3
Las Marismas, *Spain* 37 H4
Las Minas, *Spain* 39 G3
Las Navas de la Concepción, *Spain* 37 H5
Las Navas del Marqués, *Spain* 36 E6
Las Palmas, *Argentina* 126 B4
Las Palmas, *Canary Is.* 48 F4
Las Palmas →, *Mexico* 111 N10
Las Palmas ✕ (LPA), *Canary Is.* 48 G4
Las Palmas de Cocalán △, *Chile* 126 C1
Las Pedroñas, *Spain* 39 F2
Las Piedras, *Uruguay* 127 C4
Las Pipinas, *Argentina* 126 D4
Las Plumas, *Argentina* 128 E3
Las Rosas, *Argentina* 126 C3
Las Rozas, *Spain* 36 E7
Las Tablas, *Panama* 120 E3
Las Termas, *Argentina* 126 B3
Las Toscas, *Argentina* 126 B4
Las Truchas, *Mexico* 118 D4
Las Varillas, *Argentina* 126 C3
Las Vegas, *N. Mex., U.S.A.* 109 J11
Las Vegas, *Nev., U.S.A.* 111 J11
Las Vegas McCarran International ✕ (LAS), *U.S.A.* 111 J11
Lasarte, *Spain* 38 B2
Lascano, *Uruguay* 127 C5
Lash-e Joveyn, *Afghan.* 66 D2
Lashburn, *Canada* 103 C7
Lashio, *Burma* 67 H20
Lashkar, *India* 68 F8
Łasin, *Poland* 30 E6
Lasíthi, *Greece* 49 D7
Lasíthi □, *Greece* 49 D7
Lāsjerd, *Iran* 71 C7
Lask, *Poland* 31 G6
Łaskarzew, *Poland* 31 G8
Laško, *Slovenia* 41 B12
Lassay-les-Châteaux, *France* 18 D6
Lassen Pk., *U.S.A.* 108 F3
Lassen Volcanic △, *U.S.A.* 108 F3
Last Mountain L., *Canada* 103 C7
Lastchance Cr. →, *U.S.A.* 110 E5
Lastoursville, *Gabon* 84 E2
Lastovo, *Croatia* 41 F13
Lastovski Kanal, *Croatia* 41 F14
Lat Yao, *Thailand* 64 E2
Latacunga, *Ecuador* 124 D3
Latakia = Al Lādhiqīyah, *Syria* 70 C2
Latchford, *Canada* 104 C4
Latehar, *India* 69 H11
Laterza, *Italy* 43 B9
Latham, *Australia* 93 E2
Lathen, *Germany* 24 C3
Lathi, *India* 68 F4
Lathrop Wells, *U.S.A.* 111 J10
Latiano, *Italy* 43 B10
Latina, *Italy* 42 A5
Latisana, *Italy* 41 C10
Latium = Lazio □, *Italy* 41 F9
Laton, *U.S.A.* 110 J7
Latorytsya →, *Slovak Rep.* 27 C14
Latouche Treville, C., *Australia* 92 C3
Latrobe, *Australia* 95 G4
Latrobe, *U.S.A.* 116 F5
Latrónico, *Italy* 43 B9
Latvia ■, *Europe* 9 H20
Lau, *Nigeria* 83 D7
Lau Group, *Fiji* 91 C9
Lauchhammer, *Germany* 24 D9
Lauda-Königshofen, *Germany* 25 F5
Lauenburg, *Germany* 24 B6
Lauenburgische Seen ⌓, *Germany* 24 B6
Lauf, *Germany* 25 F7
Laughlin, *U.S.A.* 109 J6
Laujar de Andarax, *Spain* 39 H2
Laukaa, *Finland* 9 E21
Launceston, *Australia* 95 G4
Launceston, *U.K.* 15 G3
Laune →, *Ireland* 12 D2
Launglon Bok, *Burma* 64 F1
Laupheim, *Germany* 25 G5
Laura, *Australia* 94 B3
Laureana di Borrello, *Italy* 43 D9
Laurel, *Miss., U.S.A.* 113 K10
Laurel, *Mont., U.S.A.* 108 D9
Laurencekirk, *U.K.* 13 E6
Laurens, *U.S.A.* 115 H4
Laurentian Plateau, *Canada* 105 B6
Lauria, *Italy* 43 B8
Laurie L., *Canada* 103 B8
Laurinburg, *U.S.A.* 115 H6
Laurium, *U.S.A.* 114 B1
Lausanne, *Switz.* 25 J2
Laut, *Indonesia* 62 D3
Laut, Pulau, *Indonesia* 62 E5
Laut Kecil, Kepulauan, *Indonesia* 62 E5
Lauterbach, *Germany* 24 E5
Lauterecken, *Germany* 25 F3
Lautoka, *Fiji* 91 C7
Lauzès, *France* 20 D5
Lava Beds ⌓, *U.S.A.* 108 F3
Lavagh More, *Ireland* 12 B3
Lavagna, *Italy* 40 D6
Laval, *France* 18 D6
Lavalle, *Argentina* 126 B2
Lavant Station, *Canada* 117 A8
Lāvar Meydān, *Iran* 71 D7
Lávara, *Greece* 45 E10
Lavardac, *France* 20 D4
Lavaur, *France* 20 E5
Lavelanet, *France* 20 F5
Lavello, *Italy* 43 A8
Laverton, *Australia* 93 E3
Lavìs, *Italy* 40 B8
Lávkos, *Greece* 46 B5
Lavos, *Portugal* 36 E2
Lavradio, *Portugal* 37 G1
Lavras, *Brazil* 127 A7
Lavre, *Portugal* 37 G2
Lávrion, *Greece* 46 D6
Lávris, *Greece* 49 D6
Lavumisa, *Swaziland* 89 D5
Lavushi Manda △, *Zambia* 87 E3
Lawas, *Malaysia* 62 D5
Lawele, *Indonesia* 63 F6
Lawn Hill △, *Australia* 94 B2
Lawng Pit, *Burma* 67 G20
Lawqah, *Si. Arabia* 70 D4
Lawra, *Ghana* 82 C4
Lawrence, *N.Z.* 91 L2
Lawrence, *Kans., U.S.A.* 112 F7
Lawrence, *Mass., U.S.A.* 117 D13
Lawrenceburg, *Ind., U.S.A.* 114 F3
Lawrenceburg, *Tenn., U.S.A.* 115 H2
Lawrenceville, *Ga., U.S.A.* 115 J4
Lawrenceville, *Pa., U.S.A.* 116 E7
Laws, *U.S.A.* 110 H8
Lawton, *U.S.A.* 113 H5
Lawu, *Indonesia* 63 G14
Lawz, J. al, *Si. Arabia* 80 B4
Laxå, *Sweden* 11 F8
Laxford, L., *U.K.* 13 C3
Laxou, *France* 19 D13
Lay →, *France* 20 B2
Layla, *Si. Arabia* 75 C4
Laylān, *Iraq* 70 C5
Layon →, *France* 18 E6
Layton, *U.S.A.* 108 F7
Laytonville, *U.S.A.* 108 G2
Lazarevac, *Serbia & M.* 44 B4
Lazarevskoye, *Russia* 35 J4
Lazarivo, *Madag.* 89 C8
Lazdijai, *Lithuania* 30 D10
Lazio □, *Italy* 41 F9
Lazo, *Moldova* 29 C13
Lazo, *Russia* 54 C6
Le Beausset, *France* 21 E9
Le Bic, *Canada* 105 C6
Le Blanc, *France* 20 B5
Le Bleymard, *France* 20 D7
Le Bourgneuf-la-Fôret, *France* 18 D6
Le Bugue, *France* 20 D4
Le Canourgue = La Canourgue, *France* 20 D7
Le Cateau Cambrésis, *France* 19 B10
Le Caylar, *France* 20 E7
Le Chambon-Feugerolles, *France* 21 C8
Le Châtelet, *France* 19 F9
Le Chesne, *France* 19 C11
Le Cheylard, *France* 21 D8
Le Conquet, *France* 18 D2
Le Creusot, *France* 19 F11
Le Croisic, *France* 18 E4
Le Donjon, *France* 19 F10
Le Dorat, *France* 20 B5
Le François, *Martinique* 120 c
Le Grand-Lucé, *France* 18 E7
Le Grand-Pressigny, *France* 18 F7
Le Grand-Quevilly, *France* 18 C8
Le Havre, *France* 18 C7
Le Lamentin, *Martinique* 120 c
Le Lavandou, *France* 21 E10
Le Lion-d'Angers, *France* 18 E6
Le Louroux-Béconnais, *France* 18 E6
Le Luc, *France* 21 E10
Le Lude, *France* 18 E7
Le Mans, *France* 18 E7
Le Marin, *Martinique* 120 c
Le Mars, *U.S.A.* 112 D6
Le Mayet-de-Montagne, *France* 19 F10
Le Mêle-sur-Sarthe, *France* 18 D7
Le Monastier-sur-Gazeille, *France* 20 D7
Le Monêtier-les-Bains, *France* 21 D10
Le Mont-Dore, *France* 20 C6
Le Mont-St-Michel, *France* 18 D5
Le Muy, *France* 21 E10
Le Palais, *France* 18 E3
Le Perthus, *France* 20 F6
Le Prêcheur, *Martinique* 120 c
Le Puy-en-Velay, *France* 20 C7
Le Robert, *Martinique* 120 c
Le St-Esprit, *Martinique* 120 c
Le Sueur, *U.S.A.* 112 C8
Le Teil, *France* 21 D8
Le Teilleul, *France* 18 D6
Le Theil, *France* 18 D7
Le Thillot, *France* 19 E13
Le Thuy, *Vietnam* 64 D6
Le Touquet-Paris-Plage, *France* 19 B8
Le Tréport, *France* 18 B8
Le Val-d'Ajol, *France* 19 E13
Le Verdon-sur-Mer, *France* 20 C2
Le Vigan, *France* 20 E7
Lea →, *U.K.* 15 F8
Leach, *Cambodia* 65 F4
Lead, *U.S.A.* 112 C3
Leader, *Canada* 103 C7
Leadville, *U.S.A.* 109 G10
Leaf →, *U.S.A.* 113 K10
Leaf Rapids, *Canada* 103 B9
Leamington, *Canada* 116 D2
Leamington, *U.S.A.* 108 G7
Leamington Spa = Royal Leamington Spa, *U.K.* 15 E6
Le'an, *China* 59 D10
Leandro Norte Alem, *Argentina* 127 B4
Leane, L., *Ireland* 12 D2
Learmonth, *Australia* 92 D1
Leask, *Canada* 103 C7
Leatherhead, *U.K.* 15 F7
Leavenworth, *Kans., U.S.A.* 112 F7
Leavenworth, *Wash., U.S.A.* 108 C3
Łeba, *Poland* 30 D4
Łeba →, *Poland* 30 D4
Lebach, *Germany* 25 F2
Lebak, *Phil.* 61 H6
Lebam, *U.S.A.* 110 D3
Lebane, *Serbia & M.* 44 D5
Lebanon, *Ind., U.S.A.* 114 E2
Lebanon, *Kans., U.S.A.* 112 F5
Lebanon, *Ky., U.S.A.* 114 G3
Lebanon, *Mo., U.S.A.* 113 G8
Lebanon, *N.H., U.S.A.* 117 C12
Lebanon, *Oreg., U.S.A.* 108 D2
Lebanon, *Pa., U.S.A.* 117 F8
Lebanon, *Tenn., U.S.A.* 115 G2
Lebanon ■, *Asia* 74 B5
Lebec, *U.S.A.* 111 L8
Lebedyan, *Russia* 33 F10
Lebedyn, *Ukraine* 33 G8
Lebel-sur-Quévillon, *Canada* 104 C4
Lebomboberge, *S. Africa* 89 C5
Lębork, *Poland* 30 D4
Lebrija, *Spain* 37 J4
Łebsko, Jezioro, *Poland* 30 D4
Lebu, *Chile* 126 D1
Leca da Palmeira, *Portugal* 36 D2
Lecce, *Italy* 43 B11
Lecco, *Italy* 40 C6
Lecco, L. di, *Italy* 40 C6
Lécera, *Spain* 38 D4
Lech, *Austria* 26 D3
Lech →, *Germany* 25 G6
Lechang, *China* 59 E9
Lechtaler Alpen, *Austria* 26 D3
Lecontes Mills, *U.S.A.* 116 E6
Lectoure, *France* 20 E4
Łęczna, *Poland* 31 G9
Łęczyca, *Poland* 31 F6
Ledesma, *Spain* 36 D5
Ledong, *China* 64 C7
Leduc, *Canada* 102 C6
Lee, *U.S.A.* 117 D11
Lee →, *Ireland* 12 E3
Lee Vining, *U.S.A.* 110 H7
Leech L., *U.S.A.* 112 B7
Leechburg, *U.S.A.* 116 F5
Leeds, *U.K.* 14 D6
Leeds, *U.S.A.* 115 J2
Leek, *Neths.* 17 A6
Leek, *U.K.* 14 D5
Leeman, *Australia* 93 E1
Leeper, *U.S.A.* 116 E5
Leer, *Germany* 24 B3
Leesburg, *U.S.A.* 115 L5
Leesville, *U.S.A.* 113 K8
Leeton, *Australia* 95 E4
Leetonia, *U.S.A.* 116 F4
Leeu Gamka, *S. Africa* 88 E3
Leeuwarden, *Neths.* 17 A5
Leeuwin, C., *Australia* 93 F2
Leeuwin Naturaliste △, *Australia* 93 F2
Leeward Is., *Atl. Oc.* 121 C7
Lefka, *Cyprus* 49 D11
Lefkoniko, *Cyprus* 49 D12
Lefroy, *Canada* 116 B5
Lefroy, L., *Australia* 93 F3
Łeg →, *Poland* 31 H8
Leganés, *Spain* 36 E7
Legazpi, *Phil.* 61 E5
Lège-Cap-Ferret, *France* 20 D2
Lege Hida, *Ethiopia* 81 F5
Legendre I., *Australia* 92 D2
Leghorn = Livorno, *Italy* 40 E7
Legionowo, *Poland* 31 F7
Legnago, *Italy* 41 C8
Legnano, *Italy* 40 C5
Legnica, *Poland* 31 G3
Legrad, *Croatia* 41 B13
Leh, *India* 69 B7
Lehigh Acres, *U.S.A.* 115 M5
Lehighton, *U.S.A.* 117 F9
Lehliu, *Romania* 29 F11
Leho, *Sudan* 81 F3
Lehrte, *Germany* 24 C5
Lehututu, *Botswana* 88 C3
Lei Shui →, *China* 59 D9
Leiah, *Pakistan* 68 D4
Leibnitz, *Austria* 26 E8
Leibo, *China* 58 C4
Leicester, *U.K.* 15 E6
Leicester City □, *U.K.* 15 E6
Leicestershire □, *U.K.* 15 E6
Leichhardt →, *Australia* 94 B2
Leichhardt Ra., *Australia* 94 C4
Leiden, *Neths.* 17 B4
Leie →, *Belgium* 17 C3
Leifers = Láives, *Italy* 41 B8
Leimen, *Germany* 25 F4
Leine →, *Germany* 24 C5
Leinefelde, *Germany* 24 D6
Leinster, *Australia* 93 E3
Leinster □, *Ireland* 12 C4
Leinster, Mt., *Ireland* 12 D5
Leipalingis, *Lithuania* 30 D10
Leipzig, *Germany* 24 D8
Leiria, *Portugal* 36 F2
Leiria □, *Portugal* 36 F2
Leirvik, *Norway* 9 G11
Leishan, *China* 58 D7
Leisler, Mt., *Australia* 92 D4
Leith, *U.K.* 13 F5
Leith Hill, *U.K.* 15 F7
Leitha →, *Europe* 27 D10
Leitrim, *Ireland* 12 B3
Leitrim □, *Ireland* 12 B4
Leitza, *Spain* 38 B3
Leiyang, *China* 59 D9
Leizhou, *China* 59 G8
Leizhou Bandao, *China* 58 G7
Leizhou Wan, *China* 59 G8
Lek →, *Neths.* 17 C4
Leka, *Norway* 8 D14
Lekáni, *Greece* 45 E8
Lekbibaj, *Albania* 44 D3
Lekeitio, *Spain* 38 B2
Lekhainá, *Greece* 46 D3
Lekoui, *Burkina Faso* 82 C4
Leksand, *Sweden* 10 D9
Lékva Óros, *Greece* 49 D6
Leland, *Mich., U.S.A.* 114 C3
Leland, *Miss., U.S.A.* 113 J9
Lelång, *Sweden* 10 E6
Leleque, *Argentina* 128 E2
Lelystad, *Neths.* 17 B5
Lem, *Denmark* 11 H2
Lema, *Nigeria* 83 C5
Lema Shilindi, *Ethiopia* 81 G5
Léman, L., *Europe* 19 F13
Lembar, *Indonesia* 63 K19
Lembuak, *Indonesia* 63 K19
Lemera, *Dem. Rep. of the Congo* 86 C2
Lemery, *Phil.* 61 E4
Lemhi Ra., *U.S.A.* 108 D7
Lemmer, *Neths.* 17 B5
Lemmon, *U.S.A.* 112 C3
Lemon Grove, *U.S.A.* 111 N9
Lemoore, *U.S.A.* 110 J7
Lempdes, *France* 20 C7
Lemvig, *Denmark* 11 H2
Lena →, *Russia* 53 B13
Lenart, *Slovenia* 41 B12
Lenartovce, *Slovak Rep.* 27 C13
Lencloître, *France* 18 F7
Léndas, *Greece* 49 E6
Lendava, *Slovenia* 41 B13
Lendeh, *Iran* 71 D6
Lendinara, *Italy* 41 C8
Lengerich, *Germany* 24 C3
Lenggong, *Malaysia* 65 K3
Lenggries, *Germany* 25 H7
Lengshuijiang, *China* 59 D8
Lengshuitan, *China* 59 D8
Lengua de Vaca, Pta., *Chile* 126 C1
Lengwe △, *Malawi* 87 F3
Lengyeltóti, *Hungary* 28 D2
Lenhovda, *Sweden* 11 G9
Lenina, Kanal →, *Russia* 35 J7
Leninabad = Khŭjand, *Tajikistan* 52 E7
Leninakan = Gyumri, *Armenia* 35 K6
Leningrad = Sankt-Peterburg, *Russia* 32 C6
Lenino, *Ukraine* 33 K8
Leninogorsk, *Kazakhstan* 52 D9
Leninsk, *Russia* 35 F7
Leninsk-Kuznetskiy, *Russia* 52 D9
Leninskoye, *Russia* 34 A8
Lenk, *Switz.* 25 J3
Lenkoran = Länkäran, *Azerbaijan* 71 B6
Lenmalu, *Indonesia* 63 E8
Lenne →, *Germany* 24 D3
Lennestadt, *Germany* 24 D4
Lennox, *U.S.A.* 112 D6
Lennoxville, *Canada* 117 A13
Leno, *Italy* 40 C7
Lenoir, *U.S.A.* 115 H5
Lenoir City, *U.S.A.* 115 H3
Lenore L., *Canada* 103 C8
Lenox, *U.S.A.* 117 D11
Lens, *France* 19 B9
Lensahn, *Germany* 24 A6
Lensk, *Russia* 53 C12
Lentekhi, *Georgia* 35 J6
Lenti, *Hungary* 28 D1
Lentini, *Italy* 43 E8
Lenwood, *U.S.A.* 111 L9
Lenya, *Burma* 62 B1
Lenzen, *Germany* 24 B7
Léo, *Burkina Faso* 82 C4
Leoben, *Austria* 26 D8
Leodhas = Lewis, *U.K.* 13 C2
Leola, *U.S.A.* 112 C5
Leominster, *U.K.* 15 E5
Leominster, *U.S.A.* 117 D13
Léon, *France* 20 E2
León, *Mexico* 118 C4
León, *Nic.* 120 D2
León, *Spain* 36 C5
Leon, *U.S.A.* 112 E8
León □, *Spain* 36 C5
Leon →, *U.S.A.* 113 K6
León, Montes de, *Spain* 36 C4
Leonardo da Vinci, Rome ✕ (FCO), *Italy* 41 G9
Leonardtown, *U.S.A.* 114 F7
Leonardville, *Namibia* 88 C2
Leonberg, *Germany* 25 G5
Leonding, *Austria* 26 C7
Leonessa, *Italy* 41 F9
Leonforte, *Italy* 43 E7
Leongatha, *Australia* 95 F4
Leonídhion, *Greece* 46 D4
Leonora, *Australia* 93 E3
Leopoldina, *Brazil* 127 A7
Leopoldsburg, *Belgium* 17 C5
Leoti, *U.S.A.* 112 F4
Leova, *Moldova* 29 D13
Leoville, *Canada* 103 C7
Lepe, *Spain* 37 H3
Lepel = Lyepyel, *Belarus* 32 E5
Lepenoú, *Greece* 46 C3
Leping, *China* 59 C11
Lépo, L. do, *Angola* 88 B2
Lepontine, Alpi, *Italy* 40 B5
Leppävirta, *Finland* 9 E22
Lepsény, *Hungary* 28 D3
Lequeitio = Lekeitio, *Spain* 38 B2
Lercara Friddi, *Italy* 42 E6
Lerdo, *Mexico* 118 B4
Léré, *Chad* 83 D7
Léré, *Mali* 82 B4
Lere, *Bauchi, Nigeria* 83 D6
Lere, *Kaduna, Nigeria* 83 C6
Leribe, *Lesotho* 89 D4
Lérici, *Italy* 40 D6
Lérida = Lleida, *Spain* 38 D5
Lérins, Îs. de, *France* 21 E11
Lerma, *Spain* 36 C7
Léros, *Greece* 47 D8
Lérouville, *France* 19 D12
Lerum, *Sweden* 11 G6
Lerwick, *U.K.* 13 A7
Leş, *Romania* 28 D6
Les Abrets, *France* 21 C9
Les Andelys, *France* 18 C8
Les Borges Blanques, *Spain* 38 D5
Les Cayes, *Haiti* 121 C5
Les Coteaux, *Canada* 117 A10
Les Essarts, *France* 18 F5
Les Herbiers, *France* 18 F5
Les Minquiers, Plateau des, *Chan. Is.* 18 D4
Les Pieux, *France* 18 C5
Les Ponts-de-Cé, *France* 18 E6
Les Riceys, *France* 19 E11
Les Sables-d'Olonne, *France* 20 B2
Les Vans, *France* 21 D8
Lesbos = Lésvos, *Greece* 47 B8
L'Escala, *Spain* 38 C8
Leshan, *China* 58 C4
Leshwe ⌓, *Dem. Rep. of the Congo* 87 E2
Lésina, *Italy* 41 G12

Lésina, L. di, *Italy* 41 G12
Lesjöfors, *Sweden* 10 E8
Lesko, *Poland* 31 J9
Leskov I., *Antarctica* 5 B1
Leskovac, *Serbia & M.* 44 C5
Leskovik, *Albania* 44 F4
Leśna, *Poland* 31 G2
Lesneven, *France* 18 D2
Leśnica, *Poland* 31 H5
Lešnica, *Serbia & M.* 44 B3
Lesnoye, *Russia* 32 C8
Lesopilnoye, *Russia* 54 A7
Lesotho ■, *Africa* 89 D4
Lesozavodsk, *Russia* 53 E14
Lesparre-Médoc, *France* 20 C3
Lessay, *France* 18 C5
Lesse →, *Belgium* 17 D4
Lesse et Lomme ⌂, *Belgium* 17 D5
Lessebo, *Sweden* 11 H9
Lesser Antilles, *W. Indies* 121 D7
Lesser Slave L., *Canada* 102 B5
Lesser Sunda Is., *Indonesia* 63 F6
Lessines, *Belgium* 17 D3
Lester, *U.S.A.* 110 C5
Lester B. Pearson International, Toronto ✕ (YYZ), *Canada* 116 C5
Lestock, *Canada* 103 C8
Lesuer I., *Australia* 92 B4
Lesueur △, *Australia* 93 F2
Lésvos, *Greece* 47 B8
Leszno, *Poland* 31 G3
Letaba, *S. Africa* 89 C5
Letälven, *Sweden* 10 E8
Létavértes, *Hungary* 28 C6
Letchworth, *U.K.* 15 F7
Letea, Ostrov, *Romania* 29 E14
Lethbridge, *Canada* 102 D6
Lethem, *Guyana* 124 C7
Leti, Kepulauan, *Indonesia* 63 F7
Leti Is. = Leti, Kepulauan, *Indonesia* 63 F7
Letiahau →, *Botswana* 88 C3
Leticia, *Colombia* 124 D5
Leting, *China* 57 E10
Letjiesbos, *S. Africa* 88 E3
Letlhakane, *Botswana* 88 C4
Letlhakeng, *Botswana* 88 C3
Letong, *Indonesia* 62 D3
Letpadan, *Burma* 67 L19
Letpan, *Burma* 67 K19
Letsôk-aw Kyun, *Burma* 65 G2
Letterkenny, *Ireland* 12 B4
Leu, *Romania* 29 F9
Leucadia, *U.S.A.* 111 M9
Leucate, *France* 20 F7
Leucate, Étang de, *France* 20 F7
Leuchars, *U.K.* 13 E6
Leuk, *Switz.* 25 J3
Leuşeni, *Moldova* 29 D13
Leuser, G., *Indonesia* 62 D1
Leutkirch, *Germany* 25 H6
Leuven, *Belgium* 17 D4
Leuze-en-Hainaut, *Belgium* 17 D3
Lev Tolstoy, *Russia* 32 F10
Levádhia, *Greece* 46 C4
Levan, *Albania* 44 F3
Levanger, *Norway* 8 E14
Levant, Î. du, *France* 21 E10
Lévanto, *Italy* 40 D6
Lévanzo, *Italy* 42 E5
Levelland, *U.S.A.* 113 J3
Leven, *U.K.* 13 E6
Leven, L., *U.K.* 13 E5
Leven, Toraka, *Madag.* 89 A8
Leveque C., *Australia* 92 C3
Leverano, *Italy* 43 B10
Leverkusen, *Germany* 24 D3
Levice, *Slovak Rep.* 27 C11
Lévico Terme, *Italy* 41 C8
Levie, *France* 21 G13
Levier, *France* 19 F13
Levin, *N.Z.* 91 J5
Lévis, *Canada* 105 C5
Levis, L., *Canada* 102 A5
Levítha, *Greece* 47 D8
Levittown, *N.Y., U.S.A.* 117 F11
Levittown, *Pa., U.S.A.* 117 F10
Levka, *Bulgaria* 45 E10
Levkás, *Greece* 46 C2
Levkás □, *Greece* 46 C2
Levkímmi, *Greece* 49 B4
Levkímmi, Ákra, *Greece* 49 B4
Levkôsia = Nicosia, *Cyprus* 49 D12
Levoča, *Slovak Rep.* 27 B13
Levroux, *France* 19 F8
Levski, *Bulgaria* 45 C9
Levskigrad = Karlovo, *Bulgaria* 45 D8
Lewes, *U.K.* 15 G8
Lewes, *U.S.A.* 114 F8
Lewin Brzeski, *Poland* 31 H4
Lewis, *U.K.* 13 C2
Lewis →, *U.S.A.* 110 E4
Lewis, Butt of, *U.K.* 13 C2
Lewis Ra., *Australia* 92 D4
Lewis Range, *U.S.A.* 108 C7
Lewis Run, *U.S.A.* 116 E6
Lewisburg, *Pa., U.S.A.* 116 F8
Lewisburg, *Tenn., U.S.A.* 115 H2
Lewisburg, *W. Va., U.S.A.* 114 G5
Lewisporte, *Canada* 105 C8
Lewiston, *Idaho, U.S.A.* 108 C5
Lewiston, *Maine, U.S.A.* 115 C11
Lewiston, *N.Y., U.S.A.* 116 C5
Lewistown, *Mont., U.S.A.* 108 C9
Lewistown, *Pa., U.S.A.* 116 F7
Lexington, *Ill., U.S.A.* 112 E10
Lexington, *Ky., U.S.A.* 114 F3
Lexington, *Mich., U.S.A.* 116 C2
Lexington, *Mo., U.S.A.* 112 F8
Lexington, *N.C., U.S.A.* 115 H5
Lexington, *N.Y., U.S.A.* 117 D10
Lexington, *Nebr., U.S.A.* 112 E5
Lexington, *Ohio, U.S.A.* 116 F2
Lexington, *Tenn., U.S.A.* 115 H1
Lexington, *Va., U.S.A.* 114 G6
Lexington Park, *U.S.A.* 114 F7
Leyburn, *U.K.* 14 C6
Leye, *China* 58 E6
Leyland, *U.K.* 14 D5
Leyre →, *France* 20 D2
Leyte □, *Phil.* 61 F6
Leyte Gulf, *Phil.* 61 F6
Leżajsk, *Poland* 31 H9
Lezay, *France* 20 B3
Lezhë, *Albania* 44 E3
Lezhi, *China* 58 B5
Lézignan-Corbières, *France* 20 E6
Lezoux, *France* 20 C7
Lgov, *Russia* 33 G8
Lhasa, *China* 60 D4
Lhazê, *China* 60 D3
Lhokkruet, *Indonesia* 62 D1
Lhokseumawe, *Indonesia* 62 C1
L'Hospitalet de Llobregat, *Spain* 38 D7
Li, *Thailand* 64 D2
Li Shui →, *China* 59 C9
Li Xian, *Gansu, China* 56 G3
Li Xian, *Hebei, China* 56 E8
Li Xian, *Hunan, China* 59 C8
Liádhoi, *Greece* 47 E8
Liancheng, *China* 59 E11
Liancourt Rocks = Tok-do, *Asia* 55 F5
Lianga, *Phil.* 61 G7
Liangcheng, *Nei Monggol Zizhiqu, China* 56 D7
Liangcheng, *Shandong, China* 57 G10
Liangdang, *China* 56 H4
Lianghe, *China* 58 E2
Lianghekou, *China* 58 C7
Liangping, *China* 58 B6
Liangpran, *Indonesia* 62 D4
Lianhua, *China* 59 D9
Lianjiang, *Fujian, China* 59 D12
Lianjiang, *Guangdong, China* 59 G8
Lianping, *China* 59 E10
Lianshan, *China* 59 E9
Lianshanguan, *China* 57 D12
Lianshui, *China* 57 H10
Lianyuan, *China* 59 D8
Lianyungang, *China* 57 G10
Lianzhou, *China* 59 E9
Liao He →, *China* 57 D11
Liaocheng, *China* 56 F8
Liaodong Bandao, *China* 57 E12
Liaodong Wan, *China* 57 D11
Liaoning □, *China* 57 D12
Liaoyang, *China* 57 D12
Liaoyuan, *China* 57 C13
Liaozhong, *China* 57 D12
Liapádhes, *Greece* 46 B1
Liard →, *Canada* 102 A4
Liard River, *Canada* 102 B3
Liari, *Pakistan* 68 G2
Libau = Liepāja, *Latvia* 9 H19
Libby, *U.S.A.* 108 B6
Libenge, *Dem. Rep. of the Congo* 84 D3
Liberal, *U.S.A.* 113 G4
Liberec, *Czech Rep.* 26 A8
Liberecký □, *Czech Rep.* 26 A8
Liberia, *Costa Rica* 120 D2
Liberia ■, *W. Afr.* 82 D3
Liberty, *Mo., U.S.A.* 112 F7
Liberty, *N.Y., U.S.A.* 117 E10
Liberty, *Pa., U.S.A.* 116 E7
Liberty, *Tex., U.S.A.* 113 K7
Libiąż, *Poland* 31 H6
Lībīya, Sahrâ', *Africa* 79 C10
Libo, *China* 58 E6
Libobo, Tanjung, *Indonesia* 63 E7
Libode, *S. Africa* 89 E4
Libohovë, *Albania* 44 F4
Libourne, *France* 20 D3
Libramont, *Belgium* 17 E5
Librazhd, *Albania* 44 E4
Libreville, *Gabon* 84 D1
Libya ■, *N. Afr.* 79 C9
Libyan Desert = Lībīya, Sahrâ', *Africa* 79 C10
Libyan Plateau = Ed-Déffa, *Egypt* 80 A2
Licantén, *Chile* 126 D1
Licata, *Italy* 42 E6
Lice, *Turkey* 73 C9
Licheng, *China* 56 F7
Lichfield, *U.K.* 15 E6
Lichinga, *Mozam.* 87 E4
Lichtenburg, *S. Africa* 88 D4
Lichtenfels, *Germany* 25 E7
Lichuan, *Hubei, China* 58 B7
Lichuan, *Jiangxi, China* 59 D11
Licking →, *U.S.A.* 114 F3
Licosa, Punta, *Italy* 43 B7
Licungo →, *Mozam.* 87 F4
Lida, *Belarus* 9 K21
Liden, *Sweden* 10 B10
Lidhoríkion, *Greece* 46 C4
Lidhult, *Sweden* 11 H7
Lidköping, *Sweden* 11 F7
Lido, *Italy* 41 C9
Lido, *Niger* 83 C5
Lido di Roma = Óstia, Lido di, *Italy* 41 G9
Lidzbark, *Poland* 31 E6
Lidzbark Warmiński, *Poland* 30 D7
Liebenwalde, *Germany* 24 C9
Lieberose, *Germany* 24 D10
Liebig, Mt., *Australia* 92 D5
Liebling, *Romania* 28 E6
Liechtenstein ■, *Europe* 25 H5
Liège, *Belgium* 17 D5
Liège □, *Belgium* 17 D5
Liegnitz = Legnica, *Poland* 31 G3
Lienart, *Dem. Rep. of the Congo* 86 B2
Lienyünchiangshih = Lianyungang, *China* 57 G10
Lienz, *Austria* 26 E5
Liepāja, *Latvia* 9 H19
Liepāja □, *Latvia* 30 B8
Liepājas ezers, *Latvia* 30 B8
Lier, *Belgium* 17 C4
Liernais, *France* 19 E11
Lieşti, *Romania* 29 E12
Liévin, *France* 19 B9
Lièvre →, *Canada* 104 C4
Liezen, *Austria* 26 D7
Liffey →, *Ireland* 12 C5
Lifford, *Ireland* 12 B4
Liffré, *France* 18 D5
Lifudzin, *Russia* 54 B7
Ligao, *Phil.* 61 E5
Lightning Ridge, *Australia* 95 D4
Lignano Sabbiadoro, *Italy* 41 C10
Ligny-en-Barrois, *France* 19 D12
Ligonha →, *Mozam.* 87 F4
Ligonier, *U.S.A.* 116 F5
Ligoúrion, *Greece* 46 D5
Ligueil, *France* 18 E7
Liguria □, *Italy* 40 D5
Ligurian Sea, *Medit. S.* 6 G7
Lihou Reefs and Cays, *Australia* 94 B5
Lihue, *U.S.A.* 106 H15
Lihué Calel △, *Argentina* 126 D2
Lijiang, *China* 58 D3
Likasi, *Dem. Rep. of the Congo* 87 E2
Likenäs, *Sweden* 10 D8
Likhoslavl, *Russia* 32 D8
Likhovskoy, *Russia* 33 H11
Likoma I., *Malawi* 87 E3
Likumburu, *Tanzania* 87 D4
L'Île-Bouchard, *France* 18 E7
L'Île-Rousse, *France* 21 F12
Liling, *China* 59 D9
Lilla Edet, *Sweden* 11 F6
Lille, *France* 19 B10
Lille Bælt, *Denmark* 11 J3
Lillebonne, *France* 18 C7
Lillehammer, *Norway* 9 F14
Lillesand, *Norway* 9 G13
Lillhärdal, *Sweden* 10 C8
Lillian Pt., *Australia* 93 E4
Lillo, *Spain* 36 F7
Lillooet, *Canada* 102 C4
Lillooet →, *Canada* 102 D4
Lilongwe, *Malawi* 87 E3
Liloy, *Phil.* 63 C6
Lim →, *Bos.-H.* 44 C3
Lim Chu Kang, *Singapore* 65 d
Lima, *Indonesia* 63 E7
Lima, *Peru* 124 F3
Lima, *Mont., U.S.A.* 108 D7
Lima, *Ohio, U.S.A.* 114 E3
Lima →, *Portugal* 36 D2
Liman, *Indonesia* 63 G14
Liman, *Russia* 35 H8
Limanowa, *Poland* 31 J7
Limassol, *Cyprus* 49 E12
Limavady, *U.K.* 12 A5
Limay →, *Argentina* 128 D3
Limay Mahuida, *Argentina* 126 D2
Limbach-Oberfrohna, *Germany* 24 E8
Limbang, *Brunei* 62 D5
Limbara, Mte., *Italy* 42 B2
Limbaži, *Latvia* 9 H21
Limbdi, *India* 68 H4
Limbe, *Cameroon* 83 E6
Limburg, *Germany* 25 E4
Limburg □, *Belgium* 17 C5
Limburg □, *Neths.* 17 C5
Limedsforsen, *Sweden* 10 D7
Limeira, *Brazil* 127 A6
Limenária, *Greece* 45 F8
Limerick, *Ireland* 12 D3
Limerick, *U.S.A.* 117 C14
Limerick □, *Ireland* 12 D3
Limestone, *U.S.A.* 116 D6
Limestone →, *Canada* 103 B10
Limfjorden, *Denmark* 11 H3
Limia = Lima →, *Portugal* 36 D2
Limín Khersonísou, *Greece* 47 F7
Limingen, *Norway* 8 D15
Limmared, *Sweden* 11 G7
Limmen Bight, *Australia* 94 A2
Limmen Bight →, *Australia* 94 B2
Límni, *Greece* 46 C5
Límnos, *Greece* 47 B7
Limoges, *Canada* 117 A9
Limoges, *France* 20 C5
Limón, *Costa Rica* 120 E3
Limon, *U.S.A.* 112 F3
Limone Piemonte, *Italy* 40 D4
Limousin, *France* 20 C5
Limousin, Plateaux du, *France* 20 C5
Limoux, *France* 20 E6
Limpopo □, *S. Africa* 89 C4
Limpopo →, *Africa* 89 D5
Limuru, *Kenya* 86 C4
Lin Xian, *China* 56 F6
Lin'an, *China* 59 B12
Linapacan I., *Phil.* 61 F3
Linapacan Str., *Phil.* 61 F3
Linares, *Chile* 126 D1
Linares, *Mexico* 119 C5
Linares, *Spain* 37 G7
Linaro, Capo, *Italy* 41 F8
Línas Mte., *Italy* 42 C1
Linate, Milan ✕ (LIN), *Italy* 40 C6
Lincang, *China* 58 F3
Lincheng, *China* 56 F8
Linchuan, *China* 59 D11
Lincoln = Beamsville, *Canada* 116 C5
Lincoln, *Argentina* 126 C3
Lincoln, *N.Z.* 91 K4
Lincoln, *U.K.* 14 D7
Lincoln, *Calif., U.S.A.* 110 G5
Lincoln, *Ill., U.S.A.* 112 E10
Lincoln, *Kans., U.S.A.* 112 F5
Lincoln, *Maine, U.S.A.* 115 C11
Lincoln, *N.H., U.S.A.* 117 B13
Lincoln, *N. Mex., U.S.A.* 109 K11
Lincoln, *Nebr., U.S.A.* 112 E6
Lincoln City, *U.S.A.* 108 D1
Lincoln Hav = Lincoln Sea, *Arctic* 4 A5
Lincoln Sea, *Arctic* 4 A5
Lincolnshire □, *U.K.* 14 D7
Lincolnshire Wolds, *U.K.* 14 D7
Lincolnton, *U.S.A.* 115 H5
L'Incudine, *France* 21 G13
Lind, *U.S.A.* 108 C4
Linda, *U.S.A.* 110 F5
Lindau, *Germany* 25 H5
Lindeman I., *Australia* 94 J7
Linden, *Guyana* 124 B7
Linden, *Ala., U.S.A.* 115 J2
Linden, *Calif., U.S.A.* 110 G5
Linden, *Tex., U.S.A.* 113 J7
Lindenhurst, *U.S.A.* 117 F11
Lindesberg, *Sweden* 10 E9
Lindesnes, *Norway* 9 H12
Líndhos, *Greece* 49 C10
Líndhos, Ákra, *Greece* 49 C10
Lindi, *Tanzania* 87 D4
Lindi □, *Tanzania* 87 D4
Lindi →, *Dem. Rep. of the Congo* 86 B2
Lindö, *Sweden* 11 F10
Lindome, *Sweden* 11 G6
Lindoso, *Portugal* 36 D2
Lindow, *Germany* 24 C8
Lindsay, *Canada* 116 B6
Lindsay, *Calif., U.S.A.* 110 J7
Lindsay, *Okla., U.S.A.* 113 H6
Lindsborg, *U.S.A.* 112 F6
Lindsdal, *Sweden* 11 H10
Linesville, *U.S.A.* 116 E4
Linfen, *China* 56 F6
Ling Xian, *Hunan, China* 59 D9
Ling Xian, *Shandong, China* 56 F9
Lingao, *China* 64 C7
Lingayen, *Phil.* 63 A6
Lingayen G., *Phil.* 61 C4
Lingbi, *China* 57 H9
Lingbo, *Sweden* 10 C10
Lingchuan, *Guangxi Zhuangzu, China* 59 E8
Lingchuan, *Shanxi, China* 56 G7
Lingen, *Germany* 24 C3
Lingga, *Indonesia* 62 E2
Lingga, Kepulauan, *Indonesia* 62 E2
Lingga Arch. = Lingga, Kepulauan, *Indonesia* 62 E2
Linghem, *Sweden* 11 F9
Lingle, *U.S.A.* 112 D2
Lingqiu, *China* 56 E8
Lingshan, *China* 58 F7
Lingshi, *China* 56 F6
Lingshou, *China* 56 E8
Lingshui, *China* 64 C8
Lingtai, *China* 56 G4
Linguère, *Senegal* 82 B1
Lingui, *China* 59 E8
Lingwu, *China* 56 E4
Lingyuan, *China* 57 D10
Lingyun, *China* 58 E6
Linhai, *China* 59 C13
Linhares, *Brazil* 125 G10
Linhe, *China* 56 D4
Linjiang, *China* 57 D14
Linköping, *Sweden* 11 F9
Linkou, *China* 57 B16
Linli, *China* 59 C8
Linnhe, L., *U.K.* 13 E3
Linqi, *China* 56 G7
Linqing, *China* 56 F8
Linqu, *China* 57 F10
Linru, *China* 56 G7
Lins, *Brazil* 127 A6
Linshui, *China* 58 B6
Linstead, *Jamaica* 120 a
Linta →, *Madag.* 89 D7
Linth →, *Switz.* 25 H5
Linthal, *Switz.* 25 J5
Linton, *Ind., U.S.A.* 114 F2
Linton, *N. Dak., U.S.A.* 112 B4
Lintong, *China* 56 G5
Linwood, *Canada* 116 C4
Linwu, *China* 59 E9
Linxi, *China* 57 C10
Linxia, *China* 60 C5
Linxiang, *China* 59 C9
Linyanti →, *Africa* 88 B4
Linyi, *China* 57 G10
Linz, *Austria* 26 C7
Linz, *Germany* 24 E3
Linzhenzhen, *China* 56 F5
Linzi, *China* 57 F10
Lion, G. du, *France* 20 E7
Lionárisso, *Cyprus* 49 D13
Lioni, *Italy* 43 B8
Lions, G. of = Lion, G. du, *France* 20 E7
Lion's Den, *Zimbabwe* 87 F3
Lion's Head, *Canada* 116 B3
Liozno = Lyozna, *Belarus* 32 E6
Lipa, *Phil.* 61 E4
Lipali, *Mozam.* 87 F4
Lipany, *Slovak Rep.* 27 B13
Lípari, *Italy* 43 D7
Lípari, I., *Italy* 43 D7
Lípari, Is. = Eólie, Ís., *Italy* 43 D7
Lipcani, *Moldova* 29 B11
Lipetsk, *Russia* 33 F10
Lipiany, *Poland* 31 E1
Liping, *China* 58 D7
Lipkany = Lipcani, *Moldova* 29 B11
Lipljan, *Serbia & M.* 44 D5
Lipník nad Bečvou, *Czech Rep.* 27 B10
Lipno, *Poland* 31 F6
Lipova, *Romania* 28 D6
Lipovcy Manzovka, *Russia* 54 B6
Lipovets, *Ukraine* 33 H5
Lippe →, *Germany* 24 D2
Lippstadt, *Germany* 24 D4
Lipscomb, *U.S.A.* 113 G4
Lipsk, *Poland* 30 E10
Lipsko, *Poland* 31 G8
Lipsói, *Greece* 47 D8
Liptovský Hrádok, *Slovak Rep.* 27 B12
Liptovský Milkuláš, *Slovak Rep.* 27 B12
Liptrap, C., *Australia* 95 F4
Lipu, *China* 59 E8
Liquillo, Sierra de, *Puerto Rico* 121 d
Lira, *Uganda* 86 B3
Liri →, *Italy* 42 A6
Liria = Llíria, *Spain* 39 F4
Lisala, *Dem. Rep. of the Congo* 84 D4
Lisboa, *Portugal* 37 G1
Lisboa □, *Portugal* 37 F1
Lisbon = Lisboa, *Portugal* 37 G1
Lisbon, *N. Dak., U.S.A.* 112 B6
Lisbon, *N.H., U.S.A.* 117 B13
Lisbon, *Ohio, U.S.A.* 116 F4
Lisbon ✕ (LIS), *Portugal* 37 G1
Lisbon Falls, *U.S.A.* 115 D10
Lisburn, *U.K.* 12 B5
Lisburne, C., *U.S.A.* 4 C17
Liscannor B., *Ireland* 12 D2
Liscia →, *Italy* 42 A2
Lishe Jiang →, *China* 58 E3
Lishi, *China* 56 F6
Lishu, *China* 57 C13
Lishui, *Jiangsu, China* 59 B12
Lishui, *Zhejiang, China* 59 C12
Lisianski I., *Pac. Oc.* 96 E10
Lisichansk = Lysychansk, *Ukraine* 33 H10
Lisieux, *France* 18 C7
Liski, *Russia* 33 G10
L'Isle-Jourdain, *Gers, France* 20 E5
L'Isle-Jourdain, *Vienne, France* 20 B4
L'Isle-sur-la-Sorgue, *France* 21 E9
Lisle-sur-Tarn, *France* 20 E5
Lismore, *Australia* 95 D5
Lismore, *Ireland* 12 D4
Lista, *Norway* 9 G12
Lister, Mt., *Antarctica* 5 D11
Liston, *Australia* 95 D5
Listowel, *Canada* 116 C4
Listowel, *Ireland* 12 D2
Lit, *Sweden* 10 A8
Lit-et-Mixe, *France* 20 D2
Litang, *Guangxi Zhuangzu, China* 58 F7
Litang, *Sichuan, China* 58 B3
Litang Qu →, *China* 58 C3
Litani →, *Lebanon* 74 B4
Litchfield, *Calif., U.S.A.* 110 E6
Litchfield, *Conn., U.S.A.* 117 E11
Litchfield, *Ill., U.S.A.* 112 F10
Litchfield, *Minn., U.S.A.* 112 C7
Litchfield △, *Australia* 92 B5
Liteni, *Romania* 29 C11
Lithgow, *Australia* 95 E5
Líthinon, Ákra, *Greece* 49 E6
Lithuania ■, *Europe* 9 J20
Litija, *Slovenia* 41 B11
Lititz, *U.S.A.* 117 F8
Litókhoron, *Greece* 44 F6
Litoměřice, *Czech Rep.* 26 A7
Litomyšl, *Czech Rep.* 27 B9
Litschau, *Austria* 26 C8
Little Abaco I., *Bahamas* 120 A4
Little Barrier I., *N.Z.* 91 G5
Little Belt Mts., *U.S.A.* 108 C8
Little Bighorn Battlefield ⌂, *U.S.A.* 108 D10
Little Blue →, *U.S.A.* 112 F6
Little Buffalo →, *Canada* 102 A6
Little Cayman, *Cayman Is.* 120 C3
Little Churchill →, *Canada* 103 B9
Little Colorado →, *U.S.A.* 109 H8
Little Current, *Canada* 104 C3
Little Current →, *Canada* 104 B3
Little Falls, *Minn., U.S.A.* 112 C7
Little Falls, *N.Y., U.S.A.* 117 C10
Little Fork →, *U.S.A.* 112 A8
Little Grand Rapids, *Canada* 103 C9
Little Humboldt →, *U.S.A.* 108 F5
Little Inagua I., *Bahamas* 121 B5
Little Karoo, *S. Africa* 88 E3
Little Lake, *U.S.A.* 111 K9
Little Laut Is. = Laut Kecil, Kepulauan, *Indonesia* 62 E5
Little Mecatina = Petit-Mécatina →, *Canada* 105 B8
Little Minch, *U.K.* 13 D2
Little Missouri →, *U.S.A.* 112 B3
Little Ouse →, *U.K.* 15 E9
Little Rann, *India* 68 H4
Little Red →, *U.S.A.* 113 H9
Little River, *N.Z.* 91 K4
Little Rock, *U.S.A.* 113 H8
Little Ruaha →, *Tanzania* 86 D4
Little Sable Pt., *U.S.A.* 114 D2
Little Scarcies →, *S. Leone* 82 D2
Little Sioux →, *U.S.A.* 112 E6
Little Smoky →, *Canada* 102 C5
Little Snake →, *U.S.A.* 108 F9
Little Tobago, *Trin. & Tob.* 125 J16
Little Valley, *U.S.A.* 116 D6
Little Wabash →, *U.S.A.* 114 G1
Little White →, *U.S.A.* 112 D4
Little Zab = Zāb aş Şaghīr →, *Iraq* 70 C4
Littlefield, *U.S.A.* 113 J3
Littlehampton, *U.K.* 15 G7
Littleton, *U.S.A.* 117 B13
Litvinov, *Czech Rep.* 26 A6
Liu He →, *China* 57 D11
Liu Jiang →, *China* 58 F7
Liuba, *China* 56 H4

Liucheng, *China* 58 E7
Liugou, *China* 57 D10
Liuhe, *China* 57 C13
Liuheng Dao, *China* 59 C14
Liujiang, *China* 58 E7
Liukang Tenggaja = Sabalana, Kepulauan, *Indonesia* 63 F5
Liuli, *Tanzania* 87 E3
Liuwa Plain, *Zambia* 85 G4
Liuyang, *China* 59 C9
Liuzhou, *China* 58 E7
Liuzhuang, *China* 57 H11
Livada, *Romania* 28 C8
Livadherón, *Greece* 44 F5
Livadhia, *Cyprus* 49 E12
Livádhion, *Greece* 46 A4
Livarot, *France* 18 D7
Live Oak, *Calif., U.S.A.* 110 F5
Live Oak, *Fla., U.S.A.* 115 K4
Liveras, *Cyprus* 49 D11
Livermore, *U.S.A.* 110 H5
Livermore, Mt., *U.S.A.* 113 K2
Livermore Falls, *U.S.A.* 115 C11
Liverpool, *Canada* 105 D7
Liverpool, *U.K.* 14 D4
Liverpool, *U.S.A.* 117 C8
Liverpool Bay, *U.K.* 14 D4
Liverpool Ra., *Australia* 95 E5
Livigno, *Italy* 40 B7
Livingston, *Guatemala* 120 C2
Livingston, *U.K.* 13 F5
Livingston, *Ala., U.S.A.* 115 J1
Livingston, *Calif., U.S.A.* 110 H6
Livingston, *Mont., U.S.A.* 108 D8
Livingston, *S.C., U.S.A.* 115 J5
Livingston, *Tenn., U.S.A.* 115 G3
Livingston, *Tex., U.S.A.* 113 K7
Livingston, L., *U.S.A.* 113 K7
Livingston Manor, *U.S.A.* 117 E10
Livingstone, *Zambia* 87 F2
Livingstone Mts., *Tanzania* 87 D3
Livingstonia, *Malawi* 87 E3
Livno, *Bos.-H.* 28 G2
Livny, *Russia* 33 F9
Livonia, *Mich., U.S.A.* 114 D4
Livonia, *N.Y., U.S.A.* 116 D7
Livorno, *Italy* 40 E7
Livradois-Forez ⌂, *France* 20 E7
Livramento, *Brazil* 127 C4
Livron-sur-Drôme, *France* 21 D8
Liwale, *Tanzania* 87 D4
Liwiec →, *Poland* 31 F8
Liwonde △, *Malawi* 87 E4
Lixi, *China* 58 D3
Lixian, *China* 58 B4
Lixoúrion, *Greece* 46 C2
Liyang, *China* 59 B12
Lizard I., *Australia* 94 A4
Lizard Pt., *U.K.* 15 H2
Lizzano, *Italy* 43 B10
Ljig, *Serbia & M.* 44 B4
Ljubija, *Bos.-H.* 41 D13
Ljubinje, *Bos.-H.* 44 D2
Ljubljana, *Slovenia* 41 B11
Ljubljana ✈ (LJU), *Slovenia* 41 B11
Ljubno, *Slovenia* 41 B11
Ljubovija, *Serbia & M.* 44 B3
Ljugarn, *Sweden* 11 G12
Ljung, *Sweden* 11 G7
Ljungan →, *Sweden* 10 B11
Ljungaverk, *Sweden* 10 B10
Ljungby, *Sweden* 9 H15
Ljungbyholm, *Sweden* 11 H10
Ljungdalen, *Sweden* 10 B6
Ljungsbro, *Sweden* 11 F9
Ljungskile, *Sweden* 11 F5
Ljusdal, *Sweden* 10 C10
Ljusfallshammar, *Sweden* 11 F9
Ljusnan →, *Sweden* 10 C11
Ljusne, *Sweden* 10 C11
Ljutomer, *Slovenia* 41 B13
Llagostera, *Spain* 38 D7
Llancanelo, Salina, *Argentina* 126 D2
Llandeilo, *U.K.* 15 F4
Llandovery, *U.K.* 15 F4
Llandrindod Wells, *U.K.* 15 E4
Llandudno, *U.K.* 14 D4
Llanelli, *U.K.* 15 F3
Llanes, *Spain* 36 B6
Llangollen, *U.K.* 14 E4
Llanidloes, *U.K.* 15 E4
Llano, *U.S.A.* 113 K5
Llano →, *U.S.A.* 113 K5
Llano Estacado, *U.S.A.* 113 J3
Llanos, *S. Amer.* 124 C4
Llanos de Challe △, *Chile* 126 B1
Llanquihue, L., *Chile* 128 E1
Llanwrtyd Wells, *U.K.* 15 E4
Llebeig, C. des, *Spain* 48 B9
Lleida, *Spain* 38 D5
Lleida □, *Spain* 38 C6
Llentrisca, C., *Spain* 48 C7
Llera, *Mexico* 119 C5
Llerena, *Spain* 37 G5
Lleyn Peninsula, *U.K.* 14 E3
Llico, *Chile* 126 C1
Lliria, *Spain* 39 F4
Llobregat →, *Spain* 38 D7
Llodio, *Spain* 38 B2
Lloret de Mar, *Spain* 38 D7
Lloyd B., *Australia* 94 A3
Lloyd L., *Canada* 103 B7
Lloydminster, *Canada* 103 C7
Llucena del Cid, *Spain* 38 E4
Llucmajor, *Spain* 48 B9
Llullaillaco △, *Chile* 126 A2
Llullaillaco, Volcán, *S. Amer.* 126 A2
Lo →, *Vietnam* 64 B5
Loa, *U.S.A.* 109 G8
Loa →, *Chile* 126 A1
Loaita I., *S. China Sea* 62 B4
Loange →, *Dem. Rep. of the Congo* 84 E4
Loano, *Italy* 40 D5
Lobatse, *Botswana* 88 D4
Löbau, *Germany* 24 D10
Lobenstein, *Germany* 24 E7
Lobería, *Argentina* 126 D4
Löberöd, *Sweden* 11 J7
Łobez, *Poland* 30 E2
Lobito, *Angola* 85 G2
Lobo →, *Ivory C.* 82 D3
Lobos, *Argentina* 126 D4
Lobos, I., *Mexico* 118 B2
Lobos, I. de, *Canary Is.* 48 F6
Łobżenica, *Poland* 31 E4
Loc Binh, *Vietnam* 64 B6
Loc Ninh, *Vietnam* 65 G6
Locarno, *Switz.* 25 J4
Loch Baghasdail = Lochboisdale, *U.K.* 13 D1
Loch Garman = Wexford, *Ireland* 12 D5
Loch Lomond and the Trossachs △, *U.K.* 13 E4
Loch Nam Madadh = Lochmaddy, *U.K.* 13 D1
Lochaber, *U.K.* 13 E3
Locharbriggs, *U.K.* 13 F5
Lochboisdale, *U.K.* 13 D1
Loche, L. La, *Canada* 103 B7
Lochem, *Neths.* 17 B6
Loches, *France* 18 E7
Lochgilphead, *U.K.* 13 E3
Lochinvar △, *Zambia* 87 F2
Lochinver, *U.K.* 13 C3
Lochmaddy, *U.K.* 13 D1
Lochnagar, *Australia* 94 C4
Lochnagar, *U.K.* 13 E5
Łochów, *Poland* 31 F8
Lochy, L., *U.K.* 13 E4
Lock, *Australia* 95 E2
Lock Haven, *U.S.A.* 116 E7
Lockeford, *U.S.A.* 110 G5
Lockeport, *Canada* 105 D6
Lockerbie, *U.K.* 13 F5
Lockhart, *U.S.A.* 113 L6
Lockhart, L., *Australia* 93 F2
Lockhart River, *Australia* 94 A3
Lockney, *U.S.A.* 113 H4
Lockport, *U.S.A.* 116 C6
Locminé, *France* 18 E4
Locri, *Italy* 43 D9
Locronan, *France* 18 D2
Lod, *Israel* 74 D3
Lodeinoye Pole, *Russia* 32 B7
Lodève, *France* 20 E7
Lodge Bay, *Canada* 105 B8
Lodge Grass, *U.S.A.* 108 D10
Lodgepole Cr. →, *U.S.A.* 112 E2
Lodhran, *Pakistan* 68 E4
Lodi, *Italy* 40 C6
Lodi, *Calif., U.S.A.* 110 G5
Lodi, *Ohio, U.S.A.* 116 E3
Lodja, *Dem. Rep. of the Congo* 86 C1
Lodosa, *Spain* 38 C2
Lödöse, *Sweden* 11 F6
Lodwar, *Kenya* 86 B4
Łódź, *Poland* 31 G6
Łódzkie □, *Poland* 31 G6
Loei, *Thailand* 64 D3
Loengo, *Dem. Rep. of the Congo* 86 C2
Loeriesfontein, *S. Africa* 88 E2
Lofa →, *Liberia* 83 D2
Lofa Mano △, *Liberia* 82 D2
Lofer, *Austria* 26 D5
Lofoten, *Norway* 8 B15
Lofsdalen, *Sweden* 10 B7
Lofsen →, *Sweden* 10 B7
Loftahammar, *Sweden* 11 G10
Loga, *Niger* 83 C5
Logan, *Iowa, U.S.A.* 112 E7
Logan, *Ohio, U.S.A.* 114 F4
Logan, *Utah, U.S.A.* 108 F8
Logan, *W. Va., U.S.A.* 114 G5
Logan, Mt., *Canada* 100 B5
Logandale, *U.S.A.* 111 J12
Logansport, *Ind., U.S.A.* 114 E2
Logansport, *La., U.S.A.* 113 K8
Logirim, *Sudan* 81 G3
Logo, *Sudan* 81 F3
Logone →, *Chad* 79 F9
Logroño, *Spain* 38 C2
Logrosán, *Spain* 37 F5
Løgstør, *Denmark* 11 H3
Løgumkloster, *Denmark* 11 J2
Lohals, *Denmark* 11 J4
Lohardaga, *India* 69 H11
Loharia, *India* 68 H6
Loharu, *India* 68 E6
Lohja, *Finland* 9 F21
Löhne, *Germany* 24 C4
Lohr, *Germany* 25 F5
Lohri Wah →, *Pakistan* 68 F2
Loi-kaw, *Burma* 67 K20
Loimaa, *Finland* 9 F20
Loir →, *France* 18 E6
Loir-et-Cher □, *France* 18 E8
Loire □, *France* 21 C8
Loire →, *France* 18 E4
Loire Anjou Touraine ⌂, *France* 18 E6
Loire-Atlantique □, *France* 18 E5
Loiret □, *France* 19 E9
Loitz, *Germany* 24 B9
Loja, *Ecuador* 124 D3
Loja, *Spain* 37 H6
Loji = Kawasi, *Indonesia* 63 E7
Løjt Kirkeby, *Denmark* 11 J3
Lojung, *China* 58 E7
Loka, *Sudan* 81 G3
Lokandu, *Dem. Rep. of the Congo* 86 C2
Lokeren, *Belgium* 17 C3
Lokgwabe, *Botswana* 88 C3
Lokhvitsa, *Ukraine* 33 G7
Lokichokio, *Kenya* 86 B3
Lokitaung, *Kenya* 86 B4
Lokkan tekojärvi, *Finland* 8 C22
Løkken, *Denmark* 11 G3
Loknya, *Russia* 32 D6
Loko, *Nigeria* 83 D6
Lokoja, *Nigeria* 83 D6
Lokot, *Russia* 33 F8
Lol →, *Sudan* 81 F2
Lola, *Guinea* 82 D3
Lola, Mt., *U.S.A.* 110 F6
Lolibai, Gebel, *Sudan* 81 G3
Lolimi, *Sudan* 81 G3
Loliondo, *Tanzania* 86 C4
Lolland, *Denmark* 11 K5
Lollar, *Germany* 24 E4
Lolo, *U.S.A.* 108 C6
Lolodorf, *Cameroon* 83 E7
Lom, *Bulgaria* 44 C7
Lom →, *Bulgaria* 44 C7
Lom Kao, *Thailand* 64 D3
Lom Sak, *Thailand* 64 D3
Loma, *U.S.A.* 108 C8
Loma Linda, *U.S.A.* 111 L9
Lomami →, *Dem. Rep. of the Congo* 86 B1
Lomas de Zamóra, *Argentina* 126 C4
Lombadina, *Australia* 92 C3
Lombárdia □, *Italy* 40 C6
Lombardy = Lombárdia □, *Italy* 40 C6
Lombez, *France* 20 E4
Lomblen, *Indonesia* 63 F6
Lombok, *Indonesia* 62 F5
Lombok, Selat, *Indonesia* 63 K18
Lomé, *Togo* 83 D5
Lomela, *Dem. Rep. of the Congo* 84 E4
Lomela →, *Dem. Rep. of the Congo* 84 E4
Lomianki, *Poland* 31 F7
Lomma, *Sweden* 11 J7
Lommel, *Belgium* 17 C5
Lomond, *Canada* 102 C6
Lomond, L., *U.K.* 13 E4
Lomonosov Ridge, *Arctic* 4 A
Lomphat, *Cambodia* 64 F6
Lompobatang, *Indonesia* 63 F5
Lompoc, *U.S.A.* 111 L6
Łomża, *Poland* 31 E9
Lon, Ko, *Thailand* 65 a
Loncoche, *Chile* 128 D2
Londa, *India* 66 M9
Londiani, *Kenya* 86 C4
Londinières, *France* 18 C8
London, *Canada* 116 D3
London, *U.K.* 15 F7
London, *Ky., U.S.A.* 114 G3
London, *Ohio, U.S.A.* 114 F4
London, Greater □, *U.K.* 15 F7
London Gatwick ✈ (LGW), *U.K.* 15 F7
London Heathrow ✈ (LHR), *U.K.* 15 F7
London Stansted ✈ (STN), *U.K.* 15 F8
Londonderry, *U.K.* 12 B4
Londonderry □, *U.K.* 12 B4
Londonderry, C., *Australia* 92 B4
Londonderry, I., *Chile* 128 H2
Londres, *Argentina* 128 B3
Londrina, *Brazil* 127 A5
Lone Pine, *U.S.A.* 110 J8
Lonely Mine, *Zimbabwe* 89 B4
Long B., *U.S.A.* 115 J6
Long Beach, *Calif., U.S.A.* 111 M8
Long Beach, *N.Y., U.S.A.* 117 F11
Long Beach, *Wash., U.S.A.* 110 D2
Long Branch, *U.S.A.* 117 F11
Long Creek, *U.S.A.* 108 D4
Long Eaton, *U.K.* 14 E6
Long I., *Australia* 94 J6
Long I., *Bahamas* 121 B4
Long I., *Canada* 104 B4
Long I., *Ireland* 12 E2
Long I., *U.S.A.* 117 F11
Long Island Sd., *U.S.A.* 117 E12
Long L., *Canada* 104 C2
Long Lake, *U.S.A.* 117 C10
Long Point B., *Canada* 116 D4
Long Prairie →, *U.S.A.* 112 C7
Long Pt., *Canada* 116 D4
Long Range Mts., *Canada* 105 C8
Long Reef, *Australia* 92 B4
Long Spruce, *Canada* 103 B10
Long Str. = Longa, Proliv, *Russia* 4 C16
Long Thanh, *Vietnam* 65 G6
Long Xian, *China* 56 G4
Long Xuyen, *Vietnam* 65 G5
Longá, *Greece* 46 E3
Longa, Proliv, *Russia* 4 C16
Long'an, *China* 58 F6
Longarone, *Italy* 41 B9
Longbenton, *U.K.* 14 B6
Longboat Key, *U.S.A.* 115 M4
Longchang, *China* 58 C5
Longchi, *China* 58 C4
Longchuan, *Guangdong, China* 59 E10
Longchuan, *Yunnan, China* 58 E1
Longde, *China* 56 G4
Longeau, *France* 19 E12
Longford, *Australia* 95 G4
Longford, *Ireland* 12 C4
Longford □, *Ireland* 12 C4
Longhai, *China* 59 E11
Longhua, *China* 57 D9
Longhui, *China* 59 D8
Longido, *Tanzania* 86 C4
Longiram, *Indonesia* 62 E5
Longkou, *Jiangxi, China* 59 D10
Longkou, *Shandong, China* 57 F11
Longlac, *Canada* 104 C2
Longli, *China* 58 D6
Longlin, *China* 58 E5
Longling, *China* 58 E2
Longmeadow, *U.S.A.* 117 D12
Longmen, *China* 59 F10
Longming, *China* 58 F6
Longmont, *U.S.A.* 112 E2
Longnan, *China* 59 E10
Longnawan, *Indonesia* 62 D4
Longobucco, *Italy* 43 C9
Longquan, *China* 59 C12
Longreach, *Australia* 94 C3
Longshan, *China* 58 C7
Longsheng, *China* 59 E8
Longué-Jumelles, *France* 18 E6
Longueau, *France* 19 C9
Longueuil, *Canada* 117 A11
Longuyon, *France* 19 C12
Longvic, *France* 19 E12
Longview, *Tex., U.S.A.* 113 J7
Longview, *Wash., U.S.A.* 110 D4
Longwy, *France* 19 C12
Longxi, *China* 56 G3
Longyan, *China* 59 E11
Longyearbyen, *Norway* 4 B8
Longyou, *China* 59 C12
Longzhou, *China* 58 F6
Lonigo, *Italy* 41 C8
Löningen, *Germany* 24 C3
Lonja →, *Croatia* 41 C13
Lonoke, *U.S.A.* 113 H9
Lonquimay, *Chile* 128 D2
Lons-le-Saunier, *France* 19 F12
Lönsboda, *Sweden* 11 H8
Looe, *U.K.* 15 G3
Lookout, C., *Canada* 104 A3
Lookout, C., *U.S.A.* 115 H7
Loolmalasin, *Tanzania* 86 C4
Loon →, *Alta., Canada* 102 B5
Loon →, *Man., Canada* 103 B8
Loon Lake, *Canada* 103 C7
Loongana, *Australia* 93 F4
Loop Hd., *Ireland* 12 D2
Lop Buri, *Thailand* 64 E3
Lop Nor = Lop Nur, *China* 60 B4
Lop Nur, *China* 60 B4
Lopare, *Bos.-H.* 28 F3
Lopatin, *Russia* 35 J8
Lopatina, Gora, *Russia* 53 D15
Lopaye, *Sudan* 81 F3
Lopez, *Phil.* 61 E5
Lopez, *U.S.A.* 117 E8
Lopez, C., *Gabon* 84 E1
Lopphavet, *Norway* 8 A19
Lora →, *Afghan.* 66 D4
Lora, Hāmūn-i-, *Pakistan* 66 E4
Lora Cr. →, *Australia* 95 D2
Lora del Río, *Spain* 37 H5
Lorain, *U.S.A.* 116 E2
Loralai, *Pakistan* 68 D3
Lorca, *Spain* 39 H3
Lord Howe I., *Pac. Oc.* 96 L7
Lord Howe Ridge, *Pac. Oc.* 96 L8
Lordsburg, *U.S.A.* 109 K9
Lorestan □, *Iran* 71 C6
Loreto, *Brazil* 125 E9
Loreto, *Italy* 41 E10
Loreto, *Mexico* 118 B2
Lorgues, *France* 21 E10
Lorhosso, *Burkina Faso* 82 C4
Lorient, *France* 18 E3
Lőrinci, *Hungary* 28 C4
Lormi, *India* 69 H9
Lorn, *U.K.* 13 E3
Lorn, Firth of, *U.K.* 13 E3
Lorne, *Australia* 95 F3
Loronyo, *Sudan* 81 G3
Lorovouno, *Cyprus* 49 D11
Lörrach, *Germany* 25 H3
Lorraine ⌂, *France* 19 D12
Lorraine □, *France* 19 D13
Los, *Sweden* 10 C9
Los, Îles de, *Guinea* 82 D2
Los Alamos, *Calif., U.S.A.* 111 L6
Los Alamos, *N. Mex., U.S.A.* 109 J10
Los Alcornocales ⌂, *Spain* 37 J5
Los Altos, *U.S.A.* 110 H4
Los Andes, *Chile* 126 C1
Los Angeles, *Chile* 126 D1
Los Angeles, *U.S.A.* 111 M8
Los Angeles, Bahia de, *Mexico* 118 B2
Los Angeles Aqueduct, *U.S.A.* 111 K9
Los Angeles International ✈ (LAX), *U.S.A.* 111 M8
Los Banos, *U.S.A.* 110 H6
Los Barrios, *Spain* 37 J5
Los Blancos, *Argentina* 126 A3
Los Cardones △, *Argentina* 126 B2
Los Chiles, *Costa Rica* 120 D3
Los Corrales de Buelna, *Spain* 36 B6
Los Cristianos, *Canary Is.* 48 F3
Los Gallardos, *Spain* 39 H3
Los Gatos, *U.S.A.* 110 H5
Los Haïtises △, *Dom. Rep.* 121 C6
Los Hermanos Is., *Venezuela* 121 D7
Los Islotes, *Canary Is.* 48 E6
Los Llanos de Aridane, *Canary Is.* 48 F2
Los Loros, *Chile* 126 B1
Los Lunas, *U.S.A.* 109 J10
Los Mochis, *Mexico* 118 B3
Los Monegros, *Spain* 38 D4
Los Nietos, *Spain* 39 H4
Los Olivos, *U.S.A.* 111 L6
Los Palacios, *Cuba* 120 B3
Los Palacios y Villafranca, *Spain* 37 H5
Los Reyes, *Mexico* 118 D4
Los Roques Is., *Venezuela* 121 D6
Los Santos de Maimona, *Spain* 37 G4
Los Teques, *Venezuela* 124 A5
Los Testigos, Is., *Venezuela* 124 A6
Los Vilos, *Chile* 126 C1
Los Yébenes, *Spain* 37 F7
Łosice, *Poland* 31 F9
Loskop Dam, *S. Africa* 89 D4
Løsning, *Denmark* 11 J3
Lossiemouth, *U.K.* 13 D5
Lostwithiel, *U.K.* 15 G3
Lot □, *France* 20 D5
Lot →, *France* 20 D4
Lot-et-Garonne □, *France* 20 D4
Lota, *Chile* 126 D1
Lotagipi Swamp, *Sudan* 81 G3
Loṭfābād, *Iran* 71 B8
Lothair, *S. Africa* 89 D5
Lotorp, *Sweden* 11 F9
Lötschbergtunnel, *Switz.* 25 J3
Löttorp, *Sweden* 11 G11
Lotung, *Taiwan* 59 E13
Loubomo, *Congo* 84 E2
Loudéac, *France* 18 D4
Loudi, *China* 59 D8
Loudonville, *U.S.A.* 116 F2
Loudun, *France* 18 E7
Loue →, *France* 19 E12
Louga, *Senegal* 82 B1
Loughborough, *U.K.* 14 E6
Loughrea, *Ireland* 12 C3
Loughros More B., *Ireland* 12 B3
Louhans, *France* 19 F12
Louis Trichardt, *S. Africa* 89 C4
Louis XIV, Pte., *Canada* 104 B4
Louisa, *U.S.A.* 114 F4
Louisbourg, *Canada* 105 C8
Louise I., *Canada* 102 C2
Louiseville, *Canada* 104 C5
Louisiade Arch., *Papua N. G.* 96 J7
Louisiana, *U.S.A.* 112 F9
Louisiana □, *U.S.A.* 113 K9
Louisville, *Ky., U.S.A.* 114 F3
Louisville, *Miss., U.S.A.* 113 J10
Louisville, *Ohio, U.S.A.* 116 F3
Loulay, *France* 20 B3
Loulé, *Portugal* 37 H3
Louny, *Czech Rep.* 26 A6
Loup City, *U.S.A.* 112 E5
Loups Marins, Lacs des, *Canada* 104 A5
Lourdes, *France* 20 E3
Lourinhã, *Portugal* 37 F1
Lousã, *Portugal* 36 E2
Louta, *Burkina Faso* 82 C4
Louth, *Australia* 95 E4
Louth, *Ireland* 12 C5
Louth, *U.K.* 14 D7
Louth □, *Ireland* 12 C5
Loutrá Aidhipsoú, *Greece* 46 C5
Loutráki, *Greece* 46 D4
Louvain = Leuven, *Belgium* 17 D4
Louviers, *France* 18 C8
Louwsburg, *S. Africa* 89 D5
Lovat →, *Russia* 32 C6
Lovćen, *Serbia & M.* 44 D2
Lovćen △, *Serbia & M.* 44 D2
Lovech, *Bulgaria* 45 C8
Lovech □, *Bulgaria* 45 C8
Loveland, *U.S.A.* 112 E2
Lovell, *U.S.A.* 108 D9
Lovelock, *U.S.A.* 108 F4
Lóvere, *Italy* 40 C7
Lövestad, *Sweden* 11 J7
Loviisa, *Finland* 9 F22
Loving, *U.S.A.* 113 J2
Lovington, *U.S.A.* 113 J3
Lovisa = Loviisa, *Finland* 9 F22
Lovosice, *Czech Rep.* 26 A7
Lovran, *Croatia* 41 C11
Lovrin, *Romania* 28 E5
Lövstabruk, *Sweden* 10 D11
Lövstabukten, *Sweden* 10 D11
Low, L., *Canada* 104 B4
Low Pt., *Australia* 93 F4
Low Tatra = Nízké Tatry, *Slovak Rep.* 27 C12
Lowa, *Dem. Rep. of the Congo* 86 C2
Lowa →, *Dem. Rep. of the Congo* 86 C2
Lowell, *U.S.A.* 117 D13
Lowellville, *U.S.A.* 116 E4
Löwen →, *Namibia* 88 D2
Lower Alkali L., *U.S.A.* 108 F3
Lower Arrow L., *Canada* 102 D5
Lower Austria = Niederösterreich □, *Austria* 26 C8
Lower California = Baja California, *Mexico* 118 A1
Lower Hutt, *N.Z.* 91 J5
Lower Lake, *U.S.A.* 110 G4
Lower Manitou L., *Canada* 103 D10
Lower Post, *Canada* 102 B3
Lower Red L., *U.S.A.* 112 B7
Lower Saxony = Niedersachsen □, *Germany* 24 C4
Lower Tunguska = Tunguska, Nizhnyaya →, *Russia* 53 C9
Lower Zambezi △, *Zambia* 87 F2
Lowestoft, *U.K.* 15 E9
Lowgar □, *Afghan.* 66 B6
Łowicz, *Poland* 31 F6
Lowville, *U.S.A.* 117 C9
Loxton, *Australia* 95 E3
Loxton, *S. Africa* 88 E3
Loyalton, *U.S.A.* 110 F6
Loyalty Is. = Loyauté, Îs., *N. Cal.* 96 K8
Loyang = Luoyang, *China* 56 G7
Loyauté, Îs., *N. Cal.* 96 K8
Loyev = Loyew, *Belarus* 33 G6
Loyew, *Belarus* 33 G6
Loyoro, *Uganda* 86 B3
Lož, *Slovenia* 41 C11
Lozère □, *France* 20 D7
Loznica, *Serbia & M.* 44 B3
Lozova, *Ukraine* 33 H9
Lü Shan, *China* 59 C11
Lü-Tao, *Taiwan* 59 F13
Luachimo, *Angola* 84 F4
Luajan →, *India* 69 G11

Lualaba →, *Dem. Rep. of the Congo* 86 B2
Luampa, *Zambia* 87 F1
Lu'an, *China* 59 B11
Luan Chau, *Vietnam* 58 G4
Luan He →, *China* 57 E10
Luan Xian, *China* 57 E10
Luancheng, *Guangxi Zhuangzu, China* 58 F7
Luancheng, *Hebei, China* 56 F8
Luanco, *Spain* 36 B5
Luanda, *Angola* 84 F2
Luang, Thale, *Thailand* 65 J3
Luang Prabang, *Laos* 58 H4
Luangwa, *Zambia* 87 F3
Luangwa →, *Zambia* 87 E3
Luangwa Valley, *Zambia* 87 E3
Luanne, *China* 57 D9
Luanping, *China* 57 D9
Luanshya, *Zambia* 87 E2
Luapula □, *Zambia* 87 E2
Luapula →, *Africa* 87 D2
Luarca, *Spain* 36 B4
Luashi, *Dem. Rep. of the Congo* 87 E1
Luau, *Angola* 84 G4
Lubaczów, *Poland* 31 H10
Lubań, *Poland* 31 G2
Lubana, Ozero = Lubānas Ezers, *Latvia* 9 H22
Lubānas Ezers, *Latvia* 9 H22
Lubang, *Phil.* 61 E4
Lubang Is., *Phil.* 63 B6
Lubango, *Angola* 85 G2
Lubao, *Dem. Rep. of the Congo* 86 D2
Lubartów, *Poland* 31 G9
Lubawa, *Poland* 30 E6
Lübbecke, *Germany* 24 C4
Lübben, *Germany* 24 D9
Lübbenau, *Germany* 24 D9
Lubbock, *U.S.A.* 113 J4
Lübeck, *Germany* 24 B6
Lübecker Bucht, *Germany* 24 A6
Lubefu, *Dem. Rep. of the Congo* 86 C1
Lubefu →, *Dem. Rep. of the Congo* 86 C1
Lubelskie □, *Poland* 31 G9
Lubero = Luofu, *Dem. Rep. of the Congo* 86 C2
Luberon ⌓, *France* 21 E9
Lubersac, *France* 20 C5
Lubicon L., *Canada* 102 B5
Lubień Kujawski, *Poland* 31 F6
Lubilash →, *Dem. Rep. of the Congo* 84 F4
Lubin, *Poland* 31 G3
Lublin, *Poland* 31 G9
Lubliniec, *Poland* 31 H5
Lubnān, Jabal, *Lebanon* 74 B4
Lubniewice, *Poland* 31 F2
Lubny, *Ukraine* 33 G7
Lubomierz, *Poland* 31 G2
Luboń, *Poland* 31 F3
Lubongola, *Dem. Rep. of the Congo* 86 C2
L'ubotín, *Slovak Rep.* 27 B13
Lubraniec, *Poland* 31 F5
Lubsko, *Poland* 31 G1
Lübtheen, *Germany* 24 B7
Lubuagan, *Phil.* 61 C4
Lubudi, *Dem. Rep. of the Congo* 84 F5
Lubudi →, *Dem. Rep. of the Congo* 87 D2
Lubuklinggau, *Indonesia* 62 E2
Lubuksikaping, *Indonesia* 62 D2
Lubumbashi, *Dem. Rep. of the Congo* 87 E2
Lubunda, *Dem. Rep. of the Congo* 86 D2
Lubungu, *Zambia* 87 E2
Lubuskie □, *Poland* 31 F2
Lubutu, *Dem. Rep. of the Congo* 86 C2
Luc An Chau, *Vietnam* 64 A5
Luc-en-Diois, *France* 21 D9
Lucan, *Canada* 116 C3
Lucania, Mt., *Canada* 100 B5
Lucas Channel, *Canada* 116 A3
Lucban, *Phil.* 61 D4
Lucca, *Italy* 40 E7
Lucé, *France* 18 D8
Luce Bay, *U.K.* 13 G4
Lucea, *Jamaica* 120 a
Lucedale, *U.S.A.* 115 K1
Lucena, *Phil.* 61 E4
Lucena, *Spain* 37 H6
Lučenec, *Slovak Rep.* 27 C12
Lucera, *Italy* 43 A8
Lucerne = Luzern, *Switz.* 25 H4
Lucerne, *U.S.A.* 110 F4
Lucerne Valley, *U.S.A.* 111 L10
Lucero, *Mexico* 118 A3
Luchena →, *Spain* 39 H3
Lucheng, *China* 56 F7
Lucheringo →, *Mozam.* 87 E4
Lüchow, *Germany* 24 C7
Luchuan, *China* 59 F8
Lucia, *U.S.A.* 110 J5
Lucinda, *Australia* 94 B4
Luckau, *Germany* 24 D9
Luckenwalde, *Germany* 24 C9
Luckhoff, *S. Africa* 88 D3
Lucknow, *Canada* 116 C3
Lucknow, *India* 69 F9
Luçon, *France* 20 B2
Lüda = Dalian, *China* 57 E11
Luda Kamchiya →, *Bulgaria* 45 C11
Ludbreg, *Croatia* 41 B13
Lüdenscheid, *Germany* 24 D3
Lüderitz, *Namibia* 88 D2
Lüderitzbaai, *Namibia* 88 D2
Ludhiana, *India* 68 D6
Ludian, *China* 58 D4
Luding Qiao, *China* 58 C4
Lüdinghausen, *Germany* 24 D3
Ludington, *U.S.A.* 114 D2
Ludlow, *U.K.* 15 E5
Ludlow, *Calif., U.S.A.* 111 L10
Ludlow, *Pa., U.S.A.* 116 E6
Ludlow, *Vt., U.S.A.* 117 C12
Ludus, *Romania* 29 D9
Ludvika, *Sweden* 10 D9
Ludwigsburg, *Germany* 25 G5
Ludwigsfelde, *Germany* 24 C9
Ludwigshafen, *Germany* 25 F4
Ludwigslust, *Germany* 24 B7
Ludza, *Latvia* 32 D4
Lueki, *Dem. Rep. of the Congo* 86 C2
Luena, *Dem. Rep. of the Congo* 87 D2
Luena, *Zambia* 87 E3
Luenha = Ruenya →, *Africa* 87 F3
Lüeyang, *China* 56 H4
Lufeng, *Guangdong, China* 59 F10
Lufeng, *Yunnan, China* 58 E4
Lufira →, *Dem. Rep. of the Congo* 87 D2
Lufkin, *U.S.A.* 113 K7
Lufupa, *Dem. Rep. of the Congo* 87 E1
Luga, *Russia* 32 C5
Luga →, *Russia* 32 C5
Lugano, *Switz.* 25 J4
Lugano, L. di, *Switz.* 40 C6
Lugansk = Luhansk, *Ukraine* 33 H10
Lugard's Falls, *Kenya* 86 C4
Lugela, *Mozam.* 87 F4
Lugenda →, *Mozam.* 87 E4
Lugh Ganana, *Somali Rep.* 75 G3
Lugnaquillia, *Ireland* 12 D5
Lugo, *Italy* 41 D8
Lugo, *Spain* 36 B3
Lugo □, *Spain* 36 C3
Lugoj, *Romania* 28 E6
Lugovoy = Qulan, *Kazakhstan* 52 E8
Luhansk, *Ukraine* 33 H10
Luhe, *China* 59 A12
Luhe →, *Germany* 24 B6
Luhuo, *China* 58 B3
Luiana, *Angola* 88 B3
Luimneach = Limerick, *Ireland* 12 D3
Luing, *U.K.* 13 E3
Luino, *Italy* 40 C5
Luís Correia, *Brazil* 125 D10
Luitpold Coast, *Antarctica* 5 D1
Luiza, *Dem. Rep. of the Congo* 84 F4
Luizi, *Dem. Rep. of the Congo* 86 D2
Luján, *Argentina* 126 C4
Lujiang, *China* 59 B11
Lukang, *Taiwan* 59 E13
Lukanga Swamp, *Zambia* 87 E2
Lukavac, *Bos.-H.* 28 F3
Lukenie →, *Dem. Rep. of the Congo* 84 E3
Lukhisaral, *India* 69 G12
Lŭki, *Bulgaria* 45 E8
Lukolela, *Dem. Rep. of the Congo* 86 D1
Lukosi, *Zimbabwe* 87 F2
Lukovë, *Albania* 44 G3
Lukovit, *Bulgaria* 45 C8
Łuków, *Poland* 31 G9
Lukoyanov, *Russia* 34 C7
Lukusuzi △, *Zambia* 87 E3
Lule älv →, *Sweden* 8 D19
Luleå, *Sweden* 8 D20
Lüleburgaz, *Turkey* 45 E11
Luliang, *China* 58 E4
Luling, *U.S.A.* 113 L6
Lulong, *China* 57 E10
Lulonga →, *Dem. Rep. of the Congo* 84 D3
Lulua →, *Dem. Rep. of the Congo* 84 E4
Lumajang, *Indonesia* 63 H15
Lumbala N'guimbo, *Angola* 85 G4
Lumberton, *U.S.A.* 115 H6
Lumsden, *Canada* 103 C8
Lumsden, *N.Z.* 91 L2
Lumut, *Malaysia* 65 K3
Lumut, Tanjung, *Indonesia* 62 E3
Luna, *India* 68 H3
Lunan, *China* 58 E4
Lunavada, *India* 68 H5
Lunca, *Romania* 29 C10
Lunca Corbului, *Romania* 29 F9
Lund, *Sweden* 11 J7
Lundazi, *Zambia* 87 E3
Lunderskov, *Denmark* 11 J3
Lundi →, *Zimbabwe* 87 G3
Lundu, *Malaysia* 62 D3
Lundy, *U.K.* 15 F3
Lune →, *U.K.* 14 C5
Lüneburg, *Germany* 24 B6
Lüneburg Heath = Lüneburger Heide, *Germany* 24 B6
Lüneburger Heide, *Germany* 24 B6
Lunel, *France* 21 E8
Lünen, *Germany* 24 D3
Lunenburg, *Canada* 105 D7
Lunéville, *France* 19 D13
Lunga →, *Zambia* 87 E2
Lungi Airport, *S. Leone* 82 D2
Lunglei, *India* 67 H18
Luni, *India* 68 G5
Luni →, *India* 68 G4
Luninets = Luninyets, *Belarus* 33 F4
Luning, *U.S.A.* 108 G4
Lunino, *Russia* 34 D7
Luninyets, *Belarus* 33 F4
Lunkaransar, *India* 68 E5
Lunsemfwa →, *Zambia* 87 E3
Lunsemfwa Falls, *Zambia* 87 E2
Luo He →, *China* 56 G6
Luocheng, *China* 58 E7
Luochuan, *China* 56 G5
Luoci, *China* 58 E4
Luodian, *China* 58 E6
Luoding, *China* 59 F8
Luofu, *Dem. Rep. of the Congo* 86 C2
Luohe, *China* 56 H8
Luojiang, *China* 58 B5
Luonan, *China* 56 G6
Luoning, *China* 56 G6
Luoshan, *China* 59 A10
Luotian, *China* 59 B10
Luoxiao Shan, *China* 59 D10
Luoyang, *China* 56 G7
Luoyuan, *China* 59 D12
Luozigou, *China* 57 C16
Lupanshui, *China* 58 D5
Lupeni, *Romania* 29 E8
Lupilichi, *Mozam.* 87 E4
Łupków, *Poland* 31 J9
Lupoing, *China* 58 E5
Luquan, *China* 58 E4
Luque, *Paraguay* 126 B4
Lúras, *Italy* 42 B2
Luray, *U.S.A.* 114 F6
Lure, *France* 19 E13
Lurgan, *U.K.* 12 B5
Lusaka, *Zambia* 87 F2
Lusambo, *Dem. Rep. of the Congo* 86 C1
Lusangaye, *Dem. Rep. of the Congo* 86 C2
Luseland, *Canada* 103 C7
Lusenga Plain △, *Zambia* 87 D2
Lushan, *Henan, China* 56 H7
Lushan, *Sichuan, China* 58 B4
Lushi, *China* 56 G6
Lushnjë, *Albania* 44 F3
Lushoto, *Tanzania* 86 C4
Lushui, *China* 58 E2
Lüshun, *China* 57 E11
Lusignan, *France* 20 B4
Lusigny-sur-Barse, *France* 19 D11
Lusk, *U.S.A.* 112 D2
Lussac-les-Châteaux, *France* 20 B4
Lustenau, *Austria* 26 D2
Lūt, Dasht-e, *Iran* 71 D8
Luta = Dalian, *China* 57 E11
Lutherstadt Wittenberg, *Germany* 24 D8
Luton, *U.K.* 15 F7
Luton □, *U.K.* 15 F7
Łutselk'e, *Canada* 103 A6
Lutsk, *Ukraine* 33 G3
Lützow Holmbukta, *Antarctica* 5 C4
Lutzputs, *S. Africa* 88 D3
Luuq = Lugh Ganana, *Somali Rep.* 75 G3
Luverne, *Ala., U.S.A.* 115 K2
Luverne, *Minn., U.S.A.* 112 D6
Luvua, *Dem. Rep. of the Congo* 87 D2
Luvua →, *Dem. Rep. of the Congo* 86 D2
Luvuvhu →, *S. Africa* 89 C5
Luwegu →, *Tanzania* 87 D4
Luwuk, *Indonesia* 63 E6
Luxembourg, *Lux.* 17 E6
Luxembourg □, *Belgium* 17 E5
Luxembourg ■, *Europe* 7 F7
Luxembourg ✕ (LUX), *Lux.* 17 E6
Luxeuil-les-Bains, *France* 19 E13
Luxi, *Hunan, China* 59 C8
Luxi, *Yunnan, China* 58 E4
Luxi, *Yunnan, China* 58 E2
Luxor = El Uqsur, *Egypt* 80 B3
Luy-de-Béarn →, *France* 20 E3
Luy-de-France →, *France* 20 E3
Luyi, *China* 56 H8
Luz-St-Sauveur, *France* 20 F4
Luzern, *Switz.* 25 H4
Luzern □, *Switz.* 25 H3
Luzhai, *China* 58 E7
Luzhi, *China* 58 D5
Luzhou, *China* 58 C5
Luziânia, *Brazil* 125 G9
Lužnice →, *Czech Rep.* 26 B7
Luzon, *Phil.* 61 D4
Luzy, *France* 19 F10
Luzzi, *Italy* 43 C9
Lviv, *Ukraine* 33 H3
Lvov = Lviv, *Ukraine* 33 H3
Lwówek, *Poland* 31 F3
Lwówek Śląski, *Poland* 31 G2
Lyakhavichy, *Belarus* 33 F4
Lyakhovskiye, Ostrova, *Russia* 53 B15
Lyaki = Läki, *Azerbaijan* 35 K8
Lyal I., *Canada* 116 B3
Lyallpur = Faisalabad, *Pakistan* 68 D5
Lyaskovets, *Bulgaria* 45 C9
Lybster, *U.K.* 13 C5
Lycaonia, *Turkey* 72 D5
Lychen, *Germany* 24 B9
Lychkova, *Russia* 32 D7
Lycia, *Turkey* 47 E11
Lyckebyån →, *Sweden* 11 H9
Lycksele, *Sweden* 8 D18
Lycosura, *Greece* 46 D4
Lydda = Lod, *Israel* 74 D3
Lydenburg, *S. Africa* 89 D5
Lydia, *Turkey* 47 C10
Łydynia →, *Poland* 31 F7
Lyell, *N.Z.* 91 J4
Lyell I., *Canada* 102 C2
Lyepyel, *Belarus* 32 E5
Lygnern, *Sweden* 11 G6
Lykens, *U.S.A.* 117 F8
Lyman, *U.S.A.* 108 F8
Lyme B., *U.K.* 15 G4
Lyme Regis, *U.K.* 15 G5
Lymington, *U.K.* 15 G6
Łyna →, *Poland* 9 J19
Lynchburg, *U.S.A.* 114 G6
Lynd →, *Australia* 94 B3
Lynd Ra., *Australia* 95 D4
Lynden, *Canada* 116 C4
Lynden, *U.S.A.* 110 B4
Lyndhurst, *Australia* 95 E2
Lyndon →, *Australia* 93 D1
Lyndonville, *N.Y., U.S.A.* 116 C6
Lyndonville, *Vt., U.S.A.* 117 B12
Lyngen, *Norway* 8 B19
Lynher Reef, *Australia* 92 C3
Lynn, *U.S.A.* 117 D14
Lynn Lake, *Canada* 103 B8
Lynnwood, *U.S.A.* 110 C4
Lynton, *U.K.* 15 F4
Lyntupy, *Belarus* 9 J22
Lynx L., *Canada* 103 A7
Lyon, *France* 21 C8
Lyon St-Exupery ✕ (LYS), *France* 21 C9
Lyonnais, *France* 21 C8
Lyons = Lyon, *France* 21 C8
Lyons, *Ga., U.S.A.* 115 J4
Lyons, *Kans., U.S.A.* 112 F5
Lyons, *N.Y., U.S.A.* 116 C8
Lyons →, *Australia* 93 E2
Lyons Falls, *U.S.A.* 117 C9
Lyozna, *Belarus* 32 E6
Lys = Leie →, *Belgium* 17 C3
Lysá nad Labem, *Czech Rep.* 26 A7
Lysekil, *Sweden* 11 F5
Lyskovo, *Russia* 34 B7
Lystrup, *Denmark* 11 H4
Lysvik, *Sweden* 10 D7
Lysychansk, *Ukraine* 33 H10
Lytham St. Anne's, *U.K.* 14 D4
Lyttelton, *N.Z.* 91 K4
Lytton, *Canada* 102 C4
Lyuban, *Russia* 32 C6
Lyubertsy, *Russia* 32 E9
Lyubim, *Russia* 32 C11
Lyubimets, *Bulgaria* 45 E10
Lyuboml, *Ukraine* 33 G3
Lyubotyn, *Ukraine* 33 H8
Lyubytino, *Russia* 32 C7
Lyudinovo, *Russia* 32 F8

M

M.R. Gomez, Presa, *Mexico* 119 B5
M.R. Stefanik, Bratislava ✕ (BTS), *Slovak Rep.* 27 C10
Ma →, *Vietnam* 58 H5
Ma'adaba, *Jordan* 74 E4
Maamba, *Zambia* 88 B4
Ma'ān, *Jordan* 74 E4
Ma'ān □, *Jordan* 74 F5
Maanselkä, *Finland* 8 C23
Ma'anshan, *China* 59 B12
Maarianhamina, *Finland* 9 F18
Ma'arrat an Nu'mān, *Syria* 70 C3
Maas →, *Neths.* 17 C4
Maaseik, *Belgium* 17 C5
Maasin, *Phil.* 63 B6
Maastricht, *Neths.* 17 D5
Maave, *Mozam.* 89 C5
Mababe Depression, *Botswana* 88 B3
Mabalane, *Mozam.* 89 C5
Mabel L., *Canada* 102 C5
Mabenge, *Dem. Rep. of the Congo* 86 B1
Maberly, *Canada* 117 B8
Mabian, *China* 58 C4
Mabil, *Ethiopia* 81 E4
Mablethorpe, *U.K.* 14 D8
Mably, *France* 19 F11
Maboma, *Dem. Rep. of the Congo* 86 B2
Mabonto, *S. Leone* 82 D2
Mabrouk, *Mali* 83 B4
Mabuasehube ⌓, *Botswana* 88 D3
Mac Bac, *Vietnam* 65 H6
Macachín, *Argentina* 126 D3
Macaé, *Brazil* 127 A7
Macael, *Spain* 39 H2
McAlester, *U.S.A.* 113 H7
McAllen, *U.S.A.* 113 M5
MacAlpine L., *Canada* 100 B9
Macamic, *Canada* 104 C4
Macao = Macau, *China* 59 F9
Mação, *Portugal* 37 F3
Macapá, *Brazil* 125 C8
Macarao △, *Venezuela* 121 D6
McArthur →, *Australia* 94 B2
McArthur, Port, *Australia* 94 B2
Macau, *Brazil* 125 E11
Macau, *China* 59 F9
McBride, *Canada* 102 C4
McCall, *U.S.A.* 108 D5
McCamey, *U.S.A.* 113 K3
McCammon, *U.S.A.* 108 E7
McCauley I., *Canada* 102 C2
McCleary, *U.S.A.* 110 C3
Macclenny, *U.S.A.* 115 K4
Macclesfield, *U.K.* 14 D5
M'Clintock Chan., *Canada* 100 A9
McClintock Ra., *Australia* 92 C4
McCloud, *U.S.A.* 108 F2
McCluer I., *Australia* 92 B5
McClure, *U.S.A.* 116 F7
McClure, L., *U.S.A.* 110 H6
M'Clure Str., *Canada* 98 B8
McClusky, *U.S.A.* 112 B4
McComb, *U.S.A.* 113 K9
McConaughy, L., *U.S.A.* 112 E4
McCook, *U.S.A.* 112 E4
McCreary, *Canada* 103 C9
McCullough Mt., *U.S.A.* 111 K11
McCusker →, *Canada* 103 B7
McDame, *Canada* 102 B3
McDermitt, *U.S.A.* 108 F5
McDonald, *U.S.A.* 116 F4
Macdonald, L., *Australia* 92 D4
McDonald Is., *Ind. Oc.* 3 G13
MacDonnell Ranges, *Australia* 92 D5
MacDowell L., *Canada* 104 B1
Macduff, *U.K.* 13 D6
Maceda, *Spain* 36 C3
Macedonia, *U.S.A.* 116 E3
Macedonia ■, *Europe* 44 E5
Maceió, *Brazil* 125 E11
Maceira, *Portugal* 36 F2
Macenta, *Guinea* 82 D3
Macerata, *Italy* 41 E10
McFarland, *U.S.A.* 111 K7
McFarlane →, *Canada* 103 B7
Macfarlane, L., *Australia* 95 E2
McGehee, *U.S.A.* 113 J9
McGill, *U.S.A.* 108 G6
Macgillycuddy's Reeks, *Ireland* 12 E2
McGraw, *U.S.A.* 117 D8
McGregor, *U.S.A.* 112 D9
McGregor Ra., *Australia* 95 D3
McGuire, Mt, *Australia* 94 J6
Mach, *Pakistan* 66 E5
Māch Kowr, *Iran* 71 E9
Machado = Jiparaná →, *Brazil* 124 E6
Machagai, *Argentina* 126 B3
Machakos, *Kenya* 86 C4
Machala, *Ecuador* 124 D3
Machanga, *Mozam.* 89 C6
Machattie, L., *Australia* 94 C2
Machault, *France* 19 C11
Machava, *Mozam.* 89 D5
Machece, *Mozam.* 87 F4
Machecoul, *France* 18 F5
Macheke, *Zimbabwe* 89 B5
Macheng, *China* 59 B10
Machero, *Spain* 37 F6
Machhu →, *India* 68 H4
Machias, *Maine, U.S.A.* 115 C12
Machias, *N.Y., U.S.A.* 116 D6
Machichi →, *Canada* 103 B10
Machico, *Madeira* 48 D3
Machilipatnam, *India* 67 L12
Machiques, *Venezuela* 124 A4
Machupicchu, *Peru* 124 F4
Machynlleth, *U.K.* 15 E4
Macia, *Mozam.* 89 D5
Maciejowice, *Poland* 31 G8
McIlwraith Ra., *Australia* 94 A3
Măcin, *Romania* 29 E13
Macina, *Mali* 82 C4
McInnes L., *Canada* 103 C10
McIntosh, *U.S.A.* 112 C4
McIntosh L., *Canada* 103 B8
Macintosh Ra., *Australia* 93 E4
Macintyre →, *Australia* 95 D5
Macizo Galaico, *Spain* 36 C3
Mackay, *Australia* 94 K7
Mackay, *U.S.A.* 108 E7
MacKay →, *Canada* 102 B6
Mackay, L., *Australia* 92 D4
McKay Ra., *Australia* 92 D3
McKeesport, *U.S.A.* 116 F5
McKellar, *Canada* 116 A5
McKenna, *U.S.A.* 110 D4
Mackenzie, *Canada* 102 B4
McKenzie, *U.S.A.* 115 G1
Mackenzie →, *Australia* 94 C4
Mackenzie →, *Canada* 100 B6
McKenzie →, *U.S.A.* 108 D2
Mackenzie Bay, *Canada* 4 B1
Mackenzie City = Linden, *Guyana* 124 B7
Mackenzie Mts., *Canada* 100 B6
Mackinaw City, *U.S.A.* 114 C3
McKinlay, *Australia* 94 C3
McKinlay →, *Australia* 94 C3
McKinley, Mt., *U.S.A.* 100 B4
McKinley Sea, *Arctic* 4 A7
McKinney, *U.S.A.* 113 J6
Mackinnon Road, *Kenya* 86 C4
McKittrick, *U.S.A.* 111 K7
Macklin, *Canada* 103 C7
Macksville, *Australia* 95 E5
McLaughlin, *U.S.A.* 112 C4
Maclean, *Australia* 95 D5
McLean, *U.S.A.* 113 H4
McLeansboro, *U.S.A.* 112 F10
Maclear, *S. Africa* 89 E4
Maclear, C., *Malawi* 87 E3
Macleay →, *Australia* 95 E5
McLennan, *Canada* 102 B5
McLeod →, *Canada* 102 C5
MacLeod, B., *Canada* 103 A7
McLeod, L., *Australia* 93 D1
MacLeod Lake, *Canada* 102 C4
McLoughlin, Mt., *U.S.A.* 108 E2
McMechen, *U.S.A.* 116 G4
McMinnville, *Oreg., U.S.A.* 108 D2
McMinnville, *Tenn., U.S.A.* 115 H3
McMurdo Sd., *Antarctica* 5 D11
McMurray = Fort McMurray, *Canada* 102 B6
McMurray, *U.S.A.* 110 B4
Macodoene, *Mozam.* 89 C6
Macomb, *U.S.A.* 112 E9
Macomer, *Italy* 42 B1
Mâcon, *France* 19 F11
Macon, *Ga., U.S.A.* 115 J4
Macon, *Miss., U.S.A.* 115 J1
Macon, *Mo., U.S.A.* 112 F8
Macossa, *Mozam.* 87 F3
Macoun L., *Canada* 103 B8
Macovane, *Mozam.* 89 C6
McPherson, *U.S.A.* 112 F6
McPherson Pk., *U.S.A.* 111 L7
McPherson Ra., *Australia* 95 D5
Macquarie →, *Australia* 95 E4
Macquarie Harbour, *Australia* 95 G4
Macquarie Is., *Pac. Oc.* 96 N7
MacRobertson Land, *Antarctica* 5 D6
Macroom, *Ireland* 12 E3
MacTier, *Canada* 116 A5
Macubela, *Mozam.* 87 F4
Macugnaga, *Italy* 40 C4
Macuira △, *Colombia* 121 D5
Macuiza, *Mozam.* 87 F3

Macuro, *Venezuela* 125 K15
Macusani, *Peru* 124 F4
Macuse, *Mozam.* 87 F4
Macuspana, *Mexico* 119 D6
Macusse, *Angola* 88 B3
Mada →, *Nigeria* 83 D6
Ma'dabā □, *Jordan* 74 D4
Madadeni, *S. Africa* 89 D5
Madagali, *Nigeria* 83 C7
Madagascar ■, *Africa* 89 C8
Madā'in Sālih, *Si. Arabia* 70 E3
Madama, *Niger* 79 D8
Madame, I., *Canada* 105 C7
Madan, *Bulgaria* 45 E8
Madaoua, *Niger* 83 C6
Madara, *Nigeria* 83 C7
Madaripur, *Bangla.* 67 H17
Madauk, *Burma* 67 L20
Madawaska, *Canada* 116 A7
Madawaska →, *Canada* 116 A8
Madaya, *Burma* 67 H20
Madbar, *Sudan* 81 F3
Maddalena, *Italy* 42 A2
Maddaloni, *Italy* 43 A7
Madeira, *Atl. Oc.* 48 D3
Madeira →, *Brazil* 124 D7
Madeleine, Îs. de la, *Canada* 105 C7
Maden, *Turkey* 73 C8
Madera, *Mexico* 118 B3
Madera, *Calif., U.S.A.* 110 J6
Madera, *Pa., U.S.A.* 116 F6
Madha, *India* 66 L9
Madhavpur, *India* 68 J3
Madhepura, *India* 69 F12
Madhubani, *India* 69 F12
Madhupur, *India* 69 G12
Madhya Pradesh □, *India* 68 J8
Madidi →, *Bolivia* 124 F5
Madikeri, *India* 66 N9
Madikwe ⌂, *S. Africa* 89 D5
Madill, *U.S.A.* 113 H6
Madimba, *Dem. Rep. of the Congo* 84 E3
Ma'din, *Syria* 70 C3
Madina, *Mali* 82 C3
Madinani, *Ivory C.* 82 D3
Madingou, *Congo* 84 E2
Madirovalo, *Madag.* 89 B8
Madison, *Calif., U.S.A.* 110 G5
Madison, *Fla., U.S.A.* 115 K4
Madison, *Ind., U.S.A.* 114 F3
Madison, *Nebr., U.S.A.* 112 E6
Madison, *Ohio, U.S.A.* 116 E3
Madison, *S. Dak., U.S.A.* 112 D6
Madison, *Wis., U.S.A.* 112 D10
Madison →, *U.S.A.* 108 D8
Madison Heights, *U.S.A.* 114 G6
Madisonville, *Ky., U.S.A.* 114 G2
Madisonville, *Tex., U.S.A.* 113 K7
Madista, *Botswana* 88 C4
Madiun, *Indonesia* 63 G14
Madoc, *Canada* 116 B7
Madol, *Sudan* 81 F2
Madon →, *France* 19 D13
Madona, *Latvia* 9 H22
Madonie, *Italy* 42 E6
Madonna di Campíglio, *Italy* 40 B7
Madra Dağı, *Turkey* 47 B9
Madrakah, Ra's al, *Oman* 75 D6
Madras = Chennai, *India* 66 N12
Madras = Tamil Nadu □, *India* 66 P10
Madras, *U.S.A.* 108 D3
Madre, Laguna, *U.S.A.* 113 M6
Madre, Sierra, *Phil.* 61 C5
Madre de Dios →, *Bolivia* 124 F5
Madre de Dios, I., *Chile* 128 G1
Madre del Sur, Sierra, *Mexico* 119 D5
Madre Occidental, Sierra, *Mexico* 118 B3
Madre Oriental, Sierra, *Mexico* 118 C5
Madri, *India* 68 G5
Madrid, *Spain* 36 E7
Madrid, *U.S.A.* 117 B9
Madrid □, *Spain* 36 E7
Madrid Barajas ✕ (MAD), *Spain* 36 E7
Madridejos, *Spain* 37 F7
Madrigal de las Altas Torres, *Spain* 36 D6
Madrona, Sierra, *Spain* 37 G6
Madroñera, *Spain* 37 F5
Madu, *Sudan* 81 E2
Madura, *Australia* 93 F4
Madura, *Indonesia* 63 G15
Madura, Selat, *Indonesia* 63 G15
Madurai, *India* 66 Q11
Madurantakam, *India* 66 N11
Madzhalis, *Russia* 35 J8
Mae Chan, *Thailand* 64 B2
Mae Hong Son, *Thailand* 64 C2
Mae Khlong →, *Thailand* 64 F3
Mae Phrik, *Thailand* 64 D2
Mae Ping △, *Thailand* 64 D2
Mae Ramat, *Thailand* 64 D2
Mae Rim, *Thailand* 64 C2
Mae Sot, *Thailand* 64 D2
Mae Suai, *Thailand* 58 H2
Mae Tha, *Thailand* 64 C2
Mae Wong △, *Thailand* 64 E2
Mae Yom △, *Thailand* 64 C3
Maebashi, *Japan* 55 F9
Maella, *Spain* 38 D5
Maesteg, *U.K.* 15 F4
Maestra, Sierra, *Cuba* 120 B4
Maevatanana, *Madag.* 89 B8
Mafeking = Mafikeng, *S. Africa* 88 D4
Mafeking, *Canada* 103 C8
Maféré, *Ivory C.* 82 D4
Mafeteng, *Lesotho* 88 D4
Maffra, *Australia* 95 F4
Mafia I., *Tanzania* 86 D4
Mafikeng, *S. Africa* 88 D4
Mafra, *Brazil* 127 B6
Mafra, *Portugal* 37 G1
Mafungabusi Plateau, *Zimbabwe* 87 F2
Magadan, *Russia* 53 D16
Magadi, *Kenya* 86 C4
Magadi, L., *Kenya* 86 C4
Magaliesburg, *S. Africa* 89 D4
Magallanes, Estrecho de, *Chile* 128 G2
Magaluf, *Spain* 39 F7
Magangué, *Colombia* 124 B4
Magaria, *Niger* 83 C6
Magburaka, *S. Leone* 82 D2
Magdalen Is. = Madeleine, Îs. de la, *Canada* 105 C7
Magdalena, *Argentina* 126 D4
Magdalena, *Bolivia* 124 F6
Magdalena, *Mexico* 118 A2
Magdalena, *U.S.A.* 109 J10
Magdalena →, *Colombia* 124 A4
Magdalena →, *Mexico* 118 A2
Magdalena, B., *Mexico* 118 C2
Magdalena, Llano de la, *Mexico* 118 C2
Magdeburg, *Germany* 24 C7
Magdelaine Cays, *Australia* 94 B5
Magdub, *Sudan* 81 E2
Magee, *U.S.A.* 113 K10
Magelang, *Indonesia* 63 G14
Magellan's Str. = Magallanes, Estrecho de, *Chile* 128 G2
Magenta, *Italy* 40 C5
Magenta, L., *Australia* 93 F2
Magerøya, *Norway* 8 A21
Maggia →, *Switz.* 25 J4
Maggiorasca, Mte., *Italy* 40 D6
Maggiore, Lago, *Italy* 40 C5
Maggotty, *Jamaica* 120 a
Maghâgha, *Egypt* 80 B3
Maghama, *Mauritania* 82 B2
Magherafelt, *U.K.* 12 B5
Maghreb, *N. Afr.* 78 B5
Maghreb, *N. Afr.* 78 B5
Magione, *Italy* 41 E9
Magistralnyy, *Russia* 53 D11
Maglaj, *Bos.-H.* 28 F3
Magliano in Toscana, *Italy* 41 F8
Máglie, *Italy* 43 B11
Magnac-Laval, *France* 20 B5
Magnetic Pole (North), *Canada* 4 A2
Magnetic Pole (South), *Antarctica* 5 C9
Magnisía □, *Greece* 46 B5
Magnitogorsk, *Russia* 52 D6
Magnolia, *Ark., U.S.A.* 113 J8
Magnolia, *Miss., U.S.A.* 113 K9
Magny-en-Vexin, *France* 19 C8
Mago △, *Ethiopia* 81 F4
Magog, *Canada* 117 A12
Magoro, *Uganda* 86 B3
Magosa = Famagusta, *Cyprus* 49 D12
Magouládhes, *Greece* 49 A3
Magoye, *Zambia* 87 F2
Magozal, *Mexico* 119 C5
Magpie, L., *Canada* 105 B7
Magrath, *Canada* 102 D6
Magre →, *Spain* 39 F4
Magrur, *Sudan* 81 E3
Magrur, Wadi →, *Sudan* 81 D2
Magta Lahjar, *Mauritania* 82 B2
Maguan, *China* 58 F5
Maguarinho, C., *Brazil* 125 D9
Magude, *Mozam.* 89 D5
Magurski △, *Poland* 31 J8
Mağusa = Famagusta, *Cyprus* 49 D12
Maguse L., *Canada* 103 A9
Maguse Pt., *Canada* 103 A10
Magvana, *India* 68 H3
Magwe, *Burma* 67 J19
Magwe, *Sudan* 81 G3
Maha Sarakham, *Thailand* 64 D4
Mahābād, *Iran* 70 B5
Mahabharat Lekh, *Nepal* 69 E10
Mahabo, *Madag.* 89 C7
Mahadeo Hills, *India* 69 H8
Mahaffey, *U.S.A.* 116 F6
Mahagi, *Dem. Rep. of the Congo* 86 B3
Mahajamba →, *Madag.* 89 B8
Mahajamba, Helodranon' i, *Madag.* 89 B8
Mahajan, *India* 68 E5
Mahajanga, *Madag.* 89 B8
Mahajanga □, *Madag.* 89 B8
Mahajilo →, *Madag.* 89 B8
Mahakam →, *Indonesia* 62 E5
Mahalapye, *Botswana* 88 C4
Mahale Mts., *Tanzania* 86 D3
Mahale Mts. △, *Tanzania* 86 D2
Maḩallāt, *Iran* 71 C6
Māhān, *Iran* 71 D8
Mahan →, *India* 69 H10
Mahanadi →, *India* 67 J15
Mahananda →, *India* 69 G12
Mahanoro, *Madag.* 89 B8
Mahanoy City, *U.S.A.* 117 F8
Maharashtra □, *India* 66 J9
Mahasham, W. →, *Egypt* 74 E3
Mahasoa, *Madag.* 89 C8
Mahasolo, *Madag.* 89 B8
Mahattat ash Shīdīyah, *Jordan* 74 F4
Mahattat 'Unayzah, *Jordan* 74 E4
Mahavavy →, *Madag.* 89 B8
Mahaxay, *Laos* 64 D5
Mahbubnagar, *India* 66 L10
Maḩḑah, *Oman* 71 E7
Mahdia, *Tunisia* 79 A8
Mahe, *India* 69 C8
Mahendragarh, *India* 68 E7
Mahenge, *Tanzania* 87 D4
Maheno, *N.Z.* 91 L3
Mahesana, *India* 68 H5
Maheshwar, *India* 68 H6
Mahgawan, *India* 69 F8
Mahi →, *India* 68 H5
Mahia Pen., *N.Z.* 91 H6
Mahilyow, *Belarus* 32 F6
Mahmiya, *Sudan* 81 D3
Mahmud Kot, *Pakistan* 68 D4
Mahmudia, *Romania* 29 E14
Mahmudiye, *Turkey* 47 B12
Mahmutbey, *Turkey* 45 E12
Mahnomen, *U.S.A.* 112 B7
Mahoba, *India* 69 G8
Mahón = Maó, *Spain* 48 B11
Mahon, Menorca ✕ (MAH), *Spain* 38 F9
Mahone Bay, *Canada* 105 D7
Mahopac, *U.S.A.* 117 E11
Mahuta, *Nigeria* 83 C5
Mahuva, *India* 68 J4
Mahya Dağı, *Turkey* 45 E11
Mai-Ndombe, L., *Dem. Rep. of the Congo* 84 E3
Mai-Sai, *Thailand* 58 G2
Mai Thon, Ko, *Thailand* 65 a
Maia, *Portugal* 36 D2
Maia, *Spain* 38 B3
Maials, *Spain* 38 D5
Maîche, *France* 19 E13
Maicurú →, *Brazil* 125 D8
Máida, *Italy* 43 D9
Maidan Khula, *Afghan.* 68 C3
Maidenhead, *U.K.* 15 F7
Maidstone, *Canada* 103 C7
Maidstone, *U.K.* 15 F8
Maiduguri, *Nigeria* 83 C7
Maiella △, *Italy* 41 F11
Măieruş, *Romania* 29 E10
Maigatari, *Nigeria* 83 C6
Maignelay Montigny, *France* 19 C9
Maigo, *Phil.* 61 G5
Maigudo, *Ethiopia* 81 F4
Maihar, *India* 69 G9
Maijdi, *Bangla.* 67 H17
Maikala Ra., *India* 67 J12
Maiko △, *Dem. Rep. of the Congo* 86 C2
Mailani, *India* 69 E9
Maillezais, *France* 20 B3
Mailsi, *Pakistan* 68 E5
Main →, *Germany* 25 F4
Main →, *U.K.* 12 B5
Main Range △, *Australia* 95 D5
Main Ridge, *Trin. & Tob.* 125 J16
Mainburg, *Germany* 25 G7
Maine, *France* 18 D6
Maine □, *U.S.A.* 115 C11
Maine →, *Ireland* 12 D2
Maine-et-Loire □, *France* 18 E6
Maïne-Soroa, *Niger* 83 C7
Maingkwan, *Burma* 67 F20
Mainit, L., *Phil.* 61 G6
Mainland, *Orkney, U.K.* 13 C5
Mainland, *Shet., U.K.* 13 A7
Mainoru, *Australia* 94 A1
Mainpuri, *India* 69 F8
Maintal, *Germany* 25 E4
Maintenon, *France* 19 D8
Maintirano, *Madag.* 89 B7
Mainz, *Germany* 25 E4
Maipú, *Argentina* 126 D4
Maiquetía, *Venezuela* 124 A5
Máira →, *Italy* 40 D4
Mairabari, *India* 67 F18
Maisí, *Cuba* 121 B5
Maisí, Pta. de, *Cuba* 121 B5
Maitland, *N.S.W., Australia* 95 E5
Maitland, *S. Austral., Australia* 95 E2
Maitland →, *Canada* 116 C3
Maitri, *Antarctica* 5 D3
Maiyema, *Nigeria* 83 C5
Maiyuan, *China* 59 E11
Maiz, Is. del, *Nic.* 120 D3
Maizuru, *Japan* 55 G7
Majalengka, *Indonesia* 63 G13
Majene, *Indonesia* 63 E5
Majete ⌂, *Malawi* 87 F3
Majevica, *Bos.-H.* 28 F3
Maji, *Ethiopia* 81 F4
Majiang, *China* 58 D6
Majorca = Mallorca, *Spain* 48 B10
Maka, *Senegal* 82 C2
Makaha, *Zimbabwe* 89 B5
Makak, *Cameroon* 83 E7
Makalamabedi, *Botswana* 88 C3
Makale, *Indonesia* 63 E5
Makamba, *Burundi* 86 C2
Makari, *Cameroon* 83 C7
Makarikari = Makgadikgadi Salt Pans, *Botswana* 88 C4
Makarov Basin, *Arctic* 4 A
Makarovo, *Russia* 53 D11
Makarska, *Croatia* 41 E14
Makaryev, *Russia* 34 B6
Makasar = Ujung Pandang, *Indonesia* 63 F5
Makasar, Selat, *Indonesia* 63 E5
Makasar, Str. of = Makasar, Selat, *Indonesia* 63 E5
Makat, *Kazakhstan* 52 E6
Makedonija = Macedonia ■, *Europe* 44 E5
Makeni, *S. Leone* 82 D2
Makeyevka = Makiyivka, *Ukraine* 33 H9
Makgadikgadi △, *Botswana* 88 C3
Makgadikgadi Salt Pans, *Botswana* 88 C4
Makhachkala, *Russia* 35 J8
Makharadze = Ozurgeti, *Georgia* 35 K5
Makhfar al Buşayyah, *Iraq* 70 D5
Makhmūr, *Iraq* 70 C4
Makian, *Indonesia* 63 D7
Makindu, *Kenya* 86 C4
Makinsk, *Kazakhstan* 52 D8
Makiyivka, *Ukraine* 33 H9
Makkah, *Si. Arabia* 75 C2
Makkovik, *Canada* 105 A8
Makó, *Hungary* 28 D5
Mako, *Senegal* 82 C2
Makokou, *Gabon* 84 D2
Makongo, *Dem. Rep. of the Congo* 86 B2
Makoro, *Dem. Rep. of the Congo* 86 B2
Maków Mazowiecki, *Poland* 31 F8
Maków Podhalański, *Poland* 31 J6
Makrá, *Greece* 47 E7
Makrai, *India* 66 H10
Makran Coast Range, *Pakistan* 66 G4
Makrana, *India* 68 F6
Mákri, *Greece* 45 F9
Makriyialos, *Greece* 49 D7
Mākū, *Iran* 70 B5
Makunda, *Botswana* 88 C3
Makung, *Taiwan* 59 F12
Makurazaki, *Japan* 55 J5
Makurdi, *Nigeria* 83 D6
Makūyeh, *Iran* 71 D7
Makwassie, *S. Africa* 88 D4
Makwiro, *Zimbabwe* 89 B5
Mâl, *Mauritania* 82 B2
Mal B., *Ireland* 12 D2
Mala, Pta., *Panama* 120 E3
Mala Belozërka, *Ukraine* 33 J8
Malá Fatra △, *Slovak Rep.* 27 B12
Mala Kapela, *Croatia* 41 D12
Mała Panew →, *Poland* 31 H4
Mala Vyska, *Ukraine* 33 H6
Malabang, *Phil.* 61 H6
Malabar Coast, *India* 66 P9
Malabo = Rey Malabo, *Eq. Guin.* 83 E6
Malabon, *Phil.* 61 D4
Malabu, *Nigeria* 83 D7
Malacca, Str. of, *Indonesia* 65 L3
Malacky, *Slovak Rep.* 27 C10
Malad City, *U.S.A.* 108 E7
Maladeta, *Spain* 38 C5
Maladzyechna, *Belarus* 32 E4
Málaga, *Spain* 37 J6
Málaga □, *Spain* 37 J6
Malagarasi, *Tanzania* 86 D3
Malagarasi →, *Tanzania* 86 D2
Malagasy Rep. = Madagascar ■, *Africa* 89 C8
Malagón, *Spain* 37 F7
Malagón →, *Spain* 37 H3
Malahide, *Ireland* 12 C5
Malaimbandy, *Madag.* 89 C8
Malakâl, *Sudan* 81 F3
Malakand, *Pakistan* 68 B4
Malakwal, *Pakistan* 68 C5
Malamala, *Indonesia* 63 E6
Malanda, *Australia* 94 B4
Malang, *Indonesia* 63 G15
Malangen, *Norway* 8 B18
Malanje, *Angola* 84 F3
Mälaren, *Sweden* 10 E11
Malargüe, *Argentina* 126 D2
Malartic, *Canada* 104 C4
Malaryta, *Belarus* 33 G3
Malatya, *Turkey* 70 B3
Malawi ■, *Africa* 87 E3
Malawi, L. = Nyasa, L., *Africa* 87 E3
Malay Pen., *Asia* 65 J3
Malaya Belozërka = Mala Belozërka, *Ukraine* 33 J8
Malaya Vishera, *Russia* 32 C7
Malaya Viska = Mala Vyska, *Ukraine* 33 H6
Malaybalay, *Phil.* 61 G6
Malāyer, *Iran* 71 C6
Malaysia ■, *Asia* 65 K4
Malazgirt, *Turkey* 70 B4
Malbaza, *Niger* 83 C6
Malbon, *Australia* 94 C3
Malbooma, *Australia* 95 E1
Malbork, *Poland* 30 D6
Malcésine, *Italy* 40 C7
Malchin, *Germany* 24 B8
Malchow, *Germany* 24 B8
Malcolm, *Australia* 93 E3
Malcolm, Pt., *Australia* 93 F3
Malczyce, *Poland* 31 G3
Maldah, *India* 69 G13
Maldegem, *Belgium* 17 C3
Malden, *Mass., U.S.A.* 117 D13
Malden, *Mo., U.S.A.* 113 G10
Malden I., *Kiribati* 97 H12
Maldives ■, *Ind. Oc.* 50 J11
Maldon, *U.K.* 15 F8
Maldonado, *Uruguay* 127 C5
Maldonado, Punta, *Mexico* 119 D5
Malè, *Italy* 40 B7
Male, *Maldives* 51 J11
Malé Karpaty, *Slovak Rep.* 27 C10
Maléa, Ákra, *Greece* 46 E5
Malegaon, *India* 66 J9
Malei, *Mozam.* 87 F4
Malek, *Sudan* 81 F3
Malek Kandī, *Iran* 70 B5
Malela, *Dem. Rep. of the Congo* 86 C2
Malema, *Mozam.* 87 E4
Maléme, *Greece* 49 D5
Maleny, *Australia* 95 D5
Målerås, *Sweden* 11 H9
Malerkotla, *India* 68 D6
Máles, *Greece* 49 D7
Malesherbes, *France* 19 D9
Maleshevska Planina, *Europe* 44 E7
Malesína, *Greece* 46 C5
Malestroit, *France* 18 E4
Malfa, *Italy* 43 D7
Malgobek, *Russia* 35 J7
Malgomaj, *Sweden* 8 D17
Malgrat = Malgrat de Mar, *Spain* 38 D7
Malgrat de Mar, *Spain* 38 D7
Malha, *Sudan* 81 D2
Malhargarh, *India* 68 G6
Malheur →, *U.S.A.* 108 D5
Malheur L., *U.S.A.* 108 E4
Mali, *Guinea* 82 C2
Mali ■, *Africa* 82 B4
Mali →, *Burma* 67 G20
Mali Kanal, *Serbia & M.* 28 E4
Mali Kyun, *Burma* 64 F2
Malibu, *U.S.A.* 111 L8
Maliku, *Indonesia* 63 E6
Malili, *Indonesia* 63 E6
Målilla, *Sweden* 11 G9
Malimba, Mts., *Dem. Rep. of the Congo* 86 D2
Malin Hd., *Ireland* 12 A4
Malin Pen., *Ireland* 12 A4
Malindi, *Kenya* 86 C5
Malines = Mechelen, *Belgium* 17 C4
Malino, *Indonesia* 63 D6
Malinyi, *Tanzania* 87 D4
Malipo, *China* 58 F5
Maliq, *Albania* 44 F4
Malita, *Phil.* 63 C7
Maliwun, *Burma* 62 B1
Maliya, *India* 68 H4
Maljenik, *Serbia & M.* 44 C5
Malka Mari △, *Kenya* 86 B5
Malkara, *Turkey* 45 F10
Małkinia Górna, *Poland* 31 F9
Malko Tŭrnovo, *Bulgaria* 45 E11
Mallacoota Inlet, *Australia* 95 F4
Mallaig, *U.K.* 13 D3
Mallaoua, *Niger* 83 C6
Mallawan, *India* 69 F9
Mallawi, *Egypt* 80 B3
Mallemort, *France* 21 E9
Málles Venosta, *Italy* 40 B7
Mállia, *Greece* 49 D7
Mallión, Kólpos, *Greece* 49 D7
Mallorca, *Spain* 48 B10
Mallorytown, *Canada* 117 B9
Mallow, *Ireland* 12 D3
Malmbäck, *Sweden* 11 G8
Malmberget, *Sweden* 8 C19
Malmédy, *Belgium* 17 D6
Malmesbury, *S. Africa* 88 E2
Malmköping, *Sweden* 10 E10
Malmö, *Sweden* 11 J6
Malmslätt, *Sweden* 11 F9
Malmyzh, *Russia* 34 B10
Malnaş, *Romania* 29 D10
Malo Konare, *Bulgaria* 45 D8
Maloarkhangelsk, *Russia* 33 F9
Malolos, *Phil.* 63 B6
Malolotja ⌂, *Swaziland* 89 D5
Malombe L., *Malawi* 87 E4
Małomice, *Poland* 31 G2
Malomir, *Bulgaria* 45 D10
Malone, *U.S.A.* 117 B10
Malong, *China* 58 E4
Małopolskie □, *Poland* 31 J7
Malorad, *Bulgaria* 44 C7
Måløy, *Norway* 9 F11
Maloyaroslovets, *Russia* 32 E9
Malpartida, *Spain* 37 F4
Malpaso, *Canary Is.* 48 G1
Malpelo, I. de, *Colombia* 124 C2
Malpica de Bergantiños, *Spain* 36 B2
Malpur, *India* 68 H5
Malpura, *India* 68 F6
Mals = Málles Venosta, *Italy* 40 B7
Malta, *Idaho, U.S.A.* 108 E7
Malta, *Mont., U.S.A.* 108 B10
Malta ■, *Europe* 49 D2
Maltahöhe, *Namibia* 88 C2
Maltepe, *Turkey* 45 F13
Malton, *Canada* 116 C5
Malton, *U.K.* 14 C7
Maluku, *Indonesia* 63 E7
Maluku □, *Indonesia* 63 E7
Maluku Sea = Molucca Sea, *Indonesia* 63 E6
Malumfashi, *Nigeria* 83 C6
Malung, *Sweden* 10 D7
Malungsfors, *Sweden* 10 D7
Maluwe, *Ghana* 82 D4
Malvan, *India* 66 L8
Malvern, *U.S.A.* 113 H8
Malvern Hills, *U.K.* 15 E5
Malvinas, Is. = Falkland Is. ☑, *Atl. Oc.* 128 G5
Malý Dunaj →, *Slovak Rep.* 27 D11
Malya, *Tanzania* 86 C3
Malye Derbety, *Russia* 35 G7
Malyn, *Ukraine* 33 G5
Malyy Lyakhovskiy, Ostrov, *Russia* 53 B15
Mama, *Russia* 53 D12
Mamadysh, *Russia* 34 C10
Mamanguape, *Brazil* 125 E11
Mamarr Mitlā, *Egypt* 74 E1
Mamasa, *Indonesia* 63 E5
Mambasa, *Dem. Rep. of the Congo* 86 B2
Mamberamo →, *Indonesia* 63 E9
Mambilima Falls, *Zambia* 87 E2
Mambirima, *Dem. Rep. of the Congo* 87 E2
Mambo, *Tanzania* 86 C4
Mambrui, *Kenya* 86 C5
Mamburao, *Phil.* 61 E4
Mameigwess L., *Canada* 104 B2
Mamers, *France* 18 D7
Mamfé, *Cameroon* 83 D6
Mammoth, *U.S.A.* 109 K8
Mammoth Cave △, *U.S.A.* 114 G3
Mamoré →, *Bolivia* 124 F5
Mamou, *Guinea* 82 C2
Mamoudzou, *Mayotte* 77 H8
Mampatá, *Guinea-Biss.* 82 C2
Mampikony, *Madag.* 89 B8
Mampong, *Ghana* 83 D4
Mamry, Jezioro, *Poland* 30 D8

Mamuju, Indonesia 63 E5
Mamuno, Botswana 88 C3
Mamuras, Albania 44 E3
Man, Ivory C. 82 D3
Man, I. of, U.K. 14 C3
Man-Bazar, India 69 H12
Man Na, Burma 67 H20
Mana →, Fr. Guiana 125 B8
Mana Pools △, Zimbabwe 87 F2
Manaar, G. of = Mannar, G. of, Asia 66 Q11
Manacapuru, Brazil 124 D6
Manacor, Spain 48 B10
Manado, Indonesia 63 D6
Managua, Nic. 120 D2
Managua, L. de, Nic. 120 D2
Manakara, Madag. 89 C8
Manali, India 68 C7
Manama = Al Manāmah, Bahrain 71 E6
Manambao →, Madag. 89 B7
Manambato, Madag. 89 A8
Manambolo →, Madag. 89 B7
Manambolosy, Madag. 89 B8
Mananara, Madag. 89 B8
Mananara ⌓, Madag. 89 B8
Mananara →, Madag. 89 C8
Mananjary, Madag. 89 C8
Manankoro, Mali 82 C3
Manantenina, Madag. 89 C8
Manaos = Manaus, Brazil 124 D7
Manapire →, Venezuela 124 B5
Manapouri, N.Z. 91 L1
Manapouri, L., N.Z. 91 L1
Manaqil, Sudan 81 E3
Manār, Jabal, Yemen 75 E3
Manaravolo, Madag. 89 C8
Manas, China 60 B3
Manas →, India 67 F17
Manaslu, Nepal 69 E11
Manasquan, U.S.A. 117 F10
Manassa, U.S.A. 109 H11
Manatí, Puerto Rico 121 d
Manaung, Burma 67 K18
Manaus, Brazil 124 D7
Manavgat, Turkey 72 D4
Manawan L., Canada 103 B8
Manay, Phil. 61 H7
Manbij, Syria 70 B3
Mancha Real, Spain 37 H7
Manche □, France 18 C5
Manchegorsk, Russia 52 C4
Manchester, U.K. 14 D5
Manchester, Calif., U.S.A. 110 G3
Manchester, Conn., U.S.A. 117 E12
Manchester, Ga., U.S.A. 115 J3
Manchester, Iowa, U.S.A. 112 D9
Manchester, Ky., U.S.A. 114 G4
Manchester, N.H., U.S.A. 117 D13
Manchester, N.Y., U.S.A. 116 D7
Manchester, Pa., U.S.A. 117 F8
Manchester, Tenn., U.S.A. 115 H2
Manchester, Vt., U.S.A. 117 C11
Manchester International ✕ (MAN), U.K. 14 D5
Manchester L., Canada 103 A7
Manchhar L., Pakistan 68 F2
Manchuria = Dongbei, China 53 E13
Manchurian Plain, China 50 E16
Manciano, Italy 41 F8
Mancifa, Ethiopia 81 F5
Mand →, India 69 J10
Mand →, Iran 71 D7
Manda, Ludewe, Tanzania 87 E3
Manda, Mbeya, Tanzania 86 D3
Manda, Mbeya, Tanzania 87 D3
Mandabé, Madag. 89 C7
Mandaguari, Brazil 127 A5
Mandah = Töhöm, Mongolia 56 B5
Mandal, Norway 9 G12
Mandala, Puncak, Indonesia 63 E10
Mandalay, Burma 67 J20
Mandale = Mandalay, Burma 67 J20
Mandalgarh, India 68 G6
Mandalgovi, Mongolia 56 B4
Mandalī, Iraq 70 C5
Mandan, U.S.A. 112 B4
Mandaon, Phil. 61 E5
Mandar, Teluk, Indonesia 63 E5
Mándas, Italy 42 C2
Mandaue, Phil. 61 F5
Mandelieu-la-Napoule, France 21 E10
Mandera, Kenya 86 B5
Mandeville, Jamaica 120 a
Mandi, India 68 D7
Mandi Dabwali, India 68 E6
Mandiana, Guinea 82 C3
Mandimba, Mozam. 87 E4
Mandioli, Indonesia 63 E7
Mandla, India 69 H9
Mandø, Denmark 11 J2
Mandorah, Australia 92 B5
Mandoto, Madag. 89 B8
Mandoúdhion, Greece 46 C5
Mándra, Greece 46 C5
Mandra, Pakistan 68 C5
Mandrákhi, Greece 47 E9
Mandrare →, Madag. 89 D8
Mandritsara, Madag. 89 B8
Mandronarivo, Madag. 89 C8
Mandsaur, India 68 G6
Mandurah, Australia 93 F2
Mandúria, Italy 43 B10
Mandvi, India 68 H3
Mandya, India 66 N10
Mandzai, Pakistan 68 D2
Mané, Burkina Faso 83 C4
Maneh, Iran 71 B8
Manengouba, Mts., Cameroon 83 E6
Manera, Madag. 89 C7
Manérbio, Italy 40 C7
Maneroo Cr. →, Australia 94 C3
Manfalût, Egypt 80 B3
Manfredónia, Italy 41 G12
Manfredónia, G. di, Italy 41 G13
Manga, Burkina Faso 83 C4
Manga, Niger 83 C7
Mangabeiras, Chapada das, Brazil 125 F9
Mangalia, Romania 29 G13
Mangalore, India 66 N9
Mangan, India 69 F13
Mangaung, S. Africa 85 K5
Mangawan, India 69 G9
Mangaweka, N.Z. 91 H5
Manggar, Indonesia 62 E3
Manggawitu, Indonesia 63 E8
Manggis, Indonesia 63 J18
Mangindrano, Madag. 89 A8
Mangkalihat, Tanjung, Indonesia 63 D5
Mangla, Pakistan 68 C5
Mangla Dam, Pakistan 69 C5
Manglaur, India 68 E7
Mangnai, China 60 C4
Mango, Togo 83 C5
Mangoche, Malawi 87 E4
Mangoky →, Madag. 89 C7
Mangole, Indonesia 63 E6
Mangombe, Dem. Rep. of the Congo 86 C2
Mangonui, N.Z. 91 F4
Mangoro →, Madag. 89 B8
Mangrol, Mad. P., India 68 J4
Mangrol, Raj., India 68 G6
Mangualde, Portugal 36 E3
Mangueira, L. da, Brazil 127 C5
Mangum, U.S.A. 113 H5
Mangyshlak Poluostrov, Kazakhstan 52 E6
Manhattan, U.S.A. 112 F6
Manhiça, Mozam. 89 D5
Mania →, Madag. 89 B8
Maniago, Italy 41 B9
Manica, Mozam. 89 B5
Manica □, Mozam. 89 B5
Manicaland □, Zimbabwe 87 F3
Manicoré, Brazil 124 E6
Manicouagan →, Canada 105 C6
Manicouagan, Rés., Canada 105 B6
Maniema □, Dem. Rep. of the Congo 86 C2
Manīfah, Si. Arabia 71 E6
Manifold, C., Australia 94 C5
Maniganggo, China 58 B2
Manigotagan, Canada 103 C9
Manigotagan →, Canada 103 C9
Manihari, India 69 G12
Manihiki, Cook Is. 97 J11
Manika, Plateau de la, Dem. Rep. of the Congo 87 E2
Manikpur, India 69 G9
Manila, Phil. 61 D4
Manila, U.S.A. 108 F9
Manila B., Phil. 61 D4
Manilla, Australia 95 E5
Manimpé, Mali 82 C3
Maningrida, Australia 94 A1
Maninian, Ivory C. 82 C3
Manipur □, India 67 G19
Manipur →, Burma 67 H19
Manisa, Turkey 47 C9
Manisa □, Turkey 47 C9
Manistee, U.S.A. 114 C2
Manistee →, U.S.A. 114 C2
Manistique, U.S.A. 114 C2
Manitoba □, Canada 103 B9
Manitoba, L., Canada 103 C9
Manitou, Canada 103 D9
Manitou, L., Canada 105 B6
Manitou Is., U.S.A. 114 C3
Manitou L., Canada 103 C7
Manitou Springs, U.S.A. 112 F2
Manitoulin I., Canada 104 C3
Manitouwadge, Canada 104 C2
Manitowoc, U.S.A. 114 C2
Manizales, Colombia 124 B3
Manja, Madag. 89 C7
Manjacaze, Mozam. 89 C5
Manjakandriana, Madag. 89 B8
Manjhand, Pakistan 68 G3
Manjil, Iran 71 B6
Manjimup, Australia 93 F2
Manjra →, India 66 K10
Mankato, Kans., U.S.A. 112 F5
Mankato, Minn., U.S.A. 112 C8
Mankayane, Swaziland 89 D5
Mankera, Pakistan 68 D4
Mankim, Cameroon 83 D7
Mankono, Ivory C. 82 D3
Mankota, Canada 103 D7
Manlay = Üydzin, Mongolia 56 B4
Manlleu, Spain 38 C7
Manmad, India 66 J9
Mann Ranges, Australia 93 E5
Manna, Indonesia 62 E2
Mannahill, Australia 95 E3
Mannar, Sri Lanka 66 Q11
Mannar, G. of, Asia 66 Q11
Mannar I., Sri Lanka 66 Q11
Mannheim, Germany 25 F4
Manning, Canada 102 B5
Manning, Oreg., U.S.A. 110 E3
Manning, S.C., U.S.A. 115 J5
Mannu →, Italy 42 C2
Mannu, C., Italy 42 B1
Mannum, Australia 95 E2
Mano, S. Leone 82 D2
Mano →, Liberia 82 D2
Mano River, Liberia 82 D2
Manoharpur, India 69 H11
Manokwari, Indonesia 63 E8
Manolás, Greece 46 C3
Manombo, Madag. 89 C7
Manono, Dem. Rep. of the Congo 86 D2
Manoppello, Italy 41 F11
Manosque, France 21 E9
Manotick, Canada 117 A9
Manouane →, Canada 105 C5
Manouane, L., Canada 105 B5
Manp'o, N. Korea 57 D14
Manpojin = Manp'o, N. Korea 57 D14
Manpur, Chhattisgarh, India 69 H10
Manpur, Mad. P., India 68 H6
Manresa, Spain 38 D6
Mansa, Gujarat, India 68 H5
Mansa, Punjab, India 68 E6
Mansa, Zambia 87 E2
Månsåsen, Sweden 10 A8
Mansehra, Pakistan 68 B5
Mansel I., Canada 101 B11
Mansfield, Australia 95 F4
Mansfield, U.K. 14 D6
Mansfield, La., U.S.A. 113 J8
Mansfield, Mass., U.S.A. 117 D13
Mansfield, Ohio, U.S.A. 116 F2
Mansfield, Pa., U.S.A. 116 E7
Mansfield, Mt., U.S.A. 117 B12
Mansilla de las Mulas, Spain 36 C5
Mansle, France 20 C4
Mansoa, Guinea-Biss. 82 C1
Manson Creek, Canada 102 B4
Manta, Ecuador 124 D2
Mantadia △, Madag. 89 B8
Mantalingajan, Mt., Phil. 61 G2
Mantare, Tanzania 86 C3
Manteca, U.S.A. 110 H5
Manteo, U.S.A. 115 H8
Mantes-la-Jolie, France 19 D8
Manthani, India 66 K11
Manti, U.S.A. 108 G8
Mantiqueira, Serra da, Brazil 127 A7
Manton, U.S.A. 114 C3
Mantorp, Sweden 11 F9
Mántova, Italy 40 C7
Mänttä, Finland 9 E21
Mantua = Mántova, Italy 40 C7
Manturovo, Russia 34 A7
Manu, Peru 124 F4
Manu →, Peru 124 F4
Manu'a Is., Amer. Samoa 91 B14
Manuel Alves →, Brazil 125 F9
Manui, Indonesia 63 E6
Manukau, N.Z. 91 G5
Manuripi →, Bolivia 124 F5
Many, U.S.A. 113 K8
Manyara, L., Tanzania 86 C4
Manyas, Turkey 45 F11
Manych →, Russia 35 G5
Manych-Gudilo, Ozero, Russia 35 G6
Manyonga →, Tanzania 86 C3
Manyoni, Tanzania 86 D3
Manzai, Pakistan 68 C4
Manzala, Bahra el, Egypt 80 H7
Manzanar ⌓, U.S.A. 110 J7
Manzanares, Spain 37 F7
Manzaneda, Spain 36 C3
Manzanillo, Cuba 120 B4
Manzanillo, Mexico 118 D4
Manzanillo, Pta., Panama 120 E4
Manzano Mts., U.S.A. 109 J10
Manzarīyeh, Iran 71 C6
Manzhouli, China 60 B6
Manzini, Swaziland 89 D5
Mao, Chad 79 F9
Maó, Spain 48 B11
Maoke, Pegunungan, Indonesia 63 E9
Maolin, China 57 C12
Maoming, China 59 G8
Maopi T'ou, China 59 G13
Maouri, Dallol →, Niger 83 C5
Maoxian, China 58 B4
Maoxing, China 57 B13
Mapam Yumco, China 60 C3
Mapastepec, Mexico 119 D6
Maphrao, Ko, Thailand 65 a
Mapia, Kepulauan, Indonesia 63 D8
Mapimí, Mexico 118 B4
Mapimí, Bolsón de, Mexico 118 B4
Maping, China 59 B9
Mapinga, Tanzania 86 D4
Mapinhane, Mozam. 89 C6
Maple Creek, Canada 103 D7
Maple Valley, U.S.A. 110 C4
Mapleton, U.S.A. 108 D2
Mapuera →, Brazil 124 D7
Mapulanguene, Mozam. 89 C5
Maputo, Mozam. 89 D5
Maputo ⌓, Mozam. 89 D5
Maputo □, Mozam. 89 D5
Maputo, B. de, Mozam. 89 D5
Maqiaohe, China 57 B16
Maqnā, Si. Arabia 70 D2
Maquan He = Brahmaputra →, Asia 69 H13
Maqueda, Spain 36 E6
Maquela do Zombo, Angola 84 F3
Maquinchao, Argentina 128 E3
Maquoketa, U.S.A. 112 D9
Mar, Serra do, Brazil 127 B6
Mar Chiquita, L., Argentina 126 C3
Mar del Plata, Argentina 126 D4
Mar Menor, Spain 39 H4
Mara, Tanzania 86 C3
Mara □, Tanzania 86 C3
Maraã, Brazil 124 D5
Marabá, Brazil 125 E9
Maracá, I. de, Brazil 125 C8
Maracaibo, Venezuela 124 A4
Maracaibo, L. de, Venezuela 124 B4
Maracaju, Brazil 127 A4
Maracas Bay Village, Trin. & Tob. 125 K15
Maracay, Venezuela 124 A5
Maracena, Spain 37 H7
Maradi, Niger 83 C6
Marāgheh, Iran 70 B5
Marāh, Si. Arabia 70 E5
Marahoue △, Ivory C. 82 D3
Marais du Cotentin et du Bessin ⌓, France 18 C5
Marais Poitevin, Val de Sèvre et Vendée ⌓, France 20 B3
Marajó, I. de, Brazil 125 D9
Marākand, Iran 70 B5
Marakele △, S. Africa 89 E4
Maralal, Kenya 86 B4
Maralinga, Australia 93 F5
Maramaraereğlisi, Turkey 45 F11
Marambio, Antarctica 5 C18
Marampa, S. Leone 82 D2
Maramureş □, Romania 29 C9
Maran, Malaysia 65 L4
Marana, U.S.A. 109 K8
Maranboy, Australia 92 B5
Maranchón, Spain 38 D2
Marand, Iran 70 B5
Marang, Malaysia 65 K4
Maranguape, Brazil 125 D11
Maranhão = São Luís, Brazil 125 D10
Maranhão □, Brazil 125 E9
Marano, L. di, Italy 41 C10
Maranoa →, Australia 95 D4
Marañón →, Peru 124 D4
Marão, Mozam. 89 C5
Maraş = Kahramanmaraş, Turkey 70 B3
Mărăşeşti, Romania 29 E12
Maratea, Italy 43 C8
Marateca, Portugal 37 G2
Marathasa, Cyprus 49 E11
Marathókambos, Greece 47 D8
Marathon, Australia 94 C3
Marathon, Canada 104 C2
Marathón, Greece 46 C5
Marathon, N.Y., U.S.A. 117 D8
Marathon, Tex., U.S.A. 113 K3
Marathóvouno, Cyprus 49 D12
Maratua, Indonesia 63 D5
Maraval, Trin. & Tob. 125 K15
Maravatío, Mexico 118 D4
Marawi City, Phil. 61 G6
Marāwih, U.A.E. 71 E7
Marbella, Spain 37 J6
Marble Bar, Australia 92 D2
Marble Falls, U.S.A. 113 K5
Marblehead, U.S.A. 117 D14
Marburg, Germany 24 E4
Marcal →, Hungary 28 C2
Marcali, Hungary 28 D2
Marcaria, Italy 40 C7
Mărcăuţi, Moldova 29 B12
March, U.K. 15 E8
Marche, France 20 B5
Marche □, Italy 41 E10
Marche-en-Famenne, Belgium 17 D5
Marchena, Spain 37 H5
Marches = Marche □, Italy 41 E10
Marchesale ⌓, Italy 43 D9
Marciana Marina, Italy 40 F7
Marcianise, Italy 43 A7
Marcigny, France 19 F11
Marcillat-en-Combraille, France 19 F9
Marck, France 19 B8
Marckolsheim, France 19 D14
Marco, U.S.A. 115 N5
Marcos Juárez, Argentina 126 C3
Mărculeşti, Moldova 29 C13
Marcus I. = Minami-Tori-Shima, Pac. Oc. 96 E7
Marcus Necker Ridge, Pac. Oc. 96 F9
Marcy, Mt., U.S.A. 117 B11
Mardan, Pakistan 68 B5
Mardin, Turkey 70 B4
Mårdsjön, Sweden 10 A9
Marécchia →, Italy 41 D9
Maree, L., U.K. 13 D3
Mareeba, Australia 94 B4
Mareetsane, S. Africa 88 D4
Maremma, Italy 41 F8
Maremma ⌓, Italy 40 F8
Maréna, Kayes, Mali 82 C2
Maréna, Koulikouro, Mali 82 C3
Marengo, U.S.A. 112 E8
Marennes, France 20 C2
Marerano, Madag. 89 C7
Marettimo, Italy 42 E5
Mareuil, France 20 C4
Marfa, U.S.A. 113 K2
Marfa Pt., Malta 49 D1
Marganets = Marhanets, Ukraine 33 J8
Margaret →, Australia 92 C4
Margaret Bay, Canada 102 C3
Margaret L., Canada 102 B5
Margaret River, Australia 93 F2
Margarita, I. de, Venezuela 124 A6
Margarítion, Greece 46 B2
Margaritovo, Russia 54 C7
Margate, S. Africa 89 E5
Margate, U.K. 15 F9
Margeride, Mts. de la, France 20 D7
Margherita di Savóia, Italy 43 A9
Margherita Pk., Uganda 86 B3
Marghita, Romania 28 C7
Margonin, Poland 31 F4
Margosatubig, Phil. 61 H5
Margow, Dasht-e, Afghan. 66 D3
Marguerite, Canada 102 C4
Marhanets, Ukraine 33 J8
Mari El □, Russia 34 B8
Mari Indus, Pakistan 68 C4
Mari Republic = Mari El □, Russia 34 B8
María, Sa. de, Spain 39 H2
María Elena, Chile 126 A2
María Grande, Argentina 126 C4
Maria I., N. Terr., Australia 94 A2
Maria I., Tas., Australia 95 G4
Maria Island △, Australia 95 G4
Maria van Diemen, C., N.Z. 91 F4
Mariager, Denmark 11 H3
Mariager Fjord, Denmark 11 H4
Mariakani, Kenya 86 C4
Mariala △, Australia 95 D4
Marian, Australia 94 K6
Marian L., Canada 102 A5
Mariana Trench, Pac. Oc. 96 F6
Marianao, Cuba 120 B3
Marianna, Ark., U.S.A. 113 H9
Marianna, Fla., U.S.A. 115 K3
Mariannelund, Sweden 11 G9
Mariánské Lázně, Czech Rep. 26 B5
Marias →, U.S.A. 108 C8
Mariato, Punta, Panama 120 E3
Mariazell, Austria 26 D8
Maribo, Denmark 11 K5
Maribor, Slovenia 41 B12
Marico →, Africa 88 C4
Maricopa, Ariz., U.S.A. 109 K7
Maricopa, Calif., U.S.A. 111 K7
Marîdî, Sudan 81 G2
Marîdî, Wadi →, Sudan 81 F2
Marié →, Brazil 124 D5
Marie Byrd Land, Antarctica 5 D14
Marie-Galante, Guadeloupe 120 b
Mariecourt = Kangiqsujuaq, Canada 101 B12
Mariefred, Sweden 10 E11
Marieholm, Sweden 11 J7
Mariembourg, Belgium 17 D4
Marienbad = Mariánské Lázně, Czech Rep. 26 B5
Marienberg, Germany 24 E9
Mariental, Namibia 88 C2
Marienville, U.S.A. 116 E5
Mariestad, Sweden 11 F7
Marietta, Ga., U.S.A. 115 J3
Marietta, Ohio, U.S.A. 114 F5
Marieville, Canada 117 A11
Mariga →, Nigeria 83 C6
Marignane, France 21 E9
Marihatag, Phil. 61 G7
Mariinsk, Russia 52 D9
Mariinskiy Posad, Russia 34 B8
Marijampolė, Lithuania 9 J20
Marijampolės □, Lithuania 30 D10
Marília, Brazil 127 A6
Marín, Spain 36 C2
Marina, U.S.A. 110 J5
Marinduque, Phil. 63 B6
Marine City, U.S.A. 116 D2
Marineo, Italy 42 E6
Marinette, U.S.A. 114 C2
Maringá, Brazil 127 A5
Marinha Grande, Portugal 36 F2
Marino, Italy 41 G9
Marion, Ala., U.S.A. 115 J2
Marion, Ill., U.S.A. 113 G10
Marion, Ind., U.S.A. 114 E3
Marion, Iowa, U.S.A. 112 D9
Marion, Kans., U.S.A. 112 F6
Marion, N.C., U.S.A. 115 H5
Marion, Ohio, U.S.A. 114 E4
Marion, S.C., U.S.A. 115 H6
Marion, Va., U.S.A. 115 G5
Marion, L., U.S.A. 115 J5
Mariposa, U.S.A. 110 H7
Mariscal Estigarribia, Paraguay 126 A3
Maritime Alps = Maritimes, Alpes, Europe 21 D11
Maritimes, Alpes, Europe 21 D11
Maritsa = Évros →, Greece 72 B2
Maritsá, Greece 49 C10
Mariupol, Ukraine 33 J9
Mariusa △, Venezuela 121 E7
Marīvān, Iran 70 C5
Marj 'Uyūn, Lebanon 74 B4
Marka = Merca, Somali Rep. 75 G3
Marka, Si. Arabia 80 D5
Markam, China 58 C2
Markaryd, Sweden 11 H7
Markdale, Canada 116 B4
Marked Tree, U.S.A. 113 H9
Markelsdorfer Huk, Germany 24 A7
Market Drayton, U.K. 14 E5
Market Harborough, U.K. 15 E7
Market Rasen, U.K. 14 D7
Markham, Canada 116 C5
Markham, Mt., Antarctica 5 E11
Marki, Poland 31 F8
Märkische Schweiz ⌓, Germany 24 C10
Markkleeberg, Germany 24 D8
Markleeville, U.S.A. 110 G7
Markoupoulon, Greece 46 D5
Markovac, Serbia & M. 44 B5
Markovo, Russia 53 C17
Markoye, Burkina Faso 83 C5
Marks, Russia 34 E8
Marksville, U.S.A. 113 K8
Markt Schwaben, Germany 25 G7
Marktoberdorf, Germany 25 H6
Marktredwitz, Germany 25 E8
Marl, Germany 24 D3
Marla, Australia 95 D1
Marlbank, Canada 116 B7
Marlboro, Mass., U.S.A. 117 D13
Marlboro, N.Y., U.S.A. 117 E11
Marlborough, Australia 94 C4
Marlborough, U.K. 15 F6
Marlborough Downs, U.K. 15 F6
Marle, France 19 C10
Marlin, U.S.A. 113 K6
Marlow, Germany 24 A8
Marlow, U.K. 15 F7
Marlow, U.S.A. 113 H6
Marmagao, India 66 M8
Marmande, France 20 D4
Marmara, Turkey 45 F11
Marmara, Sea of = Marmara Denizi, Turkey 45 F12

Marmara Denizi, *Turkey* 45 F12
Marmara Gölü, *Turkey* 47 C10
Marmaris, *Turkey* 47 E10
Marmaris Limanı, *Turkey* 47 E10
Marmion, Mt., *Australia* 93 E2
Marmion L., *Canada* 104 C1
Marmolada, Mte., *Italy* 41 B8
Marmolejo, *Spain* 37 G6
Marmora, *Canada* 116 B7
Mármora, La, *Italy* 42 C2
Marnay, *France* 19 E12
Marne, *Germany* 24 B5
Marne □, *France* 19 D11
Marne →, *France* 19 D9
Marneuli, *Georgia* 35 K7
Maroala, *Madag.* 89 B8
Maroantsetra, *Madag.* 89 B8
Maroelaboom, *Namibia* 88 B2
Marofandilia, *Madag.* 89 C7
Marojejy ⌂, *Madag.* 89 A8
Marolambo, *Madag.* 89 C8
Maromandia, *Madag.* 89 A8
Maromokotro, *Madag.* 89 A8
Marondera, *Zimbabwe* 87 F3
Maroni →, *Fr. Guiana* 125 B8
Marónia, *Greece* 45 F9
Maronne →, *France* 20 C5
Maroochydore, *Australia* 95 D5
Maroona, *Australia* 95 F3
Maros →, *Hungary* 28 D5
Marosakoa, *Madag.* 89 B8
Maroseranana, *Madag.* 89 B8
Maróstica, *Italy* 41 C8
Marotandrano, *Madag.* 89 B8
Marotaolano, *Madag.* 89 A8
Maroua, *Cameroon* 83 C7
Marovato, *Madag.* 89 B8
Marovoay, *Madag.* 89 B8
Marquard, *S. Africa* 88 D4
Marquesas Is. = Marquises, Is., *Pac. Oc.* 97 H14
Marquette, *U.S.A.* 114 B2
Marquis, *St. Lucia* 121 f
Marquise, *France* 19 B8
Marquises, Is., *Pac. Oc.* 97 H14
Marra, Djebel, *Sudan* 79 F10
Marra, Gebel, *Sudan* 81 F2
Marracuene, *Mozam.* 89 D5
Marradi, *Italy* 41 D8
Marrakech, *Morocco* 78 B4
Marratxi, *Spain* 38 F7
Marrawah, *Australia* 95 G3
Marree, *Australia* 95 D2
Marrero, *U.S.A.* 113 L9
Marrimane, *Mozam.* 89 C5
Marromeu, *Mozam.* 89 B6
Marromeu ⌂, *Mozam.* 89 B6
Marroquí, Punta, *Spain* 37 K5
Marrowie Cr. →, *Australia* 95 E4
Marrubane, *Mozam.* 87 F4
Marrúbiu, *Italy* 42 C1
Marrupa, *Mozam.* 87 E4
Mars Hill, *U.S.A.* 115 B12
Marsá 'Alam, *Egypt* 80 B3
Marsá Matrûh, *Egypt* 80 A2
Marsá Sha'b, *Sudan* 80 C4
Marsabit, *Kenya* 86 B4
Marsabit △, *Kenya* 86 B4
Marsala, *Italy* 42 E5
Marsalforn, *Malta* 49 C1
Mârşani, *Romania* 29 F9
Marsberg, *Germany* 24 D4
Marsciano, *Italy* 41 F9
Marsden, *Australia* 95 E4
Marseillan, *France* 20 E7
Marseille, *France* 21 E9
Marseille ✕ (MRS), *France* 21 E9
Marseilles = Marseille, *France* 21 E9
Marsh I., *U.S.A.* 113 L9
Marshall, *Liberia* 82 D2
Marshall, *Ark., U.S.A.* 113 H8
Marshall, *Mich., U.S.A.* 114 D3
Marshall, *Minn., U.S.A.* 112 C7
Marshall, *Mo., U.S.A.* 112 F8
Marshall, *Tex., U.S.A.* 113 J7
Marshall →, *Australia* 94 C2
Marshall Is. ■, *Pac. Oc.* 96 G9
Marshalltown, *U.S.A.* 112 D8
Marshbrook, *Zimbabwe* 89 B5
Marshfield, *Mo., U.S.A.* 113 G8
Marshfield, *Vt., U.S.A.* 117 B12
Marshfield, *Wis., U.S.A.* 112 C9
Marshūn, *Iran* 71 B6
Mársico Nuovo, *Italy* 43 B8
Märsta, *Sweden* 10 E11
Marstal, *Denmark* 11 K4
Marstrand, *Sweden* 11 G5
Mart, *U.S.A.* 113 K6
Marta →, *Italy* 41 F8
Martaban, *Burma* 67 L20
Martaban, G. of, *Burma* 67 L20
Martano, *Italy* 43 B11
Martapura, *Kalimantan, Indonesia* 62 E4
Martapura, *Sumatera, Indonesia* 62 E2
Marte, *Nigeria* 83 C7
Martel, *France* 20 D5
Martelange, *Belgium* 17 E5
Martellago, *Italy* 41 C9
Martés, Sierra, *Spain* 39 F4
Martfű, *Hungary* 28 C5
Martha's Vineyard, *U.S.A.* 117 E14
Martigné-Ferchaud, *France* 18 E5
Martigny, *Switz.* 25 J3
Martigues, *France* 21 E9
Martin, *Slovak Rep.* 27 B11
Martin, *S. Dak., U.S.A.* 112 D4
Martin, *Tenn., U.S.A.* 113 G10
Martín →, *Spain* 38 D4
Martin, L., *U.S.A.* 115 J3
Martina Franca, *Italy* 43 B10
Martinborough, *N.Z.* 91 J5
Martinez, *Calif., U.S.A.* 110 G4
Martinez, *Ga., U.S.A.* 115 J4
Martinique ⊠, *W. Indies* 120 c
Martinique Passage, *W. Indies* 121 C7
Martínon, *Greece* 46 C5
Martinópolis, *Brazil* 127 A5
Martin's Bay, *Barbados* 121 g
Martins Ferry, *U.S.A.* 116 F4
Martinsberg, *Austria* 26 C8
Martinsburg, *Pa., U.S.A.* 116 F6
Martinsburg, *W. Va., U.S.A.* 114 F7
Martinsicuro, *Italy* 41 F10
Martinsville, *Ind., U.S.A.* 114 F2
Martinsville, *Va., U.S.A.* 115 G6
Marton, *N.Z.* 91 J5
Martorell, *Spain* 38 D6
Martos, *Spain* 37 H7
Martuni, *Armenia* 35 K7
Maru, *Nigeria* 83 C6
Marudi, *Malaysia* 62 D4
Maruf, *Afghan.* 66 D5
Marugame, *Japan* 55 G6
Marunga, *Angola* 88 B3
Marungu, Mts., *Dem. Rep. of the Congo* 86 D3
Marv Dasht, *Iran* 71 D7
Marvast, *Iran* 71 D7
Marvejols, *France* 20 D7
Marvel Loch, *Australia* 93 F2
Marwar, *India* 68 G5
Mary, *Turkmenistan* 52 F7
Maryborough = Port Laoise, *Ireland* 12 C4
Maryborough, *Queens., Australia* 95 D5
Maryborough, *Vic., Australia* 95 F3
Maryfield, *Canada* 103 D8
Maryland □, *U.S.A.* 114 F7
Maryland Junction, *Zimbabwe* 87 F3
Maryport, *U.K.* 14 C4
Mary's Harbour, *Canada* 105 B8
Marystown, *Canada* 105 C8
Marysville, *Canada* 102 D5
Marysville, *Calif., U.S.A.* 110 F5
Marysville, *Kans., U.S.A.* 112 F6
Marysville, *Mich., U.S.A.* 116 D2
Marysville, *Ohio, U.S.A.* 114 E4
Marysville, *Wash., U.S.A.* 110 B4
Maryville, *Mo., U.S.A.* 112 E7
Maryville, *Tenn., U.S.A.* 115 H4
Marzūq, *Libya* 79 C8
Masahunga, *Tanzania* 86 C3
Masai, *Malaysia* 65 d
Masai Mara △, *Kenya* 86 C4
Masai Steppe, *Tanzania* 86 C4
Masaka, *Uganda* 86 C3
Masalembo, Kepulauan, *Indonesia* 62 F4
Masalima, Kepulauan, *Indonesia* 62 F5
Masallı, *Azerbaijan* 73 C13
Masamba, *Indonesia* 63 E6
Masan, *S. Korea* 57 G15
Masandam, Ra's, *Oman* 71 E8
Masasi, *Tanzania* 87 E4
Masaya, *Nic.* 120 D2
Masba, *Nigeria* 83 C7
Masbate, *Phil.* 61 E5
Máscali, *Italy* 43 E8
Mascara, *Algeria* 78 A6
Mascota, *Mexico* 118 C4
Masela, *Indonesia* 63 F7
Maseru, *Lesotho* 88 D4
Mashaba, *Zimbabwe* 87 G3
Mashābih, *Si. Arabia* 70 E3
Mashan, *China* 58 F7
Mashar, *Sudan* 81 F2
Mashatu ⌂, *Botswana* 89 C4
Mashegu, *Nigeria* 83 D6
Masherbrum, *Pakistan* 69 B7
Mashhad, *Iran* 71 B8
Mashi, *Nigeria* 83 C6
Mashīz, *Iran* 71 D8
Māshkel, Hāmūn-i-, *Pakistan* 66 E3
Mashki Chāh, *Pakistan* 66 E3
Mashonaland, *Zimbabwe* 85 H6
Mashonaland Central □, *Zimbabwe* 89 B5
Mashonaland East □, *Zimbabwe* 89 B5
Mashonaland West □, *Zimbabwe* 89 B4
Mashrakh, *India* 69 F11
Mashtaga = Maştağa, *Azerbaijan* 35 K10
Masindi, *Uganda* 86 B3
Masindi Port, *Uganda* 86 B3
Maşīrah, *Oman* 75 C6
Maşīrah, Khalīj, *Oman* 75 C6
Masisi, *Dem. Rep. of the Congo* 86 C2
Masjed Soleyman, *Iran* 71 D6
Mask, L., *Ireland* 12 C2
Maskin, *Oman* 71 F8
Maslen Nos, *Bulgaria* 45 D11
Maslinica, *Croatia* 41 E13
Masnou = El Masnou, *Spain* 38 D7
Masoala △, *Madag.* 89 B9
Masoala, Tanjon' i, *Madag.* 89 B9
Masoarivo, *Madag.* 89 B7
Masohi = Amahai, *Indonesia* 63 E7
Masomeloka, *Madag.* 89 C8
Mason, *Nev., U.S.A.* 110 G7
Mason, *Tex., U.S.A.* 113 K5
Mason City, *U.S.A.* 112 D8
Maspalomas, *Canary Is.* 48 G4
Maspalomas, Pta., *Canary Is.* 48 G4
Masqat, *Oman* 75 C6
Massa, *Italy* 40 D7
Massa Maríttima, *Italy* 40 E7
Massachusetts □, *U.S.A.* 117 D13
Massachusetts B., *U.S.A.* 117 D14
Massafra, *Italy* 43 B10
Massakory, *Chad* 79 F9
Massanella, *Spain* 48 B9
Massangena, *Mozam.* 89 C5
Massango, *Angola* 84 F3
Massat, *France* 20 F5
Massawa = Mitsiwa, *Eritrea* 81 D4
Massena, *U.S.A.* 117 B10
Massénya, *Chad* 79 F9
Masset, *Canada* 102 C2
Masseube, *France* 20 E4
Massiac, *France* 20 C7
Massiah Street, *Barbados* 121 g
Massif Central, *France* 20 D7
Massif des Bauges ⌂, *France* 19 G13
Massigui, *Mali* 82 C3
Massillon, *U.S.A.* 116 F3
Massinga, *Mozam.* 89 C6
Massingir, *Mozam.* 89 C5
Mässlingen, *Sweden* 10 B6
Masson-Angers, *Canada* 117 A9
Masson I., *Antarctica* 5 C7
Maştağa, *Azerbaijan* 35 K10
Mastanli = Momchilgrad, *Bulgaria* 45 E9
Masterton, *N.Z.* 91 J5
Mastic, *U.S.A.* 117 F12
Mástikho, Ákra, *Greece* 47 C8
Mastuj, *Pakistan* 69 A5
Mastung, *Pakistan* 66 E5
Mastūrah, *Si. Arabia* 80 C4
Masty, *Belarus* 32 F3
Masuda, *Japan* 55 G5
Masvingo, *Zimbabwe* 87 G3
Masvingo □, *Zimbabwe* 87 G3
Maswa ⌂, *Tanzania* 86 C3
Maşyāf, *Syria* 70 C3
Maszewo, *Poland* 30 E2
Mat →, *Albania* 44 E3
Matabeleland, *Zimbabwe* 85 H5
Matabeleland North □, *Zimbabwe* 87 F2
Matabeleland South □, *Zimbabwe* 87 G2
Matachel →, *Spain* 37 G4
Matachewan, *Canada* 104 C3
Matadi, *Dem. Rep. of the Congo* 84 F2
Matagalpa, *Nic.* 120 D2
Matagami, *Canada* 104 C4
Matagami, L., *Canada* 104 C4
Matagorda B., *U.S.A.* 113 L6
Matagorda I., *U.S.A.* 113 L6
Matak, *Indonesia* 62 D3
Mátala, *Greece* 49 E6
Matam, *Senegal* 82 B2
Matameye, *Niger* 83 C6
Matamoros, *Campeche, Mexico* 119 D6
Matamoros, *Coahuila, Mexico* 118 B4
Matamoros, *Tamaulipas, Mexico* 119 B5
Ma'ṭan as Sarra, *Libya* 79 D10
Matandu →, *Tanzania* 87 D3
Matane, *Canada* 105 C6
Matang, *China* 58 F5
Matankari, *Niger* 83 C5
Matanomadh, *India* 68 H3
Matanzas, *Cuba* 120 B3
Matapa, *Botswana* 88 C3
Matapan, C. = Taínaron, Ákra, *Greece* 46 E4
Matapédia, *Canada* 105 C6
Matapo △, *Zimbabwe* 87 G2
Matara, *Sri Lanka* 66 S12
Mataram, *Indonesia* 63 K19
Matarani, *Peru* 124 G4
Mataranka, *Australia* 92 B5
Matarma, Râs, *Egypt* 74 E1
Mataró, *Spain* 38 D7
Matarraña →, *Spain* 38 D5
Mataruška Banja, *Serbia & M.* 44 C4
Matatiele, *S. Africa* 89 E4
Mataura, *N.Z.* 91 M2
Matehuala, *Mexico* 118 C4
Mateke Hills, *Zimbabwe* 87 G3
Matelot, *Trin. & Tob.* 125 K15
Matera, *Italy* 43 B9
Matese ⌂, *Italy* 43 A7
Matese, Monti del, *Italy* 43 A7
Mátészalka, *Hungary* 28 C7
Matetsi, *Zimbabwe* 87 F2
Matfors, *Sweden* 10 B11
Matha, *France* 20 C3
Matheniko ⌂, *Uganda* 86 B3
Mathis, *U.S.A.* 113 L6
Mathráki, *Greece* 49 A3
Mathura, *India* 68 F7
Mati, *Phil.* 61 H7
Matiakoali, *Burkina Faso* 83 C5
Matiali, *India* 69 F13
Matías Romero, *Mexico* 119 D5
Matibane, *Mozam.* 87 E5
Matiri Ra., *N.Z.* 91 J4
Matjiesfontein, *S. Africa* 88 E3
Matla →, *India* 69 J13
Matlamanyane, *Botswana* 88 B4
Matli, *Pakistan* 68 G3
Matlock, *U.K.* 14 D6
Matna, *Sudan* 81 E4
Mato Grosso □, *Brazil* 125 F8
Mato Grosso, Planalto do, *Brazil* 125 G8
Mato Grosso do Sul □, *Brazil* 125 G8
Matobo = Matapo △, *Zimbabwe* 87 G2
Matochkin Shar, *Russia* 52 B6
Matopo Hills, *Zimbabwe* 87 G2
Matopos, *Zimbabwe* 87 G2
Matosinhos, *Portugal* 36 D2
Matour, *France* 19 F11
Matroosberg, *S. Africa* 88 E2
Maţruḩ, *Oman* 75 C6
Matsena, *Nigeria* 83 C7
Matsesta, *Russia* 35 J4
Matsu Tao, *Taiwan* 59 E13
Matsue, *Japan* 55 G6
Matsum, Ko, *Thailand* 65 b
Matsumae, *Japan* 54 D10
Matsumoto, *Japan* 55 F9
Matsusaka, *Japan* 55 G8
Matsuura, *Japan* 55 H4
Matsuyama, *Japan* 55 H6
Mattagami →, *Canada* 104 B3
Mattancheri, *India* 66 Q10
Mattawa, *Canada* 104 C4
Matterhorn, *Switz.* 25 K3
Mattersburg, *Austria* 27 D9
Matthew Town, *Bahamas* 121 B5
Matthew's Ridge, *Guyana* 124 B6
Mattice, *Canada* 104 C3
Mattituck, *U.S.A.* 117 F12
Mattō, *Japan* 55 F8
Mattoon, *U.S.A.* 114 F1
Matuba, *Mozam.* 89 C5
Matucana, *Peru* 124 F3
Matūn = Khowst, *Afghan.* 68 C3
Matura B., *Trin. & Tob.* 125 K15
Maturín, *Venezuela* 124 B6
Matusadona △, *Zimbabwe* 87 F2
Matveyev Kurgan, *Russia* 33 J10
Matxitxako, C., *Spain* 38 B2
Mau, *Mad. P., India* 69 F8
Mau, *Ut. P., India* 69 G10
Mau, *Ut. P., India* 69 G9
Mau Escarpment, *Kenya* 86 C4
Mau Ranipur, *India* 69 G8
Maubeuge, *France* 19 B10
Maubourguet, *France* 20 E4
Maud, Pt., *Australia* 92 D1
Maude, *Australia* 95 E3
Maudin Sun, *Burma* 67 M19
Maués, *Brazil* 124 D7
Mauganj, *India* 67 G12
Maughold Hd., *U.K.* 14 C3
Mauguio, *France* 20 E7
Maui, *U.S.A.* 106 H16
Maulamyaing = Moulmein, *Burma* 67 L20
Maule □, *Chile* 126 D1
Mauléon-Licharre, *France* 20 E3
Maumee, *U.S.A.* 114 E4
Maumee →, *U.S.A.* 114 E4
Maumere, *Indonesia* 63 F6
Maumusson, Pertuis de, *France* 20 C2
Maun, *Botswana* 88 C3
Mauna Kea, *U.S.A.* 106 J17
Mauna Loa, *U.S.A.* 106 J17
Maungmagan Kyunzu, *Burma* 64 E1
Maupin, *U.S.A.* 108 D3
Maure-de-Bretagne, *France* 18 E5
Maurepas, L., *U.S.A.* 113 K9
Maures, *France* 21 E10
Mauriac, *France* 20 C6
Maurice, L., *Australia* 93 E5
Mauricie △, *Canada* 104 C5
Maurienne, *France* 21 C10
Mauritania ■, *Africa* 78 E3
Mauritius ■, *Ind. Oc.* 77 J9
Mauron, *France* 18 D4
Maurs, *France* 20 D6
Mauston, *U.S.A.* 112 D9
Mauterndorf, *Austria* 26 D6
Mauthen, *Austria* 26 E6
Mauvezin, *France* 20 E4
Mauzé-sur-le-Mignon, *France* 20 B3
Mavli, *India* 68 G5
Mavrovë, *Albania* 44 F3
Mavrovo △, *Macedonia* 44 E4
Mavuradonha Mts., *Zimbabwe* 87 F3
Mawa, *Dem. Rep. of the Congo* 86 B2
Mawai, *India* 69 H9
Mawana, *India* 68 E7
Mawand, *Pakistan* 68 E3
Mawk Mai, *Burma* 67 J20
Mawlaik, *Burma* 67 H19
Mawlamyine = Moulmein, *Burma* 67 L20
Mawqaq, *Si. Arabia* 70 E4
Mawson Base, *Antarctica* 5 C6
Mawson Coast, *Antarctica* 5 C6
Max, *U.S.A.* 112 B4
Maxcanú, *Mexico* 119 C6
Maxesibeni, *S. Africa* 89 E4
Maxhamish L., *Canada* 102 B4
Maxixe, *Mozam.* 89 C6
Maxville, *Canada* 117 A10
Maxwell, *U.S.A.* 110 F4
Maxwelton, *Australia* 94 C3
May, C., *U.S.A.* 114 F8
May Pen, *Jamaica* 120 a
Maya →, *Russia* 53 D14
Maya Mts., *Belize* 119 D7
Mayaguana, *Bahamas* 121 B5
Mayagüez, *Puerto Rico* 121 d
Mayahi, *Niger* 83 C6
Mayals = Maials, *Spain* 38 D5
Mayāmey, *Iran* 71 B7
Mayang, *China* 58 D7
Mayanup, *Australia* 93 F2
Mayapán, *Mexico* 119 C7
Mayapan, *Yucatán, Mexico* 119 C7
Mayarí, *Cuba* 121 B4
Mayaro B., *Trin. & Tob.* 125 K16
Maybell, *U.S.A.* 108 F9
Maybole, *U.K.* 13 F4
Maychew, *Ethiopia* 81 E4
Maydān, *Iraq* 70 C5
Maydena, *Australia* 95 G4
Mayen, *Germany* 25 E3
Mayenne, *France* 18 D6
Mayenne □, *France* 18 D6
Mayenne →, *France* 18 E6
Mayer, *U.S.A.* 109 J7
Mayerthorpe, *Canada* 102 C5
Mayfield, *Ky., U.S.A.* 115 G1
Mayfield, *N.Y., U.S.A.* 117 C10
Mayhill, *U.S.A.* 109 K11
Maykop, *Russia* 35 H5
Maymyo, *Burma* 64 A1
Maynard, *Mass., U.S.A.* 117 D13
Maynard, *Wash., U.S.A.* 110 C4
Maynard Hills, *Australia* 93 E2
Mayne →, *Australia* 94 C3
Maynooth, *Ireland* 12 C5
Mayo, *Canada* 100 B6
Mayo □, *Ireland* 12 C2
Mayo Daga, *Nigeria* 83 D7
Mayo Faran, *Nigeria* 83 D7
Mayon Volcano, *Phil.* 61 E5
Mayor I., *N.Z.* 91 G6
Mayorga, *Spain* 36 C5
Mayotte, *Ind. Oc.* 85 G9
Mayraira Pt., *Phil.* 61 B4
Maysān □, *Iraq* 70 D5
Mayskiy, *Russia* 35 J7
Maysville, *U.S.A.* 114 F4
Mayu, *Indonesia* 63 D7
Mayville, *N. Dak., U.S.A.* 112 B6
Mayville, *N.Y., U.S.A.* 116 D5
Mayya, *Russia* 53 C14
Mazabuka, *Zambia* 87 F2
Mazagán = El Jadida, *Morocco* 78 B4
Mazagão, *Brazil* 125 D8
Mazamet, *France* 20 E6
Mazán, *Peru* 124 D4
Māzandarān □, *Iran* 71 B7
Mazapil, *Mexico* 118 C4
Mazara del Vallo, *Italy* 42 E5
Mazarrón, *Spain* 39 H3
Mazarrón, G. de, *Spain* 39 H3
Mazaruni →, *Guyana* 124 B7
Mazatán, *Mexico* 118 B2
Mazatenango, *Guatemala* 120 D1
Mazatlán, *Mexico* 118 C3
Mažeikiai, *Lithuania* 9 H20
Māzhān, *Iran* 71 C8
Mazīnān, *Iran* 71 B8
Mazoe, *Mozam.* 87 F3
Mazoe →, *Mozam.* 87 F3
Mazowe, *Zimbabwe* 87 F3
Mazowieckie □, *Poland* 31 F8
Mazrûb, *Sudan* 81 E2
Mazu Dao, *China* 59 D12
Mazurian Lakes = Mazurski, Pojezierze, *Poland* 30 E7
Mazurski, Pojezierze, *Poland* 30 E7
Mazyr, *Belarus* 33 F5
Mbaba, *Senegal* 82 C1
Mbabane, *Swaziland* 89 D5
Mbagne, *Mauritania* 82 B2
M'bahiakro, *Ivory C.* 82 D4
Mbaïki, *C.A.R.* 84 D3
Mbala, *Zambia* 87 D3
Mbalabala, *Zimbabwe* 89 C4
Mbale, *Uganda* 86 B3
Mbalmayo, *Cameroon* 83 E7
Mbam →, *Cameroon* 83 E7
Mbamba Bay, *Tanzania* 87 E3
Mbandaka, *Dem. Rep. of the Congo* 84 D3
Mbanga, *Cameroon* 83 E6
Mbanza Congo, *Angola* 84 F2
Mbanza Ngungu, *Dem. Rep. of the Congo* 84 F2
Mbarangandu, *Tanzania* 87 D4
Mbarara, *Uganda* 86 C3
Mbashe →, *S. Africa* 89 E4
Mbatto, *Ivory C.* 82 D4
Mbenkuru →, *Tanzania* 87 D4
Mberengwa, *Zimbabwe* 87 G2
Mberengwa, Mt., *Zimbabwe* 87 G2
Mberubu, *Nigeria* 83 D6
Mbesuma, *Zambia* 87 E3
Mbeya, *Tanzania* 87 D3
Mbeya □, *Tanzania* 86 D3
M'bili, *Sudan* 81 F2
Mbinga, *Tanzania* 87 E4
Mbini = Río Muni □, *Eq. Guin.* 84 D2
Mboki, *C.A.R.* 81 F2
M'bonge, *Cameroon* 83 E6
Mboro, *Senegal* 82 B1
M'boukou, Rés. de, *Cameroon* 83 D7
Mboune, *Senegal* 82 C2
Mbour, *Senegal* 82 C1
Mbout, *Mauritania* 82 B2
Mbuji-Mayi, *Dem. Rep. of the Congo* 86 D1
Mbulu, *Tanzania* 86 C4
Mburucuyá, *Argentina* 126 B4
McCarran International, Las Vegas ✕ (LAS), *U.S.A.* 111 J11
Mchinja, *Tanzania* 87 D4
Mchinji, *Malawi* 87 E3
McMurdo, *Antarctica* 5 D11
Mdantsane, *S. Africa* 85 L5
Mead, L., *U.S.A.* 111 J12
Meade, *U.S.A.* 113 G4
Meadow Lake, *Canada* 103 C7
Meadow Lake ⌂, *Canada* 103 C7
Meadow Valley Wash →, *U.S.A.* 111 J12
Meadville, *U.S.A.* 116 E4
Meaford, *Canada* 116 B4
Mealhada, *Portugal* 36 E2
Mealy Mts., *Canada* 105 B8
Meander River, *Canada* 102 B5
Meares, C., *U.S.A.* 108 D2
Mearim →, *Brazil* 125 D10
Meath □, *Ireland* 12 C5
Meath Park, *Canada* 103 C7
Meaulne, *France* 19 F9
Meaux, *France* 19 D9
Mebechi-Gawa →, *Japan* 54 D10
Mebulu, Tanjung, *Indonesia* 63 K18
Mecanhelas, *Mozam.* 87 F4
Mecca = Makkah, *Si. Arabia* 75 C2
Mecca, *U.S.A.* 111 M10
Mechanicsburg, *U.S.A.* 116 F8
Mechanicville, *U.S.A.* 117 D11
Mechara, *Ethiopia* 81 F5
Mechelen, *Belgium* 17 C4
Mecheria, *Algeria* 78 B5
Mechernich, *Germany* 24 E2
Mechetinskaya, *Russia* 35 G5
Mecidiye, *Turkey* 45 F10

Mecitözü, *Turkey* 72 B6
Mecklenburg-Vorpommern □, *Germany* 24 B8
Mecklenburger Bucht, *Germany* 24 A7
Meconta, *Mozam.* 87 E4
Mecsek, *Hungary* 28 D3
Meda, *Portugal* 36 E3
Medan, *Indonesia* 62 D1
Médanos de Coro △, *Venezuela* 121 D6
Medanosa, Pta., *Argentina* 128 F3
Mede, *Italy* 40 C5
Médéa, *Algeria* 78 A6
Mededa, *Bos.-H.* 28 G4
Medellín, *Colombia* 124 B3
Medelpad, *Sweden* 10 B10
Medemblik, *Neths.* 17 B5
Mederdra, *Mauritania* 82 B1
Medford, *Mass., U.S.A.* 117 D13
Medford, *Oreg., U.S.A.* 108 E2
Medford, *Wis., U.S.A.* 112 C9
Medgidia, *Romania* 29 F13
Medi, *Sudan* 81 F3
Media Agua, *Argentina* 126 C2
Media Luna, *Argentina* 126 C2
Medianeira, *Brazil* 127 B5
Mediaş, *Romania* 29 D9
Medicina, *Italy* 41 D8
Medicine Bow, *U.S.A.* 108 F10
Medicine Bow Pk., *U.S.A.* 108 F10
Medicine Bow Ra., *U.S.A.* 108 F10
Medicine Hat, *Canada* 103 D6
Medicine Lake, *U.S.A.* 112 A2
Medicine Lodge, *U.S.A.* 113 G5
Medina = Al Madīnah, *Si. Arabia* 70 E3
Medina, *N. Dak., U.S.A.* 112 B5
Medina, *N.Y., U.S.A.* 116 C6
Medina, *Ohio, U.S.A.* 116 E3
Medina →, *U.S.A.* 113 L5
Medina de Pomar, *Spain* 36 C7
Medina de Ríoseco, *Spain* 36 D5
Medina del Campo, *Spain* 36 D6
Medina L., *U.S.A.* 113 L5
Medina Sidonia, *Spain* 37 J5
Medinaceli, *Spain* 38 D2
Medinipur, *India* 69 H12
Mediterranean Sea, *Europe* 6 H7
Médoc, *France* 20 C3
Medulin, *Croatia* 41 D10
Medveđa, *Serbia & M.* 44 D5
Medvedevo, *Russia* 34 B8
Medveditsa →, *Tver, Russia* 32 D9
Medveditsa →, *Volgograd, Russia* 34 F6
Medvedok, *Russia* 34 B10
Medvezhi, Ostrava, *Russia* 53 B17
Medvezhyegorsk, *Russia* 52 C4
Medway □, *U.K.* 15 F8
Medway →, *U.K.* 15 F8
Medzev, *Slovak Rep.* 27 C13
Medzilaborce, *Slovak Rep.* 27 B14
Medžitlija, *Macedonia* 44 F5
Meekatharra, *Australia* 93 E2
Meeker, *U.S.A.* 108 F10
Meelpaeg Res., *Canada* 105 C8
Meersburg, *Germany* 25 H5
Meerut, *India* 68 E7
Meeteetse, *U.S.A.* 108 D9
Mega, *Ethiopia* 81 G4
Megálo Khorío, *Greece* 47 E9
Megálo Petalí, *Greece* 46 D6
Megalópolis, *Greece* 46 D4
Meganísi Nisís, *Greece* 46 C2
Mégara, *Greece* 46 D5
Megasini, *India* 69 J12
Megdhova →, *Greece* 46 B3
Megève, *France* 21 C10
Meghalaya □, *India* 67 G17
Meghezez, *Ethiopia* 81 F4
Meghna →, *Bangla.* 67 H17
Mégiscane, L., *Canada* 104 C4
Megiste, *Greece* 47 E11
Megra, *Russia* 32 B9
Mehadia, *Romania* 28 F7
Meharry, Mt., *Australia* 92 D2
Mehedeby, *Sweden* 10 D11
Mehedinţi □, *Romania* 28 F7
Meheisa, *Sudan* 80 D3
Mehlville, *U.S.A.* 112 F9
Mehndawal, *India* 69 F10
Mehr Jān, *Iran* 71 C7
Mehrābād, *Iran* 70 B5
Mehrān, *Iran* 70 C5
Mehrīz, *Iran* 71 D7
Mehun-sur-Yèvre, *France* 19 E9
Mei Jiang →, *China* 59 E11
Mei Xian, *China* 56 G4
Meicheng, *China* 59 C12
Meichengzhen, *China* 59 C8
Meichuan, *China* 59 B10
Meigu, *China* 58 C4
Meiktila, *Burma* 67 J19
Meinerzhagen, *Germany* 24 D3
Meiningen, *Germany* 24 E6
Meira, Serra de, *Spain* 36 B3
Meiringen, *Switz.* 25 J4
Meishan, *China* 58 B4
Meissen, *Germany* 24 D9
Meissner, *Germany* 24 D5
Meissner-Kaufunger Wald ⌂, *Germany* 24 D5
Meitan, *China* 58 D6
Meizhou, *China* 59 E11
Meja, *India* 69 G10
Mejillones, *Chile* 126 A1
Mekdela, *Ethiopia* 81 E4
Mekele, *Ethiopia* 81 E4
Mekhtar, *Pakistan* 66 D6
Meknès, *Morocco* 78 B4
Meko, *Nigeria* 83 D5
Mekong →, *Asia* 65 H6
Mekongga, *Indonesia* 63 E6
Mekrou →, *Benin* 83 C5
Mekvari = Kür →, *Azerbaijan* 73 C13
Mel, *Italy* 41 B9
Melagiri Hills, *India* 66 N10
Melaka, *Malaysia* 65 L4
Melalap, *Malaysia* 62 C5
Mélambes, *Greece* 49 D6
Melanesia, *Pac. Oc.* 96 H7
Melaya, *Indonesia* 63 J17
Melbourne, *Australia* 95 F4
Melbourne, *U.S.A.* 115 L5
Melchor Múzquiz, *Mexico* 118 B4
Melchor Ocampo, *Mexico* 118 C4
Méldola, *Italy* 41 D9
Meldorf, *Germany* 24 A5
Melegnano, *Italy* 40 C6
Melenci, *Serbia & M.* 28 E5
Melenki, *Russia* 34 C5
Mélèzes →, *Canada* 104 A5
Melfi, *Italy* 43 B8
Melfort, *Canada* 103 C8
Melfort, *Zimbabwe* 87 F3
Melgaço, *Portugal* 36 C2
Melgar de Fernamental, *Spain* 36 C6
Melhus, *Norway* 8 E14
Melide, *Spain* 36 C2
Meligalá, *Greece* 46 D3
Melilla, *N. Afr.* 78 A5
Melilli, *Italy* 43 E8
Melipilla, *Chile* 126 C1
Mélissa, Ákra, *Greece* 49 D6
Mélissa Óros, *Greece* 47 D8
Melita, *Canada* 103 D8
Mélito di Porto Salvo, *Italy* 43 E8
Melitopol, *Ukraine* 33 J8
Melk, *Austria* 26 C8
Mellan Fryken, *Sweden* 10 E7
Mellansel, *Sweden* 8 E18
Mellbystrand, *Sweden* 11 H6
Melle, *France* 20 B3
Melle, *Germany* 24 C4
Mellen, *U.S.A.* 112 B9
Mellerud, *Sweden* 11 F6
Mellette, *U.S.A.* 112 C5
Mellid = Melide, *Spain* 36 C2
Mellieha, *Malta* 49 D1
Mellit, *Sudan* 81 E2
Mellrichstadt, *Germany* 24 E6
Melnik, *Bulgaria* 44 E7
Mělník, *Czech Rep.* 26 A7
Melo, *Uruguay* 127 C5
Melolo, *Indonesia* 63 F6
Melouprey, *Cambodia* 64 F5
Melrose, *Australia* 95 E4
Melrose, *U.K.* 13 F6
Melrose, *Minn., U.S.A.* 112 C7
Melrose, *N. Mex., U.S.A.* 113 H3
Melstone, *U.S.A.* 108 C10
Melsungen, *Germany* 24 D5
Melton Mowbray, *U.K.* 14 E7
Melun, *France* 19 D9
Melut, *Sudan* 81 E3
Melville, *Canada* 103 C8
Melville, C., *Australia* 94 A3
Melville, L., *Canada* 105 B8
Melville B., *Australia* 94 A2
Melville I., *Australia* 92 B5
Melville I., *Canada* 98 B8
Melville Pen., *Canada* 101 B11
Mélykút, *Hungary* 28 D4
Memaliaj, *Albania* 44 F3
Memba, *Mozam.* 87 E5
Memboro, *Indonesia* 63 F5
Membrilla, *Spain* 37 G7
Memel = Klaipėda, *Lithuania* 9 J19
Memel, *S. Africa* 89 D4
Memmingen, *Germany* 25 H6
Mempawah, *Indonesia* 62 D3
Memphis, *Egypt* 80 J7
Memphis, *Mich., U.S.A.* 116 D2
Memphis, *Tenn., U.S.A.* 113 H10
Memphis, *Tex., U.S.A.* 113 H4
Memphremagog, L., *U.S.A.* 117 B12
Mena, *Ukraine* 33 G7
Mena, *U.S.A.* 113 H7
Mena →, *Ethiopia* 81 F5
Menai Strait, *U.K.* 14 D3
Ménaka, *Mali* 83 B5
Menan = Chao Phraya →, *Thailand* 64 F3
Menarandra →, *Madag.* 89 D7
Menard, *U.S.A.* 113 K5
Menawashei, *Sudan* 81 E1
Mendawai →, *Indonesia* 62 E4
Mende, *France* 20 D7
Mendebo Mts., *Ethiopia* 81 F4
Mendeleyev Ridge, *Arctic* 4 B17
Menden, *Germany* 24 D3
Menderes, *Turkey* 47 C9
Mendez, *Mexico* 119 B5
Mendhar, *India* 69 C6
Mendi, *Ethiopia* 81 F4
Mendip Hills, *U.K.* 15 F5
Mendocino, *U.S.A.* 108 G2
Mendocino, C., *U.S.A.* 108 F1
Mendota, *Calif., U.S.A.* 110 J6
Mendota, *Ill., U.S.A.* 112 E10
Mendoyo, *Indonesia* 63 J17
Mendoza, *Argentina* 126 C2
Mendoza □, *Argentina* 126 C2
Mene Grande, *Venezuela* 124 B4
Menemen, *Turkey* 47 C9
Menen, *Belgium* 17 D3
Menfi, *Italy* 42 E5
Mengdingjie, *China* 58 F2
Mengeš, *Slovenia* 41 B11
Menggala, *Indonesia* 62 E3
Menghai, *China* 58 G3
Mengíbar, *Spain* 37 H7
Mengjin, *China* 56 G7
Mengla, *China* 58 G3
Menglian, *China* 58 F2
Mengshan, *China* 59 E8
Mengyin, *China* 57 G9
Mengzhe, *China* 58 F3
Mengzi, *China* 58 F4
Menihek, *Canada* 105 B6
Menihek L., *Canada* 105 B6
Menin = Menen, *Belgium* 17 D3
Menindee, *Australia* 95 E3
Menindee L., *Australia* 95 E3
Meningie, *Australia* 95 F2
Menjangan, Pulau, *Indonesia* 63 J17
Menlo Park, *U.S.A.* 110 H4
Menominee, *U.S.A.* 114 C2
Menominee →, *U.S.A.* 114 C2
Menomonie, *U.S.A.* 112 C9
Menongue, *Angola* 85 G3
Menorca, *Spain* 48 B11
Menorca ✕ (MAH), *Spain* 38 F9
Mentakab, *Malaysia* 65 L4
Mentawai, Kepulauan, *Indonesia* 62 E1
Menton, *France* 21 E11
Mentor, *U.S.A.* 116 E3
Menzies, *Australia* 93 E3
Meob B., *Namibia* 88 C1
Me'ona, *Israel* 74 B4
Meoqui, *Mexico* 118 B3
Mepaco, *Mozam.* 87 F3
Meppel, *Neths.* 17 B6
Meppen, *Germany* 24 C3
Mequinenza, *Spain* 38 D5
Mequinenza, Embalse de, *Spain* 38 D5
Mer, *France* 18 E8
Merabéllou, Kólpos, *Greece* 49 D7
Merak, *Indonesia* 63 F12
Meramangye, L., *Australia* 93 E5
Meran = Merano, *Italy* 41 B8
Merano, *Italy* 41 B8
Merate, *Italy* 40 C6
Merauke, *Indonesia* 63 F10
Merbein, *Australia* 95 E3
Merbuk, Gunung, *Indonesia* 63 J17
Merca, *Somali Rep.* 75 G3
Mercantour △, *France* 21 D10
Mercato Saraceno, *Italy* 41 E9
Merced, *U.S.A.* 110 H6
Merced →, *U.S.A.* 110 H6
Merced Pk., *U.S.A.* 110 H7
Mercedes, *Buenos Aires, Argentina* 126 C4
Mercedes, *Corrientes, Argentina* 126 B4
Mercedes, *San Luis, Argentina* 126 C2
Mercedes, *Uruguay* 126 C4
Mercedes, *U.S.A.* 113 M6
Merceditas, *Chile* 126 B1
Mercer, *N.Z.* 91 G5
Mercer, *U.S.A.* 116 E4
Mercer Island, *U.S.A.* 110 C4
Mercury, *U.S.A.* 111 J11
Mercy, C., *Canada* 101 B13
Merdrignac, *France* 18 D4
Mere, *U.K.* 15 F5
Meredith, C., *Falk. Is.* 128 G4
Meredith, L., *U.S.A.* 113 H4
Merefa, *Ukraine* 33 H9
Merei, *Romania* 29 E11
Merga = Nukheila, *Sudan* 80 D2
Mergui, *Burma* 64 F2
Mergui Arch. = Myeik Kyunzu, *Burma* 65 G1
Méribel-les-Allues, *France* 21 C10
Meriç, *Turkey* 45 E10
Meriç →, *Turkey* 45 F10
Mérida, *Mexico* 119 C7
Mérida, *Spain* 37 G4
Mérida, *Venezuela* 124 B4
Mérida, Cord. de, *Venezuela* 124 B4
Meriden, *U.K.* 15 E6
Meriden, *U.S.A.* 117 E12
Meridian, *Calif., U.S.A.* 110 F5
Meridian, *Idaho, U.S.A.* 108 E5
Meridian, *Miss., U.S.A.* 115 J1
Mérignac, *France* 20 D3
Mérinaghène, *Senegal* 82 B1
Merinda, *Australia* 94 C4
Mering, *Germany* 25 G6
Meringa, *Nigeria* 83 C7
Merir, *Pac. Oc.* 63 D8
Merirumã, *Brazil* 125 C8
Merkel, *U.S.A.* 113 J5
Mermaid Reef, *Australia* 92 C2
Merowe, *Sudan* 80 D3
Merredin, *Australia* 93 F2
Merrick, *U.K.* 13 F4
Merrickville, *Canada* 117 B9
Merrill, *Oreg., U.S.A.* 108 E3
Merrill, *Wis., U.S.A.* 112 C10
Merrimack →, *U.S.A.* 117 D14
Merriman, *U.S.A.* 112 D4
Merritt, *Canada* 102 C4
Merritt Island, *U.S.A.* 115 L5
Merriwa, *Australia* 95 E5
Merry I., *Canada* 104 A4
Merryville, *U.S.A.* 113 K8
Mersa Fatma, *Eritrea* 81 E5
Mersch, *Lux.* 17 E6
Merse →, *Italy* 41 E8
Mersea I., *U.K.* 15 F8
Merseburg, *Germany* 24 D7
Mersey →, *U.K.* 14 D4
Merseyside □, *U.K.* 14 D4
Mersin, *Turkey* 70 B2
Mersing, *Malaysia* 65 L4
Merta, *India* 68 F6
Merta Road, *India* 68 F5
Merthyr Tydfil, *U.K.* 15 F4
Merthyr Tydfil □, *U.K.* 15 F4
Mértola, *Portugal* 37 H3
Mertzon, *U.S.A.* 113 K4
Méru, *France* 19 C9
Meru, *Kenya* 86 B4
Meru, *Tanzania* 86 C4
Meru △, *Kenya* 86 B4
Merville, *France* 19 B9
Méry-sur-Seine, *France* 19 D10
Merzifon, *Turkey* 72 B6
Merzig, *Germany* 25 F2
Mesa, *U.S.A.* 109 K8
Mesa Verde △, *U.S.A.* 109 H9
Mesagne, *Italy* 43 B10
Mesanagrós, *Greece* 49 C9
Mesaoría, *Cyprus* 49 D12
Mesarás, Kólpos, *Greece* 49 D6
Meschede, *Germany* 24 D4
Mescit, *Turkey* 73 B9
Mesfinto, *Ethiopia* 81 E4
Mesgouez, L., *Canada* 104 B5
Meshchovsk, *Russia* 32 E8
Meshed = Mashhad, *Iran* 71 B8
Meshoppen, *U.S.A.* 117 E8
Meshra er Req, *Sudan* 81 F2
Mesilinka →, *Canada* 102 B4
Mesilla, *U.S.A.* 109 K10
Meslay-du-Maine, *France* 18 E6
Mesocco, *Switz.* 25 J5
Mesolóngion, *Greece* 46 C3
Mesopotamia = Al Jazirah, *Iraq* 70 C5
Mesopotamia, *U.S.A.* 116 E4
Mesopótamon, *Greece* 46 B2
Mesoraca, *Italy* 43 C9
Mésou Volímais = Volímai, *Greece* 46 D2
Mesquite, *U.S.A.* 109 H6
Messaad, *Algeria* 78 B6
Messac, *France* 18 E5
Messalo →, *Mozam.* 87 E4
Méssaména, *Cameroon* 83 E7
Messeue, *Greece* 46 D3
Messina = Musina, *S. Africa* 89 C5
Messina, *Italy* 43 D8
Messina, Str. di, *Italy* 43 D8
Messíni, *Greece* 46 D4
Messinía □, *Greece* 46 D3
Messiniakós Kólpos, *Greece* 46 E4
Messkirch, *Germany* 25 H5
Messonghi, *Greece* 49 B3
Mesta →, *Bulgaria* 44 E7
Mestá, Ákra, *Greece* 47 C7
Mestanza, *Spain* 37 G6
Mestre, *Italy* 41 C9
Mesudiye, *Turkey* 72 B7
Meta →, *S. Amer.* 124 B5
Meta Incognita Pen., *Canada* 101 B13
Metabetchouan, *Canada* 105 C5
Metairie, *U.S.A.* 113 L9
Metalici, Munţii, *Romania* 28 D7
Metaline Falls, *U.S.A.* 108 B5
Metallifere, Colline, *Italy* 40 E8
Metán, *Argentina* 126 B3
Metangula, *Mozam.* 87 E3
Metauro →, *Italy* 41 E10
Metema, *Ethiopia* 81 E4
Metengobalame, *Mozam.* 87 E3
Méthana, *Greece* 46 D5
Methóni, *Greece* 46 E3
Methven, *N.Z.* 91 K3
Metil, *Mozam.* 87 F4
Metkovets, *Bulgaria* 44 C7
Metković, *Croatia* 41 E14
Metlakatla, *U.S.A.* 100 C6
Metlika, *Slovenia* 41 C12
Metropolis, *U.S.A.* 113 G10
Métsovon, *Greece* 46 B3
Metu, *Ethiopia* 81 F4
Metz, *France* 19 C13
Metzingen, *Germany* 25 G5
Meulaboh, *Indonesia* 62 D1
Meung-sur-Loire, *France* 19 E8
Meureudu, *Indonesia* 62 C1
Meurthe →, *France* 19 D13
Meurthe-et-Moselle □, *France* 19 D13
Meuse □, *France* 19 C12
Meuse →, *Europe* 17 D5
Meuselwitz, *Germany* 24 D8
Mexia, *U.S.A.* 113 K6
Mexiana, I., *Brazil* 125 D9
Mexicali, *Mexico* 111 N11
Mexican Plateau, *Mexico* 98 G9
Mexican Water, *U.S.A.* 109 H9
México, *Mexico* 119 D5
Mexico, *Maine, U.S.A.* 117 B14
Mexico, *Mo., U.S.A.* 112 F9
Mexico, *N.Y., U.S.A.* 117 C8
México □, *Mexico* 119 D5
Mexico ■, *Cent. Amer.* 118 C4
Mexico, G. of, *Cent. Amer.* 119 C7
Mexico B., *U.S.A.* 117 C8
Meydān-e Naftūn, *Iran* 71 D6
Meydani, Ra's-e, *Iran* 71 E8
Meyenburg, *Germany* 24 B8
Meymac, *France* 20 C6
Meymaneh, *Afghan.* 66 B4
Meyrueis, *France* 20 D7
Meyssac, *France* 20 C5
Meyzieu, *France* 21 C8
Mezdra, *Bulgaria* 44 C7
Mèze, *France* 20 E7
Mezen, *Russia* 52 C5
Mezen →, *Russia* 52 C5
Mézenc, Mt., *France* 21 D8
Mezeş, Munţii, *Romania* 28 C8
Mezha →, *Russia* 32 E6
Mezhdurechenskiy, *Russia* 52 D7
Mézidon-Canon, *France* 18 C6
Mézières-en-Brenne, *France* 20 B5
Mézilhac, *France* 21 D8
Mézin, *France* 20 D4
Mezőberény, *Hungary* 28 D6
Mezőfalva, *Hungary* 28 D3
Mezőhegyes, *Hungary* 28 D5
Mezőkövácsháza, *Hungary* 28 D5
Mezőkövesd, *Hungary* 28 C5
Mézos, *France* 20 D2
Mezőtúr, *Hungary* 28 C5
Mezquital, *Mexico* 118 C4
Mezzolombardo, *Italy* 40 B8
Mfolozi →, *S. Africa* 89 D5
Mgeta, *Tanzania* 87 D4
Mglin, *Russia* 33 F7
Mhlaba Hills, *Zimbabwe* 87 F3
Mhow, *India* 68 H6
Miahuatlán, *Mexico* 119 D5
Miajadas, *Spain* 37 F5
Miami, *Fla., U.S.A.* 115 N5
Miami, *Okla., U.S.A.* 113 G7
Miami, *Tex., U.S.A.* 113 H4
Miami Beach, *U.S.A.* 115 N5
Mian Xian, *China* 56 H4
Mianchi, *China* 56 G6
Mīāndarreh, *Iran* 71 C7
Mīāndowāb, *Iran* 70 B5
Miandrivazo, *Madag.* 89 B8
Mīāneh, *Iran* 70 B5
Mianning, *China* 58 C4
Mianwali, *Pakistan* 68 C4
Mianyang, *China* 58 B5
Mianzhu, *China* 58 B5
Miaoli, *Taiwan* 59 E13
Miarinarivo, *Antananarivo, Madag.* 89 B8
Miarinarivo, *Toamasina, Madag.* 89 B8
Miariravaratra, *Madag.* 89 C8
Miass, *Russia* 52 D7
Miasteczko Krajeńskie, *Poland* 31 E4
Miastko, *Poland* 30 E3
Mica, *S. Africa* 89 C5
Micăsasa, *Romania* 29 D9
Michalovce, *Slovak Rep.* 27 C14
Michigan □, *U.S.A.* 114 C3
Michigan, L., *U.S.A.* 114 D2
Michigan City, *U.S.A.* 114 E2
Michika, *Nigeria* 83 C7
Michipicoten I., *Canada* 104 C2
Michoacan □, *Mexico* 118 D4
Michurin, *Bulgaria* 45 D11
Michurinsk, *Russia* 34 D5
Mico, Pta., *Nic.* 120 D3
Micoud, *St. Lucia* 121 f
Micronesia, *Pac. Oc.* 96 G7
Micronesia, Federated States of ■, *Pac. Oc.* 96 G7
Midai, *Indonesia* 62 D3
Midale, *Canada* 103 D8
Middelburg, *Neths.* 17 C3
Middelburg, *Eastern Cape, S. Africa* 88 E4
Middelburg, *Mpumalanga, S. Africa* 89 D4
Middelfart, *Denmark* 11 J3
Middelpos, *S. Africa* 88 E3
Middelwit, *S. Africa* 88 C4
Middle Alkali L., *U.S.A.* 108 F3
Middle Bass I., *U.S.A.* 116 E2
Middle East, *Asia* 50 F7
Middle Fork Feather →, *U.S.A.* 110 F5
Middle I., *Australia* 93 F3
Middle Loup →, *U.S.A.* 112 E5
Middle Sackville, *Canada* 105 D7
Middleboro, *U.S.A.* 117 E14
Middleburg, *Fla., U.S.A.* 115 K5
Middleburg, *N.Y., U.S.A.* 117 D10
Middleburg, *Pa., U.S.A.* 116 F7
Middlebury, *U.S.A.* 117 B11
Middlemount, *Australia* 94 C4
Middleport, *N.Y., U.S.A.* 116 C6
Middleport, *Ohio, U.S.A.* 114 F4
Middlesboro, *U.S.A.* 115 G4
Middlesbrough, *U.K.* 14 C6
Middlesbrough □, *U.K.* 14 C6
Middlesex, *Belize* 120 C2
Middlesex, *N.J., U.S.A.* 117 F10
Middlesex, *N.Y., U.S.A.* 116 D7
Middleton, *Australia* 94 C3
Middleton, *Canada* 105 D6
Middleton Cr. →, *Australia* 94 C3
Middletown, *U.K.* 12 B5
Middletown, *Calif., U.S.A.* 110 G4
Middletown, *Conn., U.S.A.* 117 E12
Middletown, *N.Y., U.S.A.* 117 E10
Middletown, *Ohio, U.S.A.* 114 F3
Middletown, *Pa., U.S.A.* 117 F8
Midge Point, *Australia* 94 J6
Midhurst, *U.K.* 15 G7
Midī, *Yemen* 81 D5
Midi, Canal du →, *France* 20 E5
Midi d'Ossau, Pic du, *France* 20 F3
Midi-Pyrénées □, *France* 20 E5
Midland, *Canada* 116 B5
Midland, *Calif., U.S.A.* 111 M12
Midland, *Mich., U.S.A.* 114 D3
Midland, *Pa., U.S.A.* 116 F4
Midland, *Tex., U.S.A.* 113 K3
Midlands □, *Zimbabwe* 87 F2
Midleton, *Ireland* 12 E3
Midlothian, *U.S.A.* 113 J6
Midlothian □, *U.K.* 13 F5
Midongy, Tangorombohitr' i, *Madag.* 89 C8
Midongy Atsimo, *Madag.* 89 C8
Midou →, *France* 20 E3
Midouze →, *France* 20 E3
Midsayap, *Phil.* 61 H6
Midu, *China* 58 E3
Midway Is., *Pac. Oc.* 96 E10
Midway Wells, *U.S.A.* 111 N11
Midwest, *U.S.A.* 107 B9
Midwest, *Wyo., U.S.A.* 108 E10
Midwest City, *U.S.A.* 113 H6
Midyat, *Turkey* 70 B4
Midzŏr, *Bulgaria* 44 C6
Mie □, *Japan* 55 G8
Miechów, *Poland* 31 H7
Miedwie, Jezioro, *Poland* 31 E1
Międzybórz, *Poland* 31 G4

Międzychód, *Poland* 31 F2
Międzylesie, *Poland* 31 H3
Międzyrzec Podlaski, *Poland* 31 G9
Międzyrzecz, *Poland* 31 F2
Międzyzdroje, *Poland* 30 E1
Miejska Górka, *Poland* 31 G3
Miélan, *France* 20 E4
Mielec, *Poland* 31 H8
Mienga, *Angola* 88 B2
Miercurea-Ciuc, *Romania* 29 D10
Miercurea Sibiului, *Romania* 29 E8
Mieres, *Spain* 36 B5
Mieroszów, *Poland* 31 H3
Mieso, *Ethiopia* 81 F5
Mieszkowice, *Poland* 31 F1
Mifflintown, *U.S.A.* 116 F7
Mifraz Ḥefa, *Israel* 74 C4
Migennes, *France* 19 E10
Migliarino, *Italy* 41 D8
Migliarino-San Rossore-Massaciuccoli ⌓, *Italy* 40 E7
Miguel Alemán, Presa, *Mexico* 119 D5
Miguelturra, *Spain* 37 G7
Mihăileni, *Romania* 29 C11
Mihăileşti, *Romania* 29 F10
Mihailovca, *Moldova* 29 D13
Mihalgazi, *Turkey* 47 A12
Mihaliççık, *Turkey* 72 C4
Mihara, *Japan* 55 G6
Miheşu de Cîmpie, *Romania* 29 D9
Mijas, *Spain* 37 J6
Mikese, *Tanzania* 86 D4
Mikha-Tskhakaya = Senaki, *Georgia* 35 J6
Mikhailovka = Mykhaylivka, *Ukraine* 33 J8
Mikhaylov, *Russia* 32 E10
Mikhaylovgrad = Montana, *Bulgaria* 44 C7
Mikhaylovka, *Russia* 34 E6
Mikhnevo, *Russia* 32 E9
Mikínai, *Greece* 46 D4
Mikkeli, *Finland* 9 F22
Mikkwa →, *Canada* 102 B6
Mikniya, *Sudan* 81 D3
Mikołajki, *Poland* 30 E8
Míkonos, *Greece* 47 D7
Mikrí Préspa, Límni, *Greece* 44 F5
Mikrón Dhérion, *Greece* 45 E10
Mikstat, *Poland* 31 G4
Mikulov, *Czech Rep.* 27 C9
Mikumi, *Tanzania* 86 D4
Mikumi △, *Tanzania* 86 D4
Milaca, *U.S.A.* 112 C8
Milagro, *Ecuador* 124 D3
Milagros, *Phil.* 61 E5
Milan = Milano, *Italy* 40 C6
Milan, *Mo., U.S.A.* 112 E8
Milan, *Tenn., U.S.A.* 115 H1
Milan Linate ✈ (LIN), *Italy* 40 C6
Milange, *Mozam.* 87 F4
Milano, *Italy* 40 C6
Milanoa, *Madag.* 89 A8
Milâs, *Turkey* 47 D9
Mílatos, *Greece* 49 D7
Milazzo, *Italy* 43 D8
Milbank, *U.S.A.* 112 C6
Milbanke Sd., *Canada* 102 C3
Milden, *Canada* 103 C7
Mildenhall, *U.K.* 15 E8
Mildmay, *Canada* 116 B3
Mildura, *Australia* 95 E3
Mile, *China* 58 E4
Miléai, *Greece* 46 B5
Miles, *Australia* 95 D5
Miles City, *U.S.A.* 112 B2
Mileşti, *Moldova* 29 C13
Milestone, *Canada* 103 D8
Mileto, *Italy* 43 D9
Miletto, Mte., *Italy* 43 A7
Miletus, *Turkey* 47 D9
Milevsko, *Czech Rep.* 26 B7
Milford, *Calif., U.S.A.* 110 E6
Milford, *Conn., U.S.A.* 117 E11
Milford, *Del., U.S.A.* 114 F8
Milford, *Mass., U.S.A.* 117 D13
Milford, *N.H., U.S.A.* 117 D13
Milford, *Pa., U.S.A.* 117 E10
Milford, *Utah, U.S.A.* 109 G7
Milford Haven, *U.K.* 15 F2
Milford Sd., *N.Z.* 91 L1
Milford Sound, *N.Z.* 91 L1
Milḥ, Baḥr al = Razāzah, Buḥayrat ar, *Iraq* 70 C4
Milicz, *Poland* 31 G4
Milikapiti, *Australia* 92 B5
Miling, *Australia* 93 F2
Militello in Val di Catánia, *Italy* 43 E7
Milk →, *U.S.A.* 108 B10
Milk, Wadi el →, *Sudan* 80 D3
Milk River, *Canada* 102 D6
Mill I., *Antarctica* 5 C8
Mill Valley, *U.S.A.* 110 H4
Millárs →, *Spain* 38 F4
Millau, *France* 20 D7
Millbridge, *Canada* 116 B7
Millbrook, *Canada* 116 B6
Millbrook, *U.S.A.* 117 E11
Mille Lacs, L. des, *Canada* 104 C1
Mille Lacs L., *U.S.A.* 112 B8
Milledgeville, *U.S.A.* 115 J4
Millen, *U.S.A.* 115 J5
Millennium I. = Caroline I., *Kiribati* 97 H12
Miller, *U.S.A.* 112 C5
Millerovo, *Russia* 35 F5
Millersburg, *Ohio, U.S.A.* 116 F3
Millersburg, *Pa., U.S.A.* 116 F8
Millerton, *U.S.A.* 117 E11
Millerton L., *U.S.A.* 110 J7
Millet, *St. Lucia* 121 f
Millevaches, Plateau de, *France* 20 C6
Millheim, *U.S.A.* 116 F7
Millicent, *Australia* 95 F3
Millington, *U.S.A.* 113 H10
Millinocket, *U.S.A.* 115 C11
Millmerran, *Australia* 95 D5
Millom, *U.K.* 14 C4
Mills L., *Canada* 102 A5
Millsboro, *U.S.A.* 116 G5
Millstream-Chichester △, *Australia* 92 D2
Milltown Malbay, *Ireland* 12 D2
Millville, *N.J., U.S.A.* 114 F8
Millville, *Pa., U.S.A.* 117 E8
Millwood L., *U.S.A.* 113 J8
Milna, *Croatia* 41 E13
Milne →, *Australia* 94 C2
Milo, *U.S.A.* 115 C11
Mílos, *Greece* 46 E6
Miłosław, *Poland* 31 F4
Milot, *Albania* 44 E3
Milparinka, *Australia* 95 D3
Miltenberg, *Germany* 25 F5
Milton, *N.S., Canada* 105 D7
Milton, *Ont., Canada* 116 C5
Milton, *N.Z.* 91 M2
Milton, *Calif., U.S.A.* 110 G6
Milton, *Fla., U.S.A.* 115 K2
Milton, *Pa., U.S.A.* 116 F8
Milton, *Vt., U.S.A.* 117 B11
Milton-Freewater, *U.S.A.* 108 D4
Milton Keynes, *U.K.* 15 E7
Milton Keynes ☐, *U.K.* 15 E7
Miluo, *China* 59 C9
Milverton, *Canada* 116 C4
Milwaukee, *U.S.A.* 114 D2
Milwaukee Deep, *Atl. Oc.* 121 C6
Milwaukie, *U.S.A.* 110 E4
Mim, *Ghana* 82 D4
Mimizan, *France* 20 D2
Mimoň, *Czech Rep.* 26 A7
Min Jiang →, *Fujian, China* 59 E12
Min Jiang →, *Sichuan, China* 58 C5
Min Xian, *China* 56 G3
Mina Pirquitas, *Argentina* 126 A2
Mīnā Su'ud, *Si. Arabia* 71 D6
Mīnā'al Aḥmadī, *Kuwait* 71 D6
Minago →, *Canada* 103 C9
Minaki, *Canada* 103 D10
Minamata, *Japan* 55 H5
Minami-Arapusa △, *Japan* 55 G9
Minami-Tori-Shima, *Pac. Oc.* 96 E7
Minas, *Uruguay* 127 C4
Minas, Sierra de las, *Guatemala* 120 C2
Minas Basin, *Canada* 105 C7
Minas de Rio Tinto = Minas de Riotinto, *Spain* 37 H4
Minas de Riotinto, *Spain* 37 H4
Minas Gerais ☐, *Brazil* 125 G9
Minatitlán, *Mexico* 119 D6
Minbu, *Burma* 67 J19
Minchinabad, *Pakistan* 68 D5
Mincio →, *Italy* 40 C7
Minčol, *Slovak Rep.* 27 B13
Mindanao, *Phil.* 61 H6
Mindanao Sea = Bohol Sea, *Phil.* 63 C6
Mindanao Trench, *Pac. Oc.* 61 F7
Mindel →, *Germany* 25 G6
Mindelheim, *Germany* 25 G6
Minden, *Canada* 116 B6
Minden, *Germany* 24 C4
Minden, *La., U.S.A.* 113 J8
Minden, *Nev., U.S.A.* 110 G7
Mindiptana, *Indonesia* 63 F10
Mindoro, *Phil.* 61 E4
Mindoro Str., *Phil.* 61 E4
Mine, *Japan* 55 G5
Minehead, *U.K.* 15 F4
Mineola, *N.Y., U.S.A.* 117 F11
Mineola, *Tex., U.S.A.* 113 J7
Mineral King, *U.S.A.* 110 J8
Mineral Wells, *U.S.A.* 113 J5
Mineralnyye Vody, *Russia* 35 H6
Minersville, *U.S.A.* 117 F8
Minerva, *U.S.A.* 116 F3
Minervino Murge, *Italy* 43 A9
Minetto, *U.S.A.* 117 C8
Mingäçevir, *Azerbaijan* 35 K8
Mingäçevir Su Anbarı, *Azerbaijan* 35 K8
Mingan, *Canada* 105 B7
Mingechaur = Mingäçevir, *Azerbaijan* 35 K8
Mingechaurskoye Vdkhr. = Mingäçevir Su Anbarı, *Azerbaijan* 35 K8
Mingela, *Australia* 94 B4
Mingenew, *Australia* 93 E2
Mingera Cr. →, *Australia* 94 C2
Minggang, *China* 59 A10
Mingguang, *China* 59 A11
Mingin, *Burma* 67 H19
Mingir, *Moldova* 29 D13
Minglanilla, *Spain* 39 F3
Minglun, *China* 58 E7
Mingo Junction, *U.S.A.* 116 F4
Mingorria, *Spain* 36 E6
Mingshan, *China* 58 B4
Mingteke Daban = Mintaka Pass, *Pakistan* 69 A6
Mingxi, *China* 59 D11
Mingyuegue, *China* 57 C15
Minho = Miño →, *Spain* 36 D2
Minhou, *China* 59 E12
Minićevo, *Serbia & M.* 28 G7
Minidoka, *U.S.A.* 108 E7
Minigwal, L., *Australia* 93 E3
Minilya →, *Australia* 93 D1
Minilya Roadhouse, *Australia* 93 D1
Minipi L., *Canada* 105 B7
Mink L., *Canada* 102 A5
Minkammen, *Sudan* 81 F3
Minna, *Nigeria* 83 D6
Minneapolis, *Kans., U.S.A.* 112 F6
Minneapolis, *Minn., U.S.A.* 112 C8
Minnedosa, *Canada* 103 C9
Minnesota ☐, *U.S.A.* 112 B8
Minnesota →, *U.S.A.* 112 C8
Minnewaukan, *U.S.A.* 112 A5
Minnipa, *Australia* 95 E2
Minnitaki L., *Canada* 104 C1
Mino, *Japan* 55 G8
Miño, *Spain* 36 B2
Miño →, *Spain* 36 D2
Minoa, *Greece* 47 F7
Minorca = Menorca, *Spain* 48 B11
Minot, *U.S.A.* 112 A4
Minqin, *China* 56 E2
Minqing, *China* 59 D12
Minsen, *Germany* 24 B3
Minsk, *Belarus* 32 F4
Mińsk Mazowiecki, *Poland* 31 F8
Mintabie, *Australia* 95 D1
Mintaka Pass, *Pakistan* 69 A6
Minto, *Canada* 105 C6
Minto, L., *Canada* 104 A5
Minton, *Canada* 103 D8
Minturn, *U.S.A.* 108 G10
Minturno, *Italy* 42 A6
Minûf, *Egypt* 80 H7
Minusinsk, *Russia* 53 D10
Minutang, *India* 67 E20
Minya el Qamh, *Egypt* 80 H7
Mionica, *Bos.-H.* 28 F3
Mionica, *Serbia & M.* 44 B4
Miquelon, *Canada* 104 C4
Miquelon, *St- P. & M.* 105 C8
Mir, *Niger* 83 C7
Mīr Kūh, *Iran* 71 E8
Mīr Shahdād, *Iran* 71 E8
Mira, *Italy* 41 C9
Mira, *Portugal* 36 E2
Mira →, *Portugal* 37 H2
Mira por vos Cay, *Bahamas* 121 B5
Mirabella Eclano, *Italy* 43 A7
Mirador-Río Azul △, *Guatemala* 120 C2
Miraj, *India* 66 L9
Miram Shah, *Pakistan* 68 C4
Miramar, *Argentina* 126 D4
Miramar, *Mozam.* 89 C6
Miramas, *France* 21 E8
Mirambeau, *France* 20 C3
Miramichi, *Canada* 105 C6
Miramichi B., *Canada* 105 C7
Miramont-de-Guyenne, *France* 20 D4
Miranda, *Brazil* 125 H7
Miranda →, *Brazil* 124 G7
Miranda de Ebro, *Spain* 38 C2
Miranda do Corvo, *Portugal* 36 E2
Miranda do Douro, *Portugal* 36 D4
Mirande, *France* 20 E4
Mirandela, *Portugal* 36 D3
Mirándola, *Italy* 40 D8
Mirandópolis, *Brazil* 127 A5
Mirango, *Malawi* 87 E3
Mirani, *Australia* 94 K6
Mirano, *Italy* 41 C9
Miras, *Albania* 44 F4
Mirassol, *Brazil* 127 A6
Mirbāṭ, *Oman* 75 D5
Mirear, *Egypt* 80 C4
Mirebeau, *Côte-d'Or, France* 19 E12
Mirebeau, *Vienne, France* 18 F7
Mirecourt, *France* 19 D13
Mirgorod = Myrhorod, *Ukraine* 33 H7
Miri, *Malaysia* 62 D4
Miriam Vale, *Australia* 94 C5
Miribel, *France* 19 G11
Mirim, L., *S. Amer.* 127 C5
Mirnyy, *Russia* 53 C12
Miroč, *Serbia & M.* 44 B6
Mirokhan, *Pakistan* 68 F3
Mirond L., *Canada* 103 B8
Mirosławiec, *Poland* 30 E3
Mirpur, *Pakistan* 69 C5
Mirpur Batoro, *Pakistan* 68 G3
Mirpur Bibiwari, *Pakistan* 68 E2
Mirpur Khas, *Pakistan* 68 G3
Mirpur Sakro, *Pakistan* 68 G2
Mirria, *Niger* 83 C6
Mirsk, *Poland* 31 H2
Mirtağ, *Turkey* 70 B4
Miryang, *S. Korea* 57 G15
Mirzaani, *Georgia* 35 K8
Mirzapur, *India* 69 G10
Mirzapur-cum-Vindhyachal = Mirzapur, *India* 69 G10
Misantla, *Mexico* 119 D5
Misawa, *Japan* 54 D10
Miscou I., *Canada* 105 C7
Mish'āb, Ra's al, *Si. Arabia* 71 D6
Mishan, *China* 60 B8
Mishawaka, *U.S.A.* 114 E2
Mishbih, Gebel, *Egypt* 80 C3
Mishima, *Japan* 55 G9
Misión, *Mexico* 111 N10
Misiones ☐, *Argentina* 127 B5
Misiones ☐, *Paraguay* 126 B4
Miskah, *Si. Arabia* 70 E4
Miskitos, Cayos, *Nic.* 120 D3
Miskolc, *Hungary* 28 B5
Misoke, *Dem. Rep. of the Congo* 86 C2
Misool, *Indonesia* 63 E8
Mişrātah, *Libya* 79 B9
Missanabie, *Canada* 104 C3
Missinaibi →, *Canada* 104 B3
Missinaibi L., *Canada* 104 C3
Mission, *Canada* 102 D4
Mission, *S. Dak., U.S.A.* 112 D4
Mission, *Tex., U.S.A.* 113 M5
Mission Beach, *Australia* 94 B4
Mission Viejo, *U.S.A.* 111 M9
Missirah, *Senegal* 82 C1
Missisa L., *Canada* 104 B2
Missisicabi →, *Canada* 104 B4
Mississagi →, *Canada* 104 C3
Mississauga, *Canada* 116 C5
Mississippi ☐, *U.S.A.* 113 J10
Mississippi →, *U.S.A.* 113 L10
Mississippi L., *Canada* 117 A8
Mississippi River Delta, *U.S.A.* 113 L9
Mississippi Sd., *U.S.A.* 113 K10
Missoula, *U.S.A.* 108 C7
Missouri ☐, *U.S.A.* 112 F8
Missouri →, *U.S.A.* 112 F9
Missouri City, *U.S.A.* 113 L7
Missouri Valley, *U.S.A.* 112 E7
Mist, *U.S.A.* 110 E3
Mistassibi →, *Canada* 105 B5
Mistassini →, *Canada* 105 C5
Mistassini, L., *Canada* 104 B5
Mistastin L., *Canada* 105 A7
Mistelbach, *Austria* 27 C9
Misterbianco, *Italy* 43 E8
Mistinibi, L., *Canada* 105 A7
Mistissini, *Canada* 105 C5
Mistretta, *Italy* 43 E7
Misty L., *Canada* 103 B8
Misurata = Mişrātah, *Libya* 79 B9
Mît Ghamr, *Egypt* 80 H7
Mitatib, *Sudan* 81 D4
Mitchell, *Australia* 95 D4
Mitchell, *Canada* 116 C3
Mitchell, *Nebr., U.S.A.* 112 E3
Mitchell, *Oreg., U.S.A.* 108 D3
Mitchell, *S. Dak., U.S.A.* 112 D6
Mitchell →, *Australia* 94 B3
Mitchell, Mt., *U.S.A.* 115 H4
Mitchell and Alice Rivers △, *Australia* 94 B3
Mitchell Ranges, *Australia* 94 A2
Mitchelstown, *Ireland* 12 D3
Mitha Tiwana, *Pakistan* 68 C5
Mithi, *Pakistan* 68 G3
Míthimna, *Greece* 47 B8
Mithrao, *Pakistan* 68 F3
Mitilíni, *Greece* 47 B8
Mitilinoí, *Greece* 47 D8
Mito, *Japan* 55 F10
Mitrofanovka, *Russia* 33 H10
Mitrovica = Kosovska Mitrovica, *Serbia & M.* 44 D4
Mitsinjo, *Madag.* 89 B8
Mitsiwa, *Eritrea* 81 D4
Mitsiwa Channel, *Eritrea* 81 D5
Mitsukaidō, *Japan* 55 F9
Mittagong, *Australia* 95 E5
Mittelberg, *Austria* 26 D3
Mittelfranken ☐, *Germany* 25 F6
Mittellandkanal →, *Germany* 24 C4
Mittenwalde, *Germany* 24 C9
Mittersill, *Austria* 26 D5
Mitterteich, *Germany* 25 F8
Mittimatalik = Pond Inlet, *Canada* 101 A12
Mittweida, *Germany* 24 E8
Mitú, *Colombia* 124 C4
Mitumba, *Tanzania* 86 D3
Mitumba, Mts., *Dem. Rep. of the Congo* 86 D2
Mitwaba, *Dem. Rep. of the Congo* 87 D2
Mityana, *Uganda* 86 B3
Mixteco →, *Mexico* 119 D5
Miyagi ☐, *Japan* 54 E10
Miyāh, W. el →, *Egypt* 80 C3
Miyāh, W. el →, *Syria* 70 C3
Miyake-Jima, *Japan* 55 G9
Miyako, *Japan* 54 E10
Miyako-Jima, *Japan* 55 M2
Miyako-Rettō, *Japan* 55 M2
Miyakonojō, *Japan* 55 J5
Miyani, *India* 68 J3
Miyanoura-Dake, *Japan* 55 J5
Miyazaki, *Japan* 55 J5
Miyazaki ☐, *Japan* 55 H5
Miyazu, *Japan* 55 G7
Miyet, Bahr el = Dead Sea, *Asia* 74 D4
Miyi, *China* 58 D4
Miyoshi, *Japan* 55 G6
Miyun, *China* 56 D9
Miyun Shuiku, *China* 57 D9
Mizan Teferi, *Ethiopia* 81 F4
Mizdah, *Libya* 79 B8
Mizen Hd., *Cork, Ireland* 12 E2
Mizen Hd., *Wick., Ireland* 12 D5
Mizhi, *China* 56 F6
Mizil, *Romania* 29 F11
Mizoram ☐, *India* 67 H18
Miẓpe Ramon, *Israel* 74 E3
Mizuho, *Antarctica* 5 D5
Mizusawa, *Japan* 54 E10
Mjällby, *Sweden* 11 H8
Mjöbäck, *Sweden* 11 G6
Mjölby, *Sweden* 11 F9
Mjörn, *Sweden* 11 G6
Mjøsa, *Norway* 9 F14
Mkata, *Tanzania* 86 D4
Mkhaya ⌓, *Swaziland* 89 D5
Mkokotoni, *Tanzania* 86 D4
Mkomazi, *Tanzania* 86 C4
Mkomazi ⌓, *Tanzania* 86 C3
Mkomazi →, *S. Africa* 89 E5
Mkulwe, *Tanzania* 87 D3
Mkumbi, Ras, *Tanzania* 86 D4
Mkushi, *Zambia* 87 E2
Mkushi River, *Zambia* 87 E2
Mkuze, *S. Africa* 89 D5
Mkuze ⌓, *S. Africa* 89 D4
Mladá Boleslav, *Czech Rep.* 26 A7
Mladenovac, *Serbia & M.* 44 B4
Mlala Hills, *Tanzania* 86 D3
Mlange = Mulanje, *Malawi* 87 F4
Mlanje, Pic, *Malawi* 85 H7
Mlava →, *Serbia & M.* 44 B5
Mława, *Poland* 31 E7
Mlawula ⌓, *Swaziland* 89 D5
Mlinište, *Bos.-H.* 41 D13
Mljet, *Croatia* 41 F14
Mljet △, *Croatia* 41 F14
Mljetski Kanal, *Croatia* 41 F14
Młynary, *Poland* 30 D6
Mmabatho, *S. Africa* 88 D4
Mme, *Cameroon* 83 D7
Mnichovo Hradiště, *Czech Rep.* 26 A7
Mo i Rana, *Norway* 8 C16
Moa, *Cuba* 121 B4
Moa, *Indonesia* 63 F7
Moa →, *S. Leone* 82 D2
Moab, *U.S.A.* 109 G9
Moala, *Fiji* 91 D8
Moama, *Australia* 95 F3
Moamba, *Mozam.* 89 D5
Moapa, *U.S.A.* 111 J12
Moate, *Ireland* 12 C4
Moba, *Dem. Rep. of the Congo* 86 D2
Mobārakābād, *Iran* 71 D7
Mobaye, *C.A.R.* 84 D4
Mobayi, *Dem. Rep. of the Congo* 84 D4
Moberley Lake, *Canada* 102 B4
Moberly, *U.S.A.* 112 F8
Mobile, *U.S.A.* 115 K1
Mobile B., *U.S.A.* 115 K2
Mobridge, *U.S.A.* 112 C4
Mobutu Sese Seko, L. = Albert, L., *Africa* 86 B3
Moc Chau, *Vietnam* 64 B5
Moc Hoa, *Vietnam* 65 G5
Mocabe Kasari, *Dem. Rep. of the Congo* 87 D2
Moçambique, *Mozam.* 87 F5
Moçâmedes = Namibe, *Angola* 85 H2
Mocanaqua, *U.S.A.* 117 E8
Mochima △, *Venezuela* 121 D7
Mochudi, *Botswana* 88 C4
Mocimboa da Praia, *Mozam.* 87 E5
Mociu, *Romania* 29 D9
Möckeln, *Sweden* 11 H8
Mockfjärd, *Sweden* 10 D8
Moclips, *U.S.A.* 110 C2
Mocoa, *Colombia* 124 C3
Mococa, *Brazil* 127 A6
Mocorito, *Mexico* 118 B3
Moctezuma, *Mexico* 118 B3
Moctezuma →, *Mexico* 119 C5
Mocuba, *Mozam.* 87 F4
Mocúzari, Presa, *Mexico* 118 B3
Modane, *France* 21 C10
Modasa, *India* 68 H5
Modder →, *S. Africa* 88 D3
Modderrivier, *S. Africa* 88 D3
Módena, *Italy* 40 D7
Modena, *U.S.A.* 109 H7
Modesto, *U.S.A.* 110 H6
Módica, *Italy* 43 F7
Modimolle, *S. Africa* 89 C4
Mödling, *Austria* 27 C9
Modo, *Sudan* 81 F3
Modra, *Slovak Rep.* 27 C10
Modriča, *Bos.-H.* 28 F3
Moe, *Australia* 95 F4
Moebase, *Mozam.* 87 F4
Moëlan-sur-Mer, *France* 18 E3
Moengo, *Suriname* 125 B8
Moffat, *U.K.* 13 F5
Moga, *India* 68 D6
Mogadishu = Muqdisho, *Somali Rep.* 75 G4
Mogador = Essaouira, *Morocco* 78 B4
Mogadouro, *Portugal* 36 D4
Mogalakwena →, *S. Africa* 89 C4
Mogami-Gawa →, *Japan* 54 E10
Mogán, *Canary Is.* 48 G4
Mogaung, *Burma* 67 G20
Mogente = Moixent, *Spain* 39 G4
Mogho, *Ethiopia* 81 G5
Mogi das Cruzes, *Brazil* 127 A6
Mogi-Guaçu →, *Brazil* 127 A6
Mogi-Mirim, *Brazil* 127 A6
Mogielnica, *Poland* 31 G7
Mogige, *Ethiopia* 81 F4
Mogilev = Mahilyow, *Belarus* 32 F6
Mogilev-Podolskiy = Mohyliv-Podilskyy, *Ukraine* 33 H4
Mogilno, *Poland* 31 F4
Mogincual, *Mozam.* 87 F5
Mogliano Véneto, *Italy* 41 C9
Mogocha, *Russia* 53 D12
Mogok, *Burma* 67 H20
Mogollon Rim, *U.S.A.* 109 J8
Mógoro, *Italy* 42 C1
Mograt, *Sudan* 80 D3
Moguer, *Spain* 37 H4
Mogumber, *Australia* 93 F2
Mohács, *Hungary* 28 E3
Mohales Hoek, *Lesotho* 88 E4
Mohall, *U.S.A.* 112 A4
Moḥammadābād, *Iran* 71 B8
Mohammedia, *Morocco* 78 B4
Mohana →, *India* 69 G11
Mohanlalganj, *India* 69 F9
Mohave, L., *U.S.A.* 111 K12
Mohawk →, *U.S.A.* 117 D11
Moheda, *Sweden* 11 G8
Mohenjodaro, *Pakistan* 68 F3
Moher, Cliffs of, *Ireland* 12 D2
Mohicanville Reservoir, *U.S.A.* 116 F3
Möhne →, *Germany* 24 D3
Mohoro, *Tanzania* 86 D4
Mohyliv-Podilskyy, *Ukraine* 33 H4
Moia, *Sudan* 81 F2
Moidart, L., *U.K.* 13 E3
Moineşti, *Romania* 29 D11
Moira →, *Canada* 116 B7
Moirans, *France* 21 C9
Moirans-en-Montagne, *France* 19 F12
Moíres, *Greece* 49 D6

Moisaküla, *Estonia* 9 G21
Moisie, *Canada* 105 B6
Moisie →, *Canada* 105 B6
Moissac, *France* 20 D5
Moita, *Portugal* 37 G2
Moixent, *Spain* 39 G4
Möja, *Sweden* 10 E12
Mojácar, *Spain* 39 H3
Mojados, *Spain* 36 D6
Mojave, *U.S.A.* 111 K8
Mojave ⌂, *U.S.A.* 111 K11
Mojave Desert, *U.S.A.* 111 L10
Mojiang, *China* 58 F3
Mojjo →, *Ethiopia* 81 F5
Mojkovac, *Serbia & M.* 44 D3
Mojo, *Bolivia* 126 A2
Mojo, *Ethiopia* 81 F4
Mojokerto, *Indonesia* 63 G15
Mokai, *N.Z.* 91 H5
Mokambo, *Dem. Rep. of the Congo* 87 E2
Mokameh, *India* 69 G11
Mokau, *N.Z.* 91 H5
Mokelumne →, *U.S.A.* 110 G5
Mokelumne Hill, *U.S.A.* 110 G6
Mokhós, *Greece* 49 D7
Mokhotlong, *Lesotho* 89 D4
Möklinta, *Sweden* 10 D10
Mokokchung, *India* 67 F19
Mokolo, *Cameroon* 83 C7
Mokolo →, *S. Africa* 89 C4
Mokopane, *S. Africa* 89 C4
Mokp'o, *S. Korea* 57 G14
Mokra Gora, *Serbia & M.* 44 D4
Mokronog, *Slovenia* 41 C12
Moksha →, *Russia* 34 C6
Mokshan, *Russia* 34 D7
Mokwa, *Nigeria* 83 D6
Mol, *Belgium* 17 C5
Mola di Bari, *Italy* 43 A10
Molale, *Ethiopia* 81 E4
Moláoi, *Greece* 46 E4
Molara, *Italy* 42 B2
Molat, *Croatia* 41 D11
Molchanovo, *Russia* 52 D9
Mold, *U.K.* 14 D4
Moldava nad Bodvou, *Slovak Rep.* 27 C14
Moldavia = Moldova ■, *Europe* 29 C13
Moldavia, *Romania* 29 D12
Molde, *Norway* 8 E12
Moldova ■, *Europe* 29 C13
Moldova Nouă, *Romania* 28 F6
Moldoveanu, Vf., *Romania* 29 E9
Moldoviţa, *Romania* 29 C10
Mole △, *Ghana* 83 D4
Mole →, *U.K.* 15 F7
Mole Creek, *Australia* 95 G4
Molepolole, *Botswana* 88 C4
Molfetta, *Italy* 43 A9
Molina de Aragón, *Spain* 38 E3
Molina de Segura, *Spain* 39 G3
Moline, *U.S.A.* 112 E9
Molinella, *Italy* 41 D8
Molinos, *Argentina* 126 B2
Moliro, *Dem. Rep. of the Congo* 86 D3
Moliterno, *Italy* 43 B8
Molkom, *Sweden* 10 E7
Mölle, *Sweden* 11 H6
Molledo, *Spain* 36 B6
Mollendo, *Peru* 124 G4
Mollerin, L., *Australia* 93 F2
Mollerussa, *Spain* 38 D5
Mollina, *Spain* 37 H6
Mölln, *Germany* 24 B6
Mölltorp, *Sweden* 11 F8
Mölnlycke, *Sweden* 11 G6
Molochansk, *Ukraine* 33 J8
Molochnoye, Ozero, *Ukraine* 33 J8
Molodechno = Maladzyechna, *Belarus* 32 E4
Molokai, *U.S.A.* 106 H16
Molong, *Australia* 95 E4
Molopo →, *Africa* 88 D3
Mólos, *Greece* 46 C4
Molotov = Perm, *Russia* 52 D6
Molsheim, *France* 19 D14
Molson L., *Canada* 103 C9
Molteno, *S. Africa* 88 E4
Molu, *Indonesia* 63 F8
Molucca Sea, *Indonesia* 63 E6
Moluccas = Maluku, *Indonesia* 63 E7
Moma, *Dem. Rep. of the Congo* 86 C1
Moma, *Mozam.* 87 F4
Mombasa, *Kenya* 86 C4
Mombetsu, *Japan* 54 B11
Mombuey, *Spain* 36 C4
Momchilgrad, *Bulgaria* 45 E9
Momi, *Dem. Rep. of the Congo* 86 C2
Mompós, *Colombia* 124 B4
Møn, *Denmark* 11 K6
Mon □, *Burma* 67 L20
Mona, Canal de la = Mona Passage, *W. Indies* 121 C6
Mona, Isla, *Puerto Rico* 121 C6
Mona, Pta., *Costa Rica* 120 E3
Mona Passage, *W. Indies* 121 C6
Monaca, *U.S.A.* 116 F4
Monaco ■, *Europe* 21 E11
Monadhliath Mts., *U.K.* 13 D4
Monadnock, Mt., *U.S.A.* 117 D12
Monaghan, *Ireland* 12 B5
Monaghan □, *Ireland* 12 B5
Monahans, *U.S.A.* 113 K3
Monapo, *Mozam.* 87 E5
Monar, L., *U.K.* 13 D3
Monarch Mt., *Canada* 102 C3
Monashee Mts., *Canada* 102 C5
Monasterevin, *Ireland* 12 C4
Monastir = Bitola, *Macedonia* 44 E5
Moncada, *Phil.* 61 D4
Moncalieri, *Italy* 40 D4
Moncalvo, *Italy* 40 C5
Moncão, *Portugal* 36 C2
Moncarapacho, *Portugal* 37 H3
Moncayo, Sierra del, *Spain* 38 D3
Mönchengladbach, *Germany* 24 D2
Monchique, *Portugal* 37 H2
Moncks Corner, *U.S.A.* 115 J5
Monclova, *Mexico* 118 B4
Moncontour, *France* 18 D4
Moncton, *Canada* 105 C7
Mondariz, *Spain* 36 C2
Mondego →, *Portugal* 36 E2
Mondego, C., *Portugal* 36 E2
Mondeodo, *Indonesia* 63 E6
Mondeville, *France* 18 C6
Mondolfo, *Italy* 41 E10
Mondoñedo, *Spain* 36 B3
Mondovì, *Italy* 40 D4
Mondragon, *Phil.* 61 E6
Mondragone, *Italy* 42 A6
Mondrain I., *Australia* 93 F3
Moneague, *Jamaica* 120 a
Monemvasía, *Greece* 46 E5
Monessen, *U.S.A.* 116 F5
Monesterio, *Spain* 37 G4
Monestier-de-Clermont, *France* 21 D9
Monett, *U.S.A.* 113 G8
Moneymore, *U.K.* 12 B5
Monfalcone, *Italy* 41 C10
Monflanquin, *France* 20 D4
Monforte, *Portugal* 37 F3
Monforte de Lemos, *Spain* 36 C3
Mong Cai, *Vietnam* 64 B6
Möng Hsu, *Burma* 58 G2
Mong Kung, *Burma* 67 J20
Mong Nai, *Burma* 67 J20
Mong Pawk, *Burma* 67 H21
Mong Ping, *Burma* 58 G2
Mong Ton, *Burma* 67 J21
Mong Wa, *Burma* 67 J22
Mong Yai, *Burma* 67 H21
Mongalla, *Sudan* 81 F3
Mongers, L., *Australia* 93 E2
Monghyr = Munger, *India* 69 G12
Mongibello = Etna, *Italy* 43 E7
Mongo, *Chad* 79 F9
Mongo →, *S. Leone* 82 D2
Mongolia ■, *Asia* 53 E10
Mongonu, *Nigeria* 83 C7
Mongu, *Zambia* 85 H4
Môngua, *Angola* 88 B2
Monifieth, *U.K.* 13 E6
Monistrol-sur-Loire, *France* 21 C8
Monkey Bay, *Malawi* 87 E4
Monkey Mia, *Australia* 93 E1
Monkey River, *Belize* 119 D7
Mońki, *Poland* 30 E9
Monkoto, *Dem. Rep. of the Congo* 84 E4
Monkton, *Canada* 116 C3
Monmouth, *U.K.* 15 F5
Monmouth, *Ill., U.S.A.* 112 E9
Monmouth, *Oreg., U.S.A.* 108 D2
Monmouthshire □, *U.K.* 15 F5
Mono L., *U.S.A.* 110 H7
Monolith, *U.S.A.* 111 K8
Monólithos, *Greece* 49 C9
Monongahela, *U.S.A.* 116 F5
Monópoli, *Italy* 43 B10
Monor, *Hungary* 28 C4
Monos I., *Trin. & Tob.* 125 K15
Monóvar, *Spain* 39 G4
Monreal del Campo, *Spain* 38 E3
Monreale, *Italy* 42 D6
Monroe, *Ga., U.S.A.* 115 J4
Monroe, *La., U.S.A.* 113 J8
Monroe, *Mich., U.S.A.* 114 E4
Monroe, *N.C., U.S.A.* 115 H5
Monroe, *N.Y., U.S.A.* 117 E10
Monroe, *Utah, U.S.A.* 109 G7
Monroe, *Wash., U.S.A.* 110 C5
Monroe, *Wis., U.S.A.* 112 D10
Monroe City, *U.S.A.* 112 F9
Monroeton, *U.S.A.* 117 E8
Monroeville, *Ala., U.S.A.* 115 K2
Monroeville, *Pa., U.S.A.* 116 F5
Monrovia, *Liberia* 82 D2
Mons, *Belgium* 17 D3
Møns Klint, *Denmark* 11 K6
Monsaraz, *Portugal* 37 G3
Monse, *Indonesia* 63 E6
Monségur, *France* 20 D4
Monsélice, *Italy* 41 C8
Mönsterås, *Sweden* 11 G10
Mont Cenis, Col du, *France* 21 C10
Mont-de-Marsan, *France* 20 E3
Mont-Joli, *Canada* 105 C6
Mont-Laurier, *Canada* 104 C4
Mont-Louis, *Canada* 105 C6
Mont Peko △, *Ivory C.* 82 D3
Mont-roig del Camp, *Spain* 38 D5
Mont-St-Michel, Le, *France* 18 D5
Mont Sangbe △, *Ivory C.* 82 D3
Mont-Tremblant ⌂, *Canada* 104 C5
Montabaur, *Germany* 24 E3
Montagnac, *France* 20 E7
Montagnana, *Italy* 41 C8
Montagne d'Ambre △, *Madag.* 89 A8
Montagne de Reims ⌂, *France* 19 C11
Montagu, *S. Africa* 88 E3
Montagu I., *Antarctica* 5 B1
Montague, *Canada* 105 C7
Montague, I., *Mexico* 118 A2
Montague Ra., *Australia* 93 E2
Montague Sd., *Australia* 92 B4
Montaigu, *France* 18 F5
Montalbán, *Spain* 38 E4
Montalbano Iónico, *Italy* 43 B9
Montalbo, *Spain* 38 F2
Montalcino, *Italy* 41 E8
Montalegre, *Portugal* 36 D3
Montalto, *Italy* 43 D8
Montalto di Castro, *Italy* 41 F8
Montalto Uffugo, *Italy* 43 C9
Montalvo, *U.S.A.* 111 L7
Montamarta, *Spain* 36 D5
Montana, *Bulgaria* 44 C7
Montaña, *Peru* 124 E4
Montana □, *Bulgaria* 44 C7
Montana □, *U.S.A.* 108 C9
Montaña Clara, I., *Canary Is.* 48 E6
Montañas de Malaga ⌂, *Spain* 37 J6
Montánchez, *Spain* 37 F4
Montargil, *Portugal* 37 F2
Montargis, *France* 19 E9
Montauban, *France* 20 D5
Montauk, *U.S.A.* 117 E13
Montauk Pt., *U.S.A.* 117 E13
Montbard, *France* 19 E11
Montbarrey, *France* 19 E12
Montbéliard, *France* 19 E13
Montblanc, *Spain* 38 D6
Montbrison, *France* 21 C8
Montcalm, Pic de, *France* 20 F5
Montceau-les-Mines, *France* 19 F11
Montcenis, *France* 21 B8
Montclair, *U.S.A.* 117 F10
Montcornet, *France* 19 C11
Montcuq, *France* 20 D5
Montdidier, *France* 19 C9
Monte Albán, *Mexico* 119 D5
Monte Alegre, *Brazil* 125 D8
Monte Azul, *Brazil* 125 G10
Monte Bello Is., *Australia* 92 D2
Monte-Carlo, *Monaco* 21 E11
Monte Caseros, *Argentina* 126 C4
Monte Comán, *Argentina* 126 C2
Monte Cristi, *Dom. Rep.* 121 C5
Monte Cucco ⌂, *Italy* 41 E9
Monte Lindo →, *Paraguay* 126 A4
Monte Patria, *Chile* 126 C1
Monte Quemado, *Argentina* 126 B3
Monte Redondo, *Portugal* 36 F2
Monte Rio, *U.S.A.* 110 G4
Monte San Giovanni Campano, *Italy* 42 A6
Monte San Savino, *Italy* 41 E8
Monte Sant' Ángelo, *Italy* 41 G12
Monte Santu, C. di, *Italy* 42 B2
Monte Sibillini △, *Italy* 41 F10
Monte Subasio ⌂, *Italy* 41 E9
Monte Vista, *U.S.A.* 109 H10
Monteagudo, *Argentina* 127 B5
Montealegre del Castillo, *Spain* 39 G3
Montebello, *Canada* 104 C5
Montebello Iónico, *Italy* 43 E8
Montebelluna, *Italy* 41 C9
Montebourg, *France* 18 C5
Montecastrilli, *Italy* 41 F9
Montecatini Terme, *Italy* 40 E7
Montecito, *U.S.A.* 111 L7
Montecristo, *Italy* 40 F7
Montefalco, *Italy* 41 F9
Montefiascone, *Italy* 41 F9
Montefrío, *Spain* 37 H7
Montegiórgio, *Italy* 41 E10
Montego Bay, *Jamaica* 120 a
Montehermoso, *Spain* 36 E4
Montejicar, *Spain* 37 H7
Montélimar, *France* 21 D8
Montella, *Italy* 43 B8
Montellano, *Spain* 37 J5
Montello, *U.S.A.* 112 D10
Montemor-o-Novo, *Portugal* 37 G2
Montemor-o-Velho, *Portugal* 36 E2
Montemorelos, *Mexico* 119 B5
Montendre, *France* 20 C3
Montenegro, *Brazil* 127 B5
Montenegro □, *Serbia & M.* 44 D3
Montenero di Bisáccia, *Italy* 41 G11
Montepuez, *Mozam.* 87 E4
Montepuez →, *Mozam.* 87 E5
Montepulciano, *Italy* 41 E8
Montereale, *Italy* 41 F10
Montereau-Faut-Yonne, *France* 19 D9
Monterey, *U.S.A.* 110 J5
Monterey B., *U.S.A.* 110 J5
Montería, *Colombia* 124 B3
Monteros, *Argentina* 126 B2
Monterotondo, *Italy* 41 F9
Monterrey, *Mexico* 118 B4
Montes Azules ⌂, *Mexico* 119 D6
Montes Claros, *Brazil* 125 G10
Montesano, *U.S.A.* 110 D3
Montesano sulla Marcellana, *Italy* 43 B8
Montesárchio, *Italy* 43 A7
Montescaglioso, *Italy* 43 B9
Montesilvano, *Italy* 41 F11
Montesinho ⌂, *Portugal* 36 D4
Montevarchi, *Italy* 41 E8
Montevideo, *Uruguay* 127 C4
Montevideo, *U.S.A.* 112 C7
Montezuma, *U.S.A.* 112 E8
Montezuma Castle ⌂, *U.S.A.* 109 J8
Montfaucon, *France* 18 E5
Montfaucon-d'Argonne, *France* 19 C12
Montfaucon-en-Velay, *France* 21 C8
Montfort, *France* 18 D5
Montfort-le-Gesnois, *France* 18 D7
Montfragüe ⌂, *Spain* 36 F5
Montgenèvre, *France* 21 D10
Montgomery = Sahiwal, *Pakistan* 68 D5
Montgomery, *U.K.* 15 E4
Montgomery, *Ala., U.S.A.* 115 J2
Montgomery, *Pa., U.S.A.* 116 E8
Montgomery, *W. Va., U.S.A.* 114 F5
Montgomery City, *U.S.A.* 112 F9
Montguyon, *France* 20 C3
Monthermé, *France* 19 C11
Monthey, *Switz.* 25 J2
Monthois, *France* 19 C11
Monti, *Italy* 42 B2
Monti Lucrétili ⌂, *Italy* 41 F9
Monti Picentini ⌂, *Italy* 43 B8
Monti Simbruini ⌂, *Italy* 41 G10
Monticelli d'Ongina, *Italy* 40 C6
Monticello, *Ark., U.S.A.* 113 J9
Monticello, *Fla., U.S.A.* 115 K4
Monticello, *Ind., U.S.A.* 114 E2
Monticello, *Iowa, U.S.A.* 112 D9
Monticello, *Ky., U.S.A.* 115 G3
Monticello, *Minn., U.S.A.* 112 C8
Monticello, *Miss., U.S.A.* 113 K9
Monticello, *N.Y., U.S.A.* 117 E10
Monticello, *Utah, U.S.A.* 109 H9
Montichiari, *Italy* 40 C7
Montier-en-Der, *France* 19 D11
Montignac, *France* 20 C5
Montigny-les-Metz, *France* 19 C13
Montigny-sur-Aube, *France* 19 E11
Montijo, *Portugal* 37 G2
Montijo, *Spain* 37 G4
Montilla, *Spain* 37 H6
Montivilliers, *France* 18 C7
Montluçon, *France* 19 F9
Montmagny, *Canada* 105 C5
Montmarault, *France* 19 F9
Montmartre, *Canada* 103 C8
Montmédy, *France* 19 C12
Montmélian, *France* 21 C10
Montmirail, *France* 19 D10
Montmoreau-St-Cybard, *France* 20 C4
Montmorillon, *France* 20 B4
Montmort-Lucy, *France* 19 D10
Monto, *Australia* 94 C5
Montoire-sur-le-Loir, *France* 18 E7
Montongbuwoh, *Indonesia* 63 K19
Montório al Vomano, *Italy* 41 F10
Montoro, *Spain* 37 G6
Montour Falls, *U.S.A.* 116 D8
Montoursville, *U.S.A.* 116 E8
Montpelier, *Idaho, U.S.A.* 108 E8
Montpelier, *Vt., U.S.A.* 117 B12
Montpellier, *France* 20 E7
Montpezat-de-Quercy, *France* 20 D5
Montpon-Ménestérol, *France* 20 D4
Montréal, *Canada* 117 A11
Montréal, *Aude, France* 20 E6
Montréal, *Gers, France* 20 E4
Montreal →, *Canada* 104 C3
Montreal L., *Canada* 103 C7
Montreal Lake, *Canada* 103 C7
Montredon-Labessonnié, *France* 20 E6
Montrésor, *France* 18 E8
Montret, *France* 19 F12
Montreuil, *Pas-de-Calais, France* 19 B8
Montreuil, *Seine-St-Denis, France* 19 D9
Montreuil-Bellay, *France* 18 E6
Montreux, *Switz.* 25 J2
Montrevel-en-Bresse, *France* 19 F12
Montrichard, *France* 18 E8
Montrose, *U.K.* 13 E6
Montrose, *Colo., U.S.A.* 109 G10
Montrose, *Pa., U.S.A.* 117 E9
Monts, Pte. des, *Canada* 105 C6
Montsalvy, *France* 20 D6
Montsant, Serra de, *Spain* 38 D6
Montsauche-les-Settons, *France* 19 E11
Montsec, Serra del, *Spain* 38 C5
Montseny ⌂, *Spain* 38 D2
Montserrat, *Spain* 38 D6
Montserrat ☒, *W. Indies* 121 C7
Montuenga, *Spain* 36 D6
Montuiri, *Spain* 48 B9
Monywa, *Burma* 67 H19
Monza, *Italy* 40 C6
Monze, *Zambia* 87 F2
Monze, C., *Pakistan* 68 G2
Monzón, *Spain* 38 D5
Mooers, *U.S.A.* 117 B11
Mooi →, *S. Africa* 89 D5
Mooi River, *S. Africa* 89 D4
Moonah →, *Australia* 94 C2
Moonda, L., *Australia* 94 D3
Moonie, *Australia* 95 D5
Moonie →, *Australia* 95 D4
Moonta, *Australia* 95 E2
Moora, *Australia* 93 F2
Moorcroft, *U.S.A.* 112 C2
Moore →, *Australia* 93 F2
Moore, L., *Australia* 93 E2
Moore Park, *Australia* 94 C5
Moore River △, *Australia* 93 F2
Moorefield, *U.S.A.* 114 F6
Moores Res., *U.S.A.* 117 B13
Moorfoot Hills, *U.K.* 13 F5
Moorhead, *U.S.A.* 112 B6
Moormerland, *Germany* 24 B3
Moorpark, *U.S.A.* 111 L8
Moorreesburg, *S. Africa* 88 E2
Moorrinya △, *Australia* 94 C3
Moosburg, *Germany* 25 G7
Moose →, *Canada* 104 B3
Moose →, *U.S.A.* 117 C9
Moose Creek, *Canada* 117 A10
Moose Factory, *Canada* 104 B3
Moose Jaw, *Canada* 103 C7
Moose Jaw →, *Canada* 103 C7
Moose Lake, *U.S.A.* 112 B8
Moose Mountain ⌂, *Canada* 103 D8
Moosehead L., *U.S.A.* 115 C11
Mooselookmeguntic L., *U.S.A.* 115 C10
Moosilauke, Mt., *U.S.A.* 117 B13
Moosomin, *Canada* 103 C8
Moosonee, *Canada* 104 B3
Moosup, *U.S.A.* 117 E13
Mopane, *S. Africa* 89 C4
Mopeia Velha, *Mozam.* 87 F4
Mopipi, *Botswana* 88 C3
Mopoi, *C.A.R.* 86 A2
Mopti, *Mali* 82 C4
Moqatta, *Sudan* 81 E4
Moqor, *Afghan.* 68 C2
Moquegua, *Peru* 124 G4
Mór, *Hungary* 28 C3
Mora, *Cameroon* 83 C7
Móra, *Portugal* 37 G2
Mora, *Spain* 37 F7
Mora, *Sweden* 10 C8
Mora, *Minn., U.S.A.* 112 C8
Mora, *N. Mex., U.S.A.* 109 J11
Mora →, *U.S.A.* 113 H2
Mora de Ebro = Mòra d'Ebre, *Spain* 38 D5
Mora de Rubielos, *Spain* 38 E4
Mòra d'Ebre, *Spain* 38 D5
Mòra la Nova, *Spain* 38 D5
Morača →, *Serbia & M.* 44 D3
Moradabad, *India* 69 E8
Morafenobe, *Madag.* 89 B7
Morąg, *Poland* 30 E6
Moral de Calatrava, *Spain* 37 G7
Moraleja, *Spain* 36 E4
Moramanga, *Madag.* 89 B8
Moran, *Kans., U.S.A.* 113 G7
Moran, *Wyo., U.S.A.* 108 E8
Moranbah, *Australia* 94 C4
Morano Cálabro, *Italy* 43 C9
Morant Bay, *Jamaica* 120 a
Morant Cays, *Jamaica* 120 C4
Morant Pt., *Jamaica* 120 a
Morar, *India* 68 F8
Morar, L., *U.K.* 13 E3
Moratalla, *Spain* 39 G3
Moratuwa, *Sri Lanka* 66 R11
Morava →, *Slovak Rep.* 27 C9
Moravia, *U.S.A.* 117 D8
Moravian Hts. = Českomoravská Vrchovina, *Czech Rep.* 26 B8
Moravica →, *Serbia & M.* 44 C4
Moraviţa, *Romania* 28 E6
Moravská Třebová, *Czech Rep.* 27 B9
Moravské Budějovice, *Czech Rep.* 26 B8
Morawa, *Australia* 93 E2
Morawhanna, *Guyana* 124 B7
Moray □, *U.K.* 13 D5
Moray Firth, *U.K.* 13 D5
Morbach, *Germany* 25 F3
Morbegno, *Italy* 40 B6
Morbi, *India* 68 H4
Morbihan □, *France* 18 E4
Mörbylånga, *Sweden* 11 H10
Morcenx, *France* 20 D3
Morcone, *Italy* 43 A7
Mordelles, *France* 18 D5
Morden, *Canada* 103 D9
Mordoğan, *Turkey* 47 C8
Mordovian Republic = Mordvinia □, *Russia* 34 C7
Mordovo, *Russia* 34 D5
Mordvinia □, *Russia* 34 C7
Mordy, *Poland* 31 F9
Morea, *Greece* 6 H10
Moreau →, *U.S.A.* 112 C4
Morecambe, *U.K.* 14 C5
Morecambe B., *U.K.* 14 C5
Moree, *Australia* 95 D4
Morehead, *U.S.A.* 114 F4
Morehead City, *U.S.A.* 115 H7
Morel →, *India* 68 F7
Morelia, *Mexico* 118 D4
Morella, *Australia* 94 C3
Morella, *Spain* 38 E4
Morelos, *Mexico* 118 B3
Morelos □, *Mexico* 119 D5
Moremi ⌂, *Botswana* 88 B3
Morena, *India* 68 F8
Morena, Sierra, *Spain* 37 G7
Moreni, *Romania* 29 F10
Moreno Valley, *U.S.A.* 111 M10
Moresby I., *Canada* 102 C2
Morestel, *France* 21 C9
Moreton I., *Australia* 95 D5
Moreton Island △, *Australia* 95 D5
Moreuil, *France* 19 C9
Morey, *Spain* 48 B10
Morez, *France* 19 F13
Morgan, *U.S.A.* 108 F8
Morgan City, *U.S.A.* 113 L9
Morgan Hill, *U.S.A.* 110 H5
Morganfield, *U.S.A.* 114 G2
Morganton, *U.S.A.* 115 H5
Morgantown, *U.S.A.* 114 F6
Morgenzon, *S. Africa* 89 D4
Morges, *Switz.* 25 J2
Morghak, *Iran* 71 D8
Morgongåva, *Sweden* 10 E10
Morhange, *France* 19 D13
Morhar →, *India* 69 G11
Mori, *Italy* 40 C7
Mori, *Japan* 54 C10
Moriarty, *U.S.A.* 109 J10
Moribaya, *Guinea* 82 D3
Morice L., *Canada* 102 C3
Moriki, *Nigeria* 83 C6
Morinville, *Canada* 102 C6
Morioka, *Japan* 54 E10
Moris, *Mexico* 118 B3
Morlaàs, *France* 20 E3
Morlaix, *France* 18 D3
Mörlunda, *Sweden* 11 G9
Mormanno, *Italy* 43 C8
Mormant, *France* 19 D9
Mornington, *Australia* 95 F4
Mornington, I., *Chile* 128 F1
Mornington I., *Australia* 94 B2
Mórnos →, *Greece* 46 C3
Moro, *Pakistan* 68 F2
Moro, *Sudan* 81 E3
Moro →, *Pakistan* 68 E2
Moro G., *Phil.* 61 H5
Morocco ■, *N. Afr.* 78 B4
Morogoro, *Tanzania* 86 D4
Morogoro □, *Tanzania* 86 D4

Moroleón, *Mexico* 118 C4
Morombe, *Madag.* 89 C7
Moron, *Argentina* 126 C4
Morón, *Cuba* 120 B4
Morón de Almazán, *Spain* 38 D2
Morón de la Frontera, *Spain* 37 H5
Morona →, *Peru* 124 D3
Morondava, *Madag.* 89 C7
Morondo, *Ivory C.* 82 D3
Morongo Valley, *U.S.A.* 111 L10
Moroni, *Comoros Is.* 77 H8
Moroni, *U.S.A.* 108 G8
Moronou, *Ivory C.* 82 D4
Morotai, *Indonesia* 63 D7
Moroto, *Uganda* 86 B3
Moroto, Mt., *Uganda* 86 B3
Morozov, *Bulgaria* 45 D9
Morozovsk, *Russia* 35 F5
Morpeth, *U.K.* 14 B6
Morphou, *Cyprus* 49 D11
Morphou Bay, *Cyprus* 49 D11
Morrilton, *U.S.A.* 113 H8
Morrinhos, *Brazil* 125 G9
Morrinsville, *N.Z.* 91 G5
Morris, *Canada* 103 D9
Morris, *Ill., U.S.A.* 112 E10
Morris, *Minn., U.S.A.* 112 C7
Morris, *N.Y., U.S.A.* 117 D9
Morris, *Pa., U.S.A.* 116 E7
Morris, Mt., *Australia* 93 E5
Morris Jesup, Kap, *Greenland* 4 A5
Morrisburg, *Canada* 117 B9
Morristown, *Ariz., U.S.A.* 109 K7
Morristown, *N.J., U.S.A.* 117 F10
Morristown, *N.Y., U.S.A.* 117 B9
Morristown, *Tenn., U.S.A.* 115 G4
Morrisville, *N.Y., U.S.A.* 117 D9
Morrisville, *Pa., U.S.A.* 117 F10
Morrisville, *Vt., U.S.A.* 117 B12
Morro, Pta., *Chile* 126 B1
Morro Bay, *U.S.A.* 110 K6
Morro del Jable, *Canary Is.* 48 F5
Morro Jable, Pta. de, *Canary Is.* 48 F5
Morrocoy △, *Venezuela* 121 D6
Morrosquillo, G. de, *Colombia* 120 E4
Mörrum, *Sweden* 11 H8
Morrumbene, *Mozam.* 89 C6
Mörrumsån →, *Sweden* 11 H8
Mors, *Denmark* 11 H2
Morshansk, *Russia* 34 D5
Mörsil, *Sweden* 10 A7
Mortagne →, *France* 19 D13
Mortagne-au-Perche, *France* 18 D7
Mortagne-sur-Gironde, *France* 20 C3
Mortagne-sur-Sèvre, *France* 18 F6
Mortain, *France* 18 D6
Mortara, *Italy* 40 C5
Morteau, *France* 19 E13
Morteros, *Argentina* 126 C3
Mortlach, *Canada* 103 C7
Mortlake, *Australia* 95 F3
Morton, *Tex., U.S.A.* 113 J3
Morton, *Wash., U.S.A.* 110 D4
Moruga, *Trin. & Tob.* 125 K15
Morundah, *Australia* 95 E4
Moruya, *Australia* 95 F5
Morvan, *France* 19 E11
Morvan ⌓, *France* 19 E11
Morven, *Australia* 95 D4
Morvern, *U.K.* 13 E3
Morwell, *Australia* 95 F4
Moryń, *Poland* 31 F1
Morzine, *France* 19 F13
Mosalsk, *Russia* 32 E8
Mosbach, *Germany* 25 F5
Moščenice, *Croatia* 41 C11
Mosciano Sant' Ángelo, *Italy* 41 F10
Moscos Is., *Burma* 64 E1
Moscow = Moskva, *Russia* 32 E9
Moscow, *Idaho, U.S.A.* 108 C5
Moscow, *Pa., U.S.A.* 117 E9
Mosel →, *Europe* 19 B14
Moselle = Mosel →, *Europe* 19 B14
Moselle □, *France* 19 D13
Moses Lake, *U.S.A.* 108 C4
Mosgiel, *N.Z.* 91 L3
Moshaweng →, *S. Africa* 88 D3
Moshi, *Tanzania* 86 C4
Moshupa, *Botswana* 88 C4
Mosina, *Poland* 31 F3
Mosjøen, *Norway* 8 D15
Moskenesøya, *Norway* 8 C15
Moskenstraumen, *Norway* 8 C15
Moskva, *Russia* 32 E9
Moskva →, *Russia* 32 E10
Moslavačka Gora, *Croatia* 41 C13
Mosomane, *Botswana* 88 C4
Mosonmagyaróvár, *Hungary* 28 C2
Mošorin, *Serbia & M.* 28 E5
Mospino, *Ukraine* 33 J9
Mosquera, *Colombia* 124 C3
Mosquero, *U.S.A.* 113 H3
Mosqueruela, *Spain* 38 E4
Mosquitia, *Honduras* 120 C3
Mosquito Coast = Mosquitia, *Honduras* 120 C3
Mosquito Creek L., *U.S.A.* 116 E4
Mosquito L., *Canada* 103 A8
Mosquitos, G. de los, *Panama* 120 E3
Moss, *Norway* 9 G14
Moss Vale, *Australia* 95 E5
Mossbank, *Canada* 103 D7
Mossburn, *N.Z.* 91 L2
Mosselbaai, *S. Africa* 88 E3
Mossendjo, *Congo* 84 E2
Mossgiel, *Australia* 95 E3
Mossingen, *Germany* 25 G5
Mossman, *Australia* 94 B4
Mossoró, *Brazil* 125 E11
Mossuril, *Mozam.* 87 E5
Most, *Czech Rep.* 26 A6
Mosta, *Malta* 49 D1
Mostaganem, *Algeria* 78 A6
Mostar, *Bos.-H.* 28 G2
Mostardas, *Brazil* 127 C5
Mostiska = Mostyska, *Ukraine* 33 H2
Móstoles, *Spain* 36 E7
Mosty = Masty, *Belarus* 32 F3
Mostyska, *Ukraine* 33 H2
Mosul = Al Mawşil, *Iraq* 70 B4
Mosŭlpo, *S. Korea* 57 H14
Mota, *Ethiopia* 81 E4
Mota del Cuervo, *Spain* 39 F2
Mota del Marqués, *Spain* 36 D5
Motagua →, *Guatemala* 120 C2
Motala, *Sweden* 11 F9
Motaze, *Mozam.* 89 C5
Moţca, *Romania* 29 C11
Moth, *India* 69 G8
Motherwell, *U.K.* 13 F5
Motihari, *India* 69 F11
Motilla del Palancar, *Spain* 39 F3
Motnik, *Slovenia* 41 B11
Motovun, *Croatia* 41 C10
Motozintla de Mendoza, *Mexico* 119 D6
Motril, *Spain* 37 J7
Motru, *Romania* 28 F7
Motru →, *Romania* 29 F8
Mott, *U.S.A.* 112 B3
Móttola, *Italy* 43 B10
Motueka, *N.Z.* 91 J4
Motueka →, *N.Z.* 91 J4
Motul, *Mexico* 119 C7
Mouchalagane →, *Canada* 105 B6
Moúdhros, *Greece* 47 B7
Mouding, *China* 58 E3
Moudjeria, *Mauritania* 82 B2
Moudon, *Switz.* 25 J2
Mouila, *Gabon* 84 E2
Moulamein, *Australia* 95 F3
Moule, *Guadeloupe* 120 b
Moule à Chique, C., *St. Lucia* 121 f
Moulianá, *Greece* 49 D7
Moulins, *France* 19 F10
Moulmein, *Burma* 67 L20
Moulouya, O. →, *Morocco* 78 B5
Moultrie, *U.S.A.* 115 K4
Moultrie, L., *U.S.A.* 115 J5
Mound City, *Mo., U.S.A.* 112 E7
Mound City, *S. Dak., U.S.A.* 112 C4
Moúnda, Ákra, *Greece* 46 C2
Moundou, *Chad* 79 G9
Moundsville, *U.S.A.* 116 G4
Moung, *Cambodia* 64 F4
Mount Airy, *U.S.A.* 115 G5
Mount Albert, *Canada* 116 B5
Mount Aspiring △, *N.Z.* 91 L2
Mount Barker, *S. Austral., Australia* 95 F2
Mount Barker, *W. Austral., Australia* 93 F2
Mount Brydges, *Canada* 116 D3
Mount Burr, *Australia* 95 F3
Mount Carmel = Ha Karmel △, *Israel* 74 C4
Mount Carmel, *Ill., U.S.A.* 114 F2
Mount Carmel, *Pa., U.S.A.* 117 F8
Mount Charleston, *U.S.A.* 111 J11
Mount Clemens, *U.S.A.* 116 D2
Mount Coolon, *Australia* 94 C4
Mount Darwin, *Zimbabwe* 87 F3
Mount Desert I., *U.S.A.* 115 C11
Mount Dora, *U.S.A.* 115 L5
Mount Edziza ⌓, *Canada* 102 B2
Mount Elgon △, *E. Afr.* 86 B3
Mount Field △, *Australia* 95 G4
Mount Fletcher, *S. Africa* 89 E4
Mount Forest, *Canada* 116 C4
Mount Gambier, *Australia* 95 F3
Mount Garnet, *Australia* 94 B4
Mount Holly, *U.S.A.* 117 G10
Mount Holly Springs, *U.S.A.* 116 F7
Mount Hope, *N.S.W., Australia* 95 E4
Mount Hope, *S. Austral., Australia* 95 E2
Mount Isa, *Australia* 94 C2
Mount Jewett, *U.S.A.* 116 E6
Mount Kaputar △, *Australia* 95 E5
Mount Kenya △, *Kenya* 86 C4
Mount Kilimanjaro △, *Tanzania* 86 C4
Mount Kisco, *U.S.A.* 117 E11
Mount Laguna, *U.S.A.* 111 N10
Mount Larcom, *Australia* 94 C5
Mount Lofty Ra., *Australia* 95 E2
Mount Magnet, *Australia* 93 E2
Mount Maunganui, *N.Z.* 91 G6
Mount Molloy, *Australia* 94 B4
Mount Morgan, *Australia* 94 C5
Mount Morris, *U.S.A.* 116 D7
Mount Pearl, *Canada* 105 C9
Mount Penn, *U.S.A.* 117 F9
Mount Perry, *Australia* 95 D5
Mount Pleasant, *Iowa, U.S.A.* 112 E9
Mount Pleasant, *Mich., U.S.A.* 114 D3
Mount Pleasant, *Pa., U.S.A.* 116 F5
Mount Pleasant, *S.C., U.S.A.* 115 J6
Mount Pleasant, *Tenn., U.S.A.* 115 H2
Mount Pleasant, *Tex., U.S.A.* 113 J7
Mount Pleasant, *Utah, U.S.A.* 108 G8
Mount Pocono, *U.S.A.* 117 E9
Mount Rainier △, *U.S.A.* 110 D5
Mount Revelstoke △, *Canada* 102 C5
Mount Robson ⌓, *Canada* 102 C5
Mount St. Helens ⌓, *U.S.A.* 110 D4
Mount Selinda, *Zimbabwe* 89 C5
Mount Shasta, *U.S.A.* 108 F2
Mount Signal, *U.S.A.* 111 N11
Mount Sterling, *Ill., U.S.A.* 112 F9
Mount Sterling, *Ky., U.S.A.* 114 F4
Mount Surprise, *Australia* 94 B3
Mount Union, *U.S.A.* 116 F7
Mount Upton, *U.S.A.* 117 D9
Mount Vernon, *Ill., U.S.A.* 114 F1
Mount Vernon, *Ind., U.S.A.* 112 F10
Mount Vernon, *N.Y., U.S.A.* 117 F11
Mount Vernon, *Ohio, U.S.A.* 116 F2
Mount Vernon, *Wash., U.S.A.* 110 B4
Mount William △, *Australia* 95 G4
Mountain Ash, *U.K.* 15 F4
Mountain Center, *U.S.A.* 111 M10
Mountain City, *Nev., U.S.A.* 108 F6
Mountain City, *Tenn., U.S.A.* 115 G5
Mountain Dale, *U.S.A.* 117 E10
Mountain Grove, *U.S.A.* 113 G8
Mountain Home, *Ark., U.S.A.* 113 G8
Mountain Home, *Idaho, U.S.A.* 108 E6
Mountain Iron, *U.S.A.* 112 B8
Mountain Pass, *U.S.A.* 111 K11
Mountain View, *Ark., U.S.A.* 113 H8
Mountain View, *Calif., U.S.A.* 110 H4
Mountain View, *Hawaii, U.S.A.* 106 J17
Mountain Zebra △, *S. Africa* 88 E4
Mountainair, *U.S.A.* 109 J10
Mountlake Terrace, *U.S.A.* 110 C4
Mountmellick, *Ireland* 12 C4
Mountrath, *Ireland* 12 D4
Moura, *Australia* 94 C4
Moura, *Brazil* 124 D6
Moura, *Portugal* 37 G3
Mourão, *Portugal* 37 G3
Mourdi, Dépression du, *Chad* 79 E10
Mourdiah, *Mali* 82 C3
Mourenx, *France* 20 E3
Mouri, *Ghana* 83 D4
Mourilyan, *Australia* 94 B4
Mourmelon-le-Grand, *France* 19 C11
Mourne →, *U.K.* 12 B4
Mourne Mts., *U.K.* 12 B5
Mourniaí, *Greece* 49 D6
Mournies = Mourniaí, *Greece* 49 D6
Mouscron, *Belgium* 17 D3
Moussoro, *Chad* 79 F9
Mouthe, *France* 19 F13
Moutier, *Switz.* 25 H3
Moûtiers, *France* 21 C10
Moutong, *Indonesia* 63 D6
Mouy, *France* 19 C9
Mouzáki, *Greece* 46 B3
Mouzon, *France* 19 C12
Movas, *Mexico* 118 B3
Moville, *Ireland* 12 A4
Mowandjum, *Australia* 92 C3
Moy →, *Ireland* 12 B2
Moyale, *Kenya* 81 G4
Moyamba, *S. Leone* 82 D2
Moyen Atlas, *Morocco* 78 B4
Moyne, L. le, *Canada* 105 A6
Moyo, *Indonesia* 62 F5
Moyobamba, *Peru* 124 E3
Moyyero →, *Russia* 53 C11
Moyynty, *Kazakhstan* 52 E8
Mozambique = Moçambique, *Mozam.* 87 F5
Mozambique ■, *Africa* 87 F4
Mozambique Chan., *Africa* 89 B7
Mozdok, *Russia* 35 J7
Mozdūrān, *Iran* 71 B9
Mozhaysk, *Russia* 32 E9
Mozhga, *Russia* 34 B11
Mozhnābād, *Iran* 71 C9
Mozirje, *Slovenia* 41 B11
Mozyr = Mazyr, *Belarus* 33 F5
Mpanda, *Tanzania* 86 D3
Mpésoba, *Mali* 82 C3
Mphoengs, *Zimbabwe* 89 C4
Mpika, *Zambia* 87 E3
Mpulungu, *Zambia* 87 D3
Mpumalanga, *S. Africa* 89 D5
Mpumalanga □, *S. Africa* 89 D5
Mpwapwa, *Tanzania* 86 D4
Mqanduli, *S. Africa* 89 E4
Mqinvartsveri = Kazbek, *Russia* 35 J7
Mrągowo, *Poland* 30 E8
Mramor, *Serbia & M.* 44 C5
Mrkonjić Grad, *Bos.-H.* 28 F2
Mrkopalj, *Croatia* 41 C11
Mrocza, *Poland* 31 E4
Msambansovu, *Zimbabwe* 87 F3
M'sila →, *Algeria* 78 A6
Msoro, *Zambia* 87 E3
Msta →, *Russia* 32 C6
Mstislavl = Mstsislaw, *Belarus* 32 E6
Mstsislaw, *Belarus* 32 E6
Mszana Dolna, *Poland* 31 J7
Mszczonów, *Poland* 31 G7
Mtama, *Tanzania* 87 E4
Mtamvuna →, *S. Africa* 89 E5
Mtilikwe →, *Zimbabwe* 87 G3
Mtsensk, *Russia* 32 F9
Mtskheta, *Georgia* 35 K7
Mtubatuba, *S. Africa* 89 D5
Mtwalume, *S. Africa* 89 E5
Mtwara-Mikindani, *Tanzania* 87 E5
Mu Gia, Deo, *Vietnam* 64 D5
Mu Ko Chang △, *Thailand* 65 G4
Mu Us Shamo, *China* 56 E5
Muang Chiang Rai = Chiang Rai, *Thailand* 58 H2
Muang Khong, *Laos* 64 E5
Muang Lamphun, *Thailand* 64 C2
Muang Mai, *Thailand* 65 a
Muang Pak Beng, *Laos* 58 H3
Muar, *Malaysia* 65 L4
Muarabungo, *Indonesia* 62 E2
Muaraenim, *Indonesia* 62 E2
Muarajuloi, *Indonesia* 62 E4
Muarakaman, *Indonesia* 62 E5
Muaratebo, *Indonesia* 62 E2
Muaratembesi, *Indonesia* 62 E2
Muaratewe, *Indonesia* 62 E4
Mubarakpur, *India* 69 F10
Mubarraz = Al Mubarraz, *Si. Arabia* 71 E6
Mubende, *Uganda* 86 B3
Mubi, *Nigeria* 83 C7
Mucajaí →, *Brazil* 124 C6
Muchachos, Roque de los, *Canary Is.* 48 F2
Mücheln, *Germany* 24 D7
Muchinga Mts., *Zambia* 87 E3
Muchkapskiy, *Russia* 34 E6
Muchuan, *China* 58 C5
Muck, *U.K.* 13 E2
Muckadilla, *Australia* 95 D4
Muckle Flugga, *U.K.* 13 A8
Mucur, *Turkey* 72 C6
Mucuri, *Brazil* 125 G11
Mucusso, *Angola* 88 B3
Muda, *Canary Is.* 48 F6
Mudanjiang, *China* 57 B15
Mudanya, *Turkey* 45 F12
Muddy Cr. →, *U.S.A.* 109 H8
Mudgee, *Australia* 95 E4
Mudjatik →, *Canada* 103 B7
Mudurnu, *Turkey* 72 B4
Muecate, *Mozam.* 87 E4
Mueda, *Mozam.* 87 E4
Mueller Ra., *Australia* 92 C4
Muende, *Mozam.* 87 E3
Muerto, Mar, *Mexico* 119 D6
Mufu Shan, *China* 59 C10
Mufulira, *Zambia* 87 E2
Mufumbiro Range, *Africa* 86 C2
Mugardos, *Spain* 36 B2
Muge →, *Portugal* 37 F2
Múggia, *Italy* 41 C10
Mughal Sarai, *India* 69 G10
Mughayrā', *Si. Arabia* 70 D3
Mugi, *Japan* 55 H7
Mugia = Muxía, *Spain* 36 B1
Mugila, Mts., *Dem. Rep. of the Congo* 86 D2
Muğla, *Turkey* 47 D10
Muğla □, *Turkey* 47 D10
Muglad, *Sudan* 81 E2
Müglizh, *Bulgaria* 45 D9
Mugu, *Nepal* 69 E10
Muhammad, Râs, *Egypt* 70 E2
Muhammad Qol, *Sudan* 80 C4
Muhammadabad, *India* 69 F10
Muhesi →, *Tanzania* 86 D4
Mühlacker, *Germany* 25 G4
Mühldorf, *Germany* 25 G8
Mühlhausen, *Germany* 24 D6
Mühlig Hofmann fjell, *Antarctica* 5 D3
Mühlviertel, *Austria* 26 C7
Muhos, *Finland* 8 D22
Muhu, *Estonia* 9 G20
Muhutwe, *Tanzania* 86 C3
Muine Bheag, *Ireland* 12 D5
Muir, L., *Australia* 93 F2
Muir of Ord, *U.K.* 13 D4
Mujnak = Muynak, *Uzbekistan* 52 E6
Muka, Tanjung, *Malaysia* 65 c
Mukacheve, *Ukraine* 33 H2
Mukachevo = Mukacheve, *Ukraine* 33 H2
Mukah, *Malaysia* 62 D4
Mukandwara, *India* 68 G6
Mukawwa, Geziret, *Egypt* 80 C4
Mukawwar, *Sudan* 80 C4
Mukdahan, *Thailand* 64 D5
Mukden = Shenyang, *China* 57 D12
Mukerian, *India* 68 D6
Mukhtolovo, *Russia* 34 C6
Mukhtuya = Lensk, *Russia* 53 C12
Mukinbudin, *Australia* 93 F2
Mukishi, *Dem. Rep. of the Congo* 87 D1
Mukomuko, *Indonesia* 62 E2
Mukomwenze, *Dem. Rep. of the Congo* 86 D2
Muktsar, *India* 68 D6
Mukur = Moqor, *Afghan.* 68 C2
Mukutawa →, *Canada* 103 C9
Mukwela, *Zambia* 87 F2
Mula, *Spain* 39 G3
Mula →, *Pakistan* 68 F2
Mulange, *Dem. Rep. of the Congo* 86 C2
Mulanje, *Malawi* 87 F4
Mulanje, Mt., *Malawi* 87 F4
Mulchén, *Chile* 126 D1
Mulde →, *Germany* 24 D8
Mule Creek Junction, *U.S.A.* 112 D2
Muleba, *Tanzania* 86 C3
Mulejé, *Mexico* 118 B2
Muleshoe, *U.S.A.* 113 H3
Muletta, Gara, *Ethiopia* 81 F5
Mulgrave, *Canada* 105 C7
Mulhacén, *Spain* 37 H7
Mülheim, *Germany* 24 D2
Mulhouse, *France* 19 E14
Muli, *China* 58 D3
Muling, *China* 57 B16
Mull, *U.K.* 13 E3
Mull, Sound of, *U.K.* 13 E3
Mullaittivu, *Sri Lanka* 66 Q12
Mullen, *U.S.A.* 112 D4
Mullens, *U.S.A.* 114 G5
Muller, Pegunungan, *Indonesia* 62 D4
Mullet Pen., *Ireland* 12 B1
Mullewa, *Australia* 93 E2
Müllheim, *Germany* 25 H3
Mulligan →, *Australia* 94 D2
Mullingar, *Ireland* 12 C4
Mullins, *U.S.A.* 115 H6
Mullsjö, *Sweden* 11 G7
Mullumbimby, *Australia* 95 D5
Mulobezi, *Zambia* 87 F2
Mulroy B., *Ireland* 12 A4
Multan, *Pakistan* 68 D4
Mulumbe, Mts., *Dem. Rep. of the Congo* 87 D2
Mulungushi Dam, *Zambia* 87 E2
Mulvane, *U.S.A.* 113 G6
Mulwad, *Sudan* 80 D3
Mumbai, *India* 66 K8
Mumbwa, *Zambia* 87 F2
Mumra, *Russia* 35 H8
Mun →, *Thailand* 64 E5
Muna, *Indonesia* 63 F6
Munabao, *India* 68 G4
Munamagi, *Estonia* 9 H22
Muncan, *Indonesia* 63 K18
Muncar, *Indonesia* 63 J17
Münchberg, *Germany* 25 E7
Müncheberg, *Germany* 24 C10
München, *Germany* 25 G7
Munchen-Gladbach = Mönchengladbach, *Germany* 24 D2
Muncho Lake, *Canada* 102 B3
Munch'ŏn, *N. Korea* 57 E14
Muncie, *U.S.A.* 114 E3
Muncoonie, L., *Australia* 94 D2
Mundabbera, *Australia* 95 D5
Munday, *U.S.A.* 113 J5
Münden, *Germany* 24 D5
Münden ⌓, *Germany* 24 D5
Mundiwindi, *Australia* 92 D3
Mundo →, *Spain* 39 G2
Mundo Novo, *Brazil* 125 F10
Mundra, *India* 68 H3
Mundrabilla, *Australia* 93 F4
Munera, *Spain* 39 F2
Mungallala, *Australia* 95 D4
Mungallala Cr. →, *Australia* 95 D4
Mungana, *Australia* 94 B3
Mungaoli, *India* 68 G8
Mungari, *Mozam.* 87 F3
Mungbere, *Dem. Rep. of the Congo* 86 B2
Mungeli, *India* 69 H9
Munger, *India* 69 G12
Mungkan Kandju △, *Australia* 94 A3
Munich = München, *Germany* 25 G7
Munich International ✕ (MUC), *Germany* 25 G7
Munising, *U.S.A.* 114 B2
Munka-Ljungby, *Sweden* 11 H6
Munkebo, *Denmark* 11 J4
Munkedal, *Sweden* 11 F5
Munkfors, *Sweden* 10 E7
Munku-Sardyk, *Russia* 53 D11
Münnerstadt, *Germany* 25 E6
Muñoz Gamero, Pen., *Chile* 128 G2
Munroe L., *Canada* 103 B9
Munsan, *S. Korea* 57 F14
Munster, *France* 19 D14
Munster, *Niedersachsen, Germany* 24 C6
Münster, *Nordrhein-Westfalen, Germany* 24 D3
Munster □, *Ireland* 12 D3
Muntadgin, *Australia* 93 F2
Muntele Mare, Vf., *Romania* 29 D8
Muntok, *Indonesia* 62 E3
Munyama, *Zambia* 87 F2
Munzur Dağları, *Turkey* 73 C8
Muong Beng, *Laos* 58 G3
Muong Boum, *Vietnam* 58 F4
Muong Et, *Laos* 64 B5
Muong Hai, *Laos* 58 G3
Muong Hiem, *Laos* 64 B4
Muong Houn, *Laos* 58 G3
Muong Hung, *Vietnam* 58 G4
Muong Kau, *Laos* 64 E5
Muong Khao, *Laos* 64 C4
Muong Khoua, *Laos* 58 G4
Muong Liep, *Laos* 64 C3
Muong May, *Laos* 64 E6
Muong Ngeun, *Laos* 58 G3
Muong Ngoi, *Laos* 58 G4
Muong Nhie, *Vietnam* 58 F4
Muong Nong, *Laos* 64 D6
Muong Ou Tay, *Laos* 58 F3
Muong Oua, *Laos* 64 C3
Muong Peun, *Laos* 58 G4
Muong Phalane, *Laos* 64 D5
Muong Phieng, *Laos* 64 C3
Muong Phine, *Laos* 64 D6
Muong Sai, *Laos* 58 G3
Muong Saiapoun, *Laos* 64 C3
Muong Sen, *Vietnam* 64 C5
Muong Sing, *Laos* 58 G3
Muong Son, *Laos* 58 G4
Muong Soui, *Laos* 64 C4
Muong Va, *Laos* 58 G4
Muong Xia, *Vietnam* 64 B5
Muonio, *Finland* 8 C20
Muonionjoki →, *Finland* 8 C20
Muping, *China* 57 F11
Mupoi, *Sudan* 81 F2
Muqaddam, Wadi →, *Sudan* 80 D3
Muqdisho, *Somali Rep.* 75 G4
Mur →, *Austria* 27 E9
Mur-de-Bretagne, *France* 18 D4
Muradiye, *Manisa, Turkey* 47 C9
Muradiye, *Van, Turkey* 73 C10
Murakami, *Japan* 54 E9
Murallón, Cerro, *Chile* 128 F2
Muranda, *Rwanda* 86 C2
Murang'a, *Kenya* 86 C4
Murashi, *Russia* 52 D5
Murat, *France* 20 C6
Murat →, *Turkey* 73 C9
Murat Dağı, *Turkey* 47 C11
Muratlı, *Turkey* 45 E11
Murato, *France* 21 F13
Murau, *Austria* 26 D7
Muravera, *Italy* 42 C2
Murayama, *Japan* 54 E10
Murça, *Portugal* 36 D3
Murchison →, *Australia* 93 E1
Murchison, Mt., *Antarctica* 5 D11
Murchison Falls, *Uganda* 86 B3
Murchison Falls △, *Uganda* 86 B3
Murchison Ra., *Australia* 94 C1

Murchison Rapids, *Malawi* 87 F3
Murcia, *Spain* 39 G3
Murcia □, *Spain* 39 H3
Murdo, *U.S.A.* 112 D4
Murdoch Pt., *Australia* 94 A3
Mürefte, *Turkey* 45 F11
Mureş □, *Romania* 29 D9
Mureş →, *Romania* 28 D5
Mureşul = Mureş →, *Romania* 28 D5
Muret, *France* 20 E5
Murewa, *Zimbabwe* 89 B5
Murfreesboro, *N.C., U.S.A.* 115 G7
Murfreesboro, *Tenn., U.S.A.* 115 H2
Murgab = Murghob, *Tajikistan* 52 F8
Murgab →, *Turkmenistan* 71 B9
Murgenella, *Australia* 92 B5
Murgeni, *Romania* 29 D13
Murgha Kibzai, *Pakistan* 68 D3
Murghob, *Tajikistan* 52 F8
Murgon, *Australia* 95 D5
Muri, *India* 69 H11
Muria, *Indonesia* 63 G14
Muriaé, *Brazil* 127 A7
Murias de Paredes, *Spain* 36 C4
Muriel Mine, *Zimbabwe* 87 F3
Müritz, *Germany* 24 B8
Müritz △, *Germany* 24 B8
Murliganj, *India* 69 G12
Murmansk, *Russia* 52 C4
Murnau, *Germany* 25 H7
Muro, *France* 21 F12
Muro, *Spain* 48 B10
Muro, C. de, *France* 21 G12
Muro de Alcoy, *Spain* 39 G4
Muro Lucano, *Italy* 43 B8
Murom, *Russia* 34 C6
Muroran, *Japan* 54 C10
Muros, *Spain* 36 C1
Muros y de Noya, Ría de, *Spain* 36 C1
Muroto, *Japan* 55 H7
Muroto-Misaki, *Japan* 55 H7
Murowana Goślina, *Poland* 31 F3
Murphy, *U.S.A.* 108 E5
Murphys, *U.S.A.* 110 G6
Murrat, *Sudan* 80 D2
Murrat Wells, *Sudan* 80 C3
Murray, *Ky., U.S.A.* 115 G1
Murray, *Utah, U.S.A.* 108 F8
Murray →, *Australia* 95 F2
Murray, L., *U.S.A.* 115 H5
Murray Bridge, *Australia* 95 F2
Murray Harbour, *Canada* 105 C7
Murray River △, *Australia* 95 E3
Murraysburg, *S. Africa* 88 E3
Murree, *Pakistan* 68 C5
Murrieta, *U.S.A.* 111 M9
Murro di Porco, Capo, *Italy* 43 F8
Murrumbidgee →, *Australia* 95 E3
Murrumburrah, *Australia* 95 E4
Murrurundi, *Australia* 95 E5
Murshid, *Sudan* 80 C3
Murshidabad, *India* 69 G13
Murska Sobota, *Slovenia* 41 B13
Murtle L., *Canada* 102 C5
Murtoa, *Australia* 95 F3
Murtosa, *Portugal* 36 E2
Murungu, *Tanzania* 86 C3
Mururoa, *Pac. Oc.* 97 K14
Murwara, *India* 69 H9
Murwillumbah, *Australia* 95 D5
Mürz →, *Austria* 26 D8
Mürzzuschlag, *Austria* 26 D8
Muş, *Turkey* 70 B4
Mûsa, Gebel, *Egypt* 70 D2
Musa Khel, *Pakistan* 68 D3
Mūsa Qal'eh, *Afghan.* 66 C4
Musafirkhana, *India* 69 F9
Musala, *Bulgaria* 44 D7
Musala, *Indonesia* 62 D1
Musan, *N. Korea* 57 C15
Musangu, *Dem. Rep. of the Congo* 87 E1
Musasa, *Tanzania* 86 C3
Musay'īd, *Qatar* 71 E6
Muscat = Masqat, *Oman* 75 C6
Muscat & Oman = Oman ■, *Asia* 75 C6
Muscatine, *U.S.A.* 112 E9
Musengezi = Unsengedsi →, *Zimbabwe* 87 F3
Musgrave Harbour, *Canada* 105 C9
Musgrave Ranges, *Australia* 93 E5
Mushie, *Dem. Rep. of the Congo* 84 E3
Mushin, *Nigeria* 83 D5
Musi →, *Indonesia* 62 E2
Musina, *S. Africa* 89 C5
Muskeg →, *Canada* 102 A4
Muskegon, *U.S.A.* 114 D2
Muskegon →, *U.S.A.* 114 D2
Muskegon Heights, *U.S.A.* 114 D2
Muskogee, *U.S.A.* 113 H7
Muskoka, L., *Canada* 116 B5
Muskwa →, *Canada* 102 B4
Muslīmiyah, *Syria* 70 B3
Musmar, *Sudan* 80 D4
Musofu, *Zambia* 87 E2
Musoma, *Tanzania* 86 C3
Musquaro, L., *Canada* 105 B7
Musquodoboit Harbour, *Canada* 105 D7
Musselburgh, *U.K.* 13 F5
Musselshell →, *U.S.A.* 108 C10
Mussidan, *France* 20 C4
Mussomeli, *Italy* 42 E6
Mussoorie, *India* 68 D8
Mussuco, *Angola* 88 B2
Mustafakemalpaşa, *Turkey* 45 F12
Mustang, *Nepal* 69 E10
Musters, L., *Argentina* 128 F3
Musudan, *N. Korea* 57 D15
Muswellbrook, *Australia* 95 E5
Muszyna, *Poland* 31 J7
Mût, *Egypt* 80 B2
Mut, *Turkey* 70 B2
Mutanda, *Mozam.* 89 C5
Mutanda, *Zambia* 87 E2
Mutare, *Zimbabwe* 87 F3
Muting, *Indonesia* 63 F10
Mutki = Mirtağ, *Turkey* 70 B4
Mutoko, *Zimbabwe* 89 B5
Mutoray, *Russia* 53 C11
Mutshatsha, *Dem. Rep. of the Congo* 87 E1
Mutsu, *Japan* 54 D10
Mutsu-Wan, *Japan* 54 D10
Muttaburra, *Australia* 94 C3
Muttalip, *Turkey* 47 B12
Mutton I., *Ireland* 12 D2
Mutuáli, *Mozam.* 87 E4
Mutum Biyu, *Nigeria* 83 D7
Muweilih, *Egypt* 74 E3
Muxía, *Spain* 36 B1
Muy Muy, *Nic.* 120 D2
Muyinga, *Burundi* 86 C3
Muynak, *Uzbekistan* 52 E6
Muzaffarabad, *Pakistan* 69 B5
Muzaffargarh, *Pakistan* 68 D4
Muzaffarnagar, *India* 68 E7
Muzaffarpur, *India* 69 F11
Muzafirpur, *Pakistan* 68 D3
Muzhi, *Russia* 52 C7
Muzillac, *France* 18 E4
Muzūra, *Egypt* 80 J7
Mvôlô, *Sudan* 81 F2
Mvuma, *Zimbabwe* 87 F3
Mvurwi, *Zimbabwe* 87 F3
Mwabvi ⌓, *Malawi* 87 F3
Mwadui, *Tanzania* 86 C3
Mwambo, *Tanzania* 87 E5
Mwandi, *Zambia* 87 F1
Mwanza, *Dem. Rep. of the Congo* 86 D2
Mwanza, *Tanzania* 86 C3
Mwanza, *Zambia* 87 F1
Mwanza □, *Tanzania* 86 C3
Mwaya, *Tanzania* 87 D3
Mweelrea, *Ireland* 12 C2
Mweka, *Dem. Rep. of the Congo* 84 E4
Mwenezi, *Zimbabwe* 87 G3
Mwenezi →, *Mozam.* 87 G3
Mwenga, *Dem. Rep. of the Congo* 86 C2
Mweru, L., *Zambia* 87 D2
Mweru Wantipa △, *Zambia* 87 D2
Mweza Range, *Zimbabwe* 87 G3
Mwilambwe, *Dem. Rep. of the Congo* 86 D2
Mwimbi, *Tanzania* 87 D3
Mwinilunga, *Zambia* 87 E1
My Tho, *Vietnam* 65 G6
Myajlar, *India* 68 F4
Myanaung, *Burma* 67 K19
Myanmar = Burma ■, *Asia* 67 J20
Myaungmya, *Burma* 67 L19
Myeik Kyunzu, *Burma* 65 G1
Myers Chuck, *U.S.A.* 102 B2
Myerstown, *U.S.A.* 117 F8
Myingyan, *Burma* 67 J19
Myitkyina, *Burma* 67 G20
Myjava, *Slovak Rep.* 27 C10
Mykhaylivka, *Ukraine* 33 J8
Mykines, *Færoe Is.* 8 E9
Mykolayiv, *Ukraine* 33 J7
Mymensingh, *Bangla.* 67 G17
Mynydd Du, *U.K.* 15 F4
Mýrdalsjökull, *Iceland* 8 E4
Myrhorod, *Ukraine* 33 H7
Myrtle Beach, *U.S.A.* 115 J6
Myrtle Creek, *U.S.A.* 108 E2
Myrtle Point, *U.S.A.* 108 E1
Myrtou, *Cyprus* 49 D12
Mysia, *Turkey* 45 G11
Myślenice, *Poland* 31 J6
Myślibórz, *Poland* 31 F1
Mysłowice, *Poland* 31 H6
Mysore = Karnataka □, *India* 66 N10
Mysore, *India* 66 N10
Mystic, *U.S.A.* 117 E13
Myszków, *Poland* 31 H6
Myszyniec, *Poland* 30 E8
Mytishchi, *Russia* 32 E9
Mývatn, *Iceland* 8 D5
Mže →, *Czech Rep.* 26 B6
Mzimba, *Malawi* 87 E3
Mzimkulu →, *S. Africa* 89 E5
Mzimvubu →, *S. Africa* 89 E4
Mzuzu, *Malawi* 87 E3

N

Na Hearadh = Harris, *U.K.* 13 D2
Na Noi, *Thailand* 64 C3
Na Phao, *Laos* 64 D5
Na Sam, *Vietnam* 58 F6
Na San, *Vietnam* 64 B5
Na Thon, *Thailand* 65 b
Naab →, *Germany* 25 F8
Na'am, *Sudan* 81 F2
Na'am →, *Sudan* 81 F2
Naantali, *Finland* 9 F19
Naas, *Ireland* 12 C5
Nababeep, *S. Africa* 88 D2
Nabadwip = Navadwip, *India* 69 H13
Nabawa, *Australia* 93 E1
Nabberu, L., *Australia* 93 E3
Nabburg, *Germany* 25 F8
Naberezhnyye Chelny, *Russia* 34 C11
Nabeul, *Tunisia* 79 A8
Nabha, *India* 68 D7
Nabīd, *Iran* 71 D8
Nabire, *Indonesia* 63 E9
Nabisar, *Pakistan* 68 G3
Nabisipi →, *Canada* 105 B7
Nabiswera, *Uganda* 86 B3
Nāblus = Nābulus, *West Bank* 74 C4
Naboomspruit, *S. Africa* 89 C4
Nabou, *Burkina Faso* 82 C4
Nabua, *Phil.* 61 E5
Nābulus, *West Bank* 74 C4
Nacala, *Mozam.* 87 E5
Nacala-Velha, *Mozam.* 87 E5
Nacaome, *Honduras* 120 D2
Nacaroa, *Mozam.* 87 E4
Naches, *U.S.A.* 108 C3
Naches →, *U.S.A.* 110 D6
Nachicapau, L., *Canada* 105 A6
Nachingwea, *Tanzania* 87 E4
Nachna, *India* 68 F4
Náchod, *Czech Rep.* 26 A9
Nacimiento L., *U.S.A.* 110 K6
Naco, *Mexico* 118 A3
Nacogdoches, *U.S.A.* 113 K7
Nácori Chico, *Mexico* 118 B3
Nacozari, *Mexico* 118 A3
Nadi, *Fiji* 91 C7
Nadi, *Sudan* 80 D3
Nadiad, *India* 68 H5
Nădlac, *Romania* 28 D5
Nador, *Morocco* 78 B5
Nadur, *Malta* 49 C1
Nadūshan, *Iran* 71 C7
Nadvirna, *Ukraine* 33 H3
Nadvornaya = Nadvirna, *Ukraine* 33 H3
Nadym, *Russia* 52 C8
Nadym →, *Russia* 52 C8
Nærbø, *Norway* 9 G11
Næstved, *Denmark* 11 J5
Nafada, *Nigeria* 83 C7
Naft-e Safīd, *Iran* 71 D6
Naftshahr, *Iran* 70 C5
Nafud Desert = An Nafūd, *Si. Arabia* 70 D4
Nag Hammâdi, *Egypt* 80 B3
Naga, *Phil.* 61 E5
Nagahama, *Japan* 55 G8
Nagai, *Japan* 54 E10
Nagaland □, *India* 67 G19
Nagano, *Japan* 55 F9
Nagano □, *Japan* 55 F9
Nagaoka, *Japan* 55 F9
Nagappattinam, *India* 66 P11
Nagar →, *Bangla.* 69 G13
Nagar Parkar, *Pakistan* 68 G4
Nagasaki, *Japan* 55 H4
Nagasaki □, *Japan* 55 H4
Nagato, *Japan* 55 G5
Nagaur, *India* 68 F5
Nagda, *India* 68 H6
Nagercoil, *India* 66 Q10
Nagina, *India* 69 E8
Nagīneh, *Iran* 71 C8
Nagir, *Pakistan* 69 A6
Naglarby, *Sweden* 10 D9
Nagod, *India* 69 G9
Nagold, *Germany* 25 G4
Nagold →, *Germany* 25 G4
Nagoorin, *Australia* 94 C5
Nagorno-Karabakh □, *Azerbaijan* 70 B5
Nagornyy, *Russia* 53 D13
Nagoya, *Japan* 55 G8
Nagpur, *India* 66 J11
Nagua, *Dom. Rep.* 121 C6
Naguabo, *Puerto Rico* 121 d
Nagyatád, *Hungary* 28 D2
Nagyecsed, *Hungary* 28 C7
Nagykálló, *Hungary* 28 C6
Nagykanizsa, *Hungary* 28 D2
Nagykáta, *Hungary* 28 C4
Nagykőrös, *Hungary* 28 C4
Naha, *Japan* 55 L3
Nahan, *India* 68 D7
Nahanni △, *Canada* 102 A4
Nahanni Butte, *Canada* 102 A4
Nahargarh, *Mad. P., India* 68 G6
Nahargarh, *Raj., India* 68 G7
Nahariyya, *Israel* 70 C2
Nahāvand, *Iran* 71 C6
Nahe →, *Germany* 25 F3
Nahîya, W. →, *Egypt* 80 B3
Nahuelbuta △, *Chile* 126 D1
Nai Yong, *Thailand* 65 a
Naicá, *Mexico* 118 B3
Naicam, *Canada* 103 C8
Naikoon ⌓, *Canada* 102 C2
Naila, *Germany* 25 E7
Naimisharanya, *India* 69 F9
Nain, *Canada* 105 A7
Nā'īn, *Iran* 71 C7
Naini Tal, *India* 69 E8
Nainpur, *India* 66 H12
Naintré, *France* 18 F7
Nainwa, *India* 68 G6
Naipu, *Romania* 29 F10
Nairn, *U.K.* 13 D5
Nairobi, *Kenya* 86 C4
Nairobi △, *Kenya* 86 C4
Naissaar, *Estonia* 9 G21
Naita, Mt., *Ethiopia* 81 F4
Naivasha, *Kenya* 86 C4
Naivasha, L., *Kenya* 86 C4
Najac, *France* 20 D5
Najaf = An Najaf, *Iraq* 70 C5
Najafābād, *Iran* 71 C6
Najd, *Si. Arabia* 75 B3
Nájera, *Spain* 38 C2
Najerilla →, *Spain* 38 C2
Najibabad, *India* 68 E8
Najin, *N. Korea* 57 C16
Najmah, *Si. Arabia* 71 E6
Najrān, *Si. Arabia* 75 D3
Naju, *S. Korea* 57 G14
Nakadōri-Shima, *Japan* 55 H4
Nakalagba, *Dem. Rep. of the Congo* 86 B2
Nakaminato, *Japan* 55 F10
Nakamura, *Japan* 55 H6
Nakano, *Japan* 55 F9
Nakano-Shima, *Japan* 55 K4
Nakashibetsu, *Japan* 54 C12
Nakfa, *Eritrea* 81 D4
Nakfa ⌓, *Eritrea* 81 D4
Nakha Yai, Ko, *Thailand* 65 a
Nakhichevan = Naxçıvan, *Azerbaijan* 70 B5
Nakhichevan Republic = Naxçıvan □, *Azerbaijan* 52 F5
Nakhl, *Egypt* 74 F2
Nakhl-e Taqī, *Iran* 71 E7
Nakhodka, *Russia* 53 E14
Nakhon Nayok, *Thailand* 64 E3
Nakhon Pathom, *Thailand* 64 F3
Nakhon Phanom, *Thailand* 64 D5
Nakhon Ratchasima, *Thailand* 64 E4
Nakhon Sawan, *Thailand* 64 E3
Nakhon Si Thammarat, *Thailand* 65 H3
Nakhon Thai, *Thailand* 64 D3
Nakhtarana, *India* 68 H3
Nakina, *Canada* 104 B2
Nakło nad Notecią, *Poland* 31 E4
Nako, *Burkina Faso* 82 C4
Nakodar, *India* 68 D6
Nakskov, *Denmark* 11 K5
Naktong →, *S. Korea* 57 G15
Nakuru, *Kenya* 86 C4
Nakuru, L., *Kenya* 86 C4
Nakusp, *Canada* 102 C5
Nal, *Pakistan* 68 F2
Nal →, *Pakistan* 68 G1
Nalázi, *Mozam.* 89 C5
Nalchik, *Russia* 35 J6
Nałęczów, *Poland* 31 G9
Nalerigu, *Ghana* 83 C4
Nalgonda, *India* 66 L11
Nalhati, *India* 69 G12
Naliya, *India* 68 H3
Nallamalai Hills, *India* 66 M11
Nallıhan, *Turkey* 72 B4
Nalón →, *Spain* 36 B4
Nam Can, *Vietnam* 65 H5
Nam-ch'on, *N. Korea* 57 E14
Nam Co, *China* 60 C4
Nam Dinh, *Vietnam* 58 G6
Nam Du, Hon, *Vietnam* 65 H5
Nam Nao △, *Thailand* 64 D3
Nam Ngum Dam, *Laos* 64 C4
Nam-Phan, *Vietnam* 65 G6
Nam Phong, *Thailand* 64 D4
Nam Tha, *Laos* 58 G3
Nam Tok, *Thailand* 64 E2
Namacunde, *Angola* 88 B2
Namacurra, *Mozam.* 89 B6
Namak, Daryācheh-ye, *Iran* 71 C7
Namak, Kavir-e, *Iran* 71 C8
Namakzār, Daryācheh-ye, *Iran* 71 C9
Namaland, *Namibia* 88 C2
Namangan, *Uzbekistan* 52 E8
Namapa, *Mozam.* 87 E4
Namaqualand, *S. Africa* 88 E2
Namasagali, *Uganda* 86 B3
Namber, *Indonesia* 63 E8
Nambour, *Australia* 95 D5
Nambucca Heads, *Australia* 95 E5
Nambung △, *Australia* 93 F2
Namche Bazar, *Nepal* 69 F12
Namchonjŏm = Nam-ch'on, *N. Korea* 57 E14
Namecunda, *Mozam.* 87 E4
Nameponda, *Mozam.* 87 F4
Náměšť nad Oslavou, *Czech Rep.* 27 B9
Námestovo, *Slovak Rep.* 27 B12
Nametil, *Mozam.* 87 F4
Namew L., *Canada* 103 C8
Namgia, *India* 69 D8
Namhkam, *Burma* 58 E1
Namib Desert, *Namibia* 88 C2
Namib-Naukluft ⌓, *Namibia* 88 C2
Namibe, *Angola* 85 H2
Namibe □, *Angola* 88 B1
Namibia ■, *Africa* 88 C2
Namibwoestyn = Namib Desert, *Namibia* 88 C2
Namīn, *Iran* 73 C13
Namlea, *Indonesia* 63 E7
Namoi →, *Australia* 95 E4
Nampa, *U.S.A.* 108 E5
Nampala, *Mali* 82 B3
Namp'o, *N. Korea* 57 E13
Nampō-Shotō, *Japan* 55 J10
Nampula, *Mozam.* 87 F4
Namrole, *Indonesia* 63 E7
Namse Shankou, *China* 67 E13
Namsen →, *Norway* 8 D14
Namsos, *Norway* 8 D14
Namtok Chat Trakan △, *Thailand* 64 D3
Namtok Mae Surin △, *Thailand* 64 C2
Namtsy, *Russia* 53 C13
Namtu, *Burma* 67 H20
Namtumbo, *Tanzania* 87 E4
Namu, *Canada* 102 C3
Namur, *Belgium* 17 D4
Namur □, *Belgium* 17 D4
Namutoni, *Namibia* 88 B2
Namwala, *Zambia* 87 F2
Namwŏn, *S. Korea* 57 G14
Namysłów, *Poland* 31 G4
Nan, *Thailand* 64 C3
Nan →, *Thailand* 64 E3
Nan-ch'ang = Nanchang, *China* 59 C10
Nan Ling, *China* 59 E8
Nan Xian, *China* 59 C9
Nana, *Romania* 29 F11
Nana Kru, *Liberia* 82 E3
Nanaimo, *Canada* 102 D4
Nanam, *N. Korea* 57 D15
Nanan, *China* 59 E12
Nanango, *Australia* 95 D5
Nan'ao, *China* 59 F11
Nanao, *Japan* 55 F8
Nanbu, *China* 58 B6
Nanchang, *Jiangxi, China* 59 C10
Nanchang, *Kiangsi, China* 59 C10
Nancheng, *China* 59 D11
Nanching = Nanjing, *China* 59 A12
Nanchong, *China* 58 B6
Nanchuan, *China* 58 C6
Nancy, *France* 19 D13
Nanda Devi, *India* 69 D8
Nanda Kot, *India* 69 D9
Nandan, *China* 58 E6
Nandan, *Japan* 55 G7
Nanded, *India* 66 K10
Nandewar Ra., *Australia* 95 E5
Nandi = Nadi, *Fiji* 91 C7
Nandigram, *India* 69 H12
Nandurbar, *India* 66 J9
Nandyal, *India* 66 M11
Nanfeng, *Guangdong, China* 59 F8
Nanfeng, *Jiangxi, China* 59 D11
Nanga-Eboko, *Cameroon* 83 E7
Nanga Parbat, *Pakistan* 69 B6
Nangade, *Mozam.* 87 E4
Nangapinoh, *Indonesia* 62 E4
Nangarhār □, *Afghan.* 66 B7
Nangatayap, *Indonesia* 62 E4
Nangeya Mts., *Uganda* 86 B3
Nangis, *France* 19 D10
Nangong, *China* 56 F8
Nanhua, *China* 58 E3
Nanhuang, *China* 57 F11
Nanhui, *China* 59 B13
Nanjeko, *Zambia* 87 F1
Nanji Shan, *China* 59 D13
Nanjian, *China* 58 E3
Nanjiang, *China* 58 A6
Nanjing, *Fujian, China* 59 E11
Nanjing, *Jiangsu, China* 59 A12
Nanjirinji, *Tanzania* 87 D4
Nankana Sahib, *Pakistan* 68 D5
Nankang, *China* 59 E10
Nanking = Nanjing, *China* 59 A12
Nankoku, *Japan* 55 H6
Nanling, *China* 59 B12
Nanning, *China* 58 F7
Nannup, *Australia* 93 F2
Nanpan Jiang →, *China* 58 E6
Nanpara, *India* 69 F9
Nanpi, *China* 56 E9
Nanping, *Fujian, China* 59 D12
Nanping, *Henan, China* 59 C9
Nanri Dao, *China* 59 E12
Nanripe, *Mozam.* 87 E4
Nansei-Shotō = Ryūkyū-rettō, *Japan* 55 M3
Nansen Basin, *Arctic* 4 A10
Nansen Cordillera, *Arctic* 4 A
Nansen Sd., *Canada* 4 A3
Nanshan I., *S. China Sea* 62 B5
Nansio, *Tanzania* 86 C3
Nant, *France* 20 D7
Nanterre, *France* 19 D9
Nantes, *France* 18 E5
Nantiat, *France* 20 B5
Nanticoke, *U.S.A.* 117 E8
Nanton, *Canada* 102 C6
Nantong, *China* 59 A13
Nantou, *Taiwan* 59 F13
Nantua, *France* 19 F12
Nantucket I., *U.S.A.* 114 E10
Nantwich, *U.K.* 14 D5
Nanty Glo, *U.S.A.* 116 F6
Nanuque, *Brazil* 125 G10
Nanusa, Kepulauan, *Indonesia* 63 D7
Nanutarra Roadhouse, *Australia* 92 D2
Nanxi, *China* 58 C5
Nanxiong, *China* 59 E10
Nanyang, *China* 56 H7
Nanyi Hu, *China* 59 B12
Nanyuki, *Kenya* 86 B4
Nanzhang, *China* 59 B8
Nao, C. de la, *Spain* 39 G5
Naococane, L., *Canada* 105 B5
Náousa, *Imathía, Greece* 44 F6
Náousa, *Kikládhes, Greece* 47 D7
Naozhou Dao, *China* 59 G8
Napa, *U.S.A.* 110 G4
Napa →, *U.S.A.* 110 G4
Napanee, *Canada* 116 B8
Napanoch, *U.S.A.* 117 E10
Nape, *Laos* 64 C5
Nape Pass = Keo Neua, Deo, *Vietnam* 64 C5
Napier, *N.Z.* 91 H6
Napier Broome B., *Australia* 92 B4
Napier Pen., *Australia* 94 A2
Napierville, *Canada* 117 A11
Naples = Nápoli, *Italy* 43 B7
Naples, *U.S.A.* 115 M5
Naples Capodichino ✕ (NAP), *Italy* 43 B7
Napo, *China* 58 F5
Napo →, *Peru* 124 D4
Napoleon, *N. Dak., U.S.A.* 112 B5
Napoleon, *Ohio, U.S.A.* 114 E3
Nápoli, *Italy* 43 B7
Nápoli, G. di, *Italy* 43 B7
Napopo, *Dem. Rep. of the Congo* 86 B2
Naqâda, *Egypt* 80 B3
Naqadeh, *Iran* 73 D11
Naqb, Ra's an, *Jordan* 74 F4
Naqqāsh, *Iran* 71 C6
Nara, *Japan* 55 G7
Nara, *Mali* 82 B3
Nara □, *Japan* 55 G8
Nara Canal, *Pakistan* 68 G3
Nara Visa, *U.S.A.* 113 H3
Naracoorte, *Australia* 95 F3
Naradhan, *Australia* 95 E4

Naraini, *India* 69 G9
Narasapur, *India* 67 L12
Narathiwat, *Thailand* 65 J3
Narayanganj, *Bangla.* 67 H17
Narayanpet, *India* 66 L10
Narberth, *U.K.* 15 F3
Narbonne, *France* 20 E7
Narcea →, *Spain* 36 B4
Nardīn, *Iran* 71 B7
Nardò, *Italy* 43 B11
Narembeen, *Australia* 93 F2
Narendranagar, *India* 68 D8
Nares Str., *Arctic* 98 A13
Naretha, *Australia* 93 F3
Narew →, *Poland* 31 F7
Nari →, *Pakistan* 68 F2
Narin, *Afghan.* 66 A6
Narindra, Helodranon' i, *Madag.* 89 A8
Narita, *Japan* 55 G10
Nariva Swamp, *Trin. & Tob.* 125 K15
Närke, *Sweden* 10 E8
Narmada →, *India* 68 J5
Narman, *Turkey* 73 B9
Narmland, *Sweden* 9 F15
Narnaul, *India* 68 E7
Narni, *Italy* 41 F9
Naro, *Ghana* 82 C4
Naro Fominsk, *Russia* 32 E9
Narodnaya, *Russia* 6 B17
Narok, *Kenya* 86 C4
Narón, *Spain* 36 B2
Narooma, *Australia* 95 F5
Narowal, *Pakistan* 68 C6
Narrabri, *Australia* 95 E4
Narran →, *Australia* 95 D4
Narrandera, *Australia* 95 E4
Narrogin, *Australia* 93 F2
Narromine, *Australia* 95 E4
Narrow Hills ⌓, *Canada* 103 C8
Narsimhapur, *India* 69 H8
Narsinghgarh, *India* 68 H7
Nartes, L. e, *Albania* 44 F3
Nartkala, *Russia* 35 J6
Naruto, *Japan* 55 G7
Narva, *Estonia* 32 C5
Narva →, *Russia* 9 G22
Narva Bay, *Estonia* 9 G19
Narvik, *Norway* 8 B17
Narvskoye Vdkhr., *Russia* 32 C5
Narwana, *India* 68 E7
Narwiański △, *Poland* 31 F9
Naryan-Mar, *Russia* 52 C6
Narym, *Russia* 52 D9
Naryn, *Kyrgyzstan* 52 E8
Nasa, *Norway* 8 C16
Năsăud, *Romania* 29 C9
Naseby, *N.Z.* 91 L3
Naselle, *U.S.A.* 110 D3
Naser, Buheirat en, *Egypt* 80 C3
Nashua, *Mont., U.S.A.* 108 B10
Nashua, *N.H., U.S.A.* 117 D13
Nashville, *Ark., U.S.A.* 113 J8
Nashville, *Ga., U.S.A.* 115 K4
Nashville, *Tenn., U.S.A.* 115 G2
Našice, *Croatia* 28 E3
Nasielsk, *Poland* 31 F7
Nasik, *India* 66 K8
Nasipit, *Phil.* 61 G6
Nasir, *Sudan* 81 F3
Nasirabad, *India* 68 F6
Nasirabad, *Pakistan* 68 E3
Nasiriyah = An Nāṣirīyah, *Iraq* 70 D5
Naskaupi →, *Canada* 105 B7
Naso, *Italy* 43 D7
Naṣrābād, *Iran* 71 C6
Naṣrīān-e Pā'īn, *Iran* 70 C5
Nass →, *Canada* 102 C3
Nassarawa, *Nigeria* 83 D6
Nassarawa □, *Nigeria* 83 D6
Nassau, *Bahamas* 120 A4
Nassau, *U.S.A.* 117 D11
Nassau, B., *Chile* 128 H3
Nasser, L. = Naser, Buheirat en, *Egypt* 80 C3
Nasser City = Kôm Ombo, *Egypt* 80 C3
Nassian, *Ivory C.* 82 D4
Nässjö, *Sweden* 11 G8
Nastapoka →, *Canada* 104 A4
Nastapoka, Is., *Canada* 104 A4
Nasugbu, *Phil.* 61 D4
Näsum, *Sweden* 11 H8
Näsviken, *Sweden* 10 C10
Nata, *Botswana* 88 C4
Nata →, *Botswana* 88 C4
Natal, *Brazil* 125 E11
Natal, *Indonesia* 62 D1
Natal, *S. Africa* 85 K6
Natal Drakensberg ⌓, *S. Africa* 89 D4
Natalinci, *Serbia & M.* 28 F5
Naṭanz, *Iran* 71 C6
Natashquan, *Canada* 105 B7
Natashquan →, *Canada* 105 B7
Natchez, *U.S.A.* 113 K9
Natchitoches, *U.S.A.* 113 K8
Nathalia, *Australia* 95 F4
Nathdwara, *India* 68 G5
Nati, Pta., *Spain* 48 A10
Natimuk, *Australia* 95 F3
Nation →, *Canada* 102 B4
National City, *U.S.A.* 111 N9
Natitingou, *Benin* 83 C5
Natividad, I., *Mexico* 118 B1
Natkyizin, *Burma* 64 E1
Natron, L., *Tanzania* 86 C4
Natrona Heights, *U.S.A.* 116 F5
Natrūn, W. el →, *Egypt* 80 H7
Nättraby, *Sweden* 11 H9
Natukanaoka Pan, *Namibia* 88 B2
Natuna Besar, Kepulauan, *Indonesia* 62 D3
Natuna Is. = Natuna Besar, Kepulauan, *Indonesia* 62 D3
Natuna Selatan, Kepulauan, *Indonesia* 62 D3
Natural Bridge, *U.S.A.* 117 B9
Natural Bridges ⌓, *U.S.A.* 109 H8
Naturaliste, C., *Australia* 95 G4
Nau Qala, *Afghan.* 68 B3
Naucelle, *France* 20 D6
Nauders, *Austria* 26 E3
Nauen, *Germany* 24 C8
Naugatuck, *U.S.A.* 117 E11
Naujaat = Repulse Bay, *Canada* 101 B11
Naujoji Akmenė, *Lithuania* 30 B9
Naumburg, *Germany* 24 D7
Nā'ūr at Tunayb, *Jordan* 74 D4
Nauru ■, *Pac. Oc.* 96 H8
Naushahra = Nowshera, *Pakistan* 66 C8
Naushahro, *Pakistan* 68 F3
Naushon I., *U.S.A.* 117 E14
Nauta, *Peru* 124 D4
Nautanwa, *India* 67 F13
Naute ⌓, *Namibia* 88 D2
Nautla, *Mexico* 119 C5
Nava, *Mexico* 118 B4
Nava, *Spain* 36 B5
Nava del Rey, *Spain* 36 D5
Navadwip, *India* 69 H13
Navahermosa, *Spain* 37 F6
Navahrudak, *Belarus* 32 F3
Navajo Reservoir, *U.S.A.* 109 H10
Navalcarnero, *Spain* 36 E6
Navalmoral de la Mata, *Spain* 36 F5
Navalvillar de Pela, *Spain* 37 F5
Navan = An Uaimh, *Ireland* 12 C5
Navapolatsk, *Belarus* 32 E5
Navarin, Mys, *Russia* 4 C16
Navarino, I., *Chile* 128 H3
Navarra □, *Spain* 38 C3
Navarre, *U.S.A.* 116 F3
Navarro →, *U.S.A.* 110 F3
Navas de San Juan, *Spain* 37 G7
Navasota, *U.S.A.* 113 K6
Navassa I., *W. Indies* 121 C5
Nävekvarn, *Sweden* 11 F10
Naver →, *U.K.* 13 C4
Navia, *Spain* 36 B4
Navia →, *Spain* 36 B4
Navia de Suarna, *Spain* 36 C3
Navibandar, *India* 68 J3
Navidad, *Chile* 126 C1
Naviraí, *Brazil* 127 A5
Navlakhi, *India* 68 H4
Navlya, *Russia* 33 F8
Năvodari, *Romania* 29 F13
Navoi = Nawoiy, *Uzbekistan* 52 E7
Navojoa, *Mexico* 118 B3
Navolato, *Mexico* 118 C3
Návpaktos, *Greece* 46 C3
Návplion, *Greece* 46 D4
Navrongo, *Ghana* 83 C4
Navsari, *India* 66 J8
Nawa Kot, *Pakistan* 68 E4
Nawab Khan, *Pakistan* 68 D3
Nawabganj, *Ut. P., India* 69 F9
Nawabganj, *Ut. P., India* 69 E8
Nawabshah, *Pakistan* 68 F3
Nawada, *India* 69 G11
Nawakot, *Nepal* 69 F11
Nawalgarh, *India* 68 F6
Nawanshahr, *India* 69 C6
Nawar, Dasht-i-, *Afghan.* 68 C3
Nawi, *Sudan* 80 D3
Nawoiy, *Uzbekistan* 52 E7
Naxçıvan, *Azerbaijan* 70 B5
Naxçıvan □, *Azerbaijan* 52 F5
Náxos, *Greece* 47 D7
Nay, *France* 20 E3
Nay, Mui, *Vietnam* 62 B3
Nāy Band, *Būshehr, Iran* 71 E7
Nāy Band, *Khorāsān, Iran* 71 C8
Nayakhan, *Russia* 53 C16
Nayarit □, *Mexico* 118 C4
Nayé, *Senegal* 82 C2
Nayong, *China* 58 D5
Nayoro, *Japan* 54 B11
Nayyāl, W. →, *Si. Arabia* 70 D3
Nazaré, *Brazil* 125 F11
Nazaré, *Portugal* 37 F1
Nazareth = Naẓerat, *Israel* 74 C4
Nazareth, *U.S.A.* 117 F9
Nazas, *Mexico* 118 B4
Nazas →, *Mexico* 118 B4
Nazca, *Peru* 124 F4
Naze, The, *U.K.* 15 F9
Naẓerat, *Israel* 74 C4
Nāzīk, *Iran* 70 B5
Nazilli, *Turkey* 47 D10
Nazko, *Canada* 102 C4
Nazko →, *Canada* 102 C4
Nazret, *Ethiopia* 81 F4
Nazwa, *Oman* 75 C6
Nchanga, *Zambia* 87 E2
Ncheu, *Malawi* 87 E3
Ndala, *Tanzania* 86 C3
Ndalatando, *Angola* 84 F2
Ndali, *Benin* 83 D5
Ndareda, *Tanzania* 86 C4
Ndélé, *C.A.R.* 84 C4
Ndiael ⌓, *Senegal* 82 B1
Ndikinimeki, *Cameroon* 83 E7
N'Dioum, *Senegal* 82 B2
Ndjamena, *Chad* 79 F8
Ndola, *Zambia* 87 E2
Ndoto Mts., *Kenya* 86 B4
Nduguti, *Tanzania* 86 C3
Ndumu ⌓, *S. Africa* 89 D5
Néa Alikarnassós, *Greece* 47 F7
Néa Ankhíalos, *Greece* 46 B4
Néa Epídhavros, *Greece* 46 D5
Néa Flippiás, *Greece* 46 B2
Néa Ionia, *Greece* 46 B4
Néa Kallikrátia, *Greece* 44 F7
Néa Mákri, *Greece* 46 C5
Néa Moudhaniá, *Greece* 44 F7
Néa Péramos, *Attikí, Greece* 46 C5
Néa Péramos, *Kavállа, Greece* 45 F8
Néa Víssi, *Greece* 45 E10
Néa Zíkhna, *Greece* 44 E7
Neagh, Lough, *U.K.* 12 B5
Neah Bay, *U.S.A.* 110 B2
Neale, L., *Australia* 92 D5
Neamţ □, *Romania* 29 C11
Neápolis, *Kozáni, Greece* 44 F5
Neápolis, *Kríti, Greece* 49 D7
Neápolis, *Lakonía, Greece* 46 E5
Near Is., *U.S.A.* 100 C1
Neath, *U.K.* 15 F4
Neath Port Talbot □, *U.K.* 15 F4
Nebbou, *Burkina Faso* 83 C4
Nebelat el Hagana, *Sudan* 81 E2
Nebine Cr. →, *Australia* 95 D4
Nebitdag, *Turkmenistan* 52 F6
Nebo, *Australia* 94 C4
Nebolchy, *Russia* 32 C7
Nebraska □, *U.S.A.* 112 E5
Nebraska City, *U.S.A.* 112 E7
Nébrodi, Monti, *Italy* 43 E7
Necedah, *U.S.A.* 112 C9
Nechako →, *Canada* 102 C4
Neches →, *U.S.A.* 113 L8
Nechisar △, *Ethiopia* 81 F4
Neckar →, *Germany* 25 F4
Neckartal-Odenwald ⌓, *Germany* 25 F5
Necochea, *Argentina* 126 D4
Neda, *Spain* 36 B2
Nedelino, *Bulgaria* 45 E9
Nedelišće, *Croatia* 41 B13
Nédha →, *Greece* 46 D3
Needles, *Canada* 102 D5
Needles, *U.S.A.* 111 L12
Needles, The, *U.K.* 15 G6
Ñeembucú □, *Paraguay* 126 B4
Neemuch = Nimach, *India* 68 G6
Neenah, *U.S.A.* 114 C1
Neepawa, *Canada* 103 C9
Neftçala, *Azerbaijan* 71 B6
Neftegorsk, *Russia* 35 H4
Neftekumsk, *Russia* 35 H7
Nefyn, *U.K.* 14 E3
Négala, *Mali* 82 C3
Negapatam = Nagappattinam, *India* 66 P11
Negara, *Indonesia* 63 J17
Negaunee, *U.S.A.* 114 B2
Negele, *Ethiopia* 81 F4
Negev Desert = Hanegev, *Israel* 74 E4
Negoiul, Vf., *Romania* 29 E9
Negombo, *Sri Lanka* 66 R11
Negotin, *Serbia & M.* 44 B6
Negotino, *Macedonia* 44 E6
Negra, Peña, *Spain* 36 C4
Negra, Pta., *Peru* 124 E2
Negrais C. = Maudin Sun, *Burma* 67 M19
Negreşti, *Romania* 29 D12
Negreşti-Oaş, *Romania* 29 C8
Negril, *Jamaica* 120 a
Negro →, *Argentina* 128 E4
Negro →, *Brazil* 124 D7
Negro →, *Uruguay* 127 C4
Negros, *Phil.* 61 G5
Negru Vodă, *Romania* 29 G13
Neguac, *Canada* 105 C6
Nehalem →, *U.S.A.* 110 E3
Nehāvand, *Iran* 71 C6
Nehbandān, *Iran* 71 D9
Nehoiu, *Romania* 29 E11
Nei Monggol Zizhiqu □, *China* 56 D7
Neijiang, *China* 58 C5
Neillsville, *U.S.A.* 112 C9
Neilton, *U.S.A.* 108 C2
Neiqiu, *China* 56 F8
Neiva, *Colombia* 124 C3
Neixiang, *China* 56 H6
Nejanilini L., *Canada* 103 B9
Nejd = Najd, *Si. Arabia* 75 B3
Nejo, *Ethiopia* 81 F4
Nekā, *Iran* 71 B7
Nekemte, *Ethiopia* 81 F4
Nêkheb, *Egypt* 80 B3
Neksø, *Denmark* 11 J9
Nelas, *Portugal* 36 E3
Nelia, *Australia* 94 C3
Nelidovo, *Russia* 32 D7
Neligh, *U.S.A.* 112 D5
Nelkan, *Russia* 53 D14
Nellore, *India* 66 M11
Nelson, *Canada* 102 D5
Nelson, *N.Z.* 91 J4
Nelson, *U.K.* 14 D5
Nelson, *Ariz., U.S.A.* 109 J7
Nelson, *Nev., U.S.A.* 111 K12
Nelson →, *Canada* 103 C9
Nelson, C., *Australia* 95 F3
Nelson, Estrecho, *Chile* 128 G2
Nelson Forks, *Canada* 102 B4
Nelson House, *Canada* 103 B9
Nelson L., *Canada* 103 B8
Nelson Lakes △, *N.Z.* 91 J4
Nelspoort, *S. Africa* 88 E3
Nelspruit, *S. Africa* 89 D5
Néma, *Mauritania* 82 B3
Neman = Nemunas →, *Lithuania* 9 J19
Neman, *Russia* 9 J20
Neméa, *Greece* 46 D4
Nemeiben L., *Canada* 103 B7
Nemërçkë, Mal, *Albania* 44 F4
Nemira, Vf., *Romania* 29 D11
Nemiscau, *Canada* 104 B4
Nemiscau, L., *Canada* 104 B4
Nemours, *France* 19 D9
Nemšová, *Slovak Rep.* 27 C11
Nemunas →, *Lithuania* 9 J19
Nemuro, *Japan* 54 C12
Nemuro-Kaikyō, *Japan* 54 C12
Nen Jiang →, *China* 57 B13
Nenagh, *Ireland* 12 D3
Nenasi, *Malaysia* 65 L4
Nene →, *U.K.* 15 E8
Nénita, *Greece* 47 C8
Nenjiang, *China* 60 B7
Neno, *Malawi* 87 F3
Neodesha, *U.S.A.* 113 G7
Neokhórion, *Aitolía kai Akarnanía, Greece* 46 C3
Neokhórion, *Árta, Greece* 46 B2
Néon Karlovásion, *Greece* 47 D8
Néon Petrítsi, *Greece* 44 E7
Neosho, *U.S.A.* 113 G7
Neosho →, *U.S.A.* 113 H7
Nepal ■, *Asia* 69 F11
Nepalganj, *Nepal* 69 E9
Nepalganj Road, *India* 69 E9
Nephi, *U.S.A.* 108 G8
Nephin, *Ireland* 12 B2
Nepi, *Italy* 41 F9
Nepomuk, *Czech Rep.* 26 B6
Neptune, *U.S.A.* 117 F10
Nera →, *Italy* 41 F9
Nera →, *Romania* 28 F6
Nérac, *France* 20 D4
Nerang, *Australia* 95 D5
Neratovice, *Czech Rep.* 26 A7
Nerchinsk, *Russia* 53 D12
Nereju, *Romania* 29 E11
Nerekhta, *Russia* 32 D11
Néret, L., *Canada* 105 B5
Neretvanski Kanal, *Croatia* 41 E14
Neringa, *Lithuania* 9 J19
Neris →, *Lithuania* 9 J21
Nerja, *Spain* 37 J7
Nerl →, *Russia* 32 D11
Nerpio, *Spain* 39 G2
Nerva, *Spain* 37 H4
Nervi, *Italy* 40 D6
Neryungri, *Russia* 53 D13
Nescopeck, *U.S.A.* 117 E8
Nesebŭr, *Bulgaria* 45 D11
Ness, L., *U.K.* 13 D4
Ness City, *U.S.A.* 112 F5
Nesterov, *Ukraine* 33 G2
Nestórion, *Greece* 44 F5
Néstos →, *Greece* 45 E8
Nesvady, *Slovak Rep.* 27 D11
Nesvizh = Nyasvizh, *Belarus* 33 F4
Netanya, *Israel* 74 C3
Netarhat, *India* 69 H11
Nete →, *Belgium* 17 C4
Netherdale, *Australia* 94 K6
Netherlands ■, *Europe* 17 C5
Netherlands Antilles ⊠, *W. Indies* 124 A5
Neto →, *Italy* 43 C10
Netrang, *India* 68 J5
Nettancourt, *France* 19 D11
Nettetal, *Germany* 24 D2
Nettilling L., *Canada* 101 B12
Nettuno, *Italy* 42 A5
Netzahualcoyotl, Presa, *Mexico* 119 D6
Neu-Isenburg, *Germany* 25 E4
Neu-Ulm, *Germany* 25 G6
Neubrandenburg, *Germany* 24 B9
Neubukow, *Germany* 24 A7
Neuburg, *Germany* 25 G7
Neuchâtel, *Switz.* 25 J2
Neuchâtel □, *Switz.* 25 J2
Neuchâtel, Lac de, *Switz.* 25 J2
Neudau, *Austria* 26 D9
Neuenhagen, *Germany* 24 C9
Neuenhaus, *Germany* 24 C2
Neuf-Brisach, *France* 19 D14
Neufahrn, *Bayern, Germany* 25 G8
Neufahrn, *Bayern, Germany* 25 G7
Neufchâteau, *Belgium* 17 E5
Neufchâteau, *France* 19 D12
Neufchâtel-en-Bray, *France* 18 C8
Neufchâtel-sur-Aisne, *France* 19 C11
Neuhaus, *Germany* 24 B6
Neuillé-Pont-Pierre, *France* 18 E7
Neuilly-St-Front, *France* 19 C10
Neukalen, *Germany* 24 B8
Neumarkt, *Germany* 25 F7
Neumünster, *Germany* 24 A5
Neung-sur-Beuvron, *France* 19 E8
Neunkirchen, *Austria* 26 D9
Neunkirchen, *Germany* 25 F3
Neuquén, *Argentina* 128 D3
Neuquén □, *Argentina* 126 D2
Neuruppin, *Germany* 24 C8
Neusäss, *Germany* 25 G6
Neuse →, *U.S.A.* 115 H7
Neusiedl, *Austria* 27 D9
Neusiedler See, *Austria* 27 D9
Neusiedler See-Seewinkel △, *Austria* 27 D9
Neuss, *Germany* 24 D2
Neussargues-Moissac, *France* 20 C7
Neustadt, *Bayern, Germany* 25 F8
Neustadt, *Bayern, Germany* 25 G7
Neustadt, *Bayern, Germany* 25 F6
Neustadt, *Bayern, Germany* 25 E7
Neustadt, *Brandenburg, Germany* 24 C8
Neustadt, *Hessen, Germany* 24 E5
Neustadt, *Niedersachsen, Germany* 24 C5
Neustadt, *Rhld-Pfz., Germany* 25 F4
Neustadt, *Sachsen, Germany* 24 D10
Neustadt, *Schleswig-Holstein, Germany* 24 A6
Neustadt, *Thüringen, Germany* 24 E7
Neustrelitz, *Germany* 24 B9
Neuvic, *France* 20 C6
Neuville-sur-Saône, *France* 21 C8
Neuvy-le-Roi, *France* 18 E7
Neuvy-St-Sépulchre, *France* 19 F8
Neuvy-sur-Barangeon, *France* 19 E9
Neuwerk, *Germany* 24 B4
Neuwied, *Germany* 24 E3
Neva →, *Russia* 32 C6
Nevada, *Iowa, U.S.A.* 112 D8
Nevada, *Mo., U.S.A.* 113 G7
Nevada □, *U.S.A.* 108 G5
Nevada City, *U.S.A.* 110 F6
Nevado, Cerro, *Argentina* 126 D2
Nevado de Colima = Volcán de Colima △, *Mexico* 118 D4
Nevado de Tres Cruces △, *Chile* 126 B2
Nevel, *Russia* 32 D5
Nevers, *France* 19 F10
Nevertire, *Australia* 95 E4
Nevesinje, *Bos.-H.* 44 C2
Neville, *Canada* 103 D7
Nevinnomyssk, *Russia* 35 H6
Nevis, *St. Kitts & Nevis* 121 C7
Nevrokop = Gotse Delchev, *Bulgaria* 44 E7
Nevşehir, *Turkey* 70 B2
New →, *U.S.A.* 114 F5
New Aiyansh, *Canada* 102 B3
New Albany, *Ind., U.S.A.* 114 F3
New Albany, *Miss., U.S.A.* 113 H10
New Albany, *Pa., U.S.A.* 117 E8
New Amsterdam, *Guyana* 124 B7
New Angledool, *Australia* 95 D4
New Baltimore, *U.S.A.* 116 D2
New Bedford, *U.S.A.* 117 E14
New Berlin, *N.Y., U.S.A.* 117 D9
New Berlin, *Pa., U.S.A.* 116 F8
New Bern, *U.S.A.* 115 H7
New Bethlehem, *U.S.A.* 116 F5
New Bloomfield, *U.S.A.* 116 F7
New Boston, *U.S.A.* 113 J7
New Braunfels, *U.S.A.* 113 L5
New Brighton, *N.Z.* 91 K4
New Brighton, *U.S.A.* 116 F4
New Britain, *Papua N. G.* 96 H7
New Britain, *U.S.A.* 117 E12
New Brunswick, *U.S.A.* 117 F10
New Brunswick □, *Canada* 105 C6
New Bussa, *Nigeria* 83 D5
New Caledonia ⊠, *Pac. Oc.* 96 K8
New Castile = Castilla-La Mancha □, *Spain* 6 H5
New Castle, *Ind., U.S.A.* 114 F3
New Castle, *Pa., U.S.A.* 116 F4
New City, *U.S.A.* 117 E11
New Concord, *U.S.A.* 116 G3
New Cumberland, *U.S.A.* 116 F4
New Cuyama, *U.S.A.* 111 L7
New Delhi, *India* 68 E7
New Denver, *Canada* 102 D5
New Don Pedro Reservoir, *U.S.A.* 110 H6
New England, *U.S.A.* 112 B3
New England Ra., *Australia* 95 E5
New Forest, *U.K.* 15 G6
New Galloway, *U.K.* 13 F4
New Glasgow, *Canada* 105 C7
New Guinea, *Oceania* 96 H5
New Hamburg, *Canada* 116 C4
New Hampshire □, *U.S.A.* 117 C13
New Hampton, *U.S.A.* 112 D8
New Hanover, *S. Africa* 89 D5
New Hartford, *U.S.A.* 117 C9
New Haven, *Conn., U.S.A.* 117 E12
New Haven, *Mich., U.S.A.* 116 D2
New Hazelton, *Canada* 102 B3
New Hebrides = Vanuatu ■, *Pac. Oc.* 96 J8
New Holland, *U.S.A.* 117 F8
New Iberia, *U.S.A.* 113 K9
New Ireland, *Papua N. G.* 96 H7
New Jersey □, *U.S.A.* 114 E8
New Kensington, *U.S.A.* 116 F5
New Lexington, *U.S.A.* 114 F4
New Liskeard, *Canada* 104 C4
New London, *Conn., U.S.A.* 117 E12
New London, *Ohio, U.S.A.* 116 E2
New London, *Wis., U.S.A.* 112 C10
New Madrid, *U.S.A.* 113 G10
New Martinsville, *U.S.A.* 114 F5
New Meadows, *U.S.A.* 108 D5
New Melones L., *U.S.A.* 110 H6
New Mexico □, *U.S.A.* 109 J10
New Milford, *Conn., U.S.A.* 117 E11
New Milford, *Pa., U.S.A.* 117 E9
New Norcia, *Australia* 93 F2
New Norfolk, *Australia* 95 G4
New Orleans, *U.S.A.* 113 L9
New Philadelphia, *U.S.A.* 116 F3
New Plymouth, *N.Z.* 91 H5
New Plymouth, *U.S.A.* 108 E5
New Port Richey, *U.S.A.* 115 L4
New Providence I., *Bahamas* 120 A4
New Quay, *U.K.* 15 E3
New Radnor, *U.K.* 15 E4
New Richmond, *Canada* 105 C6
New Richmond, *U.S.A.* 112 C8
New River Gorge △, *U.S.A.* 114 G5
New Roads, *U.S.A.* 113 K9
New Rochelle, *U.S.A.* 117 F11
New Rockford, *U.S.A.* 112 B5
New Romney, *U.K.* 15 G8
New Ross, *Ireland* 12 D5
New Salem, *U.S.A.* 112 B4
New Scone = Scone, *U.K.* 13 E5
New Siberian I. = Novaya Sibir, Ostrov, *Russia* 53 B16
New Siberian Is. = Novosibirskiye Ostrova, *Russia* 53 B15
New Smyrna Beach, *U.S.A.* 115 L5
New South Wales □, *Australia* 95 E4
New Tecumseth, *Canada* 116 B5
New Town, *U.S.A.* 112 B3
New Tredegar, *U.K.* 15 F4
New Ulm, *U.S.A.* 112 C7
New Waterford, *Canada* 105 C7
New-Wes-Valley, *Canada* 105 C9

New Westminster, *Canada* 110 A4
New York, *U.S.A.* 117 F11
New York □, *U.S.A.* 117 D9
New York J.F. Kennedy International ✈ (JFK), *U.S.A.* 117 F11
New York Mts., *U.S.A.* 109 J6
New Zealand ■, *Oceania* 91 J6
Newaj →, *India* 68 G7
Newala, *Tanzania* 87 E4
Newark, *Del., U.S.A.* 114 F8
Newark, *N.J., U.S.A.* 117 F10
Newark, *N.Y., U.S.A.* 116 C7
Newark, *Ohio, U.S.A.* 116 F2
Newark International ✈ (EWR), *U.S.A.* 117 F10
Newark-on-Trent, *U.K.* 14 D7
Newark Valley, *U.S.A.* 117 D8
Newberg, *U.S.A.* 108 D2
Newberry, *Mich., U.S.A.* 114 B3
Newberry, *S.C., U.S.A.* 115 H5
Newberry ⌓, *U.S.A.* 108 E2
Newberry Springs, *U.S.A.* 111 L10
Newboro L., *Canada* 117 B8
Newbridge = Droichead Nua, *Ireland* 12 C5
Newburgh, *Canada* 116 B8
Newburgh, *U.S.A.* 117 E10
Newbury, *U.K.* 15 F6
Newbury, *N.H., U.S.A.* 117 B12
Newbury, *Vt., U.S.A.* 117 B12
Newburyport, *U.S.A.* 115 D10
Newcastle, *Australia* 95 E5
Newcastle, *N.B., Canada* 105 C6
Newcastle, *Ont., Canada* 104 D4
Newcastle, *S. Africa* 89 D4
Newcastle, *U.K.* 12 B6
Newcastle, *Calif., U.S.A.* 110 G5
Newcastle, *Wyo., U.S.A.* 112 D2
Newcastle Emlyn, *U.K.* 15 E3
Newcastle Ra., *Australia* 92 C5
Newcastle-under-Lyme, *U.K.* 14 D5
Newcastle-upon-Tyne, *U.K.* 14 C6
Newcastle Waters, *Australia* 94 B1
Newcastle West, *Ireland* 12 D2
Newcomb, *U.S.A.* 117 C10
Newcomerstown, *U.S.A.* 116 F3
Newdegate, *Australia* 93 F2
Newell, *Australia* 94 B4
Newell, *U.S.A.* 112 C3
Newfane, *U.S.A.* 116 C6
Newfield, *U.S.A.* 117 D8
Newfound L., *U.S.A.* 117 C13
Newfoundland, *Canada* 98 E14
Newfoundland, *U.S.A.* 117 E9
Newfoundland & Labrador □, *Canada* 105 B8
Newhall, *U.S.A.* 111 L8
Newhaven, *U.K.* 15 G8
Newkirk, *U.S.A.* 113 G6
Newlyn, *U.K.* 15 G2
Newman, *Australia* 92 D2
Newman, *U.S.A.* 110 H5
Newmarket, *Canada* 116 B5
Newmarket, *Ireland* 12 D2
Newmarket, *U.K.* 15 E8
Newmarket, *U.S.A.* 117 C14
Newnan, *U.S.A.* 115 J3
Newport, *Ireland* 12 C2
Newport, *I. of W., U.K.* 15 G6
Newport, *Newp., U.K.* 15 F5
Newport, *Ark., U.S.A.* 113 H9
Newport, *Ky., U.S.A.* 114 F3
Newport, *N.H., U.S.A.* 117 C12
Newport, *N.Y., U.S.A.* 117 C9
Newport, *Oreg., U.S.A.* 108 D1
Newport, *Pa., U.S.A.* 116 F7
Newport, *R.I., U.S.A.* 117 E13
Newport, *Tenn., U.S.A.* 115 H4
Newport, *Vt., U.S.A.* 117 B12
Newport, *Wash., U.S.A.* 108 B5
Newport □, *U.K.* 15 F4
Newport Beach, *U.S.A.* 111 M9
Newport News, *U.S.A.* 114 G7
Newport Pagnell, *U.K.* 15 E7
Newquay, *U.K.* 15 G2
Newry, *U.K.* 12 B5
Newton, *Ill., U.S.A.* 112 F10
Newton, *Iowa, U.S.A.* 112 E8
Newton, *Kans., U.S.A.* 113 F6
Newton, *Mass., U.S.A.* 117 D13
Newton, *Miss., U.S.A.* 113 J10
Newton, *N.C., U.S.A.* 115 H5
Newton, *N.J., U.S.A.* 117 E10
Newton, *Tex., U.S.A.* 113 K8
Newton Abbot, *U.K.* 15 G4
Newton Aycliffe, *U.K.* 14 C6
Newton Falls, *U.S.A.* 116 E4
Newton Stewart, *U.K.* 13 G4
Newtonmore, *U.K.* 13 D4
Newtown, *U.K.* 15 E4
Newtownabbey, *U.K.* 12 B6
Newtownards, *U.K.* 12 B6
Newtownbarry = Bunclody, *Ireland* 12 D5
Newtownstewart, *U.K.* 12 B4
Newville, *U.S.A.* 116 F7
Nexon, *France* 20 C5
Neya, *Russia* 34 A6
Neyrīz, *Iran* 71 D7
Neyshābūr, *Iran* 71 B8
Nezhin = Nizhyn, *Ukraine* 33 G6
Nezperce, *U.S.A.* 108 C5
Ngabang, *Indonesia* 62 D3
Ngabordamlu, Tanjung, *Indonesia* 63 F8
N'Gage, *Angola* 84 F3
Ngala, *Nigeria* 83 C7
Ngambé, *Centre, Cameroon* 83 D7
Ngambé, *Littoral, Cameroon* 83 E7
Ngami Depression, *Botswana* 88 C3
Ngamo, *Zimbabwe* 87 F2
Ngangala, *Sudan* 81 G3
Nganglong Kangri, *China* 67 C12
Ngao, *Thailand* 64 C2
Ngaoundéré, *Cameroon* 84 C2
Ngapara, *N.Z.* 91 L3
Ngara, *Tanzania* 86 C3
Ngawi, *Indonesia* 63 G14
Nghia Lo, *Vietnam* 58 G5
Ngoboli, *Sudan* 81 G3
Ngoma, *Malawi* 87 E3
Ngomahura, *Zimbabwe* 87 G3
Ngomba, *Tanzania* 87 D3
Ngop, *Sudan* 81 F3
Ngoring Hu, *China* 60 C4
Ngorkou, *Mali* 82 B4
Ngorongoro, *Tanzania* 86 C4
Ngorongoro ⌓, *Tanzania* 86 C4
Ngozi, *Burundi* 86 C2
Ngudu, *Tanzania* 86 C3
Nguigmi, *Niger* 79 F8
Nguila, *Cameroon* 83 E7
Nguiu, *Australia* 92 B5
Ngukurr, *Australia* 94 A1
Ngunga, *Tanzania* 86 C3
Nguru, *Nigeria* 83 C7
Nguru Mts., *Tanzania* 86 D4
Ngusi, *Malawi* 87 E3
Nguyen Binh, *Vietnam* 58 F5
Nha Trang, *Vietnam* 65 F7
Nhacoongo, *Mozam.* 89 C6
Nhamaabué, *Mozam.* 87 F4
Nhamundá →, *Brazil* 125 D7
Nhangulaze, L., *Mozam.* 89 C5
Nhill, *Australia* 95 F3
Nho Quan, *Vietnam* 58 G5
Nhulunbuy, *Australia* 94 A2
Nia-nia, *Dem. Rep. of the Congo* 86 B2
Niafounké, *Mali* 82 B4
Niagara Falls, *Canada* 116 C5
Niagara Falls, *U.S.A.* 116 C6
Niagara-on-the-Lake, *Canada* 116 C5
Niah, *Malaysia* 62 D4
Niamey, *Niger* 83 C5
Niandan-Koro, *Guinea* 82 C3
Nianforando, *Guinea* 82 D2
Niangara, *Dem. Rep. of the Congo* 86 B2
Niangbo, *Ivory C.* 82 D3
Niangoloko, *Burkina Faso* 82 C4
Niantic, *U.S.A.* 117 E12
Niaro, *Sudan* 81 E3
Nias, *Indonesia* 62 D1
Niassa ⌓, *Mozam.* 87 E4
Niassa □, *Mozam.* 87 E4
Nibāk, *Si. Arabia* 71 E7
Nibe, *Denmark* 11 H3
Nicaragua ■, *Cent. Amer.* 120 D2
Nicaragua, L. de, *Nic.* 120 D2
Nicastro, *Italy* 43 D9
Nice, *France* 21 E11
Nice ✈ (NCE), *France* 21 E11
Niceville, *U.S.A.* 115 K2
Nichicun, L., *Canada* 105 B5
Nichinan, *Japan* 55 J5
Nicholás, Canal, *W. Indies* 120 B3
Nicholasville, *U.S.A.* 114 G3
Nichols, *U.S.A.* 117 D8
Nicholson, *Australia* 92 C4
Nicholson, *U.S.A.* 117 E9
Nicholson →, *Australia* 94 B2
Nicholson L., *Canada* 103 A8
Nicholson Ra., *Australia* 93 E2
Nicholville, *U.S.A.* 117 B10
Nicobar Is., *Ind. Oc.* 50 J13
Nicola, *Canada* 102 C4
Nicolls Town, *Bahamas* 120 A4
Nicopolis, *Greece* 46 B2
Nicosia, *Cyprus* 49 D12
Nicosia, *Italy* 43 E7
Nicótera, *Italy* 43 D8
Nicoya, *Costa Rica* 120 D2
Nicoya, G. de, *Costa Rica* 120 E3
Nicoya, Pen. de, *Costa Rica* 120 E2
Nida, *Lithuania* 30 C8
Nidd →, *U.K.* 14 D6
Nidda, *Germany* 25 E5
Nidda →, *Germany* 25 E4
Nidwalden □, *Switz.* 25 J4
Nidzica, *Poland* 31 E7
Niebüll, *Germany* 24 A4
Nied →, *Germany* 19 C13
Niederaula, *Germany* 24 E5
Niederbayern □, *Germany* 25 G8
Niederbronn-les-Bains, *France* 19 D14
Niedere Tauern, *Austria* 26 D7
Niederlausitz, *Germany* 24 D9
Niederösterreich □, *Austria* 26 C8
Niedersachsen □, *Germany* 24 C4
Niedersächsisches Wattenmeer △, *Germany* 24 B3
Niekerkshoop, *S. Africa* 88 D3
Niellé, *Ivory C.* 82 C3
Niemba, *Dem. Rep. of the Congo* 86 D2
Niemen = Nemunas →, *Lithuania* 9 J19
Niemodlin, *Poland* 31 H4
Nienburg, *Germany* 24 C5
Niepołomice, *Poland* 31 H7
Niers →, *Germany* 24 D1
Niesky, *Germany* 24 D10
Nieszawa, *Poland* 31 F5
Nieu Bethesda, *S. Africa* 88 E3
Nieuw Amsterdam, *Suriname* 125 B7
Nieuw Nickerie, *Suriname* 125 B7
Nieuwoudtville, *S. Africa* 88 E2
Nieuwpoort, *Belgium* 17 C2
Nieves, Pico de las, *Canary Is.* 48 G4
Nièvre □, *France* 19 E10
Niga, *Mali* 82 C3
Niğde, *Turkey* 70 B2
Nigel, *S. Africa* 89 D4
Niger □, *Nigeria* 83 D6
Niger ■, *W. Afr.* 83 B7
Niger →, *W. Afr.* 83 D6
Niger Delta, *Africa* 83 E6
Nigeria ■, *W. Afr.* 83 D6
Nighasin, *India* 69 E9
Nightcaps, *N.Z.* 91 L2
Nigríta, *Greece* 44 F7
Nii-Jima, *Japan* 55 G9
Niigata, *Japan* 54 F9
Niigata □, *Japan* 55 F9
Niihama, *Japan* 55 H6
Niihau, *U.S.A.* 106 H14
Niimi, *Japan* 55 G6
Niitsu, *Japan* 54 F9
Níjar, *Spain* 39 J2
Nijil, *Jordan* 74 E4
Nijkerk, *Neths.* 17 B5
Nijmegen, *Neths.* 17 C5
Nijverdal, *Neths.* 17 B6
Nīk Pey, *Iran* 71 B6
Nike, *Nigeria* 83 D6
Nikiniki, *Indonesia* 63 F6
Nikísiani, *Greece* 45 F8
Nikítas, *Greece* 44 F7
Nikki, *Benin* 83 D5
Nikkō, *Japan* 55 F9
Nikkō △, *Japan* 55 F9
Nikolayev = Mykolayiv, *Ukraine* 33 J7
Nikolayevsk, *Russia* 34 E7
Nikolayevsk-na-Amur, *Russia* 53 D15
Nikolsk, *Russia* 34 D8
Nikolskoye, *Russia* 53 D17
Nikopol, *Bulgaria* 45 C8
Nikopol, *Ukraine* 33 J8
Niksar, *Turkey* 72 B7
Nīkshahr, *Iran* 71 E9
Nikšić, *Serbia & M.* 44 D2
Nîl, Nahr en →, *Africa* 80 H7
Nîl el Abyad →, *Sudan* 81 D3
Nîl el Azraq →, *Sudan* 81 D3
Nila, *Indonesia* 63 F7
Niland, *U.S.A.* 111 M11
Nile = Nîl, Nahr en →, *Africa* 80 H7
Niles, *Mich., U.S.A.* 114 E2
Niles, *Ohio, U.S.A.* 116 E4
Nilüfer →, *Turkey* 45 F12
Nim Ka Thana, *India* 68 F6
Nimach, *India* 68 G6
Nimbahera, *India* 68 G6
Nîmes, *France* 21 E8
Nimfaíon, Ákra = Pínnes, Ákra, *Greece* 45 F8
Nimmitabel, *Australia* 95 F4
Nimule, *Sudan* 81 G3
Nimule △, *Sudan* 81 G3
Nin, *Croatia* 41 D12
Nīnawá, *Iraq* 70 B4
Nīnawá □, *Iraq* 70 B4
Nindigully, *Australia* 95 D4
Nineveh = Nīnawá, *Iraq* 70 B4
Ning Xian, *China* 56 G4
Ningaloo ⌓, *Australia* 92 D1
Ning'an, *China* 57 B15
Ningbo, *China* 59 C13
Ningcheng, *China* 57 D10
Ningde, *China* 59 D12
Ningdu, *China* 59 D10
Ninggang, *China* 59 D9
Ningguo, *China* 59 B12
Ninghai, *China* 59 C13
Ninghua, *China* 59 D11
Ningi, *Nigeria* 83 C6
Ningjin, *China* 56 F8
Ningjing Shan, *China* 58 C2
Ninglang, *China* 58 D3
Ningling, *China* 56 G8
Ningming, *China* 58 F6
Ningnan, *China* 58 D4
Ningpo = Ningbo, *China* 59 C13
Ningqiang, *China* 56 H4
Ningshan, *China* 56 H5
Ningsia Hui A.R. = Ningxia Huizu Zizhiqu □, *China* 56 F4
Ningwu, *China* 56 E7
Ningxia Huizu Zizhiqu □, *China* 56 F4
Ningxiang, *China* 59 C9
Ningyang, *China* 56 G9
Ningyuan, *China* 59 E8
Ninh Binh, *Vietnam* 58 G5
Ninh Giang, *Vietnam* 64 B6
Ninh Hoa, *Vietnam* 64 F7
Ninh Ma, *Vietnam* 64 F7
Nini-Suhien △, *Ghana* 82 D4
Ninove, *Belgium* 17 D4
Nioaque, *Brazil* 127 A4
Niobrara, *U.S.A.* 112 D6
Niobrara →, *U.S.A.* 112 D6
Niokolo-Koba △, *Senegal* 82 C2
Niono, *Mali* 82 C3
Nionsamoridougou, *Guinea* 82 D3
Nioro du Rip, *Senegal* 82 C1
Nioro du Sahel, *Mali* 82 B3
Niort, *France* 20 B3
Nipawin, *Canada* 103 C8
Nipfjället, *Sweden* 10 C6
Nipigon, *Canada* 104 C2
Nipigon, L., *Canada* 104 C2
Nipishish L., *Canada* 105 B7
Nipissing, L., *Canada* 104 C4
Nipomo, *U.S.A.* 111 K6
Nipton, *U.S.A.* 111 K11
Niquelândia, *Brazil* 125 F9
Nīr, *Iran* 70 B5
Nirasaki, *Japan* 55 G9
Nirmal, *India* 66 K11
Nirmali, *India* 69 F12
Niš, *Serbia & M.* 44 C5
Nisa, *Portugal* 37 F3
Nisāb, *Si. Arabia* 70 D5
Nişāb, *Yemen* 75 E4
Nišava →, *Serbia & M.* 44 C5
Niscemi, *Italy* 43 E7
Nishinomiya, *Japan* 55 G7
Nishino'omote, *Japan* 55 J5
Nishiwaki, *Japan* 55 G7
Nisíros, *Greece* 47 E9
Niška Banja, *Serbia & M.* 44 C6
Niskibi →, *Canada* 104 A2
Nisko, *Poland* 31 H9
Nisporeni, *Moldova* 29 C13
Nisqually →, *U.S.A.* 110 C4
Nissáki, *Greece* 49 A3
Nissan →, *Sweden* 11 H6
Nissum Bredning, *Denmark* 11 H2
Nissum Fjord, *Denmark* 11 H2
Nistru = Dnister →, *Europe* 33 J6
Nisutlin →, *Canada* 102 A2
Nitchequon, *Canada* 105 B5
Niterói, *Brazil* 127 A7
Nith →, *Canada* 116 C4
Nith →, *U.K.* 13 F5
Nitmiluk △, *Australia* 92 B5
Nitra, *Slovak Rep.* 27 C11
Nitra →, *Slovak Rep.* 27 D11
Nitriansky □, *Slovak Rep.* 27 C11
Nittenau, *Germany* 25 F8
Niuafo'ou, *Tonga* 91 B11
Niue, *Cook Is.* 97 J11
Niulan Jiang →, *China* 58 D4
Niut, *Indonesia* 62 D4
Niutou Shan, *China* 59 C13
Niuzhuang, *China* 57 D12
Nivala, *Finland* 8 E21
Nivelles, *Belgium* 17 D4
Nivernais, *France* 19 E10
Niwas, *India* 69 H9
Nixon, *U.S.A.* 113 L6
Nizamabad, *India* 66 K11
Nizamghat, *India* 67 E19
Nizhne Kolymsk, *Russia* 53 C17
Nizhnegorskiy = Nyzhnohirskyy, *Ukraine* 33 K8
Nizhnekamsk, *Russia* 34 C10
Nizhneudinsk, *Russia* 53 D10
Nizhnevartovsk, *Russia* 52 C8
Nizhniy Chir, *Russia* 35 F6
Nizhniy Lomov, *Russia* 34 D6
Nizhniy Novgorod, *Russia* 34 B7
Nizhniy Tagil, *Russia* 52 D6
Nizhyn, *Ukraine* 33 G6
Nizina Mazowiecka, *Poland* 31 F8
Nizip, *Turkey* 70 B3
Nízké Tatry, *Slovak Rep.* 27 C12
Nízke Tatry △, *Slovak Rep.* 27 C12
Nízký Jeseník, *Czech Rep.* 27 B10
Nizza Monferrato, *Italy* 40 D5
Njakwa, *Malawi* 87 E3
Njanji, *Zambia* 87 E3
Njegoš, *Serbia & M.* 44 D2
Njinjo, *Tanzania* 87 D4
Njombe, *Tanzania* 87 D3
Njombe →, *Tanzania* 86 D4
Njurundabommen, *Sweden* 10 B11
Nkambe, *Cameroon* 83 D7
Nkana, *Zambia* 87 E2
Nkandla, *S. Africa* 89 D5
Nkawkaw, *Ghana* 83 D4
Nkayi, *Zimbabwe* 87 F2
Nkhotakota, *Malawi* 87 E3
Nkhotakota ⌓, *Malawi* 87 E3
Nkongsamba, *Cameroon* 83 E6
Nkurenkuru, *Namibia* 88 B2
Nkwanta, *Ghana* 82 D4
Nmai →, *Burma* 58 F2
Noakhali = Maijdi, *Bangla.* 67 H17
Nobel, *Canada* 116 A4
Nobeoka, *Japan* 55 H5
Noblejas, *Spain* 36 F7
Noblesville, *U.S.A.* 114 E3
Noboribetsu, *Japan* 54 C10
Noce →, *Italy* 40 B8
Nocera Inferiore, *Italy* 43 B7
Nocera Umbra, *Italy* 41 E9
Noci, *Italy* 43 B10
Nocona, *U.S.A.* 113 J6
Nocrich, *Romania* 29 E9
Noda, *Japan* 55 G9
Nogales, *Mexico* 118 A2
Nogales, *U.S.A.* 109 L8
Nogaro, *France* 20 E3
Nogat →, *Poland* 30 D6
Nōgata, *Japan* 55 H5
Nogent, *France* 19 D12
Nogent-le-Rotrou, *France* 18 D7
Nogent-sur-Seine, *France* 19 D10
Noggerup, *Australia* 93 F2
Noginsk, *Moskva, Russia* 32 E10
Noginsk, *Tunguska, Russia* 53 C10
Nogoa →, *Australia* 94 C4
Nogoyá, *Argentina* 126 C4
Nógrád □, *Hungary* 28 C4
Noguera Pallaresa →, *Spain* 38 D5
Noguera Ribagorzana →, *Spain* 38 D5
Nohar, *India* 68 E6
Nohfelden, *Germany* 25 F3
Nohta, *India* 69 H8
Noia, *Spain* 36 C2
Noire, Montagne, *France* 20 E6
Noires, Mts., *France* 18 D3
Noirétable, *France* 20 C7
Noirmoutier, Î. de, *France* 18 F4
Noirmoutier-en-l'Île, *France* 18 F4
Nojane, *Botswana* 88 C3
Nojima-Zaki, *Japan* 55 G9
Nok Kundi, *Pakistan* 66 E3
Nok Ta Phao, Ko, *Thailand* 65 b
Nokaneng, *Botswana* 88 B3
Nokia, *Finland* 9 F20
Nokomis, *Canada* 103 C8
Nokomis L., *Canada* 103 B8
Nol, *Sweden* 11 G6
Nola, *C.A.R.* 84 D3
Nola, *Italy* 43 B7
Nolay, *France* 19 F11
Noli, C. di, *Italy* 40 D5
Nolinsk, *Russia* 34 B9
Noma Omuramba →, *Namibia* 88 B3
Nombre de Dios, *Panama* 120 E4
Nome, *U.S.A.* 100 B3
Nomo-Zaki, *Japan* 55 H4
Nonacho L., *Canada* 103 A7
Nonancourt, *France* 18 D8
Nonda, *Australia* 94 C3
None, *Italy* 40 D4
Nong Chang, *Thailand* 64 E2
Nong Het, *Laos* 64 C4
Nong Khai, *Thailand* 64 D4
Nong'an, *China* 57 B13
Nongoma, *S. Africa* 89 D5
Nongsa, *Indonesia* 65 d
Nonoava, *Mexico* 118 B3
Nonoava →, *Mexico* 118 B3
Nonthaburi, *Thailand* 64 F3
Nontron, *France* 20 C4
Nonza, *France* 21 F13
Noonamah, *Australia* 92 B5
Noord Brabant □, *Neths.* 17 C5
Noord Holland □, *Neths.* 17 B4
Noordbeveland, *Neths.* 17 C3
Noordoostpolder, *Neths.* 17 B5
Noordwijk, *Neths.* 17 B4
Nootka I., *Canada* 102 D3
Nopiming ⌓, *Canada* 103 C9
Nora, *Eritrea* 81 D5
Nora, *Sweden* 10 E9
Noralee, *Canada* 102 C3
Noranda = Rouyn-Noranda, *Canada* 104 C4
Norberg, *Sweden* 10 D9
Nórcia, *Italy* 41 F10
Norco, *U.S.A.* 111 M9
Nord □, *France* 19 B10
Nord-Kivu □, *Dem. Rep. of the Congo* 86 C2
Nord-Ostsee-Kanal, *Germany* 24 A5
Nord-Pas-de-Calais □, *France* 19 B9
Nordaustlandet, *Svalbard* 4 B9
Nordborg, *Denmark* 11 J3
Nordby, *Denmark* 11 J2
Norddeich, *Germany* 24 B3
Nordegg, *Canada* 102 C5
Norden, *Germany* 24 B3
Nordenham, *Germany* 24 B4
Norderney, *Germany* 24 B3
Norderstedt, *Germany* 24 B6
Nordfjord, *Norway* 9 F11
Nordfriesische Inseln, *Germany* 24 A4
Nordhausen, *Germany* 24 D6
Nordhorn, *Germany* 24 C3
Norðoyar, *Færoe Is.* 8 E9
Nordingrå, *Sweden* 10 B12
Nordjyllands Amtskommune □, *Denmark* 11 G4
Nordkapp, *Norway* 8 A21
Nordkapp, *Svalbard* 4 A9
Nordkinn = Kinnarodden, *Norway* 6 A11
Nordkinn-halvøya, *Norway* 8 A22
Nördlicher Teutoburger Wald-Wiehengebirge ⌓, *Germany* 24 C4
Nördlingen, *Germany* 25 G6
Nordrhein-Westfalen □, *Germany* 24 D3
Nordstrand, *Germany* 24 A4
Nordvik, *Russia* 53 B12
Nore →, *Ireland* 12 D4
Norfolk, *Canada* 116 D4
Norfolk, *Nebr., U.S.A.* 112 D6
Norfolk, *Va., U.S.A.* 114 G7
Norfolk □, *U.K.* 15 E8
Norfolk I., *Pac. Oc.* 96 K8
Norfork L., *U.S.A.* 113 G8
Norilsk, *Russia* 53 C9
Norma, Mt., *Australia* 94 C3
Normal, *U.S.A.* 112 E10
Norman, *U.S.A.* 113 H6
Norman →, *Australia* 94 B3
Norman Wells, *Canada* 100 B7
Normanby →, *Australia* 94 A3
Normandie-Maine ⌓, *France* 18 D6
Normandin, *Canada* 104 C5
Normanhurst, Mt., *Australia* 93 E3
Normanton, *Australia* 94 B3
Normétal, *Canada* 104 C4
Norquay, *Canada* 103 C8
Norquinco, *Argentina* 128 E2
Norra Dellen, *Sweden* 10 C10
Norra Kvill △, *Sweden* 11 G9
Norra Ulvön, *Sweden* 10 A12
Norrahammar, *Sweden* 11 G8
Norrbotten □, *Sweden* 8 C19
Nørre Åby, *Denmark* 11 J3
Nørre Alslev, *Denmark* 11 K5
Nørresundby, *Denmark* 11 G3
Norrhult, *Sweden* 11 G9
Norris Point, *Canada* 105 C8
Norristown, *U.S.A.* 117 F9
Norrköping, *Sweden* 11 F10
Norrland, *Sweden* 9 E16
Norrsundet, *Sweden* 10 D11
Norrtälje, *Sweden* 10 E12
Norseman, *Australia* 93 F3
Norsk, *Russia* 53 D14
Norte, Pta. del, *Canary Is.* 48 G2
Norte, Serra do, *Brazil* 124 F7
North, C., *Canada* 105 C7
North Adams, *U.S.A.* 117 D11
North Arm, *Canada* 102 A5
North Augusta, *U.S.A.* 115 J5
North Ayrshire □, *U.K.* 13 F4
North Bass I., *U.S.A.* 116 E2
North Battleford, *Canada* 103 C7
North Bay, *Canada* 104 C4
North Belcher Is., *Canada* 104 A4
North Bend, *Oreg., U.S.A.* 108 E1
North Bend, *Pa., U.S.A.* 116 E7

North Bend, *Wash., U.S.A.* 110 C5
North Bennington, *U.S.A.* 117 D11
North Berwick, *U.K.* 13 E6
North Berwick, *U.S.A.* 117 C14
North C., *Canada* 105 C7
North C., *N.Z.* 91 F4
North Canadian →, *U.S.A.* 113 H7
North Canton, *U.S.A.* 116 F3
North Cape = Nordkapp, *Norway* 8 A21
North Cape = Nordkapp, *Svalbard* 4 A9
North Caribou L., *Canada* 104 B1
North Carolina □, *U.S.A.* 115 H6
North Cascades △, *U.S.A.* 108 B3
North Channel, *Canada* 104 C3
North Channel, *U.K.* 13 F3
North Charleston, *U.S.A.* 115 J6
North Chicago, *U.S.A.* 114 D2
North Creek, *U.S.A.* 117 C11
North Dakota □, *U.S.A.* 112 B5
North Downs, *U.K.* 15 F8
North East, *U.S.A.* 116 D5
North East Frontier Agency = Arunachal Pradesh □, *India* 67 F19
North East Lincolnshire □, *U.K.* 14 D7
North Eastern □, *Kenya* 86 B5
North Esk →, *U.K.* 13 E6
North European Plain, *Europe* 6 E10
North Foreland, *U.K.* 15 F9
North Fork, *U.S.A.* 110 H7
North Fork American →, *U.S.A.* 110 G5
North Fork Feather →, *U.S.A.* 110 F5
North Fork Grand →, *U.S.A.* 112 C3
North Fork Red →, *U.S.A.* 113 H5
North Frisian Is. = Nordfriesische Inseln, *Germany* 24 A4
North Gower, *Canada* 117 A9
North Hd., *Australia* 93 F1
North Henik L., *Canada* 103 A9
North Highlands, *U.S.A.* 110 G5
North Horr, *Kenya* 86 B4
North I., *Kenya* 86 B4
North I., *N.Z.* 91 H5
North Kingsville, *U.S.A.* 116 E4
North Kitui ⌓, *Kenya* 86 C4
North Knife →, *Canada* 103 B10
North Koel →, *India* 69 G10
North Korea ■, *Asia* 57 E14
North Lakhimpur, *India* 67 F19
North Lanarkshire □, *U.K.* 13 F5
North Las Vegas, *U.S.A.* 111 J11
North Lincolnshire □, *U.K.* 14 D7
North Little Rock, *U.S.A.* 113 H8
North Loup →, *U.S.A.* 112 E5
North Luangwa △, *Zambia* 87 E3
North Magnetic Pole, *Canada* 4 A2
North Minch, *U.K.* 13 C3
North Moose L., *Canada* 103 C8
North Moose L., *Man., Canada* 103 C8
North Myrtle Beach, *U.S.A.* 115 J6
North Nahanni →, *Canada* 102 A4
North Olmsted, *U.S.A.* 116 E3
North Ossetia □, *Russia* 35 J7
North Pagai, I. = Pagai Utara, Pulau, *Indonesia* 62 E2
North Palisade, *U.S.A.* 110 H8
North Platte, *U.S.A.* 112 E4
North Platte →, *U.S.A.* 112 E4
North Pole, *Arctic* 4 A
North Portal, *Canada* 103 D8
North Powder, *U.S.A.* 108 D5
North Pt., *Barbados* 121 g
North Pt., *Trin. & Tob.* 125 J16
North Pt., *U.S.A.* 116 A1
North Rhine Westphalia = Nordrhein-Westfalen □, *Germany* 24 D3
North River, *Canada* 105 B8
North Ronaldsay, *U.K.* 13 B6
North Saskatchewan →, *Canada* 103 C7
North Sea, *Europe* 16 C8
North Seal →, *Canada* 103 B9
North Somerset □, *U.K.* 15 F5
North Sporades = Vóriai Sporádhes, *Greece* 46 B5
North Sydney, *Canada* 105 C7
North Syracuse, *U.S.A.* 117 C8
North Taranaki Bight, *N.Z.* 91 H5
North Thompson →, *Canada* 102 C4
North Tonawanda, *U.S.A.* 116 C6
North Troy, *U.S.A.* 117 B12
North Truchas Pk., *U.S.A.* 109 J11
North Twin I., *Canada* 104 B4
North Tyne →, *U.K.* 14 B5
North Uist, *U.K.* 13 D1
North Vancouver, *Canada* 102 D4
North Vernon, *U.S.A.* 114 F3
North Wabasca L., *Canada* 102 B6
North Walsham, *U.K.* 14 E9
North West = Severo-Zapadnyy □, *Russia* 52 C4
North-West □, *S. Africa* 88 D4
North West C., *Australia* 92 D1
North West Christmas I. Ridge, *Pac. Oc.* 97 G11
North West Frontier □, *Pakistan* 68 C4
North West Highlands, *U.K.* 13 D4
North West River, *Canada* 105 B7
North Western □, *Zambia* 87 E2
North Wildwood, *U.S.A.* 114 F8
North York Moors, *U.K.* 14 C7
North York Moors △, *U.K.* 14 C7
North Yorkshire □, *U.K.* 14 C6
Northallerton, *U.K.* 14 C6
Northam, *Australia* 93 F2
Northam, *S. Africa* 88 C4
Northampton, *Australia* 93 E1
Northampton, *U.K.* 15 E7
Northampton, *Mass., U.S.A.* 117 D12
Northampton, *Pa., U.S.A.* 117 F9
Northamptonshire □, *U.K.* 15 E7
Northbridge, *U.S.A.* 117 D13
Northcliffe, *Australia* 93 F2
Northeast Providence Chan., *W. Indies* 120 A4
Northeim, *Germany* 24 D6
Northern = Limpopo □, *S. Africa* 89 C4
Northern □, *Ghana* 83 D4
Northern □, *Malawi* 87 E3
Northern □, *Zambia* 87 E3
Northern Areas □, *Pakistan* 69 A5
Northern Cape □, *S. Africa* 88 D3
Northern Circars, *India* 67 L13
Northern Indian L., *Canada* 103 B9
Northern Ireland □, *U.K.* 12 B5
Northern Light L., *Canada* 104 C1
Northern Marianas ☒, *Pac. Oc.* 96 F6
Northern Province □, *S. Leone* 82 D2
Northern Province □, *S. Africa* 89 C4
Northern Range, *Trin. & Tob.* 125 K15
Northern Territory □, *Australia* 92 D5
Northfield, *Minn., U.S.A.* 112 C8
Northfield, *Vt., U.S.A.* 117 B12
Northland □, *N.Z.* 91 F4
Northome, *U.S.A.* 112 B7
Northport, *Ala., U.S.A.* 115 J2
Northport, *Wash., U.S.A.* 108 B5
Northumberland □, *U.K.* 14 B6
Northumberland, C., *Australia* 95 F3
Northumberland Is., *Australia* 94 C4
Northumberland Str., *Canada* 105 C7
Northville, *U.S.A.* 117 C10
Northwest Providence Channel, *W. Indies* 120 A4
Northwest Territories □, *Canada* 100 B9
Northwich, *U.K.* 14 D5
Northwood, *Iowa, U.S.A.* 112 D8
Northwood, *N. Dak., U.S.A.* 112 B6
Norton, *U.S.A.* 112 F5
Norton, *Zimbabwe* 87 F3
Norton Sd., *U.S.A.* 100 B3
Nortorf, *Germany* 24 A5
Norwalk, *Calif., U.S.A.* 111 M8
Norwalk, *Conn., U.S.A.* 117 E11
Norwalk, *Iowa, U.S.A.* 112 E8
Norwalk, *Ohio, U.S.A.* 116 E2
Norway, *Maine, U.S.A.* 115 C10
Norway, *Mich., U.S.A.* 114 C2
Norway ■, *Europe* 8 E14
Norway House, *Canada* 103 C9
Norwegian Sea, *Atl. Oc.* 6 B5
Norwich, *Canada* 116 D4
Norwich, *U.K.* 15 E9
Norwich, *Conn., U.S.A.* 117 E12
Norwich, *N.Y., U.S.A.* 117 D9
Norwood, *Canada* 116 B7
Norwood, *U.S.A.* 117 B10
Noshiro, *Japan* 54 D10
Nosivka, *Ukraine* 33 G6
Nosovka = Nosivka, *Ukraine* 33 G6
Noşratābād, *Iran* 71 D8
Noss Hd., *U.K.* 13 C5
Nossebro, *Sweden* 11 F6
Nossob →, *S. Africa* 88 D3
Nossombougou, *Mali* 82 C3
Nosy Barren, *Madag.* 85 H8
Nosy Be, *Madag.* 85 G9
Nosy Boraha, *Madag.* 89 B8
Nosy Lava, *Madag.* 89 A8
Nosy Varika, *Madag.* 89 C8
Noteć →, *Poland* 31 F2
Notikewin →, *Canada* 102 B5
Notio Aigaio = Notios Aiyaíon □, *Greece* 47 E7
Notios Aiyaíon □, *Greece* 47 E7
Notios Evvoïkos Kólpos, *Greece* 46 C5
Noto, *Italy* 43 F8
Noto, G. di, *Italy* 43 F8
Notodden, *Norway* 9 G13
Notre Dame B., *Canada* 105 C8
Notre-Dame-de-Koartac = Quaqtaq, *Canada* 101 B13
Notre-Dame-des-Bois, *Canada* 117 A13
Notre-Dame-d'Ivugivic = Ivujivik, *Canada* 101 B12
Notre-Dame-du-Nord, *Canada* 104 C4
Notsé, *Togo* 83 D5
Nottawasaga B., *Canada* 116 B4
Nottaway →, *Canada* 104 B4
Nottingham, *U.K.* 14 E6
Nottingham, City of □, *U.K.* 14 E6
Nottingham I., *Canada* 101 B12
Nottinghamshire □, *U.K.* 14 D6
Nottoway →, *U.S.A.* 114 G7
Notwane →, *Botswana* 88 C4
Nouâdhibou, *Mauritania* 78 D2
Nouâdhibou, Ras, *Mauritania* 78 D2
Nouakchott, *Mauritania* 82 B1
Nouâmghâr, *Mauritania* 82 B1
Nouméa, *N. Cal.* 96 K8
Nouna, *Burkina Faso* 82 C4
Noupoort, *S. Africa* 88 E3
Nouveau Comptoir = Wemindji, *Canada* 104 B4
Nouvelle-Amsterdam, I., *Ind. Oc.* 3 F13
Nouvelle-Calédonie = New Caledonia ☒, *Pac. Oc.* 96 K8
Nouzonville, *France* 19 C11
Nová Baňa, *Slovak Rep.* 27 C11
Nová Bystřice, *Czech Rep.* 26 B8
Nova Casa Nova, *Brazil* 125 E10
Nova Esperança, *Brazil* 127 A5
Nova Friburgo, *Brazil* 127 A7
Nova Gaia = Cambundi-Catembo, *Angola* 84 G3
Nova Gorica, *Slovenia* 41 C10
Nova Gradiška, *Croatia* 28 E2
Nova Iguaçu, *Brazil* 127 A7
Nova Iorque, *Brazil* 125 E10
Nova Kakhovka, *Ukraine* 33 J7
Nova Lamego, *Guinea-Biss.* 82 C2
Nova Lima, *Brazil* 127 A7
Nova Lisboa = Huambo, *Angola* 85 G3
Nova Lusitânia, *Mozam.* 87 F3
Nova Mambone, *Mozam.* 89 C6
Nova Odesa, *Ukraine* 33 J6
Nová Paka, *Czech Rep.* 26 A8
Nova Pavova, *Serbia & M.* 28 F5
Nova Scotia □, *Canada* 105 C7
Nova Siri, *Italy* 43 B9
Nova Sofala, *Mozam.* 89 C5
Nova Varoš, *Serbia & M.* 44 C3
Nova Venécia, *Brazil* 125 G10
Nova Zagora, *Bulgaria* 45 D10
Novaci, *Macedonia* 44 E5
Novaci, *Romania* 29 E8
Novaféltria, *Italy* 41 E9
Novaleksandrovskaya = Novoaleksandrovsk, *Russia* 35 H5
Novannenskiy = Novoannenskiy, *Russia* 34 E6
Novar, *Canada* 116 A5
Novara, *Italy* 40 C5
Novato, *U.S.A.* 110 G4
Novaya Kakhovka = Nova Kakhovka, *Ukraine* 33 J7
Novaya Kazanka, *Kazakhstan* 35 F9
Novaya Ladoga, *Russia* 32 B7
Novaya Lyalya, *Russia* 52 D7
Novaya Sibir, Ostrov, *Russia* 53 B16
Novaya Zemlya, *Russia* 52 B6
Nové Město, *Slovak Rep.* 27 C10
Nové Město na Moravě, *Czech Rep.* 26 B9
Nové Město nad Metují, *Czech Rep.* 27 A9
Nové Zámky, *Slovak Rep.* 27 C11
Novelda, *Spain* 39 G4
Novellara, *Italy* 40 D7
Noventa Vicentina, *Italy* 41 C8
Novgorod, *Russia* 32 C6
Novgorod-Severskiy = Novhorod-Siverskyy, *Ukraine* 33 G7
Novhorod-Siverskyy, *Ukraine* 33 G7
Novi Bečej, *Serbia & M.* 28 E5
Novi Iskar, *Bulgaria* 44 D7
Novi Kneževac, *Serbia & M.* 28 D5
Novi Lígure, *Italy* 40 D5
Novi Pazar, *Bulgaria* 45 C11
Novi Pazar, *Serbia & M.* 44 C4
Novi Sad, *Serbia & M.* 28 E4
Novi Slankamen, *Serbia & M.* 28 E5
Novi Travnik, *Bos.-H.* 28 F2
Novi Vinodolski, *Croatia* 41 C11
Novigrad, *Istra, Croatia* 41 C10
Novigrad, *Zadar, Croatia* 41 D12
Novigradsko More, *Croatia* 41 D12
Novo Hamburgo, *Brazil* 127 B5
Novo Mesto, *Slovenia* 41 C12
Novo Miloševo, *Serbia & M.* 28 E5
Novo Remanso, *Brazil* 125 E10
Novoaleksandrovsk, *Russia* 35 H5
Novoannenskiy, *Russia* 34 E6
Novoataysk, *Russia* 52 D9
Novoazovsk, *Ukraine* 33 J10
Novocheboksarsk, *Russia* 34 B8
Novocherkassk, *Russia* 35 G5
Novodevichye, *Russia* 34 D9
Novogrudok = Navahrudak, *Belarus* 32 F3
Novohrad-Volynskyy, *Ukraine* 33 G4
Novokachalinsk, *Russia* 54 B6
Novokazalinsk = Zhangaqazaly, *Kazakhstan* 52 E7
Novokhopersk, *Russia* 34 E5
Novokuybyshevsk, *Russia* 34 D9
Novokuznetsk, *Russia* 52 D9
Novomirgorod, *Ukraine* 33 H6
Novomoskovsk, *Russia* 32 E10
Novomoskovsk, *Ukraine* 33 H8
Novopolotsk = Navapolatsk, *Belarus* 32 E5
Novorossiysk, *Russia* 33 K9
Novorybnoye, *Russia* 53 B11
Novorzhev, *Russia* 32 D5
Novosej, *Albania* 44 E4
Novoselytsya, *Ukraine* 33 H4
Novoshakhtinsk, *Russia* 33 J10
Novosibirsk, *Russia* 52 D9
Novosibirskiye Ostrova, *Russia* 53 B15
Novosil, *Russia* 33 F9
Novosokolniki, *Russia* 32 D6
Novotitarovskaya, *Russia* 35 H4
Novotroitsk, *Russia* 52 D6
Novoukrayinka, *Ukraine* 33 H6
Novouljanovsk, *Russia* 34 C9
Novouzensk, *Russia* 34 E9
Novovolynsk, *Ukraine* 33 G3
Novovoronezhskiy, *Russia* 33 G10
Novozybkov, *Russia* 33 F6
Novska, *Croatia* 41 C14
Novvy Urengoy, *Russia* 52 C8
Nový Bor, *Czech Rep.* 26 A7
Novy Bug = Novyy Buh, *Ukraine* 33 J7
Nový Bydžov, *Czech Rep.* 26 A8
Novy Dwór Mazowiecki, *Poland* 31 F7
Nový Jičín, *Czech Rep.* 27 B11
Novyy Afon, *Georgia* 35 J5
Novyy Buh, *Ukraine* 33 J7
Novyy Oskol, *Russia* 33 G9
Novyy Port, *Russia* 52 C8
Now Shahr, *Iran* 71 B6
Nowa Deba, *Poland* 31 H8
Nowa Ruda, *Poland* 31 H3
Nowa Sarzyna, *Poland* 31 H9
Nowa Sól, *Poland* 31 G2
Nowata, *U.S.A.* 113 G7
Nowbarān, *Iran* 71 C6
Nowe, *Poland* 30 E5
Nowe Miasteczko, *Poland* 31 G2
Nowe Miasto, *Poland* 31 G7
Nowe Miasto Lubawskie, *Poland* 30 E6
Nowe Skalmierzyce, *Poland* 31 G4
Nowe Warpno, *Poland* 30 E1
Nowghāb, *Iran* 71 C8
Nowgong, *Assam, India* 67 F18
Nowgong, *Mad. P., India* 69 G8
Nowogard, *Poland* 30 E2
Nowogród, *Poland* 31 E8
Nowogród Bobrzanski, *Poland* 31 G2
Nowogrodziec, *Poland* 31 G2
Nowra, *Australia* 95 E5
Nowshera, *Pakistan* 66 C8
Nowy Dwór Gdański, *Poland* 30 D6
Nowy Sącz, *Poland* 31 J7
Nowy Staw, *Poland* 30 D6
Nowy Targ, *Poland* 31 J7
Nowy Tomyśl, *Poland* 31 F3
Nowy Wiśnicz, *Poland* 31 J7
Noxen, *U.S.A.* 117 E8
Noxon, *U.S.A.* 108 C6
Noyabr'sk, *Russia* 52 C8
Noyant, *France* 18 E7
Noyers, *France* 19 E10
Noyon, *France* 19 C9
Noyon, *Mongolia* 56 C2
Nozay, *France* 18 E5
Nqutu, *S. Africa* 89 D5
Nsanje, *Malawi* 87 F4
Nsawam, *Ghana* 83 D4
Nsomba, *Zambia* 87 E2
Nsukka, *Nigeria* 83 D6
Ntui, *Cameroon* 83 E7
Nu Jiang →, *China* 58 E2
Nu Shan, *China* 58 E2
Nuba Mts. = Nubah, Jibalan, *Sudan* 81 E3
Nubah, Jibalan, *Sudan* 81 E3
Nubia, *Africa* 76 D7
Nubian Desert = Nûbîya, Es Sahrâ en, *Sudan* 80 C3
Nûbîya, Es Sahrâ en, *Sudan* 80 C3
Nubledo, *Spain* 36 B5
Nuboai, *Indonesia* 63 E9
Nubra →, *India* 69 B7
Nucet, *Romania* 28 D7
Nueces →, *U.S.A.* 113 M6
Nueltin L., *Canada* 103 A9
Nueva Carteya, *Spain* 37 H6
Nueva Gerona, *Cuba* 120 B3
Nueva Palmira, *Uruguay* 126 C4
Nueva Rosita, *Mexico* 118 B4
Nueva San Salvador, *El Salv.* 120 D2
Nueva Tabarca, *Spain* 39 G4
Nuéve de Julio, *Argentina* 126 D3
Nuevitas, *Cuba* 120 B4
Nuevo, G., *Argentina* 128 E4
Nuevo Casas Grandes, *Mexico* 118 A3
Nuevo Guerrero, *Mexico* 119 B5
Nuevo Laredo, *Mexico* 119 B5
Nuevo León □, *Mexico* 118 C5
Nuevo Rocafuerte, *Ecuador* 124 D3
Nugget Pt., *N.Z.* 91 M2
Nugrus, Gebel, *Egypt* 80 C3
Nuhaka, *N.Z.* 91 H6
Nuits-St-Georges, *France* 19 E11
Nukey Bluff, *Australia* 95 E2
Nukhayb, *Iraq* 70 C4
Nukheila, *Sudan* 80 D2
Nuku'alofa, *Tonga* 91 E12
Nukus, *Uzbekistan* 52 E6
Nules, *Spain* 38 F4
Nullagine, *Australia* 92 D3
Nullagine →, *Australia* 92 D3
Nullarbor, *Australia* 93 F5
Nullarbor △, *Australia* 93 F2
Nullarbor Plain, *Australia* 93 F4
Numalla, L., *Australia* 95 D3
Numan, *Nigeria* 83 D7
Numata, *Japan* 55 F9
Numatinna →, *Sudan* 81 F2
Numaykoos Lake ⌓, *Canada* 103 B9
Numazu, *Japan* 55 G9
Numbulwar, *Australia* 94 A2
Numfoor, *Indonesia* 63 E8
Numurkah, *Australia* 95 F4
Nunaksaluk I., *Canada* 105 A7
Nunap Isua, *Greenland* 101 C15
Nunavut □, *Canada* 101 D8
Nunda, *U.S.A.* 116 D7
Nuneaton, *U.K.* 15 E6
Nungarin, *Australia* 93 F2
Nungo, *Mozam.* 87 E4
Nungwe, *Tanzania* 86 C3
Nunivak I., *U.S.A.* 100 B3
Nunkun, *India* 69 C7
Nùoro, *Italy* 42 B2
Nūrābād, *Iran* 71 E8
Nure →, *Italy* 40 C6
Nuremberg = Nürnberg, *Germany* 25 F7
Nuri, *Mexico* 118 B3
Nuri, *Sudan* 80 D3
Nuriootpa, *Australia* 95 E2
Nuristān □, *Afghan.* 66 B7
Nurlat, *Russia* 34 C10
Nurmes, *Finland* 8 E23
Nürnberg, *Germany* 25 F7
Nurpur, *Pakistan* 68 D4
Nurra, La, *Italy* 42 B1
Nurran, L. = Terewah, L., *Australia* 95 D4
Nurrari Lakes, *Australia* 93 E5
Nurri, *Italy* 42 C2
Nürtingen, *Germany* 25 G5
Nurzec →, *Poland* 31 F9
Nus, *Italy* 40 C4
Nusa Barung, *Indonesia* 63 H15
Nusa Dua, *Indonesia* 63 K18
Nusa Kambangan, *Indonesia* 63 G13
Nusa Tenggara Barat □, *Indonesia* 62 F5
Nusa Tenggara Timur □, *Indonesia* 63 F6
Nusaybin, *Turkey* 73 D9
Nushki, *Pakistan* 68 E2
Nuuk, *Greenland* 101 B14
Nuwakot, *Nepal* 69 E10
Nuweiba', *Egypt* 70 D2
Nuwerus, *S. Africa* 88 E2
Nuweveldberge, *S. Africa* 88 E3
Nuyts, C., *Australia* 93 F5
Nuyts, Pt., *Australia* 93 G2
Nuyts Arch., *Australia* 95 E1
Nxai Pan △, *Botswana* 88 B3
Nxau-Nxau, *Botswana* 88 B3
Nyaake, *Liberia* 82 E3
Nyabing, *Australia* 93 F2
Nyack, *U.S.A.* 117 E11
Nyagan, *Russia* 52 C7
Nyahanga, *Tanzania* 86 C3
Nyahua, *Tanzania* 86 D3
Nyahururu, *Kenya* 86 B4
Nyainqentanglha Shan, *China* 60 C4
Nyakanazi, *Tanzania* 86 C3
Nyakrom, *Ghana* 83 D4
Nyâlâ, *Sudan* 81 E1
Nyamandhlovu, *Zimbabwe* 87 F2
Nyambiti, *Tanzania* 86 C3
Nyamlell, *Sudan* 81 F2
Nyamwaga, *Tanzania* 86 C3
Nyandekwa, *Tanzania* 86 C3
Nyanding →, *Sudan* 81 F3
Nyandoma, *Russia* 32 B11
Nyanga △, *Zimbabwe* 87 F3
Nyangana, *Namibia* 88 B3
Nyanguge, *Tanzania* 86 C3
Nyankpala, *Ghana* 83 D4
Nyanza, *Rwanda* 86 C2
Nyanza □, *Kenya* 86 C3
Nyanza-Lac, *Burundi* 86 C2
Nyaponges, *Sudan* 81 F3
Nyasa, L., *Africa* 87 E3
Nyasvizh, *Belarus* 33 F4
Nyazura, *Zimbabwe* 87 F3
Nyazwidzi →, *Zimbabwe* 87 G3
Nyborg, *Denmark* 11 J4
Nybro, *Sweden* 11 H9
Nyda, *Russia* 52 C8
Nyeri, *Kenya* 86 C4
Nyerol, *Sudan* 81 F3
Nyhammar, *Sweden* 10 D8
Nyika △, *Malawi* 87 E3
Nyinahin, *Ghana* 82 D4
Nyíradony, *Hungary* 28 C6
Nyírbátor, *Hungary* 28 C7
Nyíregyháza, *Hungary* 28 C6
Nykøbing, *Storstrøm, Denmark* 11 K5
Nykøbing, *Vestsjælland, Denmark* 11 J5
Nykøbing, *Viborg, Denmark* 11 H2
Nyköping, *Sweden* 11 F11
Nykroppa, *Sweden* 10 E8
Nykvarn, *Sweden* 10 E11
Nyland, *Sweden* 10 A11
Nylstroom = Modimolle, *S. Africa* 89 C4
Nymagee, *Australia* 95 E4
Nymboida △, *Australia* 95 D5
Nymburk, *Czech Rep.* 26 A8
Nynäshamn, *Sweden* 11 F11
Nyngan, *Australia* 95 E4
Nyoma Rap, *India* 69 C8
Nyoman = Nemunas →, *Lithuania* 9 J19
Nyon, *Switz.* 25 J2
Nyong →, *Cameroon* 83 E6
Nyons, *France* 21 D9
Nyou, *Burkina Faso* 83 C4
Nýrsko, *Czech Rep.* 26 B6
Nysa, *Poland* 31 H4
Nysa →, *Europe* 24 C10
Nysa Kłodzka →, *Poland* 31 H4
Nysäter, *Sweden* 10 E6
Nyssa, *U.S.A.* 108 E5
Nysted, *Denmark* 11 K5
Nyunzu, *Dem. Rep. of the Congo* 86 D2
Nyurba, *Russia* 53 C12
Nyzhnohirskyy, *Ukraine* 33 K8
Nzébéla, *Guinea* 82 D3
Nzega, *Tanzania* 86 C3
Nzérékoré, *Guinea* 82 D3
Nzeto, *Angola* 84 F2
Nzilo, Chutes de, *Dem. Rep. of the Congo* 87 E2
N'Zo ⌓, *Ivory C.* 82 D3
Nzo →, *Ivory C.* 82 D3
Nzubuka, *Tanzania* 86 C3

O

O Barco, *Spain* 36 C4
O Carballiño, *Spain* 36 C2
O Corgo, *Spain* 36 C3
O Pino, *Spain* 36 C2
O Porriño, *Spain* 36 C2
Ō-Shima, *Japan* 55 G9
Oa, Mull of, *U.K.* 13 F2
Oacoma, *U.S.A.* 112 D5
Oahe, L., *U.S.A.* 112 C4
Oahe Dam, *U.S.A.* 112 C4
Oahu, *U.S.A.* 106 H16
Oak Harbor, *U.S.A.* 110 B4
Oak Hill, *U.S.A.* 114 G5
Oak Ridge, *U.S.A.* 115 G3
Oak View, *U.S.A.* 111 L7
Oakan-Dake, *Japan* 54 C12
Oakdale, *Calif., U.S.A.* 110 H6
Oakdale, *La., U.S.A.* 113 K8
Oakes, *U.S.A.* 112 B5
Oakesdale, *U.S.A.* 108 C5
Oakey, *Australia* 95 D5
Oakfield, *U.S.A.* 116 C6
Oakham, *U.K.* 15 E7
Oakhurst, *U.S.A.* 110 H7
Oakland, *U.S.A.* 110 H4
Oakley, *Idaho, U.S.A.* 108 E7
Oakley, *Kans., U.S.A.* 112 F4
Oakover →, *Australia* 92 D3
Oakridge, *U.S.A.* 108 E2

Oakville, *Canada* 116 C5
Oakville, *U.S.A.* 110 D3
Oamaru, *N.Z.* 91 L3
Oancea, *Romania* 29 E12
Oasi Faunistica di Vendicari ⌓, *Italy* 43 F8
Oasis, *Calif., U.S.A.* 111 M10
Oasis, *Nev., U.S.A.* 110 H9
Oates Land, *Antarctica* 5 C11
Oatlands, *Australia* 95 G4
Oatman, *U.S.A.* 111 K12
Oaxaca, *Mexico* 119 D5
Oaxaca □, *Mexico* 119 D5
Ob →, *Russia* 52 C7
Oba, *Canada* 104 C3
Obala, *Cameroon* 83 E7
Obama, *Japan* 55 G7
Oban, *Nigeria* 83 D6
Oban, *U.K.* 13 E3
Obbia, *Somali Rep.* 75 F4
Obera, *Argentina* 127 B4
Oberammergau, *Germany* 25 H7
Oberasbach, *Germany* 25 F6
Oberbayern □, *Germany* 25 G7
Oberdrauburg, *Austria* 26 E5
Obere Donau ⌓, *Germany* 25 G5
Oberer Bayerischer Wald ⌓, *Germany* 25 F8
Oberfranken □, *Germany* 25 E7
Oberhausen, *Germany* 24 D2
Oberkirch, *Germany* 25 G4
Oberlausitz, *Germany* 24 D10
Oberlin, *Kans., U.S.A.* 112 F4
Oberlin, *La., U.S.A.* 113 K8
Oberlin, *Ohio, U.S.A.* 116 E2
Obernai, *France* 19 D14
Oberndorf, *Germany* 25 G4
Oberon, *Australia* 95 E4
Oberösterreich □, *Austria* 26 C7
Oberpfalz □, *Germany* 25 F8
Oberpfälzer Wald, *Germany* 25 F8
Oberpfälzer Wald ⌓, *Germany* 25 F8
Oberstdorf, *Germany* 25 H6
Oberursel, *Germany* 25 E4
Oberwart, *Austria* 27 D9
Obi, *Indonesia* 63 E7
Obiaruku, *Nigeria* 83 D6
Óbidos, *Brazil* 125 D7
Óbidos, *Portugal* 37 F1
Obihiro, *Japan* 54 C11
Obilatu, *Indonesia* 63 E7
Obilnoye, *Russia* 35 G7
Obing, *Germany* 25 G8
Objat, *France* 20 C5
Obluchye, *Russia* 53 E14
Obninsk, *Russia* 32 E9
Obo, *C.A.R.* 86 A2
Oboa, Mt., *Uganda* 86 B3
Obock, *Djibouti* 81 E5
Oborniki, *Poland* 31 F3
Oborniki Śląskie, *Poland* 31 G3
Oboyan, *Russia* 33 G9
Obozerskaya = Obozerskiy, *Russia* 52 C5
Obozerskiy, *Russia* 52 C5
Obrenovac, *Serbia & M.* 44 B4
Obrovac, *Croatia* 41 D12
Obruk, *Turkey* 72 C5
Obrzycko, *Poland* 31 F3
Observatory Inlet, *Canada* 102 B3
Obshchi Syrt, *Russia* 6 E16
Obskaya Guba, *Russia* 52 C8
Obuasi, *Ghana* 83 D4
Obubra, *Nigeria* 83 D6
Obudu, *Nigeria* 83 D6
Obwalden □, *Switz.* 25 J4
Obzor, *Bulgaria* 45 D11
Ocala, *U.S.A.* 115 L4
Ocampo, *Chihuahua, Mexico* 118 B3
Ocampo, *Tamaulipas, Mexico* 119 C5
Ocaña, *Spain* 36 F7
Ocanomowoc, *U.S.A.* 112 D10
Occidental, Cordillera, *Colombia* 124 C3
Occidental, Grand Erg, *Algeria* 78 B6
Ocean City, *Md., U.S.A.* 114 F8
Ocean City, *N.J., U.S.A.* 114 F8
Ocean City, *Wash., U.S.A.* 110 C2
Ocean Falls, *Canada* 102 C3
Ocean I. = Banaba, *Kiribati* 96 H8
Ocean Park, *U.S.A.* 110 D2
Oceano, *U.S.A.* 111 K6
Oceanport, *U.S.A.* 117 F10
Oceanside, *U.S.A.* 111 M9
Ochagavía, *Spain* 38 C3
Ochakiv, *Ukraine* 33 J6
Ochamchira, *Georgia* 35 J5
Ochil Hills, *U.K.* 13 E5
Ocho Rios, *Jamaica* 120 a
Ochsenfurt, *Germany* 25 F6
Ochsenhausen, *Germany* 25 G5
Ocilla, *U.S.A.* 115 K4
Ockelbo, *Sweden* 10 D10
Ocmulgee →, *U.S.A.* 115 K4
Ocna Mureş, *Romania* 29 D8
Ocna Sibiului, *Romania* 29 E9
Ocnele Mari, *Romania* 29 E9
Ocniţa, *Moldova* 29 B12
Oconee →, *U.S.A.* 115 K4
Oconto, *U.S.A.* 114 C2
Oconto Falls, *U.S.A.* 114 C1
Ocosingo, *Mexico* 119 D6
Ocotal, *Nic.* 120 D2
Ocotlán, *Mexico* 118 C4
Ocotlán de Morelos, *Mexico* 119 D5
Ocreza →, *Portugal* 37 F3
Öcsa, *Hungary* 28 C4
Octeville, *France* 18 C5
Oda, *Ghana* 83 D4
Ōda, *Japan* 55 G6
Oda, J., *Sudan* 80 C4
Ódáðahraun, *Iceland* 8 D5
Ödåkra, *Sweden* 11 H6
Odate, *Japan* 54 D10
Odawara, *Japan* 55 G9
Odda, *Norway* 9 F12
Odder, *Denmark* 11 J4
Odei →, *Canada* 103 B9
Odemira, *Portugal* 37 H2
Ödemiş, *Turkey* 47 C9
Odendaalsrus, *S. Africa* 88 D4
Odensbacken, *Sweden* 10 E9
Odense, *Denmark* 11 J4
Odenwald = Neckartal-Odenwald ⌓, *Germany* 25 F5
Odenwald, *Germany* 25 F5
Oder →, *Europe* 24 B10
Oder-Havel Kanal, *Germany* 24 C10
Oderzo, *Italy* 41 C9
Odesa, *Ukraine* 33 J6
Ödeshög, *Sweden* 11 F8
Odessa = Odesa, *Ukraine* 33 J6
Odessa, *Canada* 117 B8
Odessa, *Tex., U.S.A.* 113 K3
Odessa, *Wash., U.S.A.* 108 C4
Odiakwe, *Botswana* 88 C4
Odiel →, *Spain* 37 H4
Odienné, *Ivory C.* 82 D3
Odintsovo, *Russia* 32 E9
Odiongan, *Phil.* 61 E4
Odobeşti, *Romania* 29 E12
Odolanów, *Poland* 31 G4
O'Donnell, *U.S.A.* 113 J4
Odorheiu Secuiesc, *Romania* 29 D10
Odoyevo, *Russia* 32 F9
Odra = Oder →, *Europe* 24 B10
Odra →, *Spain* 36 C6
Odžaci, *Serbia & M.* 28 E4
Odžak, *Bos.-H.* 28 E3
Odzi, *Zimbabwe* 89 B5
Odzi →, *Zimbabwe* 89 B5
Oebisfelde, *Germany* 24 C6
Oeiras, *Brazil* 125 E10
Oeiras, *Portugal* 37 G1
Oelrichs, *U.S.A.* 112 D3
Oelsnitz, *Germany* 25 E8
Oelwein, *U.S.A.* 112 D9
Oenpelli, *Australia* 92 B5
Oetz, *Austria* 26 D3
Of, *Turkey* 73 B9
Ofanto →, *Italy* 43 A9
Offa, *Nigeria* 83 D5
Offaly □, *Ireland* 12 C4
Offenbach, *Germany* 25 E4
Offenburg, *Germany* 25 G3
Offida, *Italy* 41 F10
Ofidhousa, *Greece* 47 E8
Ofotfjorden, *Norway* 8 B17
Ōfunato, *Japan* 54 E10
Oga, *Japan* 54 E9
Oga-Hantō, *Japan* 54 E9
Ogaden, *Ethiopia* 75 F3
Ōgaki, *Japan* 55 G8
Ogallala, *U.S.A.* 112 E4
Ogasawara Gunto, *Pac. Oc.* 96 E6
Ogbomosho, *Nigeria* 83 D5
Ogden, *U.S.A.* 108 F7
Ogdensburg, *U.S.A.* 117 B9
Ogeechee →, *U.S.A.* 115 K5
Ogilby, *U.S.A.* 111 N12
Oglio →, *Italy* 40 C7
Oglio Nord ⌓, *Italy* 40 C7
Oglio Sud ⌓, *Italy* 40 C7
Ogmore, *Australia* 94 C4
Ognon →, *France* 19 E12
Ogoja, *Nigeria* 83 D6
Ogoki, *Canada* 104 B2
Ogoki →, *Canada* 104 B2
Ogoki L., *Canada* 104 B2
Ogoki Res., *Canada* 104 B2
Ogooué →, *Gabon* 84 E1
Ogosta →, *Bulgaria* 44 C7
Ogowe = Ogooué →, *Gabon* 84 E1
Ogr = Sharafa, *Sudan* 81 E2
Ograżden, *Macedonia* 44 E6
Ogre, *Latvia* 9 H21
Ogrein, *Sudan* 80 D3
Ogulin, *Croatia* 41 C12
Ogun □, *Nigeria* 83 D5
Ogurchinskiy, Ostrov, *Turkmenistan* 71 B7
Oguta, *Nigeria* 83 D6
Ogwashi-Uku, *Nigeria* 83 D6
Ogwe, *Nigeria* 83 E6
Ohai, *N.Z.* 91 L2
Ohakune, *N.Z.* 91 H5
Ohata, *Japan* 54 D10
Ohau, L., *N.Z.* 91 L2
Ohio □, *U.S.A.* 116 F2
Ohio →, *U.S.A.* 114 G1
Ohře →, *Czech Rep.* 26 A7
Ohre →, *Germany* 24 C7
Ohrid, *Macedonia* 44 E4
Ohridsko Jezero, *Macedonia* 44 E4
Ohrigstad, *S. Africa* 89 C5
Öhringen, *Germany* 25 F5
Oi Qu, *China* 58 C2
Oiapoque, *Brazil* 125 C8
Oikou, *China* 57 E9
Oil City, *U.S.A.* 116 E5
Oil Springs, *Canada* 116 D2
Oildale, *U.S.A.* 111 K7
Oinousa, *Greece* 47 C8
Oise □, *France* 19 C9
Oise →, *France* 19 C9
Oiseaux du Djoudj △, *Senegal* 82 B1
Oistins, *Barbados* 121 g
Oistins B., *Barbados* 121 g
Ōita, *Japan* 55 H5
Ōita □, *Japan* 55 H5
Oiticica, *Brazil* 125 E10
Ojacaliente, *Mexico* 118 C4
Ojai, *U.S.A.* 111 L7
Ojcowski △, *Poland* 31 H6
Ojinaga, *Mexico* 118 B4
Ojiya, *Japan* 55 F9
Ojo de Liebre ⌓, *Mexico* 118 B2
Ojos del Salado, Cerro, *Argentina* 126 B2
Oka →, *Russia* 34 B7
Okaba, *Indonesia* 63 F9
Okahandja, *Namibia* 88 C2
Okanagan L., *Canada* 102 D5
Okanogan, *U.S.A.* 108 B4
Okanogan →, *U.S.A.* 108 B4
Okány, *Hungary* 28 D6
Okapi △, *Dem. Rep. of the Congo* 86 B2
Okaputa, *Namibia* 88 C2
Okara, *Pakistan* 68 D5
Okaukuejo, *Namibia* 88 B2
Okavango Delta, *Botswana* 88 B3
Okavango Swamp = Okavango Delta, *Botswana* 88 B3
Okaya, *Japan* 55 F9
Okayama, *Japan* 55 G6
Okayama □, *Japan* 55 G6
Okazaki, *Japan* 55 G8
Oke-Iho, *Nigeria* 83 D5
Okęcie, Warsaw ✕ (WAW), *Poland* 31 F7
Okeechobee, *U.S.A.* 115 M5
Okeechobee, L., *U.S.A.* 115 M5
Okefenokee ⌓, *U.S.A.* 115 K4
Okefenokee Swamp, *U.S.A.* 115 K4
Okehampton, *U.K.* 15 G4
Okene, *Nigeria* 83 D6
Oker →, *Germany* 24 C6
Okha, *India* 68 H3
Okha, *Russia* 53 D15
Ókhi Óros, *Greece* 46 C6
Okhotsk, *Russia* 53 D15
Okhotsk, Sea of, *Asia* 53 D15
Okhotskiy Perevoz, *Russia* 53 C14
Okhtyrka, *Ukraine* 33 G8
Oki-Shotō, *Japan* 55 F6
Okiep, *S. Africa* 88 D2
Okigwi, *Nigeria* 83 D6
Okija, *Nigeria* 83 D6
Okinawa □, *Japan* 55 L4
Okinawa-Guntō, *Japan* 55 L4
Okinawa-Jima, *Japan* 55 L4
Okino-erabu-Shima, *Japan* 55 L4
Okitipupa, *Nigeria* 83 D5
Oklahoma □, *U.S.A.* 113 H6
Oklahoma City, *U.S.A.* 113 H6
Okmulgee, *U.S.A.* 113 H7
Oknitsa = Ocniţa, *Moldova* 29 B12
Oko, W. →, *Sudan* 80 C4
Okolo, *Uganda* 86 B3
Okolona, *U.S.A.* 113 J10
Okombahe, *Namibia* 88 C2
Okonek, *Poland* 30 E3
Okotoks, *Canada* 102 C6
Okrika, *Nigeria* 83 E6
Oksibil, *Indonesia* 63 E10
Oktabrsk = Oktyabrsk, *Kazakhstan* 52 E6
Oktyabrsk, *Kazakhstan* 52 E6
Oktyabrsk, *Russia* 34 D9
Oktyabrskiy = Aktsyabrski, *Belarus* 33 F5
Oktyabrskiy, *Russia* 35 G5
Oktyabrskoy Revolyutsii, Ostrov, *Russia* 53 B10
Oktyabrskoye = Zhovtneve, *Ukraine* 33 J7
Okulovka, *Russia* 32 C7
Okuru, *N.Z.* 91 K2
Okushiri-Tō, *Japan* 54 C9
Okuta, *Nigeria* 83 D5
Okwa →, *Botswana* 88 C3
Ola, *U.S.A.* 113 H8
Ólafsfjörður, *Iceland* 8 C4
Ólafsvík, *Iceland* 8 D2
Olaine, *Latvia* 30 B10
Olancha, *U.S.A.* 111 J8
Olancha Pk., *U.S.A.* 111 J8
Olanchito, *Honduras* 120 C2
Öland, *Sweden* 11 H10
Ölands norra udde, *Sweden* 11 G11
Ölands södra udde, *Sweden* 11 H10
Olargues, *France* 20 E6
Olary, *Australia* 95 E3
Olascoaga, *Argentina* 126 D3
Olathe, *U.S.A.* 112 F7
Olavarría, *Argentina* 126 D3
Oława, *Poland* 31 H4
Olbernhau, *Germany* 24 E9
Ólbia, *Italy* 42 B2
Ólbia, G. di, *Italy* 42 B2
Olching, *Germany* 25 G7
Olcott, *U.S.A.* 116 C6
Old Bahama Chan. = Bahama, Canal Viejo de, *W. Indies* 120 B4
Old Baldy Pk. = San Antonio, Mt., *U.S.A.* 111 L9
Old Castile = Castilla y Leon □, *Spain* 36 D6
Old Crow, *Canada* 100 B6
Old Dale, *U.S.A.* 111 L11
Old Forge, *N.Y., U.S.A.* 117 C10
Old Forge, *Pa., U.S.A.* 117 E9
Old Perlican, *Canada* 105 C9
Old Shinyanga, *Tanzania* 86 C3
Old Speck Mt., *U.S.A.* 117 B14
Old Town, *U.S.A.* 115 C11
Old Washington, *U.S.A.* 116 F3
Old Wives L., *Canada* 103 C7
Oldbury, *U.K.* 15 F5
Oldcastle, *Ireland* 12 C4
Oldeani, *Tanzania* 86 C4
Oldenburg, *Niedersachsen, Germany* 24 B4
Oldenburg, *Schleswig-Holstein, Germany* 24 A6
Oldenzaal, *Neths.* 17 B6
Oldham, *U.K.* 14 D5
Oldman →, *Canada* 102 D6
Oldmeldrum, *U.K.* 13 D6
Olds, *Canada* 102 C6
Olduvai Gorge, *Tanzania* 86 C4
Oldziyt, *Mongolia* 56 B5
Olean, *U.S.A.* 116 D6
Olecko, *Poland* 30 D9
Oléggio, *Italy* 40 C5
Oleiros, *Portugal* 36 F3
Oleiros, *Spain* 36 B2
Olekma →, *Russia* 53 C13
Olekminsk, *Russia* 53 C13
Oleksandriya, *Kirovohrad, Ukraine* 33 H7
Oleksandriya, *Rivne, Ukraine* 33 G4
Oleksandrovka, *Ukraine* 33 H7
Olema, *U.S.A.* 110 G4
Olenek, *Russia* 53 C12
Olenek →, *Russia* 53 B13
Olenino, *Russia* 32 D7
Oléron, Î. d', *France* 20 C2
Oleśnica, *Poland* 31 G4
Olesno, *Poland* 31 H5
Olevsk, *Ukraine* 33 G4
Olga, *Russia* 53 E14
Olga, L., *Canada* 104 C4
Olga, Mt., *Australia* 93 E5
Ølgod, *Denmark* 11 J2
Olhão, *Portugal* 37 H3
Olib, *Croatia* 41 D11
Oliena, *Italy* 42 B2
Oliete, *Spain* 38 D4
Olifants = Elefantes →, *Africa* 89 C5
Olifants →, *Namibia* 88 C2
Olifantshoek, *S. Africa* 88 D3
Ólimbos, *Greece* 47 F9
Ólimbos, Óros, *Greece* 44 F6
Olímpia, *Brazil* 127 A6
Olimpos-Beydaglari △, *Turkey* 47 E12
Olinda, *Brazil* 125 E12
Olite, *Spain* 38 C3
Oliva, *Argentina* 126 C3
Oliva, *Spain* 39 G4
Oliva, Punta del, *Spain* 36 B5
Oliva de la Frontera, *Spain* 37 G4
Olivares, *Spain* 38 F2
Olivehurst, *U.S.A.* 110 F5
Oliveira de Azeméis, *Portugal* 36 E2
Oliveira do Douro, *Portugal* 36 D2
Olivenza, *Spain* 37 G3
Oliver, *Canada* 102 D5
Oliver L., *Canada* 103 B8
Olivet, *France* 19 E8
Olkhovka, *Russia* 34 F7
Olkusz, *Poland* 31 H6
Ollagüe, *Chile* 126 A2
Olmedo, *Spain* 36 D6
Olmeto, *France* 21 G12
Olney, *Ill., U.S.A.* 114 F1
Olney, *Tex., U.S.A.* 113 J5
Olofström, *Sweden* 11 H8
Oloma, *Cameroon* 83 E7
Olomane →, *Canada* 105 B7
Olomouc, *Czech Rep.* 27 B10
Olomoucký □, *Czech Rep.* 27 B10
Olonets, *Russia* 32 B7
Olongapo, *Phil.* 61 D4
Olonne-sur-Mer, *France* 20 B2
Oloron, Gave d' →, *France* 20 E2
Oloron-Ste-Marie, *France* 20 E3
Olot, *Spain* 38 C7
Olovo, *Bos.-H.* 28 F3
Olovyannaya, *Russia* 53 D12
Oloy →, *Russia* 53 C16
Olsberg, *Germany* 24 D4
Olshammar, *Sweden* 11 F8
Olshanka, *Ukraine* 33 H6
Olshany, *Ukraine* 33 G8
Olsztyn, *Poland* 30 E7
Olsztynek, *Poland* 30 E7
Olt □, *Romania* 29 F9
Olt →, *Romania* 29 G9
Olten, *Switz.* 25 H3
Olteniţa, *Romania* 29 F11
Olton, *U.S.A.* 113 H3
Oltu, *Turkey* 73 B9
Oluanpi, *Taiwan* 59 G13
Olula del Rio, *Spain* 39 H2
Olur, *Turkey* 73 B10
Olutanga, *Phil.* 61 H5
Olvega, *Spain* 38 D2
Olvera, *Spain* 37 J5
Olymbos, *Cyprus* 49 D12
Olympia, *Greece* 46 D3
Olympia, *U.S.A.* 110 D4
Olympic △, *U.S.A.* 110 C3
Olympic Dam, *Australia* 95 E2
Olympic Mts., *U.S.A.* 110 C3
Olympus, *Cyprus* 49 E11
Olympus, Mt. = Ólimbos, Óros, *Greece* 44 F6
Olympus, Mt. = Uludağ, *Turkey* 45 F13
Olympus, Mt., *U.S.A.* 110 C3
Olyphant, *U.S.A.* 117 E9
Om →, *Russia* 52 D8
Om Hajer, *Eritrea* 81 E4
Om Koi, *Thailand* 64 D2
Ōma, *Japan* 54 D10
Ōmachi, *Japan* 55 F8
Omae-Zaki, *Japan* 55 G9
Ōmagari, *Japan* 54 E10
Omagh, *U.K.* 12 B4
Omagh □, *U.K.* 12 B4
Omaha, *U.S.A.* 112 E7
Omak, *U.S.A.* 108 B4
Omalos, *Greece* 49 D5
Oman ■, *Asia* 75 C6
Oman, G. of, *Asia* 71 E8
Omaruru, *Namibia* 88 C2
Omaruru →, *Namibia* 88 C1
Omate, *Peru* 124 G4
Ombai, Selat, *Indonesia* 63 F6
Omboué, *Gabon* 84 E1
Ombrone →, *Italy* 40 F8
Omdurmân, *Sudan* 81 D3
Omegna, *Italy* 40 C5
Omemee, *Canada* 116 B6
Omeonga, *Dem. Rep. of the Congo* 86 C1
Ometepe, I. de, *Nic.* 120 D2
Ometepec, *Mexico* 119 D5
Ominato, *Japan* 54 D10
Omineca →, *Canada* 102 B4
Omiš, *Croatia* 41 E13
Omišalj, *Croatia* 41 C11
Omitara, *Namibia* 88 C2
Ōmiya, *Japan* 55 G9
Omme Å →, *Denmark* 11 J2
Ommen, *Neths.* 17 B6
Ömnögovĭ □, *Mongolia* 56 C3
Omo △, *Ethiopia* 81 F4
Omo →, *Ethiopia* 81 F4
Omo Valley, *Ethiopia* 81 F4
Omodeo, L., *Italy* 42 B1
Omodhos, *Cyprus* 49 E11
Omoko, *Nigeria* 83 D6
Omolon →, *Russia* 53 C16
Omono-Gawa →, *Japan* 54 E10
Omsk, *Russia* 52 D8
Omsukchan, *Russia* 53 C16
Ōmu, *Japan* 54 B11
Omul, Vf., *Romania* 29 E10
Omulew →, *Poland* 31 E8
Ōmura, *Japan* 55 H4
Omuramba Omatako →, *Namibia* 88 B2
Omuramba Ovambo →, *Namibia* 88 B2
Omurtag, *Bulgaria* 45 C10
Ōmuta, *Japan* 55 H5
Oña, *Spain* 36 C7
Onaga, *U.S.A.* 112 F6
Onalaska, *U.S.A.* 112 D9
Onancock, *U.S.A.* 114 G8
Onang, *Indonesia* 63 E5
Onaping L., *Canada* 104 C3
Oñati, *Spain* 38 B2
Onavas, *Mexico* 118 B3
Onawa, *U.S.A.* 112 D6
Oncócua, *Angola* 88 B1
Onda, *Spain* 38 F4
Ondaejin, *N. Korea* 57 D15
Ondangwa, *Namibia* 88 B2
Ondarroa, *Spain* 38 B2
Ondava →, *Slovak Rep.* 27 C14
Ondjiva, *Angola* 88 B2
Ondo, *Nigeria* 83 D5
Ondo □, *Nigeria* 83 D6
Öndörshil, *Mongolia* 56 B5
Öndverðarnes, *Iceland* 8 D1
One Tree, *Australia* 95 E3
Onega, *Russia* 52 C4
Onega →, *Russia* 6 C13
Onega, L. = Onezhskoye Ozero, *Russia* 32 B8
Oneida, *U.S.A.* 117 C9
Oneida L., *U.S.A.* 117 C9
O'Neill, *U.S.A.* 112 D5
Onekotan, Ostrov, *Russia* 53 E16
Onema, *Dem. Rep. of the Congo* 86 C1
Oneonta, *U.S.A.* 117 D9
Oneşti, *Romania* 29 D11
Onezhskoye Ozero, *Russia* 32 B8
Ongarue, *N.Z.* 91 H5
Ongers →, *S. Africa* 88 E3
Ongerup, *Australia* 93 F2
Ongjin, *N. Korea* 57 F13
Ongkharak, *Thailand* 64 E3
Ongniud Qi, *China* 57 C10
Ongoka, *Dem. Rep. of the Congo* 86 C2
Ongole, *India* 66 M12
Ongon = Havirga, *Mongolia* 56 B7
Oni, *Georgia* 35 J6
Onida, *U.S.A.* 112 C4
Onilahy →, *Madag.* 89 C7
Onitsha, *Nigeria* 83 D6
Onoda, *Japan* 55 G5
Onpyŏng-ni, *S. Korea* 57 H14
Ons, I. de, *Spain* 36 C2
Onslow, *Australia* 92 D2
Onslow B., *U.S.A.* 115 H7
Ontake-San, *Japan* 55 G8
Ontario, *Calif., U.S.A.* 111 L9
Ontario, *Oreg., U.S.A.* 108 D5
Ontario □, *Canada* 104 B2
Ontario, L., *N. Amer.* 116 C7
Ontinyent, *Spain* 39 G4
Ontonagon, *U.S.A.* 112 B10
Ontur, *Spain* 39 G3
Onyx, *U.S.A.* 111 K8
Oodnadatta, *Australia* 95 D2
Ooldea, *Australia* 93 F5
Oombulgurri, *Australia* 92 C4
Oorindi, *Australia* 94 C3
Oost-Vlaanderen □, *Belgium* 17 C3
Oostende, *Belgium* 17 C2
Oosterhout, *Neths.* 17 C4
Oosterschelde →, *Neths.* 17 C4
Oosterwolde, *Neths.* 17 B6
Ootacamund = Udagamandalam, *India* 66 P10
Ootsa L., *Canada* 102 C3
Op Luang △, *Thailand* 64 C2
Opaka, *Bulgaria* 45 C10
Opala, *Dem. Rep. of the Congo* 86 C1
Opalenica, *Poland* 31 F3
Opan, *Bulgaria* 45 D9
Opanake, *Sri Lanka* 66 R12
Opasatika, *Canada* 104 C3
Opasquia ⌓, *Canada* 104 B1
Opatija, *Croatia* 41 C11
Opatów, *Poland* 31 H8
Opava, *Czech Rep.* 27 B10
Opelika, *U.S.A.* 115 J3
Opelousas, *U.S.A.* 113 K8
Opémisca, L., *Canada* 104 C5

Opheim, *U.S.A.* 108 B10
Ophthalmia Ra., *Australia* 92 D2
Opi, *Nigeria* 83 D6
Opinaca →, *Canada* 104 B4
Opinaca, Rés., *Canada* 104 B4
Opinnagau →, *Canada* 104 B3
Opiscotéo, L., *Canada* 105 B6
Opobo, *Nigeria* 83 E6
Opochka, *Russia* 32 D5
Opoczno, *Poland* 31 G7
Opol, *Phil.* 61 G6
Opole, *Poland* 31 H4
Opole Lubelskie, *Poland* 31 G8
Opolskie □, *Poland* 31 H5
Ononono L., *Namibia* 88 B2
Oporto = Porto, *Portugal* 36 D2
Opotiki, *N.Z.* 91 H6
Opp, *U.S.A.* 115 K2
Oppdal, *Norway* 9 E13
Oppido Mamertina, *Italy* 43 D8
Opportunity, *U.S.A.* 108 C5
Oprişor, *Romania* 28 F8
Oprtalj, *Croatia* 41 C10
Opua, *N.Z.* 91 F5
Opunake, *N.Z.* 91 H4
Opuwo, *Namibia* 88 B1
Opuzen, *Croatia* 41 E14
Ora, *Cyprus* 49 E12
Oracle, *U.S.A.* 109 K8
Oradea, *Romania* 28 C6
Öræfajökull, *Iceland* 8 D5
Orahovac, *Serbia & M.* 44 D4
Orahovica, *Croatia* 28 E2
Orai, *India* 69 G8
Oraison, *France* 21 E9
Oral = Zhayyq →, *Kazakhstan* 52 E6
Oral, *Kazakhstan* 34 E10
Oran, *Algeria* 78 A5
Orange, *Australia* 95 E4
Orange, *France* 21 D8
Orange, *Calif., U.S.A.* 111 M9
Orange, *Mass., U.S.A.* 117 D12
Orange, *Tex., U.S.A.* 113 K8
Orange, *Va., U.S.A.* 114 F6
Orange →, *S. Africa* 88 D2
Orange, C., *Brazil* 125 C8
Orange Cove, *U.S.A.* 110 J7
Orange Free State = Free State □, *S. Africa* 88 D4
Orange Grove, *U.S.A.* 113 M6
Orange Walk, *Belize* 119 D7
Orangeburg, *U.S.A.* 115 J5
Orangeville, *Canada* 116 C4
Orango, *Guinea-Biss.* 82 C1
Orani, *Phil.* 61 D4
Oranienburg, *Germany* 24 C9
Oranje = Orange →, *S. Africa* 88 D2
Oranje Vrystaat = Free State □, *S. Africa* 88 D4
Oranjemund, *Namibia* 88 D2
Oranjerivier, *S. Africa* 88 D3
Oranjestad, *Aruba* 121 D5
Orapa, *Botswana* 85 J5
Orarak, *Sudan* 81 F3
Oras, *Phil.* 61 E6
Orašje, *Bos.-H.* 28 E3
Orăştie, *Romania* 29 E8
Oraşul Stalin = Braşov, *Romania* 29 E10
Orava →, *Slovak Rep.* 27 B12
Orava, Vodna nádrž, *Slovak Rep.* 27 B12
Oraviţa, *Romania* 28 E6
Orb →, *France* 20 E7
Orba →, *Italy* 40 D5
Ørbæk, *Denmark* 11 J4
Orbe, *Switz.* 25 J2
Orbec, *France* 18 C7
Orbetello, *Italy* 41 F8
Órbigo →, *Spain* 36 C5
Orbisonia, *U.S.A.* 116 F7
Orbost, *Australia* 95 F4
Örbyhus, *Sweden* 10 D11
Orcadas, *Antarctica* 5 C18
Orcas I., *U.S.A.* 110 B4
Orce, *Spain* 39 H2
Orce →, *Spain* 39 H2
Orchard City, *U.S.A.* 109 G10
Orchies, *France* 19 B10
Orchila, I., *Venezuela* 121 D6
Orchilla, Pta., *Canary Is.* 48 G1
Órcia →, *Italy* 41 F8
Orco →, *Italy* 40 C4
Orcutt, *U.S.A.* 111 L6
Ord, *U.S.A.* 112 E5
Ord →, *Australia* 92 C4
Ord, Mt., *Australia* 92 C4
Ordenes = Ordes, *Spain* 36 B2
Orderville, *U.S.A.* 109 H7
Ordes, *Spain* 36 B2
Ordesa y Monte Perido △, *Spain* 38 C4
Ording = St-Peter-Ording, *Germany* 24 A4
Ordos = Mu Us Shamo, *China* 56 E5
Ordu, *Turkey* 72 B7
Ordubad, *Azerbaijan* 73 C12
Orduña, *Álava, Spain* 38 C2
Orduña, *Granada, Spain* 37 H7
Ordway, *U.S.A.* 112 F3
Ordzhonikidze = Vladikavkaz, *Russia* 35 J7
Ordzhonikidze, *Ukraine* 33 J8
Ore, *Dem. Rep. of the Congo* 86 B2
Ore Mts. = Erzgebirge, *Germany* 24 E8
Orebić, *Croatia* 41 F14
Örebro, *Sweden* 10 E9
Örebro län □, *Sweden* 10 E8
Orecchiella ⌂, *Italy* 40 D7
Oregon, *U.S.A.* 112 D10
Oregon □, *U.S.A.* 108 E3
Oregon City, *U.S.A.* 110 E4
Oregon Dunes ⌂, *U.S.A.* 108 E1
Öregrund, *Sweden* 10 D12
Öregrundsgrepen, *Sweden* 10 D12
Orekhov = Orikhiv, *Ukraine* 33 J8
Orekhovo-Zuyevo, *Russia* 32 E10
Orel, *Russia* 33 F9
Orel →, *Ukraine* 33 H8
Orellana, *Spain* 37 F5
Orellana, Canal de, *Spain* 37 F5
Orellana, Embalse de, *Spain* 37 F5
Orem, *U.S.A.* 108 F8
Ören, *Turkey* 47 D9
Orenburg, *Russia* 52 D6
Örencik, *Turkey* 47 B11
Orense = Ourense, *Spain* 36 C3
Orense □, *Spain* 36 C3
Orepuki, *N.Z.* 91 M1
Orestiás, *Greece* 45 E10
Orestos Pereyra, *Mexico* 118 B3
Øresund, *Europe* 11 J6
Orford Ness, *U.K.* 15 E9
Organ Pipe Cactus ⌂, *U.S.A.* 109 K7
Orgañà = Organyà, *Spain* 38 C6
Organos, Pta. de los, *Canary Is.* 48 F2
Organyà, *Spain* 38 C6
Orgaz, *Spain* 37 F7
Orgeyev = Orhei, *Moldova* 29 C13
Orhaneli, *Turkey* 45 G12
Orhaneli →, *Turkey* 45 G12
Orhangazi, *Turkey* 45 F13
Orhei, *Moldova* 29 C13
Orhon Gol →, *Mongolia* 60 A5
Ória, *Italy* 43 B10
Oriental, Cordillera, *Colombia* 124 B4
Oriental, Grand Erg, *Algeria* 78 B7
Orientale □, *Dem. Rep. of the Congo* 86 B2
Oriente, *Argentina* 126 D3
Orihuela, *Spain* 39 G4
Orihuela del Tremedal, *Spain* 38 E3
Orikhiv, *Ukraine* 33 J8
Orikum, *Albania* 44 F3
Orillia, *Canada* 116 B5
Orinoco →, *Venezuela* 124 B6
Orion, *Canada* 103 D6
Oriskany, *U.S.A.* 117 C9
Orissa □, *India* 67 K14
Orissaare, *Estonia* 9 G20
Oristano, *Italy* 42 C1
Oristano, G. di, *Italy* 42 C1
Orizaba, *Mexico* 119 D5
Orizaba, Pico de, *Mexico* 119 D5
Orizare, *Bulgaria* 45 D11
Orjen, *Bos.-H.* 44 D2
Orjiva, *Spain* 37 J7
Orkanger, *Norway* 8 E13
Örkelljunga, *Sweden* 11 H7
Örken, *Sweden* 11 G9
Örkény, *Hungary* 28 C4
Orkla →, *Norway* 8 E13
Orkney, *S. Africa* 88 D4
Orkney □, *U.K.* 13 B5
Orkney Is., *U.K.* 13 B6
Orland, *U.S.A.* 110 F4
Orlando, *U.S.A.* 115 L5
Orlando, C. d', *Italy* 43 D7
Orléanais, *France* 19 E9
Orléans, *France* 19 E8
Orleans, *U.S.A.* 117 B12
Orléans, Î. d', *Canada* 105 C5
Orlice →, *Czech Rep.* 26 A8
Orlov, *Slovak Rep.* 27 B13
Orlov Gay, *Russia* 34 E9
Orlová, *Czech Rep.* 27 B11
Orlovat, *Serbia & M.* 28 E5
Orly, Paris ✕ (ORY), *France* 19 D9
Ormara, *Pakistan* 66 G4
Ormea, *Italy* 40 D4
Ormília, *Greece* 44 F7
Ormoc, *Phil.* 61 F6
Ormond, *N.Z.* 91 H6
Ormond Beach, *U.S.A.* 115 L5
Ormož, *Slovenia* 41 B13
Ormskirk, *U.K.* 14 D5
Ormstown, *Canada* 117 A11
Ornans, *France* 19 E13
Orne □, *France* 18 D7
Orne →, *France* 18 C6
Orneta, *Poland* 30 D7
Ornö, *Sweden* 10 E12
Örnsköldsvik, *Sweden* 10 A12
Oro, *N. Korea* 57 D14
Oro →, *Mexico* 118 B3
Oro Grande, *U.S.A.* 111 L9
Oro Valley, *U.S.A.* 109 K8
Orobie, Alpi, *Italy* 40 B6
Orobie Bergamasche ⌂, *Italy* 40 C6
Orobie Valtellinesi ⌂, *Italy* 40 B6
Orocué, *Colombia* 124 C4
Orodara, *Burkina Faso* 82 C4
Orodo, *Nigeria* 83 D6
Orofino, *U.S.A.* 108 C5
Orol Dengizi = Aral Sea, *Asia* 52 E7
Oromocto, *Canada* 105 C6
Oron, *Nigeria* 83 E6
Orono, *Canada* 116 C6
Orono, *U.S.A.* 115 C11
Oronsay, *U.K.* 13 E2
Oropesa, *Spain* 36 F5
Oroquieta, *Phil.* 61 G5
Orosei, *Italy* 42 B2
Orosei, G. di, *Italy* 42 B2
Orosháza, *Hungary* 28 D5
Oroszlány, *Hungary* 28 C3
Orotukan, *Russia* 53 C16
Oroville, *Calif., U.S.A.* 110 F5
Oroville, *Wash., U.S.A.* 108 B4
Oroville, L., *U.S.A.* 110 F5
Orrefors, *Sweden* 11 H9
Orroroo, *Australia* 95 E2
Orrviken, *Sweden* 10 A8
Orrville, *U.S.A.* 116 F3
Orsa, *Sweden* 10 C8
Orsara di Púglia, *Italy* 43 A8
Orsasjön, *Sweden* 10 C8
Orsha, *Belarus* 32 E6
Örsjö, *Sweden* 11 H9
Orsk, *Russia* 52 D6
Orşova, *Romania* 28 F7
Ørsted, *Denmark* 11 H4
Örsundsbro, *Sweden* 10 E11
Orta, L. d', *Italy* 40 C5
Orta Nova, *Italy* 43 A8
Ortaca, *Turkey* 47 E10
Ortakent, *Turkey* 47 D9
Ortaklar, *Turkey* 47 D9
Ortaköy, *Çorum, Turkey* 72 B6
Ortaköy, *Niğde, Turkey* 72 C6
Orte, *Italy* 41 F9
Ortegal, C., *Spain* 36 B3
Orthez, *France* 20 E3
Ortigueira, *Spain* 36 B3
Orting, *U.S.A.* 110 C4
Ortisei, *Italy* 41 B8
Ortles, *Italy* 40 B7
Ortón →, *Bolivia* 124 F5
Ortona, *Italy* 41 F11
Ortonville, *U.S.A.* 112 C6
Orūmīyeh, *Iran* 70 B5
Orūmīyeh, Daryācheh-ye, *Iran* 70 B5
Orune, *Italy* 42 B2
Oruro, *Bolivia* 124 G5
Orust, *Sweden* 11 F5
Oruzgān □, *Afghan.* 66 C5
Orvault, *France* 18 E5
Orvieto, *Italy* 41 F9
Orwell, *N.Y., U.S.A.* 117 C9
Orwell, *Ohio, U.S.A.* 116 E4
Orwell →, *U.K.* 15 F9
Orwigsburg, *U.S.A.* 117 F8
Oryakhovo, *Bulgaria* 44 C7
Orzinuovi, *Italy* 40 C6
Orzyc →, *Poland* 31 F8
Orzysz, *Poland* 30 E8
Osa →, *Poland* 30 E5
Osa, Pen. de, *Costa Rica* 120 E3
Osage, *U.S.A.* 112 D8
Osage →, *U.S.A.* 112 F9
Osage City, *U.S.A.* 112 F7
Ōsaka, *Japan* 55 G7
Osan, *S. Korea* 57 F14
Osawatomie, *U.S.A.* 112 F7
Osborne, *U.S.A.* 112 F5
Osby, *Sweden* 11 H7
Osceola, *Ark., U.S.A.* 113 H10
Osceola, *Iowa, U.S.A.* 112 E8
Oschatz, *Germany* 24 D9
Oschersleben, *Germany* 24 C7
Óschiri, *Italy* 42 B2
Oscoda, *U.S.A.* 116 B1
Osečina, *Serbia & M.* 44 B3
Ösel = Saaremaa, *Estonia* 9 G20
Osery, *Russia* 32 E10
Osgoode, *Canada* 117 A9
Osh, *Kyrgyzstan* 52 E8
Oshakati, *Namibia* 85 H3
Oshawa, *Canada* 116 C6
Oshigambo, *Namibia* 88 B2
Oshkosh, *Nebr., U.S.A.* 112 E3
Oshkosh, *Wis., U.S.A.* 112 C10
Oshmyany = Ashmyany, *Belarus* 9 J21
Oshnovīyeh, *Iran* 70 B5
Oshogbo, *Nigeria* 83 D5
Oshtorīnān, *Iran* 71 C6
Oshwe, *Dem. Rep. of the Congo* 84 E3
Osi, *Nigeria* 83 D6
Osieczna, *Poland* 31 G3
Osijek, *Croatia* 28 E3
Ósilo, *Italy* 42 B1
Ósimo, *Italy* 41 E10
Osintorf, *Belarus* 32 E6
Osipenko = Berdyansk, *Ukraine* 33 J9
Osipovichi = Asipovichy, *Belarus* 32 F5
Osiyan, *India* 68 F5
Osizweni, *S. Africa* 89 D5
Oskaloosa, *U.S.A.* 112 E8
Oskarshamn, *Sweden* 11 G10
Oskarström, *Sweden* 11 H6
Oskélanéo, *Canada* 104 C4
Öskemen, *Kazakhstan* 52 E9
Oskol →, *Ukraine* 33 H9
Oslo, *Norway* 9 G14
Oslob, *Phil.* 61 G5
Oslofjorden, *Norway* 9 G14
Osmanabad, *India* 66 K10
Osmancık, *Turkey* 72 B6
Osmaniye, *Turkey* 70 B3
Osmanlı, *Turkey* 45 E10
Ösmo, *Sweden* 10 F11
Osnabrück, *Germany* 24 C4
Ośno Lubuskie, *Poland* 31 F1
Osoblaha, *Czech Rep.* 27 A10
Osogovska Planina, *Macedonia* 44 D6
Osor, *Italy* 41 D11
Osorio, *Brazil* 127 B5
Osorno, *Chile* 128 E2
Osorno, *Spain* 36 C6
Osoyoos, *Canada* 102 D5
Osøyro, *Norway* 9 F11
Ospika →, *Canada* 102 B4
Osprey Reef, *Australia* 94 A4
Oss, *Neths.* 17 C5
Ossa, Mt., *Australia* 95 G4
Óssa, Óros, *Greece* 46 B4
Ossa de Montiel, *Spain* 39 G2
Ossabaw I., *U.S.A.* 115 K5
Osse →, *France* 20 D4
Osse →, *Nigeria* 83 D6
Ossi, *Italy* 42 B1
Ossining, *U.S.A.* 117 E11
Ossipee, *U.S.A.* 117 C13
Ossokmanuan L., *Canada* 105 B7
Ossora, *Russia* 53 D17
Ostashkov, *Russia* 32 D7
Östavall, *Sweden* 10 B9
Oste →, *Germany* 24 B5
Ostend = Oostende, *Belgium* 17 C2
Oster, *Ukraine* 33 G6
Osterburg, *Germany* 24 C7
Osterburg, *U.S.A.* 116 F6
Osterburken, *Germany* 25 F5
Österbybruk, *Sweden* 10 D11
Österbymo, *Sweden* 11 G9
Österdalälven, *Sweden* 10 C7
Østerdalen, *Norway* 9 F14
Österfärnebo, *Sweden* 10 D10
Österforse, *Sweden* 10 A11
Östergötlands län □, *Sweden* 11 F9
Osterholz-Scharmbeck, *Germany* 24 B4
Østerild, *Denmark* 11 G2
Osterode, *Germany* 24 D6
Östersund, *Sweden* 10 A8
Östervåla, *Sweden* 10 D11
Ostfriesische Inseln, *Germany* 24 B3
Ostfriesland, *Germany* 24 B3
Östhammar, *Sweden* 10 D12
Óstia, Lido di, *Italy* 41 G9
Ostíglia, *Italy* 41 C8
Östmark, *Sweden* 10 D6
Östra Husby, *Sweden* 11 F10
Ostrava, *Czech Rep.* 27 B11
Ostravský □, *Czech Rep.* 27 B10
Ostróda, *Poland* 30 E6
Ostrogozhsk, *Russia* 33 G10
Ostroh, *Ukraine* 33 G4
Ostrołęka, *Poland* 31 E8
Ostrov, *Bulgaria* 45 C8
Ostrov, *Czech Rep.* 26 A5
Ostrov, *Romania* 29 F12
Ostrov, *Russia* 32 D5
Ostrów Lubelski, *Poland* 31 G9
Ostrów Mazowiecka, *Poland* 31 F8
Ostrów Wielkopolski, *Poland* 31 G4
Ostrowiec-Świętokrzyski, *Poland* 31 H8
Ostrožac, *Bos.-H.* 28 G2
Ostrzeszów, *Poland* 31 G4
Ostseebad Kühlungsborn, *Germany* 24 A7
Osttirol □, *Austria* 26 E5
Ostuni, *Italy* 43 B10
Osum →, *Albania* 44 F4
Osŭm →, *Bulgaria* 45 C8
Ōsumi-Kaikyō, *Japan* 55 J5
Ōsumi-Shotō, *Japan* 55 J5
Osun □, *Nigeria* 83 D5
Osuna, *Spain* 37 H5
Oswegatchie →, *U.S.A.* 117 B9
Oswego, *U.S.A.* 117 C8
Oswego →, *U.S.A.* 117 C8
Oswestry, *U.K.* 14 E4
Oświęcim, *Poland* 31 H6
Otaci, *Moldova* 29 B12
Otago □, *N.Z.* 91 L2
Otago Harbour, *N.Z.* 91 L3
Otaheite B., *Trin. & Tob.* 125 K15
Ōtake, *Japan* 55 G6
Otaki, *N.Z.* 91 J5
Otaru, *Japan* 54 C10
Otaru-Wan = Ishikari-Wan, *Japan* 54 C10
Otava →, *Czech Rep.* 26 B7
Otavalo, *Ecuador* 124 C3
Otavi, *Namibia* 88 B2
Otchinjau, *Angola* 88 B1
Otelec, *Romania* 28 E5
Otelnuk, L., *Canada* 105 A6
Oţelu Roşu, *Romania* 28 E7
Otero de Rey = Outeiro de Rei, *Spain* 36 B3
Othello, *U.S.A.* 108 C4
Othonoí, *Greece* 46 B1
Óthris, Óros, *Greece* 46 B4
Oti ⌂, *Togo* 83 C5
Otjiwarongo, *Namibia* 88 C2
Otmuchów, *Poland* 31 H4
Otočac, *Croatia* 41 D12
Otoineppu, *Japan* 54 B11
Otok, *Croatia* 41 E13
Otopeni, Bucharest ✕ (OTP), *Romania* 45 B10
Otorohanga, *N.Z.* 91 H5
Otoskwin →, *Canada* 104 B2
Otra →, *Norway* 9 G13
Otradnyy, *Russia* 34 D10
Otranto, *Italy* 43 B11
Otranto, C. d', *Italy* 43 B11
Otranto, Str. of, *Italy* 43 B11
Otrokovice, *Czech Rep.* 27 B10
Otse, *S. Africa* 88 D4
Ōtsu, *Japan* 55 G7
Ōtsuki, *Japan* 55 G9
Ottawa = Outaouais →, *Canada* 104 C5
Ottawa, *Canada* 117 A9
Ottawa, *Ill., U.S.A.* 112 E10
Ottawa, *Kans., U.S.A.* 112 F7
Ottawa Is., *Canada* 101 C11
Ottélé, *Cameroon* 83 E7
Ottensheim, *Austria* 26 C7
Otter Cr. →, *U.S.A.* 117 B11
Otter L., *Canada* 103 B8
Otterndorf, *Germany* 24 B4
Otterup, *Denmark* 11 J4
Otterville, *Canada* 116 D4
Ottery St. Mary, *U.K.* 15 G4
Otto Beit Bridge, *Zimbabwe* 87 F2
Ottosdal, *S. Africa* 88 D4
Ottumwa, *U.S.A.* 112 E8
Otu, *Nigeria* 83 D5
Otukpa, *Nigeria* 83 D6
Oturkpo, *Nigeria* 83 D6
Otway, B., *Chile* 128 G2
Otway, C., *Australia* 95 F3
Otwock, *Poland* 31 F8
Ötztaler Ache →, *Austria* 26 D3
Ötztaler Alpen, *Austria* 26 E3
Ou →, *Laos* 64 B4
Ou Neua, *Laos* 58 F3
Ou-Sammyaku, *Japan* 54 E10
Ouachita →, *U.S.A.* 113 K9
Ouachita, L., *U.S.A.* 113 H8
Ouachita Mts., *U.S.A.* 113 H7
Ouagadougou, *Burkina Faso* 83 C4
Ouahigouya, *Burkina Faso* 82 C4
Ouahran = Oran, *Algeria* 78 A5
Oualâta, *Mauritania* 82 B3
Ouallam, *Niger* 83 C5
Ouallene, *Algeria* 78 D6
Ouargaye, *Burkina Faso* 83 C5
Ouargla, *Algeria* 78 B7
Ouarkoye, *Burkina Faso* 82 C4
Ouarzazate, *Morocco* 78 B4
Ouassouas, *Mali* 83 B5
Ouatagouna, *Mali* 83 B5
Oubangi →, *Dem. Rep. of the Congo* 84 E3
Ouche →, *France* 19 E12
Ouddorp, *Neths.* 17 C3
Oude Rijn →, *Neths.* 17 B4
Oudeïka, *Mali* 83 B4
Oudenaarde, *Belgium* 17 D3
Oudon →, *France* 18 E6
Oudtshoorn, *S. Africa* 88 E3
Ouellé, *Ivory C.* 82 D4
Ouémé →, *Benin* 83 D5
Ouessa, *Burkina Faso* 82 C4
Ouessant, Î. d', *France* 18 D1
Ouesso, *Congo* 84 D3
Ouest, Pte. de l', *Canada* 105 C7
Ouezzane, *Morocco* 78 B4
Ougarou, *Burkina Faso* 83 C5
Oughterard, *Ireland* 12 C2
Ouidah, *Benin* 83 D5
Ouidi, *Niger* 83 C7
Ouistreham, *France* 18 C6
Oujda, *Morocco* 78 B5
Oujeft, *Mauritania* 82 A2
Oulainen, *Finland* 8 D21
Ould Yenjé, *Mauritania* 82 B2
Oullins, *France* 21 C8
Oulu, *Finland* 8 D21
Oulujärvi, *Finland* 8 D22
Oulujoki →, *Finland* 8 D21
Oulx, *Italy* 40 C3
Oum Chalouba, *Chad* 79 E10
Oum Hadjer, *Chad* 79 F9
Oumé, *Ivory C.* 82 D3
Ounasjoki →, *Finland* 8 C21
Ounguati, *Namibia* 88 C2
Ounianga Sérir, *Chad* 79 E10
Our →, *Lux.* 17 E6
Ouranópolis, *Greece* 44 F7
Ourârene, *Niger* 83 B6
Ouray, *U.S.A.* 109 G10
Ourcq →, *France* 19 C10
Ourense, *Spain* 36 C3
Ouricuri, *Brazil* 125 E10
Ourinhos, *Brazil* 127 A6
Ourique, *Portugal* 37 H2
Ouro Fino, *Brazil* 127 A6
Ouro-Ndia, *Mali* 82 B4
Ouro Prêto, *Brazil* 127 A7
Ouro Sogui, *Senegal* 82 B2
Oursi, *Burkina Faso* 83 C4
Ourthe →, *Belgium* 17 D5
Ouse →, *E. Susx., U.K.* 15 G8
Ouse →, *N. Yorks., U.K.* 14 D7
Oust, *France* 20 F5
Oust →, *France* 18 E4
Outamba-Kilimi △, *S. Leone* 82 D2
Outaouais →, *Canada* 104 C5
Outardes →, *Canada* 105 C6
Outeiro de Rei, *Spain* 36 B3
Outer Hebrides, *U.K.* 13 D1
Outes = Serra de Outes, *Spain* 36 C2
Outjo, *Namibia* 88 C2
Outlook, *Canada* 103 C7
Outokumpu, *Finland* 8 E23
Outreau, *France* 19 B8
Ouvèze →, *France* 21 E8
Ouyen, *Australia* 95 F3
Ouzouer-le-Marché, *France* 19 E8
Ovada, *Italy* 40 D5
Ovalau, *Fiji* 91 C8
Ovalle, *Chile* 126 C1
Ovamboland, *Namibia* 88 B2
Ovar, *Portugal* 36 E2
Overath, *Germany* 24 E3
Overflakkee, *Neths.* 17 C4
Overijssel □, *Neths.* 17 B6
Overland Park, *U.S.A.* 112 F7
Overton, *U.S.A.* 111 J12
Övertorneå, *Sweden* 8 C20
Överum, *Sweden* 11 F10
Ovid, *U.S.A.* 117 D8
Ovidiopol, *Ukraine* 33 J6
Ovidiu, *Romania* 29 F13
Oviedo, *Spain* 36 B5
Oviksfjällen, *Sweden* 10 A7
Oviši, *Latvia* 9 H19
Ovoot, *Mongolia* 56 B7
Övör Hangay □, *Mongolia* 56 B2
Ovoro, *Nigeria* 83 D6
Øvre Årdal, *Norway* 9 F12
Övre Fryken, *Sweden* 10 E7
Ovruch, *Ukraine* 33 G5
Owaka, *N.Z.* 91 M2
Owambo = Ovamboland, *Namibia* 88 B2
Owasco L., *U.S.A.* 117 D8
Owase, *Japan* 55 G8
Owatonna, *U.S.A.* 112 C8
Owbeh, *Afghan.* 66 B3
Owego, *U.S.A.* 117 D8
Owen Falls Dam, *Uganda* 86 B3
Owen Sound, *Canada* 116 B4
Owens →, *U.S.A.* 110 J9
Owens L., *U.S.A.* 111 J9
Owensboro, *U.S.A.* 114 G2
Owerri, *Nigeria* 83 D6
Owl →, *Canada* 103 B10
Owo, *Nigeria* 83 D6
Owosso, *U.S.A.* 114 D3

Owyhee, *U.S.A.* 108 F5
Owyhee →, *U.S.A.* 108 E5
Owyhee, L., *U.S.A.* 108 E5
Ox Mts. = Slieve Gamph, *Ireland* 12 B3
Öxarfjörður, *Iceland* 8 C5
Oxbow, *Canada* 103 D8
Oxelösund, *Sweden* 11 F11
Oxford, *N.Z.* 91 K4
Oxford, *U.K.* 15 F6
Oxford, *Mass., U.S.A.* 117 D13
Oxford, *Miss., U.S.A.* 113 H10
Oxford, *N.C., U.S.A.* 115 G6
Oxford, *N.Y., U.S.A.* 117 D9
Oxford, *Ohio, U.S.A.* 114 F3
Oxford L., *Canada* 103 C9
Oxfordshire □, *U.K.* 15 F6
Oxía Nisís, *Greece* 46 C3
Oxie, *Sweden* 11 J7
Oxílithos, *Greece* 46 C6
Oxnard, *U.S.A.* 111 L7
Oxsjövålen, *Sweden* 10 B7
Oxus = Amudarya →, *Uzbekistan* 52 E6
Oya, *Malaysia* 62 D4
Oyama, *Japan* 55 F9
Oyambre ⌓, *Spain* 36 B6
Oyem, *Gabon* 84 D2
Oyen, *Canada* 103 C6
Oykel →, *U.K.* 13 D4
Oymyakon, *Russia* 53 C15
Oyo, *Nigeria* 83 D5
Oyo □, *Nigeria* 83 D5
Oyonnax, *France* 19 F12
Oyster Bay, *U.S.A.* 117 F11
Ōyübari, *Japan* 54 C11
Özalp, *Turkey* 73 C10
Ozamiz, *Phil.* 61 G5
Ozark, *Ala., U.S.A.* 115 K3
Ozark, *Ark., U.S.A.* 113 H8
Ozark, *Mo., U.S.A.* 113 G8
Ozark Plateau, *U.S.A.* 113 G9
Ozarks, L. of the, *U.S.A.* 112 F8
Ożarów, *Poland* 31 H8
Ózd, *Hungary* 28 B5
Ozernoye, *Russia* 34 E10
Ozette L., *U.S.A.* 110 B2
Ozieri, *Italy* 42 B2
Ozimek, *Poland* 31 H5
Ozinki, *Russia* 34 E9
Ozona, *U.S.A.* 113 K4
Ozorków, *Poland* 31 G6
Ozren, *Bos.-H.* 28 G3
Ozuluama, *Mexico* 119 C5
Ozun, *Romania* 29 E10
Ozurgeti, *Georgia* 35 K5

P

Pa, *Burkina Faso* 82 C4
Pa-an, *Burma* 67 L20
Pa Mong Dam, *Thailand* 64 D4
Pa Sak →, *Thailand* 62 B2
Paamiut, *Greenland* 101 B15
Paar →, *Germany* 25 G7
Paarl, *S. Africa* 88 E2
Pab Hills, *Pakistan* 68 F2
Pabbay, *U.K.* 13 D1
Pabianice, *Poland* 31 G6
Pabna, *Bangla.* 67 G16
Pabo, *Uganda* 86 B3
Pacaja →, *Brazil* 125 D8
Pacaraima, Sa., *S. Amer.* 124 C6
Pacasmayo, *Peru* 124 E3
Paceco, *Italy* 42 E5
Pachhar, *India* 68 G7
Pachino, *Italy* 43 F8
Pachitea →, *Peru* 124 E4
Pachmarhi, *India* 69 H8
Pachpadra, *India* 66 G8
Pachuca, *Mexico* 119 C5
Pacific, *Canada* 102 C3
Pacific-Antarctic Ridge, *Pac. Oc.* 97 M16
Pacific Grove, *U.S.A.* 110 J5
Pacific Ocean 97 G14
Pacific Rim △, *Canada* 102 D4
Pacifica, *U.S.A.* 110 H4
Pacitan, *Indonesia* 63 H14
Packwood, *U.S.A.* 110 D5
Pacov, *Czech Rep.* 26 B8
Pacy-sur-Eure, *France* 18 C8
Padaido, Kepulauan, *Indonesia* 63 E9
Padang, *Indonesia* 62 E2
Padang Endau, *Malaysia* 65 L4
Padangpanjang, *Indonesia* 62 E2
Padangsidempuan, *Indonesia* 62 D1
Padborg, *Denmark* 11 K3
Paddle Prairie, *Canada* 102 B5
Paddockwood, *Canada* 103 C7
Paderborn, *Germany* 24 D4
Padeş, Vf., *Romania* 28 E7
Padina, *Romania* 29 F12
Padma, *India* 69 G11
Pádova, *Italy* 41 C8
Padra, *India* 68 H5
Padrauna, *India* 69 F10
Padre I., *U.S.A.* 113 M6
Padre Island ⌓, *U.S.A.* 113 M6
Padrón, *Spain* 36 C2
Padstow, *U.K.* 15 G3
Padua = Pádova, *Italy* 41 C8
Paducah, *Ky., U.S.A.* 114 G1
Paducah, *Tex., U.S.A.* 113 H4
Padul, *Spain* 37 H7
Paengnyŏng-do, *S. Korea* 57 F13
Paeroa, *N.Z.* 91 G5
Paesana, *Italy* 40 D4
Pafúri, *Mozam.* 89 C5
Pag, *Croatia* 41 D12
Paga, *Ghana* 83 C4
Pagadian, *Phil.* 61 H5
Pagai Selatan, Pulau, *Indonesia* 62 E2
Pagai Utara, Pulau, *Indonesia* 62 E2
Pagalu = Annobón, *Atl. Oc.* 77 G4
Pagara, *India* 69 G9
Pagastikós Kólpos, *Greece* 46 B5
Pagatan, *Indonesia* 62 E5
Page, *U.S.A.* 109 H8
Pagėgiai, *Lithuania* 30 C8
Pago Pago, *Amer. Samoa* 91 B13
Pagosa Springs, *U.S.A.* 109 H10
Pagwa River, *Canada* 104 B2
Pahala, *U.S.A.* 106 J17
Pahang →, *Malaysia* 65 L4
Pahiatua, *N.Z.* 91 J5
Pahokee, *U.S.A.* 115 M5
Pahrump, *U.S.A.* 111 J11
Pahute Mesa, *U.S.A.* 110 H10
Pai, *Thailand* 64 C2
Paicines, *U.S.A.* 110 J5
Paide, *Estonia* 9 G21
Paignton, *U.K.* 15 G4
Paiho, *Taiwan* 59 F13
Päijänne, *Finland* 9 F21
Pailani, *India* 69 G9
Pailin, *Cambodia* 64 F4
Paimpol, *France* 18 D3
Painan, *Indonesia* 62 E2
Painesville, *U.S.A.* 116 E3
Paint Hills = Wemindji, *Canada* 104 B4
Paint L., *Canada* 103 B9
Painted Desert, *U.S.A.* 109 J8
Paintsville, *U.S.A.* 114 G4
País Vasco □, *Spain* 38 C2
Paisley, *Canada* 116 B3
Paisley, *U.K.* 13 F4
Paisley, *U.S.A.* 108 E3
Paita, *Peru* 124 E2
Paiva →, *Portugal* 36 D2
Paizhou, *China* 59 B9
Pajares, *Spain* 36 B5
Pajares, Puerto de, *Spain* 36 C5
Pajęczno, *Poland* 31 G5
Pak Lay, *Laos* 64 C3
Pak Phanang, *Thailand* 65 H3
Pak Sane, *Laos* 64 C4
Pak Song, *Laos* 64 E6
Pak Suong, *Laos* 58 H4
Pakaur, *India* 69 G12
Pakenham, *Canada* 117 A8
Pákhnes, *Greece* 49 D6
Pakhuis, *S. Africa* 88 E2
Pakistan ■, *Asia* 68 E4
Pakkading, *Laos* 64 C4
Paklenica △, *Croatia* 41 D12
Pakokku, *Burma* 67 J19
Pakość, *Poland* 31 F5
Pakowki L., *Canada* 103 D6
Pakpattan, *Pakistan* 68 D5
Pakrac, *Croatia* 28 E2
Pakruojis, *Lithuania* 30 C10
Paks, *Hungary* 28 D3
Paktīā □, *Afghan.* 66 C6
Paktīkā □, *Afghan.* 66 C6
Pakwach, *Uganda* 86 B3
Pakxe, *Laos* 64 E5
Pal Lahara, *India* 69 J11
Pala, *Chad* 79 G9
Pala, *Dem. Rep. of the Congo* 86 D2
Pala, *U.S.A.* 111 M9
Palabek, *Uganda* 86 B3
Palacios, *U.S.A.* 113 L6
Palafrugell, *Spain* 38 D8
Palagiano, *Italy* 43 B10
Palagonía, *Italy* 43 E7
Palagruža, *Croatia* 41 F13
Palaiókastron, *Greece* 49 D8
Palaiokhóra, *Greece* 49 D5
Pálairos, *Greece* 46 C2
Palaiseau, *France* 19 D9
Palam, *India* 66 K10
Palamás, *Greece* 46 B4
Palamòs, *Spain* 38 D8
Palampur, *India* 68 C7
Palamut, *Turkey* 47 C9
Palana, *Australia* 95 F4
Palana, *Russia* 53 D16
Palanan, *Phil.* 61 C5
Palanan Pt., *Phil.* 61 C5
Palandri, *Pakistan* 69 C5
Palanga, *Lithuania* 9 J19
Palangkaraya, *Indonesia* 62 E4
Palani Hills, *India* 66 P10
Palanpur, *India* 68 G5
Palapye, *Botswana* 88 C4
Palas, *Pakistan* 69 B5
Palas de Rei, *Spain* 36 C3
Palashi, *India* 69 H13
Palasponga, *India* 69 J11
Palatka, *Russia* 53 C16
Palatka, *U.S.A.* 115 L5
Palau, *Italy* 42 A2
Palau, *Mexico* 51 J17
Palau ■, *Pac. Oc.* 96 G5
Palauk, *Burma* 64 F2
Palawan, *Phil.* 61 G3
Palayankottai, *India* 66 Q10
Palazzo, Pte., *France* 21 F12
Palazzo San Gervásio, *Italy* 43 B8
Palazzolo Acréide, *Italy* 43 E7
Paldiski, *Estonia* 9 G21
Pale, *Bos.-H.* 28 G3
Paleleh, *Indonesia* 63 D6
Palembang, *Indonesia* 62 E2
Palencia, *Spain* 36 C6
Palencia □, *Spain* 36 C6
Palenque, *Mexico* 119 D6
Palenque, Ruinas de, *Mexico* 119 D6
Paleokastrítsa, *Greece* 49 A3
Paleometokho, *Cyprus* 49 D12
Palermo, *Italy* 42 D6
Palermo, *U.S.A.* 108 G3
Palermo ✕ (PMO), *Italy* 42 D6
Palestina, *Chile* 128 A3
Palestine, *Asia* 74 D4
Palestine, *U.S.A.* 113 K7
Palestrina, *Italy* 41 G9
Paletwa, *Burma* 67 J18
Palghat, *India* 66 P10
Palgrave, Mt., *Australia* 92 D2
Pali, *India* 68 G5
Palikir, *Micronesia* 96 G7
Palinuro, *Italy* 43 B8
Palinuro, C., *Italy* 43 B8
Palioúrion, Ákra, *Greece* 44 G7
Palisades Reservoir, *U.S.A.* 108 E8
Paliseul, *Belgium* 17 E5
Palitana, *India* 68 J4
Palizada, *Mexico* 119 D6
Palk Bay, *Asia* 66 Q11
Palk Strait, *Asia* 66 Q11
Palkānah, *Iraq* 70 C5
Palkot, *India* 69 H11
Palla Road = Dinokwe, *Botswana* 88 C4
Pallanza = Verbánia, *Italy* 40 C5
Pallarenda, *Australia* 94 B4
Pallasovka, *Russia* 34 E8
Pallës, Bishti i, *Albania* 44 E3
Pallinup →, *Australia* 93 F2
Pallisa, *Uganda* 86 B3
Pallu, *India* 68 E6
Palm Bay, *U.S.A.* 115 L5
Palm Beach, *U.S.A.* 115 M6
Palm Coast, *U.S.A.* 115 L5
Palm Desert, *U.S.A.* 111 M10
Palm Is., *Australia* 94 B4
Palm Springs, *U.S.A.* 111 M10
Palma, *Mozam.* 87 E5
Palma, B. de, *Spain* 48 B9
Palma de Mallorca, *Spain* 48 B9
Palma de Mallorca ✕ (PMI), *Spain* 39 F7
Palma del Río, *Spain* 37 H5
Palma di Montechiaro, *Italy* 42 E6
Palma Soriano, *Cuba* 120 B4
Palmares, *Brazil* 125 E11
Palmarola, *Italy* 42 B5
Palmas, *Brazil* 127 B5
Palmas, C., *Liberia* 82 E3
Pálmas, G. di, *Italy* 42 D1
Palmdale, *U.S.A.* 111 L8
Palmeira das Missões, *Brazil* 127 B5
Palmeira dos Índios, *Brazil* 125 E11
Palmela, *Portugal* 37 G2
Palmer, *Antarctica* 5 C17
Palmer, *U.S.A.* 100 B5
Palmer →, *Australia* 94 B3
Palmer Arch., *Antarctica* 5 C17
Palmer Lake, *U.S.A.* 112 F2
Palmer Land, *Antarctica* 5 D18
Palmerston, *Canada* 116 C4
Palmerston, *N.Z.* 91 L3
Palmerston North, *N.Z.* 91 J5
Palmerton, *U.S.A.* 117 F9
Palmetto, *U.S.A.* 115 M4
Palmi, *Italy* 43 D8
Palmira, *Argentina* 126 C2
Palmira, *Colombia* 124 C3
Palmyra = Tudmur, *Syria* 70 C3
Palmyra, *Mo., U.S.A.* 112 F9
Palmyra, *N.J., U.S.A.* 117 F9
Palmyra, *N.Y., U.S.A.* 116 C7
Palmyra, *Pa., U.S.A.* 117 F8
Palmyra Is., *Pac. Oc.* 97 G11
Palo Alto, *U.S.A.* 110 H4
Palo Seco, *Trin. & Tob.* 125 K15
Palo Verde, *U.S.A.* 111 M12
Palo Verde △, *Costa Rica* 120 D2
Paloich, *Sudan* 81 E3
Palomar Mt., *U.S.A.* 111 M10
Palompon, *Phil.* 61 F6
Palopo, *Indonesia* 63 E6
Palos, C. de, *Spain* 39 H4
Palos de la Frontera, *Spain* 37 H4
Palos Verdes, *U.S.A.* 111 M8
Palos Verdes, Pt., *U.S.A.* 111 M8
Pålsboda, *Sweden* 10 E9
Palu, *Indonesia* 63 E5
Palu, *Turkey* 70 B3
Paluke, *Liberia* 82 D3
Paluzza, *Italy* 41 B10
Palwal, *India* 68 E7
Pama, *Burkina Faso* 83 C5
Pama ⌓, *Burkina Faso* 83 C5
Pamanukan, *Indonesia* 63 G12
Pamekasan, *Indonesia* 63 G15
Pamenang, *Indonesia* 63 J19
Pamiers, *France* 20 E5
Pamir, *Tajikistan* 52 F8
Pamlico →, *U.S.A.* 115 H7
Pamlico Sd., *U.S.A.* 115 H8
Pampa, *U.S.A.* 113 H4
Pampa de las Salinas, *Argentina* 126 C2
Pampanua, *Indonesia* 63 E6
Pampas, *Argentina* 126 D3
Pampas, *Peru* 124 F4
Pamphylia, *Turkey* 72 D4
Pamplona, *Colombia* 124 B4
Pamplona, *Spain* 38 C3
Pampoenpoort, *S. Africa* 88 E3
Pamukçu, *Turkey* 47 B9
Pamukkale, *Turkey* 47 D11
Pan de Azúcar △, *Chile* 126 B1
Pan Xian, *China* 58 E5
Pana, *U.S.A.* 112 F10
Panabo, *Phil.* 61 H6
Panaca, *U.S.A.* 109 H6
Panagyurishte, *Bulgaria* 45 D8
Panaitan, *Indonesia* 63 G11
Panaji, *India* 66 M8
Panamá, *Panama* 120 E4
Panama ■, *Cent. Amer.* 120 E4
Panamá, G. de, *Panama* 120 E4
Panama Canal, *Panama* 120 E4
Panama City, *U.S.A.* 115 K3
Panamint Range, *U.S.A.* 111 J9
Panamint Springs, *U.S.A.* 111 J9
Panão, *Peru* 124 E3
Panaon I., *Phil.* 61 F6
Panare, *Thailand* 65 J3
Panarea, *Italy* 43 D8
Panaro →, *Italy* 41 D8
Panay, *Phil.* 61 F5
Panay, G., *Phil.* 63 B6
Pančevo, *Serbia & M.* 28 F5
Panch'iao, *Taiwan* 59 E13
Panciu, *Romania* 29 E12
Pancorbo, Desfiladero, *Spain* 36 C7
Pâncota, *Romania* 28 D6
Panda, *Mozam.* 89 C5
Pandan, *Malaysia* 65 d
Pandan, *Antique, Phil.* 61 F5
Pandan, *Catanduanes, Phil.* 61 D6
Pandan, Selat, *Singapore* 65 d
Pandan Tampoi = Tampoi, *Malaysia* 65 d
Pandegelang, *Indonesia* 63 G12
Pandhana, *India* 68 J7
Pandharpur, *India* 66 L9
Pando, *Uruguay* 127 C4
Pando, L. = Hope, L., *Australia* 95 D2
Pandokrátor, *Greece* 49 A3
Pandora, *Costa Rica* 120 E3
Pandrup, *Denmark* 11 G3
Panevéggio-Pale di San Martino ⌓, *Italy* 41 B8
Panevėžys, *Lithuania* 9 J21
Panfilov, *Kazakhstan* 52 E8
Panfilovo, *Russia* 34 E6
Pang-Long, *Burma* 67 H21
Pang Sida △, *Thailand* 64 E4
Pang-Yang, *Burma* 67 H21
Panga, *Dem. Rep. of the Congo* 86 B2
Pangaíon Óros, *Greece* 45 F8
Pangalanes, Canal des = Ampangalana, Lakandranon', *Madag.* 89 C8
Pangani, *Tanzania* 86 D4
Pangani →, *Tanzania* 86 D4
Pangfou = Bengbu, *China* 57 H9
Pangil, *Dem. Rep. of the Congo* 86 C2
Pangkah, Tanjung, *Indonesia* 63 G15
Pangkajene, *Indonesia* 63 E5
Pangkalanbrandan, *Indonesia* 62 D1
Pangkalanbuun, *Indonesia* 62 E4
Pangkalpinang, *Indonesia* 62 E3
Pangnirtung, *Canada* 101 B13
Pangong Tso, *India* 68 B8
Panguitch, *U.S.A.* 109 H7
Pangutaran Group, *Phil.* 61 H4
Panhandle, *U.S.A.* 113 H4
Pani Mines, *India* 68 H5
Pania-Mutombo, *Dem. Rep. of the Congo* 86 D1
Panikota I., *India* 68 J4
Panipat, *India* 68 E7
Panjal Range = Pir Panjal Range, *India* 68 C7
Panjang, Hon, *Vietnam* 65 H4
Panjgur, *Pakistan* 66 F4
Panjim = Panaji, *India* 66 M8
Panjin, *China* 57 D12
Panjinad Barrage, *Pakistan* 66 E7
Panjnad →, *Pakistan* 68 E4
Panjwai, *Afghan.* 68 D1
Pankshin, *Nigeria* 83 D6
Panmunjŏm, *N. Korea* 57 F14
Panna, *India* 69 G9
Panna Hills, *India* 69 G9
Pannawonica, *Australia* 92 D2
Pannga, Tanjung, *Indonesia* 63 K19
Pannirtuuq = Pangnirtung, *Canada* 101 B13
Pano Akil, *Pakistan* 68 F3
Pano Lefkara, *Cyprus* 49 E12
Pano Panayia, *Cyprus* 49 E11
Panorama, *Brazil* 127 A5
Pánormon, *Greece* 49 D6
Pansemal, *India* 68 J6
Panshan = Panjin, *China* 57 D12
Panshi, *China* 57 C14
Pantanal, *Brazil* 124 H7
Pantanos de Centla, Reserva de La Biósfera, *Mexico* 119 D6
Pantar, *Indonesia* 63 F6
Pante Macassar, *E. Timor* 63 F6
Pante Makasar = Pante Macassar, *E. Timor* 63 F6
Pantelleria, *Italy* 42 F4
Pantón, *Spain* 36 C3
Pánuco, *Mexico* 119 C5
Panyam, *Nigeria* 83 D6
Panyu, *China* 59 F9
Panzhihua, *China* 58 D3
Páola, *Italy* 43 C9
Paola, *Malta* 49 D2
Paola, *U.S.A.* 112 F7
Paonia, *U.S.A.* 109 G10
Paoting = Baoding, *China* 56 E8
Paot'ou = Baotou, *China* 56 D6
Paoua, *C.A.R.* 84 C3
Pápa, *Hungary* 28 C2
Papa Stour, *U.K.* 13 A7
Papa Westray, *U.K.* 13 B6
Papagayo →, *Mexico* 119 D5
Papagayo, G. de, *Costa Rica* 120 D2
Papakura, *N.Z.* 91 G5
Papantla, *Mexico* 119 C5
Papar, *Malaysia* 62 C5
Paparoa △, *N.Z.* 91 K3
Pápas, Ákra, *Greece* 46 C3
Papeete, *Tahiti* 97 J13
Papenburg, *Germany* 24 B3
Paphlagonia, *Turkey* 72 B5
Paphos, *Cyprus* 49 E11
Papien Chiang = Da →, *Vietnam* 58 G5
Papigochic →, *Mexico* 118 B3
Paposo, *Chile* 126 B1
Papoutsa, *Cyprus* 49 E12
Papua □, *Indonesia* 63 E9
Papua New Guinea ■, *Oceania* 96 H6
Papudo, *Chile* 126 C1
Papuk, *Croatia* 28 E2
Papun, *Burma* 67 K20
Papunya, *Australia* 92 D5
Pará = Belém, *Brazil* 125 D9
Pará □, *Brazil* 125 D8
Paraburdoo, *Australia* 92 D2
Paracale, *Phil.* 61 D5
Paracatu, *Brazil* 125 G9
Paracel Is., *S. China Sea* 62 A4
Parachilna, *Australia* 95 E2
Parachinar, *Pakistan* 68 C4
Paraćin, *Serbia & M.* 44 C5
Paradas, *Spain* 37 H5
Paradela, *Spain* 36 C3
Paradhísi, *Greece* 49 C10
Paradip, *India* 67 J15
Paradise, *Calif., U.S.A.* 110 F5
Paradise, *Nev., U.S.A.* 111 J11
Paradise →, *Canada* 105 B8
Paradise Hill, *Canada* 103 C7
Paradise River, *Canada* 105 B8
Paradise Valley, *U.S.A.* 108 F5
Parado, *Indonesia* 63 F5
Paragould, *U.S.A.* 113 G9
Paragua →, *Venezuela* 124 B6
Paraguaçu →, *Brazil* 125 F11
Paraguaçu Paulista, *Brazil* 127 A5
Paraguaná, Pen. de, *Venezuela* 124 A5
Paraguarí, *Paraguay* 126 B4
Paraguarí □, *Paraguay* 126 B4
Paraguay ■, *S. Amer.* 126 A4
Paraguay →, *Paraguay* 126 B4
Paraíba = João Pessoa, *Brazil* 125 E12
Paraíba □, *Brazil* 125 E11
Paraíba do Sul →, *Brazil* 127 A7
Parainen, *Finland* 9 F20
Paraiso, *Mexico* 119 D6
Parak, *Iran* 71 E7
Parakhino Paddubye, *Russia* 32 C7
Parakou, *Benin* 83 D5
Paralimni, *Cyprus* 49 D12
Parálion-Astrous, *Greece* 46 D4
Paramaribo, *Suriname* 125 B7
Paramithiá, *Greece* 46 B2
Páramos del Batallón y La Negra △, *Venezuela* 121 E5
Páramos del Batallón y La Negra △, *Venezuela* 121 E5
Paramushir, Ostrov, *Russia* 53 D16
Paran →, *Israel* 74 E4
Paraná, *Argentina* 126 C3
Paraná, *Brazil* 125 F9
Paraná □, *Brazil* 127 A5
Paraná →, *Argentina* 126 C4
Paranaguá, *Brazil* 127 B6
Paranaíba, *Brazil* 125 G8
Paranaíba →, *Brazil* 125 H8
Paranapanema →, *Brazil* 127 A5
Paranapiacaba, Serra do, *Brazil* 127 A6
Paranas, *Phil.* 61 F6
Paranavaí, *Brazil* 127 A5
Parang, *Maguindanao, Phil.* 63 C6
Parang, *Sulu, Phil.* 61 J4
Parângul Mare, Vf., *Romania* 29 E8
Paraparaumu, *N.Z.* 91 J5
Parapóla, *Greece* 46 E5
Paraspóri, Ákra, *Greece* 47 F9
Paray-le-Monial, *France* 19 F11
Parbati →, *Mad. P., India* 68 G7
Parbati →, *Raj., India* 68 F7
Parbhani, *India* 66 K10
Parchim, *Germany* 24 B7
Parczew, *Poland* 31 G9
Pardes Hanna-Karkur, *Israel* 74 C3
Pardilla, *Spain* 36 D7
Pardo →, *Bahia, Brazil* 125 G11
Pardo →, *Mato Grosso, Brazil* 127 A5
Pardubice, *Czech Rep.* 26 A8
Pardubický □, *Czech Rep.* 26 B8
Pare, *Indonesia* 63 G15
Pare Mts., *Tanzania* 86 C4
Parecis, Serra dos, *Brazil* 124 F7
Paredes de Nava, *Spain* 36 C6
Paren, *Russia* 53 C17
Parent, *Canada* 104 C5
Parent, L., *Canada* 104 C4
Parentis-en-Born, *France* 20 D2
Parepare, *Indonesia* 63 E5
Parfino, *Russia* 32 D6
Párga, *Greece* 46 B2
Pargo, Pta. do, *Madeira* 48 D2
Paria, G. de, *Venezuela* 125 K14
Pariaguán, *Venezuela* 124 B6
Paricutín, Cerro, *Mexico* 118 D4
Parigi, *Indonesia* 63 E6
Parika, *Guyana* 124 B7
Parikkala, *Finland* 32 B5
Parima, Serra, *Brazil* 124 C6
Parinari, *Peru* 124 D4
Pariñas, Pta., *S. Amer.* 122 D2
Parincea, *Romania* 29 D12
Parintins, *Brazil* 125 D7
Pariparit Kyun, *Burma* 67 M18
Paris, *Canada* 116 C4
Paris, *France* 19 D9
Paris, *Idaho, U.S.A.* 108 E8
Paris, *Ky., U.S.A.* 114 F3
Paris, *Tenn., U.S.A.* 115 G1
Paris, *Tex., U.S.A.* 113 J7
Paris, Ville de □, *France* 19 D9
Paris Charles de Gaulle ✕ (CDG), *France* 19 D9
Paris Orly ✕ (ORY), *France* 19 D9
Parish, *U.S.A.* 117 C8
Parishville, *U.S.A.* 117 B10
Park, *U.S.A.* 110 B4
Park City, *U.S.A.* 113 G6

Park Falls, *U.S.A.* 112 C9
Park Head, *Canada* 116 B3
Park Hills, *U.S.A.* 113 G9
Park Range, *U.S.A.* 108 G10
Park Rapids, *U.S.A.* 112 B7
Park River, *U.S.A.* 112 A6
Park Rynie, *S. Africa* 89 E5
Parkā Bandar, *Iran* 71 E8
Parkano, *Finland* 9 E20
Parker, *Ariz., U.S.A.* 111 L12
Parker, *Pa., U.S.A.* 116 E5
Parker Dam, *U.S.A.* 111 L12
Parkersburg, *U.S.A.* 114 F5
Parkes, *Australia* 95 E4
Parkfield, *U.S.A.* 110 K6
Parkhill, *Canada* 116 C3
Parkland, *U.S.A.* 110 C4
Parkston, *U.S.A.* 112 D6
Parksville, *Canada* 102 D4
Parla, *Spain* 36 E7
Pârliţa, *Moldova* 29 C12
Parma, *Italy* 40 D7
Parma, *Idaho, U.S.A.* 108 E5
Parma, *Ohio, U.S.A.* 116 E3
Parma →, *Italy* 40 D7
Paranaguá, *Brazil* 125 F10
Parnaíba, *Brazil* 125 D10
Parnaíba →, *Brazil* 125 D10
Parnassós, *Greece* 46 C4
Párnis, *Greece* 46 C5
Párnitha △, *Greece* 46 C5
Párnon Óros, *Greece* 46 D4
Pärnu, *Estonia* 9 G21
Paroo →, *Australia* 95 E3
Páros, *Greece* 47 D7
Parowan, *U.S.A.* 109 H7
Parpaillon, *France* 21 D10
Parral, *Chile* 126 D1
Parras, *Mexico* 118 B4
Parrett →, *U.K.* 15 F4
Parris I., *U.S.A.* 115 J5
Parrsboro, *Canada* 105 C7
Parry I., *Canada* 116 A4
Parry Is., *Canada* 98 B8
Parry Sound, *Canada* 116 A5
Parsberg, *Germany* 25 F7
Parsęta →, *Poland* 30 D2
Parsnip →, *Canada* 102 B4
Parsons, *U.S.A.* 113 G7
Parsons Ra., *Australia* 94 A2
Partanna, *Italy* 42 E5
Partenio ⌓, *Italy* 43 B7
Parthenay, *France* 18 F6
Partinico, *Italy* 42 D6
Partizánske, *Slovak Rep.* 27 C11
Partridge I., *Canada* 104 A2
Paru →, *Brazil* 125 D8
Parvān □, *Afghan.* 66 B6
Parvatipuram, *India* 67 K13
Parvatsar, *India* 68 F6
Påryd, *Sweden* 11 H9
Parys, *S. Africa* 88 D4
Pas, Pta. des, *Spain* 48 C7
Pas-de-Calais □, *France* 19 B9
Pasada, *Spain* 36 B5
Pasadena, *Canada* 105 C8
Pasadena, *Calif., U.S.A.* 111 L8
Pasadena, *Tex., U.S.A.* 113 L7
Pasaje →, *Argentina* 126 B3
Paşalimanı, *Turkey* 45 F11
Pasar, *Indonesia* 63 J17
Pasay, *Phil.* 61 D4
Pascagoula, *U.S.A.* 113 K10
Pascagoula →, *U.S.A.* 113 K10
Paşcani, *Romania* 29 C11
Pasco, *U.S.A.* 108 C4
Pasco, Cerro de, *Peru* 124 F3
Pasco I., *Australia* 92 D2
Pascoag, *U.S.A.* 117 E13
Pascua, I. de, *Chile* 97 K17
Pasewalk, *Germany* 24 B9
Pasfield L., *Canada* 103 B7
Pasha →, *Russia* 32 B7
Pashmakli = Smolyan, *Bulgaria* 45 E8
Pasinler, *Turkey* 73 C9
Pasir Mas, *Malaysia* 65 J4
Pasir Panjang, *Singapore* 65 d
Pasir Putih, *Malaysia* 65 K4
Pasirian, *Indonesia* 63 H15
Pasirkuning, *Indonesia* 62 E2
Påskallavik, *Sweden* 11 G10
Paskūh, *Iran* 71 E9
Pasłęk, *Poland* 30 D6
Pasłęka →, *Poland* 30 D6
Pasley, C., *Australia* 93 F3
Pašman, *Croatia* 41 E12
Pasni, *Pakistan* 66 G3
Paso Cantinela, *Mexico* 111 N11
Paso de Indios, *Argentina* 128 E3
Paso de los Libres, *Argentina* 126 B4
Paso de los Toros, *Uruguay* 126 C4
Paso Robles, *U.S.A.* 109 J3
Paspébiac, *Canada* 105 C6
Pasrur, *Pakistan* 68 C6
Passage West, *Ireland* 12 E3
Passaic, *U.S.A.* 117 F10
Passau, *Germany* 25 G9
Passero, C., *Italy* 43 F8
Passo Fundo, *Brazil* 127 B5
Passos, *Brazil* 125 H9
Passow, *Germany* 24 B10
Passy, *France* 21 C10
Pastavy, *Belarus* 9 J22
Pastaza →, *Peru* 124 D3
Pasto, *Colombia* 124 C3
Pastrana, *Spain* 38 E2
Pasuruan, *Indonesia* 63 G15
Pasym, *Poland* 30 E7
Pásztó, *Hungary* 28 C4
Patagonia, *Argentina* 128 F3
Patagonia, *U.S.A.* 109 L8
Patambar, *Iran* 71 D9
Patan = Lalitapur, *Nepal* 69 F11
Patan, *Gujarat, India* 66 H8
Patan, *Maharashtra, India* 68 H5
Patani, *Indonesia* 63 D7
Pătârlagele, *Romania* 29 E11
Pataudi, *India* 68 E7
Patchewollock, *Australia* 95 F3
Patchogue, *U.S.A.* 117 F11
Pate, *Kenya* 86 C5
Patea, *N.Z.* 91 H5
Pategi, *Nigeria* 83 D6
Patensie, *S. Africa* 88 E3
Paterna, *Spain* 39 F4
Paternion, *Austria* 26 E6
Paternò, *Italy* 43 E7
Pateros, *U.S.A.* 108 B4
Paterson, *U.S.A.* 117 F10
Paterson Ra., *Australia* 92 D3
Pathankot, *India* 68 C6
Pathein = Bassein, *Burma* 67 L19
Pathfinder Reservoir, *U.S.A.* 108 E10
Pathiu, *Thailand* 65 G2
Pathum Thani, *Thailand* 64 E3
Pati, *Indonesia* 63 G14
Patía →, *Colombia* 124 C3
Patiala, *Punjab, India* 68 D7
Patiala, *Ut. P., India* 69 F8
Patine Kouka, *Senegal* 82 C2
Patitírion, *Greece* 46 B5
Patkai Bum, *India* 67 F19
Pátmos, *Greece* 47 D8
Patna, *India* 69 G11
Patnos, *Turkey* 73 C10
Pato Branco, *Brazil* 127 B5
Patong, Ao, *Thailand* 65 a
Patonga, *Uganda* 86 B3
Patos, *Albania* 44 F3
Patos, *Brazil* 125 E11
Patos, L. dos, *Brazil* 127 C5
Patos, Río de los →, *Argentina* 126 C2
Patos de Minas, *Brazil* 125 G9
Patquía, *Argentina* 126 C2
Pátrai, *Greece* 46 C3
Pátraikós Kólpos, *Greece* 46 C3
Patras = Pátrai, *Greece* 46 C3
Patrocínio, *Brazil* 125 G9
Pattada, *Italy* 42 B2
Pattani, *Thailand* 65 J3
Pattaya, *Thailand* 62 B2
Patten, *U.S.A.* 115 C11
Patterson, *Calif., U.S.A.* 110 H5
Patterson, *La., U.S.A.* 113 L9
Patterson, Mt., *U.S.A.* 110 G7
Patti, *Punjab, India* 68 D6
Patti, *Ut. P., India* 69 G10
Patti, *Italy* 43 D7
Pattoki, *Pakistan* 68 D5
Patton, *U.S.A.* 116 F6
Patuakhali, *Bangla.* 67 H17
Patuanak, *Canada* 103 B7
Patuca △, *Honduras* 120 D2
Patuca →, *Honduras* 120 C3
Patuca, Punta, *Honduras* 120 C3
Pătulele, *Romania* 28 F7
Pátzcuaro, *Mexico* 118 D4
Pau, *France* 20 E3
Pau, Gave de →, *France* 20 E2
Pauillac, *France* 20 C3
Pauk, *Burma* 67 J19
Paul I., *Canada* 105 A7
Paul Smiths, *U.S.A.* 117 B10
Paulatuk, *Canada* 100 B7
Paulhan, *France* 20 E7
Paulis = Isiro, *Dem. Rep. of the Congo* 86 B2
Paulistana, *Brazil* 125 E10
Paulo Afonso, *Brazil* 125 E11
Paulpietersburg, *S. Africa* 89 D5
Pauls Valley, *U.S.A.* 113 H6
Pauma Valley, *U.S.A.* 111 M10
Pauri, *India* 69 D8
Pāveh, *Iran* 70 C5
Pavelets, *Russia* 32 F10
Pavia, *Italy* 40 C6
Pavilion, *U.S.A.* 116 D6
Pavilly, *France* 18 C7
Pāvilosta, *Latvia* 9 H19
Pavlikeni, *Bulgaria* 45 C9
Pavlodar, *Kazakhstan* 52 D8
Pavlograd = Pavlohrad, *Ukraine* 33 H8
Pavlohrad, *Ukraine* 33 H8
Pavlovo, *Russia* 34 C6
Pavlovsk, *Russia* 34 E5
Pavlovskaya, *Russia* 35 G4
Pavlovskiy-Posad, *Russia* 32 E10
Pavullo nel Frignano, *Italy* 40 D7
Pawai, Pulau, *Singapore* 65 d
Pawayan, *India* 69 E9
Pawhuska, *U.S.A.* 113 G6
Pawling, *U.S.A.* 117 E11
Pawnee, *U.S.A.* 113 G6
Pawnee City, *U.S.A.* 112 E6
Pawtucket, *U.S.A.* 117 E13
Paximádhia, *Greece* 49 E6
Paxoí, *Greece* 46 B2
Paxton, *Ill., U.S.A.* 114 E1
Paxton, *Nebr., U.S.A.* 112 E4
Payakumbuh, *Indonesia* 62 E2
Payerne, *Switz.* 25 J2
Payette, *U.S.A.* 108 D5
Paymogo, *Spain* 37 H3
Payne Bay = Kangirsuk, *Canada* 101 B13
Payne L., *Canada* 101 C12
Paynes Find, *Australia* 93 E2
Paynesville, *Liberia* 82 D2
Paynesville, *U.S.A.* 112 C7
Pays de la Loire □, *France* 18 E6
Paysandú, *Uruguay* 126 C4
Payson, *U.S.A.* 109 J8
Paz →, *Guatemala* 120 D1
Paz, B. de la, *Mexico* 118 C2
Pāzanān, *Iran* 71 D6
Pazar, *Turkey* 73 B9
Pazarcık, *Turkey* 72 D7
Pazardzhik, *Bulgaria* 45 D8
Pazarköy, *Turkey* 47 B9
Pazarlar, *Turkey* 47 C11
Pazaryeri, *Turkey* 47 B11
Pazaryolu, *Turkey* 73 B9
Pazin, *Croatia* 41 C10
Pčinja →, *Macedonia* 44 E5
Pe Ell, *U.S.A.* 110 D3
Peabody, *U.S.A.* 117 D14
Peace →, *Canada* 102 B6
Peace Point, *Canada* 102 B6
Peace River, *Canada* 102 B5
Peach Springs, *U.S.A.* 109 J7
Peachland, *Canada* 102 D5
Peachtree City, *U.S.A.* 115 J3
Peak, The = Kinder Scout, *U.K.* 14 D6
Peak Charles △, *Australia* 93 F3
Peak District △, *U.K.* 14 D6
Peak Hill, *N.S.W., Australia* 95 E4
Peak Hill, *W. Austral., Australia* 93 E2
Peak Ra., *Australia* 94 C4
Peake Cr. →, *Australia* 95 D2
Peal de Becerro, *Spain* 37 H7
Peale, Mt., *U.S.A.* 109 G9
Pearblossom, *U.S.A.* 111 L9
Pearl →, *U.S.A.* 113 K10
Pearl City, *U.S.A.* 106 H16
Pearl Harbor, *U.S.A.* 106 H16
Pearl River = Zhu Jiang →, *China* 59 F9
Pearl River, *U.S.A.* 117 E10
Pearsall, *U.S.A.* 113 L5
Peary Land, *Greenland* 4 A6
Pease →, *U.S.A.* 113 H5
Peawanuck, *Canada* 101 C11
Pebane, *Mozam.* 87 F4
Pebas, *Peru* 124 D4
Pebble Beach, *U.S.A.* 110 J5
Peć, *Serbia & M.* 44 D4
Péccioli, *Italy* 40 E7
Pechea, *Romania* 29 E12
Pechenga, *Russia* 52 C4
Pechenizhyn, *Ukraine* 33 H3
Pechiguera, Pta., *Canary Is.* 48 F6
Pechnezhskoye Vdkhr., *Ukraine* 33 G9
Pechora, *Russia* 52 C6
Pechora →, *Russia* 52 C6
Pechorskaya Guba, *Russia* 52 C6
Pecica, *Romania* 28 D6
Pecka, *Serbia & M.* 44 B3
Pécora, C., *Italy* 42 C1
Pečory, *Russia* 9 H22
Pecos, *U.S.A.* 113 K3
Pecos →, *U.S.A.* 113 L3
Pécs, *Hungary* 28 D3
Pedder, L., *Australia* 95 G4
Peddie, *S. Africa* 89 E4
Pedernales, *Dom. Rep.* 121 C5
Pedieos →, *Cyprus* 49 D12
Pedirka, *Australia* 95 D2
Pedra Azul, *Brazil* 125 G10
Pedreguer, *Spain* 39 G5
Pedreiras, *Brazil* 125 D10
Pedro Afonso, *Brazil* 125 E9
Pedro Cays, *Jamaica* 120 C4
Pedro de Valdivia, *Chile* 126 A2
Pedro Juan Caballero, *Paraguay* 127 A4
Pedro Muñoz, *Spain* 37 F8
Pedrógão Grande, *Portugal* 36 F2
Pee Dee →, *U.S.A.* 115 J6
Peebinga, *Australia* 95 E3
Peebles, *U.K.* 13 F5
Peekskill, *U.S.A.* 117 E11
Peel, *U.K.* 14 C3
Peel →, *Australia* 95 E5
Peel →, *Canada* 100 B6
Peel Sd., *Canada* 100 A10
Peene →, *Germany* 24 A9
Peera Peera Poolanna L., *Australia* 95 D2
Peerless Lake, *Canada* 102 B6
Peers, *Canada* 102 C5
Pegasus Bay, *N.Z.* 91 K4
Peggau, *Austria* 26 D8
Pegnitz, *Germany* 25 F7
Pegnitz →, *Germany* 25 F6
Pego, *Spain* 39 G4
Pegu, *Burma* 67 L20
Pegu Yoma, *Burma* 67 K20
Pehčevo, *Macedonia* 44 E6
Pehlivanköy, *Turkey* 45 E10
Pehuajó, *Argentina* 126 D3
Pei Xian = Pizhou, *China* 56 G9
Peine, *Chile* 126 A2
Peine, *Germany* 24 C6
Peip'ing = Beijing, *China* 56 E9
Peipus, L. = Chudskoye, Ozero, *Russia* 9 G22
Peissenberg, *Germany* 25 H7
Peitz, *Germany* 24 D10
Peixe, *Brazil* 125 F9
Peixe →, *Brazil* 125 H8
Pek →, *Serbia & M.* 44 B5
Pekalongan, *Indonesia* 63 G13
Pekan, *Malaysia* 65 L4
Pekan Nenas, *Malaysia* 65 d
Pekanbaru, *Indonesia* 62 D2
Pekang, *Taiwan* 59 F13
Pekin, *U.S.A.* 112 E10
Peking = Beijing, *China* 56 E9
Pekutatan, *Indonesia* 63 J17
Péla, *Guinea* 82 D3
Pelabuhan Kelang, *Malaysia* 65 L3
Pelabuhan Ratu, Teluk, *Indonesia* 63 G12
Pelabuhanratu, *Indonesia* 63 G12
Pélagos, *Greece* 46 B6
Pelaihari, *Indonesia* 62 E4
Pelat, Mt., *France* 21 D10
Pełczyce, *Poland* 31 E2
Peleaga, Vf., *Romania* 28 E7
Pelée, Mt., *Martinique* 120 c
Pelee, Pt., *Canada* 104 D3
Pelee I., *Canada* 116 E2
Pelekech, *Kenya* 86 B4
Peleng, *Indonesia* 63 E6
Pelentong, *Malaysia* 65 d
Pélézi, *Ivory C.* 82 D3
Pelhřimov, *Czech Rep.* 26 B8
Pelican, *U.S.A.* 102 B1
Pelican L., *Canada* 103 C8
Pelican Narrows, *Canada* 103 B8
Pelister △, *Macedonia* 44 F5
Pelješac, *Croatia* 41 F14
Pelkosenniemi, *Finland* 8 C22
Pella, *Greece* 44 F6
Pella, *S. Africa* 88 D2
Pella, *U.S.A.* 112 E8
Pélla □, *Greece* 44 F6
Pello, *Finland* 8 C21
Pellworm, *Germany* 24 A4
Pelly →, *Canada* 100 B6
Pelly Bay, *Canada* 101 B11
Peloponnese = Pelopónnisos □, *Greece* 46 D4
Pelopónnisos □, *Greece* 46 D4
Peloritani, Monti, *Italy* 43 D8
Pelorus Sd., *N.Z.* 91 J4
Pelotas, *Brazil* 127 C5
Pelotas →, *Brazil* 127 B5
Pelovo, *Bulgaria* 45 C8
Pelplin, *Poland* 30 E5
Pelvoux, Massif du, *France* 21 D10
Pemalang, *Indonesia* 63 G13
Pemanggil, Pulau, *Malaysia* 65 L5
Pematangsiantar, *Indonesia* 62 D1
Pemba, *Mozam.* 87 E5
Pemba, *Zambia* 87 F2
Pemba Channel, *Tanzania* 86 D4
Pemba I., *Tanzania* 86 D4
Pemberton, *Australia* 93 F2
Pemberton, *Canada* 102 C4
Pembina, *U.S.A.* 112 A6
Pembroke, *Canada* 104 C4
Pembroke, *U.K.* 15 F3
Pembrokeshire □, *U.K.* 15 F3
Pembrokeshire Coast △, *U.K.* 15 F2
Pen-y-Ghent, *U.K.* 14 C5
Peña, Sierra de la, *Spain* 38 C4
Peña de Francia, Sierra de la, *Spain* 36 E4
Penafiel, *Portugal* 36 D2
Peñafiel, *Spain* 36 D6
Peñaflor, *Spain* 37 H5
Penal, *Trin. & Tob.* 125 K15
Peñalara, *Spain* 36 E7
Penamacôr, *Portugal* 36 E3
Penang = Pinang, *Malaysia* 65 c
Penápolis, *Brazil* 127 A6
Peñaranda de Bracamonte, *Spain* 36 E5
Peñarroya, *Spain* 38 E4
Peñarroya-Pueblonuevo, *Spain* 37 G5
Penarth, *U.K.* 15 F4
Peñas, C. de, *Spain* 36 B5
Penas, G. de, *Chile* 128 F2
Peñas de San Pedro, *Spain* 39 G3
Peñas del Chache, *Canary Is.* 48 E6
Peñausende, *Spain* 36 D5
Pench'i = Benxi, *China* 57 D12
Pend Oreille →, *U.S.A.* 108 B5
Pend Oreille, L., *U.S.A.* 108 C5
Pendálofon, *Greece* 44 F5
Pendembu, *Eastern, S. Leone* 82 D2
Pendembu, *Northern, S. Leone* 82 D2
Pender B., *Australia* 92 C3
Pendik, *Turkey* 45 F13
Pendjari △, *Benin* 83 C5
Pendjari →, *Benin* 83 C5
Pendleton, *U.S.A.* 108 D4
Pendra, *India* 69 H9
Peneda-Gerês △, *Portugal* 36 D2
Penedo, *Brazil* 125 F11
Penelokan, *Indonesia* 63 J18
Penetanguishene, *Canada* 116 B5
Penfield, *U.S.A.* 116 E6
Pengalengan, *Indonesia* 63 G12
Penge, *Kasai-Or., Dem. Rep. of the Congo* 86 D1
Penge, *Sud-Kivu, Dem. Rep. of the Congo* 86 C2
P'enghu Ch'üntou, *Taiwan* 59 F12
Penglai, *China* 57 F11
Pengshan, *China* 58 B4
Pengshui, *China* 58 C7
Penguin, *Australia* 95 G4
Pengxi, *China* 58 B5
Pengze, *China* 59 C11
Penhalonga, *Zimbabwe* 87 F3
Peniche, *Portugal* 37 F1
Penicuik, *U.K.* 13 F5
Penida, Nusa, *Indonesia* 63 K18
Peninnes, Alpes = Pennine, Alpi, *Alps* 25 J3
Peninsular Malaysia □, *Malaysia* 65 L4
Peñíscola, *Spain* 38 E5
Penitente, Serra do, *Brazil* 125 E9
Penkridge, *U.K.* 14 E5
Penmarch, *France* 18 E2
Penmarch, Pte. de, *France* 18 E2
Penn Hills, *U.S.A.* 116 F5
Penn Yan, *U.S.A.* 116 D7
Penna, Punta della, *Italy* 41 F11
Pennant, *Canada* 103 C7
Penne, *Italy* 41 F10
Penner →, *India* 66 M12
Pennine, Alpi, *Alps* 25 J3
Pennines, *U.K.* 14 C5
Pennington, *U.S.A.* 110 F5
Pennington →, *Nigeria* 83 E6
Pennino, Mte., *Italy* 41 E9
Pennsburg, *U.S.A.* 117 F9
Pennsylvania □, *U.S.A.* 114 E7
Penny, *Canada* 102 C4
Peno, *Russia* 32 D7
Penobscot →, *U.S.A.* 115 C11
Penobscot B., *U.S.A.* 115 C11
Penola, *Australia* 95 F3
Penong, *Australia* 93 F5
Penonomé, *Panama* 120 E3
Penrith, *Australia* 95 E5
Penrith, *U.K.* 14 C5
Penryn, *U.K.* 15 G2
Pensacola, *U.S.A.* 115 K2
Pensacola Mts., *Antarctica* 5 E1
Pense, *Canada* 103 C8
Penshurst, *Australia* 95 F3
Penticton, *Canada* 102 D5
Pentland, *Australia* 94 C4
Pentland Firth, *U.K.* 13 C5
Pentland Hills, *U.K.* 13 F5
Pentland Hills ⌓, *U.K.* 13 F5
Penza, *Russia* 34 D7
Penzance, *U.K.* 15 G2
Penzberg, *Germany* 25 H7
Penzhino, *Russia* 53 C17
Penzhinskaya Guba, *Russia* 53 C17
Penzhou, *China* 58 B4
Penzlin, *Germany* 24 B9
Peoria, *Ariz., U.S.A.* 109 K7
Peoria, *Ill., U.S.A.* 112 E10
Pepacton Reservoir, *U.S.A.* 117 D10
Pepani →, *S. Africa* 88 D3
Pepel, *S. Leone* 82 D2
Peqin, *Albania* 44 E3
Pera Hd., *Australia* 94 A3
Perabumulih, *Indonesia* 62 E2
Perak →, *Malaysia* 65 K3
Perakhóra, *Greece* 46 C4
Perales de Alfambra, *Spain* 38 E4
Perales del Puerto, *Spain* 36 E4
Pérama, *Kérkira, Greece* 49 A3
Pérama, *Kríti, Greece* 49 D6
Perancak, *Indonesia* 63 J17
Peräpohjola, *Finland* 8 C22
Perast, *Serbia & M.* 44 D2
Percé, *Canada* 105 C7
Perche, *France* 18 D8
Perche ⌓, *France* 18 D7
Perchtoldsdorf, *Austria* 27 C9
Percival Lakes, *Australia* 92 D4
Percy, *France* 18 D5
Percy Is., *Australia* 94 C5
Perdido, Mte., *Spain* 38 C5
Perdu, Mt. = Perdido, Mte., *Spain* 38 C5
Pereira, *Colombia* 124 C3
Perelazovskiy, *Russia* 35 F6
Perenjori, *Australia* 93 E2
Peresecina, *Moldova* 29 C13
Pereslavl-Zalesskiy, *Russia* 32 D10
Peretu, *Romania* 29 F10
Pereyaslav-Khmelnytskyy, *Ukraine* 33 G6
Pérez, I., *Mexico* 119 C7
Perg, *Austria* 26 C7
Pergamino, *Argentina* 126 C3
Pergau →, *Malaysia* 65 K3
Pérgine Valsugana, *Italy* 41 B8
Pérgola, *Italy* 41 E9
Perham, *U.S.A.* 112 B7
Perhentian, Kepulauan, *Malaysia* 65 K4
Periam, *Romania* 28 D5
Péribonka →, *Canada* 105 C5
Péribonka, L., *Canada* 105 B5
Perico, *Argentina* 126 A2
Pericos, *Mexico* 118 B3
Périers, *France* 18 C5
Périgord, *France* 20 D4
Périgord-Limousin ⌓, *France* 20 C4
Périgueux, *France* 20 C4
Perijá △, *Venezuela* 121 E5
Perijá, Sierra de, *Colombia* 124 B4
Peristéra, *Greece* 46 B5
Peristerona →, *Cyprus* 49 D12
Perito Moreno, *Argentina* 128 F2
Perivol = Dragovishtitsa, *Bulgaria* 44 D6
Perkasie, *U.S.A.* 117 F9
Perković, *Croatia* 41 E13
Perlas, Arch. de las, *Panama* 120 E4
Perlas, Punta de, *Nic.* 120 D3
Perleberg, *Germany* 24 B7
Perlez, *Serbia & M.* 28 E5
Perm, *Russia* 52 D6
Përmet, *Albania* 44 F4
Pernambuco = Recife, *Brazil* 125 E12
Pernambuco □, *Brazil* 125 E11
Pernatty Lagoon, *Australia* 95 E2
Pernik, *Bulgaria* 44 D7
Peron Is., *Australia* 92 B5
Peron Pen., *Australia* 93 E1
Péronne, *France* 19 C9
Perosa Argentina, *Italy* 40 D4
Perow, *Canada* 102 C3
Perpignan, *France* 20 F6
Perris, *U.S.A.* 111 M9
Perros-Guirec, *France* 18 D3
Perry, *Fla., U.S.A.* 115 K4
Perry, *Ga., U.S.A.* 115 J4
Perry, *Iowa, U.S.A.* 112 E7
Perry, *Okla., U.S.A.* 113 G6
Perryton, *U.S.A.* 113 G4
Perryville, *U.S.A.* 113 G10
Persan, *France* 19 C9
Persberg, *Sweden* 10 E8
Perşembe, *Turkey* 72 B7
Persepolis, *Iran* 71 D7
Pershotravensk, *Ukraine* 33 G4
Persia = Iran ■, *Asia* 71 C7
Persian Gulf = Gulf, The, *Asia* 71 E6
Perstorp, *Sweden* 11 H7
Pertek, *Turkey* 73 C8
Perth, *Australia* 93 F2
Perth, *Canada* 117 B8
Perth, *U.K.* 13 E5
Perth & Kinross □, *U.K.* 13 E5
Perth Amboy, *U.S.A.* 117 F10

Perth-Andover, *Canada* 105 C6
Pertuis, *France* 21 E9
Pertusato, C., *France* 21 G13
Peru, *Ind., U.S.A.* 114 E2
Peru, *N.Y., U.S.A.* 117 B11
Peru ■, *S. Amer.* 124 D4
Peru Basin, *Pac. Oc.* 97 J18
Peru-Chile Trench, *Pac. Oc.* 124 G3
Perúgia, *Italy* 41 E9
Perušić, *Croatia* 41 D12
Pervomaysk, *Russia* 34 C6
Pervomaysk, *Ukraine* 33 H6
Pervouralsk, *Russia* 52 D6
Pésaro, *Italy* 41 E9
Pescadores = P'enghu Ch'üntou, *Taiwan* 59 F12
Pescara, *Italy* 41 F11
Pescara →, *Italy* 41 F11
Peschanokopskoye, *Russia* 35 G5
Péscia, *Italy* 40 E7
Pescina, *Italy* 41 F10
Peshawar, *Pakistan* 68 B4
Peshkopi, *Albania* 44 E4
Peshtera, *Bulgaria* 45 D8
Peshtigo, *U.S.A.* 114 C2
Peski, *Russia* 34 E6
Pêso da Régua, *Portugal* 36 D3
Pesqueira, *Brazil* 125 E11
Pessac, *France* 20 D3
Pest □, *Hungary* 28 C4
Pestovo, *Russia* 32 C8
Pestravka, *Russia* 34 D9
Péta, *Greece* 46 B3
Petah Tiqwa, *Israel* 74 C3
Petalídhion, *Greece* 46 E3
Petaling Jaya, *Malaysia* 65 L3
Petaloudhes, *Greece* 49 C10
Petaluma, *U.S.A.* 110 G4
Pétange, *Lux.* 17 E5
Petaro, *Pakistan* 68 G3
Petatlán, *Mexico* 118 D4
Petauke, *Zambia* 87 E3
Petawawa, *Canada* 104 C4
Petén Itzá, L., *Guatemala* 120 C2
Peter I., *Br. Virgin Is.* 121 e
Peter I.s Øy, *Antarctica* 5 C16
Peter Pond L., *Canada* 103 B7
Peterbell, *Canada* 104 C3
Peterborough, *Australia* 95 E2
Peterborough, *Canada* 116 B6
Peterborough, *U.K.* 15 E7
Peterborough, *U.S.A.* 117 D13
Peterborough □, *U.K.* 15 E7
Peterculter, *U.K.* 13 D6
Peterhead, *U.K.* 13 D7
Peterlee, *U.K.* 14 C6
Petermann Bjerg, *Greenland* 98 B17
Petermann Ranges, *Australia* 92 E5
Petersburg, *Alaska, U.S.A.* 100 C6
Petersburg, *Pa., U.S.A.* 116 F6
Petersburg, *Va., U.S.A.* 114 G7
Petersburg, *W. Va., U.S.A.* 114 F6
Petersfield, *U.K.* 15 F7
Petershagen, *Germany* 24 C4
Petília Policastro, *Italy* 43 C9
Petit-Canal, *Guadeloupe* 120 b
Petit Goâve, *Haiti* 121 C5
Petit Jardin, *Canada* 105 C8
Petit Lac Manicouagan, *Canada* 105 B6
Petit-Mécatina →, *Canada* 105 B8
Petit-Mécatina, Î. du, *Canada* 105 B8
Petit Piton, *St. Lucia* 121 f
Petit-Saguenay, *Canada* 105 C5
Petit Saint Bernard, Col du, *Italy* 21 C10
Petitcodiac, *Canada* 105 C6
Petite Terre, Iles de la, *Guadeloupe* 120 b
Petitot →, *Canada* 102 A4
Petitsikapau L., *Canada* 105 B6
Petlad, *India* 68 H5
Peto, *Mexico* 119 C7
Petone, *N.Z.* 91 J5
Petorca, *Chile* 126 C1
Petoskey, *U.S.A.* 114 C3
Petra, *Jordan* 74 E4
Petra, *Spain* 48 B10
Petra, Ostrova, *Russia* 4 B13
Petra Velikogo, Zaliv, *Russia* 54 C6
Petrel = Petrer, *Spain* 39 G4
Petrella, Monte, *Italy* 42 A6
Petrer, *Spain* 39 G4
Petreto-Bicchisano, *France* 21 G12
Petrich, *Bulgaria* 44 E7
Petrified Forest △, *U.S.A.* 109 J9
Petrijanec, *Croatia* 41 B13
Petrikov = Pyetrikaw, *Belarus* 33 F5
Petrila, *Romania* 29 E8
Petrinja, *Croatia* 41 C13
Petrodvorets, *Russia* 32 C5
Petrograd = Sankt-Peterburg, *Russia* 32 C6
Petrolândia, *Brazil* 125 E11
Petrolia, *Canada* 116 D2
Petrolina, *Brazil* 125 E10
Petropavl, *Kazakhstan* 52 D7
Petropavlovsk = Petropavl, *Kazakhstan* 52 D7
Petropavlovsk-Kamchatskiy, *Russia* 53 D16
Petropavlovskiy = Akhtubinsk, *Russia* 35 F8
Petrópolis, *Brazil* 127 A7
Petroşani, *Romania* 29 E8
Petrova Gora, *Croatia* 41 C12
Petrovac, *Serbia & M.* 44 D2
Petrovac, *Serbia & M.* 44 B5
Petrovaradin, *Serbia & M.* 28 E4
Petrovsk, *Russia* 34 D7
Petrovsk-Zabaykalskiy, *Russia* 53 D11
Petrovskaya, *Russia* 33 K9
Petrovskoye = Svetlograd, *Russia* 35 H6
Petrozavodsk, *Russia* 32 B8
Petrus Steyn, *S. Africa* 89 D4
Petrusburg, *S. Africa* 88 D4
Petzeck, *Austria* 26 E5
Peumo, *Chile* 126 C1
Peureulak, *Indonesia* 62 D1
Pevek, *Russia* 53 C18
Peveragno, *Italy* 40 D4
Peyrehorade, *France* 20 E2
Peyruis, *France* 21 D9
Pézenas, *France* 20 E7
Pezinok, *Slovak Rep.* 27 C10
Pfaffenhofen, *Germany* 25 G7
Pfälzerwald ⌂, *Germany* 25 F5
Pfarrkirchen, *Germany* 25 G8
Pfeffenhausen, *Germany* 25 G7
Pforzheim, *Germany* 25 G4
Pfullendorf, *Germany* 25 H5
Pfungstadt, *Germany* 25 F4
Pha Taem △, *Thailand* 64 E5
Phagwara, *India* 66 D9
Phaistós, *Greece* 49 D6
Phala, *Botswana* 88 C4
Phalera = Phulera, *India* 68 F6
Phalodi, *India* 68 F5
Phalsbourg, *France* 19 D14
Phaluai, Ko, *Thailand* 65 b
Phan, *Thailand* 64 C2
Phan Rang, *Vietnam* 65 G7
Phan Ri = Hoa Da, *Vietnam* 65 G7
Phan Thiet, *Vietnam* 65 G7
Phanae, *Greece* 47 C7
Phanat Nikhom, *Thailand* 64 F3
Phangan, Ko, *Thailand* 65 H3
Phangnga, *Thailand* 65 H2
Phangnga, Ao, *Thailand* 65 a
Phanom Sarakham, *Thailand* 64 F3
Phaphund, *India* 69 F8
Pharenda, *India* 69 F10
Pharr, *U.S.A.* 113 M5
Phatthalung, *Thailand* 65 J3
Phayao, *Thailand* 64 C2
Phelps, *U.S.A.* 116 D7
Phelps L., *Canada* 103 B8
Phenix City, *U.S.A.* 115 J3
Phet Buri, *Thailand* 64 F2
Phetchabun, *Thailand* 64 D3
Phetchabun, Thiu Khao, *Thailand* 64 E3
Phetchaburi = Phet Buri, *Thailand* 64 F2
Phi Phi, Ko, *Thailand* 65 J2
Phiafay, *Laos* 64 E6
Phibun Mangsahan, *Thailand* 64 E5
Phichai, *Thailand* 64 D3
Phichit, *Thailand* 64 D3
Philadelphia, *Miss., U.S.A.* 113 J10
Philadelphia, *N.Y., U.S.A.* 117 B9
Philadelphia, *Pa., U.S.A.* 117 G9
Philip, *U.S.A.* 112 C4
Philippeville, *Belgium* 17 D4
Philippi, *Greece* 45 E8
Philippi, *U.S.A.* 114 F5
Philippi L., *Australia* 94 C2
Philippine Sea, *Pac. Oc.* 50 H16
Philippines ■, *Asia* 61 F5
Philippolis, *S. Africa* 88 E4
Philippopolis = Plovdiv, *Bulgaria* 45 D8
Philipsburg, *Canada* 117 A11
Philipsburg, *Mont., U.S.A.* 108 C7
Philipsburg, *Pa., U.S.A.* 116 F6
Philipstown = Daingean, *Ireland* 12 C4
Philipstown, *S. Africa* 88 E3
Phillip I., *Australia* 95 F4
Phillips, *U.S.A.* 112 C9
Phillipsburg, *Kans., U.S.A.* 112 F5
Phillipsburg, *N.J., U.S.A.* 117 F9
Philmont, *U.S.A.* 117 D11
Philomath, *U.S.A.* 108 D2
Phimai, *Thailand* 64 E4
Phitsanulok, *Thailand* 64 D3
Phnom Dangrek, *Thailand* 62 B2
Phnom Penh, *Cambodia* 65 G5
Phnum Penh = Phnom Penh, *Cambodia* 65 G5
Phoenicia, *U.S.A.* 117 D10
Phoenix, *Ariz., U.S.A.* 109 K7
Phoenix, *N.Y., U.S.A.* 117 C8
Phoenix Is., *Kiribati* 96 H10
Phoenixville, *U.S.A.* 117 F9
Phon, *Thailand* 64 E4
Phon Tiou, *Laos* 64 D5
Phong →, *Thailand* 64 D4
Phong Saly, *Laos* 58 G4
Phong Tho, *Vietnam* 64 A4
Phonhong, *Laos* 64 C4
Phonum, *Thailand* 65 H2
Phosphate Hill, *Australia* 94 C2
Photharam, *Thailand* 64 F2
Phra Nakhon Si Ayutthaya, *Thailand* 64 E3
Phra Thong, Ko, *Thailand* 65 H2
Phrae, *Thailand* 64 C3
Phrom Phiram, *Thailand* 64 D3
Phrygia, *Turkey* 72 C4
Phu Chong-Na Yoi △, *Thailand* 64 E5
Phu Dien, *Vietnam* 64 C5
Phu Hin Rang Kla △, *Thailand* 64 D3
Phu Kradung △, *Thailand* 64 D3
Phu Loi, *Laos* 64 B4
Phu Luang △, *Thailand* 64 D3
Phu Ly, *Vietnam* 58 G5
Phu Phan △, *Thailand* 64 D4
Phu Quoc, Dao, *Vietnam* 65 G4
Phu Tho, *Vietnam* 58 G5
Phuc Yen, *Vietnam* 58 G5
Phuket, *Thailand* 65 a
Phuket, Ko, *Thailand* 65 a
Phul, *India* 68 D6
Phulad, *India* 68 G5
Phulchari, *Bangla.* 69 G13
Phulera, *India* 68 F6
Phulpur, *India* 69 G10
Phun Phin, *Thailand* 65 H2
Piacenza, *Italy* 40 C6
Piai, Tanjung, *Malaysia* 65 d
Pian Cr. →, *Australia* 95 E4
Pian-Upe ⌂, *Uganda* 86 B3
Piana, *France* 21 F12
Pianella, *Italy* 41 F11
Pianosa, *Puglia, Italy* 41 F12
Pianosa, *Toscana, Italy* 40 F7
Piapot, *Canada* 103 D7
Pias, *Portugal* 37 G3
Piaseczno, *Poland* 31 F8
Piaski, *Poland* 31 G9
Piastów, *Poland* 31 F7
Piatra, *Romania* 29 G10
Piatra Craiului △, *Romania* 29 E10
Piatra Neamţ, *Romania* 29 D11
Piatra Olt, *Romania* 29 F9
Piauí □, *Brazil* 125 E10
Piauí →, *Brazil* 125 E10
Piave →, *Italy* 41 C9
Piazza Ármerina, *Italy* 43 E7
Pibor →, *Sudan* 81 F3
Pibor Post, *Sudan* 81 F3
Picardie, *France* 19 C10
Picardie, Plaine de, *France* 19 C9
Picardy = Picardie, *France* 19 C10
Picayune, *U.S.A.* 113 K10
Picerno, *Italy* 43 B8
Pichhor, *India* 69 G8
Pichilemu, *Chile* 126 C1
Pichor, *India* 68 G8
Pickerel L., *Canada* 104 C1
Pickering, *U.K.* 14 C7
Pickering, Vale of, *U.K.* 14 C7
Pickle Lake, *Canada* 104 B1
Pickwick L., *U.S.A.* 115 H1
Pico Bonito △, *Honduras* 120 C2
Pico Truncado, *Argentina* 128 F3
Picos, *Brazil* 125 E10
Picos de Europa △, *Spain* 36 B6
Picton, *Australia* 95 E5
Picton, *Canada* 116 B7
Picton, *N.Z.* 91 J5
Pictou, *Canada* 105 C7
Picture Butte, *Canada* 102 D6
Pictured Rocks ⌂, *U.S.A.* 114 B2
Picún Leufú, *Argentina* 128 D3
Pidurutalagala, *Sri Lanka* 66 R12
Piechowice, *Poland* 31 H2
Piedimonte Matese, *Italy* 43 A7
Piedmont = Piemonte □, *Italy* 40 D5
Piedmont, *Ala., U.S.A.* 115 J3
Piedmont, *S.C., U.S.A.* 107 D10
Piedra →, *Spain* 38 D3
Piedrabuena, *Spain* 37 G6
Piedrahita, *Spain* 36 E5
Piedralaves, *Spain* 36 E6
Piedras Blancas, *Spain* 36 B5
Piedras Negras, *Mexico* 118 B4
Piekary Śląskie, *Poland* 31 H5
Pieksämäki, *Finland* 9 E22
Piemonte □, *Italy* 40 D5
Pienaarsrivier, *S. Africa* 89 D4
Pieniężno, *Poland* 30 D7
Pieninský △, *Europe* 27 B13
Pieńsk, *Poland* 31 G2
Piercefield, *U.S.A.* 117 B10
Pierceland, *Canada* 103 C7
Piería □, *Greece* 44 F6
Pierpont, *U.S.A.* 116 E4
Pierre, *U.S.A.* 112 C4
Pierre-Buffière, *France* 20 C5
Pierre-de-Bresse, *France* 19 F12
Pierrefontaine-les-Varans, *France* 19 E13
Pierrefort, *France* 20 D6
Pierrelatte, *France* 21 D8
Pierreville, *Trin. & Tob.* 125 K16
Pieštany, *Slovak Rep.* 27 C10
Piesting →, *Austria* 27 C9
Pieszyce, *Poland* 31 H3
Piet Retief, *S. Africa* 89 D5
Pietarsaari, *Finland* 8 E20
Pietermaritzburg, *S. Africa* 89 D5
Pietersburg = Polokwane, *S. Africa* 89 C4
Pietragalla, *Italy* 43 B8
Pietrasanta, *Italy* 40 E7
Pietroşiţa, *Romania* 29 E10
Pietrosul, Vf., *Maramureş, Romania* 29 C9
Pietrosul, Vf., *Suceava, Romania* 29 C10
Pieve di Cadore, *Italy* 41 B9
Pieve di Teco, *Italy* 40 D4
Pievepélago, *Italy* 40 D7
Pigadhítsa, *Greece* 44 G5
Pigeon L., *Canada* 116 B6
Piggott, *U.S.A.* 113 G9
Pigna, *Italy* 40 E4
Pigüe, *Argentina* 126 D3
Pihani, *India* 69 F9
Pihlajavesi, *Finland* 9 F23
Pijijiapan, *Mexico* 119 D6
Pikalevo, *Russia* 32 C8
Pikangikum Berens, *Canada* 103 C10
Pikes Peak, *U.S.A.* 112 F2
Piketberg, *S. Africa* 88 E2
Pikeville, *U.S.A.* 114 G4
Pikou, *China* 57 E12
Pikwitonei, *Canada* 103 B9
Piła, *Poland* 31 E3
Pila, *Spain* 39 G3
Pilaía, *Greece* 44 F6
Pilanesberg △, *S. Africa* 88 D4
Pilani, *India* 68 E6
Pilar, *Paraguay* 126 B4
Pilar de la Horadada, *Spain* 39 H4
Pilat ⌂, *France* 21 C8
Pilawa, *Poland* 31 G8
Pilaya →, *Bolivia* 124 H6
Pilbara, *Australia* 92 D2
Pilcomayo →, *Paraguay* 126 B4
Pilgrim's Rest, *S. Africa* 89 C5
Pilgrimstad, *Sweden* 10 B9
Píli, *Greece* 47 E9
Pilibhit, *India* 69 E8
Pilica →, *Poland* 31 G8
Pilion, *Greece* 46 B5
Pilis, *Hungary* 28 C4
Pilisvörösvár, *Hungary* 28 C3
Pilkhawa, *India* 68 E7
Pilliga, *Australia* 95 E4
Pílos, *Greece* 46 E3
Pilot Mound, *Canada* 103 D9
Pilot Point, *U.S.A.* 113 J6
Pilot Rock, *U.S.A.* 108 D4
Pilsen = Plzeň, *Czech Rep.* 26 B6
Pilštanj, *Slovenia* 41 B12
Piltene, *Latvia* 30 A8
Pilzno, *Poland* 31 J8
Pima, *U.S.A.* 109 K9
Pimba, *Australia* 95 E2
Pimenta Bueno, *Brazil* 124 F6
Pimentel, *Peru* 124 E3
Pina de Ebro, *Spain* 38 D4
Pinamalayan, *Phil.* 61 E4
Pinang, *Malaysia* 65 c
Pinar, C. des, *Spain* 48 B10
Pinar del Río, *Cuba* 120 B3
Pınarbaşı, *Çanakkale, Turkey* 47 B8
Pınarbaşı, *Kayseri, Turkey* 72 C7
Pınarhisar, *Turkey* 45 E11
Pinatubo, Mt., *Phil.* 61 D3
Pincehely, *Hungary* 28 D3
Pinchang, *China* 58 B6
Pincher Creek, *Canada* 102 D6
Pinchi L., *Canada* 102 C4
Pinckneyville, *U.S.A.* 112 F10
Pińczów, *Poland* 31 H7
Pindar, *Australia* 93 E2
Pindi Gheb, *Pakistan* 68 C5
Pindiga, *Nigeria* 83 D7
Pindos △, *Greece* 46 B3
Pindos Óros, *Greece* 46 B3
Pindus Mts. = Pindos Óros, *Greece* 46 B3
Pine →, *B.C., Canada* 102 B4
Pine →, *Sask., Canada* 103 B7
Pine, C., *Canada* 105 C9
Pine Bluff, *U.S.A.* 113 H9
Pine Bluffs, *U.S.A.* 112 E2
Pine City, *U.S.A.* 112 C8
Pine Cr. →, *U.S.A.* 116 E7
Pine Creek, *Australia* 92 B5
Pine Falls, *Canada* 103 C9
Pine Flat Res., *U.S.A.* 110 J7
Pine Grove, *U.S.A.* 117 F8
Pine Pass, *Canada* 102 B4
Pine Point, *Canada* 102 A6
Pine Ridge, *U.S.A.* 112 D3
Pine River, *Canada* 103 C8
Pine River, *U.S.A.* 112 B7
Pine Valley, *U.S.A.* 111 N10
Pinecrest, *U.S.A.* 110 G6
Pineda de Mar, *Spain* 38 D7
Pinedale, *Calif., U.S.A.* 110 J7
Pinedale, *Wyo., U.S.A.* 108 E9
Pinega →, *Russia* 52 C5
Pinehill, *Australia* 94 C4
Pinehouse L., *Canada* 103 B7
Pineimuta →, *Canada* 104 B1
Pinerolo, *Italy* 40 D4
Pineto, *Italy* 41 F11
Pinetop, *U.S.A.* 109 J9
Pinetown, *S. Africa* 89 D5
Pineville, *U.S.A.* 113 K8
Piney, *France* 19 D11
Ping →, *Thailand* 64 E3
Pingaring, *Australia* 93 F2
Pingba, *China* 58 D6
Pingbian, *China* 58 F4
Pingchuan, *China* 58 D3
Pingding, *China* 56 F7
Pingdingshan, *China* 56 H7
Pingdong, *Taiwan* 59 F13
Pingdu, *China* 57 F10
Pingelly, *Australia* 93 F2
Pingguo, *China* 58 F6
Pinghe, *China* 59 E11
Pinghu, *China* 59 B13
Pingjiang, *China* 59 C9
Pingle, *China* 59 E8
Pingli, *China* 58 A7
Pingliang, *China* 56 G4
Pinglu, *China* 56 E7
Pingluo, *China* 56 E4
Pingnan, *Fujian, China* 59 D12
Pingnan, *Guangxi Zhuangzu, China* 59 F8
Pingquan, *China* 57 D10
Pingrup, *Australia* 93 F2
Pingshan, *China* 58 C5
Pingtan, *China* 59 E12
Pingtang, *China* 58 E6
P'ingtung, *Taiwan* 59 F13
Pingwu, *China* 56 H3
Pingxiang, *Guangxi Zhuangzu, China* 58 F6
Pingxiang, *Jiangxi, China* 59 D9
Pingyao, *China* 56 F7
Pingyi, *China* 57 G9
Pingyin, *China* 56 F9
Pingyuan, *Guangdong, China* 59 E10
Pingyuan, *Shandong, China* 56 F9
Pingyuanjie, *China* 58 F4
Pinhal, *Brazil* 127 A6
Pinhal Novo, *Portugal* 37 G2
Pinheiro, *Brazil* 125 D9
Pinheiro Machado, *Brazil* 127 C5
Pinhel, *Portugal* 36 E3
Pini, *Indonesia* 62 D1
Piniós →, *Ilía, Greece* 46 D3
Piniós →, *Tríkkala, Greece* 46 B4
Pinjarra, *Australia* 93 F2
Pink Mountain, *Canada* 102 B4
Pinkafeld, *Austria* 27 D9
Pinnacles, *U.S.A.* 110 J5
Pinnacles ⌂, *U.S.A.* 110 J5
Pinnaroo, *Australia* 95 F3
Pinneberg, *Germany* 24 B5
Pínnes, Ákra, *Greece* 45 F8
Pinon Hills, *U.S.A.* 111 L9
Pinos, *Mexico* 118 C4
Pinos, Mt., *U.S.A.* 111 L7
Pinos Pt., *U.S.A.* 109 H3
Pinos Puente, *Spain* 37 H7
Pinotepa Nacional, *Mexico* 119 D5
Pinrang, *Indonesia* 63 E5
Pins, Pte. aux, *Canada* 116 D3
Pinsk, *Belarus* 33 F4
Pintados, *Chile* 124 H5
Pinyang, *China* 59 D13
Pinyug, *Russia* 52 C5
Pioche, *U.S.A.* 109 H6
Piombino, *Italy* 40 F7
Piombino, Canale di, *Italy* 40 F7
Pioner, Ostrov, *Russia* 53 B10
Pionki, *Poland* 31 G8
Piorini, L., *Brazil* 124 D6
Piotrków Trybunalski, *Poland* 31 G6
Piove di Sacco, *Italy* 41 C9
Pīp, *Iran* 71 E9
Pipar, *India* 68 F5
Pipar Road, *India* 68 F5
Piparia, *Mad. P., India* 68 H8
Piparia, *Mad. P., India* 68 J7
Pipéri, *Greece* 46 B6
Pipestone, *U.S.A.* 112 D6
Pipestone →, *Canada* 104 B2
Pipestone Cr. →, *Canada* 103 D8
Piplan, *Pakistan* 68 C4
Piploda, *India* 68 H6
Pipmuacan, Rés., *Canada* 105 C5
Pippingarra, *Australia* 92 D2
Pipriac, *France* 18 E5
Piqua, *U.S.A.* 114 E3
Piquiri →, *Brazil* 127 A5
Pir Panjal Range, *India* 68 C7
Pīr Sohrāb, *Iran* 71 E9
Pira, *Benin* 83 D5
Piracicaba, *Brazil* 127 A6
Piracuruca, *Brazil* 125 D10
Piræus = Piraiévs, *Greece* 46 D5
Piraiévs, *Greece* 46 D5
Pirajuí, *Brazil* 127 A6
Piram I., *India* 68 J5
Piran, *Slovenia* 41 C10
Pirané, *Argentina* 126 B4
Pirano = Piran, *Slovenia* 41 C10
Pirapora, *Brazil* 125 G10
Pirawa, *India* 68 G7
Pirdop, *Bulgaria* 45 D8
Pírgos, *Ilía, Greece* 46 D3
Pírgos, *Kríti, Greece* 47 F7
Pirgovo, *Bulgaria* 45 C9
Piribebuy, *Paraguay* 126 B4
Pirimapun, *Indonesia* 63 F9
Pirin △, *Bulgaria* 44 E7
Pirin Planina, *Bulgaria* 44 E7
Pírineos = Pyrénées, *Europe* 20 F4
Piripiri, *Brazil* 125 D10
Pirmasens, *Germany* 25 F3
Pirna, *Germany* 24 E9
Pirot, *Serbia & M.* 44 C6
Piru, *Indonesia* 63 E7
Piru, *U.S.A.* 111 L8
Piryatin = Pyryatyn, *Ukraine* 33 G7
Piryí, *Greece* 47 C7
Pisa, *Italy* 40 E7
Pisa →, *Poland* 31 E8
Pisa, Florence ✕ (PSA), *Italy* 40 E7
Pisagne, *Italy* 40 C7
Pisagua, *Chile* 124 G4
Pisarovina, *Croatia* 41 C12
Pisco, *Peru* 124 F3
Piscu, *Romania* 29 E12
Písek, *Czech Rep.* 26 B7
Pishan, *China* 60 C2
Pīshīn, *Iran* 71 E9
Pishin, *Pakistan* 68 D2
Pishin Lora →, *Pakistan* 68 E1
Pisidia, *Turkey* 72 D4
Pising, *Indonesia* 63 F6
Pismo Beach, *U.S.A.* 111 K6
Piso, L., *Liberia* 82 D2
Pissila, *Burkina Faso* 83 C4
Pissis, Cerro, *Argentina* 126 B2
Pissos, *France* 20 D3
Pissouri, *Cyprus* 49 E11
Pisticci, *Italy* 43 B9
Pistóia, *Italy* 40 E7
Pistol B., *Canada* 103 A10
Pisuerga →, *Spain* 36 D6
Pisz, *Poland* 30 E8
Pit →, *U.S.A.* 108 F2
Pita, *Guinea* 82 C2
Pitarpunga, L., *Australia* 95 E3
Pitcairn I., *Pac. Oc.* 97 K14
Pitch L., *Trin. & Tob.* 125 K15
Pite älv →, *Sweden* 8 D19
Piteå, *Sweden* 8 D19
Piterka, *Russia* 34 E8
Piteşti, *Romania* 29 F9
Pithapuram, *India* 67 L13
Pithara, *Australia* 93 F2
Píthion, *Greece* 45 E10
Pithiviers, *France* 19 D9
Pithoragarh, *India* 69 E9
Pithoro, *Pakistan* 68 G3
Pitigliano, *Italy* 41 F8
Pitkyaranta, *Russia* 32 B6
Pitlochry, *U.K.* 13 E5
Pitsilia, *Cyprus* 49 E12
Pitt I., *Canada* 102 C3
Pittsburg, *Calif., U.S.A.* 110 G5
Pittsburg, *Kans., U.S.A.* 113 G7
Pittsburg, *Tex., U.S.A.* 113 J7
Pittsburgh, *U.S.A.* 116 F5

Pittsfield, *Ill., U.S.A.* 112 F9
Pittsfield, *Maine, U.S.A.* 115 C11
Pittsfield, *Mass., U.S.A.* 117 D11
Pittsfield, *N.H., U.S.A.* 117 C13
Pittston, *U.S.A.* 117 E9
Pittsworth, *Australia* 95 D5
Pituri →, *Australia* 94 C2
Piura, *Peru* 124 E2
Piva →, *Serbia & M.* 44 C2
Piwniczna, *Poland* 31 J7
Pixley, *U.S.A.* 110 K7
Piyai, *Greece* 46 B3
Pizarra, *Spain* 37 J6
Pizhou, *China* 56 G9
Pizzo, *Italy* 43 D9
Placentia, *Canada* 105 C9
Placentia B., *Canada* 105 C9
Placer, *Masbate, Phil.* 61 F5
Placer, *Surigao N., Phil.* 61 G6
Placerville, *U.S.A.* 110 G6
Placetas, *Cuba* 120 B4
Plačkovica, *Macedonia* 44 E6
Plainfield, *N.J., U.S.A.* 117 F10
Plainfield, *Ohio, U.S.A.* 116 F3
Plainfield, *Vt., U.S.A.* 117 B12
Plains, *Mont., U.S.A.* 108 C6
Plains, *Tex., U.S.A.* 113 J3
Plainview, *Nebr., U.S.A.* 112 D6
Plainview, *Tex., U.S.A.* 113 H4
Plainwell, *U.S.A.* 114 D3
Plaisance, *France* 20 E4
Plaistow, *U.S.A.* 117 D13
Pláka, *Greece* 47 B7
Pláka, Ákra, *Greece* 49 D8
Plakenska Planina, *Macedonia* 44 E5
Planá, *Czech Rep.* 26 B5
Plana Cays, *Bahamas* 121 B5
Planada, *U.S.A.* 110 H6
Plancoët, *France* 18 D4
Plandište, *Serbia & M.* 28 E6
Plano, *U.S.A.* 113 J6
Plant City, *U.S.A.* 115 M4
Plaquemine, *U.S.A.* 113 K9
Plasencia, *Spain* 36 E4
Plaški, *Croatia* 41 C12
Plaster City, *U.S.A.* 111 N11
Plaster Rock, *Canada* 105 C6
Plastun, *Russia* 54 B8
Plasy, *Czech Rep.* 26 B6
Plata, Río de la, *S. Amer.* 126 C4
Plátani →, *Italy* 42 E6
Plátanos, *Greece* 49 D5
Plateau □, *Nigeria* 83 D6
Platí, Ákra, *Greece* 45 F8
Platte, *U.S.A.* 112 D5
Platte →, *Mo., U.S.A.* 112 F7
Platte →, *Nebr., U.S.A.* 112 E7
Platteville, *U.S.A.* 112 D9
Plattling, *Germany* 25 G8
Plattsburgh, *U.S.A.* 117 B11
Plattsmouth, *U.S.A.* 112 E7
Plau, *Germany* 24 B8
Plauen, *Germany* 24 E8
Plauer See, *Germany* 24 B8
Plav, *Serbia & M.* 44 D3
Plavinas, *Latvia* 9 H21
Plavnica, *Serbia & M.* 44 D3
Plavno, *Croatia* 41 D13
Plavsk, *Russia* 32 F9
Playa Blanca, *Canary Is.* 48 F6
Playa Blanca Sur, *Canary Is.* 48 F6
Playa de las Americas, *Canary Is.* 48 F3
Playa de Mogán, *Canary Is.* 48 G4
Playa del Inglés, *Canary Is.* 48 G4
Playa Esmerelda, *Canary Is.* 48 F5
Playgreen L., *Canada* 103 C9
Pleasant Bay, *Canada* 105 C7
Pleasant Hill, *U.S.A.* 110 H4
Pleasant Mount, *U.S.A.* 117 E9
Pleasanton, *Calif., U.S.A.* 110 H5
Pleasanton, *Tex., U.S.A.* 113 L5
Pleasantville, *N.J., U.S.A.* 114 F8
Pleasantville, *Pa., U.S.A.* 116 E5
Pléaux, *France* 20 C6
Plei Ku, *Vietnam* 64 F7
Plélan-le-Grand, *France* 18 D4
Pléneuf-Val-André, *France* 18 D4
Pleniţa, *Romania* 29 F8
Plenty →, *Australia* 94 C2
Plenty, B. of, *N.Z.* 91 G6
Plentywood, *U.S.A.* 112 A2
Plérin, *France* 18 D4
Plessisville, *Canada* 105 C5
Plestin-les-Grèves, *France* 18 D3
Pleszew, *Poland* 31 G4
Pleternica, *Croatia* 28 E2
Plétipi, L., *Canada* 105 B5
Pleven, *Bulgaria* 45 C8
Plevlja, *Serbia & M.* 44 C3
Plevna, *Canada* 116 B8
Plitvička Jezera △, *Croatia* 41 D12
Plješevica, *Croatia* 41 D12
Ploaghe, *Italy* 42 B1
Ploče, *Croatia* 41 E14
Płock, *Poland* 31 F6
Plöckenpass, *Italy* 41 B9
Plöckenstein, *Germany* 25 G9
Ploemeur, *France* 18 E3
Ploërmel, *France* 18 E4
Ploieşti, *Romania* 29 F11
Plomárion, *Greece* 47 C8
Plombières-les-Bains, *France* 19 E13
Plomin, *Croatia* 41 C11
Plön, *Germany* 24 A6
Plonge, Lac la, *Canada* 103 B7
Płońsk, *Poland* 31 F7
Plopeni, *Romania* 29 E10
Plopişului, Munţii, *Romania* 28 C7
Płoty, *Poland* 30 E2
Plouaret, *France* 18 D3
Plouay, *France* 18 E3
Ploučnice →, *Czech Rep.* 26 A7
Ploudalmézeau, *France* 18 D2
Plouescat, *France* 18 D2
Plougasnou, *France* 18 D3
Plougastel-Daoulas, *France* 18 D2
Plouguerneau, *France* 18 D2
Plouha, *France* 18 D4
Plouhinec, *France* 18 E2
Plovdiv, *Bulgaria* 45 D8
Plovdiv □, *Bulgaria* 45 D8
Plum, *U.S.A.* 116 F5
Plum I., *U.S.A.* 117 E12
Plumas, *U.S.A.* 110 F7
Plummer, *U.S.A.* 108 C5
Plumtree, *Zimbabwe* 87 G2
Plungė, *Lithuania* 9 J19
Pluvigner, *France* 18 E3
Plymouth, *Trin. & Tob.* 125 J16
Plymouth, *U.K.* 15 G3
Plymouth, *Calif., U.S.A.* 110 G6
Plymouth, *Ind., U.S.A.* 114 E2
Plymouth, *Mass., U.S.A.* 117 E14
Plymouth, *N.C., U.S.A.* 115 H7
Plymouth, *N.H., U.S.A.* 117 C13
Plymouth, *Pa., U.S.A.* 117 E9
Plymouth, *Wis., U.S.A.* 114 D2
Plympton-Wyoming, *Canada* 116 D2
Plynlimon = Pumlumon Fawr, *U.K.* 15 E4
Plyusa, *Russia* 32 C5
Plyusa →, *Russia* 32 C5
Plzeň, *Czech Rep.* 26 B6
Plzeňský □, *Czech Rep.* 26 B6
Pniewy, *Poland* 31 F3
Pô, *Burkina Faso* 83 C4
Pô △, *Burkina Faso* 83 C4
Po →, *Italy* 41 D9
Po, Foci del, *Italy* 41 D9
Po Hai = Bo Hai, *China* 57 E10
Pobé, *Benin* 83 D5
Pobé, *Burkina Faso* 83 C4
Pobeda, *Russia* 53 C15
Pobedy, Pik, *Kyrgyzstan* 52 E8
Pobiedziska, *Poland* 31 F4
Pobla de Segur, *Spain* 38 C5
Pobladura del Valle, *Spain* 36 C5
Pobra de Trives, *Spain* 36 C3
Pocahontas, *Ark., U.S.A.* 113 G9
Pocahontas, *Iowa, U.S.A.* 112 D7
Pocatello, *U.S.A.* 108 E7
Počátky, *Czech Rep.* 26 B8
Pochep, *Russia* 33 F7
Pochinki, *Russia* 34 C7
Pochinok, *Russia* 32 E7
Pöchlarn, *Austria* 26 C8
Pochutla, *Mexico* 119 D5
Pocito Casas, *Mexico* 118 B2
Pocking, *Germany* 25 G9
Pocomoke City, *U.S.A.* 114 F8
Poços de Caldas, *Brazil* 127 A6
Podbořany, *Czech Rep.* 26 A6
Poddębice, *Poland* 31 G5
Poděbrady, *Czech Rep.* 26 A8
Podensac, *France* 20 D3
Podenzano, *Italy* 40 D6
Podgorač, *Croatia* 28 E3
Podgorica, *Serbia & M.* 44 D3
Podgorie, *Albania* 44 F4
Podilska Vysochyna, *Ukraine* 33 H4
Podkarpackie □, *Poland* 31 H9
Podkova, *Bulgaria* 45 E9
Podlapača, *Croatia* 41 D12
Podlaskie □, *Poland* 31 E10
Podoleni, *Romania* 29 D11
Podolínec, *Slovak Rep.* 27 B13
Podolsk, *Russia* 32 E9
Podor, *Senegal* 82 B1
Podporozhye, *Russia* 32 B8
Podu Iloaiei, *Romania* 29 C12
Podu Turcului, *Romania* 29 D12
Podujevo, *Serbia & M.* 44 D5
Podyjí △, *Czech Rep.* 26 C8
Poel, *Germany* 24 B6
Pofadder, *S. Africa* 88 D2
Poggiardo, *Italy* 43 B11
Poggibonsi, *Italy* 40 E8
Póggio Mirteto, *Italy* 41 F9
Pogoanele, *Romania* 29 F12
Pogorzela, *Poland* 31 G4
Pogradec, *Albania* 44 F4
Pogranichnyy, *Russia* 54 B5
Poh, *Indonesia* 63 E6
P'ohang, *S. Korea* 57 F15
Pohjanmaa, *Finland* 8 E20
Pohnpei, *Micronesia* 96 G7
Pohorelá, *Slovak Rep.* 27 C13
Pohořelice, *Czech Rep.* 27 C9
Pohorje, *Slovenia* 41 B12
Pohri, *India* 68 G6
Poiana Mare, *Romania* 28 G8
Poiana Ruscăi, Munţii, *Romania* 28 E7
Poiana Stampei, *Romania* 29 C10
Poinsett, C., *Antarctica* 5 C8
Point Arena, *U.S.A.* 110 G3
Point Baker, *U.S.A.* 102 B2
Point Edward, *Canada* 104 D3
Point Fortin, *Trin. & Tob.* 125 K15
Point Hope, *U.S.A.* 100 B3
Point L., *Canada* 100 B8
Point Lisas, *Trin. & Tob.* 125 K15
Point Pedro, *Sri Lanka* 66 Q12
Point Pelee △, *Canada* 116 E2
Point Pleasant, *N.J., U.S.A.* 117 F10
Point Pleasant, *W. Va., U.S.A.* 114 F4
Point Reyes ⌂, *U.S.A.* 110 G2
Pointe-à-Pitre, *Guadeloupe* 120 b
Pointe-au-Pic = La Malbaie, *Canada* 105 C5
Pointe-Claire, *Canada* 117 A11
Pointe-Gatineau, *Canada* 117 A9
Pointe-Noire, *Congo* 84 E2
Pointe Noire, *Guadeloupe* 120 b
Poio, *Spain* 36 C2
Poirino, *Italy* 40 D4
Poisonbush Ra., *Australia* 92 D3
Poissonnier Pt., *Australia* 92 C2
Poitiers, *France* 18 F7
Poitou, *France* 20 B3
Poitou-Charentes □, *France* 20 B4
Poix-de-Picardie, *France* 19 C8
Poix-Terron, *France* 19 C11
Pojoaque, *U.S.A.* 109 J11
Pokaran, *India* 66 F7
Pokataroo, *Australia* 95 D4
Pokhara, *Nepal* 69 E10
Pokhvistnevo, *Russia* 34 D11
Poko, *Dem. Rep. of the Congo* 86 B2
Poko, *Sudan* 81 F3
Pokrov, *Russia* 32 E10
Pokrovsk = Engels, *Russia* 34 E8
Pokrovsk, *Russia* 53 C13
Pokrovskoye, *Russia* 33 J10
Pola = Pula, *Croatia* 41 D10
Pola, *Russia* 32 D7
Pola de Allande, *Spain* 36 B4
Pola de Lena, *Spain* 36 B5
Pola de Siero, *Spain* 36 B5
Pola de Somiedo, *Spain* 36 B4
Polacca, *U.S.A.* 109 J8
Polan, *Iran* 71 E9
Pol'ana, *Slovak Rep.* 27 C12
Poland ■, *Europe* 31 G3
Polanica-Zdrój, *Poland* 31 H3
Połaniec, *Poland* 31 H8
Polanów, *Poland* 30 D3
Polar Bear ⌂, *Canada* 104 A2
Polatlı, *Turkey* 72 C5
Polatsk, *Belarus* 32 E5
Polcura, *Chile* 126 D1
Połczyn-Zdrój, *Poland* 30 E3
Poleski △, *Poland* 31 G10
Polessk, *Russia* 9 J19
Polesye = Pripet Marshes, *Europe* 33 F5
Polgar, *Hungary* 28 C6
Pŏlgyo-ri, *S. Korea* 57 G14
Poli, *Cameroon* 83 C7
Políaigos, *Greece* 46 E6
Policastro, G. di, *Italy* 43 C8
Police, *Poland* 30 E1
Polička, *Czech Rep.* 27 B9
Policoro, *Italy* 43 B9
Polignano a Mare, *Italy* 43 A9
Poligny, *France* 19 F12
Políkhnitas, *Greece* 47 B8
Polillo Is., *Phil.* 61 D4
Polillo Strait, *Phil.* 61 D4
Polis, *Cyprus* 49 D11
Polístena, *Italy* 43 D9
Políyiros, *Greece* 44 F7
Polk, *U.S.A.* 116 E5
Polkowice, *Poland* 31 G3
Polla, *Italy* 43 B8
Pollachi, *India* 66 P10
Pollença, *Spain* 48 B10
Pollença, B. de, *Spain* 48 B10
Póllica, *Italy* 43 B8
Pollino △, *Italy* 43 C9
Pollino, Mte., *Italy* 43 C9
Polna, *Russia* 32 C5
Polnovat, *Russia* 52 C7
Pology, *Ukraine* 33 J9
Polokwane, *S. Africa* 89 C4
Polonne, *Ukraine* 33 G4
Polonnoye = Polonne, *Ukraine* 33 G4
Polski Trŭmbesh, *Bulgaria* 45 C9
Polsko Kosovo, *Bulgaria* 45 C9
Polson, *U.S.A.* 108 C6
Poltár, *Slovak Rep.* 27 C12
Poltava, *Ukraine* 33 H8
Põltsamaa, *Estonia* 9 G21
Polunochnoye, *Russia* 52 C7
Põlva, *Estonia* 9 G22
Polynesia, *Pac. Oc.* 97 J11
Polynésie française = French Polynesia ☒, *Pac. Oc.* 97 K13
Pomarance, *Italy* 40 E7
Pomaro, *Mexico* 118 D4
Pombal, *Portugal* 36 F2
Pómbia, *Greece* 49 E6
Pomene, *Mozam.* 89 C6
Pomeroy, *Ohio, U.S.A.* 114 F4
Pomeroy, *Wash., U.S.A.* 108 C5
Pomézia, *Italy* 42 A5
Pomichna, *Ukraine* 33 H6
Pomona, *Australia* 95 D5
Pomona, *U.S.A.* 111 L9
Pomorie, *Bulgaria* 45 D11
Pomorskie □, *Poland* 30 D5
Pomorskie, Pojezierze, *Poland* 30 E3
Pomos, *Cyprus* 49 D11
Pomos, C., *Cyprus* 49 D11
Pompano Beach, *U.S.A.* 115 M5
Pompei, *Italy* 43 B7
Pompey, *France* 19 D13
Pompeys Pillar, *U.S.A.* 108 D10
Pompeys Pillar ⌂, *U.S.A.* 108 D10
Pompton Lakes, *U.S.A.* 117 F10
Ponape = Pohnpei, *Micronesia* 96 G7
Ponask L., *Canada* 104 B1
Ponca, *U.S.A.* 112 D6
Ponca City, *U.S.A.* 113 G6
Ponce, *Puerto Rico* 121 d
Ponchatoula, *U.S.A.* 113 K9
Poncheville, L., *Canada* 104 B4
Pond, *U.S.A.* 111 K7
Pond Inlet, *Canada* 101 A12
Pondicherry, *India* 66 P11
Ponds, I. of, *Canada* 105 B8
Ponferrada, *Spain* 36 C4
Pongo, Wadi →, *Sudan* 81 F2
Poniatowa, *Poland* 31 G9
Poniec, *Poland* 31 G3
Ponikva, *Slovenia* 41 B12
Ponnani, *India* 66 P9
Ponoka, *Canada* 102 C6
Ponorogo, *Indonesia* 63 G14
Pons = Ponts, *Spain* 38 D6
Pons, *France* 20 C3
Ponsul →, *Portugal* 36 F3
Pont-à-Mousson, *France* 19 D13
Pont-Audemer, *France* 18 C7
Pont-Aven, *France* 18 E3
Pont Canavese, *Italy* 40 C4
Pont-d'Ain, *France* 19 F12
Pont-de-Roide, *France* 19 E13
Pont-de-Salars, *France* 20 D6
Pont-de-Vaux, *France* 19 F11
Pont-de-Veyle, *France* 19 F11
Pont-du-Château, *France* 19 G10
Pont-l'Abbé, *France* 18 E2
Pont-l'Évêque, *France* 18 C7
Pont-St-Esprit, *France* 21 D8
Pont-St-Martin, *Italy* 40 C4
Pont-Ste-Maxence, *France* 19 C9
Pont-sur-Yonne, *France* 19 D10
Ponta do Sol, *Madeira* 48 D2
Ponta Grossa, *Brazil* 127 B5
Ponta Pora, *Brazil* 127 A4
Pontacq, *France* 20 E3
Pontailler-sur-Saône, *France* 19 E12
Pontarlier, *France* 19 F13
Pontassieve, *Italy* 41 E8
Pontaumur, *France* 20 C6
Pontcharra, *France* 21 C10
Pontchartrain L., *U.S.A.* 113 K10
Pontchâteau, *France* 18 E4
Ponte da Barca, *Portugal* 36 D2
Ponte de Sor, *Portugal* 37 F2
Ponte dell'Ólio, *Italy* 40 D6
Ponte di Legno, *Italy* 40 B7
Ponte do Lima, *Portugal* 36 D2
Ponte do Pungué, *Mozam.* 87 F3
Ponte-Leccia, *France* 21 F13
Ponte nelle Alpi, *Italy* 41 B9
Ponte Nova, *Brazil* 127 A7
Ponteareas, *Spain* 36 C2
Pontebba, *Italy* 41 B10
Ponteceso, *Spain* 36 B2
Pontecorvo, *Italy* 42 A6
Pontedeume, *Spain* 36 B2
Ponteix, *Canada* 103 D7
Pontevedra, *Spain* 36 C2
Pontevedra □, *Spain* 36 C2
Pontevedra, R. de →, *Spain* 36 C2
Pontevico, *Italy* 40 C7
Pontiac, *Ill., U.S.A.* 112 E10
Pontiac, *Mich., U.S.A.* 114 D4
Pontian Kechil, *Malaysia* 65 d
Pontianak, *Indonesia* 62 E3
Pontine Is. = Ponziane, Ísole, *Italy* 42 B5
Pontine Mts. = Kuzey Anadolu Dağları, *Turkey* 72 B7
Pontínia, *Italy* 42 A6
Pontivy, *France* 18 D4
Pontoise, *France* 19 C9
Ponton →, *Canada* 102 B5
Pontorson, *France* 18 D5
Pontrémoli, *Italy* 40 D6
Pontrieux, *France* 18 D3
Ponts, *Spain* 38 D6
Pontypool, *Canada* 116 B6
Pontypool, *U.K.* 15 F4
Ponza, *Italy* 42 B5
Ponziane, Ísole, *Italy* 42 B5
Poochera, *Australia* 95 E1
Poole, *U.K.* 15 G6
Poole □, *U.K.* 15 G6
Poona = Pune, *India* 66 K8
Pooncarie, *Australia* 95 E3
Poopelloe L., *Australia* 95 E3
Poopó, L. de, *Bolivia* 124 G5
Popayán, *Colombia* 124 C3
Poperinge, *Belgium* 17 D2
Popilta L., *Australia* 95 E3
Popina, *Bulgaria* 45 B10
Popio L., *Australia* 95 E3
Poplar, *U.S.A.* 112 A2
Poplar →, *Canada* 103 C9
Poplar Bluff, *U.S.A.* 113 G9
Poplarville, *U.S.A.* 113 K10
Popocatépetl, Volcán, *Mexico* 119 D5
Popokabaka, *Dem. Rep. of the Congo* 84 F3
Pópoli, *Italy* 41 F10
Popovača, *Croatia* 41 C13
Popovo, *Bulgaria* 45 C10
Poppberg, *Germany* 25 F7
Poppi, *Italy* 41 E8
Poprad, *Slovak Rep.* 27 B13
Poprad →, *Slovak Rep.* 27 B13
Porali →, *Pakistan* 68 G2
Porbandar, *India* 68 J3
Porcher I., *Canada* 102 C2
Porcuna, *Spain* 37 H6
Porcupine →, *Canada* 103 B8
Porcupine →, *U.S.A.* 100 B5
Porcupine Gorge △, *Australia* 94 C3
Pordenone, *Italy* 41 C9
Pordim, *Bulgaria* 45 C8
Poreč, *Croatia* 41 C10
Poretskoye, *Russia* 34 C8
Pori, *Finland* 9 F19
Porí, *Greece* 46 F5
Porkhov, *Russia* 32 D5
Porlamar, *Venezuela* 124 A6
Porlezza, *Italy* 40 B6
Porma →, *Spain* 36 C5
Pornic, *France* 18 E4
Poronaysk, *Russia* 53 E15
Póros, *Greece* 46 D5
Poroshiri-Dake, *Japan* 54 C11
Poroszló, *Hungary* 28 C5
Poroto Mts., *Tanzania* 87 D3
Porpoise B., *Antarctica* 5 C9
Porquerolles, Î. de, *France* 21 F10
Porrentruy, *Switz.* 25 H3
Porreres, *Spain* 48 B10
Porsangen, *Norway* 8 A21
Porsgrunn, *Norway* 9 G13
Port Alberni, *Canada* 102 D4
Port Alfred, *S. Africa* 88 E4
Port Alice, *Canada* 102 C3
Port Allegany, *U.S.A.* 116 E6
Port Allen, *U.S.A.* 113 K9
Port Alma, *Australia* 94 C5
Port Angeles, *U.S.A.* 110 B3
Port Antonio, *Jamaica* 120 a
Port Aransas, *U.S.A.* 113 M6
Port Arthur = Lüshun, *China* 57 E11
Port Arthur, *Australia* 95 G4
Port Arthur, *U.S.A.* 113 L8
Port au Choix, *Canada* 105 B8
Port au Port B., *Canada* 105 C8
Port-au-Prince, *Haiti* 121 C5
Port Augusta, *Australia* 95 E2
Port Austin, *U.S.A.* 116 B2
Port Bell, *Uganda* 86 B3
Port Bergé Vaovao, *Madag.* 89 B8
Port Blandford, *Canada* 105 C9
Port-Bouët, *Ivory C.* 82 D4
Port Bradshaw, *Australia* 94 A2
Port Broughton, *Australia* 95 E2
Port Burwell, *Canada* 116 D4
Port Canning, *India* 69 H13
Port-Cartier, *Canada* 105 B6
Port Chalmers, *N.Z.* 91 L3
Port Charlotte, *U.S.A.* 115 M4
Port Chester, *U.S.A.* 117 F11
Port Clements, *Canada* 102 C2
Port Clinton, *U.S.A.* 114 E4
Port Colborne, *Canada* 116 D5
Port Coquitlam, *Canada* 102 D4
Port Credit, *Canada* 116 C5
Port-Cros △, *France* 21 F10
Port Curtis, *Australia* 94 C5
Port d'Alcúdia, *Spain* 48 B10
Port Dalhousie, *Canada* 116 C5
Port d'Andratx, *Spain* 48 B9
Port Darwin, *Australia* 92 B5
Port Darwin, *Falk. Is.* 128 G5
Port Davey, *Australia* 95 G4
Port-de-Bouc, *France* 21 E8
Port-de-Paix, *Haiti* 121 C5
Port de Pollença, *Spain* 48 B10
Port de Sóller, *Spain* 48 B9
Port Dickson, *Malaysia* 65 L3
Port Douglas, *Australia* 94 B4
Port Dover, *Canada* 116 D4
Port Edward, *Canada* 102 C2
Port Elgin, *Canada* 116 B3
Port Elizabeth, *S. Africa* 88 E4
Port Ellen, *U.K.* 13 F2
Port-en-Bessin, *France* 18 C6
Port Erin, *U.K.* 14 C3
Port Essington, *Australia* 92 B5
Port Etienne = Nouâdhibou, *Mauritania* 78 D2
Port Ewen, *U.S.A.* 117 E11
Port Fairy, *Australia* 95 F3
Port Fouâd = Bûr Fuad, *Egypt* 80 H8
Port Gamble, *U.S.A.* 110 C4
Port-Gentil, *Gabon* 84 E1
Port Germein, *Australia* 95 E2
Port Gibson, *U.S.A.* 113 K9
Port Glasgow, *U.K.* 13 F4
Port Harcourt, *Nigeria* 83 E6
Port Hardy, *Canada* 102 C3
Port Harrison = Inukjuak, *Canada* 101 C12
Port Hawkesbury, *Canada* 105 C7
Port Hedland, *Australia* 92 D2
Port Henry, *U.S.A.* 117 B11
Port Hood, *Canada* 105 C7
Port Hope, *Canada* 116 C6
Port Hope, *U.S.A.* 116 C2
Port Hope Simpson, *Canada* 105 B8
Port Hueneme, *U.S.A.* 111 L7
Port Huron, *U.S.A.* 116 D2
Port Iliç, *Azerbaijan* 73 C13
Port Jefferson, *U.S.A.* 117 F11
Port Jervis, *U.S.A.* 117 E10
Port-Joinville, *France* 18 F4
Port Katon, *Russia* 33 J10
Port Kelang = Pelabuhan Kelang, *Malaysia* 65 L3
Port Kenny, *Australia* 95 E1
Port-la-Nouvelle, *France* 20 E7
Port Lairge = Waterford, *Ireland* 12 D4
Port Laoise, *Ireland* 12 C4
Port Lavaca, *U.S.A.* 113 L6
Port Leyden, *U.S.A.* 117 C9
Port Lincoln, *Australia* 95 E2
Port Loko, *S. Leone* 82 D2
Port Louis, *France* 18 E3
Port-Louis, *Guadeloupe* 120 b
Port Louis, *Mauritius* 77 H9
Port MacDonnell, *Australia* 95 F3
Port McNeill, *Canada* 102 C3
Port Macquarie, *Australia* 95 E5
Port Maria, *Jamaica* 120 a
Port Matilda, *U.S.A.* 116 F6
Port Mellon, *Canada* 102 D4
Port-Menier, *Canada* 105 C7
Port Moody, *Canada* 110 A4
Port Morant, *Jamaica* 120 a
Port Moresby, *Papua N. G.* 96 H6
Port Musgrave, *Australia* 94 A3
Port-Navalo, *France* 18 E4
Port Neches, *U.S.A.* 113 L8
Port Nolloth, *S. Africa* 88 D2
Port Nouveau-Québec = Kangiqsualujjuaq, *Canada* 101 C13
Port of Spain, *Trin. & Tob.* 121 D7
Port Orange, *U.S.A.* 115 L5
Port Orchard, *U.S.A.* 110 C4
Port Orford, *U.S.A.* 108 E1
Port Pegasus, *N.Z.* 91 M1
Port Perry, *Canada* 116 B6
Port Phillip B., *Australia* 95 F3
Port Pirie, *Australia* 95 E2

Port Radium = Echo Bay, *Canada* 100 B8
Port Renfrew, *Canada* 102 D4
Port Roper, *Australia* 94 A2
Port Rowan, *Canada* 116 D4
Port Safaga = Bûr Safâga, *Egypt* 70 E2
Port Said = Bûr Sa'îd, *Egypt* 80 H8
Port St. Joe, *U.S.A.* 115 L3
Port St. Johns = Umzimvubu, *S. Africa* 89 E4
Port-St-Louis-du-Rhône, *France* 21 E8
Port St. Lucie, *U.S.A.* 115 M5
Port-Ste-Marie, *France* 20 D4
Port Sanilac, *U.S.A.* 116 C2
Port Severn, *Canada* 116 B5
Port Shepstone, *S. Africa* 89 E5
Port Simpson, *Canada* 102 C2
Port Stanley = Stanley, *Falk. Is.* 128 G5
Port Stanley, *Canada* 116 D3
Port Sudan = Bûr Sûdân, *Sudan* 80 D4
Port Sulphur, *U.S.A.* 113 L10
Port-sur-Saône, *France* 19 E13
Port Talbot, *U.K.* 15 F4
Port Taufiq = Bûr Taufiq, *Egypt* 80 J8
Port Townsend, *U.S.A.* 110 B4
Port-Vendres, *France* 20 F7
Port Vila, *Vanuatu* 96 J8
Port Wakefield, *Australia* 95 E2
Port Washington, *U.S.A.* 114 D2
Port Weld = Kuala Sepetang, *Malaysia* 65 K3
Portadown, *U.K.* 12 B5
Portaferry, *U.K.* 12 B6
Portage, *Pa., U.S.A.* 116 F6
Portage, *Wis., U.S.A.* 112 D10
Portage la Prairie, *Canada* 103 D9
Portageville, *U.S.A.* 113 G10
Portalegre, *Portugal* 37 F3
Portalegre □, *Portugal* 37 F3
Portales, *U.S.A.* 113 H3
Portarlington, *Ireland* 12 C4
Portbou, *Spain* 38 C8
Portel, *Portugal* 37 G3
Portela, Lisbon ✈ (LIS), *Portugal* 37 G1
Porter L., *N.W.T., Canada* 103 A7
Porter L., *Sask., Canada* 103 B7
Porterville, *S. Africa* 88 E2
Porterville, *U.S.A.* 110 J8
Portes-lès-Valence, *France* 21 D8
Porthcawl, *U.K.* 15 F4
Porthill, *U.S.A.* 108 B5
Porthmadog, *U.K.* 14 E3
Portile de Fier, *Europe* 28 F7
Portimão, *Portugal* 37 H2
Portishead, *U.K.* 15 F5
Portiţei, Gura, *Romania* 29 F14
Portknockie, *U.K.* 13 D6
Portland, *N.S.W., Australia* 95 E5
Portland, *Vic., Australia* 95 F3
Portland, *Canada* 117 B8
Portland, *Conn., U.S.A.* 117 E12
Portland, *Maine, U.S.A.* 101 D12
Portland, *Mich., U.S.A.* 114 D3
Portland, *Oreg., U.S.A.* 110 E4
Portland, *Pa., U.S.A.* 117 F9
Portland, *Tex., U.S.A.* 113 M6
Portland ✈ (PDX), *U.S.A.* 110 E4
Portland, I. of, *U.K.* 15 G5
Portland B., *Australia* 95 F3
Portland Bight, *Jamaica* 120 a
Portland Bill, *U.K.* 15 G5
Portland Canal, *U.S.A.* 102 B2
Portland Pt., *Jamaica* 120 a
Portmadoc = Porthmadog, *U.K.* 14 E3
Portmore, *Jamaica* 120 a
Porto, *France* 21 F12
Porto, *Portugal* 36 D2
Porto □, *Portugal* 36 D2
Porto, G. de, *France* 21 F12
Pôrto Alegre, *Brazil* 127 C5
Porto Amboim = Gunza, *Angola* 84 G2
Porto Azzurro, *Italy* 40 F7
Porto Cristo, *Spain* 48 B10
Pôrto de Móz, *Brazil* 125 D8
Porto Empédocle, *Italy* 42 E6
Pôrto Esperança, *Brazil* 124 G7
Pôrto Franco, *Brazil* 125 E9
Pórto Lágos, *Greece* 45 E9
Pôrto Mendes, *Brazil* 127 A5
Porto Moniz, *Madeira* 48 D2
Pôrto Murtinho, *Brazil* 124 H7
Pôrto Nacional, *Brazil* 125 F9
Porto-Novo, *Benin* 83 D5
Porto Petro, *Spain* 48 B10
Porto San Giórgio, *Italy* 41 E10
Porto Sant' Elpídio, *Italy* 41 E10
Porto Santo, I. de, *Madeira* 78 B2
Porto Santo Stéfano, *Italy* 40 F8
Pôrto São José, *Brazil* 127 A5
Pôrto Seguro, *Brazil* 125 G11
Porto Tolle, *Italy* 41 D9
Porto Tórres, *Italy* 42 B1
Pôrto União, *Brazil* 127 B5
Pôrto Válter, *Brazil* 124 E4
Porto-Vecchio, *France* 21 G13
Pôrto Velho, *Brazil* 124 E6
Portobelo, *Panama* 120 E4
Portoferráio, *Italy* 40 F7
Portogruaro, *Italy* 41 C9
Portola, *U.S.A.* 110 F6
Portomaggiore, *Italy* 41 D8
Portoscuso, *Italy* 42 C1
Portovénere, *Italy* 40 D6
Portoviejo, *Ecuador* 124 D2
Portpatrick, *U.K.* 13 G3
Portree, *U.K.* 13 D2
Portrush, *U.K.* 12 A5
Portsmouth, *Domin.* 121 C7
Portsmouth, *U.K.* 15 G6
Portsmouth, *N.H., U.S.A.* 115 D10
Portsmouth, *Ohio, U.S.A.* 114 F4
Portsmouth, *R.I., U.S.A.* 117 E13
Portsmouth, *Va., U.S.A.* 114 G7
Portsmouth □, *U.K.* 15 G6
Portsoy, *U.K.* 13 D6
Portstewart, *U.K.* 12 A5
Porttipahtan tekojärvi, *Finland* 8 B22
Portugal ■, *Europe* 36 F3
Portugalete, *Spain* 38 B1
Portumna, *Ireland* 12 C3
Portville, *U.S.A.* 116 D6
Porvenir, *Chile* 128 G2
Porvoo, *Finland* 9 F21
Porzuna, *Spain* 37 F6
Posada, *Italy* 42 B2
Posada →, *Italy* 42 B2
Posadas, *Argentina* 127 B4
Posadas, *Spain* 37 H5
Poschiavo, *Switz.* 25 J6
Posets, *Spain* 38 C5
Poshan = Boshan, *China* 57 F9
Posht-e Badam, *Iran* 71 C7
Posídhion, Ákra, *Greece* 44 G7
Posidium, *Greece* 47 F9
Poso, *Indonesia* 63 E6
Posong, *S. Korea* 57 G14
Posse, *Brazil* 125 F9
Possession I., *Antarctica* 5 D11
Pössneck, *Germany* 24 E7
Possum Kingdom L., *U.S.A.* 113 J5
Post, *U.S.A.* 113 J4
Post Falls, *U.S.A.* 108 C5
Postavy = Pastavy, *Belarus* 9 J22
Poste-de-la-Baleine = Kuujjuarapik, *Canada* 104 A4
Postmasburg, *S. Africa* 88 D3
Postojna, *Slovenia* 41 C11
Poston, *U.S.A.* 111 M12
Postville, *Canada* 105 B8
Potamós, *Andikíthira, Greece* 46 F5
Potamós, *Kíthira, Greece* 46 E4
Potchefstroom, *S. Africa* 88 D4
Potcoava, *Romania* 29 F9
Poteau, *U.S.A.* 113 H7
Poteet, *U.S.A.* 113 L5
Potenza, *Italy* 43 B8
Potenza →, *Italy* 41 E10
Potenza Picena, *Italy* 41 E10
Poteriteri, L., *N.Z.* 91 M1
Potgietersrus = Mokopane, *S. Africa* 89 C4
Poti, *Georgia* 35 J5
Potiskum, *Nigeria* 83 C7
Potlogi, *Romania* 29 F10
Potomac →, *U.S.A.* 114 G7
Potosí, *Bolivia* 124 G5
Potosi Mt., *U.S.A.* 111 K11
Pototan, *Phil.* 61 F5
Potrerillos, *Chile* 126 B2
Potsdam, *Germany* 24 C9
Potsdam, *U.S.A.* 117 B10
Pottenstein, *Germany* 25 F7
Pottersville, *U.S.A.* 117 C11
Pottery Hill = Abu Ballas, *Egypt* 80 C2
Pottstown, *U.S.A.* 117 F9
Pottsville, *U.S.A.* 117 F8
Pottuvil, *Sri Lanka* 66 R12
P'otzu, *Taiwan* 59 F13
Pouancé, *France* 18 E5
Pouce Coupé, *Canada* 102 B4
Poughkeepsie, *U.S.A.* 117 E11
Pouilly-sur-Loire, *France* 19 E9
Poulaphouca Res., *Ireland* 12 C5
Poulsbo, *U.S.A.* 110 C4
Poultney, *U.S.A.* 117 C11
Poulton-le-Fylde, *U.K.* 14 D5
Pouso Alegre, *Brazil* 127 A6
Pout, *Senegal* 82 C1
Pouthisat, *Cambodia* 64 F4
Pouzauges, *France* 18 F6
Pova de Sta. Iria, *Portugal* 37 G1
Považská Bystrica, *Slovak Rep.* 27 B11
Poverty B., *N.Z.* 91 H7
Povlen, *Serbia & M.* 44 B3
Póvoa de Lanhosa, *Portugal* 36 D2
Póvoa de Varzim, *Portugal* 36 D2
Povorino, *Russia* 34 E6
Povungnituk = Puvirnituq, *Canada* 101 B12
Powassan, *Canada* 104 C4
Poway, *U.S.A.* 111 N9
Powder →, *U.S.A.* 112 B2
Powder River, *U.S.A.* 108 E10
Powell, *U.S.A.* 108 D9
Powell, L., *U.S.A.* 109 H8
Powell River, *Canada* 102 D4
Powers, *U.S.A.* 114 C2
Powys □, *U.K.* 15 E4
Poyang Hu, *China* 59 C11
Poyarkovo, *Russia* 53 E13
Poysdorf, *Austria* 27 C9
Poza de la Sal, *Spain* 36 C7
Poza Rica, *Mexico* 119 C5
Pozanti, *Turkey* 72 D6
Požarevac, *Serbia & M.* 44 B5
Pozazal, Puerto, *Spain* 36 C6
Požega, *Croatia* 28 E2
Požega, *Serbia & M.* 44 C4
Poznań, *Poland* 31 F3
Poznań ✈ (POZ), *Poland* 31 F3
Pozo, *U.S.A.* 111 K6
Pozo Alcón, *Spain* 37 H8
Pozo Almonte, *Chile* 124 H5
Pozo Colorado, *Paraguay* 126 A4
Pozoblanco, *Spain* 37 G6
Pozzallo, *Italy* 43 F7
Pozzomaggiore, *Italy* 42 B1
Pozzuoli, *Italy* 43 B7
Pra →, *Ghana* 83 D4
Prabuty, *Poland* 30 E6
Prača, *Bos.-H.* 28 G3
Prachatice, *Czech Rep.* 26 B6
Prachin Buri, *Thailand* 64 E3
Prachuap Khiri Khan, *Thailand* 65 G2
Pradelles, *France* 20 D7
Prades, *France* 20 F6
Prado, *Brazil* 125 G11
Prado del Rey, *Spain* 37 J5
Præstø, *Denmark* 11 J6
Pragersko, *Slovenia* 41 B12
Prague = Praha, *Czech Rep.* 26 A7
Prague ✈ (PRG), *Czech Rep.* 26 A7
Praha, *Czech Rep.* 26 A7
Prahecq, *France* 20 B3
Prahova □, *Romania* 29 E10
Prahova →, *Romania* 29 F10
Prahovo, *Serbia & M.* 44 B6
Praia, *C. Verde Is.* 77 E1
Práia a Mare, *Italy* 43 C8
Praid, *Romania* 29 D10
Prainha, *Amazonas, Brazil* 124 E6
Prainha, *Pará, Brazil* 125 D8
Prairie, *Australia* 94 C3
Prairie City, *U.S.A.* 108 D4
Prairie Dog Town Fork →, *U.S.A.* 113 H5
Prairie du Chien, *U.S.A.* 112 D9
Prairies, L. of the, *Canada* 103 C8
Pramánda, *Greece* 46 B3
Prampram, *Ghana* 83 D5
Pran Buri, *Thailand* 64 F2
Prang, *Ghana* 83 D4
Prapat, *Indonesia* 62 D1
Prasonísi, Ákra, *Greece* 49 D9
Prästmon, *Sweden* 10 A11
Praszka, *Poland* 31 G5
Prata, *Brazil* 125 G9
Pratabpur, *India* 69 H10
Pratapgarh, *Raj., India* 68 G6
Pratapgarh, *Ut. P., India* 69 G9
Pratas Is. = Dongsha Dao, *China* 59 G11
Prato, *Italy* 40 E8
Prátola Peligna, *Italy* 41 F10
Prats-de-Mollo-la-Preste, *France* 20 F6
Pratt, *U.S.A.* 113 G5
Prattville, *U.S.A.* 115 J2
Pravdinsk, *Russia* 34 B6
Pravets, *Bulgaria* 44 D7
Pravia, *Spain* 36 B4
Praya, *Indonesia* 62 F5
Pré-en-Pail, *France* 18 D6
Precipice △, *Australia* 95 D5
Precordillera, *Argentina* 126 C2
Predáppio, *Italy* 41 D8
Predazzo, *Italy* 41 B8
Predeal, *Romania* 29 E10
Predejane, *Serbia & M.* 44 D6
Preeceville, *Canada* 103 C8
Preetz, *Germany* 24 A6
Pregrada, *Croatia* 41 B12
Preiļi, *Latvia* 9 H22
Preko, *Croatia* 41 D12
Prelog, *Croatia* 41 B13
Prémery, *France* 19 E10
Premià de Mar, *Spain* 38 D7
Premont, *U.S.A.* 113 M5
Premuda, *Croatia* 41 D11
Prentice, *U.S.A.* 112 C9
Prenzlau, *Germany* 24 B9
Preobrazheniye, *Russia* 54 C6
Preparis North Channel, *Ind. Oc.* 67 M18
Preparis South Channel, *Ind. Oc.* 67 M18
Přerov, *Czech Rep.* 27 B10
Prescott, *Canada* 117 B9
Prescott, *Ariz., U.S.A.* 109 J7
Prescott, *Ark., U.S.A.* 113 J8
Prescott Valley, *U.S.A.* 109 J7
Preservation Inlet, *N.Z.* 91 M1
Preševo, *Serbia & M.* 44 D5
Presho, *U.S.A.* 112 D4
Presicce, *Italy* 43 C11
Presidencia de la Plaza, *Argentina* 126 B4
Presidencia Roque Saenz Peña, *Argentina* 126 B3
Presidente Epitácio, *Brazil* 125 H8
Presidente Hayes □, *Paraguay* 126 A4
Presidente Prudente, *Brazil* 127 A5
Presidio, *Mexico* 118 B4
Presidio, *U.S.A.* 113 L2
Preslav, *Bulgaria* 45 C10
Preslavska Planina, *Bulgaria* 45 C10
Prešov, *Slovak Rep.* 27 B14
Prešovský □, *Slovak Rep.* 27 B13
Prespa, *Bulgaria* 45 E8
Préspa △, *Greece* 44 F5
Prespa, L. = Prespansko Jezero, *Macedonia* 44 F5
Prespansko Jezero, *Macedonia* 44 F5
Presque I., *U.S.A.* 116 D4
Presque Isle, *U.S.A.* 115 B12
Prestatyn, *U.K.* 14 D4
Prestea, *Ghana* 82 D4
Presteigne, *U.K.* 15 E5
Přeštice, *Czech Rep.* 26 B6
Preston, *Canada* 116 C4
Preston, *U.K.* 14 D5
Preston, *Idaho, U.S.A.* 108 E8
Preston, *Minn., U.S.A.* 112 D8
Preston, C., *Australia* 92 D2
Prestonburg, *U.S.A.* 114 G4
Prestwick, *U.K.* 13 F4
Pretoria, *S. Africa* 89 D4
Preuilly-sur-Claise, *France* 18 F7
Préveza, *Greece* 46 C2
Préveza □, *Greece* 46 B2
Prey Veng, *Cambodia* 65 G5
Priazovskoye, *Ukraine* 33 J8
Pribilof Is., *U.S.A.* 100 C2
Priboj, *Serbia & M.* 44 C3
Příbram, *Czech Rep.* 26 B7
Price, *U.S.A.* 108 G8
Price I., *Canada* 102 C3
Prichard, *U.S.A.* 115 K1
Priego, *Spain* 38 E2
Priego de Córdoba, *Spain* 37 H6
Priekule, *Latvia* 9 H19
Prien, *Germany* 25 H8
Prienai, *Lithuania* 9 J20
Prieska, *S. Africa* 88 D3
Priest L., *U.S.A.* 108 B5
Priest River, *U.S.A.* 108 B5
Priest Valley, *U.S.A.* 110 J6
Prievidza, *Slovak Rep.* 27 C11
Prignitz, *Germany* 24 B7
Prijedor, *Bos.-H.* 41 D13
Prijepolje, *Serbia & M.* 44 C3
Prikaspiyskaya Nizmennost = Caspian Depression, *Eurasia* 35 G9
Prikro, *Ivory C.* 82 D4
Prikubanskaya Nizmennost, *Russia* 35 H4
Prilep, *Macedonia* 44 E5
Priluki = Pryluky, *Ukraine* 33 G7
Prime Seal I., *Australia* 95 G4
Primorsk, *Russia* 32 B5
Primorsko, *Bulgaria* 45 D11
Primorsko-Akhtarsk, *Russia* 33 J10
Primorskoye, *Ukraine* 33 J9
Primrose L., *Canada* 103 C7
Prince Albert, *Canada* 103 C7
Prince Albert, *S. Africa* 88 E3
Prince Albert △, *Canada* 103 C7
Prince Albert Mts., *Antarctica* 5 D11
Prince Albert Pen., *Canada* 100 A8
Prince Albert Sd., *Canada* 100 A8
Prince Alfred, C., *Canada* 4 B1
Prince Charles I., *Canada* 101 B12
Prince Charles Mts., *Antarctica* 5 D6
Prince Edward I. □, *Canada* 105 C7
Prince Edward Is., *Ind. Oc.* 3 G11
Prince Edward Pt., *Canada* 116 C8
Prince George, *Canada* 102 C4
Prince of Wales, C., *U.S.A.* 98 C3
Prince of Wales I., *Australia* 94 A3
Prince of Wales I., *Canada* 100 A10
Prince of Wales I., *U.S.A.* 100 C6
Prince Patrick I., *Canada* 4 B2
Prince Regent Inlet, *Canada* 4 B3
Prince Rupert, *Canada* 102 C2
Princes Town, *Trin. & Tob.* 125 K15
Princess Charlotte B., *Australia* 94 A3
Princess May Ranges, *Australia* 92 C4
Princess Royal I., *Canada* 102 C3
Princeton, *Canada* 102 D4
Princeton, *Calif., U.S.A.* 110 F4
Princeton, *Ill., U.S.A.* 112 E10
Princeton, *Ind., U.S.A.* 114 F2
Princeton, *Ky., U.S.A.* 114 G2
Princeton, *Mo., U.S.A.* 112 E8
Princeton, *N.J., U.S.A.* 117 F10
Princeton, *W. Va., U.S.A.* 114 G5
Principe, I. de, *Atl. Oc.* 76 F4
Principe da Beira, *Brazil* 124 F6
Prineville, *U.S.A.* 108 D3
Prins Harald Kyst, *Antarctica* 5 D4
Prinsesse Astrid Kyst, *Antarctica* 5 D3
Prinsesse Ragnhild Kyst, *Antarctica* 5 D4
Prinzapolca, *Nic.* 120 D3
Prior, C., *Spain* 36 B2
Priozersk, *Russia* 32 B6
Pripet = Prypyat →, *Europe* 33 G6
Pripet Marshes, *Europe* 33 F5
Pripyat Marshes = Pripet Marshes, *Europe* 33 F5
Pripyats = Prypyat →, *Europe* 33 G6
Prislop, Pasul, *Romania* 29 C9
Pristen, *Russia* 33 G9
Priština, *Serbia & M.* 44 D5
Pritzwalk, *Germany* 24 B8
Privas, *France* 21 D8
Priverno, *Italy* 42 A6
Privolzhsk, *Russia* 34 B5
Privolzhskaya Vozvyshennost, *Russia* 34 E7
Privolzhskiy, *Russia* 34 E8
Privolzhskiy □, *Russia* 34 B10
Privolzhye, *Russia* 34 D9
Priyutnoye, *Russia* 35 G6
Prizren, *Serbia & M.* 44 D4
Prizzi, *Italy* 42 E6
Prnjavor, *Bos.-H.* 28 F2
Probolinggo, *Indonesia* 63 G15
Prochowice, *Poland* 31 G3
Proctor, *U.S.A.* 117 C11
Proddatur, *India* 66 M11
Prodhromos, *Cyprus* 49 E11
Proença-a-Nova, *Portugal* 36 F3
Profítis Ilías, *Greece* 49 C9
Profondeville, *Belgium* 17 D4
Progreso, *Coahuila, Mexico* 118 B4
Progreso, *Yucatán, Mexico* 119 C7
Prokhladnyy, *Russia* 35 J7
Prokletije, *Albania* 44 D3
Prokopyevsk, *Russia* 52 D9
Prokuplje, *Serbia & M.* 44 C5
Proletarsk, *Russia* 35 G5
Proletarskaya = Proletarsk, *Russia* 35 G5
Prome, *Burma* 67 K19
Prophet →, *Canada* 102 B4
Prophet River, *Canada* 102 B4
Propriá, *Brazil* 125 F11
Propriano, *France* 21 G12
Proserpine, *Australia* 94 J6
Prosna →, *Poland* 31 F4
Prospect, *U.S.A.* 117 C9
Prosser, *U.S.A.* 108 C4
Prostějov, *Czech Rep.* 27 B10
Prostki, *Poland* 30 E9
Proston, *Australia* 95 D5
Proszowice, *Poland* 31 H7
Próti, *Greece* 46 D3
Provadiya, *Bulgaria* 45 C11
Provence, *France* 21 E9
Provence-Alpes-Côte d'Azur □, *France* 21 D10
Providence, *Ky., U.S.A.* 114 G2
Providence, *R.I., U.S.A.* 117 E13
Providence Bay, *Canada* 104 C3
Providence Mts., *U.S.A.* 111 K11
Providencia, I. de, *Colombia* 120 D3
Provideniya, *Russia* 53 C19
Provins, *France* 19 D10
Provo, *U.S.A.* 108 F8
Provost, *Canada* 103 C6
Prozor, *Bos.-H.* 28 G2
Prrenjas, *Albania* 44 E4
Prudhoe Bay, *U.S.A.* 100 A5
Prudhoe I., *Australia* 94 C4
Prud'homme, *Canada* 103 C7
Prudnik, *Poland* 31 H4
Prüm, *Germany* 25 E2
Prundu, *Romania* 29 F11
Pruszcz Gdański, *Poland* 30 D5
Pruszków, *Poland* 31 F7
Prut →, *Romania* 29 E13
Pruzhany, *Belarus* 33 F3
Prvič, *Croatia* 41 D11
Prydz B., *Antarctica* 5 C6
Pryluky, *Ukraine* 33 G7
Pryor, *U.S.A.* 113 G7
Prypyat →, *Europe* 33 G6
Przasnysz, *Poland* 31 E7
Przedbórz, *Poland* 31 G6
Przedecz, *Poland* 31 F5
Przemków, *Poland* 31 G2
Przemyśl, *Poland* 31 J9
Przeworsk, *Poland* 31 H9
Przewóz, *Poland* 31 G1
Przhevalsk = Karakol, *Kyrgyzstan* 52 E8
Przysucha, *Poland* 31 G7
Psakhná, *Greece* 46 C5
Psará, *Greece* 47 C7
Psathoúra, *Greece* 46 B6
Psel →, *Ukraine* 33 H7
Pserimos, *Greece* 47 E9
Psíra, *Greece* 49 D7
Pskov, *Russia* 32 D5
Pskovskoye, Ozero, *Russia* 32 D5
Psunj, *Croatia* 28 E2
Pteleón, *Greece* 46 B4
Ptich = Ptsich →, *Belarus* 33 F5
Ptolemaís, *Greece* 44 F5
Ptsich →, *Belarus* 33 F5
Ptuj, *Slovenia* 41 B12
Ptujska Gora, *Slovenia* 41 B12
Pu Xian, *China* 56 F6
Pua, *Thailand* 64 C3
Puán, *Argentina* 126 D3
Pu'an, *China* 58 E5
Puan, *S. Korea* 57 G14
Pubei, *China* 58 F7
Pucallpa, *Peru* 124 E4
Pucheng, *China* 59 D12
Pucheni, *Romania* 29 E10
Puchheim, *Germany* 25 G7
Púchov, *Slovak Rep.* 27 B11
Pucioasa, *Romania* 29 E10
Pučišća, *Croatia* 41 E13
Puck, *Poland* 30 D5
Pucka, Zatoka, *Poland* 30 D5
Puçol, *Spain* 39 F4
Pudasjärvi, *Finland* 8 D22
Puding, *China* 58 D5
Pudozh, *Russia* 32 B9
Puduchcheri = Pondicherry, *India* 66 P11
Pudukkottai, *India* 66 P11
Puebla, *Mexico* 119 D5
Puebla □, *Mexico* 119 D5
Puebla de Alcocer, *Spain* 37 G5
Puebla de Don Fadrique, *Spain* 39 H2
Puebla de Don Rodrigo, *Spain* 37 F6
Puebla de Guzmán, *Spain* 37 H3
Puebla de la Calzada, *Spain* 37 G4
Puebla de Sanabria, *Spain* 36 C4
Puebla de Trives = Pobra de Trives, *Spain* 36 C3
Pueblo, *U.S.A.* 112 F2
Pueblo Hundido, *Chile* 126 B1
Puelches, *Argentina* 126 D2
Puelén, *Argentina* 126 D2
Puente Alto, *Chile* 126 C1
Puente-Genil, *Spain* 37 H6
Puente la Reina, *Spain* 38 C3
Puenteareas = Ponteareas, *Spain* 36 C2
Puentedeume = Pontedeume, *Spain* 36 B2
Puentes de Garcia Rodriguez = As Pontes de García Rodríguez, *Spain* 36 B3
Pu'er, *China* 58 F3
Puerca, Pta., *Puerto Rico* 121 d
Puerco →, *U.S.A.* 109 J10
Puerto Aisén, *Chile* 128 F2
Puerto Ángel, *Mexico* 119 D5
Puerto Arista, *Mexico* 119 D6
Puerto Armuelles, *Panama* 120 E3
Puerto Ayacucho, *Venezuela* 124 B5
Puerto Barrios, *Guatemala* 120 C2
Puerto Bermejo, *Argentina* 126 B4
Puerto Bermúdez, *Peru* 124 F4
Puerto Bolívar, *Ecuador* 124 D3
Puerto Cabello, *Venezuela* 124 A5
Puerto Cabezas, *Nic.* 120 D3
Puerto Cabo Gracias á Dios, *Nic.* 120 D3
Puerto Carreño, *Colombia* 124 B5
Puerto Castilla, *Honduras* 120 C2
Puerto Chicama, *Peru* 124 E3
Puerto Coig, *Argentina* 128 G3
Puerto Cortés, *Costa Rica* 120 E3
Puerto Cortés, *Honduras* 120 C2
Puerto Cumarebo, *Venezuela* 124 A5
Puerto de Alcudia = Port d'Alcúdia, *Spain* 48 B10
Puerto de Cabrera, *Spain* 48 B9
Puerto de Gran Tarajal, *Canary Is.* 48 F5
Puerto de la Cruz, *Canary Is.* 48 F3
Puerto de los Angeles ⌂, *Mexico* 118 C3
Puerto de Mazarrón, *Spain* 39 H3
Puerto de Pozo Negro, *Canary Is.* 48 F6

Puerto de Sóller = Port de Sóller, *Spain* **48 B9**
Puerto de Somosierra, *Spain* **36 D7**
Puerto del Carmen, *Canary Is.* **48 F6**
Puerto del Rosario, *Canary Is.* **48 F6**
Puerto Deseado, *Argentina* **128 F3**
Puerto Escondido, *Mexico* **119 D5**
Puerto Heath, *Bolivia* **124 F5**
Puerto Inírida, *Colombia* **124 C5**
Puerto Juárez, *Mexico* **119 C7**
Puerto La Cruz, *Venezuela* **124 A6**
Puerto Leguízamo, *Colombia* **124 D4**
Puerto Limón, *Colombia* **124 C4**
Puerto Lobos, *Argentina* **128 E3**
Puerto Lumbreras, *Spain* **39 H3**
Puerto Madryn, *Argentina* **128 E3**
Puerto Maldonado, *Peru* **124 F5**
Puerto Manotí, *Cuba* **120 B4**
Puerto Montt, *Chile* **128 E2**
Puerto Morazán, *Nic.* **120 D2**
Puerto Morelos, *Mexico* **119 C7**
Puerto Natales, *Chile* **128 G2**
Puerto Padre, *Cuba* **120 B4**
Puerto Páez, *Venezuela* **124 B5**
Puerto Peñasco, *Mexico* **118 A2**
Puerto Pinasco, *Paraguay* **126 A4**
Puerto Plata, *Dom. Rep.* **121 C5**
Puerto Pollensa = Port de Pollença, *Spain* **48 B10**
Puerto Princesa, *Phil.* **61 G3**
Puerto Quepos, *Costa Rica* **120 E3**
Puerto Real, *Spain* **37 J4**
Puerto Rico, *Canary Is.* **48 G4**
Puerto Rico ☒, *W. Indies* **121 d**
Puerto Rico Trench, *Atl. Oc.* **121 C6**
Puerto San Julián, *Argentina* **128 F3**
Puerto Sastre, *Paraguay* **126 A4**
Puerto Serrano, *Spain* **37 J5**
Puerto Suárez, *Bolivia* **124 G7**
Puerto Vallarta, *Mexico* **118 C3**
Puerto Wilches, *Colombia* **124 B4**
Puertollano, *Spain* **37 G6**
Pueyrredón, L., *Argentina* **128 F2**
Púez Odle ⌂, *Italy* **41 B8**
Puffin I., *Ireland* **12 E1**
Pugachev, *Russia* **34 D9**
Pugal, *India* **68 E5**
Puge, *China* **58 D4**
Puge, *Tanzania* **86 C3**
Puget Sound, *U.S.A.* **108 C2**
Puget-Théniers, *France* **21 E10**
Púglia □, *Italy* **43 A9**
Pugŏdong, *N. Korea* **57 C16**
Pugu, *Tanzania* **86 D4**
Pūgūnzī, *Iran* **71 E8**
Pui, *Romania* **28 E8**
Puiești, *Romania* **29 D12**
Puig Major, *Spain* **48 B9**
Puigcerdà, *Spain* **38 C6**
Puigmal, *Spain* **38 C7**
Puigpunyent, *Spain* **48 B9**
Puijiang, *China* **58 B4**
Puisaye, Collines de la, *France* **19 E10**
Puiseaux, *France* **19 D9**
Pujehun, *S. Leone* **82 D2**
Pujiang, *China* **59 C12**
Pujols, *France* **20 D3**
Pujon-chŏsuji, *N. Korea* **57 D14**
Pukaki, L., *N.Z.* **91 L3**
Pukapuka, *Cook Is.* **97 J11**
Pukaskwa △, *Canada* **104 C2**
Pukatawagan, *Canada* **103 B8**
Pukchin, *N. Korea* **57 D13**
Pukch'ŏng, *N. Korea* **57 D15**
Pukë, *Albania* **44 D3**
Pukekohe, *N.Z.* **91 G5**
Pukhrayan, *India* **69 F8**
Pukou, *China* **59 A12**
Pula, *Croatia* **41 D10**
Pula, *Italy* **42 C1**
Pulacayo, *Bolivia* **124 H5**
Pulai, *Malaysia* **65 d**
Pulandian, *China* **57 E11**
Pularumpi, *Australia* **92 B5**
Pulaski, *N.Y., U.S.A.* **117 C8**
Pulaski, *Tenn., U.S.A.* **115 H2**
Pulaski, *Va., U.S.A.* **114 G5**
Pulau →, *Indonesia* **63 F9**
Puławy, *Poland* **31 G8**
Pulga, *U.S.A.* **110 F5**
Pulicat L., *India* **66 N12**
Pullman, *U.S.A.* **108 C5**
Pulog, Mt., *Phil.* **61 C4**
Pułtusk, *Poland* **31 F8**
Pülümür, *Turkey* **73 C8**
Pumlumon Fawr, *U.K.* **15 E4**
Puná, I., *Ecuador* **124 D2**
Punakha, *Bhutan* **67 F16**
Punasar, *India* **68 F5**
Punata, *Bolivia* **124 G5**
Punch, *India* **69 C6**
Punch →, *Pakistan* **68 C5**
Punda Maria, *S. Africa* **89 C5**
Pune, *India* **66 K8**
P'ungsan, *N. Korea* **57 D15**
Pungue, Ponte de, *Mozam.* **87 F3**
Puning, *China* **59 F11**
Punjab □, *India* **68 D7**
Punjab □, *Pakistan* **68 E6**
Puno, *Peru* **124 G4**
Punpun →, *India* **69 G11**
Punta, Cerro de, *Puerto Rico* **121 d**
Punta Alta, *Argentina* **128 D4**
Punta Arenas, *Chile* **128 G2**
Punta de Díaz, *Chile* **126 B1**
Punta del Hidalgo, *Canary Is.* **48 F3**
Punta Gorda, *Belize* **119 D7**
Punta Gorda, *U.S.A.* **115 M5**
Punta Prieta, *Mexico* **118 B2**
Punta Prima, *Spain* **48 B11**
Punta Umbría, *Spain* **37 H4**
Puntarenas, *Costa Rica* **120 E3**
Punto Fijo, *Venezuela* **124 A4**
Punxsatawney, *U.S.A.* **116 F6**
Pupuan, *Indonesia* **63 J18**
Puqi, *China* **59 C9**
Puquio, *Peru* **124 F4**
Pur →, *Russia* **52 C8**
Purace, Vol., *Colombia* **124 C3**
Puračić, *Bos.-H.* **28 F3**
Puralia = Puruliya, *India* **69 H12**
Puranpur, *India* **69 E9**
Purbeck, Isle of, *U.K.* **15 G6**
Purcell, *U.S.A.* **113 H6**
Purcell Mts., *Canada* **102 D5**
Puri, *India* **67 K14**
Purmerend, *Neths.* **17 B4**
Purnia, *India* **69 G12**
Pursat = Pouthisat, *Cambodia* **64 F4**
Purukcahu, *Indonesia* **62 E4**
Puruliya, *India* **69 H12**
Purus →, *Brazil* **124 D6**
Puruvesi, *Finland* **32 B5**
Purvis, *U.S.A.* **113 K10**
Pŭrvomay, *Bulgaria* **45 D9**
Purwa, *India* **69 F9**
Purwakarta, *Indonesia* **63 G12**
Purwo, Tanjung, *Indonesia* **63 K18**
Purwodadi, *Indonesia* **63 G14**
Purwokerto, *Indonesia* **63 G13**
Puryŏng, *N. Korea* **57 C15**
Pusa, *India* **69 G11**
Pusan, *S. Korea* **57 G15**
Pushkin, *Russia* **32 C6**
Pushkino, *Moskva, Russia* **32 D9**
Pushkino, *Saratov, Russia* **34 E8**
Püspökladány, *Hungary* **28 C6**
Pustoshka, *Russia* **32 D5**
Puszczykowo, *Poland* **31 F3**
Putahow L., *Canada* **103 B8**
Putao, *Burma* **67 F20**
Putaruru, *N.Z.* **91 H5**
Putbus, *Germany* **24 A9**
Putian, *China* **59 E12**
Putignano, *Italy* **43 B10**
Puting, Tanjung, *Indonesia* **62 E4**
Putlitz, *Germany* **24 B8**
Putna, *Romania* **29 C10**
Putna →, *Romania* **29 E12**
Putnam, *U.S.A.* **117 E13**
Putnok, *Hungary* **28 B5**
Putorana, Gory, *Russia* **53 C10**
Putrajaya, *Malaysia* **65 L3**
Puttalam, *Sri Lanka* **66 Q11**
Puttgarden, *Germany* **24 A7**
Püttlingen, *Germany* **25 F2**
Putumayo →, *S. Amer.* **124 D5**
Putuo, *China* **59 C14**
Putussibau, *Indonesia* **62 D4**
Puvirnituq, *Canada* **101 B12**
Puy-de-Dôme, *France* **20 C6**
Puy-de-Dôme □, *France* **20 C7**
Puy-l'Évêque, *France* **20 D5**
Puyallup, *U.S.A.* **110 C4**
Puyang, *China* **56 G8**
Puylaurens, *France* **20 E6**
Pūzeh Rīg, *Iran* **71 E8**
Pwani □, *Tanzania* **86 D4**
Pweto, *Dem. Rep. of the Congo* **87 D2**
Pwllheli, *U.K.* **14 E3**
Pyana →, *Russia* **34 C8**
Pyapon, *Burma* **67 L19**
Pyasina →, *Russia* **53 B9**
Pyatigorsk, *Russia* **35 H6**
Pyatykhatky, *Ukraine* **33 H7**
Pydna, *Greece* **44 F6**
Pyè = Prome, *Burma* **67 K19**
Pyetrikaw, *Belarus* **33 F5**
Pyhäjoki, *Finland* **8 D21**
Pyinmana, *Burma* **67 K20**
Pyla, C., *Cyprus* **49 E12**
Pymatuning Reservoir, *U.S.A.* **116 E4**
Pyŏktong, *N. Korea* **57 D13**
Pyŏnggang, *N. Korea* **57 E14**
P'yŏngt'aek, *S. Korea* **57 F14**
P'yŏngyang, *N. Korea* **57 E13**
Pyote, *U.S.A.* **113 K3**
Pyramid L., *U.S.A.* **108 G4**
Pyramid Pk., *U.S.A.* **111 J10**
Pyramids, *Egypt* **80 J7**
Pyrénées, *Europe* **20 F4**
Pyrénées △, *France* **20 F3**
Pyrénées-Atlantiques □, *France* **20 E3**
Pyrénées-Orientales □, *France* **20 F6**
Pyryatyn, *Ukraine* **33 G7**
Pyrzyce, *Poland* **31 E1**
Pyskowice, *Poland* **31 H5**
Pytalovo, *Russia* **32 D4**
Pyu, *Burma* **67 K20**
Pyzdry, *Poland* **31 F4**

Q

Qaanaaq, *Greenland* **4 B4**
Qabirri →, *Azerbaijan* **35 K8**
Qachasnek, *S. Africa* **89 E4**
Qa'el Jafr, *Jordan* **74 E5**
Qa'emābād, *Iran* **71 D9**
Qā'emshahr, *Iran* **71 B7**
Qagan Nur, *China* **56 C8**
Qahar Youyi Zhongqi, *China* **56 D7**
Qahremānshahr = Bākhtarān, *Iran* **70 C5**
Qaidam Pendi, *China* **60 C4**
Qajarīyeh, *Iran* **71 D6**
Qala, Ras il, *Malta* **49 C1**
Qala-i-Jadid = Spīn Būldak, *Afghan.* **68 D2**
Qala Point = Qala, Ras il, *Malta* **49 C1**
Qala Viala, *Pakistan* **68 D2**
Qala Yangi, *Afghan.* **68 B2**
Qal'at al Akhḍar, *Si. Arabia* **70 E3**
Qal'at Dīzah, *Iraq* **70 B5**
Qal'at Şāliḥ, *Iraq* **70 D5**
Qal'at Sukkar, *Iraq* **70 D5**
Qalyûb, *Egypt* **80 H7**
Qamani'tuaq = Baker Lake, *Canada* **100 B10**
Qamdo, *China* **58 B1**
Qamruddin Karez, *Pakistan* **68 D3**
Qandahār, *Afghan.* **66 D4**
Qandahār □, *Afghan.* **66 D4**
Qapān, *Iran* **71 B7**
Qapshaghay, *Kazakhstan* **52 E8**
Qaqortoq, *Greenland* **101 B6**
Qâra, *Egypt* **80 B2**
Qara Qash →, *China* **69 B8**
Qarabutaq, *Kazakhstan* **52 E7**
Qaraçala, *Azerbaijan* **35 L9**
Qaraghandy, *Kazakhstan* **52 E8**
Qārah, *Si. Arabia* **70 D4**
Qarataū, *Kazakhstan* **52 E8**
Qarataū, *Kazakhstan* **52 E7**
Qardho = Gardo, *Somali Rep.* **75 F4**
Qardud, *Sudan* **81 E2**
Qareh →, *Iran* **70 B5**
Qareh Tekān, *Iran* **71 B6**
Qarqan He →, *China* **60 C3**
Qarqaraly, *Kazakhstan* **52 E8**
Qarrasa, *Sudan* **81 E3**
Qarshi, *Uzbekistan* **52 F7**
Qartabā, *Lebanon* **74 A4**
Qaryat al Gharab, *Iraq* **70 D5**
Qaryat al 'Ulyā, *Si. Arabia* **70 E5**
Qasr 'Amra, *Jordan* **70 D3**
Qaşr-e Qand, *Iran* **71 E9**
Qasr Farâfra, *Egypt* **80 B2**
Qatanā, *Syria* **74 B5**
Qatar ■, *Asia* **71 E6**
Qatlīsh, *Iran* **71 B8**
Qattâra, *Egypt* **80 A2**
Qattâra, Munkhafed el, *Egypt* **80 B2**
Qattâra Depression = Qattâra, Munkhafed el, *Egypt* **80 B2**
Qawām al Ḥamzah = Al Ḥamzah, *Iraq* **70 D5**
Qāyen, *Iran* **71 C8**
Qazaqstan = Kazakhstan ■, *Asia* **52 E7**
Qazimämmäd, *Azerbaijan* **35 K9**
Qazvin, *Iran* **71 B6**
Qazvin □, *Iran* **71 B6**
Qeissan, *Sudan* **81 E3**
Qena, *Egypt* **80 B3**
Qena, W. →, *Egypt* **80 B3**
Qeqertarsuaq, *Greenland* **101 B5**
Qeqertarsuaq, *Greenland* **101 B14**
Qeshlāq, *Iran* **70 C5**
Qeshm, *Iran* **71 E8**
Qeys, *Iran* **71 E7**
Qezel Owzen →, *Iran* **71 B6**
Qezi'ot, *Israel* **74 E3**
Qi Xian, *China* **56 G8**
Qian Gorlos, *China* **57 B13**
Qian Xian, *China* **56 G5**
Qiancheng, *China* **58 D7**
Qianjiang, *Guangxi Zhuangzu, China* **58 F7**
Qianjiang, *Hubei, China* **59 B9**
Qianjiang, *Sichuan, China* **58 C7**
Qianshan, *China* **59 B11**
Qianwei, *China* **58 C4**
Qianxi, *China* **58 D6**
Qianyang, *Hunan, China* **59 D8**
Qianyang, *Shaanxi, China* **56 G4**
Qianyang, *Zhejiang, China* **59 B12**
Qiaojia, *China* **58 D4**
Qichun, *China* **59 B10**
Qidong, *Hunan, China* **59 D9**
Qidong, *Jiangsu, China* **59 B13**
Qijiang, *China* **58 C6**
Qikiqtarjuaq, *Canada* **101 B13**
Qila Safed, *Pakistan* **66 E2**
Qila Saifullāh, *Pakistan* **68 D3**
Qilian Shan, *China* **60 C4**
Qimen, *China* **59 C11**
Qin He →, *China* **56 G7**
Qin Jiang →, *Guangxi Zhuangzu, China* **58 F7**
Qin Jiang →, *Jiangxi, China* **59 D10**
Qin Ling = Qinling Shandi, *China* **56 H5**
Qin'an, *China* **56 G3**
Qing Xian, *China* **56 E9**
Qingcheng, *China* **57 F9**
Qingdao, *China* **57 F11**
Qingfeng, *China* **56 G8**
Qinghai □, *China* **60 C4**
Qinghai Hu, *China* **60 C5**
Qinghecheng, *China* **57 D13**
Qinghemen, *China* **57 D11**
Qingjian, *China* **56 F6**
Qingjiang = Huaiyin, *China* **57 H10**
Qingliu, *China* **59 D11**
Qinglong, *China* **58 E5**
Qingping, *China* **58 D6**
Qingpu, *China* **59 B13**
Qingshui, *China* **56 G4**
Qingshuihe, *China* **56 E6**
Qingtian, *China* **59 C13**
Qingtongxia Shuiku, *China* **56 F3**
Qingxi, *China* **58 D7**
Qingxu, *China* **56 F7**
Qingyang, *Anhui, China* **59 B11**
Qingyang, *Gansu, China* **56 F4**
Qingyi Jiang →, *China* **58 C4**
Qingyuan, *Guangdong, China* **59 F9**
Qingyuan, *Liaoning, China* **57 C13**
Qingyuan, *Zhejiang, China* **59 D12**
Qingyun, *China* **57 F9**
Qingzhen, *China* **58 D6**
Qinhuangdao, *China* **57 E10**
Qinling Shandi, *China* **56 H5**
Qinshui, *China* **56 G7**
Qinyang = Jiyuan, *China* **56 G7**
Qinyuan, *China* **56 F7**
Qinzhou, *China* **58 G7**
Qionghai, *China* **64 C8**
Qionglai, *China* **58 B4**
Qionglai Shan, *China* **58 B4**
Qiongzhou Haixia, *China* **53 E13**
Qiqihar, *China* **64 B8**
Qirâiya, W. →, *Egypt* **74 E3**
Qiryat Ata, *Israel* **74 C4**
Qiryat Gat, *Israel* **74 D3**
Qiryat Mal'akhi, *Israel* **74 D3**
Qiryat Shemona, *Israel* **74 B4**
Qiryat Yam, *Israel* **74 C4**
Qishan, *China* **56 G4**
Qitai, *China* **60 B3**
Qiubei, *China* **58 E5**
Qixia, *China* **57 F11**
Qiyang, *China* **59 D8**
Qızılağac Körfäzi, *Azerbaijan* **71 B6**
Qojūr, *Iran* **70 B5**
Qom, *Iran* **71 C6**
Qom □, *Iran* **71 C6**
Qomolangma Feng = Everest, Mt., *Nepal* **69 E12**
Qomsheh, *Iran* **71 D6**
Qoraqalpoghistan □, *Uzbekistan* **52 E6**
Qorveh, *Iran* **73 E12**
Qostanay, *Kazakhstan* **52 D7**
Qoṭūr, *Iran* **73 C11**
Qu Jiang →, *China* **58 B6**
Qu Xian, *China* **58 B6**
Quabbin Reservoir, *U.S.A.* **117 D12**
Quairading, *Australia* **93 F2**
Quakenbrück, *Germany* **24 C3**
Quakertown, *U.S.A.* **117 F9**
Qualicum Beach, *Canada* **102 D4**
Quambatook, *Australia* **95 F3**
Quambone, *Australia* **95 E4**
Quamby, *Australia* **94 C3**
Quan Long = Ca Mau, *Vietnam* **65 H5**
Quanah, *U.S.A.* **113 H5**
Quang Ngai, *Vietnam* **64 E7**
Quang Tri, *Vietnam* **64 D6**
Quang Yen, *Vietnam* **58 G6**
Quannan, *China* **59 E10**
Quantock Hills, *U.K.* **15 F4**
Quanzhou, *Fujian, China* **59 E12**
Quanzhou, *Guangxi Zhuangzu, China* **59 E8**
Qu'Appelle, *Canada* **103 C8**
Quaqtaq, *Canada* **101 B13**
Quaraí, *Brazil* **126 C4**
Quarré-les-Tombes, *France* **19 E11**
Quarteira, *Portugal* **37 H2**
Quartu Sant'Élena, *Italy* **42 C2**
Quartzsite, *U.S.A.* **111 M12**
Quatsino Sd., *Canada* **102 C3**
Quba, *Azerbaijan* **35 K9**
Qūchān, *Iran* **71 B8**
Queanbeyan, *Australia* **95 F4**
Québec, *Canada* **105 C5**
Québec □, *Canada* **105 C6**
Quebrada del Condorito △, *Argentina* **126 C3**
Quedlinburg, *Germany* **24 D7**
Queen Alexandra Ra., *Antarctica* **5 E11**
Queen Charlotte City, *Canada* **102 C2**
Queen Charlotte Is., *Canada* **102 C2**
Queen Charlotte Sd., *Canada* **102 C3**
Queen Charlotte Strait, *Canada* **102 C3**
Queen Elizabeth ⌂, *U.K.* **13 E4**
Queen Elizabeth △, *Uganda* **86 C3**
Queen Elizabeth Is., *Canada* **98 B10**
Queen Mary Land, *Antarctica* **5 D7**
Queen Maud G., *Canada* **100 B9**
Queen Maud Land = Dronning Maud Land, *Antarctica* **5 D3**
Queen Maud Mts., *Antarctica* **5 E13**
Queens Chan., *Australia* **92 C4**
Queenscliff, *Australia* **95 F3**
Queensland □, *Australia* **94 C3**
Queenstown, *Australia* **95 G4**
Queenstown, *N.Z.* **91 L2**
Queenstown, *Singapore* **65 d**
Queenstown, *S. Africa* **88 E4**
Queets, *U.S.A.* **110 C2**
Queguay Grande →, *Uruguay* **126 C4**
Queimadas, *Brazil* **125 F11**
Quelimane, *Mozam.* **87 F4**
Quellón, *Chile* **128 E2**
Quelpart = Cheju do, *S. Korea* **57 H14**
Queluz, *Portugal* **37 G1**
Quemado, *N. Mex., U.S.A.* **109 J9**
Quemado, *Tex., U.S.A.* **113 L4**
Quemoy = Chinmen, *Taiwan* **59 E13**
Quemú-Quemú, *Argentina* **126 D3**
Quequén, *Argentina* **126 D4**
Querétaro, *Mexico* **118 C4**
Querétaro □, *Mexico* **118 C5**
Querfurt, *Germany* **24 D7**
Quérigut, *France* **20 F6**
Querqueville, *France* **18 C5**
Quesada, *Spain* **37 H7**
Queshan, *China* **56 H8**
Quesnel, *Canada* **102 C4**
Quesnel →, *Canada* **102 C4**
Quesnel L., *Canada* **102 C4**
Questa, *U.S.A.* **109 H11**
Questembert, *France* **18 E4**
Quetico ⌂, *Canada* **104 C1**
Quetta, *Pakistan* **68 D2**
Queyras ⌂, *France* **21 D10**
Quezaltenango, *Guatemala* **120 D1**
Quezon City, *Phil.* **61 D4**
Qufār, *Si. Arabia* **70 E4**
Qui Nhon, *Vietnam* **64 F7**
Quibaxe, *Angola* **84 F2**
Quibdo, *Colombia* **124 B3**
Quiberon, *France* **18 E3**
Quiberon, Presqu'île de, *France* **18 E3**
Quickborn, *Germany* **24 B5**
Quiet L., *Canada* **102 A2**
Quiindy, *Paraguay* **126 B4**
Quila, *Mexico* **118 C3**
Quilán, C., *Chile* **128 E2**
Quilcene, *U.S.A.* **110 C4**
Quilimarí, *Chile* **126 C1**
Quilino, *Argentina* **126 C3**
Quill Lakes, *Canada* **103 C8**
Quillabamba, *Peru* **124 F4**
Quillagua, *Chile* **126 A2**
Quillaicillo, *Chile* **126 C1**
Quillan, *France* **20 F6**
Quillota, *Chile* **126 C1**
Quilmes, *Argentina* **126 C4**
Quilon, *India* **66 Q10**
Quilpie, *Australia* **95 D3**
Quilpué, *Chile* **126 C1**
Quilua, *Mozam.* **87 F4**
Quimilí, *Argentina* **126 B3**
Quimper, *France* **18 E2**
Quimperlé, *France* **18 E3**
Quinault →, *U.S.A.* **110 C2**
Quincy, *Calif., U.S.A.* **110 F6**
Quincy, *Fla., U.S.A.* **115 K3**
Quincy, *Ill., U.S.A.* **112 F9**
Quincy, *Mass., U.S.A.* **117 D14**
Quincy, *Wash., U.S.A.* **108 C4**
Quines, *Argentina* **126 C2**
Quinga, *Mozam.* **87 F5**
Quingey, *France* **19 E12**
Quinns Rocks, *Australia* **93 F2**
Quintana de la Serena, *Spain* **37 G5**
Quintana Roo □, *Mexico* **119 D7**
Quintanar de la Orden, *Spain* **37 F7**
Quintanar de la Sierra, *Spain* **38 D2**
Quintanar del Rey, *Spain* **39 F3**
Quinte West, *Canada* **116 B7**
Quintero, *Chile* **126 C1**
Quintin, *France* **18 D4**
Quinto, *Spain* **38 D4**
Quípar →, *Spain* **39 G3**
Quirihue, *Chile* **126 D1**
Quirindi, *Australia* **95 E5**
Quirinópolis, *Brazil* **125 G8**
Quiroga, *Spain* **36 C3**
Quissac, *France* **21 E8**
Quissanga, *Mozam.* **87 E5**
Quissico, *Mozam.* **89 C5**
Quitilipi, *Argentina* **126 B3**
Quitman, *U.S.A.* **115 K4**
Quito, *Ecuador* **124 D3**
Quixadá, *Brazil* **125 D11**
Quixaxe, *Mozam.* **87 F5**
Qujing, *China* **58 E4**
Qulan, *Kazakhstan* **52 E8**
Qul'ân, Jazâ'ir, *Egypt* **70 E2**
Qumbu, *S. Africa* **89 E4**
Quneitra, *Syria* **74 B4**
Qŭnghirot, *Uzbekistan* **52 E6**
Qu'nyido, *China* **58 B2**
Quoin I., *Australia* **92 B4**
Quoin Pt., *S. Africa* **88 E2**
Quorn, *Australia* **95 E2**
Qŭqon, *Uzbekistan* **52 E8**
Qurein, *Sudan* **81 E3**
Qurnat as Sawdā', *Lebanon* **74 A5**
Qûs, *Egypt* **80 B3**
Qusar, *Azerbaijan* **35 K9**
Quşaybā', *Si. Arabia* **70 E4**
Qusaybah, *Iraq* **70 C4**
Quseir, *Egypt* **70 E2**
Qūshchī, *Iran* **70 B5**
Quthing, *Lesotho* **89 E4**
Qūṭīābād, *Iran* **71 C6**
Quwo, *China* **56 G6**
Quyang, *China* **56 E8**
Quynh Nhai, *Vietnam* **64 B4**
Quyon, *Canada* **117 A8**
Quzhou, *China* **59 C12**
Quzi, *China* **56 F4**
Qvareli, *Georgia* **35 K7**
Qytet Stalin = Kuçovë, *Albania* **44 F3**
Qyzylorda, *Kazakhstan* **52 E7**

R

Ra, Ko, *Thailand* **65 H2**
Raab, *Austria* **26 C6**
Raahe, *Finland* **8 D21**
Raalte, *Neths.* **17 B6**
Raasay, *U.K.* **13 D2**
Raasay, Sd. of, *U.K.* **13 D2**
Rab, *Croatia* **41 D11**
Raba, *Indonesia* **63 F5**
Rába →, *Hungary* **28 C2**
Raba →, *Poland* **31 H7**
Rabaçal →, *Portugal* **36 D3**
Rabah, *Nigeria* **83 C6**
Rabai, *Kenya* **86 C4**
Rabak, *Sudan* **81 E3**
Rabastens, *France* **20 E5**
Rabastens-de-Bigorre, *France* **20 E4**
Rabat = Victoria, *Malta* **49 C1**
Rabat, *Malta* **49 D1**
Rabat, *Morocco* **78 B4**
Rabaul, *Papua N. G.* **96 H7**
Rābigh, *Si. Arabia* **75 C2**
Rabka, *Poland* **31 J6**
Râbniţa, *Moldova* **29 C14**
Rābor, *Iran* **71 D8**
Rača, *Serbia & M.* **44 B4**
Răcăciuni, *Romania* **29 D11**
Răcășdia, *Romania* **28 F6**
Racconigi, *Italy* **40 D4**
Race, C., *Canada* **105 C9**
Rach Gia, *Vietnam* **65 G5**
Rachid, *Mauritania* **82 B2**
Raciąż, *Poland* **31 F7**
Racibórz, *Poland* **31 H5**
Racine, *U.S.A.* **114 D2**

Rackerby, *U.S.A.* 110 F5
Radama, Nosy, *Madag.* 89 A8
Radama, Saikanosy, *Madag.* 89 A8
Radan, *Serbia & M.* 44 D5
Rădăuţi, *Romania* 29 C10
Rădăuţi-Prut, *Romania* 29 B11
Radbuza →, *Czech Rep.* 26 B6
Radcliff, *U.S.A.* 114 G3
Radeberg, *Germany* 24 D9
Radebeul, *Germany* 24 D9
Radeče, *Slovenia* 41 B12
Radekhiv, *Ukraine* 33 G3
Radekhov = Radekhiv, *Ukraine* 33 G3
Radenthein, *Austria* 26 E6
Radew →, *Poland* 30 D2
Radford, *U.S.A.* 114 G5
Radhanpur, *India* 68 H4
Radhwa, Jabal, *Si. Arabia* 70 E3
Radika →, *Macedonia* 44 E4
Radisson, *Qué., Canada* 104 B4
Radisson, *Sask., Canada* 103 C7
Radium Hot Springs, *Canada* 102 C5
Radlje ob Dravi, *Slovenia* 41 B12
Radnevo, *Bulgaria* 45 D9
Radnice, *Czech Rep.* 26 B6
Radnor Forest, *U.K.* 15 E4
Radolfzell, *Germany* 25 H4
Radom, *Poland* 31 G8
Radomir, *Bulgaria* 44 D6
Radomka →, *Poland* 31 G8
Radomsko, *Poland* 31 G6
Radomyshl, *Ukraine* 33 G5
Radomyśl Wielki, *Poland* 31 H8
Radoszyce, *Poland* 31 G7
Radoviš, *Macedonia* 44 E6
Radovljica, *Slovenia* 41 B11
Radstadt, *Austria* 26 D6
Radstock, C., *Australia* 95 E1
Răducăneni, *Romania* 29 D12
Raduša, *Macedonia* 44 D5
Radviliškis, *Lithuania* 9 J20
Radville, *Canada* 103 D8
Raḍwá, J., *Si. Arabia* 80 C4
Radymno, *Poland* 31 J9
Radzanów, *Poland* 31 F7
Radziejów, *Poland* 31 F5
Radzyń Chełmiński, *Poland* 30 E5
Radzyń Podlaski, *Poland* 31 G9
Rae, *Canada* 102 A5
Rae Bareli, *India* 69 F9
Rae Isthmus, *Canada* 101 B11
Raeren, *Belgium* 17 D6
Raeside, L., *Australia* 93 E3
Raetihi, *N.Z.* 91 H5
Rafaela, *Argentina* 126 C3
Rafah, *Gaza Strip* 74 D3
Rafai, *C.A.R.* 86 B1
Raffadali, *Italy* 42 E6
Raffili, *Sudan* 81 F2
Rafḥā, *Si. Arabia* 70 D4
Rafsanjān, *Iran* 71 D8
Raft Pt., *Australia* 92 C3
Râgâ, *Sudan* 81 F2
Raga →, *Sudan* 81 F2
Ragachow, *Belarus* 33 F6
Ragag, *Sudan* 81 E1
Ragama, *Sri Lanka* 66 R11
Ragged, Mt., *Australia* 93 F3
Ragged Pt., *Barbados* 121 g
Raghunathpalli, *India* 69 H11
Raghunathpur, *India* 69 H12
Raglan, *N.Z.* 91 G5
Ragusa, *Italy* 43 F7
Raha, *Indonesia* 63 E6
Rahad, Nahr ed →, *Sudan* 81 E3
Rahaeng = Tak, *Thailand* 64 D2
Rahatgarh, *India* 69 H8
Rahden, *Germany* 24 C4
Raheita, *Eritrea* 81 E5
Rahimyar Khan, *Pakistan* 68 E4
Rāhjerd, *Iran* 71 C6
Rahole ⌓, *Kenya* 86 B4
Rahon, *India* 68 D7
Raichur, *India* 66 L10
Raiganj, *India* 69 G13
Raigarh, *India* 67 J13
Raijua, *Indonesia* 63 F6
Raikot, *India* 68 D6
Railton, *Australia* 95 G4
Rainbow Bridge ⌓, *U.S.A.* 109 H8
Rainbow Lake, *Canada* 102 B5
Rainier, *U.S.A.* 110 D4
Rainier, Mt., *U.S.A.* 110 D5
Rainy L., *Canada* 103 D10
Rainy River, *Canada* 103 D10
Raippaluoto, *Finland* 8 E19
Raipur, *India* 67 J12
Ra'is, *Si. Arabia* 80 C4
Raisen, *India* 68 H8
Raisio, *Finland* 9 F20
Raj Nandgaon, *India* 67 J12
Raj Nilgiri, *India* 69 J12
Raja, Ujung, *Indonesia* 62 D1
Raja Ampat, Kepulauan, *Indonesia* 63 E7
Rajahmundry, *India* 67 L12
Rajang →, *Malaysia* 62 D4
Rajanpur, *Pakistan* 68 E4
Rajapalaiyam, *India* 66 Q10
Rajasthan □, *India* 68 F5
Rajasthan Canal = Indira Gandhi Canal, *India* 68 F5
Rajauri, *India* 69 C6
Rajgarh, *Mad. P., India* 68 G7
Rajgarh, *Raj., India* 68 F7
Rajgarh, *Raj., India* 68 E6
Rajgir, *India* 69 G11
Rajgród, *Poland* 30 E9
Rajkot, *India* 68 H4
Rajmahal Hills, *India* 69 G12
Rajpipla, *India* 66 J8
Rajpur, *India* 68 H6
Rajpura, *India* 68 D7
Rajshahi, *Bangla.* 67 G16
Rajshahi □, *Bangla.* 69 G13
Rajula, *India* 68 J4
Rakaia, *N.Z.* 91 K4
Rakaia →, *N.Z.* 91 K4
Rakan, Ra's, *Qatar* 71 E6
Rakaposhi, *Pakistan* 69 A6
Rakata, Pulau, *Indonesia* 62 F3
Rakhiv, *Ukraine* 33 H3
Rakhni, *Pakistan* 68 D3
Rakhni →, *Pakistan* 68 E3
Rakitnoye, *Russia* 54 B7
Rakitovo, *Bulgaria* 45 E8
Rakoniewice, *Poland* 31 F3
Rakops, *Botswana* 88 C3
Rakovica, *Croatia* 41 D12
Rakovník, *Czech Rep.* 26 A6
Rakovski, *Bulgaria* 45 D8
Rakvere, *Estonia* 9 G22
Raleigh, *U.S.A.* 115 H6
Ralja, *Serbia & M.* 44 B4
Ralls, *U.S.A.* 113 J4
Ralston, *U.S.A.* 116 E8
Ram →, *Canada* 102 A4
Rām Allāh, *West Bank* 74 D4
Rama, *Nic.* 120 D3
Ramacca, *Italy* 43 E7
Ramakona, *India* 69 J8
Ramales de la Victoria, *Spain* 36 B7
Rāmallāh = Rām Allāh, *West Bank* 74 D4
Raman, *Thailand* 65 J3
Ramanathapuram, *India* 66 Q11
Ramanetaka, B. de, *Madag.* 89 A8
Ramanujganj, *India* 69 H10
Ramat Gan, *Israel* 74 C3
Ramatlhabama, *S. Africa* 88 D4
Ramban, *India* 69 C6
Rambervillers, *France* 19 D13
Rambipuji, *Indonesia* 63 H15
Rambouillet, *France* 19 D8
Rame Hd., *Australia* 95 F4
Ramechhap, *Nepal* 69 F12
Ramenskoye, *Russia* 32 E10
Ramganga →, *India* 69 F8
Ramgarh, *Jharkhand, India* 69 H11
Ramgarh, *Raj., India* 68 F6
Ramgarh, *Raj., India* 68 F4
Rāmhormoz, *Iran* 71 D6
Ramīān, *Iran* 71 B7
Ramingining, *Australia* 94 A2
Ramla, *Israel* 74 D3
Ramlu, *Eritrea* 81 E5
Ramm = Rum, *Jordan* 74 F4
Ramm, Jabal, *Jordan* 74 F4
Râmna →, *Romania* 29 E12
Ramnad = Ramanathapuram, *India* 66 Q11
Ramnagar, *Jammu & Kashmir, India* 69 C6
Ramnagar, *Uttaranchal, India* 69 E8
Ramnäs, *Sweden* 10 E10
Râmnicu Sărat, *Romania* 29 E12
Râmnicu Vâlcea, *Romania* 29 E9
Ramon, *Russia* 33 G10
Ramona, *U.S.A.* 111 M10
Ramonville-St-Agne, *France* 20 E5
Ramore, *Canada* 104 C3
Ramos →, *Nigeria* 83 D6
Ramotswa, *Botswana* 88 C4
Rampur, *H.P., India* 68 D7
Rampur, *Mad. P., India* 68 H5
Rampur, *Ut. P., India* 69 E8
Rampur Hat, *India* 69 G12
Rampura, *India* 68 G6
Ramrama Tola, *India* 69 J8
Ramree I., *Burma* 67 K19
Rāmsar, *Iran* 71 B6
Ramsey, *U.K.* 14 C3
Ramsey, *U.S.A.* 117 E10
Ramsey L., *Canada* 104 C3
Ramsgate, *U.K.* 15 F9
Ramsjö, *Sweden* 10 B9
Ramstein, *Germany* 25 F3
Ramtek, *India* 66 J11
Ramvik, *Sweden* 10 B11
Rana Pratap Sagar Dam, *India* 68 G6
Ranaghat, *India* 69 H13
Ranahu, *Pakistan* 68 G3
Ranau, *Malaysia* 62 C5
Rancagua, *Chile* 126 C1
Rance →, *France* 18 D5
Rancheria →, *Canada* 102 A3
Ranchester, *U.S.A.* 108 D10
Ranchi, *India* 69 H11
Rancho Cucamonga, *U.S.A.* 111 L9
Randalstown, *U.K.* 12 B5
Randan, *France* 19 F10
Randazzo, *Italy* 43 E7
Randers, *Denmark* 11 H4
Randers Fjord, *Denmark* 11 H4
Randfontein, *S. Africa* 89 D4
Randle, *U.S.A.* 110 D5
Randolph, *Mass., U.S.A.* 117 D13
Randolph, *N.Y., U.S.A.* 116 D6
Randolph, *Utah, U.S.A.* 108 F8
Randolph, *Vt., U.S.A.* 117 C12
Randsburg, *U.S.A.* 111 K9
Råne älv →, *Sweden* 8 D20
Rangae, *Thailand* 65 J3
Rangaunu B., *N.Z.* 91 F4
Rangeley, *U.S.A.* 117 B14
Rangeley L., *U.S.A.* 117 B14
Rangely, *U.S.A.* 108 F9
Ranger, *U.S.A.* 113 J5
Rangia, *India* 67 F17
Rangiora, *N.Z.* 91 K4
Rangitaiki →, *N.Z.* 91 G6
Rangitata →, *N.Z.* 91 K3
Rangkasbitung, *Indonesia* 63 G12
Rangon →, *Burma* 67 L20
Rangoon, *Burma* 67 L20
Rangpur, *Bangla.* 67 G16
Rangsit, *Thailand* 64 F3
Ranibennur, *India* 66 M9
Raniganj, *Ut. P., India* 69 F9
Raniganj, *W. Bengal, India* 67 H15
Ranikhet, *India* 69 E8
Raniwara, *India* 66 G8
Rāniyah, *Iraq* 70 B5
Ranka, *India* 69 H10
Ranken →, *Australia* 94 C2
Rankin, *U.S.A.* 113 K4
Rankin Inlet, *Canada* 100 B10
Rankins Springs, *Australia* 95 E4
Rankweil, *Austria* 26 D2
Rannoch, L., *U.K.* 13 E4
Rannoch Moor, *U.K.* 13 E4
Ranobe, Helodranon' i, *Madag.* 89 C7
Ranohira, *Madag.* 89 C8
Ranomafana, *Toamasina, Madag.* 89 B8
Ranomafana, *Toliara, Madag.* 89 C8
Ranomafana △, *Madag.* 89 C8
Ranomena, *Madag.* 89 C8
Ranong, *Thailand* 65 H2
Ranotsara Nord, *Madag.* 89 C8
Rānsa, *Iran* 71 C6
Ransiki, *Indonesia* 63 E8
Rantabe, *Madag.* 89 B8
Rantauprapat, *Indonesia* 62 D1
Rantemario, *Indonesia* 63 E5
Rantoul, *U.S.A.* 114 E1
Ranum, *Denmark* 11 H3
Ranyah, W. →, *Si. Arabia* 80 C5
Raon l'Étape, *France* 19 D13
Raoping, *China* 59 F11
Raoyang, *China* 56 E8
Rap, Ko, *Thailand* 65 b
Rapa, *Pac. Oc.* 97 K13
Rapa Nui = Pascua, I. de, *Chile* 97 K17
Rapallo, *Italy* 40 D6
Rapar, *India* 68 H4
Rāpch, *Iran* 71 E8
Raper, C., *Canada* 101 B13
Rapid City, *U.S.A.* 112 D3
Rapid River, *U.S.A.* 114 C2
Rapla, *Estonia* 9 G21
Rapti →, *India* 69 F10
Rapu Rapu I., *Phil.* 61 E6
Raqaba ez Zarqa →, *Sudan* 81 F2
Raquette →, *U.S.A.* 117 B10
Raquette Lake, *U.S.A.* 117 C10
Rarotonga, *Cook Is.* 97 K12
Ra's al 'Ayn, *Syria* 70 B4
Ra's al Khaymah, *U.A.E.* 71 E7
Râs el Mâ, *Mali* 82 B4
Râs Ghârib, *Egypt* 80 B3
Râs Mallap, *Egypt* 80 B3
Râs Muhammad △, *Egypt* 80 B3
Rasca, Pta. de la, *Canary Is.* 48 G3
Rășcani, *Moldova* 29 C12
Raseiniai, *Lithuania* 9 J20
Rashad, *Sudan* 81 E3
Rashîd, *Egypt* 80 H7
Rashîd, Masabb, *Egypt* 80 H7
Rashmi, *India* 68 G6
Rasht, *Iran* 71 B6
Rasi Salai, *Thailand* 64 E5
Raška, *Serbia & M.* 44 C4
Râsnov, *Romania* 29 E10
Rason L., *Australia* 93 E3
Rașova, *Romania* 29 F12
Rasovo, *Bulgaria* 44 C7
Rasra, *India* 69 G10
Rasskazovo, *Russia* 34 D5
Rast, *Romania* 29 G8
Rastatt, *Germany* 25 G4
Rastede, *Germany* 24 B4
Răstolița, *Romania* 29 D9
Rasul, *Pakistan* 68 C5
Raszków, *Poland* 31 G4
Rat Buri, *Thailand* 64 F2
Rat Islands, *U.S.A.* 100 C1
Rat L., *Canada* 103 B9
Ratangarh, *India* 68 E6
Rätansbyn, *Sweden* 10 B8
Raṭāwī, *Iraq* 70 D5
Rath, *India* 69 G8
Rath Luirc, *Ireland* 12 D3
Rathdrum, *Ireland* 12 D5
Rathenow, *Germany* 24 C8
Rathkeale, *Ireland* 12 D3
Rathlin I., *U.K.* 12 A5
Rathmelton, *Ireland* 12 A4
Ratibor = Racibórz, *Poland* 31 H5
Rätikon, *Austria* 26 D2
Ratingen, *Germany* 24 D2
Ratlam, *India* 68 H6
Ratnagiri, *India* 66 L8
Ratodero, *Pakistan* 68 F3
Raton, *U.S.A.* 113 G2
Rattaphum, *Thailand* 65 J3
Ratten, *Austria* 26 D8
Rattray Hd., *U.K.* 13 D7
Rättvik, *Sweden* 10 D9
Ratz, Mt., *Canada* 102 B2
Ratzeburg, *Germany* 24 B6
Raub, *Malaysia* 65 L3
Rauch, *Argentina* 126 D4
Raudales de Malpaso, *Mexico* 119 D6
Raufarhöfn, *Iceland* 8 C6
Raufoss, *Norway* 9 F14
Raukumara Ra., *N.Z.* 91 H6
Rauma, *Finland* 9 F19
Raung, Gunung, *Indonesia* 63 J17
Raurkela, *India* 69 H11
Rausu-Dake, *Japan* 54 B12
Răut →, *Moldova* 29 C14
Rava-Ruska, *Ukraine* 33 G2
Rava Russkaya = Rava-Ruska, *Ukraine* 33 G2
Ravalli, *U.S.A.* 108 C6
Ravānsar, *Iran* 70 C5
Ravanusa, *Italy* 42 E6
Rāvar, *Iran* 71 D8
Ravena, *U.S.A.* 117 D11
Ravenna, *Italy* 41 D9
Ravenna, *Nebr., U.S.A.* 112 E5
Ravenna, *Ohio, U.S.A.* 116 E3
Ravensburg, *Germany* 25 H5
Ravenshoe, *Australia* 94 B4
Ravensthorpe, *Australia* 93 F3
Ravenswood, *Australia* 94 C4
Ravenswood, *U.S.A.* 114 F5
Ravi →, *Pakistan* 68 D4
Ravna Gora, *Croatia* 41 C11
Ravna Reka, *Serbia & M.* 44 B5
Ravne na Koroškem, *Slovenia* 41 B11
Rawa Mazowiecka, *Poland* 31 G7
Rawalpindi, *Pakistan* 68 C5
Rawāndūz, *Iraq* 70 B5
Rawang, *Malaysia* 65 L3
Rawene, *N.Z.* 91 F4
Rawicz, *Poland* 31 G3
Rawka →, *Poland* 31 F7
Rawlinna, *Australia* 93 F4
Rawlins, *U.S.A.* 108 F10
Rawlinson Ra., *Australia* 93 D4
Rawson, *Argentina* 128 E3
Raxaul, *India* 69 F11
Ray, *U.S.A.* 112 A3
Ray, C., *Canada* 105 C8
Raya Ring, Ko, *Thailand* 65 a
Rayadurg, *India* 66 M10
Rayagada, *India* 67 K13
Raychikhinsk, *Russia* 53 E13
Rāyen, *Iran* 71 D8
Rayleigh, *U.K.* 15 F8
Raymond, *Canada* 102 D6
Raymond, *Calif., U.S.A.* 110 H7
Raymond, *N.H., U.S.A.* 117 C13
Raymond, *Wash., U.S.A.* 110 D3
Raymondville, *U.S.A.* 113 M6
Raymore, *Canada* 103 C8
Rayón, *Mexico* 118 B2
Rayong, *Thailand* 64 F3
Rayville, *U.S.A.* 113 J9
Raz, Pte. du, *France* 18 D2
Razan, *Iran* 71 C6
Ražana, *Serbia & M.* 44 B3
Ražanj, *Serbia & M.* 44 C5
Razāzah, Buḥayrat ar, *Iraq* 70 C4
Razazah, L. = Razāzah, Buḥayrat ar, *Iraq* 70 C4
Razdelna, *Bulgaria* 45 C11
Razdel'naya = Rozdilna, *Ukraine* 33 J6
Razdolnoye, *Russia* 54 C5
Razdolnoye, *Ukraine* 33 K7
Razeh, *Iran* 71 C6
Razgrad, *Bulgaria* 45 C10
Razim, Lacul, *Romania* 29 F14
Razlog, *Bulgaria* 44 E7
Razmak, *Pakistan* 68 C3
Ré, Î. de, *France* 20 B2
Reading, *U.K.* 15 F7
Reading, *U.S.A.* 117 F9
Reading □, *U.K.* 15 F7
Realicó, *Argentina* 126 D3
Réalmont, *France* 20 E6
Ream, *Cambodia* 65 G4
Reata, *Mexico* 118 B4
Reay Forest, *U.K.* 13 C4
Rebais, *France* 19 D10
Rebi, *Indonesia* 63 F8
Rebiana, *Libya* 79 D10
Rebiana, Sahrâ', *Libya* 79 D10
Rebun-Tō, *Japan* 54 B10
Recanati, *Italy* 41 E10
Recaș, *Romania* 28 E6
Recco, *Italy* 40 D6
Recherche, Arch. of the, *Australia* 93 F3
Rechna Doab, *Pakistan* 68 D5
Rechytsa, *Belarus* 33 F6
Recife, *Brazil* 125 E12
Recklinghausen, *Germany* 17 C7
Reconquista, *Argentina* 126 B4
Recreo, *Argentina* 126 B2
Recz, *Poland* 31 E2
Red →, *La., U.S.A.* 113 K9
Red →, *N. Dak., U.S.A.* 100 C10
Red Bank, *U.S.A.* 117 F10
Red Bay, *Canada* 105 B8
Red Bluff, *U.S.A.* 108 F2
Red Bluff L., *U.S.A.* 113 K3
Red Cliffs, *Australia* 95 E3
Red Cloud, *U.S.A.* 112 E5
Red Creek, *U.S.A.* 117 C8
Red Deer, *Canada* 102 C6
Red Deer →, *Alta., Canada* 103 C7
Red Deer →, *Man., Canada* 103 C8
Red Deer L., *Canada* 103 C8
Red Hook, *U.S.A.* 117 E11
Red Indian L., *Canada* 105 C8
Red L., *Canada* 103 C10
Red Lake, *Canada* 103 C10
Red Lake Falls, *U.S.A.* 112 B6
Red Lake Road, *Canada* 103 C10
Red Lodge, *U.S.A.* 108 D9
Red Mountain, *U.S.A.* 111 K9
Red Oak, *U.S.A.* 112 E7
Red Rock, *Canada* 104 C2
Red Rock, L., *U.S.A.* 112 E8
Red Rocks Pt., *Australia* 93 F4
Red Sea, *Asia* 75 C2
Red Slate Mt., *U.S.A.* 110 H8
Red Sucker L., *Canada* 104 B1
Red Tower Pass = Turnu Roșu, P., *Romania* 29 E9
Red Wing, *U.S.A.* 112 C8
Reda, *Poland* 30 D5
Redang, *Malaysia* 65 K4
Redange, *Lux.* 17 E5
Redcar, *U.K.* 14 C6
Redcar & Cleveland □, *U.K.* 14 C7
Redcliff, *Canada* 103 C6
Redcliffe, *Australia* 95 D5
Redcliffe, Mt., *Australia* 93 E3
Reddersburg, *S. Africa* 88 D4
Redding, *U.S.A.* 108 F2
Redditch, *U.K.* 15 E6
Redfield, *U.S.A.* 112 C5
Redford, *U.S.A.* 117 B11
Redhead, *Trin. & Tob.* 125 K16
Redkino, *Russia* 32 D9
Redlands, *U.S.A.* 111 M9
Redmond, *Oreg., U.S.A.* 108 D3
Redmond, *Wash., U.S.A.* 110 C4
Redon, *France* 18 E4
Redonda, *Antigua* 121 C7
Redondela, *Spain* 36 C2
Redondo, *Portugal* 37 G3
Redondo Beach, *U.S.A.* 111 M8
Redruth, *U.K.* 15 G2
Redvers, *Canada* 103 D8
Redwater, *Canada* 102 C6
Redwood, *U.S.A.* 117 B9
Redwood △, *U.S.A.* 108 F1
Redwood City, *U.S.A.* 110 H4
Redwood Falls, *U.S.A.* 112 C7
Ree, L., *Ireland* 12 C3
Reed, L., *Canada* 103 C8
Reed City, *U.S.A.* 114 D3
Reedley, *U.S.A.* 110 J7
Reedsburg, *U.S.A.* 112 D9
Reedsport, *U.S.A.* 108 E1
Reedsville, *U.S.A.* 116 F7
Reefton, *N.Z.* 91 K3
Rees, *Germany* 24 D2
Reese →, *U.S.A.* 108 F5
Refahiye, *Turkey* 73 C8
Reftele, *Sweden* 11 G7
Refugio, *U.S.A.* 113 L6
Rega →, *Poland* 30 D2
Regalbuto, *Italy* 43 E7
Regen, *Germany* 25 G9
Regen →, *Germany* 25 F8
Regensburg, *Germany* 25 F8
Regenstauf, *Germany* 25 F8
Reggâne = Zaouiet Reggâne, *Algeria* 78 C6
Reggello, *Italy* 41 E8
Réggio di Calábria, *Italy* 43 D8
Réggio nell'Emília, *Italy* 40 D7
Reghin, *Romania* 29 D9
Regina, *Canada* 103 C8
Regina Beach, *Canada* 103 C8
Registro, *Brazil* 127 A6
Reguengos de Monsaraz, *Portugal* 37 G3
Rehar →, *India* 69 H10
Rehli, *India* 69 H8
Rehoboth, *Namibia* 88 C2
Rehovot, *Israel* 74 D3
Reichenbach, *Germany* 24 E8
Reid, *Australia* 93 F4
Reidsville, *U.S.A.* 115 G6
Reigate, *U.K.* 15 F7
Reillo, *Spain* 38 F3
Reims, *France* 19 C11
Reina Adelaida, Arch., *Chile* 128 G2
Reina Sofia, Tenerife ✕ (TFS), *Canary Is.* 48 F3
Reinbek, *Germany* 24 B6
Reindeer →, *Canada* 103 B8
Reindeer I., *Canada* 103 C9
Reindeer L., *Canada* 103 B8
Reinga, C., *N.Z.* 91 F4
Reinosa, *Spain* 36 B6
Reitz, *S. Africa* 89 D4
Reivilo, *S. Africa* 88 D3
Rejaf, *Sudan* 81 G3
Rejmyre, *Sweden* 11 F9
Rejowiec Fabryczny, *Poland* 31 G10
Reka →, *Slovenia* 41 C11
Rekovac, *Serbia & M.* 44 C5
Reliance, *Canada* 103 A7
Rémalard, *France* 18 D7
Remarkable, Mt., *Australia* 95 E2
Rembang, *Indonesia* 63 G14
Remedios, *Panama* 120 E3
Remeshk, *Iran* 71 E8
Remetea, *Romania* 29 D10
Remich, *Lux.* 17 E6
Remiremont, *France* 19 D13
Remo, *Ethiopia* 81 F5
Remontnoye, *Russia* 35 G6
Remoulins, *France* 21 E8
Remscheid, *Germany* 17 C7
Ren Xian, *China* 56 F8
Rendang, *Indonesia* 63 J18
Rende, *Italy* 43 C9
Rendína, *Greece* 46 B3
Rendsburg, *Germany* 24 A5
Renfrew, *Canada* 117 A8
Renfrewshire □, *U.K.* 13 F4
Rengat, *Indonesia* 62 E2
Rengo, *Chile* 126 C1
Renhua, *China* 59 E9
Renhuai, *China* 58 D6
Reni, *Ukraine* 33 K5
Renk, *Sudan* 81 E3
Renmark, *Australia* 95 E3
Rennell Sd., *Canada* 102 C2
Renner Springs, *Australia* 94 B1
Rennes, *France* 18 D5
Rennie L., *Canada* 103 A7
Reno, *U.S.A.* 110 F7
Reno →, *Italy* 41 D9
Renovo, *U.S.A.* 116 E7
Renqiu, *China* 56 E9
Rens, *Denmark* 11 K3
Renshou, *China* 58 C5
Rensselaer, *Ind., U.S.A.* 114 E2
Rensselaer, *N.Y., U.S.A.* 117 D11
Rentería, *Spain* 38 B3
Renton, *U.S.A.* 110 C4
Réo, *Burkina Faso* 82 C4
Reocín, *Spain* 36 B6

Reotipur, India 69 G10
Répcelak, Hungary 28 C2
Republic, Mo., U.S.A. 113 G8
Republic, Wash., U.S.A. 108 B4
Republican →, U.S.A. 112 F6
Repulse B., Australia 94 J6
Repulse Bay, Canada 101 B11
Requena, Peru 124 E4
Requena, Spain 39 F3
Réquista, France 20 D6
Reşadiye = Datça, Turkey 47 E9
Reşadiye, Turkey 72 B7
Reşadiye Yarımadası, Turkey 47 E9
Resavica, Serbia & M. 44 B5
Resen, Macedonia 44 E5
Reserve, U.S.A. 109 K9
Resht = Rasht, Iran 71 B6
Resistencia, Argentina 126 B4
Reşiţa, Romania 28 E6
Resko, Poland 30 E2
Resolution I., Canada 101 B13
Resolution I., N.Z. 91 L1
Ressano Garcia, Mozam. 89 D5
Reston, Canada 103 D8
Reszel, Poland 30 D8
Retalhuleu, Guatemala 120 D1
Retenue, L. de, Dem. Rep. of the Congo 87 E2
Retezat △, Romania 28 E7
Retezat, Munţii, Romania 28 E8
Retford, U.K. 14 D7
Rethel, France 19 C11
Rethem, Germany 24 C5
Réthímnon, Greece 49 D6
Réthímnon □, Greece 49 D6
Reti, Pakistan 68 E3
Retiche, Alpi, Switz. 25 J6
Retiers, France 18 E5
Retortillo, Spain 36 E4
Retournac, France 21 C8
Rétság, Hungary 28 C4
Réunion ☒, Ind. Oc. 77 J9
Reus, Spain 38 D6
Reuterstadt Stavenhagen, Germany 24 B8
Reutlingen, Germany 25 G5
Reutte, Austria 26 D3
Reval = Tallinn, Estonia 9 G21
Revel, France 20 E6
Revelganj, India 69 G11
Revelstoke, Canada 102 C5
Reventazón, Peru 124 E2
Revigny-sur-Ornain, France 19 D11
Revillagigedo, Is. de, Pac. Oc. 118 D2
Revin, France 19 C11
Revúca, Slovak Rep. 27 C13
Revuè →, Mozam. 87 F3
Rewa, India 69 G9
Rewari, India 68 E7
Rexburg, U.S.A. 108 E8
Rey, Iran 71 C6
Rey, I. del, Panama 120 E4
Rey Malabo, Eq. Guin. 83 E6
Reyðarfjörður, Iceland 8 D6
Reyes, Pt., U.S.A. 110 H3
Reyhanlı, Turkey 72 D7
Reykjahlið, Iceland 8 D5
Reykjanes, Iceland 8 E2
Reykjavík, Iceland 8 D3
Reynolds Ra., Australia 92 D5
Reynoldsville, U.S.A. 116 E6
Reynosa, Mexico 119 B5
Rēzekne, Latvia 9 H22
Rezina, Moldova 29 C13
Rezovo, Bulgaria 45 D12
Rezvān, Iran 71 E8
Rgotina, Serbia & M. 44 B6
Rhamnus, Greece 46 C6
Rhayader, U.K. 15 E4
Rheda-Wiedenbrück, Germany 24 D4
Rhede, Germany 24 D2
Rhein →, Europe 17 C6
Rhein-Main-Donau-Kanal, Germany 25 F7
Rhein-Ruhr, Düsseldorf ✕ (DUS), Germany 24 D2
Rhein-Taunus ⌓, Germany 25 E4
Rhein-Westerwald ⌓, Germany 24 E3
Rheinbach, Germany 24 E2
Rheine, Germany 24 C3
Rheinfelden, Germany 25 H3
Rheinhessen-Pfalz □, Germany 25 F3
Rheinland-Pfalz □, Germany 25 E2
Rheinsberg, Germany 24 B8
Rhin = Rhein →, Europe 17 C6
Rhine = Rhein →, Europe 17 C6
Rhinebeck, U.S.A. 117 E11
Rhineland-Palatinate = Rheinland-Pfalz □, Germany 25 E2
Rhinelander, U.S.A. 112 C10
Rhinns Pt., U.K. 13 F2
Rhino Camp, Uganda 86 B3
Rhir, Cap, Morocco 78 B4
Rho, Italy 40 C6
Rhode Island □, U.S.A. 117 E13
Rhodes = Ródhos, Greece 49 C10
Rhodes ✕ (RHO), Greece 47 E10
Rhodope Mts. = Rhodopi Planina, Bulgaria 45 E8
Rhodopi Planina, Bulgaria 45 E8
Rhön, Germany 24 E5
Rhondda, U.K. 15 F4
Rhondda Cynon Taff □, U.K. 15 F4
Rhône □, France 21 C8
Rhône →, France 21 E8
Rhône-Alpes □, France 21 C9
Rhum, U.K. 13 E2
Rhyl, U.K. 14 D4
Ria-Aba, Eq. Guin. 83 E6
Ria Formosa ⌓, Portugal 37 H3
Riachão, Brazil 125 E9
Riangnom, Sudan 81 F3
Riaño, Spain 36 C6
Rians, France 21 E9
Riansáres →, Spain 37 F7
Riasi, India 69 C6
Riau □, Indonesia 62 D2
Riau, Kepulauan, Indonesia 62 D2
Riau Arch. = Riau, Kepulauan, Indonesia 62 D2
Riaza, Spain 36 D7
Riaza →, Spain 36 D7
Riba de Saelices, Spain 38 E2
Riba-Roja de Turia, Spain 39 F4
Ribadavia, Spain 36 C2
Ribadeo, Spain 36 B3
Ribadesella, Spain 36 B5
Ribado, Nigeria 83 D7
Ribao, Cameroon 83 D7
Ribas = Ribes de Freser, Spain 38 C7
Ribas do Rio Pardo, Brazil 125 H8
Ribauè, Mozam. 87 E4
Ribble →, U.K. 14 D5
Ribe, Denmark 11 J2
Ribe Amtskommune □, Denmark 11 J2
Ribeauvillé, France 19 D14
Ribécourt-Dreslincourt, France 19 C9
Ribeira = Santa Uxía, Spain 36 C2
Ribeira Brava, Madeira 48 D2
Ribeirão Prêto, Brazil 127 A6
Ribemont, France 19 C10
Ribera, Italy 42 E6
Ribérac, France 20 C4
Riberalta, Bolivia 124 F5
Ribes de Freser, Spain 38 C7
Ribnica, Slovenia 41 C11
Ribnitz-Damgarten, Germany 24 A8
Ričany, Czech Rep. 26 B7
Riccarton, N.Z. 91 K4
Riccia, Italy 43 A7
Riccione, Italy 41 E9
Rice, U.S.A. 111 L12
Rice L., Canada 116 B6
Rice Lake, U.S.A. 112 C9
Rich, C., Canada 116 B4
Richard Toll, Senegal 82 B1
Richards Bay, S. Africa 89 D5
Richardson →, Canada 103 B6
Richardson Lakes, U.S.A. 114 C10
Richardson Springs, U.S.A. 110 F5
Riche, C., Australia 93 F2
Richelieu, France 18 E7
Richey, U.S.A. 112 B2
Richfield, U.S.A. 109 G8
Richfield Springs, U.S.A. 117 D10
Richford, U.S.A. 117 B12
Richibucto, Canada 105 C7
Richland, Ga., U.S.A. 115 J3
Richland, Wash., U.S.A. 108 C4
Richland Center, U.S.A. 112 D9
Richlands, U.S.A. 114 G5
Richmond, Australia 94 C3
Richmond, N.Z. 91 J4
Richmond, U.K. 14 C6
Richmond, Calif., U.S.A. 110 H4
Richmond, Ind., U.S.A. 114 F3
Richmond, Ky., U.S.A. 114 G3
Richmond, Mich., U.S.A. 116 D2
Richmond, Mo., U.S.A. 112 F8
Richmond, Tex., U.S.A. 113 L7
Richmond, Utah, U.S.A. 108 F8
Richmond, Va., U.S.A. 114 G7
Richmond, Vt., U.S.A. 117 B12
Richmond Hill, Canada 116 C5
Richmond Ra., Australia 95 D5
Richtersveld △, S. Africa 88 D2
Richwood, U.S.A. 114 F5
Ricla, Spain 38 D3
Ridder = Leninogorsk, Kazakhstan 52 D9
Riddlesburg, U.S.A. 116 F6
Ridgecrest, U.S.A. 111 K9
Ridgefield, Conn., U.S.A. 117 E11
Ridgefield, Wash., U.S.A. 110 E4
Ridgeland, U.S.A. 115 J5
Ridgetown, Canada 116 D3
Ridgewood, U.S.A. 117 F10
Ridgway, U.S.A. 116 E6
Riding Mountain △, Canada 103 C9
Ridley, Mt., Australia 93 F3
Riebeek-Oos, S. Africa 88 E4
Ried, Austria 26 C6
Riedlingen, Germany 25 G5
Riedstadt, Germany 25 F4
Rienza →, Italy 41 B8
Riesa, Germany 24 D9
Riesi, Italy 43 E7
Riet →, S. Africa 88 D3
Rietavas, Lithuania 30 C8
Rietbron, S. Africa 88 E3
Rietfontein, Namibia 88 C3
Rieti, Italy 41 F9
Rieupeyroux, France 20 D6
Riez, France 21 E10
Rif = Er Rif, Morocco 78 A5
Riffe L., U.S.A. 110 D4
Rifle, U.S.A. 108 G10
Rift Valley, Africa 76 G7
Rift Valley □, Kenya 86 B4
Rīga, Latvia 9 H21
Riga ✕ (RIX), Latvia 30 B10
Riga, G. of, Latvia 9 H20
Rigacikun, Nigeria 83 C6
Rīgān, Iran 71 D8
Rīgas Jūras Līcis = Riga, G. of, Latvia 9 H20
Rigaud, Canada 117 A10
Rigby, U.S.A. 108 E8
Rīgestān, Afghan. 66 D4
Riggins, U.S.A. 108 D5
Rignac, France 20 D6
Rigolet, Canada 105 B8
Rihand Dam, India 69 G10
Riihimäki, Finland 9 F21
Riiser-Larsen-halvøya, Antarctica 5 C4
Rijau, Nigeria 83 C6
Rijeka, Croatia 41 C11
Rijeka Crnojevića, Serbia & M. 44 D3
Rijssen, Neths. 17 B6
Rike, Ethiopia 81 E4
Rikuchū-Kaigan △, Japan 54 E11
Rikuzentakada, Japan 54 E10
Rila, Bulgaria 44 D7
Rila Planina, Bulgaria 44 D7
Riley, U.S.A. 108 E4
Rima →, Nigeria 83 C6
Rimah, Wadi ar →, Si. Arabia 70 E4
Rimau, Pulau, Malaysia 65 c
Rimavská Sobota, Slovak Rep. 27 C13
Rimbey, Canada 102 C6
Rimbo, Sweden 10 E12
Rimersburg, U.S.A. 116 E5
Rimforsa, Sweden 11 F9
Rimi, Nigeria 83 C6
Rímini, Italy 41 D9
Rimouski, Canada 105 C6
Rimrock, U.S.A. 110 D5
Rinca, Indonesia 63 F5
Rincón de la Victoria, Spain 37 J6
Rincón de Romos, Mexico 118 C4
Rinconada, Argentina 126 A2
Rind →, India 69 G9
Ringarum, Sweden 11 F10
Ringas, India 68 F6
Ringe, Denmark 11 J4
Ringim, Nigeria 83 C6
Ringkøbing, Denmark 11 H2
Ringkøbing Amtskommune □, Denmark 11 H2
Ringkøbing Fjord, Denmark 11 H2
Ringsjön, Sweden 11 J7
Ringsted, Denmark 11 J5
Ringvassøy, Norway 8 B18
Ringwood, U.S.A. 117 E10
Rinía, Greece 47 D7
Rinjani, Indonesia 62 F5
Rinteln, Germany 24 C5
Río, Punta del, Spain 39 J2
Rio Branco, Brazil 124 E5
Río Branco, Uruguay 127 C5
Río Bravo ⌓, N. Amer. 118 B4
Río Bravo del Norte →, Mexico 119 B5
Rio Brilhante, Brazil 127 A5
Rio Claro, Brazil 127 A6
Rio Claro, Trin. & Tob. 121 D7
Río Colorado, Argentina 128 D4
Río Cuarto, Argentina 126 C3
Rio das Pedras, Mozam. 89 C6
Rio de Janeiro, Brazil 127 A7
Rio de Janeiro □, Brazil 127 A7
Rio do Sul, Brazil 127 B6
Río Dulce △, Guatemala 120 C2
Río Gallegos, Argentina 128 G3
Río Grande, Argentina 128 G3
Rio Grande, Brazil 127 C5
Río Grande, Mexico 118 C4
Río Grande, Nic. 120 D3
Río Grande, Puerto Rico 121 d
Rio Grande, U.S.A. 113 N6
Rio Grande City, U.S.A. 113 M5
Río Grande de Santiago →, Mexico 118 C3
Rio Grande do Norte □, Brazil 125 E11
Rio Grande do Sul □, Brazil 127 C5
Río Hato, Panama 120 E3
Río Lagartos, Mexico 119 C7
Rio Largo, Brazil 125 E11
Rio Maior, Portugal 37 F2
Rio Marina, Italy 40 F7
Río Mulatos, Bolivia 124 G5
Río Muni □, Eq. Guin. 84 D2
Rio Negro, Brazil 127 B6
Rio Pardo, Brazil 127 C5
Río Pilcomayo △, Argentina 126 B4
Río Platano ⌓, Honduras 120 C3
Rio Rancho, U.S.A. 109 J10
Río Segundo, Argentina 126 C3
Río Tercero, Argentina 126 C3
Rio Tinto, Portugal 36 D2
Rio Verde, Brazil 125 G8
Río Verde, Mexico 119 C5
Rio Vista, U.S.A. 110 G5
Ríobamba, Ecuador 124 D3
Ríohacha, Colombia 124 A4
Riom, France 20 C7
Riom-ès-Montagnes, France 20 C6
Rion-des-Landes, France 20 E3
Rionero in Vúlture, Italy 43 B8
Rioni →, Georgia 35 J5
Riós, Spain 36 D3
Ríosucio, Colombia 124 B3
Riou L., Canada 103 B7
Rioz, France 19 E13
Ripatransone, Italy 41 F10
Ripley, Canada 116 B3
Ripley, Calif., U.S.A. 111 M12
Ripley, N.Y., U.S.A. 116 D5
Ripley, Tenn., U.S.A. 113 H10
Ripley, W. Va., U.S.A. 114 F5
Ripoll, Spain 38 C7
Ripon, U.K. 14 C6
Ripon, Calif., U.S.A. 110 H5
Ripon, Wis., U.S.A. 114 D1
Riposto, Italy 43 E8
Risan, Serbia & M. 44 D2
Riscle, France 20 E3
Rishā', W. ar →, Si. Arabia 70 E5
Rishiri-Rebun-Sarobetsu △, Japan 54 B10
Rishiri-Tō, Japan 54 B10
Rishon le Ziyyon, Israel 74 D3
Risle →, France 18 C7
Risnjak △, Croatia 41 C11
Rison, U.S.A. 113 J8
Risør, Norway 9 G13
Rita Blanca Cr. →, U.S.A. 113 H3
Riti, Nigeria 83 D6
Ritter, Mt., U.S.A. 110 H7
Rittman, U.S.A. 116 F3
Ritzville, U.S.A. 108 C4
Riva del Garda, Italy 40 C7
Riva Lígure, Italy 40 E4
Rivadavia, Buenos Aires, Argentina 126 D3
Rivadavia, Mendoza, Argentina 126 C2
Rivadavia, Salta, Argentina 126 A3
Rivadavia, Chile 126 B1
Rivarolo Canavese, Italy 40 C4
Rivas, Nic. 120 D2
Rive-de-Gier, France 21 C8
River Cess, Liberia 82 D3
River Jordan, Canada 110 B2
Rivera, Argentina 126 D3
Rivera, Uruguay 127 C4
Riverbank, U.S.A. 110 H6
Riverdale, U.S.A. 110 J7
Riverhead, U.S.A. 117 F12
Riverhurst, Canada 103 C7
Rivers, Canada 103 C8
Rivers □, Nigeria 83 E6
Rivers Inlet, Canada 102 C3
Riversdale, S. Africa 88 E3
Riverside, U.S.A. 111 M9
Riverton, Australia 95 E2
Riverton, Canada 103 C9
Riverton, N.Z. 91 M2
Riverton, U.S.A. 108 E9
Riverton Heights, U.S.A. 110 C4
Rives, France 21 C9
Rivesaltes, France 20 F6
Riviera, U.S.A. 111 K12
Riviera di Levante, Italy 40 D6
Riviera di Ponente, Italy 40 D5
Rivière-au-Renard, Canada 105 C7
Rivière-du-Loup, Canada 105 C6
Rivière-Pentecôte, Canada 105 C6
Rivière-Pilote, Martinique 120 c
Rivière St. Paul, Canada 105 B8
Rivière-Salée, Martinique 120 c
Rivne, Ukraine 33 G4
Rívoli, Italy 40 C4
Rivoli B., Australia 95 F3
Rixheim, France 19 E14
Riyadh = Ar Riyāḍ, Si. Arabia 70 E5
Rize, Turkey 73 B9
Rizhao, China 57 G10
Rizokarpaso, Cyprus 49 D13
Rizzuto, C., Italy 43 D10
Rjukan, Norway 9 G13
Ro, Greece 47 E11
Roa, Spain 36 D7
Road Town, Br. Virgin Is. 121 e
Roan Plateau, U.S.A. 108 G9
Roanne, France 19 F11
Roanoke, Ala., U.S.A. 115 J3
Roanoke, Va., U.S.A. 114 G6
Roanoke →, U.S.A. 115 H7
Roanoke I., U.S.A. 115 H8
Roanoke Rapids, U.S.A. 115 G7
Roatán, Honduras 120 C2
Robāt Sang, Iran 71 C8
Robāṭkarīm, Iran 71 C6
Robāṭkarīm □, Iran 71 B6
Robbins I., Australia 95 G4
Róbbio, Italy 40 C5
Robe →, Australia 92 D2
Röbel, Germany 24 B8
Robert Lee, U.S.A. 113 K4
Robertsdale, U.S.A. 116 F6
Robertsganj, India 69 G10
Robertson, S. Africa 88 E2
Robertson I., Antarctica 5 C18
Robertson Ra., Australia 92 D3
Robertsport, Liberia 82 D2
Robertstown, Australia 95 E2
Roberval, Canada 105 C5
Robeson Chan., N. Amer. 4 A4
Robesonia, U.S.A. 117 F8
Robi, Ethiopia 81 F4
Robinson, U.S.A. 114 F2
Robinson →, Australia 94 B2
Robinson Ra., Australia 93 E2
Robinvale, Australia 95 E3
Robledo, Spain 39 G2
Roblin, Canada 103 C8
Roboré, Bolivia 124 G7
Robson, Canada 102 D5
Robson, Mt., Canada 102 C5
Robstown, U.S.A. 113 M6
Roca, C. da, Portugal 37 G1
Roca Partida, I., Mexico 118 D2
Rocamadour, France 20 D5
Rocas, I., Brazil 125 D12
Rocca San Casciano, Italy 41 D8
Roccadáspide, Italy 43 B8
Roccastrada, Italy 41 F8
Roccella Iónica, Italy 43 D9
Rocha, Uruguay 127 C5
Rochdale, U.K. 14 D5
Rochechouart, France 20 C4
Rochefort, Belgium 17 D5
Rochefort, France 20 C3
Rochefort-en-Terre, France 18 E4
Rochelle, U.S.A. 112 E10
Rocher River, Canada 102 A6
Rocheservière, France 18 F5
Rochester, U.K. 15 F8
Rochester, Ind., U.S.A. 114 E2
Rochester, Minn., U.S.A. 112 C8
Rochester, N.H., U.S.A. 117 C14
Rochester, N.Y., U.S.A. 116 C7
Rociu, Romania 29 F10
Rock →, Canada 102 A3
Rock Creek, U.S.A. 116 E4
Rock Falls, U.S.A. 112 E10
Rock Hill, U.S.A. 115 H5
Rock Island, U.S.A. 112 E9
Rock Rapids, U.S.A. 112 D6
Rock Sound, Bahamas 120 B4
Rock Springs, Mont., U.S.A. 108 C10
Rock Springs, Wyo., U.S.A. 108 F9
Rock Valley, U.S.A. 112 D6
Rockall, Atl. Oc. 6 D3
Rockdale, Tex., U.S.A. 113 K6
Rockdale, Wash., U.S.A. 110 C5
Rockeby = Mungkan Kandju △, Australia 94 A3
Rockefeller Plateau, Antarctica 5 E14
Rockford, U.S.A. 112 D10
Rockglen, Canada 103 D7
Rockhampton, Australia 94 C5
Rockingham, Australia 93 F2
Rockingham, U.S.A. 115 H6
Rockingham B., Australia 94 B4
Rocklake, U.S.A. 112 A5
Rockland, Canada 117 A9
Rockland, Idaho, U.S.A. 108 E7
Rockland, Maine, U.S.A. 115 C11
Rockland, Mich., U.S.A. 112 B10
Rocklin, U.S.A. 110 G5
Rockly B., Trin. & Tob. 125 J16
Rockmart, U.S.A. 115 H3
Rockport, Mass., U.S.A. 117 D14
Rockport, Mo., U.S.A. 112 E7
Rockport, Tex., U.S.A. 113 L6
Rocksprings, U.S.A. 113 K4
Rockville, Conn., U.S.A. 117 E12
Rockville, Md., U.S.A. 114 F7
Rockwall, U.S.A. 113 J6
Rockwell City, U.S.A. 112 D7
Rockwood, Canada 116 C4
Rockwood, Maine, U.S.A. 115 C11
Rockwood, Tenn., U.S.A. 115 H3
Rocky Ford, U.S.A. 112 F3
Rocky Gully, Australia 93 F2
Rocky Harbour, Canada 105 C8
Rocky Island L., Canada 104 C3
Rocky Lane, Canada 102 B5
Rocky Mount, U.S.A. 115 H7
Rocky Mountain △, U.S.A. 108 F11
Rocky Mountain House, Canada 102 C6
Rocky Mts., N. Amer. 108 G10
Rocky Point, Namibia 88 B2
Rocroi, France 19 C11
Rod, Pakistan 66 E3
Rødby, Denmark 11 K5
Rødbyhavn, Denmark 11 K5
Roddickton, Canada 105 B8
Rødding, Denmark 11 J3
Rödeby, Sweden 11 H9
Rødekro, Denmark 11 J3
Rodenkirchen, Germany 24 B4
Rodez, France 20 D6
Rodholívas, Greece 44 F7
Rodhópi □, Greece 45 E9
Rodhopoú, Greece 49 D5
Ródhos, Greece 49 C10
Rodi Gargánico, Italy 41 G12
Rodna, Romania 29 C9
Rodnei, Munţii, Romania 29 C9
Rodney, Canada 116 D3
Rodney, C., N.Z. 91 G5
Rodniki, Russia 34 B5
Rodonit, Kepi i, Albania 44 E3
Rodriguez, Ind. Oc. 3 E13
Roe →, U.K. 12 A5
Roebling, U.S.A. 117 F10
Roebourne, Australia 92 D2
Roebuck B., Australia 92 C3
Roermond, Neths. 17 C6
Roes Welcome Sd., Canada 101 B11
Roeselare, Belgium 17 D3
Rogachev = Ragachow, Belarus 33 F6
Rogačica, Serbia & M. 44 B3
Rogagua, L., Bolivia 124 F5
Rogaška Slatina, Slovenia 41 B12
Rogatec, Slovenia 41 B12
Rogatica, Bos.-H. 28 G4
Rogatyn, Ukraine 33 H3
Rogdhia, Greece 49 D7
Rogers, U.S.A. 113 G7
Rogers City, U.S.A. 114 C4
Rogersville, Canada 105 C6
Roggan →, Canada 104 B4
Roggan L., Canada 104 B4
Roggeveldberge, S. Africa 88 E3
Roggiano Gravina, Italy 43 C9
Rogliano, France 21 F13
Rogliano, Italy 43 C9
Rogoaguado, L., Bolivia 124 F5
Rogojampi, Indonesia 63 J17
Rogoźno, Poland 31 F3
Rogue →, U.S.A. 108 E1
Rohan, France 18 D4
Róhda, Greece 49 A3
Rohnert Park, U.S.A. 110 G4
Rohri, Pakistan 68 F3
Rohri Canal, Pakistan 68 F3
Rohtak, India 68 E7
Roi Et, Thailand 64 D4
Roja, Latvia 9 H20
Rojas, Argentina 126 C3
Rojişte, Romania 29 F8
Rojo, C., Mexico 119 C5
Rokan →, Indonesia 62 D2
Rokel →, S. Leone 82 D2
Rokiškis, Lithuania 9 J21
Rokitno, Russia 33 G8
Rokycany, Czech Rep. 26 B6
Rolândia, Brazil 127 A5
Rolla, U.S.A. 113 G9
Rolleston, Australia 94 C4
Rollingstone, Australia 94 B4
Rom, Sudan 81 F3
Roma, Australia 95 D4
Roma, Italy 41 G9
Roma, Sweden 11 G12
Roma, U.S.A. 113 M5
Romain C., U.S.A. 115 J6
Romaine, Canada 105 B7

Romaine →, *Canada* 105 B7
Roman, *Bulgaria* 44 C7
Roman, *Romania* 29 D11
Roman-Kosh, Gora, *Ukraine* 33 K8
Romanche →, *France* 21 C9
Romang, *Indonesia* 63 F7
Români, *Egypt* 74 E1
Romania ■, *Europe* 29 D10
Romanija, *Bos.-H.* 28 G3
Romano, Cayo, *Cuba* 120 B4
Romanovka = Basarabeasca, *Moldova* 29 D13
Romans-sur-Isère, *France* 21 C9
Romanshorn, *Switz.* 25 H5
Rombari, *Sudan* 81 G3
Romblon, *Phil.* 61 E5
Rome = Roma, *Italy* 41 G9
Rome, *Ga., U.S.A.* 115 H3
Rome, *N.Y., U.S.A.* 117 C9
Rome, *Pa., U.S.A.* 117 E8
Rome Fiumicino ✕ (FCO), *Italy* 41 G9
Rometta, *Italy* 43 D8
Romilly-sur-Seine, *France* 19 D10
Romney, *U.S.A.* 114 F6
Romney Marsh, *U.K.* 15 F8
Romny, *Ukraine* 33 G7
Rømø, *Denmark* 11 J2
Romodan, *Ukraine* 33 G7
Romodanovo, *Russia* 34 C7
Romont, *Switz.* 25 J2
Romorantin-Lanthenay, *France* 19 E8
Romsdalen, *Norway* 9 E12
Romsey, *U.K.* 15 G6
Ron, *Vietnam* 64 D6
Rona, *U.K.* 13 D3
Ronan, *U.S.A.* 108 C6
Roncador, Cayos, *Colombia* 120 D3
Roncador, Serra do, *Brazil* 125 F8
Ronciglione, *Italy* 41 F9
Ronco →, *Italy* 41 D9
Ronda, *Spain* 37 J5
Ronda, Serranía de, *Spain* 37 J5
Rondane, *Norway* 9 F13
Rondônia □, *Brazil* 124 F6
Rondonópolis, *Brazil* 125 G8
Rong, Koh, *Cambodia* 65 G4
Rong Jiang →, *China* 58 E7
Rong Xian, *Guangxi Zhuangzu, China* 59 F8
Rong Xian, *Sichuan, China* 58 C5
Rong'an, *China* 58 E7
Rongchang, *China* 58 C5
Ronge, L. la, *Canada* 103 B7
Rongjiang, *China* 58 E7
Rongshui, *China* 58 E7
Rønne, *Denmark* 11 J8
Ronne Ice Shelf, *Antarctica* 5 D18
Ronneby, *Sweden* 11 H9
Ronnebyån →, *Sweden* 11 H9
Rönneshytta, *Sweden* 11 F9
Ronsard, C., *Australia* 93 D1
Ronse, *Belgium* 17 D3
Roodepoort, *S. Africa* 89 D4
Roof Butte, *U.S.A.* 109 H9
Rooiboklaagte →, *Namibia* 88 C3
Roorkee, *India* 68 E7
Roosendaal, *Neths.* 17 C4
Roosevelt, *U.S.A.* 108 F8
Roosevelt →, *Brazil* 124 E6
Roosevelt, Mt., *Canada* 102 B3
Roosevelt I., *Antarctica* 5 D12
Ropczyce, *Poland* 31 H8
Roper →, *Australia* 94 A2
Roper Bar, *Australia* 94 A1
Roque Pérez, *Argentina* 126 D4
Roquefort, *France* 20 D3
Roquemaure, *France* 21 D8
Roquetas de Mar, *Spain* 39 J2
Roquetes, *Spain* 38 E5
Roquevaire, *France* 21 E9
Roraima □, *Brazil* 124 C6
Roraima, Mt., *Venezuela* 124 B6
Røros, *Norway* 9 E14
Rorschach, *Switz.* 25 H5
Rosa, *Zambia* 87 D3
Rosa, L., *Bahamas* 121 B5
Rosa, Monte, *Europe* 40 C4
Rosal de la Frontera, *Spain* 37 H3
Rosalia, *U.S.A.* 108 C5
Rosamond, *U.S.A.* 111 L8
Rosans, *France* 21 D9
Rosario, *Argentina* 126 C3
Rosário, *Brazil* 125 D10
Rosario, *Baja Calif., Mexico* 118 B1
Rosario, *Sinaloa, Mexico* 118 C3
Rosario, *Paraguay* 126 A4
Rosario de la Frontera, *Argentina* 126 B3
Rosario de Lerma, *Argentina* 126 A2
Rosario del Tala, *Argentina* 126 C4
Rosário do Sul, *Brazil* 127 C5
Rosarito, *Mexico* 111 N9
Rosarno, *Italy* 43 D8
Rosas = Roses, *Spain* 38 C8
Roscoe, *U.S.A.* 117 E10
Roscoff, *France* 18 D3
Roscommon, *Ireland* 12 C3
Roscommon □, *Ireland* 12 C3
Roscrea, *Ireland* 12 D4
Rose →, *Australia* 94 A2
Rose Blanche-Harbour Le Cou, *Canada* 105 C8
Rose Pt., *Canada* 102 C2
Rose Valley, *Canada* 103 C8
Roseau, *Domin.* 121 C7
Roseau, *U.S.A.* 112 A7
Rosebery, *Australia* 95 G4
Rosebud, *S. Dak., U.S.A.* 112 D4
Rosebud, *Tex., U.S.A.* 113 K6
Roseburg, *U.S.A.* 108 E2
Rosedale, *U.S.A.* 113 J9
Rosehearty, *U.K.* 13 D6
Roseland, *U.S.A.* 110 G4
Rosemary, *Canada* 102 C6
Rosenberg, *U.S.A.* 113 L7
Rosendaël, *France* 19 A9
Rosenheim, *Germany* 25 H8
Roses, *Spain* 38 C8
Roses, G. de, *Spain* 38 C8
Roseto degli Abruzzi, *Italy* 41 F11
Rosetown, *Canada* 103 C7
Rosetta = Rashîd, *Egypt* 80 H7
Roseville, *Calif., U.S.A.* 110 G5
Roseville, *Mich., U.S.A.* 116 D2
Rosewood, *Australia* 95 D5
Roshkhvār, *Iran* 71 C8
Rosières-en-Santerre, *France* 19 C9
Rosignano Maríttimo, *Italy* 40 E7
Rosignol, *Guyana* 124 B7
Roşiori de Vede, *Romania* 29 F10
Rositsa, *Bulgaria* 45 C11
Rositsa →, *Bulgaria* 45 C9
Roskilde, *Denmark* 11 J6
Roskilde Amtskommune □, *Denmark* 11 J6
Roskovec, *Albania* 44 F3
Roslavl, *Russia* 32 F7
Rosmaninhal, *Portugal* 36 F3
Rosmead, *S. Africa* 88 E4
Røsnæs, *Denmark* 11 J4
Rosolini, *Italy* 43 F7
Rosporden, *France* 18 E3
Ross, *Australia* 95 G4
Ross, *N.Z.* 91 K3
Ross Béthio, *Mauritania* 82 B1
Ross Dependency, *Antarctica* 5 D12
Ross I., *Antarctica* 5 D11
Ross Ice Shelf, *Antarctica* 5 E12
Ross L., *U.S.A.* 108 B3
Ross-on-Wye, *U.K.* 15 F5
Ross River, *Australia* 94 C1
Ross River, *Canada* 102 A2
Ross Sea, *Antarctica* 5 D11
Rossall Pt., *U.K.* 14 D4
Rossan Pt., *Ireland* 12 B3
Rossano, *Italy* 43 C9
Rossburn, *Canada* 103 C8
Rosseau, *Canada* 116 A5
Rosseau, L., *Canada* 116 A5
Rosses, The, *Ireland* 12 A3
Rossignol, L., *Canada* 104 B5
Rossignol L., *Canada* 105 D6
Rossland, *Canada* 102 D5
Rosslare, *Ireland* 12 D5
Rosslare Harbour, *Ireland* 12 D5
Rosslau, *Germany* 24 D8
Rosso, *Mauritania* 82 B1
Rosso, C., *France* 21 F12
Rossosh, *Russia* 33 G10
Røssvatnet, *Norway* 8 D16
Røst, *Norway* 8 C15
Rosthern, *Canada* 103 C7
Rostock, *Germany* 24 A8
Rostov, *Don, Russia* 33 J10
Rostov, *Yaroslavl, Russia* 32 D10
Rostrenen, *France* 18 D3
Roswell, *Ga., U.S.A.* 115 H3
Roswell, *N. Mex., U.S.A.* 113 J2
Rota, *Spain* 37 J4
Rotan, *U.S.A.* 113 J4
Rotenburg, *Hessen, Germany* 24 E5
Rotenburg, *Niedersachsen, Germany* 24 B5
Roth, *Germany* 25 F7
Rothaargebirge, *Germany* 24 D4
Rothaargebirge ⌓, *Germany* 24 E4
Rothenburg ob der Tauber, *Germany* 25 F6
Rother →, *U.K.* 15 G8
Rothera, *Antarctica* 5 C17
Rotherham, *U.K.* 14 D6
Rothes, *U.K.* 13 D5
Rothesay, *Canada* 105 C6
Rothesay, *U.K.* 13 F3
Roti, *Indonesia* 63 F6
Rotja, Pta., *Spain* 39 G6
Roto, *Australia* 95 E4
Rotondo, Mte., *France* 21 F13
Rotoroa, L., *N.Z.* 91 J4
Rotorua, *N.Z.* 91 H6
Rotorua, L., *N.Z.* 91 H6
Rott →, *Germany* 25 G9
Rottenburg, *Germany* 25 G4
Rottenmann, *Austria* 26 D7
Rotterdam, *Neths.* 17 C4
Rotterdam, *U.S.A.* 117 D10
Rottne, *Sweden* 11 G8
Rottnest I., *Australia* 93 F2
Rottumeroog, *Neths.* 17 A6
Rottweil, *Germany* 25 G4
Rotuma, *Fiji* 96 J9
Roubaix, *France* 19 B10
Roudnice nad Labem, *Czech Rep.* 26 A7
Rouen, *France* 18 C8
Rouergue, *France* 20 D5
Rouillac, *France* 20 C3
Rouleau, *Canada* 103 C8
Round Mountain, *U.S.A.* 108 G5
Round Mt., *Australia* 95 E5
Round Rock, *U.S.A.* 113 K6
Roundup, *U.S.A.* 108 C9
Rousay, *U.K.* 13 B5
Rouses Point, *U.S.A.* 117 B11
Rouseville, *U.S.A.* 116 E5
Roussillon, *Isère, France* 21 C8
Roussillon, *Pyrénées-Or., France* 20 F6
Rouxville, *S. Africa* 88 E4
Rouyn-Noranda, *Canada* 104 C4
Rovaniemi, *Finland* 8 C21
Rovato, *Italy* 40 C7
Rovenki, *Ukraine* 33 H10
Rovereto, *Italy* 40 C8
Rovigo, *Italy* 41 C8
Rovinj, *Croatia* 41 C10
Rovno = Rivne, *Ukraine* 33 G4
Rovnoye, *Russia* 34 E8
Rovuma = Ruvuma →, *Tanzania* 87 E5
Row'ān, *Iran* 71 C6
Rowena, *Australia* 95 D4
Rowley Shoals, *Australia* 92 C2
Roxa, *Guinea-Biss.* 82 C1
Roxas, *Capiz, Phil.* 61 F5
Roxas, *Isabela, Phil.* 61 C4
Roxas, *Mind. Or., Phil.* 61 E4
Roxboro, *U.S.A.* 115 G6
Roxborough, *Trin. & Tob.* 125 J16
Roxburgh, *N.Z.* 91 L2
Roxbury, *U.S.A.* 116 F7
Roxen, *Sweden* 11 F9
Roy, *Mont., U.S.A.* 108 C9
Roy, *N. Mex., U.S.A.* 113 H2
Roy, *Utah, U.S.A.* 108 F7
Royal Canal, *Ireland* 12 C4
Royal Leamington Spa, *U.K.* 15 E6
Royal Natal △, *S. Africa* 89 D4
Royal Tunbridge Wells, *U.K.* 15 F8
Royale, Isle, *U.S.A.* 112 B10
Royan, *France* 20 C2
Roye, *France* 19 C9
Royston, *U.K.* 15 E7
Rožaj, *Serbia & M.* 44 D4
Różan, *Poland* 31 F8
Rozay-en-Brie, *France* 19 D9
Rozdilna, *Ukraine* 33 J6
Rozhyshche, *Ukraine* 33 G3
Rožmitál pod Třemšínem, *Czech Rep.* 26 B6
Rožňava, *Slovak Rep.* 27 C13
Rozogi, *Poland* 30 E8
Rozoy-sur-Serre, *France* 19 C11
Roztoczański △, *Poland* 31 H10
Rozzano, *Italy* 40 C6
Rrëshen, *Albania* 44 E3
Rrogozhine, *Albania* 44 E3
Rtanj, *Serbia & M.* 44 C5
Rtishchevo, *Russia* 34 D6
Rúa = A Rúa, *Spain* 36 C3
Ruacaná, *Namibia* 88 B1
Ruaha △, *Tanzania* 86 D3
Ruahine Ra., *N.Z.* 91 H6
Ruapehu, *N.Z.* 91 H5
Ruapuke I., *N.Z.* 91 M2
Ruâq, W. →, *Egypt* 74 F2
Rub' al Khālī, *Si. Arabia* 75 D4
Rubeho Mts., *Tanzania* 86 D4
Rubezhnoye = Rubizhne, *Ukraine* 33 H10
Rubh a' Mhail, *U.K.* 13 F2
Rubha Hunish, *U.K.* 13 D2
Rubha Robhanais = Lewis, Butt of, *U.K.* 13 C2
Rubí, *Spain* 38 D7
Rubicon →, *U.S.A.* 110 G5
Rubicone →, *Italy* 41 D9
Rubik, *Albania* 44 E3
Rubino, *Ivory C.* 82 D4
Rubio, *Venezuela* 124 B4
Rubizhne, *Ukraine* 33 H10
Rubondo △, *Tanzania* 86 C3
Rubtsovsk, *Russia* 52 D9
Ruby L., *U.S.A.* 108 F6
Ruby Mts., *U.S.A.* 108 F6
Rubyvale, *Australia* 94 C4
Rucheng, *China* 59 E9
Ruciane-Nida, *Poland* 30 E8
Rūd Sar, *Iran* 71 B6
Ruda, *Sweden* 11 G10
Ruda Śląska, *Poland* 31 H5
Rudall, *Australia* 95 E2
Rudall →, *Australia* 92 D3
Rudall River △, *Australia* 92 D3
Rüdersdorf, *Germany* 24 C9
Rudewa, *Tanzania* 87 E3
Rudkøbing, *Denmark* 11 K4
Rudna, *Poland* 31 G3
Rudnik, *Bulgaria* 45 D11
Rudnik, *Poland* 31 H9
Rudnik, *Serbia & M.* 44 B4
Rudnya, *Russia* 32 E6
Rudnyy, *Kazakhstan* 52 D7
Rudo, *Bos.-H.* 28 G4
Rudolfa, Ostrov, *Russia* 52 A6
Rudolstadt, *Germany* 24 E7
Rudong, *China* 59 A13
Rudozem, *Bulgaria* 45 E8
Rudyard, *U.S.A.* 114 B3
Rue, *France* 19 B8
Ruenya →, *Africa* 87 F3
Rufa'a, *Sudan* 81 E3
Rufiji →, *Tanzania* 86 D4
Rufino, *Argentina* 126 C3
Rufisque, *Senegal* 82 C1
Rufling Pt., *Br. Virgin Is.* 121 e
Rufunsa, *Zambia* 87 F2
Rugao, *China* 59 A13
Rugby, *U.K.* 15 E6
Rugby, *U.S.A.* 112 A5
Rügen, *Germany* 24 A9
Rügen ⌓, *Germany* 24 A9
Rugles, *France* 18 D7
Ruhengeri, *Rwanda* 86 C2
Ruhla, *Germany* 24 E6
Ruhland, *Germany* 24 D9
Ruhnu, *Estonia* 9 H20
Ruhr →, *Germany* 24 D2
Ruhuhu →, *Tanzania* 87 E3
Rui'an, *China* 59 D13
Ruichang, *China* 59 C10
Ruidoso, *U.S.A.* 109 K11
Ruijin, *China* 59 E10
Ruili, *China* 58 E1
Ruivo, Pico, *Madeira* 48 D3
Ruj, *Bulgaria* 44 D6
Rujen, *Macedonia* 44 D6
Rujm Tal'at al Jamā'ah, *Jordan* 74 E4
Ruk, *Pakistan* 68 F3
Rukhla, *Pakistan* 68 C4
Ruki →, *Dem. Rep. of the Congo* 84 E3
Rukwa □, *Tanzania* 86 D3
Rukwa, L., *Tanzania* 86 D3
Rulhieres, C., *Australia* 92 B4
Rum = Rhum, *U.K.* 13 E2
Rum, *Jordan* 74 F4
Rum Cay, *Bahamas* 121 B5
Rum Jungle, *Australia* 92 B5
Ruma, *Serbia & M.* 28 E4
Ruma △, *Kenya* 86 C3
Rumāḥ, *Si. Arabia* 70 E5
Rumania = Romania ■, *Europe* 29 D10
Rumaylah, *Iraq* 70 D5
Rumbêk, *Sudan* 81 F2
Rumburk, *Czech Rep.* 26 A7
Rumford, *U.S.A.* 115 C10
Rumia, *Poland* 30 D5
Rumilly, *France* 21 C9
Rumoi, *Japan* 54 C10
Rumonge, *Burundi* 86 C2
Rumson, *U.S.A.* 117 F11
Rumuruti, *Kenya* 86 B4
Runan, *China* 56 H8
Runanga, *N.Z.* 91 K3
Runaway, C., *N.Z.* 91 G6
Runaway Bay, *Jamaica* 120 a
Runcorn, *U.K.* 14 D5
Rundu, *Namibia* 88 B2
Rungwa, *Tanzania* 86 D3
Rungwa ⌓, *Tanzania* 86 D3
Rungwa →, *Tanzania* 86 D3
Rungwe, *Tanzania* 87 D3
Rungwe, Mt., *Tanzania* 84 F6
Runka, *Nigeria* 83 C6
Runn, *Sweden* 10 D9
Runton Ra., *Australia* 92 D3
Ruokolahti, *Finland* 32 B5
Ruoqiang, *China* 60 C3
Rupa, *India* 67 F18
Rupar, *India* 68 D7
Rupat, *Indonesia* 62 D2
Rupea, *Romania* 29 D10
Rupen →, *India* 68 H4
Rupert, *U.S.A.* 108 E7
Rupert →, *Canada* 104 B4
Rupert B., *Canada* 104 B4
Rupert House = Waskaganish, *Canada* 104 B4
Rupsa, *India* 69 J12
Rur →, *Germany* 24 D1
Rurrenabaque, *Bolivia* 124 F5
Rus →, *Spain* 39 F2
Rusambo, *Zimbabwe* 87 F3
Rusape, *Zimbabwe* 87 F3
Ruschuk = Ruse, *Bulgaria* 45 C9
Ruse, *Bulgaria* 45 C9
Ruse □, *Bulgaria* 45 C10
Rusenski Lom △, *Bulgaria* 44 C7
Ruşeţu, *Romania* 29 F12
Rush, *Ireland* 12 C5
Rushan, *China* 57 F11
Rushden, *U.K.* 15 E7
Rushmore, Mt., *U.S.A.* 112 D3
Rushville, *Ill., U.S.A.* 112 E9
Rushville, *Ind., U.S.A.* 114 F3
Rushville, *Nebr., U.S.A.* 112 D3
Russas, *Brazil* 125 D11
Russell, *Canada* 103 C8
Russell, *Kans., U.S.A.* 112 F5
Russell, *N.Y., U.S.A.* 117 B9
Russell, *Pa., U.S.A.* 116 E5
Russell Cave ⌓, *U.S.A.* 115 H3
Russell L., *Man., Canada* 103 B8
Russell L., *N.W.T., Canada* 102 A5
Russellkonda, *India* 67 K14
Russellville, *Ala., U.S.A.* 115 H2
Russellville, *Ark., U.S.A.* 113 H8
Russellville, *Ky., U.S.A.* 115 G2
Rüsselsheim, *Germany* 25 F4
Russi, *Italy* 41 D9
Russia ■, *Eurasia* 53 C11
Russian →, *U.S.A.* 110 G3
Russkoye Ustie, *Russia* 4 B15
Rust, *Austria* 27 D9
Rustam, *Pakistan* 68 B5
Rustam Shahr, *Pakistan* 68 F2
Rustavi, *Georgia* 35 K7
Rustenburg, *S. Africa* 88 D4
Ruston, *U.S.A.* 113 J8
Rutana, *Burundi* 86 C3
Rute, *Spain* 37 H6
Ruteng, *Indonesia* 63 F6
Ruth, *U.S.A.* 116 C2
Rutherford, *U.S.A.* 110 G4
Rutland, *U.S.A.* 117 C12
Rutland □, *U.K.* 15 E7
Rutland Water, *U.K.* 15 E7
Rutledge →, *Canada* 103 A6
Rutledge L., *Canada* 103 A6
Rutqa, W. →, *Syria* 73 E9
Rutshuru, *Dem. Rep. of the Congo* 86 C2
Ruvo di Púglia, *Italy* 43 A9
Ruvu, *Tanzania* 86 D4
Ruvu →, *Tanzania* 86 D4
Ruvuba △, *Burundi* 86 C2
Ruvuma □, *Tanzania* 87 E4
Ruvuma →, *Tanzania* 87 E5
Ruwais, *U.A.E.* 71 E7
Ruwenzori, *Africa* 86 B2
Ruwenzori △, *Uganda* 86 B2
Ruya →, *Zimbabwe* 89 B5
Ruyigi, *Burundi* 86 C3
Ruyuan, *China* 59 E9
Ruzayevka, *Russia* 34 C7
Růzhevo Konare, *Bulgaria* 45 D8
Ružomberok, *Slovak Rep.* 27 B12
Ruzyne, Prague ✕ (PRG), *Czech Rep.* 26 A7
Rwanda ■, *Africa* 86 C3
Ryakhovo, *Bulgaria* 45 C10
Ryan, L., *U.K.* 13 G3
Ryazan, *Russia* 32 E10
Ryazhsk, *Russia* 32 F11
Rybache = Rybachye, *Kazakhstan* 52 E9
Rybachye, *Kazakhstan* 52 E9
Rybačij, *Russia* 30 C7
Rybinsk, *Russia* 32 C10
Rybinskoye Vdkhr., *Russia* 32 C10
Rybnik, *Poland* 31 H5
Rybnitsa = Râbniţa, *Moldova* 29 C14
Rybnoye, *Russia* 32 E10
Rychnov nad Kněžnou, *Czech Rep.* 27 A9
Rychwał, *Poland* 31 F5
Rycroft, *Canada* 102 B5
Ryd, *Sweden* 11 H8
Rydaholm, *Sweden* 11 H8
Ryde, *U.K.* 15 G6
Ryderwood, *U.S.A.* 110 D3
Rydzyna, *Poland* 31 G3
Rye, *U.K.* 15 G8
Rye →, *U.K.* 14 C7
Rye Bay, *U.K.* 15 G8
Rye Patch Reservoir, *U.S.A.* 108 F4
Ryegate, *U.S.A.* 108 C9
Ryki, *Poland* 31 G8
Ryley, *Canada* 102 C6
Rylsk, *Russia* 33 G8
Rylstone, *Australia* 95 E4
Rymanów, *Poland* 31 J8
Ryn, *Poland* 30 E8
Ryn Peski, *Kazakhstan* 35 G9
Ryōtsu, *Japan* 54 E9
Rypin, *Poland* 31 E6
Ryssby, *Sweden* 11 H8
Rysy, *Europe* 27 B13
Ryūgasaki, *Japan* 55 G10
Ryūkyū Is. = Ryūkyū-rettō, *Japan* 55 M3
Ryūkyū-rettō, *Japan* 55 M3
Rzepin, *Poland* 31 F1
Rzeszów, *Poland* 31 H8
Rzhev, *Russia* 32 D8

S

Sa, *Thailand* 64 C3
Sa Canal, *Spain* 48 C7
Sa Conillera, *Spain* 48 C7
Sa Dec, *Vietnam* 65 G5
Sa Dragonera, *Spain* 48 B9
Sa Mesquida, *Spain* 48 B11
Sa Pobla, *Spain* 38 F8
Sa Savina, *Spain* 48 C7
Sa'ādatābād, *Fārs, Iran* 71 D7
Sa'ādatābād, *Hormozgān, Iran* 71 D7
Sa'ādatābād, *Kermān, Iran* 71 D7
Saale →, *Germany* 24 D7
Saaler Bodden, *Germany* 24 A8
Saalfeld, *Germany* 24 E7
Saalfelden, *Austria* 26 D5
Saane →, *Switz.* 25 H3
Saanich, *Canada* 110 B3
Saar →, *Europe* 17 E6
Saar-Hunsrueck ⌓, *Germany* 25 F2
Saarbrücken, *Germany* 25 F2
Saarburg, *Germany* 25 F2
Saaremaa, *Estonia* 9 G20
Saarijärvi, *Finland* 9 E21
Saariselkä, *Finland* 8 B23
Saarland □, *Germany* 25 F2
Saarlouis, *Germany* 25 F2
Sab 'Ābar, *Syria* 70 C3
Saba, *W. Indies* 121 C7
Šabac, *Serbia & M.* 44 B3
Sabadell, *Spain* 38 D7
Sabah □, *Malaysia* 62 C5
Sabak Bernam, *Malaysia* 65 L3
Sabalān, Kūhhā-ye, *Iran* 70 B5
Sabalana, Kepulauan, *Indonesia* 63 F5
Sábana de la Mar, *Dom. Rep.* 121 C6
Sábanalarga, *Colombia* 124 A4
Sabang, *Indonesia* 62 C1
Săbăoani, *Romania* 29 C11
Sabará, *Brazil* 125 G10
Sabarmati →, *India* 68 H5
Sabattis, *U.S.A.* 117 B10
Sabáudia, *Italy* 42 A6
Saberania, *Indonesia* 63 E9
Sabhah, *Libya* 79 C8
Sabi →, *India* 68 E7
Sabidana, J., *Sudan* 80 D4
Sabie, *S. Africa* 89 D5
Sabinal, *Mexico* 118 A3
Sabinal, *U.S.A.* 113 L5
Sabiñánigo, *Spain* 38 C4
Sabinar, Punta del, *Spain* 39 J2
Sabinas, *Mexico* 118 B4
Sabinas →, *Mexico* 118 B4
Sabinas Hidalgo, *Mexico* 118 B4
Sabine →, *U.S.A.* 113 L8
Sabine L., *U.S.A.* 113 L8
Sabine Pass, *U.S.A.* 113 L8
Sabinov, *Slovak Rep.* 27 B14
Sabinsville, *U.S.A.* 116 E7
Sabirabad, *Azerbaijan* 35 K9
Sablayan, *Phil.* 61 E4
Sable, *Canada* 105 A6
Sable, C., *Canada* 105 D6
Sable, C., *U.S.A.* 107 E10
Sable I., *Canada* 105 D8
Sablé-sur-Sarthe, *France* 18 E6
Sabonkafi, *Niger* 83 C6
Sabor →, *Portugal* 36 D3
Sabou, *Burkina Faso* 82 C4
Sabres, *France* 20 D3
Sabrina Coast, *Antarctica* 5 C9
Sabugal, *Portugal* 36 E3
Sabulubbek, *Indonesia* 62 E1
Sabuncu, *Turkey* 47 B12
Sabzevār, *Iran* 71 B8
Sabzvārān, *Iran* 71 D8

Sac City, *U.S.A.* **112 D7**
Sacedón, *Spain* **38 E2**
Săcele, *Romania* **29 E10**
Sachigo →, *Canada* **104 A2**
Sachigo, L., *Canada* **104 B1**
Sachkhere, *Georgia* **35 J6**
Sachsen □, *Germany* **24 E9**
Sachsen-Anhalt □, *Germany* **24 D7**
Sächsische Schweiz △, *Germany* **24 E10**
Sacile, *Italy* **41 C9**
Sackets Harbor, *U.S.A.* **117 C8**
Sackville, *Canada* **105 C7**
Saco, *Maine, U.S.A.* **115 D10**
Saco, *Mont., U.S.A.* **108 B10**
Sacramento, *U.S.A.* **110 G5**
Sacramento →, *U.S.A.* **110 G5**
Sacramento Mts., *U.S.A.* **109 K11**
Sacramento Valley, *U.S.A.* **110 G5**
Sacratif, C., *Spain* **37 J7**
Săcueni, *Romania* **28 C7**
Sada, *Spain* **36 B2**
Sada-Misaki, *Japan* **55 H6**
Sádaba, *Spain* **38 C3**
Sadabad, *India* **68 F8**
Sadani, *Tanzania* **86 D4**
Sadao, *Thailand* **65 J3**
Sadd el Aali, *Egypt* **80 C3**
Saddle Mt., *U.S.A.* **110 E3**
Sade, *Nigeria* **83 C7**
Sadimi, *Dem. Rep. of the Congo* **87 D1**
Sadiola, *Mali* **82 C2**
Sa'dīyah, Hawr as, *Iraq* **73 F12**
Sado, *Japan* **54 F9**
Sado →, *Portugal* **37 G2**
Sadon, *Burma* **67 G20**
Sadon, *Russia* **35 J6**
Sadovoye, *Russia* **35 G7**
Sadra, *India* **68 H5**
Sadri, *India* **68 G5**
Sæby, *Denmark* **11 G4**
Saegertown, *U.S.A.* **116 E4**
Saelices, *Spain* **38 F2**
Safaalan, *Turkey* **45 E12**
Safaga, *Egypt* **80 B3**
Şafājah, *Si. Arabia* **70 E3**
Šafárikovo = Tornal'a, *Slovak Rep.* **27 C13**
Säffle, *Sweden* **10 E6**
Safford, *U.S.A.* **109 K9**
Saffron Walden, *U.K.* **15 E8**
Safi, *Morocco* **78 B4**
Şafīābād, *Iran* **71 B8**
Safīd Dasht, *Iran* **71 C6**
Safīd Kūh, *Afghan.* **66 B3**
Safīd Rūd →, *Iran* **71 B6**
Safipur, *India* **69 F9**
Safonovo, *Russia* **32 E7**
Safranbolu, *Turkey* **72 B5**
Saft Rashîn, *Egypt* **80 J7**
Şafwān, *Iraq* **70 D5**
Sag Harbor, *U.S.A.* **117 F12**
Saga, *Japan* **55 H5**
Saga □, *Japan* **55 H5**
Sagae, *Japan* **54 E10**
Sagala, *Mali* **82 C3**
Sagamartha = Everest, Mt., *Nepal* **69 E12**
Sagamore, *U.S.A.* **116 F5**
Sagar, *Karnataka, India* **66 M9**
Sagar, *Mad. P., India* **69 H8**
Sagara, L., *Tanzania* **86 D3**
Sagay, *Phil.* **61 F5**
Saginaw, *U.S.A.* **114 D4**
Saginaw →, *U.S.A.* **114 D4**
Saginaw B., *U.S.A.* **114 D4**
Sagleipie, *Liberia* **82 D3**
Saglouc = Salluit, *Canada* **101 B12**
Sagŏ-ri, *S. Korea* **57 G14**
Sagone, *France* **21 F12**
Sagone, G. de, *France* **21 F12**
Sagres, *Portugal* **37 J2**
Sagua la Grande, *Cuba* **120 B3**
Saguache, *U.S.A.* **109 G10**
Saguaro △, *U.S.A.* **109 K8**
Saguenay →, *Canada* **105 C5**
Sagunt, *Spain* **38 F4**
Sagunto = Sagunt, *Spain* **38 F4**
Sagwara, *India* **68 H6**
Sahaba, *Sudan* **80 D3**
Sahagún, *Spain* **36 C5**
Saḩam al Jawlān, *Syria* **74 C4**
Sahamandrevo, *Madag.* **89 C8**
Sahand, Kūh-e, *Iran* **70 B5**
Sahara, *Africa* **78 D6**
Saharan Atlas = Saharien, Atlas, *Algeria* **78 B6**
Saharanpur, *India* **68 E7**
Saharien, Atlas, *Algeria* **78 B6**
Saharsa, *India* **69 G12**
Sahasinaka, *Madag.* **89 C8**
Sahaswan, *India* **69 E8**
Sahel, *Africa* **78 E5**
Sahel, Canal du, *Mali* **82 C3**
Sahibganj, *India* **69 G12**
Sāḩilīyah, *Iraq* **70 C4**
Sahiwal, *Pakistan* **68 D5**
Şaḩneh, *Iran* **70 C5**
Sahrawi = Western Sahara ■, *Africa* **78 D3**
Sahuaripa, *Mexico* **118 B3**
Sahuarita, *U.S.A.* **109 L8**
Sahuayo, *Mexico* **118 C4**
Šahy, *Slovak Rep.* **27 C11**
Sai →, *India* **69 G10**
Sai Buri, *Thailand* **65 J3**
Sa'id Bundas, *Sudan* **79 G10**
Sa'īdābād = Sīrjān, *Iran* **71 D7**
Sa'īdābād, *Iran* **71 B7**
Sa'īdīyeh, *Iran* **71 B6**
Saidpur, *Bangla.* **67 G16**
Saidpur, *India* **69 G10**
Saidu, *Pakistan* **69 B5**
Saignes, *France* **20 C6**
Saigon = Thanh Pho Ho Chi Minh, *Vietnam* **65 G6**
Saijō, *Japan* **55 H6**
Saikai △, *Japan* **55 H4**
Saikanosy Masoala, *Madag.* **89 B9**
Saikhoa Ghat, *India* **67 F19**
Saiki, *Japan* **55 H5**
Sailana, *India* **68 H6**
Saillans, *France* **21 D9**
Sailolof, *Indonesia* **63 E8**
Saimaa, *Finland* **9 F23**
Saimbeyli, *Turkey* **72 D7**
Şa'in Dezh, *Iran* **70 B5**
St. Abb's Head, *U.K.* **13 F6**
St-Affrique, *France* **20 E6**
St-Agrève, *France* **21 C8**
St-Aignan, *France* **18 E8**
St. Alban's, *Canada* **105 C8**
St. Albans, *U.K.* **15 F7**
St. Albans, *Vt., U.S.A.* **117 B11**
St. Albans, *W. Va., U.S.A.* **114 F5**
St. Alban's Head, *U.K.* **15 G5**
St. Albert, *Canada* **102 C6**
St-Amand-en-Puisaye, *France* **19 E10**
St-Amand-les-Eaux, *France* **19 B10**
St-Amand-Montrond, *France* **19 F9**
St-Amarin, *France* **19 E14**
St-Amour, *France* **19 F12**
St-André-de-Cubzac, *France* **20 D3**
St-André-les-Alpes, *France* **21 E10**
St. Andrew's, *Canada* **105 C8**
St. Andrews, *U.K.* **13 E6**
St-Anicet, *Canada* **117 A10**
St. Anns B., *Canada* **105 C7**
St. Ann's Bay, *Jamaica* **120 a**
St. Anthony, *Canada* **105 B8**
St. Anthony, *U.S.A.* **108 E8**
St-Antoine, *Canada* **105 C7**
St-Antonin-Noble-Val, *France* **20 D5**
St. Arnaud, *Australia* **95 F3**
St-Astier, *France* **20 C4**
St-Aubin-du-Cormier, *France* **18 D5**
St-Augustin, *Canada* **105 B8**
St-Augustin →, *Canada* **105 B8**
St. Augustine, *U.S.A.* **115 L5**
St-Aulaye, *France* **20 C4**
St. Austell, *U.K.* **15 G3**
St-Avold, *France* **19 C13**
St. Barbe, *Canada* **105 B8**
St-Barthélemy, *W. Indies* **121 C7**
St-Béat, *France* **20 F4**
St. Bees Hd., *U.K.* **14 C4**
St. Bees I., *Australia* **94 J7**
St-Benoît-du-Sault, *France* **20 B5**
St-Bonnet, *France* **21 D10**
St-Brévin-les-Pins, *France* **18 E4**
St-Brice-en-Coglès, *France* **18 D5**
St. Bride's, *Canada* **105 C9**
St. Brides B., *U.K.* **15 F2**
St-Brieuc, *France* **18 D4**
St-Calais, *France* **18 E7**
St-Cast-le-Guildo, *France* **18 D4**
St. Catharines, *Canada* **116 C5**
St. Catherines I., *U.S.A.* **115 K5**
St. Catherine's Pt., *U.K.* **15 G6**
St-Céré, *France* **20 D5**
St-Cergue, *Switz.* **25 J2**
St-Cernin, *France* **20 C6**
St-Chamond, *France* **21 C8**
St. Charles, *Ill., U.S.A.* **114 E1**
St. Charles, *Mo., U.S.A.* **112 F9**
St. Charles, *Va., U.S.A.* **114 F7**
St-Chély-d'Apcher, *France* **20 D7**
St-Chinian, *France* **20 E6**
St. Christopher-Nevis = St. Kitts & Nevis ■, *W. Indies* **121 C7**
St-Ciers-sur-Gironde, *France* **20 C3**
St. Clair, *Mich., U.S.A.* **116 D2**
St. Clair, *Pa., U.S.A.* **117 F8**
St. Clair →, *U.S.A.* **116 D2**
St. Clair, L., *Canada* **104 D3**
St. Clair, L., *U.S.A.* **116 D2**
St. Clairsville, *U.S.A.* **116 F4**
St-Claud, *France* **20 C4**
St. Claude, *Canada* **103 D9**
St-Claude, *France* **19 F12**
St. Clears, *U.K.* **15 F3**
St-Clet, *Canada* **117 A10**
St. Cloud, *Fla., U.S.A.* **115 L5**
St. Cloud, *Minn., U.S.A.* **112 C7**
St. Cricq, C., *Australia* **93 E1**
St. Croix, *U.S. Virgin Is.* **121 C7**
St. Croix →, *U.S.A.* **112 C8**
St. Croix Falls, *U.S.A.* **112 C8**
St-Cyprien, *France* **20 F7**
St-Cyr-sur-Mer, *France* **21 E9**
St. David's, *Canada* **105 C8**
St. David's, *U.K.* **15 F2**
St. David's Head, *U.K.* **15 F2**
St-Denis, *France* **19 D9**
St-Dié, *France* **19 D13**
St-Dizier, *France* **19 D11**
St-Égrève, *France* **21 C9**
St. Elias, Mt., *U.S.A.* **100 B5**
St. Elias Mts., *N. Amer.* **102 A1**
St-Eloy-les-Mines, *France* **19 F9**
St-Émilion, *France* **20 D3**
St-Étienne, *France* **21 C8**
St-Étienne-de-Tinée, *France* **21 D10**
St-Étienne-du-Rouvray, *France* **18 C8**
St. Eugène, *Canada* **117 A10**
St. Eustatius, *W. Indies* **121 C7**
St-Exupery, Lyon ✕ (LYS), *France* **21 C9**
St-Fargeau, *France* **19 E10**
St-Félicien, *Canada* **104 C5**
St-Florent, *France* **21 F13**
St-Florent, G. de, *France* **21 F13**
St-Florent-sur-Cher, *France* **19 F9**
St-Florentin, *France* **19 E10**
St-Flour, *France* **20 C7**
St. Francis, *U.S.A.* **112 F4**
St. Francis →, *U.S.A.* **113 H9**
St. Francis, C., *S. Africa* **88 E3**
St. Francisville, *U.S.A.* **113 K9**
St-François, L., *Canada* **117 A10**
St-Fulgent, *France* **18 F5**
St-Gabriel, *Canada* **104 C5**
St. Gallen = Sankt Gallen, *Switz.* **25 H5**
St-Galmier, *France* **19 G11**
St-Gaudens, *France* **20 E4**
St-Gaultier, *France* **18 F8**
St-Gengoux-le-National, *France* **19 F11**
St-Geniez-d'Olt, *France* **20 D6**
St. George, *Australia* **95 D4**
St. George, *Canada* **105 C6**
St. George, *S.C., U.S.A.* **115 J5**
St. George, *Utah, U.S.A.* **109 H7**
St. George, C., *Canada* **105 C8**
St. George, C., *U.S.A.* **115 L3**
St. George Ra., *Australia* **92 C4**
St. George's, *Canada* **105 C8**
St-Georges, *Canada* **105 C5**
St. George's, *Grenada* **121 D7**
St. George's B., *Canada* **105 C8**
St. Georges Basin, *N.S.W., Australia* **95 F5**
St. Georges Basin, *W. Austral., Australia* **92 C4**
St. George's Channel, *Europe* **12 E6**
St. Georges Hd., *Australia* **95 F5**
St-Georges-lès-Baillargeaux, *France* **20 B4**
St-Germain-de-Calberte, *France* **20 D7**
St-Germain-en-Laye, *France* **19 D9**
St-Germain-Lembron, *France* **20 C7**
St-Gervais-d'Auvergne, *France* **19 F9**
St-Gervais-les-Bains, *France* **21 C10**
St-Gildas, Pte. de, *France* **18 E4**
St-Gilles, *France* **21 E8**
St-Girons, *Ariège, France* **20 F5**
St-Girons, *Landes, France* **20 E2**
St. Gotthard P. = San Gottardo, P. del, *Switz.* **25 J4**
St. Helena, *Atl. Oc.* **76 H3**
St. Helena, *U.S.A.* **108 G2**
St. Helena, Mt., *U.S.A.* **110 G4**
St. Helena B., *S. Africa* **88 E2**
St. Helens, *Australia* **95 G4**
St. Helens, *U.K.* **14 D5**
St. Helens, *U.S.A.* **110 E4**
St. Helens, Mt., *U.S.A.* **110 D4**
St. Helier, *U.K.* **15 H5**
St-Herblain, *France* **18 E5**
St-Hilaire-du-Harcouët, *France* **18 D5**
St-Hippolyte, *France* **19 E13**
St-Hippolyte-du-Fort, *France* **20 E7**
St-Honoré-les-Bains, *France* **19 F10**
St-Hubert, *Belgium* **17 D5**
St-Hyacinthe, *Canada* **104 C5**
St. Ignace, *U.S.A.* **114 C3**
St. Ignace I., *Canada* **104 C2**
St. Ignatius, *U.S.A.* **108 C6**
St-Imier, *Switz.* **25 H2**
St. Ives, *Cambs., U.K.* **15 E7**
St. Ives, *Corn., U.K.* **15 G2**
St-James, *France* **18 D5**
St. James, *U.S.A.* **112 D7**
St-Jean →, *Canada* **105 B7**
St-Jean, L., *Canada* **105 C5**
St-Jean-d'Angély, *France* **20 C3**
St-Jean-de-Braye, *France* **19 E8**
St-Jean-de-Luz, *France* **20 E2**
St-Jean-de-Maurienne, *France* **21 C10**
St-Jean-de-Monts, *France* **18 F4**
St-Jean-du-Gard, *France* **20 D7**
St-Jean-en-Royans, *France* **21 C9**
St-Jean-Pied-de-Port, *France* **20 E2**
St-Jean-Port-Joli, *Canada* **105 C5**
St-Jean-sur-Richelieu, *Canada* **117 A11**
St-Jérôme, *Canada* **104 C5**
St. John, *Canada* **105 C6**
St. John, *U.S.A.* **113 G5**
St. John →, *Liberia* **82 D2**
St. John →, *U.S.A.* **115 C12**
St. John, C., *Canada* **105 C8**
St. John I., *U.S. Virgin Is.* **121 e**
St. John's, *Antigua* **121 C7**
St. John's, *Canada* **105 C9**
St. Johns, *Ariz., U.S.A.* **109 J9**
St. Johns, *Mich., U.S.A.* **114 D3**
St. Johns →, *U.S.A.* **115 K5**
St. John's Pt., *Ireland* **12 B3**
St. Johnsbury, *U.S.A.* **117 B12**
St. Johnsville, *U.S.A.* **117 D10**
St-Joseph, *Martinique* **120 c**
St. Joseph, *La., U.S.A.* **113 K9**
St. Joseph, *Mo., U.S.A.* **112 F7**
St. Joseph →, *U.S.A.* **114 D2**
St. Joseph, I., *Canada* **104 C3**
St. Joseph, L., *Canada* **104 B1**
St-Jovite, *Canada* **104 C5**
St-Juéry, *France* **20 E6**
St-Julien-Chapteuil, *France* **21 C8**
St-Julien-de-Vouvantes, *France* **18 E5**
St-Julien-en-Genevois, *France* **19 F13**
St-Junien, *France* **20 C4**
St-Just-en-Chaussée, *France* **19 C9**
St-Just-en-Chevalet, *France* **20 C7**
St. Kitts & Nevis ■, *W. Indies* **121 C7**
St. Laurent, *Canada* **103 C9**
St-Laurent-de-la-Salanque, *France* **20 F6**
St-Laurent-du-Pont, *France* **21 C9**
St-Laurent-en-Grandvaux, *France* **19 F12**
St-Laurent-Médoc, *France* **20 C3**
St. Lawrence, *Australia* **94 C4**
St. Lawrence, *Canada* **105 C8**
St. Lawrence →, *Canada* **105 C6**
St. Lawrence, Gulf of, *Canada* **105 C7**
St. Lawrence I., *U.S.A.* **100 B3**
St. Lawrence Islands △, *Canada* **117 B9**
St. Leonard, *Canada* **105 C6**
St-Léonard-de-Noblat, *France* **20 C5**
St. Lewis →, *Canada* **105 B8**
St-Lô, *France* **18 C5**
St-Louis, *France* **19 E14**
St-Louis, *Guadeloupe* **120 b**
St. Louis, *Senegal* **82 B1**
St. Louis, *U.S.A.* **112 F9**
St. Louis →, *U.S.A.* **112 B8**
St-Loup-sur-Semouse, *France* **19 E13**
St. Lucia ■, *W. Indies* **121 f**
St. Lucia, L., *S. Africa* **89 D5**
St. Lucia Channel, *W. Indies* **121 D7**
St. Maarten, *W. Indies* **121 C7**
St. Magnus B., *U.K.* **13 A7**
St-Maixent-l'École, *France* **20 B3**
St-Malo, *France* **18 D4**
St-Malo, G. de, *France* **18 D4**
St-Mandrier-sur-Mer, *France* **21 E9**
St-Marc, *Haiti* **121 C5**
St-Marcellin, *France* **21 C9**
St-Marcouf, Îs., *France* **18 C5**
St. Maries, *U.S.A.* **108 C5**
St-Martin, *W. Indies* **121 C7**
St-Martin, C., *Martinique* **120 c**
St. Martin, L., *Canada* **103 C9**
St-Martin-de-Crau, *France* **21 E8**
St-Martin-de-Ré, *France* **20 B2**
St-Martin-d'Hères, *France* **21 C9**
St-Martin-Vésubie, *France* **21 D11**
St. Martins, *Barbados* **121 g**
St-Martory, *France* **20 E4**
St. Mary Pk., *Australia* **95 E2**
St. Marys, *Australia* **95 G4**
St. Marys, *Canada* **116 C3**
St. Mary's, *Corn., U.K.* **15 H1**
St. Mary's, *Orkney, U.K.* **13 C6**
St. Marys, *Ga., U.S.A.* **115 K5**
St. Marys, *Pa., U.S.A.* **116 E6**
St. Mary's, C., *Canada* **105 C9**
St. Mary's B., *Canada* **105 C9**
St. Marys Bay, *Canada* **105 D6**
St-Mathieu, Pte., *France* **18 D2**
St. Matthew I., *U.S.A.* **100 B2**
St. Matthews, I. = Zadetkyi Kyun, *Burma* **65 G1**
St-Maurice →, *Canada* **104 C5**
St. Mawes, *U.K.* **15 G2**
St-Maximin-la-Ste-Baume, *France* **21 E9**
St-Médard-en-Jalles, *France* **20 D3**
St-Méen-le-Grand, *France* **18 D4**
St-Mihiel, *France* **19 D12**
St. Moritz, *Switz.* **25 J5**
St-Nazaire, *France* **18 E4**
St. Neots, *U.K.* **15 E7**
St-Nicolas-de-Port, *France* **19 D13**
St-Niklaas, *Belgium* **17 C4**
St-Omer, *France* **19 B9**
St-Palais-sur-Mer, *France* **20 C2**
St-Pamphile, *Canada* **105 C6**
St-Pardoux-la-Rivière, *France* **20 C4**
St.-Pascal, *Canada* **105 C6**
St. Paul, *Canada* **102 C6**
St-Paul, *France* **21 D10**
St. Paul, *Minn., U.S.A.* **112 C8**
St. Paul, *Nebr., U.S.A.* **112 E5**
St-Paul →, *Canada* **105 B8**
St. Paul →, *Liberia* **82 D2**
St. Paul, I., *Ind. Oc.* **3 F13**
St-Paul-de-Fenouillet, *France* **20 F6**
St. Paul I., *Canada* **105 C7**
St-Paul-lès-Dax, *France* **20 E2**
St-Péray, *France* **21 D8**
St. Peter, *U.S.A.* **112 C8**
St-Peter-Ording, *Germany* **24 A4**
St. Peter Port, *U.K.* **15 H5**
St. Peters, *N.S., Canada* **105 C7**
St. Peters, *P.E.I., Canada* **105 C7**
St. Petersburg = Sankt-Peterburg, *Russia* **32 C6**
St. Petersburg, *U.S.A.* **115 M4**
St-Philbert-de-Grand-Lieu, *France* **18 E5**
St-Pie, *Canada* **117 A12**
St-Pierre, *Martinique* **120 c**
St-Pierre, *St- P. & M.* **105 C8**
St-Pierre, L., *Canada* **104 C5**
St-Pierre-d'Oléron, *France* **20 C2**
St-Pierre-en-Port, *France* **18 C7**
St-Pierre et Miquelon □, *N. Amer.* **105 C8**
St-Pierre-le-Moûtier, *France* **19 F10**
St-Pierre-sur-Dives, *France* **18 C6**
St-Pol-de-Léon, *France* **18 D3**
St-Pol-sur-Mer, *France* **19 A9**
St-Pol-sur-Ternoise, *France* **19 B9**
St-Pons, *France* **20 E6**
St-Pourçain-sur-Sioule, *France* **19 F10**
St-Priest, *France* **21 C8**
St-Quay-Portrieux, *France* **18 D4**
St-Quentin, *Canada* **105 C6**
St-Quentin, *France* **19 C10**
St-Rambert-d'Albon, *France* **21 C8**
St-Raphaël, *France* **21 E10**
St. Regis, *U.S.A.* **108 C6**
St-Renan, *France* **18 D2**
St-Saëns, *France* **18 C8**
St-Savin, *France* **20 B4**
St-Savinien, *France* **20 C3**
St. Sebastien, Tanjon' i, *Madag.* **89 A8**
St-Seine-l'Abbaye, *France* **19 E11**
St-Sernin-sur-Rance, *France* **20 E6**
St-Sever, *France* **20 E3**
St-Siméon, *Canada* **105 C6**
St. Simons I., *U.S.A.* **115 K5**
St. Simons Island, *U.S.A.* **115 K5**
St. Stephen, *Canada* **105 C6**
St-Sulpice, *France* **20 E5**
St-Sulpice-Laurière, *France* **20 B5**
St-Sulpice-les-Feuilles, *France* **20 B5**
St-Syprien = St-Cyprien, *France* **20 F7**
St-Thégonnec, *France* **18 D3**
St. Thomas, *Canada* **116 D3**
St. Thomas I., *U.S. Virgin Is.* **121 e**
St-Tite, *Canada* **104 C5**
St-Tropez, *France* **21 E10**
St. Troud = St. Truiden, *Belgium* **17 D5**
St. Truiden, *Belgium* **17 D5**
St-Vaast-la-Hougue, *France* **18 C5**
St-Valery-en-Caux, *France* **18 C7**
St-Valéry-sur-Somme, *France* **19 B8**
St-Vallier, *France* **19 F11**
St-Vallier-de-Thiey, *France* **21 E10**
St-Varent, *France* **18 F6**
St-Vaury, *France* **20 B5**
St. Vincent, *Italy* **40 C4**
St. Vincent, G., *Australia* **95 F2**
St. Vincent & the Grenadines ■, *W. Indies* **121 D7**
St-Vincent-de-Tyrosse, *France* **20 E2**
St. Vincent Passage, *W. Indies* **121 D7**
St-Vith, *Belgium* **17 D6**
St-Vivien-de-Médoc, *France* **20 C2**
St. Walburg, *Canada* **103 C7**
St-Yrieix-la-Perche, *France* **20 C5**
Ste-Adresse, *France* **18 C7**
Ste-Agathe-des-Monts, *Canada* **104 C5**
Ste-Anne, *Guadeloupe* **120 b**
Ste-Anne, L., *Canada* **105 B6**
Ste-Anne-des-Monts-Tourelle, *Canada* **105 C6**
Ste-Croix, *Switz.* **25 J2**
Ste-Enimie, *France* **20 D7**
Ste-Foy-la-Grande, *France* **20 D4**
Ste. Genevieve, *U.S.A.* **112 G9**
Ste-Hermine, *France* **20 B2**
Ste-Livrade-sur-Lot, *France* **20 D4**
Ste-Marguerite →, *Canada* **105 B6**
Ste-Marie, *Canada* **105 C5**
Ste-Marie, *Martinique* **120 c**
Ste-Marie-aux-Mines, *France* **19 D14**
Ste-Maure-de-Touraine, *France* **18 E7**
Ste-Maxime, *France* **21 E10**
Ste-Menehould, *France* **19 C11**
Ste-Mère-Église, *France* **18 C5**
Ste-Rose, *Guadeloupe* **120 b**
Ste. Rose du Lac, *Canada* **103 C9**
Ste-Savine, *France* **19 D11**
Ste-Sigolène, *France* **21 C8**
Saintes, *France* **20 C3**
Saintes, I. des, *Guadeloupe* **120 b**
Stes-Maries-de-la-Mer, *France* **21 E8**
Saintfield, *U.K.* **12 B6**
Saintonge, *France* **20 C3**
Saipan, *Pac. Oc.* **96 F6**
Sairang, *India* **67 H18**
Sairecábur, Cerro, *Bolivia* **126 A2**
Saitama □, *Japan* **55 F9**
Saiteli = Kadınhanı, *Turkey* **72 C5**
Saiţi, *Moldova* **29 D14**
Saiyid, *Pakistan* **68 C5**
Saja-Besaya ⌂, *Spain* **36 B6**
Sajama, *Bolivia* **124 G5**
Sajan, *Serbia & M.* **28 E5**
Sajó →, *Hungary* **28 C6**
Sajószentpéter, *Hungary* **28 B5**
Sajum, *India* **69 C8**
Sak →, *S. Africa* **88 E3**
Sakaba, *Nigeria* **83 C6**
Sakai, *Japan* **55 G7**
Sakaide, *Japan* **55 G6**
Sakaiminato, *Japan* **55 G6**
Sakākah, *Si. Arabia* **70 D4**
Sakakawea, L., *U.S.A.* **112 B4**
Sakami →, *Canada* **104 B4**
Sakami, L., *Canada* **104 B4**
Sâkâne, 'Erg i-n, *Mali* **83 A4**
Sakania, *Dem. Rep. of the Congo* **87 E2**
Sakaraha, *Madag.* **89 C7**
Sakarya, *Turkey* **72 B4**
Sakarya →, *Turkey* **72 B4**
Sakashima-Guntō, *Japan* **55 M2**
Sakassou, *Ivory C.* **82 D3**
Sakata, *Japan* **54 E9**
Sakchu, *N. Korea* **57 D13**
Sakeny →, *Madag.* **89 C8**
Sakété, *Benin* **83 D5**
Sakha □, *Russia* **53 C13**
Sakhalin, *Russia* **53 D15**
Sakhalinskiy Zaliv, *Russia* **53 D15**
Şaki, *Azerbaijan* **35 K8**
Šakiai, *Lithuania* **9 J20**
Sakon Nakhon, *Thailand* **64 D5**
Sakrand, *Pakistan* **68 F3**
Sakri, *India* **69 F12**
Sakrivier, *S. Africa* **88 E3**
Sakskøbing, *Denmark* **11 K5**
Sakti, *India* **69 H10**
Sakuma, *Japan* **55 G8**
Sakurai, *Japan* **55 G7**
Saky, *Ukraine* **33 K7**
Sal →, *Russia* **35 G5**
Sala, *Eritrea* **81 D4**
Šal'a, *Slovak Rep.* **27 C10**
Sala, *Sweden* **10 E10**
Sala →, *Eritrea* **81 D4**
Sala Consilina, *Italy* **43 B8**
Sala-y-Gómez, *Pac. Oc.* **97 K17**
Salaberry-de-Valleyfield, *Canada* **117 A10**
Salacgrīva, *Latvia* **30 A11**
Salada, L., *Mexico* **109 K6**
Saladas, *Argentina* **126 B4**
Saladillo, *Argentina* **126 D4**
Salado →, *Buenos Aires, Argentina* **126 D4**
Salado →, *La Pampa, Argentina* **128 D3**
Salado →, *Santa Fe, Argentina* **126 C3**
Salado →, *Mexico* **113 M5**
Salaga, *Ghana* **83 D4**
Sālah, *Syria* **74 C5**
Şalāḩ ad Dīn □, *Iraq* **70 C4**
Sălaj □, *Romania* **28 C8**
Sálakhos, *Greece* **49 C9**
Salala, *Liberia* **82 D2**
Salala, *Sudan* **80 C4**
Salālah, *Oman* **75 D5**

Salamanca, *Chile* 126 **C1**
Salamanca, *Spain* 36 **E5**
Salamanca, *U.S.A.* 116 **D6**
Salamanca □, *Spain* 36 **E5**
Salāmatābād, *Iran* 70 **C5**
Salamis, *Cyprus* 49 **D12**
Salamís, *Greece* 46 **D5**
Salar de Atacama, *Chile* 126 **A2**
Salar de Uyuni, *Bolivia* 124 **H5**
Sălard, *Romania* 28 **C7**
Salas, *Spain* 36 **B4**
Salas de los Infantes, *Spain* 36 **C7**
Salatiga, *Indonesia* 63 **G14**
Salaverry, *Peru* 124 **E3**
Salawati, *Indonesia* 63 **E8**
Salaya, *India* 68 **H3**
Salayar, *Indonesia* 63 **F6**
Salazar →, *Spain* 38 **C3**
Salbris, *France* 19 **E9**
Salcia, *Romania* 29 **G9**
Sălciua, *Romania* 29 **D8**
Salcombe, *U.K.* 15 **G4**
Saldaña, *Spain* 36 **C6**
Saldanha, *S. Africa* 88 **E2**
Saldanha B., *S. Africa* 88 **E2**
Saldus, *Latvia* 9 **H20**
Saldus □, *Latvia* 30 **B9**
Sale, *Australia* 95 **F4**
Sale, *Italy* 40 **D5**
Salé, *Morocco* 78 **B4**
Sale, *U.K.* 14 **D5**
Salekhard, *Russia* 52 **C7**
Salem, *India* 66 **P11**
Salem, *Ill., U.S.A.* 114 **F1**
Salem, *Ind., U.S.A.* 114 **F2**
Salem, *Mass., U.S.A.* 117 **D14**
Salem, *Mo., U.S.A.* 113 **G9**
Salem, *N.H., U.S.A.* 117 **D13**
Salem, *N.J., U.S.A.* 114 **F8**
Salem, *N.Y., U.S.A.* 117 **C11**
Salem, *Ohio, U.S.A.* 116 **F4**
Salem, *Oreg., U.S.A.* 108 **D2**
Salem, *S. Dak., U.S.A.* 112 **D6**
Salem, *Va., U.S.A.* 114 **G5**
Salemi, *Italy* 42 **E5**
Sälen, *Sweden* 10 **C7**
Salernes, *France* 21 **E10**
Salerno, *Italy* 43 **B7**
Salerno, G. di, *Italy* 43 **B7**
Salford, *U.K.* 14 **D5**
Salgir →, *Ukraine* 33 **K8**
Salgótarján, *Hungary* 28 **B4**
Salgueiro, *Brazil* 125 **E11**
Salibabu, *Indonesia* 63 **D7**
Salibea, *Trin. & Tob.* 125 **K15**
Salida, *U.S.A.* 106 **C5**
Salies-de-Béarn, *France* 20 **E3**
Salihli, *Turkey* 72 **C3**
Salihorsk, *Belarus* 33 **F4**
Salima, *Malawi* 85 **G6**
Salina, *Italy* 43 **D7**
Salina, *Kans., U.S.A.* 112 **F6**
Salina, *Utah, U.S.A.* 109 **G8**
Salina Cruz, *Mexico* 119 **D5**
Salina di Margherita di Savoia ⌂, *Italy* 43 **A9**
Salinas, *Brazil* 125 **G10**
Salinas, *Chile* 126 **A2**
Salinas, *Ecuador* 124 **D2**
Salinas, *U.S.A.* 110 **J5**
Salinas →, *Guatemala* 119 **D6**
Salinas →, *U.S.A.* 110 **J5**
Salinas, B. de, *Nic.* 120 **D2**
Salinas, Pampa de las, *Argentina* 126 **C2**
Salinas Ambargasta, *Argentina* 126 **B3**
Salinas de Hidalgo, *Mexico* 118 **C4**
Salinas Grandes, *Argentina* 126 **C3**
Salinas Pueblo Missions ⌂, *U.S.A.* 109 **J10**
Saline →, *Ark., U.S.A.* 113 **J8**
Saline →, *Kans., U.S.A.* 112 **F6**
Saline di Trapani e Paceco ⌂, *Italy* 42 **E5**
Salines, C. de ses, *Spain* 48 **B10**
Salinópolis, *Brazil* 125 **D9**
Salins-les-Bains, *France* 19 **F12**
Salir, *Portugal* 37 **H2**
Salisbury = Harare, *Zimbabwe* 87 **F3**
Salisbury, *U.K.* 15 **F6**
Salisbury, *Md., U.S.A.* 114 **F8**
Salisbury, *N.C., U.S.A.* 115 **H5**
Salisbury I., *Canada* 101 **B12**
Salisbury Plain, *U.K.* 15 **F6**
Săliște, *Romania* 29 **E8**
Salka, *Nigeria* 83 **C5**
Şalkhad, *Syria* 74 **C5**
Salla, *Finland* 8 **C23**
Sallanches, *France* 21 **C10**
Sallent, *Spain* 38 **D6**
Salles, *France* 20 **D3**
Salles-Curan, *France* 20 **D6**
Salling, *Denmark* 11 **H2**
Salliq = Coral Harbour, *Canada* 101 **B11**
Sallisaw, *U.S.A.* 113 **H7**
Sallom Junction, *Sudan* 80 **D4**
Salluit, *Canada* 101 **B12**
Salmās, *Iran* 70 **B5**
Salmerón, *Spain* 38 **E2**
Salmo, *Canada* 102 **D5**
Salmon, *U.S.A.* 108 **D7**
Salmon →, *Canada* 102 **C4**
Salmon →, *U.S.A.* 108 **D5**
Salmon Arm, *Canada* 102 **C5**
Salmon Gums, *Australia* 93 **F3**
Salmon River Mts., *U.S.A.* 108 **D6**
Salo, *Finland* 9 **F20**
Salò, *Italy* 40 **C7**
Salobreña, *Spain* 37 **J7**
Salome, *U.S.A.* 111 **M13**
Salon, *India* 69 **F9**
Salon-de-Provence, *France* 21 **E9**
Salonica = Thessaloníki, *Greece* 44 **F6**
Salonta, *Romania* 28 **D6**
Salor →, *Spain* 37 **F3**
Salou, *Spain* 38 **D6**
Salou, C. de, *Spain* 38 **D6**
Saloum →, *Senegal* 82 **C1**
Salpausselkä, *Finland* 9 **F22**
Salsacate, *Argentina* 126 **C2**
Salses, *France* 20 **F6**
Salsk, *Russia* 35 **G5**
Salso →, *Italy* 42 **E6**
Salsomaggiore Terme, *Italy* 40 **D6**
Salt, *Spain* 38 **D7**
Salt →, *Canada* 102 **B6**
Salt →, *U.S.A.* 109 **K7**
Salt Lake City, *U.S.A.* 108 **F8**
Salt Range, *Pakistan* 68 **C5**
Salta, *Argentina* 126 **A2**
Salta □, *Argentina* 126 **A2**
Saltara, *Italy* 41 **E9**
Saltash, *U.K.* 15 **G3**
Saltburn by the Sea, *U.K.* 14 **C7**
Saltcoats, *U.K.* 13 **F4**
Saltee Is., *Ireland* 12 **D5**
Saltfjellet, *Norway* 8 **C16**
Saltfjorden, *Norway* 8 **C16**
Saltholm, *Denmark* 11 **J6**
Saltillo, *Mexico* 118 **B4**
Salto, *Argentina* 126 **C3**
Salto, *Uruguay* 126 **C4**
Salto del Guaíra, *Paraguay* 127 **A5**
Salton City, *U.S.A.* 111 **M11**
Salton Sea, *U.S.A.* 111 **M11**
Saltpond, *Ghana* 83 **D4**
Saltsburg, *U.S.A.* 116 **F5**
Saltsjöbaden, *Sweden* 10 **E12**
Saluda →, *U.S.A.* 115 **J5**
Salûm, *Egypt* 80 **A2**
Salûm, Khâlig el, *Egypt* 80 **A2**
Salur, *India* 67 **K13**
Saluzzo, *Italy* 40 **D4**
Salvador, *Brazil* 125 **F11**
Salvador, *Canada* 103 **C7**
Salvador, El ■, *Cent. Amer.* 120 **D2**
Salvador, L., *U.S.A.* 113 **L9**
Salvaterra de Magos, *Portugal* 37 **F2**
Sálvora, I. de, *Spain* 36 **C2**
Salween →, *Burma* 67 **L20**
Salyan, *Azerbaijan* 52 **F5**
Salza →, *Austria* 26 **D7**
Salzach →, *Austria* 26 **C5**
Salzburg, *Austria* 26 **D6**
Salzburg □, *Austria* 26 **D6**
Salzgitter, *Germany* 24 **C6**
Salzkotten, *Germany* 24 **D4**
Salzwedel, *Germany* 24 **C7**
Sam, *India* 68 **F4**
Sam Neua, *Laos* 58 **G5**
Sam Ngao, *Thailand* 64 **D2**
Sam Rayburn Reservoir, *U.S.A.* 113 **K7**
Sam Son, *Vietnam* 64 **C5**
Sam Teu, *Laos* 64 **C5**
Sama de Langreo = Langreo, *Spain* 36 **B5**
Samagaltay, *Russia* 53 **D10**
Samales Group, *Phil.* 61 **J4**
Samâlût, *Egypt* 80 **B3**
Samana, *India* 68 **D7**
Samana Cay, *Bahamas* 121 **B5**
Samandağı, *Turkey* 72 **D6**
Samandıra, *Turkey* 45 **F13**
Samanga, *Tanzania* 87 **D4**
Samangān □, *Afghan.* 66 **B5**
Samangwa, *Dem. Rep. of the Congo* 86 **C1**
Samani, *Japan* 54 **C11**
Samanli Dağları, *Turkey* 45 **F13**
Samar, *Phil.* 61 **F6**
Samara, *Russia* 34 **D10**
Samara →, *Russia* 34 **D10**
Samara →, *Ukraine* 33 **H8**
Samaria = Shōmrōn, *West Bank* 74 **C4**
Samariá, *Greece* 49 **D5**
Samaria △, *Greece* 46 **F5**
Samarinda, *Indonesia* 62 **E5**
Samarkand = Samarqand, *Uzbekistan* 52 **F7**
Samarqand, *Uzbekistan* 52 **F7**
Sāmarrā', *Iraq* 70 **C4**
Samastipur, *India* 69 **G11**
Şamaxi, *Azerbaijan* 35 **K9**
Samba, *Dem. Rep. of the Congo* 86 **C2**
Samba, *India* 69 **C6**
Sambalpur, *India* 67 **J14**
Sambar, Tanjung, *Indonesia* 62 **E4**
Sambas, *Indonesia* 62 **D3**
Sambava, *Madag.* 89 **A9**
Sambawizi, *Zimbabwe* 87 **F2**
Sambhal, *India* 69 **E8**
Sambhar, *India* 68 **F6**
Sambhar L., *India* 68 **F6**
Sambiase, *Italy* 43 **D9**
Sambir, *Ukraine* 33 **H2**
Sambor, *Cambodia* 64 **F6**
Samborombón, B., *Argentina* 126 **D4**
Sambuca di Sicilia, *Italy* 42 **E6**
Samburu ⌂, *Kenya* 86 **B4**
Samch'ŏk, *S. Korea* 57 **F15**
Samch'onp'o, *S. Korea* 57 **G15**
Same, *Tanzania* 86 **C4**
Samer, *France* 19 **B8**
Samfya, *Zambia* 87 **E2**
Sámi, *Greece* 46 **C2**
Şämkir, *Azerbaijan* 35 **K8**
Şamlı, *Turkey* 47 **B9**
Samnah, *Si. Arabia* 70 **E3**
Samo Alto, *Chile* 126 **C1**
Samoa ■, *Pac. Oc.* 91 **B13**
Samobor, *Croatia* 41 **C12**
Samoëns, *France* 19 **F13**
Samokov, *Bulgaria* 44 **D7**
Šamorín, *Slovak Rep.* 27 **C10**
Samorogouan, *Burkina Faso* 82 **C4**
Sámos, *Greece* 47 **D8**
Samoš, *Serbia & M.* 28 **E5**
Samos, *Spain* 36 **C3**
Sámos □, *Greece* 47 **D8**
Samothráki = Mathráki, *Greece* 49 **A3**
Samothráki, *Greece* 45 **F9**
Samoylovka, *Russia* 34 **E6**
Sampa, *Ghana* 82 **D4**
Sampacho, *Argentina* 126 **C3**
Sampalan, *Indonesia* 63 **K18**
Sampang, *Indonesia* 63 **G15**
Samper de Calanda, *Spain* 38 **D4**
Sampéyre, *Italy* 40 **D4**
Sampit, *Indonesia* 62 **E4**
Sampit, Teluk, *Indonesia* 62 **E4**
Samrong, *Cambodia* 64 **E4**
Samrong, *Thailand* 64 **E3**
Samsø, *Denmark* 11 **J4**
Samsø Bælt, *Denmark* 11 **J4**
Samsun, *Turkey* 72 **B7**
Samtredia, *Georgia* 35 **J6**
Samui, Ko, *Thailand* 65 **b**
Samur →, *Russia* 35 **K9**
Samurskiy Khrebet, *Russia* 35 **K8**
Samusole, *Dem. Rep. of the Congo* 87 **E1**
Samut Prakan, *Thailand* 64 **F3**
Samut Songkhram →, *Thailand* 62 **B1**
Samwari, *Pakistan* 68 **E2**
San, *Mali* 82 **C4**
San →, *Cambodia* 64 **F5**
San →, *Poland* 31 **H8**
San Adrián, *Spain* 38 **C3**
San Adrián, C. de, *Spain* 36 **B2**
San Agustin, C., *Phil.* 61 **H7**
San Agustín de Valle Fértil, *Argentina* 126 **C2**
San Ambrosio, *Pac. Oc.* 97 **K20**
San Andreas, *U.S.A.* 110 **G6**
San Andres, *Phil.* 61 **E6**
San Andrés, I. de, *Caribbean* 120 **D3**
San Andrês del Rabanedo, *Spain* 36 **C5**
San Andres Mts., *U.S.A.* 109 **K10**
San Andrés Tuxtla, *Mexico* 119 **D5**
San Angelo, *U.S.A.* 113 **K4**
San Anselmo, *U.S.A.* 110 **H4**
San Antonio, *Belize* 119 **D7**
San Antonio, *Chile* 126 **C1**
San Antonio, *Phil.* 61 **D4**
San Antonio, *N. Mex., U.S.A.* 109 **K10**
San Antonio, *Tex., U.S.A.* 113 **L5**
San Antonio →, *U.S.A.* 113 **L6**
San Antonio, C., *Argentina* 126 **D4**
San Antonio, C., *Cuba* 120 **B3**
San Antonio, C. de, *Spain* 39 **G5**
San Antonio, Mt., *U.S.A.* 111 **L9**
San Antonio de los Baños, *Cuba* 120 **B3**
San Antonio de los Cobres, *Argentina* 126 **A2**
San Antonio Oeste, *Argentina* 128 **E4**
San Arcángelo, *Italy* 43 **B9**
San Ardo, *U.S.A.* 110 **J6**
San Augustín, *Canary Is.* 48 **G4**
San Augustine, *U.S.A.* 113 **K7**
San Bartolomé, *Canary Is.* 48 **F6**
San Bartolomé de Tirajana, *Canary Is.* 48 **G4**
San Bartolomeo in Galdo, *Italy* 43 **A8**
San Benedetto del Tronto, *Italy* 41 **F10**
San Benedetto Po, *Italy* 40 **C7**
San Benedicto, I., *Mexico* 118 **D2**
San Benito, *U.S.A.* 113 **M6**
San Benito →, *U.S.A.* 110 **J5**
San Benito Mt., *U.S.A.* 110 **J6**
San Bernardino, *U.S.A.* 111 **L9**
San Bernardino Mts., *U.S.A.* 111 **L10**
San Bernardino Str., *Phil.* 61 **E6**
San Bernardo, *Chile* 126 **C1**
San Bernardo, I. de, *Colombia* 124 **B3**
San Blas, *Mexico* 118 **B3**
San Blas, Arch. de, *Panama* 120 **E4**
San Blas, C., *U.S.A.* 115 **L3**
San Bonifacio, *Italy* 41 **C8**
San Borja, *Bolivia* 124 **F5**
San Buenaventura = Ventura, *U.S.A.* 111 **L7**
San Buenaventura, *Mexico* 118 **B4**
San Carlos = Butuku-Luba, *Eq. Guin.* 83 **E6**
San Carlos = Sant Carles, *Spain* 48 **B8**
San Carlos, *Argentina* 126 **C2**
San Carlos, *Chile* 126 **D1**
San Carlos, *Baja Calif. S., Mexico* 118 **C2**
San Carlos, *Coahuila, Mexico* 118 **B4**
San Carlos, *Nic.* 120 **D3**
San Carlos, *Neg. Occ., Phil.* 61 **F5**
San Carlos, *Pangasinan, Phil.* 61 **D4**
San Carlos, *Uruguay* 127 **C5**
San Carlos, *U.S.A.* 109 **K8**
San Carlos, *Venezuela* 124 **B5**
San Carlos de Bariloche, *Argentina* 128 **E2**
San Carlos de Bolívar, *Argentina* 128 **D4**
San Carlos de la Ràpita = Sant Carles de la Ràpita, *Spain* 38 **E5**
San Carlos del Zulia, *Venezuela* 124 **B4**
San Carlos L., *U.S.A.* 109 **K8**
San Cataldo, *Italy* 42 **E6**
San Celoni = Sant Celoni, *Spain* 38 **D7**
San Clemente, *Chile* 126 **D1**
San Clemente, *Spain* 39 **F2**
San Clemente, *U.S.A.* 111 **M9**
San Clemente I., *U.S.A.* 111 **N8**
San Cristóbal = Es Migjorn Gran, *Spain* 48 **B11**
San Cristóbal, *Argentina* 126 **C3**
San Cristóbal, *Dom. Rep.* 121 **C5**
San Cristóbal, *Venezuela* 124 **B4**
San Cristóbal de la Casas, *Mexico* 119 **D6**
San Damiano d'Asti, *Italy* 40 **D5**
San Daniele del Friuli, *Italy* 41 **B10**
San Diego, *Calif., U.S.A.* 111 **N9**
San Diego, *Tex., U.S.A.* 113 **M5**
San Diego, C., *Argentina* 128 **G3**
San Diego de la Unión, *Mexico* 118 **C4**
San Diego International ✕ (SAN), *U.S.A.* 111 **N9**
San Dimitri, Ras, *Malta* 49 **C1**
San Dimitri Point = San Dimitri, Ras, *Malta* 49 **C1**
San Donà di Piave, *Italy* 41 **C9**
San Estanislao, *Paraguay* 126 **A4**
San Esteban de Gormaz, *Spain* 38 **D1**
San Felice Circeo, *Italy* 42 **A6**
San Felice sul Panaro, *Italy* 41 **D8**
San Felipe, *Chile* 126 **C1**
San Felipe, *Mexico* 118 **A2**
San Felipe, *Venezuela* 124 **A5**
San Felipe →, *U.S.A.* 111 **M11**
San Félix, *Chile* 126 **B1**
San Félix, *Pac. Oc.* 97 **K20**
San Fernando = Sant Ferran, *Spain* 48 **C7**
San Fernando, *Chile* 126 **C1**
San Fernando, *Baja Calif., Mexico* 118 **B1**
San Fernando, *Tamaulipas, Mexico* 119 **C5**
San Fernando, *La Union, Phil.* 61 **C4**
San Fernando, *Pampanga, Phil.* 61 **D4**
San Fernando, *Spain* 37 **J4**
San Fernando, *Trin. & Tob.* 121 **D7**
San Fernando, *U.S.A.* 111 **L8**
San Fernando de Apure, *Venezuela* 124 **B5**
San Fernando de Atabapo, *Venezuela* 124 **C5**
San Fernando di Púglia, *Italy* 43 **A9**
San Francisco, *Argentina* 126 **C3**
San Francisco, *U.S.A.* 110 **H4**
San Francisco →, *U.S.A.* 109 **K9**
San Francisco, Paso de, *S. Amer.* 126 **B2**
San Francisco de Macorís, *Dom. Rep.* 121 **C5**
San Francisco del Monte de Oro, *Argentina* 126 **C2**
San Francisco del Oro, *Mexico* 118 **B3**
San Francisco International ✕ (SFO), *U.S.A.* 110 **H4**
San Francisco Javier = Sant Francesc de Formentera, *Spain* 48 **C7**
San Francisco Solano, Pta., *Colombia* 122 **C3**
San Fratello, *Italy* 43 **D7**
San Gabriel, *Chile* 126 **C1**
San Gabriel Mts., *U.S.A.* 111 **L9**
San Gavino Monreale, *Italy* 42 **C1**
San German, *Puerto Rico* 121 **d**
San Gimignano, *Italy* 40 **E8**
San Giórgio di Nogaro, *Italy* 41 **C10**
San Giórgio Iónico, *Italy* 43 **B10**
San Giovanni Bianco, *Italy* 40 **C6**
San Giovanni in Fiore, *Italy* 43 **C9**
San Giovanni in Persiceto, *Italy* 41 **D8**
San Giovanni Rotondo, *Italy* 41 **G12**
San Giovanni Valdarno, *Italy* 41 **E8**
San Giuliano Terme, *Italy* 40 **E7**
San Gorgonio Mt., *U.S.A.* 111 **L10**
San Gottardo, P. del, *Switz.* 25 **J4**
San Gregorio, *Uruguay* 127 **C4**
San Gregorio, *U.S.A.* 110 **H4**
San Guiseppe Jato, *Italy* 42 **E6**
San Ignacio, *Belize* 119 **D7**
San Ignacio, *Bolivia* 124 **G6**
San Ignacio, *Mexico* 118 **B2**
San Ignacio, *Paraguay* 120 **C2**
San Ignacio ⌂, *Mexico* 118 **B2**
San Ignacio, L., *Mexico* 118 **B2**
San Ildefonso, C., *Phil.* 61 **C5**
San Isidro, *Argentina* 126 **C4**
San Isidro, *Phil.* 61 **H7**
San Jacinto, *U.S.A.* 111 **M10**
San Jaime = Sant Jaume, *Spain* 48 **B11**
San Javier, *Misiones, Argentina* 127 **B4**
San Javier, *Santa Fe, Argentina* 126 **C4**
San Javier, *Bolivia* 124 **G6**
San Javier, *Chile* 126 **D1**
San Javier, *Spain* 39 **H4**
San Jeronimo Taviche, *Mexico* 119 **D5**
San Joaquin, *U.S.A.* 110 **J6**
San Joaquin →, *U.S.A.* 110 **G5**
San Joaquin Valley, *U.S.A.* 110 **J6**
San Jon, *U.S.A.* 113 **H3**
San Jordi = Sant Jordi, *Spain* 48 **B9**
San Jorge, *Argentina* 126 **C3**
San Jorge, B. de, *Mexico* 118 **A2**
San Jorge, G., *Argentina* 128 **F3**
San José = San Josep, *Spain* 48 **C7**
San José, *Costa Rica* 120 **E3**
San José, *Guatemala* 120 **D1**
San José, *Mexico* 118 **C2**
San Jose, *Mind. Occ., Phil.* 61 **E4**
San Jose, *Nueva Ecija, Phil.* 61 **D4**
San Jose, *U.S.A.* 110 **H5**
San Jose →, *U.S.A.* 109 **J10**
San Jose de Buenavista, *Phil.* 63 **B6**
San José de Chiquitos, *Bolivia* 124 **G6**
San José de Feliciano, *Argentina* 126 **C4**
San José de Jáchal, *Argentina* 126 **C2**
San José de Mayo, *Uruguay* 126 **C4**
San José del Cabo, *Mexico* 118 **C3**
San José del Guaviare, *Colombia* 124 **C4**
San Josep, *Spain* 48 **C7**
San Juan, *Argentina* 126 **C2**
San Juan, *Mexico* 118 **C4**
San Juan, *Phil.* 61 **F6**
San Juan, *Puerto Rico* 121 **d**
San Juan, *Trin. & Tob.* 125 **K15**
San Juan □, *Argentina* 126 **C2**
San Juan →, *Argentina* 126 **C2**
San Juan →, *Nic.* 120 **D3**
San Juan →, *U.S.A.* 109 **H8**
San Juan Bautista = Sant Joan Baptista, *Spain* 48 **B8**
San Juan Bautista, *Paraguay* 126 **B4**
San Juan Bautista, *U.S.A.* 110 **J5**
San Juan Bautista Valle Nacional, *Mexico* 119 **D5**
San Juan Capistrano, *U.S.A.* 111 **M9**
San Juan Cr. →, *U.S.A.* 110 **J5**
San Juan de Alicante, *Spain* 39 **G4**
San Juan de Guadalupe, *Mexico* 118 **C4**
San Juan de la Costa, *Mexico* 118 **C2**
San Juan de los Morros, *Venezuela* 124 **B5**
San Juan del Norte, *Nic.* 120 **D3**
San Juan del Norte, B. de, *Nic.* 120 **D3**
San Juan del Río, *Mexico* 119 **C5**
San Juan del Sur, *Nic.* 120 **D2**
San Juan I., *U.S.A.* 110 **B3**
San Juan Island △, *U.S.A.* 110 **B4**
San Juan Mts., *U.S.A.* 109 **H10**
San Just, Sierra de, *Spain* 38 **E4**
San Justo, *Argentina* 126 **C3**
San Kamphaeng, *Thailand* 64 **C2**
San Lázaro, C., *Mexico* 118 **C2**
San Lázaro, Sa., *Mexico* 118 **C3**
San Leandro, *U.S.A.* 110 **H4**
San Leonardo de Yagüe, *Spain* 38 **D1**
San Lorenzo = Sant Llorenç des Cardassar, *Spain* 48 **B10**
San Lorenzo, *Argentina* 126 **C3**
San Lorenzo, *Ecuador* 124 **C3**
San Lorenzo, *Paraguay* 126 **B4**
San Lorenzo →, *Mexico* 118 **C3**
San Lorenzo, I., *Mexico* 118 **B2**
San Lorenzo, Mte., *Argentina* 128 **F2**
San Lorenzo de la Parrilla, *Spain* 38 **F2**
San Lorenzo de Morunys = Sant Llorenç de Morunys, *Spain* 38 **C6**
San Lucas, *Bolivia* 124 **H5**
San Lucas, *Baja Calif. S., Mexico* 118 **C3**
San Lucas, *Baja Calif. S., Mexico* 118 **B2**
San Lucas, *U.S.A.* 110 **J5**
San Lucas, C., *Mexico* 118 **C3**
San Lúcido, *Italy* 43 **C9**
San Luis, *Argentina* 126 **C2**
San Luis, *Cuba* 120 **B3**
San Luis, *Guatemala* 120 **C2**
San Luis, *Ariz., U.S.A.* 109 **K6**
San Luis, *Colo., U.S.A.* 109 **H11**
San Luis □, *Argentina* 126 **C2**
San Luis, I., *Mexico* 118 **B2**
San Luis, Sierra de, *Argentina* 126 **C2**
San Luis de la Paz, *Mexico* 118 **C4**
San Luis Obispo, *U.S.A.* 111 **K6**
San Luis Potosí, *Mexico* 118 **C4**
San Luis Potosí □, *Mexico* 118 **C4**
San Luis Reservoir, *U.S.A.* 110 **H5**
San Luis Río Colorado, *Mexico* 118 **A2**
San Manuel, *U.S.A.* 109 **K8**
San Marco, C., *Italy* 42 **C1**
San Marco Argentano, *Italy* 43 **C9**
San Marco in Lámis, *Italy* 41 **G12**
San Marcos, *Guatemala* 120 **D1**
San Marcos, *Mexico* 118 **B2**
San Marcos, *Calif., U.S.A.* 111 **M9**
San Marcos, *Tex., U.S.A.* 113 **L6**
San Marino, *San Marino* 41 **E9**
San Marino ■, *Europe* 41 **E9**
San Martín, *Antarctica* 5 **C17**
San Martín, *Argentina* 126 **C2**
San Martín →, *Bolivia* 124 **F6**
San Martín, L., *Argentina* 128 **F2**
San Martín de la Vega, *Spain* 36 **E7**
San Martín de los Andes, *Argentina* 128 **E2**
San Martín de Valdeiglesias, *Spain* 36 **E6**
San Mateo = Sant Mateu, *Baleares, Spain* 48 **B7**
San Mateo = Sant Mateu, *Valencia, Spain* 38 **E5**
San Mateo, *Phil.* 61 **C4**
San Mateo, *U.S.A.* 110 **H4**
San Matías, *Bolivia* 124 **G7**
San Matías, G., *Argentina* 128 **E4**
San Miguel = Sant Miguel, *Spain* 48 **B7**
San Miguel, *El Salv.* 120 **D2**
San Miguel, *Panama* 120 **E4**
San Miguel, *U.S.A.* 110 **K6**
San Miguel →, *Bolivia* 124 **F6**
San Miguel de Tucumán, *Argentina* 126 **B2**
San Miguel del Monte, *Argentina* 126 **D4**
San Miguel I., *U.S.A.* 111 **L6**
San Miniato, *Italy* 40 **E7**
San Nicolás, *Canary Is.* 48 **G4**
San Nicolas, *Phil.* 61 **B4**
San Nicolás de los Arroyas, *Argentina* 126 **C3**
San Nicolas I., *U.S.A.* 111 **M7**
San Onofre, *U.S.A.* 111 **M9**
San Pablo, *Bolivia* 126 **A2**
San Pablo, *Phil.* 61 **D4**
San Pablo, *U.S.A.* 110 **H4**
San Páolo di Civitate, *Italy* 41 **G12**
San Pedro, *Buenos Aires, Argentina* 126 **C4**
San Pedro, *Misiones, Argentina* 127 **B5**
San Pedro, *Chile* 126 **C1**
San Pédro, *Ivory C.* 82 **E3**
San Pedro, *Mexico* 118 **C2**
San Pedro □, *Paraguay* 126 **A4**
San Pedro →, *Chihuahua, Mexico* 118 **B3**
San Pedro →, *Nayarit, Mexico* 118 **C3**
San Pedro →, *U.S.A.* 109 **K8**
San Pedro, Pta., *Chile* 126 **B1**
San Pedro, Sierra de, *Spain* 37 **F4**
San Pedro Channel, *U.S.A.* 111 **M8**
San Pedro de Atacama, *Chile* 126 **A2**
San Pedro de Jujuy, *Argentina* 126 **A3**
San Pedro de las Colonias, *Mexico* 118 **B4**
San Pedro de Macorís, *Dom. Rep.* 121 **C6**
San Pedro del Norte, *Nic.* 120 **D3**
San Pedro del Paraná, *Paraguay* 126 **B4**
San Pedro del Pinatar, *Spain* 39 **H4**
San Pedro Mártir △, *Mexico* 118 **A1**

San Pedro Mártir, Sierra, Mexico 118 A1
San Pedro Mixtepec, Mexico 119 D5
San Pedro Ocampo = Melchor Ocampo, Mexico 118 C4
San Pedro Sula, Honduras 120 C2
San Pietro, Italy 42 C1
San Pietro Vernótico, Italy 43 B11
San Quintín, Mexico 118 A1
San Rafael, Argentina 126 C2
San Rafael, Calif., U.S.A. 110 H4
San Rafael, N. Mex., U.S.A. 109 J10
San Rafael Mt., U.S.A. 111 L7
San Rafael Mts., U.S.A. 111 L7
San Ramón de la Nueva Orán, Argentina 126 A3
San Remo, Italy 40 E4
San Roque, Argentina 126 B4
San Roque, Spain 37 J5
San Rosendo, Chile 126 D1
San Saba, U.S.A. 113 K5
San Salvador, El Salv. 120 D2
San Salvador, Spain 48 B10
San Salvador de Jujuy, Argentina 126 A3
San Salvador I., Bahamas 121 B5
San Salvo, Italy 41 F11
San Sebastián = Donostia-San Sebastián, Spain 38 B3
San Sebastián, Argentina 128 G3
San Sebastian, Puerto Rico 121 d
San Sebastián de la Gomera, Canary Is. 48 F2
San Serra = Son Serra, Spain 48 B10
San Serverino Marche, Italy 41 E10
San Severo, Italy 41 G12
San Simeon, U.S.A. 110 K5
San Simon, U.S.A. 109 K9
San Stéfano di Cadore, Italy 41 B9
San Stino di Livenza, Italy 41 C9
San Telmo = Sant Telm, Spain 48 B9
San Telmo, Mexico 118 A1
San Tiburcio, Mexico 118 C4
San Valentin, Mte., Chile 128 F2
San Vicente de Alcántara, Spain 37 F3
San Vicente de la Barquera, Spain 36 B6
San Vincente del Raspeig, Spain 39 G4
San Vincenzo, Italy 40 E7
San Vito, Costa Rica 120 E3
San Vito, Italy 42 C2
San Vito, C., Italy 42 D5
San Vito al Tagliamento, Italy 41 C9
San Vito Chietino, Italy 41 F11
San Vito dei Normanni, Italy 43 B10
Sana', Yemen 75 D3
Sana →, Bos.-H. 41 C13
Sanaba, Burkina Faso 82 C4
Şanāfīr, Si. Arabia 80 B3
Sanaga →, Cameroon 83 E6
Sanaloa, Presa, Mexico 118 C3
Sanana, Indonesia 63 E7
Sanand, India 68 H5
Sanandaj, Iran 70 C5
Sanandita, Bolivia 126 A3
Sanary-sur-Mer, France 21 E9
Sanawad, India 68 H7
Sancellas = Sencelles, Spain 48 B9
Sancergues, France 19 E9
Sancerre, France 19 E9
Sancerrois, Collines du, France 19 E9
Sancha He →, China 58 D6
Sanchahe, China 57 B14
Sánchez, Dom. Rep. 121 C6
Sanchor, India 68 G4
Sancoins, France 19 F9
Sancti Spíritus, Cuba 120 B4
Sancy, Puy de, France 20 C6
Sand →, S. Africa 89 C5
Sand Hills, U.S.A. 112 D4
Sand Lakes ⌓, Canada 103 B9
Sand Springs, U.S.A. 113 G6
Sanda, Japan 55 G7
Sandakan, Malaysia 62 C5
Sandan = Sambor, Cambodia 64 F6
Sandanski, Bulgaria 44 E7
Sandaré, Mali 82 C2
Sandared, Sweden 11 G6
Sandarne, Sweden 10 C11
Sanday, U.K. 13 B6
Sandefjord, Norway 9 G14
Sanders, U.S.A. 109 J9
Sanderson, U.S.A. 113 K3
Sandersville, U.S.A. 115 J4
Sandfire Roadhouse, Australia 92 C3
Sandfly L., Canada 103 B7
Sandfontein, Namibia 88 C2
Sandhammaren, C., Sweden 11 J8
Sandía, Peru 124 F5
Sandıklı, Turkey 47 C12
Sandila, India 69 F9
Sandnes, Norway 9 G11
Sandnessjøen, Norway 8 C15
Sandoa, Dem. Rep. of the Congo 84 F4
Sandomierz, Poland 31 H8
Sândominic, Romania 29 D10
Sandover →, Australia 94 C2
Sandoway, Burma 67 K19
Sandoy, Færoe Is. 8 F9
Sandpoint, U.S.A. 108 B5
Sandray, U.K. 13 E1
Sandringham, U.K. 14 E8
Sandstone, Australia 93 E2
Sandu, China 58 E6
Sandusky, Mich., U.S.A. 116 C2
Sandusky, Ohio, U.S.A. 116 E2
Sandvig, Sweden 11 J8
Sandviken, Sweden 10 D10
Sandwich, C., Australia 94 B4
Sandwich B., Canada 105 B8
Sandwich B., Namibia 88 C1
Sandy, Oreg., U.S.A. 110 E4
Sandy, Pa., U.S.A. 116 E6
Sandy, Utah, U.S.A. 108 F8
Sandy Bay, Canada 103 B8
Sandy Bight, Australia 93 F3
Sandy C., Queens., Australia 94 C5
Sandy C., Tas., Australia 95 G3
Sandy Cay, Bahamas 121 B4
Sandy Cr. →, U.S.A. 108 F9
Sandy L., Canada 104 B1
Sandy Lake, Canada 104 B1
Sandy Valley, U.S.A. 111 K11
Sanford, Fla., U.S.A. 115 L5
Sanford, Maine, U.S.A. 115 D10
Sanford, N.C., U.S.A. 115 H6
Sanford →, Australia 93 E2
Sanford, Mt., U.S.A. 100 B5
Sang-i-Masha, Afghan. 68 C2
Sanga, Mozam. 87 E4
Sanga →, Congo 84 E3
Sangamner, India 66 K9
Sanganeb Atoll △, Sudan 80 D4
Sangar, Afghan. 68 C1
Sangar, Russia 53 C13
Sangar Sarai, Afghan. 68 B4
Sangaredi, Guinea 82 C2
Sangarh →, Pakistan 68 D4
Sangasso, Mali 82 C3
Sangatte, France 19 B8
Sangay, Ecuador 124 D3
Sange, Dem. Rep. of the Congo 86 D2
Sangeang, Indonesia 63 F5
Sângeorz-Băi, Romania 29 C9
Sanger, U.S.A. 110 J7
Sângera, Moldova 29 D13
Sangerhausen, Germany 24 D7
Sanggan He →, China 56 E9
Sanggau, Indonesia 62 D4
Sanghar, Pakistan 68 F3
Sangihe, Kepulauan, Indonesia 63 D7
Sangihe, Pulau, Indonesia 63 D7
Sangju, S. Korea 57 F15
Sangkapura, Indonesia 62 F4
Sangkhla, Thailand 64 E2
Sangkulirang, Indonesia 62 D5
Sangla, Pakistan 68 D5
Sangli, India 66 L9
Sangmélima, Cameroon 83 E7
Sangod, India 68 G7
Sangre de Cristo Mts., U.S.A. 113 G2
Sangre Grande, Trin. & Tob. 125 K15
Sangro →, Italy 41 F11
Sangrur, India 68 D6
Sangudo, Canada 102 C6
Sangue →, Brazil 124 F7
Sangüesa, Spain 38 C3
Sanguinaires, Îs., France 21 G12
Sangzhi, China 59 C8
Sanhala, Ivory C. 82 C3
Sanibel, U.S.A. 115 M4
Sanikiluaq, Canada 101 C12
Sanin-Kaigan △, Japan 55 G7
Sanirajak, Canada 101 B11
Sanjawi, Pakistan 68 D3
Sanje, Uganda 86 C3
Sanjiang, China 58 E7
Sanjo, Japan 54 F9
Sankh →, India 69 H11
Sankt Andrä, Austria 26 E7
Sankt Augustin, Germany 24 E3
Sankt Blasien, Germany 25 H4
Sankt Gallen, Switz. 25 H5
Sankt Gallen □, Switz. 25 H5
Sankt Goar, Germany 25 E3
Sankt Ingbert, Germany 25 F3
Sankt Johann im Pongau, Austria 26 D6
Sankt Johann in Tirol, Austria 26 D5
Sankt-Peterburg, Russia 32 C6
Sankt Pölten, Austria 26 C8
Sankt Ulrich = Ortisei, Italy 41 B8
Sankt Valentin, Austria 26 C7
Sankt Veit an der Glan, Austria 26 E7
Sankt Wendel, Germany 25 F3
Sankt Wolfgang, Austria 26 D6
Sankuru →, Dem. Rep. of the Congo 84 E4
Sanliurfa, Turkey 70 B3
Sanlúcar de Barrameda, Spain 37 J4
Sanluri, Italy 42 C1
Sânmartin, Romania 29 D10
Sanmen, China 59 C13
Sanmenxia, China 56 G6
Sanming, China 59 D11
Sannaspos, S. Africa 88 D4
Sannicandro Gargánico, Italy 41 G12
Sânnicolau Mare, Romania 28 D5
Sannieshof, S. Africa 88 D4
Sannīn, J., Lebanon 74 B4
Sanniquellie, Liberia 82 D3
Sannûr, W. →, Egypt 80 B3
Sanoe, Antarctica 5 D2
Sanok, Poland 31 J9
Sanquhar, U.K. 13 F5
Sans Souci, Trin. & Tob. 125 K16
Sansanding, Mali 82 C3
Sansepolcro, Italy 41 E9
Sansha, China 59 D13
Sanshui, China 59 F9
Sanski Most, Bos.-H. 41 D13
Sansui, China 58 D7
Sant Antoni Abat, Spain 48 C7
Sant Boi de Llobregat, Spain 38 D7
Sant Carles, Spain 48 B8
Sant Carles de la Ràpita, Spain 38 E5
Sant Celoni, Spain 38 D7
Sant Feliu de Guíxols, Spain 38 D8
Sant Feliu de Llobregat, Spain 38 D7
Sant Ferran, Spain 48 C7
Sant Francesc de Formentera, Spain 48 C7
Sant Jaume, Spain 48 B11
Sant Joan Baptista, Spain 48 B8
Sant Jordi, Ibiza, Spain 48 C7
Sant Jordi, Mallorca, Spain 48 B9
Sant Jordi, G. de, Spain 38 E6
Sant Llorenç de Morunys, Spain 38 C6
Sant Llorenç del Munt y l'Obac ⌓, Spain 38 D3
Sant Llorenç des Cardassar, Spain 48 B10
Sant Mateu, Baleares, Spain 48 B7
Sant Mateu, Valencia, Spain 38 E5
Sant Miguel, Spain 48 B7
Sant Telm, Spain 48 B9
Sant' Ágata Militello, Italy 43 D7
Santa Agnés, Spain 48 B7
Santa Ana, Bolivia 124 F5
Santa Ana, El Salv. 120 D2
Santa Ana, Mexico 118 A2
Santa Ana, U.S.A. 111 M9
Sant' Ángelo Lodigiano, Italy 40 C6
Sant' Antíoco, Italy 42 C1
Santa Bárbara, Chile 126 D1
Santa Barbara, Honduras 120 D2
Santa Bárbara, Mexico 118 B3
Santa Bárbara, Spain 38 E5
Santa Barbara, U.S.A. 111 L7
Santa Bárbara, Mt., Spain 39 H2
Santa Barbara Channel, U.S.A. 111 L7
Santa Barbara I., U.S.A. 111 M7
Santa Catalina, Gulf of, U.S.A. 111 N9
Santa Catalina, I., Mexico 118 B2
Santa Catalina I., U.S.A. 111 M8
Santa Catarina □, Brazil 127 B6
Santa Catarina, I. de, Brazil 127 B6
Santa Caterina di Pittinuri, Italy 42 B1
Santa Caterina Villarmosa, Italy 43 E7
Santa Cecília, Brazil 127 B5
Santa Clara, Cuba 120 B4
Santa Clara, Calif., U.S.A. 110 H5
Santa Clara, Utah, U.S.A. 109 H7
Santa Clara, El Golfo de, Mexico 118 A2
Santa Clara de Olimar, Uruguay 127 C5
Santa Clarita, U.S.A. 111 L8
Santa Clotilde, Peru 124 D4
Santa Coloma de Farners, Spain 38 D7
Santa Coloma de Gramenet, Spain 38 D7
Santa Comba, Spain 36 B2
Santa Croce Camerina, Italy 43 F7
Santa Croce di Magliano, Italy 41 G11
Santa Cruz, Argentina 128 G3
Santa Cruz, Bolivia 124 G6
Santa Cruz, Chile 126 C1
Santa Cruz, Costa Rica 120 D2
Santa Cruz, Madeira 48 D3
Santa Cruz, Phil. 61 D4
Santa Cruz, U.S.A. 110 J4
Santa Cruz →, Argentina 128 G3
Santa Cruz de la Palma, Canary Is. 48 F2
Santa Cruz de la Palma ✕ (SPC), Canary Is. 48 F2
Santa Cruz de Mudela, Spain 37 G7
Santa Cruz de Tenerife, Canary Is. 48 F3
Santa Cruz del Norte, Cuba 120 B3
Santa Cruz del Retamar, Spain 36 E6
Santa Cruz del Sur, Cuba 120 B4
Santa Cruz do Rio Pardo, Brazil 127 A6
Santa Cruz do Sul, Brazil 127 B5
Santa Cruz I., U.S.A. 111 M7
Santa Cruz Is., Solomon Is. 96 J8
Santa Cruz Mts., Jamaica 120 a
Santa Domingo, Cay, Bahamas 120 B4
Sant' Egídio alla Vibrata, Italy 41 F10
Santa Elena, Argentina 126 C4
Santa Elena, C., Costa Rica 120 D2
Sant' Eufémia, G. di, Italy 43 D9
Santa Eulàlia des Riu, Spain 48 C8
Santa Fe, Argentina 126 C3
Santa Fe, Spain 37 H7
Santa Fe, U.S.A. 109 J11
Santa Fé □, Argentina 126 C3
Santa Fé do Sul, Brazil 125 H8
Santa Filomena, Brazil 125 E9
Santa Fiora, Italy 41 F8
Santa Gertrudis, Spain 48 C7
Santa Giustina, Italy 41 B9
Santa Inês, Brazil 125 F11
Santa Inés, Spain 37 G5
Santa Inés, I., Chile 128 G2
Santa Isabel = Rey Malabo, Eq. Guin. 83 E6
Santa Isabel, Argentina 126 D2
Santa Isabel, Pico, Eq. Guin. 83 E6
Santa Isabel do Morro, Brazil 125 F8
Santa Lucía, Corrientes, Argentina 126 B4
Santa Lucía, San Juan, Argentina 126 C2
Santa Lucía, Spain 39 H4
Santa Lucía, Uruguay 126 C4
Santa Lucia Range, U.S.A. 110 K5
Santa Magdalena, I., Mexico 118 C2
Santa Margarita, Argentina 126 D3
Santa Margarita, Spain 48 B10
Santa Margarita, U.S.A. 110 K6
Santa Margarita →, U.S.A. 111 M9
Santa Margarita, I., Mexico 118 C2
Santa Margherita, Italy 42 D1
Santa Margherita Ligure, Italy 40 D6
Santa María, Argentina 126 B2
Santa Maria, Brazil 127 B5
Santa Maria, Phil. 61 C4
Santa Maria, U.S.A. 111 L6
Santa María →, Mexico 118 A3
Santa María, B. de, Mexico 118 B3
Santa Maria, C. de, Portugal 37 J3
Santa Maria Cápua Vétere, Italy 43 A7
Santa Maria da Feira, Portugal 36 E2
Santa Maria da Vitória, Brazil 125 F10
Santa Maria del Camí, Spain 48 B9
Santa Maria di Léuca, C., Italy 43 C11
Santa María la Real de Nieva, Spain 36 D6
Santa Marinella, Italy 41 F8
Santa Marta, Colombia 124 A4
Santa Marta, Sierra Nevada de, Colombia 124 A4
Santa Marta de Tormes, Spain 36 E5
Santa Marta Grande, C., Brazil 127 B6
Santa Marta Ortigueira, Ría de, Spain 36 B3
Santa Maura = Levkás, Greece 46 C2
Santa Monica, U.S.A. 111 M8
Santa Monica Mts. ⌓, U.S.A. 111 L8
Santa Olalla, Huelva, Spain 37 H4
Santa Olalla, Toledo, Spain 36 E6
Santa Paula, U.S.A. 111 L7
Santa Pola, Spain 39 G4
Santa Ponça, Spain 48 B9
Santa Rita, U.S.A. 109 K10
Santa Rosa, La Pampa, Argentina 126 D3
Santa Rosa, San Luis, Argentina 126 C2
Santa Rosa, Brazil 127 B5
Santa Rosa, Calif., U.S.A. 110 G4
Santa Rosa, N. Mex., U.S.A. 113 H2
Santa Rosa and San Jacinto Mts. ⌓, U.S.A. 111 M10
Santa Rosa de Copán, Honduras 120 D2
Santa Rosa de Río Primero, Argentina 126 C3
Santa Rosa del Sara, Bolivia 124 G6
Santa Rosa I., Calif., U.S.A. 111 M6
Santa Rosa I., Fla., U.S.A. 115 K2
Santa Rosa Range, U.S.A. 108 F5
Santa Rosalía, Mexico 118 B2
Santa Sylvina, Argentina 126 B3
Santa Tecla = Nueva San Salvador, El Salv. 120 D2
Santa Teresa, Argentina 126 C3
Santa Teresa, Australia 94 C1
Santa Teresa, Mexico 119 B5
Santa Teresa △, Uruguay 127 C5
Santa Teresa di Riva, Italy 43 E8
Santa Teresa Gallura, Italy 42 A2
Santa Uxía, Spain 36 C2
Santa Vitória do Palmar, Brazil 127 C5
Santa Ynez →, U.S.A. 111 L6
Santa Ynez Mts., U.S.A. 111 L6
Santa Ysabel, U.S.A. 111 M10
Santadi, Italy 42 C1
Santaella, Spain 37 H6
Santai, China 58 B5
Santana, Madeira 48 D3
Sântana, Romania 28 D6
Santana, Coxilha de, Brazil 127 C4
Santana do Livramento, Brazil 127 C4
Santander, Spain 36 B7
Santander Jiménez, Mexico 119 C5
Santanilla, Is., Honduras 120 C3
Santanyí, Spain 48 B10
Santaquin, U.S.A. 108 G8
Santarcángelo di Romagna, Italy 41 D9
Santarém, Brazil 125 D8
Santarém, Portugal 37 F2
Santarém □, Portugal 37 F2
Santaren Channel, W. Indies 120 B4
Santee, U.S.A. 111 N10
Santee →, U.S.A. 115 J6
Santéramo in Colle, Italy 43 B9
Santerno →, Italy 41 D8
Santhià, Italy 40 C5
Santi-Quaranta = Sarandë, Albania 44 G3
Santiago, Brazil 127 B5
Santiago, Canary Is. 48 F2
Santiago, Chile 126 C1
Santiago, Panama 120 E3
Santiago, Phil. 61 C4
Santiago □, Chile 126 C1
Santiago →, Mexico 98 G9
Santiago →, Peru 124 D3
Santiago, Punta de, Eq. Guin. 83 E6
Santiago de Compostela, Spain 36 C2
Santiago de Cuba, Cuba 120 C4
Santiago de los Cabelleros, Dom. Rep. 121 C5
Santiago del Estero, Argentina 126 B3
Santiago del Estero □, Argentina 126 B3
Santiago del Teide, Canary Is. 48 F3
Santiago do Cacém, Portugal 37 G2
Santiago Ixcuintla, Mexico 118 C3
Santiago Papasquiaro, Mexico 118 C3
Santiaguillo, L. de, Mexico 118 C4
Santiguila, Mali 82 C3
Santillana, Spain 36 B6
Santisteban del Puerto, Spain 37 G7
Santo Amaro, Brazil 125 F11
Santo Anastácio, Brazil 127 A5
Santo André, Brazil 127 A6
Santo Ângelo, Brazil 127 B5
Santo Antônio do Içá, Brazil 124 D5
Santo Antônio do Leverger, Brazil 125 G7
Santo Domingo, Dom. Rep. 121 C6
Santo Domingo, Baja Calif., Mexico 118 A1
Santo Domingo, Baja Calif. S., Mexico 118 B2
Santo Domingo, Nic. 120 D3
Santo Domingo de la Calzada, Spain 38 C2
Santo Domingo de los Colorados, Ecuador 124 D3
Santo Domingo Pueblo, U.S.A. 109 J10
Santo Stéfano di Camastro, Italy 43 D7
Santo Tirso, Portugal 36 D2
Santo Tomás, Mexico 118 A1
Santo Tomás, Peru 124 F4
Santo Tomé, Argentina 127 B4
Santo Tomé de Guayana = Ciudad Guayana, Venezuela 124 B6
Santomera, Spain 39 G3
Santoña, Spain 36 B7
Santoríni = Thíra, Greece 47 E7
Santos, Brazil 127 A6
Santos, Sierra de los, Spain 37 G5
Santos Dumont, Brazil 127 A7
Sanur, Indonesia 63 K18
Sanwer, India 68 H6
Sanxenxo, Spain 36 C2
Sanyuan, China 56 G5
São Bartolomeu de Messines, Portugal 37 H2
São Bernardo do Campo, Brazil 127 A6
São Borja, Brazil 127 B4
São Brás de Alportel, Portugal 37 H3
São Carlos, Brazil 127 A6
São Cristóvão, Brazil 125 F11
São Domingos, Brazil 125 F9
São Domingos, Guinea-Biss. 82 C1
São Francisco, Brazil 125 G10
São Francisco →, Brazil 125 F11
São Francisco do Sul, Brazil 127 B6
São Gabriel, Brazil 127 C5
São Gonçalo, Brazil 127 A7
Sao Hill, Tanzania 87 D4
São João, Guinea-Biss. 82 C1
São João da Boa Vista, Brazil 127 A6
São João da Madeira, Portugal 36 E2
São João da Pesqueira, Portugal 36 D3
São João del Rei, Brazil 127 A7
São João do Araguaia, Brazil 125 E9
São João do Piauí, Brazil 125 E10
São Joaquim, Brazil 127 B6
São Joaquim △, Brazil 127 B6
São Jorge, Pta. de, Madeira 48 D3
São José, Brazil 127 B5
São José do Norte, Brazil 127 C5
São José do Rio Prêto, Brazil 127 A6
São José dos Campos, Brazil 127 A6
São Leopoldo, Brazil 127 B5
São Lourenço, Brazil 127 A6
São Lourenço →, Brazil 125 G7
São Lourenço, Pta. de, Madeira 48 D3
São Lourenço do Sul, Brazil 127 C5
São Luís, Brazil 125 D10
São Luís Gonzaga, Brazil 127 B5
São Marcos →, Brazil 125 G9
São Marcos, B. de, Brazil 125 D10
São Martinho da Cortiça, Portugal 36 E2
São Mateus, Brazil 125 G11
São Mateus do Sul, Brazil 127 B5
São Miguel do Oeste, Brazil 127 B5
São Paulo, Brazil 127 A6
São Paulo □, Brazil 127 A6
São Paulo, I., Atl. Oc. 2 D8
São Paulo de Olivença, Brazil 124 D5
São Pedro do Sul, Portugal 36 E2
São Roque, Madeira 48 D3
São Roque, C. de, Brazil 125 E11
São Sebastião, I. de, Brazil 127 A6
São Sebastião do Paraíso, Brazil 127 A6
São Teotónio, Portugal 37 H2
São Tomé, São Tomé & Príncipe 76 F4
São Tomé, C. de, Brazil 127 A7
São Tomé & Príncipe ■, Africa 77 F4
São Vicente, Brazil 127 A6
São Vicente, Madeira 48 D2
São Vicente, C. de, Portugal 37 H1
Saona, I., Dom. Rep. 121 C6
Saône →, France 19 G11
Saône-et-Loire □, France 19 F11
Saonek, Indonesia 63 E8
Sápai, Greece 45 E9
Sapam, Ao, Thailand 65 a
Sapanca, Turkey 72 B4
Saparua, Indonesia 63 E7
Sapele, Nigeria 83 D6
Sapelo I., U.S.A. 115 K5
Şaphane, Turkey 47 B11
Sapi ⌓, Zimbabwe 87 F2
Sapiéntza, Greece 46 E3
Sapo △, Liberia 82 D3
Sapone, Burkina Faso 83 C4
Saposoa, Peru 124 E3
Sapouy, Burkina Faso 83 C4
Sapozhok, Russia 34 D5
Sapphire, Australia 94 C4
Sappho, U.S.A. 110 B2
Sapporo, Japan 54 C10
Sapri, Italy 43 B8
Sapulpa, U.S.A. 113 H6
Saqqez, Iran 70 B5
Sar Dasht, Āzarbāyjān-e Gharbī, Iran 73 D11
Sar Dasht, Khuzestān, Iran 71 C6
Sar-e Pol □, Afghan. 66 B4
Sar Gachīneh = Yāsūj, Iran 71 D6
Sar Planina, Macedonia 44 E4
Sara, Burkina Faso 82 C4
Sara, Phil. 61 F5
Šara △, Serbia & M. 44 D5
Sara Buri = Saraburi, Thailand 64 E3
Sarāb, Iran 70 B5
Sarabadi, Iraq 70 C5
Saraburi, Thailand 64 E3
Saradiya, India 68 J4
Saraféré, Mali 82 B4
Saragossa = Zaragoza, Spain 38 D4
Saraguro, Ecuador 124 D3
Sarai Naurang, Pakistan 68 C4
Saraikela, India 69 H11
Saraiu, Romania 29 F13
Sarajevo, Bos.-H. 28 G3
Sarakhs, Turkmenistan 71 B9
Saran, Gunung, Indonesia 62 E4
Saranac L., U.S.A. 117 B10
Saranac Lake, U.S.A. 117 B10
Saranda, Tanzania 86 D3
Sarandë, Albania 44 G3
Sarandí del Yi, Uruguay 127 C4
Sarandí Grande, Uruguay 126 C4
Sarangani B., Phil. 61 J6
Sarangani Is., Phil. 61 J6
Sarangarh, India 67 J13
Saransk, Russia 34 C7
Sarapul, Russia 52 D6
Sarasota, U.S.A. 115 M4
Saratoga, Calif., U.S.A. 110 H4
Saratoga, Wyo., U.S.A. 108 F10
Saratoga △, U.S.A. 117 D11

Saratoga Springs, U.S.A. 117 C11
Saratok, Malaysia 62 D4
Saratov, Russia 34 E7
Sarāvān, Iran 71 E9
Saravane, Laos 64 E6
Sarawak □, Malaysia 62 D4
Saray, Tekirdağ, Turkey 45 E11
Saray, Van, Turkey 73 C11
Saraya, Guinea 82 C2
Saraya, Senegal 82 C2
Saraycık, Turkey 47 B11
Sarayköy, Turkey 47 D10
Saraylar, Turkey 45 F11
Sarayönü, Turkey 72 C5
Sarbāz, Iran 71 E9
Sarbīsheh, Iran 71 C8
Sárbogárd, Hungary 28 D3
Sarca →, Italy 40 C7
Sarcelles, France 19 D9
Sarda →, India 67 F12
Sardarshahr, India 68 E6
Sardegna □, Italy 42 B1
Sardhana, India 68 E7
Sardina, Pta., Canary Is. 48 F4
Sardinia = Sardegna □, Italy 42 B1
Sardis, Turkey 47 C10
Sārdūīyeh = Dar Mazār, Iran 71 D8
Saren, Indonesia 63 J18
S'Arenal, Spain 37 B9
Sarentino, Italy 41 B8
Saréyamou, Mali 82 B4
Sargasso Sea, Atl. Oc. 97 D20
Sargodha, Pakistan 68 C5
Sarh, Chad 79 G9
Sarhala, Ivory C. 82 D3
Sārī, Iran 71 B7
Sari d'Orcino, France 21 F12
Sária, Greece 47 F9
Saria, India 69 J10
Sariab, Pakistan 68 D2
Sarıbeyler, Turkey 47 B9
Sarıgöl, Turkey 72 C3
Sarikamiş, Turkey 73 B10
Sarıkaya, Turkey 72 C6
Sarikei, Malaysia 62 D4
Sarıköy, Turkey 45 F11
Sarila, India 69 G8
Sarina, Australia 94 C4
Sariñena, Spain 38 D4
Sarita, U.S.A. 113 M6
Sariwŏn, N. Korea 57 E13
Sariyar Barajı, Turkey 72 B4
Sariyer, Turkey 45 E13
Sarju →, India 69 F9
Sark, U.K. 15 H5
Sarkad, Hungary 28 D6
Sarkari Tala, India 68 F4
Şarkışla, Turkey 72 C7
Şarköy, Turkey 45 F11
Sarlat-la-Canéda, France 20 D5
Sărmăşag, Romania 28 C7
Sărmaşu, Romania 29 D9
Sarmi, Indonesia 63 E9
Sarmiento, Argentina 128 F3
Sarmizegetusa, Romania 28 E7
Särna, Sweden 10 C7
Sarnano, Italy 41 E10
Sarnen, Switz. 25 J4
Sarnia, Canada 116 D2
Sarno, Italy 43 B7
Sarnthein = Sarentino, Italy 41 B8
Särö, Sweden 11 G5
Sarolangun, Indonesia 62 E2
Saronikós Kólpos, Greece 46 D5
Saronno, Italy 40 C6
Saros Körfezi, Turkey 45 F10
Sárospatak, Hungary 28 B6
Sarpsborg, Norway 9 G14
Sarracín, Spain 36 C7
Sarralbe, France 19 D14
Sarre = Saar →, Europe 17 E6
Sarre, Italy 40 C4
Sarre-Union, France 19 D14
Sarrebourg, France 19 D14
Sarreguemines, France 19 C14
Sarria, Spain 36 C3
Sarrión, Spain 38 E4
Sarro, Mali 82 C3
Sarstedt, Germany 24 C5
Sartène, France 21 G12
Sarthe □, France 18 D7
Sarthe →, France 18 E6
Sartilly, France 18 D5
Saruhanlı, Turkey 47 C9
Săruleşti, Romania 29 F11
Saruna →, Pakistan 68 F2
Sárvár, Hungary 28 C1
Sarvar, India 68 F6
Sarvestān, Iran 71 D7
Särvfjället, Sweden 10 B7
Sárviz →, Hungary 28 D3
Sary-Tash, Kyrgyzstan 52 F8
Sarych, Mys, Ukraine 33 K7
Saryshagan, Kazakhstan 52 E8
Sarzana, Italy 40 D6
Sarzeau, France 18 E4
Sasan Gir, India 68 J4
Sasaram, India 69 G11
Sasebo, Japan 55 H4
Saser, India 69 B7
Saskatchewan □, Canada 103 C7
Saskatchewan →, Canada 103 C8
Saskatoon, Canada 103 C7
Saskylakh, Russia 53 B12
Saslaya △, Nic. 120 D2
Sasolburg, S. Africa 89 D4
Sasovo, Russia 34 C5
Sassandra, Ivory C. 82 E3
Sassandra →, Ivory C. 82 E3
Sássari, Italy 42 B1
Sassnitz, Germany 24 A9
Sasso Marconi, Italy 41 D8
Sassocorvaro, Italy 41 E9
Sassoferrato, Italy 41 E9
Sasstown, Liberia 82 E3
Sassuolo, Italy 40 D7
Sástago, Spain 38 D4
Sasyk, Ozero, Ukraine 33 K5
Sata-Misaki, Japan 55 J5
Satadougou, Mali 82 C2
Satakunta, Finland 9 F20
Satama-Soukoura, Ivory C. 82 D4
Satara, India 66 L8
Satara, S. Africa 89 C5
Satbarwa, India 69 H11
Såtenäs, Sweden 11 F6
Säter, Sweden 10 D9
Satevó, Mexico 118 B3
Satilla →, U.S.A. 115 K5
Satmala Hills, India 66 J9
Satna, India 69 G9
Šator, Bos.-H. 41 D13
Sátoraljaújhely, Hungary 28 B6
Satpura Ra., India 66 J10
Satrup, Germany 24 A5
Satsuna-Shotō, Japan 55 K5
Sattahip, Thailand 64 F3
Satu Mare, Romania 28 C7
Satu Mare □, Romania 28 C8
Satui, Indonesia 62 E5
Satun, Thailand 65 J3
Saturnina →, Brazil 124 F7
Sauce, Argentina 126 C4
Sauceda, Mexico 118 B4
Saucillo, Mexico 118 B3
Sauda, Norway 9 G12
Sauðarkrókur, Iceland 8 D4
Saudi Arabia ■, Asia 70 B3
Saugeen →, Canada 116 B3
Saugerties, U.S.A. 117 D11
Saugues, France 20 D7
Saugus, U.S.A. 111 L8
Saujon, France 20 C3
Sauk Centre, U.S.A. 112 C7
Sauk Rapids, U.S.A. 112 C7
Saulgau, Germany 25 G5
Saulieu, France 19 E11
Sault, France 21 D9
Sault Ste. Marie, Canada 104 C3
Sault Ste. Marie, U.S.A. 101 D11
Saumlaki, Indonesia 63 F8
Saumur, France 18 E6
Saunders, C., N.Z. 91 L3
Saunders I., Antarctica 5 B1
Saunders Point, Australia 93 E4
Sauri, Nigeria 83 C6
Saurimo, Angola 84 F4
Sausalito, U.S.A. 110 H4
Sauveterre-de-Béarn, France 20 E3
Sauzé-Vaussais, France 20 B4
Savá, Honduras 120 C2
Sava, Italy 43 B10
Sava →, Serbia & M. 28 F5
Savage, U.S.A. 112 B2
Savage I. = Niue, Cook Is. 97 J11
Savage River, Australia 95 G4
Savai'i, Samoa 91 A12
Savalou, Benin 83 D5
Savane, Mozam. 87 F4
Savanna, U.S.A. 112 D9
Savanna-la-Mar, Jamaica 120 a
Savannah, Ga., U.S.A. 115 J5
Savannah, Mo., U.S.A. 112 F7
Savannah, Tenn., U.S.A. 115 H1
Savannah →, U.S.A. 115 J5
Savannakhet, Laos 64 D5
Savant L., Canada 104 B1
Savant Lake, Canada 104 B1
Săvârşin, Romania 28 D7
Savaştepe, Turkey 47 B9
Savé, Benin 83 D5
Save →, France 20 E5
Save →, Mozam. 89 C5
Sāveh, Iran 71 C6
Savelugu, Ghana 83 D4
Savenay, France 18 E5
Săveni, Romania 29 C11
Saverdun, France 20 E5
Saverne, France 19 D14
Savigliano, Italy 40 D4
Savigny-sur-Braye, France 18 E7
Sávio →, Italy 41 D9
Šavnik, Serbia & M. 44 D3
Savo, Finland 8 E22
Savoie □, France 21 C10
Savona, Italy 40 D5
Savona, U.S.A. 116 D7
Savonlinna, Finland 32 B5
Savoy = Savoie □, France 21 C10
Şavşat, Turkey 73 B10
Sävsjö, Sweden 11 G8
Savur, Turkey 70 B4
Sawahlunto, Indonesia 62 E2
Sawai, Indonesia 63 E7
Sawai Madhopur, India 68 G7
Sawang Daen Din, Thailand 64 D4
Sawankhalok, Thailand 64 D2
Sawara, Japan 55 G10
Sawatch Range, U.S.A. 109 G10
Sawel Mt., U.K. 12 B4
Sawi, Thailand 65 G2
Sawla, Ghana 82 D4
Sawmills, Zimbabwe 87 F2
Sawtooth ⌓, U.S.A. 108 D6
Sawtooth Range, U.S.A. 108 E6
Sawu, Indonesia 63 F6
Sawu Sea, Indonesia 63 F6
Saxby →, Australia 94 B3
Saxmundham, U.K. 15 E9
Saxony = Sachsen □, Germany 24 E9
Saxony, Lower = Niedersachsen □, Germany 24 C4
Saxton, U.S.A. 116 F6
Say, Mali 82 C4
Say, Niger 83 C5
Saya, Nigeria 83 D5
Sayabec, Canada 105 C6
Sayaboury, Laos 64 C3
Sayán, Peru 124 F3
Sayan, Vostochnyy, Russia 53 D10
Sayan, Zapadnyy, Russia 53 D10
Saydā, Lebanon 74 B4
Sayhandulaan = Oldziyt, Mongolia 56 B5
Sayḩūt, Yemen 75 D5
Saykhin, Kazakhstan 35 F8
Saylac = Zeila, Somali Rep. 75 E3
Saynshand, Mongolia 60 B6
Sayre, Okla., U.S.A. 113 H5
Sayre, Pa., U.S.A. 117 E8
Sayreville, U.S.A. 117 F10
Sayula, Mexico 118 D4
Sayward, Canada 102 C3
Sazanit, Albania 44 F3
Sázava →, Czech Rep. 26 B7
Sazin, Pakistan 69 B5
Sazlika →, Bulgaria 45 E9
Scaër, France 18 D3
Scafell Pike, U.K. 14 C4
Scalea, Italy 43 C8
Scalloway, U.K. 13 A7
Scalpay, U.K. 13 D3
Scandia, Canada 102 C6
Scandiano, Italy 40 D7
Scandicci, Italy 41 E8
Scandinavia, Europe 8 E16
Scansano, Italy 41 F8
Scapa Flow, U.K. 13 C5
Scappoose, U.S.A. 110 E4
Scarámia, Capo, Italy 43 F7
Scarba, U.K. 13 E3
Scarborough, Trin. & Tob. 121 D7
Scarborough, U.K. 14 C7
Scariff I., Ireland 12 E1
Scarp, U.K. 13 C1
Scarpe-Escaut ⌓, France 19 B10
Scebeli, Wabi →, Somali Rep. 75 G3
Šćedro, Croatia 41 E13
Schaal See, Germany 24 B6
Schaalsee ⌓, Germany 24 B6
Schaffhausen, Switz. 25 H4
Schagen, Neths. 17 B4
Schaghticoke, U.S.A. 117 D11
Schärding, Austria 26 C6
Scharhörn, Germany 24 B4
Scheessel, Germany 24 B5
Schefferville, Canada 105 B6
Scheibbs, Austria 26 C8
Schelde →, Belgium 17 C4
Schell Creek Ra., U.S.A. 108 G6
Schellsburg, U.S.A. 116 F6
Schenectady, U.S.A. 117 D11
Schenevus, U.S.A. 117 D10
Scherfede, Germany 24 D5
Schesslitz, Germany 25 F7
Schiedam, Neths. 17 C4
Schiermonnikoog, Neths. 17 A6
Schiltigheim, France 19 D14
Schio, Italy 41 C8
Schiphol, Amsterdam ✕ (AMS), Neths. 17 B4
Schladming, Austria 26 D6
Schlanders = Silandro, Italy 40 B7
Schlei →, Germany 24 A5
Schleiden, Germany 24 E2
Schleiz, Germany 24 E7
Schleswig, Germany 24 A5
Schleswig-Holstein □, Germany 24 A5
Schlüchtern, Germany 25 E5
Schmalkalden, Germany 24 E6
Schmölln, Germany 24 E8
Schneeberg, Austria 26 D8
Schneeberg, Germany 24 E8
Schneverdingen, Germany 24 B5
Schœlcher, Martinique 120 c
Schoharie, U.S.A. 117 D10
Schoharie →, U.S.A. 117 D10
Scholls, U.S.A. 110 E4
Schönberg, Mecklenburg-Vorpommern, Germany 24 B6
Schönberg, Schleswig-Holstein, Germany 24 A6
Schönbuch ⌓, Germany 25 G5
Schönebeck, Germany 24 C7
Schongau, Germany 25 H6
Schöningen, Germany 24 C6
Schopfheim, Germany 25 H3
Schorndorf, Germany 25 G5
Schortens, Germany 24 B3
Schouten I., Australia 95 G4
Schouten Is. = Supiori, Indonesia 63 E9
Schouwen, Neths. 17 C3
Schramberg, Germany 25 G4
Schrankogel, Austria 26 D4
Schreiber, Canada 104 C2
Schrems, Austria 26 C8
Schrobenhausen, Germany 25 G7
Schroffenstein, Namibia 88 D2
Schroon Lake, U.S.A. 117 C11
Schruns, Austria 26 D2
Schuler, Canada 103 C6
Schumacher, Canada 104 C3
Schurz, U.S.A. 108 G4
Schuyler, U.S.A. 112 E6
Schuylerville, U.S.A. 117 C11
Schuylkill →, U.S.A. 117 G9
Schuylkill Haven, U.S.A. 117 F8
Schwabach, Germany 25 F7
Schwaben □, Germany 25 G6
Schwäbisch-Fränkischer Wald ⌓, Germany 25 G5
Schwäbisch Gmünd, Germany 25 G5
Schwäbisch Hall, Germany 25 F5
Schwäbische Alb, Germany 25 G5
Schwabmünchen, Germany 25 G6
Schwalmstadt, Germany 24 E5
Schwandorf, Germany 25 F8
Schwaner, Pegunungan, Indonesia 62 E4
Schwanewede, Germany 24 B4
Schwarmstedt, Germany 24 C5
Schwarze Elster →, Germany 24 D8
Schwarzenberg, Germany 24 E8
Schwarzrand, Namibia 88 D2
Schwarzwald, Germany 25 G4
Schwaz, Austria 26 D4
Schwechat, Austria 27 C9
Schwechat, Vienna ✕ (VIA), Austria 27 C9
Schwedt, Germany 24 B10
Schweinfurt, Germany 25 E6
Schweizer-Reneke, S. Africa 88 D4
Schwenningen = Villingen-Schwenningen, Germany 25 G4
Schwerin, Germany 24 B7
Schweriner See, Germany 24 B7
Schwetzingen, Germany 25 F4
Schwyz, Switz. 25 H4
Schwyz □, Switz. 25 H4
Sciacca, Italy 42 E6
Scicli, Italy 43 F7
Sciliar ⌓, Italy 41 B8
Scilla, Italy 43 D8
Scilly, Isles of, U.K. 15 H1
Ścinawa, Poland 31 G3
Scione, Greece 44 G7
Scioto →, U.S.A. 114 F4
Scituate, U.S.A. 117 D14
Scobey, U.S.A. 112 A2
Scone, Australia 95 E5
Scone, U.K. 13 E5
Scordia, Italy 43 E7
Scoresbysund = Ittoqqortoormiit, Greenland 4 B6
Scorniceşti, Romania 29 F9
Scotia, Calif., U.S.A. 108 F1
Scotia, N.Y., U.S.A. 117 D11
Scotia Sea, Antarctica 5 B18
Scotland, Canada 116 C4
Scotland □, U.K. 13 E5
Scott, Antarctica 5 D11
Scott, C., Australia 92 B4
Scott City, U.S.A. 112 F4
Scott Glacier, Antarctica 5 C8
Scott I., Antarctica 5 C11
Scott Is., Canada 102 C3
Scott L., Canada 103 B7
Scott Reef, Australia 92 B3
Scottburgh, S. Africa 89 E5
Scottdale, U.S.A. 116 F5
Scottish Borders □, U.K. 13 F6
Scottsbluff, U.S.A. 112 E3
Scottsboro, U.S.A. 115 H3
Scottsburg, U.S.A. 114 F3
Scottsdale, Australia 95 G4
Scottsdale, U.S.A. 109 K7
Scottsville, Ky., U.S.A. 115 G2
Scottsville, N.Y., U.S.A. 116 C7
Scottville, U.S.A. 114 D2
Scranton, U.S.A. 117 E9
Scugog, L., Canada 116 B6
Sculeni, Moldova 29 C12
Scunthorpe, U.K. 14 D7
Scuol Schuls, Switz. 25 J6
Scutari = Shkodër, Albania 44 D3
Scutari = Üsküdar, Turkey 45 F13
Seabrook, L., Australia 93 F2
Seaford, U.K. 15 G8
Seaford, U.S.A. 114 F8
Seaforth, Australia 94 J6
Seaforth, Canada 116 C3
Seaforth, L., U.K. 13 D2
Seagraves, U.S.A. 113 J3
Seaham, U.K. 14 C6
Seal →, Canada 103 B10
Seal L., Canada 105 B7
Sealy, U.S.A. 113 L6
Searchlight, U.S.A. 111 K12
Searcy, U.S.A. 113 H9
Searles L., U.S.A. 111 K9
Seascale, U.K. 14 C4
Seaside, Calif., U.S.A. 110 J5
Seaside, Oreg., U.S.A. 110 E3
Seaspray, Australia 95 F4
Seattle, U.S.A. 110 C4
Seattle-Tacoma International ✕ (SEA), U.S.A. 110 C4
Seaview Ra., Australia 94 B4
Sebago L., U.S.A. 117 C14
Sebago Lake, U.S.A. 117 C14
Sebastián Vizcaíno, B., Mexico 118 B2
Sebastopol = Sevastopol, Ukraine 33 K7
Sebastopol, U.S.A. 110 G4
Sebba, Burkina Faso 83 C5
Sebderat, Eritrea 81 D4
Sébékoro, Mali 82 C3
Seben, Turkey 72 B4
Sebeş, Romania 29 E8
Sebeşului, Munţii, Romania 29 E8
Sebewaing, U.S.A. 114 D4
Sebezh, Russia 32 D5
Sebha = Sabhah, Libya 79 C8
Sébi, Mali 82 B4
Şebinkarahisar, Turkey 73 B8
Sebiş, Romania 28 D7
Sebnitz, Germany 24 E10
Sebring, Fla., U.S.A. 115 M5
Sebring, Ohio, U.S.A. 116 F3
Sebringville, Canada 116 C3
Sebta = Ceuta, N. Afr. 78 A4
Sebuku, Indonesia 62 E5
Sebuku, Teluk, Malaysia 62 D5
Sečanj, Serbia & M. 28 E5
Secchia →, Italy 40 C8
Sechelt, Canada 102 D4
Sechura, Desierto de, Peru 124 E2
Seclin, France 19 B10
Secondigny, France 18 F6
Sečovce, Slovak Rep. 27 C14
Secretary I., N.Z. 91 L1
Secunderabad, India 66 L11
Security-Widefield, U.S.A. 112 F2
Sedalia, U.S.A. 112 F8
Sedan, France 19 C11
Sedan, U.S.A. 113 G6
Sedano, Spain 36 C7
Sedbergh, U.K. 14 C5
Seddon, N.Z. 91 J5
Seddonville, N.Z. 91 J4
Sedé Boqér, Israel 74 E3
Sedeh, Fārs, Iran 71 D7
Sedeh, Khorāsān, Iran 71 C8
Séderon, France 21 D9
Sederot, Israel 74 D3
Sédhiou, Senegal 82 C1
Sedico, Italy 41 B9
Sedlčany, Czech Rep. 26 B7
Sedley, Canada 103 C8
Sedona, U.S.A. 109 J8
Sedova, Pik, Russia 52 B6
Sedro Woolley, U.S.A. 110 B4
Šeduva, Lithuania 30 C10
Sędziszów, Poland 31 H7
Sędziszów Małapolski, Poland 31 H8
Seebad Ahlbeck, Germany 24 B10
Seefeld in Tirol, Austria 26 D4
Seehausen, Germany 24 C7
Seeheim, Namibia 88 D2
Seeheim-Jugenheim, Germany 25 F4
Seeis, Namibia 88 C2
Seekoei →, S. Africa 88 E4
Seeley's Bay, Canada 117 B8
Seelow, Germany 24 C10
Sées, France 18 D7
Seesen, Germany 24 D6
Seevetal, Germany 24 B6
Seewinkel = Neusiedler See-Seewinkel △, Austria 27 D9
Sefadu, S. Leone 82 D2
Seferihisar, Turkey 47 C8
Séfeto, Mali 82 C3
Sefwi Bekwai, Ghana 82 D4
Segamat, Malaysia 65 L4
Şegarcea, Romania 29 F8
Ségbana, Benin 83 C5
Segbwema, S. Leone 82 D2
Seget, Indonesia 63 E8
Segonzac, France 20 C3
Segorbe, Spain 38 F4
Ségou, Mali 82 C3
Segovia = Coco →, Cent. Amer. 120 D3
Segovia, Spain 36 E6
Segovia □, Spain 36 E6
Segré, France 18 E6
Segre →, Spain 38 D5
Séguéla, Ivory C. 82 D3
Séguénéga, Burkina Faso 83 C4
Seguin, U.S.A. 113 L6
Segundo →, Argentina 126 C3
Segura →, Spain 39 G4
Segura, Sierra de, Spain 39 G2
Seh Konj, Kūh-e, Iran 71 D8
Seh Qal'eh, Iran 71 C8
Sehitwa, Botswana 88 C3
Sehlabathebe △, Lesotho 89 D4
Sehore, India 68 H7
Sehwan, Pakistan 68 F2
Şeica Mare, Romania 29 D9
Seil, U.K. 13 E3
Seiland, Norway 8 A20
Seilhac, France 20 C5
Seiling, U.S.A. 113 G5
Seille →, Moselle, France 19 C13
Seille →, Saône-et-Loire, France 19 F11
Sein, Î. de, France 18 D2
Seinäjoki, Finland 9 E20
Seine →, France 18 C7
Seine, B. de la, France 18 C6
Seine-et-Marne □, France 19 D10
Seine-Maritime □, France 18 C7
Seine-St-Denis □, France 19 D9
Seini, Romania 29 C8
Seirijai, Lithuania 30 D10
Seistan = Sīstān, Asia 71 D9
Seistan, Daryācheh-ye = Sīstān, Daryācheh-ye, Iran 71 D9
Sejerø, Denmark 11 J5
Sejerø Bugt, Denmark 11 J5
Sejny, Poland 30 D10
Seka, Ethiopia 81 F4
Sekayu, Indonesia 62 E2
Seke, Tanzania 86 C3
Sekenke, Tanzania 86 C3
Seki, Turkey 47 E11
Sekondi-Takoradi, Ghana 82 E4
Sekota, Ethiopia 81 E4
Seksna, Russia 32 C10
Sekudai, Malaysia 65 d
Sekuma, Botswana 88 C3
Selah, U.S.A. 108 C3
Selama, Malaysia 65 K3
Selárgius, Italy 42 C2
Selaru, Indonesia 63 F8
Selatan, Selat, Malaysia 65 c
Selb, Germany 25 E8
Selby, U.K. 14 D6
Selby, U.S.A. 112 C4
Selca, Croatia 41 E13
Selçuk, Turkey 47 D9
Selden, U.S.A. 112 F4
Sele →, Italy 43 B7
Selebi-Pikwe, Botswana 89 C4
Selemdzha →, Russia 53 D13
Selendi, Manisa, Turkey 47 C10
Selendi, Manisa, Turkey 47 C9
Selenga = Selenge Mörön →, Asia 60 A5
Selenge Mörön →, Asia 60 A5
Selenicë, Albania 44 F3
Selenter See, Germany 24 A6

Sélestat, *France* 19 D14
Seletan, Tanjung, *Indonesia* 62 E4
Selevac, *Serbia & M.* 44 B4
Sélibabi, *Mauritania* 82 B2
Seliger, Ozero, *Russia* 32 D7
Seligman, *U.S.A.* 109 J7
Şelim, *Turkey* 73 B10
Selîma, El Wâhât el, *Sudan* 80 C2
Selimiye, *Turkey* 47 D9
Selinda Spillway →, *Botswana* 88 B3
Selinoús, *Greece* 46 D3
Selinsgrove, *U.S.A.* 116 F8
Selizharovo, *Russia* 32 D7
Selkirk, *Canada* 103 C9
Selkirk, *U.K.* 13 F6
Selkirk I. = Horse I., *Canada* 103 C9
Selkirk Mts., *Canada* 100 C8
Sellafield, *U.K.* 14 C4
Sellama, *Sudan* 81 E2
Selliá, *Greece* 49 D6
Sellières, *France* 19 F12
Sells, *U.S.A.* 109 L8
Sellye, *Hungary* 28 E2
Selma, *Ala., U.S.A.* 115 J2
Selma, *Calif., U.S.A.* 110 J7
Selma, *N.C., U.S.A.* 115 H6
Selmer, *U.S.A.* 115 H1
Selongey, *France* 19 E12
Selous ⌂, *Tanzania* 87 D4
Selowandoma Falls, *Zimbabwe* 87 G3
Selpele, *Indonesia* 63 E8
Selsey Bill, *U.K.* 15 G7
Seltso, *Russia* 32 F8
Seltz, *France* 19 D15
Selu, *Indonesia* 63 F8
Sélune →, *France* 18 D5
Selva = La Selva del Camp, *Spain* 38 D6
Selva, *Argentina* 126 B3
Selva Lancandona = Montes Azules ⌂, *Mexico* 119 D6
Selvas, *Brazil* 124 E5
Selwyn L., *Canada* 103 B8
Selwyn Mts., *Canada* 100 B6
Selwyn Ra., *Australia* 94 C3
Seman →, *Albania* 44 F3
Semarang, *Indonesia* 63 G14
Sembabule, *Uganda* 86 C3
Sembawang, *Singapore* 65 d
Sembung, *Indonesia* 63 J18
Şemdinli, *Turkey* 73 D11
Sémé, *Senegal* 82 B2
Semeih, *Sudan* 81 E3
Semenanjung Blambangan, *Indonesia* 63 K17
Semenov, *Russia* 34 B7
Semenovka, *Chernihiv, Ukraine* 33 F7
Semenovka, *Kremenchuk, Ukraine* 33 H7
Semeru, *Indonesia* 63 H15
Semey, *Kazakhstan* 52 D9
Semikarakorskiy, *Russia* 35 G5
Semiluki, *Russia* 33 G10
Seminoe Reservoir, *U.S.A.* 108 F10
Seminole, *Okla., U.S.A.* 113 H6
Seminole, *Tex., U.S.A.* 113 J3
Seminole Draw →, *U.S.A.* 113 J3
Semipalatinsk = Semey, *Kazakhstan* 52 D9
Semirara Is., *Phil.* 61 F4
Semitau, *Indonesia* 62 D4
Semiyarka, *Kazakhstan* 52 D8
Semiyarskoye = Semiyarka, *Kazakhstan* 52 D8
Semmering P., *Austria* 26 D8
Semnān, *Iran* 71 C7
Semnān □, *Iran* 71 C7
Semporna, *Malaysia* 63 D5
Semuda, *Indonesia* 62 E4
Semur-en-Auxois, *France* 19 E11
Sen →, *Cambodia* 62 B3
Senā, *Iran* 71 D6
Sena, *Mozam.* 87 F4
Sena Madureira, *Brazil* 124 E5
Senador Pompeu, *Brazil* 125 E11
Senaki, *Georgia* 35 J6
Senang, Pulau, *Singapore* 65 d
Senanga, *Zambia* 85 H4
Senatobia, *U.S.A.* 113 H10
Sencelles, *Spain* 48 B9
Sendafa, *Ethiopia* 81 F4
Sendai, *Kagoshima, Japan* 55 J5
Sendai, *Miyagi, Japan* 54 E10
Sendai-Wan, *Japan* 54 E10
Senden, *Bayern, Germany* 25 G6
Senden, *Nordrhein-Westfalen, Germany* 24 D3
Sendhwa, *India* 68 J6
Sene →, *Ghana* 83 D4
Senec, *Slovak Rep.* 27 C10
Seneca, *U.S.A.* 115 H4
Seneca Falls, *U.S.A.* 117 D8
Seneca L., *U.S.A.* 116 D8
Senecaville L., *U.S.A.* 116 G3
Senegal ■, *W. Afr.* 82 C2
Sénégal →, *W. Afr.* 82 B1
Senegambia, *Africa* 76 E2
Senekal, *S. Africa* 89 D4
Senftenberg, *Germany* 24 D10
Senga Hill, *Zambia* 87 D3
Senge Khambab = Indus →, *Pakistan* 68 G2
Sengiley, *Russia* 34 D9
Sengua →, *Zimbabwe* 87 F2
Senhor-do-Bonfim, *Brazil* 125 F10
Senica, *Slovak Rep.* 27 C10
Senigállia, *Italy* 41 E10
Senio →, *Italy* 41 D9
Senirkent, *Turkey* 47 C12
Senise, *Italy* 43 B9
Senj, *Croatia* 41 D11
Senja, *Norway* 8 B17
Senkaku-Shotō, *Japan* 55 L1
Senkuang, *Indonesia* 65 d
Senlis, *France* 19 C9
Senmonorom, *Cambodia* 64 F6
Sennâr, *Sudan* 81 E3
Sennar □, *Sudan* 81 E3
Senneterre, *Canada* 104 C4
Senno, *Belarus* 32 E5
Sénnori, *Italy* 42 B1
Seno, *Laos* 64 D5
Senonches, *France* 18 D8
Senorbì, *Italy* 42 C2
Senožeče, *Slovenia* 41 C11
Sens, *France* 19 D10
Senta, *Serbia & M.* 28 E5
Sentani, *Indonesia* 63 E10
Sentery = Lubao, *Dem. Rep. of the Congo* 86 D2
Sentinel, *U.S.A.* 109 K7
Šentjur, *Slovenia* 41 B12
Sentosa, *Singapore* 65 d
Senya Beraku, *Ghana* 83 D4
Seo de Urgel = La Seu d'Urgell, *Spain* 38 C6
Seohara, *India* 69 E8
Seonath →, *India* 69 J10
Seondha, *India* 69 F8
Seoni, *India* 69 H8
Seoni Malwa, *India* 68 H8
Seoul = Sŏul, *S. Korea* 57 F14
Sepīdān, *Iran* 71 D7
Sepo-ri, *N. Korea* 57 E14
Sępólno Krajeńskie, *Poland* 30 E4
Sepone, *Laos* 64 D6
Sępopol, *Poland* 30 D8
Sept-Îles, *Canada* 105 B6
Septemvri, *Bulgaria* 45 D8
Sepúlveda, *Spain* 36 D7
Sequeros, *Spain* 36 E4
Sequim, *U.S.A.* 110 B3
Sequoia △, *U.S.A.* 110 J8
Serafimovich, *Russia* 34 F6
Seraing, *Belgium* 17 D5
Serakhis →, *Cyprus* 49 D11
Seram, *Indonesia* 63 E7
Seram Sea, *Indonesia* 63 E7
Seranantsara, *Madag.* 89 B8
Serang, *Indonesia* 63 G12
Serangoon, *Singapore* 65 d
Serasan, *Indonesia* 62 D3
Seravezza, *Italy* 40 E7
Şerbettar, *Turkey* 45 E10
Serbia □, *Serbia & M.* 44 C5
Serbia & Montenegro ■, *Europe* 44 C4
Şercaia, *Romania* 29 E10
Serdo, *Ethiopia* 81 E5
Serdobsk, *Russia* 34 D7
Sered', *Slovak Rep.* 27 C10
Seredka, *Russia* 32 C5
Şereflikoçhisar, *Turkey* 72 C5
Seregno, *Italy* 40 C6
Seremban, *Malaysia* 65 L3
Serengeti △, *Tanzania* 86 C3
Serengeti Plain, *Tanzania* 86 C4
Serenje, *Zambia* 87 E3
Sereth = Siret →, *Romania* 29 E12
Sergach, *Russia* 34 C7
Sergen, *Turkey* 45 E11
Sergino, *Russia* 52 C7
Sergipe □, *Brazil* 125 F11
Sergiyev Posad, *Russia* 32 D10
Seria, *Brunei* 62 D4
Serian, *Malaysia* 62 D4
Seriate, *Italy* 40 C6
Seribu, Kepulauan, *Indonesia* 62 F3
Sérifontaine, *France* 19 C8
Sérifos, *Greece* 46 D6
Sérignan, *France* 20 E7
Sérigny →, *Canada* 105 A6
Serik, *Turkey* 72 D4
Seringapatam Reef, *Australia* 92 B3
Serinhisar, *Turkey* 47 D11
Seririt, *Indonesia* 63 J17
Sermaize-les-Bains, *France* 19 D11
Sermata, *Indonesia* 63 F7
Sermersuaq, *Greenland* 4 B4
Sérmide, *Italy* 41 D8
Sernovodsk, *Russia* 34 D10
Sernur, *Russia* 34 B9
Serock, *Poland* 31 F8
Serón, *Spain* 39 H2
Serós, *Spain* 38 D5
Serov, *Russia* 52 D7
Serowe, *Botswana* 88 C4
Serpa, *Portugal* 37 H3
Serpeddí, Punta, *Italy* 42 C2
Serpentara, *Italy* 42 C2
Serpentine Lakes, *Australia* 93 E4
Serpent's Mouth = Sierpe, Bocas de la, *Venezuela* 125 L15
Serpis →, *Spain* 39 G4
Serpukhov, *Russia* 32 E9
Serra da Estrela ⌂, *Portugal* 36 E3
Serra de Outes, *Spain* 36 C2
Serra do Navio, *Brazil* 125 C8
Serra San Bruno, *Italy* 43 D9
Serradilla, *Spain* 36 F4
Sérrai, *Greece* 44 E7
Sérrai □, *Greece* 44 E7
Serramanna, *Italy* 42 C1
Serranía San Luís △, *Paraguay* 126 A4
Serras d'Aire e Candeeiros ⌂, *Portugal* 37 F2
Serravalle Scrivia, *Italy* 40 D5
Serre-Ponçon, L. de, *France* 21 D10
Serres, *France* 21 D9
Serrezuela, *Argentina* 126 C2
Serrinha, *Brazil* 125 F11
Sersale, *Italy* 43 C9
Sertã, *Portugal* 36 F2
Sertanópolis, *Brazil* 127 A5
Sêrtar, *China* 58 A3
Serua, *Indonesia* 63 F8
Serui, *Indonesia* 63 E9
Serule, *Botswana* 88 C4
Sérvia, *Greece* 44 F6
Serzedelo, *Portugal* 36 D2
Ses Salines, *Spain* 48 B10
Sese Is., *Uganda* 86 C3
Sesepe, *Indonesia* 63 E7
Sesfontein, *Namibia* 88 B1
Sesheke, *Zambia* 88 B3
Sésia →, *Italy* 40 C5
Sesimbra, *Portugal* 37 G1
S'Espalmador, *Spain* 48 C7
S'Espardell, *Spain* 48 C7
Sessa Aurunca, *Italy* 42 A6
S'Estanyol, *Spain* 48 B9
Sestao, *Spain* 38 B2
Sesto Calende, *Italy* 40 C5
Sesto San Giovanni, *Italy* 40 C6
Sestri Levante, *Italy* 40 D6
Sestriere, *Italy* 40 D3
Sestroretsk, *Russia* 32 B6
Sestrunj, *Croatia* 41 D11
Sestu, *Italy* 42 C2
Setana, *Japan* 54 C9
Sète, *France* 20 E7
Sete Lagôas, *Brazil* 125 G10
Sétif, *Algeria* 78 A7
Seto, *Japan* 55 G8
Setonaikai, *Japan* 55 G6
Setonaikai △, *Japan* 55 G6
Settat, *Morocco* 78 B4
Séttimo Torinese, *Italy* 40 C4
Setting L., *Canada* 103 C9
Settle, *U.K.* 14 C5
Settlement Pt., *Bahamas* 115 M6
Settlers, *S. Africa* 89 C4
Setúbal, *Portugal* 37 G2
Setúbal □, *Portugal* 37 G2
Setúbal, B. de, *Portugal* 37 G2
Seugne →, *France* 20 C3
Seul, Lac, *Canada* 104 B1
Seurre, *France* 19 F12
Sevan, *Armenia* 35 K7
Sevan, Ozero = Sevana Lich, *Armenia* 35 K7
Sevana Lich, *Armenia* 35 K7
Sevastopol, *Ukraine* 33 K7
Seven Sisters, *Canada* 102 C3
Sever →, *Spain* 37 F3
Sévérac-le-Château, *France* 20 D7
Severn →, *Canada* 104 A2
Severn →, *U.K.* 15 F5
Severn L., *Canada* 104 B1
Severnaya Zemlya, *Russia* 53 B10
Severo-Kurilsk, *Russia* 53 D16
Severo-Yeniseyskiy, *Russia* 53 C10
Severo-Zapadnyy □, *Russia* 52 C4
Severočeský □, *Czech Rep.* 26 A7
Severodonetsk = Syeverodonetsk, *Ukraine* 33 H10
Severodvinsk, *Russia* 52 C4
Severomoravský □, *Czech Rep.* 27 B10
Sevier, *U.S.A.* 109 G7
Sevier →, *U.S.A.* 109 G7
Sevier Desert, *U.S.A.* 108 G7
Sevier L., *U.S.A.* 108 G7
Sevilla, *Spain* 37 H5
Sevilla □, *Spain* 37 H5
Seville = Sevilla, *Spain* 37 H5
Sevlievo, *Bulgaria* 45 C9
Sevnica, *Slovenia* 41 B12
Sèvre-Nantaise →, *France* 18 E5
Sèvre-Niortaise →, *France* 20 B3
Sevsk, *Russia* 33 F8
Sewa →, *S. Leone* 82 D2
Sewani, *India* 68 E6
Seward, *Alaska, U.S.A.* 100 B5
Seward, *Nebr., U.S.A.* 112 E6
Seward, *Pa., U.S.A.* 116 F5
Seward Peninsula, *U.S.A.* 100 B3
Sewell, *Chile* 126 C1
Sewer, *Indonesia* 63 F8
Sewickley, *U.S.A.* 116 F4
Sexsmith, *Canada* 102 B5
Seychelles ■, *Ind. Oc.* 50 K9
Seyðisfjörður, *Iceland* 8 D6
Seydişehir, *Turkey* 72 D4
Seydvān, *Iran* 70 B5
Seyhan →, *Turkey* 70 B2
Seyhan Barajı, *Turkey* 72 D6
Seyitgazi, *Turkey* 47 B12
Seyitömer, *Turkey* 47 B11
Seym →, *Ukraine* 33 G7
Seymen, *Turkey* 45 E11
Seymour, *Australia* 95 F4
Seymour, *S. Africa* 89 E4
Seymour, *Conn., U.S.A.* 117 E11
Seymour, *Ind., U.S.A.* 114 F3
Seymour, *Tex., U.S.A.* 113 J5
Seyne, *France* 21 D10
Seyssel, *France* 21 C9
Sežana, *Slovenia* 41 C10
Sézanne, *France* 19 D10
Sezze, *Italy* 42 A6
Sfântu Gheorghe, *Covasna, Romania* 29 E10
Sfântu Gheorghe, *Tulcea, Romania* 29 F14
Sfântu Gheorghe, Braţul →, *Romania* 29 F14
Sfax, *Tunisia* 79 B8
Sha Xi →, *China* 59 D12
Sha Xian, *China* 59 D11
Shaanxi □, *China* 56 G5
Shaba = Katanga □, *Dem. Rep. of the Congo* 86 D2
Shaba ⌂, *Kenya* 86 B4
Shaballe = Scebeli, Wabi →, *Somali Rep.* 75 G3
Shabla, *Bulgaria* 45 C12
Shabogamo L., *Canada* 105 B6
Shabunda, *Dem. Rep. of the Congo* 86 C2
Shache, *China* 60 C2
Shackleton Ice Shelf, *Antarctica* 5 C8
Shackleton Inlet, *Antarctica* 5 E11
Shādegān, *Iran* 71 D6
Shadi, *China* 59 D10
Shadi, *India* 69 C7
Shadrinsk, *Russia* 52 D7
Shadyside, *U.S.A.* 116 G4
Shaffa, *Nigeria* 83 C7
Shafter, *U.S.A.* 111 K7
Shaftesbury, *U.K.* 15 F5
Shagamu, *Nigeria* 83 D5
Shagram, *Pakistan* 69 A5
Shah Alizai, *Pakistan* 68 E2
Shah Bunder, *Pakistan* 68 G2
Shahabad, *Punjab, India* 68 D7
Shahabad, *Raj., India* 68 G7
Shahabad, *Ut. P., India* 69 F8
Shahadpur, *Pakistan* 68 G3
Shahba, *Syria* 74 C5
Shahdād, *Iran* 71 D8
Shahdād, Namakzār-e, *Iran* 71 D8
Shahdadkot, *Pakistan* 68 F2
Shahdol, *India* 69 H9
Shahe, *China* 56 F8
Shahganj, *India* 69 F10
Shahgarh, *India* 66 F6
Shahjahanpur, *India* 69 F8
Shahpur, *India* 68 H7
Shahpur, *Baluchistan, Pakistan* 68 E3
Shahpur, *Punjab, Pakistan* 68 C5
Shahpur Chakar, *Pakistan* 68 F3
Shahpura, *Mad. P., India* 69 H9
Shahpura, *Raj., India* 68 G6
Shahr-e Bābak, *Iran* 71 D7
Shahr-e Kord, *Iran* 71 C6
Shāhrakht, *Iran* 71 C9
Shahrig, *Pakistan* 68 D2
Shahukou, *China* 56 D7
Shaikhabad, *Afghan.* 68 B3
Shajapur, *India* 68 H7
Shakargarh, *Pakistan* 68 C6
Shakawe, *Botswana* 88 B3
Shaker Heights, *U.S.A.* 116 E3
Shakhty, *Russia* 35 G5
Shakhunya, *Russia* 34 B8
Shaki, *Nigeria* 83 D5
Shākir, *Egypt* 80 B3
Shaksam Valley, *Asia* 69 A7
Shala, L., *Ethiopia* 81 F4
Shali, *Russia* 35 J7
Shallow Lake, *Canada* 116 B3
Shalqar, *Kazakhstan* 52 E6
Shalskiy, *Russia* 32 B8
Shaluli Shan, *China* 58 B2
Shām, *Iran* 71 E8
Shām, Bādiyat ash, *Asia* 70 C3
Shamâl Bahr el Ghazal □, *Sudan* 81 F2
Shamâl Dârfûr □, *Sudan* 81 E2
Shamâl Kordofân □, *Sudan* 81 E3
Shamâl Sînî □, *Egypt* 74 E2
Shamattawa, *Canada* 104 A1
Shamattawa →, *Canada* 104 A2
Shambe, *Sudan* 81 F3
Shambe △, *Sudan* 81 F3
Shambu, *Ethiopia* 81 F4
Shamīl, *Iran* 71 E8
Shamkhor = Şämkir, *Azerbaijan* 35 K8
Shāmkūh, *Iran* 71 C8
Shamli, *India* 68 E7
Shammar, Jabal, *Si. Arabia* 70 E4
Shamo = Gobi, *Asia* 56 C6
Shamo, L., *Ethiopia* 81 F4
Shamokin, *U.S.A.* 117 F8
Shamrock, *U.S.A.* 113 H4
Shamva, *Zimbabwe* 87 F3
Shan □, *Burma* 67 J21
Shan Xian, *China* 56 G9
Shanan →, *Ethiopia* 81 F5
Shanchengzhen, *China* 57 C13
Shāndak, *Iran* 71 D9
Shandon, *U.S.A.* 110 K6
Shandong □, *China* 57 G10
Shandong Bandao, *China* 57 F11
Shang Xian = Shangzhou, *China* 56 H5
Shanga, *Nigeria* 78 F6
Shangalowe, *Dem. Rep. of the Congo* 87 E2
Shangani, *Zimbabwe* 89 B4
Shangani →, *Zimbabwe* 87 F2
Shangbancheng, *China* 57 D10
Shangcheng, *China* 59 B10
Shangchuan Dao, *China* 59 G9
Shangdu, *China* 56 D7
Shanggao, *China* 59 C10
Shanghai, *China* 59 B13
Shanghai Shi □, *China* 59 B13
Shanghang, *China* 59 E11
Shanghe, *China* 57 F9
Shanglin, *China* 58 F7
Shangnan, *China* 56 H6
Shangqiu, *China* 56 G8
Shangrao, *China* 59 C11
Shangshui, *China* 60 C6
Shangsi, *China* 58 F6
Shangyou, *China* 59 E10
Shangyu, *China* 59 B13
Shangzhi, *China* 57 B14
Shangzhou, *China* 56 H5
Shanhetun, *China* 57 B14
Shani, *Nigeria* 83 C7
Shanklin, *U.K.* 15 G6
Shannon, *N.Z.* 91 J5
Shannon △, *Australia* 93 F2
Shannon →, *Ireland* 12 D2
Shannon, Mouth of the, *Ireland* 12 D2
Shannon Airport, *Ireland* 12 D3
Shansi = Shanxi □, *China* 56 F7
Shantar, Ostrov Bolshoy, *Russia* 53 D14
Shantipur, *India* 69 H13
Shantou, *China* 59 F11
Shantung = Shandong □, *China* 57 G10
Shanwei, *China* 59 F10
Shanxi □, *China* 56 F7
Shanyang, *China* 56 H5
Shanyin, *China* 56 E7
Shaodong, *China* 59 D8
Shaoguan, *China* 59 E9
Shaoshan, *China* 59 D9
Shaowu, *China* 59 D11
Shaoxing, *China* 59 C13
Shaoyang, *Hunan, China* 59 D8
Shaoyang, *Hunan, China* 59 D8
Shap, *U.K.* 14 C5
Shapinsay, *U.K.* 13 B6
Shaqq el Gi'eifer →, *Sudan* 81 D2
Shaqra', *Si. Arabia* 70 E5
Shaqrā', *Yemen* 75 E4
Sharafa, *Sudan* 81 E2
Sharafkhāneh, *Iran* 70 B5
Sharbot Lake, *Canada* 117 B8
Shari, *Japan* 54 C12
Sharjah = Ash Shāriqah, *U.A.E.* 71 E7
Shark B., *Australia* 93 E1
Shark Bay ⌂, *Australia* 93 F2
Sharm el Sheikh, *Egypt* 80 B3
Sharon, *Mass., U.S.A.* 117 D13
Sharon, *Pa., U.S.A.* 116 E4
Sharon Springs, *Kans., U.S.A.* 112 F4
Sharon Springs, *N.Y., U.S.A.* 117 D10
Sharp Pt., *Australia* 94 A3
Sharpe L., *Canada* 104 B1
Sharpsville, *U.S.A.* 116 E4
Sharq el Istiwa'iya □, *Sudan* 81 G3
Sharya, *Russia* 34 A7
Shasha, *Ethiopia* 81 F4
Shashemene, *Ethiopia* 81 F4
Shashi, *Botswana* 89 C4
Shashi, *China* 59 B9
Shashi →, *Africa* 87 G2
Shasta, Mt., *U.S.A.* 108 F2
Shasta L., *U.S.A.* 108 F2
Shatawi, *Sudan* 81 E3
Shatsk, *Russia* 34 C5
Shatskyi ⌂, *Ukraine* 31 G10
Shatt al Arab = Arab, Shatt al →, *Asia* 71 D6
Shatura, *Russia* 32 E10
Shaumyani = Shulaveri, *Georgia* 35 K7
Shaunavon, *Canada* 103 D7
Shaver L., *U.S.A.* 110 H7
Shaw →, *Australia* 92 D2
Shaw I., *Australia* 94 J7
Shawanaga, *Canada* 116 A4
Shawangunk Mts., *U.S.A.* 117 E10
Shawano, *U.S.A.* 114 C1
Shawinigan, *Canada* 104 C5
Shawnee, *U.S.A.* 113 H6
Shay Gap, *Australia* 92 D3
Shayang, *China* 59 B9
Shaybārā, *Si. Arabia* 70 E3
Shayib el Banat, Gebel, *Egypt* 80 B3
Shaykh, J. ash, *Lebanon* 74 B4
Shaykh Miskīn, *Syria* 74 C5
Shaykh Sa'īd, *Iraq* 70 C5
Shchekino, *Russia* 32 E9
Shcherbakov = Rybinsk, *Russia* 32 C10
Shchigry, *Russia* 33 G9
Shchors, *Ukraine* 33 G6
Shchuchinsk, *Kazakhstan* 52 D8
She Xian, *Anhui, China* 59 C12
She Xian, *Hebei, China* 56 F7
Shebekino, *Russia* 33 G9
Shebele = Scebeli, Wabi →, *Somali Rep.* 75 G3
Sheboygan, *U.S.A.* 114 D2
Shebshi Mts., *Nigeria* 83 D7
Shediac, *Canada* 105 C7
Sheelin, L., *Ireland* 12 C4
Sheep Haven, *Ireland* 12 A4
Sheerness, *U.K.* 15 F8
Sheet Harbour, *Canada* 105 D7
Sheffield, *U.K.* 14 D6
Sheffield, *Ala., U.S.A.* 115 H2
Sheffield, *Mass., U.S.A.* 117 D11
Sheffield, *Pa., U.S.A.* 116 E5
Shehojele, *Ethiopia* 81 E4
Shehong, *China* 58 B5
Sheikh Idris, *Sudan* 81 E3
Sheikhpura, *India* 69 G11
Shek Hasan, *Ethiopia* 81 E4
Shekhupura, *Pakistan* 68 D5
Sheki = Şaki, *Azerbaijan* 35 K8
Shelburne, *N.S., Canada* 105 D6
Shelburne, *Ont., Canada* 116 B4
Shelburne, *U.S.A.* 117 B11
Shelburne B., *Australia* 94 A3
Shelburne Falls, *U.S.A.* 117 D12
Shelby, *Mich., U.S.A.* 114 D2
Shelby, *Miss., U.S.A.* 113 J9
Shelby, *Mont., U.S.A.* 108 B8
Shelby, *N.C., U.S.A.* 115 H5
Shelby, *Ohio, U.S.A.* 116 F2
Shelbyville, *Ill., U.S.A.* 112 F10
Shelbyville, *Ind., U.S.A.* 114 F3
Shelbyville, *Ky., U.S.A.* 114 F3
Shelbyville, *Tenn., U.S.A.* 115 H2
Sheldon, *U.S.A.* 112 D7
Sheldrake, *Canada* 105 B7
Shelengo, Khawr →, *Sudan* 81 E2
Shelikhova, Zaliv, *Russia* 53 D16
Shell Lakes, *Australia* 93 E4
Shellbrook, *Canada* 103 C7
Shellharbour, *Australia* 95 E5
Shelon →, *Russia* 32 C6
Shelter I, *U.S.A.* 117 E12
Shelton, *Conn., U.S.A.* 117 E11
Shelton, *Wash., U.S.A.* 110 C3

Shemakha = Şamaxi, *Azerbaijan* 35 K9
Shëmri, *Albania* 44 D4
Shemsi, *Sudan* 80 D2
Shen Xian, *China* 56 F8
Shenandoah, *Iowa, U.S.A.* 112 E7
Shenandoah, *Pa., U.S.A.* 117 F8
Shenandoah, *Va., U.S.A.* 114 F6
Shenandoah △, *U.S.A.* 114 F6
Shenandoah →, *U.S.A.* 114 F7
Shenchi, *China* 56 E7
Shendam, *Nigeria* 83 D6
Shendî, *Sudan* 81 D3
Shenge, *S. Leone* 82 D2
Shengfang, *China* 56 E9
Shëngjergj, *Albania* 44 E4
Shëngjin, *Albania* 44 E3
Shengzhou, *China* 59 C13
Shenjingzi, *China* 57 B13
Shenmu, *China* 56 E6
Shennongjia, *China* 59 B8
Shenqiu, *China* 56 H8
Shensi = Shaanxi □, *China* 56 G5
Shenyang, *China* 57 D12
Shenzhen, *China* 59 F10
Sheo, *India* 68 F4
Sheopur Kalan, *India* 66 G10
Shepetivka, *Ukraine* 33 G4
Shepetovka = Shepetivka, *Ukraine* 33 G4
Shepparton, *Australia* 95 F4
Sheppey, I. of, *U.K.* 15 F8
Shepton Mallet, *U.K.* 15 F5
Sheqi, *China* 56 H7
Sher Qila, *Pakistan* 69 A6
Sherab, *Sudan* 81 E1
Sherborne, *U.K.* 15 G5
Sherbro →, *S. Leone* 82 D2
Sherbro I., *S. Leone* 82 D2
Sherbrooke, *N.S., Canada* 105 C7
Sherbrooke, *Qué., Canada* 117 A13
Sherburne, *U.S.A.* 117 D9
Shereik, *Sudan* 80 D3
Shergarh, *India* 68 F5
Sherghati, *India* 69 G11
Sheridan, *Ark., U.S.A.* 113 H8
Sheridan, *Wyo., U.S.A.* 108 D10
Sheringham, *U.K.* 14 E9
Sherkin I., *Ireland* 12 E2
Sherkot, *India* 69 E8
Sherman, *U.S.A.* 113 J6
Sherpur, *India* 69 G10
Sherridon, *Canada* 103 B8
Sherwood Forest, *U.K.* 14 D6
Sherwood Park, *Canada* 102 C6
Sheslay →, *Canada* 102 B2
Shethanei L., *Canada* 103 B9
Shetland □, *U.K.* 13 A7
Shetland Is., *U.K.* 13 A7
Shetrunji →, *India* 68 J5
Shewa □, *Ethiopia* 81 F4
Shewa Gimira, *Ethiopia* 81 F4
Sheyenne →, *U.S.A.* 112 B6
Shibām, *Yemen* 75 D4
Shibata, *Japan* 54 F9
Shibecha, *Japan* 54 C12
Shibetsu, *Japan* 54 B11
Shibîn el Kôm, *Egypt* 80 H7
Shibîn el Qanâtir, *Egypt* 80 H7
Shibing, *China* 58 D7
Shibogama L., *Canada* 104 B2
Shibushi, *Japan* 55 J5
Shicheng, *China* 59 D11
Shickshinny, *U.S.A.* 117 E8
Shickshock Mts. = Chic-Chocs, Mts., *Canada* 105 C6
Shidao, *China* 57 F12
Shidian, *China* 58 E2
Shido, *Japan* 55 G7
Shiel, L., *U.K.* 13 E3
Shield, C., *Australia* 94 A2
Shīeli, *Kazakhstan* 52 E7
Shifang, *China* 58 B5
Shiga □, *Japan* 55 G8
Shigu, *China* 58 D2
Shiguaigou, *China* 56 D6
Shihchiachuangi = Shijiazhuang, *China* 56 E8
Shihezi, *China* 60 B3
Shijak, *Albania* 44 E3
Shijiazhuang, *China* 56 E8
Shijiu Hu, *China* 59 B12
Shikarpur, *India* 68 E8
Shikarpur, *Pakistan* 68 F3
Shikohabad, *India* 69 F8
Shikoku □, *Japan* 55 H6
Shikoku-Sanchi, *Japan* 55 H6
Shikotsu-Ko, *Japan* 54 C10
Shikotsu-Tōya △, *Japan* 54 C10
Shiliguri, *India* 67 F16
Shilka, *Russia* 53 D12
Shilka →, *Russia* 53 D13
Shillelagh, *Ireland* 12 D5
Shillington, *U.S.A.* 117 F9
Shillong, *India* 67 G17
Shilo, *West Bank* 74 C4
Shilong, *China* 59 F9
Shilou, *China* 56 F6
Shilovo, *Russia* 34 C5
Shimabara, *Japan* 55 H5
Shimada, *Japan* 55 G9
Shimane □, *Japan* 55 G6
Shimanovsk, *Russia* 53 D13
Shimba Hills ⌂, *Kenya* 86 C4
Shimen, *China* 59 C8
Shimenjie, *China* 59 C11
Shimian, *China* 58 C4
Shimizu, *Japan* 55 G9
Shimodate, *Japan* 55 F9
Shimoga, *India* 66 N9
Shimoni, *Kenya* 86 C4
Shimonoseki, *Japan* 55 H5
Shimpuru Rapids, *Namibia* 88 B2
Shimsk, *Russia* 32 C6
Shin, L., *U.K.* 13 C4
Shinan, *China* 58 F7
Shinano-Gawa →, *Japan* 55 F9
Shināş, *Oman* 71 E8
Shīndand, *Afghan.* 66 C3
Shinglehouse, *U.S.A.* 116 E6
Shingū, *Japan* 55 H7
Shingwidzi, *S. Africa* 89 C5
Shinjō, *Japan* 54 E10
Shinkafe, *Nigeria* 83 C6
Shinshār, *Syria* 74 A5
Shinyanga, *Tanzania* 86 C3
Shinyanga □, *Tanzania* 86 C3
Shio-no-Misaki, *Japan* 55 H7
Shiogama, *Japan* 54 E10
Shiojiri, *Japan* 55 F8
Shipchenski Prokhod, *Bulgaria* 45 D9
Shiping, *China* 58 F4
Shippagan, *Canada* 105 C7
Shippensburg, *U.S.A.* 116 F7
Shippenville, *U.S.A.* 116 E5
Shiprock, *U.S.A.* 109 H9
Shiqian, *China* 58 D7
Shiqma, N. →, *Israel* 74 D3
Shiquan, *China* 56 H5
Shiquan He = Indus →, *Pakistan* 68 G2
Shīr Kūh, *Iran* 71 D7
Shiragami-Misaki, *Japan* 54 D10
Shirakawa, *Fukushima, Japan* 55 F10
Shirakawa, *Gifu, Japan* 55 F8
Shirane-San, *Gumma, Japan* 55 F9
Shirane-San, *Yamanashi, Japan* 55 G9
Shiraoi, *Japan* 54 C10
Shīrāz, *Iran* 71 D7
Shirbîn, *Egypt* 80 H7
Shire →, *Africa* 87 F4
Shiretoko-Misaki, *Japan* 54 B12
Shirinab →, *Pakistan* 68 D2
Shiriya-Zaki, *Japan* 54 D10
Shiroishi, *Japan* 54 F10
Shīrvān, *Iran* 71 B8
Shirwa, L. = Chilwa, L., *Malawi* 87 F4
Shishi, *China* 59 E12
Shishou, *China* 59 C9
Shitai, *China* 59 B11
Shivpuri, *India* 68 G7
Shixian, *China* 57 C15
Shixing, *China* 59 E10
Shiyan, *China* 59 A8
Shiyata, *Egypt* 80 B2
Shizhu, *China* 58 C7
Shizong, *China* 58 E5
Shizuishan, *China* 56 E4
Shizuoka, *Japan* 55 G9
Shizuoka □, *Japan* 55 G9
Shkhara, *Georgia* 35 J6
Shklov = Shklow, *Belarus* 32 E6
Shklow, *Belarus* 32 E6
Shkodër, *Albania* 44 D3
Shkumbini →, *Albania* 44 E3
Shmidta, Ostrov, *Russia* 53 A10
Shō-Gawa →, *Japan* 55 F8
Shoal L., *Canada* 103 D9
Shoal Lake, *Canada* 103 C8
Shōdo-Shima, *Japan* 55 G7
Sholapur = Solapur, *India* 66 L9
Shologontsy, *Russia* 53 C12
Shōmrōn, *West Bank* 74 C4
Shoreham by Sea, *U.K.* 15 G7
Shori →, *Pakistan* 68 E3
Shorkot Road, *Pakistan* 68 D5
Shoshone, *Calif., U.S.A.* 111 K10
Shoshone, *Idaho, U.S.A.* 108 E6
Shoshone L., *U.S.A.* 108 D8
Shoshone Mts., *U.S.A.* 108 G5
Shoshong, *Botswana* 88 C4
Shoshoni, *U.S.A.* 108 E9
Shostka, *Ukraine* 33 G7
Shou Xian, *China* 59 A11
Shouchang, *China* 59 C12
Shouguang, *China* 57 F10
Shouning, *China* 59 D12
Shouyang, *China* 56 F7
Show Low, *U.S.A.* 109 J9
Shpola, *Ukraine* 33 H6
Shreveport, *U.S.A.* 113 J8
Shrewsbury, *U.K.* 15 E5
Shri Mohangarh, *India* 68 F4
Shrirampur, *India* 69 H13
Shropshire □, *U.K.* 15 E5
Shū, *Kazakhstan* 52 E8
Shū →, *Kazakhstan* 50 E10
Shuangbai, *China* 58 E3
Shuangcheng, *China* 57 B14
Shuangfeng, *China* 59 D9
Shuanggou, *China* 57 G9
Shuangjiang, *China* 58 F2
Shuangliao, *China* 57 C12
Shuangshanzi, *China* 57 D10
Shuangyang, *China* 57 C13
Shuangyashan, *China* 60 B8
Shubra el Kheima, *Egypt* 80 H7
Shubra Khit, *Egypt* 80 H7
Shucheng, *China* 59 B11
Shugozero, *Russia* 32 C8
Shuguri Falls, *Tanzania* 87 D4
Shuiji, *China* 59 D12
Shuiye, *China* 56 F8
Shujalpur, *India* 68 H7
Shukpa Kunzang, *India* 69 B8
Shulan, *China* 57 B14
Shulaveri, *Georgia* 35 K7
Shule, *China* 60 C2
Shumagin Is., *U.S.A.* 100 C4
Shumen, *Bulgaria* 45 C10
Shumerlya, *Russia* 34 C8
Shumikha, *Russia* 52 D7
Shunchang, *China* 59 D11
Shunde, *China* 59 F9
Shungay, *Kazakhstan* 35 F8
Shuo Xian = Shuozhou, *China* 56 E7
Shuozhou, *China* 56 E7
Shūr →, *Fārs, Iran* 71 D7
Shūr →, *Kermān, Iran* 71 D8
Shūr →, *Yazd, Iran* 71 D7
Shūr Āb, *Iran* 71 C6
Shūr Gaz, *Iran* 71 D8
Shūrāb, *Iran* 71 C8
Shūrjestān, *Iran* 71 D7
Shurugwi, *Zimbabwe* 87 F3
Shūsf, *Iran* 71 D9
Shūsh, *Iran* 73 F13
Shūshtar, *Iran* 71 D6
Shuswap L., *Canada* 102 C5
Shuya, *Russia* 34 B5
Shuyang, *China* 57 G10
Shūzū, *Iran* 71 D7
Shwebo, *Burma* 67 H19
Shwegu, *Burma* 67 G20
Shweli →, *Burma* 67 H20
Shymkent, *Kazakhstan* 52 E7
Shyok, *India* 69 B8
Shyok →, *Pakistan* 69 B6
Si Chon, *Thailand* 65 H2
Si Kiang = Xi Jiang →, *China* 59 F9
Si Lanna △, *Thailand* 64 C2
Si-ngan = Xi'an, *China* 56 G5
Si Prachan, *Thailand* 64 E3
Si Racha, *Thailand* 64 F3
Si Xian, *China* 57 H9
Siachen Glacier, *Asia* 69 B7
Siahaf →, *Pakistan* 68 E3
Siahan Range, *Pakistan* 66 F4
Siaksriindrapura, *Indonesia* 62 D2
Sialkot, *Pakistan* 68 C6
Siam = Thailand ■, *Asia* 64 E4
Sian = Xi'an, *China* 56 G5
Sian Ka'an, Reserva de La Biósfera, *Mexico* 119 D7
Sianów, *Poland* 30 D3
Siantan, *Indonesia* 62 D3
Sīāreh, *Iran* 71 D9
Siargao I., *Phil.* 61 G7
Siari, *Pakistan* 69 B7
Siasi, *Phil.* 63 C6
Siasi I., *Phil.* 61 J4
Siátista, *Greece* 44 F5
Siau, *Indonesia* 63 D7
Šiauliai, *Lithuania* 9 J20
Šiauliai □, *Lithuania* 30 C10
Siazan = Siyäzän, *Azerbaijan* 35 K9
Sibâi, Gebel el, *Egypt* 70 E2
Sibang, *Indonesia* 63 K18
Sibayi, L., *S. Africa* 89 D5
Sibdu, *Sudan* 81 E2
Šibenik, *Croatia* 41 E12
Siberia = Sibirskiy □, *Russia* 53 D10
Siberia, *Russia* 50 C13
Siberut, *Indonesia* 62 E1
Sibi, *Pakistan* 68 E2
Sibil = Oksibil, *Indonesia* 63 E10
Sibiloi △, *Kenya* 86 B4
Sibirskiy □, *Russia* 53 D10
Sibiti, *Congo* 84 E2
Sibiu, *Romania* 29 E9
Sibiu □, *Romania* 29 E9
Sibley, *U.S.A.* 112 D7
Sibolga, *Indonesia* 62 D1
Sibsagar, *India* 67 F19
Sibu, *Malaysia* 62 D4
Sibuco, *Phil.* 61 H5
Sibuguey B., *Phil.* 61 H5
Sibut, *C.A.R.* 84 C3
Sibutu, *Phil.* 63 D5
Sibutu Group, *Phil.* 61 J3
Sibutu Passage, *E. Indies* 63 D5
Sibuyan I., *Phil.* 61 E5
Sibuyan Sea, *Phil.* 61 E5
Sic, *Romania* 29 D8
Sicamous, *Canada* 102 C5
Siccus →, *Australia* 95 E2
Sichuan □, *China* 58 B5
Sichuan Pendi, *China* 58 B5
Sicilia, *Italy* 43 E7
Sicily = Sicilia, *Italy* 43 E7
Sicuani, *Peru* 124 F4
Šid, *Serbia & M.* 28 E4
Sidamo □, *Ethiopia* 81 G4
Sidaouet, *Niger* 83 B6
Sidári, *Greece* 49 A3
Siddhapur, *India* 68 H5
Siddipet, *India* 66 K11
Sidensjö, *Sweden* 10 A12
Sidéradougou, *Burkina Faso* 82 C4
Siderno, *Italy* 43 D9
Sidhauli, *India* 69 F9
Sídheros, Ákra, *Greece* 49 D8
Sidhi, *India* 69 G9
Sidhirókastron, *Greece* 44 E7
Sîdi Abd el Rahmân, *Egypt* 80 A2
Sîdi Barrâni, *Egypt* 80 A2
Sidi-bel-Abbès, *Algeria* 78 A5
Sîdi Haneish, *Egypt* 80 A2
Sidi Ifni, *Morocco* 78 C3
Sîdi Omar, *Egypt* 80 A1
Sidlaw Hills, *U.K.* 13 E5
Sidley, Mt., *Antarctica* 5 D14
Sidmouth, *U.K.* 15 G4
Sidmouth, C., *Australia* 94 A3
Sidney, *Canada* 102 D4
Sidney, *Mont., U.S.A.* 112 B2
Sidney, *N.Y., U.S.A.* 117 D9
Sidney, *Nebr., U.S.A.* 112 E3
Sidney, *Ohio, U.S.A.* 114 E3
Sidney Lanier, L., *U.S.A.* 115 H4
Sido, *Mali* 82 C3
Sidoarjo, *Indonesia* 63 G15
Sidon = Saydā, *Lebanon* 74 B4
Sidra, G. of = Surt, Khalīj, *Libya* 79 B9
Siedlce, *Poland* 31 F9
Sieg →, *Germany* 24 E3
Siegburg, *Germany* 24 E3
Siegen, *Germany* 24 E4
Siem Pang, *Cambodia* 64 E6
Siem Reap = Siemreab, *Cambodia* 64 F4
Siemiatycze, *Poland* 31 F9
Siemreab, *Cambodia* 64 F4
Siena, *Italy* 41 E8
Sieniawa, *Poland* 31 H9
Sieradz, *Poland* 31 G5
Sieraków, *Poland* 31 F3
Sierck-les-Bains, *France* 19 C13
Sierning, *Austria* 26 C7
Sierpc, *Poland* 31 F6
Sierpe, Bocas de la, *Venezuela* 125 L15
Sierra Blanca, *U.S.A.* 109 L11
Sierra Blanca Peak, *U.S.A.* 109 K11
Sierra City, *U.S.A.* 110 F6
Sierra Colorada, *Argentina* 128 E3
Sierra de Aracena y Picas de Aroche ⌂, *Spain* 37 H4
Sierra de Bahoruco △, *Dom. Rep.* 121 C5
Sierra de Baza ⌂, *Spain* 39 H2
Sierra de Castril ⌂, *Spain* 39 H2
Sierra de España ⌂, *Spain* 39 H3
Sierra de Grazalema ⌂, *Spain* 37 J5
Sierra de Gredos ⌂, *Spain* 36 E5
Sierra de Hornachuelos ⌂, *Spain* 37 H5
Sierra de Huétor ⌂, *Spain* 37 H7
Sierra de La Culata △, *Venezuela* 121 E5
Sierra de Lancandón △, *Guatemala* 120 C1
Sierra de las Nieves ⌂, *Spain* 37 J6
Sierra de Las Quijadas △, *Argentina* 126 C2
Sierra de María-Los Vélez ⌂, *Spain* 39 H2
Sierra de San Luis △, *Venezuela* 121 D6
Sierra de Yeguas, *Spain* 37 H6
Sierra del São Mamede ⌂, *Portugal* 37 F3
Sierra Gorda, *Chile* 126 A2
Sierra Leone ■, *W. Afr.* 82 D2
Sierra Madre, *Mexico* 119 D6
Sierra Mágina ⌂, *Spain* 37 H7
Sierra Mojada, *Mexico* 118 B4
Sierra Nevada, *Spain* 37 H7
Sierra Nevada, *U.S.A.* 110 H8
Sierra Nevada ⌂, *Spain* 37 H7
Sierra Nevada △, *Venezuela* 121 E5
Sierra Nevada △, *Venezuela* 121 E5
Sierra Nevada de Santa Marta △, *Colombia* 121 D5
Sierra Nevada de Santa Marta △, *Colombia* 121 D5
Sierra Norte de Seville ⌂, *Spain* 37 H5
Sierra Subbéticas ⌂, *Spain* 37 H6
Sierra Vista, *U.S.A.* 109 L8
Sierras de Cardeña y Montoro ⌂, *Spain* 37 G6
Sierras de Cazorla, Segura y las Villas ⌂, *Spain* 39 J2
Sierraville, *U.S.A.* 110 F6
Sierre, *Switz.* 25 J3
Sifani, *Ethiopia* 81 E5
Sifié, *Ivory C.* 82 D3
Sífnos, *Greece* 46 E6
Sifton, *Canada* 103 C8
Sifton Pass, *Canada* 102 B3
Sigean, *France* 20 E6
Sighetu-Marmaţiei, *Romania* 29 C8
Sighişoara, *Romania* 29 D9
Sigli, *Indonesia* 62 C1
Siglufjörður, *Iceland* 8 C4
Sigmaringen, *Germany* 25 G5
Signa, *Italy* 40 E8
Signakhi = Tsnori, *Georgia* 35 K7
Signal, *U.S.A.* 111 L13
Signal de Botrang, *Belgium* 17 D6
Signal Pk., *U.S.A.* 111 M12
Signy I., *Antarctica* 5 C18
Signy-l'Abbaye, *France* 19 C11
Sigsig, *Ecuador* 124 D3
Sigüenza, *Spain* 38 D2
Siguiri, *Guinea* 82 C3
Sigulda, *Latvia* 9 H21
Sihanoukville = Kampong Saom, *Cambodia* 65 G4
Sihora, *India* 69 H9
Sihui, *China* 59 F9
Siikajoki →, *Finland* 8 D21
Siilinjärvi, *Finland* 8 E22
Siirt, *Turkey* 73 D9
Sijarira Ra. = Chizarira, *Zimbabwe* 87 F2
Sika, *India* 68 H3
Sikani Chief →, *Canada* 102 B4
Sikao, *Thailand* 65 J2
Sikar, *India* 68 F6
Sikasso, *Mali* 82 C3
Sikeston, *U.S.A.* 113 G10
Sikhote Alin, Khrebet, *Russia* 53 E14
Sikhote Alin Ra. = Sikhote Alin, Khrebet, *Russia* 53 E14
Sikiá., *Greece* 44 F7
Síkinos, *Greece* 47 E7
Sikkim □, *India* 67 F16
Siklós, *Hungary* 28 E3
Sil →, *Spain* 36 C3
Silacayoapan, *Mexico* 119 D5
Šilalė, *Lithuania* 30 C9
Silandro, *Italy* 40 B7
Silawad, *India* 68 J6
Silay, *Phil.* 61 F5
Silba, *Croatia* 41 D11
Silchar, *India* 67 G18
Şile, *Turkey* 45 E13
Siler City, *U.S.A.* 115 H6
Silgarhi Doti, *Nepal* 69 E9
Silghat, *India* 67 F18
Sili, *Burkina Faso* 82 C4
Silifke, *Turkey* 70 B2
Siliguri = Shiliguri, *India* 67 F16
Siling Co, *China* 60 C3
Silistea Nouă, *Romania* 29 F10
Silistra, *Bulgaria* 45 B11
Silivri, *Turkey* 45 E12
Siljan, *Sweden* 10 D8
Siljansnäs, *Sweden* 10 D8
Silkeborg, *Denmark* 11 H3
Silkwood, *Australia* 94 B4
Silla, *Spain* 39 F4
Sillajhuay, Cordillera, *Chile* 124 G5
Sillamäe, *Estonia* 9 G22
Sillé-le-Guillaume, *France* 18 D6
Silleda, *Spain* 36 C2
Silloth, *U.K.* 14 C4
Sílo, *Greece* 45 E9
Siloam Springs, *U.S.A.* 113 G7
Silopi, *Turkey* 73 D10
Silsbee, *U.S.A.* 113 K7
Siluko, *Nigeria* 83 D6
Šilutė, *Lithuania* 9 J19
Silva Porto = Kuito, *Angola* 85 G3
Silvan, *Turkey* 73 C9
Silvani, *India* 69 H8
Silver City, *U.S.A.* 109 K9
Silver Cr. →, *U.S.A.* 108 E4
Silver Creek, *U.S.A.* 116 D5
Silver L., *U.S.A.* 110 G6
Silver Lake, *Calif., U.S.A.* 111 K10
Silver Lake, *Oreg., U.S.A.* 108 E3
Silverdalen, *Sweden* 11 G9
Silverton, *Colo., U.S.A.* 109 H10
Silverton, *Tex., U.S.A.* 113 H4
Silves, *Portugal* 37 H2
Silvi Marina, *Italy* 41 F11
Silvies →, *U.S.A.* 108 E4
Silvrettahorn, *Switz.* 40 B7
Silwa Bahari, *Egypt* 80 C3
Silz, *Austria* 26 D3
Simaltala, *India* 69 G12
Simanggang = Bandar Sri Aman, *Malaysia* 62 D4
Simao, *China* 58 F3
Simard, L., *Canada* 104 C4
Şīmareh →, *Iran* 73 F12
Simav, *Turkey* 47 B10
Simav →, *Turkey* 45 F12
Simav Dağları, *Turkey* 47 B10
Simba, *Tanzania* 86 C4
Simbach, *Germany* 25 G9
Simbirsk, *Russia* 34 C9
Simbo, *Tanzania* 86 C2
Simcoe, *Canada* 116 D4
Simcoe, L., *Canada* 116 B5
Simdega, *India* 69 H11
Simeonovgrad, *Bulgaria* 45 D9
Simeria, *Romania* 28 E8
Simeto →, *Italy* 43 E8
Simeulue, *Indonesia* 62 D1
Simferopol, *Ukraine* 33 K8
Sími, *Greece* 47 E9
Simi Valley, *U.S.A.* 111 L8
Simien Mts. △, *Ethiopia* 81 E4
Simikot, *Nepal* 69 E9
Simitli, *Bulgaria* 44 E7
Simla, *India* 68 D7
Simlångsdalen, *Sweden* 11 H7
Şimleu-Silvaniei, *Romania* 28 C7
Simmern, *Germany* 25 F3
Simmie, *Canada* 103 D7
Simmler, *U.S.A.* 111 K7
Simnas, *Lithuania* 30 D10
Simojoki →, *Finland* 8 D21
Simojovel, *Mexico* 119 D6
Simonette →, *Canada* 102 B5
Simonstown, *S. Africa* 88 E2
Simontornya, *Hungary* 28 D3
Simpang Empat, *Malaysia* 65 c
Simplonpass, *Switz.* 25 J4
Simplontunnel, *Switz.* 25 J4
Simpson Desert, *Australia* 94 D2
Simpson Desert △, *Australia* 94 C2
Simpson Pen., *Canada* 101 B11
Simpungdong, *N. Korea* 57 D15
Simrishamn, *Sweden* 11 J8
Simsbury, *U.S.A.* 117 E12
Simushir, Ostrov, *Russia* 53 E16
Sin Cowe I., *S. China Sea* 62 C4
Sinabang, *Indonesia* 62 D1
Sinadogo, *Somali Rep.* 75 F4
Sinai = Es Sînâ', *Egypt* 74 F3
Sinai, Mt. = Mûsa, Gebel, *Egypt* 70 D2
Sinai Peninsula, *Egypt* 50 G7
Sinaia, *Romania* 29 E10
Sinaloa □, *Mexico* 118 C3
Sinaloa de Leyva, *Mexico* 118 B3
Sinalunga, *Italy* 41 E8
Sinan, *China* 58 D7
Sînandrei, *Romania* 28 E6
Sinarádhes, *Greece* 49 A3
Sincan, *Turkey* 72 B5
Sincanlı, *Turkey* 47 C12
Sincelejo, *Colombia* 124 B3
Sinch'ang, *N. Korea* 57 D15
Sinchang-ni, *N. Korea* 57 E14
Sinclair, *U.S.A.* 108 F10
Sinclair Mills, *Canada* 102 C4
Sinclair's B., *U.K.* 13 C5
Sinclairville, *U.S.A.* 116 D5
Sincorá, Serra do, *Brazil* 125 F10
Sind, *Pakistan* 68 G3
Sind □, *Pakistan* 68 G3
Sind →, *Jammu & Kashmir, India* 69 B6
Sind →, *Mad. P., India* 69 F8
Sind Sagar Doab, *Pakistan* 68 D4
Sindal, *Denmark* 11 G4
Sindangan, *Phil.* 61 G5
Sindangbarang, *Indonesia* 63 G12
Sinde, *Zambia* 87 F2
Sindelfingen, *Germany* 25 G4

Sindh = Sind □, *Pakistan* 68 G3
Sındırgı, *Turkey* 47 B10
Sindou, *Burkina Faso* 82 C3
Sindri, *India* 69 H12
Sine ➛, *Senegal* 82 C1
Sinegorskiy, *Russia* 35 G5
Sinekli, *Turkey* 45 E12
Sinelnikovo = Synelnykove, *Ukraine* 33 H8
Sinendé, *Benin* 83 C5
Sines, *Portugal* 37 H2
Sines, C. de, *Portugal* 37 H2
Sineu, *Spain* 48 B10
Sinfra, *Ivory C.* 82 D3
Sing Buri, *Thailand* 64 E3
Singa, *Sudan* 81 E3
Singapore ■, *Asia* 65 d
Singapore, Straits of, *Asia* 65 d
Singapore Changi ✕ (SIN), *Singapore* 65 M4
Singaraja, *Indonesia* 63 J18
Singen, *Germany* 25 H4
Singida, *Tanzania* 86 C3
Singida □, *Tanzania* 86 D3
Singitikós Kólpos, *Greece* 44 F7
Singkaling Hkamti, *Burma* 67 G19
Singkang, *Indonesia* 63 E6
Singkawang, *Indonesia* 62 D3
Singkep, *Indonesia* 62 E2
Singleton, *Australia* 95 E5
Singleton, Mt., *N. Terr., Australia* 92 D5
Singleton, Mt., *W. Austral., Australia* 93 E2
Singö, *Sweden* 10 D12
Singoli, *India* 68 G6
Singora = Songkhla, *Thailand* 65 J3
Singosan, *N. Korea* 57 E14
Sinhung, *N. Korea* 57 D14
Siniátsikon, Óros, *Greece* 44 F5
Siniscóla, *Italy* 42 B2
Sinj, *Croatia* 41 E13
Sinjai, *Indonesia* 63 F6
Sinjajevina, *Serbia & M.* 44 D3
Sinjār, *Iraq* 70 B4
Sinkat, *Sudan* 80 D4
Sinkiang Uighur = Xinjiang Uygur Zizhiqu □, *China* 60 B3
Sinmak, *N. Korea* 57 E14
Sínnai, *Italy* 42 C2
Sinnamary, *Fr. Guiana* 125 B8
Sinni ➛, *Italy* 43 B9
Sinnuris, *Egypt* 80 J7
Sinoie, Lacul, *Romania* 29 F13
Sinop, *Turkey* 72 A6
Sinor, *India* 68 J5
Sinp'o, *N. Korea* 57 E15
Sinsheim, *Germany* 25 F4
Sinsk, *Russia* 53 C13
Sintang, *Indonesia* 62 D4
Sinton, *U.S.A.* 113 L6
Sintra, *Portugal* 37 G1
Sintra-Cascais ⌓, *Portugal* 37 G1
Sinŭiju, *N. Korea* 57 D13
Sinyukha ➛, *Ukraine* 33 H6
Sinzig, *Germany* 24 E3
Sio ➛, *Hungary* 28 D3
Siocon, *Phil.* 61 H5
Siófok, *Hungary* 28 D3
Sion, *Switz.* 25 J3
Sion Mills, *U.K.* 12 B4
Sioux City, *U.S.A.* 112 D6
Sioux Falls, *U.S.A.* 112 D6
Sioux Lookout, *Canada* 104 B1
Sioux Narrows, *Canada* 103 D10
Sipalay, *Phil.* 61 G5
Šipan, *Croatia* 44 D1
Siparia, *Trin. & Tob.* 125 K15
Sipil Daği △, *Turkey* 47 C9
Siping, *China* 57 C13
Sipiwesk L., *Canada* 103 B9
Siple, *Antarctica* 5 D7
Šipovo, *Bos.-H.* 28 F2
Sipra ➛, *India* 68 H6
Sipura, *Indonesia* 62 E1
Siquia ➛, *Nic.* 120 D3
Siquijor, *Phil.* 61 G5
Siquirres, *Costa Rica* 120 D3
Şīr Abu Nu'ayr, *U.A.E.* 71 E7
Şīr Banī Yās, *U.A.E.* 71 E7
Sir Edward Pellew Group, *Australia* 94 B2
Sir Graham Moore Is., *Australia* 92 B4
Sir James MacBrien, Mt., *Canada* 100 B7
Sira ➛, *Norway* 9 G12
Siracusa, *Italy* 43 E8
Sirajganj, *Bangla.* 69 G13
Sirakoro, *Mali* 82 C3
Şiran, *Turkey* 73 B8
Sirasso, *Ivory C.* 82 D3
Sirathu, *India* 69 G9
Sīrdān, *Iran* 71 B6
Sirdaryo = Syrdarya ➛, *Kazakhstan* 52 E7
Sire, *Ethiopia* 81 F4
Siren, *U.S.A.* 112 C8
Sirente-Velino ⌓, *Italy* 41 F10
Sirer, *Spain* 48 C7
Siret, *Romania* 29 C11
Siret ➛, *Romania* 29 E12
Sirghāyā, *Syria* 74 B5
Şiria, *Romania* 28 D6
Sirinath △, *Thailand* 65 a
Sirino, Mte., *Italy* 43 B8
Sīrjān, *Iran* 71 D7
Sirmaur, *India* 69 G9
Sírna, *Greece* 47 E8
Şirnak, *Turkey* 73 D10
Sirohi, *India* 68 G5
Sironj, *India* 68 G7
Síros, *Greece* 46 D6
Sirretta Pk., *U.S.A.* 111 K8
Sīrrī, *Iran* 71 E7
Sirsa, *India* 68 E6
Sirsa ➛, *India* 69 F8
Siruela, *Spain* 37 G5
Sisak, *Croatia* 41 C13
Sisaket, *Thailand* 64 E5
Sisante, *Spain* 39 F2
Sisargas, Is., *Spain* 36 B2
Sishen, *S. Africa* 88 D3
Sishui, *Henan, China* 56 G7
Sishui, *Shandong, China* 57 G9
Sisipuk L., *Canada* 103 B8
Sisophon, *Cambodia* 64 F4
Sisseton, *U.S.A.* 112 C6
Sissonne, *France* 19 C10
Sīstān, *Asia* 71 D9
Sīstān, Daryācheh-ye, *Iran* 71 D9
Sīstān va Balūchestān □, *Iran* 71 E9
Sisteron, *France* 21 D9
Sisters, *U.S.A.* 108 D3
Siswa Bazar, *India* 69 F10
Sitakili, *Mali* 82 C2
Sitamarhi, *India* 69 F11
Sitampiky, *Madag.* 89 B8
Sitapur, *India* 69 F9
Siteki, *Swaziland* 89 D5
Sitges, *Spain* 38 D6
Sithoniá, *Greece* 44 F7
Sitía, *Greece* 49 D8
Sitka, *U.S.A.* 102 B1
Sitoti, *Botswana* 88 C3
Sitra, *Egypt* 80 B2
Sittang Myit ➛, *Burma* 67 L20
Sittard, *Neths.* 17 C5
Sittensen, *Germany* 24 B5
Sittingbourne, *U.K.* 15 F8
Sittona, *Eritrea* 81 E4
Sittoung = Sittang Myit ➛, *Burma* 67 L20
Sittwe, *Burma* 67 J18
Situbondo, *Indonesia* 63 G16
Siuna, *Nic.* 120 D3
Siuri, *India* 69 H12
Siutghiol, Lacul, *Romania* 29 F13
Sīvand, *Iran* 71 D7
Sivas, *Turkey* 70 B3
Sivaslı, *Turkey* 47 C11
Siverek, *Turkey* 70 B3
Sivrihisar, *Turkey* 72 C4
Sīwa, *Egypt* 80 B2
Sīwa, El Wâhât es, *Egypt* 80 B2
Siwa Oasis = Sīwa, El Wâhât es, *Egypt* 80 B2
Siwalik Range, *Nepal* 69 F10
Siwan, *India* 69 F11
Siwana, *India* 68 G5
Six Cross Roads, *Barbados* 121 g
Sixmilebridge, *Ireland* 12 D3
Sixth Cataract, *Sudan* 81 D3
Siyāl, Jazā'ir, *Egypt* 80 C4
Siyäzän, *Azerbaijan* 35 K9
Siziwang Qi, *China* 56 D6
Sjælland, *Denmark* 11 J5
Sjællands Odde, *Denmark* 11 J5
Sjenica, *Serbia & M.* 44 C3
Sjöbo, *Sweden* 11 J7
Sjötofta, *Sweden* 11 G7
Sjötorp, *Sweden* 11 F8
Sjumen = Shumen, *Bulgaria* 45 C10
Sjuntorp, *Sweden* 11 F6
Skadarsko Jezero, *Serbia & M.* 44 D3
Skadovsk, *Ukraine* 33 J7
Skælskør, *Denmark* 11 J5
Skærbæk, *Denmark* 11 J2
Skaftafell, *Iceland* 8 D5
Skagafjörður, *Iceland* 8 D4
Skagastølstindane, *Norway* 9 F12
Skagaströnd, *Iceland* 8 D3
Skagen, *Denmark* 11 G4
Skagern, *Sweden* 10 F8
Skagerrak, *Denmark* 11 G2
Skagit ➛, *U.S.A.* 110 B4
Skagway, *U.S.A.* 100 C6
Skala-Podilska, *Ukraine* 33 H4
Skala Podolskaya = Skala-Podilska, *Ukraine* 33 H4
Skalat, *Ukraine* 33 H3
Skalbmierz, *Poland* 31 H7
Skälderviken, *Sweden* 11 H6
Skalica, *Slovak Rep.* 27 C10
Skallingen, *Denmark* 11 J2
Skalni Dol = Kamenyak, *Bulgaria* 45 C10
Skanderborg, *Denmark* 11 H3
Skåne, *Sweden* 11 J7
Skåne län □, *Sweden* 11 H7
Skaneateles, *U.S.A.* 117 D8
Skaneateles L., *U.S.A.* 117 D8
Skänninge, *Sweden* 11 F9
Skanör med Falsterbo, *Sweden* 11 J6
Skantzoúra, *Greece* 46 B6
Skara, *Sweden* 11 F7
Skärblacka, *Sweden* 11 F9
Skardu, *Pakistan* 69 B6
Skåre, *Sweden* 10 E7
Skärhamn, *Sweden* 11 G5
Skarszewy, *Poland* 30 D5
Skaryszew, *Poland* 31 G8
Skarżysko-Kamienna, *Poland* 31 G7
Skattkärr, *Sweden* 10 E7
Skattungbyn, *Sweden* 10 C8
Skawina, *Poland* 31 J6
Skebobruk, *Sweden* 10 E12
Skeena ➛, *Canada* 102 C2
Skeena Mts., *Canada* 102 B3
Skegness, *U.K.* 14 D8
Skeldon, *Guyana* 124 B7
Skeleton Coast ⌓, *Namibia* 88 C1
Skellefte älv ➛, *Sweden* 8 D19
Skellefteå, *Sweden* 8 D19
Skelleftehamn, *Sweden* 8 D19
Skender Vakuf, *Bos.-H.* 28 F2
Skerries, The, *U.K.* 14 D3
Skhíza, *Greece* 46 E3
Skhoinoúsa, *Greece* 47 E7
Ski, *Norway* 9 G14
Skíathos, *Greece* 46 B5
Skibbereen, *Ireland* 12 E2
Skiddaw, *U.K.* 14 C4
Skidegate, *Canada* 102 C2
Skídhra, *Greece* 44 F6
Skien, *Norway* 9 G13
Skierniewice, *Poland* 31 G7
Skikda, *Algeria* 78 A7
Skillingaryd, *Sweden* 11 G8
Skillinge, *Sweden* 11 J8
Skilloura, *Cyprus* 49 D12
Skinári, Ákra, *Greece* 46 D2
Skinnskatteberg, *Sweden* 10 E9
Skipton, *U.K.* 14 D5
Skiring, C., *Senegal* 82 C1
Skirmish Pt., *Australia* 94 A1
Skiropoúla, *Greece* 46 C6
Skíros, *Greece* 46 C6
Skivarp, *Sweden* 11 J7
Skive, *Denmark* 11 H3
Skjálfandafljót ➛, *Iceland* 8 D5
Skjálfandi, *Iceland* 8 C5
Skjern, *Denmark* 11 J2
Skoczów, *Poland* 31 J5
Škofja Loka, *Slovenia* 41 B11
Skoghall, *Sweden* 10 E7
Skogstorp, *Sweden* 10 E10
Skoki, *Poland* 31 F4
Skole, *Ukraine* 33 H2
Skópelos, *Greece* 46 B5
Skopí, *Greece* 49 D8
Skopin, *Russia* 32 F10
Skopje, *Macedonia* 44 D5
Skopje ✕ (SKP), *Macedonia* 44 E5
Skórcz, *Poland* 30 E5
Skørping, *Denmark* 11 H3
Skövde, *Sweden* 11 F7
Skovorodino, *Russia* 53 D13
Skowhegan, *U.S.A.* 115 C11
Skradin, *Croatia* 41 E12
Skrea, *Sweden* 11 H6
Skrunda, *Latvia* 30 B9
Skrwa ➛, *Poland* 31 F6
Skuleskogen △, *Sweden* 10 A12
Skull, *Ireland* 12 E2
Skultorp, *Sweden* 11 F7
Skultuna, *Sweden* 10 E10
Skunk ➛, *U.S.A.* 112 E9
Skuodas, *Lithuania* 9 H19
Skurup, *Sweden* 11 J7
Skutskär, *Sweden* 10 D11
Skvyra, *Ukraine* 33 H5
Skwierzyna, *Poland* 31 F2
Skye, *U.K.* 13 D2
Skykomish, *U.S.A.* 108 C3
Skyros = Skíros, *Greece* 46 C6
Skyttorp, *Sweden* 10 D11
Slade Pt., *Australia* 94 K7
Slættaratindur, *Færoe Is.* 8 E9
Slagelse, *Denmark* 11 J5
Slamet, *Indonesia* 63 G13
Slaney ➛, *Ireland* 12 D5
Slangberge, *S. Africa* 88 E3
Slănic, *Romania* 29 E10
Slano, *Croatia* 44 D1
Slantsy, *Russia* 32 C5
Slaný, *Czech Rep.* 26 A7
Śląskie □, *Poland* 31 H6
Slätbaken, *Sweden* 11 F10
Slate Is., *Canada* 104 C2
Slatina, *Croatia* 28 E2
Slatina, *Romania* 29 F9
Slatina Timiş, *Romania* 28 E7
Slatington, *U.S.A.* 117 F9
Slaton, *U.S.A.* 113 J4
Slave ➛, *Canada* 102 A6
Slave Coast, *W. Afr.* 83 D5
Slave Lake, *Canada* 102 B6
Slave Pt., *Canada* 102 A5
Slavgorod, *Russia* 52 D8
Slavinja, *Serbia & M.* 44 C6
Slavkov u Brna, *Czech Rep.* 27 B9
Slavkovský Les ⌓, *Czech Rep.* 26 A5
Slavonija, *Europe* 28 E2
Slavonski Brod, *Croatia* 28 E3
Slavuta, *Ukraine* 33 G4
Slavyanka, *Russia* 54 C5
Slavyanovo, *Bulgaria* 45 C8
Slavyansk = Slovyansk, *Ukraine* 33 H9
Slavyansk-na-Kubani, *Russia* 33 K10
Sława, *Poland* 31 G3
Slawharad, *Belarus* 32 F6
Sławno, *Poland* 30 D3
Sławoborze, *Poland* 30 E2
Sleaford, *U.K.* 14 D7
Sleaford B., *Australia* 95 E2
Sleat, Sd. of, *U.K.* 13 D3
Sleeper Is., *Canada* 101 C11
Sleeping Bear Dunes ⌓, *U.S.A.* 114 C2
Sleepy Eye, *U.S.A.* 112 C7
Slemon L., *Canada* 102 A5
Ślesin, *Poland* 31 F5
Slide Mt., *U.S.A.* 117 E10
Slidell, *U.S.A.* 113 K10
Sliema, *Malta* 49 D2
Slieve Aughty, *Ireland* 12 C3
Slieve Bloom, *Ireland* 12 C4
Slieve Donard, *U.K.* 12 B6
Slieve Gamph, *Ireland* 12 B3
Slieve Gullion, *U.K.* 12 B5
Slieve League, *Ireland* 12 B3
Slieve Mish, *Ireland* 12 D2
Slievenamon, *Ireland* 12 D4
Sligeach = Sligo, *Ireland* 12 B3
Sligo, *Ireland* 12 B3
Sligo, *U.S.A.* 116 E5
Sligo □, *Ireland* 12 B3
Sligo B., *Ireland* 12 B3
Slippery Rock, *U.S.A.* 116 E4
Slite, *Sweden* 11 G12
Slīteres ⌓, *Latvia* 30 A9
Sliven, *Bulgaria* 45 D10
Slivnitsa, *Bulgaria* 44 D7
Sljeme, *Croatia* 41 C12
Sloan, *U.S.A.* 111 K11
Sloansville, *U.S.A.* 117 D10
Slobozia, *Moldova* 29 D14
Slobozia, *Argeş, Romania* 29 F10
Slobozia, *Ialomiţa, Romania* 29 F12
Slocan, *Canada* 102 D5
Słomniki, *Poland* 31 H7
Slonim, *Belarus* 33 F3
Slough, *U.K.* 15 F7
Slough □, *U.K.* 15 F7
Sloughhouse, *U.S.A.* 110 G5
Slovak Rep. ■, *Europe* 27 C13
Slovakia = Slovak Rep. ■, *Europe* 27 C13
Slovakian Ore Mts. = Slovenské Rudohorie, *Slovak Rep.* 27 C12
Slovenia ■, *Europe* 41 C11
Slovenija = Slovenia ■, *Europe* 41 C11
Slovenj Gradec, *Slovenia* 41 B12
Slovenska Bistrica, *Slovenia* 41 B12
Slovenske Konjice, *Slovenia* 41 B12
Slovenské Rudohorie, *Slovak Rep.* 27 C12
Slovenský Raj △, *Slovak Rep.* 27 C13
Slovyansk, *Ukraine* 33 H9
Słowiński △, *Poland* 30 D4
Słubice, *Poland* 31 F1
Sluch ➛, *Ukraine* 33 G4
Sluis, *Neths.* 17 C3
Slŭnchev Bryag, *Bulgaria* 45 D11
Slunj, *Croatia* 41 C12
Słupca, *Poland* 31 F4
Słupia ➛, *Poland* 30 D3
Słupsk, *Poland* 30 D4
Slurry, *S. Africa* 88 D4
Slutsk, *Belarus* 33 F4
Slyne Hd., *Ireland* 12 C1
Slyudyanka, *Russia* 53 D11
Småland, *Sweden* 11 G9
Smålandsfarvandet, *Denmark* 11 J5
Smålandsstenar, *Sweden* 11 G7
Smalltree L., *Canada* 103 A8
Smallwood Res., *Canada* 105 B7
Smarhon, *Belarus* 32 E4
Smarje, *Slovenia* 41 B12
Smartt Syndicate Dam, *S. Africa* 88 E3
Smartville, *U.S.A.* 110 F5
Smeaton, *Canada* 103 C8
Smedby, *Sweden* 11 H10
Smederevo, *Serbia & M.* 44 B4
Smederevska Palanka, *Serbia & M.* 44 B4
Smedjebacken, *Sweden* 10 D9
Smela = Smila, *Ukraine* 33 H6
Smerwick Harbour, *Ireland* 12 D1
Smethport, *U.S.A.* 116 E6
Smidovich, *Russia* 53 E14
Śmigiel, *Poland* 31 F3
Smila, *Ukraine* 33 H6
Smilyan, *Bulgaria* 45 E8
Smith, *Canada* 102 B6
Smith Center, *U.S.A.* 112 F5
Smith River ⌓, *U.S.A.* 108 F2
Smith Sd., *N. Amer.* 4 B4
Smithburne ➛, *Australia* 94 B3
Smithers, *Canada* 102 C3
Smithfield, *S. Africa* 89 E4
Smithfield, *N.C., U.S.A.* 115 H6
Smithfield, *Utah, U.S.A.* 108 F8
Smiths Falls, *Canada* 117 B9
Smithton, *Australia* 95 G4
Smithville, *Canada* 116 C5
Smithville, *U.S.A.* 113 K6
Smoky ➛, *Canada* 102 B5
Smoky Bay, *Australia* 95 E1
Smoky Hill ➛, *U.S.A.* 112 F6
Smoky Hills, *U.S.A.* 112 F5
Smoky Lake, *Canada* 102 C6
Smøla, *Norway* 8 E13
Smolensk, *Russia* 32 E7
Smolikas, Óros, *Greece* 44 F4
Smolník, *Slovak Rep.* 27 C13
Smolyan, *Bulgaria* 45 E8
Smooth Rock Falls, *Canada* 104 C3
Smoothstone L., *Canada* 103 C7
Smorgon = Smarhon, *Belarus* 32 E4
Smulţi, *Romania* 29 E12
Smyadovo, *Bulgaria* 45 C11
Smygehamn, *Sweden* 11 J7
Smyrna = İzmir, *Turkey* 47 C9
Smyrna, *U.S.A.* 114 F8
Snæfell, *Iceland* 8 D6
Snaefell, *U.K.* 14 C3
Snæfellsjökull, *Iceland* 8 D2
Snake ➛, *U.S.A.* 108 C4
Snake I., *Australia* 95 F4
Snake Range, *U.S.A.* 108 G6
Snake River Plain, *U.S.A.* 108 E7
Snasahögarna, *Sweden* 10 A6
Snåsavatnet, *Norway* 8 D14
Snedsted, *Denmark* 11 H2
Sneek, *Neths.* 17 A5
Sneeuberge, *S. Africa* 88 E3
Snejbjerg, *Denmark* 11 H2
Snelling, *U.S.A.* 110 H6
Snezhnoye, *Ukraine* 33 J10
Snežnik, *Slovenia* 41 C11
Śniadowo, *Poland* 31 E8
Śniardwy, Jezioro, *Poland* 30 E8
Śnieżka, *Europe* 26 A8
Snigirevka = Snihurivka, *Ukraine* 33 J7
Snihurivka, *Ukraine* 33 J7
Snina, *Slovak Rep.* 27 C15
Snizort, L., *U.K.* 13 D2
Snøhetta, *Norway* 9 E13
Snohomish, *U.S.A.* 110 C4
Snoul, *Cambodia* 65 F6
Snow Hill, *U.S.A.* 114 F8
Snow Lake, *Canada* 103 C8
Snow Mt., *Calif., U.S.A.* 110 F4
Snow Mt., *Maine, U.S.A.* 117 A14
Snow Shoe, *U.S.A.* 116 E7
Snowbird L., *Canada* 103 A8
Snowdon, *U.K.* 14 D3
Snowdonia △, *U.K.* 14 D4
Snowdrift = Łutselk'e, *Canada* 103 A6
Snowdrift ➛, *Canada* 103 A6
Snowflake, *U.S.A.* 109 J8
Snowshoe Pk., *U.S.A.* 108 B6
Snowtown, *Australia* 95 E2
Snowville, *U.S.A.* 108 F7
Snowy ➛, *Australia* 95 F4
Snowy Mt., *U.S.A.* 117 C10
Snowy Mts., *Australia* 95 F4
Snug Corner, *Bahamas* 121 B5
Snyatyn, *Ukraine* 33 H3
Snyder, *Okla., U.S.A.* 113 H5
Snyder, *Tex., U.S.A.* 113 J4
Soahanina, *Madag.* 89 B7
Soalala, *Madag.* 89 B8
Soaloka, *Madag.* 89 B8
Soamanonga, *Madag.* 89 C7
Soan ➛, *Pakistan* 68 C4
Soanierana-Ivongo, *Madag.* 89 B8
Soanindraniny, *Madag.* 89 B8
Şoarş, *Romania* 29 E9
Soavina, *Madag.* 89 C8
Soavinandriana, *Madag.* 89 B8
Soba, *Nigeria* 83 C6
Sobat, Nahr ➛, *Sudan* 81 F3
Soběslav, *Czech Rep.* 26 B7
Sobhapur, *India* 68 H8
Sobinka, *Russia* 32 E11
Sobótka, *Poland* 31 H3
Sobra, *Croatia* 41 F14
Sobradinho, Reprêsa de, *Brazil* 125 E10
Sobral, *Brazil* 125 D10
Sobrance, *Slovak Rep.* 27 C15
Sobreira Formosa, *Portugal* 36 F3
Soc Giang, *Vietnam* 58 F6
Soc Trang, *Vietnam* 65 H5
Soča ➛, *Europe* 26 E6
Socastee, *U.S.A.* 115 J6
Sochaczew, *Poland* 31 F7
Soch'e = Shache, *China* 60 C2
Sochi, *Russia* 35 J4
Société, Is. de la, *Pac. Oc.* 97 J12
Society Is. = Société, Is. de la, *Pac. Oc.* 97 J12
Socompa, Portezuelo de, *Chile* 126 A2
Socorro, *N. Mex., U.S.A.* 109 J10
Socorro, *Tex., U.S.A.* 109 L10
Socorro, I., *Mexico* 118 D2
Socotra, *Yemen* 75 E5
Socovos, *Spain* 39 G3
Socuéllamos, *Spain* 39 F2
Soda L., *U.S.A.* 109 J5
Soda Plains, *India* 69 B8
Soda Springs, *U.S.A.* 108 E8
Sodankylä, *Finland* 8 C22
Soddy-Daisy, *U.S.A.* 115 H3
Söderala, *Sweden* 10 C10
Söderåsen △, *Sweden* 11 H7
Söderbärke, *Sweden* 10 D9
Söderfors, *Sweden* 10 D11
Söderhamn, *Sweden* 10 C11
Söderköping, *Sweden* 11 F10
Södermanland, *Sweden* 9 G17
Södermanlands län □, *Sweden* 10 E10
Södertälje, *Sweden* 10 E11
Sodiri, *Sudan* 81 E2
Sodo, *Ethiopia* 81 F4
Södra Dellen, *Sweden* 10 C10
Södra Finnskoga, *Sweden* 10 D6
Södra Sandby, *Sweden* 11 J7
Södra Ulvön, *Sweden* 10 B12
Södra Vi, *Sweden* 11 G9
Sodražica, *Slovenia* 41 C11
Sodus, *U.S.A.* 116 C7
Sodwana Bay △, *S. Africa* 89 D5
Soekmekaar, *S. Africa* 89 C4
Soest, *Germany* 24 D4
Soest, *Neths.* 17 B5
Sofádhes, *Greece* 46 B4
Sofala □, *Mozam.* 89 B5
Sofara, *Mali* 82 C4
Sofia = Sofiya, *Bulgaria* 44 D7
Sofia ➛, *Madag.* 89 B8
Sofia ✕ (SOF), *Bulgaria* 44 D7
Sofievka, *Ukraine* 33 H7
Sofikón, *Greece* 46 D5
Sofiya, *Bulgaria* 44 D7
Sofiya □, *Bulgaria* 44 D7
Sōfu-Gan, *Japan* 55 K10
Sogakofe, *Ghana* 83 D5
Sogamoso, *Colombia* 124 B4
Sogār, *Iran* 71 E8
Sögel, *Germany* 24 C3
Sogndalsfjøra, *Norway* 9 F12
Søgne, *Norway* 9 G12
Sognefjorden, *Norway* 9 F11
Söğüt, *Bilecik, Turkey* 47 A12
Söğüt, *Burdur, Turkey* 47 D11
Söğüt Dağı, *Turkey* 47 D11
Söğütköy, *Turkey* 47 E10
Sŏgwipo, *S. Korea* 57 H14
Soh, *Iran* 71 C6
Sohâg, *Egypt* 80 B3
Sohagpur, *India* 68 H8
Sŏhori, *N. Korea* 57 D15
Soignies, *Belgium* 17 D4
Soin, *Burkina Faso* 82 C4
Soira, *Eritrea* 81 E4
Soissons, *France* 19 C10
Sōja, *Japan* 55 G6
Sojat, *India* 68 G5

Sok →, *Russia* 34 D10
Sokal, *Ukraine* 33 G3
Söke, *Turkey* 47 D9
Sokelo, *Dem. Rep. of the Congo* 87 D1
Sokhós, *Greece* 44 F7
Sokhumi, *Georgia* 35 J5
Soko Banja, *Serbia & M.* 44 C5
Sokodé, *Togo* 83 D5
Sokol, *Russia* 32 C11
Sokolac, *Bos.-H.* 28 G3
Sokółka, *Poland* 30 E10
Sokolo, *Ségou, Mali* 82 C3
Sokolo, *Sikasso, Mali* 82 C3
Sokolov, *Czech Rep.* 26 A5
Sokołów Małpolski, *Poland* 31 H9
Sokołów Podlaski, *Poland* 31 F9
Sokoły, *Poland* 31 F9
Sokoto, *Nigeria* 83 C6
Sokoto □, *Nigeria* 83 C6
Sokoto →, *Nigeria* 83 C5
Sol Iletsk, *Russia* 52 D6
Sola →, *Poland* 31 H6
Solai, *Kenya* 86 B4
Solan, *India* 68 D7
Solano, *Phil.* 61 C4
Solapur, *India* 66 L9
Solca, *Romania* 29 C10
Solda Gölü, *Turkey* 47 D11
Soldăneşti, *Moldova* 29 C13
Soldeu, *Andorra* 38 C6
Soldotna, *U.S.A.* 100 B4
Soléa, *Cyprus* 49 D12
Solec Kujawski, *Poland* 31 E5
Soledad, *Colombia* 124 A4
Soledad, *U.S.A.* 110 J5
Soledad, *Venezuela* 124 B6
Solent, The, *U.K.* 15 G6
Solenzara, *France* 21 G13
Solesmes, *France* 19 B10
Solfonn, *Norway* 9 F12
Solhan, *Turkey* 70 B4
Soligorsk = Salihorsk, *Belarus* 33 F4
Solihull, *U.K.* 15 E6
Solikamsk, *Russia* 52 D6
Solila, *Madag.* 89 C8
Solimões = Amazonas →, *S. Amer.* 125 D9
Solin, *Croatia* 41 E13
Solingen, *Germany* 24 D3
Sollebrunn, *Sweden* 11 F6
Sollefteå, *Sweden* 10 A11
Sollentuna, *Sweden* 10 E11
Sóller, *Spain* 48 B9
Sollerön, *Sweden* 10 D8
Solling, *Germany* 24 D5
Solling-Vogler ⌓, *Germany* 24 D5
Solnechnogorsk, *Russia* 32 D9
Solo →, *Indonesia* 63 G15
Solofra, *Italy* 43 B7
Sologne, *France* 19 E8
Solok, *Indonesia* 62 E2
Sololá, *Guatemala* 120 D1
Solomon, N. Fork →, *U.S.A.* 112 F5
Solomon, S. Fork →, *U.S.A.* 112 F5
Solomon Is. ■, *Pac. Oc.* 96 H7
Solon, *China* 60 B7
Solon Springs, *U.S.A.* 112 B9
Solor, *Indonesia* 63 F6
Solotcha, *Russia* 32 E10
Solothurn, *Switz.* 25 H3
Solothurn □, *Switz.* 25 H3
Solsona, *Spain* 38 C6
Solt, *Hungary* 28 D4
Šolta, *Croatia* 41 E13
Solṭānābād, *Khorāsān, Iran* 71 C8
Solṭānābād, *Khorāsān, Iran* 71 B8
Soltau, *Germany* 24 C5
Soltsy, *Russia* 32 C6
Solunska Glava, *Macedonia* 44 E5
Solvang, *U.S.A.* 111 L6
Solvay, *U.S.A.* 117 C8
Sölvesborg, *Sweden* 11 H8
Solway Firth, *U.K.* 14 C4
Solwezi, *Zambia* 87 E2
Sōma, *Japan* 54 F10
Soma, *Turkey* 47 B9
Somabhula, *Zimbabwe* 89 B4
Somali Pen., *Africa* 76 F8
Somali Rep. ■, *Africa* 75 F4
Somalia = Somali Rep. ■, *Africa* 75 F4
Sombernon, *France* 19 E11
Sombor, *Serbia & M.* 28 E4
Sombra, *Canada* 116 D2
Sombrerete, *Mexico* 118 C4
Sombrero, *Anguilla* 121 C7
Şomcuta Mare, *Romania* 29 C8
Somdari, *India* 68 G5
Someido ⌓, *Spain* 36 B4
Somers, *U.S.A.* 108 B6
Somerset, *Ky., U.S.A.* 114 G3
Somerset, *Mass., U.S.A.* 117 E13
Somerset, *Pa., U.S.A.* 116 F5
Somerset □, *U.K.* 15 F5
Somerset East, *S. Africa* 88 E4
Somerset I., *Canada* 100 A10
Somerset West, *S. Africa* 88 E2
Somersworth, *U.S.A.* 117 C14
Somerton, *U.S.A.* 109 K6
Somerville, *U.S.A.* 117 F10
Someş →, *Romania* 28 C7
Someşul Mare →, *Romania* 29 C8
Somme □, *France* 19 C9
Somme →, *France* 19 B8
Somme, B. de la, *France* 18 B8
Sommen, *Jönköping, Sweden* 11 F8
Sommen, *Östergötland, Sweden* 11 F9
Sommepy-Tahure, *France* 19 C11
Sömmerda, *Germany* 24 D7
Sommesous, *France* 19 D11
Sommières, *France* 21 E8
Somnath, *India* 68 J4
Somogy □, *Hungary* 28 D2
Somogyszob, *Hungary* 28 D2
Somoto, *Nic.* 120 D2
Sompolno, *Poland* 31 F5
Somport, Puerto de, *Spain* 38 C4
Son →, *India* 69 G11
Son Ha, *Vietnam* 64 E7
Son Hoa, *Vietnam* 64 F7
Son La, *Vietnam* 58 G4
Son Serra, *Spain* 48 B10
Son Servera, *Spain* 38 F8
Son Tay, *Vietnam* 58 G5
Soná, *Panama* 120 E3
Sonamarg, *India* 69 B6
Sonamukhi, *India* 69 H12
Sonar →, *India* 69 G8
Sŏnch'ŏn, *N. Korea* 57 E13
Sondags →, *S. Africa* 88 E4
Sóndalo, *Italy* 40 B7
Sondar, *India* 69 C6
Sønder Felding, *Denmark* 11 J2
Sønder Omme, *Denmark* 11 J2
Sønderborg, *Denmark* 11 K3
Sønderjyllands Amtskommune □, *Denmark* 11 J3
Sondershausen, *Germany* 24 D6
Sóndrio, *Italy* 40 B6
Sone, *Mozam.* 87 F3
Sonepur, *India* 67 J13
Song, *Nigeria* 83 D7
Song, *Thailand* 64 C3
Song Cau, *Vietnam* 64 F7
Song Xian, *China* 56 G7
Songan, *Indonesia* 63 J18
Songch'ŏn, *N. Korea* 57 E14
Songea, *Tanzania* 87 E4
Songeons, *France* 19 C8
Songhua Hu, *China* 57 C14
Songhua Jiang →, *China* 60 B8
Songimvelo ⌓, *S. Africa* 89 D5
Songjiang, *China* 59 B13
Songjin, *N. Korea* 57 D15
Songjŏng-ni, *S. Korea* 57 G14
Songkan, *China* 58 C6
Songkhla, *Thailand* 65 J3
Songming, *China* 58 E4
Songnim, *N. Korea* 57 E13
Songo, *Mozam.* 85 H6
Songo, *Sudan* 79 G10
Songpan, *China* 58 A4
Songtao, *China* 58 C7
Songwe, *Dem. Rep. of the Congo* 86 C2
Songwe →, *Africa* 87 D3
Songxi, *China* 59 D12
Songzi, *China* 59 B8
Sonhat, *India* 69 H10
Sonid Youqi, *China* 56 C7
Sonipat, *India* 68 E7
Sonkach, *India* 68 H7
Sonkovo, *Russia* 32 D9
Sonmiani, *Pakistan* 68 G2
Sonmiani B., *Pakistan* 68 G2
Sonnino, *Italy* 42 A6
Sono →, *Brazil* 125 E9
Sonoma, *U.S.A.* 110 G4
Sonora, *Calif., U.S.A.* 110 H6
Sonora, *Tex., U.S.A.* 113 K4
Sonora □, *Mexico* 118 B2
Sonora →, *Mexico* 118 B2
Sonoran Desert, *U.S.A.* 111 L12
Sonoyta, *Mexico* 118 A2
Sonqor, *Iran* 73 E12
Sŏnsan, *S. Korea* 57 F15
Sonseca, *Spain* 37 F7
Sonsonate, *El Salv.* 120 D2
Sonstorp, *Sweden* 11 F9
Sonthofen, *Germany* 25 H6
Soochow = Suzhou, *China* 59 B13
Sooke, *Canada* 110 B3
Sop Hao, *Laos* 58 G5
Sop Prap, *Thailand* 64 D2
Sopelana, *Spain* 38 B2
Sopi, *Indonesia* 63 D7
Sopo, Nahr →, *Sudan* 81 F2
Sopot, *Bulgaria* 45 D8
Sopot, *Poland* 30 D5
Sopot, *Serbia & M.* 44 B4
Sopotnica, *Macedonia* 44 E5
Sopron, *Hungary* 28 C1
Sopur, *India* 69 B6
Sør-Rondane, *Antarctica* 5 D4
Sora, *Italy* 41 G10
Sorah, *Pakistan* 68 F3
Soråker, *Sweden* 10 B11
Sorano, *Italy* 41 F8
Soraon, *India* 69 G9
Sorbas, *Spain* 39 H2
Sörbygden, *Sweden* 10 B10
Sore, *France* 20 D3
Sorel-Tracy, *Canada* 104 C5
Soresina, *Italy* 40 C6
Sörforsa, *Sweden* 10 C10
Sórgono, *Italy* 42 B2
Sorgues, *France* 21 D8
Sorgun, *Turkey* 72 C6
Soria, *Spain* 38 D2
Soria □, *Spain* 38 D2
Soriano, *Uruguay* 126 C4
Soriano nel Cimino, *Italy* 41 F9
Sorkh, Kuh-e, *Iran* 71 C8
Sorø, *Denmark* 11 J5
Soro, *Guinea* 82 C3
Soroca, *Moldova* 29 B13
Sorocaba, *Brazil* 127 A6
Soroki = Soroca, *Moldova* 29 B13
Sorong, *Indonesia* 63 E8
Soroní, *Greece* 49 C10
Soroti, *Uganda* 86 B3
Sørøya, *Norway* 8 A20
Sørøysundet, *Norway* 8 A20
Sorraia →, *Portugal* 37 G2
Sorrell, *Australia* 95 G4
Sorrento, *Italy* 43 B7
Sorsele, *Sweden* 8 D17
Sörsjön, *Sweden* 10 C7
Sorso, *Italy* 42 B1
Sorsogon, *Phil.* 61 E6
Sortavala, *Russia* 32 B6
Sortino, *Italy* 43 E8
Sortland, *Norway* 8 B16
Sorvizhi, *Russia* 34 B9
Sos = Sos del Rey Católico, *Spain* 38 C3
Sos del Rey Católico, *Spain* 38 C3
Sŏsan, *S. Korea* 57 F14
Soscumica, L., *Canada* 104 B4
Sösdala, *Sweden* 11 H7
Sosna →, *Russia* 33 F10
Sosnovka, *Kirov, Russia* 34 B10
Sosnovka, *Tambov, Russia* 34 D5
Sosnovyy Bor, *Russia* 32 C5
Sosnowiec, *Poland* 31 H6
Sospel, *France* 21 E11
Sossus Vlei, *Namibia* 88 C2
Šoštanj, *Slovenia* 41 B12
Sŏsura, *N. Korea* 57 C16
Sot →, *India* 69 F8
Sotkamo, *Finland* 8 D23
Soto del Barco, *Spain* 36 B4
Soto la Marina →, *Mexico* 119 C5
Soto y Amío, *Spain* 36 C5
Sotrondio, *Spain* 36 B5
Sotuta, *Mexico* 119 C7
Souanké, *Congo* 84 D2
Soubré, *Ivory C.* 82 D3
Souderton, *U.S.A.* 117 F9
Soúdha, *Greece* 49 D6
Soúdhas, Kólpos, *Greece* 49 D6
Souflíon, *Greece* 45 E10
Soufrière, *Guadeloupe* 120 b
Soufrière, *St. Lucia* 121 f
Soufrière Bay, *Domin.* 121 f
Souillac, *France* 20 D5
Souilly, *France* 19 C12
Soukhouma, *Laos* 64 E5
Sŏul, *S. Korea* 57 F14
Soulac-sur-Mer, *France* 20 C2
Soulougou, *Burkina Faso* 83 C5
Soultz-sous-Forêts, *France* 19 D14
Sound, The = Øresund, *Europe* 11 J6
Sound, The, *U.K.* 15 G3
Soúnion, Ákra, *Greece* 46 D6
Sources, Mt. aux, *Lesotho* 89 D4
Soure, *Brazil* 125 D9
Soure, *Portugal* 36 E2
Souris, *Man., Canada* 103 D8
Souris, *P.E.I., Canada* 105 C7
Souris →, *Canada* 112 A5
Sourou →, *Africa* 82 C4
Soúrpi, *Greece* 46 B4
Sousa, *Brazil* 125 E11
Sousel, *Portugal* 37 G3
Sousse, *Tunisia* 79 A8
Soustons, *France* 20 E2
Sout →, *S. Africa* 88 E2
South Africa ■, *Africa* 88 E3
South America 122 E5
South Atlantic Ocean 122 H7
South Aulatsivik I., *Canada* 105 A7
South Australia □, *Australia* 95 E2
South Ayrshire □, *U.K.* 13 F4
South Baldy, *U.S.A.* 109 J10
South Bass I., *U.S.A.* 116 E2
South Bend, *Ind., U.S.A.* 114 E2
South Bend, *Wash., U.S.A.* 110 D3
South Boston, *U.S.A.* 115 G6
South Branch, *Canada* 105 C8
South Brook, *Canada* 105 C8
South Carolina □, *U.S.A.* 115 J5
South Charleston, *U.S.A.* 114 F5
South China Sea, *Asia* 62 C4
South Cumberland Is. △, *Australia* 94 J7
South Dakota □, *U.S.A.* 112 C5
South Deerfield, *U.S.A.* 117 D12
South Downs, *U.K.* 15 G7
South East C., *Australia* 95 G4
South-East Indian Rise, *Ind. Oc.* 5 B10
South East Is., *Australia* 93 F3
South Esk →, *U.K.* 13 E6
South Foreland, *U.K.* 15 F9
South Fork American →, *U.S.A.* 110 G5
South Fork Feather →, *U.S.A.* 110 F5
South Fork Grand →, *U.S.A.* 112 C3
South Fork Republican →, *U.S.A.* 112 E4
South Georgia, *Antarctica* 128 G9
South Gloucestershire □, *U.K.* 15 F5
South Hadley, *U.S.A.* 117 D12
South Haven, *U.S.A.* 114 D2
South Henik L., *Canada* 103 A9
South Honshu Ridge, *Pac. Oc.* 96 E6
South Horr, *Kenya* 86 B4
South I., *Kenya* 86 B4
South I., *N.Z.* 91 L3
South Indian Lake, *Canada* 103 B9
South Invercargill, *N.Z.* 91 M2
South Island △, *Kenya* 86 B4
South Kitui ⌓, *Kenya* 86 C4
South Knife →, *Canada* 103 B10
South Koel →, *India* 69 H11
South Korea ■, *Asia* 57 G15
South Lake Tahoe, *U.S.A.* 110 G6
South Lanarkshire □, *U.K.* 13 F5
South Loup →, *U.S.A.* 112 E5
South Luangwa △, *Zambia* 87 E3
South Magnetic Pole, *Antarctica* 5 C9
South Milwaukee, *U.S.A.* 114 D2
South Molton, *U.K.* 15 F4
South Moose L., *Canada* 103 C8
South Nahanni →, *Canada* 102 A4
South Nation →, *Canada* 117 A9
South Natuna Is. = Natuna Selatan, Kepulauan, *Indonesia* 62 D3
South Negril Pt., *Jamaica* 120 a
South Orkney Is., *Antarctica* 5 C18
South Ossetia □, *Georgia* 35 J7
South Pagai, I. = Pagai Selatan, Pulau, *Indonesia* 62 E2
South Paris, *U.S.A.* 117 B14
South Pittsburg, *U.S.A.* 115 H3
South Platte →, *U.S.A.* 112 E4
South Pole, *Antarctica* 5 E
South Porcupine, *Canada* 104 C3
South Portland, *U.S.A.* 115 D10
South Pt., *Barbados* 121 g
South Pt., *U.S.A.* 116 B1
South River, *Canada* 104 C4
South River, *U.S.A.* 117 F10
South Ronaldsay, *U.K.* 13 C6
South Sandwich Is., *Antarctica* 5 B1
South Saskatchewan →, *Canada* 103 C7
South Seal →, *Canada* 103 B9
South Shetland Is., *Antarctica* 5 C18
South Shields, *U.K.* 14 C6
South Sioux City, *U.S.A.* 112 D6
South Taranaki Bight, *N.Z.* 91 H5
South Thompson →, *Canada* 102 C4
South Twin I., *Canada* 104 B4
South Tyne →, *U.K.* 14 C5
South Uist, *U.K.* 13 D1
South West Africa = Namibia ■, *Africa* 88 C2
South West C., *Australia* 95 G4
South Williamsport, *U.S.A.* 116 E8
South Yorkshire □, *U.K.* 14 D6
Southampton, *Canada* 116 B3
Southampton, *U.K.* 15 G6
Southampton, *U.S.A.* 117 F12
Southampton □, *U.K.* 15 G6
Southampton I., *Canada* 101 B11
Southaven, *U.S.A.* 113 H9
Southbank, *Canada* 102 C3
Southbridge, *N.Z.* 91 K4
Southbridge, *U.S.A.* 117 D12
Southeast Pacific Basin, *Pac. Oc.* 5 C15
Southend, *Canada* 103 B8
Southend-on-Sea, *U.K.* 15 F8
Southend-on-Sea □, *U.K.* 15 F8
Southern = Yuzhnyy □, *Russia* 35 H5
Southern □, *Malawi* 87 F4
Southern □, *S. Leone* 82 D2
Southern △, *Sudan* 81 F2
Southern □, *Zambia* 87 F2
Southern Alps, *N.Z.* 91 K3
Southern Cross, *Australia* 93 F2
Southern Indian L., *Canada* 103 B9
Southern Ocean, *Antarctica* 5 C6
Southern Pines, *U.S.A.* 115 H6
Southern Uplands, *U.K.* 13 F5
Southington, *U.S.A.* 117 E12
Southland □, *N.Z.* 91 L1
Southold, *U.S.A.* 117 E12
Southport, *Australia* 95 D5
Southport, *U.K.* 14 D4
Southport, *Fla., U.S.A.* 115 K3
Southport, *N.Y., U.S.A.* 116 D8
Southwest △, *Australia* 95 G4
Southwest C., *N.Z.* 91 M1
Southwold, *U.K.* 15 E9
Southwood △, *Australia* 95 D5
Soutpansberg, *S. Africa* 89 C4
Souvigny, *France* 19 F10
Sovata, *Romania* 29 D10
Soverato, *Italy* 43 D9
Sovetsk, *Kaliningd., Russia* 9 J19
Sovetsk, *Kirov, Russia* 34 B9
Sovetskaya Gavan = Vanino, *Russia* 53 E15
Sovicille, *Italy* 41 E8
Soweto, *S. Africa* 89 D4
Sōya-Kaikyō = La Perouse Str., *Asia* 54 B11
Sōya-Misaki, *Japan* 54 B10
Soyaux, *France* 20 C4
Sozh →, *Belarus* 33 F6
Sozopol, *Bulgaria* 45 D11
Spa, *Belgium* 17 D5
Spain ■, *Europe* 7 H5
Spalding, *Australia* 95 E2
Spalding, *U.K.* 14 E7
Spangler, *U.S.A.* 116 F6
Spanish, *Canada* 104 C3
Spanish Fork, *U.S.A.* 108 F8
Spanish Town, *Br. Virgin Is.* 121 e
Spanish Town, *Jamaica* 120 a
Sparks, *U.S.A.* 110 F7
Sparreholm, *Sweden* 10 E10
Sparta = Spárti, *Greece* 46 D4
Sparta, *Mich., U.S.A.* 114 D3
Sparta, *N.J., U.S.A.* 117 E10
Sparta, *Wis., U.S.A.* 112 D9
Spartanburg, *U.S.A.* 115 H5
Spartansburg, *U.S.A.* 116 E5
Spárti, *Greece* 46 D4
Spartivento, C., *Calabria, Italy* 43 E9
Spartivento, C., *Sard., Italy* 42 D1
Sparwood, *Canada* 102 D6
Spas-Demensk, *Russia* 32 E7
Spas-Klepiki, *Russia* 32 E11
Spassk Dalniy, *Russia* 53 E14
Spassk-Ryazanskiy, *Russia* 32 E11
Spátha, Ákra, *Greece* 49 D5
Spatsizi →, *Canada* 102 B3
Spatsizi Plateau Wilderness ⌓, *Canada* 102 B3
Spean →, *U.K.* 13 E4
Spearfish, *U.S.A.* 112 C3
Spearman, *U.S.A.* 113 G4
Speculator, *U.S.A.* 117 C10
Speia, *Moldova* 29 D14
Speightstown, *Barbados* 121 g
Speke Gulf, *Tanzania* 86 C3
Spello, *Italy* 41 F9
Spence Bay = Taloyoak, *Canada* 100 B10
Spencer, *Idaho, U.S.A.* 108 D7
Spencer, *Iowa, U.S.A.* 112 D7
Spencer, *N.Y., U.S.A.* 117 D8
Spencer, *Nebr., U.S.A.* 112 D5
Spencer, C., *Australia* 95 F2
Spencer B., *Namibia* 88 D1
Spencer G., *Australia* 95 E2
Spencerville, *Canada* 117 B9
Spences Bridge, *Canada* 102 C4
Spennymoor, *U.K.* 14 C6
Spenser Mts., *N.Z.* 91 K4
Spentrup, *Denmark* 11 H4
Sperkhiós →, *Greece* 46 C4
Sperrin Mts., *U.K.* 12 B5
Spessart, *Germany* 25 F5
Spétsai, *Greece* 46 D5
Spey →, *U.K.* 13 D5
Speyer, *Germany* 25 F4
Spezand, *Pakistan* 68 E2
Spezzano Albanese, *Italy* 43 C9
Spiekeroog, *Germany* 24 B3
Spiez, *Switz.* 25 J3
Spíli, *Greece* 49 D6
Spilimbergo, *Italy* 41 B9
Spīn Būldak, *Afghan.* 68 D2
Spinalónga, *Greece* 49 D7
Spinazzola, *Italy* 43 B9
Spineni, *Romania* 29 F9
Spirit Lake, *U.S.A.* 110 D4
Spirit River, *Canada* 102 B5
Spiritwood, *Canada* 103 C7
Spišská Nová Ves, *Slovak Rep.* 27 C13
Spišské Podhradie, *Slovak Rep.* 27 B13
Spital, *Austria* 26 D7
Spithead, *U.K.* 15 G6
Spittal an der Drau, *Austria* 26 E6
Spitzbergen = Svalbard, *Arctic* 51 B5
Spjelkavik, *Norway* 9 E12
Split, *Croatia* 41 E13
Split ✕ (SPU), *Croatia* 41 E13
Split L., *Canada* 103 B9
Split Lake, *Canada* 103 B9
Splitski Kanal, *Croatia* 41 E13
Splügenpass, *Switz.* 25 J5
Spofford, *U.S.A.* 113 L4
Spokane, *U.S.A.* 108 C5
Spoleto, *Italy* 41 F9
Spooner, *U.S.A.* 112 C9
Sporyy Navolok, Mys, *Russia* 52 B7
Sprague, *U.S.A.* 108 C5
Spratly I., *S. China Sea* 62 C4
Spratly Is., *S. China Sea* 62 C4
Spray, *U.S.A.* 108 D4
Spreča →, *Bos.-H.* 28 F3
Spree →, *Germany* 24 C9
Spreewald, *Germany* 24 D9
Spremberg, *Germany* 24 D10
Sprengisandur, *Iceland* 8 D5
Spring City, *U.S.A.* 117 F9
Spring Creek, *U.S.A.* 108 F6
Spring Garden, *U.S.A.* 110 F6
Spring Hall, *Barbados* 121 g
Spring Hill, *U.S.A.* 115 L4
Spring Mts., *U.S.A.* 109 H6
Spring Valley, *U.S.A.* 111 N10
Springbok, *S. Africa* 88 D2
Springboro, *U.S.A.* 116 E4
Springdale, *Canada* 105 C8
Springdale, *U.S.A.* 113 G7
Springe, *Germany* 24 C5
Springer, *U.S.A.* 113 G2
Springerville, *U.S.A.* 109 J9
Springfield, *Canada* 116 D4
Springfield, *N.Z.* 91 K3
Springfield, *Colo., U.S.A.* 113 G3
Springfield, *Ill., U.S.A.* 112 F10
Springfield, *Mass., U.S.A.* 117 D12
Springfield, *Mo., U.S.A.* 113 G8
Springfield, *Ohio, U.S.A.* 114 F4
Springfield, *Oreg., U.S.A.* 108 D2
Springfield, *Tenn., U.S.A.* 115 G2
Springfield, *Vt., U.S.A.* 117 C12
Springfontein, *S. Africa* 88 E4
Springhill, *Canada* 105 C7
Springhill, *U.S.A.* 113 J8
Springhouse, *Canada* 102 C4
Springs, *S. Africa* 89 D4
Springsure, *Australia* 94 C4
Springvale, *U.S.A.* 117 C14
Springville, *Calif., U.S.A.* 110 J8
Springville, *N.Y., U.S.A.* 116 D6
Springville, *Utah, U.S.A.* 108 F8
Springwater, *U.S.A.* 116 D7
Spruce-Creek, *U.S.A.* 116 F6
Spruce Knob-Seneca Rocks ⌓, *U.S.A.* 114 F6
Spruce Mt., *U.S.A.* 117 B12
Spur, *U.S.A.* 113 J4
Spurn Hd., *U.K.* 14 D8
Spuž, *Serbia & M.* 44 D3
Spuzzum, *Canada* 102 D4
Squam L., *U.S.A.* 117 C13
Squamish, *Canada* 102 D4
Square Islands, *Canada* 105 B8
Squillace, G. di, *Italy* 43 D9
Squinzano, *Italy* 43 B11
Squires, Mt., *Australia* 93 E4
Srbac, *Bos.-H.* 28 E2
Srbica, *Serbia & M.* 44 D4
Srbija = Serbia □, *Serbia & M.* 44 C5
Srbobran, *Serbia & M.* 28 E4
Sre Ambel, *Cambodia* 65 G4
Sre Khtum, *Cambodia* 65 F6
Sre Umbell = Sre Ambel, *Cambodia* 65 G4
Srebrenica, *Bos.-H.* 28 F4
Sredinny Ra. = Sredinnyy Khrebet, *Russia* 53 D16
Sredinnyy Khrebet, *Russia* 53 D16
Središče, *Slovenia* 41 B13
Sredna Gora, *Bulgaria* 45 D8

Srednekolymsk, *Russia* 53 C16
Sredni Rodopi, *Bulgaria* 45 E8
Srednogorie, *Bulgaria* 45 D8
Śrem, *Poland* 31 F4
Sremska Mitrovica, *Serbia & M.* 28 F4
Sremski Karlovci, *Serbia & M.* 28 E4
Srepok →, *Cambodia* 64 F6
Sretensk, *Russia* 53 D12
Sri Lanka ■, *Asia* 66 R12
Srikakulam, *India* 67 K13
Srinagar, *India* 69 B6
Środa Śląska, *Poland* 31 G3
Środa Wielkopolski, *Poland* 31 F4
Srono, *Indonesia* 63 J17
Srpska Crnja, *Serbia & M.* 28 E5
Srpski Itebej, *Serbia & M.* 28 E5
Staaten →, *Australia* 94 B3
Staaten River △, *Australia* 94 B3
Staberhuk, *Germany* 24 A7
Stade, *Germany* 24 B5
Stadskanaal, *Neths.* 17 A6
Stadtallendorf, *Germany* 24 E5
Stadthagen, *Germany* 24 C5
Stadtlohn, *Germany* 24 D2
Stadtroda, *Germany* 24 E7
Staffa, *U.K.* 13 E2
Staffanstorp, *Sweden* 11 J7
Stafford, *U.K.* 14 E5
Stafford, *U.S.A.* 113 G5
Stafford Springs, *U.S.A.* 117 E12
Staffordshire □, *U.K.* 14 E5
Stagnone, *Italy* 42 E5
Stagnone di Marsala ⌂, *Italy* 42 E5
Staines, *U.K.* 15 F7
Stainz, *Austria* 26 E8
Stakhanov, *Ukraine* 33 H10
Stalać, *Serbia & M.* 44 C5
Stalingrad = Volgograd, *Russia* 35 F7
Staliniri = Tskhinvali, *Georgia* 35 J7
Stalino = Donetsk, *Ukraine* 33 J9
Stalinogorsk = Novomoskovsk, *Russia* 32 E10
Stalis, *Greece* 49 D7
Stallarholmen, *Sweden* 10 E11
Ställdalen, *Sweden* 10 E8
Stalowa Wola, *Poland* 31 H9
Stalybridge, *U.K.* 14 D5
Stamford, *Australia* 94 C3
Stamford, *U.K.* 15 E7
Stamford, *Conn., U.S.A.* 117 E11
Stamford, *N.Y., U.S.A.* 117 D10
Stamford, *Tex., U.S.A.* 113 J5
Stampriet, *Namibia* 88 C2
Stamps, *U.S.A.* 113 J8
Stančevo = Kalipetrovo, *Bulgaria* 45 B11
Standerton, *S. Africa* 89 D4
Standish, *U.S.A.* 114 D4
Stanford, *S. Africa* 88 E2
Stanford, *U.S.A.* 108 C8
Stånga, *Sweden* 11 G12
Stanger, *S. Africa* 89 D5
Stanišić, *Serbia & M.* 28 E4
Stanislaus →, *U.S.A.* 110 H5
Stanislav = Ivano-Frankivsk, *Ukraine* 33 H3
Stanisławów, *Poland* 31 F8
Stanley, *Australia* 95 G4
Stanley, *Falk. Is.* 128 G5
Stanley, *U.K.* 14 C6
Stanley, *Idaho, U.S.A.* 108 D6
Stanley, *N. Dak., U.S.A.* 112 A3
Stanley, *N.Y., U.S.A.* 116 D7
Stanley Mission, *Canada* 103 B8
Stanovoy Khrebet, *Russia* 53 D13
Stanovoy Ra. = Stanovoy Khrebet, *Russia* 53 D13
Stansmore Ra., *Australia* 92 D4
Stansted, London ✕ (STN), *U.K.* 15 F8
Stanthorpe, *Australia* 95 D5
Stanton, *U.S.A.* 113 J4
Stanwood, *U.S.A.* 110 B4
Staples, *U.S.A.* 112 B7
Stąporków, *Poland* 31 G7
Star City, *Canada* 103 C8
Star Lake, *U.S.A.* 117 B9
Stará L'ubovňa, *Slovak Rep.* 27 B13
Stara Moravica, *Serbia & M.* 28 E4
Stara Pazova, *Serbia & M.* 28 F5
Stara Planina, *Bulgaria* 44 C7
Stará Turá, *Slovak Rep.* 27 C10
Stara Zagora, *Bulgaria* 45 D9
Starachowice, *Poland* 31 G8
Staraya Russa, *Russia* 32 D6
Starbuck I., *Kiribati* 97 H12
Starchiojd, *Romania* 29 E11
Starcke △, *Australia* 94 A4
Stargard Szczeciński, *Poland* 30 E2
Stari Bar, *Serbia & M.* 44 D3
Stari Trg, *Slovenia* 41 C12
Staritsa, *Russia* 32 D8
Starke, *U.S.A.* 115 L4
Starnberg, *Germany* 25 H7
Starnberger See, *Germany* 25 H7
Starobilsk, *Ukraine* 33 H10
Starodub, *Russia* 33 F7
Starogard Gdański, *Poland* 30 E5
Starokonstantinov = Starokonstyantyniv, *Ukraine* 33 H4
Starokonstyantyniv, *Ukraine* 33 H4
Starominskaya, *Russia* 33 J10
Staroshcherbinovskaya, *Russia* 33 J10
Start Pt., *U.K.* 15 G4
Stary Sącz, *Poland* 31 J7
Staryy Biryuzyak, *Russia* 35 H8
Staryy Chartoriysk, *Ukraine* 33 G3
Staryy Krym, *Ukraine* 33 K8
Staryy Oskol, *Russia* 33 G9
Stassfurt, *Germany* 24 D7
Staszów, *Poland* 31 H8
State College, *U.S.A.* 116 F7
Stateline, *U.S.A.* 110 G7
Staten, I. = Estados, I. de Los, *Argentina* 128 G4
Staten I., *U.S.A.* 117 F10
Statesboro, *U.S.A.* 115 J5
Statesville, *U.S.A.* 115 H5
Stauffer, *U.S.A.* 111 L7
Staunton, *Ill., U.S.A.* 112 F10
Staunton, *Va., U.S.A.* 114 F6
Stavanger, *Norway* 9 G11
Staveley, *N.Z.* 91 K3
Stavelot, *Belgium* 17 D5
Stavern, *Norway* 9 G14
Stavoren, *Neths.* 17 B5
Stavropol, *Russia* 35 H6
Stavros, *Cyprus* 49 D11
Stavrós, *Greece* 49 D6
Stavrós, Ákra, *Greece* 49 D6
Stavroúpolis, *Greece* 45 E8
Stawell, *Australia* 95 F3
Stawell →, *Australia* 94 C3
Stawiski, *Poland* 30 E9
Stawiszyn, *Poland* 31 G5
Stayner, *Canada* 116 B4
Stayton, *U.S.A.* 108 D2
Steamboat Springs, *U.S.A.* 108 F10
Steblevë, *Albania* 44 E4
Steele, *U.S.A.* 112 B5
Steelton, *U.S.A.* 116 F8
Steen River, *Canada* 102 B5
Steenkool = Bintuni, *Indonesia* 63 E8
Steens Mt., *U.S.A.* 108 E4
Steenwijk, *Neths.* 17 B6
Steep Pt., *Australia* 93 E1
Steep Rock, *Canada* 103 C9
Ştefan Vodă, *Moldova* 29 D14
Ştefăneşti, *Romania* 29 C12
Stefanie △, *Ethiopia* 81 G4
Stefanie L. = Chew Bahir, *Ethiopia* 81 G4
Stefansson Bay, *Antarctica* 5 C5
Stege, *Denmark* 11 K6
Ştei, *Romania* 28 D7
Steiermark □, *Austria* 26 D8
Steigerwald, *Germany* 25 F6
Steigerwald ⌂, *Germany* 25 F6
Steilacoom, *U.S.A.* 110 C4
Steilrandberge, *Namibia* 88 B1
Steinbach, *Canada* 103 D9
Steinfurt, *Germany* 24 C3
Steinhausen, *Namibia* 88 C2
Steinheim, *Germany* 24 D5
Steinhuder Meer, *Germany* 24 C5
Steinhuder Meer ⌂, *Germany* 24 C5
Steinkjer, *Norway* 8 D14
Steinkopf, *S. Africa* 88 D2
Steinwald ⌂, *Germany* 25 F8
Stellarton, *Canada* 105 C7
Stellenbosch, *S. Africa* 88 E2
Stelvio, Paso dello, *Italy* 40 B7
Stenay, *France* 19 C12
Stendal, *Germany* 24 C7
Stende, *Latvia* 30 A9
Stenhamra, *Sweden* 10 E11
Stenshuvud △, *Sweden* 11 J8
Stenstorp, *Sweden* 11 F7
Stenungsund, *Sweden* 11 F5
Steornabhaigh = Stornoway, *U.K.* 13 C2
Stepanakert = Xankändi, *Azerbaijan* 70 B5
Stepanavan, *Armenia* 35 K7
Stephens Creek, *Australia* 95 E3
Stephens I., *Canada* 102 C2
Stephens L., *Canada* 103 B9
Stephenville, *Canada* 105 C8
Stephenville, *U.S.A.* 113 J5
Stepnica, *Poland* 30 E1
Stepnoi = Elista, *Russia* 35 G7
Steppe, *Asia* 50 D9
Stereá Ellas □, *Greece* 46 C4
Sterkstroom, *S. Africa* 88 E4
Sterling, *Colo., U.S.A.* 112 E3
Sterling, *Ill., U.S.A.* 112 E10
Sterling, *Kans., U.S.A.* 112 F5
Sterling City, *U.S.A.* 113 K4
Sterling Heights, *U.S.A.* 114 D4
Sterling Run, *U.S.A.* 116 E6
Sterlitamak, *Russia* 52 D6
Sternberg, *Germany* 24 B7
Šternberk, *Czech Rep.* 27 B10
Stérnes, *Greece* 49 D6
Sterzing = Vipiteno, *Italy* 41 B8
Stettin = Szczecin, *Poland* 30 E1
Stettiner Haff, *Germany* 24 B10
Stettler, *Canada* 102 C6
Steubenville, *U.S.A.* 116 F4
Stevenage, *U.K.* 15 F7
Stevens Point, *U.S.A.* 112 C10
Stevenson, *U.S.A.* 110 E5
Stevenson L., *Canada* 103 C9
Stevensville, *U.S.A.* 108 C6
Stevns Klint, *Denmark* 11 J6
Stewart, *Canada* 102 B3
Stewart, *U.S.A.* 110 F7
Stewart →, *Canada* 100 B6
Stewart, C., *Australia* 94 A1
Stewart, I., *Chile* 128 G2
Stewart I., *N.Z.* 91 M1
Stewarts Point, *U.S.A.* 110 G3
Stewartville, *U.S.A.* 112 D8
Stewiacke, *Canada* 105 C7
Steynsburg, *S. Africa* 88 E4
Steyr, *Austria* 26 C7
Steyr →, *Austria* 26 C7
Steytlerville, *S. Africa* 88 E3
Stia, *Italy* 41 E8
Stigler, *U.S.A.* 113 H7
Stigliano, *Italy* 43 B9
Stigtomta, *Sweden* 11 F10
Stikine →, *Canada* 102 B2
Stilfontein, *S. Africa* 88 D4
Stilís, *Greece* 46 C4
Stillwater, *N.Z.* 91 K3
Stillwater, *Minn., U.S.A.* 112 C8
Stillwater, *N.Y., U.S.A.* 117 D11
Stillwater, *Okla., U.S.A.* 113 G6
Stillwater Range, *U.S.A.* 108 G4
Stillwater Reservoir, *U.S.A.* 117 C9
Stilo, Pta., *Italy* 43 D9
Stilwell, *U.S.A.* 113 H7
Stînga Nistrului □, *Moldova* 29 C14
Štip, *Macedonia* 44 E6
Stíra, *Greece* 46 C6
Stirling, *Canada* 116 B7
Stirling, *U.K.* 13 E5
Stirling □, *U.K.* 13 E4
Stirling Ra., *Australia* 93 F2
Stirling Range △, *Australia* 93 F2
Stittsville, *Canada* 117 A9
Stjernøya, *Norway* 8 A20
Stjørdalshalsen, *Norway* 8 E14
Stockach, *Germany* 25 H5
Stockaryd, *Sweden* 11 G8
Stockerau, *Austria* 27 C9
Stockholm, *Sweden* 10 E12
Stockholm Arlanda ✕ (ARN), *Sweden* 10 E11
Stockholms län □, *Sweden* 10 E12
Stockport, *U.K.* 14 D5
Stocksbridge, *U.K.* 14 D6
Stockton, *Calif., U.S.A.* 110 H5
Stockton, *Kans., U.S.A.* 112 F5
Stockton, *Mo., U.S.A.* 113 G8
Stockton-on-Tees, *U.K.* 14 C6
Stockton-on-Tees □, *U.K.* 14 C6
Stockton Plateau, *U.S.A.* 113 K3
Stoczek Łukowski, *Poland* 31 G8
Stöde, *Sweden* 10 B10
Stoeng Treng, *Cambodia* 64 F5
Stoer, Pt. of, *U.K.* 13 C3
Stogovo, *Macedonia* 44 E4
Stoholm, *Denmark* 11 H3
Stoke-on-Trent, *U.K.* 14 D5
Stoke-on-Trent □, *U.K.* 14 D5
Stokes △, *Australia* 93 E2
Stokes Pt., *Australia* 95 G3
Stokes Ra., *Australia* 92 C5
Stokksnes, *Iceland* 8 D6
Stokmarknes, *Norway* 8 B16
Stolac, *Bos.-H.* 44 C1
Stolberg, *Germany* 24 E2
Stolbovoy, Ostrov, *Russia* 53 B14
Stolbtsy = Stowbtsy, *Belarus* 32 F4
Stolin, *Belarus* 33 G4
Stöllet, *Sweden* 10 D7
Stolnici, *Romania* 29 F9
Stomíon, *Greece* 49 D5
Ston, *Croatia* 41 F14
Stone, *U.K.* 14 E5
Stoneboro, *U.S.A.* 116 E4
Stonehaven, *U.K.* 13 E6
Stonehenge, *Australia* 94 C3
Stonehenge, *U.K.* 15 F6
Stonewall, *Canada* 103 C9
Stony L., *Man., Canada* 103 B9
Stony L., *Ont., Canada* 116 B6
Stony Point, *U.S.A.* 117 E11
Stony Pt., *U.S.A.* 117 C8
Stony Rapids, *Canada* 103 B7
Stony Tunguska = Tunguska, Podkamennaya →, *Russia* 53 C10
Stonyford, *U.S.A.* 110 F4
Stopnica, *Poland* 31 H7
Storå, *Sweden* 10 E9
Storå →, *Denmark* 11 H2
Stora Gla, *Sweden* 10 E6
Stora Le, *Sweden* 10 E5
Stora Lulevatten, *Sweden* 8 C18
Storavan, *Sweden* 8 D18
Stord, *Norway* 9 G11
Store Bælt, *Denmark* 11 J4
Store Heddinge, *Denmark* 11 J6
Store Mosse △, *Sweden* 11 G7
Storebro, *Sweden* 11 G9
Storfors, *Sweden* 10 E8
Storlien, *Sweden* 10 A6
Storm B., *Australia* 95 G4
Storm Lake, *U.S.A.* 112 D7
Stormberge, *S. Africa* 88 E4
Stormsrivier, *S. Africa* 88 E3
Stornoway, *U.K.* 13 C2
Storo, *Italy* 40 C7
Storozhinets = Storozhynets, *Ukraine* 33 H3
Storozhynets, *Ukraine* 33 H3
Storrs, *U.S.A.* 117 E12
Storsjön, *Gävleborg, Sweden* 10 D10
Storsjön, *Jämtland, Sweden* 10 B7
Storsjön, *Jämtland, Sweden* 10 A8
Storstrøms Amtskommune □, *Denmark* 11 J5
Storuman, *Sweden* 8 D17
Storuman, sjö, *Sweden* 8 D17
Storvätteshågna, *Sweden* 10 B6
Storvik, *Sweden* 10 D10
Storvreta, *Sweden* 10 E11
Stouffville, *Canada* 116 C5
Stoughton, *Canada* 103 D8
Stour →, *Dorset, U.K.* 15 G6
Stour →, *Kent, U.K.* 15 F9
Stour →, *Suffolk, U.K.* 15 F9
Stourbridge, *U.K.* 15 E5
Stout L., *Canada* 103 C10
Stove Pipe Wells Village, *U.S.A.* 111 J9
Støvring, *Denmark* 11 H3
Stow, *U.S.A.* 116 E3
Stowbtsy, *Belarus* 32 F4
Stowmarket, *U.K.* 15 E9
Strabane, *U.K.* 12 B4
Stracin, *Macedonia* 44 D6
Stradella, *Italy* 40 C6
Strahan, *Australia* 95 G4
Strajitsa, *Bulgaria* 45 C9
Strakonice, *Czech Rep.* 26 B6
Straldzha, *Bulgaria* 45 D10
Stralsund, *Germany* 24 A9
Strand, *S. Africa* 88 E2
Stranda, *Møre og Romsdal, Norway* 9 E12
Stranda, *Nord-Trøndelag, Norway* 8 E14
Strandby, *Denmark* 11 G4
Strangford L., *U.K.* 12 B6
Strängnäs, *Sweden* 10 E11
Stranraer, *U.K.* 13 G3
Strasbourg, *Canada* 103 C8
Strasbourg, *France* 19 D14
Strasburg, *Germany* 24 B9
Străşeni, *Moldova* 29 C13
Stråssa, *Sweden* 10 E9
Stratford, *Canada* 116 C4
Stratford, *N.Z.* 91 H5
Stratford, *Calif., U.S.A.* 110 J7
Stratford, *Conn., U.S.A.* 117 E11
Stratford, *Tex., U.S.A.* 113 G3
Stratford-upon-Avon, *U.K.* 15 E6
Strath Spey, *U.K.* 13 D5
Strathalbyn, *Australia* 95 F2
Strathaven, *U.K.* 13 F4
Strathcona ⌂, *Canada* 102 D3
Strathmore, *Canada* 102 C6
Strathmore, *U.K.* 13 E5
Strathmore, *U.S.A.* 110 J7
Strathnaver, *Canada* 102 C4
Strathpeffer, *U.K.* 13 D4
Strathroy, *Canada* 116 D3
Strathy Pt., *U.K.* 13 C4
Strattanville, *U.S.A.* 116 E5
Stratton, *U.S.A.* 117 A14
Stratton Mt., *U.S.A.* 117 C12
Straubing, *Germany* 25 G8
Straumnes, *Iceland* 8 C2
Strausberg, *Germany* 24 C9
Strawberry →, *U.S.A.* 108 F8
Strážnice, *Czech Rep.* 27 C10
Streaky B., *Australia* 95 E1
Streaky Bay, *Australia* 95 E1
Streator, *U.S.A.* 112 E10
Středočeský □, *Czech Rep.* 26 B7
Streetsboro, *U.S.A.* 116 E3
Streetsville, *Canada* 116 C5
Strehaia, *Romania* 29 F8
Strelcha, *Bulgaria* 45 D8
Strelka, *Russia* 53 D10
Streng →, *Cambodia* 64 F4
Stresa, *Italy* 40 C5
Streymoy, *Færoe Is.* 8 E9
Strezhevoy, *Russia* 52 C8
Stříbro, *Czech Rep.* 26 A6
Strimón →, *Greece* 44 F7
Strimonikós Kólpos, *Greece* 44 F7
Strofádhes, *Greece* 46 D3
Stroma, *U.K.* 13 C5
Stromberg-Heuchelberg ⌂, *Germany* 25 F4
Strómboli, *Italy* 43 D8
Stromeferry, *U.K.* 13 D3
Stromness, *U.K.* 13 C5
Strömsbruk, *Sweden* 10 C11
Stromsburg, *U.S.A.* 112 E6
Strömsnäsbruk, *Sweden* 11 H7
Strömstad, *Sweden* 11 F5
Strömsund, *Sweden* 8 E16
Strongilí, *Greece* 47 E11
Stróngoli, *Italy* 43 C10
Strongsville, *U.S.A.* 116 E3
Stronie Śląskie, *Poland* 31 H3
Stronsay, *U.K.* 13 B6
Stropkov, *Slovak Rep.* 27 B14
Stroud, *U.K.* 15 F5
Stroud Road, *Australia* 95 E5
Stroudsburg, *U.S.A.* 117 F9
Stroumbi, *Cyprus* 49 E11
Struer, *Denmark* 11 H2
Struga, *Macedonia* 44 E4
Strugi Krasnyye, *Russia* 32 C5
Strumica, *Macedonia* 44 E6
Strumica →, *Europe* 44 E7
Struthers, *Canada* 104 C2
Struthers, *U.S.A.* 116 E4
Stryama, *Bulgaria* 45 D8
Stryker, *U.S.A.* 108 B6
Stryków, *Poland* 31 G6
Stryy, *Ukraine* 33 H2
Strzegom, *Poland* 31 H3
Strzelce Krajeńskie, *Poland* 31 F2
Strzelce Opolskie, *Poland* 31 H5
Strzelecki Cr. →, *Australia* 95 D2
Strzelin, *Poland* 31 H4
Strzelno, *Poland* 31 F5
Strzybnica, *Poland* 31 H5
Strzyżów, *Poland* 31 J8
Stuart, *Fla., U.S.A.* 115 M5
Stuart, *Nebr., U.S.A.* 112 D5
Stuart →, *Canada* 102 C4
Stuart Bluff Ra., *Australia* 92 D5
Stuart L., *Canada* 102 C4
Stuart Ra., *Australia* 95 D1
Stubbekøbing, *Denmark* 11 K6
Stuben, *Austria* 26 D3
Studen Kladenets, Yazovir, *Bulgaria* 45 E9
Studenka, *Czech Rep.* 27 B11
Stugun, *Sweden* 10 A9
Stuhr, *Germany* 24 B4
Stull L., *Canada* 104 B1
Stung Treng = Stoeng Treng, *Cambodia* 64 F5
Stupart →, *Canada* 104 A1
Stupava, *Slovak Rep.* 27 C10
Stupino, *Russia* 32 E10
Sturgeon B., *Canada* 103 C9
Sturgeon Bay, *U.S.A.* 114 C2
Sturgeon Falls, *Canada* 104 C4
Sturgeon L., *Alta., Canada* 102 B5
Sturgeon L., *Ont., Canada* 104 C1
Sturgeon L., *Ont., Canada* 116 B6
Sturgis, *Canada* 103 C8
Sturgis, *Mich., U.S.A.* 114 E3
Sturgis, *S. Dak., U.S.A.* 112 C3
Sturkö, *Sweden* 11 H9
Štúrovo, *Slovak Rep.* 27 D11
Sturt △, *Australia* 95 D3
Sturt Cr. →, *Australia* 92 C4
Stutterheim, *S. Africa* 88 E4
Stuttgart, *Germany* 25 G5
Stuttgart, *U.S.A.* 113 H9
Stuttgart Echterdingen ✕ (STR), *Germany* 25 G5
Stuyvesant, *U.S.A.* 117 D11
Stykkishólmur, *Iceland* 8 D2
Styria = Steiermark □, *Austria* 26 D8
Styrsö, *Sweden* 11 G5
Su Xian = Suzhou, *China* 56 H9
Suakin, *Sudan* 80 D4
Suan, *N. Korea* 57 E14
Suaqui, *Mexico* 118 B3
Suar, *India* 69 E8
Subang, *Indonesia* 63 G12
Subansiri →, *India* 67 F18
Subarnarekha →, *India* 69 H12
Subayhah, *Si. Arabia* 70 D3
Subcetate, *Romania* 28 E8
Subi, *Indonesia* 62 D3
Subiaco, *Italy* 41 G10
Subotica, *Serbia & M.* 28 D4
Suca, *Ethiopia* 81 F4
Suceava, *Romania* 29 C11
Suceava □, *Romania* 29 C10
Suceava →, *Romania* 29 C11
Sucha-Beskidzka, *Poland* 31 J6
Suchań, *Poland* 31 E2
Suchan, *Russia* 54 C6
Suchedniów, *Poland* 31 G7
Suchitoto, *El Salv.* 120 D2
Suchou = Suzhou, *China* 59 B13
Süchow = Xuzhou, *China* 57 G9
Suchowola, *Poland* 30 E10
Suck →, *Ireland* 12 C3
Sucre, *Bolivia* 124 G5
Sućuraj, *Croatia* 41 E14
Sucuriú →, *Brazil* 125 H8
Sud, Pte. du, *Canada* 105 C7
Sud-Kivu □, *Dem. Rep. of the Congo* 86 C2
Sud-Ouest, Pte., *Canada* 105 C7
Suda →, *Russia* 32 C9
Sudak, *Ukraine* 33 K8
Sudan, *U.S.A.* 113 H3
Sudan ■, *Africa* 81 E3
Sudbury, *Canada* 104 C3
Sudbury, *U.K.* 15 E8
Sûdd, *Sudan* 81 F3
Sudeifel = Deutsch-Luxemburgischer ⌂, *Germany* 25 F2
Süderbrarup, *Germany* 24 A5
Süderlügum, *Germany* 24 A4
Süderoogsand, *Germany* 24 A4
Sudeten Mts. = Sudety, *Europe* 27 A9
Sudety, *Europe* 27 A9
Südheide ⌂, *Germany* 24 C6
Suðuroy, *Færoe Is.* 8 F9
Sudi, *Tanzania* 87 E4
Sudirman, Pegunungan, *Indonesia* 63 E9
Sudiţi, *Romania* 29 F12
Sudogda, *Russia* 34 C5
Sudong, Pulau, *Singapore* 65 d
Sudr, *Egypt* 80 B3
Sudzha, *Russia* 33 G8
Sue →, *Sudan* 81 F2
Sueca, *Spain* 39 F4
Süedinenie, *Bulgaria* 45 D8
Suemez I., *U.S.A.* 102 B2
Suez = El Suweis, *Egypt* 80 J8
Suez, G. of = Suweis, Khalîg el, *Egypt* 80 J8
Suez Canal = Suweis, Qanâ es, *Egypt* 80 H8
Suffield, *Canada* 102 C6
Suffolk, *U.S.A.* 114 G7
Suffolk □, *U.K.* 15 E9
Şugag, *Romania* 29 E8
Sugargrove, *U.S.A.* 116 E5
Sugarive →, *India* 69 F12
Suğla Gölü, *Turkey* 72 D5
Sugluk = Salluit, *Canada* 101 B12
Suhaia, Lacul, *Romania* 29 G10
Şuḩār, *Oman* 71 E8
Sühbaatar □, *Mongolia* 56 B8
Suhl, *Germany* 24 E6
Şuhut, *Turkey* 47 C12
Sui, *Pakistan* 68 E3
Sui Xian, *China* 56 G8
Šuica, *Bos.-H.* 28 G2
Suichang, *China* 59 C12
Suichuan, *China* 59 D10
Suide, *China* 56 F6
Suifenhe, *China* 57 B16
Suihua, *China* 60 B7
Suijiang, *China* 58 C4
Suining, *Hunan, China* 59 D8
Suining, *Jiangsu, China* 57 H9
Suining, *Sichuan, China* 58 B5
Suiping, *China* 56 H7
Suippes, *France* 19 C11
Suir →, *Ireland* 12 D4
Suisun City, *U.S.A.* 110 G4
Suixi, *China* 59 G8
Suiyang, *Guizhou, China* 58 D6
Suiyang, *Heilongjiang, China* 57 B16
Suizhong, *China* 57 D11
Suizhou, *China* 59 B9
Sujangarh, *India* 68 F6
Sukabumi, *Indonesia* 63 G12
Sukadana, *Indonesia* 62 E3
Sukagawa, *Japan* 55 F10

Sukaraja, *Indonesia* 62 **E4**
Sukarnapura = Jayapura, *Indonesia* 63 **E10**
Sukawati, *Indonesia* 63 **K18**
Sukch'ŏn, *N. Korea* 57 **E13**
Sukhindol, *Bulgaria* 45 **C9**
Sukhinichi, *Russia* 32 **E8**
Sukhona →, *Russia* 52 **D4**
Sukhothai, *Thailand* 64 **D2**
Sukhumi = Sokhumi, *Georgia* 35 **J5**
Sukkur, *Pakistan* 68 **F3**
Sukkur Barrage, *Pakistan* 68 **F3**
Sukovo, *Serbia & M.* 44 **C6**
Sukri →, *India* 68 **G4**
Sukumo, *Japan* 55 **H6**
Sukunka →, *Canada* 102 **B4**
Sula →, *Ukraine* 33 **H7**
Sula, Kepulauan, *Indonesia* 63 **E7**
Sulaco →, *Honduras* 120 **C2**
Sulaiman Range, *Pakistan* 68 **D3**
Sulak →, *Russia* 35 **J8**
Sūlār, *Iran* 71 **D6**
Sulawesi, *Indonesia* 63 **E6**
Sulawesi Sea = Celebes Sea, *Indonesia* 63 **D6**
Sulawesi Selatan □, *Indonesia* 63 **E6**
Sulawesi Utara □, *Indonesia* 63 **D6**
Sulechów, *Poland* 31 **F2**
Sulęcin, *Poland* 31 **F2**
Sulejów, *Poland* 31 **G6**
Sulejówek, *Poland* 31 **F8**
Süleymanlı, *Turkey* 47 **C9**
Sulima, *S. Leone* 82 **D2**
Sulina, *Romania* 29 **E14**
Sulina, Braţul →, *Romania* 29 **E14**
Sulingen, *Germany* 24 **C4**
Suliţa, *Romania* 29 **C11**
Sulitjelma, *Norway* 8 **C17**
Sułkowice, *Poland* 31 **J6**
Sullana, *Peru* 124 **D2**
Süller, *Turkey* 47 **C11**
Sullivan, *Ill., U.S.A.* 112 **F10**
Sullivan, *Ind., U.S.A.* 114 **F2**
Sullivan, *Mo., U.S.A.* 112 **F9**
Sullivan Bay, *Canada* 102 **C3**
Sullivan I. = Lanbi Kyun, *Burma* 65 **G2**
Sullom Voe, *U.K.* 13 **A7**
Sully-sur-Loire, *France* 19 **E9**
Sulmierzyce, *Poland* 31 **G4**
Sulmona, *Italy* 41 **F10**
Süloğlu, *Turkey* 45 **E10**
Sulphur, *La., U.S.A.* 113 **K8**
Sulphur, *Okla., U.S.A.* 113 **H6**
Sulphur Pt., *Canada* 102 **A6**
Sulphur Springs, *U.S.A.* 113 **J7**
Sultan, *Canada* 104 **C3**
Sultan, *U.S.A.* 110 **C5**
Sultan Dağları, *Turkey* 72 **C4**
Sultanhisar, *Turkey* 47 **D10**
Sultaniça, *Turkey* 45 **F10**
Sultaniye, *Turkey* 45 **F12**
Sultanpur, *Mad. P., India* 68 **H8**
Sultanpur, *Punjab, India* 68 **D6**
Sultanpur, *Ut. P., India* 69 **F10**
Sulu Arch., *Phil.* 61 **J4**
Sulu Sea, *E. Indies* 61 **G4**
Sülüklü, *Turkey* 72 **C5**
Sululta, *Ethiopia* 81 **F4**
Suluova, *Turkey* 72 **B6**
Suluq, *Libya* 79 **B10**
Sulzbach, *Germany* 25 **F3**
Sulzbach-Rosenberg, *Germany* 25 **F7**
Sulzberger Ice Shelf, *Antarctica* 5 **E13**
Sumalata, *Indonesia* 63 **D6**
Sumampa, *Argentina* 126 **B3**
Sumatera □, *Indonesia* 62 **D2**
Sumatera Barat □, *Indonesia* 62 **E2**
Sumatera Utara □, *Indonesia* 62 **D1**
Sumatra = Sumatera □, *Indonesia* 62 **D2**
Sumava △, *Czech Rep.* 26 **C6**
Sumba, *Indonesia* 63 **F5**
Sumba, Selat, *Indonesia* 63 **F5**
Sumbawa, *Indonesia* 62 **F5**
Sumbawa Besar, *Indonesia* 62 **F5**
Sumbawanga □, *Tanzania* 84 **F6**
Sumbe, *Angola* 84 **G2**
Sumbu △, *Zambia* 87 **D3**
Sumburgh Hd., *U.K.* 13 **B7**
Sumdeo, *India* 69 **D8**
Sumdo, *China* 69 **B8**
Sumedang, *Indonesia* 63 **G12**
Sümeg, *Hungary* 28 **D2**
Sumeih, *Sudan* 81 **F2**
Šumen = Shumen, *Bulgaria* 45 **C10**
Sumenep, *Indonesia* 63 **G15**
Sumgait = Sumqayıt, *Azerbaijan* 35 **K9**
Summer L., *U.S.A.* 108 **E3**
Summerland, *Canada* 102 **D5**
Summerside, *Canada* 105 **C7**
Summersville, *U.S.A.* 114 **F5**
Summerville, *Ga., U.S.A.* 115 **H3**
Summerville, *S.C., U.S.A.* 115 **J5**
Summit Lake, *Canada* 102 **C4**
Summit Peak, *U.S.A.* 109 **H10**
Sumner, *Iowa, U.S.A.* 112 **D8**
Sumner, *Wash., U.S.A.* 110 **C4**
Sumoto, *Japan* 55 **G7**
Šumperk, *Czech Rep.* 27 **B9**
Sumqayıt, *Azerbaijan* 35 **K9**
Sumter, *U.S.A.* 115 **J5**
Sumy, *Ukraine* 33 **G8**
Sun City, *S. Africa* 88 **D4**
Sun City, *Ariz., U.S.A.* 109 **K7**
Sun City, *Calif., U.S.A.* 111 **M9**
Sun City Center, *U.S.A.* 115 **M4**
Sun Lakes, *U.S.A.* 109 **K8**
Sun Valley, *U.S.A.* 108 **E6**
Sunagawa, *Japan* 54 **C10**
Sunan, *N. Korea* 57 **E13**
Sunart, L., *U.K.* 13 **E3**
Sunburst, *U.S.A.* 108 **B8**
Sunbury, *Australia* 95 **F3**
Sunbury, *U.S.A.* 117 **F8**
Sunchales, *Argentina* 126 **C3**
Suncho Corral, *Argentina* 126 **B3**
Sunch'ŏn, *S. Korea* 57 **G14**
Suncook, *U.S.A.* 117 **C13**
Sunda, Selat, *Indonesia* 62 **F3**
Sunda Is., *Indonesia* 96 **H2**
Sunda Str. = Sunda, Selat, *Indonesia* 62 **F3**
Sundance, *Canada* 103 **B10**
Sundance, *U.S.A.* 112 **C2**
Sundar Nagar, *India* 68 **D7**
Sundarbans, *Asia* 67 **J16**
Sundargarh, *India* 67 **H14**
Sundays = Sondags →, *S. Africa* 88 **E4**
Sunderland, *Canada* 116 **B5**
Sunderland, *U.K.* 14 **C6**
Sundown △, *Australia* 95 **D5**
Sundre, *Canada* 102 **C6**
Sunds, *Denmark* 11 **H3**
Sundsvall, *Sweden* 10 **B11**
Sundsvallsbukten, *Sweden* 10 **B11**
Sung Hei, *Vietnam* 65 **G6**
Sungai Acheh, *Malaysia* 65 **c**
Sungai Kolok, *Thailand* 65 **J3**
Sungai Lembing, *Malaysia* 65 **L4**
Sungai Petani, *Malaysia* 65 **K3**
Sungaigerong, *Indonesia* 62 **E2**
Sungailiat, *Indonesia* 62 **E3**
Sungaipenuh, *Indonesia* 62 **E2**
Sungari = Songhua Jiang →, *China* 60 **B8**
Sunghua Chiang = Songhua Jiang →, *China* 60 **B8**
Sungikai, *Sudan* 81 **E2**
Sungurlu, *Turkey* 72 **B6**
Sunja, *Croatia* 41 **C13**
Sunland Park, *U.S.A.* 109 **L10**
Sunnansjö, *Sweden* 10 **D8**
Sunndalsøra, *Norway* 9 **E13**
Sunne, *Sweden* 10 **E7**
Sunnemo, *Sweden* 10 **E7**
Sunnyside, *U.S.A.* 108 **C3**
Sunnyvale, *U.S.A.* 110 **H4**
Suntar, *Russia* 53 **C12**
Sunyani, *Ghana* 82 **D4**
Suomenselkä, *Finland* 8 **E21**
Suomussalmi, *Finland* 8 **D23**
Suoyarvi, *Russia* 32 **A7**
Supai, *U.S.A.* 109 **H7**
Supaul, *India* 69 **F12**
Superior, *Ariz., U.S.A.* 109 **K8**
Superior, *Mont., U.S.A.* 108 **C6**
Superior, *Nebr., U.S.A.* 112 **E5**
Superior, *Wis., U.S.A.* 112 **B8**
Superior, L., *N. Amer.* 104 **C2**
Supetar, *Croatia* 41 **E13**
Suphan Buri, *Thailand* 64 **E3**
Suphan Dağı, *Turkey* 70 **B4**
Supiori, *Indonesia* 63 **E9**
Supraśl, *Poland* 31 **E10**
Supraśl →, *Poland* 31 **E9**
Supung Shuiku, *China* 57 **D13**
Sūq Suwayq, *Si. Arabia* 70 **E3**
Suqian, *China* 57 **H10**
Suquṭra = Socotra, *Yemen* 75 **E5**
Sūr, *Lebanon* 74 **B4**
Ṣūr, *Oman* 75 **C6**
Sur, Pt., *U.S.A.* 110 **J5**
Sura →, *Russia* 34 **C8**
Surab, *Pakistan* 68 **E2**
Surabaja = Surabaya, *Indonesia* 63 **G15**
Surabaya, *Indonesia* 63 **G15**
Surahammar, *Sweden* 10 **E10**
Suraia, *Romania* 29 **E12**
Surakarta, *Indonesia* 63 **G14**
Surakhany, *Azerbaijan* 35 **K10**
Šurany, *Slovak Rep.* 27 **C11**
Surat, *Australia* 95 **D4**
Surat, *India* 66 **J8**
Surat Thani, *Thailand* 65 **H2**
Suratgarh, *India* 68 **E5**
Suraż, *Poland* 31 **F9**
Surazh, *Belarus* 32 **E6**
Surazh, *Russia* 33 **F7**
Surduc, *Romania* 29 **C8**
Surduc Pasul, *Romania* 29 **E8**
Surdulica, *Serbia & M.* 44 **D6**
Surendranagar, *India* 68 **H4**
Surf, *U.S.A.* 111 **L6**
Surgères, *France* 20 **B3**
Surgut, *Russia* 52 **C8**
Sùria, *Spain* 38 **D6**
Suriapet, *India* 66 **L11**
Surigao, *Phil.* 61 **G6**
Surigao Strait, *Phil.* 61 **F6**
Surin, *Thailand* 64 **E4**
Surin Nua, Ko, *Thailand* 65 **H1**
Surinam = Suriname ■, *S. Amer.* 125 **C7**
Suriname ■, *S. Amer.* 125 **C7**
Suriname →, *Suriname* 125 **B7**
Sūrmaq, *Iran* 71 **D7**
Sürmene, *Turkey* 73 **B9**
Surovikino, *Russia* 35 **F6**
Surrey, *Canada* 110 **A4**
Surrey □, *U.K.* 15 **F7**
Sursand, *India* 69 **F11**
Sursar →, *India* 69 **F12**
Sursee, *Switz.* 25 **H4**
Sursk, *Russia* 34 **D7**
Surskoye, *Russia* 34 **C8**
Surt, *Libya* 79 **B9**
Surt, Khalīj, *Libya* 79 **B9**
Surtanahu, *Pakistan* 68 **F4**
Surte, *Sweden* 11 **G6**
Surtsey, *Iceland* 8 **E3**
Sürüç, *Turkey* 73 **D8**
Suruga-Wan, *Japan* 55 **G9**
Susa, *Italy* 40 **C4**
Susā →, *Denmark* 11 **J5**
Sušac, *Croatia* 41 **F13**
Susak, *Croatia* 41 **D11**
Susaki, *Japan* 55 **H6**
Sūsangerd, *Iran* 71 **D6**
Susanville, *U.S.A.* 108 **F3**
Susch, *Switz.* 25 **J6**
Suşehri, *Turkey* 73 **B8**
Sušice, *Czech Rep.* 26 **B6**
Susleni, *Moldova* 29 **C13**
Susner, *India* 68 **H7**
Susong, *China* 59 **B11**
Susquehanna, *U.S.A.* 117 **E9**
Susquehanna →, *U.S.A.* 117 **G8**
Susques, *Argentina* 126 **A2**
Sussex, *Canada* 105 **C6**
Sussex, *U.S.A.* 117 **E10**
Sussex, E. □, *U.K.* 15 **G8**
Sussex, W. □, *U.K.* 15 **G7**
Sustut →, *Canada* 102 **B3**
Susuman, *Russia* 53 **C15**
Susunu, *Indonesia* 63 **E8**
Susurluk, *Turkey* 47 **B10**
Susuz, *Turkey* 73 **B10**
Susz, *Poland* 30 **E6**
Sütçüler, *Turkey* 72 **D4**
Şuteşti, *Romania* 29 **E12**
Sutherland, *S. Africa* 88 **E3**
Sutherland, *U.K.* 13 **C4**
Sutherland, *U.S.A.* 112 **E4**
Sutherland Falls, *N.Z.* 91 **L1**
Sutherlin, *U.S.A.* 108 **E2**
Suthri, *India* 68 **H3**
Sutjeska △, *Bos.-H.* 28 **G3**
Sutlej →, *Pakistan* 68 **E4**
Sutter, *U.S.A.* 110 **F5**
Sutter Creek, *U.S.A.* 110 **G6**
Sutton, *Canada* 117 **A12**
Sutton, *Nebr., U.S.A.* 112 **E6**
Sutton, *W. Va., U.S.A.* 114 **F5**
Sutton →, *Canada* 104 **A3**
Sutton Coldfield, *U.K.* 15 **E6**
Sutton in Ashfield, *U.K.* 14 **D6**
Sutton L., *Canada* 104 **B3**
Suttor →, *Australia* 94 **C4**
Suttsu, *Japan* 54 **C10**
Suva, *Fiji* 91 **D8**
Suva Gora, *Macedonia* 44 **E5**
Suva Planina, *Serbia & M.* 44 **C6**
Suva Reka, *Serbia & M.* 44 **D4**
Suvorov, *Russia* 32 **E9**
Suvorov Is. = Suwarrow Is., *Cook Is.* 97 **J11**
Suvorovo, *Bulgaria* 45 **C11**
Suwałki, *Poland* 30 **D9**
Suwana, *Indonesia* 63 **K18**
Suwannaphum, *Thailand* 64 **E4**
Suwannee →, *U.S.A.* 115 **L4**
Suwanose-Jima, *Japan* 55 **K4**
Suwarrow Is., *Cook Is.* 97 **J11**
Suwayq aş Şuqban, *Iraq* 70 **D5**
Suweis, Khalîg el, *Egypt* 80 **J8**
Suweis, Qanâ es, *Egypt* 80 **H8**
Suwŏn, *S. Korea* 57 **F14**
Suzdal, *Russia* 32 **D11**
Suzhou, *Anhui, China* 56 **H9**
Suzhou, *Jiangsu, China* 59 **B13**
Suzu, *Japan* 55 **F8**
Suzu-Misaki, *Japan* 55 **F8**
Suzuka, *Japan* 55 **G8**
Suzzara, *Italy* 40 **D7**
Svalbard, *Arctic* 51 **B5**
Svalöv, *Sweden* 11 **J7**
Svaneke, *Denmark* 11 **J9**
Svängsta, *Sweden* 11 **H8**
Svanskog, *Sweden* 10 **E6**
Svappavaara, *Sweden* 8 **C19**
Svärdsjö, *Sweden* 10 **D9**
Svartå, *Sweden* 10 **E8**
Svartisen, *Norway* 8 **C15**
Svartvik, *Sweden* 10 **B11**
Svatove, *Ukraine* 33 **H10**
Svatovo = Svatove, *Ukraine* 33 **H10**
Svay Chek, *Cambodia* 64 **F4**
Svay Rieng, *Cambodia* 65 **G5**
Svealand □, *Sweden* 10 **D9**
Svedala, *Sweden* 11 **J7**
Sveg, *Sweden* 10 **B8**
Svendborg, *Denmark* 11 **J4**
Svenljunga, *Sweden* 11 **G7**
Svenstavik, *Sweden* 10 **B8**
Svenstrup, *Denmark* 11 **H3**
Sverdlovsk = Yekaterinburg, *Russia* 52 **D7**
Sverdlovsk, *Ukraine* 33 **H10**
Sverdrup Is., *Canada* 98 **B10**
Svetac, *Croatia* 41 **E12**
Sveti Nikola, Prokhad, *Europe* 44 **C6**
Sveti Nikole, *Macedonia* 44 **E5**
Sveti Rok, *Croatia* 41 **D12**
Svetlaya, *Russia* 54 **A9**
Svetlogorsk = Svyetlahorsk, *Belarus* 33 **F5**
Svetlograd, *Russia* 35 **H6**
Svetlovodsk = Svitlovodsk, *Ukraine* 33 **H7**
Svidník, *Slovak Rep.* 27 **B14**
Svilaja Planina, *Croatia* 41 **E13**
Svilajnac, *Serbia & M.* 44 **B5**
Svilengrad, *Bulgaria* 45 **E10**
Svir →, *Russia* 32 **B7**
Sviritsa, *Russia* 32 **B7**
Svishtov, *Bulgaria* 45 **C9**
Svislach, *Belarus* 33 **F3**
Svitava →, *Czech Rep.* 27 **B9**
Svitavy, *Czech Rep.* 27 **B9**
Svitlovodsk, *Ukraine* 33 **H7**
Svobodnyy, *Russia* 53 **D13**
Svoge, *Bulgaria* 44 **D7**
Svolvær, *Norway* 8 **B16**
Svratka →, *Czech Rep.* 27 **B9**
Svrljig, *Serbia & M.* 44 **C6**
Svyetlahorsk, *Belarus* 33 **F5**
Swabian Alps = Schwäbische Alb, *Germany* 25 **G5**
Swaffham, *U.K.* 15 **E8**
Swainsboro, *U.S.A.* 115 **J4**
Swakop →, *Namibia* 88 **C2**
Swakopmund, *Namibia* 88 **C1**
Swale →, *U.K.* 14 **C6**
Swan →, *Australia* 93 **F2**
Swan →, *Canada* 103 **C8**
Swan Hill, *Australia* 95 **F3**
Swan Hills, *Canada* 102 **C5**
Swan Is. = Santanilla, Is., *Honduras* 120 **C3**
Swan L., *Canada* 103 **C8**
Swan Peak, *U.S.A.* 108 **C7**
Swan Ra., *U.S.A.* 108 **C7**
Swan River, *Canada* 103 **C8**
Swanage, *U.K.* 15 **G6**
Swansea, *Australia* 95 **G4**
Swansea, *Canada* 116 **C5**
Swansea, *U.K.* 15 **F4**
Swansea □, *U.K.* 15 **F3**
Swar →, *Pakistan* 69 **B5**
Swartberge, *S. Africa* 88 **E3**
Swartmodder, *S. Africa* 88 **D3**
Swartnossob →, *Namibia* 88 **C2**
Swartruggens, *S. Africa* 88 **D4**
Swarzędz, *Poland* 31 **F4**
Swastika, *Canada* 104 **C3**
Swatow = Shantou, *China* 59 **F11**
Swaziland ■, *Africa* 89 **D5**
Sweden ■, *Europe* 9 **G16**
Swedru, *Ghana* 83 **D4**
Sweet Home, *U.S.A.* 108 **D2**
Sweetgrass, *U.S.A.* 108 **B8**
Sweetwater, *Nev., U.S.A.* 110 **G7**
Sweetwater, *Tenn., U.S.A.* 115 **H3**
Sweetwater, *Tex., U.S.A.* 113 **J4**
Sweetwater →, *U.S.A.* 108 **E10**
Swellendam, *S. Africa* 88 **E3**
Swider →, *Poland* 31 **F8**
Świdnica, *Poland* 31 **H3**
Świdnik, *Poland* 31 **G9**
Świdwin, *Poland* 30 **E2**
Świebodzice, *Poland* 31 **H3**
Świebodzin, *Poland* 31 **F2**
Świecie, *Poland* 30 **E5**
Świerzawa, *Poland* 31 **G2**
Świętokrzyski △, *Poland* 31 **H7**
Świętokrzyskie □, *Poland* 31 **H7**
Świętokrzyskie, Góry, *Poland* 31 **H7**
Swift Current, *Canada* 103 **C7**
Swift Current →, *Canada* 103 **C7**
Swilly, L., *Ireland* 12 **A4**
Swindon, *U.K.* 15 **F6**
Swindon □, *U.K.* 15 **F6**
Swinemünde = Świnoujście, *Poland* 30 **E1**
Swinford, *Ireland* 12 **C3**
Świnoujście, *Poland* 30 **E1**
Switzerland ■, *Europe* 25 **J4**
Swords, *Ireland* 12 **C5**
Swoyerville, *U.S.A.* 117 **E9**
Syasstroy, *Russia* 32 **B7**
Sychevka, *Russia* 32 **E8**
Syców, *Poland* 31 **G4**
Sydenham →, *Canada* 116 **D2**
Sydney, *Australia* 95 **E5**
Sydney, *Canada* 105 **C7**
Sydney L., *Canada* 103 **C10**
Sydney Mines, *Canada* 105 **C7**
Sydprøven = Alluitsup Paa, *Greenland* 101 **B15**
Sydra, G. of = Surt, Khalīj, *Libya* 79 **B9**
Syeverodonetsk, *Ukraine* 33 **H10**
Syke, *Germany* 24 **C4**
Sykesville, *U.S.A.* 116 **E6**
Syktyvkar, *Russia* 52 **C6**
Sylacauga, *U.S.A.* 115 **J2**
Sylarna, *Sweden* 8 **E15**
Sylhet, *Bangla.* 67 **G17**
Sylhet □, *Bangla.* 67 **G17**
Sylt, *Germany* 24 **A4**
Sylvan Beach, *U.S.A.* 117 **C9**
Sylvan Lake, *Canada* 102 **C6**
Sylvania, *U.S.A.* 115 **J5**
Sylvester, *U.S.A.* 115 **K4**
Sym, *Russia* 52 **C9**
Symón, *Mexico* 118 **C4**
Synelnykove, *Ukraine* 33 **H8**
Synevyr △, *Ukraine* 29 **B8**
Synnott Ra., *Australia* 92 **C4**
Syowa, *Antarctica* 5 **C5**
Syracuse, *Kans., U.S.A.* 113 **G4**
Syracuse, *N.Y., U.S.A.* 117 **C8**
Syracuse, *Nebr., U.S.A.* 112 **E6**
Syrdarya →, *Kazakhstan* 52 **E7**
Syria ■, *Asia* 70 **C3**
Syrian Desert = Shām, Bādiyat ash, *Asia* 70 **C3**
Sysslebäck, *Sweden* 10 **D6**
Syzran, *Russia* 34 **D9**
Szabolcs-Szatmár-Bereg □, *Hungary* 28 **B6**
Szadek, *Poland* 31 **G5**
Szamocin, *Poland* 31 **E4**
Szamos →, *Hungary* 28 **B7**
Szamotuły, *Poland* 31 **F3**
Száraz →, *Hungary* 28 **D6**
Szarvas, *Hungary* 28 **D5**
Százhalombatta, *Hungary* 28 **C3**
Szczawnica, *Poland* 31 **J7**
Szczebrzeszyn, *Poland* 31 **H9**
Szczecin, *Poland* 30 **E1**
Szczecinek, *Poland* 30 **E3**
Szczeciński, Zalew = Stettiner Haff, *Germany* 24 **B10**
Szczekociny, *Poland* 31 **H6**
Szczucin, *Poland* 31 **H8**
Szczuczyn, *Poland* 30 **E9**
Szczyrk, *Poland* 31 **J6**
Szczytna, *Poland* 31 **H3**
Szczytno, *Poland* 30 **E7**
Szechwan = Sichuan □, *China* 58 **B5**
Szécsény, *Hungary* 28 **B4**
Szeged, *Hungary* 28 **D5**
Szeghalom, *Hungary* 28 **C6**
Székesfehérvár, *Hungary* 28 **C3**
Szekszárd, *Hungary* 28 **D3**
Szendrő, *Hungary* 28 **B5**
Szentendre, *Hungary* 28 **C4**
Szentes, *Hungary* 28 **D5**
Szentgotthárd, *Hungary* 28 **D1**
Szentlőrinc, *Hungary* 28 **D3**
Szerencs, *Hungary* 28 **B6**
Szigetszentmiklós, *Hungary* 28 **C4**
Szigetvár, *Hungary* 28 **D2**
Szikszó, *Hungary* 28 **B5**
Szklarska Poreba, *Poland* 31 **H2**
Szkwa →, *Poland* 31 **E8**
Szlichtyngowa, *Poland* 31 **G3**
Szob, *Hungary* 28 **C3**
Szolnok, *Hungary* 28 **C5**
Szombathely, *Hungary* 28 **C1**
Szprotawa, *Poland* 31 **G2**
Sztum, *Poland* 30 **E6**
Sztutowo, *Poland* 30 **D6**
Szubin, *Poland* 31 **E4**
Szydłowiec, *Poland* 31 **G7**
Szypliszki, *Poland* 30 **D10**

T

Ta Khli Khok, *Thailand* 64 **E3**
Ta Lai, *Vietnam* 65 **G6**
Tab, *Hungary* 28 **D3**
Tabacal, *Argentina* 126 **A3**
Tabaco, *Phil.* 61 **E5**
Tabagné, *Ivory C.* 82 **D4**
Ţābah, *Si. Arabia* 70 **E4**
Tabanan, *Indonesia* 63 **K18**
Tabankort, *Niger* 83 **B5**
Ţabas, *Khorāsān, Iran* 71 **C9**
Ţabas, *Khorāsān, Iran* 71 **C8**
Tabasará, Serranía de, *Panama* 120 **E3**
Tabasco □, *Mexico* 119 **D6**
Tabāsīn, *Iran* 71 **D8**
Tabatinga, Serra da, *Brazil* 125 **F10**
Taber, *Canada* 102 **D6**
Taberg, *Sweden* 11 **G8**
Taberg, *U.S.A.* 117 **C9**
Tabla, *Niger* 83 **C5**
Tablas de Daimiel △, *Spain* 37 **F7**
Tablas I., *Phil.* 61 **E5**
Tablas Strait, *Phil.* 61 **E4**
Table B., *Canada* 105 **B8**
Table B., *S. Africa* 88 **E2**
Table Mt., *S. Africa* 88 **E2**
Table Rock L., *U.S.A.* 113 **G8**
Tabletop, Mt., *Australia* 94 **C4**
Tábor, *Czech Rep.* 26 **B7**
Tabora, *Tanzania* 86 **D3**
Tabora □, *Tanzania* 86 **D3**
Tabou, *Ivory C.* 82 **E3**
Tabrīz, *Iran* 70 **B5**
Tabuaeran, *Kiribati* 97 **G12**
Tabuenca, *Spain* 38 **D3**
Tabūk, *Si. Arabia* 70 **D3**
Taburno-Camposauro ⌓, *Italy* 43 **A7**
Täby, *Sweden* 10 **E12**
Tacámbaro de Codallos, *Mexico* 118 **D4**
Tacheng, *China* 60 **B3**
Tach'i, *Taiwan* 59 **E13**
Tachia, *Taiwan* 59 **E13**
Tach'ing Shan = Daqing Shan, *China* 56 **D6**
Tachov, *Czech Rep.* 26 **B5**
Tácina →, *Italy* 43 **D9**
Tacloban, *Phil.* 61 **F6**
Tacna, *Peru* 124 **G4**
Tacoma, *U.S.A.* 110 **C4**
Tacuarembó, *Uruguay* 127 **C4**
Tademaït, Plateau du, *Algeria* 78 **C6**
Tadio, L., *Ivory C.* 82 **D3**
Tadjoura, *Djibouti* 81 **E5**
Tadjoura, Golfe de, *Djibouti* 81 **E5**
Tadmor, *N.Z.* 91 **J4**
Tadoule L., *Canada* 103 **B9**
Tadoussac, *Canada* 105 **C6**
Tadrés ⌓, *Niger* 83 **B6**
Tadzhikistan = Tajikistan ■, *Asia* 52 **F8**
Taechŏn-ni, *S. Korea* 57 **F14**
Taegu, *S. Korea* 57 **G15**
Taegwan, *N. Korea* 57 **D13**
Taejŏn, *S. Korea* 57 **F14**
Taen, Ko, *Thailand* 65 **b**
Tafalla, *Spain* 38 **C3**
Tafar, *Sudan* 81 **F2**
Tafelbaai = Table B., *S. Africa* 88 **E2**
Tafermaar, *Indonesia* 63 **F8**
Tafí Viejo, *Argentina* 126 **B2**
Tafīhān, *Iran* 71 **D7**
Tafiré, *Ivory C.* 82 **D3**
Tafo, *Ghana* 83 **D4**
Tafresh, *Iran* 71 **C6**
Taft, *Iran* 71 **D7**
Taft, *Phil.* 61 **F6**
Taft, *U.S.A.* 111 **K7**
Taftān, Kūh-e, *Iran* 71 **D9**
Taga Dzong, *Bhutan* 67 **F16**
Taganrog, *Russia* 33 **J10**
Taganrogskiy Zaliv, *Russia* 33 **J10**
Tagânt, *Mauritania* 82 **B2**
Tagatay, *Phil.* 61 **D4**
Tagbilaran, *Phil.* 61 **G5**
Tággia, *Italy* 40 **E4**
Tagish, *Canada* 102 **A2**
Tagish L., *Canada* 102 **A2**

Tagliacozzo, *Italy* 41 F10
Tagliamento →, *Italy* 41 C10
Táglio di Po, *Italy* 41 D9
Tago, *Phil.* 61 G7
Tagomago, *Spain* 48 B8
Tagourâret, *Mauritania* 82 B3
Taguatinga, *Brazil* 125 F10
Tagudin, *Phil.* 61 C4
Tagum, *Phil.* 61 H6
Tagus = Tejo →, *Europe* 37 F2
Tahakopa, *N.Z.* 91 M2
Tahan, Gunong, *Malaysia* 65 K4
Tahat, *Algeria* 78 D7
Tāherī, *Iran* 71 E7
Tahiti, *Pac. Oc.* 97 J13
Tahlequah, *U.S.A.* 113 H7
Tahoe, L., *U.S.A.* 110 G6
Tahoe City, *U.S.A.* 110 F6
Tahoka, *U.S.A.* 113 J4
Taholah, *U.S.A.* 110 C2
Tahoua, *Niger* 83 C6
Tahrūd, *Iran* 71 D8
Tahsis, *Canada* 102 D3
Tahta, *Egypt* 80 B3
Tahtaköprü, *Turkey* 45 G13
Tahtalı Dağları, *Turkey* 72 C7
Tahulandang, *Indonesia* 63 D7
Tahuna, *Indonesia* 63 D7
Taï, *Ivory C.* 82 D3
Taï △, *Ivory C.* 82 D3
Tai Hu, *China* 59 B12
Tai Rom Yen △, *Thailand* 65 H2
Tai Shan, *China* 57 F9
Tai'an, *China* 57 F9
Taibei = T'aipei, *Taiwan* 59 E13
Taibique, *Canary Is.* 48 G2
Taibus Qi, *China* 56 D8
Taicang, *China* 59 B13
T'aichung, *Taiwan* 59 E13
Taieri →, *N.Z.* 91 M3
Taigu, *China* 56 F7
Taihang Shan, *China* 56 G7
Taihape, *N.Z.* 91 H5
Taihe, *Anhui, China* 56 H8
Taihe, *Jiangxi, China* 59 D10
Taihu, *China* 59 B11
Taijiang, *China* 58 D7
Taikang, *China* 56 G8
Tailem Bend, *Australia* 95 F2
Tailfingen, *Germany* 25 G5
Tailuko, *Taiwan* 59 E13
Taimyr Peninsula = Taymyr, Poluostrov, *Russia* 53 B11
Tain, *U.K.* 13 D4
T'ainan, *Taiwan* 59 F13
Taínaron, Ákra, *Greece* 46 E4
Taining, *China* 59 D11
T'aipei, *Taiwan* 59 E13
Taiping, *China* 59 B12
Taiping, *Malaysia* 65 K3
Taipingzhen, *China* 56 H6
Tairbeart = Tarbert, *U.K.* 13 D2
Taishan, *China* 59 F9
Taishun, *China* 59 D12
Taita Hills, *Kenya* 86 C4
Taitao, Pen. de, *Chile* 128 F2
T'aitung, *Taiwan* 59 F13
Taivalkoski, *Finland* 8 D23
Taiwan ■, *Asia* 59 F13
Taiwan Strait, *Asia* 59 E12
Taixing, *China* 59 A13
Taiyara, *Sudan* 81 E3
Taïyetos Óros, *Greece* 46 D4
Taiyiba, *Israel* 74 C4
Taiyuan, *China* 56 F7
Taizhong = T'aichung, *Taiwan* 59 E13
Taizhou, *China* 59 A12
Taizhou Liedao, *China* 59 C13
Ta'izz, *Yemen* 75 E3
Tājābād, *Iran* 71 D7
Tajikistan ■, *Asia* 52 F8
Tajima, *Japan* 55 F9
Tajo = Tejo →, *Europe* 37 F2
Tajrīsh, *Iran* 71 C6
Tak, *Thailand* 64 D2
Takāb, *Iran* 70 B5
Takachiho, *Japan* 55 H5
Takachu, *Botswana* 88 C3
Takada, *Japan* 55 F9
Takahagi, *Japan* 55 F10
Takaka, *N.Z.* 91 J4
Takamatsu, *Japan* 55 G7
Takaoka, *Japan* 55 F8
Takapuna, *N.Z.* 91 G5
Takasaki, *Japan* 55 F9
Takatsuki, *Japan* 55 G7
Takaungu, *Kenya* 86 C4
Takayama, *Japan* 55 F8
Take-Shima, *Japan* 55 J5
Takefu, *Japan* 55 G8
Takengon, *Indonesia* 62 D1
Takeo, *Japan* 55 H5
Tåkern, *Sweden* 11 F8
Takeshima = Tok-do, *Asia* 55 F5
Tākestān, *Iran* 71 C6
Taketa, *Japan* 55 H5
Takev, *Cambodia* 65 G5
Takh, *India* 69 C7
Takht-Sulaiman, *Pakistan* 68 D3
Takikawa, *Japan* 54 C10
Takla L., *Canada* 102 B3
Takla Landing, *Canada* 102 B3
Takla Makan = Taklamakan Shamo, *China* 60 C3
Taklamakan Shamo, *China* 60 C3
Taku →, *Canada* 102 B2
Takua Thung, *Thailand* 65 a
Takum, *Nigeria* 83 D6
Tal Halāl, *Iran* 71 D7
Tala, *Uruguay* 127 C4
Talachyn, *Belarus* 32 E5
Talacogan, *Phil.* 61 G6
Talagang, *Pakistan* 68 C5
Talagante, *Chile* 126 C1
Talak, *Niger* 83 B6
Talamanca, Cordillera de, *Cent. Amer.* 120 E3
Talant, *France* 19 E11
Talara, *Peru* 124 D2
Talas, *Kyrgyzstan* 52 E8
Talas, *Turkey* 72 C6
Talâta, *Egypt* 74 E1
Talata Mafara, *Nigeria* 83 C6
Talaud, Kepulauan, *Indonesia* 63 D7
Talaud Is. = Talaud, Kepulauan, *Indonesia* 63 D7
Talavera de la Reina, *Spain* 36 F6
Talavera la Real, *Spain* 37 G4
Talayan, *Phil.* 61 H6
Talayuela, *Spain* 36 F5
Talbandh, *India* 69 H12
Talbert, Sillon de, *France* 18 D3
Talbot, C., *Australia* 92 B4
Talbragar →, *Australia* 95 E4
Talca, *Chile* 126 D1
Talcahuano, *Chile* 126 D1
Talcher, *India* 67 J14
Talcho, *Niger* 83 C5
Taldy Kurgan = Taldyqorghan, *Kazakhstan* 52 E8
Taldyqorghan, *Kazakhstan* 52 E8
Tālesh, *Iran* 71 B6
Tālesh, Kūhhā-ye, *Iran* 71 B6
Talguharai, *Sudan* 80 D4
Tali Post, *Sudan* 81 F3
Taliabu, *Indonesia* 63 E6
Talibon, *Phil.* 63 B6
Talibong, Ko, *Thailand* 65 J2
Talihina, *U.S.A.* 113 H7
Talisayan, *Phil.* 61 G6
Taliwang, *Indonesia* 62 F5
Tall 'Afar, *Iraq* 70 B4
Tall Kalakh, *Syria* 74 A5
Talla, *Egypt* 80 B3
Talladega, *U.S.A.* 115 J2
Tallahassee, *U.S.A.* 115 K3
Tallangatta, *Australia* 95 F4
Tallard, *France* 21 D10
Tällberg, *Sweden* 10 D9
Tallering Pk., *Australia* 93 E2
Talli, *Pakistan* 68 E3
Tallinn, *Estonia* 9 G21
Tallmadge, *U.S.A.* 116 E3
Tallulah, *U.S.A.* 113 J9
Tălmaciu, *Romania* 29 E9
Talmont-St-Hilaire, *France* 20 B2
Talne, *Ukraine* 33 H6
Talnoye = Talne, *Ukraine* 33 H6
Talodi, *Sudan* 81 E3
Talovaya, *Russia* 34 E5
Taloyoak, *Canada* 100 B10
Talpa de Allende, *Mexico* 118 C4
Talparo, *Trin. & Tob.* 125 K15
Talsi, *Latvia* 9 H20
Talsi □, *Latvia* 30 A9
Taltal, *Chile* 126 B1
Taltson →, *Canada* 102 A6
Talwood, *Australia* 95 D4
Talyawalka Cr. →, *Australia* 95 E3
Tam Ky, *Vietnam* 64 E7
Tam Quan, *Vietnam* 64 E7
Tama, *U.S.A.* 112 E8
Tama ⌂, *Ethiopia* 81 F4
Tamale, *Ghana* 83 D4
Taman, *Russia* 33 K9
Taman Negara △, *Malaysia* 65 K4
Tamani, *Mali* 82 C3
Tamano, *Japan* 55 G6
Tamanrasset, *Algeria* 78 D7
Tamaqua, *U.S.A.* 117 F9
Tamar →, *U.K.* 15 G3
Tamarinda, *Spain* 48 B10
Tamarite de Litera, *Spain* 38 D5
Tamashima, *Japan* 55 G6
Tamási, *Hungary* 28 D3
Tamaské, *Niger* 83 C6
Tamaulipas □, *Mexico* 119 C5
Tamaulipas, Sierra de, *Mexico* 119 C5
Tamazula, *Mexico* 118 C3
Tamazunchale, *Mexico* 119 C5
Tamba-Dabatou, *Guinea* 82 C2
Tambacounda, *Senegal* 82 C2
Tambelan, Kepulauan, *Indonesia* 62 D3
Tambellup, *Australia* 93 F2
Tambo, *Australia* 94 C4
Tambo de Mora, *Peru* 124 F3
Tambohorano, *Madag.* 89 B7
Tambora, *Indonesia* 62 F5
Tambov, *Russia* 34 D5
Tambre →, *Spain* 36 C2
Tambuku, *Indonesia* 63 G15
Tamburâ, *Sudan* 81 F2
Tâmchekket, *Mauritania* 82 B2
Tâmega →, *Portugal* 36 D2
Tamenglong, *India* 67 G18
Tamgué, Massif du, *Guinea* 82 C2
Tamiahua, L. de, *Mexico* 119 C5
Tamil Nadu □, *India* 66 P10
Tamis →, *Serbia & M.* 28 F5
Tamluk, *India* 69 H12
Tammerfors = Tampere, *Finland* 9 F20
Tammisaari, *Finland* 9 F20
Tämnaren, *Sweden* 10 D11
Tamo Abu, Pegunungan, *Malaysia* 62 D5
Tampa, *U.S.A.* 115 M4
Tampa, Tanjung, *Indonesia* 63 K19
Tampa B., *U.S.A.* 115 M4
Tampere, *Finland* 9 F20
Tampico, *Mexico* 119 C5
Tampin, *Malaysia* 65 L4
Tampoi, *Malaysia* 65 d
Tamsweg, *Austria* 26 D6
Tamu, *Burma* 67 G19
Tamuja →, *Spain* 37 F4
Tamworth, *Australia* 95 E5
Tamworth, *Canada* 116 B8
Tamworth, *U.K.* 15 E6
Tamyang, *S. Korea* 57 G14
Tan An, *Vietnam* 65 G6
Tan Chau, *Vietnam* 65 G5
Tan-Tan, *Morocco* 78 C3
Tana →, *Kenya* 86 C5
Tana →, *Norway* 8 A23
Tana, L., *Ethiopia* 81 E4
Tana River Primate ⌂, *Kenya* 86 C5
Tanabe, *Japan* 55 H7
Tanafjorden, *Norway* 8 A23
Tanahbala, *Indonesia* 62 E1
Tanahgrogot, *Indonesia* 62 E5
Tanahjampea, *Indonesia* 63 F6
Tanahmasa, *Indonesia* 62 E1
Tanahmerah, *Indonesia* 63 F10
Tanakpur, *India* 69 E9
Tanakura, *Japan* 55 F10
Tanami, *Australia* 92 C4
Tanami Desert, *Australia* 92 C5
Tanana →, *U.S.A.* 100 B4
Tananarive = Antananarivo, *Madag.* 89 B8
Tánaro →, *Italy* 40 D5
Tancheng, *China* 57 G10
Tanch'ŏn, *N. Korea* 57 D15
Tanda, *Ut. P., India* 69 F10
Tanda, *Ut. P., India* 69 E8
Tanda, *Ivory C.* 82 D4
Tandag, *Phil.* 61 G7
Tandaia, *Tanzania* 87 D3
Tăndărei, *Romania* 29 F12
Tandaué, *Angola* 88 B2
Tandil, *Argentina* 126 D4
Tandil, Sa. del, *Argentina* 126 D4
Tandlianwala, *Pakistan* 68 D5
Tando Adam, *Pakistan* 68 G3
Tando Allahyar, *Pakistan* 68 G3
Tando Bago, *Pakistan* 68 G3
Tando Mohommed Khan, *Pakistan* 68 G3
Tandou L., *Australia* 95 E3
Tandragee, *U.K.* 12 B5
Tandsjöborg, *Sweden* 10 C8
Tane-ga-Shima, *Japan* 55 J5
Taneatua, *N.Z.* 91 H6
Tanen Tong Dan = Dawna Ra., *Burma* 64 D2
Tanew →, *Poland* 31 H9
Tanezrouft, *Algeria* 78 D6
Tang, Koh, *Cambodia* 65 G4
Tang, Ra's-e, *Iran* 71 E8
Tang Krasang, *Cambodia* 64 F5
Tanga, *Tanzania* 86 D4
Tanga □, *Tanzania* 86 D4
Tanganyika, L., *Africa* 86 D3
Tangaza, *Nigeria* 83 C5
Tanger, *Morocco* 78 A4
Tangerang, *Indonesia* 63 G12
Tangerhütte, *Germany* 24 C7
Tangermünde, *Germany* 24 C7
Tanggu, *China* 57 E9
Tanggula Shan, *China* 60 C4
Tanghe, *China* 56 H7
Tangier = Tanger, *Morocco* 78 A4
Tangorin, *Australia* 94 C3
Tangorombohitr'i Makay, *Madag.* 89 C8
Tangshan, *China* 57 E10
Tangtou, *China* 57 G10
Tanguiéta, *Benin* 83 C5
Tangxi, *China* 59 C12
Tangyan He →, *China* 58 C7
Tanimbar, Kepulauan, *Indonesia* 63 F8
Tanimbar Is. = Tanimbar, Kepulauan, *Indonesia* 63 F8
Taninthari = Tenasserim, *Burma* 65 F2
Tanjay, *Phil.* 61 G5
Tanjong Malim, *Malaysia* 65 L3
Tanjong Pelepas, *Malaysia* 65 d
Tanjore = Thanjavur, *India* 66 P11
Tanjung, *Indonesia* 63 J19
Tanjung, *Phil.* 62 E5
Tanjung Tokong, *Malaysia* 65 c
Tanjungbalai, *Indonesia* 62 D1
Tanjungbatu, *Indonesia* 62 D5
Tanjungkarang Telukbetung, *Indonesia* 62 F3
Tanjungpandan, *Indonesia* 62 E3
Tanjungpinang, *Indonesia* 62 D2
Tanjungredeb, *Indonesia* 62 D5
Tanjungselor, *Indonesia* 62 D5
Tank, *Pakistan* 68 C4
Tankhala, *India* 68 J5
Tankwa-Karoo △, *S. Africa* 88 E2
Tännäs, *Sweden* 10 B6
Tannersville, *U.S.A.* 117 E9
Tannis Bugt, *Denmark* 11 G4
Tannu-Ola, *Russia* 53 D10
Tannum Sands, *Australia* 94 C5
Tano →, *Ghana* 82 D4
Tanon Str., *Phil.* 61 F5
Tanout, *Niger* 83 C6
Tanshui, *Taiwan* 59 E13
Tansilla, *Burkina Faso* 82 C4
Tanta, *Egypt* 80 H7
Tantoyuca, *Mexico* 119 C5
Tantung = Dandong, *China* 57 D13
Tanumshede, *Sweden* 11 F5
Tanunda, *Australia* 95 E2
Tanus, *France* 20 D6
Tanzania ■, *Africa* 86 D3
Tanzilla →, *Canada* 102 B2
Tao, Ko, *Thailand* 65 G2
Tao'an = Taonan, *China* 57 B12
Tao'er He →, *China* 57 B13
Taohua Dao, *China* 59 C14
Taolanaro, *Madag.* 89 D8
Taole, *China* 56 E4
Taonan, *China* 57 B12
Taormina, *Italy* 43 E8
Taos, *U.S.A.* 109 H11
Taoudenni, *Mali* 78 D5
Taoyuan, *China* 59 C8
T'aoyüan, *Taiwan* 59 E13
Tapa, *Estonia* 9 G21
Tapa Shan = Daba Shan, *China* 58 B7
Tapachula, *Mexico* 119 E6
Tapah, *Malaysia* 65 K3
Tapajós →, *Brazil* 125 D8
Tapaktuan, *Indonesia* 62 D1
Tapanahoni →, *Suriname* 125 C8
Tapanui, *N.Z.* 91 L2
Tapauá →, *Brazil* 124 E6
Tapes, *Brazil* 127 C5
Tapeta, *Liberia* 82 D3
Taphan Hin, *Thailand* 64 D3
Tapi →, *India* 66 J8
Tapia de Casariego, *Spain* 36 B4
Tapirapecó, Serra, *Venezuela* 124 C6
Tapo-Capara △, *Venezuela* 121 E5
Tapolca, *Hungary* 28 D2
Tapuaenuku, *N.Z.* 91 K4
Tapul Group, *Phil.* 61 J4
Tapurucuará, *Brazil* 124 D5
Ţaqţaq, *Iraq* 70 C5
Taquara, *Brazil* 127 B5
Taquari →, *Brazil* 124 G7
Tara, *Australia* 95 D5
Tara, *Canada* 116 B3
Tara, *Russia* 52 D8
Tara, *Zambia* 87 F2
Tara △, *Serbia & M.* 44 C3
Tara →, *Serbia & M.* 44 C2
Taraba □, *Nigeria* 83 D7
Taraba →, *Nigeria* 83 D7
Tarābulus, *Lebanon* 74 A4
Tarābulus, *Libya* 79 B8
Taraclia, *Taraclia, Moldova* 29 E13
Taraclia, *Tighina, Moldova* 29 D14
Taradehi, *India* 69 H8
Tarajalejo, *Canary Is.* 48 F5
Tarakan, *Indonesia* 62 D5
Tarakit, Mt., *Kenya* 86 B4
Tarama-Jima, *Japan* 55 M2
Taran, Mys, *Russia* 9 J18
Taranagar, *India* 68 E6
Taranaki □, *N.Z.* 91 H5
Taranaki, Mt., *N.Z.* 91 H5
Tarancón, *Spain* 38 E1
Tarangire △, *Tanzania* 86 C4
Taransay, *U.K.* 13 D1
Táranto, *Italy* 43 B10
Táranto, G. di, *Italy* 43 B10
Tarapacá, *Colombia* 124 D5
Tarapacá □, *Chile* 126 A2
Tarapoto, *Peru* 124 E3
Tarare, *France* 21 C8
Tararua Ra., *N.Z.* 91 J5
Tarascon, *France* 21 E8
Tarascon-sur-Ariège, *France* 20 F5
Tarashcha, *Ukraine* 33 H6
Tarauacá, *Brazil* 124 E4
Tarauacá →, *Brazil* 124 E5
Taravo →, *France* 21 G12
Tarawa, *Kiribati* 96 G9
Tarawera, *N.Z.* 91 H6
Tarawera, L., *N.Z.* 91 H6
Taraz, *Kazakhstan* 52 E8
Tarazona, *Spain* 38 D3
Tarazona de la Mancha, *Spain* 39 F3
Tarbagatay, Khrebet, *Kazakhstan* 52 E9
Tarbat Ness, *U.K.* 13 D5
Tarbela Dam, *Pakistan* 68 B5
Tarbert, *Arg. & Bute, U.K.* 13 F3
Tarbert, *W. Isles, U.K.* 13 D2
Tarbes, *France* 20 E4
Tarboro, *U.S.A.* 115 H7
Tărcău, Munţii, *Romania* 29 D11
Tarcento, *Italy* 41 B10
Tarcoola, *Australia* 95 E1
Tarcoon, *Australia* 95 E4
Tardets-Sorholus, *France* 20 E3
Tardoire →, *France* 20 C4
Taree, *Australia* 95 E5
Tarfa, W. el →, *Egypt* 80 B3
Tarfaya, *Morocco* 78 C3
Târgovişte, *Romania* 29 F10
Târgu Bujor, *Romania* 29 E12
Târgu Cărbuneşti, *Romania* 29 F8
Târgu Frumos, *Romania* 29 C12
Târgu-Jiu, *Romania* 29 E8
Târgu Lăpuş, *Romania* 29 C8
Târgu Mureş, *Romania* 29 D9
Târgu Neamţ, *Romania* 29 C11
Târgu Ocna, *Romania* 29 D11
Târgu Secuiesc, *Romania* 29 E11
Târguşor, *Romania* 29 F13
Tărhăus, Vf., *Romania* 29 D11
Ţarif, *U.A.E.* 71 E7
Tarifa, *Spain* 37 J5
Tarija, *Bolivia* 126 A3
Tarija □, *Bolivia* 126 A3
Tariku →, *Indonesia* 63 E9
Tarim Basin = Tarim Pendi, *China* 60 C3
Tarim He →, *China* 60 C3
Tarim Pendi, *China* 60 C3
Taritatu →, *Indonesia* 63 E9
Tarka →, *S. Africa* 88 E4
Tarkastad, *S. Africa* 88 E4
Tarkhankut, Mys, *Ukraine* 33 K7
Tarko Sale, *Russia* 52 C8
Tarkwa, *Ghana* 82 D4
Tarlac, *Phil.* 61 D4
Tarm, *Denmark* 11 J2
Tarma, *Peru* 124 F3
Tarn □, *France* 20 E6
Tarn →, *France* 20 D5
Tarn-et-Garonne □, *France* 20 D5
Tarna →, *Hungary* 28 C4
Târnava Mare →, *Romania* 29 D8
Târnava Mică →, *Romania* 29 D8
Târnăveni, *Romania* 29 D9
Tarnica, *Poland* 31 J9
Tarnobrzeg, *Poland* 31 H8
Tarnogród, *Poland* 31 H9
Tarnos, *France* 20 E2
Târnova, *Moldova* 29 B12
Târnova, *Romania* 28 E6
Tarnów, *Poland* 31 H8
Tarnowskie Góry, *Poland* 31 H5
Tärnsjö, *Sweden* 10 D10
Táro →, *Italy* 40 C7
Ţārom, *Iran* 71 D7
Taroom, *Australia* 95 D4
Taroudannt, *Morocco* 78 B4
Tarp, *Germany* 24 A5
Tarpon Springs, *U.S.A.* 115 L4
Tarquínia, *Italy* 41 F8
Tarragona, *Spain* 38 D6
Tarragona □, *Spain* 38 D6
Tarraleah, *Australia* 95 G4
Tarrasa = Terrassa, *Spain* 38 D7
Tàrrega, *Spain* 38 D6
Tarrytown, *U.S.A.* 117 E11
Tårs, *Denmark* 11 G4
Tarshiha = Me'ona, *Israel* 74 B4
Tarsus, *Turkey* 70 B2
Tartagal, *Argentina* 126 A3
Tärtär, *Azerbaijan* 35 K8
Tärtär →, *Azerbaijan* 35 K8
Tartas, *France* 20 E3
Tartu, *Estonia* 9 G22
Ţarţūs, *Syria* 70 C2
Tarumizu, *Japan* 55 J5
Tarussa, *Russia* 32 E9
Tarutao = Ko Tarutao △, *Thailand* 65 J2
Tarutao, Ko, *Thailand* 65 J2
Tarutung, *Indonesia* 62 D1
Tarvísio, *Italy* 41 B10
Taseko →, *Canada* 102 C4
Tash-Kömür, *Kyrgyzstan* 52 E8
Tash-Kumyr = Tash-Kömür, *Kyrgyzstan* 52 E8
Tashauz = Dashhowuz, *Turkmenistan* 52 E6
Tashi Chho Dzong = Thimphu, *Bhutan* 67 F16
Ţashk, Daryācheh-ye, *Iran* 71 D7
Tashkent = Toshkent, *Uzbekistan* 52 E7
Tashtagol, *Russia* 52 D9
Tasiilaq, *Greenland* 4 C6
Tasikmalaya, *Indonesia* 63 G13
Tåsinge, *Denmark* 11 J4
Tåsjön, *Sweden* 8 D16
Taskan, *Russia* 53 C16
Tasker, *Niger* 83 C7
Taşköprü, *Turkey* 72 B6
Taşlâc, *Moldova* 29 C14
Tasman B., *N.Z.* 91 J4
Tasman Mts., *N.Z.* 91 J4
Tasman Pen., *Australia* 95 G4
Tasman Sea, *Pac. Oc.* 96 L8
Tasmania □, *Australia* 95 G4
Tăşnad, *Romania* 28 C7
Tassili n'Ajjer, *Algeria* 78 C7
Tassili Tin-Rerhoh, *Algeria* 83 A5
Tata, *Hungary* 28 C3
Tatabánya, *Hungary* 28 C3
Tatahouine, *Tunisia* 79 B8
Tatar Republic = Tatarstan □, *Russia* 34 C10
Tatarbunary, *Ukraine* 33 K5
Tatarsk, *Russia* 52 D8
Tatarstan □, *Russia* 34 C10
Tateyama, *Japan* 55 G9
Tathlina L., *Canada* 102 A5
Tathra, *Australia* 95 F4
Tatinnai L., *Canada* 103 A9
Tatla L., *Canada* 102 C4
Tatlısu, *Turkey* 45 F11
Tatnam, C., *Canada* 103 B10
Tatra = Tatry, *Slovak Rep.* 27 B13
Tatranský △, *Slovak Rep.* 27 B13
Tatry, *Slovak Rep.* 27 B13
Tatshenshini →, *Canada* 102 B1
Tatsuno, *Japan* 55 G7
Tatta, *Pakistan* 68 G2
Tatuī, *Brazil* 127 A6
Tatum, *U.S.A.* 113 J3
Tat'ung = Datong, *China* 56 D7
Tatvan, *Turkey* 70 B4
Taubaté, *Brazil* 127 A6
Tauberbischofsheim, *Germany* 25 F5
Taucha, *Germany* 24 D8
Tauern-tunnel, *Austria* 26 D6
Taufikia, *Sudan* 81 F3
Taulé, *France* 18 D3
Taumarunui, *N.Z.* 91 H5
Taumaturgo, *Brazil* 124 E4
Taung, *S. Africa* 88 D3
Taungdwingyi, *Burma* 67 J19
Taunggyi, *Burma* 67 J20
Taungup, *Burma* 67 K19
Taungup Taunggya, *Burma* 67 K18
Taunsa, *Pakistan* 68 D4
Taunsa Barrage, *Pakistan* 68 D4
Taunton, *U.K.* 15 F4
Taunton, *U.S.A.* 117 E13
Taunus, *Germany* 25 E4
Taupo, *N.Z.* 91 H6
Taupo, L., *N.Z.* 91 H5
Tauragė, *Lithuania* 9 J20
Tauragė □, *Lithuania* 30 C9
Tauranga, *N.Z.* 91 G6
Tauranga Harb., *N.Z.* 91 G6
Taureau, Rés., *Canada* 104 C5

Taurianova, Italy 43 D9
Taurus Mts. = Toros Dağları, Turkey 70 B2
Tauste, Spain 38 D3
Tauz = Tovuz, Azerbaijan 35 K7
Tavas, Turkey 47 D11
Tavda, Russia 52 D7
Tavda →, Russia 52 D7
Tavernes de la Valldigna, Spain 39 F4
Taveta, Tanzania 86 C4
Taveuni, Fiji 91 C9
Taviano, Italy 43 C11
Tavignano →, France 21 F13
Tavira, Portugal 37 H3
Tavistock, Canada 116 C4
Tavistock, U.K. 15 G3
Tavolara, Italy 42 B2
Távora →, Portugal 36 D3
Tavoy, Burma 64 E2
Tavşanlı, Turkey 47 B11
Taw →, U.K. 15 F3
Tawa →, India 68 H8
Tawas City, U.S.A. 114 C4
Tawau, Malaysia 62 D5
Taweisha, Sudan 81 E2
Tawitawi, Phil. 63 B6
Tawu, Taiwan 59 F13
Taxco de Alarcón, Mexico 119 D5
Taxila, Pakistan 68 C5
Tay ⌓, U.K. 13 E5
Tay →, U.K. 13 E5
Tay, Firth of, U.K. 13 E5
Tay, L., Australia 93 F3
Tay, L., U.K. 13 E4
Tay Ninh, Vietnam 65 G6
Tayabamba, Peru 124 E3
Tayabas Bay, Phil. 61 E4
Taylakova, Russia 52 D8
Taylakovy = Taylakova, Russia 52 D8
Taylor, Canada 102 B4
Taylor, Nebr., U.S.A. 112 E5
Taylor, Pa., U.S.A. 117 E9
Taylor, Tex., U.S.A. 113 K6
Taylor, Mt., U.S.A. 109 J10
Taylorville, U.S.A. 112 F10
Taymā, Si. Arabia 70 E3
Taymyr, Oz., Russia 53 B11
Taymyr, Poluostrov, Russia 53 B11
Tayport, U.K. 13 E6
Tayrona △, Colombia 121 D5
Tayshet, Russia 53 D10
Taytay, Phil. 61 F3
Tāyyebād, Iran 71 C9
Tayyebād □, Iran 71 C9
Taz →, Russia 52 C8
Taza, Morocco 78 B5
Tāza Khurmātū, Iraq 70 C5
Tazawa-Ko, Japan 54 E10
Tazin, Canada 103 B7
Tazin L., Canada 103 B7
Tazovskiy, Russia 52 C8
Tbilisi, Georgia 35 K7
Tchad = Chad ■, Africa 79 F8
Tchad, L., Chad 79 F8
Tchaourou, Benin 83 D5
Tch'eng-tou = Chengdu, China 58 B5
Tchentlo L., Canada 102 B4
Tchetti, Benin 83 D5
Tchibanga, Gabon 84 E2
Tchien, Liberia 82 D3
Tchin Tabaraden, Niger 83 B6
Tch'ong-k'ing = Chongqing, China 58 C6
Tczew, Poland 30 D5
Te Anau, L., N.Z. 91 L1
Te Aroha, N.Z. 91 G5
Te Awamutu, N.Z. 91 H5
Te Kuiti, N.Z. 91 H5
Te-n-Dghâmcha, Sebkhet, Mauritania 82 B1
Te Puke, N.Z. 91 G6
Te Waewae B., N.Z. 91 M1
Teaca, Romania 29 D9
Teague, U.S.A. 113 K6
Teano, Italy 43 A7
Teapa, Mexico 119 D6
Teba, Spain 37 J6
Tebakang, Malaysia 62 D4
Teberda, Russia 35 J5
Teberu, Malaysia 65 d
Tébessa, Algeria 78 A7
Tebicuary →, Paraguay 126 B4
Tebingtinggi, Riau, Indonesia 62 E2
Tebingtinggi, Sumatera Utara, Indonesia 62 D1
Tebulos, Georgia 35 J7
Tecate, Mexico 111 N10
Tecer Dağları, Turkey 72 C7
Tech →, France 20 F7
Techiman, Ghana 82 D4
Techirghiol, Romania 29 F13
Tecka, Argentina 128 E2
Tecomán, Mexico 118 D4
Tecopa, U.S.A. 111 K10
Tecoripa, Mexico 118 B3
Tecuala, Mexico 118 C3
Tecuci, Romania 29 E12
Tecumseh, Canada 116 D2
Tecumseh, Mich., U.S.A. 114 D4
Tecumseh, Okla., U.S.A. 113 H6
Tedzhen = Tejen, Turkmenistan 52 F7
Tees →, U.K. 14 C6
Tees B., U.K. 14 C6
Teeswater, Canada 116 C3
Tefé, Brazil 124 D6
Tefenni, Turkey 47 D11
Tegal, Indonesia 63 G13
Tegallalang, Indonesia 63 J18
Tegalsari, Indonesia 63 J17
Tegel, Berlin ✕ (TXL), Germany 24 C9
Tegernsee, Germany 25 H7
Teggiano, Italy 43 B8
Tegid, L. = Bala, L., U.K. 14 E4
Tegina, Nigeria 83 C6
Tegucigalpa, Honduras 120 D2
Teguidda i-n-Tessoum, Niger 83 B6
Tehachapi, U.S.A. 111 K8
Tehachapi Mts., U.S.A. 111 L8
Tehamiyam, Sudan 80 D4
Teheran = Tehrān, Iran 71 C6
Tehilla, Sudan 80 D4
Téhini, Ivory C. 82 D4
Tehoru, Indonesia 63 E7
Tehrān, Iran 71 C6
Tehran □, Iran 71 C6
Tehri, India 69 D8
Tehuacán, Mexico 119 D5
Tehuantepec, Mexico 119 D5
Tehuantepec, G. de, Mexico 119 D5
Tehuantepec, Istmo de, Mexico 119 D6
Teide, Pico de, Canary Is. 48 F3
Teifi →, U.K. 15 E3
Teign →, U.K. 15 G4
Teignmouth, U.K. 15 G4
Teiuş, Romania 29 D8
Teixeira Pinto, Guinea-Biss. 82 C1
Tejakula, Indonesia 63 J18
Tejam, India 69 E9
Tejen, Turkmenistan 52 F7
Tejen →, Turkmenistan 71 B9
Tejo →, Europe 37 F2
Tejon Pass, U.S.A. 111 L8
Tekamah, U.S.A. 112 E6
Tekapo, L., N.Z. 91 K3
Tekax, Mexico 119 C7
Teke, Turkey 45 E13
Tekeli, Kazakhstan 52 E8
Tekeze →, Ethiopia 81 E4
Tekija, Serbia & M. 44 B6
Tekirdağ, Turkey 45 F11
Tekirdağ □, Turkey 45 E11
Tekirova, Turkey 47 E12
Tekkali, India 67 K14
Tekke, Turkey 72 B7
Tekman, Turkey 73 C9
Tekoa, U.S.A. 108 C5
Tekong Besar, Pulau, Singapore 65 d
Tel Aviv ✕ (TLV), Israel 74 C3
Tel Aviv-Yafo, Israel 74 C3
Tel Lakhish, Israel 74 D3
Tel Megiddo, Israel 74 C4
Tela, Honduras 120 C2
Telanaipura = Jambi, Indonesia 62 E2
Telašćica ⌓, Croatia 41 E12
Telavi, Georgia 35 J7
Telč, Czech Rep. 26 B8
Telciu, Romania 29 C9
Telde, Canary Is. 48 G4
Telegraph Creek, Canada 102 B2
Telekhany = Tsyelyakhany, Belarus 33 F3
Telemark, Norway 9 G12
Telén, Argentina 126 D2
Teleneşti, Moldova 29 C13
Teleng, Iran 71 E9
Teleño, Spain 36 C4
Teleorman □, Romania 29 G10
Teleorman →, Romania 29 G10
Teles Pires →, Brazil 124 E7
Telescope Pk., U.S.A. 111 J9
Teletaye, Mali 83 B5
Telfer Mine, Australia 92 C3
Telford, U.K. 15 E5
Telford and Wrekin □, U.K. 14 E5
Telfs, Austria 26 D4
Télimélé, Guinea 82 C2
Teljo, J., Sudan 81 E2
Telkwa, Canada 102 C3
Tell City, U.S.A. 114 G2
Tellicherry, India 66 P9
Telluride, U.S.A. 109 H10
Teloloapán, Mexico 119 D5
Telpos Iz, Russia 6 C17
Telsen, Argentina 128 E3
Telšiai, Lithuania 9 H20
Telšiai □, Lithuania 30 C9
Teltow, Germany 24 C9
Teluk Anson = Teluk Intan, Malaysia 65 K3
Teluk Bahang, Malaysia 65 c
Teluk Betung = Tanjungkarang Telukbetung, Indonesia 62 F3
Teluk Intan, Malaysia 65 K3
Teluk Kumbar, Malaysia 65 c
Telukbutun, Indonesia 62 D3
Telukdalem, Indonesia 62 D1
Tema, Ghana 83 D5
Temax, Mexico 119 C7
Temba, S. Africa 89 D4
Tembagapura, Indonesia 63 E9
Tembe, Dem. Rep. of the Congo 86 C2
Tembe ⌓, S. Africa 89 D5
Tembleque, Spain 36 F7
Temblor Range, U.S.A. 111 K7
Teme →, U.K. 15 E5
Temecula, U.S.A. 111 M9
Temerloh, Malaysia 62 D2
Teminabuan, Indonesia 63 E8
Temir, Kazakhstan 52 E6
Temirtau, Kazakhstan 52 D8
Temirtau, Russia 52 D9
Temiscamie →, Canada 105 B5
Témiscaming, Canada 104 C4
Témiscamingue, L., Canada 104 C4
Temnikov, Russia 34 C6
Temo →, Italy 42 B1
Temosachic, Mexico 118 B3
Tempe, U.S.A. 109 K8
Témpio Pausánia, Italy 42 B2
Tempiute, U.S.A. 110 H11
Temple, U.S.A. 113 K6
Temple B., Australia 94 A3
Templemore, Ireland 12 D4
Templeton, U.S.A. 110 K6
Templeton →, Australia 94 C2
Templin, Germany 24 B9
Tempoal, Mexico 119 C5
Temryuk, Russia 33 K9
Temska →, Serbia & M. 44 C6
Temuco, Chile 128 D2
Temuka, N.Z. 91 L3
Tenabo, Mexico 119 C6
Tenaha, U.S.A. 113 K7
Tenakee Springs, U.S.A. 102 B1
Tenali, India 67 L12
Tenancingo, Mexico 119 D5
Tenango, Mexico 119 D5
Tenasserim, Burma 65 F2
Tenasserim □, Burma 64 F2
Tenby, U.K. 15 F3
Tenda, Colle di, France 21 D11
Tendaho, Ethiopia 81 E5
Tende, France 21 D11
Tendelti, Sudan 81 E3
Tendrovskaya Kosa, Ukraine 33 J6
Tendukhera, India 69 H8
Teneguía, Volcanes de, Canary Is. 48 F2
Teneida, Egypt 80 B2
Tenenkou, Mali 82 C4
Ténéré, Niger 83 B7
Tenerife, Canary Is. 48 F3
Tenerife, Pico, Canary Is. 48 G1
Tenerife Norte ✕ (TFN), Canary Is. 48 F3
Tenerife Sur ✕ (TFS), Canary Is. 48 F3
Teng Xian, Guangxi Zhuangzu, China 59 F8
Teng Xian, Shandong, China 57 G9
Tengah □, Indonesia 63 E6
Tengah, Kepulauan, Indonesia 62 F5
Tengchong, China 58 E2
Tengchowfu = Penglai, China 57 F11
Tenggara □, Indonesia 63 E6
Tenggarong, Indonesia 62 E5
Tenggol, Pulau, Malaysia 65 K4
Tengiz, Ozero, Kazakhstan 52 D7
Tenhult, Sweden 11 G8
Teniente Enciso △, Paraguay 126 A3
Teniente Rodolfo Marsh, Antarctica 5 C18
Tenino, U.S.A. 110 D4
Tenkasi, India 66 Q10
Tenke, Katanga, Dem. Rep. of the Congo 87 E2
Tenke, Katanga, Dem. Rep. of the Congo 87 E2
Tenkodogo, Burkina Faso 83 C4
Tenna →, Italy 41 E10
Tennant Creek, Australia 94 B1
Tennessee □, U.S.A. 115 H2
Tennessee →, U.S.A. 114 G1
Teno, Pta. de, Canary Is. 48 F3
Tenom, Malaysia 62 C5
Tenosique, Mexico 119 D6
Tenryū-Gawa →, Japan 55 G8
Tenterden, U.K. 15 F8
Tenterfield, Australia 95 D5
Teo, Spain 36 C2
Teófilo Otoni, Brazil 125 G10
Tepa, Indonesia 63 F7
Tepalcatepec →, Mexico 118 D4
Tepecik, Bursa, Turkey 45 F12
Tepecik, Kütahya, Turkey 47 B11
Tepehuanes, Mexico 118 B3
Tepelenë, Albania 44 F4
Tepetongo, Mexico 118 C4
Tepic, Mexico 118 C4
Teplá, Czech Rep. 26 B5
Teplice, Czech Rep. 26 A6
Tepoca, C., Mexico 118 A2
Tequila, Mexico 118 C4
Ter →, Spain 38 C8
Ter Apel, Neths. 17 B7
Téra, Niger 83 C5
Tera →, Spain 36 D5
Teraina, Kiribati 97 G11
Terakeka, Sudan 81 F3
Téramo, Italy 41 F10
Terang, Australia 95 F3
Terang, Teluk, Indonesia 63 K19
Terazit, Massif de, Niger 83 A6
Tercan, Turkey 73 C9
Tercero →, Argentina 126 C3
Terebovlya, Ukraine 33 H3
Teregova, Romania 28 E7
Tereida, Sudan 81 E3
Terek →, Russia 35 J8
Terepaima △, Venezuela 121 E6
Tereshka →, Russia 34 E8
Teresina, Brazil 125 E10
Terespol, Poland 31 F10
Terewah, L., Australia 95 D4
Terges →, Portugal 37 H3
Tergnier, France 19 C10
Teridgerie Cr. →, Australia 95 E4
Terlizzi, Italy 43 A9
Terme, Turkey 72 B7
Termez = Termiz, Uzbekistan 52 F7
Términi Imerese, Italy 42 E6
Términos, L. de, Mexico 119 D6
Termiz, Uzbekistan 52 F7
Térmoli, Italy 41 F12
Ternate, Indonesia 63 D7
Terneuzen, Neths. 17 C3
Terney, Russia 53 E14
Terni, Italy 41 F9
Ternitz, Austria 26 D9
Ternopil, Ukraine 33 H3
Ternopol = Ternopil, Ukraine 33 H3
Terowie, Australia 95 E2
Terpní, Greece 44 F7
Terra Bella, U.S.A. 111 K7
Terra Nova △, Canada 105 C9
Terrace, Canada 102 C3
Terrace Bay, Canada 104 C2
Terracina, Italy 42 A6
Terralba, Italy 42 C1
Terranova = Ólbia, Italy 42 B2
Terrasini, Italy 42 D6
Terrassa, Spain 38 D7
Terrasson-la-Villedieu, France 20 C5
Terre Haute, U.S.A. 114 F2
Terrebonne B., U.S.A. 113 L9
Terrell, U.S.A. 113 J6
Terrenceville, Canada 105 C9
Terry, U.S.A. 112 B2
Terryville, U.S.A. 117 E11
Terschelling, Neths. 17 A5
Tersko-Kumskiy Kanal →, Russia 35 H7
Tertenía, Italy 42 C2
Terter = Tärtär →, Azerbaijan 35 K8
Teruel, Spain 38 E3
Teruel □, Spain 38 E4
Tervel, Bulgaria 45 C11
Tervola, Finland 8 C21
Teryaweyna L., Australia 95 E3
Tešanj, Bos.-H. 28 F3
Teseney, Eritrea 81 D4
Tesha →, Russia 34 C6
Teshio, Japan 54 B10
Teshio-Gawa →, Japan 54 B10
Tešica, Serbia & M. 44 C5
Tesiyn Gol →, Mongolia 60 A4
Teslić, Bos.-H. 28 F2
Teslin, Canada 102 A2
Teslin →, Canada 102 A2
Teslin L., Canada 102 A2
Tessalit, Mali 83 A5
Tessaoua, Niger 83 C6
Tessin, Germany 24 A8
Tessit, Mali 83 B5
Test →, U.K. 15 G6
Testa del Gargano, Italy 41 G13
Testigos, Is. Las, Venezuela 121 D7
Tét, Hungary 28 C2
Têt →, France 20 F7
Tetachuck L., Canada 102 C3
Tetas, Pta., Chile 126 A1
Tete, Mozam. 87 F3
Tete □, Mozam. 87 F3
Teterev →, Ukraine 33 G6
Teterow, Germany 24 B8
Teteven, Bulgaria 45 D8
Tethul →, Canada 102 A6
Tetiyev, Ukraine 33 H5
Teton →, U.S.A. 108 C8
Tétouan, Morocco 78 A4
Tetovo, Macedonia 44 D4
Tetyushi, Russia 34 C9
Teuco →, Argentina 126 B3
Teulada, Italy 42 D1
Teulon, Canada 103 C9
Teun, Indonesia 63 F7
Teutoburger Wald, Germany 24 C4
Tevere ⌓, Italy 41 F9
Tevere →, Italy 41 G9
Teverya, Israel 74 C4
Teviot →, U.K. 13 F6
Tewantin, Australia 95 D5
Tewkesbury, U.K. 15 F5
Texada I., Canada 102 D4
Texarkana, Ark., U.S.A. 113 J8
Texarkana, Tex., U.S.A. 113 J7
Texas, Australia 95 D5
Texas □, U.S.A. 113 K5
Texas City, U.S.A. 113 L7
Texel, Neths. 17 A4
Texline, U.S.A. 113 G3
Texoma, L., U.S.A. 113 J6
Teykovo, Russia 32 D11
Teza →, Russia 34 B5
Tezin, Afghan. 68 B3
Teziutlán, Mexico 119 D5
Tezpur, India 67 F18
Tezzeron L., Canada 102 C4
Tha-anne →, Canada 103 A10
Tha Deua, Laos 64 D4
Tha Deua, Laos 64 C3
Tha Pla, Thailand 64 D3
Tha Rua, Thailand 64 E3
Tha Sala, Thailand 65 H2
Tha Song Yang, Thailand 64 D1
Thaba Putsoa, Lesotho 89 D4
Thabana Ntlenyana, Lesotho 89 D4
Thabazimbi, S. Africa 89 C4
Thādiq, Si. Arabia 70 E5
Thai Binh, Vietnam 58 G6
Thai Muang, Thailand 65 H2
Thai Nguyen, Vietnam 58 G5
Thailand ■, Asia 64 E4
Thailand, G. of, Asia 65 G3
Thakhek, Laos 64 D5
Thal, Pakistan 68 C4
Thal Desert, Pakistan 68 D4
Thala La = Hkakabo Razi, Burma 67 E20
Thalabarivat, Cambodia 64 F5
Thallon, Australia 95 D4
Thalu, Ko, Thailand 65 b
Thalwil, Switz. 25 H4
Thames, N.Z. 91 G5
Thames →, Canada 116 D2
Thames →, U.K. 15 F8
Thames →, U.S.A. 117 E12
Thames Estuary, U.K. 15 F8
Thamesford, Canada 116 C4
Thamesville, Canada 116 D3
Than, India 68 H4
Than Uyen, Vietnam 64 B4
Thana Gazi, India 68 F7
Thandla, India 68 H6
Thane, India 66 K8
Thanesar, India 68 D7
Thanet, I. of, U.K. 15 F9
Thangool, Australia 94 C5
Thanh Hoa, Vietnam 64 C5
Thanh Hung, Vietnam 65 H5
Thanh Pho Ho Chi Minh, Vietnam 65 G6
Thanh Thuy, Vietnam 64 A5
Thanjavur, India 66 P11
Thann, France 19 E14
Thano Bula Khan, Pakistan 68 G2
Thaolinta L., Canada 103 A9
Thaon-les-Vosges, France 19 D13
Thap Lan △, Thailand 64 E4
Thap Sakae, Thailand 65 G2
Thap Than, Thailand 64 E2
Thar Desert, India 68 F5
Tharad, India 68 G4
Thargomindah, Australia 95 D3
Tharrawaddy, Burma 67 L19
Tharthār, Buḩayrat ath, Iraq 70 C4
Tharthār, L. = Tharthār, Buḩayrat ath, Iraq 70 C4
Tharthār, W. ath →, Iraq 70 C4
Thasopoúla, Greece 45 F8
Thásos, Greece 45 F8
That Khe, Vietnam 58 F6
Thatcher, Ariz., U.S.A. 109 K9
Thatcher, Colo., U.S.A. 113 G2
Thaton, Burma 67 L20
Thau, Bassin de, France 20 E7
Thaungdut, Burma 67 G19
Thayer, U.S.A. 113 G9
Thayetmyo, Burma 67 K19
Thazi, Burma 67 J20
The Alberga →, Australia 95 D2
The Bight, Bahamas 121 B4
The Crane, Barbados 121 g
The Dalles, U.S.A. 108 D3
The English Company's Is., Australia 94 A2
The Frome →, Australia 95 D2
The Great Divide = Great Dividing Ra., Australia 94 C4
The Hague = 's-Gravenhage, Neths. 17 B4
The Hamilton →, Australia 95 D2
The Macumba →, Australia 95 D2
The Neales →, Australia 95 D2
The Officer →, Australia 93 E5
The Pas, Canada 103 C8
The Range, Zimbabwe 87 F3
The Rock, Australia 95 F4
The Salt L., Australia 95 E3
The Sandheads, India 69 J13
The Settlement, Br. Virgin Is. 121 e
The Stevenson →, Australia 95 D2
The Warburton →, Australia 95 D2
The Woodlands, U.S.A. 113 K7
Thebes = Thívai, Greece 46 C5
Thebes, Egypt 80 B3
Thedford, U.S.A. 112 E4
Theebine, Australia 95 D5
Thekulthili L., Canada 103 A7
Thelon →, Canada 103 A8
Thénezay, France 18 F6
Thenon, France 20 C5
Theodore, Australia 94 C5
Theodore, Canada 103 C8
Theodore, U.S.A. 115 K1
Theodore Roosevelt △, U.S.A. 112 B3
Theodore Roosevelt L., U.S.A. 109 K8
Thepha, Thailand 65 J3
Thérain →, France 19 C9
Theresa, U.S.A. 117 B9
Thermaïkós Kólpos, Greece 44 F6
Thermí, Greece 47 B8
Thermopolis, U.S.A. 108 E9
Thermopylae P., Greece 46 C4
Thesprotía □, Greece 46 B2
Thessalía □, Greece 46 B4
Thessalon, Canada 104 C3
Thessaloníki, Greece 44 F6
Thessaloníki □, Greece 44 F7
Thessaloníki ✕ (SKG), Greece 44 F7
Thessaloníki, Gulf of = Thermaïkós Kólpos, Greece 44 F6
Thessaly = Thessalía □, Greece 46 B4
Thetford, U.K. 15 E8
Thetford Mines, Canada 105 C5
Theun →, Laos 64 C5
Theunissen, S. Africa 88 D4
Thevenard, Australia 95 E1
Thiámis →, Greece 46 B2
Thiberville, France 18 C7
Thibodaux, U.S.A. 113 L9
Thicket Portage, Canada 103 B9
Thief River Falls, U.S.A. 112 A6
Thiel Mts., Antarctica 5 E16
Thiene, Italy 41 C8
Thiérache, France 19 C10
Thiers, France 20 C7
Thiès, Senegal 82 C1
Thiesi, Italy 42 B1
Thiet, Sudan 81 F2
Thika, Kenya 86 C4
Thikombia, Fiji 91 B9
Thille-Boubacar, Senegal 82 B1
Thimphu, Bhutan 67 F16
Þingvallavatn, Iceland 8 D3
Thionville, France 19 C13
Thíra, Greece 47 E7
Thirasía, Greece 47 E7
Third Cataract, Sudan 80 D3
Thirsk, U.K. 14 C6
Thiruvananthapuram = Trivandrum, India 66 Q10
Thisted, Denmark 11 H2
Thistle I., Australia 95 F2
Thívai, Greece 46 C5
Thiviers, France 20 C4
Thizy, France 19 F11
Þjórsá →, Iceland 8 E3
Thlewiaza →, Canada 103 A10
Thmar Puok, Cambodia 64 F4

Tho Vinh, *Vietnam* 64 C5
Thoa →, *Canada* 103 A7
Thoen, *Thailand* 64 D2
Thoeng, *Thailand* 64 C3
Thohoyandou, *S. Africa* 85 J6
Tholdi, *Pakistan* 69 B7
Thomas, *U.S.A.* 113 H5
Thomas, L., *Australia* 95 D2
Thomaston, *U.S.A.* 115 J3
Thomasville, *Ala., U.S.A.* 115 K2
Thomasville, *Ga., U.S.A.* 115 K4
Thomasville, *N.C., U.S.A.* 115 H5
Thompson, *Canada* 103 B9
Thompson, *U.S.A.* 117 E9
Thompson →, *Canada* 102 C4
Thompson →, *U.S.A.* 112 F8
Thompson Falls, *U.S.A.* 108 C6
Thompson Pk., *U.S.A.* 108 F2
Thompson Springs, *U.S.A.* 109 G9
Thompsontown, *U.S.A.* 116 F7
Thomson, *U.S.A.* 115 J4
Thomson →, *Australia* 94 C3
Thomson's Falls = Nyahururu, *Kenya* 86 B4
Thônes, *France* 21 C10
Thong Yang, *Thailand* 65 b
Thonon-les-Bains, *France* 19 F13
Thorez, *Ukraine* 33 H10
Þórisvatn, *Iceland* 8 D4
Thornaby on Tees, *U.K.* 14 C6
Thornbury, *Canada* 116 B4
Thorne, *U.K.* 14 D7
Thornhill, *Canada* 102 C3
Thorold, *Canada* 116 C5
Þórshöfn, *Iceland* 8 C6
Thouarcé, *France* 18 E6
Thouars, *France* 18 F6
Thouet →, *France* 18 E6
Thouin, C., *Australia* 92 D2
Thousand Oaks, *U.S.A.* 111 L8
Thrace, *Turkey* 45 F10
Thrakikón Pélagos, *Greece* 45 F8
Three Forks, *U.S.A.* 108 D8
Three Gorges Dam, *China* 59 B8
Three Hills, *Canada* 102 C6
Three Hummock I., *Australia* 95 G3
Three Points, C., *Ghana* 82 E4
Three Rivers, *Calif., U.S.A.* 110 J8
Three Rivers, *Tex., U.S.A.* 113 L5
Three Sisters, *U.S.A.* 108 D3
Three Springs, *Australia* 93 E2
Throssell, L., *Australia* 93 E3
Throssell Ra., *Australia* 92 D3
Thrushton △, *Australia* 95 D4
Thuan Hoa, *Vietnam* 65 H5
Thubun Lakes, *Canada* 103 A6
Thueyts, *France* 21 D8
Thuin, *Belgium* 17 D4
Thuir, *France* 20 F6
Thule = Qaanaaq, *Greenland* 4 B4
Thule Air Base = Uummannaq, *Greenland* 4 B5
Thun, *Switz.* 25 J3
Thunder B., *U.S.A.* 116 B1
Thunder Bay, *Canada* 104 C2
Thunersee, *Switz.* 25 J3
Thung Salaeng Luang △, *Thailand* 64 D3
Thung Song, *Thailand* 65 H2
Thunkar, *Bhutan* 67 F17
Thuong Tra, *Vietnam* 64 D6
Thur →, *Switz.* 25 H5
Thurgau □, *Switz.* 25 H5
Thüringen □, *Germany* 24 D6
Thüringer Wald, *Germany* 24 E6
Thurles, *Ireland* 12 D4
Thurn P., *Austria* 26 D5
Thurrock □, *U.K.* 15 F8
Thursday I., *Australia* 94 A3
Thurso, *Canada* 104 C4
Thurso, *U.K.* 13 C5
Thurso →, *U.K.* 13 C5
Thurston I., *Antarctica* 5 D16
Thury-Harcourt, *France* 18 D6
Thutade L., *Canada* 102 B3
Thy, *Denmark* 11 H2
Thyborøn, *Denmark* 11 H2
Thyolo, *Malawi* 87 F4
Thysville = Mbanza Ngungu, *Dem. Rep. of the Congo* 84 F2
Ti-n-Amzi →, *Niger* 83 B5
Ti-n-Barraouene, O. →, *Africa* 83 B5
Ti-n-Zaouatene, *Algeria* 83 B5
Ti Tree, *Australia* 94 C1
Tiadiaye, *Senegal* 82 C1
Tian Shan, *Asia* 60 B3
Tianchang, *China* 59 A12
Tiandeng, *China* 58 F6
Tiandong, *China* 58 F6
Tian'e, *China* 58 E6
Tianhe, *China* 58 E7
Tianjin, *China* 57 E9
Tiankoura, *Burkina Faso* 82 C4
Tianlin, *China* 58 E6
Tianmen, *China* 59 B9
Tianquan, *China* 58 B4
Tianshui, *China* 56 G3
Tiantai, *China* 59 C13
Tianyang, *China* 58 F6
Tianyar, *Indonesia* 63 J18
Tianzhen, *China* 56 D8
Tianzhu, *China* 58 D7
Tianzhuangtai, *China* 57 D12
Tiaret, *Algeria* 78 A6
Tiassalé, *Ivory C.* 82 D4
Tibagi, *Brazil* 127 A5
Tibagi →, *Brazil* 127 A5
Tibati, *Cameroon* 83 D7
Tibe, *Ethiopia* 81 F4
Tiber = Tevere →, *Italy* 41 G9
Tiberias = Teverya, *Israel* 74 C4
Tiberias, L. = Yam Kinneret, *Israel* 74 C4
Tibesti, *Chad* 79 D9
Tibet = Xizang Zizhiqu □, *China* 60 C3
Tibet, Plateau of, *Asia* 50 F12
Tibiao, *Phil.* 61 F5
Tibiri, *Niger* 83 C6
Ţibleş, Vf., *Romania* 29 C9
Ţibleşului, Munţii, *Romania* 29 C9
Tibnī, *Syria* 70 C3
Tibooburra, *Australia* 95 D3
Tibro, *Sweden* 11 F8
Tiburón, I., *Mexico* 118 B2
Ticao I., *Phil.* 61 E5
Tîchît, *Mauritania* 82 B3
Ticho, *Ethiopia* 81 F4
Ticino □, *Switz.* 25 J4
Ticino →, *Italy* 25 K5
Ticleni, *Romania* 29 F8
Ticonderoga, *U.S.A.* 117 C11
Ticul, *Mexico* 119 C7
Tidaholm, *Sweden* 11 F7
Tidan, *Sweden* 11 F8
Tiddim, *Burma* 67 H18
Tidioute, *U.S.A.* 116 E5
Tidjikja, *Mauritania* 82 B2
Tidore, *Indonesia* 63 D7
Tiébissou, *Ivory C.* 82 D3
Tiel, *Neths.* 17 C5
Tiel, *Senegal* 82 C1
Tieling, *China* 57 C12
Tielt, *Belgium* 17 C3
Tien Shan = Tian Shan, *Asia* 60 B3
Tien-tsin = Tianjin, *China* 57 E9
Tien Yen, *Vietnam* 64 B6
T'ienching = Tianjin, *China* 57 E9
Tienen, *Belgium* 17 D4
Tiénigbé, *Ivory C.* 82 D3
Tientsin = Tianjin, *China* 57 E9
Tieri, *Australia* 94 C4
Tierp, *Sweden* 10 D11
Tierra Amarilla, *Chile* 126 B1
Tierra Amarilla, *U.S.A.* 109 H10
Tierra Colorada, *Mexico* 119 D5
Tierra de Barros, *Spain* 37 G4
Tierra de Campos, *Spain* 36 C6
Tierra del Fuego, I. Gr. de, *Argentina* 128 G3
Tiétar →, *Spain* 36 F4
Tieté →, *Brazil* 127 A5
Tiffin, *U.S.A.* 114 E4
Tiflis = Tbilisi, *Georgia* 35 K7
Tifton, *U.S.A.* 115 K4
Tifu, *Indonesia* 63 E7
Tighina, *Moldova* 29 D14
Tigil, *Russia* 53 D16
Tignish, *Canada* 105 C7
Tigray □, *Ethiopia* 81 E4
Tigre →, *Peru* 124 D4
Tigre →, *Venezuela* 124 B6
Tigris = Dijlah, Nahr →, *Asia* 70 D5
Tigveni, *Romania* 29 E9
Tigyaing, *Burma* 67 H20
Tîh, Gebel el, *Egypt* 80 B3
Tijara, *India* 68 F7
Tijuana, *Mexico* 111 N9
Tikal, *Guatemala* 120 C2
Tikal △, *Guatemala* 120 C2
Tikamgarh, *India* 69 G8
Tikaré, *Burkina Faso* 83 C4
Tikhoretsk, *Russia* 35 H5
Tikhvin, *Russia* 32 C7
Tikiraqjuaq = Whale Cove, *Canada* 103 A10
Tiko, *Cameroon* 83 E6
Tikrīt, *Iraq* 70 C4
Tiksi, *Russia* 53 B13
Tilamuta, *Indonesia* 63 D6
Tilburg, *Neths.* 17 C5
Tilbury, *Canada* 116 D2
Tilbury, *U.K.* 15 F8
Tilcara, *Argentina* 126 A2
Tilden, *U.S.A.* 112 D6
Tilemses, *Niger* 83 B5
Tilemsi, Vallée du, *Mali* 83 B5
Tilhar, *India* 69 F8
Tilichiki, *Russia* 53 C17
Tílissos, *Greece* 49 D7
Till →, *U.K.* 14 B5
Tillabéri, *Niger* 83 C5
Tillamook, *U.S.A.* 108 D2
Tillberga, *Sweden* 10 E10
Tillia, *Niger* 83 B5
Tillsonburg, *Canada* 116 D4
Tillyeria, *Cyprus* 49 D11
Tilogne, *Senegal* 82 B2
Tílos, *Greece* 47 E9
Tilpa, *Australia* 95 E3
Tilsit = Sovetsk, *Russia* 9 J19
Tilt →, *U.K.* 13 E5
Tilton, *U.S.A.* 117 C13
Tiltonsville, *U.S.A.* 116 F4
Tim, *Denmark* 11 H2
Timagami, L., *Canada* 104 C3
Timanfaya △, *Canary Is.* 48 F6
Timaru, *N.Z.* 91 L3
Timashevo, *Russia* 34 D10
Timashevsk, *Russia* 35 H4
Timau, *Kenya* 86 B4
Timbákion, *Greece* 49 D6
Timbedgha, *Mauritania* 82 B3
Timber Creek, *Australia* 92 C5
Timber Lake, *U.S.A.* 112 C4
Timber Mt., *U.S.A.* 110 H10
Timbo, *Guinea* 82 C2
Timbo, *Liberia* 82 D3
Timbuktu = Tombouctou, *Mali* 82 B4
Timeiaouine, *Algeria* 83 A5
Timétrine, Mts., *Mali* 83 B4
Timfi Óros, *Greece* 46 B2
Timfristós, Óros, *Greece* 46 C3
Timi, *Cyprus* 49 E11
Timia, *Niger* 83 B6
Timimoun, *Algeria* 78 C6
Timirist, Râs, *Mauritania* 82 B1
Timiş = Tamis →, *Serbia & M.* 28 F5
Timiş □, *Romania* 28 E6
Timiskaming, L. = Témiscamingue, L., *Canada* 104 C4
Timişoara, *Romania* 28 E6
Timmersdala, *Sweden* 11 F7
Timmins, *Canada* 104 C3
Timok →, *Serbia & M.* 44 B6
Timor, *Indonesia* 63 F7
Timor Leste = East Timor ■, *Asia* 63 F7
Timor Sea, *Ind. Oc.* 92 B4
Timrå, *Sweden* 10 B11
Tin Can Bay, *Australia* 95 D5
Tin Ethisane, *Mali* 83 B4
Tin Gornai, *Mali* 83 B4
Tin Mt., *U.S.A.* 110 J9
Tina →, *S. Africa* 89 E4
Tîna, Khalîg el, *Egypt* 80 A3
Tinaca Pt., *Phil.* 61 J6
Tinajo, *Canary Is.* 48 E6
Tinca, *Romania* 28 D6
Tindal, *Australia* 92 B5
Tindouf, *Algeria* 78 C4
Tinée →, *France* 21 E11
Tineo, *Spain* 36 B4
Tinfunque △, *Paraguay* 126 A3
Ting Jiang →, *China* 59 E11
Tinggi, Pulau, *Malaysia* 65 L5
Tinglev, *Denmark* 11 K3
Tingo Maria, *Peru* 124 E3
Tingrela, *Ivory C.* 82 C3
Tingsryd, *Sweden* 11 H9
Tingstäde, *Sweden* 11 G12
Tinh Bien, *Vietnam* 65 G5
Tinnevelly = Tirunelveli, *India* 66 Q10
Tinogasta, *Argentina* 126 B2
Tínos, *Greece* 47 D7
Tiñoso, C., *Spain* 39 H3
Tinpahar, *India* 69 G12
Tintina, *Argentina* 126 B3
Tintinara, *Australia* 95 F3
Tintioulé, *Guinea* 82 C3
Tinto →, *Spain* 37 H4
Tioga, *N. Dak., U.S.A.* 112 A3
Tioga, *Pa., U.S.A.* 116 E7
Tioman, Pulau, *Malaysia* 65 L5
Tione di Trento, *Italy* 40 B7
Tionesta, *U.S.A.* 116 E5
Tior, *Sudan* 81 F3
Tipongpani, *India* 67 F19
Tipperary, *Ireland* 12 D3
Tipperary □, *Ireland* 12 D4
Tipton, *Calif., U.S.A.* 110 J7
Tipton, *Iowa, U.S.A.* 112 E9
Tipton Mt., *U.S.A.* 111 K12
Tiptonville, *U.S.A.* 113 G10
Tīrān, *Iran* 71 C6
Tīrān, *Si. Arabia* 80 B3
Tirana ✕ (TIA), *Albania* 43 A12
Tiranë, *Albania* 44 E3
Tirano, *Italy* 40 B7
Tiraspol, *Moldova* 29 D14
Tirdout, *Mali* 83 B4
Tire, *Turkey* 47 C9
Tirebolu, *Turkey* 73 B8
Tiree, *U.K.* 13 E2
Tiree, Passage of, *U.K.* 13 E2
Tîrgovişte = Târgovişte, *Romania* 29 F10
Tîrgu-Jiu = Târgu-Jiu, *Romania* 29 E8
Tîrgu Mureş = Târgu Mureş, *Romania* 29 D9
Tirich Mir, *Pakistan* 66 A7
Tiriolo, *Italy* 43 D9
Tiriro, *Guinea* 82 C3
Tírnavos, *Greece* 46 B4
Tirodi, *India* 66 J11
Tirol □, *Austria* 26 D3
Tirschenreuth, *Germany* 25 F8
Tirso →, *Italy* 42 C1
Tirstrup, *Denmark* 11 H4
Tiruchchirappalli, *India* 66 P11
Tirunelveli, *India* 66 Q10
Tirupati, *India* 66 N11
Tiruppur, *India* 66 P10
Tiruvannamalai, *India* 66 N11
Tisa, *India* 68 C7
Tisa →, *Serbia & M.* 28 E5
Tisdale, *Canada* 103 C8
Tishomingo, *U.S.A.* 113 H6
Tisjön, *Sweden* 10 D7
Tisnaren, *Sweden* 11 F9
Tišnov, *Czech Rep.* 27 B9
Tisovec, *Slovak Rep.* 27 C12
Tisza = Tisa →, *Serbia & M.* 28 E5
Tiszaföldvár, *Hungary* 28 D5
Tiszafüred, *Hungary* 28 C5
Tiszalök, *Hungary* 28 B6
Tiszavasvári, *Hungary* 28 C6
Tit-Ary, *Russia* 53 B13
Titaguas, *Spain* 38 F3
Titao, *Burkina Faso* 83 C4
Titel, *Serbia & M.* 28 E5
Tithwal, *Pakistan* 69 B5
Titicaca, L., *S. Amer.* 124 G5
Titisee, *Germany* 25 H4
Titiwa, *Nigeria* 83 C7
Tito, *Italy* 43 B8
Titograd = Podgorica, *Serbia & M.* 44 D3
Titova Korenica, *Croatia* 41 D12
Titu, *Romania* 29 F10
Titule, *Dem. Rep. of the Congo* 86 B2
Titusville, *Fla., U.S.A.* 115 L5
Titusville, *Pa., U.S.A.* 116 E5
Tivaouane, *Senegal* 82 C1
Tivat, *Serbia & M.* 44 D2
Tivedens △, *Sweden* 11 F8
Tiverton, *U.K.* 15 G4
Tívoli, *Italy* 41 G9
Tiyo, *Eritrea* 81 E5
Tizi-Ouzou, *Algeria* 78 A6
Tizimín, *Mexico* 119 C7
Tjæreborg, *Denmark* 11 J2
Tjällmo, *Sweden* 11 F9
Tjeggelvas, *Sweden* 8 C17
Tjirebon = Cirebon, *Indonesia* 63 G13
Tjluring, *Indonesia* 63 J17
Tjörn, *Sweden* 11 F5
Tkibuli = Tqibuli, *Georgia* 35 J6
Tkvarcheli = Tqvarcheli, *Georgia* 35 J5
Tlacotalpan, *Mexico* 119 D5
Tlahualilo, *Mexico* 118 B4
Tlaquepaque, *Mexico* 118 C4
Tlaxcala, *Mexico* 119 D5
Tlaxcala □, *Mexico* 119 D5
Tlaxiaco, *Mexico* 119 D5
Tlemcen, *Algeria* 78 B5
Tłuszcz, *Poland* 31 F8
Tlyarata, *Russia* 35 J8
To Bong, *Vietnam* 64 F7
Toa Payoh, *Singapore* 65 d
Toad →, *Canada* 102 B4
Toad River, *Canada* 102 B3
Toamasina, *Madag.* 89 B8
Toamasina □, *Madag.* 89 B8
Toay, *Argentina* 126 D3
Toba, *China* 58 B1
Toba, *Japan* 55 G8
Toba, Danau, *Indonesia* 62 D1
Toba Kakar, *Pakistan* 68 D3
Toba Tek Singh, *Pakistan* 68 D5
Tobago, *Trin. & Tob.* 121 D7
Tobarra, *Spain* 39 G3
Tobelo, *Indonesia* 63 D7
Tobermory, *Canada* 116 A3
Tobermory, *U.K.* 13 E2
Tobi, *Pac. Oc.* 63 D8
Tobin, *U.S.A.* 110 F5
Tobin, L., *Australia* 92 D4
Tobin L., *Canada* 103 C8
Toblach = Dobbiaco, *Italy* 41 B9
Toboali, *Indonesia* 62 E3
Tobol →, *Russia* 52 D7
Toboli, *Indonesia* 63 E6
Tobolsk, *Russia* 52 D7
Tobor, *Senegal* 82 C1
Tobruk = Tubruq, *Libya* 79 B10
Tobyhanna, *U.S.A.* 117 E9
Tobyl = Tobol →, *Russia* 52 D7
Tocantinópolis, *Brazil* 125 E9
Tocantins □, *Brazil* 125 F9
Tocantins →, *Brazil* 125 D9
Toccoa, *U.S.A.* 115 H4
Toce →, *Italy* 40 C5
Tochi →, *Pakistan* 68 C4
Tochigi, *Japan* 55 F9
Tochigi □, *Japan* 55 F9
Tocina, *Spain* 37 H5
Töcksfors, *Sweden* 10 E5
Toco, *Trin. & Tob.* 125 K16
Toconao, *Chile* 126 A2
Tocopilla, *Chile* 126 A1
Tocumwal, *Australia* 95 F4
Tocuyo →, *Venezuela* 124 A5
Todd →, *Australia* 94 C2
Todeli, *Indonesia* 63 E6
Todenyang, *Kenya* 86 B4
Todgarh, *India* 68 G5
Todi, *Italy* 41 F9
Todos os Santos, B. de, *Brazil* 125 F11
Todos Santos, *Mexico* 118 C2
Todtnau, *Germany* 25 H3
Toe Hd., *U.K.* 13 D1
Toecé, *Burkina Faso* 83 C4
Tofield, *Canada* 102 C6
Tofino, *Canada* 102 D3
Tofua, *Tonga* 91 D11
Tōgane, *Japan* 55 G10
Togba, *Mauritania* 82 B2
Togian, Kepulauan, *Indonesia* 63 E6
Togliatti, *Russia* 34 D9
Togo ■, *W. Afr.* 83 D5
Togtoh, *China* 56 D6
Tohma →, *Turkey* 72 C7
Tōhoku □, *Japan* 54 E10
Töhöm, *Mongolia* 56 B5
Toinya, *Sudan* 81 F2
Toiyabe Range, *U.S.A.* 108 G5
Tojikiston = Tajikistan ■, *Asia* 52 F8
Tojo, *Indonesia* 63 E6
Tōjō, *Japan* 55 G6
Tok, *U.S.A.* 100 B5
Tok-do, *Asia* 55 F5
Tokachi-Dake, *Japan* 54 C11
Tokachi-Gawa →, *Japan* 54 C11
Tokaj, *Hungary* 28 B6
Tokala, *Indonesia* 63 E6
Tōkamachi, *Japan* 55 F9
Tokanui, *N.Z.* 91 M2
Tokar, *Sudan* 80 D4
Tokara-Rettō, *Japan* 55 K4
Tokarahi, *N.Z.* 91 L3
Tokashiki-Shima, *Japan* 55 L3
Tokat, *Turkey* 72 B7
Tŏkch'ŏn, *N. Korea* 57 E14
Tokeland, *U.S.A.* 110 D3
Tokelau Is., *Pac. Oc.* 96 H10
Tokmak, *Kyrgyzstan* 52 E8
Tokmak, *Ukraine* 33 J8
Toko Ra., *Australia* 94 C2
Tokoro-Gawa →, *Japan* 54 B12
Tokuno-Shima, *Japan* 55 L4
Tokushima, *Japan* 55 G7
Tokushima □, *Japan* 55 H7
Tokuyama, *Japan* 55 G5
Tōkyō, *Japan* 55 G9
Tolaga Bay, *N.Z.* 91 H7
Tolbukhin = Dobrich, *Bulgaria* 45 C11
Toledo, *Brazil* 127 A5
Toledo, *Spain* 36 F6
Toledo, *Ohio, U.S.A.* 114 E4
Toledo, *Oreg., U.S.A.* 108 D2
Toledo, *Wash., U.S.A.* 108 C2
Toledo, Montes de, *Spain* 37 F6
Toledo Bend Reservoir, *U.S.A.* 113 K8
Tolentino, *Italy* 41 E10
Tolfa, *Italy* 41 F8
Tolga, *Australia* 94 B4
Toliara, *Madag.* 89 C7
Toliara □, *Madag.* 89 C8
Tolima, *Colombia* 124 C3
Tolitoli, *Indonesia* 63 D6
Tolkmicko, *Poland* 30 D6
Tollarp, *Sweden* 11 J7
Tollensesee, *Germany* 24 B9
Tollhouse, *U.S.A.* 110 H7
Tolmachevo, *Russia* 32 C5
Tolmezzo, *Italy* 41 B10
Tolmin, *Slovenia* 41 B10
Tolna, *Hungary* 28 D3
Tolna □, *Hungary* 28 D3
Tolo, Teluk, *Indonesia* 63 E6
Tolochin = Talachyn, *Belarus* 32 E5
Tolosa, *Spain* 38 B2
Tolox, *Spain* 37 J6
Toluca, *Mexico* 119 D5
Tom Burke, *S. Africa* 89 C4
Tom Price, *Australia* 92 D2
Toma, *Burkina Faso* 82 C4
Tomah, *U.S.A.* 112 D9
Tomahawk, *U.S.A.* 112 C10
Tomai, *Moldova* 29 D13
Tomakomai, *Japan* 54 C10
Tomales, *U.S.A.* 110 G4
Tomales B., *U.S.A.* 110 G3
Tomar, *Portugal* 37 F2
Tómaros, Óros, *Greece* 46 B2
Tomarza, *Turkey* 72 C6
Tomaszów Lubelski, *Poland* 31 H10
Tomaszów Mazowiecki, *Poland* 31 G7
Tomatlán, *Mexico* 118 D3
Tombadonkéa, *Guinea* 82 C2
Tombador, Serra do, *Brazil* 124 F7
Tombe, *Sudan* 81 F3
Tombigbee →, *U.S.A.* 115 K2
Tombouctou, *Mali* 82 B4
Tombstone, *U.S.A.* 109 L8
Tombua, *Angola* 88 B1
Tomé, *Chile* 126 D1
Tomelilla, *Sweden* 11 J7
Tomelloso, *Spain* 37 F7
Tomini, *Indonesia* 63 D6
Tomini, Teluk, *Indonesia* 63 E6
Tominian, *Mali* 82 C4
Tomiño, *Spain* 36 D2
Tomintoul, *U.K.* 13 D5
Tomislavgrad, *Bos.-H.* 28 G2
Tomkinson Ranges, *Australia* 93 E4
Tommot, *Russia* 53 D13
Tomnop Ta Suos, *Cambodia* 65 G5
Tomo →, *Colombia* 124 B5
Toms Place, *U.S.A.* 110 H8
Toms River, *U.S.A.* 117 G10
Tomsk, *Russia* 52 D9
Tomtabacken, *Sweden* 11 G8
Tona, *Spain* 38 D7
Tonalá, *Mexico* 119 D6
Tonale, Passo del, *Italy* 40 B7
Tonantins, *Brazil* 124 D5
Tonasket, *U.S.A.* 108 B4
Tonawanda, *U.S.A.* 116 D6
Tonb, *Iran* 71 E7
Tonbridge, *U.K.* 15 F8
Tondano, *Indonesia* 63 D6
Tondela, *Portugal* 36 E2
Tønder, *Denmark* 11 K2
Tondi Kiwindi, *Niger* 83 C5
Tondibi, *Mali* 83 B4
Tondoro, *Namibia* 88 B2
Tone →, *Australia* 93 F2
Tone-Gawa →, *Japan* 55 F9
Tonekābon, *Iran* 71 B6
Tong Xian, *China* 56 E9
Tôngâ, *Sudan* 81 F3
Tonga ■, *Pac. Oc.* 91 D11
Tonga Trench, *Pac. Oc.* 96 J10
Tongaat, *S. Africa* 89 D5
Tong'an, *China* 59 E12
Tongareva, *Cook Is.* 97 H12
Tongariro △, *N.Z.* 91 H5
Tongatapu Group, *Tonga* 91 E12
Tongbai, *China* 59 A9
Tongcheng, *Anhui, China* 59 B11
Tongcheng, *Hubei, China* 59 C9
Tongchŏn-ni, *N. Korea* 57 E14
Tongchuan, *China* 56 G5
Tongdao, *China* 58 D7
Tongeren, *Belgium* 17 D5
Tonggu, *China* 59 C10
Tongguan, *China* 56 G6
Tonghae, *S. Korea* 57 F15
Tonghai, *China* 58 E4
Tonghua, *China* 57 D13
Tongjiang, *China* 58 B6
Tongjosŏn Man, *N. Korea* 57 E15
Tongking, G. of = Tonkin, G. of, *Asia* 60 E5
Tongliang, *China* 58 C6
Tongliao, *China* 57 C12
Tongling, *China* 59 B11
Tonglu, *China* 59 C12
Tongnae, *S. Korea* 57 G15
Tongnan = Anyue, *China* 58 B5
Tongobory, *Madag.* 89 C7
Tongoy, *Chile* 126 C1
Tongren, *China* 58 D7
Tongres = Tongeren, *Belgium* 17 D5
Tongsa Dzong, *Bhutan* 67 F17
Tongue, *U.K.* 13 C4

Tongue →, *U.S.A.* 112 B2
Tongwei, *China* 56 G3
Tongxiang, *China* 59 B13
Tongxin, *China* 56 F3
Tongyang, *N. Korea* 57 E14
Tongyu, *China* 57 B12
Tongzi, *China* 58 C6
Tonj, *Sudan* 81 F2
Tonj →, *Sudan* 81 F2
Tonk, *India* 68 F6
Tonkawa, *U.S.A.* 113 G6
Tonkin = Bac Phan, *Vietnam* 64 B5
Tonkin, G. of, *Asia* 60 E5
Tonle Sap, *Cambodia* 64 F4
Tonnay-Charente, *France* 20 C3
Tonneins, *France* 20 D4
Tonnerre, *France* 19 E10
Tönning, *Germany* 24 A4
Tono, *Japan* 54 E10
Tonopah, *U.S.A.* 109 G5
Tonosí, *Panama* 120 E3
Tons →, *Haryana, India* 68 D7
Tons →, *Ut. P., India* 69 F10
Tønsberg, *Norway* 9 G14
Tonto ⌓, *U.S.A.* 109 K8
Tonya, *Turkey* 73 B8
Toobanna, *Australia* 94 B4
Toodyay, *Australia* 93 F2
Tooele, *U.S.A.* 108 F7
Toompine, *Australia* 95 D3
Toora, *Australia* 95 F4
Toora-Khem, *Russia* 53 D10
Toowoomba, *Australia* 95 D5
Top Springs, *Australia* 92 C5
Topalu, *Romania* 29 F13
Topaz, *U.S.A.* 110 G7
Topeka, *U.S.A.* 112 F7
Topl'a →, *Slovak Rep.* 27 C14
Topley, *Canada* 102 C3
Toplica →, *Serbia & M.* 44 C5
Toplița, *Romania* 29 D10
Topocalma, Pta., *Chile* 126 C1
Topock, *U.S.A.* 111 L12
Topola, *Serbia & M.* 44 B4
Topolčani, *Macedonia* 44 E5
Topol'čany, *Slovak Rep.* 27 C11
Topolnitsa →, *Bulgaria* 45 D8
Topolobampo, *Mexico* 118 B3
Topoloveni, *Romania* 29 F10
Topolovgrad, *Bulgaria* 45 D10
Topolvățu Mare, *Romania* 28 E6
Toppenish, *U.S.A.* 108 C3
Topraisar, *Romania* 29 F13
Topusko, *Croatia* 41 C12
Torà, *Spain* 38 D6
Tora Kit, *Sudan* 81 E3
Toraka Vestale, *Madag.* 89 B7
Torata, *Peru* 124 G4
Torbalı, *Turkey* 47 C9
Torbat-e Heydārīyeh, *Iran* 71 C8
Torbat-e Jām, *Iran* 71 C9
Torbay, *Canada* 105 C9
Torbay □, *U.K.* 15 G4
Torbjörntorp, *Sweden* 11 F7
Tordesillas, *Spain* 36 D6
Töreboda, *Sweden* 11 F8
Torekov, *Sweden* 11 H6
Torellò, *Spain* 38 C7
Toreno, *Spain* 36 C4
Torfaen □, *U.K.* 15 F4
Torgau, *Germany* 24 D8
Torgelow, *Germany* 24 B10
Torhamn, *Sweden* 11 H9
Torhout, *Belgium* 17 C3
Tori, *Ethiopia* 81 F3
Tori-Shima, *Japan* 55 J10
Torigni-sur-Vire, *France* 18 C6
Torija, *Spain* 38 E1
Torin, *Mexico* 118 B2
Torino, *Italy* 40 C4
Torit, *Sudan* 81 G3
Torkamān, *Iran* 70 B5
Torkovichi, *Russia* 32 C6
Tormac, *Romania* 28 E6
Tormes →, *Spain* 36 D4
Tornado Mt., *Canada* 102 D6
Tornal'a, *Slovak Rep.* 27 C13
Torne älv →, *Sweden* 8 D21
Torneå = Tornio, *Finland* 8 D21
Torneträsk, *Sweden* 8 B18
Tornio, *Finland* 8 D21
Tornionjoki →, *Finland* 8 D21
Tornquist, *Argentina* 126 D3
Toro, *Baleares, Spain* 48 B11
Toro, *Zamora, Spain* 36 D5
Torö, *Sweden* 11 F11
Toro ⌓, *Uganda* 86 C3
Toro, Cerro del, *Chile* 126 B2
Toro Pk., *U.S.A.* 111 M10
Törökszentmiklós, *Hungary* 28 C5
Toroníos Kólpos, *Greece* 44 F7
Toronto, *Canada* 116 C5
Toronto, *U.S.A.* 116 F4
Toronto Lester B. Pearson International ✗ (YYZ), *Canada* 116 C5
Toropets, *Russia* 32 D6
Tororo, *Uganda* 86 B3
Toros Dağları, *Turkey* 70 B2
Torpa, *India* 69 H11
Torquay, *U.K.* 15 G4
Torquemada, *Spain* 36 C6
Torrance, *U.S.A.* 111 M8
Torrão, *Portugal* 37 G2
Torre Annunziata, *Italy* 43 B7
Torre de Moncorvo, *Portugal* 36 D3
Torre del Campo, *Spain* 37 H7
Torre del Greco, *Italy* 43 B7
Torre del Mar, *Spain* 37 J6
Torre-Pacheco, *Spain* 39 H4
Torre Péllice, *Italy* 40 D4
Torreblanca, *Spain* 38 E5
Torrecampo, *Spain* 37 G6
Torrecilla en Cameros, *Spain* 38 C2
Torredembarra, *Spain* 38 D6
Torredonjimeno, *Spain* 37 H7
Torrejón de Ardoz, *Spain* 36 E7
Torrejoncillo, *Spain* 36 F4
Torrelaguna, *Spain* 36 E7
Torrelavega, *Spain* 36 B6
Torremaggiore, *Italy* 41 G12
Torremolinos, *Spain* 37 J6
Torrens, L., *Australia* 95 E2
Torrens Cr. →, *Australia* 94 C4
Torrens Creek, *Australia* 94 C4
Torrent, *Spain* 39 F4
Torrenueva, *Spain* 37 G7
Torreón, *Mexico* 118 B4
Torreperogil, *Spain* 37 G7
Torres, *Brazil* 127 B5
Torres, *Mexico* 118 B2
Torres Novas, *Portugal* 37 F2
Torres Strait, *Australia* 96 H6
Torres Vedras, *Portugal* 37 F1
Torrevieja, *Spain* 39 H4
Torrey, *U.S.A.* 109 G8
Torridge →, *U.K.* 15 G3
Torridon, L., *U.K.* 13 D3
Torrijos, *Spain* 36 F6
Tørring, *Denmark* 11 J3
Torrington, *Conn., U.S.A.* 117 E11
Torrington, *Wyo., U.S.A.* 112 D2
Torroella de Montgrì, *Spain* 38 C8
Torrox, *Spain* 37 J7
Torsås, *Sweden* 11 H9
Torsby, *Sweden* 10 D6
Torshälla, *Sweden* 10 E10
Tórshavn, *Færoe Is.* 8 E9
Torslanda, *Sweden* 11 G5
Torsö, *Sweden* 11 F7
Tortola, *Br. Virgin Is.* 121 e
Tórtoles de Esgueva, *Spain* 36 D6
Tortolì, *Italy* 42 C2
Tortona, *Italy* 40 D5
Tortorici, *Italy* 43 D7
Tortosa, *Spain* 38 E5
Tortosa, C., *Spain* 38 E5
Tortosendo, *Portugal* 36 E3
Tortue, I. de la, *Haiti* 121 B5
Tortuguero △, *Costa Rica* 120 D3
Tortum, *Turkey* 73 B9
Ţorūd, *Iran* 71 C7
Torul, *Turkey* 73 B8
Toruń, *Poland* 31 E5
Tory I., *Ireland* 12 A3
Torysa →, *Slovak Rep.* 27 C14
Torzhok, *Russia* 32 D8
Torzym, *Poland* 31 F2
Tosa, *Japan* 55 H6
Tosa-Shimizu, *Japan* 55 H6
Tosa-Wan, *Japan* 55 H6
Toscana □, *Italy* 40 E8
Toscano, Arcipelago, *Italy* 40 F7
Toshkent, *Uzbekistan* 52 E7
Tosno, *Russia* 32 C6
Tossa de Mar, *Spain* 38 D7
Tösse, *Sweden* 11 F6
Tostado, *Argentina* 126 B3
Tostedt, *Germany* 24 B5
Tostón, Pta. de, *Canary Is.* 48 F5
Tosu, *Japan* 55 H5
Tosya, *Turkey* 72 B6
Toszek, *Poland* 31 H5
Totana, *Spain* 39 H3
Totebo, *Sweden* 11 G10
Toteng, *Botswana* 88 C3
Tôtes, *France* 18 C8
Tótkomlós, *Hungary* 28 D5
Totma, *Russia* 52 C5
Totnes, *U.K.* 15 G4
Totness, *Suriname* 125 B7
Toto, *Nigeria* 83 D6
Totonicapán, *Guatemala* 120 D1
Totten Glacier, *Antarctica* 5 C8
Tottenham, *Australia* 95 E4
Tottenham, *Canada* 116 B5
Tottori, *Japan* 55 G7
Tottori □, *Japan* 55 G7
Touaret, *Niger* 83 A6
Touba, *Ivory C.* 82 D3
Touba, *Senegal* 82 C1
Toubkal, Djebel, *Morocco* 78 B4
Toucy, *France* 19 E10
Tougan, *Burkina Faso* 82 C4
Touggourt, *Algeria* 78 B7
Tougouri, *Burkina Faso* 83 C4
Tougué, *Guinea* 82 C2
Toukoto, *Mali* 82 C3
Toul, *France* 19 D12
Toulepleu, *Ivory C.* 82 D3
Toulon, *France* 21 E9
Toulouse, *France* 20 E5
Toulouse Blagnac ✗ (TLS), *France* 20 E5
Toummo, *Niger* 79 D8
Toumodi, *Ivory C.* 82 D3
Tounan, *Taiwan* 59 F13
Toungo, *Nigeria* 83 D7
Toungoo, *Burma* 67 K20
Touques →, *France* 18 C7
Touraine, *France* 18 E7
Tourane = Da Nang, *Vietnam* 64 D7
Tourcoing, *France* 19 B10
Touriñán, C., *Spain* 36 B1
Tournai, *Belgium* 17 D3
Tournan-en-Brie, *France* 19 D9
Tournay, *France* 20 E4
Tournon-St-Martin, *France* 18 F7
Tournon-sur-Rhône, *France* 21 C8
Tournus, *France* 19 F11
Tours, *France* 18 E7
Toussora, Mt., *C.A.R.* 84 C4
Touws →, *S. Africa* 88 E3
Touwsrivier, *S. Africa* 88 E3
Tovarkovskiy, *Russia* 32 F10
Tovuz, *Azerbaijan* 35 K7
Towada, *Japan* 54 D10
Towada-Hachimantai △, *Japan* 54 D10
Towada-Ko, *Japan* 54 D10
Towanda, *U.S.A.* 117 E8
Towang, *India* 67 F17
Tower, *U.S.A.* 112 B8
Towerhill Cr. →, *Australia* 94 C3
Towner, *U.S.A.* 112 A4
Townsend, *U.S.A.* 108 C8
Townshend I., *Australia* 94 C5
Townsville, *Australia* 94 B4
Towraghondi, *Afghan.* 66 B3
Towson, *U.S.A.* 114 F7
Towuti, Danau, *Indonesia* 63 E6
Toya-Ko, *Japan* 54 C10
Toyama, *Japan* 55 F8
Toyama □, *Japan* 55 F8
Toyama-Wan, *Japan* 55 F8
Toyapakeh, *Indonesia* 63 K18
Toyohashi, *Japan* 55 G8
Toyokawa, *Japan* 55 G8
Toyonaka, *Japan* 55 G7
Toyooka, *Japan* 55 G7
Toyota, *Japan* 55 G8
Tozeur, *Tunisia* 78 B7
Tozkhurmato, *Iraq* 70 C5
Tqibuli, *Georgia* 35 J6
Tqvarcheli, *Georgia* 35 J5
Trá Li = Tralee, *Ireland* 12 D2
Tra On, *Vietnam* 65 H5
Trabancos →, *Spain* 36 D5
Traben-Trarbach, *Germany* 25 F3
Trabzon, *Turkey* 73 B8
Tracadie-Sheila, *Canada* 105 C7
Tracy, *Calif., U.S.A.* 110 H5
Tracy, *Minn., U.S.A.* 112 C7
Tradate, *Italy* 40 C5
Trade Town, *Liberia* 82 D3
Trafalgar, C., *Spain* 37 J4
Traian, *Brăila, Romania* 29 E12
Traian, *Tulcea, Romania* 29 E13
Trail, *Canada* 102 D5
Trainor L., *Canada* 102 A4
Trákhonas, *Cyprus* 49 D12
Tralee, *Ireland* 12 D2
Tralee B., *Ireland* 12 D2
Tramore, *Ireland* 12 D4
Tramore B., *Ireland* 12 D4
Tran Ninh, Cao Nguyen, *Laos* 64 C4
Tranås, *Sweden* 11 F8
Tranbjerg, *Denmark* 11 H4
Trancas, *Argentina* 126 B2
Trancoso, *Portugal* 36 E3
Tranebjerg, *Denmark* 11 J4
Tranemo, *Sweden* 11 G7
Trang, *Thailand* 65 J2
Trangahy, *Madag.* 89 B7
Trangan, *Indonesia* 63 F8
Trangie, *Australia* 95 E4
Trångsviken, *Sweden* 10 A7
Trani, *Italy* 43 A9
Tranoroa, *Madag.* 89 C8
Tranqueras, *Uruguay* 127 C4
Transantarctic Mts., *Antarctica* 5 E12
Transilvania, *Romania* 29 D9
Transilvanian Alps = Carpații Meridionali, *Romania* 29 E9
Transnistria = Stînga Nistrului □, *Moldova* 29 C14
Transtrand, *Sweden* 10 C7
Transtrandsfjällen, *Sweden* 10 C6
Transylvania = Transilvania, *Romania* 29 D9
Trápani, *Italy* 42 D5
Trapper Pk., *U.S.A.* 108 D6
Traralgon, *Australia* 95 F4
Trarza, *Mauritania* 82 B2
Trasacco, *Italy* 41 G10
Trăscău, Munții, *Romania* 29 D8
Trasimeno, L., *Italy* 41 E9
Träslövsläge, *Sweden* 11 G6
Trasvase Tajo-Segura, Canal de, *Spain* 38 E2
Trat, *Thailand* 65 F4
Tratani →, *Pakistan* 68 E3
Traun, *Austria* 26 C7
Traunreut, *Germany* 25 H8
Traunsee, *Austria* 26 D6
Traunstein, *Germany* 25 H8
Traveller's L., *Australia* 95 E3
Travemünde, *Germany* 24 B6
Travers, Mt., *N.Z.* 91 K4
Traverse City, *U.S.A.* 114 C3
Travis, L., *U.S.A.* 113 K5
Travnik, *Bos.-H.* 28 F2
Trbovlje, *Slovenia* 41 B12
Trébbia →, *Italy* 40 C6
Trebel →, *Germany* 24 B9
Trébeurden, *France* 18 D3
Trebević △, *Bos.-H.* 28 G3
Třebíč, *Czech Rep.* 26 B8
Trebinje, *Bos.-H.* 44 D2
Trebisacce, *Italy* 43 C9
Trebišnjica →, *Bos.-H.* 44 D2
Trebišov, *Slovak Rep.* 27 C14
Trebižat →, *Bos.-H.* 41 E14
Trebnje, *Slovenia* 41 C12
Třeboň, *Czech Rep.* 26 B7
Trebonne, *Australia* 94 B4
Třeboňsko ⌓, *Czech Rep.* 26 B7
Trebujena, *Spain* 37 J4
Trecate, *Italy* 40 C5
Tregaron, *U.K.* 15 E4
Tregnago, *Italy* 41 C8
Tregrosse Is., *Australia* 94 B5
Tréguier, *France* 18 D3
Trégunc, *France* 18 E3
Treherne, *Canada* 103 D9
Tréia, *Italy* 41 E10
Treignac, *France* 20 C5
Treinta y Tres, *Uruguay* 127 C5
Treis-karden, *Germany* 25 E3
Treklyano, *Bulgaria* 44 D6
Trelawney, *Zimbabwe* 89 B5
Trélazé, *France* 18 E6
Trelew, *Argentina* 128 E3
Trélissac, *France* 20 C4
Trelleborg, *Sweden* 11 J7
Tremadog Bay, *U.K.* 14 E3
Trémiti, *Italy* 41 F12
Tremonton, *U.S.A.* 108 F7
Tremp, *Spain* 38 C5
Trenche →, *Canada* 104 C5
Trenčiansky □, *Slovak Rep.* 27 C11
Trenčín, *Slovak Rep.* 27 C11
Trenggalek, *Indonesia* 63 H14
Trenque Lauquen, *Argentina* 126 D3
Trent →, *Canada* 116 B7
Trent →, *U.K.* 14 D7
Trentino-Alto Adige □, *Italy* 41 B8
Trento, *Italy* 40 B8
Trenton = Quinte West, *Canada* 116 B7
Trenton, *Mo., U.S.A.* 112 E8
Trenton, *N.J., U.S.A.* 117 F10
Trenton, *Nebr., U.S.A.* 112 E4
Trepassey, *Canada* 105 C9
Trepuzzi, *Italy* 43 B11
Tres Arroyos, *Argentina* 126 D3
Três Corações, *Brazil* 127 A6
Três Lagoas, *Brazil* 125 H8
Tres Lomas, *Argentina* 126 D3
Tres Marías, Islas, *Mexico* 118 C3
Tres Montes, C., *Chile* 128 F1
Tres Pinos, *U.S.A.* 110 J5
Três Pontas, *Brazil* 127 A6
Tres Puentes, *Chile* 126 B1
Tres Puntas, C., *Argentina* 128 F3
Três Rios, *Brazil* 127 A7
Tres Valles, *Mexico* 119 D5
Tresco, *U.K.* 15 H1
Treska →, *Macedonia* 44 E5
Treskavica, *Bos.-H.* 28 G3
Trespaderne, *Spain* 36 C7
Tresticklan △, *Sweden* 11 F5
Trets, *France* 21 E9
Treuchtlingen, *Germany* 25 G6
Treuenbrietzen, *Germany* 24 C8
Trevi, *Italy* 41 F9
Trevíglio, *Italy* 40 C6
Trevinca, Peña, *Spain* 36 C4
Treviso, *Italy* 41 C9
Trévoux, *France* 21 C8
Trgovište, *Serbia & M.* 44 D6
Triabunna, *Australia* 95 G4
Triánda, *Greece* 49 C10
Triangle, *Zimbabwe* 89 C5
Triaucourt-en-Argonne, *France* 19 D12
Tribal Areas □, *Pakistan* 68 C4
Tribsees, *Germany* 24 A8
Tribulation, C., *Australia* 94 B4
Tribune, *U.S.A.* 112 F4
Tricárico, *Italy* 43 B9
Tricase, *Italy* 43 C11
Trichinopoly = Tiruchchirappalli, *India* 66 P11
Trichur, *India* 66 P10
Trida, *Australia* 95 E4
Trier, *Germany* 25 F2
Trieste, *Italy* 41 C10
Trieste, G. di, *Italy* 41 C10
Trieux →, *France* 18 D3
Triggiano, *Italy* 43 A9
Triglav, *Slovenia* 41 B10
Triglavski △, *Slovenia* 41 B10
Trigno →, *Italy* 41 F11
Trigueros, *Spain* 37 H4
Tríkeri, *Greece* 46 B5
Trikhonis, Límni, *Greece* 46 C3
Tríkkala, *Greece* 46 B3
Tríkkala □, *Greece* 46 B3
Trikomo, *Cyprus* 49 D12
Trikora, Puncak, *Indonesia* 63 E9
Trilj, *Croatia* 41 E13
Trillo, *Spain* 38 E2
Trim, *Ireland* 12 C5
Trincomalee, *Sri Lanka* 66 Q12
Trindade, *Brazil* 125 G9
Trindade, I., *Atl. Oc.* 2 F8
Třinec, *Czech Rep.* 27 B11
Trinidad, *Bolivia* 124 F6
Trinidad, *Cuba* 120 B4
Trinidad, *Trin. & Tob.* 121 D7
Trinidad, *Uruguay* 126 C4
Trinidad, *U.S.A.* 113 G2
Trinidad →, *Mexico* 119 D5
Trinidad & Tobago ■, *W. Indies* 121 D7
Trinitápoli, *Italy* 43 A9
Trinity, *Canada* 105 C9
Trinity, *U.S.A.* 113 K7
Trinity →, *Calif., U.S.A.* 108 F2
Trinity →, *Tex., U.S.A.* 113 L7
Trinity B., *Canada* 105 C9
Trinity Hills, *Trin. & Tob.* 125 K15
Trinity Is., *U.S.A.* 100 C4
Trinity Range, *U.S.A.* 108 F4
Trinkitat, *Sudan* 80 D4
Trino, *Italy* 40 C5
Trinway, *U.S.A.* 116 F2
Trionto, C., *Italy* 43 C9
Triora, *Italy* 40 D4
Tripoli = Tarābulus, *Lebanon* 74 A4
Tripoli = Tarābulus, *Libya* 79 B8
Trípolis, *Greece* 46 D4
Tripolitania, *N. Afr.* 79 B8
Tripura □, *India* 67 H18
Tripylos, *Cyprus* 49 E11
Trischen, *Germany* 24 A4
Tristan da Cunha, *Atl. Oc.* 77 K2
Trisul, *India* 69 D8
Trivandrum, *India* 66 Q10
Trivento, *Italy* 41 G11
Trnava, *Slovak Rep.* 27 C10
Trnavský □, *Slovak Rep.* 27 C10
Troarn, *France* 18 C6
Trochu, *Canada* 102 C6
Trodely I., *Canada* 104 B4
Troezen, *Greece* 46 D5
Trogir, *Croatia* 41 E13
Troglav, *Croatia* 41 E13
Tróia, *Italy* 43 A8
Troilus, L., *Canada* 104 B5
Troina, *Italy* 43 E7
Trois-Pistoles, *Canada* 105 C6
Trois-Rivières, *Canada* 104 C5
Trois-Rivières, *Guadeloupe* 120 b
Troisdorf, *Germany* 24 E3
Troitsk, *Russia* 52 D7
Troitsko Pechorsk, *Russia* 52 C6
Troitskoye, *Russia* 35 G7
Trölladyngja, *Iceland* 8 D5
Trollhättan, *Sweden* 11 F6
Trollheimen, *Norway* 8 E13
Trombetas →, *Brazil* 125 D7
Tromsø, *Norway* 8 B18
Trona, *U.S.A.* 111 K9
Tronador, Mte., *Argentina* 128 E2
Trøndelag, *Norway* 8 D14
Trondheim, *Norway* 8 E14
Trondheimsfjorden, *Norway* 8 E14
Trönninge, *Sweden* 11 H6
Tronto →, *Italy* 41 F10
Troodos, *Cyprus* 49 E11
Troon, *U.K.* 13 F4
Tropea, *Italy* 43 D8
Tropic, *U.S.A.* 109 H7
Tropojë, *Albania* 44 D4
Trosa, *Sweden* 11 F11
Trostan, *U.K.* 12 A5
Trostberg, *Germany* 25 G8
Trostyanets, *Ukraine* 33 G8
Trou Gras Pt., *St. Lucia* 121 f
Trout →, *Canada* 102 A5
Trout L., *N.W.T., Canada* 102 A4
Trout L., *Ont., Canada* 103 C10
Trout Lake, *Canada* 102 B6
Trout Lake, *U.S.A.* 110 E5
Trout River, *Canada* 105 C8
Trout Run, *U.S.A.* 116 E7
Trouville-sur-Mer, *France* 18 C7
Trowbridge, *U.K.* 15 F5
Troy, *Turkey* 47 B8
Troy, *Ala., U.S.A.* 115 K3
Troy, *Kans., U.S.A.* 112 F7
Troy, *Mo., U.S.A.* 112 F9
Troy, *Mont., U.S.A.* 108 B6
Troy, *N.Y., U.S.A.* 117 D11
Troy, *Ohio, U.S.A.* 114 E3
Troy, *Pa., U.S.A.* 117 E8
Troyan, *Bulgaria* 45 D8
Troyes, *France* 19 D11
Trpanj, *Croatia* 41 E14
Trstenik, *Serbia & M.* 44 C5
Trubchevsk, *Russia* 33 F7
Truchas Peak, *U.S.A.* 113 H2
Trucial States = United Arab Emirates ■, *Asia* 71 F7
Truckee, *U.S.A.* 110 F6
Trudfront, *Russia* 35 H8
Trudovoye, *Russia* 54 C6
Trujillo, *Honduras* 120 C2
Trujillo, *Peru* 124 E3
Trujillo, *Spain* 37 F5
Trujillo, *U.S.A.* 113 H2
Trujillo, *Venezuela* 124 B4
Truk, *Micronesia* 96 G7
Trumann, *U.S.A.* 113 H9
Trumansburg, *U.S.A.* 117 D8
Trumbull, Mt., *U.S.A.* 109 H7
Trŭn, *Bulgaria* 44 D6
Trun, *France* 18 D7
Trundle, *Australia* 95 E4
Trung-Phan = Annam, *Vietnam* 64 E7
Truro, *Canada* 105 C7
Truro, *U.K.* 15 G2
Truskavets, *Ukraine* 33 H2
Trŭstenik, *Bulgaria* 45 C8
Trustrup, *Denmark* 11 H4
Trutch, *Canada* 102 B4
Truth or Consequences, *U.S.A.* 109 K10
Trutnov, *Czech Rep.* 26 A8
Truxton, *U.S.A.* 117 D8
Truyère →, *France* 20 D6
Tryavna, *Bulgaria* 45 D9
Tryonville, *U.S.A.* 116 E5
Trzcianka, *Poland* 31 E3
Trzciel, *Poland* 31 F2
Trzcińsko Zdrój, *Poland* 31 F1
Trzebiatów, *Poland* 30 D2
Trzebiez, *Poland* 30 E1
Trzebnica, *Poland* 31 G4
Trzemeszno, *Poland* 31 F4
Tržič, *Slovenia* 41 B11
Tsagan Aman, *Russia* 35 G8
Tsamandás, *Greece* 46 B2
Tsandi, *Namibia* 88 B1
Tsangpo = Brahmaputra →, *Asia* 69 H13
Tsaratanana, *Madag.* 89 B8
Tsaratanana ⌓, *Madag.* 89 A8
Tsaratanana, Mt. de = Maromokotro, *Madag.* 89 A8
Tsarevo = Michurin, *Bulgaria* 45 D11
Tsarevo, *Bulgaria* 45 D9
Tsaritsáni, *Greece* 46 B4
Tsau, *Botswana* 88 C3
Tsavo East △, *Kenya* 86 C4
Tsavo West △, *Kenya* 86 C4
Tsebrykove, *Ukraine* 33 J6
Tselinograd = Astana, *Kazakhstan* 52 D8
Tsentralnyy □, *Russia* 34 D4

Tses, *Namibia* 88 D2
Tsetserleg, *Mongolia* 60 B5
Tsévié, *Togo* 83 D5
Tshabong, *Botswana* 88 D3
Tshane, *Botswana* 88 C3
Tshela, *Dem. Rep. of the Congo* 84 E2
Tshesebe, *Botswana* 89 C4
Tshibeke, *Dem. Rep. of the Congo* 86 C2
Tshibinda, *Dem. Rep. of the Congo* 86 C2
Tshikapa, *Dem. Rep. of the Congo* 84 F4
Tshilenge, *Dem. Rep. of the Congo* 86 D1
Tshinsenda, *Dem. Rep. of the Congo* 87 E2
Tshofa, *Dem. Rep. of the Congo* 86 D2
Tshwane, *Botswana* 88 C3
Tsigara, *Botswana* 88 C4
Tsihombe, *Madag.* 89 D8
Tsiigehtchic, *Canada* 100 B6
Tsimlyansk, *Russia* 35 G6
Tsimlyansk Res. = Tsimlyanskoye Vdkhr., *Russia* 35 F6
Tsimlyanskoye Vdkhr., *Russia* 35 F6
Tsinan = Jinan, *China* 56 F9
Tsineng, *S. Africa* 88 D3
Tsínga, *Greece* 45 E8
Tsinghai = Qinghai □, *China* 60 C4
Tsingtao = Qingdao, *China* 57 F11
Tsingy de Bemaraha ⌓, *Madag.* 89 B8
Tsingy de Namoraka ⌓, *Madag.* 89 B8
Tsinjoarivo, *Madag.* 89 B8
Tsinjomitondraka, *Madag.* 89 B8
Tsiroanomandidy, *Madag.* 89 B8
Tsiteli-Tsqaro, *Georgia* 35 K8
Tsitondroina, *Madag.* 89 C8
Tsitsikamma △, *S. Africa* 88 E3
Tsivilsk, *Russia* 34 C8
Tsivory, *Madag.* 89 C8
Tskhinvali, *Georgia* 35 J7
Tsna →, *Russia* 34 C6
Tsnori, *Georgia* 35 K7
Tso Moriri, L., *India* 69 C8
Tsobis, *Namibia* 88 B2
Tsodilo Hill, *Botswana* 88 B3
Tsogttsetsiy = Baruunsuu, *Mongolia* 56 C3
Tsolo, *S. Africa* 89 E4
Tsomo, *S. Africa* 89 E4
Tsu, *Japan* 55 G8
Tsu L., *Canada* 102 A6
Tsuchiura, *Japan* 55 F10
Tsuen Wan, *China* 59 F10
Tsugaru-Kaikyō, *Japan* 54 D10
Tsumeb, *Namibia* 88 B2
Tsumis, *Namibia* 88 C2
Tsuruga, *Japan* 55 G8
Tsurugi-San, *Japan* 55 H7
Tsuruoka, *Japan* 54 E9
Tsushima, *Gifu, Japan* 55 G8
Tsushima, *Nagasaki, Japan* 55 G4
Tsuyama, *Japan* 55 G7
Tsvetkovo, *Ukraine* 33 H6
Tsyelyakhany, *Belarus* 33 F3
Tua →, *Portugal* 36 D3
Tual, *Indonesia* 63 F8
Tuam, *Ireland* 12 C3
Tuamotu Arch. = Tuamotu Is., *Pac. Oc.* 97 J13
Tuamotu Is., *Pac. Oc.* 97 J13
Tuamotu Ridge, *Pac. Oc.* 97 K14
Tuanfeng, *China* 59 B10
Tuanxi, *China* 58 D6
Tuao, *Phil.* 61 C4
Tuapse, *Russia* 35 H4
Tuas, *Singapore* 65 d
Tuatapere, *N.Z.* 91 M1
Tuba City, *U.S.A.* 109 H8
Tuban, *Indonesia* 63 G15
Tubani, *Botswana* 88 C3
Tubarão, *Brazil* 127 B6
Tūbās, *West Bank* 74 C4
Tubas →, *Namibia* 88 C2
Tübingen, *Germany* 25 G5
Tubruq, *Libya* 79 B10
Tubuai Is., *Pac. Oc.* 97 K13
Tuc Trung, *Vietnam* 65 G6
Tucacas, *Venezuela* 124 A5
T'uch'ang, *Taiwan* 59 E13
Tuchodi →, *Canada* 102 B4
Tuchola, *Poland* 30 E4
Tuchów, *Poland* 31 J8
Tuckanarra, *Australia* 93 E2
Tucson, *U.S.A.* 109 K8
Tucumán □, *Argentina* 126 B2
Tucumcari, *U.S.A.* 113 H3
Tucupita, *Venezuela* 124 B6
Tucuruí, *Brazil* 125 D9
Tucuruí, Reprêsa de, *Brazil* 125 D9
Tuczno, *Poland* 31 E3
Tudela, *Spain* 38 C3
Tudmur, *Syria* 70 C3
Tudor, L., *Canada* 105 A6
Tudora, *Romania* 29 C11
Tuella →, *Portugal* 36 D3
Tugela →, *S. Africa* 89 D5
Tuguegarao, *Phil.* 61 C4
Tugur, *Russia* 53 D14
Tui, *Spain* 36 C2
Tuineje, *Canary Is.* 48 F5
Tukangbesi, Kepulauan, *Indonesia* 63 F6
Tukarak I., *Canada* 104 A4
Tukayyid, *Iraq* 70 D5
Tûkh, *Egypt* 80 H7
Tukkae, Ao, *Thailand* 65 a
Tukobo, *Ghana* 82 D4
Tuktoyaktuk, *Canada* 100 B6
Tukums, *Latvia* 9 H20
Tukums □, *Latvia* 30 B10
Tukuyu, *Tanzania* 87 D3
Tula, *Hidalgo, Mexico* 119 C5
Tula, *Tamaulipas, Mexico* 119 C5
Tula, *Nigeria* 83 D7
Tula, *Russia* 32 E9
Tulancingo, *Mexico* 119 C5
Tulare, *Serbia & M.* 44 D5
Tulare, *U.S.A.* 110 J7
Tulare Lake Bed, *U.S.A.* 110 K7
Tularosa, *U.S.A.* 109 K10
Tulbagh, *S. Africa* 88 E2
Tulcán, *Ecuador* 124 C3
Tulcea, *Romania* 29 E13
Tulcea □, *Romania* 29 E13
Tulchyn, *Ukraine* 33 H5
Tüleh, *Iran* 71 C7
Tulemalu L., *Canada* 103 A9
Tulgheş, *Romania* 29 D10
Tuli, *Zimbabwe* 87 G2
Tulia, *U.S.A.* 113 H4
Tuliszków, *Poland* 31 F5
Tulita, *Canada* 100 B7
Ţulkarm, *West Bank* 74 C4
Tulla, *Ireland* 12 D3
Tullahoma, *U.S.A.* 115 H2
Tullamore, *Australia* 95 E4
Tullamore, *Ireland* 12 C4
Tulle, *France* 20 C5
Tulln, *Austria* 26 C9
Tullow, *Ireland* 12 D5
Tullus, *Sudan* 81 E1
Tully, *Australia* 94 B4
Tully, *U.S.A.* 117 D8
Tulnici, *Romania* 29 E11
Tulovo, *Bulgaria* 45 D9
Tulsa, *U.S.A.* 113 G7
Tulsequah, *Canada* 102 B2
Tulu Milki, *Ethiopia* 81 F4
Tulu Welel, *Ethiopia* 81 F3
Tulua, *Colombia* 124 C3
Tulucești, *Romania* 29 E13
Tulun, *Russia* 53 D11
Tulungagung, *Indonesia* 63 H14
Tuma, *Russia* 32 E11
Tuma →, *Nic.* 120 D3
Tumacacori ⌓, *U.S.A.* 109 L8
Tumaco, *Colombia* 124 C3
Tumatumari, *Guyana* 124 B7
Tumba, *Sweden* 10 E11
Tumba, L., *Dem. Rep. of the Congo* 84 E3
Tumbarumba, *Australia* 95 F4
Tumbaya, *Argentina* 126 A2
Tumbes, *Peru* 124 D2
Tumbur, *Sudan* 81 G3
Tumbwe, *Dem. Rep. of the Congo* 87 E2
Tumby Bay, *Australia* 95 E2
Tumd Youqi, *China* 56 D6
Tumen, *China* 57 C15
Tumen Jiang →, *China* 57 C16
Tumeremo, *Venezuela* 124 B6
Tumkur, *India* 66 N10
Tump, *Pakistan* 66 F3
Tumpat, *Malaysia* 65 J4
Tumu, *Ghana* 82 C4
Tumucumaque, Serra, *Brazil* 125 C8
Tumut, *Australia* 95 F4
Tumwater, *U.S.A.* 110 C4
Tuna, *India* 68 H4
Tunadal, *Sweden* 10 B11
Tunapuna, *Trin. & Tob.* 125 K15
Tunas de Zaza, *Cuba* 120 B4
Tunbridge Wells = Royal Tunbridge Wells, *U.K.* 15 F8
Tunçbilek, *Turkey* 47 B11
Tunceli, *Turkey* 73 C8
Tuncurry, *Australia* 95 E5
Tundla, *India* 68 F8
Tundubai, *Sudan* 80 D2
Tunduru, *Tanzania* 87 E4
Tundzha →, *Bulgaria* 45 E10
Tungabhadra →, *India* 66 M11
Tungaru, *Sudan* 81 E3
Tungla, *Nic.* 120 D3
Tungsha Tao = Dongsha Dao, *China* 59 G11
Tungshih, *Taiwan* 59 E13
Tungsten, *Canada* 102 A3
Tunguska, Nizhnyaya →, *Russia* 53 C9
Tunguska, Podkamennaya →, *Russia* 53 C10
Tunica, *U.S.A.* 113 H9
Tunis, *Tunisia* 78 A7
Tunis ✕ (TUN), *Tunisia* 42 F3
Tunisia ■, *Africa* 78 B6
Tunja, *Colombia* 124 B4
Tunkhannock, *U.S.A.* 117 E9
Tunliu, *China* 56 F7
Tunnel Creek △, *Australia* 92 C4
Tunnsjøen, *Norway* 8 D15
Tunø, *Denmark* 11 J4
Tunungayualok I., *Canada* 105 A7
Tunuyán, *Argentina* 126 C2
Tunuyán →, *Argentina* 126 C2
Tuo Jiang →, *China* 58 C5
Tuolumne, *U.S.A.* 110 H6
Tuolumne →, *U.S.A.* 110 H5
Tūp Āghāj, *Iran* 70 B5
Tupã, *Brazil* 127 A5
Tupelo, *U.S.A.* 115 H1
Tupik, *Russia* 32 E7
Tupinambaranas, *Brazil* 124 D7
Tupiza, *Bolivia* 126 A2
Tupižnica, *Serbia & M.* 44 C6
Tupman, *U.S.A.* 111 K7
Tupper, *Canada* 102 B4
Tupper Lake, *U.S.A.* 117 B10
Tupungato, Cerro, *S. Amer.* 126 C2
Tuquan, *China* 57 B11
Túquerres, *Colombia* 124 C3
Tura, *Russia* 53 C11
Turabah, *Ḥā'il, Si. Arabia* 70 D4
Turabah, *Makkah, Si. Arabia* 80 C5
Tūrān, *Iran* 71 C8
Turan, *Russia* 53 D10
Ţurayf, *Si. Arabia* 70 D3
Turbacz, *Poland* 31 J7
Turbe, *Bos.-H.* 28 F2
Turčianske Teplice, *Slovak Rep.* 27 C11
Turcoaia, *Romania* 29 E13
Turda, *Romania* 29 D8
Turek, *Poland* 31 F5
Turen, *Venezuela* 124 B5
Turfan = Turpan, *China* 60 B3
Turfan Depression = Turpan Hami, *China* 50 E12
Turgeon →, *Canada* 104 C4
Tŭrgovishte, *Bulgaria* 45 C10
Turgut, *Turkey* 47 D10
Turgutlu, *Turkey* 47 C9
Turgwe →, *Zimbabwe* 89 C5
Turhal, *Turkey* 72 B7
Turia →, *Spain* 39 F4
Turiaçu, *Brazil* 125 D9
Turiaçu →, *Brazil* 125 D9
Turiec →, *Slovak Rep.* 27 B11
Turin = Torino, *Italy* 40 C4
Turkana, L., *Africa* 86 B4
Türkeli, *Turkey* 45 F11
Turkestan = Türkistan, *Kazakhstan* 52 E7
Túrkeve, *Hungary* 28 C5
Turkey ■, *Eurasia* 72 C7
Turkey Creek, *Australia* 92 C4
Turki, *Russia* 34 D6
Türkistan, *Kazakhstan* 52 E7
Türkmenbashi, *Turkmenistan* 52 E6
Turkmenistan ■, *Asia* 52 F6
Türkmenli, *Turkey* 47 B8
Türkoğlu, *Turkey* 72 D7
Turks & Caicos Is. ☒, *W. Indies* 121 B5
Turks Island Passage, *W. Indies* 121 B5
Turku, *Finland* 9 F20
Turkwel →, *Kenya* 86 B4
Turlock, *U.S.A.* 110 H6
Turnagain →, *Canada* 102 B3
Turnagain, C., *N.Z.* 91 J6
Turneffe Is., *Belize* 119 D7
Turner, *U.S.A.* 108 B9
Turner Pt., *Australia* 94 A1
Turner Valley, *Canada* 102 C6
Turners Falls, *U.S.A.* 117 D12
Turnhout, *Belgium* 17 C4
Türnitz, *Austria* 26 D8
Turnor L., *Canada* 103 B7
Turnov, *Czech Rep.* 26 A8
Tŭrnovo = Veliko Tŭrnovo, *Bulgaria* 45 C9
Turnu Măgurele, *Romania* 29 G9
Turnu Roşu, P., *Romania* 29 E9
Turobin, *Poland* 31 H9
Turpan, *China* 60 B3
Turpan Hami, *China* 50 E12
Turrës, Kala e, *Albania* 44 E3
Turriff, *U.K.* 13 D6
Tursāq, *Iraq* 70 C5
Tursi, *Italy* 43 B9
Turtle Head I., *Australia* 94 A3
Turtle Is., *S. Leone* 82 D2
Turtle L., *Canada* 103 C7
Turtle Lake, *U.S.A.* 112 B4
Turtleford, *Canada* 103 C7
Turuépano △, *Venezuela* 121 D7
Turuépano △, *Venezuela* 121 D7
Turukhansk, *Russia* 53 C9
Turzovka, *Slovak Rep.* 27 B11
Tuscaloosa, *U.S.A.* 115 J2
Tuscánia, *Italy* 41 F8
Tuscany = Toscana □, *Italy* 40 E8
Tuscarawas →, *U.S.A.* 116 F3
Tuscarora Mt., *U.S.A.* 116 F7
Tuscola, *Ill., U.S.A.* 114 F1
Tuscola, *Tex., U.S.A.* 113 J5
Tuscumbia, *U.S.A.* 115 H2
Tuskegee, *U.S.A.* 115 J3
Tustin, *U.S.A.* 111 M9
Tuszyn, *Poland* 31 G6
Tutak, *Turkey* 73 C10
Tutayev, *Russia* 32 D10
Tuticorin, *India* 66 Q11
Tutin, *Serbia & M.* 44 D4
Tutóia, *Brazil* 125 D10
Tutong, *Brunei* 62 D4
Tutova →, *Romania* 29 D12
Tutrakan, *Bulgaria* 45 B10
Tuttle Creek L., *U.S.A.* 112 F6
Tuttlingen, *Germany* 25 H4
Tutuala, *E. Timor* 63 F7
Tutuila, *Amer. Samoa* 91 B13
Tutume, *Botswana* 85 J5
Tutun, *Egypt* 80 J7
Tututepec, *Mexico* 119 D5
Tuva □, *Russia* 53 D10
Tuvalu ■, *Pac. Oc.* 96 H9
Tuxer Alpen, *Austria* 26 D4
Tuxpan, *Mexico* 119 C5
Tuxtla Gutiérrez, *Mexico* 119 D6
Tuy = Tui, *Spain* 36 C2
Tuy An, *Vietnam* 64 F7
Tuy Duc, *Vietnam* 65 F6
Tuy Hoa, *Vietnam* 64 F7
Tuy Phong, *Vietnam* 65 G7
Tuya L., *Canada* 102 B2
Tuyen Hoa, *Vietnam* 64 D6
Tuyen Quang, *Vietnam* 58 G5
Tūysarkān, *Iran* 71 C6
Tuz Gölü, *Turkey* 72 C5
Ţūz Khurmātū = Tozkhurmato, *Iraq* 70 C5
Tuzi, *Serbia & M.* 44 D3
Tuzigoot ⌓, *U.S.A.* 109 J7
Tuzla, *Bos.-H.* 28 F3
Tuzlov →, *Russia* 33 J10
Tuzluca, *Turkey* 73 B10
Tvååker, *Sweden* 11 G6
Tvardiţa, *Moldova* 29 D13
Tver, *Russia* 32 D8
Tvrdošin, *Slovak Rep.* 27 B12
Tvrdošovce, *Slovak Rep.* 27 C11
Tvŭrditsa, *Bulgaria* 45 D9
Twain, *U.S.A.* 110 E5
Twain Harte, *U.S.A.* 110 G6
Twardogóra, *Poland* 31 G4
Tweed, *Canada* 116 B7
Tweed →, *U.K.* 13 F6
Tweed Heads, *Australia* 95 D5
Tweedsmuir ⌓, *Canada* 102 C3
Twentynine Palms, *U.S.A.* 111 L10
Twillingate, *Canada* 105 C9
Twin Bridges, *U.S.A.* 108 D7
Twin Falls, *Canada* 105 B7
Twin Falls, *U.S.A.* 108 E6
Twin Valley, *U.S.A.* 112 B6
Twinsburg, *U.S.A.* 116 E3
Twistringen, *Germany* 24 C4
Twitchell Reservoir, *U.S.A.* 111 L6
Two Harbors, *U.S.A.* 112 B9
Two Hills, *Canada* 102 C6
Two Rivers, *U.S.A.* 114 C2
Two Rocks, *Australia* 93 F2
Twofold B., *Australia* 95 F4
Tyachiv, *Ukraine* 33 H2
Tychy, *Poland* 31 H5
Tyczyn, *Poland* 31 J9
Tykocin, *Poland* 31 E9
Tyler, *Minn., U.S.A.* 112 C6
Tyler, *Tex., U.S.A.* 113 J7
Tyligul →, *Ukraine* 33 J6
Týn nad Vltavou, *Czech Rep.* 26 B7
Tynda, *Russia* 53 D13
Tyndall, *U.S.A.* 112 D6
Tyne →, *U.K.* 14 C6
Tyne & Wear □, *U.K.* 14 B6
Týnec nad Sázavou, *Czech Rep.* 26 B7
Tynemouth, *U.K.* 14 B6
Tyre = Sūr, *Lebanon* 74 B4
Tyresta △, *Sweden* 10 E12
Tyrifjorden, *Norway* 9 F14
Tyringe, *Sweden* 11 H7
Tyrnyauz, *Russia* 35 J6
Tyrol = Tirol □, *Austria* 26 D3
Tyrone, *U.S.A.* 116 F6
Tyrone □, *U.K.* 12 B4
Tyrrell →, *Australia* 95 F3
Tyrrell, L., *Australia* 95 F3
Tyrrell L., *Canada* 103 A7
Tyrrhenian Sea, *Medit. S.* 6 G8
Tysfjorden, *Norway* 8 B17
Tystberga, *Sweden* 11 F11
Tytuvėnai, *Lithuania* 30 C10
Tyub Karagan, Mys, *Kazakhstan* 35 H10
Tyuleni, Ostrova, *Kazakhstan* 35 H10
Tyuleniy, *Russia* 35 H8
Tyuleniy, Mys, *Azerbaijan* 35 K10
Tyumen, *Russia* 52 D7
Tywi →, *U.K.* 15 F3
Tywyn, *U.K.* 15 E3
Tzaneen, *S. Africa* 89 C5
Tzermiádhes, *Greece* 49 D7
Tzoumérka, Óros, *Greece* 46 B3
Tzukong = Zigong, *China* 58 C5

U

U Taphao, *Thailand* 64 F3
U.S.A. = United States of America ■, *N. Amer.* 106 C7
U.S. Virgin Is. ☒, *W. Indies* 121 e
Uatumã →, *Brazil* 124 D7
Uaupés, *Brazil* 124 D5
Uaupés →, *Brazil* 124 C5
Uaxactún, *Guatemala* 120 C2
Ub, *Serbia & M.* 44 B4
Ubá, *Brazil* 127 A7
Uba, *Nigeria* 83 C7
Ubaitaba, *Brazil* 125 F11
Ubangi = Oubangi →, *Dem. Rep. of the Congo* 84 E3
Ubauro, *Pakistan* 68 E3
Ubaye →, *France* 21 D10
Ubayyiḑ, W. al →, *Iraq* 70 C4
Ube, *Japan* 55 H5
Úbeda, *Spain* 37 G7
Uberaba, *Brazil* 125 G9
Uberlândia, *Brazil* 125 G9
Überlingen, *Germany* 25 H5
Ubiaja, *Nigeria* 83 D6
Ubin, Pulau, *Singapore* 65 d
Ubolratna Res., *Thailand* 64 D4
Ubombo, *S. Africa* 89 D5
Ubon Ratchathani, *Thailand* 64 E5
Ubondo, *Dem. Rep. of the Congo* 86 C2
Ubort →, *Belarus* 33 F5
Ubrique, *Spain* 37 J5
Ubud, *Indonesia* 63 J18
Ubundu, *Dem. Rep. of the Congo* 86 C2
Ucayali →, *Peru* 124 D4
Uchab, *Namibia* 88 B2
Uchiura-Wan, *Japan* 54 C10
Uchquduq, *Uzbekistan* 52 E7
Uchte, *Germany* 24 C4
Uchur →, *Russia* 53 D14
Uckermark, *Germany* 24 B9
Ucluelet, *Canada* 102 D3
Uda →, *Russia* 53 D14
Udagamandalam, *India* 66 P10
Udainagar, *India* 68 H7
Udaipur, *India* 68 G5
Udaipur Garhi, *Nepal* 69 F12
Udala, *India* 69 J12
Udbina, *Croatia* 41 D12
Uddeholm, *Sweden* 10 D7
Uddevalla, *Sweden* 11 F5
Uddjaur, *Sweden* 8 D17
Uden, *Neths.* 17 C5
Udgir, *India* 66 K10
Udhampur, *India* 69 C6
Udi, *Nigeria* 83 D6
Údine, *Italy* 41 B10
Udmurtia □, *Russia* 52 D6
Udon Thani, *Thailand* 64 D4
Udupi, *India* 66 N9
Udvoy Balkan, *Bulgaria* 45 D10
Udzungwa △, *Tanzania* 86 D4
Udzungwa Range, *Tanzania* 87 D4
Ueckermünde, *Germany* 24 B10
Ueda, *Japan* 55 F9
Uedineniya, Os., *Russia* 4 B12
Uele →, *Dem. Rep. of the Congo* 84 D4
Uelen, *Russia* 53 C19
Uelzen, *Germany* 24 C6
Uetersen, *Germany* 24 B5
Uetze, *Germany* 24 C6
Ufa, *Russia* 52 D6
Uffenheim, *Germany* 25 F6
Ugab →, *Namibia* 88 C1
Ugalla →, *Tanzania* 86 D3
Ugalla River ⌓, *Tanzania* 86 D3
Uganda ■, *Africa* 86 B3
Ugento, *Italy* 43 C11
Ugep, *Nigeria* 83 D6
Ughelli, *Nigeria* 83 D6
Ugie, *S. Africa* 89 E4
Ugíjar, *Spain* 37 J7
Ugine, *France* 21 C10
Uglegorsk, *Russia* 53 E15
Uglich, *Russia* 32 D10
Ugljan, *Croatia* 41 D12
Ugljane, *Croatia* 41 E13
Ugra →, *Russia* 32 E9
Ugŭrchin, *Bulgaria* 45 C8
Uh →, *Slovak Rep.* 27 C15
Uherské Hradiště, *Czech Rep.* 27 B10
Uherský Brod, *Czech Rep.* 27 B10
Úhlava →, *Czech Rep.* 26 B6
Uhlenhorst, *Namibia* 88 C2
Uhrichsville, *U.S.A.* 116 F3
Uibhist a Deas = South Uist, *U.K.* 13 D1
Uibhist a Tuath = North Uist, *U.K.* 13 D1
Uig, *U.K.* 13 D2
Uíge, *Angola* 84 F2
Uijŏngbu, *S. Korea* 57 F14
Ŭiju, *N. Korea* 57 D13
Uinta Mts., *U.S.A.* 108 F8
Uis, *Namibia* 88 C1
Uitenhage, *S. Africa* 88 E4
Uithuizen, *Neths.* 17 A6
Ujazd, *Poland* 31 H5
Újfehértó, *Hungary* 28 C6
Ujh →, *India* 68 C6
Ujhani, *India* 69 F8
Uji-guntō, *Japan* 55 J4
Ujjain, *India* 68 H6
Ujście, *Poland* 31 E3
Újszász, *Hungary* 28 C5
Ujung Pandang, *Indonesia* 63 F5
Uka, *Russia* 53 D17
Ukara I., *Tanzania* 86 C3
Uke-Shima, *Japan* 55 K4
Ukerewe I., *Tanzania* 86 C3
Ukholovo, *Russia* 34 D5
Ukhrul, *India* 67 G19
Ukhta, *Russia* 52 C6
Ukiah, *U.S.A.* 110 F3
Ukmergė, *Lithuania* 9 J21
Ukraine ■, *Europe* 33 H7
Ukwi, *Botswana* 88 C3
Ulaan-Uul, *Mongolia* 56 B6
Ulaanbaatar, *Mongolia* 53 E11
Ulaangom, *Mongolia* 60 A4
Ulaanjirem, *Mongolia* 56 B3
Ulamba, *Dem. Rep. of the Congo* 87 D1
Ulan Bator = Ulaanbaatar, *Mongolia* 53 E11
Ulan Erge, *Russia* 35 G7
Ulan Khol, *Russia* 35 H8
Ulan Ude, *Russia* 53 D11
Ulanów, *Poland* 31 H9
Ulaş, *Sivas, Turkey* 72 C7
Ulaş, *Tekirdağ, Turkey* 45 E11
Ulaya, *Morogoro, Tanzania* 86 D4
Ulaya, *Tabora, Tanzania* 86 C3
Ulcinj, *Serbia & M.* 44 E3
Ulco, *S. Africa* 88 D3
Ulefoss, *Norway* 9 G13
Ulëz, *Albania* 44 E3
Ulfborg, *Denmark* 11 H2
Ulhasnagar, *India* 66 K8
Uliastay, *Mongolia* 60 B4
Uljma, *Serbia & M.* 28 E6
Ulla →, *Spain* 36 C2
Ulladulla, *Australia* 95 F5
Ullapool, *U.K.* 13 D3
Ullared, *Sweden* 11 G6
Ulldecona, *Spain* 38 E5
Ullswater, *U.K.* 14 C5
Ullŭng-do, *S. Korea* 55 F5
Ulm, *Germany* 25 G5
Ulmarra, *Australia* 95 D5
Ulmeni, *Buzău, Romania* 29 E11
Ulmeni, *Maramureş, Romania* 29 C8
Ulonguè, *Mozam.* 87 E3
Ulricehamn, *Sweden* 11 G7
Ulrika, *Sweden* 11 F9
Ulsan, *S. Korea* 57 G15
Ulsta, *U.K.* 13 A7
Ulster □, *U.K.* 12 B5
Ulstrem, *Bulgaria* 45 D10
Ulubat Gölü, *Turkey* 45 F12
Ulubey, *Turkey* 47 C11
Uluborlu, *Turkey* 47 C12

Uluçinar, Turkey 72 D6
Uludağ, Turkey 45 F13
Uludağ △, Turkey 45 F13
Uludere, Turkey 73 D10
Uluguru Mts., Tanzania 86 D4
Ulukışla, Turkey 72 D6
Ulungur He →, China 60 B3
Uluru = Ayers Rock, Australia 93 E5
Uluru-Kata Tjuta △, Australia 93 E5
Ulutau, Kazakhstan 52 E7
Uluwatu, Indonesia 63 K18
Ulva, U.K. 13 E2
Ulverston, U.K. 14 C4
Ulverstone, Australia 95 G4
Ulya, Russia 53 D15
Ulyanovsk = Simbirsk, Russia 34 C9
Ulyasutay = Uliastay, Mongolia 60 B4
Ulysses, U.S.A. 113 G4
Umag, Croatia 41 C10
Umala, Bolivia 124 G5
Uman, Ukraine 33 H6
Umaria, India 67 H12
Umarkot, Pakistan 66 G6
Umarpada, India 68 J5
Umatilla, U.S.A. 108 D4
Umbagog L., U.S.A. 117 B13
Umbakumba, Australia 94 A2
Umbértide, Italy 41 E9
Umbrella Mts., N.Z. 91 L2
Umbria □, Italy 41 F9
Ume älv →, Sweden 8 E19
Umeå, Sweden 8 E19
Umera, Indonesia 63 E7
Umfolozi ⌓, S. Africa 89 D5
Umfuli →, Zimbabwe 87 F2
Umfurudzi ⌓, Zimbabwe 87 F3
Umgusa, Zimbabwe 87 F2
Umim Urūmah, Si. Arabia 80 B4
Umka, Serbia & M. 44 B4
Umkomaas, S. Africa 89 E5
Umlazi, S. Africa 85 L6
Umm ad Daraj, J., Jordan 74 C4
Umm al Qaywayn, U.A.E. 71 E7
Umm al Qittayn, Jordan 74 C5
Umm Arda, Sudan 81 D3
Umm Bāb, Qatar 71 E6
Umm Badr, Sudan 81 E2
Umm Baiyud, Sudan 81 E3
Umm Bel, Sudan 81 E2
Umm Birkah, Si. Arabia 80 B4
Umm Boim, Sudan 81 E2
Umm Dam, Sudan 81 E3
Umm Debi, Sudan 81 E3
Umm Dubban, Sudan 81 D3
Umm Durman = Omdurmân, Sudan 81 D3
Umm el Fahm, Israel 74 C4
Umm Gafala, Sudan 81 E2
Umm Gimala, Sudan 81 E2
Umm Inderaba, Sudan 80 D3
Umm Keddada, Sudan 81 E2
Umm Koweika, Sudan 81 E3
Umm Lajj, Si. Arabia 70 E3
Umm Merwa, Sudan 80 D3
Umm Qantur, Sudan 81 E3
Umm Qurein, Sudan 81 F2
Umm Ruwaba, Sudan 81 E3
Umm Saiyala, Sudan 81 E3
Umm Shanqa, Sudan 81 E2
Umm Shutur, Sudan 81 F3
Umm Sidr, Sudan 81 E2
Umm Zehetir, Egypt 80 J8
Umnak I., U.S.A. 100 C3
Umniati →, Zimbabwe 87 F2
Umpqua →, U.S.A. 108 E1
Umreth, India 68 H5
Umtata, S. Africa 89 E4
Umuahia, Nigeria 83 D6
Umuarama, Brazil 127 A5
Umurbey, Turkey 45 F10
Umvukwe Ra., Zimbabwe 87 F3
Umzimvubu, S. Africa 89 E4
Umzingwane →, Zimbabwe 87 G2
Umzinto, S. Africa 89 E5
Una, India 68 J4
Una →, Bos.-H. 41 D13
Unac →, Bos.-H. 41 D13
Unadilla, U.S.A. 117 D9
Unalakleet, U.S.A. 100 B3
Unalaska, U.S.A. 100 C3
Unalaska I., U.S.A. 100 C3
'Unayzah, Si. Arabia 70 E4
'Unayzah, J., Asia 70 C3
Uncastillo, Spain 38 C3
Uncía, Bolivia 124 G5
Uncompahgre Peak, U.S.A. 109 G10
Uncompahgre Plateau, U.S.A. 109 G9
Undara Volcanic △, Australia 94 B3
Unden, Sweden 11 F8
Underbool, Australia 95 F3
Undersaker, Sweden 10 A7
Unecha, Russia 33 F7
Ungarie, Australia 95 E4
Ungarra, Australia 95 E2
Ungava, Pén. d', Canada 101 C12
Ungava B., Canada 101 C13
Ungeny = Ungheni, Moldova 29 C12
Unggi, N. Korea 57 C16
Ungheni, Moldova 29 C12
Unguala →, Ethiopia 81 F5
Ungwana B., Kenya 86 C5
Ungwatiri, Sudan 81 D4
Uni, Russia 34 B10
União da Vitória, Brazil 127 B5
Uničov, Czech Rep. 27 B10
Uniejów, Poland 31 G5
Unije, Croatia 41 D11
Unimak I., U.S.A. 100 C3
Union, Miss., U.S.A. 113 J10
Union, Mo., U.S.A. 112 F9
Union, S.C., U.S.A. 115 H5
Union City, Calif., U.S.A. 110 H4
Union City, N.J., U.S.A. 117 F10
Union City, Pa., U.S.A. 116 E5
Union City, Tenn., U.S.A. 113 G10
Union Gap, U.S.A. 108 C3
Union Springs, U.S.A. 115 J3
Uniondale, S. Africa 88 E3
Uniontown, U.S.A. 114 F6
Unionville, U.S.A. 112 E8
Unirea, Romania 29 F12
United Arab Emirates ■, Asia 71 F7
United Kingdom ■, Europe 7 E5
United States of America ■, N. Amer. 106 C7
Unity, Canada 103 C7
Universales, Mtes., Spain 38 E3
University Park, U.S.A. 109 K10
Unjha, India 68 H5
Unna, Germany 24 D3
Unnao, India 69 F9
Uno, Ilha, Guinea-Biss. 82 C1
Unsengedsi →, Zimbabwe 87 F3
Unst, U.K. 13 A8
Unstrut →, Germany 24 D7
Unterfranken □, Germany 25 F5
Unterschleissheim, Germany 25 G7
Unuk →, Canada 102 B2
Ünye, Turkey 72 B7
Unzen-Amakusa △, Japan 55 H5
Unzha, Russia 34 A7
Unzha →, Russia 34 B6
Uozu, Japan 55 F8
Upata, Venezuela 124 B6
Upemba △, Dem. Rep. of the Congo 87 D2
Upemba, L., Dem. Rep. of the Congo 87 D2
Upernavik, Greenland 4 B5
Upington, S. Africa 88 D3
Upleta, India 68 J4
'Upolu, Samoa 91 A13
Upper □, Ghana 83 C4
Upper Alkali L., U.S.A. 108 F3
Upper Arrow L., Canada 102 C5
Upper Austria = Oberösterreich □, Austria 26 C7
Upper Foster L., Canada 103 B7
Upper Hutt, N.Z. 91 J5
Upper Klamath L., U.S.A. 108 E3
Upper Lake, U.S.A. 110 F4
Upper Manzanilla, Trin. & Tob. 125 K15
Upper Missouri River Breaks ⌓, U.S.A. 108 C9
Upper Musquodoboit, Canada 105 C7
Upper Red L., U.S.A. 112 A7
Upper Sandusky, U.S.A. 114 E4
Upper Volta = Burkina Faso ■, Africa 82 C4
Upphärad, Sweden 11 F6
Uppland, Sweden 10 E11
Upplands-Väsby, Sweden 10 E11
Uppsala, Sweden 10 E11
Uppsala län □, Sweden 10 D11
Upshi, India 69 C7
Upstart, C., Australia 94 B4
Upton, U.S.A. 112 C2
Uqsuqtuuq = Gjoa Haven, Canada 100 B10
Ur, Iraq 70 D5
Urad Qianqi, China 56 D5
Urakawa, Japan 54 C11
Ural = Uralskiy □, Russia 52 C7
Ural = Zhayyq →, Kazakhstan 52 E6
Ural, Australia 95 E4
Ural Mts. = Uralskie Gory, Eurasia 52 D6
Uralla, Australia 95 E5
Uralsk = Oral, Kazakhstan 34 E10
Uralskie Gory, Eurasia 52 D6
Uralskiy □, Russia 52 C7
Urambo, Tanzania 86 D3
Urandangi, Australia 94 C2
Uranium City, Canada 103 B7
Uraricoera →, Brazil 124 C6
Urawa, Japan 55 G9
Uray, Russia 52 C7
'Uray'irah, Si. Arabia 71 E6
Urbana, Ill., U.S.A. 114 E1
Urbana, Ohio, U.S.A. 114 E4
Urbánia, Italy 41 E9
Urbel →, Spain 36 C7
Urbino, Italy 41 E9
Urbión, Picos de, Spain 38 C2
Urcos, Peru 124 F4
Urdinarrain, Argentina 126 C4
Urdos, France 20 F3
Urdzhar, Kazakhstan 52 E9
Ure →, U.K. 14 C6
Uren, Russia 34 B7
Ures, Mexico 118 B2
Urewera △, N.Z. 91 H6
Urfa = Sanliurfa, Turkey 70 B3
Urganch, Uzbekistan 52 E7
Urgench = Urganch, Uzbekistan 52 E7
Ürgüp, Turkey 70 B2
Uri, India 69 B6
Uri □, Switz. 25 J4
Uribia, Colombia 124 A4
Uricani, Romania 28 E8
Uriondo, Bolivia 126 A3
Urique, Mexico 118 B3
Urique →, Mexico 118 B3
Urk, Neths. 17 B5
Urkiola ⌓, Spain 38 B3
Urla, Turkey 47 C8
Urlaţi, Romania 29 F11
Urmia = Orūmīyeh, Iran 70 B5
Urmia, L. = Orūmīyeh, Daryācheh-ye, Iran 70 B5
Uroševac, Serbia & M. 44 D5
Uroyan, Montanas de, Puerto Rico 121 d
Urshult, Sweden 11 H8
Uruaçu, Brazil 125 F9
Uruapan, Mexico 118 D4
Urubamba →, Peru 124 F4
Uruçara, Brazil 124 D7
Uruçuí, Brazil 125 E10
Uruguai →, Brazil 127 B5
Uruguaiana, Brazil 126 B4
Uruguay ■, S. Amer. 126 C4
Uruguay →, S. Amer. 126 C4
Urumchi = Ürümqi, China 52 E9
Ürümqi, China 52 E9
Urup →, Russia 35 H5
Urup, Ostrov, Russia 53 E16
Uryupinsk, Russia 34 E5
Urzhum, Russia 34 B9
Urziceni, Romania 29 F11
Usa →, Russia 52 C6
Uşak, Turkey 47 C11
Uşak □, Turkey 47 C11
Usakos, Namibia 88 C2
Ušće, Serbia & M. 44 C4
Usedom, Germany 24 B10
Usedom ⌓, Germany 24 B10
Useless Loop, Australia 93 E1
'Usfān, Si. Arabia 80 C4
Ush-Tobe, Kazakhstan 52 E8
Ushakova, Ostrov, Russia 4 A12
Ushant = Ouessant, Î. d', France 18 D1
Ushashi, Tanzania 86 C3
Ushat, Sudan 81 F2
'Ushayrah, Si. Arabia 80 C5
Ushibuka, Japan 55 H5
Ushuaia, Argentina 128 G3
Ushumun, Russia 53 D13
Usk, Canada 102 C3
Usk →, U.K. 15 F5
Uska, India 69 F10
Üsküdar, Turkey 45 F13
Uslar, Germany 24 D5
Usman, Russia 33 F10
Usoke, Tanzania 86 D3
Usolye Sibirskoye, Russia 53 D11
Usoro, Nigeria 83 D6
Uspallata, P. de, Argentina 126 C2
Uspenskiy, Kazakhstan 52 E8
Ussel, France 20 C6
Usson-du-Poitou, France 20 B4
Ussuri →, Asia 54 A7
Ussuriysk, Russia 53 E14
Ussurka, Russia 54 B6
Ust-Aldan = Batamay, Russia 53 C13
Ust-Amginskoye = Khandyga, Russia 53 C14
Ust-Bolsheretsk, Russia 53 D16
Ust-Buzulukskaya, Russia 34 E6
Ust-Chaun, Russia 53 C18
Ust-Donetskiy, Russia 35 G5
Ust-Ilimpeya = Yukta, Russia 53 C11
Ust-Ilimsk, Russia 53 D11
Ust-Ishim, Russia 52 D8
Ust-Kamchatsk, Russia 53 D17
Ust-Kamenogorsk = Öskemen, Kazakhstan 52 E9
Ust-Khayryuzovo, Russia 53 D16
Ust-Kut, Russia 53 D11
Ust-Kuyga, Russia 53 B14
Ust-Labinsk, Russia 35 H4
Ust-Luga, Russia 32 C5
Ust-Maya, Russia 53 C14
Ust-Mil, Russia 53 D14
Ust-Nera, Russia 53 C15
Ust-Nyukzha, Russia 53 D13
Ust-Olenek, Russia 53 B12
Ust-Omchug, Russia 53 C15
Ust-Port, Russia 52 C9
Ust-Tsilma, Russia 52 C6
Ust Urt = Ustyurt Plateau, Asia 52 E6
Ustaritz, France 20 E2
Ustecký □, Czech Rep. 26 A7
Uster, Switz. 25 H4
Ústí nad Labem, Czech Rep. 26 A7
Ústí nad Orlicí, Czech Rep. 27 B9
Ústica, Italy 42 D6
Ustinov = Izhevsk, Russia 52 D6
Ustka, Poland 30 D3
Ustroń, Poland 31 J5
Ustrzyki Dolne, Poland 31 J9
Ustyurt Plateau, Asia 52 E6
Ustyuzhna, Russia 32 C9
Usu, China 60 B3
Usuki, Japan 55 H5
Usulután, El Salv. 120 D2
Usumacinta →, Mexico 119 D6
Usumbura = Bujumbura, Burundi 86 C2
Usure, Tanzania 86 C3
Usutuo →, Mozam. 89 D5
Uta, Indonesia 63 E9
Utah □, U.S.A. 108 G8
Utah L., U.S.A. 108 F8
Utansjö, Sweden 10 B11
Utara, Selat, Malaysia 65 c
Utarni, India 68 F4
Utatlan, Guatemala 120 C1
Ute Creek →, U.S.A. 113 H3
Utebo, Spain 38 D3
Utena, Lithuania 9 J21
Utete, Tanzania 86 D4
Uthai Thani, Thailand 64 E3
Uthal, Pakistan 68 G2
Utiariti, Brazil 124 F7
Utica, N.Y., U.S.A. 117 C9
Utica, Ohio, U.S.A. 116 F2
Utiel, Spain 39 F3
Utikuma L., Canada 102 B5
Utö, Sweden 10 F12
Utopia, Australia 94 C1
Utraula, India 69 F10
Utrecht, Neths. 17 B5
Utrecht, S. Africa 89 D5
Utrecht □, Neths. 17 B5
Utrera, Spain 37 H5
Utsjoki, Finland 8 B22
Utsunomiya, Japan 55 F9
Uttar Pradesh □, India 69 F9
Uttaradit, Thailand 64 D3
Uttaranchal □, India 69 D8
Uttoxeter, U.K. 14 E6
Utuado, Puerto Rico 121 d
Uummannaq, Greenland 4 B4
Uummannaq, Greenland 4 B5
Uummannarsuaq = Nunap Isua, Greenland 101 C15
Uusikaarlepyy, Finland 8 E20
Uusikaupunki, Finland 9 F19
Uva, Russia 34 B11
Uvac →, Serbia & M. 44 C3
Uvalde, U.S.A. 113 L5
Uvarovo, Russia 34 E6
Uvat, Russia 52 D7
Uvinza, Tanzania 86 D3
Uvira, Dem. Rep. of the Congo 86 C2
Uvs Nuur, Mongolia 60 A4
'Uwairidh, Ḥarrat al, Si. Arabia 70 E3
Uwajima, Japan 55 H6
Uwanda ⌓, Tanzania 86 D3
Uweinat, Jebel, Sudan 80 C1
Uxbridge, Canada 116 B5
Uxin Qi, China 56 E5
Uxmal, Mexico 119 C7
Uxmal, Ruinas, Mexico 119 C7
Üydzin, Mongolia 56 B4
Uyo, Nigeria 83 D6
Üyüklü Tepe, Turkey 47 D9
Uyûn Mûsa, Egypt 74 F1
Uyuni, Bolivia 124 H5
Uzbekistan ■, Asia 52 E7
Uzen, Bolshoi →, Kazakhstan 35 F9
Uzen, Mal →, Kazakhstan 35 F9
Uzerche, France 20 C5
Uzès, France 21 D8
Uzh →, Ukraine 33 G6
Uzhgorod = Uzhhorod, Ukraine 33 H2
Uzhhorod, Ukraine 33 H2
Užice, Serbia & M. 44 C3
Uzlovaya, Russia 32 F10
Üzümlü, Turkey 47 E11
Uzunköprü, Turkey 45 E10
Uzunkuyu, Turkey 47 C8

V

Vaal →, S. Africa 88 D3
Vaal Dam, S. Africa 89 D4
Vaalbos △, S. Africa 88 D3
Vaalwater, S. Africa 89 C4
Vaasa, Finland 8 E19
Vabre, France 20 E6
Vác, Hungary 28 C4
Vacaria, Brazil 127 B5
Vacaville, U.S.A. 110 G5
Vaccarès, Étang de, France 21 E8
Vach = Vakh →, Russia 52 C8
Vache, Î. à, Haiti 121 C5
Väckelsång, Sweden 11 H8
Väddö, Sweden 10 D12
Väderstad, Sweden 11 F8
Vadnagar, India 68 H5
Vado Lígure, Italy 40 D5
Vadodara, India 68 H5
Vadsø, Norway 8 A23
Vadstena, Sweden 11 F8
Vaduz, Liech. 25 H5
Værøy, Norway 8 C15
Vágar, Færoe Is. 8 E9
Vaggeryd, Sweden 11 G8
Vagney, France 19 D13
Vagnhärad, Sweden 11 F11
Vagos, Portugal 36 E2
Vågsfjorden, Norway 8 B17
Váh →, Slovak Rep. 27 D11
Vahsel B., Antarctica 5 D1
Vaï, Greece 49 D8
Vaigach, Russia 52 B6
Vaiges, France 18 D6
Vaihingen, Germany 25 G4
Vail, U.S.A. 106 C5
Vailly-sur-Aisne, France 19 C10
Vaisali →, India 69 F8
Vaison-la-Romaine, France 21 D9
Vakarel, Bulgaria 44 D7
Vakfıkebir, Turkey 73 B8
Vakh →, Russia 52 C8
Vakhtan, Russia 34 B8
Vál, Hungary 28 C3
Val-de-Marne □, France 19 D9
Val-d'Isère, France 21 C10
Val-d'Oise □, France 19 C9
Val-d'Or, Canada 104 C4
Val Grande △, Italy 40 B5
Val Marie, Canada 103 D7
Val Thorens, France 21 C10
Valaam, Russia 32 B6
Valadares, Portugal 36 D2
Valahia, Romania 29 F9
Valais □, Switz. 25 J3
Valais, Alpes du, Switz. 25 J3
Valandovo, Macedonia 44 E6
Valašské Meziříčí, Czech Rep. 27 B10
Valáxa, Greece 46 C6
Vålberg, Sweden 10 E7
Valbo, Sweden 10 D10
Valbondione, Italy 40 B7
Vălcani, Romania 28 D5
Vâlcea □, Romania 29 F9
Valcheta, Argentina 128 E3
Valdagno, Italy 41 C8
Valdahon, France 19 E13
Valdai Hills = Valdayskaya Vozvyshennost, Russia 32 D7
Valday, Russia 32 D7
Valdayskaya Vozvyshennost, Russia 32 D7
Valdeazogues →, Spain 37 G6
Valdecañas, Embalse de, Spain 36 F5
Valdemarsvik, Sweden 11 F10
Valdemoro, Spain 36 E7
Valdepeñas, Spain 37 G7
Valderaduey →, Spain 36 D5
Valdérice, Italy 42 D5
Valderrobres, Spain 38 E5
Valdés, Pen., Argentina 128 E4
Valdez, U.S.A. 100 B5
Valdivia, Chile 128 D2
Valdobbiádene, Italy 41 C8
Valdosta, U.S.A. 115 K4
Valdoviño, Spain 36 B2
Valdres, Norway 9 F13
Vale, Georgia 35 K6
Vale, U.S.A. 108 E5
Vale of Glamorgan □, U.K. 15 F4
Valea lui Mihai, Romania 28 C7
Valea Mărului, Romania 29 E12
Valemount, Canada 102 C5
Valença, Brazil 125 F11
Valença, Portugal 36 C2
Valença do Piauí, Brazil 125 E10
Valençay, France 19 E8
Valence = Valence d'Agen, France 20 D4
Valence, France 21 D8
Valence d'Agen, France 20 D4
Valencia, Spain 39 F4
Valencia, Trin. & Tob. 125 K15
Valencia, U.S.A. 109 J10
Valencia, Venezuela 124 A5
Valencia □, Spain 39 F4
Valencia ✕ (VLC), Spain 39 F4
Valencia, G. de, Spain 39 F5
Valencia de Alcántara, Spain 37 F3
Valencia de Don Juan, Spain 36 C5
Valencia I., Ireland 12 E1
Valenciennes, France 19 B10
Văleni, Romania 29 F9
Vălenii de Munte, Romania 29 E11
Valensole, France 21 E9
Valentigney, France 19 E13
Valentim, Sa. do, Brazil 125 E10
Valentin, Russia 54 C7
Valentine, U.S.A. 113 K2
Valenza, Italy 40 C5
Valera, Venezuela 124 B4
Valga, Estonia 9 H22
Valguarnera Carpepe, Italy 43 E7
Valier, U.S.A. 108 B7
Valinco, G. de, France 21 G12
Valjevo, Serbia & M. 44 B3
Valka, Latvia 9 H21
Valkeakoski, Finland 9 F20
Valkenswaard, Neths. 17 C5
Vall de Uxó = La Vall d'Uixó, Spain 38 F4
Valla, Sweden 10 E10
Valladolid, Mexico 119 C7
Valladolid, Spain 36 D6
Valladolid □, Spain 36 D6
Vallata, Italy 43 A8
Valldemossa, Spain 48 B9
Valle d'Aosta □, Italy 40 C4
Valle de Arán, Spain 38 C5
Valle de la Pascua, Venezuela 124 B5
Valle de las Palmas, Mexico 111 N10
Valle de Santiago, Mexico 118 C4
Valle de Suchil, Mexico 118 C4
Valle de Zaragoza, Mexico 118 B3
Valle del Ticino ⌓, Italy 40 C6
Valle Fértil, Sierra del, Argentina 126 C2
Valle Gran Rey, Canary Is. 48 F2
Valle Hermoso, Mexico 119 B5
Valledupar, Colombia 124 A4
Vallehermoso, Canary Is. 48 F2
Vallejo, U.S.A. 110 G4
Vallenar, Chile 126 B1
Vallentuna, Sweden 10 E12
Valleraugue, France 20 D7
Vallet, France 18 E5
Valletta, Malta 49 D2
Valley Center, U.S.A. 111 M9
Valley City, U.S.A. 112 B6
Valley Falls, Oreg., U.S.A. 108 E3
Valley Falls, R.I., U.S.A. 117 E13
Valley of the Kings, Egypt 80 B3
Valley Springs, U.S.A. 110 G6
Valley View, U.S.A. 117 F8
Valley Wells, U.S.A. 111 K11
Valleyview, Canada 102 B5
Valli di Comácchio, Italy 41 D9
Vallimanca, Arroyo, Argentina 126 D4
Vallo della Lucánia, Italy 43 B8
Vallon-Pont-d'Arc, France 21 D8
Vallorbe, Switz. 25 J2
Valls, Spain 38 D6
Valmaseda = Balmaseda, Spain 38 B1
Valmiera, Latvia 9 H21
Valnera, Spain 36 B7
Valognes, France 18 C5
Valona = Vlorë, Albania 44 F3
Valongo, Portugal 36 D2
Valozhyn, Belarus 32 E4
Valpaços, Portugal 36 D3
Valparaíso, Chile 126 C1
Valparaíso, Mexico 118 C4
Valparaiso, U.S.A. 114 E2
Valparaíso □, Chile 126 C1
Valpovo, Croatia 28 E3
Valréas, France 21 D9
Vals, Switz. 25 J5
Vals →, S. Africa 88 D4
Vals, Tanjung, Indonesia 63 F9
Vals-les-Bains, France 21 D8
Valsad, India 66 J8

Valtellina, *Italy* 40 B6
Valuyki, *Russia* 33 G10
Valverde, *Canary Is.* 48 G2
Valverde del Camino, *Spain* 37 H4
Valverde del Fresno, *Spain* 36 E4
Vama, *Romania* 29 C10
Vamdrup, *Denmark* 11 J3
Vâmhus, *Sweden* 10 C8
Vammala, *Finland* 9 F20
Vámos, *Greece* 49 D6
Van, *Turkey* 70 B4
Van, L. = Van Gölü, *Turkey* 70 B4
Van Alstyne, *U.S.A.* 113 J6
Van Blommestein Meer, *Suriname* 125 C7
Van Buren, *Canada* 105 C6
Van Buren, *Ark., U.S.A.* 113 H7
Van Buren, *Maine, U.S.A.* 115 B11
Van Buren, *Mo., U.S.A.* 113 G9
Van Canh, *Vietnam* 64 F7
Van Diemen, C., *N. Terr., Australia* 92 B5
Van Diemen, C., *Queens., Australia* 94 B2
Van Diemen G., *Australia* 92 B5
Van Gölü, *Turkey* 70 B4
Van Horn, *U.S.A.* 113 K2
Van Ninh, *Vietnam* 64 F7
Van Rees, Pegunungan, *Indonesia* 63 E9
Van Wert, *U.S.A.* 114 E3
Van Yen, *Vietnam* 58 G5
Vanadzor, *Armenia* 35 K7
Vanavara, *Russia* 53 C11
Vancouver, *Canada* 102 D4
Vancouver, *U.S.A.* 110 E4
Vancouver, C., *Australia* 93 G2
Vancouver I., *Canada* 102 D3
Vancouver International ✈ (YVR), *U.S.A.* 110 A3
Vandalia, *Ill., U.S.A.* 112 F10
Vandalia, *Mo., U.S.A.* 112 F9
Vandenburg, *U.S.A.* 111 L6
Vanderbijlpark, *S. Africa* 89 D4
Vandergrift, *U.S.A.* 116 F5
Vanderhoof, *Canada* 102 C4
Vanderkloof Dam, *S. Africa* 88 E3
Vanderlin I., *Australia* 94 B2
Vänern, *Sweden* 11 F7
Vänersborg, *Sweden* 11 F6
Vang Vieng, *Laos* 64 C4
Vanga, *Kenya* 86 C4
Vangaindrano, *Madag.* 89 C8
Vanguard, *Canada* 103 D7
Vanino, *Russia* 53 E15
Vânju Mare, *Romania* 28 F7
Vanna, *Norway* 8 A18
Vännäs, *Sweden* 8 E18
Vannes, *France* 18 E4
Vanoise, *France* 21 C10
Vanrhynsdorp, *S. Africa* 88 E2
Vansbro, *Sweden* 10 D8
Vansittart B., *Australia* 92 B4
Vantaa, *Finland* 9 F21
Vanua Balavu, *Fiji* 91 C9
Vanua Levu, *Fiji* 91 C8
Vanuatu ■, *Pac. Oc.* 96 J8
Vanwyksvlei, *S. Africa* 88 E3
Vanzylsrus, *S. Africa* 88 D3
Vapnyarka, *Ukraine* 33 H5
Var □, *France* 21 E10
Var →, *France* 21 E11
Vara, *Sweden* 11 F6
Varades, *France* 18 E5
Varáita →, *Italy* 40 D4
Varallo, *Italy* 40 C5
Varāmīn, *Iran* 71 C6
Varāmīn □, *Iran* 71 B6
Varanasi, *India* 69 G10
Varangerfjorden, *Norway* 8 A23
Varangerhalvøya, *Norway* 8 A23
Varano, Lago di, *Italy* 41 G12
Varaždin, *Croatia* 41 B13
Varazze, *Italy* 40 D5
Varberg, *Sweden* 11 G6
Vardak □, *Afghan.* 66 B6
Vardar = Axiós →, *Greece* 44 F6
Varde, *Denmark* 11 J2
Varde Å →, *Denmark* 11 J2
Vardø, *Norway* 8 A24
Varel, *Germany* 24 B4
Varella, Mui, *Vietnam* 64 F7
Varėna, *Lithuania* 9 J21
Varennes-sur-Allier, *France* 19 F10
Varennes-Vauzelles, *France* 19 E10
Vareš, *Bos.-H.* 28 F3
Varese, *Italy* 40 C5
Vârfurile, *Romania* 28 D7
Vårgårda, *Sweden* 11 F6
Varginha, *Brazil* 127 A6
Vargön, *Sweden* 11 F6
Varillas, *Chile* 126 A1
Varkaus, *Finland* 9 E22
Värmdölandet, *Sweden* 10 E12
Värmeln, *Sweden* 10 E6
Värmlands Bro, *Sweden* 10 E7
Värmlands län □, *Sweden* 10 E6
Varna, *Bulgaria* 45 C11
Varna □, *Bulgaria* 45 C11
Värnamo, *Sweden* 11 G8
Varnsdorf, *Czech Rep.* 26 A7
Várpalota, *Hungary* 28 C3
Vars, *Canada* 117 A9
Vars, *France* 21 D10
Varto, *Turkey* 73 C9
Varvarin, *Serbia & M.* 44 C5
Varysburg, *U.S.A.* 116 D6
Varzaneh, *Iran* 71 C7
Varzi, *Italy* 40 D6
Varzo, *Italy* 40 B5
Varzy, *France* 19 E10
Vas □, *Hungary* 28 C1
Vasa Barris →, *Brazil* 125 F11
Vásárosnamény, *Hungary* 28 B7
Vascão →, *Portugal* 37 H3
Vaşcău, *Romania* 28 D7
Vascongadas = País Vasco □, *Spain* 38 C2
Vasht = Khāsh, *Iran* 66 E2
Vasilevichi, *Belarus* 33 F5
Vasilikón, *Greece* 46 C5
Vasilkov = Vasylkiv, *Ukraine* 33 G6
Vaslui, *Romania* 29 D12
Vaslui □, *Romania* 29 D12
Väsman, *Sweden* 10 D9
Vassar, *Canada* 103 D9
Vassar, *U.S.A.* 114 D4
Västerås, *Sweden* 10 E10
Västerbotten, *Sweden* 8 D18
Västerdalälven →, *Sweden* 10 D8
Västergötland, *Sweden* 11 F7
Västerhaninge, *Sweden* 10 E12
Västervik, *Sweden* 11 G10
Västmanland, *Sweden* 9 G16
Västmanlands län □, *Sweden* 10 E10
Vasto, *Italy* 41 F11
Västra Götalands Län □, *Sweden* 11 F6
Vasvár, *Hungary* 28 C1
Vasylkiv, *Ukraine* 33 G6
Vatan, *France* 19 E8
Vatersay, *U.K.* 13 E1
Váthia, *Greece* 46 E4
Vatican City ■, *Europe* 41 G9
Vaticano, C., *Italy* 43 D8
Vatili, *Cyprus* 49 D12
Vatin, *Serbia & M.* 28 E6
Vatnajökull, *Iceland* 8 D5
Vatoa, *Fiji* 91 D9
Vatólakkos, *Greece* 49 D5
Vatoloha, *Madag.* 89 B8
Vatomandry, *Madag.* 89 B8
Vatra-Dornei, *Romania* 29 C10
Vatrak →, *India* 68 H5
Vättern, *Sweden* 11 F8
Vaucluse □, *France* 21 E9
Vaucouleurs, *France* 19 D12
Vaud □, *Switz.* 25 J2
Vaudreuil-Dorion, *Canada* 117 A10
Vaughn, *Mont., U.S.A.* 108 C8
Vaughn, *N. Mex., U.S.A.* 109 J11
Vaujours L., *Canada* 104 A5
Vaupés = Uaupés →, *Brazil* 124 C5
Vaupes □, *Colombia* 124 C4
Vauvert, *France* 21 E8
Vauxhall, *Canada* 102 C6
Vav, *India* 68 G4
Vavatenina, *Madag.* 89 B8
Vava'u, *Tonga* 91 D12
Vavoua, *Ivory C.* 82 D3
Vawkavysk, *Belarus* 33 F3
Vaxholm, *Sweden* 10 E12
Växjö, *Sweden* 11 H8
Våxtorp, *Sweden* 11 H7
Vaygach, Ostrov, *Russia* 52 C6
Váyia, *Greece* 46 C5
Váyia, Ákra, *Greece* 49 C10
Vechelde, *Germany* 24 C6
Vechta, *Germany* 24 C4
Vechte →, *Neths.* 17 B6
Vecsés, *Hungary* 28 C4
Veddige, *Sweden* 11 G6
Vedea →, *Romania* 29 G10
Vedia, *Argentina* 126 C3
Vedrette di Ries-Aurina ⌂, *Italy* 41 B9
Vedum, *Sweden* 11 F7
Veendam, *Neths.* 17 A6
Veenendaal, *Neths.* 17 B5
Vefsna →, *Norway* 8 D15
Vega, *Norway* 8 D14
Vega, *U.S.A.* 113 H3
Vega Baja, *Puerto Rico* 121 d
Vegadeo, *Spain* 36 B3
Vegorrítis, Límni, *Greece* 44 F5
Vegreville, *Canada* 102 C6
Veinge, *Sweden* 11 H7
Veisiejai, *Lithuania* 30 D10
Vejbystrand, *Sweden* 11 H6
Vejen, *Denmark* 11 J3
Vejer de la Frontera, *Spain* 37 J5
Vejle, *Denmark* 11 J3
Vejle Amtskommune □, *Denmark* 11 J3
Vejle Fjord, *Denmark* 11 J3
Vela Luka, *Croatia* 41 F13
Velas, C., *Costa Rica* 120 D2
Velasco, Sierra de, *Argentina* 126 B2
Velay, Mts. du, *France* 20 D7
Velbert, *Germany* 24 D3
Velddrif, *S. Africa* 88 E2
Velebit ⌂, *Croatia* 41 D12
Velebit Planina, *Croatia* 41 D12
Velebitski Kanal, *Croatia* 41 D11
Veleka →, *Bulgaria* 45 D11
Velencei-tó, *Hungary* 28 C3
Velenje, *Slovenia* 41 B12
Veles, *Macedonia* 44 E5
Velestínon, *Greece* 46 B4
Vélez-Málaga, *Spain* 37 J6
Vélez Rubio, *Spain* 39 H2
Velhas →, *Brazil* 125 G10
Velika, *Croatia* 28 E2
Velika Gorica, *Croatia* 41 C13
Velika Kapela, *Croatia* 41 C12
Velika Kladuša, *Bos.-H.* 41 C12
Velika Kruša, *Serbia & M.* 44 D4
Velika Morava →, *Serbia & M.* 44 B5
Velika Plana, *Serbia & M.* 44 B5
Velikaya →, *Russia* 32 D5
Velikaya Kema, *Russia* 54 B8
Velikaya Lepetikha, *Ukraine* 33 J7
Veliké Kapušany, *Slovak Rep.* 27 C15
Velike Lašče, *Slovenia* 41 C11
Veliki Jastrebac, *Serbia & M.* 44 C5
Veliki Kanal, *Serbia & M.* 28 E4
Veliki Popović, *Serbia & M.* 44 B5
Velikiye Luki, *Russia* 32 D6
Veliko Gradište, *Serbia & M.* 44 B5
Veliko Tŭrnovo, *Bulgaria* 45 C9
Velikonda Range, *India* 66 M11
Vélingara, *Kolda, Senegal* 82 C2
Vélingara, *Louga, Senegal* 82 B2
Velingrad, *Bulgaria* 44 D7
Velino, Mte., *Italy* 41 F10
Velizh, *Russia* 32 E6
Velké Karlovice, *Czech Rep.* 27 B11
Velké Meziříčí, *Czech Rep.* 26 B9
Vel'ký Javorník, *Slovak Rep.* 27 B11
Vel'ký Krtíš, *Slovak Rep.* 27 C12
Vel'ký Meder, *Slovak Rep.* 27 D10
Vel'ký Tribeč, *Slovak Rep.* 27 C11
Velletri, *Italy* 42 A5
Vellinge, *Sweden* 11 J6
Vellmar, *Germany* 24 D5
Vellore, *India* 66 N11
Velsk, *Russia* 32 B11
Velten, *Germany* 24 C9
Veluwezoom △, *Neths.* 17 B6
Velva, *U.S.A.* 112 A4
Velvendós, *Greece* 44 F6
Vemb, *Denmark* 11 H2
Vemdalen, *Sweden* 10 B7
Ven, *Sweden* 11 J6
Venaco, *France* 21 F13
Venado Tuerto, *Argentina* 126 C3
Venafro, *Italy* 43 A7
Venarey-les-Laumes, *France* 19 E11
Venaría, *Italy* 40 C4
Venčane, *Serbia & M.* 44 B4
Vence, *France* 21 E11
Vendas Novas, *Portugal* 37 G2
Vendée □, *France* 18 F5
Vendée →, *France* 18 F5
Vendéen, Bocage, *France* 20 B2
Vendeuvre-sur-Barse, *France* 19 D11
Vendôme, *France* 18 E8
Vendrell = El Vendrell, *Spain* 38 D6
Vendsyssel, *Denmark* 11 G4
Venelles, *France* 21 E9
Véneta, L., *Italy* 41 C9
Véneto □, *Italy* 41 C9
Venev, *Russia* 32 E10
Venézia, *Italy* 41 C9
Venézia, G. di, *Italy* 41 C10
Venezuela ■, *S. Amer.* 124 B5
Venezuela, G. de, *Venezuela* 124 A4
Vengurla, *India* 66 M8
Venice = Venézia, *Italy* 41 C9
Venice, *U.S.A.* 115 M4
Vénissieux, *France* 21 C8
Venjansjön, *Sweden* 10 D8
Venkatapuram, *India* 67 K12
Venlo, *Neths.* 17 C6
Vennesla, *Norway* 9 G12
Venosa, *Italy* 43 B8
Venray, *Neths.* 17 C6
Venta, *Lithuania* 30 B9
Venta →, *Latvia* 30 A8
Venta de Baños, *Spain* 36 D6
Venta de Cardeña = Cardeña, *Spain* 37 G6
Ventana, Punta de la, *Mexico* 118 C3
Ventana, Sa. de la, *Argentina* 126 D3
Ventersburg, *S. Africa* 88 D4
Venterstad, *S. Africa* 88 E4
Ventimíglia, *Italy* 40 E4
Ventnor, *U.K.* 15 G6
Ventoténe, *Italy* 42 B6
Ventoux, Mt., *France* 21 D9
Ventspils, *Latvia* 9 H19
Ventspils □, *Latvia* 30 A8
Ventuarí →, *Venezuela* 124 C5
Ventucopa, *U.S.A.* 111 L7
Ventura, *U.S.A.* 111 L7
Venus B., *Australia* 95 F4
Vera, *Argentina* 126 B3
Vera, *Spain* 39 H3
Veracruz, *Mexico* 119 D5
Veracruz □, *Mexico* 119 D5
Veraval, *India* 68 J4
Verbánia, *Italy* 40 C5
Verbicaro, *Italy* 43 C8
Verbier, *Switz.* 25 J3
Vercelli, *Italy* 40 C5
Verchovchevo, *Ukraine* 33 H8
Vercors ⌂, *France* 21 D9
Verdalsøra, *Norway* 8 E14
Verde →, *Argentina* 128 E3
Verde →, *Goiás, Brazil* 125 G8
Verde →, *Mato Grosso do Sul, Brazil* 125 H8
Verde →, *Chihuahua, Mexico* 118 B3
Verde →, *Oaxaca, Mexico* 119 D5
Verde →, *Veracruz, Mexico* 118 C4
Verde →, *Paraguay* 126 A4
Verde →, *U.S.A.* 106 D4
Verde, Cay, *Bahamas* 120 B4
Verde Island Pass, *Phil.* 61 E4
Verden, *Germany* 24 C5
Verdhikoúsa, *Greece* 46 B3
Verdi, *U.S.A.* 110 F7
Verdon ⌂, *France* 21 E10
Verdon →, *France* 21 E9
Verdun, *France* 19 C12
Verdun-sur-le-Doubs, *France* 19 F12
Vereeniging, *S. Africa* 89 D4
Verga, C., *Guinea* 82 C2
Vergara, *Uruguay* 127 C5
Vergato, *Italy* 40 D8
Vergemont Cr. →, *Australia* 94 C3
Vergennes, *U.S.A.* 117 B11
Vergt, *France* 20 C4
Verín, *Spain* 36 D3
Verkhnedvinsk = Vyerkhnyadzvinsk, *Belarus* 32 E4
Verkhnevilyuysk, *Russia* 53 C13
Verkhniy Baskunchak, *Russia* 35 F8
Verkhovye, *Russia* 33 F9
Verkhoyansk, *Russia* 53 C14
Verkhoyansk Ra. = Verkhoyanskiy Khrebet, *Russia* 53 C13
Verkhoyanskiy Khrebet, *Russia* 53 C13
Vermenton, *France* 19 E10
Vermilion, *Canada* 103 C6
Vermilion, *U.S.A.* 116 E2
Vermilion →, *Canada* 103 C6
Vermilion, B., *U.S.A.* 113 L9
Vermilion Bay, *Canada* 103 D10
Vermilion L., *U.S.A.* 112 B8
Vermillion, *U.S.A.* 112 D6
Vermillion →, *Canada* 104 C5
Vermont □, *U.S.A.* 117 C12
Vermosh, *Albania* 44 D3
Vernadsky, *Antarctica* 5 C17
Vernal, *U.S.A.* 108 F9
Vernalis, *U.S.A.* 110 H5
Vernazza, *Italy* 40 D6
Verner, *Canada* 104 C3
Verneuil-sur-Avre, *France* 18 D7
Verneukpan, *S. Africa* 88 E3
Vernier, *Switz.* 25 J2
Vérnio, *Italy* 40 D8
Vernon, *Canada* 102 C5
Vernon, *France* 18 C8
Vernon, *U.S.A.* 113 H5
Vernonia, *U.S.A.* 110 E3
Vernouillet, *France* 18 D8
Vero Beach, *U.S.A.* 115 M5
Véroia, *Greece* 44 F6
Véroli, *Italy* 41 G10
Verona, *Canada* 117 B8
Verona, *Italy* 40 C7
Verona, *U.S.A.* 112 D10
Verrès, *Italy* 40 C4
Versailles, *France* 19 D9
Versmold, *Germany* 24 C4
Vert, C., *Senegal* 82 C1
Vertou, *France* 18 E5
Vertus, *France* 19 D11
Verulam, *S. Africa* 89 D5
Verviers, *Belgium* 17 D5
Vervins, *France* 19 C10
Veržej, *Slovenia* 41 B13
Verzy, *France* 19 C11
Vescovato, *France* 21 F13
Veselí nad Lužnicí, *Czech Rep.* 26 B7
Veselie, *Bulgaria* 45 D11
Veselovskoye Vdkhr., *Russia* 35 G5
Veshenskaya, *Russia* 34 F5
Vesle →, *France* 19 C10
Vesoul, *France* 19 E13
Vessigebro, *Sweden* 11 H6
Vesterålen, *Norway* 8 B16
Vestfjorden, *Norway* 8 C15
Vestmannaeyjar, *Iceland* 8 E3
Vestsjællands Amtskommune □, *Denmark* 11 J5
Vestspitsbergen, *Svalbard* 4 B8
Vestvågøy, *Norway* 8 B15
Vesuvio, *Italy* 43 B7
Vesuvius, Mt. = Vesuvio, *Italy* 43 B7
Vesyegonsk, *Russia* 32 C9
Veszprém, *Hungary* 28 C2
Veszprém □, *Hungary* 28 C2
Vésztő, *Hungary* 28 D6
Vetlanda, *Sweden* 11 G9
Vetluga, *Russia* 34 B7
Vetlugu →, *Russia* 34 B8
Vetluzhskiy, *Kostroma, Russia* 34 A7
Vetluzhskiy, *Nizhniy Novgorod, Russia* 34 B7
Vetovo, *Bulgaria* 45 C10
Vetralla, *Italy* 41 F9
Vetren, *Bulgaria* 45 D8
Vettore, Mte., *Italy* 41 F10
Veurne, *Belgium* 17 C2
Veveno →, *Sudan* 81 F3
Vevey, *Switz.* 25 J2
Vévi, *Greece* 44 F5
Veynes, *France* 21 D9
Veys, *Iran* 71 D6
Vézelay, *France* 19 E10
Vézelise, *France* 19 D13
Vézère →, *France* 20 D4
Vezhen, *Bulgaria* 45 D8
Vezirköprü, *Turkey* 72 B6
Vezzani, *France* 21 F13
Vi Thanh, *Vietnam* 65 H5
Viacha, *Bolivia* 124 G5
Viadana, *Italy* 40 D7
Viamão, *Brazil* 127 C5
Viana, *Brazil* 125 D10
Viana, *Spain* 38 C2
Viana do Alentejo, *Portugal* 37 G3
Viana do Bolo, *Spain* 36 C3
Viana do Castelo, *Portugal* 36 D2
Viana do Castelo □, *Portugal* 36 D2
Vianden, *Lux.* 17 E6
Viangchan = Vientiane, *Laos* 64 D4
Vianópolis, *Brazil* 125 G9
Viar →, *Spain* 37 H5
Viaréggio, *Italy* 40 E7
Viaur →, *France* 20 D5
Vibble, *Sweden* 11 G12
Vibo Valéntia, *Italy* 43 D9
Viborg, *Denmark* 11 H3
Viborg Amtskommune □, *Denmark* 11 H3
Vibraye, *France* 18 D7
Vic, *Spain* 38 D7
Vic, Étang de, *France* 20 E7
Vic-en-Bigorre, *France* 20 E4
Vic-Fézensac, *France* 20 E4
Vic-le-Comte, *France* 19 G10
Vic-sur-Cère, *France* 20 D6
Vícar, *Spain* 39 J2
Vicenza, *Italy* 41 C8
Vich = Vic, *Spain* 38 D7
Vichada →, *Colombia* 124 C5
Vichuga, *Russia* 34 B5
Vichy, *France* 19 F10
Vicksburg, *Ariz., U.S.A.* 111 M13
Vicksburg, *Miss., U.S.A.* 113 J9
Vico, *France* 21 F12
Vico, L. di, *Italy* 41 F9
Vico del Gargano, *Italy* 41 G12
Vicovu de Sus, *Romania* 29 C10
Victor, *India* 68 J4
Victor, *U.S.A.* 116 D7
Victor Harbor, *Australia* 95 F2
Victoria = Labuan, *Malaysia* 62 C5
Victoria, *Argentina* 126 C3
Victoria, *Canada* 102 D4
Victoria, *Chile* 128 D2
Victoria, *Guinea* 82 C2
Victoria, *Malta* 49 C1
Victoria, *Phil.* 61 D4
Victoria, *Romania* 29 E9
Victoria, *Kans., U.S.A.* 112 F5
Victoria, *Tex., U.S.A.* 113 L6
Victoria □, *Australia* 95 F3
Victoria →, *Australia* 92 C4
Victoria, Grand L., *Canada* 104 C4
Victoria, L., *Africa* 86 C3
Victoria, L., *Australia* 95 E3
Victoria, Mt., *Burma* 67 J18
Victoria Beach, *Canada* 103 C9
Victoria de Durango = Durango, *Mexico* 118 C4
Victoria de las Tunas, *Cuba* 120 B4
Victoria Falls, *Zimbabwe* 87 F2
Victoria Harbour, *Canada* 116 B5
Victoria I., *Canada* 100 A8
Victoria L., *Canada* 105 C8
Victoria Ld., *Antarctica* 5 D11
Victoria Nile →, *Uganda* 86 B3
Victoria River, *Australia* 92 C5
Victoria Str., *Canada* 100 B9
Victoria West, *S. Africa* 88 E3
Victorias, *Phil.* 61 F5
Victoriaville, *Canada* 105 C5
Victorica, *Argentina* 126 D2
Victorville, *U.S.A.* 111 L9
Vicuña, *Chile* 126 C1
Vicuña Mackenna, *Argentina* 126 C3
Vidal, *U.S.A.* 111 L12
Vidal Junction, *U.S.A.* 111 L12
Vidalia, *U.S.A.* 115 J4
Vidauban, *France* 21 E10
Videbæk, *Denmark* 11 H2
Videle, *Romania* 29 F10
Vídho, *Greece* 49 A3
Vidigueira, *Portugal* 37 G3
Vidin, *Bulgaria* 44 C6
Vidio, C., *Spain* 36 B4
Vidisha, *India* 68 H7
Vidra, *Romania* 29 E11
Viduša, *Bos.-H.* 44 D2
Vidzy, *Belarus* 9 J22
Viechtach, *Germany* 25 F8
Viedma, *Argentina* 128 E4
Viedma, L., *Argentina* 128 F2
Vieira do Minho, *Portugal* 36 D2
Vielha, *Spain* 38 C5
Viella = Vielha, *Spain* 38 C5
Vielsalm, *Belgium* 17 D5
Vienenburg, *Germany* 24 D6
Vieng Pou Kha, *Laos* 58 G3
Vienna = Wien, *Austria* 27 C9
Vienna, *Ill., U.S.A.* 113 G10
Vienna, *Mo., U.S.A.* 112 F9
Vienna ✈ (VIA), *Austria* 27 C9
Vienne, *France* 21 C8
Vienne □, *France* 20 B4
Vienne →, *France* 18 E7
Vientiane, *Laos* 64 D4
Vientos, Paso de los, *Caribbean* 121 C5
Vieques, Isla de, *Puerto Rico* 121 d
Vierge Pt., *St. Lucia* 121 f
Viernheim, *Germany* 25 F4
Viersen, *Germany* 24 D2
Vierwaldstättersee, *Switz.* 25 J4
Vierzon, *France* 19 E9
Vieste, *Italy* 41 G13
Vietnam ■, *Asia* 64 C6
Vieux-Boucau-les-Bains, *France* 20 E2
Vieux Fort, *St. Lucia* 121 f
Vif, *France* 21 C9
Vigan, *Phil.* 61 C4
Vigévano, *Italy* 40 C5
Vigia, *Brazil* 125 D9
Vigía Chico, *Mexico* 119 D7
Víglas, Ákra, *Greece* 49 D9
Vignemale, *France* 20 F3
Vigneulles-lès-Hattonchâtel, *France* 19 D12
Vignola, *Italy* 40 D8
Vigo, *Spain* 36 C2
Vigo, Ría de, *Spain* 36 C2
Vigsø Bugt, *Denmark* 11 G2
Vihiers, *France* 18 E6
Vihowa, *Pakistan* 68 D4
Vihowa →, *Pakistan* 68 D4
Vijayawada, *India* 67 L12
Vijosë →, *Albania* 44 F3
Vík, *Iceland* 8 E4
Vika, *Sweden* 10 D8
Vikarbyn, *Sweden* 10 D9
Vikeke = Viqueque, *E. Timor* 63 F7
Viken, *Skåne, Sweden* 11 H6
Viken, *Västra Götaland, Sweden* 11 F8
Viking, *Canada* 102 C6
Vikmanshyttan, *Sweden* 10 D9
Vikna, *Norway* 8 D14
Vikos-Aoos △, *Greece* 46 B2
Vila da Maganja, *Mozam.* 87 F4
Vila de João Belo = Xai-Xai, *Mozam.* 89 D5

Vila de Rei, *Portugal* 36 F2
Vila do Bispo, *Portugal* 37 H2
Vila do Conde, *Portugal* 36 D2
Vila Franca de Xira, *Portugal* 37 G2
Vila Gamito, *Mozam.* 87 E3
Vila Gomes da Costa, *Mozam.* 89 C5
Vila Machado, *Mozam.* 87 F3
Vila Mouzinho, *Mozam.* 87 E3
Vila Nova de Famalicão, *Portugal* 36 D2
Vila Nova de Fos Côa, *Portugal* 36 D3
Vila Nova de Gaia, *Portugal* 36 D2
Vila Nova de Ourém, *Portugal* 36 F2
Vila Pouca de Aguiar, *Portugal* 36 D3
Vila Real, *Portugal* 36 D3
Vila Real □, *Portugal* 36 D3
Vila-real de los Infantes, *Spain* 38 F4
Vila Real de Santo António, *Portugal* 37 H3
Vila Vasco da Gama, *Mozam.* 87 E3
Vila Velha, *Brazil* 127 A7
Vila Viçosa, *Portugal* 37 G3
Vilafranca del Maestrat, *Spain* 38 E4
Vilafranca del Penedès, *Spain* 38 D6
Vilagarcía de Arousa, *Spain* 36 C2
Vilaine ➝, *France* 18 E4
Vilanandro, Tanjona, *Madag.* 89 B7
Vilanculos, *Mozam.* 89 C6
Vilanova de Castelló, *Spain* 39 F4
Vilanova i la Geltrú, *Spain* 38 D6
Vilar Formosa, *Portugal* 36 E4
Vilaseca, *Spain* 38 D6
Vilaseca-Salou = Vilaseca, *Spain* 38 D6
Vilbjerg, *Denmark* 11 H2
Vilcheka, Z., *Russia* 4 A11
Vilches, *Spain* 37 G7
Vileyka, *Belarus* 32 E4
Vilhelmina, *Sweden* 8 D17
Vilhena, *Brazil* 124 F6
Viliga, *Russia* 53 C16
Viliya = Neris ➝, *Lithuania* 9 J21
Viljandi, *Estonia* 9 G21
Vilkaviškis, *Lithuania* 30 D10
Vilkija, *Lithuania* 30 C10
Vilkitskogo, Proliv, *Russia* 53 B11
Vilkovo = Vylkove, *Ukraine* 33 K5
Villa Abecia, *Bolivia* 126 A2
Villa Ahumada, *Mexico* 118 A3
Villa Ana, *Argentina* 126 B4
Villa Ángela, *Argentina* 126 B3
Villa Bella, *Bolivia* 124 F5
Villa Bens = Tarfaya, *Morocco* 78 C3
Villa Cañás, *Argentina* 126 C3
Villa Cisneros = Dakhla, *W. Sahara* 78 D2
Villa Colón, *Argentina* 126 C2
Villa Constitución, *Argentina* 126 C3
Villa de María, *Argentina* 126 B3
Villa del Rio, *Spain* 37 H6
Villa Dolores, *Argentina* 126 C2
Villa Frontera, *Mexico* 118 B4
Villa Guillermina, *Argentina* 126 B4
Villa Hayes, *Paraguay* 126 B4
Villa Iris, *Argentina* 126 D3
Villa Juárez, *Mexico* 118 B4
Villa María, *Argentina* 126 C3
Villa Mazán, *Argentina* 126 B2
Villa Minozzo, *Italy* 40 D7
Villa Montes, *Bolivia* 126 A3
Villa Ocampo, *Argentina* 126 B4
Villa Ocampo, *Mexico* 118 B3
Villa Ojo de Agua, *Argentina* 126 B3
Villa San Giovanni, *Italy* 43 D8
Villa San José, *Argentina* 126 C4
Villa San Martín, *Argentina* 126 B3
Villa Santina, *Italy* 41 B9
Villa Unión, *Mexico* 118 C3
Villablino, *Spain* 36 C4
Villacarlos, *Spain* 48 B11
Villacarriedo, *Spain* 36 B7
Villacarrillo, *Spain* 37 G7
Villacastín, *Spain* 36 E6
Villach, *Austria* 26 E6
Villacidro, *Italy* 42 C1
Villada, *Spain* 36 C6
Villadiego, *Spain* 36 C6
Villadóssola, *Italy* 40 B5
Villafeliche, *Spain* 38 D3
Villafranca, *Spain* 38 C3
Villafranca de los Barros, *Spain* 37 G4
Villafranca de los Caballeros, *Baleares, Spain* 48 B10
Villafranca de los Caballeros, *Toledo, Spain* 37 F7
Villafranca del Cid = Vilafranca del Maestrat, *Spain* 38 E4
Villafranca del Panadés = Vilafranca del Penedès, *Spain* 38 D6
Villafranca di Verona, *Italy* 40 C7
Villafranca Tirrena, *Italy* 43 D8
Villagrán, *Mexico* 119 C5
Villaguay, *Argentina* 126 C4
Villaharta, *Spain* 37 G6
Villahermosa, *Mexico* 119 D6
Villahermosa, *Spain* 39 G2
Villaines-la-Juhel, *France* 18 D6
Villajoyosa, *Spain* 39 G4
Villalba, *Spain* 36 B3
Villalba de Guardo, *Spain* 36 C6
Villalón de Campos, *Spain* 36 C5
Villalpando, *Spain* 36 D5
Villaluenga, *Spain* 36 E7
Villamanán, *Spain* 36 C5
Villamartín, *Spain* 37 J5
Villamayor de Santiago, *Spain* 38 F2
Villamblard, *France* 20 C4
Villanova Monteleone, *Italy* 42 B1
Villanueva, *U.S.A.* 113 H2
Villanueva de Castellón = Vilanova de Castelló, *Spain* 39 F4
Villanueva de Córdoba, *Spain* 37 G6
Villanueva de la Fuente, *Spain* 39 G2
Villanueva de la Serena, *Spain* 37 G5
Villanueva de la Sierra, *Spain* 36 E4
Villanueva de los Castillejos, *Spain* 37 H3
Villanueva de los Infantes, *Spain* 37 G7
Villanueva del Arzobispo, *Spain* 39 G2
Villanueva del Fresno, *Spain* 37 G3
Villanueva y Geltrú = Vilanova i la Geltrú, *Spain* 38 D6
Villaputzu, *Italy* 42 C2
Villaquilambre, *Spain* 36 C5
Villar del Arzobispo, *Spain* 38 F4
Villar del Rey, *Spain* 37 F4
Villard-de-Lans, *France* 21 C9
Villarramiel, *Spain* 36 C6
Villarreal = Vila-real de los Infantes, *Spain* 38 F4
Villarrica, *Chile* 128 D2
Villarrica, *Paraguay* 126 B4
Villarrobledo, *Spain* 39 F2
Villarroya de la Sierra, *Spain* 38 D3
Villarrubia de los Ojos, *Spain* 37 F7
Villars-les-Dombes, *France* 19 F12
Villasayas, *Spain* 38 D2
Villaseca de los Gamitos = Villaseco de los Gamitos, *Spain* 36 D4
Villaseco de los Gamitos, *Spain* 36 D4
Villasimíus, *Italy* 42 C2
Villastar, *Spain* 38 E3
Villatobas, *Spain* 36 F7
Villavicencio, *Argentina* 126 C2
Villavicencio, *Colombia* 124 C4
Villaviciosa, *Spain* 36 B5
Villazón, *Bolivia* 126 A2
Ville-Marie, *Canada* 104 C4
Ville Platte, *U.S.A.* 113 K8
Villedieu-les-Poêles, *France* 18 D5
Villefort, *France* 20 D7
Villefranche-de-Lauragais, *France* 20 E5
Villefranche-de-Rouergue, *France* 20 D6
Villefranche-du-Périgord, *France* 20 D5
Villefranche-sur-Saône, *France* 21 C8
Villel, *Spain* 38 E3
Villemur-sur-Tarn, *France* 20 E5
Villena, *Spain* 39 G4
Villenauxe-la-Grande, *France* 19 D10
Villenave-d'Ornon, *France* 20 D3
Villeneuve-d'Ascq, *France* 19 B10
Villeneuve-l'Archevêque, *France* 19 D10
Villeneuve-lès-Avignon, *France* 21 E8
Villeneuve-sur-Allier, *France* 19 F10
Villeneuve-sur-Lot, *France* 20 D4
Villeneuve-sur-Yonne, *France* 19 D10
Villeréal, *France* 20 D4
Villers-Bocage, *France* 18 C6
Villers-Cotterêts, *France* 19 C10
Villers-sur-Mer, *France* 18 C6
Villersexel, *France* 19 E13
Villerupt, *France* 19 C12
Villeurbanne, *France* 21 C8
Villiers, *S. Africa* 89 D4
Villingen-Schwenningen, *Germany* 25 G4
Vilna, *Canada* 102 C6
Vilnius, *Lithuania* 9 J21
Vils, *Austria* 26 D3
Vils ➝, *Bayern, Germany* 25 G9
Vils ➝, *Bayern, Germany* 25 F7
Vilsbiburg, *Germany* 25 G8
Vilshofen, *Germany* 25 G9
Vilusi, *Serbia & M.* 44 D2
Vilvoorde, *Belgium* 17 D4
Vilyuy ➝, *Russia* 53 C13
Vilyuysk, *Russia* 53 C13
Vimianzo, *Spain* 36 B1
Vimioso, *Portugal* 36 D4
Vimmerby, *Sweden* 11 G9
Vimoutiers, *France* 18 D7
Vimperk, *Czech Rep.* 26 B6
Viña del Mar, *Chile* 126 C1
Vinarós, *Spain* 38 E5
Vincennes, *U.S.A.* 114 F2
Vincent, *U.S.A.* 111 L8
Vinchina, *Argentina* 126 B2
Vindelälven ➝, *Sweden* 8 E18
Vindeln, *Sweden* 8 D18
Vinderup, *Denmark* 11 H2
Vindhya Ra., *India* 68 H7
Vineland, *U.S.A.* 114 F8
Vineuil, *France* 18 E8
Vinga, *Romania* 28 D6
Vingåker, *Sweden* 10 E9
Vinh, *Vietnam* 64 C5
Vinh Linh, *Vietnam* 64 D6
Vinh Long, *Vietnam* 65 G5
Vinh Yen, *Vietnam* 58 G5
Vinhais, *Portugal* 36 D3
Vinica, *Croatia* 41 B13
Vinica, *Macedonia* 44 E6
Vinica, *Slovenia* 41 C12
Vinita, *U.S.A.* 113 G7
Vinkovci, *Croatia* 28 E3
Vinnitsa = Vinnytsya, *Ukraine* 33 H5
Vinnytsya, *Ukraine* 33 H5
Vinslöv, *Sweden* 11 H7
Vinson Massif, *Antarctica* 5 D16
Vintjärn, *Sweden* 10 D10
Vinton, *Calif., U.S.A.* 110 F6
Vinton, *Iowa, U.S.A.* 112 D8
Vinton, *La., U.S.A.* 113 K8
Vinţu de Jos, *Romania* 29 D8
Viöl, *Germany* 24 A5
Vipava, *Slovenia* 41 C10
Vipiteno, *Italy* 41 B8
Viqueque, *E. Timor* 63 F7
Vir, *Croatia* 41 D12
Virac, *Phil.* 61 E6
Virachey, *Cambodia* 64 F6
Virachey △, *Cambodia* 64 E6
Virago Sd., *Canada* 102 C2
Viramgam, *India* 68 H5
Viranşehir, *Turkey* 70 B3
Virawah, *Pakistan* 68 G4
Virbalis, *Lithuania* 30 D9
Virden, *Canada* 103 D8
Vire, *France* 18 D6
Vire ➝, *France* 18 C5
Vírgenes, C., *Argentina* 128 G3
Virgin ➝, *U.S.A.* 109 H6
Virgin Gorda, *Br. Virgin Is.* 121 e
Virgin Is. (British) ⊠, *W. Indies* 121 e
Virgin Is. (U.S.) ⊠, *W. Indies* 121 e
Virgin Islands △, *Virgin Is.* 121 C7
Virginia, *S. Africa* 88 D4
Virginia, *U.S.A.* 112 B8
Virginia □, *U.S.A.* 114 G7
Virginia Beach, *U.S.A.* 114 G8
Virginia City, *Mont., U.S.A.* 108 D8
Virginia City, *Nev., U.S.A.* 110 F7
Virginia Falls, *Canada* 102 A3
Virginiatown, *Canada* 104 C4
Virje, *Croatia* 41 B13
Viroqua, *U.S.A.* 112 D9
Virovitica, *Croatia* 28 E2
Virpazar, *Serbia & M.* 44 D3
Virpur, *India* 68 J4
Virserum, *Sweden* 11 G9
Virton, *Belgium* 17 E5
Virudunagar, *India* 66 Q10
Virunga △, *Dem. Rep. of the Congo* 86 B2
Vis, *Croatia* 41 E13
Visalia, *U.S.A.* 110 J7
Visayan Sea, *Phil.* 61 F5
Visby, *Sweden* 11 G12
Viscount Melville Sd., *Canada* 98 B9
Visé, *Belgium* 17 D5
Višegrad, *Bos.-H.* 28 G4
Viseu, *Brazil* 125 D9
Viseu, *Portugal* 36 E3
Viseu □, *Portugal* 36 E3
Vişeu de Sus, *Romania* 29 C9
Vishakhapatnam, *India* 67 L13
Vişina, *Romania* 29 G9
Vişineşti, *Moldova* 29 D13
Visingsö, *Sweden* 11 F8
Viskafors, *Sweden* 11 G6
Viskan ➝, *Sweden* 11 G6
Viški Kanal, *Croatia* 41 E13
Vislanda, *Sweden* 11 H8
Visnagar, *India* 68 H5
Višnja Gora, *Slovenia* 41 C11
Viso, Mte., *Italy* 40 D4
Viso del Marqués, *Spain* 37 G7
Visoko, *Bos.-H.* 28 G3
Visokoi I., *Antarctica* 5 B1
Visp, *Switz.* 25 J3
Vissefjärda, *Sweden* 11 H9
Visselhövede, *Germany* 24 C5
Vissenbjerg, *Denmark* 11 J4
Vista, *U.S.A.* 111 M9
Vistonikos, Ormos = Vistonís, Límni, *Greece* 45 E9
Vistonís, Límni, *Greece* 45 E9
Vistula = Wisła ➝, *Poland* 30 D5
Vit ➝, *Bulgaria* 45 C8
Vitanje, *Slovenia* 41 B12
Vitebsk = Vitsyebsk, *Belarus* 32 E6
Viterbo, *Italy* 41 F9
Vitez, *Bos.-H.* 28 F2
Viti Levu, *Fiji* 91 C7
Vitigudino, *Spain* 36 D4
Vitim, *Russia* 53 D12
Vitim ➝, *Russia* 53 D12
Vitina, *Bos.-H.* 41 E14
Vitína, *Greece* 46 D4
Vítkov, *Czech Rep.* 27 B10
Vitória, *Brazil* 125 H10
Vitória da Conquista, *Brazil* 125 F10
Vitória de São Antão, *Brazil* 125 E11
Vitoria-Gasteiz, *Spain* 38 C2
Vitosha △, *Bulgaria* 44 D7
Vitré, *France* 18 D5
Vitry-le-François, *France* 19 D11
Vitry-sur-Seine, *France* 19 D9
Vitsand, *Sweden* 10 D7
Vitsi, Óros, *Greece* 44 F5
Vitsyebsk, *Belarus* 32 E6
Vittaryd, *Sweden* 11 H7
Vitteaux, *France* 19 E11
Vittel, *France* 19 D12
Vittória, *Italy* 43 F7
Vittório Véneto, *Italy* 41 C9
Vittsjö, *Sweden* 11 H7
Viveiro, *Spain* 36 B3
Vivian, *U.S.A.* 113 J8
Viviers, *France* 21 D8
Vivonne, *France* 20 B4
Vizcaíno, Desierto de, *Mexico* 118 B2
Vizcaíno, Sierra, *Mexico* 118 B2
Vizcaya □, *Spain* 38 B2
Vize, *Turkey* 45 E11
Vizianagaram, *India* 67 K13
Vizille, *France* 21 C9
Viziňada, *Croatia* 41 C10
Viziru, *Romania* 29 E12
Vizzini, *Italy* 43 E7
Vlaardingen, *Neths.* 17 C4
Vlădeasa, Vf., *Romania* 28 D7
Vladičin Han, *Serbia & M.* 44 D6
Vladikavkaz, *Russia* 35 J7
Vladimir, *Russia* 32 D11
Vladimir Volynskiy = Volodymyr-Volynskyy, *Ukraine* 33 G3
Vladimirci, *Serbia & M.* 44 B3
Vladimirovac, *Serbia & M.* 28 E5
Vladimirovka, *Russia* 35 F8
Vladimirovo, *Bulgaria* 44 C7
Vladimirovka, *Kazakhstan* 34 E10
Vladislavovka, *Ukraine* 33 K8
Vladivostok, *Russia* 53 E14
Vlăhiţa, *Romania* 29 D10
Vlakhiótis, *Greece* 46 E4
Vlasenica, *Bos.-H.* 28 F3
Vlašić, *Bos.-H.* 28 F2
Vlašim, *Czech Rep.* 26 B7
Vlasinsko Jezero, *Serbia & M.* 44 D6
Vlasotince, *Serbia & M.* 44 D6
Vlieland, *Neths.* 17 A4
Vlissingen, *Neths.* 17 C3
Vlorë, *Albania* 44 F3
Vlorës, Gjiri i, *Albania* 44 F3
Vltava ➝, *Czech Rep.* 26 A7
Vo Dat, *Vietnam* 65 G6
Vobarno, *Italy* 40 C7
Voćin, *Croatia* 28 E2
Vöcklabruck, *Austria* 26 C6
Vodice, *Croatia* 41 E12
Vodňany, *Czech Rep.* 26 B7
Vodnjan, *Croatia* 41 D10
Voe, *U.K.* 13 A7
Vogel Pk., *Nigeria* 83 D7
Vogelkop = Doberai, Jazirah, *Indonesia* 63 E8
Vogelsberg, *Germany* 24 E5
Voghera, *Italy* 40 D6
Vohibinany, *Madag.* 89 B8
Vohilava, *Madag.* 89 C8
Vohimarina = Iharana, *Madag.* 89 A9
Vohimena, Tanjon' i, *Madag.* 89 D8
Vohipeno, *Madag.* 89 C8
Voi, *Kenya* 86 C4
Void-Vacon, *France* 19 D12
Voineşti, *Iaşi, Romania* 29 C12
Voineşti, *Prahova, Romania* 29 E10
Voiotía □, *Greece* 46 C5
Voiron, *France* 21 C9
Voisey B., *Canada* 105 A7
Voitsberg, *Austria* 26 D8
Vojens, *Denmark* 11 J3
Vojmsjön, *Sweden* 8 D17
Vojnić, *Croatia* 41 C12
Vojnik, *Italy* 41 B12
Vojvodina □, *Serbia & M.* 28 E5
Vokhtoga, *Russia* 32 C11
Volary, *Czech Rep.* 26 C6
Volborg, *U.S.A.* 112 C2
Volcán de Colima △, *Mexico* 118 D4
Volcano Is. = Kazan-Rettō, *Pac. Oc.* 96 E6
Volcans △, *Rwanda* 86 C2
Volcans d'Auvergne ⌓, *France* 20 C6
Volchansk = Vovchansk, *Ukraine* 33 G9
Volchya ➝, *Ukraine* 33 H8
Volda, *Norway* 9 E12
Volga = Privolzhskiy □, *Russia* 34 B10
Volga, *Russia* 32 C10
Volga ➝, *Russia* 35 G9
Volga Hts. = Privolzhskaya Vozvyshennost, *Russia* 34 E7
Volgo-Baltiyskiy Kanal, *Russia* 32 B9
Volgo-Donskoy Kanal, *Russia* 35 F7
Volgodonsk, *Russia* 35 G6
Volgograd, *Russia* 35 F7
Volgogradskoye Vdkhr., *Russia* 34 E8
Volgorechensk, *Russia* 34 B5
Volímai, *Greece* 46 D2
Volintiri, *Moldova* 29 D14
Volissós, *Greece* 47 C7
Volkach, *Germany* 25 F6
Völkermarkt, *Austria* 26 E7
Volkhov, *Russia* 32 C7
Volkhov ➝, *Russia* 32 B7
Völklingen, *Germany* 25 F2
Volkovysk = Vawkavysk, *Belarus* 33 F3
Volksrust, *S. Africa* 89 D4
Volnansk, *Ukraine* 33 H8
Volnovakha, *Ukraine* 33 J9
Volochanka, *Russia* 53 B10
Volodarsk, *Russia* 34 B6
Volodymyr-Volynskyy, *Ukraine* 33 G3
Vologda, *Russia* 32 C10
Volokolamsk, *Russia* 32 D8
Volokonovka, *Russia* 33 G9
Vólos, *Greece* 46 B4
Volosovo, *Russia* 32 C5
Volovets, *Ukraine* 33 H2
Volovo, *Russia* 32 F10
Volozhin = Valozhyn, *Belarus* 32 E4
Volsk, *Russia* 34 D8
Volta □, *Ghana* 83 D5
Volta ➝, *Ghana* 83 D5
Volta, L., *Ghana* 83 D5
Volta Blanche = White Volta ➝, *Ghana* 83 D4
Volta Redonda, *Brazil* 127 A7
Voltaire, C., *Australia* 92 B4
Volterra, *Italy* 40 E7
Voltri, *Italy* 40 D5
Volturno ➝, *Italy* 42 A6
Vólvi, L., *Greece* 44 F7
Volyně, *Czech Rep.* 26 B6
Volzhsk, *Russia* 34 C9
Volzhskiy, *Russia* 35 F7
Vondrozo, *Madag.* 89 C8
Vónitsa, *Greece* 46 C2
Vopnafjörður, *Iceland* 8 D6
Vorarlberg □, *Austria* 26 D2
Vóras Óros, *Greece* 44 F5
Vorbasse, *Denmark* 11 J3
Vorchdorf, *Austria* 26 C6
Vorderrhein ➝, *Switz.* 25 J5
Vordingborg, *Denmark* 11 J5
Vorë, *Albania* 44 E3
Voreio Aigaio = Vórios Aiyaíon □, *Greece* 47 C7
Voreppe, *France* 21 C9
Vóriai Sporádhes, *Greece* 46 B5
Vórios Aiyaíon □, *Greece* 47 C7
Vórios Evvoïkós Kólpos, *Greece* 46 C5
Vorkuta, *Russia* 52 C7
Vormsi, *Estonia* 9 G20
Vóroi, *Greece* 46 F6
Vorona ➝, *Russia* 34 E6
Voronezh, *Russia* 33 G10
Voronezh, *Ukraine* 33 G7
Voronezh ➝, *Russia* 33 G10
Vorontsovo-Aleksandrovskoye = Zelenokumsk, *Russia* 35 H6
Voroshilovgrad = Luhansk, *Ukraine* 33 H10
Voroshilovsk = Alchevsk, *Ukraine* 33 H10
Vorpommersche Boddenlandschaft △, *Germany* 24 A8
Vorskla ➝, *Ukraine* 33 H8
Võrtsjärv, *Estonia* 9 G22
Võru, *Estonia* 9 H22
Vosges, *France* 19 D14
Vosges □, *France* 19 D13
Vosges du Nord ⌓, *France* 19 D14
Voskopojë, *Albania* 44 F4
Voskresensk, *Russia* 32 E10
Voskresenskoye, *Russia* 34 B7
Voss, *Norway* 9 F12
Vostok, *Antarctica* 5 D8
Vostok I., *Kiribati* 97 J12
Votice, *Czech Rep.* 26 B7
Votsuri-Shima, *Japan* 55 M1
Vouga ➝, *Portugal* 36 E2
Vouillé, *France* 18 F7
Voúxa, Ákra, *Greece* 49 D5
Vouzela, *Portugal* 36 E2
Vouziers, *France* 19 C11
Vovchansk, *Ukraine* 33 G9
Voyageurs △, *U.S.A.* 112 A8
Vozhe, Ozero, *Russia* 32 B10
Vozhega, *Russia* 32 B11
Voznesensk, *Ukraine* 33 J6
Voznesenye, *Russia* 32 B8
Vrå, *Denmark* 11 G3
Vráble, *Slovak Rep.* 27 C11
Vraćevšnica, *Serbia & M.* 44 B4
Vrakhnéïka, *Greece* 46 C3
Vrancea □, *Romania* 29 E11
Vrancei, Munţii, *Romania* 29 E11
Vrangelya, Ostrov, *Russia* 53 B19
Vranica, *Bos.-H.* 28 G2
Vranje, *Serbia & M.* 44 D5
Vranjska Banja, *Serbia & M.* 44 D6
Vranov nad Topl'ou, *Slovak Rep.* 27 C14
Vransko, *Slovenia* 41 B11
Vransko Jezero, *Croatia* 41 E12
Vrapčište, *Macedonia* 44 E4
Vratsa, *Bulgaria* 44 C7
Vrbas, *Serbia & M.* 28 E4
Vrbas ➝, *Bos.-H.* 28 E2
Vrbnik, *Croatia* 41 C11
Vrbovec, *Croatia* 41 C13
Vrbovsko, *Croatia* 41 C12
Vrchlabí, *Czech Rep.* 26 A8
Vrede, *S. Africa* 89 D4
Vredefort, *S. Africa* 88 D4
Vreden, *Germany* 24 C2
Vredenburg, *S. Africa* 88 E2
Vredendal, *S. Africa* 88 E2
Vretstorp, *Sweden* 10 E8
Vrgorac, *Croatia* 41 E14
Vrhnika, *Slovenia* 41 C11
Vrīdi, *Ivory C.* 82 D4
Vrigstad, *Sweden* 11 G8
Vrindavan, *India* 68 F7
Vríses, *Greece* 49 D6
Vrnograč, *Bos.-H.* 41 C12
Vrondádhes, *Greece* 47 C8
Vrpolje, *Croatia* 28 E3
Vršac, *Serbia & M.* 28 E6
Vrsacki Kanal, *Serbia & M.* 28 E5
Vrútky, *Slovak Rep.* 27 B11
Vryburg, *S. Africa* 88 D3
Vryheid, *S. Africa* 89 D5
Vsetín, *Czech Rep.* 27 B11
Vu Liet, *Vietnam* 64 C5
Vŭcha ➝, *Bulgaria* 45 D8
Vučitrn, *Serbia & M.* 44 D4
Vukovar, *Croatia* 28 E3
Vulcan, *Canada* 102 C6
Vulcan, *Romania* 29 E8
Vulcaneşti, *Moldova* 29 E13
Vulcano, *Italy* 43 D7
Vŭlchedruma, *Bulgaria* 44 C7
Vulkaneshty = Vulcaneşti, *Moldova* 29 E13
Vunduzi ➝, *Mozam.* 87 F3
Vung Tau, *Vietnam* 65 G6
Vŭrbitsa, *Bulgaria* 45 D10
Vurshets, *Bulgaria* 44 C7
Vutcani, *Romania* 29 D12
Vuya, *Sudan* 81 F2
Vwaza ⌓, *Malawi* 87 E3
Vyartsilya, *Russia* 32 A6
Vyatka = Kirov, *Russia* 52 D5
Vyatka ➝, *Russia* 34 C10
Vyatskiye Polyany, *Russia* 34 B10
Vyazemskiy, *Russia* 53 E14
Vyazma, *Russia* 32 E8
Vyazniki, *Russia* 34 B6
Vyborg, *Russia* 32 B5
Vychegda ➝, *Russia* 52 C5
Vychodné Beskydy, *Europe* 27 B15
Vyerkhnyadzvinsk, *Belarus* 32 E4
Vyksa, *Russia* 34 C6
Vylkove, *Ukraine* 33 K5
Vynohradiv, *Ukraine* 33 H2
Vyrnwy, L., *U.K.* 14 E4
Vyshniy Volochek, *Russia* 32 D8
Vyshzha = imeni 26 Bakinskikh Komissarov, *Turkmenistan* 71 B7
Vyškov, *Czech Rep.* 27 B9
Vysoké Mýto, *Czech Rep.* 27 B9
Vysokovsk, *Russia* 32 D9
Vyšší Brod, *Czech Rep.* 26 C7
Vytegra, *Russia* 32 B9

W

W du Benin △, *Benin* 83 C5
W du Burkina Faso △, *Burkina Faso* 83 C4
W du Niger △, *Niger* 83 C5
W.A.C. Bennett Dam, *Canada* 102 B4
Wa, *Ghana* 82 C4
Waal →, *Neths.* 17 C5
Waalwijk, *Neths.* 17 C5
Waat, *Sudan* 81 F3
Wabakimi △, *Canada* 104 B2
Wabana, *Canada* 105 C9
Wabasca →, *Canada* 102 B5
Wabasca-Desmarais, *Canada* 102 B6
Wabash, *U.S.A.* 114 E3
Wabash →, *U.S.A.* 114 G1
Wabi →, *Ethiopia* 81 F5
Wabigoon L., *Canada* 103 D10
Wabowden, *Canada* 103 C9
Wąbrzeźno, *Poland* 31 E5
Wabu Hu, *China* 59 A11
Wabuk Pt., *Canada* 104 A2
Wabush, *Canada* 105 B6
Wąchock, *Poland* 31 G8
Wächtersbach, *Germany* 25 E5
Waco, *U.S.A.* 113 K6
Waconichi, L., *Canada* 104 B5
Wad Ban Naqa, *Sudan* 81 D3
Wad Banda, *Sudan* 81 E2
Wad el Haddad, *Sudan* 81 E3
Wad en Nau, *Sudan* 81 E3
Wad Hamid, *Sudan* 81 D3
Wad Medanî, *Sudan* 81 E3
Wad Thana, *Pakistan* 68 F2
Wadai, *Africa* 76 E5
Wadayama, *Japan* 55 G7
Waddeneilanden, *Neths.* 17 A5
Waddenzee, *Neths.* 17 A5
Waddi, Chappal, *Nigeria* 83 D7
Waddington, *U.S.A.* 117 B9
Waddington, Mt., *Canada* 102 C3
Waddy Pt., *Australia* 95 C5
Wadebridge, *U.K.* 15 G3
Wadena, *Canada* 103 C8
Wadena, *U.S.A.* 112 B7
Wädenswil, *Switz.* 25 H4
Wadern, *Germany* 25 F2
Wadeye, *Australia* 92 B4
Wadhams, *Canada* 102 C3
Wādī as Sīr, *Jordan* 74 D4
Wadi Gemâl, *Egypt* 80 C4
Wadi Halfa, *Sudan* 80 C3
Wadi Rum △, *Jordan* 74 F4
Wadian, *China* 59 A9
Wadlew, *Poland* 31 G6
Wadowice, *Poland* 31 J6
Wadsworth, *Nev., U.S.A.* 108 G4
Wadsworth, *Ohio, U.S.A.* 116 E3
Waegwan, *S. Korea* 57 G15
Wafangdian, *China* 57 E11
Wafrah, *Si. Arabia* 70 D5
Wageningen, *Neths.* 17 C5
Wager B., *Canada* 101 B11
Wagga Wagga, *Australia* 95 F4
Waghete, *Indonesia* 63 E9
Wagin, *Australia* 93 F2
Wagner, *U.S.A.* 112 D5
Wagon Mound, *U.S.A.* 113 G2
Wagoner, *U.S.A.* 113 H7
Wągrowiec, *Poland* 31 F4
Wah, *Pakistan* 68 C5
Wahai, *Indonesia* 63 E7
Wahiawa, *U.S.A.* 106 H15
Wâḥid, *Egypt* 74 E1
Wahnai, *Afghan.* 68 C1
Wahni, *Ethiopia* 81 E4
Wahoo, *U.S.A.* 112 E6
Wahpeton, *U.S.A.* 112 B6
Waiau →, *N.Z.* 91 K4
Waibeem, *Indonesia* 63 E8
Waiblingen, *Germany* 25 G5
Waidhofen an der Thaya, *Austria* 26 C8
Waidhofen an der Ybbs, *Austria* 26 D7
Waigeo, *Indonesia* 63 E8
Waihi, *N.Z.* 91 G5
Waihou →, *N.Z.* 91 G5
Waika, *Dem. Rep. of the Congo* 86 C2
Waikabubak, *Indonesia* 63 F5
Waikaremoana, L., *N.Z.* 91 H6
Waikari, *N.Z.* 91 K4
Waikato →, *N.Z.* 91 G5
Waikerie, *Australia* 95 E3
Waikokopu, *N.Z.* 91 H6
Waikouaiti, *N.Z.* 91 L3
Wailuku, *U.S.A.* 106 H16
Waimakariri →, *N.Z.* 91 K4
Waimate, *N.Z.* 91 L3
Wainganga →, *India* 66 K11
Waingapu, *Indonesia* 63 F6
Waini →, *Guyana* 124 B7
Wainwright, *Canada* 103 C6
Waiouru, *N.Z.* 91 H5
Waipara, *N.Z.* 91 K4
Waipawa, *N.Z.* 91 H6
Waipiro, *N.Z.* 91 H7
Waipu, *N.Z.* 91 F5
Waipukurau, *N.Z.* 91 J6
Wairakei, *N.Z.* 91 H6
Wairarapa, L., *N.Z.* 91 J5
Wairoa, *N.Z.* 91 H6
Waitaki →, *N.Z.* 91 L3
Waitara, *N.Z.* 91 H5
Waitsburg, *U.S.A.* 108 C5
Waiuku, *N.Z.* 91 G5
Wajima, *Japan* 55 F8
Wajir, *Kenya* 86 B5
Waka, *Ethiopia* 81 F4
Wakasa, *Japan* 55 G7
Wakasa-Wan, *Japan* 55 G7
Wakatipu, L., *N.Z.* 91 L2
Wakaw, *Canada* 103 C7
Wakayama, *Japan* 55 G7
Wakayama □, *Japan* 55 H7
Wake Forest, *U.S.A.* 115 H6
Wake I., *Pac. Oc.* 96 F8
WaKeeney, *U.S.A.* 112 F5
Wakefield, *Jamaica* 120 a
Wakefield, *N.Z.* 91 J4
Wakefield, *U.K.* 14 D6
Wakefield, *Mass., U.S.A.* 117 D13
Wakefield, *Mich., U.S.A.* 112 B10
Wakkanai, *Japan* 54 B10
Wakkerstroom, *S. Africa* 89 D5
Wakool, *Australia* 95 F3
Wakool →, *Australia* 95 F3
Wakre, *Indonesia* 63 E8
Wakuach, L., *Canada* 105 A6
Walamba, *Zambia* 87 E2
Wałbrzych, *Poland* 31 H3
Walbury Hill, *U.K.* 15 F6
Walcha, *Australia* 95 E5
Walcheren, *Neths.* 17 C3
Walcott, *U.S.A.* 108 F10
Wałcz, *Poland* 31 E3
Waldbröl, *Germany* 24 E3
Waldburg Ra., *Australia* 93 D2
Waldeck, *Germany* 24 D5
Walden, *Colo., U.S.A.* 108 F10
Walden, *N.Y., U.S.A.* 117 E10
Waldkirch, *Germany* 25 G3
Waldkirchen, *Germany* 25 G9
Waldkraiburg, *Germany* 25 G8
Waldport, *U.S.A.* 108 D1
Waldron, *U.S.A.* 113 H7
Waldviertel, *Austria* 26 C8
Walebing, *Australia* 93 F2
Walembele, *Ghana* 82 C4
Walensee, *Switz.* 25 H5
Wales □, *U.K.* 15 E3
Walewale, *Ghana* 83 C4
Walgett, *Australia* 95 E4
Walgreen Coast, *Antarctica* 5 D15
Walker, *U.S.A.* 112 B7
Walker, L., *Canada* 105 B6
Walker L., *Canada* 103 C9
Walker L., *U.S.A.* 108 G4
Walkerston, *Australia* 94 K7
Walkerton, *Canada* 116 B3
Wall, *U.S.A.* 112 D3
Walla Walla, *U.S.A.* 108 C4
Wallace, *Idaho, U.S.A.* 108 C6
Wallace, *N.C., U.S.A.* 115 H7
Wallaceburg, *Canada* 116 D2
Wallachia = Valahia, *Romania* 29 F9
Wallal, *Australia* 95 D4
Wallam Cr. →, *Australia* 95 D4
Wallambin, L., *Australia* 93 F2
Wallangarra, *Australia* 95 D5
Wallaroo, *Australia* 95 E2
Walldürn, *Germany* 25 F5
Wallenhorst, *Germany* 24 C4
Wallenpaupack, L., *U.S.A.* 117 E9
Wallingford, *U.S.A.* 117 E12
Wallis & Futuna, Is., *Pac. Oc.* 96 J10
Wallowa, *U.S.A.* 108 D5
Wallowa Mts., *U.S.A.* 108 D5
Walls, *U.K.* 13 A7
Walls of Jerusalem △, *Australia* 95 G4
Wallula, *U.S.A.* 108 C4
Wallumbilla, *Australia* 95 D4
Walmsley, L., *Canada* 103 A7
Walney, I. of, *U.K.* 14 C4
Walnut Canyon ⌂, *U.S.A.* 109 J8
Walnut Creek, *U.S.A.* 110 H4
Walnut Ridge, *U.S.A.* 113 G9
Walpole, *Australia* 93 F2
Walpole, *U.S.A.* 117 D13
Wals, *Austria* 26 D5
Walsall, *U.K.* 15 E6
Walsenburg, *U.S.A.* 113 G2
Walsh, *U.S.A.* 113 G3
Walsh →, *Australia* 94 B3
Walsrode, *Germany* 24 C5
Walterboro, *U.S.A.* 115 J5
Walters, *U.S.A.* 113 H5
Waltershausen, *Germany* 24 E6
Waltham, *U.S.A.* 117 D13
Waltman, *U.S.A.* 108 E10
Walton, *U.S.A.* 117 D9
Walton-on-the-Naze, *U.K.* 15 F9
Walvis Bay, *Namibia* 88 C1
Walvisbaai = Walvis Bay, *Namibia* 88 C1
Wamba, *Dem. Rep. of the Congo* 86 B2
Wamba, *Kenya* 86 B4
Wamba, *Nigeria* 83 D6
Wamego, *U.S.A.* 112 F6
Wamena, *Indonesia* 63 E9
Wamsutter, *U.S.A.* 108 F9
Wamulan, *Indonesia* 63 E7
Wan Xian, *China* 56 E8
Wana, *Pakistan* 68 C3
Wanaaring, *Australia* 95 D3
Wanaka, *N.Z.* 91 L2
Wanaka, L., *N.Z.* 91 L2
Wan'an, *China* 59 D10
Wanapitei L., *Canada* 104 C3
Wandel Sea = McKinley Sea, *Arctic* 4 A7
Wandérama, *Ivory C.* 82 D4
Wanderer, *Zimbabwe* 87 F3
Wandhari, *Pakistan* 68 F2
Wanding, *China* 58 E2
Wandoan, *Australia* 95 D4
Wanfu, *China* 57 D12
Wang →, *Thailand* 64 D2
Wang Kai, *Sudan* 81 F2
Wang Noi, *Thailand* 64 E3
Wang Saphung, *Thailand* 64 D3
Wang Thong, *Thailand* 64 D3
Wanga, *Dem. Rep. of the Congo* 86 B2
Wangal, *Indonesia* 63 F8
Wanganella, *Australia* 95 F3
Wanganui, *N.Z.* 91 H5
Wangaratta, *Australia* 95 F4
Wangary, *Australia* 95 E2
Wangcang, *China* 58 A6
Wangcheng, *China* 59 C9
Wangdu, *China* 56 E8
Wangen, *Germany* 25 H5
Wangerooge, *Germany* 24 B3
Wangiwangi, *Indonesia* 63 F6
Wangjiang, *China* 59 B11
Wangmo, *China* 58 E6
Wangolodougou, *Ivory C.* 82 D3
Wangqing, *China* 57 C15
Wankaner, *India* 68 H4
Wanless, *Canada* 103 C8
Wannian, *China* 59 C11
Wanning, *China* 64 C8
Wanon Niwat, *Thailand* 64 D4
Wanquan, *China* 56 D8
Wanrong, *China* 56 G6
Wanshan, *China* 58 D7
Wanshengchang, *China* 58 C6
Wantage, *U.K.* 15 F6
Wanyuan, *China* 58 A7
Wanzai, *China* 59 C10
Wapakoneta, *U.S.A.* 114 E3
Wapato, *U.S.A.* 108 C3
Wapawekka L., *Canada* 103 C8
Wapikopa L., *Canada* 104 B2
Wapiti →, *Canada* 102 B5
Wappingers Falls, *U.S.A.* 117 E11
Wapsipinicon →, *U.S.A.* 112 E9
Wapusk △, *Canada* 103 B10
Wapusk Nat. Park △ 103 B10
Warab □, *Sudan* 81 F2
Warangal, *India* 66 L11
Waraseoni, *India* 69 J9
Waratah, *Australia* 95 G4
Waratah B., *Australia* 95 F4
Warburg, *Germany* 24 D5
Warburton, *Vic., Australia* 95 F4
Warburton, *W. Austral., Australia* 93 E4
Warburton Ra., *Australia* 93 E4
Ward, *N.Z.* 91 J5
Ward →, *Australia* 95 D4
Ward Mt., *U.S.A.* 110 H8
Warden, *S. Africa* 89 D4
Wardha, *India* 66 J11
Wardha →, *India* 66 K11
Ware, *Canada* 102 B3
Ware, *U.K.* 15 F8
Ware, *U.S.A.* 117 D12
Waregem, *Belgium* 17 D3
Wareham, *U.S.A.* 117 E14
Waremme, *Belgium* 17 D5
Waren, *Germany* 24 B8
Warendorf, *Germany* 24 D4
Warialda, *Australia* 95 D5
Wariap, *Indonesia* 63 E8
Warin Chamrap, *Thailand* 64 E5
Warka, *Poland* 31 G8
Warkopi, *Indonesia* 63 E8
Warm Springs, *U.S.A.* 109 G5
Warman, *Canada* 103 C7
Warmbad = Bela Bela, *S. Africa* 89 C4
Warmbad, *Namibia* 88 D2
Warmińsko-Mazurskie □, *Poland* 30 D8
Warminster, *U.K.* 15 F5
Warminster, *U.S.A.* 117 F9
Warnemünde, *Germany* 24 A8
Warner Mts., *U.S.A.* 108 F3
Warner Robins, *U.S.A.* 115 J4
Warnow →, *Germany* 24 A8
Waroona, *Australia* 93 F2
Warracknabeal, *Australia* 95 F3
Warragul, *Australia* 95 F4
Warrego →, *Australia* 95 E4
Warrego Ra., *Australia* 94 C4
Warren, *Australia* 95 E4
Warren, *Ark., U.S.A.* 113 J8
Warren, *Mich., U.S.A.* 114 D4
Warren, *Minn., U.S.A.* 112 A6
Warren, *Ohio, U.S.A.* 116 E4
Warren, *Pa., U.S.A.* 116 E5
Warrenpoint, *U.K.* 12 B5
Warrensburg, *Mo., U.S.A.* 112 F8
Warrensburg, *N.Y., U.S.A.* 117 C11
Warrenton, *S. Africa* 88 D3
Warrenton, *U.S.A.* 110 D3
Warri, *Nigeria* 83 D6
Warrina, *Australia* 95 D2
Warrington, *U.K.* 14 D5
Warrington, *U.S.A.* 115 K2
Warrington □, *U.K.* 14 D5
Warrnambool, *Australia* 95 F3
Warroad, *U.S.A.* 112 A7
Warruwi, *Australia* 94 A1
Warsa, *Indonesia* 63 E9
Warsak Dam, *Pakistan* 68 B4
Warsaw = Warszawa, *Poland* 31 F8
Warsaw, *Ind., U.S.A.* 114 E3
Warsaw, *N.Y., U.S.A.* 116 D6
Warsaw, *Ohio, U.S.A.* 116 F3
Warsaw ✕ (WAW), *Poland* 31 F7
Warstein, *Germany* 24 D4
Warszawa, *Poland* 31 F8
Warta, *Poland* 31 G5
Warta →, *Poland* 31 F1
Warthe = Warta →, *Poland* 31 F1
Waru, *Indonesia* 63 E8
Warwick, *Australia* 95 D5
Warwick, *U.K.* 15 E6
Warwick, *N.Y., U.S.A.* 117 E10
Warwick, *R.I., U.S.A.* 117 E13
Warwickshire □, *U.K.* 15 E6
Wasaga Beach, *Canada* 116 B4
Wasagaming, *Canada* 103 C9
Wasatch Ra., *U.S.A.* 108 F8
Wasbank, *S. Africa* 89 D5
Wasco, *Calif., U.S.A.* 111 K7
Wasco, *Oreg., U.S.A.* 108 D3
Wase, *Nigeria* 83 D6
Waseca, *U.S.A.* 112 C8
Wasekamio L., *Canada* 103 B7
Wash, The, *U.K.* 14 E8
Washago, *Canada* 116 B5
Washburn, *N. Dak., U.S.A.* 112 B4
Washburn, *Wis., U.S.A.* 112 B9
Washim, *India* 66 J10
Washington, *U.K.* 14 C6
Washington, *D.C., U.S.A.* 114 F7
Washington, *Ga., U.S.A.* 115 J4
Washington, *Ind., U.S.A.* 114 F2
Washington, *Iowa, U.S.A.* 112 E9
Washington, *Mo., U.S.A.* 112 F9
Washington, *N.C., U.S.A.* 115 H7
Washington, *N.J., U.S.A.* 117 F10
Washington, *Pa., U.S.A.* 116 F4
Washington, *Utah, U.S.A.* 109 H7
Washington □, *U.S.A.* 108 C3
Washington, Mt., *U.S.A.* 117 B13
Washington Court House, *U.S.A.* 114 F4
Washington I., *U.S.A.* 114 C2
Washougal, *U.S.A.* 110 E4
Washpool △, *Australia* 95 D5
Wasian, *Indonesia* 63 E8
Wasilków, *Poland* 31 E10
Wasilla, *U.S.A.* 100 B5
Wasior, *Indonesia* 63 E8
Wāsiţ □, *Iraq* 70 C5
Waskaganish, *Canada* 104 B4
Waskaiowaka, L., *Canada* 103 B9
Waskesiu Lake, *Canada* 103 C7
Wasserburg, *Germany* 25 G8
Wasserkuppe, *Germany* 24 E5
Wassy, *France* 19 D11
Waswanipi, *Canada* 104 C4
Waswanipi, L., *Canada* 104 C4
Watampone, *Indonesia* 63 E6
Watamu, *Kenya* 86 C5
Watarrka △, *Australia* 92 D5
Water Park Pt., *Australia* 94 C5
Water Valley, *U.S.A.* 113 H10
Waterberg Plateau ⌂, *Namibia* 88 C2
Waterberge, *S. Africa* 89 C4
Waterbury, *Conn., U.S.A.* 117 E11
Waterbury, *Vt., U.S.A.* 117 B12
Waterbury L., *Canada* 103 B8
Waterdown, *Canada* 116 C5
Waterford, *Canada* 116 D4
Waterford, *Ireland* 12 D4
Waterford, *Calif., U.S.A.* 110 H6
Waterford, *Pa., U.S.A.* 116 E5
Waterford □, *Ireland* 12 D4
Waterford Harbour, *Ireland* 12 D5
Waterhen L., *Canada* 103 C9
Waterloo, *Belgium* 17 D4
Waterloo, *Ont., Canada* 116 C4
Waterloo, *Qué., Canada* 117 A12
Waterloo, *S. Leone* 82 D2
Waterloo, *Ill., U.S.A.* 112 F9
Waterloo, *Iowa, U.S.A.* 112 D8
Waterloo, *N.Y., U.S.A.* 116 D8
Watersmeet, *U.S.A.* 112 B10
Waterton Lakes △, *Canada* 102 D6
Watertown, *Conn., U.S.A.* 117 E11
Watertown, *N.Y., U.S.A.* 117 C9
Watertown, *S. Dak., U.S.A.* 112 C6
Watertown, *Wis., U.S.A.* 112 D10
Waterval-Boven, *S. Africa* 89 D5
Waterville, *Canada* 117 A13
Waterville, *Maine, U.S.A.* 115 C11
Waterville, *N.Y., U.S.A.* 117 D9
Waterville, *Pa., U.S.A.* 116 E7
Waterville, *Wash., U.S.A.* 108 C3
Watervliet, *U.S.A.* 117 D11
Wates, *Indonesia* 63 G14
Watford, *Canada* 116 D3
Watford, *U.K.* 15 F7
Watford City, *U.S.A.* 112 B3
Wathaman →, *Canada* 103 B8
Wathaman L., *Canada* 103 B8
Watheroo, *Australia* 93 F2
Watheroo △, *Australia* 93 F2
Wating, *China* 56 G4
Watkins Glen, *U.S.A.* 116 D8
Watling I. = San Salvador I., *Bahamas* 121 B5
Watonga, *U.S.A.* 113 H5
Watrous, *Canada* 103 C7
Watrous, *U.S.A.* 113 H2
Watsa, *Dem. Rep. of the Congo* 86 B2
Watseka, *U.S.A.* 114 E2
Watson, *Australia* 93 F5
Watson, *Canada* 103 C8
Watson Lake, *Canada* 102 A3
Watsontown, *U.S.A.* 116 E8
Watsonville, *U.S.A.* 110 J5
Wattiwarriganna Cr. →, *Australia* 95 D2
Wattwil, *Switz.* 25 H5
Watuata = Batuata, *Indonesia* 63 F6
Watubela, Kepulauan, *Indonesia* 63 E8
Watubela Is. = Watubela, Kepulauan, *Indonesia* 63 E8
Wau = Wâw, *Sudan* 81 F2
Waubamik, *Canada* 116 A4
Waubay, *U.S.A.* 112 C6
Wauchope, *N.S.W., Australia* 95 E5
Wauchope, *N. Terr., Australia* 94 C1
Wauchula, *U.S.A.* 115 M5
Waukarlycarly, L., *Australia* 92 D3
Waukegan, *U.S.A.* 114 D2
Waukesha, *U.S.A.* 114 D1
Waukon, *U.S.A.* 112 D9
Waupaca, *U.S.A.* 112 C10
Waupun, *U.S.A.* 112 D10
Waurika, *U.S.A.* 113 H6
Wausau, *U.S.A.* 112 C10
Wautoma, *U.S.A.* 112 C10
Wauwatosa, *U.S.A.* 114 D2
Waveney →, *U.K.* 15 E9
Waverley, *N.Z.* 91 H5
Waverly, *Iowa, U.S.A.* 112 D8
Waverly, *N.Y., U.S.A.* 117 E8
Wavre, *Belgium* 17 D4
Wâw, *Sudan* 81 F2
Wāw al Kabīr, *Libya* 79 C9
Wawa, *Canada* 104 C3
Wawa, *Nigeria* 83 D5
Wawa, *Sudan* 80 C3
Wawanesa, *Canada* 103 D9
Wawona, *U.S.A.* 110 H7
Waxahachie, *U.S.A.* 113 J6
Way, L., *Australia* 93 E3
Waycross, *U.S.A.* 115 K4
Wayi, *Sudan* 81 F3
Wayland, *U.S.A.* 116 D7
Wayne, *Nebr., U.S.A.* 112 D6
Wayne, *W. Va., U.S.A.* 114 F4
Waynesboro, *Ga., U.S.A.* 115 J4
Waynesboro, *Miss., U.S.A.* 115 K1
Waynesboro, *Pa., U.S.A.* 114 F7
Waynesboro, *Va., U.S.A.* 114 F6
Waynesburg, *U.S.A.* 114 F5
Waynesville, *U.S.A.* 115 H4
Waynoka, *U.S.A.* 113 G5
Wazirabad, *Pakistan* 68 C6
Wda →, *Poland* 30 E5
We, *Indonesia* 62 C1
Weald, The, *U.K.* 15 F8
Wear →, *U.K.* 14 C6
Weatherford, *Okla., U.S.A.* 113 H5
Weatherford, *Tex., U.S.A.* 113 J6
Weaverville, *U.S.A.* 108 F2
Webb City, *U.S.A.* 113 G7
Webequie, *Canada* 104 B2
Webo = Nyaake, *Liberia* 82 E3
Webster, *Mass., U.S.A.* 117 D13
Webster, *N.Y., U.S.A.* 116 C7
Webster, *S. Dak., U.S.A.* 112 C6
Webster City, *U.S.A.* 112 D8
Webster Springs, *U.S.A.* 114 F5
Weda, *Indonesia* 63 D7
Weda, Teluk, *Indonesia* 63 D7
Weddell I., *Falk. Is.* 128 G4
Weddell Sea, *Antarctica* 5 D1
Wedderburn, *Australia* 95 F3
Wedel, *Germany* 24 B5
Wedemark, *Germany* 24 C5
Wedgeport, *Canada* 105 D6
Wedza, *Zimbabwe* 87 F3
Wee Waa, *Australia* 95 E4
Weed, *U.S.A.* 108 F2
Weed Heights, *U.S.A.* 110 G7
Weedsport, *U.S.A.* 117 C8
Weedville, *U.S.A.* 116 E6
Weenen, *S. Africa* 89 D5
Weener, *Germany* 24 B3
Weert, *Neths.* 17 C5
Węgierska-Górka, *Poland* 31 J6
Węgliniec, *Poland* 31 G2
Węgorzewo, *Poland* 30 D8
Węgorzyno, *Poland* 30 E2
Węgrów, *Poland* 31 F9
Wehda □, *Sudan* 81 F3
Wei He →, *Hebei, China* 56 F8
Wei He →, *Shaanxi, China* 56 G6
Weichang, *China* 57 D9
Weichuan, *China* 56 G7
Weida, *Germany* 24 E8
Weiden, *Germany* 25 F8
Weifang, *China* 57 F10
Weihai, *China* 57 F12
Weil, *Germany* 25 H3
Weilburg, *Germany* 24 E4
Weilheim, *Germany* 25 H7
Weimar, *Germany* 24 E7
Weinan, *China* 56 G5
Weingarten, *Germany* 25 F4
Weinheim, *Germany* 25 F4
Weining, *China* 58 D5
Weipa, *Australia* 94 A3
Weir →, *Australia* 95 D4
Weir →, *Canada* 103 B10
Weir River, *Canada* 103 B10
Weirton, *U.S.A.* 116 F4
Weiser, *U.S.A.* 108 D5
Weishan, *Shandong, China* 57 G9
Weishan, *Yunnan, China* 58 E3
Weissenburg, *Germany* 25 F6
Weissenfels, *Germany* 24 D7
Weisswasser, *Germany* 24 D10
Wéitra, *Austria* 26 C7
Weixi, *China* 58 D2
Weixin, *China* 58 D5
Weiyuan, *China* 56 G3
Weiz, *Austria* 26 D8
Weizhou Dao, *China* 58 G7
Wejherowo, *Poland* 30 D5
Wekusko L., *Canada* 103 C9
Welch, *U.S.A.* 114 G5
Weldya, *Ethiopia* 81 E4
Welega □, *Ethiopia* 81 F3
Welford △, *Australia* 94 D3
Welkite, *Ethiopia* 81 F4
Welkom, *S. Africa* 88 D4
Welland, *Canada* 116 D5
Welland →, *U.K.* 15 E7
Wellesley Is., *Australia* 94 B2
Wellingborough, *U.K.* 15 E7
Wellington, *Australia* 95 E4
Wellington, *Canada* 116 C7
Wellington, *N.Z.* 91 J5
Wellington, *S. Africa* 88 E2
Wellington, *Somst., U.K.* 15 G4
Wellington, *Telford & Wrekin, U.K.* 15 E5
Wellington, *Colo., U.S.A.* 112 E2
Wellington, *Kans., U.S.A.* 113 G6

Wellington, *Nev., U.S.A.* **110 G7**
Wellington, *Ohio, U.S.A.* **116 E2**
Wellington, *Tex., U.S.A.* **113 H4**
Wellington, I., *Chile* **128 F2**
Wellington, L., *Australia* **95 F4**
Wells, *U.K.* **15 F5**
Wells, *Maine, U.S.A.* **117 C14**
Wells, *N.Y., U.S.A.* **117 C10**
Wells, *Nev., U.S.A.* **108 F6**
Wells, L., *Australia* **93 E3**
Wells, Mt., *Australia* **92 C4**
Wells Gray ⌓, *Canada* **102 C4**
Wells-next-the-Sea, *U.K.* **14 E8**
Wells River, *U.S.A.* **117 B12**
Wellsboro, *U.S.A.* **116 E7**
Wellsburg, *U.S.A.* **116 F4**
Wellsville, *N.Y., U.S.A.* **116 D7**
Wellsville, *Ohio, U.S.A.* **116 F4**
Wellsville, *Utah, U.S.A.* **108 F8**
Wellton, *U.S.A.* **109 K6**
Welmel, Wabi →, *Ethiopia* **81 F5**
Welo □, *Ethiopia* **81 E4**
Wels, *Austria* **26 C7**
Welshpool, *U.K.* **15 E4**
Welwyn Garden City, *U.K.* **15 F7**
Wem, *U.K.* **14 E5**
Wembere →, *Tanzania* **86 C3**
Wemindji, *Canada* **104 B4**
Wen Xian, *China* **56 G7**
Wenatchee, *U.S.A.* **108 C3**
Wenchang, *China* **64 C8**
Wencheng, *China* **59 D13**
Wenchi, *Ghana* **82 D4**
Wenchow = Wenzhou, *China* . . . **59 D13**
Wenchuan, *China* **58 B4**
Wenden, *U.S.A.* **111 M13**
Wendeng, *China* **57 F12**
Wendesi, *Indonesia* **63 E8**
Wendo, *Ethiopia* **81 F4**
Wendover, *U.S.A.* **108 F6**
Weng'an, *China* **58 D6**
Wengcheng, *China* **59 E9**
Wengyuan, *China* **59 E10**
Wenjiang, *China* **58 B4**
Wenling, *China* **59 C13**
Wenlock →, *Australia* **94 A3**
Wenshan, *China* **58 F5**
Wenshang, *China* **56 G9**
Wenshui, *China* **56 F7**
Wensleydale, *U.K.* **14 C6**
Wensu, *China* **60 B3**
Wensum →, *U.K.* **14 E8**
Wentworth, *Australia* **95 E3**
Wentzel L., *Canada* **102 B6**
Wenut, *Indonesia* **63 E8**
Wenxi, *China* **56 G6**
Wenxian, *China* **56 H3**
Wenzhou, *China* **59 D13**
Weott, *U.S.A.* **108 F2**
Wepener, *S. Africa* **88 D4**
Werda, *Botswana* **88 D3**
Werdau, *Germany* **24 E8**
Werder, *Germany* **24 C8**
Werdohl, *Germany* **24 D3**
Wereilu, *Ethiopia* **81 E4**
Weri, *Indonesia* **63 E8**
Werneck, *Germany* **25 F6**
Wernigerode, *Germany* **24 D6**
Werra →, *Germany* **24 D5**
Werrimull, *Australia* **95 E3**
Werris Creek, *Australia* **95 E5**
Wertach →, *Germany* **25 G6**
Wertheim, *Germany* **25 F5**
Wertingen, *Germany* **25 G6**
Wesel, *Germany* **24 D2**
Weser →, *Germany* **24 B4**
Weser-Ems □, *Germany* **24 C3**
Weserbergland, *Germany* **24 C5**
Weserbergland Schaumburg
Hameln ⌓, *Germany* **24 C5**
Wesiri, *Indonesia* **63 F7**
Weslemkoon L., *Canada* **116 A7**
Wesleyville, *U.S.A.* **116 D4**
Wessel, C., *Australia* **94 A2**
Wessel Is., *Australia* **94 A2**
Wesselburen, *Germany* **24 A4**
Wessington Springs, *U.S.A.* **112 C5**
West, *U.S.A.* **113 K6**
West →, *U.S.A.* **117 D12**
West Antarctica, *Antarctica* **5 D15**
West Baines →, *Australia* **92 C4**
West Bank ☒, *Asia* **74 C4**
West Bend, *U.S.A.* **114 D1**
West Bengal □, *India* **69 H13**
West Berkshire □, *U.K.* **15 F6**
West Beskids = Západné
Beskydy, *Europe* **27 B12**
West Branch, *U.S.A.* **114 C3**
West Branch Susquehanna →,
U.S.A. **117 F8**
West Bromwich, *U.K.* **15 E6**
West Burra, *U.K.* **13 A7**
West Canada Cr. →, *U.S.A.* **117 C10**
West Cape Howe, *Australia* **93 G2**
West Chazy, *U.S.A.* **117 B11**
West Chester, *U.S.A.* **117 G9**
West Coast ⌓, *Namibia* **88 C1**
West Coast △, *S. Africa* **88 E2**
West Columbia, *U.S.A.* **113 L7**
West Covina, *U.S.A.* **111 L9**
West Des Moines, *U.S.A.* **112 E8**
West Dunbartonshire □, *U.K.* . . **13 F4**
West End, *Bahamas* **120 A4**
West Falkland, *Falk. Is.* **128 G5**
West Fargo, *U.S.A.* **112 B6**
West Farmington, *U.S.A.* **116 E4**
West Fjord = Vestfjorden,
Norway **8 C15**
West Fork Trinity →, *U.S.A.* . . . **113 J6**
West Frankfort, *U.S.A.* **112 G10**
West Hartford, *U.S.A.* **117 E12**
West Haven, *U.S.A.* **117 E12**
West Hazleton, *U.S.A.* **117 F9**
West Helena, *U.S.A.* **113 H9**
West Hurley, *U.S.A.* **117 E10**
West Ice Shelf, *Antarctica* **5 C7**
West Indies, *Cent. Amer.* **121 D7**
West Jordan, *U.S.A.* **108 F8**
West Lorne, *Canada* **116 D3**
West Lothian □, *U.K.* **13 F5**
West Lunga →, *Zambia* **87 E1**
West MacDonnell △, *Australia* . . **92 D5**
West Memphis, *U.S.A.* **113 H9**
West Midlands □, *U.K.* **15 E6**
West Mifflin, *U.S.A.* **116 F5**
West Milton, *U.S.A.* **116 E8**
West Monroe, *U.S.A.* **113 J8**
West Newton, *U.S.A.* **116 F5**
West Nicholson, *Zimbabwe* **87 G2**
West Palm Beach, *U.S.A.* **115 M5**
West Plains, *U.S.A.* **113 G9**
West Point, *N.Y., U.S.A.* **117 E11**
West Point, *Nebr., U.S.A.* **112 E6**
West Point, *Va., U.S.A.* **114 G7**
West Pt. = Ouest, Pte. de l',
Canada **105 C7**
West Pt., *Australia* **95 F2**
West Road →, *Canada* **102 C4**
West Rutland, *U.S.A.* **117 C11**
West Schelde =
Westerschelde →, *Neths.* **17 C3**
West Seneca, *U.S.A.* **116 D6**
West Siberian Plain, *Russia* **50 C11**
West Sussex □, *U.K.* **15 G7**
West-Terschelling, *Neths.* **17 A5**
West Valley City, *U.S.A.* **108 F8**
West Virginia □, *U.S.A.* **114 F5**
West-Vlaanderen □, *Belgium* . . . **17 D2**
West Walker →, *U.S.A.* **110 G7**
West Wyalong, *Australia* **95 E4**
West Yellowstone, *U.S.A.* **108 D8**
West Yorkshire □, *U.K.* **14 D6**
Westall, Pt., *Australia* **95 E1**
Westbrook, *U.S.A.* **115 D10**
Westbury, *Australia* **95 G4**
Westby, *U.S.A.* **112 A2**
Westend, *U.S.A.* **111 K9**
Westerland, *Germany* **9 J13**
Westerly, *U.S.A.* **117 E13**
Western □, *Ghana* **82 D4**
Western □, *Kenya* **86 B3**
Western □, *S. Leone* **82 D2**
Western □, *Zambia* **87 F1**
Western Australia □, *Australia* . . **93 E2**
Western Cape □, *S. Africa* **88 E3**
Western Dvina = Daugava →,
Latvia **9 H21**
Western Ghats, *India* **66 N9**
Western Isles □, *U.K.* **13 D1**
Western Sahara ■, *Africa* **78 D3**
Western Samoa = Samoa ■,
Pac. Oc. **91 B13**
Westernport, *U.S.A.* **114 F6**
Westerschelde →, *Neths.* **17 C3**
Westerstede, *Germany* **24 B3**
Westerwald, *Germany* **24 E3**
Westfield, *Mass., U.S.A.* **117 D12**
Westfield, *N.Y., U.S.A.* **116 D5**
Westfield, *Pa., U.S.A.* **116 E7**
Westhill, *U.K.* **13 D6**
Westhope, *U.S.A.* **112 A4**
Westland △, *N.Z.* **91 K2**
Westland Bight, *N.Z.* **91 K3**
Westlock, *Canada* **102 C6**
Westmar, *Australia* **95 D4**
Westmeath □, *Ireland* **12 C4**
Westminster, *U.S.A.* **114 F7**
Westmont, *U.S.A.* **116 F6**
Westmoreland, *Barbados* . . . . **121 g**
Westmorland, *U.S.A.* **111 M11**
Weston, *Oreg., U.S.A.* **108 D4**
Weston, *W. Va., U.S.A.* **114 F5**
Weston I., *Canada* **104 B4**
Weston-super-Mare, *U.K.* **15 F5**
Westover, *U.S.A.* **116 F6**
Westport, *Canada* **117 B8**
Westport, *Ireland* **12 C2**
Westport, *N.Z.* **91 J3**
Westport, *N.Y., U.S.A.* **117 B11**
Westport, *Oreg., U.S.A.* **110 D3**
Westport, *Wash., U.S.A.* **110 D2**
Westray, *Canada* **103 C8**
Westray, *U.K.* **13 B5**
Westree, *Canada* **104 C3**
Westville, *U.S.A.* **110 F6**
Westwood, *U.S.A.* **108 F3**
Wetar, *Indonesia* **63 F7**
Wetaskiwin, *Canada* **102 C6**
Wete, *Tanzania* **84 F7**
Wetherby, *U.K.* **14 D6**
Wethersfield, *U.S.A.* **117 E12**
Wetteren, *Belgium* **17 D3**
Wetzlar, *Germany* **24 E4**
Wewoka, *U.S.A.* **113 H6**
Wexford, *Ireland* **12 D5**
Wexford □, *Ireland* **12 D5**
Wexford Harbour, *Ireland* **12 D5**
Weyburn, *Canada* **103 D8**
Weyer Markt, *Austria* **26 D7**
Weyhe, *Germany* **24 C4**
Weyib →, *Ethiopia* **81 F5**
Weymouth, *Canada* **105 D6**
Weymouth, *U.K.* **15 G5**
Weymouth, *U.S.A.* **117 D14**
Weymouth, C., *Australia* **94 A3**
Wha Ti, *Canada* **100 B8**
Whakatane, *N.Z.* **91 G6**
Whale →, *Canada* **105 A6**
Whale Cove, *Canada* **103 A10**
Whales, B. of, *Antarctica* **5 D12**
Whalsay, *U.K.* **13 A8**
Whangamomona, *N.Z.* **91 H5**
Whanganui △, *N.Z.* **91 H5**
Whangarei, *N.Z.* **91 F5**
Whangarei Harb., *N.Z.* **91 F5**
Wharfe →, *U.K.* **14 D6**
Wharfedale, *U.K.* **14 C5**
Wharton, *N.J., U.S.A.* **117 F10**
Wharton, *Pa., U.S.A.* **116 E6**
Wharton, *Tex., U.S.A.* **113 L6**
Wheatland, *Calif., U.S.A.* **110 F5**
Wheatland, *Wyo., U.S.A.* **112 D2**
Wheatley, *Canada* **116 D2**
Wheaton, *Md., U.S.A.* **114 F7**
Wheaton, *Minn., U.S.A.* **112 C6**
Wheelbarrow Pk., *U.S.A.* **110 H10**
Wheeler, *Oreg., U.S.A.* **108 D2**
Wheeler, *Tex., U.S.A.* **113 H4**
Wheeler →, *Canada* **105 A6**
Wheeler L., *U.S.A.* **115 H2**
Wheeler Pk., *N. Mex., U.S.A.* . . . **109 H11**
Wheeler Pk., *Nev., U.S.A.* **109 G6**
Wheeler Ridge, *U.S.A.* **111 L8**
Wheeling, *U.S.A.* **116 F4**
Whernside, *U.K.* **14 C5**
Whiskey Jack L., *Canada* **103 B8**
Whiskeytown-Shasta-Trinity ⌓,
U.S.A. **108 F2**
Whistleduck Cr. →, *Australia* . . . **94 C2**
Whistler, *Canada* **102 C4**
Whitby, *Canada* **116 C6**
Whitby, *U.K.* **14 C7**
White →, *Ark., U.S.A.* **113 J9**
White →, *Ind., U.S.A.* **114 F2**
White →, *S. Dak., U.S.A.* **112 D5**
White →, *Tex., U.S.A.* **113 J4**
White →, *Utah, U.S.A.* **108 F9**
White →, *Vt., U.S.A.* **117 C12**
White →, *Wash., U.S.A.* **110 C4**
White, L., *Australia* **92 D4**
White B., *Canada* **105 C8**
White Bird, *U.S.A.* **108 D5**
White Butte, *U.S.A.* **112 B3**
White City, *U.S.A.* **108 E2**
White Cliffs, *Australia* **95 E3**
White Hall, *U.S.A.* **112 F9**
White Haven, *U.S.A.* **117 E9**
White Horse, Vale of, *U.K.* **15 F6**
White I., *N.Z.* **91 G6**
White L., *Canada* **117 A8**
White L., *U.S.A.* **113 L8**
White Mountain Peak, *U.S.A.* . . . **109 G4**
White Mts., *Calif., U.S.A.* **110 H8**
White Mts., *N.H., U.S.A.* **117 B13**
White Mts. △, *Australia* **94 C4**
White Nile = Nîl el Abyad →,
Sudan **81 D3**
White Nile Dam = Khazzān Jabal
al Awliyā, *Sudan* **81 D3**
White Otter L., *Canada* **104 C1**
White Pass, *U.S.A.* **110 D5**
White Plains, *U.S.A.* **117 E11**
White River, *Canada* **104 C2**
White River, *S. Africa* **89 D5**
White River, *U.S.A.* **112 D4**
White Rock, *Canada* **110 A4**
White Russia = Belarus ■,
Europe **32 F4**
White Sands ⌓, *U.S.A.* **109 K10**
White Sea = Beloye More, *Russia* **52 C4**
White Sulphur Springs, *Mont.,*
U.S.A. **108 C8**
White Sulphur Springs, *W. Va.,*
U.S.A. **114 G5**
White Swan, *U.S.A.* **110 D6**
White Volta →, *Ghana* **83 D4**
Whitecliffs, *N.Z.* **91 K3**
Whitecourt, *Canada* **102 C5**
Whiteface Mt., *U.S.A.* **117 B11**
Whitefield, *U.S.A.* **117 B13**
Whitefish, *U.S.A.* **108 B6**
Whitefish L., *Canada* **103 A7**
Whitefish Point, *U.S.A.* **114 B3**
Whitegull, L. = Goélands, L. aux,
Canada **105 A7**
Whitehall, *Mich., U.S.A.* **114 D2**
Whitehall, *Mont., U.S.A.* **108 D7**
Whitehall, *N.Y., U.S.A.* **117 C11**
Whitehall, *Wis., U.S.A.* **112 C9**
Whitehaven, *U.K.* **14 C4**
Whitehorse, *Canada* **102 A1**
Whitemark, *Australia* **95 G4**
Whiteplains, *Liberia* **82 D2**
Whiteriver, *U.S.A.* **109 K9**
Whitesand →, *Canada* **102 A5**
Whitesands, *S. Africa* **88 E3**
Whitesboro, *N.Y., U.S.A.* **117 C9**
Whitesboro, *Tex., U.S.A.* **113 J6**
Whiteshell ⌓, *Canada* **103 D9**
Whitesville, *U.S.A.* **116 D7**
Whiteville, *U.S.A.* **115 H6**
Whitewater, *U.S.A.* **114 D1**
Whitewater Baldy, *U.S.A.* **109 K9**
Whitewater L., *Canada* **104 B2**
Whitewood, *Australia* **94 C3**
Whitewood, *Canada* **103 C8**
Whithorn, *U.K.* **13 G4**
Whitianga, *N.Z.* **91 G5**
Whitman, *U.S.A.* **117 D14**
Whitney, *Canada* **116 A6**
Whitney, Mt., *U.S.A.* **110 J8**
Whitney Point, *U.S.A.* **117 D9**
Whitstable, *U.K.* **15 F9**
Whitsunday I., *Australia* **94 J7**
Whitsunday Islands △, *Australia* **94 J7**
Whitsunday Passage, *Australia* . . **94 J6**
Whittier, *U.S.A.* **111 M8**
Whittlesea, *Australia* **95 F4**
Wholdaia L., *Canada* **103 A8**
Whyalla, *Australia* **95 E2**
Wiang Kosai △, *Thailand* **64 D2**
Wiarton, *Canada* **116 B3**
Wiawso, *Ghana* **82 D4**
Wiay, *U.K.* **13 D1**
Wiązów, *Poland* **31 H4**
Wibaux, *U.S.A.* **112 B2**
Wichian Buri, *Thailand* **64 E3**
Wichita, *U.S.A.* **113 G6**
Wichita Falls, *U.S.A.* **113 J5**
Wick, *U.K.* **13 C5**
Wicked Pt., *Canada* **116 C7**
Wickenburg, *U.S.A.* **109 K7**
Wickepin, *Australia* **93 F2**
Wickham, *Australia* **92 D2**
Wickham, C., *Australia* **95 F3**
Wickliffe, *U.S.A.* **116 E3**
Wicklow, *Ireland* **12 D5**
Wicklow □, *Ireland* **12 D5**
Wicklow Hd., *Ireland* **12 D6**
Wicklow Mts., *Ireland* **12 C5**
Wicklow Mts. △, *Ireland* **12 C5**
Widawa, *Poland* **31 G5**
Widawka →, *Poland* **31 G5**
Widgeegoara Cr. →, *Australia* . . **95 D4**
Widgiemooltha, *Australia* **93 F3**
Widnes, *U.K.* **14 D5**
Więcbork, *Poland* **31 E4**
Wiehengebirge = Nördlicher
Teutoburger Wald-
Wiehengebirge ⌓, *Germany* . . **24 C4**
Wiehl, *Germany* **24 E3**
Wiek, *Germany* **24 A9**
Wielbark, *Poland* **30 E7**
Wieleń, *Poland* **31 F3**
Wielichowo, *Poland* **31 F3**
Wieliczka, *Poland* **31 J7**
Wielkopolski △, *Poland* **31 F3**
Wielkopolskie □, *Poland* **31 F4**
Wieluń, *Poland* **31 G5**
Wien, *Austria* **27 C9**
Wiener Neustadt, *Austria* **27 D9**
Wieprz →, *Poland* **31 G8**
Wieprza →, *Poland* **30 D3**
Wieruszów, *Poland* **31 G5**
Wiesbaden, *Germany* **25 E4**
Wiesental, *Germany* **25 F4**
Wiesloch, *Germany* **25 F4**
Wiesmoor, *Germany* **24 B3**
Wieżyca, *Poland* **30 D5**
Wigan, *U.K.* **14 D5**
Wiggins, *Colo., U.S.A.* **112 E2**
Wiggins, *Miss., U.S.A.* **113 K10**
Wight, I. of □, *U.K.* **15 G6**
Wigierski △, *Poland* **30 D10**
Wigry, Jezioro, *Poland* **30 D10**
Wigston, *U.K.* **15 E6**
Wigton, *U.K.* **14 C4**
Wigtown, *U.K.* **13 G4**
Wigtown B., *U.K.* **13 G4**
Wil, *Switz.* **25 H5**
Wilamowice, *Poland* **31 J6**
Wilber, *U.S.A.* **112 E6**
Wilberforce, *Canada* **116 A6**
Wilberforce, C., *Australia* **94 A2**
Wilburton, *U.S.A.* **113 H7**
Wilcannia, *Australia* **95 E3**
Wilcox, *U.S.A.* **116 E6**
Wildbad, *Germany* **25 G4**
Wildeshausen, *Germany* **24 C4**
Wildeshauser Geest ⌓, *Germany* **24 C4**
Wildon, *Austria* **26 E8**
Wildrose, *U.S.A.* **111 J9**
Wildspitze, *Austria* **26 E3**
Wilga →, *Poland* **31 G8**
Wilge →, *S. Africa* **89 D4**
Wilhelm II Coast, *Antarctica* **5 C7**
Wilhelmsburg, *Austria* **26 C8**
Wilhelmshaven, *Germany* **24 B4**
Wilhelmstal, *Namibia* **88 C2**
Wilkes-Barre, *U.S.A.* **117 E9**
Wilkes Land, *Antarctica* **5 D9**
Wilkie, *Canada* **103 C7**
Wilkinsburg, *U.S.A.* **116 F5**
Wilkinson Lakes, *Australia* **93 E5**
Willandra Creek →, *Australia* . . . **95 E4**
Willapa B., *U.S.A.* **108 C2**
Willapa Hills, *U.S.A.* **110 D3**
Willard, *N.Y., U.S.A.* **116 D8**
Willard, *Ohio, U.S.A.* **116 E2**
Willcox, *U.S.A.* **109 K9**
Willemstad, *Neth. Ant.* **121 D6**
Willet, *U.S.A.* **117 D9**
William →, *Canada* **103 B7**
William 'Bill' Dannely Res.,
U.S.A. **115 J2**
William Creek, *Australia* **95 D2**
Williams, *Australia* **93 F2**
Williams, *Ariz., U.S.A.* **109 J7**
Williams, *Calif., U.S.A.* **110 F4**
Williams Harbour, *Canada* **105 B8**
Williams Lake, *Canada* **102 C4**
Williamsburg, *Ky., U.S.A.* **115 G3**
Williamsburg, *Pa., U.S.A.* **116 F6**
Williamsburg, *Va., U.S.A.* **114 G7**
Williamson, *N.Y., U.S.A.* **116 C7**
Williamson, *W. Va., U.S.A.* **114 G4**
Williamsport, *U.S.A.* **116 E7**
Williamston, *U.S.A.* **115 H7**
Williamstown, *Australia* **95 F3**
Williamstown, *Ky., U.S.A.* **114 F3**
Williamstown, *Mass., U.S.A.* **117 D11**
Williamstown, *N.Y., U.S.A.* **117 C9**
Willimantic, *U.S.A.* **117 E12**
Willingboro, *U.S.A.* **114 E8**
Williston, *S. Africa* **88 E3**
Williston, *Fla., U.S.A.* **115 L4**
Williston, *N. Dak., U.S.A.* **112 A3**
Williston L., *Canada* **102 B4**
Willits, *U.S.A.* **108 G2**
Willmar, *U.S.A.* **112 C7**
Willmore Wilderness ⌓, *Canada* **102 C5**
Willoughby, *U.S.A.* **116 E3**
Willow Bunch, *Canada* **103 D7**
Willow L., *Canada* **102 A5**
Willow Wall, The, *China* **57 C12**
Willowick, *U.S.A.* **116 E3**
Willowlake →, *Canada* **102 A4**
Willowmore, *S. Africa* **88 E3**
Willows, *U.S.A.* **110 F4**
Willowvale = Gatyana, *S. Africa* **89 E4**
Wills, L., *Australia* **92 D4**
Wills Cr. →, *Australia* **94 C3**
Willsboro, *U.S.A.* **117 B11**
Willunga, *Australia* **95 F2**
Wilmette, *U.S.A.* **114 D2**
Wilmington, *Australia* **95 E2**
Wilmington, *Del., U.S.A.* **114 F8**
Wilmington, *N.C., U.S.A.* **115 H7**
Wilmington, *Ohio, U.S.A.* **114 F4**
Wilmington, *Vt., U.S.A.* **117 D12**
Wilmslow, *U.K.* **14 D5**
Wilpena Cr. →, *Australia* **95 E2**
Wilsall, *U.S.A.* **108 D8**
Wilson, *N.C., U.S.A.* **115 H7**
Wilson, *N.Y., U.S.A.* **116 C6**
Wilson, *Pa., U.S.A.* **117 F9**
Wilson →, *Australia* **92 C4**
Wilson Bluff, *Australia* **93 F4**
Wilson Inlet, *Australia* **93 G2**
Wilsons Promontory, *Australia* . . **95 F4**
Wilster, *Germany* **24 B5**
Wilton, *U.S.A.* **112 B4**
Wilton →, *Australia* **94 A1**
Wiltshire □, *U.K.* **15 F6**
Wiltz, *Lux.* **17 E5**
Wiluna, *Australia* **93 E3**
Wimborne Minster, *U.K.* **15 G6**
Wimereux, *France* **19 B8**
Wimmera →, *Australia* **95 F3**
Winam G., *Kenya* **86 C3**
Winburg, *S. Africa* **88 D4**
Winchendon, *U.S.A.* **117 D12**
Winchester, *U.K.* **15 F6**
Winchester, *Conn., U.S.A.* **117 E11**
Winchester, *Idaho, U.S.A.* **108 C5**
Winchester, *Ind., U.S.A.* **114 E3**
Winchester, *Ky., U.S.A.* **114 G3**
Winchester, *N.H., U.S.A.* **117 D12**
Winchester, *Nev., U.S.A.* **111 J11**
Winchester, *Tenn., U.S.A.* **115 H2**
Winchester, *Va., U.S.A.* **114 F6**
Wind →, *U.S.A.* **108 E9**
Wind Cave △, *U.S.A.* **112 D3**
Wind River Range, *U.S.A.* **108 E9**
Windau = Ventspils, *Latvia* **9 H19**
Windber, *U.S.A.* **116 F6**
Winder, *U.S.A.* **115 J4**
Windermere, *U.K.* **14 C5**
Windhoek, *Namibia* **88 C2**
Windischgarsten, *Austria* **26 D7**
Windom, *U.S.A.* **112 D7**
Windorah, *Australia* **94 D3**
Window Rock, *U.S.A.* **109 J9**
Windrush →, *U.K.* **15 F6**
Windsor, *Australia* **95 E5**
Windsor, *N.S., Canada* **105 D7**
Windsor, *Ont., Canada* **116 D2**
Windsor, *U.K.* **15 F7**
Windsor, *Colo., U.S.A.* **112 E2**
Windsor, *Conn., U.S.A.* **117 E12**
Windsor, *Mo., U.S.A.* **112 F8**
Windsor, *N.Y., U.S.A.* **117 D9**
Windsor, *Vt., U.S.A.* **117 C12**
Windsor & Maidenhead □, *U.K.* . **15 F7**
Windsorton, *S. Africa* **88 D3**
Windward Is., *W. Indies* **121 D7**
Windward Passage = Vientos,
Paso de los, *Caribbean* **121 C5**
Winefred L., *Canada* **103 B6**
Winejok, *Sudan* **81 F2**
Winfield, *U.S.A.* **113 G6**
Wingate Mts., *Australia* **92 B5**
Wingham, *Australia* **95 E5**
Wingham, *Canada* **116 C3**
Winisk, *Canada* **104 A2**
Winisk →, *Canada* **104 A2**
Winisk L., *Canada* **104 B2**
Wink, *U.S.A.* **113 K3**
Winkler, *Canada* **103 D9**
Winklern, *Austria* **26 E5**
Winlock, *U.S.A.* **110 D4**
Winneba, *Ghana* **83 D4**
Winnebago, L., *U.S.A.* **114 D1**
Winnecke Cr. →, *Australia* **92 C5**
Winnemucca, *U.S.A.* **108 F5**
Winnemucca L., *U.S.A.* **108 F4**
Winnett, *U.S.A.* **108 C9**
Winnfield, *U.S.A.* **113 K8**
Winnibigoshish, L., *U.S.A.* **112 B7**
Winnipeg, *Canada* **103 D9**
Winnipeg →, *Canada* **103 C9**
Winnipeg, L., *Canada* **103 C9**
Winnipeg Beach, *Canada* **103 C9**
Winnipegosis, *Canada* **103 C9**
Winnipegosis L., *Canada* **103 C9**
Winnipesaukee, L., *U.S.A.* **117 C13**
Winnisquam L., *U.S.A.* **117 C13**
Winnsboro, *La., U.S.A.* **113 J9**
Winnsboro, *S.C., U.S.A.* **115 H5**
Winnsboro, *Tex., U.S.A.* **113 J7**
Winokapau, L., *Canada* **105 B7**
Winona, *Minn., U.S.A.* **112 C9**
Winona, *Miss., U.S.A.* **113 J10**
Winooski, *U.S.A.* **117 B11**
Winooski →, *U.S.A.* **117 B11**
Winschoten, *Neths.* **17 A7**
Winsen, *Germany* **24 B6**
Winsford, *U.K.* **14 D5**
Winslow, *Ariz., U.S.A.* **109 J8**
Winslow, *Wash., U.S.A.* **110 C4**
Winsted, *U.S.A.* **117 E11**
Winston-Salem, *U.S.A.* **115 G5**
Winter Garden, *U.S.A.* **115 L5**
Winter Haven, *U.S.A.* **115 M5**
Winter Park, *U.S.A.* **115 L5**

Winterberg, *Germany* 24 D4
Winterhaven, *U.S.A.* 111 N12
Winters, *U.S.A.* 110 G5
Wintersville, *U.S.A.* 116 F4
Winterswijk, *Neths.* 17 C6
Winterthur, *Switz.* 25 H4
Winthrop, *U.S.A.* 108 B3
Winton, *Australia* 94 C3
Winton, *N.Z.* 91 M2
Wipper →, *Germany* 24 D7
Wirrulla, *Australia* 95 E1
Wisbech, *U.K.* 15 E8
Wisconsin □, *U.S.A.* 112 C10
Wisconsin →, *U.S.A.* 112 D9
Wisconsin Rapids, *U.S.A.* 112 C10
Wisdom, *U.S.A.* 108 D7
Wishaw, *U.K.* 13 F5
Wishek, *U.S.A.* 112 B5
Wisła, *Poland* 31 J5
Wisła →, *Poland* 30 D5
Wisłok →, *Poland* 31 H9
Wisłoka →, *Poland* 31 H8
Wismar, *Germany* 24 B7
Wisner, *U.S.A.* 112 E6
Wissant, *France* 19 B8
Wissembourg, *France* 19 C14
Wisznice, *Poland* 31 G10
Witbank, *S. Africa* 89 D4
Witdraai, *S. Africa* 88 D3
Witham, *U.K.* 15 F8
Witham →, *U.K.* 14 E7
Withernsea, *U.K.* 14 D8
Witjira △, *Australia* 95 D2
Witkowo, *Poland* 31 F4
Witney, *U.K.* 15 F6
Witnica, *Poland* 31 F1
Witnossob →, *Namibia* 88 D3
Wittdün, *Germany* 24 A4
Witten, *Germany* 24 D3
Wittenberge, *Germany* 24 B7
Wittenburg, *Germany* 24 B7
Wittenheim, *France* 19 E14
Wittenoom, *Australia* 92 D2
Wittingen, *Germany* 24 C6
Wittlich, *Germany* 25 F2
Wittmund, *Germany* 24 B3
Wittow, *Germany* 24 A9
Wittstock, *Germany* 24 B8
Witvlei, *Namibia* 88 C2
Witzenhausen, *Germany* 24 D5
Wkra →, *Poland* 31 F7
Władysławowo, *Poland* 30 D5
Wleń, *Poland* 31 G2
Wlingi, *Indonesia* 63 H15
Włocławek, *Poland* 31 F6
Włodawa, *Poland* 31 G10
Włoszczowa, *Poland* 31 H6
Woburn, *U.S.A.* 117 D13
Wodian, *China* 56 H7
Wodonga = Albury-Wodonga, *Australia* 95 F4
Wodzisław Śląski, *Poland* 31 H5
Wœrth, *France* 19 D14
Woinbogoin, *China* 58 A2
Woippy, *France* 19 C13
Wojcieszow, *Poland* 31 H2
Wokam, *Indonesia* 63 F8
Woking, *U.K.* 15 F7
Wokingham, *U.K.* 15 F7
Wokingham □, *U.K.* 15 F7
Wolbrom, *Poland* 31 H6
Wołczyn, *Poland* 31 G5
Woldegk, *Germany* 24 B9
Wolf →, *Canada* 102 A2
Wolf Creek, *U.S.A.* 108 C7
Wolf L., *Canada* 102 A2
Wolf Point, *U.S.A.* 112 A2
Wolfe I., *Canada* 117 B8
Wolfeboro, *U.S.A.* 117 C13
Wolfen, *Germany* 24 D8
Wolfenbüttel, *Germany* 24 C6
Wolfratshausen, *Germany* 25 H7
Wolfsberg, *Austria* 26 E7
Wolfsburg, *Germany* 24 C6
Wolgast, *Germany* 24 A9
Wolhusen, *Switz.* 25 H4
Wolin, *Poland* 30 E1
Woliński △, *Poland* 30 E1
Wollaston, Is., *Chile* 128 H3
Wollaston L., *Canada* 103 B8
Wollaston Lake, *Canada* 103 B8
Wollaston Pen., *Canada* 100 B8
Wollongong, *Australia* 95 E5
Wolmaransstad, *S. Africa* 88 D4
Wolmirstedt, *Germany* 24 C7
Wołomin, *Poland* 31 F8
Wołów, *Poland* 31 G3
Wolseley, *S. Africa* 88 E2
Wolsey, *U.S.A.* 112 C5
Wolstenholme, C., *Canada* 98 C12
Wolsztyn, *Poland* 31 F3
Wolvega, *Neths.* 17 B6
Wolverhampton, *U.K.* 15 E5
Wondai, *Australia* 95 D5
Wongalarroo L., *Australia* 95 E3
Wongan Hills, *Australia* 93 F2
Wŏnju, *S. Korea* 57 F14
Wonosari, *Indonesia* 63 G14
Wonosobo, *Indonesia* 63 G13
Wonowon, *Canada* 102 B4
Wŏnsan, *N. Korea* 57 E14
Wonthaggi, *Australia* 95 F4
Wood Buffalo △, *Canada* 102 B6
Wood Is., *Australia* 92 C3
Wood L., *Canada* 103 B8
Woodah I., *Australia* 94 A2
Woodbourne, *U.S.A.* 117 E10
Woodbridge, *Canada* 116 C5
Woodbridge, *U.K.* 15 E9
Woodburn, *U.S.A.* 108 D2
Woodenbong, *Australia* 95 D5
Woodend, *Australia* 95 F3
Woodford, *Australia* 95 D5
Woodfords, *U.S.A.* 110 G7
Woodlake, *U.S.A.* 110 J7
Woodland, *Calif., U.S.A.* 110 G5
Woodland, *Maine, U.S.A.* 115 C12
Woodland, *Pa., U.S.A.* 116 F6
Woodland, *Wash., U.S.A.* 110 E4
Woodland Caribou ⌂, *Canada* 103 C10
Woodlands, *Singapore* 65 d
Woodridge, *Canada* 103 D9
Woodroffe, Mt., *Australia* 93 E5
Woods, L., *Australia* 94 B1
Woods, L. of the, *Canada* 103 D10
Woodstock, *Australia* 94 B4
Woodstock, *N.B., Canada* 105 C6
Woodstock, *Ont., Canada* 116 C4
Woodstock, *U.K.* 15 F6
Woodstock, *Ill., U.S.A.* 112 D10
Woodstock, *Vt., U.S.A.* 117 C12
Woodsville, *U.S.A.* 117 B13
Woodville, *N.Z.* 91 J5
Woodville, *Miss., U.S.A.* 113 K9
Woodville, *Tex., U.S.A.* 113 K7
Woodward, *U.S.A.* 113 G5
Woody, *U.S.A.* 111 K8
Woody →, *Canada* 103 C8
Woolacombe, *U.K.* 15 F3
Woolamai, C., *Australia* 95 F4
Wooler, *U.K.* 14 B5
Woolgoolga, *Australia* 95 E5
Woomera, *Australia* 95 E2
Woonsocket, *R.I., U.S.A.* 117 E13
Woonsocket, *S. Dak., U.S.A.* 112 C5
Wooramel →, *Australia* 93 E1
Wooramel Roadhouse, *Australia* 93 E1
Wooster, *U.S.A.* 116 F3
Worcester, *S. Africa* 88 E2
Worcester, *U.K.* 15 E5
Worcester, *Mass., U.S.A.* 117 D13
Worcester, *N.Y., U.S.A.* 117 D10
Worcestershire □, *U.K.* 15 E5
Wörgl, *Austria* 26 D5
Workington, *U.K.* 14 C4
Worksop, *U.K.* 14 D6
Workum, *Neths.* 17 B5
Worland, *U.S.A.* 108 D10
Wormhout, *France* 19 B9
Worms, *Germany* 25 F4
Worsley, *Canada* 102 B5
Wörth, *Germany* 25 F8
Wortham, *U.S.A.* 113 K6
Wörther See, *Austria* 26 E7
Worthing, *Barbados* 121 g
Worthing, *U.K.* 15 G7
Worthington, *Minn., U.S.A.* 112 D7
Worthington, *Pa., U.S.A.* 116 F5
Wosi, *Indonesia* 63 E7
Wou-han = Wuhan, *China* 59 B10
Wousi = Wuxi, *China* 59 B13
Wowoni, *Indonesia* 63 E6
Wrangel I. = Vrangelya, Ostrov, *Russia* 53 B19
Wrangell, *U.S.A.* 102 B2
Wrangell Mts., *U.S.A.* 100 B5
Wrath, C., *U.K.* 13 C3
Wray, *U.S.A.* 112 E3
Wrekin, The, *U.K.* 15 E5
Wrens, *U.S.A.* 115 J4
Wrexham, *U.K.* 14 D4
Wrexham □, *U.K.* 14 D5
Wriezen, *Germany* 24 C10
Wright = Paranas, *Phil.* 61 F6
Wright, *U.S.A.* 112 D2
Wright Pt., *Canada* 116 C3
Wrightson, Mt., *U.S.A.* 109 L8
Wrightwood, *U.S.A.* 111 L9
Wrigley, *Canada* 100 B7
Wrocław, *Poland* 31 G4
Wronki, *Poland* 31 F3
Września, *Poland* 31 F4
Wschowa, *Poland* 31 G3
Wu Jiang →, *China* 58 C6
Wu'an, *China* 56 F8
Wubin, *Australia* 93 F2
Wubu, *China* 56 F6
Wuchang, *China* 57 B14
Wucheng, *China* 56 F9
Wuchuan, *Guangdong, China* 59 G8
Wuchuan, *Guizhou, China* 58 C7
Wuchuan, *Nei Monggol Zizhiqu, China* 56 D6
Wudi, *China* 57 F9
Wuding, *China* 58 E4
Wuding He →, *China* 56 F6
Wudinna, *Australia* 95 E2
Wudu, *China* 56 H3
Wufeng, *China* 59 B8
Wugang, *China* 59 D8
Wugong Shan, *China* 59 D9
Wuhan, *China* 59 B10
Wuhe, *China* 57 H9
Wuhsi = Wuxi, *China* 59 B13
Wuhu, *China* 59 B12
Wujiang, *China* 59 B13
Wukari, *Nigeria* 83 D6
Wulajie, *China* 57 B14
Wulanbulang, *China* 56 D6
Wular L., *India* 69 B6
Wulehe, *Ghana* 83 D5
Wulian, *China* 57 G10
Wuliang Shan, *China* 58 E3
Wuliaru, *Indonesia* 63 F8
Wuling Shan, *China* 58 C7
Wulong, *China* 58 C6
Wulumuchi = Ürümqi, *China* 52 E9
Wum, *Cameroon* 83 D7
Wuming, *China* 58 F7
Wun Rog, *Sudan* 81 F2
Wundowie, *Australia* 93 F2
Wuning, *China* 59 C10
Wunnummin L., *Canada* 104 B2
Wunsiedel, *Germany* 25 E8
Wunstorf, *Germany* 24 C5
Wuntho, *Burma* 67 H19
Wupatki ⌂, *U.S.A.* 109 J8
Wuping, *China* 59 E11
Wuppertal, *Germany* 24 D3
Wuppertal, *S. Africa* 88 E2
Wuqing, *China* 57 E9
Wurtsboro, *U.S.A.* 117 E10
Würzburg, *Germany* 25 F5
Wurzen, *Germany* 24 D8
Wushan, *China* 56 G3
Wushishi, *Nigeria* 83 D6
Wusuli Jiang = Ussuri →, *Asia* 54 A7
Wutach →, *Germany* 25 H4
Wutai, *China* 56 E7
Wuting = Huimin, *China* 57 F9
Wutong, *China* 59 E8
Wutonghaolai, *China* 57 C11
Wutongqiao, *China* 58 C4
Wuwei, *Anhui, China* 59 B11
Wuwei, *Gansu, China* 60 C5
Wuxi, *Jiangsu, China* 59 B13
Wuxi, *Sichuan, China* 58 B7
Wuxiang, *China* 56 F7
Wuxuan, *China* 58 F7
Wuxue, *China* 59 C10
Wuyang, *China* 56 H7
Wuyi, *Hebei, China* 56 F8
Wuyi, *Zhejiang, China* 59 C12
Wuyi Shan, *China* 59 D11
Wuyishan, *China* 59 D12
Wuyo, *Nigeria* 83 C7
Wuyuan, *Jiangxi, China* 59 C11
Wuyuan, *Nei Monggol Zizhiqu, China* 56 D5
Wuzhai, *China* 56 E6
Wuzhi Shan, *China* 64 C7
Wuzhong, *China* 56 E4
Wuzhou, *China* 59 F8
Wyaaba Cr. →, *Australia* 94 B3
Wyalkatchem, *Australia* 93 F2
Wyalusing, *U.S.A.* 117 E8
Wyandotte, *U.S.A.* 114 D4
Wyandra, *Australia* 95 D4
Wyangala, L., *Australia* 95 E4
Wyara, L., *Australia* 95 D3
Wycheproof, *Australia* 95 F3
Wye →, *U.K.* 15 F5
Wyemandoo, *Australia* 93 E2
Wyk, *Germany* 24 A4
Wymondham, *U.K.* 15 E9
Wymore, *U.S.A.* 112 E6
Wyndham, *Australia* 92 C4
Wyndham, *N.Z.* 91 M2
Wynne, *U.S.A.* 113 H9
Wynyard, *Australia* 95 G4
Wynyard, *Canada* 103 C8
Wyola L., *Australia* 93 E5
Wyoming = Plympton-Wyoming, *Canada* 116 D2
Wyoming □, *U.S.A.* 108 E10
Wyomissing, *U.S.A.* 117 F9
Wyong, *Australia* 95 E5
Wyrzysk, *Poland* 31 E4
Wyśmierzyce, *Poland* 31 G7
Wysoka, *Poland* 31 E4
Wysokie, *Poland* 31 H9
Wysokie Mazowieckie, *Poland* 31 F9
Wyszków, *Poland* 31 F8
Wyszogród, *Poland* 31 F7
Wytheville, *U.S.A.* 114 G5
Wyżyna Małopolska, *Poland* 31 H7

X

Xaafuun, *Somali Rep.* 75 E5
Xaçmaz, *Azerbaijan* 35 K9
Xai-Xai, *Mozam.* 89 D5
Xainza, *China* 60 C3
Xalapa, *Mexico* 119 D5
Xangongo, *Angola* 88 B2
Xankändi, *Azerbaijan* 70 B5
Xanlar, *Azerbaijan* 35 K8
Xanten, *Germany* 24 D2
Xánthi, *Greece* 45 E8
Xánthi □, *Greece* 45 E8
Xanthos, *Turkey* 47 E11
Xanxerê, *Brazil* 127 B5
Xapuri, *Brazil* 124 F5
Xar Moron He →, *China* 57 C11
Xarrë, *Albania* 44 G4
Xátiva, *Spain* 39 G4
Xau, L., *Botswana* 88 C3
Xavantina, *Brazil* 127 A5
Xenia, *U.S.A.* 114 F4
Xeropotamos →, *Cyprus* 49 E11
Xertigny, *France* 19 D13
Xhora, *S. Africa* 89 E4
Xhumo, *Botswana* 88 C3
Xi Jiang →, *China* 59 F9
Xi Xian, *Henan, China* 59 A10
Xi Xian, *Shanxi, China* 56 F6
Xia Xian, *China* 56 G6
Xiachengzi, *China* 57 B16
Xiachuan Dao, *China* 59 G9
Xiaguan, *China* 60 D5
Xiajiang, *China* 59 D10
Xiajin, *China* 56 F9
Xiamen, *China* 59 E12
Xi'an, *China* 56 G5
Xian Xian, *China* 56 E9
Xianfeng, *China* 58 C7
Xiang Jiang →, *China* 59 C9
Xiangcheng, *Henan, China* 56 H8
Xiangcheng, *Henan, China* 56 H7
Xiangcheng, *Sichuan, China* 58 C2
Xiangdu, *China* 58 F6
Xiangfan, *China* 59 A9
Xianggang = Hong Kong □, *China* 59 F10
Xianghuang Qi, *China* 56 C7
Xiangning, *China* 56 G6
Xiangquan, *China* 56 F7
Xiangquan He = Sutlej →, *Pakistan* 68 E4
Xiangshan, *China* 59 C13
Xiangshui, *China* 57 G10
Xiangtan, *China* 59 D9
Xiangxiang, *China* 59 D9
Xiangyin, *China* 59 C9
Xiangyun, *China* 58 E3
Xiangzhou, *China* 58 F7
Xianju, *China* 59 C13
Xianning, *China* 59 C10
Xianshui He →, *China* 58 B3
Xiantao, *China* 59 B9
Xianyang, *China* 56 G5
Xianyou, *China* 59 E12
Xiao Hinggan Ling, *China* 60 B7
Xiao Xian, *China* 56 G9
Xiaofeng, *China* 59 B12
Xiaogan, *China* 59 B9
Xiaojin, *China* 58 B4
Xiaolan, *China* 59 F9
Xiaoshan, *China* 59 B13
Xiaoyi, *China* 56 F6
Xiapu, *China* 59 D12
Xiawa, *China* 57 C11
Xiayi, *China* 56 G9
Xichang, *China* 58 D4
Xichong, *China* 58 B5
Xichou, *China* 58 E5
Xichuan, *China* 56 H6
Xide, *China* 58 C4
Xiemahe, *China* 59 B8
Xieng Khouang, *Laos* 64 C4
Xifei He →, *China* 56 H9
Xifeng, *Gansu, China* 56 G4
Xifeng, *Guizhou, China* 58 D6
Xifeng, *Liaoning, China* 57 C13
Xifengzhen = Xifeng, *China* 56 G4
Xigazê, *China* 60 D3
Xihe, *China* 56 G3
Xihua, *China* 56 H8
Xilaganí, *Greece* 45 F9
Xiliao He →, *China* 57 C12
Xilin, *China* 58 E5
Xilókastron, *Greece* 46 C4
Ximana, *Mozam.* 87 F3
Xime, *Guinea-Biss.* 82 C2
Ximeng, *China* 58 F2
Xin Jiang →, *China* 59 C11
Xin Xian = Xinzhou, *China* 56 E7
Xinavane, *Mozam.* 89 D5
Xinbin, *China* 57 D13
Xincai, *China* 59 A10
Xinchang, *China* 59 C13
Xincheng, *Guangxi Zhuangzu, China* 58 E7
Xincheng, *Jiangxi, China* 59 D10
Xindu, *China* 58 B5
Xinfeng, *Guangdong, China* 59 E10
Xinfeng, *Jiangxi, China* 59 D11
Xinfeng, *Jiangxi, China* 59 E10
Xinfengjiang Skuiku, *China* 59 F10
Xing Xian, *China* 56 E6
Xing'an, *Guangxi Zhuangzu, China* 59 E8
Xingan, *Jiangxi, China* 59 D10
Xingcheng, *China* 57 D11
Xingguo, *China* 59 D10
Xinghe, *China* 56 D7
Xinghua, *China* 57 H10
Xinghua Wan, *China* 59 E12
Xinglong, *China* 57 D9
Xingning, *China* 59 E10
Xingping, *China* 56 G5
Xingren, *China* 58 E5
Xingshan, *China* 59 B8
Xingtai, *China* 56 F8
Xingu →, *Brazil* 125 D8
Xingwen, *China* 58 C5
Xingyang, *China* 56 G7
Xinhe, *China* 56 F8
Xinhua, *China* 59 D8
Xinhuang, *China* 58 D7
Xinhui, *China* 59 F9
Xining, *China* 60 C5
Xinjian, *China* 59 C10
Xinjiang, *China* 56 G6
Xinjiang Uygur Zizhiqu □, *China* 60 B3
Xinjie, *China* 58 D3
Xinjin = Pulandian, *China* 57 E11
Xinjin, *China* 58 B4
Xinkai He →, *China* 57 C12
Xinle, *China* 56 E8
Xinlitun, *China* 57 D12
Xinlong, *China* 58 B3
Xinmin, *China* 57 D12
Xinning, *China* 59 D8
Xinping, *China* 58 E3
Xinshao, *China* 59 D8
Xintai, *China* 57 G9
Xintian, *China* 59 E9
Xinxian, *China* 59 B10
Xinxiang, *China* 56 G7
Xinxing, *China* 59 F9
Xinyang, *China* 59 A10
Xinye, *China* 59 A9
Xinyi, *China* 59 F8
Xinyu, *China* 59 D10
Xinzhan, *China* 57 C14
Xinzheng, *China* 56 G7
Xinzhou, *Hubei, China* 59 B10
Xinzhou, *Shanxi, China* 56 E7
Xinzo de Limia, *Spain* 36 C3
Xiongyuecheng, *China* 57 D12
Xiping, *Henan, China* 56 H8
Xiping, *Henan, China* 56 H6
Xiping, *Zhejiang, China* 59 C12
Xique-Xique, *Brazil* 125 F10
Xisha Qundao = Paracel Is., *S. China Sea* 62 A4
Xishui, *Guizhou, China* 58 C6
Xishui, *Hubei, China* 59 B10
Xitole, *Guinea-Biss.* 82 C2
Xiu Shui →, *China* 59 C10
Xiuning, *China* 59 C12
Xiuren, *China* 59 E8
Xiushan, *China* 58 C7
Xiushui, *China* 59 C10
Xiuwen, *China* 58 D6
Xiuyan, *China* 57 D12
Xixabangma Feng, *China* 67 E14
Xixia, *China* 56 H6
Xixiang, *China* 56 H4
Xiyang, *China* 56 F7
Xizang Zizhiqu □, *China* 60 C3
Xlendi, *Malta* 49 C1
Xochob, *Mexico* 119 D7
Xu Jiang →, *China* 59 D11
Xuan Loc, *Vietnam* 65 G6
Xuan'en, *China* 58 C7
Xuanhan, *China* 58 B6
Xuanhua, *China* 56 D8
Xuanwei, *China* 58 C5
Xuanzhou, *China* 59 B12
Xuchang, *China* 56 G7
Xudat, *Azerbaijan* 35 K9
Xuefeng Shan, *China* 59 D8
Xuejiaping, *China* 59 B8
Xun Jiang →, *China* 59 F8
Xun Xian, *China* 56 G8
Xundian, *China* 58 E4
Xunwu, *China* 59 E10
Xunyang, *China* 56 H5
Xunyi, *China* 56 G5
Xupu, *China* 59 D8
Xúquer →, *Spain* 39 F4
Xushui, *China* 56 E8
Xuwen, *China* 59 G8
Xuyen Moc, *Vietnam* 65 G6
Xuyong, *China* 58 C5
Xuzhou, *China* 57 G9
Xylophagou, *Cyprus* 49 E12

Y

Ya Xian, *China* 64 C7
Yaamba, *Australia* 94 C5
Ya'an, *China* 58 C4
Yaapeet, *Australia* 95 F3
Yabassi, *Cameroon* 83 E6
Yabelo, *Ethiopia* 81 G4
Yabelo ⌂, *Ethiopia* 81 F4
Yablanitsa, *Bulgaria* 45 C8
Yablonovyy Khrebet, *Russia* 53 D12
Yablonovyy Ra. = Yablonovyy Khrebet, *Russia* 53 D12
Yabrai Shan, *China* 56 E2
Yabrūd, *Syria* 74 B5
Yabucoa, *Puerto Rico* 121 d
Yacambú △, *Venezuela* 121 E6
Yacheng, *China* 64 C7
Yacuiba, *Bolivia* 126 A3
Yacuma →, *Bolivia* 124 F5
Yadgir, *India* 66 L10
Yadkin →, *U.S.A.* 115 H5
Yadrin, *Russia* 34 C8
Yaeyama-Rettō, *Japan* 55 M1
Yagaba, *Ghana* 83 C4
Yağcılar, *Turkey* 47 B10
Yagodnoye, *Russia* 53 C15
Yahila, *Dem. Rep. of the Congo* 86 B1
Yahk, *Canada* 102 D5
Yahotyn, *Ukraine* 33 G6
Yahuma, *Dem. Rep. of the Congo* 84 D4
Yahyalı, *Turkey* 72 C6
Yaita, *Japan* 55 F9
Yaiza, *Canary Is.* 48 F6
Yajiang, *China* 58 B3
Yajua, *Nigeria* 83 C7
Yakima, *U.S.A.* 108 C3
Yakima →, *U.S.A.* 108 C3
Yako, *Burkina Faso* 82 C4
Yakobi I., *U.S.A.* 102 B1
Yakoruda, *Bulgaria* 44 D7
Yakovlevka, *Russia* 54 B6
Yaku-Shima, *Japan* 55 J5
Yakumo, *Japan* 54 C10
Yakutat, *U.S.A.* 100 C6
Yakutia = Sakha □, *Russia* 53 C13
Yakutsk, *Russia* 53 C13
Yala, *Thailand* 65 J3
Yalboroo, *Australia* 94 J6
Yale, *U.S.A.* 116 C2
Yalgoo, *Australia* 93 E2
Yalgorup △, *Australia* 93 D2
Yalinga, *C.A.R.* 84 C4
Yalkubul, Punta, *Mexico* 119 C7
Yalleroi, *Australia* 94 C4
Yalobusha →, *U.S.A.* 113 J9
Yalong Jiang →, *China* 58 D3
Yalova, *Turkey* 45 F13
Yalta, *Ukraine* 33 K8
Yalu Jiang →, *China* 57 E13
Yalvaç, *Turkey* 72 C4
Yam Ha Melaḥ = Dead Sea, *Asia* 74 D4
Yam Kinneret, *Israel* 74 C4
Yamada, *Japan* 55 H5
Yamagata, *Japan* 54 E10
Yamagata □, *Japan* 54 E10
Yamaguchi, *Japan* 55 G5
Yamaguchi □, *Japan* 55 G5
Yamal, Poluostrov, *Russia* 52 B8
Yamal Pen. = Yamal, Poluostrov, *Russia* 52 B8
Yamanashi □, *Japan* 55 G9
Yamanie Falls △, *Australia* 94 B4

Yamba, *Australia* 95 D5
Yambarran Ra., *Australia* 92 C5
Yambéring, *Guinea* 82 C2
Yâmbiô, *Sudan* 81 G2
Yambol, *Bulgaria* 45 D10
Yamdena, *Indonesia* 63 F8
Yame, *Japan* 55 H5
Yamethin, *Burma* 67 J20
Yamma-Yamma, L., *Australia* 95 D3
Yamoussoukro, *Ivory C.* 82 D3
Yampa →, *U.S.A.* 108 F9
Yampi Sd., *Australia* 92 C3
Yampil, *Moldova* 33 H5
Yampol = Yampil, *Moldova* 33 H5
Yamrat, *Nigeria* 83 C6
Yamrukchal = Botev, *Bulgaria* 45 D8
Yamuna →, *India* 69 G9
Yamunanagar, *India* 68 D7
Yamzho Yumco, *China* 60 D4
Yan, *Nigeria* 83 C7
Yana →, *Russia* 53 B14
Yanagawa, *Japan* 55 H5
Yanai, *Japan* 55 H6
Yan'an, *China* 56 F5
Yanbian, *China* 58 D3
Yanbu 'al Baḩr, *Si. Arabia* 70 F3
Yanchang, *China* 56 F6
Yancheng, *Henan, China* 56 H8
Yancheng, *Jiangsu, China* 57 H11
Yanchep Beach, *Australia* 93 F2
Yanchi, *China* 56 F4
Yanchuan, *China* 56 F6
Yanco Cr. →, *Australia* 95 F4
Yandoon, *Burma* 67 L19
Yanfeng, *China* 58 E3
Yanfolila, *Mali* 82 C3
Yang Xian, *China* 56 H4
Yang-Yang, *Senegal* 82 B1
Yangambi, *Dem. Rep. of the Congo* 86 B1
Yangbi, *China* 58 E2
Yangcheng, *China* 56 G7
Yangch'ü = Taiyuan, *China* 56 F7
Yangchun, *China* 59 F8
Yanggao, *China* 56 D7
Yanggu, *China* 56 F8
Yangjiang, *China* 59 G8
Yangliuqing, *China* 57 E9
Yangon = Rangoon, *Burma* 67 L20
Yangping, *China* 59 B8
Yangpingguan, *China* 56 H4
Yangquan, *China* 56 F7
Yangshan, *China* 59 E9
Yangshuo, *China* 59 E8
Yangtse = Chang Jiang →, *China* 59 B13
Yangtze Kiang = Chang Jiang →, *China* 59 B13
Yangudi Rassa △, *Ethiopia* 81 E5
Yangxin, *China* 59 C10
Yangyang, *S. Korea* 57 E15
Yangyuan, *China* 56 D8
Yangzhong, *China* 59 A12
Yangzhou, *China* 59 A12
Yanhe, *China* 58 C7
Yanji, *China* 57 C15
Yanjin, *China* 58 C5
Yanjing, *China* 58 C2
Yankari △, *Nigeria* 83 D7
Yankton, *U.S.A.* 112 D6
Yanonge, *Dem. Rep. of the Congo* 86 B1
Yanqi, *China* 60 B3
Yanqing, *China* 56 D8
Yanshan, *Hebei, China* 57 E9
Yanshan, *Jiangxi, China* 59 C11
Yanshan, *Yunnan, China* 58 F5
Yanshou, *China* 57 B15
Yantabulla, *Australia* 95 D4
Yantai, *China* 57 F11
Yanting, *China* 58 B5
Yantra →, *Bulgaria* 45 C9
Yanwa, *China* 58 D2
Yanyuan, *China* 58 D3
Yanzhou, *China* 56 G9
Yao Noi, Ko, *Thailand* 65 a
Yao Xian, *China* 56 G5
Yao Yai, Ko, *Thailand* 65 a
Yao'an, *China* 58 E3
Yaodu, *China* 58 A5
Yaoundé, *Cameroon* 83 E7
Yaowan, *China* 57 G10
Yap I., *Pac. Oc.* 96 G5
Yapen, *Indonesia* 63 E9
Yapen, Selat, *Indonesia* 63 E9
Yapero, *Indonesia* 63 E9
Yappar →, *Australia* 94 B3
Yaqui →, *Mexico* 118 B2
Yar-Sale, *Russia* 52 C8
Yaraka, *Australia* 94 C3
Yaransk, *Russia* 34 B8
Yarbasan, *Turkey* 47 C10
Yardımcı Burnu, *Turkey* 47 E12
Yare →, *U.K.* 15 E9
Yaremcha, *Ukraine* 33 H3
Yarensk, *Russia* 52 C5
Yarfa, *Si. Arabia* 80 C4
Yarí →, *Colombia* 124 D4
Yarkand = Shache, *China* 60 C2
Yarker, *Canada* 117 B8
Yarkhun →, *Pakistan* 69 A5
Yarlung Ziangbo Jiang = Brahmaputra →, *Asia* 69 H13
Yarmouth, *Canada* 105 D6
Yarmūk →, *Syria* 74 C4
Yaroslavl, *Russia* 32 D10
Yarqa, W. →, *Egypt* 74 F2
Yarra Yarra Lakes, *Australia* 93 E2
Yarram, *Australia* 95 F4
Yarraman, *Australia* 95 D5
Yarras, *Australia* 95 E5
Yartsevo, *Sib., Russia* 53 C10
Yartsevo, *Smolensk, Russia* 32 E7
Yarumal, *Colombia* 124 B3
Yasawa Group, *Fiji* 91 C7
Yaselda, *Belarus* 33 F4
Yashi, *Nigeria* 83 C6
Yashikera, *Nigeria* 83 D5
Yashkul, *Russia* 35 G7
Yasin, *Pakistan* 69 A5
Yasinovataya, *Ukraine* 33 H9
Yasinski, L., *Canada* 104 B4
Yasinya, *Ukraine* 33 H3
Yasothon, *Thailand* 64 E5
Yass, *Australia* 95 E4
Yāsūj, *Iran* 71 D6
Yatağan, *Turkey* 47 D10
Yatakala, *Niger* 83 C5
Yates Center, *U.S.A.* 113 G7
Yathkyed L., *Canada* 103 A9
Yatsushiro, *Japan* 55 H5
Yatta Plateau, *Kenya* 86 C4
Yauco, *Puerto Rico* 121 d
Yavari →, *Peru* 124 D4
Yávaros, *Mexico* 118 B3
Yavatmal, *India* 66 J11
Yavne, *Israel* 74 D3
Yavoriv, *Ukraine* 33 H2
Yavorov = Yavoriv, *Ukraine* 33 H2
Yavuzeli, *Turkey* 72 D7
Yawatahama, *Japan* 55 H6
Yawri B., *S. Leone* 82 D2
Yaxi, *China* 58 D6
Yazd, *Iran* 71 D7
Yazd □, *Iran* 71 D7
Yazd-e Khvāst, *Iran* 71 D7
Yazıköy, *Turkey* 47 E9
Yazman, *Pakistan* 68 E4
Yazoo →, *U.S.A.* 113 J9
Yazoo City, *U.S.A.* 113 J9
Ybbs, *Austria* 26 C8
Ybycuí △, *Paraguay* 126 B4
Ybytyruzú △, *Paraguay* 127 B4
Yding Skovhøj, *Denmark* 11 J3
Ye Xian = Laizhou, *China* 57 F10
Ye Xian, *China* 56 H7
Yebyu, *Burma* 64 E2
Yechŏn, *S. Korea* 57 F15
Yecla, *Spain* 39 G3
Yécora, *Mexico* 118 B3
Yedintsy = Edineţ, *Moldova* 29 B12
Yedseram →, *Nigeria* 83 C7
Yefremov, *Russia* 32 F10
Yeghegnadzor, *Armenia* 73 C11
Yegorlyk →, *Russia* 35 G5
Yegorlykskaya, *Russia* 35 G5
Yegoryevsk, *Russia* 32 E10
Yegros, *Paraguay* 126 B4
Yehbuah, *Indonesia* 63 J17
Yehuda, Midbar, *Israel* 74 D4
Yei, *Sudan* 81 G3
Yei, Nahr →, *Sudan* 81 F3
Yejmiadzin, *Armenia* 35 K7
Yekaterinburg, *Russia* 52 D7
Yekaterinodar = Krasnodar, *Russia* 35 H4
Yelabuga, *Russia* 34 C11
Yelan, *Russia* 34 E6
Yelarbon, *Australia* 95 D5
Yelatma, *Russia* 34 C5
Yelets, *Russia* 33 F10
Yélimané, *Mali* 82 B2
Yelizavetgrad = Kirovohrad, *Ukraine* 33 H7
Yell, *U.K.* 13 A7
Yell Sd., *U.K.* 13 A7
Yellow Sea, *China* 57 G12
Yellowhead Pass, *Canada* 102 C5
Yellowknife, *Canada* 102 A6
Yellowknife →, *Canada* 102 A6
Yellowstone △, *U.S.A.* 108 D9
Yellowstone →, *U.S.A.* 112 B3
Yellowstone L., *U.S.A.* 108 D8
Yelnya, *Russia* 32 E7
Yelsk, *Belarus* 33 G5
Yelwa, *Nigeria* 83 C5
Yemen ■, *Asia* 75 E3
Yen Bai, *Vietnam* 58 G5
Yenagoa, *Nigeria* 83 E6
Yenakiyeve, *Ukraine* 33 H10
Yenakiyevo = Yenakiyeve, *Ukraine* 33 H10
Yenangyaung, *Burma* 67 J19
Yenbo = Yanbu 'al Baḩr, *Si. Arabia* 70 F3
Yenda, *Australia* 95 E4
Yende Millimou, *Guinea* 82 D2
Yendéré, *Burkina Faso* 82 C4
Yendi, *Ghana* 83 D4
Yéni, *Niger* 83 C5
Yenice, *Ankara, Turkey* 72 C5
Yenice, *Aydın, Turkey* 47 D10
Yenice, *Çanakkale, Turkey* 47 B9
Yenice, *Edirne, Turkey* 45 F10
Yenice →, *Turkey* 72 D6
Yenifoça, *Turkey* 47 C8
Yenihisar, *Turkey* 47 D9
Yeniköy, *Bursa, Turkey* 45 F13
Yeniköy, *Çanakkale, Turkey* 47 B8
Yeniköy, *Kütahya, Turkey* 47 C11
Yenipazar, *Turkey* 47 D10
Yenisaía, *Greece* 45 E8
Yenişehir, *Turkey* 45 F13
Yenisey →, *Russia* 52 B9
Yeniseysk, *Russia* 53 D10
Yeniseyskiy Zaliv, *Russia* 52 B9
Yennádhi, *Greece* 49 C9
Yenne, *France* 21 C9
Yenotayevka, *Russia* 35 G8
Yenyuka, *Russia* 53 D13
Yeo →, *U.K.* 15 G5
Yeo, L., *Australia* 93 E3
Yeo I., *Canada* 116 A3
Yeola, *India* 66 J9
Yeoryioúpolis, *Greece* 49 D6
Yeovil, *U.K.* 15 G5
Yepes, *Spain* 36 F7
Yeppoon, *Australia* 94 C5
Yeráki, *Greece* 46 D4
Yerbent, *Turkmenistan* 52 F6
Yerbogachen, *Russia* 53 C11
Yerevan, *Armenia* 35 K7
Yerington, *U.S.A.* 108 G4
Yerkesik, *Turkey* 47 D10
Yerköy, *Turkey* 72 C6
Yermak, *Kazakhstan* 52 D8
Yermo, *U.S.A.* 111 L10
Yerólakkos, *Cyprus* 49 D12
Yeropol, *Russia* 53 C17
Yeropótamos →, *Greece* 49 D6
Yeroskipos, *Cyprus* 49 E11
Yershov, *Russia* 34 E9
Yerushalayim = Jerusalem, *Israel* 74 D4
Yerville, *France* 18 C7
Yes Tor, *U.K.* 15 G4
Yesan, *S. Korea* 57 F14
Yeşilhisar, *Turkey* 72 C6
Yeşilırmak →, *Turkey* 72 B7
Yeşilkent, *Turkey* 72 D7
Yeşilköy, *Turkey* 45 F12
Yeşilova, *Turkey* 47 D11
Yeşilyurt, *Manisa, Turkey* 47 C10
Yeşilyurt, *Muğla, Turkey* 47 D10
Yesnogorsk, *Russia* 32 E9
Yeso, *U.S.A.* 113 H2
Yessentuki, *Russia* 35 H6
Yessey, *Russia* 53 C11
Yeste, *Spain* 39 G2
Yetman, *Australia* 95 D5
Yeu, Î. d', *France* 18 F4
Yevlakh = Yevlax, *Azerbaijan* 35 K8
Yevlax, *Azerbaijan* 35 K8
Yevpatoriya, *Ukraine* 33 K7
Yeya →, *Russia* 33 J10
Yeysk, *Russia* 33 J10
Yezd = Yazd, *Iran* 71 D7
Yezerishche, *Belarus* 32 E5
Yhati, *Paraguay* 126 B4
Yhú, *Paraguay* 127 B4
Yi →, *Uruguay* 126 C4
Yi 'Allaq, G., *Egypt* 74 E2
Yi He →, *China* 57 G10
Yi Xian, *Anhui, China* 59 C11
Yi Xian, *Hebei, China* 56 E8
Yi Xian, *Liaoning, China* 57 D11
Yialí, *Greece* 47 E9
Yialiás →, *Cyprus* 49 D12
Yi'allaq, G., *Egypt* 80 A3
Yialousa, *Cyprus* 49 D13
Yiáltra, *Greece* 46 C4
Yianisádhes, *Greece* 49 D8
Yiannitsa, *Greece* 44 F6
Yibin, *China* 58 C5
Yichang, *China* 59 B8
Yicheng, *Henan, China* 59 B9
Yicheng, *Shanxi, China* 56 G6
Yichuan, *China* 56 F6
Yichun, *Heilongjiang, China* 60 B7
Yichun, *Jiangxi, China* 59 D10
Yidu, *China* 57 F10
Yidun, *China* 58 B2
Yifag, *Ethiopia* 81 E4
Yifeng, *China* 59 C10
Yihuang, *China* 59 D11
Yijun, *China* 56 G5
Yıldız Dağları, *Turkey* 45 E11
Yıldızeli, *Turkey* 72 C7
Yiliang, *Yunnan, China* 58 D5
Yiliang, *Yunnan, China* 58 E4
Yilong, *China* 58 B6
Yimen, *China* 58 E4
Yimianpo, *China* 57 B15
Yinchuan, *China* 56 E4
Yindarlgooda, L., *Australia* 93 F3
Ying He →, *China* 56 H9
Ying Xian, *China* 56 E7
Yingcheng, *China* 59 B9
Yingde, *China* 59 E9
Yingjiang, *China* 58 E1
Yingjing, *China* 58 C4
Yingkou, *China* 57 D12
Yingshan, *Henan, China* 59 B9
Yingshan, *Hubei, China* 59 B10
Yingshan, *Sichuan, China* 58 B6
Yingshang, *China* 59 A11
Yingtan, *China* 59 C11
Yining, *China* 52 E9
Yinjiang, *China* 58 C7
Yinmabin, *Burma* 67 H19
Yiofiros →, *Greece* 49 D7
Yioúra, *Nótios Aiyaíon, Greece* 46 D6
Yioúra, *Thessalía, Greece* 46 B6
Yipinglang, *China* 58 E3
Yirba Muda, *Ethiopia* 81 F4
Yirga Alem, *Ethiopia* 81 F4
Yirol, *Sudan* 81 F3
Yirrkala, *Australia* 94 A2
Yishan, *China* 58 E7
Yishui, *China* 57 G10
Yishun, *Singapore* 65 d
Yíthion, *Greece* 46 E4
Yitong, *China* 57 C13
Yiwu, *China* 59 C13
Yixing, *China* 59 B12
Yiyang, *Henan, China* 56 G7
Yiyang, *Hunan, China* 59 C9
Yiyang, *Jiangxi, China* 59 C11
Yizhang, *China* 59 E9
Yizheng, *China* 59 A12
Yli-Kitka, *Finland* 8 C23
Ylitornio, *Finland* 8 C20
Ylivieska, *Finland* 8 D21
Yngaren, *Sweden* 11 F10
Yoakum, *U.S.A.* 113 L6
Yob ⌂, *Eritrea* 81 D4
Yobe □, *Nigeria* 83 C7
Yog Pt., *Phil.* 63 B6
Yogan, *Togo* 83 D5
Yoğuntaş, *Turkey* 45 E11
Yogyakarta, *Indonesia* 63 G14
Yoho △, *Canada* 102 C5
Yojoa, L. de, *Honduras* 120 D2
Yŏju, *S. Korea* 57 F14
Yok Don △, *Vietnam* 64 F6
Yokadouma, *Cameroon* 84 D2
Yokkaichi, *Japan* 55 G8
Yoko, *Cameroon* 83 D7
Yokohama, *Japan* 55 G9
Yokosuka, *Japan* 55 G9
Yokote, *Japan* 54 E10
Yola, *Nigeria* 83 D7
Yolaina, Cordillera de, *Nic.* 120 D3
Yoloten, *Turkmenistan* 71 B9
Yom →, *Thailand* 62 A2
Yonago, *Japan* 55 G6
Yonaguni-Jima, *Japan* 55 M1
Yŏnan, *N. Korea* 57 F14
Yonezawa, *Japan* 54 F10
Yong Peng, *Malaysia* 65 L4
Yong Sata, *Thailand* 65 J2
Yongamp'o, *N. Korea* 57 E13
Yong'an, *China* 59 E11
Yongcheng, *China* 56 H9
Yŏngch'ŏn, *S. Korea* 57 G15
Yongchuan, *China* 58 C5
Yongchun, *China* 59 E12
Yongde, *China* 58 E2
Yongdeng, *China* 56 F2
Yongding, *China* 59 E11
Yŏngdŏk, *S. Korea* 57 F15
Yŏngdŭngpo, *S. Korea* 57 F14
Yongfeng, *China* 59 D10
Yongfu, *China* 58 E7
Yonghe, *China* 56 F6
Yŏnghŭng, *N. Korea* 57 E14
Yongji, *China* 56 G6
Yongjia, *China* 59 C13
Yŏngju, *S. Korea* 57 F15
Yongkang, *Yunnan, China* 58 E2
Yongkang, *Zhejiang, China* 59 C13
Yongnian, *China* 56 F8
Yongning, *Guangxi Zhuangzu, China* 58 F7
Yongning, *Ningxia Huizu, China* 56 E4
Yongping, *China* 58 E2
Yongqing, *China* 56 E9
Yongren, *China* 58 D3
Yongshan, *China* 58 C4
Yongsheng, *China* 58 D3
Yongshun, *China* 58 C7
Yongtai, *China* 59 E12
Yŏngwŏl, *S. Korea* 57 F15
Yongxin = Jinggangshan, *China* 59 D10
Yongxing, *China* 59 D9
Yongxiu, *China* 59 C10
Yongzhou, *China* 59 D8
Yonibana, *S. Leone* 82 D2
Yonkers, *U.S.A.* 117 F11
Yonne □, *France* 19 E10
Yonne →, *France* 19 D9
York, *Australia* 93 F2
York, *U.K.* 14 D6
York, *Ala., U.S.A.* 113 J10
York, *Nebr., U.S.A.* 112 E6
York, *Pa., U.S.A.* 114 F7
York, C., *Australia* 94 A3
York, City of □, *U.K.* 14 D6
York, Kap, *Greenland* 4 B4
York, Vale of, *U.K.* 14 C6
York Haven, *U.S.A.* 116 F8
York Sd., *Australia* 92 C4
Yorke Pen., *Australia* 95 E2
Yorkshire Dales △, *U.K.* 14 C5
Yorkshire Wolds, *U.K.* 14 C7
Yorkton, *Canada* 103 C8
Yorkville, *U.S.A.* 110 G3
Yoro, *Honduras* 120 C2
Yoron-Jima, *Japan* 55 L4
Yorosso, *Mali* 82 C4
Yos Sudarso, Pulau = Dolak, Pulau, *Indonesia* 63 F9
Yosemite △, *U.S.A.* 110 H7
Yosemite Village, *U.S.A.* 110 H7
Yoshino-Kumano △, *Japan* 55 H8
Yoshkar Ola, *Russia* 34 B8
Yŏsu, *S. Korea* 57 G14
Yotvata, *Israel* 74 F4
You Jiang →, *China* 58 F6
You Xian, *China* 59 D9
Youbou, *Canada* 110 B2
Youghal, *Ireland* 12 E4
Youghal B., *Ireland* 12 E4
Youkounkoun, *Guinea* 82 C2
Young, *Australia* 95 E4
Young, *Canada* 103 C7
Young, *Uruguay* 126 C4
Younghusband, L., *Australia* 95 E2
Younghusband Pen., *Australia* 95 F2
Youngstown, *Canada* 103 C6
Youngstown, *N.Y., U.S.A.* 116 C5
Youngstown, *Ohio, U.S.A.* 116 E4
Youngsville, *U.S.A.* 116 E5
Youngwood, *U.S.A.* 116 F5
Youxi, *China* 59 D12
Youyang, *China* 58 C7
Youyu, *China* 56 D7
Yozgat, *Turkey* 72 C6
Ypacaraí △, *Paraguay* 126 B4
Ypané →, *Paraguay* 126 A4
Yport, *France* 18 C7
Ypres = Ieper, *Belgium* 17 D2
Yreka, *U.S.A.* 108 F2
Yssingeaux, *France* 21 C8
Ystad, *Sweden* 11 J7
Ysyk-Köl, *Kyrgyzstan* 52 E8
Ythan →, *U.K.* 13 D7
Ytterhogdal, *Sweden* 10 B8
Ytyk-Kyuyel, *Russia* 53 C14
Yu Jiang →, *China* 58 F7
Yu Shan, *Taiwan* 59 F13
Yu Xian = Yuzhou, *China* 56 G7
Yu Xian, *Hebei, China* 56 E8
Yu Xian, *Shanxi, China* 56 E7
Yuan Jiang →, *Hunan, China* 59 C8
Yuan Jiang →, *Yunnan, China* 58 F4
Yuan'an, *China* 59 B8
Yuanjiang, *Hunan, China* 59 C9
Yuanjiang, *Yunnan, China* 58 F4
Yüanli, *Taiwan* 59 E13
Yüanlin, *Taiwan* 59 F13
Yuanling, *China* 59 C8
Yuanmou, *China* 58 E3
Yuanqu, *China* 56 G6
Yuanyang, *Henan, China* 56 G7
Yuanyang, *Yunnan, China* 58 F4
Yuba →, *U.S.A.* 110 F5
Yuba City, *U.S.A.* 110 F5
Yūbari, *Japan* 54 C10
Yubdo, *Ethiopia* 81 F4
Yūbetsu, *Japan* 54 B11
Yubo, *Sudan* 81 F2
Yucatán □, *Mexico* 119 C7
Yucatán, Canal de, *Caribbean* 120 B2
Yucatán, Península de, *Mexico* 98 H11
Yucatán Basin, *Cent. Amer.* 98 H11
Yucatan Channel = Yucatán, Canal de, *Caribbean* 120 B2
Yucca, *U.S.A.* 111 L12
Yucca Valley, *U.S.A.* 111 L10
Yucheng, *China* 56 F9
Yuci, *China* 56 F7
Yudu, *China* 59 E10
Yuechi, *China* 58 B6
Yuendumu, *Australia* 92 D5
Yueqing, *China* 59 C13
Yueqing Wan, *China* 59 D13
Yuexi, *Anhui, China* 59 B11
Yuexi, *Sichuan, China* 58 C4
Yueyang, *China* 59 C9
Yugan, *China* 59 C11
Yugoslavia = Serbia & Montenegro ■, *Europe* 44 C4
Yuhuan, *China* 59 C13
Yuhuan Dao, *China* 59 C13
Yujiang, *China* 59 C11
Yukhnov, *Russia* 32 E8
Yukon →, *U.S.A.* 100 B3
Yukon Territory □, *Canada* 100 B6
Yüksekova, *Turkey* 73 D11
Yukta, *Russia* 53 C11
Yukuhashi, *Japan* 55 H5
Yulara, *Australia* 93 E5
Yule →, *Australia* 92 D2
Yuleba, *Australia* 95 D4
Yuli, *Nigeria* 83 D7
Yuli, *Taiwan* 59 F13
Yulin, *Guangxi Zhuangzu, China* 59 F8
Yülin, *Hainan, China* 65 C7
Yulin, *Shaanxi, China* 56 E5
Yuma, *Ariz., U.S.A.* 111 N12
Yuma, *Colo., U.S.A.* 112 E3
Yuma, B. de, *Dom. Rep.* 121 C6
Yumbe, *Uganda* 86 B3
Yumbi, *Dem. Rep. of the Congo* 86 C2
Yumen, *China* 60 C4
Yumurtalık, *Turkey* 72 D6
Yun Gui Gaoyuan, *China* 58 E3
Yun Ho →, *China* 57 E9
Yun Ling, *China* 58 D2
Yun Xian, *Hubei, China* 59 A8
Yun Xian, *Yunnan, China* 58 E3
Yuna, *Australia* 93 E2
Yunak, *Turkey* 72 C4
Yunan, *China* 59 F8
Yuncheng, *Henan, China* 56 G8
Yuncheng, *Shanxi, China* 56 G6
Yunfu, *China* 59 F9
Yungas, *Bolivia* 124 G5
Yungay, *Chile* 126 D1
Yunhe, *China* 59 C12
Yunkai Dashan, *China* 59 F8
Yunlin, *Taiwan* 59 F13
Yunlong, *China* 58 E2
Yunmeng, *China* 59 B9
Yunnan □, *China* 58 E4
Yunquera de Henares, *Spain* 38 E1
Yunt Dağı, *Turkey* 47 C9
Yunta, *Australia* 95 E2
Yunxi, *China* 56 H6
Yunxiao, *China* 59 F11
Yuping, *China* 58 D7
Yupyongdong, *N. Korea* 57 D15
Yuqing, *China* 58 D6
Yuraygir △, *Australia* 95 D5
Yurga, *Russia* 52 D9
Yurimaguas, *Peru* 124 E3
Yurubí △, *Venezuela* 121 D6
Yuryev-Polskiy, *Russia* 32 D10
Yuryevets, *Russia* 34 B6
Yuscarán, *Honduras* 120 D2
Yûsef, Bahr →, *Egypt* 80 B3
Yushan, *China* 59 C12
Yushanzhen, *China* 58 C7
Yushe, *China* 56 F7
Yushu, *Jilin, China* 57 B14
Yushu, *Qinghai, China* 60 C4
Yusufeli, *Turkey* 73 B9
Yutai, *China* 56 G9
Yutian, *China* 57 E9
Yuxarı Qarabağ = Nagorno-Karabakh □, *Azerbaijan* 70 B5
Yuxi, *China* 58 E4
Yuyao, *China* 59 B13
Yuzawa, *Japan* 54 E10
Yuzha, *Russia* 34 B6
Yuzhno-Sakhalinsk, *Russia* 53 E15
Yuzhnyy □, *Russia* 35 H5
Yuzhou, *China* 56 G7
Yvelines □, *France* 19 D8
Yverdon-les-Bains, *Switz.* 25 J2
Yvetot, *France* 18 C7
Yzeure, *France* 19 F10

Z

Zaanstad, *Neths.* 17 B4
Zāb al Kabīr →, *Iraq* 70 C4
Zāb aş Şaghīr →, *Iraq* 70 C4
Žabalj, *Serbia & M.* 28 E5
Žabari, *Serbia & M.* 44 B5
Zabarjad, *Egypt* 80 C4
Zabaykalsk, *Russia* 53 E12
Ząbki, *Poland* 31 F8
Ząbkowice Śląskie, *Poland* 31 H3
Žabljak, *Serbia & M.* 44 C3
Zabłudów, *Poland* 31 F9
Żabno, *Poland* 31 H7
Zābol, *Iran* 71 D9
Zābol □, *Afghan.* 66 D5
Zābolī, *Iran* 71 E9
Zabré, *Burkina Faso* 83 C4
Zábřeh, *Czech Rep.* 27 B9
Zabrze, *Poland* 31 H5
Zabzuga, *Ghana* 83 D5
Zacapa, *Guatemala* 120 D2
Zacapu, *Mexico* 118 D4
Zacatecas, *Mexico* 118 C4
Zacatecas □, *Mexico* 118 C4
Zacatecoluca, *El Salv.* 120 D2
Zachary, *U.S.A.* 113 K9
Zachodnio-Pomorskie □, *Poland* 30 E2
Zacoalco, *Mexico* 118 C4
Zacualtipán, *Mexico* 119 C5
Zadar, *Croatia* 41 D12
Zadawa, *Nigeria* 83 C7
Zadetkyi Kyun, *Burma* 65 G1
Zadonsk, *Russia* 33 F10
Zafarqand, *Iran* 71 C7
Zafora, *Greece* 47 E8
Zafra, *Spain* 37 G4
Żagań, *Poland* 31 G2
Zagaoua, *Chad* 79 E10
Žagarė, *Lithuania* 30 B10
Zagazig, *Egypt* 80 H7
Zāgheh, *Iran* 71 C6
Zaglivérion, *Greece* 44 F7
Zagnanado, *Benin* 83 D5
Zagorá, *Greece* 46 B5
Zagorje, *Slovenia* 41 B11
Zagórów, *Poland* 31 F4
Zagorsk = Sergiyev Posad, *Russia* 32 D10
Zagórz, *Poland* 31 J9
Zagreb, *Croatia* 41 C12
Zagreb ✕ (ZAG), *Croatia* 41 C13
Zāgros, Kūhhā-ye, *Iran* 71 C6
Zagros Mts. = Zāgros, Kūhhā-ye, *Iran* 71 C6
Žagubica, *Serbia & M.* 44 B5
Zaguinaso, *Ivory C.* 82 C3
Zagyva →, *Hungary* 28 C5
Zahamena ⌂, *Madag.* 89 B8
Zāhedān, *Fārs, Iran* 71 D7
Zāhedān, *Sīstān va Balūchestān, Iran* 71 D9
Zahlah, *Lebanon* 74 B4
Zahna, *Germany* 24 D8
Záhony, *Hungary* 28 B7
Zainsk, *Russia* 34 C11
Zaïre = Congo →, *Africa* 84 F2
Zaječar, *Serbia & M.* 44 C6
Zaka, *Zimbabwe* 89 C5
Zakamensk, *Russia* 53 D11
Zakataly = Zaqatala, *Azerbaijan* 35 K8
Zakháro, *Greece* 46 D3
Zakhodnaya Dzvina = Daugava →, *Latvia* 9 H21
Zākhū, *Iraq* 70 B4
Zákinthos, *Greece* 46 D2
Zákinthos □, *Greece* 46 D2
Zakopane, *Poland* 31 J6
Zakroczym, *Poland* 31 F7
Zákros, *Greece* 49 D8
Zala, *Ethiopia* 81 F4
Zala □, *Hungary* 28 D1
Zala →, *Hungary* 28 D2
Zalaegerszeg, *Hungary* 28 D1
Zalakomár, *Hungary* 28 D2
Zalalövő, *Hungary* 28 D1
Zalamea de la Serena, *Spain* 37 G5
Zalamea la Real, *Spain* 37 H4
Zalău, *Romania* 28 C8
Žalec, *Slovenia* 41 B12
Zaleshchiki = Zalishchyky, *Ukraine* 33 H3
Zalew Wiślany, *Poland* 30 D6
Zalewo, *Poland* 30 E6
Zalingei, *Sudan* 79 F10
Zalishchyky, *Ukraine* 33 H3
Zama L., *Canada* 102 B5
Zambeke, *Dem. Rep. of the Congo* 86 B2
Zambeze →, *Africa* 87 F4
Zambezi = Zambeze →, *Africa* 87 F4
Zambezi, *Zambia* 85 G4
Zambezi △, *Zimbabwe* 87 F2
Zambezia □, *Mozam.* 87 F4
Zambia ■, *Africa* 87 F2
Zamboanga, *Phil.* 61 H5
Zambrów, *Poland* 31 F9
Zametchino, *Russia* 34 D6
Zamfara □, *Nigeria* 83 C6
Zamfara →, *Nigeria* 83 C5
Zamora, *Mexico* 118 D4
Zamora, *Spain* 36 D5
Zamora □, *Spain* 36 D5
Zamość, *Poland* 31 H10
Zamtang, *China* 58 A3
Zan, *Ghana* 83 D4
Záncara →, *Spain* 39 F1
Zandvoort, *Neths.* 17 B4
Zanesville, *U.S.A.* 116 G2
Zangābād, *Iran* 70 B5
Zangue →, *Mozam.* 87 F4
Zanjān, *Iran* 71 B6
Zanjān □, *Iran* 71 B6
Zanjān →, *Iran* 71 B6
Zannone, *Italy* 42 B6
Zante = Zákinthos, *Greece* 46 D2
Zanthus, *Australia* 93 F3
Zanzibar, *Tanzania* 86 D4
Zaouiet El-Kala = Bordj Omar Driss, *Algeria* 78 C7
Zaouiet Reggâne, *Algeria* 78 C6
Zaoyang, *China* 59 A9
Zaozhuang, *China* 57 G9
Zap Suyu = Zāb al Kabīr →, *Iraq* 70 C4
Zapadna Morava →, *Serbia & M.* 44 C5
Zapadnaya Dvina = Daugava →, *Latvia* 9 H21
Zapadnaya Dvina, *Russia* 32 D7
Západné Beskydy, *Europe* 27 B12
Zapadni Rodopi, *Bulgaria* 44 E7
Západočeský □, *Czech Rep.* 26 B6
Zapala, *Argentina* 128 D2
Zapaleri, Cerro, *Bolivia* 126 A2
Zapata, *U.S.A.* 113 M5
Zapatón →, *Spain* 37 F4
Zaporizhzhya, *Ukraine* 33 J8
Zaporozhye = Zaporizhzhya, *Ukraine* 33 J8
Zaqatala, *Azerbaijan* 35 K8
Zara, *Turkey* 70 B3
Zaragoza, *Coahuila, Mexico* 118 B4
Zaragoza, *Nuevo León, Mexico* 119 C5
Zaragoza, *Spain* 38 D4
Zaragoza □, *Spain* 38 D4
Zarand, *Kermān, Iran* 71 D8
Zarand, *Markazī, Iran* 71 C6
Zărandului, Munţii, *Romania* 28 D7
Zaranj, *Afghan.* 66 D2
Zarasai, *Lithuania* 9 J22
Zárate, *Argentina* 126 C4
Zarautz, *Spain* 38 B2
Zaraysk, *Russia* 32 E10
Zard, Kūh-e, *Iran* 71 C6
Zāreh, *Iran* 71 C6
Zari, *Nigeria* 83 C7
Zaria, *Nigeria* 83 C6
Żarki, *Poland* 31 H6
Zárkon, *Greece* 46 B4
Zarneh, *Iran* 70 C5
Zărneşti, *Romania* 29 E10
Zarós, *Greece* 49 D6
Żarów, *Poland* 31 H3
Zarqā', Nahr az →, *Jordan* 74 C4
Zarrīn, *Iran* 71 C7
Zaruma, *Ecuador* 124 D3
Żary, *Poland* 31 G2
Zarza de Granadilla, *Spain* 36 E4
Zarzis, *Tunisia* 79 B8
Zas, *Spain* 36 B2
Zaskar →, *India* 69 B7
Zaskar Mts., *India* 69 C7
Zastron, *S. Africa* 88 E4
Žatec, *Czech Rep.* 26 A6
Zaterechnyy, *Russia* 35 H7
Zator, *Poland* 31 J6
Zavala, *Bos.-H.* 44 D1
Zavāreh, *Iran* 71 C7
Zave, *Zimbabwe* 89 B5
Zavetnoye, *Russia* 35 G6
Zavidovići, *Bos.-H.* 28 F3
Zavitinsk, *Russia* 53 D13
Zavodovski, I., *Antarctica* 5 B1
Zavolzhsk, *Russia* 34 B6
Zavolzhye, *Russia* 34 B6
Zawadzkie, *Poland* 31 H5
Zawichost, *Poland* 31 H8
Zawidów, *Poland* 31 G2
Zawiercie, *Poland* 31 H6
Zāwiyat al Bayḑā = Al Bayḑā, *Libya* 79 B10
Zâwyet Shammas, *Egypt* 80 A2
Zâwyet Um el Rakham, *Egypt* 80 A2
Zâwyet Ungeîla, *Egypt* 80 A2
Zāyā, *Iraq* 70 C5
Zāyandeh →, *Iran* 71 C7
Zaysan, *Kazakhstan* 52 E9
Zaysan, Oz., *Kazakhstan* 52 E9
Zayü, *China* 58 C1
Zazafotsy, *Madag.* 89 C8
Zázrivá, *Slovak Rep.* 27 B12
Zbarazh, *Ukraine* 33 H3
Zbąszyń, *Poland* 31 F2
Zbąszynek, *Poland* 31 F2
Zblewo, *Poland* 30 E5
Žďár nad Sázavov, *Czech Rep.* 26 B8
Zdolbuniv, *Ukraine* 33 G4
Ždrelo, *Serbia & M.* 44 B5
Zduńska Wola, *Poland* 31 G5
Zduny, *Poland* 31 G4
Zeballos, *Canada* 102 D3
Zebediela, *S. Africa* 89 C4
Zebila, *Ghana* 83 C4
Zeebrugge, *Belgium* 17 C3
Zeehan, *Australia* 95 G4
Zeeland □, *Neths.* 17 C3
Zeerust, *S. Africa* 88 D4
Ẓefat, *Israel* 74 C4
Zege, *Ethiopia* 81 E4
Zeggerene, Iracher, *Mali* 83 B5
Zégoua, *Mali* 82 C3
Zehdenick, *Germany* 24 C9
Zeil, Mt., *Australia* 92 D5
Zeila, *Somali Rep.* 75 E3
Zeist, *Neths.* 17 B5
Zeitz, *Germany* 24 D8
Zelechów, *Poland* 31 G8
Zelengora, *Bos.-H.* 44 C2
Zelenodolsk, *Russia* 34 C9
Zelenogorsk, *Russia* 32 B5
Zelenograd, *Russia* 32 D9
Zelenogradsk, *Russia* 9 J19
Zelenokumsk, *Russia* 35 H6
Železná Ruda, *Czech Rep.* 26 B6
Železnik, *Serbia & M.* 44 B4
Zelienople, *U.S.A.* 116 F4
Želiezovce, *Slovak Rep.* 27 C11
Zelina, *Croatia* 41 C13
Zell, *Baden-W., Germany* 25 H3
Zell, *Rhld-Pfz., Germany* 25 E3
Zell am See, *Austria* 26 D5
Zella-Mehlis, *Germany* 24 E6
Zelów, *Poland* 31 G6
Zeltweg, *Austria* 26 D7
Žemaitijos △, *Lithuania* 30 B8
Zémio, *C.A.R.* 86 A2
Zempléni-hegység, *Hungary* 28 B6
Zemplínska šírava, *Slovak Rep.* 27 C15
Zempoala, *Mexico* 119 D5
Zemun, *Serbia & M.* 44 B4
Zengbé, *Cameroon* 83 D7
Zengcheng, *China* 59 F9
Zenica, *Bos.-H.* 28 F2
Žepče, *Bos.-H.* 28 F3
Zeraf, Bahr ez →, *Sudan* 81 F3
Zerbst, *Germany* 24 D8
Żerków, *Poland* 31 F4
Zermatt, *Switz.* 25 J3
Zernez, *Switz.* 25 J6
Zernograd, *Russia* 35 G5
Zerqan, *Albania* 44 E4
Zestaponi, *Georgia* 35 J6
Zetel, *Germany* 24 B3
Zeulenroda, *Germany* 24 E7
Zeven, *Germany* 24 B5
Zevenaar, *Neths.* 17 C6
Zévio, *Italy* 40 C8
Zeya, *Russia* 53 D13
Zeya →, *Russia* 53 D13
Zeytinbaği, *Turkey* 45 F12
Zeytindağ, *Turkey* 47 C9
Zghartā, *Lebanon* 74 A4
Zgierz, *Poland* 31 G6
Zgorzelec, *Poland* 31 G2
Zguriţa, *Moldova* 29 B13
Zhabinka, *Belarus* 33 F3
Zhailma, *Kazakhstan* 52 D7
Zhambyl = Taraz, *Kazakhstan* 52 E8
Zhangaly, *Kazakhstan* 35 G10
Zhangaqazaly, *Kazakhstan* 52 E7
Zhangbei, *China* 56 D8
Zhangguangcai Ling, *China* 57 B15
Zhangjiakou, *China* 56 D8
Zhangping, *China* 59 E11
Zhangpu, *China* 59 E11
Zhangshu, *China* 59 C10
Zhangwu, *China* 57 C12
Zhangye, *China* 60 C5
Zhangzhou, *China* 59 E11
Zhanhua, *China* 57 F10
Zhanjiang, *China* 59 G8
Zhannetty, Ostrov, *Russia* 53 B16
Zhanyi, *China* 58 E4
Zhanyu, *China* 57 B12
Zhao Xian, *China* 56 F8
Zhao'an, *China* 59 F11
Zhaocheng, *China* 56 F6
Zhaojue, *China* 58 C4
Zhaoping, *China* 59 E8
Zhaoqing, *China* 59 F9
Zhaotong, *China* 58 D4
Zhaoyuan, *Heilongjiang, China* 57 B13
Zhaoyuan, *Shandong, China* 57 F11
Zharkovskiy, *Russia* 32 E7
Zhashkiv, *Ukraine* 33 H6
Zhashui, *China* 56 H5
Zhayyq →, *Kazakhstan* 52 E6
Zhdanov = Mariupol, *Ukraine* 33 J9
Zhecheng, *China* 56 G8
Zhegao, *China* 59 B11
Zhejiang □, *China* 59 C13
Zheleznogorsk, *Russia* 33 F8
Zheleznogorsk-Ilimskiy, *Russia* 53 D11
Zheltyye Vody = Zhovti Vody, *Ukraine* 33 H7
Zhen'an, *China* 56 H5
Zhenba, *China* 58 A6
Zhenfeng, *China* 58 E5
Zheng'an, *China* 58 C6
Zhengding, *China* 56 E8
Zhenghe, *China* 59 D12
Zhengyang, *China* 59 A10
Zhengyangguan, *China* 59 A11
Zhengzhou, *China* 56 G7
Zhenhai, *China* 59 C13
Zhenjiang, *China* 59 A12
Zhenkang, *China* 58 F2
Zhenlai, *China* 57 B12
Zhenning, *China* 58 D5
Zhenping, *Henan, China* 56 H7
Zhenping, *Shaanxi, China* 58 B7
Zhenxiong, *China* 58 D5
Zhenyuan, *Gansu, China* 56 G4
Zhenyuan, *Guizhou, China* 58 D7
Zherdevka, *Russia* 34 E5
Zherong, *China* 59 D12
Zhetiqara, *Kazakhstan* 52 D7
Zhezqazghan, *Kazakhstan* 52 E7
Zhicheng, *China* 59 B8
Zhidan, *China* 56 F5
Zhigansk, *Russia* 53 C13
Zhigulevsk, *Russia* 34 D9
Zhijiang, *Hubei, China* 59 B8
Zhijiang, *Hunan, China* 58 D7
Zhijin, *China* 58 D5
Zhilinda, *Russia* 53 C12
Zhirnovsk, *Russia* 34 E7
Zhitomir = Zhytomyr, *Ukraine* 33 G5
Zhizdra, *Russia* 32 F8
Zhlobin, *Belarus* 33 F6
Zhmerinka = Zhmerynka, *Ukraine* 33 H5
Zhmerynka, *Ukraine* 33 H5
Zhob, *Pakistan* 68 D3
Zhob →, *Pakistan* 68 C3
Zhodino = Zhodzina, *Belarus* 32 E5
Zhodzina, *Belarus* 32 E5
Zhokhova, Ostrov, *Russia* 53 B16
Zhongdian, *China* 58 D2
Zhongdong, *China* 58 F6
Zhongdu, *China* 58 E7
Zhongning, *China* 56 F3
Zhongshan, *Antarctica* 5 C6
Zhongshan, *Guangdong, China* 59 F9
Zhongshan, *Guangxi Zhuangzu, China* 59 E8
Zhongtiao Shan, *China* 56 G6
Zhongwei, *China* 56 F3
Zhongxiang, *China* 59 B9
Zhongyang, *China* 56 F6
Zhoucun, *China* 57 F9
Zhouning, *China* 59 D12
Zhoushan, *China* 59 B14
Zhoushan Dao, *China* 59 C14
Zhouzhi, *China* 56 G5
Zhovti Vody, *Ukraine* 33 H7
Zhovtneve, *Ukraine* 33 J7
Zhovtnevoye = Zhovtneve, *Ukraine* 33 J7
Zhu Jiang →, *China* 59 F9
Zhuanghe, *China* 57 E12
Zhucheng, *China* 57 G10
Zhugqu, *China* 56 H3
Zhuhai, *China* 59 F9
Zhuji, *China* 59 C13
Zhukovka, *Russia* 32 F7
Zhumadian, *China* 56 H8
Zhuo Xian = Zhuozhou, *China* 56 E8
Zhuolu, *China* 56 D8
Zhuozhou, *China* 56 E8
Zhuozi, *China* 56 D7
Zhushan, *China* 59 A8
Zhuxi, *China* 58 A7
Zhuzhou, *China* 59 D9
Zhytomyr, *Ukraine* 33 G5
Zi Shui →, *China* 59 C9
Žiar nad Hronom, *Slovak Rep.* 27 C11
Zīārān, *Iran* 71 B6
Ziarat, *Pakistan* 68 D2
Zibo, *China* 57 F10
Zichang, *China* 56 F5
Zidarovo, *Bulgaria* 45 D11
Zidi = Wandhari, *Pakistan* 68 F2
Ziębice, *Poland* 31 H4
Zielona Góra, *Poland* 31 G2
Zierikzee, *Neths.* 17 C3
Ziesar, *Germany* 24 C8
Ziftá, *Egypt* 80 H7
Zigey, *Chad* 79 F9
Zigong, *China* 58 C5
Ziguinchor, *Senegal* 82 C1
Zihuatanejo, *Mexico* 118 D4
Zijin, *China* 59 F10
Zile, *Turkey* 72 B6
Žilina, *Slovak Rep.* 27 B11
Žilinský □, *Slovak Rep.* 27 B12
Zillah, *Libya* 79 C9
Zillertaler Alpen, *Austria* 26 D4
Zima, *Russia* 53 D11
Zimapán, *Mexico* 119 C5
Zimba, *Zambia* 87 F2
Zimbabwe, *Zimbabwe* 87 G3
Zimbabwe ■, *Africa* 87 F3
Zimi, *S. Leone* 82 D2
Zimnicea, *Romania* 29 G10
Zimovniki, *Russia* 35 G6
Zinave △, *Mozam.* 89 C5
Zinder, *Niger* 83 C6
Zinga, *Tanzania* 87 D4
Zingaro ⌂, *Italy* 42 D5
Zingst, *Germany* 24 A8
Ziniaré, *Burkina Faso* 83 C4
Zinnowitz, *Germany* 24 A9
Zion △, *U.S.A.* 109 H7
Zirbitzkogel, *Austria* 26 D7
Zirc, *Hungary* 28 C2
Žiri, *Slovenia* 41 B11
Žirje, *Croatia* 41 E12
Zirl, *Austria* 26 D4
Zirndorf, *Germany* 25 F6
Ziros, *Greece* 49 D8
Zirreh, Gowd-e, *Afghan.* 66 E3
Zisterdorf, *Austria* 27 C9
Zitácuaro, *Mexico* 118 D4
Žitava →, *Slovak Rep.* 27 C11
Žitište, *Serbia & M.* 28 E5
Zitong, *China* 58 B5
Zítsa, *Greece* 46 B2
Zittau, *Germany* 24 E10
Zitundo, *Mozam.* 89 D5
Živinice, *Bos.-H.* 28 F3
Ziwa Maghariba = Kagera □, *Tanzania* 86 C3
Ziway, L., *Ethiopia* 81 F4
Zixi, *China* 59 D11
Zixing, *China* 59 E9
Ziyang, *Shaanxi, China* 56 H5
Ziyang, *Sichuan, China* 58 B5
Ziyuan, *China* 59 D8
Ziyun, *China* 58 E6
Zizhong, *China* 58 C5
Zlarin, *Croatia* 41 E12
Zlatar, *Croatia* 41 B13
Zlatar, *Serbia & M.* 44 C3
Zlataritsa, *Bulgaria* 45 C9
Zlaté Moravce, *Slovak Rep.* 27 C11
Zlatibor, *Serbia & M.* 44 C3
Zlatitsa, *Bulgaria* 45 D8
Zlatna, *Romania* 29 D8
Zlatna Panega, *Bulgaria* 45 C8
Zlatni Pyasŭtsi, *Bulgaria* 45 C12
Zlatograd, *Bulgaria* 45 E9
Zlatoust, *Russia* 52 D6
Zletovo, *Macedonia* 44 E6
Zlín, *Czech Rep.* 27 B10
Zlínský □, *Czech Rep.* 27 B10
Złocieniec, *Poland* 30 E3
Złoczew, *Poland* 31 G5
Zlot, *Serbia & M.* 44 B5
Złotoryja, *Poland* 31 G2
Złotów, *Poland* 30 E4
Zmeinogorsk, *Kazakhstan* 52 D9
Żmigród, *Poland* 31 G3
Zmiyev, *Ukraine* 33 H9
Znamenka = Znamyanka, *Ukraine* 33 H7
Znamyanka, *Ukraine* 33 H7
Żnin, *Poland* 31 F4
Znojmo, *Czech Rep.* 26 C9
Zobeyrī, *Iran* 70 C5
Zobia, *Dem. Rep. of the Congo* 86 B2
Zoetermeer, *Neths.* 17 B4
Zogang, *China* 58 C1
Zogno, *Italy* 40 C6
Zogqên, *China* 58 A2
Zolochev = Zolochiv, *Ukraine* 33 H3
Zolochiv, *Ukraine* 33 H3
Zolotonosha, *Ukraine* 33 H7
Zomba, *Malawi* 87 F4
Zongo, *Dem. Rep. of the Congo* 84 D3
Zonguldak, *Turkey* 72 B4
Zongyang, *China* 59 B11
Zonqor Pt., *Malta* 49 D2
Zonza, *France* 21 G13
Zorgo, *Burkina Faso* 83 C4
Zorita, *Spain* 37 F5
Zorleni, *Romania* 29 D12
Zornitsa, *Bulgaria* 45 D10
Zorritos, *Peru* 124 D2
Żory, *Poland* 31 H5
Zorzor, *Liberia* 82 D3
Zossen, *Germany* 24 C9
Zou Xiang, *China* 56 G9
Zouan-Hounien, *Ivory C.* 82 D3
Zouar, *Chad* 79 D9
Zouérate = Zouîrât, *Mauritania* 78 D3
Zouîrât, *Mauritania* 78 D3
Zourika, *Niger* 83 B6
Zourma, *Burkina Faso* 83 C4
Zoutkamp, *Neths.* 17 A6
Zrenjanin, *Serbia & M.* 28 E5
Zuarungu, *Ghana* 83 C4
Zuba, *Nigeria* 83 D6
Zubayr, *Yemen* 81 D5
Zubtsov, *Russia* 32 D8
Zuénoula, *Ivory C.* 82 D3
Zuera, *Spain* 38 D4
Ẓufār, *Oman* 75 D5
Zug □, *Switz.* 25 H4
Zugdidi, *Georgia* 35 J5
Zugersee, *Switz.* 25 H4
Zugspitze, *Germany* 25 H6
Zuid-Holland □, *Neths.* 17 C4
Zuidbeveland, *Neths.* 17 C3
Zuidhorn, *Neths.* 17 A6
Zújar, *Spain* 37 H8
Zújar →, *Spain* 37 G5
Żukowo, *Poland* 30 D5
Zula, *Eritrea* 81 D4
Zülpich, *Germany* 24 E2
Zumaia, *Spain* 38 B2
Zumárraga, *Spain* 38 B2
Zumbo, *Mozam.* 87 F3
Zummo, *Nigeria* 83 D7
Zumpango, *Mexico* 119 D5
Zungeru, *Nigeria* 83 D6
Zunhua, *China* 57 D9
Zuni, *U.S.A.* 109 J9
Zunyi, *China* 58 D6
Zuo Jiang →, *China* 58 F6
Zuozhou, *China* 58 F6
Županja, *Croatia* 28 E3
Žur, *Serbia & M.* 44 D4
Zurbātīyah, *Iraq* 70 C5
Zürich, *Switz.* 25 H4
Zürich □, *Switz.* 25 H4
Zürichsee, *Switz.* 25 H4
Żuromin, *Poland* 31 E6
Žut, *Croatia* 41 E12
Zutphen, *Neths.* 17 B6
Zuurberg △, *S. Africa* 88 E4
Zuwārah, *Libya* 79 B8
Zūzan, *Iran* 71 C8
Žužemberk, *Slovenia* 41 C11
Zvenigorodka = Zvenyhorodka, *Ukraine* 33 H6
Zvenyhorodka, *Ukraine* 33 H6
Zverinogolovskoye, *Russia* 52 D7
Zvezdets, *Bulgaria* 45 D11
Zvishavane, *Zimbabwe* 87 G3
Zvolen, *Slovak Rep.* 27 C12
Zvonce, *Serbia & M.* 44 D6
Zvornik, *Bos.-H.* 28 F4
Zwedru = Tchien, *Liberia* 82 D3
Zweibrücken, *Germany* 25 F3
Zwelitsha, *S. Africa* 85 L5
Zwenkau, *Germany* 24 D8
Zwettl, *Austria* 26 C8
Zwickau, *Germany* 24 E8
Zwierzyniec, *Poland* 31 H9
Zwiesel, *Germany* 25 F9
Zwoleń, *Poland* 31 G8
Zwolle, *Neths.* 17 B6
Zwolle, *U.S.A.* 113 K8
Żychlin, *Poland* 31 F6
Żyrardów, *Poland* 31 F7
Zyryan, *Kazakhstan* 52 E9
Zyryanka, *Russia* 53 C16
Zyryanovsk = Zyryan, *Kazakhstan* 52 E9
Żywiec, *Poland* 31 J6
Zyyi, *Cyprus* 49 E12